HOLT

Elements of
LITERATURE
Sixth Course

Kylene Beers

Carol Jago

Deborah Appleman

Lelia Christenbury

Sara Kajder

Linda Rief

HOLT, RINEHART AND WINSTON

A Harcourt Education Company

Orlando • **Austin** • New York • San Diego • London

Requests for permission to make copies of any part of the work should be mailed to the following address: Permissions Department, Holt, Rinehart and Winston, 10801 N. MoPac Expressway, Building 3, Austin, Texas 78759.

Acknowledgments and other credits appear on pages 1548–1555, which are an extension of the copyright page.

ELEMENTS OF LITERATURE, HOLT, and the **"Owl Design"** are trademarks licensed to Holt, Rinehart and Winston, registered in the United States of America and/or other jurisdictions.

Printed in the United States of America

ISBN 978-0-03-036882-0
ISBN 0-03-036882-0

1 2 3 4 5 048 10 09 08

Program Authors

Kylene Beers is the senior program author for *Elements of Literature.* A former middle school teacher, she is now Senior Reading Advisor to Secondary Schools for Teachers College Reading and Writing Project at Columbia University. She is the author of *When Kids Can't Read: What Teachers Can Do* and co-editor (with Linda Rief and Robert E. Probst) of *Adolescent Literacy: Turning Promise into Practice.* The former editor of the National Council of Teachers of English (NCTE) literacy journal *Voices from the Middle,* Dr. Beers is the NCTE vice-president and will assume the presidency in 2008. With articles in *English Journal, Journal of Adolescent and Adult Literacy, School Library Journal, Middle Matters,* and *Voices from the Middle,* she speaks both nationally and internationally as a recognized authority on struggling readers. Dr. Beers has served on the review boards of *English Journal, The ALAN Review,* the Special Interest Group on Adolescent Literature of the International Reading Association, and the Assembly on Literature for Adolescents of the NCTE. She is the 2001 recipient of the Richard W. Halley Award given by NCTE for outstanding contributions to middle school literacy.

Carol Jago is a teacher with thirty-two years of experience at Santa Monica High School in California. The author of nine books on education, she continues to share her experiences as a writer and as a speaker at conferences and seminars across the country. Her wide and varied experience in standards assessment and secondary education in general has made her a sought-after speaker. As an author, Ms. Jago also works closely with Heinemann Publishers and with the National Council of Teachers of English. Her long-time association with NCTE led to her June 2007 election to a four-year term on the council's board. During that term she will serve for one year as president of the council. She is also active with the California Association of Teachers of English (CATE) and has edited CATE's scholarly journal *California English* since 1996. Ms. Jago served on the planning committees for the 2009 NAEP Reading Framework and the 2011 NAEP Writing Framework.

Deborah Appleman is professor and chair of educational studies and director of the Summer Writing Program at Carleton College in Northfield, Minnesota. Dr. Appleman's primary research interests include adolescent response to literature, multicultural literature, and the teaching of literary theory in high school. With a team of classroom teachers, she co-edited *Braided Lives,* a multicultural literature anthology. In addition to many articles and book chapters, she is the author of

Linda Rief, Alfred Tatum, Kylene Beers, Patrick Schwarz, and Carol Jago

PROGRAM AUTHORS continued

Critical Encounters in High School English: Teaching Literary Theory to Adolescents and co-author of *Teaching Literature to Adolescents.* Her most recent book, *Reading for Themselves,* explores the use of extracurricular book clubs to encourage adolescents to read for pleasure. Dr. Appleman was a high school English teacher, working in both urban and suburban schools. She is a frequent national speaker and consultant and continues to work weekly in high schools with students and teachers.

Leila Christenbury is a former high school English teacher and currently professor of English education at Virginia Commonwealth University, Richmond. The former editor of *English Journal,* she is the author of ten books, including *Writing on Demand, Making the Journey,* and *Retracing the Journey: Teaching and Learning in an American High School.* Past president of the National Council of Teachers of English, Dr. Christenbury is also a former member of the steering committee of the National Assessment of Educational Progress (NAEP). A recipient of the Rewey Belle Inglis Award for Outstanding Woman in English Teaching, Dr. Christenbury is a frequent speaker on issues of English teaching and learning and has been interviewed and quoted on CNN and in the *New York Times, USA Today, Washington Post, Chicago Tribune,* and *US News & World Report.*

Sara Kajder, author of *Bringing the Outside In: Visual Ways to Engage Reluctant Readers* and *The Tech-Savvy English Classroom,* is an assistant professor at Virginia Polytechnic Institute and State University (Virginia Tech). She has served as co-chair of NCTE's Conference on English Education (CEE) Technology Commission and of the Society for Information Technology and Teacher Education (SITE) English Education Committee. Dr. Kajder is the recipient of the first SITE National Technology Leadership Fellowship in English Education; she is a former English and language arts teacher for high school and middle school.

Linda Rief has been a classroom teacher for twenty-five years. She is author of *The Writer's-Reader's Notebook, Inside the Writer's-Reader's Notebook, Seeking Diversity, 100 Quickwrites,* and *Vision and Voice* as well as the co-author (with Kylene Beers and Robert E. Probst) of *Adolescent Literacy: Turning Promise into Practice.* Ms. Rief has written numerous chapters and journal articles, and she co-edited the first five years of *Voices from the Middle.* During the summer she teaches graduate courses at the University of New Hampshire and Northeastern University. She is a national and international consultant on adolescent literacy issues.

Leila Christenbury, Héctor Rivera, Sara Kajder, Eric Cooper, and Deborah Appleman

Program Consultants

Isabel L. Beck is professor of education and senior scientist at the University of Pittsburgh. Dr. Beck has conducted extensive research on vocabulary and comprehension and has published well over one hundred articles and several books, including *Improving Comprehension with Questioning the Author* (with Margaret McKeown) and *Bringing Words to Life: Robust Vocabulary Instruction* (with Margaret McKeown and Linda Kucan). Dr. Beck's numerous national awards include the Oscar S. Causey Award for outstanding research from the National Reading Conference and the William S. Gray Award from the International Reading Association for lifetime contributions to the field of reading research and practice.

Margaret G. McKeown is a senior scientist at the University of Pittsburgh's Learning Research and Development Center. Her research in reading comprehension and vocabulary has been published extensively in outlets for both research and practitioner audiences. Recognition of her work includes the International Reading Association's (IRA) Dissertation of the Year Award and a National Academy of Education Spencer Fellowship. Before her career in research, Dr. McKeown taught elementary school.

Amy Benjamin is a veteran teacher, literacy coach, consultant, and researcher in secondary-level literacy instruction. She has been recognized for excellence in teaching from the New York State English Council, Union College, and Tufts University. Ms. Benjamin is the author of several books about reading comprehension, writing instruction, grammar, and differentiation. Her most recent book (with Tom Oliva) is *Engaging Grammar: Practical Advice for Real Classrooms,* published by the National Council of Teachers of English. Ms. Benjamin has had a long association and leadership role with the NCTE's Assembly for the Teaching of English Grammar (ATEG).

Eric Cooper is the president of the National Urban Alliance for Effective Education (NUA) and co-founder of the Urban Partnership for Literacy with the IRA. He currently works with the NCTE to support improvements in urban education and collaborates with the Council of the Great City Schools. In line with his educational mission to support the improvement of education for urban and minority students, Dr. Cooper writes, lectures, and produces educational documentaries and talk shows to provide advocacy for children who live in disadvantaged circumstances.

Mabel Rivera, Harvey Daniels, Margaret McKeown, and Isabel Beck

PROGRAM CONSULTANTS continued

Harvey Daniels is a former college professor and classroom teacher, working in urban and suburban Chicago schools. Known for his pioneering work on student book clubs, Dr. Daniels is author and co-author of many books, including *Literature Circles: Voice and Choice in Book Clubs and Reading Groups* and *Best Practice: Today's Standards for Teaching and Learning in America's Schools.*

Ben Garcia is associate director of education at the Skirball Cultural Center in Los Angeles, California, where he oversees school programs and teacher professional development. He is a board member of the Museum Educators of Southern California and presents regularly at conferences in the area of visual arts integration across curricula. Prior to the Skirball, he worked with classroom teachers for six years in the *Art and Language Arts* program at the J. Paul Getty Museum. Recent publications include *Art and Science: A Curriculum for K–12 Teachers* and *Neoclassicism and the Enlightenment: A Curriculum for Middle and High School Teachers.*

Judith L. Irvin taught middle school for several years before entering her career as a university professor. She now teaches courses in curriculum and instructional leadership and literacy at Florida State University. Dr. Irvin's many publications include *Reading and the High School Student: Strategies to Enhance Literacy* and *Integrating Literacy and Learning in the Content Area Classroom.* Her latest book, *Taking Action: A Leadership Model for Improving Adolescent Literacy,* is the result of a Carnegie-funded project and is published by the Association for Supervision and Curriculum Development.

Victoria Ramirez is the interim education director at the Museum of Fine Arts, Houston, Texas, where she plans and implements programs, resources, and publications for teachers and serves as liaison to local school districts and

Amy Benjamin, Ben Garcia, Robin Scarcella, and Judith Irvin

teacher organizations. She also chairs the Texas Art Education Association's museum division. Dr. Ramirez earned a doctoral degree in curriculum and instruction from the College of Education at the University of Houston and an M.A.T. in museum education from George Washington University. A former art history instructor at Houston Community College, Dr. Ramirez currently teaches education courses at the University of Houston.

Héctor H. Rivera is an assistant professor at Southern Methodist University, School of Education and Human Development. Dr. Rivera is also the director of the SMU Professional Development/ESL Supplemental Certification Program for Math and Science Teachers of At-Risk Middle and High School LEP Newcomer Adolescents. This federally funded program develops, delivers, and evaluates professional development for educators who work with at-risk newcomer adolescent students. Dr. Rivera is also collaborating on school reform projects in Guatemala and with the Institute of Arctic Education in Greenland.

Mabel Rivera is a research assistant professor at the Texas Institute for Measurement, Evaluation, and Statistics at the University of Houston. Her current research interests include the education of and prevention of reading difficulties in English-language learners. In addition, Dr. Rivera is involved in local and national service activities for preparing school personnel to teach students with special needs.

Robin Scarcella is a professor at the University of California at Irvine, where she also directs the Program in Academic English/English as a Second Language. She has a Ph.D. in linguistics from the University of Southern California and an M.A. degree in education-second language acquisition from Stanford University. She has taught all grade levels. She has been active in shaping policies affecting language assessment, instruction, and teacher professional development. In the last four years, she has spoken to over ten thousand teachers and administrators. She has written over thirty scholarly articles that appear in such journals as the *TESOL Quarterly* and *Brain and Language*. Her most recent publication is *Accelerating Academic English: A Focus on the English Learner*.

Patrick Schwarz is professor of special education and chair of the Diversity in Learning and Development department for National-Louis University, Chicago, Illinois. He is author of *From Disability to Possibility* and *You're Welcome* (co-written with Paula Kluth), texts that have inspired teachers worldwide to reconceptualize inclusion to help all children. Other books co-written with Paula Kluth include *Just Give Him the Whale* and *Inclusion Bootcamp*. Dr. Schwarz also presents and consults worldwide through Creative Culture Consulting.

Alfred W. Tatum is an associate professor in the Department of Curriculum and Instruction at the University of Illinois at Chicago (UIC), where he earned his Ph.D. He also serves as the director of the UIC Reading Clinic. He began his career as an eighth-grade teacher, later becoming a reading specialist. Dr. Tatum has written more than twenty-five articles, chapters, and monographs and is the author of *Teaching Reading to Black Adolescent Males: Closing the Achievement Gap*. His work focuses on the literacy development of African American adolescent males, particularly the impact of texts on their lives.

Critical Reviewers

Noreen L. Abdullah
Chicago Public Schools
Chicago, Illinois

Martha Armenti
Baltimore City College High School
Baltimore, Maryland

Jessica J. Asmis-Carvajal
Coronado High School
El Paso, Texas

Susan Beechum
Apopka High School
Apopka, Florida

Nilda Benavides
Del Rio High School
Del Rio, Texas

Melissa Bowell
Ft. Walton Beach High School
Ft. Walton Beach, Florida

Stacey Chisolm
Meridian High School
Meridian, Mississippi

Vincent Contorno
L.C. Anderson High School
Austin, Texas

Rita Curington
Athens High School
Athens, Texas

Melinda Fulton
Leon High School
Tallahassee, Florida

Holly Hillgardner
South Bronx Preparatory
New York, New York

Anna Yoccabel Horton
Highland Middle School
Gilbert, Arizona

Elizabeth Ignatius
Paul R. Wharton High School
Tampa, Florida

Tim King
Mason High School
Mason, Ohio

Barbara Kimbrough
Kane Area High School
Kane, Pennsylvania

Jennifer Moore Krievs
Midlothian High School
Midlothian, Virginia

Lynn V. Mason
Newark High School
Newark, Ohio

Vivian Nida
University of Oklahoma
Norman, Oklahoma

John Kevin M. Perez
Hampton Bays Secondary
    High School
Hampton Bays, New York

Judd Pfeiffer
Bowie High School
Austin, Texas

Aimee Riordan
Sun Valley High School
Monroe, North Carolina

Celia Rocca
Western High School
Baltimore, Maryland

Kelly L. Self
Alexandria Senior High School
Alexandria, Louisiana

Dr. Rosa Smith-Williams
Booker T. Washington High School
Houston, Texas

Kelly Southern
Ouachita Parish High School
Monroe, Louisiana

Jody Steinke
Quincy Senior High School
Quincy, Illinois

Kelly Swifney
Zeeland West High School
Zeeland, Michigan

Nichole Wilson
Mason High School
Mason, Ohio

Dr. Bernard Zaidman
Greenville Senior High School
    Academy of Academic
    Excellence
Greenville, South Carolina

FIELD-TEST PARTICIPANTS

Linda Brescia
HS for Health Professions
    and Human Services
New York, New York

Katherine Burke
Timber Creek High School
Orlando, Florida

Greg Cantwell
Sheldon High School
Eugene, Oregon

Cheryl Casbeer
Del Rio High School
Del Rio, Texas

Ms. Linda Chapman
Colonel White High School
Dayton, Ohio

Kim Christiernsson
Durango High School
Las Vegas, Nevada

Amanda Cobb
Timber Creek High School
Orlando, Florida

Gwynne C. Eldridge
Royal Palm Beach Community
   High School
Royal Palm Beach, Florida

Marylea Erhart-Mack
University High School
Orlando, Florida

Yolanda Fernandez
Del Rio High School
Del Rio, Texas

Angela Ferreira
Hoover High School
San Diego, California

Dan Franke
Lemont High School
Lemont, Illinois

Ellen Geisler
Mentor High School
Mentor, Ohio

Luanne Greenberg
Coronado High School
El Paso, Texas

Colleen Hadley
Abilene High School
Abilene, Texas

Leslie Hardiman
Hoover High School
San Diego, California

Sandra Henderson
Lemont High School
Lemont, Illinois

Lee Ann Hoffman
Southeast High School
Bradenton, Florida

Jennifer Houston
Timber Creek High School
Orlando, Florida

Eva M. Lazear
Springfield North High School
Springfield, Ohio

Phil Lazzari
Lemont High School
Lemont, Illinois

Jacquelyn McLane
Cypress Creek High School
Orlando, Florida

Kathleen Mims
H. Grady Spruce High School
Dallas, Texas

Julie Moore
Monroe High School
Monroe, Wisconsin

Denise Morris
Rich Central High School
Olympia Fields, Illinois

Bunny Petty
Florence High School
Florence, Texas

Valerie Pfeffer
Durango High School
Las Vegas, Nevada

Bernadette Poulos
Reavis High School
Burbank, Illinois

Ann L. Rodgers
Currituck County High School
Barco, North Carolina

Narima Shahabudeen
East Orange Campus 9
High School
East Orange, New Jersey

Shari Simonds
Valley High School
Las Vegas, Nevada

Gail Tuelon
University High School
Orlando, Florida

Mandy Unruh
Brownsburg High School
Brownsburg, Indiana

Vanessa Vega
Irving High School
Irving, Texas

Elizabeth Weaver
Cypress Creek High School
Orlando, Florida

Tamera West
McQueen High School
Reno, Nevada

Erica White
Sherando High School
Stephens City, Virginia

Contents in Brief

UNIT 1 The Anglo-Saxon Period and
the Middle Ages 449–1485

COLLECTION 1 • The Anglo-Saxons: Songs of
Ancient Heroes

Literary Focus The Epic Tradition 17
Comparing Texts: World Literature Epics Across Cultures 87

COLLECTION 2 • The Middle Ages:
The Tales They Told

Literary Focus Medieval Narrative 113
Analyzing Visuals Analyzing a Painting 114
Writing Workshop Literary Analysis: Poetry 232

UNIT 2 The Renaissance 1485–1660:
A Flourish of Genius

COLLECTION 3 • Love, Time, and Death

Literary Focus Renaissance Poetry 267
Analyzing Visuals Analyzing an Illumination 269
Comparing Texts: World Literature Worlds of Wisdom 331
Comparing Texts Views on Education and Equality 373

COLLECTION 4 • William Shakespeare

Literary Focus Shakespeare's Sonnets and Plays 385
Writing Workshop Literary Research Paper 504

UNIT 3 The Restoration and the
Eighteenth Century 1660–1800

COLLECTION 5 • The Rise of the Novel

Literary Focus The Rise of the Novel 541
Analyzing Visuals Analyzing an Etching 543
Comparing Texts: World Literature Satirical Novels 591

COLLECTION 6 • Examined Lives

Literary Focus Form and Function in the Age of Reason 613
Comparing Texts Views on Women's Rights 665
Writing Workshop Persuasive Essay 682

UNIT 4 The Romantic Period 1798–1832

COLLECTION 7 • Truth and Imagination
Literary Focus Themes of Romantic Poetry 717
Analyzing Visuals Analyzing a Painting 719

COLLECTION 8 • The Quest for Beauty
Literary Focus Forms of Romantic Poetry 809
Comparing Texts: World Literature Japanese and Chinese Poetry 863
Writing Workshop Reflective Essay 882

UNIT 5 The Victorian Period 1832–1901

COLLECTION 9 • Love and Loss
Literary Focus Figurative Language 915

COLLECTION 10 • The Paradox of Progress
Literary Focus Realism 961
Analyzing Visuals Analyzing a Photograph 963
Comparing Texts: World Literature Realism and the Short Story 1007
Writing Workshop Fictional Narrative 1042

UNIT 6 The Modern World 1900 to the Present

COLLECTION 11 • The World at War
Literary Focus War Literature 1073
Comparing Texts Author Study: Virginia Woolf 1160

COLLECTION 12 • Modern and Contemporary Poetry
Literary Focus Themes of Modern and Contemporary Poetry 1187
Comparing Texts Author Study: William Butler Yeats 1198

COLLECTION 13 • Expectation and Reality
Literary Focus Irony 1295
Analyzing Visuals Analyzing a Sculpture 1296
Comparing Texts: World Literature Postcolonial Literature 1389
Writing Workshop Literary Analysis: Nonfiction 1426

RESOURCE CENTER
Handbook of Literary and Historical Terms 1452
World of Work 1474
Writer's Handbook 1480
Language Handbook 1492
Glossary 1531
Spanish Glossary 1539
Academic Vocabulary Glossary in English and Spanish 1546
Acknowledgments 1548
Picture Credits 1552
Index of Skills 1556
Index of Authors and Titles 1566

Maps
The British Isles A58
Map of the World A60

The Anglo-Saxon Period and the Middle Ages 449–1485

"Not the glittering weapon fights the fight, but rather the hero's heart."

—**Proverb**

What Do You Think? What moves a hero to act?

Time Line 2
Introduction to the Period . . . . .ESSAY 4
Link to Today
    J.R.R. Tolkien *from* The Lord of the Rings. . . . . NOVEL 12

COLLECTION 1 The Anglo-Saxons: Songs of Ancient Heroes

Literary Focus The Epic Tradition . . . . .ESSAY 17
Reading Focus Paraphrasing . . . . .ESSAY 19
Anonymous *from* Beowulf. . . . . .EPIC 21
        The Monster Grendel *translated by* Burton Raffel. 23
        The Arrival of the Hero 27
        Unferth's Challenge. 30
        The Battle with Grendel. 34
        The Monster's Mother 39
        The Final Battle *translated by* Seamus Heaney. 43

Link to Today

   from **The Collected Beowulf** *translated by* Francis Gummere;

   illustrated by **Gareth Hinds** . . . . GRAPHIC NOVEL **54**

Lyrics *from* **The Exeter Book** *(Introduction)* . . . . ESSAY **60**

  Anonymous The Seafarer *translated by* Burton Raffel . . . . POEM **61**

  Anonymous The Wife's Lament *translated by* Richard Hamer . . . POEM **66**

  Anonymous The Wanderer *translated by* Burton Raffel . . . . POEM **68**

  Anonymous Anglo-Saxon Riddles

               translated by Burton Raffel . . . . VERSE RIDDLES **74**

Bede *from* A History of the English Church and People

        translated by Leo Sherley-Price . . . . HISTORY **81**

Comparing Texts: World Literature

Epics Across Cultures **87**

  Anonymous *from* Gilgamesh: A Verse Narrative

          retold by Herbert Mason . . . . EPIC **89**

  Homer *from* the Iliad, Book 22: The Death of Hector

         translated by Robert Fagles . . . . EPIC **99**

COLLECTION 2 The Middle Ages: The Tales They Told

Literary Focus Medieval Narrative . . . . ESSAY 113

Analyzing Visuals Analyzing a Painting 114

Reading Focus Analyzing Style: Key Details . . . . ESSAY 115

Introduction to **The Canterbury Tales** . . . . ESSAY 118

Geoffrey Chaucer *from* The Canterbury Tales
                      translated by Nevill Coghill . . . . NARRATIVE POEM

                      The Prologue 121

                        from The Pardoner's Tale 149

                        from The Wife of Bath's Tale 161

Link to Today

 Jerry Ellis *from* Walking to Canterbury . . . . TRAVEL BOOK 178

Anonymous Lord Randall . . . . BALLAD 185

Anonymous Get Up and Bar the Door . . . . BALLAD 188

Anonymous Edward, Edward . . . . BALLAD 190

SKILLS FOCUS **Literary Skills** Understand medieval narratives; understand and analyze: characterization; the characteristics of a frame story; irony; the characteristics of a narrator; political context; the characteristics of ballads; the characteristics of a romance narrative; the archetype of the romance hero; the use of allegory.

Reading Skills Analyze style using key details; draw conclusions; interpret character; understand purpose; understand cause and effect; analyze details; make critical judgments.

Informational Text Skills Compare and contrast.

Anonymous *from* Sir Gawain and the Green Knight
                 translated by John Gardner . . . . ROMANCE NARRATIVE   195

Sir Thomas Malory *from* Le Morte d'Arthur
                 retold by Keith Baines . . . . ROMANCE NARRATIVE   207

Anonymous *from* Everyman . . . . MORALITY PLAY   217

Writing Workshop Literary Analysis: Poetry 232

Preparing for Timed Writing 241

Listening and Speaking Workshop Presenting a Literary Analysis . . . 242

Preparing for Standardized Tests 244
    Literary Skills Review

       Anonymous The Twa Corbies . . . . BALLAD   244

       Alexander Pushkin Raven doth to raven fly
                translated by Walter Arndt . . . . BALLAD   244

    Vocabulary Skills Review 246

    Writing Skills Review 247

Read On 248

The Renaissance 1485–1660: A Flourish of Genius

"So much one man can do,
That doth both act and know."

—Andrew Marvell

SKILLS FOCUS Literary Skills Evaluate and analyze the philosophical, political, religious, ethical, and social influences of a historical period.

Reading Skills Identify and understand chronological order; use text features such as overviews, headings, and graphic features to locate and categorize information; identify and understand elements of text structure (including headings and sections); read widely to increase knowledge of the student's culture, the cultures of others, and the common elements across cultures.

What Do You Think? How do our hearts and minds influence our actions?

Time Line 252
Introduction to the Period . . . . ESSAY 254
Link to Today
    Gary Fisher Another Renaissance? .WEB ARTICLE 262

COLLECTION **3** Love, Time, and Death

Literary Focus Renaissance Poetry . . . . .ESSAY 267
Analyzing Visuals Analyzing an Illumination 269
Sir Thomas Wyatt Whoso List to Hunt . . . . .SONNET 271
Edmund Spenser *from* Amoretti
                Sonnet 30 . . . . .SONNET 271
                Sonnet 75 . . . . SONNET 274
Christopher Marlowe The Passionate Shepherd to His Love . . . . . .POEM 277
Sir Walter Raleigh The Nymph's Reply to the Shepherd . . . . .POEM 277
Robert Herrick To the Virgins, to Make Much of Time . . . . .POEM 283
Andrew Marvell To His Coy Mistress . . . . .POEM 283
John Donne Song . . . . POEM 289
                A Valediction: Forbidding Mourning . . . . .POEM 291
                Meditation 17 . . . . MEDITATION 296
                Death be not proud . . . . SONNET 300

SKILLS FOCUS Literary Skills Understand and analyze: Renaissance poetry; characteristics of the speaker; characteristics of pastoral poems; carpe diem poetry; characteristics of metaphysical poetry; metaphysical conceits; the use of tone; paradox; dialogue; characteristics of lyric poetry; diction; parallelism; characteristics of parables; didactic literature; style; allusion; allegory; analyze philosophical context.

Reading Skills Draw inferences; understand inverted word order; use paraphrasing or retelling as a strategy for comprehension; identify the main idea of a text; identify comparison-contrast organization; recognize patterns of organization; analyze style; compare and contrast; understand archaic language; make inferences about theme; recognize and discuss themes and connections that cross cultures; compare main ideas across texts; compare and contrast; analyze an author's style; analyze the author's purpose or intent; make generalizations about a writer's beliefs.

Informational Skills Analyze persuasion/arguments in a text.

Link to Today

Margaret Edson *from* W;t . . . . DRAMA 304

Ben Jonson On My First Son . . . . POEM 309

Song: To Celia . . . . POEM 309

Sir John Suckling Why So Pale and Wan, Fond Lover? . . . . POEM 315

Richard Lovelace To Lucasta, on Going to the Wars . . . . POEM 315

To Althea, from Prison . . . . POEM 318

King James Bible Psalm 23 . . . . PSALM 321

Psalm 137 . . . . PSALM 321

The Parable of the Prodigal Son . . . . PARABLE 325

Comparing Texts: World Literature

Worlds of Wisdom 332

Koran Night *translated by* N. J. Dawood . . . . SACRED TEXT 332

Bhagavad-Gita *from* Philosophy and Spiritual Discipline
translated by Barbara Stoler Miller . . . . SACRED TEXT 334

Buddhist Traditional Zen Parables *compiled by* Paul Reps . . PARABLES 336

Confucius *from* The Analects of Confucius
translated and annotated by Arthur Waley . . . . MAXIMS 338

Lao Tzu *from the* Tao Te Ching
translated by Stephen Mitchell . . . . SACRED TEXT 339

Tao Traditional Taoist Anecdotes
translated and edited by Moss Roberts . . . . . ANECDOTES 340

Saadi Sayings of Saadi *translated by* Idries Shah . . . . AXIOMS 341

African Traditional African Proverbs
compiled by Charlotte *and* Wolf Leslau PROVERBS 342

Reading Focus Analyzing Milton's Style . . . . ESSAY 345

Paradise Lost: Milton's Epic *(Introduction)* 348

John Milton The Fall of Satan *from* Paradise Lost . . . . EPIC 350

 When I consider how my light is spent . . . . SONNET 363

John Bunyan *from* The Pilgrim's Progress . . . . ALLEGORY 367

Comparing Texts

Views on Education and Equality 373
 Francis Bacon Of Studies . . . . ESSAY 374
 Margaret Cavendish,
 Duchess of Newcastle *from* Female Orations . . . . DEBATE 377
 Queen Elizabeth I Tilbury Speech . . . . SPEECH 380

COLLECTION **4** William Shakespeare

Literary Focus Shakespeare's Sonnets and Plays . . . . ESSAY 385

Author Study: William Shakespeare 388

William Shakespeare Sonnet 18 . . . . SONNET 390

 Sonnet 29 . . . . SONNET 392

 Sonnet 30 . . . . SONNET 393

 Sonnet 71 . . . . SONNET 395

 Sonnet 73 . . . . SONNET 396

 Sonnet 116 . . . . SONNET 397

 Sonnet 130 . . . . SONNET 398

Reading Focus Using Questioning to Monitor Reading . . . . ESSAY 401

The Tragedy of Macbeth *(Introduction)* 402

William Shakespeare The Tragedy of Macbeth . . . . TRAGEDY 404

 Act I 407

 Act II 426

 Act III 440

 Act IV 458

 Act V 478

Link to Today

    from Macbeth: The Graphic Novel *adapted by* Arthur Byron
    Cover; *illustrated by* Tony Leonard Tamai . . . . GRAPHIC NOVEL **496**

Writing Workshop Literary Research Paper **504**

Preparing for Timed Writing **517**

Listening and Speaking Workshop Presenting a
                                 Literary Research Paper **518**

Preparing for Standardized Tests **520**
    Literary Skills Review

      Pierre de Ronsard When You Are Old
                      translated by Humbert Wolfe . . . . POEM **520**
      William Butler Yeats When You Are Old . . . . POEM **520**
    Vocabulary Skills Review **522**
    Writing Skills Review **523**

Read On **524**

The Restoration and the Eighteenth Century 1660–1800

"Good order is the foundation of all good things."
—Edmund Burke

SKILLS FOCUS **Literary Skills** Evaluate and analyze the philosophical, political, religious, ethical, and social influences of a historical period.

Reading Skills Identify and understand chronological order; use text organizers such as overviews, headings, and graphic features to locate and categorize information; read widely to increase knowledge of the student's culture, the cultures of others, and the common elements across cultures; identify and understand elements of text structure (including headings and sections).

What Do You Think? How can order and civilization affect human behavior?

Time Line 528
Introduction to the Period . . . . ESSAY 530
Link to Today
Chris Rose   1 Dead in Attic . . . . NEWSPAPER ARTICLE 536

COLLECTION **5** The Rise of the Novel

SKILLS FOCUS **Literary Skills** Evaluate and analyze the philosophical, political, religious, ethical, and social influences of a historical period; understand the rise of the novel; understand and analyze: the characteristics of a diary; narrative voice; situational irony; verbal irony; satire; parody; analyze credibility; analyze political context.

Reading Skills Evaluate an author's credibility; make critical judgments; analyze an author's purpose; recognize persuasive techniques; analyze author's style; draw inferences about character.

Informational Text Skills Identify comparison-contrast organization.

Literary Focus The Rise of the Novel . . . . ESSAY 541
Analyzing Visuals Analyzing an Etching 543
Samuel Pepys *from* The Diary of Samuel Pepys . . . . DIARY 545
Link to Today
Phil Gyford   Why I turned Pepys' Diary into a Weblog
from BBC Web site . . . . WEB ARTICLE 550
Daniel Defoe *from* A Journal of the Plague Year . . . . NOVEL 557
Jonathan Swift *from* Gulliver's Travels . . . . NOVEL 565
from Part 1: A Voyage to Lilliput 566
from Part 2: A Voyage to Brobdingnag 574
Reading Focus Recognizing Persuasive Techniques . . . . ESSAY 579
Jonathan Swift A Modest Proposal . . . . ESSAY 580

Comparing Texts: World Literature

Satirical Novels 591
Voltaire *from* Candide *translated by* Richard Aldington . . . . . . NOVEL 595
Miguel de Cervantes *from* Don Quixote
translated by Samuel Putnam . . . . NOVEL 603

COLLECTION 6 Examined Lives

Literary Focus Form and Function in the Age of Reason . . . . ESSAY 613

Alexander Pope Heroic Couplets . . . . COUPLETS 615

           from An Essay on Man . . . . PHILOSOPHICAL POEM 618

Reading Focus Identifying Tone . . . . ESSAY 620

Alexander Pope *from* The Rape of the Lock . . . . MOCK EPIC 621

Samuel Johnson *from* A Dictionary of
           the English Language . . . . DEFINITIONS 633

Link to Today
    Simon Winchester *from* The Meaning of Everything . . . . HISTORY 639

James Boswell *from* The Life of Samuel Johnson . . . . BIOGRAPHY 645

Thomas Gray Elegy Written in a Country Churchyard . . . . POEM 657

Comparing Texts

Views on Women's Rights 665
    Mary Wollstonecraft *from* A Vindication of
               the Rights of Woman . . . . PLATFORM 667

    Daniel Defoe *from* The Education of Women . . . . ESSAY 674

    Mary, Lady Chudleigh To the Ladies . . . . POEM 677

Writing Workshop Persuasive Essay 682

Preparing for Timed Writing 691

Listening and Speaking Workshop Presenting and
                    Analyzing Speeches 692

Preparing for Standardized Tests 694
    Literary Skills Review
    Aphra Behn Love Arm'd . . . . POEM 694
    Charles Baudelaire "I love you as I love . . ."
                translated by James McGowan . . . . POEM 694
    Vocabulary Skills Review 696
    Writing Skills Review 697

Read On 698

SKILLS FOCUS **Literary Skills** Evaluate and analyze the philosophical, political, religious, ethical, and social influences of a historical period; understand and analyze: elements of literature from the Restoration and the eighteenth century; antithesis; characteristics of the mock epic; diction; characteristics of biography; characteristics of an elegy; tone.

Reading Skills Identify the writer's stance; identify tone; analyze an author's point of view; analyze word choice and word order; analyze rhetorical devices in a text.

Informational Text Skills Identify and critique an author's argument.

UNIT 4

The Romantic Period 1798–1832

"The divine arts of imagination: imagination, the real & eternal world of which this vegetable universe is but a faint shadow."

—William Blake

What Do You Think? How can we use imagination to discover truth?

SKILLS FOCUS Literary Skills Evaluate and analyze the philosophical, political, religious, ethical, and social influences of a historical period.

Reading Skills Identify and understand chronological order; identify and understand graphic elements; use text organizers such as overviews, headings, and graphic features to locate and categorize information; identify and understand elements of text structure (including headings and sections).

Time Line		702
Introduction to the Period	ESSAY	704
Link to Today		
Jane Goodall *from* A Reason for Hope	MEMOIR	710

COLLECTION 7 Truth and Imagination

SKILLS FOCUS Literary Skills Understand and analyze: the themes of Romantic poetry; dialect; symbols; parallelism; theme; blank verse; meter and rhyme; personification; allusion; alliteration; the characteristics of a literary ballad.

Reading Skills Use paraphrasing as a strategy for comprehension; use context clues; draw conclusions about meaning; identify and understand patterns of organization; annotate a poem; interpret imagery; understand archaic words.

Informational Text Skills Analyze main idea and supporting details.

Literary Focus Themes of Romantic Poetry	ESSAY	717
Analyzing Visuals Analyzing a Painting		719
Robert Burns To a Mouse	POEM	721
To a Louse	POEM	724
Blake's Poems: Innocence to Experience *(Introduction)*		729
William Blake The Tyger	POEM	730
The Lamb	POEM	733
The Chimney Sweeper *from* Songs of Innocence	POEM	737
The Chimney Sweeper *from* Songs of Experience	POEM	740
A Poison Tree	POEM	742

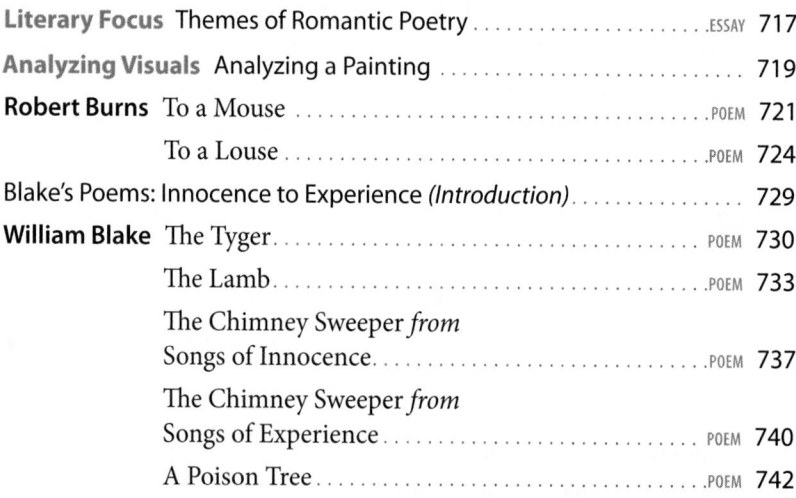

A14

Reading Focus Recognizing Patterns of Organization . . . . ESSAY 745

William Wordsworth Lines Composed a Few Miles
                          Above Tintern Abbey . . . . .POEM 747

                          from Ode: Intimations of Immortality . . . . . . .ODE 757

                          Composed upon Westminster Bridge . . . . .SONNET 761

                          The World Is Too Much with Us . . . . SONNET 763

Samuel Taylor Coleridge Kubla Khan . . . . .POEM 767

                          The Rime of the Ancient
                          Mariner . . . . NARRATIVE POEM 774

Link to Today

Timothy Foote Saving Creatures Great and Small . . . . . MAGAZINE ARTICLE 803

COLLECTION 8 The Quest for Beauty

Literary Focus Forms of Romantic Poetry . . . . ESSAY **809**

George Gordon, Lord Byron She Walks in Beauty . . . . POEM **811**

from Childe Harold's Pilgrimage,
Canto IV . . . . NARRATIVE POEM **813**

Reading Focus Comparing and Contrasting . . . . ESSAY **817**

Percy Bysshe Shelley Ozymandias . . . . SONNET **819**

Ode to the West Wind . . . . ODE **824**

To a Skylark . . . . ODE **829**

Link to Today

W. S. Merwin To a Mosquito . . . . .ODE **837**

John Keats On First Looking into Chapman's Homer . . . . SONNET **843**

When I Have Fears . . . . SONNET **843**

Ode to a Nightingale . . . . .ODE **847**

Ode on a Grecian Urn . . . . .ODE **852**

Keats's Last Letter . . . . .LETTER **859**

SKILLS FOCUS **Literary Skills** Understand forms of Romantic poetry; understand and analyze: simile; apostrophe; irony; the characteristics of an ode; symbols; diction; sonnet form; synesthesia; metaphor; imagery; mood; compare poetry across cultures.

Reading Skills Understand rhyme and rhythm; compare and contrast; make inferences as a strategy for comprehension; analyze tone; understand inverted syntax; read closely for details; visualize imagery; use text structure to understand meaning;.

Informational Text Skills Analyze primary sources.

Comparing Texts: World Literature

Japanese and Chinese Poetry 863
Introduction to Japanese and Chinese Poetry . . . . ESSAY 864
Japanese Poetry
   Tanka Poets Tanka *translated by* Geoffrey Bownas and
                Anthony Thwaite . . . . TANKA 868
   Haiku Poets Haiku *translated by* Harold G. Henderson,
                Peter Beilenson, and Harry Behn . . . . HAIKU 870
Chinese Poetry
   Tu Fu Jade Flower Palace *translated by* Kenneth Rexroth . . . . POEM 873
         Night Thoughts Afloat translated by Arthur Cooper . . . . . POEM 875
   Li Po Quiet Night Thoughts *translated by* Arthur Cooper . . . . . . POEM 877
         Question and Answer Among the Mountains
         translated by Robert Kotewall *and* Norman L. Smith . . . . . POEM 877
         Letter to His Two Small Children
         translated by Arthur Cooper . . . . POEM 877

Writing Workshop Reflective Essay 882

Preparing for Timed Writing 891

Listening and Speaking Workshop Presenting a Reflective
                                 Essay 892

Preparing for Standardized Tests 894
   Literary Skills Review
      William Blake London . . . . POEM 894
      Derek Walcott The Virgins . . . . POEM 894
   Vocabulary Skills Review 896
   Writing Skills Review 897

Read On 898

The Victorian Period 1832–1901

"For each age is a dream that is dying, / Or one that is coming to birth."
—Arthur O'Shaughnessy

What Do You Think? How can appearance be different from reality?

Time Line 902
Introduction to the Period . . . . ESSAY 904
Link to Today
Steven B. Johnson The Night-Soil Men
from The Ghost Map . . . . HISTORY 910

COLLECTION 9 Love and Loss

Literary Focus Figurative Language . . . . ESSAY 915
Alfred, Lord Tennyson The Lady of Shalott . . . . NARRATIVE POEM 917
                  Ulysses . . . . .POEM 926
                  from In Memoriam A.H.H. . . . . .POEM 931
                  Crossing the Bar . . . . .POEM 937
Reading Focus Drawing Inferences from Textual Clues . . . . .ESSAY 941
Robert Browning My Last Duchess . . . . DRAMATIC MONOLOGUE 943
                  Porphyria's Lover . . . . DRAMATIC MONOLOGUE 947
Elizabeth Barrett Browning Sonnet 43 . . . . SONNET 953
Gerard Manley Hopkins Pied Beauty . . . . .POEM 957

COLLECTION 10 The Paradox of Progress

Literary Focus Realism . . . . ESSAY 961

Analyzing Visuals Analyzing a Photograph 963

Matthew Arnold Dover Beach . . . . POEM 965

Reading Focus Making Generalizations . . . . ESSAY 971

Thomas Hardy The Darkling Thrush . . . . POEM 973

Ah, Are You Digging on My Grave? . . . . POEM 976

A. E. Housman To an Athlete Dying Young . . . . POEM 981

When I Was One-and-Twenty . . . . POEM 984

Link to Today

Jason La Canfora When Elements Go Extreme . . . . NEWSPAPER ARTICLE 988

Rudyard Kipling The Mark of the Beast . . . . SHORT STORY 993

Comparing Texts: World Literature

Realism and the Short Story 1007

Leo Tolstoy How Much Land Does a Man Need?

translated by Louise *and* Aylmer Maude . . . . SHORT STORY 1009

Anton Chekhov The Bet

translated by Constance Garnett . . . . SHORT STORY 1023

Guy de Maupassant The Jewels

translated by Roger Colet . . . . SHORT STORY 1033

Writing Workshop Fictional Narrative 1042

Preparing for Timed Writing 1051

Listening and Speaking Workshop Telling a Story 1052

Preparing for Standardized Tests 1054

Literary Skills Review

Thomas Hardy Drummer Hodge . . . . POEM 1054

Arthur Rimbaud The Sleeper of the Valley

translated by Ludwig Lewisohn . . . . POEM 1054

Vocabulary Skills Review 1056

Writing Skills Review 1057

Read On 1058

SKILLS FOCUS **Literary Skills** Evaluate and analyze the philosophical, political, religious, ethical, and social influences of a historical period; understand realism; understand and analyze: mood; the characteristics of a speaker; couplets; theme; internal and external conflict; allegory; irony; analyze historical context; analyze credibility in literature; compare realist works.

Reading Skills Visualize setting; make generalizations; analyze the relationship of form and meaning; identify conflicts and resolutions; identify theme; make predictions; draw inferences.

Informational Text Skills Analyze causes and effects.

The Modern World 1900 to the Present

"Life spends itself in the act of transformation, dissolving, bit by bit, the world as it appeared."

—Rainer Maria Rilke

What Do You Think? How does experience shape our view of the world?

Time Line 1062

Introduction to the Period . . . . ESSAY 1064

Link to Today
    Alice Oswald Spacecraft Voyager 1 Has Boldly Gone . . . SONNET 1070

COLLECTION 11 The World at War

Literary Focus War Literature . . . . ESSAY 1073

World War I

Wilfred Owen Dulce et Decorum Est . . . . POEM 1075

Rupert Brooke The Soldier . . . . SONNET 1078

Siegfried Sassoon The Rear-Guard . . . . .POEM 1081

           A Soldier's Declaration . . . . POLITICAL STATEMENT 1084

Link to Today
    Richard Norton-Taylor Under Heavy Fire in Iraq . . . . NEWSPAPER ARTICLE 1088

World War II and Aftermath

Primo Levi On the Bottom *from* Survival in Auschwitz
           translated by Stuart Woolf . . . . MEMOIR 1093

Elie Wiesel Never Shall I Forget *translated by* Marion Wiesel . . . POEM 1103

Reading Focus Identifying and Critiquing
           an Author's Argument . . . . ESSAY 1107

Winston Churchill Blood, Sweat, and Tears . . . . SPEECH 1109

Elizabeth Bowen The Demon Lover . . . . SHORT STORY 1117

Graham Greene The Destructors . . . . SHORT STORY 1127

Clashes of Culture

George Orwell Shooting an Elephant . . . . ESSAY 1141

Joseph Chamberlain "I Believe in a British Empire" . . . . .SPEECH 1151

Jawaharlal Nehru "The Noble Mansion of Free India" . . . . SPEECH 1155

Comparing Texts: Author Study

Author Study: Virginia Woolf 1160
  Virginia Woolf *from* A Room of One's Own . . . . ESSAY 1162
          from Jacob's Room . . . . NOVEL 1172
          A Haunted House . . . . SHORT STORY 1177
          from The Letters of Virginia Woolf . . . . LETTER 1181

COLLECTION **12** Modern and Contemporary Poetry

Literary Focus Themes of Modern and Contemporary Poetry . . . ESSAY 1187
T. S. Eliot The Hollow Men . . . . POEM 1189

Comparing Texts: Author Study

Author Study: William Butler Yeats 1198
  William Butler Yeats The Second Coming . . . . POEM 1200
          The Lake Isle of Innisfree . . . . POEM 1205
          The Wild Swans at Coole . . . . POEM 1208
          Sailing to Byzantium . . . . POEM 1213
          from **The Autobiography of
          William Butler Yeats** . . . . AUTOBIOGRAPHY 1216

SKILLS FOCUS **Literary Skills** Understand and analyze themes of modern and contemporary poetry; analyze philosophical context; understand and analyze: allusion; theme; alliteration and assonance; symbols; metaphor; connotations; diction; the characteristics of lyric poetry; the characteristics of an elegy; irony; the characteristics of the speaker; refrain; metaphor; imagery; poetic structure; extended metaphor; the sonnet form.

Reading Skills Draw inferences; visualize imagery; connect text to experience; analyze style; analyze author's purpose; identify theme; analyze details; analyze tone; use prior knowledge; compare and contrast; interpret imagery; draw inferences.

Informational Text Skills Analyze an author's beliefs; use graphics to understand text.

W. H. Auden Musée des Beaux Arts .... POEM 1223

Reading Focus Analyzing Details .... ESSAY 1227

Dylan Thomas Fern Hill.......................... POEM 1229

Do Not Go Gentle into That Good Night .... VILLANELLE 1235

Stevie Smith Not Waving but Drowning .... POEM 1239

Anna Akhmatova Lot's Wife *translated by* Richard Wilbur...... POEM 1243

Wislawa Szymborska Lot's Wife *translated by* Stanislaw
Baranczak *and* Clare Cavanagh.......... POEM 1247

from Nobel Lecture: The Poet and the World
translated by Stanislaw Baranczak and Clare
Cavanagh.......................... SPEECH 1251

Gabriela Mistral Fear *translated by* Doris Dana .... POEM 1257

Pablo Neruda Sonnet 79 *translated by* Stephen Tapscott....... SONNET 1261

Soneto 79 .... SONETO 1261

Philip Larkin The Explosion .... POEM 1265

Link to Today
Trapped Australian Miners Rescued .... WEB ARTICLE 1268

Ted Hughes The Horses .... POEM 1273

Seamus Heaney Digging .... POEM 1278

Margaret Atwood Mushrooms .... POEM 1285

Eavan Boland Atlantis—A Lost Sonnet..................... SONNET 1291

COLLECTION **13** Expectation and
Reality

Literary Focus Irony .... ESSAY 1295

Analyzing Visuals Analyzing a Sculpture 1296

Reading Focus Identifying Cause and Effect .... ESSAY 1297

Katherine Mansfield The Doll's House .... SHORT STORY 1299

D. H. Lawrence The Rocking-Horse Winner .... SHORT STORY 1309

James Joyce Araby.......................... SHORT STORY 1325

Jorge Luis Borges The Book of Sand
translated by Andrew Hurley.......... SHORT STORY 1335

Samuel Beckett Come and Go........................ DRAMA 1343

Harold Pinter That's All.......................... DRAMA 1351

Africa Emerges

Doris Lessing No Witchcraft for Sale . . . . SHORT STORY 1357

Nadine Gordimer Once upon a Time . . . . SHORT STORY 1369

Chinua Achebe Marriage Is a Private Affair . . . . SHORT STORY 1377

Wole Soyinka Telephone Conversation . . . . POEM 1385

Comparing Texts: World Literature

Postcolonial Literature 1389

   Derek Walcott *from* Omeros . . . . EPIC POEM 1391

   V. S. Naipaul B. Wordsworth . . . . SHORT STORY 1397

   Paul Theroux *from* Sir Vidia's Shadow . . . . MEMOIR 1407

   A Writer's Influence . . . . CARTOON 1412

   Anita Desai Games at Twilight . . . . SHORT STORY 1415

Writing Workshop Literary Analysis: Nonfiction 1426

Preparing for Timed Writing 1435

Media Workshop Analyzing Media 1436

Preparing for Standardized Tests 1444

   Literary Skills Review

      Heinrich Heine The Lorelei
                translated by Louis Untermeyer . . . . POEM 1444

      Margaret Atwood Siren Song . . . . POEM 1444

   Vocabulary Skills Review 1446

   Writing Skills Review 1447

Read On 1448

RESOURCE CENTER

Handbook of Literary and
Historical Terms 1452
World of Work 1474
Writer's Handbook 1480
Language Handbook 1492

Glossary 1531
Spanish Glossary 1539
Academic Vocabulary Glossary
in English and Spanish 1546
Acknowledgments 1548

Picture Credits 1552
Index of Skills 1556
Index of Authors and Titles 1566

Selections by Alternative Themes

Selections are listed here in alternative theme groupings.

APPEARANCE VERSUS REALITY

from **Don Quixote**
Miguel de Cervantes 603

from **A Reason for Hope**
Jane Goodall 710

To a Louse
Robert Burns 724

She Walks in Beauty
George Gordon, Lord Byron 811

Ozymandias
Percy Bysshe Shelley 819

The Night-Soil Men from **The Ghost Map**
Steven B. Johnson 910

The Lady of Shalott
Alfred, Lord Tennyson 917

The Jewels
Guy de Maupassant 1033

Araby
James Joyce 1325

The Book of Sand
Jorge Luis Borges 1335

Once upon a Time
Nadine Gordimer 1369

from **Sir Vidia's Shadow**
Paul Theroux 1407

GOOD VERSUS EVIL

from **The Lord of the Rings**
J.R.R. Tolkien 12

from **The Pardoner's Tale**
Geoffrey Chaucer 149

Edward, Edward 190

from **Everyman** 217

The Fall of Satan from **Paradise Lost**
John Milton 350

The Tragedy of Macbeth
William Shakespeare 404

My Last Duchess
Robert Browning 943

Porphyria's Lover
Robert Browning 947

The Mark of the Beast
Rudyard Kipling 993

On the Bottom from **Survival in Auschwitz**
Primo Levi 1093

Never Shall I Forget
Elie Wiesel 1103

The Second Coming
William Butler Yeats 1200

Lot's Wife
Wislawa Szymborska 1247

HEROES AND ANTIHEROES

from **Beowulf** 21

from **The Collected Beowulf**
Gareth Hinds 54

from **Gilgamesh: A Verse Narrative** 89

from the **Iliad, Book 22: The Death of Hector**
Homer 99

from **Le Morte d'Arthur**
Sir Thomas Malory 207

from **Sir Gawain and the Green Knight** 195

The Fall of Satan from **Paradise Lost**
John Milton 350

The Tragedy of Macbeth
William Shakespeare 404

Ulysses
Alfred, Lord Tennyson 926

My Last Duchess
Robert Browning 943

Dulce et Decorum Est
Wilfred Owen 1075

Under Heavy Fire in Iraq
Richard Norton-Taylor 1088

On the Bottom from **Survival in Auschwitz**
Primo Levi 1093

The Destructors
Graham Greene 1127

The Hollow Men
T. S. Eliot 1189

HUMOR AND THE STING OF SATIRE

Get Up and Bar the Door 188

Sonnet 130
William Shakespeare 398

from **Gulliver's Travels**
Jonathan Swift 565

A Modest Proposal
Jonathan Swift 580

from **Candide**
Voltaire 595

from **Don Quixote**
Miguel de Cervantes 603

from **The Rape of the Lock**
Alexander Pope 621

To a Louse
Robert Burns 724

Come and Go
Samuel Beckett 1343

That's All
Harold Pinter 1351

Telephone Conversation
Wole Soyinka 1385

THE INDIVIDUAL AND SOCIETY

from **A History of the English Church
and People**
Bede 81

The Prologue from **The Canterbury Tales**
Geoffrey Chaucer 121

Another Renaissance?
Gary Fisher 262

Meditation 17
John Donne 296

Tilbury Speech
Queen Elizabeth I 380

1 Dead in Attic
Chris Rose 536

from **The Diary of Samuel Pepys**
Samuel Pepys 545

from **Don Quixote**
Miguel de Cervantes 603

from **The Life of Samuel Johnson**
James Boswell 645

from **The Education of Women**
Daniel Defoe 674

Tanka 868

Question and Answer Among the Mountains
Li Po 877

The Night-Soil Men from **The Ghost Map**
Steven B. Johnson 910

The Mark of the Beast
Rudyard Kipling 993

The Bet
Anton Chekhov 1023

The Soldier
Rupert Brooke 1078

A Soldier's Declaration
Siegfried Sassoon 1084

Shooting an Elephant
George Orwell 1141

from **A Room of One's Own**
Virginia Woolf 1162

from **The Letters of Virginia Woolf**
Virginia Woolf 1181

Musée des Beaux Arts
W. H. Auden 1223

Not Waving but Drowning
Stevie Smith 1239

from **Nobel Lecture: The Poet and the World**
Wislawa Szymborska 1251

Digging
Seamus Heaney 1278

The Doll's House
Katherine Mansfield 1299

The Book of Sand
Jorge Luis Borges 1335

That's All
Harold Pinter 1351

No Witchcraft for Sale
Doris Lessing 1357

Games at Twilight
Anita Desai 1415

INNOCENCE AND EXPERIENCE

The Fall of Satan from **Paradise Lost**
John Milton 350

from **Candide**
Voltaire 595

from **A Reason for Hope**
Jane Goodall 710

SELECTIONS BY ALTERNATIVE THEMES continued

The Tyger
William Blake 730

The Lamb
William Blake 733

The Chimney Sweeper *from* **Songs of Innocence**
William Blake 737

The Chimney Sweeper *from* **Songs of Experience**
William Blake 740

Fern Hill
Dylan Thomas 1229

Atlantis—A Lost Sonnet
Eavan Boland 1291

The Doll's House
Katherine Mansfield 1299

The Rocking-Horse Winner
D. H. Lawrence 1309

Araby
James Joyce 1325

from **Sir Vidia's Shadow**
Paul Theroux 1407

Games at Twilight
Anita Desai 1415

LOSS AND DEATH

The Seafarer 61

The Wife's Lament 66

The Wanderer 68

from **Gilgamesh: A Verse Narrative** 89

from **The Pardoner's Tale**
Geoffrey Chaucer 149

Meditation 17
John Donne 296

Death be not proud
John Donne 300

On My First Son
Ben Jonson 309

When I consider how my light is spent
John Milton 363

Sonnet 71
William Shakespeare 395

1 Dead in Attic
Chris Rose 536

from **A Journal of the Plague Year**
Daniel Defoe 557

Elegy Written in a Country Churchyard
Thomas Gray 657

When I Have Fears
John Keats 843

Ulysses
Alfred, Lord Tennyson 926

from **In Memoriam A.H.H**
Alfred, Lord Tennyson 931

Crossing the Bar
Alfred, Lord Tennyson 937

Ah, Are You Digging on My Grave?
Thomas Hardy 976

To an Athlete Dying Young
A. E. Housman 981

Never Shall I Forget
Elie Wiesel 1103

Do Not Go Gentle into That Good Night
Dylan Thomas 1235

Lot's Wife
Anna Akhmatova 1243

Lot's Wife
Wislawa Szymborska 1247

The Explosion
Philip Larkin 1265

Atlantis—A Lost Sonnet
Eavan Boland 1291

LOVE'S SORROWS, LOVE'S TRIUMPHS

from **The Wife of Bath's Tale**
Geoffrey Chaucer 161

Lord Randall 185

Whoso List to Hunt
Sir Thomas Wyatt 271

Sonnet 30
Edmund Spenser 271

Sonnet 75
Edmund Spenser 274

The Passionate Shepherd to His Love
Christopher Marlowe 277

The Nymph's Reply to the Shepherd
Sir Walter Raleigh 277

To the Virgins, to Make Much of Time
Robert Herrick 283

To His Coy Mistress
Andrew Marvell 283

Song
John Donne 289

A Valediction: Forbidding Mourning
John Donne 291

On My First Son
Ben Jonson 309

Song: To Celia
Ben Jonson 309

Why So Pale and Wan, Fond Lover?
Sir John Suckling 315

To Lucasta, on Going to the Wars
Richard Lovelace 315

To Althea, from Prison
Richard Lovelace 318

Sonnets 18, 29, 30. 71, 73, 116, 130
William Shakespeare 391

Letter to His Two Small Children
Li Po 877

Sonnet 43
Elizabeth Barrett Browning 953

Dover Beach
Matthew Arnold 965

When I Was One-and-Twenty
A. E. Housman 984

The Demon Lover
Elizabeth Bowen 1117

from **The Autobiography of William Butler Yeats**
William Butler Yeats 1216

Sonnet 79 / Soneto 79
Pablo Neruda 1261

OPPRESSION AND FREEDOM

from **The Wife of Bath's Tale**
Geoffrey Chaucer 161

Psalm 137 321

from **Female Orations**
Margaret Cavendish, Duchess of Newcastle 377

from **A Vindication of the Rights of Woman**
Mary Wollstonecraft 667

from **The Education of Women**
Daniel Defoe 674

To the Ladies
Mary, Lady Chudleigh 677

"The Noble Mansion of Free India"
Jawaharlal Nehru 1155

from **A Room of One's Own**
Virginia Woolf 1162

Marriage Is a Private Affair
Chinua Achebe 1377

PEOPLE AND NATURE

The Seafarer 61

The Wife's Lament 66

The Wanderer 68

from **A Reason for Hope**
Jane Goodall 710

To a Mouse
Robert Burns 721

**Lines Composed a Few Miles
Above Tintern Abbey**
William Wordsworth 747

from **Ode: Intimations of Immortality**
William Wordsworth 757

Saving Creatures Great and Small
Timothy Foote 803

from **Childe Harold's Pilgrimage, Canto IV**
George Gordon, Lord Byron 813

Ode to the West Wind
Percy Bysshe Shelley 824

To a Skylark
Percy Bysshe Shelley 829

To a Mosquito
W. S. Merwin 837

Ode to a Nightingale
John Keats 847

Tanka 868

Haiku 870

Night Thoughts Afloat
Tu Fu 875

Quiet Night Thoughts
Li Po 877

SELECTIONS BY ALTERNATIVE THEMES continued

Question and Answer Among the Mountains
Li Po 877

Pied Beauty
Gerard Manley Hopkins 957

The Darkling Thrush
Thomas Hardy 973

When Elements Go Extreme
Jason La Canfora 988

The Lake Isle of Innisfree
William Butler Yeats 1205

The Wild Swans at Coole
William Butler Yeats 1208

The Explosion
Philip Larkin 1265

Trapped Australian Miners Rescued 1268

The Horses
Ted Hughes 1273

Mushrooms
Margaret Atwood 1285

POWER AND AMBITION

from **Gilgamesh: A Verse Narrative** 89

from **Everyman** 217

The Tragedy of Macbeth
William Shakespeare 404

from **Macbeth: The Graphic Novel**
Tony Leonard Tamai and Arthur Byron Cover 496

Ozymandias
Percy Bysshe Shelley 819

Jade Flower Palace
Tu Fu 873

How Much Land Does a Man Need?
Leo Tolstoy 1009

"I Believe in a British Empire"
Joseph Chamberlain 1151

The Rocking-Horse Winner
D. H. Lawrence 1309

THE QUEST AND THE PERILOUS JOURNEY

from **The Lord of the Rings**
J.R.R. Tolkien 12

from **The Collected Beowulf**
Gareth Hinds 54

The Seafarer 61

The Wanderer 68

from **Gilgamesh: A Verse Narrative** 89

from **Sir Gawain and the Green Knight** 195

from **Le Morte d'Arthur**
Sir Thomas Malory 207

from **Everyman** 217

from **The Pilgrim's Progress**
John Bunyan 367

from **Don Quixote**
Miguel de Cervantes 603

The Rime of the Ancient Mariner
Samuel Taylor Coleridge 774

Ulysses
Alfred, Lord Tennyson 926

The Rocking-Horse Winner
D. H. Lawrence 1309

Araby
James Joyce 1325

from **Omeros**
Derek Walcott 1391

THE SEARCH FOR WISDOM

Anglo-Saxon Riddles 74

from **Everyman** 217

Another Renaissance?
Gary Fisher 262

Psalm 23 321

The Parable of the Prodigal Son 325

Night 332

from **Philosophy and Spiritual Discipline** 334

Zen Parables 336

from **The Analects of Confucius** 338

from the **Tao Te Ching** 339

Taoist Anecdotes 340

Sayings of Saadi
Saadi 341

African Proverbs 342

When I consider how my light is spent
John Milton 363

from **The Pilgrim's Progress**
John Bunyan 367

Of Studies
Francis Bacon 374

Why I Turned Pepys' Diary into a Weblog
Phil Gyford 550

Heroic Couplets
Alexander Pope 615

from **An Essay on Man**
Alexander Pope 618

from **The Meaning of Everything**
Simon Winchester 639

The Bet
Anton Chekhov 1023

Spacecraft Voyager 1 Has Boldly Gone
Alice Oswald 1070

THE TRANSFORMING IMAGINATION

from **The Collected Beowulf**
Gareth Hinds 54

from **Walking to Canterbury**
Jerry Ellis 178

from **A Reason for Hope**
Jane Goodall 710

**Lines Composed a Few Miles
Above Tintern Abbey**
William Wordsworth 747

Composed upon Westminster Bridge
William Wordsworth 761

Kubla Khan
Samuel Taylor Coleridge 774

She Walks in Beauty
George Gordon, Lord Byron 811

from **Childe Harold's Pilgrimage, Canto IV**
George Gordon, Lord Byron 813

Ode to the West Wind
Percy Bysshe Shelley 824

On First Looking into Chapman's Homer
John Keats 843

Ode to a Nightingale
John Keats 847

Ode on a Grecian Urn
John Keats 852

Quiet Night Thoughts
Li Po 877

The Demon Lover
Elizabeth Bowen 1117

A Haunted House
Virginia Woolf 1177

The Lake Isle of Innisfree
William Butler Yeats 1205

Sailing to Byzantium
William Butler Yeats 1213

Fern Hill
Dylan Thomas 1229

from **Nobel Lecture: The Poet and the World**
Wislawa Szymborska 1251

Mushrooms
Margaret Atwood 1285

The Rocking-Horse Winner
D. H. Lawrence 1309

The Book of Sand
Jorge Luis Borges 1335

B. Wordsworth
V. S. Naipaul 1397

THE WAGES OF WAR

from the **Iliad, Book 22: The Death of Hector**
Homer 99

Tilbury Speech
Queen Elizabeth I 380

Dulce et Decorum Est
Wilfred Owen 1075

A Soldier's Declaration
Siegfried Sassoon 1084

Under Heavy Fire in Iraq
Richard Norton-Taylor 1088

On the Bottom *from* **Survival in Auschwitz**
Primo Levi 1093

Blood, Sweat, and Tears
Winston Churchill 1109

The Destructors
Graham Greene 1127

from **Jacob's Room**
Virginia Woolf 1172

The Hollow Men
T. S. Eliot 1189

The Second Coming
William Butler Yeats 1200

Selections By Genre

FICTION

ALLEGORY
from **The Pilgrim's Progress**
John Bunyan 367

ANECDOTES
Taoist Anecdotes 340

DEBATE
from **Female Orations**
Margaret Cavendish, Duchess of Newcastle 377

GRAPHIC NOVELS
from **The Collected Beowulf**
Gareth Hinds 54
from **Macbeth: The Graphic Novel**
Tony Leonard Tamai and Arthur Byron Cover 496

NOVEL EXCERPTS
from **The Lord of the Rings**
J.R.R. Tolkien 12
from **A Journal of the Plague Year**
Daniel Defoe 557
from **Gulliver's Travels**
Jonathan Swift 565
   from **Part 1: A Voyage to Lilliput**
   Jonathan Swift 566
   from **Part 2: A Voyage to Brobdingnag**
   Jonathan Swift 574
from **Candide**
Voltaire 595
from **Don Quixote**
Miguel de Cervantes 603
from **Jacob's Room**
Virginia Woolf 1172

PARABLES
The Parable of the Prodigal Son 325
Zen Parables 336

ROMANCE NARRATIVE
from **Sir Gawain and the Green Knight** 195
from **Le Morte d'Arthur**
Sir Thomas Malory 207

SHORT STORIES
The Mark of the Beast
Rudyard Kipling 993
How Much Land Does a Man Need?
Leo Tolstoy 1009
The Bet
Anton Chekhov 1023
The Jewels
Guy de Maupassant 1033
The Demon Lover
Elizabeth Bowen 1117
The Destructors
Graham Greene 1127
A Haunted House
Virginia Woolf 1177
The Doll's House
Katherine Mansfield 1299
The Rocking-Horse Winner
D. H. Lawrence 1309
Araby
James Joyce 1325
The Book of Sand
Jorge Luis Borges 1335
No Witchcraft for Sale
Doris Lessing 1357
Once upon a Time
Nadine Gordimer 1369
Marriage Is a Private Affair
Chinua Achebe 1377
B. Wordsworth
V. S. Naipaul 1397
Games at Twilight
Anita Desai 1415

DRAMA

from **Everyman** 217

from **W;t**
Margaret Edson 304

The Tragedy of Macbeth
William Shakespeare 404

Come and Go
Samuel Beckett 1343

That's All
Harold Pinter 1351

POETRY

from **Beowulf** 21

    The Monster Grendel 23

    The Arrival of the Hero 27

    Unferth's Challenge 30

    The Battle with Grendel 34

    The Monster's Mother 39

    The Final Battle 43

The Seafarer 61

The Wife's Lament 66

The Wanderer 68

Anglo-Saxon Riddles 74

from **Gilgamesh: A Verse Narrative** 89

from the **Iliad, Book 22: The Death of Hector**
Homer 99

from **The Canterbury Tales**
Geoffrey Chaucer 118

    The Prologue 121

    from **The Pardoner's Tale** 149

    from **The Wife of Bath's Tale** 161

Lord Randall 185

Get Up and Bar the Door 188

Edward, Edward 190

The Twa Corbies 244

Raven doth to raven fly
Alexander Pushkin 244

Whoso List to Hunt
Sir Thomas Wyatt 271

Sonnet 30
Edmund Spenser 271

Sonnet 75
Edmund Spenser 274

The Passionate Shepherd to His Love
Christopher Marlowe 277

The Nymph's Reply to the Shepherd
Sir Walter Raleigh 277

To the Virgins, to Make Much of Time
Robert Herrick 283

To His Coy Mistress
Andrew Marvell 283

Song
John Donne 289

A Valediction: Forbidding Mourning
John Donne 291

Death be not proud
John Donne 300

On My First Son
Ben Jonson 309

Song: To Celia
Ben Jonson 309

Why So Pale and Wan, Fond Lover?
Sir John Suckling 315

To Lucasta, on Going to the Wars
Richard Lovelace 315

To Althea, from Prison
Richard Lovelace 318

Psalm 23 321

Psalm 137 321

The Fall of Satan from **Paradise Lost**
John Milton 350

When I consider how my light is spent
John Milton 363

Sonnet 18
William Shakespeare 390

Sonnet 29
William Shakespeare 392

Sonnet 30
William Shakespeare 393

Sonnet 71
William Shakespeare 395

SELECTIONS BY GENRE continued

Sonnet 73
William Shakespeare 396

Sonnet 116
William Shakespeare 397

Sonnet 130
William Shakespeare 398

Sonnet 42
Francesco Petrarch 400

When You Are Old
Pierre de Ronsard 520

When You Are Old
William Butler Yeats 520

Heroic Couplets
Alexander Pope 615

from **An Essay on Man**
Alexander Pope 618

from **The Rape of the Lock**
Alexander Pope 621

Elegy Written in a Country Churchyard
Thomas Gray 657

To the Ladies
Mary, Lady Chudleigh 677

Love Arm'd
Aphra Behn 694

"I love you as I love . . ."
Charles Baudelaire 694

To a Mouse
Robert Burns 721

To a Louse
Robert Burns 724

The Tyger
William Blake 730

The Lamb
William Blake 733

The Chimney Sweeper
from **Songs of Innocence**
William Blake 737

The Chimney Sweeper
from **Songs of Experience**
William Blake 740

A Poison Tree
William Blake 742

Lines Composed a Few Miles Above Tintern Abbey
William Wordsworth 747

from **Ode: Intimations of Immortality**
William Wordsworth 757

Composed upon Westminster Bridge
William Wordsworth 761

The World Is Too Much with Us
William Wordsworth 763

Kubla Khan
Samuel Taylor Coleridge 767

The Rime of the Ancient Mariner
Samuel Taylor Coleridge 774

She Walks in Beauty
George Gordon, Lord Byron 811

from **Childe Harold's Pilgrimage, Canto IV**
George Gordon, Lord Byron 813

Ozymandias
Percy Bysshe Shelley 819

Ode to the West Wind
Percy Bysshe Shelley 824

To a Skylark
Percy Bysshe Shelley 829

To a Mosquito
W. S. Merwin 837

On First Looking into Chapman's Homer
John Keats 843

When I Have Fears
John Keats 843

Ode to a Nightingale
John Keats 847

Ode on a Grecian Urn
John Keats 852

Tanka 868

Haiku 870

Jade Flower Palace
Tu Fu 873

Night Thoughts Afloat
Tu Fu 875

Quiet Night Thoughts
Li Po 877

Question and Answer Among the Mountains
Li Po 877

Letter to His Two Small Children
Li Po 877

London
William Blake 894

The Virgins
Derek Walcott 894

The Lady of Shalott
Alfred, Lord Tennyson 917

Ulysses
Alfred, Lord Tennyson 926

from **In Memoriam A.H.H.**
Alfred, Lord Tennyson 931

Crossing the Bar
Alfred, Lord Tennyson 937

My Last Duchess
Robert Browning 943

Porphyria's Lover
Robert Browning 947

Sonnet 43
Elizabeth Barrett Browning 953

Pied Beauty
Gerard Manley Hopkins 957

Dover Beach
Matthew Arnold 965

The Darkling Thrush
Thomas Hardy 973

Ah, Are You Digging on My Grave?
Thomas Hardy 976

To an Athlete Dying Young
A. E. Housman 981

When I Was One-and-Twenty
A. E. Housman 984

Drummer Hodge
Thomas Hardy 1054

The Sleeper of the Valley
Arthur Rimbaud 1054

Spacecraft Voyager 1 Has Boldly Gone
Alice Oswald 1070

Dulce et Decorum Est
Wilfred Owen 1075

The Soldier
Rupert Brooke 1078

The Rear-Guard
Siegfried Sassoon 1081

Never Shall I Forget
Elie Wiesel 1103

The Hollow Men
T. S. Eliot 1189

The Second Coming
William Butler Yeats 1200

The Lake Isle of Innisfree
William Butler Yeats 1205

The Wild Swans at Coole
William Butler Yeats 1208

Sailing to Byzantium
William Butler Yeats 1213

Musée des Beaux Arts
W. H. Auden 1223

Fern Hill
Dylan Thomas 1229

Do Not Go Gentle into That Good Night
Dylan Thomas 1235

Not Waving but Drowning
Stevie Smith 1239

Lot's Wife
Anna Akhmatova 1243

Lot's Wife
Wislawa Szymborska 1247

Fear
Gabriela Mistral 1257

Sonnet 79 / Soneto 79
Pablo Neruda 1261

The Explosion
Philip Larkin 1265

The Horses
Ted Hughes 1273

Digging
Seamus Heaney 1278

Mushrooms
Margaret Atwood 1285

Atlantis—A Lost Sonnet
Eavan Boland 1291

Telephone Conversation
Wole Soyinka 1385

from **Omeros**
Derek Walcott 1391

The Lorelei
Heinrich Heine 1444

Siren Song
Margaret Atwood 1444

SELECTIONS BY GENRE continued

NONFICTION AND INFORMATIONAL TEXT

AUTOBIOGRAPHY

from **The Autobiography of William Butler Yeats**
William Butler Yeats 1216

AXIOMS AND MAXIMS

from **The Analects of Confucius** 338
Sayings of Saadi
Saadi. 341

BIOGRAPHY

from **The Life of Samuel Johnson**
James Boswell 645

DEFINITIONS

from **A Dictionary of the English Language**
Samuel Johnson 633

DIARY

from **The Diary of Samuel Pepys**
Samuel Pepys. 545

ESSAYS

Of Studies
Francis Bacon. 374
A Modest Proposal
Jonathan Swift. 580
from **The Education of Women**
Daniel Defoe 674
Shooting an Elephant
George Orwell 1141
from **A Room of One's Own**
Virginia Woolf. 1162

UNIT INTRODUCTIONS

Unit 1: The Anglo-Saxon Period and
the Middle Ages 449–1485 4
Unit 2: The Renaissance 1485–1660:
A Flourish of Genius. 254
Unit 3: The Restoration and
the Eighteenth Century 1660–1800 530
Unit 4: The Romantic Period 1798–1832. 704
Unit 5: The Victorian Period 1832–1901 904
Unit 6: The Modern World 1900 to the Present. . . 1064

LITERARY FOCUS ESSAYS

The Epic Tradition 17
Medieval Narrative. 113
Renaissance Poetry 267
Shakespeare's Sonnets and Plays 385
The Rise of the Novel. 541
Form and Function in the Age of Reason 613
Themes of Romantic Poetry 717
Forms of Romantic Poetry. 809
Figurative Language 915
Realism. 961
War Literature 1073
Themes of Modern and Contemporary Poetry . . 1187
Irony 1295

READING FOCUS ESSAYS

Paraphrasing 19
Analyzing Style: Key Details 115
Analyzing Milton's Style. 345
Using Questioning to Monitor Reading 401
Recognizing Persuasive Techniques 579
Identifying Tone. 620
Recognizing Patterns of Organization 745
Comparing and Contrasting 817
Drawing Inferences from Textual Clues 941
Making Generalizations. 971
Identifying and Critiquing
an Author's Argument. 1107
Analyzing Details. 1227
Identifying Cause and Effect 1297

HISTORIES

from **A History of the English Church and People**
Bede 81

from **The Meaning of Everything**
Simon Winchester 639

The Night-Soil Men *from* **The Ghost Map**
Steven B. Johnson 910

LETTERS

Keats's Last Letter
John Keats 859

from **The Letters of Virginia Woolf**
Virginia Woolf 1181

MAGAZINE ARTICLE

Saving Creatures Great and Small
Timothy Foote 803

MEDITATION

Meditation 17
John Donne 296

MEMOIRS

from **A Reason for Hope**
Jane Goodall 710

On the Bottom *from* **Survival in Auschwitz**
Primo Levi 1093

from **Sir Vidia's Shadow**
Paul Theroux 1407

NEWSPAPER ARTICLES

1 Dead in Attic
Chris Rose 536

When Elements Go Extreme
Jason La Canfora 988

Under Heavy Fire in Iraq
Richard Norton-Taylor 1088

PROVERBS

African Proverbs 342

SACRED TEXTS

Night *from* **the Koran** 332

from **Philosophy and Spiritual Discipline** 334

from the **Tao Te Ching**
Lao Tzu 339

TRAVEL BOOK

from **Walking to Canterbury**
Jerry Ellis 178

WEB ARTICLES

Another Renaissance?
Gary Fisher 262

Why I Turned Pepys' Diary into a Weblog
Phil Gyford 550

Trapped Australian Miners Rescued 1268

PUBLIC DOCUMENTS

DEBATE

from **Female Orations**
Margaret Cavendish, Duchess of Newcastle 377

PLATFORM

from **A Vindication of the Rights of Woman**
Mary Wollstonecraft 667

POLITICAL STATEMENT

A Soldier's Declaration
Siegfried Sassoon 1084

SPEECHES

Tilbury Speech
Queen Elizabeth I 380

Blood, Sweat, and Tears
Winston Churchill 1109

"I Believe in a British Empire"
Joseph Chamberlain 1151

"The Noble Mansion of Free India"
Jawaharlal Nehru 1155

from **Nobel Lecture:**
The Poet and the World
Wislawa Szymborska 1247

SELECTIONS BY REGION

AFRICA

African Proverbs 342

No Witchcraft for Sale
Doris Lessing 1357

Once upon a Time
Nadine Gordimer 1369

Marriage Is a Private Affair
Chinua Achebe 1377

Telephone Conversation
Wole Soyinka 1385

ASIA

from **Gilgamesh: A Verse Narrative** 89

Night *from* **the Koran** 332

from **Philosophy and Spiritual Discipline**
from **the Bhagavad-Gita** 334

Zen Parables 336

from **The Analects of Confucius** 338

from **the Tao Te Ching**
Lao Tzu 339

Taoist Anecdotes 340

Sayings of Saadi
Saadi 341

Tanka 868

Haiku 868

Jade Flower Palace
Tu Fu 873

Night Thoughts Afloat
Tu Fu 875

Quiet Night Thoughts
Li Po 877

**Question and Answer Among
the Mountains**
Li Po 877

Letter to His Two Small Children
Li Po 877

"The Noble Mansion of Free India"
Jawaharlal Nehru 1155

Games at Twilight
Anita Desai 1415

EUROPE

from the **Iliad, Book 22: The Death of Hector**
Homer 99

Raven doth to raven fly
Alexander Pushkin 244

When You Are Old
Pierre de Ronsard 520

When You Are Old
William Butler Yeats 520

from **Candide**
Voltaire 595

from **Don Quixote**
Miguel de Cervantes 603

"I love you as I love . . ."
Charles Baudelaire 694

How Much Land Does a Man Need?
Leo Tolstoy 1009

The Bet
Anton Chekhov 1023

The Jewels
Guy de Maupassant 1033

The Sleeper of the Valley
Arthur Rimbaud 1054

On the Bottom *from* **Survival in Auschwitz**
Primo Levi 1093

Never Shall I Forget
Elie Wiesel 1103

The Demon Lover
Elizabeth Bowen 1117

The Second Coming
William Butler Yeats 1200

The Lake Isle of Innisfree
William Butler Yeats 1205

The Wild Swans at Coole
William Butler Yeats 1208

Sailing to Byzantium
William Butler Yeats 1213

from **The Autobiography of
William Butler Yeats**
William Butler Yeats 1216

Lot's Wife
Anna Akhmatova 1233

Lot's Wife
Wislawa Szymborska 1247

from **Nobel Lecture:**
The Poet and the World
Wislawa Szymborska 1251

Digging
Seamus Heaney 1278

Atlantis—A Lost Sonnet
Eavan Boland 1291

Araby
James Joyce 1325

Come and Go
Samuel Beckett 1343

The Lorelei
Heinrich Heine 1444

GREAT BRITAIN

from **The Lord of the Rings**
J.R.R. Tolkien 12

from **Beowulf** 21

The Seafarer 61

The Wife's Lament 66

The Wanderer 68

Anglo-Saxon Riddles 74

from **A History of the English Church**
and People
Bede 81

The Prologue *from* **The Canterbury Tales**
Geoffrey Chaucer 121

from **The Pardoner's Tale**
Geoffrey Chaucer 149

from **The Wife of Bath's Tale**
Geoffrey Chaucer 161

Lord Randall 185

Get up and Bar the Door 188

Edward, Edward 190

from **Sir Gawain and the Green Knight** 195

from **Le Morte d'Arthur**
Sir Thomas Malory 207

from **Everyman** 217

The Twa Corbies 244

Whoso List to Hunt
Sir Thomas Wyatt 271

Sonnet 30
Edmund Spenser 271

Sonnet 75
Edmund Spenser 274

The Passionate Shepherd to His Love
Christopher Marlowe 277

The Nymph's Reply to the Shepherd
Sir Walter Raleigh 277

To the Virgins, to Make Much of Time
Robert Herrick 283

To His Coy Mistress
Andrew Marvell 283

Song
John Donne 289

A Valediction: Forbidding Mourning
John Donne 291

Meditation 17
John Donne 296

Death be not proud
John Donne 300

On My First Son
Ben Jonson 309

Song: To Celia
Ben Jonson 309

Why So Pale and Wan, Fond Lover?
Sir John Suckling 315

To Lucasta, on Going to the Wars
Richard Lovelace 315

To Althea, from Prison
Richard Lovelace 318

Psalm 23 321

Psalm 137 321

The Parable of the Prodigal Son 325

The Fall of Satan *from* **Paradise Lost**
John Milton 350

When I consider how my light is spent
John Milton 363

from **The Pilgrim's Progress**
John Bunyan 367

SELECTIONS BY REGION continued

Of Studies
Francis Bacon 374

Tilbury Speech
Queen Elizabeth I 380

from **Female Orations**
Margaret Cavendish, Duchess of Newcastle 377

Sonnet 18
William Shakespeare 390

Sonnet 29
William Shakespeare 392

Sonnet 30
William Shakespeare 393

Sonnet 71
William Shakespeare 395

Sonnet 73
William Shakespeare 396

Sonnet 116
William Shakespeare 397

Sonnet 130
William Shakespeare 398

The Tragedy of Macbeth
William Shakespeare 404

from **Macbeth: The Graphic Novel**
Tony Leonard Tamai and Anthony Byron Cover . . 496

from **The Diary of Samuel Pepys**
Samuel Pepys 545

Why I Turned Pepys' Diary into a Weblog
Phil Gyford 550

from **A Journal of the Plague Year**
Daniel Defoe 557

from **Gulliver's Travels**
Jonathan Swift 565

A Modest Proposal
Jonathan Swift 580

Heroic Couplets
Alexander Pope 615

from **An Essay on Man**
Alexander Pope 618

from **The Rape of the Lock**
Alexander Pope 621

from **A Dictionary of the English Language**
Samuel Johnson 633

from **The Meaning of Everything**
Simon Winchester 639

from **The Life of Samuel Johnson**
James Boswell 645

Elegy Written in a Country Churchyard
Thomas Gray 657

from **A Vindication of the Rights of Woman**
Mary Wollstonecraft 667

from **The Education of Women**
Daniel Defoe 674

To the Ladies
Mary, Lady Chudleigh 677

Love Arm'd
Aphra Behn 694

from **A Reason for Hope**
Jane Goodall 710

To a Mouse
Robert Burns 721

To a Louse
Robert Burns 724

The Tyger
William Blake 730

The Lamb
William Blake 733

The Chimney Sweeper
from **Songs of Innocence**
William Blake 737

The Chimney Sweeper
from **Songs of Experience**
William Blake 740

A Poison Tree
William Blake 742

**Lines Composed a Few Miles
Above Tintern Abbey**
William Wordsworth 747

from **Ode: Intimations of Immortality**
William Wordsworth 757

Composed upon Westminster Bridge
William Wordsworth 761

The World Is Too Much with Us
William Wordsworth 763

Kubla Khan
Samuel Taylor Coleridge 767

The Rime of the Ancient Mariner
Samuel Taylor Coleridge 774

She Walks in Beauty
George Gordon, Lord Byron 811

from **Childe Harold's Pilgrimage, Canto IV**
George Gordon, Lord Byron 813

Ozymandias
Percy Bysshe Shelley 819

Ode to the West Wind
Percy Bysshe Shelley 824

To a Skylark
Percy Bysshe Shelley 829

On First Looking into Chapman's Homer
John Keats 843

When I Have Fears
John Keats 843

Keats's Last Letter
John Keats 859

Ode to a Nightingale
John Keats 847

Ode on a Grecian Urn
John Keats 852

London
William Blake 894

The Lady of Shalott
Alfred, Lord Tennyson 917

Ulysses
Alfred, Lord Tennyson 926

from **In Memoriam A.H.H.**
Alfred, Lord Tennyson 931

Crossing the Bar
Alfred, Lord Tennyson 937

My Last Duchess
Robert Browning 943

Porphyria's Lover
Robert Browning 947

Sonnet 43
Elizabeth Barrett Browning 953

Pied Beauty
Gerard Manley Hopkins 957

Dover Beach
Matthew Arnold 965

The Darkling Thrush
Thomas Hardy 973

Ah, Are You Digging on My Grave?
Thomas Hardy 976

To an Athlete Dying Young
A. E. Housman 981

When I Was One-and-Twenty
A. E. Housman 984

The Mark of the Beast
Rudyard Kipling 993

Drummer Hodge
Thomas Hardy 1054

Spacecraft Voyager 1 Has Boldly Gone
Alice Oswald 1070

Dulce et Decorum Est
Wilfred Owen 1075

The Soldier
Rupert Brooke 1078

The Rear-Guard
Siegfried Sassoon 1081

A Soldier's Declaration
Siegfried Sassoon 1084

Under Heavy Fire in Iraq
Richard Norton-Taylor 1088

Blood, Sweat, and Tears
Winston Churchill 1109

The Destructors
Graham Greene 1127

Shooting an Elephant
George Orwell 1141

"I Believe in a British Empire"
Joseph Chamberlain 1151

from **A Room of One's Own**
Virginia Woolf 1162

from **Jacob's Room**
Virginia Woolf 1172

A Haunted House
Virginia Woolf 1177

from **The Letters of Virginia Woolf**
Virginia Woolf 1181

The Hollow Men
T. S. Eliot 1189

Musée des Beaux Arts
W. H. Auden 1223

Fern Hill
Dylan Thomas 1229

Do Not Go Gentle into That Good Night
Dylan Thomas 1235

SELECTIONS BY REGION continued

Not Waving but Drowning
Stevie Smith 1239

The Explosion
Philip Larkin 1265

Trapped Australian Miners Rescued 1268

The Horses
Ted Hughes 1273

The Rocking-Horse Winner
D. H. Lawrence 1309

That's All
Harold Pinter 1351

NORTH AMERICA

from **The Collected Beowulf**
Gareth Hinds 54

from **Walking to Canterbury**
Jerry Ellis 178

Another Renaissance?
Gary Fisher 262

from **W;t**
Margaret Edson 304

1 Dead in Attic
Chris Rose 536

Saving Creatures Great and Small
Timothy Foote 803

To a Mosquito
W. S. Merwin 837

The Night-Soil Men *from* **The Ghost Map**
Steven B. Johnson 910

When Elements Go Extreme
Jason La Canfora 988

Mushrooms
Margaret Atwood 1285

from **Sir Vidia's Shadow**
Paul Theroux 1407

Siren Song
Margaret Atwood 1444

NEW ZEALAND

The Doll's House
Katherine Mansfield 1299

SOUTH AMERICA

The Book of Sand
Jorge Luis Borges 1335

Fear
Gabriela Mistral 1257

Sonnet 79 / Soneto 79
Pablo Neruda 1261

WEST INDIES

from **Omeros**
Derek Walcott 1391

The Virgins
Derek Walcott 894

B. Wordsworth
V. S. Naipaul 1397

Skills, Workshops, and Features

SKILLS

LITERARY FOCUS ESSAYS

The Epic Tradition	17
Medieval Narrative	113
Renaissance Poetry	267
Shakespeare's Sonnets and Plays	385
The Rise of the Novel	541
Form and Function in the Age of Reason	613
Themes of Romantic Poetry	717
Forms of Romantic Poetry	809
Figurative Language	915
Realism	961
War Literature	1073
Themes of Modern and Contemporary Poetry	1187
Irony	1295

READING FOCUS ESSAYS

Paraphrasing	19
Analyzing Style: Key Details	115
Analyzing Milton's Style	345
Using Questioning to Monitor Reading	401
Recognizing Persuasive Techniques	579
Identifying Tone	620
Recognizing Patterns of Organization	745
Comparing and Contrasting	817
Drawing Inferences from Textual Clues	941
Making Generalizations	971
Identifying and Critiquing an Author's Argument	1107
Analyzing Details	1227
Identifying Cause and Effect	1297

LITERARY SKILLS

Archetype	21, 54
Elegy	61, 657, 1235
Riddles	74
Setting	81, 1127, 1397
Foil	89
Epic Simile	99
Characterization	121
Frame Story	121
Irony	149, 565, 580, 819, 1033, 1141, 1239, 1377
Narrator	161
Ballad	185
Romance	195
Romance Hero	207
Allegory	217, 367, 1009
Speaker	271, 973, 1247
Pastoral Poems	277
Carpe Diem	283
Metaphysical Poetry	289
Metaphysical Conceits	291
Tone	296, 667, 931, 1407
Paradox	300, 1335
Dialogue	304, 1351
Lyric Poetry	309
Diction	315, 633, 837, 1181, 1223, 1229
Parallelism	321, 737
Parable	325
Didactic Literature	332
Style	350, 1172
Allusion	363, 763, 1189
Sonnet	390, 843, 1291
Tragedy	404, 496

SKILLS, WORKSHOPS, AND FEATURES continued

Diary 545
Narrative Voice 557, 1299
Satire 595, 1385
Parody 603
Antithesis 615
Mock Epic 621
Biography 645
Dialect 721
Symbol 730, 829, 1208, 1369,
Theme 742, 926, 984, 1023,
                              1200, 1243, 1285, 1357

Blank Verse 747
Meter and Rhyme 757
Personification 761
Alliteration 767, 957, 1025
Literary Ballad 774
Simile 811
Apostrophe 813
Irony 819, 1033, 1141, 1239
Ode 824
Synesthesia 847
Metaphor 852, 937, 1212, 1261, 1279
Imagery 868, 877, 1081, 1177, 1265, 1415
Mood 873, 965
Sound Devices 917
Dramatic Monologue 943
Petrarchan Sonnet 953
Assonance 957, 1205
Couplet 981
Conflict 993
Figures of Speech 1075
Poetic Structure 1077, 1273
Memoir 1093
Repetition 1103
Oratory 1109

Flashback 1117
Essay 1162
Connotations 1216
Refrain 1257
Foreshadowing 1309
Epiphany 1325
Theater of the Absurd 1343
Contemporary Epic 1391

READING SKILLS FOR LITERARY TEXTS

Paraphrasing 21, 283, 721, 953
Responding to Graphics 54, 496
Identifying the Main Idea 61, 289
Using Context Clues 74, 730, 1075
Understanding Historical Context 81
Comparing and Contrasting 89, 178, 315,
                                     819, 1279, 1325
Visualizing Imagery 99, 852, 931, 1200
Analyzing Style 121, 304, 595, 1212
Drawing Conclusions 149, 737, 957
Interpreting Character 161, 1309
Understanding Purpose 185
Understanding Cause and Effect 195
Analyzing Details 207, 1229, 1415
Making Critical Judgments 217
Drawing Inferences 271, 603, 829, 943,
                                 1033, 1189, 1291, 1343
Understanding Inverted Word Order 277
Recognizing Comparisons and Contrasts 291
Recognizing Patterns of Organization . 296, 747, 1351
Understanding Archaic Language 321, 774
Making Inferences about Theme 325, 1397
Comparing Ideas Across Cultures 332
Analyzing Milton's Style 350
Analyzing Author's Purpose 363, 565, 1407

Making Generalizations about
an Author's Beliefs 367

Using Text Structures to Understand Meaning . . . 390

Using Questions to Monitor Reading 404

Evaluating an Author's Credibility 545

Making Critical Judgments 557

Recognizing Persuasive Techniques 580

Identifying the Writer's Stance 615

Identifying Tone 621, 1181

Analyzing an Author's Point of View 645

Analyzing Word Choice and Word Order 657

Analyzing Rhetorical Devices 667

Annotating a Poem 757

Interpreting Imagery 767, 1285

Understanding Rhyme and Rhythm 813

Analyzing Tone 837, 1239

Understanding Inverted Syntax 843

Reading Closely 847, 1172

Using Text Structures to
Understand Meaning 868, 873, 877

Identifying Contrasting Images 917

Summarizing 926

Visualizing Setting 965, 1177

Making Generalizations 973

Analyzing the Relationship of
Form and Meaning 981

Identifying Conflicts and Resolutions 993

Identifying Theme 1009, 1223

Making Predictions 1023, 1335

Visualizing Details 1081

Evaluating Historical Context 1093

Drawing Inferences about
an Author's Beliefs 1103

Identifying and Critiquing
an Author's Argument 1109

Making and Modifying Predictions 1117

Drawing Inferences About
a Character's Motivations 1127

Identifying the Author's Purpose 1141, 1407

Identifying the Author's Beliefs 1162

Connecting Text to Experience 1205

Analyzing Author's Perspective 1216, 1385

Using Prior Knowledge 1265

Identifying Cause and Effect 1299

Identifying Historical Context 1357

Identifying Language Structures 1369

Identifying Cultural Characteristics 1377

Using Background Knowledge 1391

INFORMATIONAL TEXT SKILLS

Comparing and Contrasting 178, 550

Analyzing Arguments 374

Critiquing an Author's Argument 639

Analyzing Details and Main Idea 802

Analyzing Primary Sources 859

Analyzing Cause and Effect 988

Analyzing Political Statements 1084

Analyzing Sequence of Events 1088

Recognizing Political Assumptions 1151

Analyzing an Author's Beliefs 1251

Using Graphics to Understand Text 1268

VOCABULARY SKILLS
ACADEMIC VOCABULARY

Talking and Writing about Literature 11, 51,
261, 360, 535, 563, 578, 589, 601, 609, 630,
654, 679, 709, 735 , 755, 772 , 800, 822, 857,
919, 924, 950, 969, 1005, 1031, 1069, 1100,
1114, 1158, 1170, 1195, 1203, 1233, 1332, 1366

SKILLS, WORKSHOPS, AND FEATURES continued

LANGUAGE COACH

Connotation . . .   21, 51, 289, 390, 763, 813, 1243, 1257

Related Words 61, 304, 761, 843

Etymology 74, 1291

Antonyms 81, 86, 374, 615, 667, 679, 852, 857,
926, 1084, 1229, 1233, 1349

Shades of Meaning 89

Verbs Used as Adjectives 99

Commonly Confused Words 121, 147, 300

Forms of Words 149

Noun Endings 161, 176

Anglo-Saxon Roots 185

Past-Tense Verbs 195, 204

Prefixes 207, 215, 367, 639, 988, 1172, 1343

Suffixes 217, 277, 296, 545, 549, 621,
630, 747, 1162, 1170

Multiple Meanings . .   271, 350, 360, 404, 730, 735, 837,
917, 924, 937, 943, 1088, 1208, 1235,
1279, 1307, 1309, 1323, 1377, 1397, 1405

Word Origins 283, 332, 363, 550, 557, 563,
633, 657, 802, 824, 873, 1075, 1151, 1158

Latin Roots 291, 321

Parts of Speech 309

Homonyms 315, 603, 609, 721, 868

Synonyms 325, 953, 993, 1005, 1261, 1268

Word Tenses 565

Verb Tenses 565, 578

Stressed Syllables 580, 589

The Sounds of C 595, 1093, 1100

Roots 633, 859, 931, 1023, 1031, 1391

Personal Definitions 645, 654

Definitions 737, 957

Pronunciation 742, 819, 822, 981, 987, 1423

Verb Forms 767, 772

Definitions and Context 774, 800

Verbs Used as Adjectives 811

Multiple Prefixes 829

Related Words 843

Word Sounds and Word Meanings 847

Specific Nouns 877

Idioms 950, 1299

Latin and French Roots 965, 969

Double Letters 973, 979

In Vain 984

Prefixes and Suffixes 1033

Proper Nouns and Proper Adjectives 1077

Prefixes -*un* and -*in* 1081, 1343, 1349

Silent Letters 1103

Suffixes-*ous* 1109, 1114

Suffix-*ly* 1117, 1125, 1357, 1366

Heteronyms 1127

Negative Prefixes 1141, 1149

Denotation/Conotation 1177

Literal and Figurative Meanings 1181

Noun Suffixes 1189, 1195

Suffix -*archy* 1200, 1203

Poetry Recitation 1205

Word Families 1212, 1251, 1385, 1407, 1415

Negating Prefixes 1216

Adverbs and Adjectives 1223

Commonly Misused Words 1239

Using *Set* and *Sit* 1247

Defining Unfamiliar words 1265

Compound Nouns 1273, 1277

Compound Words 1285

Homographs 1325, 1332

Foreign Words 1335

British Phrases 1351

Accented Syllables 1369

VOCABULARY DEVELOPMENT: VOCABULARY SKILLS

Prefixes and Suffixes 51
Anglo Saxon Words and Word Parts 52
Map Meanings 204
Etymology 86, 215, 360, 601, 755, 1125, 1203
Antonyms 147, 578
Analogies 176, 563, 800, 987, 1332, 1423
Scientific and Mathematical Words
Derived from Greek and Latin 361
Synonyms 549, 979, 1031, 1349
Context Clues 609, 772, 1195, 1307, 1366
Connotation and Intensity 589
Etymology Maps 630
Creating Definitions 654
Using a Dictionary 679
Denotation and Connotation 735
Word Origins 757
Using Print and Online Sources 822
Figurative Language 857, 969, 1277
Connotations 924, 1005, 1149, 1323
Multiple-Meaning Words 950
Synonyms and Antonyms 1100
Solving Word Analogies 1114
The Etymology of Political Science
and Historical Terms 1158
Distinguishing Word Meanings 1170
Suffixes 1233
Idioms 1405

WORKSHOPS
WRITING WORKSHOPS

Literary Analysis: Poetry 232
Literary Research Paper 504
Persuasive Essay 682
Reflective Essay 882
Fictional Narrative 1042
Literary Analysis: Nonfiction 1426

PREPARING FOR TIMED WRITING

Literary Analysis 241
Expository Essay 517
Persuasive Essay 691
Reflective Essay 891
Fictional Narrative 1051
Expository Essay: Cause and Effect 1435

LISTENING AND SPEAKING WORKSHOPS

Presenting a Literary Analysis 242
Presenting a Literary Research Paper 518
Presenting and Analyzing Speeches 692
Presenting a Reflective Essay 892
Telling a Story 1052

MEDIA WORKSHOP

Analyzing Media 1436

FEATURES
LINK TO TODAY

Women's Rights Go Wrong 8
Timepieces Across Time 258
Political Cartoons and Caricatures 532
The Coffee House Awakening 534
Long Live the Romantic Comedy 707
Urban Amusements 709
Victorian Inventions 907
The Second Sex 1069

SKILLS, WORKSHOPS, AND FEATURES continued

ANALYZING VISUALS

Analyzing a Painting 114

Analyzing an Illumination 269

Analyzing an Etching 543

Analyzing a Painting 719

Analyzing a Photograph 963

Analyzing a Sculpture 1296

CROSS-CURRICULAR LINKS

Culture Link: Grendel 35

Health Link: Deadly Dining 187

Art Link: Illustrations of *Paradise Lost* 356

Culture Link: Vanity Fair 371

Science Link: Hand Washing 481

Technology Link: From Windmills to
Wind Turbines 606

Music Link: Water Music 625

Culture Link: Real-Life Stories 661

Social Studies Link: Women's Rights Today 671

Social Studies Link: The Wye Valley 753

History Link: The Great Khan 769

Geography Link: Antarctic Convergence 787

Art Link: Ancient Greek Vase Painting 854

Culture Link: Camelot 921

Culture Link: Hanuman 1001

Technology Link: Radio Broadcasts 1111

Geography Link: Myanmar 1145

Art Link: Bruegel's *The Fall of Icarus* 1225

Social Studies Link: Agriculture in Ireland 1282

Mathematics Link: Infinity 1338

Sports Link: Games in India 1419

LITERARY PERSPECTIVES

Analyzing Historical Context 103, 407, 966, 1095

Analyzing Political Context . . 163, 582, 669, 1163, 1357

Analyzing Philosophical Context . 301, 749, 849, 1190

Analyzing Credibility in Literature 582, 776, 1024,
1327

Analyzing Biographical Information . . . 647, 927, 1230

Analyzing Style 820, 944

GRAMMAR LINKS

Subject/Verb Agreement 53

Progressive Form of Verbs 148

Transitive and Intransitive Verbs 205

Direct and Indirect Objects 295

Imperative Mood 313

Using Modifiers Correctly 330

Adjective Clauses and Adverb Clauses 362

Combining Sentences by Inserting
Words and Phrases 494

Pronoun and Antecedent Agreement 590

The Literary Present 610

Sequence of Verb Tenses 631

Irregular Verbs 655

Subjunctive Mood 680

Verb-Tense Consistency 736

Appositives 756

Prepositional Phrases 773

Infinitive Phrases 801

Sentence Structure 823, 969

Direct and Indirect Quotations 858

Adjective or Adverb? 925

Using Participles to Combine Sentences 951

Dangling Modifiers 1006

Punctuating for Clarity: Semicolons,
Colons, Dashes 1101

Connecting Ideas 1115

Independent and Subordinate Clauses . . 1171, 1333

Demonstrative Pronouns and Adjectives 1196

Active and Passive Voice Verbs 1204

Participles and Participial Phrases 1234

Effective Sentences: Parallelism 1367

Effective Sentences: Variety 1424

SKILLS REVIEW

Literary Skills 244, 520, 694, 894, 1054, 1444

Vocabulary Skills 246, 522, 696, 896, 1056, 1446

Writing Skills 247, 523, 697, 897, 1057, 1447

LANGUAGE HANDBOOK

The Parts of Speech 1492

Agreement 1493

Using Verbs 1496

Using Pronouns 1498

Using Modifiers 1500

Phrases 1502

Clauses 1504

Sentence Structure 1505

Sentence Style 1508

Sentence Combining 1511

Capitalization 1512

Punctuation 1516, 1519

Spelling 1523

Glossary of Usage 1526

WRITER'S HANDBOOK

The Writing Process 1480

Paragraphs 1482

The Writer's Language 1486

Designing Your Writing 1488

Why Be a [Reader/Writer?]

by **Kylene Beers**

THE JOURNEY

nce I had a college literature teacher who began each class by saying, "Enjoy the journey." After a couple of weeks, one student bravely responded to the now-routine comment with, "What journey?" The teacher just smiled and didn't answer the question. We were going to have to figure *that* out for ourselves.

Years later, on a long car trip with a friend, I finally figured out what my teacher meant. About every 50 miles, my friend would ask, "Are we there yet?" It didn't matter to her that we were winding our way over stunning snow-capped mountains with views of majestic waterfalls. She wanted to skip that part and *just get there!*

After hearing "Are we there yet?" one too many times, I snapped, "Enjoy the journey!!" She said, "Huh?" and I started laughing because I finally understood *exactly* what my teacher meant:

If we are only interested in doing something because of where it will get us, we miss out on too much. The journey is every bit as important as the destination.

Enjoy the journey.

Traveling via Textbook

What's the journey you ought to enjoy with a literature textbook? You know how textbooks work: There are questions to discuss, vocabulary words to learn, and essays to write.

It's easy to let finishing high school, getting into college, or landing a good job become the *reasons* why you read and write. While those are all important things, they overlook the *critical* reason to be a reader and a writer, and that reason is only found when you remember to *enjoy the journey: be* a reader and *be* a writer.

* Read *Beowulf* not just to answer the questions, but to experience his trials and to find out how his experiences might inform *your own*.

* Read the love poems in Collection 3 not only to figure out the structure of a sonnet, but to discover what love means *to you*.

As you write in response to the readings,

* Don't write merely to finish an assignment. Instead, write to discover when you stand alongside an author's ideas.

* Write to discover when you stand in opposition to an author's ideas.

If you read the assignments carefully, you'll see they are prompts that allow you—if you let them—to discover more about *yourself and the world you live in*.

The Road Ahead

Enjoy this journey. My friend on the car trip never did enjoy ours—it was far easier to complain than to pause and see what was out the window. Literature offers you an amazing window to discover more about yourself and the world you live in—

a window to worlds you might never experience
a window to people and events, struggles, and
triumphs you otherwise might never know
You just have to look.

I have great hopes that this year, more than any other year, you are open to doing just that.

Kylene Beers

Senior Author, *Elements of Literature*

How to Use Your Textbook

Each time you get a new cell phone, you find it has more features than the last one. Without looking at the instructions, you may miss out on the benefits of the phone. It's the same with your textbook. This section introduces you to your book's features, so that you can be successful from the beginning.

Unit Opener

As you look at the title and dates for each unit, think about what you might know already about that time period. Think about the **quotation**. What does it suggest about the literature of the historical period? Keep the **What Do You Think?** question in mind as you go through the unit. You may find that what you think about the period and its literature evolves as you work through the unit.

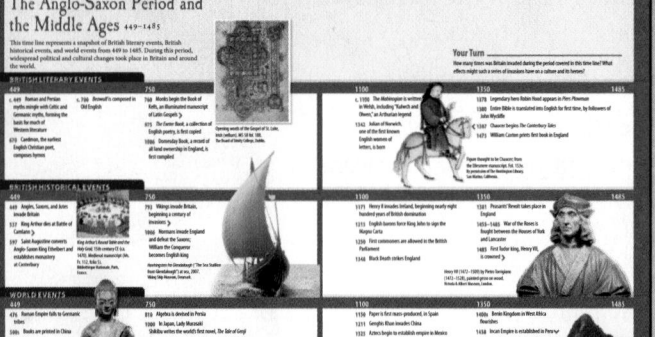

Time Line

In this book, you will study literature and events that occurred in both the recent and the distant past. The time line will help you to put it all in perspective. You'll see how history influenced literature and vice versa, including worldwide literary movements and historical events.

Introduction with Key Concepts

Often we say, "Cut to the chase," or, "Just give me the big picture." This is what **Key Concepts** does. For each unit, this feature provides the essentials about both the literature and the history of the time period. This understanding will be a foundation for your reading throughout the unit—how works of literature emerge in a time and place.

Link to Today

Though there has never been a century like this one in terms of instant communication, what makes us tick as humans hasn't really changed that much. Modern film makers draw on ancient epics, and modern history is driven by past history. **Link to Today** shows the connection and the relevance between events of the time period and our world today.

Collection Opener

A collection focuses on the major literary movements or literary works within the unit's time period. Each collection opener identifies the title of the collection—a clue to its contents—as well as a quotation that suggests a key theme or idea of the period. Try to notice the image on the opener page; consider what it suggests about the literary period.

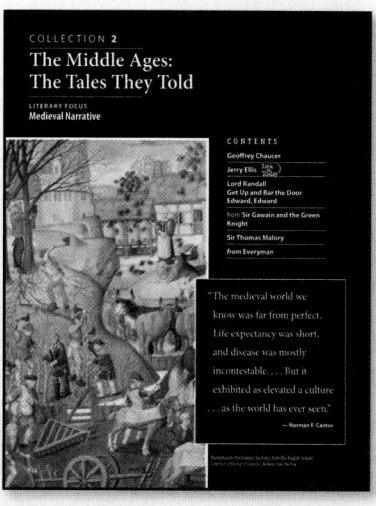

Literary Focus

The **Literary Focus** gives you necessary background on the literature and the time period you are studying. Just as Japanese animé has certain styles, themes, and techniques, the literary masters of the past had a framework within which they worked. **Literary Focus** helps you better understand that framework.

Analyzing Visuals

You are regularly immersed in images through television, magazines, street art, and billboards. Because visual media are so prevalent, you may find it challenging to think about them consciously and critically. **Analyzing Visuals** helps you apply your visual savvy to images and then connect those skills to the literary works you're reading.

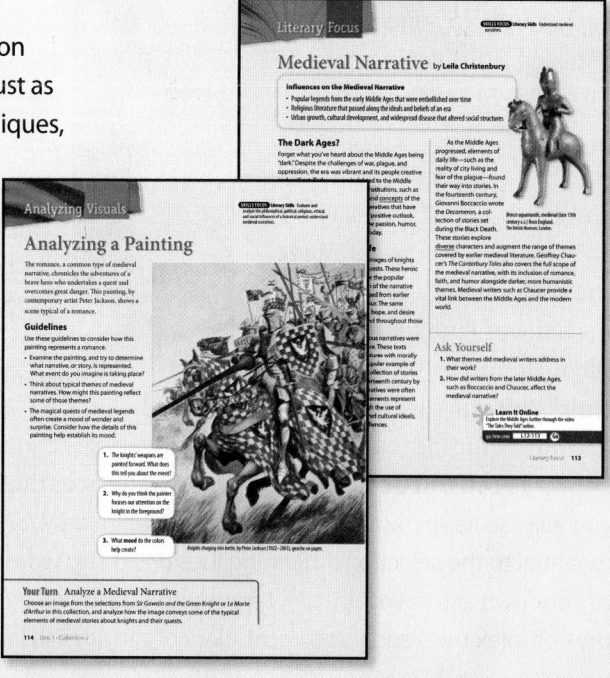

How to Use Your Textbook

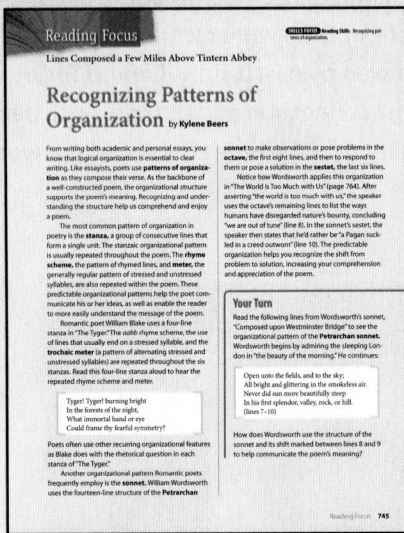

Reading Focus

Sometimes reading selections written in the past seems a little like trying to read something in another language that you barely know. **Reading Focus** gives you the keys to unlock the text. Is the word order changed in this poem? How did the writer use imagery to help the reader visualize the story in his mind? How is the sentence structure different from what we see in today's literature?

Literary Selection Pages
Preparing to Read

Before you do anything important such as playing the big game, going on a date, or taking a trip, you prepare. Do you have everything you need to make the venture successful? **Preparing to Read** ensures that you have all the important bits you need. **Meet the Writer** introduces you to the author of the selection. **What Do You Think** and **QuickWrite** give you ways to connect the ideas and themes of the literary selection to your life. The **Literary Focus, Reading Focus,** and **Writing Focus** present the skills you will use as you go through the selection. **Vocabulary** lists the words essential to the selection's meaning, besides being words you should add to your own active vocabulary. **Language Coach** will guide you through the complex rules and large vocabulary of the English language.

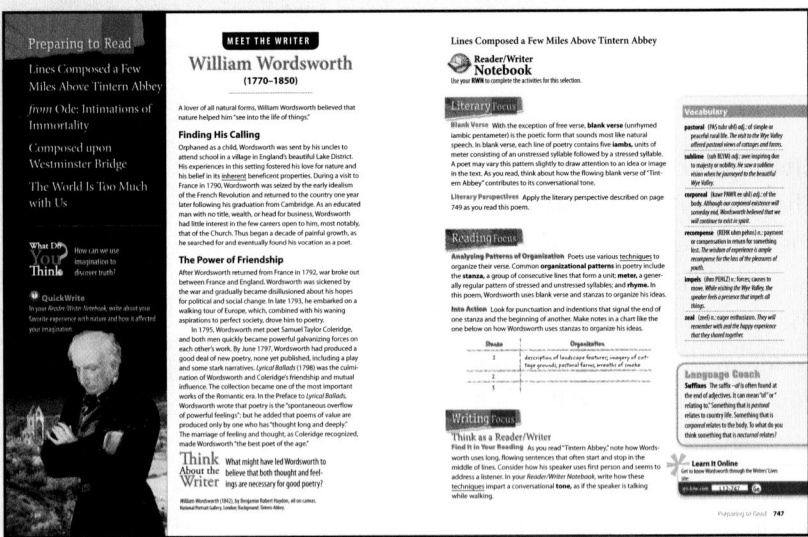

Selection

Which songs, movies, or stories from today do you think will captivate people fifty or even five hundred years from now? The few that survive will be the ones that help us grasp what it means to be human. The selections in this textbook are those universal ones that have survived. **Read with a Purpose** gives you a goal for your reading. **Build Background** provides any information you may need as context for the selection.

Literary Perspectives

Whether you are male or female, rich or poor, native or new to the U.S. influences how you see things. These same factors affect how authors write as well as how you read a piece of literature. **Literary Perspectives** helps you become aware of different perspectives, or lenses, for looking at literature to get a more complete view.

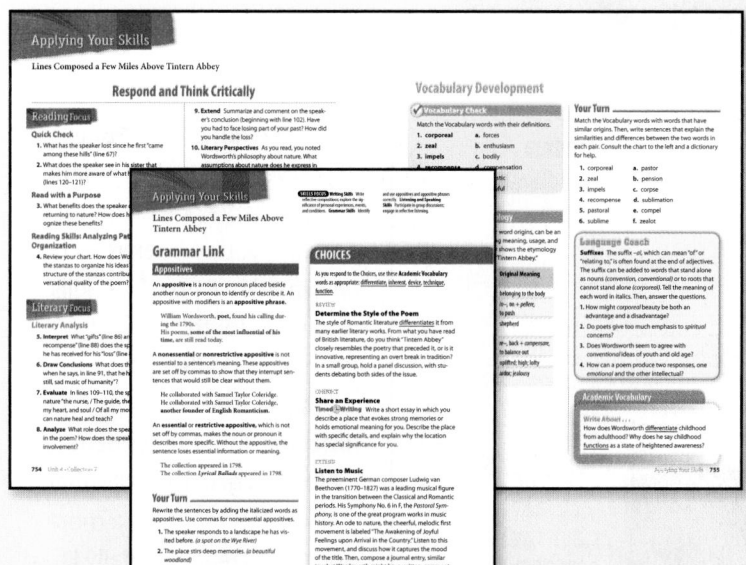

Applying Your Skills

Athletes, musicians, and artists all practice long and hard to perfect their skill. Games, performances, or exhibitions give them a venue for applying their skills. **Applying Your Skills** gives you the opportunity to apply the reading, literary and vocabulary skills you learned about before reading and then practiced throughout the selection. It shows how you are mastering the skills in each selection.

How to Use Your Textbook

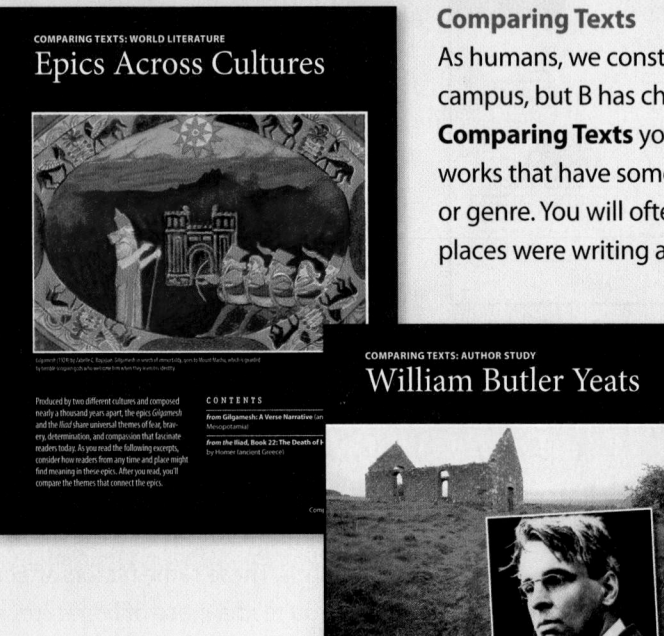

Comparing Texts

As humans, we constantly compare. College A has the prettiest campus, but B has cheaper tuition, and C is closer to home. In **Comparing Texts** you have an opportunity to compare several works that have something in common such as a subject, theme, or genre. You will often find that writers in very different times and places were writing about similar things.

Comparing Texts: Author Study

When you hear a band that you like, do you ever want to track down their earlier CDs to compare what they sound like? Well, the same applies to authors. Great authors don't write just one work of literature. They have a whole body of work for you to read and explore similarities and differences. In **Comparing Texts: Author Study** you'll dive into a number of works by an important author to make deeper connections as you read.

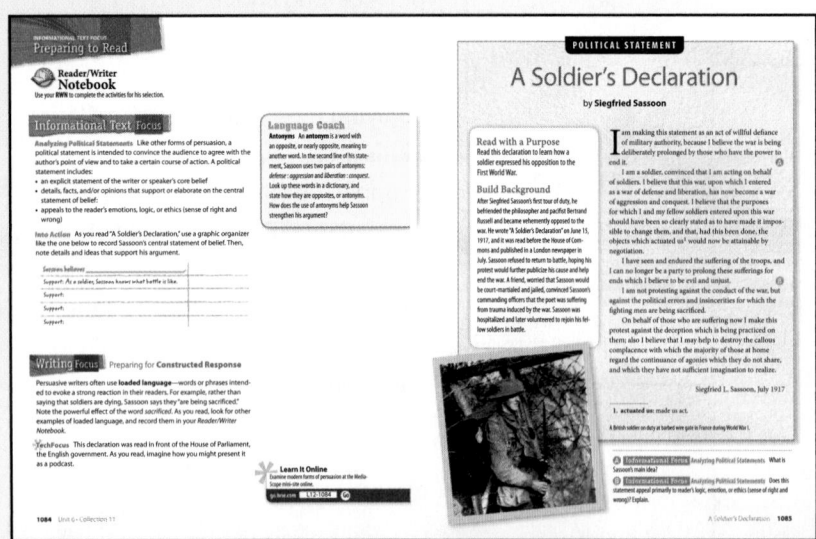

Informational Text Focus

If you've ever read an online encyclopedia or a technical manual, you've been reading informational text. The skills you need for this type of reading are different from the ones you use for literary text. **Informational Text Focus** helps you gain the skills that will enable you to be a more successful reader in daily life and on standardized tests.

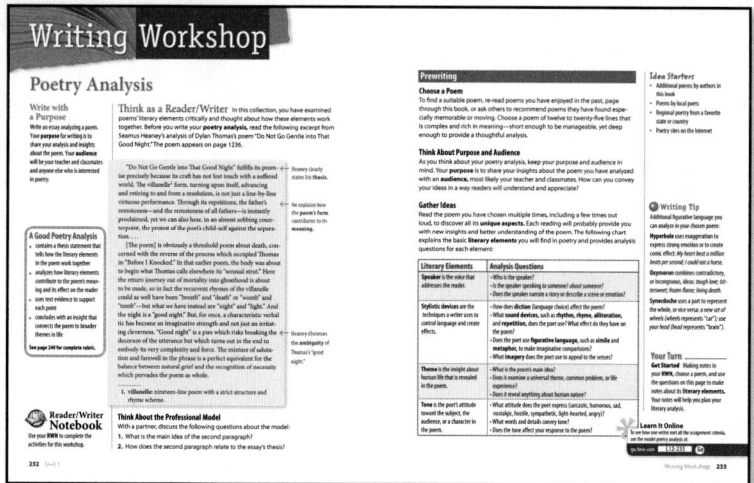

Writing Workshop

As you look forward to work, technical training, or college, you may wonder whether you'll leave writing behind in high school. The answer is most definitely "no." Any further education or career will require that you write, probably more than you have the past eleven or twelve years. **Writing Workshops** prepare you for that writing by helping you think through a piece of writing from the glimmer of an idea to the final version.

Preparing for Timed Writing

Have you ever nervously sat with a blank sheet of paper, trying to respond to a writing prompt, while the clock ticks ominously? **Preparing for Timed Writing** helps you practice for on-demand, or timed, writing so that you can realize your dreams of success.

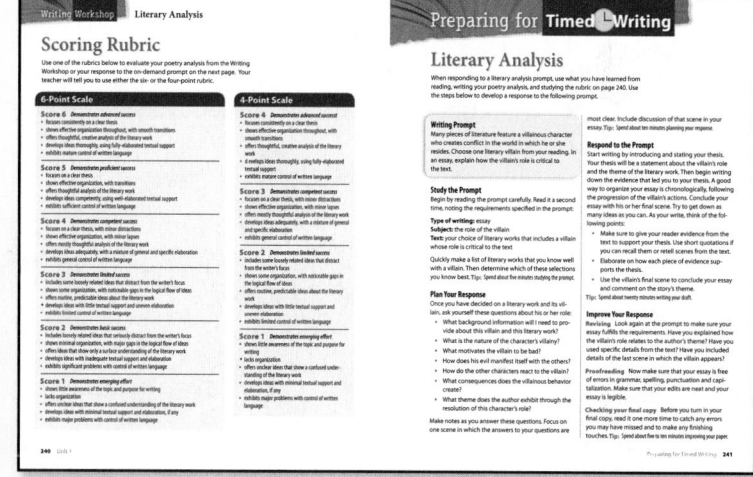

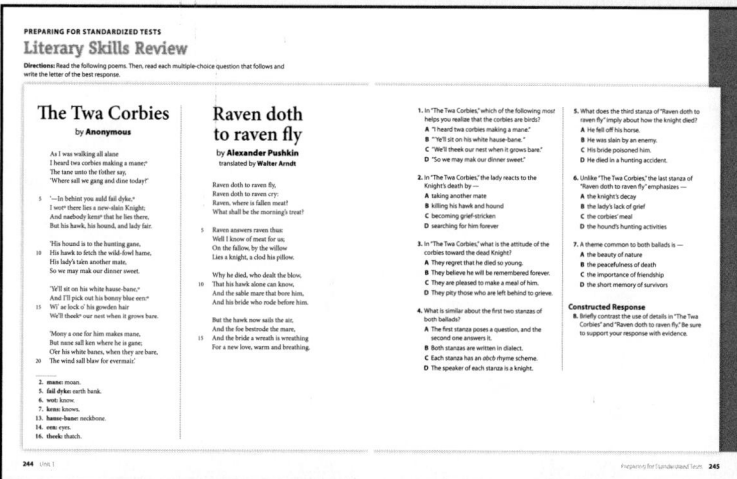

Preparing for Standardized Tests

Does the thought of taking a standardized test make you break out into a cold sweat? **Preparing for Standardized Tests** can reduce your anxiety by giving you the practice you need to feel more confident during testing.

Contents **A55**

The British Isles

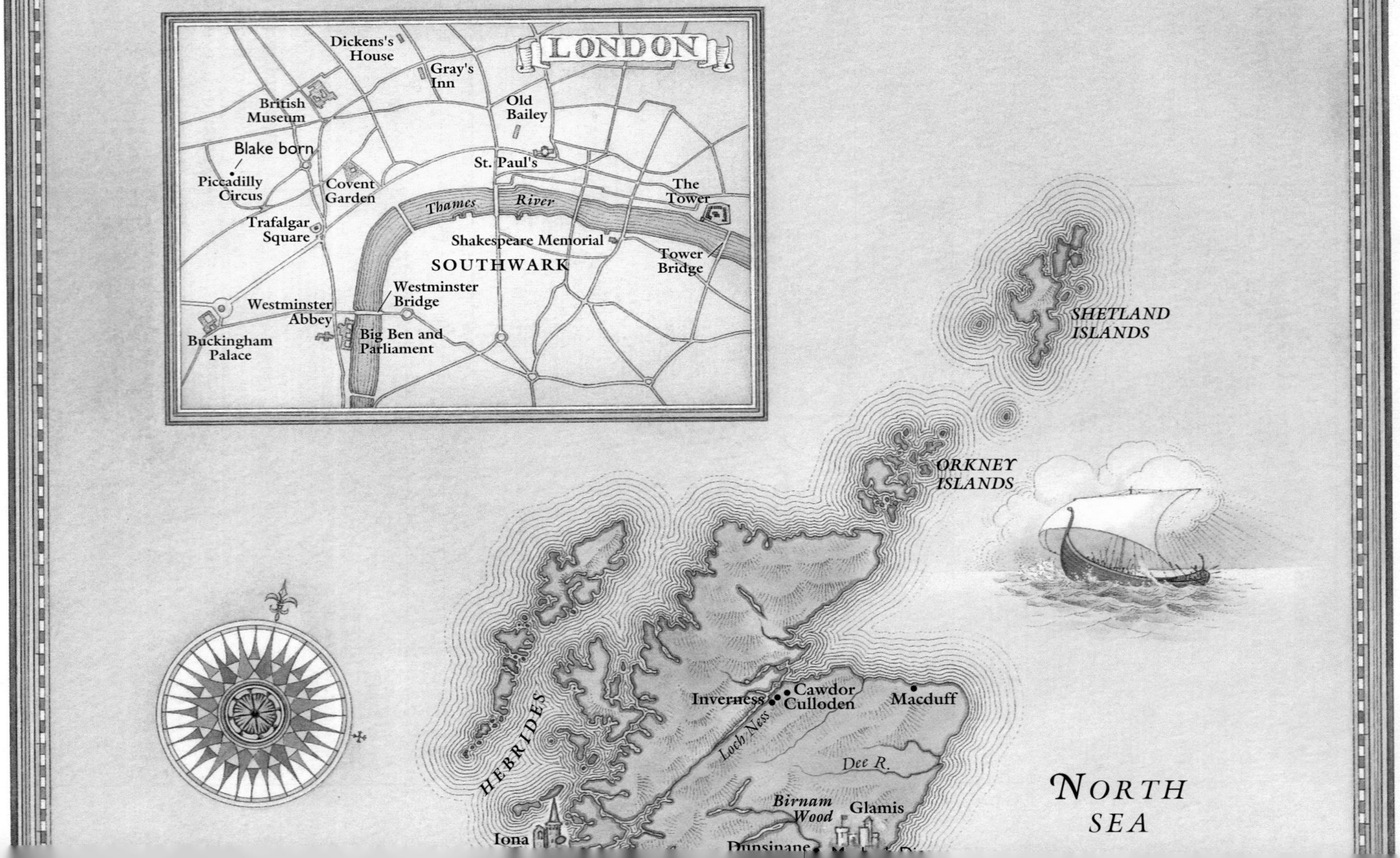

NORTH SEA

SHETLAND ISLANDS

ORKNEY ISLANDS

Macduff

Dee R.

Birnam Wood

Glamis

Cawdor
Culloden

Inverness

Loch Ness

Dunsinane

HEBRIDES

Iona

LONDON

The Tower

Tower Bridge

Old Bailey

St. Paul's

Gray's Inn

Dickens's House

Thames River

Shakespeare Memorial

SOUTHWARK

British Museum

Covent Garden

Blake born

Piccadilly Circus

Trafalgar Square

Westminster Bridge

Westminster Abbey

Big Ben and Parliament

Buckingham Palace

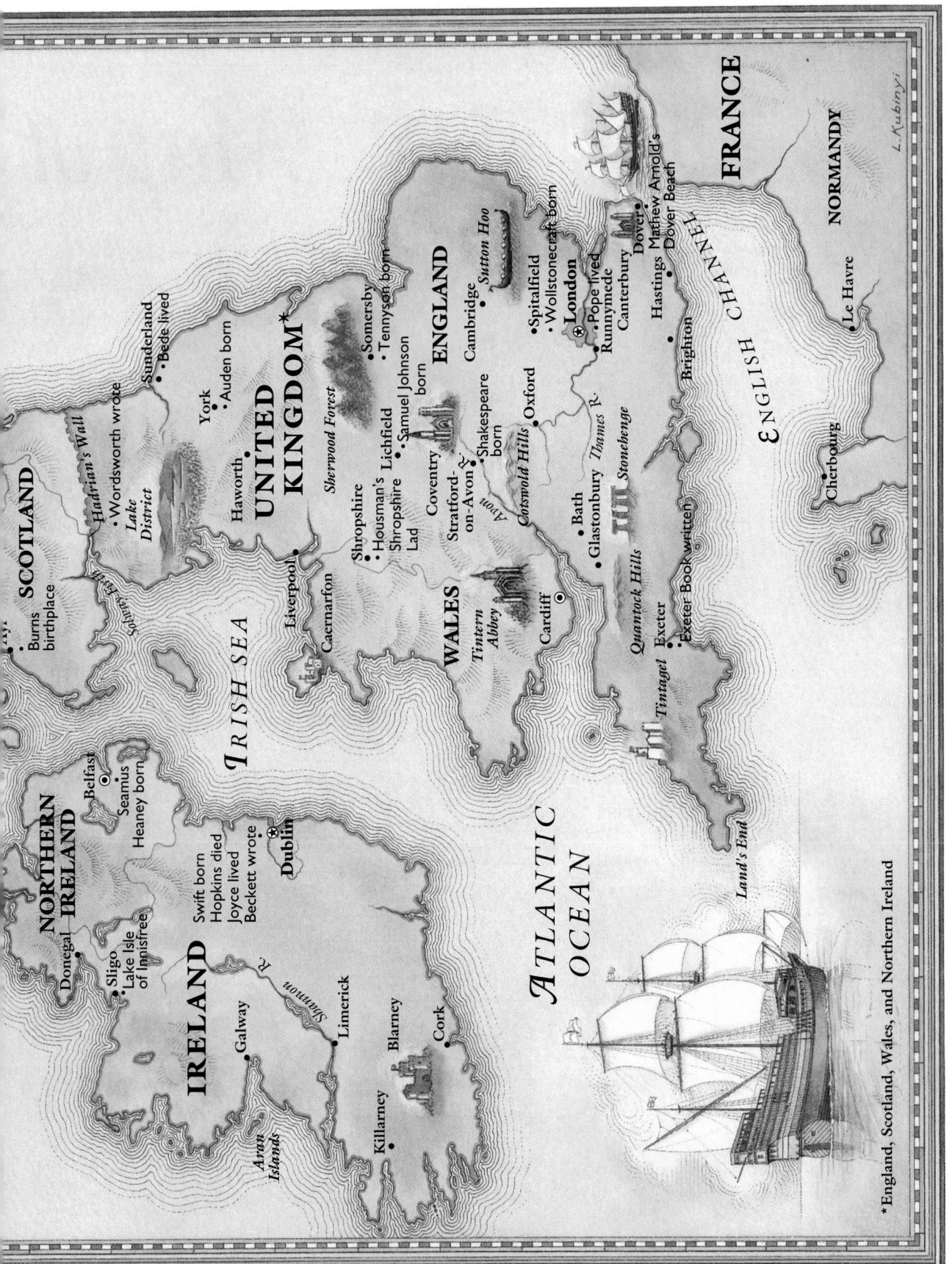

SCOTLAND

Burns birthplace

Hadrian's Wall
Wordsworth wrote
Lake District

Sunderland
Bede lived

York
Auden born

Haworth

UNITED KINGDOM*

Sherwood Forest

Somersby
Tennyson born

Shropshire
Housman's
Shropshire
Lad

Lichfield
Samuel Johnson
born

Coventry

Stratford-
on-Avon

Shakespeare
born

Cotswold Hills

Oxford

ENGLAND

Cambridge

Sutton Hoo

Spitalfield
Wollstonecraft born
London
Pope lived
Runnymede

Canterbury

Dover

Mathew Arnold's
Dover Beach

Hastings

Brighton

FRANCE

NORMANDY

ENGLISH CHANNEL

Le Havre

Cherbourg

Liverpool

Caernarfon

WALES

Tintern
Abbey

Cardiff

Avon

Thames R.

Stonehenge

Bath

Glastonbury

Quantock Hills

Exeter

Exeter Book written

Tintagel

Land's End

IRISH SEA

Belfast

Seamus
Heaney born

NORTHERN IRELAND

Donegal

Sligo
Lake Isle
of Innisfree

IRELAND

Galway

Shannon R.

Limerick

Killarney

Blarney

Cork

Swift born
Hopkins died
Joyce lived
Beckett wrote

Dublin

Aran
Islands

ATLANTIC
OCEAN

L. Kubinyi

*England, Scotland, Wales, and Northern Ireland

A57

Map of

NORTH AMERICA

Canada

Toronto
•Atwood lives

United States
St. Louis
•Eliot
born

ATLANTIC OCEAN

CARIBBEAN SEA

St. Lucia
•Walcott born

•Trinidad
and Tobago

PACIFIC OCEAN

SOUTH AMERICA

Chile

Linares
Province
•Neruda
born

Argentina
•Buenos Aires
•Borges writes

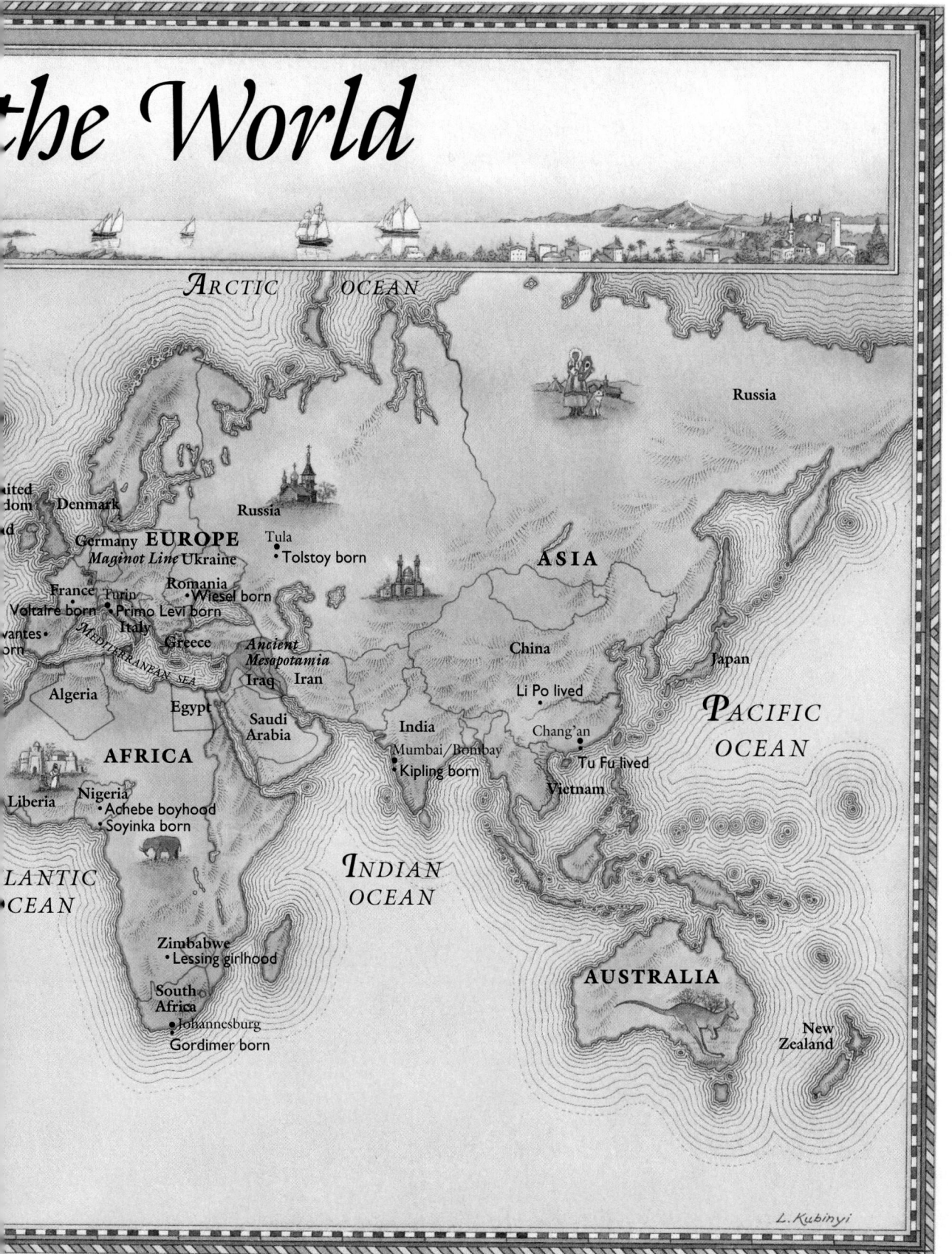

the World

ARCTIC OCEAN

Russia

 united
dom
d

Denmark

Russia

Germany **EUROPE**
Maginot Line Ukraine

Tula
• Tolstoy born

ASIA

France
Voltaire born

Turin
• Primo Levi born

Romania
• Wiesel born

Italy

China

Japan

antes •
orn

Greece

*Ancient
Mesopotamia*

Iraq   Iran

Li Po lived

P**ACIFIC**
OCEAN

MEDITERRANEAN SEA

Algeria

Egypt

Saudi
Arabia

India

Chang'an
•
Tu Fu lived

Mumbai/Bombay
• Kipling born

AFRICA

Vietnam

Liberia

Nigeria
• Achebe boyhood
• Soyinka born

I**NDIAN**
OCEAN

LANTIC
CEAN

Zimbabwe
• Lessing girlhood

AUSTRALIA

South
Africa
•Johannesburg
Gordimer born

New
Zealand

L. Kubinyi

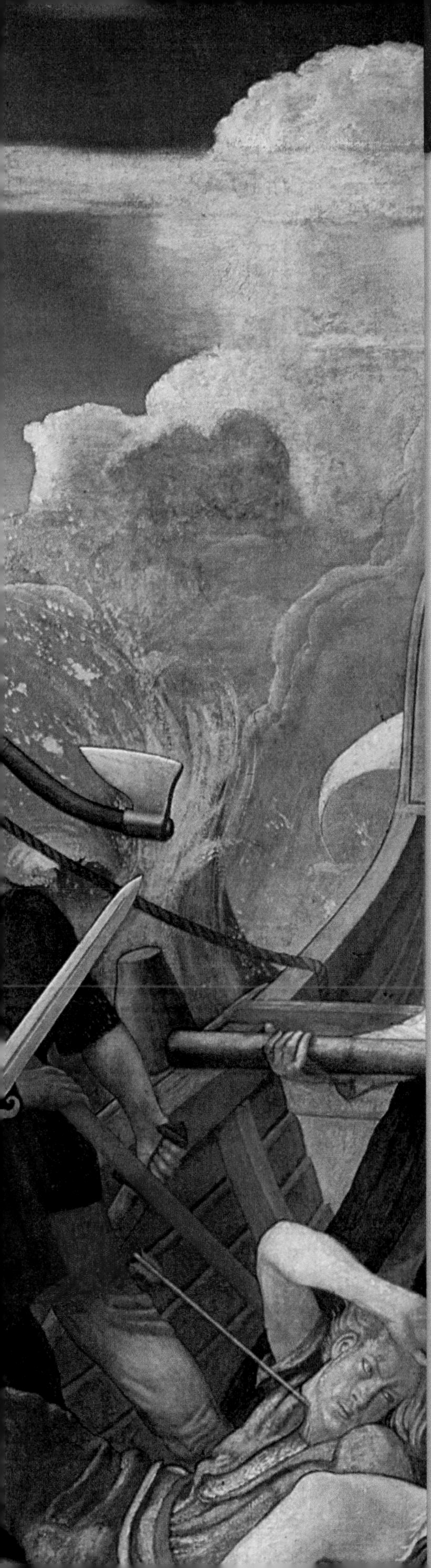

The Anglo-Saxon Period and the Middle Ages

449–1485

COLLECTION 1
The Anglo-Saxons: Songs of Ancient Heroes

COLLECTION 2
The Middle Ages: The Tales They Told

"Not the glittering weapon fights the fight, but rather the hero's heart."

—**Proverb**

What Do
You
Think

What moves a hero to act?

King Alfred's Longships, Newly Built for the Defense of the Realm, Attack Vessels of the Danish Invaders, Storm-Beaten in Swanage Bay in 877 (mural), by Colin Unwin Gill (1892–1940). Houses of Parliament, Westminster, London.

Learn It Online
Find out more about this historical period online.
go.hrw.com | L12-01 | Go

The Anglo-Saxon Period and the Middle Ages 449–1485

This time line represents a snapshot of British literary events, British historical events, and world events from 449 to 1485. During this period, widespread political and cultural changes took place in Britain and around the world.

BRITISH LITERARY EVENTS

449

c. 449 Roman and Persian myths mingle with Celtic and Germanic myths, forming the basis for much of Western literature

670 Caedmon, the earliest English Christian poet, composes hymns

c. 700 *Beowulf* is composed in Old English

750

760 Monks begin the Book of Kells, an illuminated manuscript of Latin Gospels >

975 *The Exeter Book,* a collection of English poetry, is first copied

1086 Domesday Book, a record of all land ownership in England, is first compiled

Opening words of the Gospel of St. Luke, Irish (vellum). MS 58 fol. 188. The Board of Trinity College, Dublin.

BRITISH HISTORICAL EVENTS

449

449 Angles, Saxons, and Jutes invade Britain

537 King Arthur dies at Battle of Camlann >

597 Saint Augustine converts Anglo-Saxon King Ethelbert and establishes monastery at Canterbury

King Arthur's Round Table and the Holy Grail, 15th century CE (ca. 1470). Medieval manuscript (Ms. Fr. 112, folio 5). Bibliothèque Nationale, Paris, France.

750

793 Vikings invade Britain, beginning a century of invasions >

1066 Normans invade England and defeat the Saxons; William the Conqueror becomes English king

Havhingsten fra Glendalough ("The Sea Stallion from Glendalough") at sea, 2007. Viking Ship Museum, Denmark.

WORLD EVENTS

449

476 Roman Empire falls to Germanic tribes

500s Books are printed in China

650 Official version of the Koran (Qur'an) is collected

750

810 Algebra is devised in Persia

1000 In Japan, Lady Murasaki Shikibu writes the world's first novel, *The Tale of Genji*

Seated Buddha c. 650. 19.186, Chinese, Tang dynasty (618–907). The Metropolitan Museum of Art, Rogers Fund, 1919 (19.186).

SKILLS FOCUS **Literary Skills** Evaluate the philosophical, political, religious, ethical, and social influences of a historical period. **Reading Skills** Identify and understand chronological order; use graphic sources of information; use text organizers such as overviews, headings, and graphic features to locate and categorize information.

Your Turn

How many times was Britain invaded during the period covered in this time line? What effects might such a series of invasions have on a culture and its heroes?

1100 **1350** **1485**

c. 1100 The *Mabinogion* is written in Welsh, including "Kulwch and Olwen," an Arthurian legend

1342 Julian of Norwich, one of the first known English women of letters, is born

1378 Legendary hero Robin Hood appears in *Piers Plowman*

1380 Entire Bible is translated into English for first time, by followers of John Wycliffe

< 1387 Chaucer begins *The Canterbury Tales*

1475 William Caxton prints first book in England

Figure thought to be Chaucer; from the Ellesmere manuscript. Fol. 153v. By permission of The Huntington Library, San Marino, California.

1100 **1350** **1485**

1171 Henry II invades Ireland, beginning nearly eight hundred years of British domination

1215 English barons force King John to sign the Magna Carta

1250 First commoners are allowed in the British Parliament

1348 Black Death strikes England

1381 Peasants' Revolt takes place in England

1455–1485 War of the Roses is fought between the Houses of York and Lancaster

1485 First Tudor king, Henry VII, is crowned ****

Henry VII (1472–1509) by Pietro Torrigiano (1472–1528), painted gesso on wood. Victoria & Albert Museum, London.

1100 **1350** **1485**

1150 Paper is first mass-produced, in Spain

1211 Genghis Khan invades China

1325 Aztecs begin to establish empire in Mexico

1400s Benin Kingdom in West Africa flourishes

1438 Incan Empire is established in Peru ❯

1455 Gutenberg prints first book with movable type

A general view of the Inca ruins of Machu Picchu.

3

The Anglo-Saxon Period and the Middle Ages 449–1485

The relatively small group of islands now known as Great Britain have been invaded and settled many times: first by ancient people we call the Iberians, then by the Celts (kelts), the Romans, the Angles and Saxons, the Vikings, and the Normans. Whatever we think of as British today owes something to each of these invaders. The language of the Anglo-Saxons gave this land its name—*Engla land,* or *England.* During this period a distinct form of English literature developed and helped to define the English national character.

KEY CONCEPTS

The Anglo-Saxon Legacy

History of the Times The collapse of the Roman Empire left Britain, its northernmost province, vulnerable to invasion. Angle and Saxon invaders imposed their warrior culture on the island for six centuries. Divided at first into clans, the Anglo-Saxons were later united under Alfred the Great.

Literature of the Times Anglo-Saxon literature shares common themes and ideals of conduct. The epic poem *Beowulf* reflects a society that esteemed loyalty, strength, and courage; and considered fame and glory the noblest end of a warrior.

The Normans Invade Britain

History of the Times In 1066, William the Conqueror led the Norman invasion of England and defeated the Anglo-Saxons. As king, William divided the land among his loyal barons. This system created a social structure in which every person had a place in a fixed hierarchy.

Literature of the Times Under King Alfred, the *Anglo-Saxon Chronicle* had helped make English a respected language. After 1066, literature was usually written in Latin or Norman French, reflecting the social chasm between the British masses and the Norman rulers.

Life in Medieval Society

History of the Times Under the feudal system, medieval society comprised distinctly defined social classes, including the nobility, knights, peasants, the clergy, and merchants. The contributions of each group affected how well villages and towns operated and prospered.

Literature of the Times Although monks wrote scholarly works in Latin and French, other medieval writers began to use the vernacular, or language of the common people. Works written in English, such as ballads and romances, helped to define England's national identity.

KEY CONCEPT

The Anglo-Saxon Legacy

History of the Times

After the legions of Rome conquered the Celts,[1] Roman armies and organization kept Britain free of serious invasions for four hundred years. However, by A.D. 409, the Romans had troubles at home and evacuated their troops. Without Roman control, the Angles and the Saxons from Germany swept ashore, drove out the Celts, and settled the greater part of Britain.

This period of English history is distinguished by the role of the warrior-king and his close-knit group of followers. Before the ninth century, when King Alfred united the Anglo-Saxon clans, England was the site of nearly constant invasions and battles. Not until Alfred led the Anglo-Saxons against the invading Danes did England became in any true sense a nation. The Danes were one of the fierce Viking peoples who crossed the North Sea in their dragon-prowed boats, plundering and destroying everything in their path. The constant threat of war created local communities that bonded the Anglo-Saxons through adversity and harsh living conditions.

During this period, the spread of Christianity also helped unify the Anglo-Saxons. Although it was introduced to Britain at the end of the Roman occupation, Christianity took centuries to establish itself as the main religion. Ireland's Christian monks and missionaries from continental Europe began to spread their beliefs to England during the fifth century. Elements of pagan religions persisted throughout Britain, especially in more remote areas, yet by the

The arrival of King Sweyn and Danish troops in England, Harl, 2278 f.98v. British Library, London.

late seventh century Christianity had almost entirely replaced other systems of belief. Christianity offered Anglo-Saxon people the hope of a more palatable afterlife, a comfort considering their difficult earthly existence. It also provided a common system of morality and conduct that helped to unite the different local groups throughout Britain.

Under King Alfred, Anglo-Saxons fought to protect their people, their culture, and their church from the ravages of the Danes. The struggle continued until both the Anglo-Saxons and the Danes were defeated in 1066 by William, duke of Normandy, and his invading Normans from northwestern France.

---

1. **Celts:** the groups of people originally settled in the British Isles.

Learn It Online
Go online for more information on this historical period.

go.hrw.com   L12-05   **Go**

Literature of the Times

When the Anglo-Saxons invaded Britain, they introduced a traditional Germanic ethos that celebrated the warrior and his exploits. Little evidence survives of Anglo-Saxon oral poetry, which was primarily used for telling stories and reciting magic. True English literature did not develop until Caedmon, an illiterate cowherd, began composing his own religion-inspired poetry in his native tongue. Before the sixth century there is no evidence that the Anglo-Saxons composed anything in their own language.

When Old English poetry did finally blossom, it became distinctive in several ways. Alliteration, or the use of repeated consonant sounds, gives the poetry a musical quality. Bards[2]—whom the Anglo-Saxons called *scops* (skahps)—relied on sound devices to help them remember their tales, and they repeated phrases and images that audiences would expect and understand. Single ideas are often repeated throughout a poem to create a layered effect in which each appearance adds a new depth of meaning to the whole. The *kenning*, a metaphor expressed as a compound noun—such as "whale-path" for the sea—is also Anglo-Saxon in origin and represents the literature's unique power of description.

For the Anglo-Saxons, creating poetry was as important as fighting, hunting, farming, or loving. For the non-Christian Anglo-Saxons, whose religion offered no hope of an afterlife, only fame and its commemoration in poetry could provide a defense against death. Perhaps this explains why the Anglo-Saxon bards, gifted with the skill to preserve fame in the collective memory, were honored members of society.

Many people consider the epic poem *Beowulf* to be the shining star of Old English literature. It was composed during the early eighth century, first recorded in writing nearly three hundred years later, and printed in 1815. The only surviving manuscript is from around the year 1000. In meter, style, and theme *Beowulf* adheres to the Germanic heroic tradition, yet it represents the core values of Anglo-Saxon culture. Another example of Anglo-Saxon literature is *The Exeter Book*, the largest collection of Old English poetry in existence. It was first compiled in writing around 975, includes nearly one hundred riddles, and exhibits other, diverse styles of early poetry.

Historical poems were another important genre of the time. These poems served as a historical record and were collected in the *Anglo-Saxon Chronicle*, a chronological account of events that begins with the Anglo-Saxon period and extends to Norman-controlled England. The seven manuscripts remain a primary source of early English history.

Comprehension Check

What event led to the Anglo-Saxon invasion of the British provinces?

Fast Facts

Historical Highlights

- The Romans invade Britain in 55 B.C. and create a four-hundred-year period of political stability.
- King Alfred and his descendants unite Anglo-Saxon England in the late ninth century.
- William the Conqueror defeats the Anglo-Saxons in 1066 and introduces feudalism to Britain.
- In 1215, English barons force King John to sign the Magna Carta in an attempt to curb the king's power.
- In 1348 and 1349, the Black Death, or bubonic plague, reduces England's population by a third.

Literary Highlights

- The brooding fatalism of pagan Anglo-Saxon culture gives the first British epic, *Beowulf*, its melancholy tone and stress on earthly heroism.
- The bards, or *scops*, ensure stories have an important position in early British culture.
- Christian monks copy ancient manuscripts, preserving classical and Anglo-Saxon texts.
- Chivalry gives rise to a new form of literature, the romance.

---

2. **bards:** poets, often also singers.

The Normans Invade Britain

History of the Times

In 1051, William, duke of Normandy, paid Britain's King Edward a visit. William claimed that during this visit, the king—who had no children—promised William the English throne. As Edward was dying, however, he announced that his kingdom should go to Harold, the British earl of Wessex. This betrayal, imagined or not, spurred William to lead an invasion of England by Normans in 1066.

At the Battle of Hastings, Harold was killed by a chance arrow. William, convinced of his fate, proclaimed himself ruler of England. The new king was crowned on Christmas Day, 1066.

Native revolts against Norman leadership continued until 1071, but William smothered the opposition by rapidly building castles throughout the land. The establishment of a social system called feudalism[3]—which creates a hierarchy of rulers under one lord—further secured William's reign. It also provided him with a network of thousands of knights sworn to serve him, the most powerful European army of the time.

---

3. **feudalism:** feudal system; the social, economic, and political system of Europe in the Middle Ages. Under this system, individuals gave military and other services to their overlords in return for protection and land. The ultimate overlord was the king.

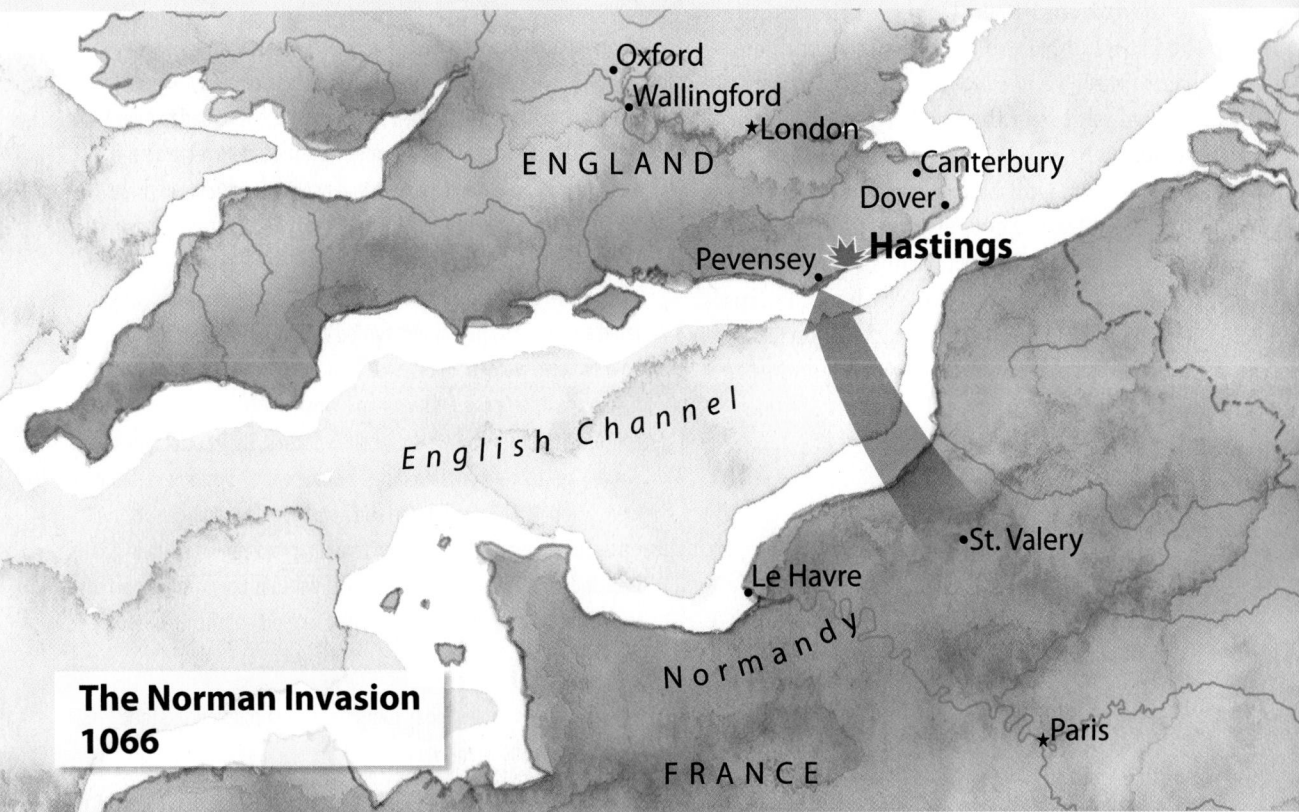

The Norman Invasion 1066

William and his army set sail near St. Valery and Le Havre in the Norman region of France, moved across the English Channel, and invaded Britain at Pevensey. About two weeks later, on October 14, 1066, the Normans defeated Harold at the Battle of Hastings. The subsequent battles at Oxford, Canterbury, and Wallingford helped secure the Normans' control of the region.

William maintained the efficient systems of government established by the Anglo-Saxons but centralized power under his own rule. To complement the Anglo-Saxon's more democratic and artistic tendencies, the Normans brought administrative ability, an emphasis on law and order, and cultural unity. William also began to replace the English nobility with Normans, modified the expectations for the behavior of the elites, and created great class divisions that oppressed the Anglo-Saxons.

Literature of the Times

The Norman conquest not only displaced the English aristocracy but also ousted the English vernacular.[4] William's rule made Norman French the language of the state. Old English became obsolete and began to disappear from the laws and literature. French—and Latin in the monasteries—would remain the official language until the Hundred Years' War, when two English kings (Edward III and Henry V) claimed the right to the French throne during the fourteenth and fifteenth centuries.

The learning boom of the twelfth and thirteenth centuries resulted in an array of literature. *The Book of Kings* is the oldest significant example of Anglo-Norman prose. Bibles and gospels created in monasteries are still celebrated for their brilliant illuminated manuscripts, which were all done by hand. Poems like *The Voyage of St. Brendan,* religious allegories such as *Castle of Love,* many morality plays, and even biographies were created during this time.

Comprehension Check

How was William the Conqueror able to form such a powerful army following his victory in 1066?

---

4. **vernacular:** a native language; the everyday language used by most people of a certain country or place.

Link to Today

Women's Rights Go Wrong

It's hard to imagine a time when women were to enjoy fewer rights in the future than they did at present, but such a time came in England of the Middle Ages. Women in Anglo-Saxon England actually fared *better* than their later medieval counterparts. Despite a culture that emphasized warfare and masculine strength, women had more rights in Anglo-Saxon society than they did after the Norman Conquest.

Evidence from wills first used during the later Anglo-Saxon period shows that women inherited and held property—even after marriage. With his proposal, a prospective husband had to offer *morgengifu,* or "morning-gift," of money and land directly to the woman. After marriage the wife had personal control over these assets. Women also had opportunities for education and power within Christianity. Some became nuns or abbesses: for example, Hild (614–680), the abbess of Whitby (in present-day Yorkshire), accumulated an immense library and turned Whitby into a center of learning.

Medieval women, in contrast, had few individual rights. They held no political power within a militaristic system and were considered subservient to their male relatives. Their social rank was entirely contingent on their father's or husband's position, and they were responsible for child care and housekeeping regardless of their class. Some women experienced temporary power when their husbands were away on business or at war, but they were expected to abdicate their leadership positions the moment the men returned.

Ask Yourself

How do women's roles today compare to their roles during the Anglo-Saxon and medieval periods?

Life in Medieval Society

History of the Times

Medieval society was dependent on the contributions of a diverse group of people. Priests held an elevated status and were responsible for the administration of the sacraments,[5] which could not be performed by any other member of the population. Knights were noblemen responsible for combat and strong leadership of their followers. The bulk of society consisted of laborers: peasants, who owned their land, and serfs, who did not. Their responsibilities were to farm the land and pledge loyalty to their feudal overlords. A great proportion of the teaching and learning in society occurred in the monasteries and convents of religious orders; these organizations were also social service institutions, functioning as orphanages and hospitals.

Villages, built around castles, were where most Europeans lived during the Middle Ages. The village was the fundamental social and economic center of medieval society. Town life was clearly different from rural life, but the lifestyles were dependent on each other. The majority of merchants and artisans lived in villages. Townspeople viewed themselves as having more freedom and opportunity for artistic expression. Rural laborers, on the other hand, were yoked to the land, and, in the case of serfs, were little more than slaves to their overlords.

---

5. **sacraments:** any of certain Christian rites, as baptism or the Eucharist.

Analyzing Visuals

Viewing and Interpreting What does this painting reveal about life in the Middle Ages?

The Month of September, from the Grimany Breviary, fl. 1515. Biblioteca Marciana, Venice, Italy.

Social mobility was nearly impossible in the Middle Ages. Regardless of how hard a merchant worked or how much money an artisan earned, social status remained fixed. Hope resided only in apprenticing a talented son to a more respected vocation or marrying a daughter "up" to a husband from a higher class.

Literature of the Times

A particular literature emerged from the turbulent history of England at this time. The works of Julian of Norwich and Sir Thomas Malory, along with the products of monasteries and universities, reflect a culture interested in the moral instruction of its population. Chaucer's *The Canterbury Tales* satirizes social classes and morality with the story of a group of pilgrims[6] traveling to the city of Canterbury. Another important work of medieval moral literature is *The Book of Margery Kempe*. Kempe, an illiterate religious mystic and spiritualist, dictated her autobiography to two clerks in a span of four years in the 1430s. The drama *Everyman,* which explores the fate of the human soul in a realistic fashion not often achieved by morality plays of the time, is another work of moral instruction.

Perhaps the most distinctive form of literature from this time period deals with the ideal of courtly love—the concept that a knight's bravery and nobility could be increased by his pure adoration of a lady. The romance narrative is a medieval genre that celebrates the adventures of a brave knight or other hero who has to overcome danger for the love of a noble lady or some other high ideal. Courtly love supported the medieval concept of chivalry, a system of social codes and ideals governing the behavior of knights and gentlewomen and guided by allegiance to an overlord. Perhaps the most famous romance narratives are *Sir Gawain and the Green Knight* and Malory's *Le Morte d'Arthur*.

Comprehension Check

Describe the trends in English literature during the Middle Ages. Were they reflective of life at the time?

___

6. **pilgrims:** those who travel to a shrine or holy place as a religious act.

Seated King, The Lewis Chessmen (about A.D. 1150–1200). Found on the Isle of Lewis, Outer Hebrides, Scotland. The chess pieces consist of elaborately worked walrus ivory and whale's teeth in the forms of seated kings and queens. ❯
The Trustees of the British Museum, London.

April, Calendar miniature from the Très Riches Heures du Duc de Berry (1416), (Engagement scene. In the background, the Chateau de Dourdan). Limbourg Brothers (15th CE), Ms.65, f .4v. Musée Condé, Chantilly, France

Wrap Up

Talk About . . .

The Anglo-Saxon heroes were exclusively male, but Celtic history and mythology record some powerful female warriors. How do these ancient views of heroism compare with contemporary ideas of greatness? With a partner or in a small group, discuss the ways in which individuals gain fame and fortune today. Try to use each Academic Vocabulary word listed below at least once in your discussion.

Write About . . .

Geoffrey Chaucer sought to teach, but he also wanted to entertain. What examples of books or movies can you think of that are both entertaining and instructive? Do you think this combination is effective? Explain.

Academic Vocabulary for Unit 1

Talking and Writing About Literature

Academic Vocabulary is the language you use to write and talk about literature. Use these words to discuss the literature you will read in this unit. These words will be underlined throughout the unit.

concept (KAHN sehpt) *n.*: notion or idea. *The concept of courtly love was a theme repeated throughout medieval literature.*

diverse (duh VURS) *adj.*: varied. *A person of diverse interests can talk on many subjects.*

emphasis (EHM fuh sihs) *n.*: stress; importance. *When writing the essay, give special emphasis to examples from the story.*

status (STAT uhs) *n.*: social or professional rank. *What was the status of women in medieval society?*

attribute (uh TRIHB yoot) *v.*: regard as being caused by something. *We attribute the core values of* Beowulf *to the Anglo-Saxon tradition.*

Your Turn

Copy the Academic Vocabulary list into your *Reader/Writer Notebook*. Try to use the words as you outline the main ideas of the selections in the collection that follows.

Link to Today

This Link to Today shows the lasting appeal of heroic adventure stories.

Build Background

In addition to echoing many elements from Anglo-Saxon and medieval literature, *The Two Towers* in particular recalls features of *Beowulf* and the Arthurian legends. These stories describe the adventures of heroes who take on formidable challenges and fight bravely against all odds. Such heroes usually have a close friend who plays an important role in the hero's experiences. Through the glory of their fame, the heroes also achieve eternal life.

Author Note

J. R. R. Tolkien (1892–1973) graduated from Oxford University and went on to become a professor of Old and Middle English at Leeds University in England. Several of his works began as stories for his children and were later expanded into the trilogy that many consider to be his masterpiece: *The Lord of the Rings* (1947). *The Two Towers* was published as the second book, between *The Fellowship of the Ring* and *The Return of the King*. The enduring stories of epic heroes and legendary creatures from Middle Earth have found a new audience in director Peter Jackson's recent films.

from THE LORD *of the* RINGS: *The Two Towers*

by **J. R. R. Tolkien**

Read with a Purpose Read this excerpt from *The Two Towers* to see how one hero's sidekick responds when the odds are overwhelmingly against him.

"Still, I wonder if we shall ever be put into songs or tales," said Sam. "We're in one, of course; but I mean: put into words, you know, told by the fireside, or read out of a great big book with red and black letters, years and years afterward. And people will say: 'Let's hear about Frodo and the Ring!' And they'll say: 'Yes, that's one of my favorite stories. Frodo was very brave, wasn't he, dad?' 'Yes, my boy, the famousest of the hobbits, and that's saying a lot.'"

"It's saying a lot too much," said Frodo, and he laughed, a long clear laugh from his heart. . . . "Why, Sam, he said, "to hear you somehow makes me as merry as if the story was already written. But you've left out one of the chief characters: Samwise the stouthearted. 'I want to hear more about Sam, dad. Why didn't they put in more of his talk, dad? That's what I like, it makes me laugh. And Frodo wouldn't have got far without Sam, would he, dad?'" . . .

Frodo was lying face upward on the ground and the monster was bending over him, so intent upon her victim that she took no heed of Sam and his cries, until he was close at hand. As he rushed up he saw that Frodo was already bound in cords, wound about him from ankle to shoulder, and the monster with her great forelegs was beginning half to lift, half to drag his body away.

On the near side of him lay, gleaming on the ground, his elven-blade, where it had fallen useless from his grasp. Sam did not wait to wonder what was to be done, or whether he was brave, or loyal, or filled with rage. He sprang forward with a yell, and seized his master's sword in his left hand. Then he charged. No onslaught more fierce was ever seen in the savage world of beasts, where some desperate small creature armed with little teeth, alone, will spring upon a tower of horn and hide that stands above its fallen mate.

"Put into words, you know, told by the fireside, or read out of a great big book with red and black letters, years and years afterward."

Disturbed as if out of some gloating dream by his small yell she turned slowly the dreadful malice of her glance upon him. But almost before she was aware that a fury was upon her greater than any she had known in countless years, the shining sword bit upon her foot and shore away the claw. Sam sprang in, inside the arches of her legs, and with a quick upthrust of his other hand stabbed at the clustered eyes upon her lowered head. One great eye went dark.

Now the miserable creature was right under her, for the moment out of the reach of her sting and of her claws. Her vast belly was above him with its putrid light, and the stench of it almost smote[1] him down. Still his fury held for one more blow, and before she could sink upon him, smothering him and all his little impudence of courage, he slashed the bright elven-blade across her with desperate strength.

But Shelob was not as dragons are, no softer spot had she save only her eyes. Knobbed and pitted with corruption was her age-old hide, but ever thickened from within with layer on layer of evil growth. The blade scored it with a dreadful gash, but those hideous folds could not be pierced by any strength of men, not though Elf or Dwarf should forge the steel or the hand of Beren or of Túrin wield it. She yielded to the stroke, and then heaved up the great bag of her belly high above Sam's head. Poison frothed and bubbled from the wound. Now splaying her legs she drove her huge bulk down on him again. Too soon. For Sam still stood upon his feet, and dropping his own sword, with both hands he held the elven-blade point upwards, fending off that ghastly roof; and so Shelob, with the driving force of her own cruel will, with strength greater than any warrior's hand, thrust herself upon a bitter spike. Deep, deep it pricked, as Sam was crushed slowly to the ground.

No such anguish had Shelob ever known, or dreamed of knowing, in all her long world of wickedness. Not the doughtiest soldier of old Gondor, nor

The Lord of the Rings: The Return of the King (2003). Sean Austin and Elijah Wood.

the most savage Orc entrapped, had ever thus endured her, or set blade to her beloved flesh. A shudder went through her. Heaving up again, wrenching away from the pain, she bent her writhing limbs beneath her and sprang backwards in a convulsive leap.

Sam had fallen to his knees by Frodo's head, his senses reeling in the foul stench, his two hands still gripping the hilt of the sword. Through the mist before his eyes he was aware dimly of Frodo's face, and stubbornly he fought to master himself and to drag himself out of the swoon that was upon him. Slowly he raised his head and saw her, only a few paces away, eyeing him, her beak drabbling a spittle of venom, and a green ooze trickling from below her wounded eye. There she crouched, her shuddering belly splayed upon the ground, the great bows of her legs quivering, as she gathered herself for another spring—this time to crush and sting to death: no little bite of poison to still the struggling of her meat; this time to slay and then to rend.

Even as Sam himself crouched, looking at her, seeing his death in her eyes, a thought came to him, as if some remote voice had spoken, and he fumbled in his breast with his left hand, and found what he sought: cold and hard and solid it seemed to his touch in a phantom world of horror, the Phial of Galadriel.

---

1. **smote:** struck, as in combat.

"Galadriel!" he said faintly, and then he heard voices far off but clear: the crying of the Elves as they walked under the stars in the beloved shadows of the Shire, and the music of the Elves as it came through his sleep in the Hall of Fire in the house of Elrond.

Gilthoniel A Elbereth!

And then his tongue was loosed and his voice cried in a language which he did not know:

*A Elbereth Gilthoniel
o menel palan-diriel,
le nallon sí di'nguruthos!
A tiro nin, Fanuilos!*

And with that he staggered to his feet and was Samwise the hobbit, Hamfast's son, again.

"Now come, you filth!" he cried. "You've hurt my master, you brute, and you'll pay for it. We're going on; but we'll settle with you first. Come on, and taste it again!"

As if his indomitable[2] spirit had set its potency in motion, the glass blazed suddenly like a white torch in

---

2. **indomitable:** incapable of being defeated.

his hand. It flamed like a star that leaping from the firmament sears the dark air with intolerable light. No such terror out of heaven had ever burned in Shelob's face before. The beams of it entered into her wounded head and scored it with unbearable pain, and the dreadful infection of light spread from eye to eye. She fell back beating the air with her forelegs, her sight blasted by inner lightnings, her mind in agony. Then turning her maimed head away, she rolled aside and began to crawl, claw by claw, toward the opening in the dark cliff behind.

Sam came on. He was reeling like a drunken man, but he came on. And Shelob cowed at last, shrunken in defeat, jerked and quivered as she tried to hasten from him. She reached the hole, and squeezing down, leaving a trail of green-yellow slime, she slipped in, even as Sam hewed a last stroke at her dragging legs. Then he fell to the ground.

Shelob was gone; and whether she lay long in her lair, nursing her malice and her misery, and in slow years of darkness healed herself from within, rebuilding her clustered eyes, until with hunger like death she spun once more her dreadful snares in the glens of the Mountains of Shadow, this tale does not tell.

Ask Yourself

1. **Read with a Purpose** In this episode, Sam comes to Frodo's rescue without thinking about the danger he risks to himself. Would you describe his actions as courageous or reckless or both? Explain your answer.

2. Tolkien emphasizes the role of a hero's friend or kinsman when he writes "Frodo wouldn't have got far without Sam, would he, dad?" Do you think that a hero's power is inherent to the individual or does it sometimes depends on the courage of his or her companions?

3. What kinds of skills, knowledge, and weapons does the hero use in this excerpt? Do you think that a hero should use just his or her body in a challenge against all odds, or is it acceptable to use weapons or tools?

COLLECTION 1

The Anglo-Saxons: Songs of Ancient Heroes

LITERARY FOCUS
The Epic Tradition

Norman calvary attacks a hill defended by Saxon infantry.
Bayeux Tapestry, embroidery (11th century).
Musée de la Tapisserie, Bayeux, France.

CONTENTS

from **Beowulf**

from **The Collected Beowulf**   Link to Today

The Seafarer

The Wife's Lament

The Wanderer

Anglo-Saxon Riddles

Bede

COMPARING TEXTS: WORLD LITERATURE
  from **Gilgamesh**
  from the **Iliad**

"And sometimes a proud old
   soldier
Who had heard songs of the
   ancient heroes
And could sing them all
   through, story after story,
Would weave a net of words."

—from *Beowulf*, translated by Burton Raffel

The Epic Tradition by **David Adams Leeming**

Characteristics of an Epic

- Long narrative poem about a quest, told in formal, elevated language
- Larger-than-life hero who embodies the values of a particular culture
- Incredible plot involving large-scale events
- Mix of myth, legend, and history that often includes gods and goddesses as characters

A Bridge from the Past to the Future

"I teach kings the history of their ancestors," declares the narrator of the African epic *Sundiata*, "for the world is old, but the future springs from the past." These words can be applied to epics from all times and places, for an epic—a long narrative poem about the exploits of a national hero—is a bridge from the past to the future. Epics carry a culture's history, values, and traditions from one generation to the next. Although epics may vary across different cultures or times, the epic tradition remains a constant social feature— where there are people, there are epics, retelling the triumphs and trials of life.

The Epic Hero

Whereas old religious stories, or myths, explain the origins and deeds of gods, the epic tradition reflects the human need to understand ourselves and bridge the gap between the human and the divine. A special kind of godlike human being, the epic hero, satisfies this need. Beowulf and other epic heroes, such as Achilles and Gilgamesh, carry the <u>status</u> and power of the gods within themselves but are also subject to the joys and hardships of the human condition.

While the heroes of the Anglo-Saxon *Beowulf,* the Mesopotamian *Gilgamesh,* and the Greek *Iliad* all embody the particular values of their cultures, we also find these values distilled in a single figure, the heroic **archetype,** the model that is somehow familiar to people of all places and times. In expressing the universal human quest for knowledge and understanding, this epic hero represents the core of the epic tradition.

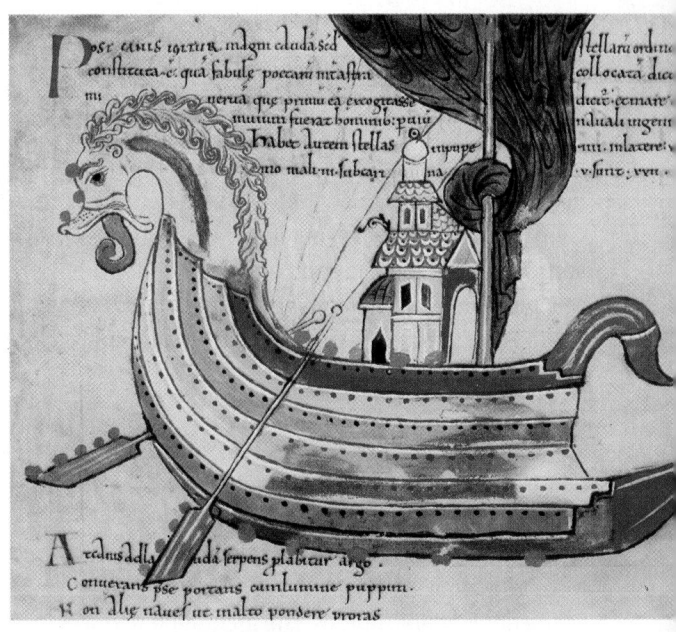

Anglo-Saxon manuscript illumination (c. 1025-1050), Viking ship of war. Ms. Cotton Tiberius. BV, part I, fol.40v. British Library, London.

When asked why there are so many hero stories in mythology, Joseph Campbell, one of the twentieth century's foremost interpreters of myths and archetypes, said, "Because that's what's worth writing about." According to Campbell,

> There is a certain typical hero sequence of actions which can be detected in stories from all over the world and from many periods of history. Essentially, it might even

Literary Focus

SKILLS FOCUS **Literary Skills** Compare epics across cultures; analyze the archetype of the epic hero.

be said that there is but one archetypal mythic hero whose life has been replicated in many lands by many, many people. A legendary hero is usually the founder of something—the founder of a new age, the founder of a new religion, the founder of a new city, the founder of a new way of life. In order to found something new, one has to leave the old and go in quest of the seed idea, a germinal idea that will have the potentiality of bringing forth that new thing.

As in our own journey through life, there are often trials and obstacles that stand between the hero and his or her goals. Like Beowulf, we must fight our own Grendels and dragons—our inner and outer demons—sometimes all alone. It is the epic hero's belief in himself, his own powers, and his cherished values, that make success possible in the face of challenges.

The Epic Lives On

Today, the epic tradition thrives in our own popular culture. In movies, comic books, fantasy novels, television shows, and video games, we meet a <u>diverse</u> array of larger-than-life, often superhuman characters—both male and female—whom we recognize as descendants of the ancient epic heroes. The archetype endures because it continues to be a universal and relevant symbol for some of the most deeply held values of humankind. In Beowulf's journey from self-seeking adventure to heroic but humble death, in Gilgamesh's transition from arrogant king to returning pilgrim, and in Achilles' passage from pouting adolescent to experienced warrior, we find a dramatic record of the personal and collective human quest.

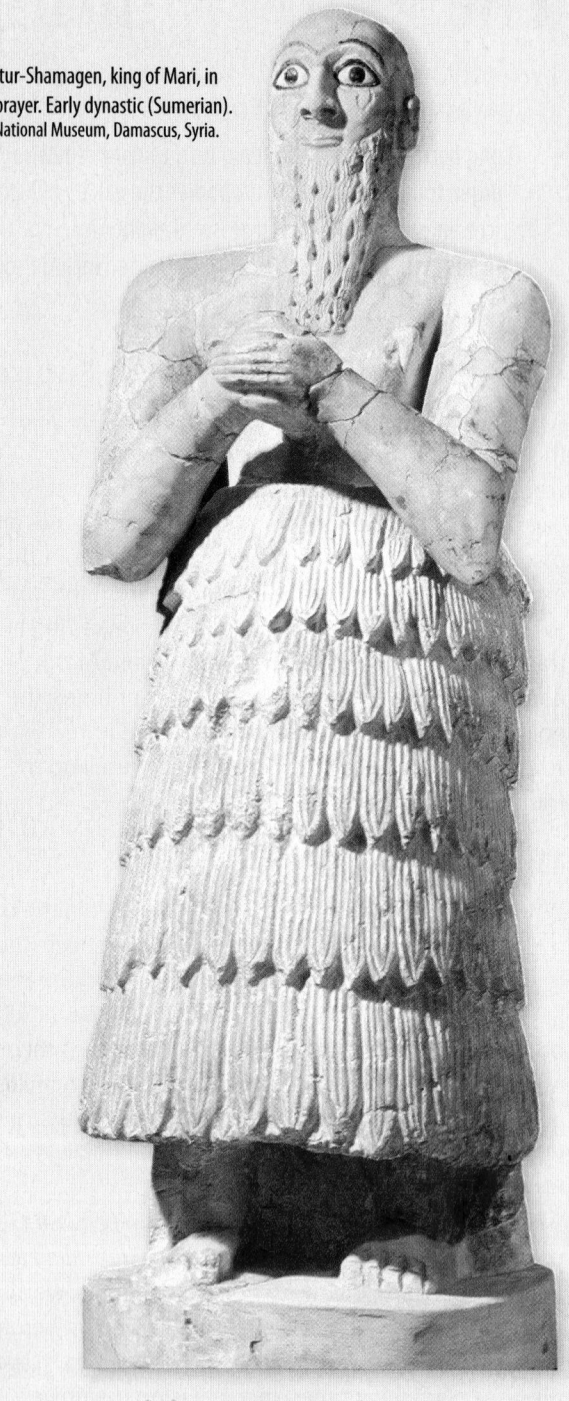

Itur-Shamagen, king of Mari, in prayer. Early dynastic (Sumerian). National Museum, Damascus, Syria.

Ask Yourself

1. Why are epics so important to a culture?

2. Think of a modern-day epic that you enjoy. How do you relate to it? How is it like ancient epics?

Learn It Online

Try the *PowerNotes* version of this lesson at

go.hrw.com   L12-18   **Go**

Reading Focus

from Beowulf

Paraphrasing by **Kylene Beers**

An efficient way of checking your own understanding of what you are reading is to paraphrase, or put into your own words, what you've read. Paraphrasing is actually a harder skill than memorizing a portion of a text, for memorization doesn't require comprehension. Rather, putting what you've read into your own words means you've figured out what the author means and now can explain it in your own way. When you paraphrase what you've read, you keep the author's intent but use language that's your own.

The author of *Beowulf* uses poetic language to share ideas about events, characters, and beliefs. The original audiences of this epic poem would have been familiar with the hero and his adventures, as well as with the conventions of style of the language. Although this style makes the poem beautiful, it can sometimes be difficult for a modern reader to understand. **Paraphrasing** is a good way to capture the meaning of the poem's details.

Your Turn

Read the following lines from an early passage of *Beowulf,* "The Monster Grendel," (lines 5–14).

> ...the poet's clear songs, sung
> Of the ancient beginnings of us all, recalling
> The Almighty making the earth, shaping
> These beautiful plains marked off by oceans,
> Then proudly setting the sun and moon
> To glow across the land and light it;
> The corners of the earth were made lovely
>   with trees
> And leaves, made quick with life, with each
> Of the nations who now move on its face.
>   And then
> As now warriors sang of their pleasure.

To paraphrase this passage, first look for words that represent people, places, and things (nouns) that you recognize. Jot them down *in order* in the column marked "Nouns." Then, read again and identify the actions or verbs that seem to go with these nouns. Note any words or phrases that complement or are related to each group of nouns and verbs. See the examples in the chart below.

Nouns	Verbs	Phrases
poet	sung	songs of the beginnings
Almighty	making	the earth, sun, moon
Corners of earth	were made	

Re-read each group of words in the chart, and then re-read the original passage. Using your chart, create the paraphrase by putting the text into your own words. It might look something like this:

> People told stories of the beginning of life when God created the earth, oceans, and sky, making them beautiful. We still celebrate that time.

Notice that a paraphrase is shorter than the original and combines repetitions into a single statement. As you read *Beowulf* or any other challenging text, use this process of paraphrasing when you come to a passage that seems unclear.

Learn It Online
Learn paraphrasing through *PowerNotes.* Find the multimedia version of this lesson at:

go.hrw.com L12-19 Go

Preparing to Read

from Beowulf

What Do You Think?

What moves a hero to act?

QuickWrite

Think about a hero you know or have read about. In your *Reader/Writer Notebook,* write down a list of situations in which a person can rise above his or her place in life to become a hero.

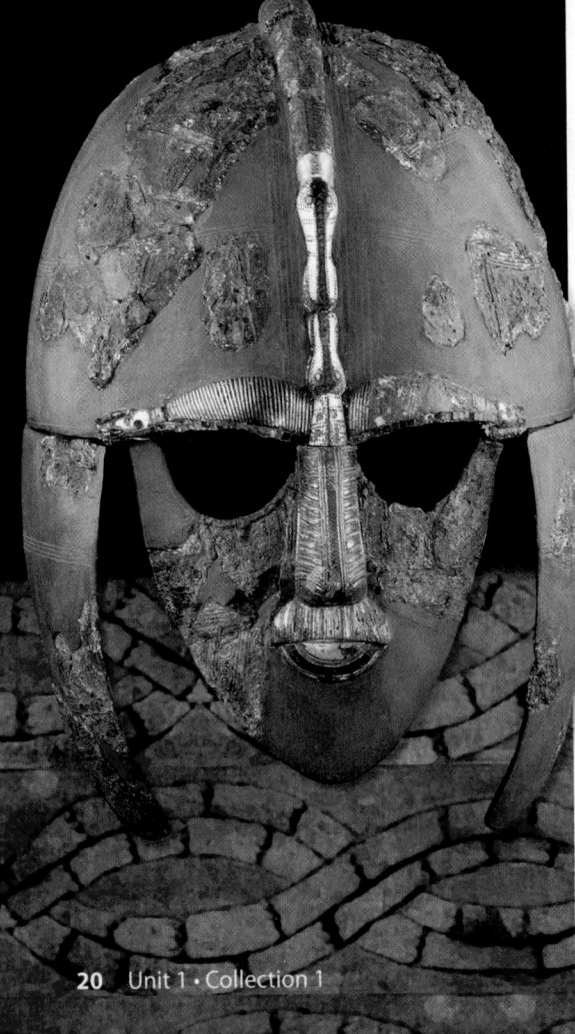

Beowulf, one of the most important and exciting epics of Western literature, features monsters, gory battles, and a brave hero.

A Classic of the Epic Tradition

Originally an oral epic, *Beowulf* was handed down with changes and embellishments from one minstrel to another. The first great work of English national literature, *Beowulf* is a celebration of the epic hero. As such, it uses a host of traditional **motifs,** or recurring elements, associated with heroic literature all over the world.

The epic tells of Beowulf (his name may mean "bear"), a Geat from Sweden who crosses the sea to Denmark in a quest to defend the Herot mead-hall and rescue King Hrothgar's people from the demonic monster Grendel. Beowulf demonstrates his bravery and strength by fighting alone and with his friend Wiglaf, and gains eternal fame through battle.

The Sources of *Beowulf*

Compared to the Homerian epics, *Beowulf* is short—approximately 3,200 lines. It was composed in Old English, probably in the northeastern part of England sometime between 700 and 750, but depicts the world of the early sixth century. Much of the poem's material is based on early Celtic and Scandinavian folk legends. Because of its geographical descriptions and emphasis on Christian elements, it has been assumed that the poet who wrote the version we know today was a Northumbrian monk.

The only surviving manuscript of *Beowulf* dates from the year 1000 and is now in the British Museum in London. Burned and stained, it was discovered in the eighteenth century. Somehow it had survived Henry VIII's destruction of the monasteries two hundred years earlier.

Part One of the text you are about to read is from Burton Raffel's popular 1963 translation of the epic. Part Two is from the Irish poet Seamus Heaney's award-winning (and bestselling) translation of the work, published in 2000.

Think About the Epic

Beowulf was originally an oral tale. What kinds of stories can be shared today by means other than books? How does telling a story out loud keep it alive?

Reader/Writer
Notebook

Use your **RWN** to complete the activities for this selection.

Literary Focus

Archetype: The Epic Hero An **archetype** is a very old imaginative pattern that appears in literature of different cultures and time periods. An archetype can be a character, a plot, an image, or a setting. One character archetype is the **epic hero,** the main character of a myth or long narrative poem. These heroes personify the values of the societies that create them, but as archetypes, they also embody universal ideals.

Reading Focus

Paraphrasing Poetry often uses literary devices and unconventional word order to enhance the rhythmic and musical qualities of its language. Paraphrasing can help you comprehend particularly difficult poetic passages. To paraphrase a passage, first group nouns, verbs, and phrases that support an idea. Then, rewrite the passage in your own words.

Into Action As you read, identify lines containing nouns, verbs, and phrases that describe the epic hero Beowulf and his actions. Use a chart like the one below to list these nouns, verbs, and phrases in these passages.

Nouns / Pronouns	Verbs	Phrases
my duty	was to go	to the Danes
I	drove / chased	giants
I	swam	hunting monsters

Writing Focus

Think as a Reader/Writer

Find It in Your Reading Although much of the epic progresses in narrative, the main characters deliver speeches to each other, establishing their credentials, their heritage, and their intentions. In your *Reader/Writer Notebook,* make notes about what characterizes these speeches.

TechFocus As you read *Beowulf,* think how its characters are similar to those you have met in modern TV shows, movies, and video games.

Vocabulary

reparation (rehp uh RAY shuhn) *n.:* payment to make up for a wrong or injury. *Hrothgar's warriors could expect no reparation from Grendel for the crimes he committed against them.*

reprisal (rih PRY zuhl) *n.:* punishment in return for an injury. *Grendel's mother attacked Herot as a reprisal for Beowulf's killing of her son.*

loathsome (LOHTH suhm) *adj.:* very hateful; disgusting. *The details of Grendel's attacks on the Geats are loathsome.*

vehemently (VEE uh muhnt lee) *adv.:* violently. *Roaring in anger, the she-wolf struck vehemently at Beowulf.*

infallible (ihn FAL uh buhl) *adj.:* unable to fail or be wrong. *The dragon's mortal blow showed that Beowulf was not an infallible hero.*

extolled (ehk STOHLD) *v.:* praised. *The Geats extolled their fallen king by constructing a great memorial to him.*

Language Coach

Connotation Some words have similar meaning but different **connotations,** the emotions or ideas evoked when you use a certain word. *Extol* means "to praise" but has particularly strong positive connotations. If you *extol* someone's good qualities, you praise them with great enthusiasm. Similarly, *loathsome* has stronger connotations than *hateful.* Saying something is *loathsome* is a powerful way to say it really disgusts you.

Learn It Online
Bring Beowulf into the twenty-first century.

go.hrw.com   L12-21   **Go**

EPIC

from Beowulf

Part One

translated by **Burton Raffel**

Read with a Purpose
Read to discover the qualities that the Anglo-Saxons considered heroic.

Building Background
The epic poem *Beowulf* was composed in the Anglo-Saxon period following the fall of the Roman Empire. The story concerns a brave and strong hero who hears tales of a fearsome beast that has laid waste to a kingdom of Danes. Note how the history and ancestry of each character is <u>emphasized</u> throughout the epic.

The Monster Grendel

I

. . . A powerful monster, living down
In the darkness, growled in pain, impatient
As day after day the music rang
Loud in that hall,° the harp's rejoicing
5   Call and the poet's clear songs, sung
Of the ancient beginnings of us all, recalling
The Almighty making the earth, shaping
These beautiful plains marked off by oceans,
Then proudly setting the sun and moon
10   To glow across the land and light it;
The corners of the earth were made lovely with trees
And leaves, made quick with life, with each
Of the nations who now move on its face. And then
As now warriors sang of their pleasure:
15   So Hrothgar's men lived happy in his hall
Till the monster stirred, that demon, that fiend,
Grendel, who haunted the moors, the wild

4. hall: guest-hall or mead-hall. (Mead is a fermented drink made from honey, water, yeast, and malt.) The hall was a central gathering place where Anglo-Saxon warriors could feast, listen to a bard's stories, and sleep in safety.

Analyzing Visuals

Viewing and Interpreting Notice the ship's ornate carvings and vibrant colors on page 22. How might the decoration serve a warlike, as well as aesthetic, function?

(opposite) *Visitors from Overseas,* by Nikolai Roerich (1874–1947). Tretyakov Gallery, Moscow, Russia.

Marshes, and made his home in a hell
Not hell but earth. He was spawned in that slime,  **Ⓐ**
20 Conceived by a pair of those monsters born
Of Cain,° murderous creatures banished
By God, punished forever for the crime
Of Abel's death. The Almighty drove
Those demons out, and their exile was bitter,
25 Shut away from men; they split
Into a thousand forms of evil—spirits
And fiends, goblins, monsters, giants,
A brood forever opposing the Lord's
Will, and again and again defeated.

2

30   Then, when darkness had dropped, Grendel
Went up to Herot, wondering what the warriors
Would do in that hall when their drinking was done.
He found them sprawled in sleep, suspecting
Nothing, their dreams undisturbed. The monster's
35 Thoughts were as quick as his greed or his claws:
He slipped through the door and there in the silence
Snatched up thirty men, smashed them
Unknowing in their beds, and ran out with their bodies,
The blood dripping behind him, back
40 To his lair, delighted with his night's slaughter.
          At daybreak, with the sun's first light, they saw
How well he had worked, and in that gray morning
Broke their long feast with tears and laments
For the dead. Hrothgar, their lord, sat joyless
45 In Herot, a mighty prince mourning
The fate of his lost friends and companions,
Knowing by its tracks that some demon had torn
His followers apart. He wept, fearing
The beginning might not be the end. And that night
50 Grendel came again, so set
On murder that no crime could ever be enough,
No savage assault quench his lust
For evil. Then each warrior tried
To escape him, searched for rest in different
55 Beds, as far from Herot as they could find,
Seeing how Grendel hunted when they slept. **Ⓑ**
Distance was safety; the only survivors

21. Cain: Grendel is the off-spring of one of the descendants of Cain, a son of Adam and Eve. Cain killed his brother, Abel, and became the first murderer. He was eternally cursed by God and, according to legend, fathered all the evil beings that plague humankind: monsters, demons, and evil spirits.

Sutton Hoo Bowls (7th century A.D.). Sutton Hoo ship burial.

? **53–58.** *Why do none of Hrothgar's men challenge Grendel?*

Ⓐ **Literary Focus** **Epic Hero** Epic heroes embody the values of the societies that create them. What values can you identify in the lines you have read so far?

Ⓑ **Literary Focus** **Epic Hero** Epic heroes perform great deeds. What do you think Beowulf's great deed will be?

Were those who fled him. Hate had triumphed.
    So Grendel ruled, fought with the righteous,
60 One against many, and won; so Herot
Stood empty, and stayed deserted for years,
Twelve winters of grief for Hrothgar, king
Of the Danes, sorrow heaped at his door
By hell-forged hands. His misery leaped **C**
65 The seas, was told and sung in all
Men's ears: how Grendel's hatred began,
How the monster relished his savage war
On the Danes, keeping the bloody feud
Alive, seeking no peace, offering
70 No truce, accepting no settlement, no price
In gold or land, and paying the living
For one crime only with another. No one
Waited for reparation from his plundering claws:
That shadow of death hunted in the darkness,
75 Stalked Hrothgar's warriors, old
And young, lying in waiting, hidden
In mist, invisibly following them from the edge
Of the marsh, always there, unseen.
    So mankind's enemy continued his crimes,
80 Killing as often as he could, coming
Alone, bloodthirsty and horrible. Though he lived
In Herot, when the night hid him, he never
Dared to touch king Hrothgar's glorious
Throne, protected by God—God,
85 Whose love Grendel could not know. But Hrothgar's
Heart was bent. The best and most noble
Of his council debated remedies, sat
In secret sessions, talking of terror
And wondering what the bravest of warriors could do.
90 And sometimes they sacrificed to the old stone gods,
Made heathen vows, hoping for Hell's
Support, the Devil's guidance in driving
Their affliction off. That was their way,
And the heathen's only hope, Hell
95 Always in their hearts, knowing neither God

? **59–64.** *How long has Grendel's reign of terror lasted?*

? **79–89.** *Why does the poem include this background information about Grendel and Hrothgar?*

C **Reading Focus** **Paraphrasing** When you read an epic poem, paraphrasing can be an effective tool to help you comprehend a passage. Paraphrase lines 59–64 in a few sentences.

Vocabulary **reparation** (rehp uh RAY shuhn) *n.:* payment to make up for a wrong or injury.

Nor His passing as He walks through our world, the Lord
Of Heaven and earth; their ears could not hear
His praise nor know His glory. Let them
Beware, those who are thrust into danger,
100　Clutched at by trouble, yet can carry no solace
In their hearts, cannot hope to be better! Hail
To those who will rise to God, drop off
Their dead bodies, and seek our Father's peace!

3

　　　　So the living sorrow of Healfdane's son°
105　Simmered, bitter and fresh, and no wisdom
Or strength could break it: That agony hung
On king and people alike, harsh
And unending, violent and cruel, and evil.
In his far-off home Beowulf, Higlac's
110　Follower° and the strongest of the Geats—greater
And stronger than anyone anywhere in this world—
Heard how Grendel filled nights with horror
And quickly commanded a boat fitted out,
Proclaiming that he'd go to that famous king,
115　Would sail across the sea to Hrothgar,
Now when help was needed. None　**D**
Of the wise ones regretted his going, much
As he was loved by the Geats: The omens were good,
And they urged the adventure on. So Beowulf
120　Chose the mightiest men he could find,

104. Healfdane's son: Hrothgar.

110. Higlac's follower: Higlac is Beowulf's uncle and feudal lord.

D **Literary Focus** **Epic Hero** What qualities of the epic hero are conveyed in lines 109–116?

The bravest and best of the Geats, fourteen
In all, and led them down to their boat;
He knew the sea, would point the prow°
Straight to that distant Danish shore. . . .

*Beowulf arrives in Denmark and is directed to Herot, the mead-hall of King
Hrothgar. The king sends Wulfgar, one of his thanes (or feudal lords), to greet
the visitors.*

123. **prow:** front part of a boat.

The Arrival of the Hero

4

125   . . . Then Wulfgar went to the door and addressed
The waiting seafarers with soldier's words:
     "My lord, the great king of the Danes, commands me
To tell you that he knows of your noble birth
And that having come to him from over the open
130 Sea you have come bravely and are welcome.
Now go to him as you are, in your armor and helmets,
But leave your battle-shields here, and your spears,
Let them lie waiting for the promises your words
May make." **E**
     Beowulf arose, with his men
135 Around him, ordering a few to remain
With their weapons, leading the others quickly
Along under Herot's steep roof into Hrothgar's
Presence. Standing on that prince's own hearth,
Helmeted, the silvery metal of his mail shirt°
140 Gleaming with a smith's° high art, he greeted
The Danes' great lord:
     "Hail, Hrothgar!
Higlac is my cousin° and my king; the days
Of my youth have been filled with glory. Now Grendel's
Name has echoed in our land: Sailors
145 Have brought us stories of Herot, the best
Of all mead-halls, deserted and useless when the moon
Hangs in skies the sun had lit,
Light and life fleeing together.
My people have said, the wisest, most knowing
150 And best of them, that my duty was to go to the Danes'
Great king. They have seen my strength for themselves, **F**

139. **mail shirt:** armored garment made of interlocking metal rings.
140. **smith's:** metalworker's.
142. **cousin:** any relative.

E Literary Focus **Epic Hero** How do Wulfgar's words show Beowulf's heroic qualities?

F Literary Focus **Epic Hero** Beowulf says that he has come to kill Grendel. What proof does he offer here that he is the right hero for the job?

Have watched me rise from the darkness of war,
Dripping with my enemies' blood. I drove
Five great giants into chains, chased
155 All of that race from the earth. I swam
In the blackness of night, hunting monsters
Out of the ocean, and killing them one
By one; death was my errand and the fate
They had earned. Now Grendel and I are called
160 Together, and I've come. Grant me, then,
Lord and protector of this noble place,
A single request! I have come so far,
Oh shelterer of warriors and your people's loved friend,
That this one favor you should not refuse me—
165 That I, alone and with the help of my men,
May purge all evil from this hall. I have heard,
Too, that the monster's scorn of men
Is so great that he needs no weapons and fears none.
Nor will I. My lord Higlac
170 Might think less of me if I let my sword
Go where my feet were afraid to, if I hid
Behind some broad linden shield:° My hands
Alone shall fight for me, struggle for life
Against the monster. God must decide **Ⓖ**
175 Who will be given to death's cold grip.
Grendel's plan, I think, will be
What it has been before, to invade this hall
And gorge his belly with our bodies. If he can,
If he can. And I think, if my time will have come,
180 There'll be nothing to mourn over, no corpse to prepare
For its grave: Grendel will carry our bloody
Flesh to the moors, crunch on our bones,
And smear torn scraps of our skin on the walls
Of his den. No, I expect no Danes
185 Will fret about sewing our shrouds,° if he wins.
And if death does take me, send the hammered
Mail of my armor to Higlac, return
The inheritance I had from Hrethel,° and he
From Wayland.° Fate will unwind as it must!"

5

190   Hrothgar replied, protector of the Danes:
       "Beowulf, you've come to us in friendship, and because
Of the reception your father found at our court.
Edgetho had begun a bitter feud,

Runic mount with animal's head, Anglo-Saxon, late 8th century. Biting head, probably part of the binding of a scabbard for a seax (Anglo-Saxon weapon or hunting knife). M&ME (1869–10,1).
The British Museum, London.

172. linden shield: shield made from wood of the linden tree.

? 180–185. *Why will Hrothgar not have to hold a funeral if Beowulf dies?*

185. shrouds: cloths used to wrap a body for burial.
188. Hrethel: Beowulf's grandfather, former king of the Geats.
189. Wayland: a smith celebrated for his skill in making swords and mail shirts.

? 191–207. *What do you think causes Hrothgar to make this speech, reminding Beowulf of the time he helped Beowulf's father? What is the probable effect of these words on Beowulf?*

Ⓖ Literary Focus **Epic Hero** To what does Beowulf <u>attribute</u> the outcome of the epic battle?

Killing Hathlaf, a Wulfing warrior:°

195 Your father's countrymen were afraid of war,
     If he returned to his home, and they turned him away.
     Then he traveled across the curving waves
     To the land of the Danes. I was new to the throne,
     Then, a young man ruling this wide
200 Kingdom and its golden city: Hergar,
     My older brother, a far better man
     Than I, had died and dying made me,
     Second among Healfdane's sons, first
     In this nation. I bought the end of Edgetho's
205 Quarrel, sent ancient treasures through the ocean's
     Furrows to the Wulfings; your father swore
     He'd keep that peace. My tongue grows heavy,
     And my heart, when I try to tell you what Grendel
     Has brought us, the damage he's done, here
210 In this hall. You see for yourself how much smaller
     Our ranks have become, and can guess what we've lost
     To his terror. Surely the Lord Almighty
     Could stop his madness, smother his lust! **Ⓗ**
     How many times have my men, glowing
215 With courage drawn from too many cups
     Of ale, sworn to stay after dark
     And stem that horror with a sweep of their swords.
     And then, in the morning, this mead-hall glittering
     With new light would be drenched with blood, the benches
220 Stained red, the floors, all wet from that fiend's
     Savage assault—and my soldiers would be fewer
     Still, death taking more and more.
     But to table, Beowulf, a banquet in your honor:
     Let us toast your victories, and talk of the future."
225   Then Hrothgar's men gave places to the Geats,
     Yielded benches to the brave visitors,
     And led them to the feast. The keeper of the mead
     Came carrying out the carved flasks,
     And poured that bright sweetness. A poet
230 Sang, from time to time, in a clear
     Pure voice. Danes and visiting Geats
     Celebrated as one, drank and rejoiced.

194. Wulfing warrior: The Wulfings were a Germanic tribe. Hrothgar's queen might have been a Wulfing.

Bronze stag atop ceremonial scepter (7th century A.D.) from the Sutton Hoo ship treasure, Suffolk, England. The British Museum, London.

Ⓗ **Reading Focus** **Paraphrasing** In your own words, paraphrase these lines about Grendel's influence.

Unferth's Challenge

6

Unferth spoke, Ecglaf's son,
Who sat at Hrothgar's feet, spoke harshly
235   And sharp (vexed by Beowulf's adventure,
By their visitor's courage, and angry that anyone
In Denmark or anywhere on earth had ever
Acquired glory and fame greater
Than his own):
            "You're Beowulf, are you—the same
240   Boastful fool who fought a swimming
Match with Brecca, both of you daring
And young and proud, exploring the deepest
Seas, risking your lives for no reason
But the danger? All older and wiser heads warned you
245   Not to, but no one could check such pride.
With Brecca at your side you swam along
The sea-paths, your swift-moving hands pulling you
Over the ocean's face. Then winter
Churned through the water, the waves ran you
250   As they willed, and you struggled seven long nights
To survive. And at the end victory was his,
Not yours. The sea carried him close
To his home, to southern Norway, near
The land of the Brondings, where he ruled and was loved,
255   Where his treasure was piled and his strength protected
His towns and his people. He'd promised to outswim you:
Bonstan's son° made that boast ring true.
You've been lucky in your battles, Beowulf, but I think
Your luck may change if you challenge Grendel,
260   Staying a whole night through in this hall,
Waiting where that fiercest of demons can find you."
            Beowulf answered, Edgetho's great son:
            "Ah! Unferth, my friend, your face
Is hot with ale, and your tongue has tried
265   To tell us about Brecca's doings. But the truth
Is simple: No man swims in the sea
As I can, no strength is a match for mine.
As boys, Brecca and I had boasted—
We were both too young to know better—that we'd risk
270   Our lives far out at sea, and so
We did. Each of us carried a naked
Sword, prepared for whales or the swift

239–252. *Why might Unferth think that Beowulf is ashamed of having taken part in the swimming race?*

257. Bonstan's son: Brecca.

Anglo-Saxon gold buckle (7th century A.D.) from the Sutton Hoo ship treasure, Suffolk, England.
British Library, London.

---

① Literary Focus **Epic Hero** An epic hero represents the ideal of his society. Here, however, Unferth challenges Beowulf's bravery. How do you think he feels about Beowulf?

Sharp teeth and beaks of needlefish.
He could never leave me behind, swim faster
275 Across the waves than I could, and I
Had chosen to remain close to his side.  **J**
I remained near him for five long nights,
Until a flood swept us apart;
The frozen sea surged around me,
280 It grew dark, the wind turned bitter, blowing
From the north, and the waves were savage. Creatures
Who sleep deep in the sea were stirred
Into life—and the iron hammered links
Of my mail shirt, these shining bits of metal
285 Woven across my breast, saved me
From death. A monster seized me, drew me
Swiftly toward the bottom, swimming with its claws
Tight in my flesh. But fate let me
Find its heart with my sword, hack myself
290 Free; I fought that beast's last battle,
Left it floating lifeless in the sea.

7

"Other monsters crowded around me,
Continually attacking. I treated them politely,
Offering the edge of my razor-sharp sword.
295 But the feast, I think, did not please them, filled
Their evil bellies with no banquet-rich food,
Thrashing there at the bottom of the sea; **K**
By morning they'd decided to sleep on the shore,
Lying on their backs, their blood spilled out
300 On the sand. Afterwards, sailors could cross
That sea-road and feel no fear; nothing
Would stop their passing. Then God's bright beacon
Appeared in the east, the water lay still,
And at last I could see the land, wind-swept
305 Cliff-walls at the edge of the coast. Fate saves
The living when they drive away death by themselves!
Lucky or not, nine was the number
Of sea-huge monsters I killed. What man,
Anywhere under Heaven's high arch, has fought

J **Literary Focus** **Epic Hero** What is Beowulf's explanation for not leaving Brecca far behind? What heroic quality does this suggest?

K **Literary Focus** **Epic Hero** How does the language of Beowulf's speech in these lines <u>emphasize</u> Beowulf's calm, confident (and perhaps arrogant) nature?

Saxon brooch (early 6th century) discovered at Mitcham, South London. Gold leaf on wood. English School.
Museum of London, UK.

310 In such darkness, endured more misery, or been harder
Pressed? Yet I survived the sea, smashed
The monsters' hot jaws, swam home from my journey.
The swift-flowing waters swept me along
And I landed on Finnish soil. I've heard
315 No tales of you, Unferth, telling
Of such clashing terror, such contests in the night!
Brecca's battles were never so bold;
Neither he nor you can match me—and I mean
No boast, have announced no more than I know
320 To be true. And there's more: You murdered your brothers,
Your own close kin. Words and bright wit
Won't help your soul; you'll suffer hell's fires,
Unferth, forever tormented. Ecglaf's
Proud son, if your hands were as hard, your heart
325 As fierce as you think it, no fool would dare
To raid your hall, ruin Herot
And oppress its prince, as Grendel has done.
But he's learned that terror is his alone,
Discovered he can come for your people with no fear
330 Of reprisal; he's found no fighting, here,
But only food, only delight.
He murders as he likes, with no mercy, gorges
And feasts on your flesh, and expects no trouble,
No quarrel from the quiet Danes. Now
335 The Geats will show him courage, soon
He can test his strength in battle. And when the sun
Comes up again, opening another
Bright day from the south, anyone in Denmark
May enter this hall: That evil will be gone!" **L**
340 *Hrothgar, gray-haired and brave, sat happily*
Listening, the famous ring-giver sure,
At last, that Grendel could be killed; he believed
In Beowulf's bold strength and the firmness of his spirit.
     There was the sound of laughter, and the cheerful clanking
345 Of cups, and pleasant words. Then Welthow,
Hrothgar's gold-ringed queen, greeted
The warriors; a noble woman who knew
What was right, she raised a flowing cup
To Hrothgar first, holding it high
350 For the lord of the Danes to drink, wishing him
Joy in that feast. The famous king
Drank with pleasure and blessed their banquet.

? 323–334. *What is Beowulf's final response to Unferth's challenge?*

Book I, from the *Beowulf* graphic novel, featuring the Francis Gummere verse translation.

L Reading Focus **Paraphrasing** How would you paraphrase the story up to this point?

Vocabulary **reprisal** (rih PRY zuhl) *n.*: punishment in return for an injury.

Then Welthow went from warrior to warrior,
Pouring a portion from the jeweled cup
355 For each, till the bracelet-wearing queen
Had carried the mead-cup among them and it was Beowulf's
Turn to be served. She saluted the Geats'
Great prince, thanked God for answering her prayers,
For allowing her hands the happy duty
360 Of offering mead to a hero who would help
Her afflicted people. He drank what she poured,
Edgetho's brave son, then assured the Danish
Queen that his heart was firm and his hands
Ready:
        "When we crossed the sea, my comrades
365 And I, I already knew that all
My purpose was this: to win the good will
Of your people or die in battle, pressed
In Grendel's fierce grip. Let me live in greatness
And courage, or here in this hall welcome
My death!" Ⓜ
370   Welthow was pleased with his words
His bright-tongued boasts; she carried them back
To her lord, walked nobly across to his side.
        The feast went on, laughter and music
And the brave words of warriors celebrating
375 Their delight. Then Hrothgar rose, Healfdane's
Son, heavy with sleep; as soon
As the sun had gone, he knew that Grendel
Would come to Herot, would visit that hall
When night had covered the earth with its net
380 And the shapes of darkness moved black and silent
Through the world. Hrothgar's warriors rose with him.
        He went to Beowulf, embraced the Geats'
Brave prince, wished him well, and hoped
That Herot would be his to command. And then
He declared:
385   "No one strange to this land
Has ever been granted what I've given you,
No one in all the years of my rule.
Make this best of all mead-halls yours, and then
Keep it free of evil, fight
390 With glory in your heart! Purge Herot
And your ship will sail home with its treasure-holds full." . . . Ⓝ

Shoulder clasp (7th century A.D.), from the
Sutton Hoo ship treasure, Suffolk, England.
The British Museum, London.

Ⓜ **Literary Focus** **Epic Hero** What does Beowulf's speech here reveal about his character?

Ⓝ **Reading Focus** **Paraphrasing** What verbs in these lines could help you paraphrase Hrothgar's speech?

The feast ends. Beowulf and his men take the place of Hrothgar's followers and lie down to sleep in Herot. Beowulf, however, is wakeful, eager to meet his enemy.

The Battle with Grendel

8

Out from the marsh, from the foot of misty
Hills and bogs, bearing God's hatred,
Grendel came, hoping to kill
395   Anyone he could trap on this trip to high Herot.  Ⓞ
He moved quickly through the cloudy night,
Up from his swampland, sliding silently
Toward that gold-shining hall. He had visited Hrothgar's
Home before, knew the way—
400   But never, before nor after that night,
Found Herot defended so firmly, his reception
So harsh. He journeyed, forever joyless,
Straight to the door, then snapped it open,
Tore its iron fasteners with a touch,
405   And rushed angrily over the threshold.
He strode quickly across the inlaid
Floor, snarling and fierce: His eyes
Gleamed in the darkness, burned with a gruesome
Light. Then he stopped, seeing the hall
410   Crowded with sleeping warriors, stuffed
With rows of young soldiers resting together.
And his heart laughed, he relished the sight,
Intended to tear the life from those bodies
By morning; the monster's mind was hot
415   With the thought of food and the feasting his belly
Would soon know. But fate, that night, intended Ⓟ
Grendel to gnaw the broken bones
Of his last human supper. Human
Eyes were watching his evil steps,
420   Waiting to see his swift hard claws.
Grendel snatched at the first Geat
He came to, ripped him apart, cut
His body to bits with powerful jaws,
Drank the blood from his veins, and bolted
425   Him down, hands and feet; death
And Grendel's great teeth came together,

The Battersea Shield, Iron Age (350–50 B.C.).
The British Museum, London.

Ⓞ **Literary Focus** Epic Hero How do these lines show us that Grendel is the opposite of the epic hero?

Ⓟ **Reading Focus** Paraphrasing What words in these lines could you omit if you wrote a paragraph paraphrasing this visit to Herot?

Eric Owens as Grendel in production of Grendel (Los Angeles).

Grendel

It is often said that "history is written by the victors," and for that reason, it is important to think objectively when we read literary and historical narratives. Like history, literature can be revised to exhibit a point of view different from that of the original author. In literature, revisionism often becomes apparent when popular stories are retold from the perspective of the antagonist, the character or force that opposes the main character. The musical *Wicked,* for example, based on the novel by Gregory Maguire, spins a new story for the wicked witch from *The Wizard of Oz* by showcasing her character's rich history prior to the beginning of the movie. John Gardner tackles a similar theme with his novel *Grendel*—later turned into an opera—which retells the epic of *Beowulf* from Grendel's point of view.

Ask Yourself

Based on your reading of "The Monster Grendel," think about what Grendel's personal reasons might have been for attacking Herot over the years. Was it truly mindless evil that drove him to murder? What could justify his slaughter of Hrothgar's people?

Snapping life shut. Then he stepped to another
Still body, clutched at Beowulf with his claws,
Grasped at a strong-hearted wakeful sleeper
430 —And was instantly seized himself, claws
Bent back as Beowulf leaned up on one arm.
That shepherd of evil,° guardian of crime,
Knew at once that nowhere on earth
Had he met a man whose hands were harder;
435 His mind was flooded with fear—but nothing **Q**
Could take his talons and himself from that tight
Hard grip. Grendel's one thought was to run
From Beowulf, flee back to his marsh and hide there:
This was a different Herot than the hall he had emptied.
440 But Higlac's follower remembered his final
Boast and, standing erect, stopped
The monster's flight, fastened those claws
In his fists till they cracked, clutched Grendel
Closer. The infamous killer fought
445 For his freedom, wanting no flesh but retreat,

Q Literary Focus Epic Hero How do we know from these lines that Beowulf is greater than the Danes?

432. shepherd of evil: a kenning for Grendel. The **kenning,** a metaphor made of compound words, is a staple of Anglo-Saxon literature. Simple kennings are compound words formed from two common nouns: *sky-candle* for sun, *battle-dew* for blood. More complex kennings are formed with compound adjectives and nouns. A ship became a *foamy-throated ship,* then a *foamy-throated sea-stallion,* and finally a *foamy-throated sea-stallion of the whale-road.* In their original language, kennings are usually written as simple compounds without hyphens or spaces between the words. In translation, kennings are often hyphenated, written as possessives (*wolf of wounds*), or written as prepositional phrases (*shepherd of evil*).

Desiring nothing but escape; his claws
Had been caught, he was trapped. That trip to Herot
Was a miserable journey for the writhing monster!
　　　　The high hall rang, its roof boards swayed,
450　And Danes shook with terror. Down
The aisles the battle swept, angry
And wild. Herot trembled, wonderfully
Built to withstand the blows, the struggling
Great bodies beating at its beautiful walls;
455　Shaped and fastened with iron, inside
And out, artfully worked, the building
Stood firm. Its benches rattled, fell
To the floor, gold-covered boards grating
As Grendel and Beowulf battled across them.
460　Hrothgar's wise men had fashioned Herot
To stand forever; only fire,
They had planned, could shatter what such skill had put
Together, swallow in hot flames such splendor
Of ivory and iron and wood. Suddenly
465　The sounds changed, the Danes started
In new terror, cowering in their beds as the terrible
Screams of the Almighty's enemy sang
In the darkness, the horrible shrieks of pain
And defeat, the tears torn out of Grendel's
470　Taut throat, hell's captive caught in the arms
Of him who of all the men on earth
Was the strongest. **ⓡ**

9

　　　　That mighty protector of men
Meant to hold the monster till its life
Leaped out, knowing the fiend was no use
475　To anyone in Denmark. All of Beowulf's
Band had jumped from their beds, ancestral
Swords raised and ready, determined
To protect their prince if they could. Their courage
Was great but all wasted: They could hack at Grendel **ⓢ**
480　From every side, trying to open
A path for his evil soul, but their points
Could not hurt him, the sharpest and hardest iron
Could not scratch at his skin, for that sin-stained demon

? 467–472. *Earlier in the epic it was explained that Grendel is a descendant of Cain, who was cursed by God. In what ways is this battle between Grendel and Beowulf really a battle between good and evil? What details in the description of the battle make this clear?*

ⓡ Literary Focus **Epic Hero** What details in these lines demonstrate Beowulf's superhuman strength?

ⓢ Reading Focus **Paraphrasing** How would you paraphrase the reasons that Beowulf's men can't harm Grendel?

Had bewitched all men's weapons, laid spells
485 That blunted every mortal man's blade.
And yet his time had come, his days
Were over, his death near; down
To hell he would go, swept groaning and helpless
To the waiting hands of still worse fiends.
490 Now he discovered—once the afflictor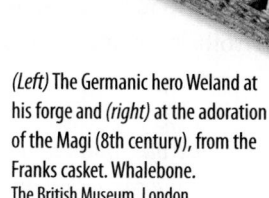
Of men, tormentor of their days—what it meant
To feud with Almighty God: Grendel
Saw that his strength was deserting him, his claws
Bound fast, Higlac's brave follower tearing at
495 His hands. The monster's hatred rose higher,
But his power had gone. He twisted in pain,
And the bleeding sinews deep in his shoulder
Snapped, muscle and bone split
And broke. The battle was over, Beowulf
500 Had been granted new glory: Grendel escaped,
But wounded as he was could flee to his den,
His miserable hole at the bottom of the marsh,
Only to die, to wait for the end
Of all his days. And after that bloody
505 Combat the Danes laughed with delight.
He who had come to them from across the sea,
Bold and strong-minded, had driven affliction
Off, purged Herot clean. He was happy,
Now, with that night's fierce work; the Danes
510 Had been served as he'd boasted he'd serve them; Beowulf,
A prince of the Geats, had killed Grendel,
Ended the grief, the sorrow, the suffering
Forced on Hrothgar's helpless people
By a bloodthirsty fiend. No Dane doubted
515 The victory, for the proof, hanging high
From the rafters where Beowulf had hung it, was the monster's
Arm, claw and shoulder and all.

10

And then, in the morning, crowds surrounded
Herot, warriors coming to that hall
520 From faraway lands, princes and leaders
Of men hurrying to behold the monster's
Great staggering tracks. They gaped with no sense
Of sorrow, felt no regret for his suffering,
Went tracing his bloody footprints, his beaten
525 And lonely flight, to the edge of the lake

(Left) The Germanic hero Weland at his forge and *(right)* at the adoration of the Magi (8th century), from the Franks casket. Whalebone. The British Museum, London.

? **514–517.** *How does Beowulf prove his victory over Grendel? Why might he do this?*

? **522–533.** *What has happened to Grendel?*

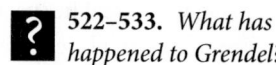 **Reading Focus** Paraphrasing In your own words, describe how Beowulf defeats Grendel.

Where he'd dragged his corpselike way, doomed
And already weary of his vanishing life.
The water was bloody, steaming and boiling
In horrible pounding waves, heat
530 Sucked from his magic veins; but the swirling
Surf had covered his death, hidden
Deep in murky darkness his miserable
End, as hell opened to receive him.
       Then old and young rejoiced, turned back
535 From that happy pilgrimage, mounted their hard-hooved
Horses, high-spirited stallions, and rode them
Slowly toward Herot again, retelling
Beowulf's bravery as they jogged along.
And over and over they swore that nowhere
540 On earth or under the spreading sky
Or between the seas, neither south nor north,
Was there a warrior worthier to rule over men.
(But no one meant Beowulf's praise to belittle
Hrothgar, their kind and gracious king!) . . .

Grendel's monstrous mother, in grief for her son, next attacks Herot, and in her dripping claws she carries off one man—Hrothgar's closest friend. The monster also carries off Grendel's arm, which Beowulf had hung high from the rafters. Beowulf is awakened and called for again. In one of the most famous verses in the epic, the old king describes where Grendel and his mother live.

I I

545   . . . "They live in secret places, windy Ⓤ
Cliffs, wolf-dens where water pours
From the rocks, then runs underground, where mist
Steams like black clouds, and the groves of trees
Growing out over their lake are all covered
550 With frozen spray, and wind down snakelike
Roots that reach as far as the water
And help keep it dark. At night that lake
Burns like a torch. No one knows its bottom,
No wisdom reaches such depths. A deer,
555 Hunted through the woods by packs of hounds,
A stag with great horns, though driven through the forest
From faraway places, prefers to die
On those shores, refuses to save its life

Purse lid, from the Sutton Hoo Ship Burial (c. 625–30 A.D.). Gold, garnets, and millefiori glass. The British Library, London.

Ⓤ **Literary Focus** **Epic Hero** How does this description of Grendel's home differ from other descriptions of the lair found in the epic?

> "Twisted gold,
> heaped-up ancient
> treasure, will reward
> you for the
> battle you
> win!"

In that water. It isn't far, nor is it
560 A pleasant spot! When the wind stirs
And storms, waves splash toward the sky,
As dark as the air, as black as the rain
That the heavens weep. Our only help,
Again, lies with you. Grendel's mother
565 Is hidden in her terrible home, in a place
You've not seen. Seek it, if you dare! Save us,
Once more, and again twisted gold,
Heaped-up ancient treasure, will reward you
For the battle you win!" **V**

Carrying the sword Hrunting, Beowulf goes to the lake where Grendel's mother has her underwater lair. Then, fully armed, he dives to the depths of this watery hell.

The Monster's Mother

12

570 . . . He leaped into the lake, would not wait for anyone's
Answer; the heaving water covered him
Over. For hours he sank through the waves;
At last he saw the mud of the bottom.
And all at once the greedy she-wolf
575 Who'd ruled those waters for half a hundred
Years discovered him, saw that a creature
From above had come to explore the bottom
Of her wet world. She welcomed him in her claws,
Clutched at him savagely but could not harm him,
580 Tried to work her fingers through the tight
Ring-woven mail on his breast, but tore
And scratched in vain. Then she carried him, armor
And sword and all, to her home; he struggled
To free his weapon, and failed. The fight
585 Brought other monsters swimming to see
Her catch, a host of sea beasts who beat at
His mail shirt, stabbing with tusks and teeth
As they followed along. Then he realized, suddenly,
That she'd brought him into someone's battle-hall,

? **570–594.** *Describe how Beowulf comes to the lair of Grendel's mother. What details remind you that Beowulf is not an ordinary man?*

V Reading Focus **Paraphrasing** How would you describe what Hrothgar is asking Beowulf to do in lines 563–569?

590 And there the water's heat could not hurt him,
Nor anything in the lake attack him through
The building's high-arching roof. A brilliant
Light burned all around him, the lake
Itself like a fiery flame.
        Then he saw
595 The mighty water witch, and swung his sword,
His ring-marked blade, straight at her head;
The iron sang its fierce song,
Sang Beowulf's strength. But her guest
Discovered that no sword could slice her evil
600 Skin, that Hrunting could not hurt her, was useless
Now when he needed it. They wrestled, she ripped
And tore and clawed at him, bit holes in his helmet,
And that too failed him; for the first time in years
Of being worn to war it would earn no glory;
605 It was the last time anyone would wear it. But Beowulf
Longed only for fame, leaped back
Into battle. He tossed his sword aside,
Angry; the steel-edged blade lay where
He'd dropped it. If weapons were useless he'd use
610 His hands, the strength in his fingers. So fame
Comes to the men who mean to win it
And care about nothing else! He raised
His arms and seized her by the shoulder; anger
Doubled his strength, he threw her to the floor.
615 She fell, Grendel's fierce mother, and the Geats'
Proud prince was ready to leap on her. But she rose
At once and repaid him with her clutching claws,
Wildly tearing at him. He was weary, that best
And strongest of soldiers; his feet stumbled
620 And in an instant she had him down, held helpless.
Squatting with her weight on his stomach, she drew
A dagger, brown with dried blood and prepared
To avenge her only son. But he was stretched
On his back, and her stabbing blade was blunted
625 By the woven mail shirt he wore on his chest.
The hammered links held; the point
Could not touch him. He'd have traveled to the bottom of the earth,
Edgetho's son, and died there, if that shining
Woven metal had not helped—and Holy

607–632. *What details in this description of the battle between Grendel's mother and Beowulf add to your suspense about the outcome? At what point do you think Beowulf may not be successful? What saves him?*

"Sigurds Helmet" (7th century) from a pre-Viking grave at Vendel.
Upplandsmuseet, Uppsala, Sweden.

W **Literary Focus** Epic Hero How is the epic hero's story or song as important as his strength and weapons?

X **Literary Focus** Epic Hero What is the role of supernatural forces in the success of the hero's journey?

630   God, who sent him victory, gave judgment
        For truth and right, Ruler of the Heavens,
        Once Beowulf was back on his feet and fighting.

13

        Then he saw, hanging on the wall, a heavy
        Sword, hammered by giants, strong
635   And blessed with their magic, the best of all weapons
        But so massive that no ordinary man could lift
        Its carved and decorated length. He drew it
        From its scabbard, broke the chain on its hilt,°
        And then, savage, now, angry
640   And desperate, lifted it high over his head
        And struck with all the strength he had left,
        Caught her in the neck and cut it through,
        Broke bones and all. Her body fell
        To the floor, lifeless, the sword was wet
645   With her blood, and Beowulf rejoiced at the sight. **Y**
        The brilliant light shone, suddenly,
        As though burning in that hall, and as bright as Heaven's
        Own candle, lit in the sky. He looked
        At her home, then following along the wall
650   Went walking, his hands tight on the sword,
        His heart still angry. He was hunting another
        Dead monster, and took his weapon with him
        For final revenge against Grendel's vicious
        Attacks, his nighttime raids, over
655   And over, coming to Herot when Hrothgar's
        Men slept, killing them in their beds,
        Eating some on the spot, fifteen
        Or more, and running to his loathsome moor
        With another such sickening meal waiting
660   In his pouch. But Beowulf repaid him for those visits,
        Found him lying dead in his corner,
        Armless, exactly as that fierce fighter
        Had sent him out from Herot, then struck off
        His head with a single swift blow. The body
665   Jerked for the last time, then lay still. . . . **Z**

638. scabbard . . . hilt: A scabbard is a case that holds the blade of a sword; a hilt is a sword's handle.

? 648–665. *What is Beowulf's final revenge against Grendel? What action of Beowulf's provides a resolution, or wrapping up, of the episode?*

Y Reading Focus **Paraphrasing** Lines 633–645 describe Beowulf killing Grendel's mother. What images in this description are essential to paraphrasing it?

Z Literary Focus **Epic Hero** What role do violence and the battle play in creating a hero's image?

Vocabulary **loathsome** (LOHTH suhm) *adj.*: very hateful; disgusting.

Applying Your Skills

from **Beowulf, Part One**

SKILLS FOCUS Literary Skills Analyze the archetype of the epic hero; analyze the universal themes of epic poetry. **Reading Skills** Paraphrase a text. **Writing Skills** Write to inform; clarify information when writing.

Respond and Think Critically

Reading Focus

Quick Check

1. Besides seeking fame and glory, why does Beowulf go to help Hrothgar and the Danes?
2. Why does Unferth challenge Beowulf?
3. Why does Grendel's mother attack Herot?

Read with a Purpose

4. Based on your observations of Beowulf's heroic qualities, what impression do you have of Anglo-Saxon society?

Reading Skills: Paraphrasing

5. As you read, you listed nouns, verbs, and phrases that describe Beowulf or his actions. Now, add another column in which you paraphrase each passage. How does paraphrasing help you see how Beowulf fits the archetype of the epic hero?

Nouns / Pronouns	Verbs	Phrases / Objects	Paraphrases
my duty	was to go	to the Danes	
I	drove /chased	giants	
I	swam	hunting monsters	

Literary Focus

Literary Analysis

6. **Analyze** Identify images of Grendel that associate him with death or darkness. How are these images supposed to make you feel about Grendel?

7. **Interpret** The battle with Grendel and the battle with Grendel's mother take place in very different settings. How do these two settings differ?
8. **Evaluate** How is Beowulf's insistence that he fight without a weapon illustrate the <u>concept</u> of an epic hero?
9. **Extend** A common occurrence in myths and legends is the hero's discovery of an evil greater than the one he has set out to destroy. Often this greater evil is a creator or parent archetype. What greater evil does Beowulf discover? How does this greater evil fit the creator archetype?

Literary Skills: Epic Hero

10. **Evaluate** How do Beowulf's heroic qualities affect your feelings about his overall character? Is it easy or difficult to relate to him? Explain.

Literary Skills Review: Universal Themes

11. **Analyze** A **universal theme** is one that occurs in literature from many different cultures around the world and throughout time. What universal themes can you find in *Beowulf*?

Writing Focus

Think as a Reader/Writer

Use It in Your Writing Review your notes about the characteristics of the speeches Beowulf and the others make. Imitating the style of the epic, write a speech of ten or more lines delivered by Beowulf at the end of the Part 1.

What Do **You Think Now** What is the main cause for Beowulf's heroic actions in Part One? Do you think his motive will be the same in Part Two?

from Beowulf

Part Two

translated by Seamus Heaney

> **Read with a Purpose** Read to discover how Beowulf rises to the heroic challenges before him.

Beowulf carries Grendel's head to King Hrothgar and then returns gift-laden to the land of the Geats, where he succeeds to the throne. After fifty winters pass, Beowulf, now an old man, faces his final task: He must fight a dragon who, angry because a thief has stolen a jeweled cup from the dragon's hoard of gold, is laying waste to the Geats' land. Beowulf and eleven warriors are guided to the dragon's lair by the thief who stole the cup. For Beowulf the price of this last victory will be great.

The Final Battle

14

Then he addressed each dear companion
one final time, those fighters in their helmets, Ⓐ
resolute and high-born: "I would rather not
use a weapon if I knew another way
670 to grapple with the dragon and make good my boast
as I did against Grendel in days gone by.
But I shall be meeting molten venom

Ⓐ **Literary Focus** **Epic Hero** Read Beowulf's speech that begins on this page. How is King Beowulf different from the younger Beowulf who defeated Grendel?

The Prow/The Oseberg Viking Ship.
Museum of Cultural History, University of Oslo, Norway

in the fire he breathes, so I go forth
in mail-shirt and shield. I won't shift a foot
675   when I meet the cave-guard: what occurs on the wall
between the two of us will turn out as fate,
overseer of men, decides. I am resolved.
I scorn further words against this sky-borne foe.

"Men at arms, remain here on the barrow,°   Ⓑ
680   safe in your armour, to see which one of us
is better in the end at bearing wounds
in a deadly fray. This fight is not yours,
nor is it up to any man except me
to measure his strength against the monster
685   or to prove his worth. I shall win the gold
by my courage, or else mortal combat,
doom of battle, will bear your lord away."

Then he drew himself up beside his shield.
The fabled warrior in his warshirt and helmet

679. barrow (BAR oh): hill.

Ⓑ **Literary Focus** **Epic Hero** How does Beowulf's resignation to his fate <u>emphasize</u> his deep responsibility to his people?

West Stow Saxon village reconstruction, Suffolk, England.

"Unyielding, the lord of his people loomed by his tall shield, sure of his ground..."

690   trusted in his own strength entirely
and went under the crag. No coward path.
Hard by the rock-face that hale veteran,
a good man who had gone repeatedly
into combat and danger and come through,
695   saw a stone arch and a gushing stream
that burst from the barrow, blazing and wafting
a deadly heat. It would be hard to survive **C**
unscathed near the hoard, to hold firm
against the dragon in those flaming depths.
700   Then he gave a shout. The lord of the Geats
unburdened his breast and broke out
in a storm of anger. Under grey stone
his voice challenged and resounded clearly.
Hate was ignited. The hoard-guard recognized
705   a human voice, the time was over
for peace and parleying.° Pouring forth
in a hot battle-fume, the breath of the monster
burst from the rock. There was a rumble under ground.
Down there in the barrow, Beowulf the warrior
710   lifted his shield: the outlandish thing
writhed and convulsed and vehemently
turned on the king, whose keen-edged sword,
an heirloom inherited by ancient right,
was already in his hand. Roused to a fury,
715   each antagonist struck terror in the other.
Unyielding, the lord of his people loomed
by his tall shield, sure of his ground,
while the serpent looped and unleashed itself.
Swaddled in flames, it came gliding and flexing
720   and racing towards its fate. Yet his shield defended **D**
the renowned leader's life and limb
for a shorter time than he meant it to:
that final day was the first time

706. parleying: discussing.

709–720. The image of a lone hero standing up to a fire-breathing dragon or other giant monster is one of the most archetypal images in Western heroic literature.

? *How does the dragon compare with Grendel and Grendel's mother?*

C **Reading Focus** **Paraphrasing** How would you reword the poetic diction in this sentence (lines 692–697)?

D **Reading Focus** **Paraphrasing** Rewrite these lines to explain what goes wrong in Beowulf's confrontation with the dragon.

Vocabulary **vehemently** (VEE uh muhnt lee) *adv.:* violently.

Gundestrup cauldron.
National Museum of Denmark.

when Beowulf fought and fate denied him
725 glory in battle. So the king of the Geats
raised his hand and struck hard
at the enamelled scales, but scarcely cut through:
the blade flashed and slashed yet the blow
was far less powerful than the hard-pressed king
730 had need of at that moment. The mound-keeper
went into a spasm and spouted deadly flames:
when he felt the stroke, battle-fire
billowed and spewed. Beowulf was foiled°
of a glorious victory. The glittering sword,
735 infallible before that day,
failed when he unsheathed it, as it never should have.
For the son of Ecgtheow, it was no easy thing
to have to give ground like that and go
unwillingly to inhabit another home
740 in a place beyond; so every man must yield
the leasehold of his days.

          It was not long
until the fierce contenders clashed again.
The hoard-guard took heart, inhaled and swelled up
and got a new wind; he who had once ruled
745 was furled° in fire and had to face the worst.
No help or backing was to be had then
from his high-born comrades; that hand-picked troop
broke ranks and ran for their lives
to the safety of the wood. But within one heart

733. foiled: prevented.

? **737–741.** *What are you led to believe about Beowulf's ultimate fate?*

745. furled: rolled up.
? **746–749.** *How do Beowulf's men react to the sight of the dragon gaining victory over Beowulf?*

Vocabulary **infallible** (ihn FAL uh buhl) *adj.:* unable to fail or be wrong.

750 sorrow welled up: in a man of worth
the claims of kinship cannot be denied.

15

His name was Wiglaf, a son of Weohstan's,
a well-regarded Shylfing warrior
related to Aelfhere. When he saw his lord
755 tormented by the heat of his scalding helmet,
he remembered the bountiful gifts bestowed on him,
how well he lived among the Waegmundings,
the freehold° he inherited from his father before him.
He could not hold back: one hand brandished
760 the yellow-timbered shield, the other drew his sword— . . . **E**

Sad at heart, addressing his companions,
Wiglaf spoke wise and fluent words:
"I remember that time when mead was flowing,
how we pledged loyalty to our lord in the hall,
765 promised our ring-giver we would be worth our price,
make good the gift of the war-gear,
those swords and helmets, as and when
his need required it. He picked us out
from the army deliberately, honoured us and judged us
770 fit for this action, made me these lavish° gifts—
and all because he considered us the best
of his arms-bearing thanes.° And now, although **F**
he wanted this challenge to be one he'd face
by himself alone—the shepherd of our land,
775 a man unequaled in the quest for glory
and a name for daring—now the day has come
when this lord we serve needs sound men

758. freehold: estate.

770. lavish (LAV ihsh): extravagant.

772. thanes (thaynz): in Anglo-Saxon England, a group of men who held land of the king in exchange for military service.

E **Reading Focus** **Paraphrasing** Paraphrase these lines about Wiglaf.

F **Literary Focus** **Epic Hero** Epic heroes almost always have a weakness or fatal flaw that causes of their downfall. According to these lines, what might Beowulf's weakness be?

Norse chessmen, from a Viking hoard, Isle of Lewis, Scotland.
The British Museum, London.

to give him their support. Let us go to him,
help our leader through the hot flame
780   and dread of the fire. As God is my witness,
I would rather my body were robed in the same
burning blaze as my gold-giver's body
than go back home bearing arms.
That is unthinkable, unless we have first
785   slain the foe and defended the life
of the prince of the Weather-Geats. I well know
the things he has done for us deserve better.
Should he alone be left exposed
to fall in battle? We must bond together,
790   shield and helmet, mail-shirt and sword."

*Together Beowulf and the young Wiglaf kill the dragon, but the old king is fatal-
ly wounded. Beowulf, thinking of his people, asks to see the monster's treasure.
Wiglaf enters the dragon's cave and finds a priceless hoard of jewels and gold.*

16

. . . Wiglaf went quickly, keen to get back,
excited by the treasure; anxiety weighed
on his brave heart, he was hoping he would find
the leader of the Geats alive where he had left him
795   helpless, earlier, on the open ground.
So he came to the place, carrying the treasure,
and found his lord bleeding profusely,
his life at an end; again he began
to swab his body. The beginnings of an utterance
800   broke out from the king's breast-cage.
The old lord gazed sadly at the gold.

"To the everlasting Lord of All,
to the King of Glory, I give thanks
that I behold this treasure here in front of me,
805   that I have been thus allowed to leave my people
so well endowed on the day I die. **G**
Now that I have bartered my last breath
to own this fortune, it is up to you
to look after their needs. I can hold out no longer.
810   Order my troop to construct a barrow
on a headland on the coast, after my pyre has cooled.
It will loom on the horizon at Hronesness

Knights on their mounts, The Lewis Chessmen
(about A.D. 1150–1200).
The British Museum, London.

? **810–816.** *Why is
constructing a memorial
important to Beowulf?*

G **Literary Focus** **Epic Hero** The death of a hero or other important characters in
literature often includes a symbolic passing on of duties. In these lines, how does Beowulf pass
on his heroic status? What do these items represent?

and be a reminder among my people—
so that in coming times crews under sail
815   will call it Beowulf's Barrow, as they steer
ships across the wide and shrouded waters."

Then the king in his great-heartedness unclasped
the collar of gold from his neck and gave it
to the young thane, telling him to use
820   it and the warshirt and the gilded helmet well.

"You are the last of us, the only one left
of the Waegmundings. Fate swept us away,
sent my whole brave high-born clan
to their final doom. Now I must follow them."
825   That was the warrior's last word.
He had no more to confide. The furious heat
of the pyre would assail° him. His soul fled from his breast
to its destined place among the steadfast ones.

Wiglaf berates the faithless warriors who did not go to the aid of their king.
With sorrow the Geats cremate the corpse of their greatest king. They place
his ashes, along with all of the dragon's treasure, in a huge burial tower
by the sea, where it can be seen by voyagers.

17

Then twelve warriors rode around the tomb,
830   chieftains' sons, champions in battle,
all of them distraught, chanting in dirges,
mourning his loss as a man and a king.
They extolled his heroic nature and exploits
and gave thanks for his greatness; which was the proper thing,
835   for a man should praise a prince whom he holds dear
and cherish his memory when that moment comes
when he has to be convoyed from his bodily home.
So the Geat people, his hearth companions,
sorrowed for the lord who had been laid low.
840   They said that of all the kings upon the earth   **H**
he was the man most gracious and fair-minded,
kindest to his people and keenest to win fame.

827. assail (uh SAYL): attack.

Knights on their mounts, The Lewis Chessmen
(about A.D. 1150–1200).
The British Museum, London

H **Literary Focus** Epic Hero According to the final lines of the poem,
what qualities make Beowulf a great hero?

Vocabulary extolled (ehk STOHLD) *v.*: praised.

from Beowulf **49**

Respond and Think Critically

Reading Focus

Quick Check

1. Why does the dragon wreak havoc upon Beowulf's land and people?

2. What is Beowulf's strategy in fighting the dragon?

3. Why does Wiglaf scold his fellow soldiers after Beowulf's death?

Read with a Purpose

4. How did Beowulf rise to the heroic challenges he had to face in Part Two? Has your impression of Anglo-Saxon society changed because of Beowulf's heroic qualities?

Reading Skills: Paraphrasing

5. While reading Part Two, you paraphrased the passages that were difficult to understand. Using a chart like the one below, chart the development of your paraphrases. Write about how the style of each passage contributed to the mood and meaning of the passage.

Passage Line Numbers	Difficult Words in Passage	Rear- range Word Order	Para- phrase	Relation- ship of Style and Meaning

Literary Focus

Literary Focus

6. **Analyze** What details does the poet use to describe the dragon? Keeping those details in mind, explain what the dragon might symbolize as Beowulf's final foe.

7. **Interpret** Grendel and the dragon wage war for different reasons. What are these reasons? How are these different motivations related to the underlying themes of the epic?

8. **Extend** Was there any way for Beowulf to defeat the dragon, or was he doomed from the start?

Literary Skills: Epic Hero

9. **Analyze** If Beowulf had a different set of heroic traits, such as great intelligence, could he still have been able to defeat the monsters? Explain.

Literary Skills Review: Alliteration

10. **Extend** The repetition of the same or similar consonant sounds in words that are close together is called **alliteration.** Look back on the selection to find passages rich in alliteration. Read these passages aloud to help you fully appreciate the importance of the sound of the epic. Form a group, and assign roles for each reader to demonstrate the dramatic qualities of the epic.

Writing Focus

Think as a Reader/Writer

Use It in Your Writing Continuing to imitate the style of the speeches in the epic, write a ten-line speech delivered by one of the time line warriors extolling Beowulf's greatness.

 What Do You Think Now

How does Beowulf's motivation change from Part One to Part Two? How would you describe his personality in Part Two as opposed to in Part One?

SKILLS FOCUS **Literary Skills** Analyze the archetype of the epic hero; analyze alliteration. **Reading Skills** Paraphrase a text. **Vocabulary Skills** Identify and use suffixes and prefixes to understand and create words. **Writing Skills** Write to entertain; develop characters.

from **Beowulf, Parts One and Two**

Vocabulary Development

✔ Vocabulary Check

Match the Vocabulary words with their definitions.

1. reparation   a. disgusting
2. loathsome   b. perfect
3. reprisal   c. penalty
4. vehemently   d. intensely
5. infallible   e. compensation
6. extolled   f. acclaimed

Vocabulary Skills: Prefixes and Suffixes

Prefixes are word parts attached to the beginning of a word, and **suffixes** are word parts attached to the end of a word. Most prefixes and suffixes alter a word's meaning or part of speech. However, some suffixes, also called inflectional endings, simply change a word's number or tense. For example, –ed changes a verb to the past tense, and –s turns a singular noun into a plural one. The table below contains examples of some common prefixes and suffixes.

Prefix or Suffix	Function / Meaning	Example
–ed	changes verb's form to past tense	planted
–ly	turns an adjective into an adverb	slowly
ex–	"out or out of; beyond; from"	exhale
in–	"not"	incapable
re–	"again; back; backward"	return
–tion	turns a verb into a noun	visualization
–some	"causes"	troublesome

Your Turn

Use the chart to help you complete the items below.

1. Use the suffix *–tion* to turn a verb into a noun.
2. Explain the difference in meaning between *infallible* and *fallible.*
3. *Reprehend* is a verb meaning "to blame." Its Latin root means "to pull back." Which Vocabulary word has the same root as *reprehend*?
4. Write a sentence using the present-tense form of *extolled.*
5. Without using a dictionary, write the definition of *expel.* Hint: Its root, *pellere,* means "to push."

Language Coach

Connotations A word's **connotations** are the ideas, emotions, or thoughts you associate with the word. A word might have strong positive or negative connotations. One way to notice a word's connotations is to imagine replacing it with another word. Describe how the meaning of each sentence changes when you alternate using the words below in parentheses.

1. The poem (*praises, extols*) the deeds of a great hero.
2. A (*hateful, loathsome*) monster attacked Beowulf and his men.
3. Beowulf struck (*strongly, vehemently*) at his enemy.
4. The hero's (*reprisal, vengeance*) was harsh.

Academic Vocabulary

Talk About . . .

Some observers believe that the <u>concept</u> of a hero forever changed after the September 11, 2001, attacks. Acts of heroism were <u>attributed</u> to a much more <u>diverse</u> group of men and women. In a small group, discuss your ideas about how one achieves hero <u>status</u> in America.

from **Beowulf, Parts One and Two**

Vocabulary Development

Vocabulary Skills: Anglo-Saxon Words and Word Parts

English has borrowed words from most of the world's languages, but many words in our basic vocabulary come to us from **Anglo-Saxon,** or Old English. The following are descendants of Old English words:

- the names of numbers ("one" for *an,* "two" for *twa,* "three" for *threo,* "four" for *feower*), words designating family relations ("father," for *faeder,* "mother" for *moder,* "son" for *sunu,* "daughter" for *dohtor*),
- names for parts of the body ("heart" for *heorte,* "foot" for *fot*)
- common, everyday things and activities ("apple" for *aeppel,* "hound" for *hund,* "weave" for *wefan*)

Many conventions in the English language can also be traced back to Anglo-Saxon times. Making nouns plural by adding *s* and creating possessives by adding *'s* come to us from Old English. Old English has given us the vowel changes in some irregular verbs, like *sing, sang, sung* (*singen, sang, sungen*) and the regular *–ed* (and sometimes *–t*) endings for the past tense and past participles of regular verbs (as in *healed, has healed*). The word endings we use to create degrees of comparison between adjectives (as in *darker, darkest*) are also Anglo-Saxon in origin.

Anglo-Saxon has contributed many important word parts—prefixes and suffixes—to the English language. Some of these affixes change the tense, person, or number of a word—often a verb. Others change the entire meaning of a word and its part of speech.

Your Turn

List examples of modern English words that use each of the Anglo-Saxon affixes shown on this page.

Prefixes from Anglo-Saxon	Meanings	Examples
a–	in; on; of; up; to	ashore, aside, atop
be–	around; about; treat as	behind, before, befriend
for–	away; off; from	forsake, forget
mis–	badly; not; wrongly	misspell, misjudge
over–	above; excessive	overtake, oversee
un–	not; reverse of	untrue, unknown

Suffixes from Anglo-Saxon	Meanings	Examples
–en	made of; like	golden, molten
–dom	state; rank; condition	wisdom, kingdom
–ful	full of; marked by	wonderful, useful
–hood	state; condition	neighborhood, childhood
–ish	suggesting; like	selfish, childish
–less	lacking; without	hopeless, helpless
–like	like; similar	dreamlike, childlike
–ly	like; characteristic of	friendly, cowardly
–ness	quality; state	kindness, tenderness
–some	apt to; showing	meddlesome, tiresome
–ward	in the direction of	forward, skyward
–y	showing; suggesting	wavy, hilly, salty

Grammar Link

Subject-Verb Agreement

Proper subject-verb agreement is essential to writing coherent, meaningful sentences but isn't always easy to recognize. Although you can often identify the correct verb form by listening to what "sounds" right, in some cases the answer isn't so clear. Consider this incorrectly written sentence:

Neither Beowulf nor his subjects *mourns* the death of Grendel.

The singular form *mourns* is incorrect because in a **compound subject** containing a singular and a plural subject joined by *or* or *nor,* the verb agrees with the subject closer to the verb. Consider another example of tricky subject-verb agreement:

Two-thirds of the audience already *know* the story of Beowulf as they watch the dramatic production.

The plural form *know* is incorrect because the verb form should match the noun to which the fraction refers (*audience*), not the fraction itself.

Your Turn

Write the correct verb forms for these incorrectly written sentences.

1. Herot's joy or his laughter anger Grendel.
2. Three-quarters of the Danish population fear Grendel's violent rampages.
3. Either Beowulf or his soldiers marches to the barrow to battle the dragon.
4. Neither the teachers nor the principal discover that one-third of the class root for Grendel.

Writing Application Review drafts in your *Reader/ Writer Notebook* to determine if you have errors in subject-verb agreemet. Change verb forms as necessary to correct your sentences.

CHOICES

As you respond to the Choices, use these **Academic Vocabulary** words as appropriate: <u>concept</u>, <u>diverse</u>, <u>emphasis</u>, <u>status</u>, <u>attribute</u>.

REVIEW
Compare Heroic Qualities
Group Discussion Although translated from Old English, *Beowulf* is considered one of the first great epics of the English language. How do Beowulf's heroic qualities compare to the qualities of heroes from other myths, such as Hercules? What do these heroic qualities <u>emphasize</u> about the values of each culture? In a group, discuss heroes from various cultures and compare them to Beowulf.

CONNECT
Make a Documentary
TechFocus In a group, plan and create a documentary about various epic heroes, including Beowulf and similar modern characters. Cast students to play the part of each epic hero; others can play interviewers, sidekicks, or even villains. Make sure your documentary examines why each epic hero is important to his or her society, as well as how the heroes are similar and different. If you have access to a video camera, film your documentary; if not, perform it live for your class.

EXTEND
Write a Sequel
Pretend that Beowulf did not die in his battle with the dragon. What might the great warrior-king do next? Write a story or outline of Beowulf's continuing adventures in a world of monsters and villains. Where would he travel? Whom and what would he fight? To what would you <u>attribute</u> his downfall?

Learn It Online
Practice Vocabulary skills with interactive tutorials at

| go.hrw.com | L12-53 | **Go** |

This Link to Today gives a classic new life with mood-drenched images.

from **The Collected Beowulf**

by **Gareth Hinds**

Reader/Writer Notebook
Use your **RWN** to complete the activities for this selection.

 **What Do You Think?** What moves a hero to act?

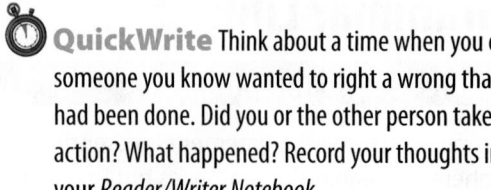 **QuickWrite** Think about a time when you or someone you know wanted to right a wrong that had been done. Did you or the other person take action? What happened? Record your thoughts in your *Reader/Writer Notebook*.

Literary Focus

Archetype: The Epic Hero The **archetype** of the **epic hero** has endured for thousands of years in serious literature and in popular culture. Today's comic books and graphic novels are particularly well suited to showing the exploits of these larger-than-life heroes who overcome great obstacles, including formidable foes and threatening monsters.

Reading Focus

Responding to Graphics Graphic novels employ a variety of visual tools to tell a story. In *The Collected Beowulf,* Gareth Hinds uses contrasting colors, separate panels, close-up pictures that display characters' emotions, and images of groups of characters. Even the text, which appears in an old-fashioned script against multicolored backgrounds, adds a visual dimension to the story. As you read, use a chart like the one below to note how images help convey Beowulf's heroic qualities.

Heroic Quality	Image
bravery	close-up of Beowulf's face as he moves forward with sword

Writing Focus

Think as a Reader/Writer

Find It in Your Reading Illustrators of previously published stories such as the *Beowulf* epic make choices about which scenes to depict visually and how to present them. As you read, use your *Reader/Writer Notebook* to comment on the graphic details and the range of colors Hinds uses to illustrate the action and the characters.

To Eastern Danes
had the valiant Geat his vaunt made good,
all their sorrow and ills assuaged,
their bale of battle borne so long,
and all the dole they erst endured,
pain a-plenty. 'Twas proof of this,
when the hardy-in-fight a hand laid down,
arm and shoulder,--all, indeed,
of Grendel's gripe,--'neath the gabled roof.

Then Beowulf's glory
eager they echoed, and all averred
that from sea to sea, or south or north,
there was no other in earth's domain,
under vault of heaven, more valiant found,
of warriors none more worthy to rule.

[S]o he conquered the foe,
felled the fiend, who fled abject,
reft of joy, to the realms of death,
mankind's foe. But his mother now,
gloomy and grim, would go that quest
of sorrow, the death of her son to avenge.
To Heorot came she, where helmeted Danes
slept in the hall. Too soon came back
old ills of the earls, when in she burst,
the mother of Grendel.

Ask not of pleasure! Pain is renewed
to Danish folk. Dead is Aeschere,
of Yrmenlaf the elder brother,
my sage adviser and stay in council,
shoulder-comrade in stress of fight.

Sorrow not, sage! It beseems us better
friends to avenge than fruitlessly mourn them
Each of us all must his end abide,
in the ways of the world, so win who may
glory ere death! When his days are told,
that is the warrior's worthiest doom.

from **The Collected Beowulf**

Respond and Think Critically

Reading Focus

Quick Check

1. At what point in the narrative of *Beowulf* does this episode take place?

2. Toward what is Beowulf diving?

3. On the last page of the selection, why is the figure on the left covering his face with his hand?

Reading Skills: Responding to Graphics

4. While reading the selection, you used a chart to note images that demonstrate Beowulf's heroic qualities. Now that you have finished reading, review the notes in your chart. Then, add a third column listing the effects each scene creates.

Heroic Quality	Image	Effects
bravery	close-up of Beowulf's face as he moves forward with sword	shows his determination to kill his foe

Literary Focus

Literary Analysis

5. **Interpret** In the scene presented on page 57, the artist uses one color to show the events narrated by the words on the page and another color to depict an event that happens later in the epic. How does the use of color help you make sense of the visual elements on the page?

6. **Draw Conclusions** This excerpt depicts a scene that is summarized in the *Beowulf* epic poem that you read. How does the graphic excerpt contribute to your overall understanding of *Beowulf*?

Literary Skills: The Epic Hero

7. **Evaluate** In this excerpt, triumphant language appears against the mysterious, frightening imagery of Beowulf's dive. How does this contrast affect your understanding of the scene? What does it suggest about Beowulf as a hero?

8. **Interpret** In a small group, create a list of epic heroes from poems, books, movies, graphic novels, and comics. How do these heroes resemble Beowulf? How are they different? What drives them to act? What makes their actions heroic?

Literary Skills Review: Sequence of Action

9. **Analyze** The **sequence of action** refers to how chronological events are presented in a narrative. How are the different panels in this excerpt like and unlike sequential events in a narrative text?

Writing Focus

Think as a Reader/Writer

Use It in Your Writing Look back at the notes you took in your *Reader/Writer Notebook* about the details and colors Hinds uses to bring *Beowulf* to life visually. Choose a single page from the excerpt reprinted here, and write a paragraph explaining how details and color enhance both character and action in the narrative.

 What Do **You Think Now**

This graphic novel makes Grendel's mother inescapably frightening. Does that change your impression of Beowulf's courage?

The Seafarer/ The Wife's Lament/ The Wanderer Anglo-Saxon Riddles

What Do You Think What moves a hero to act?

QuickWrite

Quickly jot down some ideas for a poem of loss or for a riddle in your *Reader/Writer Notebook*.

INTRODUCTION

The Exeter Book, a manuscript of Anglo-Saxon poems dating from around the middle of the tenth century, is the largest of four important collections of Anglo-Saxon poetry that have survived to the present time.

Anglo-Saxon Poetry Preserved

Containing more than thirty poems and ninety riddles, *The Exeter Book* is something of a riddle itself. Although Bishop Leofric gave the manuscript to the cathedral at Exeter (a city in southwest England) in the eleventh century, no one knows where the manuscript originated. Some of the book's leaves have been damaged by fire and, as a result, the readability of the texts has been affected. There are signs that the book's cover had been used as a chopping board, and some pages are marked by beer stains. Today, however, its "songs"—written down by monks in about 975—are our chief source of Anglo-Saxon poetry.

Poems of Loss and Puzzles for Pleasure

The dominant mood in Anglo-Saxon poetry is **elegiac,** or mournful. As you have seen in *Beowulf,* this sense of sadness over the grimness and fleetingness of earthly life occurs in the heroic epic. This mournfulness also has a place in several Old English fragments in which the speaker laments the passing of better days and greater glories. The three lyrics that follow, "The Seafarer," "The Wife's Lament," and "The Wanderer," are all elegies that have common themes including exile, a long journey, and the loss of something or someone.

Despite the grim tone of much Anglo-Saxon literature, the light tone of Anglo-Saxon riddles shows that people in those days liked to be entertained just as we do today. The compilation of riddles in *The Exeter Book* is the earliest known in England and provides clever, imaginative puzzles for its readers to solve. Their authorship and composition dates are unknown. Although some can be traced to Latin originals, the Old English riddles often differ significantly from Latin prototypes; the Old English riddles are "literary games" rather than "merely exercises in metaphor."

Think About the Poems What do the different types of literature found in *The Exeter Book* tell you about the Anglo-Saxon people?

The viking ship of King Harold II (detail) sailing against the ship of his half-brother King Olaf II of Norway (c. 1375) Fresco.

The Seafarer / The Wife's Lament / The Wanderer

Reader/Writer Notebook

Use your **RWN** to complete the activities for these selections.

Literary Focus

Elegy An **elegy** is a type of poem that mourns a person's death or laments something lost. The speakers in "The Seafarer" and "The Wanderer" yearn for a peace they used to know, while the speaker in "The Wife's Lament" mourns her separation from her exiled husband.

Reading Focus

Identifying Theme The **theme** is the central idea or insight about human experience expressed in a work of literature. Although the elegies from *The Exeter Book* were composed more than a thousand years ago, they have themes that are still relevant to our lives today. To identify these themes, pay close attention to the poems' descriptive details. Key details provide clues to the poets' ideas about life and the messages they wish to convey.

Into Action As you read each poem, use a chart like the one below to keep track of significant words and details. Add as many circles as you need. After you read, you will fill in the middle circle with the poem's theme.

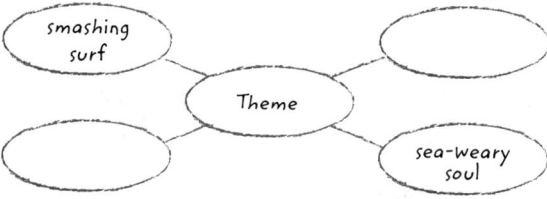

Writing Focus

Think as a Reader/Writer

Find It in Your Reading Writers of elegies use words and images that help create a sad, mournful mood. As you read, record in your *Reader/Writer Notebook* words and images that contribute to the sorrowful mood of these three elegies.

Vocabulary

wretched (REHCH ihd) *adj.*: miserable; unhappy. *Harsh conditions made the sailor's life wretched.*

desolation (dehs uh LAY shuhn) *n.*: grief; loneliness. *The sailor felt desolation after losing his friends.*

ravenous (RAV uh nuhs) *adj.*: very hungry. *The sailor says his spirit is ravenous and cannot be satisfied.*

demeanor (dih MEE nuhr) *n.*: the way in which a person behaves. *His pleasant demeanor hid his bad intentions.*

gloat (gloht) *v.*: feel or express great, often malicious, self-satisfaction or pleasure. *A wise warrior does not gloat about his victories.*

Language Coach

Related Words When you learn a new word, you may be able to learn related words that contain the same basic word part. The word *desolation* is a noun that means "loneliness." When you remove the *–ion* ending, you can find the verb and adjective *desolate*. What do you think *desolate* means? *Wretched* is an adjective that means "miserable." What do you think the noun *wretch* means?

Learn It Online
Find an interactive word web to use as you read at

go.hrw.com   L12-61   **Go**

The Seafarer

translated by **Burton Raffel**

Read with a Purpose
As you read the next three poems, discover how the authors reflect not only on loss but also on life.

Build Background
The speaker of this poem is an old sailor who has drifted through many winters on the ice-cold seas of life. Some interpreters of the poem have suggested that the poem is an allegory—a story with a literal meaning and a symbolic meaning—about the journey of life. Seafaring symbolizes the suffering necessary in the Christian way of life—the seafarer chooses the ascetic life, severe and without worldly pleasures, as a path to salvation.

This tale is true, and mine. It tells
How the sea took me, swept me back
And forth in sorrow and fear and pain,
Showed me suffering in a hundred ships,
5   In a thousand ports, and in me. It tells
Of smashing surf when I sweated in the cold
Of an anxious watch, perched in the bow
As it dashed under cliffs. My feet were cast
In icy bands, bound with frost,
10   With frozen chains, and hardship groaned
Around my heart. Hunger tore
At my sea-weary soul. No man sheltered
On the quiet fairness of earth can feel
How wretched I was, drifting through winter
15   On an ice-cold sea, whirled in sorrow,
Alone in a world blown clear of love,
Hung with icicles. The hailstorms flew.
The only sound was the roaring sea,
The freezing waves. The song of the swan
20   Might serve for pleasure, the cry of the sea-fowl,
The death-noise of birds instead of laughter,
The mewing of gulls instead of mead.
Storms beat on the rocky cliffs and were echoed
By icy-feathered terns° and the eagle's screams;
25   No kinsman could offer comfort there,

22. mead: a beverage made from fermented honey and water.

24. terns (turnz): seabirds related to gulls.

Vocabulary **wretched** (REHCH ihd) *adj.:* miserable; unhappy.

To a soul left drowning in desolation.   **A**

      And who could believe, knowing but

The passion of cities, swelled proud with wine

And no taste of misfortune, how often, how wearily,

30   I put myself back on the paths of the sea.

Night would blacken; it would snow from the north;

Frost bound the earth and hail would fall,

The coldest seeds. And how my heart

Would begin to beat, knowing once more

35   The salt waves tossing and the towering sea!

The time for journeys would come and my soul

Called me eagerly out, sent me over

The horizon, seeking foreigners' homes.   **B**

      But there isn't a man on earth so proud,

Stormy skies over Bamburgh Castle, Northumberland, England.

A **Literary Focus** **Elegy** An elegy mourns or laments the loss of something. What does the speaker seem to be lamenting in the first stanza?

B **Reading Focus** **Identifying Theme** How does the speaker describe himself in lines 30–38? What do these descriptions imply about the poem's theme?

Vocabulary **desolation** (dehs uh LAY shuhn) *n.:* grief; loneliness.

40　So born to greatness, so bold with his youth,
　　 Grown so brave, or so graced by God,
　　 That he feels no fear as the sails unfurl,
　　 Wondering what Fate has willed and will do.
　　 No harps ring in his heart, no rewards,
45　No passion for women, no worldly pleasures,
　　 Nothing, only the ocean's heave;
　　 But longing wraps itself around him.
　　 Orchards blossom, the towns bloom,
　　 Fields grow lovely as the world springs fresh,
50　And all these admonish that willing mind
　　 Leaping to journeys, always set
　　 In thoughts traveling on a quickening tide.
　　 So summer's sentinel, the cuckoo, sings
　　 In his murmuring voice, and our hearts mourn
55　As he urges. Who could understand,
　　 In ignorant ease, what we others suffer
　　 As the paths of exile stretch endlessly on?
　　　　　　　　And yet my heart wanders away,
　　 My soul roams with the sea, the whales'
60　Home,° wandering to the widest corners
　　 Of the world, returning ravenous with desire,
　　 Flying solitary, screaming, exciting me
　　 To the open ocean, breaking oaths　**C**
　　 On the curve of a wave. Thus the joys of God
65　Are fervent with life, where life itself
　　 Fades quickly into the earth. The wealth
　　 Of the world neither reaches to Heaven nor remains.
　　 No man has ever faced the dawn
　　 Certain which of Fate's three threats
70　Would fall: illness, or age, or an enemy's
　　 Sword, snatching the life from his soul.
　　 The praise the living pour on the dead
　　 Flowers from reputation: plant
　　 An earthly life of profit reaped
75　Even from hatred and rancor, of bravery
　　 Flung in the devil's face, and death
　　 Can only bring you earthly praise
　　 And a song to celebrate a place
　　 With the angels, life eternally blessed
80　In the hosts of Heaven. The days are gone
　　 When the kingdoms of earth flourished in glory;

Boat with three sailors landing on whale while it swallows fish; Ashmole 1511, folio 86 v. Bodleian Library, Oxford.

59-60. whales' home: a kenning for "the sea." In Anglo-Saxon poetry, a **kenning** is a metaphorical phrase or compound word used to name a person, place, thing, or event indirectly.

C **Literary Focus** Elegy　What is the speaker trying to find?

Vocabulary　**ravenous** (RAV uh nuhs) *adj.:* very hungry.

Now there are no rulers, no emperors,
No givers of gold, as once there were,
When wonderful things were worked among them
85 And they lived in lordly magnificence.
Those powers have vanished, those pleasures are dead.
The weakest survives and the world continues,
Kept spinning by toil. All glory is tarnished.
The world's honor ages and shrinks.
90 Bent like the men who mold it. Their faces
Blanch° as time advances, their beards
Wither and they mourn the memory of friends.
The sons of princes, sown in the dust. **D**
The soul stripped of its flesh knows nothing
95 Of sweetness or sour, feels no pain,
Bends neither its hand nor its brain. A brother
Opens his palms and pours down gold
On his kinsman's grave, strewing his coffin
With treasures intended for Heaven, but nothing
100 Golden shakes the wrath of God
For a soul overflowing with sin, and nothing
Hidden on earth rises to Heaven.
          We all fear God. He turns the earth,
He set it swinging firmly in space,
105 Gave life to the world and light to the sky.
Death leaps at the fools who forget their God.
He who lives humbly has angels from Heaven
To carry him courage and strength and belief.
A man must conquer pride, not kill it,
110 Be firm with his fellows, chaste for himself,
Treat all the world as the world deserves,
With love or with hate but never with harm,
Though an enemy seek to scorch him in hell,
Or set the flames of a funeral pyre°
115 Under his lord. Fate is stronger
And God mightier than any man's mind.
Our thoughts should turn to where our home is,
Consider the ways of coming there,
Then strive for sure permission for us
120 To rise to that eternal joy,
That life born in the love of God
And the hope of Heaven. Praise the Holy
Grace of Him who honored us,
Eternal, unchanging creator of earth. Amen.

91. blanch: turn pale.

Viking Oseberg stem/stern.

114. funeral pyre (FYOO nuhr uhl pyr): pile (usually of wood) on which a dead body is burned. *See* the burial of Beowulf, page 49.

D Reading Focus **Identifying Theme** What details does the poet use to describe the past and the present?

The Wife's Lament

translated by **Richard Hamer**

Read with a Purpose
Read to discover examples of the speaker's feelings of isolation and exile.

Build Background
The ties of kinship were such an important part of life during the Anglo-Saxon period that the threat of becoming isolated from one's community was almost unbearable. The speaker of this elegy mourns the loss of her husband and what he represents—security, comfort, and safety—although it is not clear why she has lost his favor or why she is a "friendless exile." The speaker may have been married to her husband in order to end a dispute between clans, and if the dispute were rekindled, she would have been separated from her husband and banished. Another interpretation is that the husband, too, has turned against her. Whatever the cause of her isolation, her grief represents the universal <u>concept</u> of loss and loneliness.

I sing this song about myself, full sad,
My own distress, and tell what hardships I
Have had to suffer since I first grew up,
Present and past, but never more than now;
5 I ever suffered grief through banishment.°
For since my lord departed from this people
Over the sea, each dawn have I had care
Wondering where my lord may be on land.
When I set off to join and serve my lord,
10 A friendless exile in my sorry plight,
My husband's kinsmen plotted secretly
How they might separate us from each other
That we might live in wretchedness apart
Most widely in the world: and my heart longed.
15 In the first place my lord had ordered me
To take up my abode° here, though I had
Among these people few dear loyal friends;
Therefore my heart is sad. Then had I found
A fitting man, but one ill-starred,° distressed,
20 Whose hiding heart was contemplating crime,
Though cheerful his demeanor. We had vowed
Full many a time that naught° should come between us

5. banishment: living in exile.

16. take up my abode: make this a home.

19. ill-starred: unfortunate.

22. naught: nothing.

Vocabulary   **demeanor** (dih MEEN uhr) *n.*: the way in which a person behaves.

But death alone, and nothing else at all.   **Ⓐ**
All that has changed, and it is now as though
25   Our marriage and our love had never been,
And far or near forever I must suffer
The feud of my beloved husband dear.
So in this forest grove they made me dwell,
Under the oak-tree, in this earthy barrow.°
30   Old is this earth-cave, all I do is yearn.
The dales are dark with high hills up above,
Sharp hedge surrounds it, overgrown with briars,
And joyless is the place. Full often here
The absence of my lord comes sharply to me.
35   Dear lovers in this world lie in their beds,
While I alone at crack of dawn must walk
Under the oak-tree round this earthy cave,
Where I must stay the length of summer days,
Where I may weep my banishment and all
40   My many hardships, for I never can
Contrive to set at rest my careworn heart,
Nor all the longing that this life has brought me.
A young man always must be serious,
And tough his character; likewise he should
45   Seem cheerful, even though his heart is sad
With multitude of cares. All earthly joy
Must come from his own self. Since my dear lord
Is outcast, far off in a distant land,
Frozen by storms beneath a stormy cliff
50   And dwelling in some desolate abode
Beside the sea, my weary-hearted lord
Must suffer pitiless anxiety.
And all too often he will call to mind
A happier dwelling. Grief must always be
55   For him who yearning longs for his beloved.   **Ⓑ**

29. barrow: mound of earth.

Ⓐ **Literary Focus** **Elegy** What specific words in lines 1–23 help you identify this poem as an elegy?

Ⓑ **Reading Focus** **Identifying Theme** What do the last two lines reveal about the poem's theme?

Detail of Anglo-Saxon sarcophagus lid found in crypt of St. Mary's Church in Wirksworth, Derbyshire, England.

The Wanderer

translated by **Burton Raffel**

Read with a Purpose
Read to discover how the author uses his story of wandering in the sea as a metaphor for wandering through life.

Build Background
Early Anglo-Saxon poetry often used Christian symbolism to explain the harsh conditions of life in the earthly world. In this poem, the speaker is literally on a journey across the frigid ocean. He is symbolically on the journey through a life filled with isolation, pain, and suffering. As with all journeys, however, the speaker of "The Wanderer" looks forward to coming home—in this case, to a safe harbor and a restful afterlife.

This lonely traveler longs for grace,
For the mercy of God; grief hangs on
His heart and follows the frost-cold foam
He cuts in the sea, sailing endlessly,
5 Aimlessly, in exile. Fate has opened
A single port: memory. He sees
His kinsmen slaughtered again, and cries:
      "I've drunk too many lonely dawns,
Gray with mourning. Once there were men
10 To whom my heart could hurry, hot
With open longing. They're long since dead.
My heart has closed on itself, quietly
Learning that silence is noble and sorrow
Nothing that speech can cure. Sadness
15 Has never driven sadness off;
Fate blows hardest on a bleeding heart. **A**
So those who thirst for glory smother
Secret weakness and longing, neither
Weep nor sigh nor listen to the sickness
20 In their souls. So I, lost and homeless,
Forced to flee the darkness that fell
On the earth and my lord. **B**
            Leaving everything,
Weary with winter I wandered out
25 On the frozen waves, hoping to find

A **Reading Focus** **Identifying Theme** How does the speaker describe himself?

B **Literary Focus** **Elegy** What is the speaker lamenting?

A place, a people, a lord to replace
My lost ones. No one knew me, now,
No one offered comfort, allowed
Me feasting or joy. How cruel a journey
30 I've traveled, sharing my bread with sorrow
Alone, an exile in every land,
Could only be told by telling° my footsteps.
For who can hear: "friendless and poor,"
And know what I've known since the long cheerful nights
35 When, young and yearning, with my lord I yet feasted
Most welcome of all. That warmth is dead.
He only knows who needs his lord
As I do, eager for long-missing aid;
He only knows who never sleeps
40 Without the deepest dreams of longing.
Sometimes it seems I see my lord,
Kiss and embrace him, bend my hands
And head to his knee, kneeling as though
He still sat enthroned, ruling his thanes.°
45 And I open my eyes, embracing the air,
And see the brown sea-billows heave,
See the sea birds bathe, spreading
Their white-feathered wings, watch the frost
And the hail and the snow. And heavy in heart
50 I long for my lord, alone and unloved.
Sometimes it seems I see my kin
And greet them gladly, give them welcome,
The best of friends. They fade away,
Swimming soundlessly out of sight,
55 Leaving nothing.   **C**
                    How loathsome become
The frozen waves to a weary heart.
      In this brief world I cannot wonder
That my mind is set on melancholy,
60 Because I never forget the fate
Of men, robbed of their riches, suddenly
Looted by death—the doom of earth,
Sent to us all by every rising
Sun. Wisdom is slow, and comes
65 But late. He who has it is patient;
He cannot be hasty to hate or speak,
He must be bold and yet not blind,
Nor ever too craven,° complacent, or covetous,

32. telling: here, "counting."

44. thanes (thaynz): people who, in exchange for their military service, held land of a king or lord.

68. craven (KRAY vuhn): cowardly or weak.

C Literary Focus **Elegy** What images help create a sad, elegiac mood in these lines?

Analyzing Visuals

Viewing and Interpreting   What images can you find in "The Wanderer" that correspond to details in this photograph? How do these images and details contribute to the mood of the works?

Nor ready to gloat before he wins glory.
70   The man's a fool who flings his boasts
Hotly to the heavens, heeding his spleen°
And not the better boldness of knowledge.
What knowing man knows not the ghostly,
Wastelike end of worldly wealth:
75   See, already the wreckage is there,
The windswept walls stand far and wide,
The storm-beaten blocks besmeared with frost,
The mead-halls° crumbled, the monarchs thrown down
And stripped of their pleasures. The proudest of warriors
80   Now lie by the wall: some of them war

71. spleen: archaic use meaning "whim."

78. mead-halls: Mead is an alcoholic drink made from honey and water; a mead-hall was a gathering place, usually in the home of a king or a lord.

Vocabulary   **gloat** (gloht) *v.:* feel or express great, often malicious, self-satisfaction or pleasure.

Destroyed; some the monstrous sea bird
Bore over the ocean; to some the old wolf
Dealt out death; and for some dejected
Followers fashioned an earth-cave coffin.

85 Thus the Maker of men lays waste
This earth, crushing our callow mirth,°
And the work of old giants stands withered and still.

       He who these ruins rightly sees,
And deeply considers this dark twisted life,
90 Who sagely remembers the endless slaughters
Of a bloody past, is bound to proclaim,
       "Where is the war steed? Where
                is the warrior? Where is his warlord?
Where now the feasting-places?
              Where now the mead-hall pleasures?
Alas, bright cup! Alas, brave knight!
95 Alas, you glorious princes! All gone,
Lost in the night, as you never had lived,
And all that survives you a serpentine wall,
Wondrously high, worked in strange ways.
Mighty spears have slain these men,
100 Greedy weapons have framed their fate.
       These rocky slopes are beaten by storms,
This earth pinned down by driving snow,
By the horror of winter, smothering warmth
In the shadows of night. And the north angrily
105 Hurls its hailstorms at our helpless heads.
Everything earthly is evilly born,
Firmly clutched by a fickle Fate.
Fortune vanishes, friendship vanishes,
Man is fleeting, woman is fleeting,
110 And all this earth rolls into emptiness." **D**
       So says the sage in his heart,
                sitting alone with his thought.
It's good to guard your faith,
           nor let your grief come forth
Until it cannot call
         for help, nor help but heed
The path you've placed before it.
           It's good to find your grace
115 In God, the heavenly rock
       where rests our every hope.

86. callow mirth (KAL oh murth): immature laughter.

D **Reading Focus** **Identifying Theme** What do the descriptions of earthly pleasures and concerns reveal about the poem's theme?

SKILLS FOCUS Literary Skills Analyze an elegy; analyze tone. **Reading Skills** Identify theme. **Vocabulary Skills** Demonstrate knowledge of literal meanings of words and their usage. **Writing Skills** Write poems.

The Seafarer / The Wife's Lament / The Wanderer

Respond and Think Critically

Reading Focus

Read with a Purpose

1. In what ways do the three poems reflect upon life as well as loss?

Reading Skills: Identifying Theme

2. Look back at the charts you made to record key details from the poems. Write the theme of each poem in the middle circle. How are these themes relevant to people's concerns today?

smashing surf

Theme

sea-weary soul

✓ Vocabulary Check

Match each Vocabulary word with its definition.

3. demeanor   **a.** very hungry

4. desolation   **b.** miserable

5. gloat   **c.** the way in which a person behaves

6. ravenous   **d.** loneliness

7. wretched   **e.** feel malicious self-satisfaction

Literary Focus

Literary Analysis

8. Analyze "The Seafarer" in lines 64–66 connects seafaring with religion. What is the speaker's attitude toward life on earth?

9. Extend In line 88 of "The Seafarer," the speaker says, "All glory is tarnished." Does this idea apply to today's heroes and to present-day life? Explain.

10. Evaluate Describe the place where the speaker in "The Wife's Lament" is forced to live. What words and images <u>emphasize</u> its desolation?

11. Analyze What images of winter does the speaker in "The Wanderer" use? How do these images contribute to the poem's mood?

12. Compare and Contrast Compare and contrast the experiences of the three speakers.

Literary Skills: Elegy

13. Analyze How do the contrasting descriptions of past and present contribute to the elegiac quality of each of these three poems?

Literary Skills Review: Tone

14. Analyze The attitude a writer takes toward the reader, a subject, or a character is **tone.** Writers convey tone through word choice and details. Describe the tone of each poem. Support your analysis with examples from the texts.

Writing Focus

Think as a Reader/Writer

Use It in Your Writing Review your QuickWrite about what you would lament if you were writing an elegy. Using one of the poems as a model, create a speaker and write an elegy filled with mournful images that laments the loss of something important.

What Do
You
Think?
Now

Can an everyday person be a hero? Explain.

Preparing to Read

Reader/Writer Notebook
Use your **RWN** to complete the activities for this selection.

Literary Focus

Riddles A **riddle** is a puzzling question posed as a problem to be solved. The following Anglo-Saxon riddles **personify,** or give human qualities to, the common things being described, and the descriptions include other figurative language such as metaphors and similes. Often, the personified object assumes the first-person point of view and describes itself.

Reading Focus

Using Context Clues A piece of writing consists of related details. These details, or **clues,** combine to form the **context** of the selection. When taken out of context, some details may lead in the wrong direction or no longer make sense. By considering the details as a whole, you can decipher the author's meaning. When you solve riddles, it is especially important to consider how each clue relates to other clues.

Into Action As you read each riddle, list clues in a context-clue chart like the one below. When you finish reading, use your chart to solve the riddle.

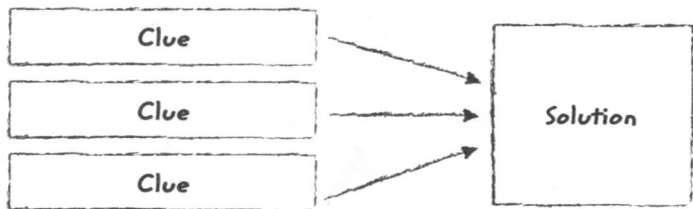

> Clue
> Clue
> Clue
> Solution

> **Language Coach**
> **Etymology** Knowing some word origins can help you figure out unfamiliar words. The Latin prefix *ex–* means "away from." In Riddle 1, the speaker says something "drives me into exile." You can use the meaning of the prefix *ex–* to help you understand the word *exile,* which means "being forced to live away from your own home." The word *abundance* in Riddle 32 comes from the Latin word for "overflowing." How does that meaning help you understand *abundance?*

Writing Focus

Think as a Reader/Writer
Find It In Your Reading A **riddle** is a series of clues that both confuse and inform the reader. As you read, pay attention to how some clues might lead you in the wrong direction. In your *Reader/Writer Notebook,* note words and phrases that lead you in the right direction and others that distract you.

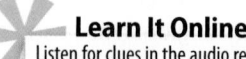

Learn It Online
Listen for clues in the audio readings of these riddles at

go.hrw.com   L12-74   **Go**

Anglo-Saxon Riddles

translated by **Burton Raffel**

Read with a Purpose

As you read the next three poems, try to discover the everyday objects or occurrences that are being described.

Build Background

The word *riddle* comes from an Old English word meaning "opinion" or "advice." Riddles exist in many ancient languages, including Sanskrit, Hebrew, Arabic, Persian, Greek, and Latin, as well as Old English. The Anglo-Saxon riddles that follow have been preserved in *The Exeter Book* and are believed to be the oldest riddles in the English language.

Riddle 1

How many men are so knowing, so wise,
That their tongues can tell Who drives me into exile,
Swells me brave and strong and fierce,
Sends me roaring across the earth,
5   Wild and cruel, burning men's homes,
Wrecking their palaces? Smoke leaps up,
Gray like a wolf, and all the world
Crackles with the sounds of pain and death.
When I shake forests, uproot peaceful
10   Groves, clouds cover me; exalted
Powers hurl me far and wide.
What once protected the world, sheltered
Men, I bear on my back, bodies
And souls whirled in the mist. Where
15   Am I swallowed down, and what is my name?   **A**

Rough Sea with Wreckage (c. 1840–1845) by Joseph Mallord William Turner (1775-1851). Oil on canvas, 92.1 x 122.6 cm. Clore Collection, Tate Gallery, London.

A Literary Focus Riddles What images are conveyed by lines 3 and 4 and by lines 9 and 10?

Riddle 14

I was a warrior's weapon, once.
Now striplings° have woven silver wires,
And gold, around me. Men have kissed me,
And I've called a field of laughing comrades
5 To war and death. I've crossed borders
On galloping steeds, and crossed the shining
Water, riding a ship. I've been filled
To the depth of my heart by girls with glittering
Bracelets, and I've lain along the bare
10 Cold planks, headless, plucked and worn. **B**
They've hung me high on a wall, bright
With jewels and beautiful, and left me to watch
Their warriors drinking. Mounted troops
Have carried me out and opened my breast
15 To the swelling wind of some soldier's lips.
My voice has invited princes to feasts
Of wine, and has sung in the night to save
What savage thieves have stolen, driving them
Off into darkness. Ask my name.

2. **striplings:** young men.

B **Reading Focus** **Using Context Clues** What objects might be used both by soldiers in battle and by young girls?

(Opposite) The Devonshire hunting tapestries. Detail of boar and bear hunt with man with horn (1424-1450). Inv.: T204-1957.   Victoria & Albert Museum, London.

Analyzing Visuals

Viewing and Interpreting What image in this fifteenth-century tapestry fits the clues in the riddle?

Riddle 32

Our world is lovely in different ways,
Hung with beauty and works of hands.
I saw an ingenious thing, made
For motion, slide against the sand,
5   Shrieking as it went. It walked swiftly
On its only foot, this odd-shaped monster,
Traveled in an open country without
Seeing, without arms, or hands,
With many ribs, and its mouth in its middle.
10 Its work is useful, and welcome, for it loads
Its belly with food, and brings abundance
To men, to poor and to rich, paying
Its tribute year after year. Solve
This riddle, if you can, and unravel its name.

C **Reading Focus** **Using Context Clues** What objects can you think of that are "made for motion" and have an odd shape that resembles a single "foot"?

SKILLS FOCUS Literary Skills Analyze characteristics of riddles; analyze alliteration. **Reading Skills** Use context clues. **Writing Skills** Write poems.

Respond and Think Critically

Reading Focus

Quick Check

1. Name some activities in which the speaker in Riddle 1 has participated.

2. How does the speaker of Riddle 14 describe himself?

3. How does the speaker of Riddle 32 describe the world?

Read with a Purpose

4. Why might someone bother to write a riddle about an everyday object or occurrence?

Reading Skills: Using Context Clues

5. As you read, you used charts to list clues. Now, review the clues for each riddle. What do you conclude is the solution for each riddle?

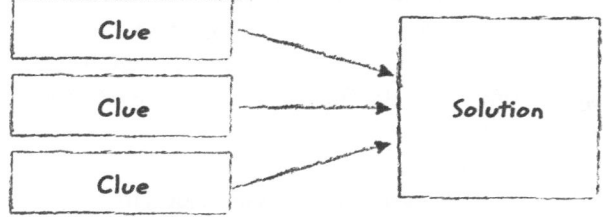

Literary Focus

Literary Analysis

6. Analyze How does personification add to the overall effect of the Anglo-Saxon riddles?

7. Analyze Find examples of vivid verbs and verb forms in the riddles. What effect do they have?

8. Hypothesize Why do you think myths of classical antiquity contain riddles for heroes to solve?

9. Extend J.R.R. Tolkien, who wrote *The Lord of the Rings,* included this riddle in *The Hobbit:*
> This thing all things devours:
> Birds, beasts, trees, flowers;
> Gnaws iron, bites steel;
> Grinds hard stones to meal;
> Slays king, ruins town,
> And beats high mountain down.

What is the solution?

Literary Skills: Riddle

10. Analyze In your *Reader/Writer Notebook*, you noted how the riddles confuse and mislead the reader. Select one of the Anglo-Saxon riddles, and explain how the author misleads the reader. Provide examples from the text.

Literary Skills Review: Alliteration

11. Analyze Authors use alliteration to create a musical quality and to unify and emphasize features in their writing. **Alliteration** is the repetition of similar consonant sounds that are near each other. "Sally sells seashells" is an example of alliteration because the *s* sound is repeated. What examples can you find of alliteration in the Anglo-Saxon riddles, and what are their effects?

Writing Focus

Think as a Reader/Writer

Use It in Your Writing Using the riddles as a model, write your own riddle with clues leading to the solution as well as distractions leading away from it.

What Do You Think Now

People have been enjoying riddles for thousands of years. What do you think explains their continuing popularity?

from
A History of the English Church and People

You?
Think

What moves a hero to act?

QuickWrite

How can an ordinary person have a positive impact on the lives of others? In your *Reader/Writer Notebook*, write a paragraph explaining your thoughts.

The Fuller Brooch, Anglo-Saxon (late 9th century). British Museum, London.

MEET THE WRITER

Bede
(c. 673–735)

Bede was the earliest English historian and the first important prose writer.

The Simple Life

Bede, a monk, was known in his own day as a person of great scholarship and learning. His <u>diverse</u> writings include grammatical handbooks, biographies, commentaries on books of the Bible, homilies, and verse.

The title "Venerable" was added to his name in recognition of his <u>status</u> and reputation for wisdom, humility, and scholarship. He seems to have traveled little and spent most of his life, beginning at the age of seven, at the monastery of Jarrow.

Our knowledge of Bede's life comes mainly from his scriptural commentaries that were found in many monastic libraries throughout western Europe. He began using *B.C.* and *A.D.* to describe dates—a method of dating that has now been used for centuries.

Early Classics

Bede completed works in three main categories: scientific, spiritual, and historical. He worked on everything from chronologies to hymns. Bede's *A History of the English Church and People,* originally written in Latin, was translated into Old English during the reign of King Alfred the Great. It quickly became a classic that helped the people of the emerging English nation take pride in their past. The *History* itself is more than a chronicle of events. It also contains legends, lives of saints, local traditions, and stories. From Bede's history we can see a fairly accurate picture of Anglo-Saxon daily life.

A selection from the *History*, "Caedmon of Whitby" tells of a miracle in the life of the first known English religious poet. Much like the scops, or professional poets of the time who celebrated the heroic deeds of their royal patrons, Caedmon celebrates the glorious works of God.

Think About the Writer

If Bede were alive today, what kinds of people might he write about? Explain.

Reader/Writer Notebook

Use your **RWN** to complete the activities for this selection.

Literary Focus

Setting The **setting** is the time and place in which a work of fiction or nonfiction takes place. It can also reflect a culture's beliefs and expectations for behavior. Bede establishes the importance of religion in people's lives to emphasize how Caedmon's verses inspired awe.

Reading Focus

Understanding Historical Context To better understand some nonfiction, you should consider the **historical context** in which it was written. Historical context refers to the issues, living conditions, and values of a period in history. In a different historical context, Caedmon's ability might have been viewed as either suspect or unimportant.

Into Action While reading the selection, find evidence in the text that describes life in late seventh-century Anglo-Saxon society. As you read, take notes in a chart like the one below to record details that relate to Bede's historical context.

Issues	Living Conditions	Values	Other Facts
		religious devotion	

Writing Focus

Think as a Reader/Writer

Find It in Your Reading Authors of nonfiction use facts, statistics, examples, and anecdotes to support the points they are making. In this excerpt, Bede uses an **anecdote,** or little story, to support the point he makes in the first paragraph—that Caedmon receives his gift from God. As you read, pay attention to how the anecdote contains the elements of a story in a very compressed form.

Vocabulary

singularly (SIHNG gyuh luhr lee) *adv.:* extraordinarily; unusually. *Bede's historical record is a singularly good one.*

frivolous (FRIHV uh luhs) *adj.:* silly or unimportant. *His serious nature prevented him from singing anything frivolous.*

profane (proh FAYN) *adj.:* irreverent; not associated with religion. *As a religious person, the young man would not write anything that was profane.*

secular (SEHK yuh luhr) *adj.:* not belonging to a religious order; worldly. *Before joining the monastery, Caedmon lived a secular life.*

doctrine (DAHK truhn) *n.:* teachings of the church. *Church doctrine is sometimes communicated with song.*

Language Coach

Antonyms A secular view focuses on issues in the world; a religious view focuses on spiritual issues. *Secular* and *religious* are antonyms—they have opposite meanings. What other Vocabulary word is also an antonym for *religious*? Does this word have exactly the same meaning as *secular*? Explain.

Learn It Online
Get to know the Vocabulary words inside and out at

go.hrw.com L12-81   **Go**

from
A History of the English Church and People

by **Bede**

translated by **Leo Sherley-Price**

Read with a Purpose
Read to discover why Caedmon's ability to create beautiful verse inspires awe.

Build Background
Considered to be the first English religious poet, Caedmon of Whitby was an illiterate herdsman who communicated religious thought and beliefs in verse, or poetic form. Caedmon's Hymn praises God by using some of the same elements used in heroic verse forms.

Caedmon of Whitby

In this monastery of [Whitby] lived a brother singularly gifted by God's grace. So skillful was he in composing religious and devotional songs that, when any passage of Scripture[1] was explained to him by interpreters, he could quickly turn it into delightful and moving poetry in his own English tongue. These verses of his have stirred the hearts of many folk to despise the world and aspire to heavenly things. Others after him tried to compose religious poems in English, but none could compare with him; for he did not acquire the art of poetry from men or through any human teacher but received it as a free gift from God. For this reason he could never compose any frivolous or profane verses; but only such as had a religious theme fell fittingly from his devout lips. He had followed a secular occupation until well advanced in years without ever learning anything about poetry. Indeed it sometimes happened at a feast that all the guests in turn would be invited to sing and entertain the company; then, when he saw the harp coming his way, he would get up from table and go home. **Ⓐ**

On one such occasion he had left the house in which the entertainment was being held and went

---

1. **passage of Scripture:** a passage from the Bible.

Ⓐ Reading Focus Understanding Historical Context What can we learn about everyday Anglo-Saxon life from reading these lines?

Vocabulary **singularly** (SIHNG gyuh luhr lee) *adv.:* extraordinarily; unusually.
frivolous (FRIHV uh luhs) *adj.:* silly or unimportant.
profane (proh FAYN) *adj.:* irreverent; not associated with religious matters.
secular (SEHK yuh luhr) *adj.:* not belonging to a religious order; worldly.

Analyzing Visuals

Viewing and Interpreting   The brightly colored, embellished images in medieval manuscripts were called illuminations (from the Latin word *illuminare,* meaning "to light up") because of the glow created by the gold and silver. How does this example, by Bede, help you understand the setting and historical context of Bede's *History*?

out to the stable, where it was his duty that night to look after the beasts. There when the time came he settled down to sleep. Suddenly in a dream he saw a man standing beside him who called him by name. "Caedmon," he said, "sing me a song." "I don't know how to sing," he replied. "It is because I cannot sing that I left the feast and came here." The man who addressed him then said: "But you shall sing to me." "What should I sing about?" he replied. "Sing about the Creation of all things," the other answered. And Caedmon immediately began to sing verses in praise of God the Creator that he had never heard before,

and their theme ran thus:

Praise we the Fashioner now of Heaven's fabric,
The majesty of his might and his mind's wisdom,
Work of the world-warden, worker of all wonders,
How he the Lord of Glory everlasting,
Wrought first for the race of men Heaven as a
   rooftree,
Then made he Middle Earth to be their mansion.

This is the general sense, but not the actual words that Caedmon sang in his dream; for verses, however masterly, cannot be translated literally from one

B

B **Literary Focus** Setting   What does this paragraph <u>emphasize</u> about life in this period?

language into another without losing much of their beauty and dignity. When Caedmon awoke, he remembered everything that he had sung in his dream, and soon added more verses in the same style to a song truly worthy of God.

Early in the morning he went to his superior, the reeve,[2] and told him about this gift that he had received. The reeve took him before the abbess,[3] who ordered him to give an account of his dream and repeat the verses in the presence of many learned men, so that a decision might be reached by common consent as to their quality and origin. All of them agreed that Caedmon's gift had been given him by our Lord. And they explained to him a passage of Scriptural history or doctrine and asked him to render it into verse if he could. He promised to do this, and returned next morning with excellent verses as they had ordered him. The abbess was delighted that God had given such grace to the man, and advised him to abandon secular life and adopt the monastic state.[4] And when she had admitted him into the Community as a brother, she ordered him to be instructed in the events of sacred history. So Caedmon stored up in his memory all that he learned, and like one of the clean animals chewing the cud, turned it into such melodious verse that his delightful renderings turned his instructors into auditors. He sang of the Creation of the world, the origin of the human race, and the whole story of Genesis. He sang of Israel's exodus from Egypt, the entry into the Promised Land, and many other events of Scriptural history. He sang of the Lord's Incarnation,[5] Passion,[6] Resurrection,[7] and Ascension into Heaven,[8] the coming of the Holy Spirit, and the teaching of the Apostles. He also made many poems on the terrors of the Last Judgment, the horrible pains of Hell, and the joys of the Kingdom of Heaven. In addition to these, he composed several others on the blessings and judgments of God, by which he sought to turn his hearers from delight in wickedness and to inspire them to love and do good. For Caedmon was a deeply religious man, who humbly submitted to regular discipline and hotly rebuked all who tried to follow another course. And so he crowned his life with a happy end. **C**

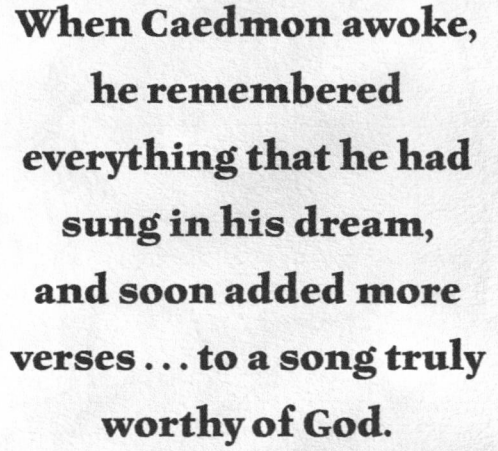

> When Caedmon awoke, he remembered everything that he had sung in his dream, and soon added more verses ... to a song truly worthy of God.

---

2. **reeve:** the manager of an estate; here, the steward in charge of the monastery.
3. **abbess** (AB ihs): the superior nun of a monastery for nuns and monks.
4. **monastic state:** Caedmon was originally a lay brother, a nonclergy member, attached to the monastery. Here, the abbess is inviting him to become a full-fledged member of the monastery by taking special vows and participating in the singing of the choir.

5. **Incarnation** (ihn kahr NAY shuhn): appearance in human form.
6. **Passion:** refers to the suffering of Jesus Christ.
7. **Resurrection** (rehz uh REHK shuhn): the condition of being restored to life after dying.
8. **Ascension into Heaven:** after his resurrection, Jesus Christ is said to have risen into heaven.

Vocabulary **doctrine** (DAHK truhn) *n.:* teachings of the church.

C **Literary Focus** Setting How does the setting contribute to the reader's understanding of the historical context?

from A History of the English Church and People

Respond and Think Critically

Reading Focus

Quick Check

1. What was Caedmon's gift?
2. Why did Caedmon leave the party?
3. What was the topic of Caedmon's first poem?
4. Why does the abbess urge Caedmon to become a monk?

Read with a Purpose

5. Why were people so moved by Caedmon's verse?

Reading Skills: Analyzing Historical Context

6. While reading, you noted how seventh-century Anglo-Saxon life was described. Review your chart, considering what it reveals about the historical context. Why did the people value Caedmon's ability and see it as a miracle?

Issues	Living Conditions	Values	Other Facts
		religious devotion	

Literary Focus

Literary Analysis

7. **Interpret** Since so few people were educated, a strong oral tradition developed over time. **Oral tradition** consists of stories and histories passed by word of mouth from one generation to the next. What clues in the selection tell you that Caedmon's story is an example of oral tradition?

8. **Evaluate** How do Caedmon's social standing and depth of knowledge change after he receives his gift from God? Cite passages from the selection to support your response.

9. **Analyze** Scholars believe that Bede's historical records are very reliable, but a certain amount of bias still exists. Evaluate the text, and identify examples of bias.

10. **Interpret** What religious purpose did Caedmon's poem's have? How were they useful for religious instruction?

Literary Skills: Setting

10. **Analyze** How does the setting emphasize the awe-inspiring quality of Caedmon's verse?

Literary Skills Review: Tone

11. **Analyze** The attitude a writer takes toward the reader, a subject, or a character or person described in the text is **tone.** What is Bede's tone in this selection about Caedmon?

Writing Focus

Think as a Reader/Writer

Use It in Your Writing Review the anecdote in paragraph 2 that supports Bede's point. Write a statement of your own about something you have observed, for example, that *speed causes traffic accidents,* and support it with an anecdote.

What Do
You Think
Now

How does Caedmon use his gifts to inspire others?

from **A History of the English Church and People**

Vocabulary Development

✓ Vocabulary Check

Match the Vocabulary words with their definitions.

1. singularly   **a.** worldly
2. frivolous   **b.** beliefs
3. profane   **c.** uniquely
4. secular   **d.** irreverent
5. doctrine   **e.** silly

Vocabulary Skills: Etymology

The English language wasn't always the language we hear and read today. It has evolved over many centuries and has been influenced by different periods in history. It has also borrowed words from other languages. We can trace many words back to their original form and use with **etymology,** or the study of word origins.

Bede uses words in his *History* that can teach us about his time. Many of these words reflect the influence of other languages on English. Other words reflect the growth of Christianity in England. Notice the origins of the words below from Bede's *History*. Though the spellings of the words have changed, note how the words were originally used.

English Word	Word Origin	Original Meaning
devout	Old French *devot,* from Latin *devotus*	(Old French) devoted, (Latin) to vow
compose	French *composer* from French *poser* and Latin *componere*	(French) to form (Latin) to put together, arrange
translate	Latin *translatus*	carried over, transferred
dignity	Old French *dignete,* from Latin *dignitas, dignus*	(Old French) high rank, (Latin) worth, worthy

Your Turn

Some of the Vocabulary words reflect the presence of Christianity during Bede's time. Using a dictionary, look up the origins of each Vocabulary word. Make a list to show the origin of each word. Why do you think religious words were so important to the people of the Anglo-Saxon period?

Language Coach

Antonyms Words with opposite meanings are called **antonyms**. For example, *good/bad, calm/nervous, young/old*. Read each word and the three answer choices. Write the letter of the antonym for each word.

1. profane
   a. wicked   **b.** ridiculous   **c.** religious
2. frivolous
   a. playful   **b.** angry   **c.** serious
3. singularly
   a. commonly   **b.** rarely   **c.** fondly
4. secular
   a. spiritual   **b.** strange   **c.** free

Academic Vocabulary

Write About . . .
The writings of Bede depict a <u>diverse</u> array of the Anglo-Saxon populace. In a short paragraph, explain how his writing <u>emphasizes</u> beliefs and values important to all the citizens. Be sure to cite specific examples from the text and use the underlined Academic Vocabulary words in your response.

Epics Across Cultures

Gilgamesh (1924) by Zabelle C. Boyajian. Gilgamesh in sesrch of immortality, goes to Mount Mashu, which is guarded by terrible scorpion gods who welcome him when they learn his identity.

Produced by two different cultures and composed nearly a thousand years apart, the epics *Gilgamesh* and the *Iliad* share universal themes of fear, bravery, determination, and compassion that fascinate readers today. As you read the following excerpts, consider how readers from any time and place might find meaning in these epics. After you read, you'll compare the themes that connect the epics.

CONTENTS

from **Gilgamesh: A Verse Narrative** (ancient Mesopotamia)

from the **Iliad, Book 22: The Death of Hector** by Homer (ancient Greece)

Preparing to Read

from Gilgamesh

What moves a hero to act?

 QuickWrite

This story is thousands of years old, but its two main characters are best friends who experience the same desire for excitement that people do today. In your *Reader/Writer Notebook,* write briefly about an adventure you have had with a friend.

INTRODUCTION

Gilgamesh reveals much about the ancient Mesopotamians' sometimes pessimistic view of life, but it also <u>emphasizes</u> the sensitivity and humanity of an ancient people—like us in their joys, sorrows, and strivings.

A Mesopotamian Epic

Like most epics, Gilgamesh is based on at least a grain of truth. Many scholars believe that Gilgamesh was an actual king who reigned over the city-state of Uruk, in Sumer, sometime between 2700 and 2500 B.C. Over the centuries, Gilgamesh became a legendary figure, rather like King Arthur in Europe. Tales of Gilgamesh's exploits grew and were probably recited in verse for centuries before they were recorded in writing. The earliest written fragments date from about 2000 B.C. Later the epic was reworked by writers from the Sumerian, Babylonian, and Assyrian cultures. Some scholars believe the epic was put into its most complete form in 1300 B.C.

The Original Epic Hero?

The Gilgamesh of the epic is a superhuman hero, two parts god and one part human. In many ways it is his human weaknesses rather than his superhuman powers that make him so interesting. He is the leader of his people and builder of a great city, yet he has excessive pride. Refusing to accept death—"the common lot of man"—Gilgamesh embarks on a quest for immortality. With superhuman strength, courage, and persistence, he confronts obstacles along the way, but ultimately he must contend with human limitations.

Gilgamesh may be the original epic hero. Versions of his epic have been found as far north as the Black Sea, as far south as Jerusalem, and from the Mediterranean coast eastward to the Persian Gulf. Many of the epic's images, events, and characters, including Gilgamesh himself, are **archetypes**—patterns that appear in literature across cultures and throughout the ages. The frequency of these patterns suggests their basis in fundamental, and even primordial, shared human experience.

Think About the Epic — What might be the reason that superhuman Gilgamesh has to contend with human limitations in the end?

A hero (Gilgamesh?) taming a young lion. Relief from the palace of Sargon II (8th century B.C.), Khorsabad, Iraq.

Reader/Writer
Notebook

Use your **RWN** to complete the activities for this selection.

Literary Focus

Foil Many heroes, such as Beowulf, "go it alone," proudly seeking glory entirely through their own efforts. Sometimes, however, a hero has a companion who serves as his **foil**—a character who sets off the other character through strong contrast. A famous example is Tom Sawyer and Huckleberry Finn, the best friends who share some wild adventures but are driven by very different motivations. In *Gilgamesh* the foil is Enkidu, who, in contrast to Gilgamesh, represents the natural man, a pure-hearted and uncomplicated person unfamiliar with the ways of civilized society.

TechFocus As you read this story, think about how the two major characters act as foils for one another. Have you ever encountered a similar relationship on an online discussion board or blog?

Reading Focus

Comparing and Contrasting Being able to **compare and contrast** situations and characters is a skill that will add depth to your reading, understanding, and enjoyment. You can see the traits of one character more sharply when they are compared or contrasted to those of another.

Into Action As you read, use a diagram like the one below to keep track of the differences and similarities between Gilgamesh and Enkidu.

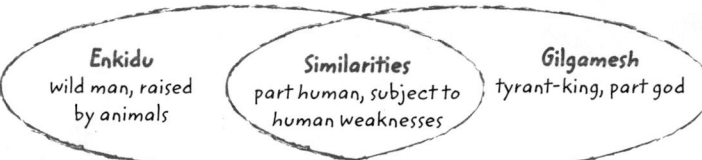

Enkidu
wild man, raised
by animals

Similarities
part human, subject to
human weaknesses

Gilgamesh
tyrant-king, part god

Writing Focus

Think as a Reader/Writer

Find It in Your Reading Even though the great early epics are full of action, they also show keen psychological insight. Gilgamesh and Enkidu are guided by internal needs and plagued by fears and doubts. In your *Reader/Writer Notebook,* take notes on thoughts and statements that reveal the characters' emotional and psychological states.

Vocabulary

austere (aw STIHR) *adj.:* spare; very plain. *Fearing for Gilgamesh's safety, the elders gave Gilgamesh an austere blessing to fight Humbaba.*

decreed (dih KREED) *v.:* ordered; commanded. *When King Gilgamesh decreed that they would go into the forest, no one could contradict him.*

contortion (kuhn TAWR shuhn) *n.:* twisted shape or motion. *Humbaba's face was a hideous contortion of what a normal face looks like.*

squall (skwawl) *n.:* brief, violent storm. *The speaker compares the monster's actions to a squall.*

Language Coach

Shades of Meaning The meaning of an adjective can change when it is used to describe different nouns. An austere room is one that is very plain. It probably has very little furniture. However, an austere blessing is not plain in the same way. Here, *austere* means "plain in the sense of not having a lot of extra words." An austere blessing is direct and to the point. What might an austere dinner be like? What about an austere warning?

Learn It Online
Learn more about this epic at

go.hrw.com   L12-89   **Go**

from Gilgamesh

A Verse Narrative

retold by **Herbert Mason**

Read with a Purpose
Read to discover what Gilgamesh's and Enkidu's attitudes toward each other reveal about their characters.

Build Background
Craving an adventure that will bring them fame, close friends Gilgamesh and Enkidu plan a journey to the cedar forest. There they will confront the monstrous and evil guardian of the forest, the giant Humbaba. As this part of the story opens, Gilgamesh is speaking to Enkidu, trying to relieve his fears of meeting the monster.

Sumerian ruins at Uruk.

Why are you worried about death?
Only the gods are immortal anyway,
Sighed Gilgamesh.
What men do is nothing, so fear is never
5   Justified. What happened to your power
That once could challenge and equal mine?
I will go ahead of you, and if I die
I will at least have the reward
Of having people say: He died in war
10   Against Humbaba. You cannot discourage me
With fears and hesitations.
I will fight Humbaba,
I will cut down his cedars.
Tell the armorers to build us two-edged swords
15   And double shields and tell them
I am impatient and cannot wait long.   Ⓐ

Thus Gilgamesh and Enkidu went
Together to the marketplace
To notify the Elders of Uruk

Ⓐ **Literary Focus** **Foil** How does Gilgamesh's opening speech to Enkidu show that Enkidu is his foil?

20 Who were meeting in their senate.
They too were talking of Humbaba,
As they often did,
Edging always in their thoughts
Toward the forbidden.

25 The one you speak of, Gilgamesh addressed them,
I now must meet. I want to prove
Him not the awesome thing we think he is
And that the boundaries set up by gods
Are not unbreakable. I will defeat him
30 In his cedar forest. The youth of Uruk
Need this fight. They have grown soft
And restless.　**B**

       The old men leaned a little forward
Remembering old wars. A flush burned on
35 Their cheeks. It seemed a little dangerous
And yet they saw their king
Was seized with passion for this fight.
Their voices gave the confidence his friend
Had failed to give; some even said
40 Enkidu's wisdom was a sign of cowardice.
You see, my friend, laughed Gilgamesh,
The wise of Uruk have outnumbered you.

Amidst the speeches in the hall
That called upon the gods for their protection,
45 Gilgamesh saw in his friend that pain
He had seen before and asked him what it was
That troubled him.

Enkidu could not speak. He held his tears
Back. Barely audibly he said:
50 It is a road which you have never traveled.　**C**

The armorers brought to Gilgamesh his weapons
And put them in his hand. He took his quiver,
Bow and ax, and two-edged sword,
And they began to march.

Gilgamesh between two demigods supporting the sun (Enkidu). Detail from a stone monument (9th century B.C.), Tell Halaf, Syria.

B **Reading Focus** Comparing and Contrasting How does Gilgamesh compare to the youth of Uruk?

C **Reading Focus** Comparing and Contrasting What is the difference in Gilgamesh's and Enkidu's moods in this scene? Whose mood does the assembly seem to share?

55 The Elders gave their austere blessing
And the people shouted: Let Enkidu lead,
Don't trust your strength, he knows the forests,
The one who goes ahead will save his friend.
May Shamash° bring you victory. . . .

60 After three days they reached the edge
Of the forest where Humbaba's watchman stood.
Suddenly it was Gilgamesh who was afraid,
Enkidu who reminded him to be fearless.
The watchman sounded his warning to Humbaba.
65 The two friends moved slowly toward the forest gate.

When Enkidu touched the gate his hand felt numb,
He could not move his fingers or his wrist,
His face turned pale like someone's witnessing

a death,
He tried to ask his friend for help
70 Whom he had just encouraged to move on,
But he could only stutter and hold out
His paralyzed hand.
It will pass, said Gilgamesh.
Would you want to stay behind because of that?
75 We must go down into the forest together.
Forget your fear of death. I will go before you
And protect you. Enkidu followed close behind
So filled with fear he could not think or speak.
Soon they reached the high cedars.

80 They stood in awe at the foot
Of the green mountain. Pleasure
Seemed to grow from fear of Gilgamesh.
As when one comes upon a path in woods
Unvisited by men, one is drawn near
85 The lost and undiscovered in himself;
He was revitalized by danger.
They knew it was the path Humbaba made.
Some called the forest "Hell," and others "Paradise";
What difference does it make? said Gilgamesh.
90 But night was falling quickly
And they had no time to call it names,
Except perhaps "The Dark,"
Before they found a place at the edge of the forest
To serve as shelter for their sleep.

59. Shamash (SHAH mahsh): god associated with the sun and human laws.

Vocabulary **austere** (aw STIHR) *adj:* spare; very plain.

95 It was a restless night for both. One snatched
    At sleep and sprang awake from dreams. The other
    Could not rest because of pain that spread
    Throughout his side. Enkidu was alone
    With sights he saw brought on by pain
100 And fear, as one in deep despair
    May lie beside his love who sleeps
    And seems so unafraid, absorbing in himself the phantoms
    That she cannot see—phantoms diminished for one
    When two can see and stay awake to talk of them
105 And search out a solution to despair,
    Or lie together in each other's arms,
    Or weep and in exhaustion from their tears
    Perhaps find laughter for their fears.
    But alone and awake the size and nature
110 Of the creatures in his mind grow monstrous,
    Beyond resemblance to the creatures he had known
    Before the prostitute° had come into his life. **D**

    He cried aloud for them to stop appearing over him
    Emerging from behind the trees with phosphorescent° eyes
115 Brought on by rain. He could not hear his voice
    But knew he screamed and could not move his arms
    But thought they tried to move
    As if a heavy weight he could raise
    Or wriggle out from underneath
120 Had settled on his chest,
    Like a turtle trapped beneath a fallen branch,
    Each effort only added to paralysis.
    He could not make his friend, his one companion, hear.

    Gilgamesh awoke but could not hear
125 His friend in agony, he still was captive to his dreams
    Which he would tell aloud to exorcise:°
    I saw us standing in a mountain gorge,
    A rockslide fell on us, we seemed no more
    Than insects under it. And then
130 A solitary graceful man appeared
    And pulled me out from under the mountain.
    He gave me water and I felt released. **E**

Clay mask of Humbaba. From Sippar, southern Iraq, (c. 1800–1600 B.C.) British Museum, London.

112. the prostitute: The first human Enkidu ever met. Before meeting her, he believed he was an animal, not a human.

114. phosphorescent (fahs fuh REHS uhnt): giving off light.

126. exorcise: to drive out.

D **Literary Focus** **Foil** What effect does the detailed description of Enkidu's suffering have on the portrayal of Gilgamesh, who is sleeping off and on?

E **Reading Focus** **Comparing and Contrasting** How do Gilgamesh and Enkidu handle their anxieties differently?

Tomorrow you will be victorious,
Enkidu said, to whom the dream brought chills
135 (For only one of them, he knew, would be released)
Which Gilgamesh could not perceive in the darkness
For he went back to sleep without responding
To his friend's interpretation of his dream.

Did you call me? Gilgamesh sat up again.
140 Why did I wake again? I thought you touched me.
Why am I afraid? I felt my limbs grow numb
As if some god passed over us drawing out our life.
I had another dream:
This time the heavens were alive with fire, but soon
145 The clouds began to thicken, death rained down on us,
The lightning flashes stopped, and everything
Which rained down turned to ashes.
What does this mean, Enkidu?

That you will be victorious against Humbaba,
150 Enkidu said, or someone said through him
Because he could not hear his voice
Or move his limbs although he thought he spoke,
And soon he saw his friend asleep beside him.

At dawn Gilgamesh raised his ax
155 And struck at the great cedar.
When Humbaba heard the sound of falling trees,
He hurried down the path that they had seen
But only he had traveled. Gilgamesh felt weak
At the sound of Humbaba's footsteps and called to Shamash
160 Saying, I have followed you in the way decreed;
Why am I abandoned now? Suddenly the winds
Sprang up. They saw the great head of Humbaba
Like a water buffalo's bellowing down the path,
His huge and clumsy legs, his flailing arms
165 Thrashing at phantoms in his precious trees.
His single stroke could cut a cedar down
And leave no mark on him. His shoulders,
Like a porter's° under building stones,
Were permanently bent by what he bore;
170 He was the slave who did the work for gods
But whom the gods would never notice.

168. porter's: a porter is a person who carries things for other people.

Vocabulary **decreed** (dih KREED) *v.*: ordered; commanded.

Monstrous in his contortion, he aroused
The two almost to pity.
But pity was the thing that might have killed.
175 It made them pause just long enough to show
How pitiless he was to them. Gilgamesh in horror saw
Him strike the back of Enkidu and beat him to the ground
Until he thought his friend was crushed to death.
He stood still watching as the monster leaned to make
180 His final strike against his friend, unable
To move to help him, and then Enkidu slid
Along the ground like a ram making its final lunge
On wounded knees. Humbaba fell and seemed
To crack the ground itself in two, and Gilgamesh,
185 As if this fall had snapped him from his daze,
Returned to life
And stood over Humbaba with his ax
Raised high above his head watching the monster plead
In strangled sobs and desperate appeals
190 The way the sea contorts under a violent squall.
I'll serve you as I served the gods, Humbaba said;
I'll build you houses from their sacred trees.

Enkidu feared his friend was weakening
And called out: Gilgamesh! Don't trust him! **F**
195 As if there were some hunger in himself
That Gilgamesh was feeling
That turned him momentarily to yearn
For someone who would serve, he paused;
And then he raised his ax up higher
200 And swung it in a perfect arc
Into Humbaba's neck. He reached out
To touch the wounded shoulder of his friend,

And late that night he reached again
To see if he was yet asleep, but there was only
205 Quiet breathing. The stars against the midnight sky
Were sparkling like mica° in a riverbed.
In the slight breeze
The head of Humbaba was swinging from a tree.

206. mica (MY kuh): kind of thin, crystalline mineral.

F Literary Focus **Foil** How are Gilgamesh's and Enkidu's traditional roles reversed in this scene? What effect does this reversal have on their roles as hero and foil?

Vocabulary **contortion** (kuhn TAWR shuhn) *n.*: twisted shape or motion.
squall (skwawl) *n.*: brief, violent storm.

SKILLS FOCUS **Literary Skills** Analyze the use of a foil; analyze the archetype of the epic hero. **Reading Skills** Compare and contrast. **Vocabulary Skills** Demonstrate knowledge of literal meanings of words and their usage. **Writing Skills** Develop characters.

Respond and Think Critically

Reading Focus

Quick Check

1. How do the elders of Uruk respond to Gilgamesh?

2. Summarize the battle with Humbaba. Do events unfold as Gilgamesh anticipated? Explain.

Read with a Purpose

3. What do you learn about Gilgamesh's strengths and weaknesses by contrasting him with his foil, Enkidu?

Reading Skills: Comparing and Contrasting

4. As you read, you compared and contrasted Gilgamesh and Enkidu. Now, add to your diagram, noting how Gilgamesh and Enkidu's differences and similarities advance the plot of the epic.

Enkidu wild man, raised by animals | *Similarities* part human, subject to human weakness | *Gilgamesh* tyrant-king, part god

✓ Vocabulary Check

Match each Vocabulary word to its definition.

5. austere   **a.** twisted shape or motion

6. decreed   **b.** brief, violent storm

7. contortion   **c.** spare; very plain

8. squall   **d.** ordered; commanded

Literary Focus

Literary Analysis

9. Analyze How do Gilgamesh and Enkidu help each other on their adventure? Are there any ways in which they hurt each other?

10. Interpret Enkidu associates Humbaba with death. How does Gilgamesh characterize Humbaba? What is Humbaba's relationship with the gods?

11. Extend Is Gilgamesh a hero worthy of unqualified admiration? What lessons, if any, do you think he still needs to learn if he is to be a true epic hero?

Literary Skills: Foil

12. Evaluate Enkidu is a foil of Gilgamesh. How is Humbaba a foil for both Gilgamesh and Enkidu?

Literary Skills Review: Epic Hero

13. Compare and Contrast To fulfill his quest, an **epic hero** must typically overcome great obstacles. How is Gilgamesh like and unlike the epic hero Beowulf? What elements of Gilgamesh's battle with Humbaba are similar to Beowulf's battles with his monsters?

Writing Focus

Think as a Reader/Writer

Use It in Your Writing Imagine what Gilgamesh or Enkidu is thinking and feeling in the hours before he confronts Humbaba. Write an interior monologue that expresses what one hero is thinking. Use the first-person pronoun.

What Do **You Think Now**   What is the most powerful force moving Gilgamesh to act against Humbaba in the end?

from the Iliad, Book 22: The Death of Hector

What Do You Think

What moves a hero to act?

QuickWrite

In the *Iliad*, characters such as Achilles and Hector strive for *arête*, or personal honor and excellence. In their eyes it is honorable to fight bravely for one's king and comrades, and dishonorable to seek personal safety when others are threatened. What do honor and personal excellence mean to you? Take notes on your own and other contemporary ideals of honor and how they compare to *arête*.

MEET THE WRITER

Homer
(c. 900–700 B.C.)

Europe's first and most enduring epics, the *Iliad* and the *Odyssey*, were composed sometime between 900 and 700 B.C. by Homer, about whom little is known. He was probably a native of the Greek district of Ionia on the western coast of Asia Minor. Homer belonged to a class of bards who played a vital role in Greek society, serving as historians and entertainers.

Homer's Epic Conventions

Features of Homer's work were so widely imitated in later written epics that they became recognizable characteristics, or conventions, of the epic genre. Many of these conventions originated in the oral tradition that gave birth to the *Iliad*. Oral poets used formulas that allowed them to summarize past events or sketch characters quickly. Conventions include the invocation, or formal plea to the gods for aid; *in medias res,* the technique of beginning the story in the middle of the action and using flashbacks; epic similes, which are extended, elaborate comparisons; and the stock epithet, a descriptive adjective or phrase repeatedly used with—or in the place of—a noun or proper name.

The Legend of the Trojan War

The *Iliad* and the *Odyssey* tell stories about the heroes and events of the Trojan War, a war that, according to Greek myth, was triggered by a beauty contest. Three goddesses—Hera, Athena, and Aphrodite—competed for a golden apple that was inscribed "To the Fairest." The gods chose Paris, a mortal, to judge the contest. Each goddess offered Paris a bribe for his vote. Paris accepted Aphrodite's bribe—Helen, the world's most beautiful woman and the wife of King Menelaus of Sparta. Paris abducted Helen and sailed for Troy. Outraged, Greek chieftains united to attack Troy. The conflict continued for ten years before the Greeks sacked the city and recaptured Helen.

The *Iliad* opens as the Trojan War enters its tenth year. The poem revolves around Achilles, the bravest Greek warrior, and his enemy Hector, the warrior-prince of Troy. In Book 22, the conflict between the two antagonists reaches its tragic climax.

Think About the Writer Homer was both historian and entertainer. What kind of job might enable him to serve both of those functions in modern society?

Homer (9th–8th century B.C.). Marble bust.   Museo Capitolino, Rome.

Reader/Writer
Notebook

Use your **RWN** to complete the activities for this selection.

Literary Focus

Epic Simile One of the most important features of the *Iliad* is Homer's use of **epic similes** (also called **Homeric similes**). These complex comparisons extend over many lines and use the words *like* and *as* to compare heroic actions to everyday events. In this excerpt, Achilles, in pursuit of Hector, is compared to a hunting dog. By using the familiar image of a hunt, Homer makes it easy for his audience to imagine Achilles racing after Hector in a relentless frenzy.

Literary Perspectives Apply the literary perspective described on page 103 as you read this epic.

Reading Focus

Visualizing Imagery Writers use imagery to help their audiences visualize, or picture, the events in a story. Before you can **visualize imagery,** you have to understand the words and ideas that convey it. You will need to pay close attention to descriptive words and the pictures they create.

Into Action As you read, use a chart like the one below to keep track of powerful imagery from epic similes in the text. In column 1, be sure to note the line numbers for each example you find.

Line Numbers	Descriptive Words	Resulting Image
Lines 1–6	"swift Achilles . . . coursing Hector, nonstop as a hound" hunts "a fawn"	simile creates image of powerful dog relentlessly hunting vulnerable fawn

Writing Focus

Think as a Reader/Writer

Find It in Your Reading Homer's heroes are driven by a desire for personal honor. As you read the *Iliad,* look for clues about what things Achilles, Hector, and Homer consider honorable. In your *Reader/Writer Notebook,* jot down particular words that convey their attitudes.

Vocabulary

groveling (GRAHV uhl ihng) *v.* used as *adj.*: crawling; begging; humiliating oneself. *The groveling Apollo was unable to convince Zeus to save Hector.*

gallant (GAL uhnt) *adj.*: noble; brave. *Risking his life for the sake of his dead son, gallant Priam crossed the enemy lines in the dark.*

scourge (skurj) *n.*: cause of serious trouble. *Hector calls Achilles, who has been his people's deadliest enemy, the scourge of the Trojans.*

fawning (FAWN ihng) *v.*: used as *adj.*: cringing and pleading. *Desperate to retrieve Hector's body, the fawning father wept at Achilles' feet.*

Language Coach

Verbs Used as Adjectives A verb expresses an action; an adjective describes a noun or a pronoun. Verbs with an *–ing* ending can sometimes be used as adjectives. **Verb:** The soldier was *groveling* to save his life. **Adjective:** The *groveling* soldier crawled on his knees. What does the verb *fawn* mean? How can it be used as a verb? as an adjective?

Learn It Online
Learn more about this epic at
go.hrw.com   L12-99   **Go**

EPIC

the Iliad

from Book 22: The Death of Hector

by **Homer**

translated by **Robert Fagles**

The Characters in the *Iliad*

The Greeks

Achilles (uh KIHL eez): son of a mortal king, Peleus, and the sea goddess Thetis; king of the Myrmidons; mightiest of the Greek warriors.
Patroclus (puh TROH kluhs): Greek warrior and dearest friend of Achilles.

The Trojans

Hector (HEHK tuhr): son of King Priam and Queen Hecuba; commander of the Trojan forces.
Paris (PAR ihs): son of King Priam and Queen Hecuba; also known as Alexandros.
Priam (PRY uhm): king of Troy; father of Hector and Paris.

Gods and Goddesses

Apollo (uh PAHL oh): god of poetry, music, and prophecy; often referred to only as the son of Zeus and Leto, the daughter of Titans. Apollo sides with the Trojans.
Athena (uh THEE nuh): goddess of wisdom. Athena takes the Greeks' side in the conflict.
Zeus (zoos): father-god. Zeus remains more or less neutral throughout the conflict.

As this excerpt opens, the exhausted Trojans take refuge behind their city walls, but Hector remains outside the gates. As Achilles races toward Troy, Hector's parents urge their son to come inside the walls, to safety. But after an inner struggle, Hector decides to fight to the death. As Achilles nears, Hector panics and flees in fear. An epic chase around the walls of Troy begins. Looking down from Mount Olympus, Zeus considers granting Apollo his wish and saving Hector from death. Athena protests vehemently, however, and Zeus grants the battle to her. Athena races down from Olympus to help Achilles, her favorite. Hector's fate is sealed.

     And swift Achilles kept on coursing Hector, nonstop
as a hound in the mountains starts a fawn from its lair,
hunting him down the gorges, down the narrow glens
and the fawn goes to ground, hiding deep in brush
5 but the hound comes racing fast, nosing him out
until he lands his kill. So Hector could never throw
Achilles off his trail, the swift racer° Achilles—
time and again he'd make a dash for the Dardan Gates,°
trying to rush beneath the rock-built ramparts, hoping
10 men on the heights might save him, somehow, raining spears
but time and again Achilles would intercept him quickly,
heading him off, forcing him out across the plain
and always sprinting along the city side himself—
endless as in a dream . . . Ⓐ
15 when a man can't catch another fleeing on ahead
and he can never escape nor his rival overtake him—
so the one could never run the other down in his speed
nor the other spring away. And how could Hector have fled
the fates of death so long? How unless one last time,
20 one final time Apollo had swept in close beside him,
driving strength in his legs and knees to race the wind?
And brilliant Achilles shook his head at the armies,
never letting them hurl their sharp spears at Hector—
someone might snatch the glory, Achilles come in second.

25 But once they reached the springs for the fourth time,
then Father Zeus held out his sacred golden scales:

Ⓐ **Literary Focus** Epic Simile Which simile emphasizes Achilles' speed?

7. swift racer: a stock epithet for Achilles.

8. Dardan Gates: gates of Troy. Dardania, a city built near the foot of Mount Ida, became part of Troy.

Menelaus and Hector fighting over the body of the Trojan Europhorbos (c. 600 B.C.). The British Museum, London.

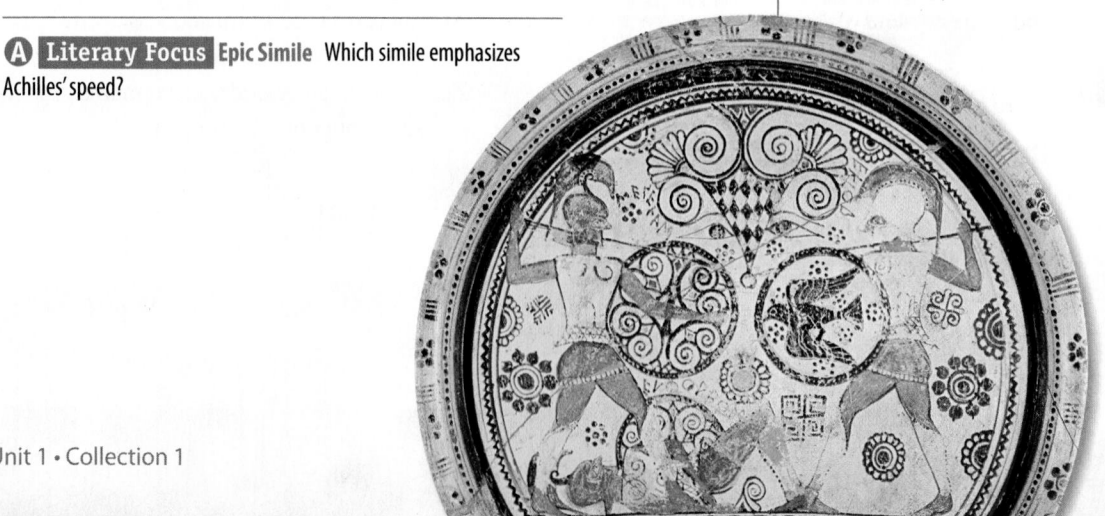

in them he placed two fates of death that lays men low—
one for Achilles, one for Hector breaker of horses°—
and gripping the beam mid-haft the Father raised it high

30 and down went Hector's day of doom, dragging him down
to the strong House of Death—and god Apollo left him. **B**
Athena rushed to Achilles, her bright eyes gleaming,
standing shoulder-to-shoulder, winging orders now:
"At last our hopes run high, my brilliant Achilles—

35 Father Zeus must love you—
we'll sweep great glory back to Achaea's fleet,
we'll kill this Hector, mad as he is for battle!
No way for him to escape us now, no longer—
not even if Phoebus the distant deadly Archer°

40 goes through torments, pleading for Hector's life,
groveling over and over before our storming Father Zeus.
But you, you hold your ground and catch your breath
while I run Hector down and persuade the man
to fight you face-to-face."

               So Athena commanded

45 and he obeyed, rejoicing at heart—Achilles stopped,
leaning against his ashen spearshaft barbed in bronze.
And Athena left him there, caught up with Hector at once,
and taking the build and vibrant voice of Deiphobus°
stood shoulder-to-shoulder with him, winging orders:

50 "Dear brother, how brutally swift Achilles hunts you—
coursing you round the city of Priam in all his
lethal   speed!
Come, let us stand our ground together—beat him
back."

    "Deiphobus!"—Hector, his helmet flashing,
          called out to her—
"dearest of all my brothers, all these warring years,

55 of all the sons that Priam and Hecuba produced!
Now I'm determined to praise you all the more,
you who dared—seeing me in these straits—
to venture out from the walls, all for *my* sake,
while the others stay inside and cling to safety."

B **Reading Focus** Visualizing Imagery What image
does Homer use to show that Zeus is deciding the fates of Hector and
Achilles?

Vocabulary **groveling** (GRAHV uhl ihng) *v.* used as *adj.*:
crawling; begging; humiliating oneself.

25–31. *How does Zeus decide the fates of Hector and Achilles? What is the final judgment?*
28. breaker of horses: a stock epithet for Hector.

34–52. *What does Athena tell Achilles she is going to do? How does Athena trick Hector?*

39. deadly Archer: a stock epithet.

48. Deiphobus (dee IHF uh buhs): one of Hector's brothers.

Literary Perspectives

Analyzing Historical Context A literary work's historical context is everything that was happening when the work was written, including the social, cultural, and political climate. Thinking about key elements of ancient Greek culture will help you interpret Homer's enduring epic. For example, the Greeks believed that each person had an assigned fate, called a *moira,* and that the boundaries of that fate should not be challenged. They felt that one should try to bear the limitations of the human condition with dignity and proper pride. A Greek hero should gain as much fame and glory as possible within the boundaries of his *moira.* Going beyond those boundaries invariably brings divine vengeance. The *Iliad* presents many examples of a character's hubris (arrogance resulting from excessive pride) leading to his downfall. Achilles succumbs to hubris when he sulkily refuses to return to battle. This hubris, combined with his friend Patroclus's own hubris over his triumph in a battle, leads to Patroclus's death. As you read, look for instances when the characters discuss or react to their fate. Think about how the idea of *moira* and hubris relate to Hector's death.

As you read, be sure to notice the questions in the text, which will guide you in using this perspective.

60   The goddess answered quickly, her eyes blazing,
"True, dear brother—how your father and mother both
implored me, time and again, clutching my knees,
and the comrades round me begging me to stay!
Such was the fear that broke them, man for man,
65 but the heart within me broke with grief for you.
Now headlong on and fight! No letup, no lance spared!
So now, now we'll *see* if Achilles kills us both
and hauls our bloody armor back to the beaked ships
or *he* goes down in pain beneath your spear."

70   Athena luring him on with all her immortal cunning—
and now, at last, as the two came closing for the kill
it was tall Hector, helmet flashing, who led off:
"No more running from you in fear, Achilles!
Not as before. Three times I fled around
75 the great city of Priam—I lacked courage then
to stand your onslaught. Now my spirit stirs me
to meet you face-to-face. Now kill or be killed!
Come, we'll swear to the gods, the highest witnesses—
the gods will oversee our binding pacts. I swear
80 I will never mutilate you—merciless as you are—
if Zeus allows me to last it out and tear your life away.
But once I've stripped your glorious armor, Achilles,
I will give your body back to your loyal comrades.
Swear you'll do the same." **C**

               A swift dark glance
85 and the headstrong runner answered, "Hector, stop!
You unforgivable, you . . . don't talk to me of pacts.
There are no binding oaths between men and lions—
wolves and lambs can enjoy no meeting of the minds—
they are all bent on hating each other to the death.
90 So with you and me. No love between us. No truce **D**
till one or the other falls and gluts with blood
Ares who hacks at men behind his rawhide shield.
Come, call up whatever courage you can muster.
Life or death—now prove yourself a spearman,
95 a daring man of war! No more escape for you—
Athena will kill you with my spear in just a moment.
Now you'll pay at a stroke for all my comrades' grief,
all you killed in the fury of your spear!"

C **Literary Perspective** **Historical Context** What does Hector's pact suggest about how Greeks valued the treatment of the human body after death?

D **Reading Focus** **Visualizing Imagery** What insulting image does Achilles present to Hector by comparing Hector and himself to lambs and wolves?

? **73–79.** *What does Hector vow? Why does he now have courage?*

? **78–98.** *What pact has Hector offered Achilles? Why does Achilles refuse the pact?*

Athena in armor. Silver tetradrachm of Ptolemy I (c. 324–323 B.C.).
Fitzwilliam Museum, Cambridge, England.

                              With that,
shaft poised, he hurled and his spear's long shadow flew
100   but seeing it coming glorious Hector ducked away,
crouching down, watching the bronze tip fly past
and stab the earth—but Athena snatched it up
and passed it back to Achilles
and Hector the gallant captain never saw her.
105   He sounded out a challenge to Peleus' princely son:
"You missed, look—the great godlike Achilles!
So you knew nothing at all from Zeus about my death—
and yet how sure you were! All bluff, cunning with words,
that's all you are—trying to make me fear you,
110   lose my nerve, forget my fighting strength.
Well, you'll never plant your lance in my back
as I flee *you* in fear—plunge it through my chest
as I come charging in, if a god gives you the chance!
But now it's for you to dodge *my* brazen spear—
115   I wish you'd bury it in your body to the hilt.
How much lighter the war would be for Trojans then
if you, their greatest scourge, were dead and gone!"

       Shaft poised, he hurled and his spear's long shadow flew
and it struck Achilles' shield—a dead-center hit—
120   but off and away it glanced and Hector seethed,
his hurtling spear, his whole arm's power poured
in a wasted shot. He stood there, cast down . . .
he had no spear in reserve. So Hector shouted out
to Deiphobus bearing his white shield—with a ringing shout
he called for a heavy lance—
                              but the man was nowhere near
125   him, vanished—
                              yes and Hector knew the truth in his heart
and the fighter cried aloud, "My time has come!
At last the gods have called me down to death.
I thought he was at my side, the hero Deiphobus—
130   he's safe inside the walls, Athena's tricked me blind.
And now death, grim death is looming up beside me,
no longer far away. No way to escape it now. This,
this was their pleasure after all, sealed long ago—
Zeus and the son of Zeus, the distant deadly Archer—
135   though often before now they rushed to my defense.
So now I meet my doom. Well let me die—

106–117. Hector is emboldened by Achilles' unsuccessful attack.

? *What do Hector's words suggest about the relationship between mortals and gods? Of what is Hector unaware?*

? **123–139.** *What truth does Hector now realize? What does he decide to do?*

Vocabulary   **gallant** (GAL uhnt) *adj:* noble; brave
scourge (skurj) *n.:* cause of serious trouble.

but not without struggle, not without glory, no,
in some great clash of arms that even men to come
will hear of down the years!"
                              And on that resolve
140 he drew the whetted sword that hung at his side,
tempered, massive, and gathering all his force
he swooped like a soaring eagle
launching down from the dark clouds to earth
to snatch some helpless lamb or trembling hare. **E**
145 So Hector swooped now, swinging his whetted sword
and Achilles charged too, bursting with rage, barbaric,
guarding his chest with the well-wrought blazoned shield,
head tossing his gleaming helmet, four horns strong
and the golden plumes shook that the god of fire
150 drove in bristling thick along its ridge.
Bright as that star amid the stars in the night sky,
star of the evening, brightest star that rides the heavens,
so fire flared from the sharp point of the spear Achilles
brandished high in his right hand, bent on Hector's death, **F**
155 scanning his splendid body—where to pierce it best?
The rest of his flesh seemed all encased in armor,
burnished, brazen—*Achilles'* armor that Hector stripped
from strong Patroclus when he killed him—true,
but one spot lay exposed,
160 where collarbones lift the neckbone off the shoulders,
the open throat, where the end of life comes quickest—*there*
as Hector charged in fury brilliant Achilles drove his spear
and the point went stabbing clean through the tender neck
but the heavy bronze weapon failed to slash the windpipe—
165 Hector could still gasp out some words, some last reply . . .
he crashed in the dust—
                              godlike Achilles gloried over him:
"Hector—surely you thought when you stripped Patroclus' armor
that you, you would be safe! Never a fear of me—
far from fighting as I was—you fool!
170 Left behind there, down by the beaked ships
his great avenger waited, a greater man by far—
that man was I, and I smashed your strength! And you—
the dogs and birds will maul you, shame your corpse
while Achaeans bury my dear friend in glory!"

156–165. Here we are reminded that Hector is wearing Achilles' old armor. Achilles had given the armor to his dear friend Patroclus, whom Hector had killed.

 How does Achilles mortally wound Hector?

E Literary Focus Epic To what is Hector compared as he runs toward Achilles?

F Reading Focus Visualizing Imagery What descriptive words does Homer use to create a vivid image of Achilles' charge?

Trojan King Priam begs Achilles to give him the body of Hector, his slain son. Hector's body lies beneath Achilles' bed. Red-figured Attic skyphos (drinking vessel) from Caere (c. 490 B.C.).
Kunsthistorisches Museum, Vienna

Analyzing Visuals

Viewing and Interpreting How does this image reflect Achilles' feelings and attitude toward Hector and the Trojans?

175   Struggling for breath, Hector, his helmet flashing,
       said, "I beg you, beg you by your life, your parents—
       don't let the dogs devour me by the Argive ships!
       Wait, take the princely ransom of bronze and gold,
       the gifts my father and noble mother will give you—
180   but give my body to friends to carry home again,
       so Trojan men and Trojan women can do me honor
       with fitting rites of fire once I am dead."

       Staring grimly, the proud runner Achilles answered,
       "Beg no more, you fawning dog—begging me by my parents!
185   Would to god my rage, my fury would drive me now
       to hack your flesh away and eat you raw—
       such agonies you have caused me! Ransom?
       No man alive could keep the dog-packs off you,
       not if they haul in ten, twenty times that ransom
190   and pile it here before me and promise fortunes more—
       no, not even if Dardan Priam should offer to weigh out
       your bulk in gold! Not even then will your noble mother
       lay you on your deathbed, mourn the son she bore . . .
       The dogs and birds will rend you—blood and bone!"

175–182. This exchange between Hector and Achilles emphasizes the importance the Greeks and Trojans placed on a proper burial. Without "fitting rites," both men believed, the soul of the departed would never find rest.

? *What does Hector plead?*

183–194. *How does Achilles react to Hector's plea?*

Vocabulary **fawning** (FAWN ihng) *v.* used as *adj:* cringing and pleading.

195   At the point of death, Hector, his helmet flashing,
       said, "I know you well—I see my fate before me.
       Never a chance that I could win you over . . .
       Iron inside your chest, that heart of yours.
       But now beware, or my curse will draw god's wrath
200   upon your head, that day when Paris and lord Apollo—
       for all your fighting heart—destroy you at the Scaean Gates!"°

       Death cut him short. The end closed in around him.
       Flying free of his limbs
       his soul went winging down to the House of Death,
205   wailing his fate, leaving his manhood far behind,
       his young and supple strength. But brilliant Achilles
       taunted Hector's body, dead as he was, "Die, die!
       For my own death, I'll meet it freely—whenever Zeus
       and the other deathless gods would like to bring it on!"

210   With that he wrenched his bronze spear from the corpse,
       laid it aside and ripped the bloody armor off the back.   **G**

200–201. Paris . . . Gates:
Hector is foretelling Achilles'
ultimate fate. Achilles will later
be slain by Paris, who will shoot
an arrow into Achilles' heel, the
only vulnerable part of his body.

G Reading Focus **Visualizing Imagery** What descriptive verbs paint the gruesome image of this scene?

Achilles and Hector. Scene from the *Iliad*. Crater by Berlin Painter (490 B.C.).

And the other sons of Achaea, running up around him,
crowded closer, all of them gazing wonder-struck
at the build and marvelous, lithe beauty of Hector.
215   And not a man came forward who did not stab his body,
glancing toward a comrade, laughing: "Ah, look here—
how much softer he is to handle now, this Hector,
than when he gutted our ships with roaring fire!"

      Standing over him, so they'd gloat and stab his body.
220   But once he had stripped the corpse the proud runner Achilles
took his stand in the midst of all the Argive troops
and urged them on with a flight of winging orders:
"Friends—lords of the Argives, O my captains!
Now that the gods have let me kill this man
225   who caused us agonies, loss on crushing loss—
more than the rest of all their men combined—
come, let us ring their walls in armor, test them,
see what recourse the Trojans still may have in mind.
Will they abandon the city heights with this man fallen?
230   Or brace for a last, dying stand though Hector's gone?
But wait—what am I saying? Why this deep debate?
Down by the ships a body lies unwept, unburied—
Patroclus . . . I will never forget him,
not as long as I'm still among the living
235   and my springing knees will lift and drive me on.
Though the dead forget their dead in the House of Death,
I will remember, even there, my dear companion.
                                              Now,
come, you sons of Achaea, raise a song of triumph!
Down to the ships we march and bear this corpse on high—
240   we have won ourselves great glory. We have brought
magnificent Hector down, that man the Trojans
glorified in their city like a god!"
                          So he triumphed
and now he was bent on outrage, on shaming noble Hector.
Piercing the tendons, ankle to heel behind both feet,
245   he knotted straps of rawhide through them both,
lashed them to his chariot, left the head to drag
and mounting the car, hoisting the famous arms° aboard,
he whipped his team to a run and breakneck on they flew,
holding nothing back. And a thick cloud of dust rose up
250   from the man they dragged, his dark hair swirling round
that head so handsome once, all tumbled low in the dust—
since Zeus had given him over to his enemies now
to be defiled in the land of his own fathers.

212–218. Achilles' comrades gather around the great warrior and the body of his victim.

  What do the Greek soldiers do to Hector's body?

Sarcophagus depicting Priam begging Achilles for the body of his son Hector. Marble.

242–253. Achilles' wrath is so great that he cannot stop at merely killing Hector.

  How is Hector's body transported from the scene of death? How do you feel as you read this description?

247. famous arms: Hector's armor.

SKILLS FOCUS Literary Skills Analyze the epic and the archetype of the epic hero; analyze the use of a foil; analyze the epic simile. **Reading Skills** Use visualization as a strategy for comprehension. **Vocabulary Skills** Demonstrate word knowledge. **Writing Skills** Write comparison-contrast essays.

from the Iliad, Book 22: The Death of Hector

Respond and Think Critically

Reading Focus

Quick Check

1. Who deceives Hector for Achilles' sake?

2. Why does Zeus decline to save Hector?

3. Why does Achilles deny Hector's dying request?

Read with a Purpose

4. Homer explores the relationship between *moira* (fate) and character. Is Hector doomed by his noble character, by fate, or by both?

Reading Skills: Visualizing Imagery

5. As you read, you noted specific, powerful images within epic similes as well as the words that described them. Now, record how the image helped you understand the epic simile.

Line Numbers	Descriptive Words	Resulting Image	How It Clarifies the Simile
Lines 1–6	"swift Achilles ... coursing Hector, nonstop as a hound" hunts "a fawn"	simile creates image of powerful dog relentlessly hunting vulnerable fawn	Shows Achilles' determination to terrify, exhaust, and capture Hector.

✓ Vocabulary Check

Use the chart for *gallant* as a model as you make charts for the other three Vocabulary words.

Word	Meaning	Example
gallant	noble; brave	Someone who suffers without complaining is gallant.

6. gallant   7. groveling   8. scourge   9. fawning

Literary Focus

Literary Analysis

10. **Evaluate** The Iliad is primarily a war epic. Does the Iliad condemn war's brutality, celebrate the heroism that war can inspire, or evenly examine both? Provide examples from the text.

11. **Extend** Hector requests that his body be left unmutilated and returned to his parents for burial. What events in wars today, or in movies or stories about war, show that we have the same concern for the bodies of our soldiers?

12. **Literary Perspective** No other warriors try to interfere in the battle between Hector and Achilles. What does this fact suggest about ancient Greek values and wartime culture?

Literary Skills: Epic Simile

13. **Analyze** How do Homer's epic similes make straightforward action—a chase, a confrontation, and a death match—seem more heroic?

Literary Skills Review: Foil

14. **Analyze** A **foil** is a character who, by contrast, emphasizes the qualities of another character. How are Achilles and Hector foils for each other?

Writing Focus

Think as a Reader/Writer

Use It in Your Writing Write an essay about two characters with contrasting views of honor. Show how each feels about what is and is not honorable.

What Do You Think Now? Do you think Achilles' behavior after Hector's death is heroic? Explain.

from Gilgamesh: A Verse Narrative
from the Iliad: The Death of Hector

Writing Focus

Analyzing Literary Criticism

The critic David Denby made this statement about the ethos, or attitudes and ethical beliefs, of the Greek and Trojan warriors of Homer's *Iliad:*

> Accepting death in battle as inevitable, the Greek and Trojan aristocrats of the *Iliad* experience the world not as pleasant or unpleasant, nor as good and evil, but as glorious or shameful.

Write an essay in which you analyze Denby's statement as it relates to either the *Iliad* or *Gilgamesh*. You will be either agreeing with Denby's perspective or disagreeing with it. To support your analysis, use specific evidence from the selection you choose to write about.

Plan Your Essay Answering the following questions may help you plan your essay.
- Why do epic heroes see their behavior in absolutes: good/evil; glorious/shameful?
- What is the role of fate in this belief?
- What is the role of a violent and uncertain world as the context for these beliefs?

Create a Thesis Statement Your thesis statement will articulate your perspective on the relationship between Denby's observation and your own analysis of either the *Iliad* or *Gilgamesh*. Sample thesis statements for this essay are:

Denby's observation that the aristocrats of the Iliad view the world as either glorious or shameful is equally true for the way Gilgamesh interacts with the world.

Denby's assertion that the Greek and Trojan aristocrats of the Iliad view the world as either glorious or shameful is not correct.

Support Your Analysis Supporting points are needed to develop an effective analysis. Use paraphrased and direct quotations from the text to support these points.

CHOICES

As you respond to the Choices, use these **Academic Vocabulary** words as appropriate: attribute, concept, diverse, emphasis, status.

REVIEW

Compare and Contrast Epics Across Cultures

In a small group, review the battle scenes from the three epics you have read. Discuss how the battle scenes in the *Iliad* compare with those in *Beowulf* and *Gilgamesh*. How does each epic hero respond to the sometimes fatal violence he faces in battle? Are the heroes equally heroic in their behaviors?

CONNECT

Connect a Common Theme

Timed ⏱ **Writing** Friendship is an important theme in both the *Iliad* and *Gilgamesh*. Achilles is fiercely loyal to Patroclus, and *Gilgamesh* stands by Enkidu to face the worst possible danger. In an essay, explain the motivations and outcomes of the friendships of these epic heroes. use specific references to the text to support your analysis.

EXTEND

Characterize a Foil

TechFocus Both *Gilgamesh* and the *Iliad* contain a set of characters that act as foils to one another: Gilgamesh and Enkidu; Achilles and Hector. With a partner, bring the foils from one of the epics alive by creating a written dialogue that might appear online on a blog or discussion board. You should each take on the persona of one of the characters from the epic you choose and then develop a discussion in which your comments help reveal the attributes of your foil. Think carefully how you can use written statements to emphasize your character's personality and the way in which it contrasts with your foil's.

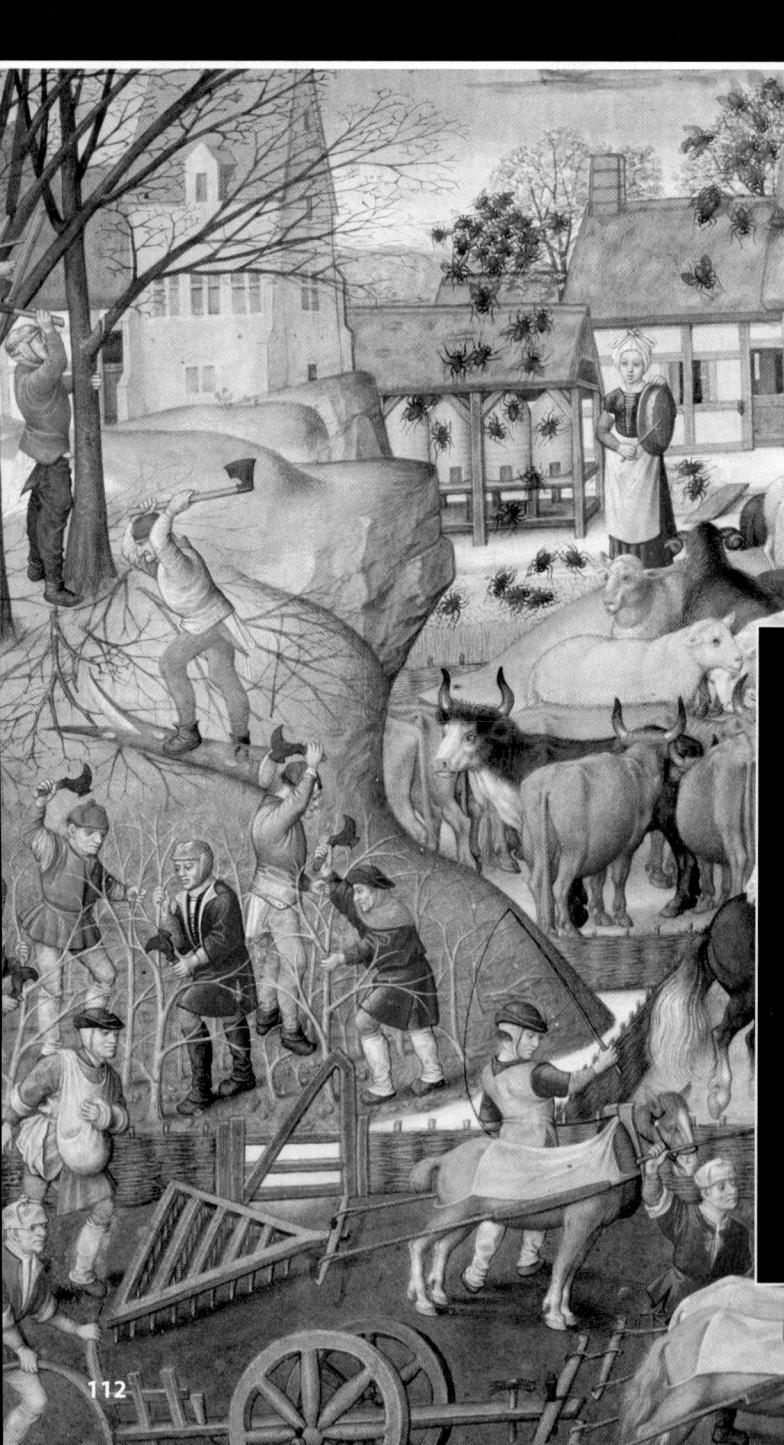

CONTENTS

Geoffrey Chaucer

Jerry Ellis Link to Today

**Lord Randall
Get Up and Bar the Door
Edward, Edward**

from **Sir Gawain and the Green Knight**

Sir Thomas Malory

from **Everyman**

"The medieval world we know was far from perfect. Life expectancy was short, and disease was mostly incontestable. . . . But it exhibited as elevated a culture . . . as the world has ever seen."

— **Norman F. Cantor**

Illustration to the Georgics by Virgil, from the English School.
Collection of the Earl of Leicester, Holkham Hall, Norfolk.

Medieval Narrative by Leila Christenbury

Influences on the Medieval Narrative

- Popular legends from the early Middle Ages that were embellished over time
- Religious literature that passed along the ideals and beliefs of an era
- Urban growth, cultural development, and widespread disease that altered social structures

The Dark Ages?

Forget what you've heard about the Middle Ages being "dark." Despite the challenges of war, plague, and oppression, the era was vibrant and its people creative and resilient. Today, we are indebted to the Middle Ages for many modern ideas and institutions, such as universities, governmental forms, and concepts of the world and of God. The medieval narratives that have survived reflect much of the time's positive outlook, and many of them contain the same passion, humor, and sense of wonder that we see today.

Adventure, Morality, Life

The term *medieval* often conjures images of knights riding off to battle or on magical quests. These heroic adventures were the foundation for the popular romance literature of the era. Much of the narrative tradition of the Middle Ages emerged from earlier legends, such as those of King Arthur. The same themes of love, betrayal, conquest, hope, and desire that consume us today can be found throughout those and other medieval stories.

In addition to romances, religious narratives were a significant part of medieval culture. These texts combine entertaining travel adventures with morally instructive religious stories. One popular example of this genre is *The Golden Legend,* a collection of stories about saints' lives, written in the thirteenth century by Jacoubs da Varagine. Religious narratives were often allegories, stories in which literal elements represent abstract or moral concepts. Through the use of allegory, medieval literature explored cultural ideals, confirmed values, and amused audiences.

As the Middle Ages progressed, elements of daily life—such as the reality of city living and fear of the plague—found their way into stories. In the fourteenth century, Giovanni Boccaccio wrote the *Decameron,* a collection of stories set during the Black Death. These stories explore diverse characters and augment the range of themes covered by earlier medieval literature. Geoffrey Chaucer's *The Canterbury Tales* also covers the full scope of the medieval narrative, with its inclusion of romance, faith, and humor alongside darker, more humanistic themes. Medieval writers such as Chaucer provide a vital link between the Middle Ages and the modern world.

Bronze aquamanile, medieval (late 13th century A.D.) from England. The British Museum, London.

Ask Yourself

1. What themes did medieval writers address in their work?
2. How did writers from the later Middle Ages, such as Boccaccio and Chaucer, affect the medieval narrative?

 Learn It Online
Explore the Middle Ages further through the video "The Tales They Told" online.

go.hrw.com | L12-113 | Go

Analyzing a Painting

The romance, a common type of medieval narrative, chronicles the adventures of a brave hero who undertakes a quest and overcomes great danger. This painting, by contemporary artist Peter Jackson, shows a scene typical of a romance.

Guidelines

Use these guidelines to consider how this painting represents a romance.

- Examine the painting, and try to determine what narrative, or story, is represented. What event do you imagine is taking place?

- Think about typical themes of medieval narratives. How might this painting reflect some of those themes?

- The magical quests of medieval legends often create a mood of wonder and surprise. Consider how the details of this painting help establish its mood.

1. The knights' weapons are pointed forward. What does this tell you about the event?

2. Why do you think the painter focuses our attention on the knight in the foreground?

3. What **mood** do the colors help create?

Knights charging into battle, by Peter Jackson (1922–2003), gouche on paper.

Your Turn Analyze a Medieval Narrative

Choose an image from the selections from *Sir Gawain and the Green Knight* or *Le Morte d'Arthur* in this collection, and analyze how the image conveys some of the typical elements of medieval stories about knights and their quests.

The Prologue to The Canterbury Tales

Analyzing Style: Key Details by **Kylene Beers**

Say It with Style

There are as many ways to say something as people can think of words to say it. An author's style is the particular way he or she says or describes something in writing. Many authors have a distinctive style: curt and to the point, exaggerated, or highly descriptive.

It is likely that as a reader you already know which styles you prefer over others. An author's choices ultimately determine style, as he or she answers questions such as "How will I describe something?" and "What details will I use?" Analyzing important descriptions and details in a writer's style can help you gain insight into what the writer is trying to express.

All in the Details

The Prologue from Chaucer's *The Canterbury Tales* is a collection of character sketches that vividly describe different individuals and their lives. To avoid getting lost in such stylistically rich literature, focus on the key details. By determining how the reader will understand the descriptions, **key details** can reveal significant insights about the characters, the setting, or the plot. Analyzing how something is described can also reveal the feelings of the author or speaker.

For example, Chaucer opens the Prologue with a description of rain. The description's key details define the tone and reveal how his speaker views the April showers.

> When in April the sweet showers fall
> And pierce the drought of March to the root,
>   and all
> The veins are bathed in liquor of such power
> As brings about the engendering of the
>   flower.

We know that the speaker is clearly admiring the rain through the set-up of the description. The second and fourth lines present fairly straightforward descriptions of drought ending and flowers growing. The first and third lines, however, include details that reveal the speaker's perspective on the rain. In the first line, the speaker describes the showers as *sweet,* and in the third line he describes the veins as *bathed.* If you imagine changing just two words, replacing *sweet* with *dark,* and *bathed* with *drowned,* you see how the tone and meaning are affected by the key details.

Your Turn

Read the following passage about the Knight's character from the Prologue. Analyze the description with a partner, and discuss how each of you perceives the Knight. Which key details affect your view of the Knight? Which details are most revealing about the Knight's character?

> Speaking of his equipment, he possessed
> Fine horses, but he was not gaily dressed.
> He wore a fustian[1] tunic stained and dark
> With smudges where his armor had left
>   mark;
> Just home from service, he had joined our
>   ranks
> To do his pilgrimage and render thanks.

---

1. **fustian** (FUHS chuhn): made of coarse cloth woven from linen and cotton.

Learn It Online

Find a *PowerNotes* interactive introduction to analyzing style online.

go.hrw.com   L12-115   **Go**

The Canterbury Tales

What Do You Think?

What moves a hero to act?

QuickWrite

If you wanted to write a story about a pilgrimage, what sorts of characters would you include, and where would they go? Write two paragraphs in your *Reader/Writer Notebook* explaining your choices.

MEET THE WRITER

Geoffrey Chaucer
(1343–1400)

Geoffrey Chaucer, using everyday language of the times, brings to life <u>diverse</u> characters from medieval society.

The Father of English Poetry

Geoffrey Chaucer made the English language respectable. Often hailed as the father of English poetry, he composed his works in the English vernacular, or everyday language, at a time when the languages of literature, science, diplomacy, and religion were Latin and French. Before Chaucer, many people thought that English couldn't possibly convey the nuances and complexities of serious literature.

A Privileged Place

Chaucer was born into a middle-class family in London in the early 1340s, not long after the beginning of the Hundred Years' War between England and France. His father was a wine merchant who had enough money to provide his son with some education. The young Chaucer read a great deal and had some legal training. He became a page to a prominent family and received the finest training in good manners. As he advanced in his career, he became attached to several noble patrons.

Chaucer was captured in France while serving as a soldier during the Hundred Years' War and was of sufficiently high social <u>status</u> to have the king contribute to his ransom. Although details of his personal life are sparse, we know that he married a woman named Philippa and had at least two children. On several occasions he was sent to Europe as the king's ambassador. In 1367, he was awarded the first of several pensions for his services to the Crown. (On April 23, 1374, he was granted the promise of a daily pitcher of wine.) In 1385, he was appointed justice of the peace in the county of Kent and later became a member of Parliament. Despite his government responsibilities, between 1374 and 1386, Chaucer composed several great allegorical poems, including *House of Fame* and *Parliament of Fowls*, and his love story *Troilus and Criseyde*.

Geoffrey Chaucer (1400), by unknown artist.
National Portrait Gallery, London.

Outside Influences

In 1372 and 1378, Chaucer traveled in Italy, where he was very likely influenced by the poems of Dante and Petrarch and by the stories of Giovanni Boccaccio. Chaucer's *The Canterbury Tales* (c. 1387–1400) shares <u>attributes</u> of Boccacio's collection of tales, the *Decameron* (c. 1348–1353). Both use a framing device within which the characters tell their tales, and both include tales based on similar plots.

Chaucer began writing *The Canterbury Tales* in 1387, during a period of unemployment when his patron was out of the country. Despite the fact that he never completed all the stories (perhaps because, some speculate, he felt that he had lost his ability to find rhymes), the collection is considered one of the greatest works in the English language. Even *The Canterbury Tales'* Prologue alone, in which each traveler is described, is sufficient to place Chaucer in the company of later giants such as Shakespeare and Milton.

Personality in Poetry

The greatness of *The Canterbury Tales* lies in Chaucer's language and the strength of spirit and personality that it effuses. John Gardner, one of Chaucer's many biographers, offers a tribute to Chaucer's lasting power:

> In a dark, troubled age, as it seems to us, he was a comfortable optimist, serene, full of faith. For all his delight in irony—and all his poetry has a touch of that—he affirmed this life, to say nothing of the next, from the bottom of his capacious heart. Joy—satisfaction without a trace of sentimental simple-mindedness—is still the effect of Chaucer's poetry and of Chaucer's personality as it emerges from the poems.

The date on Chaucer's tombstone reads October 25, 1400, but it is uncertain how he died or even if that is his correct death date. (His tombstone was erected by an admirer in 1556.) Chaucer was, quite fittingly, the first of many English writers to be buried in the famous Poets' Corner of Westminster Abbey in London. "The Father of English poetry," notes Nevill Coghill, "lies in his family vault."

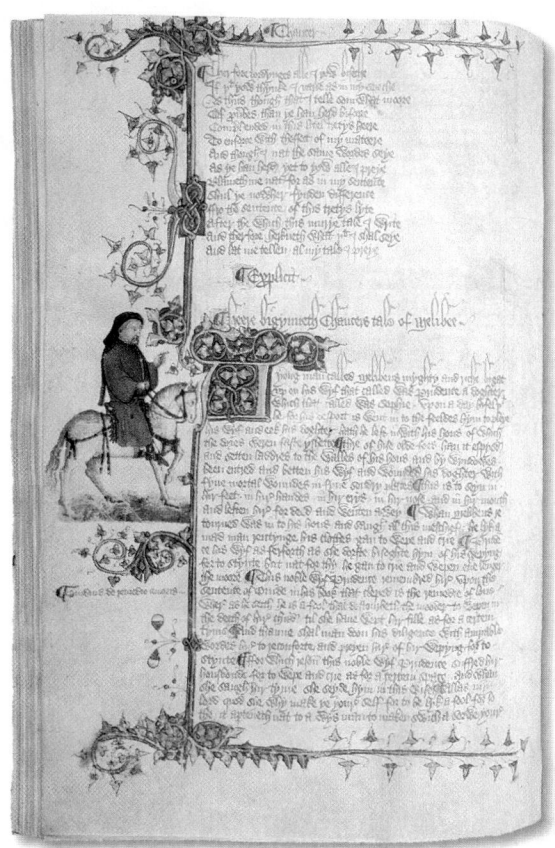

Portrait of Geoffrey Chaucer (c. 1342–1400) by English school (15th century). Huntington Library and Art Gallery, San Marino, CA.

Think About the Writer

Although the details of Chaucer's life are obscure, the colorful nature of his work is certain. What kind of life must a person lead to characterize others so richly?

Learn It Online
Find out more about Chaucer online.
go.hrw.com | L12-117 | **Go**

INTRODUCTION TO

The Canterbury Tales

Through its wide range of characters and rich collection of stories, *The Canterbury Tales* creates a snapshot of medieval society. In his poem, Chaucer brings together a group of people with varied backgrounds and beliefs and uses them to explore different aspects of life in the Middle Ages. The characters are joined in a common quest: a pilgrimage, or religious journey, from London to the shrine of the martyr Saint Thomas à Becket at Canterbury Cathedral. The group travels on horseback along their fifty-five-mile trek to Canterbury, a popular destination for pilgrims during Chaucer's time. During their pilgrimage, the characters tell each other stories that provide readers with a vivid view of the medieval world.

Preparing for a Journey

Chaucer begins his Tales with a general Prologue, which he uses to describe the spring setting and introduce the characters. Spring represents more than just the usual time for the start of pilgrimages in Chaucer's day—it is also a rich symbol of new life and a reawakening. In this opening, the pilgrim narrator, whom many consider to be Chaucer himself, sketches distinct, individual portraits of his fellow pilgrims. Through these portraits, Chaucer illuminates all classes of life in the Middle Ages, as Nevill Coghill, one of Chaucer's translators, describes:

> In all literature there is nothing that touches or resembles the Prologue. It is the concise portrait of an entire nation, high and low, old and young, male and female, lay and clerical, learned and ignorant, rogue and righteous, land and sea, town and country, but without extremes.

The Prologue takes place on the eve of the pilgrimage, as these characters first encounter each other at the Tabard Inn in Southwark, a borough in the south of London. Although most medieval inns provided only barebones accommodations, they still served as a welcome oasis during rugged travels. The pilgrims spend their evening basking in the hospitality of the inn's host, who concludes their festivities by proposing a storytelling contest as a way to pass the time along their journey to Canterbury. This proposal sets up the Tales' frame story—the main story of their pilgrimage that surrounds the individual stories told by the travelers.

Chaucer's Canterbury Pilgrims (1810), engraved and published by the artist, William Blake (1757–1827).

A Classic Medieval Narrative

Chaucer's Tales works as a brilliant depiction of his society, a timeless exploration of human nature, and a classic example of a medieval quest narrative. The poem's quest—the pilgrimage to Canterbury—begins with images of spring and awakening, winds its way through the territory of penance and death, and concludes with the Parson's reflections on eternal life. Although the Tales remains unfinished, the arc of this quest mirrors the spiritual renewal that the pilgrims themselves are seeking at the shrine of Saint Thomas à Becket. Because much of what these characters seek and ponder remains relevant to people today, the Tales presents a medieval narrative that still illuminates human nature in the modern world.

Middle English Pronunciation Guide

The version of The Canterbury Tales included in this book is a translation into Modern English by Nevill Coghill. Chaucer's original text was written in Middle English, an older version of the English language that was spoken during the medieval era. Although Coghill's translation reflects the spirit of Chaucer's text, you might try to read some of the Tales in the wonderfully musical original. Using the guide on the right to help you, practice speaking some of the lines from the opening passage that appears on the next page in the original Middle English.

Brief Pronunciation Guide to Middle English

Vowels
a: *ah,* as in *father.*
ai, ay, ei, ey: *ay,* as in *pay.*
au, aw: *ow,* as in *house.*
i: *ee,* as in *me.*
oo, o: *oh,* as in *oat.*
u: *oo,* as in *who.*
ee: *ay,* as in *pay.* For example, *eek* is pronounced *ayk.*
e: at times *ay;* also sometimes *eh,* as in *men.*
e: When it is the final letter, *e* in Middle English is a separate syllable sounded like a final *uh;* for example, *soote* (which also uses the *"oo"* rule mentioned above) rhymes with *soda.* But when the final *e* precedes a word that starts with a vowel or an *h,* it is not sounded. In "droghte of March," the final *e* in *droghte* is silent.

Consonants
g: hard *g,* as in *go,* except before *e* or *i* (in words borrowed from French), where it is sounded like *zh* or *j,* as in *garage. Pilgrimage* rhymes with *garage.*
gh: like a German *ch. Knight* is pronounced *k-nee-hkt.*
–tion, –cial: The *t* and *c* in these letter combinations are not blended with the *i* as they are in Modern English (as in the words *condition* and *special*). The *i* is sounded as a separate syllable. Therefore, in Middle English *special* would have three syllables: SPEH see al (*c* has the sound of *s* when it comes before *i*). *Condition* would have four syllables: kahn dee see AHN.

Here bygynneth the Book of the Tales of Caunterbury.

han that Aprill with his shoures soote
The droghte of March hath perced to the roote
And bathed every veyne in swich licour
Of which vertu engendred is the flour,
5   Whan Zephirus eek with his sweete breeth
Inspired hath in every holt and heeth
The tendre croppes, and the yonge sonne
Hath in the Ram his half cours y-ronne,
And smale foweles maken melodye
10   That slepen al the nyght with open eye,
So priketh hem Nature in hir corages,
Than longen folk to goon on pilgrymages,
And palmeres for to seken straunge strondes,
To ferne halwes kouthe in sondry londes.
15   And specially, from every shires ende
Of Engelond, to Caunterbury they wende,
The holy, blisful martir for to seke
That hem hath holpen whan that they were seeke
  Bifel that in that sesoun on a day
20   In Southwerk at the Tabard, as I lay
Redy to wenden on my pilgrymage
To Caunterbury with ful devout corage,
At nyght was come into that hostelrye
Wel nyne-and-twenty in a compaignye
25   Of sondry folk by aventure y-falle
In felaweshipe, and pilgrymes were they alle
That toward Caunterbury wolden ryde.
The chambres and the stables weren wyde,
And wel we weren esed atte beste;
30   And shortly, whan the sonne was to reste,
So hadde I spoken with hem everichon
That I was of hir felaweshipe anon;
And made forward erly for to ryse
To take oure wey ther as I yow devyse.
35   But, nathelees, whil I have tyme and space,
Er that I ferther in this tale pace,
Me thynketh it acordant to resoun
To telle yow al the condicioun
Of ech of hem so as it semed me,
40   And whiche they weren, and of what degree,
And eek in what array that they were inne;
And at a knyght than wol I first bigynne.

First page of *The Canterbury Tales*, by Geoffrey Chaucer (vellum), by the English School (15th century). The Huntington Library, San Marino, California.

Preparing to Read

The Prologue to The Canterbury Tales

Reader/Writer Notebook

Use your **RWN** to complete the activities for this selection.

Literary Focus

Characterization/Frame Story Writers reveal a character's personality through **characterization.** In the Prologue to *The Canterbury Tales,* Chaucer describes the main characters' appearances, actions, and thoughts to create vivid and realistic portraits. The Prologue takes place the night before the group's journey and serves as a frame story for the characters' individual stories that follow thereafter. While Chaucer uses the **frame story,** a story that contains other stories, to unite his travelers' tales, the tales themselves also have thematic unity.

Reading Focus

Analyzing Style: Key Details With twenty-nine pilgrims to introduce in the Prologue, Chaucer could not develop any one character at great length. Instead, he provides a few well-chosen details that make each character stand out vividly. Identifying **key details** concerning these characters can help you determine what Chaucer thinks about his characters and their experiences. Note that these details may undermine what the characters think of themselves or would like others to think about them.

Into Action As you read, use a chart like the one below to note one or two key details about the main characters in the Prologue. Briefly describe what you think each detail <u>emphasizes</u> about the character.

Main Character	Key Detail	What Detail <u>Emphasizes</u>
the Knight	"He had done nobly in his sovereign's war / And ridden into battle" (lines 47-48)	It tells us he's a brave man, a strong warrior, and someone of great experience.

Writing Focus

Think as a Reader/Writer

Find It in Your Reading Describing each character's appearance is one method of **characterization** used by Chaucer. As you read, consider how Chaucer describes each character's physical appearance. In your *Reader/Writer Notebook,* take notes on the different types of physical details.

Vocabulary

eminent (EHM uh nuhnt) *adj.:* great; of high-standing. *After a lifetime of glorious battles, he was the most eminent knight in the kingdom.*

benign (bih NYN) *adj.:* kind; gracious. *Even when the family was late with the rent, the benign Franklin did not harass them.*

guile (gyl) *n.:* sly dealings; skill in deceiving. *The thief used his guile to steal things before his victims could notice.*

obstinate (AHB stuh niht) *adj.:* unreasonably stubborn. *An obstinate man, the Pardoner will never admit his stubborn nature.*

frugal (FROO guhl) *adj.:* thrifty; careful with money. *The Host finds it difficult to be frugal; he likes to be generous with his money.*

Language Coach

Commonly Confused Words It is easy to confuse words that have similar sounds. *Eminent,* for example, is an adjective that describes someone or something of high standing. *Imminent* is an adjective that means "about to happen." What is the difference between an imminent leader and an eminent leader?

Learn It Online
Journey back to the time of *The Canterbury Tales* with this video introduction online.

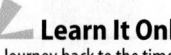
go.hrw.com L12-121 Go

THE PROLOGUE TO

The Canterbury Tales

by **Geoffrey Chaucer**

translated by **Nevill Coghill**

Read with a Purpose

Read to discover how Chaucer uses a collection of <u>diverse</u> individuals to create a vibrant picture of medieval culture and society.

Build Background

The Canterbury Tales is a group of stories told by the characters as they travel together to visit the shrine of Saint Thomas à Becket in Canterbury. The Prologue sets up the purpose of their journey, introduces all of the characters, and provides a detailed description of each member of the group. Written at the end of the fourteenth century, the poem provides a rich view of life during Chaucer's time.

John Lydgate and the Canterbury pilgrims leaving Canterbury, from a volume of Lydgate's poems (early 16th century). British Library Board. Roy. 18 D 11, fol.148.

THE PROLOGUE

When in April the sweet showers fall
And pierce the drought of March to the root, and all
The veins are bathed in liquor of such power
As brings about the engendering of the flower,
5   When also Zephyrus° with his sweet breath
Exhales an air in every grove and heath
Upon the tender shoots, and the young sun
His half-course in the sign of the *Ram°* has run,
And the small fowl are making melody
10 That sleep away the night with open eye
(So nature pricks them and their heart engages)
Then people long to go on pilgrimages
And palmers° long to seek the stranger strands
Of far-off saints, hallowed in sundry lands,
15 And specially, from every shire's end
Of England, down to Canterbury they wend°
To seek the holy blissful martyr, quick
To give his help to them when they were sick.
      It happened in that season that one day
20 In Southwark, at *The Tabard,* as I lay
Ready to go on pilgrimage and start
For Canterbury, most devout at heart,
At night there came into that hostelry°
Some nine and twenty in a company
25 Of sundry folk happening then to fall
In fellowship, and they were pilgrims all
That towards Canterbury meant to ride. **Ⓐ**

1–18. When...sick: These lines consist of a single, long sentence that is built on this structure: "When *x* occurs, then *y* happens."

? *According to the narrator, what do people long to do when spring brings new life?*

5. Zephyrus: in Greek mythology, god of the west wind.

8. Ram: Aries, first sign of the zodiac. The time is mid-April.

13. palmers: people who wore palm fronds to show that they had visited the Holy Land.

16. wend: go; travel.

23. hostelry: inn. The Tabard is a lodging place.

Ⓐ **Literary Focus** **Frame Story** How do these lines foreshadow the frame story about many different characters?

The rooms and stables of the inn were wide:
They made us easy, all was of the best.
30 And, briefly, when the sun had gone to rest,
I'd spoken to them all upon the trip
And was soon one with them in fellowship,
Pledged to rise early and to take the way
to Canterbury, as you heard me say.
35   But none the less, while I have time and space,
Before my story takes a further pace,
It seems a reasonable thing to say
What their condition was, the full array
Of each of them, as it appeared to me,
40 According to profession and degree,
And what apparel they were riding in;
And at a Knight I therefore will begin.

The Knight

There was a *Knight,* a most distinguished man,
Who from the day on which he first began
45 To ride abroad had followed chivalry,
Truth, honor, generousness, and courtesy.
He had done nobly in his sovereign's war
And ridden into battle, no man more,
As well in Christian as in heathen° places,
50 And ever honored for his noble graces.
    When we took Alexandria,° he was there.
He often sat at table in the chair
Of honor, above all nations, when in Prussia.
In Lithuania he had ridden, and Russia,
55 No Christian man so often, of his rank.
When, in Granada, Algeciras sank
Under assault, he had been there, and in
North Africa, raiding Benamarin;
In Anatolia he had been as well
60 And fought when Ayas and Attalia fell,
For all along the Mediterranean coast
He had embarked with many a noble host.
In fifteen mortal battles he had been
And jousted for our faith at Tramissene
65 Thrice in the lists, and always killed his man.
This same distinguished knight had led the van
Once with the Bey of Balat, doing work
For him against another heathen Turk;   **B**

The Knight, detail from *The Canterbury Tales,* by Geoffrey Chaucer.
The Huntington Library, San Marino, CA.

43. **There was a *Knight*...:** Note that italics will designate each new character as that character is introduced.
As you read, you might wish to create a list of all the characters introduced in the Prologue.

49. heathen: pagan. Chaucer uses the term to mean "non-Christian."

51. Zlexandria: city in Egypt captured by the Crusaders in 1365. In the next few lines, Chaucer is indicating the Knight's distinguished and extensive career.

B **Reading Focus** **Analyzing Key Details** What qualities does the Knight possess that differ from those you might expect to find in a veteran soldier?

He was of sovereign value in all eyes.
70 And though so much distinguished, he was wise
And in his bearing modest as a maid.
He never yet a boorish thing had said
In all his life to any, come what might;
He was a true, a perfect gentle-knight.
75   Speaking of his equipment, he possessed
Fine horses, but he was not gaily dressed.
He wore a fustian° tunic stained and dark
With smudges where his armor had left mark;
Just home from service, he had joined our ranks
80 To do his pilgrimage and render thanks.

The Squire

He had his son with him, a fine young Squire,
A lover and cadet, a lad of fire
With locks as curly as if they had been pressed.
He was some twenty years of age, I guessed.
85 In stature he was of a moderate length,
With wonderful agility and strength.
He'd seen some service with the cavalry
In Flanders and Artois and Picardy
And had done valiantly in little space
90 Of time, in hope to win his lady's grace.
He was embroidered like a meadow bright
And full of freshest flowers, red and white.
Singing he was, or fluting° all the day;
He was as fresh as is the month of May.
95 Short was his gown, the sleeves were long and wide;
He knew the way to sit a horse and ride.
He could make songs and poems and recite,
Knew how to joust and dance, to draw and write.
He loved so hotly that till dawn grew pale
100 He slept as little as a nightingale.
Courteous he was, lowly and serviceable,
And carved to serve his father at the table. **C**

The Yeoman

There was a Yeoman with him at his side,
No other servant; so he chose to ride.
105 This Yeoman wore a coat and hood of green,

---

77. fustian: made of coarse cloth woven from linen and cotton.

The Squire, detail from *The Canterbury Tales,* by Geoffrey Chaucer. The Huntington Library, San Marino, CA.

? **87–102.** *Summarize the narrator's description of the Squire. In what ways does the Squire appear to embody the concept of chivalry? (See page 10 for a review of chivalry.)*
93. fluting: whistling.

The Canon Yeoman, detail from *The Canterbury Tales,* by Geoffrey Chaucer. The Huntington Library, San Marino, CA.

C **Literary Focus** **Characterization** How does the portrait of the Squire differ from that of the Knight?

And peacock-feathered arrows, bright and keen
And neatly sheathed, hung at his belt the while
—For he could dress his gear in yeoman style,
His arrows never drooped their feathers low—
110 And in his hand he bore a mighty bow.
His head was like a nut, his face was brown.
He knew the whole of woodcraft up and down.
A saucy brace was on his arm to ward
It from the bow-string, and a shield and sword
115 Hung at one side, and at the other slipped
A jaunty dirk,° spear-sharp and well-equipped.
A medal of St. Christopher° he wore
Of shining silver on his breast, and bore
A hunting-horn, well slung and burnished clean,
120 That dangled from a baldrick° of bright green.
He was a proper forester, I guess.

The Nun

There also was a Nun, a Prioress,°
Her way of smiling very simple and coy.
Her greatest oath was only "By St. Loy!"°
125 And she was known as Madam Eglantyne.
And well she sang a service, with a fine
Intoning through her nose, as was most seemly,
And she spoke daintily in French, extremely,
After the school of Stratford-atte-Bowe;°
130 French in the Paris style she did not know.
At meat her manners were well taught withal;
No morsel from her lips did she let fall,
Nor dipped her fingers in the sauce too deep;
But she could carry a morsel up and keep
135 The smallest drop from falling on her breast.
For courtliness she had a special zest,
And she would wipe her upper lip so clean
That not a trace of grease was to be seen
Upon the cup when she had drunk; to eat,
140 She reached a hand sedately for the meat.
She certainly was very entertaining,
Pleasant and friendly in her ways, and straining
To counterfeit a courtly kind of grace,
A stately bearing fitting to her place,
145 And to seem dignified in all her dealings. **D**

D **Literary Focus** Characterization How does Chaucer characterize the Nun? What is your main impression of her at this point?

116. dirk: long dagger.
117. St. Christopher: patron saint of travelers.

120. baldrick: belt slung over the shoulder and chest to hold a sword.

122. prioress: head of a convent of nuns.
124. St. Loy: Saint Eligius, known for his perfect manners.

? **122–145.** *What details in the description of the Nun thus far suggest that the narrator thinks she is putting on airs— that is, trying to appear more refined and "high class" than she really is?*
129. Stratford-atte-Bowe: Benedictine convent near London where inferior French was spoken.

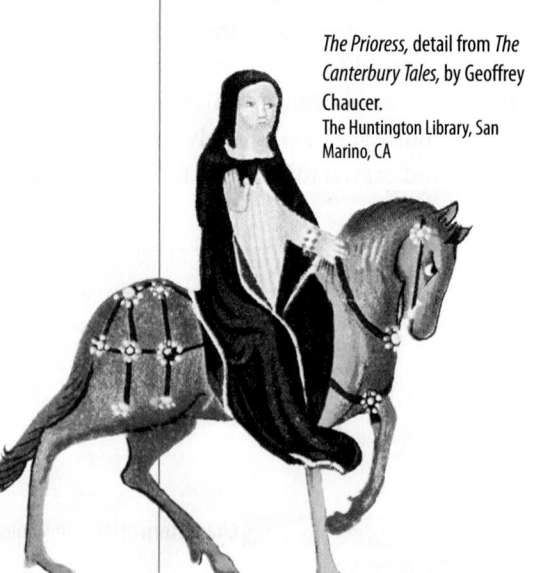

The Prioress, detail from *The Canterbury Tales,* by Geoffrey Chaucer.
The Huntington Library, San Marino, CA

As for her sympathies and tender feelings,
She was so charitably solicitous
She used to weep if she but saw a mouse
Caught in a trap, if it were dead or bleeding.
150 And she had little dogs she would be feeding
With roasted flesh, or milk, or fine white bread.
And bitterly she wept if one were dead
Or someone took a stick and made it smart;
She was all sentiment and tender heart.
155 Her veil was gathered in a seemly way,
Her nose was elegant, her eyes glass-gray;
Her mouth was very small, but soft and red,
Her forehead, certainly, was fair of spread,
Almost a span° across the brows, I own;
160 She was indeed by no means undergrown.
Her cloak, I noticed, had a graceful charm.
She wore a coral° trinket on her arm,
A set of beads, the gaudies tricked in green,°
Whence hung a golden brooch of brightest sheen
165 On which there first was graven a crowned A,
And lower, *Amor vincit omnia.*°
    Another *Nun,* the secretary at her cell,°
Was riding with her, and *three Priests* as well.

The Monk

    A *Monk* there was, one of the finest sort
170 Who rode the country; hunting was his sport.
A manly man, to be an Abbott able;
Many a dainty horse he had in stable.
His bridle, when he rode, a man might hear
Jingling in a whistling wind as clear,
175 Aye, and as loud as does the chapel bell
Where my lord Monk was Prior of the cell.
The Rule of good St. Benet or St. Maur°
As old and strict he tended to ignore;
He let go by the things of yesterday
180 And took the modern world's more spacious way.
He did not rate that text at a plucked hen
Which says that hunters are not holy men
And that a monk uncloistered is a mere
Fish out of water, flapping on the pier,
185 That is to say a monk out of his cloister.
That was a text he held not worth an oyster;
And I agreed and said his views were sound;
Was he to study till his head went round
Poring over books in cloisters? Must he toil

The Nun's Priest, detail from *The Canterbury Tales,* by Geoffrey Chaucer. The Huntington Library, San Marino, CA.

159. span: nine inches. A span was supposed to be the distance between the extended thumb and little finger.

162. coral: In the Middle Ages, coral was a defense against worldly temptations as well as a love charm.

163. a set of beads . . . green: Beads are a rosary, or a set of prayer beads and a crucifix on a string or chain. Every eleventh bead is a gaud, a large bead indicating when the Lord's Prayer is to be said.

166. *Amor vincit omnia* (AH mawr WIHN kiht AWM nee uh): Latin for "Love conquers all."

167. cell: small convent connected to a larger one.

177. St. Benet or St. Maur: Saint Benet is Benedict (c. 480– c. 547), who founded numerous monasteries and wrote a famous code of regulations for monastic life. Saint Maur is Maurice, a follower of Benedict.

190   As Austin° bade and till the very soil?
Was he to leave the world upon the shelf?
Let Austin have his labor to himself.
    This Monk was therefore a good man to horse;
Greyhounds he had, as swift as birds, to course.°
195   Hunting a hare or riding at a fence
Was all his fun, he spared for no expense.
I saw his sleeves were garnished at the hand
With fine gray fur, the finest in the land,
And on his hood, to fasten it at his chin
200   He had a wrought-gold, cunningly fashioned pin;
Into a lover's knot it seemed to pass.
His head was bald and shone like looking-glass;
So did his face, as if it had been greased.
He was a fat and personable priest;
205   His prominent eyeballs never seemed to settle.
They glittered like the flames beneath a kettle;
Supple his boots, his horse in fine condition.
He was a prelate fit for exhibition,
He was not pale like a tormented soul.
210   He liked a fat swan best, and roasted whole.
His palfrey° was as brown as is a berry. **E**

The Friar, detail from *The Canterbury Tales*, by Geoffrey Chaucer. The Huntington Library, San Marino, CA.

The Friar

    There was a *Friar*, a wanton one and merry,
A Limiter,° a very festive fellow.
In all Four Orders° there was none so mellow,
215   So glib with gallant phrase and well-turned speech.
He'd fixed up many a marriage, giving each
Of his young women what he could afford her.
He was a noble pillar to his Order.
Highly beloved and intimate was he
220   With County folk within his boundary,
And city dames of honor and possessions;
For he was qualified to hear confessions,
Or so he said, with more than priestly scope;
He had a special license from the Pope.
225   Sweetly he heard his penitents° at shrift°
With pleasant absolution,° for a gift.
He was an easy man in penance-giving
Where he could hope to make a decent living;
It's a sure sign whenever gifts are given
230   To a poor Order that a man's well shriven,°

**E** **Reading Focus** **Analyzing Key Details** How do the details in this portrait of the Monk imply that he is not serious about his vocation?

190. Austin: Saint Augustine (354–430), bishop of Hippo in North Africa. He criticized lazy monks and suggested they do hard manual labor.
194. course: cause to chase game.

211. palfrey: horse.

213. limiter: friar having the exclusive right to beg and preach in an assigned (limited) district.
214. Four Orders: The four orders of mendicant (beggar) friars are the Franciscans, the Dominicans, the Carmelites, and the Augustinians.

225. penitents: people seeking the sacrament of confession so that their sins can be forgiven. **shrift:** confession.
226. absolution: forgiveness of sins, given by a priest.
230. well shriven: confessed and forgiven of sins.

And should he give enough he knew in verity
The penitent repented in sincerity.
For many a fellow is so hard of heart
He cannot weep, for all his inward smart.
235 Therefore instead of weeping and of prayer
One should give silver for a poor Friar's care.
He kept his tippet° stuffed with pins for curls,
And pocket-knives, to give to pretty girls.
And certainly his voice was gay and sturdy,
240 For he sang well and played the hurdy-gurdy.°
At sing-songs he was champion of the hour.
His neck was whiter than a lily-flower
But strong enough to butt a bruiser down.
He knew the taverns well in every town
245 And every innkeeper and barmaid too
Better than lepers, beggars and that crew,
For in so eminent a man as he
It was not fitting with the dignity
Of his position, dealing with a scum
250 Of wretched lepers; nothing good can come
Of commerce with such slum-and-gutter dwellers,
But only with the rich and victual-sellers.°
But anywhere a profit might accrue
Courteous he was and lowly of service too. **F**
255 Natural gifts like his were hard to match.
He was the finest beggar of his batch,
And, for his begging-district, paid a rent;
His brethren did no poaching where he went.
For though a widow mightn't have a shoe,
260 So pleasant was his holy how-d'ye-do
He got his farthing° from her just the same
Before he left, and so his income came
To more than he laid out. And how he romped,
Just like a puppy! He was ever prompt
265 To arbitrate disputes on settling days°
(For a small fee) in many helpful ways,
Not then appearing as your cloistered scholar
With threadbare habit hardly worth a dollar,
But much more like a Doctor or a Pope.
270 Of double-worsted° was the semi-cope°

237. tippet: hood or long sleeve of a robe.

240. hurdy-gurdy: instrument played by turning a crank.

252. victual-sellers: merchants, especially of food.

? 256–279. *What details in these lines show the Friar's love of luxury? How does this Friar compare with your expectations of a religious figure?*

261. farthing: former British coin worth one fourth of a penny.

265. settling days: days on which disputes could be settled out of court by independent negotiators. Though friars often acted as negotiators (for a fee), they were officially forbidden to do so.

270. double-worsted: a high-quality woven wool. **semi-cope:** capelike garment.

F **Literary Focus** **Characterization** What do lines 212–254 reveal about the Friar's character?

Vocabulary **eminent** (EHM uh nuhnt) *adj.*: great; high-standing.

Upon his shoulders, and the swelling fold
About him, like a bell about its mould
When it is casting, rounded out his dress.
He lisped a little out of wantonness°
275 To make his English sweet upon his tongue.
When he had played his harp, or having sung,
His eyes would twinkle in his head as bright
As any star upon a frosty night.
This worthy's name was Hubert, it appeared.

274. wantonness: here, pretense.

The Merchant

280   There was a *Merchant* with a forking beard
And motley° dress; high on his horse he sat,
Upon his head a Flemish beaver hat
And on his feet daintily buckled boots.
He told of his opinions and pursuits
285 In solemn tones, he harped on his increase
Of capital; there should be sea-police
(He thought) upon the Harwich-Holland ranges;°
He was expert at dabbling in exchanges.
This estimable Merchant so had set
290 His wits to work, none knew he was in debt,
He was so stately in administration,
In loans and bargains and negotiation.
He was an excellent fellow all the same;
To tell the truth I do not know his name.

281. **motley:** multicolored.

287. **Harwich-Holland ranges:** sea route between Harwich (port city on the southeastern coast of England) and Holland.

The Oxford Cleric

295   An *Oxford Cleric*, still a student though,
One who had taken logic long ago,
Was there; his horse was thinner than a rake,
And he was not too fat, I undertake,
But had a hollow look, a sober stare;
300 The thread upon his overcoat was bare.
He had found no preferment in the church
And he was too unworldly to make search
For secular employment. By his bed
He preferred having twenty books in red
305 And black, of Aristotle's° philosophy,
Than costly clothes, fiddle, or psaltery.°
Though a philosopher, as I have told,
He had not found the stone for making gold.°
Whatever money from his friends he took
310 He spent on learning or another book
And prayed for them most earnestly, returning
Thanks to them thus for paying for his learning.

The Oxford Cleric, detail from *The Canterbury Tales,* by Geoffrey Chaucer. The Huntington Library, San Marino, CA.

305. **Aristotle's:** reference to the Greek philosopher (384–322 B.C.).
306. **psaltery:** stringed instrument that is plucked.
308. **stone . . . gold:** Alchemists at the time were searching for a stone that was supposed to turn ordinary metals into gold.

His only care was study, and indeed
He never spoke a word more than was need,
315 Formal at that, respectful in the extreme,
Short, to the point, and lofty in his theme.
A tone of moral virtue filled his speech
And gladly would he learn, and gladly teach. **G**

The Lawyer

A *Sergeant at the Law* who paid his calls,
320 Wary and wise, for clients at St. Paul's°
There also was, of noted excellence.
Discreet he was, a man to reverence,
Or so he seemed, his sayings were so wise.
He often had been Justice of Assize
325 By letters patent,° and in full commission.
His fame and learning and his high position
Had won him many a robe and many a fee.
There was no such conveyancer° as he;
All was fee-simple° to his strong digestion,
330 Not one conveyance could be called in question.
Though there was nowhere one so busy as he,
He was less busy than he seemed to be.
He knew of every judgment, case, and crime
Ever recorded since King William's time.
335 He could dictate defenses or draft deeds;
No one could pinch a comma from his screeds°
And he knew every statute off by rote.
He wore a homely parti-colored° coat,
Girt with a silken belt of pin-stripe stuff;
340 Of his appearance I have said enough.

The Franklin

There was a *Franklin*° with him, it appeared;
White as a daisy-petal was his beard.
A sanguine° man, high-colored and benign,
He loved a morning sop of cake in wine.
345 He lived for pleasure and had always done,
For he was Epicurus'° very son,
In whose opinion sensual delight
Was the one true felicity in sight.

G **Reading Focus** Analyzing Key Details Which details in the sketch of the Oxford Cleric match the stereotype of the poor student?

Vocabulary **benign** (bih NYN) *adj.*: kind; gracious.

? **295–318.** *In what ways is the Oxford Cleric significantly different from the Nun, the Monk, and the Friar?*

320. St. Paul's: London cathedral. Lawyers often met outside it to discuss their cases when courts were closed.
325. letters patent: letters from the king permitting people to act as judges at the Assizes, court sessions held periodically.

328. conveyancer: person who draws up documents transferring ownership of land. The Lawyer is transferring the ownership to himself.
329. fee-simple: absolute ownership of real property; in other words, he took absolute possession of everything.
336 screeds: tiresome, lengthy writings.
338. parti-colored: multicolored.

341. franklin: well-to-do landowner who is not of the nobility.
343. sanguine: ruddy complexioned. In Chaucer's day this was considered a sign of a cheerful temperament; today the word signifies optimism.
346. Epicurus': Epicurus (341–270 B.C.), an ancient Greek philosopher, taught that the goal of life is pleasure, which is achieved through virtue and moderation. Most people came to think of Epicureans as pleasure seekers.

As noted as St. Julian° was for bounty
350 He made his household free to all the County.
His bread, his ale were finest of the fine
And no one had a better stock of wine.
His house was never short of bake-meat pies,
Of fish and flesh, and these in such supplies
355 It positively snowed with meat and drink
And all the dainties that a man could think.
According to the seasons of the year
Changes of dish were ordered to appear.
He kept fat partridges in coops, beyond,
360 Many a bream and pike were in his pond.
Woe to the cook unless the sauce was hot
And sharp, or if he wasn't on the spot!
And in his hall a table stood arrayed
And ready all day long, with places laid.
365 As Justice at the Sessions° none stood higher;
He often had been Member for the Shire.°
A dagger and a little purse of silk
Hung at his girdle, white as morning milk.
As Sheriff he checked audit, every entry.
370 He was a model among landed gentry.

The Guildsmen

A *Haberdasher,*° a *Dyer,* a *Carpenter,*
A *Weaver,* and a *Carpet-maker* were
Among our ranks, all in the livery°
Of one impressive guild-fraternity.
375 They were so trim and fresh their gear would pass
For new. Their knives were not tricked out with brass
But wrought with purest silver, which avouches°
A like display on girdles and on pouches.
Each seemed a worthy burgess,° fit to grace
380 A guild-hall with a seat upon the dais.
Their wisdom would have justified a plan
To make each one of them an alderman;°
They had the capital and revenue,
Besides their wives declared it was their due.
385 And if they did not think so, then they ought;
To be called "*Madam*" is a glorious thought,
And so is going to church and being seen
Having your mantle carried, like a queen. **H**

349. **St. Julian:** patron saint of hospitality.
365. **Justice at the Sessions:** judge at a court meeting.
366. **Member for the Shire:** county representative in Parliament.

The Franklin, detail from *The Canterbury Tales,* by Geoffrey Chaucer.
The Huntington Library, San Marino, CA.

371. **haberdasher:** seller of men's clothing and accessories.
373. **livery:** traditional uniform associated with a particular trade.

377. **avouches:** guarantees.

379. **burgess:** citizen.

382. **alderman:** head of a guild and therefore a member of the town council.

? **371–388.** *What characters do you learn more about in these lines: the guildsmen or their wives? Explain.*

H **Literary Focus** **Characterization** How are the guildsmen's wives characterized in this section?

The Cook

They had a *Cook* with them who stood alone
390 For boiling chicken with a marrow-bone,
Sharp flavoring-powder and a spice for savor.
He could distinguish London ale by flavor,
And he could roast and seethe and broil and fry,
Make good thick soup, and bake a tasty pie.
395 But what a pity—so it seemed to me,
That he should have an ulcer on his knee.
As for blancmange,° he made it with the best.

The Skipper

There was a *Skipper* hailing from far west;
He came from Dartmouth, so I understood.
400 He rode a farmer's horse as best he could,
In a woollen gown that reached his knee.
A dagger on a lanyard° falling free
Hung from his neck under his arm and down.
The summer heat had tanned his color brown,
405 And certainly he was an excellent fellow.
Many a draught of vintage, red and yellow,
He'd drawn at Bordeaux, while the trader snored.
The nicer rules of conscience he ignored.
If, when he fought, the enemy vessel sank,
410 He sent his prisoners home; they walked the plank.
As for his skill in reckoning his tides,
Currents, and many another risk besides,
Moons, harbors, pilots, he had such dispatch
That none from Hull to Carthage was his match.
415 Hardy he was, prudent in undertaking;
His beard in many a tempest had its shaking,
And he knew all the havens as they were
From Gottland to the Cape of Finisterre,
And every creek in Brittany and Spain;
420 The barge he owned was called *The Maudelayne.*

The Doctor

A *Doctor* too emerged as we proceeded;
No one alive could talk as well as he did
On points of medicine and of surgery,
For, being grounded in astronomy,
425 He watched his patient closely for the hours
When, by his horoscope, he knew the powers

397. blancmange: French for "white food." In Chaucer's day blancmange was a sweet dish made from diced chicken, milk, sugar, and almonds.

402. lanyard: cord.

The Cook, detail from *The Canterbury Tales,* by Geoffrey Chaucer.
The Huntington Library, San Marino, CA.

❶ **Reading Focus** Analyzing Key Details Read lines 408–410 carefully. They reveal an important detail about the Skipper. What does "sent his prisoners home" actually mean?

Of favorable planets, then ascendent,
Worked on the images for his dependent.
The cause of every malady you'd got
430 He knew, and whether dry, cold, moist, or hot;°
He knew their seat, their humor and condition.
He was a perfect practicing physician.
These causes being known for what they were,
He gave the man his medicine then and there.
435 All his apothecaries° in a tribe
Were ready with the drugs he would prescribe
And each made money from the other's guile;
They had been friendly for a goodish while. **Ⓙ**
He was well-versed in Aesculapius° too
440 And what Hippocrates and Rufus knew
And Dioscorides, now dead and gone,
Galen and Rhazes, Hali, Serapion,
Averroes, Avicenna, Constantine,
Scotch Bernard, John of Gaddesden, Gilbertine.
445 In his own diet he observed some measure;
There were no superfluities° for pleasure,
Only digestives, nutritives and such.
He did not read the Bible very much.
In blood-red garments, slashed with bluish gray
450 And lined with taffeta, he rode his way;
Yet he was rather close as to expenses
And kept the gold he won in pestilences.
Gold stimulates the heart, or so we're told.
He therefore had a special love of gold.

The Wife of Bath

455   A worthy *woman* from beside *Bath* city
Was with us, somewhat deaf, which was a pity.
In making cloth she showed so great a bent
She bettered those of Ypres and of Ghent.°
In all the parish not a dame dared stir
460 Towards the altar steps in front of her,
And if indeed they did, so wrath was she
As to be quite put out of charity.
Her kerchiefs were of finely woven ground;°
I dared have sworn they weighed a good ten pound,
465 The ones she wore on Sunday, on her head.

Ⓙ Literary Focus Characterization How does the description of the Doctor's dealings in lines 435–438 change how he is characterized?

Vocabulary guile (gyl) *n.:* sly dealings; skill in deceiving.

430. dry . . . hot: People of the time believed that one's physical and mental conditions were influenced by the balance of four major humors, or fluids, in the body—blood (hot and wet); yellow bile (hot and dry); phlegm (cold and wet); and black bile (cold and dry).
435. apothecaries: pharmacists.
439. Aesculapius: in Greek and Roman mythology, the god of medicine. The names that follow were early Greek, Roman, Middle Eastern, and medieval medical authorities.

446. superfluities: excesses.

? **451–454.** *How did the Doctor get his gold?*

458. Ypres . . . Ghent: Flemish centers of the wool trade.

463. ground: type of cloth.

Her hose were of the finest scarlet red
And gartered tight; her shoes were soft and new.
Bold was her face, handsome, and red in hue.
A worthy woman all her life, what's more
470 She'd had five husbands, all at the church door,
Apart from other company in youth;
No need just now to speak of that, forsooth.
And she had thrice been to Jerusalem,
Seen many strange rivers and passed over them;
475 She'd been to Rome and also to Boulogne,
St. James of Compostella and Cologne,
And she was skilled in wandering by the way.
She had gap-teeth,° set widely, truth to say.
Easily on an ambling horse she sat
480 Well wimpled° up, and on her head a hat
As broad as is a buckler or a shield;
She had a flowing mantle that concealed
Large hips, her heels spurred sharply under that.
In company she liked to laugh and chat
485 And knew the remedies for love's mischances,
An art in which she knew the oldest dances.

The Parson

A holy-minded man of good renown
There was, and poor, the *Parson* to a town,
Yet he was rich in holy thought and work. **K**
490 He also was a learned man, a clerk,
Who truly knew Christ's gospel and would preach it
Devoutly to parishioners, and teach it.
Benign and wonderfully diligent,
And patient when adversity was sent
495 (For so he proved in much adversity)
He hated cursing to extort a fee,
Nay rather he preferred beyond a doubt
Giving to poor parishioners round about
Both from church offerings and his property;
500 He could in little find sufficiency.
Wide was his parish, with houses far asunder,
Yet he neglected not in rain or thunder,
In sickness or in grief, to pay a call
On the remotest, whether great or small,
505 Upon his feet, and in his hand a stave.°

? **455–486.** *Does the Wife of Bath evoke any comic female stereotypes? Explain.*

478. gap-teeth: In Chaucer's time, gap-teeth on a woman were considered a sign of boldness and were said to indicate an aptitude for love and travel.

480. wimpled: A wimple is a linen covering for the head and neck.

The Parson, detail from *The Canterbury Tales,* by Geoffrey Chaucer.
The Huntington Library, San Marino, CA.

505. stave: staff.

K **Reading Focus** Analyzing Key Details How do the details contained in these opening lines contrast with the descriptions of the previous religious figures—the Nun, the Monk, and the Friar?

This noble example to his sheep° he gave
That first he wrought, and afterward he taught;
And it was from the Gospel he had caught
Those words, and he would add this figure too,
510   That if gold rust, what then will iron do?
For if a priest be foul in whom we trust
No wonder that a common man should rust;
And shame it is to see—let priests take stock—
A shitten shepherd and a snowy flock.
515   The true example that a priest should give
Is one of cleanness, how the sheep should live.
He did not set his benefice to hire°
And leave his sheep encumbered in the mire
Or run to London to earn easy bread
520   By singing masses for the wealthy dead,
Or find some Brotherhood and get enrolled.°
He stayed at home and watched over his fold
So that no wolf should make the sheep miscarry.
He was a shepherd and no mercenary.°
525   Holy and virtuous he was, but then
Never contemptuous of sinful men,
Never disdainful, never too proud or fine,
But was discreet in teaching and benign.
His business was to show a fair behavior
530   And draw men thus to Heaven and their Savior,
Unless indeed a man were obstinate;
And such, whether of high or low estate,°
He put to sharp rebuke, to say the least.
I think there never was a better priest.
535   He sought no pomp or glory in his dealings,
No scrupulosity had spiced his feelings.
Christ and His Twelve Apostles and their lore
He taught, but followed it himself before.

The Plowman

There was a *Plowman* with him there, his brother;
540   Many a load of dung one time or other
He must have carted through the morning dew.
He was an honest worker, good and true,
Living in peace and perfect charity,
And, as the gospel bade him, so did he,
545   Loving God best with all his heart and mind
And then his neighbor as himself, repined

506. **sheep:** his parishioners.

517. **He . . . benefice to hire:** He did not hire someone else to perform his duties.

521. **find . . . enrolled:** He did not take a job as a paid chaplain to a guild.
524. **mercenary:** someone who will agree to do anything for money.

532. **estate:** rank; social standing.

? 539–555. *How is the Plowman like his brother, the Parson? How can you tell that the narrator approves of him?*

Vocabulary **obstinate** (AHB stuh niht) *adj.:* unreasonably stubborn.

At no misfortune, slacked for no content,
For steadily about his work he went
To thrash his corn, to dig or to manure
550 Or make a ditch; and he would help the poor
For love of Christ and never take a penny
If he could help it, and, as prompt as any,
He paid his tithes in full when they were due
On what he owned, and on his earnings too.
555 He wore a tabard smock° and rode a mare. **Ⓛ**
     There was a *Reeve,*° also a *Miller,* there,
A College *Maniple*° from the Inns of Court,
A papal *Pardoner*° and, in close consort,
A Church-Court *Summoner,*° riding at a trot,
560 And finally myself—that was the lot.

The Miller

     The *Miller* was a chap of sixteen stone,°
A great stout fellow big in brawn and bone.
He did well out of them, for he could go
And win the ram at any wrestling show.
565 Broad, knotty, and short-shouldered, he would boast
He could heave any door off hinge and post,
Or take a run and break it with his head.
His beard, like any sow or fox, was red
And broad as well, as though it were a spade;
570 And, at its very tip, his nose displayed
A wart on which there stood a tuft of hair
Red as the bristles in an old sow's ear.
His nostrils were as black as they were wide.
He had a sword and buckler at his side,
575 His mighty mouth was like a furnace door.
A wrangler and buffoon, he had a store
Of tavern stories, filthy in the main.
His was a master-hand at stealing grain.
He felt it with his thumb and thus he knew
580 Its quality and took three times his due—
A thumb of gold, by God, to gauge an oat!°
He wore a hood of blue and a white coat.
He liked to play his bagpipes up and down
And that was how he brought us out of town.

555. tabard smock: short jacket.

556. reeve: serf who was the steward of a manor. A reeve saw that the estate's work was done and that everything was accounted for.

557. maniple: minor employee whose principal duty was to purchase provisions for a college or law firm.

558. pardoner: minor member of the Church who bought and sold pardons for sinners.

559. summoner: low-ranking officer who summoned people to appear in Church court.

561. sixteen stone: 224 pounds.

The Miller, detail from *The Canterbury Tales,* by Geoffrey Chaucer.
The Huntington Library, San Marino, CA.

❓ **568–575.** *Do any of the comparisons that the narrator makes flatter the character of the Miller? Explain.*

581. thumb . . . oat: In other words, he pressed on the scale with his thumb to increase the weight of the grain.

Ⓛ **Literary Focus** **Characterization** To which other character is the Plowman very similar? Why is this similarity unsurprising?

The Manciple

585   The *Manciple* came from the Inner Temple;°
All caterers might follow his example
In buying victuals; he was never rash
Whether he bought on credit or paid cash.
He used to watch the market most precisely
590 And got in first, and so he did quite nicely.
Now isn't it a marvel of God's grace
That an illiterate fellow can outpace
The wisdom of a heap of learned men?
His masters—he had more than thirty then—
595 All versed in the abstrusest° legal knowledge,
Could have produced a dozen from their College
Fit to be stewards in land and rents and game
To any Peer in England you could name,
And show him how to live on what he had
600 Debt-free (unless of course the Peer were mad)
Or be as frugal as he might desire,
And make them fit to help about the Shire
In any legal case there was to try;
And yet this Manciple could wipe their eye.°

The Reeve

605   The *Reeve* was old and choleric° and thin;
His beard was shaven closely to the skin,
His shorn hair came abruptly to a stop
Above his ears, and he was docked° on top
Just like a priest in front; his legs were lean,
610 Like sticks they were, no calf was to be seen.
He kept his bins and garners° very trim;
No auditor could gain a point on him.
And he could judge by watching drought and rain
The yield he might expect from seed and grain.
615 His master's sheep, his animals and hens,
Pigs, horses, dairies, stores, and cattle-pens
Were wholly trusted to his government.
He had been under contract to present
The accounts, right from his master's earliest years.
620 No one had ever caught him in arrears.°
No bailiff,° serf, or herdsman dared to kick,
He knew their dodges, knew their every trick;
Feared like the plague he was, by those beneath.

The Manciple, detail from *The Canterbury Tales*, by Geoffrey Chaucer. The Huntington Library, San Marino, CA.

585. Inner Temple: one of the four legal societies in London composing the Inns of Court. Only the Inns were permitted to license lawyers.
595. abstrusest: most complex; hardest to understand.

604. wipe their eye: outdo them. This medieval idiom means something like "steal their thunder" or "show them up."
605. choleric: having too much choler, or yellow bile, and thus (supposedly) bad-tempered.
608. docked: clipped short.
611. garners: granaries.

620. in arrears: behind schedule in repaying debts.
621. bailiff: here, farm manager.

Vocabulary   **frugal** (FROO guhl) *adj.:* thrifty; careful with money.

He had a lovely dwelling on a heath,
625 Shadowed in green by trees above the sward.°
A better hand at bargains than his lord,
He had grown rich and had a store of treasure
Well tucked away, yet out it came to pleasure
His lord with subtle loans or gifts of goods,
630 To earn his thanks and even coats and hoods.
When young he'd learnt a useful trade and still
He was a carpenter of first-rate skill.
The stallion-cob° he rode at a slow trot
Was dapple-gray and bore the name of Scot.
635 He wore an overcoat of bluish shade
And rather long; he had a rusty blade
Slung at his side. He came, as I heard tell,
From Norfolk, near a place called Baldeswell.
His coat was tucked under his belt and splayed.
640 He rode the hindmost of our cavalcade. Ⓜ

The Summoner

There was a *Summoner*° with us at that Inn,
His face on fire, like a cherubim,°
For he had carbuncles.° His eyes were narrow,
He was as hot and lecherous as a sparrow.
645 Black scabby brows he had, and a thin beard.
Children were afraid when he appeared.
No quicksilver, lead ointment, tartar creams,
No brimstone, no boracic, so it seems,
Could make a salve that had the power to bite,
650 Clean up, or cure his whelks° of knobby white
Or purge the pimples sitting on his cheeks.
Garlic he loved, and onions too, and leeks,
And drinking strong red wine till all was hazy.
Then he would shout and jabber as if crazy,
655 And wouldn't speak a word except in Latin
When he was drunk, such tags as he was pat in;
He only had a few, say two or three,
That he had mugged up out of some decree;
No wonder, for he heard them every day.
660 And, as you know, a man can teach a jay°
To call out "Walter" better than the Pope.
But had you tried to test his wits and grope
For more, you'd have found nothing in the bag.
Then *"Questio quid juris"*° was his tag.

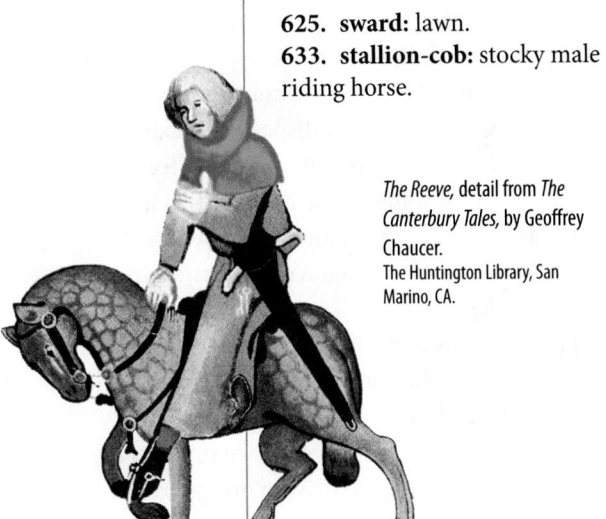

625. **sward:** lawn.
633. **stallion-cob:** stocky male riding horse.

The Reeve, detail from *The Canterbury Tales,* by Geoffrey Chaucer.
The Huntington Library, San Marino, CA.

642. **cherubim:** in medieval art, a little angel with a rosy face.
643. **carbuncles:** pus-filled skin inflammations, similar to boils.

650. **whelks:** pus-filled sores.

? 641–666. *How does the Summoner's physical appearance (lines 642–651) match his inner character? How do you know that Chaucer is being ironic in lines 665–666?*

660. **jay:** type of bird.

664. ***Questio quid juris:*** Latin for "I ask what point of the law [applies]." The Summoner uses this phrase to stall and dodge the issue.

Ⓜ **Literary Focus** Characterization Based on this sketch, what is the narrator's opinion of the Reeve?

665   He was a noble varlet° and a kind one,
        You'd meet none better if you went to find one.
        Why, he'd allow—just for a quart of wine—
        Any good lad to keep a concubine
        A twelvemonth and dispense him altogether!
670   And he had finches of his own to feather:°
        And if he found some rascal with a maid
        He would instruct him not to be afraid
        In such a case of the Archdeacon's curse
        (Unless the rascal's soul were in his purse)
675   For in his purse the punishment should be.
        "Purse is the good Archdeacon's Hell," said he.
        But well I know he lied in what he said;
        A curse should put a guilty man in dread,
        For curses kill, as shriving brings, salvation.
680   We should beware of excommunication.
        Thus, as he pleased, the man could bring duress
        On any young fellow in the diocese.
        He knew their secrets, they did what he said.
        He wore a garland set upon his head
685   Large as the holly-bush upon a stake
        Outside an ale-house, and he had a cake,
        A round one, which it was his joke to wield
        As if it were intended for a shield.

The Pardoner

        He and a gentle *Pardoner* rode together,
690   A bird from Charing Cross of the same feather,
        Just back from visiting the Court of Rome.
        He loudly sang *"Come hither, love, come home!"*
        The Summoner sang deep seconds° to this song,
        No trumpet ever sounded half so strong.
695   This Pardoner had hair as yellow as wax,
        Hanging down smoothly like a hank of flax.
        In driblets fell his locks behind his head
        Down to his shoulders which they overspread;
        Thinly they fell, like rat-tails, one by one.
700   He wore no hood upon his head, for fun;
        The hood inside his wallet had been stowed,
        He aimed at riding in the latest mode;
        But for a little cap his head was bare
        And he had bulging eye-balls, like a hare.
705   He'd sewed a holy relic° on his cap;

665. varlet: scoundrel.

670. finches . . . feather: taking care of his own interests.

The Summoner, detail from *The Canterbury Tales,* by Geoffrey Chaucer. The Huntington Library, San Marino, CA.

689. pardoner: one dispensed pardons granted by the pope.

? **689–704.** *How do such details as "yellow as wax," "driblets," "like rat-tails," and "bulging eye-balls, like a hare" affect the way you feel about this man?*

693. deep seconds: harmonies.

705. relic: remains of a saint.

N **Literary Focus** **Characterization** What final impression of the Summoner is created through the description in lines 684–688?

His wallet lay before him on his lap,
Brimful of pardons° come from Rome, all hot.
He had the same small voice a goat has got.
His chin no beard had harbored, nor would harbor,
710 Smoother than ever chin was left by barber.
I judge he was a gelding, or a mare.
As to his trade, from Berwick down to Ware
There was no pardoner of equal grace,
For in his trunk he had a pillow-case
715 Which he asserted was Our Lady's veil.
He said he had a gobbet° of the sail
Saint Peter had the time when he made bold
To walk the waves, till Jesu Christ took hold.
He had a cross of metal set with stones
720 And, in a glass, a rubble of pigs' bones.
And with these relics, any time he found
Some poor up-country parson to astound,
In one short day, in money down, he drew
More than the parson in a month or two,   **O**
725 And by his flatteries and prevarication°
Made monkeys of the priest and congregation.
But still to do him justice first and last
In church he was a noble ecclesiast.°
How well he read a lesson or told a story!
730 But best of all he sang an Offertory,°
For well he knew that when that song was sung
He'd have to preach and tune his honey-tongue
And (well he could) win silver from the crowd.
That's why he sang so merrily and loud.
735   Now I have told you shortly, in a clause,
The rank, the array, the number, and the cause
Of our assembly in this company
In Southwark, at that high-class hostelry
Known as *The Tabard*, close beside *The Bell.*
740 And now the time has come for me to tell
How we behaved that evening; I'll begin
After we had alighted at the Inn,
Then I'll report our journey, stage by stage,
All the remainder of our pilgrimage.
745 But first I beg of you, in courtesy,
Not to condemn me as unmannerly
If I speak plainly and with no concealings
And give account of all their words and dealings,

707. pardons: small strips of parchment with papal seals attached. They were sold as indulgences (pardons for sins), with the proceeds supposedly going to a religious house.

716. gobbet: fragment.

? 714–734. *These lines depict the Pardoner as a scam artist. If this is the case, why do people fall for his tricks?*

725. prevarication: telling lies.

728. ecclesiast: practitioner of Church ritual.

730. Offertory: hymn sung while offerings are collected in church.

The Pardoner, detail from *The Canterbury Tales,* by Geoffrey Chaucer.
The Huntington Library, San Marino, CA.

? 740–744. *How will the narrator organize the rest of his narrative?*

O Reading Focus Analyzing Key Details Why do you think the poet chooses to include a comparison to the Parson here?

Analyzing Visuals

Viewing and Interpreting Why does the painter use contrasting colors in the dress of the pilgrims? How might different colors be used to suggest different character traits?

Using their very phrases as they fell.
750　For certainly, as you all know so well,
He who repeats a tale after a man
Is bound to say, as nearly as he can,
Each single word, if he remembers it,
However rudely spoken or unfit,
755　Or else the tale he tells will be untrue,
The things pretended and the phrases new.
He may not flinch although it were his brother,
He may as well say one word as another.
And Christ Himself spoke broad in Holy Writ,
760　Yet there is no scurrility° in it,
And Plato says, for those with power to read,
"The word should be as cousin to the deed."
Further I beg you to forgive it me
If I neglect the order and degree
765　And what is due to rank in what I've planned.
I'm short of wit as you will understand.

745–766. *What is the narrator apologizing for in advance?*

760. scurrility: indecency.

Canterbury Pilgrims, by Alfred George Webster (fl. 1876–1917).
Lincolnshire County Council, Usher Gallery, Lincoln, UK.

The Host

Our *Host* gave us great welcome; everyone
Was given a place and supper was begun.
He served the finest victuals you could think,
770   The wine was strong and we were glad to drink.
A very striking man our Host withal,
And fit to be a marshal in a hall.
His eyes were bright, his girth a little wide;
There is no finer burgess in Cheapside.°
775   Bold in his speech, yet wise and full of tact,
There was no manly attribute he lacked,
What's more he was a merry-hearted man.
After our meal he jokingly began
To talk of sport, and, among other things   ⓟ
780   After we'd settled up our reckonings,
He said as follows: "Truly, gentlemen,
You're very welcome and I can't think when
—Upon my word I'm telling you no lie—
I've seen a gathering here that looked so spry,

774. Cheapside: district of medieval London.

ⓟ **Literary Focus** **Characterization** What do you learn about the Host in lines 771–779? How do you think the narrator feels about the Host? Explain.

785 No, not this year, as in this tavern now.
     I'd think you up some fun if I knew how.
     And, as it happens, a thought has just occurred
     To please you, costing nothing, on my word.
     You're off to Canterbury—well, God speed!
790 Blessed St. Thomas answer to your need!
     And I don't doubt, before the journey's done
     You mean to while the time in tales and fun.
     Indeed, there's little pleasure for your bones
     Riding along and all as dumb as stones.
795 So let me then propose for your enjoyment,
     Just as I said, a suitable employment.
     And if my notion suits and you agree
     And promise to submit yourselves to me
     Playing your parts exactly as I say
800 Tomorrow as you ride along the way,
     Then by my father's soul (and he is dead)
     If you don't like it you can have my head!
     Hold up your hands, and not another word."
     Well, our opinion was not long deferred,
805 It seemed not worth a serious debate;
     We all agreed to it at any rate
     And bade him issue what commands he would.
     "My lords," he said, "now listen for your good,
     And please don't treat my notion with disdain.
810 This is the point. I'll make it short and plain.
     Each one of you shall help to make things slip
     By telling two stories on the outward trip
     To Canterbury, that's what I intend,
     And, on the homeward way to journey's end
815 Another two, tales from the days of old;
     And then the man whose story is best told,
     That is to say who gives the fullest measure
     Of good morality and general pleasure,
     He shall be given a supper, paid by all,
820 Here in this tavern, in this very hall,
     When we come back again from Canterbury.
     And in the hope to keep you bright and merry
     I'll go along with you myself and ride
     All at my own expense and serve as guide.
825 I'll be the judge, and those who won't obey
     Shall pay for what we spend upon the way.
     Now if you all agree to what you've heard
     Tell me at once without another word,
     And I will make arrangements early for it."
830   Of course we all agreed, in fact we swore it
     Delightedly, and made entreaty° too

781–803. *What do words like fun (line 786), pleasure (line 793), and enjoyment (line 795) suggest about the Host's character?*

Figure thought to be Chaucer, detail from *The Canterbury Tales,* by Geoffrey Chaucer. The Huntington Library, San Marino, CA.

811–829. *Summarize the rules the Host proposes for the storytelling competition. What is the prize? Who will be the judge?*

825. those who won't obey: refers to those who won't play the game of telling a story when it's their turn. Lines 853–854 further clarify their penalty: Those who won't obey must pay the cost of the entire journey.

831. entreaty: urgent request.

That he should act as he proposed to do,
  Become our Governor in short, and be
Judge of our tales and general referee,
835   And set the supper at a certain price.
We promised to be ruled by his advice
Come high, come low; unanimously thus
We set him up in judgment over us.
More wine was fetched, the business being done;
840   We drank it off and up went everyone
To bed without a moment of delay.
    Early next morning at the spring of day
Up rose our Host and roused us like a cock,
Gathering us together in a flock,
845   And off we rode at slightly faster pace
Than walking to St. Thomas' watering-place;
And there our Host drew up, began to ease
His horse, and said, "Now, listen if you please,
My lords! Remember what you promised me.
850   If evensong and matins will agree°
Let's see who shall be first to tell a tale.
And as I hope to drink good wine and ale
I'll be your judge. The rebel who disobeys,
However much the journey costs, he pays.
855   Now draw for cut° and then we can depart;
The man who draws the shortest cut shall start." **Q**

850. if . . . agree: in other words, if you feel the same way in the evening (at evensong, or evening prayers) as you do in the morning (at matins, or morning prayers).
855. draw for cut: in other words, draw straws.

Q **Literary Focus** **Frame Story** Why are lines 848–856 an important element of the frame story of *The Canterbury Tales*?

Respond and Think Critically

Reading Focus

Quick Check

1. How does the April setting help motivate the travelers to go on their journey?

2. Where is the narrator at the beginning of the Prologue? Who joins him, and why?

3. Why is the Parson so poor?

4. How does the Host encourage the travelers to tell their stories?

Read with a Purpose

5. How important do you think someone's occupation was in medieval society?

Reading Skills: Analyzing Style: Key Details

6. In your chart, you recorded key details Chaucer uses to describe each main character. Add a new column in which you describe how and why each detail made you feel a certain way about the character.

Main Character	Key Detail	What Detail Emphasizes	What It Makes You Feel
the Knight	"He had done nobly in his sovereign's war / And ridden into battle"	He's a brave man, a strong warrior, and someone of great experience.	I admire him because he was willing to risk his life for the people of his kingdom.

Literary Focus

Literary Analysis

7. **Analyze** What aspects of medieval society does Chaucer satirize in his portrayals of the Merchant, Franklin, Doctor, and Miller?

8. **Compare and Contrast** Some of the poem's characters contrast strikingly with each other, and others display strong similarities. Choose a contrasting pair and a similar pair. Explain the differences and similarities in each pair.

9. **Evaluate** Which pilgrims does Chaucer idealize?

10. **Interpret** What do the narrator's descriptions of others reveal about his biases and values?

Literary Skills: Characterization

11. **Evaluate** Chaucer uses physical details to reveal character. Describe three pilgrims whose inner natures are revealed by their appearance.

Literary Skills: Frame Story

12. **Analyze** Describe the Prologue's frame story and how it sets up the rest of the *Tales*.

Literary Skills Review: Foil

13. **Make Judgments** A **foil** is a character who emphasizes another character's qualities by sharp contrast. Which two characters are the most striking opposites? How do they act as foils for each other?

Writing Focus

Think as a Reader/Writer

Use It in Your Writing Chaucer's descriptions create strong impressions of each character's appearance. Write a paragraph describing the appearance of a fictional character. Use details that reveal characteristics, such as status, habits, self-image, and inner nature.

 What Do You Think Now

What motivated the Host to join the group of travelers and serve as their leader?

Vocabulary Development

✓ Vocabulary Check

Choose the Vocabulary word that best completes each sentence.

1. Convincing the guard to let them past the gate was going to require some _____.

2. If he was going to save up enough money for the trip, he'd have to be _____ for the next couple of months.

3. Even though the players were right, the bullheaded coach was too _____ to agree with them.

4. His long tenure and impressive collection of awards made him the university's _____ professor.

5. She was always sympathetic to others' troubles, and she approached everyone with a _____ attitude.

Vocabulary Skills: Antonyms

Antonyms are words that are have opposite meanings, such as *smooth* and *rough*. Antonyms are also usually the same part of speech. For example, although the noun *sorrow* and the adjective *joyful* are associated with contrasting ideas, they are not antonyms. An antonym for *sorrow* would be another noun, such as *joy*. The following chart show pairs of antonyms and their parts of speech.

Word	Part of Speech	Antonym
seller	*noun*	buyer
yell	*verb*	whisper
mournful	*adjective*	cheerful
rapidly	*adverb*	slowly

Your Turn

Create an antonym chart like the one at the left for the Vocabulary words. Be sure to include the part of speech of each Vocabulary word and match it to that of its antonym.

Language Coach

Commonly Confused Words Practice with tricky words can help you use them correctly. Choose the best word to complete each sentence. Use a dictionary to understand how each word is used. Then, explain your choices.

1. Today, Chaucer is one of the most (*eminent, imminent*) writers of the Middle Ages.

2. He believed that people would (*accept, except*) tales written in English instead of Latin.

3. One (*affect, effect*) of writing in English was that more people could understand his tales.

4. He (*preceded, proceeded*) other great English writers, such as Shakespeare and Milton.

Academic Vocabulary

Write About . . .

Chaucer creates characters who reflect the richness and diversity of human nature. In a short essay, analyze the character who most intrigues you. Describe the character's attributes, social status, and role. Explain what Chaucer emphasizes about him or her and the techniques Chaucer uses to characterize this person. Cite specific examples from the Prologue, and use the underlined Academic Vocabulary words in your analysis.

The Prologue to The Canterbury Tales

Grammar Link

Progressive Form of Verbs

Each verb has a **progressive form,** which expresses a continuing action or state of being. The progressive form consists of the appropriate tense of the verb *be* plus the *–ing* form of a verb. Progressive forms exist for present, present perfect, past, past perfect, future, and future perfect verbs.

I am traveling to Canterbury.
PRESENT PROGRESSIVE

The page has been playing his lute all day.
PRESENT PERFECT PROGRESSIVE

They were telling tales to entertain each other.
PAST PROGRESSIVE

The Wife of Bath had been telling us a story.
PAST PERFECT PROGRESSIVE

We will be deciding the winner on the way back.
FUTURE PROGRESSIVE

By the time the trip ends, they will have been traveling for days. FUTURE PERFECT PROGRESSIVE

Your Turn

Rewrite the following sentences using a progressive form of a verb.

1. The Host enjoys a rowdy tale.
2. The pilgrims will converse on their way to Canterbury tomorrow.
3. The guildsmen hoped to advance in society.
4. The Oxford Cleric will return to Oxford after this trip to Canterbury.

Writing Application When might it make sense to use the progressive form of verbs in your writing? Experiment by replacing the verbs with the progressive form in a paragraph you have already written.

SKILLS FOCUS **Writing Skills** Plan writing by creating an outline; plan writing by organizing ideas and information. **Grammar Skills** Identify and use verbs; understand the use of progressive tense. **Listening and Speaking Skills** Adapt to task when speaking.

CHOICES

As you respond to the Choices, use these **Academic Vocabulary** words as appropriate: attribute, concept, diverse, emphasis, status.

REVIEW

Define Past Lives

Timed Writing Chaucer's descriptions of the pilgrims correspond to the strict classifications of social status observed in the Middle Ages. Choose two of the pilgrims that represent distinctly different social classes. Explain in an essay how Chaucer's portraits of the individuals convey his feelings about the social classes each represents. Use textual evidence to support your response.

CONNECT

Write a Frame Story

Timed Writing Write your own prologue to a modern frame story. Set your story in an airport or bus station or on a tour or pilgrimage. You might establish your frame by featuring characters who are stranded by a storm or waiting for rescue from an accident. Select a narrator, and describe the travelers with diverse characteristics, roles, and professions. Emphasize attributes that reveal characters' inner natures.

EXTEND

Tell Your Own Story

By the Prologue's end, the Host has convinced everyone to tell a story. What story might you tell in such a competition? Think of an event from your own life that might make an entertaining story, and write notes to help you recall the key details. Outline your notes, and practice telling your story. Then, tell your story to the whole class or in a small group.

Learn It Online
Tell your story in a twenty-first-century form— through a digital story. Learn how online.

go.hrw.com | L12-148 | **Go**

Preparing to Read

from The Pardoner's Tale

Reader/Writer Notebook

Use your **RWN** to complete the activities for this selection.

Literary Focus

Verbal and Situational Irony A discrepancy between appearance and reality is called **irony.** Chaucer uses irony throughout *The Canterbury Tales.* **Situational irony** occurs when what actually happens is the opposite of what is expected. **Verbal irony** occurs when someone says one thing but really means something else. The contrast seen in the Pardoner, who preaches against vice and should be helping people, but in reality is selfish and corrupt, creates both situational and verbal irony.

Reading Focus

Drawing Conclusions When you **draw a conclusion,** you form a concept that is based on the text but not explicitly stated. In "The Pardoner's Tale," characters refer to Death as if he is an actual person. By noticing, however, how events are described, you can conclude that Death represents the idea of dying.

Into Action As you read, record your conclusions in the first column of a chart like the one below. In the second column, explain how the text supports those conclusions.

Conclusion	How Conclusion Is Supported
Death is the idea or presence of death, not an actual person.	The characters speak of Death as a character, so we expect to meet him as a character. However, we never see him personified.

Writing Focus

Think as a Reader/Writer

Find It In Your Reading "The Pardoner's Tale" is filled with devious characters, and what they say is often very different from what they actually mean. As you read, notice the **verbal irony** that results from this contrast between a character's words and meaning. In your *Reader/Writer Notebook*, record the examples of verbal irony that you find most interesting.

TechFocus As you read, think about the different ways you encounter stories in the modern world.

Vocabulary

avarice (AV uhr ihs) *n.:* uncontrolled desire for wealth. *His avarice led him to seek riches at the expense of others.*

abominable (uh BAHM uh nuh buhl) *adj.:* disgusting; hateful. *Poisoning the friend who trusted him was an abominable act.*

adversary (AD vuhr sehr ee) *n.:* enemy; opponent. *Sin should have been the Pardoner's adversary, but it seemed to be one of his closest friends.*

pallor (PAL uhr) *n.:* paleness. *Death is traditionally pictured with a sickening pallor.*

absolve (ab SAHLV) *v.:* forgive; make free from blame. *After the man confesses his sins, the Pardoner should absolve him.*

Language Coach

Forms of Words The word *absolve* is a verb that means "to forgive." It is related to the noun *absolution*, which means "forgiveness." Notice that the *v* changes to a *u* in the noun form. How can you follow the same pattern and change the verbs *solve* and *revolve* into nouns? What do the new words mean?

Learn It Online
Delve deeper into the Vocabulary words with Word Watch online.

go.hrw.com   L12-149   **Go**

HAR

FROM
The Pardoner's Tale

by **Geoffrey Chaucer**

translated by **Nevill Coghill**

Read with a Purpose
Read to discover how Chaucer uses the Pardoner's tale to explore the impulses that lead people to be destructive.

Build Background
In the medieval Church, a pardoner was a clergyman with the power to forgive sins and grant indulgences, the Church's relief from temporal and purgatorial punishments for sins. Forgiving sins and granting indulgences were powers the pope bestowed upon the clergy to spiritually benefit believers. Such benefits were not supposed to be bought and sold, but greedy clergy sometimes took advantage of people's fear of punishment and demanded money. Some, like Chaucer's Pardoner, kept the money for themselves.

The Pardoner, detail from *The Canterbury Tales,* by Geoffrey Chaucer. The Huntington Library, San Marino, CA.

FROM *The Pardoner's Prologue*

"But let me briefly make my purpose plain;
I preach for nothing but for greed of gain
And use the same old text, as bold as brass,
Radix malorum est cupiditas.°
5   And thus I preach against the very vice
I make my living out of—avarice.
And yet however guilty of that sin
Myself, with others I have power to win
Them from it, I can bring them to repent;
10 But that is not my principal intent. **Ⓐ**
Covetousness° is both the root and stuff
Of all I preach. That ought to be enough.
   "Well, then I give examples thick and fast
From bygone times, old stories from the past.

4. *Radix malorum est cupiditas* (RAH dihks mah LOH rum ehst koo PIH dih tahs). Latin: literally, "The root of evil is desire" (1 Timothy 6:10). The Pardoner has been telling the pilgrims about his preaching methods.

11. covetousness: quality of craving wealth or possessions; greed.

Ⓐ **Reading Focus** Drawing Conclusions Why does the Pardoner admit he preaches to make a personal profit?

Vocabulary **avarice** (AV uhr ihs) *n.:* uncontrolled desire for wealth.

(Opposite) The Knight and the Squire from "The Pardoner's Prologue" from The Canterbury Tales, by Henry Milham (1873–1957).

15   A yokel° mind loves stories from of old,
Being the kind it can repeat and hold.
What! Do you think, as long as I can preach
And get their silver for the things I teach,
That I will live in poverty, from choice?
20   That's not the counsel of my inner voice!
No! Let me preach and beg from kirk° to kirk
And never do an honest job of work,
No, nor make baskets, like St. Paul, to gain
A livelihood. I do not preach in vain.
25   There's no apostle I would counterfeit;
I mean to have money, wool and cheese and wheat
Though it were given me by the poorest lad
Or poorest village widow, though she had
A string of starving children, all agape.°
30   No, let me drink the liquor of the grape
And keep a jolly wench in every town!
     "But listen, gentlemen; to bring things down
To a conclusion, would you like a tale?
Now as I've drunk a draft of corn-ripe ale,
35   By God it stands to reason I can strike
On some good story that you all will like.
For though I am a wholly vicious° man
Don't think I can't tell moral tales. I can!
Here's one I often preach when out for winning;
40   Now please be quiet. Here is the beginning."

The Pardoner's Tale

In Flanders once there was a company
Of youngsters haunting vice and ribaldry,°
Riot and gambling, stews and public-houses
Where each with harp, guitar, or lute carouses,°
45   Dancing and dicing° day and night, and bold
To eat and drink far more than they can hold,
Doing thereby the devil sacrifice
Within that devil's temple of cursed vice,
Abominable in superfluity,
50   With oaths so damnable in blasphemy°
That it's a grisly thing to hear them swear.
Our dear Lord's body they will rend and tear.° . . .
It's of three rioters° I have to tell
Who, long before the morning service bell,
55   Were sitting in a tavern for a drink.

15. yokel: rustic; of the country.

21. kirk: Scottish for "church."

29. agape: open-mouthed.

37. vicious: here, possessing many faults.

42. ribaldry: vulgar language or humor.
44. carouses: drinks and celebrates noisily.
45. dicing: gambling (throwing dice).

50. blasphemy: mockery of God.

52. Our . . . tear: Their oaths refer to "God's arms" and "God's blessed bones."
53. rioters: people living a wild, unrestrained lifestyle.

Vocabulary **abominable** (uh BAHM uh nuh buhl) *adj.*: disgusting; hateful.

And as they sat, they heard the hand-bell clink
Before a coffin going to the grave;
One of them called the little tavern-knave°
And said "Go and find out at once—look spry!—
60 Whose corpse is in that coffin passing by;
And see you get the name correctly too."
"Sir," said the boy, "no need, I promise you;
Two hours before you came here I was told.
He was a friend of yours in days of old,
65 And suddenly, last night, the man was slain,
Upon his bench, face up, dead drunk again.
There came a privy° thief, they call him Death,
Who kills us all round here, and in a breath
He speared him through the heart, he never stirred.
70 And then Death went his way without a word.
He's killed a thousand in the present plague,°
And, sir, it doesn't do to be too vague
If you should meet him; you had best be wary.
Be on your guard with such an adversary,
75 Be primed to meet him everywhere you go,
That's what my mother said. It's all I know."
    The publican° joined in with, "By St. Mary,
What the child says is right; you'd best be wary,
This very year he killed, in a large village
80 A mile away, man, woman, serf at tillage,°
Page in the household, children—all there were.
Yes, I imagine that he lives round there.
It's well to be prepared in these alarms,°
He might do you dishonor." "Huh, God's arms!"
85 The rioter said, "Is he so fierce to meet?
I'll search for him, by Jesus, street by street.
God's blessed bones! I'll register a vow!
Here, chaps! The three of us together now,
Hold up your hands, like me, and we'll be brothers
90 In this affair, and each defend the others,
And we will kill this traitor Death, I say! **B**
Away with him as he has made away
With all our friends. God's dignity! Tonight!"
    They made their bargain, swore with appetite,
95 These three, to live and die for one another
As brother-born might swear to his born brother.
And up they started in their drunken rage

58. **tavern-knave:** serving boy.

67. **privy:** archaic usage meaning "secretive; furtive."

71. **present plague:** the Black Death, which killed nearly one third of the population of England during the mid-fourteenth century.

77. **publican:** tavern keeper; from *public house,* a tavern or inn.
80. **tillage:** working the land.

83. **alarms:** here, anxious times.

B **Literary Focus** **Irony** Why is it ironic that the rioters vow as brothers to kill Death? Would you categorize this irony as verbal or situational?

Vocabulary **adversary** (AD vuhr sehr ee) *n.:* enemy; opponent.

And made towards this village which the page
And publican had spoken of before.
100 Many and grisly were the oaths they swore,
Tearing Christ's blessed body to a shred;
"If we can only catch him, Death is dead!"
    When they had gone not fully half a mile,
Just as they were about to cross a stile,°
105 They came upon a very poor old man
Who humbly greeted them and thus began,
"God look to you, my lords, and give you quiet!" **C**
To which the proudest of these men of riot
Gave back the answer, "What, old fool? Give place!
110 Why are you all wrapped up except your face?
Why live so long? Isn't it time to die?"
    The old, old fellow looked him in the eye
And said, "Because I never yet have found,
Though I have walked to India, searching round
115 Village and city on my pilgrimage,
One who would change his youth to have my age
And so my age is mine and must be still
Upon me, for such time as God may will.
    "Not even Death, alas, will take my life;
120 So, like a wretched prisoner at strife
Within himself, I walk alone and wait
About the earth, which is my mother's gate,°
Knock-knocking with my staff from night to noon
And crying, 'Mother, open to me soon!
125 Look at me, mother, won't you let me in?
See how I wither, flesh and blood and skin!
Alas! When will these bones be laid to rest?
Mother, I would exchange—for that were best—
The wardrobe in my chamber, standing there
130 So long, for yours! Aye, for a shirt of hair°
To wrap me in!' She has refused her grace,
Whence comes the pallor of my withered face.
    "But it dishonored you when you began
To speak so roughly, sir, to an old man,
135 Unless he had injured you in word or deed.
It says in holy writ,° as you may read,
'Thou shalt rise up before the hoary° head
And honor it.' And therefore be it said,
'Do no more harm to an old man than you,

---

104. **stile:** steps used for climbing over a wall.

122. **mother's gate:** The old man refers to Death as a mother, her house surrounded by a gate (the earth). Thus, "mother's gate" is the entrance to a grave.

130. **shirt of hair:** Coarse shirts of woven horsehair were worn as penance. Here, the old man refers to such a shirt to be used to wrap his body for burial.

136. **holy writ:** the Bible.
137. **hoary:** white.

C **Reading Focus** Drawing Conclusions Who is this old man? What might he represent, or what purpose might he serve in the story?

Vocabulary **pallor** (PAL uhr) *n*.: paleness.

140   Being now young, would have another do
      When you are old'—if you should live till then.
      And so may God be with you, gentlemen,
      For I must go whither I have to go."
          "By God," the gambler said, "you shan't do so,
145   You don't get off so easy, by St. John!
      I heard you mention, just a moment gone,
      A certain traitor Death who singles out
      And kills the fine young fellows hereabout.
      And you're his spy, by God! You wait a bit.
150   Say where he is or you shall pay for it,
      By God and by the Holy Sacrament!
      I say you've joined together by consent
      To kill us younger folk, you thieving swine!"
          "Well, sirs," he said, "if it be your design
155   To find out Death, turn up this crooked way
      Towards that grove, I left him there today
      Under a tree, and there you'll find him waiting.
      He isn't one to hide for all your prating.°
      You see that oak? He won't be far to find.
160   And God protect you that redeemed mankind,
      Aye, and amend° you!" Thus that ancient man.
          At once the three young rioters began
      To run, and reached the tree, and there they found
      A pile of golden florins° on the ground,
165   New-coined, eight bushels of them as they thought.
      No longer was it Death those fellows sought,   **D**
      For they were all so thrilled to see the sight,
      The florins were so beautiful and bright,
      That down they sat beside the precious pile.
170   The wickedest spoke first after a while.
      "Brothers," he said, "you listen to what I say.
      I'm pretty sharp although I joke away.
      It's clear that Fortune has bestowed this treasure
      To let us live in jollity and pleasure.
175   Light come, light go! We'll spend it as we ought.
      God's precious dignity! Who would have thought
      This morning was to be our lucky day?
          "If one could only get the gold away,
      Back to my house, or else to yours, perhaps—
180   For as you know, the gold is ours, chaps—
      We'd all be at the top of fortune, hey?
      But certainly it can't be done by day.
      People would call us robbers—a strong gang,
      So our own property would make us hang.

Death with his spear, from "The Pardoner's Tale." The Bodleian Library, University of Oxford. MS Douce, 105r.

158. prating: chattering.

161. amend: improve.

164. florins: coins worth twenty-four pence. *Pence* is the British plural of *penny*.

French Psalter and Prayer Book of Bonne of Luxembourg, Duchess of Normandy (before 1349), probably by Jean Le Noir, his daughter Bourgot, and his workshop.
The Metropolitan Museum of Art. The Cloisters Collection 1969 (69.86) 69.86, folio 321v–322r.

D Literary Focus **Irony** What is ironic about the rioters' discovery?

185 No, we must bring this treasure back by night
Some prudent way, and keep it out of sight.
And so as a solution I propose
We draw for lots and see the way it goes;
The one who draws the longest, lucky man,
190 Shall run to town as quickly as he can
To fetch us bread and wine—but keep things dark°—
While two remain in hiding here to mark
Our heap of treasure. If there's no delay,
When night comes down we'll carry it away,
195 All three of us, wherever we have planned."
            He gathered lots and hid them in his hand
Bidding them draw for where the luck should fall.
It fell upon the youngest of them all,
And off he ran at once towards the town.
200 As soon as he had gone the first sat down
And thus began a parley° with the other:
"You know that you can trust me as a brother;
Now let me tell you where your profit lies;
You know our friend has gone to get supplies
205 And here's a lot of gold that is to be
Divided equally among us three.
Nevertheless, if I could shape things thus
So that we shared it out—the two of us—
Wouldn't you take it as a friendly act?"
210   "But how?" the other said. "He knows the fact
That all the gold was left with me and you;
What can we tell him? What are we to do?"
"Is it a bargain," said the first, "or no?
For I can tell you in a word or so
215 What's to be done to bring the thing about."
"Trust me," the other said, "you needn't doubt
My word. I won't betray you, I'll be true."
      "Well," said his friend, "you see that we are two,
And two are twice as powerful as one.
220 Now look; when he comes back, get up in fun
To have a wrestle; then, as you attack,
I'll up and put my dagger through his back
While you and he are struggling, as in game;
Then draw your dagger too and do the same.
225 Then all this money will be ours to spend,
Divided equally of course, dear friend.
Then we can gratify our lusts and fill
The day with dicing at our own sweet will." **E**

191. keep things dark: do it in secret.

201. parley: discussion.

E **Literary Focus** Irony Why is this discussion between the two rioters ironic? Is this verbal or situational irony?

The three Rogues search in the woods for Death

Analyzing Visuals

Viewing and Interpreting Briefly describe what is happening in this illustration. What irony does this scene convey?

The Pardoner's Tale: The three rogues search in the woods for Death (1907), illustration by Walter Appleton Clark.

Thus these two miscreants° agreed to slay
230   The third and youngest, as you heard me say.
     The youngest, as he ran towards the town,
Kept turning over, rolling up and down
Within his heart the beauty of those bright
New florins, saying, "Lord, to think I might
235   Have all that treasure to myself alone!
Could there be anyone beneath the throne
Of God so happy as I then should be?"
     And so the Fiend,° our common enemy,
Was given power to put it in his thought
240   That there was always poison to be bought,
And that with poison he could kill his friends.
To men in such a state the Devil sends
Thoughts of this kind, and has a full permission
To lure them on to sorrow and perdition;°
245   For this young man was utterly content
To kill them both and never to repent.
     And on he ran, he had no thought to tarry,
Came to the town, found an apothecary°
And said, "Sell me some poison if you will,

229. miscreants: criminals; literally, "unbelievers."

238. Fiend: the devil.

244. perdition: damnation.

248. apothecary: druggist. Formerly, apothecaries made and prescribed medications.

250 I have a lot of rats I want to kill
And there's a polecat too about my yard
That takes my chickens and it hits me hard;
But I'll get even, as is only right,
With vermin that destroy a man by night." **F**

255 The chemist answered, "I've a preparation
Which you shall have, and by my soul's salvation
If any living creature eat or drink
A mouthful, ere° he has the time to think,
Though he took less than makes a grain of wheat,

260 You'll see him fall down dying at your feet;
Yes, die he must, and in so short a while
You'd hardly have the time to walk a mile,
The poison is so strong, you understand."
This cursed fellow grabbed into his hand

265 The box of poison and away he ran
Into a neighboring street, and found a man
Who lent him three large bottles. He withdrew
And deftly poured the poison into two.
He kept the third one clean, as well he might,

270 For his own drink, meaning to work all night
Stacking the gold and carrying it away.
And when this rioter, this devil's clay,
Had filled his bottles up with wine, all three,
Back to rejoin his comrades sauntered° he.

275 Why make a sermon of it? Why waste breath?
Exactly in the way they'd planned his death
They fell on him and slew him, two to one.
Then said the first of them when this was done,
"Now for a drink. Sit down and let's be merry,

280 For later on there'll be the corpse to bury."
And, as it happened, reaching for a sup,
He took a bottle full of poison up
And drank; and his companion, nothing loth,°
Drank from it also, and they perished both.

285 There is, in Avicenna's° long relation
Concerning poison and its operation,
Trust me, no ghastlier section to transcend
What these two wretches suffered at their end.
Thus these two murderers received their due,

290 So did the treacherous young poisoner too. . . .
"One thing I should have mentioned in my tale,
Dear people. I've some relics in my bale°
And pardons too, as full and fine, I hope,

258. ere: before.

Pilgrims on the road to Canterbury, Canterbury Cathedral, England. (stained glass).

274. sauntered: strolled.

283. loth: reluctant; unwilling; alternative spelling of *loath.*
285. Avicenna's: Avicenna (A.D. 980–1037), a famous Islamic philosopher and doctor, wrote several medical books.

292. relics in my bale: Relics are objects considered holy because of association with a saint—hair, bones, teeth, or clothing. A *bale* is a bundle of goods. In the Middle Ages, many relics were faked.

F **Literary Focus** Irony What is ironic about the reason the young man gives for buying the poison?

As any in England, given me by the Pope. **G**

295 If there be one among you that is willing
To have my absolution° for a shilling°
Devoutly given, come! and do not harden
Your hearts but kneel in humbleness for pardon;
Or else, receive my pardon as we go.
300 You can renew it every town or so
Always provided that you still renew
Each time, and in good money, what is due.
It is an honor to you to have found
A pardoner with his credentials sound
305 Who can absolve you as you ply the spur°
In any accident that may occur.
For instance—we are all at Fortune's beck°—
Your horse may throw you down and break your neck.
What a security it is to all
310 To have me here among you and at call
With pardon for the lowly and the great
When soul leaves body for the future state!
And I advise our Host here to begin,
The most enveloped of you all in sin.
315 Come forward, Host, you shall be the first to pay,
And kiss my holy relics right away.
Only a groat.° Come on, unbuckle your purse!"
    "No, no," said he,° "not I, and may the curse
Of Christ descend upon me if I do! . . ."

320 The Pardoner said nothing, not a word;
He was so angry that he couldn't speak.
"Well," said our Host, "if you're for showing pique,°
I'll joke no more, not with an angry man."
    The worthy Knight immediately began,
325 Seeing the fun was getting rather rough,
And said, "No more, we've all had quite enough.
Now, Master Pardoner, perk up, look cheerly!
And you, Sir Host, whom I esteem so dearly,
I beg of you to kiss the Pardoner.
330   "Come, Pardoner, draw nearer, my dear sir.
Let's laugh again and keep the ball in play."
They kissed, and we continued on our way.

296. absolution: forgiveness.
shilling: coin worth twelve pence.

305. ply the spur: In today's terms, this idiom means something like "rev it up" or "put on speed." It refers to the action of a rider digging his spurs into a horse to make it go faster.
307. beck: summons; in other words, subject to Fortune's will.

317. groat: silver coin worth four pence.
318. he: the Host.

322. pique: resentment and ill humor.

331. keep the ball in play: continue.

G **Reading Focus** **Drawing Conclusions** Do you think the Pardoner's relics are authentic or fake? Explain your reasoning.

Vocabulary **absolve** (ab SAHLV) *v.*: forgive; make free from blame.

Applying Your Skills

SKILLS FOCUS Literary Skills Analyze irony, including verbal and situational irony; analyze alliteration. **Reading Skills** Draw conclusions. **Vocabulary Skills** Demonstrate knowledge of literal meanings of words and their usage. **Writing Skills** Employ literary devices for effective writing.

from **The Pardoner's Tale**

Respond and Think Critically

Reading Focus

Quick Check

1. How does the Pardoner describe himself in the Prologue to his tale?

2. Why are the three rioters looking for Death?

Read with a Purpose

3. What moral does the Pardoner want us to draw from his tale? What moral does Chaucer want us to draw from "The Pardoner's Tale"?

Reading Skills: Drawing Conclusions

4. Review the conclusions you recorded as you read. Sometimes what you read later will contradict your earlier conclusions. Record whether or not you agree with your initial conclusions, and explain any changes you make.

Conclusion	How Conclusion Is Supported	Reviewing the Conclusion
Death is the idea or presence of death, not an actual person.	The characters speak of Death as a character, so we expect to meet him as a character. However, we never see him personified.	The description in the tavern of the man's death makes me wonder, but I still think Death is just symbolic in this poem.

✓ Vocabulary Check

Demonstrate your knowledge of Vocabulary words by answering the following questions.

5. Who is more likely to act out of **avarice:** someone self-centered or someone charitable?

6. Is your **adversary** on your team or on the team you are playing?

7. Is it **abominable** to help someone in need?

8. How is blushing related to **pallor?**

9. When might you need to **absolve** your friends: when they help you or when they upset you?

Literary Focus

Literary Analysis

10. Evaluate What attributes of medieval society (and human nature in general) do you think Chaucer is satirizing in "The Pardoner's Tale"?

11. Extend Do people with the Pardoner's ethics exist today—in all sorts of professions? Explain.

12. Analyze Is greed or desire the root of all evil? Discuss the Pardoner's moral.

Literary Skills: Verbal and Situational Irony

13. Analyze Use evidence from the tale to explain the ending's verbal and situational irony.

Literary Skills Review: Alliteration

14. Analyze In each of the first three lines of "The Pardoner's Tale," Chaucer uses **alliteration,** the repetition of the same consonant sounds in words close to each other. Identify and explain three other examples of alliteration in the poem.

Writing Focus

Think as a Reader/Writer

Use It in Your Writing Verbal irony can occur when one character deceives another. Write a short scene with dialogue in which a character misleads another by saying one thing but meaning something else.

 What Do You Think Now

After finding the gold, the "wickedest" young man takes the lead and devises a plan for the group. Why do the other two agree to follow his lead?

Preparing to Read

from The Wife of Bath's Tale

Reader/Writer Notebook

Use your **RWN** to complete the activities for this selection.

Literary Focus

Narrator The **narrator,** the teller of the story, has a distinct voice or character that is revealed through the story's subject matter, tone, and language. The narrator may be the author speaking or may be a character or persona created by the author. Chaucer masterfully matches his narrators and their stories: The Wife of Bath reveals as much about herself as she does about medieval society or women's desires. However, we can't be sure that her views are those of Chaucer or of the majority of women in her day.

Literary Perspectives Apply the literary perspective described on page 163 as you read this narrative poem.

Reading Focus

Interpreting Character We can **interpret characters** by noting details about them. While some characters are elusive, the Wife of Bath is not: She clearly expresses her ideas about women, men, and marriage.

Into Action As you read, use a chart like the one below to note details of the Wife's views on women, marriage, and true gentility. How do her views help you understand her role as a narrator and her story selection?

Topics	Details
Women	"A woman wants...sovereignty over her husband; he must not be above her"
Marriage	
Goodness / True Gentility	

Writing Focus

Think as a Reader/Writer

Find It In Your Reading As you read, take notes in your *Reader/Writer Notebook* on how the Wife reveals her nature through **details** and **tone** and where she interrupts herself with her own opinion.

Vocabulary

disperses (dihs PURS ihz) *v.*: breaks up and scatters. *The party disperses at the end of the trip.*

bequest (bih KWEHST) *n.*: gift left through a will. *The Wife of Bath wants a rich and sickly husband who can leave her widowed with a large bequest.*

prowess (PROW ihs) *n.*: outstanding ability. *The Wife rode quite comfortably and showed great prowess on the horse.*

temporal (TEHM puhr uhl) *adj.*: limited to this world; not spiritual. *Material goods are only temporal, but love endures forever.*

pestilence (PEHS tuh luhns) *n.*: plague. *The Wife of Bath believes the greatest pestilence to married women is cheap and long-lived husbands.*

Language Coach

Noun Endings The endings *–ence* and *–ance* usually tell you that a word is a noun. Nouns name people, places, or things, including intangible things, such as *independence, resistance,* and *nonsense.* Which listed Vocabulary word has an ending that indicates it is a noun?

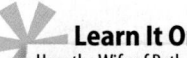

Learn It Online
Hear the Wife of Bath—or an actor playing her—tell you this tale online.

go.hrw.com   L12-161   **Go**

Preparing to Read   **161**

NARRATIVE POEM

FROM

The Wife of Bath's Tale

by **Geoffrey Chaucer**

translated by **Nevill Coghill**

Read with a Purpose
Read to discover the nature of women according to the Wife of Bath.

Build Background
In this tale, the Wife explores the relationship between men and women with her winding story about a knight's unusual quest. Like many of the stories in *The Canterbury Tales*, the Wife's tale works much like a fable, using its characters and plot to reveal human nature.

FROM *The Wife of Bath's Prologue*

The Pardoner started up,° and thereupon
"Madam," he said, "by God and by St. John,
That's noble preaching no one could surpass!
I was about to take a wife; alas!
5   Am I to buy it on my flesh so dear?
There'll be no marrying for me this year!"
    "You wait," she said, "my story's not begun.
You'll taste another brew before I've done;
You'll find it doesn't taste as good as ale;
10   And when I've finished telling you my tale
Of tribulation° in the married life
In which I've been an expert as a wife,
That is to say, myself have been the whip. **Ⓐ**
So please yourself whether you want to sip
15   At that same cask of marriage I shall broach.
Be cautious before making the approach,
For I'll give instances, and more than ten.
And those who won't be warned by other men,
By other men shall suffer their correction,
20   So Ptolemy° has said, in this connection.
You read his *Almagest;*° you'll find it there."
    "Madam, I put it to you as a prayer,"
The Pardoner said, "go on as you began!
Tell us your tale, spare not for any man.
25   Instruct us younger men in your technique."
"Gladly," she said, "if you will let me speak,
But still I hope the company won't reprove me
Though I should speak as fantasy may move me,
And please don't be offended at my views;
30   They're really only offered to amuse." … **Ⓑ**

Ⓐ Reading Focus Interpreting Character What is the tone of the Wife's reply to the Pardoner? What does it say about her character?

Ⓑ Literary Perspectives Analyzing Political Context Why might Chaucer have the Wife of Bath make this disclaimer here?

The Pilgrims at the Table, woodcut from William Caxton's second edition of Chaucer's *The Canterbury Tales* (c. 1484).

1. The Pardoner started up...: The Pardoner is responding to comments made by the Wife of Bath about wanting a sixth husband who will be both her debtor and her slave.

11. tribulation: distress; suffering.

20. Ptolemy (A.D. 100?–165?): ancient geographer, astronomer, and mathematician from Alexandria, Egypt.
21. *Almagest:* word meaning "the greatest"; another title for Ptolemy's major work, *Mathematical Composition,* in which he argues that Earth is the center of the universe, a view held in Europe until 1543.

Literary Perspectives

Analyzing Political Context In Chaucer's time, women had few political and legal rights. Women primarily tended their children and their homes, and peasant women also labored in the fields. Overt exercises of female power were uncommon. The free-spirited and childless Wife of Bath, as you can imagine, is unusual. In a society in which the Church demanded that women be subservient, her notions of women's equality could be considered heretical.

As you read, be sure to notice the questions in the text, which will guide you in using this perspective.

The Wife of Bath's Tale

When good King Arthur ruled in ancient days
(A king that every Briton loves to praise)
This was a land brim-full of fairy folk.
The Elf-Queen and her courtiers° joined and broke
35   Their elfin dance on many a green mead,°
Or so was the opinion once, I read,
Hundreds of years ago, in days of yore.
But no one now sees fairies any more.
For now the saintly charity and prayer
40   Of holy friars seem to have purged the air;
They search the countryside through field and stream
As thick as motes° that speckle a sun-beam,
Blessing the halls, the chambers, kitchens, bowers,
Cities and boroughs, castles, courts and towers,
45   Thorpes,° barns and stables, outhouses and dairies,
And that's the reason why there are no fairies.
Wherever there was wont° to walk an elf
To-day there walks the holy friar himself
As evening falls or when the daylight springs,
50   Saying his matins° and his holy things,
Walking his limit round from town to town.
Women can now go safely up and down
By every bush or under every tree;
There is no other incubus° but he,
55   So there is really no one else to hurt you
And he will do no more than take your virtue. **C**

    Now it so happened, I began to say,
Long, long ago in good King Arthur's day,
There was a knight who was a lusty liver.°
60   One day as he came riding from the river
He saw a maiden walking all forlorn
Ahead of him, alone as she was born.
And of that maiden, spite of all she said,
By very force he took her maidenhead.°
65   This act of violence made such a stir,
So much petitioning to the king for her,
That he condemned the knight to lose his head
By course of law. He was as good as dead
(It seems that then the statutes° took that view)
70   But that the queen, and other ladies too,
Implored the king to exercise his grace
So ceaselessly, he gave the queen the case

C **Literary Focus** **Narrator** What is the narrator trying to accomplish in this opening of the tale?

34. courtiers: attendants.
35. mead: meadow.

42. motes: dust particles.

45. thorpes: villages.

47. wont: accustomed.

50. matins: morning prayers.

54. incubus: evil spirit believed to descend on a sleeping woman and make her pregnant.

59. liver: In medieval times, the liver—not the heart—was believed to be the source of all desires and emotions.

64. maidenhead: virginity.

69. statutes: laws.

And granted her his life, and she could choose
Whether to show him mercy or refuse.
75   The queen returned him thanks with all her might,
And then she sent a summons to the knight
At her convenience, and expressed her will:
"You stand, for such is the position still,
In no way certain of your life," said she,
80   "Yet you shall live if you can answer me:
What is the thing that women most desire?   **D**
Beware the axe and say as I require.
      "If you can't answer on the moment, though,
I will concede you this: You are to go
85   A twelvemonth and a day to seek and learn
Sufficient answer, then you shall return.
I shall take gages° from you to extort
Surrender of your body to the court."
      Sad was the knight and sorrowfully sighed,
90   But there! All other choices were denied,
And in the end he chose to go away
And to return after a year and day
Armed with such answer as there might be sent
To him by God. He took his leave and went.
95   He knocked at every house, searched every place,
Yes, anywhere that offered hope of grace.
What could it be that women wanted most?
But all the same he never touched a coast,
Country, or town in which there seemed to be
100   Any two people willing to agree.
      Some said that women wanted wealth and treasure,
"Honor," said some, some "Jollity and pleasure,"
Some "Gorgeous clothes" and others "Fun in bed,"
"To be oft widowed and remarried," said
105   Others again, and some that what most mattered
Was that we should be cossetted° and flattered.
That's very near the truth, it seems to me;
A man can win us best with flattery.
To dance attendance on us, make a fuss,
110   Ensnares us all, the best and worst of us.
      Some say the things we most desire are these:
Freedom to do exactly as we please,
With no one to reprove our faults and lies,
Rather to have one call us good and wise.
115   Truly there's not a woman in ten score°
Who has a fault, and someone rubs the sore,

The Wife of Bath, detail from *The Canterbury Tales* by Geoffrey Chaucer. The Huntington Library and Art Gallery, San Marino, CA.

87. gages: pledges.

106. cossetted: pampered.

115. ten score: two hundred. A score is twenty.

D **Reading Focus** | **Interpreting Character** Why do you think the queen chooses this question for the knight?

But she will kick if what he says is true; **ⓔ**
You try it out and you will find so too.
However vicious we may be within
120   We like to be thought wise and void of sin.
Others assert we women find it sweet
When we are thought dependable, discreet
And secret, firm of purpose and controlled,
Never betraying things that we are told.
125   But that's not worth the handle of a rake;
Women conceal a thing? For Heaven's sake!
Remember Midas?° Will you hear the tale?
    Among some other little things, now stale,
Ovid° relates that under his long hair
130   The unhappy Midas grew a splendid pair
Of ass's ears; as subtly as he might,
He kept his foul deformity from sight;

127. Midas: mythical king blessed so that everything he touched turned to gold, but cursed by having a donkey's ears.
129. Ovid (43 B.C.–c. A.D. 17): Roman poet. Ovid's *Metamorphoses,* a collection of tales, includes one version of the Midas story.

ⓔ **Literary Focus** **Narrator** What point is the Wife of Bath making about women in lines 115–117?

Royal Shakespeare Company's production of *The Canterbury Tales* in the Gielgud Theatre, London (2006).

Save for his wife, there was not one that knew.
He loved her best, and trusted in her too.
135 He begged her not to tell a living creature
That he possessed so horrible a feature.
And she—she swore, were all the world to win,
She would not do such villainy and sin
As saddle her husband with so foul a name;
140 Besides to speak would be to share the shame.
Nevertheless she thought she would have died
Keeping this secret bottled up inside;
It seemed to swell her heart and she, no doubt,
Thought it was on the point of bursting out.
145   Fearing to speak of it to woman or man,
Down to a reedy marsh she quickly ran
And reached the sedge.° Her heart was all on fire
And, as a bittern° bumbles in the mire,
She whispered to the water, near the ground,
150 "Betray me not, O water, with thy sound!
To thee alone I tell it: It appears
My husband has a pair of ass's ears!

147. **sedge:** grasslike plant.
148. **bittern:** type of wading bird.

Analyzing Visuals

Viewing and Interpreting In this staging of *The Canterbury Tales,* what do the costumes and props convey about the tone and emphasis of the production and the status and diversity of the characters?

from The Wife of Bath's Tale   **167**

Ah! My heart's well again, the secret's out!
I could no longer keep it, not a doubt."
155   And so you see, although we may hold fast
A little while, it must come out at last,
We can't keep secrets; as for Midas, well,
Read Ovid for his story;° he will tell.   **F**
This knight that I am telling you about
160   Perceived at last he never would find out
What it could be that women loved the best.
Faint was the soul within his sorrowful breast,
As home he went, he dared no longer stay;
His year was up and now it was the day.
165   As he rode home in a dejected mood
Suddenly, at the margin° of a wood,
He saw a dance upon the leafy floor
Of four and twenty ladies, nay, and more.
Eagerly he approached, in hope to learn
170   Some words of wisdom ere he should return;
But lo! Before he came to where they were,
Dancers and dance all vanished into air!
There wasn't a living creature to be seen
Save one old woman crouched upon the green.
175   A fouler-looking creature I suppose
Could scarcely be imagined. She arose
And said, "Sir knight, there's no way on from here.
Tell me what you are looking for, my dear,
For peradventure° that were best for you;
180   We old, old women know a thing or two."   **G**
"Dear Mother," said the knight, "alack the day!
I am as good as dead if I can't say
What thing it is that women most desire;
If you could tell me I would pay your hire."
185   "Give me your hand," she said, "and swear to do
Whatever I shall next require of you
—If so to do should lie within your might—
And you shall know the answer before night."
"Upon my honor," he answered, "I agree."
190   "Then," said the crone, "I dare to guarantee
Your life is safe; I shall make good my claim.
Upon my life the queen will say the same.

158. Read Ovid. . .story: In Ovid's version, it is Midas's barber, not his wife, who tells the secret to a hole in the ground. Reeds grow up from the spot and whisper the secret whenever the wind rustles them.

166. margin: edge.

179. peradventure: perhaps.

F **Reading Focus** **Interpreting Character** What does this digression say about the Wife of Bath's nature?

G **Literary Perspectives** **Analyzing Political Context** How does the Wife of Bath's view of women's ability to contribute compare to the knight's view? What might the knight's opinion represent?

Show me the very proudest of them all
In costly coverchief or jeweled caul°

195   That dare say no to what I have to teach.
Let us go forward without further speech."
And then she crooned her gospel in his ear
And told him to be glad and not to fear.
    They came to court. This knight, in full array,

200   Stood forth and said, "O Queen, I've kept my day
And kept my word and have my answer ready."
    There sat the noble matrons and the heady
Young girls, and widows too, that have the grace
Of wisdom, all assembled in that place,

205   And there the queen herself was throned to hear
And judge his answer. Then the knight drew near
And silence was commanded through the hall.
    The queen gave order he should tell them all
What thing it was that women wanted most.

210   He stood not silent like a beast or post,
But gave his answer with the ringing word
Of a man's voice and the assembly heard:
    "My liege° and lady, in general," said he,
"A woman wants the self-same sovereignty°

215   Over her husband as over her lover,
And master him; he must not be above her.
That is your greatest wish, whether you kill
Or spare me; please yourself. I wait your will."
    In all the court not one that shook her head

220   Or contradicted what the knight had said;
Maid, wife, and widow cried, "He's saved his life!" **H**
    And on the word up started the old wife,
The one the knight saw sitting on the green,
And cried, "Your mercy, sovereign lady queen!

225   Before the court disperses, do me right!
'Twas I who taught this answer to the knight,
For which he swore, and pledged his honor to it,
That the first thing I asked of him he'd do it,
So far as it should lie within his might.

230   Before this court I ask you then, sir knight,
To keep your word and take me for your wife;
For well you know that I have saved your life.
If this be false, deny it on your sword!"
    "Alas!" he said, "Old lady, by the Lord

194. coverchief . . . caul: women's headgear. The coverchief covered the entire head; the caul, a small, netted cap, was sometimes ornamented.

213. liege: lord.
214. sovereignty: power.

The Knight and the Old Lady. The Bodleian Library, University of Oxford. Ms Douce 195, folio 105r.

H **Literary Focus** Narrator How does the narrator create suspense in this moment of the story?

Vocabulary **disperses** (dihs PURS ihz) *v.:* breaks up and scatters.

235 I know indeed that such was my behest,°
    But for God's love think of a new request,
    Take all my goods, but leave my body free."
    "A curse on us," she said, "if I agree!
    I may be foul, I may be poor and old,
240 Yet will not choose to be, for all the gold
    That's bedded in the earth or lies above,
    Less than your wife, nay, than your very love!"
        "My love?" said he. "By heaven, my damnation!
    Alas that any of my race and station
245 Should ever make so foul a misalliance!"°
    Yet in the end his pleading and defiance
    All went for nothing, he was forced to wed.
    He takes his ancient wife and goes to bed.
        Now peradventure some may well suspect
250 A lack of care in me since I neglect
    To tell of the rejoicings and display
    Made at the feast upon their wedding-day.
    I have but a short answer to let fall;
    I say there was no joy or feast at all,
255 Nothing but heaviness of heart and sorrow.
    He married her in private on the morrow
    And all day long stayed hidden like an owl,
    It was such torture that his wife looked foul.
        Great was the anguish churning in his head
260 When he and she were piloted to bed;
    He wallowed° back and forth in desperate style.
    His ancient wife lay smiling all the while;
    At last she said "Bless us! Is this, my dear,
    How knights and wives get on together here?
265 Are these the laws of good King Arthur's house?
    Are knights of his all so contemptuous?
    I am your own beloved and your wife,
    And I am she, indeed, that saved your life;
    And certainly I never did you wrong.
270 Then why, this first of nights, so sad a song?
    You're carrying on as if you were half-witted
    Say, for God's love, what sin have I committed?
    I'll put things right if you will tell me how."
        "Put right?" he cried. "That never can be now!
275 Nothing can ever be put right again!
    You're old, and so abominably plain,
    So poor to start with, so low-bred to follow;
    It's little wonder if I twist and wallow!
    God, that my heart would burst within my breast!"
280   "Is that," said she, "the cause of your unrest?"
        "Yes, certainly," he said, "and can you wonder?"

235. behest: command; order.

245. misalliance: here, a marriage that is unsuitable or inappropriate.

261. wallowed: tossed and turned.

Medieval knight on horseback, from medieval collection of Minnelieder.

"I could set right what you suppose a blunder,
That's if I cared to, in a day or two,
If I were shown more courtesy by you.
285 Just now," she said, "you spoke of gentle birth,
Such as descends from ancient wealth and worth.
If that's the claim you make for gentlemen
Such arrogance is hardly worth a hen.
Whoever loves to work for virtuous ends,
290 Public and private, and who most intends
To do what deeds of gentleness he can,
Take him to be the greatest gentleman.
Christ wills we take our gentleness from Him,
Not from a wealth of ancestry long dim,
295 Though they bequeath their whole establishment
By which we claim to be of high descent.
Our fathers cannot make us a bequest
Of all those virtues that became them best
And earned for them the name of gentlemen,
300 But bade us follow them as best we can.
      "Thus the wise poet of the Florentines,
Dante° by name, has written in these lines,
For such is the opinion Dante launches:
'Seldom arises by these slender branches
305 Prowess of men, for it is God, no less,
Wills us to claim of Him our gentleness.'
For of our parents nothing can we claim
Save temporal things, and these may hurt and maim.
      "But everyone knows this as well as I;
310 For if gentility were implanted by
The natural course of lineage° down the line,
Public or private, could it cease to shine
In doing the fair work of gentle deed?
No vice or villainy could then bear seed.
315   "Take fire and carry it to the darkest house
Between this kingdom and the Caucasus,°
And shut the doors on it and leave it there,
It will burn on, and it will burn as fair
As if ten thousand men were there to see,
320 For fire will keep its nature and degree,
I can assure you, sir, until it dies.
      "But gentleness, as you will recognize,
Is not annexed in nature to possessions.

302. **Dante:** Dante Alighieri (1265–1321), Italian poet who wrote *The Divine Comedy*.

311. **lineage:** ancestry.

316. **Caucasus:** mountain range in southeastern Europe, between the Black Sea and the Caspian Sea; in other words, far away.

Vocabulary **bequest** (bih KWEHST) *n.*: gift left through a will.
prowess (PROW ihs) *n.*: outstanding ability.
temporal (TEHM puhr uhl) *adj.*: limited to this world; not spiritual.

Men fail in living up to their professions;°
325   But fire never ceases to be fire.
       God knows you'll often find, if you inquire,
       Some lording° full of villainy and shame.
       If you would be esteemed for the mere name
       Of having been by birth a gentleman
330   And stemming from some virtuous, noble clan,
       And do not live yourself by gentle deed
       Or take your father's noble code and creed,
       You are no gentleman, though duke or earl.
       Vice and bad manners are what make a churl.°
335   "Gentility is only the renown
       For bounty that your fathers handed down,
       Quite foreign to your person, not your own;
       Gentility must come from God alone.
       That we are gentle comes to us by grace
340   And by no means is it bequeathed with place.
           "Reflect how noble (says Valerius)°
       Was Tullius surnamed Hostilius,°
       Who rose from poverty to nobleness.
       And read Boethius,° Seneca° no less,   ❶
345   Thus they express themselves and are agreed:
       'Gentle is he that does a gentle deed.'
       And therefore, my dear husband, I conclude
       That even if my ancestors were rude,
       Yet God on high—and so I hope He will—
350   Can grant me grace to live in virtue still,
       A gentlewoman only when beginning
       To live in virtue and to shrink from sinning.
           "As for my poverty which you reprove,
       Almighty God Himself in whom we move,
355   Believe, and have our being, chose a life
       Of poverty, and every man or wife
       Nay, every child can see our Heavenly King
       Would never stoop to choose a shameful thing.
       No shame in poverty if the heart is gay,
360   As Seneca and all the learned say.
       He who accepts his poverty unhurt
       I'd say is rich although he lacked a shirt.
       But truly poor are they who whine and fret
       And covet what they cannot hope to get.
365   And he that, having nothing, covets not,
       Is rich, though you may think he is a sot.°
           "True poverty can find a song to sing.

324. professions: promises.

327. lording: young lord.

334. churl: ill-mannered person.

341. Valerius: Roman writer who collected historical anecdotes that public speakers could use.
342. Tullius surnamed Hostilius: legendary king of Rome who rose from humble origins.
344. Boethius (c. A.D. 480–c. 524): Roman philosopher. In his *Consolation of Philosophy,* he argues that rank is no guarantee of honorable conduct.
Seneca (c. 4 B.C.–A.D. 65): Roman philosopher whose works were popular in the Middle Ages.

366. sot: fool.

❶ **Reading Focus** **Interpreting Character** What is the old woman's purpose in mentioning all of these famous figures?

Juvenal° says a pleasant little thing:
'The poor can dance and sing in the relief
370   Of having nothing that will tempt a thief.'
Though it be hateful, poverty is good,
A great incentive to a livelihood,
And a great help to our capacity
For wisdom, if accepted patiently.
375   Poverty is, though wanting in estate,
A kind of wealth that none calumniate.°
Poverty often, when the heart is lowly,
Brings one to God and teaches what is holy,
Gives knowledge of oneself and even lends
380   A glass by which to see one's truest friends.
And since it's no offense, let me be plain;
Do not rebuke my poverty again.
       "Lastly you taxed me, sir, with being old.
Yet even if you never had been told
385   By ancient books, you gentlemen engage
Yourselves in honor to respect old age.
To call an old man 'father' shows good breeding,
And this could be supported from my reading.
       "You say I'm old and fouler than a fen.°
390   You need not fear to be a cuckold,° then.
Filth and old age, I'm sure you will agree,
Are powerful wardens over chastity.
Nevertheless, well knowing your delights,
I shall fulfill your worldly appetites.
395   "You have two choices; which one will you try?
To have me old and ugly till I die,
But still a loyal, true, and humble wife
That never will displease you all her life,
Or would you rather I were young and pretty
400   And chance your arm what happens in a city
Where friends will visit you because of me,
Yes, and in other places too, maybe.
Which would you have? The choice is all your own."
       The knight thought long, and with a piteous groan
405   At last he said, with all the care in life,
"My lady and my love, my dearest wife,
I leave the matter to your wise decision.
You make the choice yourself, for the provision
Of what may be agreeable and rich
410   In honor to us both, I don't care which;
Whatever pleases you suffices° me."   **J**

J **Reading Focus** **Interpreting Character** What does this response reveal about
the knight?

368. Juvenal (c. A.D. 60–c. 140):
Roman satirist.

376. calumniate: slander.

389. fen: swamp.
390. cuckold: man whose wife
has cheated on him.

411. suffices: satisfies.

"And have I won the mastery?" said she,
"Since I'm to choose and rule as I think fit?"
"Certainly, wife," he answered her, "that's it."
415 "Kiss me," she cried. "No quarrels! On my oath
And word of honor, you shall find me both,
That is, both fair and faithful as a wife;
May I go howling mad and take my life
Unless I prove to be as good and true
420 As ever wife was since the world was new!
And if to-morrow when the sun's above
I seem less fair than any lady-love,
Than any queen or empress east or west,
Do with my life and death as you think best.
425 Cast up the curtain, husband. Look at me!"
    And when indeed the knight had looked to see,
Lo, she was young and lovely, rich in charms.
In ecstasy he caught her in his arms,
His heart went bathing in a bath of blisses
430 And melted in a hundred thousand kisses,
And she responded in the fullest measure
With all that could delight or give him pleasure.
    So they lived ever after to the end
In perfect bliss; and may Christ Jesus send
435 Us husbands meek and young and fresh in bed,
And grace to overbid them when we wed.
And—Jesu hear my prayer!—cut short the lives
Of those who won't be governed by their wives;
And all old, angry niggards of their pence,°
440 God send them soon a very pestilence!

439. niggards of their pence: stingy with their money.

Vocabulary **pestilence** (PEHS tuh luhns) *n.:* plague.

Applying Your Skills

from The Wife of Bath's Tale

Respond and Think Critically

Reading Focus

Quick Check

1. Identify (a) the knight's crime; (b) his original punishment; and (c) his second punishment.

2. What payment for her help does the old woman demand? What is the knight's response?

3. What final choice does the old woman offer the knight? How does he respond?

Read with a Purpose

4. Does the Wife of Bath's tale describe the characteristics she values in women? Why or why not?

Reading Skills: Interpreting Character

5. As you read, you noted details that reveal the Wife's opinions. Add a column to your chart, and explain how her views define her as a narrator.

Topics	Details	How Her Views Define Her as a Narrator
Women	"a woman wants sovereignty over her husband; he must not be above her"	
Marriage		
Goodness / True Gentility		

Literary Focus

Literary Analysis

6. **Draw Conclusions** Why do you think the queen takes a special interest in the knight's case?

7. **Evaluate** Does the Wife of Bath's character show that Chaucer had progressive views on women?

8. **Analyze** During the Wife's story, the poet hints at, or **foreshadows,** the old woman's transformation. Explain how Chaucer sets up this twist in the story, and cite evidence in the text.

9. **Literary Perspectives** How does the Wife of Bath's perspective on women contrast with the political status of women in her day? How does her perspective fit into the political structure of today's society?

Literary Skills: Narrator

10. **Evaluate** Consider what the Wife, as narrator, says about people's perceptions of women's desires. What do you think of these proposals?

Literary Skills Review: Irony

11. **Analyze** A contrast or discrepancy between what is said and what is really meant, or between what is expected and what really happens is **irony.** The knight's quest—forced upon him by the queen—is to find out what women want. What irony do you see in this punishment?

Writing Focus

Think As a Reader/Writer

Use It in Your Writing As you read, you noted aspects of the Wife's narration, such as her word choices, tone, and subject matter. Now, write a brief story of your own with a first-person narrator. Reveal your narrator's attributes through your word choices, tone, and subject matter.

 What Do You Think Now Why do you think the knight agrees at the end of the story to let the old woman decide their fate together?

from The Wife of Bath's Tale

Vocabulary Development

✓ Vocabulary Check

Answer the following questions about Vocabulary words.

1. Do rain clouds **disperse** before or after a storm?
2. If something is a **bequest**, is it given or taken away?
3. Who is more likely to have physical **prowess**, an athlete or a professor?
4. Are **temporal** things sacred or everyday?
5. Is an insect an example of **pestilence?**

Vocabulary Skills: Analogies

In word analogies, the relationship between one pair of words is similar to the relationship between another pair of words. For example:

LETTER : ENVELOPE :: hand : glove

In other words, a *letter* is to an *envelope* as a *hand* is to a *glove*. How are the paired items similarly related? *A letter goes into an envelope as a hand goes into a glove.*

Common relationships in analogies include whole/part or part/whole; cause and effect; synonyms; and antonyms. Study the examples in the chart below.

Relationship Type	Example	Explanation
Part to whole	cow : herd	A cow is part of a herd.
Cause and Effect	lightning : forest fire	Lightning can cause a forest fire.
Synonyms	rough : coarse	"Rough" and "coarse" are synonyms.
Antonyms	rough : smooth	"Rough" and "smooth" are antonyms.

Your Turn

In each of the examples below, choose the Vocabulary word that best completes the analogy.

1. BLUNDERER : INABILITY :: expert : ————
2. RAIN : FLOOD :: virus : ————
3. HOT : COLD :: ————: collect
4. ETERNAL : IMMORTAL :: ———— : mortal
5. AGREEMENT : CONTRACT :: ————: will

Language Coach

Noun Endings The ending of a word often indicates whether it is a noun or an adjective. Words that end in –*ance* and –*ence* are usually nouns, which name people, places, or things. Words that end in –*ant* and –*ent* are usually adjectives, which can describe nouns. Sort the following words into a chart like the one below. Then, use each word in a sentence.

defiance   arrogance   evident   defiant
pestilence   evidence   pestilent   arrogant

Nouns	Adjectives

Academic Vocabulary

Talk About . . .
Consider how the knight initially gets into trouble and how things turn out for him. Do you find the conclusion satisfying? Is the outcome attributed to an adequate transformation in the knight? How does the tale reflect the status of men and women in medieval society? Explain.

CHOICES

As you respond to the Choices, use these **Academic Vocabulary** words as appropriate: attribute, concept, diverse, emphasis, status.

REVIEW

Listen to the Women

During his quest, the knight receives many responses to his query about women. Review the Wife's description of the women's opinions. Note what these responses have in common and how they differ. What does this passage convey about the relationship between men and women? about the status of women? In a small group, discuss your interpretations of this passage.

Get in Touch with Midas

Timed ⌛Writing In the middle of her tale, the Wife tells a story about Midas. Review Midas's story, and consider these questions: Why do you think the Wife tells this story? Is the story more about Midas's vanity or his wife's ability to keep a secret? Are his wife's actions a betrayal even though she did not tell a person? Write an essay explaining your opinions with supporting details from the text.

CONNECT

Seek Out Chivalry

During Chaucer's time, knights were expected to adhere to the ideals of chivalry, and much of the period's literature explores this concept. Online or in the library, research the medieval code of chivalry. Consider these questions: How does the Wife's story explore these ideals? How does the knight's behavior follow or contradict the chivalric code? After completing your research, discuss in a small group how the chivalric code relates to the Wife's tale.

Find the Past in the Present

TechFocus In Chaucer's time, the way an ordinary person was most likely to encounter a story was through oral narratives. Make a list of all the ways that you could read, see, or hear a story today (for example, a magazine article, a song, a commercial). Then, retell "The Wife of Bath's Tale" using one of these modern methods. What are the advantages and disadvantages of expressing a story in this modern form?

EXTEND

Take Your Turn at Teaching

In the Wife's story, the queen challenges the knight to answer a question to save himself. Recall a wrongdoer from something else you've read. Think of a question to ask the wrongdoer to help him or her understand his or her error. Write down what the character did wrong, what your question is, and why you chose the question. In a small group, discuss your character's situations and questions and whether they might help someone learn or change.

Create a Character

In the Wife's tale, the old woman explores the discrepancy between appearance and reality and how people come to misjudge each other. Write a character sketch describing someone whose appearance does not reflect the nature of his or her character. Explain why the character's appearance may be misleading about his or her personality. Create a picture, collage, or computer graphic representing the differences between the character's physical and internal qualities.

from **Walking to Canterbury**

What moves a hero to act?

⏱ **QuickWrite**

Like Chaucer's pilgrims, people today often travel to a place important to their family, culture, or country. In your *Reader/Writer Notebook,* write about an important place that you would like to visit.

Informational Text Focus

Comparing and Contrasting A popular topic in nonfiction writing is the exploration of the past. Such works often provide a fresh perspective on historic people, places, and events by **comparing** and **contrasting** them to the contemporary world. Reflecting on these comparisons can help you identify common elements across time, as well as the differences between past and present.

Into Action As you read, use a chart like the one below to note some of the main similarities and differences between medieval London and modern London as described by the author.

Similarities	Differences
Both are bustling places crowded with people.	Modern London has many more types of transportation available.

Writing Focus   Preparing for **Constructed Response**

The author of *Walking to Canterbury* describes modern London with imagery that creates a panorama of the sights, sounds, and smells of the city today. Use your *Reader/Writer Notebook* to record the most vivid images.

Vocabulary

ingrained (ihn GRAYND) *adj.:* deeply and firmly fixed in one's nature or being. *Some of the same feelings of the medieval town are ingrained in modern London's atmosphere.*

enticing (ehn TYS ihng) *adj.:* attracting by arousing hopes or desires; tempting. *The promise of adventure on the journey was enticing.*

perplexed (puhr PLEHKSD) *v.:* troubled with doubt; puzzled. *The author's appearance clearly perplexed the customs agent.*

notorious (noh TAWR ee uhs) *adj.:* well known because of something bad; having a bad reputation. *The original inn where the pilgrims stayed was notorious for its shady clientele.*

concocted (kahn KAHKT ihd) *v.:* prepared (food or drink) by mixing a variety of ingredients. *While hiking he concocted what dinner he could from his small supply of food.*

Language Coach

Roots The Latin root *perplexus* means "tangled." How does the meaning of the root help you understand one of the listed words?

Link to Today

This Link to Today gives a new perspective on the idea of a pilgrimage.

Read with a Purpose

Read to discover how the author uses his own journey to explore the ways in which a historical setting can change over time.

Build Background

Geoffrey Chaucer's famous work *The Canterbury Tales* follows a group of characters along their religious journey from London to Canterbury in fourteenth-century England. In the book *Walking to Canterbury*, contemporary author Jerry Ellis describes his own journey along the same path to Canterbury. Using the poem as his guide, Ellis examines Chaucer's setting from a modern perspective.

from Walking to Canterbury

by **Jerry Ellis**

When I presented my passport to the immigration officer at Heathrow Airport,[1] she studied me as if I were an international oddity. I wore tennis shoes, a blue cotton shirt, a brown leather jacket, and jeans. My hat was stained from years of sun, rain, and sweat. Dove and blue jay feathers stuck from one side of the hat, while a rattlesnake rattle rode snug in the back of the band. My backpack bulged with clothes, a camera, a journal, cooking utensils, a tent, toiletries, and personal items.

"On a hike?" she said, taking a closer look at the rattlesnake rattle.

"A pilgrimage," I said, hoping that the trek would be charged with extraordinary experiences. "From London to Canterbury. I plan to do it in the same amount of time it took medieval pilgrims. Seven days."

She now seemed all the more intrigued with my attire, which was notably different from that of a pilgrim in the Middle Ages. The only thing I had in common with Chaucer's pilgrims[2] was my hat.

Like mine, decorated with feathers and the snake's rattle, which I had collected on my walks, a pilgrim would have worn a big floppy hat, decorated with badges or shells to offer proof of his journeys. He might also have worn a "sclavein," which was a long, russet-colored tunic with big sleeves,

---

1. **Heathrow Airport:** an airport located near London, England.
2. **Chaucer's pilgrims:** the characters in Chaucer's poem *The Canterbury Tales.*

The chapel at St. Aldhelm, at St. Aldhelm's head, Dorset, UK.

sometimes patched with crosses. A soft pouch, a "scrip," would have hung from a leather belt strung over his shoulder. The pouch was small, to indicate that the pilgrim had little money or none at all. A rosary of beads might have dangled from his arm or neck, and he could have carried a wooden staff with a metal toe. Leather shoes probably covered his feet.

The pilgrim's dress was symbolic as well as practical. The staff defended the traveler against wild dogs and wolves, which represented the Devil. It also served as a third leg and suggested the Trinity[3] as well as the wood of the Cross. The tunic, similar to the clothes Jesus wore, reflected the pilgrim's humanity. The medieval imagery became so ingrained into the British psyche that Sir Walter Raleigh used it two hundred years later in his poem "His Pilgrimage": **Ⓐ**

> Give me my scallop shell of quiet
> My staff of faith to walk upon;
> My scrip of joy, immortal diet;
> My bottle of salvation;
> My gown of glory, hopes true gauge,
> And thus I'll take my pilgrimage.

Dressed in my modern pilgrim attire, I took a train from the airport to Victoria Station in London and there boarded the tube (British for subway) to Russell Square near the British Museum to look for an affordable bed-and-breakfast for the night. The sun was setting, and the streets smelled of Indian curry, Chinese food, and fish-and-chips. Red phone booths stood like monuments on the sidewalk, where two men wearing double-length hair rocked their hips as each paraded with a blaring boom box on his shoulder. A bobbie (British for cop) at the corner motioned for two sleek black taxis to hurry on, and three teenagers on Rollerblades played follow the leader as the first jumped over a garbage can. No rain fell, but so many people carried umbrellas that it seemed a Mary Poppins party simmered in the approaching night's pot. My mouth watered just to walk new streets, and enchanting British accents fell on my ears like notes of an exotic song being born in the very air I breathed.

A pub's window revealed two women throwing darts, and the sound of a whacked tennis ball erupted from a small park. Images on televisions flickered inside shadowy apartments, and somewhere down an alley a car shrieked. The enticing smell of perfume from a woman strolling in front of me lingered as a lone jet streaked the sky, its red wing lights blinking. The sights and sounds of modern London were in sharp contrast to the Middle Ages.

In the 1300s, if a renegade medieval serf[4] could cross the Thames[5] into London and stay here one year and a day without being caught by his lord, he became a free man. The city itself occupied only one square mile then. About thirty-five thousand people populated London, and they ranged from ragged serfs and students to members of the craft guilds (like carpenters and weavers), clergymen, and nobles. **Ⓑ** Regardless of whether they survived on scraps of cabbage snatched from the common marketplace or dined on roasted pigs in rooms hung with tapestries, all of the populace lived surrounded by the smell of open sewers. At sundown all were also locked within London when the walled city closed its gates.…

Night had fallen when I checked into a third-story room at the Avalon Hotel, overlooking a grove of trees in a public park. A lone figure strummed a guitar as he

---

3. **the Trinity:** the Christian "Holy Trinity" of God the Father, the Son (Jesus), and the Holy Spirit.
4. **serf:** a peasant in the feudal system who ranked between a freeman and a slave.
5. **Thames:** a major river that flows through southern England and runs through London.

Ⓐ **Informational Focus** Comparing and Contrasting How is what the author is carrying different from what the pilgrims carried?

Ⓑ **Informational Focus** Comparing and Contrasting How are these elements of medieval London similar to those of a modern city?

Vocabulary **ingrained** (ihn GRAYND) *adj.*: deeply and firmly fixed in one's nature or being.
enticing (ehn TYS ihng) *adj.*: attracting by arousing hopes or desires; tempting.

Chaucer's Canterbury Pilgrims, Tabard Inn, by Edward Henry Corbould.

"Give me my scallop shell of quiet
My staff of faith to walk upon;
My scrip of joy, immortal diet;
My bottle of salvation;
My gown of glory, hopes true gauge,
And thus I'll take my pilgrimage."

—Sir Walter Raleigh

Three Pilgrim Badges (tin-lead alloy), by English School. Museum of London, UK.

(*above*) Sign for The George Inn in Southwark, a public house in London, England. (*right*) University of Kent, Canterbury, Great Britain.

Modern-day Canterbury

perched atop a bench near the tallest tree. A car horn sounded, and two cooing pigeons fluttered from my windowsill.

My tiny room, reached by a narrow flight of squeaky wooden stairs, smelled of freshly ground coffee, which perplexed me until I discovered that the bag of Guatemalan in my backpack had spilled. The bathroom was across the hall, but my room had a washbasin, hot and cold water, and a mirror on the wall. A television, receiving only three channels, sat atop a table next to a chest of drawers. Two cups, decorated with hand-painted red tulips, rested on the table with a porcelain pot and tea bags. Though as modest as my budget, the room felt cozy, safe, and warm. The £25 (about $40) for the night included a full breakfast, one I planned to make good use of before embarking on my pilgrimage the next morning.

Most medieval pilgrims sought food and shelter in monasteries, where the monks gave freely and, when they obeyed the Benedictine rule,[6] even washed the travelers' feet. But often there were more pilgrims than there was room, and the pilgrims were forced to sleep outside on the ground or in an inn, where as many as three or four people shared a bed for a penny apiece— a whole day's wages. Such medieval inns were infested with rats and fleas, and innkeepers were notorious for serving spoiled food and cheating their patrons. Robbery was easily committed after putting a pilgrim

C

to sleep with a drugged drink, concocted by mixing equal parts of seed of henbane, darnel, black poppy, and dried bryony root, which were pounded into a powder and added to ale.

The characters in *The Canterbury Tales* gathered in Tabard Inn the night before beginning their pilgrimage, and within minutes of checking into my hotel room, I took a subway to the site of the inn. It was located in Southwark, which was a red-light district in the Middle Ages. Today it is a collection of shops, pubs, and offices.

D

A real place in the Middle Ages near the foot of London Bridge, Tabard Inn burned centuries ago. Now only a plaque in a stone wall informs passersby of its existence.

Just up the street a sign designating The George pictured a knight in armor on horseback slaying a dragon. The Globe Theatre[7] was only blocks away down by the river, and Shakespeare himself frequented The George, the only pub in the same block where the Tabard Inn once stood....

Back on the streets, I started walking to my hotel. Big Ben's giant hands told time in the near distance, and Westminster Abbey towered against the night with its heavenly steeples. The Thames reflected moonlight as the tide shifted, just as it had done when Chaucer lived here.

E

---

6. **Benedictine rule:** the standard code of conduct for monks living in monasteries, written by Saint Benedictine in the sixth century.

---

7. **Globe Theatre:** London theatre where William Shakespeare presented his plays during his lifetime.

C **Informational Focus** Comparing and Contrasting In what ways is this scene similar to what a guest in a medieval inn might have experienced? In what ways is it different?

D **Informational Focus** Comparing and Contrasting According to the author, how has Southwark changed since the Middle Ages?

E **Informational Focus** Comparing and Contrasting What is the author using the Thames to represent or symbolize here?

Vocabulary **perplexed** (puhr PLEHKSD) *v.:* troubled with doubt; puzzled.
notorious (noh TAWR ee uhs) *adj.:* well known because of something bad; having a bad reputation.
concocted (kahn KAHKT ihd) *v.:* prepared (food or drink) by mixing a variety of ingredients.

SKILLS FOCUS **Informational**
Skills Compare and contrast.
Vocabulary Skills Identify and correctly
use antonyms. **Listening and Speaking**

Skills Participate in group discussions.
Writing Skills Support ideas with evidence
and details.

Respond and Think Critically

Informational Text Focus

Quick Check

1. Why does the author at first seem unusual to the immigration officer?

2. What kinds of scents does the author encounter while walking the streets of London?

3. Where did most medieval pilgrims seek lodging? Why was this usually their first choice?

4. What became of the real Tabard Inn from Chaucer's *Tales*?

Read with a Purpose

5. How does the author try to make his first night in London similar to the pilgrims' night before their journey?

Informational Skills: Comparing and Contrasting

6. Look back at the chart in which you recorded the main similarities and differences between medieval London and modern London. Overall, do you think the author believes that the two eras have more similarities than differences, or just the opposite? Explain your response.

✓ Vocabulary Check

Match each Vocabulary word with its antonym.

7. ingrained
8. enticing
9. perplexed
10. notorious
11. concocted

a. unknown
b. superficial
c. disassembled
d. repulsed
e. clarified

Text Analysis

12. **Interpret** What does the attire of the medieval pilgrims reflect about their interests and beliefs?

13. **Analyze** How does the author use his walk from the tube to the Avalon Hotel to depict modern London?

14. **Evaluate** In this passage, the author mixes medieval history with the recounting of his travels in London. Is this an effective storytelling method, or does jumping back and forth make it more difficult to follow his story? Explain.

Listening and Speaking

15. **Extend** While reading, you listed the different clothing and accessories worn or carried by travelers in the different eras. In a small group, discuss what items you would wear or bring on an important journey. Make a list of all the items mentioned. How do these items differ from those the medieval pilgrims brought along?

Writing Focus **Constructed Response**

In a paragraph, discuss how the author of *Walking to Canterbury* uses imagery to depict a modern, bustling London. Be sure to support your response with evidence from the text.

What Do **You Think Now**? How does the author's motivation for his journey to Canterbury compare to the original pilgrims' reasons for taking the journey? Support your response with evidence from the text.

Preparing to Read

Lord Randall
Get Up and Bar the Door
Edward, Edward

What Do You Think? What moves a hero to act?

QuickWrite

Think of songs you know that tell stories about heroism, such as heroic people, actions, or qualities. Choose the song you know best, and retell it in your own words.

INTRODUCTION

Ballads

Using a strong beat and repetition, ballads are a type of story passed from performer to performer, from generation to generation.

Poetry of the People

In the Middle Ages, just as today, certain forms of entertainment tended toward the sensational. Like today's popular music, medieval ballads were the poetry of the people, and their subjects were predictably popular—domestic tragedy, false love, true love, the absurdity in husband-wife relationships, and the supernatural. Unlike today's music, ballads were not copyrighted by a composer but were passed down orally from singer to singer.

Song and Dance

We often associate popular songs with dancing. The word *ballad* is in fact derived from an Old French word meaning "dancing song." Although the English ballads' connection with dance has been lost, it is clear from their meter and structure that the original ballads were written to be accompanied by music.

The meter of the old ballads is characterized by a strong, simple beat. The verse forms are relatively uncomplicated and have a primitive freshness that appeals to a general, rather than to an elitist, audience. Only later, in the era of literary ballads (more sophisticated poems that artfully evoked the atmosphere of the originals), did the rhyme scheme (*abcb*) and meter of the ballad stanza become standard.

The ballads as we know them today probably took their form in the fifteenth century, but they were not printed until Sir Thomas Percy published a number of them in 1765. Inspired by Percy, Sir Walter Scott and others traveled around the British Isles and copied down such folk songs from the people who still sang them. These ballads represent the rich history of the time.

Think About the Ballads Think about popular songs today as well as songs you might know from when your parents were growing up. How do popular songs or ballads reflect the culture and attitudes of a particular era?

Young musician, folio 47R of 14th century manuscript of De Musica by Anicius Boetius, c. 450-524 Biblioteca Nazionale, Naples

Reader/Writer
Notebook
Use your **RWN** to complete the activities for these selections.

Literary Focus

Ballad **Ballads** are songs or songlike poems that tell stories in simple, rhythmic language. Virtually every ballad includes certain predictable features, including sensational or tragic subject matter, omitted details, supernatural events, and a **refrain**—a repeated word, line, or group of lines.

Reading Focus

Understanding Purpose Although we do not know who wrote these ballads, we can still determine the authors' **purpose** from details in the text. We can look at details such as dialogue, images, or repetition. In "Lord Randall," for example, the mother repeats "my son" and "my handsome young man" in each stanza. We can see that she loves her boy and that she is upset about his behavior. We can guess that the purpose of this ballad is to share a tragic event with the listeners. The author of "Get Up and Bar the Door," in contrast, wants to share a humorous tale. We learn this purpose from details found at the very beginning of the ballad: This story will take place during a holiday inside a home full of comforting food. Even though we don't know the status of the author, we can still understand his or her purpose by paying attention to clues in the text.

Into Action As you read, use a chart like the one below to record details that help you determine the purposes of the ballads.

	"Lord Randall"	"Get Up and Bar the Door"	"Edward, Edward"
Details	mother's pleading tone		
Purpose:	to move to sadness		

Writing Focus

Think as a Reader/Writer

Find It in Your Reading Repetition is an essential feature of ballads. **Incremental repetition**—a phrase or sentence that is repeated with a new element each time—helps advance the story until the climax is reached. As you read, pay special attention to the use of repetition in each ballad.

TechFocus As you read these ballads, think about what a music video version of them might look like.

Language Coach

Anglo-Saxon Roots Many English words have changed their spelling and pronunciation since the Middle Ages. For example, the modern pronoun *you* was commonly written as *ye*. Today's English verb *have* was written often as *hae*. What familiar words can you discover in these words from the Middle Ages: *gat, nae, wi, sae, doun, mither*?

Learn It Online
Explore web links for these ballads online.

go.hrw.com | L12-185 | **Go**

LORD RANDALL

Read with a Purpose
Read this ballad to discover what happened to Lord Randall in the "wild wood."

Build Background
This ballad is sung in <u>diverse</u> versions in several countries. The basic story varies little, but Randall is variously known as Donald, Randolph, Ramsay, Ransome, and Durango. Sometimes his last meal consists of fish, sometimes snakes. The dialect of the version below is Scottish. This ballad, like many others, is sung entirely as a conversation in a question-and-answer format that builds suspense.

"O where hae ye been, Lord Randall, my son?
O where hae ye been, my handsome young man?"
"I hae been to the wild wood; mother, make my bed soon,
For I'm weary wi' hunting, and fain° wald lie down."

> **4. fain:** gladly.

5 "Where gat ye your dinner, Lord Randall, my son?
Where gat ye your dinner, my handsome young man?"
"I din'd wi' my true-love; mother, make my bed soon,
For I'm weary wi' hunting, and fain wald lie down." **A**

"What gat ye to your dinner, Lord Randall, my son?
10 What gat ye to° your dinner, my handsome young man?"
"I gat eels boil'd in broo;° mother, make my bed soon,
For I'm weary wi' hunting, and fain wald lie down."

> **10. gat ye to:** did you have for.
> **11. broo:** archaic form of "broth."

"What became of your bloodhounds, Lord Randall, my son?
What became of your bloodhounds, my handsome young man?"
15 "O they swell'd and they died; mother, make my bed soon,
For I'm weary wi' hunting, and fain wald lie down."

"O I fear ye are poison'd, Lord Randall, my son!
O I fear ye are poison'd, my handsome young man!"
"O yes! I am poison'd; mother, make my bed soon,
20 For I'm sick at the heart, and I fain wald lie down." **B**

A **Literary Focus** **Ballad** What lines here could be considered a refrain?

B **Reading Focus** **Understanding Purpose** What does Lord Randall's response to his mother's suspicion tell you about the purpose of the ballad?

"Bedford Hours" (detail). Lower margin. Calendar page for May. Man riding a horse, hunting with a hawk; Gemini. Workshop of the Master of the Duke of Bedford, Paris; 1414-1423.
The British Library Board, f.5 Add.18850

GET UP AND BAR THE DOOR

Read with a Purpose
Read to discover who wins the "battle of the sexes" in this ballad of medieval England.

Build Background
The story in this ballad exists in many versions in Europe, Asia, and the Middle East—perhaps illustrating the universal theme sometimes called the battle of the sexes. *Goodman* and *goodwife* are terms that were commonly applied to married men and women, something like *Mr.* and *Mrs.* today. The story takes place around November 11, Martinmas, or the feast of Saint Martin of Tours, which was usually celebrated with a big meal.

It fell about the Martinmas time,
   And a gay time it was then,
When our goodwife got puddings° to make,
   And she's boild them in the pan.

5   The wind sae cauld blew south and north,
   And blew into the floor;
Quoth our goodman to our goodwife,
   "Gae out and bar the door."

"My hand is in my hussyfskap,°
10   Goodman, as ye may see;
An° it should nae be barrd this hundred year,
   It's no be barrd for me." Ⓐ

They made a paction tween them twa,
   They made it firm and sure,
15   That the first word whaeer should speak,
   Should rise and bar the door.

Then by there came two gentlemen,
   At twelve o clock at night,
And they could neither see house nor hall,
20   Nor coal nor candle-light.

3. puddings: soft foods usually for special occasions; during this time, often meaning sausages.

9. hussyfskap: archaic word meaning "household chores."
11. an: archaic form of "if."

Ⓐ **Literary Focus** Ballad What story elements are introduced in these first three stanzas?

"Now whether is this a rich man's house,
    Or whether it is a poor?"
But neer a word ane° o them speak,
    For barring of the door.

25 And first they ate the white puddings,
    And then they ate the black;
Tho muckle° thought the goodwife to hersel,
    Yet neer a word she spake.

Then said the one unto the other,
30   "Here, man, tak ye my knife;
Do ye tak aff the auld man's beard,
    And I'll kiss the goodwife."

"But there's nae water in the house,°
    And what shall we do than?"
35 "What ails ye at the pudding-broo,°
    That boils into the pan?"

O up then started our goodman,
    An angry man was he:
"Will ye kiss my wife before my een,
40   And scad° me wi pudding-bree?"°

Then up and started our goodwife,
    Gied three skips on the floor:
"Goodman, you've spoken the foremost word,
    Get up and bar the door." **B**

23. ane: archaic form of "one."

27. muckle: archaic form of "much."

33. but . . . house: He probably wants water to soften the husband's beard.
35. What . . . pudding-broo: What's wrong with using the pudding broth?
40. scad: archaic form of "scald." **pudding-bree:** *Bree* is archaic form of "broth."

B Reading Focus **Understanding Purpose** What clues to the comic nature of this ballad are given in the final stanza?

January, from the *Da Costa Book of Hours* (c. 1515) by Simon Bening (1483–1561), Flemish (Bruges). The Pierpont Morgan Library, NY, c. 1515. MS. M. 399, f.2v

EDWARD, EDWARD

Read with a Purpose
Read this ballad to discover why Edward has blood on his sword.

Build Background
Like "Lord Randall," this tragic ballad exists in similar versions in different countries. Sir Thomas Percy, who in the 1760s compiled many popular ballads, found the same characters in a Swedish ballad and noted that a different version appeared with the title "Son Davie, Son Davie."

"Why does your brand sae drop wi' blude,° **A**
    Edward, Edward?
Why does your brand sae drop wi' blude,
    And why sae sad gang ye,° O?"—
5 "O I hae kill'd my hawk sae gude,°
    Mither, mither;
O I hae kill'd my hawk sae gude,
    And I had nae mair° but he, O."

"Your hawk's blude was never sae red,
10   Edward, Edward;
Your hawk's blude was never sae red,
    My dear son, I tell thee, O."—
"O I hae kill'd my red-roan steed,
    Mither, mither;
15 O I hae kill'd my red-roan steed,
    That erst° was sae fair and free, O."

"Your steed was auld,° and ye hae got mair,
    Edward, Edward;
Your steed was auld, and ye hae got mair;
20   Some other dule ye dree,° O."— **B**
"O I hae kill'd my father dear,
    Mither, mither;
O I hae kill'd my father dear,
    Alas, and wae is me, O!"

1. **brand . . . blude:** sword so drip with blood.

4. **gang ye:** go you.
5. **gude:** good.

8. **nae mair:** no more.

16. **erst:** before.

17. **auld:** old.

20. **dule ye dree:** grief you suffer.

A Reading Focus **Understanding Purpose** What clues to the tragic nature of this ballad are given in the first sentence?

B Reading Focus **Understanding Purpose** Why does Edward's mother mention that his hawk's blood wasn't so red and his steed was old and not his only horse?

25 "And whatten penance will ye dree° for that,
       Edward, Edward?
Whatten penance will ye dree for that?
       My dear son, now tell me, O."—
"I'll set my feet in yonder boat,
30   Mither, mither;
I'll set my feet in yonder boat,
       And I'll fare over the sea, O."

"And what will ye do wi' your tow'rs and your ha',°
       Edward, Edward?
35 And what will ye do wi' your tow'rs and your ha',
       That were sae fair to see, O?"—
"I'll let them stand till they doun fa',°
       Mither, mither;
I'll let them stand till they doun fa',
40   For here never mair maun° I be, O."

"And what will ye leave to your bairns° and your wife,
       Edward, Edward?
And what will ye leave to your bairns and your wife,
       When ye gang owre the sea, O?"—
45 "The warld's room: let them beg through life,
       Mither, mither;
The warld's room: let them beg through life;
       For them never mair will I see, O."

"And what will ye leave to your ain° mither dear,
50   Edward, Edward?
And what will ye leave to your ain mither dear,
       My dear son, now tell me, O?"—
"The curse of hell frae me sall ye bear°,
       Mither, mither;
55 The curse of hell frae me saw
       Sic counsels° ye gave to me, O!"   **C**

25. Whatten . . . dree: What punishment for sin will you suffer?

33. ha': hall; that is, ancestral home.

37. doun fa': fall down.

40. maun: must.

41. bairns: children.

49. ain: own.
53. frae me sall ye bear: you will carry for me.
56. sic counsels: such advice.

C **Literary Focus** **Ballad**   What is the surprise ending here?

The Sin of Worldly Vanities (c. 1300–c. 1320). The consequences of worldly vanities such as hunting and hawking are shown here as a rider with his hawk and hound is approached by a devil. One of a set illustrating the temptations, from poems by Matfre Ermengau. British Library, London.

Applying Your Skills

Ballads

Respond and Think Critically

Reading Focus

Quick Check

1. Where has Lord Randall been while away from his home?

2. In "Get Up and Bar the Door," what do the husband and wife argue about? What pact do they make?

3. What is the response of Edward's mother when he announces that he killed his father?

Read with a Purpose

4. What common view of life is represented in the three ballads?

Reading Skills: Understanding Purpose

5. While you read the ballads, you made note of details in the text that gave you clues to the author's purpose. Now that you have finished reading, review your conclusions. Then, add a row to your chart and identify, for each ballad, the most powerful and significant detail that led to your interpretation of the ballad's purpose.

	"Lord Randall"	"Get Up and Bar the Door"	"Edward, Edward"
Details:	mother's pleading tone		
Purpose:	to move to sadness		
Most powerful and significant detail:			

Literary Focus

Literary Analysis

6. **Infer** How did Lord Randall become ill?

7. **Analyze** Typical of ballads, "Lord Randall" ends with only half the story told. Why do you suppose the young man's lover has poisoned him? What other questions regarding the plot are left unanswered?

8. **Interpret** How is the word *dear* used differently by Edward and his mother in "Edward, Edward"? How do you interpret this difference?

9. **Make Judgments** In "Get Up and Bar the Door," what does the battle between the goodwife and goodman reveal about their characters?

Literary Skills: Ballad

10. **Compare** Questions and answers are often used by ballad authors. How does the series of questions and answers move the narratives of "Lord Randall" and "Edward, Edward" forward?

Literary Skills Review: Irony

11. **Evaluate** The contrast between what is expected and what really happens is called **irony.** How is each of these ballads ironic?

Writing Focus

Think as a Reader/Writer

Use It in Your Writing Review your notes on the use of repetition in each ballad. Using one of the ballads as a model, write a dialogue (it may or may not be a ballad) that uses repetition, including incremental repetition, to build to a climax and create a surprise ending. Use quotations to indicate who is speaking.

 What Do You Think Now

How can a popular song turn an everyday person into a hero?

CHOICES

As you respond to the Choices, use the **Academic Vocabulary** words as appropriate: <u>attribute</u>, <u>concept</u>, <u>diverse</u>, <u>emphasis</u>, <u>status</u>.

REVIEW

Identify Modern Ballads

With a partner, write down all the characteristics of ballads that you've learned in class and from reading the selections (the use of repetition, dialogue, and so on). Search the Internet for ballad lyrics on a specific topic appropriate for what you are studying in class—for example, "modern ballad lyrics" or "modern English ballad lyrics." Use your list as a guide for judging whether or not songs you find are ballads.

Compare Interpretations

Suppose that everything Edward predicts in "Edward, Edward" comes true. Create an illustration of the situation two years after the conversation in the ballad takes place. <u>Emphasize</u> elements that speak to each prediction Edward makes. Compare and contrast your interpretations with those of a classmate.

CONNECT

Understand Purpose

Timed ⏱ Writing Ballads depict the culture that produced them. In an essay, explain at least three characteristics of medieval English life as it is depicted in the ballads in this unit. Cite examples from the ballads to support your analysis.

Create a Music Video

TechFocus In a small group, create a music video to accompany one of these ballads. Search for a recording of the ballad you choose, or perform your own. Then, find or film images to go along with the ballad. Use the images to reveal your impressions of the ballad. Show your video to your class, and discuss how what your group created was similar to or different from how others visualized the ballad.

EXTEND

Perform a Ballad

Group Activity The comic "Get Up and Bar the Door" is just one example of how ballads handle the battle of the sexes. In a small group, find the ballad "The Old Man Who Lived in the Woods" (available in A *Treasury of New England Folklore* by B. A. Botkin) or a slightly different version called "Father Grumble" (located in *Folk Songs of the American People* edited by Alan Lomax). At what point in this new ballad do you know who's going to win the battle? How does this ballad

use repetition to create humor? Use these insights as you decide how to sing the ballad, and perform it as a group for your class.

Write News Stories

The simplicity and shortness of most ballads mean they focus on the big picture. Transform one of the ballads you read into a news story for the front page of a newspaper, and add realistic details that fit and fill out the narrative. Get together with members of your class, and arrange the stories to form a front page.

Preparing to Read

from Sir Gawain and the Green Knight

What Do You Think?

What moves a hero to act?

QuickWrite

Many heroes are tempted on their journeys. For example, Sir Gawain is tempted to steal from his host. In your *Reader/Writer Notebook,* write about why you think people may be tempted to steal.

About nine hundred years ago Chrétien de Troyes, a French court poet, began to craft tales of knightly adventures focusing on the exploits of King Arthur and the Knights of the Round Table. Between 1160 and 1190, Chrétien invented the style of narrative that is known today as **Arthurian romance.**

Not Just a Love Story

The medieval **romance** is a long narrative of prose or poetry that tells the adventures of a hero on a quest for something valuable. Love can play a role in Arthurian romance, but the hero is the focus. Because the romance hero is bound by the code of chivalry, which emphasizes loyalty to his lord and service to those who are oppressed, many romances are about seeking justice and helping people in need. The romance hero almost always encounters a series of trials, sometimes with dragons or supernatural beings such as witches or fairies. Today the term *romance* means any story that presents a happier, more perfect, or more heroic world.

Gawain the Gallant

One of the most famous Arthurian romances is *Sir Gawain and the Green Knight,* an anonymous narrative probably written around 1375. At this time, the ideals of knightly conduct were beginning to fade, and the poem is filled with romantic conventions that cling to those <u>concepts</u>.

As the poem opens, King Arthur and his knights are celebrating Christmas in Camelot. Suddenly, an enormous green stranger armed with a huge ax rides into the hall where the knights are dining. He challenges any knight to hit him immediately and says that he will return the hit after a year and a day. Gawain, the best of the knights, accepts the terms and beheads the challenger. But the Green Knight calmly picks up his own head, repeats his challenge, and gallops off with his head in his hand. The following selection tells what happens when Gawain encounters the Green Knight on the appointed day.

Think About the Poem

What contemporary story or movie can you think of that fits most of the criteria for a medieval romance?

Suit of Armor made for Christian I (1560–91) *of Saxony* (c. 1590) by Anton Peffenhauser (c. 1525–1602).

Reader/Writer Notebook

Use your **RWN** to complete the activities for this selection.

SKILLS FOCUS Literary Skills Understand the characteristics of a romance. **Reading Skills** Understand cause
and effect.

Literary Focus

The Romance The medieval **romance** narrative, which can be prose or poetry, features an idealized hero who undertakes a quest and overcomes danger for the sake of a noble lady or high ideal. The hero faces trials and adventures, often encountering supernatural or magical beings. Arthurian romance includes stories of Camelot and King Arthur's Knights of the Round Table.

Reading Focus

Understanding Cause and Effect A **cause** is the event that makes something happen. An **effect** is the result of that event. Recognizing causes and effects will help you understand the relationship between events in a narrative. Sometimes one action follows another but is not caused by it. Two events that are wrongly labeled as cause and effect create a **logical fallacy.**

Into Action As you read, use a diagram like the one below to record a cause for each of the important events of the selection. Be sure not to create incorrect relationships, or logical fallacies.

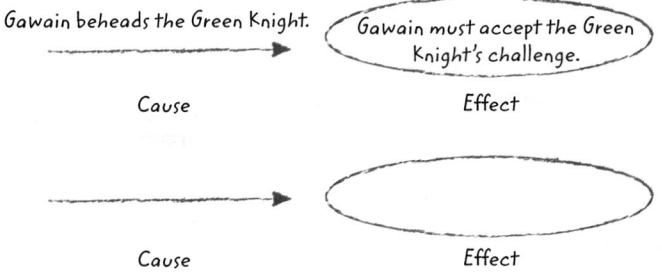

Gawain beheads the Green Knight. → Gawain must accept the Green Knight's challenge.

Cause   Effect

Cause   Effect

Vocabulary

whetting (HWEHT ihng) *v.* used as *adj.*: sharpening a blade on a stone made for the purpose. *He sharpened the blade on a whetting stone.*

daunted (DAWNT ihd) *v.* used as *adj.*: made to lose courage. *Gawain had never before been daunted by anything.*

shied (shyd) *v.*: shrank or flinched away. *Gawain shied from the blow of the ax.*

efficacious (ehf uh KAY shuhs) *adj.*: effective or useful. *Gawain's brave and boastful voice proves to be efficacious in his confrontation with the Green Knight.*

covetousness (KUHV uh tuhs nihs) *n.*: desire for what belongs to others. *Gawain accused himself of covetousness.*

Language Coach

Past-Tense Verbs Most verbs add the *–ed* ending to show action in the past. Verbs that end in *y* change the *y* to *i* before adding *–ed*. The verb *shied* is the past-tense form of the verb *shy*. What other Vocabulary word ends in *–ed*?

Writing Focus

Think as a Reader/Writer

Find It in Your Reading Writers often use **imagery** to share their ideas with readers. A writer might present a visual picture of a dream, for example, to share a character's innermost feelings in a dramatic way. As you read, note in your *Reader/Writer Notebook* passages in the selection in which imagery helps you understand and "experience" the romance hero's challenges.

 **Learn It Online**
Find interactive cause-and-effect graphic organizers online.

go.hrw.com L12-195   **Go**

from Sir Gawain and the Green Knight

translated by **John Gardner**

Read with a Purpose
Read this selection from an Arthurian romance to find out if Gawain keeps his promises.

Build Background
Gawain has come upon a mysterious castle, where for three days he is tempted by the absent lord's wife. On the last day he accepts more than just her kisses and takes a magical green sash that she claims will protect him from harm. Gawain leaves the castle with the green sash wrapped around his armor, intent on finding the Green Chapel and the dreaded Green Knight. He is certain he is headed for his death.

He put his spurs to Gringolet,° plunged down the path,
Shoved through the heavy thicket grown up by the woods
And rode down the steep slope to the floor of the valley;
He looked around him then—a strange, wild place,
5   And not a sign of a chapel on any side
But only steep, high banks surrounding him,
And great, rough knots of rock and rugged crags
That scraped the passing clouds, as it seemed to him. **Ⓐ**
He heaved at the heavy reins to hold back his horse
10 And squinted in every direction in search of the Chapel,
And still he saw nothing except—and this was strange—
A small green hill all alone, a sort of barrow,°
A low, smooth bulge on the bank of the brimming creek
That flowed from the foot of a waterfall,
15 And the water in the pool was bubbling as if it were boiling.
Sir Gawain urged Gringolet on till he came to the mound
And lightly dismounted and made the reins secure
On the great, thick limb of a gnarled and ancient tree;
Then he went up to the barrow and walked all around it,
20 Wondering in his wits what on earth it might be.
It had at each end and on either side an entrance,
And patches of grass were growing all over the thing,
And all the inside was hollow—an old, old cave
Or the cleft of some ancient crag, he couldn't tell which
25   it was.

1. **Gringolet:** Gawain's horse.

12. **barrow:** grave mound.

Ⓐ Literary Focus The Romance How does this scenery fit in with the elements of the romance?

"Whoo, Lord!" thought the knight,
"Is this the fellow's place?
Here the Devil might
Recite his midnight mass. **B**

30 "Dear God," thought Gawain, "the place is deserted enough!
And it's ugly enough, all overgrown with weeds!
Well might it amuse that marvel of green
To do his devotions here, in his devilish way! **C**
In my five senses I fear it's the Fiend himself
35 Who's brought me to meet him here to murder me.
May fire and fury befall this fiendish Chapel,
As cursed a kirk° as I ever yet came across!"
With his helmet on his head and his lance in hand
He leaped up onto the roof of the rock-walled room
40 And, high on that hill, he heard, from an echoing rock
Beyond the pool, on the hillside, a horrible noise.
Brrrack! It clattered in the cliffs as if to cleave them,
A sound like a grindstone grinding on a scythe!°
Brrrack! It whirred and rattled like water on a mill wheel!
45 *Brrrrrack!* It rushed and rang till your blood ran cold.

B **Reading Focus** **Understanding Cause and Effect** In these two stanzas, Gawain describes a disturbing and frightening place. What causes him to stay in such a place?

C **Literary Focus** **The Romance** What particular convention, or element, of romances does Gawain's description of whom—or what—he expects to meet call to mind?

Analyzing Visuals

Viewing and Interpreting In this painting, who appears to take the role of the romantic hero? What other elements of the romance can you find in this painting?

Sir Gawain and the Green Knight. Illustration by William McLaren.

37. kirk: Scottish word for "church."

43. scythe: long-handled cutting tool.

And then: "Oh God," thought Gawain, "it grinds, I think,
For me—a blade prepared for the blow I must take
                    as my right!
                God's will be done! But here!
50   He may well get his knight,
                But still, no use in fear;
                I won't fall dead of fright!"

And then Sir Gawain roared in a ringing voice,
"Where is the hero who swore he'd be here to meet me?
55 Sir Gawain the Good is come to the Green Chapel!
If any man would meet me, make it now,
For it's now or never, I've no wish to dawdle here long."
"Stay there!" called someone high above his head,
"I'll pay you promptly all that I promised before."
60 But still he went on with that whetting noise a while,
Turning again to his grinding before he'd come down.
At last, from a hole by a rock he came out into sight,
Came plunging out of his den with a terrible weapon,
A huge new Danish ax to deliver his blow with,
65 With a vicious swine of a bit bent back to the handle,
Filed to a razor's edge and four foot long,
Not one inch less by the length of that gleaming lace.
The great Green Knight was garbed as before,
Face, legs, hair, beard, all as before but for this:
70 That now he walked the world on his own two legs,
The ax handle striking the stone like a walking-stave.°
When the knight came down to the water he would not wade
But vaulted across on his ax, then with awful strides
Came fiercely over the field filled all around
75   with snow.
                Sir Gawain met him there
                And bowed—but none too low!
                Said the other, "I see, sweet sir,
                You go where you say you'll go!

80 "Gawain," the Green Knight said, "may God be your guard!
You're very welcome indeed, sir, here at my place;
You've timed your travel, my friend, as a true man should.
You recall the terms of the contract drawn up between us:
At this time a year ago you took your chances,
85 And I'm pledged now, this New Year, to make you my payment. **D**

Gawain, directed by Di Trevis

71. walking-stave: walking stick
or staff.

D Reading Focus **Understanding Cause and Effect** The Green Knight is going to
give Gawain an ax blow to the back of his neck. What do you expect the result to be?

Vocabulary **whetting** (HWEHT ihng) *v.* used as *adj.:* sharpening a blade on a
stone made for the purpose.

And here we are in this valley, all alone,
And no man here to part us, proceed as we may;
Heave off your helmet then, and have here your pay;
And debate no more with me than I did then
90   When you severed my head from my neck with a single swipe."
"Never fear," said Gawain, "by God who gave
Me life, I'll raise no complaint at the grimness of it;
But take your single stroke, and I'll stand still
And allow you to work as you like and not oppose
95   you here."
              He bowed toward the ground
              And let his skin show clear;
              However his heart might pound,
              He would not show his fear.

100 Quickly then the man in the green made ready,
Grabbed up his keen-ground ax to strike Sir Gawain;
With all the might in his body he bore it aloft
And sharply brought it down as if to slay him;
Had he made it fall with the force he first intended
105 He would have stretched out the strongest man on earth.
But Sir Gawain cast a side glance at the ax
As it glided down to give him his Kingdom Come,°
And his shoulders jerked away from the iron a little,
And the Green Knight caught the handle, holding it back,
110 And mocked the prince with many a proud reproof:°
"You can't be Gawain," he said, "who's thought so good,
A man who's never been daunted on hill or dale!   **E**
For look how you flinch for fear before anything's felt!
I never heard tell that Sir Gawain was ever a coward!
115 *I* never moved a muscle when *you* came down;
In Arthur's hall I never so much as winced.
My head fell off at my feet, yet I never flickered;
But you! You tremble at heart before you're touched!
I'm bound to be called a better man than you, then,
120   my lord."
              Said Gawain, "I shied once:
              No more. You have my word.
              But if my head falls to the stones
              It cannot be restored.

125 "But be brisk, man, by your faith, and come to the point!

107. his Kingdom Come: life after death.

110. reproof: rebuke; scolding.

E | Literary Focus | The Romance   What does Gawain's glance reveal about him?

Vocabulary **daunted** (DAWNT ihd) *v.* used as *adj.*: made to lose courage.
shied (shyd) *v.*: shrank or flinched away.

Deal out my doom if you can, and do it at once,
For I'll stand for one good stroke, and I'll start no more
Until your ax has hit—and that I swear."
"Here goes, then," said the other, and heaves it aloft

130 And stands there waiting, scowling like a madman;
He swings down sharp, then suddenly stops again,
Holds back the ax with his hand before it can hurt,
And Gawain stands there stirring not even a nerve;
He stood there still as a stone or the stock of a tree

135 That's wedged in rocky ground by a hundred roots. **F**
O, merrily then he spoke, the man in green:
"Good! You've got your heart back! Now I can hit you.
May all that glory the good King Arthur gave you
Prove efficacious now—if it ever can—

140 And save your neck." In rage Sir Gawain shouted,
"*Hit* me, hero! I'm right up to here with your threats!
Is it *you* that's the cringing coward after all?"
"Whoo!" said the man in green, "he's wrathful, too!
No pauses, then; I'll pay up my pledge at once,

145   I vow!"

                    He takes his stride to strike
                    And lifts his lip and brow;
                    It's not a thing Gawain can like,
                    For nothing can save him now!

150 He raises that ax up lightly and flashes it down,
And that blinding bit bites in at the knight's bare neck—
But hard as he hammered it down, it hurt him no more
Than to nick the nape of his neck, so it split the skin;
The sharp blade slit to the flesh through the shiny hide,

155 And red blood shot to his shoulders and spattered the ground.
And when Gawain saw his blood where it blinked in the snow
He sprang from the man with a leap to the length of a spear;
He snatched up his helmet swiftly and slapped it on,
Shifted his shield into place with a jerk of his shoulders,

160 And snapped his sword out faster than sight; said boldly—
And, mortal born of his mother that he was,
There was never on earth a man so happy by half—
"No more strokes, my friend; you've had your swing!
I've stood one swipe of your ax without resistance;

Sir Gawain and the Green Knight. Illustration by
William McLaren.

G Reading Focus Understanding Cause and Effect What causes Gawain to be
able to survive the Green Knight's stroke?

F Reading Focus Understanding Cause and Effect Why does the Green Knight
stop his ax before it hits Gawain?

Vocabulary **efficacious** (ehf uh KAY shuhs) *adj.*: effective or useful.

165 If you offer me any more, I'll repay you at once
With all the force and fire I've got—as you

will see. Ⓖ
I take one stroke, that's all,
For that was the compact we

170
Arranged in Arthur's hall;
But now, no more for me!"

The Green Knight remained where he stood, relaxing on his ax—
Settled the shaft on the rocks and leaned on the sharp end—
And studied the young man standing there, shoulders hunched,

175 And considered that staunch° and doughty° stance he took,
Undaunted yet, and in his heart he liked it;
And then he said merrily, with a mighty voice—
With a roar like rushing wind he reproved the knight—
"Here, don't be such an ogre on your ground!

180 Nobody here has behaved with bad manners toward you
Or done a thing except as the contract said.
I owed you a stroke, and I've struck; consider yourself
Well paid. And now I release you from all further duties.
If I'd cared to hustle, it may be, perchance, that I might

185 Have hit somewhat harder, and then you might well be cross!
The first time I lifted my ax it was lighthearted sport,
I merely feinted and made no mark, as was right,
For you kept our pact of the first night with honor
And abided by your word and held yourself true to me,

190 Giving me all you owed as a good man should. Ⓗ
I feinted a second time, friend, for the morning
You kissed my pretty wife twice and returned me the kisses;
And so for the first two days, mere feints, nothing more

severe.

195
A man who's true to his word,
There's nothing he needs to fear;
You failed me, though, on the third
Exchange, so I've tapped you here.

"That sash you wear by your scabbard° belongs to me;

200 My own wife gave it to you, as I ought to know.
I know, too, of your kisses and all your words
And my wife's advances, for I myself arranged them.
It was I who sent her to test you. I'm convinced
You're the finest man that ever walked this earth.

205 As a pearl is of greater price than dry white peas,
So Gawain indeed stands out above all other knights.
But you lacked a little, sir; you were less than loyal;

175. **staunch:** steadfast;
stubborn. **doughty:** courageous.

199. **scabbard:** carrying case
that covers the blade of a sword;
sheath.

Ⓗ Reading Focus **Understanding Cause and Effect** To what does the Green
Knight attribute his actions?

But since it was not for the sash itself or for lust
But because you loved your life, I blame you less."

210 Sir Gawain stood in a study° a long, long while,
So miserable with disgrace that he wept within,
And all the blood of his chest went up to his face
And he shrank away in shame from the man's gentle words.
The first words Gawain could find to say were these:

215 "Cursed be cowardice and covetousness both,
Villainy and vice that destroy all virtue!"
He caught at the knots of the girdle° and loosened them
And fiercely flung the sash at the Green Knight.
"There, there's my fault! The foul fiend vex it!

220 Foolish cowardice taught me, from fear of your stroke,
To bargain, covetous, and abandon my kind,
The selflessness and loyalty suitable in knights;
Here I stand, faulty and false, much as I've feared them,
Both of them, untruth and treachery; may they see sorrow

225   and care!
                    I can't deny my guilt;
                    My works shine none too fair!
                    Give me your good will
                    And henceforth I'll beware." **I**

230 At that, the Green Knight laughed, saying graciously,
"Whatever harm I've had, I hold it amended
Since now you're confessed so clean, acknowledging sins
And bearing the plain penance of my point;
I consider you polished as white and as perfectly clean

235 As if you had never fallen since first you were born.
And I give you, sir, this gold-embroidered girdle,
For the cloth is as green as my gown. Sir Gawain, think
On this when you go forth among great princes;
Remember our struggle here; recall to your mind

240 This rich token. Remember the Green Chapel. **J**
And now, come on, let's both go back to my castle
And finish the New Year's revels° with feasting and joy,
                    not strife,
                    I beg you," said the lord,

245   And said, "As for my wife,
                    She'll be your friend, no more
                    A threat against your life."

Gawain, directed by Di Trevis

I **Literary Focus** **The Romance** Why is Gawain so angry with himself?

J **Reading Focus** **Understanding Cause and Effect** What is the effect of Gawain's choice to take the blow, of his confession, and of his apology?

Vocabulary **covetousness** (KUHV uh tuhs nihs) *n.:* desire for what belongs to others.

210. stood in a study: stood thinking deeply.

217. girdle: a sash worn as a belt.

242. revels: festivities, often as part of a celebration.

Applying Your Skills

from **Sir Gawain and the Green Knight**

SKILLS FOCUS Literary Skills Analyze the characteristics of the romance narrative; analyze climax. **Reading Skills** Analyze cause and effect. **Writing Skills** Develop descriptions with sensory details.

Respond and Think Critically

Reading Focus

Quick Check

1. Why did Sir Gawain go to the Green Chapel?

2. What reasons did Sir Gawain have to be concerned about the outcome of the meeting?

3. What prevents Gawain's death?

Read with a Purpose

4. Does Gawain keep his promises?

Reading Skills: Understanding Cause and Effect

5. As you read *Sir Gawain and the Green Knight,* you noted effects and their causes. Now, review your conclusions. Add more arrows to your diagrams, and identify which effects had multiple causes.

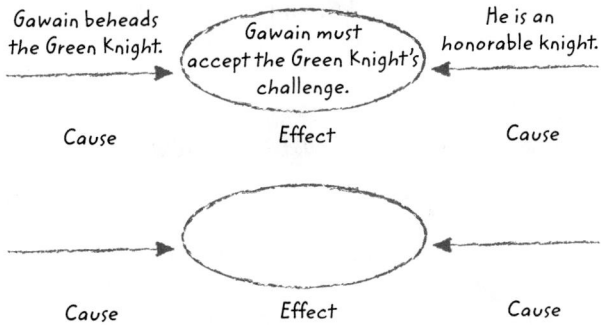

Gawain beheads the Green Knight.   He is an honorable knight.

Gawain must accept the Green Knight's challenge.

Cause   Effect   Cause

Cause   Effect   Cause

Literary Focus

Literary Analysis

6. Draw Conclusions What images make the setting of the confrontation seem demonic?

7. Evaluate The Green Knight believes that Gawain has restored himself completely by his confession of his fault and acceptance of the blow. Do you agree? Explain.

8. Make Judgments How would you describe the writer's **tone**—or attitude—in this tale? Is he entirely serious, or do you find moments of humor? Find passages in the text to support your answer.

9. Extend What meaning will the gift Gawain receives have for him in the future?

Literary Skills: The Romance

10. Interpret How is Gawain a superhuman romance hero? How is he weak or flawed, just as an ordinary person might be? Cite details from the poem to support your response.

Literary Skills Review: Climax

11. Draw Conclusions The **climax** of a story is the point when the major conflict reaches its greatest moment of tension—the resolution is unknown, but the end is in sight. What do you think is the climax of this story?

Writing Focus

Think as a Reader/Writer

Use It in Your Writing Review your notes on how the poem uses imagery to convey Gawain's challenges. Write a short paragraph about a time when you or someone you know faced a challenge. Use imagery to make your description come alive for your readers.

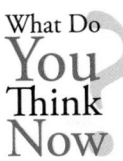

What Do You Think Now

How does the chivalric code of honor and heroism affect Gawain?

from **Sir Gawain and the Green Knight**

Vocabulary Development

✓ Vocabulary Check

Match the Vocabulary words with their synonyms.

1. whetting
2. daunted
3. shied
4. efficacious
5. covetousness

a. flinched
b. envious
c. sharpening
d. made afraid
e. effective

Vocabulary Skills: Map Meanings

A word map can help you learn a word's relationship to other words. You can use word maps to identify a word's **synonyms,** which are words with similar meanings, and **antonyms,** which are words with opposite meanings. When you know a word's synonyms and antonyms, you can use them in your writing. Here is a sample word map:

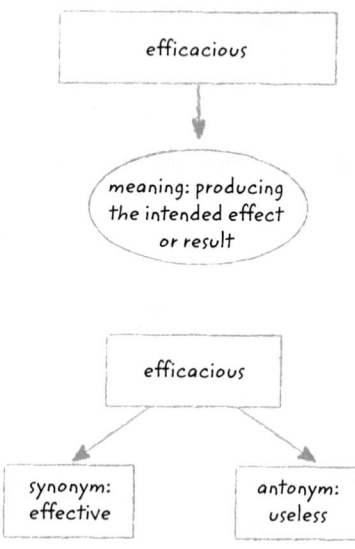

Your Turn

For each of the other Vocabulary words, create a word map like the one in the lefthand column. Not every Vocabulary word will have an antonym.

Language Coach

Past-Tense Verbs Follow spelling rules to help you recognize verbs. Most verbs add *–ed* to form the past tense. If the verb ends in *y*, the *y* is changed to *i* before adding *–ed*. For example: *cried* is the past tense of the verb *cry*. Write the present-tense form of each verb below. Then, define each word or look up its meaning in a dictionary.

1. shied
2. plied
3. pried

4. complied
5. denied
6. supplied

Academic Vocabulary

Talk About . . .

In a small group, discuss the modern concept of a hero. What qualities do we attribute to heroes? How might qualities vary among diverse cultures? What qualities are universal? What might be a modern hero's quest, and what form would the tests of the hero's honor or courage take?

Learn It Online
Find out more about synonyms at

go.hrw.com   L12-204   **Go**

SKILLS FOCUS **Vocabulary Skills** Identify and correctly use synonyms; identify and correctly use antonyms. **Grammar Skills** Understand transitive and intransitive verbs.

Viewing and Representing Skills Prepare a multimedia presentation.
Writing Skills Write a parody.

Grammar Link

Transitive and Intransitive Verbs

A **transitive** verb has a direct object—a word or word group that tells who or what receives the action of the verb. You could say, "I studied my geometry notes for an hour." In this sentence, *studied* is transitive because it has a direct object: *my geometry notes*. In contrast, an **intransitive** verb does not have a direct object. You could say, "Luis also studied for an hour." Here, *studied* is intransitive because it has no direct object. When you want to decide whether a verb is transitive or intransitive, look at the entire sentence for a clue. If you are still not sure whether a verb is transitive or intransitive, look in a dictionary. Most dictionaries group the definitions of verbs according to whether the verbs are used transitively (*v.t.*) or intransitively (*v.i.*).

Your Turn

Identify each italicized verb below as transitive or intransitive.

1. "It *whirred* and *rattled* like water on a mill wheel!"

2. "Sir Gawain *met* him there
   And *bowed*."

3. "And his shoulders *jerked* away from the iron a little,
   And the Green Knight *caught* the handle."

4. "Said Gawain, 'I *shied* once:
   No more.'"

5. "He *takes* his stride to strike
   And *lifts* his lip and brow."

Writing Application Select a paragraph you have written, and identify the verbs as either transitive or intransitive.

CHOICES

As you respond to the Choices, use these **Academic Vocabulary** words as appropriate: attribute, concept, diverse, emphasis, status.

REVIEW
Set the Scene
TechFocus At the beginning of this selection, the sights and sounds Gawain encounters fill him with foreboding. In a short multimedia presentation, create your own representation of what Gawain saw and heard. You can use still images combined with sound, create an animation, or film a live scenario.

CONNECT
Present a Romance
Modern tales of quests feature many elements of the medieval romance. With a partner, select a contemporary tale told in a movie, television show, book, or other medium that reflects the elements of romance. You might consider the genres of adventure (such as the Indiana Jones series) and space quests (such as the Star Wars series). Make an oral presentation to the class in which you show the relevant scene and emphasize how it reflects elements of romance. Explain the similarities and differences between Sir Gawain and the Green Knight and your contemporary example.

EXTEND
Write a Parody
Group Activity The strong elements of romance make it ripe for **parody**—a work that makes fun of another work by imitating some aspect of the writer's style. With a group, brainstorm ways in which you can parody a medieval or Arthurian romance. Think carefully about setting, characters, and plot as you work. Your parody can take the form of a prose narrative, a poem, skit, play, video, or recorded song or ballad.

from Le Morte d'Arthur

What Do You Think? What moves a hero to act?

QuickWrite

Why must every hero have an antagonist or enemy? Would the hero be considered heroic without an enemy. Write your ideas in your *Reader/Writer Notebook.*

Tournament of Knights of the Round Table watched by King Arthur and Queen Guinevere, from 15th-century French manuscript of *Le roman du roi Arthur et les compagnons de la Table Ronde (Book of King Arthur and the Knights of the Round Table)* by Chrétien de Troyes (died c. 1183). Biblioteca Nazionale, Turin..

Sir Thomas Malory
(c. 1405–1471)

The historical identity of Sir Thomas Malory is a mystery that has puzzled scholars and historians for centuries.

Mysterious Malory

All we know for sure about Malory is that he was a knight familiar with chivalric romances who was writing in the years 1469–1470. There was more than one Sir Thomas Malory at the time, but it is generally presumed that an imprisoned knight from Warwickshire is the Malory on the manuscript. This Malory served in France during the Hundred Years' War and apparently fought at the siege of Calais in 1436. He was elected to Parliament at least once. The record of this war hero also includes a series of arrests for theft, burglary, and assault, including the robbing of an abbey in which he allegedly broke down eighteen doors and roughed up the monks. However, since there is no record of any trials or convictions, the accusations against Malory may have been politically motivated.

A Fascination with King Arthur

The Arthur in Malory's work is not the historical sixth-century general who helped his fellow Britons defend themselves against the invading Saxons. No, Malory's Arthur is a consolidation of later legends that developed in England and on the Continent. Using Celtic and Continental sources, Malory created a mythic Arthur who later became the very embodiment of British values.

Coming as it does at the end of the fifteenth century, Malory's work serves as a kind of swan song to the feudal order of the Middle Ages with its castles, knights, and chivalric codes. Malory's readers lived in a different world. Cities were growing, and money and competition were replacing the old feudal ways of barter and mutual obligation. With the death of the ideal King Arthur, Malory is recording the death of the entire way of life that the legendary King Arthur represents.

Think About the Writer What other literary heroes of any time period might have attracted Malory's interest?

Reader/Writer Notebook

Use your **RWN** to complete the activities for this selection.

Literary Focus

The Romance Hero A **romance hero** in medieval literature is someone who embarks on an adventure that ends in some sort of fulfillment or reward. Throughout the journey, the hero strives to prove his worth, often by helping others in need. Malory's Arthur is in many ways the model, or **archetypal,** romance hero—the medieval descendant of the epic hero. He is handsome, strong, and noble and has a strict moral code. He grows up in obscurity and undergoes a childhood initiation involving a magic weapon. As an adult, he fights to defeat evil and promote peace. Throughout his life he is aided by magical weapons and mysterious events. Even his departure implies that he may return to help his people when they are in need.

Reading Focus

Analyzing Details As you read, pay close attention to the **details** describing the characters, their dialogue, and the interactions between them. There is almost nothing in the reading that doesn't teach us something about the romance hero. Malory's story begins with a dream, which <u>emphasizes</u> the supernatural or superhuman experiences of the romance hero. We see details of Arthur's clothing, his room, his enemies, and his response to the challenge of being attacked by mysterious creatures. All of these descriptions help us understand Arthur's character and values. We know that this story and this hero will be larger than life.

Into Action Complete a chart like the one below to note details you notice in the story that help you understand the romance hero.

Key Detail	Significance
Arthur's clothes ("gold cloth")	shows us that our hero is royal

Writing Focus

Think as a Reader/Writer

Find It in Your Reading As you read, note in your *Reader/Writer Notebook* places in the story where Malory's use of **dialogue** draws you in emotionally and gives you a better picture of what is happening to the romance hero.

Vocabulary

righteous (RY chuhs) *adj.:* virtuous. *Arthur felt that he was the more righteous fighter.*

prevailed (prih VAYLD) *v.:* won out; persuaded. *Gawain prevailed on Arthur to propose a truce to Mordred.*

dissuade (dih SWAYD) *v.:* deter from or advise against. *The faithful knight tried to dissuade the old king from fighting a losing battle.*

brandishing (BRAN dihsh ihng) *v.* used as *adj.:* shaking in a threatening way. *Brandishing his sword, the knight charged at his opponent.*

piteous (PIHT ee uhs) *adj.:* evoking pity. *Arthur's death was sad and piteous.*

Language Coach

Prefixes A **prefix** is a word part that comes at the beginning of the word and changes its meaning. The word *dissuade* includes the prefix *dis–*, which can mean "against" or "the opposite of." You can see the meaning of this prefix in the word's definition: "advise against." Explain how the prefix *dis–* affects the meanings of these words: *disagree, disappear, distrust, distract.*

Learn It Online
Read more about these vocabulary words on

go.hrw.com L12-207 **Go**

from Le Morte d'Arthur

by **Sir Thomas Malory**
retold by **Keith Baines**

Read with a Purpose

As you read the selection, think about how Malory presents King Arthur as a victim of circumstances that ultimately make him a hero.

Build Background

Le Morte d'Arthur is not about Arthur's death, as the title implies, but about his glorious life. Arthur's goal is to unite the knights of his realm in the fellowship of the Round Table. He does, and for a time there is peace. Ultimately, human weaknesses lead to the disintegration of his rule. Sir Modred is Arthur's illegitimate son and now his enemy. In this section, Arthur is about to confront his son on the battlefield.

Then, on the night of Trinity Sunday, Arthur was vouchsafed[1] a strange dream:

He was appareled in gold cloth and seated in a chair which stood on a pivoted[2] scaffold. Below him, many fathoms deep, was a dark well, and in the water swam serpents, dragons, and wild beasts. Suddenly the scaffold tilted and Arthur was flung into the water, where all the creatures struggled toward him and began tearing him limb from limb.

Arthur cried out in his sleep and his squires hastened to waken him. Later, as he lay between waking and sleeping, he thought he saw Sir Gawain, and with him a host of beautiful noblewomen. Arthur spoke:

"My sister's son! I thought you had died; but now I see you live, and I thank the lord Jesu! I pray you, tell me, who are these ladies?"

"My lord, these are the ladies I championed in righteous quarrels when I was on earth. Our lord God has vouchsafed that we visit you and plead with you not to give battle to Sir Modred tomorrow,

1. **vouchsafed:** graciously given.
2. **pivoted:** turned; able to be turned.

Vocabulary **righteous** (RY chuhs) *adj.:* virtuous.

for if you do, not only will you yourself be killed, but all your noble followers too. We beg you to be warned, and to make a treaty with Sir Modred, calling a truce for a month, and granting him whatever terms he may demand. In a month Sir Launcelot will be here, and he will defeat Sir Modred." **Ⓐ**

Thereupon Sir Gawain and the ladies vanished, and King Arthur once more summoned his squires and his counselors and told them his vision. Sir Lucas and Sir Bedivere were commissioned to make a treaty

---

Ⓐ Reading Focus **Analyzing Details** Arthur considers Gawain's advice to hold back from battle. What does this tell us about Arthur's <u>status</u> as a leader?

with Sir Modred. They were to be accompanied by two bishops and to grant, within reason, whatever terms he demanded.

The ambassadors found Sir Modred in command of an army of a hundred thousand and unwilling to listen to overtures of peace. However, the ambassadors eventually prevailed on him, and in return for the truce granted him suzerainty[3] of Cornwall and Kent, and succession to the British throne when King Arthur died. The treaty was to be signed by King Arthur and Sir Modred the next day. They were to meet between the two armies, and each was to be accompanied by no more than fourteen knights. **Ⓑ**

Both King Arthur and Sir Modred suspected the other of treachery, and gave orders for their armies to attack at the sight of a naked sword. When they met at the appointed place, the treaty was signed and both drank a glass of wine.

Then, by chance, one of the soldiers was bitten in the foot by an adder which had lain concealed in the brush. The soldier unthinkingly drew his sword to kill it, and at once, as the sword flashed in the light, the alarums were given, trumpets sounded, and both armies galloped into the attack.

"Alas for this fateful day!" exclaimed King Arthur, as both he and Sir Modred hastily mounted and galloped back to their armies. There followed one of those rare and heartless battles in which both armies fought until they were destroyed. King Arthur, with his customary valor, led squadron after squadron of cavalry into the attack, and Sir Modred encountered him unflinchingly. As the number of dead and

---

3. **suzerainty:** position of feudal lord.

Ⓑ Literary Focus **The Romance Hero** What power or asset does Sir Modred possess that gives him the ability to challenge Arthur?

Vocabulary **prevailed** (prih VAYLD) *v.*: won out; persuaded.

King Arthur (2004) Keira Knightley, Clive Owen.

wounded mounted on both sides, the active combatants continued dauntless until nightfall, when four men alone survived.

King Arthur wept with dismay to see his beloved followers fallen; then, struggling toward him, unhorsed and badly wounded, he saw Sir Lucas the Butler and his brother, Sir Bedivere.

"Alas!" said the king, "that the day should come when I see all my noble knights destroyed! I would prefer that I myself had fallen. But what has become of the traitor Sir Modred, whose evil ambition was responsible for this carnage?" **C**

Looking about him King Arthur then noticed Sir Modred leaning with his sword on a heap of the dead.

"Sir Lucas, I pray you give me my spear, for I have seen Sir Modred."

"Sire, I entreat you, remember your vision—how Sir Gawain appeared with a heaven-sent message to dissuade you from fighting Sir Modred. Allow this fateful day to pass; it is ours, for we three hold the field, while the enemy is broken." **D**

"My lords, I care nothing for my life now! And while Sir Modred is at large I must kill him: there may not be another chance."

"God speed you, then!" said Sir Bedivere.

When Sir Modred saw King Arthur advance with his spear, he rushed to meet him with drawn sword. Arthur caught Sir Modred below the shield and drove his spear through his body; Sir Modred, knowing that the wound was mortal, thrust himself up to the handle of the spear, and then, brandishing his sword in both hands, struck Arthur on the side of the helmet, cutting through it and into the skull beneath; then he crashed to the ground, gruesome and dead.

King Arthur fainted many times as Sir Lucas and Sir Bedivere struggled with him to a small chapel nearby, where they managed to ease his wounds a little. When Arthur came to, he thought he heard cries coming from the battlefield.

"Sir Lucas, I pray you, find out who cries on the battlefield," he said.

Wounded as he was, Sir Lucas hobbled painfully to the field, and there in the moonlight saw the camp followers stealing gold and jewels from the dead, and murdering the wounded. He returned to the king and reported to him what he had seen, and then added:

On the set of the movie *King Arthur* (2004). Ioan Gruffudd, Keira Knightly, and Clive Owen.

C Literary Focus The Romance Hero What role do Arthur and Modred both play in the carnage?

D Literary Focus The Romance Hero How might Sir Lucas be thought of as a hero, if even in a small way?

Vocabulary **dissuade** (dih SWAYD) v.: deter from or advise against.
brandishing (BRAN dihsh ihng) v. used as adj.: shaking in a threatening way.

Viewing and Interpreting How does the romantic hero depicted here match Malory's description of Arthur and Arthur's view of himself in his dream?

"My lord, it surely would be better to move you to the nearest town?" **E**

"My wounds forbid it. But alas for the good Sir Launcelot! How sadly I have missed him today! And now I must die—as Sir Gawain warned me I would—repenting our quarrel with my last breath."

Sir Lucas and Sir Bedivere made one further attempt to lift the king. He fainted as they did so. Then Sir Lucas fainted as part of his intestines broke through a wound in the stomach. When the king came to, he saw Sir Lucas lying dead with foam at his mouth.

"Sweet Jesu, give him succor!"⁴ he said. "This noble knight has died trying to save my life—alas that this was so!"

Sir Bedivere wept for his brother.

"Sir Bedivere, weep no more," said King Arthur, "for you can save neither your brother nor me; and I would ask you to take my sword Excalibur⁵ to the shore of the lake and throw it in the water. Then return to me and tell me what you have seen."

"My lord, as you command, it shall be done." **F**

Sir Bedivere took the sword, but when he came to the water's edge, it appeared so beautiful that he could not bring himself to throw it in, so instead he hid it by a tree, and then returned to the king.

"Sir Bedivere, what did you see?"

"My lord, I saw nothing but the wind upon the waves."

"Then you did not obey me; I pray you, go swiftly again, and this time fulfill my command."

Sir Bedivere went and returned again, but this time too he had failed to fulfill the king's command.

"Sir Bedivere, what did you see?"

"My lord, nothing but the lapping of the waves."

"Sir Bedivere, twice you have betrayed me! And for the sake only of my sword: it is unworthy of you! Now I pray you, do as I command, for I have not long to live."

This time Sir Bedivere wrapped the girdle around the sheath and hurled it as far as he could into the water. A hand appeared from below the surface, took the sword, waved it thrice, and disappeared again. Sir Bedivere returned to the king and told him what he had seen.

"Sir Bedivere, I pray you now help me hence, or I fear it will be too late."

Sir Bedivere carried the king to the water's edge, and there found a barge in which sat many beautiful ladies with their queen. All were wearing black hoods, and when they saw the king, they raised their voices in a piteous lament.

"I pray you, set me in the barge," said the king.

Sir Bedivere did so, and one of the ladies laid the king's head in her lap; then the queen spoke to him:

"My dear brother, you have stayed too long: I fear that the wound on your head is already cold." **G**

Thereupon they rowed away from the land and Sir Bedivere wept to see them go.

"My lord King Arthur, you have deserted me! I am alone now, and among enemies."

"Sir Bedivere, take what comfort you may, for my time is passed, and now I must be taken to Avalon⁶ for my wound to be healed. If you hear of me no more, I beg you pray for my soul."

The barge slowly crossed the water and out of sight while the ladies wept. Sir Bedivere walked alone into the forest and there remained for the night.

In the morning he saw beyond the trees of a copse a small hermitage.⁷ He entered and found a hermit kneeling down by a fresh tomb. The hermit was weeping as he prayed, and then Sir Bedivere recognized him as the Archbishop of Canterbury, who had been banished by Sir Modred.

"Father, I pray you, tell me, whose tomb is this?"

"My son, I do not know. At midnight the body was brought here by a company of ladies. We buried it,

---

4. **succor:** help.
5. **Excalibur:** Arthur's sword, given to him by the mysterious Lady of the Lake.

6. **Avalon:** legendary island, sometimes identified with the earthly Paradise.
7. **hermitage:** secluded home.

E **Reading Focus** Analyzing Details Why does Sir Lucas suggest moving King Arthur to a nearby town?

F **Literary Focus** The Romance Hero Why doesn't King Arthur keep his sword with him?

G **Reading Focus** Analyzing Details What does the woman seem to mean by saying that Arthur's wound is "already cold"?

Vocabulary **piteous** (PIHT ee uhs) *adj.*: evoking pity.

they lit a hundred candles for the service, and rewarded me with a thousand bezants."[8]

"Father, King Arthur lies buried in this tomb."

Sir Bedivere fainted when he had spoken, and when he came to he begged the Archbishop to allow him to remain at the hermitage and end his days in fasting and prayer.

"Father, I wish only to be near to my true liege."[9]

"My son, you are welcome; and do I not recognize you as Sir Bedivere the Bold, brother to Sir Lucas the Butler?"

Thus the Archbishop and Sir Bedivere remained at the hermitage, wearing the habits of hermits and devoting themselves to the tomb with fasting and prayers of contrition.[10]

Such was the death of King Arthur as written down by Sir Bedivere. By some it is told that there were three queens on the barge: Queen Morgan le Fay, the Queen of North Galys, and the Queen of the Waste Lands; and others include the name of Nyneve, the Lady of the Lake who had served King Arthur well in the past, and had married the good knight Sir Pelleas.

In many parts of Britain it is believed that King Arthur did not die and that he will return to us and win fresh glory and the Holy Cross[11] of our Lord Jesu Christ; but for myself I do not believe this, and would leave him buried peacefully in his tomb at Glastonbury, where the Archbishop of Canterbury and Sir Bedivere humbled themselves, and with prayers and fasting honored his memory. And inscribed on his tomb, men say, is this legend:

HIC IACET ARTHURUS, REX QUONDAM REXQUE FUTURUS.[12]

---

8. **bezants:** gold coins of Byzantium.
9. **liege:** lord or sovereign.
10. **contrition:** here, remorse for having offended God.

11. **Holy Cross:** cross on which Jesus was crucified.
12. *Hic . . . futurus:* Latin for "Here lies Arthur, the once and future king."

H Literary Focus **The Romance Hero** Why might Sir Bedivere want to stay at the hermitage?

I Reading Focus **Analyzing Details** What does "the once and future king" mean in terms of Arthur's legacy?

Respond and Think Critically

Reading Focus

Quick Check

1. Why is a truce called between King Arthur and Sir Modred?

2. Why do the armies spring to attack after telling each other they wouldn't do so?

3. Why doesn't Sir Bedivere throw the sword into the lake at first, as King Arthur requests?

Read with a Purpose

4. How is King Arthur a victim of circumstances? Which circumstances help make him a hero?

Reading Skills: Analyzing Details

5. Many details in stories add to the mood or atmosphere. Other details are connected to the big picture of the story. In Malory's tale, the portrayal of Arthur as a romance hero becomes more meaningful when we find out that Arthur dies for his values. Add another column to the chart below. Analyze the purpose of each key detail. Does the detail contribute to the general mood of the story, or does it have more meaning when we read the end of the story?

Key Detail	Significance	Analysis
Arthur's clothes ("gold cloth")	shows us that our hero is royal	shows the royal setting but also contrasts with Arthur's bloody appearance in battle and death

Literary Focus

Literary Analysis

6. **Analyze** What is the significance of the adder bite? Why doesn't the knight that the adder bites have a name?

7. **Evaluate** Think about the relationship between King Arthur and his people. Would you say he was a respected leader? Why or why not?

8. **Extend** What supernatural elements can you find in this story? Are any of these elements similar to those used in contemporary movies, television stories, and science fiction novels?

Literary Skills: The Romance Hero

9. **Analyze** If a romance hero dies at the end of his story, it is in glory after finding fulfillment of some kind. Does King Arthur die gloriously? What suggests that he might not have died?

Literary Skills Review: Foil

10. **Extend** A **foil** is a character who sets off another character by strong contrast. This contrast brings out the distinctive qualities of each character. How is Sir Bedivere a foil for Arthur?

Writing Focus

Think as a Reader/Writer

Use It in Your Writing Look back at your notes on Malory's use of dialogue. Choose a narrative you have written and add dialogue to it that will help you portray the characters more fully.

 **What Do You Think Now** Why does Arthur take the chance to kill Modred, even though it causes his own death?

Vocabulary Development

✓ Vocabulary Check

Match each Vocabulary word with its antonym.

1. righteous
2. prevailed
3. dissuade
4. brandishing
5. piteous

a. failed
b. dropped
c. enviable
d. persuade
e. evil

Vocabulary Skills: Etymology

Etymology is the study of word origins and word development over time. Knowing a word's etymology can help you understand and remember the word. Just as some words are created to describe new concepts, other words change meaning or drop from use.

Many words with ancient etymologies are laced throughout Malory's story. What is the etymology of *Excalibur,* Arthur's legendary sword? One theory suggests the word means "steel-cutter," perhaps implying its strength against an opponent's armor. Another says the word means "freed from the stone." Yet another says it may mean "hard-bellied; voracious."

Your Turn

Read the etymologies in the following chart to learn the origins of the Vocabulary words. In the first column, write the word you think matches each etymology. Then, look up the Vocabulary words in a dictionary that shows word origins to check the meanings of the underlined words in the etymology column.

Word	Etymology
	Old English rihtwis
	Latin praevalere
	Latin dis + suadere
	Old French brandiss
	Latin pietas

Language Coach

Prefixes A prefix comes at the beginning of the word and changes the word's meaning. The prefix *dis–* can mean "against" or "the opposite of." For example, *disallow* means "the opposite of allow" or "forbid." Use what you know about this prefix to match each word with its antonym, or word of opposite meaning.

1. dissuade
2. disloyal
3. disinterested
4. discourage
5. dispel

a. attract
b. biased
c. encourage
d. convince
e. faithful

Academic Vocabulary

Write About
In your *Reader/Writer Notebook,* write about the difference between heroism and celebrity. How might our fascination with celebrity interfere with our concepts of heroism? What makes a true hero? What attributes should our society emphasize as desirable for a hero? What is the relationship between social status and heroism?

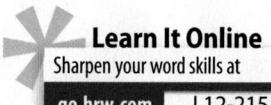

Learn It Online
Sharpen your word skills at

go.hrw.com   L12-215   Go

Preparing to Read

from Everyman

What moves a hero to act?

QuickTalk

Discuss these questions with a partner: Think about heroes you have read about in stories. What kinds of journeys do these characters take, and what do they learn about themselves on their travels?

The Haywain, with closed panels showing Everyman walking the Path of Life, by Hieronymus Bosch (c. 1450–1516). Oil on panel. Museo del Prado, Madrid, Spain.

INTRODUCTION

Morality plays, including *Everyman*, were a popular theatrical form in fifteenth- and sixteenth-century Europe that celebrated the rewards of living a moral life. Before the fifteenth century, Church leaders generally opposed public entertainment and permitted only short dialogues during the Christian religious ceremony known as the Mass. Eventually, these dialogues included props, costumes, and sets and moved outside the church walls. Adopting the vernacular, or common language, dramatists performed their plays in public places. These plays stayed true to their sacred roots by making the teaching of moral values their primary goal.

Later, acting troupes began to depend more upon the support of the public than the Church, and morality plays became a bridge between the sacred and the secular.

The Journey Through Life

Writers of morality plays wrote **allegories**—stories that have both a literal and a symbolic meaning. Characters take a physical journey, for example, that represents their spiritual journey on earth and in the afterlife. Typically, characters personify either good or bad qualities, such as justice and mercy, or greed and envy, and they battle for control of the **protagonist's,** or main character's, soul.

Everyman, the best-known morality play, is probably a translation of *Elckerlijk,* a Dutch play that was first printed in 1495. The play's protagonist learns of his approaching death and is deserted by his faithless companions. In the process, he moves from fear and despair to Christian faith. In the end, only one friend—Good Deeds—accompanies him to the grave.

Other Medieval Drama Forms

Mystery plays were elaborate productions performed to dramatize Christian history from Creation to the Second Coming. Groups of performers called guilds traveled on pageant wagons and made several stops to perform Biblical stories. Together, the group of plays was called the mystery cycle. The cycle, which ran for days, attracted large crowds with music, comedy, and special effects. **Miracle plays** focused on the lives of saints. The most famous form of the miracle play is the passion play, which retells the death of Jesus.

Think About the Play

How might the influence of the Church have affected the creativity of writers of morality plays?

Reader/Writer Notebook

Use your **RWN** to complete the activities for this selection.

Literary Focus

Allegory An **allegory** is a story in which characters, plot events, and settings stand for abstract or moral <u>concepts</u>. Allegorical stories operate on two levels of meaning: a surface level and a deeper, below-the-surface level. Because the main purpose of allegories is to instruct, the surface story is a way of conveying a symbolic story with an important moral lesson. Authors of allegories often use personification to give human form to abstract <u>concepts</u> and qualities.

Reading Focus

Making Critical Judgments When you read, you should take note of the characters and events and make judgments about them. **Making critical judgments** will help you understand the allegorical purpose and meaning of *Everyman*. In an allegory, the actions and words of the characters have symbolic meaning.

Into Action As you read, jot down the actions of each character as each responds to Everyman's request. From these actions, form a critical judgment about the characters.

Character	Action	My Judgment
Everyman		
Death		
Fellowship	Refuses to go on the journey	Will not risk death for Everyman

Writing Focus

Think as a Reader/Writer

Find It in Your Reading As you read the excerpt from *Everyman*, pay close attention to the writer's use of **personification.** In your *Reader/Writer Notebook*, write down examples of how giving human qualities to <u>concepts</u> like fellowship and knowledge helps achieve the story's allegorical purpose.

Vocabulary

reverence (REHV uhr uhns) *n.:* feeling of great respect and awe. *Life should be treated with reverence.*

transitory (TRAN suh tawr ee) *adj.:* impermanent. *Material goods are only transitory.*

reckoning (REHK uh nihng) *n.:* calculation; accounting. *Everyman wonders if he will be ready for the final reckoning of his life.*

lechery (LEHCH uhr ee) *n.:* indulgence in lust. *Lechery is most disturbing in those who have sworn to avoid it.*

commendable (kuh MEHN duh buhl) *adj.:* deserving of admiration. *Everyman's quest to live a moral life is commendable.*

Language Coach

Suffixes A suffix comes at the end of a word and often changes its part of speech. *Commend* is a verb that means "to praise or admire." When you add the suffix *–able*, you get the adjective *commendable*, which means "deserving of admiration." Identify the verb you in each of these adjectives: *lovable, predictable, imaginable, comparable.* What does each adjective mean?

Learn It Online
Let voice actors bring this play excerpt to life for you.

go.hrw.com   L12-217   **Go**

from Everyman

Read with a Purpose
Read to identify how Everyman represents all human beings.

Build Background
Typical of its time period, *Everyman* is written mainly in rhyming couplets, and the stage directions are much simpler than those of modern plays. The emphasis is not on action as much as it is on the speeches and dialogues of the play.

Characters

Messenger
God
Death
Everyman
Fellowship
Kindred

Cousin
Goods
Good Deeds
Knowledge
Confession
Beauty

Strength
Discretion
Five-Wits
Angel
Doctor

Here begineth a treatise how the High Father of Heaven sendeth Death to summon every creature to come and give account of their lives in this world, and is in manner of a moral play.

[*Enter* MESSENGER.]

Messenger.
> I pray you all give your audience,
> And hear this matter with reverence,
> By figure a moral play.
> The *Summoning of Everyman* called it is,
> 5 That of our lives and ending shows
> How transitory we be all day.
> The matter is wonder precious,
> But the intent of it is more gracious

Vocabulary **reverence** (REHV uhr uhns) *n.:* feeling of great respect and awe.
transitory (TRAN suh tawr ee) *adj.:* not permanent.

And sweet to bear away.

10　The story saith: Man, in the beginning
Look well, and take good heed to the ending,
Be you never so gay.
You think sin in the beginning full sweet,
Which in the end causeth the soul to weep,
15　When the body lieth in clay.
Here shall you see how fellowship and jollity,
Both strength, pleasure, and beauty,
Will fade from thee as flower in May.
For ye shall hear how our Heaven-King
20　Calleth Everyman to a general reckoning. 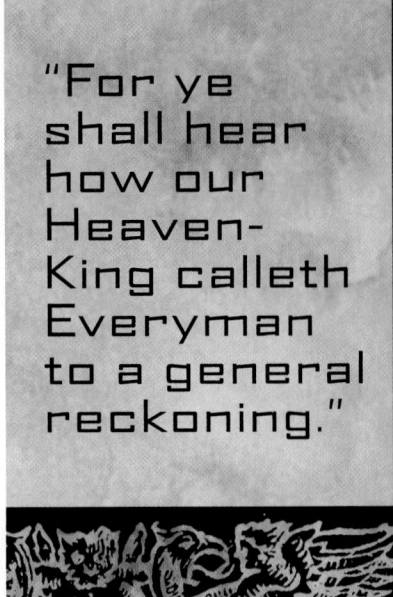 **Ⓐ**
Give audience and hear what he doth say.

[*Exit* MESSENGER.—*Enter* GOD.]

God.

I perceive, here in my majesty,
How that all the creatures be to me unkind,
Living without dread in worldly prosperity.
25　Of ghostly sight the people be so blind,
Drowned in sin, they know me not for their God.
In worldly riches is all their mind:
They fear not my righteousness, the sharp rod;
My law that I showed, when I for them died
30　They forget clean, and shedding of my blood red.
I hanged between two, it cannot be denied:
To get them life I suffered to be dead.°
I healed their feet, with thorns hurt was my head.
I could do no more than I did, truly— **Ⓑ**
35　And now I see the people do clean forsake me.
They use the seven deadly sins damnable,
As pride, covetise, wrath, and lechery
Now in the world be made commendable.
And thus they leave of angels the heavenly company.
40　Every man liveth so after his own pleasure,
And yet of their life they be nothing sure.
I see the more that I them forbear,
The worse they be from year to year:
All that liveth appaireth° fast.

"For ye shall hear how our Heaven-King calleth Everyman to a general reckoning."

29–32. when I for them died …I suffered to be dead: God is referring here to the crucifixion of Jesus.

44. appaireth: degenerates.

Ⓐ **Literary Focus** **Allegory** What does the character Everyman symbolize?

Ⓑ **Reading Focus** **Critical Judgments** Why does God sound frustrated here?

Vocabulary **reckoning** (REHK uh nihng) *n.:* calculation; accounting.
lechery (LEHCH uhr ee) *n.:* indulgence in lust.
commendable (kuh MEHN duh buhl) *adj.:* deserving of admiration.

45 Therefore I will, in all the haste,
    Have a reckoning of every man's person. **C**
    For, and I leave the people thus alone
    In their life and wicked tempests,
    Verily they will become much worse than beasts;
50 For now one would by envy another up eat.
    Charity do they all clean forgeet.
    I hoped well that every man
    In my glory should make his mansion,
    And thereto I had them all elect.
55 But now I see, like traitors deject,
    They thank me not for the pleasure that I to them meant,
    Nor yet for their being that I them have lent.
    I proffered the people great multitude of mercy,
    And few there be that asketh it heartily.
60 They be so cumbered with worldly riches
    That needs on them I must do justice—
    On every man living without fear.
    Where art thou, Death, thou mighty messenger?

[*Enter* DEATH.]

Death.

    Almighty God, I am here at your will,
65 Your commandment to fulfill.

God.

    Go thou to Everyman,
    And show him, in my name,
    A pilgrimage he must on him take,
    Which he in no wise° may escape;
70 And that he bring with him a sure reckoning
    Without delay or any tarrying.

69. wise: ways.

Death.

    Lord, I will in the world go run over all,
    And cruelly out-search both great and small.

                                    [*Exit* GOD.]

    Everyman will I beset that liveth beastly
75 Out of God's laws, and dreadeth not folly.
    He that loveth riches I will strike with my dart,
    His sight to blind, and from heaven to depart
    Except that Almsdeeds° be his good friend—
    In hell for to dwell, world without end.
80 Lo, yonder I see Everyman walking:

78. almsdeeds: good deeds.

C Reading Focus **Critical Judgments** What does God plan to do?

Full little he thinketh on my coming;   **D**
His mind is on fleshly lusts and his treasure,
And great pain it shall cause him to endure
Before the Lord Heaven-King.

[*Enter* EVERYMAN.]

85   Everyman, stand still! Whither art thou going
     Thus gaily? Hast thou thy Maker forgeet?

Everyman.
     Why askest thou?
     Why wouldest thou weet?°

Death.
     Yea, sir, I will show you:
90   In great haste I am sent to thee
     From God out of his majesty.

Everyman.
     What! sent to me?

Death.
     Yea, certainly.
     Though thou have forget him here,
95   He thinketh on thee in the heavenly sphere,
     As, ere we depart, thou shalt know.

Everyman.
     What desireth God of me?

Death.
     That shall I show thee:
     A reckoning he will needs have
100 Without any longer respite.

Everyman.
     To give a reckoning longer leisure I crave.
     This blind matter troubleth my wit.

Death.
     On thee thou must take a long journay:
     Therefore thy book of count with thee thou bring,
105 For turn again thou cannot by no way.
     And look thou be sure of thy reckoning,
     For before God thou shalt answer and shew°
     Thy many bad deeds and good but a few—
     How thou hast spent thy life and in what wise,
110 Before the Chief Lord of Paradise.
     Have ado that we were in that way,°
     For weet thou well, thou shalt make none attornay.°

D **Literary Focus** Allegory Everyman is not aware of God's presence. What does this tell us about Everyman's moral state?

88. Why wouldest thou weet: What do you want?

107. shew: archaic form of *showed*.

111. Have ado . . . in that way: Let's see about making that journey.
112. For weet . . . none attornay: You know you will have no support.

Everyman.

> Full unready I am such reckoning to give.
> I know thee not. What messenger art thou?

Death.

115   I am Death that no man dreadeth,
> For every man I 'rest, and no man spareth;
> For it is God's commandment
> That all to me should be obedient.

Everyman.

> O Death, thou comest when I had thee least in mind.

120   In thy power it lieth me to save:
> Yet of my good will I give thee, if thou will be kind,
> Yea, a thousand pound shalt thou have—
> And defer this matter till another day.   **E**

Death.

> Everyman, it may not be, by no way.

125   I set nought by gold, silver, nor riches,
> Nor by pope, emperor, king, duke, nor princes,
> For, and I would receive gifts great,
> All the world I might get.
> But my custom is clean contrary:

130   I give thee no respite. Come hence, and not tarry! . . .

Everyman.

> O wretched caitiff!° Whither shall I flee
> That I might 'scape this endless sorrow?
> Now, gentle Death, spare me till tomorrow,
> That I may amend me

135   With good advisement.

Death.

> Nay, thereto I will not consent,
> Nor no man will I respite,
> But to the heart suddenly I shall smite,
> Without any advisement.   **F**

140   And now out of thy sight I will me hie:
> See thou make thee ready shortly,
> For thou mayst say this is the day
> That no man living may 'scape away.

> [*Exit* DEATH.]

Everyman.

> Alas, I may well weep with sighs deep:

131. caitiff: coward.

E **Literary Focus** **Allegory** Why does Everyman think he can make a deal with Death?

F **Reading Focus** **Critical Judgments** Why doesn't Death permit Everyman to bargain with him?

145   Now have I no manner of company
       To help me in my journey and me to keep.
       And also my writing is full unready—
       How shall I do now for to excuse me?
       I would to God I had never be geet!°
150   To my soul a full great profit it had be.
       For now I fear pains huge and great.
       The time passeth: Lord, help, that all wrought!
       For though I mourn, it availeth nought.
       The day passeth and is almost ago:
155   I wot not well what for to do.
       To whom were I best my complaint to make?
       What and I to Fellowship thereof spake,°
       And showed him of this sudden chance?
       For in him is all mine affiance,°
160   We have in the world so many a day
       Be good friends in sport and play.
       I see him yonder, certainly.
       I trust that he will bear me company.
       Therefore to him will I speak to ease my sorrow.

     [*Enter* FELLOWSHIP.]

165   Well met, good Fellowship, and good morrow!
Fellowship.
       Everyman, good morrow, by this day!
       Sir, why lookest thou so piteously?
       If anything be amiss, I pray thee me say,
       That I may help to remedy.
Everyman.
170   Yea, good Fellowship, yea:
       I am in great jeopardy.
Fellowship.
       My true friend, show to me your mind.
       I will not forsake thee to my life's end
       In the way of good company.
Everyman.
175   That was well spoken, and lovingly!
Fellowship.
       Sir, I must needs know your heaviness.
       I have pity to see you in any distress.
       If any have you wronged, ye shall revenged be,
       Though I on the ground be slain for thee,
180   Though that I know before that I should die.
Everyman.
       Verily, Fellowship, gramercy.°

149. geet: born.

157. spake: archaic form of *spoke*.
159. affiance: trust.

181. Verily . . . gramercy: Truly . . . thank you.

Death and Man II (1911) by Egon Schiele
(1890–1918).
Museum Leopold, Vienna, Austria.

Fellowship.

Tush! by thy thanks I set not a stree.°
Show me your grief and say no more.

Everyman.

If I my heart should to you break,
185 And then you to turn your mind fro me,
And would not me comfort when ye hear me speak,
Then should I ten times sorrier be.

Fellowship.

Sir, I say as I will do, indeed.

Everyman.

Then be you a good friend at need.
190 I have found you true herebefore.

Fellowship.

And so ye shall evermore.
For, in faith, and thou go to hell,
I will not forsake thee by the way.

Everyman.

Ye speak like a good friend. I believe you well.
195 I shall deserve it, and I may.

Fellowship.

I speak of no deserving, by this day!
For he that will say and nothing do

182. stree: straw.

Is not worthy with good company to go.
Therefore show me the grief of your mind,
200 As to your friend most loving and kind.

Everyman.

I shall show you how it is:
Commanded I am to go a journay,
A long way, hard and dangerous,
And give a strait count, without delay,
205 Before the high judge Adonai.
Wherefore I pray you bear me company,
As ye have promised, in this journay.

Fellowship.

That is matter indeed! Promise is duty—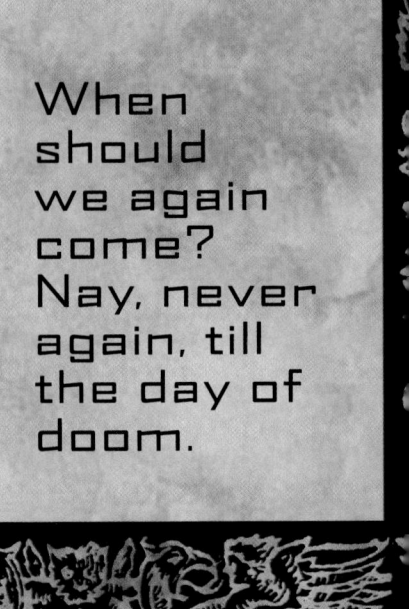
But, and I should take such a voyage on me,
210 I know it well, it should be to my pain.
Also it maketh me afeard, certain.
But let us take counsel here, as well we can—
For your words would fear a strong man.

Everyman.

Why, ye said, if I had need,
215 Ye would me never forsake, quick ne° dead,
Though it were to hell, truly.

215. ne: nor.

Fellowship.

So I said, certainly,
But such pleasures be set aside, the sooth to say.
And also, if we took such a journay,
220 When should we again come?

Everyman.

Nay, never again, till the day of doom.

Fellowship.

In faith, then will not I come there!
Who hath you these tidings brought?

Everyman.

Indeed, Death was with me here.

Fellowship.

225 Now by God that all hath bought,
If Death were the messenger,
For no man that is living today
I will not go that loath journay—
Not for the father that begat me!

Everyman.

230 Ye promised otherwise, pardie.

G **Reading Focus** **Critical Judgments** What does the statement "promise is duty" mean?

> When should we again come? Nay, never again, till the day of doom.

Fellowship.

I wot well I said so, truly.
And yet, if thou wilt eat and drink and make good cheer,
Or haunt to women the lusty company,
I would not forsake you while the day is clear,

235   Trust me verily! . . .

Everyman.

Whither away, Fellowship? Will thou forsake me?

Fellowship.

Yea, by my fay! To God I betake thee.

Everyman.

Farewell, good Fellowship! For thee my heart is sore.
Adieu forever—I shall see thee no more.

Fellowship.

240   In faith, Everyman, farewell now at the ending:
For you I will remember that parting is mourning. . . .

[*Exit* FELLOWSHIP.]

*[Kindred, Cousin, and Goods also decline to go with Everyman. Good Deeds
offers to help but cannot walk. Good Deeds calls on Knowledge, who offers to
go with Everyman and be his guide. Knowledge leads Everyman to Confession.
After Everyman confesses his sins and gives penance, Good Deeds is able to
walk and accompany Everyman. Then Everyman calls on Discretion, Strength,
Beauty, and Five-Wits to help him. On the advice of Five-Wits and Knowledge,
Everyman goes to a priest to receive holy sacraments. When Everyman returns,
Beauty and Strength depart. Discretion, Five-Wits, Knowledge, and Good
Deeds remain.]*

Everyman.

I had weened surer I should you have found.
He that trusteth in his Strength
She him deceiveth at the length.

245   Both Strength and Beauty forsaketh me—
Yet they promise, me fair and lovingly.

Discretion.

Everyman, I will after Strength be gone:
As for me, I will leave you alone.

Everyman.

Why Discretion, will ye forsake me?

Discretion.

250   Yea, in faith, I will go from thee.
For when Strength goeth before,
I follow after evermore.

Everyman.

Yet I pray thee, for the love of the Trinity,
Look in my grave once piteously.

Discretion.

255 Nay, so nigh will I not come.
Farewell everyone!

[Exit DISCRETION.]

Everyman.

O all thing faileth save God alone—
Beauty, Strength, and Discretion.
For when Death bloweth his blast
260 They all run fro me full fast.

Five-Wits.

Everyman, my leave now of thee I take.
I will follow the other, for here I thee forsake.

Everyman.

Alas, then may I wail and weep,
For I took you for my best friend.

Five-Wits.

265 I will no longer thee keep.
Now farewell, and there an end!

[Exit FIVE-WITS.]

Everyman.

O Jesu, help, all hath forsaken me!

Good Deeds.

Nay, Everyman, I will bide with thee:
I will not forsake thee indeed;
270 Thou shalt find me a good friend at need.

Everyman.

Gramercy, Good Deeds! Now may I true friends see.
They have forsaken me every one—
I loved them better than my Good Deeds alone.
Knowledge, will ye forsake me also?

Knowledge.

275 Yea, Everyman, when ye to Death shall go,
But not yet, for no manner of danger.

Everyman.

Gramercy, Knowledge, with all my heart!

H **Reading Focus** **Critical Judgments** What change does Everyman begin to experience? What causes this change?

I **Literary Focus** **Allegory** What would you expect a character called Five-Wits to symbolize?

J **Literary Focus** **Allegory** Why might Five-Wits have been Everyman's "best friend"?

The comicall Satyre of

EVERY MAN
OVT OF HIS
HVMOR.

As it was first composed by the Author B. L

Containing more then hath been publikely
spoken or acted.

With the seuerall Character of euery person

Non aliena meo pressi pede | * si propius stes
Te capiem magis | * & decies repetita placebunt.

LONDON,
Printed for Nicholas Linge.
1600.

Everyman out of his Humor. Frontispiece of 1600 edition.

Knowledge.

Nay, yet will I not depart from hence depart
Till I see where ye shall become.

Everyman.

280 Methink, alas, that I must be gone
To make my reckoning and my debts pay,
For I see my time is nigh spent away.
Take example, all ye that this do hear or see,
How they that I best loved do forsake me,
285 Except my Good Deeds that bideth truly.

Good Deeds.

All earthly things is but vanity. **Ⓚ**
Beauty, Strength, and Discretion do man forsake,
Foolish friends and kinsmen that fair spake—
All fleeth save Good Deeds, and that am I.

Everyman.

290 Have mercy on me, God most mighty,
And stand by me, thou mother and maid, holy Mary! **Ⓛ**

Good Deeds.

Fear not: I will speak for thee. **Ⓜ**

Everyman.

Here I cry God mercy!

Good Deeds.

Short our end, and 'minish° our pain.
295 Let us go, and never come again.

Everyman.

Into thy hands, Lord, my soul I commend:
Receive it, Lord, that it be not lost.
As thou me boughtest, so me defend,
And save me from the fiend's boast,
300 That I may appear with that blessed host
That shall be saved at the day of doom.
In manus tuas,° of might's most
Forever *commendo spiritum meum.°*

[Everyman *and* Good Deeds *descend into the grave.*]

Knowledge.

Now hath he suffered that we all shall endure,

294. 'minish: lessen.

302. *in manus tuas:* Latin,
meaning "into your hands"
(speaking to God).
**303. *commendo spiritum
meum:*** Latin, meaning "I commend my spirit."

Ⓚ Literary Focus **Allegory** What are "earthly things" here?

Ⓛ Reading Focus **Critical Judgments** Why does Everyman ask God to have mercy on him?

Ⓜ Literary Focus **Allegory** What does it mean when Good Deeds assures Everyman that he will speak for him?

305　The Good Deeds shall make all sure.
　　　Now hath he made ending,
　　　Methinketh that I hear angels sing
　　　And make great joy and melody
　　　Where Everyman's soul received shall be.

Angel.

310　[*within*] Come, excellent elect spouse to Jesu!
　　　Here above thou shalt go
　　　Because of thy singular virtue.　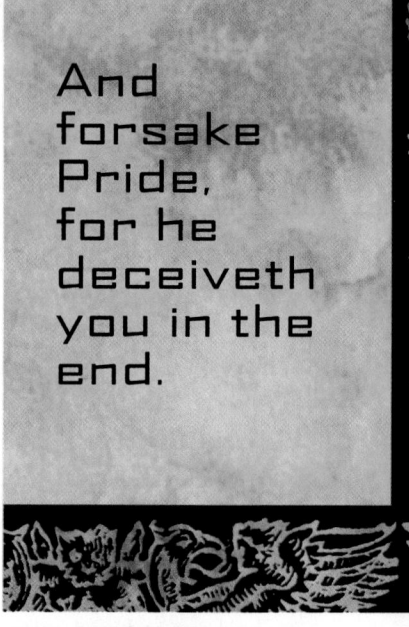
　　　Now the soul is taken the body fro,
　　　Thy reckoning is crystal clear:
315　Now shalt thou into the heavenly sphere—
　　　Unto the which all ye shall come
　　　That liveth well before the day of doom.

[*Enter* DOCTOR.]

Doctor.

　　　This memorial men may have in mind:
　　　Ye hearers, take it of worth, old and young,
320　And forsake Pride, for he deceiveth you in the end.
　　　And remember Beauty, Five-Wits, Strength, and Discretion,
　　　They all at the last do Everyman forsake,
　　　Save his Good Deeds there doth he take—
　　　But beware, for and they be small,
325　Before God he hath no help at all—
　　　None excuse may be there for Everyman.
　　　Alas, how shall he do than?
　　　For after death amends may no man make,　**O**
　　　For then mercy and pity doth him forsake.
330　If his reckoning be not clear when he doth come,
　　　God will say, *"Ite, maledicti, in ignem eternum!"*°
　　　And he that hath his account whole and sound,
　　　High in heaven he shall be crowned,
　　　Unto which place God bring us all thither,
335　That we may live body and soul togither.
　　　Thereto help, the Trinity!
　　　Amen, say ye, for saint charity.

And forsake Pride, for he deceiveth you in the end.

331. *Ite, maledicti, in ignem eternum:* Latin, meaning "Go, cursed ones, into the eternal fire!"

N Literary Focus **Allegory** What is the singular virtue to which the Angel refers?

O Reading Focus **Critical Judgments** What might it mean that "after death amends may no man make"?

from Everyman

Respond and Think Critically

Reading Focus

Quick Check

1. Who sends Death to Everyman?

2. What does Everyman do first after meeting with Death?

3. Who stays with Everyman until he dies?

Read with a Purpose

4. What is the author saying about the nature and fate of every human being?

Reading Skills: Making Critical Judgments

5. When you read, you took note of the characters' actions and made judgments about them. Add another column to your chart. In it, explain the allegorical meaning of each character.

Character	Actions	My Judgment	Allegorical Meaning
Everyman			
Death			
Fellowship	Refuses to go on the journey	Will not risk death for Everyman	

✔ Vocabulary Check

Match each Vocabulary word to its definition.

6. reverence
7. transitory
8. reckoning
9. lechery
10. commendable

a. impermanent
b. deserving of admiration
c. indulgence in lust
d. feeling of great respect and awe
e. calculation; accounting

Literary Focus

Literary Analysis

11. **Evaluate** Why do Strength, Beauty, Discretion, and Five-Wits leave Everyman in the order that they do?

12. **Interpret** What is the reason for Doctor's speech at the end of the play? Why is it significant that the speaker is a doctor? Explain.

Literary Skills: Allegory

13. **Analyze** How does the personification of abstract concepts and qualities help convey the moral lesson of this allegory? Explain.

Literary Skills Review: Characterization

14. **Make Judgments** The process by which the writer reveals the personality of a character is called **characterization**. How is Death characterized in *Everyman*? How is this portrayal similar to or different from your expectations for such a character who represents death?

Writing Focus

Think as a Reader/Writer

Use It in Your Writing As you read, you noted how the author of *Everyman* uses personification to create allegorical meaning. Write a short allegory—just a few paragraphs—in which you **personify** abstract concepts to teach a moral lesson.

What Do **You Think Now** Is Everyman a hero in this play? Why or why not?

Writing Workshop

Poetry Analysis

Write with a Purpose

Write an essay analyzing a poem. Your **purpose** for writing is to share your analysis and insights about the poem. Your **audience** will be your teacher and classmates and anyone else who is interested in poetry.

Think as a Reader/Writer

In this collection, you have examined poems' literary elements critically and thought about how these elements work together. Before you write your **poetry analysis,** read the following excerpt from Seamus Heaney's analysis of Dylan Thomas's poem "Do Not Go Gentle into That Good Night." The poem appears on page 1236.

> "Do Not Go Gentle into That Good Night" fulfills its promise precisely because its craft has not lost touch with a suffered world. The villanelle[1] form, turning upon itself, advancing and retiring to and from a resolution, is not just a line-by-line virtuoso performance. Through its repetitions, the father's remoteness—and the remoteness of all fathers—is instantly proclaimed, yet we can also hear, in an almost sobbing counterpoint, the protest of the poet's child-self against the separation. . . .
>
> [The poem] is obviously a threshold poem about death, concerned with the reverse of the process which occupied Thomas in "Before I Knocked." In that earlier poem, the body was about to begin what Thomas calls elsewhere its "sensual strut." Here the return journey out of mortality into ghosthood is about to be made, so in fact the recurrent rhymes of the villanelle could as well have been "breath" and "death" or "womb" and "tomb"—but what we have instead are "night" and "light." And the night is a "good night." But, for once, a characteristic verbal tic has become an imaginative strength and not just an irritating cleverness. "Good night" is a pun which risks breaking the decorum of the utterance but which turns out in the end to embody its very complexity and force. The mixture of salutation and farewell in the phrase is a perfect equivalent for the balance between natural grief and the recognition of necessity which pervades the poem as whole.
>
> ---
> 1. **villanelle:** nineteen-line poem with a strict structure and rhyme scheme.

← Heaney clearly states his **thesis.**

← He explains how the **poem's form** contributes to its **meaning.**

← Heaney discusses the **ambiguity** of Thomas's "good night."

A Good Poetry Analysis

- contains a thesis statement that tells how the literary elements in the poem work together
- analyzes how literary elements contribute to the poem's meaning and its effect on the reader
- uses text evidence to support each point
- concludes with an insight that connects the poem to broader themes in life

See page 240 for complete rubric.

Reader/Writer Notebook

Use your **RWN** to complete the activities for this workshop.

Think About the Professional Model

With a partner, discuss the following questions about the model:

1. What is the main idea of the second paragraph?
2. How does the second paragraph relate to the essay's thesis?

Prewriting

Choose a Poem

To find a suitable poem, re-read poems you have enjoyed in the past, page through this book, or ask others to recommend poems they have found especially memorable or moving. Choose a poem of twelve to twenty-five lines that is complex and rich in meaning—short enough to be manageable, yet deep enough to provide a thoughtful analysis.

Think About Purpose and Audience

As you think about your poetry analysis, keep your purpose and audience in mind. Your **purpose** is to share your insights about the poem you have analyzed with an **audience,** most likely your teacher and classmates. How can you convey your ideas in a way readers will understand and appreciate?

Gather Ideas

Read the poem you have chosen multiple times, including a few times out loud, to discover all its **unique aspects.** Each reading will probably provide you with new insights and better understanding of the poem. The following chart explains the basic **literary elements** you will find in poetry and provides analysis questions for each element:

Literary Elements	Analysis Questions
Speaker is the voice that addresses the reader.	• Who is the speaker? • Is the speaker speaking *to* someone? *about* someone? • Does the speaker narrate a story or describe a scene or emotion?
Stylistic devices are the techniques a writer uses to control language and create effects.	• How does **diction** (language choice) affect the poem? • What **sound devices,** such as **rhythm, rhyme, alliteration,** and **repetition,** does the poet use? What effect do they have on the poem? • Does the poet use **figurative language,** such as **simile** and **metaphor,** to make imaginative comparisons? • What **imagery** does the poet use to appeal to the senses?
Theme is the insight about human life that is revealed in the poem.	• What is the poem's main idea? • Does it examine a universal theme, common problem, or life experience? • Does it reveal anything about human nature?
Tone is the poet's attitude toward the subject, the audience, or a character in the poem.	• What attitude does the poet express (sarcastic, humorous, sad, nostalgic, hostile, sympathetic, light-hearted, angry)? • What words and details convey tone? • Does the tone affect your response to the poem?

Idea Starters

- Additional poems by authors in this book
- Poems by local poets
- Regional poetry from a favorite state or country
- Poetry sites on the Internet

● Writing Tip

Additional figurative language you can analyze in your chosen poem:

Hyperbole uses exaggeration to express strong emotion or to create comic effect: *My heart beat a million beats per second; I could eat a horse.*

Oxymoron combines contradictory, or incongruous, ideas: *tough love; bittersweet; frozen flame; living death.*

Synecdoche uses a part to represent the whole, or vice versa: *a new set of wheels (wheels* represents "car"); *use your head (head* represents "brain").

Your Turn _____

Get Started Making notes in your **RWN,** choose a poem, and use the questions on this page to make notes about its **literary elements.** Your notes will help you plan your literary analysis.

Learn It Online

To see how one writer met all the assignment criteria, see the model poetry analysis at:

go.hrw.com   L12-233   **Go**

Poetry Analysis

Choose a Topic

Once you have an understanding of the significant ideas in the poem and how the literary elements help communicate those ideas, you can decide which of the literary elements are most significant. To determine which elements to include as the **topic** of your analysis, consider these questions:

- What elements are most critical to the poem you chose?
- What elements do you feel dominate the poem?
- Which elements best support the author's intentions in writing the poem?

Create a Thesis Statement

Next, write a **thesis statement**—one or two sentences that identify the poem's key elements and sums up your insights about how they work together to create meaning. Keep in mind as you write your thesis statement:

- Your thesis statement is basically a one- or two-sentence preview of what you are going to examine, discuss, and prove in your poetry analysis.
- Be flexible—your thesis statement will probably change as you write and revise your drafts.

Gather Supporting Evidence

Your analysis must support each of your major points with **textual evidence** from the poem—direct quotations and details from the poem expressed in your own words. You must **elaborate,** or explain thoroughly, how each piece of evidence supports the point you are making. You can add depth to your poetry analysis by elaborating on the **ambiguities, nuances,** and **complexities** that make good poetry rich and meaningful.

- **Ambiguities** are words or lines that can be interpreted in more than one way or that have more than one meaning. For example, in the professional model on page 232, Seamus Heaney elaborates on the ambiguity of Dylan Thomas's "good night," which can be either a simple farewell or a very solemn final goodbye.
- **Complexities** result when a poem is rich in meaning and requires some thought to understand or interpret. Heaney points out that Thomas's poem both criticizes fathers for their remoteness and mourns their loss.
- **Nuances** are changes in the tone or meaning of the poem. "Do Not Go Gentle into That Good Night" begins with rage that turns to sorrow and desperation as the speaker turns his attention from the more general *wise, good, wild,* and *grave* men to the specific man—the speaker's dying father.

As you gather your evidence, create a chart like the one that follows.

Literary Element	Quotation or Detail	Elaboration
1.		
2.		
3.		

Your Turn

Complete Your Analysis Using the instructions on this page, complete your personal analysis of the poem—your ideas about how its elements work together to create meaning. Write your ideas in your **RWN.** You will base your literary analysis on these ideas.

Drafting

Organize and Draft Your Analysis

Your essay's focus will help you determine how to organize your ideas.

- If your essay focuses on a single literary element, you may want to use **chronological order,** tracing the development of the element from its first appearance in the poem to its last.

- If your essay focuses on two or more literary elements, you may want to organze them by **order of importance,** discussing the elements from most significant to least, or vice versa.

Use your prewriting notes and the **Writer's Framework** to the right to draft your analysis.

Framework of a Poetry Analysis

Introduction
- Start with an attention-getting quotation or bold statement.
- Introduce the poem's title and author.
- State your thesis, including the key elements you will discuss.

Body
- Organize literary elements in chronological order or by order of importance.
- Discuss each literary element.
- Provide textual evidence for each element, and elaborate.

Conclusion
- Restate your thesis.
- Summarize your main points.
- Show how the poem relates to broader themes in life.

⬤ Writing Tip

When discussing poetry, use the **literary present tense.** For example, on page 232, Seamus Heaney writes "the father's remoteness . . . **is** instantly proclaimed. . . ." and "what Thomas **calls** elsewhere . . ." Even though Dylan Thomas has been dead for several decades, Heaney uses the present tense to talk about what Thomas continues to do through his writing.

Grammar Link Punctuating Poetry Quotations

Because your poetry analysis will include direct quotations from the poem, follow these guidelines for **quoting poetry.** Look at these examples:

Quoting words or phrases (less than a line): Punctuate as needed in your sentence.

> Thomas repeats the phrase "dying of the light."

Quoting one line: Punctuate the line as needed in your sentence, keeping the original capitalization and punctuation of the line.

> A good example of Thomas's use of assonance is the long *l* sound in "Good men, the last wave by, crying how bright."

Quoting more than one line: Use a slash (/) with a space on both sides to show where one line stops and the next starts.

> Thomas's mixed feelings toward death are present in the poem's last stanza: "And you, my father, there on the sad height, / Curse, bless, me now with your fierce tears, I pray."

Your Turn _____

Draft Your Poetry Analysis Using the notes from prewriting and the **Writer's Framework,** create your first draft. Remember to do the following:

- Clearly state your **thesis.**
- Think of **main points** that prove your thesis.
- Support your main points with **evidence** from the poem.
- **Elaborate** on your evidence.

Peer Review

Review your draft with a peer, using this chart to check that all the contents of a poetry analysis are present and organized logically. Be sure any suggestions you make about your partner's piece are specific. Ask your partner to clarify any suggestions he or she makes that you don't understand completely.

Evaluating and Revising

All good writers revise to make sure that their words actually express the ideas they intended and to improve their work. Read the evaluation questions in the left-hand column, and use the tips in the middle column to help you make revisions to your poetry analysis. Then, use the suggested techniques in the right-hand column to make any necessary revisions to your draft.

Poetry Analysis: Guidelines for Content and Organization

Evaluation Question	Tip	Revision Technique
1. Does the introduction engage the reader's interest and introduce the poem?	**Put parentheses around** the engaging opening. **Circle** the title of the poem and the name of the author.	If necessary, **add** an interest-catching opening, such as a provocative quotation or a bold statement. **Add** the name of the poem and its author.
2. Does the introduction include a thesis statement that identifies the literary elements and states a main idea about them?	**Highlight** the thesis statement. **Bracket** the literary elements and the main idea.	If needed, **add** a thesis statement that identifies the poem's literary elements and states your main idea about them.
3. Are the major points clear? Do they support the thesis?	**Underline** the major points. **Draw an arrow** from the major points to the thesis.	**Rewrite** major points that are not clearly expressed. **Replace** points that don't support the thesis.
4. Does textual evidence support each major point?	**Draw a wavy line** under each quotation or detail from the poem.	**Add** quotations or details from the poem. **Elaborate** on how the evidence supports the point being made.
5. Is the discussion of literary elements arranged logically?	**Review** the underlined major points to make sure their arrangement is logical.	**Rearrange** major points by order of importance or chronological order.
6. Does the conclusion restate the thesis and make a closing connection between the poem and life in general?	**Highlight** the sentence restating the thesis. **Double-underline** the sentence or sentences connecting the poem to life.	**Add** a sentence that restates the thesis or, **add** a closing connection, if needed.

Read this student's draft with comments on its structure; note the suggestions for how it could be made even stronger. The poem this student analyzes appears on the right.

Absence and Loss in "Missing the Sea"

by Robert Scott, Sea View High School

Born in 1930 on the island of Saint Lucia, and later living in Jamaica and Trinidad, the poet Derek Walcott reveals the influence of countless sailors in his poem "Missing the Sea." The speaker laments the terrible emptiness of a house when occupied by a person who loves the freedom of the sea.

The poem's speaker expresses his loss in images of sound or absence of the sound of the wind. The wind is an effective synecdoche (using parts to represent the whole) because it represents attributes associated with the sea: water, salt, and vastness. Although absent from the house, this wind becomes "something removed [that] roars in the ears of this house." Strong verbs ("roars," "hangs," "stuns") describe a wind so strong it "weighs this mountain." Every image is harsh. Even those that emphasize the silence at the same time create a grating noise, "sound like the gnashing of windmills ground / To a dead halt." An oxymoron is also used to illustrate its power: "a deafening absence, a blow." It is this absent force that propels the sailor-poet to write his lament: "pushes this pencil." The present state of the house-bound speaker is "thick nothing now," emphasizing the negative and empty conditions through alliteration.

Missing the Sea
by Derek Walcott

Something removed roars in the ears of this house,
Hangs its drapes windless, stuns mirrors
Till reflections lack substance.

Some sound like the gnashing of windmills ground
To a dead halt;
A deafening absence, a blow.

It hoops this valley, weighs this mountain,
Estranges gesture, pushes this pencil
Through a thick nothing now,

Freights cupboards with silence, folds sour laundry
Like the clothes of the dead left exactly
As the dead behaved by the beloved,

Incredulous, expecting occupancy.

Robert's introduction identifies the **poet** and **poem** but does not have a clear **thesis statement.**

Robert uses **direct quotations** from the poem to support his ideas.

His analysis includes **figurative language: synecdoche** and **oxymoron.**

How to Write a Thesis Statement

Although Robert's essay introduces the poet and poem, it does not have a clear **thesis statement.** His thesis statement should connect the literary elements (images of absence and loss) to the meaning of the poem (the expression of the agony of the land-bound sailor). Each of the supporting points in his essay should, then, directly support his thesis.

Robert's Revision of Paragraph 1

The speaker laments the terrible emptiness of a house when occupied by a person who loves the freedom of the sea. ʌ *In "Missing the Sea," Walcott uses images of absence and loss to express the agony of a shore-bound sailor.*

Your Turn
Revise Your Thesis Statement
Read your draft, and then ask yourself,

- Could my thesis be stated more clearly?
- Is my thesis supported by the rest of my essay, or does my evidence support a different thesis?

Student Draft *continues*

The essay is arranged **chronologically,** moving from the poem's beginning to its end.

In the last full stanza, Walcott uses the images of objects found in the house (silent cupboards and "sour laundry"), again using synecdoche. The lack of sound is emphasized with the cupboard, and the negative sensory images continue with the laundry.

Instead of a direct quotation, Robert **paraphrases** and **elaborates** on the content of the last stanza.

These domestic images grow even stronger through the simile of the clothes of the dead. The deceased person's clothes are left exactly as in life. So too, the memory of the sea occupies the mind of the speaker, exactly as it did when he lived on the sea. He expects the sound of the wind but is left bereft and incredulous at its absence, just as one would feel looking at the clothes of a loved one who has passed away; the living, remaining person expresses his grief at the

Robert's analysis ends without an effective **conclusion.**

sight, just as the poem's speaker expresses his loss. By comparing the absence of the wind to the death of a loved one, Walcott emphasizes the depth of his passion and longing for the sea.

MINI-LESSON ▶ How to Conclude an Analysis

A poetry analysis must come to a definite conclusion, not just stop with the last line of the poem. At the conclusion, readers should feel a sense that the analysis is complete, that all the ideas discussed have been tied together neatly. An effective conclusion echoes the thesis statement, summarizes the key points, and leaves readers with a final thought that offers some insight readers can apply to their own experiences or future reading.

Robert ends his analysis with his examination of the poem's last stanza. To improve his essay, he decides to add another paragraph in order to leave readers with a final thought and a sense of closure.

Robert's Draft of Paragraph 4

By comparing the absence of the wind to the death of a loved one, Walcott emphasizes the depth and passion of his longing.

Robert's Revision of Paragraph 4

By comparing the absence of the wind to the death of a loved one, Walcott emphasizes the depth and passion of his longing. ∧¶ *Although many readers have not experienced a sailor's life, most have suffered the personal loss of something or someone cherished. In "Missing the Sea," Derek Walcott uses concrete images and strong figurative language to exemplify the universality of losing what you love most.*

Your Turn ——————
Conclude Your Analysis
- Re-read your analysis. Do you have an effective closing paragraph?
- Does your conclusion address the thesis and leave the reader with an insight and a new perspective?

Proofreading and Publishing

Proofread

You have worked hard to express your literary insights. Now you need to **proofread,** or **edit,** your final draft one more time before you make your final copy.

Proofreading Tip

Ask a classmate to help you by reading your analysis backward, one sentence at a time, making sure that each sentence is structured and punctuated correctly.

Grammar Link Using Quotation Marks

Always use **quotation marks** to enclose direct quotations. Many of the quotations in your poetry analysis will be only parts, or fragments, of a line or sentence. If the quotation is obviously a fragment, it can begin with a lowercase letter.

> In the last full stanza, Walcott uses the images of objects found in the house (silent cupboards and "sour laundry"), again using synecdoche.

If the quoted fragment is at the end of the sentence in which it appears, the end punctuation for the sentence is often inside the closing quotation mark, as shown in this example:

> An oxymoron is also used to illustrate its power: "a deafening absence, a blow."

Remember these additional rules:

 • Commas and periods are placed *inside* the closing quotation mark; question marks and exclamation points are placed *inside* the closing quotation mark only if the quotation is a question or an exclamation.

 • Semicolons, colons, and dashes are placed *outside* the closing quotation mark. Question marks and exclamation points are placed *outside* the closing quotation mark if the sentence (not the quotation) is a question or an exclamation.

Publishing

Share the knowledge and insight you have gained from writing your analysis. Here are some ideas for publishing your work:

- Create and distribute a poetry pamphlet. Include graphics, background information, the poem, and your analysis. Before distributing pamphlets on school grounds, be sure to get approval from your school's administration.

- Recite your poem at a poetry slam, and share your insights about the poem with your audience. For more on **reciting literature,** see page 242.

Submission Ideas

- Web sites
- Scholarly journals
- Poetry magazines

Reflect on the Process

In your **RWN,** write a short response to each of the following questions:

1. How did writing an analysis improve your understanding of the poem?
2. What parts of your analysis will you apply to other poems?
3. How will your literary analysis relate to other kinds of writing?

Your Turn _____
Proofread and Publish

Proofread your essay for errors in organization as well as in grammar, usage, and mechanics. As you proofread, note in particular the punctuation of quotations from the poem. If you find any errors, correct them. Then, publish your essay to share your insights.

Scoring Rubric

Use one of the rubrics below to evaluate your poetry analysis from the Writing Workshop or your response to the on-demand prompt on the next page. Your teacher will tell you to use either the six- or the four-point rubric.

6-Point Scale

Score 6 *Demonstrates advanced success*
- focuses consistently on a clear thesis
- shows effective organization throughout, with smooth transitions
- offers thoughtful, creative analysis of the literary work
- develops ideas thoroughly, using fully-elaborated textual support
- exhibits mature control of written language

Score 5 *Demonstrates proficient success*
- focuses on a clear thesis
- shows effective organization, with transitions
- offers thoughtful analysis of the literary work
- develops ideas competently, using well-elaborated textual support
- exhibits sufficient control of written language

Score 4 *Demonstrates competent success*
- focuses on a clear thesis, with minor distractions
- shows effective organization, with minor lapses
- offers mostly thoughtful analysis of the literary work
- develops ideas adequately, with a mixture of general and specific elaboration
- exhibits general control of written language

Score 3 *Demonstrates limited success*
- includes some loosely related ideas that distract from the writer's focus
- shows some organization, with noticeable gaps in the logical flow of ideas
- offers routine, predictable ideas about the literary work
- develops ideas with little textual support and uneven elaboration
- exhibits limited control of written language

Score 2 *Demonstrates basic success*
- includes loosely related ideas that seriously distract from the writer's focus
- shows minimal organization, with major gaps in the logical flow of ideas
- offers ideas that show only a surface understanding of the literary work
- develops ideas with inadequate textual support and elaboration
- exhibits significant problems with control of written language

Score 1 *Demonstrates emerging effort*
- shows little awareness of the topic and purpose for writing
- lacks organization
- offers unclear ideas that show a confused understanding of the literary work
- develops ideas with minimal textual support and elaboration, if any
- exhibits major problems with control of written language

4-Point Scale

Score 4 *Demonstrates advanced successt*
- focuses consistently on a clear thesis
- shows effective organization throughout, with smooth transitions
- offers thoughtful, creative analysis of the literary work
- d evelops ideas thoroughly, using fully-elaborated textual support
- exhibits mature control of written language

Score 3 *Demonstrates competent success*
- focuses on a clear thesis, with minor distractions
- shows effective organization, with minor lapses
- offers mostly thoughtful analysis of the literary work
- develops ideas adequately, with a mixture of general and specific elaboration
- exhibits general control of written language

Score 2 *Demonstrates limited success*
- includes some loosely related ideas that distract from the writer's focus
- shows some organization, with noticeable gaps in the logical flow of ideas
- offers routine, predictable ideas about the literary work
- develops ideas with little textual support and uneven elaboration
- exhibits limited control of written language

Score 1 *Demonstrates emerging effort*
- shows little awareness of the topic and purpose for writing
- lacks organization
- offers unclear ideas that show a confused understanding of the literary work
- develops ideas with minimal textual support and elaboration, if any
- exhibits major problems with control of written language

Preparing for Timed Writing

Literary Analysis

When responding to a literary analysis prompt, use what you have learned from reading, writing your poetry analysis, and studying the rubric on page 240. Use the steps below to develop a response to the following prompt.

Writing Prompt

Many pieces of literature feature a villainous character who creates conflict in the world in which he or she resides. Choose one literary villain from your reading. In an essay, explain how the villain's role is critical to the text.

Study the Prompt

Begin by reading the prompt carefully. Read it a second time, noting the requirements specified in the prompt:

Type of writing: essay
Subject: the role of the villain
Text: your choice of literary works that includes a villain whose role is critical to the text

Quickly make a list of literary works that you know well with a villain. Then determine which of these selections you know best. **Tip:** Spend about five minutes studying the prompt.

Plan Your Response

Once you have decided on a literary work and its villain, ask yourself these questions about his or her role:

- What background information will I need to provide about this villain and this literary work?
- What is the nature of the character's villainy?
- What motivates the villain to be bad?
- How does his evil manifest itself with the others?
- How do the other characters react to the villain?
- What consequences does the villainous behavior create?
- What theme does the author exhibit through the resolution of this character's role?

Make notes as you answer these questions. Focus on one scene in which the answers to your questions are most clear. Include discussion of that scene in your essay. **Tip:** Spend about ten minutes planning your response.

Respond to the Prompt

Start writing by introducing and stating your thesis. Your thesis will be a statement about the villain's role and the theme of the literary work. Then begin writing down the evidence that led you to your thesis. A good way to organize your essay is chronologically, following the progression of the villain's actions. Conclude your essay with his or her final scene. Try to get down as many ideas as you can. As your write, think of the following points:

- Make sure to give your reader evidence from the text to support your thesis. Use short quotations if you can recall them or retell scenes from the text.
- Elaborate on how each piece of evidence supports the thesis.
- Use the villain's final scene to conclude your essay and comment on the story's theme.

Tip: Spend about twenty minutes writing your draft.

Improve Your Response

Revising Look again at the prompt to make sure your essay fulfills the requirements. Have you explained how the villain's role relates to the author's theme? Have you used specific details from the text? Have you included details of the last scene in which the villain appears?

Proofreading Now make sure that your essay is free of errors in grammar, spelling, punctuation and capitalization. Make sure that your edits are neat and your essay is legible.

Checking your final copy Before you turn in your final copy, read it one more time to catch any errors you may have missed and to make any finishing touches. **Tip:** Spend about five to ten minutes improving your paper.

Presenting a Literary Analysis

Think as a Reader/Writer

When you write, you have to think as a reader and determine how to make your thoughts and ideas clear to your audience. As a speaker, you must also be aware of your audience. When you adapt a piece of writing into an oral presentation, you have to determine how to convey your ideas effectively without simply reading your words out loud.

Reading and writing about poetry probably helped you learn more about that genre. Now, you can share your understanding with your classmates by adapting your essay for an oral presentation.

Adapt Your Analysis

Adapt the Text

Writing your literary analysis was the hard part. Now, with a few basic adaptations to your essay, you can create a dynamic and interesting presentation. The organization of your presentation can be the same as that used in your essay: You just need to add some interesting features to captivate your audience.

Grabbing the attention of your audience is critical. The **introduction** to an oral presentation must be more dramatic than your written introduction. Some of this drama will arise from the way you present and verbalize your introduction, but it is also important to add a few extra touches, such as beginning your introduction with one of the unique aspects of the work you are discussing. When speaking about "The Wife of Bath's Tale," for example, you might mention Geoffrey Chaucer's use of a strong and very liberated woman as his main character. Another way to get your listener's attention is with a dramatic interpretation of lines from the poem. End your introduction with a strong but simple thesis statement that leaves listeners with a clear idea about the poem, the literary elements, and/or the author whose works you plan to discuss.

The **body** of your oral presentation should cover the main points of your essay. Elaborate on the evidence just as you did in your essay. Explain for your listeners the effects of stylistic devices that the authors use, such as imagery. To help listeners understand your analysis, include many lines from the poem. Be sure to add additional explanations of any events or passages that are difficult to understand (**complexities**), have multiple interpretations (**ambiguities**), or show subtle shades of meaning (**nuances**).

The **conclusion** of an oral presentation, like the conclusion of a written work, serves as a wrap-up of your ideas. To leave a lasting impression on your listeners, make your conclusion memorable. You can use a rhetorical question, repetition, or parallelism when restating your thesis. Consider framing your final observation in terms of universal themes. For example, a universal theme in the works of Chaucer and Tolkien is that of good versus evil. To exemplify the points you made, consider ending with a dynamic quotation from the poem.

Rehearse and Deliver Your Analysis

Speak Naturally

To speak effectively, you need to sound as natural and as relaxed as possible. Rather than memorizing your presentation, use the following steps to help you speak extemporaneously.

Step 1 Make concise notes on notecards.

Step 2 In your notes, write down key words and phrases about the main points of your analysis.

Step 3 Include reminders of specific points you want to make in your presentation.

Step 4 Carefully copy the quotations and lines from the work you will be presenting, and be certain you can read them.

Step 5 Arrange your notecards in the right order for a smooth presentation.

Polish Your Presentation

Standing still and staring straight ahead don't contribute to an effective presentation. Use the following techniques to deliver an engaging presentation.

- **Pronunciation and Enunciation** It's easy to be nervous when speaking to a group, so focus on pronouncing words correctly. Speak clearly (enunciate), and speak at a natural pace so each word is understandable.

- **Emphasis and Pauses** To get your main points across to your audience, change your tone and volume for emphasis. Pausing is also an effective way to emphasize something you've just said. It allows your listeners time to digest a point you made and lends suspense to a point you are about to make.

- **Facial Expressions and Gestures** Change your facial expressions as you deliver your presentation. A blank face is like a monotone speaking tone; it almost guarantees that your audience will tune out. Although many of us do not use hand gestures when speaking casually, in oral presentations, relaxed gestures can help emphasize our words and make the presentation seem more natural. Moving around further helps to keep your audience's attention.

- **Eye Contact** Continually make eye contact with members of your audience. Eye contact will engage your listeners and convey that the message you are sharing is one they need to hear.

Rehearse

Rehearse your presentation to practice these techniques and to become thoroughly familiar with the content of your presentation. If possible, present your response to an audience of friends and family and ask them for feedback.

A Good Oral Presentation

- sounds natural and relaxed, not memorized
- is delivered in a natural-sounding voice
- is rehearsed to perfect the content and delivery of the presentation

---

Speaking Tip

Be sure to use standard American English when you deliver your presentation. Avoid slang and colloquialisms in an oral response to literature. Your listeners could misunderstand your language or your message.

Literary Skills Review

Directions: Read the following poems. Then, read each multiple-choice question that follows and write the letter of the best response.

The Twa Corbies
by **Anonymous**

As I was walking all alane
I heard twa corbies making a mane;°
The tane unto the t'other say,
'Where sall we gang and dine today?'

5 '—In behint you auld fail dyke,°
I wot° there lies a new-slain Knight;
And naebody kens° that he lies there,
But his hawk, his hound, and lady fair.

'His hound is to the hunting gane,
10 His hawk to fetch the wild-fowl hame,
His lady's ta'en another mate,
So we may mak our dinner sweet.

'Ye'll sit on his white hause-bane,°
And I'll pick out his bonny blue een:°
15 Wi' ae lock o' his gowden hair
We'll theek° our nest when it grows bare.

'Mony a one for him makes mane,
But nane sall ken where he is gane;
O'er his white banes, when they are bare,
20 The wind sall blaw for evermair.'

---

2. **mane:** moan.
5. **fail dyke:** earth bank.
6. **wot:** know.
7. **kens:** knows.
13. **hause-bane:** neckbone.
14. **een:** eyes.
16. **theek:** thatch.

Raven doth to raven fly
by **Alexander Pushkin**
translated by **Walter Arndt**

Raven doth to raven fly,
Raven doth to raven cry:
Raven, where is fallen meat?
What shall be the morning's treat?

5 Raven answers raven thus:
Well I know of meat for us;
On the fallow, by the willow
Lies a knight, a clod his pillow.

Why he died, who dealt the blow,
10 That his hawk alone can know,
And the sable mare that bore him,
And his bride who rode before him.

But the hawk now sails the air,
And the foe bestrode the mare,
15 And the bride a wreath is wreathing
For a new love, warm and breathing.

1. In "The Twa Corbies," which of the following *most* helps you realize that the corbies are birds?

   A "I heard twa corbies making a mane."

   B "'Ye'll sit on his white hause-bane.'"

   C "We'll theek our nest when it grows bare."

   D "So we may mak our dinner sweet."

2. In "The Twa Corbies," the lady reacts to the Knight's death by —

   A taking another mate

   B killing his hawk and hound

   C becoming grief-stricken

   D searching for him forever

3. In "The Twa Corbies," what is the attitude of the corbies toward the dead Knight?

   A They regret that he died so young.

   B They believe he will be remembered forever.

   C They are pleased to make a meal of him.

   D They pity those who are left behind to grieve.

4. What is similar about the first two stanzas of both ballads?

   A The first stanza poses a question, and the second one answers it.

   B Both stanzas are written in dialect.

   C Each stanza has an *abcb* rhyme scheme.

   D The speaker of each stanza is a knight.

5. What does the third stanza of "Raven doth to raven fly" imply about how the knight died?

   A He fell off his horse.

   B He was slain by an enemy.

   C His bride poisoned him.

   D He died in a hunting accident.

6. Unlike "The Twa Corbies," the last stanza of "Raven doth to raven fly" emphasizes —

   A the knight's decay

   B the lady's lack of grief

   C the corbies' meal

   D the hound's hunting activities

7. A theme common to both ballads is —

   A the beauty of nature

   B the peacefulness of death

   C the importance of friendship

   D the short memory of survivors

Constructed Response

8. Briefly contrast the use of details in "The Twa Corbies" and "Raven doth to raven fly." Be sure to support your response with evidence.

Vocabulary Skills Review

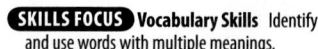

SKILLS FOCUS Vocabulary Skills Identify and use words with multiple meanings.

Multiple Meanings   **Directions:** Choose the answer in which the italicized word is used in the same way as it is used in the lines from *The Canterbury Tales.*

1. "He stood not silent like a beast or *post,*
   But gave his answer with the ringing word."
   A The student planned to *post* an ad.
   B The soldier would not leave her *post.*
   C All that's left of that old barn is a rotted *post.*
   D She gladly accepted the *post* when her boss offered it to her.

2. "'But let me briefly make my purpose *plain.*'"
   A The wind-swept *plain* stretched far and wide.
   B I prefer *plain* yogurt.
   C He's not handsome; his face is very *plain.*
   D I thought she has made it *plain* that she would be leaving tomorrow.

3. "'I preach for nothing but for greed of *gain.*'"
   A The doctor will *gain* nothing but respect for all her charity work.
   B Too many crimes have been committed for petty *gain.*
   C If I could just *gain* their interest, I know they'd hire me.
   D We could probably *gain* more speed if we shift gears.

4. "Become our Governor in short, and be Judge of our tales and *general* referee."
   A In the armed forces, a *general* ranks higher than a colonel.
   B There's a *general* feeling that we're being too strict.
   C He buys his supplies at the *general* store.
   D In *general,* the salesperson preferred to work weekends.

5. "And *set* the supper at a certain price."
   A Once Mira has *set* her mind on a goal, there's no way to stop her.
   B The fine was *set* at five hundred dollars.
   C Is there a *set* number of players needed for this game?
   D We need help getting this *set* ready for the play.

Academic Vocabulary

Directions: Choose the correct synonym for each Academic Vocabulary word.

6. Emphasis
   A sympathy
   B antagonism
   C stress
   D reduction

7. Diverse
   A varied
   B identical
   C separate
   D reduced

8. Concept
   A order
   B idea
   C thesis
   D contrast

SKILLS FOCUS Writing Skill Analyze a poem.

Writing Skills Review

Literary Analysis **Directions:** Read the following paragraph from a draft of a student's literary analysis. Then, answer the questions that follow.

(1) The Anglo-Saxon poem "The Wanderer" laments a rough physical and metaphorical journey through this life, with hope for the next. (2) By telling of his exile wandering the sea, the speaker is expressing his feelings of wandering through life, where everything is fleeting. (3) The greater theme of the poem is obvious in the very first and last lines. (4) The speaker of the poem wanders through his own narrative, beginning and ending in the same place but in the meantime traveling through his memories, disappointments, and desires. (5) He explains that he is alone because all of his friends and family are dead and gone. (6) He must rely on himself in his wanderings but declares that the only one he can really rely on is God.

1. Which sentence should be moved to follow sentence 6 to improve the style of the passage?

  A Sentence 2

  B Sentence 3

  C Sentence 4

  D Sentence 5

2. To strengthen support for the main idea, the writer could —

  A provide a few more sentences describing the speaker's journey

  B include excerpts from the poem that express the speaker's loneliness

  C tell what was his or her favorite part of the poem and why

  D include excerpts from the poem that show both the speaker's loneliness and faith

3. Which sentence could be added to support the idea in sentence 3?

  A The speaker cements his longing for his kinsmen when he cries, "Alas, you glorious princes! All gone, Lost in the night, as you never had lived." (lines 93–94)

  B The speaker begins by saying that what he wants is grace and mentions God and God's laying waste to the earth throughout the poem.

  C When the speaker says, "Fate blows hardest on a bleeding heart," he is expressing his anger at God for allowing all of the speaker's kinsmen to be slaughtered and for sending the speaker to sail aimlessly across the sea.

  D The speaker begins with longing for God's grace and mercy and returns to it at the end when he says, "It's good to find your grace in God . . . here rests our every hope." (lines 113–114)

4. Which of the following revisions best improves sentence 2?

  A Changing the first comma to a semicolon

  B Deleting the second comma

  C Making the sentence more concise: "By telling of his exile wandering the sea, the speaker expresses his feeling that life is fleeting."

  D Combining sentences 2 and 3 into a single sentence, separated by a semicolon

5. To present this passage best as an oral presentation, the writer should —

  A pause to emphasize important ideas

  B make eye contact as he or she speaks

  C rehearse thoroughly before presenting the speech

  D all of the above

Read On

FICTION
Grendel

How does it feel to be the most dreaded monster in the world? In John Gardner's contemporary novel, the ancient tale of *Beowulf* is retold from the perspective of Grendel, who shows there is more to him than his frightening appearance. Through flashbacks and stories wrought with painstaking detail, he chronicles the forces that have shaped his identify, and provides insight into the motivation behind his violent actions. After searching for meaning and questioning the heroic values that depend upon his own demise, Grendel still falls in defeat—but with his own ending to tell.

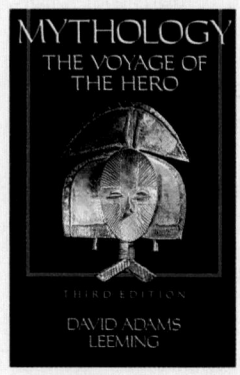

FOLKLORE/MYTHOLOGY
Mythology: The Voyage of the Hero

With narratives from English, Chinese, African, Indian, Indonesian, and Navajo cultures, David Adam Leeming's anthology demonstrates the diversity and universality of mythic tales. The collection, which explores both the hero and the heroine, is arranged by the universal hero's typical rites of passage, such as birth, quest, death, and rebirth. Philosophical and sociological influences on the meaning of myth and hero are considered in Leeming's examination of these enduring tales.

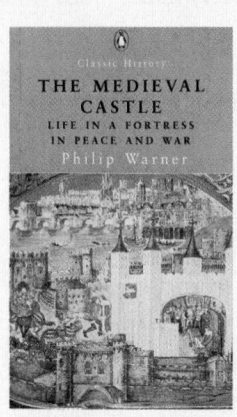

NONFICTION
The Medieval Castle

What was life really like inside á fortress? This book provides an in-depth look at everyday life in peace and war for residents of medieval castles. It also explores the effect of the castle in medieval society and the types of warfare that resulted from it. As Philip Warner describes the weapons, clothes, food, and leisure pastimes of the inhabitants of these magnificent structures, he creates a vivid portait of the medieval castle dwellers themselves, as well as shows us what they have in common with people today.

DRAMA
Becket

In *The Canterbury Tales*, a motley crew of determined pilgrims travel to the shrine of Saint Thomas á Becket. This French play by Jean Anouilh, translated into English, explores the relationship between Becket and King Henry II, who in 1162 appointed Becket as the Archbishop of Canterbury. A once cordial relationship between the two men deteriorates when Becket refuses to serve the king over God. Becket finds himself in the midst of fierce opposition, which ultimately drives him make the sacrifice that would earn him his sainthood.

FICTION
The Hobbit *and* The Lord of The Rings

J. R. R. Tolkien's *Lord of the Rings* is a three-volume fantasy epic that recounts the Great War of the Ring and the ending of the Third Age of Middle-Earth. The hobbit Frodo is called upon to embark on a dangerous mission: to destroy the One Ring by casting it into Mount Doom. To do so, Frodo and a brave group of companions must travel to the realm of the Dark Lord. *The Hobbit* (precursor to *The Ring* trilogy) follows Bilbo Baggins, Frodo's uncle, on a hazardous quest to recover stolen treasure from a dragon.

NONFICTION
Stonehenge Complete

Stonehenge, the prehistoric ruin of massive stone blocks, stands in a circle on a desolate plain in central southern England. The mysteries of Stonehenge will probably never be solved, but writers, mystics, and scholars continue to speculate about how and why Stonehenge was built and who built it. In this lavishly illustrated book, Christopher Chippindale explores the many theories about builders (Romans, Merlin, Druids) and their possible motivations (religious, astronomical, agricultural) for erecting this ancient monument.

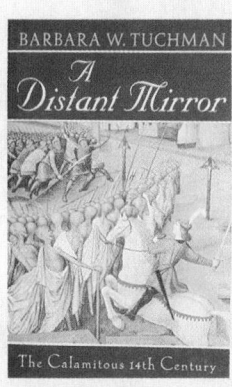

NONFICTION
A Distant Mirror

Life in the Middle Ages included its fair share of harrowing events: the Little Ice Age, which froze the Baltic Sea and shortened the growing season; the bubonic plague, which killed more than one-third of the population; and the battle between the English and French at Poitiers, in which the arrows of the English archers were so thick they darkened the sky. There were also the concerns of day-to-day life: what to wear, whom to marry, how to pay taxes, where to speak English instead of French, and when to travel. Barbara Tuchman explains all this and more in great detail.

DRAMA
Murder in the Cathedral

Culminating in the brutal assassination of Archbishop Thomas á Becket in Canterbury Cathedral on December 29, 1170, T. S. Eliot's poetic play recounts the internal struggles of Becket in his conflict with King Henry II over the role of the Church in England. Written in the 1930s, as Fascists gained power in Europe, the play seeks to warn its audience about against the propensity of political power and ideologies to undermine religious, ethical, and moral principles.

Learn It Online
Explore novels—and find tips for choosing, reading, and studying novels—at

go.hrw.com   L12-249   **Go**

THE RENAISSANCE:
A Flourish of Genius

1485–1660

COLLECTION 3
Love, Time, and Death

COLLECTION 4
William Shakespeare

"So much one man can do,

That does both act and know."

—**Andrew Marvell**

What Do
You
Think   How do our hearts
and minds influence
our actions?

The French Ambassadors of King Henry II at the court of the English King Henry VIII (1533), by Hans Holbein the Younger (1497–1543), oil on canvas. National Gallery, London.

Learn It Online
Find out more about this historical period online.

go.hrw.com | L12-251 | Go

251

THE RENAISSANCE:
A Flourish of Genius
1485–1660

This time line represents a snapshot of British literary events, British historical events, and world events from 1485 to 1660. This period is known as the Renaissance—a cultural revolution marked by scientific progress and artistic and literary achievement.

BRITISH LITERARY EVENTS

1485

c. 1516 Thomas More's *Utopia* is published >

"De optimo reip. statu, deque noua insula Utopia," (Thomas More) in *Apud inclyta Basileam* (1518). Woodcut by Ambrosius Holbein. The New York Public Library, NY.

1530

1538 Book-licensing laws are implemented in England

1557 *Tottel's Miscellany,* a collection of poetry, including poems by Wyatt and Surrey, is published

1564 William Shakespeare is born

Elizabeth I, Armada Jewel, by Nicholas Hilliard (1547–1619). Victoria & Albert Museum, London.

BRITISH HISTORICAL EVENTS

1485

1485 Richard III is defeated and killed in battle; Henry Tudor becomes King Henry VII

1492 Henry VII rejects all historic rights to French territory

1530

1534 Henry VIII declares himself head of the Church of England through the Act of Supremacy >

1558 Elizabeth I is crowned Queen of England

Henry VIII, from the original returns, transcripts, and abstracts of the Valor Ecclesiaticus (1535). National Archives, London/HIP.

WORLD EVENTS

1485

1492 Columbus reaches the Americas >

1517 Martin Luther begins the Protestant Reformation

1517 First Africans are taken to the Americas as slaves

1530

1543 Nicolaus Copernicus issues theory that planets orbit the sun

1572 Montaigne begins to compose the essays

Caravel similar to the "Santa Maria." Colored woodcut from the illustrated edition of the Colombus letter to Gabriel Sanchez (1493).

SKILLS FOCUS **Literary Skills** Evaluate and analyze the philosophical, political, religious, ethical, and social influences of a historical period. **Reading Skills** Identify and understand chronological order; use text features such as overviews, headings, and graphic features to locate and categorize information; identify and understand elements of text structure (including headings and sections).

Your Turn

With a partner, choose two British literary events from this time line. Then, locate British or world events that might be related to these literary events. In a short paragraph, explain the connection between the historical events and the literary events.

1590	1620	1660

1590 Edmund Spenser publishes first three books of *The Faerie Queene*

1604 Marlowe's *The Tragical History of Doctor Faustus* is published

1605–1606 Shakespeare writes *King Lear* and *Macbeth* ❯

1610–1611 John Donne writes *Holy Sonnets*

1611 King James Bible is published

1621 Publication of newspapers begins in London

1658 Milton begins writing *Paradise Lost*

Ian Holm as "King Lear." Cottesloe Theatre/ National Theatre, London (1997).

1590	1620	1660

1600 Elizabeth I awards a charter to the British East India Company, opening British trade with Asia

1605 Guy Fawkes and others attempt to blow up Parliament and assassinate James I in the failed Gunpowder Plot

1607 First English colony is founded in Jamestown, Virginia

1642–1651 English Civil Wars

1649 Charles I is beheaded

1653–1658 Oliver Cromwell rules England as Lord Protector ❯

1655 Jewish people, expelled in 1290, are readmitted to England

1660 Charles II is restored to the throne

Crown of Oliver Cromwell (1599–1658), London Mint, 1658 (obverse; gold) by English School (17th century). Fitzwilliam Museum, University of Cambridge, UK.

1590	1620	1660

1566–1590 Mogul ruler Akbar presides over a Golden Age in what is now India

1609 Galileo is the first person to study the sky with a telescope ❯

1620 Pilgrims on the *Mayflower* land at Plymouth Rock, Massachusetts

1639 Japan expels all Europeans except the Dutch

1649 Taj Mahal, in Agra, India, is completed

1652 Dutch traders establish a settlement in South Africa

Galileo's Telescope.

THE RENAISSANCE:
A Flourish of Genius
1485–1660

The Renaissance era in Europe and in England was marked by a change in the way people thought about themselves and the world. No longer content with the fixed religious beliefs of the Middle Ages, people became more interested in expanding their knowledge of history, art, science, and especially the classic texts of ancient Greece and Rome. The Roman Catholic Church was challenged on a number of fronts. By the end of the sixteenth century, the Church had lost its position as the supreme moral and political power in Europe.

KEY CONCEPTS

The Beginnings of Tudor Rule

History of the Times Henry Tudor defeated the Yorkist king Richard III at Bosworth Field and established the Tudor dynasty, which ruled for 118 years. Under Henry Tudor the middle class gained more power, commerce expanded, and the country prospered.

Literature of the Times The invention of the printing press in Germany spread throughout Europe. Literacy increased, and Europe experienced a creative rebirth of the arts.

The Protestant Reformation

History of the Times Henry VIII declared himself head of the English church when the pope refused to annul Henry's marriage to Catherine of Aragon. Great social and religious upheaval swept across in England.

Literature of the Times The Renaissance encouraged individual curiosity and creativity. During this time, bold new thoughts, beautiful poetry, and powerful dramatic works emerged.

England's Greatest Monarch

History of the Times Henry VIII was succeeded by his sickly son Edward. His two daughters, Mary and Elizabeth, ultimately changed English history. To this day, Elizabeth I is generally considered England's greatest ruler.

Literature of the Times The Renaissance was a golden age for literature. Poetry and drama flourished alongside religious allegory and philosophical works.

Main gatehouse of Hampton Court Palace, London.

SKILLS FOCUS **Literary Skills** Evaluate and analyze the philosophical, political, religious, ethical, and social influences of a historical period. **Reading Skills** Read widely to increase knowledge of the student's culture, the cultures of others, and the common elements across cultures; identify and understand elements of text structure (including headings and sections).

KEY CONCEPT

The Beginnings of Tudor Rule

History of the Times

The transition from the medieval period to the modern period took place primarily during the reign of the Tudors. When the Tudor line eventually ended in 1603, many modern institutions had replaced medieval ones.

Henry Tudor was a Welsh nobleman who seized the throne after the long struggle known as the Wars of the Roses. Once in power in 1485, Henry submitted his claim to Parliament, which granted him the title of king but not by hereditary right. To strengthen his position and place the Tudor line on a secure foundation, Henry married Elizabeth of York, the daughter of Edward IV, and dealt swiftly with the pretenders[1] who claimed a right to the throne.

Aware that he needed the support of the people, Henry acted to ensure peace with foreign powers. He also expanded commerce, giving his support to the English merchant class and reducing the power of the nobles. He awarded offices to men from the middle class who were loyal to him, and guaranteed Tudor law throughout the country.

By the time Henry died in 1509, England had changed considerably. The land was prosperous, the people were moderately united, and the throne was protected. The new king, Henry VIII, would mostly battle with the Church for authority and worry about producing an heir for England.

Analyzing Visuals

Viewing and Interpreting The title of this painting is *The Family of Henry VIII: An Allegory of the Tudor Succession.* Consider that an allegory operates on both a literal level and a symbolic level. What elements in the painting do you think might symbolize Tudor succession?

The Family of Henry VIII: An Allegory of the Tudor Succession (c. 1570–1575), panel by Lucas de Heere (1534–1584). National Museum and Gallery of Wales, Cardiff.

---

1. **pretenders:** individuals who claim to be rightful heirs to a position of power, but whose claim is largely denied.

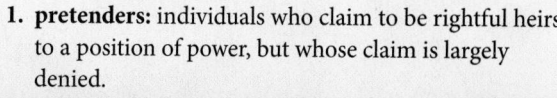
Learn It Online
Go online to learn more about this historical period.

go.hrw.com L12-255   Go

Literature of the Times

The fifteenth century was a key period for the growth of literacy in England. William Caxton introduced the printing press to the country in 1485, the same year that Henry Tudor took the throne.

Humanism was a major influence on English literature during this time. This intellectual movement looked not only to the Bible but also to Latin and Greek scholarship for wisdom and knowledge. Humanists combined classical ideals with traditional Christian thought to teach people how to live and rule. The foremost humanist in England was unquestionably Sir Thomas More, who wrote *Utopia* (1516), a famous treatise on human society. Hundreds of writers have imitated or parodied *Utopia*, which has provided us with a useful adjective for describing impractical social schemes: *utopian*. More himself, however, was far from impractical; he rose to the very top of his profession, was knighted, and became one of the king's chief ministers.

Comprehension Check

How did Henry Tudor increase the authority of the monarchy?

Fast Facts

Historical Highlights

- The Protestant Reformation begins in England in 1534, when King Henry VIII rejects the authority of the pope in Rome and declares himself head of the English Church.
- In 1553, Mary Tudor becomes queen and restores the pope's power in England.
- Elizabeth I assumes the throne in 1558 and reestablishes the Church of England.
- In 1588, the Royal Navy defeats the Spanish Armada.

Literary Highlights

- Humanists use Latin and Greek classics along with the Bible to answer fundamental questions about life.
- In 1611, the King James Bible is published.
- Dramas, including the plays of William Shakespeare, are the greatest literary achievement of the English Renaissance.

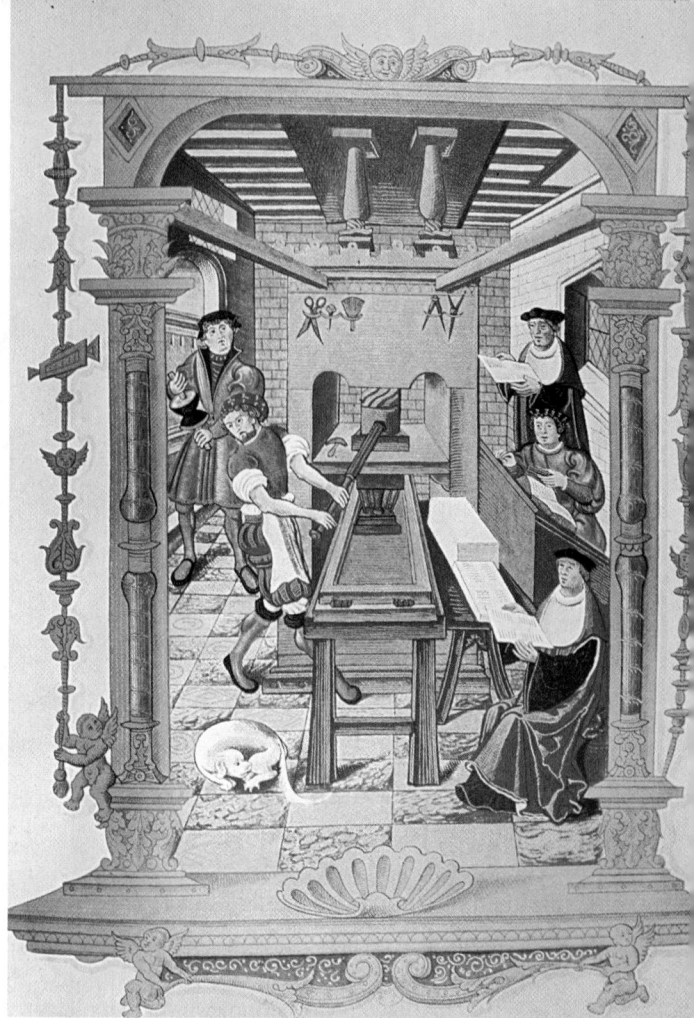

Printing press from the beginning of the 16th century.
Bibliothèque Nationale, Paris, France.

The Protestant Reformation

History of the Times

Henry VIII, who reigned from 1509 to 1547, is perhaps most famous for his six wives. The fates of these women are summarized in a jingle:

Divorced, beheaded, died,
Divorced, beheaded, survived.

Like his father, Henry VIII knew that a male heir was essential to securing the throne. His first wife, Catherine of Aragon, had failed to give him a son after twenty-four years of marriage. (Her sole surviving child was a daughter, Mary.) Henry appealed to Pope Clement VII to annul his marriage or to declare that it was never a proper union. Henry claimed that because Catherine had originally been married to his older brother Arthur—for five months before Arthur died—she could not rightfully be married to Henry. (It was against Church law to marry a dead sibling's spouse.) Because the original marriage between Catherine and Arthur had itself been annulled on the grounds that it was never consummated (so that Henry to marry Catherine in the first place), Clement refused to grant a second annulment. If Henry's new annulment were granted, a great dilemma would be created for the Church, for the original annulment would therefore have been based on a lie. Further pressure from Catherine's powerful nephew, the king of Spain, also prompted Clement to reject Henry's request.

In response, Henry appointed a new archbishop of Canterbury, who obligingly granted the annulment. In 1534, Henry finalized the break from Rome by declaring himself head of the English Church. He seized the vast and wealthy resources of the Catholic Church in England, and filled his treasury with the profit he made from selling off Church land.

Henry's decision to overthrow the Catholic Church in England was widely supported. The financial demands of the Church on the English people incited resentment, and corruption was widespread among the clergy. New religious ideas, specifically

Portrait of Henry VIII c. 1525–30 by English School, 16th c.

those of Martin Luther, were being debated, and change was inevitable. Henry's assertion, however, that he was the head of the Church of England was not tolerated universally, and many subjects remained faithful to the pope. The most famous of these was Henry's own friend, Sir Thomas More, author of *Utopia* and then lord chancellor of England. For his protests against Henry's claim to religious authority, More was beheaded in 1535.

After Henry's marriage to Catherine was declared invalid, he married Anne Boleyn, who bore a daughter, Elizabeth. Henry had Anne beheaded because she did not give him sons, and then married Jane Seymour, his third wife. She died giving birth to Henry's son, Edward. All three of Henry's children had different mothers.

Despite the controversies of his thirty-eight year reign, Henry left an important legacy. He created the Royal Navy, which is credited with protecting England from foreign invasion. He also helped England spread its political power, language, and literature over the globe. Henry was a true Renaissance man—a poet, musician, athlete, hunter, and supporter of humanistic learning. Much of what we recall about Henry VIII—his tendency to send friends and wives to the chopping block—stemmed from his desperate desire to have a male heir. He died without knowing that Elizabeth, the child he ignored because she was female, would become England's greatest ruler.

---

2. **vernacular:** native language.

Literature of the Times

The Renaissance had started in Italy in the fourteenth century and began to flourish in England after Henry VIII ascended to the throne. The Tudors, whose claim to the throne through Henry VII was based more on successful warfare than divine right and established bloodline, needed to distinguish themselves socially and politically as rightful English rulers. They also required a class of cultivated officials who would remain loyal to them. Supporting the growth of humanism allowed Tudor monarchs to accomplish both goals, as well as to patronize the development of English literature.

Humanists scholars wrote in Latin, but gradually English writers began to use the vernacular[2] and started translating Greek and Roman classics into English. Henry VIII authorized the translation of the Bible into English.

Comprehension Check

Why was Henry VIII's decision to overthrow the Church so widely embraced? What did he gain from breaking with Rome?

Link to Today

Timepieces Across Time

Do you tell time by wearing a watch, checking a clock, or looking at your cell phone? In the last century, remarkable innovations have been made in temporal technologies. The Renaissance was also a period of great advances in timekeeping. While many types of clocks existed in the ancient world, the Renaissance saw the first development of

Cathedral clock made for the tower in Salisbury Cathedral, (1386) by English School (14th century). Salisbury Cathedral, Wiltshire, UK.

modern clocks. Clocks first appeared in town centers, usually in church towers: England's oldest surviving clock, which dates from around 1386, is on Salisbury Cathedral. Before the invention of revolving hands, clocks announced themselves audibly, clanging out the hour, day and night. As individuals increasingly sought to use time to regulate their lives, clocks became privately owned possessions. As technology became more refined, timepieces became more common, more portable, and much smaller. Soon almost everyone felt the need to wear or carry a personal clock. Furthermore, as clocks proliferated, so did references to time and timekeeping in literature.

Ask Yourself

What can we learn about human beings by studying the history of inventions?

England's Greatest Monarch

History of the Times

Elizabeth I—possibly the most brilliant monarch in English history—inherited the kingdom only after her brother, Edward VI, died of tuberculosis[3] and her sister, "Bloody" Mary, died of a fever.

Edward VI's reign was short and uneventful. Crowned at age nine, Edward, though intelligent, was controlled for the remaining six years of his life by manipulative relatives. Mary, however, was a far more formidable force. A devout Catholic, she wanted to avenge the wrongs committed against her mother and her Church. When she took the throne in 1553, Mary restored power to English Catholics. She earned the name Bloody Mary for executing Protestants at the stake. Her support waned when she married Philip II, king of Spain, at a time when fear and hatred of Spain were escalating. Because Mary died childless, her sister Elizabeth succeeded to the throne.

Elizabeth's first task was to restore law and order to a kingdom torn by fierce religious feuds. Elizabeth reestablished the Church of England and refused to acknowledge the pope's authority. As a result, she was excommunicated, that is to say, officially expelled from the Roman Catholic Church. Because Elizabeth knew that taking a husband would put her under male authority, she eluded marriage for her entire reign despite much external pressure. When

Elizabeth I, so-called "Armada Portrait," (1588) by Marcus Geerarts the Younger.

Parliament begged her to marry, she said, "I am your anointed Queen. I will never be by violence constrained to do anything." She remained "the Virgin Queen," from which the American colony Virginia got its name.

Elizabeth foiled several plots against her life, some of which were engineered by her cousin Mary Stuart, Queen of Scots, also a direct descendant of Henry VII. Mary Stuart, who was a Catholic, was deposed[4] from her throne in Protestant Scotland,

---

3. **tuberculosis:** a contagious and eventually fatal lung disease.

---

4. **deposed:** removed from power, dethroned.

Renaissance Dance, La Volta (16th century).

and lived under house arrest as a royal exile in England. Because Elizabeth was childless, Mary had a claim to the English crown. When Elizabeth had Mary beheaded in 1588, Philip of Spain—irritated by Elizabeth's refusal to marry him as much as by the execution of another Catholic ally—found reason to invade England. He subsequently sent the Spanish Armada, a fleet of warships, to conquer England, which ultimately destroyed the Armada with the help of some strong storms in the Irish Sea. Without this victory, Spain may well have conquered Britain and later occupied North America.

In 1603, Elizabeth was succeeded by James VI of Scotland, her second cousin and the son of Mary Stuart. As James I, he reigned until 1625, leaving behind a weakened crown for his despotic son, Charles I, who was beheaded in 1649. England was governed by Parliament, and the Puritan leader Oliver Cromwell until 1660. When Charles II emerged from exile to assume power, the Renaissance was ending, and England was a different country.

Literature of the Times

The defeat of the Armada was an impetus[5] for Renaissance writers, for with this victory Elizabeth had confirmed the national identity of her kingdom. Writers celebrated her as a beloved symbol of peace, security, and prosperity, frequently dedicating their works to her. She also appeared mythologically as Cynthia, Diana, Gloriana, and the Faerie Queene in a host of literary works. The sixteenth century saw a great deal of publishing, and, particularly in the 1590s, an astounding outpouring of manuscripts.

Elizabeth's court became the center of a literary culture that included many gifted writers and courtiers who wrote only for a select circle of friends. Edmund Spenser, who considered himself a professional writer, published his masterpiece *The Faerie Queene* and dedicated it to Elizabeth. Even in the reign of James, poets like John Donne did not seek to have their work published.

The greatest literary achievement of the Renaissance in England is its body of dramatic work. The plays of Shakespeare and his contemporaries were written for public theaters rather than for aristocratic patrons. The last great writer of the English Renaissance is John Milton, who lived past the period of the Commonwealth and into the Restoration.

Quick Check

Describe the historical and literary impact of the defeat of the Spanish Armada.

___

5. **impetus:** a catalyst; a cause for action.

(*opposite*) *Elizabeth I, Armada Jewel* by Nicholas Hilliard (1547–1619).
Victoria & Albert Museum, London.

Wrap Up

Talk About...

Discuss the merits of a monarchy versus a democracy. Which form of government makes the most sense to you? Use each Academic Vocabulary word **listed below** at least once in your discussion.

Write About...

The invention of the printing press and the Internet changed the world. Write a paragraph comparing the influence of the printing press on society since its invention in the fifteenth century and the influence of the Internet on contemporary society.

Academic Vocabulary for Unit 2

Talking and Writing About Literature

Academic Vocabulary is the language you use to talk and write about literature. Use these words to discuss the literature you read in this unit. These words will be underlined throughout the unit.

established   (ehs TAB lihsht) *v.*: set up; caused to happen.: *Henry VII established the Tudor bloodline.*

ensure   (ehn SHOOR) *v.*: to make certain. *During his reign, Henry VII acted to ensure that the Tudor line would continue.*

widespread   (wyd SPREHD) *adj.*: occurring over a wide area. *Henry had widespread support for his decision to overthrow the Church in England.*

controversies   (KAHN truh vur seez) *n.*: lengthy disagreement. *Despite its controversies, Henry's reign saw great achievements.*

contradiction   (kahn truh DIHK shuhn) *n.*: statement in opposition to another; inconsistency. *The Catholic Church felt it would be a contradiction to annul Henry VIII's marriage to Catherine.*

Your Turn

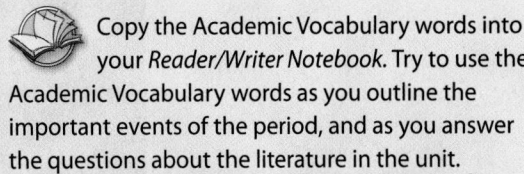

Copy the Academic Vocabulary words into your *Reader/Writer Notebook*. Try to use the Academic Vocabulary words as you outline the important events of the period, and as you answer the questions about the literature in the unit.

File Edit View Favorites Tools Help

Back Forward Stop Refresh Home Search Favorites History Mail Print

Address http://www.bbc.co.uk

Link to Today

This Link to Today claims that, thanks to the Internet, we are currently living in the midst of another Renaissance.

Read with a Purpose
Read to see what makes your world as creative as Shakespeare's.

Build Background
Leon Battista Alberti, an accomplished thinker and artist of the Renaissance, first put forth the idea of the Renaissance man. Alberti wrote that "a man can do all things if he will," including achievements in the fields of art, science, and sports. The idea of the Renaissance man follows from humanism, a philosophy that places humans at the center of the universe and encourages the development of human knowledge and excellence.

Interior of a printing shop, copper engraving by Matthaeus Marien the Elder (1593–1650).

Another Renaissance?

by **Gary Fisher**
Electronic Engineering Time

It must have been exciting to live during the Renaissance. This period, beginning in the fourteenth century, saw perhaps the most significant growth of literature, technology and the arts in history to that time. Particular advances, such as the development of printing and oil-based inks, permitted large numbers of individuals not only to see and to even own works produced by creative minds, but to produce and distribute their own work for others to see and judge.

And produce they did.

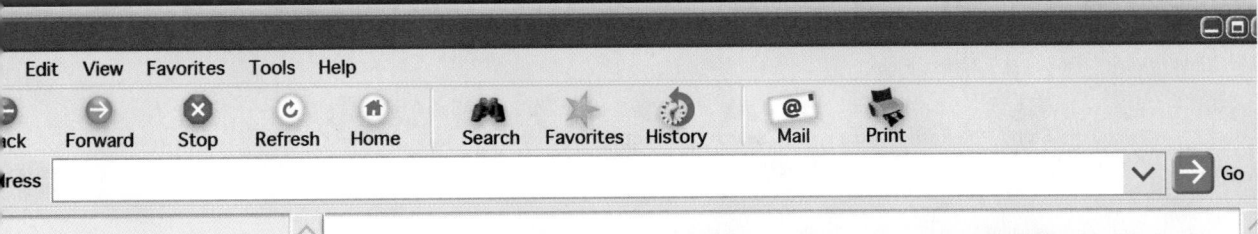

The printing presses of the printers Plantin-Moretus in Antwerp.
Museum Plantin-Moretus, Antwerp, Belgium.

During the Renaissance, in brilliant contrast to an age in which literature and art required a wealthy patron to achieve any hope of a wide audience, it became possible for almost anyone who could learn the necessary skills and acquire access to the required technology to see their ideas—the results of their creative talents—spread to the four winds.

Much of the work, of course, was produced for personal satisfaction, and much for limited distribution among very specific audiences—societies, guilds[1] and members of other groups were sometimes united by little more than their published works. For all, the technologies of the Renaissance suddenly transformed the ability to read and write from the specialized domain of clerics[2] into a skill useful to anyone, and gave anyone "touched by the muse"[3] an outlet for their creative works.

---

1. **guilds:** associations of artists or craftsmen, organized to maintain standards and to protect the interests of their members.
2. **clerics:** members of the clergy such as priests and monks.
3. **muse:** goddess who inspires a poet or artist. "Touched by the muse" means inspired by a creative force.

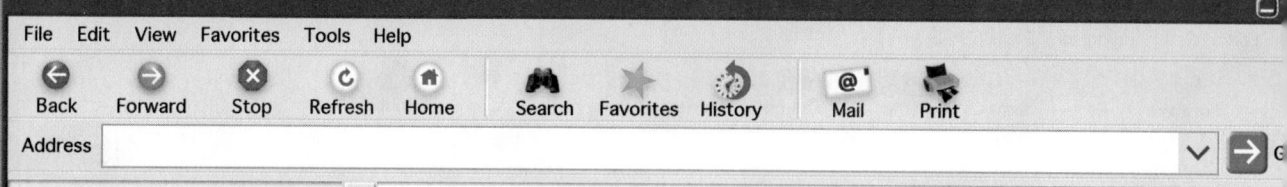

Link to Today

Perhaps the most significant effect of the Renaissance was the widespread access it opened to ideas. One of the most persistent concepts we still associate with the period is that of "Renaissance men," individuals who harnessed the technologies and creative energy of the time to put most of the current body of knowledge at their fingertips. These people wrote, but just as importantly they read and corresponded with others, building on that interaction and exchange of ideas to synthesize and develop their own.

We may be standing in the midst of another "Renaissance." Computers, the Internet and other forms of online communications, and a widespread spirit of creativity have come together during our time to give anyone with the desire to connect a worldwide audience for their talents, and millions are taking advantage of the opportunity. Many whose fifth-grade teachers might have considered them both illiterate and devoid of artistic talent are today busily learning to organize and publish the products of their creative energies in electronic form, daring to offer their ideas to a potential audience of millions.

"The Gathering," the world's largest convention of computer enthusiasts. Hamar, Norway.

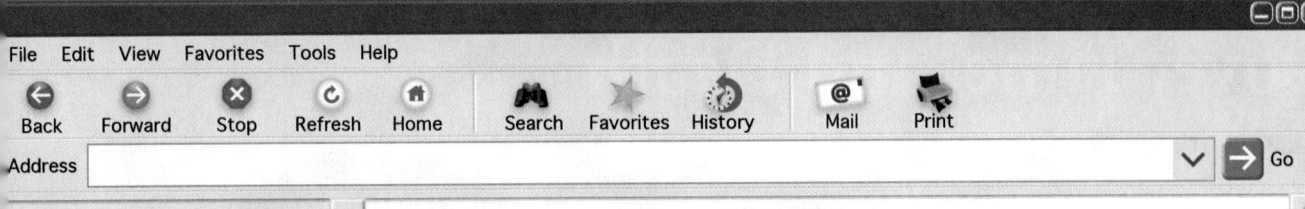

The Proportions of the Human Body (1996), by Electros aka Babis Vekri.

The age of the **Renaissance person** may have returned; the sum of human thought and knowledge, from classical literature to the most recent discoveries of science, can be literally at the fingertips of anyone with the desire to master the skills and a little technology. The spirit of the Renaissance seems also to be returning; just as the "men of arts and letters"[4] of that former era were willing—sometimes even eager—to correspond with those interested in their ideas, many of today's leading philosophers, writers and researchers participate in electronic discussion groups and gladly respond to thoughtful e-mail.

Who will be the next Da Vinci, the next Bacon, the next Jefferson?[5] It's very possible they're online today.

---

4. **letters:** literature and other written forms of communication.
5. **Da Vinci:** Leonardo da Vinci (1452–1519), Italian artist and scientist; **Bacon:** Francis Bacon (1561–1626), British statesman and philosopher; **Jefferson:** Thomas Jefferson (1743–1846), American statesman and philosopher. Da Vinci, Bacon, and Jefferson are all considered Renaissance men.

Ask Yourself

1. **Read with a Purpose** According to Gary Fisher, what does our world today have in common with the Renaissance?

2. How did Renaissance technology affect reading and writing?

3. What specific features distinguished the Renaissance from prior ages?

4. Why might someone disagree with Fisher that "the sum of human thought and knowledge . . . can be literally at the fingertips of anyone with the desire to master the skills and a little technology"? Explain.

Love, Time, and Death

LITERARY FOCUS
Renaissance Poetry

Fall of the Rebel Angels, by Pieter Brueghel the Elder.
Musée d'Art Ancien, Musées Royaux des Beaux-Arts, Brussels, Belgium.

CONTENTS

Sir Thomas Wyatt

Edmund Spenser

Christopher Marlowe

Sir Walter Raleigh

Robert Herrick

Andrew Marvel

John Donne

Margaret Edson Link to Today

Ben Jonson

Sir John Suckling

Richard Lovelace

from the **King James Bible**

COMPARING TEXTS: WORLD LITERATURE
Worlds of Wisdom

John Milton

John Bunyan

COMPARING TEXTS: VIEWS ON
EDUCATION AND EQUALITY **Frances
Bacon, Queen Elizabeth I,
Margaret Cavendish**

"Man is but earth; 'Tis true; but earth is the centre. That man who dwells upon himself, who is always conversant in himself, rests in his true centre."

—John Donne

Renaissance Poetry by Leila Christenbury

Influences on Renaissance Poetry

- Humanism, a belief in the central importance and dignity of human beings
- A new interest in ancient Greek and Roman writings, including drama and poetry
- Italian verse forms, including the sonnet
- Powerful patrons of the arts, such as Elizabeth I

The Renaissance's explosion of faith in the preeminence of the individual is often seen as the turning point between the Middle Ages and the modern world. Such confidence found a fitting outlet in poetry.

The Spirit of the Age

During the Renaissance (a term meaning "rebirth") people began to see life in an entirely new way. In the Middle Ages, people had been taught to focus not on the pleasures of this world but on the rewards of the next. With the surge of new ideas in the Renaissance, people began to question the beliefs of the past. Writers created poems that focused on their own lives, their relationships, and the physical world around them.

The widespread belief in personal ability and the potential of the individual has its roots in **humanism,** an intellectual movement in which writers and artists sought to synthesize the lessons of Latin and Greek classics with the teachings of Christianity. Humanism grew into a powerful philosophical and educational trend that shaped much Renaissance art and philosophy. Drawing on ideas from the ancient Greeks and Romans, Renaissance writers became optimistic about the power of human thought and action. They wanted to educate others and cultivate the ability of individuals to understand the natural world and live virtuously.

The humanist focus on the classics had a strong influence on Renaissance poetry. Poets admired the elaborate poetic patterns of ancient writers who composed poems that followed complicated rules regarding subject matter, line length, and **rhyme scheme.**

The Development of the Sonnet

In addition to imitating classical forms of poetry, Renaissance poets expressed their ideas in the **sonnet,** a verse form that had developed in Italy during the late Middle Ages. The word *sonnet* is derived from the Italian word *sonetto,* meaning "little sound or song." A sonnet is a fourteen-line lyric poem, which is written in **iambic pentameter** and adheres to one of several strict rhyme schemes. In Italy, the sonnet form was perfected by Francesco Petrarca (1304–1374), known in English as Petrarch. Petrarch believed that the sonnet, with its brevity and musical rhymes, was a perfect medium for the expression of emotion, especially love. An example of the form he popularized, called the **Italian,** or **Petrarchan sonnet,** is on p. 400.

The Petrarchan sonnet has two parts: an eight-line section called the octave, with a rhyme scheme of *abbaabba,* followed by a six-line section called the sestet, with a rhyme scheme of *cdecde* or *cdcdcd.* Typically, the octave establishes the speaker's situation, and the sestet resolves, draws conclusions about, or expresses a reaction to that situation. The transition from octave to sestet is called the **turn.** Like many literary terms, the *turn* is a metaphor; the speaker is, figuratively speaking, turning from one thought to another.

During the English Renaissance, Sir Thomas Wyatt, a diplomat in the court of King Henry VIII, translated some of Petrarch's sonnets and wrote a few of his own, slightly modifying the Italian form. Building on Wyatt's modifications, Henry Howard, Earl of Surrey, changed the rhyme scheme of the Italian sonnet to adapt it to the rhyme-poor English language. Surrey's innovations distinguished the English sonnet from the Italian sonnet. The English sonnet ultimately became known as the Shakespearean sonnet because William Shakespeare used it with such distinction.

Although the Shakespearean sonnet adheres to the fixed requirement of fourteen iambic pentameter lines, its organization differs from that of a Petrarchan sonnet. While a Petrarchan sonnet uses the octave and sestet to pose a question and answer or a problem and solution, a Shakespearean sonnet is divided into three quatrains, or groups of four lines, and a couplet, which consists of two lines. The three quatrains express related ideas and the couplet sums up the poet's message. The turn, or shift in thought, often occurs at the third quatrain or at the couplet. The Shakespearean sonnet's rhyme scheme is *abab cdcd efef gg*.

Edmund Spenser developed a third type of sonnet, accordingly called the Spenserian sonnet. Like the Shakespearean sonnet, the Spenserian sonnet has three quatrains and a couplet, but it uses an interlocking rhyme scheme: *abab bcbc cdcd ee*. This rhyme scheme reinforces the relationship of ideas between the quatrains and helps emphasize the closing comment in the couplet.

Poetry and Society

Social life among the upper classes required men and women to know many forms of poetry. To be popular and well received, you had to able to write in verse and sing it, too—sometimes accompanying yourself on a stringed instrument. This trend was greatly influenced by the remarkable wit and literary skills of Elizabeth I, who wrote and admired good poetry. Her courtiers often wrote verses in her honor, and her court was noted for its dramatic presentations and music. Other people imitated court behavior, writing to appear more learned or fashionable, or simply for their own enjoyment. Poetry during the Renaissance was woven into people's lives and, for the literate, represented an important aspect of the everyday world—much as music and lyrics are an integral part of our world today.

Analyzing Visuals

Viewing and Interpreting What do the activities of each of the three subjects in the painting suggest about Renaissance lifestyle?

Three Musicians, fl (c. 1500–1533)

Ask Yourself

1. How did the rediscovery of classical literature shape Renaissance poetry?

2. How did people use poetry during the Renaissance?

Learn It Online

Learn about Renaissance poetry through *PowerNotes.*

go.hrw.com   L12-268   **Go**

SKILLS FOCUS Literary Skills Evaluate and analyze the philosophical, political, religious, ethical, and social influences of a historical period; analyze Renaissance poetry.

Analyzing an Illumination

Renaissance poetry celebrates individuals, their relationships, and their natural surroundings. This image is an early Renaissance illumination, or illustration, of a medieval story about courtly love—a topic that continued to be popular during the Renaissance.

Guidelines

Use these guidelines to consider how this illumination expresses ideas typical of Renaissance poetry.

- How does the **setting** reflect ideas associated with Renaissance poetry?
- What event appears to be taking place?
- To what social class do the people belong? How can you tell?

1. What is occurring at the center of the illumination? What Renaissance value does this scene reflect?

2. What are the people in the foreground doing? What can you determine about their relationship?

3. Examine the depiction of nature, and describe the relationship of the people to the natural world.

Lutenist and Singers in a garden outside the garden walls, taken from *Roman de la Rose* (c. 1490–1500). The British Library, London.

Your Turn Analyze Renaissance Poetry

Choose another image in this collection, and write a short paragraph explaining how it reflects some of the themes of Renaissance poetry.

SIR THOMAS WYATT
Whoso List to Hunt

EDMUND SPENSER
Sonnet 30
Sonnet 75

What Do You Think?

How do our hearts and minds influence our actions?

QuickWrite

Declare your love (real or imagined) for another person in a short piece of writing. What words will best convey your feelings of love? Record your work in your *Reader/Writer Notebook*.

Sir Thomas Wyatt (c. 1540), after Hans Holbein the Younger. National Portrait Gallery, London.

MEET THE WRITERS

Sir Thomas Wyatt
(1503–1542)

Sir Thomas Wyatt is remembered today as a literary innovator. Before Wyatt, English poetry was essentially medieval in subject, style, and form. Wyatt brought the Italian sonnet to England, where it soon became <u>established</u> as a staple of Elizabethan lyric poetry.

A courtier and diplomat, Thomas Wyatt served as an ambassador to Henry VIII. He may have been in love with Anne Boleyn, future queen and mother of Elizabeth I. Several of Wyatt's works are thought to have been written in her honor.

Like most courtiers, Wyatt did not publish his poems, and circulated his works chiefly among his friends. The first book to feature Wyatt's sonnets was published fifteen years after his death.

Edmund Spenser
(1552–1599)

Edmund Spenser was one of the most influential poets of his day. His major works include *The Shepheardes Calendar,* a series of pastoral poems that combine many different forms and meters, and *The Faerie Queene,* the longest epic poem in the English language. Spenser invented a sonnet form based on an intricate pattern of rhymes, called the Spenserian sonnet, and a special stanza form called the Spenserian stanza. Both influenced later poets.

Spenser attended Cambridge University as a "sizar," or poor scholar. When he served as personal secretary to the earl of Leicester, he met Sir Philip Sidney, another gifted poet, to whom he dedicated *The Shepheardes Calendar.* Later, Spenser became a landowner in Ireland, where he wrote *The Faerie Queene.* His castle burned in 1598, and he died in London the following year. He is buried next to Chaucer in the Poets' Corner at Westminster Abbey.

Think About the Writers

Wyatt and Spenser are considered innovators. What writers or musicians today are creating new forms and influencing other artists?

Edmund Spenser by Henry Bone.

Whoso List to Hunt / Sonnet 30 / Sonnet 75

SKILLS FOCUS Literary Skills Understand characteristics of the speaker. **Reading Skills** Draw inferences.

Reader/Writer Notebook

Use your **RWN** for completing the activities on this page.

Literary Focus

Speaker The **speaker** is the voice that addresses the reader in a poem. The speaker may be the poet or a created character whose voice and concerns do not necessarily reflect those of the poet. The speaker may even be an animal or an inanimate object. Even if a poem uses the pronoun *I*, readers cannot assume that the speaker is the poet.

Reading Focus

Drawing Inferences Forming logical conclusions from details in a text and from your own experiences is known as **drawing inferences.** As you read, look for clues, such as images, word choice, and shifts in tone, which will help you better understand an author's message.

Into Action In these poems, contrasting images can help you make inferences about the speakers and the poems' messages. When reading the selections, take note of the contrasting, or <u>contradictory</u> images. Using a chart like the one below for each sonnet, record the lines and the contrasting words you find. Be sure to note verbs as well as nouns.

Lines	Contrasting Words
My love is like to ice, and I to fire;	ice and fire

Writing Focus

Think as a Reader/Writer

Find It in Your Reading As you read these three poems, pay attention to the structure of each **sonnet.** Note that Wyatt uses the Petrarchan form while Spenser uses his own modification of the English sonnet, known as the Spenserian sonnet. Keep track of each poem's stanza structure and rhyme scheme. Where does the turn, or shift in thought, occur in each sonnet? Take notes on these questions in your *Reader/Writer Notebook*.

Learn It Online
Listen to these poems read aloud online.

go.hrw.com   L12-271   **Go**

WHOSO LIST TO HUNT

by **Sir Thomas Wyatt**

Read with a Purpose
Read to discover the speaker's feelings about the creature he pursues.

Build Background
As a courtier, Wyatt was expected to compose songs, battle for the king, dance, joust in tournaments, and carry on intrigues with the ladies. According to traditional gossip, this poem is about Wyatt's longing for Anne Boleyn, a beautiful young woman at court. When he realized that King Henry VIII also fancied Anne, Wyatt gave up the pursuit to whoever else wanted to "hunt" her. In the poem below, it is thought that the deer with the jeweled collar refers to Anne.

Whoso list° to hunt, I know where is an hind,°
But as for me, alas, I may no more.
The vain travail° hath wearied me so sore
I am of them that farthest cometh behind. **A**
5 Yet may I, by no means, my wearied mind
Draw from the deer, but as she fleeth afore,
Fainting I follow. I leave off therefore,
Since in a net I seek to hold the wind.

Who list her hunt, I put him out of doubt,°
10 As well as I, may spend his time in vain.
And graven with diamonds in letters plain
There is written, her fair neck round about,
"*Noli me tangere,* for Caesar's I am,
And wild for to hold, though I seem tame." **B**

1. **whoso list:** whoever desires. **hind:** female deer.
3. **travail:** hard work.

9. **put him out of doubt:** assure him.

A **Literary Focus** Speaker The speaker places himself last in the hunt. What does this say about his view of himself?

B **Reading Focus** Drawing Inferences What can you infer from the image of diamonds?

Analyzing Visuals

Viewing and Interpreting How well does this portrait of Anne Boleyn represent the woman described in the poem? Explain.

Anne Boleyn (late 16th century) by an unknown artist. Oil on panel (21 3/8" x 16 3/8"). National Portrait Gallery, London.

SONNET

SONNET 30

by **Edmund Spenser**

Read with a Purpose
Read to learn why the speaker thinks love can bend the rules of nature.

Build Background
This sonnet was part of a larger group of sonnets known as the *Amoretti* ("little love poems"), published in 1595. Spenser wrote these sonnets to his wife, Elizabeth. The poems are about their courtship.

My love is like to ice, and I to fire;
How comes it then that this her cold so great
Is not dissolved through my so hot desire,
But harder grows the more I her entreat? **A**

5   Or how comes it that my exceeding heat
Is not delayed° by her heart frozen cold,
But that I burn much more in boiling sweat,
And feel my flames augmented manifold?°
What more miraculous thing may be told

10   That fire which all thing melts, should harden ice,
And ice which is congealed° with senseless cold,
Should kindle fire by wonderful device?°
Such is the power of love in gentle mind,
That it can alter all the course of kind.° **B**

6. **delayed:** tempered.

8. **augmented manifold:** increased in many ways.

11. **congealed:** thickened.
12. **device:** trick.

14. **kind:** nature.

A Literary Focus **Speaker** Why do you think the speaker asks direct questions of the reader?

B Reading Focus **Drawing Inferences** Note the turn, or shift in thought, in the final couplet. Based on this shift, what can you infer about the poet's message?

SONNET 75

by **Edmund Spenser**

Read with a Purpose
Read to discover what happens in the exchange between the speaker and the woman he loves.

Build Background
In this sonnet, Spenser uses the image of the sea and its eternal tides to emphasize the cyclical nature of life and the immortality brought by his poetry.

One day I wrote her name upon the strand,°
But came the waves and washèd it away;
Again I wrote it with a second hand,   **A**
But came the tide, and made my pains his prey.
5 "Vain man," said she, "that doest in vain assay,°
A mortal thing so to immortalize,
For I myself shall like to this decay,
And eke° my name be wipèd out likewise."   **B**
"Not so," quod° I, "let baser things devise°
10 To die in dust, but you shall live by fame:
My verse your virtues rare shall eternize,
And in the heavens write your glorious name.
Where whenas death shall all the world subdue,
Our love shall live, and later life renew."   **C**

1. **strand:** beach.

5. **assay:** try.

8. **eke:** also.
9. **quod:** said. **devise:** plan.

A **Reading Focus** Drawing Inferences What does "second hand" mean?

B **Literary Focus** Speaker Why do you think Spenser uses two voices in this poem?

C **Reading Focus** Drawing Inferences In the poem, the male speaker wants to immortalize his love. Why does he think she is worthy of fame?

SKILLS FOCUS Literary Skills Analyze characteristics of the speaker; analyze metaphor. **Reading Skills** Draw inferences. **Writing Skills** Write a poem.

Whoso List to Hunt
Sonnet 30 / Sonnet 75

Respond and Think Critically

Reading Focus

Quick Check

1. What might the deer represent in "Whoso List to Hunt"?

2. What is the "miraculous thing" in Sonnet 30?

3. In Sonnet 75, how does the poet plan to immortalize his love?

Read with a Purpose

4. What do the speakers' ideas about romantic love have in common?

Reading Skills: Drawing Inferences

5. Add a third column to the chart you made about contrasting images. List inferences these images help you draw about the speakers and messages.

Lines	Contrasting Words	Inferences I Can Draw
My love is like to ice, and I to fire;	ice and fire	The speaker and his love are opposites, or she doesn't love him at all.

Literary Focus

Literary Analysis

6. **Interpret** In "Whoso List to Hunt," what warning does the speaker give? What image shows that the speaker considers the chase hopeless?

7. **Analyze** What **paradoxes,** or contradictions that are actually true can you find in Sonnet 30?

8. **Evaluate** In what sense has the love of the two people in Sonnet 75 survived today?

9. **Summarize** In your own words, write brief prose summaries of two of the three sonnets. Describe each sonnet's mood, scene, and story.

10. **Extend** Some attitudes concerning love and men and women have changed since these sonnets were written. Do you think the speakers' feelings are still relevant? Cite details from the poems to explain your response.

Literary Skills: Speaker

11. **Synthesize** All three sonnets have male speakers. How might the sonnets change if they had female speakers?

Literary Skills Review: Metaphor

12. **Analyze** One of the most common figures of speech is **metaphor,** a comparison between two unlike things without the use of a connective word such as *like* or *as*. Write down at least one metaphor from each poem. How do these metaphors contribute to the poems' meanings?

Writing Focus

Think as a Reader/Writer

Use It in Your Writing As you read, you took notes on the structure of each sonnet. Where does the turn, or shift in thought, occur ? In your *Reader/Writer Notebook,* write a sonnet that explains a situation or expresses a problem and then comments on that situation or states a solution to the problem.

 What Do You Think Now

How is each of these sonnets an expression of the heart and the mind?

Preparing to Read

CHRISTOPHER MARLOWE

The Passionate Shepherd to His Love

SIR WALTER RALEIGH

The Nymph's Reply to the Shepherd

What Do You Think?

How do our hearts and minds influence our actions?

QuickWrite

In your *Reader/Writer Notebook*, explain why the idea of romantic escape is so appealing to human beings of any time period.

Reputed portrait of Christopher Marlowe (1585). French School, oil. The Master and Fellows of Corpus Christi College, Cambridge, England

MEET THE WRITERS

Christopher Marlowe
(1564–1593)

Playwright, poet, brawler, and spy, Christopher Marlowe was the rebel of the Elizabethan writers. In 1587, he began doing espionage for England, but his government affiliation did not keep him on the right side of the law. He was arrested in 1593 on charges of making scandalous and <u>controversial</u> speeches. Days before the court date, Marlowe died instantly from a stab wound sustained in a brawl. While his assailant was acquitted on grounds of self-defense, it is possible that the testimony was fabricated and Marlowe was assassinated for political reasons.

Marlowe's best-known play is *The Tragicall History of Dr. Faustus,* the story about a man who bargains with Satan. Marlowe's heroes are driven, power-hungry men who refuse to recognize their own limits as humans or their responsibilities to others. To express these themes, Marlowe created wild and soaring poetry, like nothing heard before on the stage.

Sir Walter Raleigh
(1552–1618)

Handsome, arrogant, and dashing, Sir Walter Raleigh was a colorful figure in a very colorful era. His powerful poems reflect the courage of a man who was ready to accept his fate without self-pity.

Raleigh, who called himself a "seafaring man, a soldier, a courtier," was a favorite of Queen Elizabeth I. After Elizabeth died, however, his enemies convicted him of treason on trumped-up evidence and sentenced him to death.

Even in prison, Raleigh dreamed of a final expedition to South America. In 1617, still under a death sentence, he was granted this last voyage. It was a disaster. His men attacked a Spanish settlement, and the Spanish king pressed King James to execute Raleigh. Raleigh's words upon seeing the executioner's ax reflect both his courage and wit: "This is a sharp medicine, but it is a physician for all diseases."

Think About the Writers

What effect do you think Marlowe's and Raleigh's adventures might have had on their poetry?

Sir Walter Raleigh (c. 1585) by Nicholas Hilliard. National Portrait Gallery, London.

The Passionate Shepherd to His Mistress /
The Nymph's Reply to the Shepherd

Reader/Writer Notebook

Use your **RWN** for completing the activities on this page.

Literary Focus

Pastoral Poems Marlowe's "The Passionate Shepherd to His Love" is a **pastoral,** a poem depicting country life in idealized terms. In pastoral poems, handsome shepherds and beautiful nymphs live in harmony with nature. Absent are harsh and gritty images of rural labor. Sometimes called an **antipastoral,** Raleigh's "The Nymph's Reply to the Shepherd" mocks the pastoral poem's idyllic, idealistic descriptions of rural life.

Reading Focus

Understanding Inverted Word Order Inversion, or **inverted word order,** is the rearrangement of standard word order in a phrase or sentence. The normal word order in English is subject, verb, and then object or complement: *We will read poetry.* Inverted word order reverses the word order: *Poetry we will read.* Inversion can affects **tone,** by emphasizing a particular word or idea. Poets may invert word order so that a line fits the poem's meter or rhyme scheme.

Into Action When you read a phrase or sentence with inverted word order, restate it in normal order to understand it better. For each poem, use a chart like the one below to record phrases and sentences in inverted word order and to rewrite them in normal word order.

Inverted Word Order	Normal Word Order
And we will all the pleasures prove	And we will prove all the pleasures.
wool/ Which from our pretty lambs we pull,	

Vocabulary

melodious (muh LOH dee uhs) *adj.:* producing pleasant sounds. *The shepherd awoke to the melodious sounds of the birds.*

fragrant (FRAY gruhnt) *adj.:* sweet-smelling. *We walked with the lambs through a meadow of fragrant grass and flowers.*

embroidered (ehm BROY duhrd) *v.* used as *adj.:* ornamented with needlework or as if with needlework. *She wore a beautiful dress embroidered with flowers.*

folly (FAHL ee) *n.:* foolishness. *It would be folly for a shepherd to play all the time and never work.*

Language Coach

Suffixes When you add the suffix *–ous* to the noun *melody,* you get the adjective *melodious.* Notice that the *y* changes to *i* when you add this suffix. Explain the meanings of the following adjectives and tell how they were formed from nouns: *mysterious, envious, industrious, rigorous, scandalous.*

Writing Focus

Think as a Reader/Writer

Find It in Your Reading A **refrain** is a repeated word, phrase, line, or group of lines. Refrains are used to <u>establish</u> rhythm, build suspense, or emphasize important words or ideas. As you read the poems, note in your *Reader/Writer Notebook* the refrains and their effects.

TechFocus As you read these poems, consider how modern writers might use images and sound effects to complement their words.

Learn It Online
Plunge into these poems with a video introduction online.

go.hrw.com   L12-277   Go

The Passionate Shepherd to His Love

by Christopher Marlowe

Young man leaning against a tree, miniature by Nicholas Hilliard. Victoria & Albert Museum, London.

Read with a Purpose
Read to find out what promises the shepherd makes to his beloved.

Build Background
Seventeenth-century London was growing rapidly. At the beginning of the century, the city's population swelled to 220,000 and pollution was an increasing problem. Not far from the city's borders lay the countryside, a refuge from the trials of urban life. Perhaps it is not surprising then that city dwellers enjoyed and sought out pastoral poetry, music, and painting.

Probably the most famous of the English pastorals, Marlowe's poem is also part of the carpe diem tradition, a call to "seize the day" by living life to the fullest. This poem has often been set to music, and several poets have written answers or sequels to it. Sir Walter Raleigh's reply is the most famous.

Come live with me, and be my love,
And we will all the pleasures prove° **Ⓐ**
That valleys, groves, hills, and fields,
Woods, or steepy mountain yields.

5   And we will sit upon the rocks,
Seeing the shepherds feed their flocks
By shallow rivers, to whose falls
Melodious birds sing madrigals.°

And I will make thee beds of roses,
10 And a thousand fragrant posies,
A cap of flowers, and a kirtle,°
Embroidered all with leaves of myrtle.

A gown made of the finest wool
Which from our pretty lambs we pull,
15 Fair linèd slippers for the cold,
With buckles of the purest gold.

A belt of straw and ivy buds,
With coral clasps and amber studs,
And if these pleasures may thee move,
20 Come live with me, and be my love. **Ⓑ**

The shepherd swains° shall dance and sing
For thy delight each May morning.
If these delights thy mind may move,
Then live with me, and be my love.

---

2. **prove:** experience.
8. **madrigals:** complicated songs for several voices.
11. **kirtle:** archaic word meaning "dress," "gown," or "skirt."

21. **swains:** young boys.

Ⓐ **Reading Focus** Understanding Inverted Word Order Why does Marlowe invert the word order in line 2?

Ⓑ **Literary Focus** Pastoral Poems What promised gifts seem least likely to be possessed by real shepherds?

Vocabulary **melodious** (muh LOH dee uhs) *adj.:* producing pleasant sounds.
fragrant (FRAY gruhnt) *adj.:* sweet-smelling.
embroidered (ehm BROY duhrd) *v.* used as *adj.:* ornamented with needlework or as if with needlework.

The Nymph's Reply to the Shepherd

by **Sir Walter Raleigh**

Read with a Purpose
Read the following poem to see if the nymph accepts the shepherd's offer.

If all the world and love were young,
And truth in every shepherd's tongue,
These pretty pleasures might me move
To live with thee and be thy love.

5   But Time drives flocks from field to fold,°
When rivers rage and rocks grow cold,
And Philomel° becometh dumb; **B**
The rest complains of cares to come.

The flowers do fade, and wanton° fields
10   To wayward winter reckoning yields;
A honey tongue, a heart of gall°
Is fancy's spring, but sorrow's fall.

Thy gowns, thy shoes, thy beds of roses,
Thy cap, thy kirtle, and thy posies.
15   Soon break, soon wither, soon forgotten,
In folly ripe, in reason rotten.

Thy belt of straw and ivy buds,
Thy coral clasps and amber studs,
All these in me no means can move
20   To come to thee and be thy love.

But could youth last and love still breed,
Had joys no date, nor age no need,
Then these delights my mind might move
To live with thee and be thy love.

---

5. **fold:** pen where sheep are kept in winter.
7. **Philomel:** the nightingale.
9. **wanton:** luxuriant.
11. **gall:** bitter substance.

The Hireling shepherd (1851) by William Holman Hunt.
Manchester Art Gallery, UK.

A **Reading Focus** **Understanding Inverted Word Order** How would the rhyme and meter of the poem be affected if this line were in normal word order?

B **Literary Focus** **Pastoral Poems** What season does the speaker describe in this stanza? Why does she use such harsh language in her description?

Vocabulary **folly** (FAHL ee) *n.*: foolishness.

Applying Your Skills

The Passionate Shepherd to His Love
The Nymph's Reply to the Shepherd

Respond and Think Critically

Reading Focus

Quick Check

1. In "The Passionate Shepherd," what pleasant entertainment does the shepherd offer his love?

2. In line 2 of "The Nymph's Reply," what does the nymph accuse the shepherd of doing?

3. According to the nymph, what will happen to the shepherd's lovely gifts?

Read with a Purpose

4. Describe the promises that the shepherd makes. How would the nymph describe the promises?

Reading Skills: Understanding Inverted Word Order

5. As you read, you rewrote lines that use inverted word order. Now, add a column to each poem's chart and explain the effects created by the inverted word order. Note that there may be several effects.

Inverted Word Order	Normal Word Order	Effect in Poem
And we will all the pleasures prove	And we will prove all the pleasures.	1. maintains rhyme with line above
wool/Which from our pretty lambs we pull,		

✔ Vocabulary Check

Choose the synonym for each Vocabulary word.

6. melodious   **a.** ornamented

7. fragrant   **b.** foolishness

8. embroidered   **c.** pleasant-sounding

9. folly   **d.** sweet-smelling

Literary Focus

Literary Analysis

10. **Compare and Contrast** What details in "The Passionate Shepherd to His Love" enable it to be categorized as pastoral poetry? How does the description of rural life in "The Nymph's Reply" mock the first poem's idealistic details?

11. **Evaluate** How persuasive are the shepherd and the nymph as they make their cases? With whom are you more inclined to agree? Why?

Literary Skills: Pastoral Poetry

12. **Interpret** How does the description of the pastoral world in "The Passionate Shepherd" reflect the Renaissance view of country life?

Literary Skills Review: Tone

13. **Analyze** The attitude a writer takes toward the reader or the subject is called **tone.** What is Raleigh's tone in "The Nymph's Reply"? How does his tone compare to Marlowe's?

Writing Focus

Think as a Reader/Writer

Use It in Your Writing Review how the poems' speakers repeat words, phrases, and lines to emphasize their arguments. In your *Reader/Writer Notebook,* write a poem or song in which you use a refrain to persuade your readers to think in a certain way.

What Do
You
Think
Now
Whose poem is influenced more by the heart, and whose poem is influenced more by the mind?

Grammar Link

Sentence Fragments and Run-on Sentences

A **sentence fragment** is a word group that does not express a complete thought. Some fragments are **phrase fragments,** which lack either a subject or a verb: *Herding the sheep.* Others are **subordinate clauses,** which have a subject and verb but do not express a complete thought on their own: *While they herded the sheep.* To correct a fragment, add the missing part: *While they herded the sheep, the shepherds sang.*

A **run-on sentence** is two or more complete sentences run together as one. Many run-ons are **comma splices,** two or more complete thoughts linked only with a comma: *The clouds dispersed, the moonlight revealed the sheep.* Other run-ons, called **fused sentences,** lack punctuation or a connecting word between the thoughts: *The clouds dispersed the moonlight revealed the sheep.* You can correct a run-on in three ways:

1. Use periods or semicolons to divide the sentences. *The clouds dispersed. The moonlight revealed the sheep.*

2. Use a comma and a coordinating conjunction. *The clouds dispersed,* ***and*** *the moonlight revealed the sheep.*
   <small>coordinating conjunction</small>

3. Make one sentence the subordinate clause of the other: ***When the clouds dispersed,*** *the moonlight revealed the sheep.*
   <small>subordinate clause</small>

Your Turn

Identify and correct the fragments and run-ons.

1. Although the shepherd offers a leisurely life.

2. The nymph's response to the shepherd's words?

3. Flowers bloom birds sing.

4. Still, winter comes, icy rain falls.

Writing Application Review a piece of writing in your *Reader/Writer Notebook* for fragments and run-on sentences. Correct any you find using the three methods described above.

CHOICES

As you respond to the Choices, use these **Academic Vocabulary** words as appropriate: establish, ensure, widespread, controversy, contradiction.

REVIEW
Accept the Offer

Write a formal letter from the nymph to the shepherd in which she accepts his request to be his love. In your letter, explain why the nymph has changed her mind. What kind of life does she hope to have with the shepherd? What conditions must the shepherd meet to ensure that she will join him? Use details from both poems to develop your letter.

CONNECT
Advertise the Pastoral Life

TechFocus Marlowe's poem reads almost like an advertisement for rural life. With a partner, convert this poem into a commercial or print advertisement that the shepherd might have created. If you make a commercial, use images and sounds to accompany Marlowe's words. Use persuasive techniques to encourage your viewers to consider the widespread benefits of country life. How do you think the nymph might have responded if given this advertisement?

EXTEND
Stage a Debate

Group Activity In a small group, use reason, evidence, and persuasive techniques to prepare an argument that either states it is better to live solely for today, as the shepherd claims to do, or to plan and work for the future, as the nymph advises. Choose a debater to act as the shepherd or the nymph to present each group's argument.

Preparing to Read

What Do You Think? How do our hearts and minds influence our actions?

QuickTalk

Do you think the drive to make the most of one's youth comes from the heart or the mind? Discuss your responses in a small group.

Robert Herrick after the frontispiece to Herrick's *Hesperides* (1648).

MEET THE WRITERS

Robert Herrick
(1591–1674)

Robert Herrick wrote some of his best poems while he was the vicar of Dean Prior in Devonshire, in the West Country. Herrick's lyrical poetry covers a wide range; he composed poems in imitation of the Latin love poets as well as wrote about his small house, his cat, his spaniel, or whatever else came into his mind. Herrick's poems create a portrait of "Merrie England," a timeless, idealized pastoral state full of innocent pleasures. Behind the innocent guise of his pastoral poetry, however, often lurk Herrick's particular, and sometimes contradictory, political views.

Herrick's stay in Dean Prior abruptly ended in 1647 with the arrival of Cromwell's army, which seized his parish and replaced him with a more puritanical clergyman. He spent the next thirteen years in London, where he published a poetry collection called *Hesperides*, a title from classical mythology that alludes to the treasures within Herrick's work. When Charles II was restored to power, so was Herrick, who lived on at Dean Prior until his death.

Andrew Marvell
(1621–1678)

Andrew Marvell's poems capture much of what is admirable in Renaissance lyric poetry. His poems display precision, sophistication, and lightness of touch. Educated at Cambridge, Marvell traveled through much of Europe as a young man. He managed to move between political parties through the upheaval of the Civil Wars, befriending pro-Puritan John Milton as well as several supporters of the royal family. From 1659 until his death, he served in Parliament, establishing sufficient influence with the Royalists to save Milton's life after the Restoration.

Marvell's poetry was largely unpublished during his lifetime but was read and circulated among his friends. His work demonstrates an artistic control of language that appears at once to be graceful and complex.

Think About the Writers How might political turmoil have influenced these poets to write poetry that calls on readers to live life to the fullest?

Andrew Marvell (c. 1655-1660), by unknown artist. National Portrait Gallery, London.

To the Virgins, to Make Much of Time / To His Coy Mistress

Reader/Writer
Notebook

Use your **RWN** to complete the activities for these selections.

Literary Focus

Carpe Diem Sprung from the pen of the classical Latin poet Horace, *carpe diem* (literally "seize the day") is an admonition to "make the most of your life while you can." The *carpe diem* theme became increasingly popular in Renaissance English poetry, and "To the Virgins, to Make Much of Time" and "To His Coy Mistress" are some of the greatest and most famous examples. As you read, look for each speaker's warning to young women who ignore the advice to "seize the day."

Reading Focus

Paraphrasing Readers **paraphrase** when they restate in their own words something they have read. Paraphrasing helps you clarify or simplify what you are reading. To paraphrase, pause after a paragraph, an important scene, or a stanza, and reword what you have just read.

Into Action While reading "To the Virgins, to Make Much of Time," take a moment after reading each stanza to paraphrase what the speaker has said. Use a chart like the one below to write your paraphrases. Continue this for "To His Coy Mistress." This poem has no stanzas, but you can pause to paraphrase after every sentence or complete thought.

Stanzas/Lines	My Paraphrase
Herrick, Stanza 1	Enjoy the pleasures of today while you can. Time moves on; like flowers, these pleasures will soon fade.

Writing Focus

Find It in Your Reading Writers, especially poets, use **figurative language**—language that describes one thing in terms of another—to communicate ideas effectively. Herrick and Marvell, for instance, use **personification,** a kind of metaphor in which a nonhuman thing or quality is talked about as if it were human. As you read, look for examples of personification, and think about how it helps establish the *carpe diem* theme.

Learn It Online
Let a voice actor bring these poems alive for you.

go.hrw.com   L12-283   **Go**

To the Virgins, to Make Much of Time

by **Robert Herrick**

Read with a Purpose
Read this poem to identify the reasons the speaker gives to "seize the day."

Build Background
Herrick and Marvell both used a graceful and polished style to write about love, pleasure, and honor. Herrick, a priest, addresses all young women in "To the Virgins, to Make Much of Time," while Marvell argues that even immoral behavior while alive is preferable to being good but dead.

Spring (1595), by Lucas van Valckenborch.

Gather ye rosebuds while ye may, 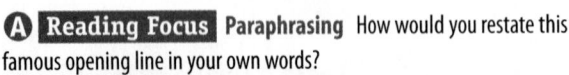 **A**
    Old Time is still a-flying;
And this same flower that smiles today,
    Tomorrow will be dying.

5 The glorious lamp of heaven, the sun,
    The higher he's a-getting,
The sooner will his race be run,
    And nearer he's to setting.

That age is best which is the first,
10   When youth and blood are warmer;
But being spent, the worse, and worst
    Times still° succeed the former.

Then be not coy,° but use your time;
    And while ye may, go marry:
15 For having lost but once your prime,
    You may forever tarry.° **B**

12. still: always.

13. coy: cold; inaccessible; aloof.

16. tarry: delay; linger.

A **Reading Focus** **Paraphrasing** How would you restate this famous opening line in your own words?

B **Literary Focus** *Carpe Diem* What images does the speaker draw from the natural world to describe how quickly one's youth passes?

To His Coy Mistress

by **Andrew Marvell**

Read with a Purpose
Read to discover how this speaker is like the speaker of Herrick's poem, and how he is different.

Had we but world° enough, and time,
This coyness,° Lady, were no crime.
We would sit down, and think which way
To walk, and pass our long love's day.

5   Thou by the Indian Ganges' side
Shouldst rubies find; I by the tide
Of Humber° would complain.° I would
Love you ten years before the Flood,°
And you should, if you please, refuse

10   Till the conversion of the Jews.°
My vegetable° love should grow
Vaster than empires and more slow;
An hundred years should go to praise
Thine eyes, and on thy forehead gaze;

15   Two hundred to adore each breast,
But thirty thousand to the rest;
An age at least to every part,
And the last age should show your heart.
For, Lady, you deserve this state,°

20   Nor would I love at lower rate.   **Ⓐ**
     But at my back I always hear
Time's wingèd chariot hurrying near;
And yonder all before us lie
Deserts of vast eternity.

25   Thy beauty shall no more be found,
Nor, in thy marble vault, shall sound
My echoing song; then worms shall try
That long-preserved virginity,
And your quaint honor turn to dust,

30   And into ashes all my lust:

1. world: geographical space.
2. coyness: reluctance to make a commitment.

7. Humber: muddy river in Marvell's hometown of Hull; here, ironically compared to the grand Ganges in India.
complain: utter complaints about not being loved.
8. Flood: Biblical flood, described in Genesis.
10. conversion of the Jews: Christians once believed that all Jews would be converted to Christianity immediately before the Last Judgment.
11. vegetable: plantlike; having the power to grow very large, like oak trees.
19. state: ceremony.

Ⓐ **Reading Focus** **Paraphrasing** Paraphrase what the speaker says he would do to demonstrate his love, if he had all the time in the world.

The Month of July, detail of a couple (c. 1400) by Italian School, fresco. Castello del Buonconsiglio, Trent, Italy.

Analyzing Visuals

Viewing and Interpreting Viewing and Interpreting "To His Coy Mistress" is one the most famous invitations to love in English literature. How does the body language of the subjects express some of the poem's ideas?

> The grave's a fine and private place,
> But none, I think, do there embrace.
>   Now therefore, while the youthful hue
> Sits on thy skin like morning dew,
> 35 And while thy willing soul transpires°
> At every pore with instant fires,
> Now let us sport us while we may,
> And now, like amorous birds of prey,
> Rather at once our time devour
> 40 Than languish in his slow-chapped° power.
> Let us roll all our strength and all
> Our sweetness up into one ball,
> And tear our pleasures with rough strife
> Through the iron gates of life;
> 45 Thus, though we cannot make our sun
> Stand still, yet we will make him run. **B**

35. transpires: breathes out.

40. slow-chapped: slow-jawed. Time is seen as consuming life.

B **Literary Focus** **Carpe Diem** What is humorous about the speaker's description of the grave in lines 31–32? How does this use of humor support the *carpe diem* theme?

Applying Your Skills

SKILLS FOCUS Literary Skills Analyze *carpe diem* poetry; analyze hyperbole. **Reading Skills** Use paraphrasing or retelling as a strategy for comprehension. **Writing Skills** Write to express.

To the Virgins, to Make Much of Time
To His Coy Mistress

Respond and Think Critically

Reading Focus

Quick Check

1. According to both speakers, what occurs when someone's youth has passed?

2. According to Herrick's speaker, what may happen to a woman who refuses to fall in love?

3. Of what "crime" does the speaker in Marvell's poem accuse his love?

Read with a Purpose

4. Why, according to the speakers in the poems, should young women "seize the day"?

Reading Skills: Paraphrasing

5. As you read, you paraphrased sections of each poem to check your comprehension of the poet's ideas. Now, add a new column to your chart for each poem. Explain how the particular line or stanza supports the *carpe diem* theme.

Stanzas/Lines	My Paraphrase	Support for Theme
Herrick, Stanza 1	Enjoy the pleasures of today while you can. Time moves on; like flowers, these pleasures will soon fade.	Gives a direct command, doesn't waste time getting to the point, which is what "act before it's too late" is all about.

Literary Focus

Literary Analysis

6. **Infer** What can you infer about the speakers' attitudes toward marriage from these poems?

7. **Evaluate** The sun appears in both "To the Virgins" (line 6) and "To His Coy Mistress" (line 45).

How does each poet use the image of the sun?

8. **Compare and Contrast** Herrick, in "To the Virgins," and Marvell, in "To His Coy Mistress," have similar objectives but different approaches. Is one poet more persuasive than the other? How are their arguments similar and different?

9. **Extend** How would you describe the tone of each poem's speaker? Are their warnings to "seize the day" motivated purely by good inentions?

Literary Skills: *Carpe Diem*

10. **Interpret** How does the advice the speakers give reflect the *carpe diem* theme?

Literary Skills Review: Hyperbole

11. **Analyze** Marvell uses both **hyperbole**—extreme exaggeration, or overstatement—as well as understatement in his argument. Identify examples of each device. Then, explain how each contributes to the poem's exploration of the subjects of youth/beauty and age/death.

Writing Focus

Think as a Reader/Writer

Use It in Your Writing Review how the poems' speakers use personification to describe how short and sweet youth, and even all of life, can be. Then, use personification to write a paragraph in your *Reader/Writer Notebook* in which you describe what it is like to be young. In your writing, you might personify youth, time, or some other abstract aspect of life, such as death or aging.

What Do **You Think Now** Does *carpe diem* appeal more to the mind or to the heart?

Song

A Valediction: Forbidding Mourning

Meditation 17

Death be not proud

What Do You Think?

How do our hearts and minds influence our actions?

⏱ QuickWrite

When people have a close bond, can they ever really be separated—even by death? Jot down your thoughts in your *Reader/Writer Notebook*.

MEET THE WRITER

John Donne
(1572–1631)

As a brash young man, Donne wrote worldly, cynical lyrics; as a reverent preacher, he composed magnificent sermons and sacred poetry. His writings reflect a complex individuality.

A Life of Contrasts

Though now considered the foremost metaphysical poet, Donne never wished to be known publicly as a poet. Born a Catholic, Donne aspired in his youth to be a courtier. He was later appointed to one of the highest positions in the Anglican Church and established himself as a great preacher.

At age twelve, Donne was already studying at Oxford. Because of his religion, he was barred from taking a degree, so he returned to London to study law. The man known as "Jack" Donne, a handsome, well-dressed youth who devoted mornings to reading and afternoons to socializing, soon emerged. One friend described him as "a great visitor of ladies, a great frequenter of plays, a great writer of …[metaphorical] verses."

Undone Ambitions

After many adventures, including two naval expeditions, Donne became secretary to Thomas Egerton, lord keeper of the great seal. This post might have been the start of a brilliant government career; however, in 1601, Donne sparked controversy when he married seventeen-year-old Anne More. Marriage with a minor, without her father's consent, was a serious crime. Anne's father had Donne jailed and dismissed from his position.

Although Donne was not in prison long, he was never able to recover his position. For years, he and Anne had to live off the bounty of friends and relatives. In the early 1600s, Donne continued to write poetry in private and prose for the public. He now wrote against the Church of Rome and became known as an important defender of the Church of England. In 1615, James I persuaded Donne to become a clergyman. His brilliant, theatrical sermons soon won him advancement in the Church, and he rose to be dean of St. Paul's, the principal cathedral of England, in London.

Think About the Writer

How might Donne's contrasting life experiences have influenced and enriched his writings?

John Donne (1522–1631).

Song

Reader/Writer Notebook

Use your **RWN** to complete the activities for this selection.

Literary Focus

Metaphysical Poetry The term **metaphysical poetry** has been applied to the work of John Donne, Andrew Marvell, and other seventeenth century poets whose detached, intellectual style sharply contrasts with the emotional extravagance of most of the Elizabethan love poets who preceded them. Metaphysical poetry is known for its startling **imagery,** intricate figures of speech, irregular **meter,** sheer verbal wit, philosophical musings, and references to esoteric fields of knowledge.

Reading Focus

Identifying the Main Idea The **main idea** of a text is the central thought or message that the writer communicates. In metaphysical poetry, the main idea often focuses on the poet's thoughts on an intellectual or philosophical problem. Donne's "Song" presents the poet's opinion on whether or not it is possible to find a beautiful, yet faithful, woman.

Into Action As you read, use a chart like the one below to summarize each stanza of the poem and note each stanza's images.

Stanza	Summary	Images
Stanza 1	The speaker asks the reader to complete several impossible and absurd tasks.	catching a falling star; mandrake root; the devil's cleft foot; singing mermaids

Vocabulary

advance (ad VANS) *v.*: bring or move forward; promote. *What habits advance learning and build character?*

pilgrimage (PIHL gruh mihj) *n.*: journey. *The poem's speaker doubts the success of a pilgrimage to find a faithful woman.*

Language Coach

Connotation Some words have strong connotations—ideas that people often think of automatically when they hear the word. A *pilgrimage* is a journey with a special significance. The connotations of the word are religious because most pilgrimages are journeys to holy places. Why might a poet decide to use a word with religious connotations in a nonreligious poem?

Writing Focus

Think as a Reader/Writer

Find It in Your Reading In "Song," Donne uses **hyperbole,** or exaggeration, to illustrate how difficult it is to find a beautiful, faithful woman. As you read, take notes in your *Reader/Writer Notebook* on Donne's use of exaggerated images.

TechFocus As you read, think about what personal experiences in Donne's life might have contributed to these poems.

Learn It Online
Learn more about Donne's life online.

go.hrw.com   L12-289   **Go**

POEM

Song

by **John Donne**

Read with a Purpose
Read to discover one man's attitude about the possibility of finding a faithful woman.

Build Background
Unlike the multitude of Renaissance songs idealizing women, the following song by Donne satirizes women using hyperbole, or gross exagerration. As you read this poem, imagine a lover who has fallen for the "perfect woman" one too many times, and, as a result, now has a cynical view of all women.

Go, and catch a falling star,
    Get with child a mandrake° root,
Tell me, where all past years are,
    Or who cleft° the devil's foot,
5 Teach me to hear mermaids singing,
Or to keep off envy's stinging,
        And find
        What wind
Serves to advance an honest mind.

10 If thou be'st born to strange sights,
    Things invisible to see,
Ride ten thousand days and nights,
    Till age snow white hairs on thee,
Thou, when thou return'st, wilt tell me
15 All strange wonders that befell thee,
        And swear
        Nowhere
Lives a woman true, and fair.

---

2. mandrake: plant whose forked root is said to resemble a human being's torso and legs.
4. cleft: split.

If thou find'st one, let me know,
20   Such a pilgrimage were sweet;
Yet do not, I would not go,
    Though at next door we might meet,
Though she were true, when you met her,
And last, till you write your letter,
25   Yet she
        Will be
False, ere I come, to two, or three. (C)

Norway Siren of Kjosfoss.

(A) **Literary Focus** Metaphysical Poetry How would you describe the imagery used in the commands in the first stanza?

(B) **Reading Focus** Identifying the Main Idea What main idea does the speaker express in lines 16–18?

(C) **Literary Focus** Metaphysical Poetry What example of hyperbole appears in the last six lines of the poem?

Vocabulary **advance** (ad VANS) *v.*: bring forward; promote.
pilgrimage (PIHL gruh mihj) *n.*: journey.

Preparing to Read

A Valediction Forbidding Mourning

Reader/Writer
Notebook
Use your **RWN** to complete the activities for this selection.

Literary Focus

Metaphysical Conceits The metaphysical poets were known for their intellectual and often unexpected comparisons. A **metaphysical conceit** is an elaborate, clever figure of speech that makes connections between two things that are startlingly different. "A Valediction: Forbidding Mourning" contains the most famous of all metaphysical conceits, a comparison of lovers to the two prongs of a drafter's compass.

Reading Focus

Recognizing Comparisons and Contrasts A **comparison** looks at similarities; a **contrast** considers differences. Comparison and contrast may be used to help structure a poem. Analyze the comparisons and contrasts in each stanza of this poem. For example, in stanza 1, the speaker compares parting from his lover to souls passing from virtuous men at death. In stanza 2, the speaker contrasts the quiet parting of the lovers with a tumultuous parting marked by floods of tears and tempestuous sighs.

Into Action As you read, use a chart like the one below to record the comparisons and contrasts in the poem.

Comparisons	Contrasts
the way virtuous men die / the way the lovers should part	the quiet way the lovers will part / floods and tempests

Vocabulary

virtuous (VUR choo uhs) *adj.*: moral; righteous. *Donne implies that virtuous men need not fear death because their souls will go to heaven.*

reckon (REHK uhn) *v.*: estimate; consider. *When confronted with a puzzling phenomenon, humans often reckon its cause and significance.*

endure (ehn DOOR) *v.*: undergo; bear. *Many people are forced to endure loneliness when separated from those they love.*

Language Coach

Latin Roots *Endure* comes from the Latin root that means "to harden." To *endure* something difficult is to make yourself hard against it. The same root appears in these words: *enduring, durable, unendurable.* How does the Latin root affect the meaning of each word?

Writing Focus

Think as a Reader/Writer
Find It in Your Reading Donne's poetry includes ideas and images from scholarly disciplines and from everyday life. In your *Reader/Writer Notebook*, note the unusual images and metaphors that Donne employs.

Learn It Online
Prepare to read this poem the multimedia way—through *PowerNotes* online.

go.hrw.com   L12-291   **Go**

A Valediction:
FORBIDDING MOURNING
by **John Donne**

Read with a Purpose
Read to discover the speaker's attitude about being separated from his lover.

Build Background
A valediction is a farewell. Izaak Walton, an acquaintance of Donne, claimed that this poem was written when Donne was called away to France on a diplomatic mission. His wife, pregnant at the time, did not want him to leave, but he felt obligated to the mission's leader, Sir Robert Drury. Two days after arriving in Paris, Donne had a vision, which he described to Sir Robert: "I have seen my dear wife pass twice by me through this room, with her hair hanging about her shoulders, and a dead child in her arms." A messenger from England brought the news that "Mrs. Donne . . . after a long and dangerous labor . . . [had given birth to] a dead child" on the very day Donne had the vision.

As virtuous men pass mildly away,
   And whisper to their souls, to go,
Whilst some of their sad friends do say,
   The breath goes now, and some say, no:

5 So let us melt, and make no noise,
   No tear-floods, nor sigh-tempests move,
'Twere profanation° of our joys
   To tell the laity° our love.

Moving of th' earth° brings harms and fears,
10   Men reckon what it did and meant,°
But trepidation of the spheres,°
   Though greater far, is innocent.° **A**

Dull sublunary° lovers' love
   (Whose soul° is sense°) cannot admit
15 Absence, because it doth remove
   Those things which elemented° it.

7. profanation: lack of reverence or respect.
8. laity: laypersons; here, those unable to understand the "religion" of true love.
9. moving of th' earth: earthquake.
10. meant: "What does it mean?" was a question usually asked of any unusual phenomenon.
11. trepidation of the spheres: irregularities in the movements of remote heavenly bodies.
12. innocent: unobserved and harmless compared with earthquakes.
13. sublunary: under the moon, therefore subject to change.
14. soul: essence. **sense:** the body with its five senses; that is, purely physical rather than spiritual.
16. elemented: constituted; composed.

A **Reading Focus** Recognizing Comparisons and Contrasts How do the movements of Earth and the other planets differ?

Vocabulary **virtuous** (VUR choo uhs) *adj.:* moral; righteous.
reckon (REHK uhn) *v.:* estimate; consider.

But we by a love, so much refined,
    That ourselves know not what it is,
Interassurèd of the mind,
20   Care less eyes, lips, and hands to miss.

Our two souls therefore, which are one,
    Though I must go, endure not yet
A breach°, but an expansion,
    Like gold to airy thinness beat.   **B** **C**

25 If they be two, they are two so
        As stiff twin compasses are two,
Thy soul the fixed foot, makes no show
        To move, but doth, if th' other do.   **D**

And though it in the center sit,
30   Yet when the other far doth roam,
It leans, and hearkens after it,
        And grows erect, as that comes home.

Such wilt thou be to me, who must
    Like th' other foot, obliquely° run;
35 Thy firmness° makes my circle just,°
    And makes me end, where I begun.

23. **breach:** break; split.

34. **obliquely:** off course.
35. **firmness:** fidelity.
just: perfect. A circle symbolizes perfection, hence wedding rings.

B **Literary Focus** **Metaphysical Conceits** What makes the comparison in line 24 a metaphysical conceit?

C **Reading Focus** **Recognizing Comparisons and Contrasts** What comparison does Donne use in the sixth stanza to express the separation of the lovers' souls?

D **Literary Focus** **Metaphysical Conceits** What makes the use of the word *circle* in the final two lines such a perfect word choice at the end of this poem?

Vocabulary **endure** (ehn DOOR) *v.:* undergo; bear.

Analyzing Visuals

Viewing and Interpreting How does a stained glass image of lovers blend two different sorts of imagery? What aspects of this image convey a mood and theme similar to those of the poem?

From *King Rene's Honeymoon* series (1862), William Morris.
Stained glass. Morris, Marshall, Faulkener & Co.
Victoria & Albert Museum, London.

Applying Your Skills

Song

A Valediction: Forbidding Mourning

Respond and Think Critically

Reading Focus

Read with a Purpose

1. Contrast the tones of the two poems.

Reading Skills: Identifying the Main Idea

2. Review your chart for "Song." In a new column, state each stanza's main idea, and explain how the images in the stanza support the main idea.

Stanza	Summary	Images	How Images Support Main Idea
Stanza 1	The speaker asks the reader to complete several impossible and absurd tasks.	catching a falling star; mandrake root; the devil's cleft foot; singing mermaids	shows the impossibility of finding a beautiful and faithful woman

Reading Skills: Recognizing Comparisons and Contrasts

3. Review your chart on comparisons and contrasts in "A Valediction" and add a column in which you describe the emotions expressed by the comparisons and contrasts you identified.

✓ Vocabulary Check

Match the Vocabulary words with their synonyms.

4. advance
5. pilgrimage
6. virtuous
7. reckon
8. endure

a. moral; righteous
b. promote
c. undergo; bear
d. consider; estimate
e. journey

Literary Focus

Literary Analysis

9. **Analyze** Donne uses the word *true* twice in "Song," then ends with the word *false*. How does this contrast affect the meaning of the poem?

10. **Interpret** In "Valediction," line 5, how is the image of melting relevant to the poem?

Literary Skills: Metaphysical Poetry

11. **Evaluate** In "Song," what hyperbole does the speaker use?

Literary Skills: Metaphysical Conceits

12. **Analyze** Explain the conceit in lines 25–36 of "A Valediction" and what it suggests about love.

Literary Skills Review: Allusion

13. **Analyze** A reference to something from literature, history, or other familiar cultural areas is an **allusion.** "Song" alludes to the mythological mermaid singing that lures sailors to crash their ships. What does this allusion signify in "Song"?

Writing Focus

Think as a Reader/Writer

Use It in Your Writing Review your notes on Donne's use of unusual, exaggerated images to convey ideas. In your *Reader/Writer Notebook*, write a paragraph in which you use hyperbole and unusual comparisons to describe an impossible goal.

 What Do You Think Now

How can positive thinking influence our feelings and actions?

Grammar Link

Direct and Indirect Objects

A **complement** is a word or word group that completes the meaning of a verb. A **direct object** is a complement that tells who or what receives the verb's action or shows the result of the action. A direct object may be a noun, pronoun, or word group that functions as a noun. To find a direct object, ask "whom?" or "what?" after a transitive verb. A direct object may be compound.

> John Donne wrote **poems.**
> He also wrote **meditations** and **sermons.**

An **indirect object** is a complement that often appears in sentences containing direct objects and that tells to whom or to what (or for whom or for what) the action of a transitive verb is done. An indirect object may be a noun, a pronoun, or a word group that functions as a noun. An indirect object may be compound.

> In "Valediction" the speaker tells the **woman** goodbye.
> Friends gave **Donne** and **his wife** financial support.

Your Turn

Identify each direct and indirect object in the following sentences.

1. Metaphysical Poets revolutionized poetry.

2. Most Renaissance poets gave readers sweet, musical verse.

3. Donne based the rhythms and sounds of his poems on spoken English.

Writing Application Write a paragraph describing an activity or event. Include at least five direct objects and two indirect objects in your description.

CHOICES

As you respond to the Choices, use these **Academic Vocabulary** words as appropriate: establish, ensure, widespread, controversy, contradiction.

REVIEW
Create a Visual Image
Images fill "Song" and "A Valediction." Choose one of these images, and incorporate it into a painting, drawing, or other artwork. Ensure that your design establishes the connection between the image and the ideas it represents. For example, how could a painting contain the elements of a compass and represent the souls of two lovers?

CONNECT
Document the Story Behind the Poem
TechFocus What real events might have affected Donne's views as they are represented in "Song" and "A Valediction"? Research Donne's life to see what he experienced during the times he wrote the poems. In a small group, prepare a documentary script explaining your findings. Dramatize events, or cast group members as "experts" to explore Donne's motives. If you can't videotape your documentary, perform it live for your class.

EXTEND
Explain a Worldview
Partner Activity During the Renaissance many people thought Earth was the center of the universe. With a

World Map, from the Portolan Atlas of the World (c. 1540), by Battista Agnese of Venice. Royal Geographic Society, London.

partner, research the Elizabethan worldview reflected in the imagery of "A Valediction." Create a poster with visuals and text explaining how Donne uses Renaissance cosmology in the poem.

Meditation 17

Reader/Writer Notebook

Use your **RWN** to complete the activities for this selection.

Literary Focus

Tone In literature, **tone** reflects an author's attitude toward the reader, a subject, or a character. Identifying tone can help you figure out the author's **purpose** and the work's **theme**. Spoken language has vocal inflections as well as nonverbal signals such as facial expressions that help the listener determine the speaker's tone. A writer achieves similar effects through words, images, and details. In "Meditation 17," Donne writes on the significance of the tolling bell: "As therefore the bell that rings . . . calls not upon the preacher only, but upon the congregation to come; so this bell calls us all." The tone of this sentence is serious and melancholy.

Reading Focus

Recognizing Patterns of Organization The organization of Donne's "Meditation 17" is based on several metaphors that develop the theme that everyone is part of a common humanity.

Into Action As you read, use a chart like the one below to record each metaphor. Then show how Donne extends or develops the metaphor.

Metaphor	Development
Humanity is a book and God is the author.	Each person is a chapter in the book. When a person dies, his or her chapter is translated into the afterlife. God rebinds the pages for the Library, or heaven.

Writing Focus

Think as a Reader/Writer

Find It in Your Reading The tolling bell that begins the meditation with its ringing continues to ring throughout the piece. The bell image acts as the connecting thread for the various sections and is a constant reminder that Donne is talking about death. As you read, note instances of the bell image. How does it function as a transition from one section of the text to another?

TechFocus Imagine the music that might accompany the following two selections by Donne.

Vocabulary

diminishes (duh MIHN ihsh ehz) v.: makes smaller; lessens; reduces. *The grief arising from death does not necessarily diminish over time for Donne.*

affliction (uh FLIHK shuhn) n.: suffering; something that causes distress or hardship. *Donne believes affliction brings humans closer to God.*

tribulation (trihb yuh LAY shuhn) n.: great trouble or misery. *Donne believes that trial and tribulation can benefit a person.*

contemplation (kahn tuhm PLAY shuhn) n.: deep thought; meditation. *Ringing church bells triggers Donne's contemplation of his own mortality.*

Language Coach

Suffixes When you add the suffix –*tion* to the verb *afflict*, you get the noun *affliction*. What verb can you find in the noun *contemplation*? Explain how the spelling of the verb changes when you add the suffix –*tion*. Name three other verbs that become nouns when this suffix is added.

Learn It Online

Explore these Vocabulary words further through Word Watch online.

go.hrw.com   L12-296   **Go**

Meditation 17

by John Donne

Read with a Purpose
Read to discover how recognizing another person's suffering can help us through difficult times.

Build Background
In 1624, prompted by a serious illness, Donne wrote a series of meditations—thoughtful reflections on a particular theme. The opening of "Meditation 17" refers to the practice in Donne's time of ringing church bells to announce the death of a church member.

Nunc lento sonitu dicunt, Morieris.	Now, this bell tolling softly for another, says to me, Thou must die. 

Perchance he for whom this bell tolls, may be so ill, as that he knows not it tolls for him; and perchance I may think myself so much better than I am, as that they who are about me, and see my state, may have caused it to toll for me, and I know not that. The Church is catholic, universal, so are all her actions; all that she does belongs to all. When she baptizes a child, that action concerns me; for that child is thereby connected to that Head[1] which is my Head too, and engrafted into that body, whereof I am a member. And when she buries a man, that action concerns me: All mankind is of one Author, and is one volume; when one man dies, one chapter is not torn out of the book, but translated[2] into a better language; and every chapter must be so translated; God employs several translators; some pieces are translated by age, some by sickness, some by war, some by justice; but God's hand is in every translation; and his hand shall bind up all our scattered leaves[3] again, for that Library where every book shall lie open to one another: As therefore the bell that rings to a sermon, calls not upon the preacher only, but upon the congregation to come; so this bell calls us all: but how much more me, who am brought so near the door by this sickness. 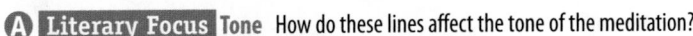 There was a contention as far as a suit[4] (in which both piety and dignity, religion

---

1. **Head:** Christ.
2. **translated:** spiritually carried across from one realm to another.
3. **leaves:** pages.
4. **contention . . . suit:** argument that went as far as a lawsuit.

A **Literary Focus** Tone How do these lines affect the tone of the meditation?

B **Reading Focus** Recognizing Patterns of Organization Donne has introduced the idea of God as Author. How is this idea developed through these following lines?

Funeral Effigy of John Donne, St. Paul's Cathedral, London.

and estimation,[5] were mingled), which of the religious orders should ring to prayers first in the morning; and it was determined, that they should ring first that rose earliest. If we understand aright the dignity of this bell that tolls for our evening prayer, we would be glad to make it ours, by rising early, in that application, that it might be ours, as well as his, whose indeed it is. The bell doth toll for him that thinks it doth; and though it intermit[6] again, yet from that minute, that that occasion wrought upon him, he is united to God. Who casts not up his eye to the sun when it rises? but who takes off his eye from a comet when that breaks out?[7] Who bends not his ear to any bell, which upon any occasion rings? but who can remove it from that bell, which is passing a piece of himself out of this world?

No man is an island, entire of itself; every man is a piece of the continent, a part of the main;[8] if a clod be washed away by the sea, Europe is the less, as well as if a promontory were, as well as if a manor of thy friends or of thine own were; any man's death diminishes me, because I am involved in mankind; and therefore never send to know for whom the bell tolls; it tolls for thee.   **C**   Neither can we call this a begging of misery or a borrowing of misery, as though we were not miserable enough of ourselves, but must fetch in more from the next house, in taking upon us the misery of our neighbors. Truly it were an excusable covetousness if we did; for affliction is a treasure, and scarce any man hath enough of it. No man hath affliction enough that is not matured, and ripened by it, and made fit for God by that affliction. If a man carry treasure in bullion, or in a wedge of gold, and have none coined into current monies, his treasure will not defray[9] him as he travels. Tribulation is treasure in the nature of it, but it is not current money in the use of it, except we get nearer and nearer our home, Heaven, by it. Another man may be sick too, and sick to death, and this affliction may lie in his bowels, as gold in a mine, and be of no use to him; but this bell, that tells me of his affliction, digs out, and applies that gold to me; if by this consideration of another's danger I take mine own into contemplation, and so secure myself by making my recourse[10] to my God, who is our only security.   **D**

---

5. **estimation:** self-esteem.
6. **intermit:** cease.
7. **comet . . . out:** Comets were regarded as signs of disaster to come.
8. **main:** mainland.
9. **defray:** pay for.
10. **making my recourse:** turning for aid.

C **Reading Focus** Recognizing Patterns of Organization How does the famous quotation "No man is an island, entire of itself" clarify the idea that we are all connected to each other?

D **Literary Focus** Tone How would you describe the tone of the last lines of the meditation?

Vocabulary **diminishes** (duh MIHN ihsh ehz) *v.:* makes smaller; lessens; reduces.
affliction (uh FLIHK shuhn) *n.:* suffering; something that causes distress or hardship.
tribulation (trihb yuh LAY shuhn) *n.:* great trouble or misery.
contemplation (kahn tuhm PLAY shuhn) *n.:* deep thought; meditation.

"Now, this bell tolling softly for another, says to me, Thou must die."

The Bells of Rostov (1983), by Sergei Chepik. Courtesy of the artist.

SKILLS FOCUS **Literary Skills** Analyze the use of tone; analyze onomatopoeia. **Reading Skills** Recognize patterns of organization. **Vocabulary Skills** Identify and correctly use synonyms. **Writing Skills** Enhance meaning by employing images.

Meditation 17

Respond and Think Critically

Reading Focus

Read with a Purpose

1. According to Donne, how can the suffering of one person benefit others?

Reading Skills: Recognizing Patterns of Organization

2. Review your notes about Donne's use of metaphor in "Meditation 17." Add a column to your chart, and summarize the main idea of each comparison.

Metaphor	Development	Main Idea
Humanity is a book, and God is the author.	Each person is a chapter in the book. When a person dies, his or her chapter is translated into the afterlife. God rebinds the pages for the Library, or heaven.	All people are interconnected because God made them.

✓ Vocabulary Check

Match each Vocabulary word with its synonym.

3. diminishes   **a.** thought

4. affliction   **b.** misery

5. tribulation   **c.** lessens

6. contemplation   **d.** suffering

Literary Focus

Literary Analysis

7. Interpret How are the comparisons in the meditation examples of a metaphysical conceit?

8. Analyze Which images best support Donne's point that all people are connected?

9. Evalute What do you think of Donne's opinion that suffering can bring good?

Literary Skills: Tone

10. Analyze Using the text to support your answer, choose a word to describe the meditation's tone.

Literary Skills Review: Onomatopoeia

11. Evaluate The use of words whose sounds suggest or imitate their meaning is called **onomatopoeia.** Where does onomatopoeia appear in the meditation? What is its effect?

Writing Focus

Think as a Reader/Writer

Use It in Your Writing You noted how Donne uses the bell image to connect the sections and to affect the piece's tone and organization. Utilize a recurring image in your own writing. Choose a sound, such as waves on the shore, cars on the highway, or ambulance sirens, and use it as your starting point for writing your own meditation. Return to the image at least twice, and be sure to end your piece with it.

 **What Do You Think Now** Donne says that suffering can be valuable. How might you act differently in a difficult situation if you could think of suffering as an opportunity rather than a challenge?

For **CHOICES** see page 303 >

Preparing to Read

Death be not proud

Reader/Writer
Notebook
Use your **RWN** to complete the activities for this selection.

Literary Focus

Paradox A **paradox** is a statement that at first glance seems impossible or illogical: "The child is father of the man." When examined more closely, a paradox expresses a deeper truth than was first apparent: "What we are as adults is very much influenced by our childhood experiences." Many writers use paradox to express things in life that seem <u>contradictory</u> yet are true. In "Death be not proud," Donne uses a paradox to communicate his belief that the death of a person's body leads to one's eternal life. Pardoxes capture our attention and force us to think more deeply about something we might otherwise take for granted.

Literary Perspectives Apply the literary perspective described on page 301 as you read this poem.

Writing Focus

Think as a Reader/Writer

Find It in Your Reading Like a riddle, a paradox invites you to look beneath the surface of the words and search for a hidden meaning. As you read "Death be not proud," use your *Reader/Writer Notebook* to keep track of ideas or images that you find <u>contradictory</u>. To help organize your notes, record the contradictory text in the left column and in the right column, explain why it seems contradictory.

Contradictory text	Why it seems contradictory

Vocabulary

dreadful (DREHD fuhl) *adj.*: terrible; causing fear. *The speaker does not think death is dreadful because he believes in life after death.*

desperate (DEHS puhr iht) *adj.*: driven by hopelessness; moved to use extreme means to try to escape frustration and loss. *Desperate men may fear, court, or cause death.*

Language Coach

Commonly Confused Words When Donne describes "desperate men," he refers to men who are reckless because they have no hope. They feel *desperation*, anxiety brought on by a great sense of urgency. Take care not to confuse the word *desperate* with *disparate*, which means "unlike" or "not similar."

Learn It Online
Find out more about Donne, his work, and his world through these Web links online.

go.hrw.com L12-300 **Go**

Death be not proud

by John Donne

Read with a Purpose

This poem begins with an **apostrophe,** a direct address to Death as if it were a person. Read to discover why the poet thinks Death should not be proud.

Build Background

This famous poem is from a sonnect collection called the *Holy Sonnets*, which were written between 1609 and 1611 before Donne took orders. The poems remained unpublished until 1633, two years after Donne's death.

Death be not proud, though some have callèd thee
Mighty and dreadful, for thou art not so,
For those whom thou think'st thou dost overthrow,
Die not, poor Death, nor yet canst thou kill me.
5   From rest and sleep, which but thy pictures° be,
Much pleasure,° then from thee, much more must flow, Ⓐ
And soonest our best men with thee do go,
Rest of their bones, and soul's delivery.°
Thou art slave to fate, chance, kings, and desperate men,
10 And dost with poison, war, and sickness dwell,
And poppy,° or charms° can make us sleep as well,
And better than thy stroke; why swell'st° thou then?
One short sleep past, we wake eternally,
And death shall be no more; Death, thou shalt die. Ⓑ

5. pictures: images. A sleeping person can resemble a dead person.
6. much pleasure: That is, rest and sleep give much pleasure.
8. rest . . . delivery: Death gives the body rest and delivers the soul from the bondage of the body.
11. poppy: opium.
charms: magic; hypnotism.
12. swell'st: swell with pride.

Ⓐ **Literary Focus** **Paradox** How does Donne explain that Death causes pleasure?

Ⓑ **Literary Perspectives** **Analyzing Philosophical Context** The speaker personifies Death, addressing it as if it were a person. What does this action indicate about the poet's philosophical stance toward Death?

Vocabulary **dreadful** (DREHD fuhl) *adj.:* terrible; causing fear.
desperate (DEHS puhr iht) *adj.:* driven by hopelessness; moved to use extreme means to try to escape frustration and loss.

Literary Perspectives

Analyzing Philosophical Context Philosophical context refers to an author's underlying assumptions about life and its meaning, for *philosophy* refers to the conscious search for truth. An author's personal philosophy influences various aspects of a literary text, including the credibility of its characters, its literary form, and its overarching themes or messages. Death is one of the most common themes in Donne's poetry. How does "Death be not proud" reflect Donne's struggle with the meaning of life and death?

As you read, be sure to notice the questions in the text, which will guide you in using this perspective.

Applying Your Skills

SKILLS FOCUS Literary Skills Analyze paradox; analyze theme; analyze philosophical context. **Vocabulary Skills** Demonstrate knowledge of literal meanings of words. **Writing Skills** Analyze literary elements; write reflective essays.

Death be not proud

Respond and Think Critically

Reading Focus

Quick Check

1. What pleasures can Death bring?

2. How is Death a slave to desperate men?

Read with a Purpose

3. According to the poem, what are the reasons Death should not be proud?

✓ Vocabulary Check

Answer the questions about the Vocabulary words.

4. Which experience might you describe as **dreadful,** being chased by a vicious dog or being startled by a sudden noise?

5. Which person is more likely to feel **desperate,** the one who has failed a quiz or the one who has lost his job?

Literary Focus

Literary Analysis

6. **Infer** What does the speaker assume about Death's self-image?

7. **Analyze** How would you describe the tone of this poem? What attitude does the speaker take toward Death?

8. **Interpret** According to the poem, how are rest and sleep like Death? What point does Donne make by using this comparison?

9. **Evaluate** As the sonnet develops, how does the speaker shift the grounds of his attack on death?

10. **Literary Perspectives** An important part of one's philosophy toward life is, ironically, one's philosophy toward death. How would you summarize the poet's attitude toward death, as conveyed in this poem?

Literary Skills: Paradox

11. **Analyze** How does the sonnet resolve its paradoxes: that those who die do not die and that Death itself will die?

Literary Skills Review: Theme

12. **Infer** The central idea or insight about human experience revealed in a work of literature is called **theme.** Some themes are stated directly, but most are implied. Write a sentence expressing the theme of "Death be not proud."

Writing Focus

Think as a Reader/Writer

Use It in Your Writing As you read the poem, you noted ideas and images that seemed <u>contradictory</u>. Now, choose one of these <u>contradictions</u>. Using it as a starting point, write an essay or meditation in your *Reader/Writer Notebook* that brings out the meaning behind the paradox.

What Do **You Think Now** Many people feel powerless when confronted by death. Do you think Donne is able to regain some kind of power over his own mortality in these poems? Explain.

Applying Your Skills

Meditation 17

Death be not proud

CHOICES

As you respond to the Choices, use these **Academic Vocabulary** words as appropriate: contradiction, controversy, ensure, establish, widespread.

REVIEW

Compare and Contrast

In "Death be not proud," Donne personifies Death. How does Donne's treatment compare with that of the personified Death in Chaucer's "The Pardoner's Tale" (see page 151)? In an essay compare and contrast the two portrayals of death. Consider Death's character and power and how people respond to Death. Cite examples from both texts to support your points.

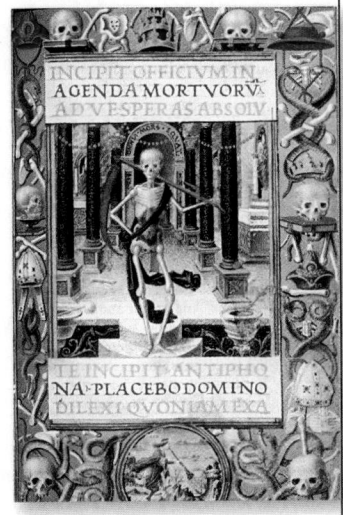

Death, the Grim Reaper, c1468–c1506. From the Office of the Dead, Mirandola Hours. British Library, London/HIP, Add. 50002. Folio No: 85.

Make a Time Line

During Donne's lifetime, the religious and political landscape of England was in constant upheaval. With a partner, research the life of John Donne as well as the political and cultural events that took place during his lifetime. Who was in power? What was the source of tension between the Roman Catholic and Anglican churches? What was going on in the rest of the world? Create a time line that puts Donne's work in historical and cultural perspective.

CONNECT

Write a Script

Though written by the same person, "Meditation 17" and "Death be not proud" have different voices. Imagine a conversation between the speakers in the two works. Establish the topic and whether the topic is a debate or agreement; then write a dialogue that recreates the conversation.

Think about Rituals

The tolling of church bells has traditionally been part of a religious funeral. For many people, rituals and customs are an important part of grieving. What rituals are commonly used to mark the death of a loved one? With a partner, discuss ways that people in our society approach funerals. What kinds of choices must be made when a person dies? How do our different cultural backgrounds influence these choices?

EXTEND

Swap Forms

Timed Writing Think about your own experiences with loss of life or death. Perhaps these experiences are through the media or they are far more personal, involving family and friends. In an expository essay, explain your experience and how it has affected your thinking and your behavior.

Set It to Music

TechFocus With a partner, choose a passage from either "Meditation 17" or "Death be not proud." Using instruments, computer software, or your voices, compose music that expresses the passage's emotions. You may set the words from your passage to the music, or read the passage aloud as an introduction. Share your composition with your classmates.

Preparing to Read

 **Link to Today** *from* **W;t**

 **What Do You Think** How do our hearts and minds influence our actions?

 **QuickWrite**
Think about a sport, activity, or type of art that is important to you. What draws you to it? Write a paragraph that describes this activity and its importance.

Literary Focus

Dialogue The majority of what we know about a play's characters is based on what they say or do. **Dialogue,** the directly quoted words of people speaking to one another, bears the burden of plot exposition, pacing, and character development. Even for a talented writer, creating dialogue that sounds natural and accomplishes these goals is a challenge.

Reading Focus

Analyzing Style Playwrights give their characters unique voices by varying speaking **styles**—phrasing, choice of words, and pacing.

Into Action Describe the dialogue in this scene, focusing on each speaker's style and the emotions expressed by the dialogue.

	Vivian	E. M.
Speaking style	hesitant; easily interrupted	
Emotional Expression		angry; dislike's Vivian's essay

Writing Focus

Think as a Reader/Writer

Find It in Your Reading As you read, note the ways in which the writer "directs" the action of the play, including stage directions, references to action in the dialogue, and punctuation.

Vocabulary

veneer (vuh NIHR) *n.:* surface appearance or show. *To understand a poem by Donne, you need more than a veneer of scholarship.*

insufficient (ihn suh FIHSH uhnt) *adj.:* not enough. *Analytical methods that might work for the writing of other poets are insufficient for understanding Donne.*

valiant (VAL yuhnt) *adj.:* brave; courageous. *"Death be not proud" depicts a valiant struggle with death.*

vanquish (VANG kwihsh) *v.:* defeat in battle or conflict. *Donne believed that through faith we can vanquish death.*

Language Coach

Related Words The Latin prefix *in–* means "non or not," so *insufficient* means "not sufficient" or "not enough." Without this prefix, *sufficient* simply means "enough." What do you think the related verb *suffice* means? What about the adverb *sufficiently*?

 Learn It Online
Listen to Edson's dialogue with the audio version of this excerpt.

go.hrw.com | L12-304 | **Go**

Link to Today

This link to today emphasizes the importance of little things.

Read with a Purpose
Read to discover why the professor believes so strongly in her way of reading a poem.

Build Background
Margaret Edson's Pulitzer Prize–winning play *W;t* tells the story of Vivian Bearing, an English professor who has devoted her career to studying John Donne's *Holy Sonnets*. At the beginning of the play, Bearing has been diagnosed with terminal cancer. In this scene, a flashback to Bearing's college days, she recalls a confrontational meeting with one of her English literature professors (E. M. Ashford) about Donne's Holy Sonnet Six, or "Death be not proud."

Author Note
Margaret Edson (1961–) considers herself first and foremost a teacher, even though she won much acclaim for her first play, *W;t*. Born in Washington, D.C., Edson's educational background is in Renaissance history and English literature, but her writing has also been influenced by her professional experiences, including the two years she spent working in a cancer ward for AIDS patients. Edson drew from this experience when she wrote *W;t* in 1991.

from W;t

by **Margaret Edson**

E.M. Please sit down. Your essay on Holy Sonnet Six, Miss Bearing, is a melodrama, with a veneer of scholarship unworthy of you—to say nothing of Donne. Do it again. **Ⓐ**

Vivian. I, ah . . . **Ⓑ**

E.M. You must begin with a text, Miss Bearing, not with a feeling.

> *Death be not proud, though some have called thee*
> *Mighty and dreadfull, for, thou art not soe.*

You have entirely missed the point of the poem, because, I must tell you, you have used an edition of the text that is inauthentically punctuated. In the Gardner edition—

Vivian. That edition was checked out of the library—

E.M. Miss Bearing! **Ⓒ**

Vivian. Sorry.

E.M. You take this too lightly, Miss Bearing. This is Metaphysical Poetry, not The Modern Novel. The standards of scholarship and critical reading which one would apply to any other text are simply insufficient. The effort must be total for the results to be meaningful. Do you think the punctuation of the last line of this sonnet is merely an insignificant detail?

The sonnet begins with a valiant struggle with death, calling on all the forces of intellect and drama to vanquish the enemy. But it is ultimately about overcoming the seemingly insuperable barriers separating life, death, and eternal life.

Ⓐ **Reading Focus** Analyzing Style What is the tone of E. M.'s opening lines?

Ⓑ **Literary Focus** Dialogue Why do Vivian's words trail off?

Ⓒ **Reading Focus** Analyzing Style What does E. M. communicate by exclaiming "Miss Bearing!"?

Vocabulary **veneer** (vuh NIHR) *n.:* surface appearance or show.
insufficient (ihn suh FIHSH uhnt) *adj.:* not enough.
valiant (VAL yuhnt) *adj.:* brave; courageous.
vanquish (VANG kwihsh) *v.:* defeat in battle or conflict.

In the edition you chose, this profoundly simple meaning is sacrificed to hysterical punctuation:

> And Death—*capital D*—shall be no more—*semicolon!*

> Death—*capital D*—*comma*—thou shalt die—*exclamation point!*

If you go in for this sort of thing, I suggest you take up Shakespeare.

Gardner's edition of the Holy Sonnets returns to the Westmoreland manuscript source of 1610—not for sentimental reasons, I assure you, but because Helen Gardner is a *scholar.* It reads:

> And death shall be no more, *comma,* Death thou shalt die.

[*As she recites this line, she makes a little gesture at the comma.*]

Nothing but a breath—a comma—separates life from life everlasting. It is very simple really. With the original punctuation restored, death is no longer something to act out on a stage, with exclamation points. It's a comma, a pause.

This way, the *uncompromising* way, one learns something from this poem, wouldn't you say? Life, death. Soul, God. Past, present. Not insuperable barriers, not semicolons, just a comma. **Ⓓ**

"Nothing but a breath—a comma—separates life from life everlasting."

Ⓓ **Literary Focus** **Dialogue** What do you think Vivian might say if she were given a few more lines in this scene?

Applying Your Skills

from **W;t**

SKILLS FOCUS **Literary Skills** Analyze dialogue; analyze internal conflict and external conflict. **Reading Skills** Analyze style. **Vocabulary Skills** Identify and correctly use antonyms. **Writing Skills** Develop characters using dialogue.

Respond and Think Critically

Reading Focus

Quick Check

1. What does E. M. think is "the point" of Donne's sonnet? Explain your answer.

2. Why does E. M. regard the Gardner edition of Donne's Holy Sonnets as superior?

Read with a Purpose

3. Why is the punctuation of the last line of Donne's sonnet so important to the professor? Explain.

Reading Skills: Analyzing Style

4. As you read, you noted speaking styles and emotions in the dialogue. Now, add a row to your chart briefly describing each character.

	Vivian	E. M.
Speaking style	hesitant; easily interrupted	
Emotional Expression		angry; dislike's Vivian's essay . . .
Character	shy; uncertain	

✔ Vocabulary Check

Match each Vocabulary word with its antonym.

5. veneer   **a.** cowardly
6. insufficient   **b.** surrender
7. valiant   **c.** depth
8. vanquish   **d.** excessive

Literary Focus

Literary Analysis

9. **Draw Conclusions** What is E. M.'s opinion of the modern novel? How do you know?

10. **Evaluate** How important is punctuation? Do you think the difference between a semicolon and a comma is that important? Explain.

Literary Skills: Dialogue

11. **Analyze** What kind of behavior does the dialogue suggest for E. M.? Defend your answer by quoting from her part of the dialogue.

Literary Skills Review: Conflict

12. **Evaluate** A struggle between opposing forces inside a person is **internal conflict. External conflict** is a struggle between people, between a person and a force of nature, or between a person and society. Does this scene have an internal conflict, an external conflict, or both? Explain.

Writing Focus

Think as a Reader/Writer

Use It in Your Writing While you read the poem, you noted strategies Edson used to "direct" the play. Now, work in a small group to write the dialogue for a short scene between two people. Add necessary stage directions in brackets. Use italics and punctuation to help the actors know how to perform each line.

 **What Do You Think Now** In this selection, the professor is passionate even about details of punctuation. Think of an activity you are passionate about. Why are even the details important to you?

Preparing to Read

On My First Son
Song: To Celia

What Do You Think?

How do our hearts and minds influence our actions?

QuickTalk

In a small group, discuss a piece of literature you have read or seen enacted in the media that closely resembles the author's feelings about that topic. How does knowing the author's feelings affect you as the reader or viewer?

Canon, with circular staves and rose at center.
British Library, London, Roy 11 E XI f.2v.

MEET THE WRITER

Ben Jonson
(1572–1637)

If his friend William Shakespeare had never existed, Jonson would probably be regarded as the chief dramatist of the age.

A Complete Londoner

Jonson overcame humble beginnings to create tragedies and comedies for the public theater, to devise masques (dramatic performances including music and lavish costumes) for the court of James I, and to be honored as poet laureate in 1616.

As a boy, Jonson met the headmaster of the elite Westminster School in London, who enrolled the boy at Westminster at his own expense. There Jonson studied Latin and Greek and learned a poetic trick he would use for the rest of his life—to write poems in prose before turning them into verse.

Jonson joined the army and fought the Spanish at Flanders—while the two armies watched, he engaged in single combat with the Spanish champion and killed him. Back in England he became a playwright and an actor. He had two brushes with the law: Once he killed a fellow actor in a duel, and once he went to jail for insulting Scotland in a play. At the Mermaid Tavern he held combats of wit with Shakespeare and others.

Writer and Literary Dictator

In 1616, Jonson astonished the reading public by publishing plays and poems under the title *Works*—a label traditionally used for intellectual subjects such as theology and history. He believed that poems and plays are serious works of art, as serious in their own way as theology and history and as worthy of high regard.

At the height of his career, Jonson was a sort of literary dictator—opinionated and quick-tempered but admired by a number of younger writers, known as "the tribe of Ben" or "the sons of Ben." They stood by an elderly, poor, and neglected Jonson whose blunt manner had <u>ensured</u> him many enemies. Jonson was buried near Chaucer in the Poets' Corner of Westminster Abbey. His inscription reads: "O rare Ben Jonson."

Think About the Writer

Jonson was famous for his rivalry with Shakespeare. How might this competition have influenced his work?

Benjamin Jonson (early 17th century) by Abraham van Blyenberch
National Portrait Gallery, London.

On My First Son / Song: To Celia

Reader/Writer
Notebook
Use your **RWN** for completing the activities on this page.

Literary Focus

Lyrics A **lyric,** from the Greek word *lurikos,* from *lura,* meaning "lyre," is a poem that imaginatively and melodically expresses a speaker's personal thoughts and feelings. Among the early Greeks, the lyric expressed the emotion of an individual singer accompanied by a lyre, a stringed harp-like instrument. Generally the lyric poem no longer has musical accompaniment, but it conveys melody through the musical effects of language, such as **rhyme**, **rhythm**, **alliteration**, and **onomatopoeia**. It also remains distinguished by subjectivity, emotion, and imagination. The lyric's forms are varied. One of its most expressive forms is the **sonnet**. Other forms of lyrics are elegies, odes, and songs.

Ben Jonson wrote some of the finest lyrics in the English language, several of which appear in his plays and masques. Note the musical effects in the two poems included here. In addition to end rhyme, look for other techniques of repetition that create verbal music.

Writing Focus

Think as a Reader/Writer
Find It in Your Reading Throughout "On My First Son" and "Song: To Celia," Jonson uses descriptive words and phrases to reveal his speakers' feelings. Some of these descriptive words and phrases are metaphors, others contain imagery. As you read the poems, create a chart in your *Reader/Writer Notebook* to record particular lines and examples. In the far right column, record how these lines of descriptive phrases evoke a particular feeling.

Line #	Example	Feeling expressed or evoked
1	Drink to me only with thine eyes	tender and warmhearted devotion

Vocabulary

lament (luh MEHNT) *v.:* mourn or grieve for. *Jonson laments his son's death.*

misery (MIHZ uh ree) *n.:* wretchedness; suffering. *The plague brought misery to many people in England.*

pledge (plehj) *v.:* solemnly promise; drink a toast to. *The speaker will pledge his love to Celia.*

divine (dih VYN) *adj.:* of or like God or a god; given or inspired by God. *The speaker is so in love with Celia that he thinks she is divine.*

Language Coach

Parts of Speech Some words can be used as different parts of speech. The verb *lament* means "to mourn or grieve for." The same word can also be used as a noun. A lament is an expression of grief or sorrow. What other Vocabulary words can be used as different parts of speech? What do they mean?

Learn It Online
Get the inside story on the Vocabulary words through Word Watch online.

go.hrw.com   L12-309   **Go**

POEM

On My First Son

by **Ben Jonson**

Read with a Purpose
Read this poem to understand how a father grieves over his son's death.

Build Background
This poem is about Ben Jonson's son Benjamin, who died of the plague on his seventh birthday. Jonson wrote "On My First Son" as a farewell to his child. The name *Benjamin* in Hebrew means "child of the right hand" and, ironically, connotes a "lucky, clever child." The **epigraph,** or inscription that appears on a grave, is in quotation marks at the end of the poem.

Farewell, thou child of my right hand,° and joy;
   My sin was too much hope of thee, loved boy:
Seven years thou wert lent to me, and I thee pay,°
   Exacted° by thy fate, on the just° day.
5 Oh, could I lose all father° now! for why
   Will man lament the state he should envy—
To have so soon 'scaped world's and flesh's rage, **Ⓐ**
   And if no other misery, yet age?
Rest in soft peace, and asked, say, "Here doth lie
10   Ben Jonson his best piece of poetry;
For whose sake henceforth all his vows be such
   As what he loves may never like too much."

1. child of my right hand: The name Benjamin in Hebrew means "child of the right hand."
3. thee pay: pay with you, give you back.
4. exacted: forced. **just:** exact. Loans were often made for exactly seven years.
5. father: sense of fatherhood; the need to mourn like a father.

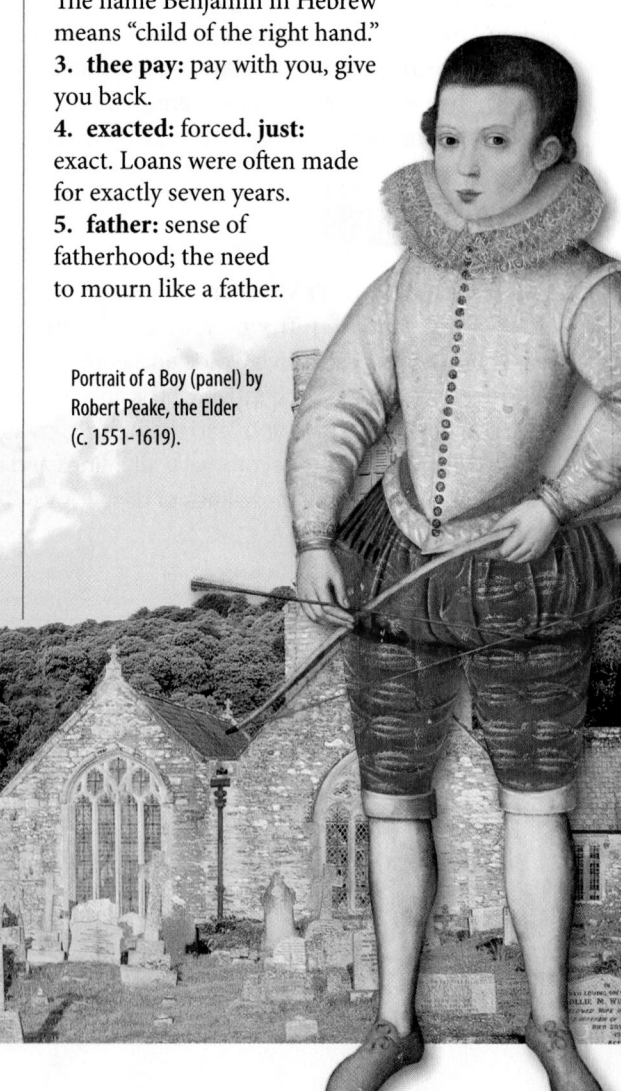

Portrait of a Boy (panel) by Robert Peake, the Elder (c. 1551-1619).

Ⓐ **Literary Focus** **Lyrics** What lyrical effect does the use of alliteration create in this line?

Vocabulary **lament** (luh MEHNT) *v*.: mourn or grieve for.
misery (MIHZ uh ree) *n*.: wretchedness; suffering.

Analyzing Visuals
Viewing and Interpreting How might this child represent Jonson's "best piece of poetry"?

Song: To Celia

by **Ben Jonson**

Read with a Purpose

Read to discover how the speaker uses surprising comparisons to describe his love.

Build Background

"Song: To Celia" celebrates the rejuvenating powers of love. It is associated with a famous tune that many people still know. Thomas Arne (1710–1778), who also wrote the British national anthem, composed music for Jonson's poem and titled it "Drink to Me Only with Thine Eyes."

Drink to me only with thine eyes,
    And I will pledge with mine;
Or leave a kiss but in the cup,
    And I'll not look for wine. **A**
5 The thirst that from the soul doth rise
    Doth ask a drink divine;
But might I of Jove's nectar° sup,
    I would not change° for thine.
I sent thee late a rosy wreath,
10   Not so much honoring thee
As giving it a hope, that there
    It could not withered be.
But thou thereon didst only breathe,
    And sent'st it back to me;
15 Since when it grows, and smells, I swear,
    Not of itself but thee.

Gathering Rosebuds by John William Waterhouse (1849-1917)

---

7. **Jove's nectar:** Jove, more commonly called Jupiter, is the supreme god in Roman mythology. Nectar was the drink that kept the gods immortal.
8. **change:** exchange.

A Literary Focus **Lyrics** What grammatical structures are repeated in the first four lines? What lyrical effect does this parallelism create?

Vocabulary **pledge** (plehj) *v.:* solemnly promise.
divine (dih VYN) *adj.:* of or like God or a god; given or inspired by God.

Applying Your Skills

On My First Son / Song: To Celia

Respond and Think Critically

Reading Focus

Quick Check

1. What is the speaker's sin in "On My First Son"?

2. To what does the speaker of "On My First Son" compare his son?

3. What does the speaker of "Song: To Celia" ask his beloved to leave for him in a cup?

4. What does the speaker of "Song: To Celia" send to his beloved?

Read with a Purpose

5. What different kinds of love are described in the poems "On My First Son" and "Song: To Celia"?

Vocabulary Check

Match the Vocabulary words with their synonyms.

6. lament
7. misery
8. pledge
9. divine

a. promise
b. godly; godlike
c. mourn; grieve
d. distress; suffering

Literary Focus

Literary Analysis

10. **Interpret** How would you describe the **tone** of "On My First Son"?

11. **Draw Conclusions** In "On My First Son," why does Jonson say we might envy the dead?

12. **Analyze** Explain the metaphor Jonson uses in lines 3–4 of "On My First Son." What does this comparison say about how Jonson views life?

13. **Infer** In "Song: To Celia," how does the speaker use the idea of drinking a cup of wine to praise his lady?

14. **Hypothesize** What might the wreath represent to the speaker in "Song: To Celia"?

Literary Skills: Lyric

15. **Analyze** A lyric expresses a speaker's personal thoughts and feelings. Describe the emotional impression created by each poem.

Literary Skills Review: Rhyme Scheme

16. **Analyze** The pattern of rhymed lines in a poem is called its **rhyme scheme**. Describe the rhyme scheme in each poem. Give each new rhyme a new letter of the alphabet. What do you discover about the rhymes in Jonson's poems?

Writing Focus

Think as a Reader/Writer

Use It in Your Writing While you read, you noticed how Jonson uses descriptive language to reveal feelings about the son or the beloved. Using descriptive language, write a poem in your *Reader/Writer Notebook* about someone or something important to you.

 What Do You Think Now

How does love lead us to a deeper understanding of ourselves and our role in the world?

SKILLS FOCUS **Literary Skills** Evaluate the philosophical, political, religious, ethical, and social influences of a historical period; analyze lyric poetry; analyze meter and rhyme. **Vocabulary Skills** Expand vocabulary through systematic word study. **Writing**

Skills Write comparison-contrast essays; compare characters or historical figures; compare literary works; compare themes or literary elements. **Grammar Skills** Identify and use imperative sentences.

Grammar Link

Imperative Mood

When a verb is used to express a direct command, a request, or an instruction, it is considered to be in the **imperative mood**:

> **Try** another approach.
> **Enclose** a stamped, self-addressed envelope.

The imperative is used with the second person. The subject is usually not expressed but is understood to be *you.* The command "Go to the board" means "(You) go to the board." The *you* is implied, not stated expressly.

In poetry, an apostrophe often begins with an imperative verb. An **apostrophe** is a figure of speech in which something that is absent is addressed as if it were present and could answer. An apostrophe can add immediacy or excitement to a poem. John Donne uses an apostrophe in his sonnet "Death be not proud" when he addresses Death as if it were a person. There, the verb *be* is in the imperative mood.

Your Turn

Identify the imperative mood in these lines by circling the imperative verbs. Not all lines will have imperative verbs.

1. "My sin was too much hope of thee, loved boy"
2. "Rest in soft peace"
3. "Drink to me only with thine eyes"
4. "Or leave a kiss but in the cup"
5. "It could not withered be"

Writing Application Write a short speech in which you try to persuade someone to do something—for example, to vote, to volunteer for a cause, or to help fund a project. In your speech, use some imperative verbs to help give force to your argument.

CHOICES

As you respond to the Choices, use these **Academic Vocabulary** words as appropriate: contradiction, controversy, ensure, establish, widespread.

REVIEW

Analyze Imperative Mood and Apostrophe

Both poems include striking examples of the imperative mood and of apostrophe. Write a comparison-contrast essay analyzing the effect of the imperative mood and apostrophe on tone in the two poems.

The Ben Jonson Pub

RESEARCH

Explore Jonson's Influence

Timed Writing A group of writers met regularly with Jonson at London taverns. This "tribe of Ben" included Robert Herrick, Thomas Carew, John Suckling, and Richard Lovelace. Jonson established standards for clarity and precision in writing. In an essay, explain Jonson's influence on one of the poets in the group. Cite examples from both poets to support your points.

EXTEND

Make Music

The British composer Thomas Arne set Jonson's "Song: To Celia" to music in a composition titled "Drink to Me Only With Thine Eyes." Find a recording of this song, using library resources or an online search. Listen to the music, and re-read the poem. Then, re-read "On My First Son," and compose music that interprets it. Record your song, and play it for your classmates. Explain how you created your melody and what you hope to convey with it.

SIR JOHN SUCKLING

Why So Pale and Wan, Fond Lover?

RICHARD LOVELACE

To Lucasta, on Going to the Wars
To Althea, from Prison

What Do You Think? How do our hearts and minds influence our actions?

QuickWrite

Write about the saying "Better to burn out than to fade away." Do you agree? Does it relate more to decisions prompted by the heart or the mind?

Sir John Suckling after Sir Anthony Van Dyck. (circa 1640) National Portrait Gallery, London.

MEET THE WRITERS

Sir John Suckling
(1609–1642)

Sir John Suckling was born rich, but he lost his fortune through gambling and extravagant living. When war broke out, he raised a company of one hundred men, outfitted in scarlet coats and white doublets, to fight for the king. He plotted to deliver one of the king's chief advisors from imprisonment in the Tower of London. However, the plot was discovered, and Suckling was forced to flee to France. There, at the age of thirty-three, he died. Historians are not sure whether he took his own life or was murdered.

Suckling's poetry belongs to the Cavalier school, so named for its writers who were Royalists or supporters of the king. His poetry was witty, charming, and graceful, earning him the praise of being "natural, easy Suckling."

Richard Lovelace
(1618–1657)

Like his fellow Cavalier poets, Richard Lovelace (pronounced "love-less") came from a wealthy family. His good looks and elegant manners created a stir when he was at Oxford University. After Oxford, Lovelace became a favorite courtier to King Charles and Queen Henrietta Maria. Lovelace became an ardent Royalist and, when the Civil Wars broke out, he fought bravely for King Charles. He was imprisoned twice by the opposing Parliamentary forces. Like Suckling, he lost all his wealth and land, and he died in poverty at age thirty-nine.

Lovelace's work is considered to be more serious than Suckling's. The poetry is tinged with a slight element of desperation and melancholy—suggesting that beneath a façade of gallantry and elegance, the careless, aristocratic life was crumbling away.

Think About the Writer How do these courtier-poets' careers compare with those of earlier courtiers such as Wyatt and Raleigh?

Richard Lovelace portrait attributed to William Dobson. Dulwich Picture Gallery, London.

Reader/Writer Notebook

Use your **RWN** to complete the activities for these selections.

Literary Focus

Diction A writer's or speaker's choice of words is called **diction**. Diction can be formal, informal, colloquial, poetic, ornate, plain, abstract, or concrete. Diction depends on the writer's subject, purpose, and audience. **Connotations**—meanings, associations, and emotions attached to words—are an important aspect of diction. Some words, for example, are suited to informal conversations but are inappropriate in a formal speech. Diction is an essential element of **style**. Diction is a critical element in conveying an author's tone or attitude about a subject.

Reading Focus

Comparing and Contrasting Comparing and contrasting literary works can help you better understand each one. When you **compare and contrast**, you focus on how important elements are similar and different.

Into Action As you read, compare the persons being addressed, the speakers themselves, the images employed, and the tone and themes conveyed. Record your observations using a chart like the one below.

Elements for comparing/ contrasting	"Why So Pale ..."	"To Lucasta ..."	"To Althea ..."
person addressed	a man in love	a woman the speaker loves	a woman the speaker loves
speaker			
images			
tone			
theme			

Writing Focus

Think as a Reader/Writer

Find It in your Reading **Imagery** is language that appeals to the five senses—sight, sound, taste, smell, and touch. Most imagery is visual—it establishes pictures in the reader's mind. Some images appeal to more than one sense. As you read, use your *Reader/Writer Notebook* to record some of the images, the words the authors choose to convey them, and the senses to which they appeal.

Vocabulary

wan (wahn) *adj.:* faint or weak. *Lovesickness has made the young man wan.*

mute (myoot) *adj.:* not speaking; silent. *Normally talkative, he has become mute as he dreams of the woman he loves.*

chaste (chayst) *adj.:* pure or modest in nature. *The man loves the woman's gentle, chaste nature.*

embrace (ehm BRAYS) *v.:* accept readily; adopt. *The soldiers patriotically embrace their solemn duty.*

inconstancy (ihn KAHN stuhn see) *n.:* changeability. *The soldier explains his inconstancy to his love: He must leave her to serve his country.*

Language Coach

Homonyms Words that have the same pronunciation but not the same spelling are called **homonyms**. Homonyms have different meanings. Some homonym pairs include verbs in the past tense. The adjective *chaste* means "pure." Its homonym is the past-tense verb *chased*, which means "ran after." Spell a homonym for each of these words: guessed, discussed, leased, missed, passed.

Learn It Online
Hear these poems read aloud online.

go.hrw.com | L12-315 | **Go**

Why So Pale and Wan, Fond Lover?

by **Sir John Suckling**

Read with a Purpose
Read to discover the speaker's advice to a young man in love.

Build Background
One convention of Renaissance love poetry is that young men suffer from unrequited love. Part of this convention is that the women who are the objects of admiration show no pity or interest. The speaker in this poem addresses someone who is suffering, a fond, or foolish, lover who looks "pale and wan."

Why so pale and wan, fond lover?
    Prithee,° why so pale?
Will, when looking well can't move her,
    Looking ill prevail? **Ⓐ**
5   Prithee, why so pale?

Why so dull and mute, young sinner?
    Prithee, why so mute?
Will, when speaking well can't win her,
    Saying nothing do't?
10   Prithee, why so mute?

Quit, quit, for shame; this will not move,
    This cannot take her.
If of herself she will not love,
    Nothing can make her:
    The devil take her!

2. prithee: contraction of "I pray thee"; I ask you.

Henry Percy, 9th earl of Northumberland (c. 1595) by Nicholas Hilliard (1547-1619). Fitzwilliam Museum, University of Cambridge, U.K.

Ⓐ **Literary Focus** Diction What words reveal the speaker's attitude toward the lover?

Vocabulary **wan** (wahn) *adj.*: faint or weak.
mute (myoot) *adj.*: not speaking; silent.

POEM

To Lucasta, on Going to the Wars

by **Richard Lovelace**

Read with a Purpose
Read to determine the speaker's attitude toward war.

Build Background
The English Civil Wars are the backdrop for this poem. It takes the form of a lover's farewell to his beloved. The poem is famous for applying the language of love and courtship to warfare.

Tell me not, sweet, I am unkind,
   That from the nunnery°
Of thy chaste breast and quiet mind
   To war and arms I fly.

5 True, a new mistress now I chase,
   The first foe in the field;
And with a stronger faith embrace
   A sword, a horse, a shield. **A**

Yet this inconstancy is such
10   As you too shall adore;
I could not love thee, dear, so much,
   Loved I not honor more. **B**

2. **nunnery:** a building where nuns live; here, used as a metaphor for a pure, safe place.

La Belle Dame Sans Merci (1902) by Sir Frank Dicksee (1853-1928). Bristol City Museum and Art Gallery, U.K.

Analyzing Visuals

Viewing and Interpreting Discuss how the image relates to the tone and mood of the poem.

A Literary Focus Diction Which words in this stanza contribute to its sad, melancholy tone?

B Reading Focus Comparing and Contrasting How does the treatment of love in these final lines differ from the lighthearted approach taken in "Why So Pale and Wan, Fond Lover?"

Vocabulary **chaste** (chayst) *adj.:* pure or modest in nature.
embrace (ehm BRAYS) *v.:* accept readily; adopt.
inconstancy (ihn KAHN stuhn see) *n.:* changeability.

To Althea, from Prison

by **Richard Lovelace**

Read with a Purpose
Read to discover how this poem illustrates Cavalier ideals.

Build Background
On two different occasions, Lovelace was imprisoned for his loyalty to the English king. Lovelace was said to be a handsome man with many admirers, but whether or not this poem is autobiographical remains a mystery.

When Love with unconfinèd wings
    Hovers within my gates,
And my divine Althea brings
    To whisper at the grates;
5 When I lie tangled in her hair
    And fettered to her eye,
The gods that wanton° in the air
    Know no such liberty. **Ⓐ** **Ⓑ**

When flowing cups run swiftly round,
10   With no allaying Thames,°
Our careless heads with roses bound,
    Our hearts with loyal flames;
When thirsty grief in wine we steep,
    When healths and drafts° go free,
15 Fishes that tipple° in the deep
    Know no such liberty.

When, like committed linnets,° I
    With shriller throat shall sing
The sweetness, mercy, majesty,
20   And glories of my King;°
When I shall voice aloud how good
    He is, how great should be,
Enlargèd winds that curl the flood
    Know no such liberty. **Ⓒ**

25 Stone walls do not a prison make,
    Nor iron bars a cage:
Minds innocent and quiet take
    That for an hermitage.°
If I have freedom in my love,
30   And in my soul am free,
Angels alone, that soar above,
    Enjoy such liberty.

---

7. **wanton:** frolic.
10. **allaying Thames:** the wine is not diluted with water from the Thames, a river that flows through London.
14. **healths and drafts go free:** generously toasting one another's health and drinking.
15. **tipple:** to drink too much alcohol; here, the fish "get drunk" on water.

---

17. **committed linnets:** caged birds.
20. **my King:** Charles I, king of England from 1625 to 1649.
28. **hermitage:** a quiet, secluded retreat.

Ⓐ **Literary Focus** Diction Find two words in the first stanza that refer to freedom and two words that refer to imprisonment. How do they set up a **paradox,** or an apparent contradiction that is actually true?

Ⓑ **Literary Focus** Diction How do the words from the first stanza contribute to the joyful or passionate atmosphere?

Ⓒ **Reading Focus** Comparing and Contrasting Why does the speaker compare himself to fishes and the winds?

Applying Your Skills

Why So Pale and Wan, Fond Lover?
To Lucasta, on Going to the Wars
To Althea, from Prison

Respond and Think Critically

Reading Focus

Quick Check

1. In "Why So Pale and Wan," how has the woman responded to the man?

2. In "To Lucasta," who is the "new mistress"?

3. In "To Althea," who is admired for being "good" and "great"?

Read with a Purpose

4. What does the speaker conclude in each poem?

Reading Skills: Comparing and Contrasting

5. Now that you have noted the poems' similarities and differences, write a paragraph about how diction affects these similarities and differences.

✓ Vocabulary Check

Answer the questions about the Vocabulary words.

6. Would a **wan** smile be a big grin?

7. Is a person keeping a secret likely to be **mute** about it?

8. Would a **chaste** person lie and cheat?

9. Is a person set in his ways likely to **embrace** change?

10. Would it seem reasonable to accuse a traitor of **inconstancy**?

Literary Focus

Literary Analysis

11. **Analyze** In "Why So Pale and Wan," what advice does the speaker give the pale lover? What is the speaker's **tone**, or attitude toward his subject?

How does his tone change? How does it differ from the tone of Lovelace's two poems?

12. **Analyze** In "To Lucasta," what metaphors of love are used to describe war? What do you think of these romantic ways of talking about war?

13. **Infer** The speaker in "To Lucasta" implies two paradoxes: that his inconstancy (line 9) is really constancy; and that to be loyal he must be disloyal. How can these contradictions be true?

14. **Interpret** In "To Althea" what do the paradoxical lines "Stone walls do not a prison make, / Nor iron bars a cage" suggest about the idea of freedom?

Literary Skills: Diction

15. **Analyze** How is each poet's **diction** suited to his subject? Explain your reasoning, and support it with examples from the text.

Literary Skills Review: Refrain

16. **Analyze** A **refrain** is a word, phrase, line, or group of lines repeated to create rhythm and suspense and to organize and emphasize ideas. What are the poems' refrains and their effects?

Writing Focus

Think as a Reader/Writer

Use It in Your Writing The imagery used by Lovelace and Suckling appeals to many of the senses. Write a poem describing a place you know well. Use adjectives that appeal to the senses to describe your place.

What Do You Think Now

How might trying to achieve an impossible goal affect a person's life?

from the King James Bible

King James I of England and Scotland
Schloss Ambras, Innsbruck, Austria.

INTRODUCTION

The King James Bible
(1611)

One of the first acts of James I after he was crowned king of
England was to sponsor a new translation of the Bible.

A Masterpiece by a Committee

There were many translations of the Bible available, but King
James and others disliked the interpretive comments included
in the existing translations. Moreover, Renaissance scholarship
had made people more historically minded and sensitive to
textual inaccuracies. The king appointed a team of clergymen
to work on the translation. Seven years later, after a final review
by a committee of bishops, the translation was published. It has
been known variously as the King James Bible, because James
sponsored it; as the Authorized Version, because the Anglican
Church authorized its use; and simply as the English Bible, for
its widespread influence on the civilization and literature of the
English-speaking world.

A Lasting Presence

If English-speaking people living before our time read anything,
they read the English Bible. And if they didn't read, they regularly heard the Bible read in church. For nearly four centuries,
most writers in English have been influenced, consciously
or unconsciously, by the English Bible. They have quoted it,
echoed it, paraphrased it, alluded to it, imitated it, and retold its
fascinating stories.

Everyday English is full of words and phrases from the English Bible: "lovingkindness," "tender mercy," "long-suffering," "the
patience of Job." We "cast pearls before swine" and "wait until
the eleventh hour before acting." Many Biblical words (such as
scapegoat) are so embedded in our language that we use them
without knowing we are using Biblical language.

Think
About the
Translation

If you had the chance to pick any
book and translate it into another
language, which book and language
would you pick? Why?

Reader/Writer
Notebook
Use your **RWN** for completing the activities on this page.

Literary Focus

Parallelism The repetition of words, phrases, or sentences that have the same grammatical structure or restate a similar idea is called **parallelism**. Here is an example of parallelism from Psalm 98 of the King James Bible:

> Let the floods clap their hands,
> Let the hills be joyful together.

Often found in literature meant to be sung or recited, parallelism establishes a sense of rhythm, balance, and order.

Language Coach

Latin Roots The adjective *captive* means "held by force." It comes from a Latin root that means "to take hold of." The adjective *capable*, which means "able to do something well," comes from the same root. Here, the root refers to taking hold of something in a figurative sense. Someone who is capable is "able to hold much." The verb *incapacitate* includes the same Latin root. What do you think it means?

Reading Focus

Understanding Archaic Language Old-fashioned language that is no longer used except in special situations is **archaic language**. Several verb forms in the psalms are archaic. For example, the ending *–eth* is the archaic equivalent of the modern third-person present-tense *–s* ending: *maketh/makes*.

Into Action As you read, use a chart like the one below to record each archaic verb in the psalms. Change each verb to the form that is in use today.

Psalm and Line Numbers	Archaic Verbs	Contemporary Forms
Psalm 23, Line 2	maketh	makes

Writing Focus

Think as a Reader/Writer
Find It in Your Reading Psalm 23 contains several **metaphors**—figures of speech that compare two unlike things without using a connective word such as *like, as, than,* or *resembles*. As you read, note in your *Reader/Writer Notebook* the metaphors used for *God*.

Learn It Online
Learn more about the King James Bible through these Internet links.

go.hrw.com   L12-321   **Go**

Psalm 23

from the KING JAMES BIBLE

Read with a Purpose
Read this psalm to discover how the speaker expresses trust in God.

Build Background
Psalm 23 may be the best-known religious poem in the Western world. It is a song of trust that affirms the speaker's confidence in God. The poem uses two extended metaphors. Its imagery reflects the pastoral way of life of the Israelite people.

The Lord is my shepherd; I shall not want.
He maketh me to lie down in green pastures:
He leadeth me beside the still waters.
He restoreth my soul:
5   He leadeth me in the paths of righteousness for his name's sake.° **Ⓐ**
Yea, though I walk through the valley of the shadow of death,
I will fear no evil: For thou art with me;
Thy rod and thy staff ° they comfort me.
Thou preparest a table before me in the presence of mine
        enemies: **Ⓑ**
10 Thou anointest my head with oil; my cup runneth over.°
Surely goodness and mercy shall follow me all the days of my life:
And I will dwell in the house of the Lord forever.

5. his name's sake: not because the speaker has earned it, but for the glory of God.
8. Thy rod and thy staff: The shepherd's tools: the first to defend the sheep from enemies; the second to guide the sheep.
10. anointest my head with oil: a custom to show respect or hospitality.

Ⓐ Literary Focus Parallelism What grammatical structure is repeated in lines 2–5 to develop the metaphor in line 1? How does the repetition enhance the psalm's message?

Ⓑ Reading Focus Understanding Archaic Language This line includes several archaic expressions. Restate the line's meaning in modern English.

Ivory carving of herders

Psalm 137

from the KING JAMES BIBLE

Read with a Purpose

Read to discover the speaker's feelings about being separated from his homeland.

Build Background

This psalm connects directly to the history of the people of Israel. In the sixth century B.C., King Nebuchadnezzar of Babylon conquered Jerusalem. Many Israelites were sent to Babylon, where they were held as captives. This lament over a remembered home has been recited by many captives in the centuries since it was first sung.

By the rivers of Babylon, there we sat down, yea, we wept,
When we remembered Zion.°
We hanged our harps
Upon the willows in the midst thereof.

5   For there they that carried us away captive required of us a song;
And they that wasted us required of us mirth,   **A**
Saying, "Sing us one of the songs of Zion."
How shall we sing the Lord's song
In a strange land?

10 If I forget thee, O Jerusalem,
Let my right hand forget her cunning.
If I do not remember thee,
Let my tongue cleave° to the roof of my mouth;
If I prefer not Jerusalem above my chief joy.   **B**

15 Remember, O Lord, the children of Edom° in the day of
        Jerusalem;
Who said, "Raze it,° raze it, even to the foundation thereof."
O daughter of Babylon,° who art to be destroyed;
Happy shall he be, that rewardeth thee
As thou hast served us.

20 Happy shall he be, that taketh
And dasheth thy little ones against the stones.

2. Zion: a hill in Jerusalem that is often a symbol for the whole of Israel.

13. cleave: adhere; stick.

15. children of Edom: The Edomites, neighbors of the Israelites, rejoiced when the Israelites' kingdom was conquered and most of its population was deported.
16. Raze it: Level it to the ground.
17. daughter of Babylon: the Babylonian people.

A Literary Focus Parallelism How does the parallelism in lines 5–6 help us to understand the speaker's sorrow?

B Literary Focus Parallelism What structure is repeated in lines 10–14? How does this repetition help you understand the speaker's feelings?

Applying Your Skills

Psalm 23 / Psalm 137

SKILLS FOCUS Literary Skills Analyze parallelism; analyze imagery. **Reading Skills** Analyze archaic language. **Writing Skills** Write poetry; use figurative language.

Respond and Think Critically

Reading Focus

Quick Check

1. Why is the speaker of Psalm 23 unafraid?

2. In Psalm 137, what did the captors request? Why is the speaker reluctant to participate in their request?

3. What do lines 18–19 in Psalm 137 mean?

Read with a Purpose

4. What different emotions do the speakers of these psalms express?

Reading Skills: Understanding Archaic Language

5. You noted archaic verbs in the psalms. Now, make a chart for archaic pronouns. The personal pronoun *thou* is the archaic form of the second-person singular pronoun *you*. *Thy* is the possessive form for *your*. *Thee* is the objective form for *you*.

Psalms and Line Numbers	Archaic Pronouns	Contemporary Forms
Psalm 23, Line 7	thou	you

Literary Focus

Literary Analysis

6. **Analyze** What metaphors are used to portray God in Psalm 23? What feelings do they evoke?

7. **Interpret** Which lines in Psalm 23 hint at the idea that life is a perilous journey?

8. **Analyze** In Psalm 23 how does the shift from speaking about God in the third person to speaking to God in the second person affect the psalm's tone?

9. **Evaluate** What emotions does the speaker express in Psalm 137? Which lines convey these emotions? How do you react to the psalm's final line?

10. **Extend** On what occasions might Psalm 137 be sung? What relevance might the text have for people today?

Literary Skills: Parallelism

11. **Analyze** These psalms have no rhyme or meter, yet they are often praised for their literary beauty. How does the use of parallelism enhance the poems' lyrical quality? Use examples from the text to support your answer.

Literary Skills Review: Imagery

12. **Analyze** Language that appeals to the senses is called **imagery**. Identify examples of imagery in the two psalms, and analyze their effects.

Writing Focus

Think as a Reader/Writer

Use It in Your Writing Review the use of metaphor in Psalm 23. In your *Reader/Writer Notebook*, write a ten-line poem in which you convey someone's positive qualities through descriptive metaphors.

What Do **You Think Now** Do these songs come from the heart or mind of the speaker, or both? Explain.

For **CHOICES** see page 330 >

SKILLS FOCUS **Literary Skills** Understand the characteristics of parables. **Reading Skills** Make inferences about
theme.

The Parable of the Prodigal Son

Reader/Writer
Notebook

Use your **RWN** to complete the activities for this selection.

Literary Focus

Parable A **parable** is a short, allegorical story that teaches a moral or
religious lesson about life. In an **allegory** the characters, settings, and
events stand for abstract or moral concepts. Because symbols can be
interpreted in multiple ways, even a brief allegory can yield more than
one meaning. The parables in the Gospels are attributed to Jesus. In "The
Parable of the Prodigal Son" the father is (literally) a parent to his sons and
is (symbolically) a parent to all who seek forgiveness and a fresh start.

Reading Focus

Making Inferences about Theme The central idea about human
experience revealed in a work is its **theme**. A parable's theme is tied to
its allegorical structure. On a literal level, this story is about two sons, an
inheritance, and a loving father. On a symbolic level, the parable carries
messages about God, sin, and forgiveness. To state the theme, you need
to understand how the symbolic level is related to the literal meaning.

Into Action As you read, use a chart like the one below. Identify the
parable's literal features, such as characters, events, and settings, and
make an educated guess about each feature's symbolic meaning.

Literal Features of the Parable	Symbolic Meaning
father's gift to his sons	God's gifts to humanity

> ### Language Coach
>
> **Synonyms** Synonyms are words with
> similar meanings. However, two synonyms
> usually do not have exactly the same
> meaning. Here is a list of synonyms for
> the word *prodigal*:
>
> - wasteful
> - reckless
> - extravagant
> - uncontrolled
>
> What is the meaning of each word? Which
> one do you think is the best synonym for
> *prodigal*? Why?

Writing Focus

Think as a Reader/Writer

Find It in Your Reading The **settings** in this story are each <u>established</u>
more by characters and events than by a physical description. In your
Reader/Writer Notebook, jot down the elements that indirectly reveal the
settings and note how they help give each setting an allegorical meaning.

Learn It Online
Listen to this parable online.

go.hrw.com L12-325 **Go**

The Parable of the Prodigal Son

from the KING JAMES BIBLE

Read with a Purpose
Read this parable to discover how characters can represent ideas such as forgiveness and sin.

Build Background
This story is about inheritance, justice, and fairness. In ancient Israel, the oldest son in a family usually inherited a major share of his father's wealth and became the head of the family upon his father's death. Note that the word *prodigal*—which never occurs in the story—means "recklessly extravagant" and "wasteful" but also "abundantly generous."

And he[1] said, A certain man had two sons:

And the younger of them said to his father, Father, give me the portion of goods that falleth to me. And he divided unto them his living.

And not many days after the younger son gathered all together, and took his journey into a far country, and there wasted his substance with riotous living.

And when he had spent all, there arose a mighty famine in that land; and he began to be in want.

And he went and joined himself to a citizen of that country; and he sent him into his fields to feed swine.[2] **Ⓐ**

And he would fain have filled his belly with the husks that the swine did eat: and no man gave unto him.

And when he came to himself, he said, How many hired servants of my father's have bread enough and to spare, and I perish with hunger!

I will arise and go to my father, and will say unto him, Father, I have sinned against heaven, and before thee,

1. he: Jesus.

2. swine: pigs. The ancient Israelites considered swine ritually taboo, or unclean, and they avoided any contact with them. Tending pigs would have been considered degrading work.

Ⓐ Literary Focus Parable What might the settings of "a far country" and "fields to feed swine" symbolize?

Analyzing Visuals

Viewing and Interpreting Which elements of the parable can you identify in this image? What do the colors represent?

And am no more worthy to be called thy son: make me as one of thy hired servants.

B

And he arose, and came to his father. But when he was yet a great way off, his father saw him, and had compassion, and ran, and fell on his neck, and kissed him.

And the son said unto him, Father, I have sinned against heaven, and in thy sight, and am no more worthy to be called thy son.

But the father said to his servants, Bring forth the best robe, and put it on him; and put a ring on his hand, and shoes on his feet:

And bring hither the fatted calf, and kill it; and let us eat, and be merry:

For this my son was dead, and is alive again; he was lost, and is found. And they began to be merry.

Now his elder son was in the field: and as he came and drew nigh to the house, he heard music and dancing.

And he called one of the servants, and asked what these things meant.

And he said unto him, Thy brother is come; and thy father hath killed the fatted calf, because he hath received him safe and sound.

And he was angry, and would not go in: therefore came his father out, and entreated him.

And he answering said to his father, Lo, these many years do I serve thee, neither transgressed I at any time thy commandment: and yet thou never gavest me a kid,[3] that I might make merry with my friends:

But as soon as this thy son was come, which hath devoured thy living with harlots,[4] thou hast killed for him the fatted calf.

And he said unto him, Son, thou art ever with me, and all that I have is thine.

It was meet that we should make merry, and be glad: for this thy brother was dead, and is alive again; and was lost, and is found.

C

—Luke 15:11–32

3. **kid: baby** goat.

4. **harlots:** prostitutes.

B Literary Focus **Parable** How would you characterize the words and actions of the younger son? What or whom might the son represent?

C Reading Focus **Making Inferences about Theme** What does the father's reply tell you about the theme of the parable?

Respond and Think Critically

Reading Focus

Quick Check

1. How did the younger son get his money? How does he lose it?

2. Why does the younger son return home?

3. How does the father greet the returning son?

4. Why does the older brother become angry?

Read with a Purpose

5. How do the father and his sons represent ideas of forgiveness and sin?

Reading Skills: Making Inferences About Theme

6. Now that you have interpreted the symbolic meaning of the parable's characters, settings, and events, record your inferences about the parable's theme in a new column of your chart.

Literal features of the Parable	Symbolic Meaning	Inferences about Theme
father's gift to his sons	God's gifts to humanity	God gives everyone gifts.

Literary Focus

Literary Analysis

7. **Summarize** In your own words, summarize the older brother's complaints.

8. **Analyze** Why didn't the father discipline the older son for his attitude toward his brother?

9. **Make Judgments** At the end of the parable, whose position do you understand better, that of the father or that of the older son? Why?

10. **Analyze** The word *prodigal* usually means "recklessly extravagant or wasteful," but it can also mean "lavish" and "abundant." Which characters could be called prodigal? Why?

11. **Extend** What contemporary situations could the parable apply to?

Literary Skills: Parable

12. **Analyze** Parables use allegories to teach a moral lesson. On a literal level, what might be the message of "The Prodigal Son"? What is the message on a symbolic level?

Literary Skills Review: Characterization

13. **Analyze** A writer's method of revealing characters' personalities is called **characterization**. Writers reveal their characters by letting us hear how they speak, by describing their appearance, actions, thoughts, and feelings, and by telling us directly what they are like. Which characterization techniques are used in this parable? Why are these techniques particularly well suited to teaching a moral lesson?

Writing Focus

Think as a Reader/Writer

Use It in Your Writing The setting in "The Parable of the Prodigal Son" is <u>established</u> more through references to people and events than by direct description. In your *Reader/Writer Notebook*, write a brief story in which you convey the setting without directly describing it.

What Do **You Think Now** Which characters in this story were influenced by their hearts? Which were influenced by their minds?

Psalm 23 / Psalm 137
The Parable of the Prodigal Son

Grammar Link

Using Modifiers Correctly

Use the comparative form when comparing two things. Use the superlative form when comparing more than two things.

SUPERLATIVE FORM: The King James Bible was the *most scholarly* Biblical translation of its time.

COMPARATIVE FORM: Later scholars revised the King James Bible in the 1880s to make it *more accurate, more consistent, and more modern.*

Include the word *other* or *else* when you are comparing one member of a group with the rest of the group.

The King James Bible stands with Shakespeare as an exemplar of English when the language was *more flexible and eloquent* than at any *other* time.

Avoid using double comparisons. A double comparison results from using two comparative forms (usually *–er* and *more*) or using two superlative forms (usually *–est* and *most*) to modify the same word.

NONSTANDARD: Shakespeare's works display a vocabulary almost three times *more broader* than the vocabulary of the King James Bible.

STANDARD: Shakespeare's works display a vocabulary almost three times *broader* than the vocabulary of the King James Bible.

Your Turn

Correct the comparative and superlative forms below.

1. Psalm 23 may be better known than any psalm.
2. He is less likelier to forgive than his father.

Writing Application Write a paragraph in which you use comparative and superlative forms to compare and contrast your subject with other things.

CHOICES

As you respond to the Choices, use these **Academic Vocabulary** words as appropriate: contradiction, controversy, ensure, establish, widespread.

REVIEW

Compare and Contrast Translations

Timed ⌐Writing In an essay, compare and contrast the following lines from other translations of Psalm 23 with the King James translation, lines 3 and 10.

• He leads me to water in places of repose; …You anoint my head with oil; my drink is abundant.

• He … leads me beside the waters of peace; …Thou hast richly bathed my head with oil, and my cup runs over.

Consider the variations in connotation, rhythm, and musicality, and cite examples from the three translations in your essay.

CONNECT

Judge Music for the Psalms

Use the Internet to find musical recordings of Franz Schubert's and John Rutter's music for Psalm 23. Play recordings for your classmates, and discuss how the music enhances the psalm's meaning.

Prodigal Son. Stained glass cartoon for church in Oretoro, Sweden (1952) by Einar Forseth
Victoria & Albert Museum, London

EXTEND

Evaluate Prodigal Images

Using the Internet or art books, find a work of art that illustrates "The Parable of the Prodigal Son." Then, write a brief essay in which you analyze how the art's visual images establish a tone, represent the parable's ideas, and help convey a moral lesson. Use examples from the artwork and from the parable to support your analysis.

Worlds of Wisdom

From age to age, people have wrestled with the same fundamental questions about life. Ever society creates its own "wisdom literature"—poems, stories, and sayings that provide guidance on everything from rearing children to preparing for the afterlife.

CONTENTS

Night *from the* **Koran**
translated by N.J. Dawood

from **Philosophy and Spiritual Discipline** *from the* **Bhagavad-Gita**
translated by Barbara Stoler Miller

Zen Parables
compiled by Paul Reps

from **The Analects of Confucius**
translated by Arthur Waley

from the **Tao Te Ching** *by* **Lao Tzu**
translated by Stephen Mitchell

Taoist Anecdotes
translated and edited by Moss Roberts

Sayings of Saadi
translated by Idries Shah

African Proverbs

orlds of Wisdom

Reader/Writer
Notebook

e your **RWN** to complete the activities for these selections.

iterary Focus

idactic Literature Literature that is meant to instruct, give advice, or nvey a philosophical or moral message is known as **didactic literature**. uch wisdom literature comes in the form of sacred texts. Secular works ch as proverbs, fables, anecdotes, folk tales, and maxims can also serve didactic literature. Most didactic literature ultimately comes from an al tradition.

eading Focus

omparing Ideas Across Cultures Even in cultures that seem very fferent, didactic literature frequently addresses similar questions: What good, and what is evil? What are the consequences of good and bad ehavior? The answers to these questions are often similar as well. For xample, good is rewarded, and evil is punished.

to Action As you read, note the major characteristics and the mes- ges of each selection.

election	Characteristics	Messages
rom Koran	Sacred text; repetition, parallelism; serious, commanding tone	Charitable acts done in God's name lead to salvation
rom Bhagavad-Gita	Sacred text from epic poem in form of dialogue; parallelism; serious tone	Self-discipline and detachment from material world leads to serenity

riting Focus

hink as a Reader/Writer

ind It in Your Reading Didactic literature often uses **metaphor** as a ool to clarify ideas and engage the reader's imagination. A metaphor is

Learn It Online
Explore the Worlds of Wisdom further with these web

Night *from the* Koran

translated by **N. J. Dawood**

Read with a Purpose
Read this excerpt from the Koran to discover some guiding principles of faith.

Build Background
The word *Koran (qu'ran)* is Arabic for "recitation." Followers of Islam believe that the Koran—first written down in Arabic in the middle of the seventh century—contains God's revelation to the prophet Mohammad through the angel Gabriel. The Koran declares that Allah is the one all-powerful God who created the world. Allah is merciful and compassionate, but he is also the God of Judgment Day. Each of the Koran's 114 chapters—called *suras*—begins, "In the Name of Allah, the Compassionate, the Merciful."

In the Name of Allah, the Compassionate, the Merciful

By the night, when she lets fall her darkness, and by the radiant day! By Him that created the male and the female, your endeavors have different ends!

For him that gives in charity and guards himself against evil and believes in goodness, We shall smooth the path of salvation; but for him that neither gives nor takes and disbelieves in goodness, We shall smooth the path of affliction. When he breathes his last, his riches will not avail him. **Ⓐ**

It is for Us to give guidance. Ours is the life of this world, Ours the life to come. I warn you, then, of the blazing fire, in which none shall burn save the hardened sinner, who denies the truth and gives no heed. But the good man who purifies himself by almsgiving[1] shall keep away from it: and so shall he that does good works for the sake of the Most High only, not in recompense[2] for a favor. Such men shall be content. **Ⓑ**

Leaf from a Qur'an manuscript, Eastern kufic calligraphy, (1940)
The Metropolitan Museum of Art, Rogers Fund, 1940 (40.164.2a).
Image © The Metropolitan Museum of Art.

---

1. **almsgiving:** performing deeds of charity.
2. **recompense:** repayment.

Ⓐ Literary Focus Didactic Literature How does this paragraph instruct people to behave?

Ⓑ Reading Focus Comparing Ideas Across Cultures In this paragraph, what similarities do you notice between Islam and other religions you might have read about or might know?

from Philosophy and Spiritual Discipline

from the Bhagavad-Gita

translated by **Barbara Stoler Miller**

Read with a Purpose
Read this excerpt from an ancient poem to discover what advice a god can give to a warrior.

Build Background
The Bhagavad-Gita, or "Song of the Lord," is part of what may be the longest poem ever written—a Hindu epic called the *Mahabharata*. It influenced Mahatma Gandhi (1869–1948), the charismatic social reformer who led India to independence from Britain in 1947. The Gita consists of a dialogue between Arjuna and his charioteer, Krishna. In this excerpt, Krishna, an earthly embodiment of a major god, and the warrior Arjuna argue just before a great battle with Arjuna's relatives. Krishna urges Arjuna to fulfill his *dharma* (sacred duty) by waging battle, but Arjuna hesitates to fight members of his family.

Lord Krishna
When he gives up desires in his mind,
is content with the self within himself,
then he is said to be a man
whose insight is sure, Arjuna.

5 When suffering does not disturb his mind,
when his craving for pleasures has vanished,
when attraction, fear, and anger are gone,
he is called a sage whose thought is sure.

When he shows no preference
10 in fortune or misfortune
and neither exults nor hates,
his insight is sure.

When, like a tortoise retracting
its limbs, he withdraws his senses
15 completely from sensuous objects,
his insight is sure.

Sensuous objects fade
when the embodied self abstains from food;
the taste lingers, but it too fades
20 in the vision of higher truth.

Even when a man of wisdom
tries to control them, Arjuna,
the bewildering senses
attack his mind with violence.

 Literary Focus Didactic Literature What is Lord Krishna's attitude toward wisdom?

25   Controlling them all,
    with discipline he should focus on me;
    when his senses are under control,
    his insight is sure.

    Brooding about sensuous objects
30   makes attachment to them grow;
    from attachment desire arises,
    from desire anger is born. **B**

    From anger comes confusion;
    from confusion memory lapses;
35   from broken memory understanding is lost;
    from loss of understanding, he is ruined. **C**

    But a man of inner strength
    whose senses experience objects
    without attraction and hatred,
40   in self-control, finds serenity.

B Literary Focus **Didactic Literature** What is Krishna saying in this stanza about the relationship between material objects and anger?

C Reading Focus **Comparing Ideas Across Cultures** According to Krishna, what is the worst thing that can happen to a person? According to the excerpt from the Koran, what is the worst thing that could happen to a person?

Analyzing Visuals

Viewing and Interpreting Discuss the relationship between the image and the text. Consider the background information about the text. How does the image reflect the message and tone of the text? How might the image seem ironic in relation to the text? Paradoxical?

Arjuna and His Charioteer Lord Krishna Confront Karna (1820), India.
Philadelphia Museum of Art. Purchased with the Edith H. Bell Fund, 1975.

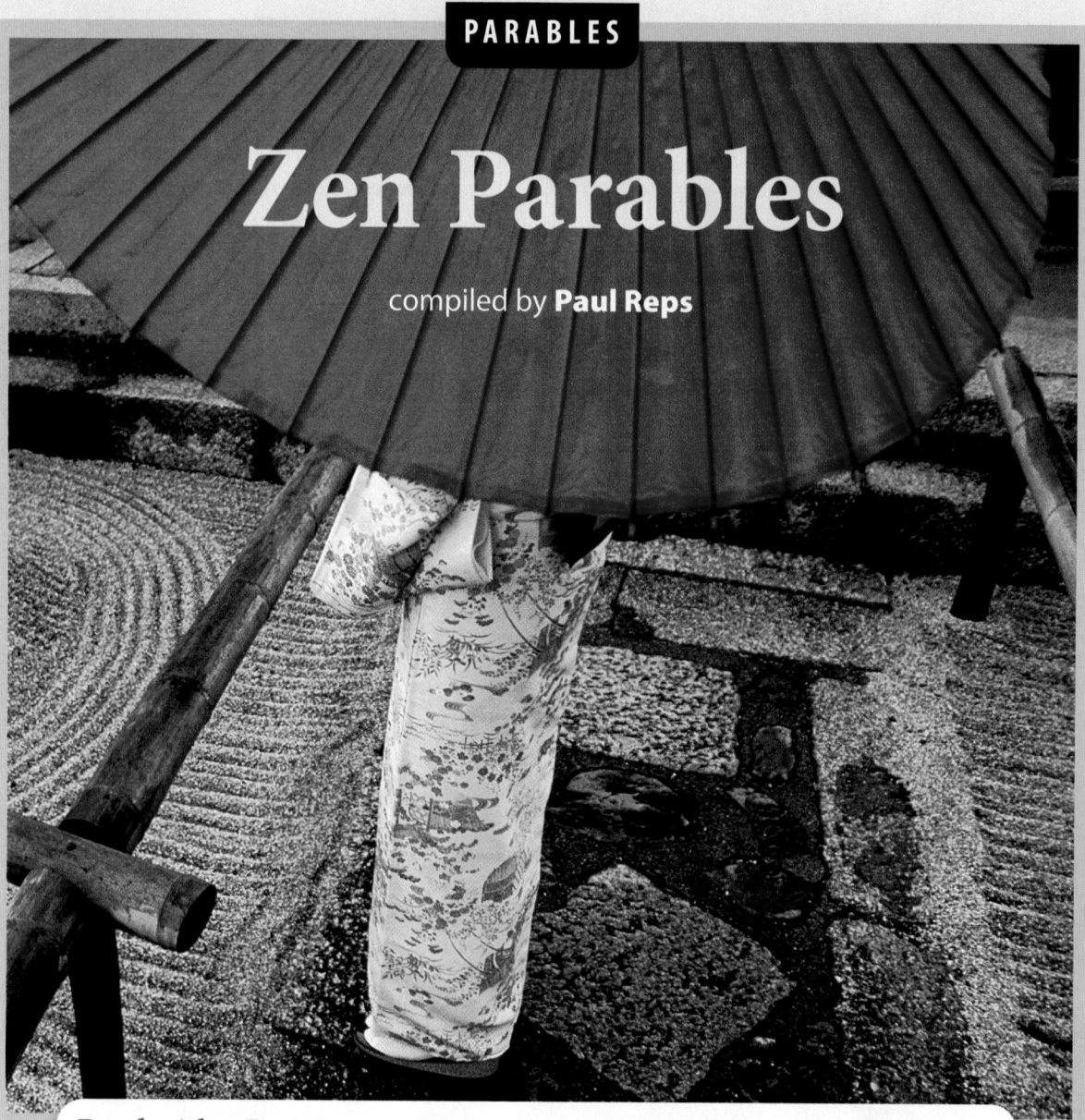

Zen Parables

compiled by **Paul Reps**

Read with a Purpose
Read to discover the philosophy that underlies Zen Buddhism.

Build Background
The Zen parables illustrate the insights of Zen Buddhism. The object of Zen is to free the mind of everyday, conventional logic through meditation. Instead of imparting facts in a clear and logical way, the Zen master first tries to confuse his students, to force them to abandon all preconceived notions of what knowledge is. He might ask a nonsensical question that has no answer, such as "What is the sound of one hand clapping?" This technique prepares students to understand the lessons inherent in the deceptively simple **parables**, or brief allegorical stories.

The Moon Cannot Be Stolen

Ryokan, a Zen master, lived the simplest kind of life in a little hut at the foot of a mountain. One evening a thief visited the hut only to discover there was nothing in it to steal.

Ryokan returned and caught him. "You may have come a long way to visit me," he told the prowler, "and you should not return empty-handed. Please take my clothes as a gift."

The thief was bewildered. He took the clothes and slunk away.

Ryokan sat naked, watching the moon. "Poor fellow," he mused, "I wish I could give him this beautiful moon." **(A)**

Temper

A Zen student came to Bankei and complained: "Master, I have an ungovernable temper. How can I cure it?"

"You have something very strange," replied Bankei. "Let me see what you have."

"Just now I cannot show it to you," replied the other.

"When can you show it to me?" asked Bankei.

"It arises unexpectedly," replied the student.

"Then," concluded Bankei, "it must not be your own true nature. If it were, you could show it to me at any time. When you were born, you did not have it, and your parents did not give it to you. Think that over."

The Gates of Paradise

A soldier named Nobushige came to Hakuin, and asked: "Is there really a paradise and a hell?"

"Who are you?" inquired Hakuin.

"I am a samurai," the warrior replied.

"You, a soldier!" exclaimed Hakuin. "What kind of ruler would have you as his guard? Your face looks like that of a beggar."

Nobushige became so angry that he began to draw his sword, but Hakuin continued: "So you have a sword! Your weapon is probably much too dull to cut off my head."

As Nobushige drew his sword, Hakuin remarked: "Here open the gates of hell!"

At these words the samurai, perceiving the master's discipline, sheathed his sword and bowed.

"Here open the gates of paradise," said Hakuin.

The First Principle

When one goes to Obaku temple in Kyoto, he sees carved over the gate the words "The First Principle." The letters are unusually large, and those who appreciate calligraphy[1] always admire them as being a masterpiece. They were drawn by Kosen two hundred years ago.

When the master drew them he did so on paper, from which workmen made the larger carving in wood. As Kosen sketched the letters, a bold pupil was with him who had made several gallons of ink for the calligraphy and who never failed to criticize his master's work.

"That is not good," he told Kosen after the first effort.

"How is that one?"

"Poor. Worse than before," pronounced the pupil. **(B)**

Kosen patiently wrote one sheet after another until eighty-four First Principles had accumulated, still without the approval of the pupil.

Then, when the young man stepped outside for a few moments, Kosen thought: "Now is my chance to escape his keen eye," and he wrote hurriedly, with a mind free from distraction:

"The First Principle."

"A masterpiece," pronounced the pupil.

---

1. **calligraphy:** the art of beautiful handwriting.

(A) Literary Focus Didactic Literature What is the master trying to teach the thief?

(B) Reading Focus Comparing Ideas Across Cultures How does the master's attitude toward the pupil compare to Krishna's attitude toward Arjuna in the Bhagavad-Gita?

from The Analects of Confucius

translated and annotated by **Arthur Waley**

Read with a Purpose
Read these brief statements, or **maxims**, to discover Confucius's attitude toward learning.

Build Background
Confucius, who <u>established</u> an important and lasting Chinese philosophical system, left no written works. After his death around 479, his disciples gathered his sayings in a collection known as *The Analects*—"selected sayings." Here, Confucius describes a concept called *chung-yung*, or "the golden mean," that emphasizes virtues such as loyalty, obedience, integrity, and obligation to one's parents and ancestors.

The Master said, "Yu, shall I teach you what knowledge is? When you know a thing, to recognize that you know it, and when you do not know a thing, to recognize that you do not know it. That is knowledge."

The Master said, "Even when walking in a party of no more than three I can always be certain of learning from those I am with. There will be good qualities that I can select for imitation and bad ones that will teach me what requires correction in myself." Ⓐ

Tzu-kung asked, saying, "Is there any single saying that one can act upon all day and every day?" The Master said, "Perhaps the saying about consideration: 'Never do to others what you would not like them to do to you.'" Ⓑ

Statue of Confucius, Chinatown, New York.

Ⓐ **Literary Focus** **Didactic Literature** What lesson is Confucius teaching here?

Ⓑ **Reading Focus** **Comparing Ideas Across Cultures** Where did you first hear of a concept similar to this? Why do you think this concept appears in so many different cultures?

from the Tao Te Ching

by **Lao Tzu**

translated by **Stephen Mitchell**

Read with a Purpose
Read to discover how the philosophy of Taoism finds wisdom in nature.

Build Background
The *Tao Te Ching*, or "Classic of the Way of Power," is a book of sayings and poems that teach the nature of Taoism. It is attributed to Lao Tzu, who, according to legend, was born as an old, bearded, white-haired man and lived to the age of 160. Broadly defined, Taoism consists of the joyful acceptance of life and a willingness to yield to the natural world, becoming one with it.

The supreme good is like water,
which nourishes all things without trying to.
It is content with the low places that people
    disdain.
Thus it is like the Tao.

5 In dwelling, live close to the ground.
In thinking, keep to the simple.
In conflict, be fair and generous.
In governing, don't try to control. **A**
In work, do what you enjoy.
10 In family life, be completely present.

When you are content to be simply yourself
and don't compare or compete,
everybody will respect you. **B**

Lao-Tzu on his buffalo, (18th century), Chinese Bibliotheque Nationale, Paris.

A Literary Focus **Didactic Literature** What is this saying about how to be a good leader?
B Reading Focus **Comparing Ideas Across Cultures** Compare these three lines with the first four lines in the excerpt from the Bhagavad-Gita. How is the focus of these passages similar?

Taoist Anecdotes

translated and edited by **Moss Roberts**

Read with a Purpose
Read to discover what makes certain characters either clever or unwise.

Build Background
Followers of Taoism have long used **anecdotes,** or brief stories, to convey their philosophy indirectly. The stories are intended to impart the spiritual teachings of Taoism, with its focus on oneness with the world and the unchangeable nature of the Way.

Gold, Gold

Many, many years ago there was a man of the land of Ch'i who had a great passion for gold. One day at the crack of dawn he went to the market—straight to the gold dealers' stalls, where he snatched some gold and ran. The market guards soon caught him. "With so many people around, how did you expect to get away with it?" a guard asked.

"When I took it," he replied, "I saw only the gold, not the people." **Ⓐ**

—Lieh Tzu

A Clever Judge

In the days when Ch'en Shu-ku was a magistrate[1] in Chienchou, there was a man who had lost an article of some value. A number of people were arrested, but no one could discover exactly who the thief was. So Shu-ku laid a trap for the suspects. "I know of a temple," he told them, "whose bell can tell a thief from an honest man. It has great spiritual powers."

The magistrate had the bell fetched and reverently enshrined in a rear chamber. Then he had the suspects brought before the bell to stand and testify to their guilt or innocence. He explained to them that if an innocent man touched the bell it would remain silent, but that if the man was guilty it would ring out.

---

1. **magistrate:** judge.

Then the magistrate led his staff in solemn worship to the bell. The sacrifices concluded, he had the bell placed behind a curtain, while one of his assistants secretly smeared it with ink. After a time he took the suspects to the bell and had each one in turn extend his hands through the curtain and touch the bell. As each man withdrew his hands, Shu-ku examined them. Everyone's hands were stained except for those of one man, who confessed to the theft under questioning. He had not dared touch the bell for fear it would ring. **Ⓑ**

—Chang Shih-nan

Moral teaching for shop boys, giving good and bad examples of behavior, (1857) by Kuniyoshi, Utagawa   School of Oriental & African Studies Library, University of London.

Ⓐ **Reading Focus** Comparing Ideas Across Cultures How does the message of this passage compare to Lord Krishna's argument from the Bhagavad-Gita?

Ⓑ **Literary Focus** Didactic Literature What does this anecdote tell you about the effects of fear and guilt?

Sayings of Saadi

translated by **Idries Shah**

Read with a Purpose
Read to understand how Saadi uses animals to teach lessons that humans can use.

Build Background
The poet Saadi lived in thirteenth-century Persia (now Iran). He followed Sufism (SOO fihz uhm), a sect of Islam that believes humans can transcend the physical world through proper philosophy and practice. Even today, Sufis are not attached to belongings and places, and they are not driven by concerns of time, money, or achievement. They concentrate instead on walking the *tariqah,* or path toward the Divine Nature. The path comprises repentance, abstinence, renunciation, poverty, patience, gratitude, and acceptance.

The Unfed Dervish
When I see the poor dervish[1] unfed
My own food is pain and poison to me. **A**

Information and Knowledge
However much you study, you cannot know
    without action.
    A donkey laden with books is neither an
    intellectual nor a wise man.
    Empty of essence, what learning has he—
    Whether upon him is firewood or book?

The Elephant Keeper
Make no friendship with an elephant keeper
If you have no room to entertain an elephant. **B**

Safety and Riches
Deep in the sea are riches beyond compare.
But if you seek safety, it is on the shore.

---

1. **dervish:** Muslim monk dedicated to a life of poverty.

A Reading Focus **Comparing Ideas Across Cultures** How is Saadi's attitude here similar to or different from the Zen master's in "The Moon Cannot Be Stolen"?

B Literary Focus **Didactic Literature** How does the humor in this proverb make it effective for teaching about friendships?

The Fox and the Camels
A fox was seen running away in terror. Someone asked what was troubling it. The fox answered:
 "They are taking camels for forced labor."
"Fool!" he was told, "the fate of camels has nothing to do with you, who do not even look like one." "Silence!" said the fox, "for if an intriguer were to state that I was a camel, *who* would work for my release?"

Portrait of a Sufi, (17th century), Islamic, India
The Metropolitan Museum of Art, Bequest of Cora Timken Burnett, 1956 (57.51.30).
Image © The Metropolitan Museum of Art.

African Proverbs

compiled by **Charlotte** and **Wolf Leslau**

Read with a Purpose
Read to discover how the proverbs of a region reflect its landscape and culture.

Build Background
In the oral literatures of Africa, **proverbs** represent a poetic form that achieves great depth of meaning using very few words. In cultures without written language, proverbs function as the distilled essence of people's values and knowledge. They are used to entertain, settle legal disputes, resolve ethical dilemmas, and teach children the philosophy of their people. The following proverbs are from Ashanti, the Democratic Republic of the Congo, and Ethiopia. Ashanti, known for its gold and its bright kente cloth, is located in the rainforests of central Ghana. The Democratic Republic of the Congo is a country of many great rivers and is bordered by the Atlantic Ocean and Lake Tanganyika. Ethiopia, in the Horn of Africa, is one of the oldest civilizations in the world. This region has a dramatic landscape of desert, mountains, and fertile plateau savannahs.

Only when you have crossed the river, can you say the crocodile has a lump on his snout. —*Ashanti*

When a man is wealthy, he may wear an old cloth. —*Ashanti*

The ruin of a nation begins in the homes of its people. —*Ashanti*

He who cannot dance will say: "The drum is bad." **A** —*Ashanti*

It is the fool's sheep that break loose twice. —*Ashanti*

No one tests the depth of a river with both feet. —*Ashanti*

Wood may remain ten years in the water, but it will never become a crocodile. **B** —*Zaire*

Evil enters like a needle and spreads like an oak tree. —*Ethiopia*

The witness of a rat is another rat. —*Ethiopia*

The frog wanted to be as big as the elephant, and burst. —*Ethiopia*

When the heart overflows, it comes out through the mouth. —*Ethiopia*

When spider webs unite, they can tie up a lion. —*Ethiopia*

Confiding a secret to an unworthy person is like carrying grain in a bag with a hole. —*Ethiopia*

I have a cow in the sky, but cannot drink her milk. —*Ethiopia*

If you offend, ask for pardon; if offended, forgive. —*Ethiopia*

A fool and water will go the way they are diverted. —*Ethiopia*

Headpiece in the form of a crocodile, (20th century) West African
Indianapolis Museum of Art

A Literary Focus Comparing Ideas Across Cultures Does this remind you of any common sayings from your everyday life?

B Reading Focus Didactic Literature What lesson is this simple proverb teaching about trying to be something you are not?

Applying Your Skills

Worlds of Wisdom

Respond and Think Critically

Reading Focus

Quick Check

1. In the Zen parable "Temper," what conclusion does master Bankei draw about the student's "ungovernable temper"?

2. In the Taoist anecdote "A Clever Judge," how does the thief get caught?

3. What is the message of Saadi's saying "Safety and Riches"?

Read with a Purpose

4. What do these examples of didactic literature tell you about how people seek wisdom?

Reading Skills: Comparing Ideas across Cultures

5. As you read, you noted major characteristics of each piece of wisdom literature and summarized each message. Now compare and contrast the form and content of the messages.

Selection	Character-istics	Messages	Similarities and Differences
from the Koran	Sacred text; repetition, parallelism; serious, commanding tone	Charitable acts done in God's name lead to salvation	Charity's role in salvation; Belief in afterlife; punishment in afterlife
from the Bhagavad-Gita	Sacred text from epic poem in form of dialogue; parallelism; serious tone	Self-discipline and detachment from material world leads to serenity	Focus on self-discipline and detachment; No discussion of charity or afterlife.

Literary Focus

Literary Analysisw

6. **Contrast** Describe one important difference between the Hindu philosophy described by Krishna and the ideas described in the excerpt from the Koran.

7. **Evaluate** Which excerpt do you think teaches most effectively? Explain your answer.

8. **Analyze** According to Saadi's saying "Information and Knowledge," what is the difference between information and knowledge?

9. **Extend** Explain how three of these pieces of literature might directly relate to our lives today.

Literary Skills: Didactic Literature

10. **Interpret** Which selection teaches in the most direct, or explicit, way? Which selection is most indirect in its approach?

Literary Skills Review: Tone

11. **Compare** The attitude of a writer toward the subject or audience is called **tone**. Choose two selections and compare their tones. How does the tone affect each selection's message?

Writing Focus

Think as a Reader/Writer

Use It in Your Writing As you read, you noted the use of metaphors. Create several instructive and entertaining proverbs of your own, and add them to your *Reader/Writer Notebook*.

 What Do You Think Now

What does didactic literature teach about the how our hearts and minds influence our actions?

SKILLS FOCUS **Literary Skills** Analyze didactic literature; evaluate the philosophical, political, religious, ethical, and social influences of a historical period. **Writing Skills** Write comparison-contrast essays.

World Literature: Worlds of Wisdom

Writing Focus

Writing a Comparison-Contrast Essay

All of the selections you have just read deal with issues of morality. Which of the authors express similar views? How is each author's argument unique? Which pieces express attitudes toward life that you find surprising, baffling, contradictory, controversial, or in conflict with your own views and beliefs? Which pieces strike you as accurately reflecting your beliefs? Write an essay in which you compare the views on morality expressed in two or three of the selections.

Prewriting

To start writing, consider the following points:

- How is the issue of morality discussed in the selections? Which selections focus more on behavior in this world? Which focus more on an afterlife?

- How does each author reveal opinions on morality? What viewpoints does the author include? (Are they the author's own viewpoints, or the viewpoints of others?)

- Which selections did you find most convincing, and why?

Gather Details Create an H-chart to record your ideas about the two or three selections you choose to compare. In the center of the H, record the main similarity. Then, write the title of each selection you have chosen at the top of the H. Record your notes about each selection. Then, examine the notes looking for other similarities and differences. From your notes, develop a thesis statement that includes the similarities and the points of difference that you can support with text evidence in an essay.

Drafting

Since you are writing a comparison-contrast essay, use the Point-by-Point method, using at least one body paragraph to develop the basis of similarity. Then continue with similarities or move to differences in the selections you have chosen to analyze.

Point-by-Point Method

Topic Sentence/Paragraph
- Selection 1
- Selection 2

Topic Sentence/Paragraph
- Selection 1
- Selection 2

Revising and Editing

- Read your paper. Identify your thesis. Have you proven the thesis in the rest of your paper? Do you return to it in the closing paragraph?

- Add text evidence if each point is not supported.

- Proofread your essay and correct any errors in spelling, mechanics and usage. Use details and examples from the texts to support your ideas, and make sure that your essay has a clear structure from beginning to end.

An effective comparison-contrast essay

- clearly states in the opening paragraph what is being compared and contrasted

- uses a thesis statement to convey the main idea

- has an effective and logical organization that includes similarities and differences

- cites and explains text passages to support ideas

- contains no errors in spelling, punctuation, and grammar

What Do **You** **Think** **Now** Do you think these pieces of wisdom literature appeal more to the heart or to the mind as a means of teaching people how to live? Explain.

The Fall of Satan *from* Paradise Lost

Analyzing Milton's Style by **Kylene Beers**

Analyzing an author's style in a work of literature can sometimes feel artificial. Why pick a poem apart? If you approach this process with a sense of exploration, you will see that analysis can improve your comprehension of a complex text by sending you back to the poem to re-read passages and by focusing your attention on the literary tools the poet has employed.

It is common for readers to be intimidated by Milton's style when they first encounter it. As it grows more familiar to you, however, you will begin to follow the meaning of the text. You will discover a story that overflows with fantastic imagery, epic drama, and profound ideas. Through his unique use of language, Milton elevates his poem into the realm of the sacred and gives its voice an air of divine authority.

Careful reading and re-reading of challenging passages is the key to getting the most out of Milton's work. For example, many modern readers are challenged by the numerous references, called **allusions,** to classic literature, Christian theology, and Renaissance culture within Milton's work. Use the footnotes to think about these references, and then re-read the passages with new knowledge.

Below is an excerpt from the opening of *Paradise Lost* and some accompanying footnotes. Read the lines and the footnotes, and then read the lines again.

> Restore us, and regain the blissful seat,
> Sing, Heavenly Muse, that on the secret top
> Of Oreb, or of Sinai,[1] didst inspire
> That shepherd,[2] who first taught the chosen seed[3]

If you don't understand the Biblical allusion, you might not understand the comparison in these lines.

1. **Oreb . . . Sinai:** names for the mountain where Moses received God's inspiration.
2. **shepherd:** Moses, a Jewish prophet.
3. **chosen seed:** the Hebrews.

However, once it is clear that Milton is comparing himself to Moses, and his words to Moses' reception of the word of God, you can understand that Milton wants his poem to feel divinely inspired. Re-read the lines one more time. Does the language seem clearer now than when you initially encountered it?

You can use the same strategy of reading and re-reading to better understand passages with challenging syntax or inverted word order. Milton often uses unusual sentence structure, placing sentence parts in unexpected places. In these cases, first locate the sentence's subject and verb to find out who is doing what.

Your Turn

In this excerpt from *Paradise Lost,* the speaker poses a question throughout six lines. Examine the text carefully, and briefly **paraphrase**—restate in your own words—the speaker's basic question.

> Say first, for Heaven hides nothing from thy view,
> Nor the deep tract of Hell, say first what cause
> Moved our grand parents[1] in that happy state,
> Favored of Heaven so highly, to fall off
> From their Creator, and transgress his will
> For one restraint,[2] lords of the world besides?[3]

1. **grand parents:** Adam and Eve.
2. **one restraint:** the command not to eat of the fruit of the tree of knowledge. 3. **besides:** in every other way.

Learn It Online
For more on Milton's style, see *PowerNotes.*

go.hrw.com L12-345 **Go**

Preparing to Read

The Fall of Satan
from Paradise Lost

When I consider how my light is spent

What Do You Think? How do our hearts and minds influence our actions?

QuickWrite

Do you think an uneducated person can be as accomplished a poet as an educated one? What might an uneducated person be able to bring to poetry that an educated person might not? Write an entry in your *Reader/Writer Notebook* that answers these questions.

John Milton (c., 1629) by unknown artist. National Portrait Gallery, London.

John Milton
(1608–1674)

Like Chaucer and Shakespeare, Milton is one of the towering figures of English literature.

The Scholar Poet

John Milton showed an early talent for languages, mastering the ancient languages of Latin, Greek, and Hebrew, and achieving fluency in many European tongues. After attaining distinction during his education at Cambridge University, Milton spent six years at his father's country house, where he read ancient and modern writing and became thoroughly acquainted with the Bible. During this period of private study, he wrote poetry, including *Lycidas*, an elegy for a Cambridge classmate. In 1638, Milton left England for two years of travel in Europe. When he returned, England was soon to be ravaged by civil war.

Political Career

In the 1640s, an ongoing struggle between King Charles and his Parliament came to a head. A believer in the Puritan cause, Milton enaged in the paper warfare that accompanied the conflict and started publishing controversial prose works—some of them very elaborate and a few of them very insulting—in support of the Parliamentary party. Although Milton shared some Puritan ideas and attitudes, such as a dislike of kings and bishops, he also differed greatly from orthodox thinking in other important ways. For instance, he advocated divorce for incompatible married couples and argued that the press should be free from government censorship and interference. Although we take these freedoms for granted today, most people in the seventeenth century—particularly most Puritans—would have considered them dangerously radical.

Milton served in the government under Oliver Cromwell, who ruled England as lord protector after the Parliamentary party had won the Civil Wars and executed King Charles. As Latin secretary to the Council of State, Milton was responsible for translating all correspondence with foreign countries, as Latin was then the language of diplomacy.

In his later years, Milton's eyesight began to fail. By 1652, he could only distinguish day from night; by the age of forty-four, before he had finished his life's work, Milton was totally blind.

A Change of Leadership

Milton believed that the ideal government was a republic in which the most capable, intelligent, and virtuous men would be <u>established</u> as leaders. In 1660, the cause for which he had worked twenty years became totally discredited; the English restored to power the son of their dead king and crowned him King Charles II. Milton was stripped of his possessions and arrested as a traitor. Fortunately, thanks to influential friends such as Andrew Marvell, Milton was allowed to go into retirement rather than to the scaffold. From that point forward, he lived in seclusion with his three daughters and his third wife (his first two wives and only son had died). By reading aloud to him, his daughters enabled Milton to carry on the studies he thought necessary for a poet.

The Road to *Paradise Lost*

Being a poet, in Milton's view, meant imitating the great writers of antiquity: the epic poets Homer and Virgil and the Greek dramatists Aeschylus, Sophocles, and Euripides. Because those writers chose subjects drawn from their own nations' histories, Milton considered various English subjects for his works, especially King Arthur and the knights of the Round Table. After years of thinking and reading, however, Milton decided that King Arthur's exploits were mainly fictitious, and so he settled on subjects drawn from the Bible.

Milton began publishing his writing while still at Cambridge. Even after his retirement from politics, and before the Restoration of Charles II, Milton continued to write political pamphlets about education, freedom of the press, divorce, and religion. He also worked simultaneously on the epic that would become *Paradise Lost*.

A Profound Work of Art

Milton published *Paradise Lost* twice: first in a ten-book version in 1667 and then in twelve books in 1674, the year of his death. Throughout his life he composed many different plans for the epic, and even once thought of it as a tragedy with Satan—the fallen archangel turned chief devil—as its protagonist. In the

Milton's First Meeting with Mary Powell, Accompanied by her Brother (1862), by Alfred Rankley.

finished poem, Satan remains very conspicuous. The first two books are devoted mainly to him (he appears frequently in Books III–X) and Milton lavishes on Satan some of his most glorious writing. Thus, it's unsurprising that many readers regard Satan as the hero of the poem. The poet and artist William Blake asserted that Milton was "of the Devil's party without knowing it."

This argument is convincing, however, only to those who concentrate on certain parts of the poem and ignore the remainder. Although the setting of the poem alternates between Hell and Heaven, the most important action takes place on Earth, where the first human beings, Adam and Eve, are given the choice of obeying or disobeying God. They choose to disobey and, having done so, they accept their punishment and make the best of the life that is left to them. They are the heroes of Milton's epic, and, in some ways, they represent us all.

Think About the Writer — Milton was closely involved in the political scene of his time. What role do you think literature and the arts should take in political or social debates?

INTRODUCTION TO
Paradise Lost
MILTON'S EPIC

When Milton wrote *Paradise Lost*, his intent was clear: to create literature's greatest epic poem. His allusions to Homer, Virgil, Dante, and a host of lesser epic poets leave no doubt that Milton wanted *Paradise Lost* to encompass and also surpass all previous epics. Milton asserts this bold ambition at the very beginning of the poem, describing its content as "things unattempted yet in prose or rhyme" (line 16). Unlike an **oral epic** or a **primary epic** such as *Beowulf*, which is performed by generations of storytellers, *Paradise Lost* is a **literary epic,** the product of an individual writer.

Milton plants *Paradise Lost* firmly in the epic tradition by following the standard conventions of the form. He begins with an invocation to the Muse; he starts the action *in media res* ("in the middle of things"); and he writes in an elevated style on a grand subject. Milton's unique style and the cosmic scale of his subject help distinguish his poem from earlier literary epics. Milton's epic does not deal with earthly matters, and instead tells a story from the dawn of Creation, depicting a conflict between good and evil. In *Paradise Lost,* the battle is not fought between people, but between Satan and God. Milton's style matches the grandeur of this story. He combines ornate language, complex syntax, blank verse, multiple allusions, and elaborate comparisons called **epic similes.** The result is a text rich in beauty, power and drama, very much the epic masterpiece that Milton so passionately hoped to create.

The Angel Michael Binding Satan (c. 1850), by William Blake. Harvard University Art Museums, Fogg Art Museum. Gift of W. A. White (1915).

Setting a Grand Stage

Paradise Lost begins in a manner that is traditional for epics: the speaker invokes the Muse and states the subject of the poem. The Muse is traditionally one of the nine Greek goddesses of inspiration. In "invoking" the Muse, the speaker essentially asks the divine being to speak through the poet. In *Paradise Lost,* Milton uses the first sixteen lines—which are one long, complex sentence—to invoke the Muse. Grammatically, the sentence begins in line 6 with the command "Sing, Heavenly Muse." To understand what he wants the Muse to sing about, we must move back to line 1, which is a reference to Adam and Eve's "first disobedience" against God in the Garden of Eden. This story of the act of disobedience, expulsion from Paradise, and the possibility of redemption is what Milton wants the Muse to relate through him. He completes the statement of his subject in lines 24–26, in which he boldly declares that he is going to "justify the ways of God to men." This declaration is Milton's great argument, or theme.

Posing an Ancient Question

If evil exists in a universe ruled by God, why does God allow that evil to exist? This question is what Milton feels he must explain. In exploring this question, the poet attempts to resolve a dilemma that has puzzled people throughout the ages. Milton asserts that God is not responsible for these evils. As he points out in the first few lines, it was Adam and Eve's own disobedient actions that "Brought death into the world, and all our woe" (line 3). Milton argues that Adam and Eve were given a choice—good or evil—and provided with the freedom to make their own decision. According to the poet, it was their choice that allowed evil and its consequences to be unleashed on the world.

Adam and Eve's fateful choice is commonly referred to in Christian theology as the *original sin,* but readers do not need to accept this traditional explanation of evil in order to enjoy the poem or find it thought provoking. The poem is rich enough to provide support for many different interpretations.

Bringing Hope to the Struggle

In "The Fall of Satan" at the beginning of *Paradise Lost,* Milton depicts Satan just after he has been banished to Hell. According to the poem, God purposely decides to let Satan escape and establish himself on Earth so that goodness can triumph. Milton argues that goodness can only be true goodness if it results from a struggle to overcome evil. Therefore, by releasing Satan to do his evil work, God gives human beings

A Dungeon Horrible (1979), by Terrance Lindall, 1979. Williamsburg Art and Historical Center, and the Yuko Nii Foundation.

something to fight against, a struggle that can allow them to be redeemed. Milton's view of life is heroic and optimistic. He suggests that Adam and Eve's tragic loss of Paradise actually enabled a greater beauty to emerge: the grace of human beings engaged in a noble struggle against darkness. The Archangel Michael tells Adam and Eve how to live in their new imperfect world. Practice good deeds, he says, and patience, temperance, faith, and love, and

> then wilt thou be not loath
> To leave this Paradise, but shalt possess
> A Paradise within thee, happier far."
> —Book XII, lines 585–587

Preparing to Read

The Fall of Satan *from* Paradise Lost

Reader/Writer Notebook

Use your **RWN** to complete the activities for this selection.

Literary Focus

Style The way in which writers use language to express ideas is called **style.** An author's style is closely connected to **diction,** or word choice, and **syntax,** or sentence construction. Milton writes in **blank verse** (unrhymed iambic pentameter), the form Shakespeare uses in his plays. With the exception of free verse, blank verse reflects the natural rhythm of English speech more than any other form. Milton also uses **epic similes,** extended comparisons that draw parallels between dissimilar things.

Reading Focus

Analyzing Milton's Style Milton includes many references to the Bible and to classical literature. The footnotes will help you with unfamiliar names and terms. Use **context clues** for unfamiliar words. Because Milton's constructions do not always follow the standard subject-verb-object order, analyze long sentences by **paraphrasing** them in your own words.

Into Action Use a chart like the one below to note the phrases or lines that you find challenging and paraphrase them in your own words.

Difficult lines	Paraphrase
(44–47) Him the Almighty Power Hurled headlong flaming from the ethereal sky With hideous ruin and combustion down To bottomless perdition,	Almighty God (subject) threw (verb) Satan headfirst from Heaven (ethereal sky) in a streak of flames and debris, to a bottomless pit of suffering (perdition).

Writing Focus

Think as a Reader/Writer

Find It in Your Reading Milton's **epic similes** enhance his descriptions of Satan and Hell. As you read, list them in your *Reader/Writer Notebook*.

TechFocus In line 74, Milton describes Earth as the center of ten concentric spheres. How can you learn more about the study of astronomy in Milton's day? Discuss ways to investigate this topic with classmates.

Vocabulary

transgress (trans GREHS) *v.:* sin against; violate a limit. *He roused the others to fight and transgress God's will.*

infernal (ihn FUR nuhl) *adj.:* hellish; fiendish. *Humanity is prey to the whims of the infernal demons.*

contention (kuhn TEHN shuhn) *n.:* struggle. *The angels were in contention for power.*

impetuous (ihm PEHCH u uhs) *adj.:* forceful; violent. *The impetuous angels tried to take over heaven but were driven out.*

desolation (dehs uh LAY shuhn) *n.:* utter misery; extreme loneliness. *Satan vows to lead humans into a state of desolation.*

Language Coach

Multiple Meanings When Milton uses the word *impetuous* in this selection, it means "forceful." The same word can often mean "acting rashly, without considering the consequences." Similarly, *contention* can refer to a struggle or to the opinion a person forms as part of an argument. Explain how both meanings are used in this sentence: *It is my contention that contention between people is inevitable.*

 **Learn It Online**
Meet this famous poem via a video introduction.

go.hrw.com | L12-350 | **Go**

The Fall of Satan
from *Paradise Lost*

by **John Milton**

Read with a Purpose
Read to discover how Satan is depicted with good and evil characteristics.

Build Background
At the opening of *Paradise Lost,* Milton states that his intention is to "justify the ways of God to men." He seeks to illuminate the consequences of Adam's action, that is to say, the misuse of reason and free will and its effect on all succeeding generations of human beings. After the invocation, the action starts *in medias res* ("in the middle of things"). The rebellious angels led by Satan have been defeated and thrown into Hell. Milton vividly depicts Satan and the horrors of Hell.

Of man's first disobedience, and the fruit
Of that forbidden tree, whose mortal taste
Brought death into the world, and all our woe,
With loss of Eden, till one greater Man°
5 Restore us, and regain the blissful seat,
Sing, Heavenly Muse,° that on the secret top
Of Oreb, or of Sinai,° didst inspire
That shepherd,° who first taught the chosen seed°
In the beginning how the Heavens and Earth
10 Rose out of Chaos; or if Sion hill°
Delight thee more, and Siloa's brook° that flowed
Fast by the oracle of God, I thence
Invoke thy aid to my adventurous song,
That with no middle flight intends to soar
15 Above the Aonian mount,° while it pursues
Things unattempted yet in prose or rhyme. **Ⓐ**
And chiefly thou, O Spirit,° that dost prefer
Before all temples the upright heart and pure,
Instruct me, for thou know'st; thou from the first
20 Wast present, and with mighty wings outspread
Dove-like sat'st brooding on the vast abyss
And mad'st it pregnant: what in me is dark

? **1–16.** *Paraphrase the first sentence of the epic. What will the subject of Milton's story be? (See lines 1–5.)*

4. one greater Man: Christ.
6. Heavenly Muse: Urania, muse of astronomy and sacred poetry. Milton hopes to be inspired by Urania, just as Moses was inspired to receive God's word for the Hebrews.
7. Oreb . . . Sinai: names for the mountain where Moses received God's inspiration.
8. shepherd: Moses. **chosen seed:** the Hebrews.
10. Sion hill: Zion, a hill near Jerusalem.
11. Siloa's brook: stream that flowed past the Temple, "the oracle of God," on Mount Zion.
15. Aonian mount: in Greek mythology, Mount Helicon, the home of the Muses.
17. Spirit: Holy Spirit; divine inspiration.

Ⓐ **Reading Focus** **Analyzing Milton's Style** How would you describe Milton's sentence structure in these opening lines?

Illumine, what is low raise and support;
That to the height of this great argument
25 I may assert Eternal Providence,
And justify the ways of God to men.
        Say first, for Heaven hides nothing from thy view,
Nor the deep tract of Hell, say first what cause
Moved our grand parents° in that happy state,
30 Favored of Heaven so highly, to fall off
From their Creator, and transgress his will
For one restraint,° lords of the world besides?°
Who first seduced them to that foul revolt?
The infernal Serpent;° he it was, whose guile,
35 Stirred up with envy and revenge, deceived
The mother of mankind, what time his pride
Had cast him out from Heaven, with all his host
Of rebel angels, by whose aid aspiring
To set himself in glory above his peers,°
40 He trusted to have equaled the Most High,
If he opposed; and with ambitious aim
Against the throne and monarchy of God,
Raised impious war in Heaven and battle proud
With vain attempt. Him the Almighty Power **B**
45 Hurled headlong flaming from the ethereal° sky
With hideous ruin and combustion down
To bottomless perdition,° there to dwell
In adamantine° chains and penal° fire,
Who durst° defy the Omnipotent to arms.
50 Nine times the space that measures day and night
To mortal men, he with his horrid crew
Lay vanquished, rolling in the fiery gulf,
Confounded though immortal. But his doom
Reserved him to more wrath; for now the thought
55 Both of lost happiness and lasting pain
Torments him; round he throws his baleful eyes,
That witnessed huge affliction and dismay
Mixed with obdurate° pride and steadfast hate.
At once as far as angels ken° he views
60 The dismal situation waste and wild:
A dungeon horrible on all sides round
As one great furnace flamed, yet from those flames

B **Reading Focus** **Analyzing Milton's Style** What is Milton describing in lines 37–44?

Vocabulary **transgress** (trans GREHS) *v.:* sin against; violate a limit.
infernal (ihn FUR nuhl) *adj.:* hellish; fiendish.

? **26.** *According to line 26, what is Milton's purpose? State this purpose in your own words.*

29. grand parents: Adam and Eve.

32. one restraint: the command not to eat of the fruit of the tree of knowledge. **besides:** in every other way.
34. Serpent: Milton is referring to Satan's final form.

39. peers: equals; the other archangels.

45. ethereal: heavenly.

47. perdition: damnation.
48. adamantine (ad uh MAN tihn): unbreakable. **penal:** punishing.
49. durst: dared.
52–56. Milton explains that the archangel Satan, jealous of God's power, has rebelled against the Almighty and thus been expelled from Heaven. The action of the poem begins at this point, *in medias res* ("in the middle of things"), the customary starting point of classical epics.
? *What most torments Satan in Hell?*
58. obdurate: stubborn; unrepentant.
59. ken: range of view.

The Great Day of His Wrath (1857), by John Martin.

Analyzing Visuals

Viewing and Interpreting How do contrasts between light and dark contribute to the emotional atmosphere surrounding Satan's expulsion from heaven?

No light, but rather darkness visible
Served only to discover sights of woe,
65 Regions of sorrow, doleful shades, where peace
And rest can never dwell, hope never comes
That comes to all; but torture without end
Still urges,° and a fiery deluge, fed
With ever-burning sulfur unconsumed:
70 Such place Eternal Justice had prepared
For those rebellious, here their prison ordained
In utter darkness, and their portion set
As far removed from God and light of Heaven
As from the center thrice to the utmost pole.° **C**
75 O how unlike the place from whence they fell!
There the companions of his fall, o'erwhelmed
With floods and whirlwinds of tempestuous fire,
He soon discerns, and weltering° by his side
One next himself in power, and next in crime,
80 Long after known in Palestine, and named

68. still urges: always afflicts.

74. center . . . pole: three times the distance from Earth, or "center," to the outermost point in the universe. In Milton's cosmos, Earth is the center of ten concentric spheres.
78. weltering: rolling about.

C **Literary Focus** **Style** Notice Milton's use of words with contrasting meanings in lines 61–74. What effect do these contrasts create?

Beelzebub.° To whom the Arch-Enemy,
And then in Heaven called Satan,° with bold words
Breaking the horrid silence thus began:
    "If thou beest he—but O how fallen! how changed
85 From him, who in the happy realms of light
Clothed with transcendent brightness didst outshine
Myriads though bright—if he whom mutual league,
United thoughts and counsels, equal hope
And hazard in the glorious enterprise,
90 Joined with me once, now misery hath joined
In equal ruin: into what pit thou seest
From what height fallen! so much the stronger proved
He with his thunder;° and till then who knew
The force of those dire arms? Yet not for those,
95 Nor what the potent Victor in his rage
Can else inflict, do I repent or change,
Though changed in outward luster, that fixed mind
And high disdain, from sense of injured merit, **D**
That with the Mightiest raised me to contend,
100 And to the fierce contention brought along
Innumerable force of spirits armed
That durst dislike his reign, and, me preferring,
His utmost power with adverse power opposed
In dubious battle on the plains of Heaven,
105 And shook his throne. What though the field be lost?
All is not lost; the unconquerable will,
And study° of revenge, immortal hate,
And courage never to submit or yield:
And what is else not to be overcome?
110 That glory never shall his wrath or might
Extort from me. To bow and sue for grace
With suppliant° knee, and deify his power
Who from the terror of this arm so late
Doubted° his empire, that were low indeed,
115 That were an ignominy and shame beneath
This downfall; since by fate the strength of gods
And this empyreal substance° cannot fail,
Since through experience of this great event,
In arms not worse, in foresight much advanced,
120 We may with more successful hope resolve
To wage by force or guile eternal war

D **Literary Focus** Style Lines 94–98 illustrate nonstandard syntax. The subject of the sentence occurs in the middle of the sentence (the *I* in line 96). Re-read these lines carefully; what does Satan say he will not do?

Vocabulary **contention** (kuhn TEHN shuhn) *n.:* struggle.

Irreconcilable to our grand Foe,
Who now triumphs, and in the excess of joy
Sole reigning holds the tyranny of Heaven."

125   So spake the apostate° Angel, though in pain,
Vaunting° aloud, but racked with deep despair;
And him thus answered soon his bold compeer:°
      "O Prince, O Chief of many thronèd Powers,
That led the embattled Seraphim° to war
130   Under thy conduct, and in dreadful deeds
Fearless, endangered Heaven's perpetual King,
And put to proof his high supremacy,
Whether upheld by strength, or chance, or fate;   **E**
Too well I see and rue the dire event,°
135   That with sad overthrow and foul defeat
Hath lost us Heaven, and all this mighty host
In horrible destruction laid thus low,
As far as gods and heavenly essences
Can perish: for the mind and spirit remains
140   Invincible, and vigor soon returns,
Though all our glory extinct, and happy state
Here swallowed up in endless misery.
But what if he our Conqueror (whom I now
Of force° believe almighty, since no less
145   Than such could have o'erpowered such force as ours)
Have left us this our spirit and strength entire
Strongly to suffer and support our pains,
That we may so suffice° his vengeful ire,
Or do him mightier service as his thralls°
150   By right of war, whate'er his business be,
Here in the heart of Hell to work in fire,
Or do his errands in the gloomy deep?
What can it then avail,° though yet we feel
Strength undiminished, or eternal being
155   To undergo eternal punishment?"
      Whereto with speedy words the Arch-Fiend replied:
"Fallen Cherub, to be weak is miserable,
Doing or suffering:° But of this be sure,
To do aught° good never will be our task,
160   But ever to do ill our sole delight,
As being the contrary to his high will
Whom we resist. If then his providence
Out of our evil seek to bring forth good,
Our labor must be to pervert that end,

125. apostate: guilty of abandoning one's beliefs. Satan is apostate.
126. vaunting: boasting.
127. compeer: companion; equal. Now Beelzebub speaks.
129. Seraphim: highest order of angels.

134. event: archaic word meaning "outcome."

? 143–145. *What does Beelzebub admit about God? How is his attitude different from Satan's?*

144. of force: of necessity.
148. suffice: archaic for "satisfy."
149. thralls: slaves.

153. avail: be of help or advantage.

? 156–168. *What does Satan vow? In what ways might this be considered the essence of evil?*

158. doing or suffering: whether active or passive.
159. aught: anything; whatever.

E Reading Focus Analyzing Milton's Style The formality of lines 128–133 adds to the exalted tone of Milton's style. What does Beelzebub reveal in these lines?

165 And out of good still° to find means of evil;
      Which oftimes may succeed, so as perhaps
      Shall grieve him, if I fail not, and disturb
      His inmost counsels from their destined aim.
      But see the angry Victor° hath recalled
170 His ministers of vengeance and pursuit
      Back to the gates of Heaven; the sulfurous hail
      Shot after us in storm, o'erblown hath laid
      The fiery surge, that from the precipice
      Of Heaven received us falling, and the thunder,
175 Winged with red lightning and impetuous rage,
      Perhaps hath spent his shafts, and ceases now
      To bellow through the vast and boundless deep.
      Let us not slip° the occasion, whether scorn
      Or satiate° fury yield it from our Foe.
180 Seest thou yon dreary plain, forlorn and wild,
      The seat of desolation, void of light,
      Save what the glimmering of these livid flames
      Casts pale and dreadful? Thither let us tend
      From off the tossing of these fiery waves,
185 There rest, if any rest can harbor there,

165. still: always.

169. angry Victor: God.

178. slip: lose.
179. satiate: satisfied

> **Vocabulary impetuous** (ihm PEHCH u uhs) *adj.*: forceful; violent.
> **desolation** (dehs uh LAY shuhn) *n.*: utter misery; extreme loneliness.

ART LINK

Depicting the fall of the rebel angels. Illustration by Gustav Doré to John Milton's Paradise Lost.

Illustrations of *Paradise Lost*

The rich imagery of Milton's epic has tempted many artists, some of whom are also considered visionaries. English poet William Blake (1757–1827) responded to Milton's writing in 12 intense watercolor illustrations that reflect his own mystical ideas and mercurial passions. French artist Gustave Doré (1832–1883) presented a very different vision of Milton's world in 40 highly detailed engravings that gave the poem's religious figures a more solid presence in the observable world. Twentieth-century philosopher and painter Terrance Lindall (1944–   ) created a series of surrealist illustrations that included such startling images as lizard-like demons, floating eyes, and a magical woman with snakes for legs.

Ask Yourself
What attracts artists to Milton's poem? What kind of artwork inspired by Milton's visions and themes might you create?

And reassembling our afflicted powers,
Consult how we may henceforth most offend
Our Enemy, our own loss how repair,
How overcome this dire calamity,
190 What reinforcement we may gain from hope,
If not, what resolution from despair."
　　　Thus Satan talking to his nearest mate
With head uplift above the wave, and eyes
That sparkling blazed; his other parts besides,
195 Prone on the flood, extended long and large,
Lay floating many a rood,° in bulk as huge
As whom the fables name of monstrous size,
Titanian or Earth-born, that warred on Jove,
Briareos or Typhon,° whom the den
200 By ancient Tarsus held, or that sea-beast
Leviathan,° which God of all his works
Created hugest that swim the ocean stream:
Him haply slumbering on the Norway foam,
The pilot of some small night-foundered° skiff,
205 Deeming some island, oft, as seamen tell,
With fixèd anchor in his scaly rind
Moors by his side under the lee, while night
Invests° the sea, and wishèd morn delays:
So stretched out huge in length the Arch-Fiend lay
210 Chained on the burning lake; nor ever thence **F**
Had risen or heaved his head, but that the will
And high permission of all-ruling Heaven
Left him at large to his own dark designs,
That with reiterated crimes he might
215 Heap on himself damnation, while he sought
Evil to others, and enraged might see
How all his malice served but to bring forth
Infinite goodness, grace, and mercy shown
On man by him seduced, but on himself
220 Treble confusion, wrath, and vengeance poured.
　　　Forthwith upright he rears from off the pool
His mighty stature; on each hand the flames
Driven backward slope their pointing spires, and rolled
In billows, leave in the midst a horrid vale. **G**
225 Then with expanded wings he steers his flight
Aloft, incumbent° on the dusky air

196. rood: old unit of measure varying locally from about six to eight yards.

198–199. Titanian . . . Typhon: In an epic simile, Milton compares Satan to the Titans and giants of Greek mythology. Briareos, a hundred-handed giant, helped Zeus (Jove) battle the Titans. Typhon, a hundred-headed serpent-monster from Cilicia (near Tarsus), attacked heaven and was imprisoned by Zeus.

201. Leviathan: biblical sea monster, either a reptile or a whale.

204. night-foundered: overtaken by night.

208. invests: covers.

214–220. Milton reminds his readers that Satan remains at the mercy of God and that God plans to use Satan's evil to bring good into the world.

? *Why has God left Satan "to his own dark designs"? Paraphrase what Milton says in lines 214–220.*

226. incumbent: lying.

F **Literary Focus** **Style** In lines 192–210, Milton employs epic similes to describe Satan lying on the lake of fire. To what is Satan being compared and what do the comparisons suggest about Satan?

G **Reading Focus** **Analyzing Milton's Style** In lines 221–238, Milton uses vivid language to depict Satan. What impression do the comparisons create?

That felt unusual weight, till on dry land
He lights, if it were land that ever burned
With solid, as the lake with liquid fire;
230 And such appeared in hue, as when the force
Of subterranean wind transports a hill
Torn from Pelorus,° or the shattered side
Of thundering Etna,° whose combustible
And fueled entrails thence conceiving fire,
235 Sublimed° with mineral fury, aid the winds,
And leave a singèd bottom all involved°
With stench and smoke: such resting found the sole
Of unblest feet. Him followed his next mate,
Both glorying to have scaped the Stygian° flood
240 As gods, and by their own recovered strength,
Not by the sufferance° of supernal° power.
      "Is this the region, this the soil, the clime,"
Said then the lost Archangel, "this the seat
That we must change for Heaven, this mournful gloom
245 For that celestial light? Be it so, since he
Who now is sovereign can dispose and bid
What shall be right: farthest from him is best,
Whom reason hath equaled, force hath made supreme
Above his equals. Farewell, happy fields,
250 Where joy forever dwells! Hail, horrors! hail,
Infernal world! and thou, profoundest° Hell,
Receive thy new possessor; one who brings
A mind not to be changed by place or time.
The mind is its own place, and in itself
255 Can make a Heaven of Hell, a Hell of Heaven. **Ⓗ**
What matter where, if I be still the same,
And what I should be, all but less than he
Whom thunder hath made greater? Here at least
We shall be free; the Almighty hath not built
260 Here for his envy, will not drive us hence:
Here we may reign secure, and in my choice
To reign is worth ambition, though in Hell:
Better to reign in Hell than serve in Heaven.
But wherefore let we then our faithful friends,
265 The associates and copartners of our loss,
Lie thus astonished° on the oblivious° pool,
And call them not to share with us their part
In this unhappy mansion, or once more
With rallied arms to try what may be yet
270 Regained in Heaven, or what more lost in Hell?"

Ⓗ **Reading Focus** Analyzing Milton's Style Paraphrase lines 254–255. How does
Milton's style make these lines memorable?

232. **Pelorus:** headland in Sicily, Italy; now called Cape Faro.
233. **Etna:** volcano in Sicily, Italy.
235. **sublimed:** vaporized.
236. **involved:** enveloped.

239. **Stygian** (STIHJ ee uhn): of or like the river Styx; infernal, hellish. In Greek mythology, the river Styx encircles the underworld.
241. **sufferance:** permission.
supernal: heavenly.

251. **profoundest:** lowest; deepest.

266. **astonished:** dazed.
oblivious: causing forgetfulness.

Applying Your Skills

SKILLS FOCUS Literary Skills Analyze style; analyze irony. Reading Skills Analyze an author's style. Writing Skills Employ literary devices for effective writing.

The Fall of Satan *from* Paradise Lost

Respond and Think Critically

Reading Focus

Quick Check

1. In the poem's opening, what does the speaker ask of the Heavenly Muse? Why?

2. With whom does Satan discuss his plans?

3. Near the end of the excerpt, what shows that Satan has fully accepted living in Hell?

Read with a Purpose

4. In what ways might Satan be seen as heroic?

Reading Skills: Analyzing Milton's Style

5. As you read, you analyzed some of the poem's challenging lines. Review these lines and your restatement of what Milton is saying. Add another column to your chart, and analyze the elements of style in the lines you paraphrased.

Difficult Lines	Paraphrase	Analysis of Style.
(44–47) Him the Almighty Power Hurled headlong flaming from the ethereal sky With hideous ruin and combustion down To bottomless perdition	Almighty God (subject) threw (verb) Satan, head-first from Heaven (ethereal sky) in a streak of flames and debris, to a bottomless pit of suffering (perdition).	Inversion: sentence begins with Him (object) followed by Almighty Power (subject). Grand diction: ethereal, perdition. Alliteration: hurled headlong, hideous. Vivid visual imagery: headlong flaming; bottomless perdition.

Literary Focus

Literary Analysis

6. **Interpret** Re-read the description of Hell in lines 53–74. How is Hell both a psychological state and a physical place?

7. **Analyze** A famous phrase in this poem is the description of Hell in line 63 as "darkness visible." This phrase is an **oxymoron**, a figure of speech that relies on **paradox**, or a self-contradictory idea. Why is this an effective image?

8. **Evaluate** How effective is Milton in creating a setting that is terrifying and an embodiment of evil? Explain your answer using textual details.

Literary Skills: Style

9. **Interpret** How does Milton create the elevated, epic style that gives *Paradise Lost* its power?

Literary Skills Review: Dramatic Irony

10. **Draw Conclusions** When the reader knows something that a character does not, **dramatic irony** is occurring. In lines 210–220 the speaker says that despite Satan's power and grandeur, the devil is still subject to God's purposes. How do these lines contribute to the dramatic irony in Satan's assertion of freedom in lines 242–270?

Writing Focus

Think as a Reader/Writer

Use It in Your Writing Milton's epic similes of Satan and Hell add depth to the poem through their wealth of details. Write an epic simile of your own, describing the larger-than-life nature of something that would not normally be seen in an extraordinary way.

What Do You Think Now

Is Milton's Satan influenced more by his heart or his mind? What governs his actions?

The Fall of Satan *from* Paradise Lost

Vocabulary Development

✔ Vocabulary Check

Choose the Vocabulary word that best completes each sentence.

a. transgress   **c.** contention   **e.** desolation

b. infernal   **d.** impetuous

1. They were the best two teams in the league, so everyone assumed they would be in _____ for the championship.

2. As all of his companions started slowly disappearing, _____ began to set in.

3. The rushing, _____ waters tore through the canyon.

4. His commander had drawn the line and to _____ it would be a serious mistake.

5. They all felt as though they might melt under the blistering heat of that _____ summer.

Vocabulary Skills: Etymologies

Exploring **etymologies,** or word origins, can give you a deeper understanding of how a word is used in a text. Particularly in a complex work like *Paradise Lost,* researching the etymologies of words can give you greater understanding of a text's meaning.

Let's see how this works. In line 81, Milton introduces Beelzebub. The name Beelzebub comes from Hebrew words meaning "god of flies." Literally, he is the "lord of filth." The word is also connected to *baal,* a false god or idol. Knowing this etymology gives the reader a deeper understanding of Milton's purpose.

Your Turn

Use a dictionary to explore the etymologies of the Vocabulary words. Use a chart like this one to list each Vocabulary word, its origin, and the relationship of the word's current meaning to its etymology.

Word	Etymology	Relationship between word and etymology
transgress		

Language Coach

Multiple Meanings Words often have more than one meaning. Notice how the word is used in a sentence to decide which meaning is intended. In the sentences that follow, choose the correct meaning of the word:

impetuous a. *(adj.)* forceful; violent; b. *(adj.)* acting rashly, without considering the consequences

contention c. *(n.)* struggle; d. *(n.)* opinion as made as part of an argument

1. The heated discussion led to *contention* among the angels.

2. Do you think Satan made an *impetuous* decision without thinking about its impact?

3. The *impetuous* enemies fought in a sweeping battle.

4. It is Satan's *contention* that he will never surrender.

Academic Vocabulary

Write About

The depiction of Satan in *Paradise Lost* is <u>controversial</u> because certain virtues he possesses suggest that Milton seeks to <u>establish</u> him as the epic's hero. Write a short paragraph examining the <u>contradiction</u> that occurs when an "evil" character like Satan becomes admirable to the reader. Consider how Milton <u>ensures</u> that readers objectively consider Satan's point of view.

Vocabulary Skills: Scientific and Mathematical Words Derived from Greek and Latin

Many of the scientific and mathematical terms that we use today are derived from ancient Greek and Latin, the classical languages that were rediscovered during the Renaissance. Developing a knowledge of Greek and Latin roots and affixes can help you understand complex scientific and mathematical words.

Words are built on a base, or **root,** which contains the core of the word's meaning. The root *bio,* for instance, comes from a Greek word meaning "life." The words *biorhythm, biome,* and *biodegradable* contain this root. These words also contain **affixes**—word parts added to the beginning (prefixes) or end (suffixes) of a root to modify its meaning. For instance, by adding the **suffix** *–logy,* meaning "study of," to the root *bio,* the word biology—"the study of life"—is formed. The **prefix** *micro* added to *biology* creates the word *microbiology,* "the study of very small [*microscopic*] life-forms."

Study these charts to learn some Greek and Latin word parts common to scientific and mathematical terms.

Greek and Latin Roots	Meaning	Examples
anthro– / andro–	human	anthropology; android
geo–	earth	geography; geology
hydr–, hydro–	water	hydrogen; hydration
iso–	alike; equal	isosceles; isometric
patho–	disease	pathology
psyche–	mind	psychology

Greek and Latin Affixes	Meaning	Examples
anti–	against	antibiotic; antidote
–gen–	something that produces or is produced	generate; oxygen; hydrogen
hemi–	half	hemisphere
hypo–	under; below	hypodermic
meta–	change; over	metamorphosis
–osis	state; condition	mitosis; symbiosis
sub–	under	subtract

Your Turn

The words below are scientific terms that have Greek or Latin origins. Using these charts and your own word knowledge, guess at each word's meaning. Identify which word parts helped you to guess the word's meaning. Then, look up the words in a dictionary and check your guesses. If your guess is incorrect, explain how the actual definition differs from yours.

1. anthropomorphic
2. aerobiology
3. pathogen
4. psychopathology
5. metamorphosis
6. suborbital

Applying Your Skills

SKILLS FOCUS Reading Skills Recognize and discuss themes and connections that cross cultures. **Writing Skills** Plan writing by creating an outline; develop descriptions with sensory details.

Grammar Skills Understand adjective and adverb clauses; understand and analyze subordinate clauses; use subordinate adjective and adverb clauses.

Grammar Link

Adjective Clauses and Adverb Clauses

To combine choppy sentences use adjective and adverb clauses. An **adjective clause** is a subordinate clause that modifies a noun or pronoun. It usually begins with a **relative pronoun**—*who, whom, whose, which,* or *that*—or a **relative adverb**—*where or when.*

An **adverb clause** is a subordinate clause that modifies a verb, an adjective, or an adverb. It tells how, when, where, why, to what extent, or under what condition. An adverb clause begins with a **subordinating conjunction:** *after, although, because, if, since, when.*

In the example below, four choppy sentences are combined into one longer sentence by using both an adjective and an adverb clause.

Without subordinate clauses
The captain gave the signal. This started the soldiers running. They ran to the cave. It was dark and wet inside.

adverb clause
When the captain gave the signal, the soldiers ran to the
adjective clause
cave, which was dark and wet inside.

In the sentence above, the adjective and adverb clauses add information about the soldiers.

Your Turn

Rewrite the following paragraph by combining the ideas through the use of adjective and adverb clauses. Try to vary sentence structure and avoid repetition.

First the rocks were moved aside. Then men tried pushing the truck. The truck was heavier than they thought. Jim gathered the men. They were exhausted. He pulled out a watch. He had been carrying the watch in his pocket. The darkness would begin. It would begin when it got late.

Writing Application Choose a paragraph you previously wrote, and, whenever possible, condense the shorter sentences using adjective and adverb clauses.

CHOICES

As you respond to the Choices, use these **Academic Vocabulary** words as appropriate: establish, ensure, widespread, controversy, contradiction.

REVIEW
Plot for Inspiration
In *Paradise Lost,* Satan refuses to accept his defeat and uses it to fuel his desire for revenge. Although Satan is motivated by evil, in real life people often use setbacks as positive inspiration. Think of a story that follows this pattern, and outline the plot of an epic based on the story. In your outline, divide the epic into three sections. In the first, include details of the person's defeat or setback; in the second, include the person's reaction to the setback; in the third, include what the person is inspired to do.

CONNECT
Explore the Cosmos
TechFocus Three of the most famous astronomers of all time—Copernicus, Gallileo, and Newton—lived during the Renaissance. Conduct research to learn what widespread advances they made in the field of astronomy. Then, design a Web page providing facts and images showing how people perceived the universe at the time Milton wrote *Paradise Lost.*

EXTEND
Describe the View from the Middle *Paradise Lost* begins its narrative *in media res,* or in the middle of the action. Review the passage beginning at line 53, when Satan just has just been cast into Hell. Beginning to read at this point feels like walking into the room in the middle of an argument—you meet the characters in a moment of high emotion. Recall a time when you stepped into the middle of an intense discussion or a strange circumstance. Describe the scene from your point of view and explain how you think entering in the middle affected your perception of the people involved.

Preparing To Read

When I consider how my light is spent

Reader/Writer Notebook

Use your **RWN** to complete the activities for this selection.

Literary Focus

Allusion An **allusion** is a reference to a statement, person, place, event, or thing from literature, history, religion, mythology, politics, or popular culture. Literary works frequently allude to past literary classics: Hemingway's novel *For Whom the Bell Tolls* takes its title from a poem by John Donne. In ordinary conversation, allusions frequently take the form of **eponyms,** whereby the name of a famous person known for a particular attribute is substituted for that attribute. For example, we may call an intelligent person an Einstein or a good baseball player a Babe Ruth.

> ### Language Coach
> **Word Origins** Some words develop their meanings because they sound like what they describe. The word *murmur* means "something spoken very softly or unclearly." When you say the word aloud, you can hear that the word itself can sound soft and unclear. Explain how the sound of the these words relates to their meanings: *mumble, rattle, gobble, chitchat.*

Reading Focus

Analyzing Author's Purpose Milton felt that his role as a poet was a divine calling. In the sonnet on his blindness, he struggles to understand and accept his condition as part of God's plan. Notice how the structure of his sonnet conforms to his purpose of serving God. In the first part of the sonnet, he asks a question. In the last six lines, he receives his answer.

Into Action As you read, use a chart to state the problem that Milton tries to resolve. Then, fill in the answer that comes after the turn in line 8.

Problem	Resolution
The speaker doesn't know how he can serve God because he is blind. He fears that he will be unable to use his one talent, writing. How can he continue to serve God if light (sight) is denied?	

Writing Focus

Think as a Reader/Writer

Find It in Your Reading Recognizing allusions as you read can help broaden your understanding of a text. In your *Reader/Writer Notebook,* note any allusions that you encounter as you read the poem.

Learn It Online
Listen to this sonnet read aloud online.

go.hrw.com   L12-363   **Go**

When I consider how my light is spent

by **John Milton**

Read with a Purpose
Read to discover how the speaker faces a turning point in his life.

Build Background
"When I consider how my light is spent," sometimes titled "On His Blindness," dramatizes the loss of sight Milton experienced in middle age. Long before he accomplished his life's work, Milton was almost completely blind. Deeply religious and believing firmly in man's accountability to God, Milton asks in the first part of the sonnet, "How can I continue to do the work that God expects of me?" He proposes an answer in the remainder of the sonnet.

When I consider how my light is spent
   Ere° half my days in this dark world and wide,
   And that one talent° which is death to hide **Ⓐ**
   Lodged with me useless, though my soul more bent
5 To serve therewith my Maker, and present
   My true account, lest He returning chide,
   "Doth God exact day-labor, light denied?"
   I fondly° ask. But Patience, to prevent
That murmur, soon replies, "God doth not need
10   Either man's work or His own gifts. Who best
   Bear His mild yoke, they serve Him best. His state **Ⓑ**
Is kingly: Thousands° at His bidding speed,
   And post o'er land and ocean without rest;
   They also serve who only stand and wait."

2. ere: before.
3. talent: reference to the parable of the talents (Matthew 25:14–30), in which a servant is scolded for burying his one talent, or coin, in the earth instead of putting it to good use.
8. fondly: foolishly.
12. thousands: of angels.

Ⓐ **Literary Focus** **Allusion** Milton uses Biblical allusions throughout his work. How does his use of allusion help to reveal his purpose?

Ⓑ **Reading Focus** **Analyzing Author's Purpose** Milton's phrase "mild yoke" refers to the burdens that a person must bear in life. Why might he refer to his blindness as a merely a "mild yoke" here, rather than as something more difficult to handle?

John Milton Composing Poetry, by Leon Botarel.

When I consider how my light is spent

Respond and Think Critically

Reading Focus

Quick Check

1. What frustration or disappointment does Milton express in the poem's first two lines?

2. What famous religious parable does Milton allude to in the first part of the sonnet?

3. By the end of the poem, how has Milton decided to respond to his worries?

Read with a Purpose

4. The tone of the poem changes about half-way through, around line 8. How does Milton's attitude in the second half compare with his attitude in the first half?

Reading Skills: Analyzing Author's Purpose

5. While you read, you analyzed the structure of Milton's poem. Now, return to your chart and add another column explaining how the sonnet's structure suits Milton's purpose.

Problem	Resolution	Milton's Purpose
The speaker doesn't know how he can serve God because he is blind. He fears that he will be unable to use his one talent, writing. How can he continue to serve God if light (sight) is denied?	He realizes that God does not need man's work. He can best serve God by bearing his burdens with patience and maintaining his faith.	

Literary Focus

Literary Analysis

6. **Analyze** In line 8, what do you think Milton means when he says that "Patience" replies to his question?

7. **Make Judgments** In the opening line, how does Milton's metaphor give us insight into how he perceives his blindness?

8. **Evaluate** In fourteen lines, Milton experiences a significant change in his point of view. Do you think this change is convincing or do you suspect that Milton still has doubts? Explain your opinion and support it with evidence from the text.

Literary Skills: Allusion

9. **Infer** Early in the sonnet, Milton alludes to a Biblical parable. How does this reference explain Milton's anxiety in the first half of the poem?

Literary Skills Review: Rhyme Scheme

10. **Evaluate** The pattern of rhymed lines in a poem is called its **rhyme scheme.** How does the rhyme scheme of Milton's sonnet reinforce his ideas?

Writing Focus

Use It in Your Writing Allusions range from direct quotations to minor hints to characters or events in another literary work. In your *Reader/Writer Notebook*, write a paragraph about a problem or event in your life and include at least two literary allusions.

What Do **You Think Now** In this sonnet, is Milton more influenced by his heart or his mind? Explain.

Preparing to Read

from The Pilgrim's Progress

What Do You Think? How do our hearts and minds influence our actions?

 **QuickTalk**

Think about a time when you stood up for something in which you believed. What did you learn about yourself as a result? In a small group, discuss how other people's rules (fair or unfair) have helped you determine what is important to you. Record your thoughts in your *Reader/Writer Notebook*.

John Bunyan, The Pilgrim's Progress (1683).
Rare book and special collection library, Sidney University.

John Bunyan
(1628–1688)

John Bunyan came from humble beginnings, originally working as a tinker, a maker and mender of pots and pans. Despite being impoverished and poorly educated, he wrote a book that for many years was second only to the Bible as the most widely read book among English readers: *The Pilgrim's Progress from This World to That Which Is to Come* (1678), commonly called *The Pilgrim's Progress*. Over time it has become <u>established</u> as one of the best-known allegories in English.

Unyielding Faith

As a young soldier in the Parliamentary army during the English Civil Wars, Bunyan met many Christians who questioned the authority of the Anglican Church. Anglicans called them Nonconformists or Dissenters. After an intense spiritual struggle, Bunyan joined a Nonconformist Puritan sect and began preaching for a Baptist congregation. Because England had no monarch during this time (1649–1660), Puritan religious sects like the Baptists flourished. When the monarchy was restored, however, so were laws against Dissenters.

Amidst much <u>controversy</u>, Bunyan defied these laws. In 1660, he was arrested for preaching without a license and imprisoned for twelve years. While in prison, Bunyan wrote about his inner life in *Grace Abounding to the Chief of Sinners* (1666). He recorded how God's grace had transformed him from an obscure, sinful man to a preacher. During his second confinement in 1677, he finished *The Pilgrim's Progress*, which traced the life journey of Christian, an allegorical character. The story's popularity led Bunyan to publish a sequel that depicts Christian's wife and children. Several phrases in our language originated in Bunyan's allegory, including "Vanity Fair," "the house beautiful," and "the slough of despond."

Released from prison again after the laws against Dissenters were relaxed, Bunyan returned to preaching, attracting thousands of listeners. King Charles II himself expressed astonishment that a tinker could draw such crowds.

Think About the Writer How do you think Bunyan's time in prison shaped his faith?

Reader/Writer
Notebook
Use your **RWN** to complete the activities for this selection.

Literary Focus

Allegory An **allegory** is a story in which the characters, settings, and events stand for abstract or moral concepts. An allegory can be read on one level for its literal meaning and on a second level for its symbolic meaning. One of the best-known allegories in the English language is Bunyan's *The Pilgrim's Progress*. It recounts the journey of a character named Christian as he travels through an earthly world toward the spiritual world. The dual levels of storytelling are reflected in the names of the people, places, and events in the story.

Reading Focus

Making Generalizations About a Writer's Beliefs A **generalization** is a statement that can be supported by different kinds of evidence. The episode of Vanity Fair depicts a town fair on market day. What beliefs can you infer from the narrator's attitude toward the merchandise, diversions, and people at Vanity Fair? Use this evidence to draw generalizations about the writer's beliefs.

Into Action As you read, use a chart like the one below to note the many examples of vanity in this allegory. What kinds of things, people, or behaviors does Bunyan's dreaming narrator consider to be vain?

Types of Things	Types of People	Types of Actions
houses	jugglers	theft

Writing Focus

Think as a Reader/Writer

Find It in Your Reading The jury described by Bunyan's narrator represents a long list of vices. As you read, notice the qualities and behaviors attributed to the members of the jury. In your *Reader/Writer Notebook*, list the vices represented by the jury and note their negative characteristics as described or suggested by the narrator.

TechFocus Use a computer drawing program to create illustrations that represent three of the characters in *The Pilgrim's Progress*. Compare your illustrations with those of your classmates. Discuss how visual clues can help clarify the representations Bunyan is making in his allegory.

Vocabulary

reproachfully (rih PROHCH fuhl ee) *adv.:* accusingly. *The crowd yelled reproachfully at the two travelers.*

confounded (kahn FOWN dihd) *v.* used as *adj.:* confused. *The citizens of Vanity were confounded by Christian and Faithful's behavior.*

malice (MAL ihs) *n.:* active ill will; spite. *The townspeople acted with malice toward Christian and Faithful.*

implacable (ihm PLAK uh buhl) *adj.:* unyielding. *Faithful faced an implacable man on the jury.*

respite (REHS piht) *n.:* postponement; reprieve. *Christian was granted a respite when he was sent to prison instead of being killed.*

Language Coach

Prefixes The prefix *im–*, meaning "not," is often attached to words that begin with *p*. *Implacable* is a common English word that means "impossible to please." *Placable* was once a common word that meant "easily pleased" but today is rarely used. What new words can you form by adding the *im–* prefix to these words: *passive, partial, personal, possibility?*

Learn It Online
Advance your vocabulary with Word Watch.

go.hrw.com | L12-367 | **Go**

from The Pilgrim's Progress

by **John Bunyan**

Read with a Purpose
Read to discover how one man's journey can reflect humanity's salvation.

Build Background
Bunyan's narrator in *The Pilgrim's Progress* recounts a dream in which a man named Christian travels from the City of Destruction to the Celestial City. At this point in the story, Christian and his companion, Faithful, enter a town called Vanity in which the local fair, or outdoor market, is in full swing. In Bunyan's day, merchants from all over Europe would sell goods at such fairs, where the buying and selling would be accompanied by eating, drinking, and general merriment. Bunyan had little formal education but studied the Bible on his own, and, accordingly, his writing style reflects the King James Version of the Bible.

Then I saw in my dream that when they were got out of the wilderness they presently saw a town before them, and the name of that town is Vanity; and at the town there is a fair kept called Vanity-Fair. It is kept all the year long; it beareth the name of Vanity-Fair, because the town where 'tis kept is lighter than vanity; and also, because all that is there sold, or that cometh thither, is Vanity. As is the saying of the wise, *All that cometh is vanity.*

This Fair is no new erected business, but a thing of ancient standing; I will show you the original of it. **A**

Almost five thousand years agone, there were pilgrims walking to the Celestial City, as these two honest persons are; and Beelzebub, Apollyon, and Legion,[1] with their companions, perceiving by the path that the Pilgrims made that their way to the City lay through this town of Vanity, they contrived here to set up a fair; a fair wherein should be sold of all sorts of vanity, and that it should last all the year long. Therefore at this Fair are all such merchandise sold, as houses, lands, trades, places, honours, preferments,[2] titles, countries, kingdoms, lusts, pleasures, and delights of all sorts, as whores, bawds, wives, husbands, children, masters, servants, lives, blood, bodies, souls, silver, gold, pearls, precious stones, and what not.

And moreover, at this Fair there is at all times to be seen jugglings, cheats, games, plays, fools, apes, knaves, and rogues, and that of all sorts.

Here are to be seen too, and that for nothing, thefts, murders, adulteries, false-swearers, and that of a blood-red colour.

And as in other fairs of less moment there are the several rows and streets under their proper names, where such and such wares are vended: so here likewise, you have the proper places, rows, streets (*viz.*[3] countries and kingdoms), where the wares of this Fair are soonest to be found: here is the Britain Row, the French Row, the Italian Row, the Spanish Row, the German Row, where several sorts of vanities are to be

---

1. **Beelzebub:** Satan. **Apollyon:** the angel of the bottomless pit in the book of Revelation. **Legion:** unclean spirits or devils.

2. **preferments:** appointments to political or religious positions.
3. **viz.:** namely.

A Literary Focus **Allegory** What does this paragraph say about the relationship of people to vanity?

Viewing and Interpreting Note how circular shapes give a sense of motion to the map of the pathway to Jerusalem. What does the orientation of the picture's features say about the significance of Vanity Fair?

Plan of the road from the City of Destruction to the Celestial City (19th century), engraved for William's elegant edition of *The Pilgrim's Progress*.

sold. But as in other fairs, some one commodity is as the chief of all the fair, so the ware of Rome and her merchandise is greatly promoted in this Fair: only our English nation, with some others, have taken a dislike thereat.[4]

Now, as I said, the way to the Celestial City lies just through this town, where this lusty Fair is kept; and he that will go to the City, and yet not go through this town, must needs go out of the world. The Prince of Princes himself, when here, went through this

Town[5] to his own country, and that upon a fair-day too. Yea, and as I think it was Beelzebub, the chief lord of this Fair, that invited him to buy of his vanities; yea, would have made him lord of the Fair, would he but have done him reverence as he went through the town. Yea, because he was such a person of honour, Beelzebub had him from street to street, and showed him all the kingdoms of the world in a little time, that he might if possible allure that Blessed One, to cheapen[6] and buy some of his vanities. But he had no

---

4. **the ware of Rome ...a dislike thereat:** reference to the Church of Rome, and the Church of England's separation from it. Rome is the center of the Catholic Church's hierarchy.

5. **The Prince of Princes . . . :** reference to the temptation of Christ (Matthew 4:11–11).
6. **cheapen:** ask the price of.

mind to the merchandise, and therefore left the town without laying out so much as one farthing upon these vanities. This Fair therefore is an ancient thing, of long standing, and a very great Fair. **(B)**

Now these pilgrims, as I said, must needs go through this Fair: well, so they did; but behold, even as they entered into the Fair, all the people in the Fair were moved, and the town itself as it were in a hubbub about them; and that for several reasons: for,

First, the pilgrims were clothed with such kind of raiment as was diverse from the raiment of any that traded in that Fair. The people therefore of the Fair made a great gazing upon them: Some said they were fools, some they were bedlams,[7] and some 'They are outlandish-men.'[8]

Secondly, and as they wondered at their apparel so they did likewise at their speech; for few could understand what they said; they naturally spoke the language of Canaan;[9] but they that kept the Fair, were the men of this world: so that from one end of the Fair to the other, they seemed barbarians each to the other.

Thirdly, but that which did not a little amuse the merchandisers was that these pilgrims set very light by all their wares, they cared not so much as to look upon them; and if they called upon them to buy, they would put their fingers in their ears, and cry, *Turn away mine eyes from beholding vanity;* and look upwards, signifying that their trade and traffic was in Heaven.

One chanced mockingly, beholding the carriages of the men, to say unto them, 'What will ye buy?' but they, looking gravely upon him, said, 'We buy the truth.' At that there was an occasion taken to despise the men the more; some mocking, some taunting, some speaking reproachfully, and some calling upon others to smite them. At last things came to a hub-

---

7. **bedlams:** mental patients from Bethlehem Hospital, the notorious hospital for the insane in London.
8. **outlandish-men:** foreigners.
9. **Canaan:** Promised Land. The "language of Canaan" is the language of the Bible.

bub and great stir in the Fair; insomuch that all order was confounded. Now was word presently brought to the great one of the Fair, who quickly came down and deputed some of his most trusty friends to take these men into examination about whom the Fair was almost overturned. . . .

The townspeople at Vanity Fair are immediately suspicious of Christian and Faithful, and they arrest the two pilgrims and bring them to trial. Three witnesses, Envy, Superstition, and Pick-thank, a favor-seeker, testify against Faithful. His fate is turned over to a jury of townspeople.

Then went the jury out, whose names were Mr. Blind-man, Mr. No-good, Mr. Malice, Mr. Love-lust, Mr. Live-loose, Mr. Heady, Mr. High-mind, Mr. Enmity, Mr. Liar, Mr. Cruelty, Mr. Hate-light, and Mr. Implacable, who every one gave in his private verdict against him among themselves, and afterwards unanimously concluded to bring him in guilty before the Judge. And first Mr. Blind-man, the foreman, said, "I see clearly that this man is an heretic." **(C)**

Then said Mr. No-good, "Away with such a fellow from the earth." "Ay," said Mr. Malice, "for I hate the very looks of him." Then said Mr. Love-lust, "I could never endure him." "Nor I," said Mr. Live-loose, "for he would always be condemning my way." "Hang him, hang him," said Mr. Heady. "A sorry scrub," said Mr. High-mind. "My heart riseth against him," said Mr. Enmity. "He is a rogue," said Mr. Liar. "Hanging is too good for him," said Mr. Cruelty. "Let's dispatch him out of the way," said Mr. Hate-light. Then said Mr. Implacable, "Might I have all the world given me, I could not be reconciled to him, therefore let us forthwith bring him in guilty of death." And so they did, therefore he was presently condemned to be had from the place where he was, to the place from whence he came, and there to be put to the most cruel death that could be invented.

(B) Reading Focus **Making Generalizations About a Writer's Beliefs** What fundamental beliefs of Bunyan's can you infer from his attitude toward "vanity," "merchandise," and "all the kingdoms of the world"?

(C) Literary Focus **Allegory** Why is Mr. Blind-man's name allegorical? Why is his statement ironic?

Vocabulary **reproachfully** (rih PROHCH fuhl ee) *adv.:* accusingly.
confounded (kahn FOWN dihd) *v.* used as *adj.:* confused.
malice (MAL ihs) *n.:* active ill will; spite.
implacable (ihm PLAK uh buhl) *adj.:* unyieldiing.

They therefore brought him out to do with him according to their law; and first they scourged him, then they buffeted him, then they lanced his flesh with knives; after that they stoned him with stones, then pricked him with their swords; and last of all they burned him to ashes at the stake. Thus came Faithful to his end. **(D)**

Now, I saw that there stood behind the multitude a chariot and a couple of horses, waiting for Faithful, who (so soon as his adversaries had dispatched him) was taken up into it, and straightway was carried up through the clouds, with sound of trumpet, the nearest way to the Celestial Gate. But as for Christian, he had some respite, and was remanded back to prison; so he there remained for a space: but he that over-rules all things, having the power of their rage in his own hand, so wrought it about that Christian for that time escaped them, and went his way. . . .

Christian continues on his journey and finds another companion, the convert Hopeful. After more trials and tests of faith, the two reach their long-awaited destination: the Gates of the Celestial City.

Now I saw in my dream, that these two men went in at the Gate; and lo, as they entered they were transfigured, and they had raiment put on that shone like gold. There was also that met them with harps and crowns, and gave them to them, the harp to praise withal, and the crowns in token of honour. Then I heard in my dream, that all the bells in the City rang again for joy; and that it was said unto them, *"Enter ye into the joy of your Lord."* I also heard the men themselves, that they sang with a loud voice, saying, *"Blessing, honour, glory, and power, be to him that sitteth upon the throne, and to the Lamb for ever and ever."*

Now just as the Gates were opened to let in the men, I looked in after them; and behold, the City shone like the sun, the streets also were paved with gold, and in them walked many men with crowns on their heads, palms in their hands, and golden harps to sing praises withal.

(D) Reading Focus **Making Generalizations about a Writer's Beliefs** What is Bunyan suggesting by providing these details of Faithful's death? What do we learn about Bunyan's own views from these details?

Vocabulary **respite** (REHS piht) *n.:* postponement; reprieve.

Romola Garay and Jonathan Rhys-Meyers in Vanity Fair *(2004).*

Vanity Fair

John Bunyan painted an image of Vanity Fair so powerful that the term *Vanity Fair* earned a place in the dictionary, where it is defined as "a place or scene of ostentation or empty, idle amusement and frivolity." The term was later used by William Makepeace Thackeray as the title for his 1847 satiric novel about selfish members of London society who follow their own desires. Throughout the years, the term retained its strength, but it began to have more favorable connotations by 1860 when *Vanity Fair* became the title of a British society magazine. Condé Nast then bought the name and launched the twentieth-century version of *Vanity Fair* magazine, a publication focused on contemporary society, celebrities, and style.

Ask Yourself

Think about the definition of the word "vanity." Why was Vanity Fair such an effective name for Bunyan's fictional market? Explain.

Applying Your Skills

SKILLS FOCUS **Literary Skills** Analyze allegory; analyze setting. **Reading Skills** Make generalizations about a writer's beliefs and support them using text. **Vocabulary Skills** Demonstrate knowledge of literal meanings of Vocabulary words and their usage. **Writing Skills** Describe a place.

from **The Pilgrim's Progress**

Respond and Think Critically

Reading Focus

Quick Check

1. Where are Christian and Faithful traveling?

2. What happens to Christian and Hopeful when they reach their final destination?

Read with a Purpose

3. What traits are necessary for humans (such as Christian, Faithful and Hopeful) to reach the Celestial City, or salvation?

Reading Skills: Making Generalizations About a Writer's Beliefs

4. While reading, you made lists of the vices that the narrator cites as examples of vanity. Now, return to your chart, and add notes to each column, explaining how each item represents some aspect of vanity.

Types of Things	Types of People	Types of Actions
Houses—people build fancy houses to show off	Jugglers—people care too much about entertainment	Theft—people are greedy and will take what isn't theirs

✔ Vocabulary Check

Match the Vocabulary words with their definitions.

5. reproachfully   **a.** spite

6. confounded   **b.** unyielding

7. malice   **c.** postponement

8. implacable   **d.** confused

9. respite   **e.** accusingly

Literary Focus

Literary Analysis

10. **Summarize** In your own words, summarize the paragraph that describes the visit of the Prince of Princes to the town.

11. **Draw Conclusions** What do you think is the primary reason the jury sentences Faithful to death?

12. **Analyze** Bunyan incorporates both Biblical language and common speech into his writing. Identify examples of common speech in the text. Then, identify examples of Biblical language. Why does Bunyan use each type of speech?

Literary Skills: Allegory

13. **Evaulate** How do Bunyan's final paragraphs reinforce the idea that the Celestial City represents heaven and salvation?

Literary Skills Review: Setting

14. **Hypothesize** The time and location in which a story takes place is its **setting.** How does the setting of Vanity Fair influence the actions of the characters?

Writing Focus

Think as a Reader/Writer

Use It in Your Writing Bunyan uses his description of the fair and jury to list various vices. Write a one-page description of a modern day place or event. Include references to at least two modern virtues or vices.

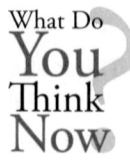 What Do **You Think Now** How do the hearts and minds of Christian, Faithful, and Hopeful influence their actions in this selection?

Views on Education and Equality

Saint Magdalene reading.
Louvre, Paris, France. Inv. 2156.

The essay, debate, and speech in this section show Renaissance views on the value of education. Sir Francis Bacon's essay praises formal education, which was unavailable to most people and particularly to women. The debate by Margaret Cavendish and the speech by Queen Elizabeth I express the views of women who were as intellectually accomplished as their male peers. Compare the views in all three selections and consider the relationship between education and equality today.

CONTENTS

Of Studies
by Francis Bacon

from **Female Orations**
by Margaret Cavendish

Tilbury Speech
by Queen Elizabeth I

Preparing to Read

Of Studies / *from* Female Orations
Tilbury Speech

Reader/Writer
Notebook

Use your **RWN** to complete the activities for the selection.

Informational Text Focus

Analyzing Arguments Speech or writing that uses logic to try to change the way people think is called an **argument**. A good argument is stated clearly and is supported by details, examples, or reasons. Any debate, real or fictional, requires each side to analyze the specific points of the opposing side. Contrasting ideas and arguments are often presented in a **parallel structure.** The repetition of words, phrases, or sentences that have a similar grammatical structure is **parallelism.**

Into Action As you read each selection, focus on how each author uses parallelism in presenting arguments. For each work, make a chart like the one below. Note the main arguments that are <u>established</u>. Then, jot down a few examples of parallelism.

Selection	"Of Studies"
Main Arguments	Learning and studying helps us think clearly and judge wisely.
Instances of Parallelism	1. 2. 3.

Writing Focus   Preparing for **Constructed Response**

In your *Reader/Writer Notebook,* jot down **metaphors** and **similes** you encounter in the following selections. Note the persuasive appeal of these figures of speech.

TechFocus As you read, consider your own opinion on the value of education. Think about what and how you learn in school and in other environments. How might you express your opinions in a blog?

Vocabulary

sloth (slawth) *n.:* laziness; idleness. *Bacon argues against sloth or inactivity.*

affectation (af ehk TAY shuhn) *n.:* artificial behavior designed to impress others. *Elizabeth's speech comes across as sincere, without a trace of affectation.*

diligence (DIHL uh juhns) *n.:* carefulness. *Bacon recommends diligence in reading.*

impediment (ihm PEHD uh muhnt) *n.:* obstacle; stumbling block. *The author argues that being female is not an impediment to learning.*

industrious (ihn DUHS tree uhs) *adj.:* hard-working. *Women have been industrious in their efforts to prove that they are capable.*

treachery (TREHCH uhr ee) *n.:* breaking of faith; betrayal of trust. *Many of Bacon's readers seem to think that educating women is a form of treachery against men.*

Language Coach

Antonyms *Slothful* and *industrious* are antonyms, words with opposite meanings. Which Vocabulary word above is an antonym for <u>carelessness</u>?

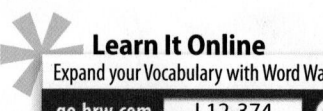

Learn It Online
Expand your Vocabulary with Word Watch.

go.hrw.com   L12-374   **Go**

Of Studies

by **Francis Bacon**

Read with a Purpose
Read this essay to discover the author's attitude toward reading and study. Do you agree with him?

Build Background
A true Renaissance man, Francis Bacon (1561–1626) was involved in politics, science, law, architecture, literature, and economics. Bacon's *Essays,* his best-known literary works, are intended to help people get ahead in life. Bacon was the first Englishman to use the word *essay* to designate a brief discourse in prose, and borrowed the word from the French writer Michel de Montaigne.

Bacon's essays are written in a terse, compact style that demands a reader's full attention. His essay on the value of studies brims with specific proposals and bold assertions. Take note of the details, examples, and reasons that Bacon uses to <u>establish</u> his arguments and persuade his readers.

S tudies serve for delight, for ornament, and for ability. Their chief use for delight is in privateness and retiring;[1] for ornament, is in discourse; and for ability, is in the judgment and disposition[2] of business. For expert men can execute, and perhaps judge of particulars, one by one; but the general counsels, and the plots and marshaling of affairs, come best from those that are learned. To spend too much time in studies is sloth; to use them too much for ornament is affectation; to make judgment wholly by their rules is the humor[3] of a scholar. They perfect nature and are perfected by experience; for natural abilities are like natural plants that need pruning by study; and studies themselves do give forth directions too much at large, except they be bounded in by experience. Crafty men contemn[4] studies; simple men admire them; and wise men use them: For they teach not their own use; but that is a wisdom without them[5] and above them, won by observation. Read not to contradict and confute;[6] nor to believe and take for granted; nor to find

Sir Francis Bacon, Viscount of St. Albans (early 17th century), detail by Paul van Somer.

---

1. **privateness and retiring:** privacy and leisure.
2. **disposition:** thoughtful placement.
3. **humor:** temperament.
4. **contemn:** despise.
5. **without them:** separate from them; outside them.
6. **confute:** dispute.

Vocabulary **sloth** (slawth) *n.:* laziness; idleness.
affectation (af ehk TAY shuhn) *n.:* artificial behavior designed to impress others.

talk and discourse; but to weigh and consider. Some books are to be tasted, others to be swallowed, and some few to be chewed and digested: That is, some books are to be read only in parts; others to be read, but not curiously; and some few to be read wholly, and with diligence and attention. Some books also may be read by deputy, and extracts made of them by others; but that would be only in the less important arguments, and the meaner sort of books; else distilled books are like common distilled waters,[7] flashy[8] things. Reading maketh a full man; conference a ready man; and writing an exact man. And therefore, if a man write little, he had need have a great memory; if he confer little, he had need have a present wit;[9] and if he read little, he had need have much cunning, to seem to know that he doth not. Ⓐ

Histories make men wise; poets witty; the mathematics subtle; natural philosophy deep; moral grave; logic and rhetoric able to contend. *Abeunt studia in mores.*[10] Nay, there is no stond[11] or impediment in the wit but may be wrought out by fit studies: like as diseases of the body may have appropriate exercises. Bowling is good for the stone and reins;[12] shooting for the lungs and breast; gentle walking for the stomach; riding for the head; and the like. So if a man's wit be wandering, let him study the mathematics; for in demonstrations, if his wit be called away never so little, he must begin again: If his wit be not apt to distinguish or find differences, let him study the Schoolmen;[13] for they are *cymini sectores:*[14] If he be not apt to beat over[15] matters, and to call one thing to prove and illustrate another, let him study the lawyers' cases; so every defect of the mind may have a special receipt.[16]

---

7. **common distilled waters:** homemade remedies.
8. **flashy:** superficial; empty.
9. **present wit:** ability to think fast.
10. *Abeunt . . . mores:* Latin for "Studies help to form character," from *Heroides* by Ovid (43 B.C.–c. A.D. 17).
11. **stond:** obstruction.
12. **stone and reins:** archaic form of "kidney stones and the kidneys."
13. **schoolmen:** medieval philosophers.
14. *cymini sectores:* Latin for "hairsplitters"; literally, dividers of the cumin seed.
15. **beat over:** thoroughly discuss.
16. **receipt:** remedy.

Ⓐ **Informational Focus** **Analyzing Arguments** Bacon lists three things in this passage that make a person complete. What difficulties result if a man lacks any of the three, or does them "little"?

Vocabulary **diligence** (DIHL uh juhns) *n.:* carefulness.
impediment (ihm PEHD uh muhnt) *n.:* obstacle; stumbling block.

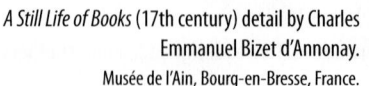

A Still Life of Books (17th century) detail by Charles Emmanuel Bizet d'Annonay.
Musée de l'Ain, Bourg-en-Bresse, France.

from Female Orations

by **Margaret Cavendish, Duchess of Newcastle**

Read with a Purpose
Read to discover how one author uses debate to express different views on the roles of men and women.

Build Background
Margaret Cavendish (1623–1673) wrote *Female Orations* as a fictional debate between women representing a range of viewpoints on the role of women in society. Cavendish, an eccentric gentlewoman, had both access to education and the freedom to write about what she pleased. Cavendish openly tackles <u>controversial</u> topics such as the situation of women in a male-dominated society. Her writings offer insight into the complexities of the cultural and political climate women experienced in the mid-seventeenth century.

I

Ladies, gentlewomen, and other inferior women, but not less worthy: I have been industrious to assemble you together, and wish I were so fortunate as to persuade you to make frequent assemblies, associations, and combinations amongst our own sex, that we may unite in prudent counsels, to make ourselves as free, happy, and famous as men; whereas now we live and die as if we were produced from beasts, rather than from men; for men are happy, and we women are miserable; they possess all the ease, rest, pleasure, wealth, power, and fame; whereas women are restless with labor, easeless with pain, melancholy for want of pleasures, helpless for want of power, and die in oblivion, for want of fame. Nevertheless, men are so unconscionable and cruel against us that they endeavor to bar us of all sorts of liberty, and will not suffer us freely to associate amongst our own sex; but would fain[1] bury us in their houses or beds, as in a grave. The truth is, we live like bats or owls, labor like beasts, and die like worms. **A**

Margaret Cavendish, Duchess of Newcastle, by Samuel Cooper.

---

1. **fain:** eagerly; gladly

A **Informational Focus** **Analyzing Arguments** What is the function of the parallel structure within the long sentence that opens this paragraph?

Vocabulary **industrious** (ihn DUHS tree uhs) *adj.:* hardworking.

II

Ladies, gentlewomen, and other inferior women: The lady that spoke to you hath spoken wisely and eloquently, in expressing our unhappiness; but she hath not declared a remedy, or showed us a way to come out of our miseries; but, if she could or would be our guide, to lead us out of the labyrinth[2] men have put us into, we should not only praise and admire her, but adore and worship her as our goddess: but alas! men, that are not only our tyrants but our devils, keep us in the hell of subjection, from whence I cannot perceive any redemption or getting out; we may complain and bewail our condition, yet that will not free us; we may murmur and rail against men, yet they regard not what we say. In short, our words to men are as empty sounds; our sighs, as puffs of winds; and our tears, as fruitless showers; and our power is so inconsiderable, that men laugh at our weakness. **B**

III

Ladies, gentlewomen, and other inferior women: The former orations were exclamations against men, repining[3] at their condition and mourning for our own; but we have no reason to speak against men, who are our admirers and lovers; they are our protectors, defenders, and maintainers; they admire our beauties, and love our persons; they protect us from injuries, defend us from dangers, are industrious for our subsistence, and provide for our children; they swim great voyages by sea, travel long journeys by land, to get us rarities and curiosities; they dig to the center of the earth for gold for us; they dive to the bottom of the sea for jewels for us: they build to the skies houses for us: they hunt, fowl, fish, plant, and reap for food for us. All which, we could not do ourselves; and yet we complain of men, as if they were our enemies, whenas[4] we could not possibly live without them, which shows we are as ungrateful as inconstant. But we have more reason to murmur against Nature, than against men, who hath made men more ingenious, witty, and wise than women; more strong, industrious, and laborious than women; for women are witless and strengthless, and unprofitable creatures, did they not bear children.

Wherefore, let us love men, praise men, and pray for men; for without men, we should be the most miserable creatures that Nature hath made or could make.…

Several other viewpoints are expressed as the debate continues in parts IV–VI. Part VII, which follows, is the last section of the debate. **C**

---

2. **labyrinth:** maze.
3. **repining:** complaining.
4. **whenas:** while on the other hand.

B **Informational Focus** **Analyzing Arguments** How would you summarize the argument of this speaker?

C **Informational Focus** **Analyzing Arguments** How does the argument of this speaker differ from those of the previous two?

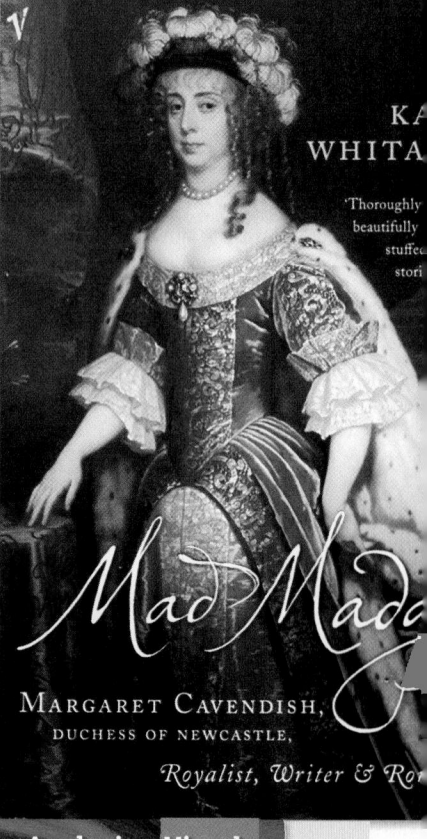

KA
WHITA

'Thoroughly
beautifully
stuffed
stori

Mad Mad

MARGARET CAVENDISH,
DUCHESS OF NEWCASTLE,
Royalist, Writer & Ro

Analyzing Visuals

Viewing and Interpreting Examine the painting and the title on this book cover. After reading the excerpts from *Female Orations,* why do you think Margaret Cavendish would have been called "Mad Madge" during her lifetime?

VII

Noble ladies, honorable gentlewomen, and worthy female-commoners: The former oratoress's speech was to persuade us out of ourselves and to be that which Nature never intended us to be, to wit, masculine. But why should we desire to be masculine, since our own sex and condition is far the better? For if men have more courage, they have more danger; and if men have more strength, they have more labor than women have; if men are more eloquent in speech, women are more harmonious in voice; if men be more active, women are more graceful; if men have more liberty, women have more safety; for we never fight duels nor battles; nor do we go long travels or dangerous voyages; we labor not in building nor digging in mines, quarries, or pits, for metal, stone, or coals; neither do we waste or shorten our lives with university or scholastical studies, questions, and disputes; we burn not our faces with smiths' forges or chemists' furnaces; and hundreds of other actions which men are employed in; for they would not only fade the fresh beauty, spoil the lovely features, and decay the youth of women, causing them to appear old, when they are young; but would break their small limbs, and destroy their tender lives. Wherefore women have no reason to complain against Nature or the god of Nature, for although the gifts are not the same as they have given to men, yet those gifts they have given to women are much better; for we women are much more favored by Nature than men, in giving us such beauties, features, shapes, graceful demeanor, and such insinuating[5] and enticing attractives, that men are forced to admire us, love us, and be desirous of us; insomuch that rather than not have and enjoy us, they will deliver to our disposals their power, persons, and lives, enslaving themselves to our will and pleasures; also, we are their saints, whom they adore and worship; and what can we desire more than to be men's tyrants, destinies, and goddesses? **Ⓓ**

---

5. **insinuating:** suggesting something in an indirect way.

Ⓓ **Informational Focus** **Analyzing Arguments** How does Cavendish use parallelism on a larger scale in this last argument?

Tilbury Speech

by Queen Elizabeth I

Read with a Purpose
Read this speech to discover how Elizabeth summons loyalty and courage in her subjects.

Build Background
Queen Elizabeth I (reigned 1558–1603) wrote poems, letters, prayers, sermons, and translations, and, at the same time, governed the country, conducted foreign policy, fostered the arts, and dedicated herself fervently to the newly established religion of her realm. She also wrote masterful speeches and political addresses. One of her best-known orations is the Tilbury Speech, given in 1588 before news of the destruction of the Spanish Armada reached England. With this speech, Elizabeth aimed to rouse her land forces to defend England against Spanish invasion.

Helen Mirren, Jeremy Irons, and Hugh Dancy in *Elizabeth I* (2005).

The arrival of Queen Elizabeth I at Tilbury; and the Defeat of the Spanish Armada (17th century), left hand panel by English School. St. Faith's Church, Gaywood, Norfolk, UK.

My loving people: We have been persuaded by some that are careful of our safety to take heed how we commit ourself to armed multitudes for fear of treachery, but I assure you I do not desire to live to distrust my faithful and loving people. Let tyrants fear. I have always so behaved myself that, under God, I have placed my chiefest strength and safeguard in the loyal hearts and goodwill of my subjects. And therefore I am come amongst you, as you see, at this time, not for my recreation and disport,[1] but being resolved in the midst and heat of the battle to live or die amongst you all, to lay down for my God, and for my kingdom, and for my people,

my honor and my blood, even in the dust. **Ⓐ** I know I have the body but of a weak and feeble woman, but I have the heart and stomach of a king— and of a king of England too—and think foul scorn that Parma, or Spain, or any prince of Europe should dare to invade the borders of my realm. To which, rather than any dishonor shall grow by me, I myself will take up arms, I myself will be your general, judge, and rewarder of every one of your virtues in the field. I know already for your forwardness you have deserved rewards and crowns, and we do assure you, in the word of a prince, they shall be duly paid you. **Ⓑ**

---

1. **disport:** pleasant diversion; entertainment.

Ⓐ Informational Focus **Analyzing Arguments** How does Elizabeth's use of parallelism create a relationship between God, England, and the English people?

Ⓑ Informational Focus **Analyzing Arguments** How would you summarize the argument of this speaker?

Vocabulary treachery (TREHCH uhr ee) *n*.: breaking of faith; betrayal of trust.

SKILLS FOCUS Informational **Skills** Analyze persuasion/arguments in a text; analyze parallelism. **Vocabulary Skills** Identify and correctly use synonyms. **Listening and Speaking Skills** Demonstrate effective gestures when speaking. **Writing Skills** Write brief constructed responses with specific support.

Of Studies / *from* Female Orations
Tilbury Speech

Respond and Think Critically

Informational Text Focus

Quick Check

1. What does Elizabeth say to assert her power?

2. How do the different speakers address their audience in Cavendish's debate?

Read with a Purpose

3. Each selection presents different attitudes about education and gender. Which writer's ideas are closest to yours? Explain.

Informational Skills: Analyzing Arguments

4. Return to the charts in which you recorded the main arguments and instances of parallelism. Now add a new row, analyzing how each use of parallelism directly supports the speaker's argument.

Selection	"Of Studies"
Main Arguments	Learning and studying helps us think clearly and judge wisely.
Instances of Parallelism	1. 2. 3.
How Parallelism Supports the Argument	

✔ Vocabulary Check

Match each Vocabulary word to its synonym.

5. affectation   a. obstacle
6. treachery   b. laziness
7. sloth   c. betrayal
8. impediment   d. artificiality
9. diligence   e. hardworking
10. industrious   f. care

Text Analysis

11. **Evaluate** Do you think Francis Bacon intended to use the word *man* throughout "Of Studies" to refer just to men, or to any human being?

12. **Compare** Review the excerpts from Cavendish's *Female Orations*. Characterize the speaker of each section. Are all the speakers meant to be serious, or are some of them trying for humor?

13. **Infer** In the Tilbury Speech, Elizabeth says that she has the body of "a weak and feeble woman" but "the heart and stomach of a king." What inferences can you draw about gender assumptions during her time?

Listening and Speaking

14. **Extend** Although Queen Elizabeth's Tilbury Speech is a carefully crafted piece of writing, it was written to be spoken and heard. Make a photocopy of this speech. Then, read it aloud several times, underlining words and phrases your voice emphasizes as you speak. Practice the speech, using gestures to reinforce what you emphasize with your voice. Consider sharing your reading with your class.

Writing Focus   Constructed Response

In one or two paragraphs, briefly discuss the persuasive appeal of metaphors and similes in the selections by Francis Bacon, Margaret Cavendish, and Queen Elizabeth I. Be sure to support your response with specific evidence from the texts.

What Do You Think Now

How can a person's attitude toward study and learning influence his or her actions?

SKILLS FOCUS **Literary Skills** Evaluate the philosophical, political, religious, ethical, and social influences of a historical period. **Writing Skills** Write comparison-contrast essays; write persuasive essays or articles. **Listening and Speaking Skills** Adapt to purpose when speaking: to inform; prepare and present oral messages; adapt to occasion when speaking: group presentations.

Of Studies / *from* Female Orations
Tilbury Speech

Writing Focus

Writing a Comparison-Contrast Essay

The selections you have just read all address <u>controversial</u> issues of education and gender equality. Which of the selections express similar views? How is each argument unique? Write an essay in which you compare the points of view on education and gender equality expressed in two of the selections. Before you begin writing, consider the following points:

1. How are the issues of education and gender equality combined in the selections? Which selection focuses more on education? Which focuses more on equality?

2. How does the writer or speaker reveal his or her opinion on education and/or equality? Are things directly stated, or are they implied? What viewpoints are included, and whose viewpoints are they?

3. Which selection did you find most convincing as an argument, and why?

Use details and examples from the texts to support your ideas, and make sure that your essay has a clear structure.

Review the elements of a successful comparison-contrast essay.

An effective comparison- contrast essay should

- clearly state what is being compared and contrasted in the opening paragraph
- use a thesis statement to establish the main idea
- be organized logically and effectively
- include quotations or references to text passages to support ideas
- include a conclusion that restates the thesis and demonstrates how it has been proved
- contain few or no errors in spelling, punctuation, and grammar

CHOICES

As you respond to the Choices, use these **Academic Vocabulary** words as appropriate: <u>contradiction</u>, <u>controversy</u>, <u>ensure</u>, <u>establish</u>, <u>widespread</u>.

REVIEW

Evaluate Education

Write an essay of your own in response to Bacon's reflections on studies. Your response may range from total disagreement to total approval of his ideas. Include examples and experiences from real life to support your response.

CONNECT

Write a Blog

TechFocus Write your own blog about the value of your education, both inside and outside school. Use personal anecdotes, images, and links to enhance your blog. (You can write your blog on paper if you don't have access to an Internet blog forum.) Then, ask two or three friends to read your blog and post responses to it. War?

EXTEND

Women in Renaissance Society

Research Activity The debates in *Female Orations* present a various viewpoints from fictional women of the time. What impression do you get from these debates about women's lives in seventeenth-century Europe? Do some outside research on the role of women in Renaissance society, and compare your findings to the portrayal Cavendish presents in her debates. Present your results to the class.

What Do You Think Now Each of the writers in this section bases opinions on personal experience. How do you think people form their opinions about equality and education today?

William Shakespeare

LITERARY FOCUS
Shakespeare's Sonnets and Plays

A Midsummer Night's Dream, Globe Theatre.

CONTENTS

**Author Study:
William Shakespeare**

from **Macbeth:
The Graphic Novel** Link to Today

"Soul of the Age!
The applause,
delight, the wonder
of our stage."

—Ben Jonson

Shakespeare's Sonnets and Plays

by **Leila Christenbury**

Characteristics of Shakespeare's Sonnets and Plays

- Reflect influences from mythology and ancient history
- Primarily use iambic pentameter
- Display an immense range of human emotions
- Represent cornerstones of centuries of English literature

The Sonnets of Shakespeare

William Shakespeare lived for just over fifty years, but he created some of the most influential literature ever written in English. Shakespeare's work still fascinates us: His characters are complex, his ideas are illuminating, and his language is as precise as it is poetic. Whether writing about love or ambition, marriage or murder, Shakespeare produced poems and plays that engage, entertain, and sustain us.

Even if Shakespeare had written no plays, his reputation as a poet, as the author of the *Sonnets,* would have been immense. Published in 1609, his series of 154 sonnets features a male speaker and a recurring subject: love. Beyond these points there is little agreement and widespread debate among critics concerning the sonnets. Is the sonnets' speaker a dramatic character invented by Shakespeare, like Romeo or Hamlet, or is the speaker the poet himself? The speaker does refer to himself as "Will" a few times, as well as makes puns on his name, but what evidence exists to prove that all the sonnets are spoken by this Will?

If the sonnets are, in fact, about the real man Shakespeare, then who are the real people behind the characters in the sonnets: the beloved young man who may be the subject of either many of the first 126 sonnets, or of some of the later sonnets? Who is the rival poet referred to in several sonnets? Are the speaker, fair young man, dark lady, and other poet the only four characters, or are there others?

Is the order in which the sonnets were originally published (probably without Shakespeare's consent) the intended sequence? Could they be rearranged to tell a more coherent story? *Should* they be rearranged?

These issues continue to generate controversy among critics. There is consensus, however, about the undeniable artistic merit of the sonnets. With great style and emotion, these poems express profound observations about important human experiences.

The Shakespearean Sonnet's Form

As established by the rules of the sonnet form, each of Shakespeare's sonnets has a formal organization and a logical organization of ideas.

As discussed on page 269, the **Shakespearean sonnet** is a fourteen-line poem that uses **iambic pentameter,** has three quatrains followed by a final couplet, and adheres to a strict rhyme scheme. The iambic pentameter meter consists of five iambs. Iambs are **metrical feet,** or units of measure, in which one unstressed syllable is followed by one stressed syllable. The Shakespearean sonnet's **rhyme scheme** is *abab cdcd efef gg.*

The logical organization of ideas in Shakespeare's sonnet varies from poem to poem. Sonnet 18 (page 391), for example, offers a twist on the standard love poem, in which the attributes of a loved one are compared to something—in this case, a summer's day. The first two quatrains present the imperfections of the summer's day rather than the more standard recitation of the loved one's perfect qualities. As often happens in Shakespeare's sonnets, the **turn,** a shift in focus or thought, occurs at the beginning of the third quatrain in line 9.

The Rise of the Renaissance Theater

The English had been writing and performing plays for centuries before the Renaissance. Most scholars believe that early medieval drama originated in the ceremonies of the Roman Catholic liturgy. Eventually, drama moved out of the churches and into the marketplaces, where in the 1300s and 1400s various workers' guilds staged cycles of plays that dramatized the history of the human race.

Although religious themes were still important, dramatic productions eventually became less about religion, Several types of plays were written and produced before the Renaissance: **miracle** and **mystery plays** taught people stories from the Bible and saints' lives, and **morality plays** provided instruction on how to live and die according to Christian principles. Beginning in the 1500s, a new type of play called an **interlude** developed. Interludes were one-act plays, some of them indistinguishable from moralities, others rowdy and farcical. With the advent of interludes, playwrights stopped being anonymous. Even before the new humanist learning emerged, there were strong dramatic traditions with which the great Renaissance playwrights were familiar.

Shakespeare's Plays

Written mostly in the 1590s, Shakespeare's early plays were some of his most performed and admired. This immensely varied group contains a history play about a deformed usurper who becomes the king of England (*Richard III*), a rowdy farce about mistaken identity (*The Comedy of Errors*), a blood-and-thunder tragedy (*Titus Andronicus*), and a poetic tragedy about ill-fated lovers (*Romeo and Juliet*).

In the late 1590s, Shakespeare entered a period of great prosperity. Elizabeth I was near the end of her reign when Shakespeare completed his cycle of plays about England during the Wars of the Roses: *Richard II*, both parts of *Henry IV,* and *Henry V.* He also wrote one of his most frequently performed tragedies, *Julius Caesar,* the magical comedy *A Midsummer Night's Dream,* and the darker comedy *A Merchant of Venice.*

As the seventeenth century began, Shakespeare was writing his greatest tragedies: *Hamlet, Othello, King Lear, Macbeth,* and *Antony and Cleopatra.* These plays are preoccupied with evil, violence, and death, but there is no evidence that Shakespeare himself was unhappy or depressed when he wrote them. Happily for us, Shakespeare's productivity was at its peak during the years 1600–1607.

Although we might think of Shakespeare as primarily a writer, we must remember that he was the consummate man of the theater, a man of business and action. He staged productions, managed the playhouse, and coordinated the actors. He had to provide good parts in every play for the principal performers in his company. His actors often played more than one character in a play, so he had to arrange for doubling or even tripling of roles. He planned his scenes carefully so that nobody would ever have to be onstage in two different roles at the same time.

Shakespeare also had to work within the conventions of the Renaissance stage. For example, there were no female actors during Shakespeare's time, so he worked to <u>establish</u> female characters that were accessible to the male actors playing these roles. Shakespeare's expertise with the page and the stage made him a complete man of the drama *and* theater.

The Globe

By the mid-sixteenth century, the art of drama in England was three centuries old, but the idea of housing it in a permanent building was new. Even after theaters had been built, plays were still performed in improvised spaces—particularly when acting companies toured the provinces or played in the large houses of royalty and nobility. The first public theater, called the Theater, in London was built in 1576. When the Theater was demolished in 1599, the timbers were used to build the Globe.

The Globe is probably the most famous public theater from Shakespeare's time, because Shakespeare's company owned it. Many of Shakespeare's plays were first performed in the Globe. Unfortunately, the original theater was destroyed by fire in 1613, and plans for the Globe have not survived. Most scholars agree that the depiction of the Globe by C. Walter Hodges is accurate. According to Hodges, the theater had three main sections: the building proper, the stage, and the tiring house, or backstage area. The main building, a wooden structure three stories high and roughly circular in shape, surrounded a spacious yard open to the sky. The public theater housed an amazingly large crowd: three

Shakespeare books.

thousand, according to two contemporary accounts.

The stage projected halfway out into the yard, so actors performed very close to the audience. The actors were highly trained and were expected to be able to sing, dance, wrestle, fence, and clown.

Special effects were also in high demand. Audiences loved to see witches or devils emerge through the trapdoor in the stage, which everybody knew led down to Hell, just as everybody knew that the ceiling over part of the stage represented Heaven.

The third section of the theater was the tiring house, a tall building that contained machinery and dressing rooms and provided a two-story back wall for the stage. A gallery was contained above this wall and a curtained space lay below. In the gallery, the audience could sit, musicians could perform, and parts of the play could be staged. At any given time, the gallery might serve as Macbeth's tower or the perch of the mysterious players in *The Taming of the Shrew*. The curtained area below the gallery was used mainly for "discoveries" of things hidden from the audience until the proper time.

Although the Globe Theater (rebuilt after the 1613 fire) was closed down in 1642, a full-scale model of the original was constructed in 1997. American actor and director Sam Wanamaker spearheaded the recontruction project, which took nearly ten years to complete. Today, the new Globe Theater (or, as it is called, "Shakespeare's Globe Theater) houses a professional theater company, historical exhibits, and an education center.

The Power of Imagination

Renaissance audiences took for granted that whatever happens on the stage is make-believe. When the people in the audience saw actors carrying lanterns, they knew it was night, even though the sun was shining brightly overhead. A few bushes became a forest. Furthermore, often instead of seeing a scene, they heard it described, as when Shakespeare has a character exclaim over a sunrise:

But look, the morn in russet mantle clad
Walks o'er the dew of yon high eastward hill.
  —*Hamlet*, Act I, Scene 1, lines 166–167

Music for the Masses

When people went to the London theater, they expected not only to see a play but also to hear music. Trumpets announced the beginning of a play and important arrivals and departures within the drama. Although most of the original music has been lost, Shakespeare's works include a great variety of sad, happy, comic, and thoughtful songs that advance the play's action, help establish a scene's mood, or reveal character.

Ask Yourself

1. What are the required elements of the Shakespearean sonnet?

2. How were outdoor settings created on the Renaissance stage?

Learn It Online
Try the PowerNotes version of this lesson.

go.hrw.com L12-387 Go

William Shakespeare
(1564–1616)

What Do You Think How do our hearts and minds influence our actions?

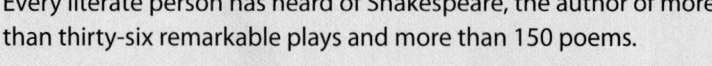

⏱ **QuickWrite**

Think of someone you know or have read about who was in love. Did love make the person see the world more clearly, or did it cloud his or her vision? Explain your answer in a paragraph in your *Reader/Writer Notebook*.

Every literate person has heard of Shakespeare, the author of more than thirty-six remarkable plays and more than 150 poems.

The Early Years

"The Bard" was born in Stratford-on-Avon, a prosperous market town in England, and was christened in the parish church on April 26, 1564. His parents came from respected families in the area, and, as a young man, Shakespeare probably attended the King's New School. He may have become a teacher; however, because his plays demonstrate knowledge of many diverse fields, some people have speculated he may have held a number of different occupations.

At eighteen, Shakespeare married Anne Hathaway. They had three children: a daughter, Susanna, and twins, Hamnet and Judith. In 1587, Shakespeare moved to London for a career in the theater.

A Life in the Theater

In the late 1590s, near the end of Elizabeth I's reign, Shakespeare completed his cycle of plays about England during the Wars of the Roses: *Richard II,* both parts of *Henry IV,* and *Henry V.* Also in this period he wrote the tragedy *Julius Caesar* and the comedies most frequently performed today such as *A Midsummer Night's Dream* and *The Merchant of Venice.* He also wrote or rewrote *Hamlet,* the tragedy that, of all his works, has provoked the most varied and controversial interpretations from critics, scholars, and actors.

By 1592, Shakespeare was active in the London scene, writing and performing in a theater troupe called the Lord Chamberlain's

A Shakespeare Time Line

Anne Hathaway Shakespeare (c.1556–1623). The Grander Collection, NY.

1582 Married Anne Hathaway

1560

1585

c. 1564 Born in Stratford-on-Avon

1587 Leaves family and moves to London; begins career in dramatic arts

Statue of William Shakespeare.

Men. He stayed with this group—though its name changed—until his retirement, enjoying the patronage of noblemen and royalty. Six of his plays were performed at the court of Queen Elizabeth; in fact, according to an old tradition, she asked him to write *The Merry Wives of Windsor* because she wanted to see the merry old knight John Falstaff in love.

Shakespeare achieved <u>widespread</u> success under Elizabeth's successor, James I. As the troupe's patron, James renamed it the King's Men, gave it license to perform anywhere in the British realm, raised its salaries, and appointed its highest members, including Shakespeare, to serve as grooms of the royal chamber.

The Twilight Years

Shakespeare seems to have retired to Stratford around 1610, although he continued to write for the London stage. His last English history play, *Henry VIII*, contained a tribute to the late queen. During the play's first performance in June 1613, the firing of the cannon at the end of Act I set the Globe's thatched roof on fire, and the building burned to the ground. No injuries were recorded, although a bottle of ale had to be poured on a man whose breeches were burning.

Shakespeare's last recorded visit to London was made in November 1614. He probably spent most of the last two years of his life in Stratford. He died on April 23, 1616, and was buried under the floor of Stratford Church. His epitaph is a warning not to move his remains to the churchyard—a common practice in his time to make room for the newly deceased:

> Good friend, for Jesus' sake forbear
> To dig the dust enclosèd here!
> Blest be the man that spares these stones,
> And curst be he that moves my bones.

Think About the Writer

Because he lacked a university education, some critics question whether Shakespeare is the author of all his works. How essential do you think education would have been for writing his works?

Key Elements of Shakespeare's Writing

- Plays written in **blank verse,** which is unrhymed **iambic pentameter**
- Sonnets written in **rhymed iambic pentameter**
- Striking **metaphors** and poetic turns of phrase
- Heartbreaking **tragedies** and uproarious **comedies**
- Profound insights into human nature

1590s Writes many of his plays, including *Henry V, Romeo and Juliet, A Midsummer Night's Dream,* and *The Merchant of Venice*

1594 Joins dramatic company, the Lord Chamberlain's Men, which includes tragic actor Richard Burbage and clown Will Kemp

Anonymous Portrait of Richard Burbage, English School, Seventeenth Century Dulwich Picture Gallery, London.

1603 The Lord Chamberlain's Men perform for King James; with the king's patronage, company name becomes the King's Men

1590

1600

1616

1592 Achieves success in London theater; from this point forward his work is well documented

1610 Retires and moves back to Stratford; continues to help manage the Globe and Blackfriars theaters

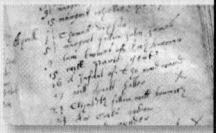

1616 Dies on April 23 in Stratford; buried beneath Stratford Church

Preparing to Read

Sonnets 18, 29, 30, 71, 73, 116, and 130

Reader/Writer Notebook

Use your **RWN** to complete the activities for these selections.

Literary Focus

Shakespearean Sonnets The **Shakespearean sonnet** is fourteen lines with three four-line units, called **quatrains;** a final two-line unit, called a **couplet;** and the **rhyme scheme** *abab cdcd efef gg.* The **meter,** or rhythmic pattern, is **iambic pentameter,** with each line consisting of five iambs. An **iamb** is an unstressed syllable followed by a stressed syllable.

Reading Focus

Using Text Structure to Understand Meaning The organization of thought in a Shakespearean sonnet usually corresponds to its structure. The three quatrains often express related ideas and the couplet summarizes the message. As you read, look for the **turn,** or shift in thought, in each sonnet. Does it occur at the beginning of the third quatrain, in the final couplet, or in a different place? Can the couplet be considered a second turn?

Into Action Track each sonnet's train of thought, and corresponding turn or turns.

Poem	Turn, or Shift in Thought
Sonnet 18	In line 9, focus shifts from nature's faults to the beloved
Sonnet 29	

Writing Focus

Think as a Reader/Writer

Find It in Your Reading Shakespeare's sonnets are characterized by their clever **metaphors**—comparisons between two unlike things. As you read, note Shakespeare's metaphors in your *Reader/Writer Notebook.*

TechFocus As you read these sonnets, think about the different ways in which modern people send messages to their loved ones.

Vocabulary

temperate (TEHM puhr iht) *adj.:* moderate. *The temperate woman was much admired for her self-restraint.*

scorn (skawrn) *v.:* refuse; reject by showing contempt. *The young man scorns the idea of marrying beneath his class.*

summon (SUHM uhn) *v.:* call. *By concentrating, she can summon childhood memories.*

surly (SUR lee) *adj.:* bad-tempered; unfriendly. *The surly dog even bit his loving master.*

expire (ehk SPYR) *v.:* die; come to an end. *The soldier feared he would expire in battle.*

impediments (ihm PEHD uh muhnts) *n. pl.:* obstacles; obstructions. *The many impediments to their union discouraged the couple.*

reeks (reeks) *v.:* has a strong, bad smell. *The kitchen reeks whenever the cook burns the bread.*

Language Coach

Connotations Good writers choose vivid verbs to create strong images. These verbs have stronger connotations—associated ideas—than neutral verbs. In one sonnet, Shakespeare describes an odor that *reeks.* Why might he have chosen this verb instead of a more neutral word, such as *smells?* Which Vocabulary words are vivid verbs that describe these actions: *call, die, refuse?*

Learn It Online
Hear a professional actor read these sonnets at

go.hrw.com   L12-390   **Go**

Sonnet 18

by **William Shakespeare**

Read with a Purpose
Read to discover how the speaker feels about trying to describe his beloved's beauty.

Build Background
In the Northern Hemisphere, summer begins on June 21, the day of the summer solstice. Shakespeare probably used the word *summer* in Sonnet 18 to mean "spring and summer," as evidenced by his reference to the "buds of May."

Shall I compare thee to a summer's day?
Thou art more lovely and more temperate.
Rough winds do shake the darling buds of May,
And summer's lease hath all too short a date.
5   Sometime too hot the eye of heaven shines,
And often is his gold complexion dimmed;
And every fair from fair sometime declines,
By chance, or nature's changing course untrimmed.
But thy eternal summer shall not fade, **A**
10   Nor lose possession of that fair thou owest,
Nor shall Death brag thou wander'st in his shade
When in eternal lines to time thou grow'st.
So long as men can breathe, or eyes can see,
So long lives this, and this gives life to thee. **B**

Summer (1895), by Walter Crane.

A Literary Focus Shakespearean Sonnets How does the ninth line provide a different view of the sonnet's central theme?

B Reading Focus Using Text Structure to Understand Meaning What new idea is introduced in the last two lines? What does Shakespeare mean when he uses the word *this*?

Vocabulary temperate (TEHM pur iht) *adj.:* moderate.

SONNET

Sonnet 29

by **William Shakespeare**

Read with a Purpose
Read this sonnet to discover how Shakespeare's speaker motivates himself when he feels unworthy.

Build Background
Even famous writers have their bad days. In this sonnet, the speaker describes a time when he feels depressed, jealous, and frustrated. He goes on to tell how he regains his confidence and creativity.

When, in disgrace with Fortune and men's eyes,
I all alone beweep my outcast state,
And trouble deaf heaven with my bootless° cries,
And look upon myself and curse my fate,   **A**
5   Wishing me like to one more rich in hope,
Featured like him, like him° with friends possessed,
Desiring this man's art,° and that man's scope,°
With what I most enjoy contented least;
Yet in these thoughts myself almost despising,
10 Haply° I think on thee, and then my state,
Like to the lark° at break of day arising
From sullen earth, sings hymns at heaven's gate;
　　For thy sweet love remembered such wealth brings
　　That then I scorn to change my state with kings.   **B**

3. **bootless:** useless; futile.

5–6. **one . . . him . . . him:** three men whom the speaker envies.
7. **art:** literary ability. **scope:** power.

10. **haply:** by chance.

A Literary Focus **Shakespearean Sonnets** What problems does the speaker describe in the first quatrain?

B Reading Focus **Using Text Structure to Understand Meaning** What prompts a change in the speaker's mood? Where in the sonnet does this shift take place?

Vocabulary **scorn** (skawrn) v.: refuse; reject by showing contempt.

Analyzing Visuals

Viewing and Interpreting Note the contrast between the subject's elaborate formal dress and his natural surroundings. In what ways do the sonnets of Shakespeare comment on natural and environmental beauty?

Sir Brooke Boothby (1781), by Joseph Wright of Derby. Tate Gallery, London.

Sonnet 30

by **William Shakespeare**

Read with a Purpose
Read this sonnet to understand how the speaker overcomes feelings of loss and regret.

Build Background
Shakespeare begins this sonnet with a strikingly original metaphor. Periods of quiet meditation are called **sessions,** as though they were court trials in which one's thoughts come to the bar of justice to hear their cases tried. (*Sessions* is a British legal term that refers to minor court cases.)

When to the sessions of sweet silent thought
I summon up remembrance of things past,
I sigh the lack of many a thing I sought,
And with old woes new wail° my dear time's waste.°
5   Then can I drown an eye (unused to flow)
For precious friends hid in death's dateless° night,
And weep afresh love's long since canceled woe,
And moan th' expense° of many a vanished sight.°
Then can I grieve at grievances foregone,   **Ⓐ**
10   And heavily from woe to woe tell° o'er
The sad account of fore° bemoanèd moan,
Which I new pay as if not paid before.
      But if the while I think on thee, dear friend,
      All losses are restored and sorrows end.   **Ⓑ**

4. **new wail:** again lament. **my . . . waste:** the damage that time has done to things dear to me.
6. **dateless:** endless.

8. **expense:** loss. **vanished sight:** things gone, such as dead friends.
10. **tell:** count.
11. **fore:** already.

Ⓐ **Literary Focus** **Shakespearean Sonnets** What sorrows trouble the speaker in the second quatrain?

Ⓑ **Reading Focus** **Using Text Structure to Understand Meaning** How does the speaker's attitude change in the final couplet?

Vocabulary **summon** (SUHM uhn) *v.*: call forth; send for.

The Happy Lovers, by Gustav Courbet (1844). Musée des Beaux-Arts, Lyon, France.

SKILLS FOCUS **Literary Skills** Analyze the characteristics of Shakespearean sonnets; analyze alliteration. **Reading Skills** Analyze text structure. **Vocabulary Skills** Identify and correctly use antonyms. **Writing Skills** Write poems.

Respond and Think Critically

Reading Focus

Read with a Purpose

1. What is the speaker's attitude toward his loved one in each of these sonnets?

Reading Skills: Using Text Structure to Understand Meaning

2. As you read, you tracked the turn, or shift in thought in each sonnet. Now, use clues from the turn and couplet to determine the overall theme.

Poem	Turn, or Shift in Thought	Theme
Sonnet 18	In line 9, focus shifts from nature's thoughts to the beloved	Art that describes love can make love eternal.
Sonnet 29		

✓ Vocabulary Check

Match each Vocabulary word with its antonym.

3. scorn   **a.** extreme

4. summon   **b.** appreciate

5. temperate   **d.** dismiss

Literary Focus

Literary Analysis

6. Interpret In the first two quatrains of Sonnet 18, what are the speaker's feelings about summer?

7. Compare and Contrast What similarities can you find in the main ideas in Sonnets 29 and 30?

8. Evaluate Shakespeare's sonnets use **conceits,** elaborate figures of speech that draw a surprising connection between two seemingly dissimilar things. In these sonnets, which conceit makes the most unexpected comparison? Explain.

Literary Skills: Shakespearean Sonnets

9. Analyze Shakespeare adheres to basic sonnet structure, but he plays with the rules. For example, one quatrain may not contain a complete thought, or the turn may not occur on a single line. Find an example of Shakespeare's deviation from structure, and explain its effect.

Literary Skills Review: Alliteration

10. Extend The repetition of consonant sounds in words close to one another, **alliteration,** increases a poem's musical effects and the connection between words. Find an example of alliteration in the sonnet and tell how it contributes to the poem's sound and meaning.

Writing Focus

Think as a Reader/Writer

Use It in Your Writing As you read, you noted Shakespeare's metaphors. Choose one or two that you found particularly powerful. What is unexpected and striking about the comparisons? Now, write out several metaphors that you could use in a poem.

What Do You Think Now

In each sonnet, how do the speaker's emotions affect how he thinks about the world?

For **CHOICES** see page 400. ❯

Sonnet 71

by **William Shakespeare**

Read with a Purpose
Read this sonnet to learn how the speaker wants his beloved to act after his death.

Build Background
In several of his sonnets, Shakespeare emphasizes the age difference between the speaker and his lover. The speaker is often portrayed as older than his beloved and will presumably die first.

No longer mourn for me when I am dead
Than you shall hear the surly sullen bell
Give warning to the world that I am fled
From this vile world, with vilest worms to dwell.  **A**
5 Nay, if you read this line, remember not
The hand that writ it; for I love you so **B**
That I in your sweet thoughts would be forgot
If thinking on me then should make you woe.
O, if, I say, you look upon this verse
10 When I, perhaps, compounded am with clay,
Do not so much as my poor name rehearse,
But let your love even with my life decay,
    Lest the wise world should look into your moan
    And mock you with me after I am gone.

A Reading Focus Using Text Structure to Understand Meaning What poetic device does Shakespeare use in lines 4–5 to emphasize the idea of a vile world?

B Literary Focus Shakespearean Sonnets How do the speaker's tone and focus shift in line 6?

Vocabulary **surly** (SUR lee) *adj.:* unfriendly; sullen.

St. Catherine's Parish Church, Eskdale Cumbria, England.

Sonnet 73

by **William Shakespeare**

Read with a Purpose
Read this sonnet to see how the speaker's aging affects his beloved.

Build Background
As in Sonnet 71, the speaker of Sonnet 73 dwells on the fact that he is growing older. Each quatrain creates and develops a different metaphor for aging.

That time of year thou mayst in me behold
When yellow leaves, or none, or few, do hang
Upon those boughs which shake against the cold,
Bare ruined choirs° where late the sweet birds sang.
5 In me thou see'st the twilight of such day
As after sunset fadeth in the west,
Which by and by black night doth take away,
Death's second self, that seals up all in rest.
In me thou see'st the glowing of such fire, **A**
10 That on the ashes of his youth doth lie
As the deathbed whereon it must expire,
Consumed with that which it was nourished by.°
    This thou perceivest, which makes thy love more strong,
    To love that well which thou must leave ere long. **B**

4. choirs: parts of a church or cathedral in which services are held. The landscape of Shakespeare's England was dotted with church ruins, a result of Henry VIII's destruction of monasteries.

12. consumed . . . nourished by: choked by the ashes of the wood that once fed its flame.

A **Reading Focus** Using Text Structure to Understand Meaning What parallel structures does Shakespeare use to introduce each metaphor for age and death?

B **Literary Focus** Shakespearean Sonnets Find the turn, or shift in thought, in this sonnet. What does the speaker tell his beloved in the final couplet?

Vocabulary **expire** (ehk SPYR) *v.:* die; come to an end.

Members of the Gozzadini family, Emilian School (15th century).
The Metropolitan Museum of Art, Robert Lehman Collection, 1975.1.96.

SONNET

Sonnet 116

by **William Shakespeare**

Read with a Purpose
Read to discover the speaker's feelings about the constancy of love.

Build Background
In this sonnet, Shakespeare asserts that true love is firm against all "impediments." *Impediments* is a word taken from the wedding ceremony of the Church of England: "If any of you know cause or just impediment why these persons should not be joined together . . ."

Let me not to the marriage of true minds
Admit impediments. Love is not love
Which alters when it alteration finds,
Or bends with the remover to remove. **A**
5   Oh no! It is an ever-fixèd mark°
That looks on tempests and is never shaken.
It is the star to every wandering bark,°
Whose worth's unknown, although his height be taken.°
Love's not Time's fool, though rosy lips and cheeks
10   Within his bending sickle's compass° come.
Love alters not with his brief hours and weeks,
But bears it out° even to the edge of doom.
        If this be error and upon me proved,
        I never writ, nor no man ever loved. **B**

5. mark: seamark; a prominent object onshore that serves as a guide to sailors.
7. bark: boat.
8. height be taken: altitude measured to determine a ship's position.
10. compass: range; reach.
12. bears it out: survives.

A **Reading Focus** Using Text Structure to Understand Meaning What argument, or thesis, does Shakespeare establish in the first quatrain?

B **Literary Focus** Shakespearean Sonnets What does the speaker conclude in the final couplet?

Vocabulary **impediments** (ihm PEHD uh muhnts) *n. pl.:* obstacles; obstructions.

Sonnet 130

by **William Shakespeare**

Read with a Purpose
Read this sonnet to see how and why the speaker shuns describing his mistress in unconventional ways.

Build Background
In this sonnet, Shakespeare ridicules the fashionable, exaggerated metaphors some of his fellow poets were using to describe the women they loved: "Your eyes are suns that set me on fire, your cheeks are roses, your breasts are white as snow." These overwrought metaphors, known as **conceits,** are traceable to Petrarch, but by 1600 they had become tiresome or laughable due to excessive use. Note that in Renaissance usage, the word *mistress* simply meant "girlfriend."

My mistress' eyes are nothing like the sun,
Coral is far more red than her lips' red.
If snow be white, why then her breasts are dun,°
If hairs be wires, black wires grow on her head.
5   I have seen roses damasked,° red and white,
But no such roses see I in her cheeks.
And in some perfumes is there more delight
Than in the breath that from my mistress reeks,
I love to hear her speak, yet well I know
10   That music hath a far more pleasing sound.
I grant I never saw a goddess go,
My mistress, when she walks, treads on the ground.   Ⓐ
    And yet, by Heaven, I think my love as rare
    As any she belied° with false compare.   Ⓑ

3. dun: dull, grayish brown.

5. damasked: marked or streaked in two colors.

14. belied: misrepresented.

Ⓐ **Literary Focus** Shakespearean Sonnets What is unusual about the speaker's description of his beloved in this sonnet?

Ⓑ **Reading Focus** Using Text Structure to Understand Meaning How does the final couplet clarify the speaker's attitude toward his mistress?

Vocabulary **reeks** (reeks) *v.:* has a strong, bad smell.

The Lady with the Ermine, by Leonardo da Vinci (1496).
Czartoryski Museum, Krakow, Poland.

Applying Your Skills

Sonnets 71, 73, 116, and 130

Respond and Think Critically

Reading Focus

Read with a Purpose

1. According to the speaker in these poems, what effects do time and nature have on love?

Reading Skills: Using Text Structure to Understand Meaning

2. As you read, you noted the location of the turn in each of the sonnets. Now, add your conclusions about theme and the details that support those conclusions.

Poem	Turn, or Shift in Thought	Theme	Supporting Details
Sonnet 71			
Sonnet 73			

✓ Vocabulary Check

Match each Vocabulary word with its synonym.

3. surly   **a.** sullen

4. reeks   **b.** hindrances

5. impediments   **b.** perish

6. expire   **d.** stinks

Literary Focus

Literary Analysis

7. **Analyze** In Sonnet 71, is the speaker sincere when he calls the world *wise?* Explain.

8. **Interpret** In Sonnet 73, how does the speaker's age affect his beloved?

9. **Compare and Contrast** How do the sentiments expressed in Sonnets 116 and 130 differ?

10. **Evaluate** Which sonnet expresses the most profound thoughts about love? Which has the greatest emotional impact? Use details in your answer.

Literary Skills: Shakespearean Sonnets

11. **Analyze** Shakespeare adheres to the basic sonnet structure but plays with the rules. Give an example of something he does that is unexpected in one of these four sonnets. What is the effect of the deviation?

Literary Skills Review: Tone

12. **Analyze** The writer's attitude toward the subject or the reader is called **tone.** Compare and contrast the tones of these four sonnets.

Writing Focus

Think as a Reader/Writer

Use It in Your Writing What metaphors are used to describe love in Sonnet 116? How do these metaphors express the poem's theme? Using your own metaphors, write a short essay about the fleetingness or the permanence of love.

What Do You Think Now?

In each sonnet, how do the speaker's emotions affect how he thinks about the world?

Applying Your Skills

Sonnets 71, 73, 116, and 130

CHOICES

As you respond to the Choices, use these **Academic Vocabulary** words as appropriate: establish, ensure, widespread, controversy, contradiction.

REVIEW
Compare Petrarch and Shakespeare
Unlike the Shakespearean sonnet, the Petrarchan sonnet is divided into an eight-line octave and a six-line sestet. In a Petrarchan sonnet, the turn or shift usually occurs on or near the ninth line. Read Sonnet 42 by Petrarch. Write a brief essay comparing his sonnet to one of Shakespeare's. Consider the structure of the poems as well as the language, imagery, themes, and poetic devices.

Sonnet 42
by **Petrarch**

The spring returns, the spring wind softly blowing	*a*
Sprinkles the grass with gleam and glitter of showers,	*b*
Powdering pearl and diamond, dripping with flowers,	*b*
Dropping wet flowers, dancing the winters going;	*a*
The swallow twitters, the groves of midnight are glowing	*a*
With nightingale music and madness; the sweet fierce powers	*b*
Of love flame up through the earth; the seed-soul towers	*b*
And trembles; nature is filled to overflowing …	*a*
The spring returns, but there is no returning	*c*
Of spring for me. O heart with anguish burning!	*c*
She that unlocked all April in a breath	*d*
Returns not … And these meadows, blossoms, birds	*e*
These lovely gentle girls—words, empty words	*e*
As bitter as the black estates of death!	*d*

—*translated by Joseph Auslander*

CONNECT
Compose Modern Messages
TechFocus Many of these sonnets function as messages from the speaker to a loved one. Today, people can send personal messages through various avenues, such as e-mail, voice mail, songs, and greeting cards. Choose two of the sonnets, and re-create their messages in one of these modern forms. Present your revised message to your class. Which form do you think is more effective at establishing and conveying its message? Which form is more powerful? Why do you think so?

EXTEND
Sing a Song of Shakespeare
Over the years, setting Shakespeare's poems to music has become a widespread practice. Choose two of your favorite sonnets from this collection, and search for melodies for each. If you can, write original music for them. Alternatively, you can pick famous existing melodies that you feel express the tone and mood of the sonnet. Play the melodies for your class, enlisting the help of a musical classmate to sing for you. Explain why you picked those particular sonnets and melodies and why you feel they express the mood of Shakespeare's poems.

Chateau de Chaumont Tapestry Set (c. 1500–1510), Tapestry weave: silk and wool. The Cleveland Museum of Art, Leonard C. Hanna, Jr. Fund.

Learn It Online
Find out how media literate you are at

go.hrw.com L12-400 **Go**

Reading Focus

The Tragedy of Macbeth

Using Questioning to Monitor Reading by **Kylene Beers**

When we say someone is lost in a book, we usually mean that he or she is totally absorbed by a good story. It is also possible to get lost in a book in quite a different way if—for one reason or another—you are confused about what the text means.

Some texts are more challenging than others to read. Works written in a different culture or time period often use unfamiliar settings, expressions, and archaic vocabulary. Use the footnotes provided to explain the meanings of words that are unfamiliar to you.

When a text is written in poetic verse, the meter (iambic pentameter in the case of Shakespeare's *Macbeth*) can be intimidating. Remember that iambic pentameter imitates the natural rhythm of human speech; when a section is confusing, read it aloud.

In addition to using footnotes and reading aloud, read the summary provided for each scene. Also, read the stage directions. Both will provide you with background information and context that you need.

Even with these aids, sometimes you need to ask yourself questions when you feel lost in a challenging text. For example, read the following excerpt from Act I, Scene 2 of *Macbeth*.

> **Malcolm:** This is the sergeant
>   Who like a good and hardy soldier
>   fought
>   'Gainst my captivity. Hail, brave
>   friend!
>   Say to the king the knowledge of
>   the broil
>   As thou didst leave it.

The stage directions and summary for the scene explain that Malcolm is with King Duncan and a bleeding captain fresh from the battlefield. The footnote defines *broil* as "quarrel." Using these clues, you can form a good question: What is Malcolm asking the wounded soldier (whom he calls *sergeant*) to do? The answer is that Malcolm asks him to give the king current information about the battle.

Let's use this technique again with this passage from Act I, Scene 3 (lines 39–43).

> **Banquo:** What are these
>   So withered, and so wild in their
>   attire,
>   That look not like th' inhabitants o'
>   th' earth,
>   And yet are on't? Live you, or are
>   you aught
>   That man may question?

The summary and scene directions tell you that Banquo and Macbeth have met three witches. Using clues from the text ("withered, and wild"; they "look not like" inhabitants of the earth), you can infer that Banquo is asking whether or not the witches are real.

Your Turn

Read this passage from Act I, Scene 3, and then ask yourself questions to monitor your understanding. Which of your own questions can you answer?

> **Ross:**
> And for an earnest of a greater honor,
> He bade me, from him, call thee Thane of
>   Cawdor;
> In which addition, hail, most worthy thane!
> For it is thine.

Learn It Online
For more information on this historical period, go to

go.hrw.com L12-401 **Go**

INTRODUCTION TO
THE TRAGEDY of MACBETH
SOURCES OF THE PLAY

Shakespeare's play *Macbeth* conforms to the general rule of Renaissance tragedies that states that the drama had to be about real people whose deeds are recorded in history. (Renaissance comedies, on the other hand, concerned the imaginary doings of fictitious characters.) Shakespeare took the main events of Macbeth's career as king of Scotland (1040–1057) from Raphael Holinshed's *Chronicles of England, Scotland, and Ireland* (1577), Shakespeare's source for historical material for many of his plays.

There are striking differences, however, between Shakespeare's account of Macbeth and Holinshed's. The historical Macbeth had a much more legitimate claim to King Duncan's throne than did the Macbeth of Shakespeare. The historical Macbeth gained the throne with the help of other nobles dissatisfied with King Duncan, and he ruled rather successfully. In contrast, Shakespeare's Macbeth has no supporters except his wife, whose strong and ambitious nature Shakespeare develops from a brief moment in history. Furthermore, in the play, the reign of Macbeth and his

Ellen Terry as Lady Macbeth (1885-1886), by John Singer Sargent.
Tate Gallery, London.

wife brings nothing but violence and disaster to Scotland.

One explanation for these changes to Holinshed's story is that Shakespeare wanted to explore—from a safe distance—the events and attitudes of his own time. Contemporary audiences have all but lost sight of the scandal that was a backdrop for the play: the Gunpowder Plot of 1605, in which several Catholic zealots plotted to blow up King James I and his Protestant Parliament. Garry Wills, a professor and political columnist, says that for its Elizabethan audience, *Macbeth* was a thriller. (According to Wills, the Gunpowder Plot would compare to a plan to bomb the U.S. Capitol building during a presidential address.) The threat to an anointed king, and the perceived evil behind it, was relived in Macbeth's imperilment of the social order in a Scotland of the distant past.

Shakespeare altered his source text, in ways both small and large, in order to pay homage to his own king and country; his changes were intended for an audience of his particular moment in history. If King James, the patron of Shakespeare's company, ever saw the play, it must have pleased him. Since he had recently survived the Gunpowder Plot, James was especially interested in attacks on kings; he always defended the idea that he ruled by divine right. Moreover, James was a Scot and claimed to be a direct descendant of Banquo, to whom the third witch says, "Thou shalt get kings, though thou be none." For these reasons, scholars have long considered *Macbeth* a play written for a command performance at court, despite having no direct evidence. James reportedly refused to sit through long plays, and this royal shortcoming has even been used to explain the fact that *Macbeth* is one of Shakespeare's shortest plays.

We can also say that Shakespeare made many changes in Holinshed's story because Shakespeare was much more interested in psychological truth than in historical fact. In this sense, *Macbeth* is also about *real* people, men and women tempted by ambition and power, caught up in a web of wants and needs. In playing out these real feelings and desires, Shakespeare's *Macbeth* transcends the historical Macbeth and gives us a portrait and a play for all times. As the critic Sylvan Barnet notes, "When one reads or sees *Macbeth,* one cannot help feeling that one is experiencing a re-creation or representation of what a man is, in the present, even in the timeless."

Three Witches, by Johann Heinrich Fuessli, oil on canvas. Royal Shakespeare Theater Collection, London.

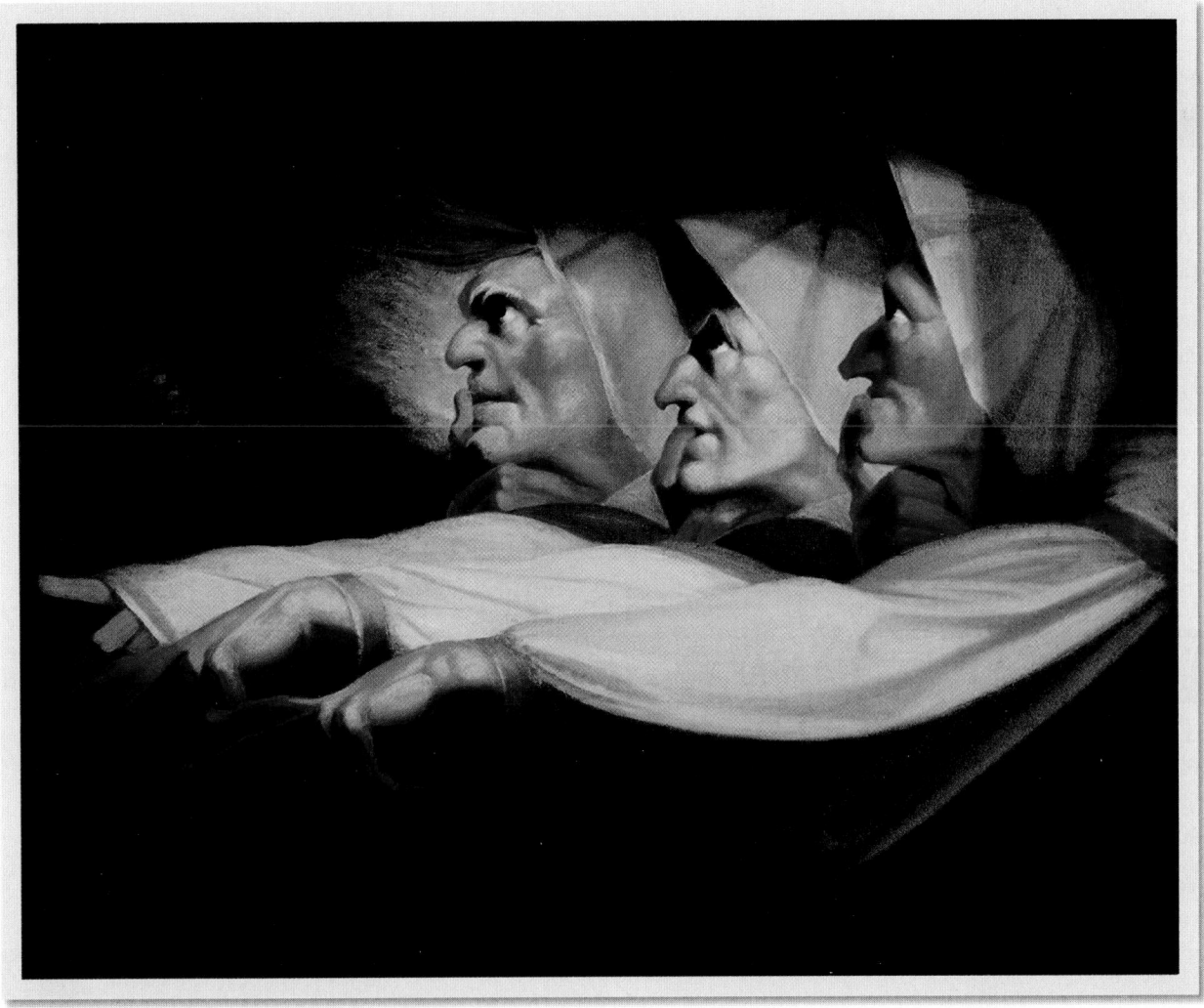

Preparing to Read

The Tragedy of Macbeth, Act I

Reader/Writer
Notebook
Use your **RWN** to complete the activities for this selection.

Literary Focus

Tragedy A **tragedy** is a story in which a heroic character dies or comes to another unhappy end. The main character in most tragedies is digni-fied, courageous, and often high ranking. The downfall of the character occurs because of a **tragic flaw**—a character weakness or error in judg-ment—or because of circumstances beyond his or her control. The tragic hero usually gains wisdom by the end of the story.

Literary Perspectives Apply the literary perspective described on page 407 as you read this play.

Reading Focus

Using Questioning to Monitor Reading Because it was written four centuries ago, *Macbeth* contains language and ideas that may be unfa-miliar to you. As you read the play, you can clarify your understanding by pausing to ask yourself questions.

Into Action As you read, use a chart like the one below to follow the development of the plot. Note one question for every major scene.

Act, Scene, Line	Questions I Have
Act I, Scene 1, line 10	What might the witches mean by something both "foul" and "fair"?

Writing Focus

Think as a Reader/Writer
Find It in Your Reading In your *Reader/Writer Notebook,* note how Shakespeare reveals his characters through their speech, thoughts, actions, and appearance.

TechFocus As you read *Macbeth,* take notes on how you imagine the setting for each scene. Think about how you could convey the setting in a media presentation.

Language Coach
Multiple Meanings Repeated words can carry many shades of meaning. The adjective *strange* is used sixteen times in *Macbeth;* the adverb *strangely* appears twice. *Strange* can have several meanings:

- not normal or ordinary; odd
- not previously experienced
- hard to explain
- out of place
- coming from another place; alien

When you read this word, pause to consider which meaning is being used. Ask yourself: Why might Shakespeare have repeated *strange* so frequently in *Macbeth?*

(Opposite)
Liev Schreiber and Jennifer Ehle star in Moises Kaufman's production of *Macbeth,* at the Delacorte Theater in NY (June 13th, 2006).

Learn It Online
Meet Macbeth through this video introduction:

go.hrw.com	L12-404	**Go**

THE TRAGEDY of MACBETH

by WILLIAM SHAKESPEARE

Read with a Purpose
Read to discover what tragic flaw ensures Macbeth's downfall.

Build Background
Some of the strongest and most widespread ideas about tragedy come from the Greek philosopher Aristotle. Aristotle observed that tragic drama of his time centered on a hero—usually of high status—who possesses a tragic flaw. As a result of this flaw, the hero's choices bring about personal and universal catastrophes. Shakespeare's tragedies are written in this ancient tradition, but with attention to his own audience.

For example, in Shakespeare's time, audiences would have expected special effects in his plays. Thunder, produced by rolling cannonballs in the area above the stage, and lightning would have set the mood in the first scene, when witches might have made their appearance from a trapdoor on the stage.

THE TRAGEDY of MACBETH
CHARACTERS

Duncan, king of Scotland

Malcolm } his sons
Donalbain

Macbeth
Banquo
Macduff
Lennox
Ross } noblemen of Scotland
Menteith
Angus
Caithness

Fleance, son to Banquo

Siward, earl of Northumberland, general of the English forces

Young Siward, his son

Seyton, an officer attending on Macbeth

Son to Macduff
An English Doctor
A Scottish Doctor
A Porter
An Old Man
Three Murderers
Lady Macbeth
Lady Macduff
A Gentlewoman attending on Lady Macbeth
Hecate
Witches
Apparitions
Lords, Officers, Soldiers, Attendants, and Messengers

Setting: Scotland; England

Glamis Castle, Angus, Scotland. Macbeth is referred to as the thane, or lord, of Glamis. The castle is believed by some to be the fictional setting for the play.

Act I

Scene 1. *An open place.*

Thunder and lightning. Enter three WITCHES.

First Witch.
   When shall we three meet again?
   In thunder, lightning, or in rain?
Second Witch.
   When the hurlyburly's done,
   When the battle's lost and won.
Third Witch.
5   That will be ere the set of sun.
First Witch.
   Where the place?
Second Witch.   Upon the heath.
Third Witch.
   There to meet with Macbeth.
First Witch.
   I come, Graymalkin.°
Second Witch.
   Paddock° calls.
Third Witch.   Anon!°
All.
10   Fair is foul, and foul is fair.
   Hover through the fog and filthy air.   *[Exeunt.]*

---

8. Graymalkin: the first witch's attendant or familiar, a gray cat.
9. Paddock: a toad, the second witch's familiar. **Anon!:** Soon!

A **Literary Focus** **Tragedy** What elements in the first scene lay the foundation for the tragedy to come?

Literary Perspectives

Analyzing Historical Context Knowledge of the ideas and events of Shakespeare's time can help you understand *Macbeth*'s themes of bloodshed, violence, and political turmoil. Perhaps the most important historical event surrounding *Macbeth* was the ascension of a new monarch in charge of the British Isles. James I, king of Britain and Shakespeare's patron when *Macbeth* was written, had ruled Scotland since he was an infant. His path to ruling all of Britain was not direct, for he followed in the footsteps of his ancestors, assuming the throne when Queen Elizabeth I died childless in 1603. Political struggles had taxed Britain for centuries, and Henry VIII had overthrown the religious system as well as killed two wives in the pursuit of a male heir. Because of this unrest, English citizens had a strong belief in the need for social order and a fear of the disorder that could result from an abuse of power.

As you read, be sure to notice the questions in the text, which will guide you in using this perspective.

Scene 2. *A camp.*

Alarum within.° Enter KING DUNCAN, MALCOLM, DONALBAIN,
    LENNOX, *with* ATTENDANTS, *meeting a bleeding* CAPTAIN.

King.
    What bloody man is that? He can report,
    As seemeth by his plight, of the revolt
    The newest state.
Malcolm.   This is the sergeant
    Who like a good and hardy soldier fought
5   'Gainst my captivity. Hail, brave friend!
    Say to the king the knowledge of the broil°
    As thou didst leave it.
Captain.   Doubtful it stood,
    As two spent swimmers, that do cling together
    And choke their art.° The merciless Macdonwald—
10   Worthy to be a rebel for to that
    The multiplying villainies of nature
    Do swarm upon him—from the Western Isles°
    Of kerns and gallowglasses° is supplied;
    And Fortune, on his damnèd quarrel smiling,
15   Showed like a rebel's whore: but all's too weak:
    For brave Macbeth—well he deserves that name—
    Disdaining Fortune, with his brandished steel,
    Which smoked with bloody execution,
    Like valor's minion° carved out his passage
20   Till he faced the slave;
    Which nev'r shook hands, nor bade farewell to him,
    Till he unseamed him from the nave to th' chops,°
    And fixed his head upon our battlements.
King.
    O valiant cousin! Worthy gentleman!
Captain.
25   As whence the sun 'gins his reflection°
    Shipwracking storms and direful thunders break,
    So from that spring whence comfort seemed to come
    Discomfort swells. Mark, King of Scotland, mark:
    No sooner justice had, with valor armed,
30   Compelled these skipping kerns to trust their heels
    But the Norweyan° lord, surveying vantage,°
    With furbished arms and new supplies of men,
    Began a fresh assault.
King.   Dismayed not this

Alarum within: trumpets offstage.

6. broil: quarrel.

? **Staging the Play**
7. *The captain is bloody and could be carried in or supported by others. How would he speak his lines?*

9. choke their art: hinder each other's ability to swim.

12. Western Isles: a region of western Scotland comprising the Outer Hebrides.

13. kerns and gallowglasses: lightly armed Irish soldiers and heavily armed soldiers.

19. minion: favorite.

22. unseamed . . . chops: split him from navel to jaws.

? **23.** *Notice that this horrible action is described by a messenger, not shown onstage. What did Macbeth do to the rebellious Macdonwald?*

25. 'gins his reflection: rises.

31. Norweyan: Norwegian. **surveying vantage:** seeing an opportunity.

Our captains, Macbeth and Banquo? **B**

Captain.   Yes;

35 As° sparrows eagles, or the hare the lion.
If I say sooth,° I must report they were
As cannons overcharged with double cracks;
So they doubly redoubled strokes upon the foe.
Except° they meant to bathe in reeking wounds,
40 Or memorize another Golgotha,°   **C**
I cannot tell—
But I am faint; my gashes cry for help.

King.
So well thy words become thee as thy wounds;
They smack of honor both. Go get him surgeons.

> [*Exit* CAPTAIN *attended.*]

[*Enter* ROSS *and* ANGUS.]

Who comes here?

45 **Malcolm.**   The worthy Thane° of Ross.

Lennox.
What a haste looks through his eyes! So should he look
That seems to° speak things strange.

Ross.   God save the king!

King.
Whence cam'st thou, worthy thane?

Ross.   From Fife, great king;
Where the Norweyan banners flout the sky
50 And fan our people cold.
Norway himself,° with terrible numbers,   **D**
Assisted by that most disloyal traitor
The Thane of Cawdor, began a dismal conflict;
Till that Bellona's bridegroom,° lapped in proof,°
55 Confronted him with self-comparisons,°
Point against point, rebellious arm 'gainst arm,
Curbing his lavish° spirit: and, to conclude,
The victory fell on us.

King.   Great happiness!

---

35. As: no more than.

? 35. *This line can be delivered in several ways. How do you imagine the captain speaks it?*

36. sooth: truth.

39. Except: unless.

40. memorize another Golgotha: make the place as memorable as Golgotha, where Christ was crucified.

? 44. *Duncan can be portrayed in several ways: as a strong but aging king, as a frail old man, or as a kind but foolish old man who doesn't understand what's going on. As the play goes on, decide how you interpret Duncan's character.*

45. Thane: Scottish title of nobility.

47. seems to: seems about to.

51. Norway himself: that is, the king of Norway.

54. Bellona's bridegroom: Bellona is the goddess of war. Macbeth, who is a great soldier, is called her mate. **lapped in proof:** clad in armor.

55. self-comparisons: counter-movements.

57. lavish: insolent; rude.

B **Reading Focus** **Using Questioning to Monitor Reading** This line closely links Macbeth and Banquo, yet the title of the play is *The Tragedy of Macbeth*. What questions does this raise for you about the relationship between these two characters?

C **Literary Perspectives** **Analyzing Historical Context** What does this reference to Golgotha tell you about the religious beliefs of the time?

D **Literary Perspectives** **Analyzing Historical Context** What traditional relationship between rulers and the military—quite different from what we expect today—is revealed in both the Scottish and the Norwegian approach to warfare in this scene?

Peter Lindford as Macbeth and Gerard Logan as Banquo.

Ross.   That now
        Sweno, the Norways' king, craves composition;°
60   Nor would we deign him burial of his men
        Till he disbursèd, at Saint Colme's Inch,°
        Ten thousand dollars to our general use.
King.
        No more that Thane of Cawdor shall deceive   **E**
        Our bosom interest:° go pronounce his present° death,
65   And with his former title greet Macbeth.
Ross.
        I'll see it done.
King.
        What he hath lost, noble Macbeth hath won.   **F**   [*Exeunt.*]

E **Reading Focus** **Using Questioning to Monitor Reading** King Duncan states that he was deceived by the Thane of Cawdor. What questions does this raise for you about Duncan's personality?

F **Literary Focus** **Tragedy** What evidence in this scene supports the idea of Macbeth as a high-ranking, dignified, and courageous man?

59. composition: peace terms.

61. Saint Colme's Inch: island off the coast of Scotland.

64. bosom interest: heart's trust. present: immediate.

? **Staging the Play**
67. *As you read, notice how later events relate to the king's words. How would you have him say these lines?*

Scene 3. *A heath.*

Thunder. Enter the three WITCHES.

First Witch.
　Where hast thou been, sister?
Second Witch.
　Killing swine.
Third Witch.
　Sister, where thou?
First Witch.
　A sailor's wife had chestnuts in her lap,
5　And mounched, and mounched, and mounched. "Give me,"
　　quoth I.
　"Aroint thee,° witch!" the rump-fed ronyon° cries.
　Her husband's to Aleppo gone, master o' th' *Tiger:*
　But in a sieve° I'll thither sail,
　And, like a rat without a tail,
10　I'll do, I'll do, and I'll do.
Second Witch.
　I'll give thee a wind.
First Witch.
　Th' art kind.
Third Witch.
　And I another.
First Witch.
　I myself have all the other;
15　And the very ports they blow,°
　All the quarters that they know
　I' th' shipman's card.°
　I'll drain him dry as hay:
　Sleep shall neither night nor day
20　Hang upon his penthouse lid;°
　He shall live a man forbid:°
　Weary sev'nights nine times nine
　Shall he dwindle, peak,° and pine:
　Though his bark cannot be lost,
25　Yet it shall be tempest-tossed.
　Look what I have.
Second Witch.
　Show me, show me.
First Witch.
　Here I have a pilot's thumb,
　Wracked as homeward he did come.

[Drum within.]

6. Aroint thee: begone. **rump-fed ronyon:** fat-rumped, scabby creature.
8. But in a sieve: Witches were believed to have the power to sail in sieves.

15. ports they blow: harbors they blow into.
17. card: compass.

20. penthouse lid: eyelid.
21. forbid: cursed.

23. peak: grow pale.

Third Witch.

30   A drum, a drum!
       Macbeth doth come.

All.

       The weird sisters, hand in hand,
       Posters° of the sea and land,
       Thus do go about, about:

35   Thrice to thine, and thrice to mine,
       And thrice again, to make up nine.
       Peace! The charm's wound up.

       [*Enter* MACBETH *and* BANQUO.]

Macbeth.

       So foul and fair a day I have not seen.   **G**

Banquo.

       How far is't called to Forres?° What are these
40   So withered, and so wild in their attire,
       That look not like th' inhabitants o' th' earth,
       And yet are on't? Live you, or are you aught
       That man may question? You seem to understand me,
       By each at once her choppy° finger laying
45   Upon her skinny lips. You should° be women,
       And yet your beards forbid me to interpret
       That you are so.

Macbeth.   Speak, if you can: what are you?

First Witch.

       All hail, Macbeth! Hail to thee, Thane of Glamis!

Second Witch.

       All hail, Macbeth! Hail to thee, Thane of Cawdor!

Third Witch.

50   All hail, Macbeth, that shalt be king hereafter!

Banquo.

       Good sir, why do you start, and seem to fear   **H**
       Things that do sound so fair? I' th' name of truth,
       Are ye fantastical, or that indeed
       Which outwardly ye show? My noble partner

33. Posters: travelers.

? **38.** *What words is Macbeth echoing here? Why, given the weather, does Macbeth think the day is "fair"?*

39. Forres: town in northeastern Scotland and site of King Duncan's castle.

? **Staging the Play**
39. *What should Banquo do as he sees the witches? How should his voice change between the words* Forres *and* What?
44. choppy: chapped; sore.
45. should: must.

? **51.** *Banquo's words give a clue as to how Macbeth reacts to the witches. What is Macbeth doing? When Banquo asks, "Are ye fantastical," whom is he addressing?*

G **Reading Focus** **Using Questioning to Monitor Reading** This line echoes the witches' line in Act I, Scene 1, line 10. What questions does it bring up for you about Macbeth and the witches?

H **Literary Focus** **Tragedy** Why might a high-ranking noble—who is related to the king ("cousin"; Act I, Scene 1, line 24) and presumably in line for the throne—"start, and seem to fear" when he hears the prediction that he will, in fact, become king?

412   Unit 2 • Collection 4

55   You greet with present grace and great prediction
     Of noble having and of royal hope,
     That he seems rapt withal:° to me you speak not.
     If you can look into the seeds of time,
     And say which grain will grow and which will not,
60   Speak then to me, who neither beg nor fear
     Your favors nor your hate.

First Witch. Hail!

Second Witch. Hail!

Third Witch. Hail!

First Witch.

65   Lesser than Macbeth, and greater.

Second Witch.

     Not so happy,° yet much happier.

Third Witch.

     Thou shalt get° kings, though thou be none.
     So all hail, Macbeth and Banquo!

First Witch.

     Banquo and Macbeth, all hail!

Macbeth.

70   Stay, you imperfect° speakers, tell me more:
     By Sinel's death I know I am Thane of Glamis;
     But how of Cawdor? The Thane of Cawdor lives,
     A prosperous gentleman; and to be king
     Stands not within the prospect of belief,
75   No more than to be Cawdor. Say from whence
     You owe° this strange intelligence?° Or why
     Upon this blasted heath you stop our way
     With such prophetic greeting? Speak, I charge you.   **J**

                              [WITCHES *vanish.*]

Banquo.

     The earth hath bubbles as the water has,
80   And these are of them. Whither are they vanished?

---

57. rapt withal: entranced by it.

? **61.** *What does Banquo ask the witches?*

66. happy: lucky.

67. get: beget.

70. imperfect: unfinished.

? **Elements of Drama**
71. *Sinel is Macbeth's father. What do you think Macbeth's tone is here? Is he overeager? or just casually curious?*

76. owe: own; have. **intelligence:** information.

? **Staging the Play**
Stage direction: The witches on Shakespeare's stage would have vanished through the trapdoor. Is Banquo, in his next speech, intrigued or disturbed? How does Macbeth feel?

---

① **Reading Focus** **Using Questioning to Monitor Reading** Macbeth and Banquo are again linked, this time by the witches. What questions does this second connection raise?

① **Literary Perspective** **Analyzing Historical Context** The portrayal of the witches reveals beliefs about witches in Shakespeare's time. What traits are displayed here?

Macbeth.
Into the air, and what seemed corporal° melted
As breath into the wind. Would they had stayed!
Banquo.
Were such things here as we do speak about?
Or have we eaten on the insane root°
85 That takes the reason prisoner?
Macbeth.
Your children shall be kings.
Banquo.   You shall be king.
Macbeth.
And Thane of Cawdor too. Went it not so?
Banquo.
To th' selfsame tune and words. Who's here?

[*Enter* ROSS *and* ANGUS.]

Ross.
The king hath happily received, Macbeth,
90 The news of thy success; and when he reads°
Thy personal venture in the rebels' fight,
His wonders and his praises do contend
Which should be thine or his. Silenced with that,
In viewing o'er the rest o' th' selfsame day,
95 He finds thee in the stout Norweyan ranks,
Nothing afeard of what thyself didst make,
Strange images of death.° As thick as tale
Came post with post,° and every one did bear
Thy praises in his kingdom's great defense,
And poured them down before him.
100 **Angus.**   We are sent
To give thee, from our royal master, thanks;
Only to herald thee into his sight,
Not pay thee.
Ross.
And for an earnest° of a greater honor,
105 He bade me, from him, call thee Thane of Cawdor;
In which addition,° hail, most worthy thane!
For it is thine.
Banquo.   What, can the devil speak true?
Macbeth.
The Thane of Cawdor lives: why do you dress me
In borrowed robes?
Angus.   Who was the thane lives yet,
110 But under heavy judgment bears that life
Which he deserves to lose. Whether he was combined
With those of Norway, or did line° the rebel

81. **corporal:** corporeal (bodily; physical).

84. **insane root:** henbane, believed to cause insanity.

90. **reads:** considers.

96–97. **Nothing . . . death:** killing, and not being afraid of being killed.
98. **post with post:** messenger with a message.

104. **earnest:** pledge.

106. **addition:** title.

112. **line:** support.

With hidden help and vantage, or that with both
He labored in his country's wrack, I know not;
115 But treasons capital,° confessed and proved,
Have overthrown him.

Macbeth (*aside*).   Glamis, and Thane of Cawdor:
The greatest is behind. (*To* ROSS *and* ANGUS.) Thanks for your
   pains.
(*Aside to* BANQUO.) Do you not hope your children shall be kings,
When those that gave the Thane of Cawdor to me
Promised no less to them?

120 **Banquo** (*aside to* MACBETH). That, trusted home,°
Might yet enkindle you unto the crown,°
Besides the Thane of Cawdor. But 'tis strange:
And oftentimes, to win us to our harm,
The instruments of darkness tell us truths,
125 Win us with honest trifles, to betray 's   Ⓚ
In deepest consequence.
Cousins,° a word, I pray you.

Macbeth (*aside*).   Two truths are told
As happy prologues to the swelling act
Of the imperial theme.—I thank you, gentlemen.—
130 (*Aside.*) This supernatural soliciting
Cannot be ill, cannot be good. If ill,
Why hath it given me earnest of success,
Commencing in a truth? I am Thane of Cawdor:
If good, why do I yield to that suggestion
135 Whose horrid image doth unfix my hair
And make my seated heart knock at my ribs,
Against the use of nature? Present fears
Are less than horrible imaginings.
My thought, whose murder yet is but fantastical,   Ⓛ
140 Shakes so my single° state of man that function
Is smothered in surmise, and nothing is
But what is not.°

Banquo.   Look, how our partner's rapt.

Macbeth (*aside*).
If chance will have me king, why, chance may crown me,   Ⓜ
Without my stir.

---

115. capital: deserving death.

❓ 117. Behind *here means "to follow." How should this important aside be spoken? What is Macbeth's mood?*

120. trusted home: trusted all the way.
121. enkindle . . . crown: arouse in you the ambition to become king.

❓ 126. *How does this speech show Banquo as part of the conscience of the play?*
127. Cousins: This word is used frequently by Shakespeare to mean "fellows" or "relatives" of some sort.

❓ Staging the Play
Stage direction: A character's private comments on what is happening, asides, are spoken for the benefit of the audience. When a character is delivering an aside, the director or the playwright must arrange for the others onstage to be involved in some way so that it would be natural for them not to notice the character delivering the aside. Where should Macbeth go onstage to deliver this important aside? Where are Banquo, Angus, and Ross?

140. single: unaided; weak.
141–142. nothing . . . not: Nothing is real to me except my imaginings.

Ⓚ **Literary Focus** **Tragedy** What do Banquo's words about the witches indicate about Macbeth's fate?

Ⓛ **Reading Focus** **Using Questioning to Monitor Reading** Macbeth describes different paths to the throne. What questions can you ask to determine his fears and concerns?

Ⓜ **Reading Focus** **Using Questioning to Monitor Reading** This last speech seems to contradict the previous one. What questions can you ask to clarify his motives?

Banquo.   New honors come upon him,
145   Like our strange° garments, cleave not to their mold
       But with the aid of use.
       Macbeth (*aside*).   Come what come may,
       Time and the hour runs through the roughest day.
       Banquo.
       Worthy Macbeth, we stay upon your leisure.
       Macbeth.
       Give me your favor.° My dull brain was wrought
150   With things forgotten. Kind gentlemen, your pains
       Are registered where every day I turn
       The leaf to read them. Let us toward the king.
       (*Aside to* BANQUO.) Think upon what hath chanced, and at
           more time,
       The interim having weighed it, let us speak
       Our free hearts each to other.
155   **Banquo.**   Very gladly.
       Macbeth.
       Till then, enough. Come, friends.   [*Exeunt.*]

Scene 4. *Forres. The palace.*

Flourish.° Enter KING DUNCAN, LENNOX, MALCOLM, DONALBAIN, *and*
    ATTENDANTS.

       King.
       Is execution done on Cawdor? Are not
       Those in commission yet returned?
       Malcolm.   My liege,
       They are not yet come back. But I have spoke
       With one that saw him die, who did report
5   That very frankly he confessed his treasons,
       Implored your highness' pardon and set forth
       A deep repentance: nothing in his life
       Became him like the leaving it. He died **N**
       As one that had been studied in his death
10   To throw away the dearest thing he owed°
       As 'twere a careless trifle.
       King.   There's no art
       To find the mind's construction in the face:

N **Reading Focus** Using Questioning to Monitor Reading Shakespeare might
have described Cawdor's death in many different ways. What questions do you have about
Shakespeare's decision to describe the traitor's death as honorable?

Right column notes:

145. strange: new.

? 145. *To what does Banquo compare Macbeth and his new honors? Is Banquo's mood different from Macbeth's?*

149. favor: pardon.

Flourish: of trumpets.

? 8. *What does this famous line mean: "nothing in his life / Became him like the leaving it"?*
10. owed: owned.

? Elements of Drama
12. *What irony do you detect here? What does Duncan fail to realize about another face?*

"ONLY I HAVE LEFT TO SAY,
MORE IS THY DUE THAN MORE THAN ALL CAN PAY."

Macbeth (Peter Lindford) with King Duncan (Daid Pearson), Ludlow Festival, England.

He was a gentleman on whom I built
An absolute trust.

[*Enter* MACBETH, BANQUO, ROSS, *and* ANGUS.]

                        O worthiest cousin!
15   The sin of my ingratitude even now
Was heavy on me: thou art so far before,
That swiftest wing of recompense is slow
To overtake thee. Would thou hadst less deserved,
That the proportion° both of thanks and payment
20   Might have been mine! Only I have left to say,
More is thy due than more than all can pay.

Macbeth.
The service and the loyalty I owe,
In doing it, pays itself.° Your highness' part
Is to receive our duties: and our duties
25   Are to your throne and state children and servants;
Which do but what they should, by doing everything
Safe toward° your love and honor.

King.   Welcome hither.

19. proportion: greater amount.

23. pays itself: is its own reward.

27. Safe toward: safeguarding.

I have begun to plant thee, and will labor
To make thee full of growing. Noble Banquo,
30 That hast no less deserved, nor must be known
No less to have done so, let me enfold thee
And hold thee to my heart.

Banquo.   There if I grow,
The harvest is your own.

King.   My plenteous joys,
Wanton in fullness, seek to hide themselves
35 In drops of sorrow. Sons, kinsmen, thanes,
And you whose places are the nearest, know,
We will establish our estate upon
Our eldest, Malcolm, whom we name hereafter
The Prince of Cumberland: which honor must
40 Not unaccompanied invest him only,
But signs of nobleness, like stars, shall shine
On all deservers. From hence to Inverness,°
And bind us further to you.

Macbeth.
The rest is labor, which is not used for you.°
45 I'll be myself the harbinger,° and make joyful
The hearing of my wife with your approach;
So, humbly take my leave.

King.   My worthy Cawdor!

Macbeth (*aside*).
The Prince of Cumberland! That is a step
On which I must fall down, or else o'erleap,
50 For in my way it lies. Stars, hide your fires;
Let not light see my black and deep desires:
The eye wink at the hand;° yet let that be
Which the eye fears, when it is done, to see.   [*Exit.*]

King.
True, worthy Banquo; he is full so valiant,
55 And in his commendations° I am fed;
It is a banquet to me. Let's after him,
Whose care is gone before to bid us welcome.
It is a peerless kinsman.   [*Flourish. Exeunt.*]

Scene 5. *Inverness. Macbeth's castle.*

Enter Macbeth's wife, LADY MACBETH, *alone, with a letter.*

Lady Macbeth (*reads*). "They met me in the day of success;
    and I have learned by the perfect'st report they have more in

---

⓪ **Literary Focus** Tragedy How do you think Macbeth would have reacted to this
news had he not met the witches and heard their prophecy?

? **32.** *You know Macbeth's thoughts. How do you feel about him as the king lavishes praise on him? Is the king's reception of Banquo even warmer? How might Macbeth react here?*

? **35.** *There's a clue in this line that shows how moved the king is. What is the king doing as he says the words "drops of sorrow"?*

42. Inverness: Macbeth's castle.
? **43.** *Who is to inherit Duncan's crown?*
44. The rest . . . you: When rest is not used for you, it is labor.
45. harbinger: sign of something to come.

52. wink . . . hand: be blind to the hand's deed.
? **53.** *Where in this speech do we begin to hear Macbeth talk in terms of darkness?*
55. his commendations: praises of him.

Glamis Castle, Angus, Scotland.

418 Unit 2 • Collection 4

them than mortal knowledge. When I burned in desire to
question them further, they made themselves air, into which
5   they vanished. Whiles I stood rapt in the wonder of it, came
missives° from the King, who all-hailed me 'Thane of Cawdor'; by which title, before, these weird sisters saluted me,
and referred me to the coming on of time, with 'Hail, king
that shalt be!' This have I thought good to deliver thee, my
10 dearest partner of greatness, that thou mightst not lose the
dues of rejoicing, by being ignorant of what greatness is
promised thee. Lay it to thy heart, and farewell."

Glamis thou art, and Cawdor, and shalt be
What thou art promised. Yet do I fear thy nature;
15 It is too full o' th' milk of human kindness
To catch the nearest way. Thou wouldst be great,
Art not without ambition, but without
The illness° should attend it. What thou wouldst highly,
That wouldst thou holily; wouldst not play false,
20 And yet wouldst wrongly win. Thou'dst have, great Glamis,
That which cries, "Thus thou must do" if thou have it;
And that which rather thou dost fear to do
Than wishest should be undone. Hie thee hither,
That I may pour my spirits in thine ear,
25 And chastise with the valor of my tongue
All that impedes thee from the golden round
Which fate and metaphysical° aid doth seem
To have thee crowned withal. **P**

[*Enter* MESSENGER.]

                              What is your tidings?
Messenger.
      The king comes here tonight.
Lady Macbeth.   Thou'rt mad to say it!
30 Is not thy master with him, who, were't so,
Would have informed for preparation?
Messenger.
      So please you, it is true. Our thane is coming.
One of my fellows had the speed of him,°
Who, almost dead for breath, had scarcely more
Than would make up his message.
35 **Lady Macbeth.**   Give him tending;
He brings great news.   [*Exit* MESSENGER.]
                  The raven himself is hoarse

? Staging the Play
Stage direction: As you
picture Lady Macbeth reading
this letter, try to imagine what she
would be doing onstage and what
her mood would be, especially at
the words "Thane of Cawdor."
6. missives: messengers.

? 13. *What does Lady
Macbeth do with the letter?
Whom is she addressing here with
"thou" and "thy"? How would you
explain "th' milk of human kindness"?*
18. illness: wickedness; evil
nature.

? 26. *What do you guess the
"golden round" is?*
27. metaphysical: supernatural.

33. had . . . him: had more speed
than he did.

? 36. *Who is the raven she
refers to as being hoarse?
Why does she call him a raven?*

P Reading Focus Using Questioning to Monitor Reading What questions do you
have about Lady Macbeth's analysis of her husband's personality?

That croaks the fatal entrance of Duncan
Under my battlements. Come, you spirits
That tend on mortal° thoughts, unsex me here,
40   And fill me, from the crown to the toe, top-full
Of direst cruelty! Make thick my blood,
Stop up th' access and passage to remorse,
That no compunctious visitings of nature°
Shake my fell° purpose, nor keep peace between
45   Th' effect and it! Come to my woman's breasts,
And take my milk for gall,° you murd'ring ministers,°
Wherever in your sightless° substances
You wait on nature's mischief! Come, thick night,
And pall° thee in the dunnest° smoke of hell,
50   That my keen knife see not the wound it makes,
Nor heaven peep through the blanket of the dark,
To cry "Hold, hold!" **Q**

[*Enter* MACBETH.]

                    Great Glamis! Worthy Cawdor!
Greater than both, by the all-hail hereafter!
Thy letters have transported me beyond
55   This ignorant present, and I feel now
The future in the instant.
Macbeth.   My dearest love,
Duncan comes here tonight.
Lady Macbeth.   And when goes hence?
Macbeth.
Tomorrow, as he purposes.
Lady Macbeth.   O, never
Shall sun that morrow see!
60   Your face, my thane, is as a book where men
May read strange matters. To beguile the time,°
Look like the time; bear welcome in your eye,
Your hand, your tongue: look like th' innocent flower,
But be the serpent under't. He that's coming
65   Must be provided for: and you shall put
This night's great business into my dispatch;°
Which shall to all our nights and days to come
Give solely sovereign sway and masterdom.
Macbeth.
We will speak further.
Lady Macbeth.   Only look up clear.°
70   To alter favor ever is to fear.°
Leave all the rest to me.   [*Exeunt.*]

Q **Reading Focus** **Using Questioning to Monitor Reading** What questions can you ask about Lady Macbeth's role in Macbeth's downfall?

39. mortal: deadly.

43. compunctious . . . nature: natural feelings of compassion.
44. fell: savage.
46. gall: a bitter substance; bile.
murd'ring ministers: agents of murder.
47. sightless: invisible.
49. pall: cover with a shroud, a burial cloth. **dunnest:** darkest.

? **52.** *How has Lady Macbeth reinforced the witches' statement: "Fair is foul, and foul is fair"?*

? **Staging the Play**
57. *Is their passion for each other as great as their passion for power? If you feel it is, how might a director illustrate it here?*

61. beguile the time: deceive those around you.

66. dispatch: management.

69. clear: undisturbed.
? **69.** *How is Macbeth feeling?*
70. To alter . . . fear: To show an altered face is dangerous.

"TO ALTER FAVOR EVER IS TO FEAR.
LEAVE ALL THE REST TO ME."

Sean Bean and Samantha Bond in the production of *Macbeth* showing at the Albery Theatre, St. Martins Lane, London.

Scene 6. *Before Macbeth's castle.*

Hautboys° and torches. Enter KING DUNCAN, MALCOLM, DONALBAIN,
BANQUO, LENNOX, MACDUFF, ROSS, ANGUS, *and* ATTENDANTS.

King.
This castle hath a pleasant seat;° the air
Nimbly and sweetly recommends itself
Unto our gentle senses.
Banquo.   This guest of summer,
The temple-haunting martlet,° does approve°
5   By his loved mansionry° that the heaven's breath
Smells wooingly here. No jutty,° frieze,
Buttress, nor coign of vantage,° but this bird
Hath made his pendent bed and procreant° cradle.
Where they most breed and haunt, I have observed
The air is delicate.

[*Enter* LADY MACBETH.]

10   **King.**   See, see, our honored hostess!

Hautboys: oboes.

1. **seat:** situation; setting.

4. **martlet:** bird that builds nests in churches. **approve:** prove.
5. **mansionry:** nest (dwelling).
6. **jutty:** projection.
7. **coign of vantage:** advantageous corner (of the castle).
8. **procreant:** breeding.

? Elements of Drama
9. *This scene contrasts strongly with the previous one. Again, what irony do you feel as Duncan admires the castle? How do you imagine Lady Macbeth acts as she now enters to greet her guests?*

The Tragedy of Macbeth, Act I, Scene 6   **421**

The love that follows us sometime is our trouble,
Which still we thank as love. Herein I teach you
How you shall bid God 'ield° us for your pains
And thank us for your trouble.

Lady Macbeth.   All our service
15   In every point twice done, and then done double,
Were poor and single business to contend
Against those honors deep and broad wherewith
Your majesty loads our house: for those of old,
And the late dignities heaped up to them,
We rest your hermits.°

20   **King.**   Where's the Thane of Cawdor?
We coursed° him at the heels, and had a purpose
To be his purveyor:° but he rides well,
And his great love, sharp as his spur, hath holp° him
To his home before us. Fair and noble hostess,
We are your guest tonight.

25   **Lady Macbeth.**   Your servants ever
Have theirs, themselves, and what is theirs, in compt,°
To make their audit at your highness' pleasure,
Still° to return your own.

King.   Give me your hand.
Conduct me to mine host: we love him highly,
30   And shall continue our graces toward him.
By your leave, hostess.   [*Exeunt.*]

Scene 7. *Macbeth's castle.*

Hautboys. Torches. Enter a SEWER,° *and diverse* SERVANTS *with dishes
and service, and pass over the stage. Then enter* MACBETH.

Macbeth.
If it were done when 'tis done, then 'twere well
It were done quickly. If th' assassination
Could trammel up the consequence, and catch,
With his surcease,° success; that but this blow
5   Might be the be-all and the end-all—here,
But here, upon this bank and shoal of time,
We'd jump the life to come. But in these cases   ®
We still have judgment here; that we but teach
Bloody instructions, which, being taught, return
10   To plague th' inventor: this even-handed justice
Commends th' ingredients of our poisoned chalice
To our own lips. He's here in double trust:

® **Literary Focus** Tragedy What does Macbeth reveal that he believes about his fate?

13. 'ield: reward.

20. We rest your hermits: We'll remain dependents who will pray for you.
21. coursed: chased.
22. purveyor: advance man.
23. holp: helped.

26. in compt: in trust.

28. Still: always.

? **31.** *How do you imagine the scene ends?*

sewer: butler.

? **1.** *In this speech, one of Shakespeare's great soliloquies, Macbeth voices his indecision and possibly reveals his conscience. A **soliloquy** is a meditative kind of speech in which a character, alone on stage and usually pretending that the audience is not present, thinks out loud. The audience is meant to understand that the speaker tells the truth freely and openly, however discreditable that truth may be. What are Macbeth's conflicts here?*
4. his surcease: Duncan's death.

First, as I am his kinsman and his subject,
Strong both against the deed; then, as his host,
15 Who should against his murderer shut the door,
Not bear the knife myself. Besides, this Duncan
Hath borne his faculties° so meek, hath been
So clear° in his great office, that his virtues
Will plead like angels trumpet-tongued against
20 The deep damnation of his taking-off;°
And pity, like a naked newborn babe,
Striding the blast, or heaven's cherubin horsed
Upon the sightless couriers° of the air,
Shall blow the horrid deed in every eye,
25 That° tears shall drown the wind. I have no spur
To prick the sides of my intent, but only
Vaulting ambition, which o'erleaps itself
And falls on th' other——

[*Enter* LADY MACBETH.]

How now! What news?
Lady Macbeth.
He has almost supped. Why have you left the chamber?
Macbeth.
Hath he asked for me?
30 **Lady Macbeth.**   Know you not he has?
Macbeth.
We will proceed no further in this business:
He hath honored me of late, and I have bought
Golden opinions from all sorts of people,
Which would be worn now in their newest gloss,
Not cast aside so soon.
35 **Lady Macbeth.**   Was the hope drunk
Wherein you dressed yourself? Hath it slept since?
And wakes it now, to look so green° and pale
At what it did so freely? From this time
Such I account thy love. Art thou afeard
40 To be the same in thine own act and valor
As thou art in desire? Wouldst thou have that
Which thou esteem'st the ornament of life,°
And live a coward in thine own esteem,
Letting "I dare not" wait upon° "I would,"
Like the poor cat i' th' adage?°
45 **Macbeth.**   Prithee, peace!
I dare do all that may become a man;
Who dares do more is none.
Lady Macbeth.   What beast was't then
That made you break° this enterprise to me?

17. **faculties:** powers.
18. **clear:** clean.

20. **taking-off:** murder.

23. **sightless couriers:** winds.

25. **That:** so that.
? 26. *Macbeth says he has no spur to prick the sides of his intent. Is that true?*

37. **green:** sickly.

42. **ornament of life:** crown.

44. **wait upon:** follow.
45. **poor . . . adage:** a saying about a cat who wants fish but won't wet its paws.

48. **break:** disclose; reveal.

When you durst do it, then you were a man;
50 And to be more than what you were, you would
    Be so much more the man. Nor time nor place
    Did then adhere,° and yet you would make both.
    They have made themselves, and that their fitness now
    Does unmake you. I have given suck, and know
55 How tender 'tis to love the babe that milks me:
    I would, while it was smiling in my face,
    Have plucked my nipple from his boneless gums,
    And dashed the brains out, had I so sworn as you
    Have done to this.

Macbeth.   If we should fail?

Lady Macbeth.   We fail?
60 But° screw your courage to the sticking-place,°
    And we'll not fail. When Duncan is asleep—
    Whereto the rather shall his day's hard journey
    Soundly invite him—his two chamberlains
    Will I with wine and wassail° so convince,°
65 That memory, the warder of the brain,
    Shall be a fume, and the receipt of reason
    A limbeck only:° when in swinish sleep
    Their drenchèd natures lie as in a death,
    What cannot you and I perform upon
70 Th' unguarded Duncan, what not put upon
    His spongy officers, who shall bear the guilt
    Of our great quell?

Macbeth.   Bring forth men-children only;
    For thy undaunted mettle° should compose
    Nothing but males. Will it not be received,
75 When we have marked with blood those sleepy two
    Of his own chamber, and used their very daggers,
    That they have done't?

Lady Macbeth.   Who dares receive it other,
    As we shall make our griefs and clamor roar
    Upon his death?

Macbeth.   I am settled, and bend up
80 Each corporal agent to this terrible feat.
    Away, and mock the time° with fairest show:
    False face must hide what the false heart doth know. **T**

                                        [*Exeunt.*]

---

52. **adhere:** suit.

? 54. *How does Lady Macbeth try to intimidate her husband in this speech? Watch what she says about herself in the next lines. There has been some question as to whether "We fail?" (line 59) should be a question. How does the meaning change if the line is spoken as a statement?*

60. **But:** only. **sticking-place:** the notch in a crossbow.

64. **wassail:** drinking. **convince:** overcome.

66–67. **the receipt . . . only:** The reasoning part of the brain would become like a limbeck (or still), distilling only confused thoughts.

? 72. Quell *is "murder." What are Lady Macbeth's plans?*

73. **mettle:** spirit.

81. **mock the time:** deceive the world.

? **Staging the Play**
81. *Should Macbeth pause here? How should these key words be spoken?*

? 82. *How is this yet another echo of the witches' words in Scene 1?*

S **Literary Focus** **Tragedy** Lady Macbeth argues that following through with his murderous plans would make Macbeth more of a man. Based on these lines, what does she think of her husband?

T **Reading Focus** **Using Questioning to Monitor Reading** As Act I ends, Lady Macbeth has, at least for the moment, the upper hand in the argument. What questions about their relationship does this raise for you?

Applying Your Skills

SKILLS FOCUS **Literary Skills** Analyze characteristics of a tragedy; analyze paradox; analyze historical context. **Reading Skills** Use questioning to monitor

reading. **Writing Skills** Explore the significance of personal experiences, events, and conditions; develop characters; employ precise language for effective writing.

The Tragedy of Macbeth
Act I

Respond and Think Critically

Reading Focus

Quick Check

1. What does the king determine to do for Macbeth? Why?

2. What do the witches predict for Banquo and Macbeth in Scene 3?

Read with a Purpose

3. What flaw pushes Macbeth from his stunning victory toward a tragic downfall?

Reading Skills: Using Questions to Monitor Reading

4. While reading Act I, you recorded questions that you had about the text. Now, add another column, record your answers, and note how you found those answers.

Act, Scene, Line	Questions I Have	My Answers
Act I, Scene 1, line 10	What might the witches mean by something both "foul" and "fair"?	Being king is "fair", but murder is "foul," and the whole thing is confusing for Macbeth, who is unsure what to do.

Literary Focus

Literary Analysis

5. Analyze How can Banquo be both "lesser than Macbeth, and greater"?

6. Interpret How does Banquo's reaction to the witches differ from Macbeth's? What do you think Macbeth's reaction suggests about his character?

7. Evaluate What conflict does Macbeth experience after he hears the witches' prophecy?

8. Make Judgments In Scene 7, lines 31–35, Macbeth presents an argument to Lady Macbeth for abandoning their plot. What do these lines indicate about what he really values?

9. Literary Perspectives English citizens in Shakespeare's time believed in the need for social order. What evidence can you find that Macbeth himself believes in order despite his "vaulting ambition"?

Literary Skills: Tragedy

10. Interpret Which characteristics of a tragic hero does Macbeth possess and Banquo lack?

Literary Skills Review: Paradox

11. Extend A **paradox** is an apparent <u>contradiction</u> that is actually true. The witches' prediction that Banquo will be "lesser than Macbeth, and greater" is a paradox. Find other examples of paradox in Act I, and explain the hidden truths they reveal.

Writing Focus

Think as a Reader/Writer

Use It in Your Writing As you read Act I, you noted how Shakespeare reveals his characters' personalities through their speech, thoughts, actions, and appearance. Now, write a description of any character's thoughts as he or she struggles to make an important decision. Try to use your character's words and thoughts to reveal his or her personality.

What Do You Think Now

In Act I, how does Macbeth respond to the impulses of his heart and mind?

For more activities see page 494-495.

Act II

Scene 1. *Inverness. Court of Macbeth's castle.*

Enter BANQUO, *and* FLEANCE, *with a torch before him (on the way to bed).*

Banquo.
How goes the night, boy?

Fleance.
The moon is down; I have not heard the clock.

Banquo.
And she goes down at twelve

Fleance.   I take't, 'tis later, sir.

Banquo.
Hold, take my sword. There's husbandry° in heaven.
5   Their candles are all out. Take thee that too.
A heavy summons° lies like lead upon me, **Ⓐ**
And yet I would not sleep. Merciful powers,
Restrain in me the cursèd thoughts that nature
Gives way to in repose! **Ⓑ**

[*Enter* MACBETH, *and a* SERVANT *with a torch.*]

                         Give me my sword!
10   Who's there?

Macbeth.
A friend.

Banquo.
What, sir, not yet at rest? The king's a-bed:
He hath been in unusual pleasure, and
Sent forth great largess to your offices:°
15   This diamond he greets your wife withal,
By the name of most kind hostess; and shut up°
In measureless content. **Ⓒ**

Macbeth.   Being unprepared,
Our will became the servant to defect,°
Which else should free have wrought.

Staging the Play
Stage direction: Who
is Fleance? What would you
remember of the witches'
prophecy when you see him here?
Do we know if Macbeth and his
wife have any children?

4. husbandry: economizing
(that is, putting out the lights to
save money on candles).
6. summons: call to sleep.

14. largess to your offices: gifts
to your servants' quarters.
16. shut up: concluded.

18. to defect: to insufficient
preparations.

Ⓐ Literary Focus Tragedy The first scene of Act I established a dark, ominous mood for the tragedy with the appearance of the witches in a thunderstorm. How do the first lines of Act II contribute to the mood?

Ⓑ Literary Focus Tragedy Based on these lines, what does Banquo fear?

Ⓒ Reading Focus Using Questioning to Monitor Reading Duncan's generosity suggests that he remains ignorant of Macbeth's character and thoughts. What questions arise about how his failing leadership contributes to Macbeth's ambition?

Banquo.   All's well.

20   I dreamt last night of the three weird sisters:
      To you they have showed some truth.

Macbeth.   I think not of them.

      Yet, when we can entreat an hour to serve,
      We would spend it in some words upon that business,
      If you would grant the time.

Banquo.   At your kind'st leisure.

Macbeth.

25   If you shall cleave to my consent, when 'tis,°
      It shall make honor for you.

Banquo.   So° I lose none
      In seeking to augment it, but still keep
      My bosom franchised° and allegiance clear,°
      I shall be counseled.   **D**

Macbeth.   Good repose the while!

Banquo.

30   Thanks, sir. The like to you!

                              [*Exit* BANQUO, *with* FLEANCE.]

Macbeth.

      Go bid thy mistress, when my drink is ready,
      She strike upon the bell. Get thee to bed.

                              [*Exit* SERVANT.]

      Is this a dagger which I see before me,
      The handle toward my hand? Come, let me clutch thee.

35   I have thee not, and yet I see thee still.
      Art thou not, fatal vision, sensible°
      To feeling as to sight, or art thou but
      A dagger of the mind, a false creation,
      Proceeding from the heat-oppressèd brain?

40   I see thee yet, in form as palpable°
      As this which now I draw.
      Thou marshal'st me the way that I was going;
      And such an instrument I was to use.
      Mine eyes are made the fools o' th' other senses,

45   Or else worth all the rest. I see thee still;
      And on thy blade and dudgeon° gouts° of blood,
      Which was not so before. There's no such thing.
      It is the bloody business which informs°
      Thus to mine eyes. Now o'er the one half-world

50   Nature seems dead, and wicked dreams abuse°
      The curtained sleep; witchcraft celebrates
      Pale Hecate's° offerings; and withered murder,

D **Literary Focus** **Tragedy** In the conversation between Macbeth and Banquo, to what does the pronoun *it* refer?

❓ **24.** *This is the second time Macbeth has suggested he and Banquo talk. Do you think he might want to confide in Banquo? Does he want to get Banquo on his side? How would you characterize his motives?*

25. cleave . . . 'tis: join my cause, when the time comes.
26. So: provided that.
28. franchised: free (from guilt). **clear:** clean.

❓ **32.** *What is to happen upon the ringing of the bell?*

36. sensible: perceptible to the senses.

40. palpable: obvious.

❓ **Staging the Play**
41. *This soliloquy is a key moment in revealing Macbeth's character. What does Shakespeare have Macbeth do at this moment?*

46. dudgeon: hilt. **gouts:** large drops.
48. informs: gives shape.

50. abuse: deceive.

52. Hecate's: Hecate (HEHK uh tee) is the goddess of sorcery.

Alarumed° by his sentinel, the wolf,
Whose howl's his watch, thus with his stealthy pace,
55   With Tarquin's° ravishing strides, towards his design
Moves like a ghost. Thou sure and firm-set earth,
Hear not my steps, which way they walk, for fear
Thy very stones prate of my whereabout,
And take the present horror from the time,
60   Which now suits with it.° Whiles I threat, he lives:
Words to the heat of deeds too cold breath gives. **E**

[A bell rings.]

I go, and it is done: the bell invites me.
Hear it not, Duncan, for it is a knell
That summons thee to heaven, or to hell.

[Exit.]

Scene 2. *Macbeth's castle.*

Enter LADY MACBETH.

Lady Macbeth.
That which hath made them drunk hath made me bold;
What hath quenched them hath given me fire. Hark! Peace!
It was the owl that shrieked, the fatal bellman,
Which gives the stern'st good-night.° He is about it.
5   The doors are open, and the surfeited grooms
Do mock their charge with snores. I have drugged their possets,°
That death and nature do contend about them,
Whether they live or die.
Macbeth *(within).*   Who's there? What, ho?
Lady Macbeth.
Alack, I am afraid they have awaked.
10   And 'tis not done! Th' attempt and not the deed
Confounds° us. Hark! I laid their daggers ready;
He could not miss 'em. Had he not resembled
My father as he slept, I had done't.

[Enter MACBETH.*]*

                         My husband!
Macbeth.
I have done the deed. Didst thou not hear a noise?
Lady Macbeth.

53. Alarumed: called to action.

55. Tarquin's: Tarquin was a Roman tyrant who raped a woman named Lucrece.

60. now suits with it: now seems suitable to it.

? Staging the Play
64. *What should the audience be feeling as Macbeth exits?*

? 3. *What sound would you hear at this point? In this soliloquy, who are the "them," and who is "He"?*
4. stern'st good-night: The owl's call is supposed to portend death. The bellman was a person who rang a bell outside a condemned person's cell the night before his execution to warn him to confess his sins.
6. possets: bedtime drinks.

11. Confounds: ruins.

? Staging the Play
13. *How should Lady Macbeth say this last line, which reveals why the plans have changed? Do you think she is beginning to show remorse?*

Glamis Castle, Angus, Scotland.

E **Reading Focus** **Using Questioning to Monitor Reading** Macbeth's speech is a combination of hallucination, imagery, allusion, and fact. What questions could you ask to clarify the meaning of his words?

15   I heard the owl scream and the crickets cry.
       Did not you speak?

Macbeth.   When?

Lady Macbeth.   Now.

Macbeth.   As I descended?

Lady Macbeth. Ay.

Macbeth. Hark!
       Who lies i' th' second chamber?

Lady Macbeth.   Donalbain.

20   **Macbeth.** This is a sorry sight.

Lady Macbeth.
       A foolish thought, to say a sorry sight.

Macbeth.
       There's one did laugh in 's sleep, and one cried "Murder!"
       That they did wake each other. I stood and heard them.
       But they did say their prayers, and addressed them
       Again to sleep.

25   **Lady Macbeth.**   There are two lodged together.

Macbeth.
       One cried "God bless us!" and "Amen" the other,
       As they had seen me with these hangman's hands:
       List'ning their fear, I could not say "Amen,"
       When they did say "God bless us!"

Lady Macbeth.   Consider it not so deeply.

Macbeth.

30   But wherefore could not I pronounce "Amen"?
       I had most need of blessing, and "Amen"
       Stuck in my throat.

Lady Macbeth.   These deeds must not be thought
       After these ways; so, it will make us mad.

Macbeth.
       Methought I heard a voice cry "Sleep no more!

35   Macbeth does murder sleep"—the innocent sleep,
       Sleep that knits up the raveled sleave° of care,
       The death of each day's life, sore labor's bath,
       Balm of hurt minds, great nature's second course,°
       Chief nourisher in life's feast——

Lady Macbeth.   What do you mean?

Macbeth.

40   Still it cried "Sleep no more!" to all the house:
       "Glamis hath murdered sleep, and therefore Cawdor
       Shall sleep no more: Macbeth shall sleep no more."

Falcon Square, Inverness City.

33. *Is Lady Macbeth fighting for control here?*

36. raveled sleave: tangled thread.

38. second course: sleep (the less substantial first course is food).

41. *Who else complained about sleep? In what way has Glamis "murdered sleep"?*

F **Literary Focus** **Tragedy** The sentence breaks and interruptions in the middle of these lines create a choppy effect. Why is this effect appropriate for Macbeth and Lady Macbeth's conversation?

Lady Macbeth.
    Who was it that thus cried? Why, worthy thane,
    You do unbend your noble strength, to think
45   So brainsickly of things. Go get some water,
    And wash this filthy witness from your hand.
    Why did you bring these daggers from the place?
    They must lie there: go carry them, and smear
    The sleepy grooms with blood.

Macbeth.   I'll go no more.
50   I am afraid to think what I have done;
    Look on 't again I dare not.

Lady Macbeth.   Infirm of purpose!
    Give me the daggers. The sleeping and the dead   **G**
    Are but as pictures. 'Tis the eye of childhood
    That fears a painted devil. If he do bleed,
55   I'll gild the faces of the grooms withal,
    For it must seem their guilt.   [*Exit. Knock within.*]

Macbeth.   Whence is that knocking?
    How is 't with me, when every noise appalls me?
    What hands are here? Ha! They pluck out mine eyes!

? **Staging the Play**
46. *What is the "filthy witness"? What actions are the couple engaged in here? In the next line, Lady Macbeth discovers the daggers. Why is she so alarmed at seeing them in her husband's hands? How could Macbeth have been carrying them so they weren't visible before?*

G **Reading Focus** **Using Questioning to Monitor Reading** Act II contains a number of links between sleep and death. What might you ask yourself to clarify why Shakespeare makes this connection?

Helen Baxendale as Lady Macbeth (1997).

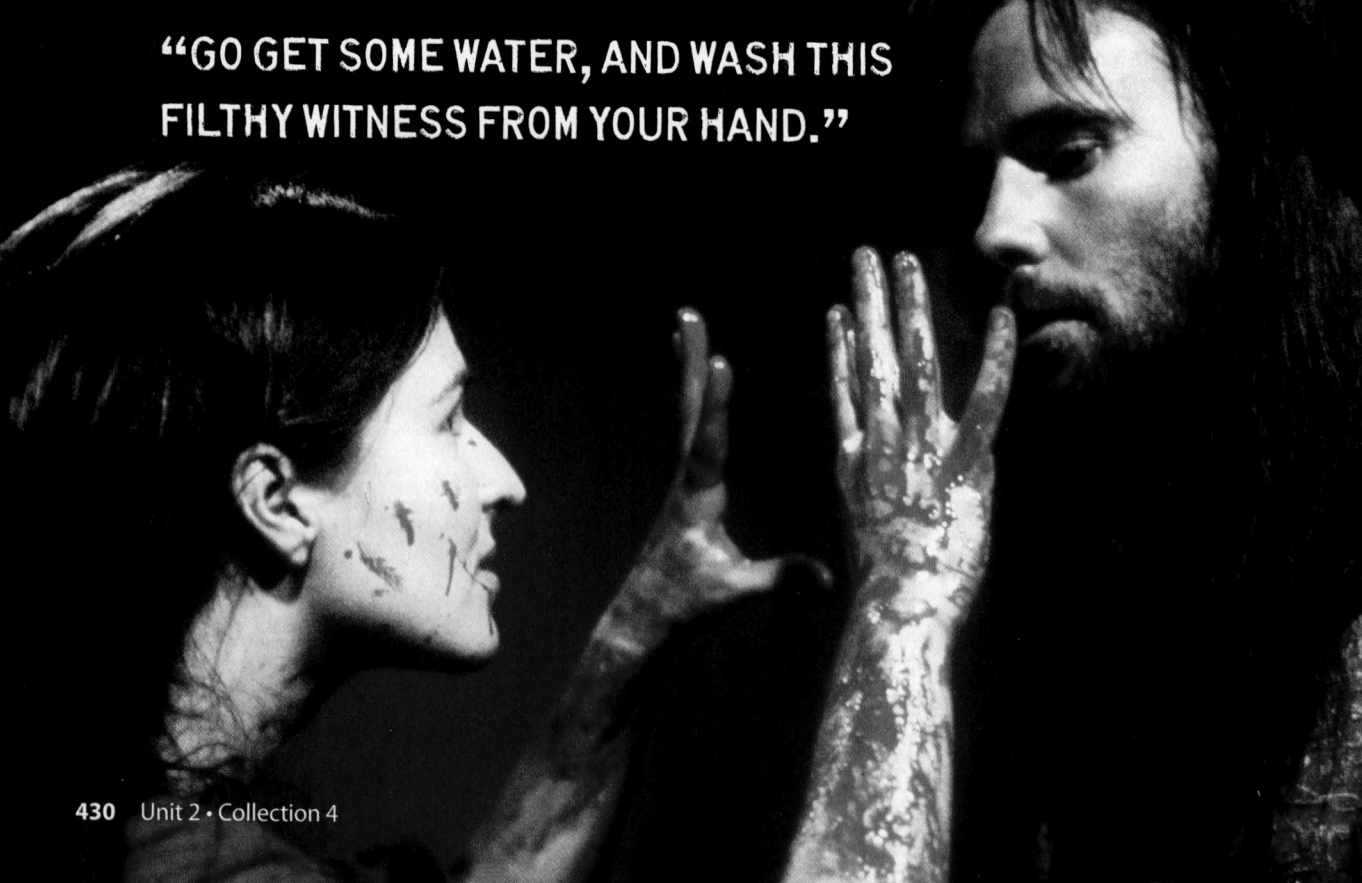

"GO GET SOME WATER, AND WASH THIS FILTHY WITNESS FROM YOUR HAND."

Will all great Neptune's ocean wash this blood
60 Clean from my hand? No; this my hand will rather
The multitudinous seas incarnadine,°
Making the green one red.

[*Enter* LADY MACBETH.]

Lady Macbeth.
My hands are of your color, but I shame
To wear a heart so white. (*Knock.*) I hear a knocking
65 At the south entry. Retire we to our chamber.
A little water clears us of this deed:
How easy is it then! Your constancy
Hath left you unattended.° (*Knock.*) Hark! more knocking.
Get on your nightgown, lest occasion call us
70 And show us to be watchers.° Be not lost **H**
So poorly in your thoughts.

Macbeth.
To know my deed, 'twere best not know myself.

[*Knock.*]

Wake Duncan with thy knocking! I would thou couldst! **I**

[*Exeunt.*]

Scene 3. *Macbeth's castle.*

Enter a PORTER. *Knocking within.*

Porter. Here's a knocking indeed! If a man were porter of hell
gate, he should have old° turning the key. (*Knock.*) Knock,
knock, knock! Who's there, i' th' name of Beelzebub?°
Here's a farmer, that hanged himself on th' expectation of
5   plenty. Come in time! Have napkins enow° about you; here
you'll sweat for 't. (*Knock.*) Knock, knock! Who's there, in
th' other devil's name? Faith, here's an equivocator,° that
could swear in both the scales against either scale; who
committed treason enough for God's sake, yet could not
10   equivocate to heaven. O, come in, equivocator. (*Knock.*) **J**
Knock, knock, knock! Who's there? Faith, here's an English

61. incarnadine: make red.

63. *Based on this speech, what does Lady Macbeth look like?*

67–68. Your . . . unattended: Your firmness has deserted you.

70. watchers: that is, up late.

71. *How is Macbeth behaving?*

Staging the Play
Stage direction: In the theater, this sharp, loud knocking is frightening. In the next line, what might Macbeth wish the knocking could awake in himself?

Staging the Play
Stage direction: Note that the Porter is drunk. What would he be doing during this long speech while the knocking persists?

2. have old: grow old.

3. Beelzebub: the Devil.

5. enow: enough.

7. equivocator: The Porter means a Jesuit, a member of the Society of Jesus, a religious order. (Jesuits were believed by some to use false arguments in their zeal for souls.)

H Literary Focus **Tragedy** The actions that constitute the murder and its coverup are not told in sequence. Make a list, in the correct order, of what Macbeth and Lady Macbeth did.

I Reading Focus **Using Questioning to Monitor Reading** Now that Macbeth has murdered Duncan, what questions can you ask to understand Macbeth's current state of mind?

J Literary Perspectives **Analyzing Historical Context** These lines refer to the failed Gunpowder Plot, a conspiracy to blow up King James and Parliament. What significance would this reference have had for Shakespeare's audience in the early seventeenth century?

tailor come hither for stealing out of a French hose:° come in, tailor. Here you may roast your goose.° (*Knock.*) Knock, knock; never at quiet! What are you? But this place is too cold for hell. I'll devil-porter it no further. I had thought to have let in some of all professions that go the primrose way to th' everlasting bonfire. (*Knock.*) Anon, anon! (*Opens an entrance.*) I pray you, remember the porter.

[*Enter* MACDUFF *and* LENNOX.]

Macduff.
Was it so late, friend, ere you went to bed,
That you do lie so late?
Porter. Faith, sir, we were carousing till the second cock:° and drink, sir, is a great provoker of three things.
Macduff. What three things does drink especially provoke?
Porter. Marry, sir, nose-painting, sleep, and urine. Lechery, sir, it provokes and unprovokes; it provokes the desire, but it takes away the performance: therefore much drink may be said to be an equivocator with lechery: it makes him and it mars him; it sets him on and it takes him off; it persuades him and disheartens him; makes him stand to and not stand to; in conclusion, equivocates him in a sleep, and giving him the lie, leaves him.
Macduff. I believe drink gave thee the lie° last night.
Porter. That it did, sir, i' the very throat on me: but I requited him for his lie, and, I think, being too strong for him, though he took up my legs sometime, yet I make a shift to cast° him.
Macduff. Is thy master stirring? **K**

[*Enter* MACBETH.]

Our knocking has awaked him; here he comes.
Lennox.
Good morrow, noble sir.
Macbeth.   Good morrow, both.
Macduff.
Is the king stirring, worthy thane?
Macbeth.   Not yet.
Macduff.
He did command me to call timely° on him:
I have almost slipped the hour.
Macbeth.   I'll bring you to him.
Macduff.

15

20

25

30

35

40

K **Literary Focus** **Tragedy** Why would Shakespeare focus on the Porter just after the murder of the king?

432 Unit 2 • Collection 4

12. **French hose:** tightfitting stocking.
13. **goose:** iron used by a tailor for pressing.

21. **second cock:** about 3:00 A.M.

32. **gave thee the lie:** pun meaning "called you a liar" and "stretched you out, lying in bed."
35. **cast:** here, a pun meaning "to cast in plaster" and "to vomit" (cast out).

? 36. *All the time this humorous bantering is going on, what do we know these king's men are about to discover?*

40. **timely:** early.

Glamis Castle, Angus, Scotland.

I know this is a joyful trouble to you;
But yet 'tis one.

Macbeth.
The labor we delight in physics° pain.
This is the door.

45 **Macduff.**   I'll make so bold to call,
For 'tis my limited service.°

[Exit MACDUFF.]

Lennox.
Goes the king hence today?

Macbeth.   He does: he did appoint so.

Lennox.
The night has been unruly. Where we lay,
Our chimneys were blown down, and, as they say,
50 Lamentings heard i' th' air, strange screams of death,
And prophesying with accents terrible
Of dire combustion° and confused events
New hatched to th' woeful time: the obscure bird
Clamored the livelong night. Some say, the earth
Was feverous and did shake.

55 **Macbeth.**   'Twas a rough night.

Lennox.
My young remembrance cannot parallel
A fellow to it.

[<i>Enter</i> MACDUFF.]

Macduff.
O horror, horror, horror! Tongue nor heart
Cannot conceive nor name thee.

Macbeth and Lennox.   What's the matter?

Macduff.
60 Confusion now hath made his masterpiece.
Most sacrilegious murder hath broke ope
The Lord's anointed temple,° and stole thence   **L**
The life o' th' building.

Macbeth.   What is't you say? The life?

Lennox.
Mean you his majesty?

Macduff.
65 Approach the chamber, and destroy your sight
With a new Gorgon:° do not bid me speak;
See, and then speak yourselves. Awake, awake!

[Exeunt MACBETH and LENNOX.]

L Literary Perspectives Analyzing Historical Context   What Renaissance belief about the relationship of the king to the divine is expressed through this speech?

---

44. physics: cures.

46. limited service: appointed duty.

? 47. *How must Macbeth be feeling?*

52. combustion: tumult; uproar.

? 54. *In Elizabethan times, people often believed that nature mirrored terrible things happening to human beings, especially to kings. How did this weather mirror what was happening to the king in Macbeth's castle?*

? Staging the Play
55. *This single line is full of irony. How might Macbeth say it?*

62. Lord's anointed temple: body of the king.

? 63. *How would you explain Macduff's metaphors?*

66. Gorgon: creature from Greek mythology whose face could turn an onlooker to stone.

Ring the alarum bell. Murder and treason!
Banquo and Donalbain! Malcolm! Awake!
70   Shake off this downy sleep, death's counterfeit,
And look on death itself! Up, up, and see
The great doom's image! Malcolm! Banquo!
As from your graves rise up, and walk like sprites,
To countenance° this horror. Ring the bell.

[*Bell rings. Enter* LADY MACBETH.]

Lady Macbeth.
75   What's the business,
That such a hideous trumpet calls to parley°
The sleepers of the house? Speak, speak!
Macduff.   O gentle lady,
'Tis not for you to hear what I can speak:
The repetition, in a woman's ear,
Would murder as it fell.

[*Enter* BANQUO.]

80   O Banquo, Banquo!
Our royal master's murdered.
Lady Macbeth.   Woe, alas!
What, in our house?
Banquo.   Too cruel anywhere.
Dear Duff, I prithee, contradict thyself,
And say it is not so.

[*Enter* MACBETH, LENNOX, *and* ROSS.]

Macbeth.
85   Had I but died an hour before this chance,
I had lived a blessèd time; for from this instant
There's nothing serious in mortality:°
All is but toys. Renown and grace is dead,
The wine of life is drawn, and the mere lees°
90   Is left this vault° to brag of.

[*Enter* MALCOLM *and* DONALBAIN.]

Donalbain.
What is amiss?
Macbeth.   You are, and do not know't.
The spring, the head, the fountain of your blood
Is stopped; the very source of it is stopped.
Macduff.
Your royal father's murdered.
Malcolm.   O, by whom?

---

74. countenance: be in keeping with.

76. parley: conference of war.

? Staging the Play
82. *The emphasis on Lady Macbeth's gentleness and fairness when we know the foulness underneath might well merit a snicker from the audience. The snicker might be expected to grow into a laugh when she says, "What, in our house?" These are difficult moments to act. How do you think Lady Macbeth should be behaving?*

87. mortality: life.

89. lees: dregs.
90. vault: pun on "wine vault" and the "vault of heaven."

? 94. *Macbeth and Lady Macbeth might well look at each other at this moment. Does Lennox draw the conclusion they intended: that the servants killed Duncan?*

Lennox.

95   Those of his chamber, as it seemed, had done't:
    Their hands and faces were all badged° with blood;
    So were their daggers, which unwiped we found
    Upon their pillows. They stared, and were distracted.
    No man's life was to be trusted with them.

Macbeth.

100   O, yet I do repent me of my fury,
    That I did kill them.

Macduff.   Wherefore did you so?

Macbeth.

    Who can be wise, amazed, temp'rate and furious,
    Loyal and neutral, in a moment? No man.
    The expedition° of my violent love

105   Outrun the pauser, reason. Here lay Duncan,
    His silver skin laced with his golden blood,
    And his gashed stabs looked like a breach in nature
    For ruin's wasteful entrance: there, the murderers,
    Steeped in the colors of their trade, their daggers

110   Unmannerly breeched with gore.° Who could refrain,°
    That had a heart to love, and in that heart
    Courage to make 's love known? **Ⓜ**

Lady Macbeth.   Help me hence, ho! **Ⓝ**

Macduff.

    Look to the lady.

Malcolm (*aside to* DONALBAIN). Why do we hold our tongues,
    That most may claim this argument for ours?°

Donalbain (*aside to* MALCOLM).

115   What should be spoken here,
    Where our fate, hid in an auger-hole,°
    May rush, and seize us? Let's away:
    Our tears are not yet brewed.

Malcolm (*aside to* DONALBAIN). Nor our strong sorrow
    Upon the foot of motion.°

Banquo.   Look to the lady.

               [LADY MACBETH *is carried out.*]

120   And when we have our naked frailties hid,°
    That suffer in exposure, let us meet
    And question° this most bloody piece of work,

---

96. badged: marked.

104. expedition: haste.

110. Unmannerly breeched with gore: unbecomingly covered with blood, as if wearing red trousers. **refrain:** check oneself.

114. That . . . ours: who are the most concerned with this topic.

116. auger-hole: unsuspected place.

118–119. Our tears . . . motion: We have not yet had time for tears nor to express our sorrows in action.

120. naked frailties hid: poor bodies clothed.
122. question: discuss.

Ⓜ **Reading Focus** Using Questioning to Monitor Reading What questions could you ask to help you understand the various characters' eulogies?

Ⓝ **Reading Focus** Using Questioning to Monitor Reading What questions do you have about Lady Macbeth's plan in this scene?

To know it further. Fears and scruples° shake us.
In the great hand of God I stand, and thence
125   Against the undivulged pretense° I fight
Of treasonous malice.

Macduff.   And so do I.

All.   So all.

Macbeth.

  Let's briefly° put on manly readiness,
And meet i' th' hall together.   **O**

All.   Well contented.

              [*Exeunt all but* MALCOLM *and* DONALBAIN.]

Malcolm.

  What will you do? Let's not consort with them.
130   To show an unfelt sorrow is an office°
Which the false man does easy. I'll to England.

Donalbain.

  To Ireland, I; our separated fortune
Shall keep us both the safer. Where we are
There's daggers in men's smiles; the near in blood,
The nearer bloody.   **P**

135 **Malcolm.**   This murderous shaft that's shot
Hath not yet lighted, and our safest way
Is to avoid the aim. Therefore to horse;
And let us not be dainty of° leave-taking,
But shift away. There's warrant° in that theft
140   Which steals itself° when there's no mercy left.

                             [*Exeunt.*]

Scene 4. *Outside Macbeth's castle.*

Enter ROSS *with an* OLD MAN.

Old Man.

  Threescore and ten I can remember well:
Within the volume of which time I have seen
Hours dreadful and things strange, but this sore° night
Hath trifled former knowings.°

Ross.   Ha, good father,
5   Thou seest the heavens, as troubled with man's act,
Threatens his bloody stage. By th' clock 'tis day,
And yet dark night strangles the traveling lamp:°

---

123. **scruples:** suspicions.

125. **undivulged pretense:** hidden purpose.

127. **briefly:** quickly.

130. **office:** function.

138. **dainty of:** fussy about.
139. **warrant:** justification.
140. **steals itself:** steals oneself away.

3. **sore:** grievous.
4. **trifled former knowings:** made trifles of former experiences.

7. **traveling lamp:** sun.

O Literary Focus **Tragedy** Macbeth refers to "manly readiness" in Act II, Scene 3, line 127, suggesting that masculine strength will be important for catching the murderers. How do Macbeth's ideas about masculine qualities affect his behavior in the play?

P Literary Perspectives **Analyzing Historical Context** Why would these words have had special meaning for King James?

The Alarm (Act II), Macbeth *production at the Princess's Theatre* (1901), by Anonymous.
Victoria & Albert Museum, London.

    Is't night's predominance,° or the day's shame,
    That darkness does the face of earth entomb,
    When living light should kiss it?
10 **Old Man.**   'Tis unnatural,
    Even like the deed that's done. On Tuesday last
    A falcon, tow'ring in her pride of place,°
    Was by a mousing° owl hawked at and killed.
    Ross.
    And Duncan's horses—a thing most strange and certain—
15   Beauteous and swift, the minions° of their race,
    Turned wild in nature, broke their stalls, flung out,°
    Contending 'gainst obedience, as they would make
    War with mankind.
    Old Man.   'Tis said they eat° each other.
    Ross.
    They did so, to th' amazement of mine eyes,
    That looked upon't.

8. predominance: astrological supremacy.

12. tow'ring . . . place: soaring at her summit.
13. mousing: usually mouse-eating.
15. minions: darlings.
16. flung out: lunged wildly.

18. eat: ate.

[*Enter* MACDUFF.]

20   Here comes the good Macduff.
     How goes the world, sir, now?
Macduff.   Why, see you not?
Ross.
     Is't known who did this more than bloody deed?
Macduff.
     Those that Macbeth hath slain.
Ross.   Alas, the day!
     What good could they pretend?°
Macduff.   They were suborned:°

25   Malcolm and Donalbain, the king's two sons,
     Are stol'n away and fled, which puts upon them
     Suspicion of the deed.
Ross.   'Gainst nature still.
     Thriftless° ambition, that will ravin up°
     Thine own life's means!° Then 'tis most like

30   The sovereignty will fall upon Macbeth.
Macduff.
     He is already named,° and gone to Scone°
     To be invested.°
Ross.   Where is Duncan's body?
Macduff.
     Carried to Colmekill,°
     The sacred storehouse of his predecessors
     And guardian of their bones.

35   **Ross.**   Will you to Scone?
Macduff.
     No, cousin, I'll to Fife.
Ross.   Well, I will thither. **Q**
Macduff.
     Well, may you see things well done there. Adieu,
     Lest our old robes sit easier than our new!
Ross.
     Farewell, father.
Old Man.

40   God's benison° go with you, and with those
     That would make good of bad, and friends of foes! **R**

                              [*Exeunt omnes.*]

Chapel Stained Glass.
Glamis Castle, Angus,
Scotland.

24. pretend: hope for.
suborned: bribed.

28. Thriftless: wasteful. **ravin up:** greedily devour.
29. own life's means: parent.
31. named: elected. **Scone** (skoon).
32. invested: installed as king.

33. Colmekill: Iona Island, the ancient burying place of Scottish kings. (It was founded by St. Colm.)

40. benison: blessing.

Q **Reading Focus** **Using Questioning to Monitor Reading** The act's last bit of dialogue concerns Ross's and Macduff's plans. What questions might you ask to better understand their plans?

R **Literary Focus** **Tragedy** Why do you think Shakespeare ends the act with the Old Man's statement?

Applying Your Skills

The Tragedy of Macbeth

Act II

Respond and Think Critically

Reading Focus

Quick Check

1. Describe Macbeth's vision at the end of Scene 1.

2. What reason does Macbeth give for killing Duncan's two guards?

3. Where do Malcolm, Donalbain, Ross, and Macduff go at the end of the act, and why?

Read with a Purpose

4. How does Macbeth's flaw continue to push him toward a tragic ending?

Reading Skills: Using Questions to Monitor Reading

5. While reading Act II, you recorded questions that you had about the text. Continue the answers you added to your chart after Act I.

Act, Scene, Line	Questions I have	My Answers
Act II, Scene 2, line 46	What is the "filthy witness"?	It is the blood all over Macbeth's hands (lines 45, 46); blood doesn't lie, but it is messy, and so is their crime—a dirty truth.

Literary Focus

Literary Analysis

6. **Analyze** Who suspects Macbeth? Support your answer with lines from Act II.

7. **Interpret** What message do you think Lady Macbeth wants her fainting spell to convey?

8. **Evaluate** The end of this act does not give us a feeling of justice. Why do you think Shakespeare ends Act II where he did?

9. **Extend** What hints can you find in Act II that suggest the fate of Macbeth and Lady Macbeth?

10. **Literary Perspectives** Why do you think Shakespeare chose not to show the murder of Duncan directly to his audience?

Literary Skills: Tragedy

11. **Analyze** How does Shakespeare continue to use Banquo to emphasize Macbeth's tragic flaw?

Literary Skills Review: Motifs

12. **Extend** A **motif** is a word, image, metaphor, or idea that occurs repeatedly in a work of literature. Two important motifs in *Macbeth* are the image of blood and the idea of sleep. What examples of these motifs can you find in Act II?

Writing Focus

Think as a Reader/Writer

Use It in Your Writing Although most of *Macbeth* is in **blank verse**, or unrhymed iambic pentameter, Shakespeare occasionally varies this pattern. Look back at the Porter's speech in Scene 3. You may have noticed that the Porter—a character of low status—doesn't speak in verse at all. Notice other ways that Shakespeare differentiates the Porter's speech from the speech of other characters. Then, write a brief dialogue between a serious character and a comic one. Use specific language to <u>establish</u> their personalities.

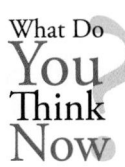

What Do You Think Now

In Act II, how does Macbeth respond to the impulses of his heart and mind?

For more activities see page 494-495. ❯

Act III

Scene 1. *Forres. The palace.*

Enter BANQUO.

Banquo.
    Thou hast it now: king, Cawdor, Glamis, all,
    As the weird women promised, and I fear
    Thou play'dst most foully for't. Yet it was said   **Ⓐ**
    It should not stand° in thy posterity,
5   But that myself should be the root and father
    Of many kings. If there come truth from them—
    As upon thee, Macbeth, their speeches shine—
    Why, by the verities on thee made good,
    May they not be my oracles as well
10   And set me up in hope? But hush, no more!   **Ⓑ**

    [*Sennet*° *sounded. Enter* MACBETH *as king,* LADY MACBETH, LENNOX,
      ROSS, LORDS, *and* ATTENDANTS.]

Macbeth.
    Here's our chief guest.
Lady Macbeth.   If he had been forgotten,
    It had been as a gap in our great feast,
    And all-thing° unbecoming.
Macbeth.
    Tonight we hold a solemn supper, sir,
    And I'll request your presence.
15 **Banquo.**   Let your highness
    Command upon me, to the which my duties
    Are with a most indissoluble tie
    For ever knit.
Macbeth.
    Ride you this afternoon?
Banquo.   Ay, my good lord.
Macbeth.
20 We should have else desired your good advice
    (Which still° hath been both grave and prosperous°)
    In this day's council; but we'll take tomorrow.
    Is't far you ride?

4. stand: continue.

? 10. *How would you describe Banquo's mood?*
Sennet: trumpet.

13. all-thing: altogether.

21. still: always. **grave and prosperous:** weighty and profitable.

Ⓐ Literary Perspectives **Analyzing Historical Context** King James claimed to be a direct descendant of Banquo. How might that claim have affected Shakespeare's portrayal of Banquo in these lines?

Ⓑ Literary Focus **Tragedy** Compare the beginning lines of Acts II and III. What is similar? What has changed?

Banquo.

    As far, my lord, as will fill up the time

25   'Twixt this and supper. Go not my horse the better,°

    I must become a borrower of the night

    For a dark hour or twain.

Macbeth.   Fail not our feast.

Banquo.

    My lord, I will not.

Macbeth.

    We hear our bloody cousins are bestowed°

30   In England and in Ireland, not confessing

    Their cruel parricide, filling their hearers

    With strange invention.° But of that tomorrow, **C**

    When therewithal we shall have cause of state

    Craving us jointly.° Hie you to horse. Adieu,

35   Till you return at night. Goes Fleance with you?

Banquo.

    Ay, my good lord: our time does call upon 's. **D**

Macbeth.

    I wish your horses swift and sure of foot,

    And so I do commend you to their backs.

    Farewell.   [*Exit* BANQUO.]

40   Let every man be master of his time

    Till seven at night. To make society

    The sweeter welcome, we will keep ourself

    Till supper-time alone. While° then, God be with you!

           [*Exeunt* LORDS *and all but* MACBETH *and a* SERVANT.]

    Sirrah, a word with you: attend° those men

45   Our pleasure?

Attendant.

    They are, my lord, without the palace gate.

Macbeth.

    Bring them before us.   [*Exit* SERVANT.]

    To be thus° is nothing, but° to be safely thus—

    Our fears in Banquo stick deep,

50   And in his royalty of nature reigns that

    Which would be feared. 'Tis much he dares;

    And, to° that dauntless temper° of his mind,

    He hath a wisdom that doth guide his valor

---

25. Go not my horse the better: unless my horse goes faster than I expect.

29. are bestowed: have taken refuge.

32. invention: lies.

34. us jointly: our joint attention.

? **42.** *Notice that Macbeth uses the "royal we"; that is, he speaks of himself as "we," as a representative of all the people.*
43. While: until.
44. attend: await.

48. thus: king. **but:** unless.

52. to: added to. **temper:** quality.

C **Literary Focus** Tragedy What is Macbeth trying to accomplish when he says that his "bloody cousins" have fled to England and Ireland?

D **Reading Focus** Using Questioning to Monitor Reading In the conversation with Banquo, Macbeth wants to know about Banquo's plans. What questions do you have about Macbeth's curiosity?

To act in safety. There is none but he
55 Whose being I do fear: and under him
My genius is rebuked,° as it is said   **E**
Mark Antony's was by Caesar. He chid the sisters,
When first they put the name of king upon me,
And bade them speak to him; then prophetlike
60 They hailed him father to a line of kings.
Upon my head they placed a fruitless crown
And put a barren scepter in my gripe,
Thence to be wrenched with an unlineal hand,
No son of mine succeeding. If't be so,
65 For Banquo's issue have I filed° my mind;
For them the gracious Duncan have I murdered;
Put rancors° in the vessel of my peace
Only for them, and mine eternal jewel°
Given to the common enemy of man,°
70 To make them kings, the seeds of Banquo kings!
Rather than so, come, fate, into the list,°
And champion me to th' utterance!° Who's there?

E **Literary Focus** **Tragedy** How does this passage develop the theme "Fair is foul, and foul is fair"?

56. genius is rebuked: guardian spirit is cowed.

? 63. *What is an "unlineal hand"? What is a "barren scepter"? What now is bothering Macbeth?*

65. filed: defiled; dirtied.
67. rancors: bitter enmity.
68. eternal jewel: immortal soul.
69. common enemy of man: Satan.
71. list: battle.
72. champion me to th' utterance: fight against me till I give up.

? 72. *In this important soliloquy, why exactly is Macbeth so angry? How does this compare to the previous soliloquy?*

(standing, right) Cathy Owen (Lady Macbeth) and Peter Lindford (Macbeth). Ludlow Festival, UK (2001).

"UPON MY HEAD THEY PLACED A FRUITLESS CROWN"

[*Enter* SERVANT *and* TWO MURDERERS.]

Now go to the door, and stay there till we call.

[*Exit* SERVANT.]

Was it not yesterday we spoke together?

Murderers.
　　It was, so please your highness.

75 **Macbeth.**　　　　　　　Well then, now
　　Have you considered of my speeches? Know
　　That it was he in the times past, which held you
　　So under fortune,° which you thought had been
　　Our innocent self: this I made good to you
80　In our last conference; passed in probation° with you,
　　How you were borne in hand,° how crossed; the instruments,°
　　Who wrought with them, and all things else that might
　　To half a soul° and to a notion° crazed
　　Say "Thus did Banquo."

First Murderer.　　　　You made it known to us.

Macbeth.
85　I did so; and went further, which is now
　　Our point of second meeting. Do you find
　　Your patience so predominant in your nature,
　　That you can let this go? Are you so gospeled,°
　　To pray for this good man and for his issue,
90　Whose heavy hand hath bowed you to the grave
　　And beggared yours forever?

First Murderer.　　　　　We are men, my liege.

Macbeth.
　　Ay, in the catalogue ye go for° men;
　　As hounds and greyhounds, mongrels, spaniels, curs,
　　Shoughs, water-rugs° and demi-wolves, are clept°
95　All by the name of dogs: the valued file°
　　Distinguishes the swift, the slow, the subtle,
　　The housekeeper, the hunter, every one
　　According to the gift which bounteous nature
　　Hath in him closed,° whereby he does receive
100　Particular addition, from the bill°
　　That writes them all alike: and so of men.
　　Now if you have a station in the file,
　　Not i' th' worst rank of manhood, say't,
　　And I will put that business in your bosoms
105　Whose execution takes your enemy off,
　　Grapples you to the heart and love of us,
　　Who wear our health but sickly in his life,°
　　Which in his death were perfect.

Second Murderer.　　　　　I am one, my liege,
　　Whom the vile blows and buffets of the world

Staging the Play
74. *What do you imagine the murderers would be like: the all-too-common "hit men" of contemporary movies? Or could they simply be officers who have a grudge against Banquo? (They have been portrayed in many ways.)*

77–78. held you / So under fortune: kept you from good fortune.
80. probation: review.
81. borne in hand: deceived.
instruments: tools.
83. soul: brain. **notion:** mind.

88. gospeled: so meek from reading the Gospel (of Jesus).

91. *What techniques is Macbeth using on the murderers?*

92. go for: pass as.

94. Shoughs, water-rugs: shaggy dogs and long-haired water dogs.
clept: called.
95. valued file: classification by valuable traits.

99. closed: enclosed.
100. bill: list.

107. Who wear . . . life: who are "sick" while he (Banquo) still lives.

110   Hath so incensed that I am reckless what
               I do to spite the world.

First Murderer.   And I another
               So weary with disasters, tugged with fortune,
               That I would set° my life on any chance,
               To mend it or be rid on't.

Macbeth.   Both of you
115   Know Banquo was your enemy.

Both Murderers.   True, my lord.

Macbeth.
               So is he mine, and in such bloody distance°
               That every minute of his being thrusts
               Against my near'st of life:° and though I could
               With barefaced power sweep him from my sight
120   And bid my will avouch° it, yet I must not,
               For° certain friends that are both his and mine,
               Whose loves I may not drop, but wail his fall
               Who I myself struck down: and thence it is
               That I to your assistance do make love,
125   Masking the business from the common eye
               For sundry weighty reasons.

Second Murderer.   We shall, my lord,
               Perform what you command us.

First Murderer.   Though our lives— **F**

Macbeth.
               Your spirits shine through you. Within this hour at most
               I will advise you where to plant yourselves,
130   Acquaint you with the perfect spy° o' th' time,
               The moment on't; for't must be done tonight,
               And something° from the palace; always thought°
               That I require a clearness:° and with him—
               To leave no rubs° nor botches in the work—
135   Fleance his son, that keeps him company,
               Whose absence is no less material to me
               Than is his father's, must embrace the fate **G**
               Of that dark hour. Resolve yourselves apart:°
               I'll come to you anon.

Murderers.   We are resolved, my lord.

Macbeth.

---

113. set: risk.

116. distance: quarrel.

118. near'st of life: vital spot.

120. avouch: justify.
121. For: because of.

? 126. *How does Macbeth justify to the murderers the fact that he has to ask them to kill Banquo?*

130. perfect spy: exact information.
132. something: some distance. thought: remembered.
133. clearness: freedom from suspicion.
134. rubs: flaws.

138. apart: alone (make up your minds by yourselves).

Glamis Castle, Angus, Scotland.

F **Reading Focus** Using Questions to Monitor Reading Macbeth apparently cuts off the First Murderer's speech. What questions do you have about this exchange?

G **Literary Focus** Tragedy In Act III, Scene 1, lines 54–55, Macbeth says of Banquo, "There is none but he / Whose being I do fear." Later that scene, lines 135–136, Macbeth says to the murderers, "Fleance his son, that keeps him company, / Whose absence is no less material to me / Than is his father's." How has Macbeth's view of murder changed since he killed Duncan?

140   I'll call upon you straight. Abide within.
        It is concluded: Banquo, thy soul's flight,
        If it find heaven, must find it out tonight.   [*Exeunt.*]

Scene 2. *The palace.*

Enter LADY MACBETH *and a* SERVANT.

Lady Macbeth.
    Is Banquo gone from court?
Servant.
    Ay, madam, but returns again tonight.
Lady Macbeth.
    Say to the king, I would attend his leisure
    For a few words.
Servant.   Madam, I will.   [*Exit.*]
Lady Macbeth.   Nought's had, all's spent,
5   Where our desire is got without content:
        'Tis safer to be that which we destroy
        Than by destruction dwell in doubtful joy.

[*Enter* MACBETH.]

    How now, my lord! Why do you keep alone,
    Of sorriest fancies your companions making,
10   Using those thoughts which should indeed have died
        With them they think on? Things without° all remedy
        Should be without regard: what's done is done.   Ⓗ
Macbeth.
    We have scorched° the snake, not killed it:
    She'll close° and be herself, whilst our poor malice°
15   Remains in danger of her former tooth.
        But let the frame of things disjoint,° both the worlds° suffer,
        Ere we will eat our meal in fear, and sleep
        In the affliction of these terrible dreams
        That shake us nightly: better be with the dead,
20   Whom we, to gain our peace, have sent to peace,
        Than on the torture of the mind to lie
        In restless ecstasy.° Duncan is in his grave;
        After life's fitful fever he sleeps well.
        Treason has done his worst: nor steel, nor poison,
25   Malice domestic,° foreign levy,° nothing,
        Can touch him further.
Lady Macbeth.   Come on.

Ⓗ **Reading Focus** Using Questioning to Monitor Reading   Lady Macbeth's response is based on her interpretation of Macbeth's thoughts. What questions do you have about her insight into his mind?

140. *What has Macbeth arranged with the murderers? What is his mood here? Does Lady Macbeth have any part in arranging these next murders?*

7. *What reversal of attitudes takes place here?*

11. without: beyond.

Staging the Play
12. *This scene can be played in several ways. Is Lady Macbeth hostile to her husband and angry with him? Or can she be shown to have some tenderness in this scene?*

13. scorched: slashed.
14. close: heal. **malice:** enmity; hatred.
16. frame of things disjoint: universe collapse. **worlds:** heaven and earth.
22. ecstasy: frenzy.
25. Malice domestic: domestic war (civil war). **foreign levy:** exaction of tribute by a foreign country.

Staging the Play
26. *What do you picture the couple doing in this scene? Are they sitting together? Are they close, or is there a distance between them?*

Gentle my lord, sleek° o'er your rugged° looks;
Be bright and jovial among your guests tonight.
Macbeth.
So shall I, love; and so, I pray, be you:
30   Let your remembrance apply to Banquo;°
Present him eminence,° both with eye and tongue:
Unsafe the while, that we must lave°
Our honors in these flattering streams
And make our faces vizards° to our hearts,
Disguising what they are.
35   **Lady Macbeth.**   You must leave this.
Macbeth.
O, full of scorpions is my mind, dear wife!
Thou know'st that Banquo, and his Fleance, lives.
Lady Macbeth.
But in them nature's copy's not eterne.°
Macbeth.
There's comfort yet; they are assailable.
40   Then be thou jocund. Ere the bat hath flown
His cloistered flight, ere to black Hecate's summons
The shard-borne° beetle with his drowsy hums
Hath rung night's yawning peal, there shall be done
A deed of dreadful note.
Lady Macbeth.   What's to be done?
Macbeth.
45   Be innocent of the knowledge, dearest chuck,°   ❶
Till thou applaud the deed. Come, seeling° night,
Scarf up° the tender eye of pitiful day,
And with thy bloody and invisible hand
Cancel and tear to pieces that great bond
50   Which keeps me pale! Light thickens, and the crow
Makes wing to th' rooky° wood.
Good things of day begin to droop and drowse,
Whiles night's black agents to their preys do rouse.
Thou marvel'st at my words: but hold thee still;
55   Things bad begun make strong themselves by ill:
So, prithee, go with me.   [*Exeunt.*]

Scene 3. *Near the palace.*

Enter three MURDERERS.

First Murderer.
But who did bid thee join with us?

27. **sleek:** smooth. **rugged:** furrowed.

30. **Let . . . Banquo:** That is, focus your thoughts on Banquo.
31. **eminence:** honors.
32. **lave:** wash.
34. **vizards:** masks.

? **Staging the Play**
35. *With what degree of urgency must Lady Macbeth say this line?*

38. **nature's copy's not eterne:** That is, they won't live forever.

42. **shard-borne:** carried on scaly wings.

45. **chuck:** chick (a term of endearment).
46. **seeling:** eye-closing; blinding.
47. **Scarf up:** blindfold.

51. **rooky:** full of rooks, or crows.

❶ **Literary Focus** Tragedy How has the relationship between Lady Macbeth and Macbeth changed? How does this change help develop Macbeth's character as a tragic hero?

Third Murderer.   Macbeth.

Second Murderer.

    He needs not our mistrust; since he delivers

    Our offices and what we have to do

    To the direction just.°

First Murderer.   Then stand with us.

5   The west yet glimmers with some streaks of day.

    Now spurs the lated° traveler apace

    To gain the timely inn, and near approaches

    The subject of our watch.

Third Murderer.   Hark! I hear horses.

Banquo (*within*). Give us a light there, ho!

Second Murderer.   Then 'tis he. The rest

10   That are within the note of expectation°

    Already are i' th' court.

First Murderer.   His horses go about.

Third Murderer.

    Almost a mile: but he does usually—

    So all men do—from hence to th' palace gate

    Make it their walk.

[*Enter* BANQUO *and* FLEANCE, *with a torch.*]

Second Murderer.

    A light, a light!

Third Murderer. 'Tis he.

15 **First Murderer.**   Stand to't.

Banquo.

    It will be rain tonight.

First Murderer.   Let it come down.

[*They set upon* BANQUO.]

Banquo.

    O, treachery! Fly, good Fleance, fly, fly, fly!

                           [*Exit* FLEANCE.]

    Thou mayst revenge. O slave!   [*Dies.*]

Third Murderer.

    Who did strike out the light?

First Murderer.   Was't not the way?°

Third Murderer.

20   There's but one down; the son is fled.   Ⓙ

Second Murderer.

    We have lost best half of our affair.

First Murderer.

Ⓙ **Literary Focus** **Tragedy** How does the Third Murderer differ from the other murderers? Was Macbeth wise to send him?

? **1.** *The identity of the Third Murderer is not made clear. Whom would you name as possible suspects?*

2–4. He needs . . . just: We need not mistrust him (the Third Murderer) since he describes our duties exactly according to our directions.
6. lated: belated.

10. within . . . expectation: on the list of expected guests.

Statue at Glamis Castle.

19. way: thing to do.
? **Staging the Play**
19. *What might the murderers be doing as the light goes out?*
? **Staging the Play**
21. *Disposal of bodies is always a problem for directors of Shakespeare's plays. How would you have Banquo's body carried off? By whom?*

Well, let's away and say how much is done.   [*Exeunt.*]

Scene 4. *The palace.*

Banquet prepared. Enter MACBETH, LADY MACBETH, ROSS, LENNOX,
        LORDS, *and* ATTENDANTS.

Macbeth.
    You know your own degrees;° sit down:
    At first and last, the hearty welcome.
Lords.
    Thanks to your majesty.
Macbeth.
    Oneself will mingle with society°
5   And play the humble host.
    Our hostess keeps her state,° but in best time
    We will require° her welcome.
Lady Macbeth.
    Pronounce it for me, sir, to all our friends,
    For my heart speaks they are welcome.

[*Enter* FIRST MURDERER.]

Macbeth.
10 See, they encounter° thee with their hearts' thanks.
    Both sides are even: here I'll sit i' th' midst:
    Be large in mirth; anon we'll drink a measure°
    The table round. (*Goes to* FIRST MURDERER.) There's blood
        upon thy face.
First Murderer.
    'Tis Banquo's then.
Macbeth.
15 'Tis better thee without than he within.°
    Is he dispatched?
First Murderer.   My lord, his throat is cut;
    That I did for him.
Macbeth.   Thou art the best o' th' cutthroats.
    Yet he's good that did the like for Fleance;
    If thou didst it, thou art the nonpareil.
First Murderer.
20 Most royal sir, Fleance is 'scaped.
Macbeth (*aside*).
    Then comes my fit again: I had else been perfect,   **K**
    Whole as the marble, founded° as the rock,

K **Literary Focus** **Tragedy** Some people have argued that Macbeth was the Third
Murderer. How does this speech support or <u>contradict</u> that theory? Explain your answer.

? **Elements of Drama**
22. *This scene, so essential to the play, is often called the play's turning point or technical climax. What have been Macbeth's good fortunes so far?*

1. degrees: ranks.
? **Elements of Drama**
2. *This crucial scene is often called the dramatic climax of the play; it is tremendously exciting when staged well. Notice where Macbeth's subjects become aware of his capacity for irrational behavior.*
4. society: the company.
6. keeps her state: remains seated in her chair of state.
7. require: request.

10. encounter: meet.

12. measure: goblet.

15. thee . . . within: outside you than inside him.

? **Staging the Play**
20. *How would Macbeth react to this line?*

As broad and general as the casing air:°
But now I am cabined, cribbed,° confined, bound in
25 To saucy° doubts and fears.—But Banquo's safe?

First Murderer.
Ay, my good lord: safe in a ditch he bides,
With twenty trenchèd° gashes on his head,
The least a death to nature.

Macbeth.   Thanks for that.
(*Aside.*) There the grown serpent lies; the worm° that's fled
30 Hath nature that in time will venom breed,
No teeth for th' present. Get thee gone. Tomorrow
We'll hear ourselves° again.   [*Exit* FIRST MURDERER.]

Lady Macbeth.   My royal lord,
You do not give the cheer.° The feast is sold
That is not often vouched, while 'tis a-making,
35 'Tis given with welcome. To feed were best at home;°
From thence, the sauce to meat° is ceremony;
Meeting were bare without it.

22. **founded:** firmly based.
23. **broad . . . casing air:** uncon-fined as the surrounding air.
24. **cribbed:** penned up.
25. **saucy:** insolent.

27. **trenchèd:** trenchlike.

29. **worm:** serpent.

32. **hear ourselves:** talk it over.

33. **cheer:** sense of cordiality.

33–35. **The feast . . . home:** The feast seems sold (not given) when the host fails to welcome the guests. Mere eating is best done at home.
36. **meat:** food.

Act III/IV: The Banquet. Derek Jacobi (rear) as Macbeth.
Royal Shakespeare Company (1993).

[*Enter the* GHOST OF BANQUO, *and sits in Macbeth's place.*]

Macbeth.   Sweet remembrancer!°
   Now good digestion wait on appetite,
   And health on both!
Lennox.   May't please your highness sit.
Macbeth.
40   Here had we now our country's honor roofed,°
   Were the graced person of our Banquo present—
   Who may I rather challenge for unkindness
   Than pity for mischance!°
Ross.   His absence, sir,
   Lays blame upon his promise. Please't your highness
45   To grace us with your royal company?
Macbeth.
   The table's full.
Lennox.   Here is a place reserved, sir.
Macbeth.
   Where?
Lennox.
   Here, my good lord. What is't that moves your highness?
Macbeth.
   Which of you have done this?
Lords.   What, my good lord?
Macbeth.
50   Thou canst not say I did it. Never shake
   Thy gory locks at me.
Ross.
   Gentlemen, rise, his highness is not well. **Ⓛ**
Lady Macbeth.
   Sit, worthy friends. My Lord is often thus,
   And hath been from his youth. Pray you, keep seat.
55   The fit is momentary; upon a thought°
   He will again be well. If much you note him,
   You shall offend him and extend his passion.°
   Feed, and regard him not.—Are you a man?
Macbeth.
   Ay, and a bold one, that dare look on that
   Which might appall the devil.
60 **Lady Macbeth.**   O proper stuff!
   This is the very painting of your fear.
   This is the air-drawn dagger which, you said,
   Led you to Duncan. O, these flaws° and starts,

Ⓛ **Literary Focus** Tragedy How does this scene mark the beginning of Macbeth's actual deterioration?

37. remembrancer: reminder.
❓ 37. *Lady Macbeth has summoned her husband to her area of the stage. How would you describe her mood?*
❓ Stage direction: *The ghost is crucial to this scene. Should the ghost be imagined? Or should it actually appear onstage? If so, how should it look?*
40. our . . . roofed: our nobility under one roof.
42–43. Who . . . mischance: whom I hope I may reprove because he is unkind rather than pity because he has encountered an accident.
❓ 46. *When Macbeth says this line, what does he see?*

❓ Staging the Play
49. *How should Macbeth ask this question? Whom should he address?*
❓ Staging the Play
51. *According to Macbeth's speech here, what is the ghost doing? Does anyone else see the ghost? How should the others be acting?*
❓ 53. *Do you think this statement is true? Or is Lady Macbeth desperately trying to cover for her husband?*
55. upon a thought: as quick as a thought.
57. extend his passion: lengthen his fit.
❓ Staging the Play
58. *Where do you think Lady Macbeth has taken her husband so that she can whisper this intimidating line?*
63. flaws: gusts; outbursts.

450   Unit 2 • Collection 4

Imposters to° true fear, would well become

65 A woman's story at a winter's fire,
Authorized° by her grandam. Shame itself!
Why do you make such faces? When all's done,
You look but on a stool.

Macbeth. Prithee, see there!
Behold! Look! Lo! How say you?

70 Why, what care I? If thou canst nod, speak too.
If charnel houses° and our graves must send
Those that we bury back, our monuments
Shall be the maws of kites.° [*Exit* GHOST.]

Lady Macbeth. What, quite unmanned in folly?

Macbeth.
If I stand here, I saw him.

Lady Macbeth. Fie, for shame!

Macbeth.
75 Blood hath been shed ere now, i' th' olden time,
Ere humane statute purged the gentle weal;°
Ay, and since too, murders have been performed
Too terrible for the ear. The time has been
That, when the brains were out, the man would die,
80 And there an end; but now they rise again,
With twenty mortal murders on their crowns,°
And push us from our stools. This is more strange
Than such a murder is.

Lady Macbeth. My worthy lord,
Your noble friends do lack you.

Macbeth. I do forget.
85 Do not muse at me, my most worthy friends;
I have a strange infirmity, which is nothing
To those that know me. Come, love and health to all!
Then I'll sit down. Give me some wine, fill full.

[*Enter* GHOST.]

I drink to th' general joy o' th' whole table,
90 And to our dear friend Banquo, whom we miss;
Would he were here! To all and him we thirst,°
And all to all.°

Lords. Our duties, and the pledge.

Macbeth.
Avaunt! and quit my sight! Let the earth hide thee!
Thy bones are marrowless, thy blood is cold;
95 Thou hast no speculation° in those eyes
Which thou dost glare with.

Lady Macbeth. Think of this, good peers,
But as a thing of custom; 'tis no other.

64. to: compared with.

66. Authorized: vouched for.

Staging the Play
68. *What could the actor playing Banquo do here in mockery of Macbeth?*

Elements of Drama
70. *What action is Macbeth engaged in here? What is his tone?*

71. charnel houses: vaults containing bones.
72–73. our . . . kites: Our tombs shall be the bellies of rapacious birds.

75. *To whom is Macbeth talking?*
76. purged . . . weal: cleansed the state and made it gentle.

81. mortal . . . crowns: deadly wounds on their heads.

85. *What impression is Macbeth trying to create?*

91. thirst: desire to drink.
92. all to all: Let everybody drink to everybody.

93. *Whom is Macbeth addressing now? According to this speech, what might the ghost be doing?*
95. speculation: sight.

Only it spoils the pleasure of the time.

Macbeth.

What man dare, I dare.

100 Approach thou like the rugged Russian bear,
The armed rhinoceros, or th' Hyrcan° tiger;
Take any shape but that, and my firm nerves°
Shall never tremble. Or be alive again,
And dare me to the desert° with thy sword.
105 If trembling I inhabit then, protest me
The baby of a girl.° Hence, horrible shadow!
Unreal mock'ry, hence!   [*Exit* GHOST.]
                    Why, so: being gone,
I am a man again. Pray you, sit still.

Lady Macbeth.

You have displaced the mirth, broke the good meeting,
With most admired° disorder.   Ⓜ

110 **Macbeth.**   Can such things be,
And overcome us° like a summer's cloud,
Without our special wonder? You make me strange
Even to the disposition that I owe,°
When now I think you can behold such sights,
115 And keep the natural ruby of your cheeks,
When mine is blanched with fear.

Ross.   What sights, my lord?

Lady Macbeth.

I pray you, speak not: he grows worse and worse;
Question enrages him: at once, good night.
Stand not upon the order of your going,°
But go at once.

120 **Lennox.**   Good night; and better health
Attend his majesty!

Lady Macbeth.   A kind good night to all!

                    [*Exeunt* LORDS.]

Macbeth.

It will have blood, they say: blood will have blood.
Stones have been known to move and trees to speak;
Augurs and understood relations° have
125 By maggot-pies and choughs and rooks brought forth°
The secret'st man of blood. What is the night?°

Lady Macbeth.

Almost at odds with morning, which is which.

Ⓜ **Reading Focus** Using Questioning to Monitor Reading Based on Macbeth's behavior here, Lady Macbeth decides that the plan is beginning to unravel. What questions does her decision to break up the party raise for you?

101. Hyrcan: of Hyrcania (near the Caspian Sea).
102. nerves: sinews.
104. desert: lonely place.
105–106. If . . . girl: If then I tremble, proclaim me a baby girl.

❓ **Staging the Play**
108. *How "brave" should Macbeth appear to be with all the "brave" talk in these lines? What is his mood when he says, "I am a man again"?*

110. admired: amazing.
❓ **110.** *Lady Macbeth and her husband converse in private again. What would the other guests be doing?*

111. overcome us: come over us.
112–113. You . . . owe: You make me wonder what my nature is.

❓ **Staging the Play**
117. *What clue here would tell the actor playing Macbeth how he should behave?*

119. Stand . . . going: Do not insist on departing in the order of your rank.

❓ **Staging the Play**
122. *Read this speech carefully, and decide how Macbeth would deliver it: slowly? quickly? What is his mood?*

124. Augurs . . . relations: auguries (omens) and comprehended reports.
125. By . . . forth: by magpies, crows, and rooks (telltale birds) revealed.
126. What . . . night: What time of night is it?

Macbeth.

How say'st thou, that Macduff denies his person
At our great bidding?

Lady Macbeth. Did you send to him, sir?

Macbeth.

130   I hear it by the way,° but I will send:
There's not a one of them but in his house
I keep a servant fee'd.° I will tomorrow,
And betimes° I will, to the weird sisters:
More shall they speak, for now I am bent° to know
135   By the worst means the worst. For mine own good
All causes° shall give way. I am in blood
Stepped in so far that, should I wade no more,
Returning were as tedious as go o'er.
Strange things I have in head that will to hand,
140   Which must be acted ere they may be scanned.°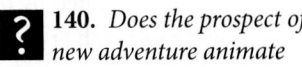

Lady Macbeth.

You lack the season of all natures,° sleep.

Macbeth.

Come, we'll to sleep. My strange and self-abuse°
Is the initiate fear that wants hard use.°
We are yet but young in deed.   [*Exeunt.*]

Scene 5. *A witches' haunt.*

Thunder. Enter the three WITCHES, *meeting* HECATE.

First Witch.

Why, how now, Hecate! you look angerly.

Hecate.

Have I not reason, beldams° as you are,
Saucy and overbold? How did you dare
To trade and traffic with Macbeth
5   In riddles and affairs of death;
And I, the mistress of your charms,
The close contriver° of all harms,
Was never called to bear my part,
Or show the glory of our art?
10   And, which is worse, all you have done
Hath been but for a wayward son,
Spiteful and wrathful; who, as others do,
Loves for his own ends, not for you.
But make amends now: get you gone,

130. by the way: incidentally.

132. fee'd: that is, paid to spy.
133. betimes: quickly.
134. bent: determined.

136. causes: considerations.

❓ 140. *Does the prospect of a new adventure animate Macbeth? Or is he spent and exhausted?*
140. may be scanned: can be examined.
141. season . . . natures: seasoning (preservative) of all living creatures.
142. self-abuse: delusion.
143. initiate . . . use: beginner's fear that lacks hardening practice.

❓ 144. *How might Lady Macbeth react to this last line?*

❓ Scene 5. *Macbeth was published in the first folio in 1623, seven years after Shakespeare's death. Some people think that this scene was written by someone else because the play was short and needed fleshing out. After you read the scene, decide if you think it "sounds" like the rest of the play.*
2. beldams: hags.

7. close contriver: secret inventor.

Ⓝ **Literary Focus** **Tragedy** What new information about Macbeth's state of mind is revealed in this speech?

15	And at the pit of Acheron°		**15. Acheron:** river of Hades.
	Meet me i' th' morning: thither he		
	Will come to know his destiny.		
	Your vessels and your spells provide,		
	Your charms and everything beside.		
20	I am for th' air; this night I'll spend		
	Unto a dismal and a fatal end:		
	Great business must be wrought ere noon.		
	Upon the corner of the moon		
	There hangs a vap'rous drop profound;°		**24. profound:** heavy.
25	I'll catch it ere it come to ground:		
	And that distilled by magic sleights°		**26. sleights:** arts.
	Shall raise such artificial sprites°		**27. artificial sprites:** spirits created by magic arts.
	As by the strength of their illusion		**29. confusion:** ruin.

Josette Simon (Witch) in *Macbeth*.
Barbican Theatre, London (1983).

"I AM FOR TH' AIR;
THIS NIGHT I'LL
SPEND UNTO A
DISMAL AND
FATAL END."

Shall draw him on to his confusion.°
30 He shall spurn fate, scorn death, and bear
    His hopes 'bove wisdom, grace, and fear:
    And you all know security°
    Is mortal's chiefest enemy. **⓪**   [*Music and a song.*]
    Hark! I am called; my little spirit, see,
35 Sits in a foggy cloud and stays for me.

                                                    [*Exit.*]

[*Sing within,* "Come away, come away," *etc.*]

First Witch.
    Come, let's make haste; she'll soon be back again.

                                                    [*Exeunt.*]

Scene 6. *The palace.*

Enter LENNOX *and another* LORD.

Lennox.
    My former speeches have but hit your thoughts,°
    Which can interpret farther. Only I say
    Things have been strangely borne.° The gracious Duncan
    Was pitied of Macbeth: marry, he was dead.
5   And the right-valiant Banquo walked too late;
    Whom, you may say, if't please you, Fleance killed,
    For Fleance fled. Men must not walk too late.
    Who cannot want the thought,° how monstrous
    It was for Malcolm and for Donalbain
10 To kill their gracious father? Damnèd fact!°
    How it did grieve Macbeth! Did he not straight,
    In pious rage, the two delinquents tear,
    That were the slaves of drink and thralls° of sleep?
    Was not that nobly done? Ay, and wisely too;
15 For 'twould have angered any heart alive
    To hear the men deny't. So that I say **ℙ**
    He has borne all things well: and I do think
    That, had he Duncan's sons under his key—
    As, an 't° please heaven, he shall not—they should find
20 What 'twere to kill a father. So should Fleance.
    But, peace! for from broad words,° and 'cause he failed

32. security: overconfidence.

1. My . . . thoughts: My recent words have only coincided with what you have in your mind.
3. borne: managed.

8. cannot . . . thought: cannot help thinking.
10. fact: evil deed.

13. thralls: slaves.

19. an 't: if it.

21. for . . . words: because of frank talk.

⓪ Reading Focus Using Questioning to Monitor Reading What questions can you ask to determine what draws Macbeth "on to his confusion"?

ℙ Literary Focus Tragedy What does Lennox suggest about Macbeth?

His presence at the tyrant's feast, I hear,
Macduff lives in disgrace. Sir, can you tell
Where he bestows himself?

Lord.   The son of Duncan,
25   From whom this tyrant holds the due of birth,°   **Q**
Lives in the English court, and is received
Of the most pious Edward° with such grace
That the malevolence of fortune nothing
Takes from his high respect.° Thither Macduff
30   Is gone to pray the holy king, upon his aid°
To wake Northumberland° and warlike Siward;°
That by the help of these, with Him above
To ratify the work, we may again
Give to our tables meat, sleep to our nights,
35   Free from our feasts and banquets bloody knives,
Do faithful homage and receive free° honors:
All which we pine for now. And this report
Hath so exasperate the king that he
Prepares for some attempt of war.

Lennox.   Sent he to Macduff?

Lord.
40   He did: and with an absolute "Sir, not I,"   **R**
The cloudy° messenger turns me his back,
And hums, as who should say "You'll rue the time
That clogs° me with this answer."

Lennox.   And that well might
Advise him to a caution, t' hold what distance
45   His wisdom can provide. Some holy angel
Fly to the court of England and unfold
His message ere he come, that a swift blessing
May soon return to this our suffering country
Under a hand accursed!

Lord.   I'll send my prayers with him.

[*Exeunt.*]

---

25. due of birth: birthright.

27. Edward: Edward the Confessor (reigned 1042–1066).
28–29. nothing . . . respect: does not diminish the high respect in which he is held.
30. upon his aid: to aid him (Malcolm).
31. To wake Northumberland: that is, to arouse the people in Northumberland, an English county near Scotland. **Siward:** Earl of Northumberland.
36. free: freely granted.

41. cloudy: disturbed.
43. clogs: burdens.
? **Elements of Drama**
49. *This is basically an "information" scene. Can you summarize what it tells you about the plot?*

Q **Literary Perspectives** Analyzing Historical Context In the time of Macbeth, Scottish laws prevented lineal succession (from parent to child) of the throne. Instead, rule was passed between families. In light of the historical situation in Shakespeare's time, why might Shakespeare have changed this concept?

R **Literary Focus** Tragedy Given how Macbeth's plans develop in this act, how would you expect him to respond to Macduff's refusal?

Applying Your Skills

SKILLS FOCUS **Literary Skills** Analyze characteristics of a tragedy; analyze irony, including verbal and situational irony; analyze historical context. **Reading Skills** Use questioning to monitor reading. **Writing Skills** Write drama.

The Tragedy of Macbeth
Act III

Respond and Think Critically

Reading Focus

Quick Check

1. Macbeth publicly announces that he will be alone until dinner. What does he really do during this time?

2. Why does Macbeth refuse to sit in the chair that is offered to him at dinner?

3. Where is Macduff during Act III? Why?

Read with a Purpose

4. How does Shakespeare portray Macbeth's tragic flaw in this act?

Reading Skills: Using Questions to Monitor Reading

5. While reading Act III, you continued to record your questions about the text. Now, record and explain your answers.

Act, Scene, Line	Questions I Have	My Answers
Act III, Scene 2, lines 16–26	Why is Macbeth talking about Duncan as if he envies the dead king?	Suffering from nightmares (lines 18, 19), Macbeth wishes his distress would end.

Literary Focus

Literary Analysis

6. **Analyze** In Act I, Lady Macbeth attacks Macbeth's masculinity and thereby convinces him to murder Duncan. How does the question of manhood come up in Act III?

7. **Analyze** How do lines 27–34 in Act III, Scene 2 express the "foul is fair" theme?

8. **Interpret** When the two murderers explain their criminal behavior, what do we learn about them?

9. **Interpret** The events during the dinner entrance (Act III, 4, 1–2) and exit (lines 119–120) are quite different. Why is this difference significant?

10. **Evaluate** How does Macbeth's situation at the end of Act III compare to his situation at the end of Act II? Explain your answer.

11. **Literary Perspectives** Why does Shakespeare portray Banquo as a good man and good father?

Literary Skills: Tragedy

12. **Analyze** In Act III, we see a darker side of Macbeth. When does he reach a turning point that <u>ensures</u> his tragic end? Provide examples from the text.

Literary Skills Review: Irony

13. **Analyze** There are several types of irony. **Verbal irony** occurs when someone says one thing but means something quite different. **Situational irony** occurs when what happens is the opposite of what is expected. **Dramatic irony** occurs when the audience or reader knows something important that a character does not. Give examples of each type of irony from Act III.

Writing Focus

Think as a Reader/Writer

Use It in Your Writing In your *Reader/Writer Notebook,* you noted Shakespeare's use of characterization. Find an example in Act III where other characters describe Macbeth. Use this example as a model to write your own brief scene in which two characters describe a third character who is not present.

What Do **You Think Now**

In Act III, how does Macbeth respond to the impulses of his heart and mind?

For more activities see page 494-495. ›

Act IV

Scene 1. *A witches' haunt.*

Thunder. Enter the three WITCHES.

First Witch.
    Thrice the brinded° cat hath mewed.
Second Witch.
    Thrice and once the hedge-pig° whined.
Third Witch.
    Harpier° cries, 'Tis time, 'tis time.
First Witch.
    Round about the caldron go:
5   In the poisoned entrails throw.
    Toad, that under cold stone
    Days and nights has thirty-one
    Swelt'red venom sleeping got,°
    Boil thou first i' th' charmèd pot.
All.
10   Double, double, toil and trouble;
    Fire burn and caldron bubble.

❓ Staging the Play
Stage direction: *This scene usually begins in darkness. In Shakespeare's day, the caldron might have risen through the trapdoor. How would you have the witches act: gleeful? lamenting?*

1. brinded: brindled.

2. hedge-pig: hedgehog.

3. Harpier: an attendant spirit like Graymalkin and Paddock in Act I, Scene 1.

8. Swelt'red . . . got: venom sweated out while sleeping.

The Witches, The Royal Opera, Covent Garden, London (2002).

"DOUBLE, DOUBLE, TOIL AND TROUBLE; FIRE BURN AND CALDRON BUBBLE."

Second Witch.

    Fillet° of a fenny° snake,

    In the caldron boil and bake;

    Eye of newt and toe of frog,

15   Wool of bat and tongue of dog,

    Adder's fork° and blindworm's° sting,

    Lizard's leg and howlet's° wing,

    For a charm of pow'rful trouble,

    Like a hell-broth boil and bubble.

All.

20   Double, double, toil and trouble;

    Fire burn and caldron bubble.

Third Witch.

    Scale of dragon, tooth of wolf,

    Witch's mummy,° maw and gulf°

    Of the ravined° salt-sea shark,

25   Root of hemlock digged i' th' dark,

    Liver of blaspheming Jew,

    Gall of goat, and slips of yew

    Slivered in the moon's eclipse,

    Nose of Turk and Tartar's lips,

30   Finger of birth-strangled babe

    Ditch-delivered by a drab,°

    Make the gruel thick and slab:°

    Add thereto a tiger's chaudron,°

    For th' ingredients of our caldron.

All.

35   Double, double, toil and trouble;

    Fire burn and caldron bubble. **Ⓐ**

Second Witch.

    Cool it with a baboon's blood,

    Then the charm is firm and good.

[*Enter* HECATE *and the other three* WITCHES.]

Hecate.

    O, well done! I commend your pains;

40   And every one shall share i' th' gains:

    And now about the caldron sing,

    Like elves and fairies in a ring,

    Enchanting all that you put in.

[*Music and a song:* "Black Spirits," *etc.*]

[*Exeunt* HECATE *and the other three* WITCHES.]

12. **Fillet:** slice. **fenny:** from a swamp.

16. **fork:** forked tongue. **blindworm's:** legless lizard's.
17. **howlet's:** owl's.

23. **Witch's mummy:** mummified flesh of a witch. **maw and gulf:** stomach and gullet.
24. **ravined:** ravenous.

31. **drab:** harlot.
32. **slab:** slimy.
33. **chaudron:** entrails.

Ⓐ **Literary Focus** **Tragedy** Compare the beginnings of Acts I and IV. What is similar? What has changed?

Second Witch.

45   By the pricking of my thumbs,
      Something wicked this way comes:
          Open, locks,
          Whoever knocks!

[*Enter* MACBETH.]

Macbeth.

      How now, you secret, black, and midnight hags!   **B**
      What is't you do?
All.   A deed without a name.
Macbeth.

50   I conjure you, by that which you profess,
      Howe'er you come to know it, answer me:
      Though you untie the winds and let them fight
      Against the churches; though the yesty° waves
      Confound° and swallow navigation up;
55   Though bladed corn be lodged° and trees blown down;
      Though castles topple on their warders' heads;
      Though palaces and pyramids do slope°
      Their heads to their foundations; though the treasure
      Of nature's germens° tumble all together,
60   Even till destruction sicken,° answer me
      To what I ask you.   **C**
First Witch.   Speak.
Second Witch.   Demand.
Third Witch.   We'll answer.
First Witch.

      Say, if th' hadst rather hear it from our mouths,
      Or from our masters?
Macbeth.   Call 'em, let me see 'em.
First Witch.

      Pour in sow's blood, that hath eaten
65   Her nine farrow;° grease that's sweaten°
      From the murderer's gibbet° throw
      Into the flame.
All.   Come, high or low,
      Thyself and office° deftly show!

[*Thunder.* FIRST APPARITION: *an Armed Head.°*]

Macbeth.

      Tell me, thou unknown power——

? *This exciting scene has five major sections, each with its own intensity. See if you can identify them when you're finished.*

53. **yesty:** foamy.
54. **Confound:** destroy.
55. **bladed . . . lodged:** grain in the ear be beaten down.
57. **slope:** bend.

59. **nature's germens:** seeds of all life.
60. **sicken:** sicken at its own work.

? **Staging the Play**
61. *These exchanges are spoken rapidly. Do the witches now see Macbeth as a participant in evil?*

65. **farrow:** young pigs.
sweaten: sweated.
66. **gibbet:** gallows.

? 67. *What are the witches doing all during this scene?*
68. **office:** function.

Armed Head: helmeted head.

Analyzing Visuals

Viewing and Interpreting How does the image on the opposite page illustrate Macbeth's relationship with the witches?

B Literary Focus **Tragedy** How has Macbeth's attitude toward the witches changed since his earlier encounters with them?

C Literary Focus **Tragedy** How has Macbeth's attitude about risk changed?

First Witch. He knows thy thought:
Hear his speech, but say thou nought.

First Apparition.
Macbeth! Macbeth! Macbeth! Beware Macduff!
Beware the Thane of Fife. Dismiss me: enough.

[*He descends.*]

Macbeth.
Whate'er thou art, for thy good caution thanks:
Thou hast harped° my fear aright. But one word more—

First Witch.
He will not be commanded. Here's another, **D**
More potent than the first.

D **Literary Focus** **Tragedy** Why does Macbeth hope to control the witches?

? **71.** *Why does the "Armed Head" deliver this message? How does the form of the apparition support the warning the apparition gives?*

74. harped: hit upon; struck the note of.

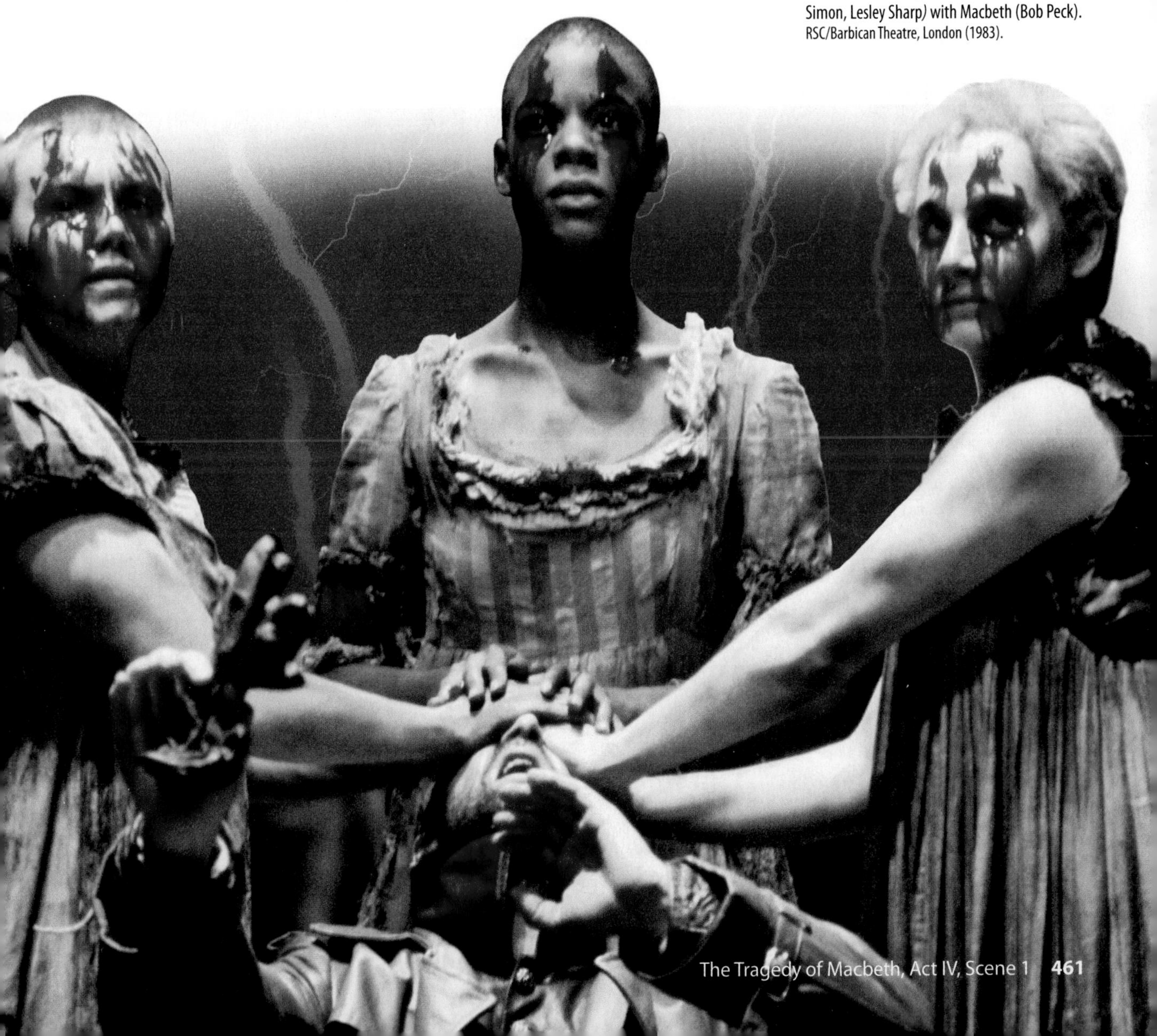

The Witches *(left-right:* Katy Behean, Josette Simon, Lesley Sharp*)* with Macbeth (Bob Peck). RSC/Barbican Theatre, London (1983).

[*Thunder.* SECOND APPARITION: *a Bloody Child.*]

Second Apparition.

Macbeth! Macbeth! Macbeth!

Macbeth.

Had I three ears, I'd hear thee.

Second Apparition.

Be bloody, bold, and resolute! Laugh to scorn
80   The pow'r of man, for none of woman born
Shall harm Macbeth.   [*Descends.*]

Macbeth.

Then live, Macduff: what need I fear of thee?
But yet I'll make assurance double sure,
And take a bond of fate.° Thou shalt not live;
85   That I may tell pale-hearted fear it lies,
And sleep in spite of thunder.

Greg Hicks as Macbeth *(2nd right)* stars with *(left-right)* Meg Fraser, Louise Bagay, and Ruth Gemmell as the Three Witches in the Royal Shakespeare Company production of *Macbeth* at the Royal Shakespeare Theatre, Stratford-upon-Avon.

? **82.** *Macbeth takes the child's message to mean he need not fear Macduff. Nonetheless, why should the Second Apparition's message be approached with caution?*

84. take . . . fate: get a guarantee from fate (that is, he will kill Macduff and thus will compel fate to keep its word).

"WHY SINKS THAT CALDRON?
AND WHAT NOISE IS THIS?"

[*Thunder.* THIRD APPARITION: *a Child Crowned, with a tree in his hand.*]

What is this,
That rises like the issue° of a king,
And wears upon his baby-brow the round
And top of sovereignty?°

All.   Listen, but speak not to't.

Third Apparition.

90   Be lion-mettled, proud, and take no care
Who chafes, who frets, or where conspirers are:
Macbeth shall never vanquished be until
Great Birnam Wood to high Dunsinane Hill
Shall come against him.   [*Descends.*]

Macbeth.   That will never be.

95   Who can impress° the forest, bid the tree
Unfix his earth-bound root? Sweet bodements,° good!
Rebellious dead, rise never, till the Wood
Of Birnam rise, and our high-placed Macbeth
Shall live the lease of nature,° pay his breath

100   To time and mortal custom.° Yet my heart
Throbs to know one thing. Tell me, if your art
Can tell so much: shall Banquo's issue ever
Reign in this kingdom?

All.   Seek to know no more. **F**

Macbeth.

I will be satisfied.° Deny me this,

105   And an eternal curse fall on you! Let me know.
Why sinks that caldron? And what noise° is this?

[*Hautboys.*]

First Witch. Show!
Second Witch. Show!
Third Witch. Show!
All.

110   Show his eyes, and grieve his heart;
Come like shadows, so depart!

---

87. issue: offspring.

88–89. round . . . sovereignty: that is, crown.

? **93.** *What does the Third Apparition prophesy? What must be Macbeth's mental state at this point?*
95. impress: conscript; draft.
96. bodements: prophecies.

99. lease of nature: natural life span.
100. mortal custom: natural death.
? **Elements of Drama**
102. *What is Macbeth's mood? How might his tone change when he asks about Banquo's issue, or children?*
104. satisfied: that is, fully informed.
106. noise: music.

E **Literary Focus** **Tragedy** Macbeth's deepest desire has changed over time. First, he just wished to remove Duncan; then, he wanted Banquo dead because he thought Banquo was suspicious of him. What does he want now?

F **Reading Focus** **Using Questioning to Monitor Reading** The witches tell Macbeth that he should "seek to know no more" (Act IV, Scene 1, line 103). Since they have (seemingly) been cooperating with Macbeth, what questions would help you clarify this apparent change in their approach?

[*A show of eight* KINGS *and* BANQUO, *last* KING *with a glass° in his hand.*]

Macbeth.
Thou art too like the spirit of Banquo. Down!
Thy crown does sear mine eyelids. And thy hair,
Thou other gold-bound brow, is like the first.

115   A third is like the former. Filthy hags!
Why do you show me this? A fourth! Start,° eyes!
What, will the line stretch out to th' crack of doom?°
Another yet! A seventh! I'll see no more.
And yet the eighth° appears, who bears a glass

120   Which shows me many more; and some I see
That twofold balls and treble scepters° carry: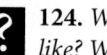
Horrible sight! Now I see 'tis true;
For the blood-boltered° Banquo smiles upon me,
And points at them for his.° What, is this so?

First Witch.
125   Ay, sir, all this is so. But why
Stands Macbeth thus amazedly?
Come, sisters, cheer we up his sprites,°
And show the best of our delights:
I'll charm the air to give a sound,

130   While you perform your antic round,°
That this great king may kindly say
Our duties did his welcome pay.

[*Music. The* WITCHES *dance, and vanish.*]

Macbeth.
Where are they? Gone? Let this pernicious hour
Stand aye accursèd in the calendar!
Come in, without there!

[*Enter* LENNOX.] **H**

135   **Lennox.**   What's your grace's will?
Macbeth.
Saw you the weird sisters?
Lennox.   No, my lord.
Macbeth.
Came they not by you?
Lennox.   No indeed, my lord.

G **Literary Perspectives** **Analyzing Historical Context** How does this final apparition symbolically honor James I?

H **Literary Focus** **Tragedy** Why do you think Lennox is still attending Macbeth?

? Staging the Play
Stage direction: A parade of eight Stuart kings passes before Macbeth. These are the kings of Banquo's line. The last king, Banquo, holds up a mirror (glass) to suggest an infinite number of descendants. According to the next speech, how does Banquo act toward Macbeth?

116. Start: that is, from the sockets.
117. crack of doom: blast (of a trumpet) at Doomsday.
119. eighth: King James I of England (the present king).
121. twofold . . . scepters: coronation emblems.
123. blood-boltered: matted with blood.
124. his: his descendants.

? 124. *What does Banquo look like? What must be Macbeth's mental state now?*
127. sprites: spirits.
130. antic round: grotesque, circular dance.

? Elements of Drama
136. *How would the mood onstage change as Lennox appears? What crucial information does he give Macbeth?*

Macbeth.
Infected by the air whereon they ride,
And damned all those that trust them! I did hear

140   The galloping of horse.° Who was't came by?

Lennox.
'Tis two or three, my lord, that bring you word
Macduff is fled to England.

Macbeth.   Fled to England?

Lennox.
Ay, my good lord.

Macbeth *(aside).*
Time, thou anticipat'st° my dread exploits.

145   The flighty purpose never is o'ertook
Unless the deed go with it.° From this moment
The very firstlings of my heart° shall be
The firstlings of my hand. And even now,
To crown my thoughts with acts, be it thought and done:

150   The castle of Macduff I will surprise;°
Seize upon Fife; give to th' edge o' th' sword
His wife, his babes, and all unfortunate souls
That trace him in his line.° No boasting like a fool;
This deed I'll do before this purpose cool:

155   But no more sights!—Where are these gentlemen?
Come, bring me where they are.   [*Exeunt.*]

Scene 2. *Macduff's castle.*

Enter Macduff's wife LADY MACDUFF, *her* SON, *and* ROSS.

Lady Macduff.
What had he done, to make him fly the land?

Ross.
You must have patience, madam.

Lady Macduff.   He had none:
His flight was madness. When our actions do not,
Our fears do make us traitors.

Ross.   You know not

5   Whether it was his wisdom or his fear.

---

140. horse: horses (or horsemen).

144. anticipat'st: foretold.
145–146. The flighty . . . it: The fleeting plan is never accomplished unless an action accompanies it.
147. firstlings . . . heart: that is, first thoughts, impulses.
150. surprise: attack suddenly.

153. trace . . . line: are of his lineage.

Staging the Play
Stage direction: *In many productions, the mood of this scene contrasts dramatically with the previous scenes of horror. How would you stage this domestic scene to suggest the vulnerability of Lady Macduff and her children?*

Glamis Castle, Angus, Scotland.

---

❶ **Reading Focus** **Using Questioning to Monitor Reading** Lennox tells Macbeth something he apparently doesn't know: Macduff's location. What questions can you ask to clarify Lennox's motives?

❿ **Literary Focus** **Tragedy** How does Macbeth's attitude here differ from his response to the murders of Banquo and Fleance?

Lady Macduff.

    Wisdom! To leave his wife, to leave his babes,

    His mansion and his titles,° in a place

    From whence himself does fly? He loves us not;

    He wants the natural touch:° for the poor wren,

10   The most diminutive of birds, will fight,

    Her young ones in her nest, against the owl.

    All is the fear and nothing is the love;

    As little is the wisdom, where the flight

    So runs against all reason.

    Ross.   My dearest coz,°

15   I pray you, school° yourself. But, for your husband,

    He is noble, wise, judicious, and best knows

    The fits o' th' season.° I dare not speak much further:

    But cruel are the times, when we are traitors

    And do not know ourselves; when we hold rumor

20   From what we fear,° yet know not what we fear,

    But float upon a wild and violent sea

    Each way and move. I take my leave of you.

    Shall not be long but I'll be here again.

    Things at the worst will cease,° or else climb upward

7. titles: possessions.

9. wants . . . touch: that is, lacks natural affection for his wife and children.

14. coz: cousin.
15. school: control.

Staging the Play
17. *How could Ross show his fear in line 17?*
17. fits . . . season: disorders of the time.
19–20. hold . . . fear: believe rumors because we fear.

24. cease: cease worsening.

Child actor in *Macbeth,* Royal Shakespeare Company (1993).

25   To what they were before. My pretty cousin,
     Blessing upon you! **Ⓚ**

Lady Macduff.
     Fathered he is, and yet he's fatherless.

Ross.
     I am so much a fool, should I stay longer,
     It would be my disgrace° and your discomfort.
     I take my leave at once.   **Ⓛ**   [*Exit* ROSS.]

30 **Lady Macduff.**   Sirrah,° your father's dead:
     And what will you do now? How will you live?

Son.
     As birds do, mother.

Lady Macduff.   What, with worms and flies?

Son.
     With what I get, I mean; and so do they.

Lady Macduff.
     Poor bird! thou'dst never fear the net nor lime,°
35   The pitfall nor the gin.°

Son.
     Why should I, mother? Poor birds they are not set for.
     My father is not dead, for all your saying.

Lady Macduff.
     Yes, he is dead: how wilt thou do for a father?

Son. Nay, how will you do for a husband?

40 **Lady Macduff.** Why, I can buy me twenty at any market.

Son. Then you'll buy 'em to sell° again.

Lady Macduff.
     Thou speak'st with all thy wit, and yet, i' faith,
     With wit enough for thee.°

Son.
     Was my father a traitor, mother?

45 **Lady Macduff.** Ay, that he was.

Son. What is a traitor?

Lady Macduff. Why, one that swears and lies.°

Son. And be all traitors that do so?

Lady Macduff. Every one that does so is a traitor, and must be
     hanged.

50 **Son.** And must they all be hanged that swear and lie?

Lady Macduff. Every one.

Son. Who must hang them?

Lady Macduff. Why, the honest men.

---

29. It . . . disgrace: That is, I would weep.

30. Sirrah: here, an affectionate address to a child.

❓ Staging the Play
30. *In taking his leave, how would Ross show affection for Lady Macduff and her young son? Would you have Ross be younger or older than Lady Macduff?*

❓ Staging the Play
31. *How would you have Lady Macduff act in this scene: frightened? bitter? loving? resigned?*

34. lime: birdlime (smeared on branches to catch birds).

35. gin: trap.

41. sell: betray.

43. for thee: for a child.

47. swears and lies: takes an oath and breaks it.

Ⓚ Literary Focus **Tragedy** What has changed in Ross's behavior?

Ⓛ Reading Focus **Using Questioning to Monitor Reading** Ross offers several reasons for why he should leave (Act IV, Scene 2, lines 28–30). What questions would you ask to explain his behavior?

Son. Then the liars and swearers are fools; for there are liars
55   and swearers enow° to beat the honest men and hang up them.
Lady Macduff. Now, God help thee, poor monkey! But
      how wilt thou do for a father?
Son. If he were dead, you'd weep for him. If you would not, it
      were a good sign that I should quickly have a new father.
60 **Lady Macduff.** Poor prattler, how thou talk'st!

[*Enter a* MESSENGER.]

Messenger.
      Bless you, fair dame! I am not to you known,
      Though in your state of honor I am perfect.°
      I doubt° some danger does approach you nearly:
      If you will take a homely° man's advice,
65   Be not found here; hence, with your little ones.
      To fright you thus, methinks I am too savage;
      To do worse to you were fell° cruelty,
      Which is too nigh your person. Heaven preserve you!
      I dare abide no longer.   [*Exit* MESSENGER.]
Lady Macduff.   Whither should I fly?
70   I have done no harm. But I remember now
      I am in this earthly world, where to do harm
      Is often laudable, to do good sometime
      Accounted dangerous folly. Why then, alas,
      Do I put up that womanly defense,
75   To say I have done no harm?—What are these faces?

[*Enter* MURDERERS.]

Murderer.
      Where is your husband?
Lady Macduff.
      I hope, in no place so unsanctified
      Where such as thou mayst find him.
Murderer.   He's a traitor.
Son.
      Thou li'st, thou shag-eared° villain!
Murderer.   What, you egg!

[*Stabbing him.*]

      Young fry° of treachery!
80 **Son.**   He has killed me, mother:

 Reading Focus **Using Questioning to Monitor Reading** The stage direction in
this scene reads "Enter Murderers," without numbering them or giving further identification.
What questions does this raise for you?

55. enow: enough.

62. in . . . perfect: That is, I am
fully informed of your honorable rank.
63. doubt: fear.
64. homely: plain.

67. fell: fierce.

? Elements of Drama
69. *Some readers think
that Lady Macbeth has sent this
messenger. Is there any support
for this theory? Would it be typical of her character? What must
Lady Macduff do when she hears
this terrible message?*

? Staging the Play
75. *What would Lady
Macduff and her son do as they
see the murderers enter the
room?*

79. shag-eared: hairy-eared.

80. fry: spawn.

Glamis Castle, Angus, Scotland.

Run away, I pray you! [*Dies.*]

[*Exit* LADY MACDUFF, *crying* "Murder!"
followed by MURDERERS.]

Scene 3. *England. Before the king's palace.*

Enter MALCOLM *and* MACDUFF.

Malcolm.
Let us seek out some desolate shade, and there
Weep our sad bosoms empty.
Macduff. Let us rather
Hold fast the mortal° sword, and like good men
Bestride our down-fall'n birthdom.° Each new morn
5 New widows howl, new orphans cry, new sorrows
Strike heaven on the face, that° it resounds
As if it felt with Scotland and yelled out
Like syllable of dolor.°
Malcolm. What I believe, I'll wail;
What know, believe; and what I can redress,

3. **mortal:** deadly.
4. **Bestride . . . birthdom:** protectively stand over our native land.
6. **that:** so that.

8. **Like . . . dolor:** similar sound of grief.

N **Literary Focus** **Tragedy** How does Macduff describe the expanded scope of
Macbeth's destruction in these lines?

10	As I shall find the time to friend,° I will.
	What you have spoke, it may be so perchance.
	This tyrant, whose sole° name blisters our tongues,
	Was once thought honest:° you have loved him well;
	He hath not touched you yet. I am young; but something
15	You may deserve of him through me;° and wisdom°
	To offer up a weak, poor, innocent lamb
	T' appease an angry god. **Ⓞ**

Macduff.
I am not treacherous.

Malcolm.   But Macbeth is.
A good and virtuous nature may recoil
20 In° an imperial charge. But I shall crave your pardon;
That which you are, my thoughts cannot transpose:°
Angels are bright still, though the brightest° fell:
Though all things foul would wear° the brows of grace,
Yet grace must still look so.°

Macduff.   I have lost my hopes.

Malcolm.
25 Perchance even there where I did find my doubts.
Why in that rawness° left you wife and child,
Those precious motives, those strong knots of love,
Without leave-taking? I pray you,
Let not my jealousies° be your dishonors,
30 But mine own safeties. You may be rightly just°
Whatever I shall think.

Macduff.   Bleed, bleed, poor country:
Great tyranny, lay thou thy basis° sure,
For goodness dare not check° thee: wear thou thy wrongs;
The title is affeered.° Fare thee well, lord:
35 I would not be the villain that thou think'st
For the whole space that's in the tyrant's grasp
And the rich East to boot.

Malcolm.   Be not offended:
I speak not as in absolute fear of you.
I think our country sinks beneath the yoke;
40 It weeps, it bleeds, and each new day a gash
Is added to her wounds. I think withal°
There would be hands uplifted in my right;°
And here from gracious England° have I offer
Of goodly thousands: but, for° all this,
45 When I shall tread upon the tyrant's head,
Or wear it on my sword, yet my poor country

Ⓞ Literary Focus **Tragedy** What does Malcolm seem to suspect about Macbeth and Macduff? Why is this suspicion ironic?

10. to friend: to be friendly, favorable.
12. sole: very.
13. honest: good.

? Elements of Drama
14. *What great irony would the audience feel upon hearing this line, given what has just taken place in the previous scene?*
15. deserve . . . me: that is, earn by betraying me to Macbeth. **wisdom:** it may be wise.
19–20. recoil / In: give way under.
21. transpose: transform.
22. the brightest: Lucifer, the angel who led the revolt of the angels and was thrown out of heaven; Satan.
23. would wear: desire to wear.
24. so: like itself.
26. rawness: unprotected condition.

29. jealousies: suspicions.
30. rightly just: perfectly honorable.

32. basis: foundation.
33. check: restrain.
34. affeered: legally confirmed.

? Staging the Play
37. *This speech might present a problem for the actor playing Macduff because it does not clearly relate to what has gone before it. It seems too grand and philosophical at this point in the play. How would you have the actor deliver this speech?*
41. withal: moreover.
42. in my right: on behalf of my claim.
43. England: the king of England.
44. for: despite.

Shall have more vices than it had before,
More suffer, and more sundry ways than ever,
By him that shall succeed.

Macduff.   What should he be?

Malcolm.

50   It is myself I mean, in whom I know
All the particulars° of vice so grafted°
That, when they shall be opened,° black Macbeth
Will seem as pure as snow, and the poor state
Esteem him as a lamb, being compared
With my confineless harms.°

55 **Macduff.**   Not in the legions
Of horrid hell can come a devil more damned
In evils to top Macbeth.

Malcolm.   I grant him bloody,
Luxurious,° avaricious, false, deceitful,
Sudden,° malicious, smacking of every sin

60   That has a name: but there's no bottom, none,
In my voluptuousness:° your wives, your daughters,
Your matrons and your maids, could not fill up
The cistern of my lust, and my desire
All continent° impediments would o'erbear,

65   That did oppose my will. Better Macbeth
Than such an one to reign.

Macduff.   Boundless intemperance
In nature° is a tyranny; it hath been
Th' untimely emptying of the happy throne,
And fall of many kings. But fear not yet

70   To take upon you what is yours: you may
Convey° your pleasures in a spacious plenty,
And yet seem cold, the time° you may so hoodwink.
We have willing dames enough. There cannot be
That vulture in you, to devour so many

75   As will to greatness dedicate themselves,
Finding it so inclined.

Malcolm.   With this there grows
In my most ill-composed affection° such
A stanchless° avarice that, were I king,
I should cut off the nobles for their lands,

80   Desire his jewels and this other's house:
And my more-having would be as a sauce
To make me hunger more, that I should forge
Quarrels unjust against the good and loyal,
Destroying them for wealth.

Macduff.   This avarice

85   Sticks deeper, grows with more pernicious root
Than summer-seeming° lust, and it hath been

---

51. particulars: special kinds. **grafted:** engrafted.

52. opened: in bloom (that is, revealed).

55. confineless harms: unbounded evils.

? **57.** *How has Macduff responded to this speech?*

58. Luxurious: lecherous.
59. Sudden: violent.

61. voluptuousness: lust.

64. continent: restraining.

? **66.** *Why do you think Malcolm is drawing attention to his vices? What could he hope to accomplish?*

67. nature: man's nature.

71. Convey: secretly manage.
72. time: here, people.

77. ill-composed affection: evilly compounded character.
78. stanchless: never ending.

? **Staging the Play**
84. *How do you imagine Malcolm delivering this speech? How could his delivery affect Macduff's response?*

86. summer-seeming: youthful, or transitory.

"NOT IN TH ELEGIONS OF HORRID HELL CAN COME A DEVIL MORE DAMNED IN EVILS TO TOP MACBETH"

The sword of our slain kings.° Yet do not fear.
Scotland hath foisons to fill up your will
Of your mere own.° All these are portable,°
90 With other graces weighed.

Malcolm.
But I have none: the king-becoming graces,
As justice, verity, temp'rance, stableness,
Bounty, perseverance, mercy, lowliness,
Devotion, patience, courage, fortitude,
95 I have no relish of° them, but abound
In the division of each several crime,°
Acting it many ways. Nay, had I pow'r, I should
Pour the sweet milk of concord into hell,
Uproar° the universal peace, confound
All unity on earth. **ⓟ**

100 **Macduff.**   O Scotland, Scotland!

Malcolm.
If such a one be fit to govern, speak:
I am as I have spoken.

Macduff.   Fit to govern!
No, not to live. O nation miserable!
With an untitled° tyrant bloody-sceptered,
105 When shalt thou see thy wholesome days again,
Since that the truest issue of thy throne
By his own interdiction° stands accursed,
And does blaspheme his breed?° Thy royal father
Was a most sainted king: the queen that bore thee,
110 Oft'ner upon her knees than on her feet,
Died° every day she lived. Fare thee well!
These evils thou repeat'st upon thyself
Hath banished me from Scotland. O my breast,
Thy hope ends here! **ⓠ**

Malcolm.   Macduff, this noble passion,
115 Child of integrity, hath from my soul
Wiped the black scruples,° reconciled my thoughts
To thy good truth and honor. Devilish Macbeth
By many of these trains° hath sought to win me
Into his power; and modest wisdom° plucks me
120 From over-credulous haste: but God above

87. **sword . . . kings:** the cause of death to our kings.
88–89. **foisons . . . own:** enough abundance of your own to satisfy your covetousness. **portable:** bearable.

95. **relish of:** taste for.
96. **division . . . crime:** variations of each kind of crime.

99. **Uproar:** put into a tumult.

104. **untitled:** having no right to the throne.

107. **interdiction:** curse; exclusion.
108. **breed:** ancestry.

111. **Died:** that is, prepared for heaven.

? **Elements of Drama**
114. *How might the tone change here? How has Macduff proved himself?*

116. **scruples:** suspicions.

118. **trains:** plots.
119. **modest wisdom:** prudence.

The roof of Glamis Castle, Angus, Scotland.

ⓟ **Reading Focus** **Using Questioning to Monitor Reading** This very dense exchange between Macbeth and Malcolm contains many archaic terms. What questions could help you summarize each character's words?

ⓠ **Literary Focus** **Tragedy** How does Macduff's harsh judgment of Malcolm suggest problems for Macbeth?

Deal between thee and me! For even now
I put myself to° thy direction, and
Unspeak mine own detraction;° here abjure
The taints and blames I laid upon myself,
125   For° strangers to my nature. I am yet
Unknown to woman, never was forsworn,
Scarcely have coveted what was mine own,
At no time broke my faith, would not betray
The devil to his fellow, and delight
130   No less in truth than life. My first false speaking
Was this upon myself. What I am truly,
Is thine and my poor country's to command:
Whither indeed, before thy here-approach,
Old Siward, with ten thousand warlike men,
135   Already at a point,° was setting forth.
Now we'll together, and the chance of goodness
Be like our warranted quarrel!° Why are you silent? **Ⓡ**

Macduff.
Such welcome and unwelcome things at once
'Tis hard to reconcile.

[*Enter a* DOCTOR.]

Malcolm.
140   Well, more anon. Comes the king forth, I pray you?
Doctor.
Ay, sir. There are a crew of wretched souls
That stay° his cure: their malady convinces
The great assay of art;° but at his touch,
Such sanctity hath heaven given his hand,
145   They presently amend.°
Malcolm.   I thank you, doctor.

[*Exit* DOCTOR.]

Macduff.
What's the disease he means?
Malcolm.   'Tis called the evil:°
A most miraculous work in this good king,
Which often since my here-remain in England
I have seen him do. How he solicits heaven,
150   Himself best knows: but strangely visited° people,
All swoll'n and ulcerous, pitiful to the eye,

---

122. to: under.
123. detraction: slander.

125. For: as.

135. at a point: prepared.
136–137. the chance . . . quarrel: May our chance of success equal the justice of our cause.

❓ Staging the Play
137. *Where should Malcolm pause in this line? Should he act puzzled, or matter-of-fact?*

142. stay: await.
142–143. convinces . . . art: defies the efforts of medical science.

145. presently amend: immediately recover.

146. evil: scrofula, called "the king's evil" because it allegedly could be cured by the king's touch.

150. strangely visited: oddly afflicted.

Ⓡ Reading Focus **Using Questioning to Monitor Reading** Malcolm has withheld the good news that Siward and ten thousand men are ready to fight Macbeth. What questions can explain this omission?

The mere° despair of surgery, he cures,
Hanging a golden stamp° about their necks,
Put on with holy prayers: and 'tis spoken,
155   To the succeeding royalty he leaves
The healing benediction. With this strange virtue°
He hath a heavenly gift of prophecy,
And sundry blessings hang about his throne
That speak° him full of grace.   **Ⓢ**

[*Enter* ROSS.]

Macduff.   See, who comes here?
Malcolm.
160   My countryman; but yet I know him not.
Macduff.
My ever gentle° cousin, welcome hither.
Malcolm.
I know him now: good God, betimes° remove
The means that makes us strangers!
Ross.   Sir, amen.
Macduff.
Stands Scotland where it did?
Ross.   Alas, poor country!
165   Almost afraid to know itself! It cannot
Be called our mother but our grave, where nothing°
But who knows nothing is once seen to smile;
Where sighs and groans, and shrieks that rent the air,
Are made, not marked;° where violent sorrow seems
170   A modern ecstasy.° The dead man's knell
Is there scarce asked for who, and good men's lives
Expire before the flowers in their caps,
Dying or ere they sicken.
Macduff.   O, relation
Too nice,° and yet too true!
Malcolm.   What's the newest grief?
Ross.
175   That of an hour's age doth hiss the speaker;°
Each minute teems° a new one.
Macduff.   How does my wife?
Ross.
Why, well.
Macduff.   And all my children?
Ross.   Well too.

Ⓢ **Literary Perspectives** **Analyzing Historical Context** These lines refer to
Edward the Confessor, king of England from 978 to 1016. Edward was believed to be capable of
healing people by touching them. Why do you think Shakespeare mentions him here?

152. mere: utter.
153. stamp: coin.

156. virtue: power.

159. speak: proclaim.

❓ *Stage direction:* *Ross is
Macduff's countryman.
What news do you anticipate he
brings with him?*

161. gentle: noble.

162. betimes: quickly.

166. nothing: no one.

169. marked: noticed.
170. modern ecstasy: ordinary
emotion.

173–174. relation / Too nice:
tale too accurate.

175. That . . . speaker: The
report of the grief of an hour
ago is hissed as stale news.
176. teems: gives birth to.
❓ **176.** *Does Ross look at
Macduff while speaking
this line, or does he turn away?*

Macduff.

The tyrant has not battered at their peace?

Ross.

No; they were well at peace when I did leave 'em.

Macduff.

180   Be not a niggard of your speech: how goes't?

Ross.

When I came hither to transport the tidings,
Which I have heavily° borne, there ran a rumor
Of many worthy fellows that were out;°
Which was to my belief witnessed° the rather,

185   For that I saw the tyrant's power° afoot.
Now is the time of help. Your eye in Scotland
Would create soldiers, make our women fight,
To doff their dire distresses.

Malcolm.   Be't their comfort
We are coming thither. Gracious England hath

190   Lent us good Siward and ten thousand men;
An older and a better soldier none
That Christendom gives out.°

Ross.   Would I could answer
This comfort with the like! But I have words
That would° be howled out in the desert air,

195   Where hearing should not latch° them.

Macduff.   What concern they?
The general cause or is it a fee-grief
Due to some single breast?°

Ross.   No mind that's honest
But in it shares some woe, though the main part
Pertains to you alone.

Macduff.   If it be mine,

200   Keep it not from me, quickly let me have it.

Ross.

Let not your ears despise my tongue forever,
Which shall possess them with the heaviest sound
That ever yet they heard.

Macduff.   Humh! I guess at it.

Ross.

Your castle is surprised;° your wife and babes

205   Savagely slaughtered. To relate the manner,
Were, on the quarry° of these murdered deer,
To add the death of you.

Malcolm.   Merciful heaven!
What, man! Ne'er pull your hat upon your brows;
Give sorrow words. The grief that does not speak

210   Whispers the o'er-fraught heart,° and bids it break.

 179. *What is the double meaning of this line?*

182. heavily: sadly.
183. out: up in arms.
184. witnessed: attested.
185. power: army.

192. gives out: reports.

194. would: should.
195. latch: catch.

196–197. fee-grief . . . breast: that is, personal grief belonging to an individual.

Staging the Play
203. *Macduff's pain becomes visible. How should we see it?*

204. surprised: suddenly attacked.
206. quarry: heap of slaughtered game.

210. Whispers . . . heart: whispers to the overburdened heart.

Macduff.

My children too?

Ross.   Wife, children, servants, all

That could be found.

Macduff.   And I must be from thence!

My wife killed too?

Ross.   I have said.

Malcolm.   Be comforted.

Let's make us med'cines of our great revenge,

215   To cure this deadly grief.

Macduff.

He has no children. All my pretty ones?

Did you say all? O hell-kite!° All?

What, all my pretty chickens and their dam°

At one fell swoop?

Malcolm.

Dispute° it like a man.

220   **Macduff.**   I shall do so;

But I must also feel it as a man.

I cannot but remember such things were,

That were most precious to me. Did heaven look on,

And would not take their part? Sinful Macduff,

225   They were all struck for thee! Naught° that I am,

Not for their own demerits but for mine

Fell slaughter on their souls. Heaven rest them now!

Malcolm.

Be this the whetstone of your sword. Let grief

Convert to anger; blunt not the heart, enrage it.

Macduff.

230   O, I could play the woman with mine eyes,

And braggart with my tongue! But, gentle heavens,

Cut short all intermission;° front to front°

Bring thou this fiend of Scotland and myself;

Within my sword's length set him. If he 'scape,

Heaven forgive him too!

235   **Malcolm.**   This time goes manly.

Come, go we to the king. Our power is ready;

Our lack is nothing but our leave.° Macbeth

Is ripe for shaking, and the pow'rs above

Put on their instruments.° Receive what cheer you may.

240   The night is long that never finds the day.   [*Exeunt.*]

Staging the Play
211. *How full, or soft, a voice would you have Macduff use in this line?*

Staging the Play
216. *How would Macduff say this line: "He has no children"?*

217. hell-kite: hellish bird of prey.
218. dam: mother.

220. *Is Malcolm being critical or encouraging here?*
220. Dispute: counter.

225. Naught: wicked.

232. intermission: interval.
front to front: forehead to forehead (that is, face to face).

237. Our lack . . . leave: We need only to take our leave.
239. Put . . . instruments: arm themselves.

Literary Focus **Tragedy** Macduff could be referring to either Malcolm or Macbeth in this line. Why might it be significant that Macbeth has no children?

Applying Your Skills

SKILLS FOCUS **Literary Skills** Analyze
characteristics of a tragedy; analyze foil; analyze historical context. **Reading Skills** Use
questioning to monitor reading. **Writing
Skills** Write drama.

The Tragedy of Macbeth

Act IV

Respond and Think Critically

Reading Focus

Quick Check

1. What does Macbeth ask the witches, and how do they respond?

2. At the end of Scene 1, what does Macbeth vow? How does he fulfill his vow in Scene 2?

3. According to Macduff and Malcolm in Scene 3, how has Macbeth's reign affected Scotland?

Read with a Purpose

4. How does Macbeth show more than one tragic flaw in Act IV?

Reading Skills: Using Questions to Monitor Reading

5. As you read, you recorded your questions about Act IV. Now, record and explain your answers.

Act, Scene, Line	Questions I Have	My Answers
Act IV, Scene 1, line 81	Why does the Second Apparition tell Macbeth no one can harm him, if the first told him to fear Macduff?	This may be a riddle that will lead to his tragic end. Macbeth has already fulfilled the witches' Act I prophecies.

Literary Focus

Literary Analysis

6. Interpret How does Macbeth explain the meaning of the first three apparitions?

7. Analyze How has Macbeth's moral character deteriorated since he last met the witches?

8. Analyze Have the witches caused any of the changes in Macbeth's moral character? Explain.

9. Make Judgments In Scene 3, Malcolm deliberately lies to Macduff. What does this behavior, and the reason for it, reveal about his character?

10. Literary Perspectives What does the conversation between Macduff and Malcolm in Scene 3 imply about the qualities that Shakespeare's audience would have considered acceptable— and unacceptable—in a king?

Literary Skills: Tragedy

11. Analyze In Act IV, what does Macbeth do that seems to <u>ensure</u> his tragic downfall?

Literary Skills Review: Foil

12. Analyze A **foil** is a character who sets off another character by sharp contrast. Banquo serves as a foil for Macbeth. How are Macduff or Malcolm foils to Macbeth?

Writing Focus

Think as a Reader/Writer

Use It in Your Writing Review your notes about Macbeth's conversation with the witches in Scene 1. Although Macbeth normally speaks in **blank verse,** in lines 94–106 he speaks in rhymed couplets—the speaking pattern of the witches. This shift reveals that Macbeth is becoming as sinister as the witches. In your *Reader/Writer Notebook,* write a short scene in which one character begins to imitate another character's way of speaking.

What Do You Think Now

In Act IV, how does Macbeth respond to the impulses of his heart and mind?

ACT V

Scene 1. *Dunsinane. In the castle.*

Enter a DOCTOR *of physic and a waiting* GENTLEWOMAN.

Doctor. I have two nights watched with you, but can perceive
no truth in your report. When was it she last walked?

Gentlewoman. Since his majesty went into the field, I have
seen her rise from her bed, throw her nightgown upon her,
5   unlock her closet,° take forth paper, fold it, write upon't,
read it, afterwards seal it, and again return to bed; yet all this
while in a most fast sleep.

Doctor. A great perturbation in nature, to receive at once the
benefit of sleep and do the effects of watching!° In this
10   slumb'ry agitation, besides her walking and other actual
performances,° what, at any time, have you heard her say?

Gentlewoman. That, sir, which I will not report after her.

Doctor. You may to me, and 'tis most meet° you should.

Gentlewoman. Neither to you nor anyone, having no witness
15   to confirm my speech.

[*Enter* LADY MACBETH, *with a taper.*]

Lo you, here she comes! This is her very guise,° and, upon
my life, fast asleep! Observe her; stand close.°

Doctor. How came she by that light?

Gentlewoman. Why, it stood by her. She has light by her
20   continually. 'Tis her command.

Doctor. You see, her eyes are open.

Gentlewoman. Ay, but their sense° are shut.

Doctor. What is it she does now? Look, how she rubs her
hands.

25   **Gentlewoman.** It is an accustomed action with her, to seem
thus washing her hands: I have known her continue in this a
quarter of an hour.   **B**

Lady Macbeth. Yet here's a spot.

Doctor. Hark! she speaks. I will set down what comes from
30   her, to satisfy° my remembrance the more strongly.

Lady Macbeth. Out, damned spot! Out, I say! One: two: why,
then 'tis time to do't. Hell is murky. Fie, my lord, fie! A soldier,

---

5. closet: chest.

9. effects of watching: deeds of one awake.
10–11. actual performances: deeds.

13. meet: suitable.

16. guise: custom.
17. close: hidden.

22. sense: powers of sight.

? Staging the Play
28. *After setting down the taper on a table, what does Lady Macbeth do with her hands?*
30. satisfy: confirm.

A Literary Focus **Tragedy** How does the idea of unnatural sleep contribute to the play's tragic themes?

B Literary Focus **Tragedy** Where has the subject of hand washing arisen previously? What do Lady Macbeth's actions tell us about the nature of evil?

and afeard? What need we fear who knows it, when none can call our pow'r to accompt?° Yet who would have

35 thought the old man to have had so much blood in him?

Doctor. Do you mark that?

Lady Macbeth. The Thane of Fife had a wife. Where is she now? What, will these hands ne'er be clean? No more o' that, my lord, no more o' that! You mar all with this starting.

40 **Doctor.** Go to,° go to! You have known what you should not.

Gentlewoman. She has spoke what she should not, I am sure of that. Heaven knows what she has known.

Lady Macbeth. Here's the smell of the blood still. All the perfumes of Arabia will not sweeten this little hand. Oh, oh, oh!

45 **Doctor.** What a sigh is there! The heart is sorely charged.°

Gentlewoman. I would not have such a heart in my bosom for the dignity° of the whole body.

Doctor. Well, well, well——

Gentlewoman. Pray God it be, sir.

50 **Doctor.** This disease is beyond my practice.° Yet I have known those which have walked in their sleep who have died holily in their beds.

Lady Macbeth. Wash your hands; put on your nightgown; look not so pale! I tell you yet again, Banquo's buried. He

55 cannot come out on 's° grave.

Doctor. Even so?

Lady Macbeth. To bed, to bed! There's knocking at the gate.

---

34. to accompt: to account.

? 35. *What does she think is still on her hands?*

? 37. *Who is the Thane of Fife?*

40. Go to: an exclamation.

? Staging the Play
43. *What does this line suggest?*

45. charged: burdened.

47. dignity: worth; rank.

50. practice: professional skill.

55. on 's: of his.
? 55. *To whom does she think she is speaking here?*

Sally Dexter as Lady Macbeth, Queens Theatre, Shaftsbury Avenue (1999).

Come, come, come, come, give me your hand! What's done
cannot be undone. To bed, to bed, to bed!   **C**

[*Exit* LADY MACBETH.]

60   **Doctor.** Will she go now to bed?
     Gentlewoman. Directly.
     Doctor.
        Foul whisp'rings are abroad. Unnatural deeds
        Do breed unnatural troubles. Infected minds
        To their deaf pillows will discharge their secrets.
65   More needs she the divine° than the physician.   **D**
        God, God forgive us all! Look after her;
        Remove from her the means of all annoyance,°
        And still° keep eyes upon her. So good night.
        My mind she has mated° and amazed my sight:
        I think, but dare not speak.
70   **Gentlewoman.**   Good night, good doctor.

[*Exeunt.*]

Scene 2. *The country near Dunsinane.*

Drum and colors. Enter MENTEITH, CAITHNESS, ANGUS, LENNOX,
     SOLDIERS.

Menteith.
   The English pow'r° is near, led on by Malcolm,
   His uncle Siward and the good Macduff.   **E**
   Revenges burn in them; for their dear° causes
   Would to the bleeding and the grim alarm°
   Excite the mortified° man.
5   **Angus.**   Near Birnam Wood
   Shall we well meet them; that way are they coming.
Caithness.
   Who knows if Donalbain be with his brother?
Lennox.
   For certain, sir, he is not. I have a file°
   Of all the gentry: there is Siward's son,
10   And many unrough° youths that even now
   Protest° their first of manhood.
Menteith.   What does the tyrant?

C Literary Focus **Tragedy** Lady Macbeth recounts not only the crimes she committed with Macbeth but also those crimes he committed himself. Identify each of these crimes.

D Literary Perspectives **Analyzing Historical Context** What do the doctor's words imply about Renaissance Christian beliefs?

E Literary Focus **Tragedy** Macbeth has moved from being a ruler to being a tyrant. How does this contrast with the leadership of those who rise against him?

Side notes:

? **Staging the Play**
59. *Once again there is a sudden dramatic change. What echo from the past brings it about? How do you think Lady Macbeth leaves the stage?*

65. **divine:** priest.

67. **annoyance:** injury.
68. **still:** continuously.
69. **mated:** baffled.

1. **pow'r:** army.

3. **dear:** heartfelt.
4. **alarm:** call to arms.
5. **mortified:** half dead.

? **5.** *Where have you heard about Birnam Wood before?*

8. **file:** list.

10. **unrough:** beardless.
11. **Protest:** assert.

Cynthia Makris (Lady Macbeth) Savonlinna Opera Festival Festival, Finland (2001).

Hand Washing

Being named after someone is usually an honor, though perhaps not if that "someone" is Lady Macbeth. At the University of Toronto and Northwestern University, researchers have found that people who have done something wrong often have an uncontrollable urge to clean themselves. This phenomenon is called the Macbeth Effect.

The connection between moral and physical cleanliness is <u>widespread</u> in both ancient and contemporary societies. Immoral behavior may be considered "dirty," and for many religions physical cleanliness is associated with virtuousness. In the King James Bible (Psalm 51:2), for example, salvation is associated with cleanliness: "Wash me thoroughly from mine iniquity, / and cleanse me from my sin."

Apparently, even pretending to be immoral has its consequences. The actor Liev Schreiber, who played Macbeth in New York in 2006, reported that although actors typically do not use the theater showers after a play, actors lined up to use them after performances of *Macbeth*. It may have been the effect of the humidity and summer heat; or, perhaps it was an example of the Macbeth Effect in action!

Ask Yourself

How does knowing that Shakespeare's portrayal of guilty behavior was proved to be accurate four hundred years later affect your understanding of the play?

Caithness.
    Great Dunsinane he strongly fortifies.
    Some say he's mad; others, that lesser hate him,
    Do call it valiant fury: but, for certain,
15   He cannot buckle his distempered° cause
    Within the belt of rule.°
Angus.   Now does he feel
    His secret murders sticking on his hands;
    Now minutely revolts upbraid° his faith-breach.
    Those he commands move only in command,
20   Nothing in love. Now does he feel his title
    Hang loose about him, like a giant's robe
    Upon a dwarfish thief.
Menteith.   Who then shall blame
    His pestered° senses to recoil and start,
    When all that is within him does condemn
    Itself for being there?

15. distempered: swollen with disease.
16. rule: self-control.

18. minutely revolts upbraid: rebellions every minute rebuke.

23. pestered: tormented.

25 **Caithness.**   Well, march we on,
       To give obedience where 'tis truly owed.
       Meet we the med'cine° of the sickly weal,°
       And with him pour we, in our country's purge,
       Each drop of us.°
    Lennox.   Or so much as it needs
30   To dew° the sovereign° flower and drown the weeds.
       Make we our march towards Birnam.

[Exeunt, marching.]

> **27. med'cine:** that is, Malcolm. **weal:** commonwealth.
> **29. Each . . . us:** that is, every last drop of our blood.
> **30. dew:** bedew; water (and thus make grow). **sovereign:** royal; also, remedial.

Scene 3. *Dunsinane. In the castle.*

Enter MACBETH, DOCTOR, *and* ATTENDANTS.

Macbeth.
       Bring me no more reports; let them fly all!
       Till Birnam Wood remove to Dunsinane
       I cannot taint° with fear. What's the boy Malcolm? **G**
       Was he not born of woman? The spirits that know
5   All mortal consequences° have pronounced me thus:
       "Fear not, Macbeth; no man that's born of woman
       Shall e'er have power upon thee." Then fly, false thanes,
       And mingle with the English epicures.
       The mind I sway° by and the heart I bear
10   Shall never sag with doubt nor shake with fear.

[*Enter* SERVANT.]

       The devil damn thee black, thou cream-faced loon!°
       Where got'st thou that goose look?
Servant.
       There is ten thousand——
Macbeth.   Geese, villain?
Servant.   Soldiers, sir.
Macbeth.
       Go prick thy face and over-red° thy fear,
15   Thou lily-livered boy. What soldiers, patch?°
       Death of° thy soul! Those linen° cheeks of thine
       Are counselors to fear. What soldiers, whey-face?
Servant.
       The English force, so please you.

> **3. taint:** become infected.
> **5. mortal consequences:** future human events.
> **9. sway:** move.
> **11. loon:** fool.
> **14. over-red:** cover with red.
> **15. patch:** fool.
> **16. of:** upon. **linen:** pale.

F **Literary Focus** **Tragedy** Here, the Scottish thanes discuss joining forces with Malcolm. Is Macbeth's impending fall that of a tragic hero, or is he a villain?

G **Literary Focus** **Tragedy** In these lines, how does Macbeth explain his irrational behavior?

Macbeth.

Take thy face hence.   [*Exit* SERVANT.]

           Seyton!—I am sick at heart,

20   When I behold—Seyton, I say!—This push°

Will cheer me ever, or disseat° me now.

I have lived long enough. My way of life

Is fall'n into the sear,° the yellow leaf,

And that which should accompany old age,

25   As honor, love, obedience, troops of friends,

I must not look to have; but, in their stead,

Curses not loud but deep, mouth-honor, breath,

Which the poor heart would fain deny, and dare not.   Ⓗ

Seyton!

[*Enter* SEYTON.]

Seyton.

       What's your gracious pleasure?

30   **Macbeth.**   What news more?

Seyton.

All is confirmed, my lord, which was reported.

Macbeth.

I'll fight, till from my bones my flesh be hacked.

Give me my armor.

Seyton.   'Tis not needed yet.

Macbeth.

I'll put it on.

35   Send out moe° horses, skirr° the country round.

Hang those that talk of fear. Give me mine armor.

How does your patient, doctor?

Doctor.   Not so sick, my lord,

As she is troubled with thick-coming fancies

That keep her from her rest.

Macbeth.   Cure her of that.

40   Canst thou not minister to a mind diseased,

Pluck from the memory a rooted sorrow,

Raze out° the written troubles of the brain,

And with some sweet oblivious° antidote

Cleanse the stuffed bosom of that perilous stuff

Which weighs upon the heart?

45   **Doctor.**   Therein the patient

Must minister to himself.   Ⓘ

---

20. push: effort.
21. disseat: unthrone (with wordplay on *cheer*, pronounced *chair*).
? 22. *What is Macbeth's mood now?*
23. sear: withered.

35. moe: more. **skirr:** scour.

? 37. *Who is the doctor's patient?*

42. Raze out: erase.
43. oblivious: causing forgetfulness.

Ⓗ **Literary Focus** Tragedy Some argue that Macbeth shows increased insight here; others believe he is merely acknowledging reality. Which position do you agree with, and why?

Ⓘ **Reading Focus** Using Questioning to Monitor Reading Macbeth demands a cure for Lady Macbeth. What questions would help you identify what she needs?

Macbeth.
Throw physic° to the dogs, I'll none of it.
Come, put mine armor on. Give me my staff.
Seyton, send out.—Doctor, the thanes fly from me.—
50   Come, sir, dispatch.° If thou couldst, doctor, cast
The water° of my land, find her disease
And purge it to a sound and pristine health,
I would applaud thee to the very echo,
That should applaud again.—Pull't off, I say.—
55   What rhubarb, senna, or what purgative drug,
Would scour these English hence? Hear'st thou of them?
Doctor.
Ay, my good lord; your royal preparation
Makes us hear something.
Macbeth.   Bring it° after me.
I will not be afraid of death and bane°
60   Till Birnam Forest come to Dunsinane.
Doctor (*aside*).
Were I from Dunsinane away and clear,
Profit again should hardly draw me here.   [*Exeunt.*]

Scene 4. *Country near Birnam Wood.*

Drum and colors. Enter MALCOLM, SIWARD, MACDUFF,
    Siward's son YOUNG SIWARD, MENTEITH, CAITHNESS,
    ANGUS, *and* SOLDIERS, *marching.*

Malcolm.
Cousins, I hope the days are near at hand
That chambers will be safe.°
Menteith.   We doubt it nothing.°
Siward.
What wood is this before us?
Menteith.   The Wood of Birnam.
Malcolm.
Let every soldier hew him down a bough
5   And bear't before him. Thereby shall we shadow
The numbers of our host, and make discovery°
Err in report of us.
Soldiers.   It shall be done.
Siward.
We learn no other but° the confident tyrant

 Literary Focus **Tragedy** What does Malcolm's command indicate about Macbeth's fate?

Keeps still in Dunsinane, and will endure°
Our setting down before't.

10 **Malcolm.**   'Tis his main hope,
For where there is advantage to be given°
Both more and less° have given him the revolt,
And none serve with him but constrainèd things
Whose hearts are absent too.

Macduff.   Let our just censures
15 Attend the true event,° and put we on
Industrious soldiership.

Siward.   The time approaches,
That will with due decision make us know
What we shall say we have and what we owe.°
Thoughts speculative their unsure hopes relate,
20 But certain issue strokes must arbitrate:°
Towards which advance the war.°   [*Exeunt, marching.*]

Scene 5. *Dunsinane. Within the castle.*

Enter MACBETH, SEYTON, *and* SOLDIERS, *with drum and colors.*

Macbeth.
Hang out our banners on the outward walls.
The cry is still "They come!" Our castle's strength
Will laugh a siege to scorn. Here let them lie
Till famine and the ague° eat them up.
5 Were they not forced° with those that should be ours,
We might have met them dareful,° beard to beard,
And beat them backward home.

[*A cry within of women.*]

                              What is that noise?
Seyton.
It is the cry of women, my good lord.   [*Exit.*]
Macbeth.
I have almost forgot the taste of fears:
10 The time has been, my senses would have cooled
To hear a night-shriek, and my fell° of hair
Would at a dismal treatise° rouse and stir
As life were in't. I have supped full with horrors.
Direness, familiar to my slaughterous thoughts,
Cannot once start° me.

[*Enter* SEYTON.]

15   Wherefore was that cry?
Seyton.

9. **endure:** allow.

11. **advantage . . . given:** afforded an opportunity.
12. **more and less:** high and low.

14–15. **just . . . event:** true judgments await the actual outcome.

18. **owe:** own. The contrast is between "what we shall say we have" and "what we shall really have."
20. **certain . . . arbitrate:** The definite outcome must be decided by battle.
21. **war:** army.

4. **ague:** fever.
5. **forced:** reinforced.
6. **met them dareful:** that is, met them on the battlefield boldly.

Staging the Play
7. *Macbeth should contrast with Malcolm now. How should Macbeth be acting?*

11. **fell:** pelt.
12. **treatise:** story.

15. **start:** startle.

Lady Macbeth, by Odilon Redon, pastel drawing.

The queen, my lord, is dead.
Macbeth.
    She should° have died hereafter;
    There would have been a time for such a word.°
    Tomorrow, and tomorrow, and tomorrow
20   Creeps in this petty pace from day to day,
    To the last syllable of recorded time;
    And all our yesterdays have lighted fools
    The way to dusty death. Out, out, brief candle!
    Life's but a walking shadow, a poor player
25   That struts and frets his hour upon the stage
    And then is heard no more. It is a tale
    Told by an idiot, full of sound and fury,
    Signifying nothing. **Ⓚ**

[*Enter a* MESSENGER.]

17. **should:** inevitably would.
18. **word:** message.

Ⓚ **Literary Focus** Tragedy Compare Macbeth's and Macduff's reactions to the death of their wives. What does this contrast tell us about Macbeth's downfall?

Thou com'st to use thy tongue; thy story quickly!

Messenger.
30   Gracious my lord,
        I should report that which I say I saw,
        But know not how to do't.

Macbeth.   Well, say, sir.

Messenger.
        As I did stand my watch upon the hill,
        I looked toward Birnam, and anon, methought,
        The wood began to move.

35   **Macbeth.**   Liar and slave!

Messenger.
        Let me endure your wrath, if't be not so.
        Within this three mile may you see it coming;
        I say a moving grove.

Macbeth.   If thou speak'st false,
        Upon the next tree shalt thou hang alive,
40   Till famine cling° thee. If thy speech be sooth,°
        I care not if thou dost for me as much.
        I pull in resolution,° and begin
        To doubt° th' equivocation of the fiend
        That lies like truth: "Fear not, till Birnam Wood
45   Do come to Dunsinane!" And now a wood
        Comes toward Dunsinane. Arm, arm, and out!
        If this which he avouches° does appear,
        There is nor flying hence nor tarrying here.
        I 'gin to be aweary of the sun,
50   And wish th' estate° o' th' world were now undone.
        Ring the alarum bell! Blow wind, come wrack!
        At least we'll die with harness° on our back.   [*Exeunt.*]

Scene 6. *Dunsinane. Before the castle.*

Drum and colors. Enter MALCOLM, SIWARD, MACDUFF, *and their* ARMY,
        with boughs.

Malcolm.
        Now near enough. Your leavy° screens throw down,
        And show like those you are. You, worthy uncle,
        Shall, with my cousin, your right noble son,
        Lead our first battle.° Worthy Macduff and we°
5   Shall take upon 's what else remains to do,
        According to our order.°

L **Literary Focus** Tragedy Why does Macbeth respond so violently to the
Messenger's report?

"LIFE... IS A TALE TOLD BY AN IDIOT, FULL OF SOUND AND FURY, SIGNIFYING NOTHING."

40. cling: wither. **sooth:** truth.

42. pull in resolution: restrain confidence.
43. doubt: suspect.

47. avouches: asserts.

50. th' estate: the orderly condition.

52. harness: armor.
? **Elements of Drama**
52. *Macbeth ends the scene in a state of great emotion. How would you characterize his mental state?*

1. leavy: leafy.

4. battle: battalion. **we:** Malcolm uses the "royal we."
6. order: plan.

Siward. Fare you well.
Do we° but find the tyrant's power° tonight,
Let us be beaten, if we cannot fight.

Macduff.
Make all our trumpets speak; give them all breath,

10 Those clamorous harbingers of blood and death.

[*Exeunt. Alarums continued.*]

Scene 7. *Another part of the field.*

Enter MACBETH.

Macbeth.
They have tied me to a stake; I cannot fly,
But bearlike I must fight the course.° What's he
That was not born of woman? Such a one
Am I to fear, or none.

2. **course:** bout; round. (He has in mind an attack of dogs or men upon a bear chained to a stake.)

[*Enter* YOUNG SIWARD.]

Young Siward.
What is thy name?

5 **Macbeth.**   Thou'lt be afraid to hear it.
Young Siward.
No; though thou call'st thyself a hotter name
Than any is in hell.
Macbeth.   My name's Macbeth.
Young Siward.
The devil himself could not pronounce a title
More hateful to mine ear.
Macbeth.   No, nor more fearful.
Young Siward.
10 Thou liest, abhorrèd tyrant; with my sword
I'll prove the lie thou speak'st.

? 4. *What is Macbeth desperately clinging to now?*

[*Fight, and* YOUNG SIWARD *slain.*]

Macbeth.   Thou wast born of woman.
But swords I smile at, weapons laugh to scorn,
Brandished by man that's of a woman born.   [*Exit.*]

[*Alarums. Enter* MACDUFF.]

Macduff.
That way the noise is. Tyrant, show thy face!

Coat of Armor at Glamis Castle, Angus, Scotland.

M **Literary Focus** **Tragedy** What does the image of Macbeth as a captive animal show us about his situation?

15　If thou be'st slain and with no stroke of mine,
　　My wife and children's ghosts will haunt me still.
　　I cannot strike at wretched kerns,° whose arms
　　Are hired to bear their staves.° Either thou, Macbeth,　Ⓝ
　　Or else my sword, with an unbattered edge,
20　I sheathe again undeeded.° There thou shouldst be;
　　By this great clatter, one of greatest note
　　Seems bruited.° Let me find him, Fortune!
　　And more I beg not.　　　　　　　　　　[*Exit. Alarums.*]

[*Enter* MALCOLM *and* SIWARD.]

Siward.
　　This way, my lord. The castle's gently rend'red:°
25　The tyrant's people on both sides do fight;
　　The noble thanes do bravely in the war;
　　The day almost itself professes° yours,
　　And little is to do.
Malcolm.　　　　　We have met with foes
　　That strike beside us.°
Siward.　　　　　Enter, sir, the castle.　　[*Exeunt. Alarum.*]

17. **kerns:** foot soldiers.
18. **staves:** spears.

20. **undeeded:** that is, having done nothing.
22. **bruited:** reported.

24. **gently rend'red:** surrendered without a struggle.

27. **itself professes:** declares itself.

29. **That . . . us:** that is, who deliberately miss us.

Scene 8. *Another part of the field.*

Enter MACBETH.

Macbeth.
　　Why should I play the Roman fool, and die
　　On mine own sword? Whiles I see lives,° the gashes
　　Do better upon them.

[*Enter* MACDUFF.]

Macduff.　　　　　Turn, hell-hound, turn!
Macbeth.
　　Of all men else I have avoided thee.
5　But get thee back! My soul is too much charged°
　　With blood of thine already.
Macduff.　　　　　I have no words:
　　My voice is in my sword, thou bloodier villain
　　Than terms can give thee out!°

　　　　　　　　　　　　　　　[*Fight. Alarum.*]

Macbeth.　　　　　Thou losest labor:
　　As easy mayst thou the intrenchant° air

2. **Whiles . . . lives:** so long as I see living men.

5. **charged:** burdened.

8. **terms . . . out:** words can describe you.

9. **intrenchant:** incapable of being cut.

Ⓝ **Literary Focus** **Tragedy** How does Macduff's motivation to fight contrast with Macbeth's?

The Tragedy of Macbeth, Act V, Scene 7–8　**489**

10   With thy keen sword impress° as make me bleed:
        Let fall thy blade on vulnerable crests;°
        I bear a charmèd life, which must not yield
        To one of woman born.

Macduff.   Despair° thy charm,
        And let the angel° whom thou still hast served
15   Tell thee, Macduff was from his mother's womb
        Untimely ripped.

Macbeth.
        Accursèd be that tongue that tells me so,
        For it hath cowed my better part of man!°
        And be these juggling fiends no more believed,
20   That palter° with us in a double sense;
        That keep the word of promise to our ear,
        And break it to our hope. I'll not fight with thee.

Macduff.
        Then yield thee, coward,
        And live to be the show and gaze o' th' time:°
25   We'll have thee, as our rarer monsters° are,
        Painted upon a pole,° and underwrit,
        "Here may you see the tyrant."

Macbeth.   I will not yield,
        To kiss the ground before young Malcolm's feet,
        And to be baited° with the rabble's curse.
30   Though Birnam Wood be come to Dunsinane,
        And thou opposed, being of no woman born,
        Yet I will try the last. Before my body
        I throw my warlike shield. Lay on, Macduff;
        And damned be him that first cries "Hold, enough!" **Ⓞ**

                                [*Exeunt, fighting. Alarums.*]

        [*Reenter fighting, and* MACBETH *slain. Exit* MACDUFF,
                with MACBETH. *Retreat and flourish.*° *Enter, with drum
                and colors,* MALCOLM, SIWARD, ROSS, THANES, *and* SOLDIERS.]

Malcolm.
35   I would the friends we miss were safe arrived.

Siward.
        Some must go off;° and yet, by these I see,
        So great a day as this is cheaply bought.

Malcolm.
        Macduff is missing, and your noble son.

Ⓞ Literary Focus **Tragedy** To arouse pity for a fallen tragic hero, the playwright must remind the audience of the hero's potential for greatness. How do these lines accomplish that purpose?

10. impress: make an impression on.
11. vulnerable crests: heads that can be wounded.

13. Despair: despair of.
14. angel: that is, fallen angel; fiend.

? **16.** *What is the meaning of lines 15–16? How do they relate to the prophecy?*

18. better . . . man: manly spirit.
20. palter: equivocate.

24. gaze . . . time: spectacle of the age.
25. monsters: freaks.
26. Painted . . . pole: pictured on a banner set by a showman's booth.

29. baited: assailed (like a bear by dogs).

Retreat and flourish: trumpet call to withdraw, and fanfare.

36. go off: die (theatrical metaphor).

"BEFORE MY BODY
I THROW MY WARLIKE SHIELD."

John Finch *(right)* as Macbeth in the film *Macbeth* (1971), directed by Roman Polanski.

Ross.
　　Your son, my lord, has paid a soldier's debt:
40　He only lived but till he was a man;
　　The which no sooner had his prowess confirmed
　　In the unshrinking station° where he fought,
　　But like a man he died.
Siward.　　　　　　　Then he is dead?
Ross.
　　Ay, and brought off the field. Your cause of sorrow
45　Must not be measured by his worth, for then
　　It hath no end.
Siward.　　　　Had he his hurts before?
Ross.
　　Ay, on the front.
Siward.　　　　Why then, God's soldier be he!
　　Had I as many sons as I have hairs,
　　I would not wish them to a fairer death:

42. unshrinking station: that is, place at which he stood firmly.

And so his knell is knolled.

50 **Malcolm.**   He's worth more sorrow,
And that I'll spend for him.

Siward.   He's worth no more:
They say he parted well and paid his score:°
And so God be with him! Here comes newer comfort. **P**

[*Enter* MACDUFF, *with Macbeth's head.*]

Macduff.
Hail, king! for so thou art: behold, where stands
55 Th' usurper's cursèd head. The time is free.°
I see thee compassed° with thy kingdom's pearl,
That speak my salutation in their minds,
Whose voices I desire aloud with mine:
Hail, King of Scotland!

All.   Hail, King of Scotland!

[*Flourish.*]

Malcolm.
60 We shall not spend a large expense of time
Before we reckon with your several loves,°
And make us even with you. My thanes and kinsmen,
Henceforth be earls, the first that ever Scotland
In such an honor named. What's more to do,
65 Which would be planted newly with the time°—
As calling home our exiled friends abroad
That fled the snares of watchful tyranny,
Producing forth the cruel ministers°
Of this dead butcher and his fiendlike queen,
70 Who, as 'tis thought, by self and violent hands°
Took off her life—this, and what needful else
That calls upon us,° by the grace of Grace
We will perform in measure, time, and place:°
So thanks to all at once and to each one,
75 Whom we invite to see us crowned at Scone. **Q**

[*Flourish. Exeunt omnes.*]

P **Reading Focus** **Using Questioning to Monitor Reading** The exchange between Siward and Malcolm recalls the conversation between Macduff and Malcolm after the news of the death of Macduff's family reached them (Act IV, Scene 3, lines 220–235). What can you ask yourself to explain this connection?

Q **Literary Perspectives** **Analyzing Historical Context** Why would the restoration of order be important to Shakespeare's audience?

---

52. parted . . . score: departed well and settled his account.

? **Elements of Drama**
53. *What character traits does Malcolm show in this scene? How is old Siward like a military man to the end?*

55. The time is free: The world is liberated.

56. compassed: surrounded.

? **Staging the Play**
Stage direction: Macduff enters with Macbeth's head on a pole. A great shout goes up. What is Macduff's tone in the next speech?

61. reckon . . . loves: reward the devotion of each of you.
64–65. What's . . . time: what else must be done that should be newly established in this age.

68. ministers: agents.

70. self . . . hands: her own violent hands.
72. calls upon us: demands my attention.
73. in . . . place: fittingly, at the appropriate time and place.

? **Staging the Play**
75. *Scone is a village in Scotland. For centuries, all Scottish kings were crowned in Scone on the Stone of Destiny. The stone was taken to England in 1296 and was returned to Scotland, to Edinburgh Castle, in 1996. How would you have the characters exit? Who would exit last?*

Applying Your Skills

The Tragedy of Macbeth
Act V

Respond and Think Critically

Reading Focus

Quick Check

1. Why, according to the Doctor, is Lady Macbeth walking in her sleep?

2. When does Lady Macbeth die?

3. How does Birnam Wood come to Dunsinane?

4. What happens to Macbeth? Who becomes king?

Read with a Purpose

5. How do Macbeth's flaws lead to his tragic end?

Reading Skills: Using Questions to Monitor Reading

6. As you read, you recorded your questions about Act V. Now, record and explain your answers.

Act, Scene, Line	Questions I Have	My Answers
Act V, Scene 1, line 12	Why won't the Gentlewoman tell the doctor what she's heard Lady Macbeth say?	The woman may be afraid to report what she knows because she fears for her life.

Literary Focus

Literary Analysis

7. **Analyze** Why do you think Shakespeare has Lady Macbeth walk in her sleep? How is this scene related to the remarks Macbeth makes in Act II, Scene 2, just after he kills Duncan?

8. **Make Judgments** Act V contains the play's **climax,** the most emotional and suspenseful part of the action and the moment when the characters' conflict is finally resolved. Which part of Act V do you consider the climax? Explain.

9. **Make Judgments** Shakespeare gave most of his tragic heroes impressive dying speeches that say something significant about their own life and death. Although Shakespeare didn't give such a speech to Macbeth, which speech in the play would serve best as his dying speech? Explain.

10. **Extend** In Act V, Macbeth says that life "is a tale / Told by an idiot, full of sound and fury, / Signifying nothing." Do you agree or disagree? Explain.

11. **Literary Perspectives** How does the ending of *Macbeth* meet the expectations of Shakespeare's Renaissance audience—including King James?

Literary Skills: Tragedy

12. **Analyze** Is Macbeth's downfall caused solely by a tragic flaw, or do other factors also help bring him to a tragic end? Explain.

Literary Skills Review: Imagery

13. **Analyze** Language that appeals to the senses—sight, hearing, smell, taste, and touch—is called **imagery.** Identify two images in Act V, and analyze how they contribute to the play's mood.

Writing Focus

Think as a Reader/Writer

Use It in Your Writing As you read, you noted how Shakespeare reveals his characters' personalities through their actions. What does Macbeth's final action reveal about him? Write a brief dramatic scene in which a character refuses to give up when facing great danger. Let your character's actions show his or her true nature. You may include stage directions.

What Do **You Think Now**

In Act V, how does Macbeth respond to the impulses of his heart and mind?

Applying Your Skills

The Tragedy of Macbeth
Acts I–V

SKILLS FOCUS Literary Skills Analyze characteristics of tragedy; analyze archetypes; analyze character. **Grammar Skills** Demonstrate control of grammar and sentence structure.

Respond and Think Critically

Literary Focus

Literary Analysis

1. **Analyze** What is Macbeth's tragic flaw at the play's start? How does it change?

2. **Analyze** How does Lady Macbeth evolve?

3. **Interpret** How does the relationship between Macbeth and Lady Macbeth change? Why? Use examples from the text to support your ideas.

4. **Infer** What is the play's strongest lesson about human nature? Explain your answer with examples from the text.

5. **Literary Perspectives** As you read, you considered how historical context shaped Shakespeare's writing of *Macbeth*. Explain how this perspective affected your interpretation of the play. How did it influence your understanding of characters, plot events, or scenes? How might you have approached the text differently without any historical background information?

Literary Skills: Tragedy

6. **Analyze** The philosopher Aristotle argued that a bad man cannot be the principal character of a tragedy. Does Shakespeare <u>ensure</u> that you retain sympathy for Macbeth? Did you lose sympathy for Macbeth? If so, where?

Literary Skills Review: Archetype

7. **Analyze** An **archetype** is a pattern that appears in literature across cultures and throughout the ages. An archetype may be a character, plot, image, or setting. A familiar pattern from the Bible is the archetype of the fall, in which someone is banished from an ideal world because of a sin or great failing. Explain how the archetype of the fall is developed in *Macbeth*.

Grammar Link

Combining Sentences by Inserting Words and Phrases

No matter what type of writing you do, you will want your writing to be clear, effective, and interesting. Short sentences can be effective, but too many of them make writing choppy. You can combine these sentences in various ways. One approach is to take a key word from one sentence and insert it into another. (You may have to alter the form of the word, such as by changing a noun to an adjective.) Here is an example:

> *Macbeth* is one of Shakespeare's plays. *Macbeth* is a tragedy.
> *Macbeth* is one of Shakespeare's tragic plays.

Drop *Macbeth is a,* and change *tragedy* to *tragic* to combine the sentences.

You can also combine sentences by turning a short sentence into a phrase and inserting it into another sentence. Here is an example:

> Have you read *The Tragedy of Macbeth?* It was written by William Shakespeare.
> Have you read *The Tragedy of Macbeth* by William Shakespeare?

The circled words mean the same thing, so you can drop *It*, delete *was written,* and insert the phrase *by William Shakespeare* into the first sentence.

Your Turn

Combine each pair of sentences by adapting a key word or phrase from one and adding it to the other.

1. The Jacobean period began in 1603. The Jacobean period began with King James I's reign.

2. The play alludes to Edward, a king of England. Edward was called "the Confessor."

3. The witches are ruled by the Queen of the Night. The Queen of the Night is Hecate.

CHOICES

As you respond to the Choices, use these **Academic Vocabulary** words as appropriate: establish, ensure, widespread, controversy, contradiction.

REVIEW
Create a Time Line
Using the Internet or books from the library, find out more about the widespread social and political unrest in England during the fifteenth, sixteenth, and early seventeenth centuries. Create a time line showing important disruptions, battles, and changes in the monarchy. Then, write two paragraphs explaining how these events would have affected a Renaissance audience's interpretation of *Macbeth*.

Write a Character Sketch
Timed Writing *Macbeth* is full of vivid characters, both static (or unchanging) and dynamic (changing). Static characters, like the witches, serve a plot purpose but do not undergo any type of growth themselves; dynamic characters, like Lady Macbeth, change throughout the course of the play. Select one dynamic character from *Macbeth,* and write a brief essay analyzing the significance of the character's changes. Be sure to include a discussion of how and when the character changes, and support your argument with evidence from the play.

CONNECT
Connect to Critical Commentary
Shakespeare has been the focus of many scholarly books, magazines, and critical reviews over the centuries. Pick a theme in the play that interests you—such as the role of women, the power of fate and the supernatural, or a historical controversy—and, using the Internet and books from the library, research what scholars have to say on your topic. Find at least three sources of scholarly opinions, and then write a brief report that discusses your findings.

Connect to the Stage
Group Activity *Macbeth* has been performed in many different ways over the centuries. A number of versions have been made into movies that range from strictly Shakespearean-style productions to modern-day or futuristic adaptations. There is even a famous version of *Macbeth* set in feudal Japan. With a small group, head to the library to find a movie version of *Macbeth*. Watch it with your group, and then put together a presentation in which you display how the movie is different from the original script and what effect you think this difference has on the story overall. If the movie is a strict interpretation with few differences, focus your presentation on how the actors handle Shakespeare's stage directions and famous lines.

EXTEND
Create a Visual
Macbeth presents a wide range of human emotions, from the witches' calculated evil, to Macduff's grief for his family, to the Porter's comic banter. Create a collage, painting, or drawing that explores the emotional range of the play. In keeping with the contrasts, show characters at moments when they feel very different emotions. You might show the emotional range of one character or the contrasting emotions of several. Present your visual to the class. Explain your imagery and choice of emotions.

Set the Scene
TechFocus Shakespeare says very little about scenery in the text of *Macbeth*. Consequently, modern producers are at liberty to set the stage in whatever way will help create the tragic mood. How would you design the set? Pick an act from *Macbeth,* and create a slide show or PowerPoint presentation showing how you would set each scene in the act. Practice your presentation, and then deliver it to your class.

SKILLS FOCUS **Literary Skills** Understand and analyze the characteristics of tragedy. **Reading Skills** Respond to graphics.

Link to Today

This Link to Today gives Shakespeare's classic a fresh visual update.

from Macbeth: The Graphic Novel

adapted by Arthur Byron Cover

illustrated by Tony Leonard Tamai

What Do You Think

How do our hearts and minds influence our actions?

 QuickTalk

With a partner, discuss the advantages of seeing a text, particularly a play, represented as a graphic novel.

Literary Focus

Tragedy Tales of murderous ambition are <u>widespread</u> outside the pages of Shakespeare's tragedies. Similar stories abound in operas, movies, and even graphic novels. In this excerpt, murder and tragedy translate well into the larger-than-life fantasy world of powerful dragon lords.

Reading Focus

Responding to Graphics Adapted graphic novels make numerous changes to original sources in order to <u>ensure</u> the visual appeal and momentum. In *Macbeth: The Graphic Novel* the author-illustrator team Arthur Byron Cover and Tony Leonard Tamai use very short pieces of Shakespeare's dialogue and rely on the graphic elements to convey the bulk of the action.

Into Action As you read, think about the changes that this combination of words and images creates for *Macbeth*. Make a list like the one below of visual details that enhance the story for you.

Visual Detail	How the Detail Enhances the Story
Banquo has a goatee and unruly hair.	The details make it easy to identify him in each frame.

Writing Focus

Think as a Reader/Writer

Find It in Your Reading As you read, notice the graphic details used to illustrate the text. In your *Reader/Writer Notebook*, make notes about images that convey emotion.

Reader/Writer Notebook

Use your **RWN** to complete the activities for this selection.

Learn It Online
Explore other ways that this classic play lives on in the twenty-first century through these Internet links.

go.hrw.com | L12-496 | **Go**

from **Macbeth: The Graphic Novel**

Respond and Think Critically

Reading Focus

Quick Check

1. What is Banquo's mood in the opening frame? Explain.

2. In the first frame on the third page, Macbeth's hands are depicted in the foreground, grasping at something. What is he reaching for? How do you know?

3. Summarize the action on the last page.

Reading Skills: Responding to Graphics

4. Look over your chart of visual details and how they enhance the story. Then, write a short paragraph summarizing the difference between reading Shakespeare's play and reading this graphic version of the story. Use your chart for examples and support.

Visual Detail	How the Detail Enhances the Story
Banquo has a goatee and unruly hair.	The details make it easy to identify him in each frame.

Literary Focus

Literary Analysis

5. **Analyze** Identify one advantage and one disadvantage of shortening Shakespeare's dialogue for this graphic novel. Explain.

6. **Interpret** Readers of Shakespeare usually take Banquo's diamond as a metaphor for Lady Macbeth's role as hostess. Why do you think the illustrator chose to show a real diamond in the graphic version of the scene? Explain.

7. **Interpret** The last page of this excerpt depicts Macbeth on his way to murdering Duncan—an action that takes place offstage in Shakespeare's play. What advantage does the addition of this action offer to readers of the graphic novel? Explain.

Literary Skills: Tragedy

8. **Evaluate** This graphic novel moves Shakespeare's tragedy to a dragon-riding world in the distant future. How does the change of setting affect the story? Explain.

Literary Skills Review: Mood

9. **Evaluate** The **mood** in a work of literature is the atmosphere or feeling it creates for a reader. How might the mood of this graphic novel change if all the frames were depicted in color instead of black and white? Explain.

Writing Focus

Think as a Reader/Writer

Use It in Your Writing Look back at the notes you took in your *Reader/Writer Notebook* about graphic details used to convey characters' emotions and the words they accompany. Using the illustrations in the graphic novel as your guide, rewrite the dialogue for one page. Create new captions to express the emotions that are visually depicted in each frame.

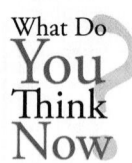
What Do **You Think Now**

In the frames devoted to Macbeth's soliloquy about an invisible dagger, how does the graphic novel depict his internal conflict? Is he experiencing a conflict of the heart or of the mind? Or both? Explain.

SKILLS FOCUS Writing Skills: Use appropriate organization; support ideas/theses with relevant evidence and details; compare literary works; compare themes or literary elements.

Author Study: William Shakespeare

Writing Focus

Writing a Comparison-Contrast Essay

Choose two of Shakespeare's sonnets, two characters from *Macbeth,* or two passages from *Macbeth* that show a striking similarity or a revealing contrast. Write an essay in which you compare and contrast your choices, focusing on Shakespeare's language, tone, or theme. Consider one of the following approaches for your essay:

- Compare and contrast Sonnets 18 and 116. What is the poet's attitude toward love in these sonnets, and what belief does he reveal about the power of the written word?

- Compare and contrast Sonnets 29 and 30. What kind of problem does each sonnet present, what is the poet's attitude toward the problem, and how does the final couplet resolve the problem?

- Compare and contrast Sonnets 71 and 73. What kind of attitude does each sonnet express toward aging and death? How does the poet convey his attitude?

- Compare and contrast Sonnets 18 and 130. What methods does the poet use to describe his beloved, and what kind of thematic statement does he make about love?

- Compare and contrast Macbeth and Lady Macbeth in a single act of *Macbeth.* What traits do you see in them, and how does Shakespeare reveal these traits? You might wish to focus on a single revealing scene for this essay.

- Compare and contrast two of Macbeth's soliloquies. What does he reveal about himself in each soliloquy, and how does Shakespeare use language to convey Macbeth's character?

- Compare and contrast Lady Macbeth in Act I and Act V of *Macbeth.* What kind of language does she use in each act, and what does her language reveal about her character?

Guidelines for a Comparison-Contrast Essay

The following guidelines will <u>ensure</u> a successful essay:

- Begin by introducing the two subjects of your essay. If your essay focuses on two sonnets, consider a brief overview of the Shakespearean sonnet. Then, briefly introduce each sonnet by letting your reader know the situation and theme.

- Close your introduction with a thesis statement that explicitly identifies the similarities and/or differences you intend to discuss in the body of your essay.

- Follow one of the two proven methods for a comparison-contrast essay: (1) Devote a section of your essay to each major point you want to make. Discuss first one subject and then the next. If your subjects are Sonnets 18 and 116, you will discuss Sonnet 18 first for each part of your paper. (2) Divide the body of your paper into two major sections—one for each subject. If your subjects are Sonnets 18 and 116, you will discuss all the points you wish to make about Sonnet 18 before moving on to Sonnet 116.

- Use quotations from Shakespeare to illustrate the point you are trying to make.

- Conclude by discussing what your comparison and contrast reveals about Shakespeare as a writer or about human nature.

 What Do **You Think Now** Do you think that Shakespeare's work was influenced more by his heart or his mind? Explain your answer, and cite examples from his work.

Writing Workshop

Literary Research Paper

Write with a Purpose

Write a formal research paper on a topic that links literature and historical investigation. Your **purpose** for writing is to convey the results of your research to your **audience**—your teacher and classmates.

> **A Good Literary Research Paper**
>
> - answers questions about a text's historical and cultural relevance
> - uses multiple, reliable sources
> - documents sources of information
> - follows an outline to support a clear thesis
> - uses formal but accessible language
>
> **See page 516 for complete rubric.**

Reader/Writer Notebook

Use your **RWN** to complete the activities for this workshop.

Think as a Reader/Writer

In this workshop, you will investigate a particular connection between history and literature. Before you write your **literary research paper,** read twentieth-century poet W. H. Auden's examination of Shakespeare's play *Love's Labour's Lost*.

> *Love's Labour's Lost* is not the greatest of Shakespeare's plays, but it is one of the most perfect. Its subject, education and culture, is interesting. The forms of culture it deals with are those prevalent in Shakespeare's time and include neo-Platonic humanism,[1] courtly manners, courtly love,[2] and Euphuism.[3] All humanism and learning is made fun of in the play, all social life is made fun of, all art is made fun of—it is not specific satire. The play begins with the scheme of four young men to found a kind of neo-Platonic academy. They already have a certain education in social manners. . . . .
>
> *Auden discusses neo-Platonic humanism and courtly manners in the paragraphs omitted here.*
>
> The courtly manners in the play are also affected by the medieval and Renaissance traditions of courtly love, which began with the Troubadours in eleventh-century Provence and were codified in the thirteenth century by Andreas Capellanus in a Latin work, *De Arte Honeste Amandi.* Andreas stipulated a number of rules of courtly love. First, the lovers must not be married. They must endure great difficulties in the achievement of their love, and must be jealous of a rival, which is undesirable in marriage, but is an essential proof of courtly love. Finally, the beloved noble lady must be treated as God.
>
> ---
>
> 1. **neo-Platonic humanism:** a belief that through the study of human life, people can reach a oneness with God.
> 2. **courtly manners and courtly love:** refined behavior expected of people in the royal court.
> 3. **Euphuism:** an overly ornate Elizabethan literary style.

← Auden clearly states his **thesis.**

← He provides **background information** about the play.

← Auden traces the historical origin of courtly love.

Think About the Professional Model

With a partner, discuss the following questions about the model.

1. How does paragraph two help to support the writer's thesis?
2. What else could he add to paragraph two to better support its main idea?

Prewriting

Choose a Research Topic

Literary research is a labor-intensive process that can be rewarding for what you can learn about a literary subject. If a topic do not immediately come to mind, search your textbook, jotting down a list of several authors and works that look interesting. Use the Internet and general reference works to do preliminary research on the authors and works in your list. Then, choose a general topic.

To decide on an appropriate historical approach to your topic, review the information provided in your textbook (especially the unit introductions) or ask your school's librarian or media specialist to direct you to appropriate resources. Here are some sample topics, appropriate for literary and historical investigation.

- How accurately *Beowulf* reflects the history and culture of the ancient Germanic tribes who populate its pages
- How Geoffrey Chaucer's life as a civil servant in fourteenth-century England influenced his writing
- How the writing of John Stuart Mill or Charles Dickens influenced social and economic reforms of the Victorian period

Narrow your subject so that you can cover it adequately. Keep challenging yourself to be more specific by asking yourself increasingly specific questions.

Make a Research Plan

Develop a list of research questions by using the *5W-How?* method: Answer the questions *Who? What? When? Where? Why?* and *How?* The following are questions one writer asked to investigate Shakespeare's source for *Julius Caesar.*

- Who was Julius Caesar?
- What account of Caesar's life did Shakespeare use as his model?
- When did the original historical events take place?
  —how do they reflect themes that were important to Shakespeare's audience?
- Where does the action of the play occur?
  —Why would the historical setting have meaning for Shakespeare's audience?
- Why was the audience interested in what happened after the death of a strong ruler?
- How did Shakespeare's audience view Caesar and his assassins?

Think About Purpose and Audience

As you plan your literary research paper, think about your purpose and audience. Your **purpose** is to convey the results of your research to your **audience**—usually your teacher and classmates. What does your audience already know about the literary work, author, and historical period? What will you need to explain?

Idea Starters

- favorite authors
- favorite works of literature
- favorite historical time period

⬤ Writing Tip

Start with what you know and what interests you. Expand on your knowledge and interests by using your school's library or media center. Many schools subscribe to online databases designed to support literary and historical investigations. Ask your librarian or media specialist how to use these valuable research tools and how best to use the Internet for preliminary research on the questions that interest you.

Your Turn _____

Get Started Making notes in your **RWN**, choose a research **topic** and develop **research questions** to guide your investigation. Keep your **purpose** and **audience** in mind as you look for answers to your research questions.

Learn It Online
For an example of a complete, double-spaced literary research paper, visit:

go.hrw.com | L12-505 | **Go**

Writing Tip

Check the **reliability** and **validity** of your sources. A source is reliable and valid when its information is accurate and its ideas are presented objectively. Take special care in choosing Internet sources. Make sure that the site is sponsored by a trustworthy organization that has some expertise in the field.

Begin Research

Start your search for answers to your research questions by consulting general reference works or by doing keyword searches using an online search engine. Ask your school's librarian how to find works that will give an **overview** of your topic. An adequate overview will enable you to explore a variety of both print and nonprint sources. Use the chart below as a general resource guide.

Information Sources	
Library Sources	**What to Look For**
Library or online catalog	Books, records, audiotapes, videotapes, and digital media
Readers' Guide to Periodical Literature	Magazines and some journal articles indexed by subject and author
Indexes to newspapers, essays, and articles	Articles from major newspapers, such as *The New York Times*; possibly local newspapers
Specialized reference books and CD-ROMs	Encyclopedias of special subjects, such as *Contemporary Authors*; biographical references, such as *Current Biography*
Online databases, microfilm, and microfiche	Collections of specialized material such as literary criticism; indexes to major newspapers; back issues of some newspapers and magazines
Community Resources	**What to Look For**
Internet and online services	Articles, interviews, pictures, video and audio recordings
Museums, historical societies, and government offices	Exhibits, experts, and records
Schools and colleges	Libraries, experts, exhibits, and special collections
TV and radio; video stores	Documentary and instructional programs and videos

Research Guidelines As you seek sources, keep these guidelines in mind:

- **Balance primary and secondary sources. Primary sources** include firsthand, original information, such as letters, autobiographies, historical documents, and works of literature and art. **Secondary sources** consist of information derived from, or about, primary sources or other secondary sources. Examples include reference works, documentary films, biographies, and history books.
- **Cover all relevant perspectives.** Your literary research paper will be an original **synthesis,** or combination, of information you gather from research, the conclusions you draw from that research information, and your own insights into the topic. Look for sources that reveal the perspectives of a variety of literary and historical authorities on your subject.

Your Turn

Begin Your Research Refer to the research questions in your **RWN** as you look at sources to find the information you need. Then, make a list of sources that might have information you can use.

Record Sources

Keep track of all your source information, which will later be included in a *Works Cited* list in your paper. For each source, make a **source card,** like the one below.

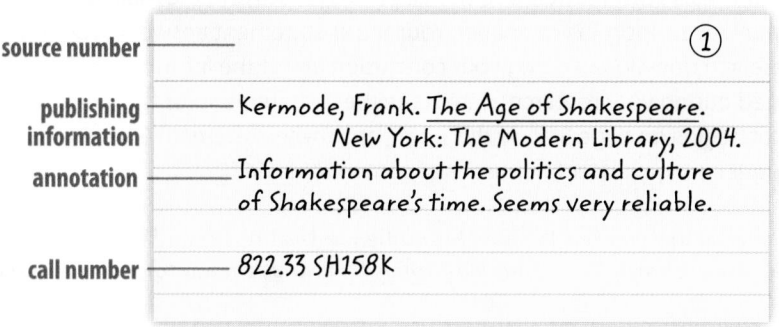

source number ——— ①

publishing information ———
Kermode, Frank. <u>The Age of Shakespeare.</u>
New York: The Modern Library, 2004.

annotation ———
Information about the politics and culture of Shakespeare's time. Seems very reliable.

call number ——— 822.33 SH158K

Research and Take Notes

Now you are ready to search for specific information to answer your research questions. As you take notes, use the following guidelines to decide how to record each piece of information—direct quotation, paraphrase, or summary.

- **Direct Quotation** When a passage is phrased in a memorable way or if you want to capture its technical accuracy, quote the author directly and exactly, word for word. Enclose the passage in quotation marks.
- **Paraphrase** Paraphrasing means that you completely rewrite a passage, using your own words and style. A paraphrase is usually about the same length as the original.
- **Summary** When you want to use the main ideas presented in a passage, summarize the information. A typical summary is highly condensed—much shorter than the original passage.

Avoid **plagiarizing,** or failing to give credit to an author whose words or ideas you have used. When you paraphrase or summarize, be sure to completely rewrite the original passages. Simply subsituting synonyms for some of the words from your source is not enough. See page 509 for information on giving credit by documenting your sources. The following is a sample **notecard.**

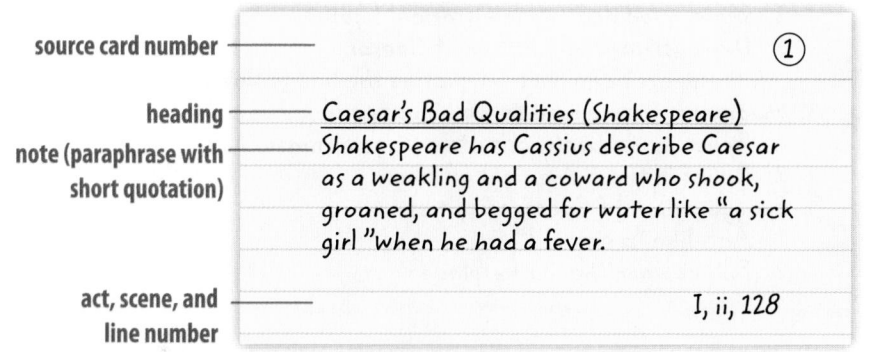

source card number ——— ①

heading ———
<u>Caesar's Bad Qualities (Shakespeare)</u>

note (paraphrase with short quotation) ———
Shakespeare has Cassius describe Caesar as a weakling and a coward who shook, groaned, and begged for water like "a sick girl" when he had a fever.

act, scene, and line number ——— I, ii, 128

Writing Tip

- Number your sources. Use the number, rather than the author and title, when you take notes from a given source.
- Record all publishing information (author, title, city, publisher, and date). This workshop uses The Modern Language Association (MLA) format, but your teacher may prefer another.
- Annotate each card with a short note about the contents of the source and your evaluation of it.
- Note the call number or location of the source. This information will save you time if you need to return to the source later.

Your Turn

Cite Sources and Take Notes
Create **source cards,** using the correct format, for each source you use. Skim your sources for information you can use in your essay. When you find relevant information, write it on a **notecard** like the one on this page.

Literary Research Paper

Analyze your information to see if it's relevant and useful.

- Divide your notes into categories based on their headings. Do more research for headings where you don't have enough information. Discard notes that turn out to be irrelevant to your topic.

- Analyze your notes for consistency. If sources do not agree on the facts, evaluate each source and use information from the one that is more reliable and valid.

- If two reliable and valid sources disagree on an important point, consider presenting this difference as part of your paper.

Drafting

Write a Thesis Statement

Your **thesis statement** is a sentence or two identifying the main idea that you intend to support in your paper. Your thesis statement answers your original research questions, stating your conclusion about the information you have analyzed during your research. Here is the thesis statement for the student model that begins on page 512. At this point, any thesis statement is preliminary. You might change it later for reasons of content or style.

Shakespeare wanted to show his audience that unlike in Plutarch's account, the main characters of his play Julius Caesar are a mixture of good and evil.

Make an Outline

Develop an outline by arranging your notecards according to your main-idea headings. Rearrange the headings until you have an order that makes sense. You will probably end up using a combination of organizational patterns—chronological order, order of importance, and logical order—for both your main ideas and your specific examples and supporting details.

- **Chronological order** can be used to discuss events in an author's or character's life in the order in which the events occurred.

- **Order of importance** can be used to discuss main ideas about an author's work. The most important idea is often discussed last for greatest effect.

- **Logical order** groups ideas by the relationships among them. Cause-effect and comparison-contrast are common examples.

Organizing your notes and creating a **formal outline** simplifies the process of writing your paper in its final form. Your outline can also serve as a table of contents for the finished paper. Look at this partial outline of the student model:

I. Introduction
    A. Shakespeare's source
    B. Thesis statement
II. Plutarch: Shakespeare's source
    A. Historian and biographer
    B. Lives of Noble Grecians and Romans
        1. Shows good and bad in historical figures
        2. Demonstrates admiration of Caesar
III. Shakespeare's challenge: depicting the bad in Caesar
    A. Audience was inclined to see him as good
        1. Belief in monarchy as system of government
        2. Belief in the divine right of kings
    B. Exaggerations of Caesar's frailties
        1. Acts like "a sick girl"
        2. Falls down in the marketplace

Document Sources

To **document** a paper means to identify the sources for the information in your paper. In general, document all quotations; all theories, ideas, and opinions other than your own; all data from surveys, research studies, and interviews; and all facts and statistics. Do not document common knowledge—information that can be found in several sources or standard reference works.

Place **parenthetical citations** (sources enclosed in parentheses) within the body of your paper as close as possible to the information they document. These citations direct readers to more complete information in the *Works Cited* list, located at the end of the paper. The chart below gives some guidelines.

Guidelines For Parenthetical Documentation

Type of Source	Content of Citation and Example
Sources with one author	Author's last name and a page number, if any: (Kermode 32)
Sources with more than one author	Authors' last names and page number: (Wells and Johnson 322) If more than three, use first author's last name and *et al.* (and others): (Anderson, et al. 313)
Same source, two citations	Author's last name and page numbers, if any: (Bullough 37, 39)
Multivolume sources	Author's last name, volume, and page number: (Prucha 2: 214)
Sources with a title only	Title (often abbreviated) and page number: (Lives 38)
Literary sources published in many editions	Author's last name, title, and division references (act, scene, canto, book, chapter, part, and line numbers) in place of page numbers: (Shakespeare, JC 1.2.128) (Note: JC abbreviates Julius Caesar)
Indirect sources	Abbreviation *qtd. in* (quoted in) before source: (qtd. in Morrow 29)

⬤ **Writing Tip**

If you have clearly indicated the author and title of your source in the text leading up to a citation, you do not need to list that information in your parenthetical citation.
For example:
In *Shakespeare's Canary,* Kuemmel and Lanier make very clear the Bard's love of songbirds (34).

Grammar Link Punctuating Parenthetical Citations

Here are some rules for adding parenthetical citations to your paper—

- Place citations *after* the closing quotation mark.

- Place citations *before* punctuation (such as periods) at the end of sentences.

> Cassius describes Caesar as "a sick girl" (Shakespeare, JC 1.2.128).

One exception to these rules is **block quotations**—quotations that run more than four lines, which are indented and do not have quotation marks. Instead, place *all* citations *after* of the end punctuation.

> . . . Difficult battles, long and swift
> marches, coarse diet, hard work, and sleeping in the open
> field conditioned him against his diseases. (McFarland, 233)

Your Turn

Write Your Draft Using your **outline** as a guide, write the first draft of your literary research paper. Remember to write a **thesis statement** and **document** your sources, using **parenthetical citations.**

Reference Note

For more on **formatting Works Cited lists,** see the model on page 514.

Assemble the *Works Cited* list

The *Works Cited* list, final section of your paper lists all the sources—both print and nonprint—that you used in your paper. If you do not cite a source in your paper, do not include it in your *Works Cited* list.

The following sample entries are a reference for preparing your *Works Cited* list. Notice that you include page numbers only for sources that are part of a larger work, such as an essay in a book of essays.

Sample *Works Cited* Entries

Standard Reference Works If an author is credited in a standard reference work, cite that person's name first in an entry. Otherwise, the title of the book or article appears first. You do not need to cite the editor. Page and volume numbers aren't needed if the work alphabetizes entries. For common reference works, use only the edition (if listed) and the year of publication.

Print Encyclopedia Article
"Plutarch." The World Book Encyclopedia. 2006 ed.

Books
One Author
Kermode, Frank. The Age of Shakespeare. New York: The Modern Library, 2004.
Two or More Authors
Kuemmel, Scott, and Terry Lanier. Shakespeare's Canary. New York: Harcourt, 2009.
For four or more authors, list the first author followed by "et al."

Selections Within Books
From a Book of Works by Several Authors
Bullough, Geoffrey. "Julius Caesar and Plutarch." Twentieth Century Interpretations of Julius Caesar.
        Ed. Leonard F. Dean. New Jersey: Prentice, 1968. 90–94.

Articles from Magazines, Newspapers, and Journals
From a Monthly or Quarterly Magazine
Morrow, Lance. "Plutarch's Exemplary Lives." Smithsonian 1 July 2004: 107–111.
From a Daily Newspaper
Jones, Chris. "Shaw Festival Debuts in Chicago Shakespeare's New Season." Chicago Tribune 18 Apr.
        2007: E4.

Other Sources
Film or Video Recording
Julius Caesar. Dir. Mankiewicz. 1953. DVD. Warner Home Video, 2006.
Material Accessed Through the Internet
Jackson, Dana. From History to the Stage: An Account of Shakespeare's Adaptation of Julius Caesar.
        2000. Shakespeare Online. 25 Sept. 2009 <www.shakespeare-online.com/essays/
        fromhistorytostage.html>.
Interviews
Keeling, Nichole. Telephone interview. 20 Sept. 2009.
E-mail Message or Personal Letter
Trahn, Linda. E-mail to the author. 27 Sept. 2009.

Evaluating and Revising

Use the guidelines in the following chart to evaluate and revise the content and organization of your paper. Ask yourself the questions in the left-hand column, and then use the tips in the middle column. Finally, use the revision techniques suggested in the right-hand column as necessary.

Literary Research Paper: Guidelines for Content and Organization

Evaluation Question	Tip	Revision Technique
1. Does the introduction hook the reader's attention, give background information, and clearly state the thesis?	**Circle** the hook, **underline** background information, and **bracket** the thesis statement.	**Add** a quotation or interesting detail to hook readers. **Add** necessary background. **Add** a thesis statement.
2. Does the body include only main ideas and supporting details that are relevant to the thesis?	With a colored marker, **highlight** the main ideas. **Number** supporting details for each.	**Delete** irrelevant ideas and details. **Add** details to support ideas with fewer than three supporting details.
3. Are facts and ideas stated mainly in your own words?	**Star** sentences containing direct quotations. If more than one third of the sentences are starred, revise.	**Replace** unnecessary direct quotations with paraphrases and summaries.
4. Are sources credited when necessary? Are citations correctly placed and punctuated?	**Place check marks** by material that came from outside sources and requires documentation.	**Add** parenthetical citations. **Correct** placement and punctuation of citations.
5. Does the conclusion restate the thesis?	**Bracket** the restatement of the thesis.	**Add** a sentence or two restating the thesis.
6. Is the *Works Cited* list complete and correctly formatted?	**Compare** citations that have checks with the entries in your *Works Cited* list.	**Add** *Works Cited* entries, and **revise** incorrectly formatted entries.

Peer Review

Ask a peer to use the evaluation questions and tips in the chart to the left to evaluate your draft and suggest revisions. Make notes about your partner's observations and suggestions.

511

Read the following portions of a student draft, and notice the comments on its strengths and suggestions for how it could be improved.

Student Draft

Shakespeare's Caesar

by Susan Chang, Reagan High School

Susan's **opening statement** is vague. →

Her **thesis statement** is clear. →

When Shakespeare wrote *Julius Caesar,* he made some changes. By looking at these changes, we can tell something about Shakespeare's purpose. The changes show that Shakespeare wanted to show his audience that all three main characters—Caesar, Brutus, and Mark Antony—are a mixture of good and evil.

To contrast Shakespeare's portrayal of Caesar, Susan **summarizes** Plutarch's view. →

Plutarch was a Greek historian and biographer. He wrote *Lives* not so much to record history as to show how the moral character—both good and bad—shaped the lives and destinies of the famous people he wrote about. His biography clearly shows admiration for Caesar, who he portrays as a natural-born orator, great soldier and general, and statesman who was beloved by his soldiers and people.

MINI-LESSON ▷ **Providing Background Information**

Susan's opening statement is vague. Readers may ask, "What did Shakespeare change?" Writers sometimes incorrectly assume that the reader is as familiar with their topic as they are. To make sure readers can follow your historical research, include background information that the average reader—someone who has *not* done the same amount of research on the topic as you have—needs. Susan added background information to help readers understand the changes she is going to discuss.

Susan's Revision of Paragraph 1

Most people know that Shakespeare's play Julius Caesar is based on history.

What many people don't know is tht he took the story from a particular source:

Plutarch's Lives of Noble Grecians and Romans. Most of the events— and

even some of the language—in Shakespeare's play is the same as in Plutarch's

account. However, ʷWhen Shakespeare wrote *Julius Caesar,* he did make ~~made~~ some

changes. By looking at these changes, we can tell something about Shakespeare's

Your Turn ———

Provide Background Information Read your draft, and ask yourself whether you give your readers sufficient information about the following:

- the writer
- the writer's sources
- the writer's time and place
- the literary work

Shakespeare faced a challenge in depicting the evil in Caesar. Many English people of the Renaissance believed that kings and queens ruled by divine right, so they were horrified by the kingly ruler's assassination (Jackson). To keep his audience from siding entirely with Caesar, Shakespeare had to show him in a worse light than Plutarch did. For instance, Plutarch describes Caesar's weaknesses but makes clear that he overcame them to do great deeds.

> In spite of his brave fighting and displays of energy, Caesar was physically weak. He was subject to epilepsy, and his slender physique and soft white skin made his courage and perseverance unusually remarkable. Difficult battles, long and swift marches, coarse diet, hard work, and sleeping in the open field conditioned him against his diseases. (McFarland, 233)

In contrast, Shakespeare exaggerates Caesar's frailties. He has Cassius describe Caesar as a weakling and a coward who shook, groaned, and begged for water like "a sick girl" when he had a fever (1.2.128). Despite the fact that these words come from Cassius, who is not always reliable, they still color the audience's opinion of Caesar. Shakespeare follows this information by having Casca report that at the marketplace, "Caesar fell down and foamed at the mouth and was speechless" (1.2.250–251). Shakespeare paints Caesar not as a man who overcame illness but as a man who feared and gave in to it. The Caesar of the play may be powerful, but he is also a hypocrite who pretends to a valor he lacks. This hypocrisy makes his death seem less tragic and his assassins less clearly in the wrong.

*Susan states a **main idea** and then gives **supporting details**. She uses a **parenthetical citation** to credit an online source without page numbers.*

*She quotes a long passage from a source, using **block quotation style**, but introduces the quotation incorrectly.*

Because the text clearly states that the quotes come from Shakespeare and Julius Caesar, *Susan does not need to include the author or title in this paragraph's citations.*

MINI-LESSON ▶ Introducing Quotations

Quotations should not disrupt the flow of your paper. Introduce them gracefully either with an introductory sentence followed by a colon or by weaving them in—making them a part of your sentence. Susan corrected her introduction to the block quotation.

Susan's Revision of Paragraph 3

light than Plutarch did. For instance, Plutarch describes Caesar's weaknesses but makes clear that he overcame them to do great deeds:

> In spite of his brave fighting and displays of energy, Caesar was physically weak. He was subject to epilepsy, and his slender physique and soft white skin made his courage and perseverance unusually remarkable. Difficult

Susan *correctly* weaves this quote into her sentence:

> He has Cassius describe Caesar as a weakling and a coward who shook, groaned, and begged for water like **"a sick girl"** when he had a fever…

Your Turn _____

Introduce Quotations Read your draft, making sure the introduction of quotations doesn't interrupt the flow of your paper and ideas. Ask a peer to review your draft and to suggest ways to introduce your quotations more smoothly.

In her conclusion, Susan restates her thesis. →

By showing Caesar, Brutus, and Mark Antony each as a blending of good and evil traits, Shakespeare makes the story of Caesar's assassination a story of the human struggle with our internal faults and failings. Caesar's arrogance and love of power first arouses Brutus's concern for the republic and then leads Caesar to ignore the warnings that would have saved him. Brutus's simple, trusting nature leads him to overlook the dishonorable agendas of his co-conspirators and misread the mood of the people. Finally, Mark Antony's nobility in avenging Caesar is tainted with cynical self-interest. None of the play's main characters are blameless, but each has a measure of nobility.

🔵 Writing Tip

Notice how the writer uses these rules for formatting his *Works Cited* list. Be sure to follow them when making your own.

- *Works Cited* pages usually begin on a separate page.
- The words *Works Cited* are centered above the list of sources.
- Each source entry begins on a separate line.
- The first line of the entry is left-aligned; additional lines have a hanging indent of a half inch.
- Sources are sorted alphabetically by authors' last names. Source with no author are sorted by title.
- If an author is cited for more than one source, his or her name appears only in the first entry. Additional entries use three hyphens (---) in place of the author's name.

Works Cited

Bullough, Geoffrey. "Julius Caesar and Plutarch." Twentieth Century Interpretations of Julius Caesar. Ed. Leonard F. Dean. New Jersey: Prentice, 1968.

"Caesar, Julius." Encyclopedia Britannica. 2007. Encyclopedia Britannica Online. 25 Sept. 2009 <http://www/britannica.com/eb/articles 9000074>.

Delaney, Bill. "Shakespeare's Julius Caesar." The Explicator Summer 2002: 188.

Jackson, Dana. From History to the Stage: An Account of Shakespeare's Adaptation of Julius Caesar. 2000. Shakespeare Online. 28 Sept. 2009 <http://www.shakespeare-online.com/essays/fromhistorytostage.html>.

Kermode, Frank. The Age of Shakespeare. New York: The Modern Library, 2004.

McFarlands, John W., and Pleasant and Audrey Graves, eds. Lives from Plutarch. New York: Random House, 1966.

Morrow, Lance. "Plutarch's Exemplary Lives." Smithsonian 1 July 2004: 107–111.

"Plutarch." The World Book Encyclopedia. 2006 ed.

Shakespeare, William. Julius Caesar. Ed. S. F. Johnson. New York: Penguin Books, 1960.

Proofreading and Publishing

Proofreading

Don't allow careless errors in grammar, usage, and mechanics to destroy your credibility. **Proofread,** or **edit,** your paper carefully to be sure that you have followed the **conventions** of standard American English.

Grammar Link Punctuating Quotations

When weaving a quotation into your text, you must sometimes add words or phrases to make the quotation clearer to readers. When you add to a quotation, you must place your addition in brackets ([ ]). At other times, you may want to quote some—but not all—of a writer's words so that you can better get at the main idea you are pointing out to your reader. When you leave words or phrases out of a quotation, you must replace them with ellipses (. . .).

Susan wove a quotation into her first draft but punctuated it incorrectly, possibly misleading readers about what Shakespeare's lines actually say. She revised her quotation to indicate where she added and deleted text.

> Shakespeare follows this information by having Casca report that at the marketplace
>
> "[Caesar] fell down **. . .** and foamed at the mouth and was speechless" (1.2.250–251).

Publishing

Consider these publishing ideas to share your hard work and insight:

- Ask your school librarian or media specialist to make your work available in the library or media center.
- Offer to present the paper to another class, either another English class or possibly a history class. You may wish to conduct additional research to find interesting and relevant audio and video support.
- Work collaboratively with your classmates to create a Web site that features your research findings. Include a space for reader feedback, if your teacher and school allow it.

Reflect on the Process Consider what you've learned about the topic, the research and writing processes, and yourself as a writer. In your **RWN,** write short responses to these questions.

1. What questions did your research answer that you had not asked or anticipated? Describe them.
2. What passage in your paper was the most effective combination of research and conclusions drawn from the research? Why?

⬤ Proofreading Tip

Your proofreading partner needs you to be honest, so that he or she can recognize the paper's strengths and weaknesses. However, try to be tactful—it can be hard to receive criticism on something that you have put so much effort into.

- Start with positive comments ("I liked the way that you . . ." or "I can tell you have put a lot of thought into . . .").
- Provide specific suggestions ("Your introduction could use more background because I didn't understand . . .") rather than vague judgments ("This introduction was terrible!").

Your Turn
Proofread and Publish

As you proofread your draft, check all your quotations against the original texts from which they come. If you have added or deleted words or phrases, be sure you have correctly used brackets and ellipses. When you are finished, make a final copy of your paper and publish it.

Scoring Rubric

Use one of the rubrics below to evaluate your literary research paper from the Writing Workshop or your response to the on-demand prompt on the next page. Your teacher will tell you to use either the six- or four-point rubric.

6-Point Scale

Score 6 *Demonstrates advanced success*
- focuses consistently on a clear thesis
- shows effective organization throughout, with smooth transitions
- offers thoughtful, creative ideas
- develops ideas thoroughly, using examples, details, and fully elaborated explanation
- exhibits mature control of written language

Score 5 *Demonstrates proficient success*
- focuses on a clear thesis
- shows effective organization, with transitions
- offers thoughtful ideas
- develops ideas competently, using examples, details, and well-elaborated explanation
- exhibits sufficient control of written language

Score 4 *Demonstrates competent success*
- focuses on a clear thesis, with minor distractions
- shows effective organization, with minor lapses
- offers mostly thoughtful ideas
- develops ideas adequately, with a mixture of general and specific elaboration
- exhibits general control of written language

Score 3 *Demonstrates limited success*
- includes some loosely related ideas that distract from the writer's expository focus
- shows some organization, with noticeable gaps in the logical flow of ideas
- offers routine, predictable ideas
- develops ideas with uneven elaboration
- exhibits limited control of written language

Score 2 *Demonstrates basic success*
- includes loosely related ideas that seriously distract from the writer's expository focus
- shows minimal organization, with major gaps in the logical flow of ideas
- offers ideas that merely skim the surface
- develops ideas with inadequate elaboration
- exhibits significant problems with control of written language

Score 1 *Demonstrates emerging effort*
- shows little awareness of the topic and purpose for writing
- lacks organization
- offers unclear and confusing ideas
- develops ideas in only a minimal way, if at all
- exhibits major problems with control of written language

4-Point Scale

Score 4 *Demonstrates advanced success*
- focuses consistently on a clear thesis
- shows effective organization throughout, with smooth transitions
- offers thoughtful, creative ideas
- develops ideas thoroughly, using examples, details, and fully elaborated explanation
- exhibits mature control of written language

Score 3 *Demonstrates competent success*
- focuses on a clear thesis, with minor distractions
- shows effective organization, with minor lapses
- offers mostly thoughtful ideas
- develops ideas adequately, with a mixture of general and specific elaboration
- exhibits general control of written language

Score 2 *Demonstrates limited success*
- includes some loosely related ideas that distract from the writer's expository focus
- shows some organization, with noticeable gaps in the logical flow of ideas
- offers routine, predictable ideas
- develops ideas with uneven elaboration
- exhibits limited control of written language

Score 1 *Demonstrates emerging effort*
- shows little awareness of the topic and purpose for writing
- lacks organization
- offers unclear and confusing ideas
- develops ideas in only a minimal way, if at all
- exhibits major problems with control of written language

Preparing for Timed Writing

Expository Essay

When responding to an expository prompt, use what you have learned from reading, writing your literary research paper, and studying the rubric on page 516. Use the steps below to develop a response to the following prompt.

Writing Prompt

Although ambition can be a good thing, too much ambition can be harmful both to the ambitious individual and to others. Write an essay explaining the harmful effects of excessive ambition.

Study the Prompt

Read the prompt carefully. Then, read it a second time, underlining words that will help you approach the prompt effectively: *ambition, harmful effects, individual,* and *others.* The prompt asks you to explain, which means you will be answering two questions in your essay: *why?* and *how?* The *why* question asks you to explain the reasons the ambition was harmful. *How?* asks you to show the harmful effects of the ambition. **Tip:** Spend about five minutes studying the prompt.

Plan Your Response

Decide quickly if you will use a personal example of ambition and its effects or if you will use hypothetical examples, drawing supporting details from your reading or other media. Try to be as specific as possible.

When you decide on the examples you will use, ask and answer the following questions:

- What is the evidence of the ambition?
- Who or what did this ambition affect?
- What was the result of the ambition?
- Why was it harmful? How? To whom?
- What did you and others learn as a result?

Using your answers, draw a conclusion and write a **thesis statement** about ambition's harmful effects. **Tip:** Spend about ten minutes planning your response.

Respond to the Prompt

Begin writing to start the flow of ideas. You might begin by defining *ambition* in your own words and then introducing your thesis statment. Create a brief scene to illustrate your definition. In the body text, explain the reasons *why* ambition is harmful and relate the reasons to your definition. For each harmful effect, provide examples of *how* it is harmful. In your conclusion, relate what your essay says about ambition to human nature in general. **Tip:** Spend about twenty minutes writing your draft.

Improve Your Response

Revising Check your response against the prompt. Does your response explain that too much ambition can be harmful and explain its harmful effects to the ambitious person and to others? Have you used specific examples to illustrate the harmful effects? Have you restated your thesis in the conclusion? Have you thought about lessons learned?

Proofreading Take a few minutes to edit your response to correct errors in grammar, usage, and mechanics. Check your usage of two key words that you will likely use in your essay:

- *Affect* is a verb that means "to influence."
  Praise can *affect* your self-image.
- *Effect* is a noun that means "the result of an action."
  The *effect* of his pride was loneliness.

Make sure that your paper is legible and neat and that any edits are easy to read.

Checking Your Final Copy Finally, read your response once more before you turn it in. You may catch an important mistake or think of the perfect last sentence! **Tip:** Save five or ten minutes to improve your paper.

Presenting a Literary Research Paper

Think as a Reader/Writer Scholars in fields such as science, history, literature, and anthropology publish their research in scholarly or professional journals. You have probably encountered such writings in your research. These same scholars also make oral presentations of their research at professional conferences. In this workshop, you will do the same: transform your written report into an oral presentation for your peers.

Adapt Your Literary Research Paper

Simple and Clear

Reading a paper is quite different from listening to a presentation. As readers, we have the opportunity to go back and re-read to clear up any confusion. Listeners don't have that opportunity. When adapting a written work into an oral presentation, it's important to think about what parts you may need to simplify and clarify for your audience. It's also important to hold your audience's attention with speaking techniques and interesting content. Use some of these tips to adjust the content:

- Grab your audience's interest by jazzing up your introduction with an interesting fact or a powerful quotation.
- Teach your audience about your main idea by stating your thesis clearly and repeating certain points for emphasis.
- End your presentation with a bang. Your conclusion should be as engaging as your introduction. Restate your thesis, and finish with a compelling quotation or anecdote.
- Simplify vocabulary, and break up longer sentences into shorter ones.
- Inform and entertain your audience by using exposition, narration, and description.
- Share as much information from primary and secondary sources as you can during the time allotted for your presentation.
- Do not cite sources except to identify the author of important quotations, facts, or ideas. In your introduction, let your audience know your report is drawn from a variety of sources.

Deliver Your Literary Research Paper

Speaking Formally

When you are giving a presentation about a topic you know well, plan to deliver it extemporaneously. Instead of memorizing your presentation, rehearse it until you are thoroughly familiar with your material. Make notecards with reminders of important points and the full text of important quotations. Number your notecards, and keep them in order. As you rehearse your presentation, maintain a formal, objective tone suitable to serious research. When you become comfortable with your material, allow yourself to vary your phrasing. Don't read your presentation from your notes; instead, use your notecards to guide you.

The Eyes Have It

If possible, enhance your presentation with visuals such as charts, graphs, photographs, or exhibits. Visuals should be large enough for the entire audience to see and should also make a relevant contribution to your presentation. Think carefully about how you want to incorporate your visuals. Practice using them when you rehearse.

Practice Makes Perfect

After you have adapted the content of your paper, made your notecards, and determined how you want to use visuals, you will need to get comfortable with your presentation. To make sure you really "know your stuff," videotape your presentation, practice in front of a mirror, or present your report to your family or friends. As you rehearse, work to perfect the content of your report and use the following tips to improve your delivery.

- Speak clearly, using standard American English. Avoid using overly technical terms and slang.
- Modulate your voice to emphasize important points.
- Pause, for emphasis, before an important point. Pause also to give your audience time to absorb important information.
- Use natural, relaxed gestures, and make eye contact with your audience.

Ready, Set, Go!

You are now prepared to give a successful oral presentation of your literary research paper. If you feel anxious or unprepared, re-read the advice presented above. Remember, too, that the more times you rehearse, the more comfortable with your presentation you will become.

A Good Oral Presentation

- follows a clear, step-by-step plan
- uses effective verbal and nonverbal speaking techniques
- uses visuals appropriately
- exhibits confidence and enthusiasm
- reveals that care and practice went into planning and rehearsing the presentation

---

Speaking Tip

If you have speaker's anxiety, take several slow, deep breaths just before your presentation. Then, look for friendly faces in the audience and make eye contact with them. If you lose your place, pause and use your notecards to get started again.

Literary Skills Review

Comparing Literature **Directions:** Read the poems that follow. Then, read each multiple-choice question and write the letter of the best response.

When You Are Old

by **Pierre de Ronsard**
translated by **Humbert Wolfe**

When you are old, at evening candle-lit
beside the fire bending to your wool,
read out my verse and murmur, "Ronsard writ
this praise for me when I was beautiful."

5 And not a maid but, at the sound of it,
though odding at the stitch on broidered stool,
will start awake, and bless love's benefit
whose long fidelities bring Time to school.

I shall be thin and ghost beneath the earth
10 by myrtle shade in quiet after pain,
but you, a crone,° will crouch beside the hearth
mourning my love and all your proud disdain.
And since what comes tomorrow who can say?
Live, pluck the roses of the world today.

11. **crone:** old woman.

When You Are Old

by **William Butler Yeats**

When you are old and grey and full of sleep,
And nodding by the fire, take down this book,
And slowly read, and dream of the soft look
Your eyes had once, and of their shadows deep;

5 How many loved your moments of glad grace,
And loved your beauty with love false or true,
But one man loved the pilgrim soul in you,
And loved the sorrows of your changing face;

10 And bending down beside the glowing bars,
Murmur, a little sadly, how Love fled
And paced upon the mountains overhead
And hid his face amid a crowd of stars.

1. The speaker in both poems is asking the woman he is addressing to imagine that she —

   A is happy in her solitude

   B is still beautiful in old age

   C has not been forgotten

   D is old and reading his poetry

2. The last two lines of Ronsard's poem are an example of the literary theme known as —

   A carpe diem

   B caesura

   C metaphysical conceit

   D kenning

3. What do the last two lines of Ronsard's poem reveal about the speaker's purpose in addressing the woman?

   A He wishes to get even with her for rejecting him.

   B He is trying to persuade her to give in to his advances now.

   C He wishes to immortalize her in a love poem.

   D He is trying to stop her from pursuing him.

4. The roses in the last line of Ronsard's poem symbolize —

   A broken promises

   B flowers

   C worldly pleasures

   D compliments

5. Ronsard's poem is an example of which poetic form?

   A Shakespearean sonnet

   B literary epic

   C Petrarchan sonnet

   D ballad

6. What emotion do both poets hope to evoke in the women they are addressing?

   A pity

   B revenge

   C regret

   D joy

7. How does the attitude toward time expressed in Ronsard's poem reflect Renaissance attitudes on that subject?

   A Ronsard's speaker is acutely aware of the brevity of youth, beauty, and earthly life.

   B Ronsard's speaker is focused on the afterlife rather than earthly life.

   C Ronsard's speaker feels he has enough time to accomplish what he wants in life.

   D Ronsard's speaker expects that time inevitably will bring greater happiness.

Constructed Response

8. In a short essay, compare and contrast these two poems. Focus on tone and the methods the poets use to convey tone.

Vocabulary Skills Review

Denotation and Connotation **Directions:** A word's **denotation** is its dictionary definition. **Connotation,** by contrast, refers to a word's emotional overtones—positive, negative, or neutral. Read each of the following short passages, and identify the connotation of the italicized word as positive, neutral, or negative.

1. John was deep in *contemplation* about which college to attend. Calmly, he gave the decision his complete attention.
   A positive
   B neutral
   C negative

2. The puzzle *confounded* me. The situation was so frustrating that I had to ask two friends for help.
   A positive
   B neutral
   C negative

3. An envious rival *insinuated* that I hadn't earned my good grades honestly. I was so insulted!
   A positive
   B neutral
   C negative

4. This country experienced severe *tribulation* over the assassination of President John F. Kennedy. There are few things worse for a nation than the violent loss of a leader.
   A positive
   B neutral
   C negative

5. Barb's *diligence* and attention to detail paid off when she took first prize in the science fair.
   A positive
   B neutral
   C negative

6. The villain's *treachery* was a powerful, frighteningly realistic part of the movie.
   A positive
   B neutral
   C negative

7. Many drivers think of speeding as a minor *transgression,* but even a minor violation of the speed limit can cause a fatal accident.
   A positive
   B neutral
   C negative

Academic Vocabulary

Directions: Choose the best definition for the italicized word in each sentence.

8. Macbeth's excessive ambition leads to *widespread* violence.
   A occurring in many places
   B happening too often
   C malicious
   D politically motivated

9. The six marriages of Henry VIII made him a *controversial* figure not only in England but in all of Europe.
   A unpopular
   B deplorable
   C subject to disagreement or argument
   D subject to ridicule

Writing Skills Review

Write a Historical Research Paper   **Directions:** Read the following paragraph from a draft of a student's historical research paper. Then, answer the questions that follow.

(1) The Globe Theater experienced a great many problems in its first few years of existence. (2) First, the theater was closed during plague epidemics in 1603 and 1609. (3) Then, in 1613 it was destroyed by a fire that broke out during a performance of *Henry VIII*. (4) It was rebuilt the following year and flourished for over twenty-eight years.

(5) In 1642, the Puritans closed the theater because they believed that plays were the work of the devil. (6) The theater was torn down in 1644 to make room for tenement housing. (7) The exact location of the theater was unknown until 1989, when parts of its original foundation were found beneath Anchor Terrace on Park Street.

1. Which of these transitions could be added to the beginning of sentence 5?
   A However,
   B As a result,
   C For example,
   D Consequently,

2. Which of the following facts would improve a reader's understanding of the time frame?
   A The Globe experienced five major setbacks during its time.
   B The Globe was built in 1599.
   C Citizens were not happy about the theater's location.
   D The Globe was built by the Burbage family.

3. Which statement would appropriately develop one of the paragraph's supporting facts?
   A The Globe was located in Southwark, on the south bank of the Thames River.
   B If the theater had lasted through Cromwell's Puritan administration, it might have survived well into the next century.
   C Fire broke out at the end of the first act of *Henry VIII*, when the firing of a cannon set the thatched roof of the theater ablaze.
   D The original theater was only in use for forty-five years, yet its place as home for Shakespeare's plays made it immortal.

4. Which of the following sources would most likely include additional information on the early history of the Globe?
   A a copy of *Henry VIII*
   B architectural drawings of the Globe Theater
   C a book about the history of London in the 1600s
   D a critical study of Shakespeare's plays

5. What might the next paragraph in this paper logically discuss?
   A the plays that were performed in the Globe Theater during its early years
   B the cause of the fire in 1613
   C Puritan attitudes toward theater and the arts
   D Shakespeare's early years, before he arrived in London

6. During an oral presentation of this passage, the speaker should —
   A pause to emphasize important ideas
   B avoid making eye contact in order to focus on the message
   C stand perfectly still while talking
   D speak softly so others may practice their presentations

Read On

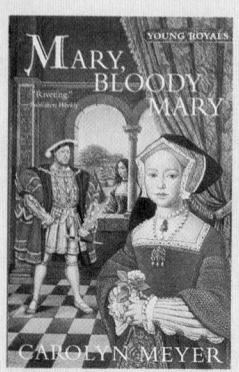

FICTION

Mary, Bloody Mary

The story of Mary Tudor's childhood reads like a classic fairy tale. A princess who was to inherit the throne of England, she is suddenly banished by her father, Henry VIII, then abused by an evil stepmother (who has enchanted her father), and finally, forced to care for her baby stepsister, who inherits Mary's right to the throne. Told in the voice of the young Mary, this novel by Carolyn Meyer explores the history and intrigue of the dramatic rule of Henry VIII and its venomous effect on Mary who, when she becomes Queen of England, is called Bloody Mary for good reason.

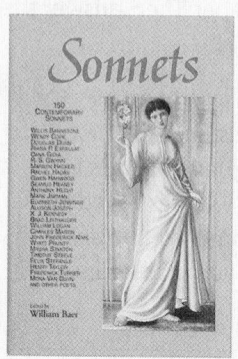

POETRY

Sonnets: 150 Contemporary Sonnets

The poetic form made famous by Shakespeare is making a comeback. This wide-ranging collection of contemporary sonnets showcases the beauty and power of the sonnet structure as employed by some of our most celebrated living poets including Seamus Heaney, Marilyn Hacker, and Wyatt Prunty. Exploring subjects as diverse as nature, movies, family, politics, and school, these poems show that the sonnet is making its mark on twenty-first-century literature.

NONFICTION

Zen and the Art of Motorcycle Maintenance: An Inquiry into Values

What is the nature of the universe? What is our place in it? Robert Pirsig follows a cross-country road trip, during which the author tours two thousand years of Western philosophy. Focusing on questions that intrigued Francis Bacon and John Milton, Pirsig invites the reader to consider his or her own place in a rapidly changing world.

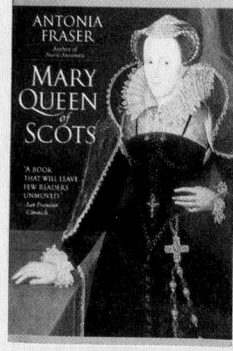

NONFICTION

Mary, Queen of Scots

Antonia Fraser's goal in this detailed biography is to separate the facts from the fiction surrounding Mary, Queen of Scots, whose life makes most fictional thrillers seem tame. As an infant, she becomes Queen of Scotland and at six years old is sent to live in France as a pawn to secure a Scot-French Catholic alliance against Protestant England. Her French husband dies, and her second husband is murdered. She then marries the man responsible for his murder. The Pope severs relations with Mary and she is deposed. Frantically hoping for help from Elizabeth, she flees to England.

DRAMA
Hamlet

"To be or not to be—that is the question." Often considered Shakespeare's greatest tragedy, *Hamlet* follows the obsession of a young man plagued by his father's death. After a visit from his father's ghost, Hamlet, the prince of Denmark, becomes determined to seek justice at any cost, and a catastrophic chain of events that shatters the royal court soon follows. Shakespeare's masterpiece features some of the most famous and emotionally wrenching soliloquies and poetry in the history of theater.

DRAMA
Rosencrantz and Guildenstern Are Dead

This is the play that turned Tom Stoppard into an overnight sensation. He has taken two minor characters from Hamlet and made them the center of a play that deals with the illusion of reality, the nature of identity, and how much or how little control we have over an inevitable destiny. The play is both comic and tragic and although we know the outcome, Stoppard keeps us in suspense until the final lines. This is a play that you will be thinking about for days after you read or see it.

DRAMA
Cyrano de Bergerac

Edmond Rostand used the famous 17th-century French playwright, soldier, and swordsman Cyrano de Bergerac as the inspiration for this boisterous tragicomedy. Cyrano is brilliant, witty (he can compose a poem in the middle of a duel), brave, and hopelessly in love with the beautiful, intelligent Roxane. Fearful of rejection because of his extremely long nose, he can confess his love for Roxane only by putting words into the mouth of Christian, the handsome young man she loves. This love triangle takes readers through one plot twist after another without a dull moment.

WEB SITE
Folger Shakespeare Library

Thou brave tiger-booted wafer-cake! Thou yeasty lily-livered hedge-pig! Learn to distinguish a Shakespearean compliment from a Shakespearean insult. Hear and see audio-video clips with acting tips on expressing anger, amazement, sorrow, love. Check out the radio documentary "Shakespeare Is a Black Woman." Read sonnets written by high-school students. Find out more about Shakespeare's life and work, and follow the links to all things Shakespeare at the Folger Shakespeare Library Web site.

Learn It Online
Explore novels at

go.hrw.com   L12-525   Go

The Restoration and the Eighteenth Century

1660–1800

COLLECTION 5
The Rise of the Novel

COLLECTION 6
Examined Lives

"Good order is the foundation of all good things."

—Edmund Burke

What Do
You?
Think

How can order and civilization affect human behavior?

Aerial view of Holkham Hall and gardens, home of Lord Leicester. Norfolk, UK.

Learn It Online
Find out more about this historical period online.

go.hrw.com   L12-527   Go

The Restoration and the Eighteenth Century 1660–1800

This time line represents a snapshot of British literary events, British historical events, and world events from 1660 to 1800. During this time, England saw the monarchy restored and Protestant succession secured. An interest in rationality emerged and the arts flourished.

BRITISH LITERARY EVENTS

1660

1660 Samuel Pepys begins his diary

1660s London theaters reopen after being closed by Puritans; actresses appear onstage for the first time

1668 John Dryden is named poet laureate of England

1678 John Bunyan publishes Part 1 of *The Pilgrim's Progress*

1680

1709 Richard Steele starts *The Tatler*, an early newspaper; he and Joseph Addison start *The Spectator* in 1711 ❯

Sir Richard Steele by Sir Godfrey Kneller, 1711. The Granger Collection.

1712 Alexander Pope publishes part of his mock epic, *The Rape of the Lock*

1719 Daniel Defoe publishes *Robinson Crusoe*

1729 Jonathan Swift publishes *A Modest Proposal*, protesting English treatment of the Irish poor

BRITISH HISTORICAL EVENTS

1660

1660 Charles II assumes the British throne, beginning the Restoration

1665 More than 68,000 Londoners die from the plague

1666 The Great Fire of London destroys much of the city

Illustration of Sir Isaac Newton and his telescope.

1680

1687 Sir Isaac Newton ❮ publishes *Mathematical Principles of Natural Philosophy*, establishing scientific laws of motion and gravity

1689 Glorious (Bloodless) Revolution; James II, a Catholic, is succeeded by Protestant monarchs William and Mary

1690 John Locke publishes an *Essay Concerning Human Understanding*, a landmark of rationalist philosophy

1695 The Penal Laws and the Test Act of 1673 deprive Catholics of civil rights

1707 England, Scotland, and Wales are unified politically as Great Britain

WORLD EVENTS

1660

1661–1715 Louis XIV rules in France, the center of cultural influence for the time

1660s Moliere stages *The School for Wives*, *Tartuffe*, and *The Misanthrope* to scandal and acclaim in Paris

1670s Ashanti Empire is formed in Africa

1675 King Philip's War erupts between colonists and Native Americans in New England

1680

1700s Spain establishes colonies in South America, Mexico, and the Philippines

1721 Russian ruler Peter the Great takes over Sweden as he expands the Russian Empire ❯

Peter the Great defeating the Swedes at Poltava in 1709. 1764, tapestry.

Your Turn

In a small group, review the time line and discuss which British literary and historical events probably had the most impact on other cultures, including American culture.

1740	1780	1800

1740 Samuel Richardson publishes *Pamela, or Virtue Rewarded*

1751 Thomas Gray writes *Elegy Written in a Country Churchyard,* one of the most influential English poems

1755 Samuel Johnson publishes his *Dictionary of the English Language*

1773 Oliver Goldsmith writes the comedy of manners *She Stoops to Conquer*

1791 James Boswell's *The Life of Samuel Johnson* is published

1792 Mary Wollstonecraft publishes *A Vindication of the Rights of Woman*

1793 William Blake begins work on his prophetic books and introduces his personal mythology

1798 William Wordsworth and Samuel Taylor Coleridge publish early Romantic work *Lyrical Ballads*

1740	1780	1800

1754 Seven Years' War ends; Britain controls most territories throughout North America

1765 James Watt invents steam engine, which powers Industrial Revolution ❯

1775 War with American colonies begins

1776 Adam Smith's early economic work *Wealth of Nations* appears

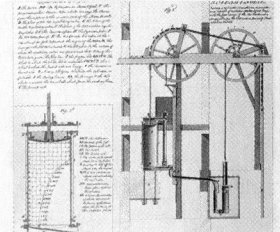

Patent drawing by James Watt of a steam engine.

1780 British put down Irish nationalist rebellion

1798 Edward Jenner develops smallpox vaccine ❯

Edward Jenner (1749–1823) performing the first vaccination against smallpox in 1796 (1879). Academie Nationale de Medicine, Paris, France.

1740	1780	1800

1742 George Frederic Handel's *Messiah* is first performed in Dublin, Ireland

1759 Voltaire's *Candide* is published

1762 Catherine the Great becomes czarina of Russia; expands Russian Empire into Poland

1765 Mozart writes *Symphony No. 1* at age nine

1780s Slave trade peaks in Africa

1789 French Revolution begins

1799 Rosetta Stone, the key to deciphering Egyptian hieroglyphs, is discovered in Egypt ❯

The Rosetta Stone, from Fort St. Julien, El-Rashid (Rosetta) 196 B.C. British Museum, London.

Unit Introduction **529**

The Restoration and the Eighteenth Century
1660–1800

The Restoration followed nearly twenty years of civil war and Puritan rule. The Church of England regained its power, and ushered in a sophisticated age of taste, refinement, and luxury. Reaction to the Roman Catholicism of James II brought about the Glorious Revolution of 1688, and Protestant succession to the throne of England was secured. In literature, the genius of the age was satire, addressed chiefly to the educated and leisured classes. A growing base of middle-class readers encouraged new forms of popular literature.

KEY CONCEPTS

Order and Reason

History of the Times With the restoration of the monarchy, stability returned to England after years of war. Fire and disease ravaged London in the 1660s, but by the middle of the eighteenth century, calm and order reigned. A new scientific and rational age emerged.

Literature of the Times Theater reflected the life of the upper classes. Satirists attacked the immorality and bad taste of the age. Journalism began. Writers of the neoclassical school revived standards of order and balance found in the classical literature of ancient Rome.

Social Classes

History of the Times The social order of England was based on a class system, with the hereditary nobility at the top and a large impoverished class at the bottom. Toward the end of the period, the Industrial Revolution was creating overcrowded slums and wretched working conditions.

Literature of the Times On the stage, comedies of manners appealed to men and women of fashion. Writers were still dependent on patrons, but this system gave way to large numbers of professional writers who created works for the middle classes.

Values and Beliefs

History of the Times The labels *Age of Enlightenment* and *Age of Reason* reveal how people viewed themselves. Religious views were influenced by the philosophy of rationalism. A movement called deism proposed that God could be discovered through the use of reason and the observation of nature.

Literature of the Times Writers used satire to expose moral corruption and commercialism. Journalists also advocated reforms. At the end of the period, focus shifted from elegance, taste, and reason toward emotional expression.

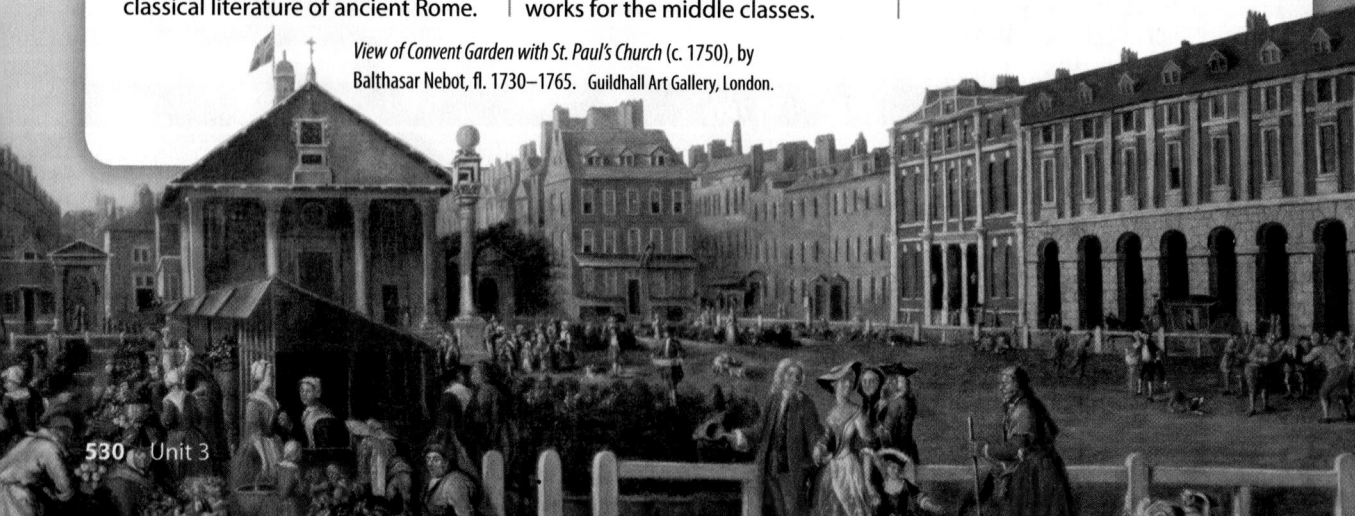

View of Convent Garden with St. Paul's Church (c. 1750), by Balthasar Nebot, fl. 1730–1765. Guildhall Art Gallery, London.

KEY CONCEPT

Order and Reason

History of the Times

In 1660, after twenty years of civil war and Puritan dictatorship, England was ready for stability and the return of Charles II. Five years later, London suffered an outbreak of plague, and the Great Fire of 1666 destroyed much of the city. By the middle of the 1700s, however, England had reached a time of peace and calm. The Glorious Revolution of 1688 that enabled William and Mary to take the throne occurred without bloodshed. During this era, Parliament became more powerful, and a two-party political system emerged.

This period of order allowed Britain's great thinkers to excel in their fields. Because at the time rational thought was considered the most powerful way to approach the world, this era is often called the Enlightenment or the Age of Reason. The work of Sir Isaac Newton and others fostered the concept that the universe was a perfect mechanism, set in motion by God, that could be understood through observation and reason. Many fields benefited from this new way of thinking.

Literature of the Times

Literature in the Restoration was influenced by French classical ideas and preferences. An emphasis on brilliance and cleverness, known as **wit,** is characteristic of literature written for the privileged classes. Satire became a dominant form in the works of English writers such as Alexander Pope and Jonathan Swift.

Writers who worked in the neoclassic tradition used forms imitating the Latin classics. For this reason, the age has also been called the Augustan Age after the Roman emperor Augustus, who was a patron of writers and artists. Pope adopted the classic epic form for his mock epic, *The Rape of the Lock.* He used the traditional literary devices found in serious epics to compose his comic narrative poem. Augustan poets are also known for their preference for public themes. It wasn't until the end of the period that a new kind of poetry expressing private themes appeared.

Comprehension Check

How do the labels *Age of Reason, Enlightenment,* and *Augustan Age* summarize this period?

Fast Facts

Historical Highlights

- Charles II is restored to the throne in 1660, ushering in an era of stability.
- William and Mary assume the throne in 1689, securing Protestant succession.
- Great Britain is formed in 1707 when Scotland and Wales are politically aligned with England
- War erupts between Britain and the American colonies in 1775

Literary Highlights

- After closure by Puritan leaders in 1642, theaters reopen in the 1660s, paving the way for Restoration dramatists.
- Alexander Pope and Jonathan Swift write accomplished satires in verse and in prose.
- A new profession, journalism, emerges.
- The novel finds an audience in the middle class. *Robinson Crusoe* (1719) by Daniel Defoe may be the first English novel.

Learn It Online
Go online for information on this historical period.

go.hrw.com   L12-531   Go

Social Classes

History of the Times

When Charles II returned from exile in France, he brought with him the lavish and leisured culture of the French aristocrats. Formal and artificial fashions included makeup, powdered wigs, and elaborate clothing. The upper classes attended balls, dances, plays, gambling soirees, and dinner parties. They retreated to seaside spas during the summer, spent the social season in town, and lived intermittently at their country houses. Change in fashion, however, was inevitable, and by the end of the eighteenth century, the period of elegance and excess was coming to an end.

During this same time, the indigent suffered from bad health, inadequate living conditions, and a lack of education. Excrement littered the city streets, rapidly spreading disease. Tenements in London, where entire families could live in a single rat-infested room, were overcrowded and filthy. Poor people often died young; at one point, 74 percent of children in London died before they turned five.

Children were expected to work, and abuse was common. Industrialization transformed towns into gritty manufacturing centers. As merchants grew rich, lower-class workers were left behind. Charities and the government offered little help, and debtors who were unable to pay their bills were frequently sent to prison.

Because physicians practiced medicine almost exclusively with the rich, little was known about the illnesses of the poor. Lack of personal hygiene contributed to their general state of bad health.

Literature of the Times

After the return of Charles II, English writers were receptive to French wit and French literary taste. The literary form that had the greatest success during the period following the Restoration was the drama, which reflected the sophistication of Charles's court.

The first half of the eighteenth century was memorable for the satire of Alexander Pope and

Link to Today

Political Cartoons and Caricatures

Satire was not confined to writers during the eighteenth century. Visual artists were also sharp social critics. William Hogarth (1697–1764) satirized contemporary life in his paintings and engravings.

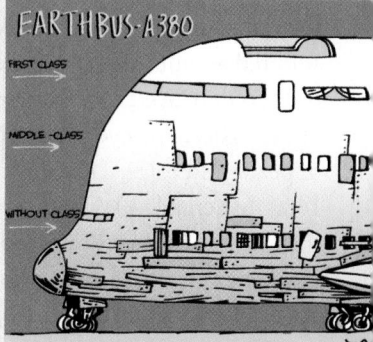

Earthly Airbus, by Alen Lauzan Falcon.

One form of visual satire with a long history is the political cartoon. Today, political cartoons appear in newspapers and magazines. They often include **caricatures**— portraits that exaggerate notable physical characteristics of a person. The leading caricaturist of the eighteenth century was the Englishman James Gillray (1756–1815), who ridiculed George III and the French Revolution. His work continues to influence today's satirists.

As an art form, caricature dates back to the fifteenth and sixteenth centuries. Italian artists Leonardo da Vinci and Annibale Carracci produced portraits of public figures with exaggerated physical features to satirize ridiculous behavior. During the Protestant Reformation, Martin Luther used editorial cartoons to reach illiterate peasants with his criticisms of the Catholic Church.

Political cartoons and caricatures are still meaningful. They use visual appeal and humor to entertain and comment on social and political conditions. Just look at the editorial pages of today's newspapers—you'll see a brand of satire that echoes James Gillray and the 1700s.

Ask Yourself

With a partner, analyze William Hogarth's engraving on the next page. What is being satirized? What is the message?

Jonathan Swift and the essays of Richard Steele and Joseph Addison. All of these writers proclaimed the need for traditional values and saw in literature a means of asserting good sense and controlling folly and vice. These writers did not hesitate to criticize their own upper-class audience. Pope's mock epic, *The Rape of the Lock,* ridiculed the lifestyle of the aristocracy by treating a petty quarrel as an epic battle.

The dominant literary figure during the second half of the eighteenth century was Samuel Johnson, considered the most learned man of his day. Johnson represents a transition from the Augustan

The enraged musician (1741), by William Hogarth.

period to the Romantic period. He is responsible for the first comprehensive dictionary of the English language, which became the basis for all subsequent English dictionaries.

By the middle of the century, new genres were becoming popular with a growing middle-class readership. Women as well as men were in the ranks of new readers. The familiar periodical essay made its appearance in the *Tatler* and later in the *Spectator.*

The novel had differentiated itself from travel narratives and journalistic writing. Writers were creating longer fictional works that often were filled with adventures. Daniel Defoe's *Robinson Crusoe,* a series of fictional letters written by a shipwrecked sailor, is considered by some to be the first English novel. Experiments in prose fiction resulted in other early novels such as Henry Fielding's raucous *Tom Jones,* Samuel Richardson's tragic Clarissa, and Laurence Sterne's hilarious hodge-podge *The Life and Opinions of Tristram Shandy, Gentleman.* Women writers also entered the literary arena for the first time and in large numbers, led by Aphra Behn, Eliza Haywood, and Fanny Burney.

Comprehension Check

How did the different social and economic classes in English society lead to the development of various types of literature?

Values and Beliefs

History of the Times

Church and state were tightly interwoven during the Restoration and the eighteenth century. When Charles II began his rule in 1660, he immediately reopened the theaters, which had been closed by Puritan leaders in 1642 because the Puritans believed plays were immoral. Theatergoing again became popular, and for the first time women were allowed to perform on stage.

Although Charles was a Protestant, his brother and heir, James II, was Roman Catholic. British leaders, who recalled both the Catholic backlash of Bloody Mary Tudor and the strict Puritanism of Cromwell's dictatorship, feared a monarch who favored alliances with the Catholic powers of Europe. For that reason, Parliament expelled James in the Glorious Revolution (so called because it occurred without any bloodshed) and offered the monarchy to his Protestant daughter, Mary, and her Dutch husband, William of Orange. They accepted, ruling equally as William III and Mary II. The Anglican Church was the official church of England.

Although William and Mary were a safe choice for a Parliament fearing religious turmoil, they were not a choice that provided religious freedom. William and Mary and succeeding monarchs restricted the rights of Catholics, Puritans, and others who did not belong to the Church of England. The Test Act of 1673 deprived Catholics of the right to hold office, and the Penal Laws of 1695 withheld civil rights from Irish Catholics. Persecution of religious minorities continued well into the eighteenth century.

The rise of rationalism in the eighteenth century created another form of spirituality called **deism,** a belief system based on reason and the observation of nature. Deists, such as Newton and Locke, believed a creator had set an orderly universe in motion and then allowed it to run its own course without divine intervention. Although many intellectuals embraced deism, Christianity continued to dominate Europe, as it had in the Middle Ages and the Renaissance.

Literature of the Times

The Anglican Church dominated religious life as the state religion. Protestants who remained outside the Anglican Church were known as Dissenters. Like Roman Catholics, they were subject to various civil restrictions. Prominent writers of this period were Roman Catholics and Dissenters.

John Dryden, a Catholic, was England's poet laureate for nearly twenty years, but he had to resign his post in 1688 following the expulsion of James II because Catholics were deprived of public office.

Link to Today

The Coffeehouse Awakening

In many urban areas today, a coffeehouse appears on almost every corner. Coffeehouses have become popular spots for refreshment, relaxation, conversation, and reading.

Dickens coffeehouse in London, England.

Coffeehouses were also exceedingly popular in Restoration England. In fact, 3,000 coffeehouses opened in London after Charles II was restored to the throne. The times were more lighthearted after years of dour Puritan rule, and the Age of Reason promoted lively philosophical and intellectual debates, which often occurred in those coffeehouses.

Ask Yourself

How might you design a coffeehouse today that promotes philosophical and intellectual discussions?

Portrait of William and Mary, c. late 18th century? Eg. 2572.
Page/Folio No: 16 British Museum, London.

Alexander Pope's Roman Catholic faith excluded him from a university education and a public position despite his prodigious talents.

Because Daniel Defoe was a Presbyterian, he was not permitted to attend Oxford or Cambridge. He reacted to the religious intolerance of his time by writing *The Shortest Way with Dissenters,* which reduced the position of the authorities to absurdity. Defoe pretended to support the Anglican policy against Dissenters. The authorities at first took his writing literally, but when they discovered that he was actually being ironic, they decided to punish him. He was arrested, tried, and sentenced to three appearances in the pillory. While crowds usually further degraded criminals in the pillory by throwing rotten vegetables and rocks at them, in this case, a group of Defoe's friends instead sang a satiric song he had composed, threw flowers at him, and cheered him for defying the government.

Comprehension Check

What influence did religion and morality have during this era, which is sometimes called the Age of Satire?

Wrap Up

Talk About ...

With a partner, discuss what injustices or follies satirists are likely to ridicule. Try to use each **Academic Vocabulary** word at least once in your discussion.

Write About ...

Alexander Pope said "Satire's my weapon." How effective is satire compared to other weapons of criticism? Explain your response in two paragraphs.

Academic Vocabulary for Unit 3

Talking and Writing About Literature
Academic Vocabulary is the language you use to write and talk about literature. Use these words to discuss the works you read in this unit. These words are underlined throughout the unit.

approach (uh PROHCH) *n.:* way of addressing something. *The satiric approach sometimes exaggerates a flaw to ridicule it.*

convince (kuhn VIHNS) *v.:* persuade; cause to believe. *Writers of satire try to convince readers to correct social problems.*

dominate (DAHM uh nayt) *v.:* hold a commanding position. *What philosophies dominate the Age of Reason?*

enhance (ehn HANS) *v.:* improve the quality of. *Pope's skillful epic similes enhance the mock epic,* The Rape of the Lock.

participate (pahr TIHS uh payt) *v:* take part in. *William and Mary restricted the rights of Catholics to participate in government.*

Your Turn

Copy the Academic Vocabulary list into your *Reader/Writer Notebook.* Then, use the information you have learned from the unit introduction to write a sentence for each word, discussing some aspect of English literature from 1660 to 1800.

Link to Today

This Link to Today provides contemporary insight into how people cope with a massive disaster.

Read with a Purpose

Read to see how one New Orleans resident reacted to the devastation of Hurricane Katrina.

Build Background

Hurricane Katrina slammed New Orleans and the Gulf Coast in August 2005, leaving more than 1,800 people dead and thousands homeless. It was one of the most destructive and costly natural disasters in United States history. This column appeared on November 17, 2005, less than three months after Katrina hit.

Author Note

Chris Rose (1960–   ) is a columnist for the New Orleans *Times-Picayune* newspaper, where he writes on a variety of subjects, including New Orleans life and entertainment. He was named a finalist for a Pulitzer Prize for his post-Katrina columns, which are collected under the title *1 Dead in Attic*. He was born in Washington, D.C. and graduated from the University of Wisconsin.

1 Dead in Attic

by CHRIS ROSE

The New Orleans *Times-Picayune*

I live on The Island,[1] where much has the appearance of Life Goes On. Gas stations, bars, pizza joints, joggers, strollers, dogs, churches, shoppers, neighbors, even garage sales. Sometimes trash and mail service, sometimes not. It sets to mind a modicum of complacency that maybe everything is all right.

But I have this terrible habit of getting into my car every two or three days and driving into the Valley Down Below, that vast wasteland below sea level that was my city, and it's mind-blowing A) how vast it is and B) how wasted it is.

My wife questions the wisdom of my frequent forays into the massive expanse of blown-apart lives and property that local street maps used to call Gentilly, Lakeview, the East and the Lower 9th. She fears that it contributes to my unhappiness and general instability and I suspect she is right. Perhaps I should just stay on the stretch of safe, dry land Uptown where we live and try to move on, focus on pleasant things, quit making myself miserable, quit reliving all those terrible things we saw on TV that first week.

That's advice I wish I could follow, but I can't. I am compelled for reasons that are not entirely clear to me. And so I drive. I drive around and try to figure out those Byzantine[2] markings and symbols that the cops and the National Guard[3] spray-painted on all the houses around here, cryptic communications that tell the story of who or what was or wasn't inside the house when the floodwater rose to the ceiling.

In some cases, there's no interpretation needed. There's one I pass on St. Roch Avenue in the 8th Ward at least once a week. It says: "1 Dead in Attic." That certainly sums up the situation. No mystery there. It's spray-painted there on the front of the house and it probably will remain spray-painted there for weeks, months, maybe years, a perpetual reminder of the untimely passing of a citizen, a resident, a New Orleanian. One of us.

---

1. **The Island:** a part of New Orleans that escaped flooding.
2. **Byzantine:** complex, intricate, and confusing.
3. **National Guard:** the reserve militia of each state of the United States.

(*Above*) Houses flooded by Hurricane Katrina, New Orleans, September 2005. (*Left*) View of London during the Great Fire, which started on September 2nd, 1666.

You'd think some numerical coding could have conveyed this information on this house, so that I—we all—wouldn't have to drive by places like this every day and be reminded: "1 Dead in Attic."

I have seen plenty of houses in worse shape than the one where 1 Dead in Attic used to live, houses in Gentilly and the Lower 9th that yield the most chilling visual displays in town: low-rider shotgun rooftops with holes that were hacked away from the inside with an ax, leaving small, splintered openings through which people sought escape. Imagine if your life came to that point, and remained there, on display, all over town for us to see, day after day.

Amazingly, those rooftops are the stories with happy endings. I mean, they got out, right?

But where are they now? Do you think they have trouble sleeping at night?

The occasional rooftops still have painted messages: "HELP US." I guess they had paint cans in their attic. And an ax, like Margaret Orr and Aaron Broussard[4] always told us we should have if we weren't going to evacuate. Some people thought Orr and Broussard were crazy. Alarmists. Extremists. Well, maybe they are crazy. But they were right.

Perhaps 1 Dead in Attic should have heeded this advice. But judging from the ages on the

---

4. **Margaret Orr and Aaron Broussard:** a New Orleans weather forecaster and the president of Jefferson Parish, which includes part of New Orleans.

state's official victims list, he or she was probably up in years. And stubborn. And unafraid. And now a statistic.

I wonder who eventually came and took 1 Dead in Attic away. Who knows? Hell, with the way things run around here—I wonder if anyone has come to take 1 Dead in Attic away. And who claimed him or her? Who grieved over 1 Dead in Attic and who buried 1 Dead in Attic?

Was there anyone with him or her at the end and what was the last thing they said to each other? How did 1 Dead in Attic spend the last weekend in August of the year 2005? What were their plans? Maybe dinner at Mandich on St. Claude?[5] Maybe a Labor Day family reunion in City Park—one of those raucous picnics where everybody wears matching T-shirts to mark the occasion and they rent a DJ and a SpaceWalk and a couple of guys actually get there the night before to secure a good, shady spot?

I wonder if I ever met 1 Dead in Attic. Maybe in the course of my job or maybe at a Saints[6] game or maybe we once stood next to each other at a Mardi Gras[7] parade . . . . 1 Dead in Attic could have been my mail carrier, a wait-

Mardi Gras Indian Headdress, New Orleans, 2005.
Eliot Kamenitz ©2007 The Times-Picayune Publishing Co.

ress at my favorite restaurant or the guy who burglarized my house a couple years ago. Who knows?

My wife, she's right. I've got to quit just randomly driving around. This can't be helping anything. But I can't stop. I return to the Valley Down Below over and over, looking for signs of progress in all that muck, some sign that things are getting better, that things are improving, that we don't all have to live in a state of abeyance forever but—you know what? I just don't see them there.

I mean, in the 8th Ward, tucked down there behind St. Roch Cemetery, life looks pretty much like it did when the floodwater first receded 10 weeks ago, with lots of cars pointing this way and that, kids' yard toys caked in mire, portraits of despair, desolation and loss. And hatchet holes in rooftops.

But there's something I've discovered about the 8th Ward in this strange exercise of mine: Apparently, a lot of Mardi Gras Indians[8] are from there. Or were from there; I'm not sure what the proper terminology is. On several desolate streets that I drive down, I see where some folks have returned to a few of the homes and they haven't bothered to put their

---

5. **Mandich on St. Claude:** a famous New Orleans restaurant.
6. **Saints:** New Orleans Saints, a professional football team.
7. **Mardi Gras:** a season of carnival in New Orleans, which occurs before Lent begins.

---

8. **Mardi Gras Indians:** in New Orleans, members of African American organizations, called tribes, that wear elaborate costumes and parade on Mardi Gras day.

furniture and appliances out on the curb—what's the point, really?—but they have retrieved their tattered and muddy Indian suits and sequins and feathers and they have nailed them to the fronts of their houses.

The colors of these displays is startling because everything else in the 8th is gray. The streets, the walls, the cars, even the trees. Just gray. So the oranges and blues and greens of the Indian costumes are something beautiful to behold, like the first flowers to bloom after the fallout. I don't know what the significance of these displays is, but they hold a mystical fascination for me. They haunt me, almost as much as the spray paint on the front of a house that says 1 Dead in Attic. They look like ghosts hanging there. They are reminders of something. Something very New Orleans.

Do these memorials mean these guys—the Indians—are coming back? I mean, they have to, don't they? Where else could they do what they do? And—maybe this is a strange time to ask—but who are these guys, anyway? Why do they do what they do with all those feathers

and beads that take so much time and money to make? What's with all the Big Chief and Spy Boy[9] role-playing?

As many times as I have reveled in their rhythmic, poetic and sometimes borderline absurd revelry in the streets of our city, I now realize that if you asked me to explain the origins and meaning of the Mardi Gras Indians—I couldn't do it. I have no clue. And that makes me wish I'd been paying more attention for the past 20 years. I could have learned something.

I could have learned something about a people whose history is now but a sepia mist over back-of-town streets and neighborhoods that nobody's ever heard of and where nobody lives and nothing ever happens anymore; a freeze frame still life in the air, a story of what we once were.

---

9. **Big Chief and Spy Boy:** two of the ranks of New Orleans Indians. Spy Boy leads the procession for a tribe, and Big Chief is the head.

Ask Yourself

1. **Read with a Purpose** After reading these comments, how would you describe the author's state of mind as he drove the streets of New Orleans in the months after Hurricane Katrina? Explain.

2. The author's neighborhood was not badly damaged by the hurricane, and he could have stayed away from New Orleans' devastated areas. Why, then, did he make a point of driving the damaged neighborhoods? Explain.

3. Where did the author get the title for this article, and why do you think he focuses so much of the essay on this phrase? Explain.

4. How did the costumes of Mardi Gras Indians attract the author's attention, and how did they affect his state of mind as he thought about New Orleans and the hurricane? Explain.

5. In this article's conclusion, the author wishes he had been paying more attention in the decades before Hurricane Katrina. Explain why.

COLLECTION 5

The Rise of the Novel

LITERARY FOCUS
The Rise of the Novel

The Reverend Randall Burroughs and his son Ellis.
Louvre, Paris, France.

CONTENTS

Samuel Pepys

Phil Gyford

Daniel Defoe   Link to Today

Jonathan Swift

COMPARING TEXTS: WORLD LITERATURE
Voltaire, Miguel de Cervantes

" 'Oh! it is only a novel!'
. . . or, in short, only some work in which the most thorough knowledge of human nature, the happiest delineation of its varieties, the liveliest effusions of wit and humour are conveyed to the world in the best chosen language."

— Jane Austen, *Northanger Abbey*

SKILLS FOCUS Literary Skills Evaluate and analyze the philosophical, political, religious, ethical, and social influences of a historical period; understand the rise of the novel.

The Rise of the Novel by **Leila Christenbury**

Influences on the Rise of the Novel

- Tradition of narratives, allegories, and satires
- New interest in biographies and journals as historical documents
- Increases in leisure time and literacy rates

What's New About the Novel?

The novel is a long fictional prose narrative; it is literature that tells a story. In this collection, you will read excerpts from some of the precursors to novels, such as *The Diary of Samuel Pepys*, and from some of the earliest examples of novels, such as *Gulliver's Travels*. If the word *novel* means "new," we are led to ask: What exactly was new about this form of writing?

Compared with stories from earlier times, the emerging novels conveyed a sense of realism. The **protagonist,** or main character, of a novel differed from the superhuman or godlike persons in myths and epics such as *Beowulf* and the brave and noble figures in romances such as *Le Morte d'Arthur*. The novel's main character could be anyone—a person's nobility, wealth, or education might become part of the plot, but the lack of these advantages did not keep a character out of the story's spotlight. Early novels told the stories of many different kinds of lives.

A novel's plot followed the adventures and misadventures of the hero or heroine and the characters he or she encountered. Some early critics of the novel mused that the novel failed to offer adequate moral instruction for readers. Samuel Johnson, an eighteenth-century writer and notable creator of *A Dictionary of the English Language,* commenting on the new fiction, worried that readers might develop sympathy for rascally heroes: "As we accompany them through their adventures with delight, and are led by degrees to interest ourselves in their favour . . . we lose the abhorrence of their faults, because they do not hinder our pleasure." Then as now, most readers read novels for fun. Much as movies today are usually intended to entertain their audiences, early novels used intriguing plots to provide enjoyment for readers.

Newspapers, Diaries, and Travel Writing

Early novels grew out of several different sources—many of which were nonfiction. Readers had tasted the excitement of scandalous urban gossip in the newspapers. The growing popularity of diaries and epistolary correspondance created an audience that expected intimate details. This development also created a desire for insight into characters' motivations, hopes, and fears. The growth in trade between England and countries throughout the world created popular interest in other countries and cultures and particularly in travel logs. Early novel writers used elements from all these genres to lend excitement, alternative voices, and energy to their writing. In this collection, you will read an excerpt from an actual diary and an excerpt from a fictional journal written to seem like an actual diary.

Early Novelists

Although the English novel did not emerge until the eighteenth century, writers in other parts of the world experimented with forms similar to the novel centuries earlier. The Greek *Daphnis and Chloe* (third century) can be considered a novel, as can *The Tale of Genji,* a vast chronicle of court life written in about 1000 by Murasaki Shikibu, a lady-in-waiting to the Japanese empress Akito. In Europe, the novel first emerged with the publication of Miguel Cervantes' *Don Quixote*. Drawing on the traditions of regal chivalric romances, only to satirize them via a bumbling but well-intentioned protagonist, Cervantes ultimately created a new textual structure through the hybridization of tragic and comic forms.

Lady Aphra Behn's *Oroonoko, or the History of the Royal Slave* (1688) is called by some the first English novel and by others a "protonovel." A combination of fiction, history, and travelogue, it presents a realistic account of the British slave trade. Daniel Defoe's *Robinson Crusoe* (1719), the loosely structured narrative of the courage and ingenuity of a castaway and his Man Friday, gets the nod from other critics as the first English novel. Nearly all readers agree, however, that Samuel Richardson's book *Pamela* (1740) is a novel. Richardson (1689–1761) was perhaps the first novelist to explore in great detail the emotional life of his characters, especially his heroines (in *Pamela* and *Clarissa*).

The novels of the prominent eighteenth-century novelist Henry Fielding (1707–1754) are crammed with rough and rowdy incidents, and though Fielding makes his characters seem good, they are never soft or sentimental. Fielding's rollicking novel *Tom Jones* has even been made into an Oscar-winning movie, proof that his high-spirited characters are still fresh and funny today. Laurence Sterne (1713–1768) produced the landmark fictional autobiography *Tristram Shandy,* an experimental novel which, despite the efforts of many imitators, remains uniquely whimsical.

These novels of Sterne, Richardson, Behn and others tell us about life at a particular time and help us understand that the joys and disappointments of human experience transcend time periods.

Tom Jones *(1963), starring Susannah York, Hugh Griffith, Albert Finney.*

Ask Yourself

1. Why might the hero of a novel appeal more to readers than a godlike or noble hero from a myth or epic poem?

2. To what extent do you think Johnson's observation—that we lose disgust for the moral flaws of main characters because we enjoy reading about them—applies to us as modern novel-readers or moviegoers?

Learn It Online

Find out more about novels, and scope out modern novels on the NovelWise site.

go.hrw.com | L12-542 | Go

SKILLS FOCUS Literary Skills Evaluate and analyze the philosophical, political, religious, ethical, and social influences of a historical period; analyze characteristics of a satire.

Analyzing an Etching

Early novels, which could be satirical and more realistic than previous fictional writings, told the stories of many different types of lives. This etching from the eighteenth century has several characteristics in common with the first novels.

Guidelines

An etching is an image produced by carving a picture or design on a metal plate and then pressing that plate onto paper. Use the guidelines below to consider how this etching reflects concerns of the novel.

- What satirical elements do you see in this etching?
- How are the people portrayed? Would you say the etching is realistic or not realistic? Explain.
- How do both the etching and the text beneath it convey a sense of plot?

1. Who or what are the heads at the left of the etching? What are they saying and why?

2. How do the relative sizes of the people and objects express the artist's **point of view?**

3. **Irony,** a contrast between expectation and reality, is characteristic of **satire.** What ironic elements can you find?

Midas Transmuting All into Gold Paper, published by Hannah Humphrey (1797). Courtesy of Warden and Scholars of New College, Oxford.

Your Turn Analyze a Satirical Image

Choose a satirical image or a cartoon from this unit, and discuss with a partner how the image displays some satirical elements.

Preparing to Read

from The Diary of Samuel Pepys

What Do You Think? How can order and civilization affect human behavior?

QuickTalk

Think about a natural disaster, such as a fire or damaging storm, that you've read about or experienced. How did people respond to the challenge? In a small group, discuss the disaster as well people's response to it.

Portrait of Samuel Pepys (1666). Oil on canvas.
National Portrait Gallery, London.

Samuel Pepys
(1633–1703)

From 1660 to 1669, Samuel Pepys (pronounced "peeps") kept a private diary about life and events in London.

The Curious Londoner

Pepys was a hardworking, accomplished naval administrator whose constant desire to learn and to <u>participate</u> in new experiences led him to explore the cultural and intellectual life of London. Music, art, literature, science, mathematics, the theater—Pepys enjoyed them all. He was the confidant of the kings Charles II and James II, and he counted among his friends many of London's influential architects, artists, mathematicians, and scientists. His diary reflects his broad interests and endless curiosity.

Historians find the *Diary* useful because Pepys was a first-hand observer of seventeenth-century life, both public and private. In 1660, he took part in bringing the exiled king Charles II back to England. He witnessed joyous occasions such as Charles's coronation in 1661 and disasters such as the plague of 1665 and the Great Fire of 1666. He recorded these important public happenings in his diary along with trivial personal experiences. For example, on one occasion he wrote: "I went to . . . the theater, where I saw again *The Lost Lady,* which doth please me better than before. And here, I sitting behind in a dark place, a lady spat backward upon me by mistake, not seeing me. But after seeing her to be a very pretty lady, I was not troubled at all." The *Diary* is full of unexpected little anecdotes such as this one.

The Diary Goes Public

Housed at Cambridge University since 1723, Pepys's diary, which fills six 282-page notebooks in shorthand, is the longest intimate eyewitness account of life in seventeenth-century London. Its contents remained unknown until the shorthand was first transcribed in 1825. A complete transcription of the most intimate parts was not published until the 1970s and 1980s.

Think About the Writer What events or aspects of daily life in your city might intrigue a curious person such as Samuel Pepys?

 Reader/Writer
Notebook

Use your **RWN** to complete the activities for this selection.

Literary Focus

Diary A **diary** is a record a person keeps of feelings, impressions, and events. Diaries are usually written for the writer's eyes only. Pepys intended his diary to be private—at least during his lifetime. He wrote it in shorthand and encoded especially personal passages in a mix of Spanish, Latin, and French. However, because Pepys carefully preserved his diary and willed it, along with other books, to Cambridge University, it is likely he imagined that someone, someday, would read his entries.

Reading Focus

Evaluating an Author's Credibility Pepys witnessed some of the events he wrote about in his diary, and heard and recorded information about others. How do these methods of obtaining information affect his **credibility,** or believability? In this excerpt, Pepys relates not only facts about the Great Fire of London but also his opinions and emotional reactions. Think about his statements and his sources of information as you evaluate his credibility.

Into Action Use a chart to analyze Pepys's statements. Record the source of his information for each statement, and note whether it is a fact, an opinion, or an emotional response.

Statement About the Fire	Source of the Information	Fact, Opinion, or Emotional Response?
Pepys saw the fire far off and was not worried.	Pepys is an eyewitness; he also hears about the fire from Jane.	The fire is a fact, but Pepys also feels relief that it is far off.

Writing Focus

Think as a Reader/Writer

Find It in Your Reading A skillful observer, Pepys provides hundreds of snapshots of life in London. His entries are not a carefully constructed narrative but rather a series of quick descriptions of what he saw, thought, and felt. Notice details that make Pepys's account a valuable historical and interesting personal record. In your *Reader/Writer Notebook*, jot down details that you think are effective and explain why you chose them.

Vocabulary

lamentable (luh MEHN tuh buhl) *adj.*: deserving of or inspiring sorrow. *Pepys regarded the fire's destruction as lamentable.*

flinging (FLIHNG ihng) *v.*: throwing forcefully. *The people were flinging their possessions into the river to protect them from the fire.*

quench (kwehnch) *v.*: put out; extinguish. *Londoners were unable to quench the fire before it destroyed four-fifths of the city.*

combustible (kuhm BUHS tuh buhl) *adj.*: easy to set on fire; fast-burning. *Built of wood and crowded against each other on narrow streets, the houses of London were highly combustible.*

dismayed (dihs MAYD) *v.*: upset; alarmed. *News that the fire was out of control and had burned hundreds of houses dismayed the people of London.*

Language Coach

Suffixes The suffixes *–able* and *–ible* can change verbs to adjectives. *Lament* is a verb that means "to show sorrow." When you add the suffix *–able*, you get the adjective *lamentable*, which means "deserving of or inspiring sorrow." Which Vocabulary word includes the *–ible* suffix? What related verb do you get if you remove the suffix? What does the verb mean?

 **Learn It Online**
Listen to this diary with the audio version online.

go.hrw.com L12-545   **Go**

from The Diary of Samuel Pepys

by **Samuel Pepys**

Read with a Purpose
Read this diary entry to observe Pepys's emotional and practical reactions to the Great Fire.

Build Background
The Great Fire of London started in the house of the king's baker on September 2, 1666. Strong eastern winds fanned it into the city's streets, where it burned until September 5, when it was finally contained and extinguished. The fire razed a large part of the city. It destroyed many city buildings, dozens of churches, a cathedral, and about 13,000 houses, leaving many Londoners homeless.

September 2, 1666

The First Day of the Great Fire of London

Lord's Day. Some of our maids sitting up late last night to get things ready against our feast today, Jane called us up, about three in the morning, to tell us of a great fire they saw in the City. So I rose, and slipped on my nightgown and went to her window, and thought it to be on the back-side of Mark Lane at the furthest; but being unused to such fires as followed, I thought it far enough off, and so went to bed again and to sleep. About seven rose again to dress myself, and there looked out at the window and saw the fire not so much as it was, and further off. So to my closet[1] to set things to rights after yesterday's cleaning. By and by Jane comes and tells me that she hears that above three hundred houses have been burned down tonight by the fire we saw, and that it was now burning down all Fish Street by London Bridge. So I made myself ready presently, and walked to the Tower[2] and there got up upon one of the high places, Sir. J. Robinson's little son going up with me; and there I did see the houses[3]

at that end of the bridge all on fire, and an infinite great fire on this and the other side of the end of the bridge—which, among other people, did trouble me for poor little Michell and our Sarah[4] on the bridge. So down, with my heart full of trouble, to the Lieutenant of the Tower, who tells me that it begun this morning in the King's baker's house in Pudding Lane, and that it hath burned down St. Magnes Church and most part of Fish Street already. So I down to the waterside and there got a boat and through bridge, and there saw a lamentable fire. Poor Michell's house, as far as the Old Swan,[5] already burned that way and the fire running further, that in a very little

4. **Sarah:** maid whom Mrs. Pepys discharged on December 5, 1662. Pepys wrote: "The wench cried, and I was ready to cry too."
5. **Michell's house . . . Old Swan:** Betty Michell, a former sweetheart of Pepys, lost her house in the fire. The Old Swan was a tavern on Thames Street, near London Bridge.

Ⓐ **Literary Focus Diary** How do these lines show us both a factual recording of events and Pepys's personal opinion about those facts?

Vocabulary lamentable (luh MEHN tuh buhl) *adj.:* deserving of or inspiring sorrow.

---

1. **closet:** private room.
2. **Tower:** Tower of London, close to Pepys' house.
3. **houses:** shops and dwellings built on London Bridge.

time it got as far as the Steelyard while I was there. Everybody endeavoring to remove their goods, and flinging into the river or bringing them into lighters[6] that lay off. Poor people staying in their houses as long as till the very fire touched them, and then running into boats or clambering from one pair of stair by the waterside to another. And among other things, the poor pigeons I perceive were loath to leave their houses, but hovered about the windows and balconies till they were some of them burned, their wings, and fell down.

Having stayed, and in an hour's time seen the fire rage every way, and nobody to my sight endeavoring to quench it, but to remove their goods and leave all to the fire; and having seen it get as far as the Steelyard, and the wind mighty high and driving it into the City, and everything, after so long a drought, proving combustible, even the very stones of churches, and among other things, the poor steeple by which pretty Mrs.—lives, and whereof my old schoolfellow Elborough is parson, taken fire in the very top and there burned till it fall down—I to Whitehall with a gentleman with me who desired to go off from the Tower to see the fire in my boat—to Whitehall, and there up to the King's closet in the chapel, where people came about me and I did give them an account dismayed them all; and word was carried in to the King, so I was called for and did tell the King and Duke of York what I saw, and that unless his Majesty did command houses to be pulled down, nothing could stop the fire. . . . **B**

---

6. lighters: large, open barges.

B **Reading Focus** Evaluating an Author's Credibility How does knowing that Pepys will speak with the king make his account more credible?

Vocabulary **flinging** (FLIHNG ihng) *v.:* throwing forcefully.
quench (kwehnch) *v.:* put out; extinguish.
combustible (kuhm BUHS tuh buhl) *adj.:* easy to set on fire; fast-burning.
dismayed (dihs MAYD) *v.:* upset; alarmed.

The Great Fire of London, September 1666, with Ludgate and Old St. Paul's (c. 1670). Oil on canvas. Yale Center for British Art, Paul Mellon Collection, USA.

Respond and Think Critically

Reading Focus

QuickCheck

1. Where did the fire start, and what caused it to spread through London?

2. How did the king learn about the extent of the fire?

3. What did Pepys think should be done to stop the fire? Why?

Read with a Purpose

4. When Pepys realized the extent of the fire, what were his emotional and practical responses?

Reading Skills: Evaluating an Author's Credibility

5. You analyzed Pepys's statements about the fire. Now, evaluate Pepys's credibility. Review your chart, and consider the author's purpose, audience, background, attitude toward his subject, and any bias you think he might have. Do you find Pepys's account credible? Why? When might an eyewitness account not be credible?

Statement About the Fire	Source of the Information	Fact, Opinion, or Emotional Response?
Pepys saw the fire far off and was not worried.	Pepys is an eyewitness; he also hears about the fire from Jane.	The fire is a fact, but Pepys also feels relief that it is far off.

Literary Focus

Literary Analysis

6. Draw Conclusions What do you learn about Pepys from his movements during the fire?

7. Infer What can you infer about Pepys's character from the concerns he expresses during the fire?

8. Analyze Pepys's probably wrote this entry after, not as, the fire took place. What details appear to be omitted from his description of the fire?

Literary Skills: Diary

9. Analyze How is this diary entry organized? Why is this structure effective for a diarist?

Literary Skills Review: Diction

10. Interpret A writer's choice of words is called **diction.** Writers choose words depending on their audience, subject, and purpose. Diction may be simple or flowery, concrete or abstract, modern or old-fashioned, general or specific, casual or formal. How would you describe Pepys's diction? Give examples to support your answer.

Writing Focus

Think as a Reader/Writer

Use It in Your Writing Now that you have seen how details can enrich an account in a diary, use the same technique to write a diary entry about an event in your own life. What would you like to remember about the event? Include details to show what you saw, thought, and felt.

What Do You Think Now

Disasters can create chaos and disorder. How did the people of London, including Pepys, respond to the fire that disrupted their lives?

Vocabulary Development

✓ Vocabulary Check

Match the Vocabulary words with their definitions.

1. lamentable   **a.** flammable

2. flinging   **b.** pitiable

3. quench   **c.** upset

4. combustible   **d.** throwing

5. dismayed   **e.** put out

Vocabulary Skills: Synonyms

Were you able to match the Vocabulary words and definitions above correctly? If so, you know some synonyms for those words. The term *synonym* comes from a Greek word combining the meanings "similar" and "name." **Synonyms** are words that have the same or nearly the same meaning. Synonyms often reflect subtle differences, or shades of, meaning. English is a language rich with synonyms. When you write, you can explore synonyms to vary your writing or to choose the word that communicates exactly what you mean.

Consider the word *flinging*. One synonym is *throwing*. But what other synonyms can you find for *flinging*? You can use a dictionary or thesaurus to complete a word web to show some synonyms for *flinging*.

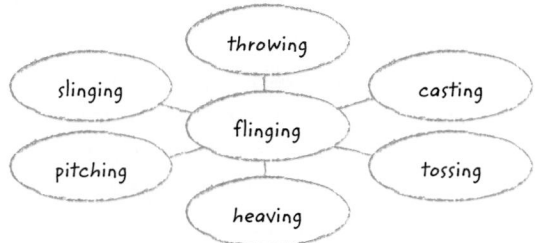

Each of these choices conveys a similar idea with a different shade of meaning. Understanding those shades of meaning helps you choose a word to say something specific or exact. For example, *throwing* is a general synonym for *flinging*. *Flinging* suggests throwing forcefully, *heaving* suggests throwing with effort, *tossing* suggests throwing casually, and *pitching* suggests throwing carefully.

Your Turn

Use a dictionary or thesaurus to find synonyms for the Vocabulary words. Create a word web for each word. Then, use a synonym from each web to replace the Vocabulary words in the following sentences. Discuss with a partner whether changing the word alters the sentence's meaning.

1. He is *flinging* the papers into the trash.

2. *Quench* the fire before you go to bed.

3. News of the tragedy *dismayed* us.

Language Coach

Suffixes You can form adjectives from some verbs by adding the suffixes *–able* or *–ible,* which mean "worthy of" or "capable of." Create adjectives by combining the verbs and suffixes listed below. Then, tell the meaning of each adjective.

1. combust + *–ible*   **3.** access + *–ible*

2. respect + *–able*   **4.** manage + *–able*

Academic Vocabulary

Write About

Consider how keeping a diary might <u>enhance</u> your life and help you <u>participate</u> in life more fully. Then, write a paragraph to <u>convince</u> a friend to keep a diary.

For **CHOICES** *see page 555* >

Link to Today

from Why I turned Pepys' Diary into a Weblog

What Do You Think

How can order and civilization affect human behavior?

QuickWrite

Do you keep a journal, diary, or blog? What motivates you to take the time to write? With a small group, discuss at least three advantages to keeping a record of your thoughts and activities.

Informational Text Focus

Comparing and Contrasting A writer compares ideas by explaining what they have in common and contrasts them by explaining how they are different. In this article, Gyford explains an idea that occurred to him because he began to compare and contrast diaries and weblogs.

Into Action As you read, use a Venn diagram like the one below to work through the same thought process that Gyford used as he designed his popular blog. The center circle identifies similarities; the two outer ovals list unique characteristics of a diary and a blog.

Diary was private | Same words in diary and blog | Blog is public

Writing Focus Preparing for **Constructed Response**

Gyford's article compares Pepys online to Pepys on paper, but it also includes a sequence of events—the story of how Gyford developed his blog. As you read, note in your *Reader/Writer Notebook* the steps Gyford took to turn his idea into something real. How does Gyford's organization of the article help you understand the information he conveys?

TechFocus As you read this article, think about other ways modern technology might bring Pepys's diary to life.

Vocabulary

domain (doh MAYN) *n.:* sphere of influence due to ownership or expertise. *Literature like Pepys's Diary is not just the domain of English professors—everyone can enjoy it.*

hefty (HEHF tee) *adj.:* heavy, considerable. *Ten years of diary entries make a hefty book.*

copyright (KAHP ee ryt) *n.:* legal right to use, sell, or distribute material that can be printed or published. *Pepys's Diary is no longer under a copyright; it is free to use.*

annotated (AN uh tayt id) *adj.:* marked with explanations in the form of notes. *Annotated blog entries help people understand Pepys's references to seventeenth-century life.*

albeit (awl BEE iht) *conj.:* although it is. *Pepys's Diary is a treasure of English literature that, albeit old, is still relevant to modern life.*

Language Coach

Word Origins *Albeit* was formed as a contraction for the phrase "although it be." Today, it is used as a single word, without any apostrophes.

Reader/Writer Notebook

Use your **RWN** to complete the activities for this selection.

Learn It Online
Check out an interactive Venn diagram online.

go.hrw.com | L12-550 | Go

Link to Today

This Link to Today updates a diary from the seventeenth century by posting it as a weblog.

Read with a Purpose

Read to discover how Pepys's writings have found new life, and a new audience, in an on-line environment.

Build Background

When Samuel Pepys began the private diary he would write for ten years, London was a thriving city. About 500,000 people lived in and around the city proper, and it was the center of England's political, business, and entertainment worlds. Pepys sought out contact with his fellow Londoners and took full advantage of all that the city offered. Gyford's weblog reaches out to today's readers who can travel through cyberspace to the time of Pepys's London.

The Tower of London.

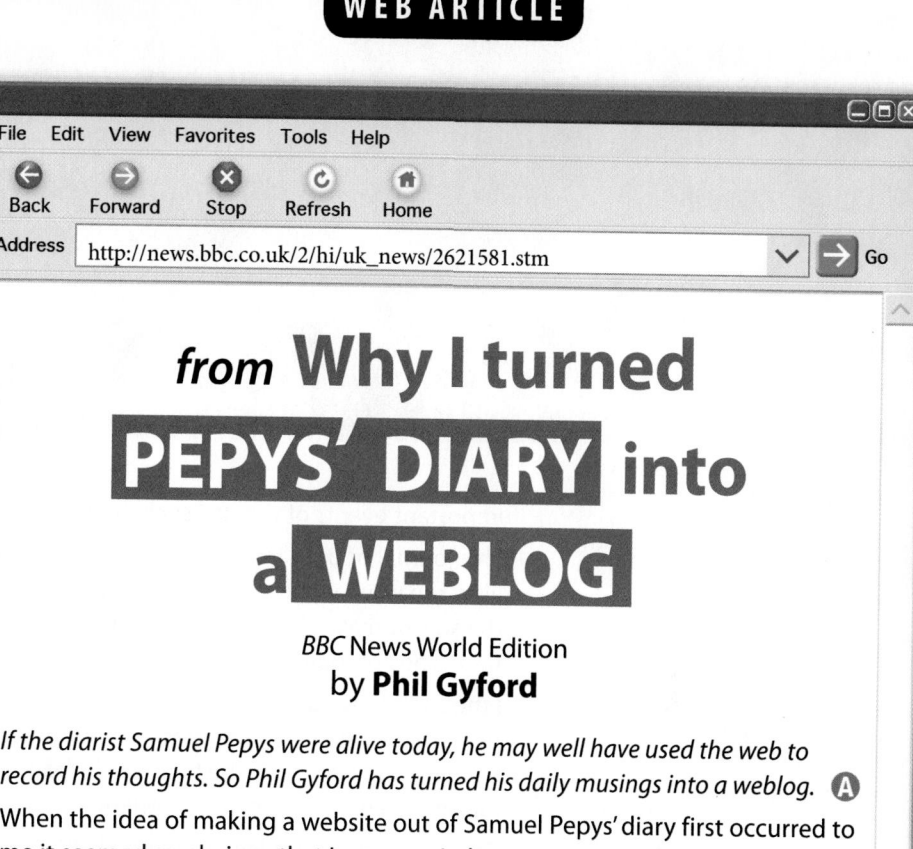

| File | Edit | View | Favorites | Tools | Help |

Back Forward Stop Refresh Home

Address http://news.bbc.co.uk/2/hi/uk_news/2621581.stm Go

from Why I turned PEPYS' DIARY into a WEBLOG

BBC News World Edition
by **Phil Gyford**

If the diarist Samuel Pepys were alive today, he may well have used the web to record his thoughts. So Phil Gyford has turned his daily musings into a weblog. **Ⓐ**

When the idea of making a website out of Samuel Pepys' diary first occurred to me it seemed so obvious that I was worried someone would beat me to it.

For nearly 10 years from 1660 Pepys wrote about his experiences day by day: his own intriguing private life, his professional rise through the ranks and

Ⓐ Informational Focus Comparing and Contrasting How might the language someone uses in a blog compare to that used in a private diary?

Old London bridge, detail from Vischer's London *(17th century).*

important events of the day such as The Great Fire and the Plague.

This journal of both large and small scale events often happens in public view today, on weblogs. Known as blogs, a few years ago these sites were the sole domain of web geeks but now an ever-increasing number cover thousands of topics.

I thought Pepys' diary could make a great weblog. The published diary takes the form of nine hefty volumes—a daunting prospect. Reading it day by day on a website would be far more manageable, with the real-time aspect making it a more involving experience.

Copyright isn't a problem; the remarkable Project Gutenberg, a community effort to make electronic texts of copyright-free books available to everyone, has produced a version of the diary dating from 1893. This Victorian edition misses out a few of the juiciest phrases but it is free to use and comes with explanatory footnotes.   **B**

Bring past to life

One of the reasons for the recent boom in weblogs is that the tools to create and manage them are generally free and increasingly easy to use. I chose Movable Type because it allows readers to post comments next to each entry.

B **Informational Focus** **Comparing and Contrasting** How does the 1893 edition of the *Diary* likely contrast to Pepys's original?

Vocabulary **domain** (doh MAYN) *n.:* a sphere of influence due to ownership or expertise.
hefty (HEHF tee) *adj.:* heavy, considerable.
copyright (KAHP ee ryt) *n.:* legal right to use, sell, or distribute any material that can be printed or published.

 Internet

It all seemed too perfect: this could be a fascinating site and would be simple and cheap to create. I couldn't believe I was alone in thinking this, so I didn't tell even my closest friends about it.

After a few months thinking about how best to tackle it, I spent a few weekends and evenings creating the site, which was ready a week before Pepys' first entry on 1 January.

Although the diary text came with footnotes, these assume a level of knowledge about British history, geography and language that few have in the 21st Century.

This is where the ability to post comments on the site has proved crucial. Entries and footnotes are already being annotated by readers who provide explanations and additional information, creating a more communal experience than conventional publishing allows. So rather than simply publishing a dead—albeit fascinating—text, I now find myself in charge of a far more exciting living read. **C**

Big book club

Only a week in, it's been fascinating to hear the thoughts of readers. Some have called Pepys the world's first blogger, which wrongly assumes no-one before 1660 kept a diary.

And because it is a personal diary, the thrill of reading it is different to that of a weblog; had Pepys been writing for publication he would undoubtedly have left out his most controversial or revealing thoughts.

Some readers have wondered if the site says anything about the state of blogging. Are conventional weblogs unexciting and we're craving novelty? I disagree—weblogging has never been healthier or more vibrant; the more people involved, the better the net is. Now the format is established and familiar, it's far easier to create innovative ways of using it.

Others have marveled at my apparent level of commitment; I have 10 years of weblogging ahead of me. But with the site built, preparing new diary entries should take little more than an evening or two each month.
But I'm sure I'll spend more time reading the diary and readers' annotations and contributing my own—this is what excites me the most. Not only will I finally read the diary, I'll do so at the same time as people all over the world. It's like the world's largest book club.

Tower of London.

C **Informational Focus** **Comparing and Contrasting** How does the "living read" experience compare to reading a published book? How might it enhance or detract from the experience?

Vocabulary **annotated** (AN uh tayt id) *adj.:* marked with explanatory notes.
albeit (awl BEE iht) *conj.:* although it is.

🌐 Internet

Why I turned Pepys' Diary into a Weblog

Respond and Think Critically

Informational Text Focus

Quick Check

1. Why didn't Gyford talk to friends about his idea?

2. Why did Gyford plan a ten-year time line for posting his blog entries?

3. How have people responded to Gyford's project?

Read with a Purpose

4. How do online readers of Pepys's diary entries experience the diary differently than someone reading the "nine hefty volumes"?

Informational Text Skills: Comparing and Contrasting

5. Look back at the Venn diagram in which you recorded comparisons and contrasts between diaries and weblogs. Now, write a short paragraph responding to the following question: Are diaries and blogs more similar or more different? Explain.

✓ Vocabulary Check

Match these Vocabulary words with their definitions.

6. domain   a. although
7. hefty   b. field of belonging
8. copyright   c. considerable
9. annotated   d. right to use or sell
10. albeit   e. explained with notes

Text Analysis

11. **Interpret** How has Gyford's blog helped make the Internet "the world's largest book club"?

12. **Infer** What is one important difference between Pepys's original audience and the audience of Gyford's blog? Explain.

13. **Extend** In what way does Gyford's blog reinvent or update Pepys's diary entries?

Listening and Speaking

14. **Analyze** Since a weblog is open to millions of Internet users, critics have questioned the wisdom of posting uncensored thoughts. With a trusted adult, discuss if people should limit what they post on personal blogs. Share both of your thoughts with a small group, and ask group members for their own responses. If time allows, share the group's ideas with your class.

Writing Focus Constructed Response

Write a paragraph in which you discuss how Gyford's organization of his article helps you understand the information he presents. Cite examples from the article.

What Do You Think Now

How can participating in the "book club" that has gathered around Pepys's *Diary* online enhance readers' understanding of both Pepys's world and today's world?

Why I turned Pepys' Diary into a Weblog / *from* The diary of Samuel Pepys

SKILLS FOCUS Informational **Skills** Identify, compare, and contrast organization; locate information from print and non-print sources. **Vocabulary Skills** Demonstrate knowledge of literal meanings of words and their usage. **Listening and Speaking Skills** Adapt to occasion when speaking: discussions. **Writing Skills** Write a brief constructed response, with specific support.

CHOICES

As you respond to the Choices, use these **Academic Vocabulary** words as appropriate: approach, convince, dominate, enhance, participate.

REVIEW
Compare Diary and Blog
With a partner, use the Internet to visit the Web site where Phil Gyford is posting Samuel Pepys's diaries in weblog form. Find an entry that interests you and read it closely. Click on some of the links in the entry. Discuss with your partner how does this experience differs from reading a printed diary entry like the one on page 546. Then, read the comments that blog visitors have added to the diary entry. Discuss this experience with your partner. How does it enhance your appreciation of what Pepys wrote in the entry itself?

CONNECT
Log On
Use a search engine to locate Gyford's blog. Read the current entries posted, and then participate further by adding a comment, perhaps to explain a word or reference in the entry or to answer another reader's question. You may also wish to ask a question of your own and see how others in this "book club" respond.

The Diary Today
TechFocus Phil Gyford brought Pepys's diary into the modern age by transforming it into a blog. What other forms might a modern version of the diary take? In a small group, turn Pepys's diary entry on pages 546–547 into another form in which a modern person might share a similar personal experience: for example, a digital story, a video diary, or even a series of cellphone text messages. Share your updated version of Pepys's diary with your class.

EXTEND
Diary and Poem
British poet John Dryden wrote a poem about the year 1666 in London, including the excerpt below about the Great Fire. Read the stanzas closely that depict the panic triggered by the spreading fire. With a small group, discuss the following question: How does Dryden's imagery enhance what you learned about the fire from Pepys (pages 546–547)?

---

from **Annus Mirabilis: The Year of Wonders**

At length the crackling noise and dreadful blaze
    Call'd up some waking lover to the sight;
And long it was ere he the rest could raise,
    Whose heavy eyelids yet were full of night.

The next to danger, hot pursued by fate,
    Half-clothed, half-naked, hastily retire:
And frighted mothers strike their breasts too late,
    For helpless infants left amidst the fire.

Their cries soon waken all the dwellers near;
    Now murmuring noises rise in every street:
The more remote run stumbling with their fear,
    And in the dark men jostle as they meet.

Paintings of the Great Fire
Timed Writing Study the painting of the Great Fire of London on page 547. How does it add to what you learned from the Pepys diary entry and the Dryden stanzas above? Write an essay responding to the following question: Which of the three depictions of the fire is the most effective, and why? Cite examples.

Preparing to Read

from A Journal of the Plague Year

What Do You Think?

How can order and civilization affect human behavior?

QuickWrite

Science fiction often depicts plagues or bio-terrorist plots that use contagious diseases as a weapon. Why do human beings find that so frightening? Do you consider this a science fiction plot or a real threat? Write a paragraph in your *Reader/Writer Notebook,* explaining your perspective.

MEET THE WRITER

Daniel Defoe
(1660–1731)

A skillful journalist and pamphleteer, Defoe wrote hundreds of works. We remember Defoe chiefly for the writing he produced late in life, *Robinson Crusoe* and *Moll Flanders,* books we now consider early examples of the realistic English novel.

A Crowded Career

Defoe had a complicated career and was at various times a tradesman, a political agent, a reformer, and a journalist. Born Daniel Foe, he added the aristocratic prefix *De* to his name when he was about thirty-five. As a Dissenter, a Nonconformist who did not belong to the Anglican Church, Defoe was barred from attending Oxford or Cambridge University. Nevertheless, he received an excellent education at a Dissenters' academy. As a merchant dealing in wool, real estate, diving bells, and other commodities, he made and lost fortunes. He participated in politics, sometimes offending the government, at other times serving as a spy or propagandist. Throughout these experiences, he wrote frequently—all together over five hundred works, in prose and verse, including a news pamphlet, *The Review,* which he published three times a week for over seven years. He addressed a broad range of subjects, including the choosing of a wife, the history of the devil, and the manufacture of glass.

Fiction or Nonfiction?

Defoe penned his best-known tales after years of writing as a journalist. Though fiction, *Robinson Crusoe, Moll Flanders,* and *A Journal of the Plague Year* appear to be true autobiographical accounts. Defoe's plain, vigorous style suits his characters and subject matter well. He uses idiomatic English and fills his stories with detailed practical knowledge. For *A Journal of the Plague Year,* presented as an eyewitness account of the London plague of 1665, Defoe sought convincing details in reports, pamphlets, mortality records, and sermons from the time of the plague, and in the memories of his uncle, Henry Foe (perhaps the H. F. who narrates the journal). A masterpiece, the *Journal* is a realistic work of fiction that grips readers even today.

Think About the Writer What current or recent events might appeal to Defoe as sources for a fictional journal or a realistic novel?

Portrait of Daniel Defoe

 **Reader/Writer**
Notebook
Use your **RWN** to complete the activities for this selection.

Literary Focus

Narrative Voice A **narrator** is the storyteller in a work of fiction. *A Journal of the Plague Year* has a first-person narrator who sees and <u>participates</u> in the events described. The narrator's voice or character is revealed through the subject matter, the tone, and the narrator's language.

Less personal and intimate than a diary, a **journal** is a record of events kept regularly by a person who sees or takes part in the events—is The words *journalism* and *journal* are related. Like newspapers, journals report facts. Journals also record the writer's reaction to events. As you read, think about how you would describe the narrator's voice. What does he think about his subject, and how does he express his thoughts?

Reading Focus

Making Critical Judgments Defoe creates a character, H. F., to report his experiences of the plague. As you read, you will critically judge this character's nature, beliefs, and credibility. To judge critically is not to correct or complain about a work; rather, it is to analyze what the narrator says and how, when, and why he says it.

Into Action Use a chart like the one below to note what details the narrator relates, whether they are facts or reactions, and why the narrator chooses to include them.

Detail H. F. Relates	Fact or Reaction?	Why H. F. Includes the Detail
how the plague spread	H. F. thinks it's a fact	to inform but also to build credibility

Writing Focus

Think as a Reader/Writer
Find It in Your Reading Defoe uses dialogue to capture what H. F. overhears in Bell Alley. In your *Reader/Writer Notebook,* note details in the dialogue and the description surrounding the dialogue that make the passage vivid. How does Defoe's use of dialogue and description of what H. F. hears affect the account and its narrative voice?

Vocabulary

infect (ihn FEHKT) *v.:* spread a disease to. *Londoners believed contact with the sick could infect the healthy.*

proportion (pruh POHR shuhn) *n.:* ratio; relative amount. *The proportion of Londoners sick with the plague decreased as people fled to the country.*

consequently (KAHN suh kwehnt lee) *adv.:* as a result of something. *H. F. had to go to his brother's house in the city; consequently, he passed houses where people were sick.*

credible (KREHD uh buhl) *adj.:* believable. *The journal's many details of London life during the plague make the account credible.*

torment (TAWR mehnt) *n.:* great pain. *What torment the survivors of the plague suffered as they grieved lost friends!*

quarantine (KWAWR uhn teen) *n.:* enforced isolation of ill people to prevent the spread of sickness. *Placing people in quarantine did not stop the spread of plague because rats carried the disease.*

Language Coach

Word Origins The word *quarantine* comes from the Italian word for *forty*. In the 14th century, there was a rule in Italy that ships from other nations had to wait forty days before they could unload passengers or cargo. What might have inspired this rule? How does this word origin help you remember the meaning of *quarantine*?

 Learn It Online
Use Word Watch online to meet these words these Vocabulary words the interactive way.

go.hrw.com | L12-557 | **Go**

from A Journal of the Plague Year

by Daniel Defoe

Read with a Purpose
Read to learn how the fear of infectious disease and death can affect daily life.

Build Background
A Journal of the Plague Year is set in 1665, during the last terrible visitation of the bubonic plague in London. (Pepys survived and recorded the event in his *Diary*.) When Defoe published his work in 1722, the plague had reappeared in Europe, reaching Marseilles in France. Fearful that merchant ships would bring infection to England, the English government placed a temporary embargo on shipping. Although nearly sixty years had been enough time for the English to lose their fear of the plague, Defoe's *Journal*—possibly published at his government's request—reminded them of its terrors. The *Journal's* narrator identifies himself only as "H. F.," a citizen of London.

1. The Infection Spreads

Here the opinion of the physicians agreed with my observation afterward, namely, that the danger was spreading insensibly, for the sick could infect none but those that came within reach of the sick person; but that one man who may have really received the infection and knows it not, but goes abroad and about as a sound person, may give the plague to a thousand people, and they to greater numbers in proportion, and neither the person giving the infection or the persons receiving it know anything of it, and perhaps not feel the effects of it for several days after. **Ⓐ**

For example, many persons in the time of this visitation never perceived that they were infected till they found to their unspeakable surprise, the tokens come out upon them; after which they seldom lived six hours; for those spots they called the tokens were really gangrene spots, or mortified flesh[1] in small knobs as broad as a little silver penny, and hard as a piece of callus or horn; so that, when the disease was come up to that length, there was nothing could follow but certain death; and yet, as I said, they knew nothing of their being infected, nor found themselves so much as out of order, till those mortal[2] marks were upon them. But everybody must allow that they were infected in a high degree before, and must have been so some time, and consequently their breath, their sweat, their very clothes, were contagious for many days before. . . .

2. Dismal Scenes

I had some little obligations, indeed, upon me to go to my brother's house, which was in Coleman Street[3]

---

1. **gangrene . . . flesh:** decay of soft tissues from a blockage of blood flow.
2. **mortal:** fatal.
3. **Coleman Street:** This place and other places Defoe names are all within the old City of London, unless otherwise noted.

Ⓐ **Literary Focus** Narrative Voice How does H. F. lend his own narrative voice authority in this paragraph?

Vocabulary **infect** (ihn FEHKT) *v.:* spread a disease to.
proportion (pruh POHR shuhn) *n.:* ratio; relative amount.
consequently (KAHN suh kwehnt lee) *adv.:* as a result of something.

Multituds flying from London by water in boats & barges.

Flying by land.

Burying the dead with a bell before them.   Searchers

Carts full of dead to bury.

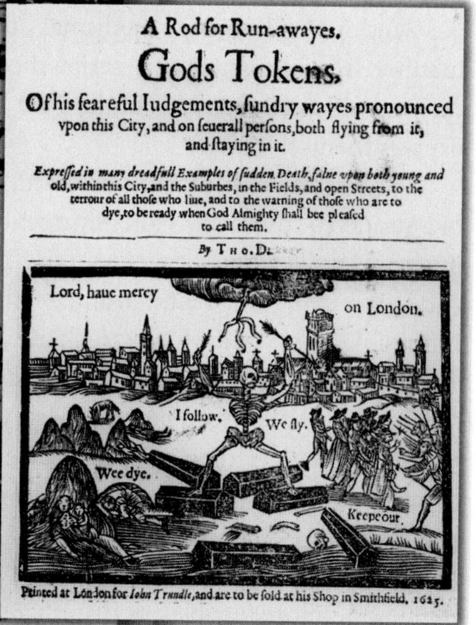

God's Tokens, A Rod for Runaways (1625), woodcut.
The Granger Collection, NY.

A Rod for Run-awayes.
Gods Tokens.
Of his fearefull Iudgements, sundry wayes pronounced vpon this City, and on seuerall persons, both flying from it, and staying in it.

Expressed in many dreadfull Examples of sudden Death, falne vpon both young and old, within this City, and the Suburbes, in the Fields, and open Streets, to the terrour of all those who liue, and to the warning of those who are to dye, to be ready when God Almighty shall bee pleased to call them.

By Tho. D——

Lord, haue mercy   on London.

I follow.   We fly.

Wee dye.   Keepe our

Printed at London for *Iohn Trundle*, and are to be sold at his Shop in Smithfield. 1625.

Analyzing Visuals

Viewing and Interpreting
How do the images and captions convey the terror and magnitude of the plague Defoe describes in the selection?

Aspects of the Great Plague of London, 1665.

parish and which he had left to my care, and I went at first every day, but afterward only once or twice a week.

In these walks I had many dismal scenes before my eyes, as particularly of persons falling dead in the streets, terrible shrieks and screechings of women, who, in their agonies, would throw open their chamber windows and cry out in a dismal, surprising manner. It is impossible to describe the variety of postures in which the passions of the poor people would express themselves.

Passing through Tokenhouse Yard, in Lothbury, of a sudden a casement[4] violently opened just over my head, and a woman gave three frightful screeches, and then cried, "Oh! death, death, death!" in a most inimitable[5] tone, and which struck me with horror and a chillness in my very blood. There was nobody to be seen in the whole street, neither did any other window open, for people had no curiosity now in any case, nor could anybody help one another, so I went on to pass into Bell Alley. **B** **C**

Just in Bell Alley, on the right hand of the passage, there was a more terrible cry than that, though it was not so directed out at the window; but the whole family was in a terrible fright, and I could hear women and children run screaming about the rooms like distracted, when a garret[6] window opened and somebody from a window on the other side the alley called and asked, "What is the matter?" upon which, from the first window, it was answered, "Oh Lord, my old master has hanged himself!" The other asked again, "Is he quite dead?" and the first answered, "Ay, ay, quite dead; quite dead and cold!" This person was a merchant and a deputy alderman, and very rich. I care not to mention the name, though I knew his name too, but that would be an hardship to the family, which is now flourishing again.

---

4. **casement:** hinged window.
5. **inimitable:** difficult or impossible to imitate.
6. **garret:** attic.

B **Literary Focus** Narrative Voice In what tone does H. F. report the terrible sights he encounters as he walks about the city? How does this tone help create narrative voice?

C **Reading Focus** Making Critical Judgments Comment on or expand upon H. F.'s explanation for the absence of a reaction from anyone else to the cries of the woman at Tokenhouse Yard.

But this is but one; it is scarce credible what dreadful cases happened in particular families every day. People in the rage of the distemper, or in the torment of their swellings, which was indeed intolerable, running out of their own government,[7] raving and distracted, and oftentimes laying violent hands upon themselves, throwing themselves out at their windows, shooting themselves, etc.; mothers murdering their own children in their lunacy,[8] some dying of mere grief as a passion, some of mere fright and surprise without any infection at all, others frighted into idiotism and foolish distractions, some into despair and lunacy, others into melancholy madness.

The pain of the swelling was in particular very violent, and to some intolerable; the physicians and surgeons may be said to have tortured many poor creatures even to death. The swellings in some grew hard, and they applied violent drawing plasters or poultices[9] to break them, and if these did not do they cut and scarified[10] them in a terrible manner. In some those swellings were made hard partly by the force of the distemper and partly by their being too violently drawn, and were so hard that no instrument could cut them, and then they burnt them with caustics,[11] so that many died raving mad with the torment, and some in the very operation. In these distresses, some, for want of help to hold them down in their beds, or to look to them, laid hands upon themselves as above. Some broke out into the streets, perhaps naked, and would run directly down to the river if they were not stopped by the watchman or other officers, and plunge themselves into the water wherever they found it.

It often pierced my very soul to hear the groans and cries of those who were thus tormented, but of the two this was counted the most promising particular in the whole infection, for if these swellings

---

7. **out of their own government:** unable to control themselves.
8. **lunacy:** madness.
9. **drawing plasters or poultices:** hot packs used to soften sores and draw infection to the skin's surface.
10. **scarified:** punctured.
11. **caustics:** chemicals that can burn or eat away flesh.

Vocabulary **credible** (KREHD uh buhl) *adj.:* believable.
torment (TAWR mehnt) *n.:* great pain.

---

could be brought to a head, and to break and run, or, as the surgeons call it, to digest, the patient generally recovered; whereas those who, like the gentlewoman's daughter, were struck with death at the beginning, and had the tokens come out upon them, often went about indifferent easy till a little before they died, and some till the moment they dropped down, as in apoplexies[12] and epilepsies is often the case. Such would be taken suddenly very sick, and would run to a bench or bulk,[13] or any convenient place that offered itself, or to their own houses if possible, as I mentioned before, and there sit down, grow faint, and die. This kind of dying was much the same as it was with those who die of common mortifications,[14] who die swooning, and, as it were, go away in a dream. Such as died thus had very little notice of their being infected at all till the gangrene was spread through their whole body; nor could physicians themselves know certainly how it was with them till they opened their breasts or other parts of their body and saw the tokens. **Ⓓ**

3. Escape from Quarantine

I remember one citizen who, having thus broken out of his house in Aldersgate Street or thereabout, went along the road to Islington;[15] he attempted to have gone in at the Angel Inn, and after that the White Horse, two inns known still by the same signs, but was refused; after which he came to the Pied Bull, an inn also still continuing the same sign. He asked them for lodging for one night only, pretending to be going into Lincolnshire,[16] and assuring them of his being very sound and free from the infection, which also at that time had not reached much that way.

They told him they had no lodging that they could spare but one bed up in the garret, and that they could spare that bed for one night, some drovers being expected the next day with cattle; so, if he would accept of that lodging, he might have it, which he did. So a servant was sent up with a candle with him to show him the room. He was very well dressed, and looked like a person not used to lie in a garret; and when he came to the room he fetched a deep sigh, and said to the servant, "I have seldom lain in such a lodging as this." However, the servant assuring him again that they had no better, "Well," says he, "I must make shift; this is a dreadful time; but it is but for one night." So he sat down upon the bedside, and bade the maid, I think it was, fetch him up a pint of warm ale. Accordingly the servant went for the ale, but some hurry in the house, which perhaps employed her other ways, put it out of her head, and she went up no more to him.

The next morning, seeing no appearance of the gentleman, somebody in the house asked the servant that had showed him upstairs what was become of him. She started. "Alas!" says she, "I never thought more of him. He bade me carry him some warm ale, but I forgot." Upon which, not the maid, but some other person was sent up to see after him, who, coming into the room, found him stark dead and almost cold, stretched out across the bed. His clothes were pulled off, his jaw fallen, his eyes open in a most frightful posture, the rug of the bed being grasped hard in one of his hands, so that it was plain he died soon after the maid left him; and 'tis probable, had she gone up with the ale, she had found him dead in a few minutes after he sat down upon the bed. The alarm was great in the house, as anyone may suppose, they having been free from the distemper till that disaster, which, bringing the infection to the house, spread it immediately to other houses round about it. . . . **Ⓔ**

---

12. **apoplexies:** strokes.
13. **bulk:** archaic word for a low stall projecting from a wall or storefront.
14. **mortifications:** archaic word for gangrene.
15. **Islington:** suburb north of London.

---

16. **Lincolnshire:** county on the east coast of England.

Ⓓ **Literary Focus** **Narrative Voice** What emotions does H. F. convey as he lists the effects of the plague on the people? What might his purpose in conveying these emotions be?

Vocabulary **quarantine** (KWAWR uhn teen) *n.*: enforced isolation of ill people to prevent the spread of sickness.

Ⓔ **Reading Focus** **Making Critical Judgments** In this entry, rather than describing numerous cases of suffering, H. F. tells at length the story of one man. What does H. F. gain by changing his approach in this passage?

from **A Journal of the Plague Year**

Respond and Think Critically

Reading Focus

QuickCheck

1. What were the symptoms of the plague?

2. Why does H. F. risk infection to go into the city?

3. What attempts were made to cure people?

4. Why doesn't the maid take ale to the lodger?

Read with a Purpose

5. How does the fear of infectious disease affect many Londoners? How does it affect H. F.?

Reading Skills: Making Critical Judgments

6. Defoe's description of the plague in London appears to be nonfiction but is actually historical fiction. As you read, you recorded and analyzed details. In a new column of your chart, judge whether the detail increases the journalistic (nonfiction) tone of the entries, builds the fictional story of the entries, or both.

Detail H. F. Relates	Fact or Reaction?	Why H. F. Includes the Detail	Nonfiction and Fiction
how the plague spread	H. F. thinks it's a fact	to inform but also to build credibility	nonfiction—this detail sounds clinical and scientific and makes the entry sound serious, like a report

Literary Focus

Literary Analysis

7. **Analyze** What effect does Defoe create by using the first-person point of view? Cite examples from the text to support your response.

8. **Infer** What can you infer about H. F.'s opinion of the man who escaped from quarantine?

9. **Extend** What is meant by "morbid curiosity"? Does H. F. possess this kind of curiosity? Where does morbid curiosity appear in modern life?

Literary Skills: Narrative Voice

10. **Analyze** H. F. concludes his journal with these lines: "A dreadful plague in London was / In the year sixty-five, / Which swept an hundred thousand souls / Away; yet I alive!" What amazement does H. F. express toward his subject in these lines?

Literary Skills Review: Tone

11. **Analyze** How might the journal's **tone,** the writer's attitude toward the events he is recounting, have been different if the work actually had been written during the London plague?

Writing Focus

Think as a Reader/Writer

Use It in Your Writing You have noted how Defoe uses dialogue and the description surrounding the dialogue to make an account vivid and to shape the narrative voice. Now, write your own narrative paragraph about an important event in your life. Use vivid descriptions and interesting, expressive dialogue.

 What Do You Think Now

What might have been the response of Londoners to the inability of city physicians and authorities to treat suffering victims or stop the spread of the plague?

Vocabulary Development

Vocabulary Check

Match the Vocabulary words with their definitions.

1. infect
2. proportion
3. consequently
4. credible
5. torment
6. quarantine

a. isolation for health reasons
b. sicken; contaminate
c. convincing; likely
d. therefore; thus
e. suffering
f. ratio

Vocabulary Skills: Analogies

In a word **analogy,** the relationship between the first pair of words is the same as the relationship between the second pair of words. Look at the pair of words below:

GREEN LIGHT : GO :: RED LIGHT : STOP

This is an abbreviated way of saying:

A green light has the same relationship to the action of going as a red light has to the action of stopping.

The analogy form shows the relationship and allows you to extend the analogy to another similar idea:

GREEN LIGHT : GO :: RED LIGHT : STOP :: YELLOW LIGHT : PREPARE TO STOP

Analogies help you learn new vocabulary because they show you how words are related to other words that you already know. Here's another example:

CREDIBLE : BELIEVABLE :: CREDULOUS : BELIEVING

You know that *credible* and *believable* are synonyms, and you can see that *credulous,* having the same root as *credible,* probably has a meaning related to *credible.* This analogy confirms your guess: *Credulous* has the same relationship to *believing* as *credible* has to *believable:* they're synonyms.

Your Turn

For each Vocabulary word, construct an analogy to broaden your understanding of the word. Analogies can point out many kinds of relationships: similarities and differences, actors and actions, tools and uses, synonyms and antonyms, and so on. Complete the table below, using a variety of relationships. Be prepared to explain the relationship each analogy demonstrates.

| word | : | word | :: | word | : | word |

Language Coach

Word Origins Choose the phrase you think describes the origin of each word below. Check your answers with a dictionary.

1. torment
    a. from the Latin word for *twist*
    b. from the Latin word for *wind*
2. infect
    a. from the Latin word for *move*
    b. from the Latin word for *spoil*
3. credible
    a. from the Latin word for *trust*
    b. from the Latin word for *true*

Academic Vocabulary

Talk About
With a partner, compare modern <u>approaches</u> to infectious disease with the responses Defoe records. What factors <u>enhance</u> our modern understanding of disease?

Preparing to Read

from Gulliver's Travels

A Modest Proposal

What Do You Think?
How can order and civilization affect human behavior?

QuickWrite

Think about social problems in your community or in the world in general. In your *Reader/Writer Notebook*, write down a list of social problems that you consider to be most in need of attention.

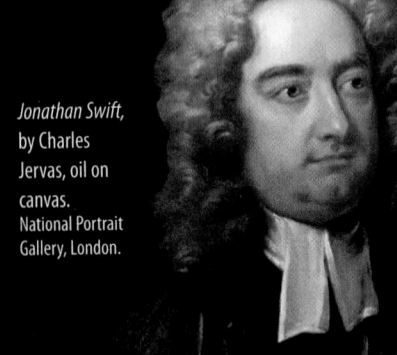

Jonathan Swift, by Charles Jervas, oil on canvas. National Portrait Gallery, London.

Jonathan Swift
(1667–1745)

Jonathan Swift is the principal prose writer of the early eighteenth century and England's greatest satirist. He once said that the secret of good prose is "proper words in proper places." He is a master of precise and clear writing.

Both Irish and English

Jonathan Swift was born in Dublin, Ireland, to English parents. His father died seven months before his birth, at which time Swift was abducted by his nurse. He spent three years in England before being returned to Ireland, where he was cared for by his uncle. He regarded himself as more English than Irish.

After studying at Trinity College, Dublin, Swift went to England, where he worked as a private secretary to Sir William Temple, a distant relative, writer, and wealthy statesman. Swift hoped his relationship to Temple would <u>enhance</u> his own chances for a political career in England, but that never came to pass. Eventually Swift received a master's degree from Oxford University and was ordained a priest. Although he wanted to be made an English bishop, the only appointment he could get was back in Ireland as the dean of St. Patrick's Cathedral in Dublin. Swift returned to his native city, was installed as dean, and held that office for the remaining thirty years of his life.

National Hero

Swift did not write for fame or money. His aim in writing was to improve human conduct, to make people more decent and humane toward one another. *Gulliver's Travels* (1726) attacks many different varieties of human misbehavior, vice, and folly. Swift's experiences in Ireland gave him firsthand knowledge of the abject poverty and suffering of the lower classes. Swift even became an Irish patriot in his pamphlets, defending the Irish against the oppressive policies of their English rulers. In *A Modest Proposal* (1729), his most famous pamphlet, he uses irony to offer an outrageous solution to Irish poverty.

Think About the Writer
How do you think Swift's ties to both England and Ireland influenced his perspective on the social issues of his time?

from Gulliver's Travels

Reader/Writer Notebook

Use your **RWN** to complete the activities for this selection.

Literary Focus

Situational Irony When what actually happens is the opposite of what is expected or appropriate, we say that **situational irony** occurs. "The Necklace," a short story by Guy de Maupassant, contains a famous example of situational irony: A couple struggle for years to pay for an expensive diamond necklace they have lost only to discover that it was made of paste. Situational irony, which is often accompanied by surprise, reminds us that life is unpredictable.

Reading Focus

Analyzing an Author's Purpose Swift uses **satire** to make fun of human weakness, vice, and folly, hoping to motivate his readers to change themselves and society. In "A Voyage to Lilliput," his target is political institutions. For example, the politicians in Lilliput obtain their positions by dancing on a tightrope. What does this say about Swift's opinion of politicians? of his country's political system?

Into Action As you read, use a chart like the one below. List important events, actions, or images in the first column. In the second column, explain what Swift is suggesting through each event, action, or image?

Event, Action, Image	Institution	Satirical Point
Gulliver is entertained by rope dancers.	politics	These political leaders "danced" around issues instead of solving the country's problems.

Vocabulary

conjectured (kuhn JEHK chuhrd) *v.*: reasoned; guessed. *When Gulliver first saw a Lilliputian, he conjectured that the rest of the population must be about the same size.*

schism (SKIHZ uhm) *n.*: division. *The disagreement caused a schism between Lilliput and Blefuscu.*

quelled (kwehld) *v.*: subdued. *The troops quelled the civil uprising of the protesters.*

copious (KOH pee uhs) *adj.*: wordy; profuse. *Gulliver gave the King and Queen a copious amount of information about England.*

odious (OH dee uhs) *adj.*: hateful; offensive. *Despite Gulliver's efforts to be likable, the King still called him an "odious vermin."*

Language Coach

Verb Tenses When learning a verb in the past tense, be sure also to learn the present tense form. *Conjecture,* the present tense of *conjectured,* takes a *–d* to form the past tense. Note, however, that *quelled* (present tense, *quell*) has assumed an *–ed.*

Writing Focus

Think as a Reader/Writer

Find It in Your Reading In *Gulliver's Travels,* Swift uses **satire** to expose the follies and vices of human behavior. As you read, take note of the words and images he uses to emphasize the extremes he sees in people and record them in your *Reader/Writer Notebook.*

Learn It Online
Find out more about Jonathan Swift with this online biography.

go.hrw.com L12-573 **Go**

from *Gulliver's Travels*

from **Part 1:** A Voyage to Lilliput

by **Jonathan Swift**

Read with a Purpose
Read to discover what Gulliver's travels reveal about human nature.

Build Background
Swift's best-known work, *Gulliver's Travels,* was published anonymously in 1726 under the original title of *Travels into Several Remote Nations of the World.* The narrator, Lemuel Gulliver, is a well-meaning but simple Englishman who describes innocently whatever he sees. Gulliver is aptly named, for a *gull* was a term for someone easily duped, or gullible. It is up to the reader to see the truths that Gulliver misses.

The first voyage, describing the visit to Lilliput, opens with an account of Gulliver's early life: his birth, parentage, and scholarship. After studying medicine, Gulliver becomes a ship's doctor and embarks on a long voyage; when the ship breaks up in a storm somewhere in the South Pacific, he manages to swim ashore and, exhausted, falls into a deep sleep.

I lay down on the grass, which was very short and soft, where I slept sounder than ever I remember to have done in my life, and, as I reckoned, above nine hours; for when I awaked, it was just daylight. I attempted to rise, but was not able to stir: For as I happened to lie on my back, I found my arms and legs were strongly fastened on each side to the ground; and my hair, which was long and thick, tied down in the same manner. I likewise felt several slender ligatures[1] across

---

1. **ligatures:** ties or bonds.

my body, from my armpits to my thighs. I could only look upward; the sun began to grow hot, and the light offended my eyes. I heard a confused noise about me, but in the posture I lay, could see nothing except the sky.

In a little time I felt something alive moving on my left leg, which advancing gently forward over my breast, came almost up to my chin; when bending my eyes downward as much as I could, I perceived it to be a human creature not six inches high, with a bow and arrow in his hands, and a quiver at his back. In the meantime, I felt at least forty more of the same kind (as I conjectured) following the first. I was in the utmost astonishment, and roared so loud, that they all ran back in a fright; and some of them, as I was afterward told, were hurt with the falls they got by leaping from my sides upon the ground. However, they soon returned, and one of them, who ventured so far as to get a full sight of my face, lifting up his hands and eyes

Vocabulary **conjectured** (kuhn JEHK chuhrd) *v.:* reasoned; guessed.

by way of admiration, cried out in a shrill, but distinct voice, *Hekinah degul:*[2] The others repeated the same words several times, but then I knew not what they meant. I lay all this while, as the reader may believe, in great uneasiness: At length, struggling to get loose, I had the fortune to break the strings, and wrench out the pegs that fastened my left arm to the ground; for, by lifting it up to my face, I discovered the methods they had taken to bind me, and at the same time with a violent pull, which gave me excessive pain, I a little loosened the strings that tied down my hair on the left side, so that I was just able to turn my head about two inches. But the creatures ran off a second time, before I could seize them; whereupon there was a great shout in a very shrill accent, and after it ceased, I heard one of them cry aloud, *Tolgo phonac;* when in an instant I felt above an hundred arrows discharged on my left hand, which pricked me like so many needles; and

besides, they shot another flight into the air, as we do bombs in Europe, whereof many, I suppose, fell on my body (though I felt them not), and some on my face, which I immediately covered with my left hand. When this shower of arrows was over, I fell a-groaning with grief and pain, and then striving again to get loose, they discharged another volley larger than the first, and some of them attempted with spears to stick me in the sides; but, by good luck, I had on me a buff jerkin,[3] which they could not pierce. I thought it the most prudent method to lie still, and my design was to continue so till night, when, my left hand being already loose, I could easily free myself: And as for the inhabitants, I had reason to believe I might be a match for the greatest armies they could bring against me, if they were all of the same size with him that I saw. But fortune disposed otherwise of me. Ⓐ

---

2. **Hekinah degul:** This and other examples of the Lilliputian language are mainly nonsense words.

3. **buff jerkin:** short, close-fitting leather jacket, often without sleeves.

Ⓐ **Literary Focus** Situational Irony What is ironic about the soldiers' actions toward Gulliver?

Television production of Gulliver's Travels.

When the people observed I was quiet, they discharged no more arrows; but, by the noise increasing, I knew their numbers were greater; and about four yards from me, over against my right ear, I heard a knocking for above an hour, like that of people at work; when turning my head that way, as well as the pegs and strings would permit me, I saw a stage erected, about a foot and a half from the ground, capable of holding four of the inhabitants, with two or three ladders to mount it: From whence one of them, who seemed to be a person of quality, made me a long speech, whereof I understood not one syllable. But I should have mentioned, that before the principal person began his oration, he cried out three times, *Langro dehul san* (these words and the former were afterward repeated and explained to me). Whereupon immediately about fifty of the inhabitants came and cut the strings that fastened the left side of my head, which gave me the liberty of turning it to the right, and of observing the person and gesture of him who was to speak. He appeared to be of a middle age, and taller than any of the other three who attended him, whereof one was a page who held up his train, and seemed to be somewhat longer than my middle finger; the other two stood one on each side to support him. He acted every part of an orator, and I could observe many periods of threatenings, and others of promises, pity, and kindness.

I answered in a few words, but in the most submissive manner, lifting up my left hand, and both my eyes to the sun, as calling him for a witness; and being almost famished with hunger, having not eaten a morsel for some hours before I left the ship. I found the demands of nature so strong upon me, that I could not forbear showing my impatience (perhaps against the strict rules of decency) by putting my finger frequently on my mouth, to signify that I wanted food. The *Hurgo*[4] (for so they call a great lord, as I afterward learnt) understood me very well. He descended from the stage, and commanded that several ladders should be applied to my sides, on which above an hundred of the inhabitants mounted and walked toward my mouth, laden with baskets full of meat,[5] which had been provided and sent thither by the King's orders, upon the first intelligence he received of me. I observed there was the flesh[6] of several animals, but could not distinguish them by the taste. There were shoulders, legs, and loins, shaped like those of mutton, and very well dressed, but smaller than the wings of a lark. I ate them by two or three at a mouthful, and took three loaves at a time, about the bigness of musket bullets. They supplied me as fast as they could, showing a thousand marks of wonder and astonishment at my bulk and appetite. **Ⓑ**

I then made another sign that I wanted drink. They found by my eating, that a small quantity would not suffice me; and being a most ingenious people, they slung up with great dexterity one of their largest hogsheads,[7] then rolled it toward my hand, and beat out the top; I drank it off at a draft, which I might well do, for it hardly held half a pint, and tasted like a small wine of Burgundy, but much more delicious. They brought me a second hogshead, which I drank in the same manner, and made signs for more, but they had none to give me. When I had performed these wonders, they shouted for joy, and danced upon my breast, repeating several times as they did at first, *Hekinah degul.* They made me a sign that I should throw down the two hogsheads, but first warned the people below to stand out of the way, crying aloud, *Borach mivola,* and when they saw the vessels in the air, there was an universal shout of *Hekinah degul.* I confess I was often tempted, while they were passing backward and forward on my body, to seize forty or fifty of the first that came in my reach, and dash them against the ground. But the remembrance of what I had felt, which probably might not be the worst they could do, and the

---

4. ***Hurgo:*** This Lilliputian word is perhaps a partial anagram (a word formed by rearranging the letters of another word) of the English word *rogue.* It would be characteristic of Swift to call a "great lord" a rogue.

---

5. **meat:** food.
6. **flesh:** meat.
7. **hogsheads:** barrels.

Ⓑ **Literary Focus** **Situational Irony** What is ironic about the Lilliputians feeding Gulliver?

> ## "When I had performed these wonders, they shouted for joy, and danced upon my breast."

Television production of Gulliver's Travels.

promise of honor I made them, for so I interpreted my submissive behavior, soon drove out those imaginations. Besides, I now considered myself as bound by the laws of hospitality to a people who had treated me with so much expense and magnificence. However, in my thoughts, I could not sufficiently wonder at the intrepidity of these diminutive mortals, who durst venture to mount and walk on my body, while one of my hands was at liberty, without trembling at the very sight of so prodigious a creature as I must appear to them. **C**

After some time, when they observed that I made no more demands for meat, there appeared before me a person of high rank from his Imperial Majesty. His Excellency, having mounted on the small of my right leg, advanced forward up to my face, with about a dozen of his retinue. And producing his credentials under the Signet Royal,[8] which he applied close to

my eyes, spoke about ten minutes, without any signs of anger, but with a kind of determinate resolution; often pointing forward, which, as I afterward found, was toward the capital city, about half a mile distant, whither it was agreed by his Majesty in council that I must be conveyed. I answered in few words, but to no purpose, and made a sign with my hand that was loose, putting it to the other (but over his Excellency's head for fear of hurting him or his train) and then to my own head and body, to signify that I desired my liberty. It appeared that he understood me well enough, for he shook his head by way of disapprobation, and held his hand in a posture to show that I must be carried as a prisoner. However, he made other

---

8. **Signet Royal:** royal seal that marks official documents.

C **Reading Focus** Analyzing an Author's Purpose
Gulliver imagines himself hurting the Lilliputians but restrains himself.
What point might Swift be making here?

signs to let me understand that I should have meat and drink enough, and very good treatment. Whereupon I once more thought of attempting to break my bonds; but again, when I felt the smart of their arrows, upon my face and hands, which were all in blisters, and many of the darts still sticking in them, and observing likewise that the number of my enemies increased, I gave tokens[9] to let them know that they might do with me what they pleased. Upon this, the *Hurgo* and his train withdrew, with much civility and cheerful countenances.

Soon after I heard a general shout, with frequent repetitions of the words, *Peplom selan,* and I felt great numbers of people on my left side relaxing the cords to such a degree, that I was able to turn upon my right, and to ease myself with making water; which I very plentifully did, to the great astonishment of the people, who conjecturing by my motions what I was going to do, immediately opened to the right and left on that side, to avoid the torrent which fell with such noise and violence from me. But before this, they had daubed my face and both my hands with a sort of ointment very pleasant to the smell, which in a few minutes removed all the smart of their arrows. These circumstances, added to the refreshment I had received by their victuals and drink, which were very nourishing, disposed me to sleep. I slept about eight hours, as I was afterward assured; and it was no wonder, for the physicians, by the Emperor's order, had mingled a sleeping potion in the hogshead of wine. ... **D**

My gentleness and good behavior had gained so far on the Emperor and his court, and indeed upon the army and people in general, that I began to conceive hopes of getting my liberty in a short time. I took all possible methods to cultivate this favorable disposition. The natives came by degrees to be less apprehensive of any danger from me. I would sometimes lie down, and let five or six of them dance on my hand. And at last the boys and girls would venture to come and play at hide-and-seek in my hair. I had now made

a good progress in understanding and speaking their language. The Emperor had a mind one day to entertain me with several of the country shows, wherein they exceed all nations I have known, both for dexterity and magnificence. I was diverted with none so much as that of the rope dancers,[10] performed upon a slender white thread, extended about two foot, and twelve inches from the ground. Upon which I shall desire liberty, with the reader's patience, to enlarge a little.

This diversion is only practiced by those persons who are candidates for great employments, and high favor, at court. They are trained in this art from their youth, and are not always of noble birth, or liberal education. When a great office is vacant, either by death or disgrace (which often happens), five or six of those candidates petition the Emperor to entertain his Majesty and the court with a dance on the rope, and whoever jumps the highest without falling, succeeds in the office. Very often the chief ministers themselves are commanded to show their skill, and to convince the Emperor that they have not lost their faculty. Flimnap, the Treasurer, is allowed to cut a caper on the straight rope, at least an inch higher than any other lord in the whole empire. I have seen him do the summerset[11] several times together upon a trencher fixed on the rope, which is no thicker than a common packthread[12] in England. My friend Reldresal, principal Secretary for Private Affairs, is, in my opinion, if I am not partial, the second after the Treasurer; the rest of the great officers are much upon a par. **E**

These diversions are often attended with fatal accidents, whereof great numbers are on record. I myself have seen two or three candidates break a limb. But the danger is much greater when the ministers themselves are commanded to show their dexterity; for, by contending to excel themselves and their fellows, they strain so far, that there is hardly one of them who hath

---

9. **gave tokens:** signaled.

10. **rope dancers:** tightrope dancers.
11. **summerset:** somersault.
12. **packthread:** twine.

D **Reading Focus** Analyzing an Author's Purpose What might be Swift's purpose for including this humorous scene?

E **Reading Focus** Analyzing an Author's Purpose Gulliver is impressed by the officeholders' rope-dancing skills instead of by their skills as government ministers. What might Swift be telling the reader about politicians?

not received a fall, and some of them two or three. I was assured that a year or two before my arrival, Flimnap would have infallibly broke his neck, if one of the King's cushions, that accidentally lay on the ground, had not weakened the force of his fall.

There is likewise another diversion, which is only shown before the Emperor and Empress, and first minister, upon particular occasions. The Emperor lays on the table three fine silken threads of six inches long. One is blue, the other red, and the third green. These threads are proposed as prizes for those persons whom the Emperor hath a mind to distinguish by a peculiar mark of his favor. The ceremony is performed in his Majesty's great chamber of state, where the candidates are to undergo a trial of dexterity very different from the former, and such as I have not observed the least resemblance of in any other country of the Old or the New World. The Emperor holds a stick in his hands, both ends parallel to the horizon, while the candidates advancing one by one, sometimes leap over the stick, sometimes creep under it backward and forward several times, according as the stick is advanced or depressed. Sometimes the Emperor holds one end of the stick, and his first minister the other; sometimes the minister has it entirely to himself. Whoever performs his part with most agility, and holds out the longest in leaping and creeping, is rewarded with the blue-colored silk; the red is given to the next, and the green to the third, which they all wear girt[13] twice round about the middle; and you see few great persons about this court, who are not adorned with one of these girdles. …

One morning, about a fortnight after I had obtained my liberty, Reldresal, principal Secretary (as they style him) of Private Affairs, came to my house attended only by one servant. He ordered his coach to wait at a distance, and desired I would give him an hour's audience; which I readily consented to, on account of his quality and personal merits, as well as of the many good offices he had done me during my solicitations at court. I offered to lie down, that he might the more conveniently reach my ear; but he chose rather to let me hold him in my hand during our conversation. He began with compliments on my liberty, said

he might pretend to some merit in it; but, however, added, that if it had not been for the present situation of things at court, perhaps I might not have obtained it so soon. "For," said he, "as flourishing a condition as we appear to be in to foreigners, we labor under two mighty evils: a violent faction at home, and the danger of an invasion by a most potent enemy from abroad. As to the first, you are to understand, that for about seventy moons past there have been two struggling parties in this empire, under the names of *Tramecksan* and *Slamecksan,* from the high and low heels on their shoes, by which they distinguish themselves. It is alleged indeed, that the high heels are most agreeable to our ancient constitution: But however this be, his Majesty hath determined to make use of only low heels in the administration of the government, and all offices in the gift of the Crown, as you cannot but observe; and particularly, that his Majesty's Imperial heels are lower at least by a *drurr* than any of his court; (*drurr* is a measure about the fourteenth part of an inch). The animosities between these two parties run so high, that they will neither eat nor drink, nor talk with each other. We compute the *Tramecksan,* or High-Heels, to exceed us in number; but the power is wholly on our side. We apprehend his Imperial Highness, the Heir to the Crown, to have some tendency toward the High-Heels; at least we can plainly discover one of his heels higher than the other, which gives him a hobble in his gait. Now, in the midst of these intestine[14] disquiets, we are threatened with an invasion from the island of Blefuscu, which is the other great empire of the universe, almost as large and powerful as this of his Majesty. For as to what we have heard you affirm, that there are other kingdoms and states in the world inhabited by human creatures as large as yourself, our philosophers are in much doubt, and would rather conjecture that you dropped from the moon, or one of the stars; because it is certain, that an hundred mortals of your bulk would, in a short time, destroy all the fruits and cattle of his Majesty's dominions. Besides, our histories of six thousand moons make no mention of any other regions, than the two great empires of Lilliput and Blefuscu. Which two mighty powers have, as I was going to tell you, been engaged in a most obstinate war for six and thirty

---

13. **girt:** encircled.

14. **intestine:** internal.

moons past. It began upon the following occasion. It is allowed on all hands, that the primitive way of breaking eggs[15] before we eat them, was upon the larger end: But his present Majesty's grandfather, while he was a boy, going to eat an egg, and breaking it according to the ancient practice, happened to cut one of his fingers. Whereupon the Emperor his father published an edict, commanding all his subjects, upon great penalties, to break the smaller end of their eggs. The people so highly resented this law, that our histories tell us there have been six rebellions raised on that account; wherein one Emperor lost his life, and another his crown. These civil commotions were constantly fomented by the monarchs of Blefuscu; and when they were quelled, the exiles always fled for refuge to that empire. It is computed, that eleven thousand persons have, at several times, suffered death, rather than submit to break their eggs at the smaller end. Many hundred large volumes have been published upon this controversy: But the books of the Big-Endians have been long forbidden, and the whole party rendered incapable by law of holding employments. During the course of these troubles, the emperors of Blefuscu did frequently expostulate by their ambassadors, accusing us of making a schism in religion, by offending against a fundamental doctrine of our great prophet Lustrog, in the fifty-fourth chapter of the Brundrecal (which is their Alcoran).[16] This, however, is thought to be a mere strain upon the text, for the words are these: *That all true believers shall break their eggs at the convenient end;* and which is the convenient end, seems, in my humble opinion, to be left to every man's

conscience, or at least in the power of the chief magistrate to determine. Now the Big-Endian exiles have found so much credit in the Emperor of Blefuscu's court, and so much private assistance and encouragement from their party here at home, that a bloody war has been carried on between the two empires for six and thirty moons with various success; during which time we have lost forty capital ships, and a much greater number of smaller vessels, together with thirty thousand of our best seamen and soldiers; and the damage received by the enemy is reckoned to be somewhat greater than ours. However, they have now equipped a numerous fleet, and are just preparing to make a descent upon us; and his Imperial Majesty, placing great confidence in your valor and strength, has commanded me to lay this account of his affairs before you." **F**

I desired the Secretary to present my humble duty to the Emperor, and to let him know, that I thought it would not become me, who was a foreigner, to interfere with parties; but I was ready, with the hazard of my life, to defend his person and state against all invaders.

Analyzing Visuals

Viewing and Interpreting   Consider the two perspectives in Part I, that of the Lilliputian and that of Gulliver, as exemplified in this photograph. In what ways does the presence of each subject affect the overall composition of the photograph? Try looking at the photograph again, but this time alternate covering either Gulliver or the Lilliputian with your hand. How do your impressions of the photograph and the text change when you alternate perspectives?

---

15. **primitive way of breaking eggs:** The English eat a boiled egg by standing it up in an egg cup, cutting off one end with a knife, and scooping out the contents with a spoon.
16. **Alcoran:** archaic English name for the Koran, the sacred book of Islam.

F **Reading Focus** Analyzing an Author's Purpose   What is ironic about the argument between the Big-Endians and the rest of the Lilliputians?

Vocabulary   schism (SKIHZ uhm) *n.:* division.
quelled (kwehld) *v.:* subdued.

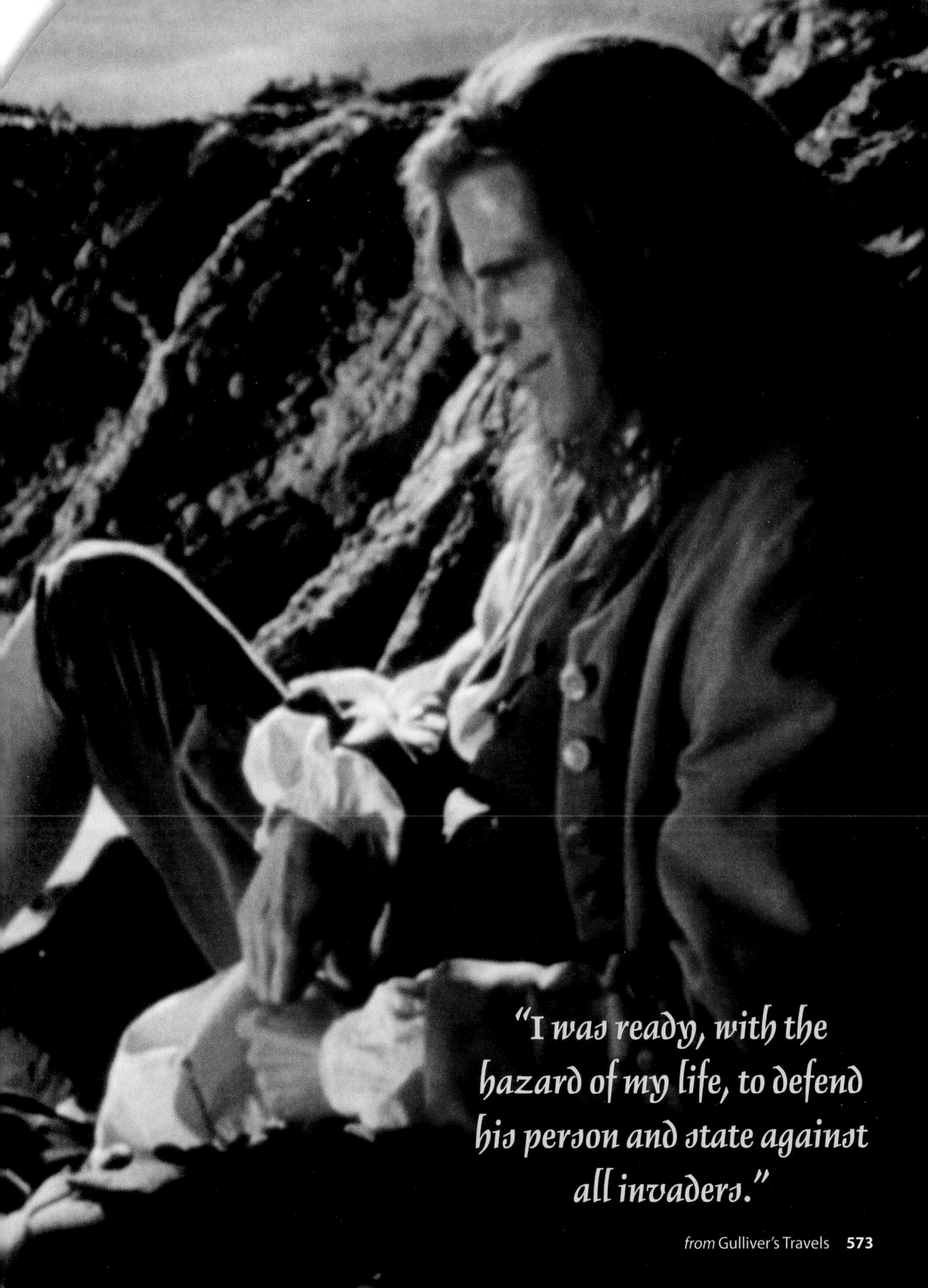

"I was ready, with the hazard of my life, to defend his person and state against all invaders."

from Part 2:
A Voyage to Brobdingnag

On his second voyage, Gulliver finds himself in Brobdingnag (BRAHB dihng nag), a country Swift locates in Alaska. Here everything is twelve times larger than in England. The situation in Part I is now reversed, and Gulliver discovers what it is like to be an insignificant, timid creature among giants. At court he tries to impress the king and queen with his importance and the importance of England and its civilization. Although its inhabitants look like large and ugly brutes, Brobdingnag is a kind of utopia, a model society with an enlightened and benevolent king. Note how the king treats Gulliver despite his opinion of Gulliver's size and civilization.

It is the custom that every Wednesday (which, as I have before observed, was their Sabbath) the King and Queen, with the royal issue of both sexes, dine together in the apartment of his Majesty, to whom I was now become a favorite; and at these times my little chair and table were placed at his left hand, before one of the saltcellars.[1] This prince took a pleasure in conversing with me, inquiring into the manners, religion, laws, government, and learning of Europe; wherein I gave him the best account I was able. His apprehension was so clear, and his judgment so exact, that he made very wise reflections and observations upon all I said. But, I confess, that after I had been a little too copious in talking of my own beloved country, of our trade, and wars by sea and land, of our schisms in religion, and parties in the state; the prejudices of his education prevailed[2] so far, that he could not forbear taking me up in his right hand, and stroking me gently with the other, after an hearty fit of laughing, asked me, whether I were a Whig or a Tory.[3] Then turning to his first minister, who waited behind him with a white staff, near as tall as the mainmast of the *Royal Sovereign*,[4] he observed how contemptible a thing was human grandeur, which could be mimicked by such diminutive insects as I. "And yet," said he, "I dare engage, those creatures have their titles and distinctions of honor, they contrive little nests and burrows, that they call houses and cities; they make a figure in dress and equipage[5]; they love, they fight, they dispute, they cheat, they betray." And thus he continued on, while my color came and went several times, with indignation to hear our noble country, the mistress of arts and arms, the scourge of France, the arbitress of Europe, the seat of virtue, piety, honor, and truth, the pride and envy of the world, so contemptuously treated. **Ⓐ**

But as I was not in a condition to resent injuries, so, upon mature thoughts, I began to doubt whether I were injured or no. For, after having been accustomed several months to the sight and converse of

---

1. **saltcellars:** dishes of salt.

2. **prevailed:** predominated; held sway.
3. **Whig . . . Tory:** the two chief political parties of eighteenth-century Great Britain.
4. **Royal Sovereign:** one of the largest British warships of Swift's age. A white staff is the symbol of the office of the British treasurer.
5. **equipage:** carriage and horses with servants.

Vocabulary **copious** (KOH pee uhs) *adj.*: wordy; profuse.

Ⓐ Reading Focus Analyzing an Author's Purpose What is Swift's attitude toward the king? What details tell you this?

this people, and observed every object upon which I cast my eyes, to be of proportionable magnitude, the horror I had first conceived from their bulk and aspect was so far worn off, that if I had then beheld a company of English lords and ladies in their finery and birthday clothes,[6] acting their several parts in the most courtly manner, of strutting, and bowing, and prating;[7] to say the truth, I should have been strongly tempted to laugh as much at them as this King and his grandees[8] did at me. Neither indeed could I forbear smiling at myself, when the Queen used to place me upon her hand toward a looking glass, by which both our persons appeared before me in full view together; and there could be nothing more ridiculous than the comparison; so that I really began to imagine myself dwindled many degrees below my usual size. . . .

I was frequently rallied[9] by the Queen upon account of my fearfulness, and she used to ask me whether the people of my country were as great cowards as myself. The occasion was this: The kingdom is much pestered with flies in summer; and these odious insects, each of them as big as a Dunstable lark, hardly gave me any rest while I sat at dinner, with their continual humming and buzzing about my ears. They

6. **birthday clothes:** new outfits worn on a royal's birthday.
7. **prating:** talking pompously.
8. **grandees:** important persons; from the Spanish *grande*.

9. **rallied:** teased.

Vocabulary **odious** (OH dee uhs) *adj.*: hateful; offensive.

Television production of Gulliver's Travels.

would sometimes alight upon my victuals, and leave their loathsome excrement or spawn behind, which to me was very visible, though not to the natives of that country, whose large optics were not so acute as mine in viewing smaller objects. Sometimes they would fix upon my nose or forehead, where they stung me to the quick, smelling very offensively, and I could easily trace that viscous[10] matter, which our naturalists tell us enables those creatures to walk with their feet upward upon a ceiling. I had much ado to defend myself against these detestable animals, and could not forbear starting when they came on my face. It was the common practice of the dwarf to catch a number of these insects in his hand, as schoolboys do among us, and let them out suddenly under my nose, on purpose to frighten me, and divert the Queen. My remedy was to cut them in pieces with my knife as they flew in the air, wherein my dexterity was much admired. . . . **B**

He [the King] was perfectly astonished with the historical account I gave him of our affairs during the last century, protesting it was only an heap of conspiracies, rebellions, murders, massacres, revolutions, banishments; the very worst effects that avarice, faction, hypocrisy, perfidiousness, cruelty, rage, madness, hatred, envy, lust, malice, and ambition, could produce.

His Majesty, in another audience, was at the pains to recapitulate the sum of all I had spoken; compared the questions he made with the answers I had given; then taking me into his hands, and stroking me gently, delivered himself in these words, which I shall never forget, nor the manner he spoke them **C**

10. **viscous:** sticky.

in. "My little friend Grildrig,[11] you have made a most admirable panegyric[12] upon your country. You have clearly proved that ignorance, idleness, and vice, are the proper ingredients for qualifying a legislator: that laws are best explained, interpreted, and applied by those whose interest and abilities lie in perverting, confounding, and eluding them. I observe among you some lines of an institution, which in its original might have been tolerable, but these half erased, and the rest wholly blurred and blotted by corruptions. It doth not appear from all you have said, how any one perfection[13] is required toward the procurement of any one station among you; much less that men are ennobled on account of their virtue, that priests are advanced for their piety or learning, soldiers for their conduct or valor, judges for their integrity, senators for the love of their country, or counselors for their wisdom. As for yourself (continued the King), who have spent the greatest part of your life in traveling, I am well disposed to hope you may hitherto have escaped many vices of your country. But by what I have gathered from your own relation, and the answers I have with much pains wringed and extorted from you, I cannot but conclude the bulk of your natives to be the most pernicious[14] race of little odious vermin that nature ever suffered to crawl upon the surface of the earth."

11. **Grildrig:** the Brobdingnagians' name for Gulliver.
12. **panegyric:** speech full of praise.
13. **perfection:** here, virtue.
14. **pernicious:** wicked; extremely harmful.

B **Literary Focus** Situational Irony Although Gulliver bravely defends himself against the gigantic flies, the queen calls him a coward. Why don't the Brobdingnagians admire Gulliver's bravery?

C **Reading Focus** Analyzing an Author's Purpose Why might Swift use physical size to illustrate Gulliver's feelings about himself and his society?

SKILLS FOCUS Literary Skills Analyze situational irony; analyze characteristics of satire. **Reading Skills** Analyze an author's purpose. **Writing Skills** Develop characters.

from Gulliver's Travels

Respond and Think Critically

Reading Focus

Quick Check

1. How does Gulliver feel he is treated by the Lilliputians?

2. How does the Brobdingnagian king regard Gulliver's home country?

3. After several months with the Brobdingnagians, how does Gulliver feel about himself?

Read with a Purpose

4. How is what the reader learns about human nature different from what Gulliver learns?

Reading Skills: Understanding the Author's Purpose

5. Review the chart you prepared before reading. Now add another column to your chart, noting how each example supports the author's purpose in the work as a whole.

Event, Action, Image	Institution	Satirical Point	Author's Purpose
Gulliver is entertained by rope dancers.	Politics	These political leaders "danced" around issues instead of solving the country's problems.	This example targets the use of influence and favoritism in political appointments.

Literary Focus

Literary Analysis

6. **Summarize** Write a description of what happens to Gulliver in either Part I or Part II.

7. **Interpret** How would you describe Swift's **tone,** or his attitude toward the Lilliputians? toward the Brobdingnagians? What words or passages support your answer?

8. **Analyze** Is there any relationship between the physical size of the Lilliputians and the Brobdingnagians and the way Swift wants us to evaluate their behavior? Does size **symbolize** moral value? Explain.

Literary Skills: Situational Irony

9. **Draw Conclusions** How does Swift's use of situational irony help you understand his opinion about events in his own time period?

Literary Skills Review: Satire

10. **Make Judgments** Writing that attacks or ridicules the shortcomings of people or institutions in an attempt to bring about change is called **satire.** How is *Gulliver's Travels* effective as a satire?

Writing Focus

Think as a Reader/Writer

Use It in Your Writing Previously, you noted the words and images Swift uses to emphasize the extremes he sees in people. Using your *Reader/Writer Notebook* and similar words and images, create your own character sketch of another extreme character that Gulliver might encounter on his journeys.

What Do You Think Now? How do the social orders in Lilliput and Brobdingnag affect the behavior of their inhabitants?

Applying Your Skills

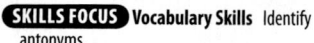

from Gulliver's Travels

Vocabulary Development

✓ Vocabulary Check

Answer these questions to test your knowledge of the Vocabulary words.

1. If you have **conjectured** something, has it been considered or purchased?

2. Are you more likely to see a **schism** in a political party or at a tea party?

3. If your opinions and rights are **quelled,** are you likely to be happy or angry?

4. Will you be satisfied or hungry after **copious** amounts of food?

5. Are you repelled or attracted by things that are **odious** to you?

Vocabulary Skills: Antonyms

An **antonym** is a word that has the opposite or nearly the opposite meaning of another word. An unabridged dictionary may list antonyms as well as synonyms for certain words. Familiarity with a word's antonym can help us better understand the word's meaning in the following ways:

• By contrasting qualities and meanings, we can form a more complete picture of what a word does and does not represent.

• Using antonyms in everyday speaking and writing adds a level of depth and interest to our language.

• Knowing antonyms allows us to give expression to one of the undeniable and intriguing facts of life—the existence of opposites.

Your Turn

In a chart like the one below, list antonyms for the Vocabulary words. Then, write a sentence using each Vocabulary word and its antonym.

Vocabulary Word	Antonym	Sentence Using Both Words
copious	meager	The critic took copious notes about the play but gave it very meager praise.
quelled		
schism		
conjectured		
odious		

Language Coach

Verb Tenses When you read a verb in the past tense, take time to identify the present tense form. For regular verbs, you will remove –ed or –d from the past tense form. Write and define the present tense for each of the following past tense verbs.

1. conjectured
2. disposed
3. interpreted
4. conveyed
5. determined

Academic Vocabulary

Talk About

With a partner, discuss how Gulliver's travels <u>enhances</u> his understanding of his world. How does his <u>approach</u> to people change after meeting and <u>participating</u> in cultures different than his own?

Reading Focus

SKILLS FOCUS Reading Skills Understand persuasive techniques (logical, emotional, and ethical appeals).

A Modest Proposal

Recognizing Persuasive Techniques by **Kylene Beers**

Warning! If you read Jonathan Swift's *A Modest Proposal* or Voltaire's *Candide* without recognizing persuasive techniques, you will miss the whole point. Swift and Voltaire seek not only to entertain their readers but also to make them believe that their views are correct.

What makes you believe someone? Is it because he or she shows you convincing evidence? Is it because you like the person? The most effective persuasive writers combine a variety of techniques to <u>convince</u> you to accept their messages.

Three major types of appeals are used in effective persuasive writing. In a **logical appeal,** an author supports an argument through reason, facts, and statistics. In an **emotional appeal,** an author uses moving language and vivid descriptions to arouse strong feelings in readers. Lastly, in an **ethical appeal,** an author establishes credibility, sharing his or her own experiences, qualifications, and motivations, to gain readers' confidence and support.

Sometimes Swift uses logic to address the problem of poverty and starvation. In the following passage, note his use of logical supporting evidence.

> Supposing that one thousand families in this city, would be constant customers for infants' flesh, besides others who might have it at merry meetings, particularly weddings and christenings, I compute that Dublin would take off annually about twenty thousand carcasses, and the rest of the kingdom (where probably they will be sold somewhat cheaper) the remaining eighty thousand.

Swift is, of course, being ironic in his suggestion that babies should be sold as meat, but his appeal to logic is clear. He mentions actual numbers, specific situations, and real places to give his argument credibility.

Your Turn

Look at the following sentences from *A Modest Proposal*. Using the questions as a guide, identify the type of appeal in each example.

In sentence 1, what scene is described and what effect does the author hope it will have on the reader? What language evokes an emotional appeal?

> It is a melancholy object to those, who walk through this great town, or travel in the country, when they see the streets, the roads, and cabin doors, crowded with beggars of the female sex, followed by three, four, or six children, all in rags, and importuning every passenger for an alms.

In sentence 2, why does the author mention that he has spent many years thinking about this subject? What appeal is he using when his cites his experience?

> As to my own part, having turned my thoughts, for many years, upon this important subject, and maturely weighed the several schemes of other projectors, I have always found them grossly mistaken in their computation.

 Learn It Online
Explore modern persuasive techniques on the MediaScope mini-site.

go.hrw.com | L12-587 | **Go**

Preparing To Read

A Modest Proposal

Reader/Writer Notebook

Use your **RWN** to complete the activities for this selection.

Literary Focus

Verbal Irony Sometimes writers and speakers use words that mean the opposite of what they really seem to be saying. **Verbal irony** is a contrast between what is said and what is really meant. Saying "thanks a lot" to someone who refuses to help you is an example of verbal irony. In speech, you can often recognize verbal irony by a person's tone of voice. In writing, the voice of the speaker is revealed in the choice of words and details.

Reading Focus

Recognizing Persuasive Techniques An effective persuasive message appeals to an audience on many levels. In a **logical appeal,** an author supports a position with evidence, whereas in an **emotional appeal,** an author uses language and descriptions to arouse strong feelings. In an **ethical appeal,** an author establishes himself or herself as a reliable and trustworthy source.

Into Action Use a chart like the one below to keep track of some of the persuasive techniques in this essay. When you encounter a persuasive appeal, write down its page number or line, and a brief paraphrase. Check the appropriate column to indicate the type of appeal.

Page	Example	Logical	Emotional	Ethical
589	In the first paragraph the speaker describes the sad sight of crowds of beggars asking for help for themselves and their children.		✓	

Writing Focus

Think as a Reader/Writer

Find It in Your Reading As you read, use your *Reader/Writer Notebook* to make note of the places in the text that most clearly indicate this essay's nature as satire.

Tech Connect Choose an ad from television or the Internet and note the persuasive qualities that you believe make the ad effective or not.

Language Coach

Stressed Syllables Read the Vocabulary words aloud to become familiar with how they sound. Which syllables are accented?

Learn It Online

Meet *A Modest Proposal* through this video introduction online.

go.hrw.com L12-588 **Go**

A Modest Proposal

by **Jonathan Swift**

FOR PREVENTING THE CHILDREN OF POOR PEOPLE IN IRELAND FROM BEING A BURDEN TO THEIR PARENTS OR COUNTRY, AND FOR MAKING THEM BENEFICIAL TO THE PUBLIC

Read with a Purpose
Read to discover who will benefit from Swift's proposal.

Build Background
In this essay, Swift does not write in his own voice but rather uses a **persona,** that of a "projector" who is an economic planner. Swift pretends to be objective, sensible, even sensitive and kind. The difference between the essay's sober, straightforward style and its appalling content, however, gives the proposal its ironic force. At times, Swift seems to drop the persona and speak in his own voice, expressing his fury and indignation.

It is a melancholy object to those, who walk through this great town,[1] or travel in the country, when they see the streets, the roads, and cabin doors, crowded with beggars of the female sex, followed by three, four, or six children, all in rags, and importuning every passenger for an alms.[2] These mothers instead of being able to work for their honest livelihood, are forced to employ all their time in strolling, to beg sustenance for their helpless infants, who, as they grow up either turn thieves for want of work, or leave their dear native country to fight for the Pretender[3] in Spain, or sell themselves to the Barbadoes.[4]

I think it is agreed by all parties, that this prodigious number of children, in the arms, or on the backs, or at the heels of their mothers, and frequently of their fathers, is in the present deplorable state of the kingdom, a very great additional grievance; and therefore whoever could find out a fair, cheap, and easy method of making these children sound and useful members of the commonwealth would deserve so well of the public, as to have his statue set up for a preserver of the nation.

---

1. **town:** Dublin.
2. **importuning . . . alms:** begging passersby for a handout.

3. **the Pretender:** Some Irishmen who left their country due to poverty went to fight for James Francis Edward Stuart (1688–1766), son of England's last Catholic king, the deposed James II. He was known as the "Pretender" because he kept trying to gain the throne.
4. **sell . . . Barbadoes:** Some Irish went to the West Indies to work as indentured servants.

Vocabulary **sustenance** (SUHS tuh nuhns) *n.:* food or provisions needed to support life.
prodigious (proh DIHJ uhs) *adj.:* huge; very great.

View of Old Chapel Lane or High Street in Skibbereen, Ireland.
The Granger Collection, NY.

But my intention is very far from being confined to provide only for the children of professed beggars; it is of a much greater extent, and shall take in the whole number of infants at a certain age, who are born of parents in effect as little able to support them, as those who demand our charity in the streets.

As to my own part, having turned my thoughts, for many years, upon this important subject, and maturely weighed the several schemes of other projectors, I have always found them grossly mistaken in their computation. It is true a child, just dropped from its dam,[5] may be supported by her milk, for a solar year with little other nourishment, at most not above the value of two shillings, which the mother may certainly get, or the value in scraps, by her lawful occupation of begging, and it is exactly at one year old that I propose to provide for them, in such a manner, as, instead of being a charge upon their parents, or the parish, or wanting food and raiment[6] for the rest of their lives, they shall, on the contrary, contribute to the feeding and partly to the clothing of many thousands. **Ⓐ**

There is likewise another great advantage in my scheme, that it will prevent those voluntary abortions, and that horrid practice of women murdering their bastard children, alas! too frequent among us, sacrificing the poor innocent babes, I doubt, more to avoid the expense, than the shame, which would move tears and pity in the most savage and inhuman breast. **Ⓑ**

The number of souls in Ireland being usually reckoned one million and a half, of these I calculate there may be about two hundred thousand couples whose wives are breeders, from which number I subtract thirty thousand couples, who are able to maintain their own children, although I apprehend there cannot be so many under the present distresses of the kingdom, but this being granted, there will remain an hundred and seventy thousand breeders. I again subtract fifty thousand for those women who miscarry, or whose children

---

5. **dam:** mother (ordinarily used only of animals).
6. **raiment:** clothing.

die by accident, or disease within the year. There only remain an hundred and twenty thousand children of poor parents annually born: The question therefore is, how this number shall be reared, and provided for, which, as I have already said, under the present situation of affairs, is utterly impossible by all the methods hitherto proposed, for we can neither employ them in handicraft, or agriculture; we neither build houses (I mean in the country) nor cultivate land: They can very seldom pick up a livelihood by stealing until they arrive at six years old, except where they are of towardly parts,[7] although, I confess they learn the rudiments much earlier, during which time, they can however be properly looked upon only as probationers,[8] as I have been informed by a principal gentleman in the county of Cavan,[9] who protested to me, that he never knew above one or two instances under the age of six, even in

---

7. **of towardly parts:** exceptionally advanced for their age.
8. **they can . . . probationers:** Children younger than six are apprentices in the profession of stealing.
9. **Cavan:** inland county in Ireland that is remote from Dublin.

Literary Perspectives

Analyzing Credibility in Literature When the way a story is told doesn't match what we know about the person telling it, we may question the narrator's credibility. Consider the fact that *A Modest Proposal* is not narrated purely by its author, for in it Swift uses a persona, that of a learned, judicious economic planner who seems to care sincerely for the Irish poor. How does that persona's inconceivable and preposterous proposal affect his (and Swift's) credibility? Why might Swift have intentionally created this effect?

Analyzing Political Context Literary texts are influenced by the particular worldview of the author, whether it is his or her political perspective, gender, or social class. Explore the way Swift represents the disparity between rich and poor in *A Modest Proposal.* How does he convey to his audience the urgency of this issue? **As you read, be sure to notice the questions in the text that will guide you in using each perspective.**

Ⓐ **Reading Focus** **Recognizing Persuasive Techniques** How does Swift use an ethical appeal in this paragraph?

Ⓑ **Reading Focus** **Recognizing Persuasive Techniques** What kind of persuasive appeal is the author using in this paragraph? How does the word choice enhance the effectiveness of the appeal?

a part of the kingdom so renowned for the quickest proficiency in that art. **C**

I am assured by our merchants, that a boy or girl, before twelve years old, is no saleable commodity, and even when they come to this age, they will not yield above three pounds, or three pounds and half a crown at most on the exchange, which cannot turn to account[10] either to the parents or the kingdom, the charge of nutriment and rags having been at least four times that value.

I shall now therefore humbly propose my own thoughts, which I hope will not be liable to the least objection.

I have been assured by a very knowing American[11] of my acquaintance in London, that a young healthy child well nursed is at a year old a most delicious, nourishing, and wholesome food, whether stewed, roasted, baked, or boiled, and I make no doubt that it will equally serve in a fricassee, or ragout.[12]

I do therefore humbly offer it to public consideration, that of the hundred and twenty thousand children, already computed, twenty thousand may be reserved for breed, whereof only one-fourth part to be males, which is more than we allow to sheep, black cattle, or swine, and my reason is that these children are seldom the fruits of marriage, a circumstance not much regarded by our savages; therefore one male will be sufficient to serve four females. That the remaining hundred thousand may at a year old be offered in sale to the persons of quality, and fortune, through the kingdom, always advising the mother to let them suck plentifully in the last month, so as to render them plump, and fat for a good table. A child will make two dishes at an entertainment for friends, and when the family dines alone, the fore or hind quarter will make a reasonable dish, and seasoned with a little pepper or salt will be very good boiled on the fourth day, especially in winter.

---

10. **turn to account:** be profitable.
11. **American:** To Swift's readers this label would have suggested a barbaric person.
12. **fricassee, or ragout** (frihk uh SEE, ra GOO): different kinds of meat stew.

I have reckoned upon a medium, that a child just born will weigh twelve pounds, and in a solar year if tolerably nursed increaseth to twenty-eight pounds.

I grant this food will be somewhat dear,[13] and therefore very proper for landlords, who, as they have already devoured[14] most of the parents, seem to have the best title to the children.

Infant's flesh will be in season throughout the year, but more plentiful in March, and a little before and after, for we are told by a grave author,[15] an eminent French physician, that fish being a prolific diet, there are more children born in Roman Catholic countries about nine months after Lent, than at any other season, therefore reckoning a year after Lent, the markets will be more glutted than usual, because the number of popish infants, is at least three to one in this kingdom, and therefore it will have one other collateral advantage by lessening the number of papists[16] among us.

I have already computed the charge of nursing a beggar's child (in which list I reckon all cottagers,[17] laborers, and four-fifths of the farmers) to be about two shillings per annum,[18] rags included, and I believe no gentleman would repine to give ten shillings for the carcass of a good fat child, which, as I have said will make four dishes of excellent nutritive meat, when he hath only some particular friend, or his own family to dine with him. Thus the squire will learn to be a good landlord, and grow popular among his tenants, the mother will have eight shillings net profit, and be fit for work until she produceth another child.

Those who are more thrifty (as I must confess the times require) may flay[19] the carcass; the skin of

---

13. **dear:** expensive.
14. **devoured:** made poor by charging high rents.
15. **grave author:** The French satirist François Rabelais produced works that are comic rather than "grave."
16. **popish . . . papists:** derogatory terms for Roman Catholics.
17. **cottagers:** tenant farmers.
18. **per annum:** per year.
19. **flay:** remove the skin of.

C **Literary Focus** **Verbal Irony** What is the "art" that Swift is referring to? What is ironic about the way the author discusses this topic?

which, artificially dressed, will make admirable gloves for ladies, and summer boots for fine gentlemen. **D**

As to our city of Dublin, shambles[20] may be appointed for this purpose, in the most convenient parts of it, and butchers we may be assured will not be wanting, although I rather recommend buying the children alive, and dressing them hot from the knife,[21] as we do roasting pigs. **E**

A very worthy person, a true lover of his country, and whose virtues I highly esteem, was lately pleased, in discoursing on this matter, to offer a refinement upon my scheme. He said, that many gentlemen of this kingdom, having of late destroyed their deer, he conceived that the want of venison might be well supplied by the bodies of young lads and maidens, not exceeding fourteen years of age, nor under twelve, so great a number of both sexes in every country being now ready to starve, for want of work and service:[22] and these to be disposed of by their parents if alive, or otherwise by their nearest relations. But with due deference to so excellent a friend, and so deserving a patriot, I cannot be altogether in his sentiments, for as to the males, my American acquaintance assured me from frequent experience, that their flesh was generally tough and lean, like that of our schoolboys, by continual exercise, and their taste disagreeable, and to fatten them would not answer the charge. Then as to the females, it would, I think with humble submission, be a loss to the public, because they soon would become breeders themselves: And besides it is not improbable that some scrupulous people might be apt to censure such a practice (although indeed very unjustly) as a little bordering upon cruelty, which, I confess, hath always been with me the strongest objection against any project, how well soever intended.

---

20. **shambles:** slaughterhouses.
21. **dressing them hot from the knife:** killing the infant only moments before cooking it.
22. **service:** employment as servants.

But in order to justify my friend, he confessed that this expedient was put into his head by the famous Sallmanaazor,[23] a native of the island Formosa, who came from thence to London, above twenty years ago, and in conversation told my friend, that in his country when any young person happened to be put to death, the executioner sold the carcass to persons of quality, as a prime dainty, and that, in his time, the body of a plump girl of fifteen, who was crucified for an attempt to poison the emperor, was sold to his imperial majesty's prime minister of state, and other great mandarins[24] of the court, in joints[25] from the gibbet,[26] at four hundred crowns. Neither indeed can I deny, that if the same use were made of several plump young girls in this town, who, without one single groat[27] to their fortunes, cannot stir abroad without a chair,[28] and appear at the playhouse, and assemblies in foreign fineries, which they never will pay for; the kingdom would not be the worse.

Some persons of a desponding spirit are in great concern about that vast number of poor people, who are aged, diseased, or maimed, and I have been desired to employ my thoughts what course may be taken, to ease the nation of so grievous an encumbrance. But I am not in the least pain upon that matter, because it is very well known, that they are every day dying, and rotting, by cold, and famine, and filth, and vermin,[29] as fast as can be reasonably expected. And as to the younger laborers they are now in almost as hopeful a

---

23. **Sallmanaazor:** George Psalmanazar (c. 1679–1763) was a Frenchman who pretended to be from Formosa, or modern Taiwan, and wrote a fraudulent account of it.
24. **mandarins:** Chinese officials.
25. **joints:** large cuts of meat, including the bone.
26. **gibbet:** wooden frame used for hanging criminals.
27. **groat:** fourpence, or a very small sum.
28. **chair:** sedan chair; a covered seat carried by servants.
29. **vermin:** pests such as lice, fleas, and bedbugs.

D **Literary Focus** Analyzing Political Context Note how the speaker uses language usually associated with descriptions of animals. Why does the speaker talk of the children of the poor as if they were livestock?

E **Reading Focus** Recognizing Persuasive Techniques When the speaker suggests "dressing" children "hot from the knife," what effect does he expect his word choice to create?

Vocabulary **scrupulous** (SKROO pyoo luhs) *adj.:* extremely careful in deciding what is right or wrong.
censure (SEHN shuhr) *v.:* express disapproval of.
expedient (ehk SPEE dee uhnt) *n.:* way of getting something; a means for achieving an end.

condition. They cannot get work, and consequently pine away for want of nourishment, to a degree, that if at any time they are accidentally hired to common labor, they have not strength to perform it, and thus the country and themselves are in a fair way of being soon delivered from the evils to come. **F**

I have too long *digressed*, and therefore shall return to my subject. I think the advantages by the proposal which I have made are obvious and many as well as of the highest importance.

For first, as I have already observed, it would greatly lessen the number of papists, with whom we are yearly overrun, being the principal breeders of the nation, as well as our most dangerous enemies, and who stay at home on purpose with a design to deliver the kingdom to the Pretender, hoping to take their advantage by the absence of so many good

Protestants,[30] who have chosen rather to leave their country, than stay at home, and pay tithes[31] against their conscience, to an idolatrous Episcopal curate.

Secondly, the poorer tenants will have something valuable of their own, which by law may be made liable to distress,[32] and help to pay their landlord's rent, their corn and cattle being already seized, and money a thing unknown.

Thirdly, whereas the maintenance of an hundred

---

30. **good Protestants:** used ironically to mean bad Protestants because they object to the Church of Ireland's bishops and regard them as "idolatrous."
31. **tithes:** monetary gifts to the church equivalent to one tenth of each donor's income.
32. **distress:** The money from the sale of their children may be seized by their landlords as payment for debt.

F **Literary Focus** **Verbal Irony** What is ironic about the use of the word *hopeful* in this paragraph?

Vocabulary **digressed** (dy GREHSD) *v.*: wandered away from the subject.

Bridget O'Donnell with her children, potato famine in the mid 19th century.

thousand children, from two years old, and upwards, cannot be computed at less than ten shillings apiece per annum, the nation's stock will be thereby increased fifty thousand pounds per annum, besides the profit of a new dish, introduced to the tables of all gentlemen of fortune in the kingdom, who have any refinement in taste, and the money will circulate among ourselves, the goods being entirely of our own growth and manufacture. **G**

Fourthly, the constant breeders, besides the gain of eight shillings sterling per annum, by the sale of their children, will be rid of the charge of maintaining them after the first year.

Fifthly, this food would likewise bring great custom to taverns, where the vintners[33] will certainly be so prudent as to procure the best receipts[34] for dressing it to perfection, and consequently have their houses frequented by all the fine gentlemen, who justly value themselves upon their knowledge in good eating, and a skillful cook, who understands how to oblige his guests will contrive to make it as expensive as they please.

Sixthly, this would be a great inducement to marriage, which all wise nations have either encouraged by rewards, or enforced by laws and penalties. It would increase the care and tenderness of mothers toward their children, when they were sure of a settlement for life to the poor babes, provided in some sort by the public to their annual profit instead of expense, we should soon see an honest emulation[35] among the married women, which of them could bring the fattest child to the market, men would become as fond of their wives, during the time of their pregnancy, as they are now of their mares in foal, their cows in calf, or sows when they are ready to farrow,[36] nor offer to beat or kick them (as is too frequent a practice) for fear of a miscarriage.

Many other advantages might be enumerated. For instance, the addition of some thousand carcasses in our exportation of barreled beef. The propagation of swine's flesh, and improvement in the art of making good bacon, so much wanted among us by the great destruction of pigs, too frequent at our tables, which are no way comparable in taste, or magnificence to a well-grown, fat yearling child, which roasted whole will make a considerable figure at a Lord Mayor's feast, or any other public entertainment. But this, and many others I omit being studious of brevity.

Supposing that one thousand families in this city, would be constant customers for infants' flesh, besides others who might have it at merry meetings, particularly weddings and christenings, I compute that Dublin would take off annually about twenty thousand carcasses, and the rest of the kingdom (where probably they will be sold somewhat cheaper) the remaining eighty thousand. **H**

I can think of no one objection, that will possibly be raised against this proposal, unless it should be urged that the number of people will be thereby much lessened in the kingdom. This I freely own, and it was indeed one principal design in offering it to the world. I desire the reader will observe, that I calculate my remedy for this one individual kingdom of Ireland, and for no other that ever was, is, or, I think, ever can be upon earth. Therefore let no man talk to me of other expedients: *Of taxing our absentees[37] at five shillings a pound; of using neither clothes, nor household furniture, except what is of our own growth and manufacture; of utterly rejecting the materials and instruments that promote foreign luxury; of curing the expensiveness of pride, vanity, idleness, and gaming[38] in our women; of introducing a vein of parsimony,[39] prudence, and temperance; of learning to love our country, wherein we differ even from Laplanders, and the*

---

33. **vintners:** wine merchants.
34. **receipts:** recipes.
35. **emulation:** competition.
36. **farrow:** produce piglets.

37. **absentees:** English landowners who refused to live on their Irish property.
38. **gaming:** gambling.
39. **parsimony:** thriftiness; economy.

G **Literary Perspective** Analyzing Credibility in Literature What might you assume about the background of the speaker, given his discussion of Irish children in economic and monetary terms?

H **Reading Focus** Recognizing Persuasive Techniques What kind of persuasive appeal is used in this paragraph? What is also ironic about this appeal—in particular, with the mention of "christenings"?

inhabitants of Topinamboo;[40] *of quitting our* animosi-ties, *and factions,*[41] *nor act any longer like the Jews, who were murdering one another at the very moment their city*[42] *was taken; of being a little cautious not to sell our country and consciences for nothing; of teaching landlords to have at least one degree of mercy toward their tenants. Lastly of putting a spirit of honesty, indus-try, and skill into our shopkeepers, who, if a resolution could now be taken to buy only our native goods, would immediately unite to cheat and exact*[43] *upon us in the price, the measure, and the goodness, nor could ever yet be brought to make one fair proposal of just dealing, though often and earnestly invited to it.* **I**

Therefore I repeat, let no man talk to me of these and the like expedients, till he hath at least a glimpse of hope, that there will ever be some hearty and sin-cere attempt to put them in practice.

But as to myself, having been wearied out for many years with offering vain, idle, visionary thoughts, and at length utterly despairing of success, I fortu-nately fell upon this proposal, which as it is wholly new, so it hath something solid and real, of no expense and little trouble, full in our own power, and whereby we can incur no danger in disobliging England. For this kind of commodity will not bear exportation, the flesh being of too tender a consistence, to admit a long continuance in salt, although perhaps I could name a country,[44] which would be glad to eat up our whole nation without it.

After all I am not so violently bent upon my own opinion, as to reject any offer, proposed by wise men, which shall be found equally innocent, cheap, easy, and effectual. But before something of that kind shall be advanced in contradiction to my scheme, and offering a better, I desire the author, or authors will be pleased maturely to consider two points. First, as things now stand, how they will be able to find food and raiment for a hundred thousand useless mouths and backs. And secondly, there being a round million of creatures in human figure, throughout this king-dom, whose whole subsistence[45] put into a common stock would leave them in debt two millions of pounds sterling, adding those who are beggars by profession to the bulk of farmers, cottagers, and laborers, with their wives and children, who are beggars in effect; I desire those politicians, who dislike my overture, and may perhaps be so bold to attempt an answer, that they will first ask the parents of these mortals, whether they would not at this day think it a great happiness to have been sold for food at a year old, in the manner I prescribe, and thereby have avoided such a perpetual scene of misfortunes, as they have since gone through, by the oppression of landlords, the impossibility of paying rent without money or trade, the want of com-mon sustenance, with neither house nor clothes to cover them from inclemencies of weather, and the most inevitable prospect of entailing the like, or great miseries, upon their breed forever.

I profess in the sincerity of my heart that I have not the least personal interest in endeavoring to promote this necessary work, having no other motive than the public good of my country, by advancing our trade, pro-viding for infants, relieving the poor, and giving some pleasure to the rich. I have no children, by which I can propose to get a single penny; the youngest being nine years old, and my wife past childbearing. **J**

---

40. **Laplanders . . . Topinamboo:** Lapland is a region encompassing some parts of northern Europe, and Topinamboo is a region of Brazil. Swift suggests that if Brazilians and Laplanders can love their seemingly inhospitable lands, the Irish should love Ireland.
41. **factions:** political groups that work against the interests of other groups.
42. **their city:** Jerusalem, which the Roman emperor Titus destroyed in A.D. 70 while Jewish factions fought one another.
43. **exact:** force payment.
44. **a country:** England.

---

45. **subsistence:** all means of keeping alive; possessions.

I **Reading Focus** Recognizing Persuasive Techniques What objection does the speaker anticipate? What counterargument does he make?

J **Literary Focus** Verbal Irony How is the speaker's claim that he hasn't "the least personal interest" ironic?

Vocabulary **animosities** (an ih MAHS uh teez) *n. pl.*: hostili-ties; violent hatreds or resentments.

Respond and Think Critically

Reading Focus

Quick Check

1. How would you state the purpose of this essay? Whom or what is Swift trying to reform?

2. What is the speaker's real meaning when he asserts that England will not mind if Ireland kills and eats its babies?

3. How does assuming the persona of an economic planner help Swift achieve his purpose?

Read with a Purpose

4. In your own words, list the six advantages of the speaker's proposal. Who would benefit or suffer from the proposal?

Reading Skills: Recognizing Persuasive Techniques

5. As you read *A Modest Proposal,* you recorded some logical, emotional, and ethical appeals. Refer to your chart to write a few sentences explaining how Swift uses each type of appeal to make his points in the essay as a whole.

Literary Focus

Literary Analysis

6. **Analyze** One technique used to deny people rights is language that dehumanizes them. List several examples of dehumanizing language that Swift uses (ironically) about the Irish.

7. **Summarize** Before writing this pamphlet, Swift had recommended many of the "other expedients" he lists. In your own words, summarize some of the other proposals, and explain why the speaker ultimately dismisses them.

8. **Hypothesize** Swift doesn't reveal his plan until later in the essay. What is the effect of this delay?

9. **Literary Perspectives** While reading the proposal, you have considered the writing from both credibility and political perspectives. How do these contexts individually and collectively contribute to how you perceive Swift's argument?

Literary Skills: Verbal Irony

10. **Evaluate** Is Swift's use of irony effective, or does it risk being taken seriously by readers who might be outraged by his apparent cruelty?

11. **Analyze** Swift lists several advantages of his proposal. Who really profits from these "advantages"? Who actually suffers?

Literary Skills Review: Tone

12. **Analyze** A writer's attitude toward a subject or the reader is called tone. How would you describe Swift's tone in *A Modest Proposal?*

Writing Focus

Think as a Reader/Writer

Use It in Your Writing Using your notes and experience reading *A Modest Proposal,* write a short satire with a created persona who attempts to solve one of today's problems. Share your satirical essay with classmates.

What Do **You Think Now** How can injustices hide behind the appearance of civilization?

SKILLS FOCUS **Literary Skills** Analyze verbal irony; analyze tone; analyze credibility; analyze political context. **Reading Skills** Analyze persuasive techniques.

Writing Skills Write a persuasive essay. **Vocabulary Skills** Understand denotation and connotation; identify and use synonyms correctly.

Vocabulary Development

✔ Vocabulary Check

Match each Vocabulary word with its synonym.

1. animosities
2. censure
3. digressed
4. expedient
5. prodigious
6. scrupulous
7. sustenance

a. nourishment
b. huge
c. careful
d. criticize
e. wandered
f. hatreds
g. means

Vocabulary Skills: Connotation and Intensity

In addition to a word's literal, dictionary meaning, or **denotation,** it has **connotations,** the emotional ideas and feelings that people may connect to it. Words can have positive, negative, or neutral connotations. Look at the line scale below. The words have a similar literal meaning, but their connotations vary depending on the context in which they are used.

Positive	Neutral	Negative
youthful	young	immature

Words can also differ in terms of **intensity,** or degree of strength, as the line scale below depicts.

High Intensity		Low Intensity
adore	love	like

Your Turn

Read each example, and use the line scales as tools to answer the questions.

1. "And besides it is not improbable that some **scrupulous** people might be apt to **censure** such a practice (although indeed very unjustly) as a little bordering upon cruelty."

   What word with a negative connotation could you substitute for *scrupulous?* What word of higher intensity could you use for *censure?*

2. "I think it is agreed by all parties, that this **prodigious** number of children … is … a very great additional grievance."

   What word of lesser intensity could be substituted for *prodigious?*

3. "therefore reckoning a year after Lent, the markets will be more **glutted** than usual …."

   What is the connotation of the word *glutted?*

Language Coach

Stressed Syllables When pronouncing words of three, four, and five syllables, you must decide which syllable receives the stress. Words such as *scrupulous* and *sustenance* have a stress on the first syllable, while *expedient* and *prodigious* have a stress on the second syllable. *Animosities* has a main stress on the third syllable, with a softer stress on the first syllable. Practice saying these words aloud to get a feel for the placement of stress.

Academic Vocabulary

Talk About…
With a partner, discuss how you would <u>approach</u> a good friend if you wanted to <u>convince</u> him or her that the status quo should be changed.

Grammar Link

Pronoun and Antecedent Agreement

A **pronoun** usually takes the place of a noun or another pronoun. **Antecedents** are the words to which pronouns refer. Pronouns should agree with, or match, their antecedents in number and gender. Look at the sentences below.

1. Give Tasha her book.
2. The cats are meowing for their dinner.
3. Either Luis or Jake has left his jacket.

In the first example, the singular, feminine pronoun *her* agrees with the feminine antecedent *Tasha*. In the second example, the plural pronoun *their* agrees with the plural antecedent cats. The third example demonstrates how the singular pronoun *his* should be used when *or* or *nor* connects two singular subjects of the same gender, in this case, masculine.

Your Turn

The following sentences may contain pronouns that do not agree with their antecedents. If a pronoun is incorrect, replace it with the correct pronoun. If the pronoun is correct, write *C.*

1. A woman who cannot provide for their children is forced to resort to begging.
2. Many children learn to steal the things that he or she need to live.
3. Poor tenants will profit from this proposal since they will have money to pay their rents.
4. Neither a landowner nor a tenant could object to a proposal that would only benefit him.

Writing Application Choose a piece of your own writing, and check to make sure that all pronouns agree with their antecedents. Mark any errors you find, and rewrite for clarity and correctness.

CHOICES

As you respond to the Choices activities, use these **Academic Vocabulary** words as appropriate: approach, convince, dominate, enhance, participate.

REVIEW
Understand Irony in Language
Class Presentation With a partner, return to some of the most ironic passages of *A Modest Proposal.* Work together to analyze and paraphrase Swift's sentences. Then, present your findings to the class. Explain how his outlandish logic would be offensive if taken at face value.

CONNECT
Recreating Irish Life
Timed Writing Using *A Modest Proposal* as the primary source, write an expository essay about the living conditions of the Irish poor in the early 1700s. Use evidence from the text to support your analysis.

EXTEND
Creating Another "Modest" Proposal
TechFocus Create a "modest" proposal of your own. Choose a modern social or political problem, and propose an outrageous solution. Your proposal should take an idea to its most ridiculous extent in order to highlight the seriousness of the problem. Instead of writing a pamphlet as Swift did, create a podcast in which you try to convince your viewers to agree with your solution.

Satirical Novels

INTRODUCTION

THE STING OF SATIRE

by **Robert DeMaria, Jr.**

A **satire** is a piece of writing designed to make its readers feel critical—of themselves, of their fellow human beings, of their society. Some satires, like Alexander Pope's *The Rape of the Lock,* are intended to make us laugh at human foolishness and weakness; these satires are good-natured and laugh-provoking. Other satires, like Swift's *A Modest Proposal,* may make us laugh, but it is often a bitter kind of laughter, arising from anger and indignation at human vices and crimes.

Neither Nice nor Neutral: The Purposes of Satire

No matter how humorous a satire may be, its ultimate purpose is most often serious: Satirists are dissatisfied with the status quo, and want to change things. Instead of giving constructive advice, though, satirists focus solely on what is wrong with the world and its inhabitants. They use exaggeration to make folly, vice, and vanity appear ridiculous and therefore unattractive. We must not expect satirists to be objective or neutral, to present both sides of a question, or to show the good and bad traits of a character. Instead, we must understand that satire is fueled by extravagant exaggeration and wild generalization: Lawyers are greedy, politicians are corrupt, scholars are boring. Satirists make fun of vicious, selfish, mean-spirited people in the hope that we will see aspects of ourselves in such people and mend our ways. Thus, satirists perform an important function in society: They expose errors and absurdities that we no longer notice because custom and familiarity have blinded us to them.

The Uses of Satire

Satire is the most prevalent of all literary forms, appearing in fiction, nonfiction, poetry, and drama. It is also one of the oldest. In its crudest form, invective (another word for name-calling) satire is probably as old as civilization. The more formal satire found in the literature of the West was mostly influenced by ancient Greek and Roman writers.

The Royal Academy Exhibition, by Thomas Rowlandson.

Throughout history, satire has traditionally thrived whenever repressive governments are in power and their obvious corruptions can be ridiculed. Times of prosperity and indulgence, when reckless spending and greed prevail—when upper classes "sup" while the lower classes starve—are likewise eras when satirists flourish.

Scathing Humor: The Weapon of the Satirist

One of the most useful techniques available to the satirist is parody, a mocking imitation of a writer's style or of a particular genre. Often, the style being parodied is applied to a trivial subject. Pope's *The Rape of the Lock,* for example, parodies the epic style to describe the theft of a lock of hair. Likewise, Miguel de Cervantes's *Don Quixote* parodies the chivalric romance, finding its satire in the incongruity that arises from the clash between the romantic and the real. Parody can only be used successfully by writers who are familiar with many works of literature and who understand and appreciate style.

Mick Jagger, by Petar Pismestrovic.

The Great Age of Satire

Satire thrived across western Europe, beginning early in Italy and cropping up later in Spain, most famously in Cervantes's parody of medieval romances, *Don Quixote* (1605). Throughout his comic novel, Cervantes ridicules the often tangled and confusing passages that are hallmarks of chivalric romances. The narrator tells us that Don Quixote read so many romances that "his brain dried up." Many passages from such tales are so convoluted that "Aristotle himself would not have been able to understand them, even if he had been resurrected for that sole purpose." Wickedly, Cervantes quotes literally from a tale by a sixteenth-century writer whose language is so exaggerated that Cervantes does not need to embellish

it further: "The reason of the unreason that afflicts my reason, in such a manner weakens my reason that I with reason lament me of your comeliness."

The great age of Western satire began in the latter half of the seventeenth century and lasted until the middle of the eighteenth century—a time of great social stability, especially in England and France.

The Fate of Satire: Make Way for Romanticism

At the end of the eighteenth century, the American Revolution, the French Revolution, and several other events shattered the peaceful climate that had thus far prevailed. Most European governments became less restrictive, and the sort of oppositional temper that marks satire and parody became harder for writers to invoke. Amid the efforts to build new nations, satire and parody gave way to attempts to recapture the grandeur of the old epics and romances. Human nature was celebrated as naturally good and noble rather than criticized as inherently corrupt and mean.

While some later writers, such as Lord Byron and Charles Dickens, did write masterful satirical works, people, for the most part, sought to glorify the achievements of their cultures. The Romantic lyric, the extended elegy, and the epic narrative became the most popular literary forms in the West in the early part of the nineteenth century. Too much critical honesty finally seemed to be more than society could bear. As one character in Molière's play *The Misanthrope* says:

> "In certain cases, it would be uncouth
> And most absurd to speak the naked truth;
> With all respect for your exalted notions,
> It's often best to veil one's true emotions.
> Wouldn't the social fabric come undone
> If we were wholly frank with everyone?"

Preparing to Read

from Candide

What Do You Think?

How can order and civilization affect human behavior?

QuickTalk

What social injustices exist today? With a small group, discuss how people in your community or in the country are working to solve these problems.

Portrait of Voltaire (1694–1778) after 1718, by Nicholas de Largilliere, oil on canvas, Musée de la Ville de Paris, Musée Carnavalet, Paris, France.

Voltaire
(1694–1778)

François-Marie Arouet, better known by his pen name, Voltaire, was a soldier who fought with words. As a satirist, philosopher, historian, dramatist, and poet, Voltaire wrote works that criticized the wastefulness of war, the intolerance of organized religion, and society's indifferent <u>approach</u> toward the plight of the poor.

A Dangerous Mind

Born in Paris to middle-class parents, Voltaire studied law for a time but soon gave it up to become a writer. His reputation was quickly established based on his classical tragedies and political satires. Voltaire's sharp words were not always well received, however, and a violent encounter with an offended nobleman left Voltaire battered, bruised, and imprisoned. He was exiled to England in 1726.

In London, Voltaire met Jonathan Swift and Alexander Pope and was deeply influenced by the works of Bacon, Newton, and Locke. When Voltaire returned to Paris, he wrote philosophical essays about how people live and work according to their moral principles. Once again, the nobility was not amused. Voltaire's most formidable work, "Essay on the Morals and the Spirit of the Nations from Charlemagne to Louis XIII," was banned, and the controversial author was forced to flee Paris.

The Practical Life

Of Voltaire's numerous romances and tales, *Candide* is his most famous and enduring. Voltaire had little patience for theory and idle speculation. His emphasis on modest but practical action is reflected in the last page of *Candide*: "Let us work without arguing…it's the only way to make life endurable."

Although Voltaire lived much of his later life near the French-Swiss border, he died in Paris at the age of eighty-three on a visit to see his last play produced. He was refused a Christian burial, but his remains were interred in Paris with great ceremony thirteen years later.

Think About the Writer What injustices of today's world would Voltaire criticize? Explain.

Wewelsburg Castle, Germany.

Reader/Writer Notebook

Use your **RWN** to complete the activities for this selection.

Literary Focus

Satire The type of writing known as **satire** ridicules the shortcomings of human beings or institutions in order to bring about change. Satires often try to <u>convince</u> the reader to do or believe something by showing the opposing view as absurd, vicious, or inhumane. Writers use exaggeration, irony, understatement, ridiculous situations, and many other tools to create satire. As you read, learn about Voltaire's beliefs by noting the objects of Voltaire's satire and whether his commentary is gentle or vicious.

Reading Focus

Analyzing an Author's Style An author's **style** is the distinctive way he or she uses language. A style can be casual or formal, plain or elaborate, concrete or abstract, and so on. Elements of style include word choice, syntax, and use of imagery and figurative language. As you read, notice how Voltaire's style <u>enhances</u> his satire.

Into Action As you read, use a chart like the one below to find examples of Voltaire's style. Then, write a brief assessment of each example.

Element of Style	Example	Assessment
Word Choice	Describes Pangloss as an "oracle" and Candide as "little."	Fancy word emphasizes Pangloss's scholarly nature; simple word emphasizes Candide's innocence.
Syntax		
Figurative Language		
Imagery		

Vocabulary

endowed (ehn DOWD) *v.* used as *adj.:* provided with. *Candide was endowed with a simple, trusting nature.*

rendered (REHN duhrd) *v.:* made; caused to be. *The baroness's extreme weight rendered her more respectable to the people of Westphalia.*

candor (KAN duhr) *n.:* honesty; directness. *Innocent Candide reacts to life's unfortunate situations with great candor.*

pensive (PEHN sihv) *adj.* reflective; thoughtful. *Dr. Pangloss's philosophy inspired Cunegonde and made her feel deeply pensive.*

vivacity (vy VAS uh tee) *n.:* liveliness; energetic spirit. *Candide expresses his love for Cunegonde with enthusiasm and vivacity.*

Language Coach

The Sounds of C Use the pronunciation guides to read the Vocabulary words. In which word does the letter *c* have the sound of /k/? In which word does the same letter have the sound of /s/? Notice what vowel follows the letter *c* in each word. Can you make a general pronunciation rule based on what you notice?

Writing Focus

Think as a Reader/Writer

Find It in Your Reading To create effective satire, writers use a variety of tools, including outrageous exaggerations and bizarre statements that are delivered as if they make sense. While reading *Candide,* use your *Reader/Writer Notebook* to track how Voltaire uses these two particular tools of satire within the dialogues between characters.

Learn It Online
Get to know the Vocabulary words inside and out through Word Watch.

go.hrw.com   L12-603   Go

from

CANDIDE

by **Voltaire**   translated by **Richard Aldington**

Read with a Purpose
Candide's name comes from the word *candor,* meaning "honesty" or "direct-ness." Read to discover how Candide lives up to his name.

Build Background
In this excerpt, Voltaire satirizes the nobility, the military, and the ideas of German philos-opher Gottfried Leibniz. Leibniz claimed that a rational God had created a rational world in which everything has a place and a purpose. Voltaire's Dr. Pangloss directly echoes Leibniz every time he proclaims, "In the best of all possible worlds, . . . all is for the best."

Daniel Evans (Candide) and Alex Kelley (Cunegonde) in Candide.

Wewelsburg Castle, Germany

CHAPTER I

How Candide was brought up in a noble castle and how he was expelled from the same

In the castle of Baron Thunder-ten-tronckh in Westphalia[1] there lived a youth, endowed by Nature with the most gentle character. His face was the expression of his soul. His judgment was quite honest and he was extremely simple-minded; and this was the reason, I think, that he was named Candide. Old servants in the house suspected that he was the son of the Baron's sister and a decent honest gentleman of the neighborhood, whom this young lady would never marry because he could only prove seventy-one quarterings,[2] and the rest of his genealogical tree was lost, owing to the injuries of time. The Baron was one of the most powerful lords in Westphalia, for his castle possessed a door and windows. His Great Hall was even decorated with a piece of tapestry. The dogs in his stableyards formed a pack of hounds when necessary; his grooms were his huntsmen; the village curate was his Grand Almoner.[3] They all called him "My Lord," and laughed heartily at his stories. The Baroness weighed about three hundred and fifty pounds, was therefore greatly respected, and did the honors of the house with a dignity which rendered her still more respectable. Her daughter Cunegonde, aged seventeen, was rosy-cheeked, fresh, plump, and tempting. The Baron's son appeared   **B**

A

in every respect worthy of his father. The tutor Pangloss[4] was the oracle of the house, and little Candide followed his lessons with all the candor of his age and character. Pangloss taught metaphysico-theologo-cosmolonigology.[5] He proved admirably that there is no effect without a cause and that in this best of all possible worlds, My Lord the Baron's castle was the best of castles and his wife the best of all possible Baronesses. "'Tis demonstrated," said he, "that things cannot be otherwise; for, since everything is made for an end, everything is necessarily for the best end. Observe that noses were made to wear spectacles; and so we have spectacles. Legs were visibly instituted to be breeched, and we have breeches. Stones were formed to be quarried and to build castles; and My Lord has a very noble castle; the greatest Baron in the province should have the best house; and as pigs were made to be eaten, we eat pork all the year round; consequently, those who have asserted that all is well talk nonsense; they ought to have said that all is for the best." Candide listened attentively and believed innocently; for he thought Mademoiselle Cunegonde extremely beautiful, although he was never bold enough to tell her so. He decided that after the happiness of being born Baron of Thunder-ten-tronckh, the second degree of happiness was to be Mademoiselle Cunegonde; the third, to see her every day; and the fourth to listen to Doctor Pangloss, the greatest philosopher of the province and therefore of the whole world. One day when Cunegonde was walking near the castle, in a little

---

1. **Westphalia:** region in western Germany noted for its excellent ham. In a letter to his niece, Voltaire described Westphalia as "vast, sad, sterile, detestable."
2. **quarterings:** divisions on a coat of arms or family tree. Seventy-one is an absurdly high number, tracing a person's genealogy over two thousand years.
3. **Grand Almoner:** member of a noble household responsible for allotting charity to the poor.

4. **Pangloss:** Greek for "all tongue."
5. **metaphysico-theologo-cosmolonigology:** This nonsense term is a satirical poke at the philosopher Leibniz and his followers, especially the embedded syllable *–nig–*, which is a shortened form of *nigaud*, the French word for "simpleton."

A **Literary Focus** Satire What technique of satire does Voltaire use to describe Candide's genealogy?

B **Reading Focus** Analyzing an Author's Style What words does Voltaire use to describe Cunegonde? How does this word choice affect your image of her?

Vocabulary **endowed** (ehn DOWD) *v.* used as *adj.:* provided with.
rendered (REHN duhrd) *v.:* made; caused to be.
candor (KAN duhr) *n.:* honesty; directness.

wood which was called The Park, she observed Doctor Pangloss in the bushes, giving a lesson in experimental physics to her mother's waiting-maid, a very pretty and docile brunette. Mademoiselle Cunegonde had a great inclination for science and watched breathlessly the reiterated experiments she witnessed; she observed clearly the Doctor's sufficient reason, the effects and the causes, and returned home very much excited, pensive, filled with the desire of learning, reflecting that she might be the sufficient reason of young Candide and that he might be hers. On her **C** way back to the castle she met Candide and blushed; Candide also blushed. She bade him good morning in a hesitating voice; Candide replied without knowing what he was saying. Next day, when they left the table after dinner, Cunegonde and Candide found themselves behind a screen; Cunegonde dropped her handkerchief, Candide picked it up; she innocently held his hand; the young man innocently kissed the young lady's hand with remarkable vivacity, tenderness, and grace; their lips met, their eyes sparkled, their knees trembled, their hands wandered. Baron Thunder-ten-tronckh passed near the screen, and, observing this cause and effect, expelled Candide from the castle by kicking him in the backside frequently and hard. Cunegonde swooned; when she recovered her senses, the Baroness slapped her in the face; and all was in consternation[6] in the noblest and most agreeable of all possible castles. **D**

---

6. **consternation:** bewilderment; dismay.

 **C** Reading Focus Analyzing an Author's Style What techniques does Voltaire use to disguise Pangloss's improper activities in the bushes?

D Literary Focus Satire How does Voltaire use irony to ridicule the Baron's family?

Vocabulary

pensive (PEHN sihv) *adj.* reflective; thoughtful.
vivacity (vy VAS uh tee) *n.:* liveliness; energetic spirit.

Daniel Evans as Candide and Alex Kelley as Cunegonde.

CHAPTER II

What happened to Candide among the Bulgarians

Candide, expelled from the earthly paradise, wandered for a long time without knowing where he was going, turning up his eyes to Heaven, gazing back frequently at the noblest of castles which held the most beautiful of young Baronesses; he lay down to sleep supperless between two furrows in the open fields: It snowed heavily in large flakes. The next morning the shivering Candide, penniless, dying of cold and exhaustion, dragged himself toward the neighboring town, which was called Waldberghoff-trarbk-dikdorff. He halted sadly at the door of an inn. Two men dressed in blue noticed him. "Comrade," said one, "there's a well-built young man of the right height."[7] They went up to Candide and very civilly invited him to dinner. "Gentlemen," said Candide with charming modesty, "you do me a great honor, but I have no money to pay my share." "Ah, sir," said one of the men in blue, "persons of your figure and merit never pay anything; are you not five feet five tall?" "Yes, gentlemen," said he,

---

7. **height:** Voltaire is making fun of the recruiting practices of the "King of the Bulgarians"—Voltaire's satiric name for King Frederick the Great of Prussia—who chose and organized soldiers according to their height.

bowing, "that is my height." "Ah, sir, come to table; we will not only pay your expenses, we will never allow a man like you to be short of money; men were only made to help each other." "You are in the right," said Candide, "that is what Doctor Pangloss was always telling me, and I see that everything is for the best." They begged him to accept a few crowns,[8] he took them and wished to give them an IOU, they refused to take it, and all sat down to table. "Do you not love tenderly ..." "Oh, yes," said he. "I love Mademoiselle Cunegonde tenderly." "No," said one of the gentlemen. "We were asking if you do not tenderly love the King of the Bulgarians." "Not a bit," said he, "for I have never seen him." "What! He is the most charming of kings, and you must drink his health." "Oh, gladly, gentlemen." And he drank. "That is sufficient," he was told. "You are now the support, the aid, the defender, the hero of the Bulgarians, your fortune is made, and your glory assured." They immediately put irons on his legs and took him to a regiment. He was made to turn to the right and left, to raise the ramrod and return the ramrod, to take aim, to fire, to march double time, and he was given thirty strokes with a stick; the next day he drilled not quite so badly, and received only twenty strokes; the day after, he only had ten and was looked on as a prodigy[9] by his comrades. **(E)** Candide was completely mystified and could not make out how he was a hero. One fine spring day he thought he would take a walk, going straight ahead, in the belief that to use his legs as he pleased was a privilege of the human species as well as of animals. He had not gone two leagues[10] when four other heroes, each six feet tall, fell upon him, bound him,

and dragged him back to a cell. He was asked by his judges whether he would rather be thrashed thirty-six times by the whole regiment or receive a dozen lead bullets at once in his brain. Although he protested that men's wills are free and that he wanted neither one nor the other, he had to make a choice; by virtue of that gift of God which is called liberty, he determined to run the gauntlet[11] thirty-six times and actually did so twice. There were two thousand men in the regiment. That made four thousand strokes which laid bare the muscles and nerves from his neck to his backside. As they were about to proceed to a third turn, Candide, utterly exhausted, begged as a favor that they would be so kind as to smash his head; he obtained this favor; they bound his eyes and he was made to kneel down. At that moment the King of the Bulgarians came by and inquired the victim's crime, and as this King was possessed of a vast genius, he perceived from what he learned about Candide that he was a young metaphysician[12] very ignorant in worldly matters, and therefore pardoned him with a clemency[13] which will be praised in all newspapers and all ages. An honest surgeon healed Candide in three weeks with the ointments recommended by Dioscorides.[14] He had already regained a little skin and could walk when the King of the Bulgarians went to war with the King of the Abares.[15] **(F)**

---

8. **crowns:** units of money.
9. **prodigy:** someone gifted from childhood with an exceptional quality or talent.
10. **leagues:** units of distance equal to about three miles.

---

11. **run the gauntlet:** run between two rows of soldiers who strike the victim with clubs or other weapons.
12. **metaphysician:** philosopher who studies the nature of reality and the origin and structure of the universe.
13. **clemency:** tendency to be merciful when deciding a punishment.
14. **Dioscorides:** Greek army physician who wrote a treatise on medicine in the first century a.d. Even in Voltaire's day, Dioscorides' work was out-of-date.
15. **Abares:** that is, the French, who fought against the "Bulgarians," or Prussians, in the Seven Years' War (1756–1763).

(E) Literary Focus Satire What element of satire does Voltaire use to make fun of the military?

(F) Reading Focus Analyzing an Author's Style How does Voltaire use understatement to satirize Candide's "walk" and subsequent arrest?

Respond and Think Critically

Reading Focus

Quick Check

1. How did Candide acquire his name?
2. Explain Doctor Pangloss's philosophy.
3. Why is Candide punished by the Bulgarian army?

Read with a Purpose

4. How does Candide react to his difficulties?

Reading Skills: Analyzing Author's Style

5. As you read, you assessed examples of Voltaire's style. Now add a column to your chart in which you explain how each element of his style <u>enhances</u> the satire of the novel.

Element of Style	Example	Assessment	How It Enhances Satire
Word Choice	Describes Pangloss as an "oracle" and Candide as "little."	Fancy word emphasizes Pangloss's scholarly nature; simple word emphasizes Candide's innocence.	Describing Pangloss as an oracle creates humor since his philosophy turns out to be foolish.
Syntax			
Figurative Language			
Imagery			

Literary Focus

Literary Analysis

6. **Analyze** Do people like Doctor Pangloss exist in today's world of education, politics, or religion?

7. **Evaluate** Based on what you've read of *Candide,* why do you think Voltaire sends Candide through such a damaging series of trials and tribulations?

8. **Interpret** As Chapter II illustrates, Candide suffers every time he exercises what he believes to be his free will. According to Voltaire, what forces get in the way of a person's exercise of free will?

Literary Skills: Satire

9. **Infer** Part of the purpose of satire is to bring about a change in an institution or way of life. What changes do you think Voltaire wanted to influence in French society by writing *Candide*?

Literary Skills Review: Archetype

10. **Compare** An **archetype** is a pattern that has appeared in literature across cultures and times. A common archetype is the journey: A hero is thrust into an strange world to face dangers and wonders. How does this excerpt from *Candide* express the archetype of the journey?

Writing Focus

Think As a Reader/Writer

Use It in Your Writing Review your notes on how Voltaire creates satire. In your *Reader/Writer Notebook,* write a brief dialogue between two characters that uses exaggeration and bizarre statements to highlight a current social problem you'd like to change.

What Do You Think Now How does social order affect the characters in *Candide*?

SKILLS FOCUS Literary Skills Analyze the characteristics of satire. Reading Skills Analyze author's style. Writing Skills Develop characters using

dialogue. Vocabulary Skills Research word origins, including Greek, Latin, and Anglo-Saxon words; demonstrate knowledge of literal meanings of words and their usage.

Vocabulary Development

✓ Vocabulary Check

Match the words with their definitions.

1. endowed
2. rendered
3. candor
4. pensive
5. vivacity

a. liveliness
b. thoughtful
c. innocence in manner
d. made
e. provided with

Vocabulary Skills: Etymology

In some ways, words are like people—they have ancestors and descendants, sisters and brothers, even distant relatives. Knowing a word's **etymology,** or origin and history, will not only help you understand the word itself, but can help you learn definitions of related words without having to find them in a dictionary.

Review the following chart to see how some English words passed into the language from Latin. Also note related words in the third column.

Word	Etymology	Related Words
quarter	Latin *quartus,* "four"	quartering, quarterly, quartet
provide	Latin *pro–,* "before" + *videre,* "to see"	provider, provident, providence
office	Latin *officium,* "duty, service"	official, officer, officiate
prodigy	Latin *prodigium,* "an omen"	prodigious, prodigiously

Your Turn

Make a chart like the one on the left. Then, use a dictionary to list the etymology and related words for each Vocabulary word.

Language Coach

The Sounds of C The letter *c* can have the sound of /k/ or /s/. When a *c* is followed by *a, o, or u,* it usually has the /k/ sound. When it is followed by *i* or *e,* it usually has the /s/ sound. Use a chart like the one below to classify each of the following words: *cosmos, reticent, civility, incognito, campaign, recipient, incumbent, despicable, sincerely, recurring.*

/k/ sound	/s/ sound

Academic Vocabulary

Write About
What techniques did Voltaire use to convince readers that society needed to change? How could the same approach be used today?

Preparing to Read

from Don Quixote

What Do You Think?

How can order and civilization affect human behavior?

QuickWrite

Think of a book, movie, or TV show that made you laugh because it represented ideas, fashions, or styles that were out of date. Why do we consider these things funny? Write your response in your *Reader/Writer Notebook*.

Portrait of Miguel de Cervantes, by Juan de Jaurequi y Aguilar.

MEET THE WRITER

Miguel de Cervantes
(1547–1616)

Unlike his famous protagonist, Miguel de Cervantes fought in many battles and survived many real adventures. He is best remembered, however, for his hilarious novel *Don Quixote*, now considered a cornerstone of Western literature, about a fictional gentleman's imaginary exploits.

Cervantes the Prisoner

In 1569, the young Cervantes, seeing no opportunities at home, joined the army and was wounded at the Battle of Lepanto in 1571. Cervantes hoped to be promoted to an army captain after the war, but he was captured by a band of Barbary pirates. After five years of enslavement in Algeria, Cervantes returned to Spain in 1580 with no hope of resuming his military career. Over the years he worked as a playwright, bureaucrat, and tax collector before landing in jail for failure to pay his debts.

According to legend, Cervantes was in jail when he was struck with the idea for *Don Quixote*. Don Quixote is a poor, aging landowner who reads nothing but romantic tales of chivalry. Teetering on the edge of madness, the old man becomes <u>convinced</u> that he is a knight-errant, even though the age of knights is long past.

Quixote the Conqueror

The Ingenious Gentleman Don Quixote of La Mancha was a smash hit when it was published in 1605. Translations into French and English appeared within ten years.

Despite his book's widespread success, Cervantes remained poor. At the time, authors were at the mercy of publishers and were seldom able to retain the copyrights on their books, a situation that was common until the nineteenth century. *Don Quixote's* publisher, not Cervantes, reaped the lion's share of the book's profits. Cervantes died in poverty on April 22, 1616—one day before Shakespeare. He left the world a comic masterpiece that earned him the title "father of the modern novel."

Think About the Writer *Don Quixote* is a parody of medieval romances. If Cervantes were alive today, what literary genre might he parody? Why?

Reader/Writer Notebook

Use your **RWN** to complete the activities for this selection.

Literary Focus

Parody A **parody** is an imitation of a work of literature, art, or music for amusement or instruction. Parodies often borrow characteristics of the original work and transfer them to a ridiculous subject. Writers take this approach by using exaggeration, verbal irony (saying one thing and meaning another), incongruity (purposefully pairing things that don't belong together), and humorous imitation. Cervantes's object of parody in *Don Quixote* is the medieval romance, which featured chivalrous knights on epic quests, often to win the love of a beautiful noblewoman.

Reading Focus

Drawing Inferences About Character A **character** is an individual in a story or play. Although sometimes writers tell us directly what a character is like, other times we must draw inferences about a character by paying attention to the character's words, appearance, actions, thoughts and feelings, and effect on other characters.

Into Action As you read, use a chart like the one below to note examples of the characters' words and behavior. In the second column, write down the inference you draw from each example.

Words and Behaviors	Inference About Character
"'...it is a great service to God to remove so accursed a breed from the face of the earth.'" (Don Quixote's words)	Quixote believes he is a servant of God on a divine mission.
"Sancho upon his donkey..." (Sancho's actions)	

Vocabulary

vile (vyl) *adj.*: evil, disgusting. *Don Quixote vows to rid the world of the vile giants.*

succor (SUHK uhr) *v.*: to help in time of distress. *Quixote prays that his beloved Dulcinea will succor him as he takes on the great giants.*

enmity (EHN muh tee) *n.*: hostility. *Quixote believes that a powerful magician who bears enmity for him is responsible for turning the giants back into windmills.*

flaccid (FLAS ihd) *adj.*: limp; flabby. *Their water bag had gone flaccid, indicating they would need to find water soon.*

disposition (dihs puh ZIHSH uhn) *n.*: natural qualities of personality. *Sancho Panza claims that he has a gentle and peaceful disposition.*

Language Coach

Homonyms *Vile* is an adjective that means "evil." A *vial* is a small glass bottle. In what kind of story or movie might someone find a vile vial?

Writing Focus

Think as a Reader/Writer

Find It in Your Reading Throughout the novel, Cervantes uses **exaggeration** to create parody. For example, Quixote does not just call out to the windmills, he shouts "at the top of his lungs." As you read, use your *Reader/Writer Notebook* to note how Cervantes uses exaggeration to create his master parody.

TechFocus As you read this selection, think about contemporary parodies you've seen on television, in movies, or on the Internet.

Learn It Online

Let this online video introduction set you off into the world of Don Quixote.

go.hrw.com   L12-603   **Go**

from
Don Quixote

by **Miguel de Cervantes**
translated by **Samuel Putnam**

Read with a Purpose
Read to discover why Don Quixote's imagination is an "affliction."

Build Background
Don Quixote is a middle-aged gentleman who spends all his time reading books about chivalry. Quixote's obsessive reading sends him close to madness when he comes to believe that he himself is a knight-errant. He takes down the family's rusty armor and names his bony old nag Rocinante. He chooses a country girl named Aldonza Lorenzo as his fair lady and renames her Dulcinea del Toboso. As he sets out to right the injustices in the world, he rides alongside his trusty squire, a poor farmer named Sancho Panza. The excerpt you are about to read from Chapter 8 relates what happens when Don Quixote and Sancho catch sight of thirty or forty windmills.

Metal sculpture of Don Quixote, by Windmills in Spain.

from **Chapter 8**

Of the good fortune which the valorous Don Quixote had in the terrifying and never-before-imagined adventure of the windmills, along with other events that deserve to be suitably recorded.

At this point they caught sight of thirty or forty windmills which were standing on the plain there, and no sooner had Don Quixote laid eyes upon them than he turned to his squire and said, "Fortune is guiding our affairs better than we could have wished; for you see there before you, friend Sancho Panza, some thirty or more lawless giants with whom I mean to do battle. I shall deprive them of their lives, and with the spoils from this encounter we shall begin to enrich ourselves; for this is righteous warfare, and it is a great service to God to remove so accursed a breed from the face of the earth."

"What giants?" said Sancho Panza.

"Those that you see there," replied his master, "those with the long arms, some of which are as much as two leagues in length."

"But look, your Grace, those are not giants but windmills, and what appear to be arms are their wings which, when whirled in the breeze, cause the millstone to go."

"It is plain to be seen," said Don Quixote, "that you have had little experience in this matter of adventures. If you are afraid, go off to one side and say your prayers while I am engaging them in fierce, unequal combat." **Ⓐ**

Saying this, he gave spurs to his steed Rocinante, without paying any heed to Sancho's warning that these were truly windmills and not giants that he was riding forth to attack. Nor even when he was close upon them did he perceive what they really were, but shouted at the top of his lungs, "Do not seek to flee, cowards and vile creatures that you are, for it is but a single knight with whom you have to deal!"

At that moment a little wind came up and the big wings began turning.

"Though you flourish as many arms as did the giant Briareus,"[1] said Don Quixote when he perceived this, "you still shall have to answer to me."

He thereupon commended himself with all his heart to his lady Dulcinea, beseeching her to succor him in this peril; and, being well covered with his shield and with his lance at rest, he bore down upon them at a full gallop and fell upon the first mill that stood in his way, giving a thrust at the wing, which was whirling at such a speed that his lance was broken into bits and both horse and horseman went rolling over the plain, very much battered indeed. Sancho upon his donkey came hurrying to his master's assistance as fast as he could, but when he reached the spot, the knight was unable to move, so great was the shock with which he and Rocinante had hit the ground. **Ⓑ**

"God help us!" exclaimed Sancho, "did I not tell your Grace to look well, that those were nothing but windmills, a fact which no one could fail to see unless he had other mills of the same sort in his head?"

"Be quiet, friend Sancho," said Don Quixote. "Such are the fortunes of war, which more than any other are subject to constant change. What is more, when I come to think of it, I am sure that this must be the work of that magician Frestón, the one who robbed me of my study and my books, and who has thus changed the giants into windmills in order to deprive me of the glory of overcoming them, so great is the enmity that he bears me; but in the end his evil arts shall not prevail against this trusty sword of mine."

"May God's will be done," was Sancho Panza's response. And with the aid of his squire the knight was once more mounted on Rocinante, who stood there with one shoulder half out of joint. And so, speaking of the adventure that had just befallen them, they

---

1. **Briareus:** in Greek mythology, a giant with a hundred arms who helped Zeus overthrow the Titans.

Ⓐ Reading Focus Drawing Inferences About Character What do Quixote's words here tell you about his character?

Ⓑ Literary Focus Parody How does Cervantes parody the knight's assault on the giants?

Vocabulary **vile** (vyl) *adj.*: evil, disgusting.
succor (SUHK uhr) *v.*: help in time of distress.
enmity (EHN muh tee) *n.*: hostility.

continued along the Puerto Lápice highway; for there, Don Quixote said, they could not fail to find many and varied adventures, this being a much-traveled thoroughfare. The only thing was, the knight was exceedingly downcast over the loss of his lance.

"I remember," he said to his squire, "having read of a Spanish knight by the name of Diego Pérez de Vargas, who, having broken his sword in battle, tore from an oak a heavy bough or branch and with it did such feats of valor that day, and pounded so many Moors, that he came to be known as Machuca,[2] and he and his descendants from that day forth have been called Vargas y Machuca. I tell you this because I too, intend to provide myself with just such a bough as the one he wielded, and with it I propose to do such exploits that you shall deem yourself fortunate to have been found worthy to come with me and behold and witness things that are almost beyond belief."

_____
2. **Machuca:** literally, "the pounder," the hero of an old ballad.

"God's will be done," said Sancho. "I believe everything that your Grace says; but straighten yourself up in the saddle a little, for you seem to be slipping down on one side, owing, no doubt, to the shaking up that you received in your fall."

"Ah, that is the truth," replied Don Quixote, "and if I do not speak of my sufferings, it is for the reason that it is not permitted knights-errant to complain of any wound whatsoever, even though their bowels may be dropping out."

"If that is the way it is," said Sancho, "I have nothing more to say; but, God knows, it would suit me better if your Grace did complain when something hurts him. I can assure you that I mean to do so, over the least little thing that ails me—that is, unless the same rule applies to squires as well."

Don Quixote laughed long and heartily over Sancho's simplicity, telling him that he might complain as much as he liked and where and when he liked, whether he had good cause or not; for he had read nothing to the contrary in the ordinances[3] of

C **Reading Focus** **Drawing Inferences About Character** What does Sancho's observation that Quixote is sliding off his horse reveal about Sancho?

TECHNOLOGY LINK

Windmill farm, Palm Springs, California.

From Windmills to Wind Turbines

The windmills that Don Quixote battled were wooden structures that used wind to produce energy. Windmills were common throughout Europe beginning in the twelfth century, but by the twentieth century, coal and oil were the <u>dominant</u> fuels, and many people had begun to look for alternative sources of energy that would create less pollution. Wind turbines are modern-day windmills used to generate electricity. They work the same way as traditional windmills: Wind strikes tilted blades, causing them to spin and rotate a central shaft. Unlike old wooden windmills, wind turbines are massive, often towering more than three hundred feet high.

Ask Yourself
Do you think Don Quixote would have done battle with a wind turbine? What other modern technology might he select? Why?

chivalry. Sancho then called his master's attention to the fact that it was time to eat. The knight replied that he himself had no need of food at the moment, but his squire might eat whenever he chose. Having been granted this permission, Sancho seated himself as best he could upon his beast, and, taking out from his saddlebags the provisions that he had stored there, he rode along leisurely behind his master, munching his victuals[4] and taking a good, hearty swig now and then at the leather flask in a manner that might well have caused the biggest-bellied tavern-keeper of Málaga to envy him. Between drafts he gave not so much as a thought to any promise that his master might have made him, nor did he look upon it as any hardship, but rather as good sport, to go in quest of adventures however hazardous they might be.

The short of the matter is, they spent the night under some trees, from one of which Don Quixote tore off a withered bough to serve him as a lance, placing it in the lance head from which he had removed the broken one. He did not sleep all night long for thinking of his lady Dulcinea; for this was in accordance with what he had read in his books, of men of arms in the forest or desert places who kept a wakeful vigil,[5] sustained by the memory of their ladies fair. Not so with Sancho, whose stomach was full, and not with chicory water.[6] He fell into a dreamless slumber, and had not his master called him, he would not have been awakened either by the rays of the sun in his face or by the many birds who greeted the coming of the new day with their merry song.

Upon arising, he had another go at the flask, finding it somewhat more flaccid than it had been the night before, a circumstance which grieved his heart, for he could not see that they were on the way to remedying the deficiency within any very short space of time. Don Quixote did not wish any breakfast; for, as has been said, he was in the habit of nourishing himself on savorous memories. They then set out once more along the road to Puerto Lápice, and around three in the afternoon they came in sight of the pass that bears that name.

"There," said Don Quixote as his eyes fell upon it, "we may plunge our arms up to the elbow in what are known as adventures. But I must warn you that even though you see me in the greatest peril in the world, you are not to lay hand upon your sword to defend me, unless it be that those who attack me are rabble and men of low degree, in which case you may very well come to my aid; but if they be gentlemen, it is in no wise permitted by the laws of chivalry that you should assist me until you yourself shall have been dubbed a knight."

"Most certainly, sir," replied Sancho, "your Grace shall be very well obeyed in this; all the more so for the reason that I myself am of a peaceful disposition and not fond of meddling in the quarrels and feuds of others. However, when it comes to protecting my own person, I shall not take account of those laws of which you speak, seeing that all laws, human and divine, permit each one to defend himself whenever he is attacked."

"I am willing to grant you that," assented Don Quixote, "but in this matter of defending me against gentlemen you must restrain your natural impulses."

"I promise you I shall do so," said Sancho. "I will observe this precept as I would the Sabbath day...." **D**

---

3. **ordinances:** authoritative commands.
4. **victuals:** provisions; food.
5. **vigil:** staying watchfully awake.
6. **chicory water:** inexpensive coffee substitute.

D | **Literary Focus** | Parody What is ironic about Sancho's promise to restrain his "natural impulses" if Don Quixote is attacked?

Vocabulary flaccid (FLAS ihd) *adj.:* limp; flabby. disposition (dihs puh ZIHSH uhn) *n.:* natural qualities of personality.

Respond and Think Critically

Reading Focus

Quick Check

1. After being knocked off his horse, how does Don Quixote explain the fact that the giants are, in fact, windmills?

2. What natural needs does Don Quixote ignore?

Read with a Purpose

3. What point is Cervantes making when he lets Quixote have delusions of knighthood?

Reading Skills: Drawing Inferences About Character

4. Review the examples and inferences in the chart you created. Then, add a column in which you summarize how the inference you made supports the humor and the genre of parody.

Words and Behaviors	Inference About Character	How It Fits the Parody
"'...it is a great service to God to remove so accursed a breed from the face of the earth.'" (Don Quixote's words)	Quixote believes he is a servant of God on a divine mission.	It seems funny that anyone given a divine mandate would fail so miserably all the time.
"Sancho upon his donkey . . ." (Sancho's actions)		

Literary Focus

Literary Analysis

5. **Extend** The word *quixotic,* which means "a well-intentioned but impractical dreamer," comes from Don Quixote. What quixotic characters can you think of? What do they have in common?

6. **Analyze** In his parody, Cervantes uses the techniques of exaggeration, irony, incongruity, and humorous imitation. List one example of each technique used in this selection.

7. **Evaluate** An idealist sees the world as he or she thinks it should be. A realist sees the world as it is. Is Don Quixote an idealist or a realist? Which role does Sancho Panza play? Use examples from the text to support your answer.

Literary Skills: Parody

8. **Infer** Cervantes chose to parody previously idealized concepts such as chivalry and heroism. What does the focus of his parody tell you about his beliefs and philosophies?

Literary Skills Review: Foil

9. **Analyze** A **foil** is a character that is used as a contrast to another character. In what ways is Sancho Panza a foil to Don Quixote? Identify the behaviors that suggest they are opposites.

Writing Focus

Think as a Reader/Writer

Use It in Your Writing Review the notes you took in your *Reader/Writer Notebook* about Cervantes's use of irony and incongruity. Then, write a few paragraphs, using these two devices in a <u>convincing</u> parody of a book, movie, or TV show.

 What Do You Think Now

Why does Cervantes use a fictional character to poke fun at the outdated ideals of chivalry and medieval romance?

Vocabulary Development

✓ Vocabulary Check

Match each Vocabulary word with its synonym.

1. vile   **a.** temperament
2. succor   **b.** droopy
3. enmity   **c.** assist
4. flaccid   **d.** gross
5. disposition   **e.** hostility

Vocabulary Skills: Context Clues

One way to learn the meaning of a new word while reading is to search for context clues. A **context clue** is a word or phrase near an unfamiliar word that provides a hint to the meaning of the unfamiliar word. Clues might be (1) a clause or an adjective that seems related to the unknown word, (2) the subject or topic of the sentence or surrounding sentences, or (3) the object of the verb. Consider this excerpt from the *Don Quixote:*

> He thereupon commended himself with all his heart to his lady Dulcinea, beseeching her to succor him in this peril. (page 605)

The context clues for the Vocabulary word *succor* can be found in the verb *beseeching* and the prepositional phrase *in this peril*. If Quixote is begging or praying for something in a situation of peril, then help or assistance is probably what he wants. Therefore, *succor* must have something to do with relief or assistance.

When searching for context clues, look for words you already know. Also consider the overall meaning of the sentence and the paragraph. These wider contexts can often give you general ideas about the word and point to its likely meaning.

Your Turn

Find each Vocabulary word in the selection. Using a table like the one below, write down the Vocabulary words and the context clues that hint at the meanings of the words. One word has been done for you.

Word	Context Clues
succor	"beseeching," "in this peril"

Language Coach

Homonyms English has many words that sound the same but are spelled differently. These are called **homonyms.** For example, many English speakers pronounce the word *dawn* the same as *Don.* Identify the homonyms for each word below.

1. affect   **4.** mane
2. stair   **5.** male
3. rein   **6.** slay

Academic Vocabulary

Talk About
How does Quixote <u>approach</u> his quest? How does he <u>convince</u> Sancho and those around him that he is a great warrior?

from Don Quixote

Grammar Link

The Literary Present

Correct verb tense is a vital element of effective writing. When writing about events of the past, you write in the past tense. One exception to this rule is the **literary present,** a usage of present tense reserved for writing about events that take place in a literary work. Consider the following sentence:

In the early seventeenth century, Cervantes published *Don Quixote*, a parody in which a middle-aged gentleman comes to believe that he is a noble knight in search of great adventure.

Because Cervantes published *Don Quixote* in the past, you write about that event in the past tense. However, when talking about what happens in the story, you use the literary present tense because the action is still occurring for readers. One exception is when you are writing about events that the characters describe in the past tense, for in that case you use the past tense:

literary present tense
Quixote (tells) Sancho about the magician who (robbed) Quixote of his study and his books.
past tense

Your Turn

Correct the tense in the following sentences, using the literary present when necessary.

1. *Don Quixote* is published in the early seventeenth century.

2. The book described the adventures of a delusional man named Don Quixote and his squire, Sancho.

3. At one point in the story, Quixote spotted an army of giants, which he decided to vanquish from the earth.

Writing Application Write a review or summary of this section of *Don Quixote,* and maintain the literary present tense.

CHOICES

As you respond to the Choices, use these **Academic Vocabulary** words as appropriate: <u>approach</u>, <u>convince</u>, <u>dominate</u>, <u>enhance</u>, <u>participate</u>.

REVIEW
Write a Song
In *Man of La Mancha,* Dale Wasserman's musical adaptation of *Don Quixote,* Quixote sings of his need to "dream the impossible dream." Review the excerpt from *Don Quixote,* and write some lyrics for your own song about this famous character who literally follows his dream.

CONNECT
Create Your Own Parody
TechFocus In a small group, work together to choose a popular song, movie, television show, or video game and create your own parody of it. Think carefully about what piece to choose and what elements of it you want to parody and why. Record your parody, or perform it live for your class. Then, ask the class to <u>participate</u> by discussing what social criticism, if any, they detected in your parody and whether or not the parody form allowed your group to make observations that would not be as easily accepted if said in a more direct way.

EXTEND
Continue the Story
Class Presentation Borrow a copy of Cervantes's *Don Quixote* from your school or local library. Read a few more chapters of the story or the entirety of Quixote's wild adventures. Summarize the chapters you read, and continue to take notes on Cervantes' use of parody. Present your summary of the continued adventures of Don Quixote and Sancho Panza to the class.

World Literature: Satirical Novels

SKILLS FOCUS **Literary Skills** Compare works from different cultures and literary periods. **Writing Skills** Use appropriate organization; support ideas/theses with relevant evidence and details; compare literary works; compare characters or historical figures; compare themes or literary elements.

Writing Focus

Writing a Comparison-Contrast Essay

French writer, Voltaire, broadly criticized his contemporaries. Cervantes, one of the masters of Spanish literature, makes particular fun of the genre of medieval romances. Their works stand today as exemplars of the genre of satire. Using notes from your *Reader/Writer Notebook,* plan and write a comparison-contrast essay about these two examples of satire from *Candide* and from *Don Quixote.*

Review the elements of a comparison-contrast essay before you begin writing.

An Effective Comparison-Contrast Essay
• States the basis of the comparison and contrast in a thesis
• Organizes ideas using the point-by-point method
• Uses and cites text evidence to support each point of comparison and contrast
• Contains few or no errors in spelling, punctuation, and usage

Prewriting

Begin a comparison-contrast essay with a strong basis of comparison. Then, look for differences that will reflect your close reading of the texts and provide additional points of discussion.

Gather Ideas Use a Venn diagram to record your notes about each selection. The major similarities will appear in the middle circle. Unique aspects of each selection will appear in the two outside circles, labeled A and B. Categorize the differences into topics that form the basis of contrast.

Consider the following ideas as you review your notes:

- Compare and contrast the objects of each writer's satire
- Compare and contrast the nature of the humor and tone in the selections
- Compare and contrast the authors' styles
- Compare and contrast the selections' themes
- Compare and contrast the national perspective or interests revealed in each selection.

Develop a Thesis Statement Using your notes, develop a thesis statement that makes an assertion about both the similarities and differences in the two satires. Always begin with a basis of similarity (such as the use of exaggeration) and then focus on the differences in the two pieces.

Sample Thesis:

Although Cervantes and Voltaire are separated by a century, they both use exaggeration as a primary tool of their satire, creating works with very different tones and structures.

Drafting

Because you are using the **point by point** method of organization, begin with the strongest comparison linking the two selections. Develop it in your first body paragraph. Then your next body paragraphs will develop *either* additional similarities or differences. Discuss both selections in each paragraph. Your final body paragraph will focus on the differences between the two satires.

Text Evidence Use direct quotations from both selections to support each point. Punctuate the quotations correctly and interweave them into your own sentences.

Revising and Editing

Reread your draft to determine if you have fully supported your thesis with explanation and text evidence. Read again for grammatical and mechanics errors. Prepare a final copy that is error–free and publish it.

What Do You Think Now How are Candide and Don Quixote affected by their own ideas of what order and civilization should be?

COLLECTION 6

Examined Lives

LITERARY FOCUS
Form and Function in the Age of Reason

The Sharp Family (1779–1781) by Johann Zoffany (1733–1810). Oil on canvas. National Portrait Gallery, London.

CONTENTS

Alexander Pope

Samuel Johnson

Simon Winchester   Link to Today

James Boswell

Thomas Gray

COMPARING TEXTS: VIEWS ON WOMEN'S RIGHTS **Mary Wollstonecraft, Daniel Defoe, Mary, Lady Chudleigh**

"True ease in writing
comes from art, not
chance,
As those move easiest
who have learned to
dance." — **Alexander Pope**

Literary Focus

SKILLS FOCUS **Literary Skills** Evaluate and analyze the philosophical, political, religious, ethical, and social influences of a historical period; understand and analyze elements of literature from the restoration and the eighteenth century.

Form and Function in the Age of Reason by **Leila Christenbury**

Influences on Form and Function in the Age of Reason

- Emphasis on reason, order, science, and philosophy
- Respect for classical forms
- Growth of the middle-class reading public
- Rise in the popularity of prose

The Age of Reason was characterized by the belief that rational thought could improve society. The conservative values of order, decorum, and clarity were of the utmost importance. Nothing during this time was what we would today call *natural*—neither dress, nor manners, nor poetry. Whether the topic was behavior (Alexander Pope), language (Samuel Johnson), or rights (Mary Wollstonecraft and Daniel Defoe), the writers of the eighteenth century relied on logic and structure to instruct their readers.

The Beauty of Order

Today when we think of great poetry, we often think of great feeling: the sonnets of Shakespeare, the private poems of Emily Dickinson, the works of Pablo Neruda or Robert Frost. These poems reveal the poets' innermost thoughts and emotions. Eighteenth-century poets, on the other hand, thought of poetry as having a public function, and they relied on well-defined poetic structures to share their ideas. If, for example, an important person died, a poet might celebrate the deceased in an **elegy,** a poem that mourns the loss of something or someone and often glorifies its subject.

At the opposite extreme, a poet might use satire to expose a certain behavior or person to public ridicule. Alexander Pope's *Rape of the Lock* uses classical epic format to mock the behaviors of the aristocracy. By presenting a frivolous subject in a form typically reserved for lofty characters and ideals, Pope made the structure of his poem a key factor in its satire.

Another poetic genre popular in the eighteenth century was the **ode,** a complex lyric poem on a serious subject. Poets used odes to express a public emotion, such as jubilation over a great victory, or to reflect on a single praiseworthy object or person in a more personal and meditative way.

Common to all of these variations of poetry were carefully constructed rhyme schemes and meter. Poems were never spontaneous and casual—just as people were never to appear in public except in fancy dress.

New Genres for a New Audience

The Age of Reason also produced genres that would appeal to the growing middle class. Newspapers such as the *Tattler* and the *Spectator* contained essays about politics, science, philosophy, literature, and, of course, gossip. Journalists, essayists, and novelists wrote in prose and treated their subjects realistically.

Although all genres emphasized reason, the literature of the eighteenth century is not without feeling. Sentimental dramas and the novels of this era often portray human beings as essentially noble and good, an optimistic view of humanity that pervades many of the period's literary forms.

Ask Yourself

1. How did the literature of the eighteenth century appeal to the intellects of its readers and writers?
2. How does eighteenth-century literature reflect the interests of different social groups?

Learn It Online
Explore the Age of Reason online with *PowerNotes*.

go.hrw.com | L12-613 | Go

Heroic Couplets

from An Essay on Man

from The Rape of the Lock

How can order and civilization affect human behavior?

QuickTalk

Pope believed that education from an early age is essential. Discuss with classmates how formal education can play a role in teaching people about society's expectations for orderly and civil behavior.

MEET THE WRITER

Alexander Pope
(1688–1744)

Alexander Pope, the most important poet of the eighteenth century, was a child prodigy who could speak in meter even before he could pronounce English properly.

This Long Disease

As a Roman Catholic in Protestant England, Pope was prohibited from attending a university. Fortunately, his father was a retired linen merchant who could afford to educate his son at home, an arrangement that suited Pope because of his delicate health. Early in life, Pope had contracted an illness that stunted his growth and disfigured his body. His servants laced him into a canvas brace so that he could sit upright. With the pains he continually suffered in his head, bones, and joints, it is no wonder Pope spoke of his life as "this long disease."

Success at a Young Age

In spite of his poor health, Pope led a remarkably productive life. At age twenty-three, he published *An Essay on Criticism*, a poem partially inspired by the Roman poet Horace's *Art of Poetry*. *The Rape of the Lock*, Pope's satiric classical epic, followed one year later. During his thirties, Pope translated into English two enormous Greek epics, Homer's *Iliad* and, with the help of two assistants, Homer's *Odyssey*. In these works, Pope was not limited by his classical models, but instead enhanced them by creating fresh and original works. For this reason, he is sometimes referred to as a neoclassical (that is, new classical) poet.

Pope's early successes inspired envy in lesser writers who then ridiculed him. To defend himself, Pope turned to satire. *The Dunciad* attacks dull writers and shows the forces of stupidity, ignorance, and folly in the world, while *Moral Essays* passes judgment on certain immoral men and women as well as on very rich people who lack common sense and good taste.

During his lifetime, Pope had a reputation for being cruel and ill-natured, but his many friends, including some of the best writers of the day, found him brilliant in conversation, affable, and generous.

Think About the Writer — What do you think might have inspired Pope to be so productive despite his many difficulties?

Alexander Pope, self-portrait. Bryn Mawr College Art Collection. Bryn Mawr, PA.

Heroic Couplets / *from* **An Essay on Man**

Reader/Writer Notebook

Use your **RWN** to complete the activities for these selections.

Literary Focus

Antithesis Pope frequently uses antitheses. An **antithesis** (an TIHTH uh sihs) expresses contrasting ideas in a grammatically balanced statement: "Give me liberty, or give me death." ("Give me liberty, or kill me" fails as an antithesis because it is not parallel or balanced.) Similarly, Pope balances infinitive against infinitive and adjective against adjective in this line from "Heroic Couplets": "To err is human, to forgive, divine." By compressing elements of similarity and difference, antithesis makes a statement forceful and memorable.

Reading Focus

Identifying the Writer's Stance As a writer, Pope intended to inspire and delight his readers. Thus, his poetry reflects his moral and social values as well as his brilliant ability to entertain. In the selections that follow, Pope uses the structure of heroic couplets (two rhyming lines of iambic pentameter) to concisely and explicitly express his **stance**—his opinion or position—on various topics. In some couplets, he uses antithesis to convey his stance in a more powerful way.

Into Action As you read these selections by Pope, **paraphrase** them, or restate them in your own words. Later, you will use your paraphrases to decipher Pope's stance on each of the topics he addresses.

Passage	Paraphrase
Couplet 1	Making music and writing poetry cannot be taught; these activities are divinely inspired.

Language Coach

Antonyms Words with opposite meanings are called **antonyms**. Some antonym pairs are obvious, such as *good* and *bad*. Others are more subtle. In one couplet, Pope uses *art* and *chance* as antonyms. If in this comparison, art refers to "skill" and chance means "luck," then how are these meanings opposite? How are the words *human* and *divine* antonyms? Are the words *thought* and *passion* antonyms?

Writing Focus

Think as a Reader/Writer

Find It in Your Reading An **antithesis** uses parallel structure to balance contrasting ideas. For example, in couplet six, "To err is human, to forgive, divine," Pope creates antithesis. As you read, record examples of antithesis in your *Reader/Writer Notebook*.

Learn It Online
Follow Pope across the Web with these links.

go.hrw.com   L12-615   **Go**

Heroic Couplets

by **Alexander Pope**

Read with a Purpose
Read to discover the author's views on subjects such as human nature, proper education, and good writing.

Build Background
Pope is the greatest master of the **heroic couplet,** two rhymed lines of iambic pentameter. (For variety, Pope occasionally introduces a triplet.) Though first used extensively by Chaucer, the heroic couplet derives its name from its appearances in Dryden's and Pope's translations of epic poems. Pope's couplets can stand alone, but they are so carefully arranged that they are more like links of a chain than separable units.

1 Music resembles poetry: in each
   Are nameless graces° which no methods° teach,
   And which a master hand alone can reach.
                    —*An Essay on Criticism*, lines 143–145

2 A little learning is a dangerous thing;
   Drink deep, or taste not the Pierian° spring. Ⓐ
                    —*An Essay on Criticism*, lines 215–216

3 Be not the first by whom the new are tried,
   Nor yet the last to lay the old aside.
                    —*An Essay on Criticism*, lines 335–336

4 True ease in writing comes from art, not chance,
   As those move easiest who have learned to dance.
                    —*An Essay on Criticism*, lines 362–363

5 Be thou the first true merit to befriend;
   His praise is lost, who stays till all commend.
                    —*An Essay on Criticism*, lines 474–475

6 Good nature and good sense must ever join;
   To err is human, to forgive, divine.
                    —*An Essay on Criticism*, lines 524–525

1. **nameless graces:** pleasing passages that cannot be explained; **methods:** instruction books for writing poetry.

2. **Pierian** (py IHR ee uhn): an allusion to the Muses, Greek goddesses of the arts and literature. The Muses were said to live in a district of Greece called Pieria.

Ⓐ **Literary Focus** **Antithesis** What examples of parallel structure do you find in this couplet? Describe the structure.

View Across Greenwich Park Toward London by Jean Rigaud (c. 1700–1757). Painted for the King Louis XV of France.
Roy Miles Fine Paintings, London.

7   Hope springs eternal in the human breast:
    Man never is, but always to be blest. **Ⓑ**
          —*An Essay on Man,* Epistle I, lines 95–96

8   'Tis education forms the common mind,
    Just as the twig is bent, the tree's inclined.
          —*Moral Essays,* Epistle I, lines 149–150

9   But when to mischief mortals bend their will,
    How soon they find fit instruments of ill! **Ⓒ**
          —*The Rape of the Lock,* Canto III, lines 125–126

10   Satire's my weapon, but I'm too discreet
    To run amuck, and tilt° at all I meet.
    —*Imitations of Horace, Satire I,* Book II, lines 69–70

10. tilt: charge at or thrust a weapon toward an opponent.

Ⓑ Literary Focus **Antithesis** What is the purpose of the comma in the second line of this couplet? How does this comma affect the antithesis?

Ⓒ Reading Focus **Identifying the Writer's Stance** What does this couplet indicate about Pope's view of his fellow human beings?

from An Essay on Man

by **Alexander Pope**

Read with a Purpose
Read to discover why Pope calls humanity the "glory, jest, and riddle of the world."

Build Background
Published when he was forty-five, *An Essay on Man* is Pope's long (1,304 lines) philosophical poem. Pope's lifetime of reading, in both English and foreign languages, greatly influenced its composition. The poem is concerned with "man," by which Pope means the whole human race, as well as the entire universe. Keep in mind that the ideas in the poem are not merely the private opinions of Pope and his friends but reflections that can be traced in the works of many authors, including Plato, Aristotle, St. Thomas Aquinas, Dante, Erasmus, Shakespeare, Bacon, and Milton.

Know then thyself,° presume not God to scan;°
The proper study of mankind is man.
Placed on this isthmus of a middle state,°   **A**
A being darkly wise, and rudely great:
5 With too much knowledge for the skeptic° side,
With too much weakness for the Stoic's pride,°
He hangs between; in doubt to act, or rest;
In doubt to deem himself a god, or beast;
In doubt his mind or body to prefer;
10 Born but to die, and reasoning but to err;
Alike in ignorance, his reason such,
Whether he thinks too little, or too much:
Chaos of thought and passion, all confused;
Still° by himself abused, or disabused;°
15 Created half to rise, and half to fall;   **B**
Great lord of all things, yet a prey to all;
Sole judge of truth, in endless error hurled:
The glory, jest, and riddle of the world!

1. Know then thyself: moral rule of Socrates and other ethical philosophers. **scan:** pry into; speculate about.
3. Placed . . . middle state: having the rational intellect of angels and the physical body of beasts.
5. skeptic: The ancient Skeptics doubted that humans can gain accurate knowledge of anything. They emphasized the limitations of human knowledge.
6. Stoic's pride: The ancient Stoics' ideal was a calm acceptance of life and an indifference to both pain and pleasure. Stoics are called proud because they refused to recognize human limitations.
14. still: always; continually. **disabused:** undeceived.

A **Reading Focus** **Identifying the Writer's Stance** What does Pope's choice of the word *isthmus* reveal about his thoughts on the place of humankind in the universe?

B **Literary Focus** **Antithesis** How is this line an example of antithesis? What does the antithesis reveal about humanity?

Analyzing Visuals

Viewing and Interpreting Eton College is an elite British high school founded by Henry VI and attended by many prominent people, including members of the royal family. In this photograph, boys from Eton are celebrating a school holiday. How might these boys exemplify Pope's line "The glory, jest, and riddle of the world"?

Applying Your Skills

Heroic Couplets / *from* An Essay on Man

SKILLS FOCUS **Literary Skills** Analyze
antithesis; analyze tone. **Reading Skills**
Analyze the writer's stance. **Writing
Skills** Use parallelism correctly.

Respond and Think Critically

Reading Focus

Quick Check

1. To what does Pope compare an educated mind?

2. What is the "proper study of mankind"?

3. Who is "lord of all things, yet a prey to all"?

Read with a Purpose

4. After reading both selections, how do you think Pope sees human beings as the "glory" of this world? as its "jest"? as its "riddle"?

Reading Skills: Identifying the Writer's Stance

5. Add a column to your chart, explaining what Pope's ideas reveal about his beliefs and values.

Passage	Paraphrase	Writer's Stance
Couplet 1	Making music and writing poetry cannot be taught; these activities are divinely inspired.	Artistic inspiration comes from God.

Literary Focus

Literary Analysis

6. Extend Think of some examples of how a little learning could be a dangerous thing (couplet 2).

7. Interpret How is satire a weapon? According to couplet 10, why does Pope show restraint in using satire?

8. Infer In *An Essay on Man,* Pope often says something flattering about humanity, only to follow it with something critical. Of what characteristics does he think we should be proud or ashamed?

9. Compare How does Pope's view of humanity compare with Hamlet's view in the following lines from *Hamlet,* Act II, Scene 2? How does it compare with your own view?

> What a piece of work is man! how noble in reason! how infinite in faculties! in form and moving how express and admirable! in action how like an angel! in apprehension how like a god! the beauty of the world, the paragon of animals!

Literary Skills: Antithesis

10. Analyze How is antithesis used in line 4 of the excerpt from *An Essay on Man*?

11. Evaluate How does Pope's use of antithesis help you understand his opinions about human nature?

Literary Skills Review: Tone

12. Analyze The attitude a writer takes toward his or her subject is called **tone.** Tone can usually be described with an adjective, such as *pessimistic* or *humorous.* Describe Pope's tone in the excerpt from *An Essay on Man.* Explain your answer, using evidence from the text.

Writing Focus

Think as a Reader/Writer

Use It in Your Writing What are your beliefs about human nature, education, writing, giving praise, and other topics that Pope addresses? Use antithesis to write three statements that express your beliefs about some of these topics.

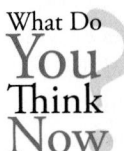 What Do **You Think Now**

Would Pope say that people are essentially civilized and ordered or essentially chaotic? Explain your answer.

from **The Rape of the Lock**

Identifying Tone by **Kylene Beers**

Tone can describe a person's voice, a piece of music, shades of color, or the tension in a muscle. In literature, **tone** reflects an author's attitude toward the subject, a character, or the reader. Authors do not always directly state what they think about what they write. Instead, they choose words and include details that imply their stance. These words and details contribute to the tone of a work of literature. Identifying tone can help you determine the author's purpose and lead you to the work's theme.

In *The Rape of the Lock*, Alexander Pope mocks the way aristocrats behave when they are "seeing and being seen." In the following passage, for example, Pope describes a group of wealthy, attractive young men and women as they meet at a fashionable court.

> In various talk th' instructive hours they
>   passed,
> Who gave the ball, or paid the visit last;
> One speaks the glories of the British queen,
> And one describes a charming Indian screen;
> A third interprets motions, looks, and eyes;
> At every word a reputation dies.
> Snuff, or the fan, supply each pause of chat,
> With singing, laughing, ogling, and all that.

Notice the details Pope includes, and consider what they imply. The young people gossip about recent social events, flatter the queen, and anticipate each others' social mistakes, but what is their goal? Why are these behaviors and attitudes important to the young people? "At every word," Pope observes, "a reputation dies." Pope's wry language indicates that the young people vie for status and approval while hoping for the downfall of others. He renders their conversation superficial and their actions insignificant through his choice of the word *chat* and his use of the direct rhyme "and all that." Given the details he includes and the words he uses, what does Pope think about his characters? His tone indicates he finds them silly and more than a little phony. Pope's characters resemble today's celebrities who are "famous for being famous" rather than for anything they produce or do.

The Author and His Publisher (1784) by Thomas Rowlandson (1756–1827). Gray wash and watercolor over pencil on laid paper.   Yale Center for British Art, Paul Mellon Collection, U.S.

Your Turn

Read the following lines from *The Rape of the Lock*, and then discuss with a partner the tone of the Baron's victory speech. Which words reveal the Baron's values? Which words express Pope's views about the Baron's behavior? (In the third line, "nymphs" are lovely young women.) What is Pope's tone in this passage?

> "Let wreaths of triumph now my
>   temples twine,"
> The victor cried, "the glorious prize is
>   mine! …
> While nymphs take treats, or assigna-
>   tions give,
> So long my honor, name, and praise
>   shall live!"

Learn It Online
Learn how to identify tone through *PowerNotes*.

go.hrw.com   LE9-91   **Go**

Preparing to Read

from The Rape of the Lock

Reader/Writer
Notebook
Use your **RWN** to complete the activities for this selection.

SKILLS FOCUS Literary Skills Understand characteristics of the mock epic. **Reading Skills** Identify tone.

Literary Focus

Mock Epic *The Rape of the Lock* is a **mock epic,** a poem that takes the form of an epic and treats a trivial subject in a lofty manner. Humor arises from the discrepancy between the insignificant subject (in this case, the snipping of a piece of hair) and the grandiose treatment. Pope combines the classic with the absurd by putting traditional devices found in serious epics into a tame, domestic context. For example, classical epics have deities who intervene in human affairs. Following these models, Pope creates "sylphs," tiny, airy spirits who try to prevent the assault on Belinda's curl.

Reading Focus

Identifying Tone The attitude a writer takes toward the reader, a subject, or a character is called **tone.** Pope conveys a satirical tone through the mock epic form, contrasting lofty style with trivial subjects.

Into Action As you read, use a chart like the one below to record words and details that will help you identify Pope's tone.

Person or Event	Line Number(s)	Words and Details Pope Uses
Queen Anne	7–8	Pope describes the queen as taking "counsel," or advice, and "tea" as if they are equally important.

Writing Focus

Think as a Reader/Writer

Find It in Your Reading Pope borrows the epic's convention of the **catalog,** a long list of objects or qualities. In an epic, a catalog details a warrior's weapons, qualities, and victories, or lists the characters' noble ancestry. Pope uses catalogs to lend a grandiose flare to his work, as when he describes how aristocrats pass their time. In your *Reader/Writer Notebook*, note Pope's catalogs and how they influence the poem's tone.

TechFocus As you read this selection, notice how Pope conveys his tone. How does he show that he is speaking satirically?

Vocabulary

reputation (rehp yoo TAY shuhn) *n.:* people's opinion of a person. *One young lady strives to maintain her reputation while ruining those of her rivals.*

stratagems (STRAT uh juhmz) *n. pl.:* clever plans to achieve a goal. *Belinda's stratagems help her win the card game.*

ambitious (am BIHSH uhs) *adj.:* aiming for a goal that is hard to reach. *The man who tries to win the affection of indifferent Belinda is ambitious indeed.*

radiant (RAY dee uhnt) *adj.:* shining with beams of light. *The many candles of Hampton Court projected a radiant glow on the fashionable crowd.*

consecrate (KAHN suh krayt) *v.:* make honorable and sacred. *A true gentleman would consecrate his affection for his lady by treating her well.*

Language Coach

Suffixes A suffix at the end of a word can help you identify the word's part of speech. The suffix *—ant* is found at the end of many adjectives, such as *radiant*. You can form a related verb by changing the suffix to *—ate*. What do you think the verb *radiate* means? What Vocabulary word shares the same suffix?

Learn It Online
Get to know the Vocabulary words online through *Word Watch.*

go.hrw.com | L12-621 | **Go**

from The Rape of the Lock

by **Alexander Pope**

Read with a Purpose

Read to experience Alexander Pope's amusing look at the battle of the sexes in eighteenth-century England.

Build Background

The title of Pope's comic masterpiece means "the violent theft of a lock of hair." The poem is based on a real incident in which a lock belonging to a rich and fashionable young lady named Arabella Fermor was stolen by an equally rich and fashionable young man named Robert, Lord Petre. When Robert snipped a curl of Arabella's hair, he set off a quarrel between the Fermor and Petre families. As it turned out, the feud subsided into laughter, thanks largely to Alexander Pope.

Pope's poem is divided into five sections called cantos. *Canto I begins like a proper epic, with a statement of the subject and an invocation to the Muse—a female deity who was supposed to inspire poets and other artists. Pope, however, clearly signals his comic intentions in the very first couplet:*

> What dire offense from amorous causes springs,
>   What mighty contests rise from trivial things,
>   I sing—

In Canto II, Belinda and her friends take a boat up the river Thames to a party. All who see her admire the two beautiful curled locks that hang down her back. And despite the small army of sprites (spirits) assigned to protect Belinda's beautiful hair, the Baron resolves to possess these locks.

A Woman in Blue (Portrait of the Duchess of Beaufort) (late 1770s) by Thomas Gainsborough (1727–1788). Hermitage, St. Petersburg, Russia.

from **Canto III**

Close by those meads, forever crowned with flowers,
Where Thames with pride surveys his rising towers,
There stands a structure° of majestic frame,
Which from the neighboring Hampton takes its name.
5 Here Britain's statesmen oft the fall foredoom
Of foreign tyrants, and of nymphs° at home;
Here thou, great Anna!° whom three realms obey,
Dost sometimes counsel take—and sometimes tea.
  Hither the heroes and the nymphs resort,
10 To taste awhile the pleasures of a court;
In various talk th' instructive hours they passed,
Who gave the ball, or paid the visit last;
One speaks the glory of the British queen,
And one describes a charming Indian screen;
15 A third interprets motions, looks, and eyes;
At every word a reputation dies. **Ⓐ**
Snuff,° or the fan,° supply each pause of chat,
With singing, laughing, ogling, and all that.
  Meanwhile, declining from the noon of day,
20 The sun obliquely shoots his burning ray;
The hungry judges soon the sentence sign,
And wretches hang that jurymen may dine. . . . **Ⓑ**
Belinda now, whom thirst of fame invites,
Burns to encounter two adventurous knights,
25 At omber° singly to decide their doom;
And swells her breast with conquests yet to come. . . .
The nymph exulting fills with shouts the sky;
The walls, the woods, and long canals reply.
  Oh thoughtless mortals! ever blind to fate,
30 Too soon dejected and too soon elate.
Sudden, these honors shall be snatched away,
And cursed forever this victorious day.
  For lo! the board with cups and spoons is crowned,
The berries° crackle, and the mill° turns round;
35 On shining altars of Japan° they raise

Ⓐ **Literary Focus** Mock Epic How is the epic form mocked in Canto III, lines 11–16?

Ⓑ **Reading Focus** Identifying Tone The central action of the poem is trivial. Lines 21–22, however, describe some real life-and-death situations. What tone does Pope use in these lines?

Vocabulary **reputation** (rehp yoo TAY shuhn) *n.*: people's opinion of a person.

---

3. **structure:** Hampton Court, a royal residence on the river Thames, upstream from London.
6. **nymphs:** young ladies.
7. **Anna:** Queen Anne (1665–1714), who ruled England, Ireland, and Scotland.
1–16. *In lines 1–8, notice how Pope juxtaposes, or places side by side, the grandiose and the trivial: At Hampton Court, statesmen discuss the fall of tyrants—and also of young ladies. Meanwhile, Queen Anne is sometimes served political counsel—and at other times, tea.*
? *What does line 16 tell you about life at the court?*
17. **snuff:** powdered tobacco product sniffed or rubbed on the teeth and gums. **fan:** standard equipment for a lady.
21–22. *These clever lines have been quoted for centuries.*
? *What do these two lines mean?*
25. **omber:** card game for three players, popular in the eighteenth century.
? **23–28.** *What is Belinda's ambition? How does Pope describe Belinda?*
33–52. *In this verse paragraph, Pope sets the scene for the grand offense. The rich are gathered in a sitting room at Hampton Court, drinking endless cups of coffee.*
? *What are Belinda's companions doing? What is the Baron doing?*
34. **berries:** coffee beans. **mill:** coffee grinder.
35. **altars of Japan:** small, lacquered tables.

The silver lamp; the fiery spirits blaze:
From silver spouts the grateful liquors glide,
While China's earth° receives the smoking tide.°
At once they gratify their scent and taste,
40 And frequent cups prolong the rich repast.
Straight hover round the fair her airy band;
Some, as she sipped, the fuming liquor fanned,
Some o'er her lap their careful plumes displayed,
Trembling, and conscious of the rich brocade.
45 Coffee (which makes the politician wise,
And see through all things with his half-shut eyes)
Sent up in vapors to the Baron's brain
New stratagems, the radiant lock to gain.
Ah, cease, rash youth! desist ere 'tis too late,
50 Fear the just gods, and think of Scylla's fate!°
Changed to a bird, and sent to flit in air,
She dearly pays for Nisus' injured hair!
　　But when to mischief mortals bend their will,
How soon they find fit instruments of ill!
55 Just then, Clarissa drew with tempting grace
A two-edged weapon from her shining case:
So ladies in romance assist their knight,
Present the spear, and arm him for the fight.
He takes the gift with reverence, and extends
60 The little engine° on his fingers' ends;
This just behind Belinda's neck he spread,
As o'er the fragrant steams she bends her head.
Swift to the lock a thousand sprites repair,
A thousand wings, by turns, blow back the hair;
65 And thrice they twitched the diamond in her ear;
Thrice she looked back, and thrice the foe drew near.
Just in that instant, anxious Ariel° sought
The close recesses of the virgin's thought;
As on the nosegay in her breast reclined,
70 He watched th' ideas rising in her mind,
Sudden he viewed, in spite of all her art,
An earthly lover lurking at her heart.°
Amazed, confused, he found his power expired,
Resigned to fate, and with a sigh retired.
75 　　The peer now spreads the glittering *forfex*° wide,
T' enclose the lock; now joins it, to divide.

---

38. China's earth: cups made of earthenware. **smoking tide:** coffee.

50. Scylla's fate: In Greek mythology, Scylla (SIHL uh) is turned into a seabird by the gods after she betrays her father, Nisus, by cutting off his purple lock of hair, on which his life and kingdom depend.

? 55–62. *What action is described in these lines?*

60. engine: instrument.

63–74. *Having been armed by an accomplice, the Baron advances toward Belinda's back and then retreats three times in rapid sequence. This comical image mimics the rhythms of fencing.*

67. Ariel: chief of the heavenly sprites sent to protect Belinda.

72. earthly lover . . . heart: If in her heart Belinda wants the Baron to succeed, the sprites cannot protect her.

75. *forfex*: Latin for "scissors."

? 75–82. *How is the theft of the lock accomplished?*

 Literary Focus Mock Epic In what ways is this treatment of coffee-making characteristic of a mock epic?

Vocabulary **stratagems** (STRAT uh juhmz) *n. pl.:* clever plans to achieve a goal.

Even then, before the fatal engine closed,
A wretched sylph too fondly interposed;
Fate urged the shears, and cut the sylph in twain,
80   (But airy substance soon unites again).
The meeting points the sacred hair dissever
From the fair head, forever, and forever!
    Then flashed the living lightning from her eyes,
And screams of horror rend th' affrighted skies.
85   Not louder shrieks to pitying Heaven are cast,
When husbands, or when lapdogs breathe their last;
Or when rich china vessels fallen from high,
In glittering dust, and painted fragments lie!
    "Let wreaths of triumph° now my temples twine,"
90   The victor cried, "the glorious prize is mine!
While fish in streams, or birds delight in air,
Or in a coach and six° the British fair,
As long as *Atalantis*° shall be read,
Or the small pillow grace a lady's bed,
95   While visits shall be paid on solemn days,
When numerous wax lights in bright order blaze,
While nymphs take treats, or assignations give,
So long my honor, name, and praise shall live!
What time would spare, from steel receives its date,°
100 And monuments, like men, submit to fate!"…

83–88. *Belinda screams in horror at the abduction of her lock.*

? *To what three kinds of shrieks is Belinda's shriek compared?*

89–100. *Like a victorious epic hero, the Baron sings of his mighty conquest, observing that while men and monuments shall pass away, his name shall live forever.*

? *Why is the Baron's attitude amusing? How long will the Baron's reputation really last—and how can you tell?*

89. wreaths of triumph: like the ones worn by athletic and military heroes in ancient times.

92. coach and six: coach with six horses.

93. *Atalantis:* *The New Atalantis* (1709), a fashionable novel by Mrs. Delarivière Manley, which thinly disguises some contemporary scandals.

99. date: destruction.

MUSIC LINK

A View of the Fireworks and Illuminations at his Grace the Duke of Richmond's at Whitehall and on the River Thames on Monday, May 15, 1749. Colored engraving.

Water Music

In *The Rape of the Lock,* Belinda rides a "painted Vessel," a decorated barge, down the river, "While melting Musick steals upon the Sky." During Pope's time, noble families hired musicians to accompany their journeys along the Thames river. In 1717, German composer George Frideric Handel (1685–1759), composed his famous *Water Music* for a celebratory boat ride for the new king, George I. The debut was a hit with the King, who enjoyed the one-hour composition so much that he insisted it be played three times. In 2005, a London documentary team recreated the original performance, with musicians wearing authentic costumes and playing period instruments.

Ask Yourself
Do you think the aristocrats in Pope's poem would have appreciated Handel's music? Why or why not?

In Canto IV, Pope describes an incident that occurs in all proper epics: a descent into the underworld. Just as Virgil had Aeneas travel down to Hades, Pope has Umbriel, a "melancholy sprite," fly down to a dismal, imaginary place called the Cave of Spleen. (Spleen is the eighteenth-century term for depression; rich, idle people were particularly subject to spleen in Pope's day.) In the cave, Umbriel obtains a vial of "soft sobs, melting griefs, and flowing tears," as well as an immense bag full of "sighs, sobs, and passions," which somewhat resembles the bag of unfavorable winds in Homer's Odyssey, *given to Odysseus to keep tightly closed so his ship won't be blown off course. Umbriel then returns to the earth's surface and empties the contents of the bag and vial over Belinda and her friend, who is even angrier than Belinda. The canto ends with Belinda lamenting to the Baron:*

> "O, hadst thou, cruel! been content to seize
> Hairs less in sight, or any hairs but these!"

The others in Belinda's tea-party audience shed tears of pity, but the Baron ignores her pleas: "Fate and Jove had stopped the Baron's ears."

from Canto V

…"To arms, to arms!" the fierce virago° cries,
And swift as lightning to the combat flies.
All side in parties, and begin th' attack;
Fans clap, silks rustle, and tough whalebones° crack;
5   Heroes' and heroines' shouts confus'dly rise,
And bass and treble voices strike the skies.   **D**
No common weapons in their hands are found,
Like gods they fight, nor dread a mortal wound. . . .°
    See, fierce Belinda on the Baron flies,
10 With more than usual lightning in her eyes:
Nor feared the chief th' unequal fight to try,
Who sought no more than on his foe to die.
But this bold lord with manly strength endued,
She with one finger and a thumb subdued:
15 Just where the breath of life his nostrils drew,
A charge of snuff the wily virgin threw;
The gnomes direct, to every atom just,
The pungent grains of titillating dust.
Sudden with starting tears each eye o'erflows,

D **Literary Focus** Mock Epic How do the first six lines of Canto V parody a classical epic?

1. virago: ferocious woman; here, Belinda's friend, who leads the attack on the Baron and his friends.

4. whalebones: Whalebones were used to shape and stiffen women's clothing.

8. Like gods . . . mortal wound: Like gods, who are immortal and do not fear physical wounds, these fighters do not fear wounds inflicted by words.

? **1–8.** *What is being described in these lines?*

9–20. *Belinda avenges herself by throwing snuff in the Baron's face to make him sneeze.*

? *How does this silly action reflect the mock epic genre?*

Sir Plume Demands the Restoration of the Lock (1854) by C. R. Leslie. Oil.

20   And the high dome re-echoes to his nose.
   "Now meet thy fate," incensed Belinda cried,
And drew a deadly bodkin° from her side. ...   **E**
   "Boast not my fall," he cried, "insulting foe!
Thou by some other shalt be laid as low.
25   Nor think, to die dejects my lofty mind:
All that I dread is leaving you behind!
Rather than so, ah, let me still survive,
And burn in Cupid's flames—but burn alive."
   "Restore the lock!" she cries; and all around
30   "Restore the lock!" the vaulted roofs rebound.

E Literary Focus Mock Epic What other form of revenge does Belinda threaten to take? How do her weapons compare to those used in a traditional epic?

22. bodkin: long, ornamental hairpin shaped like a dagger.

? 29–38. *Paraphrase this verse paragraph. Why, according to the speaker, is the lock unable to be found?*

from The Rape of the Lock   **627**

Not fierce Othello° in so loud a strain
Roared for the handkerchief that caused his pain.
But see how oft ambitious aims are crossed,
And chiefs contend till all the prize is lost!

35 The lock, obtained with guilt, and kept with pain,
In every place is sought, but sought in vain:
With such a prize no mortal must be blessed,
So Heaven decrees! with Heaven who can contest?
    Some thought it mounted to the lunar sphere,

40 Since all things lost on earth are treasured there.
There heroes' wits are kept in ponderous vases,
And beaux'° in snuffboxes and tweezer cases. **F**
There broken vows and deathbed alms are found,
And lovers' hearts with ends of riband bound. …

45   But trust the Muse—she saw it upward rise,
Though marked by none but quick, poetic eyes: …
A sudden star, it shot through liquid air,
And drew behind a radiant trail of hair.°…
    Then cease, bright nymph! to mourn thy ravished hair,

50 Which adds new glory to the shining sphere!
Not all the tresses that fair head can boast,
Shall draw such envy as the lock you lost.
For, after all the murders° of your eye,
When, after millions slain, yourself shall die;

55 When those fair suns shall set, as set they must,
And all those tresses shall be laid in dust,
This lock, the Muse shall consecrate to fame,
And midst the stars inscribe Belinda's name. **G**

31. Othello: Shakespeare's tragic hero Othello gave his wife a handkerchief, which his enemy stole and then used as false evidence of the wife's unfaithfulness.

42. beaux': fashionable gentlemen's.

45–48. *What has become of the lock?*

48. trail of hair: The word *comet* derives from a Greek word for "long-haired."

53. murders: Just as Belinda's eyes are said to "eclipse the day" (Canto I, line 14), here they are said to murder the young men who admire her. Both compliments are ancient and overused in love poetry.

49–58. *Even though the lock is gone forever, its very loss will ensure Belinda's lasting fame.*
Who, according to the poet, is the true (though comic) hero?

F **Reading Focus** **Identifying Tone** What does Pope seem to imply about the intelligence of beaux in Canto V, lines 41–42?

G **Literary Focus** **Mock Epic** What does Pope describe in Canto V, lines 51–58? What consolation does he offer?

Vocabulary **ambitious** (am BIHSH uhs) *adj.*: aiming at a goal that is hard to reach.
radiant (RAY dee uhnt) *adj.*: shining with beams of light.
consecrate (KAHN suh krayt) *v.*: make honorable and sacred.

Applying Your Skills

from **The Rape of the Lock**

Respond and Think Critically

Reading Focus

Quick Check

1. How do the heroes of this mock epic differ from the conventional epic hero?

2. Why have "the heroes and the nymphs" gathered at Hampton Court?

3. What events serve as "epic battles"?

Read with a Purpose

4. Who and what is Pope mocking in this epic?

Reading Skills: Identifying Tone

5. Add a column labeled "Tone" to the right side of your chart. For each row, decide what Pope's choice of words and details suggests about his attitude toward the person or event that he describes. Write an adjective describing the tone and a short sentence explaining your choice. When you are finished, discuss with a partner the overall tone of the selection.

Person or Event	Line Number(s)	Words and Details Pope Uses	Tone
Queen Anne	7–8	Pope describes the queen as taking "counsel," or advice, and "tea" as if they are equally important.	Comic. By elevating the act of drinking to the level of talking to a royal counselor, Pope establishes a comic tone.

Literary Focus

Literary Analysis

6. **Analyze** The worlds outside and inside the poem come together in Canto III (lines 7–8). What is the effect of the three words after the dash?

7. **Interpret** In Canto III, line 86, Pope **juxtaposes,** or places side by side, "dying husbands" and "dying lapdogs." What is the effect of this juxtaposition? Find other surprising juxtapositions in the poem, and describe their effects.

8. **Extend** How does the poem apply to contemporary life? What passages could serve as satirical commentaries on people's behavior today?

Literary Skills: Mock Epic

9. **Analyze** Who, if anyone, is victorious at the end of the poem? How does the victor compare to the victor in a conventional epic? Cite lines from the poem to support your opinion.

Literary Skills Review: Epic Simile

10. **Analyze** A mock epic parodies the classic epic's style and conventions. Since Homer, the epic's hallmark has been the **epic simile,** or extended comparison between two unlike things. What things are compared in Canto III (lines 57–58 and 85–88) and Canto V (lines 31–32)?

Writing Focus

Think as a Reader/Writer

Use It in Your Writing As you read, you noted how Pope uses catalogs to influence the poem's tone. In your *Reader/Writer Notebook*, write a short essay that incorporates a catalog. You might describe something common, such as a student's day, incorporating a list of activities. Include humorous and unexpected items to create a light-hearted tone, or scholarly items to convey a serious tone.

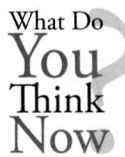
What Do **You Think Now** What emotions provoke the breakdown in orderly behavior that leads to the fighting at Hampton Court?

Applying Your Skills

from **The Rape of the Lock**

Vocabulary Development

✓ Vocabulary Check

Match the Vocabulary words with their definitions.

1. reputation
2. strategems
3. ambitious
4. radiant
5. consecrate

a. make worthy of honor
b. clever plans
c. glowing
d. people's opinion of a person
e. eager for great things

Vocabulary Skills: Etymology Maps

One important piece of information you find when you look up a word in the dictionary is its **etymology**—the word's origin and development over time. If you look up the word *etymology,* for instance, you will learn that it comes from the Greek word *etymos,* meaning "true," and the Greek suffix *logos,* meaning "word." So, to know a word's etymology is to know its true meaning in the sense that you know its history—where it came from and how it came to its current usage.

An etymology map will help you organize information about a word's origin and development. It will also help you connect the word with ideas you already know so that you can remember it more easily. Look at this etymology map for *exulting,* a word Pope uses in his poem:

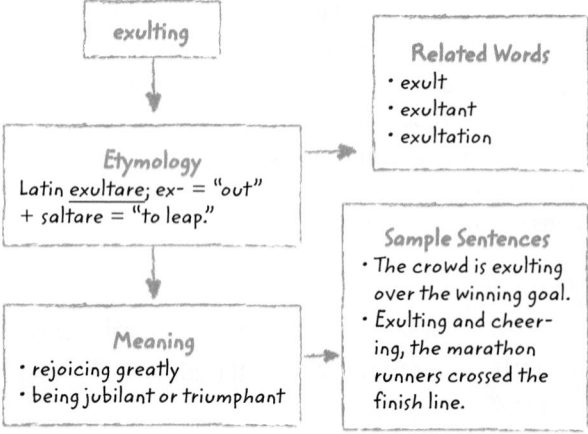

Your Turn

Use a dictionary to create an etymology map for each Vocabulary word. If you are ambitious, like the Baron, and want to know more about these words, consult the *Oxford English Dictionary* online or in a library. Compare your sample sentences with those of your classmates.

Language Coach

Suffixes Some adjectives are formed using the suffix *–ant.* Some verbs are formed using the suffix *–ate.* Choose the best word to complete each sentence. Consider whether the missing word should be an adjective or a verb. Use a dictionary to find the meanings of unfamiliar words.

1. The Baron was captivated by Belinda's (radiate, radiant) smile.
2. It seems that Belinda must (tolerant, tolerate) his advances.
3. Who do you think is the (dominant, dominate) fighter in their battle?
4. Their conflict would probably (stagnate, stagnant) if just one of them lost interest.

Academic Vocabulary

Talk About
In a small group, talk about how a mock epic might <u>convince</u> people that their behavior is silly or inappropriate by <u>enhancing</u> their self-awareness. Use the underlined Academic Vocabulary words as you <u>participate</u> in the discussion.

Grammar Link

Sequence of Verb Tenses

When writing about events that occur at the same time, use verbs in the same tense. When writing about events that occur at different times, use verbs in different tenses to show the **sequence** of events.

I swim while Bill lifts weights. (The actions occur at the same time.)

Maria told Tim that she had mentioned the concert to John. (She mentioned the concert to John before she told Tim that she had mentioned it.)

Tense	Usage	Example
Past Perfect	happening before a specific time in the past	I had saved; she had saved
Past	happening in the past	I saved; he saved
Present Perfect	happening sometime before now; may be continuing now	I have saved; she has saved
Present	existing or happening now	I save; he saves
Future Perfect	happening before a specific time in the future	I will have saved; she will have saved
Future	happening in the future	I will save; he will save

Your Turn

Revise each sentence to correct the error in verb tense.

1. We appreciated Pope's saying that to err was human.

2. Would Pope have been cruel if he knew how his cruelty would affect his reputation?

Writing Application Look over a few paragraphs of an essay you have written. Circle any incorrect verb tenses and revise those sentences appropriately.

CHOICES

As you respond to the Choices activities, use these **Academic Vocabulary** words as appropriate: approach, convince, dominate, enhance, participate.

REVIEW

Illustrate the Scene

How might an illustration capture Pope's satirical tone? Choose a scene from the poem, along with lines to serve as a caption to incorporate into an illustration or place below it. Choose a medium, and use composition, line, space, color, or other artistic elements to convey Pope's tone through your illustration. Write a brief essay explaining your approach to expressing satire visually. What problems did you encounter, and how did you solve them?

CONNECT

Compose a Letter

Recall that Pope based his mock epic on a real incident: Robert, Lord Petre's snipping of a lock of Arabella Fermor's hair. Assume that Robert regretted his action. Write a letter from Robert to Arabella in which he sincerely tries to convince her that he is sorry for his behavior. Use a tone that conveys the formality and decorum associated with the social standing of the parties concerned. Then, rewrite the letter to give it a satirical tone.

EXTEND

Analyze and Compare Strategies

TechFocus Today, people sometimes have difficulty deciphering the tone of e-mail communications. Think of some examples, from your own experiences if possible, in which an e-mail's tone could be ambiguous. What strategies do people use in e-mails to convey their tones or their emotions about what they are writing? Compare these strategies with the ways Pope reveals his tone in *The Rape of the Lock*. Which way is more effective? Why? Share your conclusions with your class.

Preparing to Read

from
A Dictionary of the English Language

What Do You Think? How can order and civilization affect human behavior?

QuickTalk

Who, in your opinion, should determine a word's meaning and pronunciation? In a small group, discuss whether you think the rules of language should be maintained and changed by certain individuals or by society as a whole.

MEET THE WRITER

Samuel Johnson
(1709–1784)

An engaging speaker and a respected writer and critic, Samuel Johnson was so beloved that his century is often called the Age of Johnson.

Humble Beginnings

Johnson is famous primarily for three large and important projects: *A Dictionary of the English Language* (1755); an edition of Shakespeare with an important critical preface and useful notes (1765); and *The Lives of the English Poets* (1779–1781). His early life, however, did not seem to mark him for greatness. The son of an unsuccessful bookseller, he was small and sickly, and he lost his sight in one eye from an infection. As Johnson grew, however, his health improved and he developed a strong personality, although he retained the disfiguring scars of medical treatments and numerous personal ticks that may have been symptoms of Tourette syndrome. Anecdotes abound of his immense height, size, and strength—and of his sometimes odd behavior—but his most impressive feature was his intellect.

An English Institution

In 1737, Johnson moved to London, the city he came to admire above all others. In London, Johnson became the <u>dominant</u> literary figure of his day. He was considered an English institution not only because of his great circle of friends and forceful personality, but because of his numerous essays, poems, and magazine contributions. Johnson's literary output, even before he began his major projects, is impressive.

In 1763, Johnson met James Boswell, who would soon begin recording Johnson's conversations for posterity. Johnson remains a vivid figure because Boswell and many of Johnson's other contemporaries recorded their impressions of him.

Though one of the most learned men of his day, Johnson always insisted that knowledge was useless unless it helped people live in the real world.

Think About the Writer Which of Johnson's qualities do you think made him so interesting to Boswell and others?

Dr. Samuel Johnson by Sir Joshua Reynolds (1723-92). Oil on canvas.

Reader/Writer Notebook

Use your **RWN** to complete the activities for this selection.

Literary Focus

Diction A writer's or speaker's choice of words is called **diction.** Speakers and writers use different types of words depending on the context—that is, their audience, subject, and purpose. Thus, diction can be formal, informal, colloquial, poetic, ornate, plain, and so on. For example, casual slang that would be suitable in a conversation with a friend would be unsuitable in a formal speech. Diction is an essential element of a writer's style and has a powerful effect on the tone of a piece of writing.

Through his diction in the *Dictionary of the English Language,* Johnson reveals his character and opinions. Some entries—"catsup. A kind of pickle, made from mushrooms"—are fairly straightforward and objective. They give us a direct description of the word. Other entries—"essay. A loose sally of the mind; an irregular indigested piece; not a regularly and orderly composition"—<u>enhance</u> the dictionary with Johnson's unique word choices and create memorable phrases. As you read, note thelanguage and style of each dictionary entry, and analyze Johnson's diction in order to determinehis opinion of the word.

Writing Focus

Think as a Reader/Writer

Find It in Your Reading In *A Dictionary of the English Language,* Johnson often uses examples to clarify a word's meaning. Some examples involve synonyms; others replace the word with a phrase or an illustrative point; still others, as with the word *bedpresser,* employ examples of usage from famous authors such as Shakespeare. In your *Reader/Writer Notebook,* create a chart like the one below to keep track of the many kinds of examples Johnson uses.

Word	Example
to romp	A stool is the first weapon taken up in a general romping or skirmish. —Swift, Rules to Servants

Vocabulary

discourse (DIHS kawrs) *n.:* conversation or speech. *Johnson was much admired for his witty discourse and banter.*

sanguine (SANG gwihn) *adj.:* reddish in color; red-faced from effort. *The runner's face was sanguine from sprinting.*

servile (SUR vuhl) *adj.:* slavishly devoted. *The members of the court made servile bows whenever the king walked by them.*

countenances (KOWN tuh nuhns ehz) *v.:* extends approval to; favors. *Johnson countenances those who work vigorously, but he dislikes lazy people.*

eminence (EHM uh nuhns) *n.:* high rank or position. *Johnson was a man of eminence, beloved by many in the city of London.*

Language Coach

Word Origins The word *servile* comes from a Latin word meaning "slave." The word *eminence* comes from Latin words that mean "to stand out" and "to jut out." Explain how these roots relate to the current meanings of these words: *service, servant, disservice, eminent, pre-eminent.*

Learn It Online
Listen to this selection online.

go.hrw.com   L12-633   **Go**

from

A Dictionary of the English Language

by **Samuel Johnson**

Read with a Purpose

Read to see how Johnson reveals his character and expresses his personality in his dictionary.

Build Background

Johnson's *Dictionary,* published in 1755, was the first comprehensive and authoritative dictionary in English. Johnson gathered information from many literary, religious, philosophical, scientific, and technical books, marking passages and underlining key words. Then, he had six copyists write out the marked passages on slips of paper, which were later pasted into eighty notebooks. Finally, using the passages, Johnson wrote definitions of the key words.

Johnson's *Dictionary* was the basis of all subsequent English dictionaries. The dictionary lives on today because it reflects its author's interesting character and sense of humor.

Natasha McEnroe, curator of the Museum at Dr. Samuel Johnson's House, holds up the revolutionary dictionary written by Johnson in the 17th century.

alligator. The crocodile. This name is chiefly used for the crocodile of America, between which, and that of Africa, naturalists have laid down this difference, that one moves the upper, and the other the lower jaw; but this is now known to be chimerical,[1] the lower jaw being equally moved by both.

athletick. Strong of body; vigorous; lusty; robust.

> Science distinguishes a man of honor from one of those *athletick* brutes, whom undeservedly we call heroes.
>
> —Dryden. Ⓐ

autopsy. Ocular demonstration; seeing a thing oneself.

balderdash. Anything jumbled together without judgment; rude mixture; a confused discourse.

bedpresser. A heavy lazy fellow.

> This *sanguine* coward, *this bedpresser,* this horse-back-breaker, this huge hill of flesh.
>
> —Shakespeare, *Henry IV,* Part 1.

catsup. A kind of pickle, made from mushrooms.

companion. A familiar term of contempt; a fellow.

> I scorn you, scurvy *companion!* What? you poor, base, rascally, cheating, lack-linen mate: Away, you moldy rogue, away.
>
> —Shakespeare, *Henry IV,* Part 2.

cough. A convulsion of the lungs, vellicated by some sharp serosity. It is pronounced *coff.*

dedication. A servile address to a patron.

dull. Not exhilarating; not delightful; as, to *make dictionaries is* dull *work.*

essay. A loose sally of the mind; an irregular indigested piece; not a regular and orderly composition.

excise. A hateful tax levied upon commodities, and adjudged not by the common judges of property, but wretches hired by those to whom excise is paid.

---

1. **chimerical** (*kuh MEHR uh kuhl*): fanciful.

favorite. One chosen as a companion by his superior; a mean wretch whose whole business is by any means to please.

fillip. A jerk of the finger let go from the thumb.

frightfully. Disagreeably; not beautifully. A woman's word.

fun. (A low cant[2] word.) Sport; high merriment; frolicsome delight.

goose. A large waterfowl proverbially noted, I know not why, for foolishness.

gravy. The serous juice that runs from flesh not much dried by the fire.

> They usually boil and roast their meat until it falls almost off from the bones; but we love it half raw, with the blood trickling down from it, delicately terming it the *gravy,* which in truth looks more like an ichorous or raw bloody matter.
>
> —Harvey, *On Consumptions.*

to hiss. To utter a noise like that of a serpent and some other animals. It is remarkable, that this word cannot be pronounced without making the noise which it signifies.

immaterial. (1) Incorporeal; void of matter. (2) Unimportant; without weight; impertinent; without relation. This sense has crept into the conversation and writings of barbarians; but ought to be utterly rejected.

jogger. One who moves heavily and dully.

lexicographer. A writer of dictionaries; a harmless drudge, that busies himself in tracing the original, and detailing the signification of words. Ⓑ

lingo. Language; tongue; speech. A low cant word.

lunch, luncheon. As much food as one's hand can hold.

merrythought. A forked bone on the body of fowls; so called because boys and girls pull in play at the two sides, the longest part broken off betokening priority of marriage.

---

2. **cant:** a word Johnson uses to describe language he perceives to be of base origins.

Ⓐ **Literary Focus** Diction How does Johnson's diction differ from Dryden's in the example provided for this word?

Ⓑ **Literary Focus** Diction Johnson satirizes many people and political groups in his witty definitions. Why might he refer to a maker of dictionaries as "a harmless drudge"? Whom does he satirize here?

Vocabulary **discourse** (DIHS kawrs) *n.:* conversation or speech.

sanguine (SANG gwihn) *adj.:* reddish in color; red-faced from effort.

servile (SUR vuhl) *adj.:* slavishly devoted.

mushroom. An upstart; a wretch risen from the dunghill; a director of a company.

network. Anything reticulated or decussated, at equal distances, with interstices between the intersections.

osprey. The sea-eagle, of which it is reported, that when he hovers in the air, all the fish in the water turn up their bellies, and lie still for him to seize which he pleases.

parody. A kind of writing, in which the words of an author or his thoughts are taken, and by a slight change adapted to some new purpose.

patron. One who countenances, supports, or protects. Commonly a wretch who supports with insolence, and is paid with flattery.

pension. An allowance made to anyone without an equivalent. In England it is generally understood to mean pay given to a state hireling for treason to his country.

to period. To put an end to. A bad[3] word.

rhinoceros. A vast beast in the East Indies armed with a horn in his front.

romance. A tale of wild adventures in war and love.

to romp. To play rudely, noisily, and boisterously.

---

3. **bad:** used here to mean "low" or "vulgar."

A stool is the first weapon taken up in a general *romping or skirmish.*

—Swift, *Rules to Servants.*

to sneeze. To emit wind audibly by the nose.

sonnet. A short poem consisting of fourteen lines, of which the rhymes are adjusted by a particular rule. It is not very suitable to the English language, and has not been used by any man of eminence since Milton.

stammel. Of this word I know not the meaning.

tittletattle. Idle talk; prattle; empty gabble.

torpedo. A fish which while alive, if touched even with a long stick, benumbs the hand that so touches it, but when dead is eaten safely.

tory. (A cant term, derived, I suppose, from an Irish word signifying a savage.) One who adheres to the ancient constitution of the state, and the apostolical hierarchy of the Church of England, opposed to a whig. **C**

unkindly. Unnatural; contrary to nature.

vivacious. Long-lived.

whale. The largest of fish.

whig. The name of a faction.

to worm. To deprive a dog of something, nobody knows what, under his tongue, which is said to prevent him, nobody knows why, from running mad.

zed. The name of the letter *z.*

C **Literary Focus** Diction How does Johnson add his opinion to this entry, even before he defines the word?

Vocabulary **countenances** (KOWN tuh nuhns ehz) *v.:* extends approval to; favors.
eminence (EHM uh nuhns) *n.:* high rank or position.

Samuel Johnson's *Dictionary.* Dr. Johnson's House Trust, London.

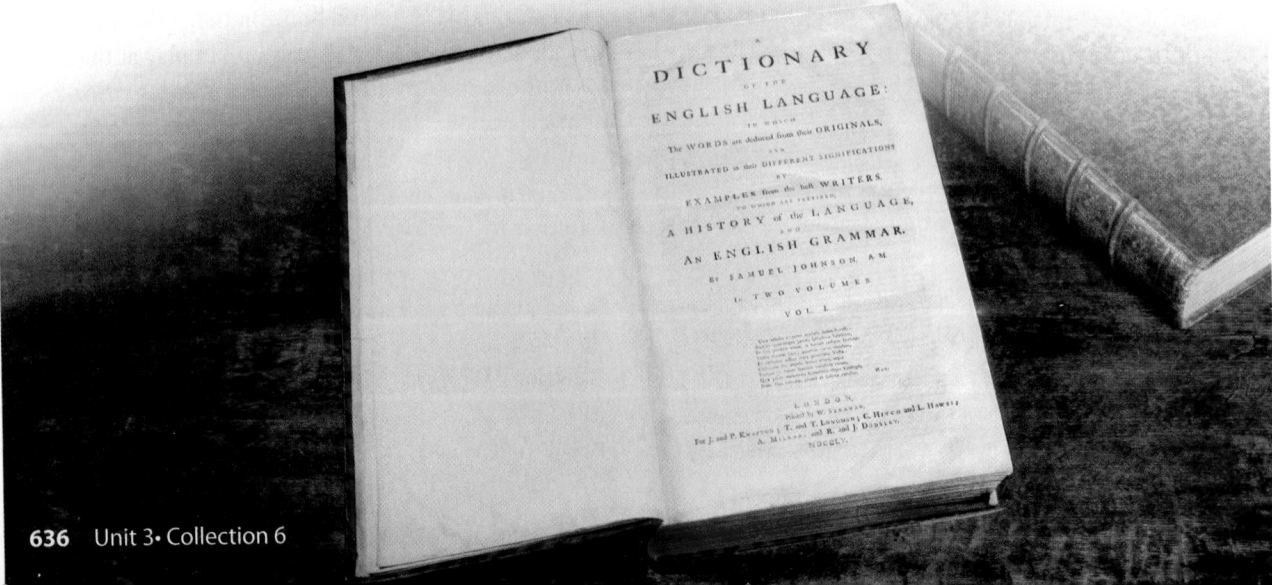

Respond and Think Critically

Reading Focus

Quick Check

1. How does Johnson define *essay?* How does his definition differ from a modern definition?

2. Which word is listed without a definition? Why might Johnson have included this word?

3. Which definitions contain what we would regard as errors of fact?

Read with a Purpose

4. How does Johnson's voice in the *Dictionary* reveal his personality? Which definitions show the writer's sense of humor? Which show his political bias, religious preferences, and independence of mind?

✔ Vocabulary Check

Match the Vocabulary words with their definitions.

5. discourse   **a.** slavish

6. sanguine   **b.** conversation

7. servile   **c.** approves

8. countenances   **d.** superiority

9. eminence   **e.** reddish

Literary Focus

Literary Analysis

10. **Compare and Contrast** Choose one word that Johnson defines in his *Dictionary.* Re-read Johnson's definition, and then read the definition of that word in a modern dictionary. How are the new and old entries alike and different?

11. **Draw Conclusions** What does Johnson think of patrons, or those who use their wealth to sup-

port artists and writers? Is a similar bias revealed in other entries? Which ones?

12. **Interpret** What is Johnson's attitude toward slang, which he calls "low" or "cant" words?

13. **Analyze** How do the dictionary entries reflect Johnson's insistence on thinking for himself?

Literary Skills: Diction

14. **Analyze** What effect does Johnson's diction create? How does his word choice help you learn about his political and social views?

Literary Skills Review: Style

15. **Analyze** Closely related to diction and syntax, **style** is the manner in which writers say what they wish to say. Describe Johnson's style. Is it consistent throughout the entries? Support your answer with examples from the text.

Writing Focus

Think as a Reader/Writer

Use It in Your Writing The definitions in Johnson's *Dictionary* show us how words were used during his time. Look back at the chart you created of definitions and examples in Johnson's *Dictionary.* In your *Reader/ Writer Notebook,* write your own one-page dictionary that includes words used frequently by your friends and family. Choose examples from your life that will help a reader to understand the meanings of the words you define.

What Do **You Think Now**? Johnson's *Dictionary* was the first comprehensive dictionary in English. How do you think this thorough and authoritative book affected the way people used language?

from The Meaning of Everything

What Do You Think?

How can order and civilization affect human behavior?

QuickTalk

In a small group, share some examples of how language confusions and misunderstandings have caused comical or even serious situations that you or others have experienced.

MEET THE WRITER

Simon Winchester
(1944–   )

Link to Today Simon Winchester's curiosity has taken him to countries around the world and deep into the history of people and language.

World Traveler

When British writer Simon Winchester was twenty-one years old, he finished a degree in geology at Oxford University and headed to Uganda to research copper. In his free time, he read a book about the first successful ascent of Mt. Everest and decided that he wanted to be a writer. Winchester now travels the world to learn about subjects for his writing, often to out-of-the-way places that might not have the comforts of hotels and regular modes of transportation. Winchester has worked as a journalist since 1967, writing articles, books, and film scripts on the many peoples, places, and languages he has encountered around the world.

The stress and demands of world travel do not discourage Winchester. He traveled over 100,000 miles during the three years he spent researching a book on the former British Empire. Another book resulted from the three months he spent in prison after he was incorrectly accused of being a spy. Despite such hardships, Winchester is delighted that interested readers make it possible for him to continue to travel and write.

The Lure of Language

Whenever Winchester travels, he observes the land and the people that inhabit it. He is fascinated by their stories, histories, and languages. He also appreciates the specificity of words—how each word means something unique—and believes that there are no true synonyms. With a geologist's scientific eye, he studies the history, use, and meaning of words. In his own detailed writing, he evokes a sense of place and time through painstakingly careful word choice—because only the *right* word will do.

Think About the Writer If Winchester traveled in your community, what might he observe about your culture and language? What stories might he choose to tell about your community?

Reader/Writer
Notebook
Use your **RWN** to complete the activities for this selection.

Informational Text Focus

Critiquing an Author's Argument What makes an argument valid and compelling? An argument consists of claims, which must be explained thoroughly and supported by evidence in order to be <u>convincing</u>. When you read nonfiction, you critique an author's **argument** to judge its effectiveness.

In the selection that follows, Winchester argues that the English language is constantly evolving, and that Samuel Johnson understood the ever-changing nature of the language when he wrote his *Dictionary*. As a reader, it is your job to decide whether Winchester presents his argument clearly and supports his claims effectively.

Into Action As you read, use a flow chart like the one below to record each claim that Winchester makes in his argument. Beside each claim, list the evidence or examples that Winchester uses to support it. When you finish reading, you should have more than one flow chart.

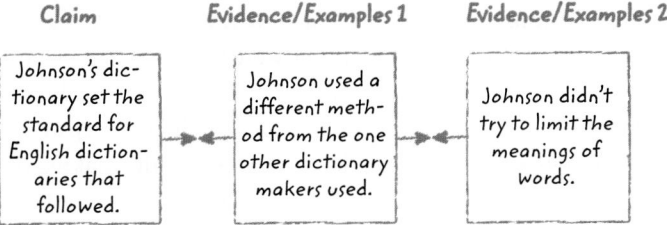

Writing Focus   Preparing for **Constructed Response**

As you read, notice how Winchester explains the contrast between descriptive and prescriptive dictionaries. Make a two-column chart in your *Reader/Writer Notebook,* and jot down ideas that help you understand these two <u>approaches</u> to defining words.

Descriptive	Prescriptive

Vocabulary

reiterate (ree IHT uh rayt) *v.:* repeat. *The author reiterates the main ideas.*

punctiliousness (puhngk TIHL ee uhs nuhs) *n.:* care for following rules and traditions exactly. *His careful speech and impeccable manners reflect his punctiliousness.*

prescribe (prih SKRYB) *v.:* limit by rules or laws; order. *Some grammar books prescribe English usage.*

copious (KOH pee uhs) *adj.:* plentiful; abundant. *Johnson compiled his dictionary from the copious notes that he and his assistants wrote about the English language.*

Language Coach

Prefixes A prefix is a word part that is added to the beginning of a word and changes its meaning. The prefix *re–* can mean "again." How is this meaning present in *reiterate*? The prefix *pre–* can mean "in advance or in preparation." How is this meaning present in *prescribe*? Explain how these prefixes affect the meanings of these words: *rearrange, prearrange, presume, resume.*

 **Learn It Online**
Find an interactive flow chart online.

go.hrw.com L12-639   **Go**

Link to Today

This Link to Today explains how Samuel Johnson's *Dictionary* set the standard for all future English dictionaries.

Read with a Purpose

Read this selection to find out why Samuel Johnson's dictionary recorded English words as they were used instead of prescribing how they should be used.

Build Background

Dictionaries appear authoritative, so it's easy to think of them as filled with rules for language users to follow. But most English dictionaries *describe* rather than *prescribe* language; they tell us how words are used rather than how they should be used. Samuel Johnson planned his *Dictionary* following a time when many authors despaired over the state of English. Many wanted a book that would set down rules for English and, in the words of Swift, "fix our language forever." Initially, Johnson agreed, but soon realized that English, by its nature, could not be fixed. His aim became not "to form, but to register" the language. The following excerpt discusses Johnson's descriptive *Dictionary* and its impact on English speakers everywhere.

from

The Meaning of Everything

by **Simon Winchester**

The magisterially[1] famous Dr Johnson created his great dictionary in 1755—in two volumes, in scores of editions, the book that all educated households possessed and took down whenever anyone asked simply for 'the dictionary,' set the standard for the following century, and some still think for all time, of just what an English dictionary should be. **Ⓐ**

It is important to reiterate in this context that Johnson's work set standards for all future *English* dictionaries. For the way that English had developed, and the way that in the eighteenth century it was coming to be recognized at home, was profoundly different from the way that other languages were then being seen, and were being recognized and then collated and corralled into dictionaries elsewhere. The point is an obvious one: but it bears repeating, as it underlies—indeed, is vital in every way to—the making of the book that plays the central role in this story.

For English is not to be regarded in the same way as, say, French or Italian, and in one crucially important way. It is not a *fixed* language, the meaning of its words established, approved, and firmly set by some official committee charged with preserving its dignity and integrity. The French have had their Académie Française, a body made up of the much-feared Forty Immortals,

---

1. **magisterially:** with dignity and authority, perhaps so much as to be overbearing.

Ⓐ **Informational Focus** **Critiquing an Author's Argument** What does Winchester's use of the phrase "magisterially famous" reveal about his opinion of Johnson? How might Winchester's opinion of Johnson affect his argument?

Vocabulary **reiterate** (ree IHT uh rayt) *v.:* to repeat.

which has done precisely this (and with an extreme punctiliousness and absolute want of humor) since 1634. The Italians have also had their Accademia della Crusca in Florence since 1582—since long before, in other words, there was even a nation called Italy. The task of both bodies was to preserve linguistic purity, to prevent the languages' ruin by permitting inelegant importations, and to guide the public on just how to write and speak. The two bodies were established, in short, to prescribe the use of the language. No such body has ever been set up in England, nor in any English-speaking country.[2] . . .

For English is a language that simply cannot be fixed, nor can its use ever be absolutely laid down. It changes constantly; it grows with an almost exponential joy. It evolves eternally; its words alter their senses and their meanings subtly, slowly, or speedily according to fashion and need. Dictionaries that record and catalogue the language thus cannot ever be *prescriptive*; they must always be entirely *descriptive*, telling of the language as it is, not as it should be. Samuel Johnson's majestic *Dictionary of the English Language*, published first in 1755 and remaining in print for well over the century following, is a classic of this kind. It is as full a record as Johnson and the six serving men who worked with him as amanuenses[3] for six years in cramped rooms south of Fleet Street could determine, of the entire assemblage of words that were employed by all who lived in the realm—the words used by the learned, the nobly born, the doctor, the dandy, and the divine and, most important of all, the words used by the common man of the street, the slum, the farm, and the field.... **B**

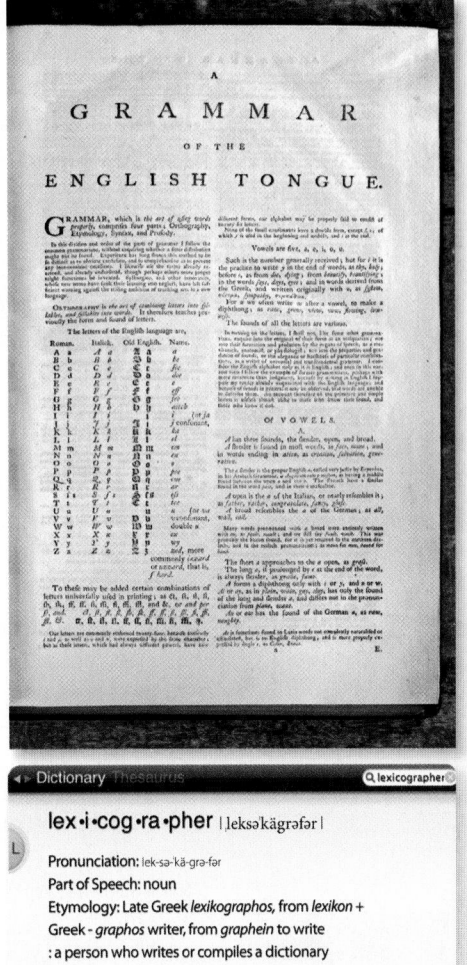

(top) Samuel Johnson's *Dictionary*, grammar page. Dr. Johnson's House Trust, London.

(bottom) An entry from an online dictionary.

---

2. Except South Africa, which has its own 'English Academy' based in Johannesburg, charged with promoting 'the effective use of English as a dynamic language'. The French and Italians would deny the use of the word 'dynamic', urging upon their respective peoples the need for linguistic stability and an abhorrence of change.

3. **amanuenses:** (uh man yu EHN seez) people who copy notes or take dictation.

B **Informational Focus** Critiquing an Author's Argument Re-read the first two sentences in this paragraph. What examples can you think of to support Winchester's claims that English constantly changes, grows, and evolves? Might Winchester's opinion of Johnson affect his argument?

Vocabulary **punctiliousness** (puhngk TIHL ee uhs nuhs) *n.*: care for following rules and traditions exactly.
prescribe (prih SKRYB) *v.*: limit by rules or laws; order.

The approach that Johnson took was not to decide for himself what words meant, not (to reiterate the point) to *prescribe* how they should be used—but instead to let the printed record of centuries-worth of writing and literature illustrate how words had actually been used in the past, and tease from the record the variety of historic meanings, from the time each was invented and first introduced, and as their various senses shifted like silverfish over the succeeding centuries. 'When I took the first survey of my undertaking,' he wrote in his famous Preface,

I found our speech copious without order, and energetick without rules: wherever I turned my view, there was perplexity to be disentangled, and confusion to be regulated. Having therefore no assistance but from general grammar I applied myself to the perusal of our writers; and noting whatever might be used to ascertain or illustrate any word or phrase, accumulated in time the materials of a dictionary which, by degrees, I reduced to method. **C**

This was a method which Johnson perhaps honored more in the breach than the observance. But it nonetheless set the pattern for all the best dictionaries for all time to come: no better means has ever been developed for producing as near as possible a complete record of a language.

C **Informational Focus** **Critiquing an Author's Argument** Why do you think Winchester includes Johnson's own words? Which of Johnson's lines support Winchester's argument that English is constantly changing? How?

Vocabulary **copious** (KOH pee uhs) *adj.*: plentiful; abundant.

Simon Winchester, atop Mount Pinatubo, Pampanga Province, Luzon, Philippines, 2002.

Applying Your Skills

from The Meaning of Everything

Respond and Think Critically

Informational Text Focus

Quick Check

1. Who are the Forty Immortals? What is their job?

2. Why does Winchester find English unique?

3. How did Johnson get the words and definitions that he included in his *Dictionary?*

Read with a Purpose

4. Why did Samuel Johnson make his dictionary descriptive instead of prescriptive?

Informational Skills: Critiquing an Author's Argument

5. Review your reading chart, and write a sentence that expresses Winchester's overall argument. Then, explain in a paragraph whether or not Winchester <u>convincingly</u> supports his argument with evidence and examples.

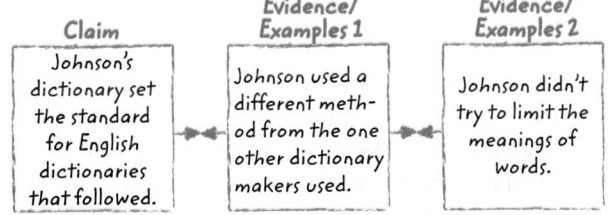

Claim	Evidence/ Examples 1	Evidence/ Examples 2
Johnson's dictionary set the standard for English dictionaries that followed.	Johnson used a different method from the one other dictionary makers used.	Johnson didn't try to limit the meanings of words.

✓ Vocabulary Check

Match each Vocabulary word with its definition.

6. reiterate   a. care about following rules

7. punctiliousness b. order

8. prescribe   c. abundant

9. copious   d. repeat

Text Analysis

10. **Compare and Contrast** Explain how a prescriptive definition of a word differs from a descriptive definition of a word.

11. **Analyze** Winchester uses the simile "shifted like silverfish" to describe English words and their meanings. Locate this simile in the selection, and explain its meaning.

12. **Extend** Why do you think English borrows so many words from other languages? How do words from other languages <u>enhance</u> English?

13. **Extend** Winchester says that English "simply cannot be fixed." What might happen if a committee tried to fix the meanings of English words? Would they succeed? Why or why not?

Listening and Speaking

14. **Analyze** With a partner, discuss your understanding of how language changes. How and when might new words come into common use in English? What effect do you think newspapers, television, radio, and the Internet have on language? Include examples from your own experiences.

Writing Focus Constructed Response

As you read, you noted the differences between descriptive and prescriptive dictionaries. In an essay, briefly discuss the advantages and disadvantages of each way of defining words. Be sure to cite specific evidence in your response.

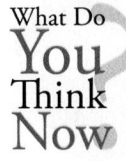
What Do You Think Now How do descriptive dictionaries simultaneously impose order on language and reflect how language changes?

Preparing to Read

from The Life of Samuel Johnson

What Do You Think?

How can order and civilization affect human behavior?

QuickWrite

If you were to write a biography, about whom would you write? Why? What would be the most interesting aspect of your biography?

Background: Perspective view of Covent Garden Flower Market. Color engraving. Science Museum, London.

MEET THE WRITER

James Boswell
(1740–1795)

James Boswell admired Samuel Johnson's writing long before the two met. Based on their twenty-year friendship, Boswell authored what many people consider the world's greatest biography—*The Life of Samuel Johnson,* published in 1791. Boswell's methods for gathering information about his subject have influenced countless other biographers.

The Young Man from Scotland

Born in Scotland, Boswell was heir to a large fortune. His father, a stern judge who wanted Boswell to practice law, disapproved of Boswell's ambitions to travel, write, and meet great people. When Boswell was twenty-two years old, however, his father relented and allowed him to go to London. In 1763, Boswell met Johnson, who was then fifty-three and famous for his *Dictionary of the English Language.* Boswell returned to Scotland to practice law, but he maintained his friendship with Johnson and aspired to become Johnson's biographer—a task he completed nearly thirty years later. In the book's opening pages, Boswell explains, "I will venture to say that [Johnson] will be seen in this work more completely than any man who has ever yet lived."

A Biographer's Method

Early in their friendship, Johnson advised Boswell to "read diligently the great book of mankind." Boswell took this advice to heart. He trained his memory to recall exact details of an event, and he later wrote these observations down in private. Thus, over the years, Boswell kept a written record of his own and other people's behavior and conversation. To write Johnson's biography, begun four years after his friend's death, Boswell used as sources his own journals, Johnson's writings and letters, and information collected from Johnson's friends. Boswell's *Life* reveals more than Johnson's character; the biography also offers us a window into the literary world of London during the second half of the eighteenth century.

Think About the Writer If Boswell were looking for someone to write about today, whom might he choose? Why?

Portrait of James Boswell by George Willison. Scottish National Portrait Gallery, Edinburgh, Scotland.

Reader/Writer
Notebook
Use your **RWN** to complete the activities for this selection.

Literary Focus

Biography A **biography** is an account of a person's life written by another person. Biographers cannot tell every detail about a person's life—no book could contain that many pages—so they choose certain details to record about their subjects. As you read, consider why Boswell chose the details, conversations, and events he includes.

Literary Perspectives Apply the literary perspective described on page 647 as you read this selection.

Reading Focus

Analyzing an Author's Point of View An author's **point of view** is the vantage point from which he or she tells a story. Boswell narrates from a **first-person point of view,** telling us only what he sees, hears, and experiences as a character in Johnson's life story. Boswell initially writes as an outsider; gradually, though, he moves into Johnson's circle of friends. This shift broadens his experiences and the range of details he can convey.

Into Action Use a chart like the one below to note the changes in Boswell's attitude as a narrator as his friendship with Johnson deepens and his vantage point changes.

Section Title	Boswell's Vantage Point
Boswell's First Meeting with Johnson, 1763	Boswell is a nervous guest, observing Johnson's circle from outside.

Writing Focus

Think as a Reader/Writer
Find It in Your Reading In this biography, Boswell often includes **dialogue**—conversation between two or more people. In your *Reader/Writer Notebook,* record instances in which the dialogue reveals the characters' personalities, such as when Mr. Davies blurts that Boswell is from Scotland, although Boswell has asked him not to do so.

Vocabulary

reverence (REHV uhr uhns) *n.:* deep respect. *Boswell developed a reverence for Johnson's wisdom.*

apprehensive (ap rih HEHN sihv) *adj.:* feeling anxious, worried. *Boswell was apprehensive about making a good impression on Johnson.*

slovenly (SLUHV uhn lee) *adj.:* untidy. *Boswell was initially surprised by Johnson's slovenly apartment.*

whimsical (HWIHM zuh kuhl) *adj.:* fanciful. *Johnson took part in whimsical arguments simply because he enjoyed debate.*

singularities (sihng gyoo LAR uh teez) *n. pl.:* characteristics that make a person unique. *Johnson's personality, with its many singularities, charmed his friends.*

candor (KAN duhr) *n.:* honesty, openness. *Johnson believed candor was essential for successful communication.*

ingenuity (ihn juh NOO uh tee) *n.:* cleverness, inventiveness. *Boswell demonstrated great ingenuity by memorizing all the details he recorded about Johnson.*

Language Coach
Personal Definitions One way to remember the meaning of new words is to associate them with someone or something in your own life. For whom or what do you feel *reverence*? Give a specific answer that uses the word *reverence*. This association will help you remember the word's definition.

 Learn It Online
Practice your vocabulary knowledge online with Word Watch.

go.hrw.com | L12-645 | **Go**

from
THE LIFE OF SAMUEL JOHNSON

by **James Boswell**

Read with a Purpose
Read this selection to discover Johnson's wit and intellect and to understand Boswell's growing admiration for his mentor and friend.

Build Background
Throughout the biography we often see Boswell provoking Johnson to speak out on a topic. Boswell also manipulates the conversation for dramatic effect, in much the same way a playwright manages the dialogue of his or her characters. This amazing level of detail, drawn from the large number of conversations Boswell reports, sets *The Life of Samuel Johnson* apart from other early biographies.

Statue of Samuel Johnson.
(Background) Perspective view of Covent Garden Flower Market (19th century) by French School. Color engraving. Science Museum, London.

Boswell's First Meeting with Johnson, 1763

This is to me a memorable year; for in it I had the happiness to obtain the acquaintance of that extraordinary man whose memoirs I am now writing; an acquaintance which I shall ever esteem as one of the most fortunate circumstances in my life. Though then but two-and-twenty, I had for several years read his works with delight and instruction, and had the highest reverence for their author, which had grown up in my fancy into a kind of mysterious veneration, by figuring to myself a state of solemn elevated abstraction, in which I supposed him to live in the immense metropolis of London. ...Mr. Thomas Davies the actor, who then kept a bookseller's shop in Russel Street, Covent Garden, told me that Johnson was very much his friend, and came frequently to his house, where he more than once invited me to meet him; but by some unlucky accident or other he was prevented from coming to us. . . .

At last, on Monday the 16th of May, when I was sitting in Mr. Davies's back parlor, after having drunk tea with him and Mrs. Davies, Johnson unexpectedly came into the shop; and Mr. Davies having perceived him through the glass door in the room in which we were sitting, advancing toward us—he announced his awful[1] approach to me, somewhat in the manner of an actor in the part of Horatio, when he addresses Hamlet on the appearance of his father's ghost, "Look, my Lord, it comes." I found that I had a very perfect idea of Johnson's figure, from the portrait of him painted by Sir Joshua Reynolds soon after he had published his *Dictionary*, in the attitude of sitting in his easy chair in deep meditation, which was the first picture his friend did for him, which Sir Joshua very kindly presented to me, and from which an engraving has been made for this work. Mr. Davies mentioned my name, and

---

1. **awful:** used here to mean producing awe; now, the more common term is "awesome."

respectfully introduced me to him. I was much agitated; and recollecting his prejudice against the Scotch, of which I had heard much, I said to Davies, "Don't tell where I come from."—"From Scotland," cried Davies roguishly. "Mr. Johnson (said I), I do indeed come from Scotland, but I cannot help it." I am willing to flatter myself that I meant this as light pleasantry to soothe and conciliate him, and not as an humiliating abasement at the expense of my country. But however that might be, this speech was somewhat unlucky; for with that quickness of wit for which he was so remarkable, he seized the expression "come from Scotland," which I used in the sense of being of that country, and, as if I had said that I had come away from it, or left it, retorted, "That, Sir, I find, is what a very great many of your countrymen cannot help." This stroke stunned

Literary Perspectives

Analyzing Biographical Information Knowing biographical information about a writer may help you understand and evaluate the writer's work. How did James Boswell's background prepare him to become Samuel Johnson's biographer, and how does his perspective shape the biography? What does he reveal about himself in his biography of Johnson? As a young man, Boswell admired Johnson's intellect and wit and aspired to the kind of life that Johnson enjoyed. Boswell wished to befriend Johnson not only because he admired the great writer, but also because Johnson could introduce him to the prominent intellectuals, artists, and politicians in London. Consider, then, how Boswell's admiration for and friendship with Johnson, as well as Boswell's interest in London's intellectual society, affect the content and tone of his biography of Johnson.

As you read, be sure to notice the questions in the text, which will guide you in using this perspective.

Vocabulary **reverence** (REHV uhr uhns) *n.*: deep respect.

me a good deal; and when we had sat down, I felt myself not a little embarrassed, and apprehensive of what might come next. He then addressed himself to Davies. "What do you think of Garrick?[2] He has refused me an order for the play for Miss Williams, because he knows the house will be full, and that an order would be worth three shillings." Eager to take any opening to get into conversation with him, I ventured to say, "O, Sir, I cannot think Mr. Garrick would grudge such a trifle to you." "Sir (said he, with a stern look), I have known David Garrick longer than you have done: and I know no right you have to talk to me on the subject." Perhaps I deserved this check; for it was rather presumptuous in me, an entire stranger, to express any doubt of the justice of his animadversion[3] upon his old acquaintance and pupil. I now felt myself much mortified, and began to think that the hope which I had long indulged of obtaining his acquaintance was blasted. And, in truth, had not my ardor been uncommonly strong, and my resolution uncommonly persevering, so rough a reception might have deterred[4] me forever from making any further attempts. Fortunately, however, I remained upon the field not wholly discomfited…. **(A)**

I was highly pleased with the extraordinary vigor of his conversation, and regretted that I was drawn away from it by an engagement at another place. I had, for a part of the evening, been left alone with him, and had ventured to make an observation now and then, which he received very civilly; so that I was satisfied that though there was a roughness in his manner, there was no ill nature in his disposition. Davies followed me to the door, and when I complained to him a

little of the hard blows which the great man had given me, he kindly took upon him to console me by saying, "Don't be uneasy. I can see he likes you very well." **(B)**

Boswell's First Visit to Johnson

A few days afterward I called on Davies, and asked him if he thought I might take the liberty of waiting on Mr. Johnson at his Chambers in the Temple.[5] He said I certainly might, and that Mr. Johnson would take it as a compliment. So upon Tuesday the 24th of May, . . . I boldly repaired to Johnson. His Chambers were on the first floor of No. 1, Inner-Temple-lane, and I entered them with an impression given me by the Reverend Dr. Blair,[6] of Edinburgh, who had been introduced to him not long before, and described his having "found the Giant in his den," an expression, which, when I came to be pretty well acquainted with Johnson, I repeated to him, and he was diverted at this picturesque account of himself….

He received me very courteously; but, it must be confessed, that his apartment, and furniture, and morning dress, were sufficiently uncouth. His brown suit of clothes looked very rusty; he had on a little old shriveled unpowdered wig, which was too small for his head; his shirtneck and knees of his breeches were loose; his black worsted stockings ill drawn up; and he had a pair of unbuckled shoes by way of slippers. But all these slovenly particularities were forgotten the moment that he began to talk. Some gentlemen, whom I do not recollect, were sitting with him; and when they went away, I also rose; but he said to me, "Nay, don't go." "Sir (said I), I am afraid that I intrude

---

2. **Garrick:** the English actor David Garrick (1717–1779), a former pupil of Johnson's.
3. **animadversion** (an uh mad VUR zhuhn): critical comment.
4. **deterred:** prevented.

5. **Temple:** area in London where lawyers and other professional people lived and worked.
6. **Blair:** Hugh Blair (1718–1800), a Presbyterian clergyman and writer.

(A) **Literary Perspectives** Analyzing Biographical Information What is Boswell's hope for himself during this first interview with Johnson? What do his words and actions suggest about his ambition?

(B) **Reading Focus** Analyzing an Author's Point of View What point of view has Boswell chosen? How does Boswell's point of view affect his portrayal of Samuel Johnson?

Vocabulary **apprehensive** (ap rih HEHN sihv) *adj.:* feeling anxious, worried.
slovenly (SLUHV uhn lee) *adj.:* untidy.

James Boswell, Oliver Goldsmith, and Samuel Johnson at the Mitre Tavern in London (19th century). Color engraving.

upon you. It is benevolent to allow me to sit and hear you." He seemed pleased with this compliment, which I sincerely paid him, and answered, "Sir, I am obliged to any man who visits me." . . . **C**

Boswell Quizzes Johnson

I know not how so whimsical a thought came into my mind, but I asked, "If, Sir, you were shut up in a castle, and a newborn child with you, what would you do?" Johnson. "Why, Sir, I should not much like my company." Boswell. "But would you take the trouble of rearing it?" He seemed, as may well be supposed, unwilling to pursue the subject: but upon my persevering in my question, replied, "Why yes, Sir, I would; but I must have all conveniences. If I had no garden,

C **Literary Focus** Biography Identify some of the details that Boswell uses in his description of Johnson in this paragraph. How do these details affect your perception of Johnson?

Vocabulary **whimsical** (HWIHM zuh kuhl) *adj.:* fanciful.

I would make a shed on the roof, and take it there for fresh air. I should feed it, and wash it much, and with warm water to please it, not with cold water to give it pain." BOSWELL. "But, Sir, does not heat relax?" JOHNSON. "Sir, you are not to imagine the water is to be very hot. I would not *coddle*[7] the child. No, Sir, the hardy method of treating children does no good. I'll take you five children from London, who shall cuff[8] five Highland children. Sir, a man bred in London will carry a burden, or run, or wrestle, as well as a man brought up in the hardiest manner in the country." BOSWELL. "Good living, I suppose, makes the Londoners strong." JOHNSON. "Why, Sir, I don't know that it does. Our chairmen[9] from Ireland, who are as strong men as any, have been brought up upon potatoes. Quantity makes up for quality." BOSWELL. "Would you teach this child that I have furnished you with, anything?" JOHNSON. "No, I should not be apt to teach it." BOSWELL. "Would not you have a pleasure in teaching it?" JOHNSON. "No, Sir, I should *not* have a pleasure in teaching it." BOSWELL. "Have you not a pleasure in teaching men? *There* I have you. You have the same pleasure in teaching men, that I should have in teaching children." JOHNSON. "Why, something about that." ...

Johnson's Eccentricities

... Talking to himself was, indeed, one of his singularities ever since I knew him. I was certain that he was frequently uttering pious ejaculations; for fragments of the Lord's Prayer have been distinctly overheard. His friend Mr. Thomas Davies, of whom

---

7. **coddle:** cook in hot water. Johnson is having fun with the two distinct meanings of the word, the other being "treat tenderly."
8. **cuff:** win a fight or scuffle with.
9. **chairmen:** here, porters who transported people through the London streets in sedan chairs (covered seats).

D **Literary Focus** **Biography** What motivates Boswell to ask the "whimsical" question during this visit to Johnson?

Vocabulary **singularities** (sihng gyoo LAR uh teez) *n. pl.*: characteristics that make a person unique.

Analyzing Visuals

Viewing and Interpreting
How does this painting reflect the atmosphere of conversation that Johnson and Boswell seem to enjoy? What can you infer about the characters in this scene?

Churchill[10] says, "That Davies hath a very pretty wife," when Dr. Johnson muttered "lead us not into temptation," used with waggish and gallant humor to whisper [to] Mrs. Davies, "You, my dear, are the cause of this."

He had another particularity, of which none of his friends ever ventured to ask an explanation. It appeared to me some superstitious habit, which he had contracted early, and from which he had never called upon his reason to disentangle him. This was his anxious care to go out or in at a door or passage by a certain number of steps from a certain point, or at least so as that either his right or his left foot (I am not certain which) should constantly make the first actual movement when he came close to the door or passage. Thus I conjecture: For I have, upon innumerable occasions, observed him suddenly stop, and then seem to count his steps with a deep earnestness; and when he had neglected or gone wrong in this sort of magical movement, I have seen him go back again, put himself in a proper posture to begin the ceremony, and, having gone through it, break from his abstraction, walk briskly on, and join his companion. A strange instance of something of this nature, even when on horseback, happened when he was in the Isle of Skye.[11] Sir Joshua Reynolds has observed him to go a good way about rather than cross a particular alley in Leicesterfields;[12] but this Sir Joshua imputed to his having had some disagreeable recollection associated with it.

That the most minute singularities which belonged to him, and made very observable parts of his appearance and manner, may not be omitted, it is requisite to mention, that while talking or even musing as he sat in his chair, he commonly held his head to one side toward his right shoulder, and shook it in a tremulous manner, moving his body backward and

An Early London Coffeehouse, c. 1705.
British Museum, London.

10. **Churchill:** Charles Churchill (1731–1764), writer of satirical and comic poems.
11. **Isle of Skye:** largest of the Inner Hebrides, a group of islands off the west coast of Scotland.
12. **Leicesterfields** (LEHS tuhr feeldz): square in London.

E Literary Perspectives Analyzing Biographical Information With what sort of men does Boswell come into contact through his friendship with Johnson? How does his knowledge of these men affect the authority of his biography?

forward, and rubbing his left knee in the same direction, with the palm of his hand. In the intervals of articulating he made various sounds with his mouth, sometimes as if ruminating, or what is called chewing the cud, sometimes giving a half whistle, sometimes making his tongue play backward from the roof of his mouth, as if clucking like a hen, and sometimes protruding it against his upper gums in front, as if pronouncing quickly under his breath, *too, too, too:* all this accompanied sometimes with a thoughtful look, but more frequently with a smile. Generally when he had concluded a period, in the course of a dispute, by which time he was a good deal exhausted by violence and vociferation, he used to blow out his breath like a whale. This I supposed was a relief to his lungs; and seemed in him to be a contemptuous mode of expression, as if he had made the arguments of his opponent fly like chaff before the wind.

I am fully aware how very obvious an occasion I here give for the sneering jocularity of such as have no relish of an exact likeness; which to render complete, he who draws it must not disdain the slightest strokes. But if witlings[13] should be inclined to attack this account, let them have the candor to quote what I have offered in my defense.… **F**

Johnson's Love of Argument

…I mentioned a new gaming club,[14] of which Mr. Beauclerk[15] had given me an account, where the members played to a desperate extent. JOHNSON. "Depend upon it, Sir, this is mere talk. *Who* is ruined by gaming? You will not find six instances in an age. There is a strange rout made about deep play: Whereas you have many more people ruined by adventurous trade,[16] and yet we do not hear such an outcry against it." THRALE. "There may be few people absolutely ruined by deep play; but very many are much hurt in their circumstances by it." JOHNSON. "Yes, Sir, and so are very many by other kinds of expense." I had heard him talk once before in the same manner; and at Oxford he said, "he wished he had learnt to play at cards." The truth, however, is, that he loved to display his ingenuity in argument; and therefore would sometimes in conversation maintain opinions which he was sensible were wrong, but in supporting which, his reasoning and wit would be most conspicuous. He would begin thus: "Why, Sir, as to the good or evil of card playing—" "Now (said Garrick), he is thinking which side he shall take." He appeared to have a pleasure in contradiction, especially when any opinion whatever was delivered with an air of confidence; so that there was hardly any topic, if not one of the great truths of religion and morality, that he might not have been incited to argue, either for or against.… **G**

---

16. **trade:** business.

---

13. **witlings:** people who think they are witty.
14. **gaming club:** gambling club.
15. **Beauclerk:** Topham Beauclerk (1739–1780), a fashionable gentleman descended from King Charles II.

F **Reading Focus** Analyzing an Author's Point of View   What reasons does Boswell give to justify including a discussion of Johnson's odd personal habits? Why might he feel the need to explain his motives?

G **Literary Focus** Biography   According to Boswell, what does Johnson enjoy most about argument? What does this information tell you about Johnson's personality?

Vocabulary **candor** (KAN duhr) *n.:* honesty, openness.
ingenuity (ihn juh NOO uh tee) *n.:* cleverness, inventiveness.

SKILLS FOCUS Literary Skills Analyze the characteristics of biography; analyze diction; analyze biographical information. **Reading Skills** Analyze author's point of view. **Writing Skills** Develop characters using dialogue.

Respond and Think Critically

Reading Focus

Quick Check

1. In the first paragraph, how does Boswell convey Johnson's significance to Boswell's own life?

2. What peculiar mannerisms did Johnson exhibit when he talked?

3. Why, according to Boswell, did Johnson sometimes express opinions that he did not believe?

Read with a Purpose

4. Cite specific details from the biography that reflect Johnson's wit and intellect. Where can you find examples of Boswell's growing admiration for his mentor and friend?

Reading Skills: Analyzing an Author's Point of View

5. Review the chart that you made as you read. In a paragraph, explain how Boswell's attitude as a narrator changes as his relationship with Johnson changes. Do the changes in Boswell's attitude make him more credible as an authority on Johnson? Support your opinion with examples from your chart.

Literary Focus

Literary Analysis

6. **Analyze** Cite specific details from the biography that reflect Samuel Johnson's independent attitudes.

7. **Extend** Do you think Johnson would have been more or less interesting had his behavior been more conventional? Why is eccentric behavior important to society? How is eccentricity regarded in our society today?

8. **Make Judgments** What was Johnson's greatest strength and greatest fault as a person?

9. **Interpret** Why does it require several encounters before Boswell befriends Johnson? Why doesn't Boswell consider their first meeting a success?

10. **Literary Perspectives** How did Boswell benefit from his friendship with Johnson?

Literary Skills: Biography

11. **Analyze** In the biography, Boswell often mentions himself—his own feelings, impressions, and conclusions about Johnson. Do you think these references contribute to Boswell's work, or should he have maintained a more detached and objective view of his subject? Explain.

Literary Skills Review: Diction

12. **Analyze** A writer or speaker's choice of words is called **diction**. In the biography, Boswell often quotes Johnson's exact words. Read Johnson's words, and write a sentence about his diction.

Writing Focus

Think as a Reader/Writer

Use It in Your Writing Imagine you were able to talk for an hour with someone you admire. In your *Reader/Writer Notebook,* write a one-page excerpt of this imaginary dialogue. Take care to communicate your subject's personality through the dialogue, just as Boswell's dialogues reveal Johnson's character.

 What Do You Think Now

Based on what you read, which elements of Johnson's life and thinking were orderly? Which were not? How do you think these elements contributed to Johnson's fame?

from **The Life of Samuel Johnson**

Vocabulary Development

✓ Vocabulary Check

Match each Vocabulary word to its antonym.

1. reverence
2. slovenly
3. apprehensive
4. whimsical
5. singularities
6. ingenuity
7. candor

a. commonalities
b. disdain
c. deceit
d. carefree
e. tidy
f. matter-of-fact
g. dullness

Vocabulary Skills: Create Definitions

One way to remember a new word is to teach it to another person. You can do this by creating a definition of the new word. A definition includes everything a reader needs to know in order to use the word correctly while speaking or writing. Here's an example of a definition using a word from the selection:

abasement
How to pronounce it: uh BAYS muhnt
Part of speech: noun
What it means: a lowering in rank, importance, or esteem
Words I associate it with: basement (the lowest room in a house), base (not noble; unworthy)
Synonyms: belittlement, humiliation
Antonyms: advancement, elevation, promotion
Sample sentence: I don't want my friends to feel abasement, so I try not to make a big deal out of embarrassing situations.

Before creating your own definition of a word, look up the word in a dictionary to make sure you understand its meaning. Then, fill out the items listed on the note card above. To help yourself remember the new word, use everyday language that makes you comfortable.

Keep your note cards in a file for future reference. You can use them to review words on your own or to study with a partner.

Your Turn

Create your own definition for each of the Vocabulary words. Use the format you have just studied to create a complete and helpful definition.

Language Coach

Personal Definitions Linking words with people and things in your life will help you remember their definitions. Answer each question, being sure to use the vocabulary word in your answer.

1. What might happen if you do one of your chores in a *slovenly* way?
2. Who do you know that is *apprehensive* about tests?
3. What book, movie, or poem would you call *whimsical*?
4. Whose *singularities* set him or her apart from other people?
5. Who do you know that speaks with *candor*?
6. Whose *ingenuity* helped you to solve a problem?

Academic Vocabulary

Talk About
How does Johnson initially <u>dominate</u> conversations with Boswell? How does Boswell learn to <u>participate</u> in these conversations?

Grammar Link

Irregular Verbs

Unlike a regular verb, an irregular verb forms its past and past participle in some way other than by adding -d or -ed to its base form. Look at the examples below featuring the irregular verb write.

Past: We *wrote* an essay about English literature.
Past participle: We have *written* many essays about English literature.

The chart below contains some common irregular verbs and their past and past participle forms.

Base Form	Past	Past Participle
do	did	[have *or* had] done
leave	left	[have *or* had] left
teach	taught	[have *or* had] taught
come	came	[have *or* had] come
shake	shook	[have *or* had] shaken
read	read	[have *or* had] read
eat	ate	[have *or* had] eaten

Your Turn

Complete each of the following sentences, using the correct past or past participle form of the italicized verb.

1. *write* Boswell _____ a memoir about Samuel Johnson, a man for whom he had great respect.

2. *leave* Mr. and Mrs. Davies _____ Boswell and Johnson alone to talk, which Boswell very much enjoyed.

3. *come* Johnson _____ to Mr. Davies' shop while Boswell was having tea in the parlor.

Writing Application Choose a piece of your own writing that includes an irregular verb, and then change the form of the verb. How does the irregular verb change?

CHOICES

As you respond to the Choices, use these **Academic Vocabulary** words as appropriate: approach, convince, dominate, enhance, participate.

REVIEW
Use Historical Perspective

Partner Activity The Age of Johnson is also called the Age of Reason. During this time, the scientific method came into full use, and writers, scientists, and philosophers valued clear, logical thought. With a partner, find out what *empiricism* is and what qualifies as *empirical evidence*. Then, discuss how Johnson modeled the empirical approach. Note also the instances in Boswell's biography in which Johnson fell short of clear, logical thought, and suggest why you think he might have done so.

CONNECT
Make a Documentary

TechFocus With a small group, create a documentary scene based on Boswell's *Life*. Using the text as a script, rehearse and film one scene from the biography. To determine how to act, use Boswell's comments about his and Johnson's moods. Then, organize a "Johnson Documentary Film Festival" so you can watch various groups' documentary scenes.

EXTEND
Write a Letter from the Good Doctor

Although Boswell's biography of Johnson is often considered the best biography in the English language, Johnson himself never had a chance to read it. Imagine that Johnson could read Boswell's biography. Write a letter to Boswell from Johnson's point of view. In your letter, explain Johnson's reaction to the biography. Which parts did he like, which did he dislike, and what reasons does he give for his opinions?

Preparing to Read

Elegy Written in a Country Churchyard

What Do You Think?

How can order and civilization affect human behavior?

QuickWrite

Rules often help maintain an orderly society. Think of the rules you must follow in school or at home. How do these rules affect your everyday life in particular and society in general? Record your thoughts in your *Reader/Writer Notebook*.

Thomas Gray
(1716–1771)

Thomas Gray was considered England's premier lyric poet by his contemporaries. Even Samuel Johnson, who found much of Gray's poetry dull, recognized the universal appeal of Gray's famous "Elegy Written in a Country Churchyard." Johnson wrote, "The Churchyard abounds with images which find a mirror in every mind, and with sentiments to which every bosom returns an echo."

A Quiet Life

Painfully shy, Gray led a quiet life as a scholar at Cambridge University, reading literature in a variety of languages, studying assorted subjects, painting landscapes, and playing the harpsichord. Gray led such a secluded life that he did not <u>participate</u> in many activities considered customary for late eighteenth-century men. For example, he never rode a horse—a primary mode of transportation at that time. Furthermore, unlike all other professors at Cambridge, Gray never gave lectures.

The great crisis of Gray's life came when his close friend Richard West died of tuberculosis. Gray sought consolation in writing poetry. Reluctant to publish his work, he carefully and fastidiously revised and rewrote his verses. It took him nine years to complete "Elegy," which was published in 1751.

Gestures Toward Romanticism

Although his verse has ties to the neoclassical tradition that tended to <u>dominate</u> eighteenth-century literature, Gray is sometimes designated as a forerunner of Romantic poetry, and his "Elegy" combines elements from several literary traditions. Like the Romantic poets, Gray turns to subjects of country life and nature. His poems express sympathy with common humanity, and he uses the first-person point of view.

Although it is important never to assume that the speaker of a poem is the same person as the writer, it is not unwise to assume that parts of Gray's poem are autobiographical. Gray is buried alongside his mother in the cemetery immortalized in his "Elegy."

Think About the Writer

Why do you think the subjects of country life and nature appealed to Thomas Gray?

Thomas Gray by John Giles Eccardt. National Portrait Gallery, London.

Reader/Writer Notebook

Use your **RWN** to complete activities for this selection

Literary Focus

Elegy An **elegy** is a poem that mourns the death of a person or laments something lost. A type of **lyric,** an elegy may lament the passing of life and beauty or may meditate on the nature of death. An elegy usually uses formal language and structure and possesses a solemn or even melancholy **tone.** As you read, keep in mind that English poetry has a strong elegiac tradition—from the poems of the Anglo-Saxons, to the works of Ben Jonson, to the more modern poetry of A. E. Housman and Dylan Thomas. Although Gray was working within this long-standing poetic tradition when he wrote his "Elegy Written in a Country Churchyard," he still managed, in large part through his vivid **imagery** and word choice, to create a unique poem celebrated for its beauty.

Reading Focus

Analyzing Word Choice and Word Order A poet creates the tone of a poem through his or her **word choice** and **word order.** For example, the tone of an elegy is usually solemn and melancholy. In his "Elegy," Gray chose words for their sounds, meanings, and **connotations**—the feelings and emotions associated with the word—to create images that recall quietness, solitude, and death. Gray's word order reflects his **meter** (iambic pentameter) and his **rhyme scheme** *(abab).*

Into Action As you read, use a chart like the one below to record your observations about word choice and word order in each stanza.

Stanza	Word Choice	Word Order
first	The connotations of words such as "curfew" and "parting" imply limits and ends.	word order in third line is inverted to fit <u>abab</u> rhyme scheme

Writing Focus

Think as a Reader/Writer

Find It in Your Reading In "Elegy," Gray **personifies,** or gives human qualities to, abstract ideas and elements of the natural world, such as ambition and grandeur. As you read, note in your *Reader/Writer Notebook* other things that Gray personifies. How does this personification <u>enhance</u> the poem?

Vocabulary

annals (AN uhlz) *n. pl.:* records, organized by year, that tell someone or something's history. *The speaker knows that the annals of the poor would contain information about farming.*

impute (ihm PYOOT) *v.:* attribute to someone or something, usually negatively. *Impute the poor's failure to succeed to society, not to the poor.*

sequestered (sih KWEHS tuhrd) *v.* used as *adj.:* set apart from; isolated. *The sequestered graves were at the cemetery's far end.*

uncouth (uhn KOOTH) *adj.:* unsophisticated; awkward. *These forgettable gravestones are carved with uncouth rhymes that use simplistic language.*

tribute (TRIHB yoot) *n.:* something done to show respect. *This plain gravestone offers a moving tribute to the person buried here.*

Language Coach

Word Origins The noun *annals* comes from the Latin word for "year," as do other common English words such as *annual, bi-annual, semi-annual, annuity, anniversary,* and *Anno Domini,* usually abbreviated *A.D.* What does *annual* mean? What does it mean in relation to books? to plants? What do the other italicized words mean?

 Learn It Online
Listen to this elegy for yourself through the online audio.

| go.hrw.com | L12-657 | Go |

ELEGY WRITTEN IN A COUNTRY CHURCHYARD

by **Thomas Gray**

Read with a Purpose
Read to discover Gray's observations about life and death.

Build Background
Gray's "Elegy" combines elements from several literary traditions. First, it can be considered a **pastoral** elegy, in that its setting is a beautiful outdoor landscape that features idealized rural people. Second, the poem borrows from the **Gothic,** a literary mode that uses wild, mysterious, or natural elements (such as the "moping owl" and the graveyard) to help create atmosphere. Third, Gray follows the convention of other writers of the time by including yet another element, **generalizations** about life and death.

> The curfew tolls the knell of parting day,
> The lowing herd wind slowly o'er the lea,°
> The plowman homeward plods his weary way,
> And leaves the world to darkness, and to me. Ⓐ
>
> 5   Now fades the glimmering landscape on the sight,
> And all the air a solemn stillness holds;
> Save where the beetle wheels his droning flight,
> And drowsy tinklings lull the distant folds.
>
>   Save that from yonder ivy-mantled tower
> 10   The moping owl does to the moon complain
> Of such, as wand'ring near her secret bower,
> Molest her ancient solitary reign.
>
>   Beneath those rugged elms, that yew tree's shade,
> Where heaves the turf in many a mold'ring heap,
> 15   Each in his narrow cell forever laid,
> The rude° forefathers of the hamlet sleep. Ⓑ

2. lea: meadow.

16. rude: uneducated; unpolished.

Ⓐ **Literary Focus** **Elegy** Which images in this stanza convey emotions characteristic of an elegy?

Ⓑ **Reading Focus** **Understanding Word Choice and Word Order** What words are inverted in this stanza? What is the effect of inverting these words?

The breezy call of incense-breathing morn,
The swallow twitt'ring from the straw-built shed,°
The cock's shrill clarion, or the echoing horn,°
20 No more shall rouse them from their lowly bed.

For them no more the blazing hearth shall burn,
Or busy housewife ply her evening care:
No children run to lisp their sire's return,
Or climb his knees the envied kiss to share.

25 Oft did the harvest to their sickle yield,
Their furrow oft the stubborn glebe° has broke;
How jocund did they drive their team afield!
How bowed the woods beneath their sturdy stroke! **C**

18. shed: nest.
19. horn: hunting horn.

26. glebe: soil.

C **Reading Focus** **Understanding Word Choice and Word Order** Think about the connotations of the words "yield" and "broke." What tone is created by ending these lines with these words?

Churchyard and chapel, South Devon, England.

Let not Ambition mock their useful toil,
30   Their homely joys and destiny obscure;
Nor Grandeur hear with a disdainful smile,
The short and simple annals of the poor.

The boast of heraldry,° the pomp of power,
And all that beauty, all that wealth e'er gave,
35   Awaits alike th' inevitable hour.
The paths of glory lead but to the grave.

Nor you, ye proud, impute to these the fault,
If Mem'ry o'er their tomb no trophies raise,
Where through the long-drawn aisle and fretted vault°
40   The pealing anthem swells the note of praise.

Can storied urn° or animated bust
Back to its mansion call the fleeting breath?
Can Honor's voice provoke° the silent dust,
Or Flatt'ry soothe the dull cold ear of Death?

45   Perhaps in this neglected spot is laid
Some heart once pregnant with celestial fire,
Hands that the rod of empire might have swayed,
Or waked to ecstasy the living lyre.

But Knowledge to their eyes her ample page
50   Rich with the spoils of time did ne'er unroll;
Chill Penury° repressed their noble rage,°
And froze the genial current° of the soul.

Full many a gem of purest ray serene,
The dark unfathomed caves of ocean bear:
55   Full many a flower is born to blush unseen,
And waste its sweetness on the desert air.

Some village Hampden° that with dauntless breast
The little tyrant of his fields withstood;
Some mute inglorious Milton here may rest,
60   Some Cromwell° guiltless of his country's blood.

33. boast of heraldry: pride in one's ancestry. Heraldry is the study of family coats of arms.

39. fretted vault: elaborately decorated church ceiling.

41. storied urn: an urn with an inscription on it.
43. provoke: evoke; call forth.

51. Penury: poverty. **rage:** emotion; feeling.
52. genial current: warm impulses.

57. village Hampden: an obscure person who, with opportunity, might have been famous like John Hampden (1594–1643), an English statesman who defied the king over unjust taxation shortly before the English Civil Wars.
60. Cromwell: Lord Protector Oliver Cromwell, who ruled England from 1653 to 1658.

Vocabulary **annals** (AN uhlz) *n. pl.:* records, organized by year, that tell someone or something's history.
impute (ihm PYOOT) *v.:* attribute to someone or something, usually negatively.

Real-Life Stories

Although Gray's elegy commemorates the lives of ordinary people buried in a country churchyard, the poem's speaker can only speculate about the particulars of their lives. While they lived, their humble circumstances prevented them from leaving a permanent record of their stories. Today, many people wish to honor the dignity—and to preserve the stories—of individual lives. The StoryCorps Project provides one means to this end.

StoryCorps enables people to preserve their stories through free broadcast-quality audio recordings. Since 2003, thousands of people have recorded interviews. At the end of each session, contributors get a CD of their interview, which also becomes part of the StoryCorps Archive, housed in the Library of Congress. The project's goal is to create an oral history of American life. (For more information, visit www.storycorps.net.)

Ask Yourself

What might we learn about the eighteenth century if people then had left behind recorded interviews?

The StoryCorps StoryBooth in Grand Central Station in New York City.

> Th' applause of list'ning senates to command,
> The threats of pain and ruin to despise,
> To scatter plenty o'er a smiling land,
> And read their hist'ry in a nation's eyes
>
> 65 Their lot forbade: nor circumscribed alone
> Their growing virtues, but their crimes confined;
> Forbade to wade through slaughter to a throne,
> And shut the gates of mercy on mankind,
>
> The struggling pangs of conscious° truth to hide,
> 70 To quench the blushes of ingenuous° shame,
> Or heap the shrine of Luxury and Pride
> With incense, kindled at the Muse's flame.°
>
> Far from the madding° crowd's ignoble strife,
> Their sober wishes never learned to stray;
> 75 Along the cool sequestered vale of life
> They kept the noiseless tenor° of their way.

69. conscious: having an awareness; aware of oneself as a thinking being.
70. ingenuous: naively innocent.

72. incense . . . flame: tributes paid to them by poets.
73. madding: frenzied.

76. tenor: course.

Vocabulary **sequestered** (sih KWEHS tuhrd) *v.* used as *adj.*: set apart ; isolated.

Yet ev'n these bones from insult to protect
Some frail memorial° still erected nigh,
With uncouth rhymes and shapeless sculpture decked,
80 Implores the passing tribute of a sigh. **D**

Their name, their years, spelt by th' unlettered muse,°
The place of fame and elegy supply:
And many a holy text around she strews,
That teach the rustic moralist to die.

85 For who to dumb Forgetfulness a prey,
This pleasing anxious being e'er resigned,
Left the warm precincts of the cheerful day,
Nor cast one longing ling'ring look behind?

On some fond breast the parting soul relies,
90 Some pious drops° the closing eye requires;
Ev'n from the tomb the voice of Nature cries,
Ev'n in our ashes live their wonted fires.

For thee,° who mindful of th' unhonored dead
Dost in these lines their artless tale relate;
95 If chance, by lonely Contemplation led,
Some kindred spirit shall inquire thy fate,

Haply° some hoary-headed swain° may say,
"Oft have we seen him at the peep of dawn
Brushing with hasty steps the dews away
100 To meet the sun upon the upland lawn.

"There at the foot of yonder nodding beech
That wreathes its old fantastic roots so high,
His listless length at noontide would he stretch,
And pore upon the brook that babbles by.

105 "Hard° by yon wood, now smiling as in scorn,
Mutt'ring his wayward fancies he would rove,
Now drooping, woeful wan, like one forlorn,
Or crazed with care, or crossed in hopeless love.

78. frail memorial: modest tombstone, in contrast to the elaborate tombs inside the church.
81. unlettered muse: humble engraver of the tombstone.
90. drops: mourners' tears.

93. thee: Gray himself.

97. haply: perhaps. **hoary-headed swain:** white-haired countryman.

105. hard: close.

D Literary Focus **Elegy** What words and images in this stanza are elegiac?

Vocabulary **uncouth** (uhn KOOTH) *adj.:* unsophisticated; awkward.
tribute (TRIHB yoot) *n.:* something done to show respect.

"One morn I missed him on the customed hill,
110 Along the heath, and near his fav'rite tree;
Another came; nor yet beside the rill,°
Nor up the lawn, nor at the wood was he.

"The next with dirges due in sad array
Slow through the churchway path we saw him borne.
115 Approach and read (for thou canst read)° the lay,
Graved on the stone beneath yon aged thorn."° **E**

The Epitaph

Here rests his head upon the lap of Earth
A youth to Fortune and to Fame unknown:
Fair Science frowned not on his humble birth,°
120 *And Melancholy marked him for her own.*

Large was his bounty, and his soul sincere,
Heaven did a recompense as largely send:
He gave to Mis'ry all he had, a tear:
He gained from Heaven ('twas all he wished) a friend.

125 *No farther seek his merits to disclose,*
Or draw his frailties from their dread abode,
(There they alike in trembling Hope repose)
The bosom of his Father and his God.

111. rill: brook.

115. thou canst read: The speaker apparently cannot read.
116. thorn: hawthorn bush.

119. fair . . . birth: He was educated—*science* meant learning in general—despite his modest beginnings.

E **Literary Focus** **Elegy** What images in this stanza evoke a somber mood?

St. Mary's Churchyard, Rostheme, England.

SKILLS FOCUS **Literary Skills** Analyze the characteristics of an elegy; analyze figures of speech. **Reading Skills** Analyze word choice and word order.

Vocabulary Skills Demonstrate knowledge of literal meanings of words and their usage. **Writing Skills** Write poetry.

Elegy Written in a Country Churchyard

Respond and Think Critically

Reading Focus

Read with a Purpose

1. How are Gray's views of life and death related? Cite one example.

Reading Skills: Analyzing Word Choice and Word Order

2. As you read, you analyzed word choice and word order within each stanza. Now, review your charts, and pick three stanzas that you analyzed. Write a paragraph explaining how the word choices and word order in the three stanzas affect the poem's tone.

✓ Vocabulary Check

Match each Vocabulary word with its definition.

3. annals
4. impute
5. sequestered
6. uncouth
7. tribute

a. unsophisticated
b. secluded
c. historical records
d. payment, praise
e. attribute

Literary Focus

Literary Analysis

8. Evaluate What ideas in the poem relate to ideas and feelings people have today?

9. Make Judgments In lines 53–56, what might a "gem of purest ray serene" and the "flower . . . born to blush unseen" symbolize?

10. Interpret The poet personifies Ambition and Grandeur in lines 29 and 31. What does he warn them not to do?

11. Infer According to lines 77–92, what evidence on the gravestones shows that humble, ordinary people also wish to be remembered?

12. Analyze How do the poem's rhyme scheme and meter enhance its meaning?

Literary Skills: Elegy

13. Interpret How does the famous line "The paths of glory lead but to the grave" (line 36) reflect the characteristics of an elegy?

14. Extend Many readers of the "Elegy" have assumed that Gray himself is the poet whose epitaph is given in the final lines. Is this assumption necessary to understanding the poem? Why might a reader like to make this assumption?

Literary Skills Review: Figures of Speech

15. Analyze A **figure of speech** is a word or phrase that describes one thing in terms of a dissimilar thing. Work with a partner to find and explain a figure of speech in Gray's poem.

Writing Focus

Think as a Reader/Writer

Use It in Your Writing As you read, you noted Gray's use of personification. Now, write your own ten-line poem in which you personify an abstract idea, such as love or death, that is central to your poem's theme.

 What Do **You Think Now** When dealing with death, why might people find comfort through established customs and traditions?

Views on Women's Rights

Painting on the Terrace by Jules Frederic Ballavoine (1855-1901). Oil on canvas. Private Collection.

The women's rights movement, an ongoing series of political movements aimed at attaining educational, social, and political equality for women, arose primarily in England and the United States. Its roots lay both in humanistic thought and in the Industrial Revolution of the eighteenth and nineteenth centuries.

According to the dictates of both theology and law, married women of the eighteenth century could not own property, run a business, or control their own lives or those of their children. Social critics (male and female) began to contrast this state of affairs with the ideal of freedom that inspired the American and French Revolutions. The readings in this Comparing Texts section present some of the earliest shots fired in the battle for women's rights.

CONTENTS

from **A Vindication of the Rights of Woman**
by Mary Wollstonecraft

from **The Education of Women**
by Daniel Defoe

To the Ladies
by Mary, Lady Chudleigh

MARY WOLLSTONECRAFT

from A Vindication of the Rights of Woman

DANIEL DEFOE

from The Education of Women

MARY, LADY CHUDLEIGH

To The Ladies

What Do You Think?

How can order and civilization affect human behavior?

QuickWrite

Supporters of women's rights believe that men and women are equal as human beings and so should have equal respect and treatment in society. What rights do women in this country have now that they did not have in the past? In what areas are men and women still not treated equally? Write a brief paragraph responding to these questions.

MEET THE WRITERS

Mary Wollstonecraft
(1759–1797)

Mary Wollstonecraft demanded "JUSTICE for one half of the human race"—that is, women. She stands as the English pioneer of the women's movement. Inspired by the slogan of the French Revolution, "liberty, equality, fraternity," Wollstonecraft published her most famous work, *A Vindication of the Rights of Woman*, in 1792. This document is a passionate criticism of the social and economic institutions that promoted women's inequality. Wollstonecraft's daughter, Mary Shelley, penned the novel *Frankenstein* (1818) and is perhaps more well-known than Wollstonecraft.

Daniel Defoe
(1660–1731)

Daniel Defoe was at various times a businessman and a spy, but he was always a man who wrote—more than five hundred works in many forms and on many subjects, from choosing a wife to manufacturing glass. During Defoe's lifetime, his political writings led to notoriety, arrests, public punishment, and even jail time. It is a great irony of literary history that the prolific Defoe is now primarily remembered as the author of only one book, his novel about a survivor—a shipwrecked sailor named Robinson Crusoe.

Mary, Lady Chudleigh
(1656–1710)

The poems and essays of Mary, Lady Chudleigh address the concerns of women of her time and explore a philosophy of how to live a peaceful life. She adamantly opposed the idea that wives should submit to the will of their husbands, and she expressed this view in many of her works.

Think About the Writers

How would these writers feel about the state of women's rights today?

Views on Women's Rights

Reader/Writer
Notebook

Use your **RWN** to complete the activities for these selections.

Literary Focus

Tone The attitude a writer takes toward the reader or a topic is **tone**. One way that writers control tone is through the use of words with specific **connotations**—associations and emotions that have become attached to a word. As you read, pay attention to words with strong connotations, and note the tone these words convey.

Literary Perspectives Apply the Literary Perspective described on page 669 as you read the excerpt from *A Vindication of the Rights of Woman*.

Reading Focus

Analyzing Rhetorical Devices **Rhetorical devices** are methods writers or speakers use to make their language more effective. One device is the **rhetorical question**, asked to make a point the author assumes the audience will agree with. **Argument by analogy** reveals a parallel between two situations. **Historical allusion** is a reference to a person, place, or event from history that relates to the topic. **Repetition** emphasizes an author's point. **Appeals to authority** support an author's argument.

Into Action As you read, use a chart like the one below to record examples of the rhetorical devices each author uses and how each device supports his or her main point.

Device	Example	How It Supports the Main Point
rhetorical question	"Where are the masculine women?" (Vindication)	makes the point that equality does not make women into men

Vocabulary

fastidious (fas TIHD ee uhs) *adj.:* picky; overly fussy. *The author says that men look at women with fastidious eyes.*

specious (SPEE shuhs) *adj.:* showy but false. *She says that men have fooled women with specious tributes to womanhood.*

cursory (KUR suhr ee) *adj.:* hasty; superficial. *The introduction contains a cursory summary of the author's arguments.*

propensity (pruh PEHN suh tee) *n.:* natural inclination. *The author believes that women have developed a propensity to assert their power in subtle ways.*

manifest (MAN uh fehst) *adj.:* evident; obvious. *Defoe claims it is manifest that the human soul separates civilized people from barbarians.*

vie (vy) *v.:* compete. *According to Defoe, men fear that educated women would vie with men to achieve great things.*

Language Coach

Antonyms Adjectives give specific descriptions that can apply to people, places, or things. One way to learn a new adjective is to think of a word that has an opposite meaning. A man who is fastidious in his habits is the opposite of careless. What is an adjective that means the opposite of *specious*? Can you name adjectives that are antonyms for *cursory* and *manifest*?

Writing Focus

Think as a Reader/Writer
Find It In Your Reading The **analogies** in these works add power to the writers' arguments. As you read, make note of such analogies in your *Reader/Writer Notebook*.

Learn It Online
Jump into this discussion through an online video introduction.

go.hrw.com L12-667   **Go**

Preparing to Read **667**

Marriage a' la Mode: The Marriage Settlement (c. 1743)
by William Hogarth (1697-1764). Oil on canvas.
National Gallery, London.

PLATFORM

from A Vindication of the Rights of Woman

by **Mary Wollstonecraft**

Read with a Purpose
Read to discover how the author justifies her arguments
in favor of women's rights.

Build Background
In much of the world today, the same educational opportunities are
available to both men and women. Women have the right to vote,
and they may study for and pursue virtually any career they wish.

These opportunities, often taken for granted, were not always available to women. In England during the Restoration, the educated
woman was the exception to the rule, and women were not allowed
to vote. Keep these facts in mind as you read this excerpt from this
famous essay.

Note that Wollstonecraft's use of the word *vindication* means
"justification."

Introduction

After considering the historic page, and viewing the living world with anxious solicitude,[1] the most melancholy emotions of sorrowful indignation have depressed my spirits, and I have sighed when obliged to confess, that either nature has made a great difference between man and man, or that the civilization which has hitherto taken place in the world has been very partial.[2] I have turned over various books written on the subject of education, and patiently observed the conduct of parents and the management of schools; but what has been the result?—a profound conviction that the neglected education of my fellow-creatures is the grand source of the misery I deplore; and that women, in particular, are rendered weak and wretched by a variety of concurring causes, originating from one hasty conclusion. The conduct and manners of women, in fact, evidently prove that their minds are not in a healthy state; for, like the flowers which are planted in too rich a soil, strength and usefulness are sacrificed to beauty; and the flaunting leaves, after having pleased a fastidious eye, fade, disregarded on the stalk, long before the season when they ought to have arrived at maturity. —One cause of this barren blooming I attribute to a false system of education, gathered from the books written on this subject by men who, considering females rather as women than human creatures, have been more anxious to make them alluring mistresses than affectionate wives and rational mothers; and the understanding of the sex has been so bubbled[3] by this specious homage, that the civilized women of the present century, with a few exceptions,

1. **solicitude:** care; concern.
2. **partial:** biased.
3. **bubbled:** be deluded with or distracted by flimsy evidence.

are only anxious to inspire love, when they ought to cherish a nobler ambition, and by their abilities and virtues exact[4] respect.　　**A**　**B**

In a treatise, therefore, on female rights and manners, the works which have been particularly written for their improvement must not be overlooked; especially when it is asserted, in direct terms, that the minds of women are enfeebled by false refinement; that the books of instruction, written by men of genius, have had the same tendency as more frivolous productions; and that, in the true style of Mahometanism,[5] they are treated as a kind of subor-

4. **exact:** demand; require.
5. **Mahometanism:** Islam, the religion of Muslims. Europeans mistakenly thought that the Koran teaches that women have no souls. In actuality, the Koran teaches that women are to be treated as equals to men.

Literary Perspectives

Analyzing Political Context Literary texts reflect social beliefs and practices and are influenced by the author's worldview, derived from his or her political perspective, gender, or social class. As you read this selection, consider the factors that shaped Mary Wollstonecraft's worldview. Wollstonecraft—as a woman in eighteenth century England—was not allowed to attend college or to vote. Her father's violence toward her mother had left Wollstonecraft disillusioned about marriage. Nineteen and self-educated, Wollstonecraft left home to work in some of the few occupations legally available to single women. As a young woman during the American and French Revolutions, she was influenced by radical political thinkers such as Thomas Paine and inspired by the French slogan "liberty, equality, fraternity."

As you read, be sure to notice questions in the text, which will guide you in using this perspective.

A **Literary Perspectives** Analyzing Political Context In the first sentence, Mary Wollstonecraft invokes both "the historic page" and "the living world." How does this first sentence help establish a political context for the text?

B **Reading Focus** Analyzing Rhetorical Devices What analogy does Wollstonecraft use in the lines starting with "The conduct and manners of women . . . " and ending with "maturity"? What point does Wollstonecraft make?

Vocabulary **fastidious** (fas TIHD ee uhs) *adj.:* picky; overly fussy.
specious (SPEE shuhs) *adj.:* showy but false.

dinate beings, and not as a part of the human species, when improvable[6] reason is allowed to be the dignified distinction which raises men above the brute creation, and puts a natural scepter[7] in a feeble hand.

Yet, because I am a woman, I would not lead my readers to suppose that I mean violently to agitate the contested question respecting the equality or inferiority of the sex; but as the subject lies in my way, and I cannot pass it over without subjecting the main tendency of my reasoning to misconstruction,[8] I shall stop a moment to deliver, in a few words, my opinion.—In the government of the physical world it is observable that the female in point of strength is, in general, inferior to the male. This is the law of nature; and it does not appear to be suspended or abrogated[9] in favor of woman. A degree of physical superiority cannot, therefore, be denied—and it is a noble prerogative![10] But not content with this natural pre-eminence, men endeavor to sink us still lower, merely to render us alluring objects for a moment; and women, intoxicated by the adoration which men, under the influence of their senses, pay them, do not seek to obtain a durable interest in their hearts, or to become the friends of the fellow creatures who find amusement in their society. **(C)**

I am aware of an obvious inference:—from every quarter have I heard exclamations against masculine women; but where are they to be found? If by this appellation[11] men mean to inveigh[12] against their ardour in hunting, shooting, and gaming, I shall most cordially join in the cry; but if it be against the imitation of manly virtues, or, more properly speaking, the

---

6. **improvable:** capable of being improved.
7. **scepter** (SEHP tuhr): symbol of authority.
8. **misconstruction:** misunderstanding.
9. **abrogated:** abolished; repeated.
10. **prerogative:** privilege.
11. **appellation:** name.
12. **inveigh:** complain loudly.

(C) **Literary Focus** Tone What is the tone of Wollstonecraft's insistence that she does not want to stir up controversy about gender equality?

(D) **Reading Focus** Analyzing Rhetorical Devices Here, Wollstonecraft poses the rhetorical question *Where are the masculine women?* What is her point?

attainment of those talents and virtues, the exercise of which ennobles the human character, and which raise females in the scale of animal being, when they are comprehensively termed mankind;—all those who view them with a philosophic eye must, I should think, wish with me, that they may every day grow more and more masculine. **(D)**

This discussion naturally divides the subject. I shall first consider women in the grand light of human creatures, who, in common with men, are placed on this earth to unfold their faculties; and afterwards I shall more particularly point out their peculiar designation.

I wish also to steer clear of an error which many respectable writers have fallen into; for the instruction which has hitherto been addressed to women, has rather been applicable to *ladies,* if the little indirect advice, that is scattered through Sandford and Merton,[13] be excepted; but, addressing my sex in a firmer tone, I pay particular attention to those in the middle class, because they appear to be in the most natural state. Perhaps the seeds of false refinement, immorality, and vanity, have ever been shed by the great. Weak, artificial beings, raised above the common wants and affections of their race, in a premature unnatural manner, undermine the very foundation of virtue, and spread corruption through the whole mass of society! As a class of mankind they have the strongest claim to pity; the education of the rich tends to render them vain and helpless, and the unfolding mind is not strengthened by the practice of those duties which dignify the human character.—They only live to amuse themselves, and by the same law which in nature invariably produces certain effects, they soon only afford barren amusement. **(E)**

---

13. **Sandford and Merton:** reference to *The History of Sandford and Merton,* a children's book. A character in the book often cites the moral superiority of a poor boy over a rich one.

(E) **Literary Focus** Tone In earlier English writings, *ladies* meant "upper-class women." How would you describe Wollstonecraft's attitude toward these women? What connotative words help to establish this tone?

Women's Rights Today

Since Mary Wollstonecraft wrote her plea for women's equality, opportunities for women, including access to education, have improved. Colleges in many countries admit women. In fact, in the United States, more women than men attend college. Nevertheless, in some regions of the world, women's access to education remains as restricted as it was to English women in Wollstonecraft's time. Globally, 90 million girls of school age do not receive a primary education. Some are prevented by poverty, others by traditional beliefs. Of all children who do not attend school, two-thirds are girls. But through financial support and strategic counseling, grass-roots organizations are providing educational opportunities to girls who have been denied them.

Other crucial issues remain to be solved, including attaining constitutional equality for women in all nations and ending violence against women. Today, many organizations continue to promote Wollstonecraft's ideals for women.

Ask Yourself

If Wollstonecraft were alive today, what issues do you think would concern her most? Why?

But as I purpose[14] taking a separate view of the different ranks of society, and of the moral character of women in each, this hint is, for the present, sufficient; and I have only alluded to the subject, because it appears to me to be the very essence of an introduction to give a cursory account of the contents of the work it introduces.

My own sex, I hope, will excuse me, if I treat them like rational creatures, instead of flattering their *fascinating* graces, and viewing them as if they were in a state of perpetual childhood, unable to stand alone. I earnestly wish to point out in what true dignity and human happiness consists—I wish to persuade women to endeavor to acquire strength, both of mind and body, and to convince them that the soft phrases, susceptibility of heart, delicacy of sentiment, and refine-

ment of taste, are almost synonymous with epithets[15] of weakness, and that those beings who are only the objects of pity and that kind of love, which has been termed its sister, will soon become objects of contempt.

F

Dismissing then those pretty feminine phrases, which the men condescendingly use to soften our slavish dependence, and despising that weak elegancy of mind, exquisite sensibility, and sweet docility of manners, supposed to be the sexual characteristics of the weaker vessel, I wish to shew[16] that elegance is inferior to virtue, that the first object of laudable[17] ambition is to obtain a character as a human being, regardless of

---

14. **purpose:** intend.

15. **epithets** (EHP uh thehts): names.
16. **shew:** archaic spelling of *show*.
17. **laudable:** praiseworthy.

F Literary Focus Tone These characteristics of women are examples of the "fascinating graces" that the author mentions in the first sentence of the paragraph. What is her attitude toward these graces?

Vocabulary **cursory** (KUR suhr ee) *adj.:* hasty; superficial.

Mr. B. Finds Pamela Writing by Joseph Highmore (1692-1780). Illustration for *Pamela* (1740) by Samuel Richardson. Oil on canvas. Victoria and Albert Museum, London.

disdain to cull[19] my phrases or polish my style;—I aim at being useful, and sincerity will render me unaffected; for, wishing rather to persuade by the force of my arguments, than dazzle by the elegance of my language, I shall not waste my time in rounding periods, or in fabricating the turgid bombast[20] of artificial feelings, which, coming from the head, never reach the heart.—I shall be employed about things, not words!—and, anxious to render my sex more respectable members of society, I shall try to avoid that flowery diction which has slided from essays into novels, and from novels into familiar letters and conversation.

These pretty superlatives,[21] dropping glibly from the tongue, vitiate[22] the taste, and create a kind of sickly delicacy that turns away from simple unadorned truth; and a deluge of false sentiments and overstretched feelings, stifling the natural emotions of the heart, render the domestic pleasures insipid,[23] that ought to sweeten the exercise of those severe duties, which educate a rational and immortal being for a nobler field of action. **(H)**

the distinction of sex; and that secondary views should be brought to this simple touchstone.[18] **(G)**

This is a rough sketch of my plan; and should I express my conviction with the energetic emotions that I feel whenever I think of the subject, the dictates of experience and reflection will be felt by some of my readers. Animated by this important object, I shall

---

18. **touchstone:** criterion; originally a stone used for testing the quality of gold and silver alloys by noting the color of the streak produced by rubbing the metals upon it.

---

19. **cull:** sort out.
20. **turgid bombast:** pompous rant or utterance.
21. **superlatives:** exaggerations.
22. **vitiate:** impair; weaken; spoil.
23. **insipid:** dull; flat.

The education of women has, of late, been more attended to than formerly; yet they are still reckoned a frivolous sex, and ridiculed or pitied by the writers who endeavor by satire or instruction to improve them. It is acknowledged that they spend many of the first years of their lives in acquiring a smattering of accomplishments; meanwhile strength of body and mind are sacrificed to libertine[24] notions of beauty, to the desire of establishing themselves,—the only way women can rise in the world,—by marriage. And this desire making mere animals of them, when they marry they act as such children may be expected to act:—they dress; they paint, and nickname God's creatures. —Surely these weak beings are only fit for a seraglio![25] —Can they be expected to govern a family with judgment, or take care of the poor babes whom they bring into the world? **O**

If then it can be fairly deduced from the present conduct of the sex, from the prevalent fondness for pleasure which takes place of ambition and those nobler passions that open and enlarge the soul; that the instruction which women have hitherto received has only tended, with the constitution of civil society, to render them insignificant objects of desire—mere propagators[26] of fools!—if it can be proved that in aiming to accomplish them, without cultivating their understandings, they are taken out of their sphere of duties, and made ridiculous and useless when the short-lived bloom of beauty is over,* I presume that *rational* men will excuse me for endeavoring to persuade them to become more masculine and respectable. **J**

Indeed the word masculine is only a bugbear:[27] there is little reason to fear that women will acquire too much courage or fortitude; for their apparent inferiority with respect to bodily strength, must render them, in some degree, dependent on men in the various relations of life; but why should it be increased by prejudices that give a sex to virtue, and confound simple truths with sensual reveries?[28]

Women are, in fact, so much degraded by mistaken notions of female excellence, that I do not mean to add a paradox when I assert, that this artificial weakness produces a propensity to tyrannize, and gives birth to cunning, the natural opponent of strength, which leads them to play off those contemptible infantine airs that undermine esteem even whilst they excite desire. Let men become more chaste and modest, and if women do not grow wiser in the same ratio, it will be clear that they have weaker understandings. It seems scarcely necessary to say, that I now speak of the sex in general. Many individuals have more sense than their male relatives; and, as nothing preponderates[29] where there is a constant struggle for equilibrium, without it has naturally more gravity, some women govern their husbands without degrading themselves, because intellect will always govern. **K**

*A lively writer, I cannot recollect his name, asks what business women turned of forty have to do in the world?

---

28. **reveries:** musings.
29. **preponderates:** predominates.

---

24. **libertine:** sensual.
25. **seraglio** (suh RAL yoh): a place in a Middle Eastern house where wives live; a harem.
26. **propagators:** breeders.
27. **bugbear:** anything causing needless fear.

O Reading Focus **Analyzing Rhetorical Devices** What rhetorical device concludes this paragraph? What point does this device make?

J Literary Perspectives **Analyzing Political Context** What social distinctions between men and women can be drawn from Wollstonecraft's discussion?

K Literary Focus **Tone** What paradox does Wollstonecraft discuss in the final paragraph? What words reveal her attitude toward this paradox?

Vocabulary **propensity** (pruh PEHN suh tee) *n.:* natural inclination.

from

The Education of Women

by **Daniel Defoe**

Read with a Purpose
Read to find out why Defoe supported the controversial issue of education for women.

Build Background
Ironically, Defoe himself did not receive the standard education for young gentlemen of his era. His parents were Dissenters—Protestants who disapproved of the Church of England—so he was barred from attending the universities in Oxford and Cambridge. Instead, he studied law, history, economics, geography, and natural science at an alternative academy. When he was about twenty, he set himself up as a merchant, trading in haberdashery (men's hats, shirts, ties, and so on), wool, real estate, and at one point civet "cats" (cat-like animals that resemble a mongoose). By the time he married, at age twenty-four, he was already writing and publishing. "The Education of Women" is one of his numerous pamphlets on religious and political controversies. Some of his contemporaries apparently considered him a nuisance: Jonathan Swift wrote in 1708, "there is no enduring him," and Joseph Addison in 1713 called him "a false, shuffling, prevaricating rascal—unqualified to give his testimony in a Court of Justice."

I have often thought of it as one of the most barbarous customs in the world, considering us as a civilized and a Christian country, that we deny the advantages of learning to women. We reproach the sex every day with folly and impertinence; while I am confident, had they the advantages of education equal to us, they would be guilty of less than ourselves.

One would wonder, indeed, how it should happen that women are conversible[1] at all; since they are only beholden to natural parts, for all their knowledge. Their youth is spent to teach them to stitch and sew or make baubles. They are taught to read, indeed, and perhaps to write their names, or so; and that is the height of a woman's education. And I would but ask any who slight the sex for their understanding, what is a man (a gentleman, I mean) good for, that is taught no more? I need not give instances, or examine the character of a gentleman, with a good estate, or a good family, and with tolerable parts; and examine what figure he makes for want of education.

The soul is placed in the body like a rough diamond; and must be polished, or the luster of it will never appear. And 'tis manifest, that as the rational soul distinguishes us from brutes; so education carries on the distinction, and makes some less brutish than others. This is too evident to need any demonstration. But why then should women be denied the benefit of instruction? If knowledge and understanding had been useless additions to the sex, GOD Almighty would never have given them capacities; for he made

---

1. **conversible:** able to interact socially.

Vocabulary   **manifest** (MAN uh fehst) *adj.:* evident; obvious.

A Dame's School (1845) by Thomas Webster (1800-1886).
Tate Gallery, London.

nothing needless. Besides, I would ask such, What they can see in ignorance, that they should think it a necessary ornament to a woman? or how much worse is a wise woman than a fool? or what has the woman done to forfeit the privilege of being taught? Does she plague us with her pride and impertinence? Why did we not let her learn, that she might have had more wit? Shall we upbraid[2] women with folly, when 'tis only the error of this inhuman custom, that hindered them from being made wiser? **A** **B**

The capacities of women are supposed to be greater, and their senses quicker than those of the men; and what they might be capable of being bred to, is plain from some instances of female wit, which this age is not without. Which upbraids us with Injustice, and looks as if we denied women the advantages of education, for fear they should *vie* with the men in their improvements. …

[They] should be taught all sorts of breeding suitable both to their genius and quality. And in particular, Music and Dancing; which it would be cruelty to bar the sex of, because they are their darlings. But besides this, they should be taught languages, as particularly French and Italian: and I would venture the injury[3] of

---

2. **upbraid:** criticize.

3. **venture the injury:** take the risk.

A Literary Focus **Tone** What are the connotations of the words "useless," "needless," "ignorance," "plague," "folly," and "inhuman?" How do they contribute to the tone of Defoe's argument?

B Reading Focus **Analyzing Rhetorical Devices** What analogy does Defoe use in this paragraph? What impact does the analogy make on his main idea?

Vocabulary **vie** (vy) *v.:* compete.

giving a woman more tongues than one. They should, as a particular study, be taught all the graces of speech, and all the necessary air of conversation; which our common education is so defective in, that I need not expose it. They should be brought to read books, and especially history; and so to read as to make them understand the world, and be able to know and judge of things when they hear of them. **C**

To such whose genius would lead them to it, I would deny no sort of learning; but the chief thing, in general, is to cultivate the understandings of the sex, that they may be capable of all sorts of conversation; that their parts and judgments being improved, they may be as profitable in their conversation as they are pleasant.

Women, in my observation, have little or no difference in them, but as they are or are not distinguished by education. Tempers, indeed, may in some degree influence them, but the main distinguishing part is their Breeding....

The great distinguishing difference, which is seen in the world between men and women, is in their education; and this is manifested by comparing it with the difference between one man or woman, and another.

And herein it is that I take upon me to make such a bold assertion, That all the world are mistaken in their practice about women. For I cannot think that GOD Almighty ever made them so delicate, so glorious creatures; and furnished them with such charms, so agreeable and so delightful to mankind; with souls capable of the same accomplishments with men: and all, to be only Stewards of our Houses, Cooks, and Slaves.

Not that I am for exalting the female government in the least: but, in short, *I would have men take women for companions, and educate them to be fit for it.* A woman of sense and breeding will scorn as much to encroach upon the prerogative of man, as a man of sense will scorn to oppress the weakness of the woman. But if the women's souls were refined and improved by teaching, that word would be lost. To say, the *weakness* of the sex, as to judgment, would be nonsense; for ignorance and folly would be no more to be found among women than men. **D**

I remember a passage, which I heard from a very fine woman. She had wit and capacity enough, an extraordinary shape and face, and a great fortune: but had been cloistered up all her time; and for fear of being stolen, had not had the liberty of being taught the common necessary knowledge of women's affairs. And when she came to converse in the world, her natural wit made her so sensible of the want of education, that she gave this short reflection on herself: "I am ashamed to talk with my very maids," says she, "for I don't know when they do right or wrong. I had more need go to school, than be married." . . .

'Tis a thing will be more easily granted than remedied....

C Literary Focus **Tone** When Defoe plays on stereotypes of women as sharp-tongued and overly talkative and says that he will "venture the injury" (take the risk) of "giving a women more tongues than one," what is his tone?

D Reading Focus **Analyzing Rhetorical Devices** What rhetorical device does Defoe use in this paragraph? How effective is this device?

To the Ladies

by **Mary, Lady Chudleigh**

Read with a Purpose
Read to find out why the author compares a wife's position to that of a servant.

Build Background
"To the Ladies" is Chudleigh's most anthologized poem; it appeared in print in 1703 and was so popular that it has been found copied onto the flyleaves of other books. Lady Chudleigh's marriage may have been somewhat unrewarding, which perhaps contributed to the bitter tone of this poem.

Wife and Servant are the same,
But only differ in the Name:
For when that fatal Knot is ty'd,
Which nothing, nothing can divide:
5   When she the word *obey* has said,
And Man by Law supreme has made,
Then all that's kind is laid aside,
And nothing left but State° and Pride:
Fierce as an Eastern Prince he grows,
10   And all his innate Rigor shows:
Then but to look, to laugh, or speak,
Will the Nuptial Contract break.
Like Mutes she Signs alone must make,
And never any Freedom take:
15   But still be govern'd by a Nod,
And fear her Husband as her God:
Him still must serve, him still obey,
And nothing act, and nothing say,
But what her haughty Lord thinks fit,
20   Who with the Pow'r, has all the Wit.   **A**
Then shun, oh! shun that wretched State,
And all the fawning Flatt'rers hate:
Value your selves, and Men despise,
You must be proud, if you'll be wise.   **B**

8. **State:** ostentation; pretentiousness.

The Betrothal (1774) by Jacobus Buys (1724-1801). Oil on canvas. Tatton Park, Cheshire, England.

A **Reading Focus** **Analyzing Rhetorical Devices** In line 9, the speaker begins an analogy, extending it through line 19. To what does she compare a husband?

B **Literary Focus** **Tone** The use of hyperbole is one mark of a satirical tone. Where is the hyperbole in lines 13–19? What is the speaker satirizing in these lines?

Applying Your Skills

from **A Vindication of the Rights of Woman /**
from **The Education of Women / To the Ladies**

Respond and Think Critically

Quick Check

1. According to Wollstonecraft, why are women considered inferior to men?

2. What does Defoe say about the "capacities of women"? Why does he say that men are afraid of educating women?

3. According to Chudleigh, what should women learn to value?

Read with a Purpose

4. What strategies do Wollstonecraft, Defoe, and Lady Chudleigh use to justify their arguments? Why does each advocate women's rights?

Reading Skills: Analyzing Rhetorical Devices

5. Review your chart of rhetorical devices. Does each author seem to favor one rhetorical device over other devices? Choose one of the selections that uses a particular rhetorical device more than once. Explain in a paragraph how the use of that device affects the author's argument and the overall tone of the piece.

Literary Focus

Literary Analysis

6. Compare What arguments are advanced by Wollstonecraft and Defoe for granting women "the advantages of learning"? What arguments are advanced only by one writer or the other?

7. Interpret Why might readers in the eighteenth century have found the opening line of Lady Chudleigh's poem shocking? What details of the poem support the meaning of this line?

8. Literary Perspectives Wollstonecraft was a strong advocate of women's rights. How does viewing this text through a political lens enhance your understanding of the historical context as well as help you understand the focus of her argument?

Literary Skills: Tone

9. Evaluate What is the overall tone of each selection? What particular words, phrases, and passages contribute to each selection's tone?

Literary Skills Review: Satire

10. Infer A **satire** mocks the failings and flaws of people or social institutions in an attempt to bring about a change. In *Vindication*, Wollstonecraft satirizes the idea that certain intellectual qualities can be strictly masculine or feminine. How does she satirize the notion that educating women will make them masculine?

Writing Focus

Think as a Reader/Writer

Use It in Your Writing Look back at the analogies you identified while reading. Using at least two original analogies, write a paragraph in your *Reader/Writer Notebook* explaining your views about one of the selections or about the topic of gender equality.

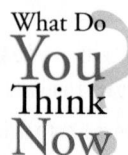
What Do **You Think Now**

How did social rules and order affect the lives of women in eighteenth-century Britain? How did these writers respond to those rules and social order?

Vocabulary Development

✓ Vocabulary Check

Match each Vocabulary word with its synonym.

1. fastidious
2. specious
3. cursory
4. propensity
5. manifest
6. vie

a. apparent
b. superficial
c. particular
d. compete
e. fake
f. inclination

Vocabulary Skills: Using a Dictionary

Scholarly documents such as Wollstonecraft's *A Vindication of the Rights of Woman* often contain difficult, specialized, or abstract vocabulary. If you find yourself puzzled by a word, look the word up in a dictionary. A dictionary can provide information about the word's meaning, part of speech, and etymology, or history.

In *Vindication,* for example, Wollstonecraft writes, "If by this appellation men mean to inveigh against their ardour . . . ." The chart below gives information about *appellation* that you may find in a dictionary.

Word: *appellation*	
Meaning	name or title
Part of speech	noun
Etymology	Latin ("a naming")

Your Turn

Use a dictionary to look up the following italicized words from the text. Using the chart as an example, fill out a similar chart for each word.

1. "After considering the historic page, and viewing the living world with anxious *solicitude*…

2. "…and it does not appear to be suspended or *abrogated* in favor of woman."

3. "If by this appellation men mean to *inveigh* against their ardour [*ardor*]…

Language Coach

Antonyms Words with opposite meanings are antonyms. Identifying antonyms can help you remember the meanings of new words. Replace each Vocabulary word in italics with one of the following antonyms: *thorough, relaxed, obscure, valid.* Read the new sentence aloud and explain how the meaning changes with the new word in place.

1. Men can be just as *fastidious* as women when it comes to their appearance.
2. She insists that the arguments for the new law are utterly *specious*.
3. A *cursory* review of the essay reveals several shifts in tone.
4. The writer's ideas are *manifest* to her readers.

Academic Vocabulary

Talk About
With a partner, discuss how educating girls and women affects individuals and societies. How can it <u>enhance</u> lives and lead people to <u>participate</u> more fully in life? Who might oppose education for girls and women? Why? How might you <u>convince</u> someone to support education for girls and women?

from **A Vindication of the Rights of Woman** /
from **The Education of Women / To the Ladies**

Grammar Link

Subjunctive Mood

You use the **subjunctive mood** when you want to express a suggestion, a necessity, a condition contrary to fact, or a wish. The **present subjunctive** expresses a necessity or suggestion. The present subjunctive form of a verb is the same as the base form of the verb, such as *be* or *have*. As you can see in the examples below, the present subjunctive often occurs in subordinate clauses beginning with *that*.

> The author suggested that women **be given** a chance to achieve equality in society.
>
> Her husband recommended that the conversation **be postponed** until the next morning.

The **past subjunctive** expresses a condition contrary to fact or expresses a wish. The past subjunctive form is *were*. Note that the past subjunctive form is used in clauses beginning with *if, as if,* or *as though*.

> If I **were** you, I'd be more careful.
>
> I wish she **were** at the beach with us.

Your Turn

Read each sentence. If the sentence is written in the subjunctive mood, write down the subjunctive phrase and identify it as present or past subjunctive.

1. If the author's style were any more inflammatory, the book would be too hot to touch.
2. The men were at work all day, making money and interacting with their peers.
3. The author requested that her book be sold in stores where women shop.

Writing Application Write a paragraph in which you use the subjunctive mood to express a wish.

CHOICES

As you respond to the Choices, use these **Academic Vocabulary** words as appropriate: approach, convince, dominate, enhance, participate.

REVIEW

Create a Visual

Today, social activists participate in protests to convince others of their views. Many carry signs and pictures to communicate their messages to passersby. Review the works by Wollstonecraft, Defoe, and Chudleigh, and create a sign that communicates the message of one of the authors. Present your work to the class, explaining the imagery in your visual and how it relates to the selection you chose.

CONNECT

Evaluate for Relevance

Timed Writing In an expository essay, analyze the relevance of Wollstonecraft's essay for our time. Do her observations about the role of women hold true today, or are her arguments limited to the social realities of the eighteenth century? Which, if any, of her observations about men and women remain valid in the twenty-first century? Use textual details and real-life examples to support your response.

EXTEND

Research the Women's Movement

Group Activity Form a group and have each member research different aspects of the fight for women's rights in the twentieth century. Search reference sources, view documentaries, or conduct interviews with women who lived through eras important to the women's movement, such as the 1960s, 1970s, and 1980s. Who are leaders in the movement for women's rights? What does the women's movement have in common with the civil rights movement? Assemble a multimedia presentation to share your findings with the class.

SKILLS FOCUS **Literary Skills** Compare works from different cultures and literary periods.; analyze and compare points of view on a topic. **Writing Skills** Use appropriate organization; support ideas/theses with relevant evidence and details; compare literary works; compare characters or historical figures; compare literary elements.

Views on Women's Rights

Writing Focus

Writing a Comparison-Contrast Essay

Establish Similarities The selections "A Vindication of the Rights of Woman," "The Education of Women," and "To the Ladies" have many similarities, and yet each is unique. Where do the authors' viewpoints on women's rights intersect? Do they use similar techniques?

Identify Differences Think about these questions and the suggestions below as you choose an approach to comparing and contrasting these selections.

Here are some specific topic ideas for your comparison-and-contrast essay:

- How is Chudleigh's poem different from the two essays, in content as well as in structure? What do the essays express that the poem does not?
- Compare and contrast the overall effectiveness of the selections. Which of the three selections is the most successful in making its point? Why?
- Compare and contrast the enduring relevance of the selections. Which of the three selections is most relevant for today's audiences? Why?

Create a Trifold Chart Create a chart to organize your thoughts. Write the title of one selection at the top of each column. As you analyze the theme, context, historical and modern relevance, and language use of each selection, record your notes in the appropriate column. Then, review your notes, looking for at least one major similarity. Begin your comparison-contrast essay with a basis of similarity beyond the obvious fact that all three address women's issues. Look closely for more insight. Use examples from the selections to support your arguments.

Create a Thesis Statement Using your notes, develop a thesis statement for your essay that makes an assertion about the similarities and differences in the three selections.

Organize your Essay The most important element of organization in a comparison-contrast essay is to begin with your basis of similarity, and then move to differences. Conclude with differences to stress that each selection is unique. Use a point-by-point organizational method by discussing each selection in each body paragraph.

Provide Text Evidence The body paragraphs focus on an element of similarity or difference and use sample quotations from each selection to prove the idea asserted in the paragraph. Be sure to follow each quotation with elaboration and explanation, linking the quotation to the main point of the essay.

Think About Today Since the topic of women's rights is still discussed today, one way to conclude is by relating the selections to current issues. If you choose that approach, think about the What Do You Think Now question that follows the chart below.

An effective comparison-contrast essay
• clearly states what is being compared and contrasted
• conveys a main idea through a thesis statement
• is organized logically and effectively
• cites text passages to support ideas
• contains few or no errors in spelling, punctuation, and grammar

What Do **You** **Think** **Now** Do you think it would be worth the risk of ridicule, punishment, or even imprisonment to speak out against an inequality today? Explain.

Writing Workshop

Persuasive Essay

Write with a Purpose

Write a persuasive essay supporting your position on an issue that is important to you. Your **purpose** for writing is to persuade your **audience**—your teacher and classmates or others who are affected by this issue.

A Good Persuasive Essay

- addresses an issue important to you and others
- demonstrates evidence and reasoning to support your position
- addresses counterarguments opposing your position
- convinces readers to agree with your opinion, take a stand, or take action

See page 690 for a complete rubric.

Reader/Writer Notebook

Use your **RWN** to complete the activities for this workshop.

Think as a Reader/Writer

In this unit, you have read many works with persuasive elements. Before you write your own **persuasive essay,** take a few minutes to read this excerpt from Desmond Tutu's "Easy Praise, Empty Words." Tutu addresses human rights violations by the military government of the Southeast Asian country of Burma, also known as Myanmar. Among these violations is the house arrest of 1991 Nobel Peace Prize winner Aung San Suu Kyi.

I make a direct call here to our friends on the UNSC [United Nations Security Council], many of whom fought hard against apartheid in South Africa, to help us now to support the people of Burma. As happened with the apartheid regime in South Africa, the people of Burma have unequivocally rejected their illegitimate rulers; and the legitimate representatives of Burma's people have urged the world to support them. I call upon my brothers and sisters on the UNSC to pass a resolution that binds Burma's regime into an irreversible contract— one that commits it to a transition to democratic government and ensures the release, not only of Aung San Suu Kyi, but of all those who have endured the darkness of a Burmese prison for the sake of freedom.

> ← Tutu urges action to help Burma.

If we commit ourselves wholeheartedly to this end, Burma will one day have a leader whose commitment to her people is unwavering, and whose integrity and vision have already been proven by her courage, sacrifice and vision. Just as Nelson Mandela no longer belongs only to South Africans, I believe that in the future Aung San Suu Kyi will be a shining light for Asia and the world.

> ← He compares Aung San Suu Kyi to another great leader, Nelson Mandela.

History has shown us that neither systems, nor governments, nor dictators are eternal, but the spirit of freedom is. Freedom then is our dangerous message, our potent weapon. We must ensure that it rings loud in the dark hallways of the dictators in Rangoon. Easy praise, empty words.

> ← Tutu restates his call to action and echoes the title.

Think About the Professional Model

With a partner, discuss the following questions about the model.

1. What effect does the comparison of the situation in Burma with that in South Africa have on Tutu's argument?
2. What language appeals to your emotions most powerfully?

Prewriting

Choose an Issue

In your essay, you will discuss an **issue,** a topic about which reasonable people can disagree. Is there an **occasion,** or real life reason, that gives you a reason to write? Look around you at the places you go regularly. Is there something in your school or community that you would like to see accomplished or changed? List several potential issues, and then evaluate each one. Your final choice should be an issue that

- you really feel strongly about, though not so strongly that your feelings interfere with your ability to argue reasonably
- has both positive and negative aspects, enabling you not only to argue your own opinion, but effectively respond to **opposing arguments**
- you can discuss using convincing evidence to support your opinion

Identify Your Thesis

Once you have an issue, write a sentence that defines your **perspective,** or **position,** on that issue. This will be your **thesis statement,** sometimes called a **position statement** or **opinion statement.** In persuasive writing, your thesis will include what you believe about the issue and how you propose to address it. Here's how the writer of the student model that begins on page 687 created his thesis statement, which identifies his opinion.

> Topic: drug and alcohol abuse
> Perspective: mentoring of various kinds can help
> Thesis statement: We can combat the United States's addiction problem by building relationships that teach kids the negative effects of drugs and alcohol.

Think About Purpose and Audience

Since your **purpose** for writing is to convince others that your perspective has merit, you will need to consider the knowledge and beliefs of your audience. In order to succeed in persuading your **audience,** you'll need to tailor your argument to their needs. Use these questions to analyze your audience members:

1. **What are their ages, interests, education levels, and values?** Use this information to determine what reasons, evidence, and language your readers will find most persuasive.

2. **What do they already know about the issue?** If your readers are not familiar with your issue, you'll need to add background information to your essay.

3. **Where do they stand on the issue?** Readers who strongly disagree with your position will require much more convincing than those who share your views or who are undecided. Be prepared to address any objections they have to your ideas.

Idea Starters

- Talk to friends and classmates about issues that concern them.
- Talk to your family about issues in your community.
- Read local and national newspapers for current issues.
- Watch local and national news programs.
- Attend meetings of your school's student council, your school district's board of education, or your local city council.

Your Turn

Get Started Making notes in your **RWN,** choose an **issue.** Then draft a **thesis statement** that shows your position. Finally make notes about your **audience** and their needs.

Learn It Online

To see how one writer completed this assignment, see the model persuasive essay at:

go.hrw.com   L12-683   Go

● Writing Tip

If the connection between a reason and its supporting evidence is not self-evident, **elaborate** upon the evidence, showing how it connects to the reason.

Support Your Position

A tightly-built argument depends on effective **support.** In your essay, include solid **reasons** why your readers should believe or act as you suggest in your thesis statement. Reasons may include appeals to logic, emotion, or ethics.

- **Logical appeals** engage your readers' ability to think clearly. Logical appeals should be the foundation of your essay.
- **Emotional appeals** stir readers' feelings and personalize the issue for your audience.
- **Ethical appeals** establish you as a fair and knowledgeable speaker and call upon your readers' sense of right and wrong.

Gather Solid Evidence

In order to persuade your audience, you must prove to them that your reasons are valid. You can do this by using relevant **evidence**—precise and pertinent facts, examples, expert opinions, analogies, case studies, and anecdotes.

Types of Evidence	
Facts	**information** that can be proven true
Examples	**specific** instances of an idea or situation
Expert opinions	**quotations** or paraphrases by respected and knowledgeable individuals or institutions
Analogies	**comparisons** showing the similarities between two otherwise unrelated concepts
Case studies	**examples** from scientific studies
Anecdotes	**brief,** personal stories that illustrate a point

Use a graphic organizer like the one below to plan each supporting paragraph in your essay.

Your Turn

Organize Your Support Making notes in your **RWN,** use the **evidence chart** and the **graphic organizer** on this page to gather and organize **support** for your thesis. Share your organizer with a peer. Think about the feedback he or she provides, and consider adding, deleting, or reorganizing evidence. Remember to keep your **purpose** and **audience** in mind.

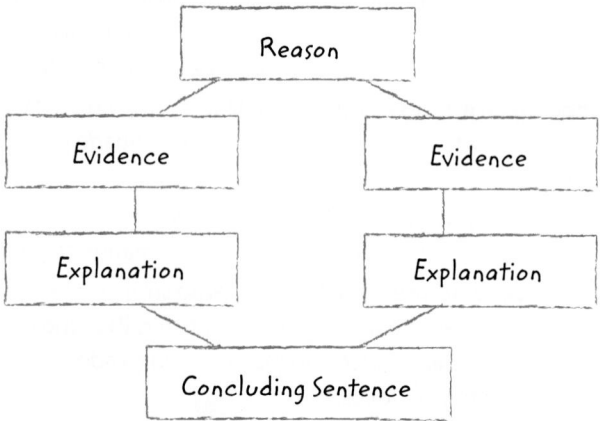

Reason

Evidence   Evidence

Explanation   Explanation

Concluding Sentence

Drafting

Follow the Writer's Framework

Use your **graphic organizer** and the **Writer's Framework** on the right to help you write the first draft of your essay.

Add Rhetorical Devices

Rhetorical devices can make your writing more colorful and convincing.

- A **rhetorical question** is a question that gets readers to think about the issue—it's not meant to be answered, because the answer is obvious. For example, "Do you care about America's future?"

- **Argument by analogy** compares two situations in order to make a point. For example, Desmond Tutu compares Aung San Suu Kyi to Nelson Mandela and the situation in Burma to apartheid in South Africa.

- **Parallelism** supports important ideas by repeating words, phrases, or sentences that have the same grammatical structure or that restate a similar idea. Parallel words or word groups are often joined by **correlative conjunctions** (both . . . and; either . . . or; neither . . . nor; not only . . . but also; whether . . . or).

Framework for a Persuasive Essay

Introduction

- Tell how the issue affects readers.
- Give background information.
- Include a clear thesis statement.

Body

- Support your position with reasons and evidence.
- Use rhetorical devices.
- Organize evidence by strength.

Conclusion

- Restate your opinion and summarize your reasons.
- Call readers to action.

Grammar Link Using Correlative Conjunctions

One rhetorical strategy employed by Desmond Tutu in his speech is **parallelism,** including the use of the **correlative conjunctions** *neither . . . nor:*

> History has shown us that **neither** systems, **nor** governments, **nor** dictators are eternal, but the spirit of freedom is.

Two other pairs of correlative conjunctions help writers show relationships between ideas: *either . . . or* and *both . . . and.* The relationship of the ideas determines which word pair works best.

In the example above, the correlative conjunctions appear in a series and are separated by commas. When using correlative conjunctions, remember that the subject closest to the verb determines if the verb is singular or plural. A plural subject requires a plural verb.

Reference Note For more on **correlative conjunctions,** see the Language Handbook.

Writing Tip

Most persuasive essays are arranged by **order of importance.** To capture your audience's attention immediately, begin your essay with your strongest reason; or, to make a strong final impression, end with your strongest reason.

Your Turn

Write Your Draft Use your **graphic organizer** and the **Writer's Framework** to write a **draft** of your persuasive essay. As you write, think about:

- Which is your strongest piece of evidence?
- Would it be more effective to begin or end with your strongest piece of evidence?
- What rhetorical devices can you employ?
- Where can you use correlative conjunctions as a rhetorical strategy?

Peer Review

Working with a peer, review your draft. Answer each question in the chart at the right to evaluate how your drafts can be improved. Then use the tips and revision techniques to revise your draft.

Evaluating and Revising

Now that you have written a draft of your persuasive essay, it is time to polish it by reading and evaluating. Check your use of rhetorical devices and evidence to make your essay as convincing as possible. The chart below will help you evaluate your draft and think of ways to revise it.

Persuasive Essay: Guidelines for Content and Organization

Evaluation Question	Tip	Revision Technique
1. Does the introduction grab readers' attention? Does it include necessary background information?	**Put brackets** around any sentence or sentences that are intended to draw reader interest. **Put a check mark** by any background information.	**Add** a question, anecdote, quotation, or provocative statement that will capture readers' interest. **Add** background facts the reader would need to understand the issue. **Elaborate** on background.
2. Does the introduction contain a clear thesis statement, or opinion statement?	**Circle** the thesis statement, or opinion statement.	**Add** a statement that expresses a clear position on the issue.
3. Does the essay include reasons and evidence to support the opinion?	**Underline** the reasons in the essay. **Double underline** sentences used as evidence for each reason.	**Add** reasons or **elaborate** on reasons already given. **Add** evidence (facts and statistics, examples, expert opinions, analogies, case studies, or anecdotes) that supports them.
4. Is there a mixture of logical, emotional, and ethical appeals?	**Put the letters _L_** by logical appeals, **_EM_** by emotional appeals, and **_ETH_** by ethical appeals. If your support uses only one kind of appeal, revise.	**Add** words and examples that engage your readers' minds, hearts, or sense of right and wrong.
5. Do rhetorical devices help shape the support for the opinion?	**Put a star** by any rhetorical questions, arguments by analogy, or use of parallelism.	**Add** rhetorical devices, such as rhetorical questions, argument by analogy, or parallelism.
6. Does the conclusion restate the writer's opinion? If appropriate, does the conclusion include a call to action?	**Circle** the restatement of the position. **Highlight** the call to action.	**Add** a statement that restates your opinion. **Add** a call to action.

Read this student's draft with comments on its structure and suggestions for how it could be made even stronger.

The Plague Upon the Land
by Stephen Lain, McCallum High School

According to Nora D. Volkow, the director of the National Institute on Drug Abuse, addiction affects nine percent of the United States population. This epidemic must be addressed where it begins—with our young people. The effects are too widespread and too many people are susceptible to the black hole of drug and alcohol addiction for us to ignore the problem. We can combat America's addiction problem by building relationships that teach kids the negative effects of drugs and alcohol.

← Stephen introduces his **issue** with a **statistic** and then states his **position.**

One way to create and nurture these relationships is through a mentoring program. Children who lack relationships with positive adult role models are more at risk to become drug and alcohol users. When kids connect with a responsible, caring mentor who engages them in productive and fun activities, they experience an alternative to drug use. A mentor can warn them about the power of peer pressure. Many kids who have avoided drinking and drugs will eventually try it. "It's just one sip; it can't hurt." But many times, that one sip will lead to one more, and then one more. A mentor can steer kids away from drugs, alcohol and peer pressure in the drug culture.

← He offers one way to approach and solve this problem.

MINI-LESSON ▸ How to Grab Your Reader's Attention

You won't interest your audience in your issue if your introduction lacks appeal. To grab your reader's attention, add an interesting or startling fact, statistic, quotation, or anecdote, or ask a rhetorical question. Stephen found additional statistics that he wanted to use to emphasize the problem and draw readers into his essay.

Stephen's Draft of Paragraph 1

...This epidemic must be addressed where it begins—with our young people. The effects are too widespread and too many people are susceptible to the black ole of drug and alcohol addiction for us to ignore the problem.

Stephen's Revision of Paragraph 1

...This epidemic must be addressed where it begins—with our young people. The effects are too widespread and too many people are susceptible to the black hole of drug and alcohol addiction for us to ignore the problem. *According to the national PTA, every day approximately 4,700 American youth under the age of eighteen try marijuana for the first time. This equals the enrollment in six average-sized high schools.*

Your Turn

Grab Your Reader's Attention Re-read the introduction of your draft to see if it is attention-grabbing. Ask yourself the following questions:

- Do I give a clear idea of the extent of the problem?
- Could I be more specific?
- What strategy did I use to get the reader's attention?

Student Draft *continues*

Stephen **develops** the role of parents and guardians in the fight against drug abuse and **cites an authoritative source.**

→ Another way to combat drug use is to make a concerted effort in each household to teach kids that drugs and alcohol can ruin your life. The American Academy of Pediatrics states that parents or guardians are the most important influence in a teen's decisions about drug use. Children can be taught at an early age that drug use will lead to a life of destruction. Caring adults can teach children the facts: alcohol abuse will lead to liver failure and ultimately death, and drugs such as crack cocaine can decimate your body and mind. The government can create standardized teaching tools to address the dangers of addiction, but the most important tool is the parents' or guardians' interest, communication, and role as a model for their children. Communication in homes may be the best weapon we have to fight drug abuse in kids.

He uses **parallel structure** at the end to emphasize his points. However, his **call to action** is vague, giving no specific actions readers can take on the issue.

→ We can take action against this epidemic of drug abuse and addiction. We can urge the community to teach schools, churches, clubs, and families how to approach the subject of drug and alcohol abuse. We can create meaningful relationships with children through effective mentoring programs.

MINI-LESSON ▸ How to Add Emotional Appeal to a Conclusion

A good conclusion to a persuasive essay should stir the readers' emotions and prompt them to act on the issue. Stephen's conclusion lacks a strong emotional appeal, which he could make by adding a stirring, specific call to action and effective, moving language.

Stephen's Draft of the Conclusion

We can take action against this epidemic of drug abuse and addiction. We can urge the community to teach schools, churches, clubs, and families how to approach the subject of drugs and alcohol abuse. We can create meaningful relationships with children though effective mentoring programs.

Stephen's Revision of Conclusion

We can take action against this epidemic of drug abuse and addiction. We can urge the community to teach schools, churches, clubs, and families how to approach the subject of drugs and alcohol abuse. We can create meaningful relationships with children though effective mentoring programs. ∧*As a society, we can attack this invader in our land if we work together to educate and mentor our young people. If you are a student, mentor younger children. If you are a teacher, ask about the opportunities in your school or community. If you are a parent or guardian, take action now. Our country's children are suffering from this plague upon our land.*

Your Turn _____

Add Emotional Appeal to Your Conclusion Re-read your draft's conclusion to assess whether it has maximum impact. Ask yourself these questions:

- Does my conclusion stir emotions in the reader?
- Is my call to action clear, inspiring readers to take specific action?

Proofreading and Publishing

Proofread

Do not undermine your authority with mistakes in grammar, usage, or mechanics. Follow these tips to **proofread,** or **edit,** your essay. Read it aloud to catch missing words or awkward constructions. Refer to a grammar, usage, and mechanics handbook to ensure you have avoided common errors, such as forgetting to include a comma after an **introductory phrase** or **clause.**

> ### Grammar Link Using Commas After Introductory Elements
>
> **Introductory phrases and clauses** create transitions that help writers lead their readers through their arguments and supporting ideas. They also enliven writing by adding variety to sentence beginnings. When you use introductory phrases and clauses, be sure to separate them from the main clause of the sentence with a comma. Stephen correctly uses commas after introductory elements in these examples from the student model.
>
> > **When kids connect with a responsible, caring mentor who engages them in productive and fun activities,** they experience an alternative to drug use. [introductory clause]
> >
> > **But many times,** that one sip will lead to one more, and then one more. [introductory phrase]
>
> **Reference Note** For more on **phrases** and **clauses,** see the Language Handbook.

Publishing

To persuade readers, you first have to reach them. Here are some ways you can share your essay with a wider audience.

- Submit your essay to the school or local newspaper.
- Submit your essay to a Web site that focuses on your issue.
- Present your essay in a meeting of your school's student council, your school district's board of education, or your local city council.
- Conduct a panel discussion about this issue.
- Submit your essay to specialized periodicals, including newsletters and online magazines.

Reflect on the Process Thinking about how you researched and wrote your persuasive essay will help you with your future writing. In your **RWN,** write short response to the following questions:

1. What sources were most helpful in learning about your issue?
2. What evidence or rhetorical device do you feel contributed most to your essay's persuasive power, and why?

● Proofreading Tip

If you write your essay on a computer, use all the tools available to you, such as grammar and spell-checkers. However, do not expect these tools to take the place of close, personal proofreading and peer review. You will often catch mistakes that your computer does not; for example, incorrect usage of *there, their,* and *they're* or *its* and *it's.*

● Writing Tip

Ask yourself the following questions to identify introductory phrases and clauses.

- Does the phrase or clause come before the sentence's subject?
- Do the words in the phrase or clause work together as an adverb to tell when, where, or how often?

Your Turn

Proofread and Publish As you proofread your draft, circle any introductory phrases and clauses you have used. Check to make sure each one is followed by a comma. Read your paper one more time to make finishing touches, and then publish it.

Scoring Rubric

Use one of the rubrics below to evaluate your persuasive essay from the Writing Workshop or your response to the on-demand prompt on the next page. Your teacher will tell you to use either the six- or the four-point rubric.

6-Point Scale

Score 6 *Demonstrates advanced success.*
- focuses consistently on a clear and reasonable position
- shows effective organization throughout, with smooth transitions
- offers thoughtful, creative ideas and reasons
- supports a position thoroughly, using convincing, fully elaborated reasons and evidence
- exhibits mature control of written language

Score 5 *Demonstrates proficient success.*
- focuses on a clear and reasonable position
- shows effective organization, with transitions
- offers thoughtful ideas and reasons
- supports a position competently, using convincing, well-elaborated reasons and evidence
- exhibits sufficient control of written language

Score 4 *Demonstrates competent success.*
- focuses on a reasonable position, with minor distractions
- shows effective organization, with minor lapses
- offers mostly thoughtful ideas and reasons
- elaborates reasons and evidence with a mixture of the general and the specific
- exhibits general control of written language

Score 3 *Demonstrates limited success.*
- includes some loosely related ideas that distract from the writer's position
- shows some organization, with noticeable gaps in the logical flow of ideas
- offers routine, predictable ideas and reasons
- supports ideas with uneven reasoning and elaboration
- exhibits limited control of written language

Score 2 *Demonstrates basic success.*
- includes loosely related ideas that seriously distract from the writer's persuasive purpose
- shows minimal organization, with major gaps in the logical flow of ideas
- offers ideas and reasons that merely skim the surface
- supports ideas with inadequate reasoning and elaboration
- exhibits significant problems with control of written language

Score 1 *Demonstrates emerging effort.*
- shows little awareness of the topic and purpose for writing
- lacks organization
- offers unclear and confusing ideas
- demonstrates minimal persuasive reasoning or elaboration
- exhibits major problems with control of written language

4-Point Scale

Score 4 *Demonstrates advanced success.*
- focuses consistently on a clear and reasonable position
- shows effective organization throughout, with smooth transitions
- offers thoughtful, creative ideas and reasons
- supports a position thoroughly, using convincing, fully elaborated reasons and evidence
- exhibits mature control of written language

Score 3 *Demonstrates competent success.*
- focuses on a reasonable position, with minor distractions
- shows effective organization, with minor lapses
- offers mostly thoughtful ideas and reasons
- elaborates reasons and evidence with a mixture of the general and the specific
- exhibits general control of written language

Score 2 *Demonstrates limited success.*
- includes some loosely related ideas that distract from the writer's position
- shows some organization, with noticeable gaps in the logical flow of ideas
- offers routine, predictable ideas and reasons
- supports ideas with uneven reasoning and elaboration
- exhibits limited control of written language

Score 1 *Demonstrates emerging effort.*
- shows little awareness of the topic and purpose for writing
- lacks organization
- offers unclear and confusing ideas
- demonstrates minimal persuasive reasoning or elaboration
- exhibits major problems with control of written language

Preparing for Timed Writing

Persuasive Essay

When responding to a prompt, use what you have learned from reading, writing your persuasive essay, and studying the rubric on page 690. Use the steps below to develop a response to the following prompt.

Writing Prompt
Imagine that your school board is thinking of implementing a graduation requirement mandating that students do part-time volunteer work. Write a persuasive essay convincing readers to support or oppose the requirement.

Study the Prompt
Read the prompt carefully. Then read it again, underlining the words that tell the type of writing, the topic, and the purpose.
Type of writing: *persuasive essay*
Topic: *a graduation requirement mandating that students do part-time volunteer work*
Purpose: *convincing readers to support or oppose the requirement*
Tip: Spend about five minutes studying the prompt.

Plan Your Response
Think about the **reasons** for each side of the **argument.** Make a list of pros and cons for the volunteering requirement. Then decide which side of the debate to **support.** Narrow your reasons down to your top three, and use the organizer below to help you gather support. List your reasons in the first column. In the second column, list at least two pieces of **evidence** (facts, statistics, anecdotes, examples) for each reason.

Reasons	Evidence

Now draft a one-sentence **thesis statement** that states your position on the topic and lists your three main reasons. **Tip:** Spend about ten minutes planning your response.

Respond to the Prompt
Begin drafting your essay. You may want to start by simply stating your **thesis,** your opinion on the issue. As you write, keep the following points in mind:

- In the introduction, grab your readers' attention and state your position, including a preview of the reasons that support your opinion.
- In each body paragraph, give one reason for your position, with valid and specific evidence to support that reason. You can use examples from your experience or someone else's experience. Specific names, dates, and places add convincing detail to your argument.
- Conclude your essay with a statement of strong conviction and a call to action.

Tip: Spend about twenty minutes writing your persuasive essay.

Improve Your Response
Revising Review your response to compare it to the prompt. Does your response state your position on the graduation requirement? Does it give evidence to back up your position? Do you conclude with a call to action? Is anything you can add to your paper to make your argument more convincing?

Proofreading Now spend a few minutes finding and correcting any errors in grammar, usage, and mechanics. Pay careful attention to the words on the page to make sure they are grammatically correct and accurately convey your meaning. Make sure that your paper and any edits are neatly written and legible.

Checking Your Final Copy Before you turn in your paper, examine it once more to make sure that you have done your best work. **Tip:** Save five or ten minutes to improve your paper.

Presenting and Analyzing Speeches

Speak with a Purpose

Adapt your persuasive essay for a persuasive speech. Then, present it to an audience.

Think as a Reader/Writer Effective persuasive speeches incorporate the same techniques that are used to write persuasive essays. Presenting your position for listeners, rather than readers, however, can offer you another advantage—you can use your voice as well as your body language to make your point. In this workshop you will learn how to use the techniques of persuasion in a speech.

Adapt Your Essay

A persuasive speech consists of the same introduction, body, and conclusion as your written essay. However, you might need to make alterations to each of these parts of your essay so they will be better suited for a speech.

- The **introduction** to an effective persuasive speech is dramatic. Consider using a thought-provoking literary quotation, a touching anecdote that illustrates an aspect of the issue you're dealing with, or a reference to an authority on the subject of your speech. Then, state your distinct perspective on the issue in a strong but simple opinion statement.

- The **body** of a persuasive speech supports the opinion statement and must consist of solid reasoning. To fit within your time limits, choose only the most effective reasons from your written essay, based on your audience. For example, an audience of classmates might respond favorably to reasons that appeal to their emotions. An audience of city council members might best respond to reasons that appeal to logic or ethics.

- The **conclusion** to an effective speech should be memorable. First, summarize the main points and restate your opinion. Finally, call the audience to action, using specific language.

As you adapt your essay, decide which of the following four basic types of persuasive speech you want to present. This will drive the wording of your opinion statement, which presents your distinct perspective.

1. A **proposition of fact** speech argues that a thesis can be seen as true or false.
2. A **proposition of policy** speech attempts to get the audience to support a particular plan of action, by offering a series of steps to follow.
3. A **proposition of problem** speech tries to persuade an audience that a specific problem exists and is serious enough to act on.
4. A **proposition of value** speech argues the relative merit of a person, place, or thing. You can't prove a proposition of value, but you can provide evidence to support your belief.

Reader/Writer Notebook

Use your **RWN** to complete the activities in this workshop.

SKILLS FOCUS Listening and
Speaking Skills Deliver a persuasive speech.

Present Your Speech

Because your persuasive speech is on an issue about which you care deeply, consider delivering it as a formal speech. Write your speech out completely, and practice it until you have it memorized. On your written speech, note the pitch and volume that you intend to use at various points in the speech. Do the same thing for gestures, pauses, and eye contact. Also, don't forget to adopt a serious tone while presenting your appeals by avoiding slang, colloquialisms, and contractions.

Notes for Good Sense

If your speech includes facts, expert opinions, or statistics, it's important that you convey them accurately. It's helpful to have these items in writing in case you forget them while giving your speech. Write all facts, quotations, and statistics carefully on note cards, and number your cards in the order that they arise in your speech. Move each card to the back of the pile as you cover it, so the next card is ready for you exactly when you might need it. You don't want to lose time or face fumbling in your pile for the right quotation.

Practice Makes Perfect

Practice your speech for family or friends or in front of a mirror. You can also get a good idea of what is working and what needs work in your presentation if you record yourself practicing on camera. Pay special attention to the sound of your voice and the movements of your body. Are all of your words audible? Are you speaking at a normal rate? When you deliver your speech, stand in a natural, relaxed position, and use subtle but appropriate hand gestures to highlight points and ideas. Remember to look around the room at your audience and use your voice to emphasize specific points in the speech. As you practice, use the checklists below to evaluate your verbal and nonverbal techniques.

Voice

Audible volume	
Normal rate	
Varied pitch emphasizes important points	

Body

Natural, relaxed standing position	
Subtle and appropriate hand gestures	
Varied eye contact	

A Good Oral Presentation

- opens with a strong, powerful introduction that gets your audience's attention
- includes specific, valid reasons and evidence
- moves at a reasonable pace—not so slow as to bore the audience or so fast as to lose listeners
- relates well to the audience
- shows the time and care that went into planning and rehearsing the speech

Speaking Tip

If you falter while speaking, don't draw attention to it in a distracting way, which can cause your audience to forget your last point. If you suddenly forget what you wanted to say, pause and take a deep breath. Look at the written copy of your speech for guidance. It's okay to backtrack a little or even to skip ahead to keep yourself from rambling. When you look back up at your audience, smile confidently and resume speaking.

 Learn It Online

Pictures, music, and animation can make your argument more compelling. See how on MediaScope, on

go.hrw.com   L12-693   **Go**

Literary Skills Review

Comparing Literature **Directions:** Read the following poems. Then, read each multiple-choice question that follows, and write the letter of the best response.

The following poems provide two accounts of unrequited love—a topic chosen by poets throughout the centuries. Aphra Behn's (1640–1689) "Love Arm'd" offers a rare glimpse into the experiences of a female speaker. Charles Baudelaire's (1821–1867) "'I love you as I love . . .'" shows how even suffering can be pleasurable if one is truly in love.

Love Arm'd

by **Aphra Behn**

Love in Fantastique Triumph satt,
Whilst Bleeding Hearts a round him flow'd,
For whom Fresh paines he did Create,
And strange Tyranick power he show'd
5   From thy Bright Eyes he took his fire,
Which round about, in sport he hurl'd;
But 'twas from mine, he took desire,
Enough to undo the Amorous World.

From me he took his sighs and tears,
10   From thee his Pride and Crueltie;
From me his Languishments and Feares,
And every Killing Dart from thee;
Thus thou and I, the God have arm'd,
And sett him up a Deity;
But my poor Heart alone is harm'd,
Whilst thine the Victor is, and free.

"I love you as I love . . ."

by **Charles Baudelaire**
translated by **James McGowan**

I love you as I love the night's high vault
O silent one, o sorrow's lachrymal,°
And love you more because you flee from me,
And temptress of my nights, ironically
5   You seem to hoard the space, to take to you
What separates my arms from heaven's blue.

I climb to the assault, attack the source,
A choir of wormlets pressing towards a
    corpse,
And cherish your unbending cruelty,
10   This iciness so beautiful to me.

---

2. lachrymal: a type of vase common to ancient Roman
   tombs, once thought to be meant for the tears of
   mourners.

1. In "Love Arm'd" what literary device does Aphra Behn use to illustrate love's power over humans?

   A onomatopoeia

   B simile

   C synecdoche

   D personification

2. In "Love Arm'd" which phrase illustrates that love has won and the speaker has lost?

   A "And sett him up a Deity"

   B "For whom Fresh paines he did Create"

   C "Love in Fantastique Triumph satt"

   D "From me he took his sighs and tears"

3. In the first stanza in "'I love you as I love…'" what does the speaker mean by the phrase "And love you more because you flee from me"?

   A He both loves and hates his beloved.

   B He is attracted by his beloved's coldness.

   C His beloved loves heaven just as he does.

   D His beloved is silent.

4. In "'I love you as I love…'" which of the following illustrates that the speaker's love does not return his affections?

   A "You seem to hoard the space"

   B "night's high vault"

   C "temptress of my nights"

   D "O silent one"

5. Which poem illustrates the disappointment and failure of love?

   A "I love you as I love…"

   B "Love Arm'd"

   C both poems

   D neither poem

6. In which poem is the speaker mourning a lost love?

   A "'I love you as I love…'"

   B "Love Arm'd"

   C both poems

   D neither poem

7. What words best describe the tone of both poems?

   A romantic and amorous

   B sorrowful and lamenting

   C peaceful and calm

   D warm-hearted and sentimental

Constructed Response

8. These poems both concern the experience of unrequited love—a love that is not returned. Write a brief essay comparing and contrasting the emotional effect of unrequited love on the speaker of each poem. Do the speakers feel the same way about their situations? How can you tell? Cite examples from the poems to support your answer.

Vocabulary Skills Review

Analogies   Directions: For each item, choose the lettered pair of words that expresses a relationship that is most similar to the relationship between the pair of capitalized words.

1. FLACCID : FLABBY ::
   A timid : outspoken
   B restful : restless
   C tardy : punctual
   D empty : vacant

2. SPECIOUS : GENUINE ::
   A interested : bored
   B limber : flexible
   C aggressive : hostile
   D flavorful : tasty

3. FASTIDIOUS : PICKY ::
   A eager : indifferent
   B freed : liberated
   C calm : distressed
   D thankful : ungrateful

4. TRIBUTE : INSULT ::
   A mansion : castle
   B liability : debt
   C conflict : accord
   D validation : support

5. IMPERTINENCE : RESPECT ::
   A suppression : release
   B slander : slur
   C infection : illness
   D mercy : compassion

6. VIE : STRUGGLE ::
   A congratulate : commiserate
   B release : snare
   C avoid : pursue
   D modify : alter

7. SEQUESTERED : HIDDEN ::
   A scrupulous : careful
   B miserly : generous
   C serious : funny
   D hopeless : optimistic

8. DISCOURSE : SILENCE ::
   A fidelity : loyalty
   B solicitude : negligence
   C crimes : misdeeds
   D truth : certainty

9. EMINENCE : DISTINCTION ::
   A anticipation : despair
   B sentiment : logic
   C hatred : scorn
   D neutrality : bias

Academic Vocabulary

10. DOMINATE : PREVAIL ::
    A repel : attract
    B hinder : facilitate
    C provoke : annoy
    D loathe : tolerate

11. ENHANCE : IMPROVE ::
    A console : comfort
    B recede :   advance
    C ignite : extinguish
    D separate : combine

PREPARING FOR STANDARDIZED TESTS

Writing Skills Review

Persuasive Essay **Directions:** Read the following paragraph from a draft of a student's persuasive essay. Then, answer the questions below it.

(1) Jonathan Swift's "A Modest Proposal" employs many persuasive techniques to offer various solutions to the poverty problem in Ireland. (2) Although Swift uses logical and ethical persuasion to influence his audience, his most effective persuasive technique is his appeal to emotion. (3) He offers evidence to show how many poor people live in Ireland, plucking the heart-strings of his readers by describing how desperately the poor mothers have to live. (4) Swift then gains readers' trust by seeming to be open to others' opinions: "I am not so violently bent upon my own opinion, as to reject any offer, proposed by wise men, which shall be found equally innocent, cheap, easy, and effectual." (5) This seems like an ethical appeal, but his words—*innocent,* *cheap, easy,* and *effectual*—when referring to the wholesale slaughter of helpless babies, stir a powerful emotional response. (6) They are repulsive. (7) Swift also evokes an emotional reaction when he says that "A young healthy child well nursed is at a year old a most delicious, nourishing, and wholesome food, whether stewed, roasted, baked, or boiled." (8) The graphic image of a roasted infant helps the reader to conclude that Swift cannot seriously mean for the English to eat Irish babies. (9) His verbal irony makes the reader recoil in horror—quite an emotional reaction! (10) Everyone should be required to read "A Modest Proposal" before graduating.

1. The writer's main purpose in writing this essay is to convince readers
   A that reading Swift's essay should be a graduation requirement
   B that Swift's essay would not be effective without its emotional appeals
   C that Swift was a genius at using verbal irony
   D that Swift's most effective persuasive technique is his appeal to emotion

2. To adapt this passage for an oral speech, the speaker might
   A copy all direct quotes from Swift onto note cards in order to recite them correctly
   B cut out the first two sentences to keep within the time limits of the presentation
   C eliminate reasons that address listeners' concerns
   D explain why Swift uses statistics

3. What evidence could the writer add to support the idea in sentence 3?
   A a lengthy description of how the poor live
   B an example of a reader who was emotionally moved by Swift's essay
   C a quote of the evidence that Swift provides
   D a specific number of people living in Ireland

4. Which persuasive technique does the writer of the essay use most in the passage?
   A logical persuasion
   B emotional persuasion
   C ethical persuasion
   D none of the above

5. Which sentence should be deleted because it does not support the essay's main idea?
   A sentence 2
   B sentence 6
   C sentence 9
   D sentence 10

DRAMA

The Misanthrope *and* Tartuffe

The French playwright Moliere had a remarkable genius for exposing and satirizing the ills of society. In Richard Wilbur's translation of *Tartuffe* and *The Misanthrope,* you'll meet two men whom Moliere considered representative of his age: one a roguish hypocrite who charms everyone he meets and the other an eccentric recluse who shuns hypocrisy at a great cost to himself. Moliere's comedies of manners, so relevant when they were written, have not lost their potency and humor today.

FICTION

Pamela

Samuel Richardson's early modern novel gives voice to a young servant who resists the improper advances of her employer. Among eighteenth century Londoners, the book became a controversial best-seller both praised for its morality and vilified for its scandalous subject matter. Richardson intended fo it to instruct and entertain. Through its examination of virtue and impropriety among the social classes, it remains a study in the abuse of power and an amusing artifact of eighteenth century life.

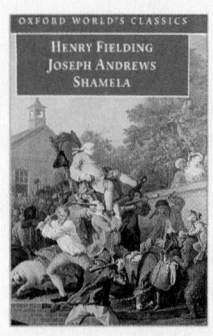

FICTION

Shamela *and* Joseph Andrews

Henry Fielding wrote his short epistolary novel, *Shamela,* as a hilarious parody and satire of Samuel Richardson's famous novel *Pamela*. Richardson tells how the exceptionally virtuous Pamela Andrews deftly avoids the clutches of one Squire B., but in *Shamela* Fielding turns the tables. In his hands, Squire B. becomes the naïve Squire Booby, who is tricked by the con artist Shamela. In *Joseph Andrews,* Fielding invented the English novel as we readers know and love it today—with an intrusive, witty narrator commenting on the zany exploits of young Joseph and his dotty friend Parson Adams.

FICTION

Mutiny on the Bounty

Considered by many readers to be the most exciting sea adventure ever written, this novel by Charles Nordhoff and James Norman Hall is based on the true story of a mutiny aboard the H.M.S. *Bounty* during its 1788–1789 voyage to Tahiti to gather breadfruit trees. Fletcher Christian leads the mutiny against the tyrannical Captain Bligh, and then sets him and his few loyal crew members adrift in a small boat. Bligh, who is too mean to die, finally makes his way back to England and reports the uprising. Now the search begins for the mutineers and the *Bounty*.

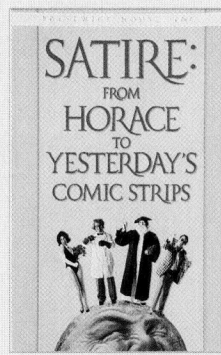

FICTION AND NONFICTION
Satire: From Horace to Yesterday's Comic Strips

Satire and its sidekick irony have been ridiculing human foibles for thousands of years. The jury is still out deciding just how effectively satire influences people to change their ways, but no one doubts satire's ability to make us laugh and cry at the same time. James Scott has compiled a variety of genres that satirize people from Roman times to the present. He also includes helpful questions with each selection to guide readers in understanding the point of the satire.

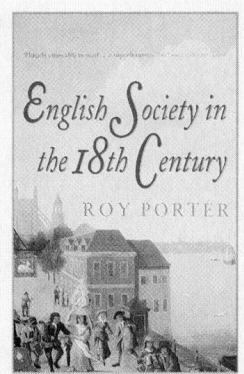

NONFICTION
English Society in the Eighteenth Century

Tired of reading about the pampered life of English royalty at Buckingham Palace? Want to know what life was like for everybody else, what "public" schools (which were private) taught, what people ate and why it was fashionable to be fat, how people dressed and why cosmetics could literally kill you, where people worked and why the Industrial Revolution changed everything? Then you should read Roy Porter's witty account of the joys and horrors of English life in the eighteenth century and how the English persevered no matter what the odds.

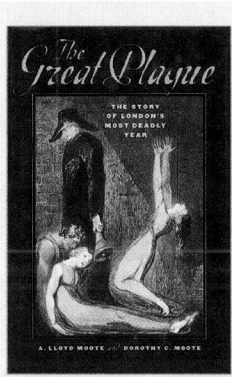

NONFICTION
The Great Plague

The comet that blazed across the London sky in the fall of 1664 inspired awe and dread. Many Londoners thought the comet boded ill. "This comet portends pestiferous and horrible windes and tempest," wrote one observer. Within a year nearly 100,000 residents of London and surrounding areas would be dead from the plague. Historian A. Lloyd Moote and microbiologist Dorothy C. Moote tell the tale of London's Great Plague, interweaving the experiences of people living in and around London during that horrible year.

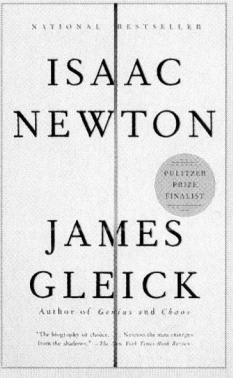

NONFICTION
Isaac Newton

Alexander Pope summed up Isaac Newton's achievement in this witty couplet: "Nature and nature's laws lay hid in night; / God said, Let Newton be! And all was light." Newton, probably the most famous scientist who ever lived, formulated the laws of motion and explained the force of gravity. In this brief biography, James Gleick tells about Newton's lonely childhood and how Newton found solace in books and began to develop his scientific theories. Gleick also clearly explains the significance of Newton's discoveries.

Learn It Online
Found out more at *NovelWise*.

go.hrw.com   L12-699   Go

The Romantic Period 1798–1832

COLLECTION 7

Truth and Imagination

COLLECTION 8

The Quest for Beauty

"The divine arts of imagination: imagination, the real & eternal world of which this vegetable universe is but a faint shadow."

—**William Blake**

What Do **You** Think

How can we use imagination to discover truth?

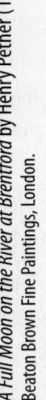

A Full Moon on the River at Brentford by Henry Pether (1828–1865). Beaton Brown Fine Paintings, London.

Learn It Online
Learn more about the Romantics online.
go.hrw.com L12-701 Go

The Romantic Period 1798–1832

This time line represents a snapshot of British literary events, British historical events, and world events from 1789 to 1832. During this tumultuous period, the Industrial Revolution transformed Britain, the French Revolution galvanized France, and Romantic literature dominated Europe.

Charles Dickens (1830) by Janet Roos. Dickens House Museum, London.

BRITISH LITERARY EVENTS

1789

1789 William Blake publishes *Songs of Innocence*

1792 Mary Wollstonecraft, in *A Vindication of the Rights of Woman*, critiques female educational restrictions ◄

1800 Maria Edgeworth's *Castle Rackrent*, the first historical novel in English, satirizes absentee landowners in Ireland

Mary Godwin, née Wollstonecraft. Portrait by John Opie. Oil on canvas. Inv. 1237. National Portrait Gallery, London.

1805

1807 Charles and Mary Lamb publish *Tales from Shakespeare*

1812 Charles Dickens, author of *A Christmas Carol,* is born ►

1813 Jane Austen publishes *Pride and Prejudice*

BRITISH HISTORICAL EVENTS

1789

1793 France declares war on England

1801 Act of Union creates United Kingdom of Great Britain and Ireland

1803 John Dalton develops modern atomic theory

1804 The steam engine is first used to drive a locomotive ▼

Richard Trevithick's locomotive. The Granger Collection, NY

1805

1811 English artisans called Luddites, fearing that industrialism threatens their livelihoods, riot and destroy textile machines

1811 Charles Bell publishes *New Idea of Anatomy of the Brain,* which explores the connection between the brain and nervous system

WORLD EVENTS

1789

1789 U.S. Congress approves its Constitution

1789 French Revolution begins with the storming of the Bastille ►

Storming of the Bastille, July 14, 1789, by Charles Thevenin. Musee de la Ville de Paris, Musee Carnavalet, Paris, France.

1803 United States purchases Louisiana Territory from France

1805

1805–1815 Napoleonic Wars lead to France's conquest of most of Europe

1808 Johann Wolfgang von Goethe publishes Part 1 of *Faust*

1810 Simón Bolivar begins series of South American rebellions against Spain ►

SKILLS FOCUS **Literary Skills** Evaluate the philosophical, political, religious, ethical, and social influences of a historical period. **Reading Skills** Identify and understand chronological order; identify and understand graphic elements; use text organizers such as overviews, headings, and graphic features to locate and categorize information.

Your Turn

Review the time line with a partner. What historical events might have driven Romantic writers to turn away from the eighteenth-century emphasis on reason and instead embrace naturalness and imagination? Explain.

1815	1822	1832

1818 Mary Shelley, daughter of Mary Wollstonecraft, publishes *Frankenstein* ➤

1819 Sir Walter Scott publishes *Ivanhoe*

1819 John Keats writes his greatest poems between January and September

1824 Percy Bysshe Shelley's complete works are published after his death

1824 George Gordon, Lord Byron dies in Greece

Cover of *Frankenstein* by Mary Shelley, late 19th century.

1815	1822	1832

1815 Napoleon surrenders to the British at Waterloo

1820 George III, mentally unstable since 1810, dies

1821 Michael Faraday publishes research that leads to the first electric motor

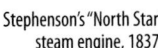
Stephenson's "North Star" steam engine, 1837.

1825 George Stephenson invents the railroad locomotive

1829 Catholic Emancipation Act allows British Roman Catholics to hold public office

1831 Charles Darwin serves as naturalist on HMS *Beagle* during an expedition along the coast of South America

1833 Slavery is abolished in the British Empire ➤

Slaves planting cane cuttings, from *Ten Views in the Island of Antigua* (1823) by William Clark. Color engraving. British Library Board, London.

1815	1822	1832

1816 Shaka becomes king and expands the Zulu nation ⌄

1817 Beethoven begins composing his Ninth Symphony

1821 Sequoyah develops a Cherokee system of writing

1822 Liberia is founded as a home for former U.S. slaves

1823 Alexander Pushkin begins his novel in verse, *Eugene Onegin*

1829 Ottoman Empire recognizes Greek independence

Zulu Kraal near Umlazi Natal, plate 27 from *The Kafirs Illustrated* (1849) by George French Angas. Color lithograph. Stapleton Collection, U.K.

The Romantic Period
1798–1832

Beginning in the late eighteenth century, great political, economic, and social changes rocked English society. The neoclassical faith in reason and its reverence for order and tradition, which had dominated English thought and literature for more than a century, seemed inadequate in the face of these profound upheavals. People needed new ways of thinking, feeling, and responding to change.

KEY CONCEPTS

Revolution Spreads

History of the Times An age of revolution began in America in 1776 and then swept across western Europe, releasing political, economic, and social forces that produced some of the most radical changes ever experienced in human life. The violence of the French Revolution shocked Europe and spread fear that other monarchies would also fall.

Literature of the Times Idealistic British writers who embraced the French Revolution rebelled against eighteenth-century rationalism. Rejecting restraint and refinement, they created a literature based on imagination.

Conservatives Clamp Down

History of the Times After the French Revolution, the English people suffered from repressive government policies enacted by conservatives who feared political change. When England and its allies defeated Napoleon in 1815, many early supporters of the French Revolution felt that it was the defeat of one tyrant by another.

Literature of the Times Six poets led the Romantic movement: William Blake, William Wordsworth, Samuel Taylor Coleridge, Lord Byron, Percy Bysshe Shelley, and John Keats. Their works are marked by imagination, idealism, and emotion, as well as an interest in nature, simplicity, and the past.

Industrialization Finds a Foothold

History of the Times England led the Industrial Revolution and replaced much human labor with machinery. The business class adopted the policy of laissez-faire economics, which allowed owners to operate factories without government interference. The result was devastating exploitation of the working poor.

Literature of the Times Gothic literature had an unmistakable appeal during the Romantic era. With its eerie, supernatural style, this type of literature reflects the renewed interest in mysticism during the Romantic period.

KEY CONCEPT

Revolution Spreads

History of the Times

The end of the eighteenth century was marked by revolution and violence. With its defeat in the American Revolution, England suffered a great economic blow and lost prestige and confidence as its thirteen American Colonies established their independence. It was the more radical revolution in France, which started with the storming of the Bastille prison on July 14, 1789, that had far more ominous effects. For the ruling classes in England, the French Revolution came to represent their worst fears: the overthrow of an anointed king by a democratic mob. To English conservatives, the French Revolution meant the triumph of radical principles, and they feared that the revolutionary fever would spread across the Channel.

Nevertheless, many British liberals supported the Revolution's purported ideals of "liberty, fraternity, and equality" until escalating violence and terror, such as the September 1792 massacre of hundreds of the nobility and clergy in France, disillusioned them.

In 1793, France and England declared war on each other. In the midst of the blood and turmoil, control of the French government again changed hands. Napoleon Bonaparte, an officer in the French army, emerged as dictator and then, in 1804, as emperor of France. In the end, Napoleon became just as ruthless as the executed king himself had been.

Literature of the Times

In 1798, two young, idealistic British poets, Samuel Taylor Coleridge and William Wordsworth, published *Lyrical Ballads, with a Few Other Poems.* Among the "few other poems" was Coleridge's long narrative, *The Rime of the Ancient Mariner* (see page 774) and a last-minute addition, Wordsworth's "Lines Composed a Few Miles Above Tintern Abbey" (see page 749). Both of these works are now among the most important poems in English literature.

Thus began in England what is now called the Romantic period. The Romantics turned to nature, to the past, or to a dream world that they felt was more genuine than the ugly, turbulent age in which they lived.

Comprehension Check

How did conservatives and democratic idealists respond differently to the French Revolution? Why?

Fast Facts

Historical Highlights

- The American and French Revolutions in the late 1700s deeply affect England. Conservative economic and political measures and a lengthy war against Napoleon strengthen the power of the rich.
- The growing industrialization of Britain leads to burgeoning urban populations and a rise in the number of poor workers.

Literary Highlights

- Romanticism arises as a response to social and economic changes caused by the Industrial Revolution.
- Wordsworth and Coleridge publish *Lyrical Ballads* in 1798.
- Keats, Byron, and Shelley write their greatest poems in the early nineteenth century.

Learn It Online
Find out more about this historical period online.

go.hrw.com | L12-705 | **Go**

(Opposite) James Watt's steam engine at an English coal mine in the 1790s. Contemporary painting by an unknown artist.
The Granger Collection, NY

Conservatives Clamp Down

History of the Times

The bewildering changes in western Europe made conservatives in England more rigid than ever. England instituted severe and repressive measures, outlawing collective bargaining and holding suspected spies or agitators in prison without a trial. After a brief peace from 1802 to 1803, England began a long war against Napoleon. English guns first defeated Napoleon's navy at the Battle of Trafalgar and with the help of allies and finally sent Napoleon's army packing at Waterloo, Belgium.

Although the conservatives in England felt they had saved their country from a tyrant and from chaos, the early supporters of the Revolution felt betrayed. For them, Waterloo was simply the defeat of one tyrant by another.

The Battle of Waterloo, 18th June 1815, published by Ackermann, 1815–1820. Color engraving by the English School (19th century). Bibliotheque Nationale, Paris, France.

Literature of the Times

The Romantic poets of the early nineteenth century were deeply aware of their revolutionary times and dedicated to bringing about change. They harbored no illusions about their very limited political power, but they believed in the force of literature. Frustrated by England's resistance to political and social change that they thought was certain to improve conditions, the Romantic poets turned from the formal, public verse of the eighteenth-century Augustans to a more private, spontaneous lyric poetry. These lyrics expressed the Romantics' belief that imagination,

Analyzing Visuals

Viewing and Interpreting   The bright dress and playful postures of the figures suggest a comic overtone, despite their overtly violent movements. Who or what might the artist be parodying in this picture?

Long Live the Romantic Comedy

Picnic scene from *Sense and Sensibility* (1995). Kate Winslet, Gemma Jones, Emilie Francois, and Emma Thompson.

Jane Austen is one of the most beloved of all British authors. Her subject matter, ordinary people in everyday life, is hailed by many scholars as a direct influence on the modern novel. During Austen's life she saw four of her novels published within four years of each other; two were published after her death. The titles of Austen's novels, *Sense and Sensibility* (1811), *Pride and Prejudice* (1813), *Mansfield Park* (1814), *Emma* (1815), *Northanger Abbey* (1803), and *Persuasion* (1817), may be more recognizable to you as the titles of box-office hits and celebrated mini-series. Many of her works have been made into movies, of which the most famous and funny, *Emma* and *Pride and Prejudice,* have been adapted several times for movies and television—even as teen comedies and musicals.

Ask Yourself

Why might people continue to find humor and value in two-hundred-year-old novels?

rather than mere reason, was the best response to the forces of change.

Much of the literature of the Romantic period—as represented by *Lyrical Ballads*—is Romantic poetry. The Romantics thought of poets as extraordinary people, necessary to humanity and society. A poet has "a greater knowledge of human nature and a more comprehensive soul, than are supposed to be common among mankind," Wordsworth said. His compatriots agreed. Blake referred to poets as teachers, Keats called them "physicians," and Shelley saw them as "unacknowledged legislators of the world." The poet, wrote Coleridge, "brings the whole soul of

man into activity" by employing "that synthetic and magical power… the imagination."

Although poetry dominated the literary scene, the novel also continued to thrive during the Romantic period. Key novelists included Jane Austen, Maria Edgeworth, and Sir Walter Scott. A leading author of great reputation, Austen wrote with humor and irony about English country life. Her works include *Pride and Prejudice, Sense and Sensibility,* and *Emma.*

Comprehension Check

What new values and responses to change did the Romantic poets offer?

Industrialization Finds a Foothold

History of the Times

England was the first nation in the world to experience the effects of the Industrial Revolution. Previously, goods had been made by hand, at home. Now, production switched to factories, where machines worked many times faster than human beings could. Since factories were in cities, the urban populations increased, creating desperate living conditions that would appall us today.

In addition, the communal land once shared by small farmers was taken over by individual owners. Some of these owners transformed the fields into vast private parks, while others divided the land into privately held fields. As a result, large numbers of landless people migrated to cities in search of work or relied on the charity of the time: the poorhouse and begging.

The economic philosophy that propelled much of this misery was a policy called **laissez faire,** "let (people) do (as they please)." According to this policy, the new economic forces should be allowed to operate freely without government interference. Laissez faire enabled the rich to grow richer and caused the poor people to suffer even more. The system had its most tragic effects on those who were helpless, especially children. Small children of poor families were often used as beasts of burden. In the coal pits, for example, very small children were harnessed to carts for dragging coal, just as if they had been small donkeys.

Literature of the Times

Wars, revolutions, industrialization, and economic upheaval made the British feel adrift and frightened. One way of responding to this sense of unease was to explore the dark side of life in literature and art. For that reason, literature of the Romantic period is filled with examples of the eerie and supernatural. The

View of Sheffield, England, showing the city's many factories and steelworks. English engraving, 1879.   The Granger Collection, NY

Romantics' taste for terror grew from a sensibility called Gothic that set stories in gloomy medieval castles.

The Gothic was one way in which people of the age expressed a sense of helplessness about forces beyond their control. Gothic literature uses devices such as ghosts, the supernatural, death, violence, and decay to terrorize readers and allow them to purge their fears and worries within the safety of fantasy. Mary Shelley's *Frankenstein,* a pivotal Gothic novel, highlights the era's anxiety over the powers of science and technology.

The Gothic style also extended to art. A melancholy painting or a desolate landscape was thought to enhance spiritual awareness. Ann Radcliffe (1764–1823), one of the best-known Gothic novelists, describes this ideal awareness in *The Mysteries of Udolpho* (1794). In twilight gloom, a character finds "that delicious melancholy which no person, who had felt it once, would resign for the gayest pleasures. They awaken our best and purest feelings; disposing us to benevolence, pity, and friendship."

Comprehension Check

How did Gothic literature provide readers and writers in the Romantic period a new way to deal with the political and social upheavals around them?

Link to Today

Urban Amusements

Many people today associate cities with a great variety of entertainment—from restaurants and shopping to zoos and amusement parks, as well as movies, music, and theater. Although the liberal philosopher Josiah Tucker called London under Kings George I, II, and III "no better than a wen," or wart, London was a veritable playground for those who could afford it. Ballooning was popular. Puppet shows, waxwork museums, and music halls attracted large audiences. One of the most frequented type of entertainment was boxing. (Lord Byron himself was taught to box by Gentleman Jackson, one of the leading fighters of the day.) Most families, whether aristocratic or common, had their portraits done. The upper class shopped at the new shopping arcades—the eighteenth-century version of malls—especially the Burlington Arcade in Piccadilly. In short, life in London during this time was as full of exciting diversions as city life is today.

Ask Yourself

How do the types of entertainment available in cities today compare to those available during the Romantic period?

The London Eye and County Hall on the bank of the River Thames, London.

Wrap Up

Talk About…

With a group, compare the poet's role in the Romantic period and in today's society. Try to use each Academic Vocabulary word **listed below** at least once in your discussion.

Write About…

Percy Bysshe Shelley wrote that the "great instrument of moral good is the imagination." Do you agree or disagree? Why?

Academic Vocabulary for Unit 4

Talking and Writing About Literature

Academic Vocabulary is the language you use to write and talk about literature. Use these words to discuss the literature you read in this unit. These words are underlined throughout the unit.

device (dih VYS) *n.*: something made for a particular purpose. *Imagery is a predominant literary device in Romantic poetry.*

differentiate (dihf uh REHN shee ayt) *v.*: distinguish; identify differences. *It is not difficult to differentiate between the styles of Romantic and Restoration poetry.*

function (FUHNGK shuhn) *n.*: the action for which a person or thing is specially fitted; purpose. *The Romantics believed the function of poets was to enlighten and lift up the masses.*

inherent (ihn HIHR uhnt) *adj.*: existing in something as a fixed, essential quality. *Many people now feel that exploitation is inherent to laissez-faire economics.*

technique (tehk NEEK) *n.*: method; way of using skills. *Evoking the powerful, emotionally rejuvenating effect of nature was a popular Romantic technique.*

Your Turn

In your *Reader/Writer Notebook*, compose a brief description of Romantic writing, using each of the Academic Vocabulary words.

Read with a Purpose
Read to discover how the natural world leads the author to a state of heightened awareness.

Build Background
When Jane Goodall studied chimpanzees at Gombe National Park in Tanganyika (now Tanzania), she defied the research conventions by giving each animal a name instead of a number. Goodall found that chimpanzees make and use tools, express distinct personalities, and engage in complex social behaviors.

Author Note
British born, Jane Goodall (1934–   ) abandoned formal schooling at age eighteen and joined a film crew that brought her to Africa, where she worked with anthropologist Louis Leakey. Their work studying chimpanzees in the early 1960s revolutionized our understanding of these animals. Like the Romantic poets, Goodall finds wonder and truth in nature—human and nonhuman alike.

MEMOIR

from A Reason for Hope

by Jane Goodall

Back in Gombe.[1] It was early in the morning and I sat on the steps of my house by the lakeshore. It was very still. Suspended over the horizon, where the mountains of the Congo fringed Lake Tanganyika,[2] was the last quarter of the waning moon and her path danced and sparkled toward me across the gently moving water. After enjoying a banana and a cup of coffee, I was off, climbing up the steep slopes behind my house, carrying only my little binoculars, a notebook, a pencil, and a handful of raisins for lunch. I never feel the need for food, and seldom for water, when I am roaming the forests. How good it felt to be alone at last, reveling in the simple life that had nourished my spirit for so long.

In the faint light from the moon reflected by the dew-laden grass, it was not difficult to find my way up the mountain. All around, the trees were shrouded with the last mysteries of the night's dreaming. It was quiet, utterly peaceful. The only sounds were the occasional chirp of a cricket, and the soft murmur where the waves caressed the stones on the beach below. Suddenly there was a burst of song, the duet of a pair of robin chats, hauntingly beautiful. I realized that the intensity of the light had changed; dawn had crept upon me unawares. The coming brightness of the sun had all but vanquished the silvery, indefinite illumination of its own radiance reflected by the moon.

1. **Gombe:** an African state located in northeastern Nigeria; founded in 1804.
2. **Lake Tanganyika** (tan GUHN yee kuh): the longest freshwater lake in the world (410 miles).

Viewing and Interpreting How does the Romantic depiction of a solitary figure facing the ocean compare to the experience Jane Goodall narrates in this excerpt from *A Reason for Hope*?

Left: *The Wanderer Above the Sea of Fog* (1818) by Caspar David Friedrich. Oil on canvas.
Hamburg Kunsthalle, Germany.
Below: Researcher Jane Goodall, on a peak overlooking Gombe, scans the forest through binoculars searching for chimpanzees.
The Jane Goodall Institute

Five minutes later I heard the rustlings of leaves overhead. I looked up and saw the branches moving against the lightening sky. The chimps had awakened. It was Fifi and her offspring, Freud, Frodo, and little Fanni. I followed when they moved off up the slope. Fanni riding on her mother's back like a diminutive[3] jockey. Presently they climbed into a tall fig tree and began to feed. I heard the occasional soft thuds as skins and seeds of figs fell to the ground.

For several hours we moved leisurely from one food tree to the next, gradually climbing higher and higher. On an open grassy ridge the chimps climbed into a massive mbula tree,[4] where Fifi, replete[5] from the morning's feasting, made a large comfortable nest high above me. She dozed through a midday siesta, little Fanni asleep in her arms, Frodo and Freud playing nearby. How healing it was to be back at Gombe again, and by myself with the chimpanzees and their forest. I had left the busy, materialistic world so full of greed and selfishness and, for a little while, could feel myself, as in the early days, a part of nature. I felt very much in tune with the chimpanzees, for I was spending time with them not to observe, but simply because I needed their company, undemanding and free of pity. From where I sat I could look out over the Kasakela Valley. Just below me to the west was the Peak. A surge of memories flooded through me: from that vantage point I had learned so much in the early days, sitting and watching while, gradually, the chimpanzees had lost their fear of the strange white ape who had invaded their world. I recaptured some of my long-ago feelings as I sat there, reflecting. The old excitement of discovery, of seeing things quite unknown to Western eyes. And the serenity[6] that had come from living, day after day, as a part of the natural world. A world that dwarfs yet somehow enhances human emotions.

As I reflected on these things I had been only partly conscious of the approach of a storm. Suddenly, I realized that it was no longer growling in the distance but was right above. The sky was dark, almost black, and the rain clouds had obliterated[7] the higher peaks. With the growing darkness came the stillness, the hush, that so often precedes a tropical downpour. Only the rumbling of the thunder, moving closer and closer, broke this stillness; the thunder and the rustling movements of the chimpanzees. All at once came a blinding flash of lightning, followed, a split second later, by an incredibly loud clap of thunder, that seemed almost to shake the solid

---

3. **diminutive:** small; tiny.
4. **mbula tree:** a medium-sized gnarled tree whose fruit, a plum-sized, custardlike apple, is a staple of the Gombe chimps' diet.
5. **replete:** stuffed with food and drink.
6. **serenity:** a feeling of peace or calm.
7. **obliterated:** completely blotted out.

Dr. Jane Goodall, touched by Jou Jou.

rock before it rumbled on, bouncing from peak to peak. Then the dark and heavy clouds let loose such torrential rain that sky and earth seemed joined by moving water. I sat under a palm whose fronds, for a while, provided some shelter. Fifi sat hunched over, protecting her infant; Frodo pressed close against them in the nest; Freud sat with rounded back on a nearby branch. As the rain poured endlessly down, my palm fronds no longer provided shelter and I got wetter and wetter. I began to feel first chilly and then, as a cold wind spring up, freezing; soon, turned in on myself, I lost all track of time. I and the chimpanzees formed a unit of silent, patient, and uncomplaining endurance.

It must have been an hour or more before the rain began to ease as the heart of the storm swept away to the south. At four-thirty the chimps climbed down, and we moved off through the soaked, dripping vegetation, back down the mountainside. Presently we arrived on a grassy ridge overlooking the lake. A pale, watery sun had appeared and its light caught the raindrops so that the world seemed hung with diamonds, sparkling on every leaf, every blade of grass. I crouched low to avoid destroying a jeweled spider's web that stretched, exquisite and fragile, across the trail.

I heard sounds of greeting as Fifi and her family joined Melissa and hers. They all climbed into a low tree to feed on fresh young leaves. I moved to a place where I could stand and watch as they enjoyed their last meal of the day. Down below, the lake was still dark and angry with white flecks where the waves broke, and rain clouds remained black in the south. To the north the sky was clear with only wisps of gray clouds still lingering. The scene was breathtaking in its beauty. In the soft sunlight, the chimpanzees' black coats were shot with coppery brown, the branches on which they sat were wet and dark as ebony, the young leaves a pale but brilliant green. And behind was the dramatic backcloth of the indigo sky where lightning flickered and distant thunder growled and rumbled.

Lost in awe at the beauty around me, I must have slipped into a state of heightened awareness. It is hard—impossible, really—to put into words the moment of truth that suddenly came upon me then. Even the mystics are unable to describe their brief flashes of spiritual ecstasy. It seemed to me, as I struggled afterward to recall the experience, that *self* was utterly absent: I and the chimpanzees, the earth and trees and air, seemed to merge, to become one with the spirit power of life itself. The air was filled with a feathered symphony, the evensong of birds. I heard new frequencies in their music and also in the singing insects' voices—notes so high and sweet I was amazed. Never had I been so intensely aware of the shape, the color of the individual leaves, the varied patterns of the veins that made each one unique. Scents were clear as well, easily identifiable: fermenting, overripe fruit; waterlogged earth; cold, wet bark; the damp odor of chimpanzee hair and, yes, my own too. And the aromatic scent of young, crushed leaves was almost overpowering. I sensed a new presence, then saw a bushbuck,[8] quietly browsing upwind, his spiraled horns gleaming and his chestnut coat dark with rain.

Suddenly a distant chorus of pant-hoots[9] elicited a reply from Fifi. As though wakening from some vivid dream I was back in the everyday world, cold, yet intensely alive. When the chimpanzees left, I stayed in that place—it seemed a most sacred place—scribbling some notes, trying to describe what, so briefly, I had experienced. I had not been visited by the angels or other heavenly beings that characterize the visions of the great mystics or the saints, yet for all that I believe it truly was a mystical experience.

Time passed. Eventually I wandered back along the forest trail and scrambled down behind my house to the beach. The sun was a huge red orb just vanishing behind the Congo hills and I sat on the beach watching the ever-changing sunset as it painted the sky red and gold and dark purple. The surface of the lake, calm after the storm, glinted with gold and violet and red ripples below the flaming sky.

Later, as I sat by my little fire, cooking my dinner of beans, tomatoes, and an egg, I was still lost in the wonder of my experience. Yes, I thought, there are my windows through which we humans, searching for meaning, can look out into the world around us. There are those carved

---

8. **bushbuck:** a reddish brown, white-striped African antelope.
9. **pant-hoots:** panting and hooting sounds chimpanzees make to communicate.

out by Western science, their panes polished by a succession of brilliant minds. Through them we can see ever farther, ever more clearly, into areas which until recently were beyond human knowledge. Through such a scientific window I had been taught to observe the chimpanzees. For more than twenty-five years I had sought, through careful recording and critical analysis, to piece together their complex social behavior, to understand the workings of their minds. And this had not only helped us to better understand their place in nature but also helped to understand a little better some aspects of our own human behavior, our own place in the natural world.

Yet there are other windows through which we humans can look out into the world around us, windows through which the mystics and the holy men of the East, and the founders of the great world religions, have gazed as they searched for the meaning and purpose of our life on earth, not only in the wondrous beauty of the world, but also in its darkness and ugliness. And those Masters contemplated the truths that they saw, not with their minds only but with their hearts and souls too. From those revelations came the spiritual essence of the great scriptures, the holy books, and the most beautiful mystic poems and writings. That afternoon, it had been as though an unseen hand had drawn back a curtain and, for the briefest moment, I had seen through such a window. In a flash of "outsight" I had known timelessness and quiet ecstasy, sensed a truth of which mainstream science is merely a small fraction. And I knew that the revelation would be with me for the rest of my life, imperfectly remembered yet always within. A source of strength on which I could draw when life seemed harsh or cruel or desperate.

Ask Yourself

1. **Read with a Purpose** Goodall says, "Lost in awe at the beauty around me, I must have slipped into a state of heightened awareness." What does Goodall mean by "a state of heightened awareness," and how did her experience in nature lead her to such a state?

2. How does Goodall's use of details affect your understanding of the experiences she relates here? Explain.

3. Goodall describes two types of "windows" through which humans can search for meaning. Explain these two types of windows. Through which window do you think most people look? Through which window do you look? Why?

4. Consider the mystical experience Goodall describes. Think about a time when something in the natural world, perhaps a dazzling sunset or a powerful storm, led you to a new understanding. Describe your experience, and explain how attention to the natural world can help us see the world in a new way.

Truth and Imagination

LITERARY FOCUS
Themes of Romantic Poetry

CONTENTS

Robert Burns

William Blake

William Wordsworth

Samuel Taylor Coleridge

Timothy Foote Link to Today

"Spiritual love acts not nor can exist
Without imagination, which, in truth,
Is but another name for absolute power
And clearest insight, amplitude of mind,
And Reason in her most exalted mood."

— **William Wordsworth**

Themes of Romantic Poetry by **Leila Christenbury**

Influences on Romantic Poetry

- Spread of democratic ideals through the American and French Revolutions and the disillusionment created by the failure of the French Revolution
- Reactions against the harsh living and working conditions created for poor people in urban areas by the Industrial Revolution and laissez-faire economics
- Fascination with nature and country life, which seemed a blissful retreat compared to the squalor of city slums

A New Focus in Poetry

Inviting readers to feel power and passion, the poetry of the Romantic period looks at the world with new eyes and tries to capture the magic of personal experience. The poets of the Restoration wrote in an age when order had just been restored to a society that badly needed it, and, accordingly, the Augustans celebrated order, hierarchy, and enlightened rule. The Romantics, on the other hand, lived in a society desperately in need of social change, even revolution. They rebelled by writing about personal feelings, supporting individual rights, and using common, everyday language.

The word *romantic* comes from the term *romance,* one of the most popular medieval genres. Romantic writers consciously used the elements of romance in an attempt to transcend the refinements of neoclassical literature and explore more psychological and mysterious aspects of human experience.

Romantic poets are distinguished by three main characteristics:

- They were fascinated with youth and innocence, particularly the freshness and wonder of a child's perspective of the world.
- They saw history as a cycle in which people must constantly question tradition and authority to improve living conditions.

- They saw change as part of life. In the context of an industrialized world, people had to accept change if they were to survive.

Romantic themes still resonate with readers today. As you read the poems in this collection, record down the themes that you find meaningful.

Imagination: The Inspired Guide

The beginning of the Romantic movement in poetry is often dated to the 1798 publication of *Lyrical Ballads,* by William Wordsworth and Samuel Taylor Coleridge. Because many of these poems deal with nature, the Romantics are often mistakenly seen merely as nature poets. The Romantics should instead be considered "mind poets," for they sought a deeper understanding of the bond between human beings and the world of the senses.

Their search led them to a third, more mysterious element linking the mind to nature. In "Lines Composed a Few Miles Above Tintern Abbey," Wordsworth describes this link as "something far more deeply interfused." This "something" is a sort of creative inertia, a power that makes things happen. The Romantics identified this power as the imagination, a faculty they believed was superior to human reasoning. For that reason, Romantic poems usually present imaginative experiences as especially powerful or moving.

Learn It Online
Learn more about the themes of Romantic poetry through *PowerNotes* online.

go.hrw.com   L12-717   Go

(opposite) *Dudley, Worcester* by Joseph Mallord William Turner. Watercolor on paper. Lady Lever Art Gallery, National Museums Liverpool

While each of the six major Romantic poets had his own view of imagination, all believed that the imagination could be stimulated by nature and the mind. The poets had a strong sense of nature's mysterious forces, which inspire writers—such as in Shelley's "Ode to the West Wind" (see page 824)—and hint at the causes of the great changes taking place in the world.

Nature: The Wise Teacher

If imagination is the Romantic poet's guide to seeking truth, nature is the teacher who can deliver the lesson. Romantic poets considered themselves special people who were, as Wordsworth wrote, "endowed with a more lively sensibility … a greater knowledge of human nature, and a more comprehensive soul, than are supposed to be common among mankind." Identifying themselves as bards, Romantics felt responsible for helping other people see the world in all its beauty and tenderness, as well as reflecting on the sadder subjects of human experience. They were, according to John Keats, to "pour out a balm upon the world."

For the Romantic poets, nature was a balm to soothe the relentless hounding of an industrialized world. The poets had a strong sense of nature's mysterious, transformative properties. A poet translated into words what he or she sensed from waves beating against the coastline, mountains shrouded in clouds, or silent groves, so that readers might perceive the power of natural forces to shape thought and feeling.

This inclination toward natural images and themes is one reason that the Gothic tradition in literature also thrived during this period. Novels such as Mary Shelley's *Frankenstein* drew attention to the mysterious side of nature and the power of the imagination through their eerie settings, supernatural events, and questions about the human ability to manipulate nature.

Experience: The Worthy Subject

Because they looked to nature for inspiration, Romantic poets favored idealized rural settings. The city, with its oppressive, crowded streets, held little appeal. However, the people who crowded those city streets were a source of fascination for some Romantic poets, who celebrated all types of human experience. The Romantic period was, historically, a time of growing awareness of the rights of individuals—including the right to healthful living conditions, the right to relief from political or economic oppression, and the right to self-expression.

Across Europe and in the former American Colonies, democracy grew stronger, and oppressive governments grew weaker. At the same time, economic oppression was on the rise as industrial factories drew workers away from small farms and family-run businesses. Burgeoning **laissez-faire** policies allowed businesses to <u>function</u> freely and with little restriction. As a result, workers, including young children, labored for long hours under dangerous conditions because no governmental regulations existed to protect them. It was of little consequence to employers when workers injured themselves and couldn't work, for there were always desperate people ready to replace them.

Some Romantic poets dreamed that poetry could improve these horrific conditions by offering an example of model behavior. Wordsworth wrote in *The Prelude*:

> What we have loved,
> Others will love, and we will teach them how;
> Instruct them how the mind of man becomes
> A thousand times more beautiful than the earth
> On which he dwells.

With the ability to cultivate the sensibilities of mankind, the poet thus becomes necessary to human beings and society.

Ask Yourself

1. Where did Romantic poets look for inspiration? Why?

2. Why do you think Romantic poets wrote about nature during a time of change?

Analyzing a Painting

Themes of Romantic poetry in the eighteenth and nineteenth centuries include the imagination, the inspiration of nature, and the questioning of tradition. This modern painting by Norman Adams shares some of those themes.

Guidelines

Use these guidelines to consider how this modern painting reflects some of the themes of Romantic poetry.

- Romantic poetry often focuses on the power of the imagination. In what way does this painting reflect a similar focus?
- How can nature be seen as an inspiration in this painting?
- In what ways does this painting question tradition?

Rainbow Painting (I) (1966) by Norman Adams (1927-2005). Oil on canvas. Tate, London, Presented by the Trustees of the Chantrey Bequest, 1969

1. Why do you think the artist chose this color for the background? What might the background represent?

2. What might the shape of the rainbow express about the artist's view of nature?

3. How does this painting represent a nontraditional view of nature?

Your Turn Analyze Romantic Themes

Look through this book, and choose an image from any historical period. Discuss with a partner what themes the image has in common with themes of Romantic poetry.

Preparing to Read

To a Mouse
To a Louse

How can we use imagination to discover truth?

QuickTalk

What fables, songs, stories, and poems do you know in which humans learn a wise lesson from animals? With a partner, list these stories and share what you recall about each story's lesson.

Robert Burns
(1759–1796)

Hardworking farmer Robert Burns gained literary fame as a poet of the ordinary people. Hailed as the national poet of Scotland, Burns used the people's own way of speaking to celebrate their lives.

The Humble Plowman

Despite long hours of toil on his family's farm, Burns found time to study, often propping a book up on the table to read during meals. His father encouraged him in his studies, and his mother taught him old Scottish songs and stories, many of which he later turned into poems.

An acquaintance noted that Burns liked to pass himself off as an "illiterate ploughman who wrote from pure inspiration," when, in fact, he could write perfectly well in standard formal English. In his writing, Burns employed heavy Scottish dialect as well as combinations of folk idioms and literary language. His talent with dialects allowed him to assume the persona of the humble plowman while achieving great feats.

Symbol of Scottish Literature

Burns was catapulted to fame with the 1786 publication of *Poems, Chiefly in the Scottish Dialect*. The immediate popularity of this collection—the first edition sold out in a month—took Burns from his rural town of Ayrshire in southwestern Scotland to urban Edinburgh, where he became a celebrity.

After his first collection was published, Burns wrote relatively few new poems and instead collected, adapted, and wrote more than three hundred songs, including "Auld Lang Syne." He helped preserve Scotland's poetic heritage and established his reputation as an accomplished lyricist. Only ten years after the success of the 1786 *Poems*, Burns died of heart disease. His reputation continued to grow, however, and by the early nineteenth century, he was well on the way to becoming the single most important poet of Scottish literature.

Think About the Writer Burns wrote about everyday people doing everyday things. What do you think attracted him to these topics?

Robert Burns (1759–1796), by Alexander Nasmyth (1758–1840). Scottish National Portrait Gallery, Edinburgh, Scotland

To a Mouse / To a Louse

Reader/Writer Notebook

Use your **RWN** to complete the activities for these selections.

Literary Focus

Dialect When you watch a movie or television show, or listen to a radio broadcast, you may notice differences in the way people from various places speak. What you hear when you note the unique speech of people from New York, London, Dallas, or Chicago is **dialect,** speech that is characteristic of a particular region or group of people. Dialects of a language may have a distinct vocabulary, pronunciation system, and grammar. Writers who use dialect are often praised for their ability to capture the true expressions of everyday people. For his celebration of Scottish dialects, Robert Burns earned the love and respect of other Scots.

Reading Focus

Paraphrasing When you **paraphrase** text, you restate its meaning in your own words. Paraphrasing is an important step in mastering new knowledge and information. Paraphrasing can be a particularly helpful technique when you read something written in an unfamiliar dialect.

Into Action As you read each stanza of the poems, ask yourself, "How might I express the same idea?" Use a chart like the one below to paraphrase each poem, stanza by stanza.

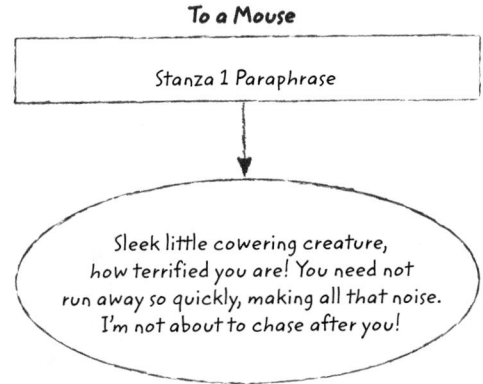

To a Mouse

Stanza 1 Paraphrase

Sleek little cowering creature, how terrified you are! You need not run away so quickly, making all that noise. I'm not about to chase after you!

Language Coach

Homonyms Words that sound alike but have different spellings and meanings are called **homonyms.** The adjective *wee,* which means "small," should not be confused with the pronoun *we.* Can you explain the different meanings of these homonyms?

> bare, bear
> forward, foreword
> poor, pour
> airs, heirs

Read on to find out which word in each group Burns uses in one of the two poems.

Writing Focus

Think as a Reader/Writer

Find It in Your Reading Burns uses **apostrophe,** a device in which a speaker directly addresses an absent person or thing as if it could respon. Record uses of apostrophe in your *Reader/Writer Notebook*.

Learn It Online
Listen to the dialect in these poems through the audio versions online.

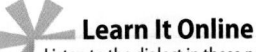

go.hrw.com   L12-721   Go

To a Mouse

by Robert Burns

Read with a Purpose
Read to discover the speaker's feelings about accidentally destroying another living creature's home.

Build Background
Burns was a man of tremendous physical strength, as well as of great intellect, as this quotation by Allan Cunningham suggests: "I saw him one evening match himself with a number of masons; and out of five-and-twenty practised hands, the most vigorous young men in the parish, there was only one that could lift the same weight as Burns." Despite his own physical prowess, Burns understood and sympathized with the vulnerabilities of the smallest creatures. In this poem, the speaker addresses a mouse whose nest he has uncovered with his plow.

On Turning Her Up in Her Nest, with the Plow, November, 1785.

      Wee, sleeket,° cowran, tim'rous beastie, **Ⓐ**
O, what a panic's in thy breastie!
Thou need na start awa sae hasty,
      Wi' bickering brattle!°
5 I wad be laith° to rin an' chase thee,
      Wi' murd'ring pattle!°

      I'm truly sorry man's dominion
Has broken Nature's social union,
An' justifies that ill opinion,
10   Which makes thee startle
At me, thy poor, earth-born companion,
      An' fellow mortal! **Ⓑ**

      I doubt na, whyles,° but thou may thieve;
What then? poor beastie, thou maun° live!
15 A daimen-icker in a thrave°
      'S a sma request:
I'll get a blessin wi' the lave,°
      An' never miss 't!

1. **sleeket:** sleek.

4. **bickering brattle:** rattling sounds.
5. **laith:** loath; unwilling.
6. **pattle:** plow staff.

13. **whyles:** sometimes.
14. **maun:** must.
15. **daimen-icker in a thrave:** occasional ear of grain out of a bundle.
17. **lave:** remainder.

Ⓐ Literary Focus Dialect What kind of creature is described in the first line? Which words used in this description sound like words we use today?

Ⓑ Reading Focus Paraphrasing Paraphrase lines 7–12. What conflict exists between "man's dominion" and "Nature's social union"?

Thy wee-bit housie, too, in ruin!
20 It's silly wa's° the win's are strewin!
An' naething, now, to big° a new ane,
      O' foggage° green!
An' bleak December's winds ensuin,
      Baith snell° an' keen!

25   Thou saw the fields laid bare an' wast,
An' weary winter comin fast,
An' cozie here, beneath the blast,
      Thou thought to dwell,
Till crash! the cruel coulter° past
30   Out thro' thy cell.

      That wee-bit heap o' leaves an' stibble, C
Has cost thee monie a weary nibble!
Now thou's turn'd out, for a' thy trouble,
      But° house or hald,°
35 To thole° the winter's sleety dribble,
      An' cranreuch° cauld!

      But Mousie, thou art no thy-lane,°
In proving foresight may be vain:
The best laid schemes o' mice an' men
40   Gang aft agley,°
An' lea'e us nought but grief an' pain,
      For promis'd joy!

      Still, thou art blest, compar'd wi' me!
The present only toucheth thee:
45 But och! I backward cast my e'e,
      On prospects drear!
An' forward, tho' I canna see,
      I guess an' fear! D

C Literary Focus Dialect What is the effect of
the repetition of *wee* and *wee-bit* in lines 1, 19, and 31?

D Reading Focus Paraphrasing First, put
lines 45–48 into normal word order. Then, restate them
in your own words. How are these lines a fitting
conclusion to the poem?

20. silly wa's: feeble walls.
21. big: build.
22. foggage: moss.

24. snell: bitter.

29. coulter: plow blade.

34. but: without. **hald:** land.
35. thole: endure.
36. cranreuch: frost.

37. no thy-lane: not alone.

40. gang aft agley: often go
amiss.

Dormouse (1996) by James Lynch. Tempera on
panel.

To a Mouse **723**

To a Louse

by **Robert Burns**

Read with a Purpose
Read to discover what the speaker appreciates about a creature that most people view with disgust.

Build Background
In "To a Louse," the speaker addresses a louse that is crawling across a lady's expensive bonnet. The speaker initially seems to be filled with indignation at the sight of the pest, but by the end of the poem, his true feelings are revealed.

On Seeing One on a Lady's Bonnet at Church.

Ha! wh'are ye gaun, ye crowlin' ferlie!°
Your impudence protects you sairly:°
I canna say but ye strunt° rarely,
    Owre gauze and lace;
5 Tho' faith! I fear ye dine but sparely
    On sic a place.

Ye ugly, creepin', blastit wonner,°
Detested, shunn'd by saunt an' sinner!
How dare ye set your fit° upon her,
10   Sae fine a lady?
Gae somewhere else, and seek your dinner
    On some poor body. **Ⓐ**

Swith, in some beggar's haffet squattle;°
There ye may creep, and sprawl, and sprattle°
15 Wi' ither kindred jumping cattle,
    In shoals and nations;
Where horn nor bane° ne'er dare unsettle
    Your thick plantations. **Ⓑ**

1. **crowlin' ferlie:** crawling wonder.
2. **sairly:** greatly; sorely.
3. **strunt:** strut.

7. **blastit wonner:** blasted wonder.
9. **fit:** foot.

13. **Swith . . . squattle:** Off! Sprawl in some beggar's temple.
14. **sprattle:** scramble; struggle.

17. **horn nor bane** (bone): materials used to make combs.

Ⓐ Literary Focus **Dialect** What words in this stanza are examples of Burns's Scottish dialect? What tone, or attitude toward his subject, does he create with these words?

Ⓑ Reading Focus **Paraphrasing** Paraphrase lines 17 and 18. Where does the speaker want the louse to go?

The Chapel of the Chateau de Versailles
(1917-19) by Edouard Vuillard (1868-1940)
Wallpaper mounted on canvas
Musee d'Orsay, Paris, France, ARS, NY

Now haud ye there,° ye're out o' sight,
20 Below the fatt'rels,° snug an' tight;
Na, faith ye yet! ye'll no be right
       Till ye've got on it,
The very tapmost tow'ring height
       O' Miss's bonnet.

25 My sooth! right bauld° ye set your nose out,
As plump and gray as onie grozet;°
O for some rank mercurial rozet,°
       Or fell red smeddum!°
I'd gie you sic a hearty doze o't,
30   Wad dress your droddum!° **C**

19. **haud ye there:** stay where you are.
20. **fatt'rels:** ribbon ends.
25. **bauld:** bold.
26. **onie grozet:** any goose-berry.
27. **rozet:** rosin, a substance derived from the resin given off by pine trees and used to make soap, varnish, and other products.
28. **fell red smeddum:** dead red powder.
30. **wad dress your droddum:** would put an end to you.

C **Literary Focus** **Dialect** In this stanza, the speaker threatens the louse. How does the speaker's word choice make the tone more comical rather than threatening?

Head louse (*Pediculus humanus capitis*) with hair egg (55x).

I wad na been surpris'd to spy
You on an auld wife's flannen toy;°
Or aiblins° some bit duddie° boy,
    On's wyliecoat;°
35 But Miss's fine Lunardi!° fie,
    How daur ye do't?

O Jenny, dinna toss your head,
An' set your beauties a' abread!°
Ye little ken what cursèd speed
40   The blastie's makin'! **D**
Thae winks and finger-ends,° I dread,
    Are notice takin'!

O wad some Pow'r the giftie gie us
To see oursels as others see us!
45 It wad frae mony a blunder free us,
    And foolish notion:
What airs in dress an' gait wad lea'e us,
    And ev'n devotion!°

32. flannen toy: flannel head-dress.
33. aiblins: perhaps.
bit duddie: small ragged.
34. wyliecoat: undershirt.
35. Lunardi: a kind of bonnet, probably with winglike ribbons, named for a balloonist of the day.
38. abread: abroad.

41. thae winks and finger-ends: those people winking and pointing.

47–48. airs in… devotion: false piety.

D **Reading Focus** **Paraphrase** Paraphrase lines 37–40. How has the speaker's attitude changed from what we've seen in previous stanzas? Why does he advise Jenny "dinna toss your head"?

To a Mouse / To a Louse

SKILLS FOCUS Literary Skills Analyze dialect; analyze characteristics of the speaker. **Reading Skills** Use paraphrasing as a strategy for comprehension. **Writing Skills** Write fiction.

Respond and Think Critically

Reading Focus

Quick Check

1. How does the speaker in "To a Mouse" feel about overturning the mouse's winter nest?

2. Why is the speaker in "To a Louse" surprised to see the louse on "sae fine a lady"?

3. Which of the louse's characteristics does the speaker mock? Which of the mouse's characteristics does the speaker praise?

Read with a Purpose

4. In "To a Mouse" and "To a Louse," the speaker addresses two creatures that most people notice with disgust or alarm. Why and how does he come to appreciate these creatures?

Reading Skills: Paraphrasing

5. Now that you have finished reading and paraphrasing the poems, re-read your paraphrases to decide what lesson each small creature conveys to the poems' speakers. Briefly explain these lessons in a paragraph, citing information from your charts to support your opinion.

Literary Focus

Literary Analysis

6. **Evaluate** What lines from "To a Mouse" indicate the speaker's understanding of the relationship between mice and farmers?

7. **Interpret** What comparison between himself and the mouse does the speaker make in the last two stanzas of "To a Mouse"?

8. **Analyze** How would you describe Burns's tone in the beginning of "To a Louse"?

9. **Make Judgments** According to Burns, what about the louse would make its presence on a "flannen toy" (line 32) or a "bit duddie boy" (line 33) more appropriate?

10. **Evaluate** What is Burns's underlying **theme,** or insight into life, in "To a Louse"? Is his main focus the louse or the lady? Explain.

Literary Skills: Dialect

11. **Analyze** How does Burns use dialect in these poems to convey strong emotions and to create memorable images?

Literary Skills Review: Speaker

12. **Make Judgments** The **speaker** is the imaginary voice assumed by the author of a poem. What does the speaker's response to plowing over a mouse's nest reveal about him?

Writing Focus

Think as a Reader/Writer

Use It in Your Writing Choose one of the stories you listed during the QuickTalk activity. In your *Reader/Writer Notebook,* write the story, using apostrophe. Use everyday language just as Burns does to communicate important events and observations.

 What Do You Think Now

How does Burns use his imagination to learn about life from even the smallest creatures?

Preparing to Read

The Tyger

The Lamb

The Chimney Sweeper
from Songs of Innocence

The Chimney Sweeper
from Songs of Experience

A Poison Tree

What Do You Think

How can we use imagination to discover truth?

QuickWrite

What are some problems or issues you observe in today's society that really bother you? Make quick notes about them in your *Reader/Writer Notebook*.

MEET THE WRITER

William Blake
(1757–1827)

Known today as much for his unique artwork as for his poetry, William Blake lived in poverty and never sought fame.

An Accomplished Artist

Compared to Coleridge, Shelley, and Keats, Blake did not live a particularly "romantic" or "poetic" life. By many accounts, he was happily married to the same woman for much of his life, never traveled, and lived outside London for only three years (1800–1803). At age ten, Blake began his artistic training when his father, a London shopkeeper, sent him to one of the best drawing schools. Apprenticed to an engraver when he was fourteen, Blake worked steadily at his craft as an engraver and an artist throughout his long life.

During his lifetime, Blake's work received little attention, and a great deal of his poetry was never published. Often when his work was noticed, readers and viewers concluded that it (and therefore Blake) was weird, confused, or insane. What we know of Blake from his vibrant and energetic poetry and artwork is that he was a great artist in the fullest sense.

"The Author of His Own Book"

The history of Blake the poet cannot be separated from that of Blake the visual artist. Not only did he provide illustrations for most of his poems, but he also printed much of his poetry himself, using engraving <u>techniques</u> he had created. One biographer writes that "the poet and his wife did everything in making the book [*Songs of Innocence* (1789)]—writing, designing, printing, engraving—everything except manufacturing the paper; the very ink, or color rather, they did make. Never before surely was a man so literally the author of his own book."

Much of what Blake wrote in addition to his poetry is cryptic and benefits from his illuminating art. However, one characteristic of the man himself clearly shines through even his most enigmatic writing: the optimism sustained by his continuous joy in the "one continued vision" of his art.

Think About the Writer

How do you think Blake's background in the visual arts might have helped him see things with a unique perspective?

William Blake, by Thomas Phillips (1807), oil on canvas. The Granger Collection, NY

INTRODUCTION TO BLAKE'S POEMS
Innocence to Experience

William Blake first published *Songs of Innocence* in 1789. In 1794, that collection and *Songs of Experience* were issued together in one volume, whose title page promised a demonstration of "the two Contrary States of the Human Soul."

Innocence and Experience

Blake conceived the first of these states, "Innocence," as a state of genuine love and naive trust toward all humankind, accompanied by unquestioned belief in Christian doctrine. Though a firm believer in Christianity, Blake thought that its doctrines were being used by the English Church and other institutions as a form of social control to encourage among the people passive obedience and acceptance of oppression, poverty, and inequality. Recognition of this social agenda marks what Blake called the state of "Experience," a profound disillusionment with human nature and society. One entering the state of "Experience" sees cruelty and hypocrisy only too clearly but is unable to imagine a way out. In his later works, Blake expressed a third, higher state of consciousness that he called "Organized Innocence." In this state, one's sense of the divinity of humanity coexists with oppression and injustice, though one continues to recognize and actively oppose both of them.

Analyzing Visuals

Viewing and Interpreting What do the details surrounding the portrait of Blake suggest about the role of the poet?

Stained glass window of William Blake, St. Mary's Church, Battersea, London

Reading Blake

When you are reading *Songs of Innocence* and, to a lesser extent, *Songs of Experience*, it is important to remember that Blake did not intend them as simple expressions of religious faith. The poems are demonstrations of viewpoints that are necessarily limited or distorted by each narrator's or speaker's state of consciousness.

Preparing to Read

The Tyger / The Lamb

Reader/Writer
Notebook

Use your **RWN** to complete the activities for these selections.

Literary Focus

Symbol A **symbol** is something that stands for both itself and something more than itself. In literature, symbols have a literal meaning, as well as a figurative, or metaphorical, meaning, which involves feelings and experiences. As you read, look for clues to help you understand what the tiger and the lamb symbolize.

Reading Focus

Using Context Clues Sometimes you can determine the meaning of an unfamiliar word by looking for **clues** in the **context,** or the surrounding words. When poets use words symbolically, context clues can help reveal the words' shades of meaning. As you read, use context clues to uncover the meanings of Blake's symbols.

Into Action Use a concept map to locate context clues to help you understand symbols. The map below is for "The Tyger." Create your own map for "The Lamb."

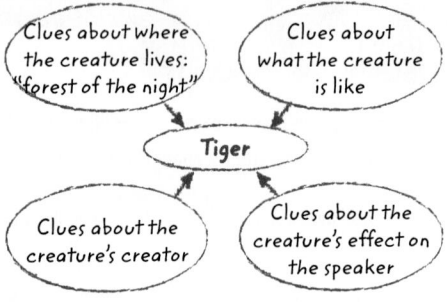

Writing Focus

Think as a Reader/Writer

Find It in Your Reading The speaker in "The Lamb" asks, "Little Lamb, who made thee?" As you read, note the speakers' rhetorical questions.

TechFocus As you read, think about what modern objects in the material world could symbolize the same things as Blake's tiger and lamb.

Vocabulary

frame (fraym) v.: shape. *Blake's love and awe of nature frame his works of art.*

aspire (uh SPYR) v.: reach upward to a goal. *His illustrated poems aspire to an understanding of human nature*

sinews (SIHN yooz) n. pl.: powerful, tough connective tissues. *Can you see the strong sinews of the tiger in Blake's illustration?*

dread (drehd) adj.: inspiring fear and awe. *The dread face of the tiger terrifies some viewers.*

bid (bihd) v.: demanded; asked. *The boy in Blake's painting of the lamb bid the gentle creature to eat from his hand.*

Language Coach

Multiple Meaning Words Many common words have more than one meaning. *Frame* can be a noun that names an underlying structure, the border around a painting, or the part of a pair of eyeglasses that holds the lenses. It can also be a verb that means "shape," "mount a picture in a frame," or "make an innocent person appear guilty." Clues in a sentence will help you figure out which meaning is being used. *Bid* can be a verb that means "command." What other meanings can this word have?

Learn It Online

Meet "The Tyger" and "The Lamb" through the introductory videos online.

go.hrw.com L12-730   **Go**

The Tyger

from Songs of Experience

by **William Blake**

Read with a Purpose
Read to discover what the tiger reveals about the source and the nature of evil.

Build Background
Blake saw the entire material world as a set of signs or symbols representing religious or mystical realities. Any one of Blake's sym-bols—the "tyger," for instance—has such a rich array of meanings that we can never expect to understand fully what such a symbol meant to him. It is possible the tiger represents a strong revolutionary energy that can enlighten and transform society: a positive but volatile force Blake believed was operating in the French Revolution. Regardless, the poem's speaker cannot comprehend such a startling energy and can only wonder whether it is demonic or godlike.

Tyger! Tyger! burning bright
In the forests of the night,
What immortal hand or eye
Could frame thy fearful symmetry?

5   In what distant deeps or skies
Burnt the fire of thine eyes?
On what wings dare he aspire?
What the hand dare seize the fire?

And what shoulder, and what art,
10 Could twist the sinews of thy heart?
And when thy heart began to beat,
What dread hand? and what dread feet?

What the hammer? what the chain?
In what furnace was thy brain?
15 What the anvil? what dread grasp
Dare its deadly terrors clasp?

When the stars threw down their spears,°
And watered heaven with their tears,
Did he smile his work to see?
20 Did he who made the Lamb make thee? **B**

Tyger! Tyger! burning bright
In the forests of the night,
What immortal hand or eye,
Dare frame thy fearful symmetry?

---

17. **stars . . . spears:** reference to the angels who fell with Satan and threw down their spears after losing the war in heaven.

A **Reading Focus** **Using Context Clues** Notice that Blake does not use the normal spelling of the word *tiger*. What other clues can you find that hint at the tiger's extraordinary nature?

B **Literary Focus** **Symbol** Think about what the lamb symbolizes, and then restate line 20 in your own words. What might the speaker be implying by this question?

Vocabulary **frame** (fraym) *v.:* shape.
aspire (uh SPYR) *v.:* reach upward to a goal.
sinews (SIHN yooz) *n. pl.:* powerful, tough connective tissues.
dread (drehd) *adj.:* inspiring fear and awe.

Above: *Songs of Innocence and of Experience: The Tyger* (ca. 1825) by William Blake. Relief etching printed in orange-brown ink and hand-colored with watercolor and gold
The Metropolitan Museum of Art, NY, Rogers Fund, 1917, 17.10.42
Right: *Songs of Innocence and Experience Plate 7: The Lamb*, (c. 1789-94), relief etching finished in pen and w/c by William Blake
Ftizwilliam Museum, University of Cambridge, U.K.

Analyzing Visuals

Viewing and Interpreting   Blake designed much of his artwork to accompany certain specific poems. What do you think is the <u>function</u> of an illustration? Is it merely background that aesthetically enhances writing, or does it play a larger role in the textual experience of reading a poem?

The Lamb

from Songs of Innocence

by **William Blake**

Read with a Purpose
Read the poem to discover what the lamb reveals about innocence and purity.

Build Background
William Blake's poetry and art reflect his fascination with the Bible and his struggle to find answers to questions that profoundly disturbed him: What is the source of evil in the world? Why does God allow the innocent to suffer? Is evil inherent or can it be transformed or transcended?

One of the *Songs of Innocence,* this poem has often been read as a statement of Christian faith. However, we know that Blake's other writings show Christ not as the "meek" and "mild" lamb (the conventional symbolic rendering of Christ) with which this innocent speaker identifies but as an active fighter against injustice. The speaker's viewpoint is thus an incomplete representation of Blake's beliefs and just one aspect of Blake's worldview.

    Little Lamb, who made thee?
    Dost thou know who made thee?
Gave thee life, and bid thee feed
By the stream and o'er the mead,°
5 Gave thee clothing of delight,
Softest clothing, wooly, bright;
Gave thee such a tender voice,
Making all the vales° rejoice?
    Little Lamb, who made thee?
10 Dost thou know who made thee?

    Little Lamb, I'll tell thee,
    Little Lamb, I'll tell thee:
He° is called by thy name,
For He calls himself a Lamb.
15 He is meek, and he is mild; **Ⓐ**
He became a little child.
I a child, and thou a lamb,
We are called by his name.
    Little Lamb, God bless thee!
20 Little Lamb, God bless thee! **Ⓑ**

---

4. **mead:** meadow.
8. **vales:** valleys.

---

13. **He:** Christ.

Ⓐ **Reading Focus** **Using Context Clues** The word *He* is defined in the footnotes. What context clues in the poem help you confirm the definition given?

Ⓑ **Literary Focus** **Symbol** Where in the second stanza does Blake make explicit the Christian symbolism of his poem?

Vocabulary **bid** (bihd) *v.*: demanded; asked.

Respond and Think Critically

Quick Check

1. What question does the speaker of "The Tyger" ask repeatedly? What answer is implied?

2. What are you told directly about the speaker of "The Lamb?" What inferences can you draw from this information?

Read with a Purpose

3. What do the tiger and the lamb tell us about the nature of good and evil?

Reading Skills: Using Context Clues

4. Review the concept maps in which you recorded context clues that help reveal the symbolic meaning of the tiger and the lamb. Write one paragraph in which you explain the symbolic meaning of the tiger, and another in which you explain the symbolic meaning of the lamb. Support your explanations with information from your concept maps.

Literary Analysis

5. Interpret The last stanza of "The Tyger" is almost identical to the first. What is the significance of the one word changed in the last stanza?

6. Evaluate Where in "The Tyger" does the speaker wonder if the tiger may have been created by God? What imagery tells us that the speaker also suspects that the tiger could be a demonic creation? List the images that suggest a human creator—like a blacksmith or a goldsmith.

7. Draw Conclusions What imagery suggests that the tiger could be a force of enlightenment? of revolutionary violence?

8. Compare and Contrast How does the second stanza of "The Lamb" respond to the questions asked in the first stanza?

9. Analyze What does the creator do for his creation in the first stanza of "The Lamb"?

10. Evaluate What differentiates the voice of the speaker in "The Tyger" from the voice of the speaker in "The Lamb"?

Literary Skills: Symbol

11. Analyze How does "The Tyger" represent people's attraction toward and repulsion from evil?

12. Infer In what ways is the lamb both a literal object and a symbol in "The Lamb"?

Literary Skills Review: Refrain

13. Interpret A **refrain** is a repeated word, phrase, line, or group of lines. Why might Blake use refrains as a technique in his poems? How do they affect each poem's meaning?

Think as a Reader/Writer

Use It in Your Writing In your *Reader/Writer Notebook,* write a paragraph in which you address a central question of "The Tyger": "Did he who made the Lamb make thee?" Include at least three thought-provoking rhetorical questions in your paragraph.

 What Do You Think Now

In a small group, discuss Blake's imaginative writing and if it is an effective way of exploring truth. How do symbols and images help us understand ideas?

Vocabulary Development

Vocabulary Check

Match the Vocabulary words with their definitions.

1. frame
2. aspire
3. sinews
4. dread
5. bid

a. inspiring fear
b. connective tissues
c. strive for
d. demand
e. form

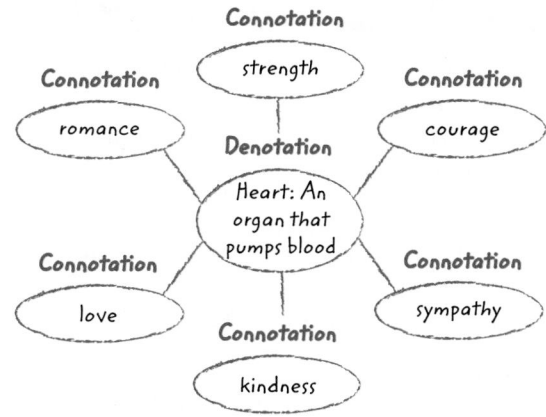

Vocabulary Skills: Denotation and Connotation

To comprehend a word fully, you must first understand its **denotation,** the literal meaning, or the dictionary definition. You must then also know a word's **connotations,** all the emotional ideas and feelings that people may ascribe to the word. For example, if you say to a friend, "Come on—have a heart!" you're not asking that friend to have an organ that pumps blood (its denotative meaning). Rather, you're asking your friend to be kind, to help you, and to show sympathy for you; you're using the word *heart* figuratively, based on its connotations of friendship, love, and kindness. Because connotations often elicit certain specific emotions, they can have powerful effects on a listener or reader. In poetry, structure often limits a poet's word choice. Every word must be denotatively and connotatively precise to convey a particular image and feeling.

Your Turn

Create a word map like the one on the right for each Vocabulary word. In the center, write the word and its denotative meaning. In the other ovals, list any connotative associations that you have for each word. Then, discuss in small groups how understanding both the denotations and connotations of these words helps you interpret Blake's poems.

Language Coach

Multiple-Meaning Words When words have more than one meaning, context clues help you decide which meaning is being used. Choose the correct meaning of *frame* in these sentences.

1. The reproduction of Blake's poem is *framed* in antique wood.
2. Our reaction is *framed* by both the words and the illustration.
3. The *frame* of "The Tyger" is four-line stanzas.
4. A thief who stole a rare book tried to get away with it by *framing* the librarian.

Academic Vocabulary

Write About...
What <u>techniques</u> does Blake use to <u>differentiate</u> between good and evil in "The Tyger" and "The Lamb"?

Learn It Online
Explore connotations online.

go.hrw.com   L12-735   **Go**

SKILLS FOCUS Literary Skills Analyze alliteration; analyze symbols. **Grammar Skills** Use consistent verb tenses. **Listening and Speaking Skills** Listen to comprehend or gain information; analyze the author's use of stylistic devices.

The Tyger / The Lamb

Grammar Link

Verb-Tense Consistency

Verbs express actions or states of being, and a verb's **tense** indicates when that action or state of being occurs. Verb tenses that vary incorrectly can be confusing and awkward:

> It is not clear when William Blake **writes** "The Lamb," but he **composed** "The Tyger" in 1793.

To correct this sentence, make the verbs all past tense:

> It is not clear when William Blake **wrote** "The Lamb," but he **composed** "The Tyger" in 1793.

Different tenses can describe events at different times:

> These poems **make** me imagine what Blake **experienced** during his life.

Writing about literature can make verb-tense consistency challenging. In general, use the **literary present tense** to discuss a literary work's subject matter:

> The speaker of the poem **expressed** ideas that Blake believed in deeply. (incorrect)
> The speaker of the poem **expresses** ideas that Blake believed in deeply. (correct)

Your Turn

Correct unnecessary verb-tense changes in the following sentences. Write *correct* if the tenses are consistent.

1. Both poems are included in collections Blake wrote in the late eighteenth century.
2. Blake illustrated the books and gives them the titles *Songs of Innocence* and *Songs of Experience*.
3. The poems Blake included are about love or life.

Writing Application Write a paragraph in which you describe from your current perspective something that happened to you in the past. Be sure to include past- and present-tense verbs and avoid unnecessary tense changes.

CHOICES

As you respond to the Choices activities, use these **Academic Vocabulary** words as appropriate: differentiate, inherent, device, technique, function.

REVIEW
Identify Sound Effects
Review the definition of *alliteration* in the Handbook of Literary and Historical Terms. Then, read "The Tyger" aloud, listening for sound effects, especially alliteration. Make a list of the consonants that Blake chooses to repeat often. With a partner, describe the sounds of these consonants and decide what effect each sound creates for the listener.

CONNECT
Digital Collage
TechFocus What objects could function as symbols similar to Blake's tiger and lamb? Create a digital collage—a collection of pictures, short video clips, and sounds—for "The Tyger" or "The Lamb" that represent the same symbolic meaning. Present your digital collage to your class, and explain the meaning that each image, video, or sound represents for you.

EXTEND
Contemporary Visionaries
Many people in Blake's day dismissed his poetry because of its unorthodox style and Blake's own eccentricities. Do you know of artists or writers today whose unusual work and personalities make it difficult for people to take them seriously? With a partner, discuss whether you think they will receive more attention from later generations.

The Chimney Sweeper *from* Songs of Innocence
The Chimney Sweeper *from* Songs of Experience

Reader/Writer
Notebook

Use your **RWN** to complete the activities for these selections.

Literary Focus

Parallelism When words, phrases, or sentences are arranged in balanced grammatical structures, they are said to be **parallel.** Poets, dramatists, preachers, and speechwriters are likely to use parallelism because the repetition it introduces enhances the rhythmic and emotional effect of their lines and makes them easier to remember. Blake's use of parallelism contributes to the childlike simplicity on the surface of his poems.

Reading Focus

Drawing Conclusions About Meaning A **conclusion** is a judgment about meaning that you make based on clues in a text. By analyzing details and literary devices within a poem, you can draw conclusions about its meaning.

Into Action Use a Venn diagram like the one below to identify parallelism within these poems. In each oval, write down words, phrases, or grammatical structures that are part of a parallel structure.

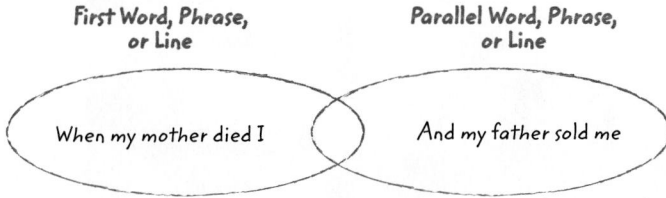

First Word, Phrase, or Line

Parallel Word, Phrase, or Line

When my mother died I

And my father sold me

> ### Language Coach
> **Definitions** The noun *woe* (woh) means "grief" or "deep sadness." The origin of the word relates to the way it sounds. Words that sound similar to *woe* are exclamations of sorrow in many languages, including Latin, Greek, German, Welsh, and Armenian. What does the common saying "woe is me!" mean?

Writing Focus

Think as a Reader/Writer

Find It in Your Reading Blake uses symbolism to create layers of meaning in his poems. As you read, take notes in your *Reader/Writer Notebook* about particular images that you think might be symbols.

Learn It Online
Use Word Watch to develop your word knowledge online.

go.hrw.com L12-737 **Go**

The Chimney Sweeper
from Songs of Innocence

by **William Blake**

Read with a Purpose
Read to discover the dreams of a child chimney sweeper.

Build Background
In this poem from *Songs of Innocence,* and in its companion poem from *Songs of Experience,* Blake speaks for the poor children of his day who were forced to do backbreaking labor. In Blake's London, buildings were heated by coal- or wood-burning fireplaces, and every building had at least one chimney that required regular cleaning. Poor children were often used to do this hazardous work because they could fit into the narrow chimney passages. Desperate for money, some poor parents sold their children to "masters" who managed—and often mistreated—crews of young sweepers. In this poem from *Songs of Innocence,* the speaker is a child who tries to cheer himself and his fellow chimney sweeper, Tom Dacre, with the thought that they will one day have endless joy in heaven.

When my mother died I was very young,
And my father sold me while yet my tongue
Could scarcely cry "'weep! 'weep! 'weep! 'weep!"°
So your chimneys I sweep, and in soot I sleep.

5   There's little Tom Dacre, who cried when his head,
That curled like a lamb's back, was shaved: so I said
"Hush, Tom! never mind it, for when your head's bare
You know that the soot cannot spoil your white hair." **Ⓐ**

And so he was quiet, and that very night,
10 As Tom was a-sleeping, he had such a sight!—
That thousands of sweepers, Dick, Joe, Ned, and Jack,
Were all of them locked up in coffins of black.

And by came an Angel who had a bright key,
And he opened the coffins and set them all free;
15 Then down a green plain leaping, laughing, they run,
And wash in a river, and shine in the Sun.

Then naked and white, all their bags left behind,
They rise upon clouds and sport in the wind;
And the Angel told Tom, if he'd be a good boy,
20 He'd have God for his father, and never want° joy.

And so Tom awoke; and we rose in the dark,
And got with our bags and our brushes to work.
Though the morning was cold, Tom was happy and warm; **Ⓑ**
So if all do their duty they need not fear harm.

3. "'weep… 'weep": the child's attempt at the chimney sweepers' cry of "Sweep! Sweep!"

20. want: lack.

Two merry chimney sweeps of St. Moritz, Switzerland

Ⓐ Literary Focus **Parallelism** What examples of parallelism can you find in the first two stanzas? What effect do they create?

Ⓑ Reading Focus **Drawing Conclusions About Meaning**
What thought keeps Tom "happy and warm," though the weather is cold and his work is hard?

(Opposite) Chimney sweeper on the roof in winter

739

The Chimney Sweeper
from Songs of Experience

by **William Blake**

Read with a Purpose
Read to discover whom the child holds responsible for his fate.

Build Background

Blake was said to be confused or insane, not only because he saw visions but also because of the way some of his poems cry out violently against social problems around him. No one should go hungry, he said, in a land as green and wealthy as England. Like Blake, and unlike the sweeper in *Songs of Innocence*, this sweeper does not accept oppression and poverty. He recognizes that the people who pray for him (his parents) are the same ones who sold him into a life of hard labor. The first three lines are spoken by an adult who comes upon the pitiful child and asks him about his parents' whereabouts. The rest of the poem is the child's bitter answer to that sad question.

A little black thing among the snow **Ⓐ**
Crying "'weep, 'weep," in notes of woe!
"Where are thy father and mother? say?"
"They are both gone up to the church to pray.

5 "Because I was happy upon the heath,
And smil'd among the winter's snow;
They clothed me in the clothes of death,
And taught me to sing the notes of woe. **Ⓑ**

"And because I am happy, and dance and sing,
10 They think they have done me no injury,
And are gone to praise God and his Priest and King,
Who make up a heaven of our misery." **Ⓒ**

Ⓐ Reading Focus Drawing Conclusions About Meaning What details about the child does Blake give in the poem's first line? What conclusion can you draw about this child's life from these details?

Ⓑ Literary Focus Parallelism What constructions in this stanza are parallel? What does the parallelism accomplish?

Ⓒ Reading Focus Drawing Conclusions About Meaning Whom does the chimney sweeper blame for his misery?

Chimney Sweep's trade sign, early nineteenth century.
Cheltenham Art Gallery & Museums, Gloucestershire

Applying Your Skills

SKILLS FOCUS Literary Skills Analyze parallelism; analyze dramatic irony. **Reading Skills** Draw conclusions about meaning. **Writing Skills** Write descriptive essays.

The Chimney Sweeper *from* Songs of Innocence
The Chimney Sweeper *from* Songs of Experience

Respond and Think Critically

Reading Focus

Quick Check

1. In the first poem, how does the angel reassure Tom Dacre in his dream?

2. How does Tom Dacre's dream contrast with the actual conditions of his daily life?

3. In the second poem, how does the young chimney sweeper answer the adult's question? What do you think his "clothes of death" are?

4. Why don't the parents of the chimney sweeper in *Songs of Experience* see the harm they have done to their child?

Read with a Purpose

5. What contributes to the distinctly different attitudes expressed in the poems?

Reading Skills: Drawing Conclusions About Meaning

6. Review the Venn diagrams you worked on as you read. In the overlapping section of each diagram, draw a conclusion about the purpose each example of parallelism serves. After you have completed each diagram, review the overlapping sections to see what your conclusions can tell you about the overall meaning of each poem as a whole.

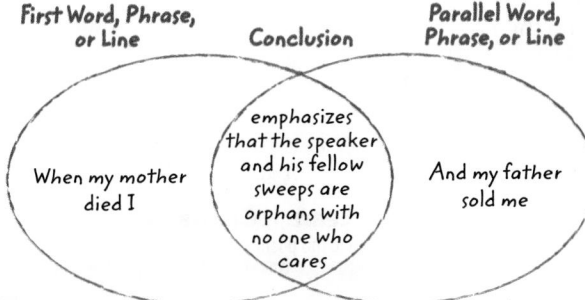

First Word, Phrase, or Line — Conclusion — Parallel Word, Phrase, or Line

When my mother died I

emphasizes that the speaker and his fellow sweeps are orphans with no one who cares

And my father sold me

Literary Focus

Literary Analysis

7. **Interpret** In the first poem, what might the "coffins of black" symbolize besides death?

8. **Evaluate** In each poem, what is the emotional effect of the child's mispronunciation of the chimney sweeper's cry?

9. **Extend** Do people today sometimes take the attitude expressed by the speaker of the first poem: If you are good, if you do your duty, you need not fear harm? Expand on your response.

Literary Skills: Parallelism

10. **Analyze** How does Blake's use of parallelism in both poems enhance their emotional effect?

Literary Skills Review: Dramatic Irony

11. **Infer** When readers understand or know something that a speaker in a literary work does not, **dramatic irony** occurs. What examples of dramatic irony can you find the first poem?

Writing Focus

Think As a Reader/Writer

Use It in Your Writing Write a short essay describing a modern-day injustice or exploitative form of employment. Include at least one symbol in your essay, and use parallelism to enhance the emotional impact of your description.

What Do You Think Now

How does Blake use his imagination to disclose the truth about child chimney sweepers to his readers?

A Poison Tree *from* Songs of Experience

Reader/Writer
Notebook

Use your **RWN** to complete the activities for this selection.

Literary Focus

Theme The **theme** of a work of literature is its central idea or main insight about human nature or human life. The theme of a work is not the same as its **subject,** or topic, but is the writer's point of view on the subject. In the case of "A Poison Tree," Blake's subject is anger, and his theme is his insight into the <u>function</u> of anger. In poetry the theme is rarely stated directly. More often, it is implied by all the details, images, and symbols of the poem and must be deciphered by the reader.

Into Action In the first column of a chart like the one below, write down the subject of the poem. In the second column, note details, images, and symbols that strike you as important.

Subject of the Poem	Details, Images, and Symbols
This poem is about . . .	The speaker waters his wrath as if it is a tree.

Language Coach

Pronunciation Reading poetry aloud can help you understand its meaning, but it is important to pronounce words correctly. Remember that some English words include silent letters, such as the w in *wrath* (meaning "anger"). Vowel combinations can have unpredictable pronunciations. Read these words aloud:

> *foe* (foh): enemy
>
> *veiled* (vayld): covered; hid

How do the following words follow similar pronunciation patterns: *wring, woe, feign?*

Writing Focus

Think as a Reader/Writer

Find It in Your Reading As you read "A Poison Tree," take note of how Blake uses **repetition.** In stanza 1, for example, the speaker repeats the word *I* four times, and begins each of the four lines with either *I was* or *I told.* This repetition contributes to the idea of growing, obsessive anger. While reading, record examples of Blake's use of repetition in your *Reader/Writer Notebook.* Think about how the repetition affects both the theme and the mood of the poem.

Learn It Online
Listen to this poem online.

go.hrw.com   L12-742   **Go**

A Poison Tree
from Songs of Experience

by **William Blake**

Read with a Purpose
Read to discover two outcomes of anger.

Build Background
This poem presents another of the "contrary states of human nature" that so intrigued Blake and appeared throughout his *Songs of Inno-* *cence* and *Songs of Experience*. Like the speaker in "The Tyger," the speaker in "A Poison Tree" is intrigued by the nature of evil.

During his informal education, Blake was immersed in the Biblical stories of good and evil, violence and forgiveness. In this poem, he describes an urge toward anger that many people confront at some time in their lives.

I was angry with my friend:
I told my wrath, my wrath did end.
I was angry with my foe:
I told it not, my wrath did grow. **A**

5 And I watered it in fears,
Night and morning with my tears;
And I sunned it with smiles,
And with soft deceitful wiles.°

And it grew both day and night,
10 Till it bore an apple bright;
And my foe beheld it shine,
And he knew that it was mine,

And into my garden stole
When the night had veiled the pole: **B**
15 In the morning glad I see
My foe outstretchd beneath the tree.

8. wiles: cunning tricks

A Literary Focus **Theme** How would you restate the poem's comment on the effects of anger?

B Literary Focus **Theme** What do the speaker and the foe have in common? How does what they share relate to the poem's theme?

SKILLS FOCUS **Literary Skills** Analyze theme; analyze symbols. **Writing Skills** Employ literary devices for effective writing.

A Poison Tree *from* Songs of Experience

Respond and Think Critically

Reading Focus

Quick Check

1. What two ways of handling anger are mentioned in the poem? In what ways do these two approaches differ?

2. Why does the speaker's wrath against his foe increase?

3. What happens to the speaker's foe in the last stanza? Of whom or what is he a victim?

Read with a Purpose

4. What causes the two different outcomes of anger?

Literary Focus

Literary Analysis

5. **Analyze** The poem differentiates between ways of handling anger. What imagery describes the second way?

6. **Make Judgments** How is the speaker of the poem a victim? Do you see the speaker as good or evil, or both? Give examples from the poem.

7. **Interpret** How does Blake compare the speaker's anger to a tree?

8. **Analyze** What sort of allusion is Blake making when in the third stanza he refers to the forbidden fruit?

9. **Evaluate** Blake's use of parallelism and simple diction gives "A Poison Tree" an air of straightforward, even childlike, simplicity. Do you think this tone supports or diminishes the points being made about anger and its consequences? Explain.

Literary Skills: Theme

10. **Draw Conclusions** Look at the chart you made showing the poem's subject, details, images, and symbols. What do they tell you about the poem's theme? Add a third column to your chart, in which you write a brief sentence stating the theme of the poem.

Subject of the Poem	Details, Images, and Symbols	Theme
This poem is about . . .	The speaker waters his wrath as if it is a tree.	The poem's theme is . . .

Literary Skills Review: Symbol

11. **Analyze** A symbol is a person, place, thing, or event that stands for both itself and something beyond itself. What might the garden, tree, and apple symbolize in "A Poison Tree"? As you answer, remember that Blake relied on Biblical allusion in much of his art.

Writing Focus

Think as a Reader/Writer

Use It in Your Writing Review your notes about repetition in Blake's poem. Now, write two paragraphs about an emotion—whether anger, fear, frustration, joy, or a different emotion—that has the potential to keep growing. Use repetition to convey the theme and mood of your description.

 What Do You Think Now

How does Blake's imaginative description of anger help you understand this powerful emotion?

Reading Focus

Lines Composed a Few Miles Above Tintern Abbey

Recognizing Patterns of Organization by Kylene Beers

From writing both academic and personal essays, you know that logical organization is essential to clear writing. Like essayists, poets use **patterns of organization** as they compose their verse. As the backbone of a well-constructed poem, the organizational structure supports the poem's meaning. Recognizing and understanding the structure help us comprehend and enjoy a poem.

The most common pattern of organization in poetry is the **stanza,** a group of consecutive lines that form a single unit. The stanzaic organizational pattern is usually repeated throughout the poem. The **rhyme scheme,** the pattern of rhymed lines, and **meter,** the generally regular pattern of stressed and unstressed syllables, are also repeated within the poem. These predictable organizational patterns help the poet communicate his or her ideas, as well as enable the reader to more easily understand the message of the poem.

Romantic poet William Blake uses a four-line stanza in "The Tyger." The *aabb* rhyme scheme, the use of lines that usually end on a stressed syllable, and the **trochaic meter** (a pattern of alternating stressed and unstressed syllables) are repeated throughout the six stanzas. Read this four-line stanza aloud to hear the repeated rhyme scheme and meter.

> Tyger! Tyger! burning bright
> In the forests of the night,
> What immortal hand or eye
> Could frame thy fearful symmetry?

Poets often use other recurring organizational features as Blake does with the rhetorical question in each stanza of "The Tyger."

Another organizational pattern Romantic poets frequently employ is the **sonnet.** William Wordsworth uses the fourteen-line structure of the **Petrarchan** **sonnet** to make observations or pose problems in the **octave,** the first eight lines, and then to respond to them or pose a solution in the **sestet,** the last six lines.

Notice how Wordsworth applies this organization in "The World Is Too Much with Us" (page 764). After asserting "the world is too much with us," the speaker uses the octave's remaining lines to list the ways humans have disregarded nature's bounty, concluding "we are out of tune" (line 8). In the sonnet's sestet, the speaker then states that he'd rather be "a Pagan suckled in a creed outworn" (line 10). The predictable organization helps you recognize the shift from problem to solution, increasing your comprehension and appreciation of the poem.

Your Turn

Read the following lines from Wordsworth's sonnet, "Composed upon Westminster Bridge" to see the organizational pattern of the **Petrarchan sonnet.** Wordsworth begins by admiring the sleeping London in "the beauty of the morning." He continues:

> Open unto the fields, and to the sky;
> All bright and glittering in the smokeless air.
> Never did sun more beautifully steep
> In his first splendor, valley, rock, or hill.
> (lines 7–10)

How does Wordsworth use the structure of the sonnet and its shift marked between lines 8 and 9 to help communicate the poem's meaning?

Preparing to Read

Lines Composed a Few Miles Above Tintern Abbey

from Ode: Intimations of Immortality

Composed upon Westminster Bridge

The World Is Too Much with Us

What Do You Think? How can we use imagination to discover truth?

QuickWrite

In your *Reader/Writer Notebook*, write about your favorite experience with nature and how it affected your imagination.

William Wordsworth
(1770–1850)

A lover of all natural forms, William Wordsworth believed that nature helped him "see into the life of things."

Finding His Calling

Orphaned as a child, Wordsworth was sent by his uncles to attend school in a village in England's beautiful Lake District. His experiences in this setting fostered his love for nature and his belief in its inherent beneficent properties. During a visit to France in 1790, Wordsworth was seized by the early idealism of the French Revolution and returned to the country one year later following his graduation from Cambridge. As an educated man with no title, wealth, or head for business, Wordsworth had little interest in the few careers open to him, most notably, that of the Church. Thus began a decade of painful growth, as he searched for and eventually found his vocation as a poet.

The Power of Friendship

After Wordsworth returned from France in 1792, war broke out between France and England. Wordsworth was sickened by the war and gradually became disillusioned about his hopes for political and social change. In late 1793, he embarked on a walking tour of Europe, which, combined with his waning aspirations to perfect society, drove him to poetry.

In 1795, Wordsworth met poet Samuel Taylor Coleridge, and both men quickly became powerful galvanizing forces on each other's work. By June 1797, Wordsworth had produced a good deal of new poetry, none yet published, including a play and some stark narratives. *Lyrical Ballads* (1798) was the culmination of Wordsworth and Coleridge's friendship and mutual influence. The collection became one of the most important works of the Romantic era. In the Preface to *Lyrical Ballads*, Wordsworth wrote that poetry is the "spontaneous overflow of powerful feelings"; but he added that poems of value are produced only by one who has "thought long and deeply." The marriage of feeling and thought, as Coleridge recognized, made Wordsworth "the best poet of the age."

Think About the Writer What might have led Wordsworth to believe that both thought and feelings are necessary for good poetry?

William Wordsworth (1842), by Benjamin Robert Haydon, oil on canvas. National Portrait Gallery, London; Background: Tintern Abbey.

Lines Composed a Few Miles Above Tintern Abbey

Reader/Writer Notebook

Use your **RWN** to complete the activities for this selection.

Literary Focus

Blank Verse With the exception of free verse, **blank verse** (unrhymed iambic pentameter) is the poetic form that sounds most like natural speech. In blank verse, each line of poetry contains five **iambs,** units of meter consisting of an unstressed syllable followed by a stressed syllable. A poet may vary this pattern slightly to draw attention to an idea or image in the text. As you read, think about how the flowing blank verse of "Tintern Abbey" contributes to its conversational tone.

Literary Perspectives Apply the literary perspective described on page 749 as you read this poem.

Reading Focus

Analyzing Patterns of Organization Poets use various <u>techniques</u> to organize their verse. Common **organizational patterns** in poetry include the **stanza,** a group of consecutive lines that form a unit; **meter,** a generally regular pattern of stressed and unstressed syllables; and **rhyme.** In this poem, Wordsworth uses blank verse and stanzas to organize his ideas.

Into Action Look for punctuation and indentions that signal the end of one stanza and the beginning of another. Make notes in a chart like the one below on how Wordsworth uses stanzas to organize his ideas.

Stanza	Organization
1	description of landscape features; imagery of cottage grounds, pastoral farms, wreaths of smoke
2	
3	

Writing Focus

Think as a Reader/Writer

Find It in Your Reading As you read "Tintern Abbey," note how Wordsworth uses long, flowing sentences that often start and stop in the middle of lines. Consider how his speaker uses first person and seems to address a listener. In your *Reader/Writer Notebook*, write how these <u>techniques</u> impart a conversational **tone,** as if the speaker is talking while walking.

Vocabulary

pastoral (PAS tuhr uhl) *adj.:* of simple or peaceful rural life. *The visit to the Wye Valley offered pastoral views of cottages and farms.*

sublime (suh BLYM) *adj.:* awe inspiring due to majesty or nobility. *He saw a sublime vision when he journeyed to the beautiful Wye Valley.*

corporeal (kawr PAWR ee uhl) *adj.:* of the body. *Although our corporeal existence will someday end, Wordsworth believed that we will continue to exist in spirit.*

recompense (REHK uhm pehns) *n.:* payment or compensation in return for something lost. *The wisdom of experience is ample recompense for the loss of the pleasures of youth.*

impels (ihm PEHLZ) *v.:* forces; causes to move. *While visiting the Wye Valley, the speaker feels a presence that impels all things.*

zeal (zeel) *n.:* eager enthusiasm. *They will remember with zeal the happy experience that they shared together.*

Language Coach

Suffixes The suffix *—al* is often found at the end of adjectives. It can mean "of" or "relating to." Something that is *pastoral* relates to country life. Something that is *corporeal* relates to the body. To what do you think something that is *nocturnal* relates?

Learn It Online

Get to know Wordsworth through the Writers' Lives site:

| go.hrw.com | L12-747 | Go |

Lines Composed a Few Miles Above Tintern Abbey

On Revisiting the Banks of the Wye During a Tour. July 13, 1798

by **William Wordsworth**

Read with a Purpose
Read to discover the benefits a city dweller finds in returning to nature.

Build Background
"Tintern Abbey" is one of the most important short lyric works in English literature. A major step in Wordsworth's writing and a definitive statement of Romantic ideals, it has inspired and guided many poets. Wordsworth wrote this landmark poem with astonishing ease during a 1798 walking tour in Wales. Soon after leaving the Wye River Valley, he composed "Tintern Abbey" in his head as he walked, finishing it, he claims, as he "was entering Bristol in the evening after a ramble of four or five days." Only then did he write it down, changing nothing.

"Tintern Abbey" demonstrates one of the most important lessons Wordsworth had learned from Coleridge: the use of a flowing blank verse and the easy maneuvering of the meditative poem.

Five years have past; five summers, with the length
Of five long winters! and again I hear   **Ⓐ**
These waters, rolling from their mountain springs
With a soft inland murmur.—Once again
5 Do I behold these steep and lofty cliffs,
That on a wild secluded scene impress
Thoughts of more deep seclusion; and connect
The landscape with the quiet of the sky.
The day is come when I again repose
10 Here, under this dark sycamore, and view
These plots of cottage ground, these orchard tufts,
Which at this season, with their unripe fruits,
Are clad in one green hue, and lose themselves
'Mid groves and copses.° Once again I see
15 These hedgerows,° hardly hedgerows, little lines

1–22. *The speaker describes a beloved place in nature to which he has returned after five years.*

[?] *Look for the verbs* hear, *behold,* view, *and* see. *What does the speaker hear? What does he see?*

14. copses: areas densely covered with shrubs and small trees.
15. hedgerows: rows of bushes, shrubs, and small trees that serve as fences.

Ⓐ **Literary Focus** **Blank Verse** Wordsworth varies the meter of his iambic pentameter at the start of the poem. How does the meter of the first two lines vary from traditional iambic pentameter, in which an unstressed syllable is immediately followed by a stressed syllable? Why do you think Wordsworth begins the poem this way?

Of sportive wood run wild: these pastoral farms,
Green to the very door; and wreaths of smoke
Sent up, in silence, from among the trees!
With some uncertain notice, as might seem
20 Of vagrant dwellers in the houseless woods,
Or of some Hermit's cave, where by his fire
The Hermit sits alone.

               These beauteous forms, **B**
Through a long absence, have not been to me
As is a landscape to a blind man's eye:
25 But oft, in lonely rooms, and 'mid the din
Of towns and cities, I have owed to them
In hours of weariness, sensations sweet,
Felt in the blood, and felt along the heart;
And passing even into my purer mind,
30 With tranquil restoration:—feelings too
Of unremembered pleasure: such, perhaps,
As have no slight or trivial influence
On that best portion of a good man's life,
His little, nameless, unremembered acts
35 Of kindness and of love. Nor less, I trust,
To them I may have owed another gift,
Of aspect more sublime; that blessed mood,
In which the burden of the mystery,
In which the heavy and the weary weight
40 Of all this unintelligible world,
Is lightened:—that serene and blessed mood,
In which the affections° gently lead us on,—
Until, the breath of this corporeal frame
And even the motion of our human blood
45 Almost suspended, we are laid asleep
In body, and become a living soul:
While with an eye made quiet by the power
Of harmony, and the deep power of joy,
We see into the life of things.

Tintern Abbey.

? **23–41.** *According to the speaker, how have memories of this beloved landscape affected him?*

42. affections: feelings.

? **49.** *What visual clue signals that a new stanza is beginning here? How does the speaker's focus or emphasis change in the new stanza?*

Literary Perspectives

Analyzing Philosophical Context Philosophical context refers to an author's underlying assumptions regarding larger questions about life and its meaning. An author's philosophy influences his or her writing in various ways, such as the form in which the text is written and the overarching themes or messages the text conveys. In this poem, the speaker retreats to nature to escape the trials of urban life. While reflecting on the landscape, he considers how he has changed since his boyhood.

As you read, be sure to notice the questions in the text, which will guide you in using this perspective.

B **Reading Focus** **Analyzing Patterns of Organization** Why does Wordsworth begin the second stanza in the middle of line 22?

Vocabulary **pastoral** (PAS tuhr uhl) *adj.:* of simple or peaceful rural life.
sublime (suh BLYM) *adj.:* awe inspiring due to nobility.
corporeal (kawr PAWR ee uhl) *adj.:* of the body.

If this

50 Be but a vain belief, yet, oh! how oft—
In darkness and amid the many shapes
Of joyless daylight; when the fretful stir
Unprofitable, and the fever of the world,
Have hung upon the beatings of my heart—
55 How oft, in spirit, have I turned to thee,
O sylvan° Wye! thou wanderer through the woods,
How often has my spirit turned to thee! **C**
    And now, with gleams of half-extinguished thought,
With many recognitions dim and faint,
60 And somewhat of a sad perplexity,
The picture of the mind° revives again:

56. sylvan: associated with the forest or woodlands.

61. picture of the mind: primarily the picture in the mind, but also the picture the individual mind has of itself.

C **Reading Focus** **Analyzing Patterns of Organization** In meditative lyrical poetry, stanzas do not have to be fixed in length. Why do you think Wordsworth made this stanza shorter than the others? How does the speaker's focus or emphasis change in this stanza?

Tintern Abbey in the Wye Valley.

Analyzing Visuals

Viewing and Interpreting What can you infer about Wordsworth's ideas of nature from this image? How might the elements of this environment represent "all in all" to him? What does it represent to you?

While here I stand, not only with the sense
Of present pleasure, but with pleasing thoughts
That in this moment there is life and food
65 For future years. And so I dare to hope,
Though changed, no doubt, from what I was when first
I came among these hills; when like a roe°
I bounded o'er the mountains, by the sides
Of the deep rivers, and the lonely streams,
70 Wherever nature led: more like a man
Flying from something that he dreads, than one
Who sought the thing he loved. For nature then
(The coarser pleasures of my boyish days,
And their glad animal movements all gone by)
75 To me was all in all.—I cannot paint
What then I was. The sounding cataract°
Haunted me like a passion: the tall rock,
The mountain, and the deep and gloomy wood,
Their colors and their forms, were then to me
80 An appetite; a feeling and a love,
That had no need of a remoter charm,°
By thought supplied, nor any interest
Unborrowed from the eye.—That time is past,
And all its aching joys are now no more,
85 And all its dizzy raptures. Not for this
Faint° I, nor mourn nor murmur; other gifts
Have followed; for such loss, I would believe,
Abundant recompense. For I have learned
To look on nature, not as in the hour
90 Of thoughtless youth; but hearing oftentimes
The still, sad music of humanity,
Nor harsh nor grating, though of ample power
To chasten and subdue. And I have felt
A presence that disturbs me with the joy
95 Of elevated thoughts; a sense sublime
Of something far more deeply interfused,
Whose dwelling is the light of setting suns,
And the round ocean and the living air,
And the blue sky, and in the mind of man:
100 A motion and a spirit, that impels
All thinking things, all objects of all thought,
And rolls through all things. Therefore am I still
A lover of the meadows and the woods,

67. roe: deer.

65–85. *With a hint of nostalgia, the speaker remembers the exhilarating times he spent in nature as a youth.*

? *How would you describe the speaker's relationship to nature when he was a boy?*

76. cataract: waterfall.

81. remoter charm: appeal other than the scene itself.

86. faint: become weak; lose heart.

? **93–102.** *Re-read these lines. In your own words, what is the "presence" (line 94) that the speaker describes?*

Vocabulary **recompense** (REHK uhm pehns) *n.:* payment or compensation in return for something lost.
impels (ihm PEHLZ) *v.:* forces; causes to move.

And mountains; and of all that we behold
105 From this green earth; of all the mighty world
Of eye, and ear, —both what they half create,
And what perceive; well pleased to recognize
In nature and the language of the sense
The anchor of my purest thoughts, the nurse,
110 The guide, the guardian of my heart, and soul
Of all my moral being.   **D**
                           Nor perchance,
If I were not thus taught, should I the more
Suffer my genial spirits° to decay:
For thou art with me here upon the banks
115 Of this fair river; thou my dearest Friend,°
My dear, dear Friend; and in thy voice I catch
The language of my former heart, and read
My former pleasures in the shooting lights
Of thy wild eyes. Oh! yet a little while
120 May I behold in thee what I was once,
My dear, dear Sister! and this prayer I make,
Knowing that Nature never did betray
The heart that loved her; 'tis her privilege,   **E**
Through all the years of this our life, to lead
125 From joy to joy: for she can so inform
The mind that is within us, so impress
With quietness and beauty, and so feed
With lofty thoughts, that neither evil tongues,
Rash judgments, nor the sneers of selfish men,
130 Nor greetings where no kindness is, nor all
The dreary intercourse° of daily life,
Shall e'er prevail against us, or disturb
Our cheerful faith, that all which we behold
Is full of blessings. Therefore let the moon   **F**
135 Shine on thee in thy solitary walk;
And let the misty mountain winds be free
To blow against thee: and, in after years,
When these wild ecstasies shall be matured
Into a sober pleasure; when thy mind

? **111–115.** *What shift takes place in this final stanza?*

113. suffer my genial spirits: allow my creative powers.

115. my dearest Friend: Wordsworth's sister, Dorothy.

? **116–134.** *What makes these lines conversational?*

? **121–159.** *What prayer does the speaker make in these concluding lines? For whom is the prayer? Paraphrase the speaker's thoughts.*

131. intercourse: dealings; social contacts.

D **Literary Perspectives** Philosophical Context In lines 93–111, the speaker finds new meanings in his surroundings. What types of philosophical, spiritual, or religious meaning do you see in his words?

E **Literary Perspectives** Philosophical Context What might the speaker mean by "Nature never did betray / The heart that loved her" (lines 122–123)?

F **Literary Focus** Blank Verse Read lines 116–134 aloud, and note the rhythm of the words. How would you describe the speaker's tone here?

The Wye Valley

Some critics have faulted Wordsworth for painting an idyllic picture of the Wye Valley and effectively glossing over its poverty. Kenneth R. Johnson in *The Hidden Wordsworth* explains that the smoke Wordsworth saw rising through the trees was a product of the area's iron industry, which burned trees to produce charcoal for the forges. Wordsworth's suggestion that smoke "might seem" to come from "vagrant dwellers in the houseless woods" touches with extreme delicacy on a fact known to everyone who visited the abbey: that vagabonds made their living by begging from tourists. Today, the British government has designated the Wye Valley a Site of Special Scientific Interest, and the region is vigilantly protected from pollution.

Ask Yourself

Why might Wordsworth have omitted descriptions of poverty from his poem? Should knowledge about the iron industry in the Wye Valley and the beggars at the abbey change the way the poem is understood? and enjoyed? Explain.

The River Wye viewed West from Monsal Head and set in limestone dales, Bridge Peak District

140   Shall be a mansion for all lovely forms,
       Thy memory be as a dwelling place
       For all sweet sounds and harmonies; oh! then,
       If solitude, or fear, or pain, or grief,
       Should be thy portion, with what healing thoughts
145   Of tender joy wilt thou remember me,
       And these my exhortations! Nor, perchance—
       If I should be where I no more can hear
       Thy voice, nor catch from thy wild eyes these gleams
       Of past existence—wilt thou then forget
150   That on the banks of this delightful stream
       We stood together; and that I, so long
       A worshipper of Nature, hither came
       Unwearied in that service: rather say
       With warmer love—oh! with far deeper zeal
155   Of holier love. Nor wilt thou then forget,
       That after many wanderings, many years
       Of absence, these steep woods and lofty cliffs,
       And this green pastoral landscape, were to me
       More dear, both for themselves and for thy sake!

Vocabulary **zeal** (zeel) *n.*: eager enthusiasm.

Applying Your Skills

Lines Composed a Few Miles Above Tintern Abbey

Respond and Think Critically

Reading Focus

Quick Check

1. What has the speaker lost since he first "came among these hills" (line 67)?

2. What does the speaker see in his sister that makes him more aware of what he "was once" (lines 120–121)?

Read with a Purpose

3. What benefits does the speaker derive from returning to nature? How does he come to recognize these benefits?

Reading Skills: Analyzing Patterns of Organization

4. Review your chart. How does Wordsworth use the stanzas to organize his ideas? How does the structure of the stanzas contribute to the conversational quality of the poem?

Literary Focus

Literary Analysis

5. **Interpret** What "gifts" (line 86) and "abundant recompense" (line 88) does the speaker believe he has received for his "loss" (line 87)?

6. **Draw Conclusions** What does the speaker mean when he says, in line 91, that he has heard "the still, sad music of humanity"?

7. **Evaluate** In lines 109–110, the speaker calls nature "the nurse, / The guide, the guardian of my heart, and soul / Of all my moral being." How can nature heal and teach?

8. **Analyze** What role does the speaker's sister play in the poem? How does the speaker regard her involvement?

9. **Extend** Summarize and comment on the speaker's conclusion (beginning with line 102). Have you had to face losing part of your past? How did you handle the loss?

10. **Literary Perspectives** As you read, you noted Wordsworth's philosophy about nature. What assumptions about nature does he express in this poem? Support your answer with examples.

Literary Skills: Blank Verse

11. **Analyze** Find two examples from the poem that sound especially conversational in tone. How does Wordsworth's use of blank verse enhance the conversational quality of the poem?

Literary Skills Review: Theme

12. **Evaluate** The central idea or insight about human experience revealed in a work of literature is called **theme.** What is this poem's theme? What do the text's structure, word choice, or imagery reveal about the theme?

Writing Focus

Think As a Reader/Writer

Use It in Your Writing In "Tintern Abbey," Wordsworth writes a deeply personal meditation in a form he and Coleridge called the "conversation poem." As you read, you noted some techniques Wordsworth uses to create a conversational tone. Using a similar conversational tone, write a poem or a brief reflective composition about a subject of your choice.

What Do **You Think Now** How can experiences with nature help us think creatively about "the dreary intercourse of daily life"?

Vocabulary Development

✓ Vocabulary Check

Match the Vocabulary words with their definitions.

1. corporeal		**a.** forces	
2. zeal		**b.** enthusiasm	
3. impels		**c.** bodily	
4. recompense		**d.** compensation	
5. pastoral		**e.** majestic	
6. sublime		**f.** peaceful	

Vocabulary Skills: Etymology

Learning about **etymology,** or word origins, can be an excellent tool for understanding meaning, usage, and related words. The chart below shows the etymology of the Vocabulary words from "Tintern Abbey."

English Word	Word Origin	Original Meaning
corporeal	Latin *corporeus*	belonging to the body
impels	Latin *impellere*	*in–,* on + *pellere,* to push
pastoral	Latin *pastoralis* < *pastor*	shepherd
recompense	Latin *recompensare*	*re–,* back + *compensare,* to balance out
sublime	Latin *sublimus*	uplifted; high; lofty
zeal	Latin *zelus* < Greek *zēlos*	ardor; jealousy

Your Turn

Match the Vocabulary words with words that have similar origins. Then, write sentences that explain the similarities and differences between the two words in each pair. Consult the chart to the left and a dictionary for help.

1. corporeal		**a.** pastor	
2. zeal		**b.** pension	
3. impels		**c.** corpse	
4. recompense		**d.** sublimation	
5. pastoral		**e.** compel	
6. sublime		**f.** zealot	

Language Coach

Suffixes The suffix *–al,* which can mean "of" or "relating to," is often found at the end of adjectives. The suffix can be added to words that stand alone as nouns *(convention, conventional)* or to roots that cannot stand alone *(corporeal).* Tell the meaning of each word in italics. Then, answer the questions.

1. How might *corporeal* beauty be both an advantage and a disadvantage?

2. Do poets give too much emphasis to *spiritual* concerns?

3. Does Wordsworth seem to agree with *conventional* ideas of youth and old age?

4. How can a poem produce two responses, one *emotional* and the other intellectual?

Academic Vocabulary

Write About . . .

How does Wordsworth <u>differentiate</u> childhood from adulthood? Why does he say childhood <u>functions</u> as a state of heightened awareness?

Lines Composed a Few Miles Above Tintern Abbey

Grammar Link

Appositives

An **appositive** is a noun or pronoun placed beside another noun or pronoun to identify or describe it. An appositive with modifiers is an **appositive phrase.**

> William Wordsworth, **poet,** found his calling during the 1790s.
> His poems, **some of the most influential of his time,** are still read today.

A **nonessential** or **nonrestrictive appositive** is not essential to a sentence's meaning. These appositives are set off by commas to show that they interrupt sentences that would still be clear without them.

> He collaborated with Samuel Taylor Coleridge.
> He collaborated with Samuel Taylor Coleridge, **another founder of English Romanticism.**

An **essential** or **restrictive appositive,** which is not set off by commas, makes the noun or pronoun it describes more specific. Without the appositive, the sentence loses essential information or meaning.

> The collection appeared in 1798.
> The collection *Lyrical Ballads* appeared in 1798.

Your Turn

Rewrite the sentences by adding the italicized words as appositives. Use commas for nonessential appositives.

1. The speaker responds to a landscape he has visited before. *(a spot on the Wye River)*

2. The place stirs deep memories. *(a beautiful woodland)*

3. We are studying the works of the romantic poet. *(William Wordsworth)*

Writing Application Write a paragraph about a friend who has had a great positive influence on you. Use appositive phrases appropriately in your description.

CHOICES

As you respond to the Choices, use these **Academic Vocabulary** words as appropriate: differentiate, inherent, device, technique, function.

REVIEW

Determine the Style of the Poem

The style of Romantic literature differentiates it from many earlier literary works. From what you have read of British literature, do you think "Tintern Abbey" closely resembles the poetry that preceded it, or is it innovative, representing an overt break in tradition? In a small group, hold a panel discussion, with students debating both sides of the issue.

CONNECT

Share an Experience

Timed └**Writing** Write a short essay in which you describe a place that evokes strong memories or holds emotional meaning for you. Describe the place with specific details, and explain why the location has special significance for you.

EXTEND

Listen to Music

The preeminent German composer Ludwig van Beethoven (1770–1827) was a leading musical figure in the transition between the Classical and Romantic periods. His Symphony No. 6 in F, the *Pastoral Symphony,* is one of the great program works in music history. An ode to nature, the cheerful, melodic first movement is labeled "The Awakening of Joyful Feelings upon Arrival in the Country." Listen to this movement, and discuss how it captures the mood of the title. Then, compose a journal entry, similar to what Wordsworth might have written, commenting on Beethoven's musical homage to nature and nature's inherent effect on the human mind and emotions.

Preparing to Read

from Ode: Intimations of Immortality

Reader/Writer Notebook

Use your **RWN** to complete the activities for this selection.

Literary Focus

Meter and Rhyme A poem's regular pattern of stressed and unstressed syllables is called its **meter.** Finding the meter, which creates the poem's rhythm, requires identifying patterns of stressed and unstressed syllables. **Rhyme** is the repetition of accented vowel sounds and all sounds following them in words close together in a poem; the most common type of rhyme, **end rhyme,** occurs at the ends of lines. **Rhyme scheme** describes a poem's overall pattern of rhyme. In "Ode," Wordsworth uses a variable meter of iambic lines of different lengths and a variable rhyme scheme.

Reading Focus

Annotating a Poem When you **annotate** a poem, you add explanatory notes—definitions, interpretations, explanations, questions, or even personal reflections—to help you analyze and feel engaged by the text.

Into Action Annotate Wordsworth's "Ode" line by line in your *Reader/Writer Notebook.* Following the example below, indicate each type of note you make and be sure to include notes on meter and rhyme.

Stanza 1	Annotations
lines 1–4	**interpretation:** rhyme scheme = abab
line 2	**explanation:** paraphrase = beauty found in common sights
lines 4–5	**definition:** "apparelled" = clothed; "celestial," "glory" suggest heaven
line 6	**reflection:** "It is not now as it hath been" = change of opinion. What happened? "Yore" brings contrast between past and present.

Writing Focus

Think as a Reader/Writer

Find It in Your Reading The use of language to evoke a concrete sensation of a person, thing, place, or experience is called **imagery.** As you read, take notes in your *Reader/Writer Notebook* on the words and phrases Wordsworth uses to create images that represent <u>inherent</u> changes that come with adulthood.

Vocabulary

piety (PY uh tee) *n.:* devotion to religion; holiness. *Wordsworth believed that children show piety through their simple acts of innocence and kindness.*

celestial (suh LEHS chuhl) *adj.:* heavenly. *According to Wordsworth, the soul is a celestial creation and therefore capable of becoming close to God.*

Language Coach

Word Origins *Piety* comes from a Latin word meaning "kind; dutiful." The adjective *pious,* which comes from the same Latin root, means someone who shows religious devotion. What do you think *impiety* and *impious* mean?

Learn It Online
Practice your Vocabulary knowledge online with Word Watch.

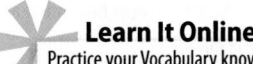 L12-757

ODE

from Ode

Intimations of Immortality *from* Recollections of Early Childhood

by **William Wordsworth**

Read with a Purpose
Read to discover the changes that occur within the human soul during the process of growing up.

Build Background

An **ode** is a complex, generally long lyric poem on a serious subject. The **epigraph,** or opening quotation, of Wordsworth's ode was taken from "My Heart Leaps Up," one of his best-loved poems. "Ode: Intimations of Immortality" is more than two hundred lines long; only three of the eleven stanzas are reprinted here. According to Wordsworth, two years passed between the writing of the first four stanzas and the remaining seven. In the poem, Wordsworth recalls the innocent joy of childhood, takes pleasure in the beauty of nature, and reflects on the rewards that come with maturity.

The Child is Father of the Man;
And I could wish my days to be
Bound each to each by natural piety.

1

There was a time when meadow, grove, and stream,
The earth, and every common sight,
> To me did seem
> Apparelled in celestial light, **A**
5 The glory and the freshness of a dream.
It is not now as it hath been of yore;—
> Turn wheresoe'er I may,
> By night or day,
The things which I have seen I now can see no more.

A **Reading Focus** **Annotating a Poem** Line 4 includes the first of several references to light, the sun, or the reflection of light. How can writing down these references help you see how light imagery is woven throughout the poem?

Vocabulary **piety** (PY uh tee) *n.:* devotion to religion.
celestial (suh LEHS chuhl) *adj.:* heavenly.

Master Hare, Francis George Hare (1788–1789) by Sir Joshua Reynolds (1723–1792). Louvre, Paris, France .

2

10   The Rainbow comes and goes,
       And lovely is the Rose,
       The Moon doth with delight
Look round her when the heavens are bare,
       Waters on a starry night
15   Are beautiful and fair;
       The sunshine is a glorious birth;
       But yet I know, where'er I go, **B**
That there hath passed away a glory from the earth.

· · · · · · · · · · · · · · · ·

5

       Our birth is but a sleep and a forgetting:
20   The Soul that rises with us, our life's Star,°
           Hath had elsewhere its setting, **C**
             And cometh from afar:
       Not in entire forgetfulness,
       And not in utter nakedness,
25   But trailing clouds of glory do we come
           From God, who is our home:
Heaven lies about us in our infancy!
Shades of the prison-house begin to close
           Upon the growing Boy,
30   But He beholds the light, and whence it flows,
           He sees it in his joy;
The Youth, who daily farther from the east
          Must travel, still is Nature's Priest,
          And by the vision splendid
35   Is on his way attended;
At length the Man perceives it die away,
And fade into the light of common day.

Master Bunbury (1780 or 1781), by Sir Joshua Reynolds (1723–1792),
oil on canvas.
The Philadelphia Museum of Art, Pennsylvania, The John Howard McFadden
Collection, 1928.

---

20. our life's Star: the sun, a metaphor for the soul.

B **Literary Focus** **Meter and Rhyme** How do the internal rhyme (rhyme within a line) and the repetition of the word I reinforce the attitude expressed by the speaker?

C **Literary Focus** **Meter and Rhyme** In line 21, Wordsworth uses a two-syllable (or feminine) rhyme for the first time. What is the effect of this shift in rhyme?

Applying Your Skills

from Ode: Intimations of Immortality *from* Recollections of Early Childhood

Respond and Think Critically

Reading Focus

Quick Check

1. According to the speaker, how does a child view the world?

2. What images describe the human soul?

3. Why does the speaker call birth a "forgetting"?

Reading Skills: Annotating a Poem

4. Circle your annotations about meter and rhyme. Where do variations occur in the meter or rhyme scheme? What do these variations reveal about the poem's meaning? Refer to your annotations and to lines from the poem to explain your response. See the example below.

> Unlike earlier stanzas, stanza 5 ends in a heroic couplet (two lines of rhymed iambic pentameter). This tidy ending seems to put the final stamp on the permanent loss of childlike innocence experienced in adulthood.

✓ Vocabulary Check

Check your understanding of the Vocabulary words by answering the following questions:

5. Where would you look to locate a **celestial** object?

6. Whom or what do you associate with **piety**?

Literary Focus

Literary Analysis

7. **Analyze** The **epigraph,** or opening quotation, presents a **paradox,** an apparent contradiction. What can our childhood experiences teach us when we are adults?

8. **Interpret** In stanza 1, the speaker describes something he has lost. What is the speaker describing? What does the image "apparelled in celestial light" (line 4) make you visualize?

9. **Interpret** According to stanza 2, how does the speaker feel now when he looks at nature?

10. **Evaluate** How is the sun used in the **extended metaphor,** or comparison, in stanza 5?

11. **Extend** Give some examples of what you think the poet means by the "prison-house" that closes in "upon the growing Boy" in lines 28–29.

Literary Skills: Meter and Rhyme

12. **Analyze** Identify instances in the poem where Wordsworth uses internal rhyme as rather than end rhyme. Is there any pattern to where and when the different types of rhyme are used?

Literary Skills Review: Imagery

13. **Analyze** Language that appeals to the senses, **imagery,** evokes a picture or concrete sensation of a person, place, thing, or experience. How are images of light and vision used to develop the poem's theme?

Writing Focus

Think as a Reader/Writer

Use It in Your Writing What memories do you have of childhood? Choose a meaningful memory, and describe it in a reflective paragraph. Use imagery to capture the feeling of childhood as you remember it.

What Do You Think Now How can we find truth by looking at the world through the imagination of a child?

Composed upon Westminster Bridge

Reader/Writer
Notebook

Use your **RWN** to complete the activities for this selection.

Literary Focus

Personification Wordsworth breathes life into his sonnet by using **personification,** a type of metaphor in which a nonhuman thing is talked about as if it were human. Inanimate objects often strike us with the seeming humanity of their sounds and movements. To a poet or anyone with imagination, the stars may look as if they are winking at people on Earth, or the wind blowing in the trees may sound as if it is whispering. As you read "Composed upon Westminster Bridge," look for instances in which Wordsworth personifies the city, the sun, the river, and even the houses of London.

Writing Focus

Think as a Reader/Writer

Find It in Your Reading In "Composed upon Westminster Bridge," Wordsworth describes a view of London in the early morning by using vivid adjectives, such as *glittering* and *smokeless,* to explain how the speaker feels and what he sees. As you read, record in your *Reader/Writer Notebook* some of the adjectives that the poet uses. What is the <u>function</u> of these adjectives? What impressions do they create?

Adjective	Noun or Pronoun Adjective Describes	Effect
silent, bare	morning	stillness and quiet

Vocabulary

majesty (MAJ uh stee) *n.*: grandeur. *Wordsworth believes that the sight of Westminster Bridge in the morning is one of pure majesty.*

splendor (SPLEHN duhr) *n.*: great brightness; brilliant light. *The rising sun bathed the city in splendor.*

Language Coach

Related Words You can find related adjectives by adding certain suffixes to nouns. Add the suffix –*ic* to the noun *majesty,* for example, to form the adjective *majestic.* Add the suffix –*id* to the root of *splendor* to form the adjective *splendid.* What do *majestic* and *splendid* mean? Can you think of other adjectives that have these endings?

Learn It Online
Explore Wordsworth's world through these Internet links:

go.hrw.com   L12-761   **Go**

Composed upon Westminster Bridge

September 3, 1802

by **William Wordsworth**

Read with a Purpose
Read to find out how the speaker feels upon viewing the city of London at daybreak.

Build Background
Published in 1807, this sonnet shows that Wordsworth, even as an ardent lover of nature, could be moved by the majesty of a sleepy city (in this case, London) as well as by mountains and waterfalls. This London, seen from a distance, is clearly a different London from the one of Blake's chimney sweepers (see pages 738–740) and the one known as the "great wen [wart]" that shocked many of Wordsworth's contemporaries with its filth and poverty. Here, London's filth and poverty are disguised and transformed by the poet's imagination.

Westminster Bridge, London.

Earth has not anything to show more fair:
Dull would he be of soul who could pass by
A sight so touching in its majesty:
This City now doth, like a garment, wear
5   The beauty of the morning; silent, bare,
Ships, towers, domes, theaters, and temples lie
Open unto the fields, and to the sky;
All bright and glittering in the smokeless air.
Never did sun more beautifully steep
10   In his first splendor, valley, rock, or hill;
Ne'er saw I, never felt, a calm so deep!
The river glideth at his own sweet will:
Dear God! the very houses seem asleep;
And all that mighty heart is lying still! Ⓐ

Ⓐ **Literary Focus** **Personification** What details in the poem personify the city?

Vocabulary **majesty** (MAJ uh stee) *n.*: grandeur.
splendor (SPLEHN duhr) *n.*: great brightness; brilliant light.

Preparing to Read

The World Is Too Much with Us

Reader/Writer
Notebook

Use your **RWN** to complete the activities for this selection.

Literary Focus

Allusion An **allusion** is a reference to a statement, person, place, event, or thing that is known from literature, history, religion, mythology, politics, science, or popular culture. Writers often use allusions to give deeper meaning to their work. In Wordsworth's "The World Is Too Much with Us," the speaker alludes to Proteus and Triton, two sea gods from Greek mythology. By making reference to these gods, Wordsworth underscores an earlier idea in the poem. Look for this connection as you read.

Writing Focus

Think as a Reader/Writer

Find It in Your Reading As you read "The World Is Too Much with Us," notice how Wordsworth uses adjectives to describe humans' relationship to the material world. Pay special attention to his use of verbal adjectives (adjectives formed from verbs). Create a chart in your *Reader/Writer Notebook* to record some of the poem's adjectives and their effect in the poem.

Adjective	Noun or Pronoun Adjective Describes	Effect
Getting and spending	we	portrays man as wasteful and careless

Vocabulary

sordid (SAWR dihd) *adj.:* foul; filthy. *Sacrificing our integrity for material things is a sordid aspect of modern life.*

pagan (PAY guhn) *n.:* person who believes in many gods or no god. *Those who worshiped the gods of ancient Greece were called pagans.*

creed (kreed) *n.:* essential points of religious belief. *His creed requires that he show respect for all creatures.*

forlorn (fawr LAWRN) *adj.:* hopeless; wretched. *He felt forlorn when he witnessed the excessive spending and waste of the modern world.*

Language Coach

Connotations The ideas or feelings associated with words are their **connotations.** Some words have strong negative or judgmental connotations. *Sordid* has a similar meaning to *dirty,* but much more negative, moralistic connotations. The word *pagan,* which means someone who believes in many or no gods, is often assigned negative connotations. When you read the word in Wordsworth's poem, consider whether or not the speaker uses the word negatively.

The World Is Too Much with Us

by **William Wordsworth**

Read with a Purpose
Read to discover what has caused us to give "our hearts away."

Build Background
Wordsworth wrote the final draft of this sonnet in 1804, at a time when he realized that his imaginative powers were beginning to fail. Although he continued to compose new works and to edit *The Pre-*lude, a long poem published after his death, he knew he was no longer responding to nature with the youthful passion that had inspired his earlier poems. This sonnet counterattacks ferocious criticism that Wordsworth was receiving from conservative reviewers who thought the poet was conspiring against society, brooding needlessly over problems "instead of contemplating the wonders and pleasures which civilization has created for mankind."

The world is too much with us; late and soon,
Getting and spending, we lay waste our powers:
Little we see in Nature that is ours;
We have given our hearts away, a sordid boon!°
5 This Sea that bares her bosom to the moon;
The winds that will be howling at all hours,
And are up-gathered now like sleeping flowers;
For this, for everything, we are out of tune;
It moves us not.—Great God! I'd rather be
10 A Pagan suckled in a creed outworn;
So might I, standing on this pleasant lea,°
Have glimpses that would make me less forlorn;
Have sight of Proteus° rising from the sea;
Or hear old Triton° blow his wreathèd horn. **A**

4. sordid boon: foul gift. That is, the act of giving our hearts away is shameful.

11. lea: meadow.

13. Proteus (PROH tee uhs): in Greek mythology, a sea god who can change shape at will.
14. Triton (TRY tuhn): in Greek mythology, a sea god who controls the waves by blowing a conch shell.

A Literary Focus **Allusion** What is Wordsworth's purpose in alluding to mythology in the final two lines? What emotions do these allusions evoke?

Vocabulary **sordid** (SAWR dihd) *adj.:* foul; filthy.
pagan (PAY guhn) *n.:* person who believes in many gods or no god.
creed (kreed) *n.:* essential points of religious belief.
forlorn (fawr LAWRN) *adj.:* hopeless; wretched.

Applying Your Skills

SKILLS FOCUS Literary Skills Analyze personification; analyze allusion; analyze theme. **Vocabulary Skills** Demonstrate knowledge of literal meanings of words. **Writing Skills** Write descriptive essays.

Composed upon Westminster Bridge
The World Is Too Much with Us

Respond and Think Critically

Reading Focus

Quick Check

1. In "Composed upon Westminster Bridge," what details and features of the city does the speaker mention?

2. How does the speaker of "The World Is Too Much with Us" feel about "getting and spending"?

Read with a Purpose

3. Compare the mood of the speaker in "Composed upon Westminster Bridge" to that of the speaker in "The World Is Too Much with Us." How does each view the possibility of future change? Would you describe their outlook as pessimistic or optimistic, realistic or idealistic? Explain.

✓ Vocabulary Check

Match the Vocabulary words with their definitions.

4. creed   a. foul
5. forlorn   b. hopeless
6. pagan   c. brilliant light
7. sordid   d. set of beliefs
8. splendor   e. grandeur
9. majesty   f. believer in many gods or no god

Literary Focus

Literary Analysis

10. **Analyze** What qualities of the scene in the first poem seem to move the speaker most deeply?

11. **Extend** How do the themes and images of "Composed upon Westminster Bridge" classify Wordsworth as a typical Romantic poet?

12. **Interpret** Why do you think the speaker in "The World Is Too Much with Us" would "rather be / A Pagan" (lines 9–10)?

13. **Evaluate** How are the ideas about materialism and progress in "The World Is Too Much with Us" relevant to today's world?

Literary Skills: Personification / Allusion

14. **Analyze** What details personify the sun in "Composed upon Westminster Bridge"? How does the image of the steeping tea bag help us visualize the movement of the light?

15. **Analyze** What examples of **allusion** did you note while reading "The World is Too Much with Us"? How do these allusions affect the theme?

Literary Skills Review: Theme

16. **Analyze** The **theme** of a literary work is the main idea or central insight into human nature. Identify and compare the themes of the two sonnets. Does Wordsworth state these themes directly, or are they implied?

Writing Focus

Think as a Reader/Writer

Use It in Your Writing Review your notes about Wordsworth's use of adjectives in "Composed upon Westminster Bridge" and "The World Is Too Much with Us." Write a descriptive paragraph about something in nature, building on one of Wordsworth's themes or addressing a theme of your own. As you write, choose adjectives to convey the images and effects you want.

What Do **You Think Now** What parts of our world limit or hinder the imagination? What parts of our world nurture or inspire the imagination? Explain.

Kubla Khan

The Rime of the Ancient Mariner

How can we use imagination to discover truth?

QuickWrite

In "Kubla Khan," Coleridge presents his vision of an earthly paradise. Imagine your own version of the perfect place. What would it look like? In your *Reader/Writer Notebook,* write a paragraph describing this fantastic place.

Samuel Taylor Coleridge
(1772–1834)

Samuel Taylor Coleridge produced some of the most memorable poems and literary criticism of the Romantic era.

A Great Friendship

As a child, Coleridge was an avid reader and immersed himself in imaginative literature such as *The Arabian Nights' Entertainments.* He impressed classmates with his extraordinary memory and powerful, persuasive expression of ideas. While a student at Cambridge during the French Revolution, Coleridge was intrigued by discussions about the nature of society and troubled by the violence that had derailed the idealism of the Revolution. He left Cambridge without a degree and instead committed himself to creating a utopian colony in America. The experiment never materialized, but Coleridge continued to deliver radical lectures and married a member of the utopian movement. In 1796, with one book of poetry published but no career prospects, he moved to a village in Somerset, England.

In the countryside, Coleridge and the poet William Wordsworth formed a strong friendship, which greatly influenced the development of Coleridge's poetic <u>techniques</u> and style. The two years that followed, before Coleridge had even reached the age of thirty, were among the most prolific of his career. In 1798, Coleridge and Wordsworth published *Lyrical Ballads,* considered the seminal work of the English Romantic era.

The Troubled Artist

Much of Coleridge's later life was marked by pain and despair. His marriage collapsed, his friendship with Wordsworth ended, and his health deteriorated. Despite his suffering, Coleridge continued writing, mostly philosophy and literary criticism, until his death in London in 1834.

Think About the Writer How do you think Coleridge's troubles might have strengthened his imagination?

The Great Khan Releases his Angle Against a Doe, by Boucicaut Master (1390–1430) Ms Fr 2810 f.31 v. Bibliotheque Nationale, Paris, France.
Samuel Taylor Coleridge (1795), by Peter Vandyke, oil on canvas. National Portrait Gallery, London.

Kubla Khan

Reader/Writer Notebook

Use your **RWN** to complete the activities for this selection.

Literary Focus

Alliteration The repetition of consonant sounds in words that are close to one another is called **alliteration.** Alliteration can give a musical quality to a poem, emphasize a line or an idea, or help establish **rhythm**. Coleridge uses alliteration throughout "Kubla Khan" to help create the poem's enchanted mood. Alliteration can also suggest movement, as in line 25: "Five miles meandering with a mazy motion." The repeated /m/ sound in the line evokes the serpentine flow of the river. As you read the poem, look and listen for other examples of alliteration.

Reading Focus

Interpreting Imagery Language that appeals to the senses is called **imagery.** While most imagery is visual, appealing to the sense of sight, imagery can also appeal to hearing, touch, taste, or smell. Study the language Coleridge uses to create and enhance his imagery in "Kubla Khan."

Into Action Record at least five striking images in your Reader/Writer Notebook. Underline examples of alliteration used in the images.

	Image in "Kubla Khan"
1	"Where Alph, the sacred river ran / Through caverns measureless to man"
2	

Writing Focus

Think as a Reader/Writer

Find It in Your Reading As you read, note the ways Coleridge uses language, including alliteration and descriptive words, to create a dreamlike effect in the poem. In your *Reader/Writer Notebook,* record examples that you find especially effective.

TechFocus As you read "Kubla Khan," notice how Coleridge combines words and imagery. Consider the ways in which modern artists use similar techniques.

Language Coach

Verb Forms When you learn a new verb, be sure to learn its base form as well as forms that end with *–s, –ed,* and *–ing.* For example, *girdled* is a past-tense verb that means "encircled." Notice how the verb is used in these phrases:

- Towers *girdle* the garden.
- A moat *girdles* the castle.
- Armed soldiers were *girdling* our camp.

What verb forms are related to *meandering*? How can you use each form in a sentence?

 Learn It Online
Find out more about Coleridge on the Writers' Lives site.

go.hrw.com L12-767   **Go**

Kubla Khan

by **Samuel Taylor Coleridge**

Read with a Purpose
Read to find out about Kubla Khan's attempt to build a paradise on earth.

Build Background
Kubla Khan (c. 1216–1294), the grandson of Genghis Khan, was the Mongol conqueror of China. Coleridge's poem about this thirteenth-century warrior has a lyrical tone and manner that resemble that of a meditative ode.

Coleridge claimed to have envisioned "Kubla Khan" during an opium-induced reverie after he had read a provocative passage in an old travel book. Upon waking from his dream, Coleridge began composing the poem but was interrupted by a visitor. After his visitor left an hour later, Coleridge could recall a mere fragment of his dream-poem.

In Xanadu did Kubla Khan
A stately pleasure-dome decree:
Where Alph,° the sacred river, ran
Through caverns measureless to man
5   Down to a sunless sea.   **A**
So twice five miles of fertile ground
With walls and towers were girdled round:
And there were gardens bright with sinuous rills,°
Where blossomed many an incense-bearing tree;
10   And here were forests ancient as the hills,
Enfolding sunny spots of greenery.   **B**

But oh! that deep romantic chasm which slanted
Down the green hill athwart a cedarn cover!°
A savage place! as holy and enchanted
15   As e'er beneath a waning moon was haunted
By woman wailing for her demon-lover!
And from this chasm, with ceaseless turmoil seething,

3. Alph: probably a reference to the Greek river Alpheus, which flows into the Ionian Sea and whose waters are fabled to rise up again in Sicily.

8. rills: streams.

13. athwart a cedarn cover: crossing diagonally under a covering growth of cedar trees.

A **Literary Focus** **Alliteration** What examples of alliteration can you find in the first five lines? What is the effect of the alliteration?

B **Reading Focus** **Interpreting Imagery** What images in the stanza evoke a sense of a fantastic, otherworldly place? Explain your answer.

Vocabulary **girdled** (GUR duhld) *v.* used as *adj.*: enclosed or circled around.
sinuous (SIHN yu uhs) *adj.*: winding; twisting.
turmoil (TUR moyl) *n.*: state of agitation or commotion.

As if this earth in fast thick pants were breathing,
A mighty fountain momently° was forced:
20 Amid whose swift half-intermitted burst
Huge fragments vaulted like rebounding hail,
Or chaffy grain beneath the thresher's flail:°
And 'mid these dancing rocks at once and ever
It flung up momently the sacred river.
25 Five miles meandering with a mazy° motion
Through wood and dale the sacred river ran,
Then reached the caverns measureless to man,
And sank in tumult to a lifeless ocean:
And 'mid this tumult Kubla heard from far
30 Ancestral voices prophesying war!
   The shadow of the dome of pleasure
   Floated midway on the waves;
   Where was heard the mingled measure°
   From the fountain and the caves.
35 It was a miracle of rare device,
A sunny pleasure-dome with caves of ice! **C**

19. momently: at each moment.

22. thresher's flail: heavy, whiplike tool used to beat grain to separate the kernels from their chaff, or husks.

25. mazy: like a maze; having many turns.

33. measure: rhythmic sound.

C **Reading Focus** **Interpreting Imagery** What do you think of when you imagine caves of ice? Why do you think Coleridge included this image in his poem?

Vocabulary **meandering** (mee AN duhr ihng) *v.* used as *adj.:* wandering with no clear direction.

HISTORY LINK

The Great Khan

In his fantasy poem, Coleridge describes Kubla Khan's magnificent pleasure-dome in the mystical city of Xanadu. The existence of the real Kubla Khan was far less fanciful; the grandson of the formidable Mongol conqueror, Genghis Khan, Kubla consolidated the Mongols' hold over China by defeating the Chinese Sung dynasty in 1279. The *khan* attached to both father and son's names comes from the Mongolian word *ruler.*

As the first Great Khan of the Yuan dynasty, Kubla undertook many projects, such as expanding road networks, maintaining granaries, and rebuilding the Grand Canal, a trade route still present in China. The name *Xanadu* comes from Coleridge's imagination, but the city may have been based on Shang-du in Inner Mongolia, where Kubla was elected khan in 1260.

Kublai Khan (1216–1294). Founder of the Mongol dynasty. Chinese silk album leaf, Yüan dynasty. The Granger Collection, NY.

Ask Yourself
How might the poem "Kubla Khan" have influenced the image and perceptions of Eastern culture in the West?

Kubla Khan **769**

A damsel with a dulcimer°
In a vision once I saw:
It was an Abyssinian° maid,
40   And on her dulcimer she played,
Singing of Mount Abora.°
Could I revive within me
Her symphony and song,
To such a deep delight 'twould win me,
45 That with music loud and long,   **D**
I would build that dome in air,
That sunny dome! those caves of ice!
And all who heard should see them there,
And all should cry, Beware! Beware!
50 His flashing eyes, his floating hair!
Weave a circle round him thrice,
And close your eyes with holy dread,
For he on honeydew hath fed,
And drunk the milk of Paradise.

D **Literary Focus** **Alliteration** Identify the examples of alliteration used in lines 37–45. How do they affect the rhythm of the poem?

37. dulcimer: musical instrument with strings that are struck with small hammers.
39. Abyssinian: Ethiopian. Ethiopia is in northeastern Africa.
41. Mount Abora: likely a reference to John Milton's (1608–1674) *Paradise Lost,* in which Mount Amara in Ethiopia is depicted as a mythical earthly paradise.

Kublai Khan's Palace, Peking. Miniature from the *Livres des Merveilles.* Manuscrits occidentaux-Francais 2810, fol 37.
Bibliothéque Nationale de France, Paris.

Analyzing Visuals

Viewing and Interpreting Note how each guard is paired with a tower. What do the guards' posture, clothing, and expressions suggest about the palace of Kubla Khan?

Respond and Think Critically

Reading Focus

Quick Check

1. In the first stanza, what images show that Xanadu is an extraordinary place?

2. What images shatter the depiction of Xanadu as peaceful and serene?

3. Why does the speaker yearn to re-create the damsel's symphony and song within himself?

Read with a Purpose

4. How does Kubla Khan build his paradise?

Reading Skills: Interpreting Imagery

5. As you read the poem, you recorded images and noted the alliteration. Add a column to the right to comment on the effect of the image on the poem as a whole.

	Image in "Kubla Khan"	Effect
1	"Where Alph, the sacred river ran / Through caverns measureless to man"	Emphasizes the enormity of the place
2		

Literary Focus

Literary Analysis

6. **Compare and Contrast** What does the imagery in lines 14–16 convey? Contrast this impression with that conveyed in lines 1–13. What phrases does Coleridge use to differentiate between the two places?

7. **Evaluate** Many ancient cultures revered poets as seers who had a special relationship with the gods. How might the last stanza allude to this?

8. **Extend** How could this poem itself be about the act of creating a poem?

9. **Make Judgments** In your opinion, does this poem celebrate the imagination or caution against its indulgence? Support your answer with evidence from the poem.

Literary Skills: Alliteration

10. **Analyze** Identify examples of alliteration, and explain their effects in the poem.

Literary Skills Review: Symbol

11. **Analyze** A **symbol** is a person, place, thing, or event that stands both for itself and for something beyond itself. What might the "dome in air" that the speaker wants to create symbolize?

Writing Focus

Think as a Reader/Writer

Use It in Your Writing Review your QuickWrite describing a perfect place and your notes about how Coleridge creates a dreamlike effect. Then, write a short poem describing your vision of paradise. Use descriptive words, alliteration, and rhyme to emphasize ideas and create a musical, dreamlike effect.

What Do You Think Now How does Coleridge's imagination reveal deeper truths?

Applying Your Skills

Kubla Khan

Vocabulary Development

 Vocabulary Check

Match each Vocabulary word with its definition.

1. girdled   **a.** wandering

2. sinuous   **b.** great disturbance

3. turmoil   **c.** having many bends or turns

4. meandering   **d.** enclosed or circled around

Vocabulary Skills: Context Clues

A word's **context**—the words and sentences that surround it—often gives clues to the word's meaning. Searching for context clues is an effective way to understand unfamiliar words as you read. When searching for context clues, start by identifying words you know. Also, consider the overall meaning of the sentence and the paragraph. Understanding the overall meaning will often allow you to make logical guesses about an unknown word.

One type of context clue is an example that illustrates a word's meaning. Consider this excerpt from the selection:

> Huge fragments *vaulted* like rebounding hail
> Or chaffy grain beneath the thresher's flail:

The phrase *like rebounding hail* contains a context clue for the word *vaulted*. If you know that rebounding hail is hail that bounces off the ground, you can infer from that clue that *vault* relates to jumping.

Another type of context clue is a word or phrase that describes the unknown word. Look for words and phrases that you do understand to see if they provide hints about the meaning of the unknown word.

Your Turn

Find each Vocabulary word in the selection. Using a table like the one below, write the context clues that

could help you determine the meaning of the Vocabulary word if you did not already know its definition. Then, explain how context clues help determine the word's meaning.

Word	Context Clues
girdled	"with walls and towers"; "round"
sinuous	
turmoil	
meandering	

Language Coach

Verb Forms When you learn a new verb, you should also try to learn its related forms. For example, *meander,* the base form of *meandering,* means "to wander with no clear direction." Choose the correct form of *meander* to complete each sentence.

   a. meander   **c.** meandered

   b. meanders   **d.** meandering

1. The ancient river _____ before it empties into the sea.

2. The caravan _____ for weeks before it arrived in Xanadu.

3. A commanding voice urges the men to stop _____ and return to camp.

4. The buzzing insects _____ through the garden in full bloom.

Academic Vocabulary

Talk About
With a partner, discuss how certain poetic techniques are more effective than others in conveying the mood, theme, or imagery. Do certain devices inherently lend themselves to specific literary functions?

Grammar Link

Prepositional Phrases

A **preposition** shows the relationship of a noun or pronoun, called the **object of the preposition,** to another word in the sentence. A **prepositional phrase** consists of a preposition, its object, and any words that modify the object. Prepositional phrases may be adjectival or adverbial.

Adjectival phrases modify nouns or pronouns, telling *what kind* or *which one.*

> Samuel Taylor Coleridge was an important poet **of the English Romantic movement.**

Adverbial phrases modify verbs, adjectives, or adverbs, telling *how, when, where, why,* or *to what extent.*

> He collaborated **with William Wordsworth.** Their work was beautiful **in a radical new way** that would change English poetry.

Your Turn

Identify the adjectival and adverbial prepositional phrases and the words they modify in the following sentences.

1. "Kubla Khan" is full of mysterious images. It brings readers on a journey, which leads to a sacred river.
2. The poem describes gardens glistening with streams and caves of ice.
3. Coleridge delivers a feverish rush of images.
4. The idea of the pleasure-dome fascinated readers of English Romanticism.

Writing Application Scan an essay you're already written, and underline all the prepositional phrases. Circle the object of the preposition, and note in the margin whether the phrase is adverbial or adjectival.

CHOICES

As you respond to the Choices, use these **Academic Vocabulary** words as appropriate: <u>differentiate</u>, <u>inherent</u>, <u>device</u>, <u>technique</u>, <u>function</u>.

REVIEW

Bring the Dream to Life

TechFocus In a small group, create a music video of "Kubla Khan." First, transform the poem into a song or dramatic reading, paying attention to musical effects created by alliteration. Then, choose or create visual images to accompany the poem's imagery. Your images need not literally represent the descriptions in "Kubla Khan" but should convey the same effect and mood. Share your video with your class.

CONNECT

Reflect on Dreams

Think about some of your past dreams, and take a few notes describing the <u>functions</u> of dreams. Are they logical or illogical? Do they tell coherent stories, or do they consist mostly of images and fragments of stories? Go over your ideas with a partner. Then, discuss how your thoughts on the <u>inherent</u> nature of dreams compare to the dreamlike flow of "Kubla Khan." Does the poem read like a dream? Cite examples from the poem to support your answer.

EXTEND

Examine the Author's Life

With a partner, use the school library or the Internet to research the life of Samuel Taylor Coleridge. Try to draw connections between biographical events and the poem "Kubla Khan." Think about possible inspirations for the poem and what meaning the images may have held for Coleridge. Present your findings to the class, and ask your peers to comment on how Coleridge's life may have affected his work.

Learn It Online
Learn more about context clues online with Word-Sharp

go.hrw.com   L12-773   **Go**

Preparing to Read

The Rime of the Ancient Mariner

Reader/Writer
Notebook

Use your **RWN** to complete the activities for this selection.

Literary Focus

Literary Ballad A **ballad** is a song or poem that tells a story. Coleridge's **literary ballad** imitates the traditional **folk ballad** in content and form, blending real events with supernatural events and using simple language, repetition, and patterns of rhythm and rhyme. To vary the meter and rhyme scheme, he uses internal rhyme, rhyming words within one line, and assonance, the repetition of vowel sounds in words close together.

Literary Perspectives Apply the literary perspective described on page 776 as you read this narrative poem.

Reading Focus

Understanding Archaic Words To make his ballad seem old, Coleridge uses many **archaic,** or out-of-date, words. The meanings of many of these words appear in the page margins. Context clues can also suggest meanings, as in "The glorious Sun *uprist*." Here, the prefix *up–* and your knowledge about the sun might lead you to guess that *uprist* means "rose."

Into Action Use a flowchart like the one below to record some of the archaic words and their meanings. List the archaic word in the first oval, its meaning in the next oval, and a modern replacement in the third.

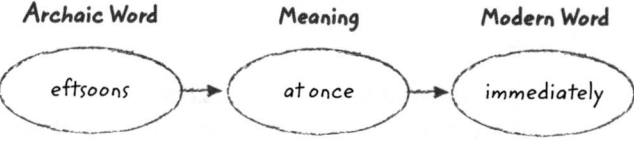

Archaic Word → Meaning → Modern Word

eftsoons → at once → immediately

Writing Focus

Think as a Reader/Writer

Find It in Your Reading Coleridge creates strong sensory **imagery** in his ballad. For example, the lines "And every tongue, through utter drought, / Was withered at the root" appeal to the sense of touch to describe tongues shriveled from lack of water. In your *Reader/Writer Notebook,* record examples of vivid sensory images from the ballad.

Language Coach
Definitions and Context One way to remember word definitions is to think about possible contexts in which you might use a word. You probably wouldn't use the adjective *dismal,* which means "gloomy," to describe someone's room unless you wanted to insult him or her. When might it be appropriate to use the word *dismal*? What kinds of settings, people, or events might it describe?

Learn It Online
Plunge into this poem with an online video introduction.

go.hrw.com   L12-774   Go

The Rime of the Ancient Mariner

by **Samuel Taylor Coleridge**

Read with a Purpose
Read to find out how the ancient Mariner's actions caused a terrible tragedy.

Build Background
Coleridge wrote *The Rime of the Ancient Mariner* as part of the collaboration with Wordsworth that culminated in the publication of *Lyrical Ballads*. Some of the poems in this volume were intended to present ordinary people and mundane events in fresh and interesting ways. Other poems, such as *The Rime of the Ancient Mariner,* were to present supernatural characters and events in a manner that would induce the reader to "procure for these shadows of imagination that willing suspension of disbelief for the moment, which constitutes poetic faith."

The poem does not explain the killing of the albatross; the results of the act, rather than the act itself, are what is important.

View of a Harbour (1815–1816) by Caspar David Friedrich. Schloss Sanssouci, Potsdam, Germany.

Argument

How a Ship having passed the Line was driven by storms to the cold Country toward the South Pole; and how from thence she made her course to the tropical Latitude of the Great Pacific Ocean; and of the strange things that befell; and in what manner the Ancient Mariner came back to his own Country.

Part I

It is an ancient Mariner,
And he stoppeth one of three.
"By thy long gray beard and glittering eye,
Now wherefore stopp'st thou me?

5   The Bridegroom's doors are opened wide,
And I am next of kin;
The guests are met, the feast is set:
May'st hear the merry din."   **Ⓐ**

He holds him with his skinny hand,
10   "There was a ship," quoth he.
"Hold off! unhand me, gray-beard loon!"
Eftsoons° his hand dropt he.

He holds him with his glittering eye—
The Wedding Guest stood still,
15   And listens like a three years' child:
The Mariner hath his will.   **Ⓑ**

The Wedding Guest sat on a stone:
He cannot choose but hear;
And thus spake on that ancient man,
20   The bright-eyed Mariner.

"The ship was cheered, the harbor cleared,
Merrily did we drop
Below the kirk,° below the hill,
Below the lighthouse top.

25   The Sun came up upon the left,
Out of the sea came he!
And he shone bright, and on the right
Went down into the sea.

An ancient Mariner meeteth three Gallants bidden to a wedding feast, and detaineth one.

12. eftsoons: archaic word meaning "at once."
The Wedding Guest is spellbound by the eye of the old seafaring man, and constrained to hear his tale.
23. kirk: church.
The Mariner tells how the ship sailed southward with a good wind and fair weather, till it reached the Line.

Literary Perspectives

Analyzing Credibility in Literature   Literature often asks us to believe in things that aren't real, and there are times when we are especially aware that a story doesn't ring true. When a story is neither fable nor fairy tale, we expect the characters and the plot to be believable or credible. Strange events and even stranger characters play a major role in *The Rime of the Ancient Mariner.* As you read, you may find yourself questioning the credibility of the Mariner's fantastic narrative, given the fact that all the objects and events described in the story are seen only through his eyes and that his frame of mind appears to be constantly shifting.

As you read, be sure to notice the questions in the text, which will guide you in using this perspective.

Ⓐ **Literary Focus** Literary Ballad   How does Coleridge use setting and character to establish background?

Ⓑ **Literary Focus** Literary Ballad   Literary ballads often focus on particular characters. What do you learn about the Mariner from his words, appearance, and actions in lines 9–16?

Higher and higher every day,
30 Till over the mast at noon°—"
The Wedding Guest here beat his breast,
For he heard the loud bassoon.

The bride hath paced into the hall,
Red as a rose is she;
35 Nodding their heads before her goes
The merry minstrelsy.°

The Wedding Guest he beat his breast,
Yet he cannot choose but hear;
And thus spake on that ancient man,
40 The bright-eyed Mariner. **C**

"And now the STORM-BLAST came, and he
Was tyrannous and strong:
He struck with his o'ertaking wings,
And chased us south along.

45 With sloping masts and dipping prow,
As who° pursued with yell and blow
Still° treads the shadow of his foe,
And forward bends his head,
The ship drove fast, loud roared the blast,
50 And southward aye° we fled.

And now there came both mist and snow,
And it grew wondrous cold:
And ice, mast-high, came floating by,
As green as emerald.

55 And through the drifts° the snowy cliffs°
Did send a dismal sheen:
Nor shapes of men nor beasts we ken°— **D**
The ice was all between.

C **Literary Focus** Literary Ballad What is the effect of the repetition in lines 20 and 40?

D **Reading Focus** Understanding Archaic Words Look at the definition of the archaic word *ken*. Did the sailors see animals and people on this stretch of their journey? Explain.

Vocabulary **tyrannous** (TIHR uh nuhs) *adj.*: harsh; oppressive.
dismal (DIHZ muhl) *adj.*: gloomy.

30. over . . . noon: The ship has reached the equator, here called the Line.

The Wedding Guest heareth the bridal music; but the Mariner continueth his tale.

36. minstrelsy: group of musicians.

The ship driven by a storm toward the South Pole.

46. who: one.
47. still: archaic word meaning "always."

50. aye: archaic word meaning "continually."

The land of ice, and of fearful sounds where no living thing was to be seen.
55. drifts: windblown snow and fog. **cliffs:** icebergs.
57. ken: archaic word meaning "saw."

The albatross lands on the ship

At length
did cross an
Albatross,
Through the
fog it came.

The ice was here, the ice was there,
60 The ice was all around:
It cracked and growled, and roared and howled,
Like noises in a swound!°

At length did cross an Albatross,
Through the fog it came;
65 As if it had been a Christian soul,
We hailed it in God's name.

It ate the food it ne'er had eat,
And round and round it flew.
The ice did split with a thunder fit;
70 The helmsman steered us through!

And a good south wind sprung up behind;
The Albatross did follow,
And every day, for food or play,
Came to the mariner's hello!

75 In mist or cloud, on mast or shroud,°
It perched for vespers° nine;
Whiles all the night, through fog-smoke white,
Glimmered the white Moonshine."

62. swound: swoon.

Till a great seabird, called the Albatross, came through the snow fog, and was received with great joy and hospitality.

And lo! the Albatross proveth a bird of good omen, and followeth the ship as it returned northward through fog and floating ice.

75. shroud: support rope that stretches from the top of the mast to the side of the ship.
76. vespers: evenings; also, evening prayers.

"God save thee, ancient Mariner!
80 From the fiends, that plague thee thus!—
Why look'st thou so?"—With my crossbow
I shot the ALBATROSS.

The ancient Mariner inhospitably killeth the pious bird of good omen.

Part II

The Sun now rose upon the right:
Out of the sea came he,
85 Still hid in mist, and on the left
Went down into the sea.

And the good south wind still blew behind,
But no sweet bird did follow,
Nor any day for food or play
90 Came to the mariner's hello!

And I had done a hellish thing,
And it would work 'em woe:
For all averred,° I had killed the bird
That made the breeze to blow.
95 Ah wretch! said they, the bird to slay,
That made the breeze to blow!

His shipmates cry out against the ancient Mariner, for killing the bird of good luck.
93. averred: asserted; claimed.

Nor dim nor red, like God's own head,
The glorious Sun uprist:
Then all averred, I had killed the bird
100 That brought the fog and mist.
'Twas right, said they, such birds to slay,
That bring the fog and mist. **E**

But when the fog cleared off, they justify the same, and thus make themselves accomplices in the crime.

The fair breeze blew, the white foam flew,
The furrow° followed free;
105 We were the first that ever burst
Into that silent sea.

The fair breeze continues; the ship enters the Pacific Ocean, and sails northward, even till it reaches the Line.
104. furrow: ship's wake.

Down dropt the breeze, the sails dropt down,
'Twas sad as sad could be;
And we did speak only to break
110 The silence of the sea!

The ship hath been suddenly becalmed.

E Literary Focus **Literary Ballad** Find three examples of internal rhyme in lines 91–102. How do these rhymes affect the meaning of the lines?

All in a hot and copper sky,
The bloody Sun, at noon,
Right up above the mast did stand,
No bigger than the Moon.

115 Day after day, day after day,
We stuck, nor breath nor motion;
As idle as a painted ship
Upon a painted ocean. **F**

Water, water, everywhere,
120 And all the boards did shrink;
Water, water, everywhere,
Nor any drop to drink.

The very deep did rot: O Christ!
That ever this should be!
125 Yea, slimy things did crawl with legs
Upon the slimy sea.

About, about, in reel and rout°
The death-fires° danced at night;
The water, like a witch's oils,
130 Burnt green, and blue and white.

And some in dreams assured were
Of the Spirit that plagued us so;
Nine fathom deep he had followed us
From the land of mist and snow. **G**

135 And every tongue, through utter drought,
Was withered at the root;
We could not speak, no more than if
We had been choked with soot.

Ah! welladay!° what evil looks
140 Had I from old and young!
Instead of the cross, the Albatross
About my neck was hung.

> **Water, water everywhere, Nor any drop to drink.**

And the Albatross begins to be avenged.

A Spirit had followed them; one of the invisible inhabitants of this planet, neither departed souls nor angels; concerning whom the learned Jew, Josephus, and the Platonic Constantinopolitan, Michael Psellus, may be consulted. They are very numerous, and there is no climate or element without one or more.

127. reel and rout: violent, whirling movement.

128. death-fires: firelike, luminous glow that is said to be seen over dead bodies.

The shipmates, in their sore distress, would fain throw the whole guilt on the ancient Mariner: in sign whereof they hang the dead seabird round his neck.

139. welladay: archaic word meaning "alas," an exclamation of sorrow.

F Literary Focus Literary Ballad How does Coleridge's use of repetition reinforce the meaning of the stanza?

G Literary Focus Literary Ballad What do this passage and its annotation reveal about the cause of the sailors' plight?

Part III

There passed a weary time. Each throat
Was parched, and glazed each eye.
145 A weary time! a weary time!
How glazed each weary eye,
When looking westward, I beheld
A something in the sky.

At first it seemed a little speck,
150 And then it seemed a mist;
It moved and moved, and took at last
A certain shape, I wist.° **H**

A speck, a mist, a shape, I wist!
And still it neared and neared:
155 As if it dodged a water sprite,
It plunged and tacked and veered.°

With throats unslaked,° with black lips baked,
We could not laugh nor wail;
Through utter drought all dumb we stood!
160 I bit my arm, I sucked the blood,
And cried, A sail! a sail!

With throats unslaked, with black lips baked,
Agape° they heard me call:
Gramercy!° they for joy did grin,
165 And all at once their breath drew in,
As they were drinking all. **I**

See! see! (I cried) she tacks no more!
Hither to work us weal;°
Without a breeze, without a tide,
170 She steadies with upright keel!

The ancient Mariner beholdeth a sign in the element afar off.

152. wist: archaic word meaning "knew."

156. tacked and veered: turned toward and then away from the wind.
At its nearer approach, it seemeth him to be a ship; and at a dear ransom, he freeth his speech from the bonds of thirst.
157. unslaked: unrelieved of thirst.

163. agape: with mouths wide open in wonder or fear.
A flash of joy;
164. gramercy: from Middle French *grand merci,* an exclamation of great thanks.
And horror follows. For can it be a ship that comes onward without wind or tide?
168. work us weal: do us good.

H **Reading Focus** Understanding Archaic Words What makes *welladay* (line 139) and *wist* (line 152) more fitting word choices for the ballad than *alas* and *knew?*

I **Reading Focus** Understanding Archaic Words Coleridge uses the word *gramercy* to give the poem an archaic quality. What other <u>devices</u> does he use to lend an archaic feel to lines 164–166?

The western wave was all aflame.
The day was well nigh done!
Almost upon the western wave
Rested the broad bright Sun;
175 When that strange shape drove suddenly
Betwixt us and the Sun.

And straight the Sun was flecked with bars,
(Heaven's Mother send us grace!)
As if through a dungeon grate he peered
180 With broad and burning face.

Alas! (thought I, and my heart beat loud)
How fast she nears and nears!
Are those *her* sails that glance in the Sun,
Like restless gossameres?°

185 Are those *her* ribs through which the Sun
Did peer, as through a grate?
And is that Woman all her crew?
Is that a DEATH? and are there two?
Is DEATH that woman's mate?

190 *Her* lips were red, *her* looks were free,
Her locks were yellow as gold:
Her skin was as white as leprosy,
The Nightmare LIFE-IN-DEATH was she,
Who thicks man's blood with cold. **J**

195 The naked hulk alongside came,
And the twain were casting dice;
"The game is done! I've won! I've won!"
Quoth she, and whistles thrice.

The Sun's rim dips; the stars rush out:
200 At one stride comes the dark;
With far-heard whisper, o'er the sea,
Off shot the specter bark.°

*It seemeth him but the skeleton
of a ship.*

*And its ribs are seen as bars on
the face of the setting Sun.*

184. gossameres: filmy cob-
webs.

*The Specter Woman and her
Deathmate, and no other
onboard the skeleton ship.*

Like vessel, like crew!

*Death and Life-in-Death have
diced for the ship's crew, and she
(the latter) winneth the ancient
Mariner.*

*No twilight within the courts of
the Sun.*

202. specter bark: ghost ship.

J Literary Focus Literary Ballad Literary ballads often contain powerful imagery.
In your own words, describe the image depicted in lines 185–194.

(right) The Death Ship nears

Analyzing Visuals

Viewing and Interpreting How does this image portray the struggle between life and death onboard the ship?

We listened and looked sideways up!
Fear at my heart, as at a cup,
205 My lifeblood seemed to sip!
The stars were dim, and thick the night,
The steersman's face by his lamp gleamed white;
From the sails the dew did drip—
Till clomb° above the eastern bar
210 The hornèd° Moon, with one bright star
Within the nether tip.°

One after one, by the star-dogged Moon,
Too quick for groan or sigh,
Each turned his face with a ghastly pang,
215 And cursed me with his eye.

Four times fifty living men,
(And I heard nor sigh nor groan)
With heavy thump, a lifeless lump,
They dropped down one by one.

220 The souls did from their bodies fly,—
They fled to bliss or woe!
And every soul, it passed me by,
Like the whizz of my crossbow!

Part IV

"I fear thee, ancient Mariner!
225 I fear thy skinny hand!
And thou art long, and lank, and brown,
As is the ribbed sea sand.

I fear thee and thy glittering eye,
And thy skinny hand, so brown."—
230 Fear not, fear not, thou Wedding Guest!
This body dropt not down.

Alone, alone, all, all alone,
Alone on a wide wide sea!
And never a saint took pity on
235 My soul in agony.

At the rising of the Moon,

209. clomb: archaic form of "climbed."
210. hornèd: crescent.
210–211. star . . . tip: A star dogging, or following, the moon is believed by sailors to be an evil omen.

One after another,

His shipmates drop down dead.

But Life-in-Death begins her work on the ancient Mariner.

The Wedding Guest feareth that a Spirit is talking to him;

But the ancient Mariner assureth him of his bodily life, and proceedeth to relate his horrible penance.

Vocabulary **ghastly** (GAST lee) *adj.:* dreadful; ghostly.

The many men, so beautiful!
And they all dead did lie:
And a thousand thousand slimy things
Lived on; and so did I.

240 I looked upon the rotting sea,
And drew my eyes away;
I looked upon the rotting deck,
And there the dead men lay.

I looked to heaven, and tried to pray;
245 But or° ever a prayer had gusht,
A wicked whisper came, and made
My heart as dry as dust.

I closed my lids, and kept them close,
And the balls like pulses beat;
250 For the sky and the sea, and the sea and the sky
Lay like a load on my weary eye,
And the dead were at my feet.

The cold sweat melted from their limbs,
Nor rot nor reek did they:
255 The look with which they looked on me
Had never passed away. Ⓚ

An orphan's curse would drag to hell
A spirit from on high;
But oh! more horrible than that
260 Is the curse in a dead man's eye!
Seven days, seven nights, I saw that curse,
And yet I could not die.

The moving Moon went up the sky,
And nowhere did abide:
265 Softly she was going up,
And a star or two beside—

He despiseth the creatures of the calm,

And envieth that they should live, and so many lie dead.

245. or: before.

But the curse liveth for him in the eye of the dead men.

In his loneliness and fixedness he yearneth toward the journeying Moon, and the stars that still sojourn, yet still move onward; and everywhere the blue sky belongs to them, and is their appointed rest, and their native country and their own natural homes, which they enter unannounced, as lords that are certainly expected and yet there is a silent joy at their arrival.

Ⓚ **Literary Focus** **Literary Ballad** How do supernatural and realistic elements work together in this stanza?

Her beams bemocked the sultry main,°
Like April hoarfrost° spread;
But where the ship's huge shadow lay,
270 The charmèd water burnt alway°
A still and awful red.

Beyond the shadow of the ship,
I watched the water snakes:
They moved in tracks of shining white,
275 And when they reared, the elfish light
Fell off in hoary° flakes.

Within the shadow of the ship
I watched their rich attire:
Blue, glossy green, and velvet black,
280 They coiled and swam; and every track
Was a flash of golden fire.

O happy, living things! no tongue
Their beauty might declare:
A spring of love gushed from my heart,
285 And I blessed them unaware:
Sure my kind saint took pity on me,
And I blessed them unaware.

The selfsame moment I could pray;
And from my neck so free
290 The Albatross fell off, and sank
Like lead into the sea. **L**

Part V

Oh sleep! it is a gentle thing,
Beloved from pole to pole!
To Mary Queen the praise be given!
295 She sent the gentle sleep from Heaven,
That slid into my soul.

The silly° buckets on the deck,
That had so long remained,
I dreamt that they were filled with dew;
300 And when I awoke, it rained.

267. main: archaic word meaning "open sea."
268. hoarfrost: frost.
270. alway: archaic form of "always."

By the light of the Moon he beholdeth God's creatures of the great calm.

276. hoary: white or gray.

Their beauty and their happiness.

He blesseth them in his heart.

The spell begins to break.

297. silly: simple; plain.

By grace of the holy Mother, the ancient Mariner is refreshed with rain.

L **Reading Focus** **Understanding Archaic Words** The word *selfsame* is rarely used today. It comes from the Middle English spelling *selue same* and is derived from the Old German *selbsama*. What do you think *selfsame* means? How is this word like the word *lifeblood*?

Antarctic Convergence

Isolated and brutally cold, Antarctica and its surrounding islands feature a climate inhospitable to humans and most mammals, with the exception of marine life such as seals, whales, dolphins, and porpoises. With an absence of indigenous land mammals and an abundance of food, Antarctica is a haven for forty-five bird species, including the albatrosses and, of course, penguins. Climatic conditions also help advance the proliferation of bird species. The Antarctic Circumpolar Current, driven by some of the most powerful winds on the planet, circles the continent of Antarctica and some of its surrounding islands. By allowing a complex exchange of water, heat, gases, salinity, and nutrients with the other oceans, the Circumpolar Current has a profound effect on the Earth's climate. In a twenty- to thirty-mile ribbon along the Southern Ocean's outer edge, the frigid waters of the current meet the fifty-degree waters of the Atlantic, Pacific, and Indian Oceans, causing a phenomenon known as the Antarctic Convergence. The convergence creates strange weather patterns and a hospitable environment for a surge of sea organisms that will feed fish, birds, and marine mammals.

Ask Yourself

Does learning about Antarctic geography and biology change your view of the events in the poem? What parts of the poem do you view differently? How does this knowledge affect your opinion of the Mariner's credibility? Explain.

The frigid waters of the Southern Ocean meet the warmer ocean waters from the north.

Native to the Northern Hemisphere, reindeer have lived on South Georgia Island near Antarctica since Norwegian sailors left some there in the early 1900s.

My lips were wet, my throat was cold,
My garments all were dank;
Sure I had drunken in my dreams,
And still my body drank.

305 I moved, and could not feel my limbs:
I was so light—almost
I thought that I had died in sleep,
And was a blessèd ghost.

And soon I heard a roaring wind:
310 It did not come anear;
But with its sound it shook the sails,
That were so thin and sere.° **M**

He heareth sounds and seeth strange sights and commotions in the sky and the element.

312. sere: archaic word meaning "worn."

M Reading Focus Understanding Archaic Words What archaic word besides *sere* appears in this stanza? Use the word's prefix to think of another archaic word that has the opposite meaning.

The upper air burst into life!
And a hundred fire flags sheen,
315 To and fro they were hurried about!
And to and fro, and in and out,
The wan stars danced between.°

And the coming wind did roar more loud,
And the sails did sigh like sedge;°
320 And the rain poured down from one black cloud;
The Moon was at its edge.

The thick black cloud was cleft,° and still
The Moon was at its side:
Like waters shot from some high crag,
325 The lightning fell with never a jag,
A river steep and wide.

The loud wind never reached the ship,
Yet now the ship moved on!
Beneath the lightning and the Moon
330 The dead men gave a groan.

They groaned, they stirred, they all uprose,
Nor spake, nor moved their eyes;
It had been strange, even in a dream,
To have seen those dead men rise. Ⓝ

335 The helmsman steered, the ship moved on;
Yet never a breeze up-blew;
The mariners all 'gan work the ropes,
Where they were wont° to do;
They raised their limbs like lifeless tools—
340 We were a ghastly crew.

The body of my brother's son
Stood by me, knee to knee:
The body and I pulled at one rope,
But he said nought to me.

313–317. The upper . . . danced between: apparently a description of the shifting lights of an aurora, which sometimes resemble waving, luminous folds of fabric.

319. sedge: reedy plants.

322. cleft: split.

The bodies of the ship's crew are inspired, and the ship moves on;

338. wont: accustomed.

Ⓝ **Literary Focus** **Literary Ballad** Describe the supernatural element that appears in lines 327–334.

345   "I fear thee, ancient Mariner!"
       Be calm, thou Wedding Guest!
       'Twas not those souls that fled in pain,
       Which to their corses° came again,
       But a troop of spirits blest: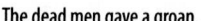

350   For when it dawned—they dropt their arms,
       And clustered round the mast;
       Sweet sounds rose slowly through their mouths,
       And from their bodies passed.

       Around, around, flew each sweet sound,
355   Then darted to the Sun;
       Slowly the sounds came back again,
       Now mixed, now one by one.

       Sometimes a-dropping from the sky
       I heard the skylark sing;
360   Sometimes all little birds that are,
       How they seemed to fill the sea and air
       With their sweet jargoning!°

       And now 'twas like all instruments,
       Now like a lonely flute;
365   And now it is an angel's song,
       That makes the heavens be mute.

       It ceased; yet still the sails made on
       A pleasant noise till noon,
       A noise like of a hidden brook
370   In the leafy month of June,
       That to the sleeping woods all night
       Singeth a quiet tune.   (P)

       Till noon we quietly sailed on,
       Yet never a breeze did breathe:
375   Slowly and smoothly went the ship,
       Moved onward from beneath.

But not by the souls of the men, nor by demons of earth or middle air, but by a blessed troop of angelic spirits, sent down by the invocation of the guardian saint.
348. corses: archaic form of "corpses."

362. jargoning: archaic word meaning "twittering."

The dead men gave a groan.

(O) **Literary Perspectives** Credibility in Literature Why does the Wedding Guest tell the ancient Mariner that he fears him? What might he believe about the Mariner and his tale?

(P) **Literary Focus** Literary Ballad How does the imagery in this stanza communicate the tone of this part of the poem?

Under the keel nine fathom deep,
From the land of mist and snow,
The spirit slid: and it was he
380 That made the ship to go.
The sails at noon left off their tune,
And the ship stood still also.

The Sun, right up above the mast,
Had fixed her° to the ocean:
385 But in a minute she 'gan stir,
With a short uneasy motion—
Backwards and forwards half her length
With a short uneasy motion.

Then like a pawing horse let go,
390 She made a sudden bound:
It flung the blood into my head,
And I fell down in a swound.   **Q**

How long in that same fit I lay,
I have not to declare;
395 But ere my living life returned,
I heard and in my soul discerned
Two voices in the air.

"Is it he?" quoth one, "Is this the man?
By him who died on cross,
400 With his cruel bow he laid full low
The harmless Albatross.

The spirit who bideth by himself
In the land of mist and snow,
He loved the bird that loved the man
405 Who shot him with his bow."

The other was a softer voice,
As soft as honeydew:
Quoth he, "The man hath penance done,
And penance more will do."   **R**

Q Reading Focus Understanding Archaic Words See line 62 for a definition of *swound*. Why might Coleridge have chosen to use this word instead of a more modern word?

R Literary Focus Literary Ballad What storytelling elements appear in lines 398–409?

The lonesome Spirit from the South Pole carries on the ship as far as the Line, in obedience to the angelic troop, but still requireth vengeance.

384. fixed her: seemed to hold the ship motionless.

The Polar Spirit's fellow demons, the invisible inhabitants of the element, take part in his wrong; and two of them relate, one to the other, that penance long and heavy for the ancient Mariner hath been accorded to the Polar Spirit, who returneth southward.

(right) I fell down in a swound.

Analyzing Visuals

Viewing and Interpreting What can you infer about the Mariner's battle from this image? How can you tell the ship's mast is making a "short uneasy motion?"

Part VI

FIRST VOICE

410   "But tell me, tell me! speak again,
     Thy soft response renewing—
     What makes that ship drive on so fast?
     What is the ocean doing?"

     SECOND VOICE

     "Still as a slave before his lord,
415   The ocean hath no blast;°
     His great bright eye most silently
     Up to the Moon is cast—

     If he may know which way to go;
     For she guides him smooth or grim.
420   See, brother, see! how graciously
     She looketh down on him."

     FIRST VOICE

     "But why drives on that ship so fast,
     Without or wave or wind?"°

     SECOND VOICE

     "The air is cut away before,
425   And closes from behind.

     Fly, brother, fly! more high, more high!
     Or we shall be belated:
     For slow and slow that ship will go,
     When the Mariner's trance is abated."

430   I woke, and we were sailing on
     As in a gentle weather:
     'Twas night, calm night, the Moon was high;
     The dead men stood together.

     All stood together on the deck,
435   For a charnel dungeon° fitter:
     All fixed on me their stony eyes,
     That in the Moon did glitter.

---

415. blast: wind.

The Mariner hath been cast into a trance; for the angelic power causeth the vessel to drive northward faster than human life could endure.
423. without . . . wind: with neither wave nor wind.

The supernatural motion is retarded; the Mariner awakes, and his penance begins anew.

435. charnel dungeon: burial vault.

Vocabulary   **abated** (uh BAYT ihd) *v.* used as *adj.*: lessened.

The pang, the curse, with which they died,
Had never passed away:
440 I could not draw my eyes from theirs,
Nor turn them up to pray.

And now this spell was snapt: once more
I viewed the ocean green,
And looked far forth, yet little saw
445 Of what had else° been seen— **S**

Like one, that on a lonesome road
Doth walk in fear and dread,
And having once turned round walks on,
And turns no more his head;
450 Because he knows, a frightful fiend
Doth close behind him tread.

But soon there breathed a wind on me,
Nor sound nor motion made:
Its path was not upon the sea,
455 In ripple or in shade.

It raised my hair, it fanned my cheek
Like a meadow gale of spring—
It mingled strangely with my fears,
Yet it felt like a welcoming.

460 Swiftly, swiftly flew the ship,
Yet she sailed softly too:
Sweetly, sweetly blew the breeze—
On me alone it blew.

Oh! dream of joy! is this indeed
465 The lighthouse top I see?
Is this the hill? is this the kirk?
Is this mine own countree? **T**

We drifted o'er the harbor bar,
And I with sobs did pray—
470 O let me be awake, my God!
Or let me sleep alway.

The curse is finally expiated
[removed, after penance is
done].

445. had else: would otherwise
have.

*And the ancient Mariner behold-
eth his native country.*

S Literary Perspectives Credibility in Literature How did the Mariner describe
the sea in line 240? How does he see it now? Why?

T Reading Focus Understanding Archaic Words How would you rewrite the
archaic words in this stanza to avoid archaic usage and spelling?

The harbor bay was clear as glass,
So smoothly it was strewn!°
And on the bay the moonlight lay,
475 And the shadow of the Moon.

The rock shone bright, the kirk no less,
That stands above the rock:
The moonlight steeped in silentness
The steady weathercock.°

480 And the bay was white with silent light,
Till rising from the same,
Full many shapes, that shadows were,
In crimson colors came.

A little distance from the prow
485 Those crimson shadows were:
I turned my eyes upon the deck—
Oh, Christ! what saw I there!

Each corse lay flat, lifeless and flat,
And, by the holy rood!°
490 A man all light, a seraph° man,
On every corse there stood.

This seraph band, each waved his hand:
It was a heavenly sight!
They stood as signals to the land,
495 Each one a lovely light; **Ⓤ**

This seraph band, each waved his hand,
No voice did they impart—
No voice; but oh! the silence sank
Like music on my heart.

500 But soon I heard the dash of oars,
I heard the Pilot's cheer;
My head was turned perforce away
And I saw a boat appear.

Ⓤ Literary Focus Literary Ballad What elements characteristic of a literary ballad
occur in this stanza?

473. strewn: stretched out; calmed.

479. weathercock: rooster-shaped weather vane.

The angelic spirits leave the dead bodies,

And appear in their own forms of light.

489. rood: crucifix.
490. seraph: angel of the highest rank.

The Pilot and the Pilot's boy,
505   I heard them coming fast:
Dear Lord in Heaven! it was a joy
The dead men could not blast.

I saw a third—I heard his voice:
It is the Hermit good!
510   He singeth loud his godly hymns
That he makes in the wood.
He'll shrieve° my soul, he'll wash away
The Albatross's blood.

Part VII

This Hermit good lives in that wood
515   Which slopes down to the sea.
How loudly his sweet voice he rears!
He loves to talk with marineres
That come from a far countree.   **V**

He kneels at morn, and noon, and eve—
520   He hath a cushion plump:
It is the moss that wholly hides
The rotted old oak stump.

The skiff boat° neared: I heard them talk,
"Why, this is strange, I trow!°
525   Where are those lights so many and fair,
That signal made but now?"

"Strange, by my faith!" the Hermit said—
"And they answered not our cheer!
The planks looked warped! and see those sails,
530   How thin they are and sere!
I never saw aught° like to them,
Unless perchance it were

512. shrieve: archaic word meaning "release from guilt after hearing confession." *The Hermit of the Wood,*

523. skiff boat: rowboat.
524. trow: archaic word meaning "believe."

Approacheth the ship with wonder.

531. aught: anything.

V **Literary Focus** **Literary Ballad** What examples of alliteration and internal rhyme can you find in this stanza? How do these sound <u>devices</u> affect the mood of the poem?

Brown skeletons of leaves that lag°
My forest brook along;
535 When the ivy tod° is heavy with snow,
And the owlet whoops to the wolf below,
That eats the she-wolf's young."

"Dear Lord! it hath a fiendish look—
(The Pilot made reply)
540 I am afeared"—"Push on, push on!"
Said the Hermit cheerily.

The boat came closer to the ship,
But I nor spake nor stirred;
The boat came close beneath the ship,
545 And straight° a sound was heard.

Under the water it rumbled on,
Still louder and more dread:
It reached the ship, it split the bay;
The ship went down like lead.

550 Stunned by that loud and dreadful sound,
Which sky and ocean smote,°
Like one that hath been seven days drowned
My body lay afloat;
But swift as dreams, myself I found
555 Within the Pilot's boat.

Upon the whirl, where sank the ship,
The boat spun round and round;
And all was still, save that the hill
Was telling of the sound.

560 I moved my lips—the Pilot shrieked
And fell down in a fit;
The holy Hermit raised his eyes,
And prayed where he did sit.

I took the oars: the Pilot's boy,
565 Who now doth crazy go,
Laughed loud and long, and all the while
His eyes went to and fro.
"Ha! ha!" quoth he, "full plain I see,
The Devil knows how to row."

533. lag: drift; move more slowly than the current.
535. ivy tod: clump of ivy.

545. straight: straightaway; at once.

The ship suddenly sinketh.

The ancient Mariner is saved in the Pilot's boat.
551. smote: struck.

> It reached the ship, it split the bay; The ship went down like lead.

570 And now, all in my own countree,
I stood on the firm land!
The Hermit stepped forth from the boat,
And scarcely he could stand.

"O shrieve me, shrieve me, holy man!"
575 The Hermit crossed° his brow.
"Say quick," quoth he, "I bid thee say—
What manner of man art thou?" **W**

Forthwith° this frame of mine was wrenched
With a woeful agony,
580 Which forced me to begin my tale;
And then it left me free. **X**

Since then, at an uncertain hour,
That agony returns:
And till my ghastly tale is told,
585 This heart within me burns.

I pass, like night, from land to land;
I have strange power of speech;
That moment that his face I see,
I know the man that must hear me:
590 To him my tale I teach.

What loud uproar bursts from that door!
The wedding guests are there:
But in the garden bower the bride
And bridemaids singing are:
595 And hark the little vesper bell,
Which biddeth me to prayer!

The ancient Mariner earnestly entreateth the Hermit to shrieve him; and the penance of life falls on him.
575. crossed: made the sign of the cross.
578. forthwith: at once.

And ever and anon throughout his future life an agony constraineth him to travel from land to land;

W Reading Focus **Understanding Archaic Words** Use a dictionary to find the meanings of *shrift* and *shrieve*. What does the Mariner request in line 574?

X Literary Focus **Literary Ballad** Like many works of fiction, a literary ballad usually has a climax. Where does the climax occur, and what is it?

Vocabulary **wrenched** (rehncht) *v.* used as *adj.*: anguished; grief-stricken.

O Wedding Guest! this soul hath been
Alone on a wide wide sea:
So lonely 'twas, that God himself
600   Scarce seemed there to be. **Y**

O sweeter than the marriage feast,
'Tis sweeter far to me,
To walk together to the kirk
With a goodly company!—

605   To walk together to the kirk,
And all together pray,
While each to his great Father bends,
Old men, and babes, and loving friends
And youths and maidens gay!

610   Farewell, farewell! but this I tell
To thee, thou Wedding Guest!
He prayeth well, who loveth well
Both man and bird and beast. **Z**

He prayeth best, who loveth best
615   All things both great and small;
For the dear God who loveth us,
He made and loveth all.

The Mariner, whose eye is bright,
Whose beard with age is hoar,
620   Is gone: and now the Wedding Guest
Turned from the bridegroom's door.

He went like one that hath been stunned,
And is of sense forlorn:°
A sadder and a wiser man,
625   He rose the morrow morn.

Alone on a wide wide sea

And to teach, by his own example, love and reverence to all things that God made and loveth.

623. forlorn: deprived.

Y Literary Perspectives **Credibility in Literature** The Mariner mentions his loneliness at sea. How might his loneliness affect his credibility as a narrator?

Z Literary Focus **Literary Ballad** Based on lines 610–617, what is the moral message or theme of the ballad?

Applying Your Skills

The Rime of the Ancient Mariner

Respond and Think Critically

Reading Focus

Quick Check

1. In Part II, what are the consequences of the Mariner's killing the albatross?

2. In Part IV, why is the Mariner unable to pray? What happens to change this situation?

3. At the end of the ballad, how does the Mariner describe his current life?

Read with a Purpose

4. What is the Mariner's tragic role? What one thing would he do differently? Explain.

Reading Skills: Understanding Archaic Words

5. Review the poem's archaic words and their meanings. For each word, add an additional circle to your chart and explain why Coleridge may have used the word instead of a modern term. Think about how the words work as sound devices and fit into the ballad's rhyme scheme.

Literary Focus

Literary Analysis

6. **Evaluate** Coleridge once said that he would have preferred to write *The Rime of the Ancient Mariner* as a work of "pure imagination." He believed that the poem had "too much" of a moral and that the moral was stated too openly. Do you agree or disagree? Explain.

7. **Make Judgments** How is death represented in the poem? What do the actions of the spirits and the bodies of the crew suggest about Coleridge's view of the supernatural?

8. **Evaluate** Coleridge added the italicized side-notes almost twenty years after he first published the poem. Do you think reading them alters the meaning of the poem? Explain.

9. **Literary Perspectives** You analyzed the credibility of the supernatural events and of the Mariner. How did this perspective affect your interpretation of the story?

Literary Skills: Literary Ballad

10. **Analyze** For the most part, this poem's form is the regular ballad stanza. Occasionally, however, Coleridge varies the lines' meter and the stanza length. Explain how one of the irregular stanzas differs from a regular one. What effects do these changes have on the poem?

Literary Skills Review: Allegory

11. **Draw Conclusions** An **allegory** is a narrative in which characters, settings, or events symbolize other people, places, or occurrences. What might be this ballad's allegorical meaning? Consider the Mariner, the wedding, the ship, and the albatross.

Writing Focus

Think as a Reader/Writer

Use It in Your Writing Review your notes about Coleridge's use of vivid figurative language and memorable sound devices. Write a paragraph or a brief poem on a subject of your choice. Include at least one example of figurative language (simile, metaphor, or personification) and one example of a sound device (alliteration, assonance, or internal rhyme).

 What Do **You Think Now**

How did Coleridge use his imagination to create a fantastic story? How does his story reveal truths about life or human nature?

The Rime of the Ancient Mariner

Vocabulary Development

✓ Vocabulary Check

Match each Vocabulary word with its synonym.

1. tyrannous
2. dismal
3. ghastly
4. abated
5. wrenched

a. bleak
b. weakened
c. tormented
d. ruthless
e. grisly

Your Turn

Select the Vocabulary word that best completes each analogy.

1. JOYFUL : GLAD :: _____ : gloomy
2. LEARNED : SCHOLAR :: _____ : dictator
3. GATHERED : COLLECTED :: _____ : lessened
4. BUOYED : HOPE :: _____ : agony
5. LOVELY : BEAUTY :: _____ : horror

Vocabulary Skills: Analogies

In literature, an **analogy** is a comparison designed to show a similarity or similarities between two things. In word analogies, the relationship between one pair of words is similar to the relationship between another pair of words. Consider this example:

ENGINE : CAR :: HORSE : CARRIAGE

To read this analogy, you say, "engine is to car as horse is to carriage." How are the paired items similarly related? An engine provides power for the car to move; similarly, a horse pulls a carriage to move it. Once you understand the relationship, you can read the analogy: "An engine is used to make a car go just as a horse is used to make a carriage go." The following chart shows other common relationships in analogies.

Relationship	Example	Analysis
Use	battery: flashlight	A battery is used to power a flashlight.
Type	puma : cat	A puma is a type of cat.
Cause/Effect	water : wet	Water causes something to be wet.
Synonyms	strange : unusual	*Strange* is synonymous with *unusual*.
Place	library: book	A library is a place where you'd find a book.
Description	mean: bully	The adjective *mean* describes a bully.

Language Coach

Definitions and Context Some neutral words fit naturally in many different contexts. Words like *object*, *place,* and *emotion* are useful in almost any situation. Other words, like *dismal,* are more specific. Thinking about how you might use these words can help you remember their definitions as you answer these questions:

1. When might you want to call a piece of writing *dismal*? When would this word be inappropriate?
2. How might the word *abated* be used on a nightly news report?
3. Do you think the word *wrenched* is more likely to appear in a poem or in daily conversation? Why?

Academic Vocabulary

Write About...

The Mariner <u>differentiates</u> himself early in his story because of his disregard for the albatross, which the crew believes <u>functions</u> as a good luck charm. Write a few paragraphs in which you discuss why you think people like to believe that certain animals or objects, such as clovers, horseshoes, or pennies, are <u>inherently</u> luckier than others.

Grammar Link

Infinitive Phrases

An **infinitive** is a verb form that can be used as a noun, an adjective, or an adverb. Most infinitives begin with *to*.

> The effect of Samuel Taylor Coleridge's poetry is **to amaze.** (noun)
> The albatross is a bird **to protect**. (adjective)
> The poem has scenes that are hard **to imagine.** (adverb)

To is left out of some infinitives.

> Careful reading can help you **(to) understand.**

An **infinitive phrase** is an infinitive and its modifiers or complements. Infinitive phrases act as nouns, adjectives, or adverbs.

> **To read this poem** is a strange experience. (noun)
> It takes a few stanzas **to cast its spell.** (adjective)
> Coleridge seems determined **to startle readers with bizarre images.** (adverb)

Do not confuse infinitive and prepositional phrases. *To* can also act as a preposition, and infinitive phrases can include prepositional phrases as modifiers.

Your Turn

Underline infinitive phrases in the following sentences, and identify each as a noun, an adjective, or an adverb.

1. A wedding guest happens to meet the Mariner.
2. The Mariner chooses to kill an albatross.
3. The sailors tie the albatross around the Mariner's neck to put the curse on his head.
4. He has many trials to face before he can be free.

Writing Application Choose a piece of your own writing. Circle the word *to* every time it appears, and identify whether it is part of an infinitive or prepositional phrase, or neither.

CHOICES

As you respond to the Choices, use these **Academic Vocabulary** words as appropriate: differentiate, inherent, device, technique, function.

REVIEW
Summarize the Poem
Re-read Part I of the ballad, and summarize it in a short paragraph. What important events occur in this part? What characters are introduced? Next, write a summary of Part II. Continue until you have a complete summary of the poem. Share your summary with a partner, and discuss whether your individual summaries are accurate and clear. How might you combine both summaries to create a better one?

CONNECT
Research Critical Comments
The supernatural events and narrative techniques of *The Rime of the Ancient Mariner* have attracted much critical attention, for the imagery lends itself to many interpretations. Use the Internet or library to research different critics' responses to the literary ballad. Summarize your findings in two or three paragraphs. Then, write a paragraph describing which critic you find most convincing and why.

EXTEND
Design a Video Game
TechFocus Create a concept for a five-level video game based on the ballad. For each level, describe a dilemma that must be solved before players can advance to the next level. Name the video game, create titles for each level, and provide a brief overview of the rules.

Preparing to Read

Saving Creatures Great and Small

What Do You Think How can we use imagination to discover truth?

 **QuickWrite**

Can animals, like the albatross, teach us lessons about life? Write a paragraph in your *Reader/Writer Notebook* explaining how an animal has taught you a lesson about life.

Informational Text Focus

Analyzing Details and Main Idea When you read an informational text for the first time, there are many clues you can use to determine the main idea. Examining the title, the tone, and the publication in which the text appears can be helpful, and details also reveal many of the key ideas.

Into Action As you read, use a chart like the one below to record details that strike you as important. In the left-hand column, enter details from the article's discussion of Coleridge's tale. In the right-hand column, enter details from the article's discussion of scientists' study of the albatross.

Coleridge Details	Scientific Details
written more than 200 years ago	spend half their lives flying over the ocean

Writing Focus   Preparing for **Constructed Response**

As you read this article, consider why an author who wishes to convey scientific information about the albatross would devote his first three paragraphs to a Romantic poet's "goofy" creation. How does the discussion of Coleridge affect what you learn about scientific study of the albatross? Record your ideas in your *Reader/Writer Notebook*.

Vocabulary

relentlessly (rih LEHNT lihs lee) *adv.:* unyielding; without pity. *He imagines the Mariner relentlessly repeating the same story.*

spontaneous (spahn TAY nee uhs) *adj.:* caused by natural impulse; not forced. *The albatross makes a spontaneous decision to fly across the Pacific in search of food.*

minuscule (mih NUHS kyool) *adj.:* extremely small. *On a map, Midway Island is minuscule.*

momentum (moh MEHN tuhm) *n.:* force with which an object moves. *Once it gathers enough acceleration, an albatross's momentum can propel it for many miles.*

conviction (kuhn VIHK shuhn) *n.:* firm belief or certainty. *The scientists trying to protect the albatross have a sincere conviction about their efforts.*

Language Coach

Word Origins The adjective *minuscule* comes from the Latin word that means "less." You might recognize this root in the word *minus*. How does the idea of "less" relate to the meaning of the word *minuscule*? How does the same Latin root affect the meaning of the word *minimum*? The word *conviction* shares a Latin root with the word *convince*. How do you think these two words are related? Use a dictionary to find out more about their origins.

Link to Today

This Link to Today provides a contemporary look at efforts to preserve the albatross species in the North Pacific Ocean.

Read with a Purpose

Read to learn how the author, a magazine editor, learns to appreciate the albatross as more than just a symbol in Coleridge's poem.

Build Background

Midway Atoll (also known as Midway Island) is an island in the North Pacific Ocean that is almost exactly "midway" between the United States and Asia. Classified as an unincorporated territory of the United States, Midway is home to thousands of species of seabirds, including the albatross, or "gooney bird." Although the albatross in Coleridge's poem was near Antarctica, the twenty different species of albatross in either the Northern or Southern Hemisphere share many of the same characteristics. Among the largest flying birds on earth, five of their species are considered endangered. Today, more than 400,000 albatross pairs nest at the National Wildlife Refuge on Midway Atoll.

Saving Creatures Great and Small

Timothy Foote, *Smithsonian* Magazine, September 2001

When I landed on Midway to do a story, I knew almost nothing about the life of the albatross. Lord of the air? Sure. Great flier? Yes. And, of course, it's really bad news if you kill one and have it hung round your neck! That last notion, I owed—like most people—not to the world of biology but to a work of Romantic literature: Samuel Taylor Coleridge's "The Rime of the Ancient Mariner," a goofy but absolutely astounding creation, written more than 200 years ago. The Ancient Mariner, who "stoppeth one of three," is still one of the most famous and most quoted poems in English.

The Mariner shoots the Albatross (1877), by Gustav Doré. Collection Kharbine-Tapabor, Paris

Nearly everyone vaguely remembers how it goes, and at least a few familiar lines. Just say aloud "It is an Ancient mariner, and he stoppeth one of three," and here comes the mariner himself, a dreadful sight, buttonholing guests late for a wedding, relentlessly telling his amazing story. How his ship sailed south and south until, with crossbow in hand, he shot an albatross that followed it, only to have the bird tied round his neck by his superstitious shipmates.

Soon natural and supernatural powers, displeased by his cruel act, begin to punish him, the crew, the ship itself, tormenting them with spectacular icebergs and huge storms followed by a deadly calm, when the helpless vessel lies for days "as idle as a painted ship upon a painted ocean." And, of course, unimaginable thirst: "Water, water everywhere, nor any drop to drink."

Vocabulary **relentlessly** (rih LEHNT lihs lee) *adv.*: unyielding; without pity.

After all sorts of horrors, all hands die—except the mariner, left alone, alone, a worse fate perhaps in store. But at the last moment the mariner is saved when, even though *in extremis,*[1] he experiences a brief moment of spontaneous joy and, indeed, reverence, at the beauty of some "water-snakes," creatures not usually associated with much charm. **A**

---

1. *in extremis:* Latin phrase meaning "in extreme circumstances."

On Midway, hip deep in fledgling albatross and busy asking dumb questions of the biologists and their helpers, I was not tempted to mention "The Ancient Mariner." They would just roll their eyes, I figured. Coleridge can seem as crazy as a hoot owl, and the poem is anything but scientific. Nevertheless, before leaving Midway, I came to think there is a revealing parallel between the words of the poet and the work of the island's committed field scientists.

A **Informational Focus** Analyzing Details and Main Idea
Why does the author include this clue about sea snakes?

Vocabulary **spontaneous** (spahn TAY nee uhs) *adj.:* caused by natural impulse; not forced.

Opposite: A pair of grey-headed albatrosses; a grey-headed albatross and chick.

Left: Bicyclist passing nesting Laysan Albatrosses (*Diomedia Immutabilis*).

Below: Black-browed Albatross nesting colony (*Thalassarche melanophris*), Saunders Island, Falklands.

Bottom: Egg of a Waved Albatross (*Diomedea irrorata*), on Española Island, one of the Galapagos Islands.

We know a great deal more about biology and the world's creatures than was the case even a few years back. Almost every week we hear that science has turned a new corner in the labyrinth of DNA. But when it comes to the study of wild creatures, especially ones like the albatross that spend half their lives flying over miles of ocean, we still rely on measuring, keeping track and slowly collecting data until it points to a specific, and maybe useful, conclusion. The main difference between then and now is that now a major aim of the work is to preserve the creatures under observation. The more you know about their habits, food and biology, the better you may be able to help them when the pinch of declining numbers comes to the shove of extinction. **B**

Today elaborate and precise descriptions abound of albatross life. Their courtship is famous, involving a stately gavotte[2] of ritual movements that include a series of mutual bowings and nibblings. Albatross couples mate for life, though some studies have noted an occasional "divorce." Once paired off, they breed pretty much every year, each year returning to the same nest site, within 20 yards or so of where the male was hatched. Sadly, they only get to dance their courtship dance once, the first time they meet.

The resulting egg—only one a year—weighs nine ounces. Parents alternate sitting on it for sometimes as long as three weeks at a stretch without relief, while the absent mate forages hundreds, even thousands of miles at sea for food. Both talk to the egg while it's incubating, with three sounds, Eh-Eh-Eh, and other varying syllables, presumably so the chick will know them after hatching.

It is only lately, with the help of minuscule new telemetric[3] devices attached to these birds, that we are beginning to have a clue about how and where they spend their months at sea. **C**

Albatross seem to be almost as dependent on wind as sailboats, which is why northern species stay in the Northern Hemisphere, and southern species keep to the Southern. Basically they are soarers and gliders, not flappers. The absence of strong sea breezes at the Equator keeps them from crossing the line. Like sailboats, they cannot sail into the wind; they have to tack. To do this they soar downwind to pick up both speed and height, then turn, using the acquired height and lingering momentum to let them glide down to the sea's surface more or less in the direction of the wind. Thus they may spend years at sea before returning to mate and rear their young on land—in our case on Midway.

The young biologists on Midway, like those who passionately advocate at-all-costs preservation of all endangered species, are driven by a conviction that is absolute. Midway folk seem to me to be close in spirit to the mariner's act of faith, as, briefly stirred by the coiled beauty of the sea snakes, he blesses them "unaware." They might even accept one of Coleridge's last lines: "He prayeth best who loveth best all things both great and small." **D**

---

3. **telemetric:** related to the science and technology of automatic measurement and transmission of data by wire, radio, or other means from remote sources.

---

2. **gavotte:** a French folk dance.

B **Informational Focus** Analyzing Details and Main Idea Based on the details in this paragraph, what do you think the main idea of the text is?

C **Informational Focus** Analyzing Details and Main Idea How does this sentence relate to the author's point about the nature of the albatross?

D **Informational Focus** Analyzing Details and Main Idea How do the quotes from Coleridge's poem support the main idea?

Vocabulary **minuscule** (mih NUHS kyool) *adj.*: extremely small.
momentum (moh MEHN tuhm) *n.*: the force with which an object moves.
conviction (kuhn VIHK shuhn) *n.*: firm belief or certainty.

Applying Your Skills

Saving Creatures Great and Small

Respond and Think Critically

Informational Text Focus

Quick Check

1. Why is the author reluctant to mention Coleridge's poem to the scientists on Midway?

2. How do researchers collect scientific data about albatrosses?

3. Why do albatrosses often spend years at sea before returning to land to mate?

Read with a Purpose

4. How does the albatross change from a symbol in Coleridge's poem to a creature worth saving in the author's experience?

Informational Skills: Analyzing Details and Main Idea

5. Look back at the chart you used to record two categories of details. For the "Coleridge" column, write a single sentence stating the idea these details support. Do the same for the "Scientific" column. Then, write a single sentence for the most important idea in the entire article.

Coleridge Details	Scientific Details
written more than 200 years ago	spend half their lives flying over the ocean

✓ Vocabulary Check

Match the Vocabulary words with their definitions.

6. relentlessly   **a.** small

7. spontaneous   **b.** certainty

8. minuscule   **c.** unyielding

9. momentum   **d.** unplanned

10. conviction   **e.** force

Text Analysis

11. **Interpret** What does the author mean by "They might even accept one of Coleridge's last lines: 'He prayeth best who loveth best all things both great and small.'"?

12. **Infer** What characteristics of albatross life does the author seem to admire most?

13. **Extend** What other lines from *The Rime of the Ancient Mariner* might apply to the scientists on Midway?

Listening and Speaking

14. **Interpret** Foote quotes directly from *The Rime of the Ancient Mariner* throughout his article. With a partner, read this article aloud, dividing it into two sections: the narrative parts from Foote's point of view and the direct quotations from Coleridge's poem. Each reader should have a distinct voice for interpreting the lines. Share your interpretive reading with the class.

Writing Focus   Constructed Response

Briefly explain how the article's closing quotation contributes to the author's main idea. Support you response with specific evidence from the article.

 What Do You Think Now

How can details about the beauty and spirit of the albatross teach us a lesson about life?

The Quest for Beauty

LITERARY FOCUS
Forms of Romantic Poetry

CONTENTS

George Gordon, Lord Byron

Percy Bysshe Shelley

W. S. Merwin Link to Today

John Keats

COMPARING TEXTS: WORLD LITERATURE
Tanka Poets, Haiku Poets, Tu Fu, Li Po

"My imagination, unbidden, possessed and guided me, gifting the successive images that arose in my mind with a vividness far beyond the usual bound of reverie."

— **Introduction to** *Frankenstein* **by Mary Shelley**

Forms of Romantic Poetry by **Leila Christenbury**

Characteristics of Romantic Poetry

- Expresses the emotions and concerns of an individual as well as of society
- Varies the structure of traditional forms to suit a poem's purpose
- Focuses on a poet's personal connection to nature

Function over Form

The Romantic poets used their art to capture individual and emotional experience. William Wordsworth defined poetry not as form (meter or rhyme or rhythm) but as "emotion recollected in tranquility." That kind of focus was startlingly different from what had been—for the order-loving eighteenth-century poets—a strictly defined literary genre. Poetry, for the Romantics, was a playground of feelings: emotional and inventive, and not necessarily written in a traditional format. Function came first for Romantic poets, who felt free to use or to abandon the forms in which poetry had previously been written. Although the Romantic poets frequently used traditional forms, such as the ode and the sonnet, they also experimented with forms, creating natural rhythms and using simple, unadorned language. In "Tintern Abbey," for example, Wordsworth used for the first time a less formal "conversational" blank verse that sounds like the flowing rhythm of natural speech.

Romantic Forms

The **ode** was a poetic form favored by the Romantics, including William Wordsworth, Percy Bysshe Shelley, and John Keats. A long, complex poem (usually a meditation on a serious topic), the ode provided the Romantics with a form suited to their introspective, philosophical subject matter. Like many Romantic odes, Percy Bysshe Shelley's "Ode to the West Wind" looks both outward and inward. It exalts an aspect of

The Interior of the British Institution Gallery (1829), by John Scarlett Davis. Oil on canvas. Yale Center for British Art, Paul Mellon Collection, U.S.

Disappointed Love (1821), by Francis Danby (1793–1861). Oil on panel. Victoria & Albert Museum, London.

nature, the powerful yet invisible wind, and contemplates the movement of unseen forces in the poet's own mind and life. However, the stanzas of "Ode to the West Wind" are unusual because they are each a variation on the **sonnet** form, a fourteen-line lyric form in iambic pentameter.

The sonnet's popularity was strong during the Renaissance after Thomas Wyatt introduced the form to England but had waned during the Restoration. Wordsworth reestablished its popularity during the Romantic period, and he and Keats were its masters.

Another Renaissance form used by Romantic poets, such as George Gordon, Lord Byron, is the nine-line **Spenserian stanza,** invented by the Renaissance poet Edmund Spenser.

Ask Yourself

1. What was more important to Romantic poets, form or function? Why?
2. What topics did Romantic poets pursue? Why?

Preparing to Read

She Walks in Beauty

from Childe Harold's Pilgrimage, Canto IV

What Do You Think? How can we use imagination to discover truth?

QuickTalk

Who is the most beautiful person you know? Is the beauty physical or emotional? In your *Reader/Writer Notebook*, write about this person, describing his or her beauty.

MEET THE WRITER

George Gordon, Lord Byron
(1788–1824)

In his Romantic poetry, Lord Byron fused aristocratic living, wild pursuits, a sensitive outlook, and precise language.

Sudden Wealth and Fame

Were it not for a twist of fate, George Gordon, Lord Byron might have grown up confined by the harsh Calvinism of Scotland. When his cousin died in battle in 1794, six-year-old George became first in line to be the sixth Baron Byron of Rochdale; four years later, he assumed the title.

Byron's rise in literary circles came no less abruptly. In 1812, the midpoint of the Romantic period, he became a celebrity when the first two cantos of his poem *Childe Harold's Pilgrimage* were published. The poem is based on Byron's travels to Europe and Asia Minor. Byron later said, "I awoke one morning and found myself famous." Four years later, he left for the Continent, never to return to Great Britain.

The Neoclassical Romantic

When Byron left England in 1816, he made contact with Percy Shelley and his wife, Mary, in Switzerland, and Byron's writing life began in earnest. He then moved to Italy, and despite the tales of debauchery that surrounded his time in Venice, there is little doubt, Byron worked hard at his writing. His wildness and aristocratic ease often obscured a period of great literary productivity.

As a poet, Byron was not a Romantic in style, for he admired the techniques of neoclassical writers who wrote with wit and precision. Yet throughout the nineteenth century, he was considered the incarnation of the "Romantic" sensibility. His premature death only reinforced this image. Byron set sail for Greece in July 1823 to support the Greek nationalists in their struggle for independence from Turkey. In a marshy Greek town called Missolonghi, he came down with fevers that took his life only a few months after his thirty-sixth birthday.

Think About the Writer How did Byron's early fame and wealth affect his lifestyle and writing? Explain.

Byron, Sixth Baron, detail by Richard Westall (1765–1836).

She Walks in Beauty

Reader/Writer Notebook

Use your **RWN** to complete the activities for this selection.

Literary Focus

Simile A **simile** is a figure of speech that makes an imaginative comparison between two seemingly unlike things by using a connective word such as *like, as, than,* or *resembles.*

Some examples of similes are: He's as helpful as a doorknob on a bathtub, She plays the flute better than the Pied Piper, and They are like two peas in a pod. Writers often use similes to encourage readers to think about something in a fresh, new way. In "She Walks in Beauty," Byron compares a beautiful woman to the night. Identify the line in which Byron makes this comparison; then, note how he develops the comparison throughout the poem.

Writing Focus

Think as a Reader/Writer

Find It in Your Reading In this short poem, Byron creates **rhythm** by using **repetition** to form pairs of phrases such as "How pure, how dear." In a chart like the one below, list pairs you find as you read the poem. Record some notes about how the pairs <u>function</u> in the poem.

Line Numbers	Paired Phrases
line 12	"How pure, how dear…"

Vocabulary

gaudy (GAW dee) *adj.:* overly bright or colorful. *During Byron's day, a woman in mourning avoided gaudy clothing and wore mostly black.*

impaired (ihm PAIRD) *v.:* marred; weakened. *The woman's dark clothing had not impaired her beauty.*

serenely (suh REEN lee) *adv.:* calmly; peacefully. *She moves serenely through the crowd and does not show her grief.*

Language Coach

Verbs Used as Adjectives Some verbs that end in *—ed* can be used as adjectives. Remember that adjectives describe a noun or pronoun. In this poem, Byron describes a woman's grace as *impaired*. The verb *impair* means "to weaken"; therefore, grace that is impaired is weakened. The poet also describes her eyes as *mellowed*. What does this verb mean? How can you tell that it is used as an adjective?

Learn It Online
Learn more about Byron and his world through these Internet links.

go.hrw.com   L12-811   **Go**

She Walks in Beauty

by **George Gordon, Lord Byron**

Read with a Purpose
Read to discover the impression a beautiful woman makes on the speaker.

Build Background
"She Walks in Beauty," one of Byron's most famous poems, was supposedly inspired by Lady Wilmot Horton, a beautiful woman whom Byron saw at a ball, perhaps in the spring of 1814. Lady Horton was in mourning and, in the fashion of the times, was wearing a black dress decorated with glittering spangles.

She walks in beauty, like the night
    Of cloudless climes° and starry skies;
And all that's best of dark and bright
    Meet in her aspect° and her eyes:
5 Thus mellowed to that tender light
    Which heaven to gaudy day denies.

One shade the more, one ray the less,
    Had half impaired the nameless grace
Which waves in every raven tress,
10   Or softly lightens o'er her face;
Where thoughts serenely sweet express
    How pure, how dear their dwelling place.

And on that cheek, and o'er that brow,
    So soft, so calm, yet eloquent,
15 The smiles that win, the tints that glow,
    But tell of days in goodness spent,
A mind at peace with all below,
    A heart whose love is innocent!

2. climes: atmospheres; climates.

4. aspect: face; look.

A **Literary Focus** Simile What is being compared in this poem? Why would these two things be linked?

Vocabulary **gaudy** (GAW dee) *adj.*: overly bright or colorful.
impaired (ihm PAIRD) *v.*: marred; weakened.
serenely (suh REEN lee) *adv.*: calmly; peacefully.

Miranda (1878), by Sir Frank Dicksee.
The Maas Gallery, London.

Preparing to Read

from Childe Harold's Pilgrimage, Canto IV

Reader/Writer Notebook

Use your **RWN** to complete the activities for this selection.

Literary Focus

Apostrophe In a figure of speech called **apostrophe,** a speaker directly addresses an absent or dead person, an abstract quality, or something nonhuman as if it were present and capable of responding. Apostrophe was a popular poetic <u>device</u> used by the Romantics. In this poem, Byron apostrophizes the ocean.

Reading Focus

Understanding Rhyme and Rhythm In *Childe Harold's Pilgrimage,* Byron uses the **Spenserian stanza,** invented by the Renaissance poet Edmund Spenser. Byron, Shelley, and Keats all employed this challenging verse form, which uses only three different end rhymes in each nine-line stanza. The rhyme scheme is *ababbcbcc.* The first eight lines of each stanza are written in **iambic pentameter,** and the ninth line adds a poetic foot, or beat, to create an **alexandrine,** a line of **iambic hexameter.** The alexandrine often summarizes a stanza or concludes it with a image.

Into Action Record each stanza's subject and how the alexandrine concludes it. Add a star if the alexandrine incorporates apostrophe.

Subject of Stanza	How Alexandrine Concludes Stanza
Stanza 1: The speaker tells of his love and enjoyment of nature.	Alexandrine explains nature's impact on speaker

Writing Focus

Think as a Reader/Writer

Find It in Your Writing In this poem, as in "She Walks in Beauty," Byron uses parallel sets of words and phrases. Sometimes he uses a series of words with a similar sound, such as "unknelled, uncoffined, and unknown." In your *Reader/Writer Notebook,* record parallel words and phrases. Note the effect this **parallelism** has on the sound of the poem.

Vocabulary

rapture (RAP chuhr) *n.:* bliss; profound joy. *As he wanders, Childe Harold seeks rapture in nature.*

intrudes (ihn TROODZ) *v.:* pushes in; interrupts. *When a crowd intrudes on his thoughts, he travels to a secluded place.*

mingle (MIHNG guhl) *v.:* mix. *He has no wish to mingle with people on the city's noisy streets.*

protracted (proh TRAK tihd) *v.* used as *adj.:* drawn out over time. *He craves solitary, protracted visits with nature.*

linger (LIHNG guhr) *v.:* stay a long while. *Upon approaching a beautiful and remote landscape, he will linger for many hours before resuming his journey.*

Language Coach

Connotations Poets choose words for both their **denotations** (dictionary definitions) and their **connotations** (the meanings associated with them). *Rapture* means "profound joy" but also has religious and spiritual connotations. Why might Byron have written about "rapture on the lonely shore" rather than "deep joy on the lonely shore"?

Learn It Online
Listen to this poem online.

go.hrw.com L12-813   Go

from
Childe Harold's Pilgrimage, Canto IV

by **George Gordon, Lord Byron**

Read with a Purpose
Read to discover what Childe Harold learns about nature and himself.

Build Background
In medieval times, *childe* probably meant "a young noble awaiting knighthood." Byron uses it as a title, like *Lord* or *Sir*, for a youth of "gentle" birth. *Childe Harold's Pilgrimage* is a long, thinly disguised autobiographical poem about Byron's own journeys.

In this excerpt from the final canto, the speaker addresses the ocean. The last two stanzas present Byron's personal conclusion to the whole poem. At this point, Byron has ceased trying to separate himself from the figure of Childe Harold.

1

There is a pleasure in the pathless woods,
There is a rapture on the lonely shore,
There is society, where none intrudes,
By the deep sea, and music in its roar:
5 I love not man the less, but Nature more,
From these our interviews, in which I steal°
From all I may be, or have been before,
To mingle with the Universe, and feel
What I can ne'er express, yet cannot all conceal. **A**

6. **steal:** remove myself.

2

10 Roll on, thou deep and dark blue Ocean—roll!
Ten thousand fleets sweep over thee in vain;
Man marks the earth with ruin—his control
Stops with the shore; upon the watery plain
The wrecks are all thy deed, nor doth remain

A Reading Focus Understanding Rhyme and Rhythm In what way does the intricate form of the Spenserian stanzas fit the poem's subject?

Vocabulary **rapture** (RAP chuhr) *n.:* bliss; profound joy.
intrudes (ihn TROODZ) *v.:* pushes in; interrupts.
mingle (MIHNG guhl) *v.:* mix.

15   A shadow of man's ravage, save his own,
       When, for a moment, like a drop of rain,
       He sinks into thy depths with bubbling groan,
  Without a grave, unknelled,° uncoffined, and unknown.

3

       And I have loved thee, Ocean! and my joy
20   Of youthful sports was on thy breast to be
       Borne, like thy bubbles, onward: From a boy
       I wantoned° with thy breakers—they to me
       Were a delight; and if the freshening° sea
       Made them a terror—'twas a pleasing fear,
25   For I was as it were a child of thee,
       And trusted to thy billows far and near,
  And laid my hand upon thy mane—as I do here. **B**

4

       My task is done, my song hath ceased, my theme
       Has died into an echo; it is fit
30   The spell should break of this protracted dream.
       The torch shall be extinguished which hath lit
       My midnight lamp—and what is writ, is writ;
       Would it were worthier! but I am not now
       That which I have been—and my visions flit
35   Less palpably° before me—and the glow
  Which in my spirit dwelt is fluttering, faint, and low.

5

       Farewell! a word that must be, and hath been—
       A sound which makes us linger;—yet—farewell!
       Ye! who have traced the Pilgrim to the scene
40   Which is his last, if in your memories dwell
       A thought which once was his, if on ye swell
       A single recollection, not in vain
       He wore his sandal shoon and scallop shell;°
       Farewell! with *him* alone may rest the pain,
45   If such there were—with *you*, the moral of his strain.° **C**

18. **unknelled** (uhn NEHLD): without the traditional ringing of a church bell to announce his death.

22. **wantoned:** frolicked; played happily.
23. **freshening:** becoming rough as the wind comes up.

35. **palpably:** clearly.

43. **sandal shoon . . . shell:** *Shoon* is archaic for "shoes." Sandals and a scallop shell worn on a hat were traditional emblems of pilgrims. The scallop shell is a symbol of Saint James, whose shrine in Spain was a great attraction to pilgrims.
45. **strain:** passage of poetry or song.

B **Literary Focus** Apostrophe How does Childe Harold profess his love as he addresses the ocean in this apostrophe?

C **Literary Focus** Apostrophe What is the tone of the speaker's address to the reader? Why might he make such an emphatic farewell?

Vocabulary **protracted** (proh TRAK tihd) *v.* used as *adj.*: drawn out over time.
linger (LIHNG guhr) *v.*: stay a long while.

Applying Your Skills

SKILLS FOCUS Literary Skills Analyze simile; analyze apostrophe; analyze alliteration. **Reading Skills** Analyze rhyme and rhythm. **Vocabulary**

Skills Demonstrate knowledge of literal meanings of words and their usage. **Writing Skills** Use parallelism correctly.

She Walks in Beauty
from Childe Harold's Pilgrimage, Canto IV

Respond and Think Critically

Reading Focus

Read with a Purpose

1. In "She Walks in Beauty," how does the woman's beauty affect the speaker?

2. In *Childe Harold's Pilgrimage,* how does the speaker reveal what he's learned about nature and himself?

Reading Skills: Understanding Rhyme and Rhythm

3. In your chart for *Childe Harold's Pilgrimage,* explain how each alexandrine helps you understand its stanza. Describe how each apostrophe affects its stanza's conclusion.

Subject of Stanza	How Alexandrine Concludes Stanza	How Alexandrine Helps Reader to Understand Stanza
Stanza 1: The speaker tells of his love and enjoyment of nature.	Alexandrine explains nature's impact on speaker	The speaker cannot fully describe his deep feelings about nature.

✔ Vocabulary Check

Match each Vocabulary word to its definition.

4. serenely
5. gaudy
6. impaired
7. intrudes
8. linger
9. mingle
10. protracted
11. rapture

a. breaks in; encroaches
b. extreme joy
c. damaged
d. move among; join in
e. lasting for a while
f. calmly
g. loud in color or style
h. hang around

Literary Focus

Literary Analysis

12. **Compare** The words "dark and bright" in line 3 of "She Walks in Beauty" suggest a balance of opposites. How is this idea developed in the poem?

13. **Analyze** In stanza 3 of *Childe Harold's Pilgrimage,* what metaphor compares the sea to a horse? What is the effect of this comparison?

Literary Skills: Simile / Apostrophe

14. **Analyze** Explain the simile in the first stanza of "She Walks in Beauty" and the emotions it evokes.

15. **Interpret** How does the use of apostrophe in line 10 of *Childe Harolde's Pilgrimage* add to the description?

Literary Skills Review: Alliteration

16. **Analyze** The repetition of consonant sounds in words that are close to one another is **alliteration.** In each poem, identify an example of alliteration, and analyze its effect.

Writing Focus

Think as a Reader/Writer

Use It in Your Writing Write a brief description of something you find beautiful or moving. Include at least three pairs or sets of parallel words and phrases to add rhythm and impact to your description.

 What Do You Think Now

How do the speakers in both poems identify and describe true beauty? Explain.

Reading Focus

Ozymandias

Comparing and Contrasting by **Kylene Beers**

The act of comparing and contrasting helps us to see more, and to see more clearly. Holding two poems side by side and looking for similarities and differences often reveals features that escaped you when you read the poems separately. Comparing and contrasting requires us to re-read and gives us a deeper understanding of the writer's message.

To **compare and contrast,** you must establish a basis for comparison by asking how the two elements are similar. Two ideas, objects, people, or events should be similar in some way or exist in similar circumstances before you can compare them.

For example, the poems, "Ode to the West Wind" by Percy Bysshe Shelley and "Ode to a Nightingale" by John Keats, share attributes that we can compare: Both were written during the Romantic period, address an element of nature, and use the characteristics and structure of an ode. With the basis of comparison established, we may discover additional similarities and also consider differences.

While poems and other pieces of literature can be compared and contrasted, we can also apply the process within a single piece. Shelley's poem "Ozymandias" provides an opportunity to do just that.

The poem's speaker recounts a memorable experience retold by a "traveler from an antique land" who has seen the ruins of the statue of King Ozymandias. He describes the "trunkless legs of stone" and "shattered visage" of the once glorious statue. He establishes the basis for comparison and contrast: the statue as originally crafted by the sculptor's hand and as it now appears to the traveler untold years later. The traveler reads the inscription that the sculptor wrought:

"My name is Ozymandias, king of kings,
Look on my works, ye Mighty, and despair!"

The contrast between the haughty king whose "sneer of cold command" was once wrought in stone and that now exists only as a "colossal wreck" creates the image Shelley uses to communicate the ironic theme in the poem. Regardless of the power and might of a man and the monuments and tributes people create to honor him, only nature is as lasting and "boundless," as represented by the desert surrounding the ruins. Shelley's use of comparison and contrast creates a powerful image that expresses an unforgettable observation about nature, life, and death.

Your Turn

Read lines 11–14 from stanza 2 and lines 31–34 from stanza 4 of Keats's "Ode on a Grecian Urn."

> 2
> Heard melodies are sweet, but those unheard
>   Are sweeter; therefore, ye soft pipes, play on;
> Not to the sensual ear, but, more endeared,
>   Pipe to the spirit ditties of no tone:…
>
> 4
> Who are these coming to the sacrifice?
>   To what green altar, O mysterious priest,
> Lead'st thou that heifer lowing at the skies,
>   And all her silken flanks with garlands dressed?…

How do the first four lines of stanza 2 compare and contrast with the first four lines of stanza 4? What hints do these similarities and differences give you about the poem's theme? Later, when you read the complete poem, check to see if you were right.

Ozymandias

Ode to the West Wind

To a Skylark

What Do You Think? How can we use imagination to discover truth?

QuickTalk

What sights (natural or manmade) prompt you to think imaginatively about life? In your *Reader/Writer Notebook,* list at least three such sights, and describe the kinds of imaginative thoughts each sight generates in you.

Percy Bysshe Shelley
(1792–1822)

Percy Bysshe Shelley lived a turbulent life, but he believed deeply that human thought and expression had the inherent power to change life for the better.

Dramatic Life

At nineteen, estranged from his family, Shelley embarked on a career of courting the unconventional. To "rescue" her from a tyrannical father, he eloped with sixteen-year-old Harriet West-brook, a classmate of his sisters. Three years later he abandoned Harriet and ran away with seventeen-year-old Mary Godwin, the daughter of two of the most important radical thinkers of the 1790s, Mary Wollstonecraft and William Godwin. Percy's alliance with Mary also involved responsibility for Mary's fifteen-year-old stepsister, Jane Clairmont, who soon changed her name to Claire and accompanied Shelley and Mary to Europe. Claire's brief affair with Byron brought Shelley and Byron together in 1816 in Switzerland in one of the age's most important literary relationships.

Shortly after the Shelleys' return to England, Harriet, only twenty-one, drowned herself in a pond in Hyde Park. Shelley could now wed Mary but was denied custody of his two children with Harriet.

Dramatic Death

Shelley and Mary fled their debts and notoriety in England and returned to the Continent. The next four years were Shelley's most productive, during which he wrote one inspired work after another.

In 1822, when he was not yet thirty, Shelley and a companion, Edward Williams, drowned when their sailboat, the *Ariel,* sank in a storm off the northwestern coast of Italy. Almost two weeks later, Shelley's body washed ashore, a copy of Sophocles' writing in one pocket and a copy of Keats's writing in the other. The body was burned in a pyre on the beach while friends (including Byron) stood by. Shelley's ashes were buried in the Protestant cemetery in Rome.

Think About the Writer What do Shelley's travels and relationships suggest about his imagination?

Percy Bysshe Shelley (1792–1822), by Joseph Severn (1845). Oil on canvas. Keats-Shelley Memorial House, Rome, Italy.

Ozymandias

Reader/Writer Notebook

Use your **RWN** to complete the activities for this selection.

Literary Focus

Irony A discrepancy between expectation and reality is called **irony.** This poem turns on a kind of irony called **situational irony,** which is created when the opposite of an expected event or outcome occurs. Although "Ozymandias" is a short poem, several characters appear in its lines. Think about which characters expect one thing to happen, only to have something else occur. How might this ironic outcome relate to Shelley's poem in particular, and with works of art in general?

Literary Perspectives Apply the literary perspective described on page 820 as you read this sonnet.

Reading Focus

Comparing and Contrasting To **compare** is to see how things are alike; to **contrast** is to see how they are different. Both skills define our world, helping us <u>differentiate</u> and categorize things around us. Irony requires us to compare and contrast, because we must compare what is expected with what really happens and note any differences.

Into Action As you read "Ozymandias," use the details in the poem to create a compare-and-contrast chart like the one below. Focus on what has changed since the statue was first completed.

Now	Then
The statue is in pieces.	The statue was whole and towered over everyone.
The statue is impressive even though it is in pieces.	The statue was impressive in its original form.

Vocabulary

antique (an TEEK) *adj.:* ancient. *The antique and decaying ruins fascinated the traveler.*

sneer (snihr) *n.:* proud, unkind facial expression. *The king's sneer caused his servants to tremble with fear.*

passions (PASH uhnz) *n. pl.:* strong emotions. *What passions led the king to command the creation of this statue?*

colossal (kuh LAHS uhl) *adj.:* magnificently huge. *Did he hope that the colossal work would endure forever?*

boundless (BOWND lihs) *adj.:* limitless. *The boundless reach of time eventually conquers mere stone.*

Language Coach

Pronunciation Read aloud the words *passions, colossal,* and *boundless.* What do you notice about the sounds the double *s* makes? Can you think of other words in which a double *s* makes the same sound as in *passions*? What general rule can you determine about when each pronunciation is used?

Writing Focus

Think as a Reader/Writer

Find It in Your Reading In "Ozymandias," Shelley chooses his words carefully to create vivid **images** and a particular **tone,** as well as a particular **rhythm** and **rhyme** pattern. In your *Reader/Writer Notebook,* note the effects of some of Shelley's word choices.

Learn It Online
Get to know this poem through the video introduction online.

go.hrw.com	L12-819	Go

OZYMANDIAS

by **Percy Bysshe Shelley**

Read with a Purpose
Read to discover what became of a mighty king's legacy.

Build Background
One of Shelley's few sonnets, "Ozymandias" was written as part of a friendly and informal poetry competition in 1817. The poetic topic was Egypt, inspired by extraordinary Egyptian fragments that had recently been displayed at the British Museum in London. Some of these fragments were from the empire of Ramses II (c. 1290–1224 B.C.), who built monuments all over Egypt. Ozymandias is the Greek name for Ramses II.

The greatest colonnaded hall ever constructed, the Great Hall at Karnak was so huge that one hundred men could stand on the capital of each column.

Statue of Ramses II at Karnak Luxor, Egypt.

I met a traveler from an antique land
Who said: Two vast and trunkless legs° of stone
Stand in the desert… Near them, on the sand,
Half sunk, a shattered visage° lies, whose frown,
5   And wrinkled lip, and sneer of cold command,
Tell that its sculptor well those passions read
Which yet survive, stamped on these lifeless things, **A**
The hand that mocked them, and the heart° that fed;
And on the pedestal these words appear:
10   "My name is Ozymandias, king of kings,
Look on my works, ye Mighty, and despair!"
Nothing beside remains. Round the decay **B**
Of that colossal wreck, boundless and bare
The lone and level sands stretch far away. **C**

---

2. **trunkless legs:** the legs without the rest of the body.
4. **visage:** face; look.
8. **hand… heart:** the hand of the sculptor, who scorned the passions to which Ozymandias gave himself wholeheartedly.

Literary Perspectives

Analyzing Style Style is the way writers say what they wish to say. Even if writers express similar ideas, each writer has a unique manner of expressing those ideas. To analyze Shelley's style in "Ozymandias," pay close attention to how he uses language: Is the diction formal or casual? plain spoken or poetic? Is the tone serious, comic, or ironic? Does he use figures of speech, such as similes or metaphors?

As you read, be sure to notice the questions in the poem, which will guide you in using this perspective.

A **Reading Focus** **Comparing and Contrasting** Choose a word from line 6 and a word from line 7 that show contrasting details in the traveler's description of the statue. What does this contrast suggest about the sculptor?

B **Literary Focus** **Irony** How does the setting described in lines 12–14 add to the irony of this inscription?

C **Literary Perspectives** **Analyzing Style** As you read this poem, what images appear in your mind? What literary techniques does the poet use to help create those images?

Vocabulary **antique** (an TEEK) *adj.:* ancient.
sneer (snihr) *n.:* proud, unkind facial expression.
passions (PASH uhnz) *n. pl.:* strong emotions.
colossal (kuh LAHS uhl) *adj.:* magnificently huge.
boundless (BOWND lihs) *adj.:* limitless.

SKILLS FOCUS Literary Skills Analyze irony; analyze sonnet; analyze the use of style. **Reading Skills** Compare and contrast. **Writing Skills** Write descriptive essays; write narratives; use appropriate word choice; develop writer's style.

Respond and Think Critically

Reading Focus

Quick Check

1. According to the poem, what was the sculptor's attitude toward the subject of his artwork?

2. If we assume his statue represents him well, what kind of king was Ozymandias?

3. Who should "despair" in this poem? Why?

Read with a Purpose

4. Would Ozymandias be surprised at what happened to his statue? What message does the statue's fate send to readers of the poem?

Reading Skills: Comparing and Contrasting

5. Circle the contrasts you noted in the chart, and underline the comparisons. Then, write a few sentences explaining how the comparisons and contrasts work together to help deliver the poem's message.

Now	Then
The statue is in (pieces).	The statue was (whole and towered) over everyone.
The statue is impressive even though it is in pieces.	The statue was impressive in its original form.

Literary Focus

Literary Analysis

6. **Summarize** Even in the brief space of a sonnet, Shelley suggests a number of narrative frames. How many speakers do you hear in this poem? Summarize what each one says.

7. **Interpret** What is the poem's message about pride?

8. **Literary Perspectives** This poem is a sonnet, one of the most timeless, constrained, and formal types of poetry. How does Shelley's choice of the sonnet form enhance the overall effect of the poem? What does it suggest about his style?

Literary Skills: Irony

9. **Analyze** What did Ozymandias expect people to see when they looked at his "works"? What do they actually see?

Literary Skills Review: Sonnet

10. **Analyze** A **sonnet** is a fourteen-line lyric poem, usually written in iambic pentameter, that has one of several rhyme schemes. Many sonnets have a **turn,** a pivotal point in the sonnet at which a question is answered, a solution is proposed, or a comment is offered. Where is the turn in "Ozymandias"? What is the function of the lines that follow the turn?

Writing Focus

Think as a Reader/Writer

Use It in Your Writing Now that you have read the poem and considered Shelley's word choices, focus on word choice in your own writing. In your *Reader/ Writer Notebook,* write a descriptive or narrative paragraph about a scene or event that is vivid in your memory. Consider how the words you choose affect the way your writing sounds, the tone it conveys, and the images it creates for your readers.

What Do **You Think Now**

Imagine that you are standing in front of the ruins of Ozymandias's statue. What could you learn about immortality, pride, and memory from the condition of the fallen monument?

Vocabulary Development

✓ Vocabulary Check

Match the Vocabulary words with their definitions.

1. antique
2. sneer
3. passions
4. colossal
5. boundless

a. infinite
b. enormously grand
c. unpleasant expression
d. old
e. strong emotions

Vocabulary Skills: Using Print and Online Sources

When you encounter an unfamiliar word, you can use print and online sources to learn about a word's meaning, use, and history. A dictionary is a good resource for finding help with words you do not know. Even if you are not sure how a word is spelled, you can usually find it in a dictionary by starting with your best guesses at its spelling. In a dictionary, you will learn the word's meaning, correct spelling, history, and related words. You can find print and online dictionaries in a library.

You can also use other online sources to study words. Several online dictionaries are free. Word lists for specific content areas are often found on specialized Web sites. If you need to differentiate the terms *ROM* and *RAM*, for example, you might check a site that explains computer terms. No matter what source you use, you can keep track of what you learn by creating vocabulary cards like this one:

new word	pedestal
meaning	support or foot of a column; base of an upright structure
part of speech	noun
related words	words with —ped— ("foot"), such as pedal
sample sentence	A strong pedestal will support a large statue.
source of info	Merriam—Webster online

Your Turn

Use five print and online sources to create vocabulary cards for the Vocabulary words. Follow the model of the vocabulary card for *pedestal*.

Language Coach

Pronunciation The double *s* in *colossal* and *boundless* is pronounced /s/. The double *s* in *passions* is pronounced /sh/. Sort the following words into a chart, and then complete the pronunciation rule below: *recession, lesson, missionary, hassle, impassable, trunkless, pressure, possessing.*

/s/ sound	/sh/ sound

The double *s* is usually pronounced as _____, but when it is followed by _____ or _____, it is pronounced as _____.

Academic Vocabulary

Write About...
How can we differentiate ourselves in a meaningful, positive way? When we die, what can we leave behind to show that our passage through life mattered? Record some thoughts about whether—and how—human beings can create something through words and work that will outlive them.

Grammar Link

Sentence Structure

Sentences are made up of **clauses,** or groups of words that contain both a subject and a verb. The kind and number of clauses in a sentence determines **sentence structure.** A **simple** sentence has one independent clause and no subordinate clauses.

> Percy Bysshe Shelley was a student at Oxford.

A **compound** sentence has two or more independent clauses but no subordinate clauses.

> Shelley was born in England, but he died in Italy.

A **complex** sentence contains one independent clause and one or more subordinate clauses.

> Although sailors encountered Shelley's boat in a storm, Shelley refused their offer to go on board.

A **compound-complex** sentence contains two or more independent clauses and one or more subordinate clauses.

> Shelley died before he was thirty, but his poems endure.

Your Turn

Identify the following sentences as simple, compound, complex, or compound-complex.

1. Shelley wrote relatively few sonnets, and "Ozymandias" is one of his best.

2. It describes the ruins of a statue that once stood in a far-off desert.

3. Although the words on the pedestal are proud, the king's mighty works have crumbled, and the barren desert surrounds them.

Writing Application Combine and revise sentences to vary the sentence structure in some paragraphs you have written in your *Reader/Writer Notebook.*

CHOICES

As you respond to the Choices, use these **Academic Vocabulary** words as appropriate: differentiate, inherent, device, technique, function.

REVIEW

Write an Inscription

The inscription on Ozymandias's statue seems ironic, given the once massive, awe-inspiring monument now lies in ruins. Write an inscription that is more in keeping with the statue's ruined condition.

CONNECT

Assess the Message

Timed └Writing In a brief essay, compare and contrast the message of "Ozymandias" with the message of Keats's "Ode on a Grecian Urn" or Shakespeare's Sonnet 18. Citing examples, explain what each poem says about the lasting power of art.

EXTEND

Documenting the Past and the Future

TechFocus With a small group, create a digital presentation of images of famous ruins from different cultures. Also, include modern buildings or other objects that you think will survive into the future. What will these objects tell future people about the world today?

Temple of Inscriptions, Palenque, Mexico.

Learn It Online
Visit the *MediaScope* mini-site online for tips on how to create a great digital presentation.

go.hrw.com | L12-823 | **Go**

Ode to the West Wind

Reader/Writer
Notebook

Use your **RWN** to complete the activities for this selection.

Literary Focus

Ode The **ode,** a complex, usually long, lyric poem written in dignified language about a serious subject, was a favorite poetic form among the Romantics. In ancient Greece and Rome, odes were written to be read in public on ceremonial occasions. In modern literature, odes tend to be more private, informal, and reflective. Like many Romantic odes, Shelley's "Ode to the West Wind" looks both outward and inward. It pays tribute to an aspect of nature—the powerful yet invisible wind—and connects the movement of the unseen wind with the power of the poet's imagination.

Shelley's ode consists of five sonnets written in a special **rhyme scheme,** or pattern, called **terza rima** (meaning "third rhyme"). This rhyme scheme uses interlocking three-line stanzas that rhyme in the pattern *aba bcb cdc ded.* The stanzas are described as interlocking because each three-line group picks up the rhyme of the second line in the previous group. In the Shakespearean manner, Shelley ends each sonnet with a rhymed **couplet:** *ee.* As you read, consider how this challenging rhyme scheme adds to the ode's elegant tone.

Writing Focus

Think as a Reader/Writer

Find It in Your Reading As you read each stanza, use a chart like the one below to write down your thoughts on how Shelley's varied sentence lengths and structures affect the flow, rhythm, pacing, and meaning.

Stanza	Observations about Sentence Structure	Effect on Flow, Rhythm, Pacing, Meaning
I	one long sentence with multiple phrases and dependent clauses, some with inverted word order; main verb, an imperative, comes at the end and is repeated twice.	provides a long, rolling list of the west wind's attributes and actions; varied length of phrases and clauses varies pace, sounds natural, despite lack of full-stop structure; establishes the wind as "destroyer and preserver," contrasted with Spring wind
II		
III		

Vocabulary

multitudes (MUHL tuh toodz) *n. pl.:* crowds; great numbers. *Multitudes of readers have experienced the powerful wind that blows through Shelley's ode.*

zenith (ZEE nihth) *n.:* highest point. *The cloud's zenith creates a mystical design against the sky.*

foliage (FOH lihj) *n.:* leafy plants. *Autumn winds strip the fall foliage from trees.*

tumult (TOO muhlt) *n.:* great noise; agitation. *The storms of autumn bring a tumult of thunder.*

withered (WIHTH uhrd) *v.* used as *adj.:* dried up. *As winter approaches, plants become withered and die in the colder winds.*

Language Coach

Word Origins The word *multitudes* comes from the Latin word meaning "many." The prefix *multi–* shares the same origin. Explain how this origin affects the meanings of these words: *multicultural, multicolor, multifaceted, multilingual, multinational.*

Learn It Online
Learn more about Shelley at the Writers' Lives site online.

go.hrw.com   L12-824   **Go**

ODE

ODE TO THE WEST WIND

by Percy Bysshe Shelley

Read with a Purpose
Read to discover the insight the speaker gains from experiencing the wind's power.

Build Background
Written in late October 1819, this major lyric was inspired by an oncoming storm near Florence, Italy, where Shelley was living at the time. The poem marks a temporary note of exaltation in Shelley's creative life after a period of intense grief over the death of his three-year-old son, William. The ode expresses Shelley's sense of purpose as a public poet and contains his personal thoughts about that role. To experience the poem's passionate and musical language, read the ode aloud.

I

O wild West Wind, thou breath of Autumn's being,
Thou, from whose unseen presence the leaves dead
Are driven, like ghosts from an enchanter fleeing,

Yellow, and black, and pale, and hectic° red,
5   Pestilence-stricken multitudes: O thou,
Who chariotest to their dark wintry bed

The winged seeds, where they lie cold and low,
Each like a corpse within its grave, until
Thine azure° sister of the Spring shall blow

10   Her clarion° o'er the dreaming earth, and fill
(Driving sweet buds like flocks to feed in air)
With living hues and odors plain and hill:

Wild Spirit, which art moving everywhere;
Destroyer and preserver; hear, O, hear!   **(A)**

II

15   Thou on whose stream, 'mid the steep sky's commotion,
Loose clouds like earth's decaying leaves are shed,
Shook from the tangled boughs of Heaven and Ocean,

4. hectic: reference to the feverish flush caused by wasting diseases, such as tuberculosis.

9. azure: sky-blue.

10. clarion: type of trumpet.

(A) Literary Focus Ode The ode traditionally focuses on a significant subject. How do the two final lines of this section make the west wind seem especially important?

Vocabulary multitudes (MUHL tuh toodz) *n. pl.*: crowds; great numbers.

Angels of rain and lightning: there are spread
On the blue surface of thine aery° surge,
20 Like the bright hair uplifted from the head

Of some fierce Maenad,° even from the dim verge
Of the horizon to the zenith's height,
The locks of the approaching storm. Thou dirge°

Of the dying year, to which this closing night
25 Will be the dome of a vast sepulcher,
Vaulted with all thy congregated might

Of vapors, from whose solid atmosphere
Black rain, and fire, and hail will burst: O, hear!

III

Thou who didst waken from his summer dreams
30 The blue Mediterranean, where he lay,
Lulled by the coil of his crystalline streams,

Beside a pumice° isle in Baiae's bay,°
And saw in sleep old palaces and towers
Quivering within the wave's intenser day,

35 All overgrown with azure moss and flowers
So sweet, the sense faints picturing them! Thou
For whose path the Atlantic's level powers

Cleave° themselves into chasms, while far below
The sea-blooms and the oozy woods which wear
40 The sapless foliage of the ocean, know

Thy voice, and suddenly grow gray with fear,
And tremble and despoil° themselves: O, hear!

IV

If I were a dead leaf thou mightest bear;   **B**
If I were a swift cloud to fly with thee;
45 A wave to pant beneath thy power, and share

B **Literary Focus** **Ode** How do the references to the earlier parts of the poem in lines 43–45 affect your overall understanding of the poem ?

Vocabulary **zenith** (ZEE nihth) *n.:* highest point.
foliage (FOH lihj) *n.:* leafy plants.

---

19. aery: archaic word meaning "airy"; unsubstantial; seen only in the mind.

21. Maenad (MEE nad): in Greek mythology, a woman who performs frenzied dances in the worship of Dionysus, the god of wine.

23. dirge: slow, solemn poem or song that expresses grief or mourning.

32. pumice: light, porous volcanic stone. **isle in Baiae's bay:** in the Bay of Naples, where pumice is found. These islands were once summer resorts for Roman nobility and, in Shelley's time, were notable for their ruins of ancient villas and monumental baths.

38. cleave: divide.

42. despoil: strip.

The impulse of thy strength, only less free
Than thou, O uncontrollable! If even
I were as in my boyhood, and could be

The comrade of thy wanderings over Heaven,
50 As then, when to outstrip thy skiey° speed
Scarce seemed a vision; I would ne'er have striven

As thus with thee in prayer in my sore need.
Oh, lift me as a wave, a leaf, a cloud!
I fall upon the thorns of life! I bleed!

55 A heavy weight of hours has chained and bowed
One too like thee: tameless, and swift, and proud. **C**

V

Make me thy lyre,° even as the forest is:
What if my leaves are falling like its own!
The tumult of thy mighty harmonies

60 Will take from both a deep, autumnal tone,
Sweet though in sadness. Be thou, Spirit fierce,
My spirit! Be thou me, impetuous° one!

Drive my dead thoughts over the universe
Like withered leaves to quicken a new birth!
65 And, by the incantation of this verse,

Scatter, as from an unextinguished hearth°
Ashes and sparks, my words among mankind! **D**
Be through my lips to unawakened earth

The trumpet of a prophecy! O, Wind,
70 If Winter comes, can Spring be far behind?

50. skiey: like the sky; also, coming from the sky.

57. lyre: Aeolian (ee OH lee uhn) harp, a stringed instrument that emits sound when the wind blows across its strings.

62. impetuous: forceful; rushing.

66. unextinguished hearth: from Shelley's "A Defense of Poetry": "The mind in creation is as a fading coal, which some invisible influence, like an inconstant wind, awakens to transitory brightness."

C Literary Focus **Ode** Until this stanza, Shelley has been describing the wind's power and actions. How is Shelley's purpose in this stanza different?

D Literary Focus **Ode** In referring to his ode as an "incantation"—words chanted in a spell or magical ceremony—what is Shelley suggesting about the power of his language?

Vocabulary **tumult** (TOO muhlt) *n.*: great noise; agitation.
withered (WIHTH uhrd) *v.* used as *adj.*: dried up.

SKILLS FOCUS **Literary Skills** Analyze the characteristics of an ode; analyze imagery. **Vocabulary Skills** Use Vocabulary appropriately. **Writing Skills** Use varied sentence structure; revise by combining text; revise by rearranging text.

Respond and Think Critically

Reading Focus

Quick Check

1. Why does the speaker identify so intensely with the wind?

2. What does the speaker regret about his adult years, as compared to his boyhood?

3. What does the speaker request of the wind in part IV?

Read with a Purpose

4. Review the poem's final sentence. Explain the insight Shelley captures in this famous line.

✓ Vocabulary Check

Complete each sentence with a Vocabulary word.

foliage
multitudes
tumult
withered
zenith

5. At noon, the sun reaches the _____ of its daily path.

6. She kept the _____ bouquet as a reminder of the prom.

7. The skiers listened for the _____ of an avalanche.

8 The dark green _____ of the ivy stood out against the white walls.

9. _____ of people stood in line to be first to see the new movie.

Literary Focus

Literary Analysis

10. **Interpret** How can the wind be both "destroyer and preserver" (line 14)? Cite evidence from the text to support your ideas.

11. **Compare and Contrast** How do stanzas IV and V differ in tone and emphasis from the first three stanzas?

12. **Draw Conclusions** What lines of this ode suggest the grief of a parent who has just lost a child? What comfort does the parent find?

13. **Interpret** How do you explain the paradox, or seeming contradiction, that words are like "ashes and sparks" (line 67)?

Literary Skills: Ode

14. **Analyze** Explain how this poem fits the definition of an ode as a serious, complex meditation.

Literary Skills Review: Imagery

15. **Analyze** Language that appeals to the senses is **imagery.** What central image and emotion is evoked in each of the first three stanzas?

Writing Focus

Think as a Reader/Writer

Use It in Your Writing Select a piece of your own writing, and analyze how its sentence lengths and structures affect its flow, pacing, rhythm, and meaning. Revise your sentences (combine, cut, use repetition and parallel structures) to improve your writing.

What Do
You
Think
Now

How can we discover truth from encounters with nature?

Preparing to Read

To a Skylark

Reader/Writer Notebook
Use your **RWN** to complete the activities for this selection.

Literary Focus

Symbol A **symbol** is a person, place, thing, or event that stands both for itself and for something beyond itself. A symbol can operate on multiple levels. For example, in "To a Skylark," a speaker praises a bird for its beautiful song. At the same time, the skylark has another level of meaning for the speaker. Can you determine what the skylark symbolizes?

Reading Focus

Making Inferences Readers **make inferences** both from information stated directly and from hints or clues in the text. When you make intelligent guesses about a text based on the evidence or clues the writer has provided, you are making inferences. Inferences combine your own knowledge and experience with the information found in the text.

Into Action As you read, use a graphic organizer like the one below to record the evidence you use to make inferences about the symbols Shelley uses in the poem.

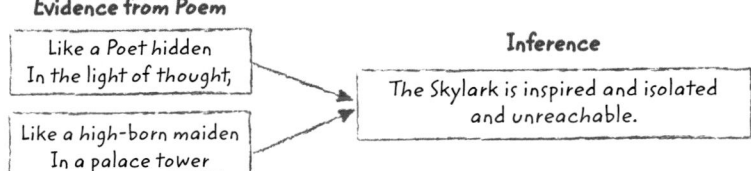

Evidence from Poem

| Like a Poet hidden In the light of thought; |
| Like a high-born maiden In a palace tower |

Inference

The Skylark is inspired and isolated and unreachable.

Writing Focus

Think as a Reader/Writer
Find It in Your Reading As you read, take notes in your *Reader/Writer Notebook* on how Shelley uses figurative language to describe the skylark and evoke its **symbolism.** In the first line, for example, the speaker calls the skylark a "blithe Spirit," asserting it as a symbol, not as a bird.

Vocabulary

blithe (blyth) *adj.:* happy and cheerful. *The bird's blithe song cheered us.*

profuse (pruh FYOOS) *adj.:* very abundant. *The skylark's profuse melodies last throughout the evening.*

unpremeditated (uhn pree MEHD uh tay tihd) *adj.:* not planned in advance. *The listener admires the spontaneity of the bird's unpremeditated songs.*

languor (LANG guhr) *n.:* lack of interest or enthusiasm. *The man's languor disappeared when he heard the invigorating song.*

satiety (suh TY uh tee) *n.:* feeling of disgust or weariness caused by excess. *Love's excessive highs and lows may lead to satiety.*

Language Coach
Multiple Prefixes The adjective *unpremeditated* contains two prefixes: *un–*, which means "not," and *pre–*, which means "in advance." Both prefixes affect the meaning of the base word *meditated*, which means "planned." An *unpremeditated* action is one that is not planned in advance. Explain the meanings of these words with double prefixes: *unprepared, unreconstructed, nondisclosure.*

Learn It Online
Explore Shelley's work and his world further through these Internet links.

go.hrw.com L12-829   **Go**

TO A SKYLARK

by **Percy Bysshe Shelley**

Read with a Purpose
Read to discover what the speaker wants to learn from the skylark.

Build Background
Shelley wrote "To a Skylark" in 1820 when he and his wife, Mary, were staying with friends near the Mediterranean coast of Italy. While on a walk, they heard the high-pitched musical song of the European skylark in flight. Mary later recalled, "It was on a beautiful summer evening, while wandering among the lanes whose myrtle hedges were the bowers of fireflies, that we heard the caroling of the skylark which inspired one of the most beautiful of his poems."

In this poem the speaker yearns to share in the skylark's joy and natural musicality.

Hail to thee, blithe Spirit!
    Bird thou never wert,
That from Heaven, or near it,
    Pourest thy full heart **A**
5 In profuse strains of unpremeditated art. **B**

    Higher still and higher
      From the earth thou springest
Like a cloud of fire;
    The blue deep thou wingest,
10 And singing still dost soar, and soaring ever singest.

    In the golden lightning
      Of the sunken sun,
O'er which clouds are bright'ning,
    Thou dost float and run;
15 Like an unbodied joy whose race is just begun.

A **Literary Focus** **Symbol** In these first few lines, why does the speaker say the skylark never was a bird?

B **Reading Focus** **Making Inferences** What does the speaker admire about the skylark? What does the speaker wish in regard to his own art?

Vocabulary **blithe** (blyth) *adj.*: happy and cheerful.
profuse (pruh FYOOS) *adj.*: very abundant.
unpremeditated (uhn pree MEHD uh tay tihd) *adj.*: not planned in advance.

The pale purple even°
    Melts around thy flight;
Like a star of Heaven,
    In the broad daylight
20 Thou art unseen, but yet I hear thy shrill delight,

    Keen as are the arrows
      Of that silver sphere,°
    Whose intense lamp narrows
      In the white dawn clear
25 Until we hardly see—we feel that it is there.

    All the earth and air
      With thy voice is loud,
    As, when night is bare,
      From one lonely cloud
30 The moon rains out her beams, and Heaven is overflowed.

    What thou art we know not;
      What is most like thee?
    From rainbow clouds there flow not
      Drops so bright to see
35 As from thy presence showers a rain of melody.

    Like a Poet hidden
      In the light of thought,
    Singing hymns unbidden,
      Till the world is wrought
40 To sympathy with hopes and fears it heeded not:

    Like a high-born maiden
      In a palace-tower,
    Soothing her love-laden
      Soul in secret hour
45 With music sweet as love, which overflows her bower:°
    Like a glow-worm golden

16. even: evening.

22. silver sphere: "a star of Heaven" (line 18).

45. bower: archaic word for a woman's bedroom.

In a dell° of dew,
   Scattering unbeholden
    Its aereal hue
50 Among the flowers and grass, which screen it from the view!

   Like a rose embowered°
    In its own green leaves,
   By warm winds deflowered,
    Till the scent it gives
55 Makes faint with too much sweet those heavy-winged thieves:

   Sound of vernal° showers
    On the twinkling grass,
   Rain-awakened flowers,
    All that ever was
60 Joyous, and clear, and fresh, thy music doth surpass:

   Teach us, Sprite° or Bird,
    What sweet thoughts are thine:
   I have never heard
    Praise of love or wine
65 That panted forth a flood of rapture so divine.

   Chorus Hymeneal,°
    Or triumphal chant,
   Matched with thine would be all
    But an empty vaunt,°
70 A thing wherein we feel there is some hidden want.

   What objects are the fountains
    Of thy happy strain?°
   What fields, or waves, or mountains?
    What shapes of sky or plain?
75 What love of thine own kind? what ignorance of pain?

   With thy clear keen joyance°
    Languor cannot be:
   Shadow of annoyance
    Never came near thee:
80 Thou lovest—but ne'er knew love's sad satiety.   **C**
   Waking or asleep,

47. dell: small valley.

51. embowered: enclosed in foliage.

56. vernal: occurring in the spring.

61. Sprite: spirit.

66. chorus Hymeneal: wedding song. *Hymeneal* is derived from Hymen, the Greek god of marriage.
69. vaunt: boast.

72. strain: melody.

76. joyance: rejoicing.

C **Literary Focus** **Symbol** What clues in this stanza point to the skylark's symbolism?

Vocabulary languor (LANG guhr) *n.*: lack of interest or enthusiasm.
satiety (suh TY uh tee) *n.*: feeling of disgust or weariness caused by excess.

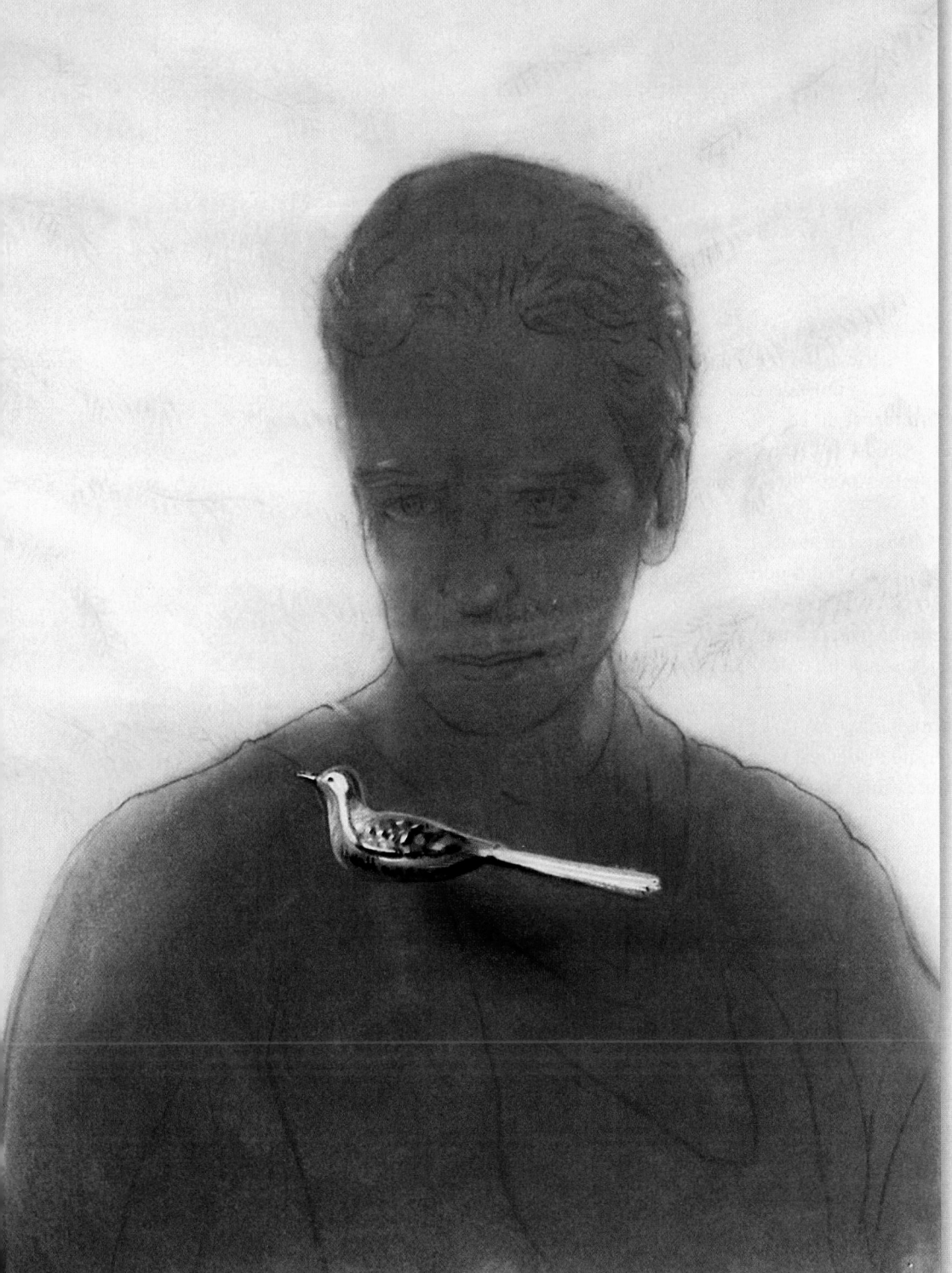

Analyzing Visuals

Viewing and Interpreting Study the illustration. To what areas are your eyes drawn? Why? How do the colors affect the mood? What effect do the image's realistic and unrealistic qualities have? How might the image connect with the ode's tone and symbolism?

Thou of death must deem
Things more true and deep
Than we mortals dream,
85   Or how could thy notes flow in such a crystal stream?

We look before and after,
And pine for what is not:
Our sincerest laughter
With some pain is fraught;
90   Our sweetest songs are those that tell of saddest thought.

Yet if we could scorn
Hate, and pride, and fear;
If we were things born
Not to shed a tear,
95   I know not how thy joy we ever should come near.

Better than all measures
Of delightful sound,
Better than all treasures
That in books are found,
100   Thy skill to poet were, thou scorner of the ground!

Teach me half the gladness
That thy brain must know,
Such harmonious madness
From my lips would flow
105   The world should listen then—as I am listening now. **D**

D **Reading Focus** Making inferences What do you think the speaker means by "harmonious madness?

Applying Your Skills

To a Skylark

Respond and Think Critically

Reading Focus

Quick Check

1. What qualities does the speaker admire in the skylark?

Read with a Purpose

2. Who or what does the speaker think will be most affected by the skylark's lessons?

Reading Skills: Making Inferences

3. Use the inferences you made from your reading to determine what the skylark symbolizes.

Evidence from Poem

> Like a Poet hidden
> In the light of thought;

> Like a high-born maiden
> In a palace tower

Inference

> The Skylark is inspired and isolated and unreachable.

Skylark Symbolizes:

✓ Vocabulary Check

Choose the synonym for each Vocabulary word.

4. blithe   **a.** abundant

5. languor   **b.** unplanned

6. profuse   **c.** cheerful

7. satiety   **d.** disinterest

8. unpremeditated   **e.** disgust

Literary Focus

Literary Analysis

9. Interpret Interpret these phrases: "unbodied joy" (line 15), "ignorance of pain" (line 75), and "scorner of the ground" (line 100).

10. Analyze A rhetorical question is asked for effect and not to elicit an answer. In lines 71–75, why does Shelley use rhetorical questions?

11. Infer What does "To a Skylark" reveal about the speaker's view of the life of an artist?

12. Extend Lines 86–90 are among the most frequently quoted in English poetry. Do the ideas expressed in these lines correspond with your own experiences? If so, explain how.

Literary Skills: Symbol

13. Analyze In what ways is the skylark an appropriate symbol for a Romantic poet to use?

Literary Skills Review: Simile

14. Analyze A **simile** is a figure of speech that compares two seemingly unlike things by using connective words such as *like, than,* or *as.* What do the similes in lines 36–55 compare, and what do they show about the skylark and the speaker?

Writing Focus

Think as a Reader/Writer

Use It in Your Writing In a paragraph, use figurative language to describe a person, place, thing, or event that has had symbolic importance in your life.

 What Do You Think Now

How can nature's smallest wonders inspire the imagination?

For **CHOICES** *see page 841.* ❯

Preparing to Read

To a Mosquito

What Do You Think?

How can we use imagination to discover truth?

QuickTalk

Merwin's writing includes many volumes of translated works, including texts in Greek, Spanish, Sanskrit, Chinese, and Japanese. In your *Reader/ Writer Notebook*, write a paragraph about how knowledge of other languages might help to stimulate someone's imagination.

MEET THE WRITER

W. S. Merwin
(1927–   )

Link to Today

American poet Merwin is deeply concerned that humans are becoming alienated from their environment. Over five decades, Merwin's spare, deceptively simple poetry has urged readers to reconnect with the world.

Man of Many Travels

Pulitzer Prize WINNER

William Stanley Merwin was born in New York City in 1927. He grew up in New Jersey and Pennsylvania. The son of a Presbyterian minister, Merwin wrote hymns during his childhood. As a young man, he attended Princeton University, where he studied writing and Romance languages. After graduation he traveled to France, England, and Spain, earning his living first as a tutor and then as a translator of Latin, Spanish, and French poetry.

Poet and Translator

Merwin's first book of poetry, *A Mask for Janus* (1952), was selected by poet W. H. Auden for the Yale Series of Younger Poets Award. Merwin continued to travel, living in Boston, London, and New York, and then settling in Hawaii in 1976.

A prolific writer, Merwin has published over fifteen books of poetry and almost twenty books of translations, in addition to plays and prose works. His translations include *Sir Gawain and the Green Knight* and Dante's *Purgatorio*. Merwin has also been honored with numerous prizes. *The Carrier of Ladders*, published in 1970, was awarded the Pulitzer Prize for Poetry. Most recently, his *Migration: Selected Poems 1951–2001,* was awarded the National Book Award for Poetry and was selected as one of *The New York Times* 100 Notable Books of the Year.

Although his early poetry was somewhat formal, his writing has evolved into a style that is more personal and freer in form. Merwin has used his poetry to explore the natural world, one of his greatest passions. Today, he continues to write and works to promote the preservation of the environment.

Think About the Writer What qualities does Merwin share with the Romantic poets?

Portrait of writer W. S. Merwin

Reader/Writer Notebook

Use your **RWN** to complete the activities for this selection.

Literary Focus

Diction A writer's choice of words is called **diction.** A writer might describe a character as "clever" instead of "smart," or "bewitching" instead of "attractive." Writers use different types of words depending on the audience they are addressing, the subject they are discussing, and the effect they are trying to produce. As you read "To a Mosquito," consider why Merwin chooses certain words and not others.

Reading Focus

Analyzing Tone A writer's attitude toward the subject or audience is called **tone.** Romantic odes usually have a serious tone. In contrast, Merwin's light tone in "To a Mosquito" takes liberties with the traditional ode.

Into Action Read the poem aloud, and listen to its words and rhythms. In the first column of a chart like the one below, record the **diction,** or word choice, that strikes you as important. In the second column, explain how each word or phrase contributes to the poem's tone.

Diction	Tone
me, me, me... me... be	simple rhymes, like rhymes in a children's book, light in tone
and rash though it may be	rhythm sounds like a nursery rhyme, light in tone

Language Coach

Multiple-Meanings Words Writers can play with words that have more than one meaning. Merwin uses the phrase "rash though it may be" to describe a mosquito's singing out loud. In this phrase, *rash* means "hasty or impetuous." However, in a poem dedicated to a mosquito, Merwin is also clearly playing with the second meaning of *rash*: "an itchy outbreak on the skin." In a single word, the poet captures a surprising range of meaning. With a partner, discuss the various meanings of the word *blood* in this poem.

Writing Focus

Think as a Reader/Writer

Find It in Your Reading Write down words and phrases that the author uses to describe the mosquito. For example, in line 6, the speaker says that the mosquito "sings out," rather than "buzzes." Use your *Reader/Writer Notebook* to record interesting descriptions of the mosquito.

TechFocus This poem is written in a casual style—without capitalization or punctuation. As you read, think about the style and tone the mosquito might use if it replied in a poem of its own.

Learn It Online
Listen to this poem online.

go.hrw.com   L12-837   Go

Link to Today

This Link to Today gives new life to an old poetic form.

Read with a Purpose

Read to discover what relation exists between the speaker and the mosquito.

Build Background

In Shelley's "To a Skylark," the speaker seeks to learn the mystery of the skylark's joyful song. In the following poem, contemporary poet W. S. Merwin ponders a different mystery: the intimate connection that exists between the human and the mosquito. Both poems employ **apostrophe**, a figure of speech in which the writer directly addresses an absent or dead person, an abstract quality, or something nonhuman as if it were present and capable of responding.

Colored scanning electron micrograph (SEM) of the head of a female yellow fever mosquito, *Aedes aegypti*.

TO A MOSQUITO

by **W. S. Merwin**

Listen to you
me me me
nothing but *me*
even without a voice
5   and rash though it may be

to sing out anyway
here I am this is me
out for your blood Ⓐ

do you mean to tell me
10   we are some kind of kin
blood relatives
your many offspring
something to me
by blood presumably
15   but with the gift of flight

on wings as fine
as light glinting across water
and with the deaths they carry Ⓑ

you need not tell me
20   that you are here
because of me
you follow me everywhere
by my breath you find me

Ⓐ **Reading Focus** Analyzing Tone What keeps the phrase "out for your blood" from making the poem's tone gloomy?

Ⓑ **Literary Focus** Diction Which words in this three-line stanza give the poem a brief Romantic tone, and why?

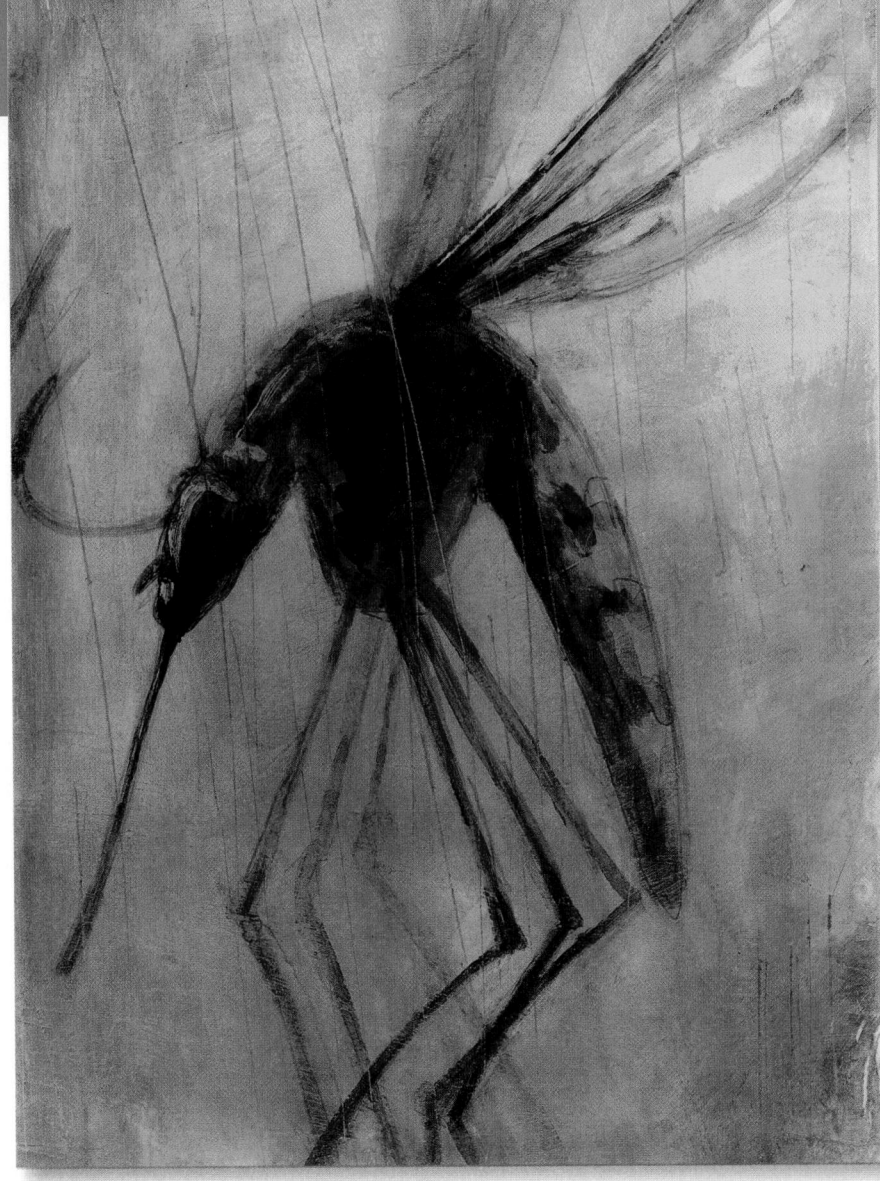

West Nile Delivery System (2007), by Jeff Faerber. Acrylic and varnish on board. Courtesy of the artist.

by the life of my body   **C**
25   you hunger to be close to me
whatever I am doing

though we do not take
each other personally
you recognize me
30   I make the world right for you
it is as though you
believe I owe you something

C **Reading Focus** **Analyzing Tone** How many words can you find that echo the opening sounds of *me* and *be?* How do these words contribute to the poet's tone?

Applying Your Skills

To a Mosquito

Respond and Think Critically

Reading Focus

Quick Check

1. How does the speaker feel about the mosquito?

2. What gift does the mosquito have that the speaker envies?

3. Why does the mosquito follow the speaker everywhere?

Read with a Purpose

4. What kind of relationship do you see between the speaker and the mosquito? Explain.

Reading Skills: Analyzing Tone

5. You have charted the connection between the poem's diction and its tone. Share your chart with a partner, and with your partner decide on a single word that you think best describes the poem's tone. Share your word with the class.

Diction	Tone
me, me, me... me... be	simple rhymes, like rhymes in a children's book, light in tone
and rash though it may be	rhythm sounds like a nursery rhyme, light in tone

Word that describes poem's tone: _____

Literary Focus

Literary Analysis

6. **Analyze** What effect is created in lines 16–18? How do these lines change or add to the poem's tone? Explain.

7. **Interpret** What is the <u>function</u> of the repetition of the word *me?*

8. **Contrast** How does Merwin's tone in "To a Mosquito" differ from Shelley's tone in "To a Skylark"?

9. **Analyze** Consider the poem's lack of punctuation and how the poem is broken into lines and stanzas. Why might Merwin have chosen to write the poem this way? What effects do these qualities create?

Literary Skills: Diction

10. **Contrast** What important differences do you see between Merwin's diction here and Shelley's diction in "To a Skylark"?

Literary Skills Review: Alliteration

11. **Analyze** The repetition of similar consonant sounds close together is **alliteration.** Why do you think Merwin repeats /m/ sounds and /b/ sounds so frequently?

Writing Focus

Think as a Reader/Writer

Use It in Your Writing In your *Reader/Writer Notebook*, write a short paragraph describing an animal of your choice. Use descriptive adjectives and verbs that characterize the animal's movements, sounds, and most interesting qualities.

What Do
You
Think
Now
How can unpleasant or annoying people, animals, or experiences serve to stimulate the imagination?

To a Skylark / To a Mosquito

CHOICES

As you respond to the Choices, use these **Academic Vocabulary** words as appropriate: device, differentiate, function, inherent, technique.

REVIEW

Compare and Contrast Two Poems

Timed ⌐Writing Write an essay in which you compare and contrast "To a Skylark" and "To a Mosquito." Analyze the ways the authors use diction, figures of speech, and sound devices. How do the poems differ in tone and theme? Use quotations from both poems to develop your essay.

Write a Dialogue About Animals

Partner Activity If the speakers of these poems could converse about the connection between humans and animals, what would they say to each other? With a partner, write a dialogue between the two speakers in which they discuss what humans receive from animals. Write the dialogue in the form of a script, and present it to your class.

CONNECT

Write a Poem to an Animal

Write your own poem to an animal. Use a unique angle or technique to describing your animal, and elaborate on it in your poem. Just as Shelley and Merwin have done, use apostrophe, addressing the animal directly within the first line of the poem. Share your poem with the class by reading it aloud.

Compose a Message

TechFocus "To a Mosquito" is written in a light, informal style. How might the mosquito reply to the speaker? Create an oral response from the mosquito to the speaker in the form of a poem or speech. Then, record your response and enhance it with sound effects to help reveal the mosquito's point of view. Share your message with your class.

EXTEND

Research Mysteries of the Animal Kingdom

Presentation In the two poems, each speaker reflects upon a mystery of an animal—the beautiful song of the soaring skylark or the minor but persistent pesting of the mosquito. What other mysteries exist in the animal kingdom? Research some other animal mysteries that interest you, and prepare a ten-minute presentation about them. Include visuals.

Discuss the Role of the Artist

Group Discussion Shelley was concerned with the role of the artist in society. Hold a group discussion on the role of the artist in the modern world. Consider some of the topics addressed in "To a Skylark," such as: From where do artists receive inspiration? How are artists regarded by others? How do they keep going when their works go unrecognized by others? You might want to expand your discussion by focusing also on musicians and their role in our society.

(above) Jackson's chameleon.
(left) Ring-tailed lemur. Madagascar.

Preparing to Read

On First Looking into Chapman's Homer

When I Have Fears

Ode to a Nightingale

Ode on a Grecian Urn

Keats's Last Letter

How can we use imagination to discover truth?

 **QuickTalk**

If your imagination could take you on an adventure, what would that adventure be? Compare adventures with other students.

John Keats
(1795–1821)

An unpropitious upbringing made it surprising that Keats became a poet at all; it is a greater wonder that when he died at twenty-five he had become one of England's major poets.

A Troubled Beginning

Keats's brief life was plagued with troubles, and he lacked the advantages most poets need to get started. His father, who ran a London stable, died when Keats was eight, and his mother died when he was fourteen. In 1811, Keats's guardian took him out of a school he loved and apprenticed him to a surgeon, a job that was then a step above that of a barber.

In 1816, Keats chose to become a poet rather than a surgeon, but harsh reviews of his first book of poetry (1817) stung him and made him doubt his commitment. By the autumn of 1818, Keats had assumed another burden: the care of his brother Tom, who was dying of tuberculosis, a disease that would soon claim Keats himself.

A Glorious Achievement

After Tom's death, Keats had a little more than two years to make what he could of his determination to lead "a literary life." Great passages and poems of near perfect technique poured from him in that miraculous time. Meanwhile, Keats had fallen in love with a woman named Fanny Brawne, but they would never marry. When he began to cough up blood, his experience nursing Tom made the truth obvious: "That drop of blood is my death warrant." Believing his only chance for survival was to live in a warmer climate, Keats made the journey to Rome in late 1820 and settled in a house near the Spanish Steps. There, in February 1821, after weeks of suffering, Keats died.

The stark sadness of Keats's own life heightens our awareness of the qualities of his poems. Rich in sensuous detail, his poems are not subdued and depressed, but rather are exciting in their representation of intense emotional experiences. Instead of being heavy with resignation, they are rich in courageous hope for what the imagination can seize and enjoy in life.

Think About the Writer Keats requested that his epitaph read: "Here lies one whose name was writ in water." What does this reveal about how Keats felt about his life work?

A portrait miniature of John Keats (c. 1818), by Joseph Severn. Ivory. No. 0713. Fitzwilliam Museum, University of Cambridge, UK.

On First Looking into Chapman's Homer / When I Have Fears

Reader/Writer Notebook

Use your **RWN** to complete the activities for these selections.

Literary Focus

Sonnet Most poets who enjoy the challenge of structure love to attempt the **sonnet** form. Sonnets, which have fourteen lines and strict rhyme schemes, are usually classified as Petrarchan (Italian) or Shakespearean (English). The **Petrarchan sonnet** is divided into two parts, an octave (eight lines) and a sestet (six lines). The octave usually presents a problem, poses a question, or expresses an idea that the sestet then resolves, answers, or drives home. The **Shakespearean sonnet** has three quatrains (four lines each) and a concluding **couplet** (a pair of rhymed lines). The three quatrains usually express related ideas or examples, while the couplet summarizes the conclusion or message. Keats wrote "On First Looking into Chapman's Homer" in the Italian, or Petrarchan, form. "When I Have Fears," however, uses the Shakespearean form.

Reading Focus

Understanding Inverted Syntax Keats often inverts the **syntax,** or word order, of his sentences to meet the demands of meter and rhyme. The usual word order in English sentences is subject-verb-complement.

Into Action Write down sentences in "On First Looking into Chapman's Homer" that do not follow standard word order. Circle the subjects, and underline the verbs. If the parts of a verb are split, as in the example below, draw an arrow from the first part of the verb to the second.

Line	Inverted Syntax
1	Much have I traveled

Writing Focus

Think as a Reader/Writer

Find It In Your Reading Much of the beauty of Keats's poems comes from their rich figurative language. Keats uses **similes** (comparisons of two unlike things, using words such as *like* and *as*) and **metaphors** (direct comparisons between unlike things, without the use of specific words of comparison). In your *Reader/Writer Notebook*, note details about the extended similes in lines 9–10 and 11–12 of "On First Looking into Chapman's Homer."

Vocabulary

realms (rehlmz) *n. pl.:* kingdoms. *Keats compares reading classical poetry to traveling in realms of gold.*

gleaned (gleend) *v.:* gathered little by little or gradually. *The speaker of "When I Have Fears" says his pen gleaned words from his brain.*

teeming (TEEM ihng) *v.* used as *adj.:* full of; alive with; fruitful. *Keats says his brain is teeming with ideas for poems.*

Language Coach

Related Words Learning the base form of verbs can help you expand your vocabulary. The base form of *teeming* is *teem,* which means "to be full of." Other related forms of this verb are *teemed* and *teems.* What do you think those verbs mean? What is the base form of *gleaned*? What are some other forms of this verb?

Learn It Online
Listen to these poems online.

go.hrw.com   L12-843   Go

SONNET

ON FIRST LOOKING INTO CHAPMAN'S HOMER

by **John Keats**

Read with a Purpose
Read to discover how reading great literature can be an exciting exploration.

Build Background
Keats wrote "On First Looking into Chapman's Homer" in 1816, just before his twenty-first birthday. The poem was inspired by an evening Keats spent with his favorite teacher, Charles Cowden Clarke. The two had stayed up all night reading a translation of Homer's *Iliad* by George Chapman, a contemporary of Shakespeare. At dawn, Keats went home and by ten that morning sent Clarke this sonnet.

Trojan Horse and Greek soldiers (640 B.C.). Relief from an earthenware amphora from Mykonos. Archaeological Museum, Mykonos, Greece.

Much have I traveled in the realms of gold,
    And many goodly states and kingdoms seen;
    Round many western islands have I been
Which bards in fealty to Apollo° hold.   **A**
5 Oft of one wide expanse had I been told
    That deep-browed Homer ruled as his demesne;°
    Yet did I never breathe its pure serene°
Till I heard Chapman speak out loud and bold:
Then felt I like some watcher of the skies
10   When a new planet swims into his ken;°
Or like stout Cortez° when with eagle eyes
    He stared at the Pacific—and all his men
Looked at each other with a wild surmise—
    Silent, upon a peak in Darien.   **B**

A **Reading Focus** **Understanding Inverted Syntax** How can you reword the first four lines to reflect standard word order? How does this change affect the sound of the poem?

B **Literary Focus** **Sonnet** What idea is presented in the octave? How does the sestet drive home the speaker's point?

Vocabulary **realms** (rehlmz) *n. pl.*: kingdoms.

4. bards in fealty to Apollo: poets in loyal service (as feudal tenants to their lord) to Apollo, the Greek god of poetry.
6. demesne (dih MEEN): domain.
7. serene: archaic word meaning "clear air."
10. ken: range of vision.
11. Cortez: sixteenth-century Spanish explorer who conquered Mexico. *Stout* means "brave, strong." Keats made a now-famous mistake in this line: It was Balboa (not Cortez) who was the first European to see the eastern shore of the Pacific Ocean from the heights of Darien, in Panama.

SONNET

WHEN I HAVE FEARS

by **John Keats**

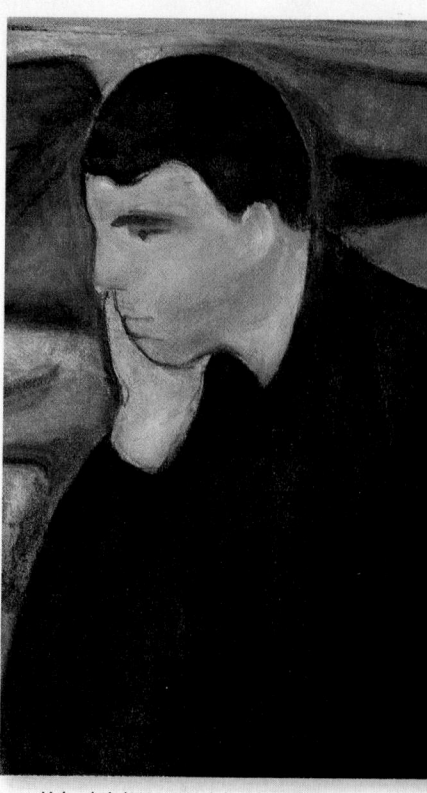

Melancholy (1894–1895), by Edvard Munch (1863–1944).
Billedgaleri (Picture Gallery), Bergen, Norway.

Read with a Purpose
As you read, think about the two things the speaker fears.

Build Background
Keats's first Shakespearean sonnet, "When I Have Fears," was written in early 1818—a year filled with disappointment in work and love and the beginning of the poet's ill health. The sonnet hauntingly anticipates Keats's death in 1821 at the age of twenty-five.

When I have fears that I may cease to be
    Before my pen has gleaned my teeming brain,
Before high-pilèd books, in charact'ry,°
    Hold like rich garners the full-ripened grain;
5 When I behold, upon the night's starred face,
    Huge cloudy symbols of a high romance,
And think that I may never live to trace
    Their shadows, with the magic hand of chance;
And when I feel, fair creature of an hour,
10   That I shall never look upon thee more, Ⓐ
Never have relish in the fairy° power
    Of unreflecting love!—then on the shore
Of the wide world I stand alone, and think
Till Love and Fame to nothingness do sink. Ⓑ

3. charact'ry: characters of the alphabet.

11. fairy: supernatural; unearthly.

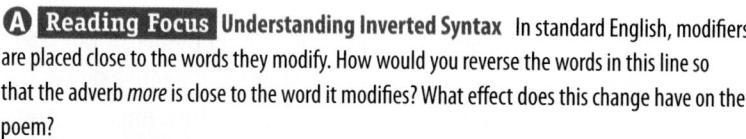

Ⓐ **Reading Focus** Understanding Inverted Syntax In standard English, modifiers are placed close to the words they modify. How would you reverse the words in this line so that the adverb *more* is close to the word it modifies? What effect does this change have on the poem?

Ⓑ **Literary Focus** Sonnet What ideas are presented in the quatrains? How does the couplet sum up the speaker's point?

Vocabulary **gleaned** (gleend) *v.*: gathered little by little or slowly.
teeming (TEEM ihng) *v.* used as *adj.*: full of; alive with; fruitful.

On First Looking into Chapman's Homer / When I Have Fears

Respond and Think Critically

Reading Focus

Quick Check

1. What experience is the basis of the poem "On First Looking into Chapman's Homer"?

2. What does the speaker fear in the poem?

3. Whom does the speaker in "When I Have Fears" address? What line tells you this?

Read with a Purpose

4. How does "On First Looking into Chapman's Homer" add to your understanding of Keats's fears in "When I Have Fears"?

Reading Skills: Understanding Inverted Syntax

5. Rewrite lines with inverted syntax from "On First Looking" so that they conform to standard English word order. How does standard word order affect the rhyme and meter?

✔ Vocabulary Check

Explain your answer to each of the following questions about the Vocabulary words.

6. Is a **realm** a kingdom or a river?

7. If you **glean** something, do you collect it bit by bit or scoop it up in a heap?

8. If something is **teeming,** is it full of life or dead?

Literary Focus

Literary Analysis

9. **Analyze** What do the images in "When I Have Fears" make you visualize? What feeling is created by the image in the final two lines?

10. **Analyze** Keats's only foreign travel was the trip to Italy he made when he was dying. What then does Keats mean in "On First Looking into Chapman's Homer" when he says he has traveled and has seen many states, kingdoms, and islands?

11. **Extend** Does the mistake at the end of "On First Looking" affect the poem's power or quality? Would substituting *Balboa* work? Explain.

Literary Skills: Sonnet

12. **Interpret** How would you sum up the octave and sestet of "On First Looking into Chapman's Homer"? How would you sum up the three quatrains and couplet in "When I Have Fears"?

Literary Skills Review: Tone

13. **Analyze** The writer's attitude toward the reader or subject is called **tone.** Describe the tone in "When I Have Fears." Does it change? Explain.

Writing Focus

Think as a Reader/Writer

Use It in Your Writing In your *Reader/Writer Notebook*, write a brief poem using similes and metaphors to describe a powerful experience. You could write an extended simile, like the two that conclude "On First Looking into Chapman's Homer."

What Do You Think Now Keats and other Romantic poets saw imagination as a creative power that made things happen. How important do you think imagination is in the world today?

Preparing to Read

Ode to a Nightingale

Reader/Writer
Notebook

Use your **RWN** to complete the activities for this selection.

Literary Focus

Synesthesia When writers use **synesthesia,** they describe one sense experience (such as smell) in terms of another sense (such as touch). For example, in "Ode to a Nightingale" the speaker remarks that he "cannot see… what soft incense hangs upon the boughs" (lines 41–42). Incense, usually perceived through smell, is here described as both something that might be soft to the touch and something that might be seen. By inviting us to use our senses in unexpected ways, Keats brings a startling new dimension to reality.

Literary Perspectives Apply the literary perspective described on page 849 as you read this poem.

Reading Focus

Reading Closely To understand complex poems and their use of sophisticated <u>techniques</u> like synesthesia, you have to **read closely.** <u>Techniques</u> for effective close reading of poetry include adjusting your reading rate, pausing to reflect on the exact meaning of words, re-reading lines that puzzle you, and letting your imagination visualize what the poet is saying.

Into Action As you read, keep a list of questions you have and the reading strategies you can use to answer them. Your list might look like this:

Questions	Reading Strategies
Stanza 1: What does the speaker mean by "Lethewards"?	I need to use the sidenotes to understand words and allusions.

Writing Focus

Think as a Reader/Writer

Find It In Your Reading In many instances in the poem, Keats **personifies** the natural world, that is to say, he gives human properties to nature. For example, when he calls the moon a queen and seats her on a throne, he is personifying the moon, as moons can't literally be crowned queen nor can they sit on thrones. Note in your *Reader/Writer Notebook* where Keats speaks of the natural world as if it has human attributes.

Vocabulary

melodious (muh LOH dee uhs) *adj.:* producing a sweet sound; tuneful. *Keats describes the plot of land where the nightingale sings as melodious.*

perplexes (pehr PLEHKS uhz) *v.:* confuses. *The nightingale fascinates and perplexes Keats, because his brain cannot understand the bird's song.*

murmurous (MUR muhr uhs) *adj.:* making consistent soft, low sounds. *The speaker enters a murmurous place where flies gather on summer evenings.*

Language Coach

Word Sounds and Word Meanings Some words sound like their meanings. (The use of a word whose sound imitates or suggests its meaning is called **onomatopoeia.**) If you read that rushing water *gurgles,* for example, you should be able to hear the sound of water in that verb. Say these Vocabulary words aloud: *melodious* and *murmurous.* Do the sounds of these words suggest what they mean?

⁎ Learn It Online
Take your study of Keats farther with these project ideas online.

go.hrw.com | L12-847 | **Go**

ODE TO A NIGHTINGALE

by **John Keats**

Read with a Purpose
As you read, think about what the speaker is saying to the nightingale.

Build Background
When Keats was twenty-three, he spent a few months at the Hampstead home of his friend Charles Brown. Keats's brother Tom had died a few months earlier. Brown remembers the scene:

In the spring of 1819 a nightingale had built her nest near my house. Keats felt a tranquil and continual joy in her song, and one morning he took his chair from the breakfast table to the grass plot under a plum tree, where he sat for two or three hours. When he came into the house, I perceived he had some scraps of paper in his hand, and these he was quietly thrusting behind the books. On inquiry, I found those scraps, four or five in number, contained his poetic feeling on the song of our nightingale.

There are no nightingales in North America. Their unearthly, sad, sweet song can only be heard in the British Isles, in central and western Europe, and in Africa during the winter.

1

My heart aches, and a drowsy numbness pains
  My sense, as though of hemlock° I had drunk,
Or emptied some dull opiate to the drains°
  One minute past, and Lethewards° had sunk: **Ⓐ**
5 'Tis not through envy of thy happy lot,
  But being too happy in thine happiness—
    That thou, light-wingèd Dryad° of the trees,
      In some melodious plot
Of beechen° green, and shadows numberless,
10   Singest of summer in full-throated ease. **Ⓑ**

2

O, for a draft of vintage!° that hath been
  Cooled a long age in the deep-delvèd earth,
Tasting of Flora° and the country green,
  Dance, and Provençal° song, and sunburnt mirth! **Ⓒ**
15 O for a beaker full of the warm South,
  Full of the true, the blushful Hippocrene,°

---

2. hemlock: poison.

3. drains: dregs, particles that settle in the bottom of a cup.

4. Lethewards (LEE thee wuhrdz): toward Lethe. In Greek and Roman mythology, Lethe is the river of forgetfulness that flows through the underworld.

7. Dryad (DRY ad): in Greek mythology, nature goddess associated with trees.

9. beechen: archaic word meaning "pertaining to beech trees."

11. vintage: wine.

13. Flora: the Roman goddess of flowers.

14. Provençal (proh vuhn SAHL): from Provence, a region in southern France known in the Middle Ages for its troubadours who sang love songs.

16. blushful Hippocrene (HIHP uh kreen): wine, which he would drink for inspiration. In Greek mythology, Hippocrene is the Muses' fountain, whose waters inspire the poets who drink from it.

Ⓐ Reading Focus **Reading Closely** Stop and rephrase in your own words what is happening in this stanza.

Ⓑ Literary Focus **Synesthesia** To what senses does the image in lines 8–10 appeal?

Ⓒ Literary Focus **Synesthesia** What images using synesthesia do you find in lines 13–14?

Vocabulary **melodious** (muh LOH dee uhs) *adj.:* producing a sweet sound; tuneful.

With beaded bubbles winking at the brim,
        And purple-stainèd mouth;
    That I might drink, and leave the world unseen,
20   And with thee fade away into the forest dim:

3

Fade far away, dissolve, and quite forget
    What thou among the leaves hast never known,
The weariness, the fever, and the fret
    Here, where men sit and hear each other groan;
25 Where palsy° shakes a few, sad, last gray hairs,
        Where youth grows pale, and specter-thin, and dies;
            Where but to think is to be full of sorrow
                And leaden-eyed despairs
        Where Beauty cannot keep her lustrous eyes,
30   Or new Love pine at them beyond tomorrow. **D**

4

Away! away! for I will fly to thee,
    Not charioted by Bacchus and his pards,°
But on the viewless wings of Poesy,°
    Though the dull brain perplexes and retards:
35 Already with thee! tender is the night,
        And haply the Queen-Moon is on her throne,
            Clustered around by all her starry Fays;°
                But here there is no light,
        Save what from heaven is with the breezes blown
40   Through verdurous° glooms and winding mossy ways. **E**

5

I cannot see what flowers are at my feet,
    Nor what soft incense hangs upon the boughs,
But, in embalmèd° darkness, guess each sweet
    Wherewith the seasonable month endows
45 The grass, the thicket, and the fruit tree wild;
        White hawthorn, and the pastoral eglantine;°
            Fast fading violets covered up in leaves;
                And mid-May's eldest child,
        The coming° musk rose, full of dewy wine,
50   The murmurous haunt of flies on summer eves.

D **Literary Perspectives** **Analyzing Philosophical Context**
What is the speaker's philosophical view of the actual world in which he lives?
E **Literary Focus** **Synesthesia** Why is the image of "light" being "blown" an example of synesthesia?

Vocabulary **perplexes** (pehr PLEHKS uhz) *v.:* confuses.
murmurous (MUR muhr uhs) *adj.:* making consistent soft, low sounds.

25. palsy: disease of the nervous system that causes partial paralysis and involuntary shaking.

32. not . . . pards: not by getting drunk. Bacchus, the Roman god of wine, had a chariot pulled by leopards, shortened here to "pards."
33. on . . . Poesy: on the invisible wings of poetry; that is, by using his poetic imagination.
37. Fays: fairies.
40. verdurous (VUR juhr uhs): full of green foliage.
43. embalmèd: perfumed.
46. eglantine (EHG luhn tyn): kind of rose.
49. coming: soon to bloom.

Literary Perspectives

Analyzing Philosophical Context Philosophy is a conscious search for truth. The philosophical context of a work refers to the writer's assumptions about life and its meaning. In this poem, the speaker searches for meaning while he listens to the sublime, almost overwhelming beauty of a nightingale's song. The poem consists of a series of propositions, each containing its own rejection, as to how the speaker might leave the world of suffering and fade away with the bird. He considers wine, poetry, and even death as ways to respond to the beauty of the bird's song. However, at the end of the poem the speaker is drawn back to his "sole self," not knowing if he has had a vision or if he has merely been asleep.

As you read, notice the questions in the text, which will guide you in using this perspective.

6

Darkling° I listen; and, for many a time
    I have been half in love with easeful Death,
Called him soft names in many a musèd rhyme,
    To take into the air my quiet breath;
55 Now more than ever seems it rich to die,
    To cease upon the midnight with no pain,
        While thou art pouring forth thy soul abroad
           In such an ecstasy!
    Still wouldst thou sing, and I have ears in vain—
60   To thy high requiem° become a sod.° **F**

7

Thou wast not born for death, immortal Bird!
    No hungry generations tread thee down;
The voice I hear this passing night was heard
    In ancient days by emperor and clown:
65 Perhaps the self-same song that found a path
    Through the sad heart of Ruth,° when, sick for home,
        She stood in tears amid the alien corn;
           The same that oft-times hath
Charmed magic casements,° opening on the foam
70   Of perilous seas, in fairy lands forlorn.

8

Forlorn! the very word is like a bell
    To toll me back from thee to my sole self!
Adieu! the fancy° cannot cheat so well
    As she is famed to do, deceiving elf. **G**
75 Adieu! adieu! thy plaintive° anthem fades
    Past the near meadows, over the still stream,
        Up the hillside; and now 'tis buried deep
           In the next valley glades:
    Was it a vision, or a waking dream?
80   Fled is that music:—Do I wake or sleep?

51. darkling: archaic word meaning "in the dark."

60. requiem (REHK wee uhm): mass or song for the dead. **sod:** piece of topsoil held together by matted roots.

66. Ruth: in the Bible, a young widow who left her own people because of famine in their land to travel with her mother-in-law to a strange country. There she gathered grain (corn) for survival.
69. casements: windows. Images of open windows intrigued Keats.
73. fancy: imagination.
75. plaintive: sad; mournful.

Lacquer box decorated with a nightingale on the branch of a gingko tree (1870–1880).
Musée des Arts Asiatiques-Guimet, Paris, France.

F **Literary Perspectives** Analyzing Philosophical Context How does the song of the bird affect the way the speaker feels about death?

G **Reading Focus** Reading Closely Pause in your reading, and put what the speaker says to the bird in lines 72–73 in your own words.

Ode to a Nightingale

SKILLS FOCUS **Literary Skills** Analyze synesthesia; analyze allusion; analzye philosophical context. **Reading Skills** Read closely. **Vocabulary Skills** Demonstrate knowledge of literal meanings of words and their usage. **Writing Skills** Write descriptive essays; describe an object or animal; use figurative language.

Respond and Think Critically

Reading Focus

Quick Check

1. What misfortunes does the speaker want to escape in the third stanza? What means of escape are considered in the fourth stanza?

2. What thoughts of death does the speaker have in stanza 6? How does he resolve these temptations?

Read with a Purpose

3. This poem is directly addressed to the nightingale. Summarize what the speaker is saying.

Reading Skills: Reading Closely

4. What reading strategies did you find most helpful for reading this poem closely?

✓ Vocabulary Check

Check your knowledge of the Vocabulary words by answering the questions below.

5. Would you describe a symphony as **melodious** or **murmurous**?

6. Would you describe the sound of two people speaking in low tones as **melodious** or **murmurous**?

7. If something **perplexes** you, how will you feel about it?

Literary Focus

Literary Analysis

8. **Analyze** How is the speaker's mood different at the poem's beginning than at its end?

9. **Identify** What <u>differentiates</u> the experience of the nightingale from that of the speaker?

10. **Make Judgments** Why does the speaker want to capture the nightingale's "ease"? Why is he "too happy in [its] happiness" (stanza 1)?

11. **Literary Perspectives** In the last stanza, the speaker points to the limits of fancy, or imagination, to fool him into forgetting himself when he is melancholy. What does this say about his belief about sadness and the power of imagination?

Literary Skills: Synesthesia

12. **Analyze** Review the uses of **synesthesia** in the poem (lines 8–10, 13–14, 28, 38–39, 41–43). What sensory experiences does each describe? What feeling or mood does the <u>device</u> help create?

Literary Skills Review: Allusions

13. **Analyze** A reference to someone or something from history, literature, religion, mythology, politics, sports, science, or pop culture is **allusion.** What allusions does Keats make to mythology and the Bible? What is the effect of the allusions?

Writing Focus

Think as a Reader/Writer

Use It in Your Writing In a paragraph in your *Reader/Writer Notebook*, describe something abstract (perhaps fame or friendship) or something from nature (perhaps an animal or a hurricane). Address your subject directly, and personify it by giving it human feelings, thoughts, and actions.

What Do You Think Now

What does Keats discover about life, death, and the force of the imagination in "Ode to a Nightingale"?

Preparing to Read

Reader/Writer Notebook

Use your **RWN** to complete the activities for this selection.

Literary Focus

Metaphor In the figure of speech known as **metaphor,** two seemingly unlike things are compared without using a connective word such as *like* or *as.* At the beginning of "Ode on a Grecian Urn," Keats uses three metaphors to describe the urn. For example, in line 1, he refers to the urn as "Thou still unravished bride of quietness…" By comparing the urn to a virgin bride, the poet implies that the urn has remained untouched throughout the ages, quietly awaiting contact with the human world. As you read, look for other metaphors that describe the urn.

Reading Focus

Visualizing Imagery Poets use **imagery,** language that appeals to the senses, to bring their subject matter to life. Most images are visual, but images can also appeal to the senses of hearing, smell, taste, and touch.

Into Action As you read "Ode on a Grecian Urn," stop after stanzas 1–3 and again after stanza 4 to write a few sentences describing how you visualize the urn's decorations. Make rough sketches of those images.

Stanza	What I Visualize
First Stanza: An urn is decorated with a rural scene showing men and gods pursuing maidens and musicians playing pipes and tambourines.	

Writing Focus

Think as a Reader/Writer

Find It in Your Reading As you read "Ode on a Grecian Urn," record in your *Reader/Writer Notebook* the words Keats repeats and the effects of that repetition.

Vocabulary

deities (DEE uh teez) *n. pl.:* gods and goddesses. *Keats wonders what story of deities or mortals is represented on the vase.*

loath (lohth) *adj.:* unwilling or reluctant. *Keats imagines that the maidens on the vase are loath to be caught by the men and gods who pursue them.*

sensual (SEHN shoo uhl) *adj.:* having to do with the five senses. *Keats says that the musicians on the vase play not for the sensual ear but for the imagination.*

Language Coach

Antonyms You can learn some word meanings by thinking about opposites. When he looks at a Greek vase, Keats wonders if the figures are "deities or mortals." This phrase suggests the two words are **antonyms,** or opposites. *Deities* are gods and goddesses. Therefore, you can figure out that *mortals* are humans. Deities live forever, but mortals will eventually die. Can you think of antonyms for the words *loath* or *sensual*?

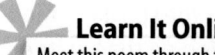 **Learn It Online**
Meet this poem through the video introduction online.

go.hrw.com   L12-852   Go

ODE ON A GRECIAN URN

by **John Keats**

Read with a Purpose
Read to discover what the speaker learns from meditating on the figures on a Greek vase.

Build Background
Many antique Greek vases show gods, goddesses, heroes, and mortals entangled in adventures. Traditionally, urns have been used as containers or for burial. The urn Keats describes is painted around with a series of mythological scenes, but no one knows exactly which urn Keats had in mind when he wrote this ode. Probably it is an imaginative combination of several vases he had seen in engravings and in the British Museum. Keats addresses the vase itself in the first stanza.

Greek red-figured hydria (c. 420–400 B.C.) by Vaspainter Meidias. British Museum, London.

1

Thou still unravished° bride of quietness,
    Thou foster child of silence and slow time,
Sylvan° historian, who canst thus express
    A flowery tale more sweetly than our rhyme:　**A**
5 What leaf-fringed legend haunts about thy shape
    Of deities or mortals, or of both,
      In Tempe or the dales of Arcady?°
    What men or gods are these? What maidens loath?
What mad pursuit? What struggle to escape?
10   What pipes and timbrels?° What wild ecstasy?　**B**

1. unravished: pure; untouched.

3. sylvan: of the forest. (The urn is decorated with a rural scene.)

7. Tempe (TEHM pee) . . . **Arcady** (AHR kuh dee): valleys in ancient Greece; ideal types of rural beauty.
10. timbrels: tambourines.

A **Literary Focus** **Metaphor** What is the urn compared to in lines 1–4?

B **Reading Focus** **Visualizing Imagery** Describe the scene you visualize when you read lines 5–10.

Vocabulary **deities** (DEE uh teez) *n. pl.:* gods and goddesses.
loath (lohth) *adj.:* unwilling or reluctant.

2

Heard melodies are sweet, but those unheard
    Are sweeter; therefore, ye soft pipes, play on;
Not to the sensual ear, but, more endeared,
    Pipe to the spirit ditties° of no tone:
15 Fair youth, beneath the trees, thou canst not leave
    Thy song, nor ever can those trees be bare;
        Bold Lover, never, never canst thou kiss,
    Though winning near the goal—yet, do not grieve;
        She cannot fade, though thou hast not thy bliss,
20   Forever wilt thou love, and she be fair!

14. ditties: short, simple songs.

Vocabulary **sensual** (SEHN shoo uhl) *adj.:* having to do with the five senses.

ART LINK

Ancient Greek Vase Painting

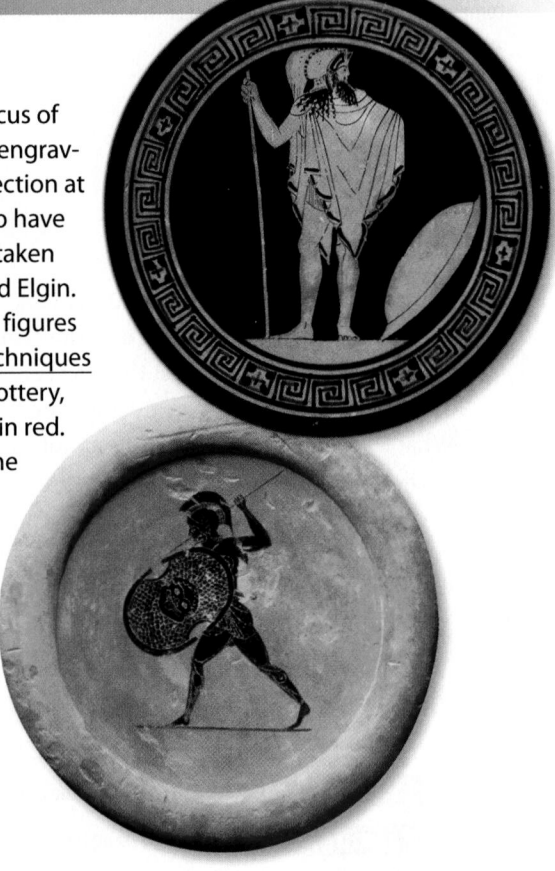

Although at one time a specific urn was thought to be the focus of this poem, critics now believe that Keats was inspired by the engravings of multiple urns and by the entire ancient Greek art collection at the British Museum in London. At the museum, he would also have seen the celebrated collection of marble sculptures recently taken from the Parthenon in Athens and brought to London by Lord Elgin.

In ancient Greece, fine pottery was often decorated with figures from mythology. Black-figure and red-figure were the two techniques used most extensively in these decorations. In black-figure pottery, the earliest form, the figures are black and details are carved in red. In red-figure pottery, the later form, the figures are red and the details are painted in black.

Black figures were drawn on the vase with a liquid form of clay called *slip,* which turned black when the clay was hardened by fire. To add detail to the design, a potter cut lines into the slip. The red showing through was simply the surface of the clay itself. Then, in about 530 B.C., a potter experimented with reversing the approach. A brush dipped in glaze was used to create red figures on the black vase. In time, the brush won over the knife, and red-figure pottery became more popular.

Ask Yourself

How do you envision the urn that Keats describes?

3

Ah, happy, happy boughs! that cannot shed
    Your leaves, nor ever bid the Spring adieu;
And, happy melodist, unwearied,
    Forever piping songs forever new;
25 More happy love! more happy, happy love!
    Forever warm and still to be enjoyed,
      Forever panting, and forever young;
All breathing human passion far above,
    That leaves a heart high-sorrowful and cloyed,°
30   A burning forehead, and a parching tongue.

29. cloyed (kloyd): wearied with excess.

4

Who are these coming to the sacrifice?
    To what green altar, O mysterious priest,
Lead'st thou that heifer lowing° at the skies,
    And all her silken flanks° with garlands dressed?
35 What little town by river or seashore,
    Or mountain-built with peaceful citadel,°
      Is emptied of this folk, this pious morn?
And, little town, thy streets forevermore
    Will silent be; and not a soul to tell
40   Why thou art desolate, can e'er return. **C**

33. lowing: mooing.
34. flanks: sides between the ribs and the hips.
36. citadel (SIHT uh duhl): fortress.

5

O Attic° shape! Fair attitude!° with brede°
    Of marble men and maidens overwrought,°
With forest branches and the trodden weed;
    Thou, silent form, dost tease us out of thought
45 As doth eternity: Cold Pastoral!°
    When old age shall this generation waste,
      Thou shalt remain, in midst of other woe
Than ours, a friend to man, to whom thou say'st,
    "Beauty is truth, truth beauty,"—that is all
50   Ye know on earth, and all ye need to know.

41. Attic: Athenian; classically elegant. **attitude:** posture. **brede:** interwoven design.
42. overwrought: decorated to excess; also, in reference to the men and maidens, overexcited.
45. Pastoral: artwork depicting idealized rural life.

C **Reading Focus** **Visualizing Imagery** Describe the scene you visualize when you read stanza 4.

Respond and Think Critically

Reading Focus

Quick Check

1. In stanzas 2 and 3, what does the speaker say to the people and even to the trees depicted on the urn?

2. What will happen to the urn when the speaker and his generation are dead? What message does the urn continue to offer?

Read with a Purpose

3. By the end of "Ode on a Grecian Urn," what has the speaker learned about the nature of life and art?

Reading Skills: Visualizing Imagery

4. Review the chart you made with sketches showing how you visualized the imagery in the ode. Put a star next to those images you found most powerful. Compare your chart with a partner's. What details can you add to your chart?

Literary Focus

Literary Analysis

5. **Make Inferences** Why do you think "unheard" melodies (lines 11–14) are "sweeter" to the speaker? Do you agree with this typically Romantic idea? Explain your response to this famous line.

6. **Analyze** What two words does the speaker repeat in stanza 3? What significance do you see in the selection of those particular words?

7. **Interpret** How do you interpret lines 28–30?

8. **Draw Conclusions** If the urn could "tease us out of thought" (line 44), what state would we be in? In what sense would this state be superior to thought?

Literary Skills: Metaphor

9. **Analyze** Discuss your understanding of the three **metaphors** used to describe the urn in lines 2–4. To what are they comparing the urn? What do the metaphors tell you about the urn?

Literary Skills Review: Setting

10. **Analyze** The time and location of an action is its **setting.** In this poem, setting is handled in an unusual way. Although the speaker might be in a museum viewing the urn, that museum setting is never mentioned. Instead, we enter the setting depicted on the urn. How would you describe the mood established by the setting the speaker sees on the urn?

Writing Focus

Think as a Reader/Writer

Use It in Your Writing In your *Reader/Writer Notebook,* write a paragraph describing a place. Use repetition to emphasize important details of the place and help create tone, mood, and rhythm.

What Do You Think Now

In what ways has the imagination brought this vase to life for the speaker?

Vocabulary Development

✓ Vocabulary Check

Check your mastery of the Vocabulary words by answering the following questions:

1. Which word is a synonym for the word **deities:** *gods* or *mortals?*
2. Which word is the opposite of the word **loath:** *willing* or *reluctant?*
3. How is the word *intellectual* opposite in meaning to the word **sensual?**

Vocabulary Skills: Figurative Language

Figurative language, such as **similes, metaphors,** and **personification,** is usually visual. Figurative language creates pictures in our minds by helping us associate one thing with another, different thing.

Similes are explicit comparisons using a connective word such as *like, as, than,* or *resembles.* **Metaphors** are comparisons that are made directly, without using connective words. **Personification** is a metaphor in which a nonhuman or nonliving thing is described as if it has human or lifelike qualities.

Figure of Speech	Example
simile	"Thou, silent form, dost tease us out of thought / As doth eternity . . ." (uses *As*)
metaphor	"Thou foster child of silence and slow time" (directly compares urn to foster child; also a personification)
personification	"Ah, happy, happy boughs!" (gives human quality of happiness to boughs)

Your Turn

Rewrite these sentences with the indicated figure of speech.

1. The urn is an unravished bride. (simile)
2. My heart is sorrowful. (metaphor)
3. The heifer lows at the skies. (personification)

Language Coach

Antonyms Words with opposite meanings are called **antonyms.** Some words, such as *winning* and *losing,* are obvious antonyms. Other antonyms may not be immediately apparent. For example, the word *pious* means "devout; religious"; its obvious antonym is *impious.* Other antonyms include *irreverent, profane,* and *blasphemous.* Choose the antonym for each Vocabulary word below, and explain your choice.

1. deities
   a. angels   b. humans   c. fools
2. loath
   a. eager   b. hated   c. uncertain
3. sensual
   a. physical   b. concrete   c. intellectual

Academic Vocabulary

Talk About
Recall that **apostrophe** is a figure of speech in which a speaker directly addresses an absent or dead person, an abstract quality, or something non-human as if it were present and capable of responding. With a partner, discuss the advantages and limitations of this technique. How does this technique function and what are its effects?

Learn It Online
Learn more about the Vocabulary words online.
go.hrw.com   L12-857   **Go**

SKILLS FOCUS **Writing Skills** Write reflective compositions; write persuasive essays; analyze a poem. **Grammar Skills** Punctuate quotations correctly.

Listening and Speaking Skills Adapt to purpose when speaking; make appropriate and meaningful comments in discussions and conversations.

Ode on a Grecian Urn

Grammar Link

Direct and Indirect Quotations

When you report a person's exact words, you use a **direct quotation.** In written language, quotation marks are used to enclose direct quotations. When a direct quotation is a question, notice that the question mark is put inside the quotation marks.

> "What men or gods are these?" asks the speaker.

At the end of a quotation, periods are placed inside closing quotation marks. Semicolons and colons are placed outside the quotation marks.

> He said, "The figures on the urn are forever frozen."

> He said "good work"; then he left the room.

Single quotation marks enclose a quotation within another quotation:

> "Let's read 'Ode on a Grecian Urn,'" he said.

An **indirect quotation** is a rewording of a person's actual words. Indirect quotations are not placed within quotation marks or set off with punctuation.

> Keats believed that unheard melodies are sweeter.

Your Turn

Rewrite the following sentences as directed.

1. Keats says in line 49 that beauty is found in truth. (Change to a direct quotation.)
2. He believes the people on the vase are "Forever panting, and forever young." (Change to an indirect quotation.)
3. "What is the main idea in "Ode on a Grecian Urn," asked the teacher. (Correct the punctuation.)

Writing Application Add direct quotations to a piece of your own writing about literature. Use passages from the literary source itself.

CHOICES

As you respond to the Choices, use these **Academic Vocabulary** words as appropriate: device, differentiate, function, inherent, technique.

REVIEW
Talk with Keats
Partner Activity Imagine that you will be talking to John Keats about "Ode on a Grecian Urn." With a partner, select at least three passages to discuss with Keats. Decide who will play the role of Keats and who will act as the questioner. Review the poem, and write out your dialogue. Include questions about Keats's devices and techniques. Present your dialogue to your class.

CONNECT
Address an Artwork
Select a work of art reproduced in this book, and, as Keats does in "Ode on a Grecian Urn," directly address it. In an essay, tell what is happening in the work, ask it questions, sum up the message you think it reveals, and tell what you think and feel about it.

EXTEND
Evaluate Two Meanings
Timed Writing Keats's poem "Ode on a Grecian Urn" presents insight into the historical period that produced the urn as well as Keats's views on art and beauty. In an expository essay, explain the historical and philosophical insight the poem provides. Use evidence from the poem to support your analysis.

Preparing to Read

Keats's Last Letter

Reader/Writer Notebook

Use your **RWN** to complete the activities for this selection.

Informational Text Focus

Analyzing Primary Sources A **primary source** is information that has been written or recorded by someone with firsthand knowledge of a topic. Primary sources include letters, autobiographies, historical documents, and eyewitness interviews. **Secondary sources** consist of information derived from, or about, primary sources or other secondary sources. Examples of secondary sources include encyclopedias, documentary films, biographies, history books, and interviews with historians. A scholar's biography about Keats is a secondary source, while Keats's letters are a primary source about Keats because they reveal his own thoughts and feelings. This last letter reflects Keats's attitude toward life and poetry as he faced imminent death.

Into Action As you read this letter, note details that tell you how Keats feels, what he thinks, and what he has been doing. Note why this information might provide valuable insights about Keats.

Information Keats reveals about his feelings, thoughts, and actions	Why this information might be valuable to a reader or researcher learning about Keats
"at my worst,...[I] summoned up more puns,... in one week than in any year of my life"	Even though Keats felt so ill, he continued to explore language. This may show Keats's commitment to the literary life, his extraordinary talent and gift with language, and his writing as a way to ease his suffering.

Writing Focus   Preparing for **Constructed Response**

Keats lived and wrote at a time when people generally wrote more formally than they do today. As you read, note in your *Reader/Writer Notebook* examples of Keats's rather formal style, which he uses even though he is writing a deeply personal letter to a close friend.

Vocabulary

habitual   (huh BIHCH oo uhl) *adj.:* regular; steady. *At the time of this letter, Keats experienced habitual feelings of sadness.*

posthumous   (PAHS choo muhs) *adj.:* happening after death. *Keats, though he was alive, felt he was living a posthumous existence.*

predominant   (prih DAHM uh nuhnt) *adj.:* having superior influence; prevailing. *Keats feels that the predominant theme of his life is that he misses people and opportunities.*

Language Coach

Root Words Within some words are common root words. For example, *habitual* contains the root word *habit*, which means "something done often or repeatedly, often without awareness." How is the meaning of this root related to the meaning of *habitual*? Identify the root word in *predominated*. Tell how its meaning relates to *predominated* and *predominant*.

Learn It Online

Learn more about the life of Keats at the Writers' Lives site online.

 L12-859

Keats's Last Letter

by **John Keats**

John Keats (1821), by Joseph Severn. Oil on canvas.
The Granger Collection, NY.

Read with a Purpose
Read to discover Keats's state of mind as he says good-bye to a dear friend.

Build Background
Keats knew that he was very ill with tuberculosis, the disease that had killed his mother and brother. His doctors said that his only hope would be to leave the cold and damp of London and move to a warmer, drier climate. Keats made plans to embark on the long and difficult journey from London to Rome. Unable to travel alone, he had hoped that his good friend Charles Brown might go with him. However, Brown learned of the plan too late and just missed saying goodbye to Keats, who sailed for Italy on September 17, 1820, accompanied by another friend, the artist Joseph Severn. Once in Italy, Keats remained in contact with Brown through letters. This letter to Brown was the last written by Keats before he died on February 23, 1821.

The "her" Keats refers to so sadly in the letter is probably Fanny Brawne, the girl in England he loved and would never be able to marry. In fact, in an earlier letter, Keats had asked Charles Brown to befriend Fanny when he was dead. Also referred to in the letter is George, Keats's brother, who had immigrated to America in 1818.

Analyzing Visuals

Viewing and Interpreting Consider the colors, the contrast between light and dark, and the lines in this painting of Keats. What mood or feeling does the painting evoke? Compare the mood of the painting to that of Keats's letter.

Rome, 30 November 1820

My dear Brown,

'Tis the most difficult thing in the world to me to write a letter. My stomach continues so bad, that I feel it worse on opening any book, yet I am much better than I was in quarantine. Then I am afraid to encounter the pro-ing and con-ing of anything interesting to me in England. I have an habitual feeling of my real life having passed, and that I am leading a post-humous existence. God knows how it would have been—but it appears to me—however, I will not speak of that subject. I must have been at Bedhampton nearly at the time you were writing to me from Chichester—how unfortunate—and to pass on the river too! There was my star predominant! I cannot answer anything in your letter, which followed me from Naples to Rome, because I am afraid to look it over again. I am so weak (in mind) that I cannot bear the sight of any handwriting of a friend I love so much as I do you. Yet I ride the little horse, and, at my worst, even in quarantine, summoned up more puns, in a sort of desperation, in one week than in any year of my life. There is one thought enough to kill me; I have been well, healthy, alert, etc., walking with her, and now—the knowledge of contrast, feeling for light and shade, all that information (primitive sense) necessary for a poem, are great enemies to the recovery of the stomach. There, you rogue, I put you to the torture; but you must bring your philosophy to bear, as I do mine, really, or how should I be able to live? Dr. Clark is very attentive to me; he says, there is very little the matter with my lungs, but my stomach, he says, is very bad. I am well disappointed in hearing good news from George, for it runs in my head we shall all die young. I have not written to Reynolds yet, which he must think very neglectful; being anxious to send him a good account of my health, I have delayed it from week to week. If I recover, I will do all in my power to correct the mistakes made during sickness; and if I should not, all my faults shall be forgiven. Severn is very well, though he leads so dull a life with me. Remember me to all friends, and tell Haslam I should not have left London without taking leave of him, but from being so low in body and mind. Write to George as soon you receive this, and tell him how I am, as far as you can guess; and also a note to my sister—who walks about my imagination like a ghost—she is so like Tom. I can scarcely bid you goodbye, even in a letter. I always made an awkward bow. **(A)**

God bless you!
John Keats

(A) **Informational Focus** Analyzing Primary Sources
Though this was his last letter, Keats lived for a few more months before dying. What does he say in the letter about his ability to write poetry?

Vocabulary **habitual** (huh BIHCH oo uhl) *adj.*: regular; steady.
posthumous (PAHS choo muhs) *adj.*: happening after death.
predominant (prih DAHM uh nuhnt) *adj.*: prevailing.

SKILLS FOCUS Informational **Skills** Analyze a primary source. **Vocabulary Skills** Demonstrate knowledge of literal meanings of words and their usage.

Listening and Speaking Skills Speak effectively; adapt to occasions when speaking: discussions. **Writing Skills** Write a brief constructed response, with specific support.

Keats's Last Letter

Respond and Think Critically

Informational Text Focus

Quick Check

1. Why is Keats unable to answer the questions from Brown's letter?

2. According to his doctor, what is Keats's most serious health problem? What is ironic, or inappropriate, about this diagnosis?

3. What does Keats mean when he says at the end, "I always made an awkward bow"?

Read with a Purpose

4. What is John Keats's state of mind as he writes this last letter to a friend? What details from the letter suggest what he is really thinking and feeling, in addition to what he writes explicitly?

Informational Skills: Analyzing Primary Sources

5. Review the chart you kept as you read this letter. Based on evidence in the letter, tell how Keats's illness affected his ability to write poetry—and letters to friends.

✓ Vocabulary Check

Be sure you can explain your answers to these questions about the Vocabulary words.

6. Keats says he has a **habitual** feeling that his real life has passed. Does this statement suggest that the feeling is fleeting or that it is always present?

7. When Keats says he feels he is leading a **posthumous** existence, does he feel healthy or ill?

8. Keats says that passing his friend on the river without knowing it showed his star **predominant.** Does this mean that Keats feels his fate, or star, has always been to miss out on joys, or that he feels his fate is ever changing?

Text Analysis

9. **Interpret** Keats writes "… the knowledge of contrast, feeling for light and shade, all that information (primitive sense) necessary for a poem, are great enemies to the recovery of the stomach." What do you think he means by this statement? Support your answer with details from the text.

10. **Analyze** Notice the pairs of contradictory words, images, and ideas in Keats's letter. Write down some of these pairs, and explain what they reveal about the author's state of mind.

11. **Evaluate** What figure of speech does Keats use to describe his sister? What effect does he create by using these particular words?

Listening and Speaking

12. **Extend** Imagine that you are writing a letter to a close friend you may not see for many years. What things would you want to mention? What feelings would you express? Write down a few things you would include in your letter, and discuss your list with a partner. Are your concerns similar to the ones Keats expresses in his letter?

Writing Focus Constructed Response

Review the notes you made in your *Reader/Writer Notebook* about Keats's formal style. Write a brief paragraph in which you contrast his style with the way a young person today would write to a close friend. Cite examples from Keats's letter.

What Do You Think Now

How has imagination now become a torment to Keats?

Japanese and Chinese Poetry

Cormorant fisherman on bamboo raft, Li River, Yangshuo.

You have just read a number of British poems from the Romantic period. In this World Literature section, you will read Japanese tanka and haiku which, like Romantic poetry, use images of nature. Unlike much Romantic poetry, these Japanese forms are concise and rigidly

CONTENTS

Tanka

Haiku

Quiet Night Thoughts
Question and Answer
    Among the Mountains
Letter to His Two Small
    Children

INTRODUCTION TO
Japanese and Chinese Poetry

Japanese Poetry

The **tanka** and the **haiku** are two of the most beloved forms of Japanese poetry. Both are very old, tanka dating from the eighth century A.D. and haiku from the thirteenth and fourteenth centuries. Both forms demand the compression of ideas and images into the space of a few words.

Japanese red-scroll garden.

The earliest-known tanka appear in a collection of poems called the *Manyoshu,* or *Collection of Ten Thousand Leaves.* **Tanka,** meaning "short songs," are brief and lyrical. Like other **lyric** poems, each tanka expresses a private emotion or thought, often on the theme of change, solitude, or love. The traditional tanka consists of exactly thirty-one syllables divided among five lines. Three of the poem's lines have seven syllables, and the other two have five. Lovers composed and exchanged tanka as expressions of affection. Aristocrats also played a game in which one person would invent the first three lines of a tanka and another person would finish it.

The Art of Haiku

Eventually, tanka inspired an even more condensed poetic form—the haiku. A **haiku** is a brief, unrhymed, three-line poem. The first and last lines each have five syllables, and the middle line has seven.

Examples of short verses similar to haiku have been found in thirteenth- and fourteenth-century Japanese literature. However, the art of haiku was not perfected until the seventeenth century, when the greatest of the classical haiku poets, Matsuo Bashō, lived. When English authors such as John Milton were composing epic, intricate poems, Bashō and his pupils were writing strikingly pure, compressed verses only a few words long. In the centuries since Bashō, the haiku form has been adopted by poets all over the world.

Unlike many Western poets, the classical haiku masters do not present similes, metaphors, or other figures of speech. Rather, haiku poets exhibit simple, unadorned images, and the reader must make an imaginative leap to understand the connection between the images.

Words Left Unsaid

With their precision, simple beauty, and economy of words, tanka and haiku embody an important principle of Japanese art and culture: What is not said is often as important as what is said. Understandably, this principle creates challenges for translators of both haiku and tanka. Form must sometimes be sacrificed, for the main work of translating any poem is to preserve its essence, the transcendent quality that stretches across distance and time to connect an author and a reader. This essence of Japanese poetry is summarized by Ki Tsurayuki, one of the editors of the great tenth-century tanka anthology, *Kokinshu,* in his preface to the collection:

> When we hear the notes of the nightingale among the blossoms, when we hear the frog in the water, we know that every living being is capable of song. Poetry, without effort, can move heaven and earth, can touch the gods and spirits. . . . [I]t turns the hearts of man and woman to each other and it soothes the soul of the fierce warrior.

Written over a thousand years ago, his comments still hold true for much of Japanese verse.

Chinese Poetry

Chinese civilization as a distinct and continuous society has existed for more than three thousand years, longer than any other culture in the world. The art of writing developed in China between 2000 and 1000 B.C., and with it came the birth of a literary tradition that dwarfs all others. More than half the books ever written have been written in Chinese.

Harmony and Balance

Chinese poetry is characterized by **lyricism,** the intensely personal expression of the speaker's thoughts and feelings. Profoundly influenced by **Confucianism, Taoism,** and **Buddhism** (see pages 331–344), Chinese poets contemplate nature and search for harmony between inner and outer forces or worlds. At its essence Chinese poetry explores passing feelings and impressions and the interplay of opposites. It sees life as a process of continual change in which opposing forces balance one another. Thus, Chinese poets muse about the changing seasons and phases of the moon, and they create vivid pictures of scenes from nature, often recalled in solitude, with imagery that is spare and lean. This minimalist, or simplified, approach engages the reader with evocative word associations and layers of meaning. So rich are these associations that Chinese poetry has inspired poetic movements in other cultures, such as the imagist movement of twentieth-century England and the United States.

The Golden Age

Chinese lyrical poetry achieved its golden age during the T'ang dynasty (618–907). Although other arts also flourished during the T'ang period, poetry was perceived as the glory of this age, and the poet Tu Fu (see page 874) is considered one of the greatest of all Chinese poets. His early poetry celebrates nature's beauty and bemoans time's passage, while his later work incorporates social criticism and compassion for those who suffer.

Rivaling Tu Fu as China's greatest poet is his contemporary, Li Po. If Tu Fu represents the classical spirit of Chinese literature, then Li Po represents its creative spirit. He is the more Romantic poet, both in his views of life and in his poetry. He often celebrates the joys of drinking wine and writes about friend-ship, solitude, the passage of time, and the glory of nature. His hallmark is brilliant freshness of expression.

Grandfather teaching calligraphy with water brush on sidewalk in Beijing.

The poems of Li Po and Tu Fu resemble the English Romantic poetry written nearly one thou-sand years later. These poems focus on nature, they use the lyric form, and they employ simple images and language. The voice of Chinese poetry, however, is quieter than the voice of a Shelley or Wordsworth. As the translator Burton Watson observes, "The Chinese poem is the voice of the poet not self-consciously addressing posterity or the world at large, but speaking quietly to a few close friends, or perhaps simply musing to himself."

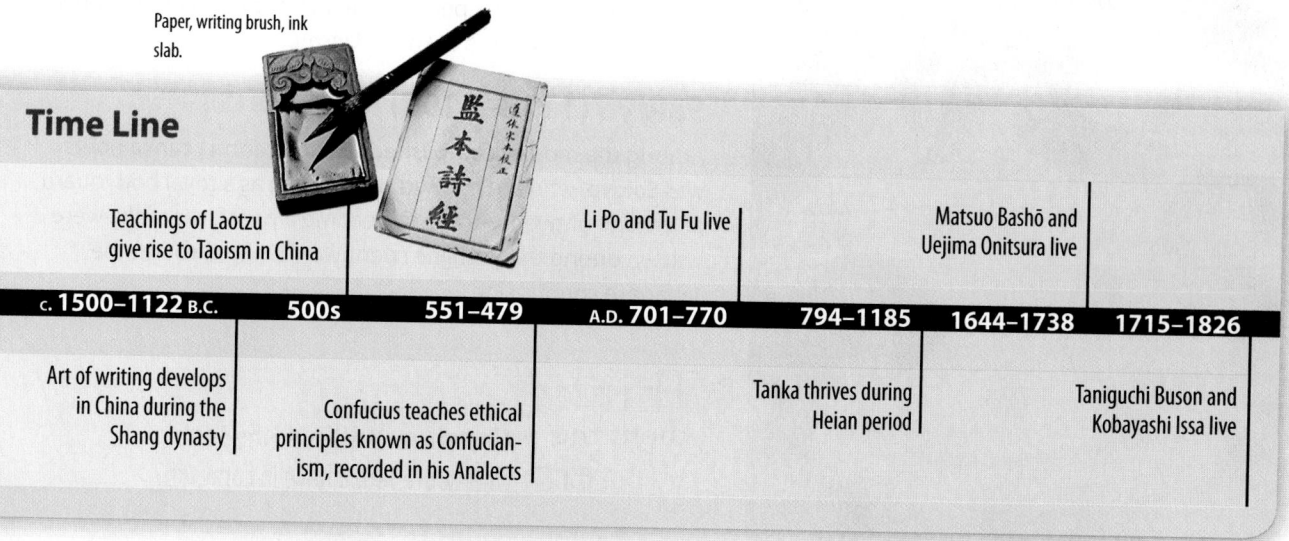

Paper, writing brush, ink slab.

Time Line

	Teachings of Laotzu give rise to Taoism in China		Li Po and Tu Fu live	Matsuo Bashō and Uejima Onitsura live		
c. 1500–1122 B.C.	**500s**	**551–479**	**A.D. 701–770**	**794–1185**	**1644–1738**	**1715–1826**
Art of writing develops in China during the Shang dynasty		Confucius teaches ethical principles known as Confucian-ism, recorded in his Analects		Tanka thrives during Heian period		Taniguchi Buson and Kobayashi Issa live

Preparing to Read

Japanese Poetry

What Do You Think?

How can we use imagination to discover truth?

QuickWrite

In your *Reader/Writer Notebook*, compose a paragraph about a memorable journey you took, perhaps to a faraway city or to a nearby neighborhood. How did you imagine your destination before you arrived? How accurate was your imagination in predicting the details about this place?

Playing karuta on New Year's Day in Kyoto, Japan.

MEET THE WRITERS

Tanka Poets

Tanka of the ancient Japanese masters are so familiar that the poems are the basis of a "poem-card" game played in Japan at the New Year. Ironically, little is known about the poets whose words have become so ingrained in Japanese culture.

Princess Nukada (seventh century)

Princess Nukada was a favorite at the court of two emperors and the most accomplished female poet of her time. The only clues we have to her character are her poems, which are delicate and passionate. Some of them, including the one reproduced here, were written for her older sister, Princess Kagami.

Oshikochi Mitsune (late ninth century)

Oshikochi Mitsune was one of the greatest poets of the early Heian era and one of the editors of the *Kokinshu,* a collection of verse. Some of his verses appear in that anthology. Many of his poems are melancholy, but they are never sentimental.

Ki Tsurayuki (884–946)

Another editor of the *Kokinshu,* Ki Tsurayuki was a high court official as well as an accomplished writer and calligrapher. He also wrote a travel diary that interwove poetry with prose. Ki Tsurayuki differentiated himself by writing in Japanese at a time when most cultured Japanese men wrote prose in Chinese. To avoid ridicule, he published the diary under a woman's name.

Ono Komachi (mid-tenth century)

Celebrated for her beauty and the emotional power of her verse, Ono Komachi is perhaps the most revered of the poets whose tanka appeared in the *Kokinshu.*

Saigyo (1118–1190)

Among the most accomplished twelfth-century tanka poets was Saigyo, who abandoned his position as a royal bodyguard at the age of twenty-three to become a priest. His tanka were written during the years he spent wandering through the Japanese countryside.

Think About the Writers

What characteristics do the poets who wrote Tanka have in common?

(background) Geothermal pool, Chinoike Jigoku (Blood Pool Hell) Beppu, Japan. (below) *Seated statue of Bashō* (1644–1694), by Ran-Koo. Wood. Edo Period (1603–1868). Musée Historique des Tissus, Lyon, France.

MEET THE WRITERS

Haiku Poets

Like the tanka poets, these haiku masters came from different backgrounds and led very different lives. They are united, however, by the striking emotion and philosophical impact of their fine verse.

Matsuo Bashō (1644–1694)

The son of a samurai, Matsuo Bashō spent his youth in the service of a local lord. He began writing verses when he was nine and soon showed remarkable promise. Before he was thirty, he had won acclaim as a poet and had started his own poetry school.

Two major influences on Bashō's poetry were his devotion to Zen Buddhism and his travels. In 1684, at the age of forty, Bashō set out on the first of his many journeys through Japan. A lone traveler, Bashō endured great discomforts and loneliness. Some of his best haiku were composed on these lonely journeys.

Uejima Onitsura (1660–1738)

One of Bashō's greatest admirers was Uejima Onitsura. Like Bashō, Onitsura came from a samurai background and began writing poetry at an early age. Though Onitsura admired Bashō, he did not imitate Bashō's style. His poems are more joyful and exuberant, and somewhat less philosophical than the verse of Bashō.

Taniguchi Buson (1715–1783)

Taniguchi Buson, a younger contemporary of Onitsura, soon established his own poetic style. His haiku are generally regarded as second only to those of Bashō. Buson was an accomplished painter, and his poems reflect his fascination with light and color.

Kobayashi Issa (1762–1826)

Kobayashi Issa is one of the most beloved of Japan's haiku masters. His life was extraordinarily sad. His mother died when he was an infant, and his relations with his stepmother were so poor that his father sent him away from home to study when he was only fourteen. His first wife bore him five children, but all of them died in infancy. Eventually his wife succumbed to illness. Possibly because of these many sorrows, Issa's verses are taut with intense emotion.

Think About the Writers — How might the writers' life experiences have affected their haiku?

Preparing to Read

Tanka / Haiku

Reader/Writer
Notebook

Use your **RWN** to complete the activities for these selections.

Literary Focus

Imagery Language that appeals to the senses (sight, hearing, touch, smell, and taste) is known as **imagery.** The Japanese tanka and haiku writers relied on imagery, often from nature, to suggest subtly and indirectly moods and themes. You, as the reader, must connect the images to the emotions they imply. Thus, the image of a fallen cherry blossom may suggest the brevity of love or even of life itself, and the image of the full moon may prompt philosophical musings about change and eternity. As you read, consider how imagery contributes to each poem's meaning.

Reading Focus

Using Text Structures to Understand Meaning In Japanese, **tanka** and **haiku** adhere to a strict structure of line lengths and syllable counts. Although some structural elements are lost in translation, these poems retain the elegant simplicity of the originals. The poems express complex ideas and powerful emotions such as yearning and loneliness in just a few short lines. Some poems develop an image across several lines; some use just a single word. As you read, examine the structure of each image for clues to help you infer the poem's meaning.

Into Action Use a chart like the one below to record each poem's imagery. Write down how each image is presented and structured.

Image	Structure
In the tree-shade of the summer mountain I stood.	Image developed over three lines.

Vocabulary

reed (reed) *n.:* kind of tall grass with a hollow, jointed stalk that grows in wet places. *The speaker's body feels as fragile as a reed.*

gourd (gawrd) *n.:* vegetable with a hard rind that can be dried, hollowed out, and used as a bowl. *When the speaker has no rice to pour in his gourd, he can put a flower in its place.*

thatched (thacht) *v.* used as *adj.:* covered with straw, leaves, or similar materials. *The image of a thatched roof with flowers makes the modest hut appear beautiful.*

Language Coach

Homonyms Words that have the same pronunciation but different spellings and meanings are called **homonyms.** You will *read* the word *reed* in one of the poems. A tanka poem by Komachi describes a body like a *reed*, which refers to a tall grass. You will find one of each of these homonym pairs in the poems: *weighted/waited, mind/mined, gourd/gored, know/no.* Can you explain the difference between the words in each pair?

Writing Focus

Think as a Reader/Writer

Find It in Your Reading In your *Reader/Writer Notebook,* record the words used by the poets to create **images** and to note which senses are invoked.

Learn It Online
Listen to these tanka and haiku online.

go.hrw.com | L12-868 | **Go**

Tanka

translated by **Geoffrey Bownas**
and **Anthony Thwaite**

Read with a Purpose
Read to discover how poets use images of nature to convey ideas.

Build Background
These poems were written by five different writers in five different centuries. Some features of the tanka form are lost in translation from Japanese to English; for example, only one of the poems retains the traditional thirty-one syllables required in tanka. Furthermore, the overall sounds of the poems differ from the sounds of the originals. The poems do, however, stay true to tanka's unrhymed style. The poems also make use of **assonance,** the repetition of vowel sounds in nearby words.

Moon over the five-story pagoda of Sensoji temple at night in Asakusa, Tokyo, Japan.

I waited and I
Yearned for you.
My blind
Stirred at the touch
Of the autumn breeze.
    —Princess Nukada

The end of my journey
Was still far off,
But in the tree-shade
Of the summer mountain
I stood, my mind floating.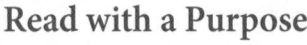
    —Oshikochi Mitsune

Now, I cannot tell
What my old friend is thinking:
But the petals of the plum
In this place I used to know
Keep their old fragrance. **B**
    —Ki Tsurayuki

How helpless my heart!
Were the stream to tempt,
My body, like a reed
Severed at the roots,
Would drift along, I think.
    —Ono Komachi

Every single thing
Changes and is changing
Always in this world.
Yet with the same light
The moon goes on shining. **C**
    —Priest Saigyo

A **Reading Focus** Using Text Structures to Understand Meaning Tanka poems are traditionally unrhymed. What structural devices help readers understand the poem's meaning?

B **Literary Focus** Imagery What does the smell of the plum blossoms suggest about friendship?

C **Literary Focus** Imagery What does the image of the moon suggest about the relationship between change and permanence?

Vocabulary **reed** (reed) *n.*: kind of tall grass with a hollow, jointed stalk that grows in wet places.

Haiku

The haiku by Bashō, Buson, and Issa are translated by Harold G. Henderson.
The haiku by Onitsura is translated by Peter Beilenson and Harry Behn.

Read with a Purpose
Read to discover how one or two simple images can suggest complex emotions or ideas.

Build Background
The first three haiku you will read are by the greatest haiku master, the seventeenth-century poet, Bashō. In all three poems, Bashō finds inherent beauty in seemingly ordinary objects or events. This practice is inspired by the Buddhist belief that anyone, through contemplation, can find great significance in even the humblest of things. Like tanka, haiku focus on only one or two images.

On a withered branch
   A crow has settled—
      autumn nightfall. **Ⓐ**
         —Matsuo Bashō

A village where they ring
   no bells!—Oh, what *do* they do
      at dusk in spring?
         —Matsuo Bashō

No rice?—In that hour
   we put into the gourd
      a maiden-flower.
         —Matsuo Bashō

Even stones in streams
   of mountain water compose
      songs to wild cherries. **Ⓑ**
         —Uejima Onitsura

Blossoms on the pear;
   and a woman in the moonlight
      reads a letter there....
         —Taniguchi Buson

A morning-glory vine
   all blossoming has thatched
      this hut of mine. **Ⓒ**
         —Kobayashi Issa

Ⓐ Reading Focus Using Text Structures to Understand Meaning How does the visual representation of the three-line poem affect your understanding of it?

Ⓑ Literary Focus Imagery What does the image of stones tell you about the beauty or importance of the wild cherries?

Ⓒ Literary Focus Imagery What does the blossoming vine on the roof suggest about the speaker's feelings for his home?

Vocabulary **gourd** (gawrd) *n.*: vegetable with a hard rind that can be dried, hollowed out, and used as a bowl.
thatched (thacht) *v.* used as *adj.*: covered with straw, leaves, or similar materials.

Applying Your Skills

SKILLS FOCUS Literary Skills Analyze imagery; analyze symbols. **Reading Skills** Use text structure to understand meaning. **Vocabulary Skills** Identify and correctly use synonyms. **Writing Skills** Write poems; develop description with sensory details.

Tanka / Haiku

Respond and Think Critically

Reading Focus

Quick Check

1. How does Saigyo use an image from nature in his tanka to contrast his thoughts on the changing world?

2. What generalization can you make about the themes of tanka poetry?

3. What images does Buson use in his haiku? What emotions do they evoke?

Read with a Purpose

4. What varied images are used to express themes common to both tanka and haiku?

Reading Skills: Using Text Structures to Understand Meaning

5. Review your charts for the poems, and connect the two boxes in each chart to a third box. How does each image and each poem's structure contribute to the meaning?

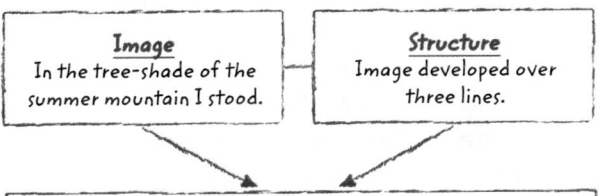

Image
In the tree-shade of the summer mountain I stood.

Structure
Image developed over three lines.

Meaning of Poem
Image emphasizes that speaker is alone on journey and is thinking ahead to when he will finish it. Description's length emphasizes importance of image. Comma after "I stood" creates a pause, shows that his body is still.

✓ Vocabulary Check

Match each Vocabulary word with its synonym.

6. reed   **a.** vessel

7. gourd   **b.** covered

8. thatched   **c.** stalk

Literary Focus

Literary Analysis

9. Compare and Contrast How do the emotions evoked in the first two tanka compare?

10. Analyze Find examples of an unexpected relationship between two things in Bashō's haiku.

11. Extend How do the six haiku translations depart from strict haiku form?

Literary Skills: Imagery

12. Make Judgments Which tanka most strongly suggests loneliness or quiet reflection? What images does the poet use to convey this mood?

13. Analyze Seasonal images are common in haiku. What seasonal images do you find in these haiku? What emotions do the images convey?

Literary Skills Review: Symbolism

14. Analyze A **symbol** is a person, place, animal, thing, or event that stands for itself and for something more than itself. What might each of the two contrasted things in Issa's haiku symbolize?

Writing Focus

Think as a Reader/Writer

Use It in Your Writing Write a tanka or haiku with images that appeal to at least two different senses.

What Do **You Think Now** What feelings and actions can nature inspire?

Preparing to Read

Chinese Poetry

What Do You Think?

How can we use imagination to discover truth?

🕐 **QuickWrite**

Imagine you are a wandering writer, like the Chinese poets described on this page. In your *Reader/Writer Notebook,* write a paragraph about how you think a life of wandering might inspire your imagination.

Ceramic sculpture on roof of Kwan Tai Temple, Tai O, Lantau Island.

Tu Fu
(712–770)

Tu Fu was born into a noble family of scholar-officials. His family connections and modest wealth would have assured him a life of relative comfort had not a violent rebellion in 755 ended the T'ang dynasty's days of glory. After the rebellion, Tu Fu was often on the road, searching for a way to make a living. Toward the end of his life, Tu Fu lived in hardship and poor health. He died in 770, on a houseboat near Hangzhou.

The uncertain course of Tu Fu's life is reflected in his poetry, which is often marked by bitterness and melancholy. In his youth, he wrote mainly about the beauty of nature and his own sorrows. As he grew older, however, Tu Fu's poems turned to more humanitarian themes. He became sensitive to people's sufferings and was the first Chinese poet to write at length about social concerns.

Although Tu Fu was not well known as a poet during his own lifetime, he wrote in an elegant style that influenced Chinese poets for centuries after his death.

Li Po
(701–762)

A well-educated youth from a good family, Li Po chose to forgo the test for imperial service taken by many young men of the upper classes. Young Li Po instead served as a wandering knight, a sword-wielding avenger of wrongs against women and children. At the age of twenty-five, he became a vagabond who wandered for most of his remaining days.

Li Po's travels in China spread his fame as a poet. Even the emperor admired him. In fact, Li Po abandoned his nomadic life for a time to serve the emperor as an imperial court poet. Li Po's traditional lyric poetry is characterized by its sense of playfulness, fantasy, and grace. The death of Li Po was sudden; an appropriately romantic legend asserts he drowned one night as he leaned from his boat to embrace the watery reflection of the moon.

Think About the Writers What aspects of these poets' lives were different and which were similar?

Jade Flower Palace / Night Thoughts Afloat

Reader/Writer Notebook

Use your **RWN** to complete the activities for these selections.

Literary Focus

Mood The overall feeling or atmosphere in a work of literature is called **mood.** A poem's mood might be cheerful or gloomy, defiant or accepting. Writers establish mood by using descriptive details and language, which evoke particular images or feelings. In traditional Chinese poetry of Tu Fu's time, a single mood usually characterized each poem. Tu Fu broke new ground by shifting the mood within a single poem.

Reading Focus

Using Text Structures to Understand Meaning Although some of their structural elements are lost in translation, Tu Fu's writings retain their original essence. "Jade Flower Palace" and "Night Thoughts Afloat" express complex ideas and powerful emotions within precisely and elegantly structured text. To create particular moods in each of his poems, Tu Fu uses different structural <u>techniques,</u> one of which is the variation of the length of complete sentences. In these sentences, he asks questions, makes declarations, states facts, and interjects his personal views. What can you infer about a poem's meaning based on its structure and how its mood is created and developed?

Into Action As you read, use a chart like the one below to record the mood or moods of each poem. For each mood, write down examples of the poem's structure that help to create that mood.

"Jade Flower Palace":

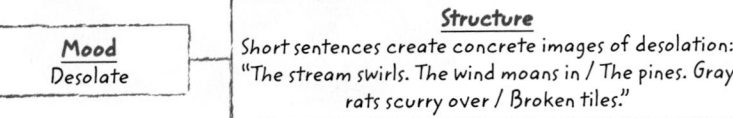

| Mood — Desolate | **Structure**
Short sentences create concrete images of desolation: "The stream swirls. The wind moans in / The pines. Gray rats scurry over / Broken tiles." |

Vocabulary

scurry (SKUR ee) v.: run away quickly. *The rats scurry across the ruins of the ancient palace.*

courtiers (KAWR tee uhrz) n.: palace attendants. *When the ruler leaves the palace, his courtiers follow him.*

pathos (PAY thahs) n.: feeling of sadness or melancholy often brought on by a work of art. *The poet is moved to pathos when he tries to describe the passing of time.*

Language Coach

Word Origins The noun *pathos* comes from the Greek word meaning "suffering, feeling, emotion." The same Greek root is found in many related words, including *sympathy, empathy, apathy, pathology,* and *pathetic.* Try to guess what each word means. Use a dictionary to find their meanings.

Writing Focus

Think as a Reader/Writer

Find It In Your Reading A writer creates **mood** through a careful choice of words and phrasing. In your *Reader/Writer Notebook,* note the language that is most effective in creating the moods in Tu Fu's poems.

Learn It Online
Learn more about Tu Fu at the Writers' Lives site online.

go.hrw.com   L12-873   **Go**

Jade Flower Palace

by **Tu Fu**

translated by **Kenneth Rexroth**

Read with a Purpose
Read to discover how hauntingly beautiful palace ruins inspire the speaker to contemplate life.

Build Background
Perhaps the most respected of all the ancient Chinese poets, Tu Fu focused on the affairs of the world and the hardships of his people. Of his goal as a poet, Tu Fu once said, "If my words aren't startling, death itself has no rest." As you read the poem, notice the vivid images and the concrete details that are hallmarks of Tu Fu's poetry.

The stream swirls. The wind moans in
The pines. Gray rats scurry over
Broken tiles. What prince, long ago, **Ⓐ**
Built this palace, standing in
5 Ruins beside the cliffs? There are
Green ghost fires in the black rooms.
The shattered pavements are all
Washed away. Ten thousand organ
Pipes whistle and roar. The storm
10 Scatters the red autumn leaves.
His dancing girls are yellow dust.
Their painted cheeks have crumbled
Away. His gold chariots
And courtiers are gone. Only
15 A stone horse is left of his
Glory. I sit on the grass and
Start a poem, but the pathos of
It overcomes me. The future
Slips imperceptibly away.
20 Who can say what the years will bring? **Ⓑ**

Painting and calligraphy from a large format Chinese album illustrating stories of Taoist immortals. One of 15 paintings. The text concerns a Taoist adept, Wang Qiao, a Han period official. ADD Ms. 22689, f16. The British Library, London.

Ⓐ Literary Focus Mood How would you describe the mood created by the setting? What images communicate this mood?

Ⓑ Literary Focus Mood What mood do the final lines create? What does this mood suggest about the relationship between the palace and the speaker?

Vocabulary **scurry** (SKUR ee) v.: run away quickly.
courtiers (KAWR tee uhrz) n.: palace attendants.
pathos (PAY thahs) n.: feeling of sadness or melancholy often brought on by a work of art.

Night Thoughts Afloat

by **Tu Fu**
translated by **Arthur Cooper**

Read with a Purpose
Read to discover the speaker's inner thoughts as he watches the night sky.

Build Background
Tu Fu wrote this poem while spending the final years of his life on a houseboat. As you read, think about how this setting could evoke conflicting emotions—a sense of peace and an awareness of failure.

Li River cormorant fisherman with lantern on his bamboo raft at night, near Yangshuo.

> By bent grasses
> in a gentle wind
>   Under straight mast
> I'm alone tonight,
>
> 5   And the stars hang
> above the broad plain
>   But moon's afloat
> in this Great River: **A**
>
>   Oh, where's my name
> 10 among the poets?
>   Official rank?
> "Retired for ill health."
>
>   Drifting, drifting,
> what am I more than
> 15   A single gull
> between sky and earth? **B**

A **Reading Focus** Using Text Structures to Understand Meaning Notice the opposition between the first and third lines in each of the first two stanzas. How does this structure contribute to the poem's meaning?

B **Literary Focus** Mood What mood does the image of the single gull suggest?

SKILLS FOCUS Literary Skills Analyze mood; analyze setting. **Reading Skills** Use text structures to understand meaning. **Vocabulary Skills** Identify antonyms. **Writing Skills** Write a poem; employ precise language for effective writing.

Respond and Think Critically

Reading Focus

Read with a Purpose

1. How does the speaker connect the ruins to the future in "Jade Flower Palace"?

2. In "Night Thoughts Afloat," why is it important that the speaker contemplates a night sky rather than a day sky?

Reading Skills: Using Text Structures to Understand Meaning

3. Connect the boxes in each chart to a third box. How do the moods contribute to each poem's meaning? How do the imagery and poem structures contribute to each poem's meaning?

"Jade Flower Palace":

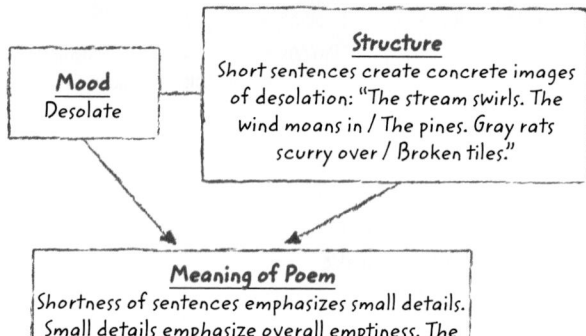

Mood
Desolate

Structure
Short sentences create concrete images of desolation: "The stream swirls. The wind moans in / The pines. Gray rats scurry over / Broken tiles."

Meaning of Poem
Shortness of sentences emphasizes small details. Small details emphasize overall emptiness. The past is desolate and crumbling.

✓ Vocabulary Check

Match the Vocabulary words with their antonyms.

4. scurry   **a.** joy

5. courtiers   **b.** plod

6. pathos   **c.** princes

Literary Focus

Literary Analysis

7. **Interpret** What does Tu Fu say about the past, present, and future in "Jade Flower Palace"?

8. **Analyze** To what does the speaker compare himself in "Night Thoughts"? What emotions does he express through the comparison?

Literary Skills: Mood

9. **Make Judgments** Find at least one mood shift in each poem. How do these shifts affect your reading?

10. **Analyze** Explain how the verbs and verbs used as adjectives contribute to the poem's mood.

Literary Skills Review: Setting

11. **Analyze** The time and location in which a piece of literature takes place is its **setting.** What differentiates the settings in these poems? How do the settings contribute to each poem's meaning?

Writing Focus

Think as a Reader/Writer

Use It in Your Writing Decide on a mood that you want to convey in an original poem. Use imagery and structure to communicate this mood in your poem. Share the poem with other students. Ask them to identify the mood you have created.

What Do You Think Now?

What truths do you find in these poems? Explain.

Preparing to Read

Quiet Night Thoughts
Question and Answer Among the Mountains
Letter to His Two Small Children

Reader/Writer Notebook

Use your **RWN** to complete the activities for these selections.

Literary Focus

Imagery To evoke readers' emotions, writers use **imagery,** language that appeals to the senses of sight, hearing, touch, smell, and taste. For example, a writer might describe an ocean as a "crashing gray tide" to build fear or as "rippling blue waves" to suggest tranquility. Instead of directly stating an emotion, Li Po's poems allow the reader to experience the emotional effect of the images.

Reading Focus

Using Text Structures to Understand Meaning Although some elements are lost in translation, Li Po's writings retain the elegant simplicity of the originals. "Quiet Night Thoughts" and "Question and Answer" express complex ideas and powerful emotions, such as freedom and homesickness, in just a few short lines. The longer "Letter" uses its precise structure to evoke thoughts and feelings. The poems may develop an image across several lines or in just a single word. Examine each image's structure. What meanings can you infer from how imagery is developed?

Into Action Use a chart like the one below to record the imagery of each poem. Write down how the image is presented and structured.

"Quiet Night Thoughts":

Image		Structure
bright moonlight	—	Image is developed across 4 lines.

Writing Focus

Think as a Reader/Writer

Find It in Your Reading In your *Reader/Writer Notebook,* record the words Li Po uses to create his **images** and note the senses they evoke.

TechFocus As you read these poems, think about the images that come into your mind. How could you share these images with others?

Language Coach

Specific Nouns Poets often use precise nouns to create sharp, specific images. Li Po describes the *sprays* of a tree. A spray, in this context, is a branch of a plant, including its leaves and flowers. The noun suggests the delicate, natural shapes found within the tree. Later, the tree's height is described as being even with the *eaves,* the part of the roof that extends beyond the wall that supports it. How does this exact noun help you create a specific image in your mind?

Learn It Online

Learn more about Chinese literature and history online.

go.hrw.com   L12-877   **Go**

Quiet Night Thoughts

by **Li Po**

translated by **Arthur Cooper**

Before my bed
there is bright moonlight
So that it seems
like frost on the ground: **A**

5   Lifting my head
I watch the bright moon,
Lowering my head
I dream that I'm home. **B**

Question and Answer Among the Mountains

by **Li Po**

translated by **Robert Kotewall** and **Norman L. Smith**

You ask me why I dwell in the green mountain;
I smile and make no reply for my heart is free of care.
As the peach-blossom flows down stream and is gone into
    the unknown,
I have a world apart that is not among men. **C**

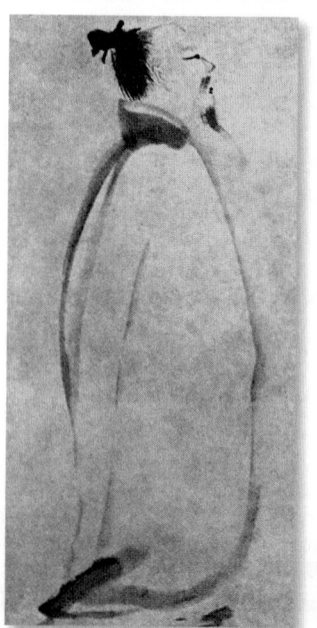

A Literary Focus Imagery What feeling is created by the image in the first four lines?

B Reading Focus Using Text Structures to Understand Meaning How does the structure of the poem help emphasize the speaker's distance from his home?

C Literary Focus Imagery How does the speaker use the image of the peach blossom to tell us something about himself?

Li Po Chanting in Stroll, by Liang Kai. The Granger Collection, NY.

Letter to His Two Small Children

by **Li Po**

translated by **Arthur Cooper**

Read with a Purpose Read to discover how the speaker expresses his feelings for his children through images of nature.

A local residence of Xidi Village, Shexian County, Anhui province, China.

Here in Wu° Land mulberry leaves are green,
Silkworms in Wu have now had three sleeps: (A)

My family, left in Eastern Lu,
Oh, to sow now Turtle-shaded fields,
5   Do the Spring things I can never join,
Sailing Yangtze° always on my own—

Let the South Wind blow you back my heart,
Fly and land it in the Tavern court
Where, to the East, there are sprays and leaves
10 Of one peach tree, sweeping the blue mist;

This is the tree I myself put in
When I left you, nearly three years past;
A peach tree now, level with the eaves,
And I sailing cannot yet turn home!

15 Pretty daughter, P'ing-yang is your name,
Breaking blossom, there beside my tree,
Breaking blossom, you cannot see me
And your tears flow like the running stream;

And little son, Po-ch'in you are called,
20 Your big sister's shoulder you must reach
When you come there underneath my peach,
Oh, to pat and pet you too, my child!   (B)

I dreamt like this till my wits went wild,
By such yearning daily burned within;
25 So tore some silk, wrote this distant pang
From me to you living at Wen Yang. . .

---

1. Wu: river in central China.

6. Yangtze: the longest river in China, flowing from Tibet to the East China Sea.

(A) **Literary Focus** Imagery What does the speaker mean when he says, "Silkworms in Wu have now had three sleeps"? What is the effect of expressing the passage of time with this image?

(B) **Literary Focus** Imagery What does the poet associate with the image of the peach tree?

Quiet Night Thoughts / Question and Answer Among the Mountains / Letter to His Two Small Children

Respond and Think Critically

Reading Focus

Quick Check

1. What is the mood of "Quiet Night Thoughts"?

2. What is the question in "Question and Answer"?

3. In "Letter to His Two Small Children," why does the speaker write to his children?

Read with a Purpose

4. In "Quiet Night Thoughts," what emotional effect does the moon have on the speaker?

5. In "Question and Answer," how does the speaker feel about living alone?

6. What feelings for his children does the speaker of "Letter" reveal in his use of nature imagery?

Reading Skills: Using Text Structures to Understand Meaning

7. Connect the two boxes in each chart to a third box. How does each image contribute to each poem's meaning? How does the structure of the image contribute to the meaning of the poem?

"Quiet Night Thoughts":

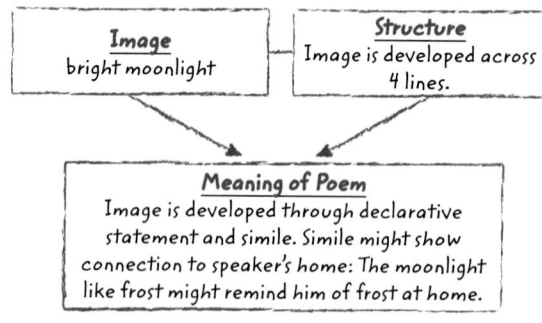

Literary Focus

Literary Analysis

8. **Analyze** How does the poet use imagery to convey the mood of "Quiet Night Thoughts"?

9. **Interpret** In "Question and Answer," the speaker answers a question by not answering it. Explain this **paradox,** or seeming contradiction.

10. **Analyze** How does Li Po use images to emphasize solitude? What emotions does he evoke?

Literary Skills: Imagery

11. **Analyze** Do the speakers effectively express their feelings by using nature images? Explain.

Literary Skills Review: Parallelism

12. **Draw Conclusions** The repetition of words, phrases, or sentences that have the same grammatical structure or that restate a similar idea is **parallelism.** Explain the effect of this technique in the last four lines of "Quiet Night Thoughts."

Writing Focus

Think as a Reader/Writer

Use It in Your Writing Review the examples of Li Po's imagery in your *Reader/Writer Notebook.* Use imagery as you write a poem about solitude.

What Do You Think Now

Why do simple nature images express feelings of solitude?

Japanese and Chinese Poetry

Writing a Comparison-Contrast Essay

In what ways is British Romantic poetry similar to and different from Japanese and Chinese poetry? Re-read the selections to clarify your ideas. Then, write an essay in which you compare and contrast the selections. Here are more specific topic ideas for your comparison-contrast essay:

- Compare and contrast the poets' use of imagery. What ideas and emotions does Romantic poetry evoke? How do these images, ideas, and emotions compare to those addressed by Japanese and Chinese poets?

- Compare and contrast the forms and structures of the poems. What differentiates the Romantic forms from those of the Japanese and Chinese? How do the poetic structures compare across cultures?

- Choose one of the Japanese or Chinese poems and a Romantic poem with a similar meaning or purpose. Compare and contrast the content, imagery, and structures of the two poems. Is one poem more effective in delivering its meaning or conveying its purpose? Explain your opinion with support from the texts.

Use examples from the selections to support your arguments. Weave your arguments together using transitional words, and remember to include a strong concluding statement.

What Do You Think Now Do poets' imaginations help them interact with the world or escape it? Explain.

CHOICES

As you respond to the Choices, use these **Academic Vocabulary** words as appropriate: device, differentiate, function, inherent, technique.

REVIEW
Create a Visual

Choose an image from a Japanese or Chinese poem in the unit and a related image from a British Romantic poem in the unit. Create a collage, painting, or drawing of each image. Present your visuals to the class, explaining the connections between them.

CONNECT
Illustrate the Poems

TechFocus Choose two or three poems that you feel have powerful imagery, and create a Web page for each. The Web pages should contain the texts of the poems as well as images and sounds that illustrate the poems' imagery and meanings. You may also read the poems aloud and place audio or video recordings of your performance on the Web pages. Then, share your Web pages with your class.

EXTEND
Compare Poets' Lives Across Cultures

With a partner, use the school library or the Internet to research more about the lives of Tu Fu or Li Po and a British Romantic poet. How are their lives similar? What differentiates them? Present your findings to the class. Offer your peers the opportunity to comment on the cross-cultural similarities and differences between the poets you chose.

Learn It Online
Explore Chinese poetry further through these Internet links.

go.hrw.com   L12-881   **Go**

Writing Workshop

Reflective Essay

Write with a Purpose

Write a reflective essay about a significant personal experience. Include the broader meaning of the experience. Your **purpose** for writing is to inspire and connect with your readers. Your **audience** is probably classmates, teacher, and others who will appreciate the significance of the experience.

A Good Reflective Essay

- focuses on one significant experience
- provides essential background information
- relates events in a clear order
- includes vivid descriptive details
- identifies the deeper meaning of the experience

See page 890 for complete rubric.

Think as a Reader/Writer

Before you write your own **reflective essay,** read the following excerpt from "A Reason to Hope" by Jane Goodall, which can be found in its entirety beginning on page 710. Observe how she describes her experience and reflects on its importance.

In the faint light from the moon reflected by the dew-laden grass, it was not difficult to find my way up the mountain. All around, the trees were shrouded with the last mysteries of the night's dreaming. It was quiet, utterly peaceful. The only sounds were the occasional chirp of a cricket, and the soft murmur where the waves caressed the stones on the beach below. Suddenly there was a burst of song, the duet of a pair of robin chats, hauntingly beautiful. I realized that the intensity of the light had changed; dawn had crept upon me unawares. . . .

← Goodall introduces the scene of the experience.

Five minutes later I heard the rustlings of leaves overhead. I looked up and saw the branches moving against the lightening sky. The chimps had awakened. It was Fifi and her offspring, Freud, Frodo, and little Fanni. I followed when they moved off up the slope. Fanni riding on her mother's back like a diminutive jockey. Presently they climbed into a tall fig tree and began to feed. I heard the occasional soft thuds as skins and seeds of figs fell to the ground.

← The chimps are introduced.

For several hours we moved leisurely from one food tree to the next, gradually climbing higher and higher. On an open grassy ridge the chimps climbed into a massive mbula tree, where Fifi . . . made a large comfortable nest high above me. She dozed through a midday siesta, little Fanni asleep in her arms, Frodo and Freud playing nearby. How healing it was to be back in Gombe again, and by myself with the chimpanzees and their forest. I had left the busy, materialistic world so full of greed and selfishness and, for a little while, could feel myself, as in the early days, a part of nature.

← Goodall begins to reflect on the meaning of the experience.

Reader/Writer Notebook

Use your **RWN** to complete the activities for this workshop.

Think About the Professional Model

1. How do Goodall's descriptions convey what she feels about the scene?
2. Summarize the reflective comments Goodall makes about the experience.

Prewriting

Choose an Experience

What experiences in your life have taught you the most important lessons? The experience could be something unusual, like a trip or a competition. Or it could be something you do every day, like visiting a friend's house. What matters most is that the experience means something to you. A trip might teach you about how other people live; a day with a friend might teach you about happiness.

If an experience does not leap immediately to mind, look through old yearbooks, photos, diaries, or journals. Also, try reading some published reflective pieces, such as poems, autobiographies and memoirs, and essays.

Gather and Record Details

To gather the details that will bring your experience and its meaning to life, list the individual events that were an integral part of your experience. The following suggestions may help you recall the events:

- Visualize the entire experience, picturing each event from beginning to end.
- Ask others who shared the experience with you to recall details.
- If you have mementos from the experience—photographs, letters, journal or diary entries—use them to help jog your memory.

Under each event in your list, record specific details about each event to help you create images in the minds of readers.

Types of Details	
Narrative details	• relate **actions, thoughts,** and **feelings** of people involved • include **dialogue** (what you or others said) • include **interior monologue** (your unspoken thoughts)
Descriptive details	• describe how **people** and **objects** look • describe the **setting** of the experience

Reflect on the Meaning

Reflective essays go beyond merely describing your personal observations and perceptions to examining **abstract ideas**—love, patience, courage, honor. When you have chosen the experience, think about these questions to help you develop your reflections and think about the **significance** of the moment:

- What did you feel at the time of the experience?
- How do you feel about it now?
- How has the experience changed the way you think and act?
- What insight about life in general did you gain from the experience?

Idea Starters

- an achievement
- a disappointment
- an experience with nature
- a friendship
- a journey
- a job

⬤ Writing Tip

Both narratives and descriptions include **concrete sensory details** that appeal to the five senses: sight, sound, taste, smell, and touch.

Your Turn _____

Get Started Making notes in your **RWN,** choose an **experience** and reflect on its **meaning** for you. Then, note **details** that will help you convey the experience and its meaning to your audience.

✳ Learn It Online

To see how one writer completed this assignment, see the model reflective essay at:

go.hrw.com | L12-883 | **Go**

Reflective Essay

Think About Purpose and Audience

Your **purpose** is to explore the connection between a personal experience and what it says about your life and, beyond that, what it says about the meaning of being human. You also share your experience with your **audience,** who will most likely be your classmates and teacher. As you think about your experience, consider what your audience needs to know to fully understand its significance to you. Also, make sure your experience is appropriate to your audience and that you'll feel comfortable telling others what happened and how you felt.

Organize Your Reflective Essay

Once you have gathered details, it is time to organize your essay. You'll organize the events in **chronological order,** the order in which they happened. You could possibly vary this order by using **flashbacks** and **flash-forwards**—jumps forward or backward in time—for effect. Take note of details you'll include and when you'll include them. Once you've finished retelling your experience, you'll conclude by **reflecting** on its importance to you.

Create an Action Plan

Your **reflective essay action plan** begins with a statement of your experience. Think about what happened and how it unfolded. Then, organize your essay by planning the introduction, body, and conclusion. What scene best begins the essay? What events will you show that lead up to the experience? How will you state the experience's significance? Here is one writer's reflective essay action plan. Use the model to help you create your own plan.

Action Plan

Experience: picking up trash after the game, leaders not showing up

Introduction:
—the night after the "powder puff game, picking up trash
—details: the sight and smell of the trash
—describe my disappointment when people didn't show up
—hint about the significance: leadership

Body:
—describe the meeting with other members of the leadership team
—tell my reaction to their "excuses"

Conclusion:
—discuss my reflections on the event; how I learned that what was important was my contribution, not what others did
—explain the idea that work should be its own reward

Your Turn

Organize Your Ideas Now that you've chosen an experience and gathered details, write a **reflective essay action plan.** Share your plan with a partner, and ask for feedback.

Drafting

Draft Your Reflective Essay

Now use your prewriting notes, including your reflective essay action plan, and the **Writer's Framework** to the right to draft your essay.

Use Language Effectively

Use the following types of descriptive language to bring your writing to life:

- Use **precise verbs:** Note the difference between *walking, ambling, strolling, sauntering,* and *hiking.* Each word has |a slightly different meaning. Choose verbs that precisely describe actions in your experience.

- Use **figurative language** to help your reader imagine what you are describing. Think about both physical resemblances and more abstract relationships to build effective comparisons and descriptions.

- Use **adverbs and adverb phrases** to help readers follow the progression of events in your essay.

Framework for a Reflective Essay

Introduction
- Engage readers' attention.
- Provide necessary background information.
- Hint at the significance.

Body
- Use narrative and descriptive details to relate events.
- Organize events chronologically.

Conclusion
- Bring narrative to an end.
- Reflect on the experience: explicitly reveal its significance.
- Identify the insight into life the experience gave you.

Grammar Link Using Adverbs and Adverb Phrases

A reflective essay often progresses over time and changes settings as the writer leads the reader to the main experience. **Adverbs and adverb phrases** help the reader follow the progression from place to place and over time. These modifiers locate action in time and space by answering the questions *where* and *when.* In the model on page 882, notice how Goodall effectively uses adverbs and adverb phrases (usually prepositional phrases used as adverbs) as she marks her progress on the mountain in Gombe.

All around, the trees were shrouded . . .

Suddenly there was a burst of song . . .

Five minutes later I heard the rustlings of leaves overhead.

For several hours we moved . . .

On an open grassy ridge the chimps climbed . . .

Reference Note For more on adverbs and adverb phrases, see the Language Handbook.

Your Turn

Write Your Draft Following your **reflective essay action plan** and the **Writer's Framework,** write a draft of your essay. Also think about how you will use **adverbs** and **adverb phrases** as transitions to help your readers follow the progression of your experience.

Reflective Essay

Peer Review

With a partner, review your draft by answering each question in the chart to the right. Begin by reading the evaluation questions in the left-hand column, studying the tips in the center column, and then revising your essay as needed using the revision techniques in the right-hand column. Encourage your partner to note any details that are missing or need more explanation.

Evaluating and Revising

To ensure your reflective essay reflects your experience with accuracy and flair, use the chart below to evaluate and revise your essay's content and organization. As you revise, pay attention to your **audience** and **purpose.**

Reflective Essay: Guidelines for Content and Organization

Evaluation Question	Tip	Revision Technique
1. Does the introduction provide necessary background information and engage the reader's attention?	**Bracket** sentences that provide background information. **Circle** the engaging opening.	**Add** background information. **Add** an engaging opener or revise existing sentences to make them more gripping.
2. Does the introduction hint at the significance of the experience?	**Underline** any sentences in the introduction that hint at the significance.	**Add** a sentence or two to hint at the significance of the experience without revealing it entirely.
3. Does the essay's body use narrative and descriptive details to relate each event?	**Put a check mark** next to each narrative or descriptive passage.	**Add** details or elaborate on events to make them clear.
4. Are the events and details in the essay arranged effectively?	**Number** events according to chronological order. If the numbers are not in sequence (unless you have purposely added a flashback or flash-forward), revise.	**Reorder** events to reflect chronological order. **Add** transitions, such as adverbs and adverb phrases, to improve the coherence of the narrative.
5. Does the essay include reflective comments in addition to those in the conclusion?	**Star** each reflective comment within the text of the essay. If there are none, look for appropriate places to add them.	**Add** reflective comments or observations that lead to and support your final reflection.
6. Does the conclusion state the significance of the experience and reveal the writer's insight about life?	**Highlight** the experience's significance. **Put a wavy line under** sentences that reveal the writer's insight about life.	**Add** one or more sentences that explicitly state the experience's significance and your insight about life.

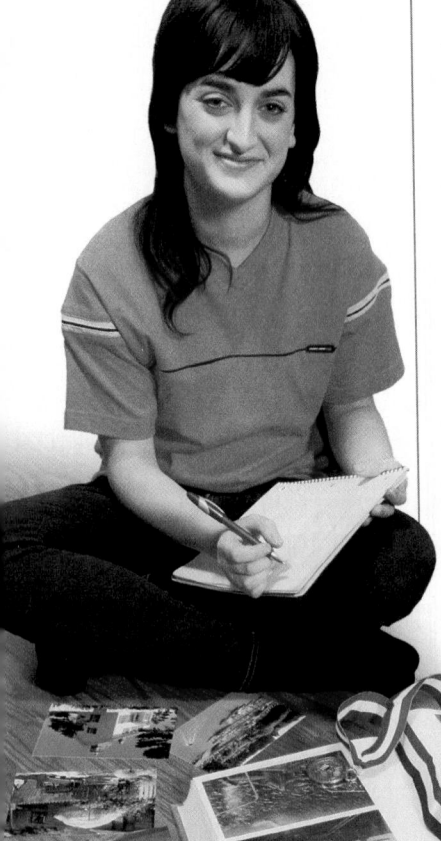

Read this student's draft with comments on its structure and suggestions for how it could be made even stronger.

On Commitment

by Steffi Yutan, Elk Grove High School

    I glanced at my watch: 11:32 P.M. I looked around the stadium and saw only five members of the leadership team after the "powder puff" game.

    Everyone had been there to watch, play, or cheer, but over half did not stay to clean up after the game. Sighing, I picked up my pace, encouraging those few around me.

    The following Monday, we discussed the disappearance of half of our leadership team after the Friday night game. Our advisor, whom I have grown to respect more than most adults in my life, let us handle the situation on our own. I sat quietly—listening to several girls who barely held back tears as they explained how hurt and abandoned they felt. I nodded in agreement, but I was more angry than hurt. I wanted to scream at my peers for being selfish, for being irresponsible, for letting me down—for letting the team down. However, I knew no amount of yelling, kicking, or screaming would get through to them. They were long gone, rolling their eyes, staring blankly into space. Instead of apologies, they made excuses. "My ride was leaving," or just "I forgot." I wondered, "How can they be so self-centered?"

← In the introduction, Steffi hints at a **conflict** that is an important part of her **experience.**

← Steffi recounts an event that leads to her realization of the **significance of her experience.**

← Steffi uses **description, dialogue,** and **interior monologue** to describe the other characters' reactions to contrast her own.

MINI-LESSON ▶ **How to Add Details to an Introduction**

Creating a vivid scene with concrete sensory details is a good way to begin a reflective essay. Since the scene after the game is a catalyst for Steffi's reflection, She decided to revise it by adding details that clearly illustrate the problem and her reaction. These details create an emotional reaction in her readers.

Steffi's Revision of Paragraph 1

I sighed deeply, bent over stiffly to pick up another dripping plastic bottle from the bleachers and dropped it in my growing-in-size-and-smell garbage bag with sticky fingers.∧ Yawning, I glanced at my watch: 11:32 P.M. I looked around the stadium and saw only five members of the leadership team *picking up trash*∧ after the "powder puff" game. Everyone had been there to watch, play, or cheer, but over half did not stay to clean up after the game. Sighing, I picked up my pace, encourage those around me∧ *; only ninety-nine bottles to go.*

Your Turn

Add Details to Your Introduction

Read your draft and then ask:

- Do I use **descriptive language** to show, rather than just tell, what happened?
- What **concrete, sensory details** can I add to allow my readers to imagine the scene?

Student Draft *continues*

Steffi explains **when** and **how** she identified the real source of the problem.

She uses **figurative language** to address apathy and its result.

The **chronological organization** moves to the present year, setting up her most reflective insight.

In her **conclusion**, Steffi uses an image of the trash to lead to her final **reflection**.

I realized then that we had different levels of ability, dedication and expectations. Not once had we discussed the commitment our team required for the laborious work of leadership. Our team did not fall apart the night of the "powder puff" game, but months before. It is the same every year. We begin excited and optimistic, proud to be campus leaders, but slowly apathy invades, leaving behind shells of good leaders tasks left undone and only a select few to pick up the slack.

This year, as vice president of the leadership team, I led a discussion on individual expectations, dedication, and commitment. The conversation has made a world of difference. Although the occasional lack of passion or poor attitudes of my peers still frustrates me, their varying degrees of commitment cannot keep me from the job that I love.

I now find myself looking forward to picking up plastic bottles after this year's "powder puff" game. But this time, with my whole team there, I know it will be worth the effort. Now I understand that real leadership is about helping others discover their own commitment.

MINI-LESSON ▶ How to Add Reflection

A good reflective essay uses reflection throughout the experience as well as in the closing paragraph. As Steffi re-read her draft, she decided that she wanted to add more reflective explanation to the fourth paragraph so that the reader is fully prepared for the conclusion. Reflective comments answer the questions: *What does this experience mean to me? What have I learned from the experience? What does my reaction say about me?*

Steffi's Revision of Paragraph 4

This year, as vice president of the leadership team, I led a discussion on

individual expectations, dedication and commitment. The dialogue has made

a world of difference. Although the occasional lack of passion or poor attitudes

of my peers frustrate me, their varying degrees of commitment cannot keep me

from the job that I love. ʌ*Being the first person on campus and the last to leave invigorates me. No matter how many hours I put in or how little acknowledgment I receive, the work is always worthwhile because I know that I am contributing something important—to myself more than anything.*

Your Turn _____

Add Reflection Re-read your draft to determine if there are **additional reflective comments** that you can make about any part of your experience. Ask yourself: *What does this experience mean to me? What does my reaction say about me?*

Proofreading and Publishing

Proofread

Now that you have evaluated and revised your reflective essay, it is time to polish and present it. Edit your essay to correct any misspellings, capitalization and punctuation errors, and problems in sentence structure.

Form proofreading teams of four, and swap papers with another team. Each person on the team can focus on a different type of error: spelling, capitalization, punctuation, and sentence structure.

Commas can be particularly challenging in your proofreading. Read carefully, applying comma rules in your writing.

> **Grammar Link** **Punctuating Words, Phrases, and Clauses in a Series**
>
> Writers often present examples or descriptions in series of three or more elements. In your own writing, be sure to use commas to separate the items in a series, including words, phrases, and clauses.
>
> Steffi often uses items in a series. As she proofread her final draft, she found places where she had omitted commas.
>
> We begin excited and optimistic, but slowly apathy invades, leaving behind shells of leaders∧
>
> tasks left undone∧and only a select few to pick up the slack.
>
> **Reference Note** For more on using commas with items in a series, see the Language Handbook.

Publishing

Your reflective essay tells a story only you can tell. Now it's time to share the story with others. Here are ways to get your essay to an audience.

- Give an oral presentation of your reflection to classmates or family members. Consider using audiovisual materials (such as presentation software) to enhance your presentation. For more on **presenting a reflection,** see page 892.
- Work with your classmates to arrange your essays by themes (for example, friendship, family, courage, sacrifice). Then, shelve this collection in your school library as a class archive for future graduating classes and for your own class to look back on at class reunions.

Reflect on the Process
Thinking about how you wrote your reflective essay will help you with other writing you will do in the future. In your **RWN,** write a short response to these questions:

1. What was the most challenging part of writing a reflective essay? Explain.
2. Would you use an action plan to help organize your ideas when writing other kinds of essays? Why or why no?

● Proofreading Tip
If you have time, set aside your paper for a day and return to it with a fresh perspective. You may catch errors that you would otherwise miss. If you are uncertain whether you've included sentence fragments, ask a classmate for help.

● Writing Tip
When the last two items in a series are joined by *and, or,* or *nor,* your teacher may prefer that you omit the comma before the conjunction, as long as the comma is not needed to make the meaning of the sentence clear.

Submission Ideas
- school newspaper
- community newspaper
- online magazine
- your personal Web page
- class or school Web page

Your Turn _____
Proofread and Publish As you are proofreading, read carefully to identify where your essay needs commas to separate items in a series. Proofread your entire paper for accuracy in spelling, punctuation, and usage. Then, print out a final copy, and publish it.

Scoring Rubric

Use one of the rubrics below to evaluate your reflective essay from the Writing Workshop or your response to the on-demand prompt on the next page. Your teacher will tell you to use either the six- or the four-point rubric.

6-Point Scale

Score 6 *Demonstrates advanced success*
- focuses consistently on narrating a single experience or a unified sequence of experiences
- shows effective narrative sequence throughout, with smooth transitions
- offers a thoughtful, creative approach to the reflection
- develops the reflection thoroughly, using vivid descriptive and narrative details
- exhibits mature control of written language

Score 5 *Demonstrates proficient success*
- focuses on narrating a single experience or a unified sequence of experiences
- shows effective narrative sequence, with transitions
- offers a thoughtful approach to the reflection
- develops the reflection competently, using descriptive and narrative details
- exhibits sufficient control of written language

Score 4 *Demonstrates competent success*
- focuses on narrating a single experience or a unified sequence of experiences, with minor distractions
- shows effective narrative sequence, with minor lapses
- offers a mostly thoughtful approach to the reflection
- develops the reflection adequately, with some descriptive and narrative details
- exhibits general control of written language

Score 3 *Demonstrates limited success*
- includes some loosely related material that distracts from the writer's narrative focus
- shows some organization, with noticeable flaws in the narrative flow
- offers a routine, predictable approach to the reflection
- develops the reflection with uneven use of descriptive and narrative detail
- exhibits limited control of written language

Score 2 *Demonstrates basic success*
- includes loosely related material that seriously distracts from the writer's narrative focus
- shows minimal organization, with major gaps in the narrative flow
- offers a reflection that merely skims the surface
- develops the reflection with inadequate descriptive and narrative detail
- exhibits significant problems with control of written language

Score 1 *Demonstrates emerging effort*
- shows little awareness of the topic and the narrative purpose
- lacks organization
- offers an unclear and confusing narrative
- develops the reflection with little or no detail
- exhibits major problems with control of written language

4-Point Scale

Score 4 *Demonstrates advanced success*
- focuses consistently on narrating a single experience or a unified sequence of experiences
- shows effective narrative sequence throughout, with smooth transitions
- offers a thoughtful, creative approach to the reflection
- develops the reflection thoroughly, using vivid descriptive and narrative details
- exhibits mature control of written language

Score 3 *Demonstrates competent success*
- focuses on narrating a single experience or a unified sequence of experiences, with minor distractions
- shows effective narrative sequence, with minor lapses
- offers a mostly thoughtful approach to the reflection
- develops the reflection adequately, with some descriptive and narrative details
- exhibits general control of written language

Score 2 *Demonstrates limited success*
- includes some loosely related material that distracts from the writer's narrative focus
- shows some organization, with noticeable flaws in the narrative flow
- offers a routine, predictable approach to the reflection
- develops the reflection with uneven use of descriptive and narrative detail
- exhibits limited control of written language

Score 1 *Demonstrates emerging effort*
- shows little awareness of the topic and the narrative purpose
- lacks organization
- offers an unclear and confusing narrative
- develops the reflection with little or no detail
- exhibits major problems with control of written language

Preparing for Timed Writing

Reflective Essay

When responding to a prompt asking you to reflect on your experiences, use what you have learned from reading, writing your reflective essay, and studying the rubric on page 890. Use the steps below to develop a response to the following prompt.

Writing Prompt
Often an unexpected experience not only surprises us but teaches us a valuable lesson. Write a reflective essay about an unexpected experience that taught you something important.

Study the Prompt
Begin by reading the prompt carefully. Circle or underline key words: *unexpected experience, surprises, teaches, valuable lesson, important*. Think carefully about what makes something valuable or important. **Tip:** Spend about three minutes studying the prompt.

Plan Your Response
Make a list of unexpected experiences from your life that you remember well. Think about what happened. Why was the experience unexpected? Why was it valuable? Once you have selected an experience, follow these steps to plan your response:

1. Write down what the experience was.
2. Describe the setting of the experience.
3. List at least two things that happened leading up to the experience.
3. List the other people who were involved.
4. Next to each event and person, note important narrative and descriptive details.
5. Beneath the details, describe your reactions to each event and person.
6. Summarize your feelings about the experience and tell what lesson you learned.

Once you have written down these essential elements, plan your essay in an outline like the one at the top of the next column.

Introduction:
- Background information
- Hint at experience's meaning

Body:
- First event of experience
- Second event of experience, and so on

Conclusion:
- Reflection on experience
- Statement of what you learned.

Tip: Spend about ten minutes planning your response.

Respond to the Prompt
Use your notes and your plan to begin writing your essay. One way to begin a reflective essay is to create a scene that leads to the important experience. You can use description or dialogue to provide readers the background information that they may need to understand the narrative of your experience. **Tip:** Spend about twenty minutes writing your reflective essay.

Improve Your Response
Revising Return to the key aspects of the prompt. Does your essay detail an important experience? Have you told what you learned and explained how the experience affected you? If not, add these elements.

Proofreading Take a few minutes to edit your response to correct errors in grammar, spelling, punctuation, and capitalization. Make sure that your edits are neat and the paper is legible.

Checking Your Final Copy Before you turn in your response, read it one more time to catch any errors you may have missed. Readers will have an easier time sharing in your experience if they don't have to plow through errors to read it. **Tip:** Save five or ten minutes to improve your response.

Presenting a Reflective Essay

Speak with a Purpose

Adapt your reflective essay for an oral presentation, and then share it with your class.

Think as a Reader/Writer When you wrote your reflective essay, you shared a significant experience in your life and told your readers how the experience affected you and what insight into life you gained from it. In this workshop, you will adapt your reflective essay for an oral presentation, which will allow you to use your voice and body language to bring the totality of the experience to life for your listeners.

Adapt Your Reflective Essay

Keep It Moving

While the techniques used in delivering an oral presentation are different to some extent from those used in writing an essay, both activities share the same purpose: to narrate an experience and to connect your insight from that experience to life in general. Here are some suggestions for adapting your essay for an oral presentation.

- **Stage your presentation.** An important part of any presentation is **dialogue** that involves narration and characters. In your oral presentation, imitate the voices of the people involved in your experience. You can also act out your **movements, facial expressions,** and **gestures** and those of other people involved in your experience. Avoid overacting and exaggerated imitations, both of which can have a negative effect on your listeners. Also, consider using **visuals** and **sound effects** to heighten the effect of your presentation, but don't overdo it. Be sure that your experience remains the center of attention.

- **Explain yourself.** You can be subtle in writing, but in your oral presentation you must provide your audience with broad hints about the significance or effect of your experience. Plan to balance those hints with the narrative and details that describe each event. At the conclusion of your presentation, make sure your explicit statements about the significance or effect of the experience and the more general insight into life that you gained are clear enough for a listening audience.

- **Use effective language.** Effective language in a reflective presentation is clear, forceful, and **aesthetic,** that is to say, artistic and tasteful. Choose **concrete images** to narrate events and to describe places. Use rhetorical questions, parallelism, figurative language, and other **rhetorical devices** to enhance the effectiveness of your language. When used appropriately, **irony** is especially effective in oral presentations because it can be communicated through your tone of voice as well as through your words.

Reader/Writer Notebook

Use your **RWN** to complete the activities for this workshop.

SKILLS FOCUS Listening and Speaking

Skills Deliver reflective presentations; rehearse oral messages; use effective verbal and nonverbal delivery techniques.

Deliver Your Reflective Essay

Speak Extemporaneously

Reading a speech word for word usually sounds stiff and unnatural. Plan to present your reflection **extemporaneously** by following these steps:

1. Outline the main points that you want to cover in your presentation.

2. Highlight any quotations or passages in your essay that you want to deliver word for word.

3. Prepare notecards with key words and phrases for your outline, as well as the text of passages you want to deliver word for word.

4. Check the order of your cards to avoid surprises.

Use Verbal and Nonverbal Techniques

Sometimes the way you say something means as much as what you say. An oral presentation gives you the opportunity to use both verbal and nonverbal techniques to engage your audience. Here are some techniques to consider.

Delivery Techniques	
Verbal Techniques	**Nonverbal Techniques**
Language: Use **standard American English** so everyone will understand your presentation, but with dialogue use **informal expressions** to capture the uniqueness of the people involved.	**Eye Contact:** Give individuals in your listening audience the impression that you are speaking directly to them by making eye contact with as many of them as you can.
Tone: Change the tone of your voice to reflect the nature of the events you are narrating. Humorous events require a light tone. Somber events require a serious tone.	**Gestures:** Use natural and unforced gestures. Be aware that overly dramatic gestures can detract from your presentation.
Volume: Vary the volume of your voice to fit the mood you want to create, but speak loudly enough to be heard.	**Facial Expressions:** Use facial expressions to convey your feelings and to characterize people involved in your experience.

Keep Practicing

Rehearsal will help you avoid nervousness and enable you to present your reflections effectively. These resources can be useful in practicing your presentation:

- Practice in front of a mirror.
- Enlist friends and family to see you rehearse and give feedback.
- Videotape yourself practicing and watch for trouble spots.

A Good Oral Presentation

- Shares the details and significance of a single experience
- Organizes ideas clearly for listeners
- Recreates the experience with dialogue, imagery, and rhetorical devices
- Uses effective verbal and nonverbal speaking techniques

Speaking Tip

Take notes after each practice session to guide your improvement.

Learn It Online

Add music and pictures to your reflective essay.

go.hrw.com | L12-893 | Go

Literary Skills Review

Comparing Literature   **Directions:** Read the poems that follow. Then, read each multiple-choice question and write the letter of the best response.

The following two poems describe cities that the poets perceive as on the verge of social ruin. William Blake's "London" depicts the poor living conditions of England in the early nineteenth century. Derek Walcott's "The Virgins" describes Frederiksted, one of the oldest port cities on the U.S. Virgin Island of St. Croix. Frederiksted is now a free port where tourists can purchase goods without paying customs duties. Its economy, once based on sugar cane, is now dependent on tourism.

London

by **William Blake**

I wander through each chartered° street,
Near where the chartered Thames does flow,
And mark° in every face I meet
Marks of weakness, marks of woe.

5   In every cry of every man,
In every infant's cry of fear,
In every voice, in every ban,°
The mind-forged manacles I hear.

How the chimney sweeper's cry
10 Every blackning church appalls,°
And the hapless soldier's sigh
Runs in blood down palace walls.

But most through midnight streets I hear
How the youthful harlot's curse°
15 Blasts the newborn infant's tear
And blights with plagues the marriage hearse.

---

1. **chartered:** controlled by law.
3. **mark:** notice.
7. **ban:** legal prohibition, public condemnation, or curse; also, a marriage announcement (spelled *bans*).
10. **appalls:** causes to lose color; also, dismays, terrifies.
14. **harlot's curse:** curse upon the harlot or prostitute by a hypocritical society that pushed women into prostitution and then condemned them for it; also the curse the harlot utters in return.

The Virgins

by **Derek Walcott**

Down the dead streets of sun-stoned
    Frederiksted,
the first free port to die for tourism,
strolling at funeral pace, I am reminded
of life not lost to the American dream;
5   but my small-islander's simplicities
can't better our new empire's civilized
exchange of cameras, watches, perfumes,
    brandies
for the good life, so cheaply underpriced
that only the crime rate is on the rise
10 in streets blighted with sun, stone arches
and plazas blown dry by the hysteria
of rumor. A condominium drowns
in vacancy; its bargains are dusted,
but only a jeweled housefly drones
15 over the bargains. The roulettes spin
rustily to the wind—the vigorous trade
that every morning would begin afresh
by revving up green water round the pierhead
heading for where the banks of silver thresh.

1. In the first stanza of "London," the speaker is —
   A describing how he loves London
   B greeting fellow citizens of London
   C noticing other people's unhappiness
   D looking at the Thames

2. Which of the following is an image of oppression and restriction used in "London"?
   A "the chartered Thames"
   B "the hapless soldier's sigh"
   C "the mind-forged manacles"
   D all of the above

3. In lines 11–12 of "London," the speaker suggests that —
   A the sighing soldier is haunted by memories of violence
   B all soldiers are poorly trained for battle
   C patriotism is worth the loss of lives
   D soldiers are rebelling

4. In lines 1–4 of "The Virgins," the speaker implies that —
   A he believes in the American dream
   B he is pleased by what tourism has done for his city
   C he doesn't remember what life was like before his city became a "new empire"
   D he thinks the American dream can be destructive

5. Which of the following literary devices does Walcott use in "The Virgins"?
   A Onomatopoeia
   B Allusion
   C Apostrophe
   D Alliteration

6. What do such images as "plazas blown dry" and "the roulettes spin rustily" suggest about the setting Walcott is describing?
   A The streets are not kept clean.
   B The tourists are not in the mood for gambling.
   C Ruin is overcoming the city.
   D The city is suffering from a drought.

7. Like the speaker in "London," the speaker in "The Virgins" sees the living conditions of his city as being —
   A recently improved
   B easily fixed
   C virtually beyond hope
   D a source of hope for everyone

8. Unlike Blake, Walcott focuses more on which aspect of his city's plight?
   A Commercial activities
   B People's hypocrisy
   C Unfair treatment of women
   D Disease and poverty

Constructed Response

9. Briefly contrast the imagery in the two poems. Support your response with specific evidence.

Vocabulary Skills Review

Context Clues

Directions: Use the clues in each sentence to help you select the definition of the italicized word.

1. The twisting of the River Wye cut a beautifully *sinuous* path through the valley. *Sinuous* means —
   A filthy
   B curving; winding
   C pure; untouched
   D dried up

2. The nightingale, hidden in the *foliage,* was just a beautiful voice among the greenery. *Foliage* means —
   A valley
   B brilliant light
   C highest point
   D leaves

3. With a cry, the toddler *wrenched* the toy from his playmate's firm grip. *Wrenched* means —
   A pulled or twisted violently
   B lessened
   C encircled; surrounded
   D commanded

4. When the Mariner's boat was stuck with no prospect of escape, the future looked *dismal*. *Dismal* means —
   A outrageous
   B hopeful
   C gloomy
   D heavenly

5. With the *tumult* of eight puppies in one room, I could not hear the radio. *Tumult* means —
   A scent
   B anxiety
   C distress
   D great noise

6. The *tyrannous* rule of the dictator struck fear in the hearts of those under his control. *Tyrannous* means —
   A oppressive
   B ghostly
   C foul
   D anxious

7. Looking at the vast desert ahead, he experienced a *forlorn* feeling as he realized he had no water. *Forlorn* means —
   A lonely; lost
   B wild; untamed
   C unkind; callous
   D hopeless; desperate

Academic Vocabulary

Directions: Use the clues in each passage to help you select the definition of the italicized word.

8. Good writers *differentiate* clearly between ideas so that readers do not confuse one concept with another. *Differentiate* means —
   A disagree; argue against
   B explain similarities
   C distinguish
   D alternate

9. The value of emotions is an *inherent* principle of Romantic poetry. It is not always stated directly, but if you read between the lines, you will find it. *Inherent* means —
   A present at birth
   B irrational
   C unexpected
   D built in; implicit

Writing Skills Review

Write a Reflective Essay **Directions:** Read the following paragraph from a draft of a student's reflective essay about the powerful natural force of fire. Then, answer the questions that follow.

(1) "There is something about fire that makes it beautiful and frightening at the same time," I thought to myself as I watched the flames engulf my home on that fateful August night. (2) Looking back, I ponder at what a peculiar thought that was to have at a time when all my worldly possessions were in the process of being destroyed. (3) I guess a person's mind does strange things when faced with traumatic events. (4) Even as I heard the sounds of firefighters shouting to each other, water spraying out of the large hose, and the gasps of curious neighbors as they arrived on the scene, my eyes were focused on the vibrant colors of red, yellow, and orange as I watched the flames dance in the night sky. (5) My trance was broken by my father, the strength of our family, as he walked up to me and put his large hand on my shoulder. (6) He squeezed firmly, wanting to say something, I imagine, but found no words to express his range of emotions. (7) I knew what he was trying to say but couldn't, and I replied, "It will be O.K., Dad. I love you, too." (8) "We're all here, we're all O.K.," I thought to myself, "and possessions can be replaced."

1. Reflective essays examine abstract ideas through the description of personal experiences. What abstract idea is explored by this author?

   A Patience

   B Gratitude

   C Hopelessness

   D Acceptance

2. What skill might the writer have used to help remember and gather the details before writing this reflective essay?

   A The writer might have visualized the events of the experience.

   B The writer might have asked a family member to help recall events from the experience.

   C The writer might have used photos or journal entries to help remember the events.

   D All of the above

3. Which sentence best helps the reader understand the writer's father's thoughts and feelings?

   A Sentence 6

   B Sentence 4

   C Sentence 1

   D Sentence 8

4. Which two sentences include the inner dialogue of the writer?

   A Sentence 2 and sentence 4

   B Sentence 7 and sentence 8

   C Sentence 1 and sentence 8

   D Sentence 1 and sentence 3

5. Which sentence best explains what the writer learned from this experience?

   A Sentence 3

   B Sentence 1

   C Sentence 2

   D Sentence 8

6. Which sentence contains an appositive?

   A Sentence 6

   B Sentence 4

   C Sentence 1

   D Sentence 5

Read On

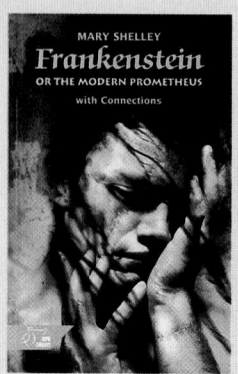

FICTION

Frankenstein

Mary Shelley said of her novel *Frankenstein* that she wanted to write a story that "would speak to the mysterious fears of our nature and awaken thrilling horror." She succeeded, writing an early science fiction novel as well as a vivid version of the Romantic mythology of the self. The wonder of Shelley's method of character development lies in the manner in which a monster, Frankenstein, simultaneously evokes our fear and our pity. As readers, we are called upon to question what we consider to be "human" and "natural."

FICTION

Pride and Prejudice

Originally published in 1813, Jane Austen's novel *Pride and Prejudice* is about five husband-hunting sisters in nineteenth-century England and the delicate tangles of love and courtship in which they ensnare themselves. What struck people then, and still strikes us now, is Austen's ability to make mundane people and events interesting and meaningful. The superficially trivial content is deceptive; it masks a deeper irony that exposes the manners and customs of the period.

FICTION

Hornblower and the *Hotspur*

Set during the Napoleonic Wars, C. S. Forester's exciting Hornblower novels are almost impossible to put down. Quick-thinking naval officer Horatio Hornblower and his crew sail from one battle to the next, each time facing a different enemy ship and adjusting to different weather conditions. Although one wrong choice can spell disaster, Hornblower must make life-or-death decisions with split-second timing. Despite his marvelous heroics, Hornblower is no superman. He often suffers from horrible seasickness and—even worse—self-doubt.

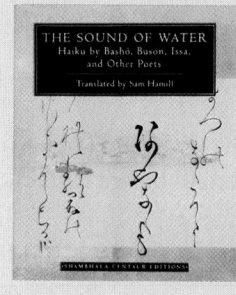

POETRY

The Sound of Water: Haiku by Bashō, Buson, Issa, and Other Poets

This pocket-sized, travel-friendly book reflects the magic of haiku: striking images, fervent emotion, and revelatory awareness in the tiniest of packages. In this masterful collection, renowned translator and poet Sam Hamill has gathered more than two hundred haiku spanning three hundred years. With their sparse yet powerful phrasing, the poems in this anthology are sure to delight and inspire new and old haiku aficionados.

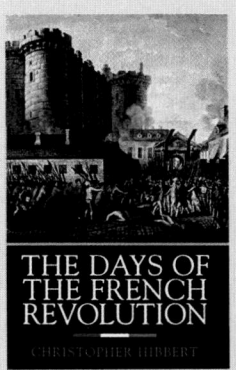

NONFICTION
The Days of the French Revolution

Christopher Hibbert's historical narrative brings all of the drama, turmoil, and bloodshed of the Reign of Terror to life. In this book, you will meet the principal players of the French Revolution—everyone from Robespierre to Marie Antoinette to Napoleon—and see their stories cast in new light, though not at the expense of truth. Swiftly plotted and gripping from start to finish, Hibbert's historical narrative reads like a good novel.

NONFICTION
The Grasmere and Alfoxden Journals

These journals reveal that Dorothy Wordsworth was as perceptive an observer of nature as was her famous brother, William. She records her responses to the natural beauty of the Lake District (the flowers, lakes, landscapes, and animals) that she sees on her daily walks as well as her reflections on the human misery (the beggars, ragged children, blind and infirm farmers, and poverty-stricken families) she encounters that stand in contrast to the region's beauty. She also informs readers of her brother's writing habits and of the visits from fellow poet Samuel Taylor Coleridge.

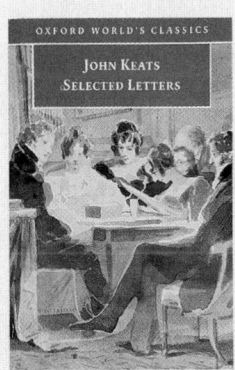

NONFICTION
The Letters of John Keats

Although John Keats died at the tragically young age of twenty-five, he left a wealth of correspondence that provides us with insight into his thoughts on a variety of topics, both spiritual and mundane. This particular collection of letters reflects the imagination and genius of the brilliant young poet. Keats candidly records many of the daily events of his life, along with, according to editor Robert Gittings, "some of the most profound comments on art, philosophy, and the human condition that any single person has produced."

NONFICTION
The Prince of Pleasure

Saul David's biography of Prince George, the future king of England and the son of George III, is a lively account of a man who was highly intelligent, articulate, literate, and a great patron of art and music. Nevertheless, George—accompanied by a menagerie of notorious members of Parliament, courtesans, fops, rakes, gamblers, and other hangers-on—led a life of unrestrained indulgence. Ever at the forefront of both fashion and scandal, this prince of pleasure is thoroughly fascinating.

Learn It Online
Go online to explore other novels, and find tips for choosing, reading, and studying books.

go.hrw.com   L12-899   **Go**

UNIT 5

The Victorian Period

1832–1901

COLLECTION 9
Love and Loss

COLLECTION 10
The Paradox of Progress

"For each age is a dream that is dying, / Or one that is coming to birth."

—**Arthur O'Shaughnessy**

What Do You Think? How can appearance be different from reality?

The Transept of The Great Exhibition of 1851 by Joseph Nash (1808-1878) Watercolor and bodycolor. Inv.:73-1898 Victoria and Albert Museum, London

Learn It Online
Find out more about this historical period online.

go.hrw.com   L12-901   Go

The Victorian Period 1832–1901

This time line represents a snapshot of British literary events, British historical events, and world events that took place primarily during the reign of Queen Victoria from 1837 to 1901. During this period, Great Britain expanded as an industrial nation and as an empire, but beneath the successes were many social and moral problems.

Alice with the Duchess, from Lewis Carroll's *Alice in Wonderland* by John Tenniel. Color lithograph.

BRITISH LITERARY EVENTS

1832

1837–1838 Charles Dickens publishes installments of *Oliver Twist,* a novel revealing the exploitation of poor children in Victorian England

1847 Emily Brontë publishes *Wuthering Heights*; her sister Charlotte Brontë publishes *Jane Eyre,* a novel about a young woman coming of age

1848 Poet Dante Gabriel Rossetti and others form the Pre-Raphaelite Brotherhood, a group of artists who reject the ugliness of modern life

1850

1857 Mary Ann Evans publishes stories, using her pen name George Eliot

1865 Charles Darwin publishes his controversial scientific study *On the Origin of Species by Means of Natural Selection*

1867 Lewis Carroll publishes *Alice in Wonderland* ⌃

1867 Matthew Arnold publishes "Dover Beach," a poem that mourns a world without faith

BRITISH HISTORICAL EVENTS

1832

1832 The First Reform Bill extends voting rights to men who own property worth ten pounds or more in annual rent

1842 Great Britain wins First Opium War, forcing China to open ports to trade in opium from British-controlled India; Hong Kong yielded to Britain

1845 Potato famine begins in Ireland; close to one million die of starvation and disease; massive emigration begins

1847 Ten Hours Act limits the number of hours women and children can work in factories

1850

1854 Florence Nightingale nurses soldiers in the Crimea

1858 Change in laws allow Lionel de Rothschild to become first Jewish member of Parliament

1867 Second Reform Bill gives the vote to most male industrial workers

1869 Suez Canal opens, allowing two-way navigation between Europe and Asia ⌄

Inaguration procession of the Suez Canal (1865) by Eduoard Riou. Bibliotheque des Arts Decoratifs, Paris.

WORLD EVENTS

1832

1836 Mexican army defeats Texans at the Alamo

1848 Women's rights convention held in Seneca Falls, New York ❯

Elizabeth Cady Stanton addressing the first Women's Rights Convention. The Granger Collection, NY.

1850

1861 U.S. Civil War begins

1867 Last Japanese shogun resigns; power returns to emperor; old feudal system abolished in 1871; severe social problems result

1869 Mohandas K. Gandhi is born in India; he later leads India to independence and inspires civil rights worldwide

1869 Leo Tolstoy completes his novel *War and Peace* in Russia

SKILLS FOCUS **Literary Skills** Evaluate and analyze the philosophical, political, religious, ethical, and social influences of a historical period. **Reading Skills** Identify and understand chronological order; identify and understand graphic elements; use text organizers such as overviews, headings, and graphic features to locate and categorize information.

Your Turn

Which details in the time line suggest the major social and moral concerns that dominated Britain during this time?

1870   **1890**   **1901**

1878 Thomas Hardy publishes *The Return of the Native*, a pessimistic novel about thwarted desire

1887 Arthur Conan Doyle introduces Sherlock Holmes in *A Study in Scarlet* ❯

Sherlock Holmes (1901). The Stapleton Collection, London.

1895 Oscar Wilde's satiric comedy *The Importance of Being Earnest* is staged, mocking an idle social class that has outlived its time ❯

1901 Rudyard Kipling publishes *Kim,* a novel that presents a picture of English colonial life in the teeming world of India

Oscar Wilde.

1870   **1890**   **1901**

1879 Zulu War against British in South Africa begins; Zulu nation eventually defeated

1889 Emmeline Parkhurst forms women's suffrage organization ❯

Pankhurst is arrested outside Buckingham Palace. The Granger Collection, NY.

1899 Second Boer War begins, leading to absorption of two African republics into British Empire

1901 Queen Victoria dies ❯

Queen Victoria, c. 1890.

1870   **1890**   **1901**

1880 Dostoyevsky publishes novels *Crime and Punishment* and *The Brothers Karamazov* in Russia

1885 Mark Twain publishes novel *Adventures of Huckleberry Finn* in the U.S.

1885 Indian National Congress is formed; begins agitating for Indian self-rule

1893 Henry Ford builds his first car in Detroit, Michigan ❯

1898 After the sinking of the battleship *Maine,* the U.S. declares war on Spain

1901 The first Nobel Prize is awarded

Henry Ford (1853–1947) photographed with his first automobile in 1896. The Granger Collection, NY.

The Victorian Period
1832–1901

The Victorian period was a time of vast social, political, and economic progress; It was also a time of great suffering among the urban poor who lived in filthy tenements in the industrial cities. The self-confidence as well as the problems and anxieties of the age are revealed in the works of the great Victorian writers. Social commentary became a trend, and the novel rose in prominence.

KEY CONCEPTS

Riots and Reforms

History of the Times The Reform Bill of 1832 answered some of the demands of the rising middle classes. When widespread unemployment and soaring bread prices gave way to a severe depression, riots broke out. The repeal of the tax that had forced bread prices up helped save England from revolution.

Literature of the Times The enormously popular novels of Charles Dickens exposed the suffering of poor people and helped move the nation toward reform.

Progress Brings Prosperity

History of the Times A spirit of optimism lifted England in the middle of the century. Free trade with Europe brought prosperity to some, while a series of factory acts improved the lives of the working class. New legislation made education free and mandatory for every child.

Literature of the Times Thomas Babington Macaulay, a representative writer of this period, based his optimism on the belief that history, technology, free enterprise, and God were working toward the betterment of human beings.

Decorum and Doubt

History of the Times Middle-class society held to strict codes of decorum and morality. Many believed that life would be improved if it were more refined and better policed. Despite the optimism of the age, some people mocked the codes of decorum and questioned the view that material comforts satisfied human needs.

Literature of the Times Matthew Arnold's poem "Dover Beach" gave voice to the doubts and anxieties of the late Victorian period.

UNIT 5 INTRODUCTION

Riots and Reforms

History of the Times

The first decade of Victoria's reign was troubled. Although the Reform Bill of 1832 appeased the middle classes by giving the vote to more landowning men, the growth of industry led to serious social problems. In 1837, the year Victoria became queen, the country entered a severe depression that by 1842 had put 1.5 million unemployed workers on some form of poverty relief. This period became known as the Hungry Forties.

Government commissions learned of children mangled when they fell asleep at machines at the end of a twelve-hour working day. They discovered young girls and boys hauling sledges of coal through narrow mine tunnels and working shifts so long that in winter they saw the sun only on Sundays.

In Ireland a potato famine (1845–1849) killed perhaps a million and forced another two million to emigrate. Some went to England, where they lived in crowded slums that had two toilets for 250 people. The cities became filthy and disorderly as the population swelled.

Massive political rallies were held in the 1840s to protest policies that kept the price of bread high and deprived most working men (and all women) of the vote. Finally, Parliament repealed the tax that had forced bread prices up. In 1867, the Second Reform Act gave the right to vote to most working-class men. A series of factory acts limited child labor by reducing the workday to ten hours.

Literature of the Times

The novels of Charles Dickens, the most important figure in Victorian literature, attacked the excesses of Victorian affluence. They also attacked the neglect and exploitation of decent people. Children in his novels endure terrible suffering, including abuse from adults.

Other early Victorian writers who contributed to social reforms include John Ruskin and William Thackery. Ruskin, a leading art and social critic, wrote on the problems of smog. Thackery, who wrote *Vanity Fair*, commented on social pretense.

Comprehension Check

What social problems in the Victorian era resulted from material progress?

Fast Facts

Historical Highlights

- Industrialization leads to the growth of slums.
- Tax reform lowers bread prices and helps prevent revolution.
- A series of reform bills eventually gives greater power to the middle class by extending the vote to more men.

Literary Highlights

- Charles Dickens uses humor in his novels to attack moral and social injustices.
- Matthew Arnold's "Dover Beach" voices doubts in the age of progress.

The General Post Office at One Minute to Six by George Elgar Hicks (1824–1914). The Museum of London, U.K.

Learn It Online
Learn more about this historical period online.

go.hrw.com   L12-905   **Go**

Progress Brings Prosperity

History of the Times

Though the Industrial Revolution created problems, it also steadily created new roads, new towns, new goods, new wealth, and new jobs for tens of thousands of people climbing up the levels of the middle class.

A new spirit of optimism lifted the nation during the middle years of the century. Reason and courage, most Victorians believed, could overcome the problems that had festered in the 1840s. In no other period of English culture before (and maybe since) were new ideas discussed and debated so vigorously by such a large segment of society. The Victorians were also voracious readers: They read not only the massive novels of Charles Dickens, William Thackeray, George Eliot, and Charlotte Brontë but also lengthy essays and religious tracts.

On the domestic front, the nation was stable and peaceful. On the world stage, Great Britain was expanding its empire, moving beyond its control of India and Ireland to China and Africa. By the beginning of the twentieth century, Great Britain's power extended to 200 million people beyond its borders.

During this era, England made great strides in improving social and political conditions. Reformers made their mark. Florence Nightingale's work in improving sanitation and nursing in hospitals during the Crimean War resulted in better medical care throughout the world. Social worker Octavia Hill worked on housing reform and conservation, and Josephine Butler campaigned for better treatment of women and girls.

In addition, education improved dramatically. With new legislation, education became free and required for every child. In 1870, Great Britain passed a law establishing state-supported schools. Schooling became mandatory in 1880, and in 1891 it was guaranteed to be free. As a result of better schooling, literacy increased, and the reading public expanded.

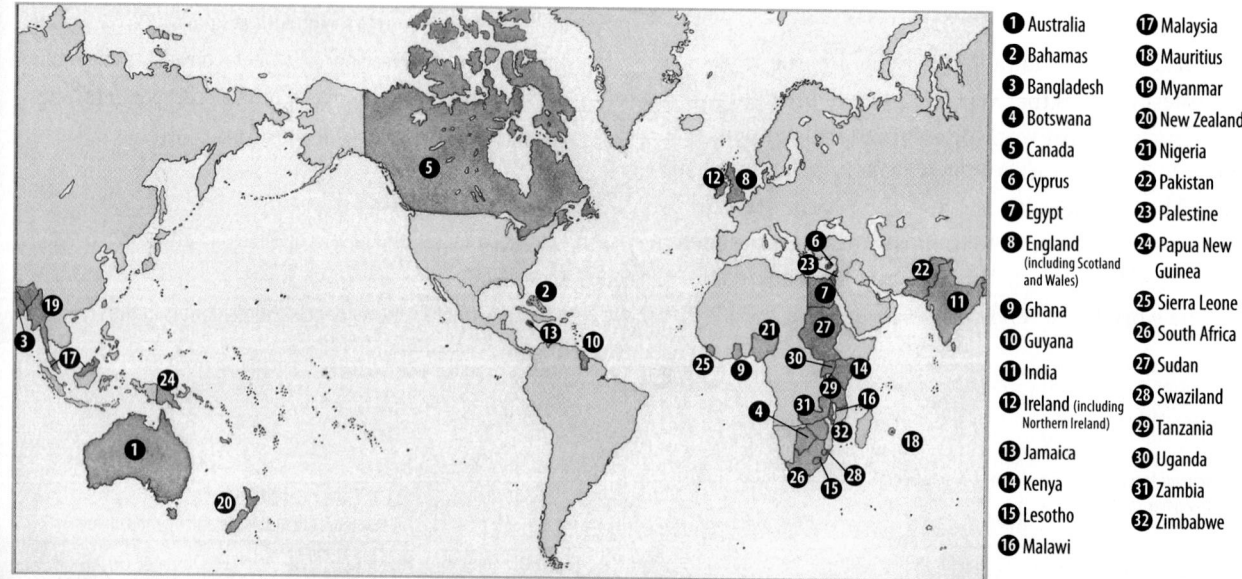

The BRITISH EMPIRE
circa 1901

1. Australia
2. Bahamas
3. Bangladesh
4. Botswana
5. Canada
6. Cyprus
7. Egypt
8. England (including Scotland and Wales)
9. Ghana
10. Guyana
11. India
12. Ireland (including Northern Ireland)
13. Jamaica
14. Kenya
15. Lesotho
16. Malawi
17. Malaysia
18. Mauritius
19. Myanmar
20. New Zealand
21. Nigeria
22. Pakistan
23. Palestine
24. Papua New Guinea
25. Sierra Leone
26. South Africa
27. Sudan
28. Swaziland
29. Tanzania
30. Uganda
31. Zambia
32. Zimbabwe

Progress was robust in science as well. Scientists came to understand the earth, its creatures, and its natural laws. Geologists worked out the history written in rocks and fossils. Darwin used his observations in the Galápagos Islands to explain the origin of species. Major advances were made in chemistry, physics, and medicine.

The showcase of the age was an enormous structure of glass and steel known as the Crystal Palace. The "palace" was designed to show, through the wonders of modern science and industry, England's confidence in its present and future accomplishments. (The Crystal Palace was destroyed by fire in 1936.)

Literature of the Times

The most eloquent spokesman for Victorian progress and optimism was Thomas Babington Macaulay. Macaulay believed that history, technology, free enterprise, and God were all working in harmony toward the betterment of human beings. Macaulay admired cleanliness and order. He wanted London streets free of garbage, drained, paved, lighted at night, and patrolled by a sober police force. He described the progress Victorian London had made in cleaning up its streets:

> We should greatly err if we were to suppose that any of the streets and squares then bore the same aspect as at present. . . . If the most fashionable parts of the capital could be placed before us, such as they then were, we should be disgusted by their squalid appearance, and poisoned by their noisome atmosphere. In Covent Garden a filthy and noisy market was held close to the dwellings of the great. Fruit women screamed, carters fought, cabbage stalks and rotten apples accumulated in heaps at the thresholds of the Countess of Berkshire and of the Bishop of Durham.

—from *A History of England* by Thomas Babington Macaulay

Comprehension Check

What specific advances in social welfare, political rights, education, and science were made in the Victorian age?

Link to Today

Victorian Inventions

The Victorian period was a time of innovation in science and technology. In fact, Victorians believed in the power of invention—that humans could solve problems in their environment by using their intellects. Many staples of life today were Victorian inventions.

antiseptic—In 1867, Joseph Lister developed antiseptic techniques for treating wounds.

bicycle—Kirkpatrick Macmillan invented the bicycle in 1869.

chloroform—James Simpson in 1848 discovered chloroform, an effective anesthetic.

fingerprinting—Sir Francis Galton in 1872 established the method of fingerprinting for identification in forensics.

Kelvin temperature scale—William Thomson (Lord Kelvin) developed this scale in 1848.

modern photography—In 1835, William Henry Fox Talbot developed modern photography by using light-sensitive paper and short exposure times.

postage stamp—Roland Hill developed the idea of a uniform postal charge, and in 1840 the first stamp was produced.

subway—In 1863, London opened the world's first subway system, the Metropolitan.

The Cyclist by Giuseppe Wulz. Museo de Storia della Fotografia Fratelli Alinari, Florence/Alinari.

Ask Yourself

What inventions have been made in the past fifty years? Do those inventions help solve problems in our environments?

Decorum and Doubt

History of the Times

Many Victorians thought of themselves as progressing morally and intellectually, as well as materially. In fact, the powerful, mainly middle-class obsession with gentility or decorum has made prudery almost a synonym for Victorianism. Book publishers and magazine editors deleted or altered words and episodes that might, in the phrase of the day, bring "a blush to the cheek" of a young person.

Sex, birth, and death were softened in art and popular fiction by sentimental conventions, made into tender courtships, joyous motherhoods, and deathbed scenes in which old people were saints and babies were angels. In the real world, people were arrested for distributing information about sexually transmitted diseases. Victorian society regarded seduced or adulterous women (but not their male partners) as "fallen" and pushed them to the margins of society.

Victorian decorum also supported powerful ideas about authority. Many Victorians were uneasy about giving strong authority to a central government. In Victorian private lives, however, the autocratic father of middle-class households is a vivid figure in both fact (Elizabeth Barrett Browning's father, for example, forbade all of his children to marry) and fiction.

Women were subject to male authority. Middle-class women especially were expected to marry and make their homes a comfortable refuge for their husbands from the male domains of business, politics, and the professions. Women who did not marry had few occupations open to them. Working-class women could find jobs as servants in prosperous households, while unmarried middle-class women could be governesses or teachers.

The Apple of their Eye by James Waite (1832–1920).

The excesses, cruelties, and hypocrisies of all these repressions were obvious to many Victorians. However, the codes and barriers of decorum changed slowly because they were part of the ideology of progress. Prudery and social order were intended to control the immorality and sexual excesses that the Victorians associated with the violent political revolutions of the eighteenth century.

Despite the confidence of the age, there were voices asking questions and raising doubts. Speaking for many of their contemporaries, and speaking to others whom they thought shallow and complacent, Victorian writers asked whether material comfort fully satisfied human needs and wishes. They questioned the cost of exploiting the earth and human beings. They protested or mocked Victorian codes of decorum and authority.

Literature of the Times

The dominant note of much mid-Victorian writing is struck by Matthew Arnold in his poem "Dover Beach." "The Sea of Faith," Arnold writes, has ebbed. There is no certainty in the world, and the dwindling of religious faith has brought about a crisis of consciousness. By the end of the century, this skepticism had become pervasive in the works of Thomas Hardy, A. E. Housman, and others. The heroes and heroines of earlier writers, such as Dickens and Eliot, find happiness in nurturing marriages and in small communities of family and friends. But there are few such marriages and communities in the fiction and poetry of Hardy and Housman. These late-Victorian writers tell of lovers and friends betrayed by unfaithfulness, war, and other troubles that we humans add to the natural trials of mortal life. Matthew Arnold responds with sadness characteristic of the century's end. His famous poem "Dover Beach" mourns the world's retreat from faith.

Comprehension Check

According to some later writers, what realities lay beneath the surface optimism and proprieties of Victorian life?

Love, Innocence.
Valentine Card, c.1870.
Color lithograph on paper.

Wrap Up

Talk About . . .

The Victorians admired material progress, but some thought progress was made at the expense of human values. With a partner, discuss how such questions are relevant today. Try to use each Academic Vocabulary word **listed below** at least once in your discussion.

Write About . . .

The Victorians disagreed on the amount of authority that should be given to the government. What responsibility should government have for social welfare; for care of the environment; and for censorship of books and television?

Academic Vocabulary for Unit 5

Talking and Writing About Literature
Academic Vocabulary is the language you use to write and talk about literature. Use these words to discuss the literature you read in this unit. These words are underlined throughout the unit.

benefit (BEHN uh fiht) *n.*: anything that is for the good of a person or thing. *How did progress in science benefit the Victorians?*

respond (rih SPAHND) *v.*: react. *Some Victorians responded critically to industrial progress.*

statistics (stuh TIHS tihks) *n. pl.*: numerical facts. *Statistics show that Victorians had a much shorter life expectancy than we do.*

publish (PUHB lihsh) *v.*: print and issue for the public. *Most of Gerard Manley Hopkins's poems were published after his death.*

complex (kuhm PLEHKS) *adj.*: hard to understand; complicated. *The factors causing the famine are complex.*

Your Turn

Copy the words into your *Reader/Writer Notebook*. Try to use these words as you answer questions about the literature in the unit that follows.

Link to Today

This Link to Today provides a look at how the people of Victorian London dealt with waste.

Read with a Purpose
Read to see how the dirty jobs of London were essential to its operation.

Build Background
In 1854, London was struck with a cholera epidemic. Dr. John Snow argued that cholera was spread via contaminated food or water. Snow plotted the locations of cholera deaths on a map and was able to isolate a water pump on Broad Street as the source of the contamination. He convinced authorities to remove the handle of the pump, effectively containing the epidemic and demonstrating that cholera was a waterborne disease. This excerpt provides a snapshot of life in London during the cholera epidemic—before the invention of safe water sewers or a public health system.

Author Note
Steven B. Johnson (1968–   ) is the author of *Everything Bad Is Good for You, Mind Wide Open,* and *Emergence.* Johnson's writing has appeared in *The New Yorker, Harper's, The Guardian, The New York Times,* and *The Wall Street Journal.*

HISTORY

The Night-Soil Men

from The Ghost Map

by **Steven B. Johnson**

It is August 1854, and London is a city of scavengers. Just the names alone read like some kind of exotic zoological catalogue: bone-pickers, rag-gatherers, pure-finders, dredg-ermen, mud-larks, sewer-hunters, dustmen, night-soil men, bunters, toshers, shoremen. These were the London underclasses, at least a hundred thousand strong. So immense were their numbers that had the scavengers broken off and formed their own city, it would have been the fifth-largest in all of England. But the diversity and precision of their routines were more remarkable than their sheer number. Early risers strolling along the Thames would see the toshers wading through the muck of low tide, dressed almost comically in flowing velveteen coats, their oversized pockets filled with stray bits of copper recovered from the water's edge. The toshers walked with a lantern strapped to their chest to help them see in the predawn gloom, and carried an eight-foot-long pole that they used to test the ground in front of them, and to pull themselves out when they stumbled into a quagmire. The pole and the eerie glow of the lantern through the robes gave them the look of ragged wizards, scouring the foul river's edge for magic coins. Beside them fluttered the mud-larks, often children, dressed in tatters and content to scavenge all the waste that the toshers rejected as below their standards: lumps of coal, old wood, scraps of rope.

Above the river, in the streets of the city, the pure-finders eked out a living by collecting dog crap (colloquially called "pure") while the bone-pickers foraged for carcasses of any stripe. Below ground, in the cramped but growing network of tunnels beneath London's streets, the sewer-hunters slogged through the flowing waste of the metropolis. Every few months, an unusually dense pocket of methane gas would be ignited by one of their kerosene lamps and the hapless soul would be incinerated twenty feet below ground, in a river of raw sewage.

The scavengers, in other words, lived in a world of excrement and death. Dickens began his last great novel, *Our Mutual Friend*, with a father-daughter team of toshers stumbling across a corpse floating in the Thames, whose coins they solemnly pocket. "What world does a dead man belong to?" the father asks rhetorically, when chided by a fellow tosher for stealing from a corpse. "Tother world. What world does money belong to? This world." Dickens' unspoken point is that the two worlds, the dead and the living, have begun to coexist in these marginal spaces. The bustling commerce of the great city has conjured up its opposite, a ghost class that somehow mimics the status markers and value calculations of the material world.

Consider the haunting precision of the bone-pickers' daily routine, as captured in Henry Mayhew's pioneering 1844 work, *London Labour and the London Poor*: "It usually takes the bone-picker from seven to nine hours to go over his rounds, during which time he travels from 20 to 30 miles with a quarter to

Bottom: An old man fashions a shovel from a scrap piece of metal in a delapidated yard (1900s).   Museum of London, U.K.
Below: A man crushes chalk into tires used to build a house made of recycled tires, cans, bottles, carpet, wood, glass, and other objects.

a half hundredweight[1] on his back. In the summer he usually reaches home about eleven of the day, and in the winter about one or two. On his return home he proceeds to sort the contents of his bag. He separates the rags from the bones, and these again from the old metal (if he be lucky enough to have found any). He divides the rags into various lots, according as they are white or colored; and if he have picked up any pieces of canvas or sacking, he makes these also into a separate parcel. When he has finished the sorting he takes his several lots to the ragshop or the marine-store dealer, and realizes upon them whatever they may be worth." …

The homeless continue to haunt today's postindustrial cities, but they rarely display the professional clarity of the bone-picker's impromptu trade, for two primary reasons. First, minimum wages and government assistance are now substantial enough that it no longer makes economic sense to eke out a living as a scavenger. (Where wages remain depressed, scavenging remains a vital occupation; witness the *pependadores* of Mexico City.) The bone collector's trade has also declined because most modern cities possess elaborate systems for managing the waste generated by their inhabitants. (In fact, the closest American equivalent to the Victorian scavengers—the aluminum-can collectors you sometimes see hovering outside supermarkets—rely on precisely those waste-management systems for their paycheck.) But

---

1. **hundredweight:** unit of measurement equal to 112 pounds; thus, a quarter to a half hundred weight is 28 to 56 pounds.

Below: Victorian rag pickers.
Right: Clothes being sorted and recycled at the Salvation Army Trading Company Wellingborough Northamptonshire, England, U.K.

London in 1854 was a Victorian metropolis trying to make do with an Elizabethan[2] public infrastructure. The city was vast even by today's standards, with two and a half million people crammed inside a thirty-mile circumference. But most of the techniques for managing that kind of population density that we now take for granted—recycling centers, public-health departments, safe sewage removal—hadn't been invented yet.

And so the city itself improvised a response—an unplanned, organic response, to be sure, but at the same time a response that was precisely contoured to the community's waste-removal needs. As the garbage and excrement grew, an underground market for refuse developed, with hooks into established trades. Specialists emerged, each dutifully carting goods to the appropriate site in the official market: the bone collectors selling their goods to the bone-boilers, the pure-finders selling their dog crap to tanners, who used the "pure" to rid their leather goods of the lime they had soaked in for weeks to remove animal hair. (A process widely considered to be, as one tanner put it, "the most disagreeable in the whole range of manufacture.")

We're naturally inclined to consider these scavengers tragic figures, and to fulminate against a system that allowed so many thousands to eke out a living by foraging through human waste. In many ways, this is the correct response. (It was, to be sure, the response of the great crusaders of the age, among them Dickens and Mayhew.) But such social outrage should be accompanied by a measure of wonder and respect: without any central planner coordinating their actions, without any education at all, this itinerant underclass managed to conjure up an entire system for processing and sorting the waste generated by two million people. The great contribution usually ascribed to Mayhew's *London Labour* is simply his willingness to see and record the details of these impoverished lives. But just as valuable was the insight that came out of that bookkeeping, once he had run the numbers: far from being unproductive vagabonds, Mayhew discovered, these people were actually performing an essential function for their community. "The removal of the refuse of a large town," he wrote, "is, perhaps, one of the most important of social operations." And the scavengers of Victorian London weren't just getting rid of that refuse—they were recycling it.

Ask Yourself

1. **Read with a Purpose** How does Johnson regard the dirty jobs of the scavengers and their role in Victorian London?

2. Why were there so many different types of scavengers in Victorian London? Why were such specific jobs necessary?

3. Why does the author state that the job of the bone-picker could not exist in today's cities?

4. Why do you suppose the bone-picker in the excerpt from Henry Mayhew's book gets home later in the day during winter?

5. What systems could a city put in place to prevent scavengers from interacting with harmful waste?

Love and Loss

LITERARY FOCUS
Figurative Language

CONTENTS

Alfred, Lord Tennyson

Robert Browning

Elizabeth Barrett Browning

Gerard Manley Hopkins

"To live is like to love—all reason is against it, and all healthy instinct for it."

—Samuel Butler

Literary Focus

Figurative Language by **Leila Christenbury**

Characteristics of Figurative Language

- Describes one thing in terms of another, dissimilar thing and is not meant to be understood literally
- Attempts to make abstract ideas concrete, such as love, life, death, and loss
- Unifies a poet's message
- Expresses universal ideas in fresh, new ways

The poets in this collection are masters of figurative language. Their writing transforms ordinary words and phrases into memorable impressions that capture an experience uniquely yet universally. It is no accident that poets use figurative language extensively in the highly compressed genre of poetry. Through metaphors, similes, personification and other images, poets can fully express ideas about death, loss, life, and love in language that is unique and memorable.

Alfred, Lord Tennyson uses figurative language to explore his complex feelings about death and loss in an elegy written to honor his friend Arthur Henry Hallam. In the poem *In Memoriam A.H.H.*, Tennyson personifies Nature as a feminine power who wields life and death without remorse. Nature says, "I bring to life, I bring to death" (Lyric 56, line 6). By **personifying** Nature, giving it human qualities and the ability to speak, Tennyson uses figurative language to depict the unexpected and seemingly capricious will that results in the death of a young man.

Tennyson uses personification throughout *In Memoriam*. The forest becomes comforting: "and the trees / Laid their dark arms about the field." Tennyson also uses a metaphor in Lyric 95, lines 21–24 to express regret that Hallam died so young:

> A hunger seized my heart; I read
>   Of that glad year which once had been,
>   In those fallen leaves which kept their green,
> The noble letters of the dead.

The Last Day in the Old Home (1862) by Robert Braithwaite Martineau 1826–1869. Tate Gallery, London.

In another memorable poem, "Crossing the Bar," Tennyson effectively uses an extended metaphor of death as one last voyage: "When I put out to sea" (line 4). The metaphor is developed with references to the sea journey that will occur "when I embark" (line 12). An **extended metaphor** uses multiple and consistent images to discuss a less familiar subject in terms of one that is more familiar to the reader. A nautical term even represents God: "I hope to see my Pilot face to face" (line 15). Tennyson's use of figurative language creates a coherent, concrete expression of the abstractions of death and heaven.

Paolo and Francesca (ca. 1887). by Charles Edward Halle.

Ask Yourself

1. How does figurative language help a reader more fully understand the complex questions and circumstances explored in poetry?
2. What is the relationship between the relatively brief length of many poems and the use of figurative language?

Learn It Online
Learn about figurative language with *PowerNotes*.
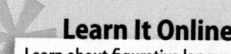 go.hrw.com L12-915 Go

The Lady of Shalott
Ulysses
from In Memoriam A.H.H.
Crossing the Bar

What Do You Think?

How can appearance be different from reality?

QuickTalk

Discuss why you think people remain enchanted with stories of castles, knights, quests, dragons, and ancient times.

Alfred, Lord Tennyson
(1809–1892)

Alfred, Lord Tennyson attained a celebrity status in England similar to what top athletes, actors, and musicians experience in our country today.

Following the Romantics

When Alfred Tennyson learned that Lord Byron had died, he went to the woods and carved on a piece of sandstone, "Byron is dead." Tennyson was fourteen years old. He felt sure that he would be a poet, and he was already practicing the dramatic gestures of the Romantic poets he admired.

Tennyson's father encouraged Alfred's interest in poetry. At Cambridge University, Tennyson's friends believed that he was destined to become the greatest poet of their generation. In 1831, lack of funds forced Tennyson to leave Cambridge. In 1832, he published his first significant book of poems, which some reviewers mocked for its melancholy themes. The next year Tennyson was devastated by the death of his closest friend, Arthur Henry Hallam. Tennyson became engaged in 1836, but the marriage was postponed because of his uncertain financial prospects.

The Melancholy Poet

During this difficult period, when both his physical and mental health suffered, Tennyson apparently never considered any career but poetry. Critics responded favorably to his two-volume *Poems* (1842), and in 1845 the government granted him an annual pension of two hundred pounds. In 1850, he published *In Memoriam,* an elegy to Hallam, was named poet laureate, and finally married.

Over the next forty years, Tennyson published nearly a dozen volumes of poetry. He became Alfred, Lord Tennyson in 1884. His poems spoke of the fragility and sadness of life, but he also believed eventually all losses would be made whole.

Think About the Writer

As poet laureate, Tennyson was extremely popular. What attracted Victorian readers so deeply to Tennyson's poetry?

Alfred Tennyson, 1st Baron Tennyson (c. 1840) by Samuel Laurence. Oil on canvas. National Portrait Gallery, London.

The Lady of Shalott

Reader/Writer Notebook

Use your **RWN** to complete the activities for this selection.

Literary Focus

Sound Devices in Poetry Poets use a range of **sound devices** to create musical effects in their poems. In "The Lady of Shalott," Tennyson uses **meter,** or rhythm, and sound repetitions such as **rhyme, alliteration,** and **assonance** to create a musical current that carries the reader through the landscape of the poem. The hypnotic force of these rhythms and repetitions also contributes to the poem's dreamy, otherworldly mood.

Reading Focus

Identifying Contrasting Images Poets sometimes use **contrasting images** to give their poems a subtle sense of tension. "The Lady of Shalott" is brimming with such images: the flat, flowing river and the upright, unchanging tower; the bustling lives of the villagers and the solitary life of the Lady; the weary whisper of the reaper and the robust song of Sir Lancelot. As you read the poem, note such oppositions in setting, actions, or imagery—and pay attention to how they affect the mood.

Into Action As you read, use a chart like the one below to record oppositions. Write down at least one opposition from each part of the poem. Then, label the opposition as setting, action, or imagery.

	Opposition	Setting, Action, or Imagery?
Part I	the barges sliding by; the Lady standing motionless in the tower window	action
Part II	the red cloaks of the passing villagers; the clear blue of the mirror	

Vocabulary

surly (SUR lee) *adj.*: rude or unfriendly. *The Lady of Shalott watches surly peasants traveling along the highway toward Camelot.*

brazen (BRAY zuhn) *adj.*: made of brass. *Sir Lancelot is clad in brazen armor.*

burnished (BUR nihsht) *v.* used as *adj.*: made bright and smooth. *The knights of Camelot wear burnished helmets.*

waning (WAYN ihng) *v.*: fading gradually. *The Lady weaves as the light is waning at nightfall.*

countenance (KOWN tuh nuhns) *n.*: facial appearance. *The Lady's blank countenance suggests that she is in a trance.*

Language Coach

Multiple-Meaning Words The word *brazen* can also mean "bold." How might this second meaning relate to a knight? Write two sentences about a medieval knight, using a different sense of the word *brazen* in each.

Writing Focus

Think as a Reader/Writer

Find It in Your Reading The musical **sounds** of "The Lady of Shalott" contrast with the poem's unsettling, haunting **images.** As you read, note in your *Reader/Writer Notebook* examples of such sounds and images.

TechFocus As you read, imagine "The Lady of Shalott" as a silent film. Keeping the poem's contrasting images in mind, think about kinds of music that might accompany each scene or the film as a whole.

 Learn It Online
Prepare to read this poem with the video introduction online.

go.hrw.com   L12-917   **Go**

The Lady of Shalott

by **Alfred, Lord Tennyson**

Read with a Purpose
Read the poem to discover how a curse affects the life of the Lady of Shalott.

Build Background
Tennyson wrote "The Lady of Shalott" in 1832 and then extensively revised it in 1842. He once commented: "I met the story first in some Italian novelle: but the web, mirror, island, etc., were my own." The symbol of Arthur's Camelot—an orderly, patriarchal kingdom in which beautiful, enchanted women languish—appealed to Tennyson and to the Victorian imagination in general. Tennyson would return to this setting in such works as "Lancelot and Elaine" and the *Idylls of the King*, a series of twelve connected poems telling the story of King Arthur and the Knights of the Round Table.

Part I

On either side the river lie
Long fields of barley and of rye,
That clothe the wold° and meet the sky;
And through the field the road runs by
5   To many-towered Camelot;°
And up and down the people go,
Gazing where the lilies blow°
Round an island there below,
        The island of Shalott.

10   Willows whiten,° aspens quiver,
Little breezes dusk and shiver
Through the wave that runs forever
By the island in the river
        Flowing down to Camelot.

15   Four gray walls, and four gray towers,
Overlook a space of flowers,
And the silent isle imbowers°
        The Lady of Shalott.

By the margin, willow-veiled,
20   Slide the heavy barges trailed
By slow horses; and unhailed
The shallop° flitteth silken-sailed
        Skimming down to Camelot:
But who hath seen her wave her hand?
25   Or at the casement seen her stand?
Or is she known in all the land,
        The Lady of Shalott?

Only reapers, reaping early
In among the bearded barley,

---

3. **wold:** rolling plain.
5. **Camelot:** legendary city, site of King Arthur's court and Round Table.
7. **blow:** blossom.
10. **whiten:** show the white undersides of their leaves when blown by the wind.

17. **imbowers:** shelters with trees, gardens, and flowers.
22. **shallop:** small, open boat.

A **Reading Focus** **Identifying Contrasting Images** What contrasting images do you find in the first stanza?

30   Hear a song that echoes cheerly°
From the river winding clearly,
    Down to towered Camelot;
And by the moon the reaper weary,
Piling sheaves in uplands airy,
35   Listening, whispers "'Tis the fairy
    Lady of Shalott." **B**

---

30. cheerly: archaic for "cheerily."

B Literary Focus **Sound Devices** What sound devices are used
to create a musical effect in this stanza?

Analyzing Visuals

Viewing and Interpreting As you read "The Lady of Shalott," look
for the scene that this painting illustrates. How do the painting's
details, including the expression on the Lady of Shalott's face, reflect
the **mood,** or atmosphere, of the poem?

The Lady of Shalott (1888) by John William Waterhouse (1849–1917).
Tate Gallery, London.

Part II

There she weaves by night and day
A magic web with colors gay.
She has heard a whisper say,
40 A curse is on her if she stay
    To look down to Camelot.
She knows not what the curse may be,
And so she weaveth steadily,
And little other care hath she,
45   The Lady of Shalott.

And moving through a mirror clear°
That hangs before her all the year,
Shadows of the world appear.
There she sees the highway near
50   Winding down to Camelot;
There the river eddy whirls,
And there the surly village churls,°
And the red cloaks of market girls,
    Pass onward from Shalott.

55 Sometimes a troop of damsels glad,
An abbot on an ambling pad,°
Sometimes a curly shepherd lad,
Or long-haired page in crimson clad,
    Goes by to towered Camelot;
60 And sometimes through the mirror blue
The knights come riding two and two:
She hath no loyal knight and true,
    The Lady of Shalott.

But in her web she still delights
65 To weave the mirror's magic sights,
For often through the silent nights
A funeral, with plumes and lights

And music, went to Camelot;
Or when the moon was overhead,
70 Came two young lovers lately wed:
"I am half sick of shadows," said
    The Lady of Shalott.

Part III

A bowshot from her bower eaves,
He rode between the barley sheaves,
75 The sun came dazzling through the leaves,
And flamed upon the brazen greaves°
    Of bold Sir Lancelot.
A red-cross knight° forever kneeled
To a lady in his shield,
80 That sparkled on the yellow field,
    Beside remote Shalott. **D**

The gemmy° bridle glittered free,
Like to some branch of stars we see
Hung in the golden Galaxy.°
85 The bridle bells rang merrily
    As he rode down to Camelot;
And from his blazoned baldric° slung
A mighty silver bugle hung,
And as he rode his armor rung,
90   Beside remote Shalott.

All in the blue unclouded weather
Thick-jeweled shone the saddle leather,
The helmet and the helmet feather
Burned like one burning flame together,

---

46. mirror clear: Weavers worked on the back of the tapestry so that they could easily knot their yarns. To see the front of their designs, weavers looked in a mirror that reflected the front of the tapestry.

52. churls: peasants; country folk.

56. pad: easy-gaited horse.

---

76. greaves: armor for the lower legs.

78. red-cross knight: The red cross is the emblem of Saint George, England's patron saint.

82. gemmy: set with jewels.

84. galaxy: Milky Way.

87. blazoned baldric: richly decorated sash worn across the chest diagonally.

C **Reading Focus** Identifying Contrasting Images What contrasting images appear in lines 55–70?

D **Literary Focus** Sound Devices Read this stanza aloud. What sound devices are used? What is the overall effect of this jumble of sounds?

Vocabulary **surly** (SUR lee) *adj.*: rude or unfriendly.
brazen (BRAY zuhn) *adj.*: made of brass.

Camelot

According to legend, Camelot was the capital city of King Arthur's realm. Arthur and his chivalrous knights would set off for their many heroic battles from Camelot, and to Camelot they would make their triumphant return. Within the castle at Camelot, the king and his knights—some versions of the legend give the number as sixteen hundred—would gather at the Round Table to make important decisions in a democratic fashion.

Though fictional, the idea of Camelot and the Round Table is so attractive and powerful that it has survived the centuries. The term *Camelot* is now used to refer to a time, a place, or a situation that seems in many ways perfect or ideal and that is governed by a strong leader and a fair, well-defined set of rules. In the 1960s, for example, the presidency of the young, charismatic John F. Kennedy was often referred to as Camelot. Both this well-loved president and the idealistic mood of that decade helped make smash hits out of the Broadway musical *Camelot* and the 1967 film of the same name.

Ask Yourself

Sir Lancelot, the most noble knight of the Round Table, ultimately contributes to the fall of Camelot. Think about the character of Lancelot in "The Lady of Shalott." What details make him seem ideal? What details make him seem less than ideal?

Top: *Camelot*, Richard Harris, 1967.
Bottom: President John F. Kennedy and the First Lady at his inaugural parade.

95   As he rode down to Camelot;
As often through the purple night,
Below the starry clusters bright,
Some bearded meteor, trailing light,
        Moves over still Shalott.

100   His broad clear brow in sunlight glowed;
On burnished hooves his war horse trode;
From underneath his helmet flowed
His coal-black curls as on he rode,
        As he rode down to Camelot.

105   From the bank and from the river
He flashed into the crystal mirror,
"Tirra lirra," by the river
        Sang Sir Lancelot.   **E**

She left the web, she left the loom,
110   She made three paces through the room,
She saw the waterlily bloom,
She saw the helmet and the plume,
        She looked down to Camelot.
Out flew the web and floated wide;

E **Reading Focus** **Identifying Contrasting Images** How do the appearance and actions of Sir Lancelot contrast with those of the Lady?

Vocabulary **burnished** (BUR nihsht) *v.* used as *adj.*: made bright and smooth.

115　The mirror cracked from side to side;
　　　"The curse is come upon me," cried
　　　　　The Lady of Shalott.

Part IV

　　In the stormy east wind straining,
　　The pale yellow woods were waning,
120　The broad stream in his banks complaining,
　　Heavily the low sky raining
　　　　　Over towered Camelot;
　　Down she came and found a boat
　　Beneath a willow left afloat,
125　And round about the prow° she wrote
　　　　　The Lady of Shalott.

　　And down the river's dim expanse
　　Like some bold seër° in a trance,
　　Seeing all his own mischance—
130　With a glassy countenance
　　　　　Did she look to Camelot.
　　And at the closing of the day
　　She loosed the chain, and down she lay;
　　The broad stream bore her far away,
135　　　　The Lady of Shalott.

　　Lying, robed in snowy white
　　That loosely flew to left and right—　**F**
　　The leaves upon her falling light—
　　Through the noises of the night
140　　　　She floated down to Camelot;
　　And as the boat head wound along
　　The willowy hills and fields among,

　　They heard her singing her last song,
　　　　　The Lady of Shalott.

145　　　　Heard a carol, mournful, holy,
　　Chanted loudly, chanted lowly,
　　Till her blood was frozen slowly,
　　And her eyes were darkened wholly,
　　　　　Turned to towered Camelot.　**G**
150　For ere she reached upon the tide
　　The first house by the waterside,
　　Singing in her song she died,
　　　　　The Lady of Shalott.

　　Under tower and balcony,
155　By garden wall and gallery,
　　A gleaming shape she floated by,
　　Dead-pale between the houses high,
　　　　　Silent into Camelot.
　　Out upon the wharfs they came,
160　Knight and burgher,° lord and dame,
　　And round the prow they read her name,
　　　　　The Lady of Shalott.

　　Who is this? and what is here?
　　And in the lighted palace near
165　Died the sound of royal cheer;
　　And they crossed themselves for fear,
　　　　　All the knights at Camelot:
　　But Lancelot mused a little space;
　　He said, "She has a lovely face;
170　God in his mercy lend her grace,
　　　　　The Lady of Shalott."　**H**

---

125. prow: front part of a boat.
128. seër: prophet.
160. burgher: townsperson.

F **Reading Focus** **Identifying Contrasting Images** How does the Lady's clothing differ from Sir Lancelot's? What might this contrast symbolize?

G **Literary Focus** **Sound Devices** How do the sounds in these lines reflect what is happening at this point in the poem?

H **Literary Focus** **Sound Devices** What musical sound effects are used in the last two stanzas?

Vocabulary **waning** (WAYN ihng) *v.:* fading gradually.
countenance (KOWN tuh nuhns) *n.:* facial appearance.

Applying Your Skills

The Lady of Shalott

Respond and Think Critically

Reading Focus

Quick Check

1. Describe where the Lady lives in relation to Camelot.

2. How can the Lady of Shalott avoid the curse?

3. After she hears Lancelot sing, what does the Lady do? What happens as a result?

Read with a Purpose

4. How does the Lady's life inside the tower differ from the life of others outside the tower?

Reading Skills: Identifying Contrasting Images

5. As you read, you recorded the poem's contrasts. Add a column to your chart, and tell what Tennyson achieves through each contrast. What central idea might the poet be trying to express?

	Opposition	Setting, Action, or Imagery?	Poet's Purpose?
Part I	the barges sliding by; the Lady standing motionless in the tower window	action	
Part II	red cloaks of the passing villagers; the clear blue of the mirror		

Literary Focus

Literary Analysis

6. Analyze Explain how lines 66–72 could **fore-shadow,** or hint at, Lancelot's arrival and the Lady's actions in the second half of the poem.

7. Summarize Summarize the plot of this poem. What moment marks the climax?

8. Interpret What role does the mirror play in the Lady's life? What might the mirror symbolize?

9. Hypothesize Why do you think Tennyson chose not to explain the curse in more detail?

Literary Skills: Sound Devices

10. Analyze Locate in the poem examples of rhyme, alliteration, and assonance. How do these sound devices help bring the poem's various contrasts to life?

Literary Skills Review: Meter and Rhyme Scheme

11. Analyze A pattern of stressed (´) and unstressed (˘) syllables in a poem is called **meter.** The pattern of rhymed lines in a poem (for example, *abab*) is called **rhyme scheme.** Scan the poem for its meter and rhyme scheme. How do these elements contribute to the poem's mood?

Writing Focus

Think as a Reader/Writer

Use It in Your Writing Review the examples of sounds and images you listed in your *Reader/Writer Notebook.* In a paragraph, rewrite the soothing sounds with more representative descriptions of their images. What words don't sound like their ideas?

 What Do You Think Now

How can a reflection in a mirror differ from reality?

Applying Your Skills

The Lady of Shalott

Vocabulary Development

✓ Vocabulary Check

Match the Vocabulary words with their definitions.

1. surly
2. brazen
3. burnished
4. waning
5. countenance

a. facial appearance
b. made bright and smooth
c. rude or unfriendly
d. fading gradually
e. made of brass

Vocabulary Skills: Connotations

Imagine the perfect pair of sunglasses. Are they a sub-dued color, such as black or brown, or are they a flashy gold or silver? Are the frames slim and streamlined, or big and round? Even though all sunglasses serve the same purpose, they express different aspects of the wearer's personality.

Words work the same way. Although two words might have the same meaning, they each carry their own connotations. **Connotations** are the feelings and associations attached to a word. For example, would you rather be described as *nerdy or bright*? If you answered *bright,* you probably are not alone. For most people, the word *bright* carries positive connotations, while the word *nerdy* carries negative ones.

The following chart contains some words from "The Lady of Shalott," the feelings and associations that go with each word, and a less powerful word the poet chose not to use.

Word	Feelings or Associations	Less Powerful Word
gazing (line 7)	dreamy, unhurried	looking
imbowers (line 17)	romantic; evokes images of the Garden of Eden	shelters
casement (line 25)	romantic, airy, antiquated	window

Your Turn

Using a table like the one below, write out the Vocabulary words from "The Lady of Shalott," the feelings or associations that go with each, and a less powerful synonym. Then, explain whether you think Tennyson made a good word choice and why.

Word	Feelings or Associations	Less Powerful Word	Good Choice? Why?

Language Coach

Multiple-Meaning Words Many words have more than one meaning, for example, the word *lie.* This word can mean "to recline or stretch out," but it can also mean "to say something that is not true."

Below are sentences from "The Lady of Shalott." Consider the meanings for the italicized word, and decide which meaning the poet intended.

1. "Little breezes *dusk* and shiver through the wave that runs forever."
   a. To make dark or shadowy
   b. The time of day right after the sun goes down
2. "By the *margin*, willow-veiled, slide the heavy barges."
   a. A blank space around the edge of a page
   b. The outer edge of something

Academic Vocabulary

Write About
Movies have been made, poems have been written, and books have been published about perfect, ideal places. In a short paragraph, describe a movie or piece of writing about an ideal place. Try to use the underlined vocabulary in your response.

Grammar Link

Adjective or Adverb?

Both adjectives and adverbs modify, or describe, other words. However, sometimes they can look suspiciously similar: *clear* and *clearly,* for example, or *merry* and *merrily.* How can you tell which is which?

An **adjective** modifies a noun or a pronoun. It tells *what kind, which one, how many,* or *how much.* An **adverb** modifies a verb, an adjective, or another adverb. It tells *where, when, how,* or *to what extent.* Often, but not always, an adverb ends in –ly. Study this sentence from "The Lady of Shallot."

> The *bridle* bells rang *merrily*
>   As he rode down to Camelot.

The first italicized word is an adjective. It modifies the noun *bells* by telling *what kind* of bells they are. The second italicized word is an adverb. It modifies the verb *rang* by telling how the bells rang.

Your Turn

For each italicized word, do the following:

• Tell whether it is an adjective or an adverb.

• Identify the word it modifies.

• Explain how it modifies that word.

1. *Long* fields of barley lie on either side of the river.
2. In a *gray* tower on an island lives a solitary Lady.
3. The lady weaves *steadily* both night and day.
4. Villagers pass *onward* toward Shalott.
5. The Lady sees in her mirror a *red-cross* knight.
6. The knight's armor glints *brightly* in the sun.

Writing Application Choose a paragraph you have already written and underline the adjectives, circle the adverbs, or put a question mark next to the word if you are not sure.

CHOICES

As you respond to the Choices, use these **Academic Vocabulary** words as appropriate: benefit, respond, publish, statistics, complex.

REVIEW

Talk About Opposites and Theme

In "The Lady of Shalott," Tennyson explores the tension between numerous opposites—for example, life and death, shadows and realities, solitude and society. Choose one of these pairs of opposites, and jot down details or images in the poem that seem related to the pair you chose. What central idea about the opposites do you think Tennyson is trying to communicate through these details? Present your evidence and your conclusion in the form of a short speech.

CONNECT

Investigate the Tragedy

Group Activity What was she thinking? Why did she do it? Do some investigative reporting to answer these questions. Have three classmates play the roles of a reaper, Sir Lancelot, and a townsperson. Before an audience, conduct "live" interviews with each character and obtain as much newsworthy information about the Lady as you can. Then, in a concluding report, speculate about why and how the Lady died. Offer observations, too, about crime statistics and how the Lady's death is affecting the community.

EXTEND

Make a Silent Movie

TechFocus Review your notes about the kinds of background music that would work well in a silent-movie version of "The Lady of Shalott." Next, work with three or four classmates to film a scene from the poem, silent-movie style. Experiment with different background music options, and analyze the effects of each. After finalizing your soundtrack, play the movie and its accompanying music for your class.

Preparing to Read

Ulysses

Reader/Writer Notebook

Use your **RWN** to complete the activities for this selection.

Literary Focus

Theme In works of literature, most writers attempt to convey a central idea or insight about a subject. This idea is called the **theme** of a work. A subject and a theme are not the same. A **subject** can be summed up in a word or two—*love* or *change,* for example. A theme, however, is a complete idea that can be stated as a sentence: *True love is an illusion,* or *Change is painful but leads to growth.* In "Ulysses," Tennyson's subject is old age. As you read, ask yourself what the theme might be.

Literary Perspectives Apply the literary perspective described on page 927 as you read this poem.

Reading Focus

Summarizing Teasing out a poem's theme is often easier if you summarize sections of the poem as you read. When you **summarize,** you use your own words to create a shortened version of a text. A summary usually includes the most important ideas in that text or section of text, along with one or two key details.

Into Action As you read, use a chart like this one to summarize each of the following sections of "Ulysses": lines 1–17, lines 18–32, lines 33–43, lines 44–56, and lines 57–70.

"Ulysses"	Summary
lines 1–17	Ulysses is tired of life at home. He fondly recalls the years of his youth, during which he sailed to distant lands and fought in wars.
lines 18–32	Ulysses' experiences have left him wanting more. He feels that . . . .

Vocabulary

hoard (hawrd) *v.:* save or store, often in secret. *Ulysses longs to spend rather than hoard his remaining years.*

vexed (vehkst) *v.:* troubled or disturbed. *Strong winds vexed the surface of the sea.*

discerning (dih SURN ihng) *v.* used as *adj.:* displaying good judgment; perceptive. *Ulysses knows his discerning son will not be blind to the people's needs.*

prudence (PROO duhns) *n.:* cautious management. *Ulysses hopes his son will use prudence rather than carelessness in his role as king.*

abides (uh BYDZ) *v.:* endures. *Ulysses has lost strength, but his adventurous spirit abides.*

Language Coach

Antonyms If you see an unfamiliar word, look at other words in the sentence. Do any of them seem to be **antonyms,** or opposites, of the unknown word? If so, they might provide a clue to the word's meaning. Examples of antonyms are *simple/difficult* and *begin/finish.* Find an antonym for one of the Vocabulary words in the sample sentences given above.

Writing Focus

Think as a Reader/Writer

Find It in Your Reading In your *Reader/Writer Notebook,* make note of lines that express the **theme** of the poem. Broad statements like "I will drink / Life to the lees" contain strong clues to the poem's theme.

Learn It Online
Listen to this poem online.

go.hrw.com   L12-926   **Go**

Ulysses

by Alfred, Lord Tennyson

Read with a Purpose
Read to discover what this "idle king" longs to do.

Build Background
Ulysses (Odysseus in Greek) is one of the Greek leaders who fought in the ten-year-long Trojan war. Homer's epic poem the *Odyssey* tells of Ulysses' equally long journey home from Troy to Ithaca. In Tennyson's poem, Ulysses, now an old king, is at home with his wife and son, Telemachus (tuh LEHM uh kuhs). After an exciting life of both marvels and horrors, the old king might finally rest, but a final journey tempts him.

It little profits that an idle king,
By this still hearth, among these barren crags,
Matched with an aged wife, I mete and dole°
Unequal laws unto a savage race,

5 That hoard, and sleep, and feed, and know not me. **A**
I cannot rest from travel; I will drink
Life to the lees.° All times I have enjoyed
Greatly, have suffered greatly, both with those
That loved me, and alone; on shore, and when

10 Through scudding drifts the rainy Hyades°
Vexed the dim sea. I am become a name;
For always roaming with a hungry heart
Much have I seen and known,—cities of men
And manners, climates, councils, governments,

15 Myself not least, but honored of them all,—
And drunk delight of battle with my peers,
Far on the ringing plains of windy Troy.
I am a part of all that I have met;
Yet all experience is an arch wherethrough

3. mete and dole: measure and give out.

7. lees: dregs or sediment.

10. Hyades (HY uh deez): stars that were thought to indicate rainy weather.

A **Reading Focus** Summarizing How would you summarize Ulysses' complaint in the first five lines?

Vocabulary **hoard** (hawrd) *v.*: save or store, often in secret.
vexed (vehkst) *v.*: troubled or disturbed.

Literary Perspectives

Analyzing Biographical Information Use biographical information to consider how events in Tennyson's own life may have helped shape "Ulysses." About the poem, Tennyson himself said: "'Ulysses' was written soon after Arthur Hallam's death, and gave my feeling about the need of going forward, and braving the struggle of life perhaps more simply than anything in *In Memoriam*." (*In Memoriam* is Tennyson's famous elegy to his beloved friend.) As you read the poem, watch for words spoken by Ulysses that echo those of Tennyson.

As you read, be sure to notice the questions in the text, which will guide you in using this perspective.

20   Gleams that untraveled world whose margin fades
       Forever and forever when I move.
       How dull it is to pause, to make an end,
       To rust unburnished, not to shine in use!   **B**
       As though to breathe were life! Life piled on life
25   Were all too little, and of one to me
       Little remains; but every hour is saved
       From that eternal silence, something more,
       A bringer of new things; and vile it were
       For some three suns to store and hoard myself,
30   And this gray spirit yearning in desire
       To follow knowledge like a sinking star,
       Beyond the utmost bound of human thought.
         This is my son, mine own Telemachus,
       To whom I leave the scepter and the isle,°—
35   Well-loved of me, discerning to fulfill
       This labor, by slow prudence to make mild
       A rugged people, and through soft degrees

Analyzing Visuals

Viewing and Interpreting In Greek mythology, Polyphemus was a famous Cyclops and the son of Poseidon, the god of the sea. Where is Polyphemus in this painting? What does this representation of Polyphemus tell you about Ulysses, who manages to defeat Polyphemus in Homer's epic poem the *Odyssey*?

34. isle: Ithaca, Ulysses' island kingdom off the west coast of Greece.

B **Literary Focus** **Theme** How does Ulysses think life should be lived?

Vocabulary **discerning** (dih SURN ihng) *v.* used as *adj.*: displaying good judgment; perceptive.
prudence (PROO duhns) *adj.*: cautious management.

Subdue them to the useful and the good.
Most blameless is he, centered in the sphere
40 Of common duties, decent not to fail
In offices of tenderness, and pay
Meet° adoration to my household gods,
When I am gone. He works his work, I mine. **C**
        There lies the port; the vessel puffs her sail;
45 There gloom the dark, broad seas. My mariners,
Souls that have toiled, and wrought, and thought with me,—
That ever with a frolic welcome took
The thunder and the sunshine, and opposed
Free hearts, free foreheads,—you and I are old;
50 Old age hath yet his honor and his toil.
Death closes all; but something ere the end,
Some work of noble note, may yet be done,
Not unbecoming men that strove with Gods. **D**
The lights begin to twinkle from the rocks;
55 The long day wanes; the slow moon climbs; the deep
Moans round with many voices. Come, my friends,
'Tis not too late to seek a newer world.
Push off, and sitting well in order smite
The sounding furrows;° for my purpose holds
60 To sail beyond the sunset, and the baths
Of all the western stars, until I die. **E**
It may be that the gulfs will wash us down;
It may be we shall touch the Happy Isles,°
And see the great Achilles,° whom we knew.
65 Though much is taken, much abides; and though
We are not now that strength which in old days
Moved earth and heaven, that which we are, we are,—
One equal temper of heroic hearts,
Made weak by time and fate, but strong in will
70 To strive, to seek, to find, and not to yield.

42. meet: proper.

Ulysses and his son Telemachus. Mosaic, 1st CE. Kunsthistorisches Museum, Vienna, Austria.

58–59. smite . . . furrows: row against the waves.

63. Happy Isles: in Greek **mythology, Elysium** (ih LIHZ ee uhm), where dead heroes lived for eternity.
64. Achilles (uh KIHL eez): Greek warrior and leader in the Trojan War.

C Reading Focus **Summarizing** What will Telemachus's job be when Ulysses is gone? Summarize this verse paragraph.

D Literary Focus **Theme** What does Ulysses believe about old age?

E Literary Perspectives **Analyzing Biographical Information** How do lines 58–61 echo Tennyson's own words about life and death?

Vocabulary abides (uh BYDZ) *v.*: endures.

SKILLS FOCUS **Literary Skills** Analyze theme; analyze imagery; analyze biographical information. **Reading Skills** Summarize as a strategy for comprehension. **Vocabulary Skills** Demonstrate knowledge of literal meanings of words and their usage. **Writing Skills** Write poems.

Respond and Think Critically

Reading Focus

Quick Check

1. Describe Ulysses' current situation as he portrays it in lines 1–11 of the poem.

2. Why is Ulysses comforted by his son's presence?

3. What other individuals does Ulysses address?

Read with a Purpose

4. What does Ulysses claim is his purpose?

Reading Skills: Summarizing

5. While reading, you summarized five different sections of the poem. Review these summaries. In a new column, choose a few words and phrases from your summaries that seem most strongly related to the poem's central meaning.

"Ulysses"	Summary	Key Words and Phrases
lines 1–17		

✓ Vocabulary Check

Match the Vocabulary words with their definitions.

6. hoard   a. endures
7. vexed   b. cautious management
8. discerning   c. disturbed
9. prudence   d. stockpile
10. abides   e. perceptive

Literary Focus

Literary Analysis

11. **Compare and Contrast** How does Ulysses contrast his past and present lives? What conclusions can you draw about his values?

12. **Interpret** What does Ulysses mean by his metaphor describing "all experience"?

13. **Infer** What do Ulysses' references to his wife and son reveal about his feelings toward them?

14. **Evaluate** What do you think of Ulysses' decision to "sail beyond the sunset"?

15. **Literary Perspectives** Tennyson's close friend Arthur Hallam died at the young age of twenty-two, and Tennyson wrote "Ulysses" shortly thereafter. How are Tennyson's feelings of loss represented in the poem?

Literary Skills: Theme

16. **Evaluate** In your view, what is the theme of "Ulysses"? Before stating the poem's theme, you may want to review the last column of your summary chart, as well the notes you made in your *Reader/Writer Notebook*.

Literary Skills Review: Imagery

17. **Analyze** Poets often use **imagery,** or language that appeals to the senses. Find three images in the last verse paragraph of "Ulysses" that describe elements of nature. What do these images tell you about the old king's attitude toward nature?

Writing Focus

Think as a Reader/Writer

Use It in Your Writing Review the grand statements made by Ulysses that you recorded in your *Reader/Writer Notebook*. Choose one with which you disagree, and write your own opposing declaration. Use this declaration in a short poem addressed to Ulysses.

What Do You Think Now

What does Ulysses say about the appearance and reality of old age?

Preparing to Read

from In Memoriam A.H.H.

Reader/Writer Notebook

Use your **RWN** to complete the activities for this selection.

Literary Focus

Tone The **tone** of a literary work is the author's attitude toward the subject. For example, the tone of a work might be reverent, sarcastic, exultant, or somber. *In Memoriam* (Latin for "in memory of") is an elegy, or a poem that mourns the death of someone important. As you might guess, the tone of such a poem is not light or playful. As you read, compare the tone at the beginning of the elegy with the tone of the later verses. As Tennyson processes his grief, his attitude toward death and loss shifts changes.

Reading Focus

Analyzing an Author's Style An **author's style** is the manner in which he or she expresses ideas. Style results from how a poet selects and uses certain tools, including words, images, sounds, rhythms, and **syntax,** or sentence structure. Look closely at what kinds of words Tennyson chooses and how he arranges them into phrases and sentences. Even as the tone of the poem shifts, what stylistic elements stay the same?

Into Action As you read, use a chart like this one to record words and phrases, images, and sound patterns that you find "uniquely Tennyson."

Words and Phrases	Images	Sounds
"dust and chaff" (l. 18)	"Nature, red in tooth and claw" (l. 15)	Alliteration: "falter where I firmly trod" (l. 13)

Vocabulary

derives (dih RYVZ) *v.*: comes from a certain source. *The poet's feeling of despair derives from his grief.*

discord (DIHS kawrd) *n.*: conflict. *There is often discord between our desires and reality.*

redress (rih DREHS) *n.*: compensation or payment for a loss. *Tennyson seeks redress for the loss of his close friend.*

diffusive (dih FYOO sihv) *adj.*: spread out; not concentrated in one place. *The poet senses the diffusive presence of his friend's spirit.*

Language Coach

Roots The Latin word *cor* means "heart." Words built on *cor* include *accord*, which means "agreement or harmony," and *cordial*, meaning "warm and friendly." Which Vocabulary word on the list above is related to these words?

Writing Focus

Think as a Reader/Writer

Find It in Your Reading If you have ever lost something or someone you loved, you know that mourning often begins with the question "Why?" As you read Lyrics 55 and 56 of *In Memoriam*, record in *your Reader/Writer Notebook* some of the **rhetorical questions** Tennyson poses.

TechFocus As you read this elegy, think about modern ways that people remember their loved ones.

Learn It Online
Learn more about the events that shaped Tennyson at the Writers' Lives site online.

go.hrw.com   L12-931   **Go**

POEM

from In Memoriam A.H.H.

by **Alfred, Lord Tennyson**

Read with a Purpose
Read to discover what Tennyson ultimately believes about life after death.

Build Background
In Memoriam is Tennyson's elegy for Arthur Henry Hallam, his closest friend at Cambridge and his sister's fiancé. In the 131 separate lyrics of this elegy, written over seventeen years, Tennyson asks and gradually answers profound questions about life and death, religion and science, and the immortality of the soul. Tennyson considered *In Memoriam* so intensely personal that he did not plan to publish it; however, in 1850 he did finally publish what is often considered his masterpiece.

55

The wish, that of the living whole
   No life may fail beyond the grave,
   Derives it not from what we have
The likest God within the soul?

5 Are God and Nature then at strife,
   That Nature lends such evil dreams?
   So careful of the type° she seems,
So careless of the single life,

  That I, considering everywhere
10   Her secret meaning in her deeds,
   And finding that of fifty seeds
She often brings but one to bear,

  I falter where I firmly trod,
   And falling with my weight of cares
15   Upon the great world's altar stairs
That slope through darkness up to God,

  I stretch lame hands of faith, and grope,
   And gather dust and chaff, and call
   To what I feel is Lord of all,
20 And faintly trust the larger hope.° **Ⓐ**

7. type: species.

20. larger hope: Tennyson explains this phrase in his Memoirs: "that the whole human race would through, perhaps, ages of suffering, be at length purified and saved."

Ⓐ Reading Focus Analyzing an Author's Style Paraphrase lines 17–20. How does the length and complexity of this single sentence reflect the idea it expresses?

Vocabulary **derives** (dih RYVZ) *v.:* comes from a certain source.

56

"So careful of the type?" but no.
 From scarpèd° cliff and quarried stone
 She° cries, "A thousand types are gone;
I care for nothing, all shall go.

5 "Thou makest thine appeal to me:
 I bring to life, I bring to death;
 The spirit does but mean the breath:
I know no more." And he, shall he, **B**

Man, her last work, who seemed so fair,
10 Such splendid purpose in his eyes,
 Who rolled the psalm to wintry skies,
Who built him fanes° of fruitless prayer,

Who trusted God was love indeed
 And love Creation's final law—
15 Though Nature, red in tooth and claw°
With ravine, shrieked against his creed—

Who loved, who suffered countless ills,
 Who battled for the True, the Just,
 Be blown about the desert dust,
20 Or sealed within the iron hills?°

2. scarpèd: eroded to a steep slope.
3. She: Nature.

12. fanes: temples.

15. red . . . claw: The phrase refers to the view of all life as a ruthless struggle for survival.

20. sealed . . . hills: preserved like fossils in rock.

B **Reading Focus** **Analyzing an Author's Style** What words, phrases, and sounds are echoed in this verse?

No more? A monster then, a dream,
   A discord. Dragons of the prime,
   That tare° each other in their slime,
Were mellow music matched with him.

25 O life as futile, then, as frail!
      O for thy° voice to soothe and bless!
      What hope of answer, or redress?   **C**
Behind the veil, behind the veil.°

95

By night we lingered on the lawn,
   For underfoot the herb was dry;
   And genial warmth; and o'er the sky
The silvery haze of summer drawn;   **D**

5   And calm that let the tapers° burn
      Unwavering: Not a cricket chirred;
      The brook alone far off was heard,
and on the board the fluttering urn.°

And bats went round in fragrant skies,
10   And wheeled or lit the filmy shapes°
      NThat haunt the dusk, with ermine capes
And woolly breasts and beaded eyes;   **E**

While now we sang old songs that pealed
      From knoll to knoll, where, couched at ease,
15   The white kine° glimmered, and the trees
Laid their dark arms about the field.

But when those others, one by one,
      Withdrew themselves from me and night,
      And in the house light after light
20 Went out, and I was all alone,

23. tare: archaic for "tore."

26. thy: Hallam's.

28. veil: veil of death.

5. tapers: candles.

8. fluttering urn: teapot or coffee urn heated by a candle.

10. filmy shapes: moths.

15. kine: archaic word meaning "cattle."

C Literary Focus **Tone** How do the exclamation points and question mark help convey a certain tone?

D Literary Focus **Tone** How do the images in this verse help signal a shift in tone?

E Reading Focus **Analyzing an Author's Style** Find seven repetitions of the word *and* in the first three stanzas of this lyric. How does this repetition help create a certain mood?

Vocabulary   **discord** (DIHS kawrd) *n.:* conflict.
redress (rih DREHS) *n.:* compensation or payment for a loss.

A hunger seized my heart; I read
    Of that glad year which once had been,
    In those fallen leaves which kept their green,
The noble letters of the dead.

25 And strangely on the silence broke
    The silent-speaking words, and strange
    Was love's dumb cry defying change
To test his worth; and strangely spoke

The faith, the vigor, bold to dwell
30   On doubts that drive the coward back,
    And keen through wordy snares to track
Suggestion to her inmost cell.

So word by word, and line by line,
    The dead man touched me from the past,
35   And all at once it seemed at last
The living soul° was flashed on mine,

And mine in this was wound, and whirled
    About empyreal° heights of thought,
    And came on that which is, and caught
40 The deep pulsations of the world,

Aeonian° music measuring out
    The steps of Time—the shocks of Chance—
    The blows of Death. At length my trance
Was canceled, stricken through with doubt.

45 Vague words! but ah, how hard to frame
    In matter-molded forms of speech,
    Or even for intellect to reach
Through memory that which I became; **F**

Till now the doubtful dusk revealed
50   The knolls once more where, couched at ease,
    The white kine glimmered, and the trees
Laid their dark arms about the field;

And sucked from out the distant gloom
    A breeze began to tremble o'er
55   The large leaves of the sycamore,
And fluctuate all the still perfume,

36. the living soul: Originally, the phrase read "his living soul." Tennyson said he changed it because he wanted the soul to be not Hallam's but the soul of "the Deity, maybe."
38. empyreal (ehm PIHR ee uhl): heavenly.
41. aeonian (ee OH nee uhn): eternal.

F Literary Focus **Tone** How does the poet express his attitude here?

And gathering freshlier overhead
    Rocked the full-foliaged elms, and swung
    The heavy-folded rose, and flung
60 The lilies to and fro, and said, **Ⓖ**

"The dawn, the dawn," and died away;
    And East and West, without a breath,
    Mixed their dim lights, like life and death,
To broaden into boundless day.

130

Thy° voice is on the rolling air;
    I hear thee where the waters run;
    Thou standest in the rising sun,
And in the setting thou art fair.

5 What art thou then? I cannot guess;
    But though I seem in star and flower
    To feel thee some diffusive power,
I do not therefore love thee less.

My love involves the love before;
10   My love is vaster passion now;
    Though mixed with God and Nature thou,
I seem to love thee more and more.

Far off thou art, but ever nigh;
    I have thee still, and I rejoice;
15   I prosper, circled with thy voice;
I shall not lose thee though I die. **Ⓗ**

1. thy: Hallam's.

Ⓖ **Reading Focus** **Analyzing an Author's Style** What poetic devices does Tennyson use in this stanza?

Ⓗ **Literary Focus** **Tone** How do words like *art, thee,* and *thy* help the poet establish a certain tone in this lyric?

Vocabulary **diffusive** (dih FYOO sihv) *adj.:* spread out; not concentrated in one place.

Autumn Morning by John Atkinson Grimshaw (1836–1893). Oil on canvas. Mallett Gallery, London.

Preparing to Read

Crossing the Bar

Reader/Writer Notebook

Use your **RWN** to complete the activities for this selection.

Literary Focus

Metaphor A **metaphor** is a comparison between two seemingly unlike things: for example, *Life is a journey*. By using metaphors, poets can make abstract ideas more concrete and understandable.

A metaphor does not use a connective word such as *like* or *as*. Instead, the comparison is either directly stated (*You are my sunshine*) or implied (*The rays of your love warm my life*). Note that in the implied metaphor, you must use the clues *rays* and *warm* to guess that your love is being compared to sunshine.

An **extended metaphor** is a comparison that is extended or developed over the course of several lines or verses, or even throughout an entire poem. "Crossing the Bar" is an example of the latter. In it, Tennyson uses a common experience—setting out to sea—as a metaphor for a profound and mysterious human experience.

Into Action Once you identify both halves of the comparison Tennyson is making, use a chart like the one below to keep track of images in the poem and the ideas they may represent.

Image	Idea
"sound and foam"	the distractions of life

SKILLS FOCUS Literary Skills Understand metaphor.

Language Coach

Multiple-Meaning Words The word *bar* has several meanings in the English language. In this poem, *bar* refers to a sandbar, or a long underwater ridge of sand near a shore. Use a dictionary to discover at least three other meanings for the word *bar*. Do any of these other meanings seem relevant to the poem?

Writing Focus

Think as a Reader/Writer

Find It in Your Reading Rather than ask questions, Tennyson forcefully declares his statements. As you read the poem, keep track of the verbs that Tennyson uses in these statements by writing them down in your *Reader/Writer Notebook*.

Learn It Online
Check out Tennyson in the twenty-first century with these Internet links.

go.hrw.com   L12-937   **Go**

POEM

Crossing the Bar

by **Alfred, Lord Tennyson**

Read with a Purpose
Read to discover what the speaker hopes to do once he has "crossed the bar."

Build Background
"Crossing the Bar" has been praised as a poem in which every image can be seen to have a double meaning. The images of a sea voyage were fresh in Tennyson's mind, because he wrote this poem in 1889, while crossing the channel that separates the Isle of Wight from the southern coast of England.

Sunset over the Needles Lighthouse and rocks, Alum Bay, Freshwater Bay, Isle of Wight, England.

Sunset and evening star,
    And one clear call for me!
And may there be no moaning of the bar,
    When I put out to sea,

5   But such a tide as moving seems asleep,
    Too full for sound and foam,
When that° which drew from out the boundless deep **Ⓐ**
    Turns again home.

Twilight and evening bell,
10   And after that the dark!
And may there be no sadness of farewell,
    When I embark;

For though from out our bourne° of Time and Place
    The flood may bear me far,
15 I hope to see my Pilot face to face **Ⓑ**
    When I have crossed the bar.

7. that: the soul.
13. bourne (bawrn): archaic word meaning "boundary."

13. bourne (bawrn): archaic word meaning "boundary."

Ⓐ Literary Focus Metaphor Metaphorically speaking, what is the "boundless deep" of the sea?

Ⓑ Literary Focus Metaphor To whom or what is Tennyson implicitly comparing the pilot of a ship?

Applying Your Skills

from **In Memoriam A.H.H. / Crossing the Bar**

Respond and Think Critically

Reading Focus

Quick Check

1. In Lyric 55 of *In Memoriam*, what complaint does the speaker voice against Nature?

2. The speaker of "Crossing the Bar" is a mariner, or sailor. What is the mariner about to do?

Read with a Purpose

3. What do these two poems reveal about Tennyson's views of life after death?

Reading Skills: Analyzing an Author's Style

4. Review the words and phrases you recorded in your chart for In *Memoriam*. Then, write a sentence or two in which you make some generalizations about Tennyson's style. Which elements of his style seem most dominant?

✔ Vocabulary Check

Complete each sentence with a Vocabulary word:
derives   discord   redress   diffusive

5. *In Memoriam* addresses the confusion and _____ that can follow the death of a loved one.

6. The speaker complains that after such a loss, adequate _____ seems impossible.

7. The speaker discovers that true joy _____ from a deep connection to nature.

8. He realizes that in nature, he can sense the _____ presences of his friend's immortal soul.

Literary Focus

Literary Analysis

9. Compare and Contrast Compare the aspects of Nature described in Lyrics 55 and 56 with those in Lyric 130. What difference is there?

10. Analyze Lyric 95 moves from a local scene to "empyreal heights of thought" (line 38) and back. How is this movement related to the speaker's **mood** in Lyrics 55 and 56, as well as in Lyric 130?

11. Interpret Paraphrase each of the speaker's wishes and hopes, and explain what they show about the speaker's feelings.

Literary Skills: Tone / Metaphor

12. Evaluate How would you characterize the poet's **tone** in Lyrics 55 and 56 of *In Memoriam?* How does this tone change in Lyrics 95 and 130?

13. Analyze In "Crossing the Bar," Tennyson uses the experience of a sailor embarking on a long voyage as a **metaphor** for death. Use details from the poem to explain how the metaphor is extended.

Literary Skills Review: Rhyme

14. Compare and Contrast The pattern of rhymed lines in a poem is called its **rhyme scheme.** How do the different rhyme schemes of the two poems contribute to the poems' moods?

Writing Focus

Think as a Reader/Writer

Use It in Your Writing Review the notes you took on Tennyson's use of questions and direct statements. Pose your own question, and use at least three of Tennyson's verbs as you try to answer the question.

What Do **You Think Now** How can we view death as a beginning instead of an ending?

from **In Memoriam A.H.H.**
Crossing the Bar

CHOICES

As you respond to the Choices, use these **Academic Vocabulary** words as appropriate: benefit, respond, publish, statistics, complex.

REVIEW
Identify Tone of Voice

Literary tone is closely linked with tone of voice. In a conversation, you can identify a person's tone by considering the topic and by listening to the rhythms and pitches of the voice. You might decide that the speaker's tone is sullen, earnest, or pleading. With a partner, take turns reading aloud "Crossing the Bar" or a lyric from *In Memoriam*. Use a different tone of voice each time. Then discuss which tone seems more consistent with Tennyson's and why.

Picture This Word Picture

A metaphor is a kind of word picture: It helps a reader envision an everyday object or idea in a fresh, surprising way. If it is a powerful metaphor, the image lingers in the reader's mind and haunts it long after the book is closed. The extended metaphor in Tennyson's "Crossing the Bar" is this kind of metaphor. Though the poem is short, the image it presents is clear, simple, and strong. Using the medium of your choice, create a visual representation of the metaphor. As you plan your rendering, consider what details you might use to suggest both the literal and the figurative meanings present in the poem.

CONNECT
Modern Elegies

TechFocus How do modern people create memorials for their loved ones? Compile a list of different types of online or modern memorials, and compare and contrast them to Tennyson's poem. What advantages are there in a poetic elegy? What benefits does technology provide? Do modern memorials also address the questions of life and death that Tennyson did? Share your findings with your class.

Argue About Life and Death

Timed ⌐**Writing** The speaker's attitude toward death in "Crossing the Bar" can be described as noble, courageous, accepting, reverent, complex—and unusual. Was the mariner able to live up to his lofty ideas about death when it came time for him to "cross"? Write an expository essay analyzing the views on death and the use of language in "Crossing the Bar." Be sure to cite passages from the text to support your response.

EXTEND
Research Victorian Grief

Tennyson's response to the death of his friend was not considered excessive at the time. Victorians took the matter of death and grieving very seriously. With a partner, research Victorian attitudes toward death and grieving. In addition to your own questions, use these questions to guide your research:

• What traditions did the Victorians follow after the death of a relative?

• How did the Victorians use art forms such as poetry, song, and sculpture to express their grief?

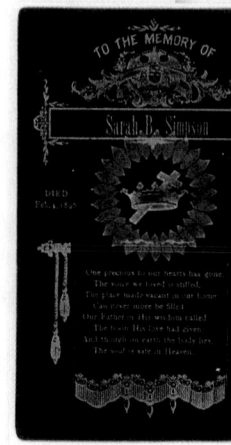

A Victorian mourning card (1896).

Research Victorian Science

Choose a natural phenomenon in the poem—such as the evening star or ocean tides—and research how it was perceived or explained by Victorian scientists. Do your findings shed additional light on Tennyson's poem? Posing as a Victorian scientist and fan of Tennyson, present your findings to the class.

Reading Focus

My Last Duchess / Porphyria's Lover

Drawing Inferences from Textual Clues by **Kylene Beers**

To understand complex poetry, you need to be a bit of a detective. Like a skilled crime-scene investigator, good readers draw inferences from clues in the poem and their own experience. You will find clues in the author's use of language, character description, and events. Putting all of the clues together will help you unravel the poem's mysteries.

The poet supplies the textual clues in the poem, and you provide the background information or internal clues from your experience. Together, this information becomes an inference—a connection between mind and text. An active reader is always making inferences and then reading further to confirm or adjust his or her inferences as information is revealed. The clues reveal the mysteries of reading poetry.

In Robert Browning's dramatic monologue "My Last Duchess," the reader has the opportunity to practice inference skills. The first character introduced is the poem's speaker, the Duke. The reader can immediately begin to infer aspects of the Duke's personality from his words (textual clues).

> But to myself they turned (since none puts by
> The curtain I have drawn for you, but I)
> And seemed as they would ask me, if they
>   durst. (lines 9–11)

The Duke's words remind us of people we have known who were arrogant ("if they durst") and controlling ("none . . . but I"). The words and our experience (internal clues) combine so that we can infer that the Duke is a domineering and haughty man who sought to control the Duchess as well as everyone else. As you continue to read, this inference may be confirmed and expanded , or you may adjust the inference about the Duke.

The Duke continues to speak in lines 31–34:

> She thanked men—good! but thanked
> Somehow—I know not how—as if she
>   ranked
> My gift of a nine-hundred-years-old name
> With anybody's gift.

These lines confirm the first inference that the Duke is an arrogant, egotistical man who expects subservience and obedience from his wife. While the Duke criticizes his late wife, his words actually confirm and expand our inference about him.

Your Turn

Re-read lines 31–34. Focus this time on making inferences about the Duchess. Combine your background experience with people (internal clues) and the words describing the Duchess (textual clues) to make an inference about her. What kind of person can we infer her to be, based on the text and our experience?

Read lines 43–45 to add clues to your inference about the Duchess.

> Oh, sir she smiled, no doubt,
> Whene'er I passed her; but who passed
>   without
> Much the same smile?

How does this additional information confirm or adjust your inferences about the Duke and his last Duchess?

My Last Duchess
Porphyria's Lover

What Do You Think How can appearance be different from reality?

QuickWrite

What does true love look like? Can you tell it when you see it? Write a quick description of how people appear when they are in love, and then think about how the appearance of love can mask real motives that have little to do with love.

Robert Browning
(1812–1889)

Robert Browning pioneered psychological portraiture in poetry by digging into fascinating and macabre characters to discover their motives.

Ambitions and Education

Robert Browning aspired to dazzle the world with his range and variety as a poet. His education allowed him to indulge his wide-ranging interests in music, art, the history of medicine, drama, literature, entomology, and other widely varying topics. Browning was mainly educated at home by tutors and by his wide reading in his banker-father's extensive library. As a teenager, Browning was brilliant, undisciplined, and determined to be a poet like his idol, Percy Bysshe Shelley. After a term at the University of London, he published (at his family's expense) several poems and plays, but not until he began writing the short dramatic monologues of the 1840s—poems like "My Last Duchess"—did he find his proper form.

A Marriage of True Minds

In 1845, Browning wrote to Elizabeth Barrett, already an established poet: "I do . . . love these books with all my heart—and I love you too." Four months after the two poets began their correspondence, they met and fell in love. They secretly married in 1846, and a week later they eloped to Italy. Mr. Barrett, who forbade his daughter to marry, estranged himself from his famous daughter for the rest of her life.

Browning's happy marriage confirmed his belief that only by acting boldly can one wrest what is good from an imperfect world. He lived in Italy until Elizabeth's death in 1861, when he returned to England with their son. During the 1860s, his fame began to grow. Readers understood that by asking them to figure out and judge wicked men like the Duke in "My Last Duchess," Browning was really challenging them to discover when love nourished and why it kills. Browning believed that human beings must act by a moral standard and that those who act bravely will be rewarded.

Think About the Writer How did Browning's ideas about love in his own life work their way into his poetry?

Robert Browning (1858) by Michele Gordigiani. Oil on canvas. National Portrait Gallery, London.

My Last Duchess / Porphyria's Lover

Reader/Writer Notebook
Use your **RWN** to complete the activities for this selection.

Literary Focus

Dramatic Monologue "My Last Duchess" and "Porphyria's Lover" are two of Browning's earliest and most popular **dramatic monologues,** poems in which a speaker who is not the poet addresses a listener who does not speak. Instead of telling us directly what the speakers and the other characters are like, Browning allows the speakers to reveal themselves, the other characters, and the situation by dropping indirect clues that we must piece together.

Literary Perspectives Apply the literary perspective described on page 944 as you read these poems.

Reading Focus

Drawing Inferences from Textual Clues Reading one of Browning's dramatic monologues is like having a curtain pulled slowly aside to reveal a portrait of the speaker. By putting what you "see"—clues from the text—together with what you already know about human behavior, you can **draw inferences,** or logical conclusions, about each speaker's motives and character traits.

Into Action As you read each poem, use a chart to record the speaker and each character he introduces. Then, write down details from the poem that give clues to each person's character and to the situation.

Character	Clues About the Character	Clues About the Situation
Duke	No one draws aside the curtain except him.	He is showing someone a portrait of his late wife.
Duchess	She is no longer the Duchess.	

Writing Focus

Think as a Reader/Writer
Find It in Your Reading Browning heightens the tension in "My Last Duchess" with **rhetorical questions,** or questions that the listener is not meant to answer. Make note of these in your *Reader/Writer Notebook*.

TechFocus As you read these poems, think about how you would present them as a podcast.

Vocabulary

officious (uh FIHSH uhs) *adj.:* eager to give unwanted help. *The Duke remembers his wife's kind response to officious young men.*

munificence (myoo NIHF uh suhns) *n.:* generosity. *The Duke views munificence as a form of weakness.*

pretense (prih TEHNS) *n.:* weakly supported claim. *The Duke's pretense that his wife was foolish goes unchallenged.*

object (AHB jihkt) *n.:* goal or purpose. *What was the Duke's true object in showing the portrait?*

displaced (dihs PLAYST) *v.* used as *adj.:* moved from its usual location. *Porphyria's displaced hair gives the speaker an evil idea.*

Language Coach

Multiple-Meaning Words The word *last* has several meanings in English. In the title "My Last Duchess," *last* means "previous" (as in "last night" or "last week") rather than "final." What does this use of the word *last* imply about the Duke and his wife or wives?

 **Learn It Online**
Meet "My Last Duchess" through the video introduction online.

go.hrw.com L12-943   **Go**

My Last Duchess

by **Robert Browning**

Read with a Purpose
Read to discover why the "last" Duchess is no longer the Duke's wife.

Build Background
Browning identified his speaker as Alfonso II d'Este (1533–1597), the fifth and last Duke of Ferrara, a powerful Italian nobleman of the Renaissance. The Duke's three marriages were all political alliances. His first wife, Lucrezia de' Medici, the fourteen-year-old daughter of the Duke of Florence, died two years into the marriage—possibly from poisoning. In the poem the Duke is negotiating to marry the daughter of a Count.

That's my last Duchess painted on the wall,
Looking as if she were alive. I call
That piece a wonder, now; Frà Pandolf's° hands
Worked busily a day, and there she stands.
5 Will 't please you sit and look at her? I said
"Frà Pandolf" by design, for never read
Strangers like you that pictured countenance,
The depth and passion of its earnest glance,
But to myself they turned (since none puts by
10 The curtain I have drawn for you, but I)
And seemed as they would ask me, if they durst,
How such a glance came there; so, not the first
Are you to turn and ask thus. Sir, 'twas not **(A)**
Her husband's presence only, called that spot
15 Of joy into the Duchess' cheek; perhaps
Frà Pandolf chanced to say, "Her mantle° laps
Over my lady's wrist too much," or, "Paint
Must never hope to reproduce the faint
Half flush that dies along her throat." Such stuff
20 Was courtesy, she thought, and cause enough
For calling up that spot of joy. She had
A heart—how shall I say?—too soon made glad,

(A) Literary Focus Dramatic Monologue What clues in lines 1–13 suggest that the poem is going to be a monologue rather than a conversation?

? **1–13.** *Paraphrase these opening lines. What are the speaker and his guest doing? What does the guest ask the speaker?*

3. Frà Pandolf's: reference to Brother Pandolf, a fictitious painter and monk.

? **13–21.** *What does the speaker think brought the "spot of joy" (line 21) to his wife's face?*

Literary Perspectives

Analyzing Style You can use this perspective to identify elements of these two poems that make them dramatic monologues—for example, a speaker and a silent listener—and to evaluate how well Browning executes the form. You can also use this perspective to identify and analyze other formal elements of the poems, such as meter, rhyme scheme, word choice, and imagery, that contribute to Browning's style. How do these elements affect the poems' overall tone and meaning?

As you read, be sure to notice the questions in each poem, which will guide you in using this perspective.

Viewing and Interpreting How does this image convey "the depth and passion of its earnest glance?" How does the woman in the painting compare with the "last" Duchess in the poem?

The Veiled Woman, or La Donna Velata (c. 1516) by Raphael (Raffaello Sanzio of Urbino) (1483–1520). Palazzo Pitti, Florence, Italy.

Too easily impressed; she liked whate'er
She looked on, and her looks went everywhere.
25 Sir, 'twas all one! My favor° at her breast,
The dropping of the daylight in the West,
The bough of cherries some officious fool
Broke in the orchard for her, the white mule   **B**
She rode with round the terrace—all and each
30 Would draw from her alike the approving speech,
Or blush, at least. She thanked men—good! but thanked
Somehow—I know not how—as if she ranked
My gift of a nine-hundred-years-old name
With anybody's gift. Who'd stoop to blame
35 This sort of trifling? Even had you skill
In speech—(which I have not)—to make your will
Quite clear to such an one, and say, "Just this
Or that in you disgusts me; here you miss,
Or there exceed the mark"—and if she let
40 Herself be lessoned so, nor plainly set
Her wits to yours, forsooth,° and made excuse,
—E'en then would be some stooping; and I choose
Never to stoop. Oh sir, she smiled, no doubt,   **C**
Whene'er I passed her; but who passed without
45 Much the same smile? This grew; I gave commands;
Then all smiles stopped together. There she stands
As if alive. Will 't please you rise? We'll meet   **D**
The company below, then. I repeat,
The Count your master's known munificence
50 Is ample warrant° that no just pretense
Of mine for dowry will be disallowed;
Though his fair daughter's self, as I avowed
At starting, is my object. Nay, we'll go
Together down, sir. Notice Neptune,° though,
55 Taming a seahorse, thought a rarity,
Which Claus of Innsbruck° cast in bronze for me!

B Literary Perspectives **Analyzing Style** What are the rhyming words in this couplet (lines 27–28)? What does this word choice imply about the speaker's attitude toward his wife?

C Reading Focus **Drawing Inferences from Textual Clues** What inferences can you draw about the Duke from these lines?

D Reading Focus **Drawing Inferences from Textual Clues** What do you suspect happened to the Duchess? On what clues do you base this guess?

Vocabulary **officious** (uh FIHSH uhs) *adj.*: eager to give unwanted help.
munificence (myoo NIHF uh suhns) *n.*: generosity.
pretense (prih TEHNS) *n.*: weakly supported claim.
object (AHB jihkt) *n.*: goal or purpose.

25. favor: gift; token of love.

? **21–34.** *What complaints does the speaker make against the Duchess's character in these lines? What most bothers him?*

41. forsooth: archaic for "in truth."

50. warrant: guarantee.

54. Neptune: in Roman mythology, god of the sea.
56. Claus of Innsbruck: imaginary sculptor.

Porphyria's Lover

by **Robert Browning**

Read with a Purpose
Read to discover the mental state of Porphyria's lover.

Build Background
Like the American writer Edgar Allan Poe, Browning had a taste for morbid psychology; he once accused his wife, Elizabeth Barrett Browning, of lacking "a scientific interest in evil." In "Porphyria's Lover," he pursues that interest, exploring the complexity of human motivation.

The rain set early in tonight,
    The sullen wind was soon awake,
It tore the elm tops down for spite,
    And did its worst to vex the lake:
5   I listened with heart fit to break.
When glided in Porphyria; straight
    She shut the cold out and the storm,
And kneeled and made the cheerless grate
    Blaze up, and all the cottage warm;
10   Which done, she rose, and from her form
Withdrew the dripping cloak and shawl,
    And laid her soiled gloves by, untied
Her hat and let the damp hair fall,
    And, last, she sat down by my side
15   And called me. When no voice replied,
She put my arm about her waist,
    And made her smooth white shoulder bare,
And all her yellow hair displaced,
    And, stooping, made my cheek lie there,
20   And spread, o'er all, her yellow hair,
Murmuring how she loved me—she
    Too weak, for all her heart's endeavor,
To set its struggling passion free

    From pride, and vainer ties dissever,°
25   And give herself to me forever. **Ⓐ**
But passion sometimes would prevail,
    Nor could tonight's gay feast restrain
A sudden thought of one so pale
    For love of her, and all in vain:
30   So, she was come through wind and rain.
Be sure I looked up at her eyes
    Happy and proud; at last I knew
Porphyria worshipped me: Surprise **Ⓑ**
    Made my heart swell, and still it grew
35   While I debated what to do.
That moment she was mine, mine, fair,
    Perfectly pure and good: I found
A thing to do, and all her hair
    In one long yellow string I wound
40   Three times her little throat around,
And strangled her. No pain felt she;
    I am quite sure she felt no pain.
As a shut bud that holds a bee,
    I warily oped° her lids; again
45   Laughed the blue eyes without a stain.

---

24. dissever: separate.
44. oped: archaic for "opened."

Vocabulary displaced (dihs PLAYST) *v.* used as *adj.*: moved from its usual location.

Ⓐ Reading Focus Drawing Inferences from Textual Clues What appears to be the main obstacle to this relationship?

Ⓑ Literary Focus Dramatic Monologue What does the speaker reveal about himself and his perceptions in lines 26–33?

Viewing and Interpreting How might this image represent the speaker's feelings about Porphyria?

Mannshode I Kviinnehar (Man's Head in Woman's Hair), 1896, by Edvard Munch (1863–1944). The Museum of Modern Art, NY.

And I untightened next the tress
    About her neck; her cheek once more
Blushed bright beneath my burning kiss:
    I propped her head up as before,
50   Only, this time my shoulder bore
Her head, which droops upon it still;
    The smiling rosy little head,
So glad it has its utmost will,
    That all it scorned at once is fled,

55   And I, its love, am gained instead! **C**
Porphyria's love: She guessed not how
    Her darling one wish would be heard.
And thus we sit together now,
    And all night long we have not stirred,
60   And yet God has not said a word! **D**

C **Literary Focus** Dramatic Monologue What do lines 46–55 suggest about the speaker?

D **Literary Perspectives** Analyzing Style Is the meter of this poem regular or irregular? How does the meter contribute to the poem's cold, detached tone?

SKILLS FOCUS Literary Skills Analyze the characteristics of dramatic monologue; analyze irony; analyze style. Reading Skills Draw inferences from textual clues. Writing Skills Write literary texts.

Respond and Think Critically

Reading Focus

Read with a Purpose

1. In "My Last Duchess," how does the Duke's version of the demise of the last Duchess differ from your interpretation of the events? Why?

2. At the end of "Porphyria's Lover," how does understanding when the monologue occurs change your understanding of the events?

Reading Skills: Drawing Inferences from Textual Clues

3. Now that you have read the poems, review the textual clues you recorded in your charts. Add another column to your chart, and record at least two inferences about each character in it.

Character	Character Clues	Situation Clues	Inferences
Duke	No one draws aside the curtain except him.	He is showing someone a portrait of his late wife.	1. 2.

Literary Focus

Literary Analysis

4. **Infer** Assume that the Count's emissary in "My Last Duchess" is an insightful person. What impression is the Duke unintentionally making?

5. **Analyze** Read the last sentence of "My Last Duchess." Is it an effective conclusion? What might the speaker intend to convey with such a comment?

6. **Evaluate** What leads the speaker in "Porphyria's Lover" to assert that Porphyria "felt no pain"? What do you think of this claim?

7. **Extend** "Porphyria's Lover" was originally published with another monologue under the title *Madhouse Cells*. How does knowing the collection's title affect your interpretation of the poem?

8. **Literary Perspectives** Choose either rhyme, meter, or word choice, and explain how Browning's use of this formal element contributes to the **mood,** or feel, of each poem. Use specific examples from the poems to support your claims.

Literary Skills: Dramatic Monologue

9. **Analyze** In a dramatic monologue, the reader sees things only through the perspective of the speaker. Summarize each speaker's attitude toward his former lover. Why might you question their assessments? Why or why not?

Literary Skills Review: Irony

10. **Analyze** A discrepancy between what is said and what is really meant, or between what appears to be true and what is really true, is irony. What irony can you find in "My Last Duchess" and "Porphyria's Lover"?

Writing Focus

Think as a Reader/Writer

Use It in Your Writing Review the rhetorical questions you recorded in your *Reader/Writer Notebook* as you read "My Last Duchess." Choose one of them, and use it as a starting point for your own dramatic monologue in response to the Duke.

What Do **You Think Now** Which speaker more successfully hides reality from us? Explain.

Vocabulary Development

✓ Vocabulary Check

Match each Vocabulary word with its meaning.

1. officious   **a.** generosity
2. munificence   **b.** eager to give unwanted help
3. pretense   **c.** weak claim
4. object   **d.** moved
5. displaced   **e.** goal or purpose

Vocabulary Skills: Multiple-Meaning Words

Many words have, over time, accumulated more than one meaning. Consider Browning's usage of the word *favor* in line 25 of "My Last Duchess." Browning uses the word *favor* in a sense that was common from the medieval period through the Victorian age—to refer to a small token of romantic love. Today, when we refer to a trinket given or received at a party—a "party favor"— we are invoking this meaning of the word. If we say, "You favor your father," we are using the word in a very different sense—to resemble someone in appearance. All of these definitions of *favor* are related, however, in that they share the same origin: They all come from a Latin word meaning "to regard with goodwill."

	Meanings:	**Word Origin:**
favor	• a small gift of love • to resemble someone	Latin <u>favere</u> meaning "regard with goodwill"

Your Turn

Using a dictionary, find two meanings for each of the following words: *object, stoop, fair*. If both the meanings share the same origin, create for that word a chart like the one for *favor*. If they have different origins, create a chart like the following.

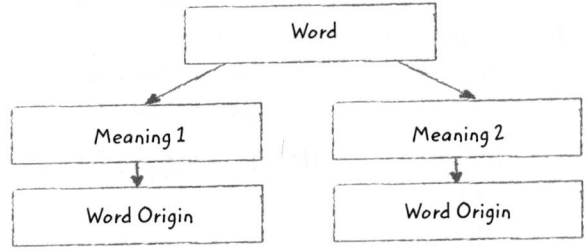

Language Coach

Idioms An **idiom** is a frequently used expression that is not meant to be taken literally. For example, the Duke says that in some of her behaviors, the Duchess *missed the mark*. This does not mean that she was literally trying to hit a target and missed. It means that her words or actions were in some way not appropriate. To help you remember the meanings of these expressions, try making a simple sketch for each that suggests both their literal and nonliteral meanings.

Academic Vocabulary

Talk About

In a small group, discuss the <u>complex</u> aspects of romantic relationships revealed in the two monologues by Browning. Do these situations exist today? Specify modern-day examples in your <u>response</u>.

SKILLS FOCUS **Literary Skills** Analyze the characteristics of a dramatic monologue. **Reading Skills** Read to research information **Vocabulary Skills** Refine vocabulary for interpersonal, academic, and workplace situations; identify and correctly use multiple- meaning words. **Grammar Skills** Identify and use participles and participial phrases correctly. **Listening and Speaking Skills** Demonstrate effective verbal techniques when speaking; demonstrate effective nonverbal techniques when speaking.

Grammar Link

Using Participles to Combine Sentences

A **participle** is a verb form that can be used as an adjective, or modifier. For example, in the phrase *falling star,* the participle *falling* modifies the noun *star.* A **participial phrase** is made up of a participle and all of its own modifiers and complements. Consider the opening sentence from "My Last Duchess":

> That's my last Duchess painted on the wall,
> **Looking as if she were alive.**

In this sentence, the participial phrase *looking as if she were alive* modifies the noun *Duchess.* Participial phrases like this one are often used to combine two sentences. For example, Browning might have expressed the same idea in this way:

> That's my last Duchess painted on the wall.
> She looks as if she were alive.

In your view, which version is more effective? Why?

Your Turn

Use a participle or a participial phrase to combine each pair of sentences.

1. The Duke drew the curtain aside. He smiled at his guest.
2. The Duke turned to leave. He pointed out a bronze sculpture of Neptune.
3. Porphyria knelt. She lit a fire in the hearth.
4. Porphyria unwrapped her shawl. She sat down next to her lover.
5. She looked in his eyes. She drew her last breath.

Writing Application Choose a composition or essay you have already written, and look for short or choppy sentences that can be combined by using participles. Rewrite a few of these sentences. How does the use of participles affect the sound and flow of your writing?

CHOICES

As you respond to the Choices, use these **Academic Vocabulary** words as appropriate: benefit, respond, publish, statistics, complex.

REVIEW

Perform a Dramatic Reading

Group Activity Because a dramatic monologue is a kind of poetic speech, it begs to be read aloud. Work with a partner to prepare two dramatic readings of either of Browning's poems, each one conveying a different interpretation of the Duke's tone. (For example, the Duke's words may sound sinister if read one way, but regretful or mournful if read another way.) Use facial expressions, gestures, and tone of voice to create two distinct impressions. Perform your dramatic readings for the class.

CONNECT

Conduct an Interview

Choose either the Duke or Porphyria's lover, and work with a partner to conduct a TV interview with that character. During the course of the interview, the speaker should be questioned about his relationship to either the Duchess or Porphyria and his role in her disappearance. Prepare some questions that can be answered by quoting directly from the poem. After rehearsing your interview, present it to the class or publish a transcript of it in your school paper.

EXTEND

Capture the Story Digitally

TechFocus Choose one of these poems, and record it as a podcast. As you read, pay attention to the tone of voice you use to bring the dramatic monologues alive. How can you use your voice to illustrate the tone and mood of the poem, as well as to reveal the character of the speaker? Share your finished podcast with your class.

Learn It Online
Explore Multiple Meaning words online.

go.hrw.com   L12-951   **Go**

Preparing to Read

Sonnet 43

What Do You Think?

How can appearance be different from reality?

QuickWrite

What kind of love do you think is most powerful—romantic love, love between friends, love of family, or some other kind of love? Record your thoughts in your *Reader/Writer Notebook*.

Elizabeth Barrett Browning (1858) by Michele Gordigiani. Oil on canvas. National Portrait Gallery, London.

Elizabeth Barrett Browning
(1806–1861)

Elizabeth Barrett Browning was one of the most famous poets of her day—more successful during her lifetime than her husband, Robert Browning.

A Renaissance Woman

Barrett Browning is remembered today for her *Sonnets from the Portuguese,* of which "How Do I Love Thee?" is the best known. During her lifetime, Barrett Browning was well known as a daring, versatile poet who frequently wrote on intellectual, religious, and political matters. When she was young, she studied Greek, Latin, French, Italian, history, and philosophy—an uncommon education for a woman in nineteenth-century England. She published long narratives, a novel in verse, translations of Greek plays, and poems that dealt with the abolition of slavery, the exploitation of children in factories, religious belief, and Italian nationalism.

Through Suffering to Freedom

Through the first half of her busy literary career, Elizabeth Barrett was a semi-invalid. Her illnesses have been variously diagnosed: She may have had a lung problem dating from childhood, as well as an injured spine from a fall she took as a teenager. It is certain, however, that her ailments were intensified by the sometime bullying protectiveness of her father and by the drugs routinely prescribed in those days for a "nervous collapse."

In 1845, she met Robert Browning. During their secret courtship, Barrett wrote forty-four sonnets tracing the development of her love for him. The next year they married secretly and eloped to the Continent. Her father never forgave her for the marriage (he had forbidden all his children to marry), nor did he ever see her again. Barrett Browning flourished in Italy and bore a son when she was forty-three years old: her own "young Florentine" with "brave blue English eyes."

Think About the Writer

How do you think childhood experiences contribute to a person's development?

Reader/Writer Notebook

Use your **RWN** to complete the activities for this selection.

Literary Focus

Petrarchan Sonnet All forty-four poems in *Sonnets from the Portuguese* are written in the form of the **Petrarchan sonnet.** This kind of sonnet, also called Italian, is organized into a group of eight lines (an octave) followed by a sestet (six lines). Each line is in **iambic pentameter** and rhymes *abbaabba cdcdcd*. Petrarchan sonnets often have a break in thought, or **turn,** between the octave and the sestet. Sonnet 43, however, lacks this feature and is instead broken into short units of thought.

Reading Focus

Paraphrasing The key to understanding what you read is being able to express it in your own words. When you **paraphrase** a sentence or passage, you not only replace the original words with your own but also use new grammar and sentence structure.

Into Action As you read, create a chart like the one below to practice paraphrasing. First, list each of the ways of loving that the speaker identifies. Then, paraphrase that statement in your own language, using your own sentence structure.

Original Sentence	Paraphrase
"I love thee to the depth and breadth and height / My soul can reach, when feeling out of sight / For the ends of Being and ideal Grace."	My love for you extends as far as my spirit can seek out the very reason for existence.

Writing Focus

Think as a Reader/Writer

Find It in Your Reading As you read, note how the writer begins the poem by asking a question and then uses **repetition** as she tries to answer it. In your *Reader/Writer Notebook,* identify where the repetition occurs and make notes about how it enhances the poem's rhythm as well as its theme.

Language Coach

Synonyms Barrett Browning uses language that would have been considered old-fashioned at the time (for example, *thee* instead of *you*) to make her work sound more serious and poetic. As you paraphrase the poem, think of modern or simpler word choices that have the same meaning. These words may literally mean the same thing as Barrett Browning's, but how do they change the tone of the poem?

Learn It Online
Listen to this famous sonnet online.

go.hrw.com   L12-953   **Go**

Sonnet 43

by **Elizabeth Barrett Browning**

Read with a Purpose
Read to discover the many aspects of mature love.

Build Background
Elizabeth Barrett Browning wrote her sonnets before her marriage but did not show them to her husband until two years later. Reluctant to <u>publish</u> the poems because they were so personal, she deliberately gave them a title that suggested that they were translated into English from an original Portuguese source.

Love Among the Ruins by Sir Edward Burne-Jones (1833–1898). Oil on canvas. Wightwick Manor Staffordshire, U.K.

How do I love thee? Let me count the ways.
I love thee to the depth and breadth and height
My soul can reach, when feeling out of sight
For the ends of Being and ideal Grace. **Ⓐ**
5   I love thee to the level of everyday's
Most quiet need, by sun and candlelight.
I love thee freely, as men strive for Right;
I love thee purely, as they turn from Praise. **Ⓑ**
I love thee with the passion put to use
10   In my old griefs, and with my childhood's faith.
I love thee with a love I seemed to lose
With my lost saints°—I love thee with the breath,
Smiles, tears, of all my life!—and, if God choose,
I shall but love thee better after death.

12. lost saints: childhood faith.

Ⓐ **Reading Focus** **Paraphrasing** Put the first four lines into your own words. How does your paraphrase help you understand the poem's theme?

Ⓑ **Literary Focus** **Petrarchan Sonnet** In a regular Petrarchan sonnet, a turn of thought would occur here. Instead of having one major division, how many units of thought does the poem contain?

SKILLS FOCUS Literary Skills Analyze the Petrarchan sonnet; analyze diction. **Reading Skills** Paraphrase a text. **Writing Skills** Enhance meaning by employing repetition.

Sonnet 43

Respond and Think Critically

Reading Focus

Quick Check

1. How many distinct ways does the speaker say that she loves her beloved?

2. In lines 2–6, what are the two contrasting levels of love that the poet expresses?

3. In lines 9–14, what are the three stages of life that the speaker contrasts?

Read with a Purpose

4. How would you define *mature love* based on the features identified by the speaker of the poem?

Reading Skills: Paraphrasing

5. As you read the poem, you paraphrased each statement in your own words. Re-read each sentence, both the original and your paraphrase, and rate how easy it is to understand by writing a number from 5 (most difficult to understand) to 1 (easiest to understand) next to it. If any of your paraphrases received less than a 5, rewrite them so that they are easier to understand and are expressed as much as possible in your own voice.

Original Sentence	Paraphrase
"I love thee to the depth and breadth and height / My soul can reach, when feeling out of sight / For the ends of Being and ideal Grace." Rating: 5	My love for you extends as far as my spirit can seek out the very reason for existence. Rating: 2

Literary Focus

Literary Analysis

6. **Infer** What do you think the poem expresses about the speaker's religious faith?

7. **Analyze** How are the pauses in the last three lines different in rhythm from those in the rest of the poem? What is the emotional effect of this change in rhythm?

8. **Evaluate** In your opinion, has Barrett Browning described all of the important emotional aspects of love? Explain your response.

Literary Skills: Petrarchan Sonnet

9. **Compare and Contrast** How would Sonnet 43 have been different if Barrett Browning had written it as a Shakespearean sonnet (see page 392)?

Literary Skills Review: Diction

10. **Analyze** A writer or speaker's choice of words is called **diction.** What examples of concrete and abstract words can you find in the poem?

Writing Focus

Think as a Reader/Writer

Use It in Your Writing. In your *Reader/Writer Notebook,* write a poem or a short speech that begins with a question. (If you choose to write a poem, you do not have to use meter and rhyme.) Then, use repetition as you try to answer your question in a variety of different ways.

What Do You Think Now

What else is love about besides creating happiness?

Pied Beauty

What Do You Think

How can appearance be different from reality?

QuickWrite

Hopkins commented that his poetry "errs on the side of oddness" by rejoicing in strange, surprising aspects of creation. What meaning do you find in small, everyday things?

Gerard Manley Hopkins (1844–1889).

MEET THE WRITER

Gerard Manley Hopkins
(1844–1889)

Throughout his short life, Gerard Manley Hopkins combined learning, service, and religious conviction with a desire to push the established bounds of poetry.

A Journey of Faith

The eldest son of highly educated parents devoted to the Church of England, Hopkins attended Highgate, a London boarding school, where he won a poetry prize and later a scholarship to study classics at Oxford. Hopkins intended to enter the Anglican ministry, but after much soul-searching, he converted to Roman Catholicism in 1866—a shocking thing to do at the time.

In 1868, Hopkins joined the Jesuits, a Roman Catholic order dedicated to teaching, and burned almost all his poetry. For seven years he wrote no poetry until, in 1875, he was asked to write an ode to five Franciscan nuns who had drowned at sea. He sent "The Wreck of the *Deutschland*" to a Jesuit periodical. The poem's form was so eccentric that the editors "dared not print it."

Poetic Innovation

Hopkins composed a small but very powerful body of poetry that he sent to his friends with explanations of his ideas for using native English vocabulary. Hopkins's poems are characterized by assonance, alliteration, internal rhyme, and what he called **sprung rhythm,** which imitates the sound of natural speech. Unlike conventional metrics, sprung rhythm does not employ only one kind of metrical unit (for example, the alternation of unstressed and stressed syllables in iambic pentameter). Despite his metrical and linguistic creativity, Hopkins shared with the Romantics a focus on nature, the transcendent, and personal struggle.

Think About the Writer

What challenges do you think Hopkins faced in going against convention in both his spiritual and artistic lives? Discuss.

Reader/Writer Notebook

Use your **RWN** to complete the activities for this selection.

Literary Focus

Alliteration and Assonance In much of his poetry, Hopkins uses two sound devices: **alliteration,** the repetition of consonant sounds, and **assonance,** the repetition of vowel sounds. Like tongue-twisters, Hopkins's poetry can be challenging to read aloud as a result. In "Pied Beauty," the repeated sounds also serve a thematic purpose. Like the creatures' colorful spots, the sounds create points of connection between otherwise unlike things—"Fresh-firecoal chestnut-falls" and "finches' wings," for example, are united by the *f* sound they share. Try reading the poem aloud, and consider the emotions these sounds conjure as you read.

Language Coach

Word Definitions Hopkins uses several words that are either archaic (that is, no longer in use) or that he invented himself. Make a list of unfamiliar words, and use context clues, definitions provided with the poem, and a dictionary to discover their meanings.

Reading Focus

Drawing Conclusions About Meaning When you read carefully, you **draw conclusions** from a text based on the evidence before you. In poetry as challenging as "Pied Beauty," you may need to re-read a line several times and draw **inferences** about words or phrases you don't understand by studying their context.

Into Action As you read, use a Venn diagram like the one below to draw conclusions about each image that Hopkins presents in lines 2–5. In the left-hand circle, record something for which the speaker is thankful. On the right, record something with which it is compared or juxtaposed. Keep in mind that some of these comparisons are made directly as **similes** but others are not.

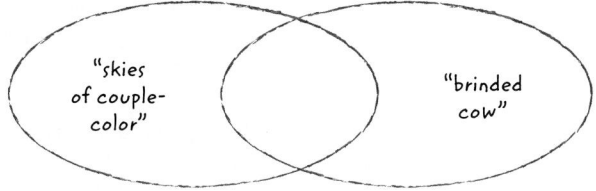

Writing Focus

Think as a Reader/Writer

Find It in Your Reading In your *Reader/Writer Notebook,* identify examples of how Hopkins uses **assonance** and **alliteration.** Record each example according to the consonant or vowel that is repeated, for example "*G:* 'Glory be to God.'"

Learn It Online
Learn more about Hopkins with these Internet links.

go.hrw.com L12-957 **Go**

POEM

Pied Beauty

by **Gerard Manley Hopkins**

Read with a Purpose
Read to discover how the speaker uses nature's diversity to praise God.

Build Background
"Pied Beauty" is a song of praise to God for all things that are pied—that is, covered with different-colored spots. Hopkins composed the poem in 1877, shortly before he was ordained a Roman Catholic priest. Before then, he had kept a "seven-year silence" by refusing to write poetry. He did, however, keep journals that provided material for much of his later verse. For example, on an 1872 vacation to the Isle of Man, Hopkins described the hillsides as "plotted and painted" with square fields, the origin of the poem's phrase "plotted and pieced."

Glory be to God for dappled things—
    For skies of couple-color as a brinded° cow;
       For rose-moles all in stipple° upon trout that swim; **Ⓐ**
Fresh-firecoal chestnut-falls;° finches' wings;
5   Landscape plotted and pieced°—fold, fallow, and plow;
       And áll trádes, their gear and tackle and trim.
All things counter, original, spare, strange;
     Whatever is fickle, freckled (who knows how?)
       With swift, slow; sweet, sour; adazzle, dim; **Ⓑ**
10   He fathers-forth° whose beauty is past change:
               Praise him.

2. brinded: archaic for "brindled"; having a light brown or gray coat streaked with a darker color.
3. stipple: random dots or spots.
4. chestnut-falls: chestnuts falling from a tree.
5. pieced: parceled into fields.
10. fathers-forth: creates.

Ⓐ Literary Focus Alliteration and Assonance In this line, what effect is created by the alliteration of *s, t,* and *z* sounds and the assonance of *o* (*rose moles*) and short *i* (*stipple/swim*)?

Ⓑ Reading Focus Drawing Conclusions About Meaning What image of creation is conveyed by listing these three pairs of opposites?

SKILLS FOCUS Literary Skills Analyze alliteration and assonance; analyze characteristics of metaphysical poetry Reading Skills Draw conclusions about meaning. Writing Skills Describe an object; illustrate beliefs about life.

Respond and Think Critically

Reading Focus

Quick Check

1. What specific examples of "pied beauty" does the poet mention in lines 2–6?

2. What do you think the poet means by saying "all things counter" (line 7)?

3. In line 10, what contrast does the poet make between the beauty of the physical world and that of God the creator?

Read with a Purpose

4. How does Hopkins's poem create a visual image or landscape in praise of God?

Reading Skills: Drawing Conclusions About Meaning

5. You created a Venn diagram to record each comparison that Hopkins makes between a thing in nature and something else. Now you can complete your understanding of how these two seemingly different things relate. Determine the meanings of any unfamiliar words. Then, in the space where the two circles overlap, write the feature that both things share.

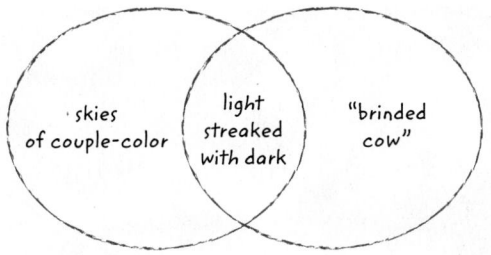

Literary Focus

Literary Analysis

6. **Interpret** Most of the poem is concerned with animals and other aspects of nature. In what line does Hopkins indirectly mention people?

7. **Make Judgments** Is the poet's praise for that which is varied and changing typical of literature written in praise of a person or of God? Explain.

Literary Skills: Alliteration and Assonance

8. **Compare and Contrast** How does the use of alliteration and assonance in "Pied Beauty" compare with that in *Sir Gawain and the Green Knight* (pages 196–202)? Do you notice any similarities in the meter of both poems?

Literary Skills Review: Metaphysical Poetry

9. **Extend** A type of poetry is known for its startling imagery, philosophical and spiritual content, verbal wit, and irregular meter is called **metaphysical poetry**. What aspects of "Pied Beauty" could qualify it for this definition?

Writing Focus

Think as a Reader/Writer

Use It in Your Writing. In your *Reader/Writer Notebook*, write a paragraph or poem in praise of a thing, not a person, whose beauty should be celebrated. Use alliteration or assonance to link images and ideas.

What Do You Think Now

How can unusual language help reveal hidden beauty?

The Paradox of Progress

LITERARY FOCUS
Realism

CONTENTS

Matthew Arnold

Thomas Hardy

A. E. Housman

Jason La Canfora Link to Today

Rudyard Kipling

COMPARING TEXTS: WORLD LITERATURE
Leo Tolstoy
Anton Chekhov
Guy de Maupassant

"There are only two tragedies in life: one is not getting what one wants, and the other is getting it."

Realism by **Leila Christenbury**

Influences on Realism

- Transition from a farming society to an industrialized nation
- Rejection of the Romantic idealism that had previously dominated literature
- Emergence of scientific objectivity as a goal in writing
- Enthusiasm of writers across the globe for the themes of realism

The Switch to Industrialization

As England moved from an agrarian society to a world force and an industrial power, its material progress and prosperity also meant change. People left the security of small villages for the urban centers where they worked in manufacturing. Industries and cities dominated, new ways of living caused upheaval, and traditional beliefs and customs were questioned. The writers in this collection felt these changes keenly and described them using factual detail and direct language, often in the context of the lives of everyday people. Look for the sense of stoic pessimism in this literature, and in particular, consider the last few lines of "Dover Beach." They are some of the most famous—and chilling—in English poetry and signal a belief that the world had entered a new era of unprecedented change.

A Reaction to Romanticism

Realism was an attempt to produce an accurate portrayal of real life without filtering it through personal feelings or Romantic idealism. Noting that liberal reforms and the revolutions of the nineteenth century had failed to bring about an era of justice, realist writers rejected the century's earlier Romantic emotionalism, seeing it as an ineffective tool for reforming—or even describing—industrial society.

Realism concerned itself with more than just the details of daily life, however. It also sought to explain why ordinary people behave the way they do. Realist novelists often relied on the emerging sciences of human and animal behavior—biology, psychology, and sociology—as well as on their own insights and observations. Realists could be divided into several different camps: Some emphasized social reform, others stressed scientific objectivity, and still others leaned toward social satire.

The values of realism, such as social satire and an unflinching factual observation of ordinary people's lives, still exert a powerful influence on literature and thought.

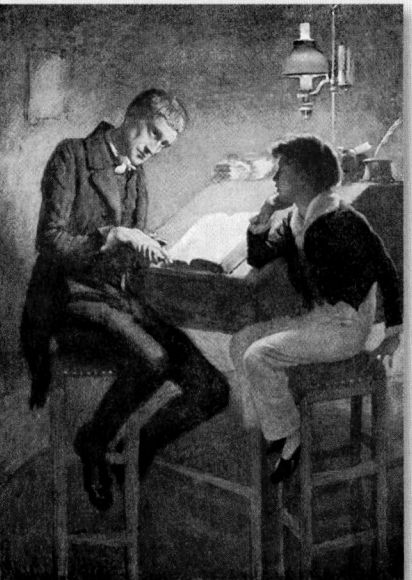

Uriah Heep and David Copperfield. Illustration by Harold Copping for "Character Sketches from Dickens," compiled ny B. W. Matz (1924).

France: Scientific Objectivity

French realists, led by novelist Gustave Flaubert, tried to make a science of their art by eliminating all sentimentality. They aimed simply to mirror life, without judgment or distortion. Nevertheless, a novel like Flaubert's *Madame Bovary* is admired today not so much for its objectivity as for its perfect prose and its satire of the middle class.

The Louth-London Royal Mail Traveling by Train from Petersborough East in December 1845 by James Pollard (1792–1867) Oil on canvas. Post conservation. Yale Center for British Art, Paul Mellon Collection, U.S.

Naturalism, a radical offshoot of realism, arose in the 1870s. Led by Emile Zola, naturalist writers considered free will an illusion and often portrayed their characters as helpless victims of heredity, fate, and circumstance. These writers tried to abolish the boundary between scientist and artist. Relying heavily on the growing scientific disciplines of psychology and sociology, they tried to dissect human behavior with as much objectivity as a scientist would dissect a frog or a cadaver. For naturalists, human life seemed a grim, losing battle against forces beyond the individual's control. The most talented naturalists, however, could not stay within the narrow ideology of their school. Guy de Maupassant (see page 1032), for example, is sometimes called a naturalist, but his work is sharpened by irony and by a gift for choosing the right details to illuminate.

Dickens: A Master at Work

In Victorian England, no one embodied realist principles more than Charles Dickens. A master storyteller, Dickens was able to combine calls for social reform with biting satire and comedy. The son of a debt-ridden clerk, Dickens lived out one of the favorite myths of the age. Through his own enormous talents and energy, he rose from poverty to become a wealthy and famous man. His success was made possible by increasing affluence and literacy, which gave him a large reading public, and by improved printing and distribution technology.

The conventional happy endings of Dickens's novels satisfied his readers', and probably his own, conviction that things usually work out well for decent people, but many of Dickens's most memorable scenes show decent people neglected, abused, and exploited. Children, especially, endure terrible suffering. The hungry Oliver Twist begs for more gruel in the workhouse; the handicapped Tiny Tim in *A Christmas Carol* cheerfully hobbles toward his possible early death; and young David Copperfield is abused by his stepfather, the cold, dark Mr. Murdstone.

Russia: Ultimate Questions

Realistic Russian novels began with those of Ivan Turgenev, whose ornate, lyrical prose brimmed with sympathy and warmth. Later Russian novelists, including Leo Tolstoy (see page 1008) and Fyodor Dostoevsky, wrote epic, sprawling novels filled with violence, love, and family crises, and populated with characters from a wide cross-section of society. The novels of these writers helped foster a powerful movement that called for the liberation of the serfs (peasants) and, later, the entire society. Yet the primary aim of Russian realists was not social reform, but a desire to answer the ultimate questions of human life. In different ways, Tolstoy and Dostoevsky repeatedly asked, "How should people live?" and "What are good and evil?"

Unlike these two giants, the playwright and short-story writer Anton Chekhov (see page 1022) worked on a much smaller scale. Chekhov found his subjects and themes in the common illusions and daily sufferings of unremarkable people. Like Tolstoy and Dostoevsky, however, Chekhov dealt with the meanings of life and death. His stories and plays are about people's attempts—usually frustrated—to find meaning and purpose in their lives.

Ask Yourself

1. Why did realists try to shed the sentimental ideas of Romantic idealism?
2. How did the struggle for social justice influence the rise of realism?
3. Why did Dickens choose to show children suffering?
4. What universal aspects of realism inspired writers around the world?

Learn It Online
Explore realism through *PowerNotes* online.

go.hrw.com   L12-962   **Go**

Analyzing Visuals

Analyzing a Photograph

As the rise of industry and science created a new, urban way of life, many writers and visual artists turned to realism, a movement that stressed the observation of the lives of ordinary people. The photograph on this page shows a scene from everyday life, without idealization or sentimentalism.

Guidelines

Use these guidelines to consider how this photograph reflects realism.

- How does the photograph's **setting** relate to concerns of realist writers?
- Realist writers used factual details to describe characters and situations. What details in the photograph help you understand the boy's daily life?
- How effective would this photograph have been for social reform? Explain.

1. What do you notice about the boy's clothing? What does this detail tell you about him?

2. Why do you think the photographer chose to show so much of the machine instead of focusing more on the boy?

Young boy working in a Lancashire cotton mill, c. 1880s.

3. What do you see on the floor? What can you infer from this evidence about working conditions?

Your Turn Analyze Realism

Choose another image in this collection, and write a short paragraph explaining how it conveys the themes and values of the realist movement.

Preparing to Read

Dover Beach

What Do **You Think?** How can appearance be different from reality?

QuickWrite

To what do people cling in times of crisis? In your *Reader/Writer Notebook*, write a short list of people, places, or things you value and depend on the most when times are tough.

MEET THE WRITER

Matthew Arnold
(1822–1888)

Unlike the other major Victorian poets, Matthew Arnold is as famous today for his essays of literary and social criticism as he is for his poetry.

An Uneven Start

In his youth Matthew Arnold had difficulty living up to the expectations of his famous father, Dr. Thomas Arnold, a leading thinker of the Victorian era and headmaster of Rugby School. Although his performance at his father's school was inconsistent, Arnold nevertheless won a scholarship to Oxford University in 1841. His performance at Oxford was a failure by Rugby standards, and he graduated without knowing what he wanted to do.

Arnold won prizes for his poetry at both Rugby and Oxford. In 1849, he published his first book of poetry, *The Strayed Reveller,* to mixed reviews. Two more volumes of poetry followed in 1852 and 1853; as a result, he was elected an Oxford professor of poetry in 1857.

Success Beyond Poetry

After his marriage in 1851, Arnold became a government inspector of schools for poor children, a job he held for thirty-five years. It became increasingly difficult for him to write poetry, and he told a friend, "My pen, it seems to me, is even stiffer and more cramped than my feelings."

After 1860, Arnold almost completely stopped writing poetry and began a separate career as a critic. His travels had given him firsthand knowledge of social problems, and he became an energetic essayist and lecturer on literary, political, social, and religious questions. In his essays, Arnold warns that without the steadying influence of culture, the nineteenth century's technological and political changes would create a grossly materialistic society. Throughout his life, Arnold knew both the excitement of trying to change the values of his age and the loneliness of not being comfortable in his own time.

Think About the Writer In what way has Arnold's warning about the influence of technology and political change come true? Explain.

Matthew Arnold (1880) by George Frederic Watts. Oil on canvas. National Portrait Gallery, London.

Reader/Writer Notebook

Use your **RWN** to complete the activities for this selection.

Literary Focus

Mood Arnold creates a mood that shifts at certain points in the poem like the ebb and flow of the tide he describes. **Mood** is the feeling, or emotional **atmosphere,** in a work created by the writer's choice of descriptive details, images, and sounds.

Literary Perspectives Apply the literary perspective described on page 966 as you read this poem.

Reading Focus

Visualizing Setting Writers like Arnold pack their writing with visual details to help you picture a particular place at a particular time. As you read, focus on descriptive words that give you a sense of the **setting**, the time and place of the events in the literary work. You may find it useful to pause every few lines and summarize the specific details of the setting. While details are often visual, the writer may appeal to other senses by indicating how the place sounds, smells, feels, or even tastes.

Into Action To visualize the setting of "Dover Beach," make an idea map like the one below. In the center circle, write the name of the place Arnold describes. Then, write each element of the setting outside the center, circle it, and draw a line connecting it to the center circle.

Writing Focus

Think as a Reader/Writer

Find It in Your Reading In your *Reader/Writer Notebook*, record words that you think help Arnold create a particular **mood**. Some of these words may be adjectives such as "calm" (line 1), but others may be nouns or verbs, like "Gleams" (line 4).

Vocabulary

blanched (blancht) *v.* used as *adj.*: made white or pale. *The pale light of the moon creates a blanched scene.*

tremulous (TREHM yuh luhs) *adj.*: quivering; wavering. *The tremulous waves beat back and forth.*

cadence (KAY duhns) *n.*: the beat of a repetitive motion; a sound that rises and falls. *The sea, which at first seemed calm, beats on the shore with a steady cadence.*

turbid (TUR bihd) *adj.*: cloudy; confused. *In the turbid waves, Sophocles sees a metaphor for human suffering.*

melancholy (MEHL uhn KAHL ee) *adj.*: sad or causing sadness. *The loss of faith leaves the speaker feeling melancholy.*

certitude (SUR tuh tood) *n.*: a feeling of sureness. *Changes in values and ideas leave the speaker without certitude.*

Language Coach

Latin and French Roots The word *blanched* comes from the French word *blanc,* meaning "white." Although English belongs to the same language family as German, Dutch, Norwegian, Danish, and Swedish, over time many words from Latin and French have come into the English language. Knowing the original meanings of some of these root words can help you understand English words that include them. Since both French and Spanish developed from Latin, knowing related Spanish words can also help you understand these roots.

Learn It Online

Meet this poem with an introductory video online.

go.hrw.com | L12-965 | Go

Dover Beach

by **Matthew Arnold**

Read with a Purpose
Read to understand the analogy Arnold makes between the physical setting that he describes and the crises of his time.

Build Background
Arnold wrote during a complex time, much like our own, when scientific discoveries threatened to undermine traditional beliefs. Political upheavals were also eroding social stability: In 1848, just three years before Arnold began writing this poem, several European countries were rocked by rebellions. Arnold believed that art should unify a culture, a function traditionally served by religion.

The sea is calm tonight.
The tide is full, the moon lies fair
Upon the straits°—on the French coast the light
Gleams and is gone; the cliffs of England stand,
5 Glimmering and vast, out in the tranquil bay. **A**
Come to the window, sweet is the night air!
Only, from the long line of spray
Where the sea meets the moon-blanched land,
Listen! you hear the grating roar
10 Of pebbles which the waves draw back, and fling,
At their return, up the high strand,°
Begin, and cease, and then again begin,
With tremulous cadence slow, and bring **B**
The eternal note of sadness in.

15 Sophocles° long ago
Heard it on the Aegean,° and it brought
Into his mind the turbid ebb and flow
Of human misery; we
Find also in the sound a thought,
20 Hearing it by this distant northern sea.

3. straits: Strait of Dover, a body of water separating southeastern England and northwestern France.

11. strand: shore.
15. Sophocles (SAHF uh kleez) (c. 496–406 B.C.): writer of tragedies in ancient Greece.
16. Aegean (ee JEE uhn): sea between Greece and Turkey.

A **Literary Focus** Mood What feelings are conveyed by the image of the sturdy cliffs standing above the calm sea?

B **Reading Focus** Visualizing Details What sounds and sights does Arnold draw attention to in lines 9–13?

Vocabulary **blanched** (blancht) *v.* used as *adj.*: made white or pale.
tremulous (TREHM yuh luhs) *adj.*: quivering; wavering.
cadence (KAY duhns) *n.*: the beat of a repetitive motion; a sound that rises and falls.
turbid (TUR bihd) *adj.*: cloudy; confused.

Literary Perspectives

Analyzing Historical Context Understanding the social climate of the mid-nineteenth century can help you appreciate the mood of alienation and uncertainty in "Dover Beach." Arnold began writing the poem in 1851, three years after revolutions in France, central Europe, the Italian peninsula, Poland, and Brazil. He did not publish the poem, however, for sixteen years. In the meantime, Charles Darwin explained his theory of evolution in *The Origin of Species by Means of Natural Selection*, published in 1859.

As you read, be sure to notice the questions in the text, which will guide you in using this perspective.

The Sea of Faith
Was once, too, at the full, and round earth's shore
Lay like the folds of a bright girdle° furled.
But now I only hear
25 Its melancholy, long, withdrawing roar,
Retreating, to the breath
Of the night wind, down the vast edges drear
And naked shingles° of the world. **C**

Ah, love, let us be true
30 To one another! for the world, which seems
To lie before us like a land of dreams,
So various, so beautiful, so new,
Hath really neither joy, nor love, nor light,
Nor certitude, nor peace, nor help for pain;
35 And we are here as on a darkling° plain
Swept with confused alarms of struggle and flight,
Where ignorant armies clash by night.

23. girdle: belt.

28. shingles: here, beaches covered with pebbles.

35. darkling: growing gloomy or dark.

C **Literary Perspectives** Analyzing Historical Context How does Arnold contrast the religious outlook of an earlier time with that of his own?

Vocabulary **melancholy** (MEHL uhn KAHL ee) *adj.:* sad or causing sadness.
certitude (SUR tuh tood) *n.:* a feeling of sureness.

Pegwell Bay, Kent—A Recollection of October 5, 1858 by William Dyce (1806–1864.) Tate Gallery, London.

967

Respond and Think Critically

Reading Focus

Quick Check

1. From where is the speaker viewing the scene (line 6)? To whom do you think he is speaking?

2. How would you paraphrase "the turbid ebb and flow / Of human misery" (lines 17–18)?

3. How does the image of "the folds of a bright girdle furled" convey a sense of safety and certainty?

Read with a Purpose

4. What analogy does Arnold make between the physical setting that he describes and the crises of his time?

Reading Skills: Visualizing Setting

5. Look back at the idea map that you drew as you read the poem. In each circle that describes an element of the setting, add words that describe it in greater detail.

Literary Focus

Literary Analysis

6. Interpret Explain the image of the "Sea of Faith" in lines 21–23.

7. Infer What do you think has happened to the speaker's faith, according to lines 24–28?

8. Summarize What does the speaker urge in the last stanza, and why?

9. Compare and Contrast What contrasting images can you find in the poem? How do these contrasts contribute to the poem's meaning?

10. Literary Perspectives You considered how Arnold responded to the scientific and political developments of his time. How does reading the poem in the context of the mid-nineteenth century affect the way you interpret it?

Literary Skills: Mood

11. Interpret How do the words "Only" (line 7) and "Listen!" (line 9) affect the mood of the opening?

12. Analyze Notice that Arnold often places commas in the middle of lines. How do these pauses contribute to the poem's mood?

13. Draw Conclusions Is the poem's mood the same throughout, or does it change? Support your answer with details from the text.

Literary Skills Review: Elegy

14. Extend An **elegy** is poem that mourns the death of a person or laments something lost. A type of lyric, an elegy is usually formal in language and structure and solemn or even melancholy in tone. In what ways is "Dover Beach" like an elegy? How is it different?

Writing Focus

Think as a Reader/Writer

Use It in Your Writing Review your response to the QuickWrite, and write a short essay about the particular person, place, or thing to which you turn in difficult times. Determine what kind of mood you want to set. How can you represent the anxiety of encountering difficulties and the relief of finding support?

What Do **You Think Now** How does Arnold see appearance as different from reality?

Vocabulary Development

✓ Vocabulary Check

Match the Vocabulary words with their definitions.

1. turbid   **a.** made white or pale
2. melancholy **b.** cloudy; confused
3. cadence   **c.** quivering; wavering
4. blanched   **d.** a feeling of sureness
5. tremulous **e.** sad or causing sadness
6. certitude   **f.** the beat of a repetitive motion; a sound that rises and falls

Vocabulary Skills: Figurative Language

If poets used language only in its most literal sense, there would not be much to poetry! Writers generate extra meaning by using words in surprising ways.

Figurative language involves bringing together seemingly unlike things, often to express a subtle or abstract meaning. Common figurative uses of language include **metaphor** and **personification**.

The dominant metaphor in "Dover Beach," for example, is the "Sea of Faith." Matthew Arnold joins the concrete noun *sea* to a very abstract one, *faith,* to conjure up the image of a time when religious belief was like an all-encompassing ocean that surrounded the world. That figurative use of language paves the way for others: If faith was once (figuratively) a sea, it now has withdrawn from the world like the withdrawing tide. The following graphic organizer charts one figurative use of language from the poem.

Example	Literal Meaning	Figurative Meaning
the grating roar / Of pebbles which the waves draw back, and fling (lines 9-10)	People usually fling objects.	The waves are personified as if they intended to fling the pebbles.

Your Turn

For each of the following uses of figurative language, complete a graphic organizer like the one on this page. Identify both the literal meaning of the boldfaced expression and its figurative use.

1. "[The waves] Begin, and cease, and then again begin, / With tremulous cadence slow, and bring / The eternal **note** of sadness in" (lines 12–15)
2. "the turbid **ebb and flow** / Of human misery" (lines 17–18)
3. "And we are here as on a **darkling plain**" (line 35)

Language Coach

Latin and French Roots Below are two Latin roots, along with related words in Spanish. Choose the Vocabulary word that is derived from each root.

Latin *certus,* "sure," related to Spanish *cierto*

Latin *cadere,* "fall," related to Spanish *cadencia*

Use a dictionary to help you find meanings for other words with Latin and French roots. You will find this information in the **etymology,** or word history, which is usually enclosed in brackets.

Academic Vocabulary

Talk About
With a partner, discuss a complex issue that causes anxiety for our time. How might we respond to the problem in a way that could benefit society?

Dover Beach

Grammar Link

Sentence Structure

As you have already learned, there are four types of sentence structures: A **simple sentence** contains one independent clause and no subordinate clauses (Matthew Arnold was a poet and critic.); a **compound sentence** contains more than one independent clause and no subordinate clauses (Matthew Arnold was a poet, and he also was a critic.); a **complex sentence** contains one independent clause and at least one subordinate clause (After he almost completely stopped writing poetry, he began a career as a critic.); and a **compound-complex sentence** contains more than one independent clause and at least one subordinate clause (When he was about forty, he began a career as a critic, but he still wrote some poetry.)

Notice that the **coordinating conjunctions** *and* and *but* are used above to join independent clauses to form compound sentences. Other compound conjunctions include *or, yet, or, nor, for,* and *so.*

The **subordinating conjunctions** *after* and *when* are used above in the subordinate clauses of complex and compound-complex sentences. Other common subordinating conjunctions are *as, before, since, until, while, because, although,* and *if.*

Your Turn

Combine the following sentences as directed.

1. The world has changed. The speaker is in doubt. (*compound*)
2. Faith is not as strong. He turns to love. (*complex*)
3. The speaker offers this hope. He still sees the world as a dark place. The poem ends on a melancholy note. (*compound-complex*)

Writing Application Choose a piece of your own writing, and revise it to add a variety of sentence structures.

CHOICES

As you respond to the Choices, use these **Academic Vocabulary** words as appropriate: benefit, complex, publish, respond, statistics.

REVIEW
Track the Mood of a Poem

The mood of "Dover Beach" pivots between contentment and anxiety, hope and despair. Re-read the poem, and identify places where the mood shifts between these extremes. Rank each section on a scale of 1 to 5, where 1 equals "very doubtful" and 5 equals "very hopeful." Then, represent the shifting emotions of the poem visually as a graph by plotting the changing values according to the lines that express each mood.

CONNECT
Examine Current Events

Timed ⏱ **Writing** Arnold wrote his poem in response to the scientific and political developments of his day. Think of an event or development in the world that causes you to feel concerned or worried and another event or development that gives you hope. Write an essay explaining the event or development and your reaction to it. Be sure to use specific details in your response.

EXTEND
Write a Poetic Sequel

The speaker of "Dover Beach" presents his thoughts to his beloved as she stands by him looking out the window at the ocean scene. Write a poem that expresses her answer to him. She may agree with the speaker and share his pessimistic mood. For an example of a response to a previously written poem, compare "The Passionate Shepherd to His Love" (page 278) and "The Nymph's Reply to the Shepherd" (page 279).

Reading Focus

The Darkling Thrush / Ah, Are You Digging on My Grave?

Making Generalizations by Kylene Beers

When you generalize, you extend the meaning of one situation to other situations or express something in general terms on the basis of specifics. For instance, after reading about several specific battles in a war, you could generalize that the cost of war, both in human terms and in economic terms, is always high.

Making generalizations from the experiences we have each day is a natural process. If the road you take to school on Monday and Tuesday is congested with traffic, making you late, you will probably conclude that it often will be congested on weekdays and that you should take another route or leave home earlier to get to school on time.

When we make generalizations about literature, we use much the same process. Instead of using clues from our environment, we use evidence from the text —language and structure—and background knowledge to help us draw conclusions about the author's purpose and theme. We combine this information with our own experience to support generalizations we then make to relate literature to universal themes and our own lives.

We can use Thomas Hardy's poem "The Darkling Thrush" to practice making generalizations.

The speaker in the poem describes winter with dismal, ghost-like images:

> When Frost was specter-gray,
> And Winter's dregs make desolate
> The weakening eye of the day

The poet compares the barren, frozen landscape to the "Century's corpse" and uses language that extends the metaphor: "crypt" and "death-lament." The poem's speaker then makes his own generalization from the clues to conclude:

> And every spirit upon earth
> Seemed fervorless as I.

Knowing that Hardy wrote the poem on December 31, 1900, the last day of the nineteenth century, allows us to observe that the poem implies a general depression among the people as they face a new century. The tone in the first half of the poem is as desolate as the landscape.

Structure also helps us make generalizations about purpose and theme. The second half of the poem shifts from winter to focus on "an aged thrush" that provides a "full-hearted evensong."

Your Turn

Read the last stanza of "The Darkling Thrush" to practice making generalizations about the purpose and theme.

> So little cause for carolings
>   Of such ecstatic sound
> Was written on terrestrial things
>   Afar or nigh around,
> That I could think there trembled through
>   His happy good-night air
> Some blessed Hope, whereof he knew
>   And I was unaware.

One caveat: We risk making invalid generalizations if we use faulty reasoning or inadequate information. Be sure to use sufficient and relevant information in your generalizations and to note exceptions.

1. How does the language in this last stanza differ from that of the first two stanzas? What images suggest a change in Hardy's tone?
2. How does the structure and language help us generalize about the way the poem's speaker and others will actually greet the new century?

The Darkling Thrush

Ah, Are You Digging on My Grave?

What Do You Think

How can appearance be different from reality?

⏱ QuickWrite

How can events change your mood? What might make you feel more optimistic or pessimistic about a situation? In your *Reader/Writer Notebook*, record a few memories about times when your mood changed unexpectedly. What caused each change?

Thomas Hardy
(1840–1928)

One of Victorian Britain's principal novelists, Hardy began and ended his literary career as a poet.

From Village to City and Back Again

Thomas Hardy was born in a small village in Dorsetshire, an area in southwestern England, which was the setting (under the ancient name of Wessex) of many of his novels and poems. He attended the village school until he was sixteen, when he was apprenticed to an architect.

In 1862, Hardy began working as an architect in London, writing poems and stories in his free time. He tried without success to <u>publish</u> his poems, but by the time he returned to Dorset in 1867, he had started to <u>publish</u> fiction. After the <u>publication</u> of his fourth novel, *Far from the Madding Crowd* (1874), Hardy was able to stop working as an architect and devote himself entirely to writing.

A Dark Vision of the World

The plots and themes of Hardy's fourteen novels express his belief in a world governed by chance and natural laws that are indifferent to what humans want and deserve. In some novels, the entire course of a character's life is determined by coincidence. People make matters worse by adding the misery of war, the cruelty of ingratitude and neglect, and the irrationality of laws and customs that frustrate talent and desire.

The bleakness, pessimism, and irony of Hardy's novels disturbed many readers. After *Tess of the D'Urbervilles* received unfavorable reviews in 1892, and *Jude the Obscure* was denounced in 1895, Hardy turned away from writing novels.

Hardy <u>published</u> *Wessex Poems* in 1898, when he was in his late fifties. The tone and style of his poems reveal a late-Victorian mood of somberness, with language that has an informal directness. He frequently uses archaic words or homely diction as a reaction against the elaborate language of some late-Victorian verse. Hardy's verse, though deceptively simple, resounds with the voice of twentieth-century poetry.

Think About the Writer — Why might it seem ironic that Hardy said he believed that humans can change for the better?

Thomas Hardy (1840–1928) by Reginald Grenville Eves (1876–1941). Oil on canvas. Towner Art Gallery, Eastbourne, East Sussex, England.

The Darkling Thrush
Ah, Are You Digging on My Grave?

Reader/Writer
Notebook

Use your **RWN** to complete the activities for this selection.

Literary Focus

Speaker You might think of every poem as talking to readers with its own unique voice. The **speaker** is the imaginary voice assumed by the author of a poem. In many poems, the speaker is close to the author, reflecting his or her personality and thoughts. You should not, however, assume that the speaker of the poem is the same as the author. Poets may shift the persona for each poem they write. The speaker of one poem might be a passionate lover; another speaker may be an isolated loner.

Reading Focus

Making Generalizations From textual clues, we can make **generalizations**, or broad assertions. The more evidence we have, the more accurate our generalization is likely to be. Limited evidence often leads to weak generalizations. For example, if you read three lines from Hardy and determine that he is a pessimist, you have generalized too quickly and with too little evidence. If you read two poems and determine that Hardy sometimes uses elements of nature to represent various moods, you have made a generalization from a larger amount of evidence. You must then prove the accuracy of your generalization by returning to the texts.

Into Action As you read the poems, take notes on the following topics.

Topic	Ah, Are You Digging	The Darkling Thrush
Death		
Winter		

Writing Focus

Think as a Reader/Writer

Find It in Your Reading Hardy chooses adjectives to create vivid images. As you read these poems, make a list in your *Reader/Writer Notebook* of adjectives that effectively create vivid mental images.

TechFocus As you read the poems, think about how the speaker of each poem might identify him- or herself on a social networking website.

Vocabulary

desolate (DEHS uh liht) *adj.*: uninhabited; barren; dreary. *The desolate landscape includes just one frail tree and nothing else.*

ecstatic (ehk STAT ihk) *adj.*: extremely joyful; showing great pleasure. *Seeing even one ray of sunshine would make me ecstatic on this gloomy, rainy day.*

prodding (PRAHD ihng) *v.*: poking; jabbing. *Someone is prodding in the dirt, looking for something lost there.*

fidelity (fy DEHL uh tee) *n.*: loyalty; faithfulness. *Dogs show their fidelity by protecting and guarding their owners.*

Language Coach

Double Letters The verb *prod* has one syllable, a short vowel sound, and ends with a single consonant. When you add *–ing* to this verb, you double the *d* and spell *prodding*. What other verbs can you think of that follow this double-letter rule?

Learn It Online
Listen to these poems online.

go.hrw.com | L12-973 | **Go**

POEM

The Darkling Thrush

by **Thomas Hardy**

Read with a Purpose
Read to discover how a small sign can lead to a surprising change of mood.

Build Background
"The Darkling Thrush" was written on December 31, 1900, the last day of the nineteenth century. As night falls, the speaker in the poem hears a thrush (a bird) singing joyfully. His thrush, like the century, is worn out and diminished—but still singing.

I leant upon a coppice° gate
    When Frost was specter-gray,
And Winter's dregs made desolate
    The weakening eye of day.
5 The tangled bine-stems° scored the sky
    Like strings of broken lyres,
And all mankind that haunted nigh
    Had sought their household fires. **Ⓐ**

The land's sharp features seemed to be
10   The Century's corpse outleant,°
His crypt the cloudy canopy,
    The wind his death-lament.
The ancient pulse of germ° and birth
    Was shrunken hard and dry,
15 And every spirit upon earth
    Seemed fervorless as I. **Ⓑ**

At once a voice arose among
    The bleak twigs overhead
In a fullhearted evensong
20   Of joy illimited;
An aged thrush, frail, gaunt, and small,
    In blast-beruffled plume,
Had chosen thus to fling his soul
    Upon the growing gloom.

25 So little cause for carolings
    Of such ecstatic sound
Was written on terrestrial things
    Afar or nigh around,
That I could think there trembled through
30   His happy good-night air
Some blessed Hope, whereof he knew
    And I was unaware.

1. coppice: thicket of small trees or shrubs.

5. bine-stems: climbing plants.

10. outleant: leaning out. Here, the word refers to leaning out of the crypt.
13. germ: seed or bud.

Ⓐ Literary Focus Speaker What image do you have of the speaker after reading the first stanza?

Ⓑ Reading Focus Making Generalizations What generalization can you make about why the speaker lacks energy?

Vocabulary **desolate** (DEHS uh liht) *adj.:* uninhabited; barren; dreary.
ecstatic (ehk STAT ihk) *adj.:* extremely joyful; showing great pleasure.

Ah, Are You Digging on My Grave?

by **Thomas Hardy**

Read with a Purpose
Read to discover the identity of an unusual speaker—and the surprising answer to her mysterious question.

Build Background
"Ah, Are You Digging on My Grave?" is written in the form of a dialogue. The poem's speaker has only limited information about her situation—and she therefore receives some very unexpected answers to her repeated questions.

"Ah, are you digging on my grave,
    My loved one?—planting rue?"° **Ⓐ**
—"No: Yesterday he went to wed
One of the brightest wealth has bred.
5 'It cannot hurt her now,' he said,
    'That I should not be true.'"

"Then who is digging on my grave?
    My nearest dearest kin?"
—"Ah, no: They sit and think, 'What use!
10 What good will planting flowers produce?
No tendance of her mound can loose
    Her spirit from Death's gin.'"°

"But some one digs upon my grave?
    My enemy?—prodding sly?"
15 —"Nay: When she heard you had passed the Gate
That shuts on all flesh soon or late,
She thought you no more worth her hate,
    And cares not where you lie." **Ⓑ**

"Then, who is digging on my grave?
20   Say—since I have not guessed!"
—"O it is I, my mistress dear,
Your little dog, who still lives near,
And much I hope my movements here
    Have not disturbed your rest?"

25 "Ah, yes! *You* dig upon my grave . . .
    Why flashed it not on me
That one true heart was left behind!
What feeling do we ever find
To equal among human kind
30   A dog's fidelity!"

"Mistress, I dug upon your grave
    To bury a bone, in case
I should be hungry near this spot
When passing on my daily trot.
35 I am sorry, but I quite forgot
    It was your resting place." **Ⓒ**

---

 2. rue: yellow-flowered herb associated with grief.
12. gin: trap.

Ⓐ Literary Focus Speaker Who is the speaker and what is her situation?

Ⓑ Reading Focus Making Generalizations What can you generalize from this stanza about how we feel about people after they die?

Ⓒ Literary Focus Speaker Who speaks in the poem's final lines? How might the speaker of the poem <u>respond</u> to these lines?

Vocabulary **prodding** (PRAHD ihng) *v.*: poking; jabbing.
fidelity (fy DEHL uh tee) *n.*: loyalty; faithfulness.

Give a Dog a Bone (1888) by William Henry
Hamilton Trood (1860–1899).

Viewing and Interpreting Does this image illustrate "a dog's fidelity" toward humans, or something else? Explain.

The Darkling Thrush / Ah, Are You Digging on My Grave?

Respond and Think Critically

Reading Focus

Quick Check

1. At what time of day and year does "The Darkling Thrush" take place?

2. What noise disturbs the speaker's train of thought, and how does he <u>respond</u> to it?

3. The speaker of "Ah, Are You Digging on My Grave?" suspects three people of disturbing her peace. Who are they?

Read with a Purpose

4. How does the speaker of each poem receive a surprise? What change does each surprise create?

Reading Skills: Making Generalizations

5. Review the notes you made while reading the two poems. Think about the broad generalizations you can make about Thomas Hardy's poetry. Write two statements that make valid generalizations that can be supported with the evidence in your notes. Choose two of the following sentence stems to help you write the statements. Be ready to support your generalizations with evidence from the poems.

   Hardy asserts that _____
   _____.

   Hardy demonstrates that _____
   _____.

   Hardy is optimistic/pessimistic (choose one)
   because _____
   _____.

Literary Focus

Literary Analysis

6. **Draw Conclusions** Does the speaker's **mood,** or emotion, change significantly in the course of "The Darkling Thrush"? If so, how?

7. **Interpret** What do you think is the significance of the word *darkling* in the title? Do you think the thrush's song seems hopeful or hopeless?

8. **Analyze** How does the character of the dog combine animal traits with human qualities?

Literary Skills: Speaker

9. **Compare and Contrast** How are the speakers of these two poems different? Which speaker do you associate more closely with Hardy? Why?

Literary Skills Review: Tone

10. **Analyze** How would you describe the **tone,** or attitude toward the subject, of each poem? How do you think Hardy feels about sentimental attitudes toward nature and death?

Writing Focus

Think as a Reader/Writer

Use It in Your Writing In your *Reader/Writer Notebook,* write a brief description of a person, place, or thing that you think creates a strong emotion or mood. Follow Hardy's model, and use precise, vivid adjectives to sharpen your description.

 What Do **You Think Now** Which speaker grows more pessimistic as the poem continues? Which speaker's mood improves? Why?

Vocabulary Development

✓ Vocabulary Check

Complete each item. Use the boldfaced Vocabulary word in your response.

1. List three reasons for **prodding** the ground.
2. Describe a **desolate** setting for a movie.
3. Identify one sign of a pet's **fidelity** to its owner.
4. Describe what makes you feel **ecstatic**.

Vocabulary Skills: Synonyms

Synonyms are words with the same or similar meanings. If you replace a word in a sentence and the meaning of the sentence does not change significantly, the words are synonyms:

Original: Show your **fidelity** to our team by coming to the game on Saturday.

Replacements: Show your **trust** to our team by coming to the game on Saturday. Show your **loyalty** to our team by coming to the game on Saturday.

The word *trust* changes the meaning of the sentence, so *fidelity* and *trust* are not synonyms. The word *loyalty* does not greatly change the meaning of the sentence, so *fidelity* and *loyalty* are synonyms.

Your Turn

Write sentences to test whether or not each pair of words are synonyms. Explain your answers.

1. desolate; deserted
2. desolate; shadowy
3. ecstatic; energetic
4. ecstatic; thrilled

Language Coach

Double Letters Recall that when you add *–ing* to the verb *prod*, you double the *d* and spell *prodding*. What other verbs in "Ah, Are You Digging on My Grave?" follow this pattern?

CHOICES

As you respond to the Choices, use these **Academic Vocabulary** words as appropriate: benefit, complex, publish, respond, statistics.

REVIEW
Retell What Happens
Review the key events in each poem by writing a short summary of what happens. For each poem, create a chart to record the basic information to include in your retellings. In one column include the language of the poem, and then write your own retelling in a second column.

CONNECT
Create a Social Networking Page
TechFocus Choose one of these poems and create a page as if on a social networking site for the poem's speaker. Use clues in the poem to identify the speaker's character and possible interests. Based on the poem, what kind of person is the speaker? How would he or she want to be presented to the world? Share your completed page with your class.

EXTEND
Draft a Response
Timed Writing The speaker in "The Darkling Thrush" seems to feel little hope that the problems of the world can be solved. Do you agree or disagree? Are there problems in today's society that you think are so complex and overwhelming that they will never go away? Write an essay in which you respond to Hardy's position.

Learn It Online
Develop your vocabulary with Word Watch online.

go.hrw.com   L12-979   Go

To an Athlete Dying Young

When I Was One-and-Twenty

A. E. Housman
(1859–1936)

A. E. Housman said that he was careful not to think of poetry while he was shaving, for "if a line of poetry strays into my memory, my skin bristles so that the razor ceases to act."

Finding Poetry in Self-Control

For Alfred Edward Housman, poetry was all feeling. He said the source of his poetry was "the pit of the stomach," but his poetry is more restrained than this comment suggests. His poems evoke a narrow range of subdued feelings that are controlled by simple, tight verse forms and clear language and syntax.

During his lifetime, Housman <u>published</u> only two books of poetry. His first collection, *A Shropshire Lad* (1896), became popular because its graceful recollection of youthful pleasures and their transience fit a late-century mood of disillusionment that had "much good, but much less good than ill." In "Terence, This Is Stupid Stuff," Housman acknowledged that his poems could be dismissed as self-indulgent whining. The test of poetry, he believed, is not what is said but how it is said. In the refined elegance of his poems, he expressed his pessimistic vision of a cold, empty world.

Overcoming Early Failure

Born in Worcestershire in western England, Housman was close to his mother, who died on his twelfth birthday. His father, a lawyer, allowed his practice to dwindle away. At sixteen, Housman won a scholarship to Oxford, where he studied classical literature. He attended classes irregularly, though, preferring to study on his own, and failed his final examination.

In 1882, Housman took a job as a clerk in the patent office, but remained determined to prove himself as a classical scholar. For the next ten years, he set for himself a rigorous program and <u>published</u> several papers on Greek and Latin literature. In 1892, he won an appointment as professor of Latin at London University. He stayed until 1911, when he moved to Cambridge University. He spent the rest of his life as a formal and rather aloof teacher and authority in classical scholarship.

What Do You Think? How can appearance be different from reality?

QuickWrite

What are some of the familiar ideas that people have about love and death? Brainstorm a list of images and ideas people commonly associate with each topic. Which of these ideas do you think are sometimes—or always—false?

Think About the Writer How might Housman's careers as a clerk and a scholar have influenced his poetry?

Alfred Edward Housman, English scholar and poet, when he was aged eighteen.

To an Athlete Dying Young

Reader/Writer
Notebook

Use your **RWN** to complete the activities for this selection.

Literary Focus

Couplet "To an Athlete Dying Young" is written entirely in couplets. A **couplet** is a pair of lines, one after another, that rhyme. The lines in a couplet usually share the same meter as well. In Housman's poem, each couplet is joined with another to form a four-line stanza. The strong rhythm created by this pattern fits the poem's somber subject matter—death—and mimics the slow, mournful tempo of a funeral procession.

Reading Focus

Analyzing the Relationship of Form and Meaning The form of a poem is the way it is structured. Most poems arrange ideas in lines and stanzas, and many poems use meter. In "To an Athlete Dying Young," Housman's form is two-line couplets paired in four-line stanzas. Each line has four stresses. Thinking about form as you read will help you understand the **meaning** the writer wants to communicate through poetry. Ask yourself: Why did the poet choose this form rather than another? How does this form support the meaning of the poem?

Into Action Use a chart like the one below to paraphrase each stanza as you read. Paying attention to the meaning of each stanza will help you understand how the poet structures ideas.

Stanza	Paraphrase
1	When you won the race, we carried you through town, celebrating your victory.
2	Today we're once again carrying you on our shoulders, but it's a much quieter occasion.
3	

Vocabulary

withers (WIHTH uhrz) v.: fades; dries up. *After it blooms, the rose soon withers and dies.*

renown (rih NOWN) n.: fame; celebrity. *He was an athlete of such great renown that everyone referred to him by his first name alone.*

Language Coach

Pronunciation Remember that poets choose words for both their meaning and their sound. Take time to learn how to pronounce unfamiliar words—it will help you hear what the poet wants you to hear. Notice that *renown* rhymes with *town*, not *own*. How does knowing how to pronounce *renown* help you appreciate "To an Athlete Dying Young"?

Writing Focus

Think as a Reader/Writer

Find It in Your Reading Housman was a master of **understatement**. He expressed deep emotions, but never exaggerated or embellished them. In his careful language, the world of the dead becomes simply "a stiller town." As you read, record in your *Reader/Writer Notebook* other examples of understatement that express strong feelings.

 Learn It Online
Take your study of this poem further with these project suggestions online.

go.hrw.com   L12-981   **Go**

To an Athlete Dying Young

by **A. E. Housman**

Read with a Purpose
Read to discover how one speaker views dying young.

Build Background
"To an Athlete Dying Young" appeared in 1896 in the first edition of *A Shropshire Lad*, a volume Housman himself paid to have <u>published</u>. The poet scarcely made a profit from this book of sixty-three verses, which often tell stories in the voice of a young soldier or farm boy. However, Housman lived to see his poems become enormously popular during the Boer War. Soldiers fighting in South Africa identified with the homesick lad from Shropshire and heard in his voice the echo of their own melancholy.

The time you won your town the race
We chaired you through the marketplace; **Ⓐ**
Man and boy stood cheering by,
And home we brought you shoulder-high.

5   Today, the road all runners come,
Shoulder-high we bring you home,
And set you at your threshold down,
Townsman of a stiller town.

Smart lad, to slip betimes° away
10 From fields where glory does not stay
And early though the laurel° grows
It withers quicker than the rose. **Ⓑ**

Eyes the shady night has shut
Cannot see the record cut,
15 And silence sounds no worse than cheers
After earth has stopped the ears:

Now you will not swell the rout
Of lads that wore their honors out,
Runners whom renown outran
20 And the name died before the man.

So set, before its echoes fade,
The fleet foot on the sill of shade, **Ⓒ**
And hold to the low lintel° up
The still-defended challenge cup.

25 And round that early-laureled head
Will flock to gaze the strengthless dead,
And find unwithered on its curls
The garland briefer than a girl's.

---

9. **betimes:** archaic for "early."
11. **laurel:** classical symbol of victory. Victorious Greek and Roman athletes were crowned with laurel wreaths.
23. **lintel:** top of a door frame.

Ⓐ Literary Focus **Couplet** Describe the rhythm of the poem's first couplet. Do the other couplets follow the same rhythm?

Ⓑ Reading Focus **Analyzing Form and Meaning** What idea does the speaker introduce in the third stanza?

Ⓒ Literary Focus **Couplet** How does the rhythm of line 22 differ from that of line 21? What effect does the poet create with this variation?

Vocabulary **withers** (WIHTH uhrz) *v.*: fades; dries up.
renown (rih NOWN) *n.*: fame; celebrity.

Viewing and Interpreting How does this image reflect the glory to which the poem's speaker refers?

Alem Techale of Ethiopia (far right) wins the World Youth title in the 1500 meter race in 2003. Techale collapsed and died during a routine training run in 2005, when she was 18.

Preparing to Read

When I Was One-and-Twenty

Reader/Writer Notebook

Use your **RWN** to complete the activities for this selection.

Literary Focus

Theme The **theme** of a poem is its central idea or insight about human experience. Most themes are implied rather than directly stated, so you need to piece together clues in order to understand the writer's message. Many themes give an insight or perspective on a topic, such as death, friendship, or family. However, keep in mind that a theme is not the same as a topic, which is simply a subject that can usually be expressed in a word or two. A theme is an idea or perspective about the topic.

Into Action You can use a chart like the one below to organize your thoughts about a poem's topics and themes. Here are examples of topics and their related themes.

Topic	Theme
death	It is better to die young than to face the miseries of aging.
education	You can learn more by doing something than by reading about it.

In the poem, "When I was One-and-Twenty," Housman presents a theme about the topic of love. As you read the poem, take notes about what the speaker experiences and learns about love. Then write a statement of the the poem's theme about love.

Writing Focus

Think as a Reader/Writer

Find It in Your Reading There are two **characters** in this poem: a wise man and the speaker. Notice how Housman uses the characters' words to reflect their personalities. Jot down examples that show how each character's words bring his personality to life.

TechFocus As you read this poem, think about how you might use technology to show that the theme of the poem is still relevant today. Think about fonts you might choose for the words or an illustration you could create to help new readers connect with the poem.

Language Coach

In Vain The word *vain* is often preceded by the preposition *in*, as in this sentence: "He gave his heart in vain because she did not return his love." Something that is done *in vain* is done unsuccessfully or without effect. When might a student have studied for a test in vain? Name three other actions that might be done in vain.

 Learn It Online
Explore more of Housman's poetry—and the inspirations behind it—with these Internet links.

go.hrw.com   L12-984   **Go**

When I Was One-and-Twenty

by **A. E. Housman**

Read with a Purpose

Read to discover how one year changes the speaker's view of life and love.

Build Background

Like "To an Athlete Dying Young," the poem "When I Was One-and-Twenty" is from *A Shropshire Lad.* Housman described the Shropshire lad as "an imaginary figure, with something of my own temper and view of life." This brief lyric is a good example of Housman's ability to compress much meaning into a few lines. The poem clearly shows Housman's characteristic directness, melodic beauty, simplicity of form, and meticulous expression of emotion.

When I was one-and-twenty
   I heard a wise man say,
"Give crowns and pounds and guineas°
   But not your heart away;
5 Give pearls away and rubies
   But keep your fancy free."
But I was one-and-twenty,
   No use to talk to me.

When I was one-and-twenty
10   I heard him say again,
"The heart out of the bosom
   Was never given in vain;
'Tis paid with sighs a plenty
   And sold for endless rue."° **Ⓐ**
15 And I am two-and-twenty,
   And oh, 'tis true, 'tis true.

---

3. crowns and pounds and guineas: units of money in Great Britain.
14. rue: sorrow; regret.

Ⓐ **Literary Focus** **Theme** What idea about love does the wise man express in his advice?

Vocabulary **fancy** (FAN see) *n.:* a liking for something or someone.
vain (vayn) *adj.:* of no use; producing no good result.

985

Applying Your Skills

To an Athlete Dying Young / When I Was One-and-Twenty

Respond and Think Critically

Reading Focus

Read with a Purpose

1. How does the speaker in each poem present a view that you might not expect?

Reading Skills: Analyzing the Relationship of Form and Meaning

2. Review the chart you made for "To an Athlete Dying Young," and add a column to note and analyze the meaning of each stanza. Identify each central image or idea. These key ideas will help you understand how Housman arranges his poem to convey his ideas.

Stanza	Paraphrase	Meaning/Analysis
1	When you won the race, we carried you through town, celebrating your victory.	Image of the athlete in the past, at the height of his glory.
2	Today we're once again carrying you on our shoulders, but it's a much quieter occasion.	Image of the athlete, now dead, being carried to his grave. Parallel shows contrast.
3		

Literary Focus

Literary Analysis

3. **Compare and Contrast** What parallel events are described in the first and second stanzas of "To an Athlete Dying Young"?

4. **Draw Conclusions** What scene do you imagine when you read the last two stanzas of "To an Athlete Dying Young"?

5. **Identify** What is the effect of Housman's use of repetition in the last line of "When I was One-and-Twenty"? What other kinds of repetition do you find in the poem?

6. **Evaluate** How would you respond to the wise man's advice in "When I was One-and-Twenty"?

Literary Skills: Couplet / Theme

7. **Interpret** Poets can use **exact** rhyme *(tune/moon)* or **half rhyme** *(moon/man)*, also called approximate rhyme. Look at the end rhymes in "To an Athlete Dying Young." What pattern of rhyming sounds do you hear?

8. **Analyze** What do you think is the theme, or message, of "When I Was One-and-Twenty"?

Literary Skills Review: Alliteration and Assonance

9. **Evaluate** Housman creates verbal music by using **alliteration**, the repetition of consonant sounds, and **assonance**, the repetition of vowel sounds. Where do you hear these sound patterns in "To an Athlete Dying Young"?

Writing Focus

Think as a Reader/Writer

Use It in Your Writing Apply Housman's uses of understatement and of characterization as you write your own description of a dramatic event you experienced or witnessed.

What Do You Think Now How do these poems present unconventional ideas about the reality of death and love?

Vocabulary Development

 Vocabulary Check

Match each Vocabulary word to its antonym.

1. fancy   **a.** obscurity
2. withers   **b.** successful
3. renown   **c.** dislike
4. vain   **d.** thrives

Vocabulary Skills: Analogies

An **analogy** shows a comparison between two pairs of words. Analogies are shown in this form:

sonnet : poem :: tragedy : drama

Here is one way to read this analogy: "*Sonnet* is related to *poem* in the same way that *tragedy* is related to *drama.*" In this analogy, a sonnet is a type of poem, and a tragedy is a type of drama.

Your Turn

Complete each analogy with a word from the box.

ages	anxious	courage	weakness

1. VAIN : INEFFECTIVE :: nervous : _____.
2. CELEBRITY : RENOWN :: hero : _____.
3. FLOWER : WITHERS :: person : _____.
4. FANCY : HATRED :: power : _____.

Language Coach

Pronunciation How does knowing how to pronounce words such as *renown* in poems affect your understanding of a poem's rhythm, rhyme, assonance, and alliteration?

CHOICES

As you respond to the Choices, use these **Academic Vocabulary** words as appropriate: benefit, complex, respond, publish, statistics.

REVIEW

Build a Topic Web

Reflect on how these poems explore the topics of love and death. Complete a web like the one below for each poem by adding details from each poem to support each category. Include your own responses to the form and theme.

CONNECT

Film Interviews

TechFocus In a small group, film a series of interviews with the speaker of this poem at age twenty-one, twenty-two, and an older age. Members of your group can act as the speaker or as friends describing him at various stages of his life. In each interview, encourage the speaker to explain his point of view on life and love.

EXTEND

Write an Essay

Timed └Writing Housman's poetry was popular with young soldiers fighting in the Boer War. In an expository essay, analyze the characteristics of Housman's poetry that might have appealed to young people in his time and those that would appeal to young people in our time. Use text evidence to support your analysis.

Learn It Online
Learn more at Word Watch.

go.hrw.com	L12-987	**Go**

Link to Today

When Elements Go Extreme

What Do You Think

How can appearance be different from reality?

QuickWrite

Suppose you see a varsity football team practicing on a hot and humid day. What assumptions might you make about the players? Which of your assumptions are mostly likely to be true? Which ones are probably unfounded?

Informational Text Focus

Analyzing Cause and Effect Many informational texts follow a cause-and-effect organization. The writer describes one event that leads to another. The first event is the cause of the second, which is its effect. The order can also be reversed: The writer first tells you what happened (effect) and then explains why (cause).

Into Action Use cause-and-effect charts as you read to understand the reasons behind key events and their impact on other events.

• If you want to know why an event was important, or how it influenced other events, write it in the Cause box. Then try to identify the effect of the event as you read.

• If you want to understand why something happened; write the event in the Effect box. Then, look for the cause as you read on.

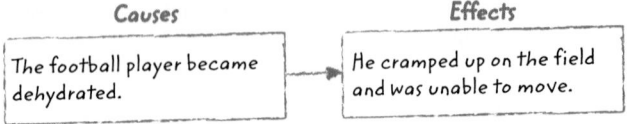

Causes

The football player became dehydrated.

Effects

He cramped up on the field and was unable to move.

Vocabulary

rendering (REHN duh rihng) *v.*: causing to be or become; making. *The extreme heat is rendering the team helpless.*

replenish (rih PLEHN ihsh) *v.*: to fill again; to renew. *When you exercise, it is important to replenish the water in your body.*

oppressive (uh PREHS ihv) *adj.*: hard to bear. *The football game was cancelled because the oppressive heat made play dangerous.*

precautions (prih KAW shuhnz) *n.*: care taken in advance; safeguards. *Stretching your muscles after you exercise is one of the precautions you can take to avoid injuries.*

supplement (SUHP luh muhnt) *n.*: something added to make complete or to enrich. *It is always wise to check with a doctor before you begin to take a dietary supplement.*

Writing Focus   Preparing for **Constructed Response**

Statistics are numerical data. Like many journalists, this writer uses statistics to support his statements. As you read, keep a list in your *Reader/Writer Notebook* of the statistics the writer presents and note why he includes each piece of information.

Language Coach

Prefixes Sometimes prefixes attach to word parts that are not words by themselves. The prefix *re–* means "again" and *replenish* means "fill again," but *plenish* on its own is not a word. Find words with the prefix *re–* in the selection. What do they mean? Can their parts stand alone?

Reader/Writer
Notebook

Use your **RWN** to complete the activities for this workshop.

Link to Today

This Link to Today looks at how hot weather can affect even the strongest athletes.

Read with a Purpose

Read this article to learn how athletes can keep playing safely when the temperature rises.

Build Background

Heatstroke is a sudden, uncontrolled increase in body temperature. It can occur when people are exposed to high temperature and humidity for several hours. A person suffering from heatstroke may feel dizzy, weak, nauseated, restless, or confused. If not treated promptly, heatstroke can lead to collapse and coma. Keeping track of outdoor temperature is one key to preventing heatstroke, but it's also important to consider the impact of the humidity. When humidity is high, the air feels hotter and the threat of heat-related illnesses such as heatstroke is greater. That's why many experts refer to the heat index (HI), which takes into account both air temperature and relative humidity. It measures how hot the air feels. An HI above 105°F is considered threatening.

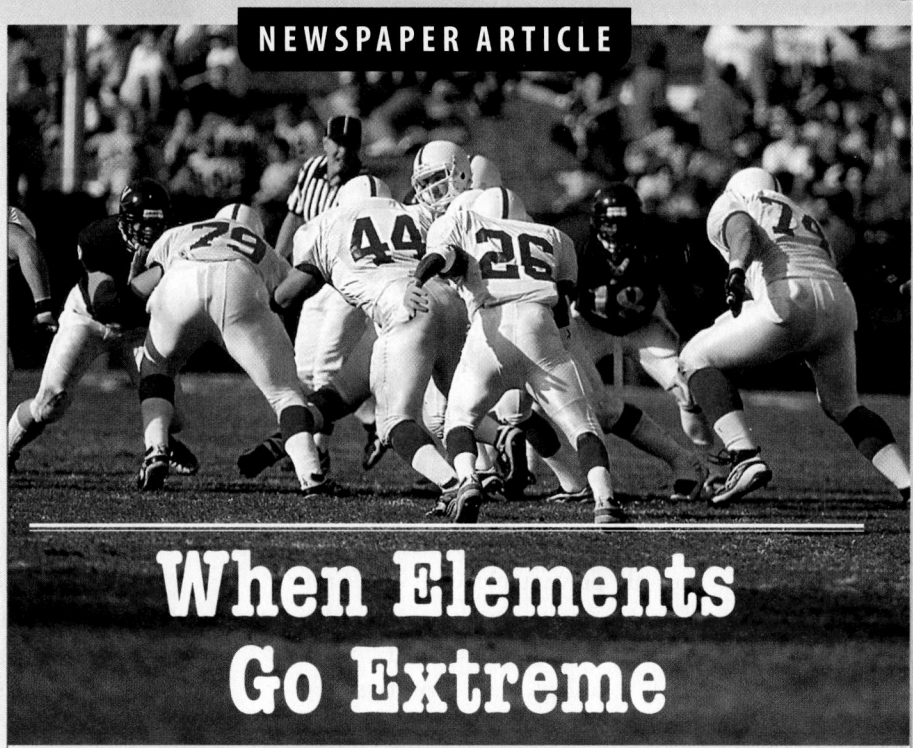

When Elements Go Extreme

by **Jason La Canfora**

Washington Post, Wednesday, August 2, 2006

Sometime during the Washington Redskins' first training camp practice in the summer of 2006, fullback Mike Sellers felt his lower body lock up. The cramps leveled him, rendering him suddenly unable to move. After being carted off the field, three intravenous treatments were required to replenish his system.

Sellers estimates he drank about a gallon of water that day, but even that was insufficient to fully hydrate him in the oppressive heat and humidity that is testing the will of Redskins players, coaches and fans. **A**

The next day Sellers was able to return for practices at Redskins Park, where the heat index reached 108 degrees, but the team's medical staff—not to mention his teammates—was watching him closely. Keeping players healthy and cool is serious business for trainers and coaches, and players are reminded frequently about the need to drink water and report any signs of discomfort, such as rapid breathing or weakness.

A **Informational Focus** Causes and Effects What cause does the second paragraph identify for the effects described in the first paragraph? Explain.

Vocabulary **rendering** (REHN duh rihng) *v.:* causing to be or become; making.
replenish (rih PLEHN ihsh) *v.:* to fill again; to renew.
oppressive (uh PREHS ihv) *adj.:* hard to bear.

In 2001, Minnesota Vikings offensive lineman Korey Stringer collapsed and died during training camp in Mankato, Minn., from complications of heatstroke. His collapse, which received intense media attention, came on a day when the heat index reached 109, and it reinforced the importance of safeguarding against dehydration and heatstroke for NFL teams. **(B)**

Although the number of deaths from heatstroke in professional, college, high school and youth football is not high, according to the University of North Carolina's National Center for Catastrophic Sport Injury Research, it says there is "no excuse for any number of heatstroke deaths since they are all preventable with the proper precautions."

The center reports that 26 football players—20 high school, 4 college, and 2 professional—have died from heat stroke over the last 10 years. Around the time of Mike Sellers's collapse, a 15-year-old high school player in suburban Atlanta died from heat stroke after collapsing one day earlier following an off-season workout.

Size can play a role, too. Korey Stringer's weight at the time of his death was 336 pounds, and, according to the Vikings' report on his death, the now-banned diet supplement ephedrine was found in his system. **(C)**

"I think it's always a concern for us," Redskins Coach Joe Gibbs said of the severe heat and humidity. "The reality is, you always start in the heat and you just do the best job you can. We're going to try to start as late [in the day] as you can and start as early as you can, and give them a rest in the middle of the day....

"But having said that, it's one of my biggest concerns and one of our concerns always, because you've got big guys there in the heat trying to be competitive and it's something you really have to watch."

Baltimore Ravens players cooling off on sidelines with water spray during training camp at McDaniel College.

"We've got a plan of weighing them in [before practice] and weighing them out, and we monitor their body weights and make sure they recover," said Bubba Tyer, the team's director of sports medicine. "And if they don't recover, we either pull them out of practice the next day or monitor them closely during practice. You see us working out there, and it's a job to work. We're icing them down and watering them down, and they get water every chance they can get."

After most practices, large tubs of freezing water are coveted spots for players, helping them quickly lower their body temperature. "The guys like it," Tyer said of the icy baths. "It's a mess of a deal, but it seems to work. It cools them off a little bit fairly quickly."

Salt tablets are available, if necessary, and "common sense" practices are best applied to all athletes training in these conditions, whether amateur or professional, Tyer said. He urges Redskins players to find a cool spot after practice, drink plenty of water and, after a brief rest, to begin moving around again to prevent cramping. It is also essential that they eat throughout the day and stay out of direct sunlight when possible, he said.

(B) Informational Focus Causes and Effects What was the cause of Mike Seller's collapse?

(C) Informational Focus Causes and Effects How did multiple causes lead to Korey Stringer's condition?

Vocabulary **precautions** (prih KAW shuhnz) *n.:* care taken in advance; safeguards.

supplement (SUHP luh muhnt) *n.:* something added to make complete or to enrich.

Informational Text
Applying Your Skills

SKILLS FOCUS Informational Skills
Analyze causes and effects. **Vocabulary
Skills** Demonstrate knowledge of literal
meanings of words and their usage.

Listening and Speaking Skills Conduct/
respond to an interview. **WritingSkills**
Write a brief constructed response, with
specific support.

When Elements Go Extreme

Respond and Think Critically

Informational Text Focus

Quick Check

1. How did Korey Stringer die? What factors contributed to his death?

2. How does Bubba Tyer help players avoid cramping after a practice?

Read with a Purpose

3. How can a coach help keep players safe when temperature and humidity rise to threatening levels?

Informational Skills: Analyzing Cause and Effect

4. As you review the cause-and-effect charts you made while reading, think again about why things happened. Many causes have more than one effect; many effects have more than one cause. Add boxes to your charts as needed to show multiple causes or effects. This chart shows two effects of one cause.

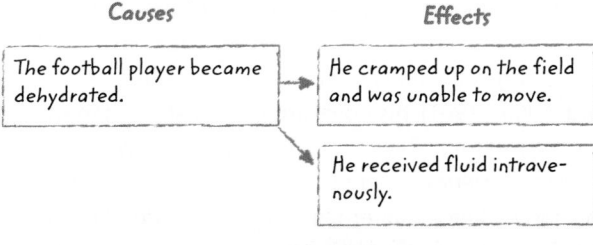

Causes

The football player became dehydrated.

Effects

He cramped up on the field and was unable to move.

He received fluid intravenously.

✓ Vocabulary Check

Match each Vocabulary word with its definition.

5. precautions   a. almost unbearable
6. supplements   b. causing to become
7. rendering   c. safeguards
8. replenish   d. additions
9. oppressive   e. renew

Text Analysis

10. **Interpret** Why do sports medicine experts at the University of North Carolina say that heatstroke deaths are "all preventable"?

11. **Infer** Why is it important to know the heat index, rather than just the temperature?

12. **Apply** What items would you put on a checklist to evaluate a team's preparations for extreme heat conditions? Explain.

Listening and Speaking

13. **Analyze** Using information from this article, conduct an interview with a classmate about the dangers of heatstroke and how to avoid them. Work with a partner to plan the questions. Decide who will be the interviewer and who will be the expert. When you present your interview, ask your audience to listen for inaccurate or incomplete answers.

Writing Focus   Constructed Response

Write a paragraph about how <u>statistics</u> in this article contribute to your understanding of heatstroke. Be sure to cite specific evidence to support your response.

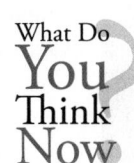

What Do You Think Now

Does this article support or challenge the assumptions you make about athletes in general, and about football players in particular.

Applying Your Skills   **991**

The Mark of the Beast

QuickWrite

Think about a time when you and a friend had different explanations for why something occurred. What caused the differences in opinion? Write down your ideas in a paragraph.

Joseph Rudyard Kipling (1899) by Sir Philip Burne-Jones. Oil on canvas. National Portrait Gallery, London.

MEET THE WRITER

Rudyard Kipling
(1865–1936)

Nobel Prize WINNER

Rudyard Kipling's popularity and public influence during his lifetime can be attributed in part to his endorsement of the British Empire. Yet his ideas about "empire" are controversial today.

Unhappy Youth and Early Success

Joseph Rudyard Kipling was born in Bombay, India, where his father was a professor at the University of Bombay. When Kipling was six years old, he and his sister were sent home to England for their education. Left in the care of foster parents, they lived in a type of boarding house, which Kipling would later refer to as "the house of desolation."

At seventeen, Kipling returned to India to work as a journalist. He quickly became popular for his stories, sketches, and poems that were <u>published</u> in newspapers and then collected in cheap editions sold at Indian railroad stations. His books were distributed in England as well, preparing the way for his return to England as a writer in 1889. By the end of Queen Victoria's reign, Kipling had become the most popular British poet since Tennyson and the most popular prose writer since Dickens. He was awarded the Nobel Prize in Literature in 1907.

Cultural Conflicts

Kipling's views about the British Empire were <u>complex</u>. He was fascinated by the conflicts between European civilization and ancient cultures. This conflict is the theme of many of his Indian works, beginning with *Plain Tales from the Hills* (1888) and continuing in *Kim* (1901), his novel about an Irish orphan submerged in the mystery of India. Kipling did not always see European culture as superior (though he nearly always presented it as such), and he knew that empires do fall. He urged readers not to trust in guns to justify their dominion over large parts of the earth. The purpose of the British Empire, he argued, was not to make the imperial nation rich, but rather to extend British efficiency, decency, and comfort throughout the world. Today, however, many readers view his argument as a rationalization of the often brutal practices of British imperialism.

Think About the Writer

What might Kipling have to say about the cultural conflicts in the world today?

Reader/Writer Notebook

Use your **RWN** to complete the activities for this selection.

Literary Focus

Conflict A **conflict** is a struggle or clash between opposing characters, forces, or emotions. When a conflict is **external,** a character or group struggles against an outside force, such as another character or group or a force of nature. When a conflict is **internal,** a struggle takes place within a character between opposing beliefs, responsibilities, desires, or emotions. As you read this story, be sure to note the conflict suggested by the proverb at the beginning of the story, and consider its thematic significance.

Reading Focus

Identifying Conflicts and Resolutions Stories are often built on a series of conflicts. To identify all the conflicts in a story, look for cause-and-effect relationships. Think about how one conflict leads to another conflict, and consider how external and internal conflicts are interrelated. Note, too, that the resolution of one conflict may lead to the resolution of another, but sometimes all the conflicts in a story are not resolved.

Into Action As you read, fill in a three-column chart. Write down the two sides of the conflict, and indicate whether each conflict is external or internal. Then, record how the conflict is—or is not—resolved.

Conflict	External or Internal?	Resolution
Providence & Church of England vs. gods and devils of Asia	external	

Writing Focus

Think as a Reader/Writer

Find It in Your Reading Like many horror stories, "The Mark of the Beast" starts normally enough, with three British civil servants drinking too much at a New Year's Eve party, but events gradually escalate to a horrible climax. As you read, record in your *Reader/Writer Notebook* the techniques Kipling uses to create **suspense** in the story.

TechFocus As you read, think about the similarities and differences between this story and horror movies you have seen. Consider the techniques Kipling and the filmmakers use to tell their stories.

Vocabulary

genial (JEEN yuhl) *adj.*: friendly. *The genial men celebrated New Year's Eve together.*

distraught (dihs TRAWT) *adj.*: extremely agitated. *The beast was distraught as it struggled to free itself from its bonds.*

redress (REE drehs) *n.*: payment or action that serves to remedy an injustice or injury. *By offering redress, Strickland tries to right a wrong committed by his friend.*

delusion (dih LOO zhuhn) *n.*: false belief. *The narrator tries to distinguish between truth and delusion.*

dispassionately (dihs PASH uh niht lee) *adv.*: without emotion; impartially. *Strickland spoke dispassionately to the doctor who was in a state of shock.*

Language Coach

Synonyms Words that have similar—but not necessarily the same—meanings are **synonyms**. They may have different shades of meaning or be used in different contexts. For example, note the difference between *genial* and *amiable,* two words that mean "friendly." *Amiable* indicates that a person is good-natured and likable, while *genial* suggests that a person is cheerful and sociable.

 Learn It Online
Learn more about Kipling and his world through these Internet links.

go.hrw.com   L12-993   Go

THE MARK OF THE BEAST

by **Rudyard Kipling**

Read with a Purpose
Read this story to explore the meaning of its title and the nature of evil.

Build Background
This story is set in colonial India during the late nineteenth century. As a member of the British ruling class, Kipling witnessed the conflicts that inevitably occur when two cultures are brought into contact by force. Although the battle lines between imperial Britain and colonial India seem clearly drawn in this story, the identity of the victor (if there is one) is less obvious.

The title of the story is an **allusion**, or reference, to the final book of the New Testament, the Book of Revelation. According to chapter 13, great evil will take over the world at some point in the future. A many-headed monster called "The Beast" will rule, and the beast's followers will be branded with its mark.

> "Your Gods and my Gods—do you or I know which are the stronger?"
>
> —*Indian Proverb*

East of Suez, some hold, the direct control of Providence ceases; Man being there handed over to the power of the Gods and Devils of Asia, and the Church of England Providence only exercising an occasional and modified supervision in the case of Englishmen.

This theory accounts for some of the more unnecessary horrors of life in India; it may be stretched to explain my story.

My friend Strickland of the Police, who knows as much of natives of India as is good for any man, can bear witness to the facts of the case. Dumoise, our doctor, also saw what Strickland and I saw. The inference which he drew from the evidence was entirely incorrect. He is dead now; he died in a rather curious manner, which has been elsewhere described.

When Fleete came to India he owned a little money and some land in the Himalayas, near a place called Dharmsala. Both properties had been left him by an uncle, and he came out to finance them. He was a big, heavy, genial, and inoffensive man. His knowledge of natives was, of course, limited, and he complained of the difficulties of the language. **Ⓐ**

He rode in from his place in the hills to spend New Year in the station, and he stayed with Strickland. On New Year's Eve there was a big dinner at the club, and the night was excusably wet.[1] When men foregather from the uttermost ends of the Empire they have a right to be riotous. The Frontier had sent down a contingent o' Catch-'em-Alive-O's[2] who had not seen twenty white faces for a year, and were used to ride fifteen miles to dinner at the

---

1. **the night was excusably wet:** In other words, the men drank a lot.
2. **Catch-'em-Alive-O's:** men who were forced into service as soldiers.

Ⓐ Literary Focus Conflict What might Fleete's lack of knowledge concerning the Indian people and his complaints about their language suggest about his attitude toward the Indian culture? What kinds of conflicts might result from this attitude?

Vocabulary **genial** (JEEN yuhl) *adj.*: friendly.

next Fort at the risk of a Khyberee[3] bullet where their drinks should lie. They profited by their new security, for they tried to play pool with a curled-up hedgehog found in the garden, and one of them carried the marker round the room in his teeth. Half a dozen planters had come in from the south and were talking "horse" to the Biggest Liar in Asia, who was trying to cap all their stories at once. Everybody was there, and there was a general closing up of ranks and taking stock of our losses in dead or disabled that had fallen during the past year. It was a very wet night, and I remember that we sang "Auld Lang Syne" with our feet in the Polo Championship Cup, and our heads among the stars, and swore that we were all dear friends. Then some of us went away and annexed Burma, and some tried to open up the Sudan and were opened up by Fuzzies[4] in that cruel scrub outside Suakim,[5] and some found stars and medals, and some were married, which was bad, and some did other things which were worse, and the others of us stayed in our chains and strove to make money on insufficient experiences.

Analyzing Visuals

Viewing and Interpreting The narrator of the story describes Hanuman as "a leading divinity worthy of respect." How does this statue convey a sense of respect and reference?

Hanuman statue at Durgiana Temple, Amritsar, Punjab, India.

Fleete began the night with sherry and bitters, drank champagne steadily up to dessert, then raw, rasping Capri with all the strength of whiskey, took benedictine with his coffee, four or five whiskeys and sodas to improve his pool strokes, beer and bones[6] at half-past two, winding up with old brandy. Consequently, when he came out, at half-past three in the morning, into fourteen degrees of frost, he was very angry with his horse for coughing, and tried to leapfrog into the saddle. The horse broke away and went to his stables; so Strickland and I formed a Guard of Dishonor to take Fleete home.

Our road lay through the bazaar, close to a little temple of Hanuman, the Monkey-god, who is a leading divinity worthy of respect. All gods have good points, just as have all priests. Personally, I attach much importance to Hanuman, and am kind to his people—the great gray apes of the hills. One never knows when one may want a friend.

There was a light in the temple, and as we passed we could hear voices of men chanting hymns. In a native temple the priests rise at all hours of the night to do honor to their god. Before we would stop him, Fleete dashed up the steps, patted two priests on the back, and was gravely grinding the ashes of his cigar butt in to the forehead of the red stone image of Hanuman. Strickland tried to drag him out, but he sat down and said solemnly:

---

3. **Khyberee:** reference to the people of Khyber, a region now part of Pakistan and Afghanistan.
4. **Fuzzies:** Sudanese natives. British soldiers gave them this name because of their long, frizzy hair. In the poem "Fuzzy-Wuzzy" (1890), Kipling calls the Sudanese soldier "a first-class fightin' man."
5. **Suakim:** Suakin, Sudan; city on the Red Sea.

---

6. **bones:** dice.

"Shee that? Mark of the B—beasht! *I* made it. Ishn't it fine?" **B**

In half a minute the temple was alive and noisy, and Strickland, who knew what came of polluting gods, said that things might occur. He, by virtue of his official position, long residence in the country, and weakness for going among the natives, was known to the priests and he felt unhappy. Fleete sat on the ground and refused to move. He said that "good old Hanuman" made a very soft pillow.

Then, without any warning, a Silver Man came out of a recess behind the image of the god. He was perfectly naked in that bitter, bitter cold, and his body shone like frosted silver, for he was what the Bible calls "a leper as white as snow." Also he had no face, because he was a leper of some years' standing, and his disease was heavy upon him. We two stooped to haul Fleete up, and the temple was filling and filling with folk who seemed to spring from the earth, when the Silver Man ran in under our arms, making a noise exactly like the mewing of an otter, caught Fleete round the body and dropped his head on Fleete's breast before we could wrench him away. Then he retired to a corner and sat mewing while the crowd blocked all the doors.

The priests were very angry until the Silver Man touched Fleete. That nuzzling seemed to sober them.

At the end of a few minutes' silence one of the priests came to Strickland and said, in perfect English, "Take your friend away. He has done with Hanuman but Hanuman has not done with him." The crowd gave room and we carried Fleete into the road. **C**

Strickland was very angry. He said that we might all three have been knifed, and that Fleete should thank his stars that he had escaped without injury.

Fleete thanked no one. He said that he wanted to go to bed. He was gorgeously drunk.

We moved on, Strickland silent and wrathful, until Fleete was taken with violent shivering fits and sweating. He said that the smells of the bazaar were overpowering, and he wondered why slaughterhouses were permitted so near English residences. "Can't you smell the blood?" said Fleete.

We put him to bed at last, just as the dawn was breaking, and Strickland invited me to have another whiskey and soda. While we were drinking he talked of the trouble in the temple, and admitted that it baffled him completely. Strickland hates being mystified by natives, because his business in life is to overmatch them with their own weapons. He has not yet succeeded in doing this, but in fifteen or twenty years he will have made some small progress.

"They should have mauled us," he said, "instead of mewing at us. I wonder what they meant. I don't like it one little bit."

I said that the Managing Committee of the temple would in all probability bring a criminal action against us for insulting their religion. There was a section of the Indian Penal Code which exactly met Fleete's offense. Strickland said he only hoped and prayed that they would do this. Before I left I looked into Fleete's room, and saw him lying on his right side, scratching his left breast. Then I went to bed cold, depressed, and unhappy, at seven o'clock in the morning.

At one o'clock I rode over to Strickland's house to inquire after Fleete's head. I imagined that it would be a sore one. Fleete was breakfasting and seemed unwell. His temper was gone, for he was abusing the cook for not supplying him with an underdone chop. A man who can eat raw meat after a wet night is a curiosity. I told Fleete this and he laughed.

"You breed queer mosquitoes in these parts," he said. "I've been bitten to pieces, but only in one place."

"Let's have a look at the bite," said Strickland. "It may have gone down since this morning."

While the chops were being cooked, Fleete opened his shirt and showed us, just over his left breast, a mark, the perfect double of the black rosettes—the five or six irregular blotches arranged in a circle—on a leopard's hide. Strickland looked and said, "It was only pink this morning. It's grown black now."

Fleete ran to a glass.

"By Jove!" he said, "this is nasty. What is it?"

We could not answer. Here the chops came in, all red and juicy, and Fleete bolted three in a most offensive manner. He ate on his right grinders only, and threw his head over his right shoulder as he snapped

---

B **Reading Focus** Identifying Conflicts and Resolutions
What conflict is set in motion here?

C **Reading Focus** Identifying Conflicts and Resolutions
What conflict might the priest's statement foreshadow?

the meat. When he had finished, it struck him that he had been behaving strangely, for he said apologetically, "I don't think I ever felt so hungry in my life. I've bolted like an ostrich."

After breakfast Strickland said to me, "Don't go. Stay here, and stay for the night."

Seeing that my house was not three miles from Strickland's, this request was absurd. But Strickland insisted, and was going to say something, when Fleete interrupted him by declaring in a shamefaced way that he felt hungry again. Strickland sent a man to my house to fetch over my bedding and a horse, and we three went down to Strickland's stables to pass the hours until it was time to go out for a ride. The man who has a weakness for horses never wearies of inspecting them; and when two men are killing time in this way they gather knowledge and lies the one from the other.

There were five horses in the stables, and I shall never forget the scene as we tried to look them over. They seemed to have gone mad. They reared and screamed and nearly tore up their pickets;[7] they sweated and shivered and lathered and were distraught with fear. Strickland's horses used to know him as well as his dogs; which made the matter more curious. We left the stable for fear of the brutes throwing themselves in their panic. Then Strickland turned back and called me. The horses were still frightened, but they let us "gentle" and make much of them, and put their heads in our bosoms.

"They aren't afraid of *us*," said Strickland. "D'you know, I'd give three months' pay if *Outrage* here could talk."

But *Outrage* was dumb, and could only cuddle up to his master and blow out his nostrils, as is the custom of horses when they wish to explain things but can't. Fleete came up when we were in the stalls, and as soon as the horses saw him, their fright broke out afresh. It was all that we could do to escape from the place unkicked. Strickland said, "They don't seem to love you, Fleete."

---

7. **pickets:** hitching posts.

The interior of the Lakshmana Temple was built during the 11th and 12th centuries. Khajuraho, Madhya Pradesh, India.

IT WAS ALL WE COULD DO TO ESCAPE FROM THE PLACE UNKICKED.

Vocabulary **distraught** (dihs TRAWT) *adj.:* extremely agitated.

"Nonsense," said Fleete; "my mare will follow me like a dog." He went to her; she was in a loose box;[8] but as he slipped the bars she plunged, knocked him down, and broke away into the garden. I laughed, but Strickland was not amused. He took his moustache in both fists and pulled at it till it nearly came out. Fleete, instead of going off to chase his property, yawned, saying that he felt sleepy. He went to the house to lie down, which was a foolish way of spending New Year's Day.

Strickland sat with me in the stables and asked if I had noticed anything peculiar in Fleete's manner. I said that he ate his food like a beast; but that this might have been the result of living alone in the hills out of the reach of society as refined and elevating as ours for instance. Strickland was not amused. I do not think that he listened to me, for his next sentence referred to the mark on Fleete's breast, and I said that it might have been caused by blister flies, or that it was possibly a birthmark newly born and now visible for the first time. We both agreed that it was unpleasant to look at, and Strickland found occasion to say that I was a fool.

"I can't tell you what I think now," said he, "because you would call me a madman; but you must stay with me for the next few days, if you can. I want you to watch Fleete, but don't tell me what you think till I have made up my mind." **D**

Blue-eyed horse.

---

8. **loose box:** stall in which the horse is free to move about.

D Literary Focus **Conflict** What explanation can you offer for Strickland's internal conflict concerning the possible cause of the mark on Fleete's chest? What larger conflict and theme might his internal conflict point to?

"But I am dining out tonight," I said.

"So am I," said Strickland, "and so is Fleete. At least if he doesn't change his mind."

We walked about the garden smoking, but saying nothing—because we were friends, and talking spoils good tobacco—till our pipes were out. Then we went to wake up Fleete. He was wide awake and fidgeting about his room.

"I say, I want some more chops," he said. "Can I get them?"

We laughed and said, "Go and change. The ponies will be round in a minute."

All right," said Fleete. "I'll go when I get the chops—underdone ones, mind."

He seemed to be quite in earnest. It was four o'clock, and we had had breakfast at one; still, for a long time, he demanded those underdone chops. Then he changed into riding clothes and went out into the veranda. His pony—the mare had not been caught— would not let him come near. All three horses were unmanageable—mad with fear—and finally Fleete said that he would stay at home and get something to eat. Strickland and I rode out wondering. As we passed the Temple of Hanuman the Silver Man came out and mewed at us.

"He is not one of the regular priests of the temple," said Strickland. "I think I should peculiarly like to lay my hands on him."

There was no spring in our gallop on the race-course that evening. The horses were stale, and moved as though they had been ridden out.

"The fright after breakfast has been too much for them," said Strickland.

That was the only remark he made through the remainder of the ride. Once or twice, I think, he swore to himself; but that did not count.

We came back in the dark at seven o'clock, and saw that there was no lights in the bungalow. "Careless ruffians my servants are!" said Strickland.

My horse reared at something on the carriage drive, and Fleete stood up under its nose.

"What are you doing, groveling about the garden?" said Strickland.

But both horses bolted and nearly threw us. We dismounted by the stables and returned to Fleete, who was on his hands and knees under the orange bushes.

"What the devil's wrong with you?" said Strickland.

"Nothing, nothing in the world," said Fleete, speaking very quickly and thickly. "I've been gardening—botanizing, you know. The smell of the earth is delightful. I think I'm going for a walk—a long walk—all night."

Then I saw that there was something excessively out of order somewhere, and I said to Strickland, "I am not dining out."

"Bless you!" said Strickland. "Here, Fleete, get up. You'll catch fever there. Come in to dinner and let's have the lamps lit. We'll dine at home."

Fleete stood up unwillingly, and said, "No lamps—no lamps. It's much nicer here. Let's dine outside and have some more chops—lots of 'em and underdone—bloody ones with gristle."

Now a December evening in Northern India is bitterly cold, and Fleete's suggestion was that of a maniac.

"Come in," said Strickland sternly. "Come in at once."

Fleete came, and when the lamps were brought, we saw that he was literally plastered with dirt from head to foot. He must have been rolling in the garden. He shrank from the light and went to his room. His eyes were horrible to look at. There was a green light behind them, not in them, if you understand, and the man's lower lip hung down.

Strickland said, "There is going to be trouble—big trouble—tonight. Don't you change your riding things."

We waited and waited for Fleete's reappearance, and ordered dinner in the meantime. We could hear him moving about his own room, but there was no light there. Presently from the room came the long-drawn howl of a wolf.

People write and talk lightly of blood running cold and hair standing up, and things of that kind. Both sensations are too horrible to be trifled with. My heart stopped as though a knife had been driven through it, and Strickland turned as white as the tablecloth.

The howl was repeated, and was answered by another howl far across the fields.

That set the gilded roof on the horror. Strickland dashed into Fleete's room. I followed, and we saw Fleete getting out of the window. He made beast noises in the back of his throat. He could not answer us when we shouted at him. He spat.

I don't quite remember what followed, but I think that Strickland must have stunned him with the long bootjack,[9] or else I should never have been able to sit on his chest. Fleete could not speak, he could only snarl, and his snarls were those of a wolf, not of a man. The human spirit must have been giving way all day and have died out with the twilight. We were dealing with a beast that had once been Fleete.

The affair was beyond any human and rational experience. I tried to say "hydrophobia,"[10] but the word wouldn't come, because I knew that I was lying.

We bound this beast with leather thongs of the punkah[11] rope, and tied its thumbs and big toes together, and gagged it with a shoehorn, which makes a very efficient gag if you know how to arrange it. Then we carried it into the dining room, and sent a man to Dumoise, the doctor, telling him to come over at

---

9. **bootjack:** device for pulling off boots, often made of cast iron.
10. **hydrophobia:** rabies. One of the effects of rabies is an inability to swallow water.
11. **punkah:** swinging fan suspended from the ceiling. It is operated by pulling an attached cord or rope.

E **Literary Focus** **Conflict** What does the narrator's use of the phrase "out of order"—instead of a word such as wrong—suggest about the nature of the conflicts and their effects in the story?

F **Reading Focus** **Identifying Conflicts and Resolutions** Explain the internal conflict described in this passage. How is it resolved?

once. After we had dispatched the messenger and were drawing breath, Strickland said, "It's no good. This isn't any doctor's work." I, also, knew that he spoke the truth.

The beast's head was free, and it threw it about from side to side. Anyone entering the room would have believed that we were curing a wolf's pelt. That was the most loathsome accessory of all.

Strickland sat with his chin in the heel of his fist, watching the beast as it wriggled on the ground, but saying nothing. The shirt had been torn open in the scuffle and showed the black rosette mark on the left breast. It stood out like a blister.

In the silence of the watching we heard something without mewing like a she-otter. We both rose to our feet, and, I answer for myself, not Strickland, felt sick—actually and physically sick. We told each other, as did the men in *Pinafore*,[12] that it was the cat.

Dumoise arrived, and I never saw a little man so unprofessionally shocked. He said that it was a heart-rending case of hydrophobia, and that nothing could be done. At least any palliative measures would only prolong the agony. The beast was foaming at the mouth. Fleete, as we told Dumoise, had been bitten by dogs once or twice. Any man who keeps half a dozen terriers must expect a nip now and again. Dumoise could offer no help. He could only certify that Fleete was dying of hydrophobia. The beast was then howling, for it had managed to spit out the shoehorn. Dumoise said that he would be ready to certify to the cause of death, and that the end was certain. He was a good little man, and he offered to remain with us; but Strickland refused the kindness. He did not wish to poison Dumoise's New Year. He would only ask him not to give the real cause of Fleete's death to the public.

So Dumoise left, deeply agitated; and as soon as the noise of the cart wheels had died away, Strickland told me, in a whisper, his suspicions. They were so wildly improbable that he dared not say them out aloud; and I, who entertained all Strickland's beliefs, was so ashamed of owning to them that I pretended to disbelieve.

"Even if the Silver Man had bewitched Fleete for polluting the image of Hanuman, the punishment could not have fallen so quickly." **G**

As I was whispering this the cry outside the house rose again, and the beast fell into a fresh paroxysm of struggling till we were afraid that the thongs that held it would give way.

"Watch!" said Strickland. "If this happens six times I shall take the law into my own hands. I order you to help me."

He went into his room and came out in a few minutes with the barrels of an old shotgun, a piece of fishing line, some thick cord, and his heavy wooden bedstead. I reported that the convulsions had followed the cry by two seconds in each case, and the beast seemed perceptibly weaker.

Strickland muttered, "But he can't take away the life! He can't take away the life!"

I said, though I knew that I was arguing against myself, "It may be a cat. It must be a cat. If the Silver Man is responsible, why does he dare to come here?"

Strickland arranged the wood on the hearth, put the gun barrels into the glow of the fire, spread the twine on the table, and broke a walking stick in two. There was one yard of fishing line, gut lapped with wire, such as is used for *mahseer*[13] fishing, and he tied the two ends together in a loop.

Then he said, "How can we catch him? He must be taken alive and unhurt."

I said that we must trust in Providence, and go out softly with polo sticks into the shrubbery at the front of the house. The man or animal that made the cry was evidently moving round the house as regularly as a night watchman. We could wait in the bushes till he came by and knock him over. **H**

---

12. **Pinafore:** *H.M.S. Pinafore* (1878), a comic operetta by W. S. Gilbert and Arthur Sullivan. Lovers in the play attempt to elope. When they are discovered, the cast sings, "Why, what was that? . . . It was—it was the cat!"

13. *mahseer* (MAH suhr): large Indian freshwater fish of the carp family.

G **Reading Focus** Identifying Conflicts and Resolutions Explain the narrator's internal conflict. How is his conflict the result of external conflicts in the story?

H **Literary Focus** Conflict To what force is the narrator referring when he says they must "trust in Providence"? What does this statement suggest about his attitude toward the conflicts in the story?

Hanuman

The Hindu deity Hanuman, an offspring of the wind god and a nymph, is usually portrayed as a red-faced monkey who stands erect like a human. Hanuman appears in the Indian epics the *Ramayana* and the *Mahabharata* as a brave and loyal aid to the hero-god Rama. Hanuman is regarded as a helpful guardian spirit, and his loyalty to Rama is considered the perfect model of *bhakti*, or human devotion to a god. Also called Mahavira, "The Great Hero," Hanuman is seen as a sympathetic helper of humans. One of the most common species of Indian monkeys is named after him and is considered sacred. Hanuman is worshipped to this day in temples devoted to him throughout India. He is often portrayed holding a mace, a symbol of strength and protection.

Ask Yourself

Of all the Hindu gods, why is it significant that Fleete is disrespectful to Hanuman in "The Mark of the Beast"?

(above) *Hanuman Revealing Rama and Sita Enshrined in his Heart* (1880) by a member of the Patua caste, Bengal School. Watercolor on paper. Victoria and Albert Museum, London.

Strickland accepted this suggestion, and we slipped out from a bathroom window into the front veranda and then across the carriage drive into the bushes.

In the moonlight we could see the leper coming round the corner of the house. He was perfectly naked, and from time to time he mewed and stopped to dance with his shadow. It was an unattractive sight, and thinking of poor Fleete, brought to such degradation by so foul a creature, I put away all my doubts and resolved to help Strickland from the heated gun barrels to the loop of twine—from the loins to the head and back again—with all tortures that might be needful.

The leper halted in the front porch for a moment and we jumped out on him with the sticks. He was wonderfully strong, and we were afraid that he might escape or be fatally injured before we caught him. We had an idea that lepers were frail creatures, but this proved to be incorrect. Strickland knocked his legs from under him and I put my foot on his neck. He mewed hideously, and even through my riding boots

I could feel that his flesh was not the flesh of a clean man.

He struck at us with his hand- and feet-stumps. We looped the lash of a dog-whip round him under the armpits, and dragged him backward into the hall and so into the dining room where the beast lay. There we tied him with trunk straps. He made no attempt to escape, but mewed.

When we confronted him with the beast the scene was beyond description. The beast doubled backward into a bow as though he had been poisoned with strychnine, and moaned in the most pitiable fashion. Several other things happened also, but they cannot be put down here.

"I think I was right," said Strickland. "Now we will ask him to cure this case."

But the leper only mewed. Strickland wrapped a towel round his hand and took the gun barrels out of the fire. I put the half of the broken walking stick through the loop of fishing line and buckled the leper comfortably to Strickland's bedstead. I understood then how men and women and little children can endure to see a witch burnt alive; for the beast was moaning on the floor, and though the Silver Man had no face, you could see horrible feelings passing through the slab that took its place, exactly as waves of heat play across red-hot iron—gun barrels, for instance.

Strickland shaded his eyes with his hands for a moment and we got to work. This part is not to be printed.

The dawn was beginning to break when the leper spoke. His mewings had not been satisfactory up to that point. The beast had fainted from exhaustion and the house was very still. We unstrapped the leper and told him to take away the evil spirit. He crawled to the beast and laid his hand upon the left breast. That was all. Then he fell face down and whined, drawing in his breath as he did so.

We watched the face of the beast, and saw the soul of Fleete coming back into the eyes. Then a sweat broke out on the forehead and the eyes—they were human eyes—closed. We waited for an hour, but Fleete still slept. We carried him to his room and bade the leper go, giving him the bedstead, and the sheet on the bedstead to cover his nakedness, the gloves and the towels with which we had touched him, and the whip that had been hooked round his body. He put the sheet about him and went out into the early morning without speaking or mewing. **I**

Strickland wiped his face and sat down. A night gong, far away in the city, made seven o'clock.

"Exactly four-and-twenty hours!" said Strickland. "And I've done enough to ensure my dismissal from the service, besides permanent quarters in a lunatic asylum. Do you believe that we are awake?"

The red-hot gun barrel had fallen on the floor and was singeing the carpet. The smell was entirely real. **J**

That morning at eleven we two together went to wake up Fleete. We looked and saw that the black leopard rosette on his chest had disappeared. He was very drowsy and tired, but as soon as he saw us, he said, "Oh! Confound you fellows. Happy New Year to you. Never mix your liquors. I'm nearly dead."

"Thanks for your kindness, but you're over time," said Strickland. "Today is the morning of the second. You've slept the clock round with a vengeance."

The door opened, and little Dumoise put his head in. He had come on foot, and fancied that we were laying out Fleete.

"I've brought a nurse," said Dumoise. "I suppose that she can come in for . . . what is necessary."

"By all means," said Fleete cheerily, sitting up in bed. "Bring on your nurses."

Dumoise was dumb. Strickland led him out and explained that there must have been a mistake in the diagnosis. Dumoise remained dumb and left the house hastily. He considered that his professional reputation had been injured, and was inclined to make a personal matter of the recovery. Strickland went out too. When he came back, he said that he had been to call on the Temple of Hanuman to offer redress for the pollution of the god, and had been solemnly assured that no white man had ever touched the idol, and that he was an incarnation of all the virtues laboring under a delusion. "What do you think?" said Strickland.

I said, "'There are more things . . .'"[14]

---

14. **"There are more things"**: reference to William Shakespeare's *Hamlet*, Act I, Scene 5, lines 166–167: "There are more things in heaven and earth, Horatio, than are dreamt of in your philosophy."

I Reading Focus Identifying Conflicts and Resolutions Which phrase or phrases in this passage indicate that at least some of the conflicts in the story have been resolved?

J Literary Focus Conflict The narrator does not respond when Strickland asks, "Do you believe that we are awake?" However, the narrator does tell the reader that the smell of the burned carpet is "entirely real." If the narrator were to answer Strickland's question, what does this detail suggest he might say?

Vocabulary **redress** (REE drehs) *n.*: payment or action that serves to remedy an injustice or injury.
delusion (dih LOO zhuhn) *n.*: false belief.

But Strickland hates that quotation. He says that I have worn it threadbare.

One other curious thing happened which frightened me as much as anything in all the night's work. When Fleete was dressed he came into the dining room and sniffed. He had a quaint trick of moving his nose when he sniffed. "Horrid doggy smell, here," said he. "You should really keep those terriers of yours in better order. Try sulfur, Strick."

But Strickland did not answer. He caught hold of the back of a chair, and, without warning, went into an amazing fit of hysterics. It is terrible to see a strong man overtaken with hysteria. Then it struck me that we had fought for Fleete's soul with the Silver Man in that room, and had disgraced ourselves as Englishmen forever, and I laughed and gasped and gurgled just as shamefully as Strickland, while Fleete thought that we had both gone mad. We never told him what we had done. **(K)**

Some years later, when Strickland had married and was a churchgoing member of society for his wife's sake, we reviewed the incident dispassionately, and Strickland suggested that I should put it before the public.

I cannot myself see that this step is likely to clear up the mystery; because, in the first place, no one will believe a rather unpleasant story, and, in the second, it is well known to every right-minded man that the gods of the heathen are stone and brass, and any attempt to deal with them otherwise is justly condemned.

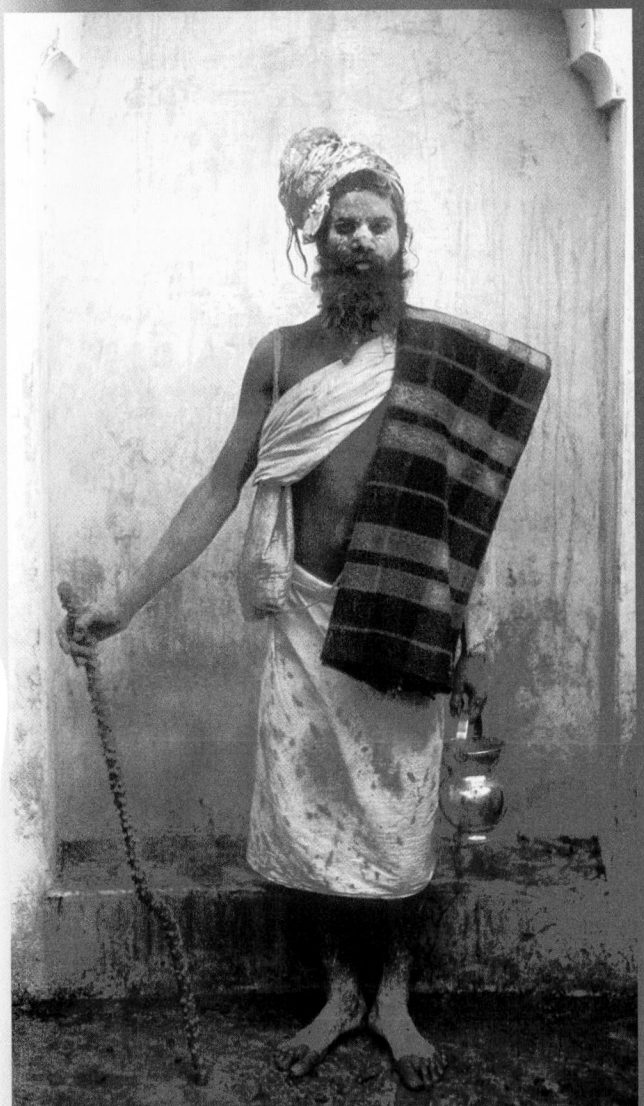

A Hindu ascetic traditionally regarded as having magical powers.

(K) Literary Focus Conflict How have Strickland and the narrator "disgraced" themselves "as Englishmen forever" as a result of the conflicts in the story?

Vocabulary dispassionately (dihs PASH uh niht lee) *adv.:* without emotion; impartially.

WE HAD FOUGHT FOR FLEETE'S SOUL WITH THE SILVER MAN IN THAT ROOM, AND HAD DISGRACED OURSELVES FOREVER

Applying Your Skills

The Mark of the Beast

Respond and Think Critically

Reading Focus

Quick Check

1. After Fleete's act of disrespect, why do the priests let the men leave the temple, seemingly unharmed?

2. What clues reveal that Fleete is becoming something nonhuman?

3. Why does the Silver Man remove the evil spirit from Fleete?

Read with a Purpose

4. The title of the story is an allusion to the Book of Revelation in the Bible. Find other places in the story where Kipling alludes to the Book of Revelation. What do these allusions suggest about Fleete's character and actions? Although the Silver Man bewitches Fleete, in what way is Fleete's wolflike behavior symbolic of the beast—or the evil—inherent in him?

Reading Skills: Identifying Conflicts and Resolutions

5. Review the chart you filled in as you read. Then, add a fourth column to the chart, and use a check mark to indicate which conflicts in the story result from cultural misunderstandings.

Conflict	External or Internal?	Resolution	Cultural Misunderstandings (√)
Providence & Church of England vs. gods and devils of Asia	external		

Literary Focus

Literary Analysis

6. **Evaluate** What does this story suggest were the issues that marked the British presence in India?

7. **Analyze** Do you think there is a clear victor in the story? Why or why not?

8. **Interpret** Re-read the Indian proverb at the beginning of the story. How does the proverb relate to the story's theme?

Literary Skills: Conflict

9. **Infer** Do Fleete, Strickland, and the narrator learn anything from the internal and external conflicts they undergo? Support your response with evidence from the story.

Literary Skills Review: Narrative Voice

10. **Make Judgments** A writer's **narrative voice** is created by tone, diction, and distinctive use of language. Describe the narrator's voice in this story. What does his voice suggest about his character, and how does it affect the telling of the tale?

Writing Focus

Think as a Reader/Writer

Use It in Your Writing Write a scene for a story in which a conflict leads to a terrible result. Use suspense to create a gripping scene and capture your reader's attention.

 What Do You Think Now

In the end, why does the narrator consider the events in the story to be a "mystery"? To support your answer, consider his actions, statements, and tone.

Vocabulary Development

✓ Vocabulary Check

Write the Vocabulary word that best completes the meaning of each sentence: **genial, distraught, redress, delusion, dispassionately.**

1. Presenting both sides of the issue, the journalist wrote _____ about the case.
2. The lost child was frightened and _____.
3. A tour guide should be _____.
4. The victims sought _____ for the crime.
5. The king's _____ that he was all powerful caused him to underestimate his enemies.

Vocabulary Skills: Connotations

To determine which word to use in a passage, writers consider a word's shades of meaning as well as its **connotations,** the emotions and associations evoked by a word. Consider, for example, why Kipling might have chosen to use the word *dispassionately* instead of *objectively* in the following passage from "The Mark of the Beast":

> Some years later,… we reviewed the incident dispassionately, and Strickland suggested that I should put it before the public.

Both *dispassionately* and *objectively* mean "in a manner free of bias; impartially." However, "emotionlessly" and "passionlessly" are also part of the **denotation** (the dictionary definition) of *dispassionately*. While *objectively* is a neutral word, *dispassionately* often connotes an emotional coldness. Kipling might have chosen to use *dispassionately* to create a contrast with the intense, <u>complex</u> emotions Strickland and the narrator experienced during their struggles years ago.

Keep in mind that although a word's denotation is objective, its connotations are subjective. A word might evoke different emotions and associations for each reader.

Your Turn

To enhance your understanding of connotations, answer the following questions:

6. The narrator comments, "We were dealing with a **beast** that had once been Fleete." What does the word *beast* suggest that *animal* does not?
7. The narrator says, "Though the Silver Man had no face, you could see horrible feelings passing through the **slab** that took its place." What images and associations does *slab* call to mind?

Language Coach

Synonyms You can find synonyms of a word in a thesaurus, but you should use a dictionary to check the precise definition of each synonym. Often a dictionary will include examples that show the contexts in which a word is used. Sometimes a dictionary entry will also include a list of synonyms and an explanation of their shades of meaning.

For each of the following words, *distraught, redress,* and *delusion,* list two synonyms, and explain the different shades of meaning of each word and its synonyms. Use a thesaurus and a dictionary to complete this activity.

Academic Vocabulary

Talk About
In a small group, discuss the <u>benefits</u> of learning about other cultures and the risks of <u>responding</u> disrespectfully to cultural differences.

Learn It Online
Learn more about connotations with *WordSharp*.
go.hrw.com   L12-1005   **Go**

The Mark of the Beast

Grammar Link

Dangling Modifiers

What would you think if you came across the following sentence in your reading?

> Fascinated by British and Indian cultural conflicts, some of Kipling's stories are set in India.

Would you wonder *who* was fascinated by the conflicts? This sentence is confusing because it contains a **dangling modifier**—a word, phrase, or clause that does not sensibly, or reasonably, modify any word or group of words in a sentence. There are three ways to correct dangling modifiers:

· Add the word that the modifier describes or qualifies, and reword the sentence as necessary:

> Fascinated by British and Indian cultural conflicts, <u>Kipling</u> set some of his stories in India.

· Add words to the modifier to make its meaning clear:

> <u>Since Kipling was</u> fascinated by British and Indian cultural conflicts, some of his stories are set in India.

· Reword the entire sentence:

> <u>Kipling was</u> fascinated by British and Indian cultural conflicts, so he set some of his stories in India.

Your Turn

Rewrite to correct the dangling modifiers.

1. Grinding cigar ashes into the image of Hanuman, it insults the god.
2. Bewitched by the leper, Fleete's presence provokes fear in the horses.
3. Transformed into a beast, the narrator and Strickland have to take action.

Writing Application Correct a dangling modifier in a paragraph you have already written.

CHOICES

As you respond to the Choices, use these **Academic Vocabulary** words as appropriate: <u>benefit</u>, <u>complex</u>, <u>publish</u>, <u>respond</u>, <u>statistics</u>.

REVIEW

Create a Horror Movie

TechFocus Think about the techniques Kipling uses to create a sense of horror in this story. Then, in a small group, create a short video adaptation of a scene from "The Mark of the Beast." Carefully consider what techniques you will use to horrify your audience, and how these techniques differ from or are the same as Kipling's.

Movie poster for *The Island of Dr Moreau* (19 based on a novel by H. G. Wells.

CONNECT

Evaluate the Story

Critics have called "The Mark of the Beast" "nasty," "poisonous," and even "sadistic." What is your evaluation of the story? Do you think it is a well-told, suspenseful horror story? Is it a <u>complex</u>, insightful examination of British imperialism? Write an essay expressing your views of the work. Be sure to support your points with evidence from the text.

EXTEND

Write a Story

In the beginning of "The Mark of the Beast," the narrator says that Dumoise "died in a rather curious manner." Write your own story telling how and why Dumoise died. Use a first-person narrator, and consider how your choice of narrator will affect the telling of your tale. Make sure the details in your story are consistent with what you know about Dumoise.

Realism and the Short Story

The Stone Breakers (1849) by Gustave Courbet (1819–1877). Oil on canvas.
Destroyed in 1945 . Formerly at Galerie Neue Meister, Dresden, Germany/ Staatliche Kunstammlungen, Dresden.

You have just read "The Mark of the Beast" by Rudyard Kipling. In this Comparing Texts: World Literature section, you will read three short stories from other countries that exemplify the style known as realism.

CONTENTS

How Much Land Does a Man Need?
by Leo Tolstoy

The Bet
by Anton Chekhov

The Jewels
by Guy de Maupassant

How Much Land Does a Man Need?

QuickWrite

Take a few notes in your *Reader/Writer Notebook* on the difference between "wants" and "needs." Do most people want more than they need?

Leo Tolstoy
(1828–1910)

The death of Count Leo Nikolayevich Tolstoy was front-page news in England and America. At the age of eighty-two, the great writer had run away from his family, seeking a place where he could lead a simple, hermit's life. He became ill in a remote train station and died of pneumonia in the stationmaster's office.

An Aristocratic Beginning

Tolstoy was born to wealthy aristocratic parents who died before Tolstoy was nine. He and his siblings were raised by his aunts on the family estate. At nineteen, Tolstoy split his inheritance with his brothers and became the master of his family's estate and its three hundred serfs. Within three years, he had gambled away about one fourth of his inheritance. Looking for adventure, he joined the Russian army and fought bravely during the Crimean War. Tolstoy's contemplative nature and serious moral outlook emerged in response to the suffering that he witnessed during the war.

In 1859, Tolstoy opened a school on his estate for his serfs' children. Soon after, he married Sonya Andreyevna Bers, who, in addition to bearing thirteen children, laboriously recopied her husband's manuscripts. She also took over the management of his estate, which freed Tolstoy to write his greatest works, *War and Peace* (1869) and *Anna Karenina* (1877).

A Spiritual Conversion

After years of moral questioning, Tolstoy underwent a shattering spiritual conversion. Convinced that the purpose of life was to do good works, he began to emulate Russia's Christian peasants. He renounced private ownership, the Orthodox Church, and the czarist government. Although Tolstoy repudiated his early works for their focus on aristocracy, his reputation today rests primarily on those early novels: *War and Peace*, a monumental telling of the lives of five aristocratic families during the Napoleonic Wars, and *Anna Karenina*, the tragic story of a woman who gives up her husband and child for what she thinks is true love.

Think About the Writer How would you describe the two distinct parts of Tolstoy's life?

Reader/Writer Notebook

Use your **RWN** to complete the activities for this selection.

Literary Focus

Allegory Tolstoy's story "How Much Land Does a Man Need?" is an **allegory,** a story that operates on both literal and symbolic levels. The characters, settings, and events of an allegory can therefore be understood both for what they are (the literal meaning) and for the abstract principles they represent (the symbolic meaning). Characters in allegories often stand for virtues and vices—pride, for example, or innocence, or greed. As you read this story, try to determine what the various elements (such as Pahom, the Devil, and the land itself) symbolize.

Reading Focus

Identifying Theme A **theme** is the central idea or insight revealed in a work of literature. Writers rarely state the theme of a story explicitly; instead, they reveal the theme by letting us see characters in action. By the end of a story, the characters have often discovered something about themselves, and, we, the readers, also participate in this discovery. That discovery about human life is the story's theme.

Into Action There are several ways to identify theme. You can ask yourself what the main character has discovered at the story's conclusion, or look for key passages that seem especially important. You can also check the story's title, which sometimes gives a clue to its theme. As you read this story, use a chart like the one below to record key details that might point to the theme.

Clues to Theme	
The peasant sister says "Gain and pain are brothers twain."	→ This statement seems to relate to the story's title.

Writing Focus

Think as a Reader/Writer

Find It in Your Reading The characters, events, and settings of an **allegory** stand for abstract things or ideas. For example, a character might stand for temptation or a setting might represent despair or happiness. In your *Reader/Writer Notebook*, write down your ideas about how this story could be made into a modern allegory by updating the characters, events, setting, and title.

Vocabulary

piqued (peekt) *v.* used as *adj.*: provoked; resentful. *The peasant woman was piqued when her older, wealthier sister boasted of the benefits of town life.*

disparaged (dihs PAR ihjd) *v.*: belittled; spoke negatively of. *The peasant woman disparaged her sister's prosperous life.*

aggrieved (uh GREEVD) *v.* used as *adj.*: offended. *Pahom felt aggrieved when the Judges acquitted Simon of any wrongdoing.*

arable (AR uh buhl) *adj.*: fit to be farmed or cultivated. *Much of Pahom's new land was arable.*

haggled (HAG uhld) *v.*: argued about a price. *Pahom haggled with the peasant to get a lower price on the land.*

prostrate (PRAHS trayt) *adj.*: lying flat. *In his dream, Pahom saw himself lying prostrate on the ground.*

 Learn It Online
Learn more about Tolstoy on the Writers' Lives site.

go.hrw.com | L12-1009 | Go

How Much Land Does a Man Need?

by **Leo Tolstoy**

translated by **Louise** and **Aylmer Maude**

Read with a Purpose
Read to discover how a man's greed consumes him.

Build Background
Until Czar Alexander II ordered their emancipation in 1861, Russian peasants, called *serfs,* were the virtual slaves of landowners and aristocrats. Serfs could be bought or sold, and were not allowed to own property. When Tolstoy wrote this story in 1886, serfs had already experienced twenty-five years of freedom. While no one (and certainly not Tolstoy the reformer) wished to see them thrown back into bondage, Tolstoy questions in this parable whether the peasants' progress had brought changes they would come to regret.

A Settler's Family (circa 1907–1915) by Sergei Mikhailovich Prokudin-Gorskii. Photograph. Digital color rendering of original tri-part glass negatives.

An elder sister came to visit her younger sister in the country. The elder was married to a tradesman in town, the younger to a peasant in the village. As the sisters sat over their tea talking, the elder began to boast of the advantages of town life: saying how comfortably they lived there, how well they dressed, what fine clothes her children wore, what good things they ate and drank, and how she went to the theater, promenades, and entertainments.

The younger sister was piqued, and in turn disparaged the life of a tradesman, and stood up for that of a peasant.

"I would not change my way of life for yours," said she. "We may live roughly, but at least we are free from anxiety. You live in better style than we do, but though you often earn more than you need, you are very likely to lose all you have. You know the proverb, 'Loss and gain are brothers twain.' It often happens that people who are wealthy one day are begging their bread the next. Our way is safer. Though a peasant's life is not a fat one, it is a long one. We shall never grow rich, but we shall always have enough to eat." **Ⓐ**

The elder sister said sneeringly:

"Enough? Yes, if you like to share with the pigs and the calves! What do you know of elegance or manners! However much your goodman may slave, you will die as you are living—on a dung heap—and your children the same."

"Well, what of that?" replied the younger. "Of course our work is rough and coarse. But, on the other hand, it is sure, and we need not bow to anyone. But you, in your towns, are surrounded by temptations; today all may be right, but tomorrow the Evil One may tempt your husband with cards, wine, or women, and all will go to ruin. Don't such things happen often enough?" **Ⓑ**

Ⓐ Reading Focus **Identifying Theme** The appearance of proverbs in a story is usually important. How would you state the proverb in this paragraph in your own words?

Ⓑ Literary Focus **Allegory** The two sisters are described as complete opposites. Which sister might stand for boastfulness? Which sister might stand for acceptance of her lot in life?

Vocabulary **piqued** (peekt) *v. used as adj.:* provoked; resentful.
disparaged (dihs PAR ihjd) *v.:* belittled; spoke negatively of.

Pahom, the master of the house, was lying on the top of the stove[1] and he listened to the women's chatter.

"It is perfectly true," thought he. "Busy as we are from childhood tilling mother earth, we peasants have no time to let any nonsense settle in our heads. Our only trouble is that we haven't land enough. If I had plenty of land, I shouldn't fear the Devil himself!"

The women finished their tea, chatted a while about dress, and then cleared away the tea things and lay down to sleep.

But the Devil had been sitting behind the stove, and had heard all that was said. He was pleased that the peasant's wife had led her husband into boasting, and that he had said that if he had plenty of land he would not fear the Devil himself.

"All right," thought the Devil. "We will have a tussle. I'll give you land enough; and by means of that land I will get you into my power." **C**

Close to the village there lived a lady, a small landowner who had an estate of about three hundred acres. She had always lived on good terms with the peasants until she engaged as her steward an old soldier, who took to burdening the people with fines. However careful Pahom tried to be, it happened again and again that now a horse of his got among the lady's oats, now a cow strayed into her garden, now his calves found their way into her meadows—and he always had to pay a fine.

Pahom paid up, but grumbled and, going home in a temper, was rough with his family. All through that summer, Pahom had much trouble because of this steward, and he was even glad when winter came and the cattle had to be stabled. Though he grudged the fodder when they could no longer graze on the pastureland, at least he was free from anxiety about them.

In the winter the news got about that the lady was going to sell her land and that the keeper of the inn on the high road was bargaining for it. When the peasants heard this they were very much alarmed.

"Well," thought they, "if the innkeeper gets the land, he will worry us with fines worse than the lady's steward. We all depend on that estate."

So the peasants went on behalf of their Commune,[2] and asked the lady not to sell the land to the innkeeper, offering her a better price for it themselves. The lady agreed to let them have it. Then the peasants tried to arrange for the Commune to buy the whole estate, so that it might be held by them all in common. They met twice to discuss it, but could not settle the matter; the Evil One sowed discord among them and they could not agree. So they decided to buy the land individually, each according to his means; and the lady agreed to this plan as she had to the other. **D**

Presently Pahom heard that a neighbor of his was buying fifty acres, and that the lady had consented to accept one half in cash and to wait a year for the other half. Pahom felt envious.

"Look at that," thought he, "the land is all being sold, and I shall get none of it." So he spoke to his wife.

"Other people are buying," said he, "and we must also buy twenty acres or so. Life is becoming impossible. That steward is simply crushing us with his fines."

So they put their heads together and considered how they could manage to buy it. They had one hundred rubles[3] laid by. They sold a colt and one half of their bees, hired out one of their sons as a laborer, and took his wages in advance; borrowed the rest from a brother-in-law, and so scraped together half the purchase money.

Having done this, Pahom chose out a farm of forty acres, some of it wooded, and went to the lady to bargain for it. They came to an agreement, and he shook hands with her upon it and paid her a deposit in advance. Then they went to town and signed the deeds, he paying half the price down, and undertaking to pay the remainder within two years.

So now Pahom had land of his own. He borrowed seed, and sowed it on the land he had bought. The harvest was a good one, and within a year he had man-

---

1. **lying… stove:** In Russian houses, large stoves made of brick or tile radiated heat to warm a room. Rich people would not lie on top of their stoves.

---

2. **Commune:** village council.
3. **rubles:** units of money in Russia

C **Reading Focus** Identifying Theme What plan does the Devil form to entrap and control Pahom?

D **Literary Focus** Allegory How does the Evil One influence the outcome of the discussion?

aged to pay off his debts both to the lady and to his brother-in-law. So he became a landowner, plowing and sowing his own land, making hay on his own land, cutting his own trees, and feeding his cattle on his own pasture. When he went out to plow his fields, or to look at his growing corn,[4] or at his grass meadows, his heart would fill with joy. The grass that grew and the flowers that bloomed there seemed to him unlike any that grew elsewhere. Formerly, when he had passed by that land, it had appeared the same as any other land, but now it seemed quite different.

So Pahom was well contented, and everything would have been right if the neighboring peasants would only not have trespassed on his cornfields and meadows. He appealed to them most civilly, but they still went on: Now the Communal herdsmen would let the village cows stray into his meadows, then horses from the night pasture would get among his corn. Pahom turned them out again and again, and forgave their owners, and for a long time he forbore to prosecute anyone. But at last he lost patience and complained to the District Court. He knew it was the peasants' want of land, and no evil intent on their part, that caused the trouble, but he thought:

"I cannot go on overlooking it or they will destroy all I have. They must be taught a lesson." **E**

So he had them up, gave them one lesson, and then another, and two or three of the peasants were fined. After a time Pahom's neighbors began to bear him a grudge for this, and would now and then let their cattle on to his land on purpose. One peasant even got into Pahom's wood at night and cut down five young lime trees[5] for their bark. Pahom passing through the wood one day noticed something white. He came nearer and saw the stripped trunks lying on the ground, and close by stood the stumps where the trees had been. Pahom was furious.

"If he had only cut one here and there it would have been bad enough," thought Pahom, "but the ras-

cal has actually cut down a whole clump. If I could only find out who did this, I would pay him out."

He racked his brain as to who it could be. Finally he decided: "It must be Simon—no one else could have done it." So he went to Simon's homestead to have a look round, but he found nothing, and only had an angry scene. However, he now felt more certain than ever that Simon had done it, and he lodged a complaint. Simon was summoned. The case was tried, and retried, and at the end of it all Simon was acquitted, there being no evidence against him. Pahom felt still more aggrieved, and let his anger loose upon the Elder and the Judges.

"You let thieves grease your palms," said he. "If you were honest folk yourselves you would not let a thief go free."

So Pahom quarreled with the Judges and with his neighbors. Threats to burn his building began to be uttered. So though Pahom had more land, his place in the Commune was much worse than before. **F**

About this time a rumor got about that many people were moving to new parts.

"There's no need for me to leave my land," thought Pahom. "But some of the others might leave our village and then there would be more room for us. I would take over their land myself and make my estate a bit bigger. I could then live more at ease. As it is, I am still too cramped to be comfortable." **G**

One day Pahom was sitting at home when a peasant, passing through the village, happened to call in. He was allowed to stay the night, and supper was given him. Pahom had a talk with this peasant and asked him where he came from. The stranger answered that he came from beyond the Volga,[6] where he had been working. One word led to another, and the man went on to say that many people were settling in those parts. He told how some people from his village had settled there. They had joined the Commune, and had had

---

4. **corn:** any plants producing grain, such as wheat or oats.
5. **lime trees:** linden trees.

6. **Volga:** river in western Russia flowing into the Caspian Sea.

E Reading Focus Identifying Theme How does Pahom become like the landowner he once resented?

F Reading Focus Identifying Theme How does land ownership ultimately harm Pahom's standing in the Commune?

G Reading Focus Identifying Theme Relate Pahom's statement to the story's title. How much land does Pahom think he needs?

Vocabulary aggrieved (uh GREEVD) v. used as *adj.*: offended.

twenty-five acres per man granted them. The land was so good, he said, that the rye sown on it grew as high as a horse, and so thick that five cuts of a sickle made a sheaf. One peasant, he said, had brought nothing with him but his bare hands, and now he had six horses and two cows of his own.

Pahom's heart kindled with desire. He thought:

"Why should I suffer in this narrow hole, if one can live so well elsewhere? I will sell my land and my homestead here, and with the money I will start afresh over there and get everything new. In this crowded place one is always having trouble. But I must first go and find out all about it myself."

Toward summer he got ready and started. He went down the Volga on a steamer to Samara,[7] then walked another three hundred miles on foot, and at last reached the place. It was just as the stranger had said. The peasants had plenty of land: Every man had twenty-five acres of Communal land given him for his use, and anyone who had money could buy, besides, at a ruble an acre as much good freehold land as he wanted.

Having found out all he wished to know, Pahom returned home as autumn came on, and began selling off his belongings. He sold his land at a profit, sold his homestead and all his cattle, and withdrew from membership in the Commune. He only waited till the spring, and then started with his family for the new settlement.

As soon as Pahom and his family reached their new abode, he applied for admission into the Commune of a large village. He stood treat to the Elders[8] and obtained the necessary documents. Five shares of Communal land were given him for his own and his sons' use: that is to say—125 acres (not all together, but in different fields) besides the use of the Communal pasture. Pahom put up the buildings he

---

7. **Samara:** city on the Volga River in southwestern Russia.
8. **stood treat to the Elders:** provided the Elders with a meal.

Analyzing Visuals

Viewing and Interpreting   Does this painting represent Pahom's ideas about land? Is farming romanticized in the painting? Explain.

needed, and bought cattle. Of the Communal land alone he had three times as much as at his former home, and the land was good corn land. He was ten times better off than he had been. He had plenty of arable land and pasturage, and could keep as many head of cattle as he liked.

At first, in the bustle of building and settling down, Pahom was pleased with it all, but when he got used to it he began to think that even here he had not enough land. The first year, he sowed wheat on his share of the Communal land and had a good crop. He wanted to go on sowing wheat, but had not enough

H **Reading Focus** Identifying Theme   How have Pahom's desires changed?

I **Literary Focus** Allegory   Events in allegories often occur in patterns. Notice how Pahom has acquired more and more land. If he follows the pattern of his past actions, what can we predict will happen next?

Vocabulary   **arable** (AR uh buhl) *adj.:* fit to be farmed or cultivated.

Harvest Time by Grigory Myasoyedov. he State Russian Museum.

Communal land for the purpose, and what he had already used was not available; for in those parts wheat is only sown on virgin soil or on fallow land. It is sown for one or two years, and then the land lies fallow till it is again overgrown with prairie grass. There were many who wanted such land and there was not enough for all; so that people quarreled about it. Those who were better off wanted it for growing wheat, and those who were poor wanted it to let to dealers, so that they might raise money to pay their taxes. Pahom wanted to sow more wheat, so he rented land from a dealer for a year. He sowed much wheat and had a fine crop, but the land was too far from the village—the wheat had to be carted more than ten miles. After a time Pahom noticed that some peasant dealers were living on separate farms and were growing wealthy; and he thought: "If I were to buy some freehold land and have a homestead on it, it would be a different thing altogether. Then it would all be nice and compact."

The question of buying freehold land recurred to him again and again.

He went on in the same way for three years, renting land and sowing wheat. The seasons turned out well and the crops were good, so that he began to lay money by. He might have gone on living contentedly, but he grew tired of having to rent other people's land every year, and having to scramble for it. Wherever there was good land to be had, the peasants would rush for it and it was taken up at once, so that unless you were sharp about it you got none. It happened in the third year that he and a dealer together rented a piece of pastureland from some peasants; and they had already plowed it up, when there was some dispute and the peasants went to law about it, and things fell out so that the labor was all lost.

"If it were my own land," thought Pahom, "I should be independent, and there would not be all this unpleasantness." **J**

J **Reading Focus** **Identifying Theme** What does Pahom want even though he "might have gone on living contentedly"?

So Pahom began looking out for land which he could buy; and he came across a peasant who had bought thirteen hundred acres, but having got into difficulties was willing to sell again cheap. Pahom bargained and haggled with him, and at last they settled the price at 1,500 rubles, part in cash and part to be paid later. They had all but clinched the matter when a passing dealer happened to stop at Pahom's one day to get a feed for his horses. He drank tea with Pahom and they had a talk. The dealer said that he was just returning from the land of the Bashkirs,[9] far away, where he had bought thirteen thousand acres of land, all for 1,000 rubles. Pahom questioned him further, and the tradesman said:

"All one need do is to make friends with the chiefs. I gave away about one hundred rubles' worth of silk robes and carpets, besides a case of tea, and I gave wine to those who would drink it; and I got the land for less than a penny an acre." And he showed Pahom the title deeds, saying:

"The land lies near a river, and the whole prairie is virgin soil."

Pahom plied him with questions, and the tradesman said:

"There is more land there than you could cover if you walked a year, and it all belongs to the Bashkirs. They are as simple as sheep, and land can be got almost for nothing."

"There now," thought Pahom, "with my one thousand rubles, why should I get only thirteen hundred acres, and saddle myself with a debt besides? If I take it out there, I can get more than ten times as much for the money." **(K)**

Pahom inquired how to get to the place, and as soon as the tradesman had left him, he prepared to go there himself. He left his wife to look after the homestead, and started on his journey taking his man with him. They stopped at a town on their way and bought a case of tea, some wine, and other presents, as the tradesman had advised. On and on they went

until they had gone more than three hundred miles, and on the seventh day they came to a place where the Bashkirs had pitched their tents. It was all just as the tradesman had said. The people lived on the steppes, by a river, in felt-covered tents. They neither tilled the ground, nor ate bread. Their cattle and horses grazed in herds on the steppe. The colts were tethered behind the tents, and the mares were driven to them twice a day. The mares were milked, and from the milk kumiss[10] was made. It was the women who prepared kumiss, and they also made cheese. As far as the men were concerned, drinking kumiss and tea, eating mutton, and playing on their pipes was all they cared about. They were all stout and merry, and all the summer long they never thought of doing any work. They were quite ignorant, and knew no Russian, but were good natured enough.

As soon as they saw Pahom, they came out of their tents and gathered round their visitor. An interpreter was found, and Pahom told them he had come about some land. The Bashkirs seemed very glad; they took Pahom and led him into one of the best tents, where they made him sit on some down cushions placed on a carpet, while they sat round him. They gave him some tea and kumiss, and had a sheep killed, and gave him mutton to eat. Pahom took presents out of his cart and distributed them among the Bashkirs, and divided the tea amongst them. The Bashkirs were delighted. They talked a great deal among themselves, and then told the interpreter to translate.

"They wish to tell you," said the interpreter, "that they like you, and that it is our custom to do all we can to please a guest and to repay him for his gifts. You have given us presents, now tell us which of the things we possess please you best, that we may present them to you."

"What pleases me best here," answered Pahom, "is your land. Our land is crowded and the soil is exhausted; but you have plenty of land and it is good land. I never saw the like of it."

---

9. **Bashkirs:** Turkish-speaking peoples who live on the Russian steppes, or plains.

10. **kumiss:** fermented drink made from mare's milk.

(K) **Reading Focus** Identifying Theme Why is Pahom tempted to go to the Bashkirs?

Vocabulary **haggled** (HAG uhld) *v.*: argued about a price.

1016 Unit 5 • Collection 10

The interpreter translated. The Bashkirs talked among themselves for a while. Pahom could not understand what they were saying, but saw that they were much amused and that they shouted and laughed. Then they were silent and looked at Pahom while the interpreter said:

"They wish me to tell you that in return for your presents they will gladly give you as much land as you want. You have only to point it out with your hand and it is yours."

The Bashkirs talked again for a while and began to dispute. Pahom asked what they were disputing about, and the interpreter told him that some of them thought they ought to ask their chief about the land and not act in his absence, while others thought there was no need to wait for his return.

While the Bashkirs were disputing, a man in a large fox-fur cap appeared on the scene. They all became silent and rose to their feet. The interpreter said, "This is our chief himself." **L**

Pahom immediately fetched the best dressing gown and five pounds of tea, and offered these to the chief. The chief accepted them, and seated himself in the place of honor. The Bashkirs at once began telling him something. The chief listened for a while, then made a sign with his head for them to be silent, and addressing himself to Pahom, said in Russian:

"Well, let it be so. Choose whatever piece of land you like; we have plenty of it."

"How can I take as much as I like?" thought Pahom. "I must get a deed to make it secure, or else they may say, 'It is yours,' and afterward may take it away again."

"Thank you for your kind words," he said aloud. "You have much land, and I only want a little. But I should like to be sure which bit is mine. Could it not be measured and made over to me? Life and death are in God's hands. You good people give it to me, but your children might wish to take it away again." **M**

"You are quite right," said the chief. "We will make it over to you."

"I heard that a dealer had been here," continued Pahom, "and that you gave him a little land, too, and signed title deeds to that effect. I should like to have it done in the same way."

The chief understood.

"Yes," replied he, "that can be done quite easily. We have a scribe, and we will go to town with you and have the deed properly sealed."

"And what will be the price?" asked Pahom.

"Our price is always the same: one thousand rubles a day."

Pahom did not understand.

"A day? What measure is that? How many acres would that be?"

"We do not know how to reckon it out," said the chief. "We sell it by the day. As much as you can go round on your feet in a day is yours, and the price is one thousand rubles a day."

Pahom was surprised.

"But in a day you can get round a large tract of land," he said.

The chief laughed.

"It will all be yours!" said he. "But there is one condition: If you don't return on the same day to the spot whence you started, your money is lost." **N**

"But how am I to mark the way that I have gone?"

"Why, we shall go to any spot you like, and stay there. You must start from that spot and make your round, taking a spade with you. Wherever you think necessary, make a mark. At every turning, dig a hole and pile up the turf; then afterward we will go round with a plow from hole to hole. You may make as large a circuit as you please, but before the sun sets you must return to the place you started from. All the land you cover will be yours."

Pahom was delighted. It was decided to start early next morning. They talked a while, and after drink-

---

L Literary Focus **Allegory** Foxes are known for their cleverness. Who do you suspect the chief might be?

M Reading Focus **Identifying Theme** When proverbs and wise sayings appear in a story, they often point to the theme. Why might Pahom's statement, "Life and death are in God's hands," be important in this story?

N Literary Focus **Allegory** In many traditional folk stories, bargains are made with the Devil. What bargain is struck with the chief?

ing some more kumiss and eating some more mutton, they had tea again, and then the night came on. They gave Pahom a featherbed to sleep on, and the Bashkirs dispersed for the night, promising to assemble the next morning at daybreak and ride out before sunrise to the appointed spot.

Pahom lay on the featherbed, but could not sleep. He kept thinking about the land.

"What a large tract I will mark off!" thought he. "I can easily do thirty-five miles in a day. The days are long now, and within a circuit of thirty-five miles what a lot of land there will be! I will sell the poorer land, or let it to peasants, but I'll pick out the best and farm it. I will buy two ox teams, and hire two more laborers. About a hundred and fifty acres shall be plow land, and I will pasture cattle on the rest."

Pahom lay awake all night, and dozed off only just before dawn. Hardly were his eyes closed when he had a dream. He thought he was lying in that same tent and heard somebody chuckling outside. He wondered who it could be, and rose and went out, and he saw the Bashkir chief sitting in front of the tent holding his sides and rolling about with laughter. Going nearer to the chief, Pahom asked: "What are you laughing at?" But he saw that it was no longer the chief, but the dealer who had recently stopped at his house and had told him about the land. Just as Pahom was going to ask, "Have you been here long?" he saw that it was not the dealer, but the peasant who had come up from the Volga, long ago, to Pahom's old home. Then he saw that it was not the peasant either, but the Devil himself with hoofs and horns, sitting there and chuckling, and before him lay a man barefoot, prostrate on the ground, with only trousers and a shirt on. And Pahom dreamt that he looked more attentively to see what sort of a man it was that was lying there, and he saw that the man was dead, and that it was himself! He awoke horror-struck. **O**

"What things one does dream," thought he.

Looking round he saw through the open door that the dawn was breaking.

"It's time to wake them up," thought he. "We ought to be starting."

He got up, roused his man (who was sleeping

Man in the Field by Vladimir Yegorovich Makovsky (1846–1920).

in his cart), bade him harness, and went to call the Bashkirs.

"It's time to go to the steppe to measure the land," he said.

The Bashkirs rose and assembled, and the chief came too. Then they began drinking kumiss again, and offered Pahom some tea, but he would not wait.

"If we are to go, let us go. It is high time," said he.

The Bashkirs got ready and they all started: some mounted on horses, and some in carts. Pahom drove in his own small cart with his servant and took a spade with him. When they reached the steppe, the morning red was beginning to kindle. They ascended a hillock

---

O **Reading Focus** Identifying Theme Dreams are often used in literature to foretell the future. What lesson is found in Pahom's dream?

Vocabulary **prostrate** (PRAHS trayt) *adj.:* lying flat.

(called by the Bashkirs a *shikhan*) and dismounting from their carts and their horses, gathered in one spot. The chief came up to Pahom and stretching out his arm toward the plain: **P**

"See," said he, "all this, as far as your eye can reach, is ours. You may have any part of it you like."

Pahom's eyes glistened: It was all virgin soil, as flat as the palm of your hand, as black as the seed of a poppy, and in the hollows different kinds of grasses grew breast high.

The chief took off his fox-fur cap, placed it on the ground, and said:

"This will be the mark. Start from here, and return here again. All the land you go round shall be yours."

Pahom took out his money and put it on the cap. Then he took off his outer coat, remaining in his sleeveless undercoat. He unfastened his girdle and tied it tight below his stomach, put a little bag of bread into the breast of his coat, and tying a flask of water to his girdle, he drew up the tops of his boots, took the spade from his man, and stood ready to start. He considered for some moments which way he had better go—it was tempting everywhere.

"No matter," he concluded, "I will go toward the rising sun."

He turned his face to the east, stretched himself, and waited for the sun to appear above the rim.

"I must lose no time," he thought, "and it is easier walking while it is still cool."

The sun's rays had hardly flashed above the horizon, before Pahom, carrying the spade over his shoulder, went down into the steppe.

Pahom started walking neither slowly nor quickly. After having gone a thousand yards he stopped, dug a hole, and placed pieces of turf one on another to make it more visible. Then he went on; and now that he had walked off his stiffness he quickened his pace. After a while he dug another hole.

Pahom looked back. The hillock could be distinctly seen in the sunlight, with the people on it, and the glittering tires of the cart wheels. At a rough guess Pahom concluded that he had walked three miles. It was growing warmer; he took off his undercoat, flung it across his shoulder, and went on again. It had grown quite warm now; he looked at the sun, it was time to think of breakfast.

"The first shift is done, but there are four in a day, and it is too soon yet to turn. But I will just take off my boots," said he to himself.

He sat down, took off his boots, stuck them into his girdle, and went on. It was easy walking now.

"I will go on for another three miles," thought he, "and then turn to the left. This spot is so fine, that it would be a pity to lose it. The further one goes, the better the land seems."

He went straight on for a while, and when he looked round, the hillock was scarcely visible and the people on it looked like black ants, and he could just see something glistening there in the sun.

"Ah," thought Pahom, "I have gone far enough in this direction, it is time to turn. Besides I am in a regular sweat, and very thirsty."

He stopped, dug a large hole, and heaped up pieces of turf. Next he untied his flask, had a drink, and then turned sharply to the left. He went on and on; the grass was high, and it was very hot.

Pahom began to grow tired: He looked at the sun and saw that it was noon.

"Well," he thought, "I must have a rest."

He sat down, and ate some bread and drank some water; but he did not lie down, thinking that if he did he might fall asleep. After sitting a little while, he went on again. At first he walked easily: The food had strengthened him; but it had become terribly hot and he felt sleepy, still he went on, thinking: "An hour to suffer, a lifetime to live."

He went a long way in this direction also, and was about to turn to the left again, when he perceived a damp hollow: "It would be a pity to leave that out," he thought. "Flax would do well there." So he went on past the hollow, and dug a hole on the other side of it before he turned the corner. Pahom looked toward the hillock. The heat made the air hazy: It seemed to be quivering, and through the haze the people on the hillock could scarcely be seen. **Q**

P **Literary Focus** **Allegory** How have the Bashkir chief, the dealer, and the peasant all furthered the Devil's plan?

Q **Reading Focus** **Identifying Theme** How does greed drive Pahom?

"Ah!" thought Pahom, "I have made the sides too long; I must make this one shorter." And he went along the third side, stepping faster. He looked at the sun: It was nearly halfway to the horizon, and he had not yet done two miles of the third side of the square. He was still ten miles from the goal.

"No," he thought, "though it will make my land lopsided, I must hurry back in a straight line now. I might go too far, and as it is I have a great deal of land."

So Pahom hurriedly dug a hole, and turned straight toward the hillock.

Pahom went straight toward the hillock, but he now walked with difficulty. He was done up with the heat, his bare feet were cut and bruised, and his legs began to fail. He longed to rest, but it was impossible if he meant to get back before sunset. The sun waits for no man, and it was sinking lower and lower.

"Oh dear," he thought, "if only I have not blundered trying for too much! What if I am too late?"

He looked toward the hillock and at the sun. He was still far from his goal, and the sun was already near the rim.

Pahom walked on and on; it was very hard walking but he went quicker and quicker. He pressed on, but was still far from the place. He began running, threw away his coat, his boots, his flask, and his cap, and kept only the spade which he used as a support.

"What shall I do," he thought again. "I have grasped too much and ruined the whole affair. I can't get there before the sun sets." **R**

And this fear made him still more breathless. Pahom went on running, his soaking shirt and trousers stuck to him, and his mouth was parched. His breast was working like a blacksmith's bellows, his heart was beating like a hammer, and his legs were giving way as if they did not belong to him. Pahom was seized with terror lest he should die of the strain.

Though afraid of death, he could not stop. "After having run all that way they will call me a fool if I stop now," thought he. And he ran on and on, and drew near and heard the Bashkirs yelling and shouting to him, and their cries inflamed his heart still more. He gathered his last strength and ran on.

The sun was close to the rim, and cloaked in mist looked large, and red as blood. Now, yes now, it was about to set! The sun was quite low, but he was also quite near his aim. Pahom could already see the people on the hillock waving their arms to hurry him up. He could see the fox-fur cap on the ground and the money on it, and the chief sitting on the ground holding his sides. And Pahom remembered his dream. **S**

"There is plenty of land," thought he, "but will God let me live on it? I have lost my life, I have lost my life! I shall never reach that spot!"

Pahom looked at the sun, which had reached the earth: One side of it had already disappeared. With all his remaining strength he rushed on, bending his body forward so that his legs could hardly follow fast enough to keep him from falling. Just as he reached the hillock it suddenly grew dark. He looked up—the sun had already set! He gave a cry: "All my labor has been in vain," thought he, and was about to stop, but he heard the Bashkirs still shouting, and remembered that though to him, from below, the sun seemed to have set, they on the hillock could still see it. He took a long breath and ran up the hillock. It was still light there. He reached the top and saw the cap. Before it sat the chief laughing and holding his sides. Again Pahom remembered his dream, and he uttered a cry: His legs gave way beneath him, he fell forward and reached the cap with his hands. **T**

"Ah, that's a fine fellow!" exclaimed the chief. "He has gained much land!"

Pahom's servant came running up and tried to raise him, but he saw that blood was flowing from his mouth. Pahom was dead!

The Bashkirs clicked their tongues to show their pity.

His servant picked up the spade and dug a grave long enough for Pahom to lie in, and buried him in it. Six feet from his head to his heels was all he needed.

R **Reading Focus** Identifying Theme What words in this paragraph might be significant in summarizing what is happening to Pahom?

S **Reading Focus** Identifying Theme What thought here might be a key to the story's theme?

T **Literary Focus** Allegory Why might the chief be holding his sides?

Respond and Think Critically

Reading Focus

Quick Check

1. What happens when Pahom buys more land?
2. How does the Devil triumph over Pahom?

Read with a Purpose

3. What does the story reveal about how we come to confuse what we want with what we need?

Reading Skill: Identifying Theme

4. Review the chart you filled out. Put an asterisk beside details that most strongly support a theme. Then, write at least one sentence summarizing what Pahom discovers.

```
+-----------------------------------------------+
|               Clues to Theme                  |
|                                               |
| +------------------+   +--------------------+ |
| | The peasant      |   | This statement     | |
| | sister says      |   | seems to relate    | |
| | "Gain and pain   |   | to the story title.| |
| | are brothers     |   |                    | |
| | twain."          |   |                    | |
| +------------------+   +--------------------+ |
|                                               |
| Theme:                                        |
+-----------------------------------------------+
```

✓ Vocabulary Check

Be sure you can justify your answers to these questions about the Vocabulary words.

5. If you are **piqued**, are you happy or irritated?
6. Would you feel honored or upset after being **disparaged**?
7. If you are **aggrieved**, do you feel wronged or flattered?
8. Would **arable** land be fertile or unproductive?
9. When two people **haggled** about something, would you say they argued or agreed?
10. Pahom found himself **prostrate**. Was he flat on the ground or sitting on the ground?

Literary Focus

Literary Analysis

11. **Analyze** Think about the discussion between the sisters at the story's beginning. How does their conversation foreshadow Pahom's end?
12. **Draw Conclusions** Based on the story's events, how do you think Tolstoy views ambition?
13. **Extend** Consider the contrast between what Pahom wants and "all he needs." How could Tolstoy's parable about materialism apply today?

Literary Skills: Allegory

14. **Summarize** Outline this story as an allegory. Follow this format: The story is about_____. The devil stands for_____, while Pahom stands for_____. Pahom's attempt to get as much land as he could cover in a day represents_____. The land itself stands for_____.

Literary Skills Review: Tone

15. **Interpret** A writer's **tone** is the attitude he or she takes toward the subject matter or the audience. How would you describe Tolstoy's tone?

Writing Focus

Think As a Reader/Writer

Use It in Your Writing You wrote in your *Reader/Writer Notebook* how this story could be set in today's world. Now, use your notes to write your own brief allegory about materialism today.

What Do You Think Now?

What did Pahom think he was winning as he gained more and more land?

Preparing to Read

The Bet

What Do You Think? How can appearance be different from reality?

QuickTalk

What sorts of powerful experiences can totally change the way someone thinks about life? With a partner, talk about some possibilities. Record your ideas in your *Reader/Writer Notebook*.

Anton Pavlovich Chekhov (1898) by Osip Emmanuilovich Braz (1873–1936). Tretyakov Gallery, Moscow, Russia.

MEET THE WRITER

Anton Chekhov
(1860–1904)

Shortly before his death, Chekhov joked that people would read his work for only seven more years. A century later, his brilliant short stories and plays show no signs of being forgotten.

A Doctor and Writer

Anton Pavlovich Chekhov was born in the seaport town of Taganrog in the south of Russia. When he was sixteen, his father went bankrupt and fled with the rest of the family to Moscow to avoid a prison sentence. Left behind as a "hostage" to his father's creditors, Chekhov tutored the creditor's son at a cheap rate, finished school, and went to Moscow to study medicine on a scholarship. To support himself and his family, who were living in a slum, Chekhov wrote comic stories to sell to periodicals. Comic stories soon gave way to more serious pieces, in which, as Chekhov said, questions were asked but not answered.

Studying medicine greatly <u>benefited</u> the young writer. As a doctor, Chekhov became acquainted with hundreds of ordinary people. He continued to write while practicing medicine and gave up his full-time practice only when it took too much time away from his writing.

Humanity, Reason, and Generosity

It was not until the last years of his brief life that Chekhov achieved some affluence. He moved his parents and sister to a large country estate, where he organized famine relief, fought cholera epidemics, and treated poor patients free of charge. Although the theme of many of his works is alienation, Chekhov's real-life activities demonstrate that humanity, reason, and generosity were among his highest values.

His finest stories were all written in the 1890s and his four great plays, *The Sea Gull* (1896), *Uncle Vanya* (1897), *Three Sisters* (1901), and *The Cherry Orchard* (1904), were written while he was fatally ill with tuberculosis. In 1901 he married the actress who played the lead role in *The Sea Gull*, but the couple spent their honeymoon in a sanitarium. Three years later Chekhov died at the age of forty-four, still at the height of his creativity.

Think About the Writer How did Chekhov's experiences as a doctor affect his writing?

Reader/Writer Notebook

Use your **RWN** to complete the activities for this selection.

Literary Focus

Theme The truth or insight about human life revealed in a story is its **theme.** For example, the theme of a story about growing up might be that disillusionment is inherently part of the maturation process. To identify theme, the reader must consider all of a story's elements, and then infer the truths or insights the story reveals. The theme is often illuminated at the end of the story in the main character's discovery about life. Identifying themes requires a tolerance for ambiguity, especially in open-ended stories like "The Bet," which raises more questions than it answers.

Literary Perspectives Apply the Literary Perspective described on page 1024 as you read this story.

Reading Focus

Making Predictions A **prediction** is a special kind of **inference,** or educated guess, about what will happen next. Some predictions turn out to be inaccurate, and modifying them is an essential—and enjoyable—part of active reading. Because Chekhov begins this story with a debate about capital punishment, you might predict that the story will explore that subject. As you read, see if you have made a correct prediction, or if Chekhov has surprised you by focusing instead on some larger issue.

Into Action As you read, make predictions based on clues that suggest or foreshadow what will happen to the characters later in the story. Use a chart like the one below to record the clues and your predictions.

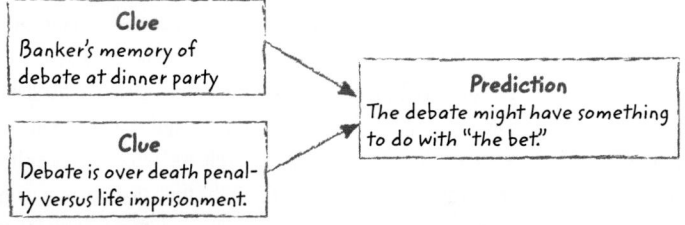

Writing Focus

Think as a Reader/Writer

Find It in Your Reading This story spans fifteen years, from the time of the bet's inception to its conclusion. As you read, record in your *Reader/Writer Notebook* how Chekhov marks the passage of time in years, hours, and minutes.

Vocabulary

frivolous (FRIHV uh luhs) *adj.:* light-minded; lacking seriousness. *The frivolous banker made a large bet without thinking.*

compulsory (kuhm PUHL suhr ee) *adj.:* required; enforced. *The banker argues that voluntary confinement is more unbearable than compulsory imprisonment.*

caprice (kuh PREES) *n.:* sudden notion or desire. *The banker realizes that the bet was the result of unwise caprice.*

zealously (ZEHL uhs lee) *adv.:* fervently; devotedly. *The prisoner spends his time zealously studying books and languages.*

indiscriminately (ihn dihs KRIHM uh niht lee) *adv.:* without making careful distinctions; randomly. *The lawyer reads indiscriminately, diving into any book he can get.*

ethereal (ih THIHR ee uhl) *adj.:* light and delicate; unearthly. *After reading the poems, the lawyer was visited by ethereal visions.*

renounce (rih NOWNS) *v.:* formally give up; reject. *The lawyer decides to renounce his claim to the money.*

Language Coach

Roots Knowing a word's root can help you figure out the meanings of related words. For example, the Vocabulary word *indiscriminately* comes from the Latin root *discrīmināre,* which means "to separate." Now that you know this word's root, can you figure out the definitions of the words *discriminate* and *discrimination?*

 Learn It Online

Explore the vocabulary words inside and out through Word Watch online.

go.hrw.com L12-1023 **Go**

The Bet

by **Anton Chekhov**

translated by **Constance Garnett**

Read with a Purpose
Read to discover the stakes and the surprising outcome of an unusual bet.

Build Background
Would you give up all human company for years to win an amazing fortune? A character in this famous Russian story bets that he can do it, and his voluntary solitude raises serious questions for him and for readers.

1

It was a dark autumn night. The old banker was walking up and down his study and remembering how, fifteen years before, he had given a party one autumn evening. There had been many clever men there, and there had been interesting conversations. Among other things, they had talked of capital punishment. The majority of the guests, among whom were many journalists and intellectual men, disapproved of the death penalty. They considered that form of punishment out of date, immoral, and unsuitable for Christian states. In the opinion of some of them, the death penalty ought to be replaced everywhere by imprisonment for life.

"I don't agree with you," said their host, the banker. "I have not tried either the death penalty or imprisonment for life, but if one may judge a priori,[1] the death penalty is more moral and more humane than imprisonment for life. Capital punishment kills a man at once, but lifelong imprisonment kills him slowly. Which executioner is the more humane, he who kills you in a few minutes or he who drags the life out of you in the course of many years?" Ⓐ

"Both are equally immoral," observed one of the guests, "for they both have the same object—to take away life. The state is not God. It has not the right to take away what it cannot restore when it wants to."

Among the guests was a young lawyer, a young man of five-and-twenty. When he was asked his opinion, he said: "The death sentence and the life sentence are equally immoral, but if I had to choose between the death penalty and imprisonment for life, I would

---

1. **a priori:** Latin for "from the first." Here, a generalization based on theory not experience.

Ⓐ **Reading Focus** Making Predictions Based on these first paragraphs, what do you think will be the main subject of the story?

Literary Perspectives

Analyzing Credibility in Literature Literature often asks us to believe in things that don't seem possible, and there are times when we are especially aware that a story doesn't ring true. A situation in a story, such as an improbable bet, might ask us to question our own beliefs, but if it causes us to question the credibility of the story or storyteller, we often lose interest and trust in the story. Samuel Taylor Coleridge coined the phrase "suspension of disbelief" to describe "dramatic truth," or the truth that operates within the work of art. As a reader, your willingness to accept the "truth" of the story hinges on the fact that you can temporarily suspend your judgment of what is possible in order to enjoy the story. However, you should still take note when you find inconsistencies within the story, or if you believe that the story is not playing by its own rules.

As you read, be sure to notice the questions in the text, which will guide you in using this perspective.

certainly choose the second. To live anyhow is better than not at all."

A lively discussion arose. The banker, who was younger and more nervous in those days, was suddenly carried away by excitement; he struck the table with his fist and shouted at the young man: "It's not true! I'll bet you two million you wouldn't stay in solitary confinement for five years."

"If you mean that in earnest," said the young man, "I'll take the bet, but I would stay not five, but fifteen years."

"Fifteen? Done!" cried the banker. "Gentlemen, I stake two million!"

"Agreed! You stake your millions and I stake my freedom!" said the young man.

And this wild, senseless bet was carried out! The banker, spoiled and frivolous, with millions beyond his reckoning, was delighted at the bet. At supper he made fun of the young man and said: "Think better of it, young man, while there is still time. To me two million is a trifle, but you are losing three or four of the best years of your life. I say three or four, because you won't stay longer. Don't forget either, you unhappy man, that voluntary confinement is a great deal harder to bear than compulsory. The thought that you have the right to step out in liberty at any moment will poison your whole existence in prison. I am sorry for you."

And now the banker, walking to and fro, remembered all this and asked himself: "What was the object of that bet? What is the good of that man's losing fifteen years of his life and my throwing away two million? Can it prove that the death penalty is better or worse than imprisonment for life? No, no. It was all nonsensical and meaningless. On my part it was the caprice of a pampered man, and on his part simple greed for money...." **Ⓑ**

Then he remembered what followed that evening.

It was decided that the young man should spend the years of his captivity under the strictest supervision in one of the lodges in the banker's garden. It was agreed that for fifteen years he should not be free to cross the threshold of the lodge, to see human beings, to hear the human voice, or to receive letters and newspapers. He was allowed to have a musical instrument and books and was allowed to write letters, to drink wine, and to smoke. By the terms of the agreement, the only relations he could have with the outer world were by a little window made purposely for that object. He might have anything he wanted—books, music, wine, and so on—in any quantity he desired, by writing an order, but could receive them only through the window. The agreement provided for every detail and every trifle that would make his imprisonment strictly

The Painter Konstantin Alekseevich Korovin (1891) by Valentin Serov (1865–1939). Tretyakov Gallery, Moscow, Russia.

Ⓑ Reading Focus **Making Predictions** How has the banker's view of the bet changed in fifteen years? What do you predict he will do next?

Vocabulary **frivolous** (FRIHV uh luhs) *adj.*: light-minded; lacking seriousness.
compulsory (kuhm PUHL suhr ee) *adj.*: required; enforced.
caprice (kuh PREES) *n.*: sudden notion or desire.

solitary, and bound the young man to stay there *exactly* fifteen years, beginning from twelve o'clock of November 14, 1870, and ending at twelve o'clock of November 14, 1885. The slightest attempt on his part to break the conditions, if only two minutes before the end, released the banker from the obligation to pay him two million.

For the first year of his confinement, as far as one could judge from his brief notes, the prisoner suffered severely from loneliness and depression. The sounds of the piano could be heard continually day and night from his lodge. He refused wine and tobacco. Wine, he wrote, excites the desires, and desires are the worst foes of the prisoner; and besides, nothing could be more dreary than drinking good wine and seeing no one. And tobacco spoiled the air of his room. In the first year the books he sent for were principally of a light character—novels with a complicated love plot, sensational and fantastic stories, and so on. **C**

In the second year the piano was silent in the lodge, and the prisoner asked only for the classics. In the fifth year music was audible again, and the prisoner asked for wine. Those who watched him through the window said that all that year he spent doing nothing but eating and drinking and lying on his bed, frequently yawning and talking angrily to himself. He did not read books. Sometimes at night he would sit down to write; he would spend hours writing and in the morning tear up all that he had written. More than once he could be heard crying.

In the second half of the sixth year the prisoner began zealously studying languages, philosophy, and history. He threw himself eagerly into these studies—so much so that the banker had enough to do to get him the books he ordered. In the course of four years, some six hundred volumes were procured at his request. It was during this period that the banker received the following letter from his prisoner: **D**

"My dear Jailer, I write you these lines in six languages. Show them to people who know the languages.

Let them read them. If they find not one mistake, I implore you to fire a shot in the garden. That shot will show me that my efforts have not been thrown away. The geniuses of all ages and of all lands speak different languages, but the same flame burns in them all. Oh, if you only knew what unearthly happiness my soul feels now from being able to understand them!" The prisoner's desire was fulfilled. The banker ordered two shots to be fired in the garden.

Then, after the tenth year, the prisoner sat immovably at the table and read nothing but the Gospels. It seemed strange to the banker that a man who in four years had mastered six hundred learned volumes should waste nearly a year over one thin book easy of comprehension. Theology[2] and histories of religion followed the Gospels.

In the last two years of his confinement, the prisoner read an immense quantity of books quite indiscriminately. At one time he was busy with the natural sciences; then he would ask for Byron or Shakespeare. There were notes in which he demanded at the same time books on chemistry, and a manual of medicine, and a novel, and some treatise on philosophy or theology. His reading suggested a man swimming in the sea among the wreckage of his ship and trying to save his life by greedily clutching first at one spar[3] and then at another.

2

The old banker remembered all this and thought: "Tomorrow at twelve o'clock he will regain his freedom. By our arrangement I ought to pay him two million. If I do pay him, it is all over with me: I shall be utterly ruined."

Fifteen years before, his millions had been beyond

---

2. **theology:** study of religious teachings concerning God and God's relation to the world.
3. **spar:** pole that supports or extends a ship's sail.

C **Literary Perspectives** Analyzing Credibility in Literature What makes the story seem believable so far?

D **Literary Focus** Theme Based on this description of the prisoner's activities, what can you infer about the story's theme?

Vocabulary **zealously** (ZEHL uhs lee) *adv.*: fervently; devotedly.

indiscriminately (ihn dihs KRIHM uh niht lee) *adv.*: without making careful distinctions; randomly.

his reckoning; now he was afraid to ask himself which were greater, his debts or his assets. Desperate gambling on the Stock Exchange, wild speculation, and the excitability which he could not get over even in advancing years had by degrees led to the decline of his fortune, and the proud, fearless, self-confident millionaire had become a banker of middling rank, trembling at every rise and fall in his investments. "Cursed bet!" muttered the old man, clutching his head in despair. "Why didn't the man die? He is only forty now. He will take my last penny from me, he will marry, will enjoy life, will gamble on the Exchange, while I shall look at him with envy like a beggar and hear from him every day the same sentence: 'I am indebted to you for the happiness of my life; let me help you!' No, it is too much! The one means of being saved from bankruptcy and disgrace is the death of that man!" **E**

It struck three o'clock. The banker listened; everyone was asleep in the house, and nothing could be heard outside but the rustling of the chilled trees. Trying to make no noise, he took from a fireproof safe the key of the door which had not been opened for fifteen years, put on his overcoat, and went out of the house.

It was dark and cold in the garden. Rain was falling. A damp, cutting wind was racing about the garden, howling and giving the trees no rest. The banker strained his eyes but could see neither the earth nor the white statues, nor the lodge, nor the trees. Going to the spot where the lodge stood,

he twice called the watchman. No answer followed. Evidently the watchman had sought shelter from the weather and was now asleep somewhere either in the kitchen or in the greenhouse.

"If I had the pluck to carry out my intention," thought the old man, "suspicion would fall first upon the watchman."

He felt in the darkness for the steps and the door and went into the entry of the lodge. Then he groped his way into a little passage and lighted a match. There was not a soul there. There was a bedstead with no bedding on it, and in the corner there was a dark

Still Life with Book Sheets and Pictures (1783) by Russian School. Oil on canvas. Tretyakov Gallery, Moscow, Russia.

E Reading Focus Making Predictions What new problem arises in this passage? What could happen next?

Analyzing Visuals

Viewing and Interpreting Note how the books and documents are tightly bound. How is this image a metaphor for the bet?

cast-iron stove. The seals on the door leading to the prisoner's rooms were intact.

When the match went out, the old man, trembling with emotion, peeped through the little window. A candle was burning dimly in the prisoner's room. He was sitting at the table. Nothing could be seen but his back, the hair on his head, and his hands. Open books were lying on the table, on the two easy chairs, and on the carpet near the table.

Five minutes passed and the prisoner did not once stir. Fifteen years' imprisonment had taught him to sit still. The banker tapped at the window with his finger, and the prisoner made no movement whatever in response. Then the banker cautiously broke the seals off the door and put the key in the keyhole. The rusty lock gave a grating sound and the door creaked. The banker expected to hear at once footsteps and a cry of astonishment, but three minutes passed and it was as quiet as ever in the room. He made up his mind to go in. **F**

At the table a man unlike ordinary people was sitting motionless. He was a skeleton with the skin drawn tight over his bones, with long curls like a woman's, and a shaggy beard. His face was yellow with an earthy tint in it, his cheeks were hollow, his back long and narrow, and the hand on which his shaggy head was propped was so thin and delicate that it was dreadful to look at it. His hair was already streaked with silver, and seeing his emaciated, aged-looking face, no one would have believed that he was only forty. He was asleep. . . . In front of his bowed head there lay on the table a sheet of paper, on which there was something written in fine handwriting.

"Poor creature!" thought the banker, "he is asleep and most likely dreaming of the millions. And I have only to take this half-dead man, throw him on the bed, stifle him a little with the pillow, and the most conscientious expert would find no sign of a violent death. But let us first read what he has written here...."

The banker took the page from the table and read as follows:

"Tomorrow at twelve o'clock I regain my freedom and the right to associate with other men, but before I leave this room and see the sunshine, I think it necessary to say a few words to you. With a clear conscience I tell you, as before God, who beholds me, that I despise freedom and life and health and all that in your books is called the good things of the world.

"For fifteen years I have been intently studying earthly life. It is true I have not seen the earth or men, but in your books I have drunk fragrant wine, I have sung songs, I have hunted stags and wild boars in the forests, I have loved women.... Beauties as ethereal as clouds, created by the magic of your poets and geniuses, have visited me at night and have whispered in my ears wonderful tales that have set my brain in a whirl. In your books I have climbed to the peaks of Elburz and Mont Blanc,[4] and from there I have seen the sun rise and have watched it at evening flood the sky, the ocean, and the mountaintops with gold and crimson. I have watched from there the lightning flashing over my head and cleaving the storm clouds. I have seen green forests, fields, rivers, lakes, towns. I have heard the singing of the sirens,[5] and the strains of the shepherds' pipes; I have touched the wings of comely devils who flew down to converse with me of God.... In your books I have flung myself into the bottomless pit, performed miracles, slain, burned towns, preached new religions, conquered whole kingdoms....

"Your books have given me wisdom. All that the unresting thought of man has created in the ages is compressed into a small compass in my brain. I know that I am wiser than all of you.

"And I despise your books, I despise wisdom and the blessings of this world. It is all worthless, fleeting, illusory, and deceptive, like a mirage. You may be proud, wise, and fine, but death will wipe you off the face of the earth as though you were no more than

---

4. **Elburz and Mont Blanc:** Elburz is a mountain range in northern Iran; Mont Blanc, in France, is the highest mountain in the Alps.
5. **sirens:** in Greek mythology, partly human female creatures who lived on an island and lured sailors to their death with their beautiful singing.

F **Literary Perspectives** Analyzing Credibility in Literature Does the banker's hesitation seem believable here? Why or why not?

Vocabulary **ethereal** (ih THIHR ee uhl) *adj.*: light and delicate; unearthly.

mice burrowing under the floor, and your posterity, your history, your immortal geniuses will burn or freeze together with the earthly globe.

"You have lost your reason and taken the wrong path. You have taken lies for truth and hideousness for beauty. You would marvel if, owing to strange events of some sort, frogs and lizards suddenly grew on apple and orange trees instead of fruit or if roses began to smell like a sweating horse; so I marvel at you who exchange heaven for earth. I don't want to understand you.

"To prove to you in action how I despise all that you live by, I renounce the two million of which I once dreamed as of paradise and which now I despise. To deprive myself of the right to the money, I shall go out from here five minutes before the time fixed and so break the compact...." **G**

When the banker had read this, he laid the page on the table, kissed the strange man on the head, and went out of the lodge, weeping. At no other time, even when he had lost heavily on the Stock Exchange, had he felt so great a contempt for himself. When he got home, he lay on his bed, but his tears and emotion kept him for hours from sleeping.

Next morning the watchmen ran in with pale faces and told him they had seen the man who lived in the lodge climb out of the window into the garden, go to the gate, and disappear. The banker went at once with the servants to the lodge and made sure of the flight of his prisoner. To avoid arousing unnecessary talk, he took from the table the writing in which the millions were renounced and, when he got home, locked it up in the fireproof safe. **H**

Analyzing Visuals

Viewing and Interpreting What might this open window symbolize to both the banker and the lawyer? Who do you think opened the window? Why?

The Veranda at Liselund by Peter Ilsted (Danish, 1861–1933). Adelson Galleries, New York.

G **Literary Focus** **Theme** In one sense, the lawyer spends his years of imprisonment searching for the meaning of life. What do you think he discovers by the story's end?

H **Reading Focus** **Making Predictions** Are you surprised at the banker's actions at the end? What ending to the story did you predict?

Vocabulary **renounce** (rih NOWNS) *v.*: formally give up; reject.

Applying Your Skills

The Bet

Respond and Think Critically

Reading Focus

Quick Check

1. Why do the lawyer and the banker make a bet?

2. At the end of the fifteen years, how has the banker's situation changed?

3. Why does the banker go to the lodge on the last night of the lawyer's imprisonment?

4. What decision does the lawyer announce in a letter? Why does he make this decision?

Read with a Purpose

5. Who wins the bet—the banker, the lawyer, or neither character? Explain your answer.

Reading Skill: Making Predictions

6. Now that you have finished reading, add a box next to your "Prediction" box. In this box, tell whether your prediction was right or wrong; if it was wrong, tell what actually happened.

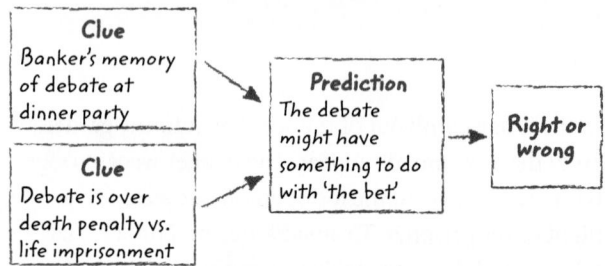

Literary Focus

Literary Analysis

7. **Interpret** In retrospect, the banker views his bet as "the caprice of a pampered man." How does he feel about himself at the end of the fifteen years? What does this reveal about Chekhov's view about what is important in life?

8. **Analyze** Like a psychiatrist, Chekhov meticulously describes the effects of the lawyer's solitary exile. How does isolation affect the prisoner at different stages over the fifteen-year period?

9. **Evaluate** Do you think the lawyer would have had such a dismal view of the world had he not been imprisoned? Explain your answer.

10. **Literary Perspectives** Whose actions did you find more credible: the banker's or the lawyer's? How would you change the story to make it more believable?

Literary Skills: Theme

11. **Interpret** State in a full sentence what you think is the story's main theme—the insight it provides about human experience. Do you think this story has more than one theme? Explain.

Literary Skills Review: Motivation

12. **Make Judgments** The reason or reasons behind a character's behavior are called **motivation.** The banker believes that "greed for money" was the lawyer's motivation for betting. Do you agree? Cite textual evidence that supports your position.

Writing Focus

Think as a Reader/Writer

Use It in Your Writing Chekhov indicates the passage of time with words and phrases. Using similar phrases, write a story of your own that involve events that take place over a large period of time.

 What Do You Think Now

What did you expect the lawyer to learn about himself and life after fifteen years in solitude? Did the reality surprise you? Explain your <u>responses</u>.

Vocabulary Development

✓ Vocabulary Check

Answer the questions about the Vocabulary words.

1. Is the lawyer **frivolous**? Explain.
2. Is attending college **compulsory**?
3. Why does the banker consider the bet a **caprice**?
4. What does it mean that the prisoner **zealously** studied books and languages in prison?
5. In the last two years, the lawyer read **indiscriminately.** What sorts of books did he read?
6. If the prisoner's visions were **ethereal,** were they delicate or nightmarish?
7. The lawyer **renounced** the money. Does that mean he claimed it, or that he rejected it?

Vocabulary Skills: Synonyms

A synonym for a word should be of the same part of speech. *Compulsory* and *obligation,* for example, (which both refer to something mandatory) are not synonyms since they are different parts of speech. The proper synonym for *compulsory (adj.)* is *obligatory (adj.)*

Your Turn

Match each Vocabulary word with its synonym.

1. frivolous   **a.** whim
2. caprice   **b.** reject
3. zealously   **c.** enthusiastically
4. renounce   **d.** silly

Language Coach

The Greek word *zêlos* means "enthusiasm for a cause." For which Vocabulary word is *zêlos* a root? What are the related noun forms for this word?

CHOICES

As you respond to the Choices, use these **Academic Vocabulary** words as appropriate: benefit, complex, publish, respond, statistics.

REVIEW

Conduct a Panel Discussion

Group Activity In this story, the lawyer's letter to his "jailer" is specific about the lawyer's philosophy of life. In a small group, read the letter and hold a round-table discussion of the lawyer's views. Choose a leader who will make sure that all who speak offer reasons and examples to support their views. At the close of the discussion, prepare a summary of the group's responses to the lawyer's philosophy.

CONNECT

Write About Solitary Confinement

Timed ⌐Writing Imagine yourself in the lawyer's place. How would solitary confinement affect you? The rules of your confinement include no human contact, no exit, no television, no access to technology. You may ask for books, musical instruments, and exercise equipment. Write a brief essay in which you tell how you might spend one year alone.

EXTEND

Debate an Issue

The question of capital punishment versus solitary confinement is a complex issue that is still debated today. Form two teams to debate the issue discussed at the party at the start of the story, one to support solitary confinement as punishment and one to support capital punishment. Find evidence to support your position.

Learn It Online
Explore Chekhov's world through these Internet links.

go.hrw.com   L12-1031   **Go**

The Jewels

How can appearance be different from reality?

QuickWrite

In your *Reader/Writer Notebook,* write a paragraph about a time when you had a false impression of someone or something. What was it like to discover the truth?

Engraved portrait of Guy de Maupassant, an illustration from *Le Monde Illustre* (1894).

MEET THE WRITER

Guy de Maupassant
(1850–1893)

Maupassant's terse, realistic stories have informed generations of American writers, from Edgar Allan Poe to Stephen King.

An Interest in Realism

Guy de Maupassant came from a wealthy family in rural Normandy. His parents separated when he was young, and Maupassant was raised by his mother, a daring woman who once raised eyebrows because she wore her skirts above her ankles. Among his mother's friends was the great realist novelist Gustave Flaubert (1821–1880), who, along with Maupassant's mother, encouraged him to write from an early age.

As a young man, Maupassant served in the army and studied law. He then took a civil service job in Paris, where he reconnected with Flaubert, who, now aging and lonely, became a mentor to the young man. Every week, leading realist writers, such as Émile Zola (1840–1902) and Russian novelist Ivan Turgenev (1818–1883), met at Flaubert's house to discuss literature. At that time, Maupassant was writing poems, historical dramas, and horror stories, but under the influence of his new friends, he turned to realistic fiction.

Later Maupassant joined a group of younger realists, or naturalists, who met at Zola's house. They were less interested in style and more intent on analyzing social conditions.

Darkly Ironic

By the time he was in his thirties, Maupassant had become one of France's best-known artists, and enjoyed the rare benefit of being able to support himself independently as a writer. In 1883 alone, he turned out two novels and seventy short stories. Those darkly ironic stories boast a knowledge of life both in rural Normandy and in seedy and fashionable Paris, and their characters are often victims of their own greed or vanity.

Few of Maupassant's friends suspected that the strong young writer was in constant pain and nearly blind from overwork and syphilis. At the end of 1891, Maupassant suffered a complete mental breakdown, from which he never recovered. He died in an asylum before his forty-third birthday.

Think About the Writer

Where did Maupassant get the material for his stories?

Reader/Writer Notebook

Use your **RWN** to complete the activities for this selection.

Literary Focus

Irony The discrepancy between appearances and reality is known as **irony.** There are three basic types of irony. In **verbal irony,** a person says something but means something very different, as when, for example, someone remarks in the middle of a hurricane, "Nice day we're having." In **situational irony,** what actually happens is different from what you would expect to happen. When it rains on the weather forecasters' picnic or when the police officer's son robs the bank, we perceive situational irony. In **dramatic irony,** a character believes something to be true, while the reader knows better. A character might think he is safe in his house, but the reader knows that a robber is approaching the back window. As you read "The Jewels," look for examples of situational and dramatic irony.

Reading Focus

Drawing Inferences An **inference** is an educated guess. As you read "The Jewels," pay close attention to what is *not* said as well as to what *is* said. Stay alert, for Maupassant often drops crucial clues in the space of one or two words. Sometimes you have to make inferences about a character, an event, or even just about the significance of a brief remark.

Into Action Use a graphic organizer like the one below to note details and then draw inferences based on those details.

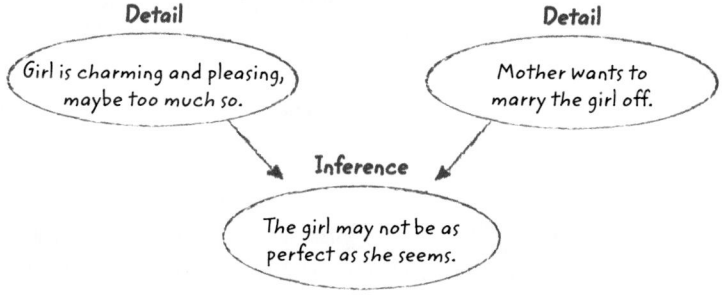

Detail: Girl is charming and pleasing, maybe too much so.

Detail: Mother wants to marry the girl off.

Inference: The girl may not be as perfect as she seems.

Vocabulary

unpretentious (uhn prih TEHN shuhs) *adj.:* modest. *Madame Lantin's dresses were simple and unpretentious.*

assuage (uh SWAYJ) *v.:* ease; calm. *Lantin was so grief-stricken that even a great expanse of time could not assuage his sorrow.*

incurred (ihn KURD) *v.:* brought upon oneself. *Monsieur Lantin incurred a number of debts that thrust him into a bad financial situation.*

surreptitiously (sur uhp TIHSH uhs lee) *adv.:* in a secret or sneaky manner. *The jewelers looked at Lantin surreptitiously to hide their amusement.*

contemptuous (kuhn TEHMP chu uhs) *adj.:* scornful. *He gave the carriages contemptuous looks because the rich would no longer look down on him.*

Language Coach

Prefixes and Suffixes Word parts added to the fronts of words to change their meaning are called **prefixes**; word parts added to the ends of words to change their meaning or part of speech are called **suffixes.** Find two Vocabulary words with prefixes. Find a word with a suffix that changes the word's tense. Find another word with a suffix that changes the word from noun to adjective.

Writing Focus

Think as a Reader/Writer

Find It in Your Reading The **dialogue** in this story is written mostly in short sentences that realistically convey information about the characters and their situation. In your *Reader/Writer Notebook*, write down two or three sentences you consider realistic. Give reasons for your choices.

Learn It Online
Learn more about Maupassant's life and work at the Writers' Lives site.

go.hrw.com   L12-1033   **Go**

The Jewels

by **Guy de Maupassant**
translated by **Roger Colet**

Read with a Purpose
Read to discover how a woman's jewelry collection is not what it seems to be.

Build Background
Guy de Maupassant, like his fellow realists, rejected the Romantic notion that the world was essentially good. Instead, Maupassant's stories reveal surprising and sometimes shocking truths about people's inner lives. Maupassant's characters are not members of the upper classes and nobility; they are ordinary people, such as peasants, minor government officials, even prostitutes.

You may notice that Maupassant uses only a few sentences to describe major events and characters. This terse style is partly attributed to the fact that many of his stories were originally published in newspapers, which restricted the length of his material.

Monsieur Lantin had met the girl at a party given one evening by his office superior and love had caught him in its net.

She was the daughter of a country tax collector who had died a few years before. She had come to Paris then with her mother, who struck up acquaintance with a few middle-class families in her district in the hope of marrying her off. They were poor and decent, quiet and gentle. The girl seemed the perfect example of the virtuous woman to whom every sensible young man dreams of entrusting his life. Her simple beauty had a modest, angelic charm and the imperceptible smile which always hovered about her lips seemed to be a reflection of her heart.

Everybody sang her praises and people who knew her never tired of saying: "Happy the man who marries her. Nobody could find a better wife." **A**

Monsieur Lantin, who was then a senior clerk at the Ministry of the Interior with a salary of three thousand five hundred francs[1] a year, proposed to her and married her.

He was incredibly happy with her. She ran his household so skillfully and economically that they gave the impression of living in luxury. She lavished attention on her husband, spoiling and coddling him,

1. **francs:** In the late nineteenth century, a franc was worth about twenty cents in American currency.

A **Reading Focus** Drawing Inferences How many times does Maupassant use a form of the word *seem* in his description of the girl? What inference can you make based on the use of this word?

The Eiffel Tower stands overlooking the promenades and fairgrounds of the Paris Exposition, 1889.

and the charm of her person was so great that six years after their first meeting he loved her even more than in the early days.

He found fault with only two of her tastes: her love for the theater and her passion for imitation jewelry.

Her friends (she knew the wives of a few petty officials) often obtained a box at the theater for her for popular plays, and even for first nights; and she dragged her husband along willy-nilly to these entertainments, which he found terribly tiring after a day's work at the office. He therefore begged her to go to the theater with some lady of her acquaintance who would bring her home afterwards. It was a long time before she gave in, as she thought that this arrangement was not quite respectable. But finally, just to please him, she agreed, and he was terribly grateful to her.

Now this love for the theater soon aroused in her a desire to adorn her person. True, her dresses remained very simple, always in good taste, but unpretentious; and her gentle grace, her irresistible, humble, smiling charm seemed to be enhanced by the simplicity of her gowns. But she took to wearing two big rhinestone earrings which sparkled like diamonds, and she also wore necklaces of fake pearls, bracelets of imitation gold, and combs set with colored glass cut to look like real stones.

Her husband, who was rather shocked by this love of show, often used to say: "My dear, when a woman can't afford to buy real jewels, she ought to appear adorned with her beauty and grace alone: those are still the rarest of gems."

But she would smile sweetly and reply: "I can't help it. I like imitation jewelry. It's my only vice.

Vocabulary **unpretentious** (uhn prih TEHN shuhs) *adj.*: modest.

I know you're right, but people can't change their natures. I would have loved to own some real jewels."

Then she would run the pearl necklaces through her fingers and make the cut-glass gems flash in the light, saying: "Look! Aren't they beautifully made? Anyone would swear they were real."

He would smile and say: "You have the taste of a gypsy."

Sometimes, in the evening, when they were sitting together by the fireside, she would place on the tea table the leather box in which she kept her "trash," as Monsieur Lantin called it. Then she would start examining these imitation jewels with passionate attention, as if she were enjoying some deep and secret pleasure; and she would insist on hanging a necklace around her husband's neck, laughing uproariously and crying: "How funny you look!" And then she would throw herself into his arms and kiss him passionately. **B**

One night in winter when she had been to the opera, she came home shivering with cold. The next morning she had a cough, and a week later she died of pneumonia.

Lantin very nearly followed her to the grave. His despair was so terrible that his hair turned white within a month. He wept from morning to night, his heart ravaged by unbearable grief, haunted by the memory, the smile, the voice, the every charm of his dead wife.

Time did nothing to assuage his grief. Often during office hours, when his colleagues came along to chat about the topics of the day, his cheeks would suddenly puff out, his nose wrinkle up, his eyes fill with tears, and with a terrible grimace he would burst out sobbing

He had left his wife's room untouched, and every day would shut himself in it and think about her. All the furniture and even her clothes remained exactly where they had been on the day she had died.

But life soon became a struggle for him. His income, which in his wife's hands had covered all their expenses, was now no longer sufficient for him on his own; and he wondered in amazement how she

had managed to provide him with excellent wines and rare delicacies which he could no longer afford on his modest salary. **C**

He incurred a few debts and ran after money in the way people do when they are reduced to desperate shifts. Finally, one morning, finding himself without a sou[2] a whole week before the end of the month, he decided to sell something; and immediately the idea occurred to him of disposing of his wife's "trash." He still harbored a sort of secret grudge against those false gems which had irritated him in the past, and indeed the sight of them every day somewhat spoiled the memory of his beloved.

He rummaged for a long time among the heap of gaudy trinkets she had left behind, for she had stubbornly gone on buying jewelry until the last days of her life, bringing home a new piece almost every evening. At last he decided on the large necklace which she had seemed to like best, and which, he thought, might well be worth six or seven francs, for it was beautifully made for a piece of paste.[3]

He put it in his pocket and set off for his Ministry, following the boulevards and looking for a jeweler's shop which inspired confidence.

At last he spotted one and went in, feeling a little ashamed of exposing his poverty in this way, and of trying to sell such a worthless article.

"Monsieur," he said to the jeweler, "I would like to know what you think this piece is worth."

The man took the necklace, examined it, turned it over, weighed it, inspected it with a magnifying glass, called his assistant, made a few remarks to him in an undertone, placed the necklace on the counter and looked at it from a distance to gauge the effect.

Monsieur Lantin, embarrassed by all this ritual, was opening his mouth to say: "Oh, I know perfectly well that it isn't worth anything," when the jeweler

---

2. **sou:** French coin worth about two cents in American currency in the late nineteenth century.
3. **paste:** kind of glass used to make fake gems.

B **Reading Focus** Drawing Inferences What inference can you make about the wife from her words and actions?

C **Reading Focus** Drawing Inferences What do you think might account for Madame Lantin's amazing ability to stretch her husband's salary?

Vocabulary **assuage** (uh SWAYJ) *v.*: ease; calm.
incurred (ihn KURD) *v.*: brought upon oneself.

said: "Monsieur, this necklace is worth between twelve and fifteen thousand francs; but I couldn't buy it unless you told me where it came from." **D**

The widower opened his eyes wide and stood there gaping, unable to understand what the jeweler had said. Finally he stammered: "What was that you said?… Are you sure?"

The other misunderstood his astonishment and said curtly: "You can go somewhere else and see if they'll offer you more. In my opinion it's worth fifteen thousand at the most. Come back and see me if you can't find a better price."

Completely dumbfounded, Monsieur Lantin took back his necklace and left the shop, in obedience to a vague desire to be alone and to think.

Once outside, however, he felt an impulse to laugh, and he thought: "The fool! Oh, the fool! But what if I'd taken him at his word? There's a jeweler who can't tell real diamonds from paste!"

And he went into another jeweler's shop at the beginning of the Rue de la Paix. As soon as he saw the necklace, the jeweler exclaimed: "Why, I know that necklace well: it was bought here."

Monsieur Lantin asked in amazement: "How much is it worth?"

"Monsieur, I sold it for twenty-five thousand. I am prepared to buy it back for eighteen thousand once you have told me, in accordance with the legal requirements, how you came to be in possession of it." **E**

This time Monsieur Lantin was dumbfounded. He sat down and said: "But… but… examine it carefully, Monsieur. Until now I thought it was paste."

"Will you give me your name, Monsieur?" said the jeweler.

"Certainly. My name's Lantin. I'm an official at the Ministry of the Interior, and I live at No. 16, Rue des Martyrs."

The jeweler opened his books, looked for the entry, and said: "Yes, this necklace was sent to Madame Lantin's address, No. 16, Rue des Martyrs, on the 20th of July 1876."

The two men looked into each other's eyes, the clerk speechless with astonishment, the jeweler scenting a thief. Finally the latter said: "Will you leave the necklace with me for twenty-four hours? I'll give you a receipt."

"Why, certainly," stammered Monsieur Lantin. And he went out folding the piece of paper, which he put in his pocket.

Then he crossed the street, walked up it again, noticed that he was going the wrong way, went back as far as the Tuileries, crossed the Seine, realized that he had gone wrong again, and returned to the Champs-Élysées,[4] his mind a complete blank. He tried to think it out, to understand. His wife couldn't have afforded to buy something so valuable—that was certain. But in that case it was a present! A present! But a present from whom? And why was it given her?

He halted in his tracks and remained standing in the middle of the avenue. A horrible doubt crossed his mind. Her? But in that case all the other jewels were presents, too! The earth seemed to be trembling under his feet and a tree in front of him to be falling; he threw up his arms and fell to the ground unconscious. **F**

He came to his senses in a chemist's shop into which the passersby had carried him. He took a cab home and shut himself up.

He wept bitterly until nightfall, biting on a handkerchief so as not to cry out. Then he went to bed worn out with grief and fatigue and slept like a log.

A ray of sunlight awoke him and he slowly got up to go to his Ministry. It was hard to think of working after such a series of shocks. It occurred to him that he could ask to be excused and he wrote a letter to his superior. Then he remembered that he had to go back to the jeweler's and he blushed with shame. He spent a long time thinking it over, but decided that he could not leave the necklace with that man. So he dressed and went out. **G**

---

4. **Champs-Élysées:** elegant boulevard in Paris.

D **Reading Focus** Drawing Inferences Why do you suppose the jeweler wants to know where the necklace came from?

E **Literary Focus** Irony What is ironic or unexpected about Lantin's discovery of the true value of the jewelry?

F **Reading Focus** Drawing Inferences What can you infer about the manner in which Madame Lantin came to possess the jewels?

G **Reading Focus** Drawing Inferences Why is Lantin feeling shameful?

Jolie Madame (Pretty Woman) (1973) by Audrey Flack.
National Gallery of Australia.

Viewing and Interpreting How do these objects suggest a person who, like Madame Lantin, enjoys the theater? How might they be something other than what they appear to be?

It was a fine day and the city seemed to be smiling under the clear blue sky. People were strolling about the streets with their hands in their pockets.

Watching them, Lantin said to himself: "How lucky rich people are! With money you can forget even the deepest of sorrows. You can go where you like, travel, enjoy yourself. Oh, if only I were rich!"

He began to feel hungry, for he had eaten nothing for two days, but his pocket was empty. Then he remembered the necklace. Eighteen thousand francs! Eighteen thousand francs! That was a tidy sum, and no mistake!

When he reached the Rue de la Paix he started walking up and down the pavement opposite the jeweler's shop. Eighteen thousand francs! A score of times he almost went in, but every time shame held him back.

He was hungry, though, very hungry, and he had no money at all. He quickly made up his mind, ran across the street so as not to have any time to think, and rushed into the shop.

As soon as he saw him the jeweler came forward and offered him a chair with smiling politeness. His assistants came into the shop, too, and glanced surreptitiously at Lantin with laughter in their eyes and on their lips.

Vocabulary **surreptitiously** (sur uhp TIHSH uhs lee) *adv.*: in a secret or sneaky manner.

"I have made inquiries, Monsieur," said the jeweler, "and if you still wish to sell the necklace, I am prepared to pay you the price I offered you."

"Why, certainly," stammered the clerk.

The jeweler took eighteen large bank notes out of a drawer, counted them and handed them to Lantin, who signed a little receipt and with a trembling hand put the money in his pocket.

Then, as he was about to leave the shop, he turned towards the jeweler, who was still smiling, and lowering his eyes said: "I have… I have some other jewels which have come to me from… from the same legacy. Would you care to buy them from me, too?"

The jeweler bowed.

"Certainly, Monsieur."

One of the assistants went out, unable to contain his laughter; another blew his nose loudly. **H**

Lantin, red faced and solemn, remained unmoved.

"I will bring them to you," he said.

And he took a cab to go and fetch the jewels.

When he returned to the shop an hour later he still had had nothing to eat. The jeweler and his assistants began examining the jewels one by one, estimating the value of each piece. Almost all of them had been bought at that shop.

Lantin now began arguing about the valuations, lost his temper, insisted on seeing the sales registers, and spoke more and more loudly as the sum increased.

The large diamond earrings were worth twenty thousand francs, the bracelets thirty-five thousand, the brooches, rings, and lockets sixteen thousand, a set of emeralds and sapphires fourteen thousand, and a solitaire pendant on a gold chain forty thousand—making a total sum of one hundred and ninety-six thousand francs.

The jeweler remarked jokingly: "These obviously belonged to a lady who invested all her savings in jewelry."

Lantin replied seriously: "It's as good a way as any of investing one's money."

And he went off after arranging with the jeweler to have a second expert valuation the next day.

Out in the street he looked at the Vendôme column[5] and felt tempted to climb up it as if it were a greasy pole. He felt light enough to play leapfrog with the statue of the Emperor perched up there in the sky. **I**

He went to Voisin's for lunch and ordered wine with his meal at twenty francs a bottle.

Then he took a cab and went for a drive in the Bois.[6] He looked at the other carriages with a slightly contemptuous air, longing to call out to the passersby: "I'm a rich man, too! I'm worth two hundred thousand francs!" **J**

Suddenly he remembered his Ministry. He drove there at once, strode into his superior's office, and said: "Monsieur, I have come to resign my post. I have just been left three hundred thousand francs."

He shook hands with his former colleagues and told them some of his plans for the future; then he went off to dine at the Café Anglais.

Finding himself next to a distinguished-looking gentleman, he was unable to refrain from informing him, with a certain coyness, that he had just inherited four hundred thousand francs.

For the first time in his life he was not bored at the theater, and he spent the night with some prostitutes.

Six months later he married again. His second wife was a very virtuous woman, but extremely bad-tempered. She made him very unhappy. **K**

---

5. **Vendôme column:** monument in Paris honoring Napoleon.
6. **Bois:** Bois de Bologne, a park in Paris.

H **Reading Focus** Drawing Inferences What do you infer is the reason the clerks are laughing at Lantin?

I **Reading Focus** Drawing Inferences Lantin and the jeweler both know that Madame Lantin did not save her money to invest in jewelry. Why does Lantin maintain this pretense?

J **Literary Focus** Irony How does Lantin change as he becomes wealthy? What is ironic about the way he feels now?

K **Literary Focus** Irony What is ironic about the description of Lantin's second wife? (Would you expect a virtuous woman to make him unhappy?)

Vocabulary contemptuous (kuhn TEHMP chu uhs) *adj.:* scornful.

Applying Your Skills

The Jewels

Respond and Think Critically

Reading Focus

Quick Check

1. Describe the Lantins' married life, including how they feel about each other and their economic circumstances.

2. How does the death of his wife affect Monsieur Lantin's standard of living?

Read with a Purpose

3. What kind of person does Madame Lantin seem to be? What is she really?

Reading Skills: Drawing Inferences

4. Look back at the inferences you made while reading the story. Add a circle above each "Inference" circle in your chart. In this circle, revise any inferences that turned out to be incorrect.

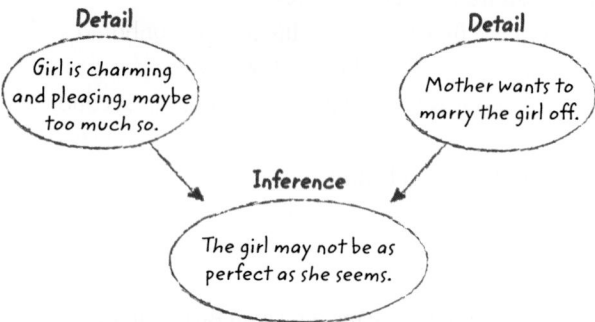

Detail
Girl is charming and pleasing, maybe too much so.

Detail
Mother wants to marry the girl off.

Inference
The girl may not be as perfect as she seems.

✔ Vocabulary Check

Match each Vocabulary word with its synonym.

5. unpretentious   **a.** disapproving
6. assuage   **b.** humble
7. incurred   **c.** soothe
8. surreptitiously   **d.** invited
9. contemptuous   **e.** secretly

Literary Focus

Literary Analysis

10. **Interpret** Why do you think Lantin hesitates to accept the eighteen thousand francs?

11. **Extend** Maupassant used fiction to examine social issues. With what particular problem does "The Jewels" deal?

12. **Draw Conclusions** What does Maupassant suggest about the connection between virtue and happiness?

Literary Skills: Irony

13. **Analyze** Re-read the last two paragraphs of the story. What is ironic about how Lantin changes after he sells the jewels?

Literary Skills Review: Symbol

14. **Evaluate** A **symbol** is a person, place, or thing that has meaning in itself and also stands for something else. What do the jewels symbolize in this story?

Writing Focus

Think as a Reader/Writer

Use It in Your Writing Using the realistic dialogue from "The Jewels" as a model, write at least six lines of realistic dialogue on your own.

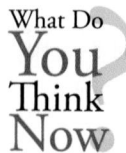

What Do You Think Now

Why might Lantin find it preferable to assume the jewels are fake? What does his decision later to sell the jewels suggest about his values?

SKILLS FOCUS Literary Skills Compare realist works. **Reading Skills** Relate literary works to themes of an era. **Writing Skills** Write a compare-and-contrast essay.

World Literature: The Rise of Realism

Writing Focus

Writing a Comparison-Contrast Essay

In what ways are these three short stories similar and different? Consider how these works exhibit some of the characteristics of realism: the use of characters from ordinary life; an unflinching look at how changes in society affect ordinary people; an examination of the motivations of human behavior; a realistic—even ironic—view of human life. Re-read the selections to determine specific points of similarity and difference.

Prewriting

Consider the following topics or develop your own:

- Compare and contrast the desires of and lessons learned by the main characters in the stories.
- Compare the use of irony in the stories.
- Compare and contrast the writers' views of life.
- Compare and contrast the ways the stories contrast appearances with reality.
- Compare and contrast themes.

Review the Elements of the Writing Form Once you have chosen a topic, review the elements of what makes a successful comparison-contrast essay before you begin.

An effective comparison / contrast essay

- states the basis of the comparison-contrast in a thesis
- organizes ideas, using the point-by-point method
- uses and cites text evidence to support each point of comparison and contrast
- contains few or no errors in spelling, punctuation, and usage

Gather Ideas Create a trifold chart like the one on the right to record your thoughts about each story. Look for patterns of similarities and differences.

"How Much Land . . .?"	"The Bet"	"The Jewels"
Pahom and devil—owning land debt free	lawyer and banker bet	clerk marries beautiful but poor woman
greed; could not stop	two million	discovers jewelry was real; she was not
irony: greed leads to death	irony: renounces and disappears	irony: wife deceived husband

Develop a Thesis Statement Using your notes and observations, develop a thesis that makes an assertion about the similarities and differences in the selections. Use a basis of similarity (such as ironic conclusions), and then focus on the differences in the three selections. Sample thesis:

The ironic endings of the three stories emphasize their realism, but the main characters have very different motives for their actions.

Drafting

Because you are using the point-by-point method of organization, begin with the strongest comparison linking the three stories. Develop it in your first body paragraph. Then, depending on your analysis, your next body paragraphs will develop either additional similarities or differences. Your final body paragraph will focus on the differences.

Revising and Editing

Re-read your draft to determine if you have fully supported your thesis with explanation and text evidence. Then read for grammatical, mechanics, and usage errors. Prepare a final copy that is error-free. Publish.

What Do **You Think Now** How does reality interfere with our expectations of how life should be?

Writing Workshop

Fictional Narrative

Write with a Purpose

Write a fictional narrative with a plot, setting, and characters of your creation. Your **purpose** for writing is to entertain readers and express an understanding of the human condition. Because your **audience** includes your teacher and classmates, make sure your narrative avoids content that is inappropriate for a school setting.

A Good Fictional Narrative

- presents realistic, well-rounded characters who undergo growth or change
- is set in a place and time that contributes to the tone and plot
- has a plot driven by a conflict that is resolved in the end
- expresses a truth about the human condition

See page 1050 for complete rubric.

Reader/Writer Notebook

Use your **RWN** to complete the activities for this workshop.

Think as a Reader/Writer

In this workshop, you'll share your imagination, experience, and insight into the human condition to write a **fictional narrative.** Before you begin writing, take a few minutes to read the following excerpt from "Games at Twilight" by Anita Desai (page 1416).

It was still too hot to play outdoors. They had had their tea, they had been washed and had their hair brushed, and after the long day of confinement in the house that was not cool but at least a protection from the sun, the children strained to get out. Their faces were red and bloated with the effort, but their mother would not open the door, everything was still curtained and shuttered in a way that stifled the children, made them feel that their lungs were stuffed with cotton wool and their noses with dust and if they didn't burst out into the light and see the sun and feel the air, they would choke.

"Please, ma, please," they begged. "We'll play on the veranda and porch—we won't go a step out of the porch."

"You will, I know you will, and then—"

"No—we won't, we won't," they wailed so horrendously that she actually let down the bolt of the front door so that they burst out like seeds from a crackling, overripe pod into the veranda, with such wild, maniacal yells that she retreated to her bath and the shower of talcum powder and the fresh sari that were to help her face the summer evening.

They faced the afternoon. It was too hot. Too bright. The white walls of the veranda glared stridently in the sun. The bougainvillea hung about it, purple and magenta, in livid balloons. The garden outside was like a tray made of beaten brass, flattened out on the red gravel and the stony soil in all shade of metal—aluminum, tin, copper, and brass.

(margin notes:)

Desai introduces the **characters** and begins to describe the **setting.**

Dialogue adds to the plot and characterization.

She uses the words *horrendously* and *maniacal* to set the story's **mood.**

She helps readers visualize the **scene** through **figurative language** and **descriptive details.**

Think About the Professional Model

With a partner, discuss the following questions about the model:

1. Where is the narrative set? What clues tell you about the setting?
2. What problem do the characters in the excerpt face?

Prewriting

Imagine a Story

Begin creating your narrative by deciding on its basic **literary elements**. Because your imagination is the only limit, deciding what to write about may require some time and thought. Use the following questions to guide your brainstorming. Start with any of the questions, but answer them all before you move on to consider these elements in detail.

- *Who* are the **characters**? Who is the **protagonist** (main character), and who is the **antagonist** (the character who blocks the protagonist)?
- *Where* does the narrative take place? Will you choose a **setting** that is familiar to you, such as your school, or one that is not, such as outer space?
- *When* does the narrative take place? Will you set your narrative in the past, the present, or the future?
- *What* problem, or **conflict,** does the main character face?
- *What* happens in the narrative?

Analyze Your Characters

The main characters in your story—especially the protagonist—should be **realistic** and **well rounded.** You should know them inside and out. For each character, ask yourself, "What is the character's name, age, and appearance? How does the character behave? What motivates him or her?" From the short excerpt of "Games at Twilight" on page 1042, you know a few things about the characters:

Names: unknown
Ages: children
Appearance: washed, hair brushed; faces "red and bloated"
Motivation: to get out of the house to play

Define the Conflict

There are two main types of conflict: **internal** and **external.** Use the flowchart below to decide what kind of conflict will drive your narrative.

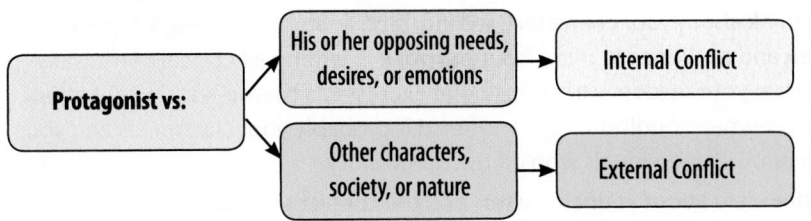

In the excerpt from "Games at Twilight," one external conflict is the children's desires versus their mother's wishes. Complex stories usually have more than one conflict, plus a mixture of internal and external conflicts.

Idea Starters

- Base characters on people you know. Be sure to change their names and some other details.
- Choose a setting based on places you have visited, read about, or seen on TV or in movies.
- Get plot ideas from real-life incidents (your own, those of people you know, or ones you have heard about).

Your Turn _____

Get Started Taking notes in your **RWN,** answer the questions on this page to determine the basic elements of your story. Then, analyze your characters, and define your narrative's conflict.

 Learn It Online
To see how one writer completed this assignment, see the model short story at:

go.hrw.com L12-1043 **Go**

Fictional Narrative

Writing Tips

- All the events in your narrative should help move the plot forward. Events not closely related to the plot may confuse readers and cause them to lose interest.
- Your narrative's plot should generate **suspense**—a feeling of uncertainty and curiosity about what will happen next.

Plot Your Narrative

Unfold the narrative events in your story chronologically, or in time order. A classic plot structure begins with the **exposition,** which introduces the characters and conflict; moves through **complications,** which arise as characters attempt to resolve the conflict; builds toward the **climax,** the moment when the conflict's outcome is imminent; and ends with the **resolution,** or **denouement,** when the problems are resolved and the narrative ends. To outline your plot, write a **plot plan** like this one, created by the writer of the student model (pages 1047-1048).

Plot Plan

Exposition	Mary attends a school in which new clothes are a status symbol. She is snubbed each year by her classmates because she is too poor to afford a new coat.
Complications	Mary sews buttons on her old coat to make it look new and fashionable. She imagines the next day at school.
Climax	Mary wears her coat to school expecting that her classmates will admire it.
Resolution/ Denouement	Frustrated and angry because of her classmates' rejection, Mary breaks down, screaming, and tears the buttons off her coat.

Choose a Point of View

Now you must choose the point of view from which your story's **narrator** will tell the story. Use the following chart to choose a point of view:

Omniscient Narrator	all-knowing and outside the action; can tell readers the thoughts and feelings of all the characters; uses third-person pronouns, such as *he, she,* and *they.*
First-Person Narrator	witness of or participant in the story; can tell only what he or she knows, thinks, or feels; uses first-person pronouns such as *I* and *we.*
Third-Person-Limited Narrator	outside of the action, but not all knowing; focuses on the thoughts and feelings of one character; uses third-person pronouns, such as *he, she,* and *they.*

Think About Purpose and Audience

As you think about your characters, setting, plot, and point of view, keep your **purpose** and **audience** in mind. Your **purpose** in writing a fictional narrative is to entertain your readers with a story that expresses a **theme**—an insight about life or the human condition. Your **audience** is probably your classmates and your teacher or other individuals who enjoy a good story.

- Will they care about your characters and the conflict they face?
- Will they identify with the events of the plot?
- Will the resolution give them a new insight into what it means to be human?

Your Turn

Plan Your Narrative Use the chart on this page to make a **plot plan** of your narrative. Share your chart with a peer, and consider the feedback he or she provides. Revise your plot as needed, keeping in mind your **purpose** and **audience.**

Drafting

Draft Your Fictional Narrative

Use your prewriting notes, **plot plan,** and the **Writer's Framework** to the right to begin writing your fictional narrative.

Use Dialogue

Your characters should speak, using realistic dialogue, for two purposes:

- to advance the action of the plot
- to reveal characters' personalities and motivations

Start a new paragraph every time the speaker changes, and use quotation marks to enclose each speaker's words.

Create Mood

Your narrative's **mood,** or **atmosphere,** is the overall emotion it creates, such as peaceful, festive, ominous, or playful. Mood is created through your choice of words and details. For instance, in the following sentence from the student model, the words *faded, worn thin,* and *coffin* create a sad, bleak mood:

And every year she pulled out the same faded red jacket, worn thin from years of hand-me-downing and cold, from its cardboard coffin. . . .

Dialogue can help set the mood, by using the natural rhythm of spoken language, including the use of **contractions.**

> ### Framework for Fictional Narrative
>
> **Beginning**
> - Describe setting.
> - Introduce characters and establish point of view.
> - Set the plot in motion with the conflict.
>
> **Middle**
> - Develop characters through actions, dialogue, description, and sensory details.
> - Introduce complications.
>
> **End**
> - Build suspense or plot intensity to the climax.
> - Resolve the conflict.
> - Reveal the final outcome.
> - Make the theme clear to readers.

● Writing Tip

To make the people, places, and things in your story come alive for the reader, use **sensory details** that appeal to sight, hearing, smell, touch, and taste as well as **figurative language,** such as simile and metaphor.

Grammar Link Using Contractions with Dialogue

While **contractions** are not usually acceptible in formal writing, such as a research paper, you can use contractions in fictional narratives to help with characterization and mood. If you're wondering whether to use a contraction, ask yourself whether the separated words sound stilted. If they do, replace them with a contraction. Look at these examples from "Games at Twilight" (page 1042):

> "Please, ma, please," they begged. "We'll play on the veranda and porch—we won't go a step out of the porch."
>
> "You will, I know you will, and then—"
>
> "No—we won't, we won't," they wailed. . . . "

The author, Desai, uses the contraction *we'll* instead of *we will* and *won't* instead of *will not* in order to replicate authentic speech for the dialogue and create an informal mood in her story.

Your Turn _____

Write Your Draft Use your **plot plan** and the **Writer's Framework** to write a draft of your fictional narrative. As you write, ask yourself,

- Where can I use **dialogue** to enhance my narrative?
- Will **contractions** make the dialogue more realistic?
- What **mood** do I want to convey in my narrative?

Peer Review

Ask a peer to read your fictional narrative, evaluating it by using the chart to the right. Then, ask the following questions to find out how well you communicated your ideas:

- Did the characters seem real?
- Did you care about the conflict?
- Was the resolution satisfying?

Use peer feedback to improve your narrative.

Evaluating and Revising

Evaluating and revising your draft is an essential step in producing a fictional narrative. Examine your characterization, descriptions, and plot to make your narrative the best it can be. The chart below will help you evaluate and revise your draft. With a partner, begin on the left side of the chart, and work through each revision question, tip, and suggestion.

Fictional Narrative: Guidelines for Content and Organization

Evaluation Question	Tip	Revision Technique
1. Do the first few paragraphs introduce the setting, characters, and conflict?	**Circle** facts about characters. **Bracket** information about the conflict. **Underline** facts about the setting.	**Add** descriptions of characters or setting or a hint about the conflict.
2. Does the narrative maintain a consistent point of view?	**Highlight** all pronouns referring to characters and make sure they are in the same person.	**Replace** pronouns as needed for consistency.
3. Do all the events move the plot forward?	**Number** each event. In the margin, write a corresponding note explaining how the event relates to the plot.	**Cut** events that are not essential to the plot.
4. Is dialogue used appropriately to advance the story's plot and to reveal character?	**Put a star** beside any dialogue.	**Add** dialogue that reveals character or forwards the plot. **Replace** unnecessary dialogue with a paraphrase.
5. Does the narrative create a consistent mood?	**Circle** words and details that create mood.	**Add** language and details that evoke the mood you are trying to achieve.
6. Is the conflict resolved at the end of the narrative?	**Underline** the sentences in which the conflict is resolved.	**Add** sentences that tell how the conflict is resolved.

Read this student's draft; note the comments on its structure and suggestions for how it could be made even stronger.

Buttons

by Tawnee Cunningham, Kane Area Senior High School

It was getting colder; everyone had new coats. Coats appeared with shiny buttons, gleaming like pebbles in a stream, wool thick and as soft as a cloud. Everyone but her. It was like that every year. The others in her class wore new sweaters and mittens, some the latest hat or skirt, showing off what they could afford and flaunting what she couldn't. And every year she pulled out the same faded red jacket, worn thin from years of hand-me-downing and cold, from its cardboard coffin, wishing immensely that it were a new tweed blazer or the handsome peacoat she'd seen in the window of a department store uptown. And every year she endured the snubbing and repulsed looks of her peers, ignoring the stares at the frayed edges and the too-short sleeves.

This year would be no different. The style of choice this fall was fancy buttons, at the seams, on the lapels; anywhere one could sew a button. Walking past the variety store, she suddenly had an idea. Into the little shop she went, searching her pockets for loose change. The bell over the door rang with happy thoughts of acceptance and contentment.

← Tawnee introduces the **protagonist** and **conflict**.

← She uses vivid **sensory details** to describe the shabby coat.

← The main character finds a possible solution to her problem.

MINI-LESSON **How to Add Interior Monologue**

One way to help readers understand characters' motivation is to use **interior monologue**—characters' unspoken internal flow of thoughts and feelings. In her draft, Tawnee doesn't tell what Mary is thinking when she goes into the variety store. The addition of interior monologue makes her motivation clearer. The revision allows the reader to "hear" her thoughts.

Tawnee's Revision of Paragraph 2

This year would be no different. The style of choice this fall was fancy buttons, at the seams, on the lapels; anywhere one could sew a button. Walking past the variety store, she suddenly had an idea. ∧*"Buttons cost little. What can it hurt?*

Just a few additions to my coat could save me from another season of torture."

Into the little shop she went, searching her pockets for loose change. The bell over the door rang with happy thoughts of acceptance and contentment.

Your Turn _____

Add Interior Monologue Reread your draft to find places where you could clarify characters' motivations by adding interior monologue. Ask yourself:

- Is it clear why the characters do what they do?
- Can readers tell what the characters think and feel about the events of the plot?

Writing Workshop Fictional Narrative

Student Draft continues

Tawnee details the **character's thoughts** as she replaces the old buttons. →

Finally at home, she brought out the little cedar box she kept her needle-work in. Carefully, she removed the tarnished buttons from their thread bindings. In each place, she attached a new one, blue and twisted in a little centipede pattern. As she sewed, she heard the compliments she would receive the next day. They would greet her as she removed her jacket, begging to know where she'd gotten such a beautiful coat. She would just smile modestly and shrug, she imagined, and accept their invitations to sit with them during lunch. That night, she could barely sleep for the excitement of it all.

She moves the conflict toward its resolution. →

She set off to the school, her head held high. The others crowded around the door, talking and gossiping, conversations whispered behind hands in expensive leather gloves. No one noticed her. It didn't matter, she knew they would.

The **denouement**, or **resolution**, is achieved. →

She uses **figurative language** to emphasize the loss of the buttons. →

But there were no shared lunches—only sarcasm and disdain. Mary Green started screaming and would not stop. When her parents finally came for her, they asked why her coat was ripped and torn. The answer lay on the sidewalk, splayed about like dropped pennies, the buttons she'd sewed the night before, glinting in the sun like round, azure tears.

MINI-LESSON How to Clarify Transitions

Tawnee's draft does not always provide sufficient **transitions**—words, phrases, and sentences that provide a smooth flow from one idea to the next. Her readers can get lost when Tawnee abruptly changes setting. Between paragraphs 3 and 4, she decided to add some transitional information to indicate that the events of paragraph 4 occur the next day. She also adds some imagery that shows the change in setting and allows the reader insight into the character's thinking.

Tawnee's Draft of Paragraphs 3 and 4

That night, she could barely sleep for the excitement of it all.
    She set off to the school, her head held high.

Tawnee's Revision of Paragraph 4

That night, she could barely sleep for the excitement of it all.
    She set off to the school, her head held high.

The next morning, the ground sparkled with a layer of white frost, making the flowers shiver in protest. It was a perfect time to debut her new jacket.

Your Turn

Clarify Transitions Look through your draft for places where transitions would be useful. Pay close attention to transitions between paragraphs, and make sure the reader can tell

- *where* the action is happening.
- *when* the action is happening.
- and *what* the characters think and feel about the actions.

Proofreading and Publishing

Proofread

Errors can distract readers from your story and ruin its effect. Follow these tips to **proofread,** or **edit,** your fictional narrative:

- Consult a style manual to answer questions of grammar, usage, and mechanics. Review the section on punctuating dialogue.
- Start proofreading at the end of your narrative and work your way back to the beginning, checking the spelling of each word.
- Look at each sentence to make sure that it contains a subject and a verb and that it expresses a single, complete thought. If a sentence contains two or more complete thoughts running together with only a comma between them, then you have a **comman splice,** which should be corrected.

Grammar Link **Avoiding Comma Splices**

In her draft, Tawnee includes a **comma splice**—a run-on sentence in which only a comma separates two independent clauses. One quick fix for a comma splice is to replace the comma with a semicolon.

Tawnee's Revision

> It didn't matter; she knew they would.

You can also correct comma splices by adding a coordinating conjunction (such as *and, but, for, nor, or, so,* and *yet*) after the comma or by turning each independent clause into a separate sentence.

Reference Note For more on comma splices, see the Language Handbook.

Publishing

You've worked hard to write an interesting, insightful fictional narrative. Try these ideas for sharing your piece with an audience outside your classroom:

- Submit your fictional narrative to a print or online literary magazine.
- Host a fiction reading at which you and your peers can read your work out loud to an audience.
- Use desktop publishing software to improve your narrative's **presentation**—how it actually looks on the page. Print, then bind it in a folder, and give it to a friend or family member as a gift.

Reflect on the Process

Thinking about the process of writing your fictional narrative will help you with your future writing. Write a short response to each of these questions in your **RWN:**

1. What prewriting technique helped you the most?
2. What is the strongest part of your fictional narrative? Why?

Proofreading Tip

Use your intuition when proofreading. When something in your draft seems wrong, stop and examine it carefully before you move on. If you can't find the problem, ask your teacher or a peer to help.

Writing Tip

To find comma splices, highlight every comma in your draft. For each one found, ask these questions:

- Does the comma come between two independent clauses that could stand on their own as separate sentences?
- If so, is the comma followed by a coordinating conjunction, such as and or but?

Your Turn _____

Proofread and Publish As you proofread your draft, check carefully for **comma splices** and other sentence flaws. After correcting any errors, publish your narrative.

Scoring Rubric

Use one of the rubrics below to evaluate your fictional narrative from the Writing Workshop or your response to the on-demand prompt on the next page. Your teacher will tell you to use either the six- or four-point rubric.

6-Point Scale

Score 6 *Demonstrates advanced success*
- focuses consistently on narrating a single incident or a unified sequence of incidents
- shows effective narrative sequence throughout, with smooth transitions
- offers a thoughtful, creative approach to the narration
- develops the story thoroughly, using precise and vivid descriptive and narrative details
- exhibits mature control of written language

Score 5 *Demonstrates proficient success*
- focuses on narrating a single incident or a unified sequence of incidents
- shows effective narrative sequence, with transitions
- offers a thoughtful approach to the narration
- develops the story competently, using descriptive and narrative details
- exhibits sufficient control of written language

Score 4 *Demonstrates competent success*
- focuses on narrating a single incident or a unified sequence of incidents, with minor distractions
- shows effective narrative sequence, with minor lapses
- offers a mostly thoughtful approach to the narration
- develops the story adequately, with some descriptive and narrative details
- exhibits general control of written language

Score 3 *Demonstrates limited success*
- includes some loosely related material that distracts from the writer's narrative focus
- shows some organization, with noticeable flaws in the narrative flow
- offers a routine, predictable approach to the narration
- develops the story with uneven use of descriptive and narrative detail
- exhibits limited control of written language

Score 2 *Demonstrates basic success*
- includes loosely related material that seriously distracts from the writer's narrative focus
- shows minimal organization, with major gaps in the narrative flow
- offers a narrative that merely skims the surface
- develops the story with inadequate descriptive and narrative detail
- exhibits significant problems with control of written language

Score 1 *Demonstrates emerging effort*
- shows little awareness of the topic and the narrative purpose
- lacks organization
- offers an unclear and confusing narrative
- develops the story with little or no detail
- exhibits major problems with control of written language

4-Point Scale

Score 4 *Demonstrates advanced success*
- focuses consistently on narrating a single incident or a unified sequence of incidents
- shows effective narrative sequence throughout, with smooth transitions
- offers a thoughtful, creative approach to the narration
- develops the story thoroughly, using precise and vivid descriptive and narrative details
- exhibits mature control of written language

Score 3 *Demonstrates competent success*
- focuses on narrating a single incident or a unified sequence of incidents, with minor distractions
- shows effective narrative sequence, with minor lapses
- offers a mostly thoughtful approach to the narration
- develops the story adequately, with some descriptive and narrative details
- exhibits general control of written language

Score 2 *Demonstrates limited success*
- includes some loosely related material that distracts from the writer's narrative focus
- shows some organization, with noticeable flaws in the narrative flow
- offers a routine, predictable approach to the narration
- develops the story with uneven use of descriptive and narrative detail
- exhibits limited control of written language

Score 1 *Demonstrates emerging effort*
- shows little awareness of the topic and the narrative purpose
- lacks organization
- offers an unclear and confusing narrative
- develops the story with little or no detail
- exhibits major problems with control of written language

Fictional Narrative

When responding to a prompt, use what you have learned from reading, writing your fictional narrative, and studying the rubric on page 1050. Use the steps below to develop a response to the following prompt:

Writing Prompt
Write a fictional narrative about a time when freedom was won or lost. In your story, create a setting, conflict, and events that illustrate the gain or loss of freedom.

Study the Prompt

Begin by reading the prompt carefully. Read it a second time, circling or underlining words that identify important information: *time, freedom, won, lost, setting, conflict,* and *events.*

Because this task requires a narrative structure, you must create characters to respond to the **conflict** (for freedom) in a distinct setting (time and place). You must decide what kind of freedom your characters will win or lose and how that happens. **Tip:** Spend about five minutes studying the prompt.

Plan Your Response

Ask yourself questions about the imaginary situation suggested by the prompt to help you create the **literary elements** that will go into your story.

- What kind of freedom is at stake in your story? personal, physical freedom? freedom of the spirit? intellectual freedom?
- What is the **setting**? Where and when will the struggle for freedom occur?
- What will the **major characters** be like?
- What **minor characters** will be in the narrative?
- What **point of view** will your narrative use?
- How will the **plot** unfold? What will the **complications** be that move the narrative action forward?
- How will the **conflict** in your narrative be resolved? Will freedom be won or lost?

Answer these questions carefully but quickly, and make some notes. **Tip:** Spend about ten minutes planning your response.

Respond to the Prompt

Start writing, even if you are unsure about how to begin. The most important thing is to get your ideas on paper. One way to begin is to create a **dialogue** between your main character and others which will reveal the setting and conflict. As you write, remember the following points:

- Use **descriptive details** to allow your reader to "see" the characters and their experience. Be as specific as you can when you describe the characters and what happens.
- Include a few **narrative details** to illustrate the conflict and lead to its resolution.
- Use **transitional phrases and sentences** to let your readers know when and where the action is happening.
- Make the **resolution** clear. One way to do that is to have the main character speak to others.

Tip: Spend about twenty minutes writing your fictional narrative.

Improve Your Response

Revising Go back to the key aspects of the prompt. Does your response include characters, a setting, a conflict, complications, and a resolution? Have you used dialogue or description to make the characters and action clear? Does your narrative have a beginning, middle, and end? Is the point of view consistent?

Proofreading Take a few minutes to proofread to correct errors in grammar, spelling, punctuation, and capitalization. Make sure that all your edits are neat, and check that your paper is legible.

Checking Your Final Copy Before you turn in your narrative, read it one more time to catch any errors you may have missed. You'll be glad you took one more look to present your best writing. **Tip:** Save five or ten minutes to improve your response.

Telling a Story

Speak with a Purpose

Adapt your short story into an oral presentation. Practice telling your story, and then present it to your class.

Think as a Reader/Writer The processes of speaking and listening are similar to those of writing and reading. Speakers, like writers, attempt to express ideas in a clear, engaging manner. Listeners, like readers, aim to absorb and understand the ideas being expressed.

Storytelling is an ancient art form, but it also takes place every day, all around us. In fact, you probably tell stories all the time. At the dinner table, you might tell your family an amusing anecdote about something that happened at school; or in line for concert tickets, you might swap "concert stories" with your friends. Now, you can share a short story of your own by adapting it as an oral presentation.

Adapt Your Short Story

Consider Your Listeners

A reader has the luxury of setting his or her own pace, re-reading for clarity or enjoyment, or pausing to answer the phone, fix a snack, or take a catnap. A listener, on the other hand, has only one chance to register what is being said. As you adapt your story for an oral presentation, consider doing your listener the following favors:

- **Keep It Simple and Vivid** On paper, that extended metaphor comparing Fido to Beowulf may have worked. In an oral presentation, though, it might confuse—or exasperate—your listeners. Read through your story, marking images that are simple, strong, and vivid for use in your presentation. Cut those that are abstract or complicated, or that require elaborate background knowledge.

- **Streamline Your Organization** Remember that listeners do not have the benefit of seeing a paragraph break on a page, or of flipping back and forth to see what happened when. To help listeners follow the progression of events, add verbal cues such as transitional words and phrases, or brief references to earlier key events. Also consider limiting your use of flashback and foreshadowing, which can wreak chronological havoc in a listener's mind.

- **Spell Out the Big Idea** In a work of literature, an implicit theme can be a lovely thing. In an oral presentation, however, you may need to guide your listeners toward your main point in language that is somewhat direct. Consider having your main character reflect aloud on a lesson learned, or take an action that clearly shows how he or she has changed.

 **Reader/Writer Notebook**

Use your **RWN** to complete the activities for this workshop.

Deliver Your Short Story

Use Effective Language

When presenting a short story orally, you probably will not read it word-for-word. Instead, you may choose words and craft sentences somewhat spontaneously. To make sure you use appropriate, effective language, keep the following in mind:

- Standard American English should be used for clarity in the bulk of your narrative.
- Informal language may be used occasionally, for effect.
- Technical language may be used for specificity, but only when no other kind of language will do.

> ### A Good Oral Presentation
> - uses vivid images that the listener can easily understand
> - organizes events so they are easy to follow
> - uses appropriate words and sentences
> - uses effective nonverbal techniques

Polish Your Performance

After you have adapted your story for listeners and decided what kinds of language to use, apply the tips in this checklist to craft and practice your performance.

Tip for Polishing Your Performance	Done?
Read your story aloud until you are very familiar with it. If you trip over certain words or phrases, practice them in isolation, or change them altogether.	
Practice adjusting your voice. Use a different pitch for each character; vary your rate to match the story's action; and change your tone of voice to convey mood.	
Use gestures and facial expressions to add interest. Practice using movements that are expressive, but not distracting.	

To Note or Not to Note?

Make a set of notecards and put them in order. Then, practice both with and without them. If they increase your comfort and confidence, use them during your presentation. If you find them difficult to handle, set them aside and trust your own storytelling instincts.

Use Nonverbal Techniques

Facial expressions and gestures add meaning to your oral narrative. Use gestures to emphasize high points of conflict or humor. Keep in mind that your eyes convey emotion—involve your listeners by making frequent eye contact with them. Be sure to tailor your gestures and tone to your audience. For instance, exaggerated facial expressions might be appropriate for small children, but not for your classmates.

Speaking Tip

You may have heard that looking above the heads of your listeners is an effective public speaking technique. It is not—especially in a small space such as a classroom. Try looking at your listeners instead. Friendly eye contact will connect you to your audience in a personal way and will keep your listeners involved in the story. Avoid extended or intense eye contact, though, which can make a listener uncomfortable.

 Learn It Online
Add music and pictures to your story.

go.hrw.com   L12-1053   **Go**

Literary Skills Review

Comparing Literature   **Directions:** Read the followingpoems Then, read each multiple-choice question that follows, and write the letter of the best response.

The following two nineteenth-century poems are examples of two different literary traditions. Thomas Hardy (1840–1928), an English novelist who became a poet late in life, was a realist and pessimist. Arthur Rimbaud (1854–1891) was a young French symbolist—one of a group of poets who reacted against the idealism of Romanticism and sought to express their ironic view of the world, using rhythmical language and sometimes shocking imagery. "Drummer Hodge" is set in South Africa during the Boer War (1899–1902) in which the British defeated the Boers, South Africans of Dutch descent. Hardy uses some words from Afrikaans, the language spoken by the Boers. "The Sleeper of the Valley" is set in an unspecified time and place.

Drummer Hodge
by **Thomas Hardy**

1

They throw in Drummer Hodge, to rest
    Uncoffined—just as found:
His landmark is a kopje°-crest
    That breaks the veldt° around;
5 And foreign constellations west°
    Each night above his mound.

2

Young Hodge the Drummer never knew—
    Fresh from his Wessex home—
The meaning of the broad Karoo,°
10 The Bush,° the dusty loam,
And why uprose to nightly view
    Strange stars amid the gloam.

3

Yet portion of that unknown plain
    Will Hodge forever be;
15 His homely Northern breast and brain
    Grow to some Southern tree,
And strange-eyed constellations reign
    His stars eternally.

---

3. **kopje** (KAHP ee): (Afrikaans) small hill.
4. **veldt** (vehlt): (Afrikaans) prairie.
5. **west:** move westward.
9. **Karoo** (kuh ROO): (Hottentot) dry plain.
10. **Bush:** uncleared, outlying area.

The Sleeper of the Valley
by **Arthur Rimbaud**
translated by **Ludwig Lewisohn**

There's a green hollow where a river sings
Silvering the torn grass in its glittering flight,
And where the sun from the proud mountain flings
Fire—and the little valley brims with light.

5 A soldier young, with open mouth, bare head,
Sleeps with his neck in the dewy watercress,
Under the sky and on the grass his bed,
Pale in the deep green and the light's excess.

He sleeps amid the iris and his smile
10 Is like a sick child's slumbering for a while.
Nature, in thy warm lap his chilled limbs hide!

The perfume does not thrill him from his rest.
He sleeps in sunshine, hand upon his breast,
Tranquil—with two red holes in his right side.

1. Hardy uses the word "throw" (line 1) to describe the manner in which Drummer Hodge is buried. What does this word suggest about the feelings of those burying him?

   A relief

   B contentment

   C indifference

   D grief

2. According to "Drummer Hodge," what will happen to Hodge in the future?

   A He will be given a formal burial.

   B He will go to heaven.

   C He will become a permanent part of the landscape.

   D He will be remembered.

3. What word *best* describes the landscape in which the soldier lies in "The Sleeper of the Valley"?

   A tropical

   B pastoral

   C urban

   D arid

4. In "The Sleeper of the Valley," the contrast between the beautiful language and imagery and the reality of the soldier's death is an example of

   A irony

   B symbolism

   C alliteration

   D Romanticism

5. Which statement about both poems is *incorrect?*

   A Both are patriotic.

   B Both are rhymed.

   C Both use irony.

   D Both use imagery.

6. In "The Sleeper of the Valley," what detail *most* strongly suggests that the soldier is dead before we read the last line?

   A The grass is torn.

   B His limbs are chilled.

   C His head is bare.

   D His mouth is open.

7. In both "Drummer Hodge" and "The Sleeper of the Valley," there is evidence that —

   A a dead soldier is deeply mourned

   B people are glad that a soldier is dead

   C some people are saddened by a soldier's death and some people are happy about it

   D a particular soldier's death can go unnoticed

Constructed Response

8. Write a brief essay about the theme of "Drummer Hodge" and "The Sleeper of the Valley." Be sure to support your response with specific evidence from the poems.

Vocabulary Skills Review

Analogies **Directions:** For each item, choose the lettered pair of words that expresses a relationship that is most similar to the relationship between the pair of capitalized words.

1. MELANCHOLY : CHEERFUL ::
 A restless : fitful
 B punctual : prompt
 C report : interpretation
 D empty : complete

2. CERTITUDE : DOUBT ::
 A anger : contentment
 B belief : faithful
 C obstinate : hostile
 D palate : flavorful

3. FIDELITY : UNWAVERING ::
 A vile : venomous
 B charity : giving
 C repudiate : confirmation
 D elementary : perplexing

4. OPPRESSIVE : OVERBEARING ::
 A hateful: demanding
 B libel : lawsuit
 C generous : giving
 D comedy : funny

5. DISTRAUGHT : CALM ::
 A mourner : joyful
 B vessel : ocean
 C wild : domesticated
 D fortitude : strength

6. DELUSION : UNCONVINCING ::
 A pulchritude : gorgeous
 B mountain : altitude
 C illness : physician
 D soil : seedling

7. GENIAL : PERSONABLE ::
 A secretive : public
 B harsh : bitter
 C dime : coin
 D allow : permit

8. OPPRESSIVE : DICTATOR ::
 A anticipatory : despair
 B obnoxious : hostess
 C hatred : dislike
 D solitary : hermit

Acacemic Vocabulary

9. RESPOND : IGNORE ::
 A energetic : animated
 B prevent : avert
 C puncture : pierce
 D retain : lose

10. COMPLEX : INTRICATE ::
 A frantic : indifferent
 B tense : anxious
 C calm : distressed
 D languid : invigorating

Writing Skills Review

Editing a Short Story   **Directions:** Read the following excerpt from a draft of a short story and the questions below it. Choose the best answer to each question, and mark your answers on your own paper.

(1) Maya glanced again at the grimy scrap of note-book paper: *twenty-four, thirty-six, twenty-four.* (2) She stuffed the paper into her pocket and began to spin the lock's dial. (3) With a downward tug, the lock opened. She was in! (4) "Excuse me," came a deep voice from behind. (5) *Oh, no,* Maya thought. (6) With a weary sigh, she turned around and began to explain to the vice principal that her sister was home sick and needed her math book.

---

1. To help establish a suspenseful tone, how could the writer change sentence 2?

  A She stuffed the paper into her pocket, carefully adjusted her headband, and began to spin the lock's dial.

  B She crumpled the paper, tossed it carelessly aside, and began to spin the lock's dial.

  C She folded the paper, stuck it in her backpack, and began to spin the lock's dial.

  D She stuffed the paper into her pocket, glanced up and down the corridor, and began to spin the lock's dial.

2. Which verb could replace the word *opened* in sentence 3 to improve the precision of the writing?

  A clicked   **C** disengaged

  B disconnected   **D** snapped

3. Which would be the best way to slow down the pace of the story after the first paragraph?

  A present and analyze various school rules

  B explain exactly where in the school the locker is located

  C flash back to another incident in which Maya broke a school rule

  D compare and contrast the inside of this locker with the inside of Maya's own locker

4. To heighten the story's conflict, which of the following could the writer add after sentence 5?

  A I should clean out my locker before I start losing things.

  B *After two detentions this month, he'll never believe me.*

  C If I close the locker quietly, maybe he won't notice me.

  D Even though I'm breaking a rule, I have a good reason for it.

5. To create irony in the story, which of the following could the writer add after sentence 6?

  A "There's no need to explain, Maya," Mr. Harvey said. "I just wanted to let you know that Tara will need her history book, too."

  B "You'll have to explain later Maya," Mr. Harvey said. "I'm late for an important meeting."

  C "There's no need to explain, Maya," Mr. Harvey said. "Just shut the locker and come with me to the front office."

  D "You'll have to explain later, Maya," Mr. Harvey said. "I'm looking forward to hearing what your excuse will be this time."

Read On

FICTION
Jane Eyre

Meet Jane Eyre, an independent young woman who defies Victorian England's superficial expectations. This classic romance tells the story of a governess who captures the heart of her employer, Mr. Rochester, despite her plain appearance. Battling a series of secrets and obstacles, Jane Eyre eventually finds the happiness she seeks through her steadfast intelligence, strong will, and moral integrity.

FICTION
David Copperfield

Charles Dickens's favorite and most autobiographical novel contains some of his most memorable characters, including the optimistic Mr. Micawber, the devoted Clara Pegotty, the brutal Mr. Creakle, headmaster of Salem House School, and of course, one of the creepiest of all Dickens's villains, the unctuous, hypocritical Uriah Heep. Told in the first person, the novel depicts David's up-and-down relationships with numerous characters and his gradual realization that his calling is to be a novelist.

FICTION
Silas Marner

Silas Marner is a recluse and miser whose gold is stolen, but then symbolically replaced by a golden-haired child who crawls into his cottage on a freezing winter night. Marner raises the little girl with the mysterious origins, and his life is changed for the better. George Eliot shows her readers that even a small English village holds enough secrets about crimes, misunderstandings, and forbidden relationships to fill a novel.

DRAMA
The Importance of Being Earnest

In his famous play *The Importance of Being Earnest*, Oscar Wilde—no friend of the British class system— satirizes the British obsession with respectability. Jack Worthing, a respectable man in his community, creates a double life and imaginary identity as a way to escape the social pressures of money and success. The result is a witty play that presents Wilde's alternative philosophy at every turn: "The truth is rarely pure and never simple."

NONFICTION
What Jane Austen Ate and Charles Dickens Knew

Welcome to nineteenth-century England! In this entertaining book, Daniel Pool gives new life to the daily routines of the Victorian period, covering the era's nitty-gritty details (How did they keep clean?) and formal etiquette (How did one address a duke?). Find out what the Victorians ate, what they wore, how they traveled, and whom they married.

NONFICTION
Dared and Done: The Marriage of Elizabeth Barrett and Robert Browning

Julia Markus shows how the courtship and marriage of the Victorian poets Elizabeth Barrett and Robert Browning were the equivalent of an A-list celebrity romance and marriage today, except that this marriage succeeded. After Robert read Elizabeth's poetry, he fell in love with her, confessing his admiration in an ardent letter that she answered. When he met her four months later, he loved her even more, but how could Elizabeth defy her tyrannical father to marry Robert?

NONFICTION
Queen Victoria

Victoria reigned longer than any British monarch (1837–1901), and as the embodiment of the Victorian Age, believed that she was capable of boundless improvement, a belief instilled in her by her devoted husband, Albert. In this brief book, Elizabeth Longford describes, with anecdotes and carefully researched facts, the events in Victoria's life before her marriage to Albert, during their happy, productive years together, and through her decades of mourning and seclusion and her gradual return to public life after Albert's death.

WEB SITE
The Victorian Web

www.victorianweb.org
This wide-ranging site includes articles on everything from political and social history to theosophy and railways. In addition to the full text of many Victorian poems, stories, plays, and reviews, the Victorian Web features paintings, sculpture, drawings, photographs, and other Victorian art. A section on what Victorians wore includes images of hairstyles, footwear, hats, coats, dresses, and children's clothing.

Learn It Online
Explore *NovelWise*.

go.hrw.com L12-1059 **Go**

UNIT 6

The Modern World

1900 to the Present

COLLECTION 11
The World at War

COLLECTION 12
Modern and Contemporary Poetry

COLLECTION 13
Expectation and Reality

"Life spends itself in the act of transformation, dissolving, bit by bit, the world as it appeared."

—**Rainer Maria Rilke**

What Do
You?
Think   How does experience shape
         our view of the world?

Learn It Online
What's this historical period all about? Watch a short
video introduction online.

go.hrw.com   L12-1061   Go

Tower Bridge and GLA City Hall. London, England, UK.

The Modern World
1900 to the Present

This time line represents a snapshot of British literary events, British historical events, and world events from 1900 to the present. During this period, two world wars, economic depression, the creation of new nations from old colonial holdings, and revolutionary developments in technology changed the world significantly.

Peggy Ashcroft in *A Passage to India* (1984).

BRITISH LITERARY EVENTS

1900

1902 Joseph Conrad publishes *Heart of Darkness*

1904 W. B. Yeats and Lady Gregory found Dublin's Abbey Theatre to produce plays by and about the Irish

1913 G. B. Shaw's *Pygmalion* is first produced; D. H. Lawrence publishes *Sons and Lovers* ❯

1916 James Joyce publishes *A Portrait of the Artist as a Young Man*

1920

1922 Joyce publishes *Ulysses;* T. S. Eliot publishes *The Waste Land*

1924 E. M. Forster publishes *A Passage to India* ⌃

1927 Virginia Woolf publishes *To the Lighthouse*

Sons and Lovers (1960), with Wendy Hiller, Dean Stockwell, and Trevor Howard.

BRITISH HISTORICAL EVENTS

1900

1901 Queen Victoria dies and is succeeded by her son Edward VII

1910 Britain loses South Africa

1914 England declares war on Germany on August 4, under a treaty to protect Belgium

1916 Easter Rebellion fails in Dublin; uprising's leaders are executed by British

1918 World War I ends; voting rights are extended to British women over age thirty

1920

1922 Britain divides Ireland by treaty, with six northern counties remaining part of United Kingdom; civil war begins in Ireland

1939 After Germany invades Poland, Britain declares war on Germany ❯

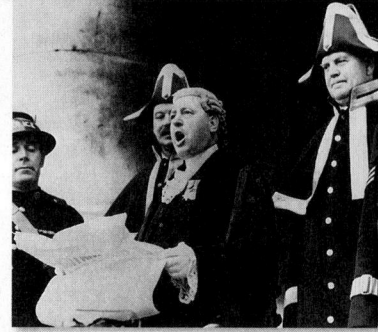

Proclamation of War by British. Mr. W. T. Boston, Saltbearer and acting town crier.

WORLD EVENTS

1900

1910 Union of South Africa is formed; racial segregation becomes governing rule

1914 World War I begins with the assassination of Austrian Archduke Franz Ferdinand

1915 Czech writer Franz Kafka publishes *The Metamorphosis*

1917 United States enters World War I; Russian Revolution begins

1918 World War I ends with nearly ten million casualties

1920

1929 United States stock market crashes, triggering a worldwide depression

1933 Adolf Hitler appointed chancellor of Germany; Germans build first concentration camp at Dachau

1934–1938 Stalinist purges in Russia force over ten million people into labor camps

1939 Germany invades Poland; World War II begins ❯

Recruitment poster from World War II (1939). Color lithography.

Your Turn

Review the time line, and discuss this question with a partner. What historical events might have prompted twentieth-century writers to reject forms and subjects of the past?

1940 — 1960 — 2010

1945 George Orwell's satire on totalitarianism, *Animal Farm,* is published

1947 W. H. Auden publishes his long poem *The Age of Anxiety*

1953 Samuel Beckett's ground-breaking play *Waiting for Godot* is first produced in Paris ❯

Johnny Murphy and Barry McGovern in *Waiting for Godot.*

1960 Harold Pinter's absurdist play *The Caretaker* is first produced

1966 Tom Stoppard's absurdist, humorous play *Rosencrantz and Guilderstern Are Dead* is staged ❯

1998 Ted Hughes publishes *Birthday Letters,* poems about his relationship with his former wife, Sylvia Plath

2005 Zadie Smith publishes *On Beauty*

Nicholas Rowe and James Wallace in *Rosencrantz and Guildenstern Are Dead.*

1940 — 1960 — 2010

1940 Battle of Britain; Royal Air Force prevents German invasion

1945 Germany surrenders; World War II ends

1948 London hosts the first Summer Olympics after the games' twelve-year hiatus

1949 Twenty-six counties in Ireland achieve full status as an independent republic; Britain retains control of six counties in the north

1960 Britain loses Nigeria

1960s British singing group The Beatles revolutionizes popular music ❯

2003 Britain joins the United States in war against Iraq

2005 Terrorists attack London's public transportation system

The Beatles at Abbey Road studios for *Our World* TV broadcast (1967).

1940 — 1960 — 2010

1941 Japan bombs United States fleet at Pearl Harbor; United States declares war on Japan, Germany, and Italy

1945 Germany surrenders; United States drops atom bombs over Hiroshima and Nagasaki, ending the war with Japan

1947 Mohandas Gandhi is assassinated in India; State of Israel is created

1948 UN partitions Palestine; Arab-Israeli war results

1961 Berlin wall is built to separate East and West Germany

1975 Fall of Saigon marks end of Vietnam War

1991 Soviet Union is dissolved

2001 Terrorists hijack planes and destroy the World Trade Towers in New York and part of the Pentagon in Washington, D.C.

2003 United States and Britain go to war with Iraq

2007 Doris Lessing wins the Nobel Prize in Literature

The Modern World 1900 to the Present

"The center cannot hold," wrote poet William Butler Yeats, and indeed, in the early twentieth century, the prosperity and stability of the Victorian era dissolved into chaos and conflict. Two world wars and a major economic depression eroded Great Britain's political and economic power and brought a slow death to the once-mighty empire.

KEY CONCEPTS

World War I: The Great War

History of the Times In early twentieth-century Europe, rising nationalism, competition for colonies, and growing military capabilities helped create an environment ripe for conflict. By its terrible end in 1918, World War I had cost Britain not only 750,000 lives but also her confidence and optimism.

Literature of the Times Writers experimented with form and content. Literature reflected the disillusionment and cynicism people felt after the war.

World War II and Its Aftermath

History of the Times Poverty caused by an economic slump in the 1930s spawned dictatorships in Germany, Italy, and Russia. The German dictator Hitler invaded Poland in 1939, igniting World War II. The horrors of this war, particularly nuclear devastation and the Nazi concentration camps, changed the world forever.

Literature of the Times Much of the literature written after World War II has been a blistering response to war and the limits set on freedom.

Identity and Diversity

History of the Times After World War II, most of Britain's remaining colonies declared independence. Many nations in Europe and Latin America were politically redefined. Formerly marginalized groups, such as women and ethnic minorities, began demanding self-determination. None of these changes were achieved without conflict.

Literature of the Times Globalization is the word in literature and in economics. World writers as well as writers from Britain's former colonies explore the political, racial, and gender issues of the time in a bitingly honest fashion.

Mature students in computer class at adult education centre, Camden, London.

KEY CONCEPT

World War I: The Great War

History of the Times

When Germany invaded Belgium in 1914, Europe was plunged into World War I, the so-called Great War. Victorian writer Rudyard Kipling was right in celebrating the British character as essentially patriotic, for when Britain then declared war on Germany, young men rushed to enlist. Six months later, many of the same young men lay slaughtered in the rain-soaked, vermin-infested trenches of France. Over the course of four years, a generation of young Englishmen was fed to the insatiable furnace of the war.

With the armistice in 1918, a new cynicism arose. The old values of national honor and glory had endorsed a devastating war. Pessimism about the state and the individual's relation to society emerged from feelings of disillusionment. In response to the "romantic nonsense" of the past, and, in particular, to the propaganda machine that had led the nation into war, a new realism began to pervade literary thought.

Literature of the Times

The carnage of war transformed poetry. Poets, including those who had served on the Western Front, now questioned or even mocked the values that had sent so many young men to their deaths.

Novelists focused on introspection. The century's most influential writer was the Irishman James Joyce, whose 1922 novel *Ulysses* appeared to a storm of controversy. In a revolutionary manner, Joyce drew on myth and symbol, Freudian explorations of sexuality, and new conceptions of time and the workings of human consciousness. Literary critics called this experimentation with form and content **modernism.**

Comprehension Check

How did the war change the way people thought about themselves and society?

Spring on the Trenches, Ridge Wood (1917), by Paul Nash.

Fast Facts

Historical Highlights

- World War I, the Great Depression, and World War II alter Great Britain's position as a world power and dramatically change its society.
- After World War II, most of Great Britain's colonies gain independence.

Literary Highlights

- Joseph Conrad, James Joyce, Virginia Woolf, and D. H. Lawrence experiment with the form and content of the novel.
- Writers from former British colonies and other countries explore the effects of cultural domination, racism, sexism, and war.

World War II and Its Aftermath

History of the Times

World War I, which had been called a war to end all wars, ironically led to another war, even more savage than the first. The League of Nations, the idealistic dream of U.S. President Woodrow Wilson, had no sooner been created than it was abandoned by a newly isolationist U.S. government. A worldwide economic depression that began in 1929 fostered the rise of dictators in German, Italy, and Russia.

In Italy and Germany the form of totalitarianism that developed was **fascism,** a type of government that is rigidly nationalistic and that relies on the rule of a single dictator whose power is absolute and backed by force. Benito Mussolini, who came to power in Italy in 1922, asserted control through brutality and manipulation. Adolf Hitler and the Nazi party capitalized on Germany's economic woes to convince many Germans that their problems were caused by Jews, Communists, and immigrants.

Russia's totalitarian government, based on the political theories of the economist Karl Marx, was Communist. Its founder, Vladimir Ilyich Lenin, had sought in the 1920s to create a society without a class system, one in which the state would distribute the country's wealth equally among the people. In reality, however, the new government became as repressive as the rule of the Russian czars. After Lenin's death in 1924, Joseph Stalin assumed power. In 1941, he became premier and continued to rule with an iron fist. Under Stalin's rule as many as fifteen million men and women were sent to the gulag, or system of forced-labor and detention camps.

By 1939, the Nazis were sweeping through Europe with their motorized army and superior air force. Hitler's plan for the systematic destruction of the Jews and other minorities, scapegoats on whom he blamed Germany's economic woes, resulted in the deaths of millions of innocent men, women, and children—including the six million Jews who were murdered in the Holocaust.

Only twenty years after the "war to end all wars," Europe had again plunged into a bloody, brutal conflict. In 1940, Germany occupied France and then prepared to invade Britain by launching devastating air attacks against London and other cities. Prime Minister Winston Churchill declared: "We shall go on to the end." The British did persevere, but only after the Soviet Union and the United States entered the war did Germany's defeat become inevitable.

For Japan, which had allied itself with Germany and Italy, the war ended in a new horror. On August 6, 1945, the entire city of Hiroshima was wiped out by a single atomic bomb dropped from an American plane. When the Japanese Emperor still did not surrender, on August 9, a second atom bomb was dropped on Nagasaki.

While recovering from the war and rebuilding its own shattered economy, Great Britain was unable to retain control of its many colonies. Most, including India, the "jewel in the crown," became independent nations.

Literature of the Times

Much world literature in the twentieth century has been a direct and bitter response to war and limits on human freedom. In *All Quiet on the Western Front* (1928), the German writer Erich Maria Remarque describes the horrors of World War I with such vehemence that the novel was banned in Germany.

Even this harrowing war novel paled in comparison to the haunting personal testaments to suffering endured during the Holocaust, such as those of the Italian writer Primo Levi (see page 1194) and the Romanian writer Elie Wiesel (see page 1104), both interned in Nazi concentration camps. Writers in the former Soviet Union—such as Aleksandr Solzhenitsyn and Anna Akhmatova (see page 1242)—made an art of defying governmental attempts to regulate their writing.

(*above*) Crowds gather in Piccadilly Circus, London, to celebrate V-E Day (May 8th, 1945). (*right*) People dancing in the streets of London during celebrations of V-E Day.

British dramatists responded to the fragmentation of the times by experimenting with form and subject matter. Samuel Beckett even went so far as to undermine the very idea of logical coherence in *Waiting for Godot* (1953), called the most significant play of the twentieth century. The plays of the prolific Tom Stoppard combine extensive comic wordplay with serious questions about philosophical issues. His recent prizewinning trilogy *Coast of Utopia* (2002) deals with the origins of modern radicalism in Russia.

Much of the work written since World War II is categorized as **postmodern** by literary critics and historians. Directly or indirectly, this body of writing is concerned with women's rights, multiculturalism, and the ever-present question of identity in postmodern society.

Comprehension Check

How did the rise of totalitarianism lead to the violence and oppression that characterize the modern world?

Identity and Diversity

History of the Times

Prior to World War II, countries such as Australia, Canada, and South Africa had already separated from the British Empire. The end of World War II sealed the empire's fate, and in the late 1940s and 1950s, most of Britain's remaining colonies declared independence.

As a result of the decline of Western imperial powers after World War II, dozens of independent states emerged in Africa and Asia, and many older nations in Europe and Latin America were politically redefined. These nations and others began to assert their own identities and reclaim territories. For example, India declared independence from Britain in 1946, and Nigeria did the same in 1960.

In 1947, the State of Israel was created to provide a homeland for the millions of Jews who had become refugees during World War II. The creation and subsequent population of Israel displaced hundreds of thousands of Palestinians from their homes, and the fighting over territory in that area continues today.

In 1989, the Berlin Wall that separated Communist East Germany from West Germany was torn down. Five years later, Nelson Mandela was elected president in the first South African election open to all races.

Despite momentous demonstrations of independence and progress, injustice, war, and genocide persist. A new world-wide threat has presented itself in the form of international terrorism, manifested in the 2001 devastating attacks on the World Trade Towers in New York City and on the Pentagon in Washington, D.C. Our human effort to understand one another has never been more challenging or more essential.

Literature of the Times

Innovations in technology and transportation have linked people in ways our ancestors couldn't have imagined. Ideas travel as fast as electronic channels can carry them, and one writer may influence another living continents away.

Current world literature frequently focuses on political and social problems. Literally hundreds of writers from former British colonies explore issues of personal identity and the effects of cultural domination and racism. Literary critics call the works of these writers **postcolonial literature.** These writers have seen their local cultures uprooted by colonialism or foreign influence, and they have had to ask themselves continually whether they are to celebrate their native traditions, imitate foreign models, or create new modes of expression.

Comprehension Check

To what does the title "Identity and Diversity" refer?

March outside British fort wall by Troops Out, a group calling for the removal of British troops from Northern Ireland.

THE TROOPS OUT MOVEMENT OF ENGLAND SCOTLAND AND WALES
END BRITISH RULE IN IRELAND NO

The Second Sex

Link to Today

Political concerns in postwar world literature are not the sole domain of nations and cultures; women's voices are some of the strongest to emerge in the postwar world. Many feminist writers work to expose women's lack of power in a world controlled by men. In the influential feminist work *The Second Sex* (1949), French writer Simone de Beauvoir analyzes women's secondary status in society and denounces the male middle class for perceiving women as objects; she demands an end to the "slavery of half of humanity." The Nigerian feminist Buchi Emecheta has informed numerous women writers from various African countries and uses motherhood (but not marriage) as a symbol for artistic creativity in her fiction. In *The Handmaid's Tale* (1985), the Canadian writer Margaret Atwood presents a grim cautionary tale that warns readers of a possible future world in which a puritanical dictatorship seeks to repress and control women.

Ask Yourself

What issues or concerns do feminist writers address today?

British technical aid worker teaching dress-making to woman in Malawi.

Wrap Up

Talk About …

What is the value in reading works of literature from other cultures? Explain. Try to use each Academic Vocabulary Word **listed below** at least once in your discussion.

Write About …

Does art continue to challenge norms, or does it reflect a new social stability? Answer this question in a brief essay, considering not only literature but also other modern technological forms of communication.

Academic Vocabulary for Unit 6

Talking and Writing About Literature
Academic Vocabulary is the language you use to write and talk about literature. These words will be underlined throughout the unit.

perspective (puhr SPEHK tihv) *n.:* particular way of looking at something. *Many poets changed their perspective on World War I when they saw the terrible suffering it caused.*

inevitable (ihn EHV uh tuh buhl) *adj.:* unavoidable. *When the United States and the Soviet Union entered World War II, Germany's defeat became inevitable.*

considerably (kuhn SIHD uhr uh blee) *adv.:* by a large amount. *Great Britain became considerably weaker after World War II.*

adapt (uh DAPT) *v.:* adjust for a new purpose. *Russia's totalitarian government adapted Karl Marx's theories to create a new society.*

exhibit (ehg ZIHB iht) *v.:* show, demonstrate. *Former British colonies still exhibit the effects of cultural domination.*

Your Turn

Copy the words from the Academic Vocabulary list into your *Reader/Writer Notebook*. Make a point of trying to use these words as you discuss the selections in the collections that follow.

Read with a Purpose

Read this poem to see how the speaker describes the journey of *Voyager 1* into the outer reaches of space.

Build Background

Two unpiloted spacecrafts, *Voyager 1* and *Voyager 2*, were launched in 1977 to explore outer space and send scientific information back to NASA. *Voyager 1* has traveled farther from Earth than any object made by humans; in 2006, its distance from the Earth was 100 times that of the sun. Guided by a ten-person flight team at NASA, *Voyager 1* is traveling about one million miles per day at the outer edge of our solar system, approaching interstellar space, which is filled with material from the explosions of stars.

Author Note

Alice Oswald (1966–   ) has worked as a gardener, and her love of the natural world permeates her poetry. It took her three years to complete her poem *Dart,* which describes the long journey of the Dart River as it flows into the sea. The speakers in Dart include the voices of the many people who work and live along the river, along with those of animals, plants, and insects. Oswald won the T. S. Eliot Prize for poetry in 2003. She lives in England with her family.

Spacecraft Voyager 1 Has Boldly Gone

by **Alice Oswald**

Spacecraft Voyager 1 has boldly gone
into Deep Silence carrying a gold-plated disc inscribed with
    whale-song
it has bleeped back a last infra-red fragment of language
and floated way way up over the jagged edge
5 of this almost endless bright and blowy enclosure of weather
to sink through a new texture as tenuous as the soft upward
    pressure of an elevator
and go on and on falling up steep flights of blackness with
    increasing swiftness
beyond the Crystalline Cloud of the Dead beyond Plato[1] beyond
    Copernicus[2]
O meticulous swivel cameras still registering events
10 among those homeless spaces gathering in that silence
that hasn't yet had time to speak in that increasing sphere
of tiny runaway stars notched in the year
now you can look closely at massless light
that is said to travel freely but is probably in full flight

---

1. **Plato:** Ancient Greek philosopher (around 428 B.C.–around 348 B.C.); the Ancient Greeks constructed the first "model" of the solar system based on mathematical theories.
2. **Copernicus:** Polish astronomer (1473–1543) who proposed a controversial idea that the sun was at the center of the universe, and the planets, including Earth, rotated around it.

Bright rings of Saturn and its northern hemisphere defined by bright features.

Ask Yourself

1. **Read with a Purpose** What imagery and vivid verbs does the poet use to describe the journey of the *Voyager*. How do her references to everyday objects help you imagine the journey?

2. The poem's first line refers to the popular science-fiction series *Star Trek,* which tells the story of a spacecraft whose mission is "to boldly go where no man has gone before." What does this allusion tell you about the journey of *Voyager 1*?

3. In what way might pictures and other data sent back from *Voyager 1* help the "Deep Silence" "speak" to people today? What "messages" might it send us?

4. To Plato and Copernicus (mentioned in line 8), the solar system was a mystery yet to be unraveled. In what way does *Voyager 1* go "beyond" them? What mysteries related to science would you like to see explained in your lifetime?

COLLECTION 11

The World at War

LITERARY FOCUS
War Literature

Dive Bomber and Tank (1940). by Jose Clement Orozco (1883–1949).
The Museum of Modern Art, NY / ARS, NY.

CONTENTS

Wilfred Owen

Rupert Brooke

Siegfried Sassoon

Richard Norton-Taylor Link to Today

Primo Levi

Elie Wiesel

Winston Churchill

Elizabeth Bowen

Graham Greene

George Orwell

Joseph Chamberlain

Jawaharlal Nehru

COMPARING TEXTS: AUTHOR STUDY
Virginia Woolf

> "We are all of us made by war, twisted and warped by war, but we seem to forget it."
>
> —**Doris Lessing**

SKILLS FOCUS **Literary Skills** Understand and analyze elements of literature from particular periods in British and World History; understand war literature.

War Literature by **Leila Christenbury**

Features of War Literature

- Poems that express the glory and horror of battle
- Memoirs that recount the experiences of soldiers and concentration camp victims
- Short stories that depict the lives of ordinary citizens affected by war
- Elegies that mourn the loss of loved ones, fellow soldiers, and civilians
- Speeches that evoke national pride and encourage citizens to keep their faith in the war cause

War from All Perspectives

As battles raged during two world wars, writers captured the horror of battle, the unfathomable suffering endured in prisoner-of-war and concentration camps, and the sacrifice, the fear, and the losses felt by civilians. Eyewitnesses to two world wars are the authors of the literature in this collection. All of them suffered terribly in war, and one, Wilfred Owen, died on the battlefield.

The poems of the World War I soldiers reflect the mood of Britain. As the war progressed, taking 750,000 British lives and leaving the soldiers who returned haunted with memories of trench warfare, the poems' themes shifted from the early idealism and patriotic glory of Rupert Brooke to the dejection and horror of Wilfred Owen and Siegfried Sassoon.

Survivors Reflect

World War II brought further horror. As British civilians lost loved ones overseas and Londoners suffered nightly bombings, Prime Minister Winston Churchill made impassioned speeches over the radio, urging fortitude and patience. The war, which did not distinguish between soldiers and civilians, took more than forty million lives. The era's literature is as vast as its suffering, encompassing the <u>perspectives</u> of soldiers, civilians, and prisoners alike. Desperate to recount their experiences and find meaning in the war, writers crafted **memoirs** and **elegies** to express the loss and grief occasioned by the twentieth century's costliest and deadliest war. Experiences in the Nazi concentration camps prompted the graphic true accounts of writers such as Primo Levi, Victor Frankl, and Elie Wiesel.

Analyzing Visuals

Viewing and Interpreting How do the colors and lines in these sketches convey the atmosphere of war?

Illustration from *All Quiet on the Western Front* (1929), by Erich Maria Remarque.

Ask Yourself

1. What can you learn about war from these civilian and soldier writers?
2. What value is there in writing and reading war literature?

Learn It Online
Explore war literature with *PowerNotes* online.

go.hrw.com | L12-1073 | **Go**

OWEN

lce et
corum Est

BROOKE

e Soldier

Do
u
nk

How does experience
shape our view of the
world?

uickTalk

n a small group why young men and
might view going to war as an adventure.
gree with this view?

MEET THE WRITERS

Wilfred Owen
(1893–1918)

Wilfred Owen is one of the most poignant figures in modern
literature. To learn his craft, he immersed himself in the history
of English poetry and studied the French modernist poets, but
these literary influences were to become secondary to the
devastating impact of a war Owen witnessed firsthand.

World War I broke out when Owen was twenty-one. He
joined the British army, and the course of his life was determined. His progress in poetry was made not in the halls of an
ancient university or in country retreats but in the muddy
purgatory of trench warfare and the twilight existence of
military hospitals. His gift for lyricism was bitterly tempered
by "the pity of war, the pity war distilled." In November 1918,
and a mere seven days before the war ended, Owen was listed
among those killed in action.

Rupert Brooke
(1887–1915)

Handsome and charismatic, Rupert Brooke was England's
golden poet. After distinguishing himself as an athlete and
scholar in private school, he studied at Cambridge and in Germany, and traveled through Italy, Canada, the United States,
and the South Seas. His popular early poems celebrated love
and nature.

When World War I broke out, Brooke received a commission in the Royal Navy. The war sonnets he wrote during a lull in
fighting in 1914 enjoyed considerable and immediate popularity. Although the poems were later criticized for being overly
sentimental and overlooking the devastating effects of war,
Brooke's works captured the hope and patriotism of a country
that believed in the war efforts. His death from blood poisoning
early in the war was mourned by all of England, including Winston Churchill, who called him one of "England's noblest sons."

Wilfred Owen (1916).

Rupert Brooke, portrait by
Sherril Schell.

**Think
About the
Writers** Owen served in the war considerably
longer than Brooke. What different
views of the war do you think their
poems might reflect? Why?

Dulce et Decorum Est

Reader/Writer Notebook

Use your **RWN** to complete the activities for this selection.

Literary Focus

Figures of Speech A **figure of speech** is a word or phrase that describes one thing in terms of another. Among the most common figures of speech are **similes, metaphors,** and **symbols.** An **oxymoron** (plural: *oxymora*) is a figure of speech that combines opposite or contradictory ideas. The phrase *sweet sorrow*, used to describe the feeling of being happy and sad at the same time, is an example of an oxymoron.

Reading Focus

Using Context Clues When you read poetry, you may encounter an unfamiliar word or a familiar word used in a new way (such as a figure of speech). You can use **context clues,** or the words, ideas, and information around the unfamiliar word, to help you guess the word's meaning. The poems in this collection refer to World War I trench warfare; therefore, if you read that the men slept underground in dark and muddy trenches, you could use context clues to guess that a trench is a hole in the ground. If you read that the men dropped into "hellish battle holes," you could use context clues to guess that this figure of speech refers to trenches.

Into Action In a chart like the one below, write unfamiliar words you find in the poem. Then, write any context clues that might help you determine the words' meanings. These clues might include other words in the poem or an explanation of the general context, or what's happening.

Unfamiliar Word	Context Clues
flound'ring	The men are stumbling to put on their gas masks.

Vocabulary

writhing [RY thihng] *v.* used as *adj.*: twisting and turning, as in pain. *The soldier was writhing from the agony of the bullet wound.*

vile [vyl] *adj.*: disgusting. *The vile, oozing sores on the man's leg made his friends turn away in horror.*

ardent [AHR duhnt] *adj.*: eager; enthusiastic. *The soldiers were ardent for victory over their enemies.*

Language Coach

Word Origins The word *writhing* comes from an Old English word meaning "to twist, wind about." Other modern English words from this root include *wreath, wreathe,* and *wry*. Using the knowledge of the root's meaning, explain the meaning of these phrases: "a wry face," "wry humor," "things gone awry."

Writing Focus

Think as a Reader/Writer

Find It in Your Reading Owen uses startling **figures of speech** to convey war's horror. Note the **simile** he uses to describe the injured man: "his hanging face, like a devil's sick of sin." In your *Reader/Writer Notebook*, note other figures of speech from the poem.

Learn It Online
Learn more with these Internet links.

go.hrw.com   L12-1075   **Go**

Dulce et Decorum Est

by **Wilfred Owen**

Two British soldiers waiting for the signal to attack at Ginchy, France (September 1916).

Read with a Purpose
Read this poem to discover how the poet conveys the horrors of war.

Build Background
This poem's title comes from the Latin statement *Dulce et decorum est pro patria mori,* which means "It is sweet and honorable to die for one's country." The statement has been used for centuries as a morale builder—and as a gravestone inscription—for soldiers.

After poison gas became a battlefield weapon during World War I, every soldier in the trenches had a gas mask. This poem describes the horrible consequences of failing to put on the mask in time.

Bent double, like old beggars under sacks,
Knock-kneed, coughing like hags, we cursed
    through sludge,
Till on the haunting flares we turned our backs
And toward our distant rest began to trudge.
5 Men marched asleep. Many had lost their boots
But limped on, blood-shod. All went lame; all
    blind;
Drunk with fatigue; deaf even to the hoots
Of tired, outstripped Five-Nines° that dropped
    behind.

Gas! GAS! Quick, boys!—An ecstasy of
    fumbling,
10 Fitting the clumsy helmets just in time;
But someone still was yelling out and stumbling
And flound'ring like a man in fire or lime° . . .
Dim, through the misty panes and thick green
    light,
As under a green sea, I saw him drowning. **A** **B**

15 In all my dreams, before my helpless sight,
He plunges at me, guttering, choking, drowning.

If in some smothering dreams you too could
    pace
Behind the wagon that we flung him in,
And watch the white eyes writhing in his face,
20 His hanging face, like a devil's sick of sin;
If you could hear, at every jolt, the blood
Come gargling from the froth-corrupted lungs,
Obscene as cancer, bitter as the cud
Of vile, incurable sores on innocent tongues,—
25 My friend, you would not tell with such high zest
To children ardent for some desperate glory,
The old Lie: *Dulce et decorum est*
Pro patria mori

---

  8. **Five-Nines:** 5.9-caliber gas shells.
12. **lime:** powder produced from heat on limestone. It can cause severe skin irritations.

A **Literary Focus** **Figures of Speech** What oxymoron appears in this stanza?

B **Reading Focus** **Using Context Clues** Use context clues to figure out what the speaker means by "misty panes." What words or details help you guess the meaning?

Vocabulary **writhing** [RY thihng] *v.* used as *adj.*: twisting and turning, as in pain.
vile [vyl] *adj.*: disgusting.
ardent [AHR duhnt] *adj.*: eager; enthusiastic.

The Soldier

Reader/Writer Notebook

Use your **RWN** to complete the activities for this selection.

Literary Focus

Poetic Structure The way a poem is constructed—its number of lines, rhyme scheme, and rhythm—is its **poetic structure**. Sonnets have similar poetic structures. They have fourteen lines, have one of several rhyme schemes, and are usually written with a meter called iambic pentameter. **Iambic pentameter** is a line of verse with five iambs. An **iamb** is a unit of measure consisting of an unstressed syllable followed by a stressed syllable. There are two major types of sonnets, each with a slightly different poetic structure. As you read "The Soldier," note how Brooke uses elements from both types.

The **Petrarchan sonnet** is divided into two parts: an eight-line octave with the rhyme scheme *abbaabba* and a six-line **sestet** with the rhyme scheme *cdecde* or *cdcdcd*. The octave usually presents a problem, poses a question, or expresses an idea, which the sestet then resolves, answers, or drives home. The transition from octave to sestet is known as the **turn**.

The **Shakespearean sonnet** has three four-line units, or **quatrains,** followed by a concluding two-line unit, or **couplet.** The three quatrains often express related ideas or examples, while the couplet sums up the message expressed in the quatrains. The turn usually occurs during the transition from the third quatrain to the couplet. The rhyme scheme of the Shakespearean sonnet is *abab cdcd efef gg.*

Writing Focus

Think as a Reader/Writer

Find It in Your Reading Poets often use sounds in their poems to emphasize message and tone. Brooke uses **alliteration,** the repetition of consonant sounds in words that are close to each other, to enhance the positive tone of his poem. In your Reader/Writer Notebook, use a chart like the one below to note examples of alliteration and the specific effects they create.

Example	Effect
"Her sights and sounds; dreams happy as her day"	The gliding sounds of /s/ and /z/ create a light tone

Vocabulary

concealed [kuhn SEELD] *v.* used as *adj.*: hidden. *The soldier's body will be concealed under the cold, hard ground.*

eternal [ih TUR nuhl] *adj.*: forever; everlasting. *The soldiers hoped the monument would be an eternal reminder of their comrades' sacrifice.*

Language Coach

Proper Nouns and Proper Adjectives
Nouns are words that name a person, place, thing, or idea *(woman, city, desk, hope).* Proper nouns are capitalized and name a specific person, place, thing, or idea: *Rupert Brooke, England, Romanticism.* Adjectives describe nouns. Proper adjectives are formed from proper nouns, and they, too, are capitalized: *English* soldiers, *Georgian* poets.

Tell whether the boldfaced words are proper nouns or proper adjectives.
1. The **German** troops marched across **Europe.**
2. Soldiers from **New Zealand** and **Australia** joined the **British** war effort.
3. **Woodrow Wilson** was the **American** president during the war.

Learn It Online
Explore the vocabulary words online with Word Watch.

go.hrw.com L12-1077   **Go**

THE SOLDIER

by **Rubert Brooke**

Read with a Purpose
Read this poem to discover how the speaker feels about dying for his country.

Build Background
When war broke out, Brooke enlisted in the navy and served briefly in Belgium. His war sonnets express idealistic patriotism. Had Brooke lived to witness the horrors of trench warfare, he might have developed a more cynical and disillusioned attitude about war; however, he died of blood poisoning en route to the Dardanelles with the British Mediterranean Expeditionary Force. He was buried on the island of Skyros in the Aegean Sea, a "corner of a foreign field that is forever England."

If I should die, think only this of me;
    That there's some corner of a foreign field
That is forever England. There shall be
    In that rich earth a richer dust concealed;
5 A dust whom England bore, shaped, made aware,
    Gave, once, her flowers to love, her ways to roam,
A body of England's breathing English air,
    Washed by the rivers, blest by suns of home. **A**

And think, this heart, all evil shed away,
10 A pulse in the eternal mind, no less
    Gives somewhere back the thoughts by England given;
Her sights and sounds; dreams happy as her day;
    And laughter, learnt of friends; and gentleness,
    In hearts at peace, under an English heaven. **B**

A **Literary Focus** Poetic Structure What idea is presented in the octave through the image of the "dust" of England?

B **Literary Focus** Poetic Structure How is the idea that is introduced by the image of the "dust" in the octave then expanded in the sestet?

Vocabulary **concealed** [kuhn SEELD] *v.* used as *adj.*: hidden.
eternal [ih TUR nuhl] *adj.*: forever; everlasting.

Applying Your Skills

SKILLS FOCUS **Literary Skills** Analyze figures of speech; analyze poetic structure; analyze theme. **Reading Skills** Understand context clues.

Vocabulary Skills Demonstrate knowledge of literal meanings of words and their usage. **Writing Skills** Write a poem; use figurative language; write to express.

Dulce et Decorum Est / The Soldier

Respond and Think Critically

Reading Focus

Read with a Purpose

1. In each poem, how does the speaker feel about the war and the cause for which he might die?

Reading Skills: Using Context Clues

2. Complete your chart for "Dulce et Decorum Est" by writing what you think each word or phrase means. Then compare your chart with a partner's, and discuss how context clues helped you guess meaning.

Unfamiliar Word	Context Clues	Meaning
flound'ring (floundering)	The men are stumbling to put on their gas masks.	making uncontrolled movements; nearly falling

✓ Vocabulary Check

Match each Vocabulary word with its definition.

3. concealed   **a.** everlasting

4. writhing   **b.** hidden

5. vile   **c.** eager

6. ardent   **d.** disgusting

7. eternal   **e.** twisting about in pain

Literary Focus

Literary Analysis

8. **Analyze** Who is the "you" addressed in the final stanza of "Dulce et Decorum Est"? What is the effect of Owen's ending the poem in this way?

9. **Interpret** How is the idea of immortality linked with the idea of patriotism in "The Soldier"?

10. **Contrast** How would you describe the difference in tone between the two poems?

Literary Skills: Figures of Speech / Poetic Structure

11. **Analyze** What oxymoron can you find in the last stanza of "Dulce et Decorum Est"? What emotions or insights does it evoke?

12. **Interpret** Explain the similes in lines 23–24 of "Dulce et Decorum Est." How do they relate to the other ideas expressed in the poem?

13. **Extend** How does "The Soldier" combine elements of both the Petrarchan and Shakespearean sonnet forms?

14. **Analyze** How does the structure of "The Soldier" contribute to the message? What ideas about death are expressed in each part of the poem?

Literary Skills Review: Theme

15. **Interpret** The central idea or insight about human experience revealed in a work is called the **theme.** Write a sentence telling the theme of each of these two poems.

Writing Focus

Think as a Reader/Writer

Use It in Your Writing Review the notes you took about figurative language in "Dulce et Decorum Est" and about alliteration in "The Soldier." Then, write a poem that uses figurative language and alliteration to convey your ideas about war.

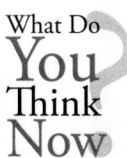

What Do **You Think Now**

How do the two poets' ideas about war differ? How might their experiences have affected their perceptions of war?

Preparing to Read

The Rear-Guard

A Soldier's Declaration

What Do You Think?

How does experience shape our view of the world?

QuickWrite

Why might the experience of war make people react to situations in ways they would not have thought possible? In your *Reader/Writer Notebook,* write a brief response to this question.

Novelist Siegfried Sassoon in military uniform England, UK (1915).

Siegfried Sassoon
(1886–1967)

World War I veteran Siegfried Sassoon's graphic and vivid poems exposed the brutal effects of the war.

From Idealism to Horror

Siegfried Sassoon had an upbringing of great privilege, his family having made its fortune in India. Like many other upper-class British men, he signed up for the war with the intention of having a great adventure, which he thought would be much like the exciting fox hunts of his youth. During Sassoon's convalescence from a riding accident that delayed his deployment, his brother was killed in battle. Despite his grief, Sassoon's initial poems during this period reflect an idealistic perspective.

However, Sassoon's own battles in the trenches shattered this idealism. Known as "Mad Jack" for his extraordinary bravery on the war front, Sassoon was awarded the Military Cross for his courage. Nevertheless, he became a pacifist and an ardent voice against the war. (For years, he was rumored to have hurled his Military Cross into the Mersey River in protest, but the Cross was discovered in his son's attic in 2007.) While he was hospitalized for shell-shock in 1917, he met and influenced the soldier and poet Wilfred Owen.

Driven by Memories

Sassoon was haunted by memories of the war. His poems caused an uproar with some readers for their graphic depiction of battle, while other readers accused him of being unpatriotic. Nevertheless, his poetry books sold well and boosted his reputation as a passionate voice for his generation. His later novels and autobiographies memorialize his fellow soldiers, exhibit the atrocities of war, and reveal his own inner wounds.

During World War II, Sassoon opened his home to British and American soldiers and war refugees. He continued to write and was awarded a Queen's Gold Medal. Much of his later work reflects his views on religion (he converted from Judaism to Catholicism in 1957), but he is best remembered for the great war poems of his youth.

Think About the Writer
How might writing about the war have helped Sassoon heal from the tragedy of his experiences?

The Rear-Guard

Reader/Writer Notebook

Use your **RWN** to complete the activities for this selection.

Literary Focus

Imagery Language that appeals to the senses is called **imagery.** Most images appeal to the sense of sight, but imagery can also appeal to the senses of hearing, touch, taste, or smell. While imagery is featured in all types of writing, it is especially important in poetry.

Reading Focus

Visualizing Details You will have a fuller, more enjoyable experience of poetry and prose if you visualize details as you read. **Visualizing details** means picturing them in your mind: using your imagination and the information you read to "see" what you are reading. You might use the following techniques to help you visualize a poem:

· Read a few lines, and then stop and consider the images the lines evoke.
· Describe the images to a peer.
· Draw a picture of what you have read.

Into Action In a chart like the one below, note the details you visualize as you read. First, write the line numbers; then, write what you visualize.

Line Numbers	What I Visualize
1—3	I visualized a man underground, making his way tentatively through the darkness with his flashlight. He sniffs, smells something terrible, and wrinkles up his nose in disgust.

Language Coach

Prefix *un–* When added to an adjective or a participle, the prefix *un–* means the absence of a quality. For example, the adjective *unwholesome* means that the quality of wholesomeness is missing. When added to a verb or a participle, *un–* means the reversal, or "undoing," of an action. For example, *unloading* in the last line represents the reversal of the action of loading a gun. What other word with the prefix *un–* can you find in the poem? What part of speech is it, and how does the prefix *un–* contribute to its meaning?

Writing Focus

Think as a Reader/Writer

Find It in Your Reading The images and words writers choose convey a **tone,** or attitude toward their subject. Note how the words and **images** in the following lines help create a bitter, tormented tone: "Dawn's ghost that filtered down a shafted stair / To the dazed, muttering creatures underground." As you read the poem, note in your *Reader/Writer Notebook* words and images that help Sassoon create a bitter tone.

TechFocus "The Rear-Guard" presents a soldier's perspective. Imagine a movie camera panning the area and then zooming in to reveal the setting. What do you see in each shot?

Learn It Online
Find graphic organizers online to help you organize your thoughts as you read.

go.hrw.com L12-1081

POEM

The Rear-Guard

by **Siegfried Sassoon**

Read with a Purpose
Read to understand one soldier's
horrifying experience in the trenches.

Build Background
During World War I, soldiers sometimes lived for years in interconnected underground
caverns infested by rats and only occasionally illuminated by dim shafts of natural light.

(Hindenburg Line,° April 1917.)
Groping along the tunnel, step by step,
He winked his prying torch° with patching glare
From side to side, and sniffed the unwholesome air.

Tins, boxes, bottles, shapes too vague to know,
5   A mirror smashed, the mattress from a bed;
And he, exploring fifty feet below
The rosy gloom of battle overhead.

Tripping, he grabbed the wall; saw someone lie
Humped at his feet, half-hidden by a rug,
10   And stooped to give the sleeper's arm a tug.   **Ⓐ**
"I'm looking for headquarters." No reply.
"God blast your neck!" (For days he'd had no sleep.)

"Get up and guide me through this stinking place."
Savage, he kicked a soft, unanswering heap,
15   And flashed his beam across the livid face
Terribly glaring up, whose eyes yet wore
Agony dying hard ten days before;
And fists of fingers clutched a blackening wound.

Alone he staggered on until he found
20   Dawn's ghost that filtered down a shafted stair
To the dazed, muttering creatures underground
Who hear the boom of shells in muffled sound.
At last, with sweat of horror in his hair,
He climbed through darkness to the twilight air,
25   Unloading hell behind him step by step.   **Ⓑ**

Hindenburg Line: German
defensive barricade running
across northern France. It
was made of massive barbed-
wire entanglements and deep
trenches.
2. torch: flashlight

Fusilier returning from
trenches during World
War I (c. 1915).

Ⓐ **Reading Focus** **Visualizing Details** What images come to mind as you read lines
5–10? What words or phrases help you visualize?
Ⓑ **Literary Focus** **Imagery** What line in the poem appeals to the sense of hearing?

Applying Your Skills

The Rear Guard

Respond and Think Critically

Reading Focus

Quick Check

1. Why might the poet describe the battle as a "rosy gloom"?

2. What details does the poet include to show that men live in this underground "hell"?

Read with a Purpose

3. What information about life in the trenches did you learn by reading this poem?

Reading Skills: Visualizing Details

4. Review your chart about visualizing details. Then, write a sentence or two describing the types of imagery Sassoon uses in the poem.

Line Numbers	What I Visualize
1–3	I visualized a man underground. He is carrying a flashlight and trying to make his way through the darkness. He sniffs, smells something terrible, and wrinkles up his nose in disgust.

Literary Focus

Literary Analysis

5. **Analyze** What reason does the speaker give for how he treats the man on the ground? What else in the poem might explain the speaker's reaction?

6. **Interpret** Who are the "dazed, muttering creatures"? How does this description, along with the speaker's description of himself and the dead man, emphasize war's dehumanizing effect?

7. **Evaluate** The speaker does not describe how he feels upon realizing the man he has kicked is dead. Does this omission add to or detract from the power of the poem? Explain your response.

8. **Extend** Many readers in England, even the leaders of the pacifist movement, were shocked by the graphic violence in Sassoon's poems. Do you think a poem such as this would have hurt or helped the pacifist cause? Explain.

Literary Skills: Imagery

9. **Evaluate** How does the poet use imagery to convey the atrocity of war? In your opinion, which image is most compelling? Why?

Literary Skills Review: Enjambment

10. **Analyze** A **run-on line,** or **enjambment,** is a line of poetry that does not stop at the end of the line but instead continues on to the next line. Poets carefully choose where they will end lines, not only for rhythm, rhyme, and meter, but also to effect meaning. Look at lines 14–17 to see how Sassoon uses enjambment to slowly reveal the state of the man lying on the ground. How does this measured revelation affect the reader?

Writing Focus

Think as a Reader/Writer

Use It in Your Writing Review your notes on the words and details Sassoon uses to convey tone. Write a short poem or paragraph about a recent news event. Decide what tone you will convey, and carefully choose words and details to help you convey it.

What Do You Think Now Given what you have learned about the trenches, do the speaker's actions in this poem make sense to you? Why or why not?

For **CHOICES** see page 1087.

Preparing to Read

Reader/Writer Notebook

Use your **RWN** to complete the activities for his selection.

Informational Text Focus

Analyzing Political Statements Like other forms of persuasion, a political statement is intended to convince the audience to agree with the author's point of view and to take a certain course of action. A political statement includes:

- an explicit statement of the writer or speaker's core belief
- details, facts, and/or opinions that support or elaborate on the central statement of belief:
- appeals to the reader's emotions, logic, or ethics (sense of right and wrong)

Into Action As you read "A Soldier's Declaration," use a graphic organizer like the one below to record Sassoon's central statement of belief. Then, note details and ideas that support his argument.

Sassoon believes _____.	
Support: As a soldier, Sassoon knows what battle is like.	
Support:	
Support:	
Support:	

> ## Language Coach
>
> **Antonyms** An **antonym** is a word with an opposite, or nearly opposite, meaning to another word. In the second line of his statement, Sassoon uses two pairs of antonyms: *defense* : *aggression* and *liberation* : *conquest*. Look up these words in a dictionary, and state how they are opposites, or antonyms. How does the use of antonyms help Sassoon strengthen his argument?

Writing Focus   Preparing for **Constructed Response**

Persuasive writers often use **loaded language**—words or phrases intended to evoke a strong reaction in their readers. For example, rather than saying that soldiers are dying, Sassoon says they "are being sacrificed." Note the powerful effect of the word *sacrificed*. As you read, look for other examples of loaded language, and record them in your *Reader/Writer Notebook*.

TechFocus This declaration was read in front of the House of Parliament, the English government. As you read, imagine how you might present it as a podcast.

 Learn It Online
Examine modern forms of persuasion at the Media-Scope mini-site online.

go.hrw.com   L12-1084   **Go**

A Soldier's Declaration

by **Siegfried Sassoon**

Read with a Purpose

Read this declaration to learn how a soldier expressed his opposition to the First World War.

Build Background

After Siegfried Sassoon's first tour of duty, he befriended the philosopher and pacifist Bertrand Russell and became vehemently opposed to the war. He wrote "A Soldier's Declaration" on June 15, 1917, and it was read before the House of Commons and published in a London newspaper in July. Sassoon refused to return to battle, hoping his protest would further publicize his cause and help end the war. A friend, worried that Sassoon would be court-martialed and jailed, convinced Sassoon's commanding officers that the poet was suffering from trauma induced by the war. Sassoon was hospitalized and later volunteered to rejoin his fellow soldiers in battle.

I am making this statement as an act of willful defiance of military authority, because I believe the war is being deliberately prolonged by those who have the power to end it. **A**

I am a soldier, convinced that I am acting on behalf of soldiers. I believe that this war, upon which I entered as a war of defense and liberation, has now become a war of aggression and conquest. I believe that the purposes for which I and my fellow soldiers entered upon this war should have been so clearly stated as to have made it impossible to change them, and that, had this been done, the objects which actuated us[1] would now be attainable by negotiation.

I have seen and endured the suffering of the troops, and I can no longer be a party to prolong these sufferings for ends which I believe to be evil and unjust. **B**

I am not protesting against the conduct of the war, but against the political errors and insincerities for which the fighting men are being sacrificed.

On behalf of those who are suffering now I make this protest against the deception which is being practiced on them; also I believe that I may help to destroy the callous complacence with which the majority of those at home regard the continuance of agonies which they do not share, and which they have not sufficient imagination to realize.

Siegfried L. Sassoon, July 1917

---

1. **actuated us:** made us act.

A British soldier on duty at barbed wire gate in France during World War I.

A **Informational Focus** Analyzing Political Statements What is Sassoon's main idea?

B **Informational Focus** Analyzing Political Statements Does this statement appeal primarily to reader's logic, emotion, or ethics (sense of right and wrong)? Explain.

A Soldier's Declaration

Respond and Think Critically

Informational Text Focus

Quick Check

1. What do you think is the difference between a war of "defense and liberation" and a war of "aggression and conquest"?

2. What generalization about the people in |England does Sassoon make in his final paragraph?

Read with a Purpose

3. Sassoon suggests that there could have been an alternative to continuing the war. What is this alternative, and what has prevented it, according to Sassoon?

Informational Skills: Analyzing Political Statements

4. Review each supporting item you recorded in your chart. Then, determine whether each appeals to logic, emotion, or ethics. (Some may appeal to more than one.) Then, choose the most persuasive part of this political statement, and discuss it with a small group of your peers.

Sassoon believes _____	Logic, emotion, or ethics
Support: As a soldier, Sassoon knows what battle is like.	fact; appeals to logic
Support:	
Support:	
Support:	

Text Analysis

5. **Analyze** What is Sassoon's **tone,** or attitude toward his subject, in this political statement? What might account for this tone?

6. **Infer** In the third paragraph, Sassoon makes a distinction between the conduct of the war and its political errors and insincerities. Why might he have been careful to make this distinction?

7. **Evaluate** Sassoon harshly criticizes those "at home." Do you think this is an effective persuasive technique? Why or why not?

8. **Make Judgments** Under what circumstances, if any, should soldiers be allowed to speak out against a war? Should they ever be permitted to refuse to serve? Explain your response.

Listening and Speaking

9. **Extend** With a partner, stage a debate in which one of you takes the part of Sassoon (against the war) and the other expresses the opposite view (for the war). Support your side as persuasively as possible. Ask another classmate to judge who is the winner of the debate.

Writing Focus   Constructed Response

In a brief essay, discuss Sassoon's use of loaded language in "A Soldier's Declaration." Be sure to cite specific evidence to support your response.

What Do You Think Now?
How might Sassoon's experiences of war have influenced his perspective about his country and its politics?

The Rear-Guard
A Soldier's Declaration

SKILLS FOCUS Informational Skills Analyze a political statement. **Reading Skills** Locate information from print and nonprint sources, including appropriate texts, periodicals, book indexes, databases, technical sources, and the Internet; produce research projects and reports in varying forms for audiences. **Listening and Speaking Skills** Adapt to purpose when speaking: persuade. **Writing Skills** Write a brief constructed response, with specific support; deliver multi-media presentations.

CHOICES

As you respond to the Choices, use these **Academic Vocabulary** words as appropriate: <u>adapt</u>, <u>considerably</u>, <u>exhibit</u>, <u>inevitable</u>, <u>perspective</u>.

REVIEW
Use Imagery to Describe a Scene
Group Activity Most of the imagery Sassoon includes in "The Rear-Guard" appeals to the sense of sight. In a small group, use your imagination and the details in the poem to describe the smells, feelings, and sounds a soldier might experience as he makes his way through the trenches. Choose a representative to present your description to the class.

Make a Podcast of a Political Statement
TechFocus Imagine that Sassoon asked you to read his declaration aloud to the English government. On a copy of the declaration, underline or highlight the words or phrases you will emphasize. Mark when you will pause, when you will make eye contact with your audience, and what gestures you will use for effect. Ask classmates to prepare responses as members of Parliament. Then, make a podcast of your statement and the responses.

CONNECT
Create Storyboards
TechFocus Imagine you are a movie director planning to shoot the scene Sassoon conveys in "The Rear-Guard." Re-read the poem, and create storyboards, brief sketches that plan the main shots for each part of a scene. Tell how you will zoom and pan the scene with a camera to slowly reveal the fate of the man on the ground. In a short paragraph, explain the scene's action and setting.

Write a Letter to the Editor
Timed └Writing In "A Soldier's Declaration," Sassoon says that people at home do not have "sufficient imagination" to realize the suffering of soldiers in World War I. Do you think that today's mass media has strengthened peoples' ability to understand the realities of war? Write your response in a brief essay. Be sure to include details to support your thesis.

EXTEND
Design a World War I Memorial
Throughout history, artists and architects have designed memorials to celebrate and honor those who served in battle. Use details from "The Rear-Guard" and the other World War I poems you have read in this collection as a springboard to design a World War I memorial to be <u>exhibited</u> in the center of your hometown. You might do research online for ideas about how other wars have been memorialized. Share your designs with the class, and explain why you included each element.

Presentation on War Memories
Ask your family and friends if they remember someone who served in World War I or who was alive during that time. Request that they tell any memories this person shared about life during that war. You might also bring in old letters from this time, provided they are not too personal. Use your notes on these memories, along with letters, photographs, or magazine clippings to create a class multimedia exhibit called "War Memories."

Statue of a World War I British soldier. Winchester, Britain, UK.

Under Heavy Fire in Iraq

How does experience shape our view of the world?

⏱ **QuickWrite**

What makes people perform extraordinary acts of bravery? How might they react to the experience afterward? Jot down some notes in your *Reader/Writer Notebook*.

Informational Text Focus

Analyzing Sequence of Events To get your attention, journalists often start with the most important part of a story. They don't necessarily tell everything that happened in the order in which it occurred. As a result, when you read news stories, you must **analyze the sequence of events,** or determine what happened when. As you read "Under Heavy Fire in Iraq," make a chart to organize information about the three main events Norton-Taylor describes. Then, determine the sequence of events by noting their relationship to one another.

Main Events:	When It Occurred	Key Events of Main Event
Beharry wins Victoria Cross	March 2005, after events in Iraq	

Vocabulary

engagements (ehn GAYJ muhnts) *n.*: military battles. *The newspaper reported three engagements between the two forces.*

incapacitated (ihn kuh PAS uh tayt ihd) *v.*: disabled; deprived of power. *The bomb blast incapacitated the commander.*

noxious (NAHK shuhs) *adj.*: very harmful, often poisonous. *The noxious gas left the soldiers violently ill and unable to move.*

oblivious (uh BLIHV ee uhs) *adj.*: unaware or paying no attention. *The brave soldier seemed oblivious to danger.*

Writing Focus Preparing for **Constructed Response**

The details the speaker uses to tell what happened, or the **narrative information,** play an important role in this article. Use your *Reader/Writer Notebook* to record details that especially impress you.

Language Coach

Multiple-Meaning Words You can use context to help you define multiple-meaning words. Find two meanings for the multiple-meaning words listed below; then, use context clues to help you determine the meaning of each word as it is used in the selection.

citation	turret	hatch
mine	lodged	brass

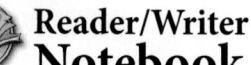

Reader/Writer
Notebook
Use your **RWN** to complete the activities for this selection.

✳ **Learn It Online**
Get to know these vocabulary words online with Word Watch.

go.hrw.com L12-1088 **Go**

Link to Today

This link to today shows the timelessness of courage under fire.

Read with a Purpose

Read to see how one soldier's bravery earned him England's highest military honor.

Build Background

In March 2003, the United States and Great Britain declared war on Iraq. Baghdad and other critical sites were bombed; 300,000 U.S. and British coalition troops entered Iraq; and, by April, Baghdad was controlled by the coalition. The operation was considered a success, but almost immediately, resistance forces in Iraq (insurgents from Iraq and other Middle Eastern countries) began attacking British and American soldiers. By 2007, more than 64,000 Iraqi civilians, 149 British soldiers, and nearly 3,500 U.S. soldiers had been killed in the war.

Under Heavy Fire in Iraq

The Guardian
Friday, March 18, 2005

A young soldier has been awarded the Victoria Cross, the highest military honor, for bravery under fire in some of the fiercest, and largely unreported, engagements between British forces and insurgents in south-eastern Iraq.

Private Johnson Beharry, 25, is the first soldier to receive the VC since the Falklands war in 1982[1] and the first living recipient since 1969, when two Australians were given the award for action in Vietnam.

The citation[2] describes his "great heroism" in two separate encounters in the town of Amara, north of Basra. In the first, the Warrior armored vehicle he was driving was hit by multiple rocket-propelled grenades (RPGs).

His company, the citation says, had been ordered to extract a foot patrol pinned down by small arms and heavy machine-gun fire and an attack by an improvised explosive device and RPGs. **(A)**

As they passed a roundabout[3] on their way to the pinned-down patrol, his platoon noticed that the road ahead was empty of civilians and traffic, an indicator of a potential ambush. The platoon commander ordered the vehicle to halt so that he could assess the situation. The vehicle was then hit by RPGs.

The citation continues: "As a result of this ferocious initial volley of fire, both the platoon commander and the vehicle's gunner were incapacitated by concussion and other wounds, and a number of the soldiers in the rear of the vehicle were also wounded."

---

1. **Falklands war:** brief war between England and Argentina over control of the Falkland Islands, located in the South Atlantic Ocean.
2. **citation:** honorable mention of a soldier in war.
3. **roundabout:** British term for a traffic circle.

(A) **Informational Focus** Analyzing Sequence of Events How does the writer use a shift in tense to show that the order occurred before the armored vehicle was hit?

Vocabulary **engagements** (ehn GAYJ muhnts) *n.*: military battles.
incapacitated (ihn kuh PAS uh tayt ihd) *v.*: disabled; deprived of power.

Private Johnson Beharry (25) at Buckingham Palace in London after receiving the Victoria Cross from Queen Elizabeth (April 27, 2005).

Private Beharry had no means of communication with the turret crew or any of the other Warriors around him. He did not know if his commander or crew were still alive or how serious their injuries were.

"On his own initiative, he closed his driver's hatch and moved forward through the ambush position to try to establish some form of communications, halting just short of a barricade across the road."

The Warrior was hit again by the RPGs. It caught fire and filled with thick, noxious smoke. **Ⓑ**

Private Beharry, continues the citation, "assessed that his best course of action to save the lives of his crew was to push through, out of the ambush. He drove his Warrior directly through the barricade, not knowing if there were mines or improvised explosive devices placed there to destroy his vehicle. By doing this he was able to lead the remaining five Warriors behind him towards safety."

Another RPG hit the Warrior. "The flames and force of the blast passed directly over him, down the driver's tunnel, further wounding the semi-conscious gunner in the turret."

Private Beharry was "forced to drive the vehicle along the rest of the ambushed route, some 1,500 meters, with his hatch opened up and his head exposed to enemy fire, all the time with no communications with any other vehicle."

A 7.62mm bullet penetrated his helmet and remained lodged on its inner surface.

Private Beharry then climbed on to the turret of the burning vehicle and, "seemingly oblivious to the incoming enemy small arms fire, manhandled his wounded platoon commander out of the turret, off the vehicle and to the safety of a nearby Warrior."

Remounting his burning vehicle for the third time, he drove it through "a complex chicane and into the security of the defended perimeter of the outpost, thus denying it to the enemy." Once inside, he collapsed from physical and mental exhaustion.

A few weeks later, on June 11, another Warrior convoy he was leading was ambushed. A grenade detonated six inches from his head. **Ⓒ**

"With the blood from his head injury obscuring his vision, Beharry managed to continue to control his vehicle and forcefully reversed the Warrior out of the ambush," says the citation. He then collapsed, unconscious.

The Grenada-born[4] private was paraded by the top brass yesterday among his comrades in the 1st Battalion, the Princess of Wales's Royal Regiment, and other recipients of high military honors. **Ⓓ**

"I was just doing my job. I was just thinking of the guys in the vehicle and the guys behind me," he said.

He was asked what was going through his mind at the time. "An RPG," Private Beharry promptly replied.

He was not afraid at the time, only afterward. Asked why he had left Grenada, he said he wanted "a change of life."

Asked if he would be Britain's first black general, he quickly replied, "No."

His wife, Lynthia, said that after he had been injured he was told he had only a 50-50 chance of surviving. She said her husband would return to Iraq "if he has to."

Private Beharry's award was described by Gary Sheffield, a leading historian of the modern British army, as "a classic in the VC mold—he was rescuing colleagues."

—*Richard Norton-Taylor is the security affairs editor for* The Guardian. *He is also a playwright.*

---

4. **Grenada-born:** Grenada is an island in the Caribbean Sea.

Ⓑ **Informational Focus** Analyzing Sequence of Events   When do the commander and gunner become incapacitated? How does the sequence of events make Beharry's behavior particularly brave?

Ⓒ **Informational Focus** Analyzing Sequence of Events   What does this paragraph tell you about when the first event occurred?

Ⓓ **Informational Focus** Analyzing Sequence of Events   Read the date of the article. On what date did Beharry receive his award?

Vocabulary **noxious** (NAHK shuhs) *adj.:* very harmful, often poisonous.
oblivious (uh BLIHV ee uhs) *adj.:* unaware or paying no attention.

INFORMATIONAL TEXT FOCUS
Applying Your Skills

SKILLS FOCUS **Informational Skills** Analyze the sequence of events in a text. **Vocabulary Skills** Demonstrate knowledge of literal meanings of words and their usage. **Listening and Speaking Skills** Prepare a script when speaking. **Writing Skills** Write a brief constructed response, with specific support.

Under Heavy Fire in Iraq

Respond and Think Critically

Informational Text Focus

Quick Check

1. What did Beharry do to earn the Victoria Cross?

2. Beharry had to make decisions without help from his commanding officer or his colleagues. What choices did he make? What do these choices suggest about his abilities as a soldier?

Read with a Purpose

3. How does Beharry's experience compare to that of the three World War I poets? What do all wars have in common? How does modern warfare differ from warfare during World War I?

Informational Skills: Analyzing Sequence of Events

4. Review the chart, and notice the amount of time between the first and second event. When was Beharry's Warrior hit in each case? What did Beharry do afterward? How does analyzing the sequence of events help you better understand Beharry's actions as a soldier?

✓ Vocabulary Check

Match the Vocabulary words to their definitions.

5. engagements   a. unaware

6. incapacitated   b. deprived of power or disabled

7. noxious   c. military battles

8. oblivious   d. very dangerous or poisonous

Text Analysis

9. **Analyze** Why did the writer include the details in the second paragraph? What do they suggest about the importance of Beharry's award?

10. **Infer** How does Beharry respond to the question about what was going through his mind at the time of the engagement? What does his response reveal about his personality?

11. **Interpret** What does the inclusion of the historian's quotation at the end of the article suggest about the writer's perspective, or point of view?

12. **Make Judgments** What was Beharry's bravest act? Cite evidence from the selection.

Listening and Speaking

13. **Extend** In a small group, plan a TV broadcast of this story. Write a script of a news anchor introducing the story and a field reporter interviewing Beharry, his commanding officer, and the historian Gary Sheffield. Include details from the article. Assign each group member a role. Present, and if possible, videotape your broadcast.

Writing Focus   Constructed Response

Briefly discuss the effect of the details included in this article. Be sure to cite evidence from the article to support your response.

What Do You Think Now   Beharry notes that he wasn't scared at the time, only afterward. Why do you think this was the case? How might his experiences have affected his perception of the world?

On the Bottom
from Survival in Auschwitz

What Do  **You Think**

How does experience shape our view of the world?

🕐 QuickWrite

Why do you think Primo Levi and others felt they had to write about their experiences in Nazi concentration camps? Why is it important that the atrocities of the Holocaust be remembered generation after generation? Write down your thoughts in your *Reader/Writer Notebook*.

Primo Levi (1919-1987)

Primo Levi
(1919–1987)

Primo Levi recorded his horrible experiences "not to weep and wail, but to be a witness, to give readers material for judgment."

The Camps

Primo Levi was studying chemistry at the University of Turin in Italy when World War II erupted in Europe. After the German army occupied northern Italy, Levi, a Jew, joined a resistance group and was soon arrested by Italian Fascists. Levi thought that he would wait out the war in a detention center, but when the Germans took over his detention camp, all Jews were immediately deported. In February 1944, Levi and 649 others were sent to Auschwitz (now called Auschwitz-Birkenau Nazi German Concentration and Death Camp). He was one of only twenty-three of the group who survived until the camp was liberated less than a year later.

After liberation, Levi returned to Italy and resumed work as a chemist. Soon he began writing, chronicling his experiences in the death camp and his journey back to Italy in his first books, *Survival in Auschwitz* (1947) and *The Reawakening* (1963).

Lessons of the Holocaust

Levi did not confine his writing to Holocaust experiences. He also published poems, essays, short stories, novels, and memoirs; he even dabbled in science fiction. Levi's last book, *The Drowned and the Saved* (1986), is a meditation on the meaning of the Nazi barbarity. To the critic Alexander Stille, who considered Levi's work "ultimately hopeful," this last book seemed to reflect a pessimistic perspective, causing the critic to speculate that "by the end of his life, Levi had become increasingly convinced that the lessons of the Holocaust were destined to be lost as it took a place among the routine atrocities of history."

On April 11, 1987, Levi fell to his death down the stairwell of his apartment. Some believe that the fall was an accident; others believe that Levi took his own life. Did Levi ultimately lose faith in humanity? That question may never be answered.

Think About the Writer

How might Levi's science career have influenced his decision to set aside emotions and write as "a witness" to Nazi atrocities?

Reader/Writer Notebook

Use your **RWN** to complete the activities for this selection.

Literary Focus

Memoir A **memoir** records the memories of its author. In this sense, a memoir is a type of autobiography, or writing about the self. Unlike an **autobiography,** a memoir usually focuses on a particular time period in the writer's life, often one of historical importance. Primo Levi's memoir describes his experience in Auschwitz, a concentration camp constructed in Poland by the Nazis. The excerpt you will read focuses on Levi's arrival at the camp in 1944, when he was twenty-four years old.

Literary Perspectives Apply the literary <u>perspective</u> described on page 1095 as you read this memoir.

Reading Focus

Evaluating Historical Context Memoirs are usually shaped by their **historical context,** that is, by the political, ethical, and social influences that characterize a particular time and place.

Into Action As you read this excerpt, think about what you know about its historical context. In a chart like the one below, note details that you think are particularly powerful. In the second column, note what each detail tells you about the Holocaust.

Historical Details	What It Tells Me
The door the prisoners go through says "Arbeit Macht Frei," meaning "work makes you free."	Shows the psychological cruelty of the Nazis, since no matter how hard the prisoners worked, they would never be free. In fact, most would die. Sign held out cruel and false hope.

Writing Focus

Think as a Reader/Writer

Find It in Your Reading Although Primo Levi writes about something that happened in the past, he primarily uses the present tense. As you read, note how his use of the present tense brings an immediacy to the writing. In your *Reader/Writer Notebook,* note three instances where Levi's use of present tense draws you into the narrative.

Vocabulary

taciturn (TAS uh turn) *adj.:* not talkative. *The taciturn soldier spoke little to the men and did not answer their questions.*

disconcerted (dihs kuhn SUR tihd) *v.* used as *adj.:* confused. *The unwillingness of the camp soldiers to tell what would happen next left the men feeling disconcerted.*

livid (LIHV ihd) *adj.:* pale; grayish. *The men's livid faces reflected their fright.*

sordid (SAWR dihd) *adj.:* filthy; foul. *The sordid conditions of the camp promoted the spread of disease.*

demolition (dehm uh LIHSH uhn) *n.:* destruction. *The demolition of the men's identity began when they lost their possessions.*

affinity (uh FIHN uh tee) *n.:* kinship; bond. *Their isolation and despair left the men feeling no affinity with one another.*

Language Coach

The Sounds of C The letter *c* in English can have a soft or a hard sound. The soft sound of /s/ is seen in words such as *center* and *cyst,* while the hard sound of /k/ occurs in words like *count* and *crib.* The general rule for pronouncing *c* is as follows: The letter *c* is sounded as /s/ when it occurs before the letters *e, i,* or *y.* Otherwise, it is sounded as /k/. Find a Vocabulary word with only one *c,* which is sounded as /s/. Find another Vocabulary word with two *c*'s, one sounded as /k/ and the other sounded as /s/.

 Learn It Online
Watch the video introduction online to learn more about the experiences that inspired this memoir.

go.hrw.com | L12-1093 | **Go**

On the Bottom

from Survival in Auschwitz

by **Primo Levi**   translated by **Stuart Woolf**

Read with a Purpose
Read to learn how humans feel and what they might do when they believe they have hit "the bottom."

Build Background
Beginning in the 1930s, Nazi Germany started to remove Jews and other so-called "undesirables"—homosexuals, gypsies, Poles, political dissidents, members of various religious groups, and the disabled—to concentration camps. By 1942, the greatest mass murder in the history of humanity had begun; by the time it ended, in 1945, perhaps eleven million human beings had been starved, tortured, and murdered. Six million of the victims were Jews. The excerpt from Primo Levi's memoir that you are about to read begins early in 1944 after Levi and 649 other Jews were packed into twelve cattle cars, with no food or water or toilets. Eleven days later the cattle cars arrived at Auschwitz, a notorious camp in German-occupied Poland.

Levi's group was quickly divided into those who were able-bodied and those who were not. In Levi's convoy, ninety-six men and twenty-nine women were selected to work in the labor camps of Auschwitz. All the others were murdered. As this excerpt begins, the prisoners have been taken by a lorry, or truck, to a room inside the camp.

The journey did not last more than twenty minutes. Then the lorry stopped, and we saw a large door, and above it a sign, brightly illuminated (its memory still strikes me in my dreams): *Arbeit Macht Frei*,[1] work gives freedom.   **A**

We climb down, they make us enter an enormous empty room that is poorly heated. We have a terrible thirst. The weak gurgle of water in the radiators makes us ferocious; we have had nothing to drink for four days. But there is also a tap—and above it a card which says that it is forbidden to drink as the water is dirty. Nonsense. It seems obvious that the card is a joke, "they" know that we are dying of thirst and they put us in a room, and there is a tap, and *Wassertrinken Verboten*.[2] I drink and I incite my companions to do likewise, but I have to spit it out, the water is tepid and sweetish, with the smell of a swamp.

This is hell. Today, in our times, hell must be like this. A huge, empty room: we are tired, standing on our feet, with a tap which drips while we cannot drink the water, and we wait for something which will certainly be terrible, and nothing happens and nothing continues to happen. What can one think about? One cannot think any more; it is like being already dead. Someone sits down on the ground. The time passes drop by drop.

We are not dead. The door is opened and an SS[3] man enters, smoking. He looks at us slowly and asks, "*Wer kann Deutsch?*"[4] One of us whom I have never seen, named Flesch, moves forward; he will be our

---

1. *Arbeit Macht Frei* (AHR byt mahkht fry).
2. *Wassertrinken Verboten* (VAHS ehr TRIHNK ehn fehr BOH tehn): German for "Drinking water is forbidden."

A **Reading Focus** **Evaluating Historical Context** Given what you know about the fate of most prisoners, how is the sign ironic?

---

3. **SS:** abbreviation for *Schutzstaffel* ("elite guard"), the Nazi units in charge of the extermination camps during World War II.
4. *Wer kann Deutsch?* (vehr kahn doych): German for "Who knows German?"

Auschwitz, by Heinrich Ehmsen, 1948. ©Horst Ehmsen, Vienna.

interpreter. The SS man makes a long, calm speech; the interpreter translates. We have to form rows of five, with intervals of two yards between man and man; then we have to undress and make a bundle of the clothes in a special manner, the woolen garments on one side, all the rest on the other; we must take off our shoes but pay great attention that they are not stolen.

Stolen by whom? Why should our shoes be stolen? And what about our documents, the few things we have in our pockets, our watches? We all look at the interpreter, and the interpreter asks the German, and the German smokes and looks him through and through as if he were transparent, as if no one had spoken.

I had never seen old men naked. Mr. Bergmann wore a truss[5] and asked the interpreter if he should

take it off, and the interpreter hesitated. But the German understood and spoke seriously to the interpreter pointing to someone. We saw the interpreter swallow and then he said: "The officer says, take off the truss, and you will be given that of Mr. Coen." One could see the words coming bitterly out of Flesch's mouth; this was the German manner of laughing. **(B)**

Now another German comes and tells us to put the shoes in a certain corner, and we put them there, because now it is all over and we feel outside this world and the only thing is to obey. Someone comes with a broom and sweeps away all the shoes, outside the door in a heap. He is crazy, he is mixing them all together, ninety-six pairs, they will be all unmatched. The outside door opens; a freezing wind enters and we are naked and cover ourselves up with our arms. The wind blows and slams the door; the German reopens it and stands watching with interest how we writhe to hide from the wind, one behind the other. Then he leaves and closes it. **(C)**

Now the second act begins. Four men with razors, soapbrushes, and clippers burst in; they have

Literary Perspectives

Analyzing Historical Context At the time Levi wrote his memoir, just after World War II ended, the full horror of the concentration camps set up by Nazi Germany and its collaborators was not yet known to the world. As Allied forces marched across Europe into Germany and Poland in 1944, they liberated Auschwitz and other camps. For the first time, outsiders bore witness to the atrocities perpetuated in the camps. While the stories told by these liberators and the photographs they took communicated unspeakable horror to the rest of the world, it was the first-person accounts told by the victims themselves that provided the more vivid and detailed testament.

As you read, be sure to notice the questions in the text, which will guide you in using this <u>perspective</u>.

(B) Literary Focus Memoir What personal details make this more than a strictly historical account?

(C) Reading Focus Evaluating Historical Context How do the Nazis' actions in this paragraph reflect their belief that their victims are less than human?

---

5. **truss:** belt with a pad, worn to support a hernia, a rupture of the intestine through the abdominal wall.

trousers and jackets with stripes, with a number sewn on the front; perhaps they are the same sort as those others of this evening (this evening or yesterday evening?), but these are robust and flourishing. We ask many questions but they catch hold of us and in a moment we find ourselves shaved and sheared. What comic faces we have without hair! The four speak a language which does not seem of this world. It is certainly not German, for I understand a little German.

Finally another door is opened: here we are, locked in, naked, sheared and standing, with our feet in water—it is a shower room. We are alone. Slowly the astonishment dissolves, and we speak, and everyone asks questions and no one answers. If we are naked in a shower room, it means that we will have a shower. If we have a shower it is because they are not going to kill us yet. But why then do they keep us standing, and give us nothing to drink, while nobody explains anything, and we have no shoes or clothes, but we are all naked with our feet in the water, and we have been traveling five days and cannot even sit down.

And our women?

Mr. Levi asks me if I think that our women are like us at this moment, and where they are, and if we will be able to see them again. I say yes, because he is married and has a daughter; certainly we will see them again. But by now my belief is that all this is a game to mock and sneer at us. Clearly they will kill us, whoever thinks he is going to live is mad, it means that he has swallowed the bait, but I have not; I have understood that it will soon all be over, perhaps in this same room, when they get bored of seeing us naked, dancing from foot to foot and trying every now and again to sit down on the floor. But there are two inches of cold water and we cannot sit down. **(D)**

We walk up and down without sense, and we talk, everybody talks to everybody else, we make a great noise. The door opens, and a German enters; it is the officer of before. He speaks briefly, the interpreter translates. "The officer says you must be quiet, because this is not a rabbinical[6] school." One sees the words

---

6. **rabbinical** (ruh BIHN uh kuhl): of or relating to rabbis, teachers of Jewish law.

which are not his, the bad words, twist his mouth as they come out, as if he was spitting out a foul taste. We beg him to ask what we are waiting for, how long we will stay here, about our women, everything; but he says no, that he does not want to ask. This Flesch, who is most unwilling to translate into Italian the hard, cold German phrases and refuses to turn into German our questions because he knows that it is useless, is a German Jew of about fifty, who has a large scar on his face from a wound received fighting the Italians on the Piave.[7] He is a closed, taciturn man, for whom I feel an instinctive respect as I feel that he has begun to suffer before us.

The German goes and we remain silent, although we are a little ashamed of our silence. It is still night and we wonder if the day will ever come. The door opens again, and someone else dressed in stripes comes in. He is different from the others, older, with glasses, a more civilized face, and much less robust. He speaks to us in Italian.

By now we are tired of being amazed. We seem to be watching some mad play, one of those plays in which the witches, the Holy Spirit, and the devil appear. He speaks Italian badly, with a strong foreign accent. He makes a long speech, is very polite, and tries to reply to all our questions.

We are at Monowitz, near Auschwitz, in Upper Silesia,[8] a region inhabited by both Poles and Germans. This camp is a workcamp, in German one says *Arbeitslager*,[9] all the prisoners (there are about ten thousand) work in a factory which produces a type of rubber called Buna, so that the camp itself is called Buna.

---

7. **Italians on the Piave:** During World War I, Austria and Germany defeated 600,000 Italian troops in the Battle of Caporetto; the Italian forces were pushed back to the Piave River near Venice.
8. **Upper Silesia:** region including parts of southwestern Poland, eastern Germany, and the northern Czech Republic. After World War I, Germany and Poland divided northern Silesia; southern Silesia fell under the rule of Czechoslovakia.
9. *Arbeitslager* (AHR byts LAHG ehr).

(D) Literary Focus Memoir What personal details in this paragraph can help readers understand the horror of the camps?

Vocabulary **taciturn** (TAS uh turn) *adj.:* not talkative.

1935 . . . 1940 (20th century), by Russian school. Color lithograph.

Viewing and Interpreting Levi describes how the prisoners were transformed into phantoms after arriving at Auschwitz. How does this image capture this idea?

We will be given shoes and clothes—no, not our own—other shoes, other clothes, like his. We are naked now because we are waiting for the shower and disinfection, which will take place immediately after the reveille,[10] because one cannot enter the camp without being disinfected. **E**

Certainly there will be work to do; everyone must work here. But there is work and work: he, for example, acts as a doctor. He is a Hungarian doctor who studied in Italy and he is the dentist of the Lager.[11] He has been in the Lager for four and a half years (not

in this one: Buna has only been open for a year and a half), but we can see that he is still quite well, not very thin. Why is he in the Lager? Is he Jewish like us? "No," he says simply, "I am a criminal."

We ask him many questions. He laughs, replies to some and not to others, and it is clear that he avoids certain subjects. He does not speak of the women: he says they are well, that we will see them again soon, but he does not say how or where. Instead he tells us other things, strange and crazy things, perhaps he too is playing with us. Perhaps he is mad—one goes mad in the Lager. He says that every Sunday there are concerts and football matches. He says that whoever boxes well can become cook. He says that whoever works well receives prize coupons with which to buy tobacco and soap. He says that the water is really not drinkable, and that instead a coffee substitute is distributed every day, but generally nobody drinks it as the soup itself is sufficiently watery to quench thirst. We beg him to find us something to drink, but he says he cannot, that

---

10. **reveille** (REHV uh lee): early-morning bugle call to waken military troops.
11. **Lager:** short for *Arbeitslager.*

E **Reading Focus** **Evaluating Historical Context** Today, thousands of shoes of the murdered prisoners are <u>exhibited</u> at Auschwitz. How might knowing about this <u>exhibit</u> affect a reader's reaction to this portion of the memoir?

he has come to see us secretly, against SS orders, as we still have to be disinfected, and that he must leave at once; he has come because he has a liking for Italians, and because, he says, he "has a little heart." We ask him if there are other Italians in the camp and he says there are some, a few, he does not know how many; and he at once changes the subject. Meanwhile a bell rang and he immediately hurried off and left us stunned and disconcerted. Some feel refreshed but I do not. I still think that even this dentist, this incomprehensible person, wanted to amuse himself at our expense, and I do not want to believe a word of what he said. **F**

At the sound of the bell, we can hear the still dark camp waking up. Unexpectedly the water gushes out boiling from the showers—five minutes of bliss; but immediately after, four men (perhaps they are the barbers) burst in yelling and shoving and drive us out, wet and steaming, into the adjoining room which is freezing; here other shouting people throw at us unrecognizable rags and thrust into our hands a pair of broken-down boots with wooden soles; we have no time to understand and we already find ourselves in the open, in the blue and icy snow of dawn, barefoot and naked, with all our clothing in our hands, with a hundred yards to run to the next hut. There we are finally allowed to get dressed.

When we finish, everyone remains in his own corner and we do not dare lift our eyes to look at one another. There is nowhere to look in a mirror, but our appearance stands in front of us, reflected in a hundred livid faces, in a hundred miserable and sordid puppets. We are transformed into the phantoms glimpsed yesterday evening.[12] **G**

---

12. **We are transformed . . . evening:** Levi is referring to the inmates at Auschwitz whom he and the other new prisoners witnessed briefly upon arriving at the camp on the previous evening.

Then for the first time we became aware that our language lacks words to express this offense, the demolition of a man. In a moment, with almost prophetic intuition, the reality was revealed to us: we had reached the bottom. It is not possible to sink lower than this; no human condition is more miserable than this, nor could it conceivably be so. Nothing belongs to us any more; they have taken away our clothes, our shoes, even our hair; if we speak, they will not listen to us, and if they listen, they will not understand. They will even take away our name: and if we want to keep it, we will have to find ourselves the strength to do so, to manage somehow so that behind the name something of us, of us as we were, still remains. **H**

We know that we will have difficulty in being understood, and this is as it should be. But consider what value, what meaning is enclosed even in the smallest of our daily habits, in the hundred possessions which even the poorest beggar owns: a handkerchief, an old letter, the photo of a cherished person. These things are part of us, almost like limbs of our body; nor is it conceivable that we can be deprived of them in our world, for we immediately find others to substitute the old ones, other objects which are ours in their personification and evocation of our memories.

Imagine now a man who is deprived of everyone he loves, and at the same time of his house, his habits, his clothes, in short, of everything he possesses: he will be a hollow man, reduced to suffering and needs, forgetful of dignity and restraint, for he who loses all often easily loses himself. He will be a man whose life or death can be lightly decided with no sense of human affinity, in the most fortunate of cases, on the basis of a pure judgment of utility. It is in this way that one can understand the double sense of the term "extermination camp," and it is now clear what we seek to express with the phrase: "to lie on the bottom." **I**

F **Literary Focus** Memoir Why do you think Levi is so cynical? Do you think the man is lying to be deceitful or for another reason? Explain.

G **Literary Focus** Memoir What details make this passage more than an impersonal recounting of historical events?

H **Literary Focus** Memoir In this passage, Levi leaves the narrative to offer extended commentary. From his perspective, how is this moment more than just the completion of the entry process?

I **Literary Perspectives** Analyzing Historical Context What knowledge helps you understand Levi's concluding sentence?

Vocabulary **disconcerted** (dihs kuhn SUR tihd) *adj.*: confused.
livid (LIHV ihd) *adj.*: pale; grayish.
sordid (SAWR dihd) *adj.*: filthy; foul.
demolition (dehm uh LIHSH uhn) *n.*: destruction.
affinity (uh FIHN uh tee) *n.*: kinship; bond.

On the Bottom *from* Survival in Auschwitz

Respond and Think Critically

Reading Focus

Quick Check

1. When Levi arrives in Auschwitz, what factors lead him to conclude that it is "hell"?

2. Describe how the prisoners are "dehumanized."

Read with a Purpose

3. What details in the memoir reveal what people will do when they "hit bottom"? How were some people able to survive the inhuman treatment that Levi and others endured?

Reading Skills: Evaluating Historical Context

4. As you read, you noted details about the political, ethical, and social background of the Holocaust. Now, in a new column, explain how these details deepened your reading experience.

Historical Detail	What It Tells Me	How knowing detail enriches my reading
The door prisoners go through says "Arbeit Macht Frei," meaning "work makes you free."	Shows the psychological cruelty of the Nazis, since no matter how hard prisoners worked, they never would be free. In fact, most would die. Sign held out cruel and false hope.	

Literary Focus

Literary Analysis

5. **Interpret** Explain Levi's reference to the double meaning of the term "extermination camp."

6. **Analyze** Why does Levi use the phrase "second act" to describe what happens to the men after they undress?

7. **Interpret** What does it mean to be "hollow"? Why does Levi conclude that it is easy to decide if a "hollow" man lives or dies?

8. **Extend** Levi says that the Nazis' offense was the "demolition of a man." At what other times in history has one group of people "demolished" other people and tried to rob them of their humanity?

9. **Literary Perspectives** How does knowing the Holocaust's massive scale of suffering and death affect your understanding of this memoir?

Literary Skills: Memoir

10. **Contrast** How is Levi's memoir different from a newspaper article about the camps?

Literary Skills Review: Setting

11. **Analyze** The time and place of a story is its **setting.** What sensory details—sight, smell, hearing, touch, and taste—help you imagine this setting?

Writing Focus

Think as a Reader/Writer

Use It in Your Writing As you read this memoir, you took notes on Levi's use of the present tense. Now, write a brief personal memoir in which you use the present tense to help your reader feel as if he or she is sharing your experience. Try to write about an incident that is set in some specific historical context.

What Do You Think Now

How would Levi's experiences in Auschwitz account for his view of the world?

On the Bottom *from* Survival in Auschwitz

Vocabulary Development

✓ Vocabulary Check

Be sure you can justify your answer to each of the following questions about the Vocabulary words.

1. Which person could be described as **taciturn**—a person who speaks a great deal or a person who is not talkative?

2. If someone is **disconcerted,** would he or she feel confused or satisfied?

3. If a face is described as **livid,** is it pale or rosy red?

4. Which setting would be described as **sordid:** a filthy tenement or a tidy farmhouse?

5. If you are going to cause the **demolition** of a building, are you going to start building it or destroy it?

6. If you have **affinity** with someone, do you feel close to him or her or do you feel envious?

Vocabulary Skills: Synonyms and Antonyms

Synonyms are words with the same or nearly the same meaning: *Sad* and *sorrowful* are both adjectives that mean "unhappy." **Antonyms** are words with opposite meanings: *Happy* and *miserable* are adjectives which have opposite meanings.

Although synonyms have more or less the same meaning, many synonyms do not share exact meanings. When you are selecting a synonym or antonym for your writing, you should refer to a good dictionary to be certain that you have chosen the most precise word. For example, *robust* and *healthy* are synonyms that mean about the same thing; however, *healthy* usually implies simply the absence of disease, while *robust* is used to describe someone who is strong and energetic.

Your Turn

Use each Vocabulary word to complete the exercise.

taciturn	sordid	livid
disconcerted	demolition	affinity

1. _____ is a synonym for *pale.*
2. _____ is an antonym for *chatty.*
3. _____ is a synonym for *connection.*
4. _____ is an antonym for *construction.*
5. _____ is an antonym for *clean.*
6. _____ is an synonym for *confuse.*

Language Coach

The Sounds of C The letter *c* can be sounded like /k/ or like /s/. The general rule governing the pronunciation of words with the letter *c* is this: The letter *c* is sounded like /s/ when it comes before the letters *e, i,* and *y.* At other times *c* is sounded like the /k/ sound.

Sound out each of these words: *scant, scent, since, tacit, tactical, census.* How is the letter *c* sounded?

There are some exceptions to the rule. How is the letter *c* pronounced in the words *soccer* and *muscle?* How would the words be pronounced if the general rule were followed?

Academic Vocabulary

Write About

Throughout history people have <u>exhibited</u> the ability to <u>adapt</u> to difficult conditions and withstand extraordinary loss. Write a paragraph about a survival experience that you have heard or read about.

Grammar Link

Punctuating for Clarity: Semicolons, Colons, Dashes

The purpose of punctuation is clarity; a misplaced mark of punctuation can cause confusion. Levi, or his transla- tor, uses several kinds of punctuation to show relation- ships among ideas within a sentence.

A **semicolon** connects independent clauses that are closely related in thought and are not joined by a coor- dinating conjunction (such as *and, but, nor*):

> One cannot think any more; it is like being already dead.

A **colon** joins two independent clauses when the sec- ond clause explains the idea of the first clause:

> Just then, with almost prophetic intuition, the real- ity was revealed to us: we had reached the bottom.

A **dash** sets off an abrupt break in thought or is used to mean *namely, in other words,* or *that is* before an expla- nation. Dashes are sharp and dramatic breaks into the main thought of a sentence.

> We will be given shoes and clothes—no, not our own—other shoes, other clothes, like his.

Your Turn

Punctuate the paragraph below with colons, semi- colons, and dashes.

> The physical abuse the concentration camp prisoners endured was terrible however, Levi also describes a horrible sort of emotional abuse a stripping away of identity. The prisoners by losing their material possessions and acquiring new uniforms became property themselves.

Writing Application Revise a piece of your writing in your *Reader/Writer Notebook* to include semicolons, colons, and dashes.

CHOICES

As you respond to the Choices, use these **Academic Vocabulary** words as appropriate: adapt, considerably, exhibit, inevitable, perspective.

REVIEW

Compare and Contrast Accounts

Visit an online Holocaust exhibit to watch an inter- view with a Holocaust survivor, or with an Allied soldier who participated in the liberation of one of the camps. Then, compare and contrast this account with Levi's. What is similar or different about the level of detail and the tone of the accounts? Is the emo- tional impact of watching an interview greater than the impact of reading a printed document?

CONNECT

Hold a Group Discussion

Group Activity Have you ever seen a bumper sticker that says, "Think globally, but act locally"? This statement suggests that people can help solve the world's problems by improving life in their own com- munities. This memoir's events reflect an extreme and tragic result of categorizing people into "us" and "them." In a group, brainstorm ideas about how to bring unity to your school and community.

EXTEND

Write about the Power of Words

Timed Writing Like many Holocaust survivors, Levi felt the need to serve as a "witness" and tell his story so that such events would never be repeated. Are such events inevitable, or do you think memoirs such as Levi's can prevent something similar from happening again? In a brief essay, explain your thoughts, citing specific examples from Levi's text.

Preparing to Read

Never Shall I Forget

What Do You Think?

How does experience shape our view of the world?

QuickWrite

How would imprisonment in a camp like Auschwitz forever affect the way a survivor would view the world? Write a brief response to this question in your *Reader/Writer Notebook*.

Writer Elie Wiesel (1984)

Elie Wiesel
(1928–   )

Nobel Prize WINNER

Elie Wiesel survived the Holocaust to write his story: to try to convey the unspeakable so that the world would not forget the horror he and millions of others had experienced. As he explained, "We [survivors] believe that if we survived, we must do something with our lives. The first task is to tell the tale."

Nightmare Youth

Wiesel was fifteen years old when he and all other Jews in his Romanian village were deported to concentration camps in German-occupied Poland in 1944. A serious student of Judaism, Wiesel had thought that he would spend his life in his small village, working at the family store and devoting his life to religious study. Instead, he and his father were taken to Auschwitz (now called Auschwitz-Birkenau Nazi German Concentration and Death Camp) and then to camps at Buna, Gleiwitz, and Buchenwald, where his father died. Wiesel's mother and younger sister were both victims of the gas chambers. Against considerable odds, Wiesel and his two older sisters survived.

A Voice for the Lost

After the war, Wiesel lived in a French orphanage and then studied philosophy and literature at the Sorbonne, in Paris, and worked as a journalist. In 1955, after breaking a self-imposed vow never to write about the Holocaust, Wiesel poured his memories into a nine-hundred-page volume, soon condensed and republished as *Night*. Wiesel has said that his works have in common "their commitment to memory." He is torn between silence and a need to communicate. "You can speak," he says, "but how can you, when the full story is beyond language?"

Wiesel now lives in the United States, where he has served as the Chairman of the President's Commission on the Holocaust and where he was awarded the Congressional Medal of Achievement. In 1986, Wiesel won the Nobel Peace Prize. He continues to write and to advocate for the remembrance of the Holocaust and for the end of racism, hatred, and genocide.

Think About the Writer

What reasons might Wiesel have had for not wanting to write about the Holocaust? What might have changed his mind?

Reader/Writer Notebook

Use your **RWN** to complete the activities for this selection.

Literary Focus

Repetition Writers, especially poets, use **repetition** for many reasons: to emphasize important ideas, to create an emotional impact, and to add rhythm to the writing. In "Never Shall I Forget," Wiesel uses repetition for all of those reasons, but his most dramatic use of repetition is a refrain that emphasizes his main idea—"Never shall I forget." Read the poem aloud to experience the emotional effect of the repetition.

Reading Focus

Drawing Inferences About an Author's Beliefs As you read some texts, you find yourself making **inferences,** or educated guesses, about the writer's beliefs or views of the world. When you discuss inferences you make about a writer, be sure you can cite passages from the text to support your inferences. You might be surprised that different readers of the same text make different inferences.

Into Action As you read "Never Shall I Forget," note key words and passages.

Key Words and Passages
Repeated 7 times "Never shall I forget"

Writing Focus

Think as a Reader/Writer

Find It in Your Reading The repetition of words, phrases, or sentences that have the same grammatical structure or that state a similar idea is called **parallelism.** Like other forms of repetition, parallelism can add emphasis and create rhythm in a text. Note how Wiesel uses parallelism by beginning each sentence with the same statement, "Never shall I forget . . . ." In your *Reader/Writer Notebook*, note another use of parallel structure in the poem.

Vocabulary

nocturnal (nahk TUR nuhl) *adj.:* occurring at night. *The terror of daily camp life was not relieved by the nocturnal silence.*

condemned (kuhn DEHMD) *v.:* doomed. *He was condemned to live with the horrible memories of the camps.*

Language Coach

Silent Letters Many words in English have silent letters, that is, one or more letters that are not pronounced. The word *condemned,* above, for example, is sounded /kuhn DEHMD/. The second *n* is silent. Here are two more words with silent *n*'s: *solemn, column.* Respond to the following items.

1. Here are words with silent *w*'s. How is each word pronounced? *who, two, answer*
2. Here are three words with silent *g*'s. How is each word pronounced? *might, sign, gnat*
3. What is the silent letter in each of these words? *know, island, business*
4. A common silent letter in English words is the final *e*. Find three words in the poem that end with a silent *e*.

Learn It Online
Listen to this powerful poem online.

go.hrw.com | L12-1103 | **Go**

POEM

Never Shall I Forget

by Elie Wiesel
translated by Marion Wiesel

Read with a Purpose
Read to learn what this survivor will never forget.

Build Background
While working as a young journalist in the 1950s, Wiesel interviewed a French novelist named Francois Mauriac, who urged Wiesel to tell his story. Wiesel's first autobiographical work, *Night,* tells the story of a teenaged boy who survives the concentration camps and is haunted by questions of how God could have allowed so many of his people to be murdered. The following excerpt from *Night,* "Never Shall I Forget," originally appeared as a prose passage in the condensed version of the book.

Never shall I forget that night, the first night in the camp, that turned my life into one long night seven times sealed.　**A**
Never shall I forget that smoke.
　　Never shall I forget the small faces of the children whose bodies I saw transformed into smoke under a silent sky.
　　Never shall I forget those flames that consumed my faith forever.
5　　Never shall I forget the nocturnal silence that deprived me for all eternity of the desire to live.
　　Never shall I forget those moments that murdered my God and my soul and turned my dreams to ashes.
　　Never shall I forget those things, even were I condemned to live as long as God Himself.
　　Never.　**B**

Visitors at the Auschwitz-Birkenau Nazi Concentration and Death Camp, Poland.

A **Reading Focus** Reading Focus Drawing Inferences What can you infer about Wiesel's beliefs about his own life?

B **Literary Focus** Repetition What does Wiesel emphasize by repeating the poem's title as a kind of refrain?

Vocabulary **nocturnal** (nahk TUR nuhl) *adj.*: occurring at night.
condemned (kuhn DEHMD) *v.*: doomed.

Analyzing Visuals

Viewing and Interpreting What is significant about a visitor selecting just one person's picture out of group of people's pictures to photograph? How does this image convey the message of the refrain "Never shall I forget"?

Applying Your Skills

Never Shall I Forget

SKILLS FOCUS **Literary Skills** Analyze repetition; analyze personification. **Reading Skills** Draw inferences about an author's beliefs. **Vocabulary Skills** Demonstrate knowledge of literal meanings of words and their usage. **Writing Skills** Enhance meaning by employing parallelism.

Respond and Think Critically

Reading Focus

Read with a Purpose

1. Cite all the things Wiesel will never forget.

Reading Skills: Drawing Inferences

2. Review your list of key words and passages from the poem. Write a few sentences explaining your inferences about the author's beliefs and worldview.

Key Words and Passages
Repeated 7 times "Never shall I forget"
What I Infer About Writer's Beliefs and Worldview

✓ Vocabulary Check

Choose the correct letter to complete these statements about Vocabulary words.

3. The **nocturnal** silence described by Wiesel is experienced (a) in the morning, (b) in the afternoon, (c) at night.

4. Choose the more likely context for *condemned*: (a) She was **condemned** to spend time with friends; (b) Her illness **condemned** her to spend hours in agony.

Literary Focus

Literary Analysis

5. **Interpret** What do you think Wiesel means when he says his life has been turned "into one long night"?

6. **Analyze** Why does Wiesel use the word *condemned* to describe living forever? What does this suggest about his state of mind?

7. **Interpret** *Seven* is symbolic in the Jewish and Christian traditions. For example, God rested on the seventh day of creation; there are seven branches on the menorah and seven blessings for a Jewish wedding. In the Christian tradition, seven sealed books foretell the end of the world. Where does Wiesel use *seven* in this poem? Why?

Literary Skills: Repetition

8. **Evaluate** Wiesel has said that his works' focus is "their commitment to memory." How does repetition in the poem emphasize this commitment?

Literary Skills Review: Personification

9. **Analyze** Talking about a nonhuman or nonliving thing or quality as if it were human or had life is **personification.** What words suggest that Wiesel sees "nocturnal silence" and "those moments" as if they were living things that acted willfully to destroy his hope and his faith?

Writing Focus

Think as a Reader/Writer

Use It in Your Writing In your *Reader/Writer Notebook,* you noted examples of Wiesel's use of parallelism. Now, write a paragraph or poem about an important event in your life or in the life of someone else. Use parallelism to emphasize your tone or feelings.

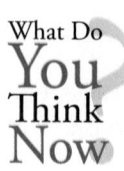

What Do You Think Now

According to the poem, how has Wiesel's experience affected his faith?

Reading Focus

Blood, Sweat, and Tears

Identifying and Critiquing an Author's Argument by **Kylene Beers**

When you read persuasive writing, you have two tasks: first, to identify the author's argument (What is he or she trying to convince you to believe?), and second, to critique, or evaluate, that argument (What kind of evidence does the author use?).

Authors of persuasive writing want to convince you that their ideas or positions are best. The writer of an advertisement, for example, wants you to buy the product; the author of a newspaper editorial wants you to agree with his or her opinion. Politicians and world leaders often use persuasion to try to gain the public's support for particular actions.

As England's prime minister during World War II, Winston Churchill had the <u>inevitably</u> difficult job of convincing English citizens that the war effort was worthwhile. He used powerful language to persuade them that they would not only be able to endure hardship but also achieve victory.

In a persuasive speech, an author usually directly states his or her arguments and may use repetition to alert listeners to important points. In Churchill's "Blood, Sweat, and Tears" speech, he states that he has "nothing to offer but blood, toil, tears, and sweat." These humble images of hard work and sacrifice support his argument urging all Englishmen to join the fight. Churchill further asserts that his sacrifice and that of Englishmen will "go forward together with our united strength." The language of effort and unity signals a major argument: Together we will be victorious.

Once you **identify the argument,** evaluate the evidence used to support it. Evidence can include **logical appeals** (reasons, facts, statistics, and other forms of evidence); **emotional appeals** (moving language and vivid descriptions that arouse strong feelings in readers); and **ethical appeals,** (statements and examples that invoke commonly held moral standards and social values).

To critique this evidence you must determine how well it supports the author's argument by asking:
- Does the evidence directly pertain to the argument?
- Is the evidence convincing? Are there facts, expert opinions, or logical reasons to support the claims?
- Are the emotional appeals effective? Is the argument also supported by logical appeals, or does the author rely solely on emotions to convince the audience?
- Is the author unbiased, credible, and knowledgeable?
- If the argument is a solution to a problem, does the author provide evidence that the solution will work?

Your Turn

Read this excerpt from Churchill's speech. Identify his argument (the main idea), and critique it by applying the above criteria. Record your thoughts in a paragraph, using evidence from the text.

> We have before us an ordeal of the most grievous kind. We have before us many, many long months of struggle and of suffering. You ask, What is our policy? I will say: "It is to wage war, by sea, land and air, with all our might and with all the strength that God can give us: to wage war against a monstrous tyranny, never surpassed in the dark, lamentable catalogue of human crime. That is our policy." You ask, What is our aim? I can answer in one word: Victory—victory at all costs, victory in spite of all terror, victory however long and hard the road may be; for without victory there is no survival.

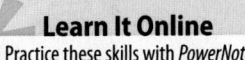

Learn It Online
Practice these skills with *PowerNotes* online.

go.hrw.com L12-1107   **Go**

Preparing to Read

Blood, Sweat, and Tears

What Do You Think?

How does experience shape our view of the world?

QuickWrite

What qualities make a good leader? What qualities are especially important for a national leader in times of war? Write your answers in a brief paragraph in your *Reader/Writer Notebook*.

Sir Winston Leonard Spencer Churchill, by Robert Elliot. National Portrait Gallery, London.

Winston Churchill
(1874–1965)

Nobel Prize WINNER

Winston Churchill was a soldier, a statesman, a man of letters, and a Nobel laureate. As prime minister during the deadliest war of the century, he inspired Britain's soldiers and civilians.

Soldier and Writer

Churchill was the son of a British politician, Lord Randolph Churchill, and his American wife, Jennie Jerome. Of his schooling, Churchill said, "I got into my bones the essential structure of the ordinary British sentence—which is a noble thing." His father, however, lacked confidence in young Winston's academic abilities and insisted he prepare for a military career.

In 1895, Churchill volunteered to visit Cuba to observe Spain's war against Cuban rebels and to send dispatches to a British newspaper. On his return, he began his simultaneous careers as a politician and a writer.

They Owe Him Liberty

Churchill became prime minister in 1940. One of his great triumphs was persuading his War Cabinet to challenge Hitler rather than negotiate with him. An unparalleled orator, Churchill rallied the nation never to surrender, especially during the "blitz," when Germany bombed London for fifty-seven successive nights. Of the British pilots who fought the Germans night after night, Churchill said, "Never in the field of human conflict has so much been owed by so many to so few." Few comments on war are as poignant or memorable.

After leaving politics, Churchill published history books, including four volumes of the *History of the English Speaking People* and five volumes of the monumental *Second World War*. In 1953, Churchill was awarded the Nobel Prize for Literature. He is best known, however, for the enviable war leadership he exhibited, of which his daughter Mary said, "I owe you what every Englishman, woman and child does—Liberty itself." Churchill's ties to the United States remained close, and in 1963, President Kennedy awarded him honorary U.S. citizenship.

Think About the Writer

How did Churchill's language skills help him in his political life, as well as in his literary life?

Reader/Writer Notebook

Use your **RWN** to complete the activities for this selection.

Literary Focus

Oratory The art of public speech is **oratory.** Because listeners cannot return to an oral speech if they miss a point, orators often state their main ideas and then use **repetition** of words, phrases, and sentence structures to emphasize their key points. Repetition also creates **rhythm** in speaking. Note Churchill's stirring use of this oratorical device as you read.

Reading Focus

Identifying and Critiquing an Author's Argument To persuade listeners or readers to agree with their arguments, orators and writers can use two types of appeals: **logical appeals,** directed to the listeners' intellect, and **emotional appeals,** directed to the listeners' feelings. Churchill begins his speech by listing the methodical, reasonable steps he took to form his government. He then arouses strong feelings in his audience by using emotionally charged words like *ordeal, struggle,* and *tyranny.*

Into Action Make a graphic organizer like the one below, and list words, phrases, and sentences that appeal to logic and emotions. Later, you will explain the purpose of the appeals and evaluate their effectiveness.

Logical Appeals	forming large Administration is "serious undertaking"
Emotional Appeals	

Vocabulary

rigor (RIHG uhr) *n.:* severity. *Churchill explained that the rigor of the situation called for speedy action.*

grievous (GREE vuhs) *adj.:* outrageous; horrible. *The grievous acts of German troops as they invaded their neighbors horrified British citizens.*

lamentable (luh MEHN tuh buhl) *adj.:* regrettable; unfortunate. *Sending young troops to war was lamentable but necessary.*

buoyancy (BOY uhn see) *n.:* lightness of spirit; cheerfulness. *Despite the hard task ahead of him, Churchill felt a sense of buoyancy about the future.*

Language Coach

Suffix –ous The suffix –ous is added to words or roots to make adjectives. The Vocabulary word *grievous*, for example, is formed by adding –ous to the verb "grieve." (Note that the e is dropped from the end of the word when the suffix is added.) Identify one Vocabulary word to which the suffix –ous could be added to form an adjective.

Writing Focus

Think as a Reader/Writer

Find It in Your Reading In his speech, Churchill uses several rhetorical devices, including **parallelism,** the repetition of sentence structures and key words. Parallelism creates a kind of rhythm in speech which Churchill's listeners would have found moving and pleasing to hear. In your *Reader/ Writer Notebook,* note some examples of parallelism in this speech.

TechFocus As you read, think about how modern technology could be used to enhance the logical and emotional appeals of this speech.

Learn It Online
Explore the Vocabulary words with Word Watch.

 L12-1109

Blood, Sweat, and Tears

by **Winston Churchill**

Read with a Purpose
Read this speech to see how a new prime minister tries to persuade his citizens to prepare for a long and difficult war.

Build Background
In September of 1939, Britain declared war on Germany after German troops invaded Poland. When Churchill gave this speech to Parliament in May of 1940, the Germans had also marched into Holland and Belgium and were driving deep into France. Churchill knew the Battle of Britain was imminent. As newly elected prime minister, Churchill had just formed a coalition government of Labour and Liberals; he knew that he had to inspire the country with an unwavering belief in its ability to survive, triumph, and endure. Few who heard Churchill's radio speeches during the war ever forgot them.

On Friday evening last I received His Majesty's Commission[1] to form a new Administration. It was the evident wish and will of Parliament and the nation that this should be conceived on the broadest possible basis and that it should include all Parties, both those who supported the last Government and also the Parties of the Opposition. I have completed the most important part of this task. A War Cabinet has been formed of five Members, representing, with the Opposition Liberals,[2] the unity of the nation. The three Party Leaders have agreed to serve, either in the War Cabinet or in high executive office. The three Fighting Services have been filled. It was necessary that this should be done in one single day, on account of the extreme urgency and rigor of events. A number of other key positions were filled yesterday, and I am submitting a further list to His Majesty tonight. I hope to complete the appointment of the principal Ministers during tomorrow. The appointment of the other Ministers usually takes a little longer, but I trust that, when Parliament meets again, this part of my task will be complete in all respects. Ⓐ Ⓑ

---

1. **His Majesty's Commission:** The king at the time was George VI. After his or her party is elected, the prime minister is officially appointed by the monarch.
2. **Opposition Liberals:** Churchill was a member of the Conservative Party; those belonging to the Liberal Party were in the opposition.

Ⓐ **Literary Focus** Oratory What main idea does Churchill express in this paragraph?

Ⓑ **Reading Focus** Identifying and Critiquing an Author's Argument What argument does Churchill make to support the necessity of creating a War Cabinet quickly? Does this argument appeal to reason or emotion?

Vocabulary rigor (RIHG uhr) *n.*: severity.

I considered it in the public interest to suggest that the House should be summoned to meet today. Mr. Speaker agreed, and took the necessary steps, in accordance with the powers conferred upon him by the Resolution of the House. At the end of the proceedings today, the Adjournment of the House will be proposed until Tuesday, 21st May, with, of course, provision for earlier meeting if need be. The business to be considered during that week will be notified to Members at the earliest opportunity. I now invite the House, by the Resolution which stands in my name, to record its approval of the steps taken and to declare its confidence in the new Government.[3]

To form an Administration of this scale and complexity is a serious undertaking in itself, but it must be remembered that we are in the preliminary stage of one of the greatest battles in history, that we are in action at many points in Norway and in Holland, that we have to be prepared in the Mediterranean, that the air battle is continuous, and the many preparations have to be made here at home. In this crisis I hope I may be pardoned if I do not address the House at

---

3. **the new Government:** that is, the recently elected administration led by Churchill.

TECHNOLOGY LINK

England: Family listening to speech by Winston Churchill (1945).

Radio Broadcasts

Private English citizens would have heard Churchill's speech on the radio. Radio waves, like sound waves, fluctuate in the air, and operate on certain frequencies. The national government typically assigns each radio station a carrier frequency, which is silent until information is added to the carrier wave by the radio station's transmitter. When you tune a radio to the station's frequency, your radio amplifies the signal many times so that you can hear the transmission. Radio broadcasting emerged around 1920, and by World War II, the English people received much of their war news via broadcast programs. The radio was an equally powerful communication tool for the Axis as well as the Allied powers. German radio broadcasts became an important part of Adolf Hitler's proganda campaigns and were successful in convincing many German citizens that the Reich was justified in invading and occupying neighboring countries.

Ask Yourself

How did leaders on both sides of the conflict use the radio to affect the way people felt about the war?

Winston Churchill (1874–1965) inspecting ruins of the House of Commons (May 1941).

any length today. I hope that any of my friends and colleagues, or former colleagues, who are affected by the political reconstruction, will make all allowance for any lack of ceremony with which it has been necessary to act. I would say to the House, as I said to those who have joined this Government: "I have nothing to offer but blood, toil, tears, and sweat." **C**

We have before us an ordeal of the most grievous kind. We have before us many, many long months of struggle and of suffering. You ask, What is our policy? I will say: "It is to wage war, by sea, land and air, with all our might and with all the strength that God can give us: to wage war against a monstrous tyranny, never surpassed in the dark, lamentable catalogue of human crime. That is our policy." You ask, What is our aim? I can answer in one word: Victory—victory at all costs, victory in spite of all terror, victory however long and hard the road may be; for without victory there is no survival. Let that be realized; no survival for the British Empire; no survival for all that the British Empire has stood for; no survival for the urge and impulse of the ages, that mankind will move forward towards its goal. But I take up my task with buoyancy and hope. I feel sure that our cause will not be suffered to fail among men. At this time I feel entitled to claim the aid of all, and I say, "Come, then, let us go forward together with our united strength." **D**

C **Literary Focus** **Oratory** What powerful words does Churchill use to persuade his listeners to support him?

D **Literary Focus** **Oratory** What words or phrases does Churchill repeat to emphasize his goal?

Vocabulary **grievous** (GREE vuhs) *adj.:* outrageous; horrible.
lamentable (luh MEHN tuh buhl) *adj.:* regrettable; unfortunate.
buoyancy (BOY uhn see) *n.:* lightness of spirit; cheerfulness.

Applying Your Skills

Blood, Sweat, and Tears

SKILLS FOCUS Literary Skills Analyze oratory; analyze symbols. **Reading Skills** Identify and critique an author's argument. **Writing Skills** Use parallelism correctly.

Respond and Think Critically

Reading Focus

Quick Check

1. Why was it important to Churchill to include members of the opposition party in his War Cabinet?

2. What did Churchill want approved?

3. How did Churchill apologize for "any lack of ceremony"?

Read with a Purpose

4. How successful would a leader be today if he or she used a similar speech to persuade citizens to prepare for a long and difficult war?

Reading Skills: Identifying and Critiquing an Author's Argument

5. Look back at the chart you created identifying the speech's logical and emotional appeals. At the bottom, summarize Churchill's purpose in making the appeals and evaluate the effectiveness of his arguments.

Literary Focus

Literary Analysis

6. **Interpret** How would you interpret Churchill's statement, "I have nothing to offer but blood, toil, tears, and sweat"? How could the statement make the people feel that their leader would suffer with them and give up his life for them?

7. **Evaluate** The credibility of a public figure is often revealed in public addresses. How would you characterize Churchill after reading his speech? Does he convince you of his competence and command of the situation? Explain.

8. **Hypothesize** Churchill knew that German leaders would read his speech. What effect do you think he wanted it to have on his enemy?

Literary Skills: Oratory

9. **Make Judgments** How does Churchill use repetition and parallelism to emphasize his points in the last two paragraphs?

10. **Analyze** What call to action does Churchill include in his speech? He uses the word *united* in the call to action. What effect do you think that word would have on his listeners?

Literary Skills Review: Symbol

11. **Interpret** A **symbol** is something that stands both for itself and for something beyond itself. In his speech, Churchill refers to the "British Empire" and all it "has stood for." What do you think the British Empire symbolized to Churchill and his English audience? In contrast, how does Churchill characterize the enemy?

Writing Focus

Think as a Reader/Writer

Use It in Your Writing As you read the speech, you noted examples of parallelism in your *Reader/Writer Notebook*. Now, with a partner, choose a topic for a short persuasive speech of your own. Work together to develop your argument with logical and emotional appeals. Try to use some examples of parallelism to give your speech a memorable and pleasing cadence, or rhythmic movement.

 What Do You Think Now

What experiences might have shaped Churchill's view of the world? How do you think people like Churchill acquire the gift of speaking with eloquence?

Applying Your Skills

Blood, Sweat, and Tears

Vocabulary Development

✓ Vocabulary Check

Be sure you can justify your answer to each of the following Vocabulary questions.

1. If a class were known for its **rigor,** would it be an easy class or a challenging one?

2. If a wound is described as **grievous,** is it a minor wound or a horrible one?

3. Churchill says that Hitler's tyranny has never been surpassed in the **lamentable** catalogue of human crime. Does *lamentable* mean understandable or regrettable?

4. When he says he takes up his post with **buoyancy,** what is Churchill suggesting about his outlook for the future?

Vocabulary Skills: Solving Word Analogies

A **word analogy** compares two pairs of words. The relationship between the first pair of words is the same as that of the second pair. Common types of relationships expressed in word analogies are **synonyms, antonyms,** and **characteristic.**

CRY: WEEP:: laugh: chuckle

[*Cry* and *weep* **are synonyms,** or words with similar meanings, as are *laugh* and *chuckle.*]

SULLEN: CHEERY:: generous: stingy

[*Sullen* and *cheery* are **antonyms,** or words with opposite meanings, as are *generous* and *stingy.*]

COMEDIANS : FUNNY : : lions : fierce.

[*Funny* is a **characteristic** of *comedians,* just as *fierce* is a characteristic of *lions.*]

To complete a word analogy, it helps to "read" the relationship. The colon [:] stands for the phrase "is/are

related to." The double colon between the pairs stands for the phrase "in the same way as." Thus, the previous analogies would be stated like this: *Cry* is related to *weep* in the same way *laugh* is related to *chuckle.* *Sullen* is related to *cheery* in the same way that *generous* is related to *stingy. Comedians* are related to *funny* in the same way that *lions* are related to *fierce.*

Your Turn

Complete each of the following analogies with one of the boldfaced words in the Vocabulary Check.

1. ARID : DRY : : _____ : horrible
2. BIRTH : JOYFUL :: death : _____
3. SILENCE : QUIET : : _____ : severity
4. WEALTH : POVERTY : : _____ : sadness

Language Coach

The Suffix –*ous* The suffix –*ous* means "full of," or "characterized by." To which of the following words from the selection can you add the suffix –*ous* to make adjectives? If necessary, use a dictionary for help. You will have to change the spelling of some words in order to add the suffix. What does each word mean when the suffix is added?

1. villain   3. struggle   5. victor
2. horror   4. monster

Academic Vocabulary

Talk About
Effective persuasive speeches and writing often require the speaker or writer to think from the perspective of his or her audience. In a small group, discuss how Churchill may have adapted his delivery and language to make a greater impact on his listeners.

Grammar Link

Connecting Ideas

In a coherent composition, ideas are connected clearly, and every sentence and paragraph flows smoothly and sensibly to the next. One way to create coherence in a composition is by using clear transitional expressions.

Transitions show *how* ideas are connected. Often transitional words show chronological or spatial relationships (for example, *next, after, nearby, adjacent*). Transitions may also show relationships of cause and effect *(because, since, as a result)* or of contrast *(but, although, on the other hand)*. In the second sentence below, *consequently* shows a cause-and-effect relationship and makes a clear transition from one sentence to another.

> During the blitz, the Germans targeted London. *Consequently,* many Londoners moved to the countryside.

Your Turn

Add coherence to the sentences that follow by inserting effective transitions as directed.

1. Churchill had a lonely childhood that haunted him all his life. He always had a close relationship with his nanny. *[Indicate contrast.]*

2. Churchill inspired his country throughout the war. He is considered a great British leader. *[Indicate cause and effect.]*

3. Churchill had ambivalent feelings toward Europe after the war. He believed that there was a special relationship between Britain and the United States. *[Indicate contrast.]*

4. Winston Churchill was Colonial Secretary in 1921. He helped create the countries of Iraq and Jordan. *[Indicate chronology.]*

Writing Application Look over a piece of your writing. Circle any transitional expressions you used and add additional transitions to make your writing clearer.

CHOICES

As you respond to the Choices, use these **Academic Vocabulary** words as appropriate: perspective, considerably, adapt, exhibit, inevitable.

REVIEW
Compose Compelling Orations

Identify an issue you think is important. Write a short speech explaining why this topic matters considerably to you as well as why it should matter to others. Use emotional, ethical, and logical appeals and make notes in the margin about tone and delivery.

CONNECT
A Multimedia Version

TechFocus Design a multimedia version of "Blood, Sweat, and Tears," using modern technology such as music and video to enhance the logical and emotional appeals of Churchill's speech. Show your presentation to your class, and then discuss the effects that modern technology had on the viewers. How do you think your presentation would have affected Churchill's listeners?

EXTEND
Conduct Research

Churchill gave many impassioned speeches during the war. Use the Internet to find another of his speeches, and determine whether he uses logical appeals, emotional appeals, or both. What is his purpose in this speech? If possible, find an audio recording of the speech, and note how listening to his delivery affects your reaction to it. Two speeches to look for are usually known as "We shall fight on the beaches" (June 4, 1940) and "Their finest hour" (June 18, 1940), both delivered to the House of Commons.

Learn It Online
Learn how to create a great multimedia presentation at the MediaScope site.

go.hrw.com   L12-1115   **Go**

Preparing to Read

The Demon Lover

What Do You Think?
How does experience shape our view of the world?

QuickTalk

You've read about how the two World Wars affected soldiers and prisoners. In a small group, discuss the impact wars might have on civilians. What losses might they suffer?

Writer Elizabeth Bowen (c. 1940–1960), by Robin Adler.

Elizabeth Bowen
(1899–1973)

Much of Elizabeth Bowen's writing is concerned with the processes of growing up, of losing innocence, and of coming to terms with reality. Her main characters are often wealthy, well-mannered women (like herself); yet her novels also reveal a sense that life cannot be trusted, that existence is a struggle.

"No Trouble"

Elizabeth Bowen was born in Dublin and spent her early years in County Cork on her family's country estate. As Bowen later wrote, her family tried "to live as though living gave them no trouble." An only child, Bowen was looked after by a governess and taught to dance, wear gloves, and <u>exhibit</u> good manners. On her mother's orders she was not taught to read until she was seven. When her father was confined to a mental hospital, Elizabeth was not allowed to dwell on his condition. Her father recovered, but her mother contracted fatal cancer. Twelve-year-old Elizabeth was not allowed to attend her mother's funeral or to mourn her.

Literature and War

After attending a boarding school in England, Bowen moved to London to write stories. There she attended readings at the Poetry Bookshop, where she made the first of the literary friendships that were to become the fabric of her life.

In 1923, Bowen published her first collection of stories, *Encounters*. She married Alan Cameron, a teacher, and moved to Oxford, where she wrote industriously, producing story collections regularly and writing nearly a novel a year.

In 1935, the couple moved back to London, where Bowen became a notable hostess of the literary world. During World War II, with its nightly air raids on London, Bowen was a dedicated air-raid warden, but she went right on giving parties. She also wrote the stories published in *The Demon Lover* (1945), a collection she called a "diary" of her reactions to the war.

After the war, Cameron died of a heart attack. Predictably, Bowen became more active than ever. She died of lung cancer in 1973 and is buried in an Irish churchyard.

Think About the Writer
How would pretending that life is no trouble affect a child?

Reader/Writer Notebook

Use your **RWN** to complete the activities for this selection.

Literary Focus

Flashback A **flashback** is a scene in a narrative or dramatic work that interrupts the present action to tell what happened at an earlier time. "The Demon Lover" uses a flashback to provide important background information about the main character, Mrs. Drover. To recognize where the flashback begins, look for the sudden appearance of a verb in the past perfect tense (that is, preceded by the helping verb *had*).

Reading Focus

Making and Modifying Predictions Making **predictions,** or educated guesses about what will happen in a story, will add to your understanding and enjoyment. As you read, you will often learn new information that will cause you to **modify your predictions.** In "The Demon Lover," the flash-back will provide you with new information about Mrs. Drover and her life. Use this information to help you modify your predictions.

Into Action Read the story up until the flashback, and then in a chart like the one below, predict what will happen next. Then, read the flashback, and modify your prediction. As you continue to read, add new informa-tion to the chart, and modify your predictions accordingly.

My prediction	A woman will meet a mysterious man.
Details in the flashback	
My modified prediction	
New information	
My modified prediction	

Writing Focus

Think as a Reader/Writer

Find It in Your Reading The descriptive details writers use to create a setting also help establish a story's **mood,** or atmosphere. As you read Bowen's description of the empty house, record in your *Reader/Writer Notebook* details that create an unsettling mood.

TechFocus Imagine you are adapting this story for a television movie. Consider how you will stage the flashback.

Vocabulary

prosaic (proh ZAY ihk) *adj.:* ordinary; dull. *The woman's life story seemed prosaic until she revealed her secret from long ago.*

assent (uh SEHNT) *n.:* acceptance. *The woman had learned to view her rather ordinary life with a feeling of assent.*

intermittent (ihn tuhr MIHT uhnt) *adj.:* starting and stopping; periodic. *The rain was not constant but intermittent.*

precipitately (prih SIHP uh tiht lee) *adv.:* suddenly. *She turned precipitately to see what had caused the noise that startled her.*

emanated (EHM uh nayt id) *v.:* flowed; came forth. *The noise emanated from downstairs.*

impassively (ihm PAS ihv lee) *adv.:* calmly; indifferently. *She set aside her anxiety and impassively descended the stairs to see what had happened.*

Language Coach

Suffix –ly The suffix –ly is added to some adjectives (words that describe people, places, things, or ideas) to form adverbs (words that describe verbs, adjectives, or other adverbs). Which two Vocabulary words are adverbs that end in –ly? To which two Vocabulary words could you add –ly to form adverbs?

 Learn It Online
Enhance your study of this story with these project ideas online.

go.hrw.com   L12-1117   **Go**

The Demon Lover

by **Elizabeth Bowen**

Read with a Purpose
Read this story to find out about one woman's strange encounter with her past.

Build Background
"The Demon Lover" takes place in London during World War II, when frequent German air raids drove many Londoners to leave the city. The story's title comes from a British ballad, in which a woman is lured away from her second husband and her children by her first husband, who has been missing at sea and has come into great wealth. She goes to sea with him—only to find that he has a demon's cloven foot. The demon lover then breaks the ship in half, sinking it, and sending the two of them to hell.

Toward the end of her day in London Mrs. Drover went round to her shut-up house to look for several things she wanted to take away. Some belonged to herself, some to her family, who were by now used to their country life. It was late August; it had been a steamy, showery day: At the moment the trees down the pavement glittered in an escape of humid yellow afternoon sun. Against the next batch of clouds, already piling up ink-dark, broken chimneys and parapets[1] stood out. In her once familiar street, as in any unused channel, an unfamiliar queerness had silted up; a cat wove itself in and out of railings, but no human eye watched Mrs. Drover's return. Shifting some parcels under her arm, she slowly forced round her latchkey in an unwilling lock, then gave the door, which had warped, a push with her knee. Dead air came out to meet her as she went in.

The staircase window having been boarded up, no light came down into the hall. But one door, she could just see, stood ajar, so she went quickly through into the room and unshuttered the big window in there.

Now the prosaic woman, looking about her, was more perplexed than she knew by everything that she saw, by traces of her long former habit of life—the yellow smoke stain up the white marble mantelpiece, the ring left by a vase on the top of the escritoire;[2] the bruise in the wallpaper where, on the door being thrown open widely, the china handle had always hit the wall. The piano, having gone away to be stored, had left what looked like claw marks on its part of the parquet.[3] Though not much dust had seeped in, each object wore a film of another kind; and, the only ventilation being the chimney, the whole drawing room smelled of the cold hearth. Mrs. Drover put down her parcels on the escritoire and left the room to proceed upstairs; the things she wanted were in a bedroom chest. **A**

She had been anxious to see how the house was—the part-time caretaker she shared with some neighbors was away this week on his holiday, known to be not yet back. At the best of times he did not look

---

1. **parapets** (PAR uh pehts): low walls around rooftops.

2. **escritoire** (es krih TWAHR): writing table.
3. **parquet** (pahr KAY): wood floor made of boards arranged in geometric patterns.

A **Reading Focus** **Making and Modifying Predictions** Re-read the title and first two paragraphs in the story. Think about the description of the setting and of Mrs. Drover. Then, predict what will happen to Mrs. Drover in this story.

Vocabulary **prosaic** (proh ZAY ihk) *adj.*: ordinary; dull.

in often, and she was never sure that she trusted him. There were some cracks in the structure, left by the last bombing, on which she was anxious to keep an eye. Not that one could do anything—

A shaft of refracted[4] daylight now lay across the hall. She stopped dead and stared at the hall table—on this lay a letter addressed to her.

She thought first—then the caretaker *must* be back. All the same, who, seeing the house shuttered, would have dropped a letter in at the box? It was not a circular, it was not a bill. And the post office redirected, to the address in the country, everything for her that came through the post. The caretaker (even if he *were* back) did not know she was due in London today—her call here had been planned to be a surprise—so his negligence in the manner of this letter, leaving it to wait in the dusk and the dust, annoyed her. Annoyed, she picked up the letter, which bore no stamp. But it cannot be important, or they would know . . . She took the letter rapidly upstairs with her, without a stop to look at the writing till she reached what had been her bedroom, where she let in light. The room looked over the garden and other gardens: The sun had gone in; as the clouds sharpened and lowered, the trees and rank lawns seemed already to smoke with dark. Her reluctance to look again at the letter came from the fact that she felt intruded upon— and by someone contemptuous of her ways. However, in the tenseness preceding the fall of rain she read it: It was a few lines.

Dear Kathleen: You will not have forgotten that today is our anniversary, and the day we said. The years have gone by at once slowly and fast. In view of the fact that nothing has changed, I shall rely upon you to keep your promise. I was sorry to see you leave London, but was satisfied that you would be back in time. You may expect me, therefore, at the hour arranged. Until then... K.

Martha (1925), by Georg Schrimpf (1889–1938), oil on canvas.

Mrs. Drover looked for the date: It was today's. She dropped the letter onto the bedsprings, then picked it up to see the writing again—her lips, beneath the remains of lipstick, beginning to go white. She felt so much the change in her own face that she went to the mirror, polished a clear patch in it, and looked at once urgently and stealthily in. She was confronted by a woman of forty-four, with eyes starting out under a hat brim that had been rather carelessly pulled down. She had not put on any more powder since she left the shop where she ate her solitary tea.[5] The pearls her husband had given her on their marriage hung loose round her now rather thinner throat, slipping in the V of the pink wool jumper her sister knitted last autumn as they sat round the fire. Mrs. Drover's most normal expression was one of controlled worry, but of assent.

---

4. **refracted:** bent by its passage from one medium to another.

5. **tea:** in Britain, a light late-afternoon meal, served with tea.

B **Reading Focus** Making and Modifying Predictions What is mysterious about the arrival of the letter? Modify your prediction about what will happen based on what you have learned so far.

Vocabulary **assent** (uh SEHNT) *n.:* acceptance.

Since the birth of the third of her little boys, attended by a quite serious illness, she had had an intermittent muscular flicker to the left of her mouth, but in spite of this she could always sustain a manner that was at once energetic and calm.

Turning from her own face as precipitately as she had gone to meet it, she went to the chest where the things were, unlocked it, threw up the lid, and knelt to search. But as rain began to come crashing down she could not keep from looking over her shoulder at the stripped bed on which the letter lay. Behind the blanket of rain the clock of the church that still stood struck six—with rapidly heightening apprehension she counted each of the slow strokes. "The hour arranged . . . My God," she said, "*what* hour? How should I . . . ? After twenty-five years . . . "

The young girl talking to the soldier in the garden had not ever completely seen his face. It was dark; they were saying goodbye under a tree. Now and then—for it felt, from not seeing him at this intense moment, as though she had never seen him at all—she verified his presence for these few moments longer by putting out a hand, which he each time pressed, without very much kindness, and painfully, on to one of the breast buttons of his uniform. That cut of the button on the palm of her hand was, principally, what she was to carry away. This was so near the end of a leave from France that she could only wish him already gone. It was August 1916. Being not kissed, being drawn away from and looked at intimidated Kathleen till she imagined spectral glitters in the place of his eyes. Turning away and looking back up the lawn she saw, through branches of trees, the drawing-room window alight: She caught a breath for the moment when she could go running back there into the safe arms of her mother and sister, and cry: "What shall I do, what shall I do? He has gone." **C**

Hearing her catch her breath, her fiancé said, without feeling: "Cold?"

"You're going away such a long way."

"Not so far as you think."

"I don't understand?"

"You don't have to," he said. "You will. You know what we said."

"But that was—suppose you—I mean, suppose."

"I shall be with you," he said, "sooner or later. You won't forget that. You need do nothing but wait."

Only a little more than a minute later she was free to run up the silent lawn. Looking in through the window at her mother and sister, who did not for the moment perceive her, she already felt that unnatural promise drive down between her and the rest of all humankind. No other way of having given herself could have made her feel so apart, lost and forsworn.[6] She could not have plighted a more sinister troth.[7]

Kathleen behaved well when, some months later, her fiancé was reported missing, presumed killed. Her family not only supported her but were able to praise her courage without stint[8] because they could not regret, as a husband for her, the man they knew

---

6. **forsworn** (fawr SWAWRN): having sworn falsely; perjured.
7. **plighted . . . troth:** made a more sinister promise of marriage.
8. **stint:** limitation.

C **Literary Focus** Flashback What are the signals that a flashback begins here?

Vocabulary **intermittent** (ihn tuhr MIHT uhnt) *adj.:* starting and stopping; periodic.
precipitately (prih SIHP uh tiht lee) *adv.:* suddenly.

Girl reading a Letter in an interior (1908), by Peter Vilhelm Ilsted (1861–1933).

almost nothing about. They hoped she would, in a year or two, console herself—and had it been only a question of consolation things might have gone much straighter ahead. But her trouble, behind just a little grief, was a complete dislocation from everything. She did not reject other lovers, for these failed to appear: For years she failed to attract men—and with the approach of her thirties she became natural enough to share her family's anxiousness on this score. She began to put herself out,[9] to wonder; and at thirty-two she was very greatly relieved to find herself being courted by William Drover. She married him, and the two of them settled down in this quiet, arboreal[10] part of Kensington: In this house the years piled up, her children were born, and they all lived till they were driven out by the bombs of the next war. Her movements as Mrs. Drover were circumscribed, and she dismissed any idea that they were still watched. **D**

As things were—dead or living the letter writer

sent her only a threat. Unable, for some minutes, to go on kneeling with her back exposed to the empty room, Mrs. Drover rose from the chest to sit on an upright chair whose back was firmly against the wall. The desuetude[11] of her former bedroom, her married London home's whole air of being a cracked cup from which memory, with its reassuring power, had either evaporated or leaked away, made a crisis—and at just this crisis the letter writer had, knowledgeably, struck. The hollowness of the house this evening canceled years on years of voices, habits, and steps. Through the shut windows she only heard rain fall on the roofs around. To rally herself, she said she was in a mood—and for two or three seconds shutting her eyes, told herself that she had imagined the letter. But she opened them—there it lay on the bed. **E**

On the supernatural side of the letter's entrance she was not permitting her mind to dwell. Who, in London, knew she meant to call at the house today? Evidently, however, this had been known. The caretaker, *had* he come back, had had no cause to expect her: He would have taken the letter in his pocket, to forward it, at his own time, through the post. There was no other sign that the caretaker had been in—but, if not? Letters dropped in at doors of deserted houses do not fly or walk to tables in halls. They do not sit on the dust of empty tables with the air of certainty that they will be found. There is needed some human hand—but nobody but the caretaker had a key. Under circumstances she did not care to consider, a house can be entered without a key. It was possible that she was not alone now. She might be being waited for, downstairs. Waited for—until when? Until "the hour arranged." At least that was not six o'clock: Six has struck.

She rose from the chair and went over and locked the door. **F**

---

9. **put herself out:** vex or distress herself.
10. **arboreal** (ahr BAWR ee uhl): full of trees.

11. **desuetude** (DEHS wih tood): disuse.

D **Literary Focus** Flashback What information about Mrs. Drover's past do you learn in the flashback?

E **Literary Focus** Flashback How does this flashback end? What signal returns the story to the present?

F **Reading Focus** Making and Modifying Predictions What do you think will happen to Mrs. Drover? What new information helps you modify your prediction?

Shepherd Returning from the War, by Peter Brook, oil on canvas.
Leeds Museums and Galleries (City Art Gallery), UK.

Analyzing Visuals

Viewing and Interpreting How might this painting represent Mrs. Drover's feelings as she returns to her closed-up house?

The thing was, to get out. To fly? No, not that: She had to catch her train. As a woman whose utter dependability was the keystone of her family life she was not willing to return to the country, to her husband, her little boys, and her sister, without the objects she had come up to fetch. Resuming work at the chest she set about making up a number of parcels in a rapid, fumbling-decisive way. These,

with her shopping parcels, would be too much to carry; these meant a taxi—at the thought of the taxi her heart went up and her normal breathing resumed. I will ring up the taxi now; the taxi cannot come too soon: I shall hear the taxi out there running its engine, till I walk calmly down to it through the hall. I'll ring up— But no: the telephone is cut off …She tugged at a knot she had tied wrong.

The idea of flight... He was never kind to me, not really. I don't remember him kind at all. Mother said he never considered me. He was set on me, that was what it was—not love. Not love, not meaning a person well. What did he do, to make me promise like that? I can't remember— But she found that she could.

She remembered with such dreadful acuteness that the twenty-five years since then dissolved like smoke and she instinctively looked for the weal[12] left by the button on the palm of her hand. She remembered not only all that he said and did but the complete suspension of *her* existence during that August week. I was not myself—they all told me so at the time. She remembered—but with one white burning blank as where acid has dropped on a photograph: *Under no conditions* could she remember his face.

So, wherever he may be waiting, I shall not know him. You have no time to run from a face you do not expect.

The thing was to get to the taxi before any clock struck what could be the hour. She would slip down the street and round the side of the square to where the square gave on the main road. She would return in the taxi, safe, to her own door, and bring the solid driver into the house with her to pick up the parcels from room to room. The idea of the taxi driver made her decisive, bold: She unlocked her door, went to the top of the staircase, and listened down.

She heard nothing—but while she was hearing nothing the *passé*[13] air of the staircase was disturbed by a draft that traveled up to her face. It emanated from the basement: Down there a door or window was being opened by someone who chose this moment to leave the house. **G**

The rain had stopped; the pavements steamily shone as Mrs. Drover let herself out by inches from her own front door into the empty street. The unoccupied houses opposite continued to meet her look with their damaged stare. Making toward the thoroughfare and the taxi, she tried not to keep looking behind. Indeed, the silence was so intense—one of those creeks of London silence exaggerated this summer by the damage of war—that no tread could have gained on hers unheard. Where her street debouched[14] on the square where people went on living, she grew conscious of, and checked, her unnatural pace. Across the open end of the square two buses impassively passed each other: Women, a perambulator,[15] cyclists, a man wheeling a barrow signalized, once again, the ordinary flow of life. At the square's most populous corner should be—and was—the short taxi rank. This evening, only one taxi—but this, although it presented its blank rump, appeared already to be alertly waiting for her. Indeed, without looking round the driver started his engine as she panted up from behind and put her hand on the door. As she did so, the clock struck seven. The taxi faced the main road: To make the trip back to her house it would have to turn—she had settled back on the seat and the taxi had turned before she, surprised by its knowing movement, recollected that she had not "said where." She leaned forward to scratch at the glass panel that divided the driver's head from her own. **H**

The driver braked to what was almost a stop, turned round, and slid the glass panel back: The jolt of this flung Mrs. Drover forward till her face was almost into the glass. Through the aperture[16] driver and passenger, not six inches between them, remained for an eternity eye to eye. Mrs. Drover's mouth hung open for some seconds before she could issue her first scream. After that she continued to scream freely and to beat with her gloved hands on the glass all round as the taxi, accelerating without mercy, made off with her into the hinterland of deserted streets.

---

12. **weal** (weel): lump; welt.
13. *passé* (pah SAY): no longer fresh; rather old.

---

14. **debouched** (dee BOOSHT): came out; emerged.
15. **perambulator** (puhr AM byoo layt uhr): chiefly British for "baby carriage." The word is often shortened to *pram.*
16. **aperture:** opening.

G Reading Focus **Making and Modifying Predictions** What do these lines suggest might happen next? Why is Mrs. Drover afraid?

H Reading Focus **Making and Modifying Predictions** How do you think the ending will resolve the story's tension?

Vocabulary **emanated** (EHM uh nayt id) *v.*: flowed; came forth.
impassively (ihm PAS ihv lee) *adv.*: calmly; indifferently.

Respond and Think Critically

Reading Focus

Quick Check

1. How does Bowen convey that Mrs. Drover's house has been empty for some time? What mood does she establish with this description?

2. Why does Kathleen feel free when the soldier goes missing? Why is the betrothal "sinister"?

Read with a Purpose

3. How does Mrs. Drover react to this undesirable encounter with her past?

Reading Skills: Making and Modifying Predictions

4. Look back at the predictions you made while reading. Complete your chart by writing in what actually happened. Write a brief description of what new information helped you modify your predictions as you read, and how closely your predictions matched what actually happened.

Literary Focus

Literary Analysis

5. **Analyze** During each war, Mrs. Drover experiences dislocation and confusion, and during each war, the demon lover is part of her life. What do these strands—the war, Mrs. Drover's inner turmoil, and the demon lover's appearances—tell you about the story's theme?

6. **Interpret** The use of an omniscient narrator allows Bowen to give readers information about Mrs. Drover's psychological makeup that Mrs. Drover herself is not consciously aware of. Identify several such passages in the text. How do you interpret Mrs. Drover's psychological state?

7. **Evaluate** How does Bowen create suspense in this story? Did you experience Mrs. Drover's fear, or do you think the story is too unrealistic to be frightening? Explain your response.

Literary Skills: Flashback

8. **Make Judgments** Do you think the abrupt shift into the past in the flashback is effective or merely confusing? Why?

9. **Interpret** Some readers believe Mrs. Drover's experience is a hallucination. Her powers of imagination have combined with the pressures of wartime to transform reality into a waking nightmare. What details in the flashback support this interpretation of the story?

Literary Skills Review: Foreshadowing

10. **Analyze** When writers use **foreshadowing,** they drop hints about what will happen later in the story. What details in the lovers' last meeting foreshadow a sinister, threatening reunion? What other details in the story foreshadow a scary ending to Mrs. Drover's day?

Writing Focus

Think as a Reader/Writer

Use It in Your Writing Look back at the notes you took about the descriptive details Bowen uses to create an unsettling mood. Then, write a descriptive paragraph in which you use details and images to create a particular mood.

What Do You Think Now? How do you think Mrs. Drover's life has been affected by the two wars? How might her <u>perspective</u> of the world have changed?

Vocabulary Development

✔ Vocabulary Check

Match the Vocabulary words with their definitions.

1. emanated   indifferently
2. assent   ordinary, dull
3. prosaic   flowed, came forth
4. impassively   acceptance
5. intermittent   suddenly
6. precipitately   periodic

Vocabulary Skills: Etymology

English is made up of words that originated in many different languages. By looking in the dictionary, you can learn a word's **etymology,** or origin. Look at this sample dictionary entry for the word *prosaic:*

Pro·sa·ic *adj.* [LL *prosaicus,* fr. L *prosa* prose]
1. dull, unimaginative   2. ordinary

The information in brackets tells you the etymology— that the word came from the Late Latin word *prosaicus,* which came from the Latin word *prosa.* The dictionary will include a key to the abbreviations.

Your Turn

Use a dictionary to determine the etymology of *assent, intermittent, precipitately,* and *emanated.*

Language Coach

Suffix –ly Remember that the suffix *–ly* is added to some words to form adverbs, words that describe verbs, adjectives, or other adverbs. Find the adverb *impassively* in the story. Tell what word it describes. Then find two other *–ly* adverbs in the story and tell what words they describe.

CHOICES

As you respond to the Choices, use these **Academic Vocabulary** words as appropriate: perspective, considerably, adapt, exhibit, inevitable.

REVIEW

Create a Story Map

Use the following chart to create a story map for "The Demon Lover." Note when the flashback occurs.

Situation	
Characters	
Conflict	
Event	
Climax	
Resolution	

CONNECT

Plan a TV Flashback

TechFocus In a group, plan a TV adaptation of the flashback in this story. Use storyboards to explain how you will use camera angles, fades, lighting, setting and costumes, and other techniques to alert the audience to the flashback and then to return them to the present. In a class presentation, have a group member share your ideas for adapting the flashback.

EXTEND

Tell What Happens Next

Some readers believe that Mrs. Drover's experience is a figment of her imagination, while others consider the story to be an out-and-out ghost tale. Choose the interpretation you prefer, or develop one of your own, and write a paragraph telling what happens next in the story.

 Learn It Online
Learn more about Bowen and her work through these Internet links.

go.hrw.com   L12-1125   **Go**

Preparing to Read

The Destructors

What Do You Think How does experience shape our view of the world?

QuickWrite

Why do you think some people are so influenced by peer pressure? Write a paragraph on this topic in your *Reader/Writer Notebook*.

Graham Greene (1904–1991) at his home in Nice (May 1982).

Graham Greene
(1904–1991)

In his serious novels as well as in his light "entertainments" and thrillers, Graham Greene's intention was always to tell the truth, which he saw as the primary duty of the artist.

An Early Literary Triumph

Henry Graham Greene was born to a comfortable family in Hertfordshire, England. As he grew into adolescence, he became depressed and unhappy at school. After trying to run away, he was sent to London for psychoanalysis. He would later recall those six months in London as among the happiest of his life.

While he was still at school, a local newspaper published one of Greene's stories, and he recalled feeling a sense of true literary triumph "for the first and last time." The experience convinced him to become a professional writer. He attended Oxford University, where he wrote a novel and published a book of poems.

A Hungry Curiosity

In 1926, Greene became engaged to Vivien Dayrell-Browning and began to take instruction in her faith, Roman Catholicism. Formerly an atheist, he became convinced of "the probable existence of something we call God." Greene later exhibited his religious concerns in his fiction with the novels *Brighton Rock* (1938) and *The Power and the Glory* (1940), in which he explored good and evil and the workings of divine grace.

Greene worked as a journalist until his first novel, *The Man Within,* was published in 1929. Although his next books received little attention, Greene came into his own with the thriller *Stamboul Train* (1932; also published as *Orient Express*).

Greene wrote more than twenty novels, as well as works in a dozen other genres, including children's stories and screenplays. In his autobiography, he revealed his motive for writing fiction as "a desire to reduce the chaos of experience to some sort of order, and a hungry curiosity. We cannot love others, so the theologians teach, unless in some degree we can love ourselves, and curiosity too begins at home."

Think About the Writer How might a hungry curiosity and a strong desire for new experiences serve a writer?

Reader/Writer Notebook

Use your **RWN** to complete the activities for this selection.

Literary Focus

Setting The **setting** is the time and place of a story. The setting of this story reflects both political and social influences of the historical period: a drab corner of a city still reeling from war. As the story progresses, though, the setting becomes not just a backdrop, but rather a key plot element that helps to shape the characters. Greene's characteristic use of coarse **imagery** and language creates a seedy, drab world full of shabby violence and a pessimistic mood.

Reading Focus

Drawing Inferences About Characters' Motivations Characters' words and actions, as well as the author's description of the characters, will help you **draw inferences about characters' motivations,** or their reasons for behaving the way they do. In "The Destructors," each of the four numbered sections gives you a bit more insight into T., the enigmatic main character. Greene slowly reveals more about the character's motivations as the story progresses.

Into Action On a spider map, note particular words and actions that you find most revealing about each of the following characters. When you have finished reading the story, you will use these clues to draw inferences about the characters' motivations.

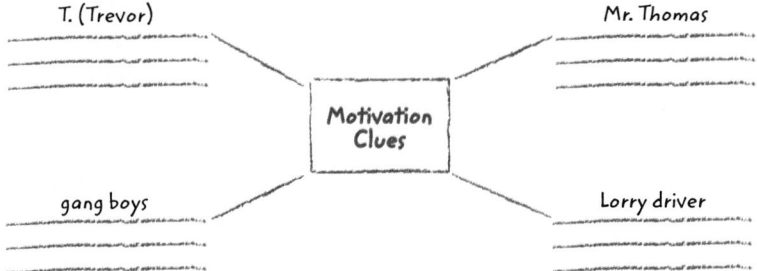

Writing Focus

Think as a Reader/Writer

Find It in Your Reading As you read, note how Greene uses dialogue to tell you about the characters. What does the dialogue reveal about the important characters in the story? In your *Reader/Writer Notebook,* record lines of dialogue you think are key to understanding the characters.

Vocabulary

ignoble (ihg NOH buhl) *adj.:* shameful; degrading. *The parents felt much distress because of the boys' ignoble behavior.*

exploit (EHKS ployt) *n.:* daring act. *The boys' exploit was more cruel than brave.*

daunted (DAWNT ihd) *v.* used as *adj.:* intimidated. *The young boy was daunted by his confident older friends.*

fickleness (FIHK uhl nuhs) *n.:* changeableness. *The young boy's fickleness annoyed the older boy.*

altruistic (al tru IHS tihk) *adj.:* unselfish. *It was unclear whether Mr. Thomas's gift was a bribe or an altruistic act.*

exhilaration (ehg zihl uh RAY shuhn) *n.:* excitement; high spirits. *Their actions caused them to feel exhilaration despite their fear.*

abstain (ab STAYN) *v.:* refrain. *Mike abstains from destroying the house.*

stealthy (STEHL thee) *adj.:* secret; sly. *The stealthy child climbed unseen over the fence.*

Language Coach

Heteronyms The word *exploit* is a **heteronym,** a word that is pronounced differently depending on its meaning and part of speech. How and when does the pronunciation of the following heteronyms change?
1. *converse* (noun meaning "the opposite"); *converse* (verb meaning "talk")
2. *contest* (noun meaning "competition"); *contest* (verb meaning "dispute")

Learn It Online
Explore the vocabulary words further with Word Watch online.

go.hrw.com   L12-1127   **Go**

THE DESTRUCTORS

by **Graham Greene**

Read with a Purpose
Read to learn how one boy incites a gang of teenagers to commit an act of destruction.

Build Background
This story is set in 1954, nine years after the end of World War II. During the war, London had been regularly "blitzed" by German planes dropping firebombs, and many of its buildings were destroyed. Years after the war, Londoners still walked among the rubble. Considerably more troubling than this physical destruction was what many people saw as the moral destruction of society, the collapse of hope, especially among gangs of young people who had never known a reality other than war and its aftermath.

It was on the eve of August Bank Holiday that the latest recruit became the leader of the Wormsley Common gang. No one was surprised except Mike, but Mike at the age of nine was surprised by everything. "If you don't shut your mouth," somebody once said to him, "you'll get a frog down it." After that Mike had kept his teeth tightly clamped except when the surprise was too great. **A**

The new recruit had been with the gang since the beginning of the summer holidays, and there were possibilities about his brooding silence that all recognized. He never wasted a word even to tell his name until that was required of him by the rules. When he said "Trevor" it was a statement of fact, not as it would have been with the others a statement of shame or defiance. Nor did anyone laugh except Mike, who finding himself without support and meeting the dark gaze of the newcomer opened his mouth and was quiet again. There was every reason why T., as he was afterward referred to, should have been an object of mockery—there was his name (and they substituted the initial because otherwise they had no excuse not

to laugh at it), the fact that his father, a former architect and present clerk, had "come down in the world" and that his mother considered herself better than the neighbors. What but an odd quality of danger, of the unpredictable, established him in the gang without any ignoble ceremony of initiation? **B**

The gang met every morning in an impromptu car-park, the site of the last bomb of the first blitz. The leader, who was known as Blackie, claimed to have heard it fall, and no one was precise enough in his dates to point out that he would have been one year old and fast asleep on the down platform of Wormsley Common Underground[1] Station. On one side of the car-park leaned the first occupied house, number 3, of the shattered Northwood Terrace—literally leaned, for it had suffered from the blast of the bomb and the side walls were supported on wooden struts. A smaller bomb and some incendiaries[2] had fallen beyond, so that the house stuck up like a jagged tooth and carried

---

1. **Underground:** British for "subway."
2. **incendiaries:** firebombs.

A **Literary Focus** Setting What is the time and place of this story?

B **Reading Focus** Drawing Inferences About Characters' Motivations What might be the cause of T.'s "brooding silence" and seeming unpredictability?

Vocabulary **ignoble** (ihg NOH buhl) *adj.*: shameful; degrading.

Soldiers look on at damage in Tralfagar Square caused by German bombs (1942).

on the further wall relics of its neighbor, a dado,[3] the remains of a fireplace. T., whose words were almost confined to voting "Yes" or "No" to the plan of operations proposed each day by Blackie, once startled the whole gang by saying broodingly, "Wren[4] built that house, father says."

"Who's Wren?"

"The man who built St. Paul's."[5]

"Who cares?" Blackie said. "It's only Old Misery's."

Old Misery—whose real name was Thomas—had once been a builder and decorator. He lived alone in the crippled house, doing for himself: Once a week you could see him coming back across the common

with bread and vegetables, and once as the boys played in the car-park he put his head over the smashed wall of his garden and looked at them.

"Been to the loo,"[6] one of the boys said, for it was common knowledge that since the bombs fell something had gone wrong with the pipes of the house and Old Misery was too mean[7] to spend money on the property. He could do the redecorating himself at cost price, but he had never learned plumbing. The loo was a wooden shed at the bottom of the narrow garden with a star-shaped hole in the door: It had escaped the blast which had smashed the house next door and sucked out the window frames of number 3.

The next time the gang became aware of Mr. Thomas was more surprising. Blackie, Mike, and a thin

---

3. **dado:** wood paneling along the lower part of the walls of a room.
4. **Wren:** Sir Christopher Wren (1632–1723), a celebrated English architect.
5. **St. Paul's:** cathedral in London.

6. **loo:** British slang for "bathroom."
7. **mean:** stingy.

C Literary Focus **Setting** How does the setting already seem fitting for the story's title?

yellow boy, who for some reason was called by his surname[8] Summers, met him on the common coming back from the market. Mr. Thomas stopped them. He said glumly, "You belong to the lot that play in the car-park?"

Mike was about to answer when Blackie stopped him. As the leader he had responsibilities. "Suppose we are?" he said ambiguously.

"I got some chocolates," Mr. Thomas said. "Don't like 'em myself. Here you are. Not enough to go round, I don't suppose. There never is," he added with somber conviction. He handed over three packets of Smarties.

D

The gang were puzzled and perturbed by this action and tried to explain it away. "Bet someone dropped them and he picked 'em up," somebody suggested.

"Pinched[9] 'em and then got in a bleeding funk," another thought aloud.

"It's a bribe," Summers said. "He wants us to stop bouncing balls on his wall."

"We'll show him we don't take bribes," Blackie said, and they sacrificed the whole morning to the game of bouncing that only Mike was young enough to enjoy. There was no sign from Mr. Thomas.   **E**

Next day T. astonished them all. He was late at the rendezvous, and the voting for that day's exploit took place without him. At Blackie's suggestion the gang was to disperse in pairs, take buses at random, and see how many free rides could be snatched from unwary conductors (the operation was to be carried out in pairs to avoid cheating). They were drawing lots for their companions when T. arrived.

"Where you been, T.?" Blackie asked. "You can't vote now. You know the rules."

"I've been *there*," T. said. He looked at the ground, as though he had thoughts to hide.

"Where?"

---

8. **surname:** last name.
9. **pinched:** British for "stole."

"At Old Misery's." Mike's mouth opened and then hurriedly closed again with a click. He had remembered the frog.

"At Old Misery's?" Blackie said. There was nothing in the rules against it, but he had a sensation that T. was treading on dangerous ground. He asked hopefully, "Did you break in?"

"No. I rang the bell."

"And what did you say?"

"I said I wanted to see his house."

"What did he do?"

"He showed it me."

"Pinch anything?"

"No."

"What did you do it for then?"

The gang had gathered round: It was as though an impromptu court were about to form and to try some case of deviation. T. said, "It's a beautiful house," and still watching the ground, meeting no one's eyes, he licked his lips first one way, then the other.

"What do you mean, a beautiful house?" Blackie asked with scorn.

"It's got a staircase two hundred years old like a corkscrew. Nothing holds it up."

"What do you mean, nothing holds it up. Does it float?"

"It's to do with opposite forces, Old Misery said."

"What else?"

"There's paneling."

"Like in the Blue Boar?"

"Two hundred years old."

"Is Old Misery two hundred years old?"

Mike laughed suddenly and then was quiet again. The meeting was in a serious mood. For the first time since T. had strolled into the car-park on the first day of the holidays his position was in danger. It only needed a single use of his real name and the gang would be at his heels.

"What did you do it for?" Blackie asked. He was just, he had no jealousy, he was anxious to retain T. in the gang if he could. It was the word "beautiful" that

---

D Reading Focus **Drawing Inferences About Characters' Motivations** Why do you think Mr. Thomas gives the boys candy?

E Reading Focus **Drawing Inferences About Characters' Motivations** What do the boys think Mr. Thomas's motive is for offering them candy? What does this suggest about their attitude toward adults?

Vocabulary **exploit** (EHKS ployt) *n.:* daring act.

worried him—that belonged to a class world that you could still see parodied at the Wormsley Common Empire by a man wearing a top hat and a monocle,[10] with a haw-haw accent. He was tempted to say, "My dear Trevor, old chap," and unleash his hell hounds. "If you'd broken in," he said sadly—that indeed would have been an exploit worthy of the gang. **F**

"This was better," T. said. "I found out things." He continued to stare at his feet, not meeting anybody's eye, as though he were absorbed in some dream he was unwilling—or ashamed—to share.

"What things?"

"Old Misery's going to be away all tomorrow and Bank Holiday."

Blackie said with relief, "You mean we could break in?"

"And pinch things?" somebody asked.

Blackie said, "Nobody's going to pinch things. Breaking in—that's good enough, isn't it? We don't want any court stuff."

"I don't want to pinch anything," T. said. "I've got a better idea."

"What is it?"

T. raised his eyes, as gray and disturbed as the drab August day. "We'll pull it down," he said. "We'll destroy it."

Blackie gave a single hoot of laughter and then, like Mike, fell quiet, daunted by the serious implacable gaze. "What'd the police be doing all the time?" he said.

"They'd never know. We'd do it from inside. I've found a way in." He said with a sort of intensity, "We'd be like worms, don't you see, in an apple. When we came out again there'd be nothing there, no staircase, no panels, nothing but just walls, and then we'd make the walls fall down—somehow." **G**

"We'd go to jug,"[11] Blackie said.

"Who's to prove? And anyway we wouldn't have

pinched anything." He added without the smallest flicker of glee, "There wouldn't be anything to pinch after we'd finished."

"I've never heard of going to prison for breaking things," Summers said.

"There wouldn't be time," Blackie said. "I've seen housebreakers at work."

"There are twelve of us," T. said. "We'd organize."

"None of us know how—"

"I know," T. said. He looked across at Blackie. "Have you got a better plan?"

"Today," Mike said tactlessly, "we're pinching free rides—"

"Free rides," T. said. "You can stand down, Blackie, if you'd rather...."

"The gang's got to vote."

"Put it up then."

Blackie said uneasily, "It's proposed that tomorrow and Monday we destroy Old Misery's house."

"Here, here," said a fat boy called Joe.

"Who's in favor?"

T. said, "It's carried."

"How do we start?" Summers asked.

"He'll tell you," Blackie said. It was the end of his leadership. He went away to the back of the car-park and began to kick a stone, dribbling it this way and that. There was only one old Morris[12] in the park, for few cars were left there except lorries:[13] Without an attendant there was no safety. He took a flying kick at the car and scraped a little paint off the rear mudguard. Beyond, paying no more attention to him than to a stranger, the gang had gathered round T.; Blackie was dimly aware of the fickleness of favor. He thought of going home, of never returning, of letting them all discover the hollowness of T.'s leadership, but suppose after all what T. proposed was possible—nothing like it had ever been done before. The fame of the Wormsley

---

10. **monocle:** eyeglass for one eye.
11. **jug:** slang for "jail."

---

12. **Morris:** car made by the Morris firm, a British automaker.
13. **lorries:** British for "trucks."

F Reading Focus Drawing Inferences About Characters' Motivations What details in this paragraph convey the boys' distrust of the upper-class world? How might this distrust motivate them to treat T.?

G Reading Focus Drawing Inferences About Characters' Motivations What do you think has led T. to devise this destructive plan?

Vocabulary daunted (DAWNT ihd) *v.* used as adj.: intimidated.
fickleness (FIHK uhl nuhs) *n.*: changeableness.

PERHAPS AFTER ALL NOBODY HAD TURNED UP: THE PLAN HAD BEEN A WILD INVENTION: THEY HAD WOKEN UP WISER.

Common car-park gang would surely reach around London. There would be headlines in the papers. Even the grown-up gangs who ran the betting at the all-in wrestling and the barrow-boys[14] would hear with respect of how Old Misery's house had been destroyed. Driven by the pure, simple, and altruistic ambition of fame for the gang, Blackie came back to where T. stood in the shadow of Misery's wall. **(H)**

T. was giving his orders with decision: It was as though this plan had been with him all his life, pondered through the seasons, now in his fifteenth year crystallized with the pain of puberty. "You," he said to Mike, "bring some big nails, the biggest you can find, and a hammer. Anyone else who can better bring a hammer and a screwdriver. We'll need plenty of them. Chisels too. We can't have too many chisels. Can anybody bring a saw?"

"I can," Mike said.

"Not a child's saw," T. said. "A real saw."

Blackie realized he had raised his hand like any ordinary member of the gang.

"Right, you bring one, Blackie. But now there's a difficulty. We want a hacksaw."[15]

What's a hacksaw?" someone asked.

----

14. **barrow-boys:** boys who sold fruit or vegetables from a barrow, or cart.

15. **hacksaw:** saw made for cutting metal.

"You can get 'em at Woolworth's," Summers said.

The fat boy called Joe said gloomily, "I knew it would end in a collection."

"I'll get one myself," T. said. "I don't want your money. But I can't buy a sledgehammer."

Blackie said, "They are working on number fifteen. I know where they'll leave their stuff for Bank Holiday."

"Then that's all," T. said. "We meet here at nine sharp."

"I've got to go to church," Mike said.

"Come over the wall and whistle. We'll let you in."

2

On Sunday morning all were punctual except Blackie, even Mike. Mike had had a stroke of luck. His mother felt ill, his father was tired after Saturday night, and he was told to go to church alone with many warnings of what would happen if he strayed. Blackie had had difficulty in smuggling out the saw, and then in finding the sledgehammer at the back of number 15. He approached the house from a lane at the rear of the garden, for fear of the policeman's beat along the main road. The tired evergreens kept off a stormy sun: Another wet Bank Holiday was being prepared over the Atlantic, beginning in swirls of dust under the trees. Blackie climbed the wall into Misery's garden. **(I)**

There was no sign of anybody anywhere. The loo stood like a tomb in a neglected graveyard. The curtains were drawn. The house slept. Blackie lumbered nearer with the saw and the sledgehammer. Perhaps after all nobody had turned up: The plan had been a wild invention: They had woken wiser. But when he came close to the back door he could hear a confusion of sound, hardly louder than a hive in swarm: a clickety-clack, a bang bang bang, a scraping, a

----

(H) Reading Focus Drawing Inferences About Characters' Motivations Why does Blackie decide to support T.'s plan?

Vocabulary **altruistic** (al tru IHS tihk) *adj.:* unselfish.

(I) Literary Focus Setting What is the effect of the story's being set on Sunday and of the references to going to church?

creaking, a sudden painful crack. He thought, It's true, and whistled.

They opened the back door to him and he came in. He had at once the impression of organization, very different from the old happy-go-lucky ways under his leadership. For a while he wandered up and down stairs looking for T. Nobody addressed him: He had a sense of great urgency, and already he could begin to see the plan. The interior of the house was being carefully demolished without touching the outer walls. Summers with hammer and chisel was ripping out the skirting-boards[16] in the ground floor dining room: He had already smashed the panels of the door. In the same room Joe was heaving up the parquet[17] blocks, exposing the soft wood floorboards over the cellar. Coils of wire came out of the damaged skirting and Mike sat happily on the floor, clipping the wires. **J**

On the curved stairs two of the gang were working hard with an inadequate child's saw on the banisters—when they saw Blackie's big saw they signaled for it wordlessly. When he next saw them a quarter of the banisters had been dropped into the hall. He found T. at last in the bathroom—he sat moodily in the least cared-for room in the house, listening to the sounds coming up from below.

"You've really done it," Blackie said with awe. "What's going to happen?"

"We've only just begun," T. said. He looked at the sledgehammer and gave his instructions. "You stay here and break the bath and the washbasin. Don't bother about the pipes. They come later."

Mike appeared at the door. "I've finished the wire, T.," he said.

"Good. You've just got to go wandering round now. The kitchen's in the basement. Smash all the china and glass and bottles you can lay hold of. Don't turn on the taps—we don't want a flood—yet. Then go into all the rooms and turn out drawers. If they are

locked get one of the others to break them open. Tear up any papers you find and smash all the ornaments. Better take a carving knife with you from the kitchen. The bedroom's opposite here. Open the pillows and tear up the sheets. That's enough for the moment. And you, Blackie, when you've finished in here crack the plaster in the passage up with your sledgehammer."

"What are you going to do?" Blackie asked.

"I'm looking for something special," T. said. **K**

It was nearly lunchtime before Blackie had finished and went in search of T. Chaos had advanced. The kitchen was a shambles of broken glass and china. The dining room was stripped of parquet, the skirting was up, the door had been taken off its hinges, and the destroyers had moved up a floor. Streaks of light came in through the closed shutters where they worked with the seriousness of creators—and destruction after all is a form of creation. A kind of imagination had seen this house as it had now become.

Mike said, "I've got to go home for dinner."

"Who else?" T. asked, but all the others on one excuse or another had brought provisions with them.

They squatted in the ruins of the room and swapped unwanted sandwiches. Half an hour for lunch and they were at work again. By the time Mike returned, they were on the top floor, and by six the superficial damage was completed. The doors were all off, all the skirtings raised, the furniture pillaged and ripped and smashed—no one could have slept in the house except on a bed of broken plaster. T. gave his orders—eight o'clock next morning—and to escape notice they climbed singly over the garden wall, into the car-park. Only Blackie and T. were left; the light had nearly gone, and when they touched a switch, nothing worked—Mike had done his job thoroughly.

"Did you find anything special?" Blackie asked.

T. nodded. "Come over here," he said, "and look." Out of both pockets he drew bundles of pound notes. "Old Misery's savings," he said. "Mike ripped out the mattress, but he missed them."

"What are you going to do? Share them?"

"We aren't thieves," T. said. "Nobody's going to steal anything from this house. I kept these for you

---

16. **skirting-boards:** baseboards; boards placed along the base of the walls of a room.
17. **parquet** (PAR kay): fancy wood floor made of boards arranged in geometric patterns.

J **Reading Focus** Drawing Inferences About Characters' Motivations What do you think motivates the gang to put so much effort into the destruction of the house?

K **Literary Focus** Setting What is T.'s attitude toward the house he is destroying? What do his actions toward this element of the setting reveal about his thoughts and feelings?

and me—a celebration." He knelt down on the floor and counted them out—there were seventy in all. "We'll burn them," he said, "one by one," and taking it in turns they held a note upward and lit the top corner, so that the flame burnt slowly toward their fingers. The gray ash floated above them and fell on their heads like age. "I'd like to see Old Misery's face when we are through," T. said. **(L)**

"You hate him a lot?" Blackie asked.

"Of course I don't hate him," T. said. "There'd be no fun if I hated him." The last burning note illuminated his brooding face. "All this hate and love," he said, "it's soft, it's hooey. There's only things, Blackie," and he looked round the room crowded with the unfamiliar shadows of half things, broken things, former things. "I'll race you home, Blackie," he said. **(M)**

3

Next morning the serious destruction started. Two were missing—Mike and another boy, whose parents were off to Southend and Brighton in spite of the slow warm drops that had begun to fall and the rumble of thunder in the estuary like the first guns of the old blitz. "We've got to hurry," T. said.

Summers was restive.[18] "Haven't we done enough?" he said. "I've been given a bob for slot machines.[19] This is like work."

"We've hardly started," T. said. "Why, there's all the floors left, and the stairs. We haven't taken out a single window. You voted like the others. We are going to *destroy* this house. There won't be anything left when we've finished."

They began again on the first floor picking up the top floorboards next the outer wall, leaving the joists[20] exposed. Then they sawed through the joists and retreated into the hall, as what was left of the floor

---

18. **restive:** impatient; nervous.
19. **a bob for slot machines:** a shilling for vending machines.
20. **joists:** parallel beams that support a floor.

(L) **Reading Focus** Drawing Inferences About Characters' Motivations Why do you think T. chooses Old Misery's money as "something special" he wants to destroy himself?

(M) **Reading Focus** Drawing Inferences About Characters' Motivations What do T.'s words reveal about his motivations?

heeled and sank. They had learned with practice, and the second floor collapsed more easily. By the evening an odd exhilaration seized them as they looked down the great hollow of the house. They ran risks and made mistakes: When they thought of the windows it was too late to reach them. "Cor,"[21] Joe said, and dropped a penny down into the dry rubble-filled well. It cracked and span among the broken glass.

"Why did we start this?" Summers asked with astonishment; T. was already on the ground, digging at the rubble, clearing a space along the outer wall. "Turn on the taps," he said. "It's too dark for anyone to see now, and in the morning it won't matter." The water overtook them on the stairs and fell through the floorless rooms.

It was then they heard Mike's whistle at the back. "Something's wrong," Blackie said. They could hear his urgent breathing as they unlocked the door.

"The bogies?"[22] Summers asked.

"Old Misery," Mike said. "He's on his way." He put his head between his knees and retched. "Ran all the way," he said with pride.

"But why?" T. said. "He told me. . . ." He protested with the fury of the child he had never been, "It isn't fair."

"He was down at Southend," Mike said, "and he was on the train coming back. Said it was too cold and wet." He paused and gazed at the water. "My, you've had a storm here. Is the roof leaking?"

"How long will he be?"

"Five minutes. I gave Ma the slip and ran."

"We better clear," Summers said. "We've done enough, anyway."

"Oh, no, we haven't. Anybody could do this—" "This" was the shattered hollowed house with nothing left but the walls. Yet walls could be preserved. Façades[23] were valuable. They could build inside

---

21. **cor:** British exclamation of strong surprise or irritation.
22. **bogies** (BOH gees): slang for "police."
23. **façades** (fuh SAHDS): fronts of buildings.

Vocabulary **exhilaration** (ehg zihl uh RAY shuhn) *n.*: excitement; high spirits.

Street Kids (c. 1949–1951), by Joan Eardley (1921–1963), oil on canvas.
Scottish National Gallery of Modern Art, Edinburgh, UK.

again more beautifully than before. This could again be a home. He said angrily, "We've got to finish. Don't move. Let me think." **N**

"There's no time," a boy said.

"There's got to be a way," T. said. "We couldn't have got thus far . . ."

"We've done a lot," Blackie said.

"No. No, we haven't. Somebody watch the front."

"We can't do any more."

"He may come in at the back."

"Watch the back too." T. began to plead. "Just give me a minute and I'll fix it. I swear I'll fix it." But his authority had gone with his ambiguity. He was only one of the gang. "Please," he said.

"Please," Summers mimicked him, and then suddenly struck home with the fatal name. "Run along home, Trevor."

T. stood with his back to the rubble like a boxer knocked groggy against the ropes. He had no words as his dreams shook and slid. Then Blackie acted before the gang had time to laugh, pushing Summers backward. "I'll watch the front, T.," he said, and cautiously he opened the shutters of the hall. The gray wet common stretched ahead, and the lamps gleamed in the puddles. "Someone's coming, T. No, it's not him. What's your plan, T.?"

"Tell Mike to go out to the loo and hide close beside it. When he hears me whistle he's got to count ten and start to shout."

"Shout what?"

"Oh, 'Help,' anything."

"You hear, Mike," Blackie said. He was the leader again. He took a quick look between the shutters. "He's coming, T."

"Quick, Mike. The loo. Stay here, Blackie, all of you till I yell."

"Where are you going, T.?"

"Don't worry. I'll see to this. I said I would, didn't I?" **O**

Old Misery came limping off the common. He had mud on his shoes and he stopped to scrape them on the pavement's edge. He didn't want to soil his house, which stood jagged and dark between the bomb sites, saved so narrowly, as he believed, from destruction. Even the fanlight had been left unbroken by the bomb's blast. Somewhere somebody whistled. Old Misery looked sharply round. He didn't trust whistles. A child was shouting: It seemed to come from his own garden. Then a boy ran into the road from the car-park. "Mr. Thomas," he called, "Mr. Thomas."

"What is it?"

"I'm terribly sorry, Mr. Thomas. One of us got taken short, and we thought you wouldn't mind, and now he can't get out."

"What do you mean, boy?"

"He's got stuck in your loo."

"He'd no business—Haven't I seen you before?"

"You showed me your house."

"So I did. So I did. That doesn't give you the right to—"

"Do hurry, Mr. Thomas. He'll suffocate."

"Nonsense. He can't suffocate. Wait till I put my bag in."

"I'll carry your bag."

"Oh, no, you don't. I carry my own."

"This way, Mr. Thomas."

"I can't get in the garden that way. I've got to go through the house."

"But you *can* get in the garden this way, Mr. Thomas. We often do."

"You often do?" He followed the boy with a scandalized fascination. "When? What right . . ."

"Do you see . . . ? The wall's low."

"I'm not going to climb walls into my own garden. It's absurd." **P**

"This is how we do it. One foot here, one foot there, and over." The boy's face peered down, an arm shot out, and Mr. Thomas found his bag taken and deposited on the other side of the wall.

"Give me back my bag," Mr. Thomas said. From the loo a boy yelled and yelled. "I'll call the police."

N **Literary Focus** Setting What do you think the house represents to T.? Why is it important to him that it is utterly destroyed?

O **Reading Focus** Drawing Inferences About Characters' Motivations What do T.'s responses in this stressful situation reveal about his motivation?

P **Literary Focus** Setting What details of the setting are emphasized here? What is the significance of these details?

"Your bag's all right, Mr. Thomas. Look. One foot there. On your right. Now just above. To your left." Mr. Thomas climbed over his own garden wall. "Here's your bag, Mr. Thomas."

"I'll have the wall built up," Mr. Thomas said. "I'll not have you boys coming over here, using my loo." He stumbled on the path, but the boy caught his elbow and supported him. "Thank you, thank you, my boy," he murmured automatically. Somebody shouted again through the dark. "I'm coming, I'm coming," Mr. Thomas called. He said to the boy beside him, "I'm not unreasonable. Been a boy myself. As long as things are done regular. I don't mind you playing round the place Saturday mornings. Sometimes I like company. Only it's got to be regular. One of you asks leave and I say Yes. Sometimes I'll say No. Won't feel like it. And you come in at the front door and out at the back. No garden walls." **Q**

"Do get him out, Mr. Thomas."

"He won't come to any harm in my loo," Mr. Thomas said, stumbling slowly down the garden. "Oh, my rheumatics,"[24] he said. "Always get 'em on Bank Holiday. I've got to go careful. There's loose stones here. Give me your hand. Do you know what my horoscope said yesterday? 'Abstain from any dealings in first half of week. Danger of serious crash.' That might be on this path," Mr. Thomas said. "They speak in parables and double meanings." He paused at the door of the loo. "What's the matter in there?" he called. There was no reply.

"Perhaps he's fainted," the boy said.

"Not in my loo. Here, you, come out," Mr. Thomas said, and giving a great jerk at the door he nearly fell on his back when it swung easily open. A hand first supported him and then pushed him hard. His head hit the opposite wall and he sat heavily down. His bag hit his feet. A hand whipped the key out of the lock and the door slammed. "Let me out," he called, and heard the key turn in the lock. "A serious crash," he thought, and felt dithery and confused and old.

---

24. **rheumatics:** type of severe arthritis.

A voice spoke to him softly through the star-shaped hole in the door. "Don't worry, Mr. Thomas," it said, "we won't hurt you, not if you stay quiet."

Mr. Thomas put his head between his hands and pondered. He had noticed that there was only one lorry in the car-park, and he felt certain that the driver would not come for it before the morning. Nobody could hear him from the road in front, and the lane at the back was seldom used. Anyone who passed there would be hurrying home and would not pause for what they would certainly take to be drunken cries. And if he did call "Help," who, on a lonely Bank Holiday evening, would have the courage to investigate? Mr. Thomas sat on the loo and pondered with the wisdom of age. **R**

After a while it seemed to him that there were sounds in the silence—they were faint and came from the direction of his house. He stood up and peered through the ventilation-hole—between the cracks in one of the shutters he saw a light, not the light of a lamp, but the wavering light that a candle might give. Then he thought he heard the sound of hammering and scraping and chipping. He thought of burglars—perhaps they had employed the boy as a scout, but why should burglars engage in what sounded more and more like a stealthy form of carpentry? Mr. Thomas let out an experimental yell, but nobody answered. The noise could not even have reached his enemies.

4

Mike had gone home to bed, but the rest stayed. The question of leadership no longer concerned the gang. With nails, chisels, screwdrivers, anything that was sharp and penetrating they moved around the inner walls worrying at the mortar between the bricks. They started too high, and it was Blackie who hit on the damp course[25] and realized the work could be halved if they weakened the joints immediately above. It was a

---

25. **damp course:** layer of waterproof material placed between two layers of brick in a house's foundation to keep moisture from rising up through the walls.

Q Reading Focus **Drawing Inferences About Characters' Motivations** What do these comments suggest about Mr. Thomas?

R Literary Focus **Setting** What message do you think is conveyed by the setting of this scene?

Vocabulary **abstain** (ab STAYN) *v.*: refrain.
stealthy (STEHL thee) *adj.*: secret; sly.

long, tiring, unamusing job, but at last it was finished. The gutted house stood there balanced on a few inches of mortar between the damp course and the bricks.

There remained the most dangerous task of all, out in the open at the edge of the bomb site. Summers was sent to watch the road for passers by, and Mr. Thomas, sitting on the loo, heard clearly now the sound of sawing. It no longer came from his house, and that a little reassured him. He felt less concerned. Perhaps the other noises too had no significance.

A voice spoke to him through the hole. "Mr. Thomas."

"Let me out," Mr. Thomas said sternly.

"Here's a blanket," the voice said, and a long gray sausage was worked through the hole and fell in swathes over Mr. Thomas's head.

"There's nothing personal," the voice said. "We want you to be comfortable tonight."

"Tonight," Mr. Thomas repeated incredulously.

"Catch," the voice said. "Penny buns—we've buttered them, and sausage-rolls. We don't want you to starve, Mr. Thomas." **(S)**

Mr. Thomas pleaded desperately. "A joke's a joke, boy. Let me out and I won't say a thing. I've got rheumatics. I got to sleep comfortable."

"You wouldn't be comfortable, not in your house, you wouldn't. Not now."

"What do you mean, boy?" but the footsteps receded. There was only the silence of night: no sound of sawing. Mr. Thomas tried one more yell, but he was daunted and rebuked by the silence—a long way off an owl hooted and made away again on its muffled flight through the soundless world.

At seven next morning the driver came to fetch his lorry. He climbed into the seat and tried to start the engine. He was vaguely aware of a voice shouting, but it didn't concern him. At last the engine responded and he backed the lorry until it touched the great wooden shore[26] that supported Mr. Thomas's house.

---

26. **shore:** beam.

That way he could drive right out and down the street without reversing. The lorry moved forward, was momentarily checked as though something were pulling it from behind, and then went on to the sound of a long rumbling crash. The driver was astonished to see bricks bouncing ahead of him, while stones hit the roof of his cab. He put on his brakes. When he climbed out the whole landscape had suddenly altered. There was no house beside the car-park, only a hill of rubble. He went round and examined the back of his car for damage, and found a rope tied there that was still twisted at the other end round part of a wooden strut. **(T)**

The driver again became aware of somebody shouting. It came from the wooden erection which was the nearest thing to a house in that desolation of broken brick. The driver climbed the smashed wall and unlocked the door. Mr. Thomas came out of the loo. He was wearing a gray blanket to which flakes of pastry adhered. He gave a sobbing cry. "My house," he said. "Where's my house?"

"Search me," the driver said. His eye lit on the remains of a bath and what had once been a dresser and he began to laugh. There wasn't anything left anywhere.

"How dare you laugh," Mr. Thomas said. "It was my house. My house."

"I'm sorry," the driver said, making heroic efforts, but when he remembered the sudden check to his lorry, the crash of bricks falling, he became convulsed again. One moment the house had stood there with such dignity between the bomb sites like a man in a top hat, and then, bang, crash, there wasn't anything left—not anything. He said, "I'm sorry. I can't help it, Mr. Thomas. There's nothing personal, but you got to admit it's funny."

(S) Reading Focus Drawing Inferences About Characters' Motivations Why do you think the boys give Mr. Thomas a blanket and some buns?

(T) Literary Focus Setting How might the phrase "the whole landscape had suddenly altered" describe many countries following World War II?

Applying Your Skills

The Destructors

Respond and Think Critically

Reading Focus

Quick Check

1. The gang's hierarchy, or leadership structure, is important at the beginning of the story. Why do you think the gang is no longer concerned with who is the leader as they destroy the house?

2. How does the destruction of the house deviate from the gang's normal activities?

Read with a Purpose

3. How could tearing down Mr. Thomas's house be seen as an expression of T.'s feelings of loss?

Reading Skills: Drawing Inferences About Characters' Motivations

4. Using the clues you collected for your spider map, draw inferences about the motivations of T., the other gang members, Mr. Thomas, and the lorry driver.

✓ Vocabulary Check

Match the Vocabulary words with their definitions.

5. altruistic   **a.** shameful

6. exploit   **b.** secret

7. abstain   **c.** daring act

8. daunted   **d.** intimidated

9. stealthy   **e.** unselfish

10. ignoble   **f.** changeableness

11. fickleness   **g.** high excitement

12. exhilaration   **h.** refrain

Literary Focus

Literary Analysis

13. Analyze A gang is a social group with a shared set of values. What are this gang's values, and where do you think they come from?

14. Interpret How would you explain T.'s response when Blackie asks if he hates Mr. Thomas? In what sense does T.'s response reveal what might happen even to children in the aftermath of war?

15. Extend Images of emptiness and internal rot appear throughout the story. Identify these images and explain how they apply to the house, to Wormsley Common, and to the characters.

Literary Skills: Setting

16. Evaluate Describe the setting of the Wormsley Common carpark and its surroundings. How does it add to the story's emotional atmosphere?

Literary Skills Review: Theme

17. Interpret A story's **theme** is the general message that it conveys. Consider the comparison the lorry driver makes between the house and a "top hat". How does this relate to the theme?

Writing Focus

Think as a Reader/Writer

Use It in Your Writing Using Greene's dialogue as a model, write a short conversation between two people that reveals important information about their personalities.

What Do You Think Now

Why do you think the young boys in this story were so eager to belong to a group?

Shooting an Elephant

What Do You Think?

How does experience shape our view of the world?

QuickWrite

What compels people to act against their better judgment? How might outside pressures affect people's decision-making? Record some thoughts in your *Reader/Writer Notebook*.

A British soldier serving in India (1912).

MEET THE WRITER

George Orwell
(1903–1950)

George Orwell is famous for his novels that depict a frightening vision of a totalitarian future. He wrote, "Every line of serious work that I have written since 1936 has been written, directly or indirectly, *against* totalitarianism and *for* democratic socialism."

Child Writer

George Orwell was born Eric Blair in Bengal, India, where his British father was a member of the Indian civil service. A few years later, his family returned to England. A lonely child, Orwell spent much time making up stories and poems. He later wrote that from an early age he knew he was going to be a writer.

After graduating from Eton College, a prep school, Orwell joined the Indian Imperial Police, serving in Burma (now Myanmar) from 1922 to 1927, when he resigned to devote more time to writing. Returning to Europe, he took part-time, ill-paying jobs in France and England. His first book, *Down and Out in Paris and London* (1933), is based on those experiences. He based his next novel, *Burmese Days* (1934), on his life in Burma.

Fighter of Fascism

Writing under his own name as a journalist, Orwell used the pseudonym George Orwell for his books. After publishing three novels, he wrote about conditions among English industrial workers for the socialist Left Book Club. *The Road to Wigan Pier* (1937) is a moving portrait of the lives of the working class.

Deeply disturbed by the rise of fascism in the 1930s, Orwell fought against the Nationalists (fascists) in the Spanish Civil War and published a book based on these experiences—*Homage to Catalonia* (1938). His most famous novels, *Animal Farm* (1945) and *1984* (1949), exhibit his dedication to political freedom. *Animal Farm* is a political allegory that reveals the dangers of totalitarianism. And *1984* has given us an entire vocabulary for the excesses of totalitarian regimes, including the terms *newspeak* and *Big Brother*. In *1984*, Orwell stresses the connections between language, thought, and power and shows how corrupt language can promote political oppression.

Think About the Writer

How might Orwell's own experiences working at low-paying jobs have affected his political views?

Reader/Writer Notebook

Use your **RWN** to complete the activities for this selection.

Literary Focus

Irony A discrepancy between expectation and reality or between appearance and reality is called **irony.** Irony is the dominant literary mode in the twentieth century. Orwell employs several strategies to create irony. He uses **verbal irony,** saying one thing and meaning something else (often just the opposite), and **situational irony,** in which something happens that is different from what is expected or appropriate.

Reading Focus

Identifying the Author's Purpose The purpose of an **informal essay,** such as this one by Orwell, is often to express the personality and opinions of its author. In the essay's first sentence, Orwell admits that he was "hated by large numbers of people" in Burma because he represented British tyranny. This hatred controlled and at times even tyrannized Orwell himself. This ironic situation was not Orwell's alone; it was shared by most colonists. The ironies Orwell points out, as well as other details, can help you **identify the author's purpose.**

Into Action Make a chart like the one below. In one column, list details describing Orwell's personal dilemma in the essay, and in the second, list details describing the cultural dilemma presented by colonialism. Think about how these dilemmas relate to his purpose for writing.

Orwell's Personal Dilemma	Colonialism's Cultural Dilemma
He's "in charge" but feels pressured by the group.	

Writing Focus

Think as a Reader/Writer

Find It in Your Reading When describing events from their past, writers often remark on their motivations at the time. In your *Reader/Writer Notebook,* note when Orwell shifts from storytelling to commenting on his own thoughts and actions. How does this technique help him reveal **situational irony?** What clarity about the situation does he have from the vantage point of the future?

TechFocus As you read, think about how Orwell shares his personal experience. What experience would you like to share in a digital story?

Vocabulary

perplexing (puhr PLEHK sihng) *v.* used as *adj.:* confusing. *Because he secretly supported the Burmese, Orwell found their hatred of him perplexing.*

wretched (REHCH ihd) *adj.:* miserable; deprived. *The convicts were wretched in their filthy prisons.*

supplant (suh PLANT) *v.:* replace; displace. *Young Orwell did not realize that one Empire could just as easily supplant another.*

squalid (SKWAHL ihd) *adj.:* foul; dirty. *Many villagers lived in squalid conditions that caused disease and unhappiness.*

unendurable (uhn ehn DOOR uh buhl) *adj.:* more than can be tolerated. *To be squashed by an elephant would be unendurable.*

innumerable (ih NOO muhr uh buhl) *adj.:* too many to count. *Orwell was overwhelmed by the innumerable crowd following him through the streets.*

pretext (PREE tehkst) *n.:* excuse. *The British used the law as a pretext for both subtle and overt forms of racism.*

Language Coach

Negative Prefixes Adding the prefixes *–in* and *–un* to the beginning of a word often produces a word with the opposite meaning. For example, *unendurable* means "not able to be tolerated or endured." What other Vocabulary word uses the prefix *–in* or *–un?* How does the prefix help you understand the meaning of the word?

Learn It Online

Learn more about Orwell at the Writers' Lives site.

 go.hrw.com   L12-1141   **Go**

Shooting an Elephant

by **George Orwell**

Read with a Purpose
Read this essay to discover how a British police officer in a British colony deals with overwhelming pressure to act against his conscience.

Build Background
This essay is set in Burma, a southeast Asian country conquered by the British in the 1800s. As a British police officer in Burma in the 1920s, George Orwell did not just symbolize foreign rule—he was its agent. His awareness of being an enemy in another culture kindled enormous conflicts within him. Though given some self-rule in 1937, Burma didn't become fully independent until 1948, after a harsh period of Japanese occupation during World War II. In 1989, the government changed the country's official name to the Union of Myanmar, the country's Burmese name since the 13th century.

A British soldier serving in India (1912).

n Moulmein, in Lower Burma, I was hated by large numbers of people—the only time in my life that I have been important enough for this to happen to me. I was subdivisional police officer of the town, and in an aimless, petty kind of way anti-European feeling was very bitter. No one had the guts to raise a riot, but if a European woman went through the bazaars alone somebody would probably spit betel juice over her dress. As a police officer I was an obvious target and was baited whenever it seemed safe to do so. When a nimble Burman tripped me up on the football field and the referee (another Burman) looked the other way, the crowd yelled with hideous laughter. This happened more than once. In the end the sneering yellow faces of young men that met me everywhere, the insults hooted after me when I was at a safe distance, got badly on my nerves. The young Buddhist priests were the worst of all. There were several thousands of them in the town and none of them seemed to have anything to do except stand on street corners and jeer at Europeans. **Ⓐ**

All this was perplexing and upsetting. For at that time I had already made up my mind that imperialism was an evil thing and the sooner I chucked up my job and got out of it the better. Theoretically—and secretly, of course—I was all for the Burmese and all against their oppressors, the British. As for the job I was doing, I hated it more bitterly than I can perhaps make clear. In a job like that you see the dirty work of Empire at close quarters. The wretched prisoners huddling in the stinking cages of the lockups, the gray, cowed faces of the long-term convicts, the scarred buttocks of the men who had been flogged with bamboos—all these oppressed me with an intolerable sense of guilt. But I could get nothing into perspective. I was young and ill-educated and I had had to think out my problems in the utter silence that is imposed on every Englishman in the East. I did not even know that the British Empire is dying, still less did I know that it is a great deal better than the younger empires that are going to supplant it. All I knew was that I was stuck

between my hatred of the empire I served and my rage against the evil-spirited little beasts who tried to make my job impossible. With one part of my mind I thought of the British Raj[1] as an unbreakable tyranny, as something clamped down, *in saecula saeculorum,*[2] upon the will of prostrate peoples; with another part I thought that the greatest joy in the world would be to drive a bayonet into a Buddhist priest's guts. Feelings like these are the normal by-products of imperialism; ask any Anglo-Indian official, if you can catch him off duty. **Ⓑ**

One day something happened which in a round-about way was enlightening. It was a tiny incident in itself, but it gave me a better glimpse than I had had before of the real nature of imperialism—the real motives for which despotic governments act. Early one morning the subinspector at a police station the other end of the town rang me up on the phone and said that an elephant was ravaging the bazaar. Would I please come and do something about it? I did not know what I could do, but I wanted to see what was happening and I got on to a pony and started out. I took my rifle, an old .44 Winchester and much too small to kill an elephant, but I thought the noise might be useful *in terrorem.*[3] Various Burmans stopped me on the way and told me about the elephant's doings. It was not, of course, a wild elephant, but a tame one which had gone "must."[4] It had been chained up, as tame elephants always are when their attack of "must" is due, but on the previous night it had broken its

---

1. **Raj** (rahj): rule over India. The word is derived from *rajya*, Hindi for "kingdom."
2. *in saecula saeculorum* (ihn SEE koo luh SEE koo LAWR uhm): Latin for "forever and ever" (literally, "into ages of ages").
3. *in terrorem* (ihn tehr AWR uhm): Latin for "for terror." In other words, the gun might serve to frighten the elephant.
4. **must:** state of frenzy in animals. The word comes from *mast,* Hindi for "intoxicated."

Ⓐ Literary Focus Irony How is the first sentence of the essay an example of situational irony?

Ⓑ Literary Focus Irony What is ironic about the statement that begins, "All I knew was that I was stuck . . ."?

Vocabulary **perplexing** (puhr PLEHK sihng) *v.* used as *adj.:* confusing.
wretched (REHCH ihd) *adj.:* miserable; deprived.
supplant (suh PLANT) *v.:* replace; displace.

chain and escaped. Its mahout,[5] the only person who could manage it when it was in that state, had set out in pursuit, but had taken the wrong direction and was now twelve hours' journey away, and in the morning the elephant had suddenly reappeared in the town. The Burmese population had no weapons and were quite helpless against it. It had already destroyed somebody's bamboo hut, killed a cow, and raided some fruit stalls and devoured the stock; also it had met the municipal rubbish van and, when the driver jumped out and took to his heels, had turned the van over and inflicted violences upon it. **C**

The Burmese subinspector and some Indian constables were waiting for me in the quarter where the elephant had been seen. It was a very poor quarter, a labyrinth of squalid bamboo huts, thatched with palm leaf, winding all over a steep hillside. I remember that it was a cloudy, stuffy morning at the beginning of the rains. We began questioning the people as to where the elephant had gone and, as usual, failed to get any definite information. That is invariably the case in the East; a story always sounds clear enough at a distance, but the nearer you get to the scene of events the vaguer it becomes. Some of the people said that the elephant had gone in one direction, some said that he had gone in another, some professed not even to have heard of any elephant. I had almost made up my mind that the whole story was a pack of lies, when we heard yells a little distance away. There was a loud, scandalized cry of "Go away, child! Go away this instant!" and an old woman with a switch in her hand came round the corner of the hut, violently shooing away a crowd of naked children. Some more women followed, clicking their tongues and exclaiming; evidently there was something that the children ought not to have seen. I

rounded the hut and saw a man's dead body sprawling in the mud. He was an Indian, a black Dravidian coolie,[6] almost naked, and he could not have been dead many minutes. The people said that the elephant had come suddenly upon him round the corner of the hut, caught him with its trunk, put its foot on his back, and ground him into the earth. This was the rainy season and the ground was soft, and his face had scored a trench a foot deep and a couple of yards long. He was lying on his belly with arms crucified and head sharply twisted to one side. His face was coated with mud, the eyes wide open, the teeth bared and grinning with an expression of unendurable agony. (Never tell me, by the way, that the dead look peaceful. Most of the corpses I have seen looked devilish.) The friction of the great beast's foot had stripped the skin from his back as neatly as one skins a rabbit. As soon as I saw the dead man I sent an orderly to a friend's house nearby to borrow an elephant rifle. I had already sent back the pony, not wanting it to go mad with fright and throw me if it smelled the elephant. **D**

The orderly came back in a few minutes with a rifle and five cartridges, and meanwhile some Burmans had arrived and told us that the elephant was in the paddy fields below, only a few hundred yards away. As I started forward practically the whole population of the quarter flocked out of the houses and followed me. They had seen the rifle and were all shouting excitedly that I was going to shoot the elephant. They had not shown much interest in the elephant when he was merely ravaging their homes, but it was different now that he was going to be shot. It was a bit of fun to them, as it would be to an English crowd;

---

5. **mahout** (muh HOWT): elephant keeper. The word derives from *mahaut,* Hindi for "great in measure" and, thus, "important officer."

6. **Dravidian coolie:** *Dravidian* denotes any of several intermixed races living chiefly in southern India and northern Sri Lanka. A coolie is an unskilled laborer. The word is derived from *quli,* Hindi for "hired servant," and is considered offensive.

C Reading Focus **Identifying the Author's Purpose** What do you learn about the setting in this paragraph? What do you think is Orwell's purpose in describing this setting?

D Reading Focus **Identifying the Author's Purpose** How does Orwell's description of the dead man make you feel? What purpose might such a description serve?

Vocabulary **squalid** (SKWAHL ihd) *adj.*: foul; dirty. **unendurable** (uhn ehn DOOR uh buhl) *adj.*: more than can be tolerated.

besides they wanted the meat. It made me vaguely uneasy. I had no intention of shooting the elephant—I had merely sent for the rifle to defend myself if necessary—and it is always unnerving to have a crowd following you. I marched down the hill, looking and feeling a fool, with the rifle over my shoulder and an ever-growing army of people jostling at my heels. At the bottom, when you got away from the huts, there was a metaled[7] road and beyond that a miry waste of paddy fields a thousand yards across, not yet plowed but soggy from the first rains and dotted with coarse grass. The elephant was standing eight yards from the road, his left side toward us. He took not the slightest notice of the crowd's approach. He was tearing up bunches of grass, beating them against his knees to clean them, and stuffing them into his mouth. **Ⓔ**

I had halted on the road. As soon as I saw the elephant I knew with perfect certainty that I ought not to shoot him. It is a serious matter to shoot a working elephant—it is comparable to destroying a huge and costly piece of machinery—and obviously one ought not to do it if it can possibly be avoided. And at that distance, peacefully eating, the elephant looked no more dangerous than a cow. I thought then and I think now that his attack of "must" was already passing off; in which case he would merely wander harmlessly about until the mahout came back and caught him. Moreover, I did not in the least want to shoot him. I decided that I would watch him for a little while to make sure that he did not turn savage again, and then go home.

But at that moment I glanced round at the crowd that had followed me. It was an immense crowd, two thousand at the least and growing every minute. It blocked the road for a long distance on either side. I looked at the sea of yellow faces above the garish clothes—faces all happy and excited over this bit of fun, all certain that the elephant was going to be shot. They were watching me as they would watch a conjurer about to perform a trick. They did not like me, but with the magical rifle in my hands I was momen-

---

7. **metaled:** paved with cinders, stones, or the like.

Ⓔ **Literary Focus** **Irony** What is the situational irony in the march of British police officer "down [a] hill, looking and feeling a fool"?

Myanmar

Workers transplanting rice fields in Mandalay, Myanmar.

The British already had colonized India when they set their sights on Burma, first gaining control of the coastline and then moving inland. In addition to harvesting the valuable teak from Burma's forests, the British also planned to extract rubies and oil. While Burma did not, as the British had hoped, contain an easy trade route to China, the opening of the Suez Canal did create a demand for rice that led to the expansion of rice farming in the Irrawaddy delta.

Burma gained full independence in 1948, and in 1989, the government changed the country's name to Myanmar (the U.S., however, only recognizes the name Burma). Although the British exhausted the ruby mines, Myanmar is still the world's primary source of teak. Rice remains a key export while oil is extracted only for domestic consumption. The subtropical and tropical forests covering half the country are home to various birds and other wildlife like monkeys, leopards, tigers, and cobras. Elephants are plentiful and still used for labor, but the rhinoceros and the wild buffalo are protected species.

Ask Yourself

What details about Britain's interest in Burma's geography explain why the Burmese people resented the British?

tarily worth watching. And suddenly I realized that I should have to shoot the elephant after all. The people expected it of me and I had got to do it; I could feel their two thousand wills pressing me forward, irresistibly. And it was at this moment, as I stood there with the rifle in my hands, that I first grasped the hollowness, the futility of the white man's dominion in the East. Here was I, the white man with his gun, standing in front of the unarmed native crowd—seemingly the leading actor of the piece; but in reality I was only an absurd puppet pushed to and fro by the will of those yellow faces behind. I perceived in this moment that when the white man turns tyrant it is his own freedom that he destroys. He becomes a sort of hollow, posing dummy, the conventionalized figure of a sahib.[8] For it is the condition of his rule that he shall spend his life in trying to impress the "natives," and so in every crisis he has got to do what the "natives" expect of him. He wears a mask, and his face grows to fit it. I had got to shoot the elephant. I had committed myself to doing it when I sent for the rifle. A sahib has got to act like a sahib; he has got to appear resolute, to know his own mind and do definite things. To come all that way, rifle in hand, with two thousand people marching at my heels, and then to trail feebly away, having done nothing—no, that was impossible. The crowd would laugh at me. And my whole life, every white man's life in the East, was one long struggle not to be laughed at.   **F**   **G**

But I did not want to shoot the elephant. I watched him beating his bunch of grass against his knees, with that preoccupied grandmotherly air that elephants have. It seemed to me that it would be murder to shoot him. At that age I was not squeamish about killing animals, but I had never shot an elephant

---

8. **sahib** (SAH ihb): master; sir. In colonial India the title was used as a sign of respect for a European gentleman.

and never wanted to. (Somehow it always seems worse to kill a *large* animal.) Besides, there was the beast's owner to be considered. Alive, the elephant was worth at least a hundred pounds; dead, he would only be worth the value of his tusks, five pounds, possibly. But I had got to act quickly. I turned to some experienced-looking Burmans who had been there when we arrived, and asked them how the elephant had been behaving. They all said the same thing: He took no notice of you if you left him alone, but he might charge if you went too close to him.

It was perfectly clear to me what I ought to do. I ought to walk up to within, say, twenty-five yards of the elephant and test his behavior. If he charged, I could shoot; if he took no notice of me, it would be safe to leave him until the mahout came back. But also I knew that I was going to do no such thing. I was a poor shot with a rifle and the ground was soft mud into which one would sink at every step. If the elephant charged and I missed him, I should have about as much chance as a toad under a steamroller. But even then I was not thinking particularly of my own skin, only of the watchful yellow faces behind. For at that moment, with the crowd watching me, I was not afraid in the ordinary sense, as I would have been if I had been alone. A white man mustn't be frightened in front of "natives"; and so, in general, he isn't frightened. The sole thought in my mind was that if anything went wrong those two thousand Burmans would see me pursued, caught, trampled on, and reduced to a grinning corpse like that Indian up the hill. And if that happened it was quite probable that some of them would laugh. That would never do. There was only one alternative. I shoved the cartridges into the magazine and lay down on the road to get a better aim.   **H**

The crowd grew very still, and a deep, low, happy sigh, as of people who see the theater curtain go up at last, breathed from innumerable throats. They were

---

F **Reading Focus** Identifying the Author's Purpose How is the comparison of the narrator to a puppet ironic? What does it reveal about the author's purpose?

G **Literary Focus** Irony What is ironic about the white man's "one long struggle" in the East?

H **Reading Focus** Identifying the Author's Purpose What comment about colonialism is Orwell making in this paragraph? How does this comment help reveal his purpose?

Vocabulary **innumerable** (ih NOO muhr uh buhl) *adj.:* too many to count.

going to have their bit of fun after all. The rifle was a beautiful German thing with cross-hair sights. I did not then know that in shooting an elephant one would shoot to cut an imaginary bar running from earhole to earhole. I ought, therefore, as the elephant was sideways on, to have aimed straight at his earhole; actually I aimed several inches in front of this, thinking the brain would be further forward. **(I)**

When I pulled the trigger I did not hear the bang or feel the kick—one never does when a shot goes home—but I heard the devilish roar of glee that went up from the crowd. In that instant, in too short a time, one would have thought, even for the bullet to get there, a mysterious, terrible change had come over the elephant. He neither stirred nor fell, but every line of his body had altered. He looked suddenly stricken, shrunken, immensely old, as though the frightful impact of the bullet had paralyzed him without knocking him down. At last, after what seemed a long time—it might have been five seconds, I dare say—he sagged flabbily to his knees. His mouth slobbered. An enormous senility seemed to have settled upon him. One could have imagined him thousands of years old. I fired again into the same spot. At the second shot he did not collapse but climbed with desperate slowness to his feet and stood weakly upright, with legs sagging and head drooping. I fired a third time. That was the shot that did for him. You could see the agony of it jolt his whole body and knock the last remnant of strength from his legs. But in falling he seemed for a moment to rise, for as his hind legs collapsed beneath him he seemed to tower upward like a huge rock toppling, his trunk reaching skyward like a tree. He trumpeted, for the first and only time. And then down he came, his belly toward me, with a crash that seemed to shake the ground even where I lay. **(J)**

I got up. The Burmans were already racing past me across the mud. It was obvious that the elephant would never rise again, but he was not dead. He was breathing very rhythmically with long rattling gasps, his great mound of a side painfully rising and falling.

His mouth was wide open—I could see far down into caverns of pale pink throat. I waited a long time for him to die, but his breathing did not weaken. Finally I fired my two remaining shots into the spot where I thought his heart must be. The thick blood welled out of him like red velvet, but still he did not die. His body did not even jerk when the shots hit him, the tortured breathing continued without a pause. He was dying, very slowly and in great agony, but in some world remote from me where not even a bullet could damage him further. I felt that I had got to put an end to that dreadful noise. It seemed dreadful to see the great beast lying there, powerless to move and yet powerless to die, and not even to be able to finish him. I sent back for my small rifle and poured shot after shot into his heart and down his throat. They seemed to make no impression. The tortured gasps continued as steadily as the ticking of a clock.

In the end I could not stand it any longer and went away. I heard later that it took him half an hour to die. Burmans were bringing dahs[9] and baskets even before I left, and I was told they had stripped his body almost to the bones by the afternoon.

Afterward, of course, there were endless discussions about the shooting of the elephant. The owner was furious, but he was only an Indian and could do nothing. Besides, legally I had done the right thing, for a mad elephant has to be killed, like a mad dog, if its owner fails to control it. Among the Europeans opinion was divided. The older men said I was right, the younger men said it was a damn shame to shoot an elephant for killing a coolie, because an elephant was worth more than any damn Coringhee[10] coolie. And afterward I was very glad that the coolie had been killed; it put me legally in the right and it gave me a sufficient pretext for shooting the elephant. I often wondered whether any of the others grasped that I had done it solely to avoid looking a fool. **(K)**

---

9. **dahs** (dahz): large carving knives.
10. **Coringhee** (kawr IHNG ee): port in southeastern India.

(I) Literary Focus Irony What is ironic about this detail of Orwell's situation?

(J) Reading Focus Identifying the Author's Purpose How do these details help Orwell achieve his purpose?

(K) Literary Focus Irony Why is Orwell glad the man died? How does the ending further Orwell's point?

Vocabulary pretext (PREE tehkst) *n.:* excuse.

Applying Your Skills

Shooting an Elephant

Respond and Think Critically

Reading Focus

Quick Check

1. What is Orwell's inner conflict, and how does he deal with it?

2. What clues in the essay suggest the outcome?

Read with a Purpose

3. Why does Orwell act against his better judgment? What role does imperialism play?

Reading Skills: Identifying the Author's Purpose

4. Add a column to the chart you made while reading. Explain the author's purpose for writing the essay. What opinions about himself and his situation compel him to write the essay?

Orwell's Personal Dilemma	Colonialism's Cultural Dilemma	Author's Purpose
He's "in charge" but feels pressured by the group.		

Literary Focus

Literary Analysis

5. Interpret What is Orwell's attitude toward the Burmese? Do his thoughts and actions embody the perspective of an imperialist?

6. Make Predictions Based on Orwell's commentary, do you think he would make the same choice to shoot the elephant if he had the chance to repeat the day? Why or why not?

7. Evaluate Orwell describes at length the shooting and the death of the elephant. Is the gruesome detail necessary? How does it add to or detract from the essay?

8. Extend What does this essay reveal about Orwell's code of ethics or behavior as a young police officer in Burma? What does it reveal about the true nature of colonialism? Are these insights related? Explain.

Literary Skills: Irony

9. Analyze Explain the meaning of Orwell's insight that tyrants destroy their own freedom, as well as the freedom of the people they oppress. Why is this insight an example of situational irony?

Literary Skills Review: Symbol

10. Analyze The elephant is an important **symbol,** a person, place, thing, or idea that stands both for itself and for something beyond itself. What political idea or assumption might the elephant symbolize? In other words, what political idea confronted, confused, and inevitably weakened Orwell? With supporting details from the text, explain the elephant's symbolic importance.

Writing Focus

Think as a Reader/Writer

Use It in Your Writing Using Orwell's essay as a guide, write a short narrative essay about when you or someone you know experienced inner conflict and had to make an important decision. Intersperse your narrative with commentary, looking back on the event from your current perspective. What do you see about the incident now that you couldn't see then?

 What Do **You Think Now**

How does a fear of appearing foolish paralyze the British colonialists? Do you think this fear often causes people to make bad decisions? Why or why not?

Vocabulary Development

Vocabulary Check

Match the Vocabulary words with their definitions.

1. supplant
2. pretext
3. perplexing
4. unendurable
5. squalid
6. innumerable
7. wretched

a. confusing
b. foul or unclean
c. too many to be counted
d. miserable
e. more than one can tolerate
f. replace
g. excuse

Vocabulary Skills: Connotations

Connotations are the ideas and feelings associated with a word that go beyond its dictionary definition. Authors carefully choose words with certain connotations that will evoke the intended response in their readers. Orwell may have chosen to use *peacefully,* as opposed to *calmly,* to describe the elephant's eating, because *peacefully* more strongly suggests the elephant is no longer dangerous.

Your Turn

Answer these questions about connotation.

1. When Orwell says that "the crowd yelled with hideous laughter," why is *hideous* an unusual word to use? What emotional response does the word evoke in you?

2. Orwell uses *agony* to describe both the death of the Indian and the death of the elephant. What does *agony* suggest that *intense pain* does not?

Language Coach

Negative Prefixes Add the prefix *–un* or *–in* to the following words to reverse the meanings. Use a dictionary if necessary.

1. breakable
2. variably
3. tolerable
4. healthy

CHOICES

As you respond to the Choices, use these **Academic Vocabulary** words as appropriate: <u>adapt</u>, <u>considerably</u>, <u>exhibit</u>, <u>inevitable</u>, <u>perspective</u>.

REVIEW
Discuss Irony

In a small group, discuss the passage in which the elephant comes into view. What is Orwell's first impression of the creature? What words does he use to describe the elephant? Then, discuss the irony in this situation. Given the elephant's demeanor, what is ironic about what ultimately happens to it?

CONNECT
Create a Blog

In addition to imperialism and its negative effects, Orwell's essay raises a number of important issues: racism and oppression, animal rights, societal pressures, and shame and its effects. Choose one of these issues, and write a short blog entry discussing your opinion. Use ideas from the essay, as well as from your own experience, to support your opinions.

EXTEND
Tell Your Own Story

TechFocus Choose an event from your life that has had a strong effect on you and create a digital story to share this event and its meaning to you with others. Include clips from home movies or scanned images, and choose music that suits the tone and message of the story. Finally, create a voice-over that uses tone to convey your message. Remember to include commentary that expresses your current <u>perspective</u> on the event.

 Learn It Online
Learn the steps of making a digital story online at the Digital Storytelling site.

go.hrw.com | L12-1149 | **Go**

JOSEPH CHAMBERLAIN

"I Believe in a British Empire"

JAWAHARLAL NEHRU

"The Noble Mansion of Free India"

What Do You Think?

How does experience shape our view of the world?

QuickWrite

Political opinions are shaped by many influences, including personal experience, family values, and individual interests. Briefly write about the influences that have shaped your political perspective.

Joseph Chamberlain (1896), by John Singer Sargent, oil on canvas. National Portrait Gallery, London.

Jawaharlal Nehru (1889–1964).

MEET THE WRITERS

Joseph Chamberlain
(1836–1914)

The son of a wealthy shoe manufacturer in London, Joseph Chamberlain began working at age 16 and used his shrewd business sense to make his fortune and retire by age 38. He began his political life as a radical liberal, supporting social reform such as free education and improved housing for the poor. He split with the Liberal party over Irish Home Rule and joined other dissident Liberals, called Liberal Unionists. Chamberlain eventually abandoned his radical perspective and turned toward imperialism. In 1895, he joined the Conservative Cabinet. He believed the British Empire should be self-reliant, looking to its own colonies—and not to foreign allies—for economic and military reinforcement. However, the tariffs he supported were unpopular with the British, who feared rising prices, and the Conservatives lost the next election. Although Chamberlain was reelected to parliament, he suffered a debilitating stroke in 1906 that ended his political career.

Jawaharlal Nehru
(1889–1964)

The son of a well-known lawyer, Nehru was educated by English and Indian tutors in India and then attended Harrow and Cambridge and studied law in England. After Nehru returned to India, his interest in gaining India's freedom from Britain led him to the great Indian leader Mohandas Gandhi, who believed that India's freedom could be attained through nonviolent resistance. Nehru joined the Indian Congress Party and worked for Indian independence from Great Britain for twenty-eight years before he saw it become a reality, in 1947. In that year, Nehru was elected the first prime minister of the newly independent nation.

Think About the Writers

How do these men's politics reflect the values and interests of their nations?

Reader/Writer Notebook

Use your **RWN** to complete the activities for this selection.

Informational Text Focus

Recognizing Political Assumptions When politicians like Chamberlain and Nehru deliver speeches, they often make **political assumptions,** or unsupported statements they believe to be true. While these assumptions are not necessarily false, they may be generalizations or statements that are difficult to prove, or they may be statements the speaker assumes the audience believes to be true. Both Chamberlain and Nehru make political assumptions in their speeches; Nehru, for example, claims that prosperity for India will benefit all countries. This statement is an assumption because Nehru believes it to be true but does not support it with evidence. As you analyze political speeches, **recognizing political assumptions** will help you identify the speaker's perspective on a subject and show you how the speaker uses unsupported claims to convince his or her audience to support a point of view.

Into Action As you read each speech, fill in a chart like the one below. Note each speaker's point of view regarding colonialism, and then note the political assumptions the speaker makes.

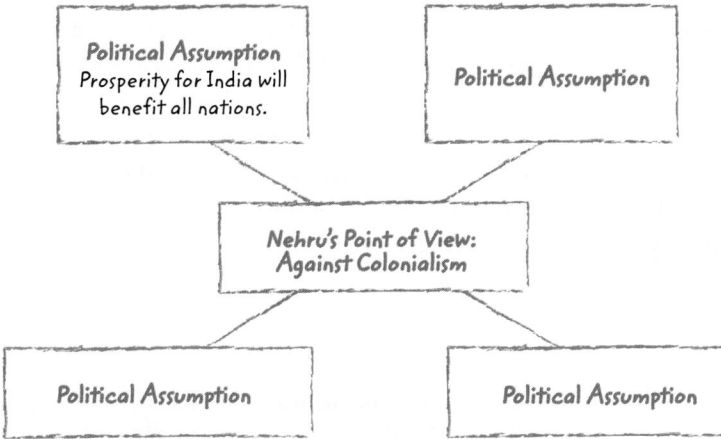

Writing Focus

Preparing for **Constructed Response**

Politicians and other persuasive writers and speakers use **loaded language**—words and phrases that have strong emotional overtones and that evoke strong emotional responses, either positive or negative. As you read the speeches by Chamberlain and Nehru, use your *Reader/ Writer Notebook* to record examples of loaded language.

Vocabulary

"I Believe in a British Empire"

obtained (uhb TAYND) *v.:* got; acquired. *Britain obtained many colonies, some by force and others peacefully.*

apathy (AP uh thee) *n.:* lack of interest. *The speaker accused his opponents of apathy.*

cultivate (KUHL tuh vayt) *v.:* develop; promote. *To prevent war, it is important to cultivate understanding between countries.*

prosperity (prahs PEHR uh tee) *n.:* wealth or good fortune. *Chamberlain believed colonialism would ensure British prosperity.*

"The Noble Mansion of Free India"

pledge (plehj) *n.:* promise or vow. *Nehru's pledge was to help India retain its glory.*

endured (ehn DOORD) *v.:* suffered, put up with. *He asserted that India had endured much hardship under British rule.*

incessant (ihn SEHS uhnt) *adj.:* constant; never ending. *Nehru claimed that India's good fortune would require incessant work.*

indivisible (ihn duh VIHZ uh buhl) *adj.:* unable to be divided or separated. *India's fortunes are indivisible from the fortunes of the rest of the world.*

Language Coach

Latin Word Origins The Latin word *dūrāre* means "to last or harden." Words derived from *dūrāre* include *duration,* "a period of time that something lasts" and *durable,* meaning "tough enough to last." Which Vocabulary word is related to these words?

 Learn It Online
Listen to these speeches online.

go.hrw.com | L12-1151 | **Go**

"I Believe in a British Empire"

by Joseph Chamberlain

Read with a Purpose

Read this speech to learn how Chamberlain supports his view that colonialism is in England's best interest.

Build Background

This speech, delivered in 1903, in Birmingham, England, was part of a Conservative party tariff-reform campaign.

Since many European countries viewed England as a bully for its aggression in the Boer War, Chamberlain believed England could not rely on European nations as allies. His speech exhibits tenets of both colonialism and isolationism, the belief that one's country should not have pacts and alliances with other nations. As he begins, Chamberlain refers to his political enemies, the Liberals who oppose tariff reform.

I cannot look forward without dread to handing over the security and existence of this great Empire to the hands of those who have made common cause with its enemies, who have charged their own countrymen with methods of barbarism,[1] and who apparently have been untouched by that pervading[2] sentiment which I found everywhere where the British flag floats, and which has done so much in recent years to draw us together. I should not require to go to South Africa in order to be convinced that this feeling has obtained deep hold on the minds and hearts of our children beyond the seas.[3] It has had a hard life of it, this feeling of Imperial patriotism. It was checked for a generation by the apathy and the indifference which were the characteristics of our former relations with our Colonies, but it was never extinguished. The embers were still alight, and when in the late war[4] this old country of ours showed that it was still possessed by the spirit of our ancestors, and that it was still prepared to count no sacrifice that was necessary in order to maintain the honor and the interests of the Empire, then you found a response from your children across the seas that astonished the whole world by a proof, an undeniable proof, of affection and regard. Ⓐ

---

1. **charged . . . barbarism:** Many British citizens were appalled by the brutal methods that were used to help win the Boer War.
2. **pervading:** spreading throughout.

3. **children beyond the seas:** the colonists—Canadians, Australians, New Zealanders, and even some black South Africans—who helped England fight and win the Boer War.
4. **the late war:** the Boer War (1899–1902) fought between Britain and the two Boer republics in South Africa. (Boers are South Africans of Dutch descent.)

Ⓐ **Informational Focus** Recognizing Political Assumptions What other reasons, besides "affection and regard," might colonies have had for fighting in the war? How is Chamberlain's statement an example of a political assumption?

Vocabulary **obtained** (uhb TAYND) *v.*: got; acquired.
apathy (AP uh thee) *n.*: lack of interest.

Is it to end there? Are we to sink back into the old policy of selfish isolation which went very far to dry and even to sap the loyalty of our colonial brethren? I do not think so. I think these larger issues touch the people of this country. I think they have awakened to the enormous importance of a

Politician Joseph Chamberlain holding loaves of bread at Bingley Hall.

creative time like the present, and of taking advantage of the opportunities offered in order to make permanent what has begun so well. Remember, we are a kingdom, an old country. We proceed here on settled lines. We have our quarrels and our disputes, and we pass legislation which may be good or bad; but we know that, whatever changes there may be, at all events the main stream will ultimately reach its appointed destination. That is the result of centuries of constitutional progress and freedom.

But the Empire is not old. The Empire is new—the Empire is in its infancy. Now is the time when we can mold that Empire and when we and those who live with us can decide its future destinies. Just let us consider what that Empire is; I am not going tonight to speak of those hundreds of millions of our Indian and native fellow subjects for whom we have become responsible. I consider for the moment only our relations to that white British population that constitutes the majority in the great self-governing colonies of the Empire. Here in the United Kingdom there are some forty millions of us. Outside there are ten millions of men either directly descended from ancestors who left this country or more probably men who themselves in their youth left this country in order to find their fortunes in our possessions abroad. How long do you suppose that this proportion of population is going to endure? The development of those colonies has been delayed by many reasons—but mainly probably by a more material reason—by the fact that the United States of America has offered a greater attraction to British emigration.

But that has changed. The United States, with all their vast territory, are filling up; and even now we hear of tens of thousands of emigrants leaving the United States in order to take up the fresh and rich lands of our colony in Canada. It seems to me not at all an impossible assumption that before the end of this present century we may find our fellow subjects beyond the seas as numerous as we are at home. I want you to look forward. I want you to consider the infinite importance of this not only to yourselves but to your descendants. Now is the time when you can exert influence. Do you wish that if these ten millions become forty millions they shall still be closely, intimately, affectionately united to you, or do you contemplate the possibility of their being separated, going off each in his own direction, under a separate flag? Think what it means to your power and influence as a country; think what it means to your position among the nations of the world; think what it means to your trade and commerce—I put that last. **B** **C**

What is the meaning of an Empire? What does it mean to us? We have had a little experience. We have had a war, a war in which the majority of our children abroad had no apparent direct interest. We had no hold over them of any kind, and yet at one time during this war, by the voluntary decision of these people, at least 50,000 Colonial soldiers were standing shoulder to shoulder with British troops, displaying a gallantry equal to their own and the keenest intelligence. It is something for a beginning, and if this country were in danger, I mean if we were, as our forefathers were, face to face some day—Heaven forfend[5]—with some great coalition of hostile nations, when we

had with our backs to the wall to struggle for our very lives, it is my firm conviction there is nothing within the power of these self-governing colonies they would not do to come to our aid. I believe their whole resources in men and in money would be at the disposal of the Mother Country in such an event. That is something—something which it is wonderful to have achieved, and which it is worth almost any sacrifice to maintain. . . . **D**

I believe in a British Empire, in an Empire which, though it should be its first duty to cultivate friendship with all the nations of the world, should yet, even if alone, be self-sustaining and self-sufficient, able to maintain itself against the competition of all its rivals. And I do not believe in a Little England which shall be separated from all those to whom it would in the natural course look for support and affection, a Little England which would then be dependent absolutely on the mercy of those who envy its present prosperity, and who have shown they are ready to do all in their power to prevent its future union with the British races throughout the world. **E**

---

5. **forfend:** prevent.

B **Informational Focus** Recognizing Political Assumptions How does Chamberlain justify and defend colonialism? How can you tell he assumes his listeners agree with him?

C **Informational Focus** Recognizing Political Assumptions What kind of relationship between Great Britain and the colonies does Chamberlain want to promote? What does he assume will be the result of this kind of relationship?

D **Informational Focus** Recognizing Political Assumptions What does Chamberlain assume the colonies would do if England were in danger and why does he think they would they do it? On what basis does he make this assumption?

E **Informational Focus** Recognizing Political Assumptions Why does Chamberlain "believe in a British Empire"? What assumption does he appear to make about the rest of the world?

Vocabulary **cultivate** (KUHL tuh vayt) *v.*: develop; promote.
prosperity (prahs PEHR uh tee) *n.*: wealth or good fortune.

"The Noble Mansion of Free India"

by Jawaharlal Nehru

Read with a Purpose

Read to find out what Nehru believes the Indian government owes its people and the world and how it can fulfill this responsibility.

Build Background

Jawaharlal Nehru was renowned for his efforts to establish a democratic government in India. He also sought to raise the standard of living for Indians, even while opposing alliances with powerful nations and adopting a policy of nonaggression. Nehru gave the following speech on the eve of Indian independence from Great Britain (August 14, 1947) to the members of the Indian Parliament.

Long years ago we made a tryst[1] with destiny, and now the time comes when we shall redeem our pledge, not wholly or in full measure, but very substantially. At the stroke of the midnight hour, when the world sleeps, India will awake to life and freedom. A moment comes, which comes but rarely in history, when we step out from the old to the new, when an age ends, and when the soul of a nation, long suppressed, finds utterance. It

1. **tryst:** rendezvous.

Vocabulary **pledge** (plehj) *n.:* promise or vow.

Indian Prime Minister Jawaharlal Nehru with his entourage at an airport in India.

is fitting that at this solemn moment we take the pledge of dedication to the service of India and her people and to the still larger cause of humanity.

At the dawn of history India started on her unending quest, and trackless centuries are filled with her striving and the grandeur of her success and her failures. Through good and ill fortune alike she has never lost sight of that quest or forgotten the ideals which gave her strength. We end today a period of ill fortune and India discovers herself again. The achievement we celebrate today is but a step, an opening of opportunity, to the greater triumphs and achievements that await us. Are we brave enough and wise enough to grasp this opportunity and accept the challenge of the future? **(A)**

Freedom and power bring responsibility. The responsibility rests upon this Assembly,[2] a sovereign body representing the sovereign people of India. Before the birth of freedom we have endured all the pains of labor and our hearts are heavy with the memory of this sorrow. Some of those pains continue even now. Nevertheless, the past is over and it is the future that beckons to us now.

That future is not one of ease or resting but of incessant striving so that we may fulfill the pledges we have so often taken and the one we shall take today. The service of India means the service of the millions who suffer. It means the ending of poverty and ignorance and disease and inequality of opportunity. The ambition of the greatest man of our generation[3] has been to wipe every tear from every eye. That may be beyond us, but as long as there are tears and suffering, so long our work will not be over. **(B)**

And so we have to labor and to work, and work hard, to give reality to our dreams. Those dreams are for India, but they are also for the world, for all the nations and peoples are too closely knit together today for any one of them to imagine that it can live apart. Peace has been said to be indivisible; so is freedom, so is prosperity now, and so also is disaster in this One World that can no longer be split into isolated fragments.

To the people of India, whose representatives we are, we make an appeal to join us with faith and confidence in this great adventure. This is no time for petty and destructive criticism, no time for ill will or blaming others. We have to build the noble mansion of free India where all her children may dwell. **(C)**

---

2. **Assembly:** Indian Parliament.
3. **greatest . . . generation:** Mohandas Gandhi.

(A) **Informational Focus** Recognizing Political Assumptions According to Nehru, how did colonialism affect India?

(B) **Informational Focus** Recognizing Political Assumptions What does "service" mean to Nehru? What assumption does he make about the role of government?

(C) **Informational Focus** Recognizing Political Assumptions What assumptions does Nehru make about the relationships among nations and peoples?

Vocabulary **endured** (ehn DOORD) *v.:* suffered, put up with. **incessant** (ihn SEHS uhnt) *adj.:* constant; never ending. **indivisible** (ihn duh VIHZ uh buhl) *adj.:* unable to be separated.

"I Believe in a British Empire"
"The Noble Mansion of Free India"

Respond and Think Critically

Informational Text Focus

Quick Check

1. In the opening sentence of his speech, how does Chamberlain establish his <u>perspective</u> on Britain's colonialism? Explain.

2. How does Nehru use a description of India's past to support his belief that "greater triumphs and achievements" are <u>inevitable</u>?

Read with a Purpose

3. Which speech is more convincing? Why?

Informational Skills: Recognizing Political Assumptions

4. Look over each chart you created as you read. Then, write a short discussion of **political assumptions** in the two speeches. What assumptions does each speaker make about the effects of colonialism? How would you describe each man's view of the role of government based on these assumptions?

Text Analysis

5. **Make Inferences** What kind of attitude toward British colonists does Chamberlain <u>exhibit</u> in the expression "our children beyond the seas?"

6. **Analyze** What group of people does Chamberlain consider when he says "The Empire"? How does he feel about the group he excludes?

7. **Evaluate** Identify some emotional appeals in Chamberlain's speech. Do you think these appeals add to or detract from his argument?

8. **Evaluate** Does Chamberlain believe one can be critical of the British Empire and still be patriotic? How can you tell?

9. **Analyze** What effect does Nehru create by personifying India? Explain.

10. **Interpret** How does the image of the "noble mansion" sum up Nehru's message?

11. **Analyze** How would you describe the tone of Nehru's speech? What historical context accounts for this tone?

12. **Extend** Which speaker's vision of the future of colonialism and the relationships among nations do you think is closer to being realized? Explain.

Listening and Speaking

13. **Extend** With a partner, examine the next to last paragraph in Nehru's speech. Discuss how peace, freedom, prosperity, and disaster might be described as indivisible in today's world.

Writing Focus   Constructed Response

In a brief essay, discuss Chamberlain and Nehru's use of loaded language in "I Believe in a British Empire" and "The Noble Mansion of Free India." Be sure to support your response with specific evidence from the speeches.

What Do
You
Think
Now   What experiences, values, and interests shaped the politics of Chamberlain and Nehru?

"I Believe in a British Empire"
"The Noble Mansion of Free India"

Vocabulary Development

✓ Vocabulary Check

Tell whether each Vocabulary word is paired with its synonym or an antonym.

1. **pledge**/promise
2. **indivisible**/inseparable
3. **obtained**/lost
4. **apathy**/interest
5. **incessant**/constant
6. **cultivate**/develop
7. **prosperity**/poverty
8. **endured**/suffered

Vocabulary Skills: The Etymology of Political Science and Historical Terms

New words and phrases are introduced into our vocabulary nearly every day. Many English political science and historical terms have been borrowed from other languages. Consider the following terms.

Term	Word Origin	Meaning
apartheid	Afrikaans, "the state of being separate," (Dutch *apart* "separate," from French *a part*, + Dutch –*heid*, "-hood")	official South African policy of strict racial segregation and discrimination (c. 1948–1991)
democracy	Greek *demokratia*, "rule by the people," (*demos*, "the people," + *kratein*, "to rule")	government in which all citizens take part and limit the power of rulers
imperialism	Latin *imperialis*, "empire," from *imperare*, "to command"	domination of a powerful nation over the political, economic, and cultural affairs of another nation or region

Your Turn

Use a dictionary to learn the history of the political science and historical terms listed below. Determine the language the word is borrowed from, its original meaning, and its current meaning.

Term	Word Origin	Meaning
coup d'état		
détente		
electorate		
fascist		
monarch		
parliament		
laissez-faire		
veto		

Language Coach

Latin Word Origins Find the Latin words from which the Vocabulary words *incessant* and *cultivate* originate. How does knowing each word's Latin origin help you understand the word's meaning? Find another word that comes from each Latin word and record its meaning.

Academic Vocabulary

Talk About
With a partner, discuss what you know about a significant conflict between groups in the world today. What characteristics does the conflict exhibit? What are the perspectives of the groups involved? How have people adapted to the problems created by the conflict? What are the inevitable effects of the conflict?

Virginia Woolf

What Do You Think

How does experience shape our view of the world?

 **QuickWrite**

What do you think contributes most to a person's success in life: opportunity, talent, confidence, or some other quality? Record your thoughts in your *Reader/ Writer Notebook.*

CONTENTS

from **A Room of One's Own**

from **Jacob's Room**

The Haunted House

from **The Letters of Virginia Woolf**

(Center) Garden at Virginia Woolf's country home of Monk's house. *(Bottom left)* Virginia Woolf with her niece Angelica Garnett (née Bell) in 1934. The Granger Collection, NY.

Virginia Woolf

(1882–1941)

Despite describing herself as "a born melancholic," Virginia Woolf was bright, passionate, and quick-witted. She battled periods of paralyzing self-doubt and severe depression and anxiety to become one of the twentieth-century's most innovative writers, conveying unlike any writer before her "an ordinary mind on an ordinary day."

From Privilege to Tragedy to Bloomsbury

Virginia Woolf was born in Victorian London to the scholar and literary critic Sir Leslie Stephen and his artistic wife, Julia. In her youth, Woolf enjoyed all the advantages of a financially comfortable and intellectually challenging environment. Too frail to attend school regularly, she was privately tutored and given the luxury of access to her father's extensive library. Her father encouraged her to read only what she liked.

When her mother died in 1895, Woolf experienced her first episode of severe depression. A few years later she suffered a series of tragedies with the death of her half sister in 1902 and her father in 1904.

After her father's death, Virginia, her sister, Vanessa, and their two brothers moved to the area of London known as Bloomsbury. Soon they and their friends began to meet in what came to be called the Bloomsbury Group, an intellectual circle whose other prominent members included the writer E. M. Forster, the artist Duncan Grant, and the economist John Maynard Keynes. An informal gathering with the highest cultural standards, the Bloomsbury Group helped provide the right environment for Virginia Woolf's sensitive, experimental fiction. One member of the group was Leonard Woolf, a journalist and economist. Although Virginia had considered in her journals the possibility that she might never choose to marry, she and Leonard Woolf wed in 1912.

Creativity and Despair

Leonard Woolf provided Virginia with encouragement and stability during her bouts of depression and through her difficult writing process, which was similar with every book she composed. She began with an inspiration, wrote for often more than a year with intermittent bouts of productivity and paralyzing writer's block, and then, after extensive revisions, worked with Leonard to prepare her books for production. She would end the process exhausted and often mentally unstable, but would <u>inevitably</u> find during this time the inspiration for her next work.

A Woolf Time Line

1895 Woolf's mother, Julia Stephen, dies

1904–1905 Moves to London; meets the members of the Bloomsbury group

1905–1907 English instructor at Morley College, London; writes reviews and feature articles for the *Times Literary Supplement*

1880 1890 1900

1882 Virginia Stephen is born to a wealthy family in London

1902 Woolf's half sister, Stella Duckworth, dies

1904 Woolf's father, Leslie Stephen, dies

1906 Woolf's beloved brother, Toby, dies

Virginia Woolf and Adrian Stephen playing cricket (c. 1886).

Virginia Woolf

Woolf had been writing since she was fourteen and reviewing books since her early twenties, but it was not until she was thirty-three, that her first novel, *The Voyage Out,* was published. The subsequent publication of *Jacob's Room* (1922) and *Mrs. Dalloway* (1925) established her position as one of the foremost writers of her time. With these novels—and with her later novels *To the Lighthouse* (1927) and *The Waves* (1931)—Woolf pursued an experimental vision that emphasizes personal impressions over external events and focuses on the experience of life as it is being lived.

Like James Joyce, Woolf employs the technique of stream of consciousness, although her version is somewhat different. For example, while *Mrs. Dalloway,* like Joyce's *Ulysses,* seeks to cover the entire lifetime of a character in the chronicle of a single day, the former work does so mainly by linking characters' thoughts of mundane, domestic tasks to related, more emotionally dense moments. Woolf was a great admirer of Joyce's *A Portrait of the Artist as a Young Man,* but she considered *Ulysses* an "illiterate, underbred book." Still, she worried that "what I am doing is probably being better done by Mr. Joyce." The novelist E. M. Forster, in writing about *Mrs. Dalloway,* disagreed with her concern, noting that "to convey the actual process of thinking is a creative feat, and I know of no one except Virginia Woolf who has accomplished it."

Woolf also wrote a great many reviews and essays, in which she explored the work of female writers, often focusing on a particular author whom she felt had been neglected. In 1917, she and her husband established the Hogarth Press, which published many of the most important male and female writers of the day.

A Tragic End

Woolf's depression, for which no medication was available at that time, deepened with the German bombing raids over England in World War II. In March of 1941, fearing she could not endure yet another bout of intense suffering, she wrote a note to Leonard expressing her love for him and then took her own life.

Think About the Writer — How might Woolf's fragile health have fueled her desire to write about the thoughts and feelings of her characters instead of about their actions?

Key Elements of Woolf's Writing

- Stream of consciousness, which follows the thoughts and feelings of characters
- Emphasis on impressions and ideas rather than on plot and action
- Experimentation with new techniques, such as conveying everyday events in elevated style

Learn It Online
Find out more about Virginia Woolf online.
go.hrw.com L12-1161 Go

Virginia Woolf with her husband Leonard Woolf in Cassis, on the French Riviera in (1928).

Nicole Kidman as Virginia Woolf in *The Hours* (2002).

1917 Establishes the Hogarth Press with Leonard Woolf

1927 Publishes *To the Lighthouse* (novel)

1931 Publishes *The Waves* (novel)

1937 Julian Bell, Woolf's beloved nephew, is killed in the Spanish Civil War

1910 **1920** **1930** **1940**

1912 Marries Leonard Woolf

1915 Publishes first novel, *The Voyage Out*

1925 Publishes *Mrs. Dalloway* (novel)

1928 Delivers feminist lectures at Cambridge University

1929 Publishes *A Room of One's Own* (essays)

1941 Dies in Sussex, England

Preparing to Read

from **A Room of One's Own**

Reader/Writer
Notebook
Use your **RWN** to complete the activities for this selection.

Literary Focus

Essay An **essay** is a short piece of nonfiction writing that explores a particular topic. Formal essays are usually impersonal in tone and tend to be highly organized and full of facts. An **informal essay** is highly subjective, usually dominated by the author's own personal <u>perspective</u> and beliefs. Although informal essays can be casual in tone, they often reveal deeply held principles and touch upon controversial aspects of society.

Literary Perspectives Apply the literary perspective described on page 1163 as you read this essay.

Reading Focus

Identifying the Author's Beliefs Note that at times Woolf states her beliefs directly, and at other times she only hints at them. To **identify the author's beliefs,** look for words such as "I think" and "I agree" that indicate an opinion. Also look for **loaded language,** language with strong emotional connotations, and for evidence that supports the author's beliefs.

Into Action Create a word web and identify four or five of Woolf's beliefs.

It was almost impossible for a woman to become a writer.

Women received disproportionate access to education.

Virginia Woolf believes that . . .

Writing Focus

Think as a Reader/Writer
Find It in Your Reading To show the effects of sexual discrimination, Woolf imagines what would have happened had Shakespeare had a talented sister named Judith. In your *Reader/Writer Notebook*, note Woolf's use of vivid details to <u>exhibit</u> the effects of discrimination on Judith's life.

Vocabulary

servile (SUR vyl) *adj.*: like a slave; submissive. *Some people believed women should set aside their own wants and be servile.*

suppressed (suh PREHST) *v.* used as *adj.*: kept from being known. *The talent of many women was suppressed because they were not given the chance to learn a craft.*

propitious (pruh PIHSH uhs) *adj.*: favorable. *The most propitious place for a writer is a quiet room of one's own.*

prodigious (pruh DIHJ uhs) *adj.*: enormous. *Woolf was often exhausted by the prodigious energy writing required.*

notorious (noh TAWR ee uhs) *adj.*: widely but unfavorably known. *Some writers are notorious for turning in manuscripts late.*

formidable (FAWR muh duh buhl) *adj.*: hard to surmount. *Finding time to write was a formidable task for women with children.*

Language Coach

Suffixes The adjectival suffixes *–ous* and *–ious* mean "full of" or "characterized by" a particular quality. Note that in the Vocabulary word *notorious* the letter *i* before *–ous* is pronounced /ee/. However, in *propitious* and *prodigious* the "i" before *–ous* is not pronounced at all. Look at the syllabic spellings for these words. How are the "t" in *propitious* and the "g" in *prodigious* pronounced?

Learn It Online
Jump into this essay with the video introduction

go.hrw.com   L12-1162   **Go**

from A Room of One's Own

by **Virginia Woolf**

Read with a Purpose
Read to discover what life might have been like for William Shakespeare's equally brilliant sister.

Build Background
A Room of One's Own is considered a pioneering work of feminist criticism. The aims of feminist criticism include exposing sexist attitudes in or toward literature, reinterpreting earlier works from a feminist perspective, uncovering neglected women writers, and analyzing how gender affects a writer's subjects, themes, and even style.

Here am I asking why women did not write poetry in the Elizabethan age, and I am not sure how they were educated; whether they were taught to write; whether they had sitting rooms to themselves; how many women had children before they were twenty-one; what, in short, they did from eight in the morning till eight at night. They had no money evidently; according to Professor Trevelyan[1] they were married whether they liked it or not before they were out of the nursery, at fifteen or sixteen very likely. It would have been extremely odd, even upon this showing, had one of them suddenly written the plays of Shakespeare, I concluded, and I thought of that old gentleman, who is dead now, but was a bishop, I think, who declared that it was impossible for any woman, past, present, or to come, to have the genius of Shakespeare. He wrote to the papers about it. He also

told a lady who applied to him for information that cats do not as a matter of fact go to heaven, though they have, he added, souls of a sort. How much thinking those old gentlemen used to save one! How the borders of ignorance shrank back at their approach! Cats do not go to heaven. Women cannot write the plays of Shakespeare. **Ⓐ** **Ⓑ**

---

1. **Professor Trevelyan:** G. M. Trevelyan, author of *The History of England* (1926).

Ⓐ **Literary Perspectives** Analyzing Political Context What information about the lives of women in the Elizabethan age do you learn here? Do you think the bishop's remark is sexist? Why or why not?

Ⓑ **Literary Focus** Essay How would you describe Woolf's tone in this paragraph? What does it suggest about her opinion of the bishop's remarks?

Literary Perspectives

Analyzing Political Context When we analyze political context from the perspective of gender, we examine patterns of thought, behavior, and power in relations between the sexes. Many pioneering women and men have worked diligently to point out how sexism, or inequality between the sexes, hurts both women and men. The struggle for equal rights for women has been long and often difficult. For example, women in England did not win the right to vote until 1918 (for women over 30) and 1928 (for women over 18), and it took marches, rallies, and thousands of women being jailed and protesting to achieve this victory. The essay you are about to read originated from two lectures Woolf delivered at women's colleges at Cambridge University in 1928.

As you read, be sure to notice the questions in the text, which will guide you in using this perspective.

Be that as it may, I could not help thinking, as I looked at the works of Shakespeare on the shelf, that the bishop was right at least in this; it would have been impossible, completely and entirely, for any woman to have written the plays of Shakespeare in the age of Shakespeare. Let me imagine, since facts are so hard to come by, what would have happened had Shakespeare had a wonderfully gifted sister, called Judith, let us say. Shakespeare himself went, very probably—his mother was an heiress—to the grammar school, where he may have learnt Latin—Ovid, Virgil, and Horace—and the elements of grammar and logic. He was, it is well known, a wild boy who poached rabbits, perhaps shot a deer, and had, rather sooner than he should have done, to marry a woman in the neighborhood, who bore him a child rather quicker than was right. That escapade sent him to seek his fortune in London. He had, it seemed, a taste for the theater; he began by holding horses at the stage door. Very soon he got work in the theater, became a successful actor, and lived at the hub of the universe, meeting everybody, knowing everybody, practicing his art on the boards, exercising his wits in the streets, and even getting access to the palace of the queen. Meanwhile his extraordinarily gifted sister, let us suppose, remained at home. She was as adventurous, as imaginative, as agog to see the world as he was. But she was not sent to school. She had no chance of learning grammar and logic, let alone of reading Horace and Virgil. She picked up a book now and then, one of her brother's perhaps, and read a few pages. But then her parents came in and told her to mend the stockings or mind the stew and not moon about with books and papers. They would have spoken sharply but kindly, for they were substantial people who knew the conditions of life for a woman and loved their daughter—indeed, more likely than not she was the apple of her father's eye. Perhaps she scribbled some pages up in an apple loft on the sly, but was careful to hide them or set fire to them. Soon, however, before she was out of her teens, she was to be betrothed to the son of a neigh-

boring wool stapler.[2] She cried out that marriage was hateful to her, and for that she was severely beaten by her father. Then he ceased to scold her. He begged her instead not to hurt him, not to shame him in this matter of her marriage. He would give her a chain of beads or a fine petticoat, he said; and there were tears in his eyes. How could she disobey him? How could she break his heart? The force of her own gift alone drove her to it. She made up a small parcel of her belongings, let herself down by a rope one summer's night, and took the road to London. She was not seventeen. The birds that sang in the hedge were not more musical than she was. She had the quickest fancy, a gift like her brother's, for the tune of words. Like him, she had a taste for the theater. She stood at the stage door; she wanted to act, she said. Men laughed in her face. The manager—a fat, loose-lipped man—guffawed. He bellowed something about poodles dancing and women acting—no woman, he said, could possibly be an actress. He hinted—you can imagine what. She could get no training in her craft. Could she even seek her dinner in a tavern or roam the streets at midnight? Yet her genius was for fiction and lusted to feed abundantly upon the lives of men and women and the study of their ways. At last—for she was very young, oddly like Shakespeare the poet in her face, with the same gray eyes and rounded brows—at last Nick Greene the actor-manager took pity on her; she found herself with child by that gentleman and so—who shall measure the heat and violence of the poet's heart when caught and tangled in a woman's body?—killed herself one winter's night and lies buried at some crossroads where the omnibuses now stop outside the Elephant and Castle.[3] **C**

That, more or less, is how the story would run, I think, if a woman in Shakespeare's day had had Shakespeare's genius. But for my part, I agree with

---

2. **wool stapler:** dealer in wool, a product sorted according to its fiber, or "staple."

3. **buried . . . Elephant and Castle:** Suicides, who were for years not permitted church burials, were commonly buried at a crossroads as a kind of punishment, perhaps to ensure that their souls would wander forever. The Elephant and Castle is a pub at a busy crossroads in south London.

C Literary Focus **Essay** What point, or main idea, is Woolf trying to prove by inventing Judith Shakespeare?

Virginia Woolf in a Deck Chair, by Vanessa Bell (1879–1961).

Analyzing Visuals

Viewing and Interpreting   Note the muted quality of the subject's face. Why might Vanessa Bell (Woolf's sister) have obscured the woman's features? How does this device contribute to the the woman's identity?

the deceased bishop, if such he was—it is unthinkable that any woman in Shakespeare's day should have had Shakespeare's genius. For genius like Shakespeare's is not born among laboring, uneducated, servile people. It was not born in England among the Saxons and the Britons. It is not born today among the working classes. How, then, could it have been born among women whose work began, according to Professor Trevelyan, almost before they were out of the nursery, who were forced to it by their parents and held to it by all the power of law and custom? Yet genius of a sort must have existed among women as it must have existed among the working classes. Now and again an Emily Brontë or a Robert Burns blazes out and proves its presence. But certainly it never got itself onto paper. When, however, one reads of a witch being ducked, of a woman possessed by devils, of a wise woman selling herbs, or even

of a very remarkable man who had a mother, then I think we are on the track of a lost novelist, a suppressed poet, of some mute and inglorious[4] Jane Austen, some Emily Brontë who dashed her brains out on the moor or mopped and mowed about the highways crazed with the torture that her gift had put her to. Indeed, I would venture to guess that Anon, who wrote so many poems without signing them, was often a woman. It was a woman Edward Fitzgerald,[5] I think, suggested who made the ballads and the folk songs, crooning them to her children, beguiling her spinning with them, or the length of the winter's night. **Ⓓ**

---

4. **mute and inglorious:** allusion to line 59 of Thomas Gray's poem "Elegy Written in a Country Churchyard."
5. **Edward Fitzgerald** (1809–1883): English and poet.

Ⓓ Literary Perspectives Analyzing Political Context How does what you have read about women's lives support the idea that "Anonymous" was likely a woman? What does Woolf mean by this statement?

Drawing room at Charleston Farm, home to the Bloomsbury Group.

This may be true or it may be false—who can say?—but what is true in it, so it seemed to me, reviewing the story of Shakespeare's sister as I had made it, is that any woman born with a great gift in the sixteenth century would certainly have gone crazed, shot herself, or ended her days in some lonely cottage outside the village, half witch, half wizard, feared and mocked at. For it needs little skill in psychology to be sure that a highly gifted girl who had tried to use her gift for poetry would have been so thwarted and hindered by other people, so tortured and pulled asunder by her own contrary instincts, that she must have lost her health and sanity to a certainty. No girl could have walked to London and stood at a stage door and forced her way into the presence of actor-managers without doing herself a violence and suffering an anguish which may have been irrational—for chastity may be a fetish invented by certain societies for unknown reasons—but were nonetheless inevitable. Chastity had then, it has even now, a religious importance in a woman's life, and has so wrapped itself round with nerves and instincts that to cut it free and bring it to the light of day demands courage of the rarest. To have lived a free life in London in the sixteenth century would have meant for a woman who was poet and playwright a nervous stress and dilemma which might well have killed her. Had she survived, whatever she had written would have been twisted and deformed, issuing from a strained and morbid imagination. And undoubtedly, I thought, looking at the shelf where there are no plays by women, her work would have gone unsigned. That refuge she would have sought certainly. It was the relic of the sense of chastity that dictated anonymity to women even so late as the nineteenth century. Currer Bell, George Eliot, George Sand,[6] all the victims of inner strife as their

6. **Currer Bell, George Eliot, George Sand:** male pseudonyms for the female writers Charlotte Brontë, Mary Ann Evans, and Amantine-Aurore-Lucile Dupin.

writings prove, sought ineffectively to veil themselves by using the name of a man. Thus they did homage to the convention, which if not implanted by the other sex was liberally encouraged by them (the chief glory of a woman is not to be talked of, said Pericles,[7] himself a much-talked-of man), that publicity in women is detestable. Anonymity runs in their blood. The desire to be veiled still possesses them. They are not even now as concerned about the health of their fame as men are, and, speaking generally, will pass a tombstone or a signpost without feeling an irresistible desire to cut their names on it, as Alf, Bert, or Chas. must do in obedience to their instinct, which murmurs if it sees a fine woman go by, or even a dog, *Ce chien est à moi.*[8] And, of course, it may not be a dog, I thought, remembering Parliament Square, the Sieges Allee,[9] and other avenues; it may be a piece of land or a man with curly black hair. It is one of the great advantages of being a woman that one can pass even a very fine negress without wishing to make an Englishwoman of her. **E F**

That woman, then, who was born with a gift of poetry in the sixteenth century, was an unhappy woman, a woman at strife against herself. All the conditions of her life, all her own instincts, were hostile to the state of mind which is needed to set free whatever is in the brain. But what is the state of mind that is most propitious to the act of creation, I asked. Can one come by any notion of the state that furthers and makes possible that strange activity? Here I opened the volume containing the Tragedies of Shakespeare. What was Shakespeare's state of mind, for instance, when he wrote *Lear* and *Antony and Cleopatra?* It was certainly the state of mind most favorable to poetry that there

7. **Pericles** (c. 495–429 B.C.): Athenian legislator and general.
8. *Ce chien est à moi* (suh shee EHN ayt ah mwah): French for "This dog is mine."
9. **Sieges Allee:** busy thoroughfare in Berlin, German for "Avenue of Victory."

E **Reading Focus** Identifying the Author's Beliefs According to Woolf, what does the women writers' use of male pseudonyms at late as the nineteenth century prove?

F **Literary Perspectives** Analyzing Political Context What impulse does Woolf attribute to men but not to women? How might political context account for this difference?

Vocabulary **propitious** (pruh PIHSH uhs) *adj.*: favorable.

has ever existed. But Shakespeare himself said nothing about it. We only know casually and by chance that he "never blotted a line." Nothing indeed was ever said by the artist himself about his state of mind until the eighteenth century perhaps. Rousseau[10] perhaps began it. At any rate, by the nineteenth century self-consciousness had developed so far that it was the habit for men of letters to describe their minds in confessions and autobiographies. Their lives also were written, and their letters were printed after their deaths. Thus, though we do not know what Shakespeare went through when he wrote *Lear,* we do know what Carlyle went through when he wrote *The French Revolution;* what Flaubert went through when he wrote *Madame Bovary;* what Keats was going through when he tried to write poetry against the coming of death and the indifference of the world.

And one gathers from this enormous modern literature of confession and self-analysis that to write a work of genius is almost always a feat of prodigious difficulty. Everything is against the likelihood that it will come from the writer's mind whole and entire. Generally material circumstances are against it. Dogs will bark; people will interrupt; money must be made; health will break down. Further, accentuating all these difficulties and making them harder to bear is the world's notorious indifference. It does not ask people to write poems and novels and histories; it does not need them. It does not care whether Flaubert finds the right word or whether Carlyle scrupulously verifies this or that fact. Naturally, it will not pay for what it does not want. And so the writer, Keats, Flaubert,

Carlyle, suffers, especially in the creative years of youth, every form of distraction and discouragement. A curse, a cry of agony, rises from those books of analysis and confession. "Mighty poets in their misery dead"[11]—that is the burden of their song. If anything comes through in spite of all this, it is a miracle, and probably no book is born entire and uncrippled as it was conceived. **G**

But for women, I thought, looking at the empty shelves, these difficulties were infinitely more formidable. In the first place, to have a room of her own, let alone a quiet room or a soundproof room, was out of the question, unless her parents were exceptionally rich or very noble, even up to the beginning of the nineteenth century. Since her pin money,[12] which depended on the goodwill of her father, was only enough to keep her clothed, she was debarred from such alleviations[13] as came even to Keats or Tennyson or Carlyle, all poor men, from a walking tour, a little journey to France, from the separate lodging which, even if it were miserable enough, sheltered them from the claims and tyrannies of their families. Such material difficulties were formidable; but much worse were the immaterial. The indifference of the world which Keats and Flaubert and other men of genius have found so hard to bear was in her case not indifference but hostility. The world did not say to her as it said to them, Write if you choose; it makes no difference to me. The world said with a guffaw, Write? What's the good of your writing? **H**

---

10. **Rousseau:** Jean-Jacques Rousseau (1712–1778), French author whose candid, autobiographical *Confessions* began a vogue in literature for confessional accounts.

---

11. **"Mighty poets . . . dead":** line from William Wordsworth's poem "Resolution and Independence."
12. **pin money:** small allowance for personal expenses.
13. **alleviations:** things that lighten or relieve burdens or suffering or make it easier to bear.

G **Reading Focus** Identifying the Author's Beliefs What evidence does Woolf offer to prove that writing a work of genius is very difficult?

H **Reading Focus** Identifying the Author's Beliefs According to Woolf, what two difficulties faced by all writers are even more formidable for women writers?

Vocabulary **prodigious** (pruh DIHJ uhs) *adj.:* enormous.
notorious (noh TAWR ee uhs) *adj.:* widely but unfavorably known.
formidable (FAWR muh duh buhl) *adj.:* hard to surmount.

Applying Your Skills

from **A Room of One's Own**

SKILLS FOCUS Literary Skills Analyze the characteristics of an essay; analyze the use of tone; analyze political context. **Reading Skills** Identify an author's beliefs. **Writing Skills** Write persuasive essays or articles.

Respond and Think Critically

Reading Focus

Quick Check

1. How would you summarize Woolf's response to the bishop's argument?

2. Why might marriage have been "hateful" to Judith Shakespeare? How does her father's reaction show how little he understands her?

Read with a Purpose

3. What might have happened to Judith if she had been allowed to develop her talents?

Reading Skills: Identifying the Author's Beliefs

4. Look over the chart you created, and place a check mark next to the belief that you think is most central to the essay. In a sentence or two, explain why this belief is the most important.

Literary Focus

Literary Analysis

5. Interpret Woolf says of women "Anonymity runs in their blood." According to Woolf, why do women shy away from the limelight? Given what you know about women's history, does her explanation make sense to you? Why or why not?

6. Infer Woolf describes the writing process in great detail. What can you infer about her experience of writing from this description?

7. Make Judgments Does Woolf make any generalizations that you think are unsupported by historical or contemporary evidence? Explain your response and cite examples of political and historical events.

8. Evaluate Is Woolf's use of an invented biography convincing to you? Why or why not?

9. Draw Conclusions In this essay, Woolf expresses several beliefs—some quite strongly, others more subtly. In your opinion, which belief is most central to the theme of the essay?

10. Literary Perspectives Woolf's essay critiques gender roles in the early twentieth century. How relevant are her concerns to men and women today? Explain.

Literary Skills: Essay

11. Analyze What elements of this essay make it informal? Consider the subject matter, humor, the subjectivity of the writer, and the language.

Literary Skills Review: Tone

12. Evaluate How would you describe this essay's **tone,** the attitude a writer takes toward the subject? Does this tone serve Woolf's purpose? Support your ideas with textual examples.

Writing Focus

Think as a Reader/Writer

Use It in Your Writing Return to a piece of persuasive writing you have composed on an important issue, or think of a new issue. Using vivid details, write an anecdote about a real or imagined person affected by the issue. Share your anecdote with a partner, and discuss whether it advances your argument.

What Do You Think Now From this essay, what can you infer that Woolf values most in life? Explain.

from **A Room of One's Own**

Vocabulary Development

✓ Vocabulary Check

Be sure you can justify your answers to the following Vocabulary questions.

1. Is a car that uses a **prodigious** amount of gasoline energy efficient or inefficient?

2. Are **servile** people submissive or combative?

3. If your opponent is **formidable,** do you consider that person easy or difficult to defeat?

4. When writers are **suppressed,** are their works widely published or censored?

5. Who is more likely to be called **notorious**—a criminal or notary public?

6. If the timing of an event is **propitious,** would it be better to postpone the event or hold it as planned?

Vocabulary Skills: Distinguishing Word Meanings

Distinguishing between the meanings of different words can be difficult. Words may have similar meanings with subtle or sometimes not-so-subtle differences. For example, consider the words *famous* and *notorious.* A person might be flattered to be called *famous,* or well known, but might not take so kindly to being called *notorious,* which also means "well known," but in an unfavorable or undesirable way. A woman who saves someone's life might become famous, while a woman who robs a string of banks would become notorious.

So how do you tell the difference? If you're uncertain, use a dictionary to help you distinguish meaning between words.

Your Turn

Answer each of the following questions. The boldfaced words are Vocabulary words.

1. What is the difference between *servile* and *helpful?*

2. What is the difference between *suppressed* and *restrained?*

3. What is the difference between *propitious* and *lucky?*

4. What is the difference between *formidable* and *insurmountable?*

5. What is the difference between *prodigious* and *large?*

Language Coach

Suffixes For each of these nouns, write a related adjective ending with the suffix *–ous* or *–ious.*

space	mischief	fame
grief	glamour	glory
nerve	capacity	adventure

If the adjective has an *i* before *–ous,* is the *i* pronounced? What consonant sounds in the adjectives are different from those in the nouns?

Academic Vocabulary

Talk About

Given Woolf's perspective, do you think the challenges faced by female writers are inevitable? Must women artists always adapt themselves to social restrictions? Discuss your thoughts with a partner.

Grammar Link

Independent and Subordinate Clauses

A clause is a group of words made up of a verb and its subject. An **independent clause** expresses a complete thought and can act as a sentence; a **subordinate clause** expresses an incomplete thought and cannot stand alone. Subordinate clauses fall under three types:

1. An **adjective clause** modifies a noun or a pronoun. It begins with a relative pronoun, such as *that, who, whom,* or *whose,* or a relative adverb, such as *where* or *when.*

   Virginia Woolf, **who wrote "Shakespeare's Sister,"** was a talented writer.

2. A **noun clause** performs the same function as a noun. Words used to introduce noun clauses include *how, that, what, who, whoever,* and *why.*

   The teacher will give extra credit **to whoever writes a paper on Virginia Woolf.**

3. An **adverb clause** modifies a verb, adjective, or adverb and tells where, how, when, why, or to what extent. Subordinating conjunctions like *as though* or *than* introduce adverb clauses.

   Woolf wrote **as if Judith Shakespeare actually existed.**

Your Turn

What type of clauses are the underlined words?

1. Despite periods of severe depression, <u>Woolf continued to write</u>.

2. <u>Whatever you write</u> should be edited carefully.

3. <u>Writers must decide</u> when to take a break.

Writing Application In your own piece of writing, find two independent clauses you can combine by making one clause subordinate.

CHOICES

As you respond to the Choices, use these **Academic Vocabulary** words as appropriate: perspective, considerably, adapt, exhibit, inevitable.

REVIEW

Determine Fact versus Opinion

Sometimes it is difficult to distinguish fact from opinion. Remember that facts can be proven, while opinions express someone's thoughts and ideas on a topic and cannot necessarily be supported with hard evidence. Return to the essay, and discuss some of Woolf's statements. Which are facts? Which are opinions veiled as facts? Which are clearly opinions?

CONNECT

Start a Classroom Blog

TechFocus With a group of classmates, start a classroom blog about the issues raised in this selection. Discuss how life for women has changed since the time Woolf wrote her essay and what issues related to feminism affect your lives. Would American culture today encourage a woman with Shakespeare's genius? Why or why not? Ask your classmates and students in other classes for their perspectives.

EXTEND

Create a Multi-Media Time Line

Learn more about the feminist movement and its leaders in the twentieth and twenty-first century. Form a group of five, and assign each member a period of time to research online. Find out who the important people were and what they achieved. Then, create a multi-media time line, using video, still images, and voiceovers. Share your time line with the rest of the class.

Preparing to Read

from Jacob's Room

Reader/Writer
Notebook

Use your **RWN** to complete the activities for this selection.

Literary Focus

Style The manner in which writers express what they want to say is **style**. With *Jacob's Room*, Woolf believed she had finally begun "to say something in my own voice." Instead of a traditional plot, Woolf provides glimpses of characters and impressionistic details of experience. As you read, note the following stylistic elements: compound phrases that link impressions; repetitions that draw unexpected connections; and a succession of images that conveys a sense of simultaneous experience.

Reading Focus

Reading Closely Virginia Woolf's style in this excerpt requires close reading. When **reading closely** you must pay attention to details and stop often to ensure you understand. You may have to re-read certain portions and monitor your comprehension by asking and answering questions.

Into Action Read the excerpt closely. Stop after each paragraph, and complete a chart like this one. Re-read if necessary to find the answers.

Question	Paragraph 1	Paragraph 2	Paragraph 3 [etc.]
What is the scene?			
What vivid details does the narrator describe?	London lamps like "burning bayonets."		
Are there people in the scene? What are they doing?			

Vocabulary

bawling (BAWL ihng) *v.* used as *adj.*: crying loudly. *Grieving women were bawling as they walked.*

contemptuous (kuhn TEHMP choo uhs) *adj.*: showing strong dislike. *The men's eyes showed their contemptuous feelings for their ill-mannered neighbors.*

feverishly (FEE vuhr ihsh lee) *adv.*: in an agitated manner. *Readers turned the pages feverishly to find out what would happen next.*

defiant (dih FY uhnt) *adj.*: rebellious; disobedient. *The little boy was defiant, refusing to obey his mother.*

immobility (ihm oh BIHL uh tee) *n.*: lack of movement. *Immobility kept the old ladies' bodies stiff and sore.*

Language Coach

Prefixes When added to some words, the prefix *im–*, like the prefixes *un–*, *in–*, *il–*, and *dis–*, means "not." *Immobility* for example, means "no mobility." Use your knowledge of prefixes to tell the meanings of these words:

immature   impurity
impatience   impartial

Writing Focus

Think as a Reader/Writer

Find It in Your Reading Woolf uses sensory details: for example, "Sticks and leaves caught in the frozen grass." In your *Reader/Writer Notebook*, identify the words she uses to appeal to the senses of sight, sound, and touch. How do these details help you "see," "hear," and "feel" each scene?

Learn It Online
Discover more about the vocabulary words online with Word Watch.

go.hrw.com   L12-1172   **Go**

from
Jacob's Room

by **Virginia Woolf**

Read with a Purpose
Read to experience impressions and images that relate to one man on one day in London.

Build Background
Woolf's novel *Jacob's Room* is set in pre-World War I London and tells the story of a young man named Jacob Flanders, who eventually dies in the war. The name Flanders was inspired by the Flanders region of Belgium, the site of prolonged fighting in World War I. The character of Flanders was inspired by Woolf's brother Toby, who had died of typhoid fever in 1906.

The lamps of London uphold the dark as upon the points of burning bayonets. The yellow canopy[1] sinks and swells over the great four-poster. Passengers in the mail-coaches running into London in the eighteenth century looked through leafless branches and saw it flaring beneath them. The light burns behind yellow blinds and pink blinds, and above fanlights, and down in basement windows. The street market in Soho[2] is fierce with light. Raw meat, china mugs, and silk stockings blaze in it. Raw voices wrap themselves round the flaring gas-jets. Arms akimbo[3], they stand on the pavement bawling— Messrs. Kettle and Wilkinson; their wives sit in the shop, furs wrapped round their necks, arms folded, eyes contemptuous. Such faces as one sees. The little man fingering the meat must have squatted before the fire in innumerable lodging-houses, and heard and seen and known so much that it seems to utter itself even volubly[4] from dark eyes, loose lips, as he fingers the meat silently, his face sad as a poet's, and never a song sung. Shawled women carry babies with purple eyelids; boys stand at street corners; girls look across the road—rude illustrations, pictures in a book whose pages we turn over and over as if we should at last find what we look for. Every face, every shop, bedroom window, public-house, and dark square is a picture feverishly turned—in search of what? It is the same with books. What do we seek through millions of pages? Still hopefully turning the pages—oh, here is Jacob's room. Ⓐ

He sat at the table reading the *Globe*. The pinkish sheet was spread flat before him. He propped his face in his hand, so that the skin of his cheek was wrinkled in deep folds. Terribly severe he looked, set, and

---

1. **canopy:** covering.
2. **Soho:** area in West-Central London.
3. **akimbo:** bent or arched.

---

4. **volubly:** fluently, talkatively.

Ⓐ **Literary Focus** Style Notice all the images of facial and body parts. What effect do these images create?

Vocabulary **bawling** (BAWL ihng) *v. used as adj.:* crying loudly.
contemptuous (kuhn TEHMP choo uhs) *adj.:* showing dislike.
feverishly (FEE vuhr ihsh lee) *adv.:* in an agitated manner.

Analyzing Visuals

Viewing and Interpreting Note the proportions of the man reclining on the sofa. What might have motivated the artist to construct the central figure in such a manner? In what ways, if any, do solo figures like the man in the painting and Jacob in Woolf's novel become defined by their surroundings?

defiant. (What people go through in half an hour! But nothing could save him. These events are features of our landscape. A foreigner coming to London could scarcely miss seeing St. Paul's[5].) He judged life. These pinkish and greenish newspapers are thin sheets of gelatine pressed nightly over the brain and heart of the world. They take the impression of the whole. Jacob cast his eye over it. A strike, a murder, football, bodies found; vociferation[6] from all parts of England simultaneously. How miserable it is that the *Globe* newspaper offers nothing better to Jacob Flanders! When a child begins to read history one marvels, sorrowfully, to hear him spell out in his new voice the ancient words.…   **B**

The snow, which had been falling all night, lay at three o'clock in the afternoon over the fields and the hill. Clumps of withered grass stood out upon the hill-top; the furze bushes were black, and now and then a black shiver crossed the snow as the wind drove flurries of frozen particles before it. The sound was that of a broom sweeping— sweeping.   **C**

The stream crept along by the road unseen by any one. Sticks and leaves caught in the frozen grass. The sky was sullen grey and the trees of black iron. Uncompromising was the severity of the country. At four o'clock the snow was again falling. The day had gone out.

A window tinged yellow about two feet across alone combatted the white fields and the black trees. … At six o' clock a man's figure carrying a lantern crossed the field. … A raft of twig stayed upon a stone, suddenly detached itself, and floated towards the culvert[7]. … A load of snow slipped and fell from a fir branch.… Later there was a mournful cry.… A motor car came along the road shoving the dark before it. . . . The dark shut down behind it.…   **D**

Spaces of complete immobility separated each of these movements. The land seemed to lie dead. . . . Then the old shepherd returned stiffly across the field. Stiffly and painfully the frozen earth was trodden under and gave beneath pressure like a treadmill. The worn voices of clocks repeated the fact of the hour all night long.   **E**

Jacob, too, heard them, and raked out the fire. He rose. He stretched himself. He went to bed.

---

5. **St. Paul's:** London cathedral where many important British ceremonies, including royal weddings and birthday celebrations, are performed.
6. **vociferation:** shouting.

---

7. **culvert:** drain that carries water underground.

B Reading Focus **Reading Closely** What do you find out about Jacob in this paragraph? List some details you have learned about him.

C Reading Focus **Reading Closely** How does the scene shift between the second and third paragraphs? What is the narrator describing in this paragraph?

D Literary Focus **Style** What effect does Woolf create by using ellipses to end her sentences?

E Literary Focus **Style** How does Woolf show the impact of time on physical surroundings?

Vocabulary **defiant** (dih FY uhnt) *adj.:* rebellious; disobedient.
immobility (ihm oh BIHL uh tee) *n.:* lack of movement.

Applying Your Skills

from **Jacob's Room**

SKILLS FOCUS **Literary Skills** Analyze the use of style; analyze point of view. **Reading Skills** Read closely. **Vocabulary Skills** Demonstrate knowledge of literal meanings of words and their usage. **Writing Skills** Describe a place.

Respond and Think Critically

Reading Focus

Quick Check

1. What is the mood of the butcher in the first paragraph? What details indicate his feelings?

2. How does reading the newspaper seem to affect Jacob? Explain your response.

Read with a Purpose

3. How do the descriptions of London and Jacob's room help you understand the excerpt?

Reading Skills: Reading Closely

4. Look over the chart you completed. Then, write a brief description of the experience of reading this excerpt closely. What parts of the selection did you have to re-read? What questions did you have after reading each paragraph? Share your experiences with a partner.

✓ Vocabulary Check

Match the Vocabulary words with their definitions.

5. bawling   a. lack of movement

6. contemptuous   b. rebellious

7. feverishly   c. crying loudly

8. defiant   d. anxiously

9. immobility   e. showing strong disrespect

Literary Focus

Literary Analysis

10. **Interpret** Critics have argued that Jacob's Room is not ultimately about Jacob but rather about the world that creates him. How would you describe this world? How does it affect Jacob?

11. **Compare and Contrast** To what does the narrator compare the experience of looking for Jacob's room? How are the two experiences similar?

12. **Extend** Do you agree that newspapers "take the impression of the whole," that is, that they reflect the experiences of all people? Why or why not?

Literary Skills: Style

13. **Analyze** What repetitions can you find in the first paragraph? What effect do they create?

14. **Evaluate** Woolf's narrator surveys the countryside by skipping from image to image. On what details does Woolf focus, and how does she describe them? What is the effect of this style?

Literary Skills Review: Point of View

15. **Analyze** The vantage point from which an author tells a story, or point of view, is often classified as **first-person** (the narrator is a character who uses the pronoun *I*); **third-person limited** (the narrator is external and tells the story from one character's perspective); or **omniscient** (the narrator is outside the story but knows everything that is going on). How would you describe the point of view in this excerpt?

Writing Focus

Think as a Reader/Writer

Use It in Your Writing Using Woolf's descriptions as a model, describe a scene. Focus on certain details and choose words with sensory appeal to help your reader "see," "hear," and "feel" the scene.

 What Do You Think Now

Woolf wrote *Jacob's Room* after World War I. How might the war have affected her world view and values? How might this explain the details included in the story?

Preparing To Read

A Haunted House

Reader/Writer
Notebook

Use your **RWN** to complete the activities for this selection.

Literary Focus

Imagery Language that appeals to the senses is called **imagery.** Although most images are visual, imagery can also appeal to your sense of hearing, touch, taste, or smell. "A Haunted House," is alive with vivid imagery conveyed in unique ways. Note how Woolf appeals to the senses in her description of this scene, allowing the reader to see, hear, and feel what she describes: "The wind roars up the avenue. Trees stoop and bend this way and that. Moonbeams splash and spill widely in the rain."

Reading Focus

Visualizing Setting Using story details to see a scene in your mind's eye is called **visualizing setting.** Try the following techniques to help you visualize the setting:

- Read a paragraph or two. Then, stop, and visualize what you've read.
- Read aloud. Sometimes hearing the words helps to visualize the scene.
- Create a picture in your mind as you read. Add to or adjust your picture as you learn more details about the setting.

Into Action Using a chart like this one, briefly summarize the reading, and note what you visualize.

What I Read	What I Visualize
It is raining, and the wind is blowing hard and bending trees. Inside the light is still, and the ghostly couple open windows.	stormy dark night; trees bending in the wind; a soft light inside a peaceful house; windows opening and shutting gently

Language Coach

Denotation / Conotation To express themselves precisely and create vivid imagery, writers rely not only on a word's **denotations,** or dictionary definitions, but also on its connotations. **Connotations,** the ideas and feelings a word evokes, can cause a description to take on a negative or positive tone. For example, describing something that does not cost much as *cheap* might imply that its quality is poor because *cheap* has more negative connotations. The word *inexpensive,* however, has more neutral connotations.

Writing Focus

Think as a Reader/Writer

Find It in Your Reading Note how Woolf chooses words and phrases that create clear, vivid **imagery** and communicate the **connotation** (or emotional meaning) she intends. In your *Reader/Writer Notebook,* record similar instances, where words and phrases, such as *gently* and *the pulse of a heart,* have clear connotations and create a vivid picture.

Learn It Online
Find graphic organizers online to help you read.

go.hrw.com L12-1177 **Go**

A Haunted House

by **Virginia Woolf**

Read with a Purpose
Read this story to find out what compels a ghostly couple to return to their home.

Build Background
A Haunted House and Other Stories was published by Leonard Woolf three years after Virginia's death. Like many of Woolf's stories, "A Haunted House" focuses on thoughts and impressions instead of on actions. In classic Woolf style, "A Haunted House" is delightfully unpredictable—a ghost story like no other.

Whatever hour you woke there was a door shutting. From room to room they went, hand in hand, lifting here, opening there, making sure—a ghostly couple.

'Here we left it,' she said. And he added, 'Oh, but here too!' 'It's upstairs,' she murmured, 'And in the garden,' he whispered. 'Quietly,' they said, 'or we shall wake them.'

But it wasn't that you woke us. Oh, no. 'They're looking for it; they're drawing the curtain,' one might say, and so read on a page or two. 'Now they've found it,' one would be certain, stopping the pencil on the margin. And then, tired of reading, one might rise and see for oneself, the house all empty, the doors standing open, only the wood pigeons bubbling with content and the hum of the threshing machine sounding from the farm. 'What did I come in here for? What did I want to find?' My hands were empty. 'Perhaps it's upstairs then?' The apples were in the loft. And so down again, the garden still as ever, only the book had slipped into the grass. **Ⓐ**

But they found it in the drawing-room. Not that one could ever see them. The window-panes reflected apples, reflected roses; all the leaves were green in the glass. If they moved in the drawing-room, the apple only turned its yellow side. Yet, the moment after, if the door was opened, spread about the floor, hung upon the walls, pendant from ceiling—what? My

hands were empty. The shadow of a thrush crossed the carpet; from the deepest wells of silence the wood pigeon drew its bubble of sound. 'Safe, safe, safe,' the pulse of the house beat softly. 'The treasure buried; the room …' the pulse stopped short. Oh, was that the buried treasure? **Ⓑ**

A moment later the light had faded. Out in the garden then? But the trees spun darkness for a wandering beam of sun. So fine, so rare, coolly sunk beneath the surface the beam I sought always burnt behind the glass. Death was the glass; death was between us; coming to the woman first, hundreds of years ago, leaving the house, sealing all the windows; the rooms were darkened. He left it, left her, went North, went East, saw the stars turned in the Southern sky; sought the house, found it dropped beneath the Downs. 'Safe, safe, safe,' the pulse of the house beat gladly, 'The treasure yours.'

The wind roars up the avenue. Trees stoop and bend this way and that. Moonbeams splash and spill wildly in the rain. But the beam of the lamp falls straight from the window. The candle burns stiff and still. Wandering through the house, opening the windows, whispering not to wake us, the ghostly couple seek their joy.

'Here we slept,' she says. And he adds, 'Kisses without number.' 'Waking in the morning—' 'Silver between the trees—' 'Upstairs—' 'In the garden—'

Ⓐ Reading Focus **Visualizing Setting** Describe the setting. What details help you visualize the scene?

Ⓑ Literary Focus **Imagery** What imagery helps you see and hear this scene?

Analyzing Visuals

Viewing and Interpreting Note how the house becomes "small" when framed by the flowers. How does Woolf use descriptions of nature to affect the reader's <u>perspective</u> of the haunted house?

'When summer came—' 'In winter snowtime—' The doors go shutting far in the distance, gently knocking like the pulse of a heart. **C**

Nearer they come; cease at the doorway. The wind falls, the rain slides silver down the glass. Our eyes darken; we hear no steps beside us; we see no lady spread her ghostly cloak. His hands shield the lantern. 'Look,' he breathes. 'Sound asleep. Love upon their lips.' **D**

Stooping, holding their silver lamp above us, long they look and deeply. Long they pause. The wind drives straightly; the flame stoops slightly. Wild beams of moonlight cross both floor and wall, and, meeting, stain the faces bent; the faces pondering; the faces that search the sleepers and seek their hidden joy. **E**

'Safe, safe, safe,' the heart of the house beats proudly. 'Long years—' he sighs. 'Again you found me.' 'Here,' she murmurs, 'sleeping; in the garden reading; laughing, rolling apples in the loft. Here we left our treasure—' Stooping, their light lifts the lids upon my eyes. 'Safe! safe! safe!' the pulse of the house beats wildly. Waking, I cry 'Oh, is this *your*—buried treasure? The light in the heart.'

C **Reading Focus** Visualizing Setting Woolf gives just a few details here as the ghostly couple remember their days in the house. Are you able to visualize the setting based on so few words? Why or why not?

D **Reading Focus** Visualizing Setting What is the setting of this scene? What is happening?

E **Literary Focus** Imagery How does the image of the ghostly couple in this scene help you get to know them?

Applying Your Skills

A Haunted House

Respond and Think Critically

Reading Focus

Quick Check

1. What can you infer about the ghostly couple's experience when they lived in the house? Provide two details that support your response.

2. How does the narrator refer to the treasure the couple has come to find? Where do they find it?

Read with a Purpose

3. What do the ghostly couple plan to do with the "buried treasure"?

Reading Skills: Visualizing Setting

4. Add a third column to your chart noting how visualizing helped you understand the story.

What I Read	What I Visualize	How It Helped Me Understand
Paragraphs 1 and 2	ghostly couple in a house with many rooms, an upstairs, and a garden	

Literary Focus

Literary Analysis

5. **Interpret** How does the narrator convey a sense that the ghostly couple's visits are ongoing?

6. **Evaluate** What details in the third paragraph show the narrator is not afraid of the couple? Describe the narrator's **tone,** or attitude.

7. **Analyze** Most stories follow the classic plot structure consisting of situation, conflict, main event, climax, and resolution. How does the structure of Woolf's story differ from this format?

8. **Evaluate** What message about life does Woolf express in this story? Why do you think she chose a "ghost story" to convey this message?

9. **Compare and Contrast** The house in this story repeats the phrase "safe, safe, safe." Read D. H. Lawrence's story "The Rocking Horse Winner" (on page 1309 of this book), another story in which a house seems to repeat a phrase. Compare the phrases that the two houses repeat. How does the repetition create very different feelings?

Literary Skills: Imagery

10. **Interpret** This story emphasizes the pleasure of lightness, both physical and emotional. How does the imagery reinforce this idea?

Literary Skills Review: Figures of Speech

11. **Analyze** A **figure of speech** is a word or phrase that describes one thing in terms of another, dissimilar thing. **Metaphors** ("the world is his oyster") make direct comparisons. **Similes** ("the world is like an oyster") use connecting words, such as *like* or *as,* to make comparisons. Find figures of speech in the story. What effects do they create?

Writing Focus

Think as a Reader/Writer

Use It in Your Writing Using Woolf's techniques as a model, describe a setting with a strange, mysterious mood. Be sure to use key details and rich images.

 What Do You Think Now

What things or experiences are important to the ghostly couple? Are these also important to the narrator? How do you know?

Preparing to Read

from **The Letters of Virginia Woolf**

Reader/Writer
Notebook

Use your **RWN** to complete the activities for this selection.

Literary Focus

Diction A writer's or speaker's choice of words, **diction,** is an essential element of his or her style. Authors select words for their **denotations,** or dictionary meanings, and their **connotations,** or emotional associations, to convey their ideas precisely. Diction is also <u>adapted</u> to fit the writer's audience, subject, and purpose. Instead of stating that Murry's eyes gave the impression that he was unpleasantly eager to please her, Woolf wrote about his "oleaginous eyes," a concise, more evocative description.

Reading Focus

Identifying Tone Paying close attention to a writer's choice of words and details is critical in **identifying tone,** or the writer's attitude toward a subject, a character, or the reader. For example, Woolf conveys a critical tone by describing the poet Byron as "tawdry and melodramatic."

Into Action In Woolf's letter, she uses different tones as she describes people and events in her life. Note each instance of tone in a chart like the one below. Tell what words express her tone, or attitude, about each.

Subject	Strachey's health	
Choice of Words	"distressed" "plagued"	
Tone	concerned, but also humorous	

Writing Focus

Think as a Reader/Writer

Find It in Your Reading Writers utilize different elements of **syntax,** the arrangement of words in a sentence. They may play with word order or emphasize sentence parts to create rhythm (see the repetition of "He said" and "I said" in Woolf's description of her conversation with Murry). In your *Reader/Writer Notebook,* take notes on Woolf's syntax, including sentence length and construction, and how she creates rhythm.

Vocabulary

plagued (playgd) *v.* used as *adj.:* afflicted. *Strachey was plagued with severe illnesses.*

sepulchral (suh PUHL kruhl) *adj.:* deep and gloomy. *Eliot's sepulchral voice boomed into the telephone.*

distorting (dihs TAWRT ihng) *v.* used as *adj.:* misshaping; deforming. *The distorting glass, broken in places, made the visitors look much taller and skinnier than they actually were.*

confounded (kahn FOWND ihd) *v.* used as *adj.:* confused. *Virginia was confounded by Murry's behavior.*

hoarding (HAWR dihng) *v.:* storing; accumulating. *She was hoarding ideas to share with Strachey when she could finally meet him.*

coherently (koh HIHR uhnt lee) *adv.:* clearly and logically. *Writers use transitions to make sure their ideas are presented coherently.*

Language Coach

Literal and Figurative Meanings Some words have both a literal (original or exact) meaning and a figurative meaning. For example, *coherent* literally means "glued or stuck together," but over time, it has also come to have a figurative meaning as well: "logically connected." What is the relationship between the literal and figurative meanings of the words?

 Learn It Online
Learn more about these vocabulary words online.

go.hrw.com   L12-1181   **Go**

from The Letters of Virginia Woolf

by **Virginia Woolf**

Read with a Purpose
Read this letter to learn how Virginia Woolf handles "moments of crisis" in her daily life.

Build Background

Biographer Lytton Strachey was a close friend of Woolf's and a member of the Bloomsbury group. Woolf wrote this letter to him after moving from Brighton to London with her husband, Leonard. The letter reflects her literary life, full of references to writers and artists: poet T. S. Eliot, writers Lord Harold Nicolson and his wife Vita Sackville-West, writer John Middleton Murry (Katherine Mansfield's husband), art critic Clive Bell, who married Woolf's sister Vanessa ("Nessa"), and painter Dora Carrington.

1454: TO LYTTON STRACHEY   52 Tavistock Square W.C.
March 21st 1924

Dearest Lytton,

I am greatly distressed to hear that you are still plagued by diseases of all kinds—just as I was snatching a few moments to read Books & Characters[1] too. Why do I always fly to your works when the electricians are in the hall, the gasmen in the basement, and the telephone ringing with Tom's [Eliot] sepulchral voice? It's a very queer fact, but in moments of crisis, I always turn to you but supply me with another book soon. I open at page 173, and say Oh but I know this by heart; and it will soon be the case with all the pages: and this is no exaggeration; and I daresay no particular praise either; only one of your peculiarities as an author. Another is to beget[2] Nicolsons. But the mixture is not appetizing to me, for all the praises of Clive and Desmond, who have drunk too many glasses of his [Harold Nicolson's] champagne to be trusted. But then Byron seems to me tawdry and melodramatic. And Claire and Trelawny[3] and so and so on—I conceive them like a cave at some Earl's Court Exhibition—a grotto[4] I mean lined with distorting mirrors and plastered with oyster shells. Do not trouble to unwind this metaphor. **(A)**

_____

1. **Books and Characters:** *Books and Characters: French and English*, a book of literary criticism by Lytton Strachey, was published in 1922.
2. **beget:** produce (used figuratively).
3. **Claire and Trelawny:** Claire Clairmont, step-sister of novelist Mary Shelley, and Edward John Trelawny, friend of poets Byron and Shelley. Trelawny wrote a literary memoir of Byron and Shelley.
4. **grotto:** fake cave.

(A) Reading Focus **Identifying Tone** What tone does Woolf use when describing her experience of reading Strachey's book? Do you think she is praising him? Explain.

Vocabulary **plagued** (playgd) *v.* used as *adj.*: afflicted.
sepulchral (suh PUHL kruhl) *adj.*: deep and gloomy.

Virginia Woolf; Giles Lytton Strachey (June 1923), by Lady Ottoline Murrell, vintage snapshot print   National Portrait Gallery, London.

I am jangled and splintered by the move, and only hook together words by the force of affection: Say one word, and I will come down, and talk in a gentle and soothing voice about—well, did you hear how I rushed into Murry's arms at the Nation dinner the other night? He forced himself upon me. He has rolling and oleaginous[5] eyes. I said we were enemies. He said we were in different camps. He said one must write with one's instincts. I said one must write with one's mind. He said Bloomsbury was a tangle of exquisite sensibilities. I said come and see me there. He said no. I said very well. He said I like you. I said come and see me then. He said no. So I got up and flounced out of the room, saying Not for ten years—Undoubtedly, he has been rolling in dung, and smells impure. **B** **C**

We live largely in the basement—The confusion is still confounded—busts of my mother standing upon rolls of carpet, chamber pots stuffed full of book binding tools, and my unfortunate books—oh never let the undertakers pack your books when you move—I haven't a single volume left whole. In compensation, Nessa and Duncan have painted me a room, where you must come instantly and sit and talk and talk and talk, and never have to catch a taxi, and so by degrees get delivered of that vast mass of communi-cation which I assure you has been hoarding up within me, and so perhaps in you, these ten years. We will sit in the Square and let Dadie [Rylands] play tennis before us. This will be in the summer, with the leaves out, and exquisite ladies—but your taste doesn't lie that way.

I will write more coherently later.

Ask Carrington to let me hear how you are.

Yr.

V.W.

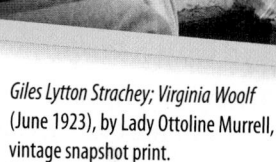

Giles Lytton Strachey; Virginia Woolf (June 1923), by Lady Ottoline Murrell, vintage snapshot print. National Portrait Gallery, London.

---

5. **oleaginous:** oily; unpleasantly eager to please.

B **Literary Focus** Diction What images come to mind from Woolf's description of herself as "jangled and splintered"? To which senses do those words appeal? How does Woolf's word choice fit the tone and style of the letter?

C **Reading Focus** Identifying Tone What words or phrases help you identify Woolf's tone, or attitude, toward Murry?

Vocabulary **distorting** (dihs TAWRT ihng) *v.* used as *adj.*: misshaping; deforming.
confounded (kahn FOWND ihd) *v.* used as *adj.*: confused.
hoarding (HAWR dihng) *v.*: storing; accumulating.
coherently (koh HIHR uhnt lee) *adv.*: clearly and logically.

Applying Your Skills

from **The Letters of Virginia Woolf**

SKILLS FOCUS Literary Skills Analyze diction; analyze the use of style. **Reading Skills** Identify tone. **Vocabulary Skills** Use vocabulary appropriately. **Writing Skills** Develop writer's style.

Respond and Think Critically

Reading Focus

Quick Check

1. What was occurring in Woolf's life at the time she wrote this letter? What details suggest why she feels so "jangled"?

2. What can you infer about Woolf's relationships with other writers from this letter?

Read with a Purpose

3. How does Woolf deal with life's "moments of crisis"? Are those solutions effective for her?

Reading Skills: Identifying Tone

4. Look back on the chart you created. What can you infer from Woolf's tone about her opinion of each subject?

✓ Vocabulary Check

Fill in each blank with one of the Vocabulary words.

> **plagued, sepulchral, distorting, confounded, hoarding, coherently**

5. The squirrel was _____ acorns for the winter.

6. Express your ideas _____.

7. The _____ mirrors twisted our reflections.

8. Woolf was _____ by depression and anxiety.

9. She was _____ by the writer's odd behavior.

10. The music's _____ tone subdued the audience.

Literary Focus

Literary Analysis

11. Infer Woolf notes that it has been ten years since she's seen Strachey. Does her letter suggest the two of them are still close? Why or why not?

12. Extend Murry says, "one must write with one's instincts," and Woolf replies, "one must write with one's mind." What is the difference between these two methods of writing?

13. Analyze What role does reading play in Woolf's life?

14. Interpret What messages is Woolf conveying to Strachey about her life and opinions? Use information from the letter to support your response.

Literary Skills: Diction

15. Analyze What is the difference between a cave and a grotto? Why did Woolf make this distinction in describing Claire, Trelawny, and the other writers? What was she saying about their work?

Literary Skills Review: Style

16. Evaluate The way a writer says what he or she wishes to say is called **style.** Style includes diction, sentence structure, imagery, rhythm, and arrangement of ideas. Style can be casual or formal, plain or ornate, as well as comic, poetic, forceful, etc. Describe Woolf's style in the letter.

Writing Focus

Think As a Reader/Writer

Use It in Your Writing Following Woolf's style, write a short letter telling about your day. In your letter, vary your syntax, use both long and short sentences to create interest, and employ repetition to create rhythm. Read your letter aloud to ensure it flows.

 What Do **You Think Now** After reading this letter, what people, things, and ideas can you infer are important to Woolf?

SKILLS FOCUS Literary Skills Analyze texts using approaches to literary criticism; understand and analyze the use of style. Writing Skills Use appropriate organization; support ideas/theses with relevant evidence and details; perform literary analysis.

Author Study: Virginia Woolf

Writing Focus

Writing a Comparison-Contrast Essay

Think about the four different selections you have read by Virginia Woolf. Choose at least two of the selections to compare and contrast. Remember to begin with a basis of comparison other than shared authorship. Re-read your notes from the four selections to determine commonalities. Once you have analyzed and compared the two selections, analyze them again to see differences.

Prewriting

Select a Topic Use your own ideas or one of the following topics in a comparison-contrast essay.

- the relationship between physical space and happiness
- the effect of the external world on the character
- descriptions of people's external worlds to hint at or reflect their inner experiences
- the freedom and restrictions of daily life

An effective comparison-contrast essay
• states what is being compared/contrasted
• conveys a main idea through a thesis statement
• has an effective and logical organization that includes similarities and differences
• cites and explains text passages to support ideas
• contains few or no errors in spelling, punctuation, and grammar

Gather Details Record your ideas in an H chart. In the center of the H, record the main similarity. At the top of the H, write the title of each selection you have chosen. Record your notes about each selection, and write a thesis statement that includes the similarities and the differences that you can support with text evidence.

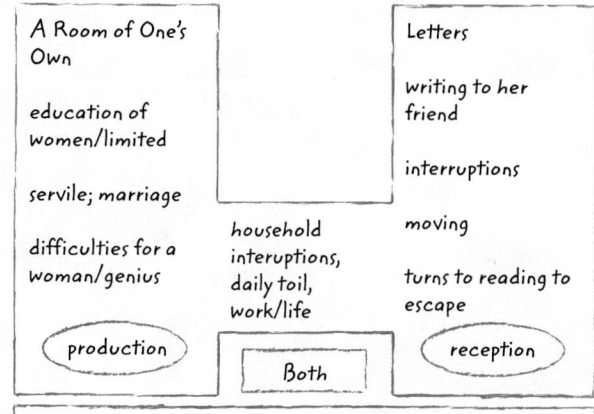

A Room of One's Own
education of women/limited
servile; marriage
difficulties for a woman/genius

household interruptions, daily toil, work/life

Letters
writing to her friend
interruptions
moving
turns to reading to escape

production   Both   reception

Thesis Statement
Although both "A Room of One's Own" and "Letters" by Virginia Woolf acknowledge the interruptions of daily life for women, the pieces differ greatly in their portrayal of the impact they have on women's lives.

Drafting

Since you are writing a comparison-contrast essay, use the Point by Point method. Include at least one body paragraph to develop the basis of similarity. Then, continue with similarities or discuss differences in the selections you have chosen to analyze.

Point by Point Method	Block Method
Topic Sentence/Paragraph: Selection 1 Section 2	Topic Sentence/Paragraph: Selection 1 Section 2

Revising and Editing

- Read your paper. Have you proven your thesis? Do you return to it in the closing paragraph?
- Add text evidence if it does not appear to support each point.
- Proofread your essay and correct any errors in spelling, mechanics and usage.

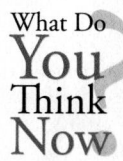

What Do You Think Now How did Woolf's experiences affect her view of the world?

COLLECTION 12

Modern and Contemporary Poetry

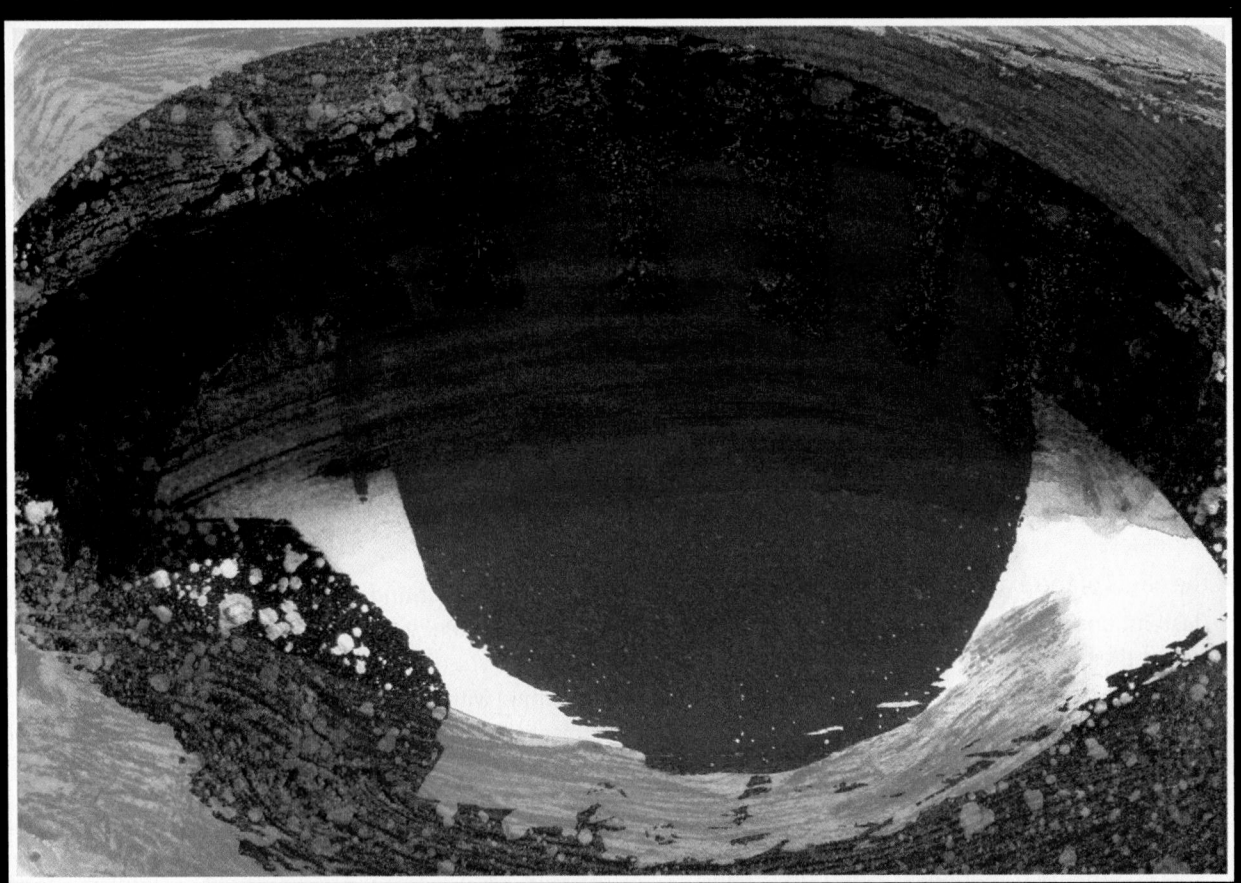

CONTENTS

T. S. Eliot

William Butler Yeats

W. H. Auden

Dylan Thomas

Stevie Smith

Anna Akhmatova

Wislawa Szymborska

Gabriela Mistral

Pablo Neruda

Philip Larkin

Trapped Australian **Link** to **Today**
Miners Rescued

Ted Hughes

Seamus Heaney

Margaret Atwood

Eavan Boland

> "All paths lead to the same goal: to convey to others what we are."
>
> —**Pablo Neruda**

Themes of Modern and Contemporary Poetry by Leila Christenbury

Characteristics of Themes in Modern and Contemporary Poetry
- Depict life as chaotic, dangerous, and uncontrollable
- Portray loss and death as universal experiences
- Value humanity and artistic expression as antidotes to despair

The Modern Age

A sense of increasing chaos, along with a feeling of alienation from nature and humanity, pervades the poetry of the modern age, an age ushered in by the turmoil of World War I. Modernist poets rejected traditional values and assumptions and the rules by which these were expressed.

This collection opens with two significant poets of the modern era: the American expatriate T. S. Eliot, whose poem *The Wasteland* was the single most important poem published in England during this period, and William Butler Yeats, whose mature poetry ranks among the best twentieth century poetry in English. With its note of despair, "The Hollow Men" by Eliot introduces this collection. The writing of Yeats is highly inventive and filled with memorable imagery, vivid language, and references not only to nature but also to a private mythology that Yeats created and to which he occasionally refers. Yeats revisits the story of "The Second Coming" from the book of Revelation in the Bible and examines the threats of modern life, showing readers what we have to fear. Then, in "Sailing to Byzantium," his focus shifts to the importance of art and its redemptive value.

As World War II approached, W. H. Auden wrote his famous poem "Musée des Beaux Arts" about human suffering. He said of poetry, "In so far as poetry, or any of the arts, can be said to have an ulterior purpose, it is, by telling the truth, to disenchant and disintoxicate." This tradition continues throughout the contemporary age.

(Opposite) *Eye* (2000) by Howard Hodgkin (b. 1932). Hand colored etching with carborundum. Alan Cristea Gallery, London.

The Contemporary Age

Following World War II, poets continued with modernist themes but moved away from elaborate symbolism and complex forms until, by the mid 1960s, the contemporary age had emerged. This collection presents a variety of contemporary poets. Philip Larkin, influenced by the Victorian poet Thomas Hardy, shaped tough and unsentimental but intensely emotional poems from ordinary experience, as in his poem "The Explosion." In "Lot's Wife," Wislawa Szymborska, like the earlier poet Anna Akhmatova, explores a woman's separation from her homeland. The Irish poet Seamus Heaney gives voice to the experience and richness of his rural heritage through his poem "Digging." These and other examples of modern and contemporary poetry embrace universal ideas about hope, fear, and loss in life and love.

Ask Yourself

1. How does modern and contemporary poetry reflect the experiences of people in the modern age?

2. In your opinion, what value is there in poetry? Do you agree with Auden that the purpose of poetry should be "to disenchant?" Explain.

Learn It Online
Explore modern themes online with *PowerNotes*.

go.hrw.com   L12-1187   **Go**

Preparing to Read

The Hollow Men

QuickWrite

"The Hollow Men" describes a world of godless despair without the promise of salvation. In your *Reader/Writer Notebook*, write your thoughts about the condition of humanity today.

T. S. Eliot
(1888–1965)

Nobel Prize WINNER

Unlike poets whose long, outstanding careers eventually turn them into cultural monuments, Thomas Stearns Eliot was a monument who later became known as a man.

Aristocratic Beginnings

Internationally famous, Eliot was the product of an aristocratic New England family that valued privacy. He saw the poet as an artisan whose work, all important, stood apart from its creator. Consequently, millions of readers knew T. S. Eliot less as a real personality than as a presence. He was remote, disciplined, and self-possessed, a man whose modest output was nevertheless the most celebrated and influential poetry written in English over a span of three decades.

T. S. Eliot was born in 1888 in St. Louis, Missouri, where his grandfather established Washington University. Despite this geographical displacement, the Eliots remained New Englanders. Eliot was educated at Harvard College, after which he attended graduate school at the Sorbonne in Paris, France. Like many young American writers of his generation, Eliot found life abroad so stimulating that he decided not to return home. Settling in London before World War I, he worked in a bank, married an Englishwoman, and became an editor and a publisher. Eliot made his expatriation complete by becoming a British citizen in 1927.

Influential Writing

Eliot had a vast influence as a poet. His techniques, along with those of his friend and fellow American expatriate, Ezra Pound, became the hallmarks of modern poetry. For over thirty years, Eliot's was the voice that expressed the dislocation and despair of the twentieth century. His world-weariness and his grave, restrained, and impersonal cadences—so much like the voices he heard in New England pulpits—were widely imitated and recognized. A Nobel Prize recipient, Eliot was so popular that 14,000 people once filled an arena to hear him speak.

Think About the Writer How do you think Eliot would view this discussion of his life as an introduction to reading his poetry?

 **Reader/Writer**
Notebook
Use your **RWN** to complete the activities for this selection.

Literary Focus

Allusion An **allusion** is a reference to a statement, person, place, event, or thing that is known from literature, history, or other subjects. "The Hollow Men" opens with two allusions. The line *"Mistah Kurtz—he dead,"* from Joseph Conrad's novel *Heart of Darkness,* refers to a character who is emotionally dead long before he is physically dead. This reference strikes a note of futility echoed throughout the entire poem. The second allusion, *A penny for the Old Guy,* refers to Guy Fawkes, the man chosen to light the fuse in the notorious Gunpowder Plot of 1605 (see Build Background on page 1190).

"The Hollow Men" <u>exhibits</u> many other allusions, especially to works by Shakespeare and Dante. As you read, think about the associations and emotions these allusions evoke.

Literary Perspectives Apply the literary perspective described on page 1190 as you read this poem.

Reading Focus

Drawing Inferences Writers often expect readers to "read between the lines." Readers must use evidence from the text, along with their own prior knowledge and experience, to **draw inferences**.

Into Action As you read, draw inferences about the hollow men and analyze their character traits to show how effectively they represent Eliot's view of human history. Use a chart like the one below to note details about the hollow men and to record your inferences.

Evidence	Inference
"headpiece filled with straw" (line 4)	If their heads are filled with straw, they can't think.

Vocabulary

supplication (suhp luh KAY shuhn) *n.:* humble plea. *The priest prayed for his supplication to be heard.*

perpetual (purh PEHCH oo uhl) *adj.:* lasting forever. *He gloomily predicted perpetual suffering.*

conception (kuhn SEHP shuhn) *n.:* the originating of something. *The conception of the new book was an elaborate vision.*

potency (POH tuhn see) *n.:* strength; power. *The potency of the vitamins was tested.*

Language Coach

Noun Suffixes The words *supplication* and *conception* both end in the suffix *–ion,* meaning "the act of." The *-ion* suffix changes the verbs *supplicate* and *conceive* into nouns. What other nouns with this suffix can you find in the poem? From what verbs are these nouns formed?

Writing Focus

Think as a Reader/Writer
Find It in Your Reading The **allusions** to works and events set the **tone** in Eliot's poem. As you read the poem, note allusions in your *Reader/Writer Notebook* and think about how each affects the poem's tone.

 Learn It Online
Prepare to read this poem through the video introduction online.

go.hrw.com | L12-1189 | **Go**

The Hollow Men by **T. S. Eliot**

Read with a Purpose
Read to discover one view of humanity after World War I.

Build Background
The allusion to "the Old Guy" in the epigraph refers to the failed Gunpowder Plot of 1605. On November 5 of that year, a band of conspirators planned to kill King James I (and others) by placing barrels of gunpowder in the cellars of Parliament. A soldier named Guy Fawkes was supposed to light the fuse, but the plot failed, and Fawkes was arrested and sentenced to be hanged, drawn, and quartered. To commemorate this grisly event, huge bonfires are set all over England every year on November 5. When these fires are lit, straw-filled effigies of Fawkes that look like scarecrows—the "stuffed men" of the poem—go up in flames, lighting the skies. Children join in the fun by carrying a "guy" and becoming beggars who ask passersby to give them "a penny for the guy" so that they can buy fireworks.

Mistah Kurtz—he dead.
A penny for the Old Guy

I

We are the hollow men°
We are the stuffed men
Leaning together
Headpiece filled with straw. Alas!
5 Our dried voices, when
We whisper together
Are quiet and meaningless
As wind in dry grass
Or rats' feet over broken glass
10 In our dry cellar. **A**

Shape without form, shade without color, **B**
Paralyzed force, gesture without motion;

1. hollow men: allusion to Shakespeare's *Julius Caesar* (Act IV, Scene 2, lines 23–27): "hollow men… sink in the trial" (fail when put to the test).
11–12. A **paradox** is an apparent contradiction that is actually true.

? *What paradoxes are listed in these lines? What do these paradoxes tell you about the hollow men?*

Literary Perspectives

Analyzing Philosophical Context Philosophical context refers to an author's underlying assumptions about larger questions of life and its meaning. To read literary works from this <u>perspective</u>, we must uncover and consider the philosophical arguments of the author. When T. S. Eliot wrote "The Hollow Men" in 1923, World War I had shaken the foundations of British society, and this once powerful nation was overcome by cynicism and hopelessness. Hundreds of thousands of people had died in combat, the British Empire and many of its traditions were disintegrating, and a new suspicion toward government had emerged. As you read, consider how these historical conditions may have influenced Eliot's philosophical approach to "modern man."

As you read, be sure to notice the questions in the text, which will guide you in using this perspective.

A **Reading Focus** Drawing Inferences What inferences can you draw about the hollow men so far?

B **Literary Perspectives** Analyzing Philosophical Context What does Eliot's description of "hollow" and "stuffed" men tell you about his outlook on humanity?

Those who have crossed
With direct eyes, to death's other Kingdom°
15 Remember us—if at all—not as lost
Violent souls, but only
As the hollow men
The stuffed men. **C**

II

Eyes I dare not meet in dreams
20 In death's dream kingdom
These do not appear:
There, the eyes are
Sunlight on a broken column
There, is a tree swinging
25 And voices are
In the wind's singing
More distant and more solemn
Than a fading star.

Let me be no nearer
30 In death's dream kingdom
Let me also wear
Such deliberate disguises
Rat's coat, crowskin, crossed staves°
In a field
35 Behaving as the wind behaves
No nearer—

Not that final meeting
In the twilight kingdom

III

This is the dead land
40 This is cactus land
Here the stone images
Are raised, here they receive
The supplication of a dead man's hand
Under the twinkle of a fading star. **D**

13–14. Those… Kingdom: Those with "direct eyes" have crossed from the world of the hollow men into Paradise. The allusion is to Dante's *Paradiso*.

Analyzing Visuals

Viewing and Interpreting Note the severe and extreme physical dimensions of the sculpture, as well as the gritty quality of its material. In what ways does the sculpture portray the hollow men described in Eliot's poem? How does it deviate?

L'Homme Qui Marche (1947) by Alberto Giacometti. Bronze. Inv. Nr. GS 30. Kunsthaus, Zurich.

33. staves: rods or staffs. "crossed staves / In a field" form a scarecrow.

? 37–38. *What might the "final meeting / In the twilight kingdom" be? How might this explain what the speaker is afraid of?*

? 39–44. *What kind of setting is described here? How is this setting appropriate to the nature of the hollow men?*

C Reading Focus Drawing Inferences What does it mean for the hollow men to be both "hollow" and "stuffed"?

D Literary Focus Allusion In line 44, the image of the star is an allusion to Dante, who used the star to symbolize God. What do "stone images" make you think of? What might "prayers to broken stone" be?

Vocabulary supplication (suhp luh KAY shuhn) *n.:* humble plea.

45   Is it like this
In death's other kingdom
Waking alone
At the hour when we are
Trembling with tenderness
50   Lips that would kiss
Form prayers to broken stone.

IV

The eyes are not here
There are no eyes here
In this valley of dying stars
55   In this hollow valley
This broken jaw of our lost kingdoms

     In this last of meeting places
We grope together
And avoid speech
60   Gathered on this beach of the tumid river°

     Sightless, unless
The eyes reappear
As the perpetual star
Multifoliate rose°
65   Of death's twilight kingdom
The hope only
Of empty men.

V

Here we go round the prickly pear°
Prickly pear prickly pear
70   *Here we go round the prickly pear*
At five o'clock in the morning.

     Between the idea
And the reality
Between the motion
75   And the act°
Falls the Shadow
                For Thine is the Kingdom°

60. tumid river: Hell's swollen river, the Acheron (AK uh rahn), in Dante's *Inferno*. The damned must cross this river to enter the land of the dead.

64. multifoliate rose: Dante describes Paradise as a rose of many leaves (*Paradiso,* Canto 32).

68. prickly pear: cactus.
68–71. These lines are a parody of a children's rhyme that begins, "Here we go 'round the mulberry bush." The mulberry bush was traditionally a symbol of fertility. To go around and around means to never reach a destination; it is a pointless action.

? *How would you interpret going around and around a prickly pear—a type of cactus?*

74–75. between... act: reference to Shakespeare's *Julius Caesar*: "Between the acting of a dreadful thing / And the first motion, all the interim is / Like a phantasma or a hideous dream" (Act II, Scene 1, lines 63–65).

77. For... Kingdom: closing lines of the Lord's Prayer: "For thine is the kingdom, and the power, and the glory, forever and ever."

Between the conception
And the creation
80 Between the emotion
And the response
Falls the Shadow

Life is very long

Between the desire
85 And the spasm
Between the potency
And the existence
Between the essence
And the descent°
90 Falls the Shadow

For Thine is the Kingdom

For Thine is
Life is
For Thine is the

95 *This is the way the world ends*
This is the way the world ends
This is the way the world ends
Not with a bang but a whimper. **E**

88–89. between… descent:
The Greek philosopher Plato defined "the essence" as an unattainable ideal and "the descent" as its imperfect expression in material or physical reality.

95–98. These lines are a continuation of the children's singsong rhyme, parodying the original words, "This is the way we clap our hands."

? *What does it mean for the world to end with a "whimper" instead of a "bang"?*

E **Literary Perspectives** **Analyzing Philosophical Context** How would you describe the view of the future expressed in the final four lines of the poem?

Vocabulary **conception** (kuhn SEHP shuhn) *n.:* the originating of something.
potency (POH tuhn see) *n.:* strength; power.

City Square (La Place) (1948) by Alberto Giacometti. Bronze. The Museum of Modern Art, New York, NY, U.S.A. © 2005 Artists' Rights Society (ARS) New York/ADAGP, Paris.

Respond and Think Critically

Reading Focus

Quick Check

1. Eliot refers to twentieth-century people as "hollow men." What is a hollow person lacking?

2. According to lines 20–28, what is "death's dream kingdom" like?

Read with a Purpose

3. What have you learned about Eliot's view of humanity after World War I?

Reading Skills: Drawing Inferences

4. As you read the poem, you recorded your inferences about the hollow men. Now, use your inferences to assess how well the hollow men represent Eliot's view of human history.

Literary Focus

Literary Analysis

5. **Compare and Contrast** In Part I, the hollow men are compared with effigies of Guy Fawkes and contrasted with the historical Fawkes. What does this comparison and contrast tell you?

6. **Analyze** In Part III, what mood—or emotional effect—does the imagery convey?

7. **Analyze** In Part IV, what is the hope of the hollow men? What might regaining sight symbolize? Why do you think the hollow men are powerless to regain sight by themselves?

8. **Analyze** In Part V, what is "the Shadow" that intervenes between thought and action? Why can the speaker not complete the Lord's Prayer?

9. **Draw Conclusions** What is ironic about the hollow men's ability to describe vividly their particular character traits and deficiencies?

10. **Literary Perspectives** Do you think Eliot effectively demonstrates his argument that contemporary history is an "immense panorama of futility and anarchy"? Use evidence from the poem to support your answer.

Literary Skills: Allusion

11. **Analyze** How do Eliot's allusions to Dante's and Shakespeare's work affect your reading of the selection? What do the allusions add to the theme or meaning of the poem?

12. **Analyze** How does Eliot's allusion to a children's rhyme affect the mood of the poem?

Literary Skills Review: Theme

13. **Interpret** The **theme** is a work's main message or insight into life. How would you state the theme of this poem? How is this theme supported by the poem's **tone**—the author's attitude toward the subject or the reader?

Writing Focus

Think As a Reader/Writer

Use It in Your Writing Now that you have seen Eliot's use of allusion, use an allusion in your own writing. Write a brief poem expressing your view of humanity today and include an allusion to reinforce your poem's message.

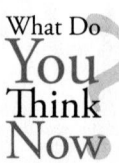
What Do You Think Now

What in Eliot's experience might account for the bleak view of humanity expressed in this poem?

Vocabulary Development

✓ Vocabulary Check

Match each Vocabulary word with its definition.

1. supplication
2. perpetual
3. conception
4. potency

a. strength
b. origination
c. humble plea
d. lasting forever

Vocabulary Skills: Context Clues

Sometimes you can determine the meaning of an unfamiliar word by looking for clues in the **context**—the surrounding words. Some of the most useful types of context clues include **restatement, comparison, contrast**, and **synonym.** The chart that follows shows some kinds of context clues, as well as definitions and examples.

Type of Context Clue	Definition	Example
restatement	A difficult word is rephrased in more accessible language.	He showed *deference*, or great respect, to his professor.
comparison	Comparison shows the likeness between an unfamiliar word and familiar words surrounding it.	He was incredibly *reserved*, as if he wanted to prevent anyone from really knowing him.
synonym	A nearby word has a similar meaning to the unfamiliar word.	He had always been *cynical* and only became more and more jaded.

Your Turn

In your *Reader/Writer Notebook,* copy any unfamiliar words from the poem. Then look back over the poem to investigate the context clues provided for each of the words. Be sure to look beyond that same stanza in order to determine the words' meanings. Record the clues, and explain your thinking process in using them.

Language Coach

Noun Suffixes The suffix *–ion* means "the act of" and can change a word's part of speech to form a noun. When changing a word that ends in *–ceive*, change the *ive* to a *p* and add *–tion*. What is the noun form of the word *receive?* What is the verb form of the word *conception?*

Academic Vocabulary

Talk About

From your <u>perspective</u>, what conditions in today's world contribute to alienation and despair? How do people <u>exhibit</u> this alienation? How might they adapt to stressful conditions so that alienation does not become <u>inevitable</u>? Discuss these questions with a partner. Use the underlined Academic Vocabulary words in your discussion.

Learn It Online
Visit *WordSharp* for another look at context clues.

go.hrw.com | L12-1195 | Go

SKILLS FOCUS **Literary Skills** Analyze allusion. **Writing Skills** Analyze a poem. **Grammar Skills** Identify and use demonstrative adjectives; identify and use demonstrative pronouns. **Listening and Speaking Skills** Participate in informal discussion and conversations; compare and contrast media genres.

Grammar Link

Demonstrative Pronouns and Adjectives

The words *this, that, these,* and *those* are called **demonstrative pronouns** when they point out (or demonstrate) a noun or pronoun.

This is a poem about the futility of existence after World War I. (*This* replaces "The Hollow Men.")

That is the writer I was telling you about. (*That* replaces the name of the writer.)

These are my favorite poems by T. S. Eliot. (*These* replaces the titles of the poems.)

Those are the famous lines that end the poem. (*Those* replaces the line numbers or the words in the lines.)

This, that, these, and *those* are called **demonstrative adjectives** when they modify nouns or pronouns.

This poem is about the futility of existence after World War I.

These poems are my favorite ones by T. S. Eliot.

Your Turn

Identify each demonstrative adjective and demonstrative pronoun in the paragraph below.

You may research the allusions in this poem. Those from literature may be found in works by Dante, Shakespeare, and Conrad, but this reference is from history, and that one is from the Bible.

Writing Application Write your own paragraph using demonstrative adjectives and demonstrative pronouns.

CHOICES

As you respond to the Choices, use these **Academic Vocabulary** words as appropriate: <u>adapt</u>, <u>considerably</u>, <u>exhibit</u>, <u>inevitable</u>, <u>perspective</u>.

REVIEW
State the Theme

Timed ╚Writing Write an essay about Eliot's use of allusions in "The Hollow Men." Be sure to discuss how the allusions contribute to the poem's theme. Include details that support your thesis, and conclude your essay with a summary of your argument.

CONNECT
Add Hypertext

TechFocus Create a hypertext version of "The Hollow Men" that provides links to explanations, illustrations, and questions regarding the poem's allusions. Compare the experiences of reading the poem with and without the hypertext. Do the links add <u>considerably</u> to the experience? In what ways do you think they detract from the reading?

EXTEND
Investigate Allusions

Choose one text that Eliot alludes to in his poem, such as *Julius Caesar, Inferno, Paradiso,* or the Bible. Investigate that work and then discuss with a partner how your experience with that work supports your reading of the poem itself. What understanding did you gain from investigating the allusions?

Learn It Online
Find out more about Eliot and his work through these Internet links.

go.hrw.com | L12-1196 | **Go**

COMPARING TEXTS: AUTHOR STUDY

William Butler Yeats

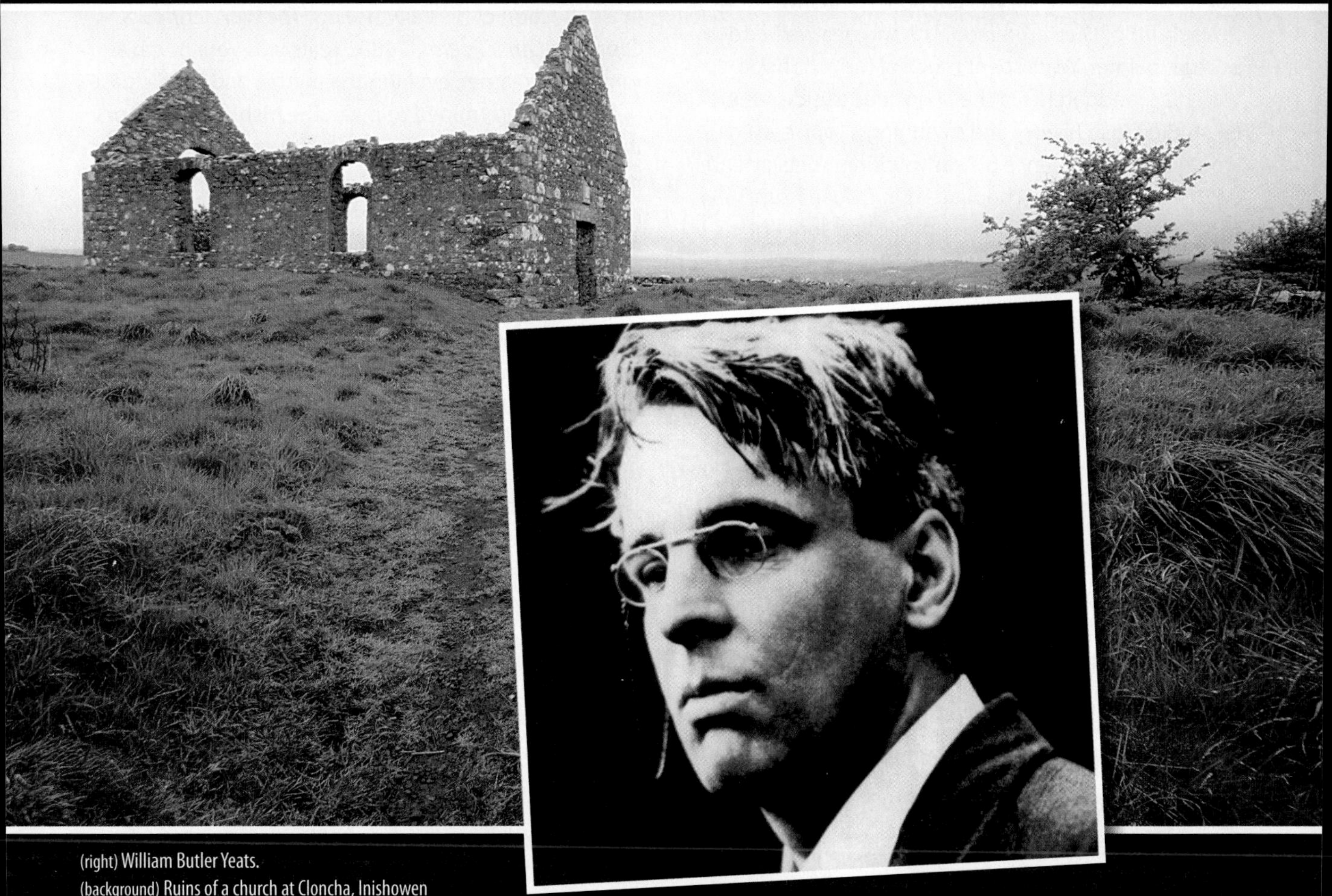

(right) William Butler Yeats.
(background) Ruins of a church at Cloncha, Inishowen Peninsula, County Donegal, Ireland.

What Do You Think? How does experience shape our view of the world?

QuickWrite

In your *Reader/Writer Notebook,* write down some of your most significant experiences and some goals you would like to achieve.

CONTENTS

The Second Coming

The Lake Isle of Innisfree

The Wild Swans at Coole

Sailing to Byzantium

from **The Autobiography of William Butler Yeats**

William Butler Yeats
(1865–1939)

Generally regarded as the twentieth century's greatest poet writing in English, William Butler Yeats was born in a suburb of Dublin, Ireland. The son of a well-known portrait painter, Yeats spent much of his childhood with his grandparents in the Sligo countryside, where he studied Irish history and mythology, topics which would heavily influence his early writing. Yeats attended the Metropolitan School of Art in Dublin from 1884 to 1886, during which time he published some of his first poems in the *Dublin University Review*.

Art Nouveau

Yeats arrived on the literary scene during the revival of the Pre-Raphaelite movement of the mid-nineteenth century. Known as Art Nouveau, this revival emphasized the mysterious and the unfathomable, especially those recesses of the mind now known as the unconscious, which was just then being scrutinized by pioneering psychologists Sigmund Freud and Carl Jung. Particularly in poetry, the revival valued suggestion above statement, symbols above facts, and musical measures above common speech. It was within this atmosphere that the young Yeats established a reputation as a lyricist of great delicacy and as a versifier of old tales drawn from Irish folklore and mythology.

Celtic Pride

In a collection of his early poems, *The Wanderings of Oisin and Other Poems* (1889), Yeats was very much a romantic dreamer, evoking the mythic and heroic past of Ireland. Determined to make the Irish conscious of their heroic past, he was a major advocate of the Celtic Revival, a movement for Ireland's social, intellectual, and political independence from England. In some ways, Yeats saw himself as the prophet-priest of Ireland's national destiny. The Celtic Revival was partially successful, and he moved from the cultural to the political side of the movement. A part of the Anglo-Irish Protestant minority, Yeats participated in the politics of the civil war that followed the annexation of Northern Ireland. From 1922 to 1928, he served as a senator of the newly formed Irish Free State. In his poem "Easter, 1916," written two years before "The Second Coming," Yeats reflected on the unsuccessful revolt of the Irish Nationalists against the British government. He asserts, "Too long a sacrifice / Can make a stone of the heart." This sentiment applied to his personal life as well.

An Irish and an English Love

For years, Yeats had idolized and yearned for Maud Gonne, the beautiful Irish political activist who rejected him and instead chose another, more politically radical suitor. Upon later reflecting on his relationship with Gonne, Yeats pronounced it a "miserable love affair."

A Yeats Time Line

William Butler Yeats by John Butler Yeats. National Gallery of Ireland.

1884–1886 Attends the Metropolitan School of Art in Dublin

1904 Helps to establish the Abbey Theatre

1860   1880   1900

1865 Born in Dublin, Ireland, the son of a well-known portrait painter

1889 Publishes *The Wanderings of Oisin and Other Poems*

The room at Lissadell House, where Yeats wrote plays and poems, County Sligo, Ireland.

Yeats finally accepted Gonne's rejection, and in 1917, at age fifty-two, he married Georgie Hyde-Lees, an Englishwoman with whom he eventually had two children. Hyde-Lees would remain his "delight and comfort" for the next twenty-two years.

Poet and Playwright

In 1914, Yeats set out to create a stark, chiseled, and eloquently resonant type of poetry. That same year, he published a volume of poetry aptly titled *Responsibilities*. Some critics have said Yeats carved out of English a language distinctly his own, one that was monumentally sparse and unadorned. This style ("cold and passionate as the dawn" in Yeats's words) confirms the basic definition of poetry as "heightened speech." W. H. Auden, a fellow poet, reflected that Yeats wrote "some of the most beautiful poetry" of the time. Yeats toured the United States, giving ritualized readings of the poems for which he was awarded the 1923 Nobel Prize in literature.

In addition to being a poet, Yeats was a dramatist and helped his friend Lady Gregory establish Dublin's Abbey Theatre as a monument to Irish culture and high literary standards. When the Abbey Theatre opened its doors in 1904, the repertory boasted three plays, two of which were by William Butler Yeats. Yeats's interest in drama waned after a few years, and he soon gave up an active role in the management of the Abbey, but the institution went on to play a critical part in the development of modern drama. Some audiences may agree with Yeats himself, who felt that some of his most memorable poems are embedded, like gems, in the scripts of his plays.

During his life, Yeats profoundly affected the history of Ireland and the canon of poetry. Ten years after his 1939 death and burial in the south of France, his body was disinterred and sent back to Ireland. Like a primitive king, with full ceremony and military pomp, Yeats returned to Ireland on the deck of a battleship.

Think About the Writer How might Yeats's involvement with the movement for Irish independence from England have affected his writing?

Key Elements of Yeats's Writing

- Lyricism and mysticism predominate
- Irish heritage is celebrated
- Style provides an example of poetry as heightened speech
- Allusions to places and literature enliven and enrich poems

Learn It Online
Learn more about Yeats at the Writers' Lives site.
go.hrw.com   L12-1199   Go

1916 Writes "The Wild Swans at Coole," while in love with Maud Gonne

1921 Writes "The Second Coming"

1939 Dies in the south of France

1910   **1920**   **1930**

1914 Publishes *Responsibilities*, a volume of poetry

1917 Marries Georgie Hyde-Lees

1923 Awarded the Nobel Prize in literature

1922–1928 Serves as a senator of the newly formed Irish Free State

William Butler Yeats with his wife Georgie Hyde Lee and their children Anne and Michael.

Preparing to Read

Reader/Writer
Notebook
Use your **RWN** to complete the activities for this selection.

Literary Focus

Theme The poem's title and many of its images allude to a Christian perspective of history, specifically, a prophecy from the Bible's Book of Revelation. (An **allusion** is a reference to something that is widely known from religion, literature, or politics.) The poem's **theme,** or central insight, relies upon this allusion and turns it inside out. Consider why Yeats refers to this Christian idea of a just, peaceful end of time, especially in the context of the chaos of World War I and the 1917 Russian Revolution. (Yeats wrote this poem in 1921.) What idea about the Second Coming, or the security of Christian hope, might Yeats be trying to express?

Reading Focus

Visualizing Imagery Poets often exhibit theme, the work's central insight, through imagery. **Imagery** is language that appeals to the senses. Although most images are visual, imagery can also appeal to the senses of hearing, touch, taste, or smell. To visualize imagery, pay attention to the details the poet uses that create a picture in your mind.

Into Action To visualize the poem's central image, note elements of its description in an idea web. In the web's center, write the word "beast." In the surrounding ovals, describe images that relate to the beast.

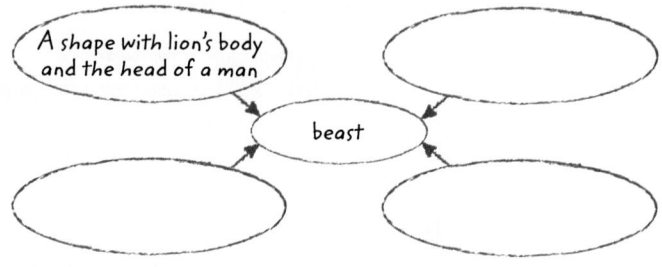

Writing Focus

Think as a Reader/Writer
Find It in Your Reading In your *Reader/Writer Notebook*, record the images Yeats uses to convey theme.

TechFocus Consider what pictures or sounds the poem evokes in your mind. How do these different elements work with, or against, each other?

Vocabulary

anarchy (AN uhr kee) *n.:* disorder and confusion. *Anarchy prevailed during the Russian Revolution.*

conviction (kuhn VIHK shuhn) *n.:* firm belief. *She was firm in her conviction that Ireland should be independent.*

intensity (ihn TEHN suh tee) *n.:* great vigor. *He embraced the task with intensity.*

revelation (rehv uh LAY shuhn*) n.:* act of making known. *The people await a revelation that will confirm their hopes.*

vexed (vehkst) *v.:* troubled. *The peace seekers were vexed by the violence.*

Language Coach

Suffix —*archy* The suffix —*archy* means "rule, government." In the word *anarchy*, it is combined with the prefix *an—*, meaning "without," to form a word that means "without rule or government." With a partner, think of other words that include the suffix —*archy* to form words that refer to different types of rule or government.

 Learn It Online
Get a different look at "The Second Coming" through the video introduction online.

go.hrw.com | L12-1200 | **Go**

The Second Coming

by **William Butler Yeats**

Twilight at the Great Sphinx of Giza, Egypt.

Read with a Purpose
Read to discover the speaker's dire predictions about the future.

Background
In Christianity, the Second Coming refers to the belief that Jesus will one day return to Earth and usher in an era of peace and justice. The "first coming" was the birth of Jesus in Bethlehem in Judea, just over two thousand years ago.

This poem addresses not only the Christian conception of the universe but also Yeats's cyclical view of history. Each cycle, known as a gyre (jyr), begins in a rational state and then gradually dissolves into chaos and irrationality.

Turning and turning in the widening gyre
The falcon cannot hear the falconer;
Things fall apart; the center cannot hold;
Mere anarchy is loosed upon the world,
5   The blood-dimmed tide is loosed, and everywhere
The ceremony of innocence is drowned;
The best lack all conviction, while the worst
Are full of passionate intensity.   **Ⓐ**

Surely some revelation is at hand;
10   Surely the Second Coming is at hand.
The Second Coming! Hardly are those words out
When a vast image out of Spiritus Mundi°
Troubles my sight: somewhere in sands of the
        desert
A shape with lion body and the head of a man,
15   A gaze blank and pitiless as the sun,
Is moving its slow thighs, while all about it
Reel shadows of the indignant desert birds.
The darkness drops again; but now I know
That twenty centuries of stony sleep
20   Were vexed to nightmare by a rocking cradle
And what rough beast, its hour come round at
        last,
Slouches towards Bethlehem to be born?   **Ⓑ**

---

12. Spiritus Mundi: Latin for "the world's soul or spirit"; for Yeats, the collective reservoir of human memory from which artists draw their images.

Ⓐ **Literary Focus** **Theme** If the falcon and the falconer represent order, what does the breakdown in their relationship suggest about Yeats's attitude toward conditions in his times?

Ⓑ **Reading Focus** **Visualizing Imagery** What details does Yeats use to help you visualize "the beast"?

Vocabulary **anarchy** (AN uhr kee) *n.:* disorder and confusion.
conviction (kuhn VIHK shuhn) *n.:* firm belief.
intensity (ihn TEHN suh tee) *n.:* great vigor.
revelation (rehv uh LAY shuhn) *n.:* act of making known.
vexed (vehkst) *v.:* troubled.

The Second Coming

Respond and Think Critically

Reading Focus

Read with a Purpose

1. What do you think Yeats foresees for the future?

Reading Skills: Visualizing Imagery

2. While reading, you noted descriptions of one of the poem's central images, the beast, in an idea web. Now, write a summary of what you see when you visualize the image of the beast described in the poem. Note some of the specific words that make this imagery especially vivid.

Literary Focus

Literary Analysis

3. Interpret What do you think the poet means by the word *center* in line 3? What condition does the phrase "the center cannot hold" describe?

4. Make Judgments To what might the "blood-dimmed tide" in line 5 refer? What could the "ceremony of innocence" in line 6 mean? Explain your interpretation.

5. Analyze If you had to name one dominant emotion expressed by the speaker, what would it be?

6. Evaluate Consider the poet's use of each of the following words: *mere* (line 4), *pitiless* (line 15), *indignant* (line 17), *stony* (line 19), and *slouches* (line 22). Think about the connotations of each word. What idea or emotion does each word help convey? How vivid or forceful do you find each word in its context?

7. Analyze Notice how the approximate rhyme of the first lines changes to unrhymed verse. Notice also the variation of the iambic pentameter. Where do the rhyme and rhythm change, and what is the effect? How does the poem's rhythm reflect the theme?

8. Extend Why might Yeats have ended the poem with a question? Explain.

Literary Skills: Theme

9. Interpret What message about the <u>inevitable</u> future does Yeats express in the poem? Do you agree with this message? Why or why not?

10. Analyze The first two lines of the poem present the image of a falconer who is unable to limit the flight of his released falcon. How does this image help convey one of the poem's central themes? (Remember that **theme** is the main message or insight of a literary work.) Consider the poem's historical context in your response.

11. Make Judgments How would you answer the poem's concluding question? How does your answer relate to the poem's theme?

Literary Skills Review: Irony

12. Analyze A discrepancy between what is expected and what happens is called **irony**. How does the idea of the Second Coming become **ironic** in the second stanza? How is this irony frightening?

Writing Focus

Think as a Reader/Writer

Use It in Your Writing Identify a message that you would like to express to readers. Then, write a poem or a paragraph that uses vivid imagery to convey this theme. Share your writing with the class.

What Do **You Think Now** What world events may have influenced Yeats to write this poem? Why?

Vocabulary Development

✓ Vocabulary Check

Match the Vocabulary words with their definitions.

1. anarchy
2. conviction
3. intensity
4. revelation
5. vexed

a. troubled
b. disorder
c. great vigor
d. act of making known
e. firm belief

Word	Language of Origin	Original Word and Meaning
anarchy	Greek	anarchos, meaning "having no ruler"
conviction		
intensity		
revelation		
vexed		

Vocabulary Skills: Etymology

Etymology is the history of a word. In many dictionaries, a precise etymology is given for each word, taking its history back to its origin. By studying etymologies, you can familiarize yourself with certain roots and their meanings. Doing so will help you determine the meanings of related words. Look at the following dictionary entry:

> **anarchy** (AN uhr kee) *n.* [ML *anarchia* < Gr *anarchos*, having no ruler < *an–*, without + *archos* ruler] a state of disorder.

The information in brackets gives the history of the word. The dictionary should have a key in the front to help you decipher the abbreviations. In this case, the word is traced back through Middle Latin (ML) to Greek (Gr). Other common abbreviations include *G* for German, *OE* for Old English, *ME* for Middle English, *F* for French, and *L* for Latin. Always check the dictionary's key to make certain you are reading the etymology properly.

Your Turn

Use a dictionary to look up the etymologies of the Vocabulary words. Use a chart like the one on the right to record the information you find.

Language Coach

Suffix –archy With a partner, look over the list of words with the suffix –*archy* that you identified. Use a dictionary to look up the meaning of each of the words. Based on their meanings, can you guess the meanings of the prefixes they include?

Academic Vocabulary

Talk About
Yeats possessed the ability to exhibit strong themes in both his poetic and his dramatic writing. With a partner, jot down reasons why Yeats might have been able to adapt to these considerably different forms.

Learn It Online
Develop your vocabulary online with Word Watch.

go.hrw.com L12-1203 **Go**

The Second Coming

Grammar Link

Active and Passive Voice Verbs

A verb in the **active voice** expresses an action performed by its subject:

> The student reads the poem.

[The subject, *student,* performs the action.]

A verb in the passive voice expresses an action performed on its subject:

> The poem is read by the student.

[The subject, *poem,* is acted upon. Notice the passive voice is a verb phrase with a *be* verb, (in this case, *is*) + the past participle, (in this case, *read*.)]

Active voice generally makes writing more powerful and precise than the passive voice does. However, sometimes writers use the passive voice for good reasons. For instance, Yeats uses the passive voice frequently in "The Second Coming" to suggest that the forces at work are beyond anyone's control.

> Mere anarchy *is loosed* upon the world,
> The blood-dimmed tide *is loosed,* and everywhere
> The ceremony of innocence *is drowned;*

Your Turn

In the following sentences, change the passive voice to the active voice. Add subjects where necessary.

1. "The Second Coming" was written by Yeats.

2. Yeats is considered one of the best poets of the twentieth century.

3. His work is studied in schools and universities.

4. His poetry and drama are appreciated by critics.

Writing Application Scan an essay you have written for sentences in which you used passive voice. Change the cases of passive voice to active voice, and read those sentences aloud. Do they sound more powerful?

CHOICES

As you respond to the Choices, use these **Academic Vocabulary** words as appropriate: perspective, considerably, adapt, exhibit, inevitable.

Great Sphinx against the pyramid of Khafra, on the Giza Plateau at the west bank of the Nile River, near Cairo, Egypt.

REVIEW
Analyze Allusion

Remember, an **allusion** is a reference in a work to another work or historical event. In this selection, Yeats alludes to the Sphinx at Giza. Review the poem and research the Sphinx. Write an essay exploring why Yeats chose this allusion.

CONNECT
Make a Digital Collage

TechFocus Make a digital collage of text, visual images, and sounds to illustrate "The Second Coming." Try to convey the poem's theme in your collage. Then, exhibit the collage for your class.

EXTEND
Give a Poetic Answer

Write a poem responding to the question posed in the final lines of "The Second Coming." You might share Yeats's perspective, or you might express a more positive viewpoint. Use vivid imagery to express your theme.

Preparing to Read

The Lake Isle of Innisfree

Reader/Writer Notebook

Use your **RWN** to complete the activities for this selection.

Literary Focus

Assonance and Alliteration **Assonance** is the repetition of vowel sounds in words that are close together; **alliteration** is the repetition of consonant sounds in words that are close together. Yeats's lyrical skills, especially his haunting use of assonance and alliteration, create poetry whose verbal music echoes in readers' memories. The lilting rhythms of the poem and the repetition of vowel and consonant sounds soothe and transport the reader. As you read, consider how these techniques affect the message and the emotional force of the poem.

Reading Focus

Connecting Text to Experience When you connect what you read with your experiences, you will better understand the ideas and feelings the text conveys. In this poem, the speaker imagines a retreat on a beautiful island. When your life becomes stressful, do you imagine a place or a time in which you feel calm and free? Have you experienced such a retreat?

Into Action Create a chart to record connections between the text and your own experience. In the first column, write details from the text about the speaker's imagined trip to Innisfree. In the second column, write details from a real or imagined peaceful retreat you have experienced.

Text	My Experience
The speaker will go to a small cabin on Innisfree.	I have spent some weekends camping outdoors in beautiful woods.

Writing Focus

Think as a Reader/Writer

Find It in Your Reading In addition to **alliteration** and **assonance,** Yeats uses inverts word order and uses repetition to create verbal music. In your *Reader/Writer Notebook,* record examples of these techniques in the poem.

Vocabulary

glade (glayd) *n.:* small open space in a forest. *The deer rested and nibbled grass in the glade.*

glimmer (GLIHM uhr) *n.:* faint, unsteady light. *He watched the glimmer of the stars in the night sky.*

Language Coach

Poetry Recitation Reading poetry aloud is sometimes difficult because the reader gets caught up in the rhythm of the poem and puts too much stress on the rhymes. Practice reading the sentences in the poem aloud. Try to read naturally and with fluency.

Learn It Online
Listen to the rhythms of this poem for yourself online.

The Lake Isle of Innisfree

by **William Butler Yeats**

Read with a Purpose
Read the poem to discover the speaker's vision of an ideal place.

Build Background
Innisfree is a real island in Sligo, a beautiful county in the west of Ireland where Yeats spent many summers as a child, visiting his grandparents. Yeats's father had once read Thoreau's *Walden* to him, and you may notice that the bean rows and cabin in this poem are straight from Thoreau's account of his life in the Walden Woods of Massachusetts.

I will arise and go now, and go to Innisfree,
And a small cabin build there, of clay and wattles° made:
Nine bean-rows will I have there, a hive for the honey-bee,
And live alone in the bee-loud glade.

5   And I shall have some peace there, for peace comes dropping slow,
Dropping from the veils of the morning to where the cricket sings;
There midnight's all a glimmer, and noon a purple glow,
And evening full of the linnet's° wings.   **Ⓐ**

I will arise and go now, for always night and day
10   I hear lake water lapping with low sounds by the shore;
While I stand on the roadway, or on the pavements gray,
I hear it in the deep heart's core.   **Ⓑ**

2. **wattles:** interwoven twigs or branches.

8. **linnet's:** A linnet is a European songbird.

Ⓐ Literary Focus Assonance and Alliteration   What examples of alliteration and assonance create verbal music in lines 5–8?

Ⓑ Reading Focus Connecting Text to Experience   When have you felt peaceful at your "heart's core"? Do you associate the feeling with a particular place and time? Explain.

Vocabulary   glade (glayd) *n.:* small open space in a forest.
glimmer (GLIHM uhr) *n.:* faint, unsteady light.

Applying Your Skills

Respond and Think Critically

Reading Focus

Read with a Purpose

1. What attributes of Innisfree does the speaker find ideal?

Reading Skills: Connecting Text to Experience

2. Look over the chart you made as you read. Add to each entry the speaker's feelings and your own feelings from your experience. How does this exercise help you connect with the text?

✔ Vocabulary Check

Fill in the blanks in the following sentence, using the Vocabulary words, *glimmer* and *glade.*

3. That evening we spread our picnic blanket in the _____ and watched the _____ of the flitting fireflies .

Literary Focus

Literary Analysis

4. Classify How would you classify the kind of life the speaker wants to lead on the island?

5. Infer To what does the speaker compare peace? Why might he have had a hard time finding peace in the city?

6. Drawing Conclusions What does the last stanza say about the speaker's relationship with nature?

7. Make Judgments The pronoun *I* appears seven times in this twelve-line poem. Why do you think the speaker so often inserts himself into the scene he describes? Does this presence make the poem more or less soothing to you? Explain.

Literary Skills: Assonance and Alliteration

8. Compare and Contrast What is Yeats's message about the future and its possibilities? How does this message compare to that of "The Second Coming"? Why do you think Yeats wrote poems with such different messages?

9. Evaluate What vowel sounds dominate the first stanza?

10. Analyze Explain how alliteration helps you experience the sights and sounds described in line 10.

11. Extend Read the poem aloud to a partner. Describe the total effect of the vowel sounds in the poem. How would the poem have been different if the poet had used more hard consonants, such as *k, d,* or *p*?

Literary Skills Review: Tone

12. Analyze The attitude a writer takes toward the reader, a subject, or a character is called **tone.** How would you describe the **tone** of the poem? Do you think it could be called a Romantic poem? Explain why or why not.

Writing Focus

Think As a Reader/Writer

Use It in Your Writing Review your notes on Yeats's use of alliteration, assonance, inversion, and repetition. Then, write a poem or a paragraph about a special place, using these techniques to create verbal music. If you like, begin with the words "I will arise and go now...."

 What role does daydreaming play in your life? Do you think the kind of daydreaming the speaker does in this poem is helpful? Why or why not?

Preparing to Read

Reader/Writer Notebook

Use your **RWN** to complete the activities for this selection.

Literary Focus

Symbol A **symbol** is a figure of speech in which a person, place, thing, or event stands both for itself and for something beyond itself. A symbol can be understood literally (for what it is) and also figuratively (as representative of something beyond itself). If Yeats's swans are to be regarded as symbols, what do they represent? As you read this poem, keep in mind that symbols are open-ended: Their meanings are various and open to interpretation.

Into Action The symbolism of the swans works well in the context in which they appear; the passing of time is central to the poem's meaning. Using a graphic organizer like the one below, track the references and images of time. Copy the words and phrases that reference time or the passing of time. Record the line number as in the examples below. What do the images suggest about time? How does the context of passing time affect your reading of the poem and the symbolism of the swans?

Images of Time	Meaning
autumn beauty (1)	Autumn suggests passing of time, getting older.
October twilight (3)	October is late in the year, and twilight is late in the day. Both suggest time passing, including aging and approaching death.

Vocabulary

clamorous (KLAM uhr uhs) *adj.:* loud and noisy. *The clamorous cries of the birds broke the stillness.*

passion (PASH uhn) *n.:* strong emotion. *Disappointments had dampened the man's passion for life.*

Language Coach

Multiple-Meaning Words Some words have more than one meaning. For example, Yeats uses the word *still* to mean "motionless" or "tranquil" in line 4. *Still* can also be used as an adverb to mean "up to this or that time." To determine which meaning is intended, study the word's context. How is *still* used in lines 19, 24, and 25?

Writing Focus

Think as a Reader/Writer

Find It in Your Reading Look for the **symbolism** that Yeats uses in "The Wild Swans at Coole." Consider what you already know about Yeats's life. Also keep in mind that swans are migratory, returning annually to the same places, and monogamous (they mate for life). As you read, note in your *Reader/Writer Notebook* details about how Yeats describes the swans in each stanza, and brainstorm ideas about what the swans might represent, or symbolize. Do the swans symbolize the same thing in each stanza of the poem, or does what they represent vary?

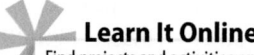

Learn It Online
Find projects and activities online to take your study of Yeats further.

go.hrw.com L12-1208   Go

POEM

The Wild Swans at Coole

by **William Butler Yeats**

Bewick's Swans over a Pearly Sea (1975) by Sir Peter Scott (1909–1989). Oil on canvas.

Read with a Purpose

Read to find out how the passage of time has affected the speaker's response to the familiar sight of the swans.

Build Background

Yeats's friend Lady Gregory lived on an estate known as Coole Park in Ireland's County Galway. When Yeats first visited there in 1897, he was in love with Maud Gonne, the political activist for Irish independence, who was more interested in politics than in Yeats. This poem, written in 1916, recalls Yeats's first view of the swans. Nineteen years later, he realizes, "All's changed."

The trees are in their autumn beauty,
The woodland paths are dry,
Under the October twilight the water
Mirrors a still sky;
5 Upon the brimming water among the stones
Are nine-and-fifty swans. **A**

The nineteenth autumn has come upon me
Since I first made my count;
I saw, before I had well finished,
10 All suddenly mount
And scatter wheeling in great broken rings
Upon their clamorous wings.

A **Literary Focus** Symbol   What does autumn often symbolize? Think about the time of year and what happens in nature.

Vocabulary **clamorous** (KLAM uhr uhs) *adj.:* loud and noisy.

I have looked upon those brilliant creatures,
And now my heart is sore.
15 All's changed since I, hearing at twilight,
The first time on this shore,
The bell-beat of their wings above my head,
Trod with a lighter tread.

Unwearied still, lover by lover,
20 They paddle in the cold
Companionable streams or climb the air;
Their hearts have not grown old;
Passion or conquest, wander where they will,
Attend upon them still.

25 But now they drift on the still water,
Mysterious, beautiful;
Among what rushes will they build,
By what lake's edge or pool
Delight men's eyes when I awake some day
30 To find they have flown away? **B**

Swan on River Wey, Sussex, England.

B Literary Focus Symbol In order to serve as a symbol, the swans must possess qualities that allow them to stand not only for themselves but also for something else. What words in lines 25–29 help establish the swans' status as symbols? What do you think the swans symbolize to the speaker?

Vocabulary **passion** (PASH uhn) *n.:* strong emotion.

Analyzing Visuals

Viewing and Interpreting What about the image might cause an observer to walk "with a lighter tread"?

SKILLS FOCUS **Literary Skills** Analyze symbols; analyze mood. **Vocabulary Skills** Demonstrate knowledge of literal meanings of words and their usage. **Writing Skills** Write poems; write descriptive essays.

Respond and Think Critically

Reading Focus

Quick Check

1. How does the speaker feel as he gazes at the swans?

2. How did he feel nineteen years earlier when he heard the beating of their wings?

3. Why do you think the speaker's heart is "sore"?

Read with a Purpose

4. How has the speaker's response to the swans changed over time? How do you account for this change?

✓ Vocabulary Check

Answer the questions about the Vocabulary words *clamorous* and *passion.*

5. Which word or words would you associate with **passion**—*love, hatred, boredom?*

6. Which would be **clamorous** near a concession stand at the beach—*gulls or crabs?*

Literary Focus

Literary Analysis

7. **Paraphrase** State in your own words the question the speaker asks in the last stanza.

8. **Interpret** The word *awake* in line 29 can be interpreted in different ways. Do you think that the speaker means it literally, as in *wake up in the morning,* or figuratively, as in *wake up from a daydream or illusion?* How might this word offer a clue about the theme of the poem?

9. **Extend** An **elegy** is a poem that mourns the death of a person or laments something that has been lost. Why might this poem be thought of as an elegy? How does the poem relate in theme, tone, and imagery to any of the other famous elegies in this book (pages 310, 982, and 1236)?

Literary Skills: Symbol

10. **Evaluate** What do you think is Yeats's message to readers in this poem about love and about the passage of time? Support your response with details from the poem.

11. **Make Judgments** What qualities of the swans do you think the speaker envies? Why? What might the swans symbolize to the speaker? Do the swans symbolize different things at different times in the speaker's life? Explain.

Literary Skills Review: Mood

12. **Analyze** The emotional atmosphere a poem evokes is called **mood.** How are the time of day and year in the poem appropriate to its **mood?**

Writing Focus

Think as a Reader/Writer

Use It in Your Writing Review your notes on Yeats's use of symbolism. Choose a common object that has qualities that could be seen as symbolic (a door, for example, might symbolize opportunity). Then, write a poem or paragraph in your *Reader/Writer Notebook* using the object as a symbol for something beyond what its literal meaning indicates.

 What Do You Think Now

Having read this poem, what are your thoughts on how the passage of time can change a person and his or her responses to familiar things?

Preparing to Read

 **Reader/Writer Notebook**
Use your **RWN** to complete the activities for this selection.

Literary Focus

Metaphor In a **metaphor,** two seemingly unlike things are compared without using a connective word, such as *like* or *as.* A metaphor talks of one thing as if it were another. Poets use metaphors to convey emotion and to suggest more than is possible with literal speech. For example, Yeats uses metaphors to speak about old age and art in the poem "Sailing to Byzantium." Look for other metaphors as you read.

Reading Focus

Analyzing Style The unique manner in which writers use language to express their ideas is called **style.** An author's style is closely connected to **diction,** or word choice, and **syntax,** or sentence construction. A writer's style may be categorized as formal, casual, plain, elevated, abstract, concrete, or any of a number of other descriptive words. A writer's use of **figurative language,** such as metaphor, is also part of his or her style.

Into Action As you read, use a spider map like the one below to analyze Yeats's style. Consider different elements of style, including diction, syntax, and figurative language.

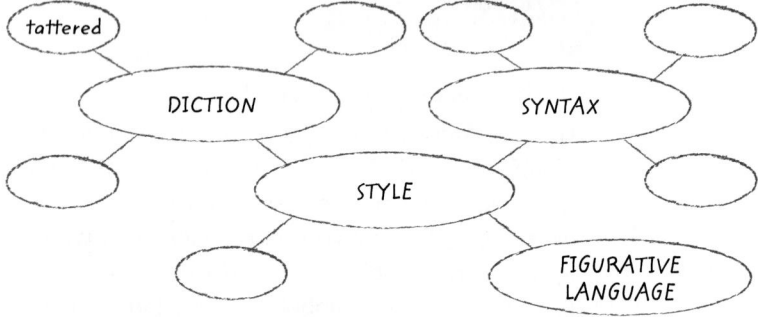

Writing Focus

Think as a Reader/Writer

Find It in Your Reading Yeats uses several **extended metaphors,** or metaphors that are developed throughout the poem. As you read, note in your *Reader/Writer Notebook* to what Yeats compares created things, including art. How are they different from "any natural thing"?

Vocabulary

sensual (SEHN shoo uhl) *adj.:* appealing to bodily senses rather than to the mind. *He distrusts sensual pleasures of food and drink.*

artifice (AHR tuh fihs) *n.:* human skill or craft, as opposed to what is natural. *He admired the artifice of the ornate buildings.*

Language Coach

Word Families Explore the word family of each Vocabulary word. Word families include words that are related because they have the same base word. For example, the word *sense* is related to *sensual,* and *artificial* is related to *artifice.* What other words can you find for each word family?

 **Learn It Online**
Explore Yeats and his work further through these Internet links.

go.hrw.com | L12-1212 | **Go**

Sailing to Byzantium

by **William Butler Yeats**

Read with a Purpose
Read to see how the speaker views art, as opposed to the natural world.

Build Background
Byzantium was an important symbol to Yeats, because the art created there during the fifth and sixth centuries represents humanity in a highly stylized and artificial way. For Yeats, the artificiality of the work shows the perfect union of form and idea and the perfect expression of spirit in a physical form that, unlike the human body, will never decay.

I

That is no country for old men. The young
In one another's arms, birds in the trees
—Those dying generations—at their song,
The salmon-falls, the mackerel-crowded seas,
5   Fish, flesh, or fowl, commend all summer long
Whatever is begotten, born, and dies.
Caught in that sensual music all neglect
Monuments of unaging intellect.   **A**

A **Literary Focus** Metaphor For what are "Monuments of unaging intellect" a metaphor?

Vocabulary **sensual** (SEHN shoo uhl) *adj.:* appealing to bodily senses rather than to the mind.

Blue Mosque and Hagia Sophia, Istanbul, Turkey. The first known name for Istanbul was Byzantium; later the city was called Constantinople, after the Roman emperor Constantine.

II

    An aged man is but a paltry thing,
10   A tattered coat upon a stick, unless
    Soul clap its hands and sing, and louder sing
    For every tatter in its mortal dress,
    Nor is there singing school but studying
    Monuments of its own magnificence;
15   And therefore I have sailed the seas and come
    To the holy city of Byzantium. **B**

III

    O sages standing in God's holy fire
    As in the gold mosaic of a wall,°
    Come from the holy fire, perne in a gyre,°
20   And be the singing-masters of my soul.
    Consume my heart away; sick with desire
    And fastened to a dying animal
    It knows not what it is; and gather me
    Into the artifice of eternity. **C**

IV

25   Once out of nature I shall never take
    My bodily form from any natural thing,
    But such a form as Grecian goldsmiths make
    Of hammered gold and gold enameling
    To keep a drowsy Emperor awake;
30   Or set upon a golden bough to sing°
    To lords and ladies of Byzantium
    Of what is past, or passing, or to come. **D**

17–18. sages… wall: Wise men and saints are depicted in gold mosaic on the walls of Byzantine churches in Ravenna, Italy, and in Sicily.

19. perne in a gyre: a spool spinning in a spiraling motion. For Yeats, this is an image of historical cycles.

29–30. a drowsy Emperor… sing: Yeats wrote, "I have read somewhere that in the Emperor's palace at Byzantium was a tree made of gold and silver, and artificial birds that sang."

B | **Literary Focus** | **Metaphor** To what does the speaker compare an "aged man"?

C | **Reading Focus** | **Analyzing Style** How would you describe the author's style in this stanza? For instance, is it formal or casual, simple or ornate, modern or antiquated, prosaic or poetic?

D | **Reading Focus** | **Analyzing Style** What do you notice about the author's diction and syntax? How do they affect the tone of the poem?

Vocabulary **artifice** (AHR tuh fihs) *n.*: human skill or craft, as opposed to what is natural.

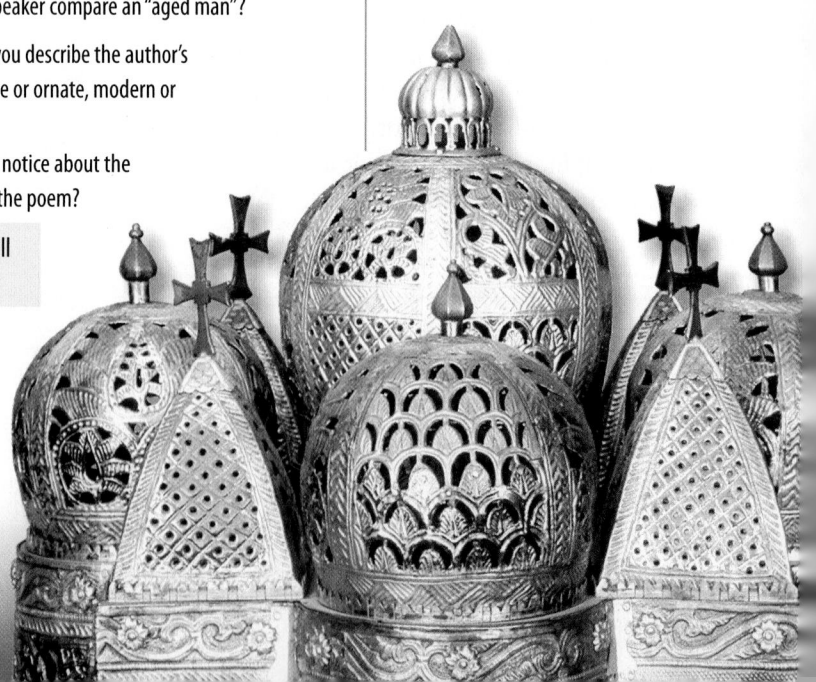

Incense burner in the form of a cupola (12th century).
St. Mark's Basilica, Venice, Italy.

Applying Your Skills

Sailing to Byzantium

Respond and Think Critically

Reading Focus

Quick Check

1. What do the "Fish, flesh, or fowl" in line 5 represent?

2. Of what is the speaker afraid? What does he seek by sailing to Byzantium?

3. What might the soul that "clap[s] its hands, and sing[s]" represent?

Read with a Purpose

4. What does art represent to the speaker? How is it a way to rise above the human condition?

Reading Skills: Analyzing Style

5. While reading "Sailing to Byzantium," you used a spider map to help analyze the writer's style. Now that you have finished reading, review your spider map and determine how you would characterize Yeats's style in this poem.

✓ Vocabulary Check

Use the Vocabulary words, **sensual** and **artifice,** to fill in the blanks in the following sentence.

6. The sculptor used eye-catching _____ and _____ materials, such as smooth, cool marble, to create fascinating statues.

Literary Focus

Literary Analysis

7. **Contrast** How is the country in the first stanza contrasted to Byzantium?

8. **Interpret** What does Yeats mean by "Monuments of unaging intellect" in line 8?

9. **Infer** What form does the speaker choose as a reflection of his soul? What does his choice tell you of his feelings about old age and death?

10. **Extend** The **rhyme scheme** is the pattern of rhymed lines in a poem. It can be indicated with the letters of the alphabet, as in *abcb*. Each new rhyme is assigned a new letter. What is the rhyme scheme of each stanza of this poem? (Consider the use of slant, or imperfect, rhyme in your answer.) How does the rhyme scheme affect your understanding and enjoyment of the poem?

Literary Skills: Metaphor

11. **Analyze** Choose a metaphor from the poem, identify the things being compared, and explain how the comparison contributes to the poem's meaning.

Literary Skills Review: Symbol

12. **Analyze** A **symbol** is a person, place, thing, or event that stands both for itself and for something beyond itself. Byzantium is a symbol in this poem. What other symbols can you find? What does each symbol represent for Yeats?

Writing Focus

Think as a Reader/Writer

Use It in Your Writing Now that you have studied how Yeats uses an extended metaphor, try using one in your own writing. Write a paragraph describing a place that you find magical. Use at least one extended metaphor in your description.

What Do **You Think Now**

How do you think Yeats's experience of aging might have shaped his views about art and his writing?

Preparing to Read

Reader/Writer
Notebook
Use your **RWN** to complete the activities for this selection.

Literary Focus

Connotations All of the associations and emotions that have come to be attached to a word are its **connotations.** For example, the word *cheap* means "economical," but it also has the negative connotation of being poor in quality. *Inexpensive* can also mean "economical" but lacks the negative connotation. Writers choose words with specific connotations to express particular ideas and to elicit certain responses from readers.

Reading Focus

Analyzing Author's Perspective The **author's perspective** is his or her viewpoint, or opinion, about the topic of the writing. The author shares his or her <u>perspective</u> by choosing precise words with just the right connotations and by including certain details. Sometimes authors state their perspective, but more often the reader must infer the author's perspective by analyzing word choice, connotations, and details.

Into Action Use a chart like the one below to record words, phrases, and details that convey the author's <u>perspective</u>. Note where these details appear in the text as in the example below.

Words, phrases, details	Perspective
"her great height" (p. 1217)	She is physically tall, but her height also serves as a metaphor. She looms large in the author's mind. She is a larger-than-life figure.

Vocabulary

disillusionment (dihs ih LOO zhehn muhnt) *n.:* being disenchanted, or freed from a false idea. *Disillusionment followed when she learned that her cause had been betrayed.*

vehemently (VEE uh muhnt lee) *adv.:* with strong feeling; passionately. *Yeats spoke vehemently in his proposal.*

incoherent (ihn koh HIHR uhnt) *adj.:* confused; rambling. *The incoherent outburst revealed the depth of her grief.*

Language Coach

Negating Prefixes Prefixes that reverse the meaning of a word are called **negating prefixes.** The prefix *in–* can work as a negating prefix, as in *incoherent,* which is the opposite of *coherent.* List two other words that start with the negating prefix *in–*. Can you identify another Vocabulary word that has a different negating prefix?

Writing Focus

Think as a Reader/Writer
Find It in Your Reading Yeats includes many adjectives to describe Maud Gonne. For instance, he describes her as "wasted," and "gentle and indolent." As you read, note in your *Reader/Writer Notebook* the adjectives Yeats uses to describe Gonne, as well as their **connotations.**

Learn It Online
Practice the Vocabulary words with Word Watch online.

go.hrw.com   L12-1216   **Go**

from

The Autobiography of William Butler Yeats

by **William Butler Yeats**

Read with a Purpose
Read to discover the intensity of Yeats's feelings for Maud Gonne, with whom he was obsessed for decades.

Build Background
This selection is mainly about Yeats's relationship with Maud Gonne, a radical political activist who spent time in prison for fighting for her country's rights. Yeats spent most of his adulthood enamored with Gonne and proposed marriage to her twice.

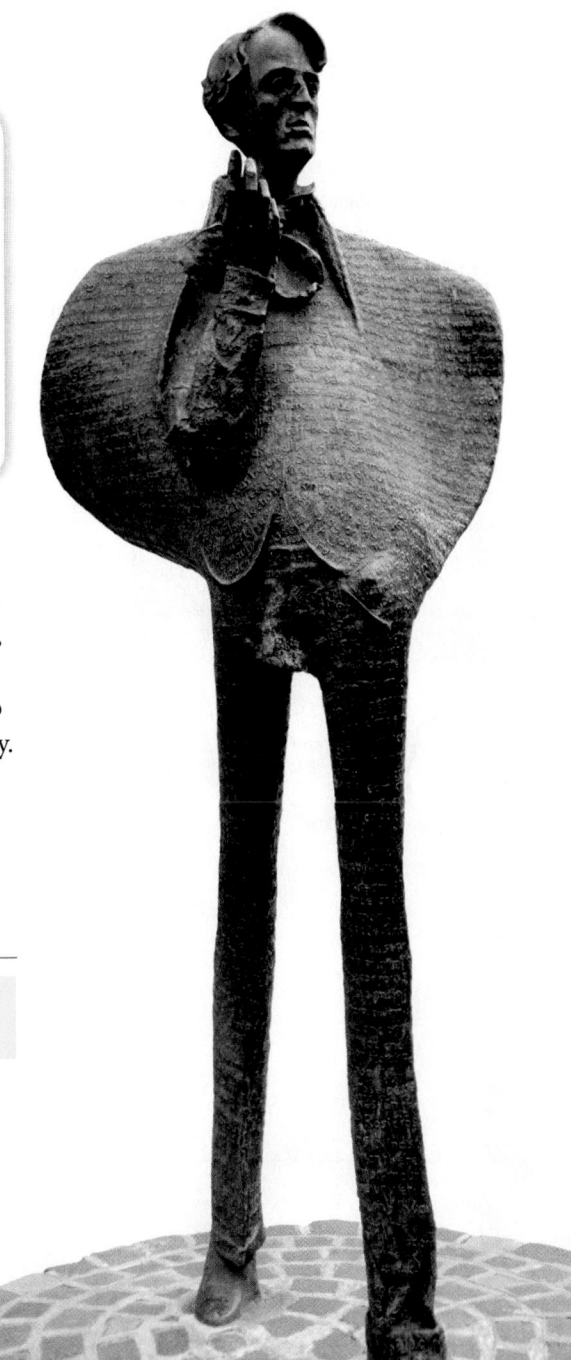

A few months later I was again in Ireland and I heard that she was in Dublin. I called and waited for her at a little hotel in Nassau Street, which no longer exists, in a room overlooking the College Park. At the first sight of her as she came through the door, her great height seeming to fill it, I was overwhelmed with emotion, an intoxication of pity. She did not seem to have any beauty, her face was wasted, the form of the bones showing, and there was no life in her manner. As our talk became intimate, she hinted at some unhappiness, some disillusionment. The old hard resonance had

Vocabulary   disillusionment (dihs ihh LOO zhehn muhnt) *n.:* being disenchanted; being freed from a false idea.

Analyzing Visuals

Viewing and Interpreting   Note the figure's exaggerated proportions. Why might an artist or writer overemphasize certain features when depicting a subject or even himself or herself?

Bronze statue of William Butler Yeats. Sligo, Ireland.

1217

gone and she had become gentle and indolent. I was in love once more and no longer wished to fight against it. I no longer thought what kind of wife would this woman make, but of her need for protection and for peace. (A) (B)

Yet I left Dublin next day to stay somewhere in Orange Ulster with the brilliant student of my old Dublin school, Charles Johnston, and spent a week or ten days with him and his elder brother, making fire balloons.[1] We made the fire balloons of tissue paper

---

1. **fire balloons:** small, unmanned hot-air balloons.

(A) **Literary Focus** Connotations What connotation does *intoxication* have in this paragraph? What does it add to Yeats's description of his feelings? What connotation does *wasted* have in this paragraph? What does it add to the description of Gonne?

(B) **Reading Focus** Analyzing Author's Perspective How does Yeats view being "in love once more"? What is his attitude toward Gonne?

and then chased them over the countryside, our chase becoming longer and longer as our skill in manufacture improved. I was not, it seems – not altogether – captive; but presently came from her a letter touching a little upon her sadness, and telling of a dream of some past life.[2] She and I had been brother and sister somewhere on the edge of the Arabian desert, and sold together into slavery. She had an impression of some long journey and of miles upon miles of the desert sand. I returned to Dublin at once, and that evening, but a few minutes after we had met, asked her to marry me. I remember a curious thing. I had come into the room with that purpose in my mind, and hardly looked at her or thought of her beauty. I sat there holding her hand and speaking vehemently. She did not take away her hand for a while. I ceased to speak, and presently as I sat in silence I felt her nearness to me and her beauty. At once I knew that my confidence had gone, and an instant later she drew her hand away. No, she could not marry – there were reasons – she would never marry; but in words that had no conventional ring she asked for my friendship. We spent the next day upon the cliff paths at Howth and dined at a little cottage near the Baily Lighthouse, where her old nurse lived, and I overheard the old nurse asking if we were engaged to be married. At the day's end I found I had spent ten shillings, which seemed to me a very great sum. (C)

---

2. **a dream of some past life:** Yeats was a believer in reincarnation.

(C) **Reading Focus** Analyzing Author's Perspective How does Yeats perceive Gonne as he enters the room? What does he think about?

Vocabulary vehemently (VEE uh muhnt lee) *adv.:* with strong feeling; passionately.

> I returned to Dublin at once, and that evening, but a few minutes after we had met, asked her to marry me.

Maud Gonne (1865–1953)

She had adopted a little girl, she told me, some three years ago, and now this child had died.

Maud Gonne

I saw her day after day. I read her my unfinished *The Countess Cathleen*,[3] and I noticed that she became moved at the passage, 'the joy of losing joy, of ceasing all resistance' –

[there is a kind of joy
In casting hope away, in losing joy,
In ceasing all resistance]

—————
3. ***The Countess Cathleen:*** play by Yeats that was first produced in 1899.

and thought, she is burdened by a sense of responsibility for herself. I told her after meeting her in London I had come to understand the tale of a woman selling her soul to buy food for a starving people as a symbol of all souls who lose their peace, or their fineness, or any beauty of the spirit in political service, but chiefly of her soul that had seemed so incapable of rest. For the moment she had no political work nor plan of any, and we saw each other continually. Suddenly she was called back to France, and she told me in confidence that she had joined a secret political society and though she had come to look upon its members as self-seekers and adventurers she could not disobey this, the first definite summons it had sent to her. I stayed in Ireland, probably at Sligo with my uncle, George Pollexfen, finishing *The Countess Cathleen* that had become but the symbolical song of my pity. Then came a letter of wild sorrow. She had adopted a little child, she told me, some three years ago, and now this child had died. Mixed into her incoherent grief were accounts of the death bird that had pecked at the nursery window the day when it was taken ill, and how at sight of the bird she had brought doctor after doctor. **D E**

D Reading Focus **Analyzing Author's Perspective** What do you make of Yeats's comparison of Gonne to a woman who sells her soul to buy food for starving people? What does it reveal about his view of Gonne?

E Reading Focus **Analyzing Author's Perspective** What does Yeats's reference to his play as the "symbolical song of my pity" tell you about his perspective on his situation with Gonne?

Vocabulary **incoherent** (ihn koh HIHR uhnt) *adj.*: confused; rambling.

Applying Your Skills

SKILLS FOCUS Literary Skills Analyze connotation; analyze paradox. **Reading Skills** Analyze author's perspective. **Vocabulary Skills** Demonstrate knowledge of literal meanings of words and their usage. **Writing Skills** Describe a person.

from **The Autobiography of William Butler Yeats**

Respond and Think Critically

Reading Focus

Quick Check

1. Why is Yeats "overwhelmed with emotion" upon first seeing Maud Gonne?

2. Why do you think Yeats returns to Dublin after reading Maud Gonne's letter about her dream?

3. How does Yeats respond to Gonne's rejection?

Read with a Purpose

4. How would you describe Yeats's relationship with Maud Gonne?

Reading Skills: Analyzing Author's Perspective

5. Review the chart you filled in as you read. Based on the words, phrases, and details you noted and the perspectives they revealed, what is Yeats's perspective on his relationship with Maud Gonne? Add a row to the bottom of the chart, analyzing his overall perspective.

✔ Vocabulary Check

Answer the questions about the Vocabulary words.

6. Are you more likely to feel **disillusionment** if your favorite athlete loses a game honestly or if you discover he or she has won by cheating?

7. Would a person who speaks **vehemently** be described as calm or excited?

8. Would you be more likely to be **incoherent** when you're exhausted or well rested? Calm or upset? Confident or nervous?

Literary Focus

Literary Analysis

9. **Analyze** What is ironic about Yeats's description of Gonne and his love for her?

10. **Infer** What is Yeats's state of mind when he asks Gonne to marry him? How do you know?

11. **Make Judgments** Based on what you've read, what do you think of Gonne's character? Explain.

Literary Skills: Connotations

12. **Analyze** Choose three words from the selection whose connotations are important to understanding Yeats's feelings about Maud Gonne. Explain how those connotations affect your understanding of the author's feelings.

Literary Skills Review: Paradox

13. **Analyze** An apparent contradiction that is actually true is called a **paradox.** What does Yeats mean by "there is a kind of joy in casting hope away, in losing joy, in ceasing all resistance" (p. 1219)? Why do you think Gonne was moved by the passage?

Writing Focus

Think as a Reader/Writer

Use It in Your Writing Review the adjectives you noted as you read. In a paragraph, describe a person who inspires you. Choose adjectives with powerful connotations to express your feelings.

 What Do **You Think Now** How do you think Yeats's experience with unrequited love might have affected him as a writer?

SKILLS FOCUS **Literary Skills** Analyze elements of poetry; analyze style. **Writing Skills** Analyze other writers' strategies; compare literary works; compare themes or literary elements. **Listening and Speaking Skills** Engage in appreciative listening; organize and present oral interpretations: poems.

Author Study: William Butler Yeats

Writing Focus

Writing a Comparison-Contrast Essay

Review the criteria for a good comparison-contrast essay before you begin.

An effective comparison-contrast essay

- states the basis of the comparison and contrast in a thesis
- organizes ideas using the point-by-point method
- uses and cites text evidence to support each point of comparison and contrast
- contains few or no errors in spelling, punctuation, and usage

Prewriting

William Butler Yeats expressed his concern for the world's future and his own personal pessimism in a unique style that marks him as one of the twentieth century's foremost poets. Choose any two of his poems to compare and contrast. First, choose poems that have a strong basis of similarity, other than having the same author. As you study the poems, also look closely for ways in which they differ. Your analysis should include both similarities and differences.

Gather Details Use a T-chart like the one below to record notes about each poem. Read the poems closely, noting Yeats's use of language and theme.

The Second Coming	Sailing to Byzantium

Re-read your T-chart to discover at least one strong basis of similarity. Circle those notes in one color. Look again to determine if there is another strong similarity. Circle those notes in another color. If there is only one major similarity, proceed to the differences. Use another color to identify at least one significant difference. You will have color-coded your close reading of the poems to discover your analysis points. Consider the following ideas or your own for analyzing two of Yeats's poems:

- Compare and contrast Yeats's view of the future.
- Compare and contrast the use of allusion.
- Compare and contrast the use of irony.
- Compare the influence of Irish heritage.

Develop a Thesis Statement Using your notes, develop a thesis statement that makes an assertion about both the similarities and differences in the poems you select. Always begin with a basis of similarity (such as the use of allusions), and then focus on the differences in the two poems. Sample thesis:

Yeats uses religious and historical allusions to express a pessimism about both the past and the future.

Drafting

Because you are using the point-by-point method of organization, begin with the strongest comparison linking the two poems. Develop it in your first body paragraph. In your following body paragraphs, develop either additional similarities or differences. Discuss both poems in each paragraph. In your final body paragraph, focus on the differences between the two poems.

Text Evidence Use direct quotations from both poems to support each point. Punctuate the quotations as the author did, and interweave them into your own sentences.

Revising and Editing

Re-read your draft to determine if you have fully supported your thesis with explanation and text evidence. Correct any grammatical and mechanics errors.

What Do
You Think Now

After reading poems that appeared throughout Yeats's life, how do you think his experiences affected his writing?

Preparing to Read

Musée des Beaux Arts

W. H. Auden (1907-1973)

MEET THE WRITER

W. H. Auden
(1907–1973)

Wystan Hugh Auden named the times in which he lived the "Age of Anxiety," but as far as poetry was concerned, that same era could have been called the Age of Auden given the breadth and depth of his influence.

The Early Influences of Religion

Auden was born in York, a city in northern England. His father was a physician and his mother a nurse. In his adolescence, Auden discovered poetry, and he studied all its forms with an analytical eye. By the time Auden entered Oxford, he was as much a teacher as a student, and quickly surrounded himself with other young poets who accepted him as their leader.

Auden's sympathies during the 1930s were with the Left, and, like many young intellectuals of the time, he went to Spain during its Civil War to serve as an ambulance driver on the left-wing Republican side. However, he was disturbed by the Republicans' looting of Roman Catholic churches and left Spain without doing anything to help the Republican cause.

Back in England Auden saw economic stagnation and mass unemployment. At first his work was influenced by Freud and Marx, but gradually his poetry reflected a more religious perspective, as he found reality more ambiguous and troubling than he had imagined.

A Move to America

Auden shocked his British compatriots when, in 1939, as Hitler's divisions were about to march into Poland and ignite World War II, he decided to make his home in the United States. Auden had received an invitation to teach at the University of Michigan, and with the rise of fascism in Europe, he believed his chances of enjoying creative freedom were greatest in America. In 1946, he became a U.S. citizen.

Auden's immigration to the United States was at the time regarded as a defection, but when he moved back to England in the last year of his life, to seek safety and companionship in a university community, the British welcomed him back.

Think About the Writer

Why do you think Auden called his times the "Age of Anxiety"?

Reader/Writer Notebook

Use your **RWN** to complete the activities for this selection.

Literary Focus

Diction In addition to the great masters of poetry and the music of British dance halls, the blues songs of America also influenced Auden. As you read this poem, note where he adopts **colloquial language,** the common language of daily life. Auden purposefully pairs this colloquial language alongside eloquent poetic language to create contrasting **diction,** or word choice. This diction works to surprise the reader, who may expect only lofty, dignified language in poetry, as well as creates an offhand tone that unnerves the reader by mirroring the randomness of the real world.

Reading Focus

Identifying Theme A theme is a central idea or insight about human experience revealed in a work of literature. Writers do not usually state their themes directly but instead imply them through subtle diction and various literary devices. As a reader, you must piece together the significant details and determine what theme those details reveal. No two readers of the same work will state its theme in exactly the same way; indeed, sometimes, literature reveals more than one theme.

Into Action As you read, use an idea web to organize theme-related details in the poem that seem especially important, even puzzling.

Writing Focus

Think as a Reader/Writer

Find It in Your Reading As you read the poem, note in your *Reader/Writer Notebook* the speaker's occasional use of colloquial, or informal, **diction** to describe what he sees. Does the informal language give you an especially vivid picture of the scene? Use examples from the text to explain your answer.

Vocabulary

reverently (REHV uhr uhnt lee) *adv.:* with reverence and respect. *Auden imagines the aged reverently waiting for a miraculous birth.*

martyrdom (MAHR tuhr duhm) *n.:* death of a martyr, someone who dies for his or her beliefs. *Auden refers to paintings of people who suffered martyrdom for their religion.*

leisurely (LEE zhuhr lee) *adv.:* without hurry; taking plenty of time. *As Icarus fell, the unhurried plowman continued to plow leisurely.*

forsaken (fawr SAY kuhn) *adj.:* forlorn; abandoned. *Auden imagines he hears the falling boy's forsaken cry.*

Language Coach

Adverbs and Adjectives Many adverbs (words that modify verbs, adjectives, or other adverbs) end in —*ly.* Adjectives (words that modify nouns or pronouns) do not often end in —*ly.* You can sometimes change an adverb to an adjective by deleting the —*ly.* Which Vocabulary word can you change to an adjective by removing the —*ly*? Is there a Vocabulary word that ends with —*ly* and that can be used as an adverb or an adjective?

✳ **Learn It Online**
Find out more about Auden and his inspiration for this poem through these Internet links.

go.hrw.com   L12-1223   **Go**

Musée des Beaux Arts by **W. H. Auden**

Read with a Purpose
Read to discover what this speaker sees in the museum that makes him think about human suffering.

Build Background
The source and inspiration for this poem are found in Pieter Bruegel's famous sixteenth-century painting *The Fall of Icarus,* which depicts a dramatic moment in the Greek legend of the great craftsman Daedalus and his son Icarus. According to the legend, the two men were imprisoned on the island of Crete. Daedalus made wings of feathers and wax, and together he and his son used these wings to fly off the island. In his excitement, Icarus flew too high. The sun's heat melted the wax in his wings, causing him to plummet into the sea, where he drowned.

About suffering they were never wrong,
The Old Masters: ° how well they understood
Its human position; how it takes place
While someone else is eating or opening a window or just walking
    dully along; **Ⓐ**
5 How, when the aged are reverently, passionately waiting
For the miraculous birth, there always must be
Children who did not specially want it to happen, skating
On a pond at the edge of the wood:
They never forgot
10 That even the dreadful martyrdom must run its course
Anyhow in a corner, some untidy spot
Where the dogs go on with their doggy life and the torturer's horse
Scratches its innocent behind on a tree. **Ⓑ**

In Bruegel's *Icarus,* for instance: how everything turns away
15 Quite leisurely from the disaster; the plowman may
Have heard the splash, the forsaken cry,
But for him it was not an important failure; the sun shone
As it had to on the white legs disappearing into the green
Water; and the expensive delicate ship that must have seen
20 Something amazing, a boy falling out of the sky,
Had somewhere to get to and sailed calmly on. **Ⓒ**

---

2. Old Masters: European painters of great skill who painted before 1800.

Ⓐ Reading Focus Identifying Theme What is the ironic contrast in the first four lines?

Ⓑ Literary Focus Diction What words in the first stanza seem colloquial or unpoetic to you?

Ⓒ Reading Focus Identifying Theme What do the plowman and the ship do when Icarus falls into the sea and drowns? How do these actions relate to details in the first four lines?

Vocabulary **reverently** (REHV uhr uhnt lee) *adv.:* with reverence and respect.
martyrdom (MAHR tuhr duhm) *n.:* death of a martyr, someone who dies for his or her beliefs.
leisurely (LEE zhuhr lee) *adv.:* without hurry; taking plenty of time.
forsaken (fawr SAY kuhn) *adj.:* forlorn; abandoned.

The Fall of Icarus by Pieter Bruegel the Elder.   Royal Museum of Fine Arts of Belgium.

Bruegel's *The Fall of Icarus*

According to one critic, Pieter Bruegel's painting *The Fall of Icarus* represents "the greatest conception of indifference" in the history of art. The indifference, whether it is that of the artist or a strategy of technique, lies in its unexpected focus. The painting's center of interest is not Icarus but a peasant plowing a field. The peasant is handsomely dressed—in medieval rather than ancient Greek costume—and the furrows he tills are richly realistic. In the lower right-hand corner, almost as an afterthought, Icarus is seen splashing into the water not far from a passing ship.

Ask Yourself

Study the painting, and find the figure of the boy falling into the sea. Has Auden expressed in words what Bruegel expressed with paint? Which expression of the theme, written or painted, do you find more compelling? Why?

SKILLS FOCUS Literary Skills Analyze diction; analyze tone. **Reading Skills** Identify and analyze theme. **Vocabulary Skills** Demonstrate knowledge of literal meanings of words and their usage. **Writing Skills** Write poems.

Respond and Think Critically

Reading Focus

Quick Check

1. According to lines 1–4, what did the Old Masters understand about suffering?

2. What example of his theory about the Old Masters does the speaker offer in lines 14–21?

Read with a Purpose

3. Why did this painting inspire the speaker?

Reading Skills: Identifying Theme

4. Remember that **theme** is the central idea or truth about life revealed in a text. In the idea web you created, highlight the details from the poem that you think are especially important. Then, in your own words, state the theme of the poem in the center circle of the web. Be sure to compare your thematic statements in class.

✓ Vocabulary Check

Match each Vocabulary word with its definition.

5. reverently   **a.** abandoned

6. martyrdom   **b.** with respect

7. leisurely   **c.** without hurry

8. forsaken   **d.** death of someone on behalf of a cause

Literary Focus

Literary Analysis

9. **Hypothesize** Lines 5–13 describe two other paintings, perhaps by Bruegel, perhaps by other Old Masters. Based on hints in these lines, what events do you think are portrayed in these two paintings? How do bystanders in the paintings respond to these events?

10. **Hypothesize** What details in lines 5–13 suggest that these other paintings to which the speaker refers might be religious in nature?

11. **Interpret** What is meant by line 17: "for [the plowman] it was not an important failure"?

12. **Evaluate** Re-read lines 14–21 of the poem. Has Auden correctly interpreted the meaning of Bruegel's painting? Use evidence from both the text and the painting to support your ideas.

13. **Make Judgments** Do you agree with Auden's view of how people respond to the suffering of others? Explain.

Literary Skills: Diction

14. **Compare and Contrast** What contrast in diction can you see between expressions such as "dreadful martyrdom" and "doggy life"? Find another example of contrasting diction and explain its effect.

Literary Skills Review: Tone

15. **Analyze** The attitude a writer takes toward a subject is called **tone.** What tone do you detect in Auden's poem? Is he sorrowful, bitter, sarcastic, cynical, humorous, or something else?

Writing Focus

Think as a Reader/Writer

Use It in Your Writing As you read, you noted Auden's use of colloquial diction to describe what is happening in Bruegel's painting. Now, select one of the paintings in this book and write a poem about it. Use colloquial diction to describe the painting.

What Do **You** **Think** **Now** What experiences did Auden have that might explain his <u>perspective</u> on the way people respond to the suffering of others?

Reading Focus

Fern Hill

Analyzing Details by **Kylene Beers**

Look through this book for a piece of artwork that you like. Go ahead. Flip through the book, and find that art, and study it.… Now, think about that piece of art. While you liked the whole picture, there were details that caught your eye—the subtle (or bold) colors, the way someone was standing or sitting, the expression on someone's face. Details provide more meaning, more substance to what we are seeing or reading. When you read, you find details in the same way that you saw details in the art: You look carefully not at the whole, but at the parts.

Poets select details that express emotions or experiences in unique and memorable ways. Carefully chosen details form the basis of vivid images and figurative language. By analyzing details you can come to a richer understanding of a poem. Follow these steps to analyze details in a poem:

First, read and re-read a poem to identify the striking details. In Dylan Thomas's "Fern Hill," for example, the poem's speaker describes himself as "green and carefree," and then as "green and dying," creating a contrasting and contradictory image. Let's focus on Thomas's use of the word *green,* which he uses repeatedly in the poem to describe the setting and the speaker.

Next, consider what the details represent literally. The word *green* denotes a color and suggests youth, vigor, freshness, and inexperience. When *green* describes a natural setting, one imagines plants, as in the spring or summer.

Because poetry expresses meaning figuratively, you next should explore meaning beyond the literal level. A young person described as green may be full of hope and potential. If the landscape is green, then it is probably fertile and fruitful. Therefore, *green* in both cases can be read as promising new life.

Finally, consider how the detail fits together with the rest of the poem. *Green* suggests the promise of

new life, yet it is ironically and paradoxically juxtaposed in the second-to-last line with the word *dying,* highlighting one of Thomas's persistent themes—the lurking presence of death in life, of the worm in the seed.

To analyze details from any poem, not only one of Thomas's, ask yourself these questions:

· What are the most striking or memorable details?
· Does the poet repeat any words or phrases?
· What do these words or images represent on a literal level? on a figurative level?
· How do they make me feel?
· Why does the poet choose these particular details?
· What is their overall meaning in the work?
· What meaning can I **infer** from these details?

Your Turn

Read the second stanza of "Fern Hill" printed below. Identify memorable details. Then use the analysis questions to help you interpret them. Write a constructed response analyzing the details you find most striking.

> And as I was green and carefree, famous
>   among the barns
> About the happy yard and singing as the farm
>   was home,
>   In the sun that is young once only,
>   Time let me play and be
>   Golden in the mercy of his means,
> And green and golden I was huntsman and
>   herdsman, the calves
> Sang to my horn, the foxes on the hills barked
>   clear and cold,
>   And the Sabbath rang slowly
>   In the pebbles of the holy streams.

 Learn It Online

Learn how to analyze details the multimedia way through *PowerNotes* online.

go.hrw.com | L12-1227 | Go

Fern Hill

Do Not Go Gentle into That Good Night

How does experience shape our view of the world?

QuickWrite

Childhood is often remembered as a time of carefree innocence. Take a few minutes to free-write about one happy childhood memory of your own in your *Reader/Writer Notebook*.

Dylan Thomas (c. 1937) by Augustus Edwin John. National Museum of Wales, Cardiff. © Courtesy of the Estate of Augustus John.

Dylan Thomas
(1914–1953)

Dylan Thomas was a prodigy, a supremely gifted youth who wrote some of his most famous works before he was twenty.

Early Success and Early Struggles

Born in Swansea, Wales, Dylan Thomas was largely self-educated, choosing the rough-and-tumble life of a newspaper reporter over the comparative serenity of a university education. His recognition by the leading poets and critics of Britain and the United States came early, and with it came international fame. Neither was enough to prevent him from living on the edge of poverty. The temporary solace he found in alcohol led to his early death.

Universally Celebrated

A man of magical presence with a transparent hunger for affection, Thomas charmed both his British and American contemporaries. When he first came to America in 1950, he was regarded as the most charismatic British visitor since Oscar Wilde in 1885, and those who attended Thomas's readings responded to his personal magnetism. They also heard something new in modern poetry, a kind of expression combining the oratorical *hywl,* or chanting eloquence, of the Welsh chapel service with the theatrical delivery of Victorian actors who thrilled audiences with recitations from Shakespeare and Marlowe.

His *Collected Poems*, published in 1952, established Thomas as a major 20th-century poet. Nevertheless, Thomas found it increasingly difficult to concentrate sufficiently to write poetry. Consequently, he turned to other genres and produced two works that became familiar around the world: the play *Under Milk Wood* (1954) and the lyrical memoir *A Child's Christmas in Wales* (1955).

Celebrated by critics, sought after by American lecture agencies, and idolized almost like a rock star, Thomas died at the height of a fame he could neither accept nor enjoy. "Once I was lost and proud," he told a *New York Times* reporter, "now I'm found and humble. I prefer that other."

Think About the Writer   What do you think Thomas meant by his statement (quoted in the last paragraph above) to the *New York Times* reporter ?

Fern Hill

Reader/Writer Notebook

Use your **RWN** to complete the activities for this selection.

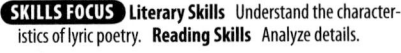
Literary Focus

Lyric Poetry Rather than telling a story, **lyric poetry** focuses on expressing emotions or thoughts. In the lyric poem "Fern Hill," Dylan Thomas uses a range of **sound effects** and **figures of speech** to convey vivid memories of a young boy's enchanted life in the Welsh countryside. Although the speaker's memories are colored by reflection and experience, the exuberance of his feelings, above all, claims our attention.

Literary Perspectives Apply the literary perspective described on page 1230 as you read this poem.

Reading Focus

Analyzing Details The details that a writer includes in his or her work are carefully chosen to convey thoughts, feelings, and impressions. In poetry, many of the details are **sensory details,** or details that appeal to the senses of sight, sound, smell, taste, and touch. **Analyzing details** can help you better understand the emotions and thoughts conveyed by lyric poetry.

Into Action As you read, use a graphic organizer like the one below to record details that help you imagine the scene and share the speaker's feelings and experiences. You might group details according to the senses to which they appeal.

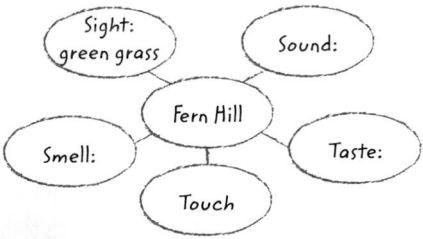

Vocabulary

lilting (LIHLT ihng) *v.* used as *adj.:* singing or speaking with a gentle rhythm. *The child's lilting voice expressed his joy.*

carefree (KAIR free) *adj.:* without worry; happy. *The speaker in "Fern Hill" recalls the happy, carefree days he spent outdoors as a child.*

heedless (HEED lihs) *adj.:* careless. *He ran heedless through the fields, unmindful of any threats or dangers.*

tuneful (TOON fuhl) *adj.:* musical; melodious. *The tuneful song of the birds filled the sky.*

Language Coach

Antonyms Pairs of words that have opposite meanings are called **antonyms.** It is relatively easy to think of antonyms for certain words. For example, you might be able to quickly decide that *worried* is an antonym for *carefree* and that *careful* is an antonym for *heedless.* What about the words *lilting* and *tuneful?* Can you find appropriate antonyms for them? What words can you think of that have meanings nearly opposite to theirs?

Writing Focus

Think as a Reader/Writer

Find It in Your Reading As you read "Fern Hill," use your *Reader/Writer Notebook* to record the concrete nouns that Thomas includes in his poem. For instance, in the first stanza these nouns include *apple boughs, house, grass, eyes, wagons, prince, trees, leaves, daisies, barley, rivers,* and *light.* Consider how these details create mental pictures as you read.

 **Learn It Online**
Discover this poem with the introductory video online.

go.hrw.com   L12-1229   **Go**

Fern Hill by **Dylan Thomas**

Read with a Purpose
Read to understand the speaker's feelings about his care-free childhood.

Build Background
As a child, Thomas spent his summers among relatives who worked on a farm that, in his poem, he refers to as Fern Hill. Set in an apple orchard, the farmhouse is constructed of the whitewashed stucco typical of Wales. Fern Hill looks down upon enormous tidal flats, an ever-changing seascape that provides a bountiful habitat for water birds.

Now as I was young and easy under the apple boughs
About the lilting house and happy as the grass was green,
  The night above the dingle° starry,
    Time let me hail and climb
5   Golden in the heydays of his eyes,
And honored among wagons I was prince of the apple towns
And once below a time I lordly had the trees and leaves
    Trail with daisies and barley
  Down the rivers of the windfall light.

10   And as I was green and carefree, famous among the barns
About the happy yard and singing as the farm was home,
  In the sun that is young once only,
    Time let me play and be
  Golden in the mercy of his means,
15 And green and golden I was huntsman and herdsman,
    the calves
Sang to my horn, the foxes on the hills barked clear
    and cold,
  And the sabbath rang slowly
In the pebbles of the holy streams.

3. dingle: little wooded valley, nestled between steep hills.

Literary Perspectives

Analyzing Biographical Information Because authors typically explore topics about which they care deeply and know well, the literary works they create often reflect the events and circumstances of their own lives. Although readers must be careful to distinguish between the author of a poem and its speaker (the imaginary voice assumed by the author), knowing particular aspects of the author's life can provide insight into the author's work. Two key elements that enrich our understanding of "Fern Hill" are: (1) the importance to Thomas of the Welsh countryside in which he grew up and (2) his inability to reconcile the adult world and its responsibilities with the idyllic world of his childhood.

As you read, be sure to notice the questions in the text, which will guide you in using this perspective.

A **Reading Focus** **Analyzing Details** To what is the speaker referring in the line "The night above the dingle starry"? What effect does the unusual word choice and word order create?

Vocabulary **lilting** (LIHLT ihng) *v.* used as *adj.:* singing or speaking with a gentle rhythm.
carefree (KAIR free) *adj.:* without worry; happy.

All the sun long it was running, it was lovely, the hay
20 Fields high as the house, the tunes from the chimneys, it was air
And playing, lovely and watery
And fire green as grass.
And nightly under the simple stars
As I rode to sleep the owls were bearing the farm away,
25 All the moon long I heard, blessed among stables, the nightjars°
Flying with the ricks,° and the horses
Flashing into the dark. **B**

And then to awake, and the farm, like a wanderer white
With the dew, come back, the cock on his shoulder: it was all
30 Shining, it was Adam and maiden,
The sky gathered again
And the sun grew round that very day.
So it must have been after the birth of the simple light
In the first, spinning place, the spellbound horses walking warm
35 Out of the whinnying green stable
On to the fields of praise. **C**

And honored among foxes and pheasants by the gay house
Under the new made clouds and happy as the heart was long,
In the sun born over and over,
40 I ran my heedless ways,
My wishes raced through the house high hay
And nothing I cared, at my sky blue trades, that time allows
In all his tuneful turning so few and such morning songs
Before the children green and golden
45 Follow him out of grace,

Nothing I cared, in the lamb white days, that time would take me
Up to the swallow thronged loft by the shadow of my hand,
In the moon that is always rising,
Nor that riding to sleep
50 I should hear him fly with the high fields
And wake to the farm forever fled from the childless land.
Oh as I was young and easy in the mercy of his means,
Time held me green and dying
Though I sang in my chains like the sea. **D**

25. nightjars: common gray-brown nocturnal birds, named for their jarring cries.
26. ricks: haystacks.

Dylan Thomas's son, Colm (c. 1950–1951).

B Literary Focus | Lyric Poetry What feelings do the images of earth, air, fire, and water in lines 19–22 evoke?

C Literary Perspectives | Analyzing Biographical Information Thomas's childhood experiences inspired this poem. How are childhood impressions sometimes distorted?

D Literary Perspectives | Analyzing Biographical Information Based on what you know of Thomas's life, why do you think he used the phrase "green and dying"? How do you interpret this phrase?

Vocabulary **heedless** (HEED lihs) *adj.:* careless.
tuneful (TOON fuhl) *adj.:* musical; melodious.

Respond and Think Critically

Reading Focus

Quick Check

1. In what ways is the experience described in the poem a universal childhood experience?

Read with a Purpose

2. How would you summarize the adult speaker's perspective on his childhood?

Reading Skills: Analyzing Details

3. Review the graphic organizer you filled in as you read. What feeling or impression do the details you noticed convey? Write a couple of sentences summarizing how the details contribute to the emotional impact of the poem.

Literary Focus

Literary Analysis

4. Infer What does the poem imply about childhood innocence? On what details do you base your inference?

5. Analyze In line 30, the speaker refers to "Adam and maiden" from the Biblical story of Adam and Eve. In what specific ways was the speaker's childhood like the life Adam and Eve led in the Biblical garden of Eden? In what ways is the boy's "waking" in the last stanza like the "waking" of Adam and Eve as they left the garden?

6. Interpret In lines 42–45, the speaker says that as a child he ignored the fact that time allows few carefree days before leading children "out of grace." What does he mean?

7. Analyze Where is time personified in the poem? Describe the different types of intentions that time seems to have regarding the boy.

8. Extend Thomas once called the line *I ran my heedless ways* "bloody bad." Why do you think Thomas felt this way about a line most people accept and even admire? Do you agree with him?

9. Literary Perspectives Thomas wrote "Fern Hill" at the end of World War II. When Swansea was bombed, his parents retreated to their cottage near Fernhill, Wales, and Thomas visited them there. How does this knowledge affect your understanding of the poem's subject and mood?

Literary Skills: Lyric Poetry

10. Evaluate The focus of lyric poetry is on expressing emotions and thoughts rather than telling a story. How does "Fern Hill" fit this definition?

Literary Skills Review: Alliteration

11. Analyze Note Thomas's use of **alliteration,** the repetition of consonant sounds, as in line 15 of the poem: "And green and golden I was huntsman and herdsman." It helps produce the musical quality of a lyric poem. Where else does Thomas use alliteration? What is its effect?

Writing Focus

Think as a Reader/Writer

Use It in Your Writing Using what you learned about the effect of concrete nouns, write a paragraph describing a childhood memory. Include plenty of concrete nouns as details. For example, if you write about a beach memory, you might include concrete nouns such as *sand, shells, waves, crabs,* and *sun.*

 What Do **You Think Now** How do our experiences in childhood affect us as adults?

SKILLS FOCUS **Literary Skills** Analyze the characteristics of lyric poetry; analyze alliteration; analyze biographical information. **Reading Skills** Analyze details. **Writing**

Skills Write descriptive paragraphs. **Vocabulary Skills** Use suffixes to interpret and create words.

Vocabulary Development

✓ Vocabulary Check

Match each Vocabulary word with its definition.

1. lilting
2. carefree
3. heedless
4. tuneful

   a. melodious
   b. without worry
   c. thoughtless
   d. singing with a gentle rhythm

Vocabulary Skills: Suffixes

A **suffix** is a word part added to the end of a word or root to create a new word.

A suffix can change a word's part of speech:

Suffix	added to	forms a(n)	Examples
–ness; –ity	adj.	noun	swiftness; timidity
–ly	adj.	adv.	thoroughly
–less; –ful	noun	adj.	heedless; tuneful
–ing	verb	verb, adj., or noun	bearing, lilting, turning

A suffix can change a word's meaning:

Suffix	Meaning	Example
–less	without	heedless: without heed or care
–ful	filled with, full of	tuneful: filled with tune or song

Adding a suffix may change the spelling of the root word:

• Most words that have two or more syllables and end in –y change the y to i before adding –ness, –less, or –ly:

   happy + –ness = happiness
   merry + –ly = merrily
   penny + –less = penniless

• Words that end in a silent e will lose the e before a suffix that begins with a vowel:

   live + –ing = living
   active + –ity = activity

• Words that end in a silent e will usually keep the silent e before a suffix that begins with a consonant:

   tune + –ful = tuneful
   care + –less = careless
   EXCEPTIONS: true + –ly = truly; awe + –ful = awful

Your Turn

Add appropriate suffixes to the following words, and make spelling changes as necessary.

1. coincide
2. grave
3. creepy
4. hope

Language Coach

Antonyms "Fern Hill" contains many adjectives that describe sensory details. List the poem's vivid adjectives, and write an antonym for each of the words. If you cannot find an antonym for a word, explain why it is difficult to find the word's opposite.

Academic Vocabulary

Write About

Thomas's childhood experiences are overtly underlined{exhibited} in his poetry. Do the events of childhood underlined{inevitably} influence the work of writers and poets? Write a short essay in which you argue whether or not it is possible to adopt a completely new underlined{perspective}.

SKILLS FOCUS **Writing Skills** Deliver multi-media presentations; write descriptive essays. **Grammar Skills** Identify and use participles and participial phrases correctly. **Listening and Speaking Skills** Present persuasive arguments and share opinions.

Grammar Link

Participles and Participial Phrases

A **participle** is a verb form that is used as an adjective. A **participial phrase** consists of a participle and all the words related to the participle. Participles are classified as either **present participles** or **past participles.**

A **present participle** ends in *–ing.*

The child played along the **curving** stream.

Playing in the orchard, the speaker is carefree. [Participial phrase *playing in the orchard* modifies *speaker.*]

Most **past participles** end in *–d* or *–ed*, but some are irregular.

The **tormented** poet acted recklessly.

Appreciated by critics, "Fern Hill" is a timeless poem. [The participial phrase *appreciated by critics* modifies the noun phrase "*Fern Hill.*"]

Written after World War II, the poem reflects Thomas's disillusionment. [The participial phrase *written after World War II* modifies *poem.*]

Your Turn

Underline each participle and participial phrase.

1. The sleeping child dreamed about the farm.
2. Running through the field, the excited boy chased the birds.
3. The girl, exhausted from her play, curled up in her mother's lap and slept.

Writing Application Circle all the participles in something you have written. Then, write in the margins whether they are past or present and what they modify.

CHOICES

As you respond to the Choices, use these **Academic Vocabulary** words as appropriate: adapt, considerably, exhibit, inevitable, perspective.

REVIEW
Illustrate the Details
Create a visual (or multimedia) representation of "Fern Hill," illustrating with color, light, and form the details that Thomas includes in his poem. You can choose any medium—water colors, collage, mosaic, oil paints, or even multimedia. When you have finished your work, share it with classmates, explaining how you chose to adapt the details from the poem to the different media.

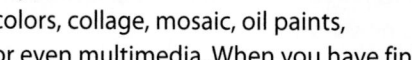

CONNECT
Make a Case
Work with a small group of students to make a case for agreeing or disagreeing with Thomas's view of childhood and time. Then, debate your group's perspective with another group. Use support from the poem and your own experience to further your case.

EXTEND
Describe a Place
Timed ⌐Writing Write a short essay in which you describe a place where you spent significant time as a child. Be sure to use details in your description.

Learn It Online
Learn how to create an eye-popping multimedia presentation! Visit *MediaScope* online.

go.hrw.com | L12-1234 | Go

Preparing to Read

Do Not Go Gentle into That Good Night

Reader/Writer Notebook

Use your **RWN** to complete the activities for this selection.

Literary Focus

Elegy An **elegy** is a poem that mourns the death of someone or laments something lost. A type of **lyric,** an elegy is usually formal in language and structure, and solemn or melancholy in tone. The typical elegy mourns a death that has already occurred. This poem is a bit different. It is an elegy spoken to a dying man, urging him not to surrender but to meet death in a spirit of challenge. As he often did in his poetry, here Thomas gives his own twist to a familiar subject. The poem may invite charges of irreverence, but its lyrical solemnity, not its argument, is what echoes most in the reader's mind.

The particular form of this elegy is called a **villanelle,** a nineteen-line poem divided into five tercets (three-line stanzas), each with the **rhyme scheme** *aba,* and a final quatrain with the rhyme scheme *abaa.* Note that the first and third lines of the first tercet alternate as the last line of tercets 2 through 5, and are combined as a final couplet in the quatrain. Villanelles typically have only two end-rhyme sounds in the entire poem. As you read, notice how the repetition of the end-rhyme sounds, skillfully blended with the iambic pentameter, helps create somber, delicate music appropriate for this elegy.

Language Coach

Multiple-Meaning Words Some words have more than one definition. One way to determine a word's meaning is to look at the word's context. For example, the word *grave* can mean "a cemetery plot" or "serious." Which meaning does Thomas intend in line 13? Is it possible that the poet intends both meanings? Explain.

Writing Focus

Think as a Reader/Writer

Find It in Your Reading In your *Reader/Writer Notebook*, create a graphic organizer like the one below. As you read the poem, record repeated words as well as strong, vivid, and even violent words and phrases. Some examples are provided to get you started. Record the line numbers as in the examples below.

Repetition	Strong, Vivid Words/Phrases
"Do not go gentle" (1, 6, 12, 18)	"Rage, rage," (3, 9)
"dying of the light" (3, 6, 15, 19)	"blaze like meteors" (14)

Do Not Go Gentle into That Good Night

by **Dylan Thomas**

Read with a Purpose
Read the poem to discover how a son advises his father to approach impending death.

Build Background
In this poem the use of *gentle* instead of the adverb *gently* may at first seem ungrammatical. However, when we read the line as "Do not go, gentle, into that good night," as Thomas insisted, we gain the additional meaning of all that is gentle, including the gentle man who was Thomas's father.

Do not go gentle into that good night,
Old age should burn and rave at close of day;
Rage, rage against the dying of the light.   **Ⓐ**

Though wise men at their end know dark is right,
5 Because their words had forked no lightning they
Do not go gentle into that good night.

Good men, the last wave by, crying how bright
Their frail deeds might have danced in a green bay,
Rage, rage against the dying of the light.

10 Wild men who caught and sang the sun in flight,
And learn, too late, they grieved it on its way,
Do not go gentle into that good night.

Grave men, near death, who see with blinding sight
Blind eyes could blaze like meteors and be gay,
15 Rage, rage against the dying of the light.

And you, my father, there on the sad height,
Curse, bless, me now with your fierce tears, I pray.
Do not go gentle into that good night.
Rage, rage against the dying of the light.

Ⓐ **Literary Focus** Elegy How does the first tercet establish the solemn, intense mood of this elegy?

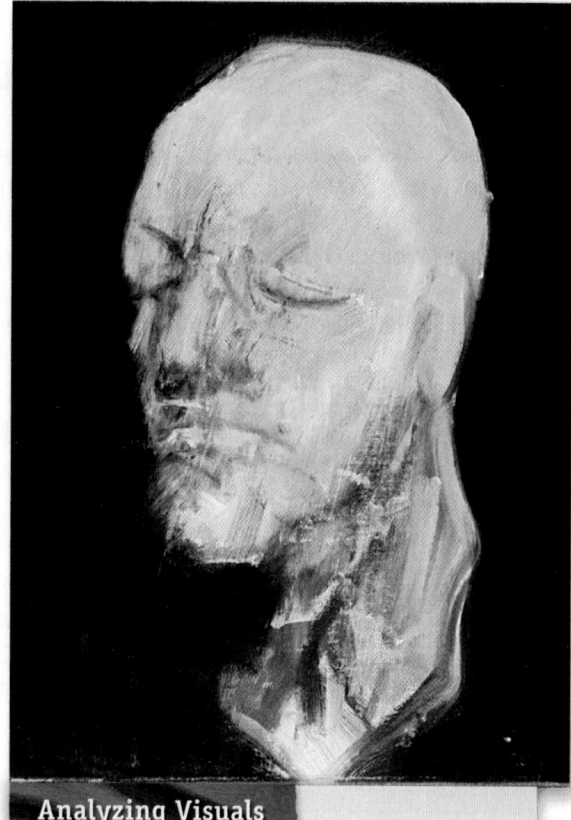

Analyzing Visuals

Viewing and Interpreting If the subject of the painting were facing death, what might his closed eyes suggest?

Study for Portrait V (after the life mask of William Blake) (1956) by Francis Bacon. Estate of Francis Bacon/Artists Rights Society (ARS), NY/DACS, London.

Applying Your Skills

Do Not Go Gentle into That Good Night

Respond and Think Critically

Reading Focus

Quick Check

1. What is the main point of this poem?

2. What does the speaker pray for at the end of the poem?

3. What is the "good night"? Explain the pun, or play on words, in this phrase.

Read with a Purpose

4. How does the speaker feel about facing death? How does he want his father to face it?

Literary Focus

Literary Analysis

5. **Interpret** Given the speaker's feelings about the "good night," do you see anything contradictory in his use of the word *good?* Explain.

6. **Analyze** What does the speaker's prayer at the end indicate about the relationship between this father and son?

7. **Compare and Contrast** How do each of the types of people described in stanzas 2–5 respond to the "dying of the light"?

8. **Extend** Soon after this poem was finished, Thomas sent it to princess Caetani in Rome, hoping she might publish it in her literary magazine. In an accompanying letter, he wrote: "The only person I can't show the little enclosed poem to is, of course, my father, who doesn't know he's dying." Given the fact that the poem became one of the most famous elegies of the century, do you think Thomas's reluctance was justified? Why or why not? What would you have done in his situation?

9. **Make Judgments** Note how Thomas features words that relate to images of light *(fire, lightning, sun, blaze, bright).* How does Thomas present a man's relationship to light in the poem? Does this relationship evolve or stay the same? Support your answer with details from the poem.

Literary Skills: Elegy

10. **Analyze** The elegy form goes back to the ancient Greeks and Romans, who used the term to refer to any serious meditation, including poems about love, war, and death. Today, *elegy* refers exclusively to poems of mourning. In what ways does Thomas's poem fit both definitions?

Literary Skills Review: Metaphor

11. **Interpret** A comparison of two seemingly unlike things is called a **metaphor.** When an author uses metaphor, he or she speaks of one thing as if it were another. Identify at least three metaphors for death or dying in this poem. How do they contribute to the elegiac tone of the poem?

Writing Focus

Think as a Reader/Writer

Use It in Your Writing Re-read the language you recorded in your graphic organizer. What is Thomas's tone? Using your own repetitions and strong, vivid verbs, write a paragraph about the way you think people should face death.

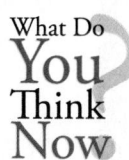

What Do You Think Now

How has this poem influenced your perspective on death?

Not Waving but Drowning

What Do You Think?

How does experience shape our view of the world?

QuickWrite

In your *Reader/Writer Notebook*, write about a time when you or another person misunderstood someone's words, gestures, or intentions. What were the consequences of the misunderstanding?

Stevie Smith
(1902–1971)

Florence Margaret Smith was nicknamed "Stevie" because she was short like the British jockey Steve Donoghue. Although all of her works reflect her offbeat outlook and writing style, it is in her poems that she fully displays her cleverness.

"Cheerfully Gruesome"

Smith was born in Yorkshire but was raised by her mother and aunt in Palmers Green, a suburb of London. Smith lived with her aunt for sixty-six years until "Auntie Lion" died in 1968 at the age of ninety-six. Smith herself died only three years later.

After finishing school, Smith worked as a secretary for a magazine publisher, a post she retained for thirty years. In her early thirties, Smith began to publish poetry and fiction. Her first publication, *Novel on Yellow Paper* (1936), is a playful monologue, which some critics have compared to the writing of Gertrude Stein. In 1937, Smith began to publish her poems. *A Good Time Was Had by All* revealed short, matter-of-fact verses and <u>exhibited</u> a childishly simple but biting tone that would become characteristic of her poems. Smith's poems often deal with death, loneliness, or despair, but she is not self-pitying. Her sometimes whimsical humor adds sparkle, allowing her to distance herself from her subject.

Smith summarized her style when she claimed that she was "straightforward, but not simple." The poet Robert Lowell described her poetic voice as "cheerfully gruesome," and the humorist Ogden Nash admired her "songs of deadly innocence."

Artist and Performer

Stevie Smith accompanied many of her poems with drawings that she called "doodles." She loved to perform her poetry, reading it on the radio and occasionally singing her verses. During the 1960s, interest in Smith's work increased <u>considerably</u>, in part because of these public readings. In 1969, she received the Queen's Gold Medal for Poetry. Since her death in 1971, she has been the subject of a play written by Hugh Whitemore called *Stevie*, later adapted as a film.

Think About the Writer

What do you think Smith means when she says her writing is "straightforward, but not simple"?

Reader/Writer Notebook

Use your **RWN** to complete the activities for this selection.

Literary Focus

Irony The discrepancy between expectations and reality or between appearances and reality is called **irony**. **Verbal irony** occurs when a writer or speaker says one thing but really means something quite different—often the opposite of what he or she has said. **Situational irony** happens when a situation unfolds differently than expected, and **dramatic irony** occurs when the reader has important information that the characters in a work do not have. In "Not Waving but Drowning," Smith explores and develops the irony inherent in a tragic misunderstanding.

Reading Focus

Analyzing Tone The attitude a writer takes toward the reader, a subject, or a character is called **tone**. Tone is conveyed through the writer's choice of words and details. In "Not Waving but Drowning," Smith provides details from three <u>perspectives</u> to create the poem's tone.

Into Action As you read "Not Waving but Drowning," use a chart like the one below to record the details and words that the poet uses to help convey tone.

Detail	Tone
"Poor chap, he always loved larking".	

Writing Focus

Think as a Reader/Writer

Find It in Your Reading Writers use different points of view to give readers different ways of thinking about a situation. As you read, take notes in your *Reader/Writer Notebook* about how Smith shifts <u>perspective</u> in this poem, from the speaker ("Nobody heard him") to the drowned man ("I was much further out") to the friends on the beach ("It must have been too cold for him"). How does she indicate a shift? What is the effect of including three different <u>perspectives</u> in such a short poem? How does presenting each one help Smith create the irony and tone of the poem?

Language Coach

Commonly Misused Words The verbs *lay* and *lie* are often misused. Here is an explanation of their different forms and tenses:

Present	Past	Past Participle
lay	laid	[has] laid
lie	lay	[has] lain

Lay (meaning "put down" or "place") is a transitive verb, which takes an object: [verb] [object]

_____ **Lay the book** on the table.

Lie (meaning "recline") is an intransitive verb, which does not take an object:

Lie on the bed and rest.

In this poem, is *lay* in the present tense, or is it the past tense of *lie?*

Learn It Online
Listen to this poem online.

go.hrw.com   L12-1239   **Go**

Not Waving but Drowning
by **Stevie Smith**

Read with a Purpose
Read this poem to see how a misunderstanding turns deadly.

Build Background
Stevie Smith said that "Not Waving but Drowning" was about "misunderstandings which may prove fatal." Smith has been called "one of the absolute originals of English literature" because her work defies classification. As you read the following poem, think about the specific ways in which it is unusual or offbeat.

Nobody heard him, the dead man,
But still he lay moaning:
I was much further out than you thought
And not waving but drowning.

5   Poor chap, he always loved larking°
And now he's dead
It must have been too cold for him his heart gave way,
They said. **Ⓐ**

Oh, no no no, it was too cold always
10 (Still the dead one lay moaning)
I was much too far out all my life
And not waving but drowning. **Ⓑ**

5. larking: playing; having a good time.

Ⓐ **Literary Focus** **Irony** How is the reaction of the people on the beach an example of dramatic irony? What do you know that these people do not?

Ⓑ **Reading Focus** **Analyzing Tone** What is the tone of the last stanza? What words does Smith use to convey this tone?

Applying Your Skills

Respond and Think Critically

Reading Focus

Quick Check

1. Explain this poem's title. What, besides a swimming disaster, might Smith be describing?

2. What does the drowned man mean by "it was too cold always" (line 9) and "I was much too far out all my life" (line 11)?

3. What is unusual or offbeat about this poem? Use details to support your opinions.

Read with a Purpose

4. What causes the misunderstanding between the man and the people on the beach?

Reading Skills: Analyzing Tone

5. The tone of this poem has been described as pessimistic, yet also humorous. Highlight details in your chart that support either or both of these tones.

Details	Tone
"Poor chap, he always loved larking"	Spectator's words convey sympathy; that the spectators thought swimmer was playing when he was drowning is darkly humorous

Literary Focus

Literary Analysis

6. **Interpret** The people on the beach refer to the drowned man's reaction to the cold. What might the "cold" associated with the drowned man's "heart" symbolize?

7. **Infer** What kind of person did the dead man appear to be? Look to the second stanza for the basis of your response.

8. **Extend** How could this poem be a summary of one's whole life? How could this poem summarize the human condition in general?

9. **Evaluate** Smith said that good writing had to be "sad, true, economical, and funny." Do you think her poem meets these criteria?

Literary Skills: Irony

10. **Evaluate** Name two instances of irony in the poem. Explain what makes them ironic, and tell whether they are examples of dramatic, verbal, or situational irony.

Literary Skills Review: Repetition

11. **Analyze** The **repetition** of lines and verses often occurs in poetry. In this poem, a variation of the couplet that ends the first stanza also ends the last stanza. What is the effect of this repetition? What is the author emphasizing?

Writing Focus

Think as a Reader/Writer

Use It in Your Writing Look at your QuickWrite that describes a misunderstanding. Now, write a short description of the event from at least two points of view. Show how the different perspectives helped cause the misunderstanding.

What Do **You Think Now** How do the poem's three different speakers influence each view of the event that takes place?

Lot's Wife

What Do You Think? How does experience shape our view of the world?

QuickWrite

Think of a time when you were sorry to leave a place. What did you value about your experience in that place, and what did you miss after leaving? Record your thoughts in your *Reader/Writer Notebook*.

Anna Akhmatova (1889–1966).

MEET THE WRITER

Anna Akhmatova
(1889–1966)

In some countries, writers who express political views in their work run into problems with government authorities. Anna Akhmatova, however, was persecuted by the Soviet government because her writing did not <u>exhibit</u> political themes.

A Poet Suppressed

Akhmatova grew up just outside St. Petersburg in a suburb that for centuries had served as the summer palace of the czars, or emperors. Here she became part of the thriving artistic community of prerevolutionary St. Petersburg. With her husband, Nikolai Gumilev, she helped found acmeism, a literary movement that rejected the vagueness and ambiguity of symbolism and focused instead on clarity and precision.

Akhmatova's early successes ended abruptly with the 1917 Russian Revolution. In the years following the revolution, only "socially useful" art was tolerated. Akhmatova was viciously attacked and her poems suppressed because they were too personal. When Gumilev, her ex-husband by that time, was executed for allegedly plotting against the Soviet government, Akhmatova was deemed guilty by association. As punishment, she was not allowed to publish at all from 1922 to 1940.

Life in Stalinist Russia

During the years of Stalinist terror (1924–1953), Akhmatova lived in one room with only a bed, desk, and four books (Pushkin, Shakespeare, Dante, and the Bible). She memorized her poetry instead of writing it down, and although not published, her poems lived in the minds of her fellow Russians. After giving a reading during one of Stalin's wartime "thaws" (periods of fewer restrictions), she received a standing ovation from three thousand people in Moscow's largest auditorium. (The thaw ended when Stalin reportedly asked who had organized the standing ovation.) In 1946, she was expelled from the Union of Soviet Writers. Her own son was imprisoned until 1953, the year of Stalin's death. In her final years, Akhmatova was again recognized officially and allowed to travel to the West.

Think About the Writer What can you infer about Akhmatova from her refusal to write "socially useful" poems despite pressure from the government?

 **Reader/Writer Notebook**

Use your **RWN** to complete the activities for this selection.

Literary Focus

Theme   The **theme** is the central idea or insight of a work of literature. The theme is different from the topic, or subject, of a poem. As you read the following poem, you might note that its subject is exile, but what does the poem express about exile? What theme does the poem convey? Remember that Akhmatova's poems were shaped by the political events of her time. As you read the poem, consider the following:

- Akhmatova was an artist suppressed by the Soviet government.
- Other artists in the Soviet Union were arrested and sent to prison camps, never to return.
- After her ex-husband's execution, Akhmatova made the difficult decision to stay in Russia rather than flee.

Into Action   Use a graphic organizer like the one below to help you identify the theme of the poem.

Vocabulary

hulking (HUHLK ihng) *adj.*: big and clumsy. *The man's hulking figure filled the doorway.*

native (NAY tihv) *adj.*: belonging to a person because of birth. *She left her native city when she was a child.*

welded (WEHLD ihd) *v.* used as *adj.*: joined; sealed. *The steel walls and doors of the safe are carefully welded to make the safe strong.*

Language Coach

Connotations   Remember that words have **connotations,** or feelings or ideas, associated with them. What feelings or ideas come to you when you hear the word *hulking?* How does this word differ from the word *massive?* If necessary, use a dictionary or thesaurus to help you figure out the different connotations of the words.

Writing Focus

Think as a Reader/Writer

Find It in Your Reading   Writers use many techniques to help them convey a message to their readers. As you read "Lot's Wife," note how Akhmatova uses a story from the Bible and then has the speaker comment on the story. In your *Reader/Writer Notebook*, record notes about the words and phrases that you think most effectively express the ideas of the story and the speaker's perspective.

 Learn It Online

Learn more about Akhmatova and her world through these Internet links.

go.hrw.com   L12-1243   **Go**

Lot's Wife

by **Anna Akhmatova**

translated by **Richard Wilbur**

Read with a Purpose
Read to discover how Lot's wife feels about her home.

Build Background
The poem is based on the Biblical incident recounted in Genesis 19. Angered by the wickedness of the city of Sodom, God sends angels to punish the inhabitants. Only one man, Lot, is looked upon favorably by God. Lot is told to flee Sodom with his family and to never look back. As Lot's family escapes, however, his wife disobeys the command and turns her head to gaze back upon the city. She is immediately turned into a pillar of salt.

The just man followed then his angel guide
Where he strode on the black highway, hulking and bright;
But a wild grief in his wife's bosom cried,
Look back, it is not too late for a last sight **A**

5 *Of the red towers of your native Sodom, the square*
Where once you sang, the gardens you shall mourn,
And the tall house with empty windows where
You loved your husband and your babes were born.

She turned, and looking on the bitter view
10 Her eyes were welded shut by mortal pain;
Into transparent salt her body grew,
And her quick feet were rooted in the plain.

Who would waste tears upon her? Is she not
The least of our losses, this unhappy wife?
15 Yet in my heart she will not be forgot
Who, for a single glance, gave up her life. **B**

Head of Akhmatova, by Natan Altman. Frauenkopf: 1916–1918. Museum Ludwig, Köln.

A **Literary Focus** Theme How does the "wild grief" that "cried" within the woman relate to the poem's theme?

B **Literary Focus** Theme Why will the speaker never forget the woman?

Vocabulary **hulking** (HUHLK ihng) *adj.:* big and clumsy.
native (NAY tihv) *adj.:* belonging to a person because of birth.
welded (WEHLD ihd) *v. used as adj.:* joined; sealed.

Applying Your Skills

Respond and Think Critically

Reading Focus

Quick Check

1. What makes Lot's wife care about Sodom, despite its evils?

2. What does the phrase "mortal pain" (line 10) suggest about how we should view the attitude of Lot's wife?

3. Why do you think the speaker is so affected by Lot's wife?

Read with a Purpose

4. How does Lot's wife feel about her home? What does "bitter view" (line 9) suggest about her feelings?

✓ Vocabulary Check

Match each Vocabulary word with its definition.

5. hulking   a. belonging to a person because of birth

6. native   b. joined; sealed

7. welded   c. big and clumsy

Literary Focus

Literary Analysis

8. **Interpret** In line 5, Akhmatova refers to the "red towers" and the "square" of Sodom. To what other square and city might she be referring?

9. **Analyze** How would you describe the tone of this poem? What words or phrases contribute to this tone?

10. **Make Judgments** Do you think that Lot's wife should be remembered and pitied? Explain.

11. **Infer** Re-read the biography of Akhmatova on page 1242. How might "Lot's Wife" have been shaped by the events of Akhmatova's life and the political situation in Russia at the time she wrote the poem?

Literary Skills: Theme

12. **Evaluate** How would you state the theme of "Lot's Wife"? What view of life does this theme reflect, and how is this view of life shaped by historical influences?

Literary Skills Review: Allusion

13. **Analyze** A reference within a literary work to another literary work or historical event is called an **allusion.** The entire poem is based on the allusion to the Biblical story of Sodom and Gomorrah. What similarities might Akhmatova have seen between Stalinist Russia and the city of Sodom? between herself and Lot's wife?

Writing Focus

Think as a Reader/Writer

Use It in Your Writing Choose a message about life you want to convey and a familiar story you can use to express this message. Using "Lot's Wife" as a model, write a short poem that retells the story. Communicate your theme by carefully choosing words that express your ideas and by commenting on the story or on one of the characters at the end of your poem.

 What Do **You Think Now** How might you feel if you had to leave your homeland because life there had become intolerable? Would you regard your departure as desertion or as a wise investment in the future? Explain.

Lot's Wife

from Nobel Lecture: The Poet and the World

What Do You Think

How does experience shape our view of the world?

QuickWrite

Think about a time when someone misinterpreted your actions. In your *Reader/Writer Notebook*, write what happened and how you felt.

1996 Nobel Prize winner Wislawa Szymborska, Zakopane (October 4, 1996).

MEET THE WRITER

Wislawa Szymborska
(1923–)

Nobel Prize WINNER

Wislawa Szymborska (vees WAH ah vah sheem BAWR skah) has said she aims to write "poems that are ambiguous, that are both happy and sad, like a coin with two sides." Her poetry appeals to young and old alike; one poem inspired a critically acclaimed film, and another became lyrics to a hit rock song.

War and Politics

Born in a small town in Poland, Szymborska began writing poems at the age of five. In 1931, her family moved to Krakow, where Szymborska has since spent much of her life. Of her family, she says, "We talked a lot about books. We read a lot." When she was sixteen, Germany's invasion of Poland ignited World War II. In Krakow, Germans executed the university staff, sent thousands to labor and death camps, and closed the schools. Although the Soviets liberated Poland in 1945, they went on to establish their own form of repression, Communism. Under the Communist policy of socialist realism, artists were expected to adapt their works to glorify the Communist system. After publication of her poems was blocked, Szymborska published two volumes that conformed to socialist realist requirements. By 1957, she had become disillusioned with Communism, and her later poetry has shunned overtly political themes, focusing instead on human relationships and details of everyday life.

World-Class Poet

Szymborska's ability to reveal simply and directly the unexpected in the ordinary has attracted a wide readership. One critic praised "the wit and clarity of Szymborska's turns of phrase. Under her pen, simple language becomes striking." Despite their often somber subjects, her poems allow, as another critic stated, "rays of light to penetrate [their] bleak landscapes." Preferring to live privately, Szymborska has never sought publicity and was not well known outside Poland until she won the Nobel Prize in Literature in 1996.

Think About the Writer

What do you think about Szymborska's commitment to writing "ambiguous" poems?

Lot's Wife

Reader/Writer Notebook

Use your **RWN** to complete the activities for this selection.

Literary Focus

Speaker The **speaker** of a poem is the voice, or persona, assumed by the author of the poem. This voice is often not identified immediately or directly. Rather, the reader gradually comes to understand that a unique voice is speaking and that this speaker's characteristics must be interpreted as they are revealed. Although the speaker is often not the poet, the poet may use the speaker's voice to express his or her ideas about a subject or to interpret an event. As you read the poem, consider how Szymborska gives voice to the possible thoughts and motivations of the speaker of this poem.

Into Action Use a graphic organizer like the one below to help you understand the characteristics of the speaker in "Lot's Wife" and any other poem you read. Answer the prompts about characteristics, using short sentences or phrases from the poem. What motivates the speaker? What does he or she want? What does he or she regret?

	Names I Have	Things I Say Often	Relation- ships I Have	Actions I Take	Emotions I Feel
Speaker #1					
Speaker #2					

Language Coach

Using *Set* and *Sit* Sometimes speakers and writers use *set* and *sit* interchangeably, but the words have distinct meanings and uses. The verb *set* means "to put [something] in a place." *Set* generally takes a direct object. The verb *sit* means "to be seated in an upright position." *Sit* generally does not have a direct object. In the following sentences, choose the correct verb form in parentheses.

1. She (*set, sat*) down her pack while she tied her shoes.

2. After he fumbled the ball, he (*set, sat*) on the bench.

3. The city (*sits, sets*) on a hill by the sea.

Writing Focus

Think as a Reader/Writer

Find It in Your Reading One way that writers, particularly poets, emphasize ideas is through **parallelism,** the repetition of words, phrases, and sentences that have the same grammatical structures. In "Lot's Wife," Szymborska uses parallelism to express and emphasize the motivations of the speaker: "I looked back for all the reasons given above. / I looked back involuntarily." In your *Reader/Writer Notebook,* take notes on the effect of this repetition. Note the different reasons the speaker gives for looking back and how the poet uses repetition to express the idea that there were many possible reasons for the speaker's actions. Then, read the poem aloud to note how the use of repetition adds rhythm to the poem. Be sure to record your impressions in your notebook.

Learn It Online

Listen to this poem's speaker for yourself online.

go.hrw.com   L12-1247   **Go**

LOT'S WIFE

by **Wislawa Szymborska**

translated by **Stanislaw Baranczak** and **Clare Cavanagh**

Read with a Purpose
Read to discover how one poet interprets the experience of Lot's wife.

Build Background
The poem is based on Chapter 19 in the Bible's Book of Genesis, in which God destroys the city and inhabitants of Sodom but spares Lot, its one righteous man. God tells Lot and his family to flee and literally never look back. Lot's wife, however, turns back to look at Sodom and is turned into a pillar of salt.

They say I looked back out of curiosity. **Ⓐ**
But I could have had other reasons.
I looked back mourning my silver bowl.
Carelessly, while tying my sandal strap.
5 So I wouldn't have to keep staring at the righteous nape
of my husband Lot's neck.
From the sudden conviction that if I dropped dead
he wouldn't so much as hesitate.
From the disobedience of the meek.
10 Checking for pursuers.
Struck by the silence, hoping God had changed his mind.
Our two daughters were already vanishing over the hilltop.
I felt age within me. Distance.
The futility of wandering. Torpor.
15 I looked back setting my bundle down.
I looked back not knowing where to set my foot.
Serpents appeared on my path,
spiders, field mice, baby vultures.
They were neither good nor evil now—every living thing
20 was simply creeping or hopping along in the mass panic.
I looked back in desolation.
In shame because we had stolen away.
Wanting to cry out, to go home. **Ⓑ**
Or only when a sudden gust of wind

Ⓐ **Literary Focus** **Speaker** Notice that the speaker refers to herself as I. Who is the speaker of this poem?

Ⓑ **Literary Focus** **Speaker** How does the speaker feel about the home she is leaving?

Croat woman prepares to flee her village in Bosnia during Yoguslavian civil war.

25   unbound my hair and lifted up my robe.
It seemed to me that they were watching from the walls of Sodom
and bursting into thunderous laughter again and again.
I looked back in anger.
To savor their terrible fate.

30   I looked back for all the reasons given above.
I looked back involuntarily.
It was only a rock that turned under foot, growling at me.
It was a sudden crack that stopped me in my tracks.
A hamster on its hind paws tottered on the edge.

35   It was then we both glanced back.
No, no. I ran on,
I crept, I flew upward
until darkness fell from the heavens
and with it scorching gravel and dead birds.

40   I couldn't breathe and spun around and around.
Anyone who saw me must have thought I was dancing. **C**
It's not inconceivable that my eyes were open.
It's possible I fell facing the city.

C **Literary Focus** **Speaker** What does the speaker imply by stating that anyone who witnessed her actions must have interpreted them as "dancing"?

Analyzing Visuals

Viewing and Interpreting What does the woman's facial expression suggest about the effects of even preparing for a long journey? With that in mind, why might have Lot's wife needed to take just one look back?

SKILLS FOCUS **Literary Skills** Analyze characteristics of the speaker; analyze internal and external conflict. **Writing Skills** Write poems.

Respond and Think Critically

Reading Focus

Quick Check

1. What clues tell you who the first-person speaker of the poem is?

2. What does the speaker mean when she says that "every living thing" was "neither good nor evil now"? What has changed?

Read with a Purpose

3. How does Szymborska interpret the motivations and experience of Lot's wife's?

Literary Focus

Literary Analysis

4. **Infer** In lines 5–6, what does Szymborska imply about Lot's wife's feelings toward Lot? Explain.

5. **Compare and Contrast** Compare and contrast the speaker's fate in the last lines of the poem with the Bible's account of the wife's fate: She "looked back … and … became a pillar of salt."

6. **Hypothesize** Why do you think Szymborska includes the image of the hamster in line 34?

7. **Evaluate** Often, characters in stories that convey a moral message are flat, built on a single dominant trait. Has Szymborska changed Lot's wife from a flat character into a round character—a character with depth and complexity? Explain.

Literary Skills: Speaker

8. **Analyze** The **speaker** of a poem is the voice, or persona, assumed by the author. From what you know about Szymborska, how does her actual persona seem to differ from that of the speaker? How, in any way, is she similar to the speaker?

9. **Hypothesize** In this poem, the speaker refers to herself as I. How does the use of first person affect the feelings the poem elicits? Look back on your graphic organizer to help you answer.

Literary Skills Review: Conflict

10. **Analyze** A struggle between opposing characters, forces, or emotions is called **conflict.** In **external conflict,** a character struggles against some outside force. An **internal conflict** is a struggle between opposing needs, desires, or emotions within a single character. Explain the conflicts Lot's wife experiences in the poem.

Writing Focus

Think as a Reader/Writer

Use It in Your Writing Review how Szymborska uses repetition, including parallelism, to emphasize her ideas. Write your own five-line poem explaining a reason that someone did something. Begin each line with the same phrase to create a rhythm to the poem.

What Do **You Think Now**

How did the experience of Lot's wife shape her worldview?

Preparing to Read

from Nobel Lecture: The Poet and the World

Reader/Writer
Notebook

Use your **RWN** to complete the activities for this selection.

Informational Text Focus

Analyzing an Author's Beliefs To **analyze an author's beliefs,** you must consider the author's ideas and how he or she expresses them. What kinds of language does the author use? What problems does he or she describe? What characters or real people does the author esteem?

Into Action As you read Szymborska's Nobel lecture, think about TOPICAL questions (questions regarding Title, Opinion, Problem, Insight, Characters, Action, and Language) to help you analyze her beliefs. Using the chart below as a guide, record your answers.

Title	What connotations/associations does the title suggest? Does the title tell you the subject?	The subject will have to do with the relationship of poets to the world.
Opinion	What is the writer's attitude about the subject? What language does she use to indicate her opinion?	
Problem	What problem or issue is this writer exploring? What is the author's solution to the problem?	
Insight	What special insight does the author have on this subject? Why?	
Characters	Who are the important characters or people that have influenced the author's attitude?	
Action	What action will she take?	
Language	What language does the author use that is particularly striking? What images support her perspective?	

Writing Focus   Preparing for **Constructed Response**

Good writers present their beliefs coherently by logically moving from one idea to the next. As you read, record in your *Reader/Writer Notebook* Szymborska's main ideas and note how she moves from one idea to the next. For example, she presents examples of scientists who said "I don't know" and then begins the next paragraph by stating, "Poets, if they're genuine, must also keep repeating 'I don't know.'" In what other ways does she create coherence and unity in her writing?

Vocabulary

inspiration (ihn spuh RAY shuhn) *n.:* influence of thought and strong feelings on actions, especially good actions. *Inspiration for the project came to the artist in a dream.*

quell (kwehl) *v.:* bring under control by subduing. *The poet had to quell her fear of rejection before sending her poems to agents.*

fervor (FUR vuhr) *n.:* intense emotion. *She expressed her beliefs with a fervor her fellow poets had never seen before.*

lethal (LEE thuhl) *adj.:* deadly. *The snake had a lethal bite.*

impotence (IHM puh tuhns) *n.:* helplessness. *Though frustrated by her impotence, the writer continued to fight for equal rights.*

epithet (EHP uh theht) *n.:* descriptive expression. *He used the epithet "honest" to describe his friend Abe, as in "Honest Abe."*

deviate (DEE vee ayt) *v.:* turn aside from a way, norm, or truth. *Writers will lose their inspiration if they deviate from their desire to learn more about the world.*

Language Coach

Word Families Words that are related by the base or root are called **word families.** For example, *lethal* and *lethally* are part of the same word family. Can you name two words that are related to *inspiration*?

Learn It Online
Get to know the Vocabulary words through Word Watch online.

go.hrw.com   L12-1251   **Go**

from Nobel Lecture:
The Poet and the World December 7, 1996

by **Wislawa Szymborska**
translated by **Stanislaw Baranczak** and **Clare Cavanagh**

Read with a Purpose
Read to discover the role Szymborska believes poets play in the world.

Build Background
In 1895, Swedish intellect Alfred Nobel signed a will leaving most of his estate to establish prizes given in physics, chemistry, peace, physiology or medicine, and literature (an award for economics was established in 1968). Szymborska was awarded the Nobel Prize in Literature in 1996 "for poetry that with ironic precision allows the historical and biographical context to come to light in fragments of human reality." She gave this lecture after receiving the prize.

Wislawa Szymborska at the Polish PEN Literary Club, where she received the Club's annual literary prize (1996).

Inspiration is not the exclusive privilege of poets or artists. There is, there has been, there will always be a certain group of people whom inspiration visits. It's made up of all those who've consciously chosen their calling and do their job with love and imagination. It may include doctors, teachers, gardeners—I could list a hundred more professions. Their work becomes one continuous adventure as long as they manage to keep discovering new challenges in it. Difficulties and setbacks never quell their curiosity. A swarm of new questions emerges from every problem that they solve. Whatever inspiration is, it's born from a continuous "I don't know." **A**

There aren't many such people. Most of the earth's inhabitants work to get by. They work because they have to. They didn't pick this or that kind of job out of passion; the circumstances of their lives did the choosing for them. Loveless work, boring work, work valued only because others haven't got even that much—this is one of the harshest human miseries. And there's no sign that coming centuries will produce any changes for the better as far as this goes.

And so, though I deny poets their monopoly on inspiration, I still place them in a select group of Fortune's darlings. **B**

At this point, though, certain doubts may arise in my audience. All sorts of torturers, dictators, fanatics, and demagogues[1] struggling for power with a few loudly shouted slogans also enjoy their jobs, and they, too, perform their duties with inventive fervor. Well, yes; but they "know," and whatever they know is enough for them once and for all. They don't want to find out about anything else, since that might diminish the force of their arguments. But any knowledge that doesn't lead to new questions quickly dies out: it fails to maintain the temperature required for sustaining life. In the most extreme cases, cases well known from ancient and modern history, it even poses a lethal threat to society. **C**

This is why I value that little phrase "I don't know" so highly. It's small, but it flies on mighty wings. It expands our lives to include spaces within us as well as the outer expanses in which our tiny Earth hangs suspended. If Isaac Newton had never said to himself, "I don't know," the apples in his little orchard might have dropped to the ground like hailstones, and at best he would have stooped to pick them up and gobble them with gusto. Had my compatriot Marie Sklodowska-

---

1. **demagogues:** leaders who try to gain power by appealing to people's emotions.

A Informational Focus Analyzing an Author's Beliefs What main idea or belief does Szymborska express in this paragraph? How does repetition help convey the main belief?

B Informational Focus Analyzing an Author's Beliefs What is Szymborska's evaluation of poets?

C Informational Focus Analyzing an Author's Beliefs What tone does Szymborska adopt toward "dictators, fanatics, and demagogues"? How does this tone reflect her beliefs?

Vocabulary inspiration (ihn spuh RAY shuhn) *n.:* influence of thought and strong feelings on actions, especially good actions.
quell (kwehl) *v.:* bring under control by subduing.
fervor (FUR vuhr) *n.:* intense emotion.
lethal (LEE thuhl) *adj.:* deadly.

Curie never said to herself, "I don't know," she probably would have wound up teaching chemistry at some private high school for young ladies from good families and ended her days performing this otherwise perfectly respectable job. But she kept on saying, "I don't know," and these words led her, not just once but twice, to Stockholm, where restless, questing spirits are occasionally rewarded with the Nobel Prize.

Poets, if they're genuine, must also keep repeating, "I don't know." Each poem marks an effort to answer this statement, but as soon as the final period hits the page, the poet begins to hesitate, starts to realize that this particular answer was pure makeshift, absolutely inadequate. So the poets keep on trying, and sooner or later the consecutive results of their self-dissatisfaction are clipped together with a giant paperclip by literary historians and called their "oeuvres."[2]...

The world—whatever we might think when we're terrified by its vastness and our own impotence or when we're embittered by its indifference to individual suffering, of people, animals, and perhaps even plants (for why are we so sure that plants feel no pain?); whatever we might think of its expanses pierced by the rays of stars surrounded by planets we've just begun to discover, planets already dead, still dead, we just don't know; whatever we might think of this measureless theater to which we've got reserved tickets, but tickets whose lifespan is laughably short, bounded as it is by two arbitrary dates; whatever else we might think of this world—it is astonishing.

But "astonishing" is an epithet concealing a logical trap. We're astonished, after all, by things that deviate from some well-known and universally acknowledged norm, from an obviousness to which we've grown accustomed. But the point is, there is no such obvious world. Our astonishment exists per se, and it isn't based on a comparison with something else. **D**

Granted, in daily speech, where we don't stop to consider every word, we all use phrases such as "the ordinary world," "ordinary life," "the ordinary course of events." But in the language of poetry, where every word is weighed, nothing is usual or normal. Not a single stone and not a single cloud above it. Not a single day and not a single night after it. And above all, not a single existence, not anyone's existence in this world.

It looks as though poets will always have their work cut out for them. **E**

---

2. **oeuvres** (UHR vruhz): the collected life works of artists.

D **Informational Focus** Analyzing an Author's Beliefs What belief about the world does Szymborska elaborate through the analysis of the word *astonishing*?

E **Informational Focus** Analyzing an Author's Beliefs How does this belief compare to her previous statement about poets being "Fortune's darlings"? Explain.

Vocabulary **impotence** (IHM puh tuhns) *n.:* helplessness.
epithet (EHP uh theht) *n.:* descriptive expression.
deviate (DEE vee ayt) *v.:* turn aside from a way, norm, or truth.

Applying Your Skills

SKILLS FOCUS **Informational Skills** Analyze an author's beliefs. **Vocabulary Skills** Demonstrate knowledge of literal meanings of words. **Listening and Speaking Skills** Deliver informative presentations. **Writing Skills** Write a brief constructed response, with specific support.

from **Nobel Lecture: The Poet and the World**

Respond and Think Critically

Informational Text Focus

Quick Check

1. How are the people the poet describes in the first paragraph different from those she describes in the second? What does she say is "one of the harshest human miseries"?

2. What counterargument to her ideas does the poet raise in the fourth paragraph? Summarize her response to the counterargument.

Read with a Purpose

3. According to Szymborska, how does knowledge endure?

Informational Skills: Analyzing an Author's Beliefs

4. Add another column to your chart, and make **inferences,** or educated guesses based on what you have read and what you already know, about the author's beliefs.

✓ Vocabulary Check

Match each Vocabulary word with its definition.

5. inspiration
6. quell
7. fervor
8. lethal
9. impotence
10. epithet
11. deviate

a. bring under control
b. helplessness
c. descriptive expression
d. turn aside
e. deadly
f. intense emotion
g. motivation

Text Analysis

12. **Interpret** What does Szymborska mean by the phrase "Fortune's darlings" (page 1253)?

13. **Analyze** Szymborska reveals extraordinary truths while speaking of everyday things. Why might it be important for a poet to recognize "nothing is usual or normal" (page 1254)?

14. **Compare and Contrast** What can be the difference between people who say, "I don't know" and people who say, "I know" (page 1253)? Why can "knowing" be negative and, at times, even deadly, according to Szymborska?

15. **Make Judgments** Do you agree with Szymborska's opinion of the phrases "I don't know" and "I know"? What exceptions might you make?

16. **Analyze** Szymborska says the world is "astonishing" (page 1254). How might viewing the world in this way lead to inspiration? What everyday elements of the world do you find astonishing?

Listening and Speaking

17. **Extend** Research a question or subject that inspires you or stimulates your curiosity. Prepare an oral presentation for your classmates about your thoughts and discoveries. Your presentation may be a report, story, poem, or discussion.

Writing Focus Constructed Response

Do you agree with Szymborska that work should be inspiring? In your *Reader/Writer Notebook,* write two short paragraphs that express your opinion. Use transitions to connect your ideas.

What Do You Think Now How does Szymborska's experience as a poet affect how she sees the world?

Preparing to Read

Fear

Gabriela Mistral (1889–1957).

MEET THE WRITER

Gabriela Mistral
(1889–1957)

Nobel Prize WINNER

In 1945, Gabriela Mistral became the first female poet and the first Latin American to win the Nobel Prize in Literature. She was of Spanish, Basque, and Indian heritage.

An Angel in the Wind

Mistral was born Lucilla Godoy Alcayaga in the village of Vicuna, Chile, high in the Andes Mountains. Her father, a schoolteacher and poet, abandoned the family when she was a small child. He left his daughter a garden, in which Mistral, as her mother remembers, sat and conversed with the birds and the trees. At the age of fifteen, Mistral began teaching school but continued to pursue a literary career and published poems under a variety of different names. In 1913, she settled on the pen name Gabriela Mistral. The first part of her pen name refers to the archangel Gabriel; the second part refers to the cold, dry *mistral,* a wind that blows across southern France.

Mistral wrote much of her early poetry in response to the suicide of a man she loved and to whom she had been engaged to marry. She received worldwide attention when Federico de Onis, a Spanish professor at Columbia University in New York "discovered" and published her poetry.

Poet and Activist

Mistral continued to write poetry while working as a principal and, later, as an international ambassador. In the 1920s, she helped reorganize the rural school systems of Mexico; and in the 1930s, she served as Chile's cultural representative to the League of Nations. After World War II, Mistral acted as the Chilean consul in Los Angeles and Italy. She was also a delegate to a United Nations subcommittee on women's rights. On her frequent trips back to Chile, Mistral was often greeted by thousands of schoolchildren singing her poems. When she received the Nobel Prize in Literature, she remarked, with a characteristically good-humored <u>perspective</u>, that she must have been voted in by women and children.

Think About the Writer

How do you think the experiences of Mistral's childhood might have inspired her later works?

Reader/Writer Notebook

Use your **RWN** to complete the activities for this selection.

Literary Focus

Refrain A **refrain** is a repeated word, phrase, line, or group of lines. Refrains are commonly used in poetry and sung to create **rhythm,** build suspense, and emphasize important words or ideas. Although they usually occur at the end of a stanza, refrains can appear elsewhere. As you read "Fear," note the location of the refrain and how often it is repeated. What effect does the refrain create?

Writing Focus

Think as a Reader/Writer

Find It in Your Reading Poets use **refrains** and organizational structure to give their poems a songlike quality to help their readers "hear" and "feel" the rhythm and music of the poem. The cause-effect structure of Mistral's poem "Fear" supports the speaker's use of three scenarios where she loses her beloved child, the essence of every parent's fear. Each possibility grows more devastating than the one preceding it. In your *Reader/Writer Notebook,* use a graphic organizer like the below to record the cause of her fear: the transformation, the images that describe it, and the feared result of each imagined transformation. Note how the cause-effect structure is repeated in each stanza.

Stanza	Transformation	Images	Effect
1	a swallow	"fly far away ... nest in the eaves"	could not comb her hair
2	a princess	"tiny golden slippers"	could never sleep by her side
3			

Language Coach

Connotations Good writers choose words with certain **connotations,** the emotions, ideas, and even specific images a word evokes. With a partner, discuss the thoughts, feelings, ideas, or images that come to mind when you read the following words. Think in particular of how this collection of words calls to mind fairy tales you have read.

swallow	straw bed
princess	glass slipper
queen	throne

Learn It Online
Hear this poem read online at

go.hrw.com L12-1257 **Go**

Fear

by **Gabriela Mistral**

translated by **Doris Dana**

Read with a Purpose
Read to discover how a mother feels about her daughter growing up.

Build Background
When Mistral won the Nobel Prize in Literature, she was called "the poet of motherhood by adoption" because of her great love for and commitment to children. This love is reflected in much of her writing, as in the poem you are about to read.

I don't want them to turn
my little girl into a swallow.
She would fly far away into the sky
and never fly again to my straw bed,
5   or she would nest in the eaves
where I could not comb her hair.
I don't want them to turn
my little girl into a swallow. Ⓐ

I don't want them to make
10 my little girl a princess.
In tiny golden slippers
how could she play on the meadow?
And when night came, no longer
would she sleep at my side.
15 I don't want them to make
my little girl a princess.

And even less do I want them
one day to make her queen.
They would put her on a throne
20 where I could not go to see her.
And when nighttime came
I could never rock her…
I don't want them to make
my little girl a queen! Ⓑ

Ⓐ **Literary Focus** Refrain What words does the speaker repeat? What is the effect of this repetition?

Ⓑ **Literary Focus** Refrain What effect does the refrain have at the end of the poem? What thoughts or emotions does it elicit?

Märchenprinzessin mit Fächer (Fairy Tale Princess with Fan; 1912), by Alexej van Jawlensky. Museum Ludwig, Köln. © Artists Rights Society (ARS), NY/VG, Bildkunst, Bonn.

Applying Your Skills

SKILLS FOCUS Literary Skills Analyze refrain; analyze theme. **Writing Skills** Write descriptive essays.

Fear

Respond and Think Critically

Reading Focus

Quick Check

1. What does the image of a "straw bed" suggest about the social and economic situation of the speaker? What else might the image suggest?

2. In the second stanza, the speaker evokes the image of "tiny golden slippers… on the meadow" as incongruous or out of place. In what other way would the slippers be incongruous in the situation?

3. Why do you think the speaker moves from the image of a bird to a princess to a queen in the poem?

Read with a Purpose

4. How do negatives words such as *don't, never,* and *not* emphasize the mother's feelings?

Literary Focus

Literary Analysis

5. **Interpret** A swallow is a bird that migrates, usually nesting in widely separated summer and winter regions. Given this information, why do you think Mistral uses the specific image of a swallow rather than simply any bird?

6. **Infer** Why do you think the speaker fears that she could no longer see her own daughter if her daughter were made a queen? (In your answer, consider the connotations of the words *queen* and *throne*.)

7. **Analyze** What is ironic about a mother's fear that her daughter will become a "queen," that is, someone who lives a life untouched by common cares and daily concerns?

8. **Make Judgments** Why do you think this poem is titled "Fear"? Does the poem match your idea of what the topic of a poem with this title would be? Explain.

9. **Extend** We are not told who the *them* of the poem are. Who do you think they are? Would the emotional impact of the poem be increased or reduced if the speaker identified *them*? Explain your response.

Literary Skills: Refrain

10. **Analyze** Remember that a **refrain** is a repeated word, phrase, line, or group of lines. Identify the refrain in the poem. Explain how the refrain helps reveal the speaker's emotional state.

Literary Skills Review: Theme

11. **Interpret** The central idea or message of a literary work is referred to as **theme.** In one sentence, state the theme of the poem. What comment on life does this theme make?

Writing Focus

Think as a Reader/Writer

Use It in Your Writing Using the images in Mistral's poem as a guide, write a brief essay describing something or someone you are afraid of losing. (If you prefer, write about someone else's fears.) Consider what words or phrases you can use to help your reader "see" the images in your essay. If you choose, use a refrain to add a musical quality to your essay.

What Do You Think Now

What experiences might have shaped the mother's fears? What advice would you give to her?

Preparing to Read

Sonnet 79 /
Soneto 79

How does experience shape our view of the world?

QuickWrite

In what ways does love empower us? In your *Reader/Writer Notebook*, record notes on your responses to this question.

Nobel Prize winning poet Pablo Neruda, Paris, France (1971).

MEET THE WRITER

Pablo Neruda
(1904–1973)

Nobel Prize WINNER

"Poetry is like bread," Neruda said, "and it must be shared by everyone, the men of letters and the peasants, by everyone in our vast, incredible, extraordinary family of man."

Poetry Is a Gift

When the Chilean poet Pablo Neruda was a boy searching for "creaturely things" behind his house, he saw a child's hand poking through a hole in the fence, offering him a toy sheep made of real wool. Thrilled, Neruda raced home to return with his most treasured possession, a fragrant pine cone, which he dropped through the hole for the unseen friend. Neruda often related this incident. From his perspective, poetry was a gift to be shared with the world—a gift that always brought something in return.

Neruda became a poet when he was still a teenager in Temuco, a frontier town in southern Chile. Born Neftali Ricardo Reyes Basoalto, Neruda adopted his pen name to avoid upsetting his father, a railroad worker who frowned on his son's poetic ambitions. A bohemian in black clothing, Neruda was only twenty years old when he published a collection of love poems that eventually sold two million copies worldwide.

The Poet as Protester

Neruda's serious involvement with politics began when he was appointed to the diplomatic service. As consul in Spain, Neruda became close friends with the Spanish poet Federico García Lorca. When García Lorca was murdered by Fascist forces in the Spanish Civil War, Neruda joined the Communist Party and wrote letters attacking Chile's repressive government. In 1946, he was accused of treason and forced to flee his homeland. Neruda returned to Chile in 1952 and began writing *Elementary Odes* (1954), poems in praise of simple things from socks to onions. In 1959, returning to his earlier themes of love and nature, he wrote *One Hundred Love Poems* for his wife, Matilde Urrutia. Neruda won the Nobel Prize in Literature in 1971.

Think About the Writer If Neruda believed that poetry should "be shared by everyone," what would you predict would be the topics of his poems?

Reader/Writer Notebook

Use your **RWN** to complete the activities for this selection.

Literary Focus

Metaphor Poets use **metaphors** to make imaginative comparisons between two basically unlike things. Because they can suggest much more than literal statements, metaphors are very useful in writing. Most metaphors are visual and convey strong emotion. For example, in the English translation of the first line of this sonnet, the speaker asks his love to "tie your heart to mine." The rope is a metaphor for love; both things tie two people together. In Spanish, the line reads "amarra tu corazón al mío." The verb *amarrar* in Spanish can specifically refer to mooring a boat to some safe harbor. Neruda could therefore be comparing his lover's heart to a boat that is moored or tied up safely alongside his heart. Note the visual picture that the metaphor creates in your mind and how the image makes you feel.

If you fail to understand a poet's metaphors, you have missed an important part of the poem. Sometimes metaphors are complex, and several interpretations are possible. When you encounter a complex metaphor, talk about it with a classmate. Discussing poetry and solving its puzzles are part of the pleasure of reading it.

Writing Focus

Think as a Reader/Writer

Find It in Your Reading Poets use comparisons to help their readers see the world in new and imaginative ways. In a **simile,** the poet compares two unlike things using a specific word of comparison, such as *like* or *as*. In a **metaphor,** the poet directly identifies two unlike things without the use of *like* or *as*. In your *Reader/Writer Notebook,* use a chart like the one below to record the metaphors and similes you find in Neruda's poem. See if you can name the two things that are being compared. Then, briefly note how you think those things are similar.

Stanza	Simile/Metaphor	What is being compared?	How are they similar?

Vocabulary

punctual (PUHNGK choo uhl) *adj.:* prompt; on time. *The poet says that sleep is as punctual as a train.*

constancy (KAHN stuhn see) *n.:* faithfulness; loyalty. *The speaker tells of the constancy that he finds in his lover's heart.*

Language Coach

Synonyms Words with the same or nearly the same meanings are called **synonyms.** In the definitions above, the word *prompt* is a synonym for *punctual,* and the words *faithfulness* and *loyalty* are synonyms for *constancy.* When writers translate a poem from one language to another, they must be aware of the slight differences in meanings among synonyms. They must choose the word that best matches the word in the original language. Neruda's translator uses *punctual* and *constancy* for the Spanish words *puntualidad* and *tenacidad.* If you speak Spanish or have access to a Spanish-English dictionary, look up the Spanish words *puntualidad* and *tenacidad.* Do you think the translator used the best English synonyms in his translation?

Learn It Online
Learn more about Neruda online at the Writers' Lives site.

 go.hrw.com L12-1261   **Go**

Read with a Purpose
Read this poem to discover what the speaker believes love can accomplish.

Build Background
Sonnet 79 comes from Neruda's book *One Hundred Love Poems*. The book is divided into four parts (morning, afternoon, evening, and night), each corresponding to a different stage in a person's life. As you read Sonnet 79, think about to which stage of life it refers.

Sonnet 79

by **Pablo Neruda**
translated by **Stephen Tapscott**

By night, Love, tie your heart to mine, and the two
together in their sleep will defeat the darkness
like a double drum in the forest, pounding
against the thick wall of wet leaves.

5 Night travel: black flame of sleep
that snips the threads of the earth's grapes,
punctual as a headlong train that would haul
shadows and cold rocks, endlessly. **A**

Because of this, Love, tie me to a purer motion,
10 to the constancy that beats in your chest
with the wings of a swan underwater, **B**

so that our sleep might answer all the sky's
starry questions with a single key,
with a single door the shadows had closed.

Soneto 79

De noche, amada, amarra tu corazón al mío
y que ellos en el sueño derroten las tinieblas
como un doble tambor combatiendo en el bosque
contra el espeso muro de las hojas mojadas.

5 Nocturna travesía, brasa negra del sueño
interceptando el hilo de las uvas terrestres
con la puntualidad de un tren descabellado
que sombra y piedras frías sin cesar arrastrara.

Por eso, amor, amárrame al movimiento puro,
10 a la tenacidad que en tu pecho golpea
con las alas de un cisne sumergido,

para que a las preguntas estrelladas del cielo
responda nuestro sueño con una sola llave,
con una sola puerta cerrada por la sombra.

A Literary Focus **Metaphor** To what does the metaphor "Night travel" refer?

B Literary Focus **Metaphor** What is being compared to the "wings of a swan"?

Vocabulary **punctual** (PUHNGK choo uhl) *adj.*: prompt; on time.
constancy (KAHN stuhn see) *n.*: faithfulness; loyalty.

SKILLS FOCUS Literary Skills Analyze metaphor; analyze a Petrarchan sonnet. **Vocabulary Skills** Identify and correctly use antonyms. **Writing Skills** Write poems; write descriptive paragraphs.

Sonnet 79 / Soneto 79

Respond and Think Critically

Reading Focus

Quick Check

1. In line 2, what does the speaker say he and his love will do together?

2. In lines 12–14, what does the speaker say their sleep will accomplish?

Read with a Purpose

3. How can love do things that seem impossible?

✓ Vocabulary Check

Answer the following questions about each Vocabulary word.

4. Antonyms are words with opposite meanings. Which of the following words is an antonym for the word *punctual?*

   a. tidy   c. prompt
   b. late   d. suitable

5. Which of the following words is an antonym for the word *constancy?*

   a. fickleness   c. devotion
   b. steadiness   d. love

Literary Focus

Literary Analysis

6. **Evaluate** Explain the extended simile in lines 2–4. How does this comparison make you feel?

7. **Make Judgments** What do you think are the "sky's / starry questions" in lines 12–13?

8. **Evaluate** Work with a classmate who speaks or reads Spanish, and evaluate the effectiveness and accuracy of the English translation. (For example, what do you think of the translation of "brasa negra" in line 5 as "black flame"?)

9. **Hypothesize** Why is the speaker so fearful of "the "darkness"?

10. **Extend** What do you think of the idea that love completes people—that it unites them so that they can be one person? In what other poems in this book have you encountered this idea?

Literary Skills: Metaphor

11. **Analyze** On what comparison is the extended metaphor in line 5–8 based? What images does this metaphor call to mind?

Literary Skills Review: Petrarchan Sonnet

12. **Make Judgments** Although this sonnet follows the form of the **Petrarchan sonnet** (see page 267), it does not follow its traditional rhyme scheme. Neruda's nontraditional sonnet does, however, contain the abrupt turn of thought of the classic sonnet. Where do you think the change, or turn, occurs in Sonnet 79?

Writing Focus

Think as a Reader/Writer

Use It in Your Writing Write a brief poem or paragraph in which you use at least two **metaphors** or **similes** to describe something the way Neruda describes love, sleep, and death—perhaps something like hope, joy, or fear. One way to begin is to identify the emotion directly with something concrete. For example, you might write, "Hope is…" or "Joy is…" Try to use metaphors or similes that create vivid images and express strong feelings.

What Do **You Think Now** Do you agree with the speaker that "tying" your heart to another person can protect you and possibly conquer fears of death?

Preparing to Read

The Explosion

What Do You Think?

How does experience shape our view of the world?

QuickWrite

Think of a local, national, or international tragedy that has made the headlines. In your *Reader/Writer Notebook,* record a brief description of how people responded to the news of the disaster.

Philip Arthur Larkin (1974), by Fay Godwin, bromide print. National Portrait Gallery, London.

MEET THE WRITER

Philip Larkin
(1922–1985)

Philip Larkin originally aspired to become a jazz drummer. After a few pivotal academic experiences, however, he gave up that ambition to pursue a literary career.

An Ordinary Life

Larkin describes his early life as middle class and ordinary. He was born in Coventry, England. His father was city treasurer, and his mother was a homemaker. Larkin was a good student, but during childhood did not <u>exhibit</u> any special talent for writing. As he approached the British equivalent of high school, he did read nearly a book a day. Then, he began writing. "I wrote ceaselessly," he said, "... now verse, which I sewed up into little books, now prose, a thousand words a night after homework."

An Unassuming Poet

Educated at Oxford, Larkin spent most of his life as librarian at the University of Hull. He maintained an uneasy and sometimes yearning bachelorhood, and he wrote of romantic love in terms of bittersweet comedy or outright farce. Although Larkin shared much of the disillusionment of his fellow postwar writers, he was <u>considerably</u> shyer about dealing with the issues they addressed with the same passionate or satiric tone.

This decision not to engage with wider social issues seemed more characteristic of Larkin's personality than indicative of a general absence of conviction. In their quiet way, his poems reflect the themes of contemporary experience. When grappling with these themes, Larkin keeps to an intimately human scale, in which the balance lies somewhere between disgust and disdain, and heartbreak and despairing humor.

Larkin was the most widely admired poet of the generation that succeeded Dylan Thomas. Unlike Thomas, Larkin scrupulously avoided public attention. He refused hundreds of invitations to read or lecture in the United States and Great Britain. He seemed content to cultivate his own talents without reference to the choruses of praise and delight that attended the publication of each of his few but flawless collections of poetry.

Think About the Writer Can someone write movingly about something he or she has not experienced? Explain.

Reader/Writer Notebook

Use your **RWN** to complete the activities for this selection.

Literary Focus

Imagery Language that evokes sensory impressions is known as **imagery.** Most imagery is visual, appealing to the sense of sight, but imagery can also appeal to the senses of hearing, touch, smell, and taste. In addition to creating sensory impressions, imagery can evoke emotion. The word *slagheap* in line 3, for example, helps you visualize the heap of debris at the pit mouth; the image also can create a sense of foreboding or even disgust. The words *freshened silence* in line 6 help you feel the fresh morning air and hear the silence; the image can also create a feeling of well-being. As you read the poem, let the imagery help you imagine this scene and understand the writer's feelings about what happened.

Language Coach

Defining Unfamiliar Words Because many poets love diverse language, they sometimes use words you do not often read or hear in regular speech. To determine the meaning of some of these words, see if the word is built from a word you recognize. For example, Larkin describes the coal miners "shouldering off" the freshened silence. You know what shoulders are: What do you think "shouldering off" might mean? Check a dictionary to see if your guess is correct.

Reading Focus

Using Prior Knowledge The information and experience you possess before you read a poem or literary work is your **prior knowledge.** For example, if you are familiar with coal mining, you might be able to picture the pithead, or opening of the coal mine, in this poem. Use whatever prior knowledge you have about the subject matter (mining) to help you understand details in the rest of this poem.

Into Action As you read, use a KWL (Know-Want-Learn) chart like the one below to record what you know, want to know, and have learned.

What I Know	What I Want to Know	What I Learned
This poem is about a coal-mine explosion. Coal mining is a dangerous job.	What happens to the miners?	

Writing Focus

Think as a Reader/Writer

Find It in Your Reading Larkin wants us to imagine vividly the coal mine, the miners coming down the lane, the cows, the dimmed sun, and the men walking toward their wives after the disaster. In your *Reader/Writer Notebook*, record the precise **imagery** Larkin uses to help you imagine the scene leading up to the disaster, the explosion itself, and what the wives saw later.

Learn It Online
Find an interactive KWL chart online.

go.hrw.com   L12-1265   **Go**

THE EXPLOSION

by **Philip Larkin**

Read with a Purpose
Read this poem to find a vision of life emerging from death.

Build Background
Mining coal is a difficult and dangerous job. Underground mines are ventilated to prevent miners from inhaling noxious gases, but these gases are flammable. Despite efforts to take safety precautions, explosions inside the mines, like the one described in the following poem, do occur. The *pithead* mentioned in line 2 is the opening to the mine; a *slagheap* (line 3) is the mountain of coal dust and mineral waste produced in the mining process. Larkin, who wrote this poem many years ago, might be referring to one of the terrible disasters that took place in the coal mines in Wales. Those mines are now almost all closed.

Miner pauses in a tunnel before starting a shift in Britain's most modern iron ore mine. Irthlinborough, Northamptonshire.

On the day of the explosion
Shadows pointed towards the pithead:
In the sun the slagheap slept.

Down the lane came men in pitboots
5 Coughing oath-edged talk and pipe-smoke,
Shouldering off the freshened silence.

One chased after rabbits; lost them;
Came back with a nest of lark's eggs;
Showed them; lodged them in the grasses.

10 So they passed in beards and moleskins,°
Fathers, brothers, nicknames, laughter,
Through the tall gates standing open. **A**

10. moleskins: trousers made of thick, durable cotton fabric.

At noon, there came a tremor; cows
Stopped chewing for a second; sun,
15 Scarfed as in a heat-haze, dimmed. **B**

The dead go on before us, they
Are sitting in God's house in comfort,
We shall see them face to face—

Plain as lettering in the chapels
20 It was said, and for a second
Wives saw men of the explosion

Larger than in life they managed—
Gold as on a coin, or walking
Somehow from the sun towards them,

25 One showing the eggs unbroken.

A Literary Focus Imagery What images so far help you "see" and "hear" the miners as they head toward work?

B Reading Focus Using Prior Knowledge What do you know about underground explosions that would explain the tremor and the dimmed sun?

Applying Your Skills

The Explosion

Respond and Think Critically

Reading Focus

Quick Check

1. What three events are described in this poem? What happened in the morning, at noon, and later in the chapels?

Read with a Purpose

2. What details in the poem indicate that the speaker sees life emerging from death? What do you think the "tall gates" (line 12) could be?

Reading Skills: Using Prior Knowledge

3. As you read the poem, you filled out a KWL chart. Now, complete the chart by filling in the "What I Learned" column.

What I Know	What I Want to Know	What I Learned
This poem is about a coal-mine explosion. Coal mining is a dangerous job.	What happens to the miners?	The miners die in the explosion.

Literary Focus

Literary Analysis

4. **Interpret** What does the description in lines 4–12 tell you about the miners? Besides the pipe-smoke, what do you think might cause the coughing?

5. **Compare and Contrast** The first part of the poem is written in an almost singsong rhythm that sounds at times like a children's rhyme. Where does the rhythm change? How does the tone of the poem in the first four stanzas contrast with the tone of the last five?

6. **Infer** Who is most likely speaking the italicized words in lines 16–18? Where are these words being spoken (or sung), and why?

Literary Skills: Imagery

7. **Evaluate** Review the images in lines 13–15 that describe the moment of impact. How do these images of the cow and sun contrast with the explosion itself and with the deaths that resulted from it? What do the images suggest about nature's response to human tragedy?

Literary Skills Review: Symbol

8. **Analyze** A **symbol** is something that stands both for itself and for something beyond itself. What might the eggs in the poem symbolize? Consider when the man finds the eggs, as well as the image of the "eggs unbroken" at the end of the poem. What message do you think this symbol conveys?

Writing Focus

Think As a Reader/Writer

Use It in Your Writing Write a short essay describing an accident or disaster that you read about or witnessed. Use imagery to help your reader imagine not only the sights at the scene but also the sounds and, possibly, the smells and tastes. (If you prefer, describe a happy event instead of an accident or disaster: You might describe a wedding or a personal triumph.) Try opening your essay with Larkin's words: "On the day of the…"

 What Do You Think Now — How do you think the speaker of this poem is affected by the tragic events he describes? What clues help you make this inference?

Preparing to Read

Link to Today Trapped Australian Miners Rescued

What Do You Think

How does experience shape our view of the world?

⏱ QuickWrite

How would you expect someone who was trapped in a mine for a week to react? Explain your thoughts in your *Reader/Writer Notebook*.

Informational Text Focus

Using Graphics to Understand Text Many informational texts include graphics to clarify the text and to add important information to help readers understand the text. Graphics should be simple enough to aid understanding but complex enough to add information.

Into Action As you view the graphic on page 1270, identify the parts of the text that it clarifies and the information it adds to the selection. Use a chart like the one below to record your responses.

Clarification	New Information
location of the cage in which the men were trapped	The miners were 1 kilometer below ground.

Writing Focus Preparing for **Constructed Response**

Good graphics include clear captions and labels to inform readers. Look at the graphic included with the text, and determine whether you think the labels are clear. Explain your opinion. Would you add other labels or a caption? Does anything seem missing? If yes, what? Record your thoughts in your *Reader/Writer Notebook*.

Vocabulary

condolences (kuhn DOH luhns ihz) *n. pl.*: expressions of sympathy offered to a grieving person. *She gave her condolences to the father of the deceased.*

thermal (THUR muhl) *adj.*: relating to heat. *The thermal-activated lamp came on with one touch.*

painstaking (PAYNZ tay kihng) *adj.*: using great care. *The painstaking surgery took hours.*

plight (plyt) *n.*: unpromising condition or situation. *The plight of the polar bear is serious.*

elation (ih LAY shuhn) *n.*: high spirits; jubilation. *His elation showed in the smile on his face.*

Language Coach

Synonyms Words that have the same or nearly the same meaning are called **synonyms.** Learning synonyms can help you expand your vocabulary. Identify a synonym for two of the Vocabulary words. Use a thesaurus or dictionary if necessary.

✳ Learn It Online
Develop your vocabulary knowledge with Word Watch online.

go.hrw.com   L12-1268   **Go**

Link to Today

Read with a Purpose

Read to find out how two miners reacted to a drastic situation.

Build Background

Gold was first discovered in Tasmania (an island southeast of Australia), in 1852. Like coal mining, gold mining is done underground and is extremely dangerous for the miners. This news article tells of three miners who were trapped underground after a small earthquake caused a cave-in.

Tasmanian miners Todd Russell *(left)* and Brant Webb *(right)* move their safety tags to "Safe" following their rescue after having been trapped for fourteen days underground in Beaconsfield gold mine.

Trapped Australian Miners Rescued

BBC News, May 9, 2006

Two Australian miners were rescued from a gold mine after being trapped deep underground for two weeks. Brant Webb, 37, and Todd Russell, 34, walked out of the lift at the mine in Tasmania and waved to cheering crowds.

Australian Prime Minister John Howard said the rescue was a "wonderful demonstration of Australian mateship."[1] He offered condolences to the family of Larry Knight, a third miner who died in the initial accident, caused when a tremor dislodged rocks. His colleagues, Mr. Webb and Mr. Russell, were trapped in a tiny cage when the tremor struck. Rescuers took a week to bring them out, drilling through hard rock, often by hand. **Ⓐ**

Residents of the town of Beaconsfield gathered at the gates of the mine as news of the rescue began to emerge. The mine's siren sounded and the town's church bell pealed in celebration.

Miners Todd Russell *(left)* and Brant Webb *(second from left)* emerge from mine at Beaconsfield, Australia.

1. **mateship:** Australian term meaning camaraderie and unconditional assistance, especially during hard times.

Ⓐ **Informational Focus** Using Graphics to Understand Text How does the diagram on the next page add to what you already know about the drilling procedure that rescued the miners?

Vocabulary **condolences** (kuhn DOH luhns ihz) *n. pl.:* expressions of sympathy offered to a grieving person.

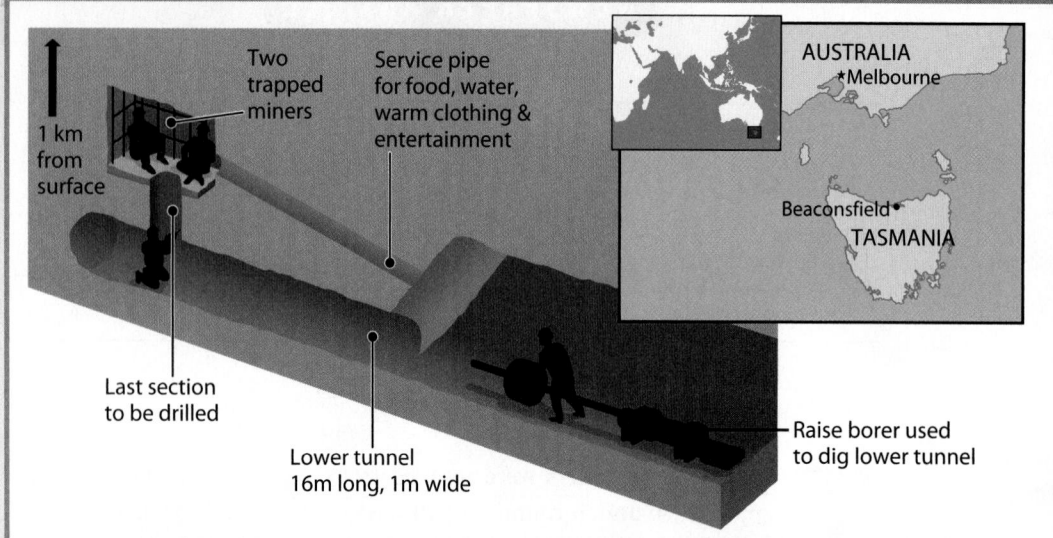

Graphic of the rescue.

Labels in graphic:
1 km from surface
Two trapped miners
Service pipe for food, water, warm clothing & entertainment
AUSTRALIA
*Melbourne
Beaconsfield•
TASMANIA
Last section to be drilled
Lower tunnel 16m long, 1m wide
Raise borer used to dig lower tunnel

Mr. Webb and Mr. Russell, wearing mining helmets and yellow jackets, walked out of the mine to a large board and shifted their name cards from red to green to signal they had finished their shift. They then waved to the crowds and hugged family and friends before being taken by ambulance to hospital for medical checks.

"They're amazing," said mine manager Matthew Gill, who is also a close friend of the two. "I said welcome and we hugged." Gill said the delicate rescue operation had involved keeping the men horizontal for as long as possible in case they were injured. They were then pulled to safety through a vertical tunnel. **B**

"I think the people responsible for the rescue were breaking new ground, but the difficult thing was breaking hard rock," Paul James Reynolds of the Tasmanian emergency services told the BBC.

Sense of Humor

Mr. Russell and Mr. Webb survived for five days on just one shared cereal bar and by licking water from the rocks around them, before rescuers discovered they were alive by using a thermal imaging camera. The painstaking and dangerous operation to free them then began as rescuers ground through rock described as five times as hard as concrete. The men were given food and water through a small plastic pipe. Rescuers also managed to get portable media players to them to help pass the time. **C**

The men's plight and the sense of humor they displayed to emergency workers gripped Australia, leading to reports of a media scramble to secure exclusive rights to their story.

"The elation is unbelievable, absolutely unbelievable," onlooker Diane Alexander told the *Sydney Morning Herald* newspaper.

"The great escape is over," said union official Bill Shorten. "A giant rock of pressure has been taken off these families."

B **Informational Focus** Using Graphics to Understand
Text   Does the graphic differentiate the horizontal and vertical rescue?

C **Informational Focus** Using Graphics to Understand
Text   Without the label, would you be able to identify the tunnel that rescuers used to get food and water to the trapped miners? Explain.

D **Informational Focus** Using Graphics to Understand
Text   Does the graphic provide additional information about the rescue?

Vocabulary   **thermal** (THUR muhl) *adj.*: relating to heat.
painstaking (PAYNZ tay kihng) *adj.*: using great care.
plight (plyt) *n.*: unpromising condition or situation.
elation (ih LAY shuhn) *n.*: high spirits; jubilation.

Applying Your Skills

SKILLS FOCUS Informational Skills Use graphics to understand text. Vocabulary Skills Demonstrate knowledge of literal meanings of words. Listening and

Speaking Skills Deliver informative presentations. Writing Skills Write a brief constructed response, with specific support.

Trapped Australian Miners Rescued

Respond and Think Critically

Informational Text Focus

Quick Check

1. Summarize what happened to the miners in Tasmania.

2. What were the miners determined to do from the beginning of the ordeal? Why do you think they had this plan?

Read with a Purpose

3. How did the miners react to the dangerous situation? Is their reaction what you would expect? Explain your opinion.

Informational Skills: Using Graphics to Understand Text

4. Look over the chart you created as you read. How does the graphic help you better understand the article? What additional information does it provide? What information does it clarify for you? Explain.

✓ Vocabulary Check

Match the Vocabulary words to their definitions.

5. condolences   a. relating to heat

6. elation   b. using great care

7. thermal   c. difficult situation

8. painstaking   d. high spirits

9. plight   e. expressions of sympathy

Text Analysis

10. **Analyze** Why did the writer include details about the miners waving to the "cheering crowd" in the article? What tone does it set?

11. **Interpret** When the miners were finally rescued days after the shift began, they changed their time cards to show that they had finished their shift. What does this action suggest about their attitude as they emerged from the mine?

12. **Make Judgments** Only one sentence refers to the miner who lost his life in the mine collapse. Do you think this is fair coverage? Explain.

Listening and Speaking

13. **Extend** Work with a small group to prepare a short news broadcast of the mining rescue. Write the story, and then have two group members work as news anchors, one person directing and another operating the video camera (if you have access to one). Share your video broadcast with the rest of the class, or if you do not have access to a video camera, present the broadcast live.

Writing Focus   Constructed Response

In a paragraph or two, discuss the importance of graphics in an informational text like this one. Be sure to use evidence from the article to support your response.

What Do You Think Now? How do you think the two miners felt after their rescue? How might the experience have affected their view of their work? of their lives?

Preparing to Read

The Horses

How does experience shape our view of the world?

QuickWrite

Think about an encounter you have had in nature with an animal or plant. In your *Reader/Writer Notebook,* write about how the encounter affected you emotionally.

Ted Hughes (1930–1998).

MEET THE WRITER

Ted Hughes
(1930–1998)

Ted Hughes often used violent nature imagery in his poetry to symbolize the human condition. Born in West Yorkshire, England, Hughes was influenced considerably by the landscape of his hometown surroundings.

A Private Life

Hughes served two years in the Royal Air Force before attending Cambridge University. In 1956, he married the American poet Sylvia Plath. Plath committed suicide in 1963 after the couple had separated. An intensely private person, Hughes was silent for decades about his relationship with Plath and the accusations that he was somehow responsible for her death. In 1998, he broke that silence with the publication of a collection of poems, *Birthday Letters*.

The Poet's Work

Hughes's recurring subjects are reflected in the titles of a number of his books: *The Hawk in the Rain* (1957), *Animal Poems* (1967), *Crow* (1970), *Cave Birds* (1975), and *Wolfwatching* (1989). The critic A. Alvarez called Hughes a "survivor-poet" because Hughes sees parallels between human beings and animals—both are creatures that will do anything to ensure survival. Although Hughes writes about nature, he has little in common with the Romantics, who saw in nature a reflection of divine providence and primeval innocence. In Hughes's poems, nature often represents the darkest impulses of the human heart; violence is not only an accepted fact of life but also a tendency that links all creatures on earth. Hughes sees humans as alienated from nature, with instincts that have been diminished by reason and civilization. To see the world from the perspective of an animal, in Hughes's thinking, is to recover a power that has been lost.

In 1984, Hughes was named Poet Laureate of the United Kingdom, a title he held until his death.

Think About the Writer

How is the term "survivor-poet" appropriate for both Hughes's poetry and his personal life?

Reader/Writer Notebook

Use your **RWN** to complete the activities for this selection.

Literary Focus

Poetic Structure The literary techniques that a writer uses to organize and create a poem make up that poem's **poetic structure.** One unit of poetic structure is the **line,** traditionally a single thought expressed on one physical line of the poem. A group of consecutive lines that form a single unit make up a **stanza,** which is itself separated by blank lines. Two-line stanzas that rhyme are called **couplets.** Hughes, however, does not follow any of these traditional organizational patterns exactly. Sometimes a line in his poem breaks in midthought and sometimes in midstanza. Although most of the stanzas in "The Horses" contain two lines, one contains a single line. Finally, Hughes does not rhyme his couplets and instead uses assonance and alliteration to give his poem a musical sound.

Vocabulary

tortuous (TAWR choo uhs) *adj.:* characterized by twists and turns. *We drove slowly down the tortuous mountain road.*

moorline (MUR lyn) *n.:* edge of a heath or wasteland. *The horses were eating grass near the moorline.*

dregs (drehgz) *n. pl.:* sediment. *The dregs of the coffee clung to the bottom of the mug.*

erupted (ih RUHPT ihd) *v.:* burst forth. *My anger erupted at the injustice.*

Writing Focus

Think as a Reader/Writer

Find It in Your Reading The line and stanza breaks in Hughes's poems are not random. As you read, ask yourself why Hughes breaks lines at certain points in the poem. Identify the effect of each break. Does it signal a change of thought? Does it emphasize some quality? Next to each break, write a short note about its effect. In your *Reader/Writer Notebook,* record your findings in a graphic organizer like the one below, making certain to use ellipsis points and quotation marks accurately.

Line #	Line	Effect of Line Break
1	"hour-before-dawn dark"	sets the scene; hyphens and alliteration emphasize time
2	"Evil air, a frost-making stillness"	reader must pause and be still
3	"A world cast in frost. . . . above the wood"	creates feeling of suspense and stillness

Language Coach

Compound Nouns Compound nouns are nouns made up of more than one word; for example, *moor* + *line* = *moorline*. Compound nouns can be closed (*moorline*), open (*ice cream*), or hyphenated (*mother-in-law*). As you read the poem, look for compound nouns. Be careful not to mistake hyphenated adjectives for compound nouns.

TechFocus As you read "The Horses," think about what other visual images, in addition to the ones Hughes evokes, might help elaborate on the **theme,** or message, of the poem. How might photographs, drawings, or even computer illustrations represent the poem's language?

Learn It Online
Listen to this poem online.

go.hrw.com   L12-1273

POEM

The Horses by Ted Hughes

Read with a Purpose Read to envision one man's encounter with nature.

I climbed through woods in the hour-before-dawn dark.
Evil air, a frost-making stillness,

Not a leaf, not a bird—
A world cast in frost. I came out above the wood

5   Where my breath left tortuous statues in the iron light.
But the valleys were draining the darkness

Till the moorline—blackening dregs of the brightening grey—
Halved the sky ahead. And I saw the horses: **Ⓐ**

Huge in the dense grey—ten together—
10 Megalith°-still. They breathed, making no move,

With draped manes and tilted hind-hooves,
Making no sound.

I passed: not one snorted or jerked its head.
Grey silent fragments

15 Of a grey silent world.   **Ⓑ**

I listened in emptiness on the moor-ridge.
The curlew's° tear turned its edge on the silence.

10. megalith: huge stone, often used in the monuments constructed by ancient people.

17. curlew's: referring to a large brown shorebird.

Ⓐ Literary Focus **Poetic Structure** What length are most of the stanzas within this poem? What do you notice about Hughes's stanzas?

Ⓑ Literary Focus **Poetic Structure** Why do you think Hughes sets line 15 alone? What is the effect of this organization?

Vocabulary **tortuous** (TAWR choo uhs) *adj.*: characterized by twists and turns.
moorline (MUR lyn) *n.*: edge of a heath or wasteland.
dregs (drehgz) *n. pl.*: sediment.

1274   Unit 6 • Collection 12

Slowly detail leafed from the darkness. Then the sun
Orange, red, red erupted

20   Silently, and splitting to its core tore and flung cloud,
Shook the gulf open, showed blue,

And the big planets hanging—.
I turned

Stumbling in the fever of a dream, down towards
25   The dark woods, from the kindling tops,

And came to the horses.
                                    There, still they stood,
But now steaming and glistening under the flow of light,   **C**

Their draped stone manes, their tilted hind-hooves
30   Stirring under a thaw while all around them

The frost showed its fires. But still they made no sound.
Not one snorted or stamped,

Their hung heads patient as the horizons,
High over valleys, in the red levelling rays—

35   In din of the crowded streets, going among the years, the faces,
May I still meet my memory in so lonely a place

Between the streams and the red clouds, hearing curlews,
Hearing the horizons endure.

C **Literary Focus** Poetic Structure How does the three-line stanza affect the
overall rhythm of the poem? How does it support the themes of the poem?

Vocabulary **erupted** (ih RUHPT ihd) *v.:* burst forth.

The Horses

Respond and Think Critically

Quick Check

1. What kind of landscape is evoked in "The Horses"? What aspects of the scene does the poet emphasize?

2. How are the horses described? What does "Megalith-still" (line 10) suggest?

3. Why do you think Hughes emphasizes the silence of the scene?

Read with a Purpose

4. What effect does the encounter with nature have on the speaker of the poem?

Literary Focus

Literary Analysis

5. **Evaluate** Do you think "The Horses" expresses the poet's union with nature or his alienation from it? Explain.

6. **Interpret** Although Hughes does not use end rhyme, he achieves subtle musical effects by employing other devices. How does he use repetition, alliteration, and other techniques of sound? What are their effects?

7. **Extend** Hughes appears to say in the poem that the horses' stillness is ominous because they do not react the way we expect, or want them to, in the presence of a stranger. What contradictions or abnormalities have you witnessed in animals or other elements of nature (for example, the silence before a storm)? How did the experience make you feel?

8. **Analyze** Hughes ends the poem with the phrase "Hearing the horizons endure." What do you think

he means by this line? Notice the incongruity of the descriptions with their subject, the horizons.

Literary Skills: Poetic Structure

9. **Make Judgments** How does Hughes's use of poetic structure contribute to the poem's meaning? Explain your answer by using examples from the poem.

Literary Skills Review: Imagery

10. **Analyze** Language that appeals to the senses is called **imagery.** Most images are visual, but imagery can also appeal to the senses of hearing, touch, taste, or smell. Identify an image from the poem that appeals to a sense other than sight.

Writing Focus

Think As a Reader/Writer

Use It in Your Writing Now that you have seen how a master poet like Ted Hughes uses line and stanza breaks to create and reinforce meaning, write your own short poem about the natural world. Think carefully about your poem's structure, and make sure you have a reason for each of your line and stanza breaks.

What Do **You Think Now** How do you think an experience with nature such as that described in this poem might affect a person's view of the world?

Vocabulary Development

✓ Vocabulary Check

Respond to the following items.

1. Identify something that can be **tortuous.**
2. Tell where you might see a **moorline.**
3. Name one thing that has **dregs.**
4. Identify something that could have **erupted.**

Vocabulary Skills: Figurative Language

Figurative language is used to describe one thing in terms of another, dissimilar thing. The following are three common types of figurative language:

Simile: a figure of speech that makes a comparison between two seemingly unlike things by using a connective word such as *like* or *as.* ("My love is like a red, red rose.")

Metaphor: the same kind of comparison without a connective word. ("Your eyes are diamonds.")

Personification: a form of metaphor in which a non-human or nonliving thing is talked about as if it were human or had life. ("Death, be not proud.")

Your Turn

Label each of the following figures of speech as simile, metaphor, or personification.

1. The road was as **tortuous** as a slithering snake.
2. The gritty **dregs** swam happily in the coffee pot.
3. The children waited like frightened deer when their neighbor's anger **erupted.**

Language Coach

Compound Nouns Look at the list of compound nouns that you found in the poem. Divide each into its component words, and write a short explanation of how the meanings of the component words combine to form the compound noun.

CHOICES

As you respond to the Choices, use these **Academic Vocabulary** words as appropriate: perspective, considerably, adapt, exhibit, inevitable.

REVIEW
Write an Essay

Timed ⏱ Writing In "The Horses," Hughes uses **free verse,** a form of poetry with no regular rhyme scheme or meter. Poets who use free verse often rely on other poetic devices, such as alliteration, internal rhyme, and imagery, to make their poems memorable. Analyze Hughes's use of poetic devices, and explain how they contribute to the poem's theme and mood.

CONNECT
Express Your Experience

Re-read the poem "The Horses," noting how the experience affected the speaker long after the event. Think of a lasting experience of your own, and record the reasons it made an impression. From your notes, construct a poem that expresses your experience. Include figurative language, meaningful stanza divisions, and sound techniques in your poem.

EXTEND
Create a Collage

TechFocus Illustrate Hughes's poem by making a collage. You might first copy the poem in your own handwriting and then draw or cut out magazine pictures. Consider using a computer graphics program to create your collage and type in the poem. Whichever medium you choose, be sure to capture not just the events but also the feelings of the poem. Exhibit your finished collage in your classroom.

Preparing to Read

Digging

What Do You Think?

How does experience shape our view of the world?

QuickWrite

How do you relate to the older generations in your family or community? In your *Reader/Writer Notebook*, write a brief description of the way the older generations have influenced your view of the world.

Seamus Heaney relaxes in a London park (1995).

MEET THE WRITER

Seamus Heaney
(1939–   )

Nobel Prize WINNER

Seamus Heaney was born to Roman Catholic parents in largely Protestant Northern Ireland. His boyhood on a farm in County Derry profoundly contributed to his identity as a poet. He earned his education as a scholarship student at Queens University in Belfast, where, still in his midtwenties, he was appointed lecturer in English.

Roots in the Bogs

Instead of leading him away from his Irish roots, Heaney's studies—particularly those regarding the history and psychology of myth—forged for him a new way of seeing both the grandeur of his native landscape and its figures who, unknowingly, unite past with present. Heaney believes that through his writing, generations of his ancestors will find a voice.

Heaney's poetry was <u>considerably</u> influenced by archaeologist P. V. Glob's book *The Bog People,* which describes several corpses found in northern European bogs. Although deposited thousands of years ago, the corpses looked newly dead—a result of the bogs' high acid content. Some of the "bog people" appeared to have been ritually sacrificed, and others seem to have been murdered. The bog people suggested to Heaney "an idea of bog as the memory of the landscape, or as a landscape that remembered everything that happened in and to it." The images of the bog people also reminded him of the atrocities, past and present, in Irish political and religious struggles.

An Ancient Epic Versus a Bestseller

The American poet Robert Lowell regarded Heaney as "the best Irish poet since William Butler Yeats." In 1995, Heaney was awarded the Nobel Prize in Literature for his works "of lyrical beauty and ethical depth, which exalt everyday miracles and the living past." Four years later, Heaney's new translation of *Beowulf* accomplished what seemed to be impossible: The ancient epic overtook *Harry Potter and the Prisoner of Azkaban* for Britain's coveted Whitbread Book of the Year Award.

Think About the Writer

How is Heaney's past reflected in the subject matter of his poetry?

Reader/Writer Notebook

Use your **RWN** to complete the activities for this selection.

Literary Focus

Extended Metaphor In a **metaphor,** two seemingly unlike things are compared without the use of a connective word, such as *like* or *as*. Poets use metaphor to help us see the world imaginatively and to suggest more than is possible with literal speech. An **extended metaphor** is developed over a few lines or throughout an entire poem. For example, if you were planning to use an extended metaphor comparing friendship to a rose, you might come up with these similarities:

- Both start out small and gradually grow larger.
- Both bring delight but sometimes also pain.
- Both can wither and die.

Until you read the last line, you may not realize "Digging" is built on an extended metaphor.

Reading Focus

Comparing and Contrasting To see the similarities between two things is **comparing;** to see the differences is **contrasting.** To understand an extended metaphor, you must be able to analyze the comparison it makes.

Into Action In your *Reader/Writer Notebook,* create a Venn diagram like this one to compare and contrast the kinds of "digging" in the poem. Write the similarities in the space where the ovals overlap.

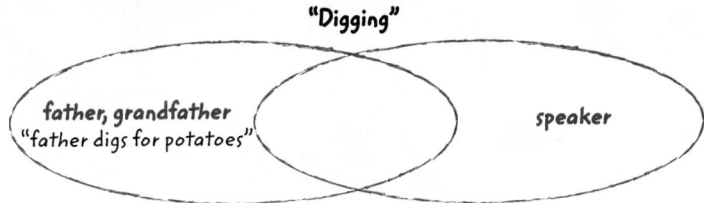

"Digging"

father, grandfather
"father digs for potatoes"

speaker

Vocabulary

coarse (kawrs) *adj.*: of low quality; rough. *The poet's father wore coarse boots.*

nestled (NEHS uhld) *v.*: snugly settled, as in a nest. *The old man's boot nestled in a mound of dirt.*

Language Coach

Multiple-Meaning Words Find where the following words are used in the poem, and put them in a list. Beside each word, indicate its part of speech as used in the poem (noun, verb, adjective, adverb). With a partner, discuss other meanings each word can have. How could the words be used as other parts of speech? Use a dictionary if necessary.

squat	ground
bends	handle

Writing Focus

Think as a Reader/Writer

Find It in Your Reading The **imagery** in this poem helps us imagine the writer sitting at his desk; his father digging in the garden and in the potato fields; and his grandfather digging turf in the bog. In your *Reader/Writer Notebook,* note the words that you think create especially vivid sensory images, not only of sight but also of sound, touch, and smell.

Learn It Online
Learn more about Heaney through these Internet links.

go.hrw.com L12-1279 **Go**

Man picking potatoes, Shea Head, Ireland.

POEM

Digging Ⓐ by **Seamus Heaney**

Read with a Purpose
Read to find out why the poem is called "Digging."

Build Background

In the not-too-distant past, Irish farmers dug two things in particular: potatoes and turf, or peat. The peat was dug from bogs, the huge soggy areas of decaying vegetable matter that have produced for Ireland, especially in previous centuries, the material that is dried and burned in fires for cooking and heat.

Between my finger and my thumb
The squat pen rests; snug as a gun.

Under my window, a clean rasping sound
When the spade sinks into gravelly ground:
5   My father, digging. I look down

Till his straining rump among the flowerbeds
Bends low, comes up twenty years away
Stooping in rhythm through potato drills°
Where he was digging.

10   The coarse boot nestled on the lug,° the shaft
Against the inside knee was levered firmly.
He rooted out tall tops, buried the bright edge deep
To scatter new potatoes that we picked
Loving their cool hardness in our hands.

15   By God, the old man could handle a spade.
Just like his old man.

8. drills: furrows or rows of planted seeds.

10. lug: piece of the spade that projects out.

Ⓐ **Literary Focus** Extended Metaphor How is the title related to the metaphor that extends to the end of the poem?

Vocabulary **coarse** (kawrs) *adj.*: of low quality; rough.
nestled (NEHS uhld) *v.*: snugly settled, as in a nest.

Analyzing Visuals

Viewing and Interpreting How does the photograph on the opposite page echo the images Heaney conveys in stanza 3?

My grandfather cut more turf in a day
Than any other man on Toner's bog.
Once I carried him milk in a bottle
20   Corked sloppily with paper. He straightened up
To drink it, then fell to right away
Nicking and slicing neatly, heaving sods
Over his shoulder, going down and down
For the good turf. Digging.

25   The cold smell of potato mould, the squelch and slap
Of soggy peat, the curt° cuts of an edge
Through living roots awaken in my head.
But I've no spade to follow men like them.

Between my finger and my thumb
30   The squat pen rests.
I'll dig with it. **Ⓑ**

26. curt: here, short.

Ⓑ **Reading Focus** **Comparing and Contrasting** In what ways is writing like digging? In what ways is it different?

Agriculture in Ireland

Most people in nineteenth-century Ireland subsisted on small family farms that grew potatoes, the main source of food for the impoverished Irish people suffering under British rule. From 1845 to 1849, Ireland experienced a colossal famine (called in Irish *An Gorta Mór*, "The Great Hunger") when a blight rendered much of the potato crop useless. One and a half million people died during the famine, and another million immigrated to America. Today, farming accounts for just 3 percent of Ireland's gross national product. Since Ireland has joined the European Union, potato production has declined—as have the small farms like the one Heaney describes.

Ask Yourself

How does Heaney feel about the farmers that had been in his family for generations?

SKILLS FOCUS **Literary Skills:** Analyze extended metaphor; analyze alliteration. **Reading Skills** Compare and contrast. **Vocabulary Skills** Demonstrate knowledge of literal meanings of words. **Writing Skills** Write descriptive essays.

Digging

Respond and Think Critically

Reading Focus

Quick Check

1. What does the speaker see from his window?

2. What does he remember about his grandfather's digging?

3. With what does the speaker say he'll dig?

Read with a Purpose

4. What is the speaker's goal for his writing?

Reading Skills: Comparing and Contrasting

5. Complete your diagram comparing the kinds of digging mentioned in the poem. How is the speaker's digging similar to and different from the digging done by his father and grandfather?

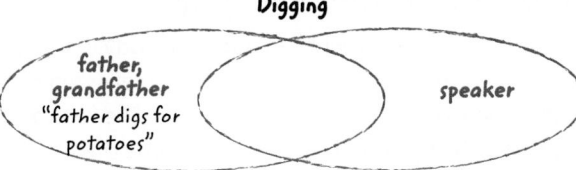

Digging

father, grandfather "father digs for potatoes"

speaker

✓ Vocabulary Check

Be sure you can justify your answers to these questions about the Vocabulary words.

6. Would you describe something that is fine and delicate as **coarse?**

7. If a baby is **nestled** in your arms, is the baby uncomfortable or snug?

Literary Focus

Literary Analysis

8. Analyze To what things does the speaker compare his pen? What is significant about these comparisons?

9. Infer In lines 25–27, the spade cuts through the "living roots." How might digging, either the kind done by the speaker's father or that done by the speaker himself, be seen as violent?

10. Analyze Identify other images of violence or destruction in the poem. What might the poet be suggesting about the relationship between creation and destruction?

Literary Skills: Extended Metaphor

11. Evaluate Note the occurrences of the verb *dig* or *digging*, and examine the poem's extended metaphor. Why is the verb *digging* a good way to describe the work of a writer?

Literary Skills Review: Alliteration

12. Analyze The repetition of initial consonant sounds of words close together in a text is called **alliteration.** Identify and analyze the effect of three uses of alliteration in the poem.

Writing Focus

Think as a Reader/Writer

Use It in Your Writing Review your notes about the images in "Digging." In your *Reader/Writer Notebook*, write a short essay in which you describe a person in a particular scene. Use words that will help your reader to imagine the sights, sounds, smells, tastes, and tactile feelings of the scene's details.

What Do You Think Now

How does the poet's family background affect his aims in writing?

For **CHOICES** see page 1289. ❯

Mushrooms

How does experience shape our view of the world?

QuickWrite

How does interacting with nature shape how you think about the world? In your *Reader/Writer Notebook*, jot down a quick list of five things in nature that you know well. Think about how you would describe each item on your list to someone who has no experience with it.

Margaret Atwood (1939).

MEET THE WRITER

Margaret Atwood
(1939–   )

The Man Booker Prize WINNER

Canadian novelist, poet, and critic Margaret Atwood applies a strict moral intelligence to her investigations of individual responsibility, social justice, and the natural world.

Choosing a Writer's Life

As a child, Margaret Atwood experienced both city and country life. Her family spent April to November living in the wilderness of Quebec and the remainder of the year in cities, including Ottawa and Toronto. Accordingly, Atwood's writings reflect insights into human society and a passionate love of nature.

Inspired by Edgar Allan Poe, Atwood began writing poetry in high school. At age sixteen, while walking home one day and drafting a poem in her head, she had a realization: Writing was "suddenly the only thing I wanted to do." Her subsequent dedication to the literary life has produced works ranging from poems and novels to book reviews and literary criticism.

A Sharp Look at Human Society

In 1972, Atwood published *Survival*, a landmark study of Canadian literature. The same year, her novel *Surfacing* reflected her growing interest in women's roles. Another novel, *The Penelopiad* (2005), retells the story of the *Odyssey* from the point of view of Penelope, Odysseus's wife.

Atwood's novels often focus on the relationship between the personal and the political. *The Handmaid's Tale* (1985), for example, is a nightmarish vision of a future dictatorship in which women are valued only for their ability to breed. In *The Blind Assassin* (2000), a Canadian family saga reflects shaping events in twentieth-century Canada, and *Oryx and Crake* (2003) explores the consequences of genetic manipulation.

Although Atwood is wary of how we use technology, she emphasizes that science is not the problem: "The driving force in the world today is the human heart—that is, human emotions…. Our tools have become very powerful. Hate, not bombs, destroys cities. Desire, not bricks, rebuilds them."

Think About the Writer How might growing up in both cities and remote wilderness have affected Atwood's views?

Reader/Writer Notebook

Use your **RWN** to complete the activities for this selection.

Literary Focus

Theme The **theme** of a poem is the central insight it expresses about human experience. Theme is not the same as the subject, for while the subject is communicated directly, the theme is usually implied. The subject of "Mushrooms" is the growth of mushrooms, but Atwood uses this subject to comment on the broader relationship between experience and poetry. Writers develop theme through imagery, form, language, tone, and style.

Reading Focus

Interpreting Imagery One tool poets use to convey theme is **imagery,** language that appeals to the five senses. Looking at a poem's images will help you understand the theme the writer wants to communicate. Many images appeal to the sense of sight, but Atwood also appeals to the senses of hearing, taste, and smell as she explores the mushrooms' growth.

Into Action As you read, list in a chart like this one the imagery in "Mushrooms." In the first column, record these images and the lines where you found them. In the next column, identify the senses to which the image appeals. Then, add your impressions about what the imagery suggests.

Imagery (lines)	Sense(s)	Impressions of Image
"tiny / bright red balloons / filling with water" (lines 6–8)	sight; touch	growing, expanding; whimsical, surprising
"a sound below sound" (line 9)	hearing	

Vocabulary

embers (EHM buhrz) *n. pl.*: glowing remains of a fire. *We tried to put out the campfire, but the embers still burned dimly in the night.*

parallel (PAR uh lehl) *adv.*: in line with, but without meeting. *I watch the bird fly parallel to the ground, and it never touched down.*

underfoot (uhn duhr FUT) *adv.*: between the feet and the ground. *After the storm, the wet lawn felt spongy underfoot.*

decay (dih KAY) *n.*: wasting away; rotting; decline in quality. *Decay had already eaten away the edges of the old tree stump.*

Language Coach

Compound Words A compound word is one word formed by putting two or more words together. Which Vocabulary word is a compound word? In this poem, Atwood invents some of her own compound words. What compound words might you invent to describe your favorite place in nature?

Writing Focus

Think as a Reader/Writer

Find It in Your Reading Atwood uses **figurative language,** primarily similes and metaphors, to compare the mushrooms with inanimate objects and natural elements. As you read, notice how the comparisons and vivid **images** combine to create sensory appeal. In your *Reader/Writer Notebook,* record two or three examples that you find most effective.

TechFocus In this poem, Atwood examines a biological subject from a poet's point of view. Notice that she refers to scientific details about the life cycle of mushrooms. What words would you type into a search engine to find out more about these references?

Learn It Online
Practice your vocabulary knowledge with Word Watch online.

go.hrw.com   L12-1285   **Go**

Mushrooms

by **Margaret Atwood**

Read with a Purpose

Read to discover how a writer connects collecting mushrooms with her own creative life.

Build Background

Mushrooms and other fungi are not plants—scientists classify them in a different kingdom of living things because they lack chlorophyll, the green material plants use to turn light energy into food. Instead, mushrooms obtain energy by absorbing nutrients from dead animal and plant materials. Mushrooms have two main parts. The first part, the threadlike, underground *mycelium*, absorbs food and can live for many years in soil or wood. The *fruiting body*, the second part, is typically what you see of a mushroom growing in the woods. It includes the stalk, cap, and gills. Often appearing after rainfall, the fruiting body usually lives only a few days. During its short lifetime, the mushroom reproduces by releasing spores from which new mycelia can grow.

White Beech mushrooms.

i

In this moist season,
mist on the lake and thunder
afternoons in the distance

they ooze up through the earth
5 during the night,
like bubbles, like tiny
bright red balloons
filling with water;
a sound below sound, the thumbs of rubber
10 gloves turned softly inside out.

In the mornings, there is the leaf mold
starred with nipples,
with cool white fishgills,
leathery purple brains,
15 fist-sized suns dulled to the color of embers,
poisonous moons, pale yellow. **A**

ii

Where do they come from?

For each thunderstorm that travels
overhead there's another storm
20 that moves parallel in the ground.
Struck lightning is where they meet.

Underfoot there's a cloud of rootlets,
shed hairs or a bundle of loose threads
blown slowly through the midsoil.
25 These are their flowers, these fingers
reaching through darkness to the sky,
these eyeblinks
that burst and powder the air with spores.

iii

They feed in shade, on halfleaves
30 as they return to water,
on slowly melting logs,
deadwood. They glow
in the dark sometimes. They taste
of rotten meat or cloves
35 or cooking steak or bruised
lips or new snow. **B**

iv

It isn't only
for food I hunt them
but for the hunt and because
40 they smell of death and the waxy
skins of the newborn,
flesh into earth into flesh. **C**

Here is the handful
of shadow I have brought back to you:
45 this decay, this hope, this mouthful of dirt, this poetry.

Fungus found in a West Sussex wood.

A **Reading Focus** **Interpreting Imagery** Why do you think
that the poet compares mushrooms to both suns and moons?

B **Literary Focus** **Theme** What key idea about mushrooms and
their place in the world is suggested by this list of images?

C **Reading Focus** **Interpreting Imagery** How would you
describe this image in your own words?

Vocabulary **embers** (EHM buhrz) *n. pl.*: glowing remains of
a fire.
parallel (PAR uh lehl) *adv.*: in line with, but without meeting.
underfoot (uhn duhr FUT) *adv.*: between the feet and the ground.
decay (dih KAY) *n.*: wasting away; rotting; decline in quality.

Respond and Think Critically

Reading Focus

Quick Check

1. In the final stanza, what does the speaker say she has brought back from her hunt?

Read with a Purpose

2. How is collecting mushrooms similar to writing poetry?

Reading Skills: Interpreting Imagery

3. Thinking about how a poem's images relate to each other is part of interpreting poetic imagery. In a new column of your chart, compare each image with other images in the poem. Using the connections you discover, write a statement of the poem's theme.

✓ Vocabulary Check

Change each sentence so that the Vocabulary word is used logically.

4. The two roads run **parallel** until they meet at a crowded intersection.
5. The fresh bouquet of flowers shows signs of **decay.**
6. A stormy gray sky spreads **underfoot.**
7. Only the icy **embers** remain from last night's blaze.

Literary Focus

Literary Analysis

8. **Identify** In lines 6–10, what repeated consonant suggests the sound of the fingers of rubber gloves turning inside out?

9. **Analyze** What uses of assonance and alliteration help create the poem's music? Where do repeated grammatical structures help create a rhythm?
10. **Interpret** To what does the speaker refer when she describes the cycle of "flesh into earth into flesh" in line 42?
11. **Analyze** Why might Atwood have chosen to break the word *mouthful* between lines 45 and 46? What is the effect of this break?

Literary Skills: Theme

12. **Draw Conclusions** Explain the poem's last four lines. How could mushrooms suggest decay, hope, a mouthful of dirt, and poetry? How do these lines contribute to the poem's theme?

Literary Skills Review: Symbol

13. **Interpret** A **symbol** is a person, place, thing, or event that stands both for itself and for something beyond itself. What might the mushrooms symbolize?

Writing Focus

Think as a Reader/Writer

Use It in Your Writing Review Atwood's use of similes and metaphors. In your *Reader/Writer Notebook*, write a paragraph in which you use imagery and figurative language, including similes and metaphors, to compare an inanimate object, such as a car, to something animate or abstract, such as freedom.

 **What Do You Think Now** What is the speaker's attitude toward new experiences? If you adopted her attitude for a day, how might it change the way you experience the natural world?

Digging / Mushrooms

CHOICES

As you respond to the Choices, use these **Academic Vocabulary** words as appropriate: adapt, considerably, exhibit, inevitable, perspective.

REVIEW

Write a Comparison Essay

Timed ⌐Writing In "Digging," Heaney compares digging to writing. In a brief essay, compare another activity or occupation to writing. Use details to support your thesis.

Prepare a Summary Chart

Use a chart like the one below to summarize the main images and ideas of each part of "Mushrooms." Compare your chart with that of another student, noting which details you each included. Talk about which ideas you think are essential and which details can be left out of your summary.

Part	Summary
i	
ii	
iii	
iv	

CONNECT

Write an E-mail Recommendation

One joy of literature is sharing it with friends and relatives. Think about your experience reading "Digging." What friend or family member do you think would most enjoy this poem? Write an e-mail or letter in which you recommend that this person read the poem. You might want to quote a few memorable lines or include an analysis of the poem's theme.

Present a Radio Program

Create a poetry reading of "Digging" or "Mushrooms" (or both) that could be broadcast over the radio. Write material for a brief introduction that will prepare listeners for the poem. Practice reading the poem aloud, and create a reading script that notes where you will pause, how you will vary your pace, and which words you will emphasize. When you record your program, be sure to read slowly enough so that your listeners can follow your presentation.

EXTEND

Create a Field Guide

TechFocus Use Internet resources to learn more about mushrooms. Then, use presentation software to exhibit the information in the form of a digital field guide, including both illustrations and text. Although your guide will have a scientific and informative tone, try to also incorporate at least a hint of Atwood's poetic sense of wonder and mystery. You might consider including a line from her poem as a caption or heading.

Plan an Anthology

Create the table of contents for a poetry anthology that includes "Digging" and "Mushrooms." Choose a theme and title for your anthology, as well as a list of other poems you would include. You might combine poems by well-known authors with those written by yourself or classmates. Create a cover that gives readers an accurate impression of what they can expect to find inside.

Preparing to Read

Atlantis—
A Lost Sonnet

What Do You Think?

How does experience shape our view of the world?

QuickWrite

What would you miss about your hometown or state if you had to move away? What people and things would you have the most trouble leaving? Record your response in your *Reader/Writer Notebook*.

Eavan Boland (1944).

Born in Dublin, Ireland, Eavan Boland was the youngest of five children. Her father was a diplomat, and her mother was a painter. When she was five, her family moved to London, and then six years later, to New York City. Returning to Ireland in her teens was difficult for Boland; she has described having to reacquaint herself with Ireland and feeling a lack of belonging—a theme that appears frequently in her poetry.

Feminist and Love Poet

Some critics call Boland a feminist writer because of her realistic look at the difficulty of obtaining and maintaining freedom as a married woman. In her verse, however, she finds balance between her love of domestic life and her feminist ideas.

"So much of European love poetry is court poetry, coming out of the glamorous traditions of the court. . . . There's little about the ordinariness of love," said Boland in an interview for *The New Yorker* magazine. In response to what she found lacking in love poetry, Boland has presented the "dailiness," as she calls it, of love and life. Although she titled her 2001 collection *Against Love Poetry,* Boland's poetry is a reaction not against love but against the portrayal of an idealized romantic love. In her poems, Boland examines from a realistic perspective the conflicts faced in life and love.

A Great Irish Poet

Early in her career Boland established herself as an important poet, but she did not receive formal recognition for several decades. After publishing several poetry collections and receiving many prizes, including the Poetry Book Society Choice award for *The Journey,* Boland became increasingly well known. By 1999, her poetry, along with that of Seamus Heaney and other great Irish poets, became a requirement for study at Irish high schools. Boland has taught at Trinity College and is currently a professor at Stanford University in California.

Think About the Writer

Considering the isolation Boland felt from Ireland in her youth, how do you think she would respond to being named among the great Irish poets?

Reader/Writer Notebook

Use your **RWN** to complete the activities for this selection.

Literary Focus

Sonnet The traditional **sonnet** form includes fourteen lines. Depending on the type of sonnet, these lines are traditionally divided into an octave and a sestet (an eight-line and a six-line stanza in a Petrarchan sonnet) or into quatrains and a couplet (three four-line stanzas and one two-line stanza in a Shakespearean sonnet). Sonnets also traditionally have an intricate rhyme scheme and are often written in iambic pentameter.

Throughout literary history, poets have experimented with the sonnet, creating new versions by manipulating length, rhyme scheme, and meter. Boland's "Atlantis—A Lost Sonnet" is a variation on the sonnet form but does contain one important element common to most sonnets: the **turn,** in which the concluding lines either answer the question posed by the speaker or summarize the message found in the beginning lines.

Reading Focus

Drawing Inferences Authors, especially poets, expect readers to **draw inferences,** or make educated guesses based on prior knowledge and clues from the text. As you read "Atlantis—A Lost Sonnet," read "between the lines" and use your own prior knowledge and experience to make inferences about the poem's subject, speaker, and theme.

Into Action In your *Reader/Writer Notebook,* use a chart like the one below to record your inferences about the poem as you read.

Prior Experience	Clues	Inference
I miss the city I used to live in and the people I knew there.	The speaker talks about the everyday things she misses about the "old city."	

Writing Focus

Think as a Reader/Writer

Find It in Your Reading As you read, notice Boland's descriptions of Atlantis and of the city that she has lost. In your *Reader/Writer Notebook,* record the details she uses to describe each place. How does she use these details to establish a general image of Atlantis and a more intimate image of her own lost city?

Vocabulary

convey (kuhn VAY) *v.:* communicate; express. *The speaker found it difficult to convey her sorrow about her loss.*

traditions (truh DIHSH uhnz) *n. pl.:* customs, values, or ideas handed down from generation to generation. *Family traditions can provide people with a sense of stability and continuity.*

Language Coach

Etymology The **etymology,** or origins of words, can help you understand more about their meaning. Use a dictionary to find the etymology of *convey* and *traditions.* From what ancient language did both words originate? Identify their original meanings, and tell how knowing this information helps you understand the current meaning of the words.

 Learn It Online
Let the online audio version of this poem bring it alive for you.

go.hrw.com | L12-1291 | Go

Atlantis—A Lost Sonnet

by **Eavan Boland**

Read with a Purpose
Read to discover how the speaker compares her loss to the loss of the legendary island of Atlantis.

Build Background
The story of the lost island of Atlantis originated about 335 B.C. with the Greek philosopher Plato. In his writings, he tells the story of an advanced society established in honor of the sea god Poseidon. Allegedly, the citizens became greedy and willful, so the island was destroyed by the sea. Many have debated whether or not such a civilization actually existed. Theories abound, but its origins and identity remain uncertain.

How on earth did it happen, I used to wonder
that a whole city—arches, pillars, colonnades,°
not to mention vehicles and animals—had all
one fine day gone under?

5 I mean, I said to myself, the world was small then.
Surely a great city must have been missed?
I miss our old city—

white pepper, white pudding,° you and I meeting
under fanlights and low skies to go home in it. Maybe
10 what really happened is ⓐ

this: the old fable-makers searched hard for a word
to convey that what is gone is gone forever and
never found it. And so, in the best traditions of

where we come from, they gave their sorrow a name
15 and drowned it. ⓑ

2. colonnades: series of columns supporting a roof.

8. white pudding: sausage made from pork and oatmeal that is part of a traditional Irish breakfast.

Underwater Roman ruins, Pamukkale, Costa del Egeo, Turkey.

ⓐ **Literary Focus** Sonnet What ideas does Boland present in the beginning lines of the sonnet?

ⓑ **Reading Focus** Drawing Inferences According to the speaker, why do the "fable-makers" want to drown Atlantis?

Vocabulary **convey** (kuhn VAY) *v.*: communicate; express.
traditions (truh DIHSH uhnz) *n. pl.*: customs, values, or ideas handed down from generation to generation.

Applying Your Skills

Respond and Think Critically

Reading Focus

Quick Check

1. What does the speaker wonder about in the first two stanzas of the poem? What does she mean when she says that "the world was small then"?

2. What does the speaker compare to Atlantis? What emotions does she convey through this comparison?

3. How would you describe the speaker's relationship to loss? What seems to be her perspective?

Read with a Purpose

4. How does the speaker regard the story of the lost island of Atlantis? Explain your opinion.

Reading Skills: Drawing Inferences

5. Complete the chart you began while reading. Write down what you can infer from your prior experience and the clues in the poem.

✔ Vocabulary Check

Answer these questions about the Vocabulary words.

6. What would you **convey** to someone who is celebrating a birthday?

7. What **traditions** does your family observe?

Literary Focus

Literary Analysis

8. **Infer** Why do you think the poet includes references to the everyday, such as "vehicles and animals," "white pepper," and "fanlights and low skies"? Explain.

9. **Extend** What do you think compels people to want to "drown" sorrows or forget their losses?

10. **Analyze** How many lines does this sonnet have? Why do you think Boland uses this number of lines?

11. **Interpret** Why do you think Boland calls her poem "A Lost Sonnet"? How does this relate to the story of Atlantis?

Literary Skills: Sonnet

12. **Analyze** Most sonnets have a **turn,** or a shift in thought that summarizes or explains the ideas presented earlier in the poem or answers a question posed in the poem. At which point does the turn occur in Boland's poem? How does she summarize or explain the ideas that she introduces in the beginning lines?

Literary Skills Review: Allusion

13. **Evaluate** An **allusion** is a reference within a literary work to another literary work or historical event. Boland bases her entire poem on an allusion to the lost island of Atlantis. How does she interpret this object of allusion? How does the story influence her poetry?

Writing Focus

Think as a Reader/Writer

Use It in Your Writing Think of three details about your hometown or state that would identify it to most readers. Then, write a short poem or a paragraph about how you would (or would not) miss your hometown if you left it. Choose details that help you establish the tone you want.

What Do You Think Now

How do you think the experience of loss has affected the speaker's view of the world?

Expectation and Reality

LITERARY FOCUS
Irony

The Evil Genius of a King (Paris, 1914–1915) by Giorgio de Chirico
(1888–1978). Oil on canvas.
The Museum of Modern Art, NY/ARS,NY.

CONTENTS

Katherine Mansfield

D. H. Lawrence

James Joyce

Jorge Luis Borges

Samuel Beckett

Harold Pinter

Doris Lessing

Nadine Gordimer

Chinua Achebe

Wole Soyinka

**COMPARING TEXTS: POSTCOLONIAL
LITERATURE   Derek Walcott,
V. S. Naipaul, Paul Theroux,
Anita Desai**

"The fact of storytelling hints at a fundamental human unease, hints at human imperfection. Where there is perfection there is no story to tell."

—Ben Okri

Irony by **Leila Christenbury**

Types of Irony

- Verbal irony: The narrator or a character says one thing but means something different.
- Situational irony: The opposite of what is expected happens.
- Dramatic irony: The reader or audience knows something a character does not.

A Response to Modern Life

Saying one thing but meaning another is one way to define **irony,** a term that also refers to the gap between what is expected or assumed and what really happens. One critic has called a person's ability to detect irony "one of the surest tests of intelligence and sophistication." In the literature in this collection, irony occurs in different forms and degrees; however, in almost all the pieces, the use of irony underscores serious and important themes. The heartbreaking incongruity between what is desired and what is realized is characteristic of much of this literature.

The first half of the twentieth century was a time when much of what people assumed to be true about the world was called into question. Darwin's theory of evolution and Freud's ideas about the subconscious made people re-examine their own identities. Two horrific world wars and the Holocaust shook people's faith in God and human kindness. It is unsurprising that many people adopted an ironic <u>perspective</u>—irony had come to reflect their experience of reality. The dissonance resulting from the fact that life was not as they expected or dreamed it to be is reflected in the irony of that period's literature.

In D. H. Lawrence's "The Rocking-Horse Winner," for example, Paul's desire to win his mother's affection by making her rich is thwarted only when she desires, "more money!—more than ever!" In such instances of **situational irony,** the opposite of one's expectations becomes the reality.

Irony in the Atmosphere

Today, it can be difficult for us to recognize irony because its influence is so pervasive. Many people we hear or interact with every day use verbal irony. Everyone from the morning DJs on our favorite radio stations, to our friends and families, to characters in our favorite TV shows and movies, says one thing and means another. The surface meaning of one statement likely has a different underlying meaning. Sarcasm, a heavy-handed manner of speaking meant to ridicule and mock, is an even stronger expression of **verbal irony.** As a part of the atmosphere of life in the twenty-first century, sarcasm is a synonym for what is cool, hip, and cynically detached.

Dramatic irony can be another way to make an individual look foolish because the reader or audience has information the character does not. The contrast in dramatic irony is not between what is stated and what is meant, but rather between what the character says or thinks and the true state of affairs. In all instances of irony, disparate information and intentions affect how we see characters, ourselves, and the world.

Ask Yourself

1. Could you go for a whole day without saying anything ironic? Why or why not?
2. Think of a favorite ironic line or moment from a book, TV show, or movie. What do you like about it?

Learn It Online

Learn about irony through *PowerNotes* online.

go.hrw.com | L12-1295 | Go

Analyzing a Sculpture

Irony, the contrast, or discrepancy, between expectation and reality, became one of the dominant literary modes in the twentieth century. Today, an ironic point of view continues to be expressed in literature as well as in the visual arts, as in, for example, this sculpture by Tony Cragg.

Guidelines

Use these guidelines to consider how this sculpture expresses irony:

- How does the sculpture show a contrast between expectation and reality?

- A re-examination of identity helped engender irony in the twentieth century. What does this sculpture suggest about identity?

- How might the sculpture's title, *Bent of Mind,* be considered ironic?

1. What might the overall shape of the sculpture represent?

2. Note that the faces are pointed away from each other. What does this positioning suggest?

3. Does the placement of this sculpture in an outdoor setting increase or decrease the ironic effect?

Bent of Mind, by Tony Cragg. Cass Sculpture Foundation, U.K.

Your Turn Analyze Irony

Choose another image in this book, and write a short paragraph explaining how the image conveys a sense of irony.

The Doll's House

Identifying Cause and Effect by **Kylene Beers**

"Why?" is the question so often on people's minds. We wonder why people behave as they do, why events turn out a certain way, why the world is the way it is. Whenever we ask why, we are trying to determine a cause, or a reason, for an effect we have witnessed or experienced: a friend's failure to speak, a team's thrilling victory, or a destructive storm.

We also ask, "Then what happened?," when we hear about an event and wonder what will happen as a result. If we find out that a popular baseball player is in a serious slump, for instance, we wonder about the effects. Will he be fired? Will he sit on the bench while a rookie takes his place? Will his team suffer losses?

As in life, literature is made up of an interlocking chain of **causes and effects.** Identifying this cause-and-effect sequence will help you understand a story's plot and characters' motivations. In stories such as "The Doll's House," you will be asked to infer causes and effects based on subtle clues.

When analyzing causes and effects, begin by identifying a circumstance that is the result of other factors (the effect). For example, in "The Doll's House" a major aspect of the plot is a clearly stated effect: " The Kelveys were shunned by everybody." The exclusion and poor treatment of children is a scenario that causes the reader to ask "Why?" A careful reader asks questions to find the causes.

Read the following passage. Three causes, or reasons, for the ostracism of the Kelvey children are mentioned in the text. Write them in a chart like this one:

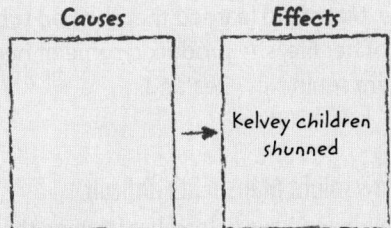

They [the Kelveys] were the daughters of a spry, hardworking little washerwoman, who went about from house to house by the day. This was awful enough. But where was Mr. Kelvey? Nobody knew for certain. But everybody said he was in prison. So they were the daughters of a washerwoman and a jailbird. . . . And they looked it! . . . The truth was they were dressed in "bits" given to her by the people for whom she worked.

Your Turn

Read the following passage from "The Doll's House." Create another chart reflecting the causes and effects.

"How dare you ask the little Kelveys into the courtyard?" said her cold, furious voice. "You know as well as I do you're not allowed to talk to them. Run away, children, run away at once. And don't come back again," said Aunt Beryl. And she stepped into the yard and shooed them out as if they were chickens. . . .

. . . They did not need telling twice. Burning with shame, shrinking together, Lil huddling along like her mother, our Else dazed, somehow they crossed the big courtyard and squeezed through the white gate.

That afternoon had been awful. A letter had come from Willie Brent, a terrifying, threatening letter, saying if she did not meet him that evening in Pulman's Bush, he' d come to the front door and ask the reason why! But now that she had frightened those little rats of Kelveys and given Kezia a good scolding, her heart felt lighter. That ghastly pressure was gone. She went back into the house humming.

Preparing to Read

The Doll's House

What Do You Think? How does experience shape our view of the world?

QuickTalk

With a partner, think of groups of people others might ridicule or tease. In your *Reader/Writer Notebook*, take notes on how the experience of bullying affects both the victims and the bullies.

Katherine Mansfield seated in a deck chair, France, 1916.
Alexander Turnbull Library, New Zealand.

MEET THE WRITER

Katherine Mansfield
(1888–1923)

Before the work of Katherine Mansfield, short stories were expected to have strong plots, and clever, tricky endings were idealized. Mansfield's stories were different. Some readers complained that nothing happened in them. Indeed, often very little happened externally in her stories, but a great deal occurred in the minds of her characters.

An Unhappy Childhood

Katherine Mansfield was born in New Zealand. A <u>considerably</u> unhappy child, she shared her mother's distaste for being "out here," oceans away from England, the source of their culture. At school she was moody and had few friends; one teacher described her as dumpy and unattractive. Although Mansfield had her father's talent for math and could memorize verse at sight, she was a careless scholar. When she was fifteen, her family enrolled her in Queen's College in London. Mansfield loved London and grieved when summoned home to New Zealand.

A New Life, an Early Death

When she was nineteen, Mansfield's family permitted her to return by herself to London. The child once regarded as homely had become a beauty, with porcelain skin and keen eyes. With almost no allowance from her father, Mansfield was painfully poor. (She called her father "the richest man in New Zealand, and the meanest.") Her first literary success came in 1910, when several of her stories were accepted by a journal. Around the same time, a man named John Middleton Murry accepted a story of hers for his literary magazine. The two began a long and stormy relationship.

When Mansfield's younger brother, Leslie, died in World War I, she was overcome with grief. From that point forward, she vowed to write about New Zealand as a "debt of love.… I shall tell everything, even of how the laundry basket squeaked."

At twenty-nine, Mansfield learned that she had tuberculosis. In the last year of her life, she produced some of her finest stories, many of them set in New Zealand.

Think About the Writer How might Mansfield's difficult childhood have helped her imagine the inner lives of other people?

Reader/Writer Notebook

Use your **RWN** to complete the activities for this selection.

Literary Focus

Narrative Voice The **narrator** is the **voice** that tells a story. The narrator can be a character in the story, in which case he or she speaks as *I*, or the narrator can be an external presence. The voice of the narrator may be ironic, sympathetic, humorous, critical, or distant. Mansfield excelled at creating distinct voices for her narrators. In almost all her stories, the narrator reveals interior moods by using evocative language. The narrator of "The Doll's House" penetrates the characters' minds so thoroughly that we feel as if we are participating with them in the action. In fact, you'll notice that the narrator's voice at times sounds like the voices of the children, and at other times, like the voices of the narrow-minded adults.

Reading Focus

Identifying Cause and Effect Most plots are built around a series of causes and their effects. A **cause** is the reason that some action takes place. An **effect** is the result, or consequence, of some action or event. Most traditional plots are built on a cause-and-effect chain: One event causes another event, which causes another event, which causes another event. Multiple causes in a plot may be responsible for a single effect, or a single event may have multiple effects.

Into Action As you read, use a graphic organizer like the one below to note the chain of causes and effects on which the story is constructed. Add circles and arrows for additional causes and effects as needed.

Writing Focus

Think as a Reader/Writer

Find It in Your Reading The **narrative voice** we hear in this story sometimes sounds like the children thinking and sometimes sounds like the adults. In your *Reader/Writer Notebook*, note the details the narrator uses to make you feel as if you are hearing these characters' thoughts.

TechFocus As you read "The Doll's House," consider how you might record this story for a radio broadcast or a podcast.

Vocabulary

congealed (kuhn JEELD) *v.* used as *adj.*: thickened. *The paint on the doll's house was congealed into big lumps.*

conspicuous (kuhn SPIHK yoo uhs) *adj.*: attracting attention. *The Kelvey children were conspicuous in their poor clothes.*

flagged (flagd) *v.*: declined; lost strength or interest. *After a few days, interest in the doll's house flagged.*

clambered (KLAM buhrd) *v.*: climbed clumsily. *Kezia clambered back onto the gate to see the Kelveys as they passed.*

Language Coach

Idioms When learning a new language, you may encounter certain phrases that seem bizarre or don't make sense. Many of these phrases are **idioms,** expressions whose actual meaning differs from their literal meaning. If you say someone "bad-mouthed" you, for example, you are using an idiom. Here are some idioms from the story. Discuss with classmates what each italicized idiom means.

1. The children *burned to tell* everybody.
2. They just had time to *fall into line*.
3. *The line had to be drawn somewhere,* so the children would not talk to the Kelveys.
4. They walked past the Kelveys *with their heads in the air.*

Learn It Online
Find projects and activities online to take your reading of "The Doll's House" further.

go.hrw.com   L12-1299   **Go**

The DOLL's HOUSE

by **Katherine Mansfield**

When dear old Mrs. Hay went back to town after staying with the Burnells, she sent the children a doll's house. It was so big that the carter[1] and Pat carried it into the courtyard, and there it stayed, propped up on two wooden boxes beside the feed-room door. No harm could come of it; it was summer. And perhaps the smell of paint would have gone off by the time it had to be taken in. For, really, the smell of paint coming from that doll's house ("Sweet of old Mrs. Hay, of course; most sweet and generous!")—but the smell of paint was quite enough to make anyone seriously ill, in Aunt Beryl's opinion. Even before the sacking was taken off. And when it was …

There stood the doll's house, a dark, oily, spinach green, picked out with bright yellow. Its two solid little chimneys, glued onto the roof, were painted red and white, and the door, gleaming with yellow varnish, was like a little slab of toffee. Four windows, real windows, were divided into panes by a broad streak of green. There was actually a tiny porch, too, painted yellow, with big lumps of congealed paint hanging along the edge.

But perfect, perfect little house! Who could possibly mind the smell? It was part of the joy, part of the newness.

"Open it quickly, someone!"

The hook at the side was stuck fast. Pat pried it open with his penknife, and the whole housefront swung back, and—there you were, gazing at one and the same moment into the drawing room and dining room, the kitchen and two bedrooms. That is the way for a house to open! Why don't all houses open like that? How much more exciting than peering through the slit of a door into a mean little hall with a hatstand and two umbrellas! That is—isn't it?—what you long to know about a house when you put your hand on the knocker. Perhaps it is the way God opens houses at dead of night when He is taking a quiet turn with an angel … **A**

---

1. **carter:** delivery person.

A Literary Focus **Narrative Voice** What details suggest that the narrator is entering into the minds of the children?

Vocabulary **congealed** (kuhn JEELD) *v. used as adj.:* thickened.

Left: Two girls with blue aprons (1904–1905), by Edvard Munch (1863–1944). Munch Museum, Oslo, Norway/ARS,NY. *Below:* View of Dining Room in the Doll's House, (c. 1735 –1740).

"O-oh!" The Burnell children sounded as though they were in despair. It was too marvelous; it was too much for them. They had never seen anything like it in their lives. All the rooms were papered. There were pictures on the walls, painted on the paper, with gold frames complete. Red carpet covered all the floors except the kitchen; red plush chairs in the drawing room, green in the dining room; tables, beds with real bedclothes, a cradle, a stove, a dresser with tiny plates, and one big jug. But what Kezia liked more than anything, what she liked frightfully, was the lamp. It stood in the middle of the dining-room table, an exquisite little amber lamp with a white globe. It was even filled all ready for lighting, though, of course, you couldn't light it. But there was something inside that looked like oil, and that moved when you shook it.

The father and mother dolls, who sprawled very stiff as though they had fainted in the drawing room, and their two little children asleep upstairs, were really too big for the doll's house. They didn't look as though they belonged. But the lamp was perfect. It seemed to smile at Kezia, to say, "I live here." The lamp was real.

The Burnell children could hardly walk to school fast enough the next morning. They burned to tell everybody, to describe, to—well—to boast about their doll's house before the school bell rang.

"I'm to tell," said Isabel, "because I'm the eldest. And you two can join in after. But I'm to tell first."

There was nothing to answer. Isabel was bossy, but she was always right, and Lottie and Kezia knew too well the powers that went with being eldest. They brushed through the thick buttercups at the road edge and said nothing.

"And I'm to choose who's to come and see it first. Mother said I might."

For it had been arranged that while the doll's house stood in the courtyard they might ask the girls at school, two at a time, to come and look. Not to stay to tea, of course, or to come traipsing[2] through the house. But just to stand quietly in the courtyard while Isabel pointed out the beauties, and Lottie and Kezia looked pleased...

But hurry as they might, by the time they had reached the tarred palings[3] of the boys' playground the bell had begun to jangle. They only just had time to whip off their hats and fall into line before the roll was called. Never mind. Isabel tried to make up for it by looking very important and mysterious and by whispering behind her hand to the girls near her, "Got something to tell you at playtime."

Playtime came and Isabel was surrounded. The girls of her class nearly fought to put their arms round her, to walk away with her, to beam flatteringly, to be her special friend. She held quite a court under the huge pine trees at the side of the playground. Nudging, giggling together, the little girls pressed up close. And the only two who stayed outside the ring were the two who were always outside, the little Kelveys. They knew better than to come anywhere near the Burnells.   **B**
For the fact was, the school the Burnell children went to was not at all the kind of place their parents would have chosen if there had been any choice. But there was none. It was the only school for miles. And the consequence was all the children in the neighborhood, the Judge's little girls, the doctor's daughters, the storekeeper's children, the milkman's, were forced to mix together. Not to speak of there being an equal number of rude, rough little boys as well. But the line had to be drawn somewhere. It was drawn at the Kelveys. Many of the children, including the Burnells, were not allowed even to speak to them. They walked past the Kelveys with their heads in the air, and as they set the fashion in all matters of behavior, the Kelveys were shunned by everybody. Even the teacher had a special voice for them, and a special smile for the other children when Lil Kelvey came up to her desk with a bunch of dreadfully common-looking flowers.

They were the daughters of a spry, hardworking little washerwoman, who went about from house to house by the day. This was awful enough. But where was Mr. Kelvey? Nobody knew for certain. But everybody said he was in prison. So they were the daughters

---

3. **palings** (PAY lihngs): fence stakes.

B **Literary Focus** **Narrative Voice** Does the narrator want us to sympathize with the Burnells? How can you tell?

---

2. **traipsing** (TRAYPS ihng): colloquial for "wandering" or "tramping about."

of a washerwoman and a jailbird. Very nice company for other people's children! And they looked it. Why Mrs. Kelvey made them so conspicuous was hard to understand. The truth was they were dressed in "bits" given to her by the people for whom she worked. Lil, for instance, who was a stout, plain child, with big freckles, came to school in a dress made from a green art-serge[4] tablecloth of the Burnells, with red plush sleeves from the Logans' curtains. Her hat, perched on top of her high forehead, was a grown-up woman's hat, once the property of Miss Lecky, the postmistress. It was turned up at the back and trimmed with a large scarlet quill.[5] What a little guy[6] she looked! It was impossible not to laugh. And her little sister, our Else, wore a long white dress, rather like a nightgown, and a pair of little boy's boots. But whatever our Else wore she would have looked strange. She was a tiny wishbone of a child, with cropped hair and enormous solemn eyes—a little white owl. Nobody had ever seen her smile; she scarcely ever spoke. She went through life holding on to Lil, with a piece of Lil's skirt screwed up in her hand. Where Lil went our Else followed. In the playground, on the road going to and from school, there was Lil marching in front and our Else holding on behind. Only when she wanted anything, or when she was out of breath, our Else gave Lil a tug, a twitch,

---

4. **art-serge** (ahrt suhrj): type of woven wool fabric.
5. **quill:** feather.
6. **guy:** British for "odd-looking person."

and Lil stopped and turned round. The Kelveys never failed to understand each other.

Now they hovered at the edge; you couldn't stop them listening. When the little girls turned round and sneered, Lil, as usual, gave her silly, shamefaced smile, but our Else only looked.

And Isabel's voice, so very proud, went on telling. The carpet made a great sensation, but so did the beds with real bedclothes, and the stove with an oven door.

When she finished Kezia broke in. "You've forgotten the lamp, Isabel."

"Oh, yes," said Isabel, "and there's a teeny little lamp, all made of yellow glass, with a white globe that stands on the dining-room table. You couldn't tell it from a real one."

"The lamp's best of all," cried Kezia. She thought Isabel wasn't making half enough of the little lamp. But nobody paid any attention. Isabel was choosing the two who were to come back with them that afternoon and see it. She chose Emmie Cole and Lena Logan. But when the others knew they were all to have a chance, they couldn't be nice enough to Isabel. One by one they put their arms round Isabel's waist and walked her off. They had something to whisper to her, a secret. "Isabel's *my* friend."

Only the little Kelveys moved away forgotten; there was nothing more for them to hear. Days passed, and as more children saw the doll's house, the fame of it spread. It became the one subject, the rage. The one

---

C **Literary Focus** Narrative Voice Whose attitude toward the "little Kelveys" are we hearing in these paragraphs?

Vocabulary **conspicuous** (kuhn SPIHK yoo uhs) *adj.:* attracting attention.

question was, "Have you seen Burnells' doll's house? Oh, ain't it lovely!" "Haven't you seen it? Oh, I say!"

Even the dinner hour was given up to talking about it. The little girls sat under the pines eating their thick mutton sandwiches and big slabs of johnny cake spread with butter. While always, as near as they could get, sat the Kelveys, our Else holding on to Lil, listening too, while they chewed their jam sandwiches out of a newspaper soaked with large red blobs …

"Mother," said Kezia, "can't I ask the Kelveys just once?"

"Certainly not, Kezia."

"But why not?"

"Run away, Kezia; you know quite well why not."

At last everybody had seen it except them. On that day the subject rather flagged. It was the dinner hour. The children stood together under the pine trees, and suddenly, as they looked at the Kelveys eating out of their paper, always by themselves, always listening, they wanted to be horrid to them. Emmie Cole started the whisper.

"Lil Kelvey's going to be a servant when she grows up."

"O-oh, how awful!" said Isabel Burnell, and she made eyes at Emmie.

Emmie swallowed in a very meaning way and nodded to Isabel as she'd seen her mother do on those occasions.

"It's true—it's true—it's true," she said.

Then Lena Logan's little eyes snapped. "Shall I ask her?" she whispered.

"Bet you don't," said Jessie May.

"Pooh, I'm not frightened," said Lena. Suddenly she gave a little squeal and danced in front of the other girls. "Watch! Watch me! Watch me now!" said Lena. And sliding, gliding, dragging one foot, giggling behind her hand, Lena went over to the Kelveys.

Lil looked up from her dinner. She wrapped the rest quickly away. Our Else stopped chewing. What was coming now?

"Is it true you're going to be a servant when you grow up, Lil Kelvey?" shrilled Lena.

Dead silence. But instead of answering, Lil only gave her silly, shamefaced smile. She didn't seem to mind the question at all. What a sell[7] for Lena! The girls began to titter. **D**

Lena couldn't stand that. She put her hands on her hips; she shot forward. "Yah, yer father's in prison!" she hissed, spitefully.

A bedroom in "Mrs. Bryant's Pleasure", doll's house (1860–1865). Bethnal Green Museum, London.

This was such a marvelous thing to have said that the little girls rushed away in a body, deeply, deeply excited, wild with joy. Someone found a long rope, and they began skipping. And never did they skip so high, run in and out so fast, or do such daring things as on that morning.

In the afternoon Pat called for the Burnell children with the buggy and they drove home. There were visitors. Isabel and Lottie, who liked visitors, went upstairs to change their pinafores.[8] But Kezia thieved out at the back. Nobody was about; she began to swing on the big white gates of the courtyard. Presently, looking along the road, she saw two little dots. They grew bigger, they were coming toward her. Now she

---

7. **sell:** slang for "trick."
8. **pinafores** (PIHN uh fawrz): sleeveless, apronlike garments that girls wore to keep their dresses clean.

Vocabulary **flagged** (flagd) *v.*: declined; lost strength or interest.

D **Reading Focus** Identifying Cause and Effect What has caused the girls to be cruel to the Kelveys? What are the effects of their cruelty?

could see that one was in front and one close behind. Now she could see that they were the Kelveys. Kezia stopped swinging. She slipped off the gate as if she was going to run away. Then she hesitated. The Kelveys came nearer, and beside them walked their shadows, very long, stretching right across the road with their heads in the buttercups. Kezia clambered back on the gate; she had made up her mind; she swung out.

"Hullo," she said to the passing Kelveys.

They were so astounded that they stopped. Lil gave her silly smile. Our Else stared.

"You can come and see our doll's house if you want to," said Kezia, and she dragged one toe on the ground. But at that Lil turned red and shook her head quickly.

"Why not?" asked Kezia.

Lil gasped, then she said, "Your ma told our ma you wasn't to speak to us."

"Oh, well," said Kezia. She didn't know what to reply. "It doesn't matter. You can come and see our doll's house all the same. Come on. Nobody's looking."

But Lil shook her head still harder.

"Don't you want to?" asked Kezia.

Suddenly there was a twitch, a tug at Lil's skirt. She turned round. Our Else was looking at her with big, imploring eyes; she was frowning; she wanted to go. For a moment Lil looked at our Else very doubtfully. But then our Else twitched her skirt again. She started forward. Kezia led the way. Like two little stray cats they followed across the courtyard to where the doll's house stood.

"There it is," said Kezia.

There was a pause. Lil breathed loudly, almost snorted; our Else was still as a stone.

"I'll open it for you," said Kezia kindly. She undid the hook and they looked inside.

"There's the drawing room and the dining room, and that's the—"

"Kezia!"

Oh, what a start they gave!

"Kezia!"

It was Aunt Beryl's voice. They turned round.

At the back door stood Aunt Beryl, staring as if she couldn't believe what she saw.

"How dare you ask the little Kelveys into the courtyard?" said her cold, furious voice. "You know as well as I do, you're not allowed to talk to them. Run away, children, run away at once. And don't come back again," said Aunt Beryl. And she stepped into the yard and shooed them out as if they were chickens.

"Off you go immediately!" she called, cold and proud.

They did not need telling twice. Burning with shame, shrinking together, Lil huddling along like her mother, our Else dazed, somehow they crossed the big courtyard and squeezed through the white gate.

"Wicked, disobedient little girl!" said Aunt Beryl bitterly to Kezia, and she slammed the doll's house to.

The afternoon had been awful. A letter had come from Willie Brent, a terrifying, threatening letter, saying if she did not meet him that evening in Pulman's Bush, he'd come to the front door and ask the reason why! But now that she had frightened those little rats of Kelveys and given Kezia a good scolding, her heart felt lighter. That ghastly pressure was gone. She went back to the house humming. **(E)**

When the Kelveys were well out of sight of Burnells', they sat down to rest on a big red drainpipe by the side of the road. Lil's cheeks were still burning; she took off the hat with the quill and held it on her knee. Dreamily they looked over the hay paddocks,[9] past the creek, to the group of wattles[10] where Logan's cows stood waiting to be milked. What were their thoughts?

Presently our Else nudged up close to her sister. But now she had forgotten the cross lady. She put out a finger and stroked her sister's quill; she smiled her rare smile.

"I seen the little lamp," she said, softly.

Then both were silent once more. **(F)**

---

9. **paddocks** (PAD uhks): enclosed pieces of land.
10. **wattles** (WAHT uhlz): here, acacia trees, used to make wattles, fences made of twisted twigs.

Vocabulary clambered (KLAM buhrd) v.: climbed clumsily.

(E) Literary Focus Narrative Voice Whose feelings are we hearing in this passage?

(F) Reading Focus Identifying Cause and Effect What is the ultimate cause of this return to silence?

Applying Your Skills

The Doll's House

Respond and Think Critically

Reading Focus

Quick Check

1. Why aren't the Burnells allowed to speak to the Kelveys?

2. What is the teacher's attitude toward the Kelveys?

3. Why do you think the Kelveys understand each other so well?

Read with a Purpose

4. According to this story, what are the causes and effects of childhood cruelty?

Reading Skills: Identifying Cause and Effect

5. As you read the story, you charted its main events with a cause-and-effect map. Review the events that occurred after the arrival of the doll's house at the Burnell's home. Sort the effects into two lists—one of positive effects and one of negative effects.

Positive Effects	Negative Effects

Literary Focus

Literary Analysis

6. **Compare and Contrast** Why does Isabel invite friends to see the doll's house? Why does Kezia invite Lil and Else to see it?

7. **Analyze** How would you state the story's theme? Use textual evidence for support.

8. **Make Judgments** How do you feel about the cruelty exhibited by Lil and Else's classmates?

9. **Interpret** At the end of the story, the narrator asks of Lil and Else, "What were their thoughts?" What do you believe they were thinking?

10. **Evaluate** Is this story realistic, that is, do events like this happen anywhere, anytime? Explain.

Literary Skills: Narrative Voice

11. **Analyze** Find details in the story that show that the narrator is able to enter into the feelings and minds of all the main characters. How would the story change if the narrator focused only on Lil and Else?

Literary Skills Review: Symbol

12. **Interpret** A **symbol** stands both for itself and for something beyond itself. Find details in the story that suggest that the doll's house might symbolize an imaginary world more perfect and more ordered than the one in which the girls live. How would this symbol make Kezia's desire to share that world with the Kelveys more significant?

Writing Focus

Think as a Reader/Writer

Use It in Your Writing Review the details you noted that helped you enter the minds and feelings of the children in this story. Then, write one or two paragraphs about an incident in which one child is cruel to another. Write as an omniscient narrator, and use details that will help your readers feel as if they are sharing the thoughts and perspective of the children.

What Do You Think Now How do you think their experience of rejection will shape the Kelveys' view of the world? What kinds of adults might the other children in the story grow up to be?

Vocabulary Development

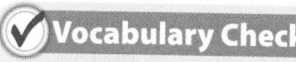

✔ Vocabulary Check

Match the Vocabulary words with their definitions.

1. congealed
2. conspicuous
3. flagged
4. clambered

a. lost momentum
b. climbed awkwardly
c. easy to spot
d. thickened

Vocabulary Skills: Context Clues

As you come across an unfamiliar word in your reading, see if context clues can help determine its meaning.

"Even before the *sacking* was taken off."

To figure out what *sacking* is, you would have these clues: (1) It is something that can cover a doll's house; (2) it can come off; (3) the word *sack* is in it.

Your Turn

Go back to the text and locate each of the Vocabulary words in the list below. On a separate sheet of paper, note any context clues that would help you define the word if it weren't defined at the bottom of the page.

congealed	flagged
conspicuous	clambered

Language Coach

Multiple Meanings If you encounter a familiar word that does not make sense in its context, the word may have more than one meaning. What do the italicized words mean in these sentences?

1. "How much more exciting than peering through the slit of a door into a *mean* little hall."
2. "They *burned* to tell everybody."
3. "They only just had time to … fall into line before the *roll* was called.

CHOICES

As you respond to the Choices, use the **Academic Vocabulary** words as appropriate: <u>perspective</u>, <u>considerably</u>, <u>adapt</u>, <u>exhibit</u>, <u>inevitable</u>.

REVIEW
Through Different Eyes

The narrator of "The Doll's House" has a strong voice that enters the thoughts of all the story's main characters. Choose a narrator with a more limited point of view, and, using the pronoun *I*, rewrite a scene from the story using that narrator's <u>perspective</u> and voice. You may choose a character in the story, or you can invent an outside narrator.

CONNECT
Record a Dramatic Reading

TechFocus Choose a section of "The Doll's House" to perform as a radio show or podcast. Before you begin, consider how your voice should sound as you read aloud different passages, and think about how you can <u>adapt</u> the story and bring to life a particular narrative voice in your pacing and tone. Play your recorded podcast for your class.

EXTEND
A Modern Schoolyard

Could the scenes in this story take place in a contemporary schoolyard? Would the snobbishness today be based on social class, as it is in this story, or might the cruelty have some other cause? Would the bullies and the victims be likely to behave the way they do in "The Doll's House"? Write a brief essay about bullies and childhood cruelty in today's times.

 Learn It Online
Explore Katherine Mansfield and her world further through these Internet links:

go.hrw.com   L12-1307   **Go**

The Rocking-Horse Winner

How does experience shape our view of the world?

How is our experience of life affected by money—or the absence of it? Record your thoughts in your *Reader/Writer Notebook*.

D.H. Lawrence (1885–1930).

MEET THE WRITER

D. H. Lawrence
(1885–1930)

David Herbert Lawrence was the frailest child of a coal miner and his disappointed wife, whose ambition was to keep her sons out of the mines and her daughters from servitude. Lawrence fulfilled his mother's wishes and became a schoolmaster.

A Scandalous Start

In 1912, Lawrence left his teaching job. In preparation for a European tour, he visited his old French professor and fell in love with the professor's wife, Frieda, a German baroness and the mother of three children. Within weeks, Frieda had fled with Lawrence to Germany and then to Italy, where Lawrence finished *Sons and Lovers* (1913).

Reviews of the novel were cautiously favorable, but the moral controversy over Lawrence's work was intensifying: One critic found the novel's amorous parts "too graphic." Lawrence began to see industrialized England as corrosive and oppressive. He embraced a belief in "blood knowledge," in balancing the animal self with the intellect. From his perspective, England was overcivilized and prudish, and now he took aim at it.

Furious Censors

When a privately printed edition of *Women in Love* was published in 1920, one critic judged it "a loathsome study of sex depravity leading youth to unspeakable disaster." Despite the uproar, or maybe because of it, Lawrence's books began selling well. In 1928, Lawrence published *Lady Chatterley's Lover,* about a wealthy woman who becomes romantically involved with her husband's gamekeeper. The novel, which became one of the most notable books of the twentieth century, drew new waves of anger from the censors. U.S. customs officers seized copies as they arrived on the docks, and the novel was banned in Britain. As a result, all of Lawrence's work, including his poetry, became considerably more popular.

Lawrence died of tuberculosis at age forty-five. He is buried in Taos, New Mexico, where he and Frieda lived for a time to treat his lung disease.

Think About the Writer
How would Lawrence's life have been different if he had been born a century later, in 1985?

Reader/Writer Notebook

Use your **RWN** to complete the activities for this selection.

Literary Focus

Foreshadowing When writers use **foreshadowing,** they provide clues that hint at what might happen later in the story. Sometimes those clues are events that immediately arouse our curiosity and create suspense. Sometimes the clues are subtle—small details that only later do we recognize as clues pointing to something that is revealed at the story's conclusion. Part of the pleasure of reading stories is spotting those elements that foreshadow what is to come.

Reading Focus

Interpreting Character Perhaps even more enjoyable than predicting what will happen next in a story is **interpreting character,** figuring out the general psychology of the people in the story. To start your analysis of character, you should pay close attention to what the characters say, what traits they exhibit, how they dress, and why they act the way they do. In some stories a character's needs or fears serve as clues.

Into Action As you read, use a chart like the one below to analyze the two main characters in "The Rocking-Horse Winner."

	The Mother	Paul
Key statements about character	"woman who was beautiful, who started with all the advantages"	Says of himself, "I'm a lucky person"
Character's actions		
Character's wants or needs		
Character's fears		

Writing Focus

Think as a Reader/Writer

Find It in Your Reading Lawrence supplies precise descriptive details in the first paragraph, as we meet Paul's mother, a key character in the story. In your *Reader/Writer Notebook*, write down some of the details Lawrence supplies to give you a sense of what this woman is like.

Vocabulary

asserted (uh SURT ihd) *v.*: declared. *The child asserted that he was lucky.*

obscure (uhb SKYUR) *adj.*: little known. *The boy wanted to bet on an obscure horse named Daffodil.*

reiterated (ree IHT uh rayt ihd) *v.*: repeated. *The gardener reiterated that the boy was lucky.*

uncanny (uhn KAN ee) *adj.*: strange; eerie; weird. *The boy's blue eyes had an uncanny cold fire in them.*

iridescent (ihr ih DEHS uhnt) *adj.*: showing rainbowlike colors. *The cushions on the sofa were covered in iridescent fabrics.*

overwrought (oh vuhr RAWT) *adj.*: overly excited. *The mother noticed that the boy was overwrought about the race.*

remonstrated (rih MAHN strayt ihd) *v.*: protested. *The mother remonstrated that the boy was too big for a rocking horse.*

arrested (uh REHST ihd) *v.* used as *adj.*: checked or stopped in motion. *The rocking horse stood in an arrested prance in the boy's bedroom.*

Language Coach

Multiple Meanings Which Vocabulary words have other meanings that are different from the definitions provided?

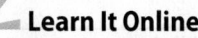
Learn It Online
Get to know the Vocabulary words inside and out through Word Watch online.

go.hrw.com   L12-1309   Go

The Rocking-Horse Winner

by D. H. Lawrence

Left: Horses and jockeys racing in the Ascot Stakes during the Royal Meeting at Ascot. Right: *The Rocking-Horse Winner* (1950), John Mills, John Howard Davies.

She married for love, and the love turned to dust.

Read with a Purpose
Read to find out if the boy in the story is really a winner.

Build Background
Lawrence saw men and women as torn between the promptings of their instincts and the demanding voices of their upbringing and education. He believed that instincts were naturally better than a forced system of education and conformity. As you read "The Rocking-Horse Winner," which is told like a modern fable, notice which voices are most dominant in the house and what effects these voices have on the characters.

Lawrence also felt that people should surmount their fear and lust for money. He once said he would advise the young not to be wage slaves.

There was a woman who was beautiful, who started with all the advantages, yet she had no luck. She married for love, and the love turned to dust. She had bonny children, yet she felt they had been thrust upon her, and she could not love them. They looked at her coldly, as if they were finding fault with her. And hurriedly she felt she must cover up some fault in herself. Yet what it was that she must cover up she never knew. Nevertheless, when her children were present, she always felt the center of her heart go hard. This troubled her, and in her manner she was all the more gentle and anxious for her children, as if she loved them very much. Only she herself knew that at the center of her heart was a hard little place that could not feel love, no, not for anybody. Everybody else said of her: "She is such a good mother. She adores her children." Only she herself, and her children themselves, knew it was not so. They read it in each other's eyes. **Ⓐ**

Ⓐ Reading Focus **Interpreting Character** What does the first paragraph specifically state about the mother?

There were a boy and two little girls. They lived in a pleasant house, with a garden, and they had discreet servants, and felt themselves superior to anyone in the neighborhood.

Although they lived in style, they felt always an anxiety in the house. There was never enough money. The mother had a small income,[1] and the father had a small income, but not nearly enough for the social position which they had to keep up. The father went into town to some office. But though he had good prospects, these prospects never materialized. There was always the grinding sense of the shortage of money, though the style was always kept up.

At last the mother said: "I will see if *I* can't make something." But she did not know where to begin. She racked her brains, and tried this thing and the other, but could not find anything successful. The failure made deep lines come into her face. Her children were growing up, they would have to go to school. There must be more money, there must be more money. The father, who was always very handsome and expensive in his tastes, seemed as if he never *would* be able to do anything worth doing. And the mother, who had a great belief in herself, did not succeed any better, and her tastes were just as expensive.

And so the house came to be haunted by the unspoken phrase: *There must be more money! There must be more money!* The children could hear it all the time, though nobody said it aloud. They heard it at Christmas, when the expensive and splendid toys filled the nursery. Behind the shining modern rocking horse, behind the smart doll's house, a voice would start whispering: "There *must* be more money! There *must* be more money!" And the children would stop playing, to listen for a moment. They would look into each other's eyes, to see if they had all heard. And each one saw in the eyes of the other two that they too had heard. "There *must* be more money! There *must* be more money!"

It came whispering from the springs of the still-swaying rocking horse, and even the horse, bending his wooden, champing head, heard it. The big doll, sitting so pink and smirking in her new pram,[2] could

hear it quite plainly, and seemed to be smirking all the more self-consciously because of it. The foolish puppy, too, that took the place of the teddy bear, he was looking so extraordinarily foolish for no other reason but that he heard the secret whisper all over the house: "There *must* be more money!" **B**

Yet nobody ever said it aloud. The whisper was everywhere, and therefore no one spoke it. Just as no one ever says: "We are breathing!" in spite of the fact that breath is coming and going all the time.

"Mother," said the boy Paul one day, "why don't we keep a car of our own? Why do we always use uncle's, or else a taxi?"

"Because we're the poor members of the family," said the mother.

"But why *are* we, mother?"

"Well—I suppose," she said slowly and bitterly, "it's because your father has no luck."

The boy was silent for some time.

"Is luck money, mother?" he asked, rather timidly.

"No, Paul. Not quite. It's what causes you to have money."

"Oh!" said Paul vaguely. "I thought when Uncle Oscar said *filthy lucker,* it meant money."

"*Filthy lucre*[3] does mean money," said the mother. "But it's lucre, not luck."

"Oh!" said the boy. "Then what is luck, mother?"

"It's what causes you to have money. If you're lucky you have money. That's why it's better to be born lucky than rich. If you're rich, you may lose your money. But if you're lucky, you will always get more money."

"Oh! Will you? And is father not lucky?"

"Very unlucky, I should say," she said bitterly.

The boy watched her with unsure eyes.

"Why?" he asked.

"I don't know. Nobody ever knows why one person is lucky and another unlucky."

"Don't they? Nobody at all? Does *nobody* know?"

"Perhaps God. But He never tells."

"He ought to, then. And aren't you lucky either, mother?"

---

3. **filthy lucre** (LOO kuhr): filthy money.

---

1. **income:** money from an inheritance or investments—not a salary.
2. **pram:** baby carriage, short for "perambulator."

B **Literary Focus** Foreshadowing What could the whispering foreshadow? What do you think will happen next?

"I can't be, if I married an unlucky husband."

"But by yourself, aren't you?"

"I used to think I was, before I married. Now I think I am very unlucky indeed."

"Why?"

"Well—never mind! Perhaps I'm not really," she said.

The child looked at her to see if she meant it. But he saw, by the lines of her mouth, that she was only trying to hide something from him.

"Well, anyhow," he said stoutly,[4] "I'm a lucky person."

"Why?" said his mother, with a sudden laugh.

He stared at her. He didn't even know why he had said it.

"God told me," he asserted, brazening it out.[5]

"I hope He did, dear!" she said, again with a laugh, but rather bitter.

"He did, mother!"

"Excellent!" said the mother, using one of her husband's exclamations.

The boy saw she did not believe him; or rather, that she paid no attention to his assertion. This angered him somewhere, and made him want to compel her attention.

---

4. **stoutly** (STOWT lee): bravely; boldly.
5. **brazening it out:** acting boldly and defiantly.

Vocabulary   **asserted** (uh SURT ihd) *v.*: declared.

He went off by himself, vaguely, in a childish way, seeking for the clue to "luck." Absorbed, taking no heed of other people, he went about with a sort of stealth, seeking inwardly for luck. He wanted luck, he wanted it, he wanted it. When the two girls were playing dolls in the nursery, he would sit on his big rocking horse, charging madly into space, with a frenzy that made the little girls peer at him uneasily. Wildly the horse careered,[6] the waving dark hair of the boy tossed, his eyes had a strange glare in them. The little girls dared not speak to him.

When he had ridden to the end of his mad little journey, he climbed down and stood in front of his rocking horse, staring fixedly into its lowered face. Its red mouth was slightly open, its big eye was wide and glassy-bright.

"Now!" he would silently command the snorting steed. "Now, take me to where there is luck! Now take me!"

And he would slash the horse on the neck with the little whip he had asked Uncle Oscar for. He *knew* the horse could take him to where there was luck, if only he forced it. So he would mount again and start on his

---

6. **careered:** rushed wildly.

He wanted luck, he wanted it, he wanted it.

furious ride, hoping at last to get there. He knew he could get there.

"You'll break your horse, Paul!" said the nurse. "He's always riding like that! I wish he'd leave off!" said his elder sister Joan.

But he only glared down on them in silence. Nurse gave him up. She could make nothing of him. Anyhow, he was growing beyond her.

One day his mother and his Uncle Oscar came in when he was on one of his furious rides. He did not speak to them.

"Hallo, you young jockey! Riding a winner?" said his uncle.

"Aren't you growing too big for a rocking horse? You're not a very little boy any longer, you know," said his mother.

But Paul only gave a blue glare from his big, rather close-set eyes. He would speak to nobody when he was in full tilt. His mother watched him with an anxious expression on her face.

C **Reading Focus** Interpreting Character What does Paul want?

At last he suddenly stopped forcing his horse into the mechanical gallop and slid down.

"Well, I got there!" he announced fiercely, his blue eyes still flaring, and his sturdy long legs straddling apart.

"Where did you get to?" asked his mother.

"Where I wanted to go," he flared back at her.

"That's right, son!" said Uncle Oscar. "Don't you stop till you get there. What's the horse's name?"

"He doesn't have a name," said the boy.

"Gets on without all right?" asked the uncle.

"Well, he has different names. He was called Sansovino last week."

"Sansovino, eh? Won the Ascot.[7] How did you know this name?"

"He always talks about horse races with Bassett," said Joan.

The uncle was delighted to find that his small nephew was posted with all the racing news. Bassett, the young gardener, who had been wounded in the left foot in the war and had got his present job through Oscar Cresswell, whose batman[8] he had been, was a perfect blade of the "turf."[9] He lived in the racing events, and the small boy lived with him.

Oscar Cresswell got it all from Bassett.

"Master Paul comes and asks me, so I can't do more than tell him, sir," said Bassett, his face terribly serious, as if he were speaking of religious matters.

"And does he ever put anything on a horse he fancies?"

"Well—I don't want to give him away—he's a young sport, a fine sport, sir. Would you mind asking him himself? He

---

7. **Ascot:** famous horse race held annually at Ascot Heath, in England. Several traditional British races are mentioned in the story.
8. **batman:** British officer's personal attendant.
9. **blade of the "turf":** stylish young racing fan.

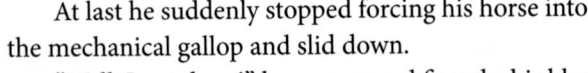

Aren't you growing too big for a rocking horse?

sort of takes a pleasure in it, and perhaps he'd feel I was giving him away, sir, if you don't mind."

Bassett was serious as a church.

The uncle went back to his nephew and took him off for a ride in the car.

"Say, Paul, old man, do you ever put anything on a horse?" the uncle asked.

The boy watched the handsome man closely.

"Why, do you think I oughtn't to?" he parried.

"Not a bit of it! I thought perhaps you might give me a tip for the Lincoln."

The car sped on into the country, going down to Uncle Oscar's place in Hampshire.

"Honor bright?" said the nephew.

"Honor bright, son!" said the uncle.

"Well, then, Daffodil."

"Daffodil! I doubt it, sonny. What about Mirza?"

"I only know the winner," said the boy. "That's Daffodil."

"Daffodil, eh?"

There was a pause. Daffodil was an obscure horse comparatively.

"Uncle!"

"Yes, son?"

"You won't let it go any further, will you? I promised Bassett."

"Bassett be damned, old man! What's he got to do with it?"

"We're partners. We've been partners from the first. Uncle, he lent me my first five shillings, which I lost. I promised him, honor bright, it was only between me and him; only you gave me that ten-shilling note I started winning with, so I thought you were lucky. You won't let it go any further, will you?"

The boy gazed at his uncle from those big, hot, blue eyes, set rather close together. The uncle stirred and laughed uneasily.

"Right you are, son! I'll keep your tip private. Daffodil, eh? How much are you putting on him?"

"All except twenty pounds," said the boy. "I keep that in reserve."

The uncle thought it a good joke.

"You keep twenty pounds in reserve, do you, you young romancer?[10] What are you betting, then?"

"I'm betting three hundred," said the boy gravely. "But it's between you and me, Uncle Oscar! Honor bright?"

The uncle burst into a roar of laughter.

"It's between you and me all right, you young Nat Gould,"[11] he said, laughing. "But where's your three hundred?"

"Bassett keeps it for me. We're partners."

"You are, are you! And what is Bassett putting on Daffodil?"

"He won't go quite as high as I do, I expect. Perhaps he'll go a hundred and fifty."

"What, pennies?" laughed the uncle.

"Pounds," said the child, with a surprised look at his uncle. "Bassett keeps a bigger reserve than I do."

Between wonder and amusement Uncle Oscar was silent. He pursued the matter no further, but he determined to take his nephew with him to the Lincoln races.

"Now, son," he said, "I'm putting twenty on Mirza, and I'll put five on for you on any horse you fancy. What's your pick?"

"Daffodil, uncle."

"No, not the fiver on Daffodil!"

"I should if it was my own fiver," said the child.

"Good! Good! Right you are! A fiver for me and a fiver for you on Daffodil."

The child had never been to a race meeting before, and his eyes were blue fire. He pursed his mouth tight and watched. A Frenchman just in front had put his money on Lancelot. Wild with excitement, he flayed his arms up and down, yelling *Lancelot! Lancelot!* in his French accent.

Daffodil came in first, Lancelot second, Mirza third. The child, flushed and with eyes blazing, was curiously serene. His uncle brought him four five-pound notes, four to one. **Ⓓ**

---

10. **romancer:** imaginative storyteller.
11. **Nat Gould:** famous British authority on racing.

Ⓓ **Literary Focus** Foreshadowing What do you think the description of the child foreshadows here?

"What am I to do with these?" he cried, waving them before the boy's eyes.

"I suppose we'll talk to Bassett," said the boy. "I expect I have fifteen hundred now; and twenty in reserve; and this twenty."

His uncle studied him for some moments.

"Look here, son!" he said. "You're not serious about Bassett and that fifteen hundred, are you?"

"Yes, I am. But it's between you and me, uncle. Honor bright?"

"Honor bright all right, son! But I must talk to Bassett."

"If you'd like to be a partner, uncle, with Bassett and me, we could all be partners. Only, you'd have to promise, honor bright, uncle, not to let it go beyond us three. Bassett and I are lucky, and you must be lucky, because it was your ten shillings I started winning with…"

Uncle Oscar took both Bassett and Paul into Richmond Park for an afternoon, and there they talked.

"It's like this, you see, sir," Bassett said. "Master Paul would get me talking about racing events, spinning yarns, you know, sir. And he was always keen on knowing if I'd made or if I'd lost. It's about a year since, now, that I put five shillings on Blush of Dawn for him: And we lost. Then the luck turned, with that ten shillings he had from you: That we put on Singhalese. And since that time, it's been pretty steady, all things considering. What do you say, Master Paul?"

"We're all right when we're sure," said Paul. "It's when we're not quite sure that we go down."

"Oh, but we're careful then," said Bassett.

"But when are you *sure*?" smiled Uncle Oscar.

"It's Master Paul, sir," said Bassett in a secret, religious voice. "It's as if he had it from heaven. Like Daffodil, now, for the Lincoln. That was as sure as eggs." **E**

"Did you put anything on Daffodil?" asked Oscar Cresswell.

"Yes, sir. I made my bit."

"And my nephew?"

Bassett was obstinately silent, looking at Paul.

"I made twelve hundred, didn't I, Bassett? I told uncle I was putting three hundred on Daffodil."

"That's right," said Bassett, nodding.

"But where's the money?" asked the uncle.

"I keep it safe locked up, sir. Master Paul he can have it any minute he likes to ask for it."

"What, fifteen hundred pounds?"

"And twenty! And *forty*, that is, with the twenty he made on the course."

"It's amazing!" said the uncle.

"If Master Paul offers you to be partners, sir, I would, if I were you: if you'll excuse me," said Bassett.

Oscar Cresswell thought about it.

"I'll see the money," he said.

They drove home again, and sure enough, Bassett came round to the garden house with fifteen hundred pounds in notes. The twenty pounds reserve was left with Joe Glee, in the Turf Commission[12] deposit.

"You see, it's all right, uncle, when I'm *sure!* Then we go strong, for all we're worth. Don't we, Bassett?"

"We do that, Master Paul."

"And when are you sure?" said the uncle, laughing.

"Oh, well, sometimes I'm *absolutely* sure, like about Daffodil," said the boy; "and sometimes I have an idea; and sometimes I haven't even an idea, have I, Bassett? Then we're careful, because we mostly go down."

"You do, do you! And when you're sure, like about Daffodil, what makes you sure, sonny?"

"Oh, well, I don't know," said the boy uneasily. "I'm sure, you know, uncle; that's all."

"It's as if he had it from heaven, sir," Bassett reiterated.

"I should say so!" said the uncle.

But he became a partner. And when the Leger was coming on Paul was "sure" about Lively Spark, which

---

12. **Turf Commission:** committee of the Jockey Club, the chief governing body for horse racing. This committee operates a bank in which bettors can deposit money for future bets.

E **Literary Focus** Foreshadowing What might the words *secret* and *religious* foreshadow about the relationship between Bassett and the boy?

Vocabulary **reiterated** (ree IHT uh rayt ihd) *v.*: repeated.

The Rocking-Horse Winner (1950), John Mills, John Howard Davies.

was a quite inconsiderable horse. The boy insisted on putting a thousand on the horse, Bassett went for five hundred, and Oscar Cresswell two hundred. Lively Spark came in first, and the betting had been ten to one against him. Paul had made ten thousand.

"You see," he said, "I was absolutely sure of him."

Even Oscar Cresswell had cleared two thousand.

"Look here, son," he said, "this sort of thing makes me nervous."

"It needn't, uncle! Perhaps I shan't be sure again for a long time."

"But what are you going to do with your money?" asked the uncle.

"Of course," said the boy, "I started it for mother. She said she had no luck, because father is unlucky, so I thought if *I* was lucky, it might stop whispering."

"What might stop whispering?"

"Our house. I *hate* our house for whispering."

"What does it whisper?"

"Why—why"—the boy fidgeted—"why, I don't know. But it's always short of money, you know, uncle."

"I know it, son, I know it."

"You know people send mother writs,[13] don't you, uncle?"

"I'm afraid I do," said the uncle.

"And then the house whispers, like people laughing at you behind your back. It's awful, that is! I thought if I was lucky——"

"You might stop it," added the uncle.

The boy watched him with big blue eyes, that had an uncanny cold fire in them, and he said never a word.

"Well, then!" said the uncle. "What are we doing?"

---

13. **writs:** legal papers; here, ones demanding payment.

Vocabulary   **uncanny** (uhn KAN ee) *adj.*: strange; eerie; weird.

"I shouldn't like mother to know I was lucky," said the boy.

"Why not, son?"

"She'd stop me."

"I don't think she would."

"Oh!"—and the boy writhed in an odd way—"I *don't* want her to know, uncle." **F**

"All right, son! We'll manage it without her knowing."

They managed it very easily. Paul, at the other's suggestion, handed over five thousand pounds to his uncle, who deposited it with the family lawyer, who was then to inform Paul's mother that a relative had put five thousand pounds into his hands, which sum was to be paid out a thousand pounds at a time, on the mother's birthday, for the next five years.

"So she'll have a birthday present of a thousand pounds for five successive years," said Uncle Oscar. "I hope it won't make it all the harder for her later."

Paul's mother had her birthday in November. The house had been "whispering" worse than ever lately, and, even in spite of his luck, Paul could not bear up against it. He was very anxious to see the effect of the birthday letter, telling his mother about the thousand pounds.

When there were no visitors, Paul now took his meals with his parents, as he was beyond the nursery control. His mother went into town nearly every day. She had discovered that she had an odd knack of sketching furs and dress materials, so she worked secretly in the studio of a friend who was the chief "artist" for the leading drapers.[14] She drew the figures of ladies in furs and ladies in silk and sequins for the newspaper advertisements. This young woman artist earned several thousand pounds a year, but Paul's mother only made several hundreds, and she was again dissatisfied. She so wanted to be first in something, and she did not succeed, even in making sketches for drapery advertisements.

---

14. **drapers:** dealers in cloth.

She was down to breakfast on the morning of her birthday. Paul watched her face as she read her letters. He knew the lawyer's letter. As his mother read it, her face hardened and became more expressionless. Then a cold, determined look came on her mouth. She hid the letter under the pile of others, and said not a word about it.

"Didn't you have anything nice in the post for your birthday, mother?" said Paul.

"Quite moderately nice," she said, her voice cold and absent. **G**

She went away to town without saying more.

But in the afternoon Uncle Oscar appeared. He said Paul's mother had had a long interview with the lawyer, asking if the whole five thousand could not be advanced at once, as she was in debt.

"What do you think, uncle?" said the boy.

"I leave it to you, son."

"Oh, let her have it, then! We can get some more with the other," said the boy.

"A bird in the hand is worth two in the bush, laddie!" said Uncle Oscar.

"But I'm sure to *know* for the Grand National; or the Lincolnshire; or else the Derby. I'm sure to know for *one* of them," said Paul.

So Uncle Oscar signed the agreement, and Paul's mother touched the whole five thousand. Then something very curious happened. The voices in the house suddenly went mad, like a chorus of frogs on a spring evening. There were certain new furnishings, and Paul had a tutor. He was *really* going to Eton,[15] his father's school, in the following autumn. There were flowers in the winter, and a blossoming of the luxury Paul's mother had been used to. And yet the voices in the house, behind the sprays of mimosa and almond blossom, and from under the piles of iridescent cushions, simply trilled and screamed in a sort of ecstasy: "There *must* be more money! Oh-h-h; there must be more money. Oh, now, now-w! Now-w-w—there *must* be

---

15. **Eton:** Eton College, exclusive prep school, near London.

F Literary Focus **Foreshadowing** What could the description of the boy's eyes and the word *odd* foreshadow about Paul?

G Reading Focus **Interpreting Character** What words in this sentence tell you something about the mother's character?

Vocabulary **iridescent** (ihr ih DEHS uhnt) *adj.:* showing rainbowlike colors.

more money!—more than ever! More than ever!"

It frightened Paul terribly. He studied away at his Latin and Greek with his tutor. But his intense hours were spent with Bassett. The Grand National had gone by: He had not "known," and had lost a hundred pounds. Summer was at hand. He was in agony for the Lincoln. But even for the Lincoln he didn't "know," and he lost fifty pounds. He became wild-eyed and strange, as if something were going to explode in him. **(H)**

"Let it alone, son! Don't you bother about it!" urged Uncle Oscar. But it was as if the boy couldn't really hear what his uncle was saying.

"I've got to know for the Derby! I've got to know for the Derby!" the child reiterated, his big blue eyes blazing with a sort of madness.

His mother noticed how overwrought he was.

"You'd better go to the seaside. Wouldn't you like to go now to the seaside, instead of waiting? I think you'd better," she said, looking down at him anxiously, her heart curiously heavy because of him.

But the child lifted his uncanny blue eyes.

"I couldn't possibly go before the Derby, mother!" he said. "I couldn't possibly!"

"Why not?" she said, her voice becoming heavy when she was opposed. "Why not? You can still go from the seaside to see the Derby with your Uncle Oscar, if that's what you wish. No need for you to wait here. Besides, I think you care too much about these races. It's a bad sign. My family has been a gambling family, and you won't know till you grow up how much damage it has done. But it has done damage. I shall have to send Bassett away, and ask Uncle Oscar not to talk racing to you, unless you promise to be reasonable about it: Go away to the seaside and forget it. You're all nerves!" **(I)**

"I'll do what you like, mother, so long as you don't send me away till after the Derby," the boy said.

"Send you away from where? Just from this house?"

"Yes," he said, gazing at her.

"Why, you curious child, what makes you care about this house so much, suddenly? I never knew you loved it."

He gazed at her without speaking. He had a secret within a secret, something he had not divulged, even to Bassett or to his Uncle Oscar.

But his mother, after standing undecided and a little bit sullen for some moments, said:

"Very well, then! Don't go to the seaside till after the Derby, if you don't wish it. But promise me you won't let your nerves go to pieces. Promise you won't think so much about horse racing and *events,* as you call them!"

"Oh no," said the boy casually, "I won't think much about them, mother. You needn't worry. I wouldn't worry, mother, if I were you."

"If you were me and I were you," said his mother, "I wonder what we *should* do!"

"But you know you needn't worry, mother, don't you?" the boy repeated.

"I should be awfully glad to know it," she said wearily.

"Oh, well, you *can,* you know. I mean, you *ought* to know you needn't worry," he insisted.

"Ought I? Then I'll see about it," she said.

Paul's secret of secrets was his wooden horse, that which had no name. Since he was emancipated from a nurse and a nursery-governess, he had had his rocking horse removed to his own bedroom at the top of the house.

"Surely you're too big for a rocking horse!" his mother had remonstrated.

"Well, you see, mother, till I can have a *real* horse, I like to have *some* sort of animal about," had been his quaint answer.

"Do you feel he keeps you company?" she laughed.

"Oh yes! He's very good, he always keeps me company, when I'm there," said Paul.

So the horse, rather shabby, stood in an arrested prance in the boy's bedroom.

The Derby was drawing near, and the boy grew

(H) Literary Focus Foreshadowing What details in these last two paragraphs seem to signal trouble?

(I) Literary Focus Foreshadowing What might the mother's remarks about gambling foreshadow?

Vocabulary **overwrought** (OH vuhr RAWT) *adj.:* overly excited.
remonstrated (rih MAWN strayt ihd) *v.:* protested.
arrested (uh REHST ihd) *v.* used as *adj.:* checked; stopped in motion.

more and more tense. He hardly heard what was spoken to him, he was very frail, and his eyes were really uncanny. His mother had sudden strange seizures of uneasiness about him. Sometimes, for half an hour, she would feel a sudden anxiety about him that was almost anguish. She wanted to rush to him at once, and know he was safe.

Two nights before the Derby, she was at a big party in town, when one of her rushes of anxiety about her boy, her firstborn, gripped her heart till she could hardly speak. She fought with the feeling, might and main, for she believed in common sense. But it was too strong. She had to leave the dance and go downstairs to telephone to the country. The children's nursery-governess was terribly surprised and startled at being rung up in the night. **J**

"Are the children all right, Miss Wilmot?"

"Oh yes, they are quite all right."

"Master Paul? Is he all right?"

"He went to bed as right as a trivet.[16] Shall I run up and look at him?"

"No," said Paul's mother reluctantly. "No! Don't trouble. It's all right. Don't sit up. We shall be home fairly soon." She did not want her son's privacy intruded upon.

"Very good," said the governess.

It was about one o'clock when Paul's mother and father drove up to their house. All was still. Paul's mother went to her room and slipped off her white fur cloak. She had told her maid not to wait up for her. She heard her husband downstairs, mixing a whiskey and soda.

And then, because of the strange anxiety at her heart, she stole upstairs to her son's room. Noiselessly she went along the upper corridor. Was there a faint noise? What was it?

She stood, with arrested muscles, outside his door, listening. There was a strange, heavy, and yet not loud noise. Her heart stood still. It was a soundless noise, yet rushing and powerful. Something huge, in violent, hushed motion. What was it? What in God's name was

it? She ought to know. She felt that she knew the noise. She knew what it was.

Yet she could not place it. She couldn't say what it was. And on and on it went, like a madness.

Softly, frozen with anxiety and fear, she turned the door handle.

The room was dark. Yet in the space near the window, she heard and saw something plunging to and fro. She gazed in fear and amazement.

Then suddenly she switched on the light, and saw her son, in his green pajamas, madly surging on the rocking horse. The blaze of light suddenly lit him up, as he urged the wooden horse, and lit her up, as she stood, blonde, in her dress of pale green and crystal, in the doorway.

"Paul!" she cried. "Whatever are you doing?"

"It's Malabar!" he screamed in a powerful, strange voice. "It's Malabar!"

His eyes blazed at her for one strange and senseless second, as he ceased urging his wooden horse. Then he fell with a crash to the ground, and she, all her tormented motherhood flooding upon her, rushed to gather him up.

But he was unconscious, and unconscious he remained, with some brain fever. He talked and tossed, and his mother sat stonily by his side. **K**

"Malabar! It's Malabar! Bassett, Bassett, I *know*! It's Malabar!"

So the child cried, trying to get up and urge the rocking horse that gave him his inspiration.

"What does he mean by Malabar?" asked the heart-frozen mother.

"I don't know," said the father stonily.

"What does he mean by Malabar?" she asked her brother Oscar.

"It's one of the horses running for the Derby," was the answer.

And, in spite of himself, Oscar Cresswell spoke to Bassett, and himself put a thousand on Malabar: at fourteen to one.

16. **trivet:** short-legged stand used for placing hot dishes on a table.

J **Literary Focus** Foreshadowing What details in this paragraph and the previous one foreshadow trouble?

K **Reading Focus** Interpreting Character What word reveals something about the mother here?

The Rocking-Horse Winner (1950), Valerie Hobson.

The third day of the illness was critical: They were waiting for a change. The boy, with his rather long, curly hair, was tossing ceaselessly on the pillow. He neither slept nor regained consciousness, and his eyes were like blue stones. His mother sat, feeling her heart had gone, turned actually into a stone.

In the evening, Oscar Cresswell did not come, but Bassett sent a message, saying could he come up for one moment, just one moment? Paul's mother was very angry at the intrusion, but on second thoughts she agreed. The boy was the same. Perhaps Bassett might bring him to consciousness.

The gardener, a shortish fellow with a little brown moustache and sharp little brown eyes, tiptoed into the room, touched his imaginary cap to Paul's mother, and stole to the bedside, staring with glittering, small-ish eyes at the tossing, dying child.

"Master Paul!" he whispered. "Master Paul! Malabar came in first all right, a clean win. I did as you told me. You've made over seventy thousand pounds, you have; you've got over eighty thousand. Malabar came in all right, Master Paul."

"Malabar! Malabar! Did I say Malabar, mother? Did I say Malabar? Do you think I'm lucky, mother? I knew Malabar, didn't I? Over eighty thousand pounds! I call that lucky, don't you, mother? Over eighty thousand pounds! I knew, didn't I know I knew? Malabar came in all right. If I ride my horse till I'm sure, then I tell you, Bassett, you can go as high as you like. Did you go for all you were worth, Bassett?"

"I went a thousand on it, Master Paul."

"I never told you, mother, that if I can ride my horse, and *get there,* then I'm absolutely sure—oh, absolutely! Mother, did I ever tell you? I *am* lucky!"

"No, you never did," said his mother.

But the boy died in the night.

And even as he lay dead, his mother heard her brother's voice saying to her: "My God, Hester, you're eighty-odd thousand to the good, and a poor devil of a son to the bad. But, poor devil, poor devil, he's best gone out of a life where he rides his rocking horse to find a winner."

The Rocking-Horse Winner

Respond and Think Critically

Reading Focus

Quick Check

1. How has the woman in the story been unlucky?

2. How is Paul confused about the word *luck*?

3. What does Paul do to ease his mother's anxiety over the family debts?

Read with a Purpose

4. Now that you have read the story, do you think Paul is a winner? Why or why not?

Reading Skills: Interpreting Character

5. Review the character chart you kept as you read. Now, add a row to the bottom called "Character's motivations for actions." In the space provided, analyze the motivations of the mother and Paul.

	The Mother	Paul
Key statements about character	"woman who was beautiful, who started with all the advantages	Says of himself, "I'm a lucky person"
Character's actions		
Character's wants or needs		
Character's fears		
Character's motivations for actions		

Literary Focus

Literary Analysis

6. **Hypothesize** How do you explain the ever louder voices in the house? Why do only Paul and his sister hear and react to the voices?

7. **Interpret** How would you explain what has really happened to Paul? What clues suggest that he has gone mad?

8. **Analyze** Think about the title of the story. What could the rocking horse symbolize?

9. **Interpret** Uncle Oscar says that Paul is best gone out of a life where he rides a rocking horse to find a winner. Do you think Uncle Oscar has been complicit in Paul's tragedy?

10. **Evaluate** Do you think Lawrence's fable is applicable to life today? Explain.

Literary Skills: Foreshadowing

11. **Evaluate** Review all the details that foreshadow Paul's tragic end. How does the foreshadowing in the story prepare you for the conclusion?

Literary Skills Review: Atmosphere

12. **Analyze** The mood or feeling created in a literary work is called **atmosphere.** How would you describe the atmosphere of this story?

Writing Focus

Think as a Reader/Writer

Use It in Your Writing Review your notes about the ways the mother is characterized in the first paragraph of the story. Then, write a one-paragraph character description of your own. In your description, tell the reader precisely what your character sees or feels.

What Do
You
Think
Now
How does an obsession with money affect each of these family members—especially Paul?

Vocabulary Development

✓ Vocabulary Check

Be sure you can justify your answers to these questions about Vocabulary words.

1. *Assert, reiterate,* and *remonstrate* all describe the way people speak to one another. Which means "to declare"? Which means "to repeat"? Which means "to protest"?

2. The boy's eyes in the story are often described as **uncanny.** If something is **uncanny,** is it likely to be a bit frightening or to be comforting?

3. Would an **obscure** book be popular or not well known?

4. How is an **iridescent** color different from a regular color?

5. Paul was often **overwrought.** Does this mean he was overexcited or depressed?

Vocabulary Skills: Connotations

Connotations are all the meanings, associations, or emotions that have come to be attached to a word. For example, Paul wonders about "filthy lucre," a negative expression that even suggests something debased. The effect would be different if Paul had said "money."

Your Turn

Which Vocabulary word in each of these pairs has a stronger connotation, that is, has more intensity?

asserted/said	uncanny/weird
overwrought/excited	remonstrated/objected

Language Coach

Multiple Meanings How many different meanings can each boldfaced word have?

She will **rack** her brains for the answer.
She wore a **smart** hat.
The **spring** in the rocking horse broke.

CHOICES

As you respond to the Choices, use the **Academic Vocabulary** words as appropriate: perspective, considerably, adapt, exhibit, inevitable.

REVIEW
Continue the Story

Now that you have analyzed the characters from "The Rocking-Horse Winner," you should have a good idea of how they might behave in another situation. Decide what you think would happen if the story were to continue. Write a follow-up scene that features at least one of the characters from the story.

Mother and Son (1990) by Vladimir Sherbakov (b. 1935). Oil on canvas.

CONNECT
Hypothesize About Motivation

Timed ⏱ Writing Write a brief essay proposing possible explanations and motivations for the behavior of Paul's mother in "The Rocking-Horse Winner." Use examples from the story to support your analysis.

EXTEND
Write a Song

Review the story again, and brainstorm ideas for lyrics to a song about Master Paul. Decide on a perspective, then come up with a title for your song. Make a list of words, phrases, and images suggested by the title. After you write the lyrics of the song, revise them and then share the song with your class.

✳ **Learn It Online**
Learn more about connotations with *WordSharp.*

go.hrw.com   L12-1323   **Go**

Preparing to Read

Araby

What Do You Think? How does experience shape our view of the world?

🕐 **QuickTalk**

With a partner, discuss a trip or event that you greatly anticipated. Did the trip or event live up to your expectations? Why or why not? Record your thoughts in your *Reader/Writer Notebook*.

James Joyce (1934) by Jacques-Émile Blanche.
Courtesy The National Gallery of Ireland/© 2006 ARS, New York/ADAGP.

James Joyce
(1882–1941)

James Joyce's controversial novel *Ulysses* (1922) changed the face of modern fiction. Based on Homer's epic poem the *Odyssey*, *Ulysses* addresses issues of cultural identity, nationhood, history, and family in the modern world by chronicling the movements of two characters on one summer day in Dublin.

Early Struggles

Born in Rathgar, Ireland, a Dublin suburb, James Joyce was one of ten children in an impoverished family. Although he was educated in Roman Catholic schools, he had lost his faith by the time he entered University College, Dublin. After graduating, Joyce went to Paris, where he gave English lessons and wrote book reviews. In 1903, he returned home to be with his dying mother. The next year, he fell in love with a student named Nora Barnacle. When Joyce's debts mounted, he persuaded Nora to leave Ireland with him. The penniless couple settled first in the Italian city of Trieste, where their two children were born. Joyce's luck began to improve when the American poet Ezra Pound favorably reviewed Joyce's short story collection *Dubliners* and persuaded a British magazine to serialize his novel *A Portrait of the Artist as a Young Man*.

Ulysses Brings Scandal and Fame

When Italy entered World War I, the Joyces left Trieste for Zurich. Gifts from anonymous patrons eased Joyce's financial troubles, but his physical problems increased <u>considerably</u>. Between 1917 and 1930, he had twenty-five operations for glaucoma and cataracts.

British publishers found *Ulysses* so scandalous, they refused to set it in type. In 1922, however, Sylvia Beach, the owner of a Paris bookstore, agreed to publish it. Despite many favorable reviews, the book was banned in Britain and the United States. In 1934, after a famous court case, *Ulysses* was published in America. A British edition soon followed, and Joyce's fame spread worldwide. He died at the age of fifty-eight.

Think About the Writer *Ulysses* describes the events of a single day in Dublin. How might living abroad have influenced Joyce to choose this topic?

Reader/Writer Notebook

Use your **RWN** to complete the activities for this selection.

Literary Focus

Epiphany Joyce called a moment of insight or a revelation experienced by one of his characters an **epiphany.** Before Joyce used the word in this manner, an *epiphany* referred solely to a religious experience, a moment during which a human being felt an intense connection with the divine or understood a spiritual truth. Since Joyce, an epiphany has come to refer to any moment of sudden insight or revelation experienced by a character in fiction. Although Joyce gave the word a modern, literary meaning, you will see that the main character's epiphany in "Araby" is described with religious language and imagery.

Literary Perspectives Apply the literary perspective described on page 1327 as you read this story.

Reading Focus

Comparing and Contrasting In "Araby," the main character's vivid imagination sometimes causes him to misunderstand the realities of his life. His perspective on life noticeably contrasts with that of the people around him. Comparing his imaginings about the world with reality will help you understand his epiphany at the end of the story.

Into Action As you read the story, look for differences between the way the character imagines things to be and the way they really are. List these differences in a comparison-and-contrast chart like the one below.

Imagination	Reality
The word "Araby" fills him with an "Eastern enchantment."	

Writing Focus

Think as a Reader/Writer

Find It in Your Reading James Joyce is a master of **imagery,** the use of words to create pictures of places and events. As you read, choose three places in the story that seem real to you. For each one, keep a list in your *Reader/Writer Notebook* of the words or phrases that are most important in helping you form a mental image.

Vocabulary

imperturbable (ihm puhr TUR buh buhl) *adj.:* calm, impassive. *The man was imperturbable in the face of the boy's excitement.*

somber (SAHM buhr) *adj.:* gloomy. *The dark, dirty street on which he lived was somber.*

impinge (ihm PIHNJ) *v.:* strike; touch. *The dropped coins impinge upon the silence.*

annihilate (uh NY uh layt) *v.:* destroy; make nonexistent. *Failure can annihilate a person's hopes.*

monotonous (muh NAHT uh nuhs) *adj.:* unvarying. *The boy found his classwork monotonous.*

garrulous (GAR uh luhs) *adj.:* talkative. *The boy became impatient with the garrulous ladies as he tried to read his book in peace.*

improvised (IHM pruh vyzd) *v.* used as *adj.:* made for the occasion with whatever is handy. *The improvised tent covered the vendor's wares.*

pervades (puhr VAYDZ) *v.:* spreads throughout. *Gloom pervades the neighborhood.*

Language Coach

Homographs Words that are spelled the same but have different meanings are called **homographs.** For example, note how the word *blind* is used in this story. As you read, use a dictionary to find all the meanings of *blind* and other homographs you find.

Learn It Online
Discover more about Joyce's world online.

 go.hrw.com L12-1325   **Go**

Araby

by **James Joyce**

Read with a Purpose
Read to discover what Araby is and what the main character finds there.

Build Background
On May 14, 1894, a five-day charity bazaar came to the city of Dublin. The bazaar was called *Araby*, a reference to Arabia, where bazaars, markets with long rows of stalls or shops, are common. For the children of Dublin, Arabia seemed a mysterious, exotic place, very different from the dreary streets of the city in which they lived.

The house in this story is based on one in which Joyce and his family actually lived. It stood on the same blind (dead-end) street as the Christian Brothers' School Joyce attended.

N orth Richmond Street, being blind, was a quiet street except at the hour when the Christian Brothers' School set the boys free. An uninhabited house of two stories stood at the blind end, detached from its neighbors in a square ground. The other houses of the street, conscious of decent lives within them, gazed at one another with brown imperturbable faces.

The former tenant of our house, a priest, had died in the back drawing-room. Air, musty from having been long enclosed, hung in all the rooms, and the waste room behind the kitchen was littered with old useless papers. Among these I found a few paper-covered books, the pages of which were curled and damp: *The Abbot,* by Walter Scott, *The Devout Communicant,* and *The Memoirs of Vidocq.*[1] I liked the last best because its leaves were yellow. The wild garden behind the house contained a

Analyzing Visuals

Viewing and Interpreting How might the characters in this story have reacted to this poster if they had seen it hanging in Dublin?

Araby poster, Dublin.
Courtesy of the National Library of Ireland.

---

1. *The Abbott . . . Vidocq* (vee DUHK): respectively, a historical romance about Mary, Queen of Scots, by Sir Walter Scott; an 1813 religious manual written by a Franciscan friar; and the memoirs (though not actually written by François Vidocq) of a French criminal who later became a detective.

Vocabulary **imperturbable** (ihm puhr TUR buh buhl) *adj.:* calm; impassive.

central apple-tree and a few straggling bushes under one of which I found the late tenant's rusty bicycle-pump. He had been a very charitable priest; in his will he had left all his money to institutions and the furniture of his house to his sister.

When the short days of winter came dusk fell before we had well eaten our dinners. When we met in the street the houses had grown somber. The space of sky above us was the color of ever-changing violet and toward it the lamps of the street lifted their feeble lanterns. The cold air stung us and we played till our bodies glowed. Our shouts echoed in the silent street. The career[2] of our play brought us through the dark muddy lanes behind the houses where we ran the gauntlet[3] of the rough tribes from the cottages, to the back doors of the dark dripping gardens where odors arose from the ashpits, to the dark odorous stables where a coachman smoothed and combed the horse or shook music from the buckled harness. When we returned to the street light from the kitchen windows had filled the areas. If my uncle was seen turning the corner we hid in the shadow until we had seen him safely housed. Or if Mangan's sister came out on the doorstep to call her brother in to his tea we watched her from our shadow peer up and down the street. We waited to see whether she would remain or go in and, if she remained, we left our shadow and walked up to Mangan's steps resignedly. She was waiting for us, her figure defined by the light from the half-opened door. Her brother always teased her before he obeyed and I stood by the railings looking at her. Her dress swung as she moved her body and the soft rope of her hair tossed from side to side.

---

2. **career:** course; path.
3. **gauntlet** (GAWNT liht): series of challenges. Derived from *gatlopp*, Swedish for "running down a lane," the term originally referred to a form of military punishment in which a wrongdoer had to run between two rows of soldiers who struck him as he passed.

A **Reading Focus** Comparing and Contrasting The word *yet* in the last sentence of this paragraph signals a contrast. What is being contrasted in this sentence?

Vocabulary **somber** (SAHM buhr) *adj.:* gloomy.

Every morning I lay on the floor in the front parlor watching her door. The blind was pulled down to within an inch of the sash so that I could not be seen. When she came out on the doorstep my heart leaped. I ran to the hall, seized my books, and followed her. I kept her brown figure always in my eye and, when we came near the point at which our ways diverged, I quickened my pace and passed her. This happened morning after morning. I had never spoken to her, except for a few casual words, and yet her name was like a summons to all my foolish blood. **A**

Her image accompanied me even in places the most hostile to romance. On Saturday evenings when my aunt went marketing I had to go to carry some of the parcels. We walked through the flaring streets, jostled by drunken men and bargaining women, amid the curses of laborers, the shrill litanies[4] of shop-boys who stood on guard by the barrels of pigs' cheeks, the nasal chanting of street-singers, who sang a *come-all-you* about O'Donovan Rossa,[5] or a ballad about the troubles in our native land. These noises converged

---

4. **litanies:** repeated sales cries. Literally, a litany is a prayer composed of a series of specific invocations and responses.
5. *come-all-you* ...**Rossa:** A come-all-you (kuhm AL yuh) is a type of Irish ballad that usually begins "Come all you [young lovers, rebels, Irishmen, and so on]." O'Donovan Rossa was Jeremiah O'Donovan (1831–1915) of County Cork. He was active in Ireland's struggle against British rule in the mid-nineteenth century.

Literary Perspectives

Analyzing Credibility in Literature You learn much of what you know about a story from its narrator. Some stories have an omniscient, or all-knowing, narrator who objectively reports "reality." Other stories, such as "Araby," attempt to depict a character's unique, imperfect way of seeing the world. In these stories, the writer often uses first-person point of view, in which the character "speaks" in the first person. It is up to the reader to decide when the character is reporting something real and when the character is imagining or misinterpreting events.

As you read, be sure to notice the questions in the text, which will guide you in using this perspective.

in a single sensation of life for me: I imagined that I bore my chalice[6] safely through a throng of foes. Her name sprang to my lips at moments in strange prayers and praises which I myself did not understand. My eyes were often full of tears (I could not tell why) and at times a flood from my heart seemed to pour itself out into my bosom. I thought little of the future. I did not know whether I would ever speak to her or not or, if I spoke to her, how I could tell her of my confused adoration. But my body was like a harp and her words and gestures were like fingers running upon the wires. **B**

One evening I went into the back drawing-room in which the priest had died. It was a dark rainy evening and there was no sound in the house. Through one of the broken panes I heard the rain impinge upon the earth, the fine incessant needles of water playing in the sodden beds. Some distant lamp or lighted window gleamed below me. I was thankful that I could see so little. All my senses seemed to desire to veil themselves and, feeling that I was about to slip from them, I pressed the palms of my hands together until they trembled, murmuring: *O love! O love!* many times.

At last she spoke to me. When she addressed the first words to me I was so confused that I did not know what to answer. She asked me was I going to *Araby.* I forget whether I answered yes or no. It would be a splendid bazaar, she said; she would love to go.

—And why can't you? I asked.

While she spoke she turned a silver bracelet round and round her wrist. She could not go, she said, because there would be a retreat that week in her convent.[7] Her brother and two other boys were fighting for their caps and I was alone at the railings. She held one of the spikes, bowing her head toward me. The light from the lamp opposite our door caught the white curve of her neck, lit up her hair that rested there and, falling, lit up the hand upon the railing. It fell over one side of her dress and caught the white border of a petticoat, just visible as she stood at ease.

—It's well for you,[8] she said.

—If I go, I said, I will bring you something.

What innumerable follies laid waste my waking and sleeping thoughts after that evening! I wished to annihilate the tedious intervening days. I chafed against the work of school. At night in my bedroom and by day in the classroom her image came between me and the page I strove to read. The syllables of the word *Araby* were called to me through the silence in which my soul luxuriated and cast an Eastern enchantment over me. I asked for leave to go to the bazaar on Saturday night. My aunt was surprised and hoped it was not some Freemason[9] affair. I answered few questions in class. I watched my master's face pass from amiability to sternness; he hoped I was not beginning to idle. I could not call my wandering thoughts together. I had hardly any patience with the serious work of life which, now that it stood between me and my desire, seemed to me child's play, ugly monotonous child's play. **C**

On Saturday morning I reminded my uncle that I wished to go to the bazaar in the evening. He was fussing at the hallstand, looking for the hat-brush, and answered me curtly:

---

6. **chalice** (CHAL ihs): cup; specifically, the cup used for Holy Communion wine. Joyce's use of the term evokes the image of a young man on a sacred mission.
7. **retreat… convent:** temporary withdrawal from worldly life by the students and teachers at the convent school, to devote time to prayer, meditation, and study.

8. **It's well for you:** "You're lucky" (usually said enviously).
9. **Freemason:** The Freemasons are a secret society whose practices were originally drawn from those of British medieval stonemasons' guilds. In Ireland its members were almost exclusively Protestant and were often hostile to Catholics. The aunt apparently associates the bazaar with the mysterious practices of Freemasonry.

B **Literary Perspectives** Analyzing Credibility in Literature How does the narrator's description contrast with what is actually going on around him? How can you tell?

C **Reading Focus** Comparing and Contrasting How do the narrator's thoughts distract him from reality? Which of his worlds, imaginary or real, do you think he prefers?

Vocabulary **impinge** (ihm PIHNJ) *v.:* strike; touch.
annihilate (uh NY uh layt) *v.:* destroy; make nonexistent.
monotonous (muh NAHT uh nuhs) *adj.:* unvarying.

—Yes, boy, I know.

As he was in the hall I could not go into the front parlor and lie at the window. I left the house in bad humor and walked slowly toward the school. The air was pitilessly raw and already my heart misgave me.

When I came home to dinner my uncle had not yet been home. Still it was early. I sat staring at the clock for some time and, when its ticking began to irritate me, I left the room. I mounted the staircase and gained the upper part of the house. The high cold empty gloomy rooms liberated me and I went from room to room singing. From the front window I saw my companions playing below in the street. Their cries reached me weakened and indistinct and, leaning my forehead against the cool glass, I looked over at the dark house where she lived. I may have stood there for an hour, seeing nothing but the brown-clad figure cast by my imagination, touched discreetly by the lamplight at the curved neck, at the hand upon the railings and at the border below the dress.

When I came downstairs again I found Mrs. Mercer sitting at the fire. She was an old garrulous woman, a pawnbroker's widow, who collected used stamps for some pious purpose. I had to endure the gossip of the tea-table. The meal was prolonged beyond an hour and still my uncle did not come. Mrs. Mercer stood up to go: She was sorry she couldn't wait any longer, but it was after eight o' clock and she did not like to be out late, as the night air was bad for her. When she had gone I began to walk up and down the room, clenching my fists. My aunt said:

—I'm afraid you may put off your bazaar for this night of Our Lord.

At nine o' clock I heard my uncle's latchkey in the halldoor. I heard him talking to himself and heard the hallstand rocking when it had received the weight of his overcoat. I could interpret these signs. When he was midway through his dinner I asked him to give me the money to go to the bazaar. He had forgotten.

St. Patrick's Day Close, Dublin, by Walter Osborne.
Courtesy The National Gallery of Ireland.

—The people are in bed and after their first sleep now, he said.

I did not smile. My aunt said to him energetically:

—Can't you give him the money and let him go? You've kept him late enough as it is.

My uncle said he was very sorry he had forgotten. He said he believed in the old saying: *All work and no play makes Jack a dull boy.* He asked me where I was going and, when I had told him a second time he asked me did I know *The Arab's Farewell to his Steed.*[10] When I left the kitchen he was about to recite the opening lines of the piece to my aunt.

I held a florin[11] tightly in my hand as I strode down Buckingham Street toward the station. The sight of the streets thronged with buyers and glaring with gas recalled to me the purpose of my journey. I took my seat in a third-class carriage of a deserted train. After an intolerable delay the train moved out of the station slowly. It crept onward among ruinous houses and over the twinkling river. At Westland Row Station a crowd of people pressed to the carriage doors; but the porters moved them back, saying that it was a special train for the bazaar. I remained alone in the bare carriage. In a few minutes the train drew up beside an improvised wooden platform. I passed out on to the road and saw by the lighted dial of a clock that it was ten minutes to ten. In front of me was a large building which displayed the magical name.

I could not find any sixpenny entrance and, fearing that the bazaar would be closed, I passed in quickly through a turnstile, handing a shilling to a weary-looking man. I found myself in a big hall girdled at half its height by a gallery. Nearly all the stalls were closed and the greater part of the hall was in darkness. I recognized a silence like that which pervades a church after a service. I walked into the center of the bazaar timidly. A few people were gathered about the stalls which were still open. Before a curtain, over

which the words *Café Chantant*[12] were written in colored lamps, two men were counting money on a salver.[13] I listened to the fall of the coins.

Remembering with difficulty why I had come I went over to one of the stalls and examined porcelain vases and flowered tea-sets. At the door of the stall a young lady was talking and laughing with two young gentlemen. I remarked their English accents and listened vaguely to their conversation.

—O, I never said such a thing!

—O, but you did!

—O, but I didn't!

—Didn't she say that?

—Yes. I heard her.

—O, there's a... fib!

Observing me the young lady came over and asked me did I wish to buy anything. The tone of her voice was not encouraging; she seemed to have spoken to me out of a sense of duty. I looked humbly at the great jars that stood like eastern guards at either side of the dark entrance to the stall and murmured:

—No, thank you.

The young lady changed the position of one of the vases and went back to the two young men. They began to talk of the same subject. Once or twice the young lady glanced at me over her shoulder.

I lingered before her stall, though I knew my stay was useless, to make my interest in her wares seem the more real. Then I turned away slowly and walked down the middle of the bazaar. I allowed the two pennies to fall against the sixpence in my pocket. I heard a voice call from one end of the gallery that the light was out. The upper part of the hall was now completely dark. **(D)**

Gazing up into the darkness I saw myself as a creature driven and derided by vanity; and my eyes burned with anguish and anger. **(E)**

---

10. ***The Arab's... Steed:*** popular sentimental poem by the English writer Caroline Norton (1808–1877).

11. **florin:** British coin at the time worth the equivalent of about fifty cents.

12. ***Café Chantant*** (ka FAY SHAHN tahn): The name refers to a coffeehouse with musical entertainment.

13. **salver** (SAL vuhr): serving tray.

Vocabulary improvised (IHM pruh vyzd) *v.* used as *adj.*: made for the occasion from whatever is handy.
pervades (puhr VAYDZ) *v.*: spreads throughout.

(D) Reading Focus Comparing and Contrasting How does the reality of the Araby bazaar differ from what the boy imagined?

(E) Literary Focus Epiphany What does the boy realize about himself?

Applying Your Skills

Araby

Respond and Think Critically

Reading Focus

Quick Check

1. What clues does the story provide that the narrator is a man remembering his childhood from a mature <u>perspective</u>?

2. How often have the narrator and Mangan's sister spoken to each other?

3. What is the purpose of the narrator's quest—his journey to the bazaar?

Read with a Purpose

4. What did Araby turn out to be? What did the narrator find there?

Reading Skills: Comparing and Contrasting

5. Look back at your chart, in which you compared what the narrator imagines with what is real. How would you summarize the difference? Add a row to the bottom of the chart you made, and summarize the comparison.

Imagination	Reality
The word "Araby" fills him with an "Eastern enchantment."	He finds that the people who work there are ordinary.
Summary of comparison:	

Literary Focus

Literary Analysis

6. **Draw Conclusions** What conclusions can you draw about the uncle? What kind of person is he, and what problems may he have?

7. **Make Judgments** In what ways are the lives of the characters narrow, or restricted?

8. **Infer** How does the narrator deal with intrusions of reality into his fantasy: at the market, for example? What do his reactions tell you about him?

9. **Extend** There are many religious references in this story—for example, a dead priest, a chalice, the narrator's prayer-like utterances, and the bazaar's churchly silence. How do these references inform your understanding of the narrator's state of mind and quest?

10. **Literary Perspectives** How would you evaluate the story's ending? Is the narrator's description of his feelings realistic or exaggerated? Explain.

Literary Skills: Epiphany

11. **Analyze** What epiphany has the narrator experienced by the end of the story? What details support your answer?

Literary Skills Review: Tone

12. **Interpret** How would you describe the writer's **tone,** or attitude toward the characters and what happens to them? Cite specific textual examples.

Writing Focus

Think as a Reader/Writer

Use It in Your Writing Review your notes on Joyce's use of imagery to create places that seem real. Think of the most enchanting place you have ever been. Then, write a paragraph using imagery to describe it. Try to make your place seem real to the reader. Finally, share your description with a classmate.

What Do You Think Now? How does the narrator's experience of life in a dreary Dublin neighborhood shape his view of the world?

Vocabulary Development

✓ Vocabulary Check

Complete each of the following sentences with one of the Vocabulary words: *imperturbable, somber, impinge, annihilate, monotonous, garrulous, improvised, pervades.*

1. Do not let this unfortunate event _____ on your happiness.

2. Krista was determined to _____ the colony of ants living in her kitchen.

3. A bad odor _____ the garage where the puppy spent the night.

4. Keisha yawned; she found the speech dull and _____.

5. The other people at the horror movie screamed and covered their eyes, but Bruce was _____.

6. Raul used a tablecloth as a(n) _____ cape and pretended to fight a bull.

7. The doctor looked _____ when he told Megan she had broken both legs.

8. The _____ man at the bus stop would not stop talking to Marco.

Vocabulary Skills: Analogies

A **word analogy** is a formally written statement that compares two pairs of words. In a word analogy, the relationship between the first pair of words is the same as the relationship between the second pair of words. For example, *cool* and *chilly* have a synonymous relationship to each other, as do the words *mad* and *angry*. To express this relationship, you would write:

> COOL : CHILLY :: mad : angry

The colon (:) stands for the phrase "is related to." The double colon (::) between the two pairs of words stands for the phrase "in the same way that."

Here are two ways to read the analogy:

> COOL is related to CHILLY in the same way that *mad* is related to *angry.*
> COOL is to CHILLY as *mad* is to *angry.*

Two types of relationships frequently expressed in word analogies are **synonyms** and **antonyms.** The example used above (COOL : CHILLY :: mad : angry) expresses a synonymous relationship. The following word analogy expresses an antonymous, or opposite, relationship:

> SOILED : CLEAN :: careless : careful

Your Turn

Work with a partner to complete each analogy below with a Vocabulary word.

imperturbable   somber   monotonous
garrulous   improvised   pervades

1. EXCITING : THRILLING :: _____ : tedious.

2. BRIGHT : DULL :: _____ : uncommunicative

3. SPICY : BLAND :: _____ : festive

4. SMART : INTELLIGENT :: _____ : calm

5. RAMSHACKLE : STURDY :: _____ : rehearsed

6. FLOWS : RUNS :: _____ : permeates

Language Coach

Homographs There is yet another homograph for one of the words from the selection: *blind.* In addition to meaning "a window covering" or "unquestioning," what else can blind mean?

Academic Vocabulary

Write About

Write about the narrative <u>perspective</u> and point of view Joyce <u>exhibits</u> in this story.

SKILLS FOCUS Vocabulary Skills
Understand word analogies. **Writing
Skills** Describe a place; write autobigraphical
narratives. **Grammar Skills** Identify and
use independent clauses; identify and use
subordinate clauses.

Grammar Link

Independent and Subordinate Clauses

James Joyce uses sophisticated sentences—grammatically complex constructions with more than one clause. A **clause** is a group of words that contains a verb and its subject and that is used as part of a sentence. There are two types of clauses.

An **independent** clause expresses a complete thought and can stand by itself as a sentence.

> SUBJECT   VERB
> James Joyce wrote *Ulysses.*

A **subordinate clause** does not express a complete thought and cannot stand alone as a sentence.

> SUBJECT   VERB
> after he moved to Zurich

To function grammatically, a subordinate clause must be combined with an independent clause:

> James Joyce wrote *Ulysses* after he moved to Zurich.

Subordinate clauses can serve as adjectives, nouns, or adverbs in a sentence.

Your Turn

Circle the subordinate clause in each sentence below.

1. Joyce lived briefly in a former military fortification, where he began to write an autobiographical novel.
2. Sylvia Beach was an American who owned a bookstore in Paris.
3. Ezra Pound believed that Joyce's writing deserved to be published.

Writing Application Choose a piece of your own writing. Underline the independent and subordinate clauses. Be sure that you have varied your sentence patterns, and revise independent and subordinate clauses as necessary.

CHOICES

As you respond to the Choices, use the **Academic Vocabulary** words as appropriate: perspective, considerably, adapt, exhibit, inevitable.

REVIEW

Compare and Contrast Through Art

Write down everything you know from the story about the narrator's real world. Then, write down his expectations for Araby. Divide a large sheet of paper or poster board in half. On one half, create a visual representation of the narrator's real world. You may draw, paint, or create a collage. On the other half, create a visual representation of the narrator's idea of Araby. Exhibit your project for the class.

CONNECT

Write a Travel Brochure

From the narrator's perspective, Araby represents a place where his dreams will come true. Is there a place that you think would transform you if you could visit or live there? Research this exciting locale in your library or on the Internet. Then, write a travel brochure encouraging people to visit. Make it sound as alluring as possible.

EXTEND

Write a "Before and After" Essay

Timed └Writing We all have experienced epiphanies, those moments when we suddenly understand things in a new way. Think of an epiphany you have experienced. Then, write a short personal essay describing you and your life before and after the epiphany. Choose an epiphany that is not too personal and that you feel comfortable sharing with your classmates.

Learn It Online
Discover Joyce's influence on the modern world through these Internet links.

go.hrw.com   L12-1333   Go

Preparing to Read

The Book of Sand

What Do You Think?

How does experience shape our view of the world?

🕐 QuickTalk

In your *Reader/Writer Notebook,* write down a dependable reality of daily life, such as gravity. What would the world would be like if that reality shifted slightly—or simply no longer existed?

Jorge Luis Borges (1899–1986).

Jorge Luis Borges
(1899–1986)

A native of Argentina, Jorge Luis Borges (BOHR hehs) announced at age six that he intended to become a writer. He began working at his chosen profession immediately. At age nine, he translated Oscar Wilde's fairy tale "The Happy Prince" into Spanish. Borges later credited his father with inspiring his writing career. He felt that his father had made him aware of poetry, specifically of the idea that words can be powerful and symbolic, and not just a means of everyday communication.

A Cosmopolitan Life

Borges learned English at an early age from his English-born grandmother, and subsequently devoured his father's extensive library. He loved the horror stories of Edgar Allan Poe, the adventures of Robert Louis Stevenson, and the fairy tales in *The Thousand and One Nights.* Ironically, Borges first read the great Spanish classics *El Cid* and *Don Quixote* in English translations. Later, when he read *Don Quixote* in its original Spanish, he said it sounded like a bad translation!

The Borges family was traveling in Europe when World War I broke out. They took refuge in neutral Switzerland, where Borges attended school and adapted quickly to his new environment by learning three more languages: French, Latin, and German. After the war the family moved first to Italy, then to Spain, and finally back to Argentina.

Creating His Own World

Borges began his career as a poet, and he always considered himself a poet first and foremost. In the 1940s, however, Borges turned to experimental prose, writing stories about transparent tigers; wizards who conjure up visions in a bowl of ink; and encyclopedias that do not record events but cause them. The stories in *The Garden of Forking Paths* (1941) and *El Aleph* (1949) ignore plot and character and most of the usual elements of fiction, and instead blend fact and fantasy in a world of games and riddles, literary mystery, and philosophical inquiry.

Think About the Writer

How might Borges's extensive travels have helped develop his imagination?

Reader/Writer Notebook

Use your **RWN** to complete the activities for this selection.

Literary Focus

Paradox Statements or situations that contain two seemingly contradictory truths are called **paradoxes.** In forcing us to conceive of reality in new and different ways, paradoxes challenge the limits of our intellect. Borges was a master of paradox, in part because he set his outrageous events in an everyday context. In the following story, Borges drops his paradox into the lap of a harmless book lover who discovers that loving a book and hating a book can be infinitely the same thing.

Reading Focus

Making Predictions A **prediction** is a type of **inference,** a guess based on evidence. In a story that presents a mystery or a puzzle, we read carefully, looking for clues. We base our predictions on the characters and their situations as well as on our own experiences and knowledge about life. We typically make initial guesses early in a work and adjust them as the story unfolds to fit new events and information. Sometimes, despite our careful reading, what seems <u>inevitable</u> can turn out to be uncertain.

Into Action As you read "The Book of Sand," jot down any predictions you form. Later, you'll see if your predictions were true.

Predictions

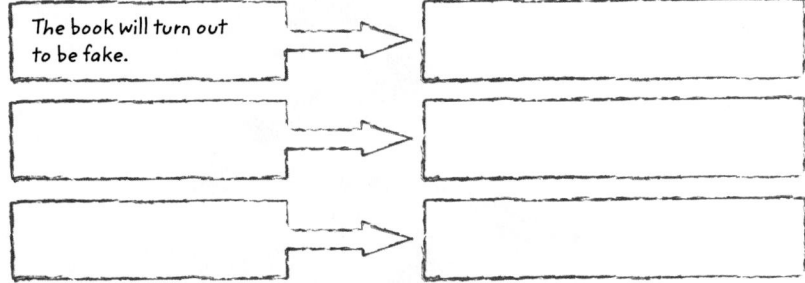

The book will turn out to be fake.

Vocabulary

pedantic (peh DAN tihk) *adj.:* showing an exaggerated concern for books, learning, and rules. *The old man adopted a pedantic tone with his visitor.*

discomfiture (dihs KUHM fih chuhr) *n.:* frustration; embarrassment. *His discomfiture was obvious from his faltering speech.*

caste (kast) *n.:* social class. *In India your caste is determined at birth.*

defiled (dih FYLD) *v.:* made unclean. *In turning the pages of the book with dirty hands, you defiled the pages.*

diabolic (dy uh BAHL ihk) *adj.:* of or having to do with evil or the devil. *Obsession can become diabolic if it causes people to lose their sanity.*

bibliophile (BIHB lee uh fyl) *n.:* one who loves books. *The old man was such a bibliophile that his apartment was filled with books.*

misanthropy (mih SAN thruh pee) *n.:* hatred for humankind. *Those who are afflicted with misanthropy often live solitary lives.*

artifice (AHRT uh fihs) *n.:* trickery; deception. *When he first saw the remarkable book, he thought there might be artifice involved.*

Writing Focus

Think as a Reader/Writer

Find It In Your Reading The mood, or feeling, in a literary work is called its **atmosphere.** In "The Book of Sand," Borges's descriptions and language evoke an atmosphere of mystery and dread. As you read, write in your *Reader/Writer Notebook* the words and phrases that you think contribute to the story's atmosphere.

Language Coach

Foreign Words Words and phrases in italics are often foreign. The phrase *more geometrico* is Latin and pronounced "MOH ray gee oh MEHT rih coh." In Latin, an *e* at the end of a word is always pronounced.

 Learn It Online
Discover more about Borges online.

go.hrw.com   L12-1335   **Go**

The Book of Sand

by **Jorge Luis Borges**   translated by **Andrew Hurley**

Read with a Purpose
Read to find out what the Book of Sand is and how it affects the narrator's life.

Build Background
Borges believed that reality consists not only of what we have actually seen and done, but also of what we have read and of what our reading has led us to imagine.

...thy rope of sands...
—George Herbert (1593–1633)

The line consists of an infinite number of points; the plane, of an infinite number of lines; the volume, of an infinite number of planes; the hypervolume, of an infinite number of volumes... No—this, *more geometrico*,[1] is decidedly not the best way to begin my tale. To say that the story is true is by now a convention of every fantastic tale; mine, nevertheless, is true. **A**

I live alone, in a fifth-floor apartment on Calle Belgrano.[2] One evening a few months ago, I heard a knock at my door. I opened it, and a stranger stepped in. He was a tall man, with blurred, vague features, or perhaps my nearsightedness made me see him that way. Everything about him spoke of honest poverty: he was dressed in gray, and carried a gray valise. I immediately sensed that he was a foreigner. At first I thought he was old; then I noticed that I had been misled by his sparse hair, which was blond, almost white, like the Scandinavians'. In the course of our conversation, which I doubt lasted more than an hour, I learned that he hailed from the Orkneys.[3]

---

1. *more geometrico:* in the geometrical manner.
2. **Calle Belgrano:** street in Buenos Aires.
3. **Orkneys:** group of islands off the northern coast of Scotland.

A **Literary Focus** **Paradox** If the opening sentences are not the best way to begin, why does the narrator begin with them anyway?

Head of a Man (Diego) (1964) by Alberto Giacometti. Konsthaus, Zurich, Switzerland, © 2006 Artists' Rights Society (ARS), New York, ADAGP, Paris.

I pointed the man to a chair. He took some time to begin talking. He gave off an air of melancholy, as I myself do now.

"I sell Bibles," he said at last.

"In this house," I replied, not without a somewhat stiff, pedantic note, "there are several English Bibles, including the first one, Wyclif's.[4] I also have Cipriano de Valera's,[5] Luther's[6] (which is, in literary terms, the worst of the lot), and a Latin copy of the Vulgate. As you see, it isn't exactly Bibles I might be needing."

After a brief silence he replied.

"It's not only Bibles I sell. I can show you a sacred book that might interest a man such as yourself. I came by it in northern India, in Bikaner."

He opened his valise and brought out the book. He laid it on the table. It was a clothbound octavo[7] volume that had clearly passed through many hands. I examined it; the unusual heft[8] of it surprised me. On the spine was printed *Holy Writ,* and then *Bombay.*

"Nineteenth century, I'd say," I observed.

"I don't know," was the reply. "Never did know."

I opened it at random. The characters were unfamiliar to me. The pages, which seemed worn and badly set, were printed in double columns, like a Bible. The text was cramped, and composed into versicles.[9]

At the upper corner of each page were Arabic numerals. I was struck by an odd fact: the even-numbered page would carry the number 40,514, let us say, while the odd-numbered page that followed it would be 999. I turned the page; the next page bore an eight-digit number. It also bore a small illustration, like those one sees in dictionaries: an anchor drawn in pen and ink, as though by the unskilled hand of a child.   **Ⓑ**

It was at that point that the stranger spoke again.

"Look at it well. You will never see it again."

There was a threat in the words, but not in the voice.

I took note of the page, and then closed the book. Immediately I opened it again. In vain I searched for the figure of the anchor, page after page. To hide my discomfiture, I tried another tack.

"This is a version of Scripture in some Hindu language, isn't that right?"

"No," he replied.

Then he lowered his voice, as though entrusting me with a secret.

"I came across this book in a village on the plain, and I traded a few rupees[10] and a Bible for it. The man who owned it didn't know how to read. I suspect he saw the Book of Books as an amulet.[11] He was of the lowest caste; people could not so much as step on his shadow without being defiled. He told me his book was called the Book of Sand because neither sand nor this book has a beginning or an end."

He suggested I try to find the first page.

I took the cover in my left hand and opened the book, my thumb and forefinger almost touching. It was impossible: several pages always lay between the

---

4. **Wyclif's Bible:** first English translation of the Bible. John Wycliffe (c. 1330–1384) took charge of the project and perhaps did some translating.

5. **Cipriano de Valera's:** Spanish translation of the Bible; Casiodoro de Reina (1520–1594) translated the Bible, and Cipriano de Valera (1531–1602) edited it.

6. **Luther's:** German translation of the Bible. Martin Luther (1483–1546) was the German priest who set in motion the Protestant Reformation.

7. **octavo:** book, the pages of which have been made from sheets of paper that have been folded eight times.

8. **heft:** heaviness.

9. **versicles:** little verses.

---

10. **rupees:** basic monetary unit of many Asian countries, including India, Pakistan, and Nepal.

11. **amulet:** ornament often inscribed with a magical incantation or symbol to protect the wearer from evil.

Vocabulary **pedantic** (peh DAN tihk) *adj.:* showing an exaggerated concern for books, learning, and rules.
discomfiture (dihs KUHM fih chuhr) *n.:* frustration; embarrassment.
caste (kast) *n.:* social class.
defiled (dih FYLD) *v.:* made unclean.

Ⓑ **Reading Focus** **Making Predictions** From the book's curious features, and from what you know of the narrator's character, what do you predict the narrator will do about the book?

cover and my hand. It was as though they grew from the very book.

"Now try to find the end."

I failed there as well.   C

"This can't be," I stammered, my voice hardly recognizable as my own.

"It can't be, yet it *is*," the Bible peddler said, his voice little more than a whisper. "The number of pages in this book is literally infinite. No page is the first page; no page is the last. I don't know why they're numbered in this arbitrary way, but perhaps it's to give one to understand that the terms of an infinite series can be numbered any way whatever."

Then, as though thinking out loud, he went on.

"If space is infinite, we are anywhere, at any point in space. If time is infinite, we are at any point in time."

His musings irritated me.

"You," I said, "are a religious man, are you not?"

C Literary Focus Paradox What is paradoxical about the book as the narrator describes it?

MATHEMATICS LINK

Infinity

In common parlance, infinity is defined as something without end, but in mathematics, infinity has a more precise definition. Although philosophers, mathematicians, and scientists have written about the concepts of infinity for more than two thousand years, infinity wasn't well defined mathematically until the late nineteenth century, when Georg Cantor developed the theory behind finite and infinite sets. In mathematical terms, infinity is something that is equal to some of its parts. For example, consider how all whole numbers (1, 2, 3, 4, and so on) can be matched with all even whole numbers (2, 4, 6, 8, and so on), implying that the number of whole numbers is equal to the number of even whole numbers.

Furthermore, infinities come in two sizes, the infinitely large and the infinitely small. The science journalist Peter Tyson explains: "As Jonathan Swift wrote, 'So, naturalists observe, a flea / Has smaller fleas that on him prey / And these have smaller still to bite 'em / And so proceed ad infinitum.' We may not be able to conceive of Swift's infinitesimal fleas, because reason insists they don't exist, but we can imagine ever smaller numbers without much trouble. It's no hardship, for example, to grasp the notion of an infinity of numbers stretching between, say, the numerals 2 and 3. Take half of the 1 that separates them,... then half of that half, then half of that half, and so proceed ad infinitum.... [Yet here's] another of those confounding paradoxes: the numerals 2 and 3 are separated by both a finite number (1) and an infinity of numbers."

Ask Yourself:

How might the study of infinity apply to science as well as to mathematics?

"Yes, I'm Presbyterian. My conscience is clear. I am certain I didn't cheat that native when I gave him the Lord's Word in exchange for his diabolic book."

I assured him he had nothing to reproach[12] himself for, and asked whether he was just passing through the country. He replied that he planned to return to his own country within a few days. It was then that I learned he was a Scot, and that his home was in the Orkneys. I told him I had great personal fondness for Scotland because of my love for Stevenson and Hume.[13]

"And Robbie Burns,"[14] he corrected.

As we talked I continued to explore the infinite book.

"Had you intended to offer this curious specimen to the British Museum, then?" I asked with feigned indifference.

"No," he replied, "I am offering it to you," and he mentioned a great sum of money.

I told him, with perfect honesty, that such an amount of money was not within my ability to pay. But my mind was working; in a few moments I had devised my plan.

"I propose a trade," I said. "You purchased the volume with a few rupees and the Holy Scripture; I will offer you the full sum of my pension, which I have just received, and Wyclif's black-letter[15] Bible. It was left to me by my parents."

"A black-letter Wyclif!" he murmured.

I went to my bedroom and brought back the money and the book. With a bibliophile's zeal he turned the pages and studied the binding.

"Done," he said.

---

12. **reproach:** criticize or censure.
13. **Stevenson and Hume:** Robert Louis Stevenson (1850–1894), Scottish author; David Hume (1711–1776), Scottish philosopher.
14. **Robbie Burns:** Robert Burns (1759–1796), Scottish poet.
15. **black-letter:** typeset used in early printed books.

I was astonished that he did not haggle. Only later was I to realize that he had entered my house already determined to sell the book. He did not count the money, but merely put the bills into his pocket.

We chatted about India, the Orkneys, and the Norwegian jarls[16] that had once ruled those islands. Night was falling when the man left. I have never seen him since, nor do I know his name.

I thought of putting the Book of Sand in the space left by the Wyclif, but I chose at last to hide it behind some imperfect volumes of the *Thousand and One Nights*.

I went to bed but could not sleep. At three or four in the morning I turned on the light. I took out the impossible book and turned its pages. On one, I saw an engraving of a mask. There was a number in the corner of the page—I don't remember now what it was—raised to the ninth power.

I showed no one my treasure. To the joy of possession was added the fear that it would be stolen from me, and to that, the suspicion that it might not be truly infinite. Those two points of anxiety aggravated my already habitual misanthropy. I had but few friends left, and those, I stopped seeing. A prisoner of the Book, I hardly left my house. I examined the worn binding and the covers with a magnifying glass, and rejected the possibility of some artifice. I found that the small illustrations were spaced at two-thousand-page intervals. I began noting them down in an alphabetized notebook, which was very soon filled. They never repeated themselves. At night, during the rare intervals spared me by insomnia,[17] I dreamed of the book. **Ⓓ**

Summer was drawing to a close, and I realized that the book was monstrous. It was cold consolation

---

16. **jarls:** Scandinavian nobles ranking directly below a king.
17. **insomnia:** inability to sleep.

Ⓓ Reading Focus **Making Predictions** Now that the narrator has acquired the book, what do you think will happen?

Viewing and Interpreting How does this painting illustrate the idea of a book with an "infinite" number of pages without depicting the book as thick or heavy?

Open Book (1930), by Paul Klee. Water-based paint and varnish over white lacquer on paper, mounted on canvas. Guggenheim Museum, New York.

to think that I, who looked upon it with my eyes and fondled it with my ten flesh-and-bone fingers, was no less monstrous than the book. I felt it was a nightmare thing, an obscene thing, and that it defiled and corrupted reality.

I considered fire, but I feared that the burning of an infinite book might be similarly infinite, and suffocate the planet in smoke.

I remembered reading once that the best place to hide a leaf is in the forest. Before my retirement I had worked in the National Library, which contained nine hundred thousand books; I knew that to the right of the lobby a curving staircase descended into the shadows of the basement, where the maps and periodicals are kept. I took advantage of the librarians' distraction to hide the Book of Sand on one of the library's damp shelves; I tried not to notice how high up, or how far from the door.

I now feel a little better, but I refuse even to walk down the street the library's on.

SKILLS FOCUS Literary Skills Analyze paradox; analyze irony. Reading Skills Make predictions as a strategy for comprehension. Vocabulary Skills

Demonstrate knowledge of literal meanings of words and their usage. Writing Skills Write to achieve a purpose; develop descriptions with sensory details.

The Book of Sand

Respond and Think Critically

Reading Focus

Quick Check

1. What can you infer about the book from its outward appearance?

2. Why doesn't the stranger give the narrator his name?

3. Why does the narrator come to feel that the book is "monstrous"?

Read with a Purpose

4. What did the Book of Sand turn out to be?

Reading Skills: Making Predictions

5. As you read "The Book of Sand," you made predictions about the story. Identify which of your predictions were true and which ones you changed because they were inaccurate.

✓ Vocabulary Check

Match the Vocabulary words with their definitions.

6. pedantic   a. evil
7. discomfiture   b. hatred of people
8. caste   c. trick
9. defiled   d. lover of books
10. diabolic   e. scholarly
11. bibliophile   f. dirtied
12. misanthropy   g. class
13. artifice   h. embarrassment

Literary Focus

Literary Analysis

14. Infer Why do you think Borges gave his story the same title as the book in the story?

15. Compare and Contrast Write two brief descriptions of the main character, one at the beginning of the story and the other at the end. What accounts for the differences in his perspective and personality?

16. Evaluate What dependable realities does Borges question in this story?

Literary Skills: Paradox

17. Analyze The illustrations in "The Book of Sand" are both there and not there. How would you explain this paradox? Identify and explain another paradox in the story.

Literary Skills Review: Situational Irony

18. Analyze When what actually happens is the opposite of what is expected or appropriate, situational irony occurs. How is the narrator's fear that the book will be stolen ironic?

Writing Focus

Think as a Reader/Writer

Use It in Your Writing Review your list of eerie words and phrases. In a paragraph, describe something scary or supernatural that you have witnessed or heard about. Try to create a spooky atmosphere in your description with carefully chosen words and phrases.

What Do
You
Think
Now   How did the narrator's experience with the Book of Sand affect his view of the world?

Come and Go

What Do You Think How does experience shape our view of the world?

 QuickTalk

With a partner, discuss what you believe makes life meaningful.

Samuel Beckett (1906–1989).

Samuel Beckett
(1906–1989)

Nobel Prize WINNER

Although Samuel Beckett was born in Ireland, he lived most of his life in France and wrote in both French and English. His plays are prime examples of the theater of the absurd.

Struggling Against Darkness

Beckett attended Trinity College in Dublin, where he was good at sports but did poorly in his studies during his first two years. In his third year he began studying French. He excelled, graduated first in his class in modern languages, and was awarded a two-year post at the École normale supérieure in Paris. Beckett seemed to be headed for a career in the classroom.

In Paris, Beckett met fellow Irishman James Joyce and joined the circle of young Irishmen who helped Joyce, whose eyesight was poor. In 1930, Beckett published his first book.

By the time Beckett returned to Dublin, he realized that he did not want to teach. He found life in Ireland with his family confining. There he suffered his first depression, a condition that was to recur over several years as he struggled for success and the means to return to Paris. In 1937, he decided that living in poverty was better than staying in Ireland, and he returned to Paris, where he met his wife, a French pianist.

After France fell to Germany in World War II, Beckett put aside his writing to join the French Resistance. His group was infiltrated, and Beckett and his wife fled for their lives. In 1945, they returned to Paris, where Beckett received the *Croix de Guerre* and the *Médaille de la Résistance.*

Success at Last

Beckett always considered himself primarily a novelist. "I turned to writing plays to relieve myself of the awful depression the prose had led me into," he explained. It was his play *Waiting for Godot* that made him famous at the age of forty-seven. He received the Nobel Prize in Literature in 1969.

Think About the Writer How do you think Beckett's depression might have affected his outlook on life?

Reader/Writer Notebook

Use your **RWN** to complete the activities for this selection.

Literary Focus

Theater of the Absurd The plays of a small group of playwrights working in the 1950s and early 1960s have come to be called the **theater of the absurd.** Although the plays are sometimes humorous, *absurd* in this context means "pointless." Absurdist playwrights believed that human life has no purpose, and their works illustrate this lack of purpose. The action of absurdist plays does not follow the familiar pattern of conflict, climax, and resolution, but circles back on itself to <u>exhibit</u> the futility of action. The point of an absurdist play's language is not to communicate the characters' thoughts and feelings, but to show that language is not adequate to communicate anything of value—or even that there is nothing of value to communicate.

Reading Focus

Drawing Inferences An **inference** is an intelligent guess based on clues in the text. *Come and Go* gives the audience or reader little information with which to work: no setting, no exposition, only the tersest possible dialogue—some of which is whispered incomprehensibly between the characters. Beckett relies on his audience to infer the meaning of his play.

Into Action As you read, use a chart like the one below to note each inference you make and the clues on which you based it.

Inference	Clues
The characters have met before.	Vi asks, "When did we three last meet?"

Writing Focus

Think as a Reader/Writer

Find It in Your Reading Beckett's language is stripped down to the bare essentials. He uses few literary devices. However, he does use **repetition**. As you read, make note of instances of repetition in the play.

TechFocus Imagine that you write a theater-review Web page or blog. As you read, take notes about the play, and then formulate an opinion about it. Try to judge it on its own terms—that is, determine what effect the playwright intended to create, and decide whether he succeeded.

Vocabulary

undeterminable (uhn dih TUR muh nuh buhl) *adj.*: not able to be measured or decided. *The setting of the play is undeterminable.*

erect (ih REHKT) *adj.*: upright. *The actresses stand erect for their entrances and exits.*

appalled (uh PAWLD) *v.* used as *adj.*: dismayed. *Many in the audience were appalled at the playwright's bleak outlook on life.*

resume (rih ZOOM) *v.*: begin again. *The play will resume after the intermission.*

successive (suhk SEHS ihv) *adj.*: following in consecutive order. *The players were so popular, they made their third successive bow.*

accommodate (uh KAHM uh dayt) *v.*: provide room for. *The theater could accommodate five hundred people.*

compatible (kuhm PAT uh buhl) *adj.*: able to exist or work together. *The two actors could not appear in the same play because their styles were not compatible.*

Language Coach

Prefixes *un*– and *in*– The prefixes *un*– and *in*– mean "not" or "the opposite of." *Un*– appears in the Vocabulary word *undeterminable*. To which Vocabulary word can you add the prefix *in*–? With the prefix, what does the word mean?

 Learn It Online
Increase your vocabulary knowledge online with Word Watch.

go.hrw.com | L12-1343 | **Go**

DRAMA

Come *and* Go

by **Samuel Beckett**

> Read with a Purpose Read to find out how the characters feel about their lives.

Cast of Characters

FLO
VI
RU
(**Age undeterminable**)

Sitting center side by side stage right to left FLO, VI, *and* RU. *Very erect, facing front, hands clasped in laps.*

Silence.

VI: Ru.
RU: Yes.
VI: Flo.
FLO: Yes.
VI: When did we three last meet?
RU: Let us not speak.

Silence.

Exit VI right.

Silence.

FLO: Ru.
RU: Yes.
FLO: What do you think of Vi?
RU: I see little change. (FLO *moves to center seat, whispers in* RU's *ear.* Appalled.)

Vocabulary **undeterminable** (uhn dih TUR muh nuh buhl) *adj.*: not able to be measured or decided.
erect (ih REHKT) *adj.*: upright.
appalled (uh PAWLD) *v.* used as *adj.*: dismayed.

1344 Unit 6 • Collection 13

Oh! (*They look at each other.* FLO *puts her finger to her lips.*) Does she not realize? **Ⓐ**

FLO: God grant not.

Enter VI. FLO and RU turn back front, resume pose. VI sits right. Silence. **Ⓑ**

FLO: Just sit together as we used to, in the playground at Miss Wade's.
RU: On the log.

Silence.

Exit FLO left.

Silence.

RU: Vi.
VI: Yes.
RU: How do you find Flo?
VI: She seems much the same. (RU *moves to center seat, whispers in* VI's *ear. Appalled.*) Oh! (*They look at each other.* RU *puts her finger to her lips.*) Has she not been told? **Ⓒ**
RU: God forbid.

Enter FLO. RU and VI turn back front, resume pose. FLO sits left.

RU: Holding hands . . . that way. **Ⓓ**
FLO: Dreaming of . . . love.

Silence.

Exit RU right.

Silence.

VI: Flo.
FLO: Yes.
VI: How do you think Ru is looking?
FLO: One sees little in this light. (VI *moves center seat, whispers in* FLO's *ear. Appalled.*) Oh! (*They look at each other.* VI *puts her finger to her lips.*) Does she not

---

Ⓐ Reading Focus **Drawing Inferences** What can you infer from this exchange and Flo's earlier question about Vi? Is your inference general or specific?

Ⓑ Literary Focus **Theater of the Absurd** How does the play so far differ from other plays you have read or seen?

Ⓒ Reading Focus **Drawing Inferences** Do these lines change or add to your inference about Vi? What can you infer about Flo?

Ⓓ Literary Focus **Theater of the Absurd** What earlier part of the conversation does this line continue? Why don't you think the playwright makes the connection clear?

Vocabulary **resume** (rih ZOOM) *v.:* begin again.

Appalled.) Oh! (*They look at each other.* VI *puts her finger to her lips.*) Does she not know? **E**

VI: Please God not.

> Enter RU. VI *and* FLO *turn back front, resume pose.* RU *sits right. Silence.*

VI: May we not speak of the old days? (*Silence.*) Of what came after? (*Silence.*) Shall we hold hands in the old way?

> *After a moment they join hands as follows :* VI's *right hand with* RU's *right hand.* VI's *left hand with* FLO's *left hand,* FLO's *right hand with* RU's *left hand,* VI's *arms being above* RU's *left arm and* FLO's *right arm. The three pairs of clasped hands rest on the three laps.*

> *Silence.*

FLO: I can feel the rings.

> *Silence.* **F**

Notes

Successive *positions*

1	FLO	VI	RU
2	FLO		RU
		FLO	RU
3	VI	FLO	RU
4	VI		RU
	VI	RU	
5	VI	RU	FLO
6	VI		FLO
		VI	FLO
7	RU	VI	FLO

E **Reading Focus** Drawing Inferences Do these lines change or add to your inferences about Vi and Flo? What do you now understand about all three characters?

F **Literary Focus** Theater of the Absurd Why do you think the play ends with silence rather than with Vi's last line? What feeling do you have about the characters' lives and about life in general at the end of the play?

Vocabulary **successive** (suhk SEHS ihv) *adj.*: following in consecutive order.

Hands

RU   VI   FLO

Analyzing Visuals

Viewing and Interpreting What is the effect of the characters' holding hands here? How can FLO "feel the rings?"

Come and Go, directed by Annie Ryan, with Barbara Brennan, Susan Fitzgerald, and Bernadette McKenna. London, 2006.

Lighting

Soft, from above only and concentrated on playing area. Rest of stage as dark as possible.

Costume

Full-length coats, buttoned high, dull violet (RU), dull red (VI), dull yellow (FLO). Drab nondescript hats with enough brim to shade faces. Apart from color differentiation three figures as alike as possible. Light shoes with rubber soles. Hands made up to be as visible as possible. No rings apparent.

Seat

Narrow bench-like seat, without back, just long enough to accommodate three figures almost touching. As little visible as possible. It should not be clear what they are sitting on.

Exits

The figures are not seen to go off stage. They should disappear a few steps from lit area. If dark not sufficient to allow this, recourse should be had to screens or drapes as little visible as possible. Exits and entrances slow, without sound of feet.

Ohs

Three very different sounds.

Voices

As low as compatible with audibility. Colorless except for three "ohs" and two lines following.

Vocabulary **accommodate** (uh KAHM uh dayt) *v.:* provide room for.
compatible (kuhm PAT uh buhl) *adj.:* able to exist or work together.

Respond and Think Critically

Reading Focus

Quick Check

1. What do you think "Miss Wade's" was?

2. How long do you think it has been since the characters last met?

3. What has happened to the three women since "the old days"?

4. Are the women close friends? Explain.

Read with a Purpose

5. How do you think the characters feel about their lives? Why do you think so?

Reading Skills: Drawing Inferences

6. As you read the play, you used a graphic organizer to note the inferences you made and the clues you used to make them. Now, add a box below the column of inferences, and use it to write a sentence that you feel expresses the theme, or meaning, of the play.

Inference	Clues
Theme	

Literary Focus

Literary Analysis

7. **Interpret** Why do you think Beckett titles his play *Come and Go*?

8. **Infer** What do you think the characters whisper to one another? Do they each whisper the same thing or something different?

9. **Draw Conclusions** Have the characters' dreams of love been fulfilled? Explain.

10. **Compare and Contrast** Do the characters differ from one another in any significant way? Give examples from the play to support your response.

11. **Make Judgments** Do you think that the phrase "less is more" applies to this play? Explain why or why not.

Literary Skills: Theater of the Absurd

12. **Evaluate** What features of the play contribute to a sense of absurdity, or pointlessness?

Literary Skills Review: Stage Directions

13. **Analyze** The playwright's instructions for staging the play—where the characters are on stage, what they wear, what they do, what the stage looks like, and so on—are called **stage directons.** Why do you think Beckett's stage directions are so specific? How do the stage directions reinforce the play's meaning? Give specific examples.

Writing Focus

Think as a Reader/Writer

Use It in Your Writing Now it's your turn to write terse dialogue like Beckett's that includes some repetition. Start by writing a conversation between two people. Then, cross out everything that is not essential to its meaning. Include, however, the repetition of a key word or phrase. Finally, rewrite your stripped-down dialogue, and share it with a partner.

What Do You Think Now? How do you think the characters' experiences shape their views of life? Remember that you will have to infer most of their experience and their current views.

SKILLS FOCUS **Literary Skills** Analyze
the theater of the absurd; analyze elements of drama. **Reading Skills** Draw
inferences. **Writing Skills** Write biographical narratives; compare literary texts; write
to express; draw conclusions when writing.
Vocabulary Skills Identify and correctly use
synonyms.

Vocabulary Development

Vocabulary Check

Complete each sentence with one
of the Vocabulary words.

undeterminable
erect
appalled
resume
successive
accommodate
compatible

1. Our team has won five
   _____ championships.

2. Jan was _____ when she saw
   that she had failed the class.

3. Dale's new software is not _____ with his old
   computer.

4. The players will _____ their computer game
   after the pizza arrives.

5. The music was so loud and distorted that the
   lyrics were _____.

6. In yoga, Kai learned to straighten his spine and
   stand _____.

7. A ramp is being added to the school's entrance
   to _____ wheelchairs.

Vocabulary Skills: Synonyms

Part of the skill of a good writer lies in choosing the
right word among many with similar meanings. Words
that have similar meanings are called synonyms.

Your Turn

Using a thesaurus, find at least one synonym for each
of the Vocabulary words listed at the top of the page.

Language Coach

Prefixes *un-* and *in-* Which prefix can be affixed
to these Vocabulary words and related words?

erect   appalled   successive   accommodating

How does the prefix change each word's meaning?

CHOICES

As you respond to the Choices, use the **Academic Vocabulary**
words as appropriate: adapt, considerably, exhibit, inevitable,
perspective.

REVIEW
Write a Psychological Profile

Based on the play and the information in Meet the
Writer, draw inferences about Beckett as a person.
What do you think he was like? Make inferences
about how his struggle with depression affected his
perspective on life and influenced his writing. Check
your inferences by researching Beckett in your library
or on the Internet. Then, write a short psychological
profile of the playwright.

CONNECT
Create a Theater Review Web Page

TechFocus Design your own theater review Web
page or blog. Then, look at your notes and opinions
about *Come and Go*. Post a short review in which
you judge the play on its own terms. Then, offer your
classmates a chance to post their comments about
your review and about the play.

EXTEND
Compare the Theater of the Absurd

Research the theater of the
absurd, and choose a representative play to read on your
own. Write a short paper
comparing and contrasting
this play with *Come and Go*,
and share your findings with
your classmates.

Poster advertising a production of
Eugene Ionesco's *Rhinoceros*.

Learn It Online
Improve your vocabulary skills with *WordSharp* at

| go.hrw.com | L12-1349 | Go |

That's All

What Do You Think?

How does experience shape our view of the world?

QuickTalk

Think of an everyday conversation that you often have with a parent, sibling, or friend. For example, perhaps you and a friend often discuss plans for the weekend. In your *Reader/Writer Notebook*, write a few lines of this conversation in dialogue form.

Harold Pinter (c. 1970).

MEET THE WRITER

Harold Pinter
(1930–   )

Nobel Prize WINNER

Harold Pinter, an avowed disciple of Beckett and probably the most influential of the contemporary English playwrights, is on the fringe of absurdist theater. While Beckett's absurdist drama often deals with grotesque characters and bizarre settings, Pinter generally gives us more or less real settings and identifiable characters speaking everyday language. The whole, however, is stylized in a manner that is now called Pinteresque.

Actor, Playwright, and Director

Pinter was born in East London. He attended drama school briefly and later worked as an actor on television and the stage. His first play, *The Room,* appeared in 1957. In 1965, his play *The Homecoming* was produced by the Royal Shakespeare Company. In addition to writing for the stage, Pinter has written many screenplays. He has adapted his plays for radio and television and has directed productions of his own plays as well as those of others.

A Different Kind of Theater

Pinter presents a world in which reality is menacing, pregnant pauses (all carefully indicated by Pinter) are frightening, and banal speech is full of mystery. Also, unlike traditional plays, Pinter's plays do not probe the complex psychology of character. Instead, Pinter's characters are often without pasts—or they have contradictory pasts.

Pinter's recurrent themes are "time, memory, and the power of the past over the present." Many of his characters are haunted by some recollection, whether true or imaginary. The director Peter Hall has said that enigma is at the heart of Pinter's plays and that audiences must piece together the story in order to judge it.

Pinter, who has been politically active throughout his career, announced in 2005 that he would no longer write plays but would devote himself to politics and poetry. Later that year, Pinter won the Nobel Prize in Literature.

Think About the Writer

How do you think Pinter's experience as an actor might have affected his playwriting?

Reader/Writer Notebook

Use your **RWN** to complete the activities for this selection.

Literary Focus

Dialogue Writers use **dialogue**—a conversation between two or more characters— to advance the plot or pattern of the work; to present an interplay of ideas and personalities; and to reveal the background, occupation, or social level of the characters through tone and dialect.

You are already an expert at analyzing dialogue. Every day you analyze conversations for a wealth of spoken and unspoken information. Here are some questions you subconsciously consider:

- What can I infer about the speaker's background?
- How does the speaker feel about what he or she is saying?
- What does the speaker avoid saying?
- What do the speaker's silences and pauses imply?
- Is the speaker saying what he or she really thinks?

The play you are about to read focuses on both what is said and unsaid.

Language Coach

British Phrases This short play contains some British phrases that may be unfamiliar to you. Take a look at these two phrases:

put on the kettle: prepare tea for a visitor

come round: come over to visit

If you are uncertain of the meaning of any idiomatic phrases in the play, check with your teacher.

Reading Focus

Understanding Patterns of Organization Pinter organizes his short play as a dialogue between two people. He primarily structures the dialogue around repetition and pauses.

Into Action As you read, use a chart to record patterns in the dialogue.

Patterns	Observations
how the sketch begins	In mid-conversation
how the conversation is balanced between speakers	
repetition and how it varies	
pattern of pauses and how the pattern shifts	

Writing Focus

Think as a Reader/Writer

Find It in Your Reading Writers <u>adapt</u> words and phrases from everyday speech to make their dialogue sound more natural. Note in your *Reader/Writer Notebook* how the sentence structure, word choice, repetition, and pauses in the play mimic everyday speech (and how they vary from it) and what they reveal about the speakers.

Learn It Online
Listen to an audio performance of this play online:

go.hrw.com   L12-1351   **Go**

Analyzing Visuals

Viewing and Interpreting How does this image reflect the ordinary nature of the dialogue in the play? How might the women respond to each other here?

That's All

by **Harold Pinter**

Read with a Purpose
Read to discover the emotion and meaning that lie beneath the surface of the mundane dialogue in this play.

Build Background
Pinter's dialogue is the hallmark of his art. He has taken everyday speech and stylized it to the point where it becomes a kind of poetry. His dialogue is filled with repetitions and pauses; it has been described as an evasion of communication. Pinter believes that people communicate by their silence—that what is not said is often more important than what is said. The following revue sketch titled *That's All* is one of five comedy sketches first presented on BBC Radio in 1964. This is the entire text.

Mrs. A. I always put the kettle on about that time.

Mrs. B. Yes. *(Pause.)*

Mrs. A. Then she comes round.

Mrs. B. Yes. *(Pause.)*

Mrs. A. Only on Thursdays.

Mrs. B. Yes. *(Pause.)*

Mrs. A. On Wednesdays I used to put it on. When she used to come round. Then she changed it to Thursdays.

Mrs. B. Oh yes.

Mrs. A. After she moved. When she used to live round the corner, then she always came in on Wednesdays, but then when she moved she used to come down to the butcher's on Thursdays. She couldn't find a butcher up there.

Mrs. B. No.

Mrs. A. Anyway, she decided she'd stick to her own butcher. Well, I thought, if she can't find a butcher, that's the best thing.

Mrs. B. Yes. *(Pause.)* Ⓐ

Ⓐ **Literary Focus** Dialogue In plays, characters are revealed through their words and actions. What have you learned about the characters of Mrs. A and Mrs. B based on their dialogue so far?

Opposite: Spectators at an archery match in the Forest of Arden (1950), Warwickshire, England.

Mrs. A. So she started to come down on Thursdays. I didn't know she was coming down on Thursdays until one day I met her in the butcher.

Mrs. B. Oh yes.

Mrs. A. It wasn't my day for the butcher. I don't go to the butcher on Thursday.

Mrs. B. No, I know. *(Pause.)*

Mrs. A. I go on Friday.

Mrs. B. Yes. *(Pause.)*

Mrs. A. That's where I see you.

Mrs. B. Yes. *(Pause.)*

Mrs. A. You're always in there on Fridays.

Mrs. B. Oh yes. *(Pause.)*

Mrs. A. But I happened to go in for a bit of meat, it turned out to be a Thursday. I wasn't going in for my usual weekly on Friday. I just slipped in, the day before.

Mrs. B. Yes. **B**

Mrs. A. That was the first time I found out she couldn't find a butcher up there, so she decided to come back here, once a week, to her own butcher.

Mrs. B. Yes.

Mrs. A. She came on Thursday so she'd be able to get meat for the weekend Lasted her till Monday, then from Monday to Thursday they'd have fish. She can always buy cold meat, if they want a change.

Mrs. B. Oh yes. *(Pause.)* **C**

Mrs. A. So I told her to come in when she came down after she'd been to the butcher's and I'd put a kettle on. So she did. *(Pause.)*

Mrs. B. Yes. *(Pause.)*

Mrs. A. It was funny because she always used to come in Wednesdays. *(Pause.)* Still, it made a break. *(Long pause.)*

Mrs. B. She doesn't come in no more, does she? *(Pause.)*

Mrs. A. She comes in. She doesn't come in so much, but she comes in. *(Pause.)*

Mrs. B. I thought she didn't come in. *(Pause.)* **D**

Mrs. A. She comes in. *(Pause.)* She just doesn't come in so much. That's all.

B Reading Focus Understanding Patterns of Organization
This dialogue is very regular. Mrs. A speaks, and then Mrs. B responds briefly. How is this pattern the same as or different from the conversations you have every day?

C Reading Focus Understanding Patterns of Organization
How do the frequent pauses contribute to the conversation?

D Literary Focus Dialogue Why do you think Mrs. B suddenly takes a more active role in the conversation? What is the meaning of her remark?

SKILLS FOCUS **Literary Skills** Analyze dialogue; analyze elements of drama. **Reading Skills** Analyze patterns of organization. **Writing Skills** Use dialogue effectively.

Respond and Think Critically

Reading Focus

Quick Check

1. Summarize Mrs. A and Mrs. B's conversation.
2. How do you picture Mrs. A and Mrs. B? Why?

Read with a Purpose

3. What is the underlying meaning and emotion in the dialogue?

Reading Skills: Understanding Patterns of Organization

You used a chart to record patterns in the dialogue. Now, add a column, and explain the effect of the patterns.

Patterns	Observations	Effect
How sketch begins	In mid-conversation	It engages us to piece together what's missing
How conversation is balanced between speakers		
Repetition and how it varies		
Pattern of pauses and how the pattern shifts		

Literary Focus

Literary Analysis

4. **Compare and Contrast** How are the two characters distinguished from each other by what they say? Why are they identified by letters of the alphabet?
5. **Analyze** What do you learn about Mrs. A, Mrs. B, and the woman they discuss?

6. **Interpret** Why do you think Pinter chose "That's All" as the title of his play?
7. **Compare and Contrast** How is the dialogue in *That's All* like and unlike conversations that you hear every day? How is the dialogue like a poem?
8. **Interpret** *That's All* was first performed on the radio. Explain how a radio performance of the sketch would differ from a stage performance.
9. **Analyze** What might be Pinter's theme?

Literary Skills: Dialogue

10. **Analyze** The play begins with a special form of dialogue called **stichomythia**, wherein two speakers in a verbal duel alternate speeches of a single line. How does this form of dialogue help characterize Mrs. A?

Literary Skills Review: Exposition

11. **Analyze** In traditional drama, much of the first scene provides **exposition**—an introduction to the play's characters, setting, and major conflict. How does the lack of exposition in this play affect the audience?

Writing Focus

Think as a Reader/Writer

Use It in Your Writing Look over your notes about sentence structure, word choice, repetition, and pauses in Pinter's dialogue. Using conversational patterns familiar to you, write a brief dialogue between two people discussing a third person. Try to shape all three characters through what is said and unsaid.

What sort of life experiences do these women discuss? How do these experiences affect their worldview?

Preparing to Read

No Witchcraft for Sale

What Do You Think?

How does experience shape our view of the world?

QuickTalk

What clashes of cultures trouble the world today? With a partner, discuss the usual causes of these cases of cultural strife. Record your thoughts in your *Reader/Writer Notebook*.

Doris Lessing at the Edinburgh International Book Festival, Edinburgh, Scotland, UK (2001).

MEET THE WRITER

Doris Lessing
(1919–)

Nobel Prize WINNER

Doris Lessing was born in Persia (now Iran) to British parents who had fled England to escape what they saw as its narrowness and provincialism. When she was five, the family moved yet again, this time to a three-thousand-acre farm in Southern Rhodesia (now Zimbabwe). The farm employed some thirty to fifty black African laborers, who each earned the equivalent of about $1.50 a month and lived in mud huts with no sanitation.

Searching for Direction

In Africa, Lessing's mother was often ill and her father grew increasingly eccentric. A lonely child, Lessing educated herself by reading the classics of European and American fiction.

At fourteen, Lessing left school and went to work in Salisbury, the capital of Southern Rhodesia, first as a nursemaid and then as a stenographer and telephone operator. Salisbury had a white population of about ten thousand and a larger black population that Lessing discovered "didn't count." When her first marriage collapsed, she entered radical politics. At twenty-six, she married again, but that marriage also ended in divorce.

An Instrument of Change

"I can't remember a time when I didn't want to come to England," she recalled. In 1949, she left Africa for England with her two-year-old son and a manuscript of her first novel, *The Grass Is Singing* (1950). The book, which depicts the complex relationship between a white farmer's wife and her black servant, was one of the earliest novels about racial inequality in Africa. Lessing's most widely read and discussed book is *The Golden Notebook* (1962), an ambitious and complex work that explores politics, mental illness, and women's issues in modern life.

Lessing was awarded the Nobel Prize in Literature in 2007. Her work reflects her belief that she has the responsibility to be "an instrument of change." "It is not merely a question of preventing evil," she says "but of strengthening a vision of a good which may defeat the evil."

Think About the Writer

How might Lessing's childhood in Africa have influenced her work?

Reader/Writer Notebook

Use your **RWN** to complete the activities for this selection.

Literary Focus

Theme Most fiction can be categorized as one of two types: escape fiction or interpretive fiction. **Escape fiction** is pure entertainment; it gives us pleasure and helps us temporarily escape from the world. Theme is not a primary element in escape fiction. **Interpretive fiction,** on the other hand, is not meant to help us escape from the world but rather to help us understand it better. Even if it is fantasy, interpretive fiction gives us a different <u>perspective</u> on what it means to be human. This truth about life revealed in a story is called **theme.**

Lessing's story is an example of interpretive fiction. As you will see, a powerful theme does not have to come from a complex story. Lessing's tale is simple but has a forceful, provocative, and timely theme.

Literary Perspectives Apply the literary <u>perspective</u> described on page 1359 as you read this story.

Reading Focus

Identifying Historical Context Regardless of whether a story is escape fiction or interpretive fiction, it has a **historical context.** (In fact, many readers choose fiction such as detective novels and romances because of their historical context.) Lessing's tale is set in Southern Rhodesia at a time when the British ruled that part of Africa. The servants in the story are black Africans; the Farquars are part of the British ruling class.

Into Action As you read, consider how the characters and their conflicts are products of a particular historical context. In your *Reader/Writer Notebook,* use an idea web like the one below to record details.

Writing Focus

Think as a Reader/Writer

Find It in Your Reading Lessing presents her characters by using a few strong descriptive words: Mrs. Farquar felt "she had achieved a very great thing"; Teddy had "miraculous fair hair and Northern blue eyes." In your *Reader/Writer Notebook,* record some of the words Lessing uses to delineate her characters.

Vocabulary

reverently (REHV uhr uhnt lee) *adv.:* with great respect or awe, as for something sacred. *Gideon reverently held the child's lustrous curls.*

efficacy (EHF uh kuh see) *n.:* ability to produce a desired effect. *Mrs. Farquar had heard of the efficacy of native herbs.*

perfunctory (puhr FUHNGK tuhr ee) *adj.:* halfhearted; disinterested. *The scientist was somewhat perfunctory as he explained the benefits of the new drug.*

annulled (uh NUHLD) *v.:* erased; canceled. *The Farquars' anger annulled the guilt they felt toward Gideon.*

perversely (puhr VURS lee) *adv.:* disagreeably; contrarily. *Because the family did not understand Gideon's culture, they considered him to be perversely obstinate.*

Language Coach

Suffix –ly The suffix –ly is added to some adjectives to form adverbs, words that describe verbs, adjectives, or other adverbs. What two Vocabulary words are adverbs formed by adding –ly to an adjective? What verb does each adverb describe in the sample sentences above? How could you form an adverb out of the adjective *inevitable*?

 Learn It Online
Jump into this story with the video introduction online.

go.hrw.com   L12-1357

No Witchcraft for Sale

by **Doris Lessing**

Read with a Purpose
As you read, think about how political realities affect human relationships.

Build Background
In her preface to *African Stories* (1964), the collection from which this story is taken, Lessing writes: "If people had been prepared to listen, two decades earlier, to the small, but shrill-enough, voices crying out for the world's attention, perhaps the present suffering in South Africa and Southern Rhodesia could have been prevented. Britain, who is responsible, became conscious of her responsibility too late; and now the tragedy must play itself out."

In 1980, after years of conflict, Southern Rhodesia emerged as the Republic of Zimbabwe under the leadership of a black African, Robert Mugabe.

This story, which is not about witchcraft at all, reads like a contemporary parable.

The Farquars had been childless for years when little Teddy was born; and they were touched by the pleasure of their servants, who brought presents of fowls and eggs and flowers to the homestead when they came to rejoice over the baby, exclaiming with delight over his downy golden head and his blue eyes. They congratulated Mrs. Farquar as if she had achieved a very great thing, and she felt that she had—her smile for the lingering, admiring natives was warm and grateful.

Later, when Teddy had his first haircut, Gideon the cook picked up the soft gold tufts from the ground, and held them reverently in his hand. Then he smiled at the little boy and said: "Little Yellow Head." That became the native name for the child. Gideon and Teddy were great friends from the first. When Gideon had finished his work, he would lift Teddy on his shoulders to the shade of a big tree, and play with him there, forming curious little toys from twigs and leaves and grass, or shaping animals from wetted soil. When Teddy learned to walk it was often Gideon who crouched before him, clucking encouragement, finally catching him when he fell, tossing him up in the air till they both became breathless with laughter. Mrs.

Vocabulary **reverently** (REHV uhr uhnt lee) *adv.*: with great respect or awe, as for something sacred.

Farquar was fond of the old cook because of his love for her child.

There was no second baby; and one day Gideon said: "Ah, missus, missus, the Lord above sent this one; Little Yellow Head is the most good thing we have in our house." Because of that "we" Mrs. Farquar felt a warm impulse toward her cook; and at the end of the month she raised his wages. He had been with her now for several years; he was one of the few natives who had his wife and children in the compound and never wanted to go home to his kraal,[1] which was some hundreds of miles away. Sometimes a small piccanin[2] who had been born the same time as Teddy, could be seen peering from the edge of the bush, staring in awe at the little white boy with his miraculous fair hair and Northern blue eyes. The two little children would gaze at each other with a wide, interested gaze, and once Teddy put out his hand curiously to touch the black child's cheeks and hair. **Ⓐ**

Gideon, who was watching, shook his head wonderingly, and said: "Ah, missus, these are both children, and one will grow up to be a baas,[3] and one will be a servant"; and Mrs. Farquar smiled and said sadly, "Yes, Gideon, I was thinking the same." She sighed. "It is God's will," said Gideon, who was a mission boy.[4] The Farquars were very religious people; and this shared feeling about God bound servant and masters even closer together.

Teddy was about six years old when he was given a scooter, and discovered the intoxications of speed. All day he would fly around the homestead, in and out of flowerbeds, scattering squawking chickens and irritated dogs, finishing with a wide dizzying arc into the kitchen door. There he would cry: "Gideon, look at me!" And Gideon would laugh and say: "Very clever, Little Yellow Head." Gideon's youngest son, who was now a herdsboy, came especially up from the compound to see the scooter. He was afraid to come near it, but Teddy showed off in front of him. "Piccanin," shouted Teddy, "get out of my way!" And he raced in circles around the black child until he was frightened, and fled back to the bush.

"Why did you frighten him?" asked Gideon, gravely reproachful.

Teddy said defiantly: "He's only a black boy," and laughed. Then, when Gideon turned away from him without speaking, his face fell. Very soon he slipped into the house and found an orange and brought it to Gideon, saying: "This is for you." He could not bring himself to say he was sorry; but he could not bear to lose Gideon's affection either. Gideon took the orange unwillingly and sighed. "Soon you will be going away to school, Little Yellow Head," he said wonderingly, "and then you will be grown up." He shook his head gently and said, "And that is how our lives go." He seemed to be putting a distance between himself and

---

1. **kraal** (krahl): South African village.
2. **piccanin** (PIHK uh nihn): black African child. Derived from *pequeno* (pay KAY noo), Portuguese for "small." The term is now considered offensive.
3. **baas** (bahs): Afrikaans for "master." Afrikaans, a language developed from seventeenth-century Dutch, is spoken in South Africa.
4. **mission boy:** one educated by Christian missionaries.

Ⓐ Reading Focus Identifying Historical Context How do you think most servants' jobs affect their families?

Literary Perspectives

Analyzing Political Context Literary texts are often shaped by the author's particular worldview, which can be influenced by his or her political perspective, gender, or social class. In "No Witchcraft for Sale," Lessing sets the story of the two men's friendship against the backdrop of a rigid racial and economic hierarchy in Africa. The political, economic, and, indeed, gender inequalities present in the society inevitably contribute to the evolution of the relationship between Gideon and the Farquars. As you read, note how the divergent social and vocational expectations for Gideon and Teddy may influence their behavior toward each other. Is the role each of these characters assumes determined by the political context or by innate character traits that remain independent of societal pressures? If born into different circumstances, how might Gideon and Teddy have related to each other? Would their friendship have been more or less likely to exist at all?

As you read, be sure to notice the questions in the text, which will guide you in using this perspective.

Teddy, not because of resentment, but in the way a person accepts something inevitable. The baby had lain in his arms and smiled up into his face: The tiny boy had swung from his shoulders and played with him by the hour. Now Gideon would not let his flesh touch the flesh of the white child. He was kind, but there was a grave formality in his voice that made Teddy pout and sulk away. Also, it made him into a man: With Gideon he was polite, and carried himself formally, and if he came into the kitchen to ask for something, it was in the way a white man uses toward a servant, expecting to be obeyed. **Ⓑ**

But on the day that Teddy came staggering into the kitchen with his fists to his eyes, shrieking with pain, Gideon dropped the pot full of hot soup that he was holding, rushed to the child, and forced aside his fingers. "A snake!" he exclaimed. Teddy had been on his scooter, and had come to a rest with his foot on the side of a big tub of plants. A tree snake, hanging by its tail from the roof, had spat full into his eyes. Mrs. Farquar came running when she heard the commotion. "He'll go blind," she sobbed, holding Teddy close against her. "Gideon, he'll go blind!" Already the eyes, with perhaps half an hour's sight left in them, were swollen up to the size of fists: Teddy's small white face was distorted by great purple oozing protuberances.[5] Gideon said: "Wait a minute, missus, I'll get some medicine." He ran off into the bush.

Mrs. Farquar lifted the child into the house and bathed his eyes with permanganate.[6] She had scarcely heard Gideon's words; but when she saw that her remedies had no effect at all, and remembered how she had seen natives with no sight in their eyes, because of the spitting of a snake, she began to look for the return of her cook, remembering what she heard of the efficacy of native herbs. She stood by the window, holding the terrified, sobbing little boy in her arms,

---

5. **protuberances** (proh TOO buhr uhns ihz): swellings; bulges.
6. **permanganate** (puhr MANG guh nayt): dark purple chemical compound used as a disinfectant.

and peered helplessly into the bush. It was not more than a few minutes before she saw Gideon come bounding back, and in his hand he held a plant.

"Do not be afraid, missus," said Gideon, "this will cure Little Yellow Head's eyes." He stripped the leaves from the plant, leaving a small white fleshy root. Without even washing it, he put the root in his mouth, chewed it vigorously, and then held the spittle there while he took the child forcibly from Mrs. Farquar. He gripped Teddy down between his knees, and pressed the balls of his thumbs into the swollen eyes, so that the child screamed and Mrs. Farquar cried out in protest: "Gideon, Gideon!" But Gideon took no notice. He knelt over the writhing child, pushing back the puffy lids till chinks of eyeball showed, and then he spat hard, again and again, into first one eye, and then the other. He finally lifted Teddy gently into his mother's arms, and said: "His eyes will get better." But Mrs. Farquar was weeping with terror, and she could hardly thank him: It was impossible to believe that Teddy could keep his sight. In a couple of hours the swellings were gone: The eyes were inflamed and tender but Teddy could see. Mr. and Mrs. Farquar went to Gideon in the kitchen and thanked him over and over again. They felt helpless because of their gratitude: It seemed they could do nothing to express it. They gave Gideon presents for his wife and children, and a big increase in wages, but these things could not pay for Teddy's now completely cured eyes. Mrs. Farquar said: "Gideon, God chose you as an instrument for His goodness," and Gideon said: "Yes, missus, God is very good." **Ⓒ**

Now, when such a thing happens on a farm, it cannot be long before everyone hears of it. Mr. and Mrs. Farquar told their neighbors and the story was discussed from one end of the district to the other. The bush is full of secrets. No one can live in Africa, or at least on the veld,[7] without learning very soon that there is an ancient wisdom of leaf and soil and season

---

7. **veld:** in South Africa, open country with very few bushes or trees; grassland. *Veld*, also spelled *veldt*, is Afrikaans for "field."

Ⓑ Literary Focus Theme This is a key moment in the story. What has happened here?

Ⓒ Reading Focus Identifying Historical Context Why might the Farquars feel unable to express their gratitude to Gideon?

Vocabulary **efficacy** (EHF uh kuh see) *n.*: ability to produce a desired effect.

Viewing and Interpreting Consider the prominence of the color white in the photograph, the positioning of the human and animal subjects, and the text of the sign. How does this image challenge or reinforce your assumptions about "witchcraft"?

Neverdie Mushwana, a South African "witch doctor," in front of his home with one of his snakes. Tzaneen, South Africa (1997).

—and, too, perhaps most important of all, of the darker tracts of the human mind—which is the black man's heritage. Up and down the district people were telling anecdotes, reminding each other of things that had happened to them.

"But I saw it myself, I tell you. It was a puff-adder bite. The kaffir's[8] arm was swollen to the elbow, like a great shiny black bladder. He was groggy after a half a minute. He was dying. Then suddenly a kaffir walked out of the bush with his hands full of green stuff. He smeared something on the place, and next day my boy was back at work, and all you could see was two small punctures in the skin."

This was the kind of tale they told. And, as always, with a certain amount of exasperation, because while all of them knew that in the bush of Africa are waiting valuable drugs locked in bark, in simple-looking leaves, in roots, it was impossible to ever get the truth about them from the natives themselves. **Ⓓ**

The story eventually reached town; and perhaps it was at a sundowner party,[9] or some such function, that a doctor, who happened to be there, challenged it. "Nonsense," he said. "These things get exaggerated in the telling. We are always checking up on this kind of story, and we draw a blank every time."

Anyway, one morning there arrived a strange car at the homestead, and out stepped one of the workers from the laboratory in town, with cases full of test tubes and chemicals.

Mr. and Mrs. Farquar were flustered and pleased and flattered. They asked the scientist to lunch, and they told the story all over again, for the hundredth time. Little Teddy was there too, his blue eyes sparkling with health, to prove the truth of it. The scientist explained how humanity might benefit if this new drug could be offered for sale; and the Farquars were even more pleased: They were kind, simple people, who liked to think of something good coming about

They were kind, simple people, who liked to think of something good coming about because of them.

because of them. But when the scientist began talking of the money that might result, their manner showed discomfort. Their feelings over the miracle (that was how they thought of it) were so strong and deep and religious, that it was distasteful to them to think of money. The scientist, seeing their faces, went back to his first point, which was the advancement of humanity. He was perhaps a trifle perfunctory: It was not the first time he had come salting the tail of a fabulous bush secret.[10]

Eventually, when the meal was over, the Farquars called Gideon into their living room and explained to him that this baas, here, was a Big Doctor from the Big City, and he had come all that way to see Gideon. At this Gideon seemed afraid; he did not understand; and Mrs. Farquar explained quickly that it was because of the wonderful thing he had done with Teddy's eyes that the Big Baas had come.

---

8. **kaffir's** (KAF uhrz): *Kaffir* is a contemptuous term for a black African, derived from *kāfir,* Arabic for "infidel."
9. **sundowner party:** British colloquial term for "cocktail party." The term derives from the colonials' custom of gathering for drinks at sunset.

---

10. **salting… bush secret:** allusion to the ironic advice given to children about catching a bird by putting salt on its tail. In other words, the scientist knows his search may be futile.

Ⓓ **Literary Focus** **Theme** What details here establish the separation between black Africans and white Africans?

Vocabulary **perfunctory** (puhr FUHNGK tuhr ee) *adj.:* half-hearted; disinterested.

Gideon looked from Mrs. Farquar to Mr. Farquar, and then at the little boy, who was showing great importance because of the occasion. At last he said grudgingly: "The Big Baas want to know what medicine I used?" He spoke incredulously, as if he could not believe his old friends could so betray him. Mr. Farquar began explaining how a useful medicine could be made out of the root, and how it could be put on sale, and how thousands of people, black and white, up and down the continent of Africa, could be saved by the medicine when that spitting snake filled their eyes with poison. Gideon listened, his eyes bent on the ground, the skin of his forehead puckering in discomfort. When Mr. Farquar had finished he did not reply. The scientist, who all this time had been leaning back in a big chair, sipping his coffee and smiling with skeptical good humor, chipped in and explained all over again, in different words, about the making of drugs and the progress of science. Also, he offered Gideon a present. **E**

There was silence after this further explanation, and then Gideon remarked indifferently that he could not remember the root. His face was sullen and hostile, even when he looked at the Farquars, whom he usually treated like old friends. They were beginning to feel annoyed; and this feeling annulled the guilt that had been sprung into life by Gideon's accusing manner. They were beginning to feel that he was unreasonable. But it was at that moment that they all realized he would never give in. The magical drug would remain where it was, unknown and useless except for the tiny scattering of Africans who had the knowledge, natives who might be digging a ditch for the municipality in a ragged shirt and a pair of patched shorts, but who were still born to healing, hereditary healers, being the nephews or sons of the old witch doctors whose ugly masks and bits of bone and all the uncouth properties of magic were the outward signs of real power and wisdom. **F**

The Farquars might tread on that plant fifty times a day as they passed from house to garden, from cow kraal to mealie[11] field, but they would never know it.

But they went on persuading and arguing, with all the force of their exasperation; and Gideon continued to say that he could not remember, or that there was no such root, or that it was the wrong season of the year, or that it wasn't the root itself, but the spit from his mouth that had cured Teddy's eyes. He said all these things one after another, and seemed not to care they were contradictory. He was rude and stubborn. The Farquars could hardly recognize their gentle, lovable old servant in this ignorant, perversely obstinate African, standing there in front of them with lowered eyes, his hands twitching his cook's apron, repeating over and over whichever one of the stupid refusals that first entered his head. **G**

And suddenly he appeared to give in. He lifted his head, gave a long, blank angry look at the circle of whites, who seemed to him like a circle of yelping dogs pressing around him, and said: "I will show you the root."

They walked single file away from the homestead down a kaffir path. It was a blazing December afternoon, with the sky full of hot rain clouds. Everything was hot: The sun was like a bronze tray whirling overhead, there was a heat shimmer over the fields, the soil was scorching underfoot, the dusty wind blew gritty and thick and warm in their faces. It was a terrible day, fit only for reclining on a veranda with iced drinks, which is where they would normally have been at that hour.

From time to time, remembering that on the day of the snake it had taken ten minutes to find the root, someone asked: "Is it much further, Gideon?" And Gideon would answer over his shoulder, with

---

11. **mealie:** corn.

E Reading Focus **Identifying Historical Context** How does the white scientist treat Gideon?

F Literary Focus **Theme** How does the balance of power shift in this conversation?

G Literary Perspectives **Analyzing Political Context** Why has the power structure changed at this point in the story?

Vocabulary annulled (uh NUHLD) v.: erased; canceled.
perversely (puhr VURS lee) adv.: disagreeably; contrarily.

"as good as the white man's doctor"

angry politeness: "I'm looking for the root, baas." And indeed, he would frequently bend sideways and trail his hand among the grasses with a gesture that was insulting in its perfunctoriness. He walked them through the bush along unknown paths for two hours, in that melting destroying heat, so that the sweat trickled coldly down them and their heads ached. They were all quite silent: the Farquars because they were angry, the scientist because he was being proved right again; there was no such plant. His was a tactful silence.

At last, six miles from the house, Gideon suddenly decided they had had enough; or perhaps his anger evaporated at that moment. He picked up, without an attempt at looking anything but casual, a handful of blue flowers from the grass, flowers that had been growing plentifully all down the paths they had come.

He handed them to the scientist without looking at him, and marched off by himself on the way home, leaving them to follow him if they chose.

When they got back to the house, the scientist went to the kitchen to thank Gideon: He was being

very polite, even though there was an amused look in his eyes. Gideon was not there. Throwing the flowers casually into the back of his car, the eminent visitor departed on his way back to his laboratory.

Gideon was back in his kitchen in time to prepare dinner, but he was sulking. He spoke to Mr. Farquar like an unwilling servant. It was days before they liked each other again.

The Farquars made inquiries about the root from their laborers. Sometimes they were answered with distrustful stares. Sometimes the natives said: "We do not know. We have never heard of the root." One, the cattle boy, who had been with them a long time, and had grown to trust them a little, said: "Ask your boy in the kitchen. Now, there's a doctor for you. He's the son of a famous medicine man who used to be in these parts, and there's nothing he cannot cure." Then he added politely: "Of course, he's not as good as the white man's doctor, we know that, but he's good for us."

After some time, when the soreness had gone from between the Farquars and Gideon, they began to joke: "When are you going to show us the snake root, Gideon?" And he would laugh and shake his head, saying, a little uncomfortably: "But I did show you, missus, have you forgotten?"

Much later, Teddy, as a schoolboy, would come into the kitchen and say: "You old rascal, Gideon! Do you remember that time you tricked us all by making us walk miles all over the veld for nothing? It was so far my father had to carry me!"

And Gideon would double up with polite laughter. After much laughing, he would suddenly straighten himself up, wipe his old eyes, and look sadly at Teddy, who was grinning mischievously at him across the kitchen: "Ah, Little Yellow Head, how you have grown! Soon you will be grown up with a farm of your own...." **H**

H **Literary Perspectives** Analyzing Political Context How is the relationship between Teddy and Gideon influenced by their social classes?

No Witchcraft for Sale

Respond and Think Critically

Reading Focus

Quick Check

1. Describe the relationship between Gideon and Teddy at the start of the story. What incident causes a change in their relationship?

2. What happens when the scientist tries to get the plant's name from Gideon?

Read with a Purpose

3. How would you describe the relationship between the Farquars and Gideon? How is the relationship affected by the political climate?

Reading Skills: Identifying Historical Context

4. As you read, you took notes on historical context, characters, and conflicts. Now, make a general statement about ways that politics and social class can affect human relationships.

Literary Focus

Literary Analysis

5. **Infer** Why do you think Gideon refuses to share his wisdom with the Farquars? Do you think his refusal is justified? Explain your response.

6. **Analyze** Re-read Gideon's comment at the end of the story. What does it reveal about his understanding of the relationship between white European and black African cultures?

7. **Interpret** In her preface to *African Stories,* Lessing reveals that she holds the British responsible for much of the suffering in Southern Rhodesia. Does she really feel the Farquars are people of goodwill, or is there some irony in her attitude? Support your answer with details from the story.

8. **Evaluate** Mrs. Farquar tells Gideon he is "an instrument for [God's] goodness." Do you think Gideon considers this statement to be a compliment? Why or why not?

9. **Literary Perspectives** The events Lessing narrates are definitely affected by their political context. However, could the basic conflict occur anywhere, at any time, in any culture? Explain.

Literary Skills: Theme

10. **Draw Conclusions** How would you state the theme of the story? Use evidence from the story to support your response.

Literary Skills Review: Characterization

11. **Analyze** The process by which a writer reveals the personality of a character, **characterization,** can be direct or indirect. What direct statements does Lessing provide to help us understand the character of Mrs. Farquar?

12. **Compare and Contrast** The writer subtly contrasts Teddy with Gideon's own little son. Find details that make you aware of the differences.

Writing Focus

Think as a Reader/Writer

Use It in Your Writing In your *Reader/Writer Notebook,* you recorded words Lessing uses to describe her characters. Now, write a description of another character who might take part in a conflict similar to the one in the story. Use direct and indirect methods to make your character come alive.

What Do You Think Now? Do Mrs. Farquar and Gideon "agree to disagree"? Do the characters in the story accept that a certain degree of social and cultural conflict is <u>inevitable</u>?

No Witchcraft for Sale

Vocabulary Development

✔ Vocabulary Check

Be sure you can justify your answer to each question below about the Vocabulary words.

1. Which word is the opposite of **reverently?**
   (a) respectively (b) mockingly

2. What word means the same as **efficacy?**
   (a) effectiveness (b) ineffectiveness

3. Which word describes someone who is **perfunctory?** (a) indifferent (b) enthusiastic

4. If something is **annulled,** is it (a) verified or (b) canceled?

5. If you say someone is acting **perversely,** do you mean that the person is acting (a) in a contrary way or (b) in an eager way?

Vocabulary Skills: Context Clues

Context refers to the words and sentences that surround a particular word. Sometimes the context of an unfamiliar word can give you a clue to the word's meaning. There are several types of context clues:

1. **Restatement clues:** The meaning of the unfamiliar word is restated somewhere in its context.

   The mother's *fortitude*—her *courage and perseverance*—saw her through the ordeal.

2. **Contrast clues:** The unfamiliar word is contrasted with a familiar word.

   One explorer's *fortitude* contrasted with the other's *weakness.*

3. **Example clues:** An example of the word is found in its context.

   Men like Gideon had to show *fortitude* to survive; for example, they had to exhibit *courage in the face of racism.*

Your Turn

What context clues might help you guess the meanings of the boldface Vocabulary words?

1. With great love and affection, Gideon **reverently** held the little boy's curls.

2. Gideon proved the **efficacy** of the root he found by using it to restore Teddy's sight.

3. They had a **perfunctory** conversation, barely saying "hello" and "goodbye."

Language Coach

Suffix –ly Remember that the suffix –ly is added to some words to create adverbs. Read the following sentences that include adverbs from the story. Name the adverb, and tell what word in the sentence it modifies, or describes.

1. She peered helplessly into the bush.
2. He chewed the root vigorously.
3. He took the child forcibly from his mother.

Academic Vocabulary

Write About...
From Gideon's perspective, the change in his relationship to Teddy is inevitable, and he seems to adapt automatically to a different role as Teddy grows older. In a short essay, analyze whether the behavior Gideon exhibits toward Teddy alters because of the Farquars' or society's expectations.

Grammar Link

Effective Sentences: Parallelism

When you use **parallelism** within sentences, you use the same grammatical form to express two or more equally important ideas. Always use the same form to:

- coordinate ideas

    Correct: The servant's duties included cooking and growing plants. *Incorrect:* The servant's duties included to cook and growing plants.

- compare and contrast ideas

    Correct: She was better at ordering her servants than at cleaning the house herself. *Incorrect:* She was better at ordering her servants than to clean the house herself.

- link ideas with correlative conjunctions (*both… and, either… or, neither… nor, not only… but also*)

    Correct: The scooter was neither new nor cheap. *Incorrect:* The scooter was neither new and it wasn't cheap.

Your Turn

Use parallelism to rewrite the following sentences.

1. Gideon was not only a kind man but also he was good at healing.
2. Teddy liked to ride his scooter and frightening Gideon's little boy.
3. Teddy loved Gideon for saving his life and because he gave the boy a lot of attention.
4. Gideon ignored the doctor, marching into the house and who demanded the herbs.

Writing Application Scan a piece of your writing, and underline any instances of parallelism. Check to see if you have used parallelism correctly to coordinate ideas, compare and contrast ideas, or link ideas with correlative conjunctions.

CHOICES

As you respond to the Choices, use these **Academic Vocabulary** words as appropriate: perspective, considerably, adapt, exhibit, inevitable.

REVIEW
Use Another Point of View

"No Witchcraft for Sale" is told by an **omniscient narrator,** a narrator who is outside the story and knows everything that is going on in the story. Rewrite a scene from the story from a first-person perspective (using the pronoun I), perhaps from the point of view of Mrs. Farquar or Gideon. You might even choose to let the scientist or doctor tell the story, or you might have Teddy tell the story years after the incident happened.

CONNECT
Make a Policy Recommendation

Timed └Writing Think of an inequity that exists in today's society. What can be done to correct it? Write a brief essay in which you suggest one way to make our society more just. Define what you see as the problem, tell why it merits attention, and propose your solution.

EXTEND
Research Colonialism in Africa

What do you know about colonialism and its lingering effects? Choose a sub-Saharan African country other than Liberia. Use library or Internet resources to learn about the country's colonial history and its effects. Write a short report to share with your class.

Learn It Online
Explore context clues with *WordSharp*.

go.hrw.com L12-1367 **Go**

Once upon a Time

Nadine Gordimer
(1923–   )

What Do You Think? How does experience shape our view of the world?

QuickWrite

People use all sorts of devices to "wall themselves off," or to keep themselves away from others. In your *Reader/Writer Notebook,* make a list of these "walls" or ways in which people separate themselves.

Nobel Prize WINNER

Nadine Gordimer, the daughter of a Lithuanian father and an English mother, grew up in a small mining town about thirty miles from Johannesburg, South Africa. Like most colonials, her family adopted European conventions and values. Gordimer spent most of her childhood reading because she found middle-class colonial society extremely dull. This society, and its injustices, later served as the inspiration for much of her writing, which explores the devastating effects of racism.

A Strong New Voice

Gordimer began writing at the age of nine during a period in which she was removed from school because of sickness. When her short story collection *The Soft Voice of the Serpent* appeared in 1952, critics hailed Gordimer as a strong new voice who drew fresh, authentic perceptions of African life. Among her best-known novels is *July's People* (1981), in which the white people in South Africa become servants of the black Africans. In 1991, she won the Nobel Prize in Literature.

A Society Out of Joint

One critic has called Gordimer "one of the very few links between white and black in South Africa…." Although much of Gordimer's writing concerns the troubles of her nation, she does not see herself as a political writer. "Here I live in a society which is fundamentally out of joint. One can't but be politically concerned," she has said. Nevertheless, she disclaims a political agenda: "I don't understand politics except in terms of what politics does to influence lives. What interests me is the infinite variety of effects apartheid has on men and women."

When apartheid was in effect, Gordimer's writing irked the government of South Africa considerably, and three of her novels were subsequently banned. Nevertheless, she has always considered herself "an intensely loyal South African. I care deeply for my country."

"Nadine Gordimer (1923).

Think About the Writer How do you think Gordimer could still love her country if it forced people to live under laws she considered unjust and destructive?

Reader/Writer Notebook

Use your **RWN** to complete the activities for this selection.

Literary Focus

Symbols A **symbol** is something that stands both for itself and for something beyond itself. Established symbols—sometimes known as public symbols—include the flags that stand for various states or nations, the dove that represents peace, and the bald eagle that stands for the United States. Writers and artists often create their own personal, unique symbols, the meanings of which are revealed in the course of a poem, story, or novel. As you read this story, note how Gordimer uses symbolism to dramatize the chilling effect of racial prejudice and inequality.

Reading Focus

Identifying Language Structures When a story begins "Once upon a time...," you assume you are about to hear a fairy tale because you recognize the characteristic language structure. In "Once upon a Time," Gordimer uses several language structures from the literature of fairy tales, and because she repeats these phrases and sentences, her story "sounds" like a fairy tale. Her insistent repetition of these language structures also adds to the story's dramatic momentum, for we soon realize this is no fairy tale.

Into Action As you read Gordimer's story, record in a chart like the one below language structures that remind you of fairy tales. You may wish to begin with the title and move chronologically through the story.

Typical Fairy-Tale Phrases and Sentences

1. Title of story is "Once upon a time"
2.
3.
4.

Writing Focus

Think as a Reader/Writer

Find It in Your Reading In addition to containing repeated language structures, fairy tales feature stock character types and plot events. As you read, record in your *Reader/Writer Notebook* details in the story that are reminiscent of fairy tales. Concentrate on character types and events.

Vocabulary

apertures (AP uhr churz) *n.:* openings. *The woman was listening so intensely that she felt as if the apertures of her ears were widening.*

distend (dihs TEHND) *v.:* expand; swell. *Having eaten both a large breakfast and lunch, the worker felt his stomach distend.*

itinerant (y TIHN uhr uhnt) *adj.:* migratory. *Itinerant workers came to the suburb looking for employment.*

audaciously (aw DAY shuhs lee) *adv.:* boldly. *Some intruders audaciously drank the whiskey in the cabinets of the houses they robbed.*

aesthetics (ehs THEHT ihks) *n.:* principles of beauty. *The writer ridiculed the homeowners by saying they tried to combine the aesthetics of prison architecture with Spanish villa style.*

serrated (SEHR ay tihd) *v.* used as *adj.:* marked along the edge with jagged, saw-like notches. *Serrated blades of steel were placed all along the metal coil in order to tear apart any intruder who tried to climb over it.*

Language Coach

Accented Syllables In the pronunciation guide to the Vocabulary words, the accented syllable is printed in capital letters. Practice pronouncing each of the Vocabulary words, paying special attention to the syllable that is accented. Which two Vocabulary words are not accented on the second syllable?

 Learn It Online
There iss more to words than just definitions. Get the whole story with Word Watch at

go.hrw.com | LE9-91 | **Go**

ONCE UPON A TIME

by **Nadine Gordimer**

Read with a Purpose
Read to find out whether this fairy tale is written for children or for adults.

Build Background
Until the 1990s, South Africa under white rule enforced a policy called apartheid (ah PAHRT hayt), the legal separation of races. Black South Africans and other people who were not white experienced brutal political and economic discrimination.

Most black South Africans were forced to live in remote areas or all-black "townships" bordering white cities. The only black people who could live in white cities were those with employment, a practice that in effect split up families. To enter cities, black and other nonwhite South Africans were required to show "passbooks" that identified them by name, residency, and race.

In 1993, after decades of riots and rebellions that left thousands of black people dead and most of their leaders jailed, the white government—under both internal and international pressure—repealed the apartheid laws. One year later, the first all-race election swept the black South African leader Nelson Mandela, a former political prisoner, into office as president. "Once upon a Time" is set during the era when apartheid was still law.

Someone has written to ask me to contribute to an anthology of stories for children. I reply that I don't write children's stories; and he writes back that at a recent congress/book fair/seminar a certain novelist said every writer ought to write at least one story for children. I think of sending a postcard saying I don't accept that I "ought" to write anything.

And then last night I woke up—or rather was wakened without knowing what had roused me.

A voice in the echo chamber of the subconscious? A sound.

A creaking of the kind made by the weight carried by one foot after another along a wooden floor. I listened. I felt the apertures of my ears distend with concentration. Again: the creaking. I was waiting for it; waiting to hear if it indicated that feet were moving from room to room, coming up the passage—to my door. I have no burglar bars, no gun under the pillow,

---

Vocabulary **apertures** (AP uhr churz) *n.*: openings. **distend** (dihs TEHND) *v.*: expand; swell.

but I have the same fears as people who do take these precautions, and my windowpanes are thin as rime,[1] could shatter like a wineglass. A woman was murdered (how do they put it) in broad daylight in a house two blocks away, last year, and the fierce dogs who guarded an old widower and his collection of antique clocks were strangled before he was knifed by a casual laborer he had dismissed without pay.

I was staring at the door, making it out in my mind rather than seeing it, in the dark. I lay quite still—a victim already—but the arrhythmia[2] of my heart was fleeing, knocking this way and that against its body-cage. How finely tuned the senses are, just out of rest, sleep! I could never listen intently as that in the distractions of the day; I was reading every faintest sound, identifying and classifying its possible threat.

But I learned that I was to be neither threatened nor spared. There was no human weight pressing on the boards, the creaking was a buckling, an epicenter[3] of stress. I was in it. The house that surrounds me while I sleep is built on undermined ground; far

beneath my bed, the floor, the house's foundations, the stopes[4] and passages of gold mines have hollowed the rock, and when some face trembles, detaches, and falls, three thousand feet below, the whole house shifts slightly, bringing uneasy strain to the balance and counterbalance of brick, cement, wood, and glass that hold it as a structure around me. The misbeats of my heart tailed off like the last muffled flourishes on one of the wooden xylophones made by the Chopi and Tsonga[5] migrant miners who might have been down there, under me in the earth at that moment. The stope where the fall was could have been disused, dripping water from its ruptured veins; or men might now be interred there in the most profound of tombs. Ⓐ

I couldn't find a position in which my mind would let go of my body—release me to sleep again. So I began to tell myself a story; a bedtime story.

In a house, in a suburb, in a city, there were a man and his wife who loved each other very much and were living happily ever after. They had a little boy, and they loved him very much. They had a cat and a dog that the little boy loved very much. They had a car and a caravan trailer for holidays, and a swimming pool which was fenced so that the little boy and

---

1. **rime:** tiny ice crystals that can form on grass and leaves.
2. **arrhythmia** (uh RIHTH mee uh): irregular beating.
3. **epicenter:** central point.

---

4. **stopes:** excavations.
5. **Chopi** (CHOH pee) **and Tsonga** (TSAHNG gah): Bantu-speaking peoples of Mozambique in southeastern Africa. *Tsonga* is often spelled *Thonga*.

Ⓐ **Literary Focus** Symbols What might be symbolic about a house that rests on shaky ground?

his playmates would not fall in and drown. They had a housemaid who was absolutely trustworthy and an itinerant gardener who was highly recommended by the neighbors. For when they began to live happily ever after they were warned, by that wise old witch, the husband's mother, not to take on anyone off the street. They were inscribed[6] in a medical benefit society, their pet dog was licensed, they were insured against fire, flood damage, and theft, and subscribed to the local Neighborhood Watch, which supplied them with a plaque for their gates lettered YOU HAVE BEEN WARNED over the silhouette of a would-be intruder. He was masked; it could not be said if he was black or white, and therefore proved the property owner was no racist. **Ⓑ**

It was not possible to insure the house, the swimming pool, or the car against riot damage. There were riots, but these were outside the city, where people of another color were quartered. These people were not allowed into the suburb except as reliable housemaids and gardeners, so there was nothing to fear, the husband told the wife. Yet she was afraid that some day such people might come up the street and tear off the plaque YOU HAVE BEEN WARNED and open the gates and stream in…. Nonsense, my dear, said the husband, there are police and soldiers and tear gas and guns to keep them away. But to please her—for he loved her very much and buses were being burned, cars stoned, and schoolchildren shot by the police in

those quarters out of sight and hearing of the suburb—he had electronically controlled gates fitted. Anyone who pulled off the sign YOU HAVE BEEN WARNED and tried to open the gates would have to announce his intentions by pressing a button and speaking into a receiver relayed to the house. The little boy was fascinated by the device and used it as a walkie-talkie in cops and robbers play with his small friends.

The riots were suppressed, but there were many burglaries in the suburb and somebody's trusted housemaid was tied up and shut in a cupboard by thieves while she was in charge of her employers' house. The trusted housemaid of the man and wife and little boy was so upset by this misfortune befalling a friend left, as she herself often was, with responsibility for the possessions of the man and his wife and the little boy that she implored her employers to have burglar bars attached to the doors and windows of the house, and an alarm system installed. The wife said, She is right, let us take heed of her advice. So from every window and door in the house where they were living happily ever after they now saw the trees and sky through bars, and when the little boy's pet cat tried to climb in by the fanlight[7] to keep him company in his little bed at night, as it customarily had done, it set off the alarm keening[8] through the house.

The alarm was often answered—it seemed—by other burglar alarms, in other houses, that had been

---

6. **inscribed:** enrolled.

7. **fanlight:** semicircular window over a door or a larger window.
8. **keening:** wailing.

Ⓑ **Reading Focus** Identifying Language Structures What fairy-tale language does Gordimer use to describe the family's situation?

Vocabulary **itinerant** (y TIHN uhr uhnt) *adj.:* migratory.

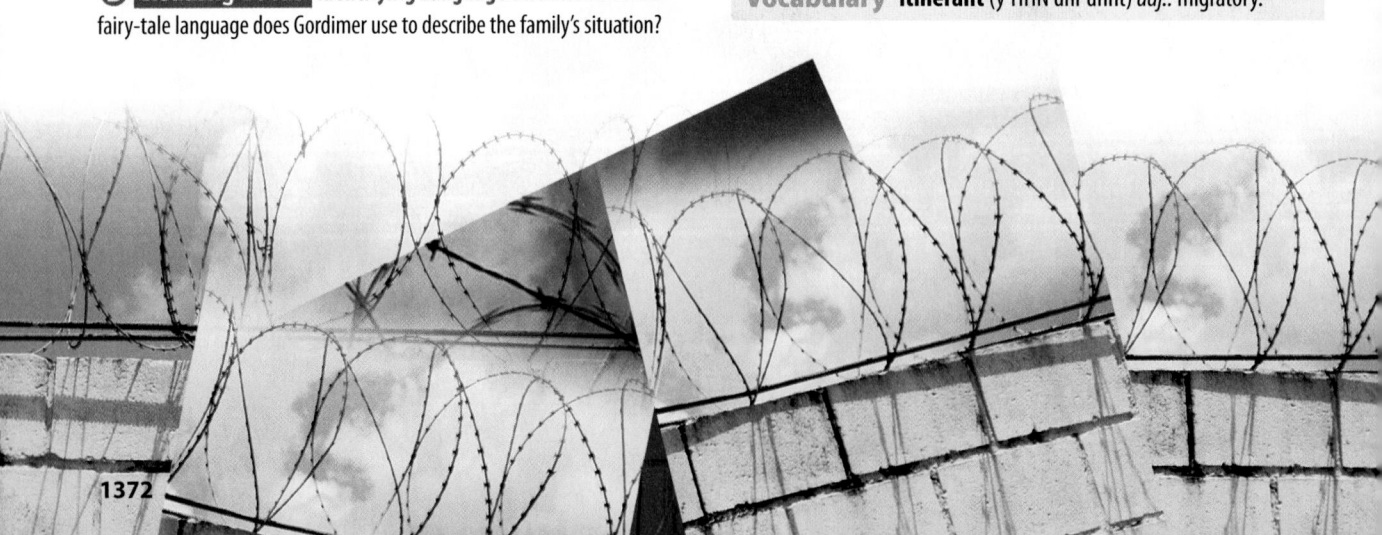

triggered by pet cats or nibbling mice. The alarms called to one another across the gardens in shrills and bleats and wails that everyone soon became accustomed to, so that the din roused the inhabitants of the suburb no more than the croak of frogs and musical grating of cicadas'[9] legs. Under cover of the electronic harpies'[10] discourse intruders sawed the iron bars and broke into homes, taking away hi-fi equipment, television sets, cassette players, cameras and radios, jewelry and clothing, and sometimes were hungry enough to devour everything in the refrigerator or paused audaciously to drink the whiskey in the cabinets or patio bars. Insurance companies paid no compensation for single malt, a loss made keener by the property owner's knowledge that the thieves wouldn't even have been able to appreciate what it was they were drinking.

Then the time came when many of the people who were not trusted housemaids and gardeners hung about the suburb because they were unemployed. Some importuned for a job: weeding or painting a roof; anything, *baas*,[11] madam. But the man and his wife remembered the warning about taking on anyone off the street. Some drank liquor and fouled the street with discarded bottles. Some begged, waiting for the man or his wife to drive the car out of the electronically operated gates. They sat about with their feet in the gutters, under the jacaranda[12] trees that made a green

tunnel of the street—for it was a beautiful suburb, spoiled only by their presence—and sometimes they fell asleep lying right before the gates in the midday sun. The wife could never see anyone go hungry. She sent the trusted housemaid out with bread and tea, but the trusted housemaid said these were loafers and *tsotsis*,[13] who would come and tie her up and shut her in a cupboard. The husband said, She's right. Take heed of her advice. You only encourage them with your bread and tea. They are looking for their chance. … And he brought the little boy's tricycle from the garden into the house every night, because if the house was surely secure, once locked and with the alarm set, someone might still be able to climb over the wall or the electronically closed gates into the garden.

You are right, said the wife, then the wall should be higher. And the wise old witch, the husband's mother, paid for the extra bricks as her Christmas present to her son and his wife—the little boy got a Space Man outfit and a book of fairy tales.

But every week there were more reports of intrusion: in broad daylight and the dead of night, in the early hours of the morning, and even in the lovely summer twilight—a certain family was at dinner while the bedrooms were being ransacked upstairs. The man and his wife, talking of the latest armed robbery in the suburb, were distracted by the sight of the little boy's pet cat effortlessly arriving over the seven-foot wall, descending first with a rapid bracing of extended forepaws down on the sheer vertical surface, and then a graceful launch, landing with swishing tail within the property. The whitewashed wall was marked with the

---

9. **cicadas'** (suh KAY duhz): Cicadas are large insects that make a shrill sound.
10. **harpies':** Harpies are hideous monsters from Greek mythology that have the head and trunk of a woman and the tail, legs, and talons of a bird. In some myths they are guardians of a treasure.
11. ***baas*** (bahs): Afrikaans for "master." Afrikaans, a language developed from seventeenth-century Dutch, is spoken in South Africa.
12. **jacaranda** (jak uh RAN duh): tropical tree with large clusters of blue or lavender flowers.

---

13. ***tsotsis*** (TSAHT sihs): colloquial expression for "flashily dressed street thugs."

Vocabulary   audaciously (aw DAY shuhs lee) *adv.:* boldly.

cat's comings and goings; and on the street side of the wall there were larger red-earth smudges that could have been made by the kind of broken running shoes, seen on the feet of unemployed loiterers, that had no innocent destination.

When the man and wife and little boy took the pet dog for its walk round the neighborhood streets they no longer paused to admire this show of roses or that perfect lawn; these were hidden behind an array of different varieties of security fences, walls, and devices. The man, wife, little boy, and dog passed a remarkable choice: There was the low-cost option of pieces of broken glass embedded in cement along the top of walls, there were iron grilles ending in lance points, there were attempts at reconciling the aesthetics of prison architecture with the Spanish Villa style (spikes painted pink) and with the plastic urns of neoclassical façades (twelve-inch pikes finned like zigzags of lightning and painted pure white). Some walls had a small board affixed, giving the name and telephone number of the firm responsible for the installation of the devices. While the little boy and the pet dog raced ahead, the husband and wife found themselves comparing the possible effectiveness of each style against its appearance; and after several weeks when they paused before this barricade or that without needing to speak, both came out with the conclusion that only one was worth considering. It was the ugliest but the most honest in its suggestion of the pure concentration-camp style, no frills, all evident efficacy. Placed the length of walls, it consisted of a continuous coil of stiff and shining metal serrated into jagged blades, so that there would be no way of climbing over it and no way through its tunnel without getting entangled in its fangs. There would be no way out, only a struggle getting bloodier and bloodier, a deeper and sharper hooking and tearing of flesh. The wife shuddered to look at it. You're right, said the husband, anyone would think twice.

… And they took heed of the advice on a small board fixed to the wall: Consult DRAGON'S TEETH The People For Total Security. **C**

Next day a gang of workmen came and stretched the razor-bladed coils all round the walls of the house where the husband and wife and little boy and pet dog and cat were living happily ever after. The sunlight flashed and slashed, off the serrations, the cornice of razor thorns encircled the home, shining. The husband said, Never mind. It will weather. The wife said, You're wrong. They guarantee it's rustproof. And she waited until the little boy had run off to play before she said, I hope the cat will take heed…. The husband said, Don't worry, my dear, cats always look before they leap. And it was true that from that day on the cat slept in the little boy's bed and kept to the garden, never risking a try at breaching security.

One evening, the mother read the little boy to sleep with a fairy story from the book the wise old witch had given him at Christmas. Next day he pretended to be the Prince who braves the terrible thicket of thorns to enter the palace and kiss the Sleeping Beauty back to life: He dragged a ladder to the wall, the shining coiled tunnel was just wide enough for his little body to creep in, and with the first fixing of its razor teeth in his knees and hands and head he screamed and struggled deeper into its tangle. The trusted housemaid and the itinerant gardener, whose "day" it was, came running, the first to see and to scream with him, and the itinerant gardener tore his hands trying to get at the little boy. Then the man and his wife burst wildly into the garden and for some reason (the cat, probably) the alarm set up wailing against the screams while the bleeding mass of the little boy was hacked out of the security coil with saws, wire cutters, choppers, and they carried it—the man, the wife, the hysterical trusted housemaid, and the weeping gardener—into the house.

C Reading Focus **Identifying Language Structures** How does the "Dragon's Teeth" advertisement link the story to older fairy tales?

SKILLS FOCUS **Literary Skills** Analyze symbols; analyze irony, including verbal and situational irony. **Reading Skills** Identify language structures. **Vocabulary**

Skills Demonstrate knowledge of literal meanings of words. **Writing Skills** Write to inform.

Respond and Think Critically

Reading Focus

Quick Check

1. What four measures do the husband and wife take to protect themselves?

Read with a Purpose

2. Is the intended audience for this story children or adults? What do you think Gordimer's purpose was in telling this "bedtime story"?

Reading Skills: Identifying Language Structures

3. As you read, you noted the fairy-tale elements of the story. Review your chart, and tell how the fairy-tale style affected your response to the story. What did you think about the way the style contrasted with the violence in the story?

✓ Vocabulary Check

Answer these questions about Vocabulary words.

4. Is an **aperture** an opening or a closing?

5. If your eyes **distend,** do they swell or contract?

6. Is an **itinerant** person someone who stays at home or wanders around?

7. If you speak **audaciously,** are you shy or bold?

8. If you are studying **aesthetics,** are you studying ideas of beauty or theories of revolution?

9. If a knife is **serrated,** is it smooth or jagged?

Literary Focus

Literary Analysis

10. **Analyze** Fairy tales often contain moral lessons. What is the moral of "Once upon a Time"?

11. **Make Judgments** Are the couple innocent homeowners who are only trying to feel secure, or are they the cause of the tragedy? Explain.

Literary Skills: Symbols

12. **Interpret** How can the security systems in the story—especially the wall—be seen as symbols? Be sure to consider the double meaning of the plaque "YOU HAVE BEEN WARNED."

Literary Skills Review: Situational Irony

13. **Analyze** When what happens is the opposite of what we expect will happen **situational irony** occurs. What is this story's central irony? What did the parents hope to accomplish with their security systems? What actually happened?

Writing Focus

Think as a Reader/Writer

Use It in Your Writing Review your notes about character types and events related to fairy tales, as well as your Into Action chart. Think of a social issue (perhaps one involving a clash of cultures) on which you could base a fairy tale with a moral lesson. Write such a fairy tale, using the appropriate character types, events, and language.

What Do You Think Now?

What experiences have given this couple their fearful view of the world? Based on their experience, what might be the worldview of the story's black African characters?

Preparing to Read

Marriage Is a Private Affair

QuickTalk

With a partner, discuss this question: "When, if ever, is it justifiable to challenge the customs of your society?" In your *Reader/Writer Notebook*, take notes on both your and your partner's thoughts.

Chinua Achebe (1930).

Chinua Achebe
(1930–   )

Nigerian writer Chinua Achebe (CHIHN wah ah CHAY bay) planned to study medicine, but literature and his country's nationalist movement changed his plans.

Redefining Africa

Achebe was born in the eastern Nigerian town of Ogidi, where his father, a Christian convert, taught at the mission school. As a student, Achebe realized the destructive effects of colonialism and dedicated himself to redefining Africa and telling the true story of Africans. According to Achebe, the European idea that "Africa was the Primordial Void, was sheer humbug.… Africa had a history, a religion, a civilization." Achebe chose to write in English, which he had begun to learn at the age of eight, in order to reach a wide audience.

Stories for a Human Purpose

Achebe's novels, beginning with the celebrated *Things Fall Apart* (1958), focus on how dramatically Nigeria changed in the twentieth century. The novels trace the evolution of life in Nigeria—sometimes presented as a fictionalized nation—from the arrival of early English missionaries, through the years of colonial rule, to the post-independence era rife with corruption and political turmoil. Although Achebe believes that "Africa's meeting with Europe must be accounted a terrible disaster in this matter of human understanding and respect," he does not idealize his African characters. He instead holds them responsible for their private decisions and for solving the problems that threaten their nation's future.

During Nigeria's civil war in the late 1960s, Achebe worked for the cause of the secessionist Biafrans. Since that time he has taught and encouraged promising young writers. He believes that at the heart of the African oral tradition is the <u>perspective</u> that art is and always was at the service of humans. "Our ancestors created their myths," he has said, "and told their stories for a human purpose." Through his fiction, nonfiction, and poetry, he has been a catalyst for an entire generation of African writers.

Think About the Writer
What do you think of Achebe's belief about the purpose of art?

Reader/Writer Notebook

Use your **RWN** to complete the activities for this selection.

Literary Focus

Verbal Irony When a writer or speaker says one thing but means something else (usually the opposite of what is stated), **verbal irony** occurs. For example, if you tell a friend that you "just love being kept waiting in the rain," you are probably using verbal irony. A classic literary example of verbal irony occurs in Jonathan Swift's essay "A Modest Proposal" (page 580), in which Swift suggests that the Irish solve their social problems by selling their babies to their English landlords as food. Verbal irony is often used to point out the lunacy of an idea. Instead of saying to a friend, "You shouldn't cheat," you might make the idea ridiculous by stating, "Sure, go ahead and cheat on the test. Then you'll feel really proud of yourself."

Reading Focus

Identifying Cultural Characteristics Reading is the least expensive way to travel. Without leaving your room, you can spend time in any country in the world, among people of widely differing cultures. When you read, just as when you travel, you encounter attitudes and behaviors different from your own.

Into Action As you read Achebe's story, make a cluster chart like the one below to identify what the story reveals about Nigerian culture. Add as many ovals as you need around the central idea.

Writing Focus

Think as a Reader/Writer

Find It in Your Reading Good writers show rather than tell; they let us draw conclusions about a character by exhibiting the character in action and by letting us hear what the character says. For example, instead of telling us directly, "Joe was a good person," the writer will show Joe in action as he does something positive for someone else or says something that demonstrates his virtues. In your *Reader/Writer Notebook,* note instances where Achebe reveals a character's traits by letting us hear the person's words and by showing the person in action.

Vocabulary

cosmopolitan (kahz muh PAHL uh tuhn) *adj.:* worldly; sophisticated. *The old Ibo customs about marriage seemed outdated in the cosmopolitan atmosphere of the city.*

rash (rash) *adj.:* foolhardy. *The father thought his son's sudden decision to marry was rash.*

commiserate (kuh MIHZ uh rayt) *v.:* feel sorrow or pity for; sympathize. *The old men came to commiserate with the father about his son's marriage plans.*

persevered (pur suh VIHRD) *v.:* persisted despite difficulty or opposition. *The old man persevered in putting his son out of his mind.*

perfunctorily (puhr FUHNGK tuhr uh lee) *adv.:* mechanically; carelessly. *The father read the letter perfunctorily.*

Language Coach

Multiple-Meaning Words Some words have more than one meaning and can be used as different parts of speech. For example, *rash* means "foolhardy" when it is used as an adjective; when it is used as a noun, it means "a red, itchy skin condition." Find the following words in the story. Use context clues to define each word and to identify its part of speech as it is used in the sentence. What other meanings can each word have?

leave	sound	engaged
spent	object	sentence
account	steel	broke

 Learn It Online

Learn more about Achebe's life online at the Writers' Lives site.

go.hrw.com L12-1377 **Go**

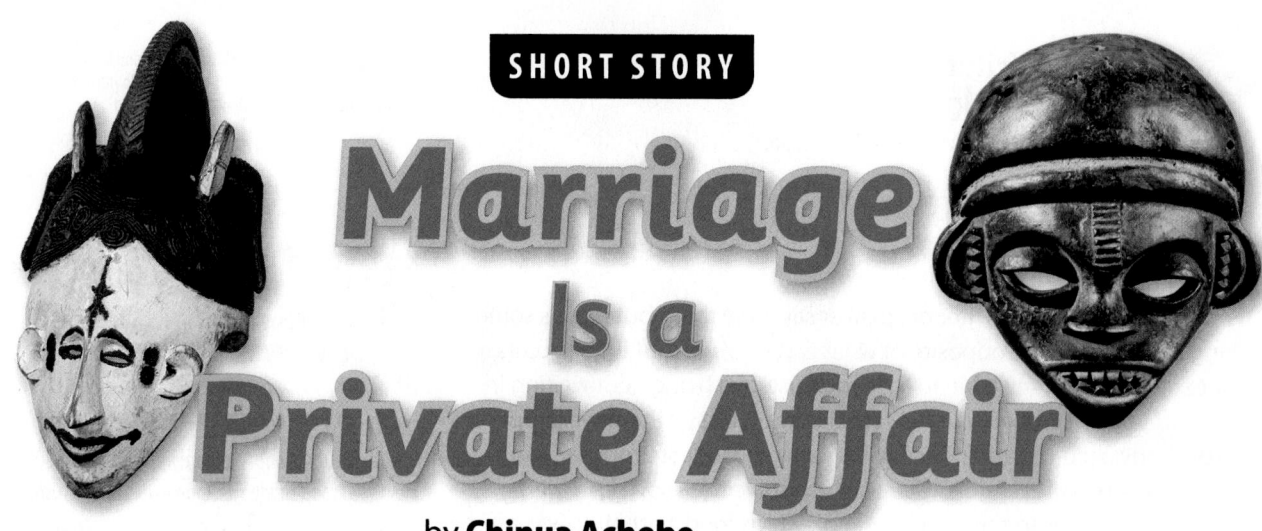

Marriage Is a Private Affair

by **Chinua Achebe**

Read with a Purpose
Read to find out if marriage really is a private affair.

Build Background
The West African nation of Nigeria has more than 250 ethnic groups, which often speak different languages and frequently differ in religion, customs, and traditions. Both the Ibo and the Ibibio people live in southeastern Nigeria but traditionally did not intermarry. In Achebe's story, a young Ibo man and a young Ibibio woman have moved from their native regions to Lagos, a large, modern city in southwestern Nigeria. Like the young man in the story, Achebe is Ibo.

"Have you written to your dad yet?" asked Nene[1] one afternoon as she sat with Nnaemeka[2] in her room at 16 Kasanga Street, Lagos.[3]

"No. I've been thinking about it. I think it's better to tell him when I get home on leave!"

"But why? Your leave is such a long way off yet—six whole weeks. He should be let into our happiness now."

Nnaemeka was silent for a while, and then began very slowly as if he groped for his words: "I wish I were sure it would be happiness to him."

"Of course it must," replied Nene, a little surprised. "Why shouldn't it?"

"You have lived in Lagos all your life, and you know very little about people in remote parts of the country."

"That's what you always say. But I don't believe anybody will be so unlike other people that they will be unhappy when their sons are engaged to marry."

"Yes. They are most unhappy if the engagement is not arranged by them. In our case it's worse—you are not even an Ibo."[4]

This was said so seriously and so bluntly that Nene could not find speech immediately. In the cosmopolitan atmosphere of the city it had always seemed to her something of a joke that a person's tribe could determine whom he married.

At last she said, "You don't really mean that he will object to your marrying me simply on that account? I had always thought you Ibos were kindly disposed to other people."

"So we are. But when it comes to marriage, well, it's not quite so simple. And this," he added, "is not

---

1. **Nene** (NAY nay).
2. **Nnaemeka** (ihn naw ay MAY kuh).
3. **Lagos** (LAY gahs): former capital of Nigeria.

---

4. **Ibo** (EE boh): member of an African ethnic group living chiefly in southeastern Nigeria.

Vocabulary **cosmopolitan** (kahz muh PAHL uh tuhn) *adj.*: worldly; sophisticated.

(Facing page, left mask): Old Ibibio mask.
The Trustees of the British Museum. (Facing page, right mask): Wood
mask. Ibo, Nigeria. The Trustees of the British Museum.
(Above painting): Couple with Leaves (1979), by Laura James, acrylic
on canvas.

Analyzing Visuals

Viewing and Interpreting How does the artist use colors, angles, and
patterns in this painting to convey that the subjects are a loving couple?

peculiar to the Ibos. If your father were alive and lived in the heart of Ibibio-land[5] he would be exactly like my father." Ⓐ

"I don't know. But anyway, as your father is so fond of you, I'm sure he will forgive you soon enough. Come on then, be a good boy and send him a nice lovely letter…"

"It would not be wise to break the news to him by writing. A letter will bring it upon him with a shock. I'm quite sure about that."

"All right, honey, suit yourself. You know your father."

As Nnaemeka walked home that evening he turned over in his mind different ways of overcoming his father's opposition, especially now that he had gone and found a girl for him. He had thought of showing his letter to Nene but decided on second thoughts not to, at least for the moment. He read it again when he got home and couldn't help smiling to himself. He remembered Ugoye[6] quite well, an Amazon[7] of a girl who used to beat up all the boys, himself included, on the way to the stream, a complete dunce at school.

I have found a girl who will suit you admirably—Ugoye Nweke,[8] the eldest daughter of our neighbor, Jacob Nweke. She has a proper Christian upbringing. When she stopped schooling some years ago her father (a man of sound judgment) sent her to live in the house of a pastor where she has received all the training a wife could need. Her Sunday school teacher has told me that she reads her Bible very fluently. I hope we shall begin negotiations when you come home in December.

On the second evening of his return from Lagos, Nnaemeka sat with his father under a cassia tree. This was the old man's retreat where he went to read his Bible when the parching December sun had set and a fresh, reviving wind blew on the leaves.

"Father," began Nnaemeka suddenly, "I have come to ask for forgiveness."

"Forgiveness? For what, my son?" he asked in amazement.

"It's about this marriage question."

"Which marriage question?"

"I can't—we must—I mean it is impossible for me to marry Nweke's daughter."

"Impossible? Why?" asked his father.

"I don't love her."

"Nobody said you did. Why should you?" he asked. Ⓑ

"Marriage today is different…"

"Look here, my son," interrupted his father, "nothing is different. What one looks for in a wife are a good character and a Christian background."

Nnaemeka saw there was no hope along the present line of argument.

"Moreover," he said, "I am engaged to marry another girl who has all of Ugoye's good qualities, and who…"

His father did not believe his ears. "What did you say?" he asked slowly and disconcertingly.

"She is a good Christian," his son went on, "and a teacher in a girls' school in Lagos."

"Teacher, did you say? If you consider that a qualification for a good wife I should like to point out to you, Emeka, that no Christian woman should teach. St. Paul in his letter to the Corinthians[9] says that women should keep silence." He rose slowly from his seat and paced forward and backward. This was his pet subject, and he condemned vehemently those church leaders who encouraged women to teach in their schools. After he had spent his emotion on a long homily he at last came back to his son's engagement, in a seemingly milder tone. Ⓒ

---

5. **Ibibio-land** (ihb uh BEE oh land): area of southeastern Nigeria that is the traditional homeland of the Ibibio, another African ethnic group.
6. **Ugoye** (oo GOH yay).
7. **Amazon**: tall, strong, aggressive woman. The Amazons were a group of warrior women in Greek mythology.
8. **Nweke** (ihn WAY kay).

---

9. **St. Paul . . . Corinthians**: reference to a passage in the Bible (1 Corinthians 14:34).

Ⓐ **Literary Focus** Verbal Irony Given what you have read so far, what is ironic about the story's title?

Ⓑ **Reading Focus** Identifying Cultural Characteristics What does this conversation suggest about traditional Ibo marriages?

Ⓒ **Reading Focus** Identifying Cultural Characteristics What is the traditional Ibo definition of a good wife?

"Whose daughter is she, anyway?"

"She is Nene Atang."

"What!" All the mildness was gone again. "Did you say Neneataga, what does that mean?"

"Nene Atang from Calabar.[10] She is the only girl I can marry." This was a very rash reply and Nnaemeka expected the storm to burst. But it did not. His father merely walked away into his room. This was most unexpected and perplexed Nnaemeka. His father's silence was infinitely more menacing than a flood of threatening speech. That night the old man did not eat.

When he sent for Nnaemeka a day later he applied all possible ways of dissuasion. But the young man's heart was hardened, and his father eventually gave him up as lost.

"I owe it to you, my son, as a duty to show you what is right and what is wrong. Whoever put this idea into your head might as well have cut your throat. It is Satan's work." He waved his son away.

"You will change your mind, Father, when you know Nene."

"I shall never see her," was the reply. From that night the father scarcely spoke to his son. He did not, however, cease hoping that he would realize how serious was the danger he was heading for. Day and night he put him in his prayers. **(D)**

Nnaemeka, for his own part, was very deeply affected by his father's grief. But he kept hoping that it would pass away. If it had occurred to him that never in the history of his people had a man married a woman who spoke a different tongue, he might have been less optimistic. "It has never been heard," was the

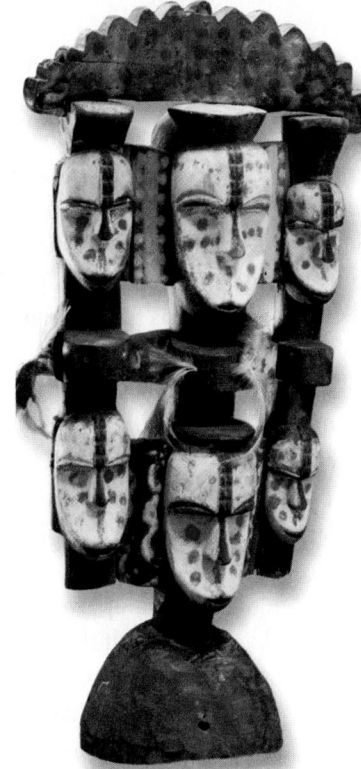

Iknega Headdress, X65.7994. Fowler Museum at UCLA.

verdict of an old man speaking a few weeks later. In that short sentence he spoke for all of his people. This man had come with others to commiserate with Okeke[11] when news went round about his son's behavior. By that time the son had gone back to Lagos.

"It has never been heard," said the old man again with a sad shake of his head.

"What did Our Lord say?" asked another gentleman. "Sons shall rise against their Fathers; it is there in the Holy Book."

"It is the beginning of the end," said another.

The discussion thus tending to become theological, Madubogwu, a highly practical man, brought it down once more to the ordinary level.

"Have you thought of consulting a native doctor about your son?" he asked Nnaemeka's father.

"He isn't sick," was the reply.

"What is he then? The boy's mind is diseased and only a good herbalist can bring him back to his right senses. The medicine he requires is *Amalile,* the same that women apply with success to recapture their husbands' straying affection."

"Madubogwu is right," said another gentleman. "This thing calls for medicine." **(E)**

"I shall not call in a native doctor." Nnaemeka's father was known to be obstinately ahead of his more superstitious neighbors in these matters. "I will not be another Mrs. Ochuba. If my son wants to kill himself let him do it with his own hands. It is not for me to help him."

"But it was her fault," said Madubogwu. "She ought to have gone to an honest herbalist. She was a clever woman, nevertheless."

---

10. **Calabar:** seaport city in southeastern Nigeria.

11. **Okeke** (oh KAY kay).

(D) **Reading Focus** **Identifying Cultural Characteristics** What do you infer about the importance of tradition from the father's reaction?

(E) **Reading Focus** **Identifying Cultural Characteristics** What do the reactions of the father's friends suggest about Ibo culture?

Vocabulary **rash** (rash) *adj.:* foolhardy.
commiserate (kuh MIHZ uh rayt) *v.:* feel sorrow or pity for; sympathize.

"She was a wicked murderess," said Jonathan, who rarely argued with his neighbors because, he often said, they were incapable of reasoning. "The medicine was prepared for her husband, it was his name they called in its preparation, and I am sure it would have been perfectly beneficial to him. It was wicked to put it into the herbalist's food, and say you were only trying it out."

Six months later, Nnaemeka was showing his young wife a short letter from his father:

It amazes me that you could be so unfeeling as to send me your wedding picture. I would have sent it back. But on further thought I decided just to cut off your wife and send it back to you because I have nothing to do with her. How I wish that I had nothing to do with you either.

When Nene read through this letter and looked at the mutilated picture her eyes filled with tears, and she began to sob.

"Don't cry, my darling," said her husband. "He is essentially good-natured and will one day look more kindly on our marriage." But years passed and that one day did not come.

For eight years, Okeke would have nothing to do with his son, Nnaemeka. Only three times (when Nnaemeka asked to come home and spend his leave) did he write to him.

"I can't have you in my house," he replied on one occasion. "It can be of no interest to me where or how you spend your leave—or your life, for that matter."

The prejudice against Nnaemeka's marriage was not confined to his little village. In Lagos, especially among his people who worked there, it showed itself in a different way. Their women, when they met at their village meeting, were not hostile to Nene. Rather, they paid her such excessive deference as to make her feel she was not one of them. But as time went on, Nene gradually broke through some of this prejudice and even began to make friends among them. Slowly and grudgingly they began to admit that she kept her home much better than most of them.

The story eventually got to the little village in the heart of the Ibo country that Nnaemeka and his young wife were a most happy couple. But his father was one of the few people in the village who knew nothing about this. He always displayed so much temper whenever his son's name was mentioned that everyone avoided it in his presence. By a tremendous effort of will he had succeeded in pushing his son to the back of his mind. The strain had nearly killed him but he had persevered, and won.

Then one day he received a letter from Nene, and in spite of himself he began to glance through it perfunctorily until all of a sudden the expression on his face changed and he began to read more carefully.

…Our two sons, from the day they learnt that they have a grandfather, have insisted on being taken to him. I find it impossible to tell them that you will not see them. I implore you to allow Nnaemeka to bring them home for a short time during his leave next month. I shall remain here in Lagos . . .

The old man at once felt the resolution he had built up over so many years falling in. He was telling himself that he must not give in. He tried to steel his heart against all emotional appeals. It was a reenactment of that other struggle. He leaned against a window and looked out. The sky was overcast with heavy black clouds and a high wind began to blow, filling the air with dust and dry leaves. It was one of those rare occasions when even Nature takes a hand in a human fight. Very soon it began to rain, the first rain in the year. It came down in large sharp drops and was accompanied by the lightning and thunder which mark a change of season. Okeke was trying hard not to think of his two grandsons. But he knew he was now fighting a losing battle. He tried to hum a favorite hymn but the pattering of large raindrops on the roof broke up the tune. His mind immediately returned to the children. How could he shut his door against them? By a curious mental process he imagined them standing, sad and forsaken, under the harsh angry weather—shut out from his house.

That night he hardly slept, from remorse—and a vague fear that he might die without making it up to them.

Vocabulary **persevered** (pur suh VIHRD) *v.:* persisted despite difficulty or opposition.
perfunctorily (puhr FUHNGK tuhr uh lee) *adv.:* mechanically; carelessly.

Applying Your Skills

SKILLS FOCUS **Literary Skills** Analyze irony, including verbal and situational irony; analyze plot. **Reading Skills** Identify cultural characteristics of a text. **Vocabulary**

Skills Demonstrate knowledge of literal meanings of words and their usage. **Writing Skills** Develop characters.

Marriage Is a Private Affair

Respond and Think Critically

Reading Focus

Quick Check

1. What is the source of the conflict in this story?

2. What details suggest the amount of time that passes between the time of the marriage and the story's end? During that time, how does Okeke act toward his son?

3. What finally resolves the conflict between father and son and daughter-in-law?

Read with a Purpose

4. How does Nnaemeka's decision to marry affect his family in the short run and in the long run?

Reading Skills: Identifying Cultural Characteristics

5. As you read the story, you noted details that revealed something about Nigerian culture. Would you describe that culture—as it is embodied in the old men of the father' village—as conservative, liberal, or both? What details suggest that the culture will change in the future?

✓ Vocabulary Check

Be ready to justify your answers to these questions.

6. Lagos is described as *cosmopolitan.* Does this mean the city is worldly or primitive?

7. If Nnaemeka gives a **rash** reply, is he being cautious or foolhardy?

8. The old men came to **commiserate** with Okeke. Were they comforting him or scolding him?

9. If the father **persevered** in trying to forget his son, did he persist or give up?

10. The father read his daughter-in-law's letter **perfunctorily.** Did he read it carelessly or carefully?

Literary Focus

Literary Analysis

11. **Analyze** In his depiction of the conflict between Nnaemeka and his father, does Achebe seem to favor strongly one side or the other? Explain.

12. **Interpret** What might the rain at the end of the story symbolize? Find a detail in the next-to-last paragraph that suggests this symbolism.

13. **Analyze** What do you think is the story's theme?

14. **Extend** How might Achebe's story relate to conflicts that exist today within a multicultural society such as the United States?

Literary Skills: Verbal Irony

15. **Interpret** The story's title is an example of **verbal irony**—it says something different from what it means. In what other ways could the title apply to the resolution at the end of the story?

Literary Skills Review: Plot

16. **Summarize** Write a summary of the **plot** of the story, detailing the exposition, conflict, complicating events, climax, and resolution.

Writing Focus

Think as a Reader/Writer

Use It in Your Writing Write a paragraph describing a fictional character from your own culture who is in the midst of a conflict. Like Achebe, use words and actions to *show* rather than tell about the character.

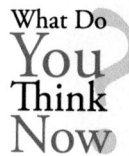 What Do You Think Now How are the views of the three main characters in the story influenced by their experiences?

Telephone Conversation

What Do You Think?

How does experience shape our view of the world?

⏱ QuickTalk

In your *Reader/Writer Notebook*, write briefly about an incident of racial discrimination you have heard about or witnessed.

Wole Soyinka (1934).

MEET THE WRITER

Wole Soyinka
(1934–   )

Nobel Prize WINNER

A voice of modern Africa, Wole Soyinka became the first African to win the Nobel Prize in Literature. Soyinka's favorite African deity is Ogun, god of both war and creative fire—a fitting muse for a multi-talented writer and performer whose plays, songs, novels, and poetry combine political activism, universal themes, and African traditions.

A Child of Two Worlds

Born Akinwande Oluwole Soyinka in a village in western Nigeria, Soyinka was the son of the principal of a Christian school and a teacher. His parents both supported European-style education, but his father also retained strong ties to his heritage as a member of the Yoruba people. As Soyinka grew up, he struggled with but respected both traditions; his 1981 autobiography, *Aké: The Years of Childhood,* relates his <u>perspective</u> on this dual heritage.

After attending University College at Ibadan, Nigeria, Soyinka studied English literature in England at the University of Leeds. In the late 1950s, he wrote plays and poetry in London for theater and radio. During this period of African nationalism and pressure for independence, Soyinka treated themes of racism, injustice, tyranny, and corruption all with satiric wit. Soyinka was also concerned with the collision of ancient traditions with modern realities, and he peppered his plays with vivid Yoruba masquerade rituals.

Suffering for Liberty

Soyinka experienced brutal despotism firsthand during Nigeria's civil war of the late 1960s, when he was imprisoned for two years for the so-called crime of meeting with secessionist leaders such as the writer Chinua Achebe. He describes these experiences in *The Man Dies: Prison Notes,* published in 1972. Today, Soyinka continues to record and dramatize, with passion and humor, the struggle and spirit of modern-day Africa.

Think About the Writer

What do you think of Soyinka's use of humor to fight oppression? Do you think this approach can be effective? Explain.

Reader/Writer Notebook

Use your **RWN** to complete the activities for this selection.

Literary Focus

Satire Writing that ridicules the foolish or even destructive actions of humans with the intention of bringing about awareness and reform is called **satire.** In satire, writers exaggerate or skew the human attitude or action that they are targeting. By making the action or attitude appear foolish, or even preposterous, satirists hope to inspire people to recognize it and make changes. In the following poem, Wole Soyinka uses satire to reveal the absurdity of racial discrimination.

Reading Focus

Analyzing Author's Perspective When you read satire, it is especially important that you have a clear notion of the writer's perspective. **Perspective** refers to a way of looking at the world, including assumptions, attitudes, biases, and insecurities. When you analyze a writer's perspective, you must remember that the person who speaks in a poem or story is not necessarily the author.

Into Action As you read, use an organizer like the one below to take notes on the perspectives of the poem's two characters, the speaker and the landlady he is addressing. Remember that perspective encompasses assumptions and attitudes, including biases and insecurities.

Speaker's Perspective	Landlady's Perspective
1. Doesn't want to waste his time talking to a landlady who won't rent a place to him because he is African.	
2.	

Vocabulary

revelation (rehv uh LAY shuhn) *n.:* something revealed. *It was a revelation to him that he might be rejected on the basis of his skin color.*

clinical (KLIHN uh kuhl) *adj.:* objective; without emotion. *The landlady took a hard, clinical look at the prospective tenant.*

impersonality (ihm pur suh NAL uh tee) *n.:* lack of human connection. *The landlady's impersonality in dealing with her prospective tenant was chilling.*

conceding (kuhn SEED ihng) *v.:* admitting as true. *The landlady was finally conceding that she did not know what West African sepia was.*

Language Coach

Word Families When you encounter an unfamiliar word, look closely to see if there is a familiar word embedded in it. For example, the word *reveal* is embedded in the word *revelation* (spelled slightly differently). This knowledge might help you guess that *revelation* means "something revealed." What words are embedded in *impersonality, clinical,* and *conceding*?

Writing Focus

Think as a Reader/Writer

Find It in Your Reading The thrust of this poem comes from a dialogue between two characters who have different perspectives: One character is in a phone booth, and the other is in her home. The dialogue is both funny and sad. As you read, make a list of the characteristics of this dialogue you find interesting or most effective. Note also the way the writer describes the voice of the woman to whom he is speaking and his surroundings in the phone booth.

 Learn It Online
Get to know the Vocabulary words online.

go.hrw.com   L12-1385

Telephone Conversation

by **Wole Soyinka**

Read with a Purpose
As you read, try to hear the two people who are having this telephone conversation. How do you picture them?

Build Background
The speaker in Soyinka's poem is talking from one of the red public telephone booths that were especially common in London years ago. Such phones had two buttons, A and B; pressing A put one through to the recipient of the call. The speaker is a well-educated black African; the woman with whom he is conversing is a white British woman who has property to rent.

When Soyinka was a college student in London in the late 1950s, millions of people from former British colonies were flooding into England in search of educational opportunities and employment. This poem records one of Soyinka's own experiences with racial discrimination during that time.

The price seemed reasonable, location
Indifferent. The landlady swore she lived
Off premises. Nothing remained
But self-confession. "Madam," I warned,
5   "I hate a wasted journey—I am African."
Silence. Silenced transmission of
Pressurized good-breeding. Voice, when it came,
Lipstick coated, long gold-rolled
Cigarette-holder pipped. Caught I was, foully.

10   "HOW DARK?"… I had not misheard… "ARE YOU LIGHT
OR VERY DARK?" Button B. Button A. Stench
Of rancid breath of public hide-and-speak.
Red booth. Red pillar-box.° Red double-tiered
Omnibus° squelching tar. It *was* real! Shamed
15   By ill-mannered silence, surrender
Pushed dumbfoundment to beg simplification.
Considerate she was, varying the emphasis—   **Ⓐ**

13. pillar-box: British for "mailbox," red like the phone booth.
13–14. double-tiered omnibus: bus with two decks, or tiers.

Ⓐ **Reading Focus** Analyzing Author's Perspective   Judging from what you've read so far, how would you say the writer feels about these two conversationalists?

Vocabulary   **revelation** (rehv uh LAY shuhn) *n.*: something revealed.
clinical (KLIHN uh kuhl) *adj.*: objective; without emotion.

The Man (2001), by Francks Deceus, mixed media on canvas.

"ARE YOU DARK? OR VERY LIGHT?" Revelation came.
"You mean—like plain or milk chocolate?"

20 Her assent was clinical, crushing in its light
Impersonality. Rapidly, wavelength adjusted,
I chose. "West African sepia"—and as an afterthought,
"Down in my passport." Silence for spectroscopic
Flight of fancy,° till truthfulness clanged her accent

25 Hard on the mouthpiece. "WHAT'S THAT?" conceding,
"DON'T KNOW WHAT THAT IS." "Like brunette." **B**

"THAT'S DARK, ISN'T IT?" "Not altogether.
Facially, I am brunette, but madam, you should see
The rest of me. Palm of my hand, soles of my feet

30 Are a peroxide blonde. Friction, caused—
Foolishly, madam—by sitting down, has turned
My bottom raven black—One moment madam!"—sensing
Her receiver rearing on the thunderclap
About my ears—"Madam," I pleaded, "wouldn't you rather

35 See for yourself?"

23–24. spectroscopic (spehk truh skahp ihk) **flight of fancy:** wide range, or spectrum, of ideas.

B **Literary Focus** Satire How does the speaker mock the woman in this exchange?

Vocabulary **impersonality** (ihm pur suh NAL uh tee) *n.*: lack of human connection.
conceding (kuhn SEED ihng) *v.*: admitting as true.

Applying Your Skills

SKILLS FOCUS **Literary Skills** Analyze the characteristics of satire; analyze imagery. **Reading Skills** Analyze author's perspective. **Vocabulary**

Skills Demonstrate knowledge of literal meanings of words and their usage. **Writing Skills** Use dialogue effectively.

Telephone Conversation

Respond and Think Critically

Reading Focus

Quick Check

1. Paraphrase (restate in your own words) what happens in each stanza of this poem.

Read with a Purpose

2. What does each person on either end of the telephone conversation "see" about the other person? What do the landlady and prospective tenant assume about each other?

Reading Skills: Analyzing Author's Perspective

3. Add a third column to your perspectives chart in which you describe the *author's* perspective in this poem. Do you think the author shares either the African man's or the landlady's perspective? Why do you think so?

✓ Vocabulary Check

Be ready to justify your responses to the questions about Vocabulary words.

4. When the writer says "**revelation** *came*," does he mean that something became clear to him or that something became obscure to him?

5. When the writer describes the landlady's agreement as *clinical*, does he mean she was emotional or that she was objective and without emotion?

6. When the writer says the landlady's agreement is crushing in its **impersonality**, does he mean she agreed in a very warm and human way or she showed a lack of human connection?

7. When the landlady is described as *conceding*, is she admitting something, or is she refusing to change her mind?

Literary Focus

Literary Analysis

8. **Analyze** What is ironic about the speaker's reference to the landlady's "good-breeding"? What is ironic about his calling her "considerate"?

9. **Evaluate** What do you think of the speaker's final question? How will it affect the landlady?

10. **Analyze** What is the **theme,** or truth about life, revealed in this poem?

Literary Skills: Satire

11. **Interpret** Who or what is the target of Soyinka's satire in this poem? What change in society does this satirist want to see occur?

12. **Evaluate** How effective do you think the methods of this satire will be in inspiring change?

Literary Skills Review: Imagery

13. **Analyze** Language that appeals to the senses is **imagery.** What colors does Soyinka use to help us visualize skin color? What is communicated by using precise colors to describe skin tones?

Writing Focus

Think as a Reader/Writer

Use It in Your Writing Re-read your notes about this poem's use of dialogue. In a poem or prose passage, write about a difficult personal encounter you've read about or experienced. Use dialogue to make the description more vivid.

 What Do **You Think Now**

What people and events might have shaped the landlady's view of the world?

Postcolonial Literature

Captain Justin Bootah of the Lifeguards from India addresses a Queen's Guard at Trooping the Color.

When European colonies gained their independence, they also began to assert their own literary voices. Brilliant writers like Derek Walcott, V. S. Naipaul, and Anita Desai began to express the experiences of their peoples and countries, while others like American writer Paul Theroux have documented postcolonial aftermath in the course of traveling and living abroad. Shaped by a dual heritage, that of the European colonizer and that of the original culture, they have struggled to forge their own identities. Because of their common experiences and themes, the works of these writers can be grouped in the category of postcolonial literature. As you read, notice how the form and content of Walcott's, Naipaul's, and Desai's texts are influenced by the colonial experience.

CONTENTS

from **Omeros** by Derek Walcott

B. Wordsworth by V. S. Naipaul

from **Sir Vidia's Shadow** by Paul Theroux

Games at Twilight by Anita Desai

Preparing to Read

from Omeros

What Do You Think?

How does experience shape our view of the world?

⏱ QuickWrite

Think about someone you know or have heard of whose good deeds you might celebrate in a poem. What did this person do to impress you? Write a few sentences about this person in your *Reader/Writer Notebook*.

Derek Walcott (1930).

MEET THE WRITER

Derek Walcott
(1930–)

Nobel Prize WINNER

Derek Walcott was born on the Caribbean island of St. Lucia, then under British rule. Walcott lost his father at a very young age. His mother, a schoolteacher, encouraged Walcott's love of reading and provided him with a thorough background in the Western classics.

Caught Between Two Worlds

With black and white grandparents on both sides of his family, Walcott grew up with a biracial heritage that often presented difficulties for him. His inability to identify completely with either black or white people was only one reason for what he called his "schizophrenic boyhood." As a lover of Western literature and his island home, Walcott lived "two lives: the interior life of poetry and the outward life of action and dialect."

Another cause of Walcott's ambivalent perspective was his knowledge of Britain's role in slavery and the oppression of his people. This awareness coexisted with Walcott's love of British poetry. As he grew older, Walcott also began to feel uncomfortable with the strict Catholic culture of St. Lucia. He fled to Kingston, Jamaica, where he earned a degree at the University of the West Indies, and quickly joined the thriving arts community. In 1957, he received a Rockefeller Foundation grant to study theater arts in New York City. Though Walcott disliked living in New York, it was later to be the site of production for his award-winning play, *Dream on Monkey Mountain*.

Classical Poet with a New Subject

During the 1960s, Walcott began to focus on writing poetry. Much of Walcott's form is derived from the British poetry he loves. He writes in a rich, expressive style and makes liberal use of classical allusions. Much of his subject matter, however, comes from the Caribbean islands.

In 1992, the quincentennial of Columbus's landing in the Caribbean, Walcott was awarded the Nobel Prize in Literature. The Swedish Academy stated, "In him, West Indian culture has found its great poet."

Think About the Writer

How do you think writing helped Derek Walcott forge an identity for himself?

Reader/Writer Notebook

Use your **RWN** to complete the activities for this selection.

Literary Focus

Contemporary Epic An **epic** is a long narrative poem that tells the story of a larger-than-life hero who embodies the values of a particular society. Originally an oral tradition, epics were memorized and recited so they could be passed from one generation to the next. Those that were written down, such as *Gilgamesh,* the *Iliad,* and the *Odyssey,* became some of the earliest works of literature. Early epics tend to be about kings or fierce warriors who fight battles or make dangerous journeys to unknown lands. Later epics, such as Milton's *Paradise Lost,* reflect the preoccupations of their times. **Contemporary epics** often focus on ordinary protagonists or even antiheroes (characters obviously lacking any heroic qualities) while retaining elements of the epic form, such as the long narrative.

Reading Focus

Using Background Knowledge To understand and enjoy a contemporary epic, such as *Omeros,* you need some **background knowledge.** First, you must understand the epic form, including its use of grandiose language and long narratives. Second, you must recognize allusions to earlier epics or other works of literature. Finally, you should know, or be able to infer, something of the culture the epic represents.

Into Action As you read, use a chart like the one below to record notes on the epic's form and allusions, as well as the culture it represents.

Epic Form	Allusions	Culture
Grandiose language: Walcott uses grandiose language and epic style to describe everyday things, such as the hero's shoes.		

Writing Focus

Think as a Reader/Writer

Find It in Your Reading Like most epic writers, Walcott uses language that combines specific, realistic detail with **figurative language** in the form of simile or metaphor. Make two columns on a sheet of paper. Label one "Realistic Detail" and the other "Figurative Language." As you read, note examples of each in the correct column.

Vocabulary

ascended (uh SEHND ihd) *v.:* went up. *The gull ascended from the beach.*

idyll (YD uhl) *n.:* short work of prose or poetry about an idealized country scene. *The poet composed an idyll about the beaches of the Caribbean.*

goblet (GAHB liht) *n.:* drinking vessel, often ornate. *The guest of honor was presented with a goblet of wine.*

epilogue (EHP uh lawg) *n.:* short section at the end of a literary work that often tells what happened after the end of the story. *In the epilogue, the audience discovered that the hero later became a dentist.*

Language Coach

Roots The word *epilogue* contains the root *logos,* meaning "speech," "word," or "reason." Use your knowledge of affixes and roots to write definitions for the following words, and tell how their meanings relate to the root *logos: prologue, illogical,* and *dialogue.*

Learn It Online
Get the scoop on the author's life and work.

go.hrw.com   L12-1391   **Go**

from Omeros

by **Derek Walcott**

Read with a Purpose
Read to find out how the speaker remembers Achille and his journey.

Build Background
The title of this poem, *Omeros,* is the modern Greek word for *Homer,* the poet who is thought to have written the *Iliad* and the *Odyssey.* The *Iliad's* main character is Achilles, a hero of the Trojan War. In the *Odyssey,* the main character, Odysseus, has many adventures traveling home from the Trojan War. The main character of Walcott's epic is a fisherman named Achille, who journeys with a friend to the West African coast from which their ancestors came. The opening of *Omeros* even echoes some of the language from the beginning of the *Iliad:*

> *Sing, O goddess, the anger of Achilles son of Peleus, that brought countless ills upon the Achaeans. Many a brave soul did it send hurrying down to Hades, and many a hero did it yield a prey to dogs and vultures.*

I sang of quiet Achille, Afolabe's son, **A**
who never ascended in an elevator,
who had no passport, since the horizon needs none,

never begged nor borrowed, was nobody's waiter, **B**
5 whose end, when it comes, will be a death by water
(which is not for this book, which will remain unknown

and unread by him). I sang the only slaughter
that brought him delight, and that from necessity—
of fish, sang the channels of his back in the sun.

A Reading Focus Using Background Knowledge How does this line echo language from the *Iliad?*

B Literary Focus Contemporary Epic What details does the poet include that make it clear this is a contemporary epic?

Vocabulary ascended (uh SEHND ihd) *v.:* went up.

Omeros book cover by Derek Walcott.
Courtesy of the Artist.

10   I sang our wide country, the Caribbean Sea.
      Who hated shoes, whose soles were as cracked as a stone,
      who was gentle with ropes, who had one suit alone,

      whom no man dared insult and who insulted no one,
      whose grin was a white breaker cresting,° but whose frown
15   was a growing thunderhead, whose fist of iron   **C**

14. a white breaker cresting: a foam-topped wave reaching its highest point.

C **Literary Focus** **Contemporary Epic** What do you learn here about this epic's hero, Achille?

would do me a greater honour if it held on
to my casket's oarlocks° than mine lifting his own
when both anchors are lowered in the one island,

but now the idyll dies, the goblet is broken,
20 and rainwater trickles down the brown cheek of a jar
from the clay of Choiseul.° So much left unspoken

by my chirping nib!° And my earth-door lies ajar.
I lie wrapped in a flour-sack sail. The clods thud
on my rope-lowered canoe. Rasping shovels scrape

25 a dry rain of dirt on its hold, but turn your head
when the sea-almond rattles or the rust-leaved grape
from the shells of my unpharaonic° pyramid

towards paper shredded by the wind and scattered
like white gulls that separate their names from the foam
30 and nod to a fisherman with his khaki dog

that skitters from the wave-crash, then frown at his form
for one swift second. In its earth-trough, my pirogue°
with its brass-handled oarlocks is sailing. Not from

but with them, with Hector,° with Maud in the rhythm   **D**
35 of her beds trowelled over, with a swirling log
lifting its mossed head from the swell; let the deep hymn

of the Caribbean continue my epilogue;
may waves remove their shawls as my mourners walk home
to their rusted villages, good shoes in one hand,

40 passing a boy who walked through the ignorant foam,
and saw a sail going out or else coming in,
and watched asterisks of rain puckering the sand.

	17. oarlocks: metal hoops in a ship or boat that hold the oars in place.
	21. Choiseul: one of the western Solomon Islands.
	22. nib: tip of a fountain pen.
	27. unpharaonic: not like or fitting for a pharaoh.
	32. pirogue: type of canoe made of a hollowed-out tree trunk.
	34. Hector: the most important warrior of the Trojan army in the *Iliad*. In the ancient epic, he is killed by Achilles.

D **Reading Focus** **Using Background Knowledge** Read the sidenote that explains the character of Hector. In what sense is the speaker of the poem "traveling" with Hector?

Vocabulary **idyll** (YD uhl) *n.*: short work of prose or poetry about an idealized country scene.
goblet (GAHB liht) *n.*: drinking vessel, often ornate.
epilogue (EHP uh lawg) *n.*: short section at the end of a literary work that often tells what happened after the end of the story.

Applying Your Skills

from **Omeros**

Respond and Think Critically

Reading Focus

Quick Check

1. How would you describe Achille? What kind of person does he seem to be? Give details to support your description. (Consider what Achille kills and why.)

2. Where is the speaker of this poem? What has happened to him?

3. Why does the speaker ask the "deep hymn / of the Caribbean" to continue his epilogue?

Read with a Purpose

4. What is the speaker's opinion of Achille and his actions?

Reading Skills: Using Background Knowledge

5. Review the chart you made as you read. Now, create a Venn diagram. Label one circle "Epic Form and Allusions," and in it write what the poem owes to ancient Western literature. Label the other circle "Culture," and in it write how the poem represents Caribbean culture. In the intersecting space, describe how the Caribbean subject matter and the classical form combine.

✓ Vocabulary Check

Match the Vocabulary words with their definitions.

6. ascended   **a.** drinking vessel

7. idyll   **b.** went up

8. goblet   **c.** final part of a story or poem

9. epilogue   **d.** pastoral poem or story

Literary Focus

Literary Analysis

10. **Analyze** To what does the poet compare the coffin in line 27? Why do you think he chose this metaphor?

11. **Compare and Contrast** How is Achille similar to and different from traditional epic heroes? Consider that most heroes have adventures, often during war.

12. **Make Judgments** How does the speaker feel about the setting? How can you tell?

Literary Skills: Contemporary Epic

13. **Interpret** Do you think the epic form enriches the meaning of this poem? Why or why not?

Literary Skills Review: Diction

14. **Analyze** What diction, or word choice, does the poet use that does not seem to belong to the world in which the poem is set?

Writing Focus

Think as a Reader/Writer

Use It in Your Writing As you read the excerpt, you noted Walcott's use of realistic detail and figurative language. Now, recall your QuickWrite. What person did you name whose deeds you might want to celebrate? Write a short poem praising this person. Use both specific, realistic detail and figurative language. Your poem does not have to rhyme.

 What Do You Think Now

How is Walcott's experience living in the Caribbean reflected in the poem?

Preparing to Read

B. Wordsworth

How does experience shape our view of the world?

🕐 **QuickWrite**

In your *Reader/Writer Notebook,* jot down four or five qualities you associate with poets. As you read, see how your image of poets corresponds with that of the poet in the story.

V. S. Naipaul (1932).

V. S. Naipaul
(1932–   )

Nobel Prize WINNER

Naipaul's works have been acclaimed for their bitter yet compassionate insights into the human struggle for identity and survival.

Escape from the Island

When V. S. (Vidiadhar Surajprasad) Naipaul was born, his homeland, the Caribbean island of Trinidad, was still under British colonial rule. His family had immigrated to Trinidad in the nineteenth century to work as indentured servants on the sugar plantations. With their Asian background and Hindu religion, the Naipauls felt like members of a transplanted society. As a result, from his earliest days, Naipaul felt a degree of rootlessness. He also found it difficult to <u>adapt</u> to life on the small island, a world that at times seemed a sort of prison.

Fortunately, Naipaul was an outstanding student. Scholastic honors won him a place at Trinidad's Queen's Royal College and gave him a chance to leave the island. Later, he was granted a scholarship to England's Oxford University, where he was one of only a few dark-skinned students at a university famous for educating England's privileged white upper classes.

When Naipaul left Oxford, he had no desire to return to Trinidad. He began working part time for the British Broadcasting Corporation (BBC) and tried his hand at writing fiction about the island life he had fled. His first short stories, which later became *Miguel Street,* went unnoticed until he was able to publish two novels set in Trinidad.

A Place in the Limelight

Naipaul's first masterpiece, *A House for Mr. Biswas,* concerns a poor Trinidadian's desperate quest for a house of his own. The book, which some critics have compared to the works of Charles Dickens, established Naipaul as a major novelist throughout the literary world.

Naipaul has won numerous awards, including the Nobel Prize in Literature. His search for roots has led him to travel back to the West Indies and then to Africa, the Middle East, and India as he pursues the meaning of his own mixed heritage.

Think About the Writer How do you think Naipaul's sense of being an outsider might affect his life and his writing?

Reader/Writer Notebook

Use your **RWN** to complete the activities for this selection.

Literary Focus

Setting The time and place of a story is known as its **setting.** The setting of this story is the back streets of Port-of-Spain, capital of Trinidad, where Naipaul lived as a child. Naipaul uses imagery and dialogue, as well as factual details, to enliven the setting. Several of the story's details, such as beggars asking for pennies, suggest it takes place during the Great Depression in the 1930s, the years of Naipaul's own childhood. As you will see, the main characters of "B. Wordsworth," a young boy and an old, self-proclaimed poet, seem to be set apart from their harsh surroundings. At arm's length from the story's other, more desperate characters, the pair are determined to find and appreciate spots of beauty in an otherwise violent—or at best indifferent—world.

Reading Focus

Making Inferences About Theme Few stories explicitly state their **theme,** or central idea or insight about human experience. The reader is expected to infer the theme from clues in the text. Every element of a story—its plot; the thoughts, feelings, and actions of its characters; its language; and its setting—work together to express a theme.

Into Action As you read, ask yourself how each element of the story reflects the theme. Write your notes in an organizer like the one below.

Plot	Characterization	Language	Setting
	B. Wordsworth describes himself as a poet.		

Writing Focus

Think as a Reader/Writer

Find It in Your Reading In this story, Naipaul uses **dialect,** or a variant form, of English. In your *Reader/Writer Notebook,* record the lines of dialect and list ways it differs from standard English. How might the story change if these lines were in standard English? What would the story lose or gain?

TechFocus Imagine that you are in charge of <u>adapting</u> this story to the big screen. Take notes describing the characters and the setting, and decide how you would convey them on film.

Vocabulary

botanical (buh TAN uh kuhl) *adj.:* of plants or plant life; relating to the science of botany. *The old man had a great deal of botanical knowledge about trees and flowers.*

rite (ryt) *n.:* formal ceremony. *A rite was held to remember those who died in the war.*

patronize (PAY truh nyz) *v.:* be a customer of. *The man and the boy considered carefully which shop to patronize.*

distill (dihs TIHL) *v.:* draw out the essence of. *The old man was able to distill all his wisdom into a few words.*

keenly (KEEN lee) *adv.:* strongly and clearly. *The boy felt the poet's pain so keenly that he was overcome with sadness.*

Language Coach

Multiple-Meaning Words The Vocabulary word *patronize* has more than one meaning. In addition to the definition provided above, *patronize* can mean "look down on or be condescending toward" or "support an art or cause." Use context clues to help you tell which meaning is used in each sentence:

1. Their friends *patronize* the ballet by buying tickets for each performance.
2. The young poets *patronize* the local bookstore.
3. The women *patronize* the teenager by pretending to like her poetry.

Learn It Online

Hear a professional actor read this story.

go.hrw.com   L12-1397   **Go**

B. WORDSWORTH

by **V. S. Naipaul**

Read with a Purpose
Read to discover what makes B. Wordsworth a poet.

Build Background
The poet in this story is a black Trinidadian who calls himself B. [Black] Wordsworth, "brother" to William Wordsworth. Recall that English poet William Wordsworth introduced a new theory of poetry that glorified everyday things and everyday language.

Three beggars called punctually every day at the hospitable houses in Miguel Street. At about ten an Indian came in his dhoti[1] and white jacket, and we poured a tin of rice into the sack he carried on his back. At twelve an old woman smoking a clay pipe came and she got a cent. At two a blind man led by a boy called for his penny.

Sometimes we had a rogue.[2] One day a man called and said he was hungry. We gave him a meal. He asked for a cigarette and wouldn't go until we had lit it for him. That man never came again.

The strangest caller came one afternoon at about four o'clock. I had come back from school and was in my home clothes. The man said to me, "Sonny, may I come inside your yard?"

He was a small man and he was tidily dressed. He wore a hat, a white shirt, and black trousers.

I asked, "What you want?"

He said, "I want to watch your bees."

We had four small gru-gru palm trees[3] and they were full of uninvited bees.

Papiamento (1987), by Julio Larraz, oil on canvas.
Marlborough Gallery, New York.

---

1. **dhoti** (DOH tee): loincloth worn by many Hindu men.
2. **rogue** (rohg): archaic for "wandering beggar."
3. **gru-gru** (GROO groo) **palm trees:** spiny-trunked West Indian palms.

Ⓐ **Literary Focus** Setting What details help you visualize the scene on Miguel Street?

I ran up the steps and shouted, "Ma, it have a man outside here. He say he want to watch the bees."

My mother came out, looked at the man, and asked in an unfriendly way, "What you want?"

The man said, "I want to watch your bees."

His English was so good, it didn't sound natural, and I could see my mother was worried.

She said to me, "Stay here and watch him while he watch the bees."

The man said, "Thank you, Madam. You have done a good deed today."

He spoke very slowly and very correctly as though every word was costing him money.

We watched the bees, this man and I, for about an hour, squatting near the palm trees.

The man said, "I like watching bees. Sonny, do you like watching bees?"

I said, "I ain't have the time."

He shook his head sadly. He said, "That's what I do, I just watch. I can watch ants for days. Have you ever watched ants? And scorpions, and centipedes, and *congorees*[4]—have you watched those?"

I shook my head.

I said, "What you does do, mister?"

He got up and said, "I am a poet."

I said, "A good poet?"

He said, "The greatest in the world."

"What your name, mister?"

"B. Wordsworth."

"B for Bill?"

"Black. Black Wordsworth. White Wordsworth was my brother. We share one heart. I can watch a small flower like the morning glory and cry."

I said, "Why you does cry?"

"Why, boy? Why? You will know when you grow up. You're a poet, too, you know. And when you're a poet you can cry for everything."

I couldn't laugh.

He said, "You like your mother?"

"When she not beating me."

He pulled out a printed sheet from his hip pocket and said, "On this paper is the greatest poem about mothers and I'm going to sell it to you at a bargain price. For four cents."

I went inside and I said, "Ma, you want to buy a poetry for four cents?"

My mother said, "Tell that blasted man to haul his tail away from my yard, you hear."

I said to B. Wordsworth, "My mother say she ain't have four cents."

B. Wordsworth said, "It is the poet's tragedy."

And he put the paper back in his pocket. He didn't seem to mind.

---

4. *congorees* (KAHNG guh reez): conger eels; long, scale-less eels found in the warm waters of the West Indies.

I said, "Is a funny way to go round selling poetry like that. Only calypsonians[5] do that sort of thing. A lot of people does buy?"

He said, "No one has yet bought a single copy."

"But why you does keep on going round, then?"

He said, "In this way I watch many things, and I always hope to meet poets."

I said, "You really think I is a poet?"

"You're as good as me," he said. **B**

And when B. Wordsworth left, I prayed I would see him again.

About a week later, coming back from school one afternoon, I met him at the corner of Miguel Street.

He said, "I have been waiting for you for a long time."

I said, "You sell any poetry yet?"

He shook his head.

He said, "In my yard I have the best mango tree in Port-of-Spain.[6] And now the mangoes are ripe and red and very sweet and juicy. I have waited here for you to tell you this and to invite you to come and eat some of my mangoes." **C**

He lived in Alberto Street in a one-roomed hut placed right in the center of the lot. The yard seemed all green. There was the big mango tree. There was a coconut tree and there was a plum tree. The place looked wild, as though it wasn't in the city at all. You couldn't see all the big concrete houses in the street. **D**

He was right. The mangoes were sweet and juicy. I ate about six, and the yellow mango juice ran down my

---

5. **calypsonians** (kuh lihp SOH nee uhnz): West Indian folk musicians who traditionally perform satirical, syncopated songs that are improvised, or composed on the spot. *Calypso* possibly comes from *kaiso,* a Trinidadian dialect word meaning "town crier."

6. **Port-of-Spain:** seaport on the island of Trinidad; capital of Trinidad and Tobago.

B **Reading Focus** **Making Inferences About Theme** What do you think B. Wordsworth means when he says that the boy is a poet? What might being a poet have to do with the theme of the story?

C **Literary Focus** **Setting** How does the tropical setting of Trinidad help form B. Wordsworth's ideas about life?

D **Literary Focus** **Setting** What can you infer about B. Wordsworth's values from this description of his home?

arms to my elbows and down my mouth to my chin and my shirt was stained.

My mother said when I got home, "Where you was? You think you is a man now and could go all over the place? Go cut a whip for me."

She beat me rather badly, and I ran out of the house swearing that I would never come back. I went to B. Wordsworth's house. I was so angry, my nose was bleeding.

B. Wordsworth said, "Stop crying, and we will go for a walk."

I stopped crying, but I was breathing short. We went for a walk. We walked down St. Clair Avenue to the Savannah[7] and we walked to the racecourse.

B. Wordsworth said, "Now, let us lie on the grass and look up at the sky, and I want you to think how far those stars are from us."

I did as he told me, and I saw what he meant. I felt like nothing, and at the same time I had never felt so big and great in all my life. I forgot all my anger and all my tears and all the blows.

When I said I was better, he began telling me the names of the stars, and I particularly remembered the constellation of Orion the Hunter,[8] though I don't really know why. I can spot Orion even today, but I have forgotten the rest.

Then a light was flashed into our faces, and we saw a policeman. We got up from the grass.

The policeman said, "What you doing here?"

B. Wordsworth said, "I have been asking myself the same question for forty years."

---

7. **Savannah** (suh VAN uh): two-hundred-acre park in the center of Port-of-Spain. The racecourse is located there.
8. **Orion** (aw RY uhn) **the Hunter:** constellation named for a hunter in Greek and Roman mythology whom Diana—the goddess of the moon and of hunting—loves but accidentally kills.

We became friends, B. Wordsworth and I. He told me, "You must never tell anybody about me and about the mango tree and the coconut tree and the plum tree. You must keep that a secret. If you tell anybody, I will know, because I am a poet."

I gave him my word and I kept it.

I liked his little room. It had no more furniture than George's front room,[9] but it looked cleaner and healthier. But it also looked lonely.

One day I asked him. "Mister Wordsworth, why you does keep all this bush in your yard? Ain't it does make the place damp?"

He said, "Listen, and I will tell you a story. Once upon a time a boy and girl met each other and they fell in love. They loved each other so much they got married. They were both poets. He loved words. She loved grass and flowers and trees. They lived happily in a single room, and then one day, the girl poet said to the boy poet, 'We are going to have another poet in the family.' But this poet was never born, because the girl died, and the young poet died with her, inside her. And the girl's husband was very sad, and he said he would never touch a thing in the girl's garden. And so the garden remained, and grew high and wild." **(E)**

I looked at B. Wordsworth, and as he told me this lovely story, he seemed to grow older. I understood his story.

We went for long walks together. We went to the Botanical Gardens and the Rock Gardens. We climbed Chancellor Hill in the late afternoon and watched the darkness fall on Port-of-Spain, and watched the lights go on in the city and on the ships in the harbor.

He did everything as though he were doing it for the first time in his life. He did everything as though he were doing some church rite. **(F)**

---

9. **George's front room:** George is a character in another story in Naipaul's book *Miguel Street.*

(E) Reading Focus Making Inferences About Theme What does B. Wordsworth's story tell you about his definition of a poet? What can you guess about the theme from his story and his definition of a poet?

(F) Reading Focus Making Inferences About Theme What do B. Wordsworth's attitudes suggest about how a poet should approach everyday life?

Vocabulary botanical (buh TAN uh kuhl) *adj.*: of plants or plant life; relating to the science of botany.
rite (ryt) *n.*: formal ceremony.

The Trial (1986), by Julio Larraz, oil on canvas.
Marlborough Gallery, New York.

Viewing and Interpreting   Note that the subject's face is blurred but his wedding ring is quite visible. How do artists and writers emphasize or downplay certain traits to construct a subject's or character's identity? What salient characteristics does Naipaul give to B. Wordsworth?

He would say to me, "Now, how about having some ice cream?"

And when I said, yes, he would grow very serious and say, "Now, which café shall we patronize?" As though it were a very important thing. He would think for some time about it, and finally say, "I think I will go and negotiate the purchase with that shop."

The world became a most exciting place. One day, when I was in his yard, he said to me, "I have a great secret which I am now going to tell you."

I said, "It really secret?"

"At the moment, yes."

I looked at him, and he looked at me. He said, "This is just between you and me, remember. I am writing a poem."

"Oh." I was disappointed.

He said, "But this is a different sort of poem. This is the greatest poem in the world."

I whistled.

He said, "I have been working on it for more than five years now. I will finish it in about twenty-two years from now, that is, if I keep on writing at the present rate."

"You does write a lot, then?"

He said, "Not any more. I just write one line a month. But I make sure it is a good line."

I asked, "What was last month's good line?"

He looked up at the sky, and said, *"The past is deep."*

I said, "It is a beautiful line."

B. Wordsworth said, "I hope to distill the experiences of a whole month into that single line of poetry.

Vocabulary   patronize (PAY truh nyz) *v.:* be a customer of.
distill (dihs TIHL) *v.:* draw out the essence of.

So, in twenty-two years, I shall have written a poem that will sing to all humanity."

I was filled with wonder.

Our walks continued. We walked along the sea wall at Docksite one day, and I said, "Mr. Wordsworth, if I drop this pin in the water, you think it will float?"

He said, "This is a strange world. Drop your pin, and let us see what will happen."

The pin sank.

I said, "How is the poem this month?"

But he never told me any other line. He merely said, "Oh, it comes, you know. It comes."

Or we would sit on the sea wall and watch the liners come into the harbor.

But of the greatest poem in the world I heard no more.

I felt he was growing older.

"How you does live, Mr. Wordsworth?" I asked him one day.

He said, "You mean how I get money?"

When I nodded, he laughed in a crooked way.

He said, "I sing calypsos in the calypso season."

"And that last you the rest of the year?"

"It is enough."

"But you will be the richest man in the world when you write the greatest poem?"

He didn't reply.

One day when I went to see him in his little house, I found him lying on his little bed. He looked so old and so weak, that I found myself wanting to cry.

He said, "The poem is not going well."

He wasn't looking at me. He was looking through the window at the coconut tree, and he was speaking as though I wasn't there. He said, "When I was twenty I felt the power within myself." Then, almost in front of my eyes, I could see his face growing older and more tired. He said, "But that—that was a long time ago."

And then—I felt it so keenly, it was as though I had been slapped by my mother. I could see it clearly on his face. It was there for everyone to see. Death on the shrinking face.

He looked at me, and saw my tears and sat up.

He said, "Come." I went and sat on his knees.

He looked into my eyes, and he said, "Oh, you can see it, too. I always knew you had the poet's eye." **G**

He didn't even look sad, and that made me burst out crying loudly.

He pulled me to his thin chest, and said, "Do you want me to tell you a funny story?" and he smiled encouragingly at me.

But I couldn't reply.

He said, "When I have finished this story, I want you to promise that you will go away and never come back to see me. Do you promise?"

I nodded.

He said, "Good. Well, listen. That story I told you about the boy poet and the girl poet, do you remember that? That wasn't true. It was something I just made up. All this talk about poetry and the greatest poem in the world, that wasn't true, either. Isn't that the funniest thing you have heard?"

But his voice broke.

I left the house, and ran home crying, like a poet, for everything I saw.

I walked along Alberto Street a year later, but I could find no sign of the poet's house. It hadn't vanished, just like that. It had been pulled down, and a big, two-storied building had taken its place. The mango tree and the plum tree and the coconut tree had all been cut down, and there was brick and concrete everywhere. **H**

It was just as though B. Wordsworth had never existed.

G **Reading Focus** Making Inferences About Theme   What does B. Wordsworth mean when he says that the boy possesses "the poet's eye"?

H **Literary Focus** Setting   What do these changes in the setting signify?

Vocabulary **keenly** (KEEN lee) *adv.*: strongly and clearly.

Applying Your Skills

B. Wordsworth

Respond and Think Critically

Reading Focus

Quick Check

1. What does B. Wordsworth mean when he says that White Wordsworth was his "brother"?

2. What did the boy find comforting about looking at the stars?

3. How does the boy feel about B. Wordsworth? What does the boy learn from him?

Read with a Purpose

4. Now that you have read the story, do you agree that B. Wordsworth is a poet? If not, why not? If so, what do you think makes him a poet?

Reading Skills: Making Inferences About Theme

5. Review the notes you made on plot, characterization, language, and setting in your chart. Think about how these elements work together, and write a sentence expressing the story's **theme,** or central idea or insight about life. Look back at your chart to make sure each element supports your interpretation of the theme.

Literary Focus

Literary Analysis

6. **Analyze** Consider what B. Wordsworth says to the policeman who asks, "What you doing here?" How is B. Wordsworth's reply significant? (Is his response what poets also seek to know?)

7. **Make Judgments** Do you think B. Wordsworth's tragic story about the boy poet and the girl poet is true? If not, why did he tell it in the first place?

8. **Draw Conclusions** Why do you think B. Wordsworth stopped writing his poem?

9. **Compare and Contrast** Consider the contrast between the mother's no-nonsense ways and the poetic vision of B. Wordsworth. What might Naipaul want to express about the nature of poetry and the role of the poet in society?

10. **Hypothesize** If we think of the story's narrator as the author's recollection of himself at that age, what does the story suggest about the influences (historical, political, cultural) that made Naipaul a writer? What does it suggest about his view of the poet's position and role in society?

Literary Skills: Setting

11. **Evaluate** What parts of the setting are most vivid in your mind? If you were going to illustrate the story, on what images would you focus?

Literary Skills Review: Characterization

12. **Analyze** Writers develop their characters through dialogue, description, expression of their feelings and actions, and other characters' reactions. Which of these methods of **characterization** made the boy most real for you? What made B. Wordsworth most real for you?

Writing Focus

Think as a Reader/Writer

Use It in Your Writing Re-read the lines of dialect you wrote in your *Reader/Writer Notebook*. Now, write a brief character sketch of an imaginary person. Use dialogue that gives your character a particular way of talking to reveal his or her background.

 What Do You Think Now What experiences do you think might have shaped B. Wordsworth's unique view of the world?

Vocabulary Development

✔ Vocabulary Check

Match the Vocabulary words with their definitions.

6. ascended   **a.** drinking vessel

7. idyll   **b.** went up

8. goblet   **c.** final part of a story or poem

9. epilogue   **d.** pastoral poem or story

Vocabulary Skills: Idioms

An **idiom** is a phrase whose meaning cannot be determined by the literal meanings of its individual words:

> I met someone who told me she was a famous violinist, but she was just pulling my leg.

To *pull someone's leg,* for example, means "to tease or play a joke on someone," not to literally pull their leg.

> The actress was a seasoned performer, but she still got butterflies in her stomach at performances.

To *have butterflies in your stomach* doesn't mean your stomach is filled with insects but that you feel nervous.

Your Turn ⎯⎯⎯⎯⎯⎯

Read each sentence below, and identify the idioms.

1. His mother had a hard time making ends meet.

2. When the boy came home late, his mother was fit to be tied and punished him severely.

3. B. Wordsworth said the story was funny, but his voice was breaking as he told it.

Language Coach

Multiple-Meaning Words Write two definitions for each of the following words from the selection: *watch, flower, fell, present, last, broke.*

CHOICES

As you respond to the Choices, use these **Academic Vocabulary** words as appropriate: <u>perspective</u>, <u>considerably</u>, <u>adapt</u>, <u>exhibit</u>, <u>inevitable</u>.

REVIEW

Videotape a Scene

TechFocus In small groups, use the notes you made as you read to create and videotape one scene from the story. Have actors use their voices, body language, and costumes to develop the characters. Be creative about setting: You might videotape your scene in a garden, for example, and use mangoes to convey the idea that you are in B. Wordsworth's garden. <u>Exhibit</u> your final product to the class.

CONNECT

Write a Journal Entry

In the story, B. Wordsworth finds poetry in the intense appreciation of life. Write a journal entry about an experience that you appreciated intensely. Use sensory details to try to re-create the moment.

EXTEND

Research Calypsos

B. Wordsworth claims to make his living singing calypsos. Use library or Internet resources to find out more about calypsos. What are they typically about? What is their structure? Then, write a calypso of your own and share it with a small group of classmates.

✳ Learn It Online
Use the *Digital Storytelling* site to help you develop a script and videotape your scene!

go.hrw.com   L12-1405   **Go**

Preparing to Read

from Sir Vidia's Shadow

What Do You Think How does experience shape our view of the world?

QuickWrite

In your *Reader/Writer Notebook,* record a few thoughts about someone you consider to be a mentor and how that person has helped you.

Paul Theroux (1941).

Paul Theroux
(1941–   )

"The quintessential explorer with a talent for noticing the odd, compelling detail," Paul Theroux is one of America's most skilled travel writers.

A World Traveler

Theroux was born in Medford, Massachusetts, into a large, working-class family. As a child, he was a voracious reader, but only after taking a creative writing class in college did he consider becoming a writer. After graduation, Theroux joined the Peace Corps and was sent to teach English in Malawi, southern Africa. After becoming connected with a political group the government distrusted, Theroux was deported. Nevertheless, he soon returned to Africa and settled in Uganda, where he met V. S. Naipaul, already an acclaimed novelist. Naipaul became Theroux's mentor, and the two writers struck up a friendship that would last for thirty years. Theroux's first novel, Waldo, was published while he was living in Uganda.

An Ironic Wit

From Uganda, Theroux moved to Singapore and then to London, where he began writing full time. In 1975, he published *The Great Railway Bazaar,* a bestselling travel book about his four-month train trip across Europe and Asia. Though set in many countries, all of Theroux's novels <u>exhibit</u> ironic wit and an acerbic <u>perspective</u>. According to Nadine Gordimer, "Paul Theroux is without peer as the merciless obituarist of colonialism. He knows his way matchlessly about the milieu where no one was ever at home. . . . Theroux novels are neither apologia nor accusation; wit is his rare medium, and that lays bare both."

Since 1967, Theroux has published more than forty-seven works of travel writing, novels, short story collections, and criticism. His work has won or been nominated for several awards, and four of his novels have been made into films. Theroux says that his main goal is to amuse his readers. "My fear is that I'll be boring. You never actually run out of ideas, but you might run out of ideas that are intelligent, amusing, original."

Think About the Writer What might the American writer Theroux have in common with postcolonial writers?

Reader/Writer Notebook

Use your **RWN** to complete the activities for this selection.

Literary Focus

Tone A writer's **tone** is the attitude he or she takes toward the reader, a subject, or a character. Writers convey tone through careful word choice, details, and interpretation of events. For example, in the sentence, "He frowned and folded his arms, looking defiant," Theroux's use of negative words to portray Naipaul's actions helps create a critical tone.

Reading Focus

Analyzing Author's Purpose In writing, authors may have many purposes: to inform, to persuade, or to express themselves. An author's purpose in writing a memoir is often mixed. Although most people write memoirs to record their lives and share their experiences, they may also want to "set the record straight" or tell their side of a particular story. You must **analyze an author's purpose** based on what the work actually accomplishes. For instance, if you read a memoir that discredits a widely believed version of events and promotes an alternate version, you may infer that the author means to persuade you to believe his or her version of how things happened.

Into Action Use a graphic organizer like this one to collect information that will help you analyze the author's purpose in the excerpt from *Sir Vidia's Shadow*. In the first column, note any information that strikes you as significant. Then, think about what the information reveals about the author and/or about Sir Vidia. When making your notes, take into account the tone in which the information is delivered.

Significant Information	What It Reveals About the Author	What It Reveals About Sir Vidia

Writing Focus

Think as a Reader/Writer

Find It in Your Reading In *Sir Vidia's Shadow*, Theroux's style is highly realistic, almost like that of a newspaper reporter. He provides many facts and details to make the scene seem real. As you read, make a list of details that help you visualize the scene.

Vocabulary

ritualistic (rihch yoo uh LIHS tihk) *adj.:* relating to a formal ceremony. *The traveler had a ritualistic method of packing that he repeated before every trip.*

compulsive (kuhm PUHL sihv) *adj.:* driven by an irresistible impulse. *The boy had a compulsive need to wash his hands dozens of times each day.*

connoisseur (kahn uh SUR) *n.:* person with highly informed and refined taste. *The writer was a connoisseur of fine wines.*

presumptuous (prih ZUHMP choo uhs) *adj.:* going beyond the proper bounds. *It was presumptuous of the interviewer to question the writer's motives.*

rebuffed (rih BUHFD) *v.:* rejected with disdain. *The writer rebuffed the rude interviewer.*

ingratiate (ihn GRAY shee ayt) *v.:* try to gain another's favor or goodwill. *The student wanted the teacher's approval and so tried to ingratiate himself.*

Language Coach

Word Families To guess the meaning of a new word, see if you know the meaning of words from the same word family (words with the same root). What words do you know with the same roots as the following words from the selection: *unmodernized uncompromising,* and *asthmatically?*

 Learn It Online
There's more to words than just definitions. Get the whole story at Word Watch.

go.hrw.com L12-1407   **Go**

MEMOIR

from
Sir Vidia's Shadow

by **Paul Theroux**

Paul Theroux and V. S. Naipaul at Hay-on-Wye (May 5th, 1996).

Read with a Purpose
Read to find out who Sir Vidia is and what the author means by his "shadow."

Build Background
Sir Vidia's Shadow is not fiction but a memoir, a book about the author's life. In this memoir, Theroux recounts his thirty-year friendship with writer V. S. Naipaul and its dissolution. This excerpt tells the author's <u>perspective</u> of an event in which the two men participated.

It happens to be a tic of mine as a traveler, on returning to any distant city, to take the same walk, make the same stops, eat the same meals at the same restaurants, look into the same stores, verify the faces of clerks or doormen, even touch the same posts and gates—go through a ritualistic renewal of familiarity along a known route before striking out and doing anything new. It is not compulsive. It eases my spirit. And in any new city I make a route and remember it.

It was a sunny morning at the end of May in England's never-disappointing springtime. I was just a tourist now. Christie's[1] salesrooms were on my London trail. I walked from Brown's Hotel to King Street in time to see the "Visions of India" pre-auction show.

"Your friend Naipaul was just here," a Christie's man said, greeting me. He knew me as a sometime bidder and Naipaul as a connoisseur. "He might still be somewhere in the building."

We looked among the pictures but didn't see him. I had wanted to surprise him, perhaps have lunch. He had agreed to go to Hay-on-Wye to do the staged dialogue. I would have enjoyed looking at these pictures with Vidia,[2] who had a discerning eye for paintings of Indian landscapes. But he had gone.

I continued on my quasi-Tourettic[3] walk, feeling like a practitioner of advanced mazecraft. I had arrived in London that morning and was happy with my first-class rail ticket to Newport, Wales, in my pocket. I left the next day from Paddington station, first reading the newspaper and then looking over the first chapter of *Kowloon Tong,* which I had just started to write. I had spent part of the winter in Hong Kong....

---

1. **Christie's:** famous London auction house that handles items of great value.

2. **Vidia:** shortened version of V. S. Naipaul's first name.

3. **quasi-Tourettic:** resembling Tourette's syndrome, a neurological disease that can cause people to move and speak involuntarily.

Vocabulary　**ritualistic** (rihch yoo uh LIHS tihk) *adj.:* relating to a formal ceremony.

compulsive (kuhm PUHL sihv) *adj.:* driven by an irresistible impulse.

connoisseur (kahn uh SUR) *n.:* person with highly informed and refined taste.

A taxi met me at Newport. The driver, a former teacher and Welsh speaker, took me to Abergavenny and across the Black Mountains past jumbled villages. Too far from London to be within commuting distance, the countryside looked unmodernized, like the England of the sixties and seventies. The village of Hay was on a hill, the river Wye below it. I dropped my bag at the innlike hotel and after lunch, on that afternoon of June 1, 1996, went to the festival.[4] **Ⓐ**

Vidia and Nadira had arrived, having left Dairy Cottage that morning. "Paul, this is Nadira."

The skinny, scowling seven-year-old girl in her little princess sari on the Nairobi verandah had become a big woman. She was dark and tall—taller than Vidia—and watchful, with the sort of frank sizing-you-up stare that is never seen on the faces of Pakistani women. Her sari was loose at the hips, as if she had just lost some weight. She was waiting for me to say something. I spoke to Vidia.

"I just missed you at that Indian show at Christie's yesterday."

Before Vidia could reply, Nadira slapped his shoulder and said, "You bad man! You did not tell me you went there!"

She slapped his arm again and scolded him. This seemed a trifle presumptuous in a woman who had been married only a month. I had never seen anyone touch Vidia before.

"You will not buy any more pictures!"

"You're telling my secrets, Paul," Vidia said quietly, looking a little grim. **Ⓑ**

Salman Rushdie[5] was being introduced to Vidia as I stepped up to a table to get myself a cup of coffee,

and then I saw Bill Buford from *The New Yorker* beckoning, and we all headed to a big white circus tent.

As I passed Salman, he was smiling and shaking his head. He said, "I have never met him before."

"What did he say?"

"He said, 'Are you all right?' I told him yes, I am all right. He said, 'Good, good, good.'" Salman began to laugh.

We took our seats, Vidia, Bill Buford, and I, on the stage in the big circus tent. The audience was large, but still the atmosphere was that of a dog show. We were being asked to perform, to walk on our hind legs, jump through hoops, create a spectacle for the readers. Buford said, "What about questions afterwards?"

"No questions," Vidia said. I felt sure he hated doing this, but he had agreed; I had not twisted his arm. His general philosophy was "The writer should never precede the work." Or even: "The writer should remain invisible." Books were the things. But there were no books in sight, only goggling faces in the sold-out tent and the sense of scrutiny, all those faces like light bulbs. **Ⓒ**

In his rambling introduction—Vidia fidgeting irritatedly as my new book was mentioned—Bill said, "Paul, you're two decades younger than Vidia," and finally asked, "What did Vidia give you as a writer?"

I thanked him and said, "A couple of corrections, Bill. I am not two decades younger than Vidia. I am fifty-five, Vidia's sixty-four. And we met over thirty years ago, when I actually did feel more than twenty years younger. I felt very young. I felt that I was meeting a much older, much wiser, much more experienced person. A person much more than nine or ten years older than I was."

Vidia sat looking meditative. He had not said a word, and we had hardly spoken beforehand. He was wearing a dark jacket and a sweater under it, dark wool trousers, dark shoes. He seemed to be listening carefully, and I was grateful to have this chance to pay tribute to him.

---

4. **festival:** the Hay Festival, an annual arts festival in Wales.
5. **Salman Rushdie:** famous and highly acclaimed contemporary writer who was under threat of death from Muslim extremists for his portrayal of Muhammad in his novel *The Satanic Verses.*

Ⓐ **Literary Focus** Tone How would you describe the author's attitude toward himself in the first two paragraphs of this excerpt? Give two details that indicate his tone.

Ⓑ **Literary Focus** Tone What is the author's attitude toward Sir Vidia and his wife? Note words and phrases that help convey his attitude.

Ⓒ **Reading Focus** Analyzing Author's Purpose What is the author's purpose in telling the reader that Sir Vidia freely agreed to come to the festival?

Vocabulary **presumptuous** (prih ZUHMP choo uhs) *adj.:* going beyond the proper bounds.

"And you ask what he gave me?" I said. "I feel that he gave me everything. The main thing that he gave me was the confidence that I was a writer. He said that every writer was different, and if you were great, you were a new man. I had to write my own book, but that it would not resemble anyone else's book. My writing had to come from inside me, and that every book needed a reason to be written."

To my left, I could see Vidia nodding. I was annoyed that I had had to speak first, and I felt that I was rambling.

"In 1966 in Kampala, when I met Vidia, I had not published a book. Vidia was the first writer I had met who had a total sense of mission, a total sense of self, an uncompromising attitude towards himself, towards the novel. If he made a rule, he kept to the rule. He said that a writer has to make his own way in the world. He asked me once or twice, 'Are you sure you're up for it? Are you sure you want to be a writer? Are you sure you want to live this terrible life?' I was twenty-four years old. I said, 'I'm up for it.'" **D**

Vidia was sitting next to me, near enough for me to hear him sighing in impatience—or perhaps he was simply breathing asthmatically. Near as he was, he was not looking at me or at the audience. He sat at an angle and stared into space while, on his other side, Bill Buford spoke to him—spoke to his shoulder, for Vidia remained turned away. His body language said bluntly that he wished he was elsewhere. **E**

Bill began to ask me another question when, out of self-consciousness—for Vidia, the star of this show, still had not spoken—I turned to Vidia and asked, "You once wrote, 'To be a victim is to be absurd.' What did you mean by this?"

Vidia cleared his throat and said, "Well, I think the word 'victim' has probably been extended. I was thinking about people who were utterly helpless politically and had no rights, no one to turn to, and I thought: They were always absurd. This was in a note to a study of slavery and revolution that I spent some years working on. The slaves had no rights—and I am thinking about the Caribbean slavery—and to be a victim is to be absurd. Slaves are absurd people. That is the truth. The current use of the word is an extension of that. I haven't thought about it like that. I was thinking about it in a very practical, realistic way. I don't make generalizations."

"So you don't mean it in the modern sense," I said.

"No, not in the sense of someone in a university who can't get a job," Vidia said with the sort of snappish energy he had when he was irritable. I had noticed the awkward way he sat and could see that he had something on his mind. "No, that's another kind of victim."

People in the audience laughed at his seeming to mock universities, and over their laughter I persisted, hoping to draw him out.

Vidia lifted his head, looked at nothing, and said, "I don't think like this about myself. I deal with material at hand and I don't make generalizations like this."

Feeling rebuffed, I said no more and let the silence descend. Time for Vidia to offer something. Perhaps he was right: it seemed in my question that I was embarrassed by his discomfort and trying to ingratiate myself.

He giggled confidently in the silence and said, "Sorry, I don't want to stump the conversation." **F**

Buford rescued the faltering moment, saying, "Paul, if I can intercept. I arrived from New York last night, and as I got here on the train I was thinking of your books. In some ways no two writers could be more different, and yet there are some similarities. And one is that both of you became writers in Britain. In your case, Vidia, you actively became a writer when you came to Britain and started studying at Oxford. And in Paul's case—you, Paul, also became a writer when you lived here. What was the effect of being in Britain for you?"

D **Reading Focus** Analyzing Author's Purpose Why does the author includes all of these complimentary remarks about Sir Vidia?

E **Literary Focus** Tone How would you describe the tone of this description of Sir Vidia and his behavior?

F **Reading Focus** Analyzing Author's Purpose How does this detail reflect upon Sir Vidia?

Vocabulary **rebuffed** (rih BUHFD) *v.*: rejected with disdain. **ingratiate** (ihn GRAY shee ayt) *v.*: try to gain another's favor or goodwill.

I gestured for Vidia to answer.

"This is a very important question," Vidia said.

He coiled in his chair, concentrating hard, and lifted his gaze again, speaking to the heights of the circus tent.

"It has to be considered," he said. "Writing is a physical business. Books are real physical objects. They have to be printed, published, reviewed, read, distributed—it's a physical object, it's a commercial enterprise. It's an effect of the industrial society. You can't beat a book out on a drum." He let this sink in. "So, in the 1950s, when I started, if you were writing in English, there was only one place where you could be a writer. It was here. It couldn't be the United States, because I had no link with America. I had a link only with here. It certainly couldn't be any other English-speaking country, because I don't think they even had publishing industries."

He frowned and folded his arms, looking defiant. "The thing was different in 1950. It has changed considerably. There's a publishing industry in Australia, Canada—India has developed a publishing industry. And to write always as an exotic is a very awful thing to have to do."

"Why is it awful? Buford asked.

"Because you seldom have people who can share your experience, your background," Vidia said. "My brother, while he lived, said to me one day that probably he was the only man who could truly understand what I was writing. And I understood a little bit more of what he was trying to do as well, because we shared the background. If we were addressing audiences of people like ourselves, we would have been different writers. I am always aware of writing in a vacuum, almost always for myself, and almost not having an audience. That wonderful relationship that I felt an American writer would always have with his American readers, or a French writer with his French readers—I was always writing for people who were indifferent to my material."

Buford said, "Why could you not return to Trinidad?"

"You cannot beat books out on the drum!" Vidia cried. "It's as simple as that. What would I have done?" He moved heavily in his chair and looked pleadingly at Buford, mocking him with incomprehension. "I mean, enter into it imaginatively—that question. Who would have published your books? Who would have read them? Who would have reviewed them? Who would have bought them? Who would have paid you for the effort? It's not a question."

Over the nervous laughter from the audience at seeing Vidia's hackles rise, Buford said that surely the source of Vidia's fiction was the richness of Trinidad.

"Yes, yes, inevitably, because that's the material you have when you're starting out," Vidia said. "It's the material you carry for your first twenty years or so. And it is very important, because it's a complete experience. Experience later will be modified. But that's very pure."

"I was just wondering, regarding this question of an audience," I said. "When did you develop this sense of people reading your work?"

"I don't have that sense at all. I've seldom met people who have," he said, and there was laughter. "I've met an awful lot of people who come and bluff their way through interviews with me." There was more laughter and silence when the laughter died down. In that silence Vidia smirked and said, "But again, I don't want to stump the conversation."

"No, you're not stumping it."

"Oh, good."

"But circumstances of writing do change," I said.

It was obvious that he had no questions for me. So I was obliged to assume the humble position of interviewer and petition him with questions. Once again his shadow fell across me. Did I mind? Not at all, for here we were, occupying a stage in front of an attentive audience of readers. Yet I had a vibration—yes, a vibration—that Vidia objected to sharing the stage. **G**

G **Literary Focus** Tone At the end of the excerpt, how has the author's attitude changed toward Sir Vidia? toward himself?

CARTOON

A Writer's Influence

Cartoon by Andrew Toos.
To analyze this cartoon, see the Comparing Texts Wrap Up on page 1425.

from **Sir Vidia's Shadow**

Respond and Think Critically

Reading Focus

Quick Check

1. Why is the author in London? How does he feel when he first arrives there?

2. Why didn't Sir Vidia begin publishing his work in Trinidad?

Read with a Purpose

3. Who is Sir Vidia? What kind of "shadow" does the author believe Sir Vidia casts on him?

Reading Skills: Analyzing Author's Purpose

4. Add a row labeled "Summary" to the bottom of the organizer you made while reading. In the second column, summarize what the excerpt reveals about the author. In the third column, summarize what it reveals about Sir Vidia. Use this information to infer the author's purpose.

✓ Vocabulary Check

Match the Vocabulary words with their definitions.

5. ritualistic   a. driven by impulse
6. compulsive   b. rejected
7. connoisseur   c. try to please
8. presumptuous   d. ceremonial
9. rebuffed   e. tasteful person
10. ingratiate   f. forward

Literary Focus

Literary Analysis

11. **Analyze** What feelings does the author express about the festival? Is his attitude consistent throughout the excerpt? Explain your answer.

12. **Interpret** What do you think Sir Vidia meant when he called the life of a writer "terrible"?

13. **Evaluate** Are Sir Vidia's actions and possible motivations described in an objective way? Give examples to support your opinion.

14. **Make Judgments** At the end of the excerpt, the author states that he did not mind Sir Vidia's uncooperative behavior. How true do you think that statement is? Explain your answer.

Literary Skills: Tone

15. **Analyze** Describe the tone the author takes toward Sir Vidia. Explain whether it changes throughout the excerpt or remains consistent.

Literary Skills Review: Point of View

16. **Analyze** The <u>perspective</u> from which a story is told is called **point of view.** From what point of view (first or third person) is this story told? How does it affect your perception of the events?

Writing Focus

Think As a Reader/Writer

Use It in Your Writing Review your list of realistic details from the excerpt. Write a paragraph about an event you have experienced. Use realistic details to help your readers visualize the event.

 What Do You Think Now

Theroux and Naipaul's friendship ended before Theroux wrote this account. How do you think this fact affected Theroux's perception of the events?

Preparing to Read

Games at Twilight

QuickWrite

In your *Reader/Writer Notebook*, describe briefly a childhood game you frequently played and what you learned from playing it.

Anita Desai
(1937–   )

Anita Desai has been described as "such a consummate artist that she [is able to suggest], beyond the confines of the plot and the machinations of her characters, the immensities that lie beyond them—the immensities of India."

Early Instincts

Born in Musoorie, India, Desai claims to have been writing "as instinctively as I breathe" since age seven. Her father was Bengali, and her mother was German, so Desai grew up hearing Hindi, English, and German spoken at home. English, however, was the language in which Desai learned to read and write. Desai was educated at the University of Delhi and began publishing her writing in 1963.

Reaching for Truth

Desai's novels often focus on the emotional and spiritual lives of wives, older women, or sisters who take responsibility for others but are unable to create satisfactory lives for themselves. Her novels include *Cry, the Peacock* (1963), *In Custody* (1984), *Baumgartner's Bombay* (1988), *Journey to Ithaca* (1995), *Fasting, Feasting* (1999), and *The Zigzag Way* (2004).

Desai's fiction also explores the trials of contemporary Indian characters as they struggle to adapt to cultural and social change. She sees her work as an attempt to discover "the truth that is nine-tenths of the iceberg that lies submerged beneath the one-tenth visible portion we call Reality." To evoke this "truth," Desai uses vivid, sensual language and intense imagery. Because of her sensuous style and use of rich imagery and symbolism, Desai has been referred to as an "imagist-novelist."

Desai has taught at Mount Holyoke and Smith Colleges and at the Massachusetts Institute of Technology. Her daughter Kiran Desai is the prize-winning author of the novel *The Inheritance of Loss.*

Think About the Writer How do you think Desai's cultural heritage might have affected her writing? Why might she have chosen to focus her writing on the experiences of women?

Kiran Desai and Anita Desai. Venice, Italy (2006).

Reader/Writer
Notebook

Use your **RWN** to complete the activities for this selection.

Literary Focus

Imagery Fiction writers use **imagery,** language that appeals to the five senses, to help readers envision a given scene. Desai does not use simple imagery but rather drenches us in the smells, textures, sounds, and colors of a summer afternoon in India. From the bursting open of a door to the crushed silence of a defeated child, Desai enables us to experience the world through the eyes and ears of her characters.

Reading Focus

Analyzing Details Although one detail may not have much meaning in itself, many details together give depth and meaning to a story. Without details, a scene can be unsatisfying to read. For example, the scene *The children played a game* requires more detail: You want to know who the children were, when and where they played, what happened, and how they felt about it.

Into Action As you read, use a chart like the one below to jot down details that help you imagine the scene and learn about the characters.

Details / Imagery	What I Learn About the Characters and the Scene
"everything was curtained and shuttered in a way that stifled the children"	

Writing Focus

Think as a Reader/Writer

Find It in Your Reading To make her fiction seem more real, Desai uses strong, active verbs. For example, the verb *to lie* tells you only the position of a person's body; the verb *to sprawl* tells you not just that the person is lying down but that he or she is lying unselfconsciously, with legs and arms flung out. As you read, note the strong, active verbs that fire your imagination.

TechFocus This story is about a group of Indian children playing games. As you read, take notes for a Web page about children's games around the world.

Vocabulary

maniacal (muh NY uh kuhl) *adj.*: crazed; wildly enthusiastic. *The boy's maniacal laughter revealed his enjoyment of the game.*

stridently (STRY duhnt lee) *adv.*: harshly; sharply. *The boy yelled stridently at the disobedient dog.*

superciliously (soo puhr SIHL ee uhs lee) *adv.*: disdainfully; scornfully. *The girl superciliously rejected her sister's request to play.*

temerity (tuh MEHR uh tee) *n.*: reckless boldness. *The girl had the temerity to stand on her bike seat while going downhill.*

intoxicating (ihn TAHK suh kay tihng) *v.* used as *adj.*: causing wild excitement, often beyond the point of self-control. *The child found hide-and-seek intoxicating.*

dogged (DAWG ihd) *adj.*: stubbornly persistent. *The boy was dogged in his determination to win the game.*

lugubrious (loo GOO bree uhs) *adj.*: solemn or mournful, especially in an excessive way. *The children made a lugubrious sound when they were forced to come in for the night.*

ignominy (IHG nuh mihn ee) *n.*: shame; disgrace. *He could hardly stand the ignominy of having lost the game.*

Language Coach

Word Families Word families group words that share the same root. Notice that *maniacal* contains the root *maniac*. What words share roots with the Vocabulary words?

Learn It Online

Learn more online about Desai's life and work.

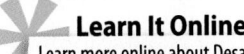

Games at Twilight

by **Anita Desai**

Read with a Purpose
Read to find out what happens during games played at twilight.

Build Background
The story is set not long after India gained its independence from Britain in 1947. During the long British rule, many upper-class Indian families had adopted Western values, behaviors, customs, and leisure pastimes.

It was still too hot to play outdoors. They had had their tea, they had been washed and had their hair brushed, and after the long day of confinement in the house that was not cool but at least a protection from the sun, the children strained to get out. Their faces were red and bloated with the effort, but their mother would not open the door, everything was still curtained and shuttered in a way that stifled the children, made them feel that their lungs were stuffed with cotton wool and their noses with dust and if they didn't burst out into the light and see the sun and feel the air, they would choke. **A** **B**

"Please, ma, please," they begged. "We'll play in the veranda and porch—we won't go a step out of the porch."

"You will, I know you will, and then——"

"No—we won't, we won't," they wailed so horrendously that she actually let down the bolt of the front door so that they burst out like seeds from a crackling, overripe pod into the veranda, with such wild, maniacal yells that she retreated to her bath and the shower of talcum powder and the fresh sari that were to help her face the summer evening.

A **Literary Focus** **Imagery** Identify the images in this passage. How does this imagery work to stimulate readers' senses?

B **Reading Focus** **Analyzing Details** What words and details help you visualize this scene and imagine the children's feelings?

Vocabulary **maniacal** (muh NY uh kuhl) *adj.*: crazed; wildly enthusiastic.

They faced the afternoon. It was too hot. Too bright. The white walls of the veranda glared stridently in the sun. The bougainvillea[1] hung about it, purple and magenta, in livid balloons. The garden outside was like a tray made of beaten brass, flattened out on the red gravel and the stony soil in all shades of metal—aluminum, tin, copper, and brass. No life stirred at this arid time of day—the birds still drooped, like dead fruit, in the papery tents of the trees; some squirrels lay limp

---

1. **bougainvillea** (boo guhn VIHL ee uh): woody, tropical vine with showy, purplish bracts, or modified leaves.

Two young girls in Rajasthan, India.

on the wet earth under the garden tap. The outdoor dog lay stretched as if dead on the veranda mat, his paws and ears and tail all reaching out like dying travelers in search of water. He rolled his eyes at the children—two white marbles rolling in the purple sockets, begging for sympathy—and attempted to lift his tail in a wag but could not. It only twitched and lay still. **C**

Then, perhaps roused by the shrieks of the children, a band of parrots suddenly fell out of the eucalyptus tree, tumbled frantically in the still, sizzling air, then sorted themselves out into battle formation and streaked away across the white sky.

The children, too, felt released. They too began tumbling, shoving, pushing against each other, frantic to start. Start what? Start their business. The business of the children's day which is—play.

"Let's play hide-and-seek."

"Who'll be It?"

"You be It."

"Why should I? You be——"

"You're the eldest——"

"That doesn't mean——"

The shoves became harder. Some kicked out. The motherly Mira intervened. She pulled the boys roughly apart. There was a tearing sound of cloth, but it was lost in the heavy panting and angry grumbling, and no one paid attention to the small sleeve hanging loosely off a shoulder.

"Make a circle, make a circle!" she shouted, firmly pulling and pushing till a kind of vague circle was formed. "Now clap!" she roared, and, clapping, they all chanted in melancholy unison: "Dip, dip, dip—my blue ship——" and every now and then one or the other saw he was safe by the way his hands fell at the

---

C **Literary Focus** Imagery What images does Desai use to create the impression of oppressive heat?

Vocabulary **stridently** (STRY duhnt lee) adv.: harshly; sharply.

crucial moment—palm on palm, or back of hand on palm—and dropped out of the circle with a yell and a jump of relief and jubilation.

Raghu was It. He started to protest, to cry "You cheated—Mira cheated—Anu cheated——" but it was too late, the others had all already streaked away. There was no one to hear when he called out, "Only in the veranda—the porch—Ma said—Ma *said* to stay in the porch!" No one had stopped to listen, all he saw were their brown legs flashing through the dusty shrubs, scrambling up brick walls, leaping over compost heaps and hedges, and then the porch stood empty in the purple shade of the bougainvillea, and the garden was as empty as before; even the limp squirrels had whisked away, leaving everything gleaming, brassy, and bare. **D**

Only small Manu suddenly reappeared, as if he had dropped out of an invisible cloud or from a bird's claws, and stood for a moment in the center of the yellow lawn, chewing his finger and near to tears as he heard Raghu shouting, with his head pressed against the veranda wall, "Eighty-three, eighty-five, eighty-nine, ninety . . ." and then made off in a panic, half of him wanting to fly north, the other half counseling south. Raghu turned just in time to see the flash of his white shorts and the uncertain skittering of his red sandals, and charged after him with such a bloodcurdling yell that Manu stumbled over the hosepipe, fell into its rubber coils, and lay there weeping, "I won't be It—you have to find them all—all—All!"

"I know I have to, idiot," Raghu said, superciliously kicking him with his toe. "You're dead," he said with satisfaction, licking the beads of perspiration off his upper lip, and then stalked off in search of worthier prey, whistling spiritedly so that the hiders should hear and tremble.

Ravi heard the whistling and picked his nose in a panic, trying to find comfort by burrowing the finger deep—deep into that soft tunnel. He felt himself too exposed, sitting on an upturned flowerpot behind the garage. Where could he burrow? He could run around

the garage if he heard Raghu come—around and around and around—but he hadn't much faith in his short legs when matched against Raghu's long, hefty, hairy footballer legs. Ravi had a frightening glimpse of them as Raghu combed the hedge of crotons and hibiscus, trampling delicate ferns underfoot as he did so. Ravi looked about him desperately, swallowing a small ball of snot in his fear.

The garage was locked with a great heavy lock to which the driver had the key in his room, hanging from a nail on the wall under his workshirt. Ravi had peeped in and seen him still sprawling on his string cot in his vest and striped underpants, the hair on his chest and the hair in his nose shaking with the vibrations of his phlegm-obstructed snores. Ravi had wished he were tall enough, big enough to reach the key on the nail, but it was impossible, beyond his reach for years to come. He had sidled away and sat dejectedly on the flowerpot. That at least was cut to his own size.

But next to the garage was another shed with a big green door. Also locked. No one even knew who had the key to the lock. That shed wasn't opened more than once a year, when Ma turned out all the old broken bits of furniture and rolls of matting and leaking buckets, and the white anthills were broken and swept away and Flit sprayed into the spider webs and rat holes so that the whole operation was like the looting of a poor, ruined, and conquered city. The green leaves of the door sagged. They were nearly off their rusty hinges. The hinges were large and made a small gap between the door and the walls—only just large enough for rats, dogs, and, possibly, Ravi to slip through.

Ravi had never cared to enter such a dark and depressing mortuary of defunct household goods seething with such unspeakable and alarming animal life but, as Raghu's whistling grew angrier and sharper and his crashing and storming in the hedge wilder, Ravi suddenly slipped off the flowerpot and through the crack and was gone. He chuckled aloud with

---

D **Reading Focus** Analyzing Details How does Desai use language to suggest physical action? Explain.

Vocabulary **superciliously** (soo puhr SIHL ee uhs lee) *adv.*: disdainfully; scornfully.

Cricket match near Rajabai Tower (c. 2003).

Games in India

Many of the games played in India, such as chess, were developed in that country: Kite flying, wrestling, hunting, and polo are all traditional Indian games. When the British colonized India, they introduced other games, such as soccer, field hockey, and track and field. Cricket, by far the most popular English athletic import, is a summer game similar to baseball. The first recorded cricket game in India was a match played by a group of sailors in 1721. In 1926, India joined the Imperial Cricket Conference, which allowed the national team to play against England and a select group of other colonies. The king of England (then emperor of India) attended the country's first match against England along with 24,000 spectators. Some historians believe facing the English in cricket was a turning point in India's struggle for independence. Today, cricket remains an obsession throughout India, and cricket players are some of the nation's wealthiest and most famous people.

Ask Yourself

In what ways has the British culture influenced the children in the story and their games? Support your answer with details and examples from the story.

astonishment at his own temerity so that Raghu came out of the hedge, stood silent with his hands on his hips, listening, and finally shouted, "I heard you! I'm coming! *Got* you——" and came charging round the garage only to find the upturned flowerpot, the yellow dust, the crawling of white ants in a mud hill against the closed shed door—nothing. Snarling, he bent to pick up a stick and went off, whacking it against the garage and shed walls as if to beat out his prey. Ravi shook, then shivered with delight, with self-congratulation. Also with fear. It was dark, spooky in the shed. It had a muffled smell, as of graves. Ravi had once got locked into the linen cupboard and sat there weeping for half an hour before he was rescued. But at least that had been a familiar place, and even smelled pleasantly of starch, laundry, and, reassuringly, of his mother. But the shed smelled of rats, anthills, dust,

and spider webs. Also of less definable, less recognizable horrors. And it was dark. Except for the white-hot cracks along the door, there was no light. The roof was very low. Although Ravi was small, he felt as if he could reach up and touch it with his fingertips. But he didn't stretch. He hunched himself into a ball so as not to bump into anything, touch or feel anything. What might there not be to touch him and feel him as he stood there, trying to see in the dark? Something cold, or slimy—like a snake. Snakes! He leapt up as Raghu whacked the wall with his stick—then, quickly realizing what it was, felt almost relieved to hear Raghu, hear his stick. It made him feel protected. **E**

But Raghu soon moved away. There wasn't a sound once his footsteps had gone around the garage and disappeared. Ravi stood frozen inside the shed. Then he shivered all over. Something had tickled the

E **Literary Focus** Imagery Identify the similes that Desai uses in this passage to suggest death.

Vocabulary **temerity** (tuh MEHR uh tee) *n.*: reckless boldness.

back of his neck. It took him a while to pick up the courage to lift his hand and explore. It was an insect—perhaps a spider—exploring *him*. He squashed it and wondered how many more creatures were watching him, waiting to reach out and touch him, the stranger. **F**

There was nothing now. After standing in that position—his hand still on his neck, feeling the wet splodge of the squashed spider gradually dry—for minutes, hours, his legs began to tremble with the effort, the inaction. By now he could see enough in the dark to make out the large solid shapes of old wardrobes, broken buckets, and bedsteads piled on top of each other around him. He recognized an old bathtub —patches of enamel glimmered at him, and at last he lowered himself onto its edge. **G**

He contemplated slipping out of the shed and into the fray. He wondered if it would not be better to be captured by Raghu and be returned to the milling crowd as long as he could be in the sun, the light, the free spaces of the garden, and the familiarity of his brothers, sisters, and cousins. It would be evening soon. Their games would become legitimate. The parents would sit out on the lawn on cane basket chairs and watch them as they tore around the garden or gathered in knots to share a loot of mulberries or black, teeth-splitting *jamun*² from the garden trees. The gardener would fix the hosepipe to the water tap, and water would fall lavishly through the air to the ground, soaking the dry yellow grass and the red gravel and arousing the sweet, the intoxicating scent of water on dry earth—that loveliest scent in the world. Ravi sniffed for a whiff of it. He half-rose from the bathtub, then heard the despairing scream of one of the girls as Raghu bore down upon her. There was the sound of a crash, and of rolling about in the bushes, the shrubs, then screams and accusing sobs of "I touched the den——" "You did not——" "I did——"

"You liar, you did *not*" and then a fading away and silence again.

Ravi sat back on the harsh edge of the tub, deciding to hold out a bit longer. What fun if they were all found and caught—he alone left unconquered! He had never known that sensation. Nothing more wonderful had ever happened to him than being taken out by an uncle and bought a whole slab of chocolate all to himself, or being flung into the soda man's pony cart and driven up to the gate by the friendly driver with the red beard and pointed ears. To defeat Raghu—that hirsute,³ hoarse-voiced football champion—and to be the winner in a circle of older, bigger, luckier children—that would be thrilling beyond imagination. He hugged his knees together and smiled to himself almost shyly at the thought of so much victory, such laurels.

There he sat smiling, knocking his heels against the bathtub, now and then getting up and going to the door to put his ear to the broad crack and listening for sounds of the game, the pursuer and the pursued, and then returning to his seat with the dogged determination of the true winner, a breaker of records, a champion.

It grew darker in the shed as the light at the door grew softer, fuzzier, turned to a kind of crumbling yellow pollen that turned to yellow fur, blue fur, gray fur. Evening. Twilight. The sound of water gushing, falling. The scent of earth receiving water, slaking its thirst in great gulps and releasing that green scent of freshness, coolness. Through the crack Ravi saw the long purple shadows of the shed and the garage lying still across the yard. Beyond that, the white walls of the house. The bougainvillea had lost its lividity, hung in dark bundles that quaked and twittered and seethed with masses of homing sparrows. The lawn was shut off from his view. Could he hear the children's voices? It seemed to him that he could. It seemed to him that

---

2. *jamun* (JAH muhn): plumlike fruit.

3. **hirsute** (HUR soot): hairy; shaggy.

F **Literary Focus** Imagery In this passage, find examples of imagery that appeals to multiple senses. To which sense does each image appeal?

G **Reading Focus** Analyzing Details What details does Desai use to make the shed seem creepy and scary?

Vocabulary **intoxicating** (ihn TAHK suh kay tihng) *v.* used as *adj.*: causing wild excitement, often beyond the point of self-control. **dogged** (DAWG ihd) *adj.*: stubbornly persistent.

he could hear them chanting, singing, laughing. But what about the game? What had happened? Could it be over? How could it when he was still not found? **H**

It then occurred to him that he could have slipped out long ago, dashed across the yard to the veranda, and touched the "den." It was necessary to do that to win. He had forgotten. He had only remembered the part of hiding and trying to elude the seeker. He had done that so successfully, his success had occupied him so wholly, that he had quite forgotten that success had to be clinched by that final dash to victory and the ringing cry of "Den!"

With a whimper he burst through the crack, fell on his knees, got up, and stumbled on stiff, benumbed legs across the shadowy yard, crying heartily by the time he reached the veranda so that when he flung himself at the white pillar and bawled, "Den! Den! Den!" his voice broke with rage and pity at the disgrace of it all, and he felt himself flooded with tears and misery.

Out on the lawn, the children stopped chanting. They all turned to stare at him in amazement. Their faces were pale and triangular in the dusk. The trees and bushes around them stood inky and sepulchral, spilling long shadows across them. They stared, wondering at his reappearance, his passion, his wild animal howling. Their mother rose from her basket chair and came toward him, worried, annoyed, saying, "Stop it, stop it, Ravi. Don't be a baby. Have you hurt yourself?" Seeing him attended to, the children went back to clasping their hands and chanting, "The grass is green, the rose is red…." **I**

But Ravi would not let them. He tore himself out of his mother's grasp and pounded across the lawn into their midst, charging at them with his head lowered so that they scattered in surprise. "I won, I won, I won," he bawled, shaking his head so that the big tears flew. "Raghu didn't find me. I won, I won——"

It took them a minute to grasp what he was saying, even who he was. They had quite forgotten him. Raghu had found all the others long ago. There had been a fight about who was to be It next. It had been so fierce that their mother had emerged from her bath and made them change to another game. Then they had played another and another. Broken mulberries from the tree and eaten them. Helped the driver wash the car when their father returned from work. Helped the gardener water the beds till he roared at them and swore he would complain to their parents. The parents had come out, taken up their positions on the cane chairs. They had begun to play again, sing and chant. All this time no one had remembered Ravi. Having disappeared from the scene, he had disappeared from their minds. Clean.

"Don't be a fool," Raghu said roughly, pushing him aside, and even Mira said, "Stop howling, Ravi. If you want to play, you can stand at the end of the line," and she put him there very firmly.

The game proceeded. Two pairs of arms reached up and met in an arc. The children trooped under it again and again in a lugubrious circle, ducking their heads and intoning

"The grass is green,
The rose is red;
Remember me
When I am dead, dead, dead, dead…" **J**

And the arc of thin arms trembled in the twilight, and the heads were bowed so sadly, and their feet tramped to that melancholy refrain so mournfully, so helplessly, that Ravi could not bear it. He would not follow them, he would not be included in this funereal game. He had wanted victory and triumph—not a funeral. But he had been forgotten, left out, and he would not join them now. The ignominy of being forgotten—how could he face it? He felt his heart go heavy and ache inside him unbearably. He lay down full length on the damp grass, crushing his face into it, no longer crying, silenced by a terrible sense of his insignificance.

Applying Your Skills

Games at Twilight

Respond and Think Critically

Quick Check

1. Briefly summarize the main events in this story.

2. How do Ravi's experiences in the shed contribute to the mood of the story?

3. What is ironic about the end of the story? (Consider what Ravi originally wanted to do and what actually ends up happening.)

Read with a Purpose

4. Are the children's games described in the story similar to or different from games you played when you were a child? Explain.

Reading Skills: Analyzing Details

5. Review the details and images you recorded in your graphic organizer. Which were most vivid to you? If you had to draw one picture to illustrate the story, what would you draw?

Literary Focus

Literary Analysis

6. Draw Conclusions Why is everyone surprised to see Ravi when he finally emerges from his hiding place?

7. Infer What kind of game are the children playing at twilight? Why might the time of day be significant?

8. Interpret What has Ravi learned by the end of the story? Cite a passage from the story that supports your answer.

9. Analyze What is the **theme** of this story; that is, what truth or insight about life does it reveal? How does the story's title reinforce its theme?

10. Evaluate Are the children in this story and childhood itself realistically portrayed? Give examples to support your view.

Literary Skills: Imagery

11. Analyze Which images in the story suggest loss and death? How do these images make you feel?

Literary Skills Review: Protagonist and Antagonist

12. Make Judgments A **protagonist** is the hero of the story, the person we focus our attention on or the person who sets the conflict in motion. The **antagonist** is the person or force that blocks the protagonist. Who is the story's protagonist? How can you tell? Who or what is the story's main antagonist? Why do you think so?

Writing Focus

Think As a Reader/Writer

Use It in Your Writing Review your list of strong, precise verbs. Write a short essay describing an activity, such as a sport or game, and then analyze the verbs you used. Can you choose more precise verbs to strengthen your description? Look for adverbs—you can often replace a verb-adverb combination with a more effective verb. For example, rather than say, "She ran quickly through the woods," you might say, "She darted through the woods."

 What Do You Think Now

How do you think Ravi's childhood experience will shape his view of the world? Many people have similar experiences. How do you think these experiences might affect people's worldviews differently?

Vocabulary Development

✓ Vocabulary Check

State whether each Vocabulary word is paired with its synonym or antonym.

1. lugubrious   cheerful
2. temerity   recklessness
3. intoxicating   boring
4. dogged   persistent
5. maniacal   crazed
6. stridently   gently
7. ignominy   honor
8. superciliously   scornfully

Vocabulary Skills: Analogies

In a word analogy, the relationship between the first pair of words is the same as the relationship between the second pair. Some relationships expressed in analogies are part and whole; action and related object; and performer and related action.

Part and Whole
CHAPTER : BOOK :: fender : car
A *chapter* is part of a *book,* as a *fender* is part of a *car.*

Action and Related Object
BOIL : EGG :: throw : ball
You *boil* an *egg;* you *throw* a *ball.*

Performer and Related Action
AUTHOR : WRITE :: chef : cook
An *author* is one who *writes;* a *chef* is one who *cooks.*

Steps for Solving Analogy Questions

- Identify the relationship between the capitalized pair of words, and note the part of speech of each word.
- Look for the same relationship and the same part of speech in the pairs of words in the answer choices.
- Choose the pair whose relationship and word order most closely match those of the capitalized pair.

Your Turn

For each numbered item, choose the pair of words that expresses a relationship that is most similar to the relationship between the pair of capitalized words.

1. PALM : HAND ::
   a. eye : face
   b. steeple : church
   c. fingernail : finger
   d. sole : foot

2. PURSUER : CHASE ::
   a. pilot : fly
   b. hunter : stalk
   c. shallow : deep
   d. instruct : teacher

3. WASH : CAR ::
   a. climb : ladder
   b. garden : lettuce
   c. garage : clean
   d. polish : shoe

Language Coach

Pronunciation Look back at the Vocabulary words on page 1415. Use the pronunciation key to say aloud each of the words. What is surprising about the pronunciation of *dogged?*

Academic Vocabulary

Talk About
Like many postcolonial writers, Desai is considerably influenced by her cultural perspective. In a small group, discuss whether a writer can "escape" his or her background. Is it inevitable that cultural heritage will inform a writer's work?

 **Learn It Online**
For more about synonyms and antonyms, visit *WordSharp.*

go.hrw.com   L12-1423   Go

Grammar Link

Effective Sentences: Variety

Desai crafts lively prose not only by using rich imagery and details but also by varying sentence structures. One way to vary your sentences is to vary the beginnings. Instead of starting with the subject, rearrange some of your sentences to begin with modifiers.

SUBJECT FIRST	*Ravi, ordinary and small, yearns to triumph over Raghu.*
SINGLE-WORD MODIFIERS FIRST	*Ordinary and small, Ravi yearns to triumph over Raghu.*
SUBJECT FIRST	*The children, unaware that Ravi is missing, continue their games.*
PARTICIPIAL PHRASE FIRST	*Unaware that Ravi is missing, the children continue their games.*
SUBJECT FIRST	*Raghu, a hefty football player, intimidates the other children.*
APPOSITIVE PHRASE FIRST	*A hefty football player, Raghu intimidates the other children.*

Your Turn

Rewrite the following sentences so that they do not start with the subject.

1. Mira, motherly and self-assured, prods the children to form a circle.
2. Manu, frightened by Raghu's shouting, dashes away.
3. Bougainvillea, a tropical plant, thrives in the sun.
4. The children, careless of Ravi's feelings, ignore him.

Writing Application Re-read a paragraph you wrote recently in your *Reader/Writer Notebook*. Look for ways to diversify sentence structure by varying the beginnings of at least two sentences.

CHOICES

As you respond to the Choices, use these **Academic Vocabulary** words as appropriate: perspective, considerably, adapt, exhibit, inevitable.

REVIEW
Write with Imagery

With five classmates, think of an experience you can all imagine that involves your five senses, such as sledding or going to the beach. Have each group member relate a different sensory perspective: The first member describes what he or she would see; the second describes what he or she would hear; the third describes what he or she would taste; the fourth describes what he or she would smell; and the fifth describes what he or she would feel. Combine your input into one imagery-rich paragraph.

CONNECT
Describe a Memory

Timed └Writing In her review of *Games at Twilight*, Victoria Glendinning calls the title story a "jewel." She believes that it "recounts something that has happened in one way or another to nearly everyone in childhood.… Mrs. Desai is a writer's writer in that anyone who has ever set pen to paper must ask himself just what it is about the writing that makes it so memorable, and there is, naturally, no simple answer to the question." In a brief essay, discuss the following questions: Do you agree that Desai is recounting something "that has happened… to nearly everyone in childhood"? How would you describe that experience? What makes Desai's story memorable?

EXTEND
Design a Web Page

TechFocus Design a Web page about children's games around the world, using the notes you took as you read as well as any additional research you did on the Internet. What, if anything, do many of the games have in common?

SKILLS FOCUS Literary Skills Compare works within a literary genre. **Writing Skills** Use appropriate organization; support ideas/theses with relevant evidence and details; compare literary works; compare characters or historical figures; compare themes or literary elements.

from Omeros / B. Wordsworth / *from* Sir Vidia's Shadow / Cartoon / Games at Twilight

Writing Focus

Analyzing Postcolonial Literature

Postcolonial literature provides readers with many avenues for reflection and analysis. Below you will find three different writing assignments to challenge and synthesize your thinking about the issues and the voices of the period.

Postcolonial Traditions

Think about what makes Walcott's, Naipaul's, and Desai's texts representative of postcolonial literature. How does each reflect the influence of colonialism? Remember that a work can be influenced by colonialism in two ways:

- The work may reflect the influence of colonialism in its **content** (what the work is about). For instance, it may describe traditions and behaviors that come from the region's colonizers.

- The work may reflect the influence of colonialism in its **form** (the structure of the work). For instance, an author might borrow a form, such as the sonnet, which comes from the colonizer's literary tradition.

Choose one of these approaches to write a comparison-contrast analysis of these writers and their works. Decide on the **content** or the **form** that you want to focus on for your analysis, and then determine how each text exhibits the content or form relevant to your analysis. Use ample evidence from each text to support your thesis.

The Role of a Mentor in Writing

Think about the thematic relationship among the three selections "from *Sir Vidia's Shadow*," the cartoon on page 1412, and "B. Wordsworth." All three explore the role of a mentor in a writer's life. What do the three have in common? How do they differ? How do they approach the subject similarly and differently? Write a comparison contrast essay in which you use the **block method** of organization to address what each has to say about mentoring. In the block method, each of your body paragraphs addresses one text. Since the cartoon is unique from the other two, begin with it for your first body paragraph. Then proceed to develop a body paragraph for the other two selections. Remember to keep your focus on how each one addresses the idea of a mentor. In each body paragraph, address the similarities and differences among the three. Use ample examples from the texts to support your points about each one.

Writing a Personal Reflection

Now that you have read the three selections "from *Sir Vidia's Shadow*," "B. Wordsworth," and the cartoon, you may be thinking about the role of a mentor in your own life. Who serves as a mentor for you? How is that role enacted? How has the mentor affected your life? How was this accomplished? How are you different now? Is the change positive or negative?

Write an essay that explains how a mentor how influenced your life. Be specific as you describe the process and the effect the mentor has had on your life.

What Do You Think Now? Now that you have read these postcolonial works, how do you think the experience of colonialism has shaped the way citizens of colonized countries view the world?

Learn It Online
There's more to the story than meets the eye.

go.hrw.com   L12-1425   **Go**

Writing Workshop

Nonfiction Analysis

Write with a Purpose

Write an essay that analyzes a nonfiction text. Your **purpose** is to explain the nonfiction selection to your **audience**—your classmates, teacher, and other readers interested in the topic or author.

Think as a Reader/Writer

In this unit, you have read nonfiction selections that demonstrate many of the literary qualities you find in fictional works. These qualities are why the texts are referred to as literary nonfiction. Before you write an **nonfiction analysis,** read an excerpt of Kenneth Keskinen's analysis of George Orwell's political essay "Shooting an Elephant" (page 1141).

> We are struck immediately by the urgent, even emotional tone of the opening of the essay. The emotionally charged words reflect the intensity of Orwell's feelings, such expressions as "sneering" and "hideous laughter." In the second paragraph he uses "guilt," "hatred," and "evil-spirited little beasts." These words, along with his use of the personal pronouns, make us aware that here is a writer who is personally and deeply concerned, a writer whose concern gives immediacy and power to his account. This is evident from the very first sentence in which he states that ". . . I was hated by large numbers of people. . . ." Indeed, most of Orwell's essays begin with such compelling sentences. . . .
>
> . . . Orwell's own abhorrence of the "unfree" society that does not let the individual be his human "off-duty" self is present in "Shooting an Elephant." It is an abhorrence that would lead to his denunciation of communism in his best-known works, *1984* and *Animal Farm*. Orwell seems always to be asking basic questions: How free can man be? What are the masks—in the name of progress, of tradition, of duty, of civilization, or of the *status quo*—that men try to wear as they deal with other men? Ultimately, Orwell decries the wearing of any mask that keeps us from recognizing that there are human needs, human strengths, human failings and feelings that we all share "off duty" in a world where the white and non-white . . . are not political entities but human beings.

← Keskinen discusses Orwell's **word choices**, quoting directly from Orwell's essay.

← Keskisen states and explains the **theme** of Orwell's essay.

Reader/Writer Notebook

Use your *RWN* to complete the activities for this workshop.

Think About the Professional Model

With a partner, discuss the following questions about the model:

1. How does Keskinen's use of direct quotations support his assertion?
2. Are the references to Orwell's *1984* and *Animal Farm* an effective way for Keskinen to support his thesis? Why or why not?

Prewriting

Choose a Text and Gain an Overview

Find a **nonfiction text,** such as an essay, speech, memoir, history, journal, or letter, whose subject matter intrigues you or whose author writes in a style you enjoy. Begin your analysis by reading the text once to gain an overview of the subject and a general understanding of the ideas expressed. Note the following:

- the work's title, author, and subject matter
- the author's purpose—to inform, persuade, express, or entertain
- any background information needed to understand the subject

Think About Purpose and Audience

As you consider which work to analyze, keep in mind your purpose and audience. Your **purpose** in analyzing a nonfiction text is to develop and support your own interpretation of the selection. Your analysis should enhance a reader's understanding and appreciation of the work. Your **audience** is your teacher, peers, and others interested in this author or subject.

Analyze the Theme

Literary nonfiction, though factual, goes beyond merely conveying information. Nonfiction texts usually express a **theme,** or insight about human nature or life. Sometimes authors directly state their themes, but at other times readers have to dig deeper to find significance beyond the surface meaning. To determine your text's theme, re-read the text, paying close attention to what the author says directly and indirectly, and to the **stylistic devices** he or she uses. The chart below provides questions that will help you identify and analyze stylistic devices.

Stylistic Devices
Diction—What effect do the author's word choices have on the reader? What connotations (as opposed to denotations, or strict, literal meanings) do the words evoke?
Figurative language—What things or ideas does the author describe through simile, metaphor, or personification? What meaning could be implied from the comparisons made?
Imagery—What sensory details does the author use? What feelings do the images evoke? Do they paint the subject in a positive or negative light?
Irony—Where do what the writer says contrast what you think he or she means? Where are your expectations of what's going to happen thwarted? Where does what appears to be true really not?
Repetition—Do repeated words, phrases, or ideas directly or indirectly say anything about human nature or life in general?
Symbol—What person, place, thing, or event seems to stand for something beyond itself? What does the symbolic meaning suggest about humanity or life in general?
Tone –What is the author's attitude toward the reader? the subject? What words or details clue you into the writer's this attitude?

Idea Starters

- nonfiction texts by writers in this textbook
- suggestions from a friend, family member, librarian, or teacher
- nonfiction texts written by writers of fiction you enjoy
- nonfiction texts written during a historical period that interests you

Your Turn

Get Started Choose a nonfiction text, and take notes in your **RWN** on the **title, author, author's purpose,** and **background information.** Then, identify the work's **theme,** and determine what **stylistic devices** the author uses to expresses it.

Learn It Online
To see how one writer completed this assignment, see the model nonfiction analysis at:

go.hrw.com L12-1427 Go

Develop a Thesis

Sum up your ideas about the nonfiction text's theme in a sentence that will guide the rest of your analysis. The **thesis statement** should identify the theme and how the author develops it. The writer of the student model that begins on page 1431 wrote the following preliminary, or draft, thesis statement:

> In "The Death of the Moth," Virginia Woolf uses the moth's struggle to live and its death as a metaphor for human existence.

Gather Support

To support your thesis statement, use two or more **key points.** These are **reasons** that readers should accept your interpretation. Use **evidence—direct quotations, paraphrases,** and **summaries**—from the text to support each key point. **Elaborate,** or explain, each piece of evidence, giving the readers your insight into what the evidence means and how it relates to your key points and thesis.

Using Direct Quotations Most of the ideas in your analysis should be expressed in your own words. However, a few well-chosen quotations from the text can provide excellent support for your ideas. When choosing quotations, ask yourself the following questions:

* Does this quotation support my thesis or one of my key ideas?
* Will the quotation make sense to someone who hasn't read the original essay, or will I need to provide a lot of additional context to explain it?
* Is the quotation short enough to support my ideas without interrupting the flow of my essay?

Organize Your Analysis

Present your ideas in a logical manner—either **chronologically** or in the **order of importance.** Create an **analysis plan,** like this one, to organize your thoughts.

> <u>Title and Author:</u> "The Death of the Moth" by Virginia Woolf
> <u>Organization:</u> Chronological order
>
> <u>Introduction:</u>
> —Thesis statement: In "The Death of the Moth," Virginia Woolf uses the moth's struggle to live and its death as a metaphor for human existence.
>
> <u>Body:</u>
> —Explain what the moth symbolizes.
> —Use evidence from the essay to show how Woolf weaves her metaphor.
> —Elaborate on details.
>
> <u>Conclusion:</u>
> —Restate the thesis.
> —Concluding thought: Use quote. "Just as life had been strange, death was now as strange."

Writing Tip

When quoting directly from a text:

* Put quotation marks around any material taken from the text.
* Introduce quotations to show how they connect to your ideas.
* Avoid quoting large blocks of text. Instead, paraphrase the important ideas, and choose a few phrases or at most one or two sentences to illustrate your point.

Your Turn _____

Plan Your Analysis In your **RWN,** write your **thesis statement,** and gather **evidence** to support it. Consider how you'll **elaborate** on your evidence. Then, organize your thoughts in a **nonfiction analysis plan.**

Draft Your Analysis

Use the notes from your *Reader/Writer Notebook*, your analysis plan, and the **Writer's Framework** to the right to create the first draft of your analysis.

Use Transitions

Your organizational pattern is not the only means through which you create **coherence,** the sense that your ideas hold together logically. You should also help your readers follow your analysis by using **transitional words and phrases** to connect ideas and tell why and how they are related.

- compare ideas: *also, and, as well as, in the same way, likewise, similarly*
- contrast ideas: *although, but, however, on the other hand, unlike, yet*
- show importance or order: *first, second, next, last, most important*
- show chronology (time): *after, before, during, finally, meanwhile, next, then*
- show support: *for example, for instance, indeed, in fact*

Framework for a Nonfiction Analysis

Introduction
- Present background information that provides context for your analysis.
- Provide the selection's author and title.
- Include a clear thesis statement.

Body
- Organize key points logically.
- Include evidence from the text
- Elaborate on how the evidence supports the key points or thesis

Conclusion
- Restate your thesis
- Summarize your key points.
- End your analysis with a final thought—an idea for your readers to ponder.

Grammar Link Punctuating Transitions

Conjunctive adverbs (such as *however, alternatively, therefore, likewise,* or *nevertheless*) serve as transitions between one idea and another. You can use conjunctive adverbs to begin a sentence or to combine two sentences. The examples below are from the professional model on page 1426 and the student model on page 1431.

Use a comma after conjunctive adverbs at the beginning of a complete sentence:

> **Indeed,** most of Orwell's essays begin with such compelling sentences. . . .

Use a semicolon before and a comma after a conjunctive adverb used to join two complete independent clauses:

> The moth becomes temporarily still**; meanwhile,** she admits, "I forgot about him."

Reference Note For more on conjunctive adverbs, see the Language Handbook.

Your Turn _____

Write Your Draft Following your nonfiction analysis action plan, write a draft of your essay. Also, think about how you will use direct quotations and transitions to support and link your ideas.

Peer Review

With a peer reviewer, read each evaluation question in the chart to the right. Look over your papers together to ensure you have both met all the guidelines. Ask for and give suggestions for improvement.

Evaluating and Revising

Read the questions in the left-hand column of the chart, and then use the tips in the middle column to help you make revisions to your essay. The right-hand column suggests techniques you can use to revise your draft. As you revise, pay attention to your **audience** and **purpose.**

Nonfiction Analysis: Guidelines for Content and Organization

Evaluation Question	Tip	Revision Technique
1. Does the introduction contain the title and author of the essay and a clear thesis statement?	**Underline** the title and author of the essay. **Double underline** the thesis statement.	If needed, **add** the essay's author and title and a thesis statement.
2. Does the essay include key points, or reasons, that support the thesis?	**Bracket** each key point.	**Add** key points that support the thesis.
3. Is there relevant evidence to support each key point?	**Put a check mark** by each relevant piece of evidence—quotation, paraphrase, summary.	**Add** evidence to back up each key point. **Replace** or **delete** any evidence that does not support the key point.
4. Is evidence clearly explained through elaboration?	**Draw an arrow** from each piece of evidence to its elaboration.	**Elaborate** by explaining what the evidence means or why it is important.
5. Is the organizational pattern of the essay easy to follow?	**Highlight** the key points, which you have already bracketed. If they are not organized in a logical order, rearrange them.	**Rearrange** body paragraphs into a logical order, such as order of importance or chronological order. **Add** transitional expressions to connect ideas.
6. Does the conclusion restate the thesis?	**Underline** the restatement of the thesis.	If needed, **add** a sentence that summarizes the thesis.

Read this student's draft; note the comments on its structure and suggestions for how it could be made even stronger.

Life and Death

by Julia Morado, Donnellon High School

Through close examination of an event that appears so common and trivial, a moth dying, Virginia Woolf explores universal questions of life and death. In her essay "The Death of the Moth," Woolf uses the moth's struggle to live and its ultimate death as an extended metaphor for the fate of every human being.

To Woolf, the moth symbolizes life and energy. She refers to the moth with the masculine pronouns "him" and "his." By doing so, she makes his struggle representative of all living things—including human beings. She explains, "The same energy which inspired the rooks, the ploughmen, the horses . . . sent the moth fluttering from side to side of his square window-pane." She describes the moth by saying, "Watching him, it seemed as if a fibre, very thin but pure, of the enormous energy of the world had but thrust into his frail and diminutive body." Woolf contemplates that perhaps the moth's purpose was "to show us the true nature of life." The first part of the extended metaphor is clear as Woolf observes that the moth represents the essence of life.

← Julia states the **title** and **author** and presents her **thesis statement**.

← Her first **key point**—the moth as a symbol of life and energy.

← Julia uses **quotations** from the text as **evidence**.

MINI-LESSON ▶ How to Interweave Quoted Material

Rather than quoting complete sentences from Woolf's essay, Julia can better incorporate quotes by identifying the strongest part of the quoted material and including only that in her own sentences. Using strong verbs and direct objects is a good way to begin **interweaving quotations** into your own syntax, as Julia's revision illustrates.

Julia's Draft of Paragraph 2

By doing so, she makes his struggle representative of all living things—including human beings. She explains, "The same energy which inspired the rooks, the ploughmen, the horses . . . sent the moth fluttering from side to side of his square window-pane." She describes the moth by saying, "Watching him, it seemed as if a fibre, very thin but pure, of the enormous energy of the world had but thrust into his frail and diminutive body." Wolf contemplates . . .

Julia's Revision of Paragraph 2

By doing so, she makes his struggle representative of all living things—including human beings. The moth's energy "inspired the rooks, the ploughmen, the horses." In him, Woolf sees "the enormous energy of the world." Woolf contemplates . . .

Your Turn _____

Interweave Quoted Material Read your draft, and then ask yourself,

- Do I quote complete sentences when a few words or a phrase would suffice?
- How can I better interweave quoted material to ensure my essay flows smoothly?

Student Draft continues

Julia makes another **key point**—humans often take life for granted.

Even when confronted with the representation of "something marvelous," Woolf confesses that she, like all human beings, "is apt to forget all about life." The moth becomes temporarily still; meanwhile, she admits, "I forgot about him." Her human preoccupation with her own tasks absorbs her attention as the moth settles and becomes still. She forgets the moth—and the marvel of life it represents—in the course of her daily activities.

Julia's analysis follows **chronological order** and uses **transitional phrases** to show this.

However, as the essay progresses, the inevitable occurs. The moth begins to die, futilely struggling and fluttering to the bottom of the window, finally resting on his back on the windowsill. Seeing his vain efforts to recover, Woolf picks up a pencil to help the moth, but realizes the presence of death. Her effort to help would be fruitless. Woolf admires the moths last heroic struggle, calling it "superb," even in its failure. Woolf's admiration for the moth's valiant fight to live contrasts with respect for death, which she calls "an oncoming doom." She states, "Nothing had any chance against death." As she observes the finally still moth, Woolf imagines him to say, "death is stronger than I am."

Julia **quotes** evidence, but doesn't **elaborate** on it.

Her conclusion **revisits the thesis** and adds a **final thought** for readers to contemplate.

Woolf uses the moth's struggle to contemplate both life and death in her essay. "Just as life had been strange," she says, "death was now as strange." She explores the mysteries of both states through the extended metaphor of the moth's short life and final fate. Human beings lives and fates mirror those of the insignificant moth.

MINI-LESSON ▶ How to Connect Text Evidence to the Thesis

Julia discusses the meaning of the moth's death in paragraph 4 and uses a quotation from the text as evidence. However, she does not elaborate on the evidence or show how it supports her thesis. It is a big temptation to let the text evidence speak for you. However, your essay expresses *your* ideas on the nonfiction work you've read. Remember to link ideas back to the thesis statement and to give your own interpretation of text evidence. Your comments can also create transition to the next paragraph, as Julia's revision does.

Julia's Draft of Paragraph 4

As she observes the finally still moth, Woolf imagines him to say, "death is stronger than I am."

Julia's Revison of Paragraph 4

As she observes the finally still moth, Woolf imagines him to say, "death is stronger than I am." As the metaphor concludes, with the moth's demise, Woolf's message is clear: All living things will succumb to the inevitability of death. In accepting that death is stronger than itself, the moth (and the humans it symbolizes) accepts that there are larger, more powerful forces in the universe that, though we may struggle against them, ultimately control our fate. Death is a part of life and equally mysterious.

Your Turn _____

Connect Text Evidence Read your draft, and then ask yourself, *What evidence needs further explanation?* Look for quotations that readers may not understand without context. If you are uncertain about a quotation, ask a peer who has not read the essay you're analyzing if he or she thinks the evidence requires elaboration and connection to the thesis.

Proofreading and Publishing

If you want readers to take your analysis seriously, make sure it is free of mistakes in grammar, spelling, and punctuation. **Proofread, or edit,** carefully, and then make any changes in your draft prior to printing your final copy.

Because your analysis discusses an author's work and your nonfiction text's effects, you may find yourself using many **possessive nouns.** You may find errors in the use of **apostrophes** that indicate possession.

Grammar Link Punctuating Possessives

An **apostrophe** used with a noun shows ownership or relationship.

To form the possessive of a **singular noun,** add an apostrophe and an *s.* If the noun ends in *s,* and adding another *s* will make the noun awkward to pronounce, add only an apostrophe.

To form the possessive of a **plural noun,** add only an appostrophe if the noun ends in an *s.* If the plural noun does not end in an *s,* add both an appostrophe and an *s.*

Julia found and corrected some possessives in her draft.

> Woolf admires the moth's last heroic struggle. . . . [singular noun]
>
> Human beings' lives and fates mirror those of the insignificant moth. [plural noun]

Reference Note   For more on possessives, see the Language Handbook.

Publishing

Look for an audience that may have an interest in reading about the nonfiction text you analyzed. Try one of these ideas for sharing your analysis:

- Ask permission to post or submit your analysis to a Web site dedicated to the author of the nonfiction text you analyzed.

- Create your own Web log, and post your essay there. Add past and future writing assignments to your blog, creating your own online portfolio. Ask readers to post responses to what you have written.

Reflect on the Process

Thinking about how you wrote your nonfiction analysis essay will help you with other writing you'll do. In your **RWN,** write a short response to these questions:

1. What was the most challenging part of writing the paper? Explain.
2. How did using a framework help you organize your ideas? Explain.
3. What have you learned from this workshop that might help you with other types of writing?

Proofreading Tip

Few mistakes are more embarrassing than misspelling an author's name or getting a work's title wrong (for example, Virginia Woolfe, "The Death of the Month," or "Death of a Moth"). Always double-check references to your author's name and the title of the work you have analyzed.

Submission Ideas

- online or print scholarly or literary magazine
- your personal Web page
- class or school newspaper or Web page

Your Turn ____

Proofread and Publish

Proofread your essay. As you are proofreading, read carefully to make sure that you have correctly punctuated possessive nouns. After checking the **presentation** of your final draft, publish it for an audience.

Scoring Rubric

Use one of the rubrics below to evaluate your nonfiction analysis from the Writing Workshop or your response to the expository on-demand prompt on the next page. Your teacher will tell you to use either the six- or the four-point rubric.

6-Point Scale

Score 6 *Demonstrates advanced success*
- focuses consistently on a clear thesis
- shows effective organization throughout, with smooth transitions
- offers thoughtful, creative ideas
- develops ideas thoroughly, using examples, details, and fully elaborated explanation
- exhibits mature control of written language

Score 5 *Demonstrates proficient success*
- focuses on a clear thesis
- shows effective organization, with transitions
- offers thoughtful ideas
- develops ideas competently, using examples, details, and well-elaborated explanation
- exhibits sufficient control of written language

Score 4 *Demonstrates competent success*
- focuses on a clear thesis, with minor distractions
- shows effective organization, with minor lapses
- offers mostly thoughtful ideas
- develops ideas adequately, with a mixture of general and specific elaboration
- exhibits general control of written language

Score 3 *Demonstrates limited success*
- includes some loosely related ideas that distract from the writer's expository focus
- shows some organization, with noticeable gaps in the logical flow of ideas
- offers routine, predictable ideas
- develops ideas with uneven elaboration
- exhibits limited control of written language

Score 2 *Demonstrates basic success*
- includes loosely related ideas that seriously distract from the writer's expository focus
- shows minimal organization, with major gaps in the logical flow of ideas
- offers ideas that merely skim the surface
- develops ideas with inadequate elaboration
- exhibits significant problems with control of written language

Score 1 *Demonstrates emerging effort*
- shows little awareness of the topic and purpose for writing
- lacks organization
- offers unclear and confusing ideas
- develops ideas in only a minimal way, if at all
- exhibits major problems with control of written language

4-Point Scale

Score 4 *Demonstrates advanced success*
- focuses consistently on a clear thesis
- shows effective organization throughout, with smooth transitions
- offers thoughtful, creative ideas
- develops ideas thoroughly, using examples, details and, fully elaborated explanation
- exhibits mature control of written language

Score 3 *Demonstrates competent success*
- focuses on a clear thesis, with minor distractions
- shows effective organization, with minor lapses
- offers mostly thoughtful ideas
- develops ideas adequately, with a mixture of general and specific elaboration
- exhibits general control of written language

Score 2 *Demonstrates limited success*
- includes some loosely related ideas that distract from the writer's expository focus
- shows some organization, with noticeable gaps in the logical flow of ideas
- offers routine, predictable ideas
- develops ideas with uneven elaboration
- exhibits limited control of written language

Score 1 *Demonstrates emerging effort*
- shows little awareness of the topic and purpose for writing
- lacks organization
- offers unclear and confusing ideas
- develops ideas in only a minimal way, if at all
- exhibits major problems with control of written language

Preparing for **Timed** **Writing**

Expository Essay: Cause and Effect

When responding to an expository prompt, use what you have learned from reading, writing your nonfiction analysis, and studying the rubric on page 1434. Use the steps below to develop a response to the following prompt.

Writing Prompt

Think about a time when you made a dramatic change in your life. This change could have been prompted by others, but it had a direct effect on you. Explain what caused the change and how you have been affected by it.

Study the Prompt

Begin by reading the prompt carefully. Circle or under-line key words: *time, dramatic change, effect on you, caused*. A **dramatic change** is one that has a deep or lasting impact on your life. You will explain that **effect** in your essay. **Tip:** Spend about five minutes studying the prompt.

Plan Your Response

The prompt asks you to explain a dramatic change. What was the **cause** of the change? Think about times when circumstances have changed for you. Perhaps you moved, changed schools, or lost someone you cared for. Perhaps you had a prolonged illness or were injured. The change of circumstances should be sig-nificant, or important. Choose one dramatic change in your life to explain. Answer these questions about the change:

- What happened? What caused the change?
- Who caused the change, me or someone else?
- Who else was involved in this event?
- How did the event affect me or change me?
- What illustration or elaboration can I use to dem-onstrate that change?
- Have others been affected by the change? If so, how?

Once you have answered the questions, plan your essay by following the outline in the next column.

Introduction:

- Tell what happened.
- Explain who was involved.
- Describe where and how it happened.

Body:

- Explain the effect of this change on your life. You may have one major effect to elaborate on or sev-eral smaller effects to illustrate.

Conclusion:

- Look ahead. Explain how the change will affect you in the future.

Tip: Spend about ten minutes planning your response.

Respond to the Prompt

Use your notes and outline to start writing your essay. Your reader needs to know about the change and then how it affected you and continues to affect you. One way to begin is to create a brief scene in which you discovered the change. Use transitions, such as *conse-quently, because,* and *therefore,* to make the connec-tions clear. **Tip:** Spend about twenty minutes writing your essay.

Improve Your Response

Revising Revisit the key aspects of the prompt. Does your essay explain the change and its effect on you and others? Do you use transitions to make clear connec-tions? If not, add these elements.

Proofreading Take a few minutes to proofread your response to correct errors in grammar, spelling, and mechanics. Make sure that your edits are neat and that the paper is legible.

Checking Your Final Copy Before you turn in your response, read it one more time to catch any errors you may have missed. **Tip:** Save five or ten minutes to improve your essay.

Analyzing Media

Listen and View with a Purpose

Analyze how various media influence your <u>perspective</u>; then, create and deliver your own multimedia presentation using words, images, and sounds.

Think as a Reader/Writer You can often choose what you read. Today, however, you are bombarded by information, images and sounds beyond your control. Television, advertisements, the Internet, and other media of the digital age have made it increasingly important to understand how media messages work. This workshop will show you how to apply analytical skills to the media that surround you and how to combine media into a presentation of your own.

Analyzing Media

It is difficult to imagine a day without e-mail, the Internet, television, radio, books, or newspapers. Clearly, receiving and decoding media messages is part of daily life. These messages reach their intended audiences through two categories of **media sources.**

- **Print media sources** include books, newspapers, magazines, pamphlets, advertising fliers, billboards, and posters.
- **Electronic media sources** include radio, television, videos, the Internet, blogs, and podcasts.

In the twenty-first century, of course, many digital media combine several kinds of information, not to mention multiple modes of delivery. Consider today's cell phone, for example. Unlike traditional telephones, which transmit voices over telephone wires, the cell phone accomplishes several functions wirelessly. It can provide phone service, voice mail, text messaging, e-mail, digital photography, digital video clips, digital music, video games, and more.

Media for the Twenty-First Century

To function successfully in today's world, you must be able to read and analyze three kinds of media:

- **Informational media** Advances in computer technology have brought with them an information explosion. Thanks to the Internet, you can access search engines, online databases, newspaper Web sites, blogs, and hundreds of thousands of other Web-based resources when you need information. Much of what is available on the Web, however, is not reliable.
- **Commercial advertisements** Every day, you are exposed to a flood of commercial images. Learning how advertisements work can help you to make informed choices.
- **Political advertisements** Our political process is shaped, in large part, by the advertising media. Understanding such political advertising can help you to participate effectively in the political process.

Reader/Writer Notebook

Use your **RWN** to complete the activities for this workshop.

SKILLS FOCUS **Reading Skills** Analyze editorials, advertisements, documentaries, and other texts for bias and use of common persuasive techniques; evaluate the credibility of information sources and their appropriateness for varied needs. **Writing Skills** Compare print media and electronic media. **Listening and Speaking Skills** Understand and identify logical fallacies and propaganda techniques.

Media Literacy

Critical readers and viewers use media literacy concepts to analyze, interpret, and evaluate media messages. The left column of the following chart will help you understand basic media literacy concepts. The suggestions in the right column will help you analyze the media messages you receive.

Media Literacy Concepts

Concept	Application
1. People—alone or in groups—write, edit, select, illustrate, or compose every media message.	When you look at a Web page, try to find who is behind the information on the page—the name of the individual or group. Always be on the alert for bias in the media you encounter.
2. Like a story or poem, a media message reflects a particular point of view—sometimes a combined point of view.	When you see an eyewitness account on televised news, remember that it reflects at least three points of view: the witness speaking in the video clip, the technician who edited the original video footage, and the television station airing it.
3. Your interpretation of a media message is based on your knowledge.	Discover as much as you can about the media that shape your world. As you learn more about how media work, you will be a more effective citizen of the digital age.
4. Every media message has a purpose—to inform, persuade, or entertain, but always to persuade.	As you observe media messages, always look for a persuasive purpose and the persuasive methods that support the purpose.
5. Media producers shape messages according to the characteristics of the medium in use.	Remember that even the most versatile cell phone is limited by its size.

A Good Media Analysis

- identifies the medium and its message
- considers the creator of the message and his or her purpose
- discerns how the form or style of the medium affects its message
- recognizes the strategies used in creating or expressing the message
- infers what may have been left out of the message and why
- evaluates the effectiveness of the message

Webpage for USDA Food Pyramid.

Learn It Online
Analyze Web pages and more at *MediaScope*.

go.hrw.com   L12-1437   Go

Media Workshop

Analyzing Media

Presentation Tip

Ensure a successful multimedia presentation by learning as much as you can about how today's media work. Before you choose a topic, examine as many print and televised ads as possible, looking for the propaganda methods presented here. If time allows, use the Internet to research other persuasive methods used by advertisers in the digital age.

Recognizing Propaganda

Media producers use the techniques of propaganda to achieve their purposes and to shape their messages for their intended audiences. To be an effective media consumer, you must be able to analyze and evaluate the use of these methods. The following chart describes some of the most common propaganda strategies in use today.

Media Strategies

Strategy	Examples
Ad Hominem Attack Also known as name-calling, this approach is common in political advertising, in which one candidate or group tries to persuade voters by smearing the reputation of another candidate or group.	In a common variation on the political attack ad, a disapproving voice repeats the name of a candidate and, with each repetition, names something supposedly negative the candidate has done or cast a vote for. Attack ads present heavily edited evidence, almost always out of context.
Bandwagon This technique appeals to the human desire to belong by suggesting that all the right people use a particular product or support a particular candidate.	Advertisements for a particular food or drink will picture a crowd of happy, attractive people consuming the product in an especially pleasant setting. The implicit message: purchase the product and join the in-crowd.
Card Stacking Advertisers stack the cards when they emphasize the appealing aspects of their product—or their candidate—and leave out any negative traits.	A snack-food ad might trumpet that the product is low in fat, and leave out the high sugar content.
Facts and Figures Propaganda exploits our tendency to see data as proof, selecting facts and figures to make the favored candidate—or product—look appealing.	"Nine out of ten doctors recommend" product X.
False Causality Suggesting that one event caused another because they occurred in sequence is a trick of advertising and political propaganda.	Advertisements regularly suggest that purchasing the "right" product will lead to success or happiness.
Glittering Generalities Abstract words with a positive emotional appeal give propaganda persuasive power.	Ads in favor of a particular candidate use phrases such as "truth, justice, and the American way." Attack ads use words and phrases that have the reverse effect.

Plain Folks / Snob Appeal Variations on the bandwagon method, Plain Folks appeals to the ordinary citizen in you, while Snob Appeal exploits the desire to be part of a select group.

Commercials for fast food products often picture ordinary people, sometimes even in rural settings. By contrast, ads for expensive designer luggage feature rich and exclusive-looking settings.

Testimonial This method uses the testimony of a well-known person to support a product, a cause, or a candidate.

Rock stars, movie stars, and famous athletes are everywhere in the world of advertising.

Transfer When advertisers create an exciting scene and place their product in it, they rely on viewers to transfer their desire for excitement from the scene to the product.

Think Carribbean vacations, white water rapids, and gorgeous views—as depicted in television ads for beverages, chewing gum, and other products.

Weasel Words Propaganda can use words to soften a harsh truth or to create the illusion of substance where there is none.

When an ad says the product has been "clinically tested," the advertiser has weaseled out of telling you what you really need to know to make an informed choice.

"Got Milk" print ad with Mia Hamm. © 1999 America's Dairy Farmers and Milk Processors.

Analyzing Visuals

Viewing and Interpreting This advertisement counts on viewers to recognize the slogan and the milk moustache common to a series of advertisements for milk. What elements of the advertisement make it visually appealing? With a partner, examine the ad closely and identify at least two strategies presented in the adjacent chart. If time allows, share your ideas with the class as a whole.

Learn It Online
Learn more about political advertisements at *MediaScope*.

go.hrw.com | L12-1439 | **Go**

Analyzing Media

Preparing a Multimedia Analysis

Now that you have studied strategies common to the propaganda of advertising, you will analyze a commercial advertisement or a group of related commercial advertisements and shape your analysis into a multimedia presentation, using words, images, and sound. In choosing a suitable subject for this presentation, consider your own interests, as well as the kinds of advertising that are prominent when you are ready to begin. You might wish to choose print and televisioni ads for a single product.

Select Words, Images, and Sound You will use words to present the major ideas in your analysis, images to illustrate your ideas, and sound to enhance what your words and images convey. Use the following chart to help you assemble the components of your presentation.

Presentation Tip

Before planning your multimedia presentation, check with your campus library or media center to see what kind of presentation equipment is available to you. Many schools also make training and support available to students. In addition, you can take advantage of interactive training software that is available for presentational software such as PowerPoint and for presentational equipment such as LCD projectors.

Media	Content	Format
Text	• the major points of your presentation • important facts, figures, or quotations	• Use PowerPoint or a similar approach to present major points in large lettering, attractively formatted. • An LCD projector will display the text of your presentation on a large screen. • A document camera will enlarge facts, figures, and quotations and display them on a large screen.
Images	• color reproductions of still images from the advertisement(s) your presentation analyzes • video clips from the advertisement(s) your presentation analyzes	• You can use PowerPoint to project still images and even video clips. • You can also use an LCD projector, a video projector, or a document camera to project images.
Sound	• video clips with sound—for advertisements that have a soundtrack • your own voice to conduct the presentation	• The methods listed above can be used to project sound. • Use speakers appropriate for the size of the room and your audience. • Practice projecting your voice; use a microphone and speakers, if appropriate.

Research Your Topic   Remember the purpose of your presentation—to analyze the persuasive methods at work in a commercial or political advertisement. You may choose to analyze a print or televised ad. If time allows, you might wish to analyze a group of related ads. Once you have chosen an advertisement, analyze it thoroughly, looking for the media strategies presented on pages 1438-39. After you identify your ad's primary methods of persuasion, do some more research on these methods so that you can explain them effectively when you make your presentation.

Consider Your Audience
As you prepare your presentation, think about the characteristics and needs of your audience. The following questions will help you analyze your audience:

- What will my audience know about my chosen subject?
- What will my audience want to know?
- What methods can I use to capture and hold my audience's attention?
- What media would work best in presenting my topic?
- What combination of media will my audience find most interesting?

Maximize Your Impact
The most appropriate text, image, or sound effect might be ineffective and even distracting if it is not designed properly. Pay close attention to the quality of the material you choose. Think carefully about how to incorporate it into your presentation. Use the following design principles to create the maximum impact on your audience.

- **Text** Limit the amount of text that you expect your audience to read. For each screen or slide, display information in list form, if possible. Present three to five listed items per slide—or one impressive quotation. Choose a plain, non-serif font in a size that your audience will be able to read from the back of the presentation area. If you begin with a list of major points, consider repeating the slide with this list, as needed, for emphasis.
- **Images** Since your purpose is to analyze the persuasive techniques at work in print or televised advertising, high-quality slides or video clips are essential. Be sure images are large enough and clear enough to be seen by everyone in the presentation area. Consider a four-step process for any image or video you analyze: 1. Introduce the image or clip. 2. Show your audience the image or clip without commenting. 3. Show and briefly discuss a slide listing the points you want to make about the image or clip. 4. Show the image or clip again, and point out the features you want your audience to notice. Use a wand-shaped pointer about the length of a yardstick to pinpoint details in any advertisement you share with your audience.
- **Sound** If you present televised advertising, be sure that your equipment is loud enough for your presentation area. Use speakers, if necessary. Practice projecting your voice to the back of the presentation area. If possible, use a microphone and speakers.

Learn It Online
Plan your multimedia presentation online with *MediaScope.*

go.hrw.com   L12-1429   **Go**

Develop a Thesis Statement The thesis statement for your presentation will identify the most important persuasive strategies at work in the advertisement or group of advertisements you have chosen to analyze. For the sake of your audience, consider presenting your thesis statement as a list of bullet points—on a single slide or screen, using large, non-serif letters, clearly visible from the back of the presentation area.

Organize Your Presentation To help ensure that the audience finds your presentation easy to follow, plan its organization carefully. Follow the steps in the chart below to effectively combine the spoken content and the multimedia support you've chosen.

Organizing a Multimedia Presentation

1. Compose your thesis statement and create a single slide or screen presenting the major points of your thesis as a bulleted list.

2. Create a single slide or screen for each of the major points listed on your thesis slide or screen. Each of these screens will introduce a major part of your presentation.

3. Plan the visual back-up for each major point in your presentation. What image or video clip will you show your audience? How will you point out the persuasive strategy you want to highlight at this point in your presentation.

4. Plan the textual support for each major point in your presentation. Set up one or more slides or screens to display the information and ideas you want your audience to remember.

5. If it would be useful to remind your audience of any major point or points, make duplicate slides or screens of these to insert in your presentation, as appropriate.

6. Plan your conclusion. Consider repeating your thesis slide. If time allows, consider showing your audience a new advertisement that uses the techniques your presentation analyzed. Ask members of the audience to identify these techniques.

7. Plan how you will integrate the components of your analysis—words, images, and sound—into a seamless presentation. Make an outline, chart, or storyboard to consult as you rehearse.

Practice Your Presentation Throughout the process of planning and developing your presentation, you've probably given serious consideration to the effect it will have on your intended audience. Now is the time to determine whether all of the elements work together as planned. Gather a group of friends or family members, and rehearse your presentation. Deliver it exactly as you would for the intended audience of your final presentation. If you need use of the school's audiovisual equipment, arrange a rehearsal before or after school.

As you rehearse, express interest in and enthusiasm about your topic. After all, your delivery holds the whole presentation together. Speak confidently, enunciate clearly, and avoid vocalized pauses, such as um or ah. Use nonverbal behavior—eye contact, facial expressions, and gestures—to your advantage. Be familiar with your presentation equipment, and don't turn your back on the audience when using it. After your rehearsal, use the questions in the chart below to ask your audience for feedback.

Audience Feedback

Which section of the spoken part of the presentation was most memorable? Why did it succeed?

Which of the multimedia elements of the presentation were most effective? Why did you think so?

How well did the presentation combine spoken words with text, images, and sounds? Explain.

What parts of the multimedia presentation, if any, did you find confusing? Why?

How did the delivery itself affect the presentation? Explain.

What did you learn about propaganda techniques in advertising? Where in the presentation would you like more information?

Revise Your Presentation Adjust the content and delivery of your presentation according to your rehearsal audience's responses. Do further research, if indicated, to strengthen the content of your analysis. If necessary, revise slides or screens for greater clarity or adjust the way you present still images or video clips. Then, practice delivering your presentation for a second time to make sure all of the problems have been eliminated. Check and double-check your presentation equipment. The effectiveness of an excellent presentation depends on your efficient management of your equipment. Because a multimedia presentation coordinates so many different parts, anticipate possible troubles and be prepared for emergencies.

Viewing Tip

As a viewer of media, don't ignore or discount your gut reaction to an image, but use your head, too. Think about why you reacted to the image as you did. Ask yourself these questions:

- What made me react that way?
- Is my reaction the one the image maker wanted me to have? Why might he or she have tried to evoke a particular reaction?
- How does my reaction to the image affect my understanding of the issue or story the image accompanies?

Learn It Online
Polish your presentation with *MediaScope*.

go.hrw.com   L12-1443   Go

Literary Skills Review

Comparing Literature   **Directions:** Read the two poems below. Then, read each multiple-choice question that follows, and write the letter of the best response.

The Lorelei

by **Heinrich Heine**
translated by **Louis Untermeyer**

I cannot tell why this imagined
   Despair has fallen on me;
The ghost of an ancient legend
   That will not let me be:

5   The air is cool, and twilight
   Flows down the quiet Rhine;
A mountain alone in the high light
   Still holds the faltering shine.

The last peak rosily gleaming
10   Reveals, enthroned in air,
A maiden, lost in dreaming,
   Who combs her golden hair.

Combing her hair with a golden
   Comb in her rocky bower,°
15   She sings the tune of an olden
   Song that has magical power.

The boatman has heard; it has bound him
   In throes of a strange, wild love;
Blind to the reefs that surround him,
20   He sees but the vision above.

And lo, hungry waters are springing—
   Boat and boatman are gone. . . .
Then silence. And this, with her singing,
   The Lorelei has done.

---

14. bower: enclosed place or retreat, usually a lady's
bedroom or private room; a natural enclosure.

Siren Song

by **Margaret Atwood**

This is the one song everyone
would like to learn: the song
that is irresistible:

the song that forces men
5   to leap overboard in squadrons
even though they see the beached skulls

the song nobody knows
because anyone who has heard it
is dead, and the others can't remember

10   Shall I tell you the secret
and if I do, will you get me
out of this bird suit?

I don't enjoy it here
squatting on this island
15   looking picturesque and mythical

with these two feathery maniacs,
I don't enjoy singing
this trio, fatal and valuable.

I will tell the secret to you,
20   to you, only to you.
Come closer. This song

is a cry for help: Help me!
Only you, only you can,
you are unique

25   at last. Alas
it is a boring song
but it works every time.

1. In lines 1–4 of "The Lorelei," the speaker —

   A is pursued by a real ghost

   B finds comfort in a legend

   C experiences real love for the first time

   D feels a compelling connection to a legend

2. The **mood** in lines 5–8 of "The Lorelei" could *best* be described as —

   A fearful

   B joyful

   C romantic

   D reckless

3. What has occurred in the final stanza of "The Lorelei"?

   A The speaker betrays the Lorelei.

   B The boatman has gone away with the woman.

   C The boatman has drowned.

   D The speaker expresses envy of the boatman.

4. The **tone** of "Siren Song" is *best* described as —

   A cynical

   B romantic

   C sorrowful

   D joyful

5. What do lines 13-16 of "Siren Song" suggest about the speaker's attitude?

   A She finds her situation ridiculous.

   B She enjoys being mythical and powerful.

   C She is proud of her beauty.

   D She does not want to find true love.

6. Who is the speaker of "Siren Song"?

   A a siren wearing a bird suit

   B Margaret Atwood

   C a sailor

   D a bitter woman

7. What implied **theme** is contained in the last two lines of "Siren Song"?

   A Help is available for those who ask.

   B Women are rarely taken seriously.

   C Men cannot be manipulated.

   D Attraction follows a predictable pattern.

8. How does the overall **imagery** in "Siren Song" differ from that in "The Lorelei"?

   A The imagery in "The Lorelei" is romantic, while the imagery in "Siren Song" is jarring.

   B The imagery in "The Lorelei" is violent, while the imagery in "Siren Song" is soothing.

   C The imagery in "The Lorelei" is powerful, while the imagery in "Siren Song" is understated.

   D The imagery in "The Lorelei" is playful, while the imagery in "Siren Song" is naïve.

9. The sirens in "The Lorelei" and "Siren Song" are alike in that they both —

   A are mermaids

   B regret their actions

   C call men to their deaths

   D feel unattractive

Constructed Response

10. Briefly contrast the concluding stanzas of "The Lorelei" and "Siren Song," focusing on tone. Use specific evidence from the poems to support your response.

Vocabulary Skills Review

Synonyms **Directions:** Words that have similar meanings are called **synonyms.** For example, *benign* and *benevolent* are synonyms meaning "kind." In the sentences below, choose the word or phrase that is closest to the meaning of the italicized word.

1. An *impetuous* person is —

 A overly helpful

 B dangerously manipulative

 C extremely impulsive

 D unreasonably stubborn

2. An *impediment* is —

 A an obstacle

 B an architectural feature

 C a commandment

 D a plea

3. *Guile* is the same as —

 A innocence

 B bitterness

 C awe

 D deceit

4. Someone who is *implacable* is —

 A fearful

 B relentless

 C attentive

 D confused

5. *Ignominy* means —

 A ignorance

 B disgrace

 C aggression

 D retaliation

6. Someone who looks at you *reproachfully* is —

 A studying you

 B admiring you

 C blaming you

 D recognizing you

7. An object with *allure* is —

 A fascinating

 B flattering

 C repulsive

 D threatening

Academic Vocabulary

Directions: Choose the word or phrase that is closest to the meaning of the italicized word.

8. If something is *inevitable*, it is —

 A enviable

 B unavoidable

 C inedible

 D not edited correctly

9. Your *perspective* is your —

 A context

 B historical period

 C anxiety level

 D point of view

Writing Skills Review

Edit an Essay on Nonfiction   **Directions:** Read the following excerpt from a draft of a student's nonfiction essay and the questions below it. Choose the best answer to each question, and mark your answers on your own paper.

(1) In his essay "Shooting an Elephant," author George Orwell ironically recalls his struggle as a keeper of the peace in Burma between doing what was right (sparing an elephant) and what was required (maintaining his authority over the Burmese). (2) Even as he prepared to kill the elephant, Orwell was completely aware of the absurdity and tragedy of his situation. (3) Throughout his life, Orwell lived a double identity of sorts. (4) As a child born in Bengal in 1903 to a British civil servant and a merchant's daughter, Orwell found himself in a position where he was socially superior to the native people and yet had no wealth or standing among the whites. (5) At school in England, he stood out. (6) As an adult, Orwell returned to Burma as a member of the imperial police force, but when he began to realize how much the Burmese resented the English, his political sympathies shifted. (7) After leaving the police force and Burma, Orwell decided to try a social experiment. (8) He dressed in rags and lived among the working poor in London and Paris. (9) His experiences as a laborer became the basis for his first recognized work, *Down and Out in Paris and London,* published in 1933. (10) The book was more fiction than essay, but readers enjoyed it.

1. The writer's main purpose in writing this essay is to explain —
   A why Orwell is a master of ironic prose
   B that Orwell experienced life as an outsider
   C events that shaped Orwell's political views
   D Orwell's reputation as a political writer

2. Which sentence in the essay states the thesis?
   A sentence 3
   B sentence 6
   C sentence 8
   D sentence 9

3. Which evidence could the writer have added to support the idea in sentence 5?
   A an example of how Orwell was different from other students
   B a lengthy quotation from a childhood letter
   C a statistic about boys' schools in early twentieth-century England
   D a fact about Orwell's education

4. Which sentence could be deleted because it does not support the excerpt's main idea?
   A sentence 1
   B sentence 2
   C sentence 7
   D sentence 10

5. Which organizational pattern does the writer use most in the essay?
   A order of importance
   B chronological order
   C cause and effect
   D problem and solution

Read On

FICTION
The Inimitable Jeeves

To say that P. G. Wodehouse is a hilarious writer is an understatement. In the course of his long career, Wodehouse wrote over ninety humor books, many of which chronicle the hijinks of Bertie Wooster and Bingo Little. Bertie's valet, Jeeves, deftly rescues Bertie from his entanglements and provides sardonic commentary on his foppish employer's antics. This volume contains several classic stories, including "The Metropolitan Touch," "The Delayed Exit of Claude and Eustace," and "The Purity of the Turf," which some consider to be the funniest story ever written by Wodehouse.

FICTION
Brave New World

Imagine a society that is perfectly harmonious, a community where everyone gets along. How terrible would it be? In his science fiction novel, Aldous Huxley presents a terrifying vision of a Utopian world gone wrong. "Community, Identity, Stability" is the motto of this future state envisioned by Huxley, and to achieve its totalitarian ideals, the government uses pleasure to subdue its citizens. It seems that everyone should be happy, yet the protagonist, Bernard Marx, feels empty and attempts to find fulfillment through love—a subversive emotion.

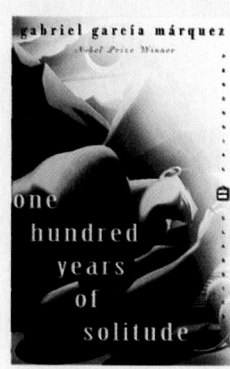

FICTION
One Hundred Years of Solitude

Stories about our origins are fascinating to storytellers and writers. In his prize-winning novel, Gabriel Garcia Márquez invents a mythical Colombian village called Macondo and recounts the history of its founding family, the Buendías. In tracing several generations over the course of a century, he weaves together reality and fantasy, exploring the development of his country's unique culture, and illuminating the wonder and strangeness of life.

FICTION
Things Fall Apart

The rise and fall of powerful people and societies inevitably makes for a compelling story, one which Chinua Achebe tells particularly well in this novel. His portrayal of Nigerian tribal life before and after the arrival of Europeans in Africa centers on the protagonist Okonkwo, a successful man who loses everything and is exiled from the tribe. How will he handle the change, both as a man and as a leader? Losing all hope as his homeland is transformed and modernized, Okonkwo, in his downfall, becomes a poignant symbol of colonial Africa.

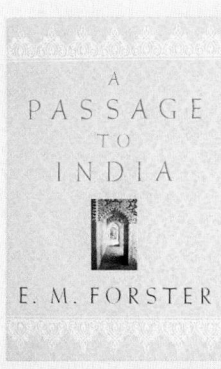

FICTION

A Passage to India

E. M. Forster's most famous novel depicts culture clashes and racial tension in British India just after the turn of the twentieth century. Adela Quested and Mrs. Moore (the mother of Adela's fiancé) come to the city of Chandrapore and befriend Dr. Aziz, who suggests that they all visit the mysterious Marabar Caves. This seemingly innocuous proposal is their undoing: In the darkness of the caves, Adela believes Aziz has assaulted her, and Mrs. Moore becomes panic-stricken. Aziz is arrested and the British and Indian communities seem even more hopelessly divided.

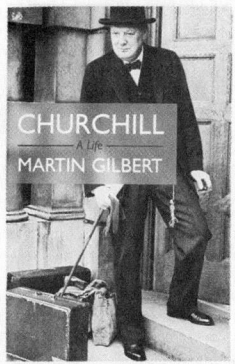

NONFICTION

Churchill: A Life

That this 1000-page biography is merely a condensed version of Martin Gilbert's eight-volume opus on Winston Churchill should give you an idea of how famous and fascinating Churchill was as both a public figure and private person. Filled with anecdotes, excerpts from letters and conversations, and comments from Churchill's family and friends, this biography traces Churchill's life as a schoolboy undergoing floggings, a soldier writing war dispatches and escaping from capture during the Boer War, a Prime Minister keeping Britain rallied during World War II, and a writer winning the Nobel Prize in Literature.

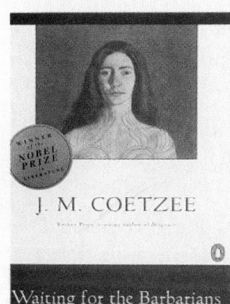

FICTION

Waiting for the Barbarians

Set in an unnamed Empire, in a remote, unnamed village overseen by an unnamed bureaucrat, this tale grapples with notions of power and justice. The Magistrate has long ignored rumors of insurgency by the natives, or "barbarians," living outside the village. He, the villagers, and the natives live peacefully together until the Empire's military arrives and the soldiers brutally and unjustly persecute the barbarians. J. M. Coetzee's fable of the misuse of power will leave you contemplating which people, after all, are really the barbarians.

NONFICTION

Unbowed

When Maathai was born in 1940, the land around her village in Kenya was lush and fertile. Thirty years later, ill-advised agricultural practices had deforested the valley and displaced food crops, leading to erosion and malnutrition. Maathai began a grass-roots movement to restore the land and improve the lives of the people. Read about why she was beaten and jailed for her work, but also about how her efforts have led to the planting of twenty million trees, winning Maathai a seat in Parliament—and the Nobel Peace Prize.

Learn It Online
Go online to find tips for choosing, reading, and studying books.

go.hrw.com   L12-1449   **Go**

Resource Center

Handbook of Literary and Historical Terms............1452
The World of Work....................................1474
Writer's Handbook...................................1480
Language Handbook 1492
Glossary..1531
Spanish Glossary....................................1539
Academic Vocabulary Glossary
in English and Spanish 1546

Handbook of Literary and Historical Terms

ALEXANDRINE A line of poetry made up of six iambs—that is, a line written in iambic hexameter. The following alexandrine is from Lord Byron's *Childe Harold's Pilgrimage* (Collection 8):

> Without a grave, unknelled, uncoffined, and
> unknown.

ALLEGORY A story in which the characters, settings, and events stand for abstract or moral concepts. Allegories thus have two meanings: a literal meaning and a symbolic meaning. Allegories were a popular literary form during the Middle Ages. The best-known English allegory is John Bunyan's *The Pilgrim's Progress* (Collection 3), which recounts the adventures of a character named Christian. The hero's journey to the Celestial City brings him up against many trials that symbolize the pitfalls facing the Christian traveling through this world toward the spiritual world.

ALLITERATION The repetition of consonant sounds in words that are close to one another. Alliteration occurs most often at the beginning of words, as in "rough and ready." But consonants within words sometimes alliterate, as in "baby blue." The echoes that alliteration creates can increase a poem's rhythmic and musical effects and make its lines especially memorable. In this line from Shakespeare's Sonnet 30 (page 393), the /w/ sounds emphasize the melancholy tone:

> And with old woes new wail my dear time's
> waste.

Alliteration is an essential feature of Anglo-Saxon poetry; in most lines, two or three of the four stressed syllables alliterate.

"Basil, do you think the center is going to hold?
Drawing by Booth; ©1984 The New Yorker Magazine, Inc.

ALLUSION A reference to a statement, person, place, event, or thing that is known from literature, history, religion, mythology, politics, sports, science, or popular culture. The concluding lines of Wilfred Owen's poem "Dulce et Decorum Est" (Collection 11) are *"Dulce et decorum est / Pro patria mori."* ("It is sweet and proper to die for one's country"). These lines allude to a line from an ode by the Latin poet Horace. The title of William Faulkner's *The Sound and the Fury* is an allusion to a line from Shakespeare's *Macbeth* (Collection 4). The cartoon above alludes to William Butler Yeats's poem "The Second Coming" (Collection 12).

ANALOGY A comparison of two things to show that they are alike in certain respects. Writers often make analogies to show how something unfamiliar is like something well-known or widely experienced. For example, people often draw an analogy between creating a work of art and giving birth to a child.

ANECDOTE **A brief and sometimes witty story that focuses on a single interesting incident or event, often in order to make a point or teach a moral lesson.** Sometimes an anecdote reveals the character of a famous person. Taoists, Zen Buddhists, and Sufis, among others, use anecdotes to convey indirectly the teachings of their philosophies.

ANIMISM **A belief that spirits or souls are present in all living things.** This belief was at the heart of the ancient Celtic religion, and it can be found in many other ancient religions.

ANTAGONIST **The character or force that opposes or blocks the protagonist, or main character, in a narrative.** Usually the antagonist is human, like Sir Modred, the villainous rebel who destroys the Round Table in Sir Thomas Malory's *Le Morte d'Arthur* (Collection 2) or the schoolgirls who mercilessly taunt the Kelvey sisters in Katherine Mansfield's "The Doll's House" (Collection 13). Sometimes the antagonist is supernatural, like Satan, who opposes God in John Milton's *Paradise Lost* (Collection 3).

ANTICLIMAX See *Climax.*

ANTITHESIS **A contrast of ideas expressed in a grammatically balanced statement.** In the following line from Canto III of *The Rape of the Lock* (Collection 6), Alexander Pope balances noun against noun and verb against verb:

> And wretches hang that jurymen may dine.

APHORISM **A concise, sometimes witty saying that expresses a principle, truth, or observation about life.** Alexander Pope's poetry contains some of the most famous aphorisms in the English language, as in this heroic couplet from *An Essay on Criticism* (Collection 6):

> To err is human, to forgive, divine.

APOSTROPHE **A figure of speech in which a speaker directly addresses an absent or dead person, an abstract quality, or something nonhuman as if it were present and capable of responding.** Apostrophe was a popular device with the Romantic poets: Wordsworth, for example, apostrophizes the river Wye in his "Tintern Abbey" (Collection 7). Among the second-generation Romantics, Shelley apostrophized the west wind; Byron apostrophized the ocean; and Keats apostrophized a nightingale and a Greek urn (all in Collection 8).

ARCHETYPE **A pattern that appears in literature across cultures and is repeated through the ages. An archetype can be a character, a plot, an image, or a setting.** All stories or myths that contain a quest, for example, share certain features, suggesting that each quest-story has been formed from a master pattern. Similarly, all epic heroes have a number of common characteristics, though each one also has culturally specific characteristics. Ignoring the culturally specific characteristics of a particular epic hero will allow you to perceive what the archetype of the epic hero is.

ASIDE **Private words that a character in a play speaks to the audience or to another character and that are not supposed to be overheard by others onstage.** Stage directions usually tell when a speech is an aside.

ASSONANCE **The repetition of similar vowel sounds followed by different consonant sounds in words that are close together.** Assonance differs from exact rhyme in that it does not repeat the consonant sound following the vowel. The words *face* and *base* rhyme, while the words *face* and *fade* are assonant. Like alliteration, assonance can create musical and rhythmic effects. In this line from Alfred, Lord Tennyson's "The Lady of Shalott" (Collection 9), the repetition of the short /a/ sounds creates a rhythmic effect that mimics the action being described:

> An abbot on an ambling pad,

ATMOSPHERE **The mood or feeling in a literary work.** Atmosphere is usually created through descriptive details and evocative language.

AUGUSTAN **Similar to the reign of Emperor Augustus (63 b.c.–a.d. 14) or having qualities or tastes that are associated with classical Rome.** In English literary history the Augustan Age dates from the Restoration to the middle of the eighteenth century. Perhaps more than anyone else, Alexander Pope (Collection 6) exhibits Augustan literary tastes in his poetry.

AUTOBIOGRAPHY **A written account of the author's own life.** Unlike **diaries, journals,** and letters, autobiographies are unified narratives usually prepared for a public audience. And unlike **memoirs,** which often focus on famous events and people, autobiographies are usually quite introspective. George Orwell's "Shooting an Elephant" (Collection 11) is a well-known autobiographical essay.

See also *Memoir.*

BALLAD **A song or songlike poem that tells a story.** Most ballads have a regular pattern of **rhythm** and **rhyme,** and they use simple language with a great deal of repetition. Ballads generally have a **refrain**—lines or words that are repeated at regular intervals. They usually tell sensational stories of tragedy, adventure, betrayal, revenge, and jealousy. **Folk ballads** are composed by anonymous singers and are passed down orally from generation to generation before they are written down (often in several different versions). "Lord Randall" (Collection 2) is an example of a folk ballad. **Literary ballads,** on the other hand, are composed and written down by known poets, usually in the style of folk ballads. Samuel Taylor Coleridge's *The Rime of the Ancient Mariner* (Collection 7) is a famous literary ballad.

The typical ballad stanza is a quatrain with the rhyme scheme *abcb.* The first and third lines have four stressed syllables, and the second and fourth lines have three. The number of unstressed syllables in each line may vary, but often the meter is primarily **iambic.**

BIOGRAPHY **An account of a person's life written by another person.** The *Life of Samuel Johnson* by James Boswell is one of the most famous biographies ever written.

BLANK VERSE **Poetry written in unrhymed iambic pentameter.** "Blank" means that the poetry is unrhymed. "Iambic pentameter" means that each line contains five iambs, or metrical feet, each consisting of an unstressed syllable followed by a stressed syllable (ˇ´). Blank verse is the most important metrical form used in English dramatic and epic poetry. It is the verse line used in Shakespeare's plays and John Milton's *Paradise Lost* (Collection 3). One of the reasons blank verse has been so popular, even among modern poets, is that it combines the naturalness of unrhymed verse with the structure of metrical verse. Except for **free verse,** it is the poetic form that sounds the most like natural speech. It also lends itself easily to slight variations within the basic pattern. Like most of the English Romantic poets, William Wordsworth made extensive use of blank verse, as in these lines from "Tintern Abbey" (Collection 7):

> And now, with gleams of half-extinguished
>   thought,
> With many recognitions dim and faint,
> And somewhat of a sad perplexity,
> The picture of the mind revives again:

CADENCE **The natural rise and fall of the voice.** Poets who write in **free verse** try to imitate the natural cadences of spoken language.

See also *Rhythm.*

CAESURA **A pause or break within a line of poetry, usually indicated by the natural rhythm of the language.** A midline, or medial, caesura is a characteristic of Anglo-Saxon poetry; it divides the four-beat line in half. Later poets use the caesura less predictably, as in the following lines from Wilfred Owen's "Dulce et Decorum Est" (Collection 11). Here, the caesuras are indicated by the symbol ||.

> Bent double, || like old beggars under sacks,
> Knock-kneed, || coughing like hags, || we
> cursed through sludge

CANTO **A subdivision in a long poem, corresponding to a chapter in a book.** Poems divided into cantos include Pope's *The Rape of the Lock* (Collection 6) and Byron's *Childe Harold's Pilgrimage* (Collection 8). Not all major subdivisions of long poems are called cantos: Milton's *Paradise Lost* (Collection 3) is divided into books, and Coleridge's *The Rime of the Ancient Mariner* (Collection 7) into parts.

The word *canto* comes from a Latin word for "song" and originally designated a section of a narrative poem that a minstrel could sing in one session.

CAPITALISM   **An economic philosophy that advocates the idea that the means of production and distribution should be owned and controlled by private individuals.** Adam Smith, an eighteenth-century economist, is one of the great theorists of capitalism, a system which helped to foster the conditions that produced the Industrial Revolution in England and the technological advances of the nineteenth and twentieth centuries.

See also *Laissez Faire.*

CARPE DIEM   **A Latin phrase that literally means "seize the day"—that is, "make the most of present opportunities."** The *carpe diem* theme is common in seventeenth-century English poetry, as in this famous line from Robert Herrick's "To the Virgins, to Make Much of Time": "Gather ye rosebuds while ye may." The theme is also forcefully expressed in Andrew Marvell's "To His Coy Mistress" (both in Collection 3)

CHARACTER   **An individual in a story or play.** A character always has human traits, even if the character is an animal, like the ravens in "The Twa Corbies" (Collection 2); or a god, as in the *Iliad* (Collection 1); or a monster, as in *Beowulf* (Collection 1). A character may also be a human with superhuman powers, like Gilgamesh (Collection 1). But most characters are ordinary human beings, like Geoffrey Chaucer's colorful pilgrims in *The Canterbury Tales* (Collection 2) and the boy in James Joyce's "Araby" (Collection 13).

The process by which the writer reveals the personality of a character is called **characterization.** A writer can reveal a character in the following ways:

1. by telling us directly what the character is like: humble, ambitious, vain, easily manipulated, and so on
2. by describing how the character looks and dresses
3. by letting us hear the character speak
4. by revealing the character's private thoughts and feelings
5. by revealing the character's effect on other people—showing how other characters feel or behave toward the character
6. by showing the character's actions

The first method of revealing a character is called **direct characterization.** When a writer uses this method, we do not have to figure out what a character's personality is like—the writer tells us directly. The other five methods of revealing a character are known as **indirect characterization.** When a writer uses these methods, we have to exercise our own judgment, putting clues together to figure out what a character is like—just as we do in real life when we are getting to know someone.

Characters can be classified as static or dynamic. A **static character** is one who does not change much in the course of a story. A **dynamic character,** on the other hand, changes in some important way as a result of the story's action. Characters can also be classified as flat or round. **Flat characters** have only one or two personality traits. They are one-dimensional—they can be summed up by a single phrase. In contrast, **round characters** have more dimensions to their personalities—they are complex, solid, and multifaceted, like real people.

CHIVALRY   **The system of ideals and social codes governing the behavior of knights and gentlewomen in feudal times.** The ideal knight was meant to be brave, honorable, and courteous; gentlewomen were meant to be chaste. The code of chivalry is reflected in medieval romance literature, particularly in Malory's *Le Morte d'Arthur* (Collection 2).

CLASSICISM   **A movement in art, literature, and music that advocates imitating the principles manifested in the art and literature of ancient ("classical") Greece and Rome.** Classicism emphasizes reason, clarity, balance, harmony, restraint, order, and universal themes. Classicism is often placed in direct opposition to **Romanticism,** with its emphasis on unrestrained emotions and personal themes. However, this opposition should be approached with caution, as it is sometimes exaggerated for effect. Classicism was particularly admired in art in the eighteenth century and is exemplified in Alexander Pope's mock heroic epic, *The Rape of the Lock* (Collection 6).

See also *Neoclassicism, Romanticism.*

CLICHÉ   **An expression that was fresh and apt when it was first coined but is now so overused that it has become hackneyed and stale.** "Busy as a bee" and "fresh as a daisy" are two examples. Clichés are often likened to dead metaphors—figures of speech ("leg of a chair," "mouth of a river") whose power to surprise has now been completely lost.

CLIMAX **The point of greatest emotional intensity or suspense in a plot when the outcome of the conflict becomes known.** In Shakespeare's plays, the climax usually occurs in the last act, just before the final scene. Following the climax, the story is **resolved,** or closed.

Some critics talk of more than one climactic moment in a long work (though usually the greatest climax occurs near the end of the plot). In drama, one such climactic moment is called the turning point, or **crisis.** At the **turning point,** something happens that seals the fate of the hero. In Shakespeare's plays, this moment usually occurs in the third act. At the turning point the hero's fortunes begin to decline or improve. All the action leading up to this turning point is **rising action,** and all the action following it is **falling action.** The turning point in Guy de Maupassant's "The Jewels" (Collection 10) occurs when Madame Lantin dies, leaving her husband alone and ravaged by grief. From that point onward, it is downhill for Monsieur Lantin—everything goes wrong, culminating in the story's climax, when Lantin, attempting to sell his wife's necklace, discovers that she has been deceptive. The sale of the jewels brings about the ironic resolution of the story: Lantin becomes wealthy and remarries, choosing a wife who is virtuous but makes him very unhappy.

In contrast, when something trivial or comical occurs at the point in a narrative when one expects something important or serious, the accompanying deflation is called an **anticlimax.** James Joyce's "Araby" (Collection 13) contains such an anticlimactic moment.
See also *Plot.*

COMEDY **In general, a story that ends happily.** The hero of a comedy is usually an ordinary character who overcomes a series of obstacles that block what he or she wants. Often a comedy pits two young people who wish to marry against parental blocking figures who want to prevent the marriage. The wedding that concludes these comedies suggests the formation of a new society and a renewal of life. Comedy is distinct from **tragedy,** in which a great person comes to an unhappy or disastrous end, usually through some lapse in judgment or character flaw. Comedies are often, but not always, intended to make us laugh. Two famous comedies are Oscar Wilde's play *The Importance of Being Earnest* and George Bernard Shaw's *Pygmalion.* Even though it contains some of the darker elements of tragedy, Shakespeare's *The Tempest* is considered a comedy because harmony and reconciliation are achieved by the end of the play.
See also *Farce, Tragedy.*

COMMUNISM **A philosophy that advocates the creation of a classless and stateless society in which economic goods are distributed equally.** The most famous communist government is, of course, the now dissolved Soviet Union, a country which one could say perverted the ideals of communism, since it had a ruling class which was better off than the working class. Human nature seems to prevent people from bringing into being a perfect communist society. George Orwell's novel *Animal Farm* satirizes the ideals of communism, showing the ruination of a farm which has been taken over by radical animal reformers.

CONCEIT **A fanciful and elaborate figure of speech that makes a surprising connection between two seemingly dissimilar things.** A conceit may be a brief metaphor, or it may form the framework of an entire poem. Two particularly important types of conceits are the **Petrarchan conceit** and the **metaphysical conceit.**

Petrarchan conceits get their name from the fourteenth-century Italian poet Petrarch (page 400), who developed their use in his influential sonnet sequence. Poets influenced by Petrarch used these conceits to describe the beauty of the lady for whom they wrote. She invariably had hair of gold, lips of cherry red, and teeth of oriental pearl. In Sonnet 130 (Collection 4), Shakespeare ridicules the use of such conceits. Petrarchan conceits were also used to describe a paradoxical state.

The metaphysical conceit is so called because it was widely used by the seventeenth-century metaphysical poets. This type of conceit is especially startling, complex, and ingenious. A famous example is John Donne's comparison of separated lovers to the legs of a compass in "A Valediction: Forbidding Mourning" (Collection 3).

CONFLICT **A struggle or clash between opposing characters, forces, or emotions.** In an **external conflict,** a character struggles against some outside force: another character, society as a whole, or some natural force. An **internal conflict,** on the other hand, is a struggle between opposing needs, desires, or emotions within a single character. Many works, especially longer ones, contain both internal and external conflicts. In Doris Lessing's "No Witchcraft for Sale" (Collection 13), the conflict between Gideon and the scientist reflects larger cultural conflicts.

See also *Plot.*

CONNOTATIONS All the meanings, associations, or emotions that have come to be attached to a word. For example, an expensive restaurant might prefer to advertise its "delicious cuisine" rather than its "delicious cooking." *Cuisine* and *cooking* have the same literal meaning—"prepared food." But *cuisine* has connotations of elegance and sophistication, while *cooking* does not. The same restaurant would certainly not describe its food as "great grub."

Notice the difference between the following pairs of words: *young/immature, ambitious/cutthroat, uninhibited/shameless, lenient/lax.* We might describe ourselves using the first words but someone else using the second ones. The English philosopher Bertrand Russell once gave a classic example of the different connotations of words: "I am firm. You are obstinate. He is a pigheaded fool."

See also *Denotation.*

CONSONANCE The repetition of final consonant sounds after different vowel sounds. The words *east* and *west, dig* and *dog, turn* and *torn,* and Shakespeare's famous *"struts* and *frets"* (from *Macbeth,* in Collection 4) are examples of consonance. The term is also sometimes used to refer to repeated consonant sounds in the middle of words, as in *solemn stillness.* (Consonance, when loosely defined, can be a form of **alliteration.** Strictly speaking, however, alliteration is the repetition of initial consonant sounds.) Like **assonance,** consonance is one form of **approximate rhyme.**

See also *Alliteration, Assonance.*

COUPLET Two consecutive lines of poetry that rhyme. The couplet has been widely used since the Middle Ages, especially to provide a sense of closure. A couplet that presents a completed thought is called a closed couplet. Shakespeare used closed couplets to end his sonnets, as in this example from Sonnet 29 (Collection 4):

> For thy sweet love remembered such wealth brings
> That then I scorn to change my state with kings.

A couplet written in **iambic pentameter** is called a **heroic couplet.** Although the heroic couplet has been used in English literature since Chaucer, it was perfected during the eighteenth century. Here is an example from Pope's *An Essay on Man* (Collection 6):

> Alike in ignorance, his reason such,
> Whether he thinks too little, or too much:

COURTLY LOVE A conventional medieval code of behavior that informed a knight of the proper way to treat his lady. The code was first developed by the troubadours (lyric poets) of southern France and extensively employed in European literature from the twelfth century throughout the medieval period.

DEISM The belief that God, after creating the universe, ceased to interfere with the laws of nature and society. Influenced by Newton's description of the universe as a great clock that was set in motion by the Creator, the deists of the mid-eighteenth century argued that people could only gain an understanding of the laws of nature and society by using their reason.

DENOTATION The literal, dictionary definition of a word. For example, a denotation, or dictionary definition, of the word *star* (as in "movie star") is an "eminent actor or actress," but the **connotation** is that of an actor or actress who is adored by fans and who leads a fascinating and glamorous life.

See also *Connotation.*

DENOUEMENT See *Plot.*

DEUS EX MACHINA Any artificial or contrived device used at the end of a plot to resolve or untangle the complications. The term is Latin and means "god from a machine." The phrase refers to a device used in ancient Greek and Roman drama: At the conclusion of the play, a god would be lowered onto the stage by a mechanical device so that he could save the hero and end the story happily. The term now refers to any device that resolves a plot in a forced or implausible way: An orphan finds that he has inherited a fortune just as he is being packed off to the poorhouse; a hero is saved because the villain has forgotten to load his gun. Oscar Wilde's *The Importance of Being Earnest* and Charles Dickens's *Oliver Twist* both contain examples of *deus ex machina.*

DIALECT A way of speaking that is characteristic of a particular region or group of people. A dialect may have a distinct vocabulary, pronunciation system, and grammar. In the Middle Ages, when Latin was the "literary" language of Europe, writers such as Geoffrey Chaucer (Collection 2) began writing for middle-class audiences in their own regional languages, or what are now interchangeably called **dialects** or **vernaculars.** Today one dialect usually becomes accepted as the standard for a country or culture. In the United States, the dialect used in formal writing and spoken by most TV and radio announcers is known as standard English.

Writers often use other dialects, however, to establish character or to create local color. For example, V. S. Naipaul (Collection 13) has used the dialect spoken by Trinidad's Asian Indian population in many of his works. The East London cockney dialect, and the lower-class background it betrays, are at the very heart of George Bernard Shaw's famous play *Pygmalion.* In this excerpt from the play, Henry Higgins, with his friend Colonel Pickering in attendance, begins to instruct the flower girl Eliza Doolittle in how to speak "proper" English:

> **Higgins.** Say your alphabet.
> **Liza.** I know my alphabet. Do you think I know nothing? I dont need to be taught like a child.
> **Higgins.** (*thundering*). Say your alphabet.
> **Pickering.** Say it, Miss Doolittle. You will understand presently. Do what he tells you; and let him teach you in his own way.
> **Liza.** Oh well, if you put it like that—Ahyee, beyee, ceyee, deyee—
> **Higgins.** (*with the roar of a wounded lion*). Stop. Listen to this, Pickering. . . . (*To Eliza*) Say A, B, C, D.
> **Liza.** (*almost in tears*). But I'm saying it. Ahyee, Bee, Ce-ee—

DIALOGUE   **Conversation between two or more people.** Writers use dialogue to advance the action of a plot, to present an interplay of ideas and personalities, and to reveal the background, occupation, or social level of the characters through **tone** and **dialect.**

DICTION   **A writer's or speaker's choice of words.** Speakers and writers use different types of words depending on the audience they're addressing, the subject they're discussing, and the effect they're trying to produce. For example, slang that would be suitable in a casual conversation with a friend ("He's a total nerd") would be unsuitable in a political debate. Similarly, the language that a nutritionist would use to describe a meal would be different from the language that a restaurant reviewer or a novelist would use.

Diction is an essential element of a writer's **style.** A writer's diction can be simple or flowery (*shop/boutique*), modern or old-fashioned (*pharmacy/apothecary*), general or specific (*sandwich/grilled cheese on rye*). Notice that the **connotations** of words (rather than their strict, literal meanings, or **denotations**) are an important aspect of diction.

DIDACTIC LITERATURE   **Literary works that are meant to instruct, give advice, or convey a philosophy or moral message.** Much didactic literature derives from religious teaching, as is the case with "The Parable of The Prodigal Son" (Collection 3) and the Taoist anecdotes (Collection 3). Secular works such as fables, folk tales and maxims are also didactic in intent.

See also *Fable, Parable.*

DISSONANCE   (DIHS·uh nuhns) **A harsh, discordant combination of sounds.** The opposite of **euphony** (YOO fuh nee), a pleasant, harmonious combination of sounds, dissonance is usually created by the repetition of harsh consonant sounds. Dissonance is often used in poetry to communicate energy. Dissonance is also called **cacophony** (kuh KAHF uh nee).

DRAMATIC MONOLOGUE   **A poem in which a character addresses one or more listeners who remain silent or whose replies are not revealed.** The occasion is usually a critical one in the speaker's life. Tennyson's "Ulysses" and Browning's "My Last Duchess" (Collection 9) are famous dramatic monologues.

DRAMATIC SONG   **A poem found in a play that serves to establish mood, reveal character, or advance action.** The songs in Shakespeare's plays are the best songs of this kind. Employing a variety of techniques and forms and relying heavily on **onomatopoeia,** Shakespeare wrote songs that can be read alone, but which are best understood within the context of the plays in which they appear.

ELEGY   **A poem that mourns the death of a person or laments something lost.** Elegies may lament the passing of life and beauty, or they may be meditations on the nature of death. A type of **lyric,** an elegy is usually formal in language and structure and solemn or even melancholy in tone. Much of English poetry is elegiac, from the Anglo-Saxon lyric "The Seafarer"

(Collection 1) to A. E. Housman's "To an Athlete Dying Young" (Collection 10) and Dylan Thomas's "Do Not Go Gentle into That Good Night" (Collection 12).

END-STOPPED LINE **A line of poetry in which the meter and the meaning conclude with the end of the line.** Often the end-of-line pause is marked with punctuation, though it need not be. These lines from Alexander Pope's *An Essay on Man* (Collection 6) are end-stopped:

> Know then thyself, presume not God to scan;
> The proper study of mankind is man.

See also *Run-on line.*

ENLIGHTENMENT; THE AGE OF REASON
Names historians have applied to the eighteenth century. The period has been called the Enlightenment and the Age of Reason because at that time, people began to rely on reason and experience, rather than superstition and church authority, to gain an understanding of the world.

EPIC **A long narrative poem that relates the great deeds of a larger-than-life hero who embodies the values of a particular society.** Most epics include elements of myth, legend, folklore, and history. Their tone is serious and their language grand. Most **epic heroes** undertake quests to achieve something of tremendous value to themselves or their society. Homer's *Odyssey* and *Iliad* (Collection 1) and Virgil's *Aeneid* are the best-known epics in the Western tradition. The two most important English epics are the Anglo-Saxon poem *Beowulf* (Collection 1) and John Milton's *Paradise Lost* (Collection 3).

Many epics share standard characteristics and formulas known as **epic conventions,** which the oral poets drew upon to help them recall the stories they were recounting and which the writers of literary epics draw upon to establish the epic quality of their poems. The conventions include: an **invocation,** or formal plea for aid, to a deity or some other spiritual power; action that begins *in medias res* (literally "in the middle of things") and then **flashes back** to events that take place before the narrative's current time setting; **epic similes,** or elaborately extended comparisons relating heroic events to simple, everyday events; a consistently predictable **metrical structure;** and **stock epithets,** or descriptive adjectives or phrases used repeatedly with—or in place of—a noun or proper name.

See also *Literary Epic.*

EPIGRAM **A brief, clever, and usually memorable statement.** Alexander Pope's writings are **epigrammatic** in style. Here is an example from his *Essay on Criticism:*

> We think our fathers fools, so wise we grow,
> Our wiser sons, no doubt, will think us so.

See also *Maxim, Proverb.*

EPIPHANY **In a literary work, a moment of sudden insight or revelation that a character experiences.** The word comes from the Greek and can be translated as "manifestation" or "showing forth." The term has religious meanings that have been transferred to literature by modern writers. James Joyce first gave the word its literary meaning in an early draft of *A Portrait of the Artist as a Young Man.* In Joyce's story "Araby" (Collection 13), the narrator experiences an epiphany at the end of the story when he recognizes the cheap vulgarity of the bazaar and the emptiness of his dream.

EPITAPH **An inscription on a tombstone or a commemorative poem written about a person who has died.** Epitaphs range from the solemn to the farcical. Ben Jonson's "On My First Son" (Collection 3) contains a famously poignant epitaph.

EPITHET **An adjective or other descriptive phrase that is regularly used to characterize a person, place, or thing.** Phrases such as "Peter the Great," "Richard the Lion-Hearted," and "America the Beautiful" are epithets. Homer created so many descriptive epithets in his *Iliad* (Collection 1) and *Odyssey* that his name has been permanently associated with a type of epithet. The **Homeric epithet** consists of a compound adjective that is regularly used to modify a particular noun. Famous examples are "the wine-dark sea," "the gray-eyed goddess Athena," and the "rosy-fingered dawn."

See also *Kenning.*

ESSAY A short piece of nonfiction prose that examines a single subject from a limited point of view. There are two major types of essays. **Informal essays** (also called **personal essays**) generally reveal a great deal about the personalities and feelings of their authors. They tend to be loosely structured, conversational, sometimes even humorous, in tone; and usually highly subjective. **Formal essays** (also called **traditional essays**) are usually serious and impersonal in tone. Because they are written to inform or persuade, they are expected to be factual, logical, and tightly organized.

In the European literary tradition the essay began in France with Michel de Montaigne, who sought to test his own judgment by analyzing it in a series of short prose pieces, which he called *essais,* a common sixteenth-century spelling of the French word *assay,* which means "trial" or "attempt." Sir Francis Bacon, who published his *Essays* (see "Of Studies" Collection 3) in the late sixteenth and early seventeenth century, brought the form into England and pioneered what we now call the formal essay. Notable twentieth-century English essayists include Virginia Woolf and George Orwell (both in Collection 11).

EXAGGERATION See *Hyperbole.*

FABLE A very brief story in prose or verse that teaches a moral, or a practical lesson about life. The characters in most fables are animals that behave and speak like humans. Some of the most popular fables are those attributed to Aesop, who was supposed to have been a slave in ancient Greece. Several of the pilgrims' tales in Geoffrey Chaucer's *The Canterbury Tales* (Collection 2) also contain fables. Other popular and widely influential fables include those collected in the Panchatantra, like "Right-Mind and Wrong-Mind".

See also *Parable.*

FALLING ACTION See *Climax.*

FARCE A type of comedy in which ridiculous and often stereotyped characters are involved in far-fetched, silly situations. The humor in farce is based on crude physical action, slapstick, and clowning. Characters may slip on banana peels, get pies thrown in their faces, and knock one another on the head with ladders. The movies featuring Abbott and Costello, Laurel and Hardy, and the Marx brothers are all examples of farces.

The word *farce* comes from a Latin word for "stuffing," and in fact farces were originally used to fill in the waiting time between the acts of a serious play. Even in tragedies, farcical elements are often included to provide **comic relief,** or a break from the pervading tension. Shakespeare frequently lets his "common" characters engage in farcical actions.

FASCISM A nationalistic philosophy that advocates rule by a single charismatic dictator. Fascism properly speaking refers to the philosophy of Benito Mussolini's political party, which was founded in 1919 to oppose communism in Italy. The word, however, was soon used to describe the philosophies of similar repressive, nationalistic political parties in other countries. The German Nazis were fascists. The regimes of Francisco Franco in Spain and Juan Peron in Argentina were fascistic.

FEUDALISM The economic, political, and social system of medieval Europe. This system was basically composed of three classes: the feudal lords, who were powerful landowners; vassals, who did work or military service for the feudal lords in exchange for land; and serfs, who were servants to the lords and vassals and who were bound to their masters' land.

FIGURE OF SPEECH A word or phrase that describes one thing in terms of another, dissimilar thing, and is not meant to be understood on a literal level. Some 250 different types of figures of speech have been identified, but the most common are the **simile** ("My love is like a red, red rose"), the **metaphor** ("The Lord is my shepherd"), and **personification** ("Death, be not proud"). These involve a comparison between unlike things, but not all figures of speech involve comparison. When one refers to the king using the word *crown,* one is not comparing the crown to the king, but associating the crown with the king.

See also *Hyperbole, Metaphor, Metonymy, Oxymoron, Personification, Simile, Symbol.*

FLASHBACK A scene in a movie, play, short story, novel, or narrative poem that interrupts the present action of the plot to "flash backward" and tell what happened at an earlier time. "The Demon Lover" by Elizabeth Bowen (Collection 11) includes a flashback that describes Mrs. Drover's farewell to her fiancé twenty-five years before the main action of the story takes place.

FOIL **A character who sets off another character by strong contrast.** This contrast emphasizes the differences between two characters, bringing out the distinctive qualities in each. In *Gilgamesh* (Collection 1), Enkidu is a foil to Gilgamesh.

FORESHADOWING **The use of clues to hint at what is going to happen later in the plot.** Foreshadowing arouses the reader's curiosity and builds up **suspense.** Foreshadowing occurs in Elizabeth Bowen's "The Demon Lover" (Collection 11) when Mrs. Drover imagines "spectral glitters in the place of" her fiancé's eyes, and when we learn that she made an "unnatural promise" to him—that she "could not have plighted a more sinister troth."

See also *Suspense.*

FRAME STORY **An introductory narrative within which one or more of the characters proceed to tell individual stories.** Perhaps the best-known example of stories contained in a frame story is the Persian collection called *The Thousand and One Nights.* In English literature, Geoffrey Chaucer's *The Canterbury Tales* (Collection 2) uses a frame story involving a group of people on a pilgrimage; within the narrative frame, each of the pilgrims then tells his or her own story.

FREE VERSE **Poetry that has no regular meter or rhyme scheme.** Free verse usually relies on the natural **rhythms** of ordinary speech. Poets writing in free verse may use **alliteration, internal rhyme, onomatopoeia,** and other musical devices to achieve their effects. They may also place great emphasis on **imagery.** Matthew Arnold's "Dover Beach" (Collection 10) is an early example of free verse, and T. S. Eliot's poems, including "The Hollow Men" (Collection 12), are especially fine and famous examples.

GOTHIC **A term used to describe literary works that contain primitive, medieval, wild, mysterious, or natural elements.** Such elements were frowned upon by eighteenth-century neoclassicists but hailed by the Romantic writers of the following era. The **Gothic novel,** a genre popular in the late eighteenth and early nineteenth centuries, is chiefly characterized by gloomy settings and an atmosphere of terror and mystery. Mary Wollstonecraft Shelley's *Frankenstein* is one of the most widely known Gothic novels.

HAIKU **A brief, unrhymed, three-line poem developed in Japan in the 1600s.** The first and third lines of a traditional haiku have five syllables each, and the middle line has seven. Haiku generally juxtapose familiar images and present them in a compressed form, forcing the reader to make an imaginative leap to understand the connection between them.

HUMANISM **An intellectual movement of the Renaissance that restored the study of the classics and focused on examining human life here and now.** Though humanists were still interested in theology and religious questions, the focus of their interest expanded to include earthly matters as well. Famous humanists include Sir Thomas More and Erasmus.

HYPERBOLE **A figure of speech that uses exaggeration to express strong emotion or create a comic effect.** While hyperbole (also known as **overstatement**) does not express the *literal* truth, it is often used in the service of truth to capture a sense of intensity or to emphasize the essential nature of something. For instance, if you claim that it was 250 degrees in the shade, you are using hyperbole to express the truth that it was miserably hot.

IAMBIC PENTAMETER **A line of poetry made up of five iambs.** An **iamb** is a metrical foot, or unit of measure, consisting of an unstressed syllable followed by a stressed syllable (˘´). The word *suggest,* for example, is made up of one iamb. *Pentameter* derives from the Greek words *penta* (five) and *meter* (measure). Here are two lines from John Keats's "Ode to a Nightingale" (Collection 8) that are written in iambic pentameter:

> Forlorn the very word is like a bell
> To toll me back from thee to my sole self!

Iambic pentameter is by far the most common verse line in English poetry. Shakespeare's sonnets and plays, for example, are written primarily in this meter. Many modern poets, such as W. H. Auden (Collection 12), have continued to use iambic pentameter. Other than **free verse,** it is the poetic meter that sounds the most like natural speech.

See also *Blank Verse.*

IMAGERY **Language that appeals to the senses.** Most images are visual—that is, they appeal to the sense of sight. But imagery can also appeal to the senses of hearing, touch, taste, or smell. While imagery is an element in all types of writing, it is especially important in poetry.

INCREMENTAL REPETITION **A device widely used in ballads whereby a line or lines are repeated with slight variations from stanza to stanza.** Each repetition advances the plot of the narrative. Incremental repetition is used in the folk ballad "Lord Randall" (Collection 2).

INDUSTRIAL REVOLUTION **The period of social and economic change following the replacement of hand tools by machines and power tools, which allowed manufacturers to increase their production and save money.** The perfection of the steam engine in the last half of the eighteenth century signaled the arrival of the age of the machine. The Industrial Revolution began on a small scale among textile manufacturers in the middle of the eighteenth century, but soon spread rapidly. Most textile products were produced by steam-engine-powered machines by the early nineteenth century. As the nineteenth century progressed, other industries began to use steam engines to produce their goods. George Eliot used the Industrial Revolution as the backdrop for *Silas Marner* (1861), and Charles Dickens satirizes its social effects in *Hard Times* (1854).

IN MEDIAS RES **The technique of starting a story in the middle and then using a flashback to tell what happened earlier.** *In medias res* is Latin for "in the middle of things." Epics traditionally begin in *medias res*. For example, John Milton's *Paradise Lost* (Collection 3) opens with Satan and his cohorts in Hell, after the war in Heaven and their fall, events that are recounted later in a flashback.

IRONY **A contrast or discrepancy between expectation and reality—between what is said and what is really meant, between what is expected and what really happens, or between what appears to be true and what really is true.**

Verbal irony occurs when a writer or speaker says one thing but really means something quite different—often the opposite of what he or she has said. If you tell your friend that you "just love being kept waiting in the rain," you are using verbal irony. A classic example of verbal irony is Jonathan Swift's suggestion in *A Modest Proposal* (Collection 5) that the Irish solve their poverty and overpopulation problems by selling their babies as food to their English landlords.

Situational irony occurs when what happens is the opposite of what is expected or appropriate. In James Joyce's story "Araby" (Collection 13), the boy hears about a bazaar called Araby and imagines that it will be a splendid, exotic place, yet when he arrives, he finds that the bazaar is cheap and commonplace.

Dramatic irony occurs when the audience or the reader knows something important that a character in a play or story does not know. Dramatic irony occurs in Elizabeth Bowen's "The Demon Lover" (Collection 11), when Mrs. Drover is riding in the taxi. The reader suspects that the taxi driver is the demon lover even though Mrs. Drover does not. Dramatic irony is a powerful device in William Blake's "The Chimney Sweeper" from *Songs of Innocence* (Collection 7). The speaker is a child who believes what he has been told—that "if all do their duty they need not fear harm." But the reader, who is not so innocent, knows this is not so.

KENNING **In Anglo-Saxon poetry, a metaphorical phrase or compound word used to name a person, place, thing, or event indirectly.** *Beowulf* (Collection 1) includes the kennings "whale-road" for the sea and "shepherd of evil" for Grendel.

See also *Epithet*.

LAISSEZ FAIRE (LEHS ay FAIR) **An economic policy based on the idea that economic forces should be allowed to operate freely and without government regulation.**

LITERARY EPIC **Literary epics are epics that have been composed by individual writers, often following earlier models.** Unlike an **oral epic** or a **primary epic,** which is performed by generations of anonymous storytellers and modified slightly with each retelling, a literary epic is the product of a single imagination working within the epic tradition.

See also *Epic*.

LYRIC POETRY **Poetry that focuses on express-ing emotions or thoughts, rather than on telling a story.** Most lyrics are short, and they usually imply rather than directly state a single strong emotion. The term *lyric* comes from the Greek. In ancient Greece, lyric poems were recited to the accompaniment of a stringed instrument called the lyre. Today, poets still try to make their lyrics melodious, but they rely only on the musical effects they can create with words (such as rhyme, **rhythm, alliteration,** and **onomato-poeia**). Samuel Taylor Coleridge's "Kubla Khan," William Wordsworth's "Tintern Abbey" (both in Collection 7), and Matthew Arnold's "Dover Beach" (Collection 10) are all lyric poems.

MAGIC REALISM **A literary style that combines in-credible events with realistic details and relates them all in a matter-of-fact tone.** Magic realism originated in Latin America, where writers such as Gabriel García Márquez and Julio Cortázar drew on elements of sur-realism and local folklore to create a style that is both timeless and innovative.

MATERIALISM **A belief that nothing exists except matter and that the operations of everything, includ-ing thought, will, and feeling, are caused by material agencies.**

MAXIM **A brief, direct statement that expresses a basic rule of human conduct or a general truth about human behavior.** "It is better to give than to receive" is an example of a well-known maxim.

See also *Epigram, Moral Tale, Proverb.*

MEMOIR **A type of autobiography that usually focuses on a single time period or historical event.** *Survival in Auschwitz* by Primo Levi (Collection 11) is a memoir about the author's experience at the death camp in 1944–1945.

METAPHOR **A figure of speech that makes a comparison between two seemingly unlike things without using a connective word such as *like, as, than,* or *resembles*.** You are using a metaphor if you say you're "at the end of your rope" or describe two political candidates as "running neck and neck."

Some metaphors are **directly** stated, like Percy Bysshe Shelley's comparison "My soul is an enchanted boat." (If he had written, "My soul is *like* an enchanted boat," he would have been using a **simile.**) Other metaphors are **implied,** like John Suckling's line "Time shall molt away his wings." The words *molt* and *wings* imply a comparison between time and a bird shedding its feathers.

An **extended metaphor** is a metaphor that is extended, or developed, over several lines of writing or even throughout an entire poem.

A **dead metaphor** is a metaphor that has become so common that we no longer even notice that it is a figure of speech. Our everyday language is filled with dead metaphors, such as *foot of the bed, bone of conten-tion,* and *mouth of the river.*

A **mixed metaphor** is the incongruous mixture of two or more metaphors. Mixed metaphors are usually unintentional and often conjure up ludicrous images: "If you put your money on that horse, you'll be barking up the wrong tree."

METAPHYSICAL POETRY **A term applied to the poetry of John Donne, Andrew Marvell, and other seventeenth-century poets who wrote in a difficult and abstract style.** Metaphysical poetry is intellectual and detached. It is characterized by ingenious, obscure imagery, philosophical meditation, verbal wit, and it often uses rough-sounding meter.

METER **A generally regular pattern of stressed and unstressed syllables in poetry.** When we want to indicate the metrical pattern of a poem, we mark the stressed syllables with the symbol ´ and the unstressed syllables with the symbol ˘. Indicating the metrical pattern of a poem in this way is called **scanning** the poem, or **scansion.** Here is how to scan these lines from William Blake's "The Tyger" (Collection 7):

> Tygĕr! Tygĕr! burnĭng bright
> In the forests of the night

Meter is measured in units called feet. A **foot** usu-ally consists of one stressed syllable and one or more unstressed syllables. The basic metrical feet used in English poetry are the **iamb** (as in *cŏnvínce*), the **trochee** (as in *bórrŏw*), the **anapest** (as in *cŏntrădíct*), the **dactyl** (as in *áccŭráte*), and the **spondee** (as in *séawéed*). A poem is described as iambic, trochaic, anapestic, dactylic, or spondaic according to what kind of foot appears most often in its lines.

A complete description of a metrical line indicates both the type and number of feet the line contains. For example, a line of iambic pentameter consists of five iambs, while a line of trochaic tetrameter consists of four trochees.

METONYMY (muh TAHN uh mee) **A figure of speech in which something closely related to a thing or suggested by it is substituted for the thing itself.** You are using metonymy if you call the judiciary "the bench," the king "the crown," the president (or presidential staff) "the White House," or the race track "the turf."

See also *Synecdoche*

MOCK EPIC **A comic narrative poem that parodies the epic by treating a trivial subject in a lofty, grand manner.** A mock epic uses dignified language, elaborate figures of speech, and supernatural intervention. The style of the mock epic is called **mock heroic** (and short mock epics are often called mock heroics). Alexander Pope's *The Rape of the Lock* (Collection 6) is considered the supreme mock epic in the English language.

MODERNISM **A broad trend in literature and other arts, from approximately 1890 to 1940, that reflected the impact of works like Sigmund Freud's writings on psychology.** In general, modernist writers rejected the forms and values of the past and sought new forms to reflect the fragmentation and uncertainty that they felt characterized modern life. Many modern poets, for example, rejected traditional poetic meters and wrote **free verse.** Novelists such as James Joyce employed a technique called **stream of consciousness** to record the randomness and free associations of their characters' thoughts.

MONOLOGUE **A long, formal speech made by a character in a play.** A monologue may be directed at another character or the audience. Shakespeare's soliloquies (Collection 3) can also be called monologues.

See also *Soliloquy.*

MOOD See *Atmosphere.*

MORAL TALE **A tale that teaches a lesson about life.** Several of the pilgrims' tales in Geoffrey Chaucer's *The Canterbury Tales* (Collection 2) are moral tales.

MOTIF **In literature, a word, a character, an object, an image, a metaphor, or an idea that recurs in a work or in several works.** The rose is a motif that runs through many love poems. *Beowulf* (Collection 1) contains many of the traditional motifs associated with heroic literature from all over the world, including a hero who does great deeds in battle or undertakes an extraordinary journey and a supernatural or fantastic being that takes part in the action. These motifs, along with others common to heroic literature, also appear in epics such as the *Iliad* (Collection 1) and Milton's *Paradise Lost* (Collection 3). A motif almost always bears an important relationship to the **theme** of a work of literature.

MOTIVATION **The reasons for or forces behind the action of a character.** Motivation is revealed through a combination of the character's desires and moral nature with the circumstances in which he or she is placed. In James Joyce's "Araby" (Collection 13), the narrator's crush on Mangan's sister and his romanticized view of the world combine to provide his motivation for attending the bazaar.

See also *Character.*

MYTH **An anonymous traditional story, rooted in a particular society, that usually serves to explain the mysteries of nature and a society's beliefs and customs.** Most myths grew out of religious rituals, and almost all of them involve the exploits of gods and heroes. Myths helped people to understand and cope with things beyond human control. Every culture has its own **mythology,** but in the Western world the most important myths have been those of ancient Greece and Rome. In twentieth-century literature, **allusions** to myths are often **ironic,** intended to reveal how diminished humanity has become in comparison with grand mythological figures.

NARRATOR **One who tells, or narrates, a story.** In fiction the narrator occupies any one of a variety of relations to the events described: from the center of the action to a distant, even objective, observer. A narrator may also be reliable or unreliable—if unreliable, the reader is made aware that the narrator's perceptions and interpretations of the action are different from those of the author. Such unreliable narrators can be deceitful or bumbling, but are often just naive or highly impressionable characters. The narrator at the beginning of James Joyce's "Araby" (Collection 13), for example, is an impressionable boy, and the story is, in part, about how the boy's point-of-view changes and becomes more reliable.

See also *Point of View.*

NEOCLASSICISM   The revival of classical standards and forms during the late seventeenth and eighteenth centuries. The neoclassicists valued the classical ideals of order, reason, balance, harmony, clarity, and restraint. In particular, they studied and tried to emulate the Latin poets Horace and Virgil. Alexander Pope (Collection 6) is one of the most celebrated English neoclassical poets.

NOVEL   A long fictional prose narrative, usually of more than fifty thousand words. In general, the novel uses the same basic literary elements as the short story: **plot, character, setting, theme,** and **point of view.** The novel's length usually permits these elements to be more fully developed than they are in the short story. However, this is not always true of the modern novel. Some modern novels are basically character studies, with only the barest plot structures. Others reveal little about their characters and concentrate instead on setting or tone or even the language of the novel itself.

Some of the greatest novels ever written are *Tom Jones* by Henry Fielding, *Pride and Prejudice* by Jane Austen, *Jane Eyre* by Charlotte Brontë, *Bleak House* and *Great Expectations* by Charles Dickens, *The Brothers Karamazov* by Fyodor Dostoyevsky, *Madame Bovary* by Gustave Flaubert, *Middlemarch* by George Eliot, *Jude the Obscure* by Thomas Hardy, *War and Peace* by Leo Tolstoy, *Lord Jim* by Joseph Conrad, *Sons and Lovers* by D. H. Lawrence, *Ulysses* by James Joyce, and *One Hundred Years of Solitude* by Gabriel García Márquez.

OCTAVE   An eight-line stanza or poem or the first eight lines of an Italian, or Petrarchan, sonnet. The usual rhyme scheme of the octave in this type of sonnet is *abbaabba.* The octave, which is sometimes called the **octet,** is followed by a six-line **sestet** with the rhyme scheme *cdecde* or *cdcdcd.*

See also *Sonnet.*

ODE   A complex, generally long lyric poem on a serious subject. In English poetry, there are basically two types of odes. One is highly formal and dignified in style and is generally written for ceremonial or public occasions. This type of ode derives from the choral odes of the classical Greek poet Pindar. The other type of ode derives from those written by the Latin poet Horace, and it is much more personal and reflective. In English poetry, it is exemplified by the intimate, meditative odes of such Romantic poets as Wordsworth, Keats, and Shelley (Collections 7 and 8).

ONOMATOPOEIA   (ahn uh mat uh PEE uh) The use of a word whose sound imitates or suggests its meaning. Many familiar words, such as *clap, squish, sizzle,* and *wheeze* are onomatopoeic. In poetry, onomatopoeia can reinforce meaning while creating evocative and musical effects. The word "lapping," in the following lines from W. B. Yeats's "The Lake Isle of Innisfree" (Collection 12), is onomatopoeic.

I will arise and go now, for always night and day
I hear lake water lapping with low sounds by the shore;

OTTAVA RIMA   An eight-line stanza in iambic pentameter with the rhyme scheme *abababcc.* The form was developed in Italy and was popularized by the fourteenth-century Italian poet Giovanni Boccaccio. The most famous example of ottava rima in English poetry is Lord Byron's *Don Juan.* William Butler Yeats's "Sailing to Byzantium" is another notable example.

OXYMORON   A figure of speech that combines apparently contradictory or incongruous ideas. "Bittersweet," "cruel kindness," and "eloquent silence" are oxymora. The classic oxymoron "wise fool" is almost a literal translation of the term from the Greek—*oxys* means "sharp" or "keen," and *moros* means "foolish." A famous oxymoron in literature is John Milton's description of Hell in *Paradise Lost* (Collection 3):

> No light, but rather darkness visible. . .

PARABLE **A short, allegorical story that teaches a moral or religious lesson about life.** The most famous parables in Western literature are those like "The Parable of the Prodigal Son" (Collection 3) told by Jesus in the Gospels of the Bible.

PARADOX **An apparent contradiction that is actually true.** A paradox may be a statement or a situation; as a statement, it is a figure of speech. The metaphysical poets of the seventeenth century (Collection 3) made brilliant use of paradoxes, as in this famous example from John Donne's "Death be not proud" (Collection 3):

> One short sleep past, we wake eternally,
> And death shall be no more; Death, thou shalt die.

The speaker in the cartoon does not understand the famous series of paradoxes that open *A Tale of Two Cities* by Charles Dickens.

"I wish you would make up your mind, Mr. Dickens. Was it the best of times or was it the worst of times? It could scarcely have been both."

Drawing by Handelsman; ©1987 The New Yorker Magazine, Inc.

PARALLELISM **The repetition of words, phrases, or sentences that have the same grammatical structure or that restate a similar idea.** Parallelism is often used in literature meant to be spoken aloud, such as poetry, drama, and speeches, because it can help make lines emotional, rhythmic, and memorable. It is also one of the most important techniques used in Biblical poetry. The parallelism in the following lines from Psalm 23 (Collection 3) heightens the emotional effect and enacts a meditative tone:

> He maketh me to lie down in green pastures:
> He leadeth me beside the still waters.
> He restoreth my soul:
> He leadeth me in the paths of righteousness for
>   his name's sake.

PARODY **The imitation of a work of literature, art, or music for amusement or instruction.** Parodies usually use exaggeration or inappropriate subject matter to make a serious style seem ridiculous. Alexander Pope's *The Rape of the Lock* (Collection 6) is a parody of such serious and sweeping epics as the *Iliad* (Collection 1) and the Aeneid. Cervantes' *Don Quixote* (Collection 5) is a parody of medieval romances.

PASTORAL **A type of literature that depicts country life in idyllic, idealized terms.** The term *pastoral* comes from the Latin word for shepherd, and originally, pastorals were about shepherds, nymphs, and rural life. Today, the term has a looser meaning and refers to any literary work that portrays an idyllic rural setting or that expresses nostalgia for an age or place of lost innocence. The most famous traditional English pastoral is Christopher Marlowe's "The Passionate Shepherd to His Love," which is satirized in Sir Walter Raleigh's "The Nymph's Reply to the Shepherd" (both in Collection 3).

PERSONIFICATION **A kind of metaphor in which a nonhuman or nonliving thing or quality is talked about as if it were human or had life.** In these lines, from William Wordsworth's "The World Is Too Much with Us" (Collection 7), the sea is given human form and the wind is given a voice:

> This Sea that bares her bosom to the moon;
> The winds that will be howling at all hours,

See also *Apostrophe, Figure of Speech, Metaphor*.

PLOT **The series of related events that make up a story or drama.** The plot is the underlying structure of a story. Most plots are built on these "bare bones": A **basic situation,** or **exposition,** introduces the characters, setting, and, usually, the story's major **conflict.** Out of this basic situation, **complications** develop that intensify the conflict. **Suspense** mounts until a **climax**—the tensest or most exciting part of the plot—is reached, where something happens to determine the outcome of the conflict. Finally, all the problems or mysteries of the plot are unraveled in the **resolution,** or **denouement.**

See also *Climax*.

POINT OF VIEW **The vantage point from which a writer tells a story.** There are three main points of view: **first person, limited third person,** and **omniscient third person.**

In the **first-person point of view,** the narrator is a character in the story. Using the pronoun *I,* this narrator tells us his or her own experiences but cannot reveal the private thoughts of other characters. When we read a story told in the first person, we hear and see only what the narrator hears and sees. We may have to interpret what this narrator says because a first-person narrator may or may not be objective, honest, or perceptive. For example, in James Joyce's "Araby" (Collection 13), the narrator is a boy who is, in the beginning of the story, a youth whose point of view is romantic, and the story is about his giving up this view.

In the **limited-third-person point of view,** the narrator is outside the story—like an omniscient narrator—but tells the story from the vantage point of only one character. The narrator can enter the mind of this chosen character but cannot tell what any other characters are thinking except by observation. This narrator also can go only where the chosen character goes. For example, "In the Shadow of War" by Ben Okri is told entirely from the point of view of Omovo, the

main character. We experience the stupefying summer heat, the mysteriousness of the veiled woman, and the horror of the gruesome river scene through Omovo's eyes alone.

In the **omniscient** (or **"all-knowing"**) **point of view,** the person telling the story knows everything that's going on in the story. This omniscient narrator is outside the story, a godlike observer who can tell us what all the characters are thinking and feeling, as well as what is happening anywhere in the story. For example, in "The Rocking-Horse Winner" by D. H. Lawrence (Collection 13), the narrator enters into the thoughts and secrets of every character, revealing both the "hard little place" in the mother's heart and Paul's determination to "compel her attention" by being lucky.

See also *Narrator, Stream of Consciousness*.

POSTMODERNISM **A trend in art and philosophy that reflects the late-twentieth-century distrust in the idea that there is a legitimate and true system of thought that can be used to understand the world and our place in it.** Postmodernists, like the modernists, see contemporary life as fragmentary, but rather than regard the fragmentary condition of our world with horror, as for instance T. S. Eliot had done in "The Hollow Men" (Collection 12), postmodernists look upon the fragments as materials that can be plundered and combined in new ways to create works of art. Postmodern writing typically experiments with nontraditional forms and allows for multiple meanings. The lines between real and imaginary worlds are often blurred, as is the boundary between fiction and nonfiction. Other characteristics of postmodern literature are cultural diversity and an often playful self-consciousness; that is, an acknowledgment that literature is not a mirror that accurately reflects the world, but a created world unto itself. Gabriel García Márquez's One *Hundred Years of Solitude,* in which reality and fantasy are blended, is an exemplary postmodern novel.

PROTAGONIST **The main character in fiction, drama, or narrative poetry.** The protagonist is the character we focus our attention on—the person whose conflict sets the plot in motion. (The character or force that blocks the protagonist is called the **antagonist.**) In *Beowulf* (Collection 1), the title character is the protagonist and the monster Grendel his antagonist. Most protagonists are **rounded, dynamic** characters who change in some important way by the end of the story. Whatever the protagonist's weaknesses, we still usually identify with his or her conflict and care about how it is resolved.

PROVERB **A short saying that expresses a common truth or experience, usually about human failings and the ways that people interact with one another.** Proverbs often incorporate such literary elements as **metaphor, alliteration, parallelism,** and **rhyme.**

See also *Epigram, Maxim.*

PUN **A play on the multiple meanings of a word or on two words that sound alike but have different meanings.** Many jokes and riddles are based on puns. ("Why was Cleopatra so negative? Answer: Because she was the queen of denial.") Shakespeare was one of the greatest punsters of all time. Dylan Thomas uses a pun in his poem, "Do Not Go Gentle into That Good Night" (Collection 12):

> Do not go gentle into that good night,
> Old age should burn and rave at the close of
>   day;
> Rage, rage against the dying of the light.

The casual farewell "good night" also means death.

QUATRAIN **A four-line stanza or poem or a group of four lines unified by a rhyme scheme.** The quatrain is the most common verse unit in English poetry. This quatrain from John Donne's "A Valediction: Forbidding Mourning" (Collection 3) has the rhyme scheme *abab:*

> As virtuous men pass mildly away,
>   And whisper to their souls, to go,
> Whilst some of their sad friends do say,
>   The breath goes now, and some say, no:

RATIONALISM **A philosophy that advocates the idea that one should use reason rather than emotion when one is attempting to discover the truth.** Rationalists believe that one must follow reason to determine what opinions are correct and what course of action one should take in any given situation. Opposed to rationalism is Romanticism, which places emphasis on the value of intuition and emotion in arriving at truth.

REALISM **In literature and art, the attempt to depict people and things as they really are, without idealization.** Realism as a movement developed during the mid–nineteenth century as a reaction against Romanticism. Realist writers believed that fiction should truthfully depict the harsh, gritty reality of everyday life without beautifying, sentimentalizing, or romanticizing it. The Norwegian playwright Henrik Ibsen was among the first to introduce realism to the stage. The English novelists Charles Dickens, George Eliot, Thomas Hardy, and Joseph Conrad are also considered realists.

See also *Romanticism.*

REFRAIN **A repeated word, phrase, line, or group of lines.** While refrains are most common in poetry and songs, they are sometimes used in prose, particularly speeches. Refrains are used to create rhythm, build suspense, or emphasize important words or ideas.

REFORMATION **The break from Catholicism and the authority of the pope that resulted in the establishment of the Protestant churches in the sixteenth century.** Most scholars date the beginning of the Reformation to 1517, the year Martin Luther nailed his *Ninety-five Theses* to the door of a church in Wittenburg, Germany. The *Theses* criticized the Catholic Church's abuse of indulgences and called for reform. In response the Church leaders condemned Luther, and he was forced to break from the Catholic Church and begin his own religious movement.

RENAISSANCE **A French word meaning "rebirth," used to designate the period in European history beginning in Italy in the fourteenth century and ending in the seventeenth century when scientific truths began to challenge long-accepted religious beliefs.** The Renaissance was characterized by a renewal of interest in classical learning and a focus on the study of human life on earth, not only on God and eternity.

RESOLUTION See *Plot.*

RHYME **The repetition of accented vowel sounds and all sounds following them in words that are close together in a poem.** *Park* and *bark* rhyme, as do *sorrow* and *borrow.* The most common type of rhyme, **end**

rhyme, occurs at the ends of lines. **Internal rhyme** occurs within lines. Both types are used throughout *The Rime of the Ancient Mariner* by Samuel Taylor Coleridge (Collection 7), contributing to the poem's bouncy, songlike rhythm:

> The fair breeze blew, the white foam flew,
> The furrow followed free;
> We were the first that ever burst
> Into that silent sea.

When words sound similar but do not rhyme exactly, they are called **approximate rhymes** (or **half rhymes, slant rhymes,** or **imperfect rhymes**).

The pattern of rhymed lines in a poem is called its **rhyme scheme.** A rhyme scheme is indicated by giving each new rhyme a new letter of the alphabet. For example, the rhyme scheme of Coleridge's lines is *abcb.*

RHYTHM   The alternation of stressed and unstressed syllables in language. Rhythm occurs naturally in all forms of spoken and written language. The most obvious kind of rhythm is produced by **meter,** the regular pattern of stressed and unstressed syllables found in some poetry. Writers can also create less structured rhythms by using rhyme, repetition, pauses, and variations in line length and by balancing long and short words or phrases. (Poetry that is written without any regular meter or rhyme scheme is called **free verse.**)

See also *Free Verse, Meter.*

ROMANCE   Historically, a medieval verse narrative chronicling the adventures of a brave knight or other hero who must undertake a quest and overcome great danger for love of a noble lady or high ideal. Such a heroic character is bound by the code of **chivalry,** which emphasizes loyalty to his lord and ready service to the oppressed. He also must adhere to the philosophy of **courtly love,** an idealized view of the relationship between the sexes in which a knight performs brave deeds to win the approval of his lady.

Today the term *romance* has come to mean any story that presents a world of wish-fulfillment, a world that is happier, more perfect, or more heroic than the real world. Characters in romances "live happily ever after" in a world where good always triumphs over evil. Many of today's most popular novels, movies, TV shows, and even cartoons are essentially romances. *Sir*

Gawain and the Green Knight and Sir Thomas Malory's *Le Morte d'Arthur* (Collection 2) are famous English romances.

ROMANTICISM   A literary, artistic, and philosophical movement that developed as a reaction against neoclassicism in the late eighteenth century and dominated the early nineteenth century. While classicism and neoclassicism emphasize reason, order, harmony, and restraint, Romanticism emphasizes emotion, imagination, intuition, freedom, personal experience, the beauty of nature, the primitive, the exotic, and even the grotesque. However, many critics feel that the traditional opposition between Romanticism and classicism is all too often forced and exaggerated.

In English literature, William Blake, Samuel Taylor Coleridge, William Wordsworth, Percy Bysshe Shelley, John Keats, Lord Byron, Mary Wollstonecraft Shelley (Collections 7 and 8), and Sir Walter Scott are the leading Romantic writers.

RUN-ON LINE   A line of poetry that does not contain a pause or conclusion at the end, but rather continues on to the next line. Run-on lines force the reader on to the next line. Only with the next line do they form a grammatical unit and thus make complete sense. Such lines are said to exhibit **enjambment** (French for "striding over"). The following lines from Margaret Atwood's "Siren Song" (Collection 13) are run-on lines:

> This is the one song everyone
> would like to learn: the song
> that is irresistible:

See also *End-stopped Line.*

SARCASM   A kind of particularly cutting irony, in which praise is used tauntingly to indicate its opposite in meaning. The speaker's tone of voice can be an important clue in understanding this kind of irony. When a mud-soaked, windblown friend arrives for dinner, one might say sarcastically, "Why, don't you look lovely!"

SATIRE   A kind of writing that ridicules human weakness, vice, or folly in order to bring about social reform. Satires often try to persuade the reader to do or believe something by showing the opposite view as absurd or—even more forcefully—vicious and inhumane. Among the most brilliant satirists in English literature are Geoffrey Chaucer, Alexander Pope, John Dryden, Jonathan Swift, Jane Austen, George Bernard Shaw, and Evelyn Waugh.

SCANSION See *Meter.*

SCOP **An Anglo-Saxon minstrel or poet.** Scops are the Anglo-Saxon equivalents to the ancient Celtic bards.

SESTET **A six-line stanza or poem or the last six lines of an Italian, or Petrarchan, sonnet.** The usual rhyme scheme of the sestet in an Italian sonnet is *cdecde* or *cdcdcd.* It follows an eight-line **octave** with the rhyme scheme *abbaabba.*

SETTING **The time and place of a story or play.** Usually the setting is established early in a story. It may be presented immediately through descriptive details, as in Anita Desai's "Games at Twilight" (Collection 13), or it may be revealed more gradually, as in Rudyard Kipling's "The Mark of the Beast" (Collection 10). Setting often contributes greatly to a story's emotional effect. The exotic setting of V. S. Naipaul's "B. Wordsworth" (Collection 13) sets the tone for its eccentric characters, while the green valley in William Wordsworth's "Tintern Abbey" (Collection 7) creates a contemplative calm. Setting may also play a role in a story's conflict, as the fortress-like suburban houses do in Nadine Gordimer's "Once upon a Time" (Collection 13). Two of the most important functions of setting are to reveal character and to suggest a theme, as the setting of blitzed London does in Graham Greene's "The Destructors" (Collection 11).

See also *Atmosphere.*

SHORT STORY **A brief work of fiction.** The short story generally has a simpler plot than a novel and often reveals character through significant moments, or **epiphanies,** rather than through the accretion of many incidents or detailed descriptions.

SIMILE **A figure of speech that makes a comparison between two seemingly unlike things by using a connective word such as *like, than,* or *resembles.*** The following simile, from George Gordon, Lord Byron's

"She Walks in Beauty" (Collection 8), is one of the most famous in English literary history:

> She walks in beauty, like the night
> Of cloudless climes and starry skies;

An **epic simile,** also called a **Homeric simile,** is an extended simile in which many parallels are made between two dissimilar things.

See also *Figure of Speech, Metaphor.*

SOCIAL DARWINISM **The notion that, in society, only the fittest will survive.** This idea is an extension of Darwin's scientific theories of natural selection—though Darwin was not involved in its development. Social Darwinism was used to justify rigid class distinctions, indifference to social ills, and doctrines of racial superiority.

SOCIALISM **A political movement that advocates the idea that the ownership and operation of the means of production and distribution should be owned by the community rather than by private individuals.** This political movement is related to communism in that it seeks to eliminate class distinctions within society.

SOLILOQUY **A long speech in which a character who is usually alone onstage expresses his or her private thoughts or feelings.** The soliloquy is an old dramatic convention that was particularly popular in Shakespeare's day. Perhaps the most famous soliloquy is the "To be, or not to be" speech in Shakespeare's play *Hamlet.* Another major soliloquy occurs in *Macbeth,* when Macbeth bewails his wife's death in the celebrated "Tomorrow, and tomorrow, and tomorrow" speech (Collection 4).

See also *Monologue.*

SONNET **A fourteen-line lyric poem, usually written in iambic pentameter, that has one of several rhyme schemes.** There are two major types of sonnets. The oldest sonnet form is the **Italian sonnet,** also called the **Petrarchan sonnet** (after the fourteenth-century Italian poet Petrarch, who popularized the form). The Petrarchan sonnet is divided into two parts: an eight-line **octave** with the rhyme scheme *abbaabba* and a six-line **sestet** with the rhyme scheme *cdecde* or *cdcdcd.* The octave usually presents a problem, poses a question, or expresses an idea, which the sestet then resolves, answers, or drives home. The transition from octave to sestet is known as the **turn.** Louise Labé's Sonnet 23, Elizabeth Barrett Browning's Sonnet 43 (Collection 9), and John Keats's "On First Looking into Chapman's Homer" (Collection 8) are written in the Petrarchan form.

The other major sonnet form, which was widely used by Shakespeare, is called the **Shakespearean sonnet,** or the **English sonnet** (Collection 4). It has three four-line units, or **quatrains,** followed by a concluding two-line unit, or **couplet.** The organization of thought in the Shakespearean sonnet usually corresponds to this structure. The three quatrains often express related ideas or examples, while the couplet sums up the poet's conclusion or message found in the first three. The turn in the Shakespearean sonnet usually occurs during the transition from the third quatrain to the couplet. The rhyme scheme of the Shakespearean sonnet is *abab cdcd efef gg.*

A third type of sonnet, the **Spenserian sonnet,** was developed by Edmund Spenser. Like the Shakespearean sonnet, the Spenserian sonnet is divided into three quatrains and a couplet, but it uses a rhyme scheme that links the quatrains: *abab bcbc cdcd ee.*

A group of sonnets on a related theme is called a **sonnet sequence** or a **sonnet cycle.**

SPEAKER The imaginary voice, or persona, assumed by the author of a poem. This voice is often not identified immediately or directly. Rather, the reader gradually comes to understand that a unique voice is speaking and that this speaker's characteristics must be interpreted as they are revealed. This process is an especially important part of reading a **lyric poem.**

SPEECH A more or less formal address delivered to an audience or assembly or the written or printed copy of this address. The use of the word *speech* to designate an address to an audience seems to have entered into the English language in the sixteenth century.

Speeches are most commonly delivered by politicians, political activists, and other public figures. .

SPENSERIAN STANZA A nine-line stanza with the rhyme scheme *ababbcbcc.* The first eight lines of the stanza are in iambic pentameter, and the ninth line is an **alexandrine**—that is, a line of iambic hexameter.

The form was created by Edmund Spenser for his long poem *The Faerie Queene.* Several English Romantic poets have used the Spenserian stanza, including John Keats, Percy Bysshe Shelley, Lord Byron (all in Collection 8), and Robert Burns.

SPRUNG RHYTHM A term coined by Gerard Manley Hopkins (Collection 9) to designate his unconventional use of poetic meter. Instead of the regular, musical **meter** of most poetry, Hopkins uses sounds that impede smooth reading and echo the sound of Anglo-Saxon poetry, which greatly influenced him. Sprung rhythm is based on the stressed syllables in a line without regard for the number of unstressed syllables; it also makes frequent use of **alliteration** and inverted syntax.

STANZA A group of consecutive lines in a poem that form a single unit. A stanza in a poem is something like a paragraph in prose: It often expresses a unit of thought. A stanza may consist of only one line or of any number of lines beyond that. The word *stanza* is Italian for "stopping place" or "place to rest."

STREAM OF CONSCIOUSNESS A writing style that tries to depict the random flow of thoughts, emotions, memories, and associations running through a character's mind. The term *interior monologue* is often used interchangeably with "stream of consciousness." James Joyce (Collection 13) and Virginia Woolf (Collection 11) were among the first to experiment with the stream-of-consciousness style in their novels.

STYLE The manner in which writers or speakers say what they wish to say. An author's style simultaneously expresses his or her ideas and reveals his or her unique way of expressing them. Style is closely connected to **diction,** or word choice, and, depending on what the author wants to communicate, can be formal or casual, plain or ornate, abstract or concrete, as well as comic, poetic, forceful, journalistic, and so on. Sir Francis Bacon (Collection 3) and James Joyce (Collection 13) are both often studied for their styles.

See also *Diction.*

SUSPENSE **The uncertainty or anxiety we feel about what is going to happen next in a story.** Writers often create suspense by dropping hints or clues that something—especially something bad—is going to happen. In "The Demon Lover" by Elizabeth Bowen (Collection 11), we begin to feel suspense when Mrs. Drover receives a mysterious letter that makes her lips "go white"; our anxiety increases sharply when the flashback reveals that the letter writer is her old fiancé; and our suspense reaches a climax when she escapes into a taxi and we discover who the driver is.

SYMBOL **A person, place, thing, or event that stands both for itself and for something beyond itself.** Many symbols have become widely recognized: A lion is a symbol of power; a dove is a symbol of peace. These established symbols are sometimes called **public symbols.** But writers often invent new, personal symbols whose meaning is revealed in their work. For example, the old house in Graham Greene's "The Destructors" (Collection 11) is a symbol of civilization and beauty.

SYMBOLISM **A literary movement that began in France during the late nineteenth century and advocated the use of highly personal symbols to suggest ideas, emotions, and moods.** The French symbolists believed that emotions are fleeting, individual, and essentially inexpressible—and that the poet is, therefore, forced to suggest meaning rather than directly express it. Many twentieth-century writers were influenced by the symbolists, including T. S. Eliot, William Butler Yeats, James Joyce, Dylan Thomas, and Virginia Woolf (Collections 11, 12, and 13).

SYNECDOCHE (sih NEHK duh kee) **A figure of speech in which a part represents the whole.** The capital city of a nation, for example, is often spoken of as though it were the government: "Washington is claiming popular support for its position." Another example is "our daily bread" meaning food. Synecdoche is closely related to **metonymy.**

See also *Metonymy.*

SYNESTHESIA (sihn ehs THEE zhuh) **In literature, a term used for descriptions of one kind of sensation in terms of another.** For example, color may be described as sound (a "loud" yellow), sound as taste (how "sweet" the sound), odor as tangible (a "sharp" smell), and so on.

TANKA **A traditional five-line form of Japanese poetry.** The tanka follows a strict form: The first and third lines have five syllables each, and the second, fourth, and fifth lines have seven syllables each.

TERCET **A triplet, or stanza of three lines, in which each line ends with the same rhyme.** It is also either of the two three-line groups forming the sestet of a **sonnet.**

TERZA RIMA **An interlocking, three-line stanza form with the rhyme scheme *aba bcb cdc ded* and so on.** Terza rima is an Italian verse form originally devised by Dante for *The Divine Comedy.* Among the many English poems that borrowed the form, Shelley's "Ode to the West Wind" (Collection 8) is one of the most famous.

THEME **The central idea or insight about human experience revealed in a work of literature.** A theme is not the same as the subject of a work, which can usually be expressed in a word or two: old age, ambition, love. The theme is the idea the writer wishes to convey about that subject—the writer's view of the world or revelation about human nature. For example, one theme of James Joyce's "Araby" (Collection 13) might be stated this way: One of the painful aspects of growing up is that some of our dreams turn out to be illusions.

A theme may also be different from a **moral,** which is a lesson or rule about how to live. The theme of "Araby" stated above, for example, would not make sense as a moral.

While some stories, poems, and plays have themes that are directly stated, most themes are **implied.** It is up to the reader to piece together all the clues the writer has provided about the work's total meaning.

TONE **The attitude a writer takes toward the reader, a subject, or a character.** Tone is conveyed through the writer's choice of words and details. For example, Jonathan Swift's *A Modest Proposal* (Collection 5) is satiric in tone, while the tone of "Pied Beauty" by Gerard Manley Hopkins (Collection 9) might be described as awed.

TOTALITARIANISM **A system of government that advocates the rule of an absolute dictator or a single political party.** Totalitarian governments forbid any opposition to the government party or ruler to emerge within the state. Consequently, free speech and other liberties guaranteed in democracies are denied to those living under a totalitarian government. George Orwell's *Animal Farm* explores the consequences of a totalitarian regime.

TRAGEDY **A play, novel, or other narrative depicting serious and important events, in which the main character comes to an unhappy end.** In a tragedy, the main character is usually dignified, courageous, and often high ranking. This character's downfall may be caused by a **tragic flaw**—an error in judgment or a character weakness—or the downfall may result from forces beyond his or her control. The **tragic hero** usually wins some self-knowledge and wisdom, even though he or she suffers defeat, possibly even death. Tragedy is distinct from **comedy,** in which an ordinary character overcomes obstacles to get what he or she wants. *Beowulf* (Collection 1), Shakespeare's *Macbeth* (Collection 4), and John Milton's *Paradise Lost* (Collection 3) are all tragedies.

See also *Comedy.*

TURN See *Sonnet.*

UNDERSTATEMENT **A figure of speech that consists of saying less than what is really meant or saying something with less force than is appropriate.** Understatement is the opposite of **hyperbole** and is a form of **irony.** You are using understatement if you come in from a torrential downpour and say, "It's a bit wet out there," or if you describe a Great Dane as "not exactly a small dog." Understatement can be used to create a kind of deadpan humor, but it can also function as a sustained ironic tone throughout a work, as in Wole Soyinka's "Telephone Conversation" (Collection 13).

See also *Hyperbole, Irony.*

VERNACULAR See *Dialect.*

VILLANELLE **A nineteen-line poem divided into five tercets (three-line stanzas), each with the rhyme scheme *aba,* and a final quatrain with the rhyme scheme *abaa.*** Line 1 is repeated entirely to form lines 6, 12, and 18, while line 3 is repeated as lines 9, 15, and 19. Thus, there are only two rhymes in the poem, and the two lines used as **refrains** (lines 1 and 3) are paired as the final couplet. The villanelle was originally used in French pastoral poetry. Dylan Thomas's "Do Not Go Gentle into That Good Night" (Collection 12) is an example of a modern villanelle.

WIT **A quality of speech or writing that combines verbal cleverness with keen perception, especially of the incongruous.** The definition of wit has undergone dramatic changes over the centuries. In the Middle Ages it meant "common sense"; in the Renaissance it meant "intelligence"; and in the seventeenth century it meant "originality of thought." The modern meaning of *wit* began to develop during the seventeenth and eighteenth centuries with the writings of John Dryden and Alexander Pope (Collection 6). In his *Essay on Criticism,* Pope said:

> True wit is Nature to advantage dressed:
> What oft was thought, but ne'er so well
> expressed

Perhaps the best examples of more modern wit can be found in the works of Oscar Wilde and George Bernard Shaw.

The World of Work

The ability to read critically and write effectively is your driver's license to navigating today's world. Without strong reading and writing skills, you will feel as frustrated and powerless as you do in a traffic jam. A future college student must be able to write application essays and understand scholarship guidelines. A mechanic must be able to read instruction manuals to use new equipment. A renter must understand a lease before getting an apartment. A supervisor must be able to write an effective memo to present ideas. In your life and in the world of work, you will rely on reading and writing skills to learn new information, communicate effectively, and get the results you want.

Reading

To avoid getting stranded in life and in the world of work, you will need to learn to read **informative documents** and **persuasive documents.**

Informative Documents

Informative documents are like road maps: They provide facts and information. They can also be good places to check when you want to verify or clarify information from other sources. If a friend writes down directions that you're uncertain about, you consult a map to verify the directions. Likewise, if you read on a Web site an angry customer's complaint about repairs on a computer you just bought, you could review the warranty to see if the information is valid. Two kinds of common informative documents are consumer documents and workplace documents.

CONSUMER DOCUMENTS You've probably already made thousands of buying decisions in your life. As you get older, however, buying decisions often carry bigger consequences. Should you sign a six- or a twelve-month apartment lease? Should you buy or lease a car? Being informed about the details of major purchases can help you avoid costly mistakes. This information can be found in **consumer documents,** such as warranties, contracts, product information, and instruction manuals.

■ **Warranties** describe what happens if the product doesn't work properly or breaks down. Warranties note how long the product is covered for repair or replacement, which repairs the warranty does and does not cover, and how to receive repair service.

> The SureFocus digital camera is guaranteed to be free of defects in material or workmanship under normal use for a period of one (1) year from the date of purchase. Equipment covered by the warranty will be repaired by SureFocus Repair Members WITHOUT CHARGE, except for insurance, transportation, and handling charges. A copy of this warranty card and proof of purchase must be enclosed when returning equipment for warranty service. The warranty does not apply in the following cases:
>
> - the camera has been damaged through abuse
> - leaking batteries or other liquids have caused damage to the camera
> - unauthorized repair technicians have attempted to service the camera

■ **Contracts** give details about an agreement that a buyer enters into with a company. A lease for an apartment or a car is a contract that defines the terms of the lease, including how long it lasts, what the responsibilities of the customer—also known as the lessee—and the landlord or car company are, how to end the lease, and what the penalties for breaking the lease are. A lease always includes a space for the customer's signature, which signifies agreement with the terms of the contract. Below is a portion of a typical apartment lease.

This apartment lease is entered into by <u>Althea Brown</u>, hereinafter "Lessee," and Sun Valley Apartments.

1. **Grant of Lease:** Sun Valley Apartments does hereby lease unto Lessee Apartment <u>#B-2</u>, located at <u>101 Saguaro Drive, El Cajon, CA</u>.

2. **Term of Lease:** This lease shall begin on the <u>first</u> day of <u>August, 2008</u>, and extend until the <u>first</u> day of <u>August, 2009</u>, after which the lessee can extend the lease month to month until terminated according to the terms described below.

3. **Rental Payments:** Lessee agrees to pay as rent the sum of <u>$800</u> per month each month during the term of this lease before the <u>fifth</u> day of each month.

■ **Product information** describes the basic features and materials of a product. A suit label would tell whether the suit is 100 percent wool or a blend of materials and would give cleaning instructions. Product information on the box of a cordless telephone would tell the frequency, number of channels, and whether it has automatic redial, memory, caller ID, voice-mail indicator light, and other features.

■ **Instruction manuals** tell the owner how to set up, operate, and troubleshoot problems with a product. Instruction manuals also include safety precautions, diagrams, and descriptions of the product's features.

WORKPLACE DOCUMENTS Two common workplace documents—**procedure manuals** and **memoranda**—can tell you how to do your job and how to stay informed so you are both knowledgeable and effective.

■ **Procedure manuals** are the step-by-step directions that tell employees how to serve customers, operate machinery, report problems, request vacation, or do anything that the company wants performed in a certain way. Procedure manuals are often used to train new employees and to clarify procedures for existing employees. As you read a procedure manual, pay attention to the specific instructions so you know exactly how to carry out the procedures.

■ **Memoranda** —or memos—are the standard form of communication in many businesses. Memos are concise messages, generally covering only one topic. For example, an employee might send a memo to a supervisor reporting on the status of a project, or a supervisor might send a brief summary of discussions and decisions made in a meeting. To read a memo effectively, first check the subject line at the top to learn the topic of the memo. As you read, notice the pattern of organization in the body of the memo. Headings or bullets may indicate the main ideas. Pay attention to the purpose of the memo to decide whether and how to respond. Is the memo summarizing information, requesting action, or providing facts, such as dates and prices?

Persuasive Documents

While informative documents are like road maps, persuasive documents are like travel brochures, trying to influence a reader's destination. Persuasive documents try to persuade readers to believe or act in a certain way. It's important for you to be able to distinguish between informative and persuasive public documents. For example, a policy statement from a county commission about recycling might quote facts, but its primary purpose is to influence citizens to support the commission's position. By critically reading persuasive public documents, you can evaluate whether you agree or disagree. Persuasive public documents include **policy statements, political platforms, speeches,** and **debates.**

■ A **policy statement** outlines a person's or group's position on an issue and sometimes provides the rationale for that position. For example, the mayor might issue a policy statement explaining why she supports or opposes a tax increase for school construction. The policy statement gives the main points for the mayor's position and may provide facts or use rhetorical devices to support the position. A policy statement may also include a **call to action,** or a request for readers to take a specific action. Some organizations issue policy statements to endorse specific legislation, hoping to win the support of the voting public or of the lawmakers who can create the legislation.

■ A **political platform** outlines a political candidate's position on a variety of issues so voters know where the candidate stands. It may also set forth the candidate's goals and describe the beliefs that guide his or her positions. The positions and goals are known as the *planks* of the platform. The audience for a political platform is usually friendly to the candidate, and the platform is intended to rouse support and to persuade undecided voters. Sometimes a platform will also address and rebut opposing viewpoints. Below is an excerpt from the political platform of a city council candidate about the issue of noise pollution.

> Rocky Mount is a quiet and peaceful place that does not need more intrusion from the local government to reduce noise levels. We are not close to a major airport, so we do not hear the regular drone of airplanes. Concertgoers hear Beethoven and Mozart, not the loud rock groups that play in larger cities. Noise pollution is an occasional, not regular or excessive, problem that can be handled without more city ordinances. Therefore, I do not support the development of laws to address the nonexistent issue of noise pollution.

■ A **persuasive speech** is designed to change an audience's attitudes or beliefs or to move an audience to action. A speaker may make persuasive arguments and address audience counterclaims by using reasoning and rhetorical devices such as repetition. (For more on **persuasive speaking,** see page 692.)

■ A **debate** involves two teams who take turns discussing a controversial topic. The topic under discussion is called the proposition. One side argues for the proposition, and the other side argues against it. Each side also refutes, or argues against, its opponent's case.

Critiquing Persuasive Documents

Persuasive documents use logical, emotional, and ethical appeals to be convincing. Notice how these appeals are used to help you critique a document's validity and truthfulness.

- ■ **Logical appeals** are based on reasons and supporting evidence. As you read, notice whether the evidence is based on reliable facts that can be confirmed through other, unbiased sources. If you are unsure, consult informative public documents, such as state laws, to verify the evidence. Notice whether the appeal makes sense and avoids fallacies, such as hasty generalizations or circular reasoning. A hasty generalization is a conclusion based on insufficient evidence. Circular reasoning occurs when the reason for an opinion is simply the opinion stated in different words.

- ■ **Emotional appeals** rely on strong feelings to persuade readers. The writer may use examples that tug on heartstrings or arouse anger. Vivid language may make either positive or negative associations with the topic. Evaluate emotional appeals based on all of the evidence. If an argument is based primarily on emotion, the case may be weak. Watch out for signs of bias and stereotypes—including words such as *always* and *never*—that suggest the reasoning is unsound.

- ■ **Ethical appeals** rely on the reader's sense of right and wrong. For example, a writer might persuade an audience to share a certain view by implying that the opposing position is unpatriotic or selfish.

Critique a persuasive document by seeing how fairly the writer treats the topic. Does the writer use credible evidence? Does he or she know enough about the topic to be believed?

Your Turn 1 Choose a persuasive public document, and critique its effectiveness and validity. Identify the appeals and the call to action, if any. Consult at least one informative public document to verify information presented in the persuasive document.

Writing

Writing is your passport to exciting places in life. A powerful résumé can win you the job of your dreams. A memo proposing cost-saving measures can earn you a promotion. A letter to your city council can lead to a new soccer field for a recreational league. Clear, effective writing is one of the best skills you can have as you enter the world of work.

Job Applications and Résumés

One of the first places you will use writing beyond school will be in a job application or résumé. To fill out a **job application** completely and accurately, first read the instructions carefully. Type or write neatly in blue or black ink. Include all information requested. If a question does not apply to you, write *N/A* or *not applicable* in the blank. Proofread your completed form and neatly correct any errors. Finally, submit the form to the correct person.

A **résumé** summarizes your skills, education, achievements, and work experience. Prepare a résumé to use when you apply for a job or when you seek admission to a college or special program. Keep in mind that a résumé should be tailored to match the target audience. Select and highlight the skills and experiences that would most appeal to the employer or college reading the résumé. For a college or academic program, for example, you would highlight a strong GPA, successful class projects, and involvement in school clubs. The language would create a sophisticated, but not artificial, tone. For an employer, on the other hand, you would highlight work experience, both paid and volunteer, and the skills you learned on the job, using clear and direct language.

Here are some more tips to help you create a résumé:

- ■ Give complete information about work experience, including job title, dates of employment, company, and location.

- ■ Do not use *I;* instead, use short, parallel phrases that describe duties and activities.

- ■ Proofread carefully. Mistakes on a résumé make the writer seem careless—not a positive quality for an employee.

Workplace Documents

Memos are the standard form of communication in many businesses. To write a concise, easy-to-understand memo, you must first understand your main purpose for writing. Are you writing to provide information or to make a request? Memos should provide all essential information—*who, what, when, where, why,* and *how*—and get quickly to the point. If you are asking for action and information, include a deadline. Memos follow a standard format that includes the date, the recipient, the sender, and the subject at the top of the document. Notice how the following memo gets right to the point and communicates information clearly and directly.

Date: February 25, 2008

To: Sophia Cervenka

From: Cole Hurley

Subject: Computer Training

Training on the new software will begin Monday, March 10, 2008. Members of your department who are interested in receiving training should call me at extension 4390 by Friday, March 7, to sign up. Training will last from 8:00 A.M.–3:00 P.M. The next training session will be held on March 18.

Word-Processing Features

A clear message is essential in workplace communication, but the appearance of workplace documents also counts. Learn to use word-processing features to your advantage by making documents that are easy on both the eyes and the mind.

■ **Margins** are the space that surrounds the text on a page. Most word-processing programs automatically set side and top margins. You can adjust these default margins to suit your purpose.

■ A **font** is a complete set of characters (including letters, numbers, and punctuation marks) in a particular size and design. For most workplace documents, use a font that is businesslike and easy to read. (For more on **fonts,** see page 1489.)

■ **Line spacing** is the white space between lines of text. Most letters and memos are single-spaced to conserve space, but longer reports are often double-spaced to allow room for handwritten edits and comments.

INTEGRATING DATABASES, GRAPHICS, AND SPREADSHEETS Workplace documents often integrate databases, graphics, and spreadsheets into text. For example, a pie chart or a spreadsheet can show budget expenses, or a list of customers in a specific ZIP Code might be integrated from a database into a report. Add features such as these to communicate your ideas more effectively. Place a graphic close to the related text, and explain the graphic's context. For help in integrating visuals and other components into documents, consult the Help section of your word-processing program or ask your teacher to help you.

RÉSUMÉ FORMAT Word-processing features can help you create an attractive format for your résumé. Here are some guidelines to remember:

■ **Make sure the résumé is not cluttered. Use wide margins for the top, bottom, and sides, and use double-spacing between sections to make the résumé easy to scan for information.**

■ **Consider using a different font, boldface, and a larger point size for your name and for headings. Be sure all the fonts are easy to read.**

The following résumé was written by a student interested in a sales job. He highlighted skills and experiences that show his interpersonal skills and initiative and used an attractive, easy-to-read format.

MIGUEL GUERRERO

1902 Greig Street

Santa Rosa, CA 95403

(707) 555-0085

E-mail: mguerrero@fhs.k12.ca.us

EDUCATION

Senior, Forsythe High School

Grade-point average: 3.3 (B)

WORK EXPERIENCE

Summer 2007–present

Waiter, Starlite Restaurant

- Serve customers quickly and efficiently
- Train new employees in effective customer service
- Twice awarded Star Employee

Summer 2006

Campaign Volunteer, Antonio Suarez Campaign for Mayor

- Assisted in door-to-door campaigns
- Collected and input data for mailing list
- Organized teen volunteers to distribute flyers

SKILLS

Communication: Telephone sales, oral presentations

Computers: Word processing, Web design

ACTIVITIES

Debate team, soccer team, student government representative

REFERENCES

Janet Matteson, Owner   David Cho, Principal

Starlite Restaurant   Forsythe High School

(707) 555-0146   (707) 555-0013

Your Turn 2   Create a résumé for your dream job. Think about what experiences and skills you have that would appeal to a potential employer. Present this information in a clear, concise, and eye-catching way.

Writer's Handbook

The Writing Process

Effective writing involves a process. The steps in this process, called a **recursive** process because you may repeat them several times, are like those of a spiral staircase—you must travel around and around, yet with each revolution you ascend toward your goal. While each writer's process is slightly different, most effective writers follow the steps below.

Stages of the Writing Process	
Prewriting	• Identify your purpose and audience. • Choose a topic and an appropriate form. • Formulate your thesis, or main idea, about the topic. • Gather information about the topic. • Organize information in a preliminary plan.
Drafting	• Draft an introduction that seizes your readers' attention and provides necessary background information. • State your thesis clearly and assertively. • Develop body paragraphs that elaborate on key ideas. • Follow an organizational plan. • Draft a conclusion that restates your thesis and leaves readers with something to think about.
Evaluating and Revising	• Evaluate your draft.
Proofreading and Publishing	• Revise to improve its content, organization, and style. • Proofread your draft, and correct errors in spelling, punctuation, grammar, and usage. • Share your final draft with readers. • Reflect on your writing experience.

Throughout the writing process, make sure you do the following:

- **Keep your ideas coherent and focused.** Keep your specific purpose in mind to help you present a tightly reasoned argument. Evaluate every idea to make sure it will focus your readers on your main point, and make that point clear in your thesis statement.

- **Share your own perspective.** You bring your own ideas to every piece you write. Share not only information you've gathered but also your viewpoint on your topic. Let your natural voice shine through to readers.

- **Keep your audience in mind.** Consider your readers' backgrounds and interests. If your form is not assigned, choose a form that will grab your readers, such as a song, editorial, screenplay, or letter.
- **Plan to publish.** Labor over every piece as though it will be published or shared with an audience. Enlist the help of a classmate when you proofread a finished piece, and use the questions in the chart below. The numbers in parentheses indicate the sections in the Language Handbook that contain instruction on each concept.

Questions for Proofreading

1. Is every sentence complete, not a fragment or run-on? (8a, 9d–e)

2. Are punctuation marks used correctly? (12a–r, 13a–o)

3. Are the first letters of sentences, proper nouns, and proper adjectives capitalized? (11a, c)

4. Does each verb agree in number with its subject? (2a) Are verb forms and tenses used correctly? (3b–c)

5. Are subject and object forms of personal pronouns used correctly? (4a–e) Does every pronoun agree with a clear antecedent in number and gender? (2j)

When revising and proofreading, use the symbols below.

Symbols for Revising and Proofreading

Symbol	Example	Meaning of Symbol
≡	805 Linden avenue	Capitalize a lowercase letter.
/	the First of May	Lowercase a capital letter.
∧	one of my friends	Insert a missing word, letter, or punctuation mark. Replace a word.
∧⁀	at the onset beginning	Replace a word.
℮	Give me a a number	Delete a word, letter, or punctuation mark.
∽	beleive	Change the order of letters.
¶	¶"Yes," she answered.	Begin a new paragraph.

Paragraphs

The Parts of a Paragraph

Paragraphs can be as different as oak trees are from pines. Some paragraphs are a single word; others run several pages. Their uses differ, too: A paragraph may present a main idea, connect one idea to another, emphasize an idea, or simply give the reader's eyes a rest in a long passage.

Many paragraphs in essays and other types of nonfiction, including workplace writing, develop one main idea. A main-idea paragraph is often built from a **topic sentence, supporting sentences,** and a **clincher sentence.**

Parts of a Paragraph	
Topic Sentence	• is an explicit statement of the paragraph's main idea or central focus • is often the first or second sentence in a paragraph, but may appear at the end to emphasize or summarize
Supporting Sentences	• provide elaboration by supporting, building, or proving the main idea • often include details of the following types: *sensory details:* information about sight, sound, taste, smell, and texture *facts:* details that can be proved true *examples:* specific instances that illustrate a general idea *anecdotes:* brief stories about people or events that illustrate a main idea *analogies:* comparisons between ideas familiar to readers and unfamiliar concepts being explained
Clincher Sentence	• may restate the topic sentence, summarize supporting details, offer a final thought, or help readers refocus on the main idea of a long paragraph

Tip Not every paragraph needs a clincher sentence. Use one for a strong or dramatic touch or for renewing a main idea in a lengthy or complicated paragraph.

Tip Not every paragraph has, or needs, a topic sentence. In fiction, paragraphs rarely have topic sentences. Paragraphs presenting time sequences (how-to instructions or histories, for example) may also lack topic sentences—the steps or events themselves focus the reader's mind. Finally, a paragraph may imply, or suggest, its main idea without directly stating it in a topic sentence. In your school writing, however, topic sentences are a help: They keep you focused on each paragraph's topic.

PUTTING THE PARTS TOGETHER You can clearly see the parts of a paragraph in the following example. Notice that its topic sentence expresses the paragraph's main idea and that the clincher sentence re-emphasizes it.

The arrival of printing in England was to be of far more importance than any of the changes of ruler during the Wars of the Roses. Up until this time books had been copied out by hand by scribes in monasteries or other workshops, a long and laborious process. As a result books were rare and very costly. Printing by machine meant that they could be cheap and plentiful. The knowledge books contained could also be spread far wider, reaching new audiences, as more people than ever before learned to read. When William Caxton set up his printing presses in the precincts of Westminster Abbey in 1476, it was to be a landmark in the history of the English language and literature, daily life, and culture.

Sir Roy Strong, *The Story of Britain*

Topic Sentence

Supporting Sentences

Clincher Sentence

Qualities of Paragraphs

Think about trees again. Each type is so distinct: a pine with its needles and cones, a magnolia with its glossy leaves and huge blossoms. Yet, while different, each is a pleasing whole. Paragraphs achieve this wholeness, too, through two major qualities: **unity** and **coherence**.

UNITY Unity means that all of a paragraph's supporting sentences really fit the main idea—no pine cones should poke out among the magnolia blooms. In other words, all of the supporting sentences must work together and stay on the topic. Unity is achieved when

- all sentences relate to the paragraph's main idea—whether it is stated in a topic sentence or implied, or
- all sentences relate to a sequence of events

COHERENCE When a paragraph has coherence, the ideas are arranged in an order that makes sense so that the reader moves easily from one idea to another. The paragraph flows; it doesn't bounce readers around or befuddle them. You can create coherence in a paragraph by paying attention to

- the order you use to arrange ideas
- the connections you make between ideas to show readers how the ideas are related

To create coherence through the arrangement of your ideas, choose the type of order that best fits your purpose. The chart below explains how to use the four main types of order.

Types of Order		
Order	**When to Use**	**How It Works**
Chronological	• to tell a story or relate an event • to explain a process • to show cause and effect	• presents events in the order they happen • shows how things change over time
Spatial	• to describe individual features • to create a complete visual picture	• arranges details by location in space—top to bottom, left to right, near to far, center to edge, and so on
Order of Importance	• to inform • to persuade	• arranges ideas and details from most important to least, or vice versa • places emphasis where the writer thinks it is most effective
Logical	• to inform or to persuade, often by classifying: defining, dividing a subject into parts, or comparing and contrasting	• groups ideas or details together in ways that illustrate the relationships between them; for example, as parts of a whole

Tip The types of order can overlap or can be used in combination. For example, to explain an effect, you might move **chronologically** through its causes, describing the first cause, which leads to the second cause, and so on. However, suppose that three simultaneous causes produce a single effect. You could discuss those causes in **order of importance.**

Guide readers through your clearly arranged ideas by pointing out the connections among them. Show connections by using **direct references** (repetition of ideas), **transitional expressions,** and **parallelism**. The chart on the next page details how you can use these three types of connections to add to the coherence of your writing.

Connecting Ideas	
Type of Connection	**How to Use It**
Direct References, or Repetition of Ideas	• Refer to a noun or pronoun used earlier in the paragraph. • Repeat a word used earlier. • Substitute synonyms for words used earlier.
Transitional Expressions	• Compare ideas (*also, and, another, in the same way, just, like, likewise, moreover, similarly, too*). • Contrast ideas (*although, but, however, in spite of, instead, nevertheless, on the other hand, still, yet*). • Show cause and effect (*accordingly, as a result, because, consequently, for, since, so, so that, therefore*). • Indicate time (*after, at last, before, early, eventually, first, later, next, then, thereafter, until, when, while*). • Show place (*above, across, adjacent, behind, beside, beyond, down, here, in, near, over, there*). • Show importance (*first, last, less significant, mainly, more important, to begin with*).
Parallelism	• Use the same grammatical forms or structures to balance related ideas in a sentence. • Sparingly, use the same sentence structures to show connections between related ideas in a paragraph or composition.

Your Turn Develop two paragraphs on a single topic that interests you. First, choose two primary methods of organizing ideas on the topic (keeping in mind that you may use a combination of orders). Then, plan a topic sentence, a variety of supporting details, and a clincher sentence for each of your two paragraphs. Finally, draft your paragraphs, clearly organizing and connecting ideas and eliminating any ideas that detract from your focus.

The Writer's Language

Revising often focuses on a piece's content and organization. However, to communicate ideas effectively, you must work just as carefully to revise a piece's **style**—how you express those ideas. When revising your style, fine-tune your writing's **sound, word choice,** and **sentence variety,** and use **rhetorical devices** to grab reader attention and make your ideas clear and interesting.

A SOUND STYLE   Keep your **audience** and **purpose** in mind to help you choose a suitable **voice, tone,** and **level of formality** for a piece of writing.

Voice   In writing, voice is your unique personality on paper. Just as you recognize a friend's spoken voice, you can recognize the work of favorite writers by the unique way they express ideas. To evaluate your own writing voice, read your work out loud. If your writing doesn't sound natural, revise it to bring your personality to life.

Tone   Tone reveals your attitude toward a topic and audience. Always use an appropriate tone for your audience and purpose. For example, if your purpose is to persuade readers to share your view on an important issue, your tone should be serious and respectful.

Level of Formality   You wouldn't don formal wear for a beach party, and neither should you use a casual, informal style for a serious essay on a subject about which you care deeply. Match the level of formality to your subject, your audience, and your purpose. Look at these examples.

INFORMAL	Some people shouldn't own pets. Period.
FORMAL	Certain people should not own pets under any circumstances.

WORD CHOICE   Make sure your words express the ideas you want them to express. Every word should help create a clear, vivid picture of what you mean and communicate the connotation you want.

Precise Language   Replace vague language in your writing with words that are distinct and strong. For example, you might describe a big boulder you saw on a hike as being as *huge as a car* or as *mammoth as a double-decker bus.* You could mention that the boulder *rumbled* down the hill or *squatted* by the path. Using **precise verbs, nouns,** and **adjectives** like these will make your writing clearer and more interesting.

Connotations   As you choose words, notice their **connotations**—the emotional effects they create. For instance, the word *cheap* means "economical," but it also has the negative connotation of being poor in quality. The word *inexpensive* expresses the same idea as *cheap* but in a more positive way. Choose words carefully by considering their effects.

SENTENCE VARIETY Readers can become bored with writing that uses the same types of sentences over and over. Create variety by varying the beginnings of your sentences and mixing simple, compound, and complex sentences.

RHETORICAL DEVICES To give your ideas a greater impact, use the rhetorical devices of **parallelism, repetition,** and **analogy.**

Parallelism Just as a train stays on its tracks because they're parallel, readers will stay on track if your written ideas are grammatically parallel.

NOT PARALLEL   More lives are saved when **drivers wear seat belts** and **motorcyclists are wearing helmets.**

PARALLEL   More lives are saved when **drivers wear seat belts** and **motorcyclists wear helmets.**

You can also use parallelism for effect by using similar sentence structures to express related ideas.

Repetition Repeating important words or phrases can create an emotional response or underscore their significance. Use this technique sparingly to make your key ideas resonate with readers.

Analogy An analogy illustrates an idea by comparing it to something with similar characteristics. For example, you could say, "The politician worked the crowd as if he were selling the Fountain of Youth."

A STYLISH MODEL Read the following passage, noting the writer's sound, word choice, sentence variety, and rhetorical devices.

A Writer's Model

Credit cards are a ticket to an unpleasant lesson for college freshmen. One in five college students will rack up $10,000 in credit card debt by graduation. That's right—$10,000! Some people use credit as recklessly as play money. Unfortunately, the consequences for misusing credit cards are staggering. A $5,000 credit card debt can take up to 30 years and $15,000 to pay off—three times the value of the items purchased. Credit cards only look good until the bill comes due. I encourage students to stand firm and refuse the temptations dangled before them by credit card companies.

Voice/tone

Repetition
Analogy
Connotation

Precise verbs

Your Turn Revise the paragraph below to improve its style. Add your own ideas as appropriate.

I think students should be allowed to bring cell phones to school. What if we need to call someone? Students have rights too. I think the school staff should quit treating us like babies. This rule just isn't fair and should be changed.

Designing Your Writing

A document must be designed to convey information in a way that is easy to understand and remember. In other words, the text arrangement and appearance and any visuals must support the content. You can create effective design and visuals by hand, or you can use advanced publishing software and graphics programs to design pages and to integrate other features into your word-processed documents.

Page Design

LAY IT ON THE LINE If you want your documents to catch readers' attention, you must design them to be visually appealing and easy to read. Use the following design elements to improve readability.

- **Columns** arrange text in separate sections printed vertically side by side. Text in reference books and newspapers usually appears in columns. A **block** is a rectangle of text shorter than a page. The text in advertisements is usually set in blocks so that it may be read quickly. Blocks and columns are separated from each other by white space.

- A **bullet** (•) is a symbol used to highlight information in a text. Bullets separate information into lists like this one. Bullets attract attention and help readers remember information.

- A **heading** appears at the beginning of a section of text to tell readers what that section is about. A **subheading** indicates a smaller section within a heading. Headings and subheadings may be set off from other text in large, **boldface**, or *italic* type or in a different font.

- **White space** is any area on a page where there is little or no text or graphics. Usually, white space is limited to the margins and the spaces between words, lines, and columns. Advertisements usually have more white space than do books or articles.

- A **caption** appears under a photograph or illustration to explain its meaning and connect it to the text. Captions may appear in italics or in a smaller type size than the main text.

- **Contrast** refers to the balance of light and dark areas on a page. Dark areas contain blocks of text or graphics. Light areas have little type. A page with high contrast, or roughly balanced light and dark areas, is easier to read than a page with low contrast.

- **Emphasis** is how a page designer indicates to a reader which information on a page is most important. Because readers' eyes are drawn naturally to color, large and bold print, and graphics, these elements are commonly used to create emphasis.

Type

LETTER PERFECT   The basic material of your document is the type. Your choice of different **cases** and **fonts** can pull the reader into the text, provide emphasis, and make your document easy to read.

Case   The two cases of type are uppercase, or capital, letters and lowercase, or small, letters. You can vary case in these ways:

- **Uppercase** letters Text in all uppercase letters attracts readers' attention and may be used in headings or titles. Because text in all capital letters can be difficult to read, use all capitals only for emphasis, not for large bodies of text.

- **Small caps** Small caps are uppercase letters that are reduced in size. They are used in abbreviations of time, such as 9:00 A.M. and A.D. 1500. Small caps may be combined with capital letters for an artistic effect.

Font   A font is one complete set of characters (such as letters, numbers, and punctuation marks) of a given size and design. The three types of fonts are explained in the chart below.

Categories of fonts		
Category	**Explanation**	**Uses**
decorative, or **script,** fonts	elaborately designed characters that convey a distinct mood or feeling	Decorative fonts are difficult to read and should be used in small amounts for an artistic effect.
serif fonts	characters with small strokes (serifs) at each end, such as the main type on this page	Because the strokes on serif characters help guide the reader's eyes from letter to letter, serif type is often used for large bodies of type.
sans serif fonts	characters such as these, formed of straight lines with no serifs	Sans serif fonts are easy to read and are used as headings, subheadings, and captions.

- **Font size** The size of the type in a document is called the font size or point size. In general, newspapers and textbooks use type measured at 12 points. Type for headings and headlines is larger, while captions are usually smaller.

- **Font style** Most text is set in roman (not slanted) style. *Italic,* or slanted, style is used for captions or book titles. Underscored or boldface type can be used for emphasis.

Visuals

SHOW, DON'T TELL If you wanted to tell about the weekly expenses and income from your summer lawn-care business, it would be more effective to show the information in a table than to list it in a paragraph. Visuals, or graphics, such as this must be accurate and appropriate. You can create visuals by hand or by using technology, such as advanced computer software and graphics programs. You can also add to a document's impact by integrating a database or spreadsheet into it. Here are some useful visuals.

- **Graphs** present numeric information and can show trends or changes over time or how one thing changes in relation to another. A **bar graph** can also compare quantities at a glance, or note the parts of a whole. A **line graph** can compare trends or show how two or more variables interact, as in this example.

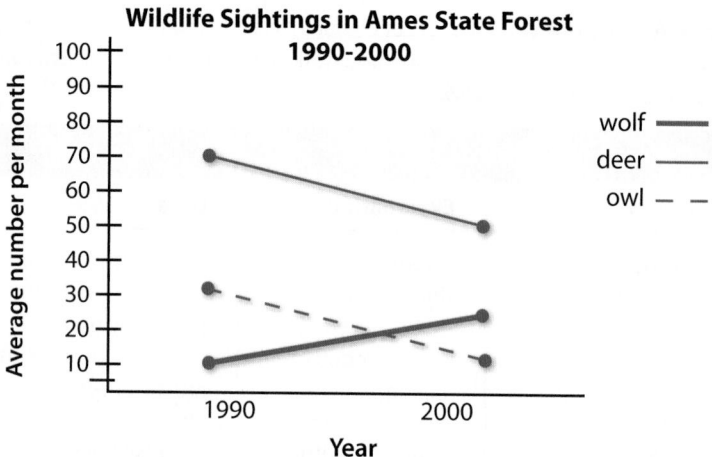

- **Tables** use rows and columns to provide detailed information arranged in an accessible way. A **spreadsheet** is a special kind of table created on a computer. The cells of a spreadsheet are associated with mathematical equations. Spreadsheets are especially useful for budgets or schedules in which the numbers are variables in an equation. In the spreadsheet below, the last column of each row calculates the average of the figures to the left of it.

First Quarter Grades					
Name	**Essay**	**Test**	**Speech**	**Project**	**Average**
Cooper, L.	84	78	81	92	84
Nguyen, H.	90	86	88	95	90
Torres, B.	88	94	91	90	91
Watt, K.	96	90	93	88	92

- **Pictures,** such as drawings and photographs, can show how something works, what something or someone looks like, or something new, unfamiliar, or indescribable. You can scan a copyright-free picture on the computer or paste it manually into your document. Place it near the reference in the text, and include a caption.

- **Charts** show relationships among ideas or data. A **flowchart** uses geometric shapes linked by arrows to show the sequence of events in a process. A **pie chart** is a circle divided into wedges. Each wedge represents a certain percentage of the total, as in this example.

How Energy Is Used Worldwide

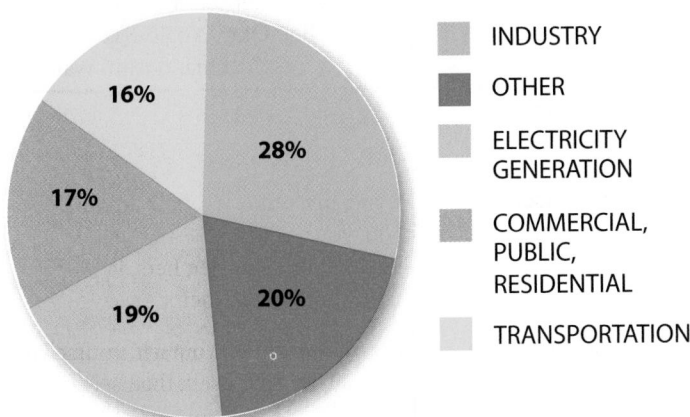

- INDUSTRY
- OTHER
- ELECTRICITY GENERATION
- COMMERCIAL, PUBLIC, RESIDENTIAL
- TRANSPORTATION

- **Time lines** identify the events that have taken place over a given period of time. (For an example of a time line, see page 2.)

Your Turn Choose and create the visual you think would most effectively communicate the following information using the guidelines in this section.

The estimated expenses for the Sanger High senior class trip are as follows: bus rental, $1,000; gas, $200; hotel, ten rooms at $45 per room for five days, or $2,250; food, $30 a day per person (ten people for five days), or $1,500. The total trip cost is $4,950

Language Handbook

1. The Parts of Speech

Part Of Speech	Definition	Examples
NOUN	Names person, place, thing, or idea	Common: writer, family, country, poem Proper: Ben Okri, Anglo-Saxons, "My Last Duchess," Romanticism, Wales
PRONOUN	Takes place of one or more nouns or pronouns	
Personal	Refers to one(s) speaking (first person), spoken to (second person), spoken about (third person)	I, me, my, mine, we, us, our, ours you, your, yours he, him, his, she, her, hers, it, its they, them, their, theirs
Reflexive	Refers to subject and directs action of verb back to subject	myself, ourselves, yourself, yourselves, himself, herself, itself, themselves
Intensive	Refers to and emphasizes noun or another pronoun	(See Reflexive.)
Demonstrative	Refers to specific one(s) of group	this, that, these, those
Interrogative	Introduces question	what, which, who, whom, whose
Relative	Introduces subordinate clause and refers to noun or pronoun outside that clause	that, which, who, whom, whose
Indefinite	Refers to one(s) not specifically named	all, any, anyone, both, each, either, everybody, many, none, nothing
ADJECTIVE	Modifies noun or pronoun by telling *what kind, which one, how many,* or *how much*	**a paperback** book, **an Anglo-Saxon** law, **this** one, **the seven brave** warriors, **less** space
VERB	Shows action or state of being	
Action	Expresses physical or mental activity	describe, travel, fight, believe, consider, remember
Linking	Connects subject with word identifying or describing it	appear, be, seem, become, feel, look, smell, sound, taste
Helping (Auxiliary)	Helps another verb express time, voice, or mood	be, have, may, can, shall, must, would
ADVERB	Modifies verb, adjective, or adverb by telling *how, when, where,* or *to what extent*	walks **slowly, quite** different, **somewhat** boldly, coming **here soon**

PREPOSITION	Relates noun or pronoun to another word	about, at, by, for, of, in, on, according to, along with, because of
CONJUNCTION	Joins words or word groups	
Coordinating	Joins words or word groups used in the same way	and, but, for, nor, or, so, yet
Correlative	A pair of conjunctions that join parallel words or word groups	both . . . and, either . . . or, neither . . . nor, not only . . . but (also)
Subordinating	Begins a subordinate clause and connects it to independent clause	although, as if, because, since, so that, unless, when, where, while
INTERJECTION	Expresses emotion	ah, wow, ugh, whew

Your Turn

The use of precise nouns and descriptive adverbs makes writing accurate, specific, and more interesting. Rewrite the following paragraph about Jonathan Swift's *Gulliver's Travels*, replacing the vague nouns with precise nouns and weak adverbs with more descriptive adverbs.

1. The book written by an English author recounts the story of an English doctor.
2. After some troubles, the man leaves town.
3. Part One of the book describes the man's trip to a place of very little people.
4. These people capture the man and bind him up with very small strings.
5. The man eventually leaves this place and returns to his home, only to sail away again.

2. Agreement

AGREEMENT OF SUBJECT AND VERB

2a. A verb should agree with its subject in number. Singular subjects take singular verbs. Plural subjects take plural verbs.

SINGULAR   **He lives** in Camelot.

PLURAL   **They live** in Camelot.

2b. The number of the subject is not changed by a phrase or a clause following the subject.

The **Lilliputians,** tiny people from the nation of Lilliput, **capture** Gulliver.

2c. Indefinite pronouns may be singular, plural, or either.

(1) The following indefinite pronouns are singular: *anybody, anyone, anything, each, either, everybody, everyone, everything, neither, nobody, no one, nothing, one, somebody, someone,* and *something.*

One of the most beautiful places in England **is** the Lake District.

(2) The following indefinite pronouns are plural: *both, few, many,* and *several.*

Both of the epics **were written** by John Milton.

(3) The indefinite pronouns *all, any, most, none,* and *some* are singular when they refer to singular words and are plural when they refer to plural words.

SINGULAR   **None** of the equipment **was damaged.** [*None refers to equipment.*]

PLURAL   **None** of the machines **were damaged.** [*None* refers to *machines.*]

2d. A *compound subject* may be singular, plural, or either.

(1) Subjects joined by *and* usually take a plural verb.

After rehearsal, **Juan, Anita,** and **Marcus are going** out to dinner.

A compound subject that names only one person or thing takes a singular verb.

His **wife** and **partner** in crime **is** Lady Macbeth.

(2) Singular subjects joined by *or* or *nor* take a singular verb.

Jill or **Jorge plans** to write a character analysis of Macduff.

(3) When a singular subject and a plural subject are joined by *or* or *nor,* the verb agrees with the subject nearer the verb.

Neither the **dancers** nor the **choreographer was** pleased with the routine.

2e. The verb agrees with its subject even when the verb precedes the subject, as in sentences beginning with *here, there,* or *where.*

SINGULAR   Where **is** [*or* where**'s**] Malcolm?

PLURAL   Here **are** [*not* here's] **Malcolm** and his **brother.**

2f. A *collective noun* (such as *audience, flock,* or *team*) is singular in form but names a group of persons or things. A collective noun takes a singular verb when the noun refers to the group as a unit and takes a plural verb when the noun refers to the parts or members of the group.

SINGULAR   The tour **group is** on the bus. [The group as a unit is on the bus.]

PLURAL   The tour **group was talking** about their plans. [The members of the group are talking to one another.]

2g. An expression of an amount (a length of time, a statistic, or a fraction, for example) is singular when the amount is thought of as a unit or when it refers to a singular word and plural when the amount is thought of as many parts or when it refers to a plural word.

SINGULAR   **Fifty years is** how long Beowulf rules Geatland. [one unit]

PLURAL   **One fourth** of the seniors **are working** on a production of *Macbeth.* [The fraction refers to *seniors.*]

Expressions of measurement (length, weight, capacity, area) are usually singular.

Four and seven-tenths inches is the diameter of a compact disc.

2h. The title of a creative work (such as a book, song, film, or painting) or the name of an organization, a country, or a city (even if it is plural in form) takes a singular verb.

"Tears, Idle Tears" was written by Alfred, Lord Tennyson.

The **United Nations was formed** in 1945.

Has the **Netherlands been flooded** recently?

2i. A verb agrees with its subject, not with its predicate nominative.

SINGULAR   The **subject** of the lecture **was** epic heroes.

PLURAL   **Epic heroes were** the subject of the lecture.

AGREEMENT OF PRONOUN AND ANTECEDENT

A pronoun usually refers to a noun or another pronoun. The word to which a pronoun refers is called its ***antecedent.***

2j. A pronoun agrees with its antecedent in number and gender. Singular pronouns refer to singular antecedents. A few singular pronouns also indicate gender (feminine, masculine, or neuter). Plural pronouns refer to plural antecedents.

William Wordsworth published *The Prelude* before **he** became poet laureate. [singular, masculine]

Lady Macbeth helps **her** husband. [singular, feminine]

The **Lilliputians** gave **their** captive food. [plural, neuter]

2k. Indefinite pronouns may be singular, plural, or either.

(1) Singular pronouns are used to refer to the indefinite pronouns *anybody, anyone, anything, each, other, everybody, everyone, everything, neither, nobody, no one, nothing, one, somebody, someone,* and *something.* The gender of any of these pronouns is determined by the word or words that the pronoun refers to.

Each of the **boys** has learned **his** part in *Macbeth.*

One of the **girls** has injured **herself**.

If the antecedent may be either masculine or feminine, use both the masculine and feminine pronouns to refer to it.

Anyone who is going on the field trip needs to bring **his** or **her** lunch.

(2) Plural pronouns are used to refer to the indefinite pronouns *both, few, many,* and *several.*

Many of the spectators leapt from **their** seats and cheered.

(3) Singular or plural pronouns may be used to refer to the indefinite pronouns *all, any, most, none,* and *some.* These indefinite pronouns are singular when they refer to singular words and are plural when they refer to plural words.

SINGULAR **None** of the renovated theater matches **its** original beauty. [*None* refers to the singular noun *theater.*]

PLURAL **None** of the geese have left on **their** annual migration. [*None* refers to the plural noun *geese.*]

2l. A plural pronoun is used to refer to two or more singular antecedents joined by *and.*

Malcolm and Donalbain left Scotland soon after **their** father was killed.

2m. A singular pronoun is used to refer to two or more singular antecedents joined by *or* or *nor.*

Neither **Malcolm nor Donalbain** felt **he** was safe.

2n. A collective noun (such as *club* or *family*) takes a singular pronoun when the noun refers to the group as a unit and takes a plural pronoun when the noun refers to the parts or members of the group.

SINGULAR The **jury** reached **its** decision less than one hour later. [The jury decided as a unit.]

PLURAL The **jury** disagreed on how much importance **they** should give to one of the defendant's statements. [The members of the jury disagree.]

2o. The title of a creative work (such as a book, song, film, or painting) or the name of an organization, a country, or a city (even if it is plural in form) takes a singular pronoun.

I read *Gulliver's Travels* and wrote a report on **it**.

The **United Arab Emirates** generates most of **its** revenue from the sale of oil.

Your Turn

Rewrite the following sentences to make sure the pronouns and their antecedents agree.
1. We recognize that each of the characters in *Macbeth* had his or her own motives.
2. With that in mind, each of the boys is carefully researching their part for the play.
3. So far not one of the girls has forgotten their lines.
4. Mrs. Talbott said that anyone who is in the play needs to provide his or her own props and costume.
5. Neither Joan nor Elizabeth has begun work on their costume yet.

3. Using Verbs

THE PRINCIPAL PARTS OF VERBS

Every verb has four basic forms called the **principal parts:** the *base form,* the *present participle,* the *past,* and the *past participle.* A verb is classified as regular or irregular depending on the way it forms its past and past participle.

3a. A *regular verb* forms the past and past participle by adding *–d* or *–ed* to the base form. An *irregular verb* forms the past and the past participle in some other way.

Common Regular And Irregular Verbs

The following examples include *is* and *have* in italics to show that helping verbs (forms of *be* and *have*) are used with the present participle and past participle forms.

BASE FORM	PRESENT PARTICIPLE	PAST	PAST PARTICIPLE
Regular			
attack	*is* attacking	attacked	*have* attacked
drown	*is* drowning	drowned	*have* drowned
occur	*is* occurring	occurred	*have* occurred
risk	*is* risking	risked	*have* risked
try	*is* trying	tried	*have* tried
use	*is* using	used	*have* used
Irregular			
be	*is* being	was, were	*have* been
bring	*is* bringing	brought	*have* brought
burst	*is* bursting	burst	*have* burst
come	*is* coming	came	*have* come
eat	*is* eating	ate	*have* eaten
go	*is* going	went	*have* gone
lead	*is* leading	led	*have* led

pay	*is* paying	paid	*have* paid
see	*is* seeing	saw	*have* seen
sing	*is* singing	sang	*have* sung
steal	*is* stealing	stole	*have* stolen
take	*is* taking	took	*have* taken
throw	*is* throwing	threw	*have* thrown

If you are not sure about the principal parts of a verb, look in a dictionary. Entries for irregular verbs give the principal parts. If no principal parts are listed, the verb is a regular verb.

TENSES AND THEIR USES

3b. The *tense* of a verb indicates the time of the action or state of being that is expressed by the verb.

(1) The ***present tense*** is used mainly to express an action or a state of being that is occurring now.

The article **compares** Beowulf with other epic heroes.

The present tense is also used

- to show a customary or habitual action or state of being
- to convey a general truth—something that is always true
- to make a historical event seem current (such use is called the ***historical present***)
- to summarize the plot or subject matter of a literary work or to refer to an author's relationship to his or her work (such use is called the ***literary present***)
- to express future time

Every Friday, our teacher **gives** us a vocabulary quiz. [customary action]

Reptiles **are** coldblooded. [general truth]

The Greeks **establish** separate city-states, which **war** among themselves. [historical present]

In the land of the Lilliputians, Gulliver **appears** gigantic. [literary present]

The two-week seminar on Shakespeare **begins** on Monday. [future time]

(2) The *past tense* is used to express an action or state of being that occurred in the past but did not continue into the present.

An expert on T. S. Eliot's poetry **spoke** to our class last Wednesday.

(3) The *future tense* (*will* or *shall* + base form) is used to express an action or a state of being that will occur.

Laura **will play** the part of Lady Macbeth.

I **will** [*or* **shall**] **serve** as her understudy.

Shall and *will* are both acceptable in forming the future tense.

(4) The *present perfect tense* (*have* or *has* + past participle) is used to express an action or a state of being that occurred at some indefinite time in the past.

Kenneth Branagh **has played** the roles of Henry V and of Iago.

The present perfect tense is also used to express an action or a state of being that began in the past and continues into the present.

Herot **has stood** empty and deserted for twelve years.

(5) The *past perfect tense* (*had* + past participle) is used to express an action or state of being completed in the past before some other past occurrence.

The kingdom **had suffered** greatly before Beowulf arrived. [The suffering occurred before the arriving.]

Be sure to use the past perfect tense in "if" clauses that express the earlier of two past actions.

If you **had read** [*not* read *or* would have read] the article for class, you would have learned about Sutton Hoo.

(6) The *future perfect tense* (*will have* or *shall have* + past participle) is used to express an action or state of being that will be completed in the future before some other future occurrence.

By this time tomorrow, I **will** [*or* **shall**] **have memorized** "The Seafarer."

3c. Avoid unnecessary shifts in tense.

INCONSISTENT	Wiglaf discovered the dragon's treasure and then brings it to Beowulf. [shift from past to present tense]
CONSISTENT	Wiglaf **discovered** the dragon's treasure and then **brought** it to Beowulf. [past tense]
CNSISTENT	Wiglaf **discovers** the dragon's treasure and then **brings** it to Beowulf. [present tense]

When describing events that occur at different times, use verbs in different tenses to show the order of events.

She **taught** school for several years, but now she **works** for a publishing company. [Because she taught at a specific time in the past, the past tense *taught* is correct. Because she works at the present time, the present tense *works* is correct.]

ACTIVE VOICE AND PASSIVE VOICE

3d. *Voice* is the form a transitive verb takes to indicate whether the subject of the verb performs or receives the action.

A verb is in the *active voice* when its subject performs the action (its object receives the action).

| ACTIVE VOICE | William Shakespeare **wrote** more than thirty-five plays. |

A verb is in the *passive voice* whenever its subject receives the action (the verb has no object). A passive verb is always a verb phrase that includes a form of *be* and the past participle of an action verb.

| PASSIVE VOICE | More than thirty-five plays **were written** by William Shakespeare. |

3e. Use the passive voice sparingly.

In general, the passive voice is less direct and less forceful than the active voice. In some cases, the passive voice also may sound awkward.

| AWKWARD PASSIVE | The sleeping grooms are smeared with King Duncan's blood by Lady Macbeth. |
| ACTIVE | Lady Macbeth **smears** the sleeping grooms with King Duncan's blood. |

Although you generally will want to use active voice rather than passive voice, the passive voice is not less correct than the active voice. In fact, the passive voice is useful in the following situations:

1. when you do not know the performer of the action

   The Globe **was built** in 1599.

2. when you do not want to reveal the performer of the action

   The actor **was criticized** for his portrayal of Macbeth.

3. when you want to emphasize the receiver of the action

   King Duncan **was murdered** while he was asleep.

Your Turn

Read the following paragraph, and decide whether it should be rewritten in the present or past tense. Then, change the verb forms to make the verb tense consistent.

1. At first the Lilliputians fear Gulliver and bound him up.
2. Then they built a huge wagon upon which to transport him to their capital city.
3. There they presented him to their emperor, a handsome little man just slightly taller than his subjects.
4. The Lilliputians find that Gulliver's size can benefit them and used him in their war against Blefuscu.
5. Eventually Gulliver offended the Lilliputians, and he escapes to Blefuscu and avoided punishment.

4. Using Pronouns

CASE

Case is the form that a noun or a pronoun takes to indicate its use in a sentence. In English, there are three cases: *nominative, objective,* and *possessive.* Most personal pronouns have a different form for each case.

THE NOMINATIVE CASE

4a. A subject of a verb is in the nominative case.

They built the tower near the sea as **he** had requested. [*They* is the subject of the verb *built. He* is the subject of the verb *had requested.*]

4b. A predicate nominative is in the nominative case.

The students who won the prize were **she** and **Carlos**. [*She* and *Carlos* are predicate nominatives that follow the linking verb *were* and identify the subject *students.*]

PERSONAL PRONOUNS			
Singular			
	NOMINATIVE	OBJECTIVE	POSSESSIVE
FIRST PERSON	I	me	my, mine
SECOND PERSON	you	you	your, yours
THIRD PERSON	he, she, it	him, her, it	his, her, hers, its
Plural			
	NOMINATIVE	OBJECTIVE	POSSESSIVE
FIRST PERSON	we	us	our, ours
SECOND PERSON	you	you	your, yours
THIRD PERSON	they	them	their, theirs

The form of a noun is the same for both the nominative case and the objective case. A noun changes its form for the possessive case, usually by adding an apostrophe and an *s* to most singular nouns and only an apostrophe to most plural nouns.

The Objective Case

4c. An object of a verb is in the objective case.

The knight's answer pleases **her**. [*Her* is a direct object that tells *whom* the answer pleases.]

The Pardoner tells **them** a story. [*Them* is an indirect object that tells to *whom* the Pardoner tells a story.]

4d. An object of a preposition is in the objective case.

Are the Lilliputians afraid of **him**? [*Him* is the object of the preposition *of*.]

The Possessive Case

4e. A noun or a pronoun preceding a gerund is in the possessive case.

We were all thrilled by **Joetta's** [*or* **her**] scoring in the top 5 percent. [*Joetta's* or *her* modifies *scoring,* a gerund used as the object of the preposition *by*.]

Do not confuse a gerund with a present participle, which is a verb form that ends in *–ing* and may function as an adjective.

Macbeth found **them** [*not* their] standing around a caldron. [*Them* is modified by the participial phrase *standing around a caldron*.]

SPECIAL PRONOUN PROBLEMS

4f. An appositive is in the same case as the noun or pronoun to which it refers.

Duncan's sons, **Malcolm and he**, leave Scotland. [The compound appositive *Malcolm and him* refers to the subject, sons.]

Macduff suspects both of them, **Malcolm and him**. [The compound appositive *Malcolm and him* refers to *them*, the object of the preposition *of*.]

4g. A pronoun following *than* or *as* in an elliptical construction is in the same case as it would be if the construction were completed.

An *elliptical construction* is a clause from which words have been omitted.

NOMINATIVE	I see him more often **than she**. [I see him more often *than she sees him. She* is the subject in the elliptical construction.]
OBJECTIVE	I see him more often **than her**. [I see him more often *than I see her. Her* is the direct object in the elliptical construction.]

4h. A pronoun ending in *–self* or *–selves* should not be used in place of a personal pronoun.

Everyone except John and **me** [*not* myself] has read *Don Juan.*

4i. The pronoun *who* (*whoever*) is in the nominative case. The pronoun *whom* (*whomever*) is in the objective case.

Who wrote "Ozymandias"? [*Who* is the subject of the verb *wrote*.]

With **whom** did Wordsworth write *Lyrical Ballads*? [*Whom* is the object of the preposition *with*.]

CLEAR PRONOUN REFERENCE

The word that a pronoun stands for or refers to is called the *antecedent* of the pronoun.

4j. A pronoun should always refer clearly to its antecedent.

Avoid an ambiguous, a general, a weak, or an indefinite reference by

1. rephrasing the sentence,
2. replacing the pronoun with an appropriate noun,
3. giving the pronoun a clear antecedent.

AMBIGUOUS	When the Green Knight was talking to Sir Gawain, he was holding his head in his head. [The antecedent of *he* and *his* is unclear. Was the Green Knight holding Sir Gawain's head or his own?]
CLEAR	The Green Knight was holding his head in his hand when he was talking to Sir Gawain.
GENERAL	Macbeth will become king. This is one of the witches' prophecies. [*This* has no specific antecedent.]
CLEAR	That Macbeth will become king is one of the witches' prophecies.

WEAK	Our dog Hank is jealous of my new baby sister. To help him get over it, I try to give him extra attention. [The antecedents of *it* is not expressed.]
CLEAR	To help our dog Hank get over his jealousy of my new baby sister, I try to give him extra attention.
INDEFINITE	In this book it includes pictures of artifacts from the Sutton Hoo ship burial. [*It* is not necessary to the meaning of the sentence.]
CLEAR	This book includes pictures of artifacts from the Sutton Hoo ship burial.

Your Turn

Rewrite the following sentences using the correct pronoun case. If a pronoun is used correctly, leave it as is.

1. Last night Mark and me studied the play together.
2. In class today our teacher asked all of we to take parts and read they out loud.
3. When Jose stood up to read the part of Lady Macbeth, the other boys laughed at he.
4. Them teased him unmercifully for the rest of the day.
5. Our teacher, whom is the world's kindest person, explained to him that him shouldn't feel embarrassed.

5. Using Modifiers

A **modifier** is a word or group of words that limits the meaning of another word or group of words. The two kinds of modifiers are *adjectives* and *adverbs*.

5a. Use an *adjective* to limit the meaning of a noun or a pronoun. Use an *adverb* to limit the meaning of a verb, an adjective, or another adverb.

COMPARISON OF MODIFIERS

5b. *Comparison* refers to the change in the form of an adjective or an adverb to show increasing or decreasing degrees in the quality the modifier expresses.

The three degrees of comparison are *positive, comparative,* and *superlative.*

1. Most one-syllable modifiers form the comparative and superlative degrees by adding *–er* and *–est.*
2. Some two-syllable modifiers form the comparative and superlative degrees by adding *–er* and *–est.* Other two-syllable modifiers form the comparative and superlative degrees by using *more* and *most.*

3. Modifiers of more than two syllables form the comparative and superlative degrees by using *more* and *most.*
4. To show a decrease in the qualities they express, all modifiers form the comparative by using *less* and the superlative by using *least.*

Positive	Comparative	Superlative
soft	softer	softest
thirsty	thirstier	thirstiest
slowly	more slowly	most slowly
skillfully	less skillfully	least skillfully

5. Some modifiers form the comparative and superlative degrees in other ways.

Positive	Comparative	Superlative
bad (ill)	worse	worst
far	farther (further)	farthest (furthest)
good (well)	better	best
little	less	least
many (much)	more	most

5c. Use the comparative degree when comparing two things. Use the superlative degree when comparing more than two.

COMPARATIVE After reading *King Lear* and *the Winter's Tale,* I can understand why *King Lear* is the **more popular** play. [comparison of two plays]

SUPERLATIVE Of the three plays I saw, I think *Macbeth* was the **most powerful.** [comparison of three plays]

5d. Avoid a double comparison or a double negative. A *double comparison* is the use of two comparative forms (usually *–er* and *more* or *less*) or two superlative forms (usually *–est* and *most* or *least*) to modify the same word. A *double negative* is the use of two negative words when one is enough.

Who is the **noblest** [*not* most noblest] of King Arthur's knights?

I know **nothing** [*not* don't know nothing] about the Wars of the Roses.

5e. Include the word *other* or *else* when comparing one member of a group with the rest of the group.

ILLOGICAL Wiglaf is bolder than any of Beowulf's followers. [Wiglaf is one of Beowulf's followers. Logically, Wiglaf cannot be bolder than himself.]

LOGICAL Wiglaf is bolder than any of Beowulf's **other** followers.

5f. Avoid comparing items that cannot logically be compared.

ILLOGICAL I think Olivier's portrayal of Hamlet is more compelling than any other actor. [The sentence makes an illogical comparison between a portrayal and an actor.]

LOGICAL I think Olivier's portrayal of Hamlet is more compelling than any other actor's [portrayal]. [The sentence makes a logical comparison between portrayals.]

PLACEMENT OF MODIFIERS

5g. Avoid using a *misplaced modifier*—a modifying word, phrase, or clause that sounds awkward because it modifies the wrong word or group of words.

To correct a misplaced modifier, place the word, phrase, or clause as close as possible to the word or words you intend it to modify.

MISPLACED The old man told the three young rioters under a tree they would find Death. [What occurred under a tree: the telling or the finding?]

CLEAR The old man told the three young rioters they would find Death **under a tree**.

MISPLACED The anxious hunter watched the raging lion come charging at him as he readied his bow and arrow.

CLEAR **As he readied his bow and arrow,** the anxious hunter watched the raging lion come charging at him.

5h. Avoid using a *dangling modifier*—a modifying word, phrase, or clause that does not sensibly modify any word or words in a sentence.

You may correct a dangling modifier by

- adding a word or words that the dangling word, phrase, or clause can sensibly refer to
- adding a word or words to the dangling word, phrase, or clause
- rewording the sentence

DANGLING After becoming poet laureate, "The Charge of the Light Brigade" was written. [Who became poet laureate?]

CLEAR After becoming poet laureate, Alfred, Lord Tennyson wrote "The Charge of the Light Brigade."

CLEAR Alfred, Lord Tennyson wrote "The Charge of the Light Brigade" after he became poet laureate.

Your Turn

For each of the following sentences, correct the error in comparison or placement of modifiers.

1. In the play *Macbeth,* it's hard to determine who was the more despicable character.
2. One could argue that of all the noblemen Macbeth was the more ambitious.
3. Surely, however, Lady Macbeth was the more ruthless and powerful woman in the land.
4. With metaphorical blood on her hands, the stain of murder cannot be removed.
5. Having gained the throne through treachery, guilt and fear consume Macbeth and his wife.

6. Phrases

WHAT IS A PHRASE?

6a. A *phrase* is a group of related words that is used as a single part of speech and that does not contain both a verb and its subject.

> *The Rime of the Ancient Mariner,* **Coleridge's best-known poem, was published in 1798.**
> [*Coleridge's best-known poem* functions as a noun, *was published* is a verb, and *in 1798* functions as an adverb.]

THE PREPOSITIONAL PHRASE

6b. A *prepositional phrase* begins with a preposition and ends with the *object of the preposition,* a word or word group that functions as a noun.

> **From the rafters of Herot** hung one **of Grendel's arms.** [The noun *rafters* is the object of the preposition *from.* The noun *Herot* is the object of the preposition *of.* The noun *arms* is the object of the preposition *of.*]

An object of a preposition may be compound.

> The three men ignored the warnings **of the tavern-knave and the publican.** [Both *tavern-knave* and *publican* are objects of the preposition *of.*]

(1) An **adjective phrase** is a prepositional phrase that modifies a noun or a pronoun. An adjective phrase tells *what kind* or *which one.*

> The three rioters found eight bushels **of gold coins.** [*Of gold coins* modifies the noun *bushels.*]

An adjective phrase usually follows the word it modifies. That word may be the object of another preposition.

> They told stories on their journey **to Canterbury.** [*To Canterbury* modifies *journey,* the object of the preposition *on.*]

More than one adjective phrase may modify the same word.

> Chaucer's trips **to Italy on important diplomatic missions** broadened his knowledge. [The phrases *to Italy* and *on important diplomatic missions* modify the noun *trips.*]

(2) An **adverb phrase** is a prepositional phrase that modifies a verb, an adjective, or an adverb. An adverb phrase tells *how, when, where, why,* or *to what extent* (*how long* or *how* far).

As you can see in the example below, more than one adverb phrase can modify the same word. The example also shows that an adverb phrase, unlike an adjective phrase, can precede the word it modifies.

> **In 1799,** Wordsworth returned **with his sister to the Lake District.** [Each phrase modifies the verb *returned. In 1799* tells *when,* with his sister tells *how,* and *to the Lake District* tells *where.*]

VERBALS AND VERBAL PHRASES

A **verbal** is a form of a verb used as a noun, an adjective, or an adverb. A **verbal phrase** consists of a verbal and its modifiers and complements.

Participles and Participial Phrases

6c. A *participle* is a verb form that is used as an adjective. A *participial phrase* consists of a participle and all the words related to the participle.

The two kinds of participles are the *present participle* and the *past participle.*

(1) **Present participles** end in *–ing.*

> Sir Gawain heard the Green Knight **sharpening his ax.** [The participial phrase modifies the noun *Green Knight.* The noun *ax* is the direct object of the present participle *sharpening.*]

(2) Most **past participles** end in *–d* or *–ed.* Others are irregularly formed.

> **Tormented by her guilt,** Lady Macbeth lost her sanity. [The participial phrase modifies the noun *Lady Macbeth.* The adverb phrase *by her guilt* modifies the past participle *tormented.*]

Gerunds and Gerund Phrases

6d. A *gerund* is a verb form ending in *-ing* that is used as a noun. A *gerund phrase* consists of a gerund and all the words related to the gerund.

> For Gulliver, **living in Brobdingnag** is quite different from **living in Lilliput.** [*Living in Brobdingnag* is the subject of the verb *is. Living in*

Lilliput is the object of the preposition *from*. The adverb phrases *in Brobdingnag* and *in Lilliput* modify the gerund *living*.]

The Miller enjoys **playing the bagpipes.** [*Playing the bagpipes* is the direct object of the verb *enjoy*. *Bagpipes* is the direct object of the gerund *playing*.]

Infinitives and Infinitive Phrases

6e. An *infinitive* is a verb form that can be used as a noun, an adjective, or an adverb. An infinitive usually begins with *to*. An *infinitive phrase* consists of an infinitive and all the words related to the infinitive.

The three rioters vow **to kill Death.** [The infinitive phrase acts as a noun and is the direct object of the verb *vow*. *Death* is the direct object of the infinitive *to kill*.]

She had a great desire **to visit Stratford-on-Avon.** [The infinitive phrase acts as an adjective and modifies the noun *desire*. *Stratford-on-Avon* is the direct object of the infinitive *to visit*.]

Macbeth goes to the witches' haunt **to talk to them.** [The infinitive phrase acts as an adverb and modifies the verb *goes*. The adverb phrase *to them* modifies the infinitive *to talk*.]

Lady Macbeth helps her husband **become king.** [The sign of the infinitive, *to,* is omitted. The infinitive has a subject, *husband,* making the entire construction an **infinitive clause.** The infinitive clause acts as a noun and is the direct object of the verb *helps*.]

APPOSITIVES AND APPOSITIVE PHRASES

6f. An *appositive* is a noun or a pronoun placed beside another noun or pronoun to identify or explain it. An *appositive phrase* consists of an appositive and its modifiers.

An appositive or appositive phrase usually follows the word it identifies or explains.

Have you read Coleridge's poem **"Kubla Khan"?** [The appositive *"Kubla Khan"* identifies the noun *poem*.]

Shakespeare was born in Stratford-on-Avon, **a market town about eighty miles from London.** [The entire appositive phrase *a market town about eighty miles from London* identifies the noun *Stratford-on-Avon*.]

For emphasis, however, an appositive or appositive phrase may precede the word that it explains or identifies.

A riot of colorful sights, intriguing aromas, and surprising noises, a Cairo bazaar is great fun to visit. [The appositive phrase explains why a Cairo bazaar is fun to visit.]

Your Turn

For each of the following items, use phrases to combine the short, choppy sentences into one smooth sentence.

1. King Arthur was a fabled Brython (ancient Briton) leader. He figures prominently in Britain's literary and legendary history.
2. The Arthurian legend was widely popular throughout Britain and elsewhere. It probably had its source in oral history.
3. The earliest literary reference to Arthur is found in Welsh poetry. He is mentioned briefly in several 6th century Welsh poems.
4. In the 12th century, Geoffrey of Monmouth wrote an account of Arthur's reign. It was the first narrative account.
5. Tennyson's poem about King Arthur was first published in the second half of the 19th century. It was called *Idylls of the King*.

7. Clauses

7a. A *clause* is a group of words that contains a verb and its subject and that is used as part of a sentence. There are two kinds of clauses: the *independent clause* and the *subordinate clause.*

THE INDEPENDENT CLAUSE

7b. An *independent* (or *main*) *clause* expresses a complete thought and can stand by itself as a sentence.

SUBJECT   VERB
William Shakespeare wrote more than 150 sonnets. [one independent clause]

THE SUBORDINATE CLAUSE

7c. A *subordinate* (or *dependent*) *clause* does not express a complete thought and cannot stand alone as a sentence.

SUBJECT VERB
that **Lord Byron swam** across the Hellespont

The thought expressed by a subordinate clause becomes complete when the clause is combined with an independent clause to create a complete sentence.

I read **that Lord Byron swam across the Hellespont.**

The Adjective Clause

7d. An *adjective clause* is a subordinate clause that modifies a noun or a pronoun.

An adjective clause always follows the word or words that it modifies. Usually, an adjective clause begins with a **relative pronoun** (such as *that, which, who, whom, whose*). A relative pronoun both relates an adjective clause to the word or words the clause modifies and performs a function within its own clause by serving as a subject, an object of a verb, an object of a preposition, or a modifier.

Mary Shelley, **who wrote** *Frankenstein,* liked reading ghost stories with her friends. [The relative pronoun *who* relates the adjective clause to the noun *Mary Shelley* and serves as the subject of the verb *wrote.*]

The knight **for whom Sir Gawain is searching** is the Knight of the Green Chapel. [The relative pronoun

whom relates the adjective clause to the noun *knight* and serves as the object of the preposition *for.*]

An adjective clause may begin with a **relative adverb,** such as *when* or *where.*

My uncle Robert told us about the time **when he backpacked across the island of Luzon.** [The adjective clause modifies the noun *time.*]

Malcolm flees to England, **where he raises an army to attack Macbeth.** [The adjective clause modifies the noun *England.*]

The Noun Clause

7e. A *noun clause* is a subordinate clause that may be used as a subject, a predicate nominative, a direct object, an indirect object, or an object of a preposition.

Words that are commonly used to introduce noun clauses include *how, that, what, whether, who, whoever,* and *why.*

That Fleance escapes the murderers troubles Macbeth. [subject]

Power is **what Macbeth** desires. [predicate nominative]

Banquo suspected **that Macbeth had murdered** Duncan. [direct object]

The teacher will give **whoever can recite the soliloquy** ten points. [indirect object]

The teacher will give ten points to **whoever can recite the soliloquy.** [object of a preposition]

The word that introduces a noun clause may or may not have another function in the clause.

The witches predict **that Macbeth will become king.** [The word *that* introduces the noun clause but does not have any function within the clause.]

The Adverb Clause

7f. An *adverb clause* is a subordinate clause that modifies a verb, an adjective, or an adverb.

An adverb clause, which may come before or after the word or words it modifies, tells *how, when, where, why, to what extent,* or *under what condition.* An adverb clause is introduced by a **subordinating conjunction**— a word or word group that relates the adverb clause to the word or words the clause modifies.

He acted **as though he had seen a ghost.** [The adverb clause modifies the verb *acted,* telling *how* he acted.]

Jane is taller **than her grandmother is.** [The adverb clause modifies the adverb *taller,* telling *to what extent* Jane is tall.]

They stayed longer **than they thought they would.** [The adverb clause modifies the adverb *longer,* telling *to what extent* their stay was lnger.]

The Elliptical Clause

7g. Part of a clause may be left out when the meaning can be understood from the context of the sentence. Such a clause is called an *elliptical clause.*

While [he was] **painting,** Rembrandt concentrated completely on his work.

Ken may ride with us **if he wants to** [ride with us].

This job took longer **than the last one.** [took]

Your Turn

In most cases, the decision of where to place an adverb clause is a matter of style, not correctness. Each of the following sentences contains an adverb clause. Decide whether each clause is placed where it reads best in context. If the adverb clause it could be better placed, revise the sentence.

1. When he was just ten years old, George Gordon Byron assumed the barony in 1798.
2. George Gordon Byron, who was better known as Lord Byron, began writing *Don Juan* in 1818.
3. Byron would be remembered as a great poet even if he had not written *Don Juan.*
4. Byron traveled throughout southern Europe with a friend after he left Cambridge.
5. Byron, while he traveled in Greece, continued to work on his autobiographical poem, *Childe Harold.*

8. Sentence Structure

SENTENCE OR FRAGMENT?

8a. A *sentence* is a group of words that has a subject and a verb and expresses a complete thought.

"My Last Duchess" is an example of a dramatic monologue.

For how many years was Winston Churchill the prime minister of Britain?

What an ambitious man Macbeth was!

Only a sentence should begin with a capital letter and end with a period, a question mark, or an exclamation point. Do not be misled by a group of words that looks like a sentence but that either does not have a subject and a verb or does not express a complete thought. Such a word group is called a **sentence fragment.**

FRAGMENT	Awakens and finds himself surrounded by people six inches tall.
SENTENCE	Gulliver awakens and finds himself surrounded by people six inches tall.

SUBJECT AND PREDICATE

8b. A sentence consists of two parts: a subject and a predicate. A *subject* tells *whom* or *what* the sentence is about. A *predicate* tells something about the subject.

In the following examples, all the words labeled *subject* make up the **complete subject,** and all the words labeled *predicate* make up the **complete predicate.**

SUBJECT	PREDICATE
My sister and I	enjoyed *Gulliver's Travels.*

PREDICATE	SUBJECT	PREDICATE
For fifty years	Beowulf	ruled Geatland.

The Simple Subject

8c. A *simple subject* is the main word or group of word that tells *whom* or *what* the sentence is about.

The first **leader** of the Wormsley Common gang was Blackie. [The complete subject is *the first leader of the Wormsley Common gang.*]

The Simple Predicate

8d. A *simple predicate* is a verb or verb phrase that tells something about the subject.

> **Have** you **read** "The Seafarer? [The complete predicate is *have read "The Seafarer."*]

The Compound Subject and the Compound Verb

8e. A *compound subject* consists of two or more subjects that are joined by a conjunction—usually *and* or *or*—and that have the same verb.

> A **nun** and three **priests** accompany the Prioress on the Canterbury pilgrimage.

8f. A *compound verb* consists of two or more verbs that are joined by a conjunction—usually *and, but,* or *or*—and that have the same subject.

> Truth **enlightens** the mind, **frees** the spirit, and **strengthens** the soul.

How to Find the Subject of a Sentence

8g. To find the subject of a sentence, ask *Who?* or *What?* before the verb.

(1) The subject of a sentence is never within a prepositional phrase.

> A **group** of pilgrims gathered at the Tabard. [Who gathered? Group gathered. *Pilgrims* is the object of the preposition *of.*]

> Out of the stillness came the loud **sound** of laughter. [What came? Sound came. *Stillness* is the object of the preposition *out of. Laughter* is the object of the preposition *of.*]

(2) The subject of a sentence expressing a command or a request is always understood to be *you*, although *you* may not appear in the sentence.

> COMMAND — Name the pilgrim accompanying the Plowman. [Who is being told to name? *You* is understood.]

The subject of a command or a request is you even when a sentence contains a **noun of direct address**—a word that names or identifies the one or ones spoken to.

> REQUEST — Maria, [**you**] please read the first stanza of "To a Skylark."

(3) The subject of a sentence expressing a question usually follows the verb or a part of the verb phrase. Turning the question into a statement will often help you find the subject.

> QUESTION — Have you read Lord Byron's poem "She Walks in Beauty"?

> STATEMENT — **You** have read Lord Byron's poem "She Walks in Beauty." [Who has read? You have read.]

> QUESTION — Were Shakespeare's plays popular during his own lifetime?

> STATEMENT — Shakespeare's **plays** were popular during his own lifetime. [What were popular? Plays were popular.]

(4) The word *there* or *here* is never the subject of a sentence.

> There is **Canterbury Cathedral**. [What is there? Canterbury Cathedral is there.]

COMPLEMENTS

8h. A *complement* is a word or a group of words that completes the meaning of a verb or a verbal. The four main kinds of complements are *direct object, indirect object, objective complement,* and *subject complement.*

The Direct Object and the Indirect Object

8i. A *direct object* is a noun, pronoun, or a word group that functions as a noun and tells *who* or *what* receives the action of a transitive verb.

> Banquo definitely suspected **him.** [Suspected whom? him]

> Beethoven's composed **sonatas** and **symphonies.** [Composed what? sonatas and symphonies]

8j. An *indirect object* is a word or word group that comes between a transitive verb and a direct object, An indirect object, which may be a noun, a pronoun, or a word group that functions as a noun, tells *to whom, to what, for whom,* or *for what* the action of the verb is done.

> The Wife of Bath told the other **pilgrims** an interesting story. [Told to whom? pilgrims]

> We should give **practicing for the concert** our full attention. [Should give our full attention to what? practicing for the concert]

The Objective Complement

8k. An *objective complement* is a word or word group that helps complete the meaning of a transitive verb by identifying or modifying the direct object. An objective complement, which may be a noun, a pronoun, an adjective, or a word group that functions as a noun or adjective, almost always follows the direct object.

> Macduff called Malcolm **king**. [The noun *king* identifies the direct object *Malcolm*.]
>
> He believed the money **his**. [The pronoun *his* modifies the direct object *money*.]
>
> Everyone considered him **chivalrous**. [The adjective *chivalrous* modifies the direct object *him*.]

A *transitive verb* is an action verb that takes an object, which tells who or what receives the action.

The Subject Complement

8l. A *subject complement* is a word or word group that completes the meaning of a linking verb or a verbal and that identifies or modifies the subject. The two kinds of subject complements are *predicate nominatives* and *predicate adjectives*.

(1) A ***predicate nominative*** is the word or group of words that follows a linking verb and refers to the same person, place, thing, or idea as the subject of the verb. A predicate nominative may be a noun, a pronoun, or a word group that functions as a noun.

> Of these three poets, Wordsworth was the most inspired **one**. [The pronoun *one* refers to the subject *Wordsworth*.]
>
> The main characters are **Paul** and his **mother**. [The two nouns *Paul* and *mother* are a compound predicate nominative that refers to the subject *characters*.]

(2) A ***predicate adjective*** is an adjective that follows a linking verb and modifies the subject of the verb.

> Did King Hrothgar feel **powerless**? [The adjective *powerless* modifies the subject *King Hrothgar*.]
>
> Iago is **sly** and **scheming**. [The two adjectives *sly* and *scheming* are a compound predicate adjective that modifies the subject *Iago*.]

SENTENCES CLASSIFIED ACCORDING TO STRUCTURE

8m. According to structure, sentences are classified as *simple*, *compound*, *complex*, or *compound-complex*.

(1) A ***simple sentence*** has one independent clause and no subordinate clauses.

> "Not Waving but Drowning" is one of my favorite poems.

(2) A ***compound sentence*** has two or more independent clauses but no subordinate clauses.

> Othello is a great man, but his character is flawed.
>
> Agatha Christie was a prolific writer; she wrote more than eighty books in less than sixty years.

(3) A ***complex sentence*** has one independent clause and at least one subordinate clause.

> The poet who wrote "Ode on a Grecian Urn" is John Keats. [The independent clause is *the poet is John Keats*. The subordinate clause is *who wrote "Ode on a Grecian Urn."*]

(4) A ***compound-complex sentence*** contains two or more independent clauses and at least one subordinate clause.

> After Macbeth killed their father, Malcolm fled to England, and Donalbain escaped to Ireland. [The two independent clauses are *Malcolm fled to England* and *Donalbain escaped to Ireland*. The subordinate clause is *after Macbeth killed their father*.]

SENTENCES CLASSIFIED ACCORDING TO PURPOSE

8n. According to their purpose, sentences are classified as *declarative*, *interrogative*, *imperative*, and *exclamatory*.

(1) A ***declarative sentence*** makes a statement. It is followed by a period.

> The lock on the front door is broken**.**

(2) An ***interrogative sentence*** asks a question. It is followed by a question mark.

> Have you read Dylan Thomas's "Fern Hill"**?**

(3) An *imperative sentence* makes a request or gives a command. It is usually followed by a period. A very strong command, however, is followed by an exclamation point.

Please return this book to the library.

Give me the name of the warrior who succeeds Beowulf.

Stop making that noise!

(4) An *exclamatory sentence* expresses strong feeling or shows excitement. It is followed by an exclamation point.

What a talented writer she was!

We won!

Your Turn

Read each of the following items that contain short sentences. Decide what type of sentence structure (simple, compound, complex, compound-complex) would best express the ideas in each item. Then, rewrite each item.

1. William Shakespeare was born in 1564. His birthplace was Stratford, a town in central England.
2. The famous dramatist and poet prospered financially. He was able to buy the largest house in Stratford.
3. Lord Byron was a major poet of the Romantic Period. Byron's friend Percy Bysshe Shelley was also a major poet of the period.
4. Wordsworth said we perceive the world around us. He also argued that we in part create it.
5. The Romantics asserted the importance of the individual. They also emphasized the imagination.

9. Sentence Style

WAYS TO ACHIEVE CLARITY
Coordinating Ideas

9a. To *coordinate* two or more ideas, or to give them equal emphasis, link them with a connecting word, an appropriate mark of punctuation, or both.

I read the novel *Frankenstein*, **and** then I saw the film.

Subordinating Ideas

9b. To *subordinate* an idea, or to show that one idea is related to but less important than another, use an adverb clause or an adjective clause.

Sir Gawain accepts the magic sash **because he wants it to protect him from the Green Knight.** [adverb clause]

Hrunting is the name of the sword **that Unferth gives Beowulf.** [adjective clause]

Using Parallel Structure

9c. Use the same grammatical form (*parallel structure*) to express ideas of equal weight.

(1) Use parallel structure when you link coordinate ideas.

In the winter I usually like **to ski** and **to skate.** [infinitive paired with infinitive]

(2) Use parallel structure when you compare or contrast ideas.

Einstein liked mathematical **research** more than laboratory **supervision.** [noun contrasted with noun]

(3) Use parallel structure when you link ideas with correlative conjunctions (such as *both . . . and, either . . . or, neither . . . nor,* or *not only . . . but also*).

Virginia Woolf was not only **a novelist** but also **an essayist.** [Note that the correlative conjunctions come directly before the parallel terms.]

When you revise for parallel structure, you may need to add an article, a preposition, or a pronoun before each of the parallel terms.

UNCLEAR	I admire the poems of Byron more than Wordsworth.
CLEAR	I admire the poems of Byron more than **those of** Wordsworth.

OBSTACLES TO CLARIFY
Sentence Fragments

9d. Avoid using a *sentence fragment*—a word or word group that either does not contain a subject and a verb or does not express a complete thought.

Here are two common ways to correct a sentence fragment.

1. Add words to make the thought complete.

FRAGEMENT	Twelve Geats around Beowulf's tower. [The verb is missing.]
SENTENCE	Twelve Geats **rode** around Beowulf's tower.

2. Attach the fragment to the sentence that comes before or after it.

FRAGEMENT	A doctor and a gentlewoman see Lady Macbeth. Walking in her sleep. [participial phrase]
SENTENCE	A doctor and a gentlewoman see Lady Macbeth **walking in her sleep.**

Sentence fragments can be effective when used in expressive and creative writing and in informal writing.

Run-On Sentences

9e. Avoid using a *run-on sentence*—two or more complete thoughts that run together as if they were one complete thought.

The two kinds of run-on sentences are *fused sentences* and *comma splices*. A **fused sentence** has no punctuation or connecting word at all between the complete thoughts. A **comma splice** has just a comma between the complete thoughts.

FUSED SENTENCE	Wiglaf helps Beowulf the other warriors retreat in fear.
COMMA SPLICE	Wiglaf helps Beowulf, the other warriors retreat in fear.

You can correct run-on sentences in several ways.

1. Make two sentences.

Wiglaf helps Beowulf. **T**he other warriors retreat in fear.

2. Use a comma and a coordinating conjunction.

Wiglaf helps Beowulf, **but** the other warriors retreat in fear.

3. Change one of the independent clauses to a subordinate clause.

Wiglaf helps Beowulf, **while the other warriors retreat in fear.**

4. Use a semicolon.

Wiglaf helps Beowulf; the other warriors retreat in fear.

5. Use a semicolon and a conjunctive adverb.

Wiglaf helps Beowulf; **however,** the other warriors retreat in fear.

Unnecessary Shifts in Sentences

9f. Avoid making unnecessary shifts in subject, in verb tense, and in voice.

AWKWARD	Grandma goes to the farmers' market, where the freshest produce is. [shift in subject]
BETTER	**Grandma** goes to the farmers' market, where **she** finds the freshest produce.
AWKWARD	Macbeth sees Banquo's ghost, but no one else did. [shift in tense]
BETTER	Macbeth **sees** Banquo's ghost, but no one else **does**.
AWKWARD	Lyle spent four hours at the library, but no books on his research topic were found. [shift in voice]
BETTER	Lyle **spent** four hours at the library, but he **found** no books on his topic.

REVISING FOR VARIETY

9g. Use a variety of sentence beginnings.

Putting the subject first in a declarative sentence is not wrong, but starting every sentence with the subject can make your writing boring. To add variety to your sentences, rearrange sentence parts to vary the beginnings. The following examples show how a writer can revise sentences to avoid beginning with the subject every time.

SUBJECT FIRST	Lady Macbeth is cunning and ruthless and goads her husband into committing murder.
SINGLE-WORD MODIFIERS FIRST	**Cunning** and **ruthless,** Lady Macbeth goads her husband into committing murder.
SUBJECT FIRST	*In Memoriam,* **which was published in 1850,** is Alfred, Lord Tennyson's elegy for his friend Arthur Hallam.
PARTICIPIAL PHRASE FIRST	**Published in 1850,** *In Memoriam* is Alfred, Lord Tennyson's elegy for his friend Arthur Hallam.
APPOSITIVE PHRASE FIRST	**An elegy for Alfred, Lord Tennyson's friend Arthur Hallam,** *In Memoriam* was published in 1850.

Varying Sentence Structure

9h. Use a mix of simple, compound, complex, and compound-complex sentences in your writing.

The three "weird sisters" greet Macbeth and Banquo with prophecies. [simple] According to the witches, Macbeth will become king, but Banquo will not, though his descendants will. [compound-complex] When Macbeth asks the witches to tell him more, they vanish. [complex] The subsequent conversation between Banquo and Macbeth lends insight into each man's character. [simple] That is, Banquo is skeptical of the witches' prophecies; however, Macbeth believes in them. [compound]

Revising to Reduce Wordiness

9i. Avoid using unnecessary words in your writing.

The following guidelines suggest some ways to revise wordy sentences.

1. Take out a whole group of unnecessary words.

| WORDY | Grendel's mother carried Beowulf to her home where she lived. |
| BETTER | Grendel's mother carried Beowulf to her home. |

2. Replace pretentious words and expressions with straightforward ones.

| WORDY | In *Lord of the Flies,* a group of males, all of whom are under thirteen years of age, is stranded on a land mass surrounded by water and totally free of inhabitants. |
| BETTER | In *Lord of the Flies,* a group of **young boys** is stranded on an **uninhabited island.** |

3. Reduce a clause to a phrase.

| WORDY | Sir Lancelot falls in love with Queen Guinevere, who is the wife of King Arthur. |
| BETTER | Sir Lancelot falls in love with Queen Guinevere, **King Arthur's wife.** |

4. Reduce a phrase or a clause to one word.

| WORDY | At that point in time, Mr. Thomas returns. |
| BETTER | **Then,** Mr. Thomas returns. |

Your Turn

Revise the following sentences by varying sentence beginnings and sentence structure and by eliminating wordiness.

1. A mariner stopped three young men who were on their way to a wedding; the mariner was grizzled and old with a glittering eye.
2. The ancient mariner grabbed the young man's arm with his bony hand and insisted on telling him a story.
3. The mariner's ship was caught in a powerful storm, the old man said, and was driven in a southward direction into a desolate land of ice and sounds that were fearful.
4. The situation seemed hopeless and bleak because they were trapped in barren place that they could not escape, and then a great seabird, an albatross, came through the hazy fog and broke the terrible spell.
5. The great bird was shot with a cross-bow by the ancient mariner bringing doom upon the hapless ship and all its crew who manned the ship; his reasons were unclear.

10. Sentence Combining

COMBINING BY INSERTING WORDS AND PHRASES

10a. Combine related sentences by taking a key word (or using another form of the key word) from one sentence and inserting it into another.

> ORIGINAL   The famous magician Harry Houdini performed impossible escapes. The escapes only seemed impossible.
>
> COMBINED   The famous magician Harry Houdini performed **seemingly** impossible escapes. [The verb *seemed* becomes the adverb *seemingly*.]

10b. Combine related sentences by taking (or creating) a phrase from one sentence and inserting it into another.

> ORIGINAL   Has your class read the poem "The Hollow Men"? It was written by T. S. Eliot.
>
> COMBINED   Has your class read the poem "The Hollow Men" **by T. S. Eliot**? [prepositional phrase]

COMBINING BY COORDINATING IDEAS

10c. Combine related sentences whose ideas are equally important by using coordinating conjunctions (*and, but, or nor, for, so, yet*) or correlative conjunctions (*both . . . and, either . . . or, neither . . . nor, not only . . . but also*).

The relationship of the ideas determines which connective will work best. When joined, the coordinate ideas form compound elements.

> ORIGINAL   *Paradise Lost* was written by John Milton. *Paradise Regained* was also written by him.
>
> COMBINED   *Paradise Lost* **and** *Paradise Regained* were written by John Milton. [compound subject]

> ORIGINAL   *Adonais* is one of Shelley's best-known poems. Many critics think that *Prometheus Unbound* is his true masterpiece.
>
> COMBINED   *Adonais* is one of Shelley's best-known poems, **but** many critics think that *Prometheus Unbound* is his true masterpiece. [compound sentence]

Another way to form a compound sentence is to link independent clauses with a semicolon or with a semicolon and a conjunctive adverb (such as *however, likewise,* or *therefore*) followed by a comma.

> Kathleen was willing to compromise**;** Jean Paul was not.

> The McCambridge family moved to Northampton shire**; however,** they stayed there only a few months before returning to Rutland.

COMBINING BY SUBORDINATING IDEAS

10d. Combine related sentences whose ideas are not equally important by placing the less important idea in a subordinate clause (adjective clause, adverb clause, or noun clause).

> ORIGINAL   My friend and I read about the life of Queen Victoria. She ruled Great Britain from 1837 to 1901.
>
> COMBINED   My friend and I read about the life of Queen Victoria, **who ruled Great Britain from 1837 to 1901**. [adjective clause]
>
> *or*
>
> COMBINED   Queen Victoria, **whose life my friend and I read about**, ruled Great Britain from 1837 to 1901. [adjective clause]

ORIGINAL	Grendel's mother attacks Herot. King Hrothgar once again asks Beowulf for his help.
COMBINED	**When Grendel's mother attacks Herot,** King Hrothgar once again asks Beowulf for his help. [adverb clause]
ORIGINAL	They will find Death under an oak tree. An old man tells the three rioters that this will happen.
COMBINED	An old man tells the three rioters **that they will find Death under an oak tree.** [noun clause]

Your Turn

Combine each pair of related sentences by inserting words or phrases, coordinating ideas, or subordinating ideas.

1. The popularity of the legendary hero Arthur waned during the Middle Ages. It experienced a revival during the 19th century.
2. The Romantics created their own literary types. Among the types created by the Romantics was the hero-artist, or poetic speaker.
3. Have you read the poems "When I Have Fears" and "Ode to a Nightingale"? They were written by John Keats.
4. The young man demanded that the ancient mariner let go of him. The old seafarer dropped his hold.
5. The young man could not get away. He was trapped by the old man's glittering stare.

11. Capitalization

11a. Capitalize the first word in every sentence.

The warrior who succeeds Beowulf as king is Wiglaf.

(1) Capitalize the first word of a sentence following a colon.

Mrs. Kelley asked me this question: **H**ow old is Beowulf when he fights Grendel?

(2) Capitalize the first word of a direct quotation.

After winning, Brian said, "**W**e couldn't have done it without the support of the good people of Raleigh."

When quoting from another writer's work, capitalize the first word of the quotation only if the writer has capitalized it in the original work.

After winning, Brian acknowledged "the support of the good people of Raleigh."

(3) Traditionally, the first word of a line of poetry is capitalized.

If all the world and love were young,
And truth in every shepherd's tongue,
These pretty pleasures might me move
To live with thee and be thy love.
— Sir Walter Raleigh, "The Nymph's
Reply to the Shepherd"

You will notice that some writers do not follow this rule. Whenever you quote from a writer's work, always use capital letters exactly as the writer uses them.

11b. Capitalize the first word in the salutation and the closing of a letter.

Dear John,   **D**ear Sir or Madam: **S**incerely,

11c. Capitalize proper nouns and proper adjectives.

A **common noun** is a general name for a person, a place, a thing, or an idea. A **proper noun** names a particular person, place, thing, or idea. A **_proper adjective_** is formed from a proper noun. Common nouns are capitalized only if they begin a sentence (also, in most cases, a line of poetry), begin a direct quotation, or are part of a title.

Common Nouns	Proper Nouns	Proper Adjectives
dramatist	Shakespeare	Shakespearean performer
country	Russia	Russia diplomat
mountains	the Alps	Alpine flora

In most proper nouns made up of two or more words, do not capitalize articles (*a, an, the*), short prepositions (those with fewer than five letters, such as *at, of, for, to, with*), the mark of the infinitive (*to*), and coordinating conjunctions (*and, but, for, nor, or, so, yet*).

Speaker of the House of Representatives

American Society for the Prevention of Cruelty to Animals

When you're not sure whether to capitalize a word, check a dictionary.

(1) Capitalize the names of most persons and animals.

GIVEN NAMES	Virginia	Geoffrey
SURNAMES	Woolf	Chaucer
ANIMALS	Lassie	Rocinante

Some names contain more than one capital letter. Usage varies in the capitalization of *van, von, du, de la,* and other parts of many multiword names. Always verify the spelling of a name with the person, or check the name in a reference source.

La Fontaine   O'Connor   al-Khansa   McEwen

Van Doren   Ibn Ezra   van Gogh   de Vega

(2) Capitalize the names of nationalities, races, and peoples.

Japanese   Caucasian   Hispanic   Celt

(3) Capitalize brand names. Notice that the noun that follows a brand name is not capitalized.

Sealtest milk   Wonder bread   Crest toothpaste

(4) Capitalize geographical names.

Type of Name	Examples
Towns, Cities	Stratford-on-Avon, Dublin, Rio de Janeiro, South Bend
Counties, Townships	Marion County, Alexandria Township, Brooklyn Borough, Lafayette Parish
States, Territories	Oklahoma, North Carolina, Yucatán, Yukon Territory
Regions	the Middle East, the Lake District Western Hemisphere, the Southwest
Countries	England, Costa Rica
Continents	South America, Europe
Islands	Long Island, British Isles
Mountains	Himalayas, Mount Rainier Pikes Peak, Sierra Nevada
Other Landforms and Features	Cape of Good Hope, Black Forest Death Valley, Isthmus of Corinth
Bodies of Water	Indian Ocean, Red Sea Bering Strait, San Francisco Bay
Parks	Hawaii Volcanoes National Park, Point Reyes National Seashore
Roads, Highways, Streets	Route 42, King Avenue, Interstate 75, Thirty-fourth Street

Words such as *city, state,* and *county* are often capitalized in official documents such as proclamations. In general usage, however, these words are not capitalized.

OFFICIAL USAGE	the State of Iowa
GENERAL USAGE	the state of Iowa

Words such as *north, western,* and *southeast* are not capitalized when they indicate direction.

north of London

heading southwest

The second word in a hyphenated number begins with a lowercase letter.

Forty-second Street

(5) Capitalize the names of organizations, teams, business firms, institutions, buildings and other structures, and government bodies.

Type of Name	Examples
Organizations	Disabled American Veterans, Professional Photographers of America
Teams	River City Eastside Bombers, Harlem Globetrotters
Business Firms	Aaron's Carpets, National Broadcasting Corporation
Institutions	Oxford University, Southern Christian Leadership Conference
Buildings and Other Structures	Lincoln Center for the Performing Arts, the Great Wall of China
Government Bodies	United States Congress, House of Commons

Do not capitalize words such as *democratic, republican,* and *socialist* when they refer to principles or forms of government. Capitalize such words only when they refer to specific political parties.

The citizens demanded **d**emocratic reforms.

Who will be the **R**epublican nominee for governor?

Do not capitalize words such as *building, hospital, theater, high school,* and *post office* unless they are part of a proper noun.

(6) Capitalize the names of historical events and periods, special events, holidays and other calendar items, and time zones.

Type of Name	Examples
Historical Events and Periods	Middle Ages, Reign of Terror
Special Events	Super Bowl, Pan-American Games
Holidays and Other Calendar Items	Monday, Memorial Day, November, National Book Week
Time Zones	Eastern Daylight Time (EDT), Central Mountain Time (CMT)

Do not capitalize the name of a season unless it is being personified or used as part of a proper noun.

We moved here last **f**all.

This month **F**all begins painting the leaves in brilliant hues.

The **F**all Festival is next week.

(7) Capitalize the names of ships, trains, aircraft, spacecraft, monuments, awards, planets and other heavenly bodies, and any other particular places and things.

Type of Name	Examples
Ships	*Merrimac,* **U.S.S.** *Nautilus*
Trains	*Zephyr, Hill Country Flyer*
Aircraft	*Enola Gay, Spruce Goose*
Spacecraft	*Columbia, Magellan*
Monuments	**Mount** Rushmore, **National Monument, Effigy Mounds National Monument**
Awards	**Nobel** Prizem, **Medal of Freedom**
Planets and Other Heavenly Bodies	**Neptune, Polaris, Big Dipper, Cassiopeia**
Other Particular Places and Things	Hurricane Alma, Silk Route Marshall Plan, Union Jack

Do not capitalize the words *sun* and *moon.* Do not capitalize the word *earth* unless it is used along with the proper names of other places, things, or events.

11d. Do not capitalize the names of school subjects, except names of languages and course names followed by a number.

French   art   Algebra **I**

11e. Capitalize titles.

(1) Capitalize a title belonging to a particular person when it comes before the person's name.

General Patton   Dr. Sanchez   President Lincoln

In general, do not capitalize a title used alone or following a name. Some titles, however, are by tradition capitalized. If you are unsure about capitalizing a title, check in a dictionary.

Who is the **p**rime **m**inister of **B**ritain?

When was Ann Richards **g**overnor of Texas?

The **P**rince of **W**ales vistited our school.

A title is usually capitalized when it is used alone in direct address.

Good afternoon, **S**ir [*or* **s**ir], may I help you?

(2) Capitalize a word showing a family relationship when the word is used before or in place of a person's name, unless a possessive comes before the word.

I asked **M**om if **U**ncle Bob is named after her **u**ncle Roberto.

(3) Capitalize the first and last words and all important words in titles of books, periodicals, poems, stories, essays, speeches, plays, historical documents, movies, radio and television programs, works of art, musical compositions, and cartoons.

NOTE Unimportant words in a title include articles (*a, an, the*), short prepositions (those with fewer than five letters, such as *of, to, in, for, from, with*), and coordinating conjunctions (*and, but, for, nor, or, so, yet*).

Type of Name	Examples
Books	*A Tale of Two Cities, Gulliver's Travels*
Periodicals	*National Geography, Time*
Poems	"**S**he **W**alks in **B**eauty," "**T**o **H**is **C**oy **M**istress"
Stories	"**T**he **R**ocking-**H**orse **W**inner," "**G**ames at **T**wilight"
Essays and Speeches	"**A** **M**odest **P**roposal," the **G**ettysburg **A**ddress
Plays	*The Tragedy of Macbeth, Pygmalion*
Historical Documents	**M**agna **C**arta, **T**reaty of **V**ersailles
Movies	*Lawrence of Arabia, Clueless*
Radio and TV Programs	*The World, Nova*
Works of Art	*The Kiss, March of Humanity*
Musical Compositions	*War Requiem*, "**T**ears in **H**eaven"
Cartoons or Comic Strips	*For Better or Worse, Jump Start*

11f. Capitalize the names of religions and their followers, holy days and celebrations, holy writings, and specific deities and venerated beings.

Type of Name	Examples
Religions and Followers	**C**hristianity, **B**uddhist, **M**uslim, **J**udaism
Holy Days and Celebrations	**E**aster, **R**amadan, **P**assover, **H**oly **W**eek
Holy Writings	**B**ible, **K**oran, **T**almud, **I** **C**hing
Specific Deities and Venerated Beings	**A**llah, **G**od, **D**alai **L**ama, **J**ehovah

The words *god* and *goddess* are not capitalized when they refer to mythological deities. The names of specific mythological deities are capitalized, however.

The Greek **g**od of the sea was **P**oseidon.

Your Turn

Have students correct the errors in capitalization in the following letter.
  [1] october 11
  [2] dear laura,
  [3] thank you so much for the illustrated edition of alfred, lord tennyson's *best loved poems.*
  [4] please also send a copy of the Book to our President, mr. jeffrey sampras, at 235 east seventy-third street, new york, ny 10021.
  [5] sincerely yours,

12. Punctuation

END MARKS

12a. A statement (or declarative sentence) is followed by a period.

> The Ancient Mariner told an amazing tale.

12b. A question (or interrogative sentence) is followed by a question mark.

> Do you know who played the leading role in the first movie version of *Hamlet***?**

12c. A request or command (or imperative sentence) is followed by either a period or an exclamation point.

> Turn the music down, please. [request]

> Name the poet who wrote "The Lady of Shalott." [mild command]

> Watch out**!** [strong command]

12d. An exclamation (or exclamatory sentence) is followed by an exclamation point.

> What an interesting story, "My Oedipus Complex" is**!**

12e. An abbreviation is usually followed by a period.

If an abbreviation with a period ends a sentence, do not add another period. However, do add a question mark or an exclamation point if one is needed.

> The store opens at 10 A.M.

> Does the store open at 10 A.M.**?**

Some abbreviations, including those for most units of measure, are written without periods.

> AM/FM, CIA, CNN, PC, NASA, SOS

> cc, ft, lb, kw, ml, psi, rpm [*but* in. *for* inch]

Type of Abbreviation	Examples
Personal Names	Howard G. Chua-Eoan W. H. Auden
Organizations, Companies	Co. Inc. Ltd.
Titles Used with Names	Ms. Sr. Dr.
Times of Day	A.M. (*or* a.m.), P.M. (*or* p.m.)

Years	B.C. (*written after the date*)
	A.D. (*written before the date*)
Addresses	St. Blvd. P.O. Box
States	S.C. Calif.

Use a two-letter state code when the ZIP Code is included. Two-letter state codes are not followed by periods, and no comma is placed between the state code and the ZIP Code.

> Lexington, **KY** 40505

COMMAS

12f. Use commas to separate items in a series.

> Virginia Woolf**,** James Joyce**,** and D. H. Lawrence are among the writers we are studying.

If all the items in a series are linked by *and, or,* or *nor,* do not use commas to separate them.

> Byron **and** Shelley **and** Keats were contemporaries.

12g. Use a comma to separate two or more adjectives preceding a noun.

> Gawain is the most gallant**,** honorable knight.

When the last adjective before a noun is thought of as part of the noun, the comma before the it is omitted.

> I've finally found a decent, affordable used car. [*Used car* is thought of as one unit.]

12h. Use a comma before *and, but, or, nor, for, so,* and *yet* when they join independent clauses.

> I read Seamus Heaney's "The Grauballe Man," and now I want to read more of his poems.

You may omit the comma before *and, but, or,* or *nor* if the clauses are very short and there is no chance of misunderstanding.

12i. Use commas to set off nonessential clauses and nonessential participial phrases.

A *nonessential* clause or phrase is one that can be left out without changing the meaning of the sentence.

> NONESSENTIAL CLAUSE
> W. H. Auden, **who was born in York, England,** became an American citizen in 1946.

NONESSENTIAL PHRASE	The little blue sports car, **leaving all the others far behind,** forged into the lead.

An ***essential*** clause or phrase is one that cannot be left out without changing the meaning of the sentence. Essential clauses and phrases are *not* set off by commas.

ESSENTIAL CLAUSE	The writer **who received the Nobel Prize in literature in 1923** was William Butler Yeats.
ESSENTIAL PHRASE	The pilgrims **riding along with the Knight** are the Squire and the Yeoman.

12j. Use a comma after certain introductory elements.

(1) Use a comma after a one-word such as *first, next, yes,* or *no* and after any mild exclamation such as *well* or *why* at the beginning of a sentence.

Yes, I have read *Don Juan.*

(2) Use a comma after an introductory participial phrase.

Looking calm, Jill walked to the podium.

(3) Use a comma after two or more introductory prepositional phrases or after a single long one.

With the help of Wiglaf, he killed the dragon.

(4) Use a comma after an introductory adverb clause.

After I had locked the car door, I remembered that the keys were still in the ignition.

12k. Use commas to set off elements that interrupt a sentence.

(1) Appositives and appositive phrases are usually set off by commas.

George Bernard Shaw's first play, ***Widowers' Houses,*** was published in 1893.

Is that she, **the one holding the sunflowers**?

Sometimes an appositive is so closely related to the word or words near it that it should not be set off by commas. Such an appositive is called a ***restrictive appositive.***

The poet **Edmund Spenser** died suddenly in 1599.

(2) Words used in direct address are set off by commas.

Your research paper, **Dylan,** is quite interesting.

(3) Parenthetical expressions are set off by commas.

Parenthetical expressions are remarks that add incidental information or that relate ideas to each other. Some common parenthetical expressions are *for example, I think, moreover,* and *on the other hand.*

Macbeth is superstitious and sensitive; Lady Macbeth, **on the other hand,** is logical and bold.

A contrasting expression introduced by *not, rather than,* or a similar term is parenthetical. Set it off by commas.

Percy Bysshe Shelley, **not John Keats,** wrote "Ode to the West Wind."

12l. Use a comma in certain conventional situations.

(1) Use a comma to separate items in dates and addresses.

On April, 1994, William Shakespeare died.

My grandparents' address is 505 King Street, Austin, TX 78701.

(2) Use a comma after the salutation of a personal letter and after the closing of any letter.

Dear Alicia,   Yours truly,

(3) Use a comma to set off an abbreviation such as *Jr., Sr., RN, M.D., Ltd.,* or *Inc.*

Is Jorge Rivera, Jr., in your class?

She is the owner of Flowers by Arthurine, Inc.

SEMICOLONS

12m. Use a semicolon between independent clauses that are closely related in thought and are not joined by *and, but, for, nor, or, so,* or *yet.*

The rain had finally stopped; a few rays of sunshine were pushing through breaks in the clouds.

12n. Use a semicolon between independent clauses joined by a conjunctive adverb or a transitional expression.

A ***conjunctive adverb***—such as *furthermore, however,* or *nevertheless*—or a ***transitional expression***—such as *for instance, in fact,* or *that is*—indicates the relationship of the independent clauses that it joins.

The snow made traveling difficult; **nevertheless,** we arrived home safely.

12o. Use a semicolon (rather than a comma) before a coordinating conjunction to join independent clauses that contain commas.

> During the seventeenth century—the era of such distinguished prose writers as Sir Thomas Browne, John Donne, and Jeremy Taylor—the balanced compound sentence using commas and semicolons reached a high degree of perfection and popularity; but the tendency today is to use a fast-moving style with shorter sentences, fewer commas, and fewer semicolons. [commas within the clauses]

12p. Use a semicolon between items in a series if the items contain commas.

> The summer reading list includes *Jude the Obscure*, by Thomas Hardy; *Lord Jim*, by Joseph Conrad; and *Lord of Flies*, by William Golding.

COLONS

12q. Use a colon to mean "note what follows."

(1) Use a colon before a list of items, especially after expressions such as *follows* and *the following*.

> That collection includes poems by the following authors: Robert Burns, William Blake, William Wordsworth, and Samuel Taylor Coleridge.

Do not use a colon before a list that directly follows a verb or a preposition.

> Collection 8 includes poems by Robert Burns, William Blake, William Wordsworth, and Samuel Taylor Coleridge. [The list directly follows the preposition *by*.]

(2) Use a colon before a quotation that lacks a speaker tag such as *he said* or *she remarked*.

> His father's response surprised him: "I'm proud of you, son."

(3) Use a colon before a long, formal statement or quotation.

> When he awoke, Gulliver found himself tied down: "I could only look upward; the sun began to grow hot, and the light offended my eyes. I heard a confused noise about me, but in the posture I lay, could see nothing except the sky."

12r. Use a colon in certain conventional situations.

12:01 P.M. [between the hour and the minute]

Mark 3:10 [between chapter and verse in referring to passages from the Bible]

To Whom It May Concern: [after the salutation of a business letter]

"A Valediction: Forbidding Mourning" [between a title and a subtitle]

Your Turn

Correct the following sentences by adding or deleting punctuation as needed.

1. George Gordon Byron, was born on January, 22, 1788, in London, England; and died on April, 19, 1824, in Missoloughi, Greece.
2. Lord Bryan's major works include: *Childe Harold's Pilgrimage*—1812–1818—and *Don Juan,* 1819–1824.
3. Byron was afflicted by a clubfoot; a constant source of embarrassment for him.
4. After year's of treatments from a quack, named Lavender, Byron, finally, received a special brace, prescribed by a reputable doctor.
5. Byrons cousin, Mary, whom he idolized, cruelly referred to him as 'that lameboy.'

13. Punctuation

ITALICS

Italics are printed characters that *slant to the right like this.* To indicate italics in handwritten or typewritten work, use underlining.

13a. Use italics (underlining) for words, letters, and symbols referred to as such and for foreign words that have not been adopted into English.

> The words *hiss* and *clang* are examples of onomatopoeia.
>
> You typed *ie* instead of *ei.*
>
> The motto *e pluribus unum* appears on all United States coins.

13b. Use italics (underlining) for titles of books, plays, long poems, periodicals, newspapers, works of art, films, television series, long musical compositions, recordings, comic strips, court cases, trains, ships, aircraft, and spacecraft.

Type of Title	Examples
Books	*The Canterbury Tales*
Plays	*The Taming of the Shrew*
Long Poems	*The Rime of the Ancient Mariner*
Periodicals	*Sports Illustrated*
Newspapers	*The Boston Globe*
Works of Art	*The Persistence of Memory*
Films	*It's a Wonderful Life*
TV Series	*American Playhouse*
Long Musical Compositions	*The Planets, The Magic Flute*
Recordings	*The Genius of Ray Charles*
Comic Strips	*Doonesbury*
Court Cases	*Marbury* v. *Madison*
Trains, Aircraft, Ships, and Spacecraft	*Orient Express, Enola Gay, Queen Elizabeth 2, Apollo 13*

NOTE The article *the* before the title of a book, periodical, or newspaper is not italicized or capitalized unless it is part of the official title. The official title of a book appears on the title page. The official title of a periodi-

cal or newspaper is the name on its masthead, usually found on the editorial page.

> What role does fate play in "The Seafarer"?
>
> I found this information in *The New York Times.*
>
> My mom looks through t**he** *Sun-Times* every morning.

QUOTATION MARKS

13c. Use quotation marks to enclose a *direct quotation*—a person's exact words.

(1) A direct quotation usually begins with a capital letter.

> Sir Francis Bacon Wrote, "**K**nowledge is power."

However, when the quotation is only part of a sentence, do not begin it with a capital letter.

> In Act I, Scene 5, Lady Macbeth describes her husband's nature as "**t**oo full o' th' milk of human kindness."

Do not use quotation marks to enclose an **indirect quotation** (a rewording of a direct quotation).

> DIRECT QUOTATION   Al said, "I'm going fishing today."
>
> INDIRECT QUOTATION   Al said that he is going fishing today.

(2) When the expression identifying the speaker divides a quoted sentence, the second part begins with a lowercase letter.

> "All good moral philosophy," according to Sir Francis Bacon, "**i**s but the handmaid to religion." [Notice that each part of a divided quotation is enclosed in quotation marks.]

When the second part of a divided quotation is a new sentence, the first word begins with a capital letter.

> "On his first voyage, Gulliver finds himself in Lilliput," explained Ms. Chávez. "**T**he people there are only six inches tall."

(3) When used with quotation marks, other marks of punctuation are placed according to the following rules.

• Commas and periods are always placed inside the closing quotation marks.

> "Read these lines," he said, "and tell me what you think they mean."

- Semicolons and colons are always placed outside the closing quotation marks.

Gloria promised, "I'll go to the dance with you"; however, she said that several weeks ago.

Find examples of the following figures of speech in Wordsworth's poem "I Wandered Lonely as a Cloud": personification, metaphor, and simile.

- Question marks and exclamation points are placed inside the closing quotation marks if the quotation itself is a question or an exclamation. Otherwise, they are placed outside.

Did Keats write "Ode on a Grecian Urn"?

"What an imagination you have!" exclaimed Beth.

(4) When quoting a passage that consists of more than one paragraph, put quotation marks at the beginning of each paragraph and at the end of only the last paragraph.

"At Mr. Bowyers's, a great deal of company; some I knew, others I did not. Here we stayed upon the leads and below till it was late, expecting to see the fireworks; but they were not performed tonight. Only, the City had a light like a glory round about it, with bonfires.

"At last I went to King Street; and there sent Crockford to my father's and my house to tell them I could not come home tonight, because of the dirt and a coach could not be had."

—Samuel Pepys, *The Diary of Samuel Pepys*

(5) Use single quotation marks to enclose a quotation within a quotation.

Ms. Markham asked us, "What do you think John Donne meant when he said, 'No man is an island, entire of itself'?"

(6) When writing **dialogue** (a conversation), begin a new paragraph every time the speaker changes, and enclose each speaker's words in quotation marks.

This frightened the fellow that attended about the work; but after some pause John Hayward, recovering himself, said, "Lord, bless us! There's somebody in the cart not quite dead!"

So another called to him and said, "Who are you?"

The fellow answered, "I am the poor piper. Where am I?"

"Where are you?" says Hayward. "Why, you are in the dead-cart, and we are going to bury you."

—Daniel Defoe, *A Journal of the Plague Year*

13d. Use quotation marks to enclose titles of short works, such as short stories, poems, essays, articles, songs, episodes of television series, and chapters and other parts of books.

Type of Name	Examples
Short Stories	"The Doll's House," "Games at Twilight"
Poems	"Ode to a Nightingale," "Thoughts of Hanoi"
Essays	"Shakespeare's Sister," "The Myth of Sisyphus"
Articles	"How to Improve Your Grades"
Songs	"Wind Beneath My Wings," "Frankie and Johnny"
TV Episodes	"Tony's Surprise Party," "Inside the Earth"
Chapters and Parts of Books	"The Age of Reform," "How Ecosystems Change"

Neither italics nor quotation marks are used for titles of major religions works or titles of legal or historical documents.

the Bible   Code of Hammurabi

Bill of Rights   Monroe Doctrine

ELLIPSIS POINTS

13e. Use three spaced periods called *ellipsis points* (. . .) to mark omissions from quoted material and pauses in a written passage.

ORIGINAL   At last she spoke to me. When she addressed the first words to me I was so confused that I did not know what to answer. She asked me was I going to *Araby.* I forget whether I answered yes or no. It would be a splendid bazaar, she said; she would love to go.

—James Joyce, "Araby"

(1) If the quoted material that comes before the ellipsis points is not a complete sentence, use three ellipsis points with a space before the first point.

Of his conversation with Mangan's sister, the narrator says, "When she addressed the first words to me . . . I did not know what to answer."

(2) If the quoted material that comes before the ellipsis points is a complete sentence, use an end mark before the ellipsis points.

According to Mangan's sister, "It would be a splendid bazaar. . . ."

(3) If one sentence or more is omitted, ellipsis points follow any end mark that precedes the omitted material.

The narrator recalls his encounter with Mangan's sister: "At last she spoke to me. . . . She asked me was I going to *Araby*."

(4) To show that a full line or more of poetry has been omitted, use a line of spaced periods that is as long as the line of poetry above it.

ORIGINAL   It fell about the Martinmas time,
And a gay time it was then,
When our goodwife got puddings to make,
And she's boild them in the pan.
    — Traditional, "Get Up and Bar the Door"

ONE LINE   It fell about the Martinmas time,
OMITTED   . . . .
When our goodwife got puddings to make,
And she's boild them in the pan.

APOSTROPHES
Possessive Case

13f. The *possessive case* of a noun or a pronoun indicates ownership or relationship. Use an apostrophe in forming the possessive case of nouns and indefinite pronouns.

(1) To form the possessive of a singular noun, add an apostrophe and an *s*.

Beowulf**'s** shield

the principal**'s** office

When forming the possessive of a singular noun ending in an s sound, add only an apostrophe if the addition of 's will make the noun awkward to pronounce. Otherwise, add 's.

Ms. Rodgers' class   the witness's testimony

(2) To form the possessive of a plural noun ending in *s,* add only the apostrophe.

the players' uniforms   the volunteers' efforts

(3) Form the possessive of only the last word in a compound word, in the name of an organization or business firm, or in a word group showing joint possession.

brother-in-law**'s** car

Ralph Merrill and Company**'s** products

Macbeth and Lady Macbeth**'s** plan

When a possessive pronoun is part of a word group showing joint possession, each noun in the word group is also possessive.

Chen**'s**, Ramona**'s**, and **my** project

(4) Form the possessive of each noun in a word group showing individual possession of similar items.

Byron**'s**, Shelley**'s**, and Keats**'s** poems

(5) Possessive forms of words indicating time, such as *minute, day, month,* and *year,* and words indicating amounts in cents or dollars require apostrophes.

four weeks' vacation   a dollar**'s** worth

(6) To form the poss essive of an indefinite pronoun, add an apostrophe and an *s*.

no one**'s** fault   somebody else**'s** jacket

Contractions

13g. Use an apostrophe to show where letters, words, or numbers have been omitted in a contraction.

let us	**let's**	she would	**she'd**
you will	**you'll**	1998	**'98**

The word *not* can be shortened to *–n't* and added to a verb, usually without changing the spelling of the verb.

do not	**don't**	should not	**shouldn't**

EXCEPTION: will not   **won't**

Plurals

13h. Use an apostrophe and an *s* to form the plurals of all lowercase letters, some uppercase letters, numerals, and some words referred to as words.

There are two *c*'s and two *m*'s in accommodate.

Try not to use so many *I*'s in your cover letter. [Without the apostrophe, the plural of the pronoun *I* would spell *Is*.]

You may add only an *s* to form the plurals of words, numerals, and capital letters if the plural forms will not cause misreading. However, it is never wrong to use an apostrophe in such cases.

James I ruled England during the early **1600s** [*or* **1600's**].

HYPHENS

13i. Use a hyphen to divide a word at the end of a line.

- Do not divide a one-syllable word.

Did the Green Knight know that Sir Gawain had **kissed** [*not* kis-sed] his wife?

- Divide a word only between syllables.

First, Macbeth was killed; then he was **decapitated** [*not* decapita-ted].

- Divide an already hyphenated word at the hyphen.

Queen Elizabeth I was ruler of England for **forty-five** [*not* for-ty five] years.

- Do not divide a word so that one letter stands alone.

Paradise Lost by John Milton is a famous English **epic** [*not* e-pic].

13j. Use a hyphen with compound numbers from twenty-one to ninety-nine and with fractions used as modifiers.

thirty-seven

a **three-fourths** majority [*but* **three fourths** of the voters]

DASHES

13k. Use dashes to set off abrupt breaks in thoughts.

The playwright handles her material—I should say lack of material—quite well.

13l. Use dashes to set off appositives or parenthetical expressions that contain commas.

Several of the Romantic poets—Keats, Shelley, and Byron, for example—led fascinating lives.

13m. Use a dash to set off an introductory list or group of examples.

Alliteration, caesuras, and kennings—these are features of Anglo-Saxon poetry.

PARENTHESES

13n. Use parentheses to enclose informative or explanatory material of minor importance.

A *roman à clef* (literally, "novel with a key") is a novel about real people to whom the novelist has assigned fictitious names.

The Globe (**s**ee the drawing on page 428) was built in 1599. [The *s* in *see* is lowercase because the parenthetical sentence is within a complete sentence.]

The Globe was built in 1599. (**S**ee the drawing on page 428.) [The *S* in *See* is capitalized and a period follows *page 428* because the parenthetical sentence is not within another sen tence but instead stands on its own.]

BRACKETS

13o. Use brackets to enclose an explanation within quoted or parenthetical material.

The newspaper article stated that "at the time of that Democratic National Convention [in Chicago in 1968] there were many protest groups operating in the United States."

Your Turn

In the following dialogue, (1) insert end marks, commas, and quotation marks; (2) correct any errors in capitalization; and (3) add new paragraphs as necessary.

[1] Didn't you study shakespeare in class this year Benjamin asked

[2] Yes we read several of his tragedies, including *Hamlet* and *Macbeth* answered Elaine

[3] Hamlet's soliloquy from act three is my favorite exclaimed Carl

[4] Is that the one that begins to be, or not to be Elaine inquired

[5] Benjamin nodded and said yes, that's it!

14. Spelling

UNDERSTANDING WORD STRUCTURE

Many English words are made up of words and affixes (prefixes and suffixes).

Roots

The **root** of a word is the part that carries the word's core meaning.

Root	Meaning	Examples
–fin–	end, limit	final, infinite
–gram–	write, writing	grammar, epigram
–tract–	pull, draw	tractor, extract
–vit–	life	vitamin, vital

Prefixes

A **prefix** is one or more letters or syllables added to the beginning of a word or word part to create a new word.

Prefix	Meaning	Examples
contra–	against	contradict, contrast
inter–	between, among	interstate, interact
mis–	not, wrongly	misfire, misspell
re–	back, again	reflect, refinance

Suffixes

A **suffix** is one or more letters or syllables added to the end of a word or word part to create a new word.

Suffix	Meaning	Examples
–fy	make, cause	verify, pacify
–ish	suggesting, like	smallish, childish
–ist	doer, believer	artist, humanist
–ty	quality, state	cruelty, certainty

SPELLING RULES

The best way to be sure you have spelled a word correctly is to look the word up in a dictionary.

ie and *ei*

14a. Write *ie* when the sound is long *e*, except after *c*.

relieve chief field conceit deceive

EXCEPTIONS

either leisure neither seize protein

14b. Write *ei* when the sound is not long *e*.

reign foreign their sovereign weight

EXCEPTIONS

ancient view friend mischief conscience

NOTE Rules 14a and 14b apply only when the *i* and the *e* are in the same syllable.

–cede, –ceed, and *–sede*

14c. The only English word ending in *–sede* is *supersede*. The only words ending in *–ceed* are *exceed, proceed,* and *succeed.* Most other words with this sound end in *–cede.*

concede precede recede secede

Adding Prefixes

14d. When adding a prefix, do not change the spelling of the original word.

over + run = **over**run   mis + spell = **mis**spell

Adding Suffixes

14e. When adding the suffix *–ness* or *–ly,* do not change the spelling of the original word.

gentle + ness = gentle**ness**   final + ly = final**ly**

EXCEPTIONS

For most words ending in *y,* change the *y* to *i* before adding *–ness* or *–ly.*

heavy + ness = heav**iness**   ready + ly = read**ily**

NOTE One-syllable adjectives ending in *y* generally follow rule 14h.

shy + ness = shy**ness**   sly + ly = sly**ly**

14f. Drop the final silent *e* before a suffix beginning with a vowel.

awake + en = awak**en**   race + ing= rac**ing**

EXCEPTIONS

Keep the final silent *e*

- in a word ending in *ce* or *ge* before a suffix beginning with *a* or *o*.

  peace**able**   courag**eous**

- in *dye* and in *singe* before *–ing*.

  dy**eing**   sing**eing**

- in *mile* before *–age*.

  mil**eage**

NOTE When adding *–ing* to words that end in *ie*, drop the *e* and change the *i* to *y*.

die + ing = d**ying**   lie + ing = l**ying**

14g. Keep the final silent *e* before a suffix beginning with a consonant.

care + less = car**eless**   sure + ty = sur**ety**

EXCEPTIONS

nine + th = nin**th**   judge + ment = judg**ment**

true + ly = tru**ly**   wise + dom = wis**dom**

14h. For words ending in *y* preceded by a consonant, change the *y* to *i* before any suffix that does not begin with *i*.

heavy + est = heav**iest**

accompany + ment = accompan**iment**

verify + ing = verif**ying**

14i. For words ending in *y* preceded by a vowel, keep the *y* when adding a suffix.

enjoy + ing = enjoy**ing**   play + ed = play**ed**

EXCEPTIONS

day + ly = da**ily**   lay + ly = la**id**

pay + ed = pa**id**   say + ed = sa**id**

14j. Double the final consonant before a suffix that begins with a vowel if the word *both* (1) has only one syllable or has the accent on the last syllable *and* (2) ends in a single consonant preceded by a single vowel.

rap + ing = ra**pping**   refer + ed = refe**rred**

EXCEPTIONS

- For words ending in *w* or *x*, do not double the final consonant.

  bow + ed = bow**ed**   tax + able = tax**able**

- For words ending in *c*, add *k* before the suffix instead of doubling the *c*.

  picnic + k + ing = picnic**king**

FORMING THE PLURALS OF NOUNS

14K. Remembering the following rules will help you spell the plural forms of nouns.

(1) For most nouns, add *–s*.

beagle**s**   senator**s**   taxi**s**   Saxon**s**

(2) For nouns ending in *s, x, z, ch,* or *sh*, add *–es*.

glass**es**   waltz**es**   brush**es**   Perez**es**

(3) For nouns ending in *y* preceded by a vowel, add *–s*.

monkey**s**   decoy**s**   Saturday**s**   Kelley**s**

(4) For nouns ending in *y* preceded by a consonant, change the *y* to *i* and add *–es*.

comed**ies**   cavit**ies**   theor**ies**   sk**ies**

EXCEPTIONS

For proper nouns, add *–s*

Gregory**s**   Kimberly**s**

(5) For some nouns ending in *f* or *fe*, add *–s*. For others, change the *f* or *fe* to *v* and add *–es*.

belief**s**   loa**ves**   giraffe**s**   wi**ves**

EXCEPTIONS

For proper nouns, add *–s*.

DeGroff**s**   Rolfe**s**

(6) For nouns ending in *o* preceded by a vowel, add *–s*.

radio**s**   cameo**s**   shampoo**s**   Matsuo**s**

(7) For nouns ending in *o* preceded by a consonant, add *–es*.

torpedo**es**   echo**es**   hero**es**   potato**es**

For some common nouns ending in *o* preceded by a consonant, especially those referring to music, and for proper nouns, add only an *–s*.

photo**s**   hairdo**s**   solo**s**   Spiro**s**

(8) The plurals of a few nouns are formed in irregular ways.

g**ee**se   men   child**ren**   mice   teeth

(9) For a few nouns, the singular and the plural forms are the same.

deer   series   Chinese   aircraft

(10) For most compound nouns, form the plural of only the last word of the compound.

courthouse**s**   seat belt**s**   four-year-old**s**

(11) For compound nouns in which one of the words is modified by the other word or words, form the plural of the noun modified.

son**s**-in-law   passer**s**by   mountain goat**s**

(12) For some nouns borrowed from other languages, the plural is formed as in the original languages. In a few cases, two plural forms are acceptable.

analysis—analys**es**

phenomenon—phenomen**a** *or* phenomenon**s**

(13) To form the plurals of figures, most uppercase letters, signs, and words used as words, add an *–s* or both an apostrophe and an *–s*.

1500**s** *or* 1500**'s**   *B***s** *or* *B***'s**

$**s** *or* $**'s**   *and***s** *or* *and***'s**

To avoid confusion, add both an apostrophe and an *–s* to form the plural of all lowercase letters, certain uppercase letters, and some words used as words.

The word *fictitious* contains three *i***'s.** [Without an apostrophe, the plural of *i* could be confused with the word *is.*]

Sebastian usually makes straight A**'s.** [without an apostrophe, the plural of *A* could be confused with the word *As.*]

Because I mistakenly thought Evelyn Waugh was a woman, I used *her***'s** instead of *his***'s** in my paragraph. [Without an apostrophe, the plural of *her* would look like the possessive pronoun hers, and the plural of *his* would look like the word *hiss.*]

In names, ***diacritical marks*** (marks that show pronunciation) and capitalization are as essential to correct spelling as the letters themselves. If you're not sure about the spelling of a name, check with the person whose name it is, or consult a reference source.

François	Lagerlöf
Van Doren	van Gogh
Márquez	Marín
de Vega	al-Khansa

Your Turn

Each of the following sentences contains two misspelled words. Correct each misspelling.

1. Nobody in our class has recieved thier books.
2. To sucede in debate, your arguements must be well thought out.
3. Lonelyness is a recuring theme in many literary works.
4. Saddly the bishop sat in judgement against him.
5. His acheivements exceded her expectations.

15. Glossary Of Usage

The **Glossary of Usage** is an alphabetical list of expressions with definitions, explanations, and examples. Some of the examples are labeled *standard, nonstandard, formal,* or *informal.* The label **standard** or **formal** identifies usage that is appropriate in serious writing and speaking (such as in compositions and speeches). The label *informal* indicates standard English that is generally used in conversation and in everyday writing such as personal letters. The label **nonstandard** identifies usage that does not follow the guidelines of standard English usage.

accept, except *Accept* is a verb meaning "to receive." *Except* may be a verb meaning "to leave out" or a preposition meaning "excluding."

> Does Sir Gawain **accept** the challenge from the Green Knight? [verb]

> Certain states **except** teachers from jury duty. [verb]

> I have read all of *Macbeth* **except** the last act. [preposition]

affect, effect *Affect* is a verb meaning "to influence." *Effect* may be either a verb meaning "to bring about or to accomplish" or a noun meaning "the result [of an action]."

> How did the murder of King Duncan **affect** Lady Macbeth? [verb]

> In this dispute, management and labor should be able to **effect** a compromise. [verb]

> What far-reaching **effects** did the *Brown v. Board of Education of Topeka* decision have? [noun]

all ready, already *All ready* means "all prepared." *Already* means "previously."

> Are you **all ready** for the audition?

> We have **already** read "The Seafarer."

all right *All right* means "satisfactory," "unhurt; safe," "correct," or, in reply to a question or to preface a remark, "yes." *Alright* is a misspelling.

> Does this look **all right** [*not* alright]?

> Oh, **all right** [*not* alright], you can go.

all the farther, all the faster Avoid using these expressions in formal situations. Use *as far as* or *as fast as.*

> Is that **as fast** [*not* all the faster] Chris can run?

all together, altogether *All together* means "everyone in the same place." *Altogether* means "entirely."

> The knights were **all together** for the celebration.

> Sir Gawain was not **altogether** honest with the Green Knight.

allusion, illusion An *allusion* is an indirect reference to something. An *illusion* is a mistaken idea or a misleading appearance.

> The speaker made an **allusion** to Emily Brontë's *Wuthering Heights.*

> Before selecting a career, he had to abandon some of his **illusions** about his own abilities.

> The director chose certain colors to create an **illusion** of depth on the small stage.

a lot Avoid this expression in formal situations by using *many* or *much.*

> **Many** [*not* a lot] of my friends work part time.

already See **all ready, already.**

altogether See **all together, altogether.**

among See between, among.

and etc. *Etc.* stands for the Latin words *et cetera,* meaning "and others" or "and so forth." Always avoid using *and* before *etc.* In general, avoid using *etc.* in formal situations. Use one of its meanings instead.

> We are comparing the main female characters in Shakespeare's tragedies: Lady Macbeth, Cleopatra, Juliet, **and others** [*or* **etc.,** *but not* and etc.].

any one, anyone The expression *any one* specifies one member of a group. *Anyone* means "one person, no matter which."

> **Any one** of you could win the poetry contest.

> **Anyone** who finishes the test early may leave.

as See **like, as.**

as if See **like, as if.**

at Avoid using *at* after a construction beginning with *where.*

NONSTANDARD	Where was Beowulf at when Grendel's mother attacked?
STANDARD	**Where** was Beowulf when Grendel's mother attacked?

a while, awhile   *A while* means "a period of time." *A while* means "for a short time."

Herot remained empty for quite **a while.**

They stayed there **awhile.**

bad, badly   *Bad* is an adjective. *Badly* is an adverb. In standard English, *bad* should follow a sense verb, such as *feel, look, sound, taste,* or *smell,* or other linking verb.

The prospects for fair weather look **bad** [*not* badly].

because   In formal situations, do not use the construction *reason . . . because.* Instead, use *reason . . . that.*

The **reason** Sir Gawain accepts the green sash is **that** [*not* because] he thinks it will protect him from the Green Knight.

being as, being that   Avoid using either of these expressions for *since* or *because.*

Because [*not* being as *or* being that] Sir Gawain is a knight, we expect him to behave chivalrously.

beside, besides   *Beside* means "by the side of" or "next to." *Besides* means "in addition to" or "other than" or "moreover."

The Geats built Beowulf's tomb **beside** the sea.

No one **besides** Wiglaf helped Beowulf battle the dragon.

I have decided that I do not want to take journalism; **besides**, I cannot fit it into my schedule.

between, among   Use *between* to refer to only two items or to more than two when comparing each item individually to each of the others.

The reward money will be divided **between** Chang and Marta.

Sasha explained the difference **between** assonance, consonance, and alliteration. [Each item is compared individually to each of the others.]

Use *among* to refer to more than two items when you are not considering each item in relation to each other item individually.

The reward money will be divided **among** the four girls.

bring, take   *Bring* means "to come carrying something." *Take* means "to go carrying something."

I'll **bring** my copy of *Gulliver's Travels* when I come over to your house.

Please **take** the model of the Globe Theater to the school library.

bust, busted   Avoid using these words as verbs. Instead, use a form of *break* or *burst,* depending on the meaning.

The window is **broken** [*not* busted].

The water main has **burst** [*not* busted] open.

can, may   Use *can* to express ability. Use *may* to express possibility.

Can you play the guitar?

It **may** rain later.

cannot (can't) help but   Avoid using *but* and the infinitive form of a verb after the expression *cannot (can't) help.* Instead, use a gerund alone.

NONSTANDARD   I can't help but laugh when I look at that photograph.

STANDARD   I can't help **laughing** when I look at that photograph.

compare, contrast   Used with *to, compare* means "to look for similarities between." Used with *with, compare* means "to look for similarities and differences between." *Contrast* is used to point out differences.

The simile at the end of the poem **compares** the eagle's fall **to** a thunderbolt.

We **compared** Shakespeare's style **with** that of Christopher Marlowe.

The tour guide also **contrasted** the two castles' provisions for defense.

could of   See **of.**

double subject   Do not use an unnecessary pronoun after the subject of a sentence.

George Bernard Shaw [*not* George Bernard Shaw he] wrote *Pygmalion.*

due to   Avoid using *due to* for "because of" or "owing to."

All schools were closed **because of** [*not* due to] inclement weather.

effect   See **affect, effect.**

either, neither   *Either* usually means "one or the other of two." In referring to more than two, use *any* one or *any* instead. *Neither* usually means "not one or the other of two." In referring to more than two use *none* instead.

Either of the two quotations would be appropriate to use at the beginning of your speech.

You should be able to find ample information about **any one** of those four poets.

Neither of the Perez twins is in school today.

None of the seniors have voted yet.

etc. See **and etc.**

every day, everyday *Every day* means "each day." *Everyday* means "daily" or "usual."

Every day presents its own challenges.

The party will be casual; wear **everyday** clothes.

every one, everyone *Every one* specifies every person or thing of those named. *Everyone* means "every person, all of the people named."

Elizabeth Bowen wrote **every one** of these stories.

Did **everyone** read "The Demon Lover"?

except See **accept, except.**

farther, further Use *farther* to express physical distance. Use *further* to express abstract relationships of degree or quantity.

Your house is **farther** from school than mine is.

The United Nations members decided that **further** debate was unnecessary.

fewer, less Use *fewer* to modify a plural noun and *less* to modify a singular noun.

Fewer students are going out for football this year.

Now I spend **less** time watching TV.

good, well Avoid using the adjective good to modify an action verb. Instead, use the adverb *well,* meaning "capably" or "satisfactorily."

We did **well** [*not* good] on the exam.

Used as an adjective, *well* means "in good health" or "satisfactory in appearance or condition."

I feel **well.**

It's eight o'clock, and all is **well.**

had of See **of.**

had ought, hadn't ought Do not use *had* or *hadn't* with *ought.*

Your application **ought** [*not* had ought] to have been sent in earlier

She **ought not** [*not* hadn't ought] to swim so soon after eating lunch.

illusion See **allusion, illusion.**

imply, infer *Imply* means "to suggest indirectly." *Infer* means "to interpret" or "to draw a conclusion."

The speaker of "To a Skylark" **implies** that the skylark is a divine being.

I **inferred** from her speech that she would support a statewide testing program.

in, in to, into *In* generally shows location. In the construction *in to,* in is an adverb followed by the preposition *to. Into* generally shows direction.

Rudyard Kipling was born **in** Bombay.

He found the treasure and turned it **in to** his king.

Sir Gawain rode **into** the wilderness to find the Green Knight.

infer See **imply, infer.**

irregardless, regardless *Irregardless* is nonstandard. Use *regardless* instead.

Regardless [*not* irregardless] of the danger, he continued his journey.

its, it's *Its* is the possessive form of *it. It's* is the contraction of *it is* or *it has.*

The community is proud of **its** school system.

It's [it is] a symbol of peace.

It's [it has] been cooler today.

kind of, sort of In formal situations, avoid using these terms for the adverb *somewhat* or *rather.*

| INFORMAL | Macbeth appeared to be kind of worried. |
| FORMAL | Macbeth appeared to be **rather** [*or* **somewhat**] worried. |

kind of a(n), sort of a(n) In formal situations, omit the *a(n).*

| INFORMAL | What kind of a poem is "The Passionate Shepherd to His Love"? |
| FORMAL | What **kind of** poem is "The Passionate Shepherd to His Love"? |

kind(s), sort(s), type(s) With the singular form of each of these nouns, use *this* or *that.* With the plural form, use *these* or *those.*

This type of engine performs more economically than any of **those types.**

less See **fewer, less.**

lie, lay The verb *lie* means "to rest" or "to stay, to recline, or to remain in a certain state or position." Its principal parts are *lie, lying, lay,* and *lain. Lie* never takes an object. The verb *lay* means "to put [something] in a place." Its principal parts are *lay, laying, laid,* and *laid. Lay* usually takes an object.

> Gulliver was **lying** on his back and could hardly move. [no object]

> The Lilliputians **laid** baskets of food near Gulliver's mouth. [*Baskets* is the object of *laid.*]

like, as   In formal situations, do not use *like* for *as* to introduce a subordinate clause.

| INFORMAL | John looks like his father looked twenty years ago. |
| FORMAL | John looks **as** his father looked twenty years ago. |

like, as if   In formal situations, avoid using the preposition *like* for the compound conjunction *as if* or *as though* to introduce a subordinate clause.

| INFORMAL | The heavy footsteps sounded like they were coming nearer. |
| FORMAL | The heavy footsteps sounded **as if** [or **as though**] they were coming nearer. |

might of, must of   See **of.**

neither   See **either, neither.**

nor   See **or, nor.**

of   *Of* is a preposition. Do not use *of* in place of *have* after verbs such as *could, should, would, might, must,* and *ought* [*to*]. Also, do not use *had of* for *had.*

> If **I had** [*not* had of] know about the shortcut, **I would have** [*not* would of] been here sooner.

Avoid using *of* after other prepositions such as *inside, off,* and *outside.*

> Flimnap fell **off** [*not* off of] the tightrope.

off, off of   Do not use *off* or *off of* for *from.*

> You can get a program **from** [*not* off of] the usher.

on to, onto   In the expression *on to, on* is an adverb and *to* is a preposition. *Onto* is a preposition.

> The lecturer moved **on to** her next main idea.

> She walked **onto** the stage.

or, nor   Use *or* with *either;* use *nor* with *neither.*

> The list of authors does not include **either** James Joyce **or** [*not* nor] D. H. Lawrence.

> **Neither** James Joyce **nor** D. H. Lawrence is on the list of authors.

ought   See **had ought, hadn't ought.**

ought to of   See **of.**

raise   See **rise, raise.**

reason . . . because   See **because.**

refer back   Since the prefix *re–* in *refer* means "back," adding *back* is generally unnecessary.

> The writer is **referring** [*not* referring back] to the years when he lived in Ireland.

rise, raise   The verb *rise* means "to go up" or "to get up." Its principal parts are *rise, rising, rose,* and *risen. Rise* never takes an object. The verb *raise* means "to cause [something] to rise" or "to lift up." Its principal parts are *raise, raising, raised,* and *raised. Raise* usually takes an object.

> Her blood pressure **rose** as she waited. [no object]

> The Green Knight **raised** the ax above his head. [*Ax* is the object of *raised.*]

should of   See **of.**

sit, set   The verb *sit* means "to rest in an upright, seated position." Its principal parts are *sit, sitting, sat,* and *sat. Sit* seldom takes an object. The verb *set* means "to put [something] in a place." Its principal parts are *set, setting, set,* and *set. Set* usually takes an object.

> Banquo's ghost **sits** in Macbeth's place. [no object]

> Please **set** the groceries on the table. [*Groceries* is the object of *set.*]

some, somewhat   In formal situations, avoid using *some* to mean "to some extent." Use *somewhat.*

> The Wedding Guest was **somewhat** shaken [*not* shaken some] by the Ancient Mariner's gaze and appearance.

sort(s)   See **kind(s), sort(s), type(s)** and **kind of a(n), sort of a(n).**

sort of   See **kind of, sort of.**

take   See **bring, take.**

than, then   *Than* is a conjunction used in comparisons. *Then* is an adverb meaning "at that time" or "next."

> Is King Macbeth more superstitious **than** Lady Macbeth?

> First, we will read "The Lamb"; **then,** we will read "The Tyger."

that   See **who, which, that.**

their, there, they're   *Their* is a possessive form of *they.* As an adverb, *there* means "at that place." *There* can also be used to begin a sentence. *They're* is the contraction of *they are.*

> They built a tomb for **their** fallen leader.
>
> Macduff was not **there** at the time.
>
> **There** is very little time left.
>
> **They're** waiting for Banquo.

theirs, there's   *Theirs* is a possessive form of the pronoun *they. There's* is the contraction for *there is.*

> The treasure is **theirs** now.
>
> **There's** an allusion to the Bible in the poem.

them   Do not use *them* as an adjective. Use *those.*

> Have you seen **those** [*not* them] murals by Judith Baca at the art museum?

then   See **than, then.**

there   See **their, there, they're.**

there's   See **theirs, there's.**

they're   See **their, there, they're.**

this here, that there   Avoid using *here* or *there* after *this* or *that.*

> **This** [*not* this here] poem was written by Robert Browning.

try and, try to   Use *try to,* not *try and.*

> I will **try to** [*not* try and] finish reading *The Diary of Samuel Pepys* tonight.

type, type of   Avoid using the noun *type* as an adjective. Add *of* after *type.*

> What **type of** [*not* type] character is the knight in "The Wife of Bath's Tale"?

type(s)   See **kind(s), sort(s), type(s).**

ways   Use *way,* not *ways,* when referring to distance.

> Is Canterbury a long **way** [*not* ways] from the Tabard Inn?

well   See **good, well.**

when, where   Avoid using *when* or *where* to begin a definition.

NONSTANDARD	A caesura is where you break or pause in a line of poetry.
STANDARD	A caesura is **a break or pause in a line of poetry.**

where   Avoid using *where* for *that.*

> I read **that** [*not* where] you won a scholarship.

where . . . at   See **at.**

who, which, that   *Who* refers to persons only. *Which* refers to things only. *That* may refer to either persons or things.

> Sir Gawain was the knight **who** [*or* **that**] accepted the Green Knight's challenge.
>
> The Globe, **which** was built in 1599, burned down in 1613.
>
> Is this the only poem **that** Sir Walter Raleigh ever wrote?

who's, whose   *Who's* is the contraction of *who is* or *who has. Whose* is the possessive form of *who.*

> Well, look **who's** [who is] here!
>
> **Who's** [who has] read all of the play?
>
> **Whose** treasure is it?

would of   See **of.**

your, you're   *Your* is a possessive form of *you. You're* is the contraction of *you are.*

> Is that **your** car?
>
> I can see that **you're** tired.

Your Turn

Revise the following sentences according to the rules of *Standard English.*

1. The reason they had to be quiet was because the performance was in progress.
2. The prompter helped the cast rehearse they're lines.
3. She was much more convincing in that role then the others.
4. In the orchestra pit, the conductor took his place, paused a moment, and than lifted his baton.
5. Percy Bysshe Shelley he wrote *Prometheus Unbound.*

Glossary

The glossary that follows is an alphabetical list of words found in the selections in this book. Use this glossary just as you would use a dictionary - to find out the meaning of unfamiliar words. (Some technical, foreign, and more obscure words in this book are not listed here but instead are defined for you in the footnotes that accompany many of the selections.)

Many words in the English language have more than one meaning. This glossary gives the meanings that apply to the words as they are used in the selections in this book. Words closely related in form and meaning are usually listed together in one entry (for instance, cower and cowered), and the definition is given for the first form.

The following abbreviations are used:

adj.	adjective
adv.	adverb
n.	noun
v.	verb

Each word's pronunciation is given in parentheses. For more information about the words in this glossary or for information about words not listed here, consult a dictionary.

A

abated (uh BAYT ihd) *v.* used as *adj.* lessened.

abides (uh BYDZ) *v.* endures.

abominable (uh BAHM uh nuh buhl) *adj.* disgusting; hateful.

abstain (ab STAYN) *v.* refrain.

accommodate (uh KAHM uh dayt) *v.* provide room for.

advance (ad VANS) *v.* promote; accelerate growth or progress of.

adversary (AD vuhr sehr ee) *n.* enemy; opponent.

aesthetics (ehs THEHT ihks) *n.* principles of beauty.

affectation (af ehk TAY shuhn) *n.* artificial behavior designed to impress others.

affinity (uh FIHN uh tee) *n.* kinship; bond.

affliction (uh FLIHK shuhn) *n.* suffering; something that causes pain or distress.

aggrieved (uh GREEVD) *v.* used as *adj.* offended.

albeit (awl BEE iht) *conj.* although it is.

altruistic (al tru IHS tihk) *adj.* unselfish.

ambitious (am BIHSH uhs) *adj.* aiming at a goal that is hard to reach.

anarchy (AN uhr kee) *n.* disorder and confusion.

animosities (an ih MAHS uh teez) *n.* pl. hostilities; violent hatreds or resentments.

annals (AN uhlz) *n.* records, organized by year, that tell someone or something's history.

annihilate (uh NY uh layt) *v.* destroy; make nonexistent.

annotated (AN uh tayt id) *adj.* marked with explanations in the form of notes.

annulled (uh NUHLD) *v.* erased; canceled.

antique (an TEEK) *adj.* ancient.

apathy (AP uh thee) *n.* lack of interest.

apertures (AP uhr churz) *n.* openings.

appalled (uh PAWLD) *v.* used as *adj.* dismayed.

apprehensive (ap rih HEHN sihv) *adj.* feeling anxious, worried.

arable (AR uh buhl) *adj.* fit to be farmed or cultivated.

ardent (AHR duhnt) *adj.* eager; enthusiastic.

arrested (uh REHST ihd) *v.* used as *adj.* checked or stopped in motion.

artifice (AHR tuh fihs) *n.* human skill or craft, as opposed to what is natural; trickery; deception.

ascended (uh SEHND ihd) *v.* went up.

aspire (uh SPYR) *v.* reach upward to a goal.

assent (uh SEHNT) *n.* acceptance.

asserted (uh SURT ihd) *v.* declared.

assuage (uh SWAYJ) *v.* ease; calm.

audaciously (aw DAY shuhs lee) *adv.* boldly.

austere (aw STIHR) *adj.* spare; very plain.

avarice (AV uhr ihs) *n.* an uncontrolled desire for wealth.

B

bawling (BAWL ihng) *v.* used as *adj.* crying loudly.

benign (bih NYN) *adj.* kind; gracious.

bequest (bih KWEHST) *n.* a gift left through a will.

bibliophile (BIHB lee uh fyl) *n.* one who loves books.

bid (bihd) *v.* demanded; asked.

blanched (blancht) *v.* used as *adj.* made white or pale.

blithe (blyth) *adj.* happy and cheerful.

botanical (buh TAN uh kuhl) *adj.* of plants or plant life; relating to the science of botany.

boundless (BOWND lihs) *adj.* limitless.

brandishing (BRAN dihsh ihng) *v.* used as *adj.* shaking in a threatening way.

brazen (BRAY zuhn) *adj.* made of brass.

buoyancy (BOY uhn see) *n.* lightness of spirit;

cheerfulness.

burnished (BUR nihsht) *v.* used as *adj.* made bright and smooth.

C

cadence (KAY duhns) *n.* the beat of a repetitive motion; a sound that rises and falls.

candor (KAN duhr) *n.* honesty; directness, openness.

caprice (kuh PREES) *n.* sudden notion or desire.

carefree (KAIR free) *adj.* without worry; happy.

caste (kast) *n.* social class.

celestial (suh LEHS chuhl) *adj.* heavenly.

censure (SEHN shuhr) *v.* to express disapproval of.

certitude (SUR tuh tood) *n.* a feeling of sureness.

chaste (chayst) *adj.* pure, decent, or modest in nature and behavior.

clambered (KLAM buhrd) *v.* climbed clumsily.

clamorous (KLAM uhr uhs) *adj.* loud and noisy.

clinical (KLIHN uh kuhl) *adj.* objective; without emotion.

coarse (kawrs) *adj.* of low quality; rough.

coherently (koh HIHR uhnt lee) *adv.* clearly and logically.

colossal (kuh LAHS uhl) *adj.* magnificently huge.

combustible (kuhm BUHS tuh buhl) *adj.* easy to set on fire; fast-burning.

commendable (kuh MEHN duh buhl) *adj.* deserving of admiration.

commiserate (kuh MIHZ uh rayt) *v.* feel sorrow or pity for; sympathize.

compatible (kuhm PAT uh buhl) *adj.* able to exist or work together.

compulsive (kuhm PUHL sihv) *adj.* driven by an irresistible impulse.

compulsory (kuhm PUHL suhr ee) *adj.* required; enforced.

concealed (kunh SEELD) *v.* used as *adj.* hidden.

conceding (kuhn SEED ihng) *v.* admitting as true.

conception (kuhn SEHP shuhn) *n.* the originating of something.

concocted (kahn KAHKT ihd) *v.* prepared (food or drink) by mixing a variety of ingredients.

condemned (kuhn DEHMD) *v.* doomed.

condolences (kuhn DOH luhns ihz) *n. pl.* expressions of sympathy offered to a grieving person.

confounded (kahn FOWN dihd) *v.* used as *adj.* confused.

congealed (kuhn JEELD) *v.* used as *adj.* thickened.

conjectured (kuhn JEHK chuhrd) *v.* reasoned; guessed.

connoisseur (kahn uh SUR) *n.* person with highly informed and refined taste.

consecrate (KAHN suh krayt) *v.* make honorable and sacred.

consequently (KAHN suh kwehnt lee) *adv.* as a result of something.

conspicuous (kuhn SPIHK yoo uhs) *adj.* attracting attention.

constancy (KAHN stuhn see) *n.* faithfulness; loyalty.

contemplation (kahn tuhm PLAY shuhn) *n.* deep thought; meditation.

contemptuous (kuhn TEHMP choo uhs) *adj.* showing strong dislike; scornful.

contention (kuhn TEHN shuhn) *n.* struggle.

contortion (kuhn TAWR shuhn) *n.* twisted shape or motion.

convey (kuhn VAY) *v.* communicate; express.

conviction (kuhn VIHK shuhn) *n.* firm belief or certainty.

copious (KOH pee uhs) *adj.* plentiful; abundant.

copyright (KAHP ee ryt) *n.* the legal right to use, sell or distribute any material, such as books, songs, and characters, that can be printed or published.

corporeal (kawr PAWR ee uhl) *adj.* of the body.

cosmopolitan (kahz muh PAHL uh tuhn) *adj.* worldly; sophisticated.

countenance (KOWN tuh nuhns) *n.* facial appearance.

countenances (KOWN tuh nuhns ehz) *v.* extends approval to; favors.

courtiers (KAWR tee uhrz) *n.* palace attendants.

covetousness (KUHV uh tuhs nihs) *n.* desire for what belongs to others.

credible (KREHD uh buhl) *adj.* believable.

creed (kreed) *n.* the essential points of religious belief.

cultivate (KUHL tuh vayt) *v.* develop; promote.

cursory (KUR suhr ee) *adj.* hasty; superficial.

D

daunted (DAWNT ihd) *v.* used as *adj.* made to lose courage; intimidated.

decay (dih KAY) *n.* wasting away; rotting; decline in quality.

decreed (dih KREED) *v.* ordered; commanded.

defiant (dih FY uhnt) *adj.* rebellious; disobedient.

defiled (dih FYLD) *v.* made unclean.

deities (DEE uh teez) *n. pl.* gods and goddesses.

delusion (dih LOO zhuhn) *n.* false belief.

demeanor (dih MEE nuhr) *n.* the way in which a person behaves.

demolition (dehm uh LIHSH uhn) *n.* destruction.

derives (dih RYVZ) *v.* comes from a certain source.

desolate (DEHS uh liht) *adj.* uninhabited; barren; dreary.

desolation (dehs uh LAY shuhn) *n.* grief; loneliness.

desperate (DEHS puhr iht) *adj.* driven by hopelessness; moved to use extreme means to try to escape frustration and loss.

deviate (DEE vee ayt) *v.* turn aside from a way, norm, or truth.

diabolic (dy uh BAHL ihk) *adj.* of or having to do with evil or the devil.

diffusive (dih FYOO sihv) *adj.* spread out; not concentrated in one place.

digressed (dy GREHSD) *v.* wandered away from the subject.

diligence (DIHL uh juhns) *n.* carefulness.

diminishes (duh MIHN ihsh ehz) *v.* makes smaller; lessens; reduces.

discerning (dih SURN ihng) *v.* used as *adj.* displaying good judgment; perceptive.

discomfiture (dihs KUHM fih chuhr) *n.* frustration; embarrassment.

disconcerted (dihs kuhn SUR tihd) *v.* used as adj confused.

discord (DIHS kawrd) *n.* conflict.

discourse (DIHS kawrs) *n.* conversation or speech.

disillusionment (dihs ih LOO zhehn muhnt) *n.* being disenchanted, or freed from a false idea.

dismal (DIHZ muhl) *adj.* gloomy.

dismayed (dihs MAYD) *v.* upset; alarmed.

disparaged (dihs PAR ihjd) *v.* belittled; spoke negatively of.

dispassionately (dihs PASH uh niht lee) *adv.* without emotion; impartially.

disperses (dihs PURS ihz) *v.* breaks up and scatters.

displaced (dihs PLAYST) *v.* moved from its usual location.

disposition (dihs puh ZIHSH uhn) *n.* natural qualities of personality.

dissuade (dih SWAYD) *v.* to *advise* against.

distend (dihs TEHND) *v.* expand; swell.

distill (dihs TIHL) *v.* draw out the essence of.

distorting (dihs TAWRT ihng) *v.* used as *adj.* misshaping; deforming.

distraught (dihs TRAWT) *adj.* extremely agitated.

divine (dih VYN) *adj.* of or like God or a god; given or inspired by God.

doctrine (DAHK truhn) *n.* teachings of the church.

dogged (DAWG ihd) *adj.* stubbornly persistent.

domain (doh MAYN) *n.* a sphere of influence due to ownership, expertise, or responsibility.

dread (drehd) *adj.* inspiring fear and awe.

dreadful (DREHD fuhl) *adj.* terrible; causing fear.

dregs (drehgz) *n.* pl. sediment.

E

ecstatic (ehk STAT ihk) *adj.* extremely joyful; showing great pleasure.

efficacious (ehf uh KAY shuhs) *adj.* effective or useful.

efficacy (EHF uh kuh see) *n.* ability to produce a desired effect.

elation (ih LAY shuhn) *n.* high spirits; jubilation.

emanated (EHM uh nayt id) *v.* flowed; came forth.

embers (EHM buhrz) *n.* pl. glowing remains of a fire.

embrace (ehm BRAYS) *v.* accept readily; take up or adopt.

embroidered (ehm BROY duhrd) *v.* used as adj. ornamented with needlework or as if with needlework.

eminence (EHM uh nuhns) *n.* high rank or position.

eminent (EHM uh nuhnt) *adj.* great; high-standing.

endowed (ehn DOWD) *v.* used as *adj.* provided with.

endure (ehn DOOR) *v.* undergo; bear.

endured (ehn DOORD) *v.* suffered, put up with.

engagements (ehn GAYJ muhnts) *n.* military battles.

enmity (EHN muh tee) *n.* hostility.

enticing (ehn TYS ihng) *adj.* attracting by arousing hopes or desires; tempting.

epilogue (EHP uh lawg) *n.* short section at the end of a literary work that often tells what happened after the end of the story.

epithet (EHP uh theht) *n.* descriptive expression.

erect (ih REHKT) *adj.* upright.

erupted (ih RUHPT ihd) *v.* burst forth.

eternal (ih TUR nuhl) *adj.* forever; everlasting.

ethereal (ih THIHR ee uhl) *adj.* light and delicate; unearthly.

exhilaration (ehg zihl uh RAY shuhn) *n.* excitement; high spirits.

expedient (ehk SPEE dee uhnt) *n.* way of getting something; a means for achieving an end.

expire (ehk SPYR) *v.* die; come to an end.

exploit (EHKS ployt) *n.* daring act.

extolled (ehk STOHLD) *v.* praised.

F

fancy (FAN see) *n.* a liking for something or someone.

fastidious (fas TIHD ee uhs) *adj.* picky; overly fussy.

fawning (FAWN ihng) *v.* used as *adj.* cringing and pleading.

fervor (FUR vuhr) *n.* intense emotion.

feverishly (FEE vuhr ihsh lee) *adv.* in an agitated manner.

fickleness (FIHK uhl nuhs) *n.* changeableness.

fidelity (fy DEHL uh tee) *n.* loyalty; faithfulness.

flaccid (FLAS ihd) *adj.* limp; flabby.

flagged (flagd) *v.* declined; lost strength or interest.

flinging (FLIHNG ihng) *v.* used as *adj.* throwing forcefully.

foliage (FOH lihj) *n.* leafy plants.

folly (FAHL ee) *n.* foolishness.

forlorn (fawr LAWRN) *adj.* hopeless; wretched.

formidable (FAWR muh duh buhl) *adj.* hard to surmount.

forsaken (fawr SAY kuhn) *adj.* forlorn; abandoned.

fragrant (FRAY gruhnt) *adj.* sweet-smelling.

frame (fraym) *v.* shape.

frivolous (FRIHV uh luhs) *adj.* silly or unimportant.

frugal (FROO guhl) *adj.* thrifty; careful with money.

G

gallant (GAL uhnt) *adj.* noble; brave.

garrulous (GAR uh luhs) *adj.* talkative.

gaudy (GAW dee) *adj.* overly bright or colorful.

genial (JEEN yuhl) *adj.* friendly.

ghastly (GAST lee) *adj.* dreadful; ghostly.

girdled (GUR duhld) *v.* used as *adj.* enclosed or circled around.

glade (glayd) *n.* small open space in a forest.

gleaned (gleend) *v.* gathered little by little or gradually.

glimmer (GLIHM uhr) *n.* faint, unsteady light.

gloat (gloht) *v.* feel or express great, often malicious, self-satisfaction or pleasure.

goblet (GAHB liht) *n.* drinking vessel, often ornate.

gourd (gawrd) *n.* a vegetable with a hard rind that can be dried, hollowed out, and used as a bowl.

grievous (GREE vuhs) *adj.* outrageous; horrible.

groveling (GRAHV uhl ihng) *v.* used as *adj.* crawling; begging; humiliating oneself.

guile (gyl) *n.* sly dealings; skill in deceiving.

H

habitual (huh BIHCH oo uhl) *adj.* regular; steady.

haggled (HAG uhld) *v.* argued about a price.

heedless (HEED lihs) *adj.* careless; thoughtless.

hefty (HEHF tee) *adj.* heavy, considerable.

hoard (hawrd) *v.* save or store, often in secret.

hoarding (HAWR dihng) *v.* storing; accumulating.

hulking (HUHLK ihng) *adj.* big and clumsy.

I

idyll (YD uhl) *n.* short work of prose or poetry about an idealized country scene.

ignoble (ihg NOH buhl) *adj.* shameful; degrading.

ignominy (IHG nuh mihn ee) *n.* shame; disgrace.

immobility (ihm oh BIHL uh tee) *n.* lack of movement.

impaired (ihm PAIRD) *v.* marred; weakened.

impassively (ihm PAS ihv lee) *adv.* calmly; indifferently.

impediment (im PEHD uh muhnt) *n.* obstacle; obstruction.

impels (ihm PEHLZ) *v.* forces; causes to move.

impersonality (ihm pur suh NAL uh tee) *n.* lack of human connection.

imperturbable (ihm puhr TUR buh buhl) *adj.* calm, impassive.

impetuous (ihm PEHCH u uhs) *adj.* forceful; violent.

impinge (ihm PIHNJ) *v.* strike; touch.

implacable (ihm PLAK uh buhl) *adj.* impossible to please, satisfy, or change; unyielding.

impotence (IHM puh tuhns) *n.* helplessness.

improvised (IHM pruh vyzd) *v.* used as *adj.* made for the occasion with whatever is handy.

impute (ihm PYOOT) *v.* attribute to someone or something, usually negatively.

incapacitated (ihn kuh PAS uh tayt ihd) *v.* disabled; deprived of power.

incessant (ihn SEHS uhnt) *adj.* constant; never ending.

incoherent (ihn koh HIHR uhnt) *adj.* confused; rambling.

inconstancy (ihn KAHN stuhn see) *n.* changeability or changeableness, specifically, a shift in loyalties ; variability.

incurred (ihn KURD) *v.* brought upon oneself.

indiscriminately (ihn dihs KRIHM uh niht lee) *adv.* without making careful distinctions; randomly.

indivisible (ihn duh VIHZ uh buhl) *adj.* unable to be divided or separated.

industrious (ihn DUHS tree uhs) *adj.* hardworking.

infallible (ihn FAL uh buhl) *adj.* unable to fail or be wrong.

infect (ihn FEHKT) *v.* spread a disease to.

infernal (ihn FUR nuhl) *adj.* hellish; fiendish.

ingenuity (ihn juh NOO uh tee) *n.* cleverness, inventiveness.

ingrained (ihn GRAYND) *adj.* deeply and firmly fixed in one's nature or being.

ingratiate (ihn GRAY shee ayt) *v.* try to gain another's favor or goodwill.

innumerable (ih NOO muhr uh buhl) *adj.* too many to count.

inspiration (ihn spuh RAY shuhn) *n.* influence of thought and strong feelings on actions, especially good actions.

insufficient (ihn suh FIHSH uhnt) *adj.* not enough.

intensity (ihn TEHN suh tee) *n.* great vigor.

intermittent (ihn tuhr MIHT uhnt) *adj.* starting and stopping; periodic.

intoxicating (ihn TAHK suh kay tihng) *v.* used as *adj.* causing wild excitement, often beyond the point of self-control.

intrudes (ihn TROODZ) *v.* pushes in; interrupts.

iridescent (ihr ih DEHS uhnt) *adj.* showing rainbowlike colors.

itinerant (y TIHN uhr uhnt) *adj.* migratory

K

keenly (KEEN lee) *adv.* strongly and clearly.

L

lament (luh MEHNT) *v.* mourn or grieve for.

lamentable (luh MEHN tuh buhl) *adj.* deserving of or inspiring sorrow; regrettable; unfortunate.

languor (LANG guhr) *n.* lack of interest or enthusiasm.

lechery (LEHCH uhr ee) *n.* indulgence in lust.

leisurely (LEE zhuhr lee) *adv.* without hurry; taking plenty of time.

lethal (LEE thuhl) *adj.* deadly.

lilting (LIHLT inhg) *v.* used as *adj.* singing or speaking with a gentle rhythm.

linger (LIHNG guhr) *v.* stay a long while.

livid (LIHV ihd) adj pale; grayish.

loath (lohth) *adj.* unwilling or reluctant.

loathsome (LOHTH suhm) *adj.* very hateful; disgusting.

lugubrious (loo GOO bree uhs) *adj.* solemn or mournful, especially in an excessive way.

M

majesty (MAJ uh stee) *n.* grandeur.

malice (MAL ihs) *n.* active ill will; spite.

maniacal (muh NY uh kuhl) *adj.* crazed; wildly enthusiastic.

manifest (MAN uh fehst) *adj.* evident; obvious.

martyrdom (MAHR tuhr duhm) *n.* death of a martyr, someone who dies for his or her beliefs.

meandering (mee AN duhr ihng) *v.* used as *adj.* wandering with no clear direction.

melancholy (MEHL uhn KAHL ee) *adj.* sad or causing sadness.

melodious (muh LOH dee uhs) *adj.* producing pleasant sounds; tuneful..

mingle (MIHNG guhl) *v.* mix.

minuscule (mih NUHS kyool) *adj.* extremely small.

misanthropy (mih SAN thruh pee) *n.* hatred for humankind.

misery (MIHZ uh ree) *n.* wretchedness; suffering

momentum (moh MEHN tuhm) *n.* the force with which an object moves.

monotonous (muh NAHT uh nuhs) *adj.* unvarying.

moorline (MUR lyn) *n.* edge of a heath or wasteland.

multitudes (MUHL tuh toodz) *n.* pl. crowds; great numbers.

munificence (myoo NIHF uh suhns) *n.* generosity.

murmurous (MUR muhr uhs) *adj.* making consistent soft, low sounds.

mute (myoot) *adj.* not speaking; silent.

N

native (NAY tihv) *adj.* belonging to a person because of birth.

nestled (NEHS uhld) *v.* snugly settled, as in a nest.

nocturnal (nahk TUR nuhl) *adj.* occurring at night.

notorious (noh TAWR ee uhs) *adj.* well known because of something bad; having a bad reputation;

noxious (NAHK shuhs) *adj.* very harmful, often poisonous.

O

object (AHB jihkt) *n.* goal or purpose.

oblivious (uh BLIHV ee uhs) *adj.* unaware or paying no attention to.

obscure (uhb SKYUR) *adj.* little known.

obstinate (AHB stuh niht) *adj.* unreasonably stubborn.

obtained (uhb TAYND) *v.* got; acquired.

odious (OH dee uhs) *adj.* hateful; offensive.

officious (uh FIHSH uhs) *adj.* eager to give unwanted help.

oppressive (uh PREHS ihv) *adj.* hard to bear.

overwrought (oh vuhr RAWT) *adj.* overly excited.

P

pagan (PAY guhn) *n.* a person who believes in many gods or no god.

painstaking (PAYNZ tay kihng) *adj.* using great care.

pallor (PAL uhr) *n.* paleness.

parallel (PAR uh lehl) *adv.* in line with, but without meeting.

passion (PASH uhn) *n.* strong emotion.

pastoral (PAS tuhr uhl) *adj.* of simple or peaceful rural life.

pathos (PAY thahs) *n.* a feeling of sadness or melancholy often brought on by a work of art.

patronize (PAY truh nyz) *v.* be a customer of.

pedantic (peh DAN tihk) *adj.* showing an exaggerated concern for books, learning, and rules.

pensive (PEHN sihv) *adj.* reflective; thoughtful.

perfunctory (puhr FUHNGK tuhr ee) *adj.* halfhearted;

disinterested. —**perfunctorily** *adv.*

perpetual (purh PEHCH oo uhl) *adj.* lasting forever.

perplexed (pehr PLEHKSD) *v.* troubled with doubt; puzzled.

perplexes (pehr PLEHKS uhz) *v.* confuses.

perplexing (puhr PLEHK sihng) *v.* used as *adj.* confusing.

persevered (pur suh VIHRD) *v.* persisted despite difficulty or opposition.

pervades (puhr VAYDZ) *v.* spreads throughout.

perversely (puhr VURS lee) *adv.* disagreeably; contrarily.

pestilence (PEHS tuh luhns) *n.* plague.

piety (PY uh tee) *n.* devotion to religion; holiness.

pilgrimage (PIHL gruh mihj) *n.* a journey, especially to a sacred place.

piqued (peekt) *v.* used as *adj.* provoked; resentful.

piteous (PIHT ee uhs) *adj.* deserving of pity.

plagued (playgd) *v.* used as *adj.* afflicted.

pledge (plehj) *n.* promise or vow.

pledge (plehj) *v.* solemnly promise; drink a toast to.

plight (plyt) *n.* unpromising condition or situation.

posthumous (PAHS choo muhs) *adj.* happening after death.

potency (POH tuhn see) *n.* strength; power.

precautions (prih KAW shuhnz) *n.* care taken in advance; safeguards.

precipitately (prih SIHP uh tiht lee) *adv.* suddenly.

predominant (prih DAHM uh nuhnt) *adj.* having superior influence; prevailing.

prescribe (prih SKRYB) *v.* limit by rules or laws; order.

presumptuous (prih ZUHMP choo uhs) *adj.* going beyond the proper bounds.

pretense (prih TEHNS) *n.* weakly supported claim.

pretext (PREE tehkst) *n.* excuse.

prevailed (prih VAYLD) *v.* gained the desired effect.

prodding (PRAHD ihng) *v.* poking; jabbing.

prodigious (proh DIHJ uhs) *adj.* huge; very great.

pprofane (proh FAYN) *adj.* irreverent; not associated with religious matters.

profuse (pruh FYOOS) *adj.* very abundant.

propensity (pruh PEHN suh tee) *n.* natural inclination.

propitious (pruh PIHSH uhs) *adj.* favorable.

proportion (pruh POHR shuhn) *n.* ratio; relative amount.

prosaic (proh ZAY ihk) *adj.* ordinary; dull.

prosperity (prahs PEHR uh tee) *n.* wealth or good fortune.

prostrate (PRAHS trayt) *adj.* lying flat.

protracted (proh TRAK tihd) *v.* used as *adj.* drawn out over time.

prowess (PROW ihs) *n.* outstanding ability.

prudence (PROO duhns) *n.* cautious management.

punctiliousness (puhngk TIHL ee uhs nuhs) *n.* care for following rules and traditions exactly.

punctual (PUHNGK choo uhl) *adj.* prompt; on time.

Q

quarantine (KWAWR uhn teen) *n.* enforced isolation of ill people so they do not spread their illness to others.

quell (kwehl) *v.* bring under control by subduing.

quench (kwehnch) *v.* put out; extinguish.

R

radiant (RAY dee uhnt) *adj.* shining with beams of light.

rapture (RAP chuhr) *n.* bliss; profound joy.

rash (rash) *adj.* foolhardy.

ravenous (RAV uh nuhs) *adj.* very hungry.

realms (rehlmz) *n. pl.* kingdoms.

rebuffed (rih BUHFD) *v.* rejected with disdain.

reckon (REHK uhn) *v.* estimate; consider; judge.

reckoning (REHK uh nihng) *n.* calculation, accounting.

recompense (REHK uhm pehns) *n.* payment or compensation in return for something lost.

redress (REE drehs) *n.* payment or action that serves to remedy an injustice or injury.

reed (reed) *n.* a kind of tall grass with a hollow, jointed stalk that grows in wet places.

reeks (reeks) *v.* has a strong, bad smell.

reiterate (ree IHT uh rayt) *v.* repeat.

relentlessly (rih LEHNT lihs lee) *adv.* unyielding; without pity.

remonstrated (rih MAHN strayt ihd) *v.* protested.

rendered (REHN duhrd) *v.* made; caused to be.

rendering (REHN duh rihng) *v.* causing to be or become; making.

renounce (rih NOWNS) *v.* formally give up; reject.

renown (rih NOWN) *n.* fame; celebrity.

reparation (rehp uh RAY shuhn) *n.* payment to make up for a wrong or injury.

replenish (rih PLEHN ihsh) *v.* to fill again; to renew.

reprisal (rih PRY zuhl) *n.* punishment in return for an injury.

reproachfully (rih PROHCH fuhl ee) *adv.* accusingly.

reputation (rehp yoo TAY shuhn) *n.* people's opinion of a person.

respite (REHS piht) *n.* postponement; reprieve.

resume (rih ZOOM) *v.* begin again.

revelation (rehv uh LAY shuhn) *n.* act of making known; something revealed.

reverence (REHV uhr uhns) *n.* feeling of great respect and awe.

reverently (REHV uhr uhnt lee) *adv.* with great respect or awe, as for something sacred.

righteous (RY chuhs) *adj.* morally right.

rigor (RIHG uhr) *n.* severity.

rite (ryt) *n.* formal ceremony.

ritualistic (rihch yoo uh LIHS tihk) *adj.* relating to a formal ceremony.

S

sanguine (SANG gwihn) *adj.* reddish in color; red-faced from effort.

satiety (suh TY uh tee) *n.* feeling of disgust or weariness caused by excess.

schism (SKIHZ uhm) *n.* division.

scorn (skawrn) *v.* refuse; reject by showing contempt.

scourge (skurj) *n.* to punish severely, usually with a whip.

scrupulous (SKROO pyoo luhs) *adj.* extremely careful in deciding what is right or wrong.

scurry (SKUR ee) *v.* run away quickly.

secular (SEHK yuh luhr) *adj.* not belonging to a religious order; worldly.

sensual (SEHN shoo uhl) *adj.* appealing to bodily senses rather than to the mind.

sepulchral (suh PUHL kruhl) *adj.* deep and gloomy.

sequestered (sih KWEHS tuhrd) *v.* used as *adj.* set apart from; isolated.

serenely (suh REEN lee) *adv.* calmly; peacefully.

serrated (SEHR ay tihd) *v.* used as *adj.* marked along the edge with jagged, sawlike notches.

servile (SUR vuhl) *adj.* like a slave; submissive.

shied (shyd) *vb.* shrank or flinched away.

sinews (SIHN yooz) *n.* powerful, tough connective tissues.

singularities (sihng gyoo LAR uh teez) *n.* pl. characteristics that make a person unique.

singularly (SIHNG gyuh luhr lee) *adv.* extraordinarily; unusually.

sinuous (SIHN yu uhs) *adj.* winding; twisted.

sloth (slawth) *n.* laziness; idleness.

slovenly (SLUHV uhn lee) *adj.* untidy.

sneer (snihr) *n.* proud, unkind facial expression.

somber (SAHM buhr) *adj.* gloomy.

sordid (SAWR dihd) *adj.* filthy; foul.

specious (SPEE shuhs) *adj.* showy but false.

splendor (SPLEHN duhr) *n.* great brightness; brilliant light.

spontaneous (spahn TAY nee uhs) *adj.* caused by natural impulse; not forced.

squalid (SKWAHL ihd) *adj.* foul; dirty.

squall (skwawl) *n.* brief, violent storm.

stealthy (STEHL thee) *adj.* secret; sly.

stratagems (STRAT uh juhmz) *n.* pl. clever plans to achieve a goal.

stridently (STRY duhnt lee) *adv.* harshly; sharply.

sublime (suh BLYM) *adj.* awe inspiring due to majesty or nobility.

successive (suhk SEHS ihv) *adj.* following in consecutive order.

succor (SUHK uhr) *v.* to help in time of distress.

summon (SUHM uhn) *v.* call.

superciliously (soo puhr SIHL ee uhs lee) *adv.* disdainfully, scornfully.

supplant (suh PLANT) *v.* replace; displace.

supplement (SUHP luh muhnt) *n.* something added to make complete or to enrich.

supplication (suhp luh KAY shuhn) *n.* humble plea.

suppressed (suh PREHST) *v.* used as *adj.* kept from being known.

surly (SUR lee) *adj.* bad-tempered; unfriendly.

surreptitiously (sur uhp TIHSH uhs lee) *adv.* in a secret or sneaky manner.

sustenance (SUHS tuh nuhns) *n.* food or provisions needed to support life.

T

taciturn (TAS uh turn) *adj.* not talkative.

teeming (TEEM ihng) *v.* used as *adj.* full of; alive with; fruitful.

temerity (tuh MEHR uh tee) *n.* reckless boldness.

temperate (TEHM puhr iht) *adj.* moderate.

temporal (TEHM puhr uhl) *adj.* limited to this world; not spiritual.

thatched (thacht) *v.* used as *adj.* covered with straw, leaves, or similar materials.

thermal (THUR muhl) *adj.* relating to heat.

torment (TAWR mehnt) *n.* great pain.

tortuous (TAWR choo uhs) *adj.* characterized by twists and turns.

traditions (truh DIHSH uhnz) *n.* pl. customs, values, or ideas handed down from generation to generation.

transgress (trans GREHS) *v.* sin against; violate a limit.

transitory (TRAN suh tawr ee) *adj.* not permanent.

treachery (TREHCH uhr ee) *n.* a breaking of faith; betrayal of trust.

tremulous (TREHM yuh luhs) *adj.* quivering; wavering.

tribulation (trihb yuh LAY shuhn) *n.* great trouble or misery.

tribute (TRIHB yoot) *n.* something done to show respect.

tumult (TOO muhlt) *n.* great noise; agitation.

tuneful (TOON fuhl) *adj.* musical; melodious.

turbid (TUR bihd) *adj.* cloudy; confused.

turmoil (TUR moyl) *n.* state of agitation or commotion.

tyrannous (TIHR uh nuhs) *adj.* harsh; oppressive.

U

uncanny (uhn KAN ee) *adj.* strange; eerie; weird.

uncouth (uhn KOOTH) *adj.* unsophisticated; awkward.

underfoot (uhn duhr FUT) *adv.* between the feet and the ground.

undeterminable (uhn dih TUR muh nuh buhl) *adj.* not able to be measured or decided.

unendurable (uhn ehn DOOR uh buhl) *adj* more than can be tolerated.

unpremeditated (uhn pree MEHD uh tay tihd) *adj.* not planned in advance.

unpretentious (uhn prih TEHN shuhs) *adj.* modest.

V

vain (vayn) *adj.* of no use; producing no good result.

valiant (VAL yuhnt) *adj.* brave; courageous.

vanquish (VANG kwihsh) *v.* defeat in battle or conflict.

vehemently (VEE uh muhnt lee) *adv.* with strong feeling; passionately.

veneer (vuh NIHR) *n.* a surface appearance or show.

vexed (vehkst) *v.* troubled or disturbed.

vie (vy) *v.* compete.

vile (vyl) *adj.* evil, disgusting.

virtuous (VUR choo uhs) *adj.* moral; righteous.

vivacity (vy VAS uh tee) *n.* liveliness; energetic spirit.

W

wan (wahn) *adj.* faint or weak in a way suggesting sadness, sickness, or weariness.

waning (WAYN ihng) *v.* fading gradually.

welded (WEHLD ihd) *v.* used as *adj.* joined; sealed.

whetting (HWEHT ihng) *v.* used as *adj.* act of sharpening a blade on a stone made for the purpose.

whimsical (HWIHM zuh kuhl) *adj.* fanciful.

withered (WIHTH uhrd) *v.* used as *adj.* dried up.

withers (WIHTH uhrz) *v.* fades; dries up.

wrenched (rehncht) *v.* used as *adj.* anguished; grief-stricken.

wretched (REHCH ihd) *adj.* miserable; unhappy.

writhing (RY thihng) *v.* used as *adj.* twisting and turning, as in pain.

Z

zeal (zeel) *n.* eager enthusiasm.

zealously (ZEHL uhs lee) *adv.* fervently; devotedly.

zenith (ZEE nihth) *n.* the highest point.

Spanish Glossary

A

abarrotar *v.* llenar con algo.

abatido *adj.* desalentado; afligido.

abolir *v.* anular; cancelar.

abominable *adj.* desagradable; odioso.

aborrecible *adj.* detestable; ofensivo.

abrazar *v.* aceptar gustosamente; adoptar.

absolver *v.* perdonar; librar de culpas.

abstener *v.* no hacer algo.

acaparar *v.* guardar o almacenar, a menudo en secreto.

acongojado *v.* abatir.

acopiar *v.* amontonar; acumular.

admitir *v.* reconocer que algo es cierto.

adular *v.* arrastrarse y suplicar.

adversario *sust.* enemigo; oponente.

afectación *sust.* comportamiento artificial planeado para impresionar a otras personas.

afilar *v.* hacer más filosa una cuchilla usando una piedra que sirve para esa función.

afinidad *sust.* similitud; lazo.

aflicción *sust.* sufrimiento; algo que causa dolor o preocupación.

agraviado *adj.* sentirse herido o maltratado.

ajeno *adj.* que no es conciente o no presta atención a algo.

alojar *v.* dar lugar.

altaneramente *adv.* con desprecio.

altruista *adj.* que no es egoísta.

amainar *v.* disminuir.

ambicioso *adj.* que aspira a un objetivo muy difícil de alcanzar.

amilanar *v.* intimidar.

anales *sust. pl.* registros, organizados por año, que cuentan la historia de alguien o algo.

anarquía *sust.* desorden y confusión.

anidar *v.* ubicarse cómodamente, como en un nido.

animosidad *sust.* hostilidad; resentimiento u odio violento.

aniquilar *v.* destruir; hacer que algo deje de existir.

anotado *adj.* que tiene notas escritas con explicaciones.

antiguo *adj.* viejo.

apatía *sust.* falta de interés.

apertura *sust.* abertura.

apesadumbrado *adj.* angustiado; afligido.

aplacar *v.* controlar.

aprensivo *adj.* ansioso y preocupado.

apuro *sust.* condición o situación poco prometedora.

arable *adj.* que puede cultivarse.

ardiente *adj.* entusiasta.

ardor *sust.* emoción intensa.

armónico *adj.* musical; melodioso.

arraigado *adj.* firmemente establecido en uno mismo o en la propia naturaleza.

artificio *sust.* destreza u oficio humano, opuesto a lo natural.

artificio *sust.* trampa; engaño.

ascender *v.* subir.

ascua *sust.* restos de una fogata que está por extinguirse.

aséptico *adj.* objetivo; sin sentimiento.

aspirar *v.* tratar de alcanzar un objetivo.

astucia *sust.* uso de métodos maliciosos; habilidad para engañar.

atribular *v.* afligir.

atroz *adj.* espantoso; terrible.

atroz *adj.* terrible; horrible.

aturdido *adj.* confundido.

aturdido *v.* used as *adj.* confundido.

audazmente *adv.* con atrevimiento.

aunque *conj.* si bien.

austero *adj.* sobrio; muy sencillo.

avaricia *sust.* deseo incontrolable de riquezas.

azotar *v.* castigar violentamente, en general con un látigo.

B

bajo los pies *loc. adv.* entre los pies y el piso.

benigno *adj.* amable; gentil.

berrear *v.* llorar en voz muy alta.

bibliófilo *sust.* persona a la que le encantan los libros.

blandir *v.* sacudir de modo amenazante.

blanquear *v.* hacer que algo se vuelva blanco o pálido.

bordado *adj.* decorado con aplicaciones de hilo o como si tuviera aplicaciones de hilo.

botánico *adj.* relativo a las plantas o la flora; que tiene que ver con la ciencia botánica.

bruñir *v.* hacer que algo luzca brillante y liso.

burdo *adj.* poco sofisticado; ordinario.

C

cadencia *sust.* ritmo de un movimiento repetitivo; sonido que se eleva y cae.

cadencioso *adj.* caracterizado por un ritmo moderado.

cáliz *sust.* recipiente para beber, a menudo ornamentado.

candor *sust.* honestidad; sinceridad.

candor *sust.* honestidad; sinceridad.

capricho *sust.* idea o deseo repentino.

casta *sust.* clase social.

casto *adj.* puro, decente o modesto de carácter y comportamiento.

celestial *adj.* relativo al cielo.

celosamente *adv.* fervientemente; devotamente.

cenit *sust.* el punto más alto.

censurar *v.* expresar desaprobación.

certeza *sust.* sentimiento de seguridad.

charlatán *adj.* conversador.

chillón *adj.* demasiado brillante o colorido.

circundar *v.* rodear o cercar.

cisma *sust.* división.

claro *sust.* pequeño espacio abierto en un bosque.

codicia *sust.* deseo de tener lo que pertenece a otros.

coherentemente *adv.* clara y lógicamente.

colosal *adj.* extraordinariamente grande.

combate *sust.* batalla militar.

combinar *v.* mezclar.

combustible *adj.* que arde con facilidad.

compadecer *v.* sentir pena o dolor por algo o alguien.

compatible *adj.* que puede existir o funcionar con otra cosa.

compromiso *sust.* promesa o juramento.

compulsivo *adj.* causado por un impulso irresistible.

cómputo *sust.* cálculo, cuenta.

concepción *sust.* el origen de algo.

condenar *v.* sentenciar.

condolencia *sust.* expresión de simpatía que se ofrece a una persona apenada.

conducta *sust.* forma en la que se comporta una persona.

congraciar *v.* intentar obtener el favor o la aprobación de otra persona.

conjeturar *v.* razonar; adivinar.

conmoción *sust.* estado de agitación o alteración.

consagrar *v.* hacer honorable y sagrado.

consecuentemente *adv.* como resultado de algo.

consentimiento *sust.* aceptacón.

conspicuo *adj.* que llama la atención.

consternado *adj.* extremadamente agitado.

contienda *sust.* lucha.

contorsión *sust.* movimiento o forma retorcido.

conturbar *v.* preocupar; alarmar.

convertir *v.* hacer que algo sea de determinada manera.

convertir *v.* causar; hacer que algo o alguien sea otra cosa.

convicción *sust.* seguridad o creencia firme.

convicción *sust.* creencia firme.

convocar *v.* llamar.

copioso *adj.* abundante; cuantioso.

copioso *adj.* abundante; cuantioso.

corpóreo *adj.* relativo al cuerpo.

corromper *v.* hacer que algo sea impuro.

cortesano *sust.* miembro del séquito de un palacio.

cosmopolita *adj.* de mucho mundo; sofisticado.

credo *sust.* puntos esenciales de una creencia religiosa.

cuarentena *sust.* aislamiento forzado de una persona enferma para que no contagie su enfermedad a otros.

cultivar *v.* desarrollar; promover.

D

deambular *v.* caminar sin rumbo definido.

decretar *v.* ordenar; mandar.

deidad *sust.* dios.

demandar *v.* ordenar; pedir.

demolición *sust.* destrucción.

denigrar *v.* arrastrarse; suplicar; humillarse.

deplorable *adj.* que inspira pena.

deplorable *adj.* lamentable; desafortunado.

derecho de autor *sust.* derecho legal a usar, vender o distribuir cualquier material que se pueda imprimir o publicar, como libros, canciones y caracteres.

derivar *v.* provenir de determinada fuente.

derrotar *v.* ganarle a alguien en una batalla o conflicto.

desafiante *adj.* rebelde; desobediente.

desaliñado *adj.* desordenado.

desapasionadamente *adv.* sin emoción; imparcialmente.

descomunal *adj.* grande y torpe.

desconcertar *v.* preocupar con dudas; confundir.

desconcertar *v.* confundir.

desconcertar *v.* confundir.

desdén *sust.* expresión orgullosa y poco amable.

desdicha *sust.* desgracia; sufrimiento.

desencanto *sust.* desilusión o abandono una idea falsa.

desesperado *adj.* dominado por la desesperanza;

impulsado a emplear medios extremos para intentar escapar a la frustración y la pérdida.

desestimar *v.* rechazar con desdén.

desierto *adj.* abandonado.

desolación *sust.* tristeza; soledad.

desolación *sust.* desdicha absoluta; soledad extrema.

desolado *adj.* inhabitado; árido; deprimente.

desorientar *v.* confundir.

despectivo *adj.* despreciativo.

despectivo *adj.* que muestra gran disgusto o es muy irrespetuoso.

desplazar *v.* mover de su ubicación habitual.

despreciar *v.* no aceptar; rechazar con desdén.

despreocupado *adj.* sin preocupaciones; feliz.

destilar *v.* extraer la esencia de algo.

desventurado *adj.* desgraciado; infeliz.

desventurado adj infeliz.

desviar *v.* apartar de un camino, norma o verdad.

deterioro *sust.* consumición, podredumbre; disminución de la calidad.

diabólico *adj.* relacionado con el mal o el demonio.

difuso *adj.* esparcido; que no está concentrado en un solo lugar.

dilatar *v.* expandir; hinchar.

diligencia *sust.* cuidado.

discordia *sust.* conflicto.

discurso *sust.* conversación o habla.

disminuir *v.* hacer más pequeño; rebajar; reducir.

disparar *v.* correr muy rápido.

dispersar *v.* separar y desparramar.

distorsionar *v.* deformar.

disuadir *v.* aconsejar en contra de algo.

divagar *v.* alejarse del asunto que se trata.

divino *adj.* similar a Dios o a un dios, o relativo a él; brindado o inspirado por Dios.

doctrina *sust.* enseñanzas de la iglesia.

dominio *sust.* territorio que pertenece a alguien, ya sea por propiedad, habilidad o responsabilidad.

dotar *v.* equipar con algo.

E

eficacia *sust.* capacidad de producir el efecto deseado.

eficaz *adj.* efectivo o útil.

elaborar *v.* preparar (comida o bebida) mezclando una variedad de ingredientes.

emanar *v.* fluir; aparecer.

embelesar *v.* causar gran excitación, a menudo más allá del autocontrol.

eminencia *sust.* alto rango o posición.

eminente *adj.* excelente, grandioso.

empajar *v.* cubrir con paja, hojas o materiales similares.

enchapado *adj.* que tiene una capa de algo en la superficie.

encomiar *v.* alabar.

enemistad *sust.* hostilidad.

engaño *sust.* falsa creencia.

engañoso *adj.* que parece cierto pero es falso.

engarabitar *v.* trepar con torpeza.

entendido *sust.* persona de gusto muy refinado que sabe mucho sobre un tema.

epílogo *sust.* sección corta al final de una obra literaria que a menudo cuenta qué pasó después del final del relato.

epíteto *sust.* expresión descriptiva.

erecto *adj.* derecho.

escandaloso *adj.* famoso por algo negativo; que tiene mala reputación.

escandaloso *adj.* famoso por su mala reputación.

escrupuloso *adj.* extremadamente cuidadoso en decidir qué está bien y qué está mal.

espantoso *adj.* terrible; que causa temor.

esplendor *sust.* brillo fuerte; luz brillante.

espontáneo *adj.* causado por un impulso natural; que no es forzado.

estallar *v.* explotar.

estética *sust.* conjunto de principios de la belleza.

estimar *v.* considerar; juzgar.

estratagema *sust.* plan inteligente para alcanzar un objetivo.

estrepitoso *adj.* ruidoso.

estridentemente *adv.* con severidad; con dureza.

etéreo *adj.* suave y delicado; de otro mundo.

euforia *n.* excitación; alegría.

exaltado *adj.* demasiado agitado.

excepcionalmente *adv.* particularmente; extraordinariamente.

expediente *sust.* modo de obtener algo; medio para alcanzar un objetivo.

expirar *verbo.* morir; terminar.

extasiado *adj.* extremadamente alegre; que demuestra gran placer.

éxtasis *sust.* alegría; felicidad absoluta.

extravagante *adj.* fuera de lo normal sin razón aparente.

F

famélico *adj.* que tiene mucha hambre.

fascinación *sust.* atracción por algo o por alguien.

febrilmente *adv.* con agitación o excitación.

fervor *sust.* entusiasmo y ansiedad.

fidelidad *sust.* lealtad.

flácido *adj.* flojo; blando.

flaquear *v.* disminuir; perder fuerza o interés.

follaje *sust.* plantas con muchas hojas.

formidable *adj.* difícil de manejar o soportar.

fragante *adj.* que tiene un aroma agradable.

frecuentar *v.* aquí, ser cliente de alguien.

frenar *v.* detener el movimiento.

frívolo *adj.* superficial o poco importante.

frívolo *adj.* superficial; que no tiene seriedad.

furtivo *adj.* secreto; disimulado.

G

gallardo *adj.* noble; valiente.

genial *adj.* simpático, agradable.

güira *sust.* fruto de cáscara dura que puede ser secado, ahuecado y usado como recipiente.

H

habitual *adj.* frecuente, constante.

hastío *sust.* sensación de disgusto o cansancio provocada por un exceso.

heder *v.* tener mal olor.

hosco *adj.* malhumorado; poco amable.

hosco *adj.* grosero o poco amistoso.

I

idilio *sust.* texto corto en prosa o verso sobre una escena ideal relacionada con el campo.

impávidamente *adv.* calmadamente; indiferentemente.

impedimento *sust.* obstáculo; dificultad.

impedimento *sust.* obstáculo; estorbo.

impeler *v.* incitar; estimular.

impersonalidad *sust.* falta de relación con los pensamientos, sentimientos, etc. de una persona.

impertinente *adj.* que sobrepasa los límites de lo correcto.

imperturbable *adj.* calmo, sereno.

impetuoso *adj.* enérgico; violento.

implacable *adj.* imposible de complacer, satisfacer o cambiar; que no cede.

importunar *v.* molestar; interrumpir.

impotencia *sust.* desesperanza.

improvisar *v.* no planificar.

improvisar *v.* hacer en el momento, con lo que se tiene a mano.

imprudente *adj.* insensato.

impulso *sust.* fuerza por la cual se mueve un objeto.

imputar *v.* atribuir algo a alguien.

incapacitar *sust.* inhabilitar, quitar el poder.

incesante *adj.* constante; que nunca termina.

incoherente *adj.* confuso; ilógico.

inconstancia *sust.* cambio o transformación, especialmente un cambio en la lealtad hacia otra persona; variabilidad.

incurrir *v.* atraer algo sobre uno mismo.

indemnización *sust.* pago en compensación por un mal o un daño hecho.

indeterminable *adj.* que no se puede medir o determinar.

indiscriminadamente *adv.* sin hacer distinciones cuidadosas, al azar.

indivisible *adj.* que no se puede separar.

inexorablemente *adv.* inflexiblemente; sin piedad.

infalible *adj.* que no falla ni se equivoca.

infernal *adj.* relativo al infierno; endemoniado.

infinito *adj.* que no tiene límites.

ingenio *sust.* inteligencia; creatividad.

inmovilidad *sust.* falta de movimiento.

innato *adj.* que pertenece a una persona de nacimiento.

innoble *adj.* vergonzoso.

innumerable *adj.* que son tantos que no se pueden contar.

inquietante *adj.* extraño; asombroso; raro.

inspiración *sust.* influencia del pensamiento y de fuertes sentimientos sobre las acciones, especialmente buenas acciones.

insuficiente *adj.* que no alcanza.

insufrible adj que no se puede tolerar.

intermitente *adj.* que empieza y se detiene a intervalos; periódico.

intimidar *v.* lograr que otra persona pierda el coraje.

irisado *adj.* que muestra colores similares a los del arco iris.

irreflexivo *adj.* descuidado; desconsiderado.

itinerante *adj.* que viaja.

J

jovialidad *sust.* ligereza de ánimo; alegría.

júbilo *sust.* ánimo; alegría.

juicioso *adj.* que muestra buen juicio, perceptivo.

junco *sust.* tipo de pasto alto con un tallo hueco que crece en lugares húmedos.

jurar *v.* prometer solemnemente.

L

laborioso *adj.* trabajador.

lamentar *v.* sentir pena o dolor por algo.

languidez *sust.* falta de interés o de entusiasmo.

lánguido *adj.* débil de una manera que expresa

tristeza, enfermedad o cansancio.

lanzar *v.* arrojar con fuerza.

lascivia *sust.* propensión a la lujuria.

lastimoso *adj.* digno de lástima.

latón *sust.* metal compuesto de cobre y cinc.

lealtad *sust.* fidelidad.

legado *sust.* aquello que se regala en un testamento.

letal *adj.* mortal.

lívido adj pálido; sin color.

loable *adj.* que merece admiración.

lúgubre *adj.* sombrío.

lúgubre *adj.* extremadamente solemne o triste.

M

majestuosidad *sust.* grandeza.

malicia *sust.* intención de hacer el mal; maldad.

maníaco *adj.* enloquecido; excesivamente entusiasta.

manifiesto *adj.* evidente; obvio.

marchitar *v.* debilitar.

marchitar *v.* desvanecer; secarse.

martirio *sust.* muerte de un mártir, alguien que muere por sus creencias.

meditabundo *adj.* pensativo; que reflexiona mucho.

melancólico *adj.* triste o que provoca tristeza.

melodioso *adj.* que produce sonidos agradables.

melodioso *adj.* que produce un sonido dulce; placentero al oído.

menguar *v* disminuir lentamente.

menospreciar *v* rebajar; hablar negativamente de algo o alguien.

mesurado *adj.* ahorrativo; cuidadoso con el dinero.

meticulosidad *sust.* atencián en seguir las reglas y las tradiciones con exactitud.

minucioso *adj.* hecho con cuidado.

minúsculo *adj.* extremadamente pequeño.

misantropía *sust.* odio a la humanidad.

mitigar *verbo.* atenuar.

modesto *adj.* sencillo; sin pretensiones.

moldear *v.* formar.

monótono *adj.* que no varía.

mudo *adj.* que no habla; silencioso.

multitud *sust.* muchedumbre; cantidad grande de algo.

munificencia *sust.* generosidad.

N

naturaleza *sust.* características naturales de la personalidad.

necedad *sust.* tontería.

nocivo *adj.* muy dañino, a menudo venenoso.

nocturno *adj.* que ocurre durante la noche.

O

objetar *v.* protestar.

objetivo *sust.* meta o propósito.

obligatorio *adj.* requerido; forzoso.

obstinado *adj.* excesivamente testarudo.

obstinado *adj.* persistente; terco.

obtener *v.* conseguir; recibir.

oficioso *adj.* ansioso de ofrecer ayuda no requerida.

opresivo *adj.* difícil de soportar.

oprobio *sust.* vergüenza; deshonra.

oscuro *adj.* poco conocido.

P

pagano *sust.* persona que cree en muchos dioses o en ninguno.

palidez *sust.* blancura.

paralelo *adj.* que está alineado con algo, pero no lo cruza.

páramo *sust.* terreno frío y desamparado.

particularidad *sust.* característica que hace a una persona única.

pasión *sust.* emoción fuerte.

pasión *sust.* emoción fuerte.

pasmar *v.* molestar.

pastoral *adj.* relativo a la vida sencilla o pacífica del campo.

patetismo *sust.* sentimiento de tristeza o melancolía a menudo provocado por una obra de arte.

pavoroso *adj.* que inspira temor y respeto.

pedante *adj.* que muestra una preocupación exagerada por los libros, el aprendizaje y las reglas.

peregrinación viaje, especialmente a un lugar sagrado.

perenne *adj.* eterno; que dura para siempre.

pereza *sust.* holgazanería; flojera.

pericia *sust.* capacidad extraordinaria.

perjudicar *v.* estropear; debilitar.

permanecer *v.* quedarse durante un largo rato.

perpetuo *adj.* que dura para siempre.

perseverar *v.* continuar a pesar de las dificultades o la oposición; persistir.

perversamente *adv.* de mala manera.

pestilencia *sust.* plaga.

piedad *sust.* devoción por la religión; santidad.

plácidamente *adv.* sin apuro; tomándose mucho tiempo.

poso *sust.* sedimento.

postrado *adj.* que yace acostado.

póstumo *adj.* que sucede después de la muerte.

potencia *sust.* fuerza, poder.

precaución *sust.* medida de cuidado que se toma de antemano.

precipitadamente *adv.* de repente.

precipitado *adj.* rápido.

predominante *adj.* que tiene una influencia superior; que prevalece.

prescribir *v.* limitar por medio de reglas y leyes; ordenar; determinar.

pretensión *sust.* reclamo débilmente respaldado.

pretexto *sust.* excusa.

prevalecer *v.* lograr el efecto deseado.

proclamar *v.* declarar.

prodigioso *adj.* extraordinario; maravilloso.

prodigioso *adj.* enorme.

proeza *n.* acto de valentía.

profano *adj.* irrespetuoso; que no se relaciona con asuntos religiosos.

profuso *adj.* muy abundante.

prolongar *v.* alargar en el tiempo.

promover acelerar el crecimiento o el progreso de algo o alguien.

propagar *v.* contagiar una enfermedad.

propagar *v.* expandirse por todos lados.

propensión *sust.* inclinación o tendencia natural.

propicio *dj.* favorable.

proporción *sust.* razón; cantidad relativa.

prórroga *sust.* postergación; retraso.

prosaico *adj.* ordinario; aburrido.

prosperidad *sust.* riqueza o buena fortuna.

prudencia *sust.* comportamiento cuidadoso.

puntilloso *adj.* manático; demasiado exigente.

puntual *adj.* sin demora; a tiempo.

punzar *v.* pinchar; clavar.

R

radiante *adj.* que irradia luz.

reacio *adj.* que no está dispuesto a hacer algo.

reanudar *v.* continuar.

recluir *v.* separar; incomunicar.

recolectar *v.* juntar de a poco o gradualmente.

recompensa *sust.* pago o compensación a cambio de algo que se había perdido y se ha encontrado.

recto *adj.* moralmente correcto.

reflexión *sust.* pensamiento profundo; meditación.

regatear *v.* discutir por un precio.

regodearse *v.* sentir o expresar gran placer y satisfacción, a menudo maliciosamente.

reino *sust.* territorio dominado por un rey.

reiterar *v.* repetir.

reiterar *v.* repetir.

renombre *sust.* fama; celebridad.

renunciar *v.* rendirse formalmente; rechazar.

reponer *v.* volver a llenar; renovar.

represalia *sust.* castigo en respuesta a una agresión u ofensa.

reproche *sust.* acusación.

repugnante *adj.* odioso; desagradable.

reputación *sust.* la buena opinión que tiene la gente sobre una persona.

resarcimiento *sust.* compensación o pago por una pérdida.

resarcimiento *sust.* pago o acción que sirve como remedio de una injusticia o de un daño.

resentirse *v.* sentir rencor o despecho.

respingar *v.* encogerse o estremecerse.

retorcer *v.* moverse o sacudirse por dolor.

revelación *sust.* acto de dar algo a conocer.

revelación *sust.* algo que se descubre.

reverencia *sust.* sentimiento de respeto o veneración.

reverencia *sust.* respeto profundo.

reverencialmente *adv.* con veneración y respeto.

reverencialmente *adv.* con gran respeto, como el que se tiene por algo sagrado.

rigor *sust.* firmeza.

risueño *adj.* feliz y despreocupado.

rito *sust.* ceremonia formal.

ritualista *adj.* relativo a una ceremonia formal.

rivalizar *v.* competir.

robusto *adj.* pesado; corpulento.

S

saciar *v.* aliviar; calmar.

sancionar *sust.* aprobar; autorizar.

sanguíneo *adj.* rojizo.

secular *adj.* que no pertenece a ninguna orden religiosa; mundano.

seducir *v.* atraer despertando esperanzas y deseos; tentar.

semblante *sust.* expresión en la cara de una persona.

sensual *adj.* relativo a los cinco sentidos.

sensual *adj.* que apela a los sentidos del cuerpo en vez de a la mente.

sepulcral *adj.* profundo y oscuro.

serenamente *adv.* calmadamente; pacíficamente.

serrado *adj.* que tiene dientes como los de una sierra a lo largo del borde.

servil *adj.* dedicado ciegamente.

servil *adj.* como un esclavo; obediente.

sinuoso *adj.* con muchas curvas; torcido.

socorrer *v.* ayudar en caso de peligro o necesidad.

sofocar *v.* apagar; extinguir.

soldar *v.* unir; sellar.

solidificar *v.* espesar.

sombrío *adj.* lúgubre.

someramente *adv.* mecánicamente; sin cuidado.

somero *adj.* poco entusiasta; indiferente.

soportar *v.* resistir.

sórdido *adj.* sucio; repugnante.

sórdido adj sucio; desagradable.

sórdido *adj.* impuro; sucio.

sublime *adj.* impresionante por ser noble o majestuoso.

subrepticiamente *adv.* en secreto o a escondidas.

sucesivo *adj.* que sigue en orden consecutivo.

suplantar *v.* reemplazar; desplazar.

suplemento *sust.* algo agregado a una dieta, a menudo para compensar una deficiencia.

súplica *sust.* humilde ruego.

suprimir *v.* evitar que se conozca.

sustento *sust.* comida o provisiones necesarias para vivir.

susurrante *adj.* que produce un ruido suave y continuo.

T

taciturno adj callado.

temeridad *sust.* atrevimiento tonto o impulsivo; insensatez.

templado *adj.* moderado.

temporal *adj.* limitado a este mundo; que no es espiritual.

tendón *sust.* tejido fibroso y fuerte de gran poder conector.

térmico *adj.* relacionado con el calor.

tirano *adj.* severo; opresivo.

tolerar *v.* soportar.

tolerar *v.* sufrir; tolerar.

tormento *sust.* gran angustia.

tortuoso *adj.* lleno de vueltas o curvas.

tosco *adj.* de baja calidad; áspero.

tradición *sust.* costumbres, valores o ideas que se pasan de generación en generación.

traición *sust.* deslealtad; abuso de confianza.

transgredir *v.* ir en contra de algo; violar un límite impuesto.

transitorio *adj.* que no es permanente.

transmitir *v.* comunicar; expresar.

trastornar *v.* inquietar o perturbar.

trémulo *adj.* que tiembla o se tambalea.

tribulación *sust.* gran preocupación o pena.

tributo *sust.* algo hecho en honor a alguien.

tumulto *sust.* ruido grande; agitación.

turbación *sust.* frustración; vergüenza.

turbio *adj.* empañado; confuso.

turbión *sust.* tormenta violenta y breve.

V

valeroso *adj.* valiente; que tiene coraje.

vano *adj.* inútil; que no produce ningún resultado bueno.

vehementemente *adv.* violentamente.

vehementemente *adv.* con gran sentimiento; apasionadamente.

velado *v.* oculto.

verosímil *adj.* creíble.

vigor *sust.* gran intensidad.

vil *adj.* malvado, desagradable.

vil *adj.* desagradable.

virtuoso *adj.* moral; recto.

vislumbre *sust.* luz débil y temblorosa.

vivacidad *sust.* animación; espíritu energético.

vivamente *adv.* con fuerza y claridad.

volubilidad *sust.* capacidad de cambio.

vulnerar *v.* golpear; afectar.

Academic Vocabulary Glossary

The Academic Vocabulary Glossary in this section is an alphabetical list of the academic vocabulary words found in this textbook. Use this glossary just as you would use a dictionary—to find out the meanings of words used in your literature class to talk about and write about literary and informational texts and to talk about and write about concepts and topics in your other academic classes.

For each word, the glossary includes the pronunciation, part of speech, and meaning. A Spanish version of the glossary immediately follows the English version. For more information about the words in the Academic Vocabulary Glossary, please consult a dictionary.

ENGLISH

A

adapt (uh DAPT) *v.* adjust for a new purpose.
approach (uh PROHCH) *n.* a way of addressing something.
attribute (uh TRIHB yoot) *v.* regard as being caused by something.

B

benefit (BEHN uh fiht) *n.* anything that is for the good of a person or thing.

C

complex (kuhm PLEHKS) *adj.* hard to understand; complicated.
concept (KAHN sehpt) *n.* notion or idea.
considerably (kuhn SIHD uhr uh blee) *adv.* by a large amount.
controversies (KAHN truh vur seez) *n.* lengthy disagreement.
convince (kuhn VIHNS) *v.* persuade; cause to believe.

D

device (dih VYS) *n.* something made for a particular purpose.
differentiate (dihf uh REHN shee ayt) *v.* distinguish; identify differences.
diverse (duh VURS) *adj.* varied.
dominate (DAHM uh nayt) *v.* hold a commanding position.

E

emphasis (EHM fuh sihs) *n.* stress; importance.
enhance (ehn HANS) *v.* improve the quality of.
ensure (ehn SHOOR) *v.* to make certain.
established (ehs TAB lihsht) *v.* set up; caused to happen.
exhibit (ehg ZIHB iht) *v.* show, demonstrate.

F

function (FUNGK shuhn) *n.* the action for which a person or thing is specially fitted; purpose.

I

inevitable (ihn EHV uh tuh buhl) *adj.* unavoidable.
inherent (ihn HIHR uhnt) *adj.* existing in something as a fixed, essential quality.

P

participate (par TIHS uh payt) *v.* take part in.
perspective (puhr SPEHK tihv) *n.* particular way of looking at something.
publish (PUHB lihsh) *v.* print and issue for the public.

R

respond (rih SPAHND) *v.* react.

S

statistics (stuh TIHS tihks) *n. pl.* numerical facts.
status (STAT uhs) *n.* social or professional rank.

T

technique (tehk NEEK) *n.* method; way of using skills.

W

widespread (WYD SPREHD) *adj.* occurring over a wide area.

SPANISH

A

adaptar *v.:* ajustar a un nuevo propósito.
artefacto *sust.* algo construido para un fin específico.
atribuir *v.* considerar que es la causa de algo.

B

beneficio *sust.* algo que sea para el bien de una persona o cosa.

C

complejo *adj.* difícil de entender; complicado.
concepto *sust.* noción o idea.
considerablemente *adv.* por gran cantidad.
controversia *sust.* desacuerdo o discusión prolongada.

D

diferenciar *v.* distinguir; reconocer lo que es distinto.
diverso *adj.* variado.
dominar *v.* tener poder.

E

énfasis *sust.* hincapié; importancia.
enfoque *v.* modo de considerar algo.
estadística *sust.* datos numéricos.
estatus *sust.* rango social o profesional.
exhibir *v.* mostrar, demostrar.

F

función *sust.* acción para la que una persona está especialmente capacitada; propósito.

G

generalizado *adj.* que ocurre en un área amplia.

I

ineludible *adj.* inevitable.
inherente *adj.* que existe como una cualidad natural e inseparable de algo.
instaurar *v.* establecer; permitir que algo ocurra.

P

participar *v.* formar parte de algo.
perfeccionar *v.* mejorar la calidad de algo.
perspectiva *sust.* modo particular de ver algo.
persuadir *v.* convencer; hacer que alguien crea algo.
publicar *v.* imprimir algo y distribuirlo al público.

R

ratificar *v.* dar certeza.
reaccionar *v.* responder.

T

técnica *sust.* método; modo de usar las destrezas.

ACKNOWLEDGMENTS

For permission to reprint copyrighted material, grateful acknowledgment is made to the following sources:

"B. Wordsworth" from *Miguel Street* by V. S. Naipaul. Copyright © 1959 by V. S. Naipaul. Reproduced by permission of **Gillon Aitken Associates Ltd.**

"Raven doth to raven fly" from *Alexander Pushkin: Collected Narrative and Lyrical Poetry,* translated by Walter Arndt. Copyright © 1984 by Walter Arndt. Reproduced by permission of **Ardis Publishers.**

From *Walking to Canterbury* by Jerry Ellis. Copyright © 2003 by Jerry Ellis. Reproduced by permission of **Ballentine Books, a division of Random House, Inc., www.randomhouse.com.**

From "The Second Teaching: Philosophy and Spiritual Decline" from *The Bhagavad-Gita,* translated by Barbara Stoler Miller. Translation copyright © 1986 by Barbara Stole Miller. Reproduced by permission of **Bantam Books, a division of Random House, Inc.** and electronic format by permission of **The Estate of Barbara Stoler Miller.**

"Why I Turned Pepys' Diary into a Weblog" by Phil Gyford from *BBC News World Edition,* January 2, 2003, from *BBC News* Web site at www.news.bbc.co.uk. Copyright © 2003 by **BBC News.** Reproduced by permission of the publisher.

From "Trapped Australian Miners Rescued" from *BBC News International Edition,* May 9, 2006, from *BBC News* Web site at www.news.bbc.co.uk. Copyright © 2006 by **BBC News.** Reproduced by permission of the publisher.

From "Introduction" to *The Life and Times of Chaucer* by John Gardner. Copyright © 1977 by Boskydell Artists, Ltd. Reproduced by permission of **Georges Borchardt, Inc.**

"Another Renaissance?" by Gary Fisher from *Electronic Engineering Times,* October 28, 1996. Copyright © 1996 by **CMP Media Inc.** Reproduced by permission of the publisher.

From "Games at Twilight" from *Games at Twilight and Other Stories* by Anita Desai. Copyright © 1978 by Anita Desai. Reproduced by permission of **Anita Desai c/o Rogers, Coleridge & White Ltd., 20 Powis Mews, London W11 1JN.**

"Marriage is a Private Affair" from *Girls at War and Other Stories* by Chinua Achebe. Copyright © 1972, 1973 by Chinua Achebe. Reproduced by permission of **Doubleday, a division of Random House, Inc.** and electronic format by permission of **Harold Ober Associates Incorporated.**

"A morning-glory vine" by Kobayashi Issa from *An Introduction to Haiku,* translated by Harold G. Henderson. Copyright © 1958 by Harold G. Henderson. Reproduced by permission of **Doubleday, a division .of Random House, Inc., www.randomhouse.com.**

From "Le Morte D'Arthur" from *Le Morte D'Arthur* by Sir Thomas Malory, translated by Keith Baines. Copyright © 1962 by Keith Baines; copyright renewed © 1990 by Francesca Evans. Introduction copyright © 1962 by Robert Graves; copyright renewed © 1990 by Beryl Graves. Reproduced by permission of **Dutton Signet, a division of Penguin Group (USA) Inc., www.penguin.com.**

From *Beowulf,* translated by Burton Raffel. Translation copyright © 1962 and renewed © 1991 by Burton Raffel. Reproduced by permission of **Dutton/Signet, a division of Penguin Group (USA) Inc.** and electronic format by permission of **Russell & Volkening as agents for the author.**

From *WIT* by Margaret Edson. Copyright © 1993, 1999 by Margaret Edson. Reproduced by permission of **Faber and Faber, Inc., an affiliate of Farrar, Straus and Giroux, LLC.**

"The Wife's Lament" from *A Choice of Anglo-Saxon Verse,* translated by Richard Hamer. Translation copyright © 1970 by Richard Hamer. Reproduced by permission of **Faber and Faber Ltd.**

"Once upon a Time" from *Jump and Other Stories* by Nadine Gordimer. Copyright 1991 by Felix Licensing, B. V. All rights reserved. Reproduced by permission of **Farrar, Straus and Giroux, LLC** and electronic format by permission of **Russell & Volkening, Inc., as agents for Nadine Gordimer.**

"Digging" from *Selected Poems 1966–1987* by Seamus Heaney. Copyright © 1990 by Seamus Heaney. All rights reserved. Reproduced by permission of **Farrar, Straus and Giroux, LLC.**

"The Horses" from *Collected Poems* by Ted Hughes. Copyright © 2003 by The Estate of Ted Hughes. All rights reserved. Reproduced by permission of **Farrar, Straus and Giroux, LLC** and electronic format by permission of **Faber and Faber Ltd.**

"The Explosion" from *Philip Larkin: Collected Poems,* edited by Anthony Thwaite. Copyright © 1988, 1989 by the Estate of Philip Larkin. All rights reserved. Reproduced by permission of **Farrar, Straus and Giroux, LLC** and electronic format by permission of **The Society of Authors as the Literary Representative of the Estate of Philip Larkin.**

"The Virgins" from *Sea Grapes* by Derek Walcott. Copyright © 1976 by Derek Walcott. All rights reserved. Reproduced by permission of **Farrar, Straus and Giroux, LLC.**

From *Omeros* by Derek Walcott. Copyright © 1990 by Derek Walcott. All rights reserved. Reproduced by permission of **Farrar, Straus and Giroux, LLC.**

From *Reason for Hope* by Jane Goodall with Phillip Berman. Copyright © 1999 by Sokc Publications Ltd. and Phillip Berman. All rights reserved. Reproduced by permission of **Grand Central Publishing.**

Come and Go from *Collected Shorter Plays* by Samuel Beckett. Copyright © 1965 by Samuel Beckett and renewed © 1999 by the Estate of Samuel Beckett. Reproduced by permission of **Grove/Atlantic Inc.**

Acknowledgments

From "That's All" from *Complete Plays: Three* by Harold Pinter. Copyright © 1966 by H. Pinter Ltd. Reproduced by permission of **Grove/Atlantic, Inc.**

Slightly adapted from "Private Twice Rescued Colleagues While Under Heavy Fire in Iraq: Soldier Wins First VC Since Falklands" by Richard Norton-Taylor from *The Guardian*, March 18, 2005. Copyright © 2005 by **Guardian News & Media Limited.** Reproduced by permission of the publisher.

"The Hollow Men" from *Collected Poems 1909–1962* by T. S. Eliot. Copyright 1936 by **Harcourt, Inc.**; copyright © 1963, 1964 by T. S. Eliot. Reproduced by permission of the publisher.

"Shooting an Elephant" from *Shooting an Elephant and Other Essays* by George Orwell. Copyright 1950 by Sonia Brownell Orwell; copyright renewed © 1978 by Sonia Pitt-Rivers. Reproduced by permission of **Harcourt, Inc.** and electronic format by permission of **Bill Hamilton as the Literary Executor of the Estate of the Late Sonia Brownell Orwell and Secker & Warburg Ltd.**

"Lot's Wife" from *View with a Grain of Sand* by Wislawa Szymborska, translated by Stanislaw Baranczak and Clare Cavanaugh. English translations copyright © 1995 by **Harcourt, Inc.** Reproduced by permission of the publisher and electronic format by permission of **Stanislaw Baranczak.**

"A Haunted House" from *The Complete Shorter Fiction of Virginia Woolf* by Susan Dick. Copyright © 1985 by Quentin Bell and Angelica Garnett. Reproduced by permission of **Harcourt, Inc.**

Letter No. 1454: "To Lytton Strachey, March 21st 1924" from *The Letters of Virginia Woolf, Volume III: 1923-1928.* Copyright ©1977 by Quentin Bell and Angelica Garnett. All rights reserved. Reproduced by permission of **Harcourt, Inc.**

From *The Civilization of the Middle Ages* by Norman F. Cantor. Copyright © 1963, 1968 1974 and 1993 by Norman F. Cantor. Reproduced by permission of **HarperCollins Publishers, Inc.**

"# 8 The supreme good is like water" from *Tao Te Ching by Lao Tzu, A New English Version*, translated by Stephen Mitchell. Translation copyright © 1988 by **Stephen Mitchell.** Reproduced by permission of **HarperCollins Publishers, Inc.** and electronic format by permission of the translator.

"Never Shall I Forget" from *Night* by Elie Wiesel, translated by Marion Wiesel. Copyright © 1972, 1985 by Elie Wiesel; translation copyright © 2006 by Marion Wiesel All rights reserved. Reproduced by permission of **Hill and Wang, a division of Farrar, Straus and Giroux, LLC.**

From The *Collected Beowulf* by Gareth Hinds. Copyright © 1999–2000 by **Gareth Hinds.** Reproduced by permission of the artist.

"Mushrooms" and "Siren Song" from *Selected Poems, 1965–1975* by Margaret Atwood. Copyright © 1976 by Margaret Atwood. Reproduced by permission of **Houghton Mifflin Company** and electronic format by permission of **Margaret Atwood.**

From *Gilgamesh: A Verse Narrative* translated by Herbert Mason. Copyright © 1970 by Herbert Mason. All rights reserved.

Reproduced by permission of **Houghton Mifflin Company,** www.hmco.com.

From *Sir Vidia's Shadow* by Paul Theroux. Copyright © 1998 by Paul Theroux. All right reserved. Reproduced by permission of **Houghton Mifflin Company,** www.hmco.com.

From *The Lord of the Rings: The Two Towers* by J.R.R. Tolkien. Copyright © 1954, 1965 by J.R.R. Tolkien; copyright renewed © 1982 by Christopher R. Tolkien, Michal H.R. Tolkien, John F.R. Tolkien and Priscilla M.A.R. Tolkien. Reproduced by permission of **Houghton Mifflin Company** and electronic format by permission of **HarperCollins Publishers, Ltd.**

"Telephone Conversation" by Wole Soyinka from *Reflections: Nigerian Prose and Verse*, edited by Frances Ademola. Copyright © 1962, 1990 by Wole Soyinka. Reproduced by permission of **Melanie Jackson Agency, L.L.C.**

"The Demon Lover" from *The Collected Stories of Elizabeth Bowen.* Copyright © 1981 by Curtis Brown Ltd., Literary Executors of the Estate of Elizabeth Bowen. Reproduced by permission of **Alfred A. Knopf, a division of Random House, Inc.** and electronic format by permission of **Curtis Brown Ltd., on behalf of the Estate of Elizabeth Bowen.**

"The Doll's House" from *The Short Stories of Katherine Mansfield.* Copyright 1923 by Alfred A. Knopf, a division of Random House, Inc.; copyright renewed 1951 by John Middleton Murry. Reproduced by permission of **Alfred A. Knopf, a division of Random House, Inc.,** www.randomhouse.com.

From speech by Jawaharlal Nehru, August 14, 1947. Reproduced by permission of **Jawaharlal Nehru Memorial Fund.**

"Dulce et Decorum Est" from *The Collected Poems of Wilfred Owen.* Copyright © 1963 by Chatto & Windus, Ltd. Reproduced by permission of **New Directions Publishing Corporation.**

"Not Waving But Drowning" from *Collected Poems of Stevie Smith.* Copyright © 1972 by Stevie Smith. Reproduced by permission of **New Directions Publishing Corporation.**

"Fern Hill" and "Do Not Go Gentle into That Good Night" from *The Poems of Dylan Thomas.* Copyright 1945 by The Trustees for the Copyrights of Dylan Thomas. Reproduced by permission of **New Directions Publishing Corporation** and electronic format by permission of **Harold Ober Associates Incorporated.**

"Jade Flower Palace" by Tu Fu from *One Hundred Poems from the Chinese*, translated by Kenneth Rexroth. Copyright © 1971 by Kenneth Rexroth. Reproduced by permission of **New Directions Publishing Corporation.**

From Nobel Lecture: "The Poet and the World" by Wislawa Szymborska. Copyright © 1996 by **The Nobel Foundation.** Reproduced by permission of the publisher.

From "Everyman" from *The Norton Anthology of English Literature, Seventh Edition*, Volume 1, edited by M.H. Abrams and Stephen Greenblatt. Copyright © 1962, 1968, 1974, 1986, 1990, 1993 and 2000 by **W. W. Norton & Company, Inc.** Reproduced by permission of the publisher.

Acknowledgments

Small") by Timothy Foote from *Smithsonian Magazine* Web site accessed May 22, 2007 at www.smithsonianmagazine.com/issues/2001/september/journeys_smitty.php. Copyright © 2001 by **Smithsonian Institute**. Reproduced by permission of the publisher.

"I waited and I," by Princess Nukada, "The end of my journey" by Oshikochi Mitsune, "Now, I cannot tell" by Ki Tsurayuki, "How helpless my heart!" by Ono Komachi, and "Every single thing" by Priest Saigyo from *The Penguin Book of Japanese Verse*, translated by Geoffrey Bownas and Anthony Thwaite (Penguin Classics, 1964). Translation copyright © 1964 by Geoffrey Bownas and Anthony Thwaite. Reproduced by permission of **Anthony Thwaite**.

"The First Principle, "The Gates of Paradise," The Moon Cannot Be Stolen," and "Temper" from *Zen Flesh, Zen Bones: A Collection of Zen and Pre-Zen Writings*, compiled by Paul Reps. Copyright © 1957 by **Charles E. Tuttle Co., Inc., Boston, MA, and Tokyo, Japan**. Reproduced by permission of the publisher.

From "Sir Gawain and the Green Knight" from *The Complete Works of the Gawain-Poet*, translated by John Gardner. Copyright © 1965 by **The University of Chicago**. Reproduced by permission of the publisher.

"Sonnet 79/Soneto 79""from *100 Love Sonnets/Cien sonetos de amor* by Pablo Neruda, translated by Stephen Tapscott. Copyright © 1959 by Pablo Neruda and Fundaciòn Pablo Neruda; translation copyright © 1986 by **The University of Texas Press**. Reproduced by permission of the publisher and electronic format by permission of **Agencia Literaria Carmen Balcells**.

"The Lorelei" from *Heinrich Heine: Paradox and Poet* by Louis Untermeyer. Copyright 1937 by Louis Untermeyer. Reproduced by permission of **Laurence S. Untermeyer on behalf of The Estate of Louis Untermeyer, Norma Anchin Untermeyer c/o Professional Publishing Services Company**.

From "The Book of Sand" from *Collected Fictions* by Jorges Luis Borges, translated by Andrew Hurley. Copyright © 1998 by Maria Kodama; translation copyright © 1998 by Penguin Putnam Inc. Reproduced by permission of **Viking Penguin, a division of Penguin Group (USA) Inc., www.penguin.com**.

From *Don Quixote* by Miguel de Cervantes Saavedra, translated by Samuel Putnam. Copyright 1949 by The Viking Press, Inc. Reproduced by permission of **Viking Penguin a division of Penguin Group (USA) Inc., www.penguin.com**.

"The Death of Hector" from *The Iliad* by Homer, translated by Robert Fagles. Copyright © 1990 by Robert Fagles. Reproduced by permission of **Viking Penguin, a division of Penguin Group (USA) Inc.** and electronic format by permission of **Georges Borchardt. Inc.**

"The Destructors" from *Collected Stories of Graham Greene*. Copyright © 1955, 1983 by Graham Greene. Reproduced by permission of **Viking Penguin, a division of Penguin Group (USA) Inc., www.penguin.com**.
"The Rocking-Horse Winner" from *Complete Short Stories of D.*

H. Lawrence. Copyrigh 1933 by the Estate of D. H. Lawrence; copyright renewed © 1961 by Angelo Ravagli and C.M. Weekley, Executors of the Estate of Frieda Lawrence Ravagli. Reproduced by permission of **Viking Penguin, a division of Penguin Group (USA) Inc.** and electronic format by permission of **Pollinger Limited and the Estate of Frieda Lawrence Ravagli.**

"On the Bottom" from *If This Is a Man (Survival in Auschwitz)* by Primo Levi, translated by Stuart Woolf. Copyright © 1958 by Guilio Einaudi editore S.P.A.; copyright © 1959 by Orion Press, Inc. Reproduced by permission of **Viking Penguin, a division of Penguin Group (USA) Inc.** and electronic format by permission of **Guilio Enaudi Editore S.P.A.**

"When Elements Go Extreme" by Jason La Canfora from *The Washington Post*, August 2, 2006. Copyright © 2006 by **The Washington Post**. Reproduced by permission of the publisher. "Fear" from *Selected Poems of Gabriela Mistral: A Bilingual Edition*, translated by Doris Dana. Copyright © 1961, 1964, 1970, 1971 by Doris Dana. Published by The Johns Hopkins University Press, Baltimore, 1971. Reproduced by permission of **Writers House, Inc., as agent for the proprietor**.

"To a Mosquito" from *Present Company* by W. S. Merwin. Copyright © 2005 by W. S. Merwin. Reproduced by permission of **The Wylie Agency, Inc.**

Riddles 1, 14, and 32, "The Seafarer," and "The Wanderer" from *Poems and Prose from the Old English*, translated by Burton Raffel. Copyright © 1960, 1964, 1998 by Burton Raffel. Reproduced by permission of **Yale University Press**.

Source Cited:

Parable of the Prodigal Son from *The New Oxford Annotated Bible*. Published by Oxford University Press, New York, NY, 1946.

(bc), The Bridgeman Art Library; (br), Shakespeare Birthplace Trust Records Office; **391** (cr), Private Collection/© Christopher Wood Gallery, London, UK/The Bridgeman Art Library; (b), Charles Gullung/Photonica/Getty Images; **392-393** (b) Bridget Webber/Photonica/Getty Images; **392** (br), Art Resource, NY; **393** (br), Giraudon/The Bridgeman Art Library; **395**, Steve Frost/Alamy; **396-397** (t), Richard Green/Photonica/Getty Images; **397** (tl, tr), Photograph ©1984 The Metropolitan Museum of Art; **398**, The Bridgeman Art Library; **402**, Art Resource, NY; **403**, Erich Lessing/Art Resource, NY; **405** (tr), Roger Holmes/Photonica/Getty Images; (b), Sara Krulwich/The New York Times/Redux; **406**, David Robertson/Alamy; **410-417**, Donald Cooper/Photostage; **418**, Dale Jorgensen/Superstock; **421**, Ben Graville/PhotoNews Service LTD.; **428**, Steve Mackins; **429**, David Gowans/Alamy; **430**, Cromwell/Lamancha/Grampian TV/The Kobal Collection; **432**, Steve Mackins; **437**, The Bridgeman Art Library, NY; **438**, David Sanger Photography/Alamy; **442**, Donald Cooper/Photostage; **444**, Steve Mackins; **447**, Vittoriano Rastelli/Corbis; **448-461**, Donald Cooper/Photostage; **462**, Robbie Jack/Corbis; **465**, Robert Holmes/Corbis; **466**, Clive Barda/ArenaPal; **469**, Robert Harding Picture Library Ltd./Alamy; **472**, Vittoriano Rastelli/Corbis; **479**, Paul Ridgeway/PhotoNews Service, LTD; **481**, Matti Kolho/Lebrecht Music & Arts; **484**, Steve Mackins; **486**, Private Collection/Pace Wildenstein Gallery, New York; **488**, David Sanger/Alamy; **491**, Columbia Pictures/Photofest, NY; **526-527**, Skyscan Photolibrary/Alamy; **528** (cl), Private Collection/Archives Charmet/The Bridgeman Art Library; (br), National Trust/Art Resource, NY; **529** (t), Donald Cooper/Photostage, UK; (cl), Bildarchiv Preussischer Kulturbesitz/Art Resource, NY; (cr), Archives Charmet/The Bridgeman Art Library; (br), British Museum, London/The Bridgeman Art Library; **530** Guildhall Art Gallery, City of London/The Bridgeman Art Library; **532** Alen Lauzan Falcon/Politicalcartoons.com; (br), Book cover from ZEN AND THE ART OF MOTORCYCLE MAINTENANCE by ROBERT PIRSIG. Copyright ©1974 by ROBERT M. PIRSIG. Reprinted by permission of HarperCollins Publishers. WILLIAM MORROW; (br), The Tragedy of Hamlet by William Shakespeare. Cover, ©HRW. Cover art by Joe Melomo; **533**, Historical Picture Archive/Corbis; **534** Jon Arnold Images/Alamy; **535** HIP/Art Resource, NY; **536** Granger Collection, NY; **537** (t), Jerry Grayson/Helifilms Australia PTY Ltd./Getty Images; (cl), AKG Images; **540**, Erich Lessing/Art Resource, NY; **542** (tr), Courtesy of Everett Collection; (cr), Lebrecht Music & Arts; **543**, Courtesy of the Warden and Scholars of New College, Oxford/The Bridgeman Art Library; **544** (bl), National Portrait Gallery, London/The Bridgeman Art Library; (cl), AKG Images; **547**, Yale Center for British Art, Paul Mellon Collection/The British Art Library; **551**, Jonathan Blair/Corbis; **552**, Private Collection/The Bridgeman Art Library; **553**, John Miller/Robert Harding Picture Library, Ltd/Alamy; **556-558**,The Granger Collection, NY; **558-559** (cr), Private Collection/The Bridgeman Art Library; **559** (cl), The Granger Collection, NY; (cr), Private Collection/The Bridgeman Art Library; **560-561** (cl), The Granger Collection, NY; (cr), Private Collection/The Bridgeman Art Library; **561** (cr), Private Collection/The Bridgeman Art Library; **564**, National Portrait Gallery, London; **567-573**, Courtesy of the Everett Collection; **575**, Alex Bailey/Corbis Sygma; **581**, The Granger Collection, NY; **585** (cr), The Granger Collection, NY; (bl), The Illustrated London News Picture Library; (br), The illustrated News Picture Library; **591**, Richard Melloul/Sygma/Corbis; **592**, Burstein Collection/CORBIS; **593**, Petar Pismestrovic/Artizan; **594** (tl), Achim Bednorz; (cl), Lauros/Giraudon/The Bridgeman

Art Library; **596** (b), Donald Cooper/Photostage; (bl), Achim Bednorz; **598**, Donald Cooper/Photostage; **602** (cl), Private Collection/The Bridgeman Art Library; **602, 604**, Hans Georg Roth/Corbis; **612** (cl), **617** (t), The Bridgeman Art Library; **618**, David Levenson/Alamy; **622**, The Bridgeman Art Library.; **625**, Visual Arts Library, London/Alamy; **627**, Robert Halsband Collection; **628**, The Bridgeman Art Library; **632**, Private Collection/The Bridgeman Art Library; **634**, AP Photo/Adam Butler; **638** (bl), Scott Eells/Getty Images; **642**, Rob Howard/Corbis; **644** (b), Bridgeman Art Library; (bl), The Bridgeman Art Library; **646** (bl), Bridgeman Art Library; (bc), Michael Nicholson/CORBIS; **649**, The Granger Collection, NY; **650-651** (c), The Bridgeman Art Library; **656** (bl), Thomas Dobner/Alamy; **659**, Thomas Dobner/Alamy; **662-663** (bc), Alan Novelli/Alamy; **665**, Private Collection/Gemalde Mensing/The Bridgeman Art Library; **668**, The Bridgeman Art Library; **669**, Christopher Weil Photography/StoryCorps; **672-673** (b), Jeremy Pardoe/Alamy; **672** (tl), The Bridgeman Art Library; **675**, Art Resource, NY; **677**, The Bridgeman Art Library; **679**, Mark Atkinson/JupiterImages/Comstock; **700-701**, Fine Art Photographic Library, London/Art Resource, NY; **702** (tl), Jochen Remmer/Bildarchiv Preussischer Kulturbesitz/Art Resource, NY; (tr), The Bridgeman Art Library; (cl), The Granger Collection, NY; (bl), Réunion des Musées Nationaux/Art Resource, NY; (br), Wim Wiskerke/Alamy; **703** (t), Ann Ronan Picture Library, London/HIP/Art Resource, NY; (cl), Private Collection/The Bridgeman Art library; (cr), The British Library, London/The Bridgeman Art Library; (bl), The Bridgeman Art Library; **704**, The Granger Collection, NY; **706**, Lauros/Giraudon/The Bridgeman Art Library; **707**, Everett Collection; **708** (tr), The Granger Collection, NY; (tr), The Misanthrope and Tartuffe by Moliére. Cover illustration by Mark English. Used by permission of Harcourt Publishers; **709**, Alex Segre/Alamy; **711** (tr), The Bridgeman Art Library; (b), The Jane Goodall Institute; **716**, The Bridgeman Art Library; **719**, Tate Picture Library, London; **720** (bl), Anna Grossman/Photonica/Getty Images; **722** (t), **723** (bc), Anna Grossman/Photonica/Getty Images; (br), The Maas Gallery, London, UK/The Bridgeman Art Library; **725**, Hervé Lewandowski/Réunion des Musées Nationaux/Art Resource, NY; **726**, Peter Arnold, Inc./Alamy; **728** (cl), Art Resource, NY; (bl), The Granger Collection, NY; **729**, Jarrold Publishing/The Art Archive; **732** (cl), Art Resource, NY; (cr), The Bridgeman Art Library; **736** (cr), Randy Wells/Corbis; (br), S.E. Arndt/Peter Arnold, Inc.; **738-739** (c), INSADCO Photography/Alamy; **739**, Bettmann/Corbis; **740**, The Bridgeman Art Library; **746** (bl), Pictorial Press Ltd./Alamy; **749**, Neil Setchfield/Alamy; **750**, Pictorial Press, Ltd/Alamy; **753**, AA World Travel Library/Alamy; **758**, Erich Lessing/Art Resource, NY; **759**, Art Resource, NY; **762** (t), Frank Rothe/Photonica/Getty Images; (cr), John Miller/Robert Harding World Imagery/Corbis; **766** (bl), The Bridgeman Art Library; **769**, Granger Collection, NY; **775**, The Bridgeman Art Library; **787, 797**, Momatiuk-Eastcott/Corbis; **803**, The Bridgeman Art Library; **804**, Art Wolfe/Photo Researchers, Inc.; **804-805** (bkgd), Art Wolfe/Photo Researchers Inc.; **805** (tl), Kevin Schafer/Corbis; (cr), David Hosking/Photo Researchers Inc.; (bc), Eric Hosking/Photo Researchers, Inc.; **808**, The Bridgeman Art Library; **809**, Art Resource, NY; **810**, Sotheby's Transparency Library, London; **812**, Private Collection/The Bridgeman Art Library; **814-815** (c), Farhad J. Parsa/Photonica/Getty Images; (b), Sharon Montrose/Stone/Getty Images; **818**, Bridgeman Art Library; **820**, Michael Juno/Alamy; **823**, World Pictures/Alamy; **825**, Terry Deroy Gruber/Photonica/Getty Images; **826-827**, Amelia P. Schaffner/

INDEX OF SKILLS

LITERARY SKILLS

Alexandrine, **813**

Allegory, **217**, 220, 222, 223, 228, 229, 230, 231, **325, 367**, 368, 370, 372, 799, **1009**, 1011, 1012, 1014, 1017, 1018, 1020, 1021

Alliteration, 50, 79, 160, 309, 394, **767**, 768, 770, 771, 816, 840, 917, **957**, 958, 959, 986, **1205**, 1206, 1207, 1232, 1273, 1283

Allusion, **294**, 345, **363**, 364, 365, **763**, 764, 765, 851, **1189**, 1191, 1194, 1200, 1245, 1293

Analysis, literary. *See* Literary analysis

Analyzing credibility, **582**, 588, **776**, 789, 793, 798, 799, **1024**, 1026, 1028, 1030, **1327**, 1328, 1331

Analyzing style, **820**, 821, **944**, 946, 948, 949
   See also Style.

Analyzing Visuals
   etchings, **543**
   paintings, **114**
   photographs, **963**
   Renaissance illuminations, **269**
   sculpture, **1296**

Anglo-Saxon legacy, **4–6**

Antagonist, **1422**

Antipastoral, **277**

Antithesis, **615**, 616, 617, 618, 619

Apostrophe, 301, **313**, 721, 727, **813**, 815, 816

Archetype, **17, 21**, 54, 88, 494, **600**

Art. *See* Analyzing Visuals.

Assonance, **774**, 917, **957**, 958, 959, 986, **1205**, 1206, 1207, 1273

Atmosphere, 1322

Autobiography, **1093**

Ballad, **184–185**, 186, 188, 190, 192
   See also Literary ballad.

Biographical information, **647**, 648, 651, 653, **927**, 929, 930, **1230**, 1231, 1232

Biography, **645**, 649, 650, 652, 653

Blank verse, **350**, 439, 477, **747**, 748, 752, 754

Carpe diem, **283**, 284, 286, 287

Character foil, **89**, 91, 94, 96, 97, 110, 146, 214

Characterization, 231, 329, 457, 603, 1365, 1404
   in narrative poetry, **121**, 125, 126, 129, 132, 134, 137, 139, 140, 143, 146

Chinese poetry, **864–865, 872–879**

Climax, 203

Colloquial language, **1223**

Conflict, **307**, 1250
   external, **307, 993**
   internal, **307, 993**
   in short story, **993**, 994, 998, 999, 1000, 1002, 1003, 1004

Connotations, **315, 667, 1216**, 1218, 1220

Constructed Response, 246, 521, 695, 895, 1055

Contemporary epic, **1391**, 1392, 1393, 1395

Contrasting images, **917**, 918, 920, 921, 922, 923

Couplet, 824, 843, **981**, 982, 1075, 1273

Credibility, **582**, 588, **776**, 789, 793, 798, 799, **1024**, 1026, 1028, 1030, **1327**, 1328, 1331

Cross-curricular links, 35, 187, 356, 371, 481, 606, 625, 661, 671, 753, 769, 787, 854, 921, 1001, 1089, 1111, 1145, 1225, 1282, 1338, 1419

Dialect, **721**, 722, 723, 724, 725, 727

Dialogue, **304**, 305, 306, 307, **1351**, 1354, 1355, 1397

Diary, **545**, 546, 548

Diction
   in letters, **1181**, 1183, 1184
   in poetry, **315**, 316, 317, 318, 319, **837**, 838, 839, 840, 955, **1223**, 1224, 1226, 1395
   and style, **315**, 316, 317, 318, 319, 548, 653
   and tone, **633**, 635, 636, 637, 839

Didactic literature, **332**, 333, 334, 335, 337, 338, 339, 340, 341, 342, 343

Drama, medieval, **216**

Drama, Renaissance, **385–386**

Dramatic irony, **359**, 457, 741, **1033**, **1239**

Dramatic monologue, **943**, 944, 947, 948, 949

Elegy, **61**, 63, 64, 67, 68, 70, 73, **657**, 658, 662, 663, 664, **931**, 968, 1073, **1235**, 1236, 1237

Elizabeth I, **254, 259–261**

End rhyme, **757**

Enjambment, **1083**

Epic, **17–18**, 20, **1391**

Epic, mock, **621**, 623, 624, 626, 627, 628, 629

Epic hero, 17, **21**, 23, 24, 26, 27, 28, 30, 31, 34, 35, 36, 38, 40, 41, 42, 43, 44, 47, 48, 49, 50, 54, **88**, 97

Epic simile, **99**, 102, 106, 110, 350, 629

Epiphany, **1325**, 1330, 1331

Escape fiction, **1355**

Essay, **1162**, 1163, 1164, 1169

Exact rhyme, 986

Exposition, 1355

Extended metaphor, 760, 915, **937**, **1279**, 1281, 1283

External conflict, **307, 993**

Figurative language, **283, 915**, 923, 930, 939, 949, 955

Figures of speech, **291, 1075**, 1076, 1079, 1180, 1229
   apostrophe, 301, **313**, 721, 727, **813**, 815, 816
   personification, **282**, 287, **761**, 762, 765, 915, 1106
   simile, **99**, 102, 106, 110, 350, **811**, 812, 816, 835, 915, 1075, 1180
   See also Metaphor; Symbol.

First-person point of view, **1176**

Flashback, **1117**, 1120, 1121, 1124

Foil, **89**, 91, 94, 96, 97, 110, 146, 214, 477

Folk ballad, 774

Foreshadowing, 214, 1124, **1309**, 1312, 1315, 1316, 1318, 1319, 1320, 1322

Frame story, 118, **121**, 123, 145, 146

Graphic novel, **54**, 59, **496**, 502

Haiku, **864**, 867, 868, **870**

Half rhyme, 986

Hero
   epic, **21**, 23, 24, 26, 27, 28, 30, 31, 34, 35, 36, 38, 40, 41, 42, 43, 44, 47, 48, 49, 50, 54, 97
   romance, **207**, 209, 210, 212,

213, 214
Historical background
  Anglo-Saxon Period and Middle
    Ages, **1–11**
  Modern World, **1061–1069**
  Renaissance, **251–261**
  Restoration and Eighteenth
    Century, **527–535**
  Victorian Period, **901–909**
Historical context, **407,** 409, 413,
  425, 431, 433, 436, 439, 440,
  456, 457, 464, 474, 477, 480,
  492, 493, 494, **966,** 967, 968,
  1095, 1098, 1099
Homeric simile, 99
Humanism, 267
Hyperbole, **287,** 294, 298
Iamb, **747, 1075**
Iambic hexameter, **813**
Iambic pentameter, 267, 385, **813,**
  1075
Identity and diversity in modern
  literature, **1064, 1068–1069**
Imagery, 271, 289, 291, 324
  contrasting, **917,** 918, 920, 921,
    922, 923
  in drama, 493
  in poetry, 657, 760, 828, **868,**
    869, 870, 871, **877,** 878, 879,
    880, 930, **1081,** 1082, 1083,
    1265, 1266, 1267, 1276
  in short story, **1177,** 1178, 1179,
    1180, 1388, 1397, **1415,** 1416,
    1417, 1419, 1420, 1421, 1422
Informal essay, **1162**
Interlude, in drama, **386**
Internal conflict, **307, 993**
Internal rhyme, **774**
Interpretive fiction, **1357**
Irony, **149,** 153, 156, 158, 175, 192,
  820, 821, 949, **1033,** 1037,
  1039, 1040, **1141,** 1143, 1145,
  1146, 1147, 1148, 1202, **1239,**
  1240, 1241, **1295**
  dramatic, **359,** 457, 741, **1033,**
    1239, 1295
  situational, **149,** 160, 457, **565,**
    567, 568, 576, 577, **819, 1033,**
    1141, 1239, 1295, 1341,
    1375
  verbal, **149,** 160, 457, **580,** 583,
    585, 587, 588, **1033, 1141,**
    1239, 1377, 1380, 1383
Japanese poetry, **864–871**
Journal, **557**
Literary analysis
  allegory, 372

argument, 382, 643, 1113
author's beliefs, 1255
ballad, 192
biography, 653
blog, 554
diary, 548
diction, 637
didactic literature, 343
drama, 307, 425, 439, 457, 477,
  493, 502, 1348, 1355
elegy, 73, 664
epic tradition, 42, 50, 97, 110,
  629
essay, 1148, 1169
figurative language, 923, 930,
  939, 949, 955
form and function, 619
graphic novel, 59
historical context, 85
Japanese and Chinese poetry,
  871, 876, 880
journal, 562
letter, 1184
medieval drama, 231
medieval narrative, 146, 160,
  175, 183
memoir, 1413
metaphysical conceits, 299
modern poetry, 1194, 1202,
  1207, 1211, 1215, 1220, 1226,
  1232, 1241, 1245, 1250, 1259,
  1263, 1267, 1276, 1283, 1288,
  1293, 1395
newspaper article, 991, 1271
novel, 1176
oral tradition, 85
parables, 329
political writing, 678, 1157
Psalms, 324
realism, 969, 978, 986
Renaissance poetry, 275, 280,
  287, 294, 302, 312, 319, 359,
  365
riddles, 79
romance, 203, 214
Romantic poetry, 727, 734, 741,
  744, 754, 760, 765, 771, 799,
  807, 816, 821, 828, 835, 840,
  846, 851, 856
satire, 577, 588, 600
short story, 1004, 1021, 1030,
  1040, 1124, 1139, 1180, 1306,
  1322, 1341, 1365, 1375, 1383,
  1388, 1404, 1422
sonnet, 394, 399
war literature, 1079, 1083, 1086,
  1091, 1099, 1106, 1124, 1139

Literary ballad, **774,** 776, 777, 779,
  780, 782, 785, 788, 789, 790,
  794, 795, 797, 798, 799
Literary Focus
  epic tradition, **17–18**
  figurative language, **915**
  form and function in Age of
    Reason, **613**
  forms of romantic poetry, **809**
  irony, **1295**
  medieval narrative, **113**
  realism, **961–962**
  Renaissance poetry, **267–268**
  rise of the novel, **541–542**
  Shakespeare's sonnets and plays,
    385–387
  themes of modern and
    contemporary poetry, **1187**
  themes of romantic poetry,
    717–718
  war literature, **1073**
Literary Perspectives
  biographical information, **647,**
    648, 651, 653, **927,** 929, 930,
    1230, 1231, 1232
  credibility, **582,** 588, **776,** 789,
    793, 798, 799, **1024,** 1026,
    1028, 1030, **1327,** 1328, 1331
  historical context, **407,** 409,
    413, 425, 431, 433, 436, 439,
    440, 456, 457, 464, 474, 477,
    480, 492, 493, 494, **966,** 967,
    968, **1095,** 1098, 1099
  philosophical context, **301,**
    302, **749,** 752, 754, **849,** 851,
    1190, 1193, 1194
  political context, **163,** 168, 175,
    582, 669, 678, **1163,** 1166,
    1167, 1169, **1357,** 1363, 1364,
    1365
  style, **820,** 821, **944,** 946, 948,
    949
Lyric, **309,** 310, 311, 312, 657, 1235
Lyric poetry, **1229,** 1231, 1232
Medieval drama, **216**
Medieval narrative, **113–115**
Medieval society, **4, 9–10**
Meet the Writer, 80, 98, 116, 206,
  270, 276, 282, 288, 308, 314,
  320, 346, 366, 388, 544, 556,
  594, 602, 614, 632, 638, 644,
  656, 666, 720, 728, 746, 810,
  818, 836, 842, 866, 867, 872,
  916, 942, 964, 972, 992, 1008,
  1022, 1032, 1074, 1080, 1092,
  1102, 1108, 1116, 1126, 1140,
  1150, 1160, 1188, 1198, 1222,

1228, 1238, 1242, 1246, 1256, 1260, 1264, 1272, 1278, 1284, 1290, 1298, 1308, 1324, 1334, 1342, 1350, 1356, 1368, 1376, 1384, 1390, 1396, 1406, 1414

Memoir, 1073, **1093**, 1095, 1096, 1098, 1099

Metaphor, **275**, 291, 321, **852**, 853, 856, 915, **937**, 938, 939, 1075, 1180, **1212**, 1213, 1214, 1215, 1237, **1261**, 1262, 1263
  extended, 760, 915, **937, 1279**, 1281, 1283

Metaphysical conceit, **291**, 293, 294

Metaphysical poetry, **289**, 290, 294, 959

Meter, 289, 745, 747, **757**, 759, 760, 774, 917, 923

Middle English, **119**

Miracle play, **216**, 386

Mock epic, **621**, 623, 624, 626, 627, 628, 629

Modern and contemporary poetry, **1187**

Monologue, dramatic, **943**, 944, 947, 948, 949

Mood, 502, **873**, 874, 875, 876, **965**, 966, 968, 1211

Morality play, **216**, 386

Motif, 20, 439

Motivation, 1030

Mystery play, **216**, 386

Narrative voice, **557**, 558, 560, 561, 562, 1004, **1299**, 1301, 1302, 1303, 1305, 1306

Narrator, **161**, 164, 166, 169, 175, **557**

Naturalism, **962**

Nonfiction, forms of
  autobiography, **1093**
  biography, **645**, 649, 650, 652, 653
  essay, **1162**, 1163, 1164, 1169
  journal, **557**
  memoir, **1093**, 1095, 1096, 1098, 1099

Norman invasion of Britain, **4, 7–8**

Novel, **541–542**

Octave, 745, 1075

Ode, 809, **824**, 825, 826, 827, 828

Omniscient point of view, **1176**

Onomatopoeia, **299**, 309

Oppositions, 917

Oratory, **1109**, 1110, 1112, 1113

Order and reason in the Restoration and eighteenth century, **530–531**

Oxymoron, **359, 1075**

Parable, **325**, 326, 328, 329

Paradox, 275, **300**, 301, 302, **359**, 425, 1220, **1335**, 1336, 1338, 1341

Parallelism, **321**, 322, 323, 324, **374**, 381, **737**, 739, 740, 741, 880

Parody, **603**, 605, 607, 608

Pastoral poetry, **277**, 278, 279, 280

Personification, **282**, 287, **761**, 762, 765, 915, 1106

Petrarchan sonnet, **745, 843, 953**, 954, 955, **1077, 1263**

Philosophical context, **301**, 302, **749**, 752, 754, **849**, 851, **1190**, 1193, 1194

Plot, 1383

Poetic structure, **1077**, 1078, 1079, **1272**, 1274, 1275, 1276

Point of view, **1176**, 1413

Political context, **163**, 168, 175, **582, 669**, 678, **1163**, 1166, 1167, 1169, **1357**, 1363, 1364, 1365

Postcolonial literature, 1068, **1387**

Progress and prosperity in the Victorian Era, **904, 906–907**

Protagonist, 216, 541, **1422**

Protestant Reformation, **254, 257–258**

Quatrain, **1075**

QuickTalk, 282, 308, 496, 545, 594, 614, 632, 638, 842, 916, 1116, 1324, 1342, 1356, 1376

Realism, **961–962**

Refrain, **185**, 277, 280, 319, 734, **1257**, 1258, 1259

Renaissance poetry, **267–268**

Repetition, **1103**, 1104, 1106, 1109, 1241

Rhetorical question, 943, 949

Rhyme, **757**, 759, 760, 774, 917

Rhyme scheme, 309, **312**, 365, 385, 745, 747, 757, 774, 824, 923, 939

Rhythm, 309, 774

Riddle, **74**, 75, 79

Riots and reforms in the Victorian Era, **904–905**

Romance, 114, **195**, 196, 197, 199, 202, 203

Romance hero, **207**, 209, 210, 212, 213, 214

Romantic poetry, **717–718, 809**

Run-on line, **1083**

Satire, 146, 565, 577, **595**, 597, 598, 599, 600, 678, **1385**, 1387, 1388

Scanning a poem, **757**

Sestet, 745, 1075

Setting, **81**, 83, 84, 85, 269, 372, 856, 876
  and details, 1099
  in photographs, 963
  of short story, **1127**, 1128, 1132, 1133, 1136, 1137, 1138, 1139, **1397**, 1398, 1400, 1403, 1404

Shakespearean sonnet, **390**, 391, 392, 393, 394, 395, 396, 397, 398, 399, **843, 1077**

Simile, **811**, 812, 816, 835, 915, 1075, 1180
  epic, **99**, 102, 106, 110, 350
  Homeric, 99

Situational irony, **149**, 160, 457, **565**, 567, 568, 576, 577, **819, 1033, 1141, 1239**, 1341, 1375

Social classes in the Restoration and eighteenth century, **530, 532–533**

Sonnet, **267**, 271, 275, 309, 363, 809, 821, **843**, 844, 845, 846, **1291**
  Petrarchan, **267**, 745, **843, 953**, 954, 955, **1077, 1263**
  Shakespearean, **268, 385, 390**, 391, 392, 393, 394, 395, 396, 397, 398, 399, **843, 1077**
  turn in, 267, 385

Sound devices, **917**, 919, 920, 922, 923, 1229

Speaker, **271**, 272, 273, 274, 275, 727, **973**, 975, 976, 978
  of a poem, 727, **973**, 975, 976, 978, **1247**, 1248, 1249, 1250

Spenserian stanza, 809

Stage directions, 1348

Stanza, 745

Style, **350**, 353, 354, 357, 359, **821**, 1184
  and diction, **315**, 316, 317, 318, 319, 548, 637
  in novel, **1172**, 1173, 1175, 1176
  in poetry, **820**, 821, **944**, 946, 948, 949
  and syntax, 350

Subject, **926**

Symbol, 871, 1040, 1113, 1148, 1215, 1267, 1288, 1306
  in modern poetry, **1208**, 1209, 1210, 1211
  in Romantic poetry, **730**, 731, 733, 734, 744, 771, **829**, 830, 834, 835
  in short story, **1369**, 1371, 1375

Synesthesia, **847,** 848, 849, 850, 851
Tanka, **864, 866,** 868, **869**
Terza rima, **824**
Theater of the absurd, **1343,** 1345, 1346, 1348
Theme, 296, 302, **926**
    in poetry, 727, **742,** 743, 744, 754, 765, 928, 929, 930, **984,** 985, 986, 1194, **1200,** 1201, 1202, **1243,** 1244, 1245, 1259, **1285,** 1287, 1288
    in short story, **1023,** 1026, 1029, 1030, 1139, **1357,** 1360, 1362, 1363, 1365
    universal, 42, 73
    war literature, 1079
Third-person limited point of view, **1176**
Tone, 85, 161, 203, 273, 296, 297, 298, 299, 562, 588, 1021
    and connotations, **667,** 670, 671, 673, 675, 676, 677, 678
    and diction, 839
    in essay, 1169
    and inversion, 277
    in memoir, **1407,** 1409, 1410, 1411, 1413
    in poetry, 280, 399, 619, 657, 846, **931,** 934, 935, 936, 939, 978, 1081, 1083, 1194, 1207, 1226
in short story, 1331
Tragedy, **404,** 407, 410, 412, 415, 418, 422, 424, 425, 426, 427, 429, 431, 432, 436, 438, 439, 440, 441, 442, 444, 446, 447, 448, 450, 453, 455, 456, 457, 459, 460, 461, 463, 464, 465, 467, 469, 470, 472, 476, 477, 478, 480, 482, 483, 484, 486, 487, 488, 489, 490, 493, 494, **496,** 502
Tragic flaw, **404**
Tragic hero, **404**
Tudor rule, **254–256**
Turn, poetic, 267, 385, 1075, 1291
Universal theme, 42, 73
Values and beliefs in the Restoration and eighteenth century, **530, 534–535**
Verbal irony, **149,** 160, 457, **580,** 583, 585, 587, 588, **1033, 1141, 1239, 1377,** 1380, 1383
Villanelle, **1235**
War literature, **1073**
World War I, **1064–1065**
World War II, **1064, 1066–1067**

INFORMATIONAL TEXT SKILLS

Analyzing argument, **374,** 376, 377, 378, 379, 381, 382
Analyzing author's beliefs, **1251,** 1253, 1254, 1255
Analyzing cause and effect, **988,** 989, 990, 991
Analyzing details and main idea, **802,** 804, 806, 807
Analyzing political statements, **1084,** 1085, 1086
Analyzing primary sources, **859,** 861, 862
Analyzing sequence of events, **1088,** 1089, 1090, 1091
Argument, analyzing, **374,** 376, 377, 378, 379, 381, 382
Author's argument, **639,** 640, 641, 642, 643
Author's beliefs, **1251,** 1253, 1254, 1255
Causes and effects, **988,** 989, 990, 991
Comparing and contrasting, **550,** 551, 552, 553, 554
Critiquing author's argument, **639,** 640, 641, 642, 643
Details and main idea, **802,** 804, 806, 807
Effects, causes and, **988,** 989, 990, 991
Graphics, using, **1268,** 1269, 1270, 1271
Main idea, **802,** 804, 806, 807
Parallelism, **374,** 381
Political assumptions, **1151,** 1152, 1154, 1156, 1157
Political statements, **1084,** 1085, 1086
Primary sources, **859,** 861, 862
Recognizing political assumptions, **1151,** 1152, 1154, 1156, 1157
Sequence of events, **1088,** 1089, 1090, 1091

READING SKILLS

Alexandrine, **813**
Analyzing details, **115,** 124, 128, 131, 133, 135, 141, 146, **207,** 212, 213, 214, **1227, 1229,** 1230, 1232, **1415,** 1416, 1418, 1420, 1421, 1422
Analyzing style, 304, 305, 307, **821**
    key details, **115,** 124, 128, 131, 133, 135, 141, 146
    poetry, **350,** 352, 355, 357, 358, 359, **931,** 932, 933, 934, 936, 939, **1212,** 1214, 1215
    satire, **595,** 597, 598, 599, 600
Analyzing tone, **837,** 838, 840, **1239,** 1240, 1241
Annotating a poem, **757,** 758, 760
Appeal, persuasive
    to authority, 667
    types of, **579, 580, 1107, 1109**
Archaic words, **321,** 322, 324, **774,** 777, 781, 786, 788, 790, 794, 797, 799
Argument by analogy, **667**
    See also Persuasive techniques.
Author's argument, identifying and critiquing, **639,** 640, 641, 642, 643, **1107, 1109,** 1110, 1113
Author's beliefs, **367,** 370, 371, 372, **1162,** 1167, 1168, 1169
Author's credibility, **545,** 547, 548
Author's perspective, **1216,** 1218, 1219, 1220, **1385,** 1386, 1388
Author's point of view, **645,** 648, 652, 653
Author's purpose, **185,** 186, 189, 190, 192, **363,** 364, 365, **565,** 569, 570, 572, 574, 576, 577, **1141,** 1144, 1146, 1147, 1148, **1407,** 1409, 1410, 1413
Author's stance, **615,** 617, 618, 619
Author's style. *See* Analyzing style.
Background knowledge, **1391,** 1392, 1394, 1395
Build background, 12, 23, 62, 66, 68, 75, 82, 90, 101, 122, 151, 162, 179, 186, 188, 190, 196, 219, 262, 272, 273, 274, 278, 284, 290, 292, 297, 301, 305, 310, 311, 316, 317, 318, 322, 323, 326, 334, 336, 338, 339, 340, 341, 342, 351, 364, 368, 375, 377, 380, 391, 392, 395, 396, 397, 398, 405, 536, 546, 551, 558, 566, 581, 596, 604, 616, 618, 622, 634, 640, 646, 658, 668, 674, 677, 722, 725, 731, 733, 738, 740, 743, 758, 762, 764, 768, 775, 803, 812, 820, 825, 830, 836, 844, 845, 853, 860, 869, 870, 874, 875, 878, 910, 918, 927, 938, 944, 947, 954, 958, 966, 974, 976, 982, 985, 989, 994, 1010, 1024, 1034, 1070, 1076, 1078, 1082, 1085, 1089, 1094, 1104, 1110, 1118, 1128, 1142, 1152, 1155, 1163, 1173, 1178, 1182, 1190,

1206, 1209, 1213, 1217, 1224, 1230, 1236, 1240, 1244, 1248, 1252, 1258, 1262, 1266, 1269, 1281, 1286, 1292, 1301, 1311, 1326, 1336, 1344, 1353, 1358, 1370, 1378, 1386, 1392, 1398, 1408, 1416

Cause and effect
  identifying, **1297, 1299,** 1304, 1305, 1306
  understanding, **195,** 197, 198, 200, 201, 202, 203
Character, interpreting, **161,** 163, 165, 168, 172, 173, 175, **1309,** 1311, 1314, 1318, 1320, 1322
Comparing and contrasting, **89,** 92, 94, 97, 315, 317, 318, 319
  epic heroes, 97
  medieval and contemporary periods, **178,** 180, 182, 183
  in poetry, **291,** 292, 293, 294, **817, 819,** 820, 821, **1279,** 1282, 1283
  in short story, **1325,** 1327, 1328, 1330, 1331
Comparing ideas across cultures, **332,** 333, 335, 337, 338, 339, 340, 341, 342, 343
Comparison, **291, 819**
Conclusions, drawing, **149,** 151, 153, 154, 159, 160
  about meaning, **737,** 739, 740, 741, **957,** 958, 959
Connecting text to experience, **1205,** 1206, 1207
Connotations, 657
Context clues, **74,** 77, 78, 79, 350, **730,** 731, 733, 734, **1075,** 1076, 1079
Contrast, **291, 819**
Credibility, author's, **545,** 547, 548
Critical judgments, **217,** 220, 221, 223, 226, 228, 229, 230, 231, **557,** 560, 561, 562
Cultural characteristics, **1377,** 1380, 1381, 1383
Details
  analyzing, **115,** 124, 128, 131, 133, 135, 141, 146, **207,** 212, 213, 214, **1227, 1229,** 1230, 1232, **1415,** 1416, 1418, 1420, 1421, 1422
  visualizing, **1081,** 1082, 1083
Diction. *See* Word order.
Drawing conclusions, **149,** 151, 153, 154, 159, 160
  about meaning, **737,** 739, 740,

741, **957,** 958, 959
Drawing inferences. *See* Making inferences.
Effect. *See* Cause and effect.
Emotional appeal, **579, 580, 1107, 1109**
Ethical appeal, **579, 580, 1107**
Evaluating historical context, **81,** 82, 85, **1093,** 1094, 1095, 1097, 1098, 1099
Form and meaning, **981,** 982, 986
Generalizations, **971, 973,** 975, 976, 978
  about writer's beliefs, **367,** 370, 371, 372
Graphic novel, responding to, **54,** 59, **496,** 502
Graphic organizers, 1229, 1235, 1243, 1257, 1273
  cause-and-effect chain, 1299
  cluster chart, 1377
  compare-and-contrast chart, 819, 821
  concept map, 767, 771, 965, 968, 969, 1033, 1040
  flow chart, 639, 643, 774, 799
  idea web, 1200, 1223, 1226, 1355
  making inferences, 829, 835
  spider map, 1127, 1212
  trifold chart, 1041
  Venn diagram, 741, 957, 959, 1395
  word map, 204, 735
  word web, 61, 73, 1162
Historical allusion, **667**
Historical context, **81,** 82, 85, **1093,** 1094, 1095, 1097, 1098, 1099, **1357,** 1359, 1360, 1363, 1364, 1365
Iambic hexameter, **813**
Iambic pentameter, **813**
Identifying cause and effect, **1297, 1299,** 1304, 1305, 1306
Identifying cultural characteristics, **1377,** 1380, 1381, 1383
Identifying historical context, **1357,** 1359, 1360, 1363, 1364, 1365
Identifying language structure, **1369,** 1372, 1374, 1375
Identifying main ideas, **61,** 73, **289,** 290, 294
Identifying theme, 63, 65, 67, 68, 72, **325,** 328, 329, **1009,** 1011, 1012, 1013, 1014, 1016, 1017, 1019, 1020, 1021, **1223,** 1224, 1225, 1226
Identifying tone, **620, 621,** 623, 628,

629, **1181,** 1182, 1183, 1184
Imagery
  interpreting, **766,** 768, 769, 771, **1285,** 1287, 1288
  visualizing, **99,** 103, 104, 106, 108, 110, 271, **852,** 853, 855, 856, **1200,** 1201, 1202
Inferences, 271, 272, 273, 274, 275
  about author's beliefs, **1103,** 1104, 1106
  about character, **603,** 605, 606, 608
  about characters' motivations, **1127,** 1128, 1130, 1131, 1132, 1133, 1134, 1136, 1137, 1138, 1139
  about drama, **1343,** 1345, 1346, 1348
  about meaning, 957
  about poetry, **829,** 830, 834, 835, **1189,** 1190, 1191, 1194, **1290,** 1292, 1293
  about short stories, **1033,** 1034, 1036, 1037, 1039, 1040
  about theme, **325,** 328, 329, **1397,** 1400, 1401, 1403, 1404
  from textual clues, **941, 943,** 946, 947, 949
  See also Predictions.
Interpreting character, **161,** 163, 165, 168, 172, 173, 175, **1309,** 1311, 1314, 1318, 1320, 1322
Interpreting imagery, **766,** 768, 769, 771, **1285,** 1287, 1288
Inverted word order, **277,** 278, 279, 280, **843,** 844, 845, 846
Language structure, **1369,** 1372, 1374, 1375
Loaded language, 1162
Logical appeal, **579, 580, 1107, 1109**
Logical fallacy, **195**
Main idea, **61,** 73, **289,** 290, 294
Making critical judgments, **217,** 220, 221, 223, 226, 228, 229, 230, 231, **557,** 560, 561, 562
Making generalizations, **971, 973,** 975, 976, 978
  about writer's beliefs, **367,** 370, 371, 372
Making inferences, **271,** 272, 273, 274, 275
  about author's beliefs, **1103,** 1104, 1106
  about character, **603,** 605, 606, 608
  about characters' motivations,

1127, 1128, 1130, 1131, 1132, 1133, 1134, 1136, 1137, 1138, 1139

about drama, **1343,** 1345, 1346, 1348

about meaning, 957

about poetry, **829,** 830, 834, 835, **1189,** 1190, 1191, 1194, **1290,** 1292, 1293

about short stories, **1033,** 1034, 1036, 1037, 1039, 1040

about theme, **325,** 328, 329, **1397,** 1400, 1401, 1403, 1404

from textual clues, **941, 943,** 946, 947, 949

Making predictions, **1023,** 1024, 1025, 1027, 1029, 1030, **1335,** 1337, 1339, 1341

Meaning and form, **981,** 982, 986

Meter, 745

Modifying predictions, **1117,** 1118, 1119, 1121, 1123, 1124

Monitoring reading, **401, 404,** 409, 410, 412, 413, 415, 416, 419, 420, 424, 425, 426, 428, 430, 431, 435, 438, 439, 441, 444, 445, 452, 455, 457, 463, 465, 467, 468, 472, 473, 477, 483, 492, 493

Octave, 745

Paraphrasing

epic, **19, 21,** 25, 29, 32, 33, 34, 36, 37, 39, 41, 42, 45, 47, 48, 49, 50, 345, 350

poetry, **283,** 284, 285, 287, **721,** 722, 723, 724, 726, 727, **953,** 954, 955

Patterns of organization, **296,** 297, 298, 299, **745,** 749, 750, 754, **1351,** 1354, 1355

Persuasive techniques, **579, 580,** 582, 584, 586, 587, 588

Petrarchan sonnet, **745**

Predictions

making, **1023,** 1024, 1025, 1027, 1029, 1030, **1335,** 1337, 1339, 1341

modifying, **1117,** 1118, 1119, 1121, 1123, 1124

See also Inferences.

Prior knowledge, **1265,** 1266, 1267

Purpose, author's, **185,** 186, 189, 190, 192, **363,** 364, 365, **565,** 569, 570, 572, 574, 576, 577, **1141,** 1144, 1146, 1147, 1148, **1407,** 1409, 1410, 1413

Questioning, **401, 404,** 409, 410, 412, 413, 415, 416, 419, 420, 424, 425, 426, 428, 430, 431, 435, 438, 439, 441, 444, 445, 452, 455, 457, 463, 465, 467, 468, 472, 473, 477, 483, 492, 493

Reading closely, **847,** 848, 850, 851, **1172,** 1175, 1176

Reading Focus

analyzing cause and effect, **1297**

analyzing details, **1227**

analyzing Milton's style, **345**

analyzing style: key details, **115**

comparing and contrasting, **817**

drawing inferences from textual clues, **941**

identifying and critiquing author's argument, **1107**

identifying cause and effect, **1297**

identifying tone, **620**

making generalizations, **971**

paraphrasing, **19**

recognizing patterns of organization, **745**

recognizing persuasive techniques, **579**

using questioning to monitor reading, **401**

Read with Purpose, 12, 15, 23, 43, 62, 66, 68, 75, 82, 90, 101, 122, 151, 162, 179, 186, 188, 190, 196, 219, 262, 272, 273, 274, 278, 279, 284, 285, 290, 292, 297, 301, 305, 310, 311, 316, 317, 318, 322, 323, 326, 334, 336, 338, 339, 340, 341, 342, 351, 364, 368, 375, 377, 380, 391, 392, 395, 396, 397, 405, 536, 546, 551, 558, 566, 581, 596, 604, 616, 618, 622, 634, 640, 646, 658, 668, 674, 677, 722, 724, 731, 733, 738, 740, 743, 758, 762, 764, 768, 775, 803, 812, 820, 825, 830, 836, 844, 845, 853, 860, 869, 870, 874, 875, 878, 879, 910, 918, 927, 932, 938, 944, 947, 954, 956, 958, 966, 974, 976, 982, 985, 989, 994, 1010, 1024, 1034, 1070, 1076, 1078, 1082, 1085, 1089, 1094, 1104, 1110, 1118, 1128, 1142, 1152, 1155, 1163, 1173, 1178, 1182, 1190, 1206, 1209, 1213, 1217, 1224, 1230, 1236, 1240, 1244, 1248, 1252, 1258, 1262, 1266, 1269, 1274, 1281, 1286, 1292, 1301, 1311, 1326, 1336, 1344, 1353, 1358, 1370, 1378, 1386, 1392, 1398, 1408, 1416

Repetition, 667

Resolution, **993,** 996, 999, 1000, 1002, 1004

Responding to graphics, **54,** 59, **496,** 502

Rhetorical devices, **667,** 669, 670, 672, 673, 675, 676, 677, 678

Rhetorical question, **667**

Rhyme scheme, 745

Rhythm and rhyme, reading, **813,** 814, 816

Satire, 565

Sensory details, **1229**

Sestet, 745

Setting, visualizing, **965,** 966, 968, **1177,** 1178, 1179, 1180

Sonnet, 745

Stanza, 745, 747

Style, analyzing, 304, 305, 307, **821**

key details, **115,** 124, 128, 131, 133, 135, 141, 146

poetry, **350,** 352, 355, 357, 358, 359, **931,** 932, 933, 934, 936, 939, **1212,** 1214, 1215

satire, **595,** 597, 598, 599, 600

Summarizing, **926,** 927, 929, 930

TechFocus, 21, 837

Text structure and meaning, **390,** 391, 392, 393, 394, 395, 396, 397, 398, 399, **868,** 869, 870, 871, **873,** 876, **877,** 880

Theme, identifying, 63, 65, 67, 68, 72, **325,** 328, 329, **1009,** 1011, 1012, 1013, 1014, 1016, 1017, 1019, 1020, 1021, **1223,** 1224, 1225, 1226

Tone

analyzing, **837,** 838, 840, **1239,** 1240, 1241

identifying, **620, 621,** 623, 628, 629, **1181,** 1182, 1183, 1184

Understanding archaic language, **321,** 322, 324, **774,** 777, 781, 786, 788, 790, 794, 797, 799

Understanding cause and effect, **195,** 197, 198, 200, 201, 202, 203

Understanding historical context, **81,** 82, 85

Visualizing details, **1081,** 1082, 1083

Visualizing imagery, **99,** 103, 104, 106, 108, 110, **852,** 853, 855, 856, **1200,** 1201, 1202

Visualizing setting, **965,** 966, 968, **1177,** 1178, 1179, 1180
Word choice, **657,** 658, 659, 663, 664
Word order, **657,** 658, 659, 663, 664
   inverted, **277,** 278, 279, 280
Writer's stance, **615,** 617, 618, 619

VOCABULARY SKILLS

Academic Vocabulary, 11, 261, 360, 535, 909, 1069
Accented syllables, **1369**
Adjectives, verbs as, **811**
Affix, 52, **361**
Analogy, **176, 563,** 696, **800, 987,** 1056, **1114, 1332, 1423**
Anglo-Saxon word roots, **52,** 185
Antonym, **81,** 86, 147, 374, 578, 615, 667, 679, 852, 857, 926, 1084, **1100,** 1114, 1229, 1233, 1349
Article, definite, **965**
British phrases, **1351**
Characteristic relationship, **1114**
Commonly confused words, **121,** 147, 300, **1247**
Commonly misused words, **1239**
Compound noun, 1273, 1277
Compound word, **1285**
Connotation, **21,** 51, 289, 315, 390, 522, **589, 735,** 813, **924, 1005, 1149,** 1243, 1257, 1323
Context clues, **772,** 896, **1195, 1307, 1366**
C sounds, **595,** 601, 1093, **1100**
Definite article, **965**
Definitions, creating, **645, 654**
Denotation, 522, **589, 735,** 1005
Dictionary, **679, 822**
Double letters, **973**
Etymology, **86,** 215, **360, 601, 630, 1125, 1158, 1203,** 1291
Figurative language, **857, 969,** 1181, **1277**
Foreign words, **1335**
Forms of words, **149**
French word roots, **969**
Greek word roots, **361**
Heteronym, **1127**
Historical terms, **1158**
Homograph, **1325, 1332**
Homonym, **315,** 603, 869
Idiom, **950, 1299, 1405**
Intensity, **589**
Latin word roots, **178,** 291, 321, **361,** 931, 969, 1151, 1158
Literal meaning, **1181**

Mathematical words, **361**
Metaphor, **857,** 969
Multiple-meaning words, 248, 271, 350, 360, 404, 802, 837, 917, 924, 937, 943, **950,** 1088, 1208, 1235, 1279, 1307, 1309, 1322, 1377, 1397
Negative prefix, **1141, 1216**
Noun
   compound, 1273, 1277
   endings, **161,** 176
   suffix, **1189, 1195**
Nouns, specific, 877
Online sources, **822**
Onomatopoeia, 847
Parts of speech, **309**
Past tense verbs, **195,** 204
Personal definitions, **645, 654**
Personification, **857,** 969
Poetry recitation, 1205
Political science terms, **1158**
Prefix, **51,** 52, 829, 988, 1033, 1081
   dis-, **207, 215**
   im-, **367, 1172**
   in- and *un-,* **1141, 1149, 1216, 1343**
   micro-, **361**
   re-, **639**
Pronunciation, 119, **819,** 822, 981, 1423
Recitation, 1205
Related words, 304, 843
Repetition, **1177**
Roots, word. *See* Word roots.
Scientific words, **361**
Shades of meaning, 89
Silent consonants, **772**
Silent letters, **1103**
Simile, **857**
Sounds, word, **847**
Specific nouns, 877
Stressed syllables, **580,** 589
Suffix, **51,** 52, 1033, 1109, **1233**
   -able and *-ible,* **217, 545, 549**
   -ant and *-ate,* **621, 630**
   -archy, **1200, 1203**
   -ion, **1189, 1195**
   -ly, **1117, 1125, 1357, 1366**
   -ology, **361**
   -ous, **277, 1114**
   -ous and *-ious,* **1162, 1170**
   -tion, **296**
Synonym, **325, 549,** 953, **979,** 993, 1005, 1031, **1100,** 1114, 1261, 1268, **1349**
Unfamiliar words, defining, **1265**
Verbs as adjectives, **811**

Verb tenses, **565,** 578
Word analogy, **176, 563,** 696, **800, 987,** 1056, **1114, 1332, 1423**
Word chart, 110
Word definitions, **957, 1265**
Word family, **1212,** 1251, 1385, 1407
Word map, **204**
Word meanings, **1170**
Word origins, **283,** 333, 363, 557, 563, 755, 824, 873
Word roots, **74,** 178, 185, 633, 859, 1023, 1391
   Anglo-Saxon, **52,** 185
   French, **969**
   Greek, **361**
   Latin, **178,** 291, 321, **361,** 931, 969, 1151, 1158
Word sounds, **847**

WRITING SKILLS

Choices
   advertisement, 281
   allusions, 1204
   anthology, 1289
   ballad, 1289
   blog, 383, 555, 940, 1149, 1171
   calypso, 1405
   character sketch, 148, 495
   compare and contrast, 111, 193, 303, 313, 330, 400, 841, 1101, 1289, 1333, 1349
   critical essay, 313, 330, 383, 680, 801, 823, 858, 1006, 1101, 1196, 1277, 1323, 1424
   debate, 1031
   diary, 555
   digital collage, 1204, 1277
   discussion, 53, 177, 1031, 1101, 1149
   documentary, 53, 655
   drama reading, 951, 1307
   expository essay, 177, 193
   fact and opinion, 1171
   field guide, 1289
   foil, 111
   frame story, 148
   graphics, 177
   group activity, 193, 205, 281, 295, 495, 555, 610, 680, 756, 823, 841, 925, 951, 1031, 1087, 1101, 1234
   hypertext, 1196
   illustration, 631
   imagery, 1087, 1424
   inscription, 823
   interior monologue, 1323

interview, 925, 951
journal entry, 1405
letters, 281, 631, 655, 1087
memorial, 1087
message, 841
mood, 971
movie, 925, 1006
music, 193, 303, 313, 330, 400, 610, 756
narrator, 1307
news story, 193
North America, 1367
orations, 1115
paraphrase, 979
parody, 205
partner activity, 295, 590, 655, 773, 841, 858, 881, 940, 1196
personal essay, 1031, 1234, 1333
persuasion, 940
photographs, 736, 951
plot outline, 362
podcast, 1087
poem, 841, 971, 987, 1204, 1277
point of view, 362
presentation, 205, 495, 823, 1087
psychological profile, 1349
radio program, 1289
recommendation, 1289, 1367
research, 177, 193, 383, 495, 590, 680, 773, 841, 881, 940, 1115, 1367
response essay, 979
rituals, 303
satire, 590
script, 303
setting, 756
slide show, 773, 979
sound effects, 736
speech, 925
storyboard, 1087
story map, 1125
storytelling, 148, 177, 1006, 1125, 1149, 1307, 1323
style, 303
summary, 610, 801, 971, 1289
symbols, 736
theme, 111
time line, 303, 495, 1171
topic web, 987
travel brochure, 1333
TV flashback, 1125
video, 193, 631, 801, 1405
visual image, 295, 495, 555, 680, 881, 940, 1234
Web page, 362, 881, 1115, 1349, 1424
Comparison/contrast essay, **344,**

382, 503, 611, 681, 881, 1041, 1185, 1221, 1425
Constructed Response, 344, 374–382, 802, 1268
Historical research paper, 531
Hyperbole, 289, 294
Parody, 205
Personification, 217, 231
Persuasive essay, 697
QuickWrite, 20, 60, 80, 88, 98, 116, 184, 194, 206, 216, 270, 288, 314, 320, 346, 366, 388, 556, 564, 602, 644, 656, 666, 720, 728, 746, 766, 810, 836, 866, 872, 942, 952, 964, 972, 980, 992, 1008, 1022, 1032, 1074, 1080, 1092, 1102, 1108, 1126, 1140, 1150, 1188, 1222, 1228, 1238, 1242, 1248, 1256, 1260, 1264, 1272, 1278, 1284, 1290, 1298, 1308, 1334, 1350, 1368, 1384, 1390, 1396, 1406, 1414
Reflective essay, 897
Short story, editing, 1057
Sonnet, 271, 275
TechConnect, 580
TechFocus, 53, 111, 149, 193, 205, 281, 289, 295, 303, 350, 362, 367, 383, 400, 404, 495, 555, 590, 610, 621, 631, 823, 881, 917, 925, 940, 950, 979, 987, 993, 1006, 1081, 1087, 1115, 1117, 1125, 1149, 1171, 1204, 1273, 1277, 1285, 1289, 1323, 1349, 1405, 1424
Think as a Reader/Writer
    active verbs, 1414, 1422
    adjectives, 761, 763, 765, 973, 978
    allegory, 1009, 1021
    alliteration and assonance, 957, 959, 1077, 1079
    allusions, 363, 365, 1189, 1194
    analogy, 667, 678
    anecdotes, 81, 85
    antithesis, 615, 619
    apostrophe, 721
    assumptions, 991
    atmosphere, 1335, 1341
    catalog, 621, 629
    characterization, 367, 372, 404, 425, 457, 493, 984, 986
    concrete nouns, 1229, 1232
    connotations, 1216, 1220
    conversational tone, 747, 754
    critical essay, 111, 1255
    description, 121, 146, 309, 312,

372, 545, 548, 580, 767, 837, 840, 1088, 1091, 1117, 1124, 1162, 1172, 1176, 1309, 1322, 1357, 1365
details, 178, 183, 1088, 1091, 1291, 1293, 1299, 1306, 1391, 1395, 1407, 1413
dialogue, 207, 214, 439, 477, 557, 562, 645, 653, 1127, 1139, 1348, 1351, 1355, 1385, 1388, 1397, 1404
diction, 633, 637, 639, 1223
elegy, 61
epics, 21, 50, 99, 110, 350, 359
examples, 633, 637
figures of speech, 291, 294, 799, 829, 835, 1077, 1079, 1391, 1395
graphics, 59, 1268, 1271
imagery, 195, 203, 291, 296, 298, 315, 319, 496, 502, 757, 760, 868, 871, 877, 880, 917, 923, 1177, 1265, 1267, 1279, 1283, 1285, 1325, 1331
interior monologue, 89, 97
irony, 1141, 1148
language structures, 1369, 1375
loaded language, 1084, 1086, 1151, 1157
main idea and details, 802, 807, 1251
metaphors and similes, 321, 332, 343, 374, 382, 390, 394, 399, 843, 846, 937, 939, 1075, 1212, 1261, 1263
mood, 61, 73, 873, 876, 965, 968, 1117, 1124, 1180
narrator, 161, 175
organization, 550, 554
paradox, 300, 302
parallelism, 615, 619, 1103, 1106, 1109, 1247
parody, 603, 608
passage of time, 1023, 1030, 1208
personification, 217, 231, 657, 664, 847, 851
poem, 271, 275, 930, 1202, 1273, 1276, 1395
point of view, 1239, 1241
present tense, 1093, 1099
questions, 931
realism, 1033, 1040
refrain, 277, 280, 1257, 1259
repetition, 185, 192, 742, 744, 811, 852, 856, 953, 955, 1205, 1207, 1235, 1247, 1250, 1343,

1348
rhetorical questions, 943, 949
riddles, 74, 79
satire, 565, 577, 595, 600
sentence structure, 824, 828
setting, 325, 329
show and tell, 1377, 1383
sound devices, 917, 923
speaker, 730
stage directions, 304, 307
statistics, 988
style, 859, 862, 1184
suspense, 993, 1004
symbols, 737, 741, 1208, 1211, 1215
syntax, 1181
theme, 926, 930, 1200, 1202, 1243, 1245
tone, 1081, 1083, 1235
understatement, 981, 986
verbal irony, 149, 160
word choice, 819, 821
Timed Writing, 111, 148, 177, 193, 303, 313, 330, 495, 680, 823, 841, 858, 881, 971, 979, 1031, 1101, 1234, 1307, 1333, 1349

STANDARDIZED TEST PRACTICE

Literary Skills Review, 244–245, 520–521, 694–695, 894–895, 1054–1055, 1444–1446
Vocabulary Skills Review, 246, 522, 696, 896, 1056, 1448
Writing Skills Review, 247, 523, 697, 897, 1057, 1449

LANGUAGE (GRAMMAR, USAGE, AND MECHANICS) SKILLS

Active voice, **1204**
Adjective
    and adverb, **925, 1223**
    clause, **362, 1171**
    demonstrative, **1196**
    proper, **1077**
    shades of meaning, 89
    verb as, **99, 811**
Adverb
    and adjective, **925, 1223**
    clause, **362, 1171**
    relative, **361**
Antecedent, **590**
Apostrophe, **313**
Appositive, **756**
Appositive phrase, **756**
Clause

    adjective, **362, 1171**
    adverb, **362, 1171**
    dependent/independent, **281, 970, 1171, 1333**
    noun, **1171**
    in sentence, **823**
    subordinate, **281, 970, 1171, 1333**
Colon, **1101**
Combining sentences, **494, 951**
Comma splice, **281**
Comparative modifier, **330**
Complement, **295**
Complex sentence, **823, 970**
Compound–complex sentence, **823, 970**
Compound sentence, **823, 970**
Conjunction, subordinating, **362**
Connecting ideas, **1115**
Dangling modifier, **1006**
Dash, **1101**
Demonstrative adjective, **1196**
Demonstrative pronoun, **1196**
Dependent clause, **281, 970, 1171**
Direct object, **295**
Direct quotation, **858**
Double comparison, **330**
Effective sentences, **1424**
Essential appositive, **756**
Fused sentences, **281**
Imperative mood, **313**
Independent clause, **970, 1171, 1333**
Indirect object, **295**
Indirect quotation, **858**
Infinitive, **801**
Infinitive phrase, **801**
Intransitive verb, **205**
Irregular verbs, **655**
Literary present tense, **610,** 736
Modifier, **330, 1006**
Nonessential appositive, **756**
Noun, proper, **1077**
Noun clause, **1171**
Noun endings, **161, 176**
Parallelism, **1367**
Participial phrase, **1234**
Participles, **951, 1234**
Passive voice, **1204**
Past participle, **1234**
Past subjunctive, **680**
Past tense verbs, **195,** 204
Phrase fragment, **281**
Preposition, **773**
Prepositional phrase, **773**
Present participle, **1234**
Present subjunctive, **680**

Present tense, **610,** 736
Progressive verb forms, **148**
Pronoun
    antecedent agreement, **590**
    demonstrative, **1196**
    relative, **361**
Proper adjective, **1077**
Proper noun, **1077**
Punctuation, **1101**
Quotation, **858**
Relative adverb, **361**
Relative pronoun, **361**
Restrictive appositive, **756**
Run-on sentence, **281**
Semicolon, **1101**
Sentence fragment, **281**
Sentences
    combining, **494, 951**
    fused/run-on, **281**
    structure, **823, 970**
    types of, **823, 970**
    variety, **1424**
Simple sentence, **823, 970**
Subject/verb agreement, **53**
Subjunctive mood, **680**
Subordinate clause, **281, 970, 1171, 1333**
Subordinating conjunction, **362**
Superlative modifier, **330**
Tense. *See* Verb tenses
Transitions, **1115**
Transitive verb, **205**
Verbs
    active/passive voice, **1204**
    as adjectives, **99, 811**
    irregular, **655**
    progressive forms of, **148**
    transitive/intransitive, **205**
Verb tenses, **565,** 578
    consistency, **736**
    literary present, **610**
    past, **195,** 204
    sequence of, **631**

READ ON

Achebe, Chinua, 1450
Anouilh, Jean, 248
Austen, Jane, 898, 1058
Baer, William, 524
Becket, 248
Brave New World, 1450
Bronte, Charlotte, 1058
Coetzee, J. M., 1451
Churchill: A Life, 1451
Dared and Done: The Marriage of Elizabeth Barrett and Robert

Browning, 1058
Jane Eyre, 1058
Forster, E. M., 1451
Frankenstein, 898
Fraser, Antonia, 524
Garcia Márquez, Gabriel, 1450
Gardner, John, 248
Gilbert, Martin, 1451
Grendel, 248
Hamlet, 525
Huxley, Aldous, 1450
The Inimitable Jeeves, 1450
Keats, John, 898
Leeming, David Adams, 248
Letters of John Keats, 898
Maathai, Wangari, 1451
Markus, Julia, 1058

Mary, Bloody Mary, 524
Mary, Queen of Scots, 524
Medieval Castle, The, 248
Meyer, Carolyn, 524
One Hundred Years of Solitude, 1450
Passage to India, A, 1451
Pirsig, Robert, 524
Pool, Daniel, 1058
Pride and Prejudice, 898
Shakespeare, William, 525
Shelley, Mary, 898
Sonnets: 150 Contemporary Sonnets, 524
Sound of Water, The, 898
Things Fall Apart, 1450
Unbowed, 1451
Voyage of the Hero, The, 248

Waiting for the Barbarians, 1451
Warner, Philip, 248
What Jane Austen Ate, 1058
Woodhouse, P. G., 1450
Zen and the Art of Motorcycle Maintenance, 524

INDEX OF AUTHORS AND TITLES

Page numbers in italics refer to the pages on which author biographies appear .

Achebe, Chinua, *1376*, 1378
African Proverbs, 342
Ah, Are You Digging on My Grave?, 976
Akhmatova, Anna, *1242*, 1244
Aldington, Richard, 596
Alfred, Lord Tennyson, *916*, 918, 927, 932, 938
Analects of Confucius, The, from, 338
Anglo-Saxon Riddles, 75–78
Another Renaissance?, 262–265
Araby, 1326–1330
Arndt, Walter, 245
Arnold, Matthew, *964*, 966
Atlantis—A Lost Sonnet, 1292
Atwood, Margaret, *1284*, 1286, 1445
Auden, W.H., *1222*, 1224
Autobiography of William Butler Yeats, The, from, 1217–1219
B. Wordsworth, 1398–1403
Bacon, Francis, 375
Baines, Keith, 208
Baranczak, Stanislaw, 1248, 1252
Bashō, Matsuo, *867*, 870
Baudelaire, Charles, 695
Beckett, Samuel, *1342*, 1344
Bede, The Venerable, *80*, 82
Behn, Aphra, 694
Behn, Harry, 870
Beilenson, Peter, 870
Beowulf, from, 23–41, 43–49
Bet, The, 1024–1029
Bhagavad-Gita, from, 334–335
Blake, William, *728*, 731, 733, 738, 740, 743, 894
Blood, Sweat, and Tears, 1110–1112
Boland, Eavan, *1290*, 1292
Book of Sand, The, 1336–1340
Borges, Jorge Luis, *1334*, 1336
Boswell, James, *644*, 646
Bowen, Elizabeth, *1116*, 1118
Bownas, Geoffrey, 869
Brooke, Rupert, *1074*, 1078
Browning, Elizabeth Barrett, *952*, 954
Browning, Robert, *942*, 944, 947
Bunyan, John, *366*, 368
Burns, Robert, *720*, 722, 724
Buson, Taniguchi, *867*, 870
Candide, from, 596–599
Canterbury Tales, The, from, 122–145, 151–159, 162–174
Cavanagh, Clare, 1248, 1252

Cavendish, Margaret, 377
Cervantes, Miguel de, *602*, 604
Chamberlain, Joseph, *1150*, 1152
Chaucer, Geoffrey, 116, 122, 151, 162
Chekhov, Anton, *1022*, 1024
Childe Harold's Pilgrimage, Canto IV, from, 814–815
Chimney Sweeper, The (Songs of Experience), 740
Chimney Sweeper, The (Songs of Innocence), 739
Chudleigh, Lady Mary, *666*, 677
Churchill, Winston, *1108*, 1110
Coghill, Nevill, 122, 151, 162
Coleridge, Samuel Taylor, *766*, 768, 775
Colet, Roger, 1034
Collected Beowulf, The, from, 55–58
Come and Go, 1344–1346
Composed Upon Westminster Bridge, 762
Cooper, Arthur, 875, 878, 879
Crossing the Bar, 938
Dana, Doris, 1258
Darkling Thrush, The, 974–975
Dawood, N. J., 333
Day of Destiny, The, from, 208–213
Death be not proud, 301
Defoe, Daniel, *556*, 558, *666*, 674
Demon Lover, The, 1118–1123
Desai, Anita, *1414*, 1416
Destructors, The, 1128–1138
Diary of Samuel Pepys, The, from, 546–547
Dictionary of the English Language, A, from, 634–636
Digging, 1281–1282
Doll's House, The, 1300–1305
Donne, John, *288*, 290, 292, 297, 301
Do Not Go Gentle into That Good Night, 1236
Don Quixote, from, 604–607
Dover Beach, 966–967
Drummer Hodge, 1054
Dulce et Decorum Est, 1076
Edson, Margaret, 305
Education of Women, The, from, 674–676
Edward, Edward, 190–191
Elegy Written in a Country Churchyard, 658–663
Eliot, T.S., *1188*, 1190

Ellis, Jerry, 179
Essay on Man, An, from, 618
Everyman, from, 218–230
Exeter Book, The, from, 60
Explosion, The, 1266
Fagles, Robert, 100
Fall of Satan, The, 351–358
Fear, 1258
Female Orations, from, 377
Fern Hill, 1230–1231
Fisher, Gary, 262
Foote, Timothy, 803
Games at Twilight, 1416–1421
Gardner, John, 196
Garnett, Constance, 1024
Get Up and Bar the Door, 188–189
Ghost Map, The, from, 910–913
Gilgamesh, from, 90–96
Gordimer, Nadine, *1368*, 1370
Gordon, George (Lord Byron), *810*, 812, 814
Gray, Thomas, *656*, 658
Greene, Graham, *1126*, 1128
Gulliver's Travels, from, 564–576
Gyford, Phil, 551
Haiku, 870
Hamer, Richard, 66
Hardy, Thomas, *972*, 974, 976, 1054
Haunted House, A, 1178–1179
Heaney, Seamus, 43, *1278*, 1281
Heine, Henrich, 1444
Henderson, Harold G., 870
Heroic Couplets, 616–617
Herrick, Robert, *282*, 284
Hinds, Gareth, 54
History of the English Church and People, A, from, 82–84
Hollow Men, The, 1190–1193
Homer, 98, 100
Hopkins, Gerard Manley, *956*, 958
Horses, The, 1274–1275
Housman, A.E., *980*, 982, 985
How Much Land Does a Man Need?, 1010–1020
Hughes, Ted, *1272*, 1274
Hurley, Andrew, 1336
"I Believe in a British Empire," 1152–1154
Iliad, from the, 101–109
"I love you as I love . . .," 694
In Memoriam A. H. H., from, 932–936
Issa, Kobayashi, *867*, 870
Jacob's Room, from, 1173–1175

Jade Flower Palace, 874
Jewels, The, 1034–1039
Johnson, Samuel, *632*, 634
Johnson, Steven B., 910
Jonson, Ben, *308*, 310, 311
Journal of the Plague Year, A, from, 558–561
Joyce, James, *1324*, 1326
Keats, John, *842*, 844, 845, 848, 853, 860
Keats's Last Letter, 860–861
King James Bible, from, 322–323, 326–328
Kipling, Rudyard, *992*, 994
Komachi, Ono, *866*, 869
Koran, from, 333
Kotewall, Robert, 878
Kubla Khan, 768–770
La Canfora, Jason, 989
Lady of Shalott, The, 918–922
Lake Isle of Innisfree, The, 1206
Lamb, The, 733
Lao Tzu, 339
Larkin, Philip, *1264*, 1266
Lawrence, D. H., *1308*, 1311
Leslau, Charlotte and Wolf, 342
Lessing, Doris, *1356*, 1358
Letters of Virginia Woolf, The, from, 1182–1183
Letter to His Two Small Children, 879
Levi, Primo, *1092*, 1094
Lewisohn, Ludwig, 1055
Li Po, *872*, 878, 879
Life of Samuel Johnson, The, from, 646–652
Lines Composed a Few Miles Above Tintern Abbey, 748–753
London, 894
Lord of the Rings, The, from, 12–15
Lord Randall, 186
Lorelei, The, 1444
Lot's Wife (Akhmatova), 1244
Lot's Wife (Szymborska), 1248–1249
Love Arm'd, 694–695
Lovelace, Richard, *314*, 317, 318
Macbeth, 405–424, 426–438, 440–456, 458–476, 478–492
Malory, Sir Thomas, 206, 208
Mansfield, Katherine, *1298*, 1301
Mark of the Beast, The, 994–1003
Marlowe, Christopher, *276*, 278
Marriage is a Private Affair, 1378–1382
Marvell, Andrew, *282*, 285
Mason, Herbert, 90
Maude, Aylmer, 1010
Maude, Louise, 1010

Maupassant, Guy de, *1032*, 1034
McGowan, James, 695
Meaning of Everything, The, from, 640–642
Meditation 17 (Donne), 297
Merwin, W.S., *836*, 838
Miller, Barbara Stoler, 334
Milton, John, *346*, 351, 364
Mistral, Gabriela, *1256*, 1258
Mitchell, Stephen, 339
Mitsune, Oshikochi, *866*, 869
Modest Proposal, A, from, 581–587
Musée des Beaux Arts, 1224–1225
Mushrooms, 1286–1287
My Last Duchess, 944–946
Naipaul, V. S., *1396*, 1398
Nehru, Jawaharlal, *1150*, 1155
Neruda, Pablo, *1260*, 1262
Never Shall I Forget, 1104
Night, 333
Night-Soil Men, The, 910–913
Night Thoughts Afloat, 875
Nobel Lecture: The Poet and the World, from, 1252–1254
Noble Mansion of Free India, The, 1155–1156
Not Waving but Drowning, 1240
No Witchcraft for Sale, 1358–1364
Nukada, Princess, *866*, 869
Nymph's Reply to the Shepherd, The, 279
Ode: Intimations of Immortality, from, 758–759
Ode To A Grecian Urn, 853–855
Ode To A Nightingale, 848–850
Ode to the West Wind, 825–827
Of Studies, 375
Omeros, 1392–1394
Once Upon a Time, 1370–1374
1 Dead in Attic, 536–539
On First Looking Into Chapman's Homer, 844
Onitsura, Uejima, *867*, 870
On My First Son, 310
Orwell, George, *1140*, 1142
Oswald, Alice, 1070
Owen, Wilfred, *1074*, 1076
Ozymandias, 820
Parable of the Prodigal Son, The, 326–328
Paradise Lost, from, 351–358
Pardoner's Tale, The, from, 151–159
Passionate Shepherd to His Love, The, 278
Pepys, Samuel, *544*, 546
Philosophy and Spiritual Discipline, from, 334–335

Pied Beauty, 958
Pilgrim's Progress, The, from, 368–371
Pinter, Harold, *1350*, 1353
Poison Tree, The, 743
Pope, Alexander, *614*, 616, 618, 622
Porphyria's Lover, 947–948
Under fire in Iraq, 1089–1090
Psalm 23, 322
Psalm 137, 323
Putnam, Samuel, 604
Queen Elizabeth I, 380
Question and Answer Among the Mountains, 878
Quiet Night Thoughts, 878
Raffel, Burton, 23, 62, 68, 75
Raleigh, Sir Walter, *276*, 279
Rape of the Lock, The, from, 622–628
Raven doth to raven fly, 245
Rear-Guard, The, 1082
Reps, Paul, 336
Rexroth, Kenneth, 874
Rimbaud, Arthur, 1055
Rime of the Ancient Mariner, The, 775–798
Roberts, Moss, 340
Rocking-Horse Winner, The, 1310–1321
Ronsard, Pierre de, 520
Room of One's Own, A, from, 1163–1168
Rose, Chris, 536
Saigyo, *866*, 869
Sailing to Byzantium, 1213–1214
Sassoon, Siegfried, *1080*, 1082, 1085
Saving Creatures Great and Small, 803–806
Sayings of Saadi, 341
Seafarer, The, 62–65
Second Coming, The, 1201
Shah, Idries, 341
Shakespeare, William, 391, 392, 393, 395, 396, 397, 398, 405
Shelley, Percy Bysshe, *818*, 820, 825, 830
Sherley-Price, Leo, 82
She Walks in Beauty, 812
Shooting an Elephant, 1142–1147
Sir Gawain and the Green Knight, from, 196–202
Sir Vidia's Shadow, from, 1408–1411
Siren Song, 1445
Sleeper of the Valley, The, 1055
Smith, Norman L., 878
Smith, Stevie, *1238*, 1240
Soldier, The, 1078
Soldier's Declaration, A, 1085
Song: To Celia, 311

Song (Donne), 290
Sonnet 43 (Browning), 954
Sonnet 79 (Neruda), 1262
Sonnet 18 (Shakespeare), 391
Sonnet 29 (Shakespeare), 392
Sonnet 30 (Shakespeare), 393
Sonnet 71 (Shakespeare), 395
Sonnet 73 (Shakespeare), 396
Sonnet 116 (Shakespeare), 397
Sonnet 130 (Shakespeare), 398
Sonnet 30 (Spenser), 273
Sonnet 75 (Spenser), 274
Soyinka, Wole, *1384*, 1386
Spacecraft Voyager 1 Has Boldly Gone, 1070–1071
Spenser, Edmund, *270*, 273, 274
Suckling, Sir John, *314*, 316
Survival in Auschwitz, from, 1094–1098
Swift, Jonathan, *564*, 566, 581
Szymborska, Wislawa, *1246*, 1248, 1252
Tanka, 869
Taoist Anecdotes, 340
Tao Te Ching, from, 339
Tapscott, Stephen, 1262
Telephone Conversation, 1386–1387
That's All, 1352–1354
Theroux, Paul, *1406*, 1408
Thomas, Dylan, *1228*, 1230, 1236
Thwaite, Anthony, 869
Tilbury Speech, 380
To a Louse, 724–726
To Althea, from Prison, 318
To a Mosquito, 838–839
To a Mouse, 722–723
To a Skylark, 830–834
To an Athlete Dying Young, 982
To His Coy Mistress, 285–286
Tolkien, J. R. R., 12
Tolstoy, Leo, *1008*, 1011
To Lucasta, on Going to the Wars, 317
To the Ladies, 677
To the Virgins, to Make Much of Time, 284
Trapped Australian Miners Rescued, 1269–1270
Tsurayuki, Ki, *866*, 869
Tu Fu, *872*, 874, 875
Twa Corbies, The, 244
Tyger, The, 731
Ulysses, 927–929
Untermeyer, Louis, 1444
Valediction: Forbidding Mourning, A, 292–293
Vindication of the Rights of Women, A, from, 668–673

Virgins, The, 895
Voltaire, *594*, 596
Walcott, Derek, 895, *1390*, 1392
Waley, Arthur, 338
Walking to Canterbury, from, 179–182
Wanderer, The, 68–72
When Elements Go Extreme, 989–990
When I consider how my light is spent, 364
When I Have Fears, 845
When I Was One-and-Twenty, 985
When You Are Old (Ronsard), 520
When You Are Old (Yeats), 521
Whoso List to Hunt, 272
Why I Turned Pepys' Diary into a Weblog, from, 551–553
Why So Pale and Wan, Fond Lover?, 316
Wiesel, Elie, *1102*, 1104
Wife of Bath, The, from, 162–174
Wife's Lament, The, 66–67
Wilbur, Richard, 1244
Wild Swans at Coole, The, 1209–1210
Winchester, Simon, *638*, 640
Wolfe, Humbert, 520
Wollstonecraft, Mary, *666*, 668
Woolf, Stuart, 1094
Woolf, Virginia, *1160*, 1163, 1173, 1178, 1182
Wordsworth, 1399–1403
Wordsworth, William, *746*, 748, 762, 764
World Is Too Much with Us, The, 764
W;t, from, 305–306
Wyatt, Sir Thomas, *270*, 272
Yeats, William Butler, 521, *1198*, 1201, 1206, 1209, 1213, 1217
Zen Parables, 336–337

DATE DUE
